Definitive L‌‌‌‌‌‌p‌‌
Football Yearbook

2022/23 Season
Volume 6
Book A (A-L)

All player data of first level leagues 2022/23 and 2022

Francisco Javier Artal Alegría

www.futboletin.com

futboletin@futboletin.com

Complete collection of the Definitive European Football Yearbook 2022/23

Volume 1: All first level leagues line-ups 2022/23 and 2022 (books A, B, C and D)
Volume 2: Team rosters of all first level leagues 2022/23 and 2022
Volume 3: All european domestic cups line-ups 2022/23 and 2022 (books A and B)
Volume 4: All international club competitions line-ups 2022/23
Volume 5: All international nations games line-ups 2022/23
Volume 6: All player data of first level leagues 2022/23 and 2022 (books A and B)

Name (and complete or original name)
(a) Date and place of birth
(b) Height (m.)
(c) Position
(d) Senior team (15/08/2023)
(e) Previous senior Teams (until 15/08/2023)

*** á Regni Højgaard - Hilmar á Regni Højgaard (a) 22/08/2003, ¿? (Faroe Islands) (b) - (c) M - right midfielder (d) B68 Toftir (e) -

*** Aabid - Rayane Aabid (a) 19/01/1992, Villeneuve-d'Ascq (France) (b) 1,78 (c) M - central midfielder (d) Hatayspor (e) Kasimpasa, Yeni Malatyaspor, Hatayspor, AS Béziers, Paris FC, AS Béziers, AC Amiens, JA Armentières

*** Aalberg - Isak Hagen Aalberg (a) 11/05/2005, Steinkjer (Norway) (b) 1,91 (c) D - central defense (d) Kristiansund BK (e) -

*** Aalto - Henri Aalto (Henri Olavi Aalto) (a) 20/04/1989, Espoo (Finland) (b) 1,84 (c) D - right back (d) FC Honka (e) VfB Oldenburg, SJK Seinäjoki, FC Honka, Grankulla IFK, FC Honka

*** Aaltonen - Anton Aaltonen (a) 28/11/2003, ¿? (Finland) (b) 1,75 (c) M - central midfielder (d) FC Inter Turku (e) HJK Klubi 04

*** Aarflot - Elias Aarflot (a) 25/11/2003, ¿? (Norway) (b) 1,86 (c) F - center forward (d) Grorud IL (e) Tromsø, Lyn, Tromsø, Grorud IL II

*** Aarons - Rolando Aarons (Rolando James Aarons) (a) 16/11/1995, Kingston (Jamaica) (b) 1,78 (c) F - left winger (d) - (e) Huddersfield Town, Motherwell FC, Huddersfield Town, Newcastle Utd., Motherwell FC, Newcastle Utd., Wycombe Wanderers, Newcastle Utd., Sheffield Wednesday, Newcastle Utd., Slovan Liberec, Newcastle Utd., Hellas Verona, Newcastle Utd.

*** Aaronson - Brenden Aaronson (Brenden Russell Aaronson) (a) 22/10/2000, Medford, New Jersey (United States) (b) 1,77 (c) M - attacking midfielder (d) 1.FC Union Berlin (e) Union Berlin, Leeds Utd., RB Salzburg, Philadelphia, Bethlehem Steel, Bethlehem Steel

*** Aaronson - Paxten Aaronson (Paxten Reid Aaronson) (a) 26/08/2003, Medford, New Jersey (United States) (b) 1,75 (c) M - attacking midfielder (d) Eintracht Frankfurt (e) Philadelphia, Union II

*** Aas - Syver Aas (a) 15/01/2004, ¿? (Norway) (b) 1,81 (c) M - central midfielder (d) Skeid Oslo (e) Odd, Odd II

*** Aasbak - Christoffer Aasbak (a) 22/07/1993, ¿? (Norway) (b) 1,87 (c) D - left back (d) Kristiansund BK (e) Hødd, Byåsen, Ranheim, Byåsen

*** Abada - Liel Abada (עבדה ליאל) (a) 03/10/2001, Petach Tikva (Israel) (b) 1,68 (c) F - right winger (d) Celtic FC (e) M. Petah Tikva

*** Abakumov - Dmitriy Abakumov (Абакумов Дмитрий Николаевич) (a) 08/07/1989, Voronezh (Soviet Union, now in Russia) (b) 1,84 (c) G (d) FC Urartu Yerevan (e) Ararat-Armenia, Luch, Orenburg, Mordovia, KamAZ, CSKA Moskva II

*** Abalora - Razak Abalora (a) 04/09/1996, Accra (Ghana) (b) 1,94 (c) G (d) FC Sheriff Tiraspol (e) Asante Kotoko, Azam FC, WAFA SC

*** Abanda - Leroy Abanda (Leroy Abanda Mfomo) (a) 07/06/2000, Le Blanc-Mesnil (France) (b) 1,80 (c) D - left back (d) OFI Creta (e) RFC Seraing, PAS Lamia, RFC Seraing, AC Milan, US Boulogne, AC Milan, Neuchâtel Xamax

*** Abankwah - James Abankwah (a) 16/01/2004, Dublin (Ireland) (b) 1,82 (c) D - central defense (d) Udinese (e) St. Patrick's Ath., Udinese, St. Patrick's Ath., Cherry Orchard FC

*** Abascal - Rodrigo Abascal (Rodrigo Abascal Barros) (a) 14/01/1994, Montevideo (Uruguay) (b) 1,90 (c) D - central defense (d) Boavista Porto FC (e) Peñarol, CA Fénix, Juventud, CA Fénix

*** Abass - Issah Abass (a) 26/09/1998, Asokwa (Ghana) (b) 1,73 (c) F - left winger (d) GD Chaves (e) Mainz 05, HNK Rijeka, Mainz 05, FC Twente, Mainz 05, FC Utrecht, Mainz 05, Olimpija, Asokwa FC, Olimpija, Asokwa FC

*** Abaz - Armin Abaz (a) 27/03/2002, Grabs SG (Switzerland) (b) 1,87 (c) G (d) FC Winterthur (e) FC St. Gallen

*** Abazaj - Kristal Abazaj (a) 06/07/1996, Elbasan (Albania) (b) 1,83 (c) F - right winger (d) KF Tirana (e) Istanbulspor, RSC Anderlecht, FK Kukësi, RSC Anderlecht, NK Osijek, RSC Anderlecht, KF Skënderbeu, FC Luftëtari, KF Skënderbeu, FC Luftëtari, KF Elbasani

*** Abazaj - Marin Abazaj (a) 31/03/2001, Pogradec (Albania) (b) 1,81 (c) M - central midfielder (d) FK Bylis (e) KF Pogradeci, FC Dinamo, KF Pogradeci

*** Abazarov - Ashqin Abazarov (a) 30/09/2003, ¿? (Azerbaijan) (b) - (c) F (d) Neftchi 2 Baku (e) -

*** Abazi - Agan Abazi (a) 09/10/2002, Skopje (North Macedonia) (b) 1,74 (c) F - right winger (d) - (e) Makedonija, Vardar

*** Abazi - Anid Abazi (a) 09/10/2002, Skopje (North Macedonia) (b) 1,76 (c) D - right back (d) Gostivar (e) FK Skopje, FC Shkupi

*** Abazi - Armend Abazi (a) 17/08/1994, Skënderaj (RF Yugoslavia, now in Kosovo) (b) - (c) M - right midfielder (d) KF Drenica (e) FC Malisheva, KF Ferizaj, KF Drenica

*** Abazi - Leonit Abazi (a) 05/07/1993, Gjilan (Yugoslavia, now in Kosovo) (b) 1,74 (c) D - left back (d) FC Ballkani (e) FC Prishtina, KF Skënderbeu, FC Drita

*** Abazi (c) D (d) KF Drenica (e) - - Arjan Abazi (c) D (d) KF Drenica (e) -

*** Abbas - Ali Abbas (עבאס עלי) (a) 31/05/2001, ¿? (Israel) (b) - (c) D - right back (d) Maccabi Bnei Reineh (e) T. Kfar Kana

*** Abbas - Asylzhan Abbas (Аббас Асылжан Бабакожаулы) (a) 11/06/1999, Arys (Kazakhstan) (b) 1,73 (c) F - right winger (d) - (e) FK Turan, Kyran, Kyran II

*** Abbasov - Mirabdulla Abbasov (Mirabdulla Miryavər oğlu Abbasov) (a) 27/04/1995, Baku (Azerbaijan) (b) 1,82 (c) F - center forward (d) - (e) FK Sabail, Neftchi Baku, FK Sabail, Neftchi Baku, Sumqayit, Neftchi Baku, Daugavpils, Neftchi Baku

*** Abbasov - Mirsahib Abbasov (Mirsahib Miryavər oğlu Abbasov) (a) 19/01/1993, Baku (Azerbaijan) (b) 1,78 (c) F - left winger (d) - (e) Zira FK, FK Sabail, Zira FK, Keshla

*** Abbasov - Rüfat Abbasov (Rüfət Ceyhun oğlu Abbasov) (a) 01/01/2005, ¿? (Azerbaijan) (b) 1,68 (c) D - central defense (d) Neftchi Baku (e) Neftchi 2 Baku

*** Abbasov - Urfan Abbasov (a) 14/10/1992, Baku (Azerbaijan) (b) 1,77 (d) FK Qabala (e) FK Sabail, FK Qabala, Qarabag FK

*** Abbruzzese - Rhys Abbruzzese (a) 28/03/1998, Trecynon (Wales) (b) 1,71 (c) D - left back (d) Haverfordwest County (e) Barry Town

*** Abd Elhamed - Hatem Abd Elhamed (אלחמיד עבד חאתם) (a) 18/03/1991, Kafr Manda (Israel) (b) 1,86 (c) D - central defense (d) Hapoel Beer Sheva (e) Hapoel Haifa, H. Beer Sheva, Celtic FC, H. Beer Sheva, FC Ashdod, KAA Gent, FC Ashdod, KAA Gent, FC Ashdod, FC Dinamo, FC Ashdod, RSC Charleroi

*** Abdallah - Amar Abdallah (Aamir Abdallah Yunis) (a) 08/05/1999, Kassala (Sudan) (b) 1,75 (c) F - right winger (d) - (e) FCI Levadia, Pärnu Vaprus, FCI Levadia, Heidelberg Utd., Northcote City

*** Abdelhamid - Yunis Abdelhamid (الحميد عبد يونس) (a) 28/09/1987, Montpellier (France) (b) 1,90 (c) D - central defense (d) Stade de Reims (e) Dijon, Valenciennes FC, AC Arles-Avignon, AC Arles B, AS Lattes

*** Abdelkadous - Billel Abdelkadous (a) 22/05/1990, Metz (France) (b) 1,92 (c) F - left winger (d) US Mondorf-Les-Bains (e) Amnéville, SAS Epinal, Amnéville, Shabab Al-Ordon, Amnéville, Vereya, RC Arbaa, RE Virton, FC Bleid-Gaume, Amnéville, Stade Reims B, Amnéville

*** Abdelli - Himad Abdelli (a) 17/11/1999, Montivilliers (France) (b) 1,85 (c) M - attacking midfielder (d) Angers SCO (e) Le Havre AC

*** Abdibek - Ali Abdibek (Абдибек Али) (a) 23/06/2003, ¿? (Kazakhstan) (b) 1,76 (c) F - left winger (d) Tobol Kostanay II (e) -

*** Abdijanovic - Amir Abdijanovic (a) 03/03/2001, Dornbirn (Austria) (b) 1,80 (c) F - center forward (d) SCR Altach (e) FC Dornbirn, SCR Altach, Wolfsburg II

*** Abdikhamitov - Asadbek Abdikhamitov (Абдихамитов Асадбек) (a) 16/03/2002, ¿? (Kazakhstan) (b) 1,92 (c) D - central defense (d) Kyran Shymkent (e) FK Turan II, Kyran, Kyran II

*** Abdikholikov - Bobur Abdikholikov (Бобур Алишер оглы Абдихоликов) (a) 23/04/1997, Koson (Uzbekistan) (b) 1,75 (c) F - center forward (d) Ordabasy Shymkent (e) Energetik-BGU, Rukh Lviv, Nasaf Qarshi

*** Abdilla - Craig Abdilla (a) 17/03/1999, ¿? (Malta) (b) 1,86 (c) G (d) St. George's FC (e) Mqabba FC, Gzira Utd., Mqabba FC, Qrendi FC, FC Swieqi Utd., Mqabba FC, Mosta FC, Pembroke

*** Abdoul Gafar - Abdoul Gafar (Abdoul Gafar Kassoum Sina Sirima) (a) 30/12/1998, ¿? (Burkina Faso) (b) 1,80 (c) F - center forward (d) FK Slutsk (e) Armavir, FC Noah, FC Sheriff, Tambov, Baltika, Entente SSG

*** Abdrakhmanov - Eldar Abdrakhmanov (Абдрахманов Эльдар Маратович) (a) 16/01/1987, Uralsk (Soviet Union, now in Russia) (b) 1,75 (c) D - right back (d) Akzhayik Uralsk (e) Atyrau, Akzhayik, Ordabasy, Akzhayik, Akzhayik II

*** Abdul Samed - Salis Abdul Samed (a) 26/03/2000, Accra (Ghana) (b) 1,79 (c) M - pivot (d) RC Lens (e) Clermont Foot, JMG Abidjan, Clermont Foot, JMG Abidjan

*** Abdulahi - Liban Abdulahi (a) 02/11/1995, Haarlem (Netherlands) (b) 1,78 (c) M - central midfielder (d) Olympia Haarlem (e) TEC, FC Locomotive, Thór, Koninklijke HFC, J-Södra IF, De Graafschap, Telstar, FC Volendam

*** Abdulai - Neat Abdulai (a) 17/07/2001, Gostivar (North Macedonia) (b) 1,86 (c) F - center forward (d) - (e) AP Brera, Levico Terme, Montebelluna, San Luigi, Trieste

*** Abdulla - Aybar Abdulla (Абдулла Айбар) (a) 22/01/2002, Karaganda (Kazakhstan) (b) 1,76 (c) F - right winger (d) Shakhter Karaganda (e) Kairat Almaty, Kairat Moskva, Kairat-Zhas

*** Abdulla - Xhelil Abdulla (a) 25/09/1991, Tetovo (North Macedonia) (b) 1,90 (c) D - central defense (d) Gostivar (e) FC Shkupi, Renova, FC Llapi, Renova, Shkëndija, Euromilk GL, MSV Duisburg, De Graafschap, Shkëndija

*** Abdullaev - Abdulla Abdullaev (Абдуллаєв Абдулла Шахюсіфович) (a) 12/02/2002, Odesa (Ukraine) (b) 1,84 (c) F - left winger (d) Metalist 1925 Kharkiv (e) Zorya Lugansk, Shakhtar II

*** Abdullahi - Ahmed Abdullahi (a) 19/06/2004, ¿? (Nigeria) (b) - (c) F (d) Jong KAA Gent (e) HB Abuja

*** Abdullahi - Fawaz Abdullahi (Olamide Fawaz Abdullahi) (a) 04/05/2003, Kano (Nigeria) (b) 1,87 (c) M - central midfielder (d) APOEL FC (e) Doxa Katokopias

*** Abdullahi - Suleiman Abdullahi (a) 10/12/1996, Kaduna (Nigeria) (b) 1,85 (c) F - center forward (d) IFK Göteborg (e) Union Berlin, Eintracht Braunschweig, Union Berlin, Eintracht Braunschweig, Union Berlin, Eintracht Braunschweig, Viking, Kanemi Warriors

*** Abdullayev - Araz Abdullayev (Araz Abdulla oğlu Abdullayev) (a) 18/04/1992, Baku (Azerbaijan) (b) 1,80 (c) F - right winger (d) - (e) Sumqayit, Ethnikos, Boluspor, Qarabag FK, FK Qabala, Anorthosis, FK Qabala, Neftchi Baku, Panionios, Everton Reserves, Neftchi Baku, Everton Reserves, Neftchi Baku

*** Abdullayev - Elshan Abdullayev (Elşən Mübariz oğlu Abdullayev) (a) 05/02/1994, Sumqayit (Azerbaijan) (b) 1,70 (c) F (d) - (e) Sumqayit, FK Sabail, Sabah FK, Qarabag FK, Zira FK, Qarabag FK, Neftchi Baku, Sumqayit, Neftchi Baku

*** Abdullayev - Samir Abdullayev (Samir Abbas oğlu Abdullayev) (a) 24/04/2002, ¿? (Azerbaijan) (b) - (c) M - right midfielder (d) FK Sabail (e) Shamakhi, FC Shamakhi 2

*** Abdullazada - Rüfat Abdullazada (Rüfət Şahin oğlu Abdullazadə) (a) 17/01/2001, Sumqayit (Azerbaijan) (b) 1,78 (c) F - right winger (d) FK Sabail (e) Sumqayit

*** Abdullazada - Sabuhi Abdullazada (Səbuhi Mübariz oğlu Abdullazadə) (a) 18/12/2001, ¿? (Azerbaijan) (b) 1,75 (c) M - central midfielder (d) Sumqayit PFK (e) -

*** Abdulmajeed - Sagir Abdulmajeed (Sagir Abdulmajeed) (a) 30/08/2002, Kaduna (Nigeria) (b) - (c) F - right winger (d) - (e) Belshina, FC Saksan

*** Abdulrazak - Ishaq Abdulrazak (a) 05/05/2002, ¿? (Nigeria) (b) 1,65 (c) M - right midfielder (d) BK Häcken (e) RSC Anderlecht, Norrköping

*** Abdumannopov - Doniyor Abdumannopov (Дониёр Бахтиёржон оглы Абдуманнопов) (a) 12/10/2000, Marhamat (Uzbekistan) (b) - (c) F - right winger (d) Navbahor Namangan (e) Bunyodkor, Navbahor, Sogdiana, Energetik-BGU, FK Andijon, FK Andijon II, Energetik-BGU

*** Abdumazhidov - Odil Abdumazhidov (Одил Абдумажидов) (a) 01/06/2001, Andijon (Uzbekistan) (b) 1,85 (c) D - central defense (d) FC Olympic (e) Metallurg Bk., Ordabasy, Metallurg Bk., FK Andijon

*** Abdurahimi - Besart Abdurahimi (a) 31/07/1990, Zagreb (Yugoslavia, now in Croatia) (b) 1,75 (c) F - right winger (d) Apollon Limassol (e) Akritas Chlor., Pafos FC, Akritas Chlor., NK Rudes, NK Bravo, FC Hermannstadt, FK Partizani, Shkëndija, KSC Lokeren, Cerezo Osaka, KSC Lokeren, FC Astana, KSC Lokeren, NK Zagreb, Hapoel Tel Aviv, NK Zagreb

*** Abdurahmanov - Zeynaddin Abdurahmanov (Zeynəddin Dəyanət oğlu Abdurahmanov) (a) 23/09/2002, Qusar (Azerbaijan) (b) 1,78 (c) M - central midfielder (d) FK Sabail 2 (e) -

*** Abdurakhmanov - Odilzhon Abdurakhmanov (Одилжон Алишерович Абдурахманов) (a) 18/03/1996, ¿? (Azerbaijan) (b) 1,85 (c) M - central midfielder (d) FK Maktaaral (e) Bunyodkor, Alay Osh, Aldiyer

*** Abdurakhmonov - Shokhrukh Abdurakhmonov (Шохрух Комил оглы Абдурахмонов) (a) 08/03/1999, Akkurgan (Uzbekistan) (b) - (c) M - attacking midfielder (d) Bunyodkor Tashkent (e) Energetik-BGU, Dinamo, Energetik-BGU, Dinamo, Pakhtakor, Dinamo, Pakhtakor

*** Abdusalamov - Magomedkhabib Abdusalamov (Абдусаламов Магомедхабиб Магомедович) (a) 01/05/2003, Makhachkala (Russia) (b) 1,83 (c) F - center forward (d) Pafos FC (e) Akritas Chlor., Pafos FC, Rodina Moskva

*** Abed - Ahmed Abed (אחמד עאבד) (a) 30/03/1990, Nazareth (Israel) (b) 1,84 (c) F - right winger (d) Maccabi Bnei Reineh (e) M. Ahi Nazareth, Kiryat Shmona, Hapoel Tel Aviv, Giresunspor, Kiryat Shmona, M. Ahi Nazareth

*** Abedini - Eris Abedini (a) 29/08/1998, Sorengo (Switzerland) (b) 1,90 (c) M - pivot (d) Neuchâtel Xamax FCS (e) FC Winterthur, FC Chiasso, Recreativo Granada, FC Lugano, FC Wil 1900, FC Lugano, FC Winterthur, FC Lugano, FC Chiasso, FC Lugano, FC Chiasso

*** Abeid - Aly Abeid (Yacoub Aly Abeid) (a) 11/12/1997, Riyadh (Saudi Arabia) (b) 1,74 (c) D - left back (d) UTA Arad (e) Valenciennes FC, At. Levante, Alcorcón, At. Levante, ASAC Concorde

*** Abela - Deacon Abela (a) 23/09/2004, ¿? (Malta) (b) - (c) D - central defense (d) Swieqi United FC (e) Valletta, FC Swieqi Utd., Valletta

*** Abels - Dirk Abels (a) 13/06/1997, Udenhout (Netherlands) (b) 1,86 (c) D - right back (d) Grasshopper Club Zürich (e) Sparta Rotterdam

*** Abena - Myenty Abena (Leo Myenty Janna Abena) (a) 12/12/1994, Paramaribo (Surinam) (b) 1,91 (c) D - central defense (d) Ferencváros TC (e) Slovan Bratislava, Spartak Trnava, De Graafschap

*** Abergel - Laurent Abergel (a) 01/02/1993, Marseille (France) (b) 1,70 (c) M - pivot (d) FC Lorient (e) AS Nancy, AC Ajaccio, Ol. Marseille, AC Ajaccio, Ol. Marseille, Ol. Marseille B

*** Abibi - Alessio Abibi (a) 04/12/1996, Umbertide (Italy) (b) 1,96 (c) G (d) AC Perugia Calcio (e) Dundalk FC, KS Kastrioti, Cavese, Avellino, KF Tirana, CD Eldense, AltoVicentino, Gavorrano, Perugia

*** Abid - Adnane Abid (a) 23/08/2003, Verviers (Belgium) (b) 1,65 (c) F - right winger (d) Jong Genk (e) KRC Genk

*** Abiken - Aybol Abiken (Айбол Ерболатұлы Әбікен) (a) 01/06/1996, Almaty (Kazakhstan) (b) 1,79 (c) M - pivot (d) Sperre (e) Kairat Almaty, FK Aksu, Kairat Almaty, Kairat II

*** Abildgaard - Oliver Abildgaard (Oliver Abildgaard Nielsen) (a) 10/06/1996, Aalborg (Denmark) (b) 1,92 (c) M - pivot (d) Como 1907 (e) Rubin Kazan, Hellas Verona, Rubin Kazan, Celtic FC, Rubin Kazan, Aalborg BK, Rubin Kazan, Aalborg BK

*** Abilgazy - Sultan Abilgazy (Абилгазы Султан) (a) 22/02/1997, Kokshetau (Kazakhstan) (b) 1,80 (c) D - central defense (d) Yelimay Semey (e) FK Turan, Tobol Kostanay, Okzhetpes, Okzhetpes II, Okzhetpes, Okzhetpes II

*** Abilmazhinov - Dzhokhangir Abilmazhinov (Абильмажинов Джохангир Ерболович) (a) 10/06/2000, Karaganda (Kazakhstan) (b) 1,72 (c) M - central midfielder (d) Shakhter-Bulat (e) -

*** Abilov - Elchan Abilov (Elcan Əbilov) (a) 09/09/2004, ¿? (Azerbaijan) (b) 1,82 (c) M - attacking midfielder (d) Neftchi 2 Baku (e) -

*** Ablade - Terry Ablade (a) 12/10/2001, Accra (Ghana) (b) - (c) F - center forward (d) - (e) AFC Wimbledon, FC Jazz

*** Abline - Matthis Abline (a) 28/03/2003, Angers (France) (b) 1,82 (c) F - center forward (d) Stade Rennais FC (e) AJ Auxerre, Stade Rennes, Le Havre AC, Stade Rennes, Stade Rennes B

*** Abner - Abner (Abner Vinícius da Silva Santos) (a) 27/05/2000, Presidente Prudente (Brazil) (b) 1,81 (c) D - left back (d) Real Betis Balompié (e) Athletico-PR, Ponte Preta

*** Abner - Douglas Abner (Douglas Abner Almeida dos Santos) (a) 30/01/1996, Brasília (Brazil) (b) 1,75 (c) M - attacking midfielder (d) - (e) UE Santa Coloma, Castelo Branco, Santarém, SC Ideal, Linköping City, Cesarense, Boavista B, Boavista, Salgueiros, Boavista, Académico Viseu, Boavista

*** Aboosah - Jacob Aboosah (a) 16/03/2002, Accra (Ghana) (b) - (c) M (d) EurAfrica FC (e) HNK Rijeka, EurAfrica FC

*** Aboubakar - Karim Aboubakar (a) 30/07/1995, Accra (Ghana) (b) 1,78 (c) F - center forward (d) - (e) Sumqayit, Bnei Yehuda, Hapoel Acre, Yeclano, Algeciras CF, CD Don Benito, UP Plasencia, CP Valdivia, CD Don Benito, UB Conquense, AD Alcorcón B, Medeama

*** Aboubakar - Vincent Aboubakar (Vincent Paté Aboubakar) (a) 22/01/1992, Garoua (Cameroon) (b) 1,84 (c) F - center forward (d) Besiktas JK (e) Al-Nassr, Besiktas, FC Porto, Besiktas, FC Porto, FC Lorient, Valenciennes FC, Coton Sport FC

*** Aboukhlal - Zakaria Aboukhlal (a) 18/02/2000, Rotterdam (Netherlands) (b) 1,79 (c) F - right winger (d) Toulouse FC (e) AZ Alkmaar

*** Abouzziane - Sami Abouzziane (a) 16/09/2001, ¿? (Morocco) (b) - (c) F - left winger (d) - (e) La Fiorita, ACD Torconca, La Fiorita, Fiorentino, United Riccione

*** Abraham - Morice Abraham (Morice Michael Abraham) (a) 13/08/2003, Nyamagana (Tanzania) (b) - (c) M - attacking midfielder (d) FK Spartak Subotica (e) -

*** Abraham - Paulos Abraham (a) 16/07/2002, Solna (Sweden) (b) 1,78 (c) F - left winger (d) FC Groningen (e) AIK, FC Groningen, AIK, Brommapojkarna

*** Abraham - Tammy Abraham (Kevin Oghenetega Tamaraebi Bakumo-Abraham) (a) 02/10/1997, Camberwell-London (England) (b) 1,94 (c) F - center forward (d) AS Roma (e) Chelsea, Aston Villa, Chelsea, Swansea City, Chelsea, Bristol City

*** Abrahamsson - Peter Abrahamsson (Peter Anders Abrahamsson) (a) 18/07/1988, Jörlanda (Sweden) (b) 1,90 (c) G (d) BK Häcken (e) Örgryte, Vallens IF

*** Abrahamyan - Gor Abrahamyan (Գոռ Աբրահամյան) (a) 07/12/2005, Vagharshapat (Armenia) (b) 1,69 (c) M - attacking midfielder (d) FC Noah Yerevan (e) -

*** Abrahamyan - Pargev Abrahamyan (Պարգեւ Աբրահամյան) (a) 26/09/1999, ¿? (Armenia) (b) 1,69 (c) D - right back (d) FC Noah Erewan II (e) Ararat II, Gandzasar, FC Sevan

*** Abrahamyan - Ruben Abrahamyan (Ռուբեն Աբրահամյան) (a) 07/08/2003, ¿? (Armenia) (b) 1,79 (c) D - left back (d) BKMA Yerevan (e) BKMA Yerevan II, Urartu II

*** Abramov - Gilad Abramov (אברמוב גלעד) (a) 30/03/2000, Hadera (Israel) (b) 1,79 (c) M - central midfielder (d) FK Qabala (e) Hapoel Hadera

*** Abramov - Yegor Abramov (Абрамов Єгор Олександрович) (a) 06/03/2006, ¿? (Ukraine) (b) 1,78 (c) D - left back (d) Metalist Kharkiv (e) -

*** Abramovich - Aleksandr Abramovich (Абрамович Александр Александрович) (a) 18/11/2001, ¿? (Belarus) (b) - (c) G (d) Falko Dzerzhinsk Region (e) Zhodino II

*** Abramovich - Anton Abramovich (Абрамович Антон Дмитриевич) (a) 27/04/1999, Minsk (Belarus) (b) 1,75 (c) M - left midfielder (d) - (e) Dzerzhinsk, BATE II, Dzerzhinsk, BATE II

*** Abramovich - Evgeniy Abramovich (Абрамович Евгений Александрович) (a) 17/09/1995, Borisov (Belarus) (b) 1,84 (c) G (d) Torpedo-BelAZ Zhodino (e) Dzerzhinsk, Torpedo Zhodino, Dzerzhinsk, Torpedo Zhodino, Smolevichi, Torpedo Zhodino, Zhodino II

*** Abramowicz - Dawid Abramowicz (a) 16/05/1991, Brzeg Dolny (Poland) (b) 1,86 (c) D - left back (d) Radomiak Radom (e) Wisla Kraków, Radomiak, GKS Tychy, GKS Katowice, P. Niepolomice, Nieciecza, Skra Czestochowa, Wisła Płock, Śląsk Wroclaw, Chojniczanka, Śląsk Wroclaw, Olimpia Grudz., Śląsk Wroclaw, Slask Wroclaw II, KP Brzeg Dolny

*** Abramowicz - Mateusz Abramowicz (a) 08/11/1992, Brzeg Dolny (Poland) (b) 1,86 (c) G (d) Miedź Legnica (e) Stadtallendorf, Chrobry Glogow, GKS Katowice, Śląsk Wroclaw, MKS Kluczbork, Nieciecza, MKS Kluczbork, Czarni Zagan, KP Brzeg Dolny

*** Abramowicz - Slawomir Abramowicz (Sławomir Abramowicz) (a) 09/06/2004, Warszawa (Poland) (b) 1,89 (c) G (d) Jagiellonia Białystok (e) Polonia, UKS Warszawa

*** Abrashi - Amir Abrashi (Amir Malush Abrashi) (a) 27/03/1990, Bischofszell (Switzerland) (b) 1,72 (c) M - pivot (d) Grasshopper Club Zürich (e) SC Freiburg, FC Basel, SC Freiburg, Grasshoppers, FC Winterthur, Grasshoppers, FC Winterthur

*** Abreu - Artur Abreu (Artur Abreu Pereira) (a) 11/08/1994, Niederkorn (Luxembourg) (b) 1,82 (c) F - left winger (d) Union Titus Petange (e) Vitória Guimarães B, Union Titus Petange, Differdange 03, Luna Oberkorn, Differdange 03
*** Abrgil - Ravid Abrgil (Ravid Hay Abergel) (a) 20/11/2003, ¿? (Israel) (b) - (c) F (d) - (e) FC Ashdod
*** Absalom - Kelland Absalom (Kelland Ellis Absalom) (a) 05/01/1998, ¿? (Wales) (b) - (c) G (d) Bala Town (e) Penybont, Barry Town, Carmarthen, Merthyr Town, Haverfordwest, Östersund, Ytterhogdals IK
*** Abu Abaid - Iyad Abu Abaid (עביד אבו איאד) (a) 31/12/1994, Meisar (Israel) (b) 1,83 (c) D - central defense (d) Hapoel Beer Sheva (e) Hapoel Tel Aviv, Kiryat Shmona, Maccabi Haifa, Hapoel Tel Aviv, Maccabi Netanya
*** Abu Akel - Fares Abu Akel (עקל אבו פראס) (a) 08/02/1997, Umm al-Fahm (Israel) (b) 1,77 (c) M - pivot (d) FK Qabala (e) FC Ashdod, Hapoel Ikhsal, H. Umm al-Fahm
*** Abu Fani - Mohammed Abu Fani (פאני אבו מוחמד) (a) 27/04/1998, Kafr-Qara (Israel) (b) 1,64 (c) M - central midfielder (d) Ferencváros TC (e) Maccabi Haifa, Hapoel Hadera, Maccabi Haifa, Hapoel Hadera, Maccabi Haifa, H. Ramat Gan, Maccabi Haifa
*** Abu Hanna - Joel Abu Hanna (חנא אבו ואל'ג) (a) 22/01/1998, Troisdorf (Germany) (b) 1,84 (c) D - central defense (d) Maccabi Netanya (e) Legia Warszawa, Lechia Gdánsk, Legia Warszawa, Zorya Lugansk, 1.FC Magdeburg, Fortuna Köln, 1.FC Magdeburg, 1.FC Kaiserslautern, Bayer Leverkusen
*** Abu Nil - Mohammed Abu Nil (ניל אבו מוחמד) (a) 03/05/2001, ¿? (Israel) (b) - (c) G (d) Ihud Bnei Sakhnin (e) M. Bnei Reineh, Bnei Sakhnin
*** Abu Rumi - Mohamad Abu Rumi (רומי אבו מוחמד) (a) 01/03/2004, Tamra (Israel) (b) 1,78 (c) M - attacking midfielder (d) Ironi Kiryat Shmona (e) -
*** Abu Yunes - Nasim Abu Yunes (יונס אבו נסים) (a) 31/05/2000, ¿? (Israel) (b) 1,86 (c) D - central defense (d) Ihud Bnei Sakhnin (e) Hapoel Kaukab, Bnei Sakhnin, Hapoel Bueine, Bnei Sakhnin, H. Kfar Kana, Bnei Sakhnin
*** Abubakar - Asumah Abubakar (Asumah Abubakar-Ankra) (a) 10/05/1997, Kumasi (Ghana) (b) 1,83 (c) F - center forward (d) FC Lucerna (e) FC Lugano, SC Kriens, MVV Maastricht, Willem II
*** Abubakar - Haruna Abubakar (a) 26/09/2000, ¿? (Ghana) (b) - (c) D - central defense (d) Atlantis FC (e) Mikkelin, HJK Klubi 04, King Faisal
*** Abubakar - Rashid Abubakar (Abdul Rashid Abubakar) (a) 16/03/2000, ¿? (Ghana) (b) 1,78 (c) M - central midfielder (d) FK Loznica (e) FK Sarajevo, Accra Lions, HLJ Ice City, Accra Lions
*** Abubakar - Sadick Abubakar (a) 02/02/1998, Accra (Ghana) (b) - (c) D - central defense (d) FK Radnik Surdulica (e) Radnicki Srem, Smederevo 1924, J-Södra IF, Nkz Warriors SC
*** Abubakari - Malik Abubakari (Abdul Malik Abubakari) (a) 10/05/2000, Tamale (Ghana) (b) 1,85 (c) F - center forward (d) Slovan Bratislava (e) Slovan Bratislava, Malmö FF, HJK Helsinki, Malmö FF, Moreirense, Casa Pia, Moreirense, Fafe, Moreirense, Charity Stars
*** Abubakari - Mohammed Abubakari (a) 15/02/1986, Kumasi (Ghana) (b) 1,78 (c) M - pivot (d) - (e) IFK Mariehamn, Helsingborgs IF, Häcken, Åtvidabergs FF, Doxa Dramas, AE Larisa, PAOK, Panserraikos, PAOK, APO Levadiakos, PAOK, Panserraikos, Feyenoord, Feyenoord Ghana
*** Abuladze - Mate Abuladze (მათე აბულაძე) (a) 30/06/2000, ¿? (Georgia) (b) - (c) D - central defense (d) FC Samtredia (e) Torpedo Kutaisi
*** Aburjania - Giorgi Aburjania (გიორგი აბურჯანია) (a) 02/01/1995, Tbilisi (Georgia) (b) 1,86 (c) M - pivot (d) Hatayspor (e) Gil Vicente, FC Cartagena, Real

Oviedo, Sevilla FC, FC Twente, Sevilla FC, CD Lugo, Sevilla FC, Gimnàstic, Anorthosis, FC Locomotive, FC Dila, Olympic Tbilisi, Metalurgi R., Metallurgist II
*** Abyshov - Ruslan Abyshov (Ruslan İbrahim oğlu Abışov) (a) 10/10/1987, Baku (Soviet Union, now in Azerbaijan) (b) 1,87 (c) D - central defense (d) - (e) Zira FK, Sabah FK, Neftchi Baku, Inter Baku, FK Qabala, Xäzär Länkäran, Rubin Kazan, FK Qabala, Rubin Kazan, Xäzär Länkäran, Neftchi Baku
*** Abzalov - Shokhan Abzalov (Абзалов Шохан) (a) 11/09/1993, Kyzylorda (Kazakhstan) (b) 1,82 (c) F - left winger (d) Okzhetpes Kokshetau (e) FK Turan, Kaysar, Baikonur
*** Abzhandadze - Bakar Abzhandadze (ბაქარ აბჟანდაძე) (a) 13/02/2003, ¿? (Georgia) (b) - (c) D (d) FC Borjomi (e) Locomotive II
*** Acapandié - Mathieu Acapandié (a) 14/12/2004, Saint-Pierre (Reunion) (b) 1,82 (c) D - right back (d) FC Nantes B (e) -
*** Accam - David Accam (a) 28/09/1990, Accra (Ghana) (b) 1,74 (c) F - right winger (d) - (e) FC Inter, Nashville, Hammarby IF, Nashville, Columbus Crew, Philadelphia, Chicago, Helsingborgs IF, Östersund, Evesham, Ledbury Town, Right to Dream
*** Accarino - Luca Accarino (a) 19/05/2004, ¿? (Malta) (b) - (c) M - central midfielder (d) Floriana FC (e) -
*** Accosta - Nicolò Accosta (a) 31/08/2004, Roma (Italy) (b) 1,85 (c) D - central defense (d) FC Fiorentino (e) -
*** Acella - Christian Acella (a) 07/07/2002, Milano (Italy) (b) - (c) M - central midfielder (d) US Cremonese (e) Giana Erminio, Cremonese
*** Acerbi - Francesco Acerbi (a) 10/02/1988, Vizzolo Pedrabissi (Italy) (b) 1,92 (c) D - central defense (d) Internazionale Milano (e) Lazio, Internazionale Milano, Lazio, Sassuolo, Genoa, Chievo Verona, Genoa, AC Milan, Chievo Verona, Genoa, Reggina, Pavia
*** Aceves - Álvaro Aceves (Álvaro Aceves Catalina) (a) 26/07/2003, Valladolid (Spain) (b) 1,90 (c) G (d) Real Valladolid Promesas (e) -
*** Achahbar - Anass Achahbar (أنس أشهبار) (a) 13/01/1994, Den Haag (Netherlands) (b) 1,73 (c) M - attacking midfielder (d) - (e) Sepsi OSK, FC Dordrecht, PEC Zwolle, NEC Nijmegen, PEC Zwolle, Feyenoord, Arminia Bielefeld, Feyenoord
*** Acheampong - Christopher Acheampong (a) 31/03/2000, ¿? (Ghana) (b) 1,70 (c) D - right back (d) CSKA 1948 II (e) Accra Lions
*** Acheampong - Geoffrey Acheampong (Geoffrey Edwin Kofi Acheampong) (a) 28/01/1997, Sunyani (Ghana) (b) 1,80 (c) M (d) Sliema Wanderers (e) Mosta FC, RoPS, Elmina Sharks, AC Kajaani, LA Galaxy II, SC Bastia, UCSB Gauchos, Santa Barbara, Right to Dream
*** Achi - Mohamed Achi (Mohamed Achi Bouakline) (a) 16/01/2002, Bondy (France) (b) 1,81 (c) M - central midfielder (d) FC Nantes (e) Paris 13 At., FC Nantes, FC Nantes B
*** Achim - Cosmin Achim (Cosmin Florin Achim) (a) 19/09/1995, Drăgăneşti-Olt (Romania) (b) 1,88 (c) D - central defense (d) - (e) Petrolul, FC Voluntari, Energeticianul, FC Voluntari, Academia Hagi, AF Gică Popescu
*** Achim - Florin Achim (Florin Vasile Achim) (a) 16/07/1991, Baia Mare (Romania) (b) 1,78 (c) D - right back (d) Concordia Chiajna (e) FCSB, Academica Clinceni, Olimpia SM, Ramat haSharon, Bregalnica Stip, H. Petah Tikva, Universitatea Cluj, Sageata Navodar, FC Maramures, Astra II, FC Maramures, Minaur
*** Achim - Vlad Achim (Vlad Alexandru Achim) (a) 07/04/1989, Constanţa (Romania) (b) 1,82 (c) M - pivot (d) FC U Craiova 1948 (e) FC Dinamo, FC Viitorul, FCSB, FC Botosani, FCSB, FC Voluntari, FC Viitorul, Ceahlăul, Ceahlaul II

*** Achinov - Egor Achinov (Егор Ачинов) (a) 11/08/2004, ¿? (Russia) (b) 1,88 (c) G (d) Shirak Gyumri C.F. (e) FDC Vista

*** Achkov - Martin Achkov (Мартин Христов Ачков) (a) 10/07/1999, Sofia (Bulgaria) (b) 1,86 (c) D - left back (d) - (e) Septemvri Sofia, Slavia Sofia, Spartak Varna, Slavia Sofia

*** Achol - Manyumow Achol (a) 10/12/2000, Wellington (New Zealand) (b) 1,93 (c) M - pivot (d) FK Auda (e) W. Phoenix Reserves, Lower Hutt City, Hawke's Bay, Kingston City, Eauze FC, Wellington Ol., W. Phoenix Reserves, Wellington Ol.

*** Achouri - Elias Achouri (Mohamed Elias Achouri) (a) 10/02/1999, Saint-Denis (France) (b) 1,77 (c) F - right winger (d) FC Copenhague (e) Viborg FF, Estoril Praia, Trofense, Estoril Praia, Vitória Guimarães B

*** Acimovic - Milos Acimovic (Miloš Aćimović) (a) 06/07/1997, Trebinje (Bosnia and Herzegovina) (b) 1,83 (c) F - left winger (d) FK Leotar Trebinje (e) FK Krupa, Zrinjski Mostar, SV Lafnitz, Zrinjski Mostar, Leotar Trebinje

*** Acka - Donaldo Acka (Ntonalnto Atska, Donaldo Açka) (a) 17/09/1997, Filippiada (Greece) (b) 1,79 (c) M - pivot (d) - (e) FC Haka, Universitatea Cluj, ACSM Poli Iasi, FC Luftëtari, AE Karaiskakis, Eth. Filippiada, AO Simantron

*** Acka - Stephane Acka (a) 11/10/1990, Abidjan (Ivory Coast) (b) 1,84 (c) D - central defense (d) Zira FK (e) Ness Ziona, Kiryat Shmona, CS U Craiova, BB Erzurumspor, CS U Craiova, FC U Craiova, Belluno, Legnago

*** Ackah - Yaw Ackah (a) 01/06/1999, Accra (Ghana) (b) 1,69 (c) M - pivot (d) Kayserispor (e) A. Keciörengücü, Kayserispor, BB Erzurumspor, Kayserispor, Boavista, Boavista B

*** Ackovski - Kristijan Ackovski (Кристијан Ацковски) (a) 15/02/1998, Skopje (North Macedonia) (b) 1,80 (c) M - pivot (d) FC Shkupi (e) Bregalnica Stip, Rabotnicki, Borec Veles, Rabotnicki

*** Acolatse - Elton Acolatse (Elton-Ofoi Acolatse) (a) 25/07/1995, Amsterdam (Netherlands) (b) 1,84 (c) F - left winger (d) Diósgyőri VTK (e) FC Ashdod, H. Beer Sheva, Bursaspor, H. Beer Sheva, Sint-Truiden, H. Beer Sheva, Sint-Truiden, KV Brugge, Sint-Truiden, KV Brugge, KVC Westerlo, Ajax B

*** Acosta - Diego Acosta (Diego Emmanuel Acosta Curtido) (a) 12/11/2002, Minga Guazú (Paraguay) (b) 1,75 (c) F - center forward (d) Sportivo Luqueño (e) Orenburg, KamAZ

*** Acosta - Federico Acosta (a) 30/03/1996, Buenos Aires (Argentina) (b) 1,85 (c) D - central defense (d) - (e) AP Brera, Baveno, Acc. Borgomanero, Palmese, Boca Gibraltar, Villa Dálmine

*** Acquah - Benjamin Acquah (a) 29/12/2000, Amasaman (Ghana) (b) 1,80 (c) M - central midfielder (d) Helsingborgs IF (e) Ebusua Dwarfs, Helsingborgs IF, Ebusua Dwarfs

*** Acquarelli - Maicol Acquarelli (a) 21/09/1993, ¿? (San Marino) (b) - (c) D - central defense (d) AC Juvenes-Dogana (e) Juvenes-Dogana, Cailungo, Tre Fiori, San Giovanni

*** Acuña - Marcos Acuña (Marcos Javier Acuña) (a) 28/10/1991, Zapala (Argentina) (b) 1,72 (c) D - left back (d) Sevilla FC (e) Sporting Lisboa, Racing, Ferro

*** Adair - Harry Adair (a) 22/01/2002, ¿? (Northern Ireland) (b) - (c) M - central midfielder (d) - (e) Larne FC, Ballyclare, Larne FC, Loughgall FC

*** Adakhadzhiev - Adam Adakhadzhiev (Адахаджиев Адам Андиевич) (a) 23/11/1998, Omsk (Russia) (b) 1,76 (c) M - central midfielder (d) FC Khan Tengri (e) Kairat Almaty, Zhetysu, Kairat Almaty, Kairat-Zhas, Kairat II

*** Adalgeirsson - Finnbogi Laxdal Adalgeirsson (Finnbogi Laxdal Aðalgeirsson) (a) 14/12/2002, ¿? (Iceland) (b) - (c) D - left back (d) Haukar Hafnarfjördur (e) Haukar, ÍA Akranes, Kári, ÍA Akranes, Kári

*** Adalsteinsson - Arnar Daniel Adalsteinsson (Arnar Daníel Aðalsteinsson) (a) 14/03/2004, ¿? (Iceland) (b) - (c) D - central defense (d) ÍF Grótta (e) Breidablik, Grótta, Breidablik, Augnablik

*** Adalsteinsson - Arnór Dadi Adalsteinsson (Arnór Daði Aðalsteinsson) (a) 06/03/1997, Reykjavík (Iceland) (b) 1,88 (c) D - left back (d) Fram Reykjavík (e) Furman Paladins, Fram Reykjavík, Furman Paladins, Fram Reykjavík, Furman Paladins, Fram Reykjavík, Furman Paladins, Fram Reykjavík

*** Adalsteinsson - Arnór Sveinn Adalsteinsson (Arnór Sveinn Aðalsteinsson) (a) 26/01/1986, Reykjavík (Iceland) (b) 1,80 (c) D - central defense (d) Breidablik Kópavogur (e) KR Reykjavík, Breidablik, Hønefoss, Breidablik, Hønefoss, Breidablik

*** Adalsteinsson - Aron Kári Adalsteinsson (Aron Kári Aðalsteinsson) (a) 09/07/1999, ¿? (Iceland) (b) 1,90 (c) D - central defense (d) Fram Reykjavík (e) Breidablik, Fram Reykjavík, Breidablik, HK Kópavogs, Breidablik, Keflavík, Breidablik, ÍR, Breidablik

*** Adalsteinsson - Bjarki Adalsteinsson (Bjarki Aðalsteinsson) (a) 10/10/1991, ¿? (Iceland) (b) 1,94 (c) D - central defense (d) UMF Grindavík (e) Leiknir, Thór, Selfoss, Breidablik, Selfoss, Breidablik, Reynir S., Breidablik, Augnablik, Breidablik

*** Adalsteinsson - Bjarni Adalsteinsson (Bjarni Aðalsteinsson) (a) 01/09/1999, ¿? (Iceland) (b) - (c) M - pivot (d) KA Akureyri (e) Magni, KA Akureyri, Magni, KA Akureyri, Dalvík/Reynir

*** Adalsteinsson - Elfar Árni Adalsteinsson (Elfar Árni Aðalsteinsson) (a) 12/08/1990, ¿? (Iceland) (b) 1,87 (c) F - center forward (d) KA Akureyri (e) Breidablik

*** Adalsteinsson - Hákon Atli Adalsteinsson (Hákon Atli Aðalsteinsson) (a) 20/08/2004, ¿? (Iceland) (b) - (c) M (d) Völsungur ÍF (e) KA Akureyri, Hamrarnir, KA Akureyri

*** Adam - David Adam (a) 15/11/1993, ¿? (Slovenia) (b) - (c) G (d) - (e) Koper, Tabor Sezana, PO Xylotymbou, Tabor Sezana, NK Radomlje, Koper, NK Dekani, Koper, NK Ankaran, Koper

*** Adamadze - Guram Adamadze (გურამ ადამაძე) (a) 31/08/1988, Kutaisi (Soviet Union, now in Georgia) (b) 1,85 (c) D - central defense (d) Kolkheti Khobi (e) Guria, Sioni Bolnisi, Torpedo Kutaisi, Dinamo Batumi, Torpedo Kutaisi, Shukura, Torpedo Kutaisi, FC Dila, Torpedo Kutaisi, WIT Georgia

*** Adambaev - Adi Adambaev (Адамбаев Ади Махамбетулы) (a) 04/04/2001, ¿? (Kazakhstan) (b) 1,85 (c) D - right back (d) FK Atyrau (e) FK Ekibastuz, Shakhter-Bulat, ZSKA Almaty

*** Adamchik - Taisir Adamchik (Адамчик Тайсир Ахмедович) (a) 11/05/2002, Zhirovichi (Belarus) (b) 1,82 (c) M - pivot (d) FK Slonim 2017 (e) Slonim City, FK Minsk, FK Minsk II, Slonim, FK Minsk II

*** Adami Martins - Adam Adami Martins (Adam Adami Martins) (a) 24/06/1992, Rio de Janeiro (Brazil) (b) - (c) M - pivot (d) CBR Carli Pietracuta (e) Tre Fiori, Pennarossa, BX Brussels, Audax-RJ, Artsul

*** Adamonis - Marius Adamonis (a) 13/05/1997, Panevezys (Lithuania) (b) 1,91 (c) G (d) SS Lazio (e) Salernitana, Lazio, Sicula Leonzio, Lazio, Catanzaro, Lazio, Casertana, Lazio, Salernitana, Lazio, Atlantas, Bournemouth, Atlantas

*** Adamov - Arsen Adamov (Адамов Арсен Русланович) (a) 20/10/1999, Nizhniy Tagil, Ekaterinburg Region (Russia) (b) 1,80 (c) D - right back (d) FK Orenburg (e) Orenburg, Zenit, Ural, Akhmat Grozny, Akhmat II

*** Adamov - Denis Adamov (Адамов Денис Андреевич) (a) 20/02/1998, Uljanovsk (Russia) (b) 1,96 (c) G (d) Zenit de San Petersburgo (e) Sochi, Krasnodar-2, Krasnodar II

*** Adamovic - Milos Adamovic (Милош Адамовић) (a) 19/06/1988, Šabac (Yugoslavia, now in Serbia) (b) 1,77 (c) M - pivot (d) FK Javor-Matis Ivanjica (e) Macva, Radnik, Vasas FC, Mladost, Ravan Baku, FC Sheriff, Sunkar Kaskelen, FC Sheriff, Taraz, FC Sheriff, Polonia, FC Sheriff, OFK Beograd

*** Adamovic - Nenad Adamovic (Ненад Адамовић) (a) 12/01/1989, Topola (Yugoslavia, now in Serbia) (b) 1,70 (c) M - attacking midfielder (d) FK Mladost Lucani (e) Neman Grodno, Taraz, Zhetysu, Vitebsk, Čukarički, M. Petah Tikva, Dinamo Minsk, Hajduk 1912, Smederevo 1924, Metalac, FK Partizan, Teleoptik, FK Partizan

*** Adams - Akor Adams (Akor Jerome Adams) (a) 29/01/2000, Kogi (Nigeria) (b) 1,90 (c) F - center forward (d) Montpellier HSC (e) Lillestrøm, Sogndal, Jamba F.A., Sogndal, Jamba F.A.

*** Adams - Ché Adams (Ché Zach Everton Fred Adams) (a) 13/07/1996, Leicester (England) (b) 1,79 (c) F - center forward (d) Southampton FC (e) Birmingham City, Sheffield Utd., Ilkeston, Oadby Town

*** Adams - Joe Adams (Joseph Anthony Adams) (a) 13/02/2001, Bolton (England) (b) 1,76 (c) M - attacking midfielder (d) Southport FC (e) Dundalk FC, Brentford B, Grimsby Town, Brentford B, Bury

*** Adams - Kasim Adams (Kasim Adams Nuhu) (a) 22/06/1995, Accra (Ghana) (b) 1,90 (c) D - central defense (d) TSG 1899 Hoffenheim (e) FC Basel, Hoffenheim, Fortuna Düsseldorf, Hoffenheim, BSC Young Boys, RCD Mallorca, BSC Young Boys, RCD Mallorca, RCD Mallorca B, Medeama

*** Adams - Mohammed Adams (a) 11/11/2000, ¿? (Ghana) (b) 1,92 (c) D - central defense (d) SC Covilhã (e) FC Honka, SC Covilhã, FC Honka, RoPS, FC Honka, Okyeman FC, Liberty Prof., Okyeman FC

*** Adams - Olubi Adams (Olubi Sirach Adams) (a) 04/01/2003, ¿? (Nigeria) (b) 1,78 (c) F - right winger (d) - (e) Zalgiris

*** Adams - Tyler Adams (Tyler Shaan Adams) (a) 14/02/1999, Wappingers Falls, New York (United States) (b) 1,75 (c) M - pivot (d) Leeds United (e) RB Leipzig, New York, NY Red Bulls II, New York, NY Red Bulls II

*** Adamsen - Tonni Adamsen (a) 15/11/1994, ¿? (Denmark) (b) 1,80 (c) F - center forward (d) Silkeborg IF (e) FC Helsingör, BK Frem, Taastrup FC

*** Adamski - Rafal Adamski (Rafał Adamski) (a) 21/11/2001, Dzierżoniów (Poland) (b) 1,90 (c) F - center forward (d) Zagłębie Lubin (e) Zaglebie Lubin II, Miedź Legnica, Miedz Legnica II

*** Adamu - Junior Adamu (Chukwubuike Junior Adamu) (a) 06/06/2001, Kano (Nigeria) (b) 1,83 (c) F - center forward (d) SC Freiburg (e) RB Salzburg, FC St. Gallen, RB Salzburg, FC Liefering

*** Adamyan - Armen Adamyan (Արմեն Ադամյան) (a) 20/01/2004, ¿? (Armenia) (b) - (c) M - central midfielder (d) FC Pyunik Yerevan B (e) -

*** Adamyan - Ashot Adamyan (Адамян Ашот Арташесович) (a) 15/06/1997, ¿? (Armenia) (b) 1,75 (c) M - attacking midfielder (d) Lernayin Artsakh Goris (e) FC Noah, Gandzasar, Gandzasar II, Banants II, Mika Erewan II

*** Adamyan - Sargis Adamyan (Սարգիս Ադամյան) (a) 23/05/1993, Yerevan (Armenia) (b) 1,84 (c) F - center forward (d) 1.FC Köln (e) Hoffenheim, KV Brugge,

Hoffenheim, Jahn Regensburg, TSV Steinbach, TSG Neustrelitz, Hansa Rostock II, Hansa Rostock, Hansa Rostock II

*** Adamyuk - Volodymyr Adamyuk (Адамюк Володимир Михайлович) (a) 17/07/1991, Sivka-Kalushska, Ivano-Frankivsk Oblast (Soviet Union, now in Ukraine) (b) 1,86 (c) D - right back (d) SK Dnipro-1 (e) PFC Lviv, Veres Rivne, Dnipro, Stal D., Krymteplytsya

*** Adan - Tiago Adan (Tiago Adan Fonseca) (a) 14/03/1988, Votorantim (Brazil) (b) 1,90 (c) F - center forward (d) Marsaxlokk FC (e) Real Kashmir, Retrô, Hibernians FC, Floriana, Hibernians FC, Novorizontino, Vila Nova FC, Atlético-PR, Oeste, Atlético-PR, Náutico, Atlético-PR, Ferroviária, Atlético-PR, Criciúma EC, Atlético-PR, Ferroviária, Atlético-PR, América-RN, Atlético-PR, Arapongas, Astra II, Arapongas, Caxias-RS, São Bento (SP), Náutico

*** Adán - Antonio Adán (Antonio Adán Garrido) (a) 13/05/1987, Madrid (Spain) (b) 1,90 (c) G (d) Sporting de Lisboa (e) Atlético Madrid, Real Betis, Cagliari, Real Madrid, RM Castilla, Real Madrid C

*** Adang - Xavier Adang (Xavier Rodrigue Adang Mveng) (a) 07/06/2004, ¿? (Cameroon) (b) 1,85 (c) M - attacking midfielder (d) MSK Zilina B (e) Gambinos Stars, MSK Zilina B, Gambinos Stars

*** Adarabioyo - Tosin Adarabioyo (Abdul-Nasir Oluwatosin Oluwadoyinsolami Adarabioyo) (a) 24/09/1997, Manchester (England) (b) 1,96 (c) D - central defense (d) Fulham FC (e) Blackburn, West Bromwich Albion

*** Adaramola - Tayo Adaramola (Omotayo Daniel Adaramola) (a) 14/11/2003, Dublin (Ireland) (b) - (c) D - left back (d) - (e) Coventry City

*** Adawi - Omar Adawi (a) 09/04/2001, ¿? (Finland) (b) - (c) M - attacking midfielder (d) Käpylän Pallo (e) SJK II, Käpylän Pallo

*** Addis - Jonny Addis (Jonathan Addis) (a) 27/09/1992, Newry (Northern Ireland) (b) 1,85 (c) D - central defense (d) Cliftonville FC (e) Ballymena, Glentoran, Carrick Rangers

*** Addo - Edmund Addo (a) 17/05/2000, Chorkor, Accra (Ghana) (b) 1,80 (c) M - pivot (d) Crvena zvezda Beograd (e) Spartak, FC Sheriff, FK Senica, Mighty Cosmos

*** Addo - Henry Addo (a) 01/05/2003, ¿? (Ghana) (b) 1,80 (c) F - left winger (d) MSK Zilina B (e) Zilina Africa

*** Addy - David Addy (David Nii Addy) (a) 21/02/1990, Prampram (Ghana) (b) 1,83 (c) D - left back (d) - (e) JK Tammeka, Ilves, Riga, RoPS, Delhi Dynamos, Waasland-Beveren, Vitória Guimarães, FC Porto, Panetolikos, FC Porto, Académica Coimbra, FC Porto, Randers FC, Wa All Stars FC

*** Adediran - Quadri Adediran (Quadri Adebayo Adediran) (a) 10/10/2000, Lagos (Nigeria) (b) 1,75 (c) F - center forward (d) SK Dynamo Ceske Budejovice (e) Dukla Praha, San Gwann FC, Novi Pazar/Mar.

*** Adedokun - Val Adedokun (Valintino Adedokun) (a) 14/02/2003, Dublin (Ireland) (b) - (c) D - left back (d) FC Brentford B (e) Dundalk FC

*** Adegbenro - Samuel Adegbenro (Samuel Adeniyi Adegbenro) (a) 03/12/1995, Osogbo (Nigeria) (b) 1,78 (c) F - left winger (d) Beijing Guoan (e) Norrköping, Rosenborg, Viking, Kwara United, Prime FC

*** Adegboyega - Emmanuel Adegboyega (a) 16/09/2003, Dundalk, Louth (Ireland) (b) 1,91 (c) D - central defense (d) - (e) Drogheda United, Dundalk FC, Glenmuir Utd.

*** Adejo - Daniel Adejo (a) 07/08/1989, Kachia Kaduna (Nigeria) (b) 1,85 (c) D - central defense (d) PAS Lamia 1964 (e) AOK Kerkyra, Salernitana, Vicenza, AEL Kalloni, Reggina, Este

*** Adekanye - Bobby Adekanye (Habeeb Omobolaji Adekanye) (a) 14/02/1999, Ibadan (Nigeria) (b) 1,75 (c) F - right winger (d) Go Ahead Eagles Deventer (e) Lazio, Crotone, Lazio, ADO Den Haag, Lazio, Cádiz CF, Lazio

*** Adekoya - Dayo Adekoya (Adekoya Adedayo Kevin Adetokunbo) (a) 17/03/2000, Tilburg (Netherlands) (b) 1,80 (c) F - center forward (d) 1874 Northwich FC (e) Airbus UK

*** Adekugbe - Sam Adekugbe (Samuel Ayomide Adekugbe) (a) 16/01/1995, London (England) (b) 1,76 (c) D - left back (d) Vancouver Whitecaps FC (e) Hatayspor, Galatasaray, Hatayspor, Vålerenga, Vancouver, IFK Göteborg, Vancouver, Brighton & Hove Albion, Vancouver, Whitecaps Reserves

*** Adekunle - Issa Adekunle (Usman Issa Adekunle) (a) 20/12/1997, Kwara (Nigeria) (b) 1,78 (c) F - left winger (d) Zemplin Michalovce (e) Podbrezova, Slavoj Trebisov, AS Trencin, Inter Bratislava, AS Trencin, Tatran Presov, AS Trencin, Niger Tornadoes

*** Adeleye - Adebayo Adeleye (a) 17/05/2000, ¿? (Nigeria) (b) 1,84 (c) G (d) Hapoel Jerusalem (e) -

*** Adelgaard - Aske Adelgaard (Aske Emil Berg Adelgaard) (a) 10/11/2003, ¿? (Denmark) (b) - (c) D - left back (d) Odense Boldklub (e) -

*** Adeline - Martin Adeline (Martin Gabriel Belaïd Adeline) (a) 02/12/2003, Épernay (France) (b) 1,80 (c) M - central midfielder (d) FC Annecy (e) FC Annecy, Stade Reims, Rodez AF, Stade Reims, Stade Reims B

*** Adem - Ali Adem (a) 01/06/2000, Skopje (North Macedonia) (b) 1,75 (c) M - pivot (d) FC Shkupi (e) Aris Thessaloniki, Veria NPS, Aris Thessaloniki, FC Shkupi, Aris Thessaloniki, Vardar

*** Adem - Ermedin Adem (Ермедин Адем) (a) 07/07/1990, Skopje (Yugoslavia, now in North Macedonia) (b) 1,79 (c) M - pivot (d) Voska Sport (e) Makedonija, Renova, FC Shkupi, Teteks Tetovo, Makedonija, FK Milano Kumanovo, FK Sloga

*** Ademi - Albion Ademi (a) 19/02/1999, Prishtinë (RF Yugoslavia, now in Kosovo) (b) 1,73 (c) F - left winger (d) IFK Värnamo (e) Värnamo, Djurgården, FC Lahti, Djurgården, IFK Mariehamn, FC Inter, Kemi Kings, FC Inter, TPS

*** Ademi - Arijan Ademi (Аријан Адеми) (a) 29/05/1991, Šibenik (Yugoslavia, now in Croatia) (b) 1,85 (c) M - pivot (d) Beijing Guoan (e) Dinamo Zagreb, NK Lokomotiva, Dinamo Zagreb, HNK Sibenik

*** Ademi - Ilirid Ademi (a) 04/03/1995, ¿? (RF Yugoslavia, now in North Macedonia) (b) 1,82 (c) F - left winger (d) - (e) KF Erzeni, KF Egnatia, KF Laçi, FC Shkupi, Renova, Makedonija, Gostivar

*** Ademi - Kemal Ademi (a) 23/01/1996, Villingen-Schwenningen (Germany) (b) 1,97 (c) F - center forward (d) FC Lucerna (e) Khimki, SV Sandhausen, Khimki, SC Paderborn, Khimki, Fenerbahce, Karagümrük, Fenerbahce, FC Basel, Neuchâtel Xamax, Hoffenheim II, Hoffenheim II

*** Ademi - Orhan Ademi (a) 28/10/1991, St. Gallen (Switzerland) (b) 1,89 (c) F - center forward (d) - (e) VfB Oldenburg, UTA Arad, MSV Duisburg, Eintracht Braunschweig, Würzb. Kickers, SV Ried, Eintracht Braunschweig, VfR Aalen, Eintracht Braunschweig, SCR Altach, Altach Juniors, Au-Berneck

*** Adénon - Khaled Adénon (Abdoul Khaled Akiola Adénon) (a) 29/07/1985, Abobo (Ivory Coast) (b) 1,81 (c) D - central defense (d) Doxa Katokopias (e) US Avranches, Al-Wehda, Amiens SC, Luçon VF, Le Mans FC, SC Bastia, Le Mans UC 72, ASEC Mimosas, ASEC Mimosas B

*** Adeola - Raymond Adeola (a) 12/05/2001, ¿? (Belarus) (b) 1,70 (c) F - left winger (d) FK Gomel (e) Gomel, Rodina Moskva, Gomel, FC Saksan

*** Adeshina - Adetunji Rasaq Adeshina (a) 02/12/2004, ¿? (Nigeria) (b) - (c) M - pivot (d) FK Novi Pazar (e) -

*** Adetunji - Sunday Adetunji (Sunday Damilare Adetunji) (a) 10/12/1997, Lagos (Nigeria) (b) 1,91 (c) F - center forward (d) - (e) FC Shkupi, Rivers United, Plateau United, Lobi Stars, Abia Warriors, 1.FK Pribram B, Lobi Stars, Enyimba Aba, Abia Warriors

*** Adewale - Derinsola Adewale (a) 28/06/2005, ¿? (Ireland) (b) - (c) M (d) Bohemian FC (e) -

*** Adewoye - Shawn Adewoye (a) 29/06/2000, Bree (Belgium) (b) 1,83 (c) D - central defense (d) RKC Waalwijk (e) KRC Genk

*** Adeyemi - Karim Adeyemi (Karim-David Adeyemi) (a) 18/01/2002, München (Germany) (b) 1,80 (c) F - left winger (d) Borussia Dortmund (e) RB Salzburg, FC Liefering, RB Salzburg

*** Adeyemo - Ola Adeyemo (Olajuwon Bamidele Adeyemo) (a) 15/01/1995, ¿? (England) (b) 1,83 (c) F - center forward (d) Longford Town FC (e) Newry City, Peterhead FC, Cove Rangers FC, Wexford FC, Ytterhogdals IK, Lewes, Valdres FK, East Fife, Leyton Orient

*** Adi - Tamir Adi (עדי תמיר) (a) 02/05/1993, Beer Sheva (Israel) (b) 1,85 (c) M - central midfielder (d) Hapoel Hadera (e) B. Jerusalem, Kiryat Shmona, B. Jerusalem, Hapoel Katamon, H. Ramat Gan, I. Kiryat Gat, FC Ashdod, Hakoah Amidar, FC Ashdod, Hakoah Amidar, FC Ashdod, M. Beer Sheva

*** Adil - Aslan Adil (Әділ Аслан Айдосұлы) (a) 13/01/1998, Taldykorgan (Kazakhstan) (b) 1,74 (c) F - right winger (d) Zhetysu Taldykorgan (e) Kaspiy Aktau, Zhetysu, Zhetysu B, Zhetysu II

*** Adil - Olzhas Adil (Әділ Олжас) (a) 01/04/2003, ¿? (Kazakhstan) (b) 1,82 (c) M - central midfielder (d) FC Zhenis Astana (e) FK Turan, Astana-M

*** Adilehou - Moise Adilehou (Moise Wilfrid Maoussé Adilehou) (a) 01/11/1995, Colombes (France) (b) 1,90 (c) D - central defense (d) Maccabi Petah Tikva (e) Zira FK, NAC Breda, Boluspor, APO Levadiakos, AOK Kerkyra, Slovan Bratislava

*** Adili - Dzihan Adili (a) 06/06/2002, Skopje (North Macedonia) (b) - (c) M - pivot (d) KF Drenica (e) Belasica, Korabi Debar

*** Adili - Mevlan Adili (a) 30/03/1994, Skopje (North Macedonia) (b) 1,86 (c) D - central defense (d) Shkëndija Tetovo (e) FK Bylis, SKA Khabarovsk, KF Vllaznia, FC Shkupi, Zalgiris, Shkëndija, UTA Arad, FC Shkupi, Shkëndija, FC Shkupi

*** Adili - Murat Adili (a) 22/09/1992, Kicevo (North Macedonia) (b) 1,91 (c) F - center forward (d) Pobeda Prilep (e) Arsimi, Besa Dobri Dol, Ohrid Lihnidos, Borec Veles, Korabi Debar, Vëllazërimi, KF Ferizaj, Renova, Vëllazërimi

*** Adilkhanov - Alvi Adilkhanov (Адилханов Альви Мусаевич) (a) 09/03/2003, ¿? (Russia) (b) 1,78 (c) M - central midfielder (d) - (e) Akhmat II, Akademia Ramzan

*** Adilkhanov - Edqar Adilkhanov (a) 26/06/2005, ¿? (Azerbaijan) (b) - (c) M - attacking midfielder (d) FC Shamakhi 2 (e) -

*** Adilov - Aldair Adilov (Альдаир Адилов) (a) 11/06/2002, Astana (Kazakhstan) (b) 1,72 (c) D - right back (d) Qyzyljar Petropavlovsk (e) Astana-Zhas, BGU Minsk II, F. Marcet

*** Adingra - Simon Adingra (a) 01/01/2002, Abobo (Ivory Coast) (b) 1,75 (c) F - left winger (d) Brighton & Hove Albion (e) Union St. Gilloise, Brighton & Hove Albion, Nordsjælland, Right to Dream

*** Adjei - Nathaniel Adjei (a) 21/08/2002, ¿? (Ghana) (b) 1,91 (c) D - central defense (d) Hammarby IF (e) Danbort FC, Hammarby TFF, Danbort FC

*** Adjetey - Jonas Adjetey (Jonas Adjei Adjetey) (a) 13/12/2003, ¿? (Ghana) (b) 1,88 (c) D - central defense (d) FC Basel (e) B. Chelsea II, Great Olympics

*** Adjijev - Mario Adjijev (Марио Аџијев) (a) 14/09/2005, Stip (North Macedonia) (b) - (c) M (d) - (e) Bregalnica Stip

*** Adjoumani - Yannick Adjoumani (a) 29/12/2002, ¿? (Ivory Coast) (b) 1,68 (c) D - left back (d) Östersunds FK (e) ASEC Mimosas, Häcken, Östersund, Häcken, ASEC Mimosas, Häcken, ASEC Mimosas

*** Adler - Adler (Adler Da Silva Parreira) (a) 28/12/1998, Genève (Switzerland) (b) 1,87 (c) F - center forward (d) Slovan Bratislava (e) Michalovce, Slovan Bratislava, Pohronie, Stade Nyonnais, Pohronie, Stade Nyonnais, Servette FC, Etoile Carouge, Servette FC, FC Vernier

*** Adli - Amine Adli (a) 10/05/2000, Béziers (France) (b) 1,80 (c) F - right winger (d) Bayer 04 Leverkusen (e) Toulouse, Toulouse B

*** Adli - Yacine Adli (عدلي ياسين) (a) 29/07/2000, Vitry-sur-Seine (France) (b) 1,86 (c) M - attacking midfielder (d) AC Milan (e) Girondins Bordeaux, AC Milan, Girondins Bordeaux, Paris Saint-Germain, Paris Saint Germain B

*** Admiraal - Luuk Admiraal (a) 15/03/2002, Zwijndrecht (Netherlands) (b) - (c) F - left winger (d) - (e) Excelsior, Spakenburg, Excelsior, ASWH

*** Adolphsson - Andri Adolphsson (a) 01/12/1992, ¿? (Iceland) (b) - (c) F - right winger (d) Stjarnan Gardabaer (e) Valur, ÍA Akranes, Valur, ÍA Akranes

*** Adoni - Zacharias Adoni (Ζαχαρίας Άδωνη) (a) 13/07/1999, Palaiometocho (Cyprus) (b) 1,90 (c) D - central defense (d) Apollon Limassol (e) Ethnikos, Nea Salamis, Ethnikos, Doxa Katokopias, ASIL Lysi, Doxa Katokopias, APOEL FC, Doxa Katokopias, APOEL FC

*** Adopo - Michel Adopo (Michel Ndary Adopo) (a) 19/07/2000, Villeneuve-Saint-Georges (France) (b) 1,87 (c) M - central midfielder (d) Atalanta de Bérgamo (e) Torino, Viterbese, Torino

*** Adrian - Samuel Adrian (Samuel Osvald Wilhelm Adrian) (a) 02/03/1998, Blentarp (Sweden) (b) 1,83 (c) M - pivot (d) Jönköpings Södra IF (e) Malmö FF, J-Södra IF, Malmö FF, Falkenbergs FF, Malmö FF, Kalmar FF, Malmö FF

*** Adrián - Adrián (Adrián San Miguel del Castillo) (a) 03/01/1987, Sevilla (Spain) (b) 1,90 (c) G (d) Liverpool FC (e) West Ham Utd., Real Betis, Betis B, Utrera, Betis B, CD Alcalá, Betis B, Betis C

*** Adriano Firmino - Adriano Firmino (Adriano Firmino dos Santos da Silva) (a) 04/11/1999, Rio de Janeiro (Brazil) (b) 1,87 (c) M - pivot (d) CD Santa Clara (e) Cruzeiro

*** Adriel - Adriel (Adriel Tadeu Ferreira da Silva) (a) 22/05/1997, São Paulo (Brazil) (b) 1,84 (c) M - pivot (d) Schwarz-Weiß Bregenz (e) Austria Lustenau, Paysandu, Corinthians B, Gainare Tottori, Audax-RJ

*** Adu - Enoch Kofi Adu (a) 14/09/1990, Kumasi (Ghana) (b) 1,73 (c) M - pivot (d) Ekenäs IF (e) Mjällby AIF, AIK, Akhisarspor, Malmö FF, KV Brugge, Stabæk, KV Brugge, Nordsjælland, OGC Nice, Liberty Prof.

*** Adu-Adjei - Daniel Adu-Adjei (Daniel William Kwabena Adu-Adjei) (a) 21/06/2005, London (England) (b) - (c) F - center forward (d) - (e) Poole Town

*** Aduev - Amir Aduev (Адуев Амир Адамович) (a) 11/05/1999, Ordzhonikidzevskaya, Ingushetia Republic (Russia) (b) 1,81 (c) M - central midfielder (d) - (e) Akhmat Grozny, Shakhter K., Akhmat Grozny, Montpellier, Montpellier B

*** Adukor - Joachim Adukor (a) 02/05/1993, Tema (Ghana) (b) 1,86 (c) M - pivot (d) - (e) Aktobe, FK Sarajevo, Diósgyőr, FK Sarajevo, OFI Creta, AS Béziers, Trofense, Gefle

*** Adukwaw - Ebenezer Adukwaw (Ebenezer Adukwaw Boadi) (a) 03/08/2001, ¿? (North Macedonia) (b) - (c) F - center forward (d) KF Trepca 89 (e) Elmina Sharks, Skyy FC

*** Adzic - Luka Adzic (Лука Аџић) (a) 17/09/1998, Beograd (RF Yugoslavia, now in Serbia) (b) 1,84 (c) F - left winger (d) FK Čukarički (e) PEC Zwolle, RSC Anderlecht, FC Emmen, RSC Anderlecht, Ankaragücü, RSC Anderlecht, FC Emmen, RSC Anderlecht, Crvena zvezda

*** Adzic - Vasilije Adzic (a) 12/05/2006, ¿? (Serbia and Montenegro, now in Kosovo) (b) - (c) M (d) Buducnost Podgorica (e) -

*** Adzic - Vladan Adzic (Vladan Adžić) (a) 05/07/1987, Cetinje (Yugoslavia, now in Montenegro) (b) 1,93 (c) D - central defense (d) Buducnost Podgorica (e) NK Varazdin, Pohang Steelers, Buducnost Podgorica, Suwon FC, OFK Beograd, Rudar Pljevlja, FK Lovcen

*** Adzovic - Adil Adzovic (Адил Аџовић) (a) 21/04/2002, Podgorica (RF Yugoslavia, Montenegro) (b) - (c) M (d) - (e) FK Decic Tuzi, FK Cetinje, FK Decic Tuzi

*** Adzovic - Aldin Adzovic (Алдин Аџовић) (a) 18/06/1994, ¿? (RF Yugoslavia, now in Montenegro) (b) - (c) M - attacking midfielder (d) OFK Petrovac (e) FK Jezero, KF Arbëria, FK Iskra, FK Decic Tuzi, FC Ballkani, Zeta Golubovac, Borac Cacak, FK Decic Tuzi, FK Mladost, FK Decic Tuzi

*** Aebischer - Michel Aebischer (a) 06/01/1997, Fribourg (Switzerland) (b) 1,83 (c) M - central midfielder (d) Bologna (e) BSC Young Boys, Bologna, BSC Young Boys

*** Aegidius - Jonathan Aegidius (Jonathan Risbjerg Ægidius) (a) 22/04/2002, ¿? (Denmark) (b) 1,90 (c) G (d) Brøndby IF (e) Hellerup IK, Brøndby IF

*** Aegisson - Heidar Aegisson (Heiðar Ægisson) (a) 10/08/1995, ¿? (Iceland) (b) 1,75 (c) D - right back (d) Stjarnan Gardabaer (e) Valur, Stjarnan, Boston Eagles, Stjarnan, Skínandi

*** Aegisson - Már Aegisson (Már Ægisson) (a) 11/01/2000, Reykjavík (Iceland) (b) - (c) M - right midfielder (d) Fram Reykjavík (e) Úlfarnir, Fram Reykjavík

*** Aer - Siim Aer (a) 22/07/2001, Paide (Estonia) (b) - (c) D - right back (d) Paide Linnameeskond (e) Pärnu Vaprus, Paide

*** Aertssen - Olivier Aertssen (a) 07/08/2004, Veldhoven (Netherlands) (b) 1,82 (c) D - central defense (d) Ajax Amsterdam B (e) -

*** Afajanyan - Petros Afajanyan (Պետրոս Աֆաջանյան) (a) 31/10/1998, Yerevan (Armenia) (b) 1,82 (c) M - pivot (d) FC Syunik (e) Ararat Yerevan, FC Noah, Shirak Gyumri, Ararat II, Pyunik Yerevan B, Pyunik Yerevan B

*** Afanasjev - Mikhail Afanasjev (Афанасьев Михаил Васильевич) (a) 04/11/1986, Minsk (Soviet Union, now in Belarus) (b) 1,74 (c) M - right midfielder (d) - (e) Torpedo Zhodino, Isloch, Fakel Voronezh, Torpedo Zhodino, Belshina, Soligorsk, Atyrau, Gomel, Dinamo Minsk, Salyut Belgorod, Kuban Krasnodar, Amkar Perm, MTZ-Ripo Minsk, BATE Borisov

*** Afanasjevs - Valerijs Afanasjevs (a) 20/09/1982, Daugavpils (Soviet Union, now in Latvia) (b) 1,70 (c) M - attacking midfielder (d) BFC Daugavpils (e) Liepaja, Metalurgs, Daugavpils, Dinaburg, Daugavpils, Riga, Ditton

*** Afena-Gyan - Felix Afena-Gyan (Felix Ohene Afena-Gyan) (a) 19/01/2003, Sunyani (Ghana) (b) 1,75 (c) F - center forward (d) US Cremonese (e) AS Roma, EurAfrica FC

*** Affamah - Joe-Loic Affamah (a) 29/06/2002, Lomé (Togo) (b) 1,75 (c) F - center forward (d) FC Nantes (e) Torreense, FC Nantes, FC Nantes B

*** Affengruber - David Affengruber (a) 19/03/2001, Scheibbs (Austria) (b) 1,85 (c) D - central defense (d) SK Sturm Graz (e) RB Salzburg, FC Liefering

*** Affi - Yann Emmanuel Affi (Yann Emmanuel Affi) (a) 11/11/1995, Tiébissou (Ivory Coast) (b) 1,85 (c) D - central defense (d) AC Oulu (e) Gomel, Dynamo Brest, SC Gagnoa, Torpedo Zhodino, SC Gagnoa

*** Afolabi - Jonathan Afolabi (Jonathan Swanson Afolabi) (a) 14/01/2000, Dublin (Ireland) (b) 1,89 (c) F - center forward (d) Bohemian FC (e) Celtic FC, Airdrieonians, Celtic FC, Ayr United, Celtic FC, Celtic Reserves, Dundee FC, Celtic Reserves, Dunfermline A., Celtic Reserves, St. Josephs Boys

*** Afonso - João Afonso (João Ricardo da Silva Afonso) (a) 28/05/1990, Castelo Branco (Portugal) (b) 1,88 (c) D - central defense (d) SC União Torreense (e) Santa Clara, Vitória Guimarães, Córdoba CF, Vitória Guimarães, Estoril Praia, Vitória Guimarães, Castelo Branco

*** Afriyie - Daniel Afriyie (Daniel Afriyie Barnieh) (a) 26/06/2001, Kumasi (Ghana) (b) 1,65 (c) F - left winger (d) FC Zürich (e) Hearts of Oak, Rahimo FC

*** Afyan - Vyacheslav Afyan (Վյաչեսլավ Աֆյան) (a) 28/10/2005, ¿? (Armenia) (b) - (c) M - right midfielder (d) FC Pyunik Yerevan B (e) -

*** Aga - Namir Aga (אגא נמיר) (a) 13/01/1995, ¿? (Israel) (b) - (c) D - central defense (d) Ironi Tiberias (e) M. Bnei Reineh, Hapoel Kaukab, Ironi Tiberias, Hapoel Kaukab, Hapoel Shefaram, Hapoel Acre, M. Zur Shalom, Hapoel Acre

*** Aga - Oscar Aga (a) 06/01/2001, Oslo (Norway) (b) 1,80 (c) F - center forward (d) Fredrikstad FK (e) Fredrikstad, Rosenborg, Elfsborg, Grorud, Stabæk, Grorud, Stabæk

*** Agachi - Sebastian Agachi (Sebastian Iulian Agachi) (a) 25/09/2000, Chișinău (Moldova) (b) 1,82 (c) G (d) FC Zimbru Chisinau (e) Dacia Buiucani, FC Bălți, FCV Farul, FC Farul 1920, Academia Hagi, FC Arges, Academia Hagi, FC Aninoasa, Academia Hagi

*** Agalarov - Gamid Agalarov (Агаларов Гамид Русланович) (a) 16/07/2000, Makhachkala (Russia) (b) 1,81 (c) F - center forward (d) Akhmat Grozny (e) Ufa, Volgar, Ufa, Anzhi, Anzhi II

*** Agamagomedov - Samur Agamagomedov (Агамагомедов Самур Вагитович) (a) 30/11/1998, Derbent, Dagestan Region (Russia) (b) 1,90 (c) G (d) - (e) FC Van, Legion, FC Van, FC Noah, Nika Moskva

*** Agamaliyev - Murad Agamaliyev (a) 27/12/2006, ¿? (Azerbaijan) (b) - (c) G (d) Sumqayit 2 (e) -

*** Aganovic - Adnan Aganovic (Adnan Aganović) (a) 03/10/1987, Dubrovnik (Yugoslavia, now in Croatia) (b) 1,81 (c) M - central midfielder (d) Sepsi OSK Sf. Gheorghe (e) AEL Limassol, Altay SK, AE Larisa, Steaua Bucuresti, AEL Limassol, FC Viitorul, FC Brasov, NK Istra, Koper, NK Varazdin, Medjimurje, Trogir 1912

*** Aganspahic - Almir Aganspahic (Almir Aganspahić) (a) 12/09/1996, Sarajevo (Bosnia and Herzegovina) (b) 1,89 (c) F - center forward (d) Shkëndija Tetovo (e) Čukarički, Sumqayit, Čukarički, Novi Pazar, Celik Zenica, FK Krupa, Mladost Kakanj, Raufoss, NK Osijek, FK Sarajevo

*** Agapov - Ilya Agapov (Агапов Илья Николаевич) (a) 21/01/2001, Kazan (Russia) (b) 1,93 (c) D - central defense (d) CSKA Moskva (e) Pari Nizhny Novgórod, Spartak-2, Rubin Kazán II, Neftekhimik, Rubin Kazán II

*** Agaptsev - Stanislav Agaptsev (Stanislav Agaptšev) (a) 08/06/2006, Tallinn (Estonia) (b) 1,78 (c) M - central midfielder (d) Kalju FC (e) -

*** Agardius - Viktor Agardius (Lars Viktor Filip Agardius) (a) 23/10/1989, Skepparslöv (Sweden) (b) 1,81 (c) D - left back (d) - (e) Brommapojkarna, Norrköping, Mjällby AIF, AS Livorno, Kalmar FF, Mjällby AIF, Kristianstad FF

*** Agarmaa - Marcus Agarmaa (a) 19/09/2003, Tartu (Estonia) (b) - (c) G (d) Tartu JK Welco (e) JK Welco, JK Tammeka

*** Agayev - Mahmud Agayev (Mahmud Seymur oğlu Ağayev) (a) 17/05/2004, Baku (Azerbaijan) (b) 1,72 (c) F - left winger (d) FK Zira 2 (e) -

*** Agayev - Salahat Agayev (Sǝlahǝt Nüsrǝt oğlu Ağayev) (a) 04/01/1991, Füzuli (Soviet Union, now in Azerbaijan) (b) 1,90 (c) G (d) FK Sabail (e) FK Qabala, Sabah FK, Neftchi Baku, Keshla, Sumqayit, Inter Baku, Sumqayit, Inter Baku, MOIK, Inter Baku

*** Agayev - Samir Agayev (Samir Ağayev) (a) 25/05/2002, ¿? (Azerbaijan) (b) - (c) M - pivot (d) FK Zira 2 (e) Qaradag

*** Agazada - Abbas Agazada (Abbas Ağazadǝ) (a) 10/02/1999, ¿? (Azerbaijan) (b) 1,77 (c) M - pivot (d) Turan-Tovuz IK (e) Sabah 2, Turan Tovuz, Sabah 2, Sabah FK, MOIK, FK Qabala

*** Agbadou - Emmanuel Agbadou (Emmanuel Elysee Djedje Agbadou Badobre) (a) 17/06/1997, Abidjan (Ivory Coast) (b) 1,92 (c) D - central defense (d) Stade de Reims (e) KAS Eupen, FC San Pedro, US Monastir, FC San Pedro

*** Agbekpornu - Michael Agbekpornu (a) 31/08/1998, Accra (Ghana) (b) 1,88 (c) M - pivot (d) Slaven Belupo Koprivnica (e) KF Egnatia, Dreams FC

*** Agbo - David Agbo (a) 01/04/2000, ¿? (Ghana) (b) 1,72 (c) M - central midfielder (d) FC Inter Turku (e) Kristiansund, Mobile Phone

*** Agbo - Uche Agbo (Uche Henry Agbo) (a) 04/12/1995, Kano City (Nigeria) (b) 1,86 (c) M - pivot (d) Slovan Bratislava (e) RC Deportivo, Standard Liège, RC Deportivo, Standard Liège, SC Braga, Standard Liège, Rayo Vallecano, Standard Liège, Watford, Granada CF, Watford, Udinese, Granada CF, Granada B, Udinese, Enyimba Aba, JUTH FC, FC Taraba

*** Agbor - Brian Agbor (Brian Emo Agbor) (a) 14/06/2001, ¿? (Belgium) (b) - (c) D - central defense (d) KAA Gent (e) Jong KAA Gent

*** Agbor - Emmanuel Agbor (a) 21/06/2003, ¿? (Cameroon) (b) 1,83 (c) F - center forward (d) Miedź Legnica (e) Miedz Legnica II, YOSA, Cinyodev FC

*** Agcabayov - Arsen Agcabayov (Arsen İlham oğlu Ağcabǝyov) (a) 11/09/2000, ¿? (Azerbaijan) (b) 1,80 (c) D - central defense (d) FC Shamakhi (e) Sabah FK, Sumqayit, Sabah FK, FK Sabail

*** Agdon - Agdon (Agdon Santos Menezes) (a) 26/01/1993, Salvador (Brazil) (b) 1,76 (c) F - center forward (d) Alashkert Yerevan CF (e) Alashkert CF, Ararat-Armenia, Varzim, Feirense, Oliveirense, Merelinense, Braga B, Vitória B

*** Ageev - Ivan Ageev (Агеев Иван Андреевич) (a) 21/04/2005, Orsha (Belarus) (b) - (c) M - pivot (d) Energetik-BGU Minsk (e) BGU Minsk II

*** Ageev - Mikhail Ageev (Агеев Михаил Андреевич) (a) 22/04/2000, Volzhskiy, Volgograd Region (Russia) (b) 1,85 (c) F - center forward (d) Ural 2 Ekaterinburg (e) Ural, Volgar, Ural, Loko-Kazanka M., Dinamo Moskva II

*** Aghasaryan - Narek Aghasaryan (Նարեկ Աղասարյան) (a) 15/07/2001, Pyatigorsk (Russia) (b) 1,74 (c) M - pivot (d) FC Urartu Yerevan (e) BKMA Yerevan, Banants III

*** Aghbalyan - Daniel Aghbalyan (Դանիել Աղբալյան) (a) 12/03/1999, Stary Oskol (Russia) (b) 1,72 (c) M - pivot (d) BKMA Yerevan (e) Pyunik Yerevan B, FC Ani, Pyunik Yerevan B, Novaya Usman

*** Agic - Tino Agic (Tino Agić) (a) 30/04/2002, Rijeka (Croatia) (b) 1,88 (c) D - central defense (d) HNK Rijeka (e) ND Gorica, HNK Rijeka, NK Tresnjevka

*** Agimanov - Tamerlan Agimanov (Агиманов Тамерлан) (a) 16/08/2006, ¿? (Kazakhstan) (b) 1,86 (c) F - right winger (d) FK Aksu (e) FK Aksu II

*** Agirrezabala - Julen Agirrezabala (Julen Agirrezabala Astúlez) (a) 26/12/2000, Donostia-San Sebastián (Spain) (b) 1,87 (c) G (d) Athletic Club (e) Bilbao Athletic, CD Basconia

*** Agius - Andrei Agius (a) 12/08/1986, Pietà (Malta) (b) 1,82 (c) D (d) - (e) Hibernians FC, Aprilia, Torres, Latina Calcio, Birkirkara FC, Melfi, Cassino, Salernitana, Igea Virtus, Martina

*** Agius - Brady Agius (a) 05/09/2002, ¿? (Malta) (b) - (c) D (d) Marsa FC (e) Santa Lucia FC

*** Agius - Daniel Agius (a) 15/11/1996, ¿? (Malta) (b) - (c) F - left winger (d) Floriana FC (e) Marsaxlokk, Floriana, Santa Lucia FC, Floriana, Sirens FC, Floriana, Sirens FC, Floriana

*** Agius - Leonardo Agius (a) 17/09/2002, ¿? (Malta) (b) - (c) M - central midfielder (d) Balzan FC (e) FC Lugano II

*** Agius - Nathan Agius (a) 16/11/2003, ¿? (Malta) (b) - (c) M (d) - (e) Mosta FC

*** Agius - Terence Agius (a) 15/01/1994, ¿? (Malta) (b) - (c) M - central midfielder (d) Swieqi United FC (e) Pietà Hotspurs, Zabbar SP, Sirens FC, Birkirkara FC, Mosta FC, Birkirkara FC, Balzan FC, Birkirkara FC, Balzan FC, Hamrun Spartans, Balzan FC, Pembroke, Balzan FC, Pietà Hotspurs

*** Agkatsev - Stanislav Agkatsev (Агкацев Станислав Витальевич) (a) 09/01/2002, Vladikavkaz (Russia) (b) 1,89 (c) G (d) FK Krasnodar (e) Krasnodar-2, Krasnodar II

*** Agnaldo - Agnaldo (Agnaldo Pinto de Moraes Júnior) (a) 11/03/1994, São Gonçalo (RJ) (Brazil) (b) 1,76 (c) M - central midfielder (d) KF Skënderbeu (e) FK Kukësi, KF Skënderbeu, KS Kastrioti, RoPS, Molde, RoPS, Molde, Vila Nova FC, Molde, Desp. Brasil, Molde, Desp. Brasil

*** Agnarsson - Erlingur Agnarsson (a) 05/03/1998, ¿? (Iceland) (b) - (c) M - attacking midfielder (d) Víkingur Reykjavík (e) -

*** Agnarsson - Hannes Agnarsson (a) 26/02/1999, Tórshavn (Faroe Islands) (b) 1,85 (c) F - right winger (d) B36 Tórshavn (e) Hellerup IK, B36 Tórshavn, Hellerup IK, B36 Tórshavn, B36 II

*** Agnarsson - Martin Agnarsson (a) 07/12/2003, Tórshavn (Faroe Islands) (b) 1,72 (c) D - left back (d) Viborg FF (e) B36 Tórshavn, B36 II

*** Agoumé - Lucien Agoumé (Lucien Jefferson Agoumé) (a) 09/02/2002, Yaoundé (Cameroon) (b) 1,85 (c) M - pivot (d) Internazionale Milano (e) Troyes, Internazionale Milano, Stade Brestois, Internazionale Milano, Spezia, Internazionale Milano, FC Sochaux

*** Agovic - Alen Agovic (a) 28/11/1997, ¿? (Luxembourg) (b) - (c) D - right back (d) FC UNA Strassen (e) Kayl-Tétange

*** Agovic - Denis Agovic (a) 12/07/1993, ¿? (Luxembourg) (b) 1,86 (c) D - central defense (d) FC UNA Strassen (e) Jeunesse Esch, FC UNA Strassen, Jeunesse Esch

*** Agovic - Edis Agovic (a) 12/07/1993, Düdelingen (Luxembourg) (b) 1,88 (c) F - left winger (d) F91 Dudelange (e) FC UNA Strassen, Jeunesse Esch, Kayl-Tétange, Jeunesse Esch

*** Agovic - Erkan Agovic (a) 24/08/2000, ¿? (Luxembourg) (b) - (c) G (d) US Mondorf-Les-Bains (e) Differdange II, Differdange 03, FC Rodange 91, Differdange 03

*** Agovic - Kevin Agovic (a) 15/08/2000 (c) F - left winger (d) US Hostert (e) Schifflange 95, Mondercange

*** Agra - Salvador Agra (Salvador José Milhazes Agra) (a) 11/11/1991, Vila do Conde (Portugal) (b) 1,66 (c) F - left winger (d) Boavista Porto FC (e) Tondela, Legia Warszawa, Benfica, Cádiz CF, Benfica, Granada CF, Benfica, Desportivo Aves, Benfica, Nacional, Real Betis, SC Braga, Real Betis, Académica Coimbra, Real Betis, SC Braga, Real Betis, AC Siena, Real Betis, Olhanense, Varzim

*** Agrafiotis - Nikolas Agrafiotis (Николас Аграфиотис) (a) 25/04/2000, 's-Hertogenbosch (Netherlands) (b) 1,91 (c) F - center forward (d) Excelsior Rotterdam (e) FC Dordrecht

*** Agu - Felix Agu (a) 27/09/1999, Osnabrück (Germany) (b) 1,80 (c) D - right back (d) SV Werder Bremen (e) VfL Osnabrück

*** Aguado - Álvaro Aguado (Álvaro Aguado Méndez) (a) 01/05/1996, Jaén (Spain) (b) 1,75 (c) M - central midfielder (d) - (e) Real Valladolid, CF Fuenlabrada, Real Valladolid, CD Numancia, Real Valladolid, Córdoba CF, Real Valladolid, Córdoba CF, Córdoba CF B, Real Jaén CF, Ontinyent

*** Agudelo - Kevin Agudelo (Kevin Andrés Agudelo Ardila) (a) 14/11/1998, Puerto Caicedo (Colombia) (b) 1,78 (c) M - attacking midfielder (d) Al-Nasr SC (UAE) (e) Spezia, Genoa, Spezia, Genoa, Spezia, Genoa, Fiorentina, Genoa, Atlético Huila, Bogotá FC

*** Agüera - Alejo Agüera (Alejandro Agüera Lasala) (a) 07/01/1999, Tarragona (Spain) (b) 1,83 (c) G (d) - (e) UE Santa Coloma, FC Ascó, AD Ceuta, UE Valls, Pobla de Mafumet CF

*** Aguerd - Nayef Aguerd (نايف أكرد) (a) 30/03/1996, Kénitra (Morocco) (b) 1,90 (c) D - central defense (d) West Ham United (e) Stade Rennes, Dijon, FUS Rabat, AM Football

*** Agüero - Sébastien Agüero (Sébastien Jacques Manuel Agüero) (a) 17/08/1993, Chenôve (France) (b) - (c) D - right back (d) Atlètic Club d'Escaldes (e) UE Engordany, Is-Selongey, Dijon FCO B

*** Aguilar - José Aguilar (José Aguilar Martinez) (a) 05/02/2001, Almería (Spain) (b) 1,72 (c) M - central midfielder (d) - (e) FC Sion

*** Aguilar - Juan Cruz Aguilar (a) 08/02/1996, San Nicolás (Argentina) (b) 1,88 (c) M - central midfielder (d) Marsaxlokk FC (e) Defensores (VR), Ind. Chivilcoy, Defensores (VR)

*** Aguilar - Ruben Aguilar (a) 26/04/1993, Grenoble (France) (b) 1,70 (c) D - right back (d) AS Mónaco (e) Montpellier, AJ Auxerre, Grenoble, Saint-Étienne B, Grenoble B

*** Aguirre - Leandro Aguirre (Leandro Damián Aguirre) (a) 08/02/1989, Rosario (Argentina) (b) 1,67 (c) D - left back (d) Marsaxlokk FC (e) Birkirkara FC, Valletta, GyE Mendoza, Valletta, Independiente Rivadavia, Aldosivi, Boca Juniors, Aldosivi, Boca Juniors, Nacional, Boca Juniors

*** Aguirregabiria - Martín Aguirregabiria (Martín Aguirregabiria Padilla) (a) 10/05/1996, Vitoria (Spain) (b) 1,80 (c) D - right back (d) FC Famalicão (e) Alavés, Depor. Alavés B

*** Agvadish - Omer Agvadish (עומר אגבדיש) (a) 30/12/2000, Jerusalem (Israel) (b) 1,78 (c) M - right midfielder (d) Hapoel Jerusalem (e) -

*** Agwata - Austin Agwata (Austin Agwata) (a) 30/06/2002, Enugu (Nigeria) (b) 1,77 (c) F - center forward (d) MFK Zvolen (e) Tiszakécske, IFK Haninge, FK Minsk, Topflight

*** Agyare - Benjamin Agyare (a) 08/05/1994, Accra (Ghana) (b) 1,81 (c) D - central defense (d) FC Drita Gjilan (e) KF Drenica, FC Drita, FK Apolonia, Hearts of Oak, Heart of Lions

*** Agyei - Enock Agyei (Enock Atta Agyei) (a) 13/01/2005, ¿? (Belgium) (b) 1,72 (c) F - right winger (d) Burnley FC (e) KV Mechelen, Burnley, RSC Anderlecht Futures

*** Agyekum - Lawrence Agyekum (a) 23/11/2003, ¿? (Austria) (b) 1,74 (c) M - central midfielder (d) FC Liefering (e) RB Salzburg, FC Liefering, RB Salzburg, WAFA SC

*** Agyiri - Ernest Agyiri (a) 06/03/1998, Accra (Ghana) (b) 1,76 (c) F - left winger (d) Randers FC (e) FCI Levadia, EN Paralimniou, AFC Tubize, Vålerenga, Right to Dream

*** Ahadi - Mosawer Ahadi (a) 08/03/2000, Mazar-i-Sharif (Afghanistan) (b) 1,76 (c) F - right winger (d) Helsinki IFK (e) Ekenäs IF, Helsinki IFK, FC Espoo, JäPS, FC Honka, Ekenäs IF, FC Honka, Pallokerho

*** Ahamada - Naouirou Ahamada (Naouirou Mohamed Ahamada) (a) 29/03/2002, Marseille (France) (b) 1,83 (c) M - central midfielder (d) Crystal Palace (e) VfB Stuttgart, VfB Stuttgart

*** Ahiabu - Prosper Ahiabu (Prosper Dayegbe Ahiabu) (a) 10/05/1999, ¿? (Ghana) (b) 1,88 (c) M - central midfielder (d) Vaasan Palloseura (e) AS Soliman, Liberty Prof., WAFA SC

*** Ahlblad - Mathias Ahlblad (a) 18/02/2003, ¿? (Finland) (b) 1,84 (c) G (d) FC Honka (e) HJK Klubi 04

*** Ahlin - August Ahlin (August Per Arnold Ahlin) (a) 06/04/1997, ¿? (Sweden) (b) 1,82 (c) G (d) - (e) Sirius, Gamla Upsala SK, Boo FK, Railsplitters

*** Ahlmann - Jakob Ahlmann (Jakob Ahlmann Nielsen) (a) 18/01/1991, Brønderslev (Denmark) (b) 1,80 (c) D - left back (d) Aalborg BK (e) -

*** Ahmadli - Tarlan Ahmadli (Tərlan Seymur oğlu Əhmədli) (a) 21/11/1994, Baku (Azerbaijan) (b) 1,73 (c) G (d) Turan-Tovuz IK (e) Sumqayit, FK Qabala, Sabah FK, FK Khazar Baku, Sumqayit

*** Ahmadov - Mirali Ahmadov (Mirəli Mirməcid oğlu Əhmədov) (a) 16/04/2003, ¿? (Azerbaijan) (b) - (c) D - left back (d) Araz-Naxcivan Nakchivan (e) FK Sabail, Shamakhi, Sabah 2, Neftchi 2 Baku

*** Ahmadov - Ramin Ahmadov (Əhmədov Ramin Ramiz) (a) 01/06/2001, ¿? (Azerbaijan) (b) 1,83 (c) M - central midfielder (d) FC Shamakhi (e) Zira FK, PFK Zaqatala

*** Ahmadov - Rüfat Ahmadov (Rüfət Pərviz oğlu Əhmədov) (a) 22/09/2002, Culfa (Azerbaijan) (b) 1,78 (c) D - left back (d) Kapaz PFK (e) Kapaz PFK, FK Qabala

*** Ahmadov - Süleyman Ahmadov (Süleyman Vüqar oğlu Əhmədov) (a) 25/11/1999, Sumqayit (Azerbaijan) (b) 1,77 (c) D - left back (d) FK Sabail (e) Sumqayit

*** Ahmadov - Tapdiq Ahmadov (Tapdıq Əhmədov) (a) 08/05/1997, ¿? (Azerbaijan) (b) - (c) F - center forward (d) - (e) FC Shamakhi 2, Qaradag, FK Zira 2

*** Ahmadzada - Nihad Ahmadzada (Nihad Rövşən oğlu Əhmədzadə) (a) 23/07/2006, ¿? (Azerbaijan) (b) - (c) M - left midfielder (d) Sumqayit 2 (e) -

*** Ahmadzada - Rustam Ahmadzada (Rüstəm Aləm oğlu Əhmədzadə) (a) 25/12/2000, Burtyn, Khmelnytskyi Oblast (Ukraine) (b) 1,84 (c) F - center forward (d) Zira FK (e) Qarabag FK, FK Minaj, Kolos II, Podillya Kh., Kolos II, Zirka Kyiv

*** Ahmed - Mubarak Mohammed Ahmed (a) 25/03/2003, Lagos (Nigeria) (b) 1,89 (c) F - center forward (d) - (e) Ceahlaul, FC Van, Right2Win SA

*** Ahmed Hassan - Ahmed Hassan (محجوب حسن أحمد, Ahmed Hassan Mahgoub) (a) 05/03/1993, Cairo (Egypt) (b) 1,91 (c) F - center forward (d) Olympiakos El Pireo (e) Alanyaspor, Olympiakos, Konyaspor, Olympiakos, SC Braga, Olympiakos, SC Braga, Olympiakos, SC Braga, Rio Ave

*** Ahmedhodzic - Anel Ahmedhodzic (Anel Ahmedhodžić) (a) 26/03/1999, Malmö (Sweden) (b) 1,90 (c) D - central defense (d) Sheffield United (e) Malmö FF, Girondins Bordeaux, Malmö FF, Hobro IK, Malmö FF

*** Ahmedi - Valon Ahmedi (Valon Ahmedi) (a) 07/10/1994, Ohrid (Yugoslavia, North Macedonia) (b) 1,75 (c) M - attacking midfielder (d) Shakhter Soligorsk (e) Shkëndija, Inter Zaprešić, Kiryat Shmona, NK Maribor, NK Celje, Südtirol

*** Ahmetaj - Alessandro Ahmetaj (a) 02/01/2000, Novafeltria (Italy) (b) 1,80 (c) M - central midfielder (d) KF Egnatia (e) ND Gorica, Koper, NK Dekani, Koper

*** Ahmeti - Berat Ahmeti (a) 26/01/1995, Prishtinë (Yugoslavia, now in Kosovo) (b) 1,77 (c) M - attacking midfielder (d) KF Drenica (e) KF Feronikeli, KF Ulpiana, KF Trepca 89, KF Feronikeli, KF Gjilani, KF Vllaznia, Újpest II, FC Prishtina, KF Flamurtari

*** Ahmeti - Ergyn Ahmeti (a) 21/12/1995, Mitrovica (RF Yugoslavia, now in Kosovo) (b) 1,85 (c) M - attacking midfielder (d) KF Llapi (e) KF Dukagjini, FC Drita, FC Prishtina, KF Trepca

*** Ahmetovic - Mersudin Ahmetovic (Mersudin Ahmetović) (a) 19/02/1985, Tuzla (Yugoslavia, now in Bosnia and Herzegovina) (b) 1,90 (c) F - center forward (d) FK Igman Konjic (e) FK Sarajevo, Sloboda Tuzla, Zhetysu, Salyut Belgorod, Volga Nizhny Novgorod, Rostov, Sloboda Tuzla

*** Ahmetovic - Muhamed Ahmetovic (a) 19/07/1999, Rimini (Italy) (b) - (c) M - pivot (d) SS Folgore/Falciano (e) Pennarossa, Dro Alto Garda, Spoleto

*** Ahmetxhekaj - Adrian Ahmetxhekaj (a) 12/11/2000, Luxembourg (Luxembourg) (b) - (c) M - central midfielder (d) Racing FC Union Luxembourg (e) Jeunesse Canach, Kayl-Tétange

*** Ahmetxhekaj - Denis Ahmetxhekaj (a) 21/02/2002, ¿? (Luxembourg) (b) - (c) D - central defense (d) Racing FC Union Luxembourg (e) CS Fola Esch, US Rumelange

*** Ahmun - Ben Ahmun (Benjamin Ahmun) (a) 02/02/1992, ¿? (Wales) (b) 1,86 (c) F - center forward (d) Pontypridd United (e) Penybont, STM Sports, Caldicot

*** Aholou - Jean-Eudes Aholou (Jean-Eudes Pascal Aholou) (a) 20/03/1994, Yopougon (Ivory Coast) (b) 1,86 (c) M - pivot (d) Racing Club Strasbourg (e) AS Monaco, Racing Club Strasbourg, AS Monaco, Racing Club Strasbourg, AS Monaco, St.-Étienne, AS Monaco, Racing Club Strasbourg, US Orléans, LOSC Lille B

*** Aidara - Mohamed Aidara (a) 06/11/1996, Abidjan (Ivory Coast) (b) 1,88 (c) D - central defense (d) Al-Taraji (e) Vizela, ASEC Mimosas

*** Aidarashvili - Dachi Aidarashvili (დაჩი აიდარაშვილი) (a) 05/11/2004, ¿? (Georgia) (b) - (c) M (d) FC Locomotive Tbilisi II (e) -

*** Aidonis - Antonis Aidonis (Αντώνης Αηδόνης) (a) 22/05/2001, Neustadt an der Weinstraße (Germany) (b) 1,86 (c) D - central defense (d) Aris Thessaloniki (e) VfB Stuttgart, Dynamo Dresden, VfB Stuttgart, Stuttgart II

*** Aidoo - Joseph Aidoo (a) 29/09/1995, Tema (Ghana) (b) 1,81 (c) D - central defense (d) RC Celta de Vigo (e) KRC Genk, Hammarby IF, Inter Allies, Hammarby IF, Inter Allies

*** Aiesh - Hosam Aiesh (عياش حسام) (a) 14/04/1995, Göteborg (Sweden) (b) 1,75 (c) F - right winger (d) FC Seoul (e) IFK Göteborg, Östersund, Varbergs BoIS, Östersund, Häcken, Varbergs BoIS, Häcken

*** Aigner - Sebastian Aigner (a) 03/01/2001, ¿? (Austria) (b) 1,80 (c) M - pivot (d) SCR Altach (e) FC Liefering

*** Äijälä - Elias Äijälä (a) 24/03/2003, ¿? (Finland) (b) 1,79 (c) D - left back (d) FC Honka (e) FC Honka II

*** Aiken - Murray Aiken (a) 14/11/2004, ¿? (Scotland) (b) 1,77 (c) M - central midfielder (d) Airdrieonians FC (e) Hibernian B

*** Aina - Ola Aina (Temitayo Olufisayo Olaoluwa Aina) (a) 08/10/1996, Southwark (England) (b) 1,84 (c) D - right back (d) Nottingham Forest (e) Torino, Fulham, Torino, Chelsea, Torino, Chelsea, Hull City, Chelsea

*** Ainsalu - Mihkel Ainsalu (a) 08/03/1996, Tartu (Estonia) (b) 1,89 (c) M - central midfielder (d) FCI Levadia (e) Telstar, FCI Levadia, TJK Legion, FC Helsingör, PFC Lviv, FC Flora, JK Nomme Kalju, Kalju Nõmme II

*** Aioani - Marian Aioani (Marian Mihai Aioani) (a) 07/11/1999, Buftea (Romania) (b) 1,86 (c) G (d) FCV Farul Constanta (e) Chindia
*** Ait El Hadj - Anouar Ait El Hadj (a) 20/04/2002, Molenbeek (Belgium) (b) 1,67 (c) M - attacking midfielder (d) KRC Genk (e) RSC Anderlecht
*** Aitchison - Jack Aitchison (a) 05/03/2000, Fauldhouse (Scotland) (b) 1,80 (c) F - center forward (d) Exeter City (e) Motherwell FC, Barnsley FC, Forest Green Rovers, Barnsley FC, Stevenage, Barnsley FC, Celtic Reserves, Forest Green Rovers, Celtic Reserves, Alloa Athletic, Celtic Reserves, Dumbarton FC, Celtic Reserves
*** Aït-Nouri - Rayan Aït-Nouri (Rayan Aït-Nouri) (a) 06/06/2001, Montreuil (France) (b) 1,80 (c) D - left back (d) Wolverhampton Wanderers (e) Angers SCO, Wolverhampton Wanderers, Angers SCO
*** Aiwu - Emanuel Aiwu (a) 25/12/2000, Innsbruck (Austria) (b) 1,85 (c) D - central defense (d) US Cremonese (e) Rapid Wien, Admira Wacker, FC Admira II
*** Aizu - Yuki Aizu (会津 雄生) (a) 01/08/1996, Setagaya, Tokyo (Japan) (b) 1,68 (c) D - right back (d) Hwaseong FC (e) Pirin, Linköping City, FC Gifu, Tsukuba Univ.
*** Aizups - Rinalds Aizups (a) 31/05/2004, ¿? (Latvia) (b) - (c) D - central defense (d) BFC Daugavpils (e) -
*** Ajazi - Spartak Ajazi (a) 03/07/1994, Laç (Albania) (b) 1,86 (c) F - center forward (d) AF Elbasani (e) KS Kastrioti, KS Burreli, Besëlidhja, KS Burreli, KF Iliria, KS Burreli, KF Laçi
*** Ajdar - Ognjen Ajdar (Огњен Ајдар) (a) 05/04/2003, Beograd (Serbia and Montenegro, now in Serbia) (b) 1,75 (c) F - left winger (d) Graficar Belgrad (e) Graficar, Radnicki Niš, BASK Beograd
*** Ajdini - Ardi Ajdini (a) 04/11/2002, Prishtinë (RF Yugoslavia, now in Kosovo) (b) 1,88 (c) D - central defense (d) FC Prishtina (e) KF 2 Korriku, FC Besa, KF 2 Korriku
*** Ajdinovic - Edin Ajdinovic (Един Ајдиновић) (a) 07/06/2001, Beograd (RF Yugoslavia, now in Serbia) (b) 1,84 (c) M - central midfielder (d) FK Vozdovac (e) -
*** Ajer - Kristoffer Ajer (Kristoffer Vassbakk Ajer) (a) 17/04/1998, Rælingen (Norway) (b) 1,98 (c) D - central defense (d) Brentford FC (e) Celtic FC, Kilmarnock FC, Celtic FC, Start
*** Ajeti - Albian Ajeti (a) 26/02/1997, Basel (Switzerland) (b) 1,83 (c) F - center forward (d) Celtic FC (e) Sturm Graz, Celtic FC, West Ham Utd., FC Basel, FC St. Gallen, FC Augsburg, FC St. Gallen, FC Augsburg, FC Basel
*** Ajhmajer - Nejc Ajhmajer (a) 22/04/2003, Maribor (Slovenia) (b) 1,83 (c) D - right back (d) NK Celje (e) -
*** Ajibade - Jamiu Ajibade (Jamiu Ola Ajibade) (a) 02/01/2003, ¿? (Nigeria) (b) - (c) F - center forward (d) - (e) Skála
*** Ajorque - Ludovic Ajorque (a) 25/02/1994, Saint-Denis (Reunion) (b) 1,96 (c) F - center forward (d) 1.FSV Mainz 05 (e) Racing Club Strasbourg, Clermont Foot, Angers SCO, Luçon VF, Angers SCO, Poiré-sur-Vie, Angers SCO, Angers SCO B
*** Ajroud - Anis Ajroud (a) 30/03/2002, M'saken (Tunisia) (b) 1,82 (c) F - left winger (d) ES Cannet Rocheville (e) Pietà Hotspurs, AC Ajaccio B
*** Ajrullahu - Izet Ajrullahu (a) 08/05/1998, ¿? (RF Yugoslavia, now in North Macedonia) (b) 1,75 (c) F - left winger (d) Teteks Tetovo (e) FK Skopje, Renova, Makedonija, FK Skopje, Genc Kalemler, Komarno, O. Secuiesc, UTA Arad
*** Ajzeraj - Almir Ajzeraj (a) 05/10/1997, Prishtinë (RF Yugoslavia, now in Kosovo) (b) 1,71 (c) F - left winger (d) FC Drita Gjilan (e) KF Skënderbeu, FC Ballkani, KF Skënderbeu, KF Flamurtari, Kek-U Kastriot, KF Flamurtari
*** Akakpo - Yaovi Akakpo (Roger Akakpo) (a) 11/03/1999, ¿? (Togo) (b) 1,77 (c) F - right winger (d) FK Qabala (e) -

*** Akan - Mahmut Akan (a) 14/07/1994, Ankara (Turkey) (b) 1,81 (c) D - left back (d) - (e) Ankaragücü, Menemenspor, Ankaragücü, Ankaraspor, Ankaragücü, Karabükspor, Bugsas Spor

*** Akanbi - Rasheed Akanbi (Rasheed Ibrahim Akanbi) (a) 09/05/1999, Lagos (Nigeria) (b) 1,89 (c) F - left winger (d) FC Sheriff Tiraspol (e) Kocaelispor, Menemenspor, Tire Belediye, Foca Belediye, Future PA

*** Akanji - Manuel Akanji (Manuel Obafemi Akanji) (a) 19/07/1995, Wiesendangen (Switzerland) (b) 1,88 (c) D - central defense (d) Manchester City (e) Borussia Dortmund, FC Basel, FC Winterthur

*** Akaydin - Samet Akaydin (a) 13/03/1994, Trabzon (Turkey) (b) 1,90 (c) D - central defense (d) Fenerbahce (e) Adana Demirspor, A. Keciörengücü, Sanliurfaspor, Sancaktepe Belediye, Arsinspor

*** Akbaba - Emre Akbaba (a) 04/10/1992, Seine-Saint Denis (France) (b) 1,80 (c) M - attacking midfielder (d) Adana Demirspor (e) Galatasaray, Alanyaspor, Galatasaray, Alanyaspor, Antalyaspor, Alanyaspor, Antalyaspor, Alanyaspor, Antalyaspor, K.Maras BB, FC Montfermeil

*** Akbashev - Roman Akbashev (Акбашев Роман Радикович) (a) 01/11/1991, Sterlitamak, Bashkortostan (Soviet Union, now in Russia) (b) 1,77 (c) M - attacking midfielder (d) FK Rostov (e) Fakel Voronezh, Neftekhimik, Rubin Kazan, Avangard Kursk, Volgar, Avangard Kursk, KamAZ, Avangard Kursk, Dinamo Kirov, Sperre) KamAZ, KamAZ II

*** Akbergen - Bakdaulet Akbergen (Акберген Бакдаулет Бахтиярулы) (a) 30/10/2000, Arys (Kazakhstan) (b) 1,72 (c) F - left winger (d) - (e) FK Turan, FK Turan II

*** Akbunar - Halil Akbunar (a) 09/11/1993, Izmir (Turkey) (b) 1,67 (c) F - right winger (d) Pendikspor (e) Pendikspor, Eyüpspor, KVC Westerlo, Göztepe, Elazigspor, Göztepe

*** Akdag - Erol Can Akdag (Erol Can Akdağ) (a) 18/08/1996, Giresun (Turkey) (b) 1,74 (c) M - pivot (d) Giresunspor (e) Tuzlaspor, Giresunspor, Agri 1970 Spor, Giresunspor, Ankara Adliye, Giresunspor, Ankara Adliye, Giresunspor

*** Akdag - Ümit Akdag (Ümit Akdağ) (a) 06/10/2003, Bucuresti (Romania) (b) 1,92 (c) D - central defense (d) Göztepe (e) Alanyaspor

*** Aké - Nathan Aké (Nathan Benjamin Aké) (a) 18/02/1995, Den Haag (Netherlands) (b) 1,80 (c) D - central defense (d) Manchester City (e) Bournemouth, Chelsea, Bournemouth, Chelsea, Watford, Chelsea, Reading, Chelsea

*** Akere - Samuel Akere (a) 16/02/2004, ¿? (Nigeria) (b) - (c) M - left midfielder (d) Botev Plovdiv (e) FDC Vista, G12 FC

*** Akgül - Hakan Akgül (a) 19/03/2003, Istanbul (Turkey) (b) - (c) M - attacking midfielder (d) AP Brera (e) -

*** Akgün - Oguzhan Akgün (Oğuzhan Akgün) (a) 13/07/2001, Kocaeli (Turkey) (b) 1,74 (c) F - left winger (d) Besiktas JK (e) Sakaryaspor, Besiktas, Ergene Velimese, Besiktas, Ergene Velimese, Altinordu, Istanbulspor

*** Akgün - Yunus Akgün (a) 07/07/2000, Istanbul (Turkey) (b) 1,73 (c) F - right winger (d) Galatasaray (e) Adana Demirspor, Galatasaray, Adana Demirspor, Galatasaray

*** Akhaev - Bauyrzhan Akhaev (Ахаев Бауыржан) (a) 26/09/2001, ¿? (Kazakhstan) (b) 1,77 (c) D - right back (d) FK Altay (e) Astana-M

*** Akhalaia - Lado Akhalaia (a) 01/07/2002, Chişinău (Moldova) (b) 1,90 (c) F - center forward (d) Swift Hesperange (e) Swift Hesperange, Torino, RE Virton

*** Akhanov - Yuri Akhanov (Аханов Юрий) (a) 31/07/2002, ¿? (Kazakhstan) (b) 1,85 (c) D - central defense (d) FC Astana-M (e) Astana-M

*** Akhmaev - Said-Ali Akhmaev (Ахмаев Саид-Али Саидович) (a) 30/05/1996, Moskva (Russia) (b) 1,82 (c) F - center forward (d) - (e) Khimki 2, SKA Khabarovsk, Torpedo Vlad., Tambov, Ararat Moskva, Kolomna, CSF Speranta, Rostov II, Chernomorets N., Rostov II, Spartak Moskva II

*** Akhmatov - Rassambek Akhmatov (Рассамбек Ахматов) (a) 31/05/1996, Atchkhoï-Martan (Russia) (b) 1,72 (c) M - pivot (d) - (e) Chindia, Maktaaral, Comuna Recea, Kansas City II, FC Miami City, Vauban S., FC Miami City, FCSR Obernai, FR Haguenau

*** Akhmet - Ali Akhmet (Ахмет Али) (a) 13/02/2003, ¿? (Kazakhstan) (b) 1,78 (c) F - center forward (d) Tobol Kostanay II (e) -

*** Akhmetov - Eldos Akhmetov (Елдос Қуанышұлы Ахметов) (a) 01/06/1990, Taraz (Soviet Union, now in Kazakhstan) (b) 1,87 (c) D - central defense (d) FK Aksu (e) Taraz, Kaysar, Kairat Almaty, Irtysh, FC Astana, Taraz, Irtysh, OSShlOSD Taraz

*** Akhmetov - Ilzat Akhmetov (Ахметов Ильзат Тоглокович) (a) 31/12/1997, Bishkek (Kyrgyzstan) (b) 1,73 (c) M - attacking midfielder (d) FK Krasnodar (e) CSKA Moskva, Rubin Kazan, Rubin Kazán II, Akron Konoplev

*** Akhomach - Ilias Akhomach (Ilias Akhomach Chakkour) (a) 16/04/2004, Hostalets de Pierola (Spain) (b) 1,75 (c) F - right winger (d) Villarreal CF (e) Barcelona Atlètic

*** Akhundov - Tural Akhundov (Tural Möhsüm oğlu Axundov) (a) 01/08/1988, Baku (Soviet Union, now in Azerbaijan) (b) 1,72 (c) D - right back (d) - (e) Kapaz PFK, Shamakhi, Neftchi Baku, Sumqayit, Kapaz PFK, Simurq, Ravan Baku, Mughan

*** Akhundzade - Nariman Akhundzade (Nəriman Əhməd oğlu Axundzadə) (a) 23/04/2004, ¿? (Azerbaijan) (b) - (c) F - right winger (d) Qarabağ FK (e) Qarabag 2

*** Akhvlediani - Ilia Akhvlediani (ილია ახვლედიანი) (a) 05/10/1998, ¿? (Georgia) (b) 1,82 (c) D - right back (d) FC Samtredia (e) Samgurali, Shukura

*** Akhvlediani - Tornike Akhvlediani (თორნიკე ახვლედიანი) (a) 24/07/1999, Tbilisi (Georgia) (b) 1,82 (c) F - center forward (d) FC Samtredia (e) Torpedo Kutaisi, Dinamo Tbilisi, FC Zestafoni, FC Gagra

*** Akieme - Sergio Akieme (Sergio Akieme Rodríguez) (a) 16/12/1997, Madrid (Spain) (b) 1,75 (c) D - left back (d) UD Almería (e) FC Barcelona B, UD Almería, FC Barcelona B, Rayo Vallecano, Rayo B

*** Akila - Jesse Akila (a) 27/12/2001, Jos (Nigeria) (b) - (c) F - center forward (d) AS Trencin (e) Ararat-Armenia, Plateau United, MFM FC

*** Akin - Furkan Akin (Furkan Akın) (a) 18/09/2000, Istanbul (Turkey) (b) 1,83 (c) M - central midfielder (d) FK Gomel (e) Dinamo-Auto, Darica GB

*** Akinfeev - Igor Akinfeev (Акинфеев Игорь Владимирович) (a) 08/04/1986, Vidnoe, Moskau Oblast (Soviet Union, now in Russia) (b) 1,87 (c) G (d) CSKA Moskva (e) CSKA Moskva II

*** Akinis - Nojus Akinis (a) 15/03/2004, ¿? (Lithuania) (b) - (c) M - left midfielder (d) FK Garliava (e) Kaunos Zalgiris B

*** Akinsanmiro - Ebenezer Akinsanmiro (a) 25/11/2004, ¿? (Nigeria) (b) 1,84 (c) M - attacking midfielder (d) - (e) Remo Stars FC

*** Akinsola - Tunde Akinsola (Babatunde Jimoh Akinsola) (a) 10/03/2003, Lagos (Nigeria) (b) 1,75 (c) F - right winger (d) Real Valladolid Promesas (e) Valiant FC

*** Akintola - David Akintola (Babajide David Akintola) (a) 13/01/1996, Oyo (Nigeria) (b) 1,78 (c) F - right winger (d) Adana Demirspor (e) Midtjylland, Hatayspor, Midtjylland, Omonia Nicosia, Midtjylland, Rosenborg, Midtjylland, Haugesund, Midtjylland, Jerv, Midtjylland, Thisted FC, Midtjylland, FC Ebedei

*** Akintunde - James Akintunde (Oluwaseun Ewerogba Akintunde) (a) 29/03/1996, London (England) (b) 1,75 (c) F - center forward (d) Bohemian FC (e) Derry City,

Maidenhead Utd., Chester, Cambridge Utd., Needham Market, Cambridge Utd., Brackley, Cambridge Utd., Histon FC, Cambridge Utd., Sudbury, Cambridge Utd.

*** Akinyemi - Adeleke Akinyemi (Adeleke Akinola Akinyemi) (a) 11/08/1998, Lagos (Nigeria) (b) 1,81 (c) F - center forward (d) MFK Karvina (e) KF Laçi, Start, HamKam, Start, JFK Ventspils, Real Sapphire, Renova, KF Skënderbeu, KF Trepca 89, KF Skënderbeu, Serdarli GB, Real Sapphire

*** Akio - William Akio (a) 23/07/1998, Nairobi (Kenya) (b) 1,80 (c) F - right winger (d) Cavalry FC (e) Ross County, Raith Rovers, Ross County, Valour FC, UTRGV Vaqueros

*** Akiotu - Jason Akiotu (a) 11/03/1998, London (England) (b) - (c) D - left back (d) 1874 Northwich FC (e) Portadown, Farsley, Hyde United

*** Akiti - Tobi Akiti (a) 20/04/2001, ¿? (Malta) (b) - (c) F - center forward (d) San Gwann FC (e) Mosta FC, Divine Praise

*** Akkal - Salim Akkal (a) 17/02/2000, Le Blanc-Mesnil (France) (b) - (c) M - central midfielder (d) Le Puy Foot 43 Auvergne (e) Angers SCO B, USM Alger, Angers SCO B

*** Akkan - Gökhan Akkan (a) 01/01/1995, Yozgat (Turkey) (b) 1,88 (c) G (d) Caykur Rizespor (e) Ankaragücü, Çaykur Rizespor, Ankaragücü

*** Akliouche - Maghnes Akliouche (a) 25/02/2002, Tremblay-en-France (France) (b) 1,83 (c) M - attacking midfielder (d) AS Mónaco (e) -

*** Akman - Hamza Akman (Hamza Yiğit Akman) (a) 27/09/2004, Istanbul (Turkey) (b) 1,70 (c) M - central midfielder (d) Galatasaray (e) -

*** Akmurzin - Timur Akmurzin (Акмурзин Тимур Андреевич) (a) 07/12/1997, Moskva (Russia) (b) 1,89 (c) G (d) Veles Moscú (e) Tobol Kostanay, Spartak-2, Rubin Kazan, Ufa, Rubin Kazan, Rubin Kazán II

*** Akobeto - Élie Akobeto (Élie Junior Akobeto) (a) 18/05/1995, Paris (France) (b) 1,75 (c) F - center forward (d) - (e) Flint Town, Gretna, East Stirlingshire FC, 1904 FC, Atlanta SC, Grimsby Town, Mansfield Town, Loughborough, Hyde FC

*** Akolo - Chadrac Akolo (a) 01/04/1995, Kinshasa (Zaire, now DR Congo) (b) 1,72 (c) F - right winger (d) FC St. Gallen 1879 (e) Amiens SC, SC Paderborn, Amiens SC, VfB Stuttgart, Amiens SC, VfB Stuttgart, FC Sion, Neuchâtel Xamax, FC Sion, FC Bex

*** Akosah-Bempah - Nana Akosah-Bempah (Nana Dwomoh Akosah-Bempah) (a) 29/08/1997, Delaware (United States) (b) 1,78 (c) F - center forward (d) Hapoel Acre (e) Pardubice, Motorlet Praha, Orlando P. Reserves, Cape Town Spurs, Orlando P. Reserves, Cape Town City, All Stars, Cape Town City

*** Akouokou - Paul Akouokou (Edgar Paul Akouokou) (a) 20/12/1997, Abidjan (Ivory Coast) (b) 1,81 (c) M - pivot (d) Real Betis Balompié (e) Betis Deportivo, Ekenäs IF, B. Jerusalem, H Rishon leZion, B. Jerusalem, Ekenäs IF

*** Akovic - Zoran Akovic (Zoran Aković) (a) 26/12/1985, Berane (Yugoslavia, now in Montenegro) (b) 1,93 (c) G (d) FK Mornar Bar (e) FK Berane, FK Bokelj, Zeta Golubovac, Novi Pazar, Rudar Pljevlja, Assyriska FF, Vasalunds IF, Husqvarna FF, Gefle, Husqvarna FF, FK Celik Niksic, Mornar Bar, Kecskeméti TE, OFK Bar

*** Akpa Akpro - Jean-Daniel Akpa Akpro (a) 11/10/1992, Toulouse (France) (b) 1,80 (c) M - central midfielder (d) SS Lazio (e) FC Empoli, Lazio, Salernitana, Toulouse, Toulouse B

*** Akpa Akpro - Jean-Louis Akpa Akpro (a) 04/01/1985, Toulouse (France) (b) 1,82 (c) F - center forward (d) Flint Town United (e) Radcliffe, Oldham Athletic, Masfout Club, Barnet, Yeovil Town, Barnet, Shrewsbury, Tranmere Rovers, Bury, Tranmere Rovers, AFC Rochdale, Grimsby Town, FC Brüssel, Toulouse, Stade Brestois, Toulouse, Toulouse B

*** Akpan - Ini Etim Akpan (a) 03/08/1984, ¿? (Malta) (b) - (c) G (d) Mosta FC (e) Floriana, Birkirkara FC, Lija Athletic, Birkirkara FC, Lija Athletic, Sliema Wanderers
*** Akpinar - Murat Cem Akpinar (Murat Cem Akpınar) (a) 24/01/1999, Düzköy (Turkey) (b) 1,73 (c) M - central midfielder (d) Trabzonspor (e) Giresunspor, Trabzonspor, Kocaelispor, Trabzonspor, Trabzonspor, Hekimoglu, Trabzonspor, 1461 Trabzon
*** Akpoguma - Kevin Akpoguma (Kevin John Ufuoma Akpoguma) (a) 19/04/1995, Neustadt an der Weinstraße (Germany) (b) 1,92 (c) D - central defense (d) TSG 1899 Hoffenheim (e) Hannover 96, Hoffenheim, Fortuna Düsseldorf, Hoffenheim, Karlsruher SC
*** Akpoveta - Oke Akpoveta (a) 12/12/1991, Warri (Nigeria) (b) 1,77 (c) F - center forward (d) Kokkolan Pallo-Veikot (e) Valletta, Höganäs BK, Kokkolan PV, Al-Thoqbah, Norrby, IK Frej Täby, FK Sabail, AFC Eskilstuna, Helsingborgs IF, Dalkurd, Lyngby BK, IK Frej Täby, Lyngby BK, Brönshöj BK, Ravan Baku, Brøndby IF, Warri Wolves FC
*** Akpudje - Joshua Akpudje (Joshua Oghene Ochuko Akpudje) (a) 23/07/1998, ¿? (Nigeria) (b) 1,92 (c) D - central defense (d) FK Jablonec (e) Daugavpils, Panevezys, Daugavpils, MFM FC
*** Akrap - Valentin Akrap (a) 13/01/2003, ¿? (Austria) (b) 2,02 (c) F - center forward (d) SV Horn (e) SV Horn, SV Ried, SV Ried II
*** Akrong - Jacob Akrong (Jacob Nii Martey Akrong) (a) 31/12/1992, Accra (Ghana) (b) 1,81 (c) D - central defense (d) Mosta FC (e) FE Grama, Zacatepec, Palamós CF, Badalona, UD Almería B, Granada B, CD Guadalajara, Granada B, San Roque Lepe, Granada B, Cádiz CF B, Granada B, Udinese
*** Akroum - Hicham Akroum (a) 21/06/1992, ¿? (France) (b) 1,85 (c) M - central midfielder (d) Glacis United (e) Racing CFF, IC de Croix, Saint-Dizier
*** Aksaka - Baran Aksaka (Özgür Baran Aksaka) (a) 29/01/2003, Tekirdag (Turkey) (b) 1,78 (c) M - pivot (d) Galatasaray (e) -
*** Aksalu - Mihkel Aksalu (a) 07/11/1984, Kuressaare (Soviet Union, now in Estonia) (b) 1,95 (c) G (d) Paide Linnameeskond (e) SJK Seinäjoki, FC Flora, Sheffield Utd., Mansfield Town, Sheffield Utd., FC Flora, Tervis Pärnu, FC Flora, HÜJK Emmaste, Kuressaare, Sörve JK, Kuressaare
*** Akselsen - Paetur Akselsen (Pætur Akselsen) (a) 24/04/2006, ¿? (Faroe Islands) (b) 1,86 (c) D - left back (d) 07 Vestur (e) -
*** Aksentijevic - Nikola Aksentijevic (Никола Аксентијевић) (a) 09/03/1993, Kragujevac (RF Yugoslavia, now in Montenegro) (b) 1,79 (c) D - right back (d) Ethnikos Achnas (e) Radnicki Niš, Napredak, Radnicki Niš, Vojvodina, Excelsior Mouscron, OFK Beograd, Vitesse, FK Partizan, Vitesse, FK Partizan, Teleoptik
*** Aksit - Nuri Emre Aksit (Nuri Emre Akşit) (a) 26/04/2002, Soest (Netherlands) (b) 1,84 (c) D - central defense (d) - (e) Turgutluspor, Konyaspor, 1922 Konya, Konyaspor, Menemenspor
*** Aksoy - Engin Can Aksoy (a) 14/11/2003, Bakirköy (Turkey) (b) - (c) D - left back (d) Hatayspor (e) Eyüpspor, Hatayspor
*** Aksoy - Fatih Aksoy (Fatih Aksoy) (a) 06/11/1997, Istanbul (Turkey) (b) 1,89 (c) D - central defense (d) Alanyaspor (e) Besiktas, Sivasspor, Besiktas
*** Aksu - Duhan Aksu (Tuncer Duhan Aksu) (a) 11/09/1997, Ankara (Turkey) (b) 1,83 (c) D - left back (d) Kasimpasa (e) Istanbulspor
*** Aktürkoglu - Kerem Aktürkoglu (Muhammed Kerem Aktürkoğlu) (a) 21/10/1998, Izmit (Turkey) (b) 1,73 (c) F - left winger (d) Galatasaray (e) 24 Erzincanspor, Karacabey Belediye, BB Bodrumspor

*** Akyol - Ufuk Akyol (a) 27/08/1997, Ravensburg (Germany) (b) 1,80 (d) Antalyaspor (e) KaragÃ¼mrÃ¼k

*** Akyüz - Furkan Akyüz (Furkan Onur Akyüz) (a) 21/09/2005, Bursa (Turkey) (b) 1,91 (c) G (d) Fenerbahce (e) -

*** Al Hamlawi - Assad Al Hamlawi (Assad Al Islam Al Hamlawi - أسد الإسلام الحملاوي) (a) 27/10/2000, ¿? (Sweden) (b) 1,8 (c) F - center forward (d) - (e) Varbergs BoIS, Helsingborgs IF, J-Södra IF, Helsingborgs IF, Ängelholms FF

*** Alaba - David Alaba (David Olatukunbo Alaba) (a) 24/06/1992, Wien (Austria) (b) 1,80 (c) D - central defense (d) Real Madrid CF (e) Bayern München, Hoffenheim, Bayern München, FC Bayern II, Austria Wien Reserves

*** Alabi - Samuel Alabi (Samuel Alabi Borquaye) (a) 06/05/2000, ¿? (Ghana) (b) 1,70 (c) M - attacking midfielder (d) FC Baden 1897 (e) FC Baden 1897, FC Luzern, FC Ashdod, FC Luzern, FC Ashdod, Dreams FC

*** Aláez - Jordi Aláez (Jordi Aláez Peña) (a) 23/01/1998, Andorra la Vella (Andorra) (b) 1,75 (c) F - left winger (d) Cerdanyola FC (e) FC Santa Coloma, Ciudad Real, Diagoras, FC Santa Coloma, FC Andorra

*** Alagbe - Oluwatobiloba Alagbe (Oluwatobiloba Adefunyibomi Alagbe) (a) 24/04/2000, ¿? (Nigeria) (b) - (c) D - central defense (d) Asteras Tripolis (e) Progrès Niederkorn, Asteras Tripoli, Jeunesse Esch, Asteras Tripoli

*** Alagic - Nermin Alagic (Nermin Alagić) (a) 03/05/2001, Sanski Most (Bosnia and Herzegovina) (b) - (c) M - right midfielder (d) FK Velez Mostar (e) Igman Konjic, Velez Mostar, Igman Konjic, Velez Mostar, Podgrmec S.

*** Alakbarov - Ildar Alakbarov (İldar Ruslan oğlu Əlәkbәrov) (a) 27/04/2001, Pskov (Russia) (b) 1,71 (c) F - right winger (d) Sabah FK (e) Neftekhimik, Strogino Moskva, SShOR Zenit, DYuSSh Kolomyag

*** Al-Ammari - Amir Al-Ammari (العماري عبود فؤاد أمير) (a) 27/07/1997, Jönköping (Sweden) (b) 1,84 (c) M - central midfielder (d) Halmstads BK (e) IFK Göteborg, Halmstads BK, IFK Göteborg, Mjällby AIF, IFK Göteborg, Halmstads BK, J-Södra IF, Husqvarna FF

*** Alampasu - Dele Alampasu (Dele Sunday Alampasu) (a) 24/12/1996, ¿? (Nigeria) (b) 1,99 (c) G (d) Jura Dolois Football (e) Pietà Hotspurs, Jelgava, JFK Ventspils, Feirense, Cesarense, Feirense, Abuja College

*** Alan Calbergue - Alan Calbergue (Alan Calbergue Leite Rodrigues) (a) 11/07/1998, Belém (Brazil) (b) 1,70 (c) M - central midfielder (d) KF Erzeni (e) Sousa, Passo Fundo, Monte Azul, Paysandu, América-RN, Paysandu, Marília, Paysandu, Aimoré, Paysandu

*** Alan Dias - Alan Dias (Alan Carlos de Paula Dias Filho) (a) 05/09/1998, ¿? (Brazil) (b) 1,91 (c) D - central defense (d) Lokomotiv Sofia (e) Criciúma EC, Brasil Pelotas, Botafogo-SP, Goiás B

*** Aland - Richard Aland (a) 15/03/1994, Tartu (Estonia) (b) 1,94 (c) G (d) Jalgpallikool Tammeka (e) FA Tartu Kalev, JK Trans Narva, FCI Levadia, FC Flora, Pärnu Vaprus, FC Flora, JK Nomme Kalju, Tartu SK 10 II, Tartu SK 10, Tartu SK 10 II

*** Alanko - Samu Alanko (a) 16/05/1998, Vaasa (Finland) (b) 1,84 (c) F - left winger (d) Vaasan Palloseura (e) AC Oulu, VPS, Young Violets, First Vienna FC, VPS, FF Jaro, VPS

*** Alarcón - Ángel Alarcón (Ángel Alarcón Galiot) (a) 15/05/2004, Castelldefels (Spain) (b) - (c) F - left winger (d) FC Barcelona Atlètic (e) -

*** Alarcón - Felipe Alarcón (Luis Felipe Alarcón Guzmán) (a) 02/02/1992, Madrid (Spain) (b) 1,60 (c) D - central defense (d) - (e) Sant Julià, Botev Vratsa II

*** Alarcón - Tomás Alarcón (Tomás Jesús Alarcón Vergara) (a) 19/01/1999, Rancagua (Chile) (b) 1,76 (c) M - pivot (d) Cádiz CF (e) Real Zaragoza, Cádiz CF, O'Higgins

*** Alaribe - Emmanuel Alaribe (Emmanuel Chinemerem Alaribe) (a) 24/08/2000, Owerri (Nigeria) (b) 1,80 (c) F - center forward (d) FC Zimbru Chisinau (e) Ramat haSharon, FC Bălți, Codru, Olympic Hybrid

*** Alario - Lucas Alario (Lucas Nicolás Alario) (a) 08/10/1992, Tostado, Santa Fe (Argentina) (b) 1,85 (c) F - center forward (d) Eintracht Frankfurt (e) Bayer Leverkusen, River Plate, Colón

*** Alasania - Gegi Alasania (გეგი ალასანია) (a) 01/06/2003, ¿? (Georgia) (b) - (c) D (d) Guria Lanchkhuti (e) FC Irao Tbilisi, Locomotive II

*** Alasgarov - Namiq Alasgarov (a) 03/02/1995, Ã‡ilÉ™gir, Qusar Region (Azerbaijan) (b) 1,73 (d) Sabah FK (e) Bursaspor, Neftchi Baku, Qarabag FK, Kapaz PFK, Qarabag FK, FK Baku

*** Alasgarov - Salman Alasgarov (Salman Sabit oğlu Ələsgərov) (a) 09/06/2001, Gandja (Azerbaijan) (b) 1,88 (c) M - central midfielder (d) FK Qabala 2 (e) PFK Zaqatala

*** Alava - Aapeli Alava (a) 05/02/2001, ¿? (Finland) (b) - (c) G (d) - (e) Kuopion Elo

*** Alaverdyan - Narek Alaverdyan (Նարեկ Ալավերդյան) (a) 19/02/2002, Yerevan (Armenia) (b) 1,76 (c) M - right midfielder (d) BKMA Yerevan (e) Ararat-Armenia, Ararat-Armenia II

*** Alavidze - Mikheil Alavidze (მიხეილ ალავიძე) (a) 05/11/1987, Batumi (Soviet Union, now in Georgia) (b) 1,82 (c) G (d) - (e) Dinamo Batumi, Rustavi, Dinamo Batumi, Guria, FK Andijon, Dinamo Batumi, Shurtan Guzar, Metalurgi R., Standard, FC Locomotive, Metalurgi R.

*** Alba - Jordi Alba (Jordi Alba Ramos) (a) 21/03/1989, L'Hospitalet de Llobregat (Spain) (b) 1,70 (c) D - left back (d) Inter Miami CF (e) FC Barcelona, Valencia CF, Gimnàstic, Valencia CF, Valencia Mestalla

*** Alba - Miguel Alba (Miguel Ángel Alba) (a) 14/08/1988, Mar del Plata (Argentina) (b) 1,85 (c) F - attacking midfielder (d) Santa Lucia FC (e) Agropoli, Trinitapoli, Valletta, Birkirkara FC, Valletta, Gimnasia y Tiro, Birkirkara FC, Ermis Aradippou, PAE Veria, Pafos FC, CD Guaraní, Santamarina, Ñublense, Alianza Petrol., Douglas Haig, Unión (MdP), Chacarita Jrs., Unión (MdP)

*** Al-Badarin - Monir Al-Badarin (Монир Хакам Ал Бадарин البدارين حكم منير) (a) 08/07/2005, Stara Zagora (Bulgaria) (b) - (c) M - attacking midfielder (d) - (e) Botev II

*** Albanese - Alessandro Albanese (a) 12/01/2000, Luik (Belgium) (b) 1,74 (c) F - left winger (d) KV Oostende (e) RE Virton, KV Oostende, Waasland-Beveren

*** Albanese - Ivan Albanese (a) 14/07/1998, Luxembourg (Luxembourg) (b) - (c) F - right winger (d) UN Käerjeng 97 (e) Swift Hesperange, Differdange 03, Swift Hesperange, Differdange 03

*** Albanis - Christos Albanis (Χρήστος Αλμπάνης) (a) 05/11/1994, Kalabaka (Greece) (b) 1,84 (c) F - left winger (d) FC Andorra (e) AEK Athína, FC Andorra, AEK Athína, Apollon Limassol, AEK Athína, Apollon Smyrnis, SC Freiburg II, E. Frankfurt II

*** Albayrak - Mehmet Albayrak (a) 05/01/2004, Adana (Turkey) (b) - (c) D - central defense (d) Sivasspor (e) -

*** Alberto Costa - Alberto Costa (Alberto Oliveira Baio) (a) 29/09/2003, Santo Tirso (Portugal) (b) 1,86 (c) D - right back (d) Vitória Guimarães SC B (e) -

*** Albertsson - Aron Thórdur Albertsson (Aron Þórður Albertsson) (a) 27/06/1996, ¿? (Iceland) (b) - (c) M - central midfielder (d) KR Reykjavík (e) Fram Reykjavík, Thróttur, HK Kópavogs, Fram Reykjavík

*** Albijanic - Milorad Albijanic (Milorad Albijanić) (a) 04/10/1998, Trebinje (Bosnia and Herzegovina) (b) 1,86 (c) F - center forward (d) FK Radnik Bijeljina (e) Simm-Bau, Leotar Trebinje, Simm-Bau, HNK Capljina, Igman Konjic, Zvijezda 09

*** Albini - Filippo Albini (a) 16/09/2000, Rimini (Italy) (b) - (c) F - center forward (d) AC Virtus Acquaviva (e) Sant'Ermete, United Riccione, Savignanese

*** Albiol - Raúl Albiol (Raúl Albiol Tortajada) (a) 04/09/1985, Vilamarxant (Spain) (b) 1,90 (c) D - central defense (d) Villarreal CF (e) Napoli, Real Madrid, Valencia CF, Getafe CF, Valencia CF, Valencia B

*** Alblas - Norbert Alblas (a) 12/12/1994, Amstelveen (Netherlands) (b) 1,86 (c) G (d) Excelsior Rotterdam (e) TOP Oss, NEC Nijmegen, Ajax, Ajax B

*** Albrighton - Marc Albrighton (Marc Kevin Albrighton) (a) 18/11/1989, Tamworth (England) (b) 1,75 (c) M - right midfielder (d) Leicester City (e) West Bromwich Albion, Leicester City, Aston Villa, Wigan Ath., Aston Villa, Aston Villa Reserves

*** Albu - Alexandru Albu (Cristian Alexandru Albu) (a) 17/08/1993, Bucuresti (Romania) (b) 1,88 (c) M - pivot (d) FC Rapid 1923 (e) Concordia, FC Rapid 1923, Concordia, UTA Arad, Concordia, Academica Clinceni, Concordia, Chiajna II, Unirea Urziceni

*** Albu - Catalin Albu (Andrei Cătălin Albu) (a) 03/06/2004, Plenița (Romania) (b) - (c) M - central midfielder (d) ACSO Filiasi (e) ACSO Filiasi, FC U Craiova, Academia Hagi

*** Albu - Dragos Albu (Constantin Dragoș Albu) (a) 15/03/2001, Plenița (Romania) (b) 1,86 (c) M - central midfielder (d) FC U Craiova 1948 (e) AF Gică Popescu

*** Alcaraz - Carlos Alcaraz (Carlos Jonás Alcaraz) (a) 30/11/2002, La Plata (Argentina) (b) 1,83 (c) M - central midfielder (d) Southampton FC (e) Racing, Racing Club II

*** Alcaraz - Rubén Alcaraz (Rubén Alcaraz Jiménez) (a) 01/05/1991, Barcelona (Spain) (b) 1,80 (c) M - central midfielder (d) Cádiz CF (e) Real Valladolid, Cádiz CF, Real Valladolid, Girona FC, UD Almería, Girona FC, CE L'Hospitalet, AE Prat, Gramenet, Gramenet B, UA Horta

*** Alceus - Bryan Alceus (a) 01/02/1996, Colombes (France) (b) 1,75 (c) M - central midfielder (d) Doxa Katokopias (e) FC Arges, Olympiakos N., FC Arges, Zira FK, Gaz Metan, Paris FC, Bastia-Borgo, Paris FC, C'Chartres, Entente SSG, Stade Bordelais, Cozes, Girondins Bordeaux B

*** Alcevski - Marko Alcevski (Марко Алчевски) (a) 16/04/2002, Bitola (North Macedonia) (b) 1,88 (c) G (d) AP Brera (e) Borec Veles, AP Brera

*** Aldair - Aldair (Aldair Djaló Baldé) (a) 31/01/1992, Vila Meã (Portugal) (b) 1,70 (c) F - right winger (d) Bodrum FK (e) Olimpija, Tabor Sezana, Onisilos Sotira, União Madeira, Gil Vicente, AEL Limassol, Olhanense, Penafiel

*** Al-Dakhil - Ameen Al-Dakhil (أمين الدخيل) (a) 06/03/2002, ¿?, Baghdad (Irak) (b) 1,87 (c) D - central defense (d) Burnley FC (e) Sint-Truiden, Standard Liège

*** Alderete - Omar Alderete (Omar Federico Alderete Fernández) (a) 26/12/1996, Asunción (Paraguay) (b) 1,88 (c) D - central defense (d) Getafe CF (e) Hertha Berlin, Getafe CF, Hertha Berlin, Valencia CF, Hertha Berlin, FC Basel, Huracán, Cerro Porteño, Gimnasia y Esgrima, Cerro Porteño

*** Alderweireld - Toby Alderweireld (Tobias Albertine Maurits Alderweireld) (a) 02/03/1989, Wilrijk (Belgium) (b) 1,87 (c) D - central defense (d) Royal Antwerp FC

(e) Al-Duhail SC, Tottenham Hotspur, Atlético Madrid, Southampton, Atlético Madrid, Ajax, Ajax B

*** Alebiosu - Ryan Alebiosu (a) 17/12/2001, London (England) (b) 1,88 (c) D - right back (d) - (e) Kilmarnock FC, Crewe Alexandra

*** Aleesami - Haitam Aleesami (a) 31/07/1991, Oslo (Norway) (b) 1,83 (c) D - left back (d) - (e) Apollon Limassol, Rostov, Amiens SC, Palermo, IFK Göteborg, Fredrikstad, Skeid, Holmlia SK

*** Alef - Alef (Alef dos Santos Saldanha) (a) 28/01/1995, Nova Odessa (Brazil) (b) 1,86 (c) M - pivot (d) São Bernardo FC (e) Fehérvár, SC Braga, APOEL FC, SC Braga, AEK Athína, SC Braga, Apollon Limassol, SC Braga, Umm Salal SC, SC Braga, Ponte Preta, Ol. Marseille B, Ponte Preta

*** Alef Santos - Alef Santos (Alef Santos de Araujo) (a) 06/11/1996, Salvador (Brazil) (b) 1,80 (c) M - pivot (d) FC Dila Gori (e) Dinamo Batumi, FC Dila, Dinamo Batumi, Maringá, Mirassol-SP, Atlântico FC, Vitória B

*** Alefirenko - Danyil Alefirenko (Алефіренко Даниїл Сергійович) (a) 19/04/2000, Kharkiv (Ukraine) (b) 1,76 (c) F - left winger (d) Zorya Lugansk (e) Chornomorets, Zorya Lugansk, Zorya II, SK Metalist

*** Alegría - Juan Alegría (Juan Diego Alegría Arango) (a) 06/06/2002, Ibagué (Colombia) (b) 1,78 (c) F - center forward (d) Jaguares de Córdoba (e) FC Honka, Rangers II, Falkirk FC, Rangers II, Partick Thistle, Rangers II, FC Honka

*** Alejo - Iván Alejo (Iván Alejo Peralta) (a) 10/02/1995, Valladolid (Spain) (b) 1,86 (c) F - right winger (d) Cádiz CF (e) Getafe CF, Cádiz CF, Getafe CF, Málaga CF, Getafe CF, SD Eibar, Alcorcón, Villarreal CF B, At. Madrid B, At. Madrid C

*** Aleksandrov - Aleksandar Aleksandrov (Александър Емилов Александров) (a) 30/07/1986, Sofia (Bulgaria) (b) 1,75 (c) D - right back (d) - (e) CSKA 1948, Tsarsko Selo, CSKA 1948, Slavia Sofia, Etar, Levski Sofia, Cherno More, Beroe, Lokomotiv SZ, Minyor Pernik, Conegliano, Septemvri Sofia

*** Aleksandrov - Aleksandar Aleksandrov (Александър Ивов Александров) (a) 28/03/1994, Pernik (Bulgaria) (b) 1,78 (c) F - right winger (d) Minyor Pernik (e) Lokomotiv Sofia, Dunav, Lokomotiv Sofia, Neftochimik, CSKA-Sofia, Minyor Pernik, Slavia Sofia, Minyor Pernik

*** Aleksandrov - Denislav Aleksandrov (Денислав Мартинов Александров) (a) 19/07/1997, Pleven (Bulgaria) (b) 1,82 (c) F - left winger (d) Slavia Sofia (e) Lokomotiv Plovdiv, CSKA 1948, Ludogorets II

*** Aleksandrov - Maksim Aleksandrov (Александров Максим Михайлович) (a) 26/01/2002, ¿? (Russia) (b) 1,83 (c) M - pivot (d) Dinamo 2 Moskva (e) Dinamo Moskva II

*** Aleksandrov - Simeon Aleksandrov (Симеон Славейков Александров) (a) 24/09/2003, ¿? (Bulgaria) (b) 1,64 (c) F - left winger (d) Pirin Blagoevgrad (e) CSKA-Sofia, Septemvri Sofia, CSKA-Sofia, Septemvri Sofia

*** Aleksandrov - Viktor Aleksandrov (Александров Виктор Сергеевич) (a) 14/02/2002, Nizhniy Novgorod (Russia) (b) 1,87 (c) D - central defense (d) FC Pari Nizhniy Novgorod (e) Rubin Kazan, Pari Nizhny Novgórod, Rubin Kazan, Rubin Kazán II, Valmiera, Rubin Kazán II

*** Aleksandrovich - Aleksandr Aleksandrovich (Александрович Александр Юрьевич) (a) 06/07/1997, ¿? (Belarus) (b) - (c) M - attacking midfielder (d) Dnepr Mogilev (e) Belshina, FC Tver, Smolevichi, Vitebsk, Orsha, Vitebsk, Orsha, Vitebsk, Vitebsk II, FK Postavy

*** Aleksandrovs - Niks Aleksandrovs (Niks Daniels Aleksandrovs) (a) 05/05/2002, ¿? (Latvia) (b) - (c) G (d) FK Auda (e) Riga II

*** Alekseev - Ivan Alekseev (Алексеев Иван Александрович) (a) 29/06/2001, St. Petersburg (Russia) (b) 1,79 (c) M - central midfielder (d) - (e) Rodina Moskva, Akritas Chlor., Rodina Moskva, Zvezda St. Peterburg, Arsenal Tula II, Algoritm SPb, DYuSSh Kolomyag

*** Alekseev - Nikita Alekseev (Алексеев Никита Сергеевич) (a) 09/01/2002, Lukino (Russia) (b) 1,94 (c) G (d) Ural 2 Ekaterinburg (e) Nosta, Master-Saturn

*** Alekseiciks - Kristers Alekseiciks (Kristers Alekseiciks (geb. Kristers Neilands)) (a) 09/09/2000, Kuldiga (Latvia) (b) 1,97 (c) D - central defense (d) Valmiera FC (e) Tukums, Valmiera, JFK Ventspils, Ventspils II

*** Aleksi - Albano Aleksi (a) 10/10/1992, Fier (Albania) (b) 1,77 (c) M - pivot (d) KF Egnatia (e) KF Tirana, KF Teuta, FC Luftëtari, KF Butrinti

*** Aleksic - Danijel Aleksic (Данијел Алексић) (a) 30/04/1991, Pula (Yugoslavia, now in Croatia) (b) 1,82 (c) M - attacking midfielder (d) Basaksehir FK (e) Al-Ahli, Yeni Malatyaspor, FC St. Gallen, Lechia Gdánsk, St.-Étienne, AC Arles-Avignon, St.-Étienne, Genoa, Greuther Fürth, Genoa, Vojvodina, Vojvodina II

*** Aleksievich - Ilya Aleksievich (Алексиевич Илья Леонидович) (a) 10/02/1991, Zhodino (Soviet Union, now in Belarus) (b) 1,72 (c) M - pivot (d) FK Gomel (e) Krumkachi, FK Minsk, Torpedo Zhodino, Soligorsk, Torpedo Zhodino, Soligorsk, Panetolikos, BATE Borisov, Gomel, Torpedo Zhodino, Zhodino II

*** Aleksovski - Filip Aleksovski (Филип Алексовски) (a) 25/03/2000, Skopje (North Macedonia) (b) 1,84 (c) F - right winger (d) Makedonija Gjorce Petrov (e) Korabi Debar, Makedonija

*** Aleksovski - Igor Aleksovski (a) 24/02/1995, Skopje (North Macedonia) (b) 1,86 (c) G (d) Rabotnicki Skopje (e) Renova, FC Shkupi, Vardar, Makedonija

*** Alemán - Antonio Alemán (Antonio Alemán Miñano) (a) 27/01/2001, Murcia (Spain) (b) - (c) M - attacking midfielder (d) Atlético Bembibre (e) Hércules CF B, Salamanca CF B, Torre Pacheco

*** Alemañ - Pedro Alemañ (Pedro Alemañ Serna) (a) 21/03/2002, Elche (Spain) (b) 1,82 (c) M - attacking midfielder (d) Sparta Rotterdam (e) Valencia Mestalla

*** Alemão - Alemão (Guilherme António de Souza) (a) 07/12/1992, Morro Agudo (Brazil) (b) 1,71 (c) D - right back (d) FC Ararat-Armenia (e) Oliveirense, Leixões, Marítimo B, Tourizense, São Carlos

*** Alemão - Alemão (João Victor Tornich) (a) 06/11/2002, Franca (Brazil) (b) 1,94 (c) D - central defense (d) Portimonense SC (e) -

*** Alemayehu Mulugeta - Isak Alemayehu Mulugeta (Isak Alexander Alemayehu Mulugeta) (a) 11/10/2006, Umeå (Sweden) (b) 1,77 (c) M - attacking midfielder (d) Djurgårdens IF (e) -

*** Alemdar - Dogan Alemdar (Doğan Alemdar) (a) 29/10/2002, Kayseri (Turkey) (b) 1,92 (c) G (d) ESTAC Troyes (e) Troyes, Stade Rennes, Kayserispor

*** Aleme - Bryan Aleme (Bryan Glenn Andrew Aleme Ondua) (a) 08/02/2001, Paris (France) (b) 1,91 (c) M - pivot (d) - (e) Penya Encarnada, Zejtun C., Esperance Paris, Salamanca CF B

*** Aleñá - Carles Aleñá (Carles Aleñá Castillo) (a) 05/01/1998, Mataró (Spain) (b) 1,80 (c) M - central midfielder (d) Getafe CF (e) FC Barcelona, Getafe CF, FC Barcelona, Real Betis, FC Barcelona, FC Barcelona B

*** Alesevic - Vehudin Alesevic (Vehudin Alešević) (a) 02/07/1997, Bihać (Bosnia and Herzegovina) (b) 1,79 (c) F - right winger (d) FK Igman Konjic (e) FK Olimpik, Slavija S., FK Olimpik, Krajisnik

*** Aléx Bruno - Aléx Bruno (Aléx Bruno de Souza Silva) (a) 07/10/1993, Queimados (Brazil) (b) 1,73 (c) F - left winger (d) - (e) Maktaaral, Atyrau, Londrina-PR, Suwon FC, Gyeongnam FC, Zimbru Chisinau, Santa Rita, Widzew Lódz,

*** Alex Júnior - Alex Júnior (Alex Júnior Christian) (a) 05/12/1993, Port-au-Prince (Haiti) (b) 1,83 (c) M - left midfielder (d) FK Aksu (e) FC Telavi, Taraz, Atyrau, Ararat-Armenia, Gandzasar, Boavista, Camacha, Boavista, Vila Real, Boavista, Vila Real, Newark, Violette AC

*** Alex Matos - Alex Matos (Alexsander Francisco de Matos Júnior) (a) 06/07/2002, ¿? (Brazil) (b) 1,69 (c) F - left winger (d) - (e) Paysandu

*** Alex Pinto - Alex Pinto (Carlos Alexandre Reis Pinto) (a) 08/07/1998, Guimarães (Portugal) (b) 1,87 (c) D - right back (d) DAC Dunajska Streda (e) Farense, Benfica B, Gil Vicente, Benfica B

*** Alex Raoul - Alex Raoul (Alex Raoul Leyi) (a) 29/09/2002, Douala (Cameroon) (b) 1,90 (c) D - central defense (d) KF Llapi (e) Santo André, Fecafoot

*** Alex Sandro - Alex Sandro (Alex Sandro Lobo Silva) (a) 26/01/1991, Catanduva (Brazil) (b) 1,81 (c) D - left back (d) Juventus de Turín (e) FC Porto, Maldonado, Santos, Maldonado, Atlético-PR

*** Alex Santana - Alex Santana (Alex Paulo Menezes Santana) (a) 13/05/1995, Atibaia (Brazil) (b) 1,82 (c) M - central midfielder (d) Club Athletico Paranaense (e) Ludogorets, Botafogo, Internacional, Paraná, Internacional, Paraná, Internacional, Guarani, Internacional, Criciúma EC, Internacional

*** Alex Souza - Alex Souza (Alex Aparecido de Souza Alcântara) (a) 24/03/2001, Tres Lagoas (MS) (Brazil) (b) 1,80 (c) F - center forward (d) FC Hegelmann (e) Boluspor, Hegelmann

*** Alexander - Uwem Alexander (a) 20/05/2002, Zagreb (Croatia) (b) 1,90 (c) D - central defense (d) NK Bjelovar (e) NK Osijek, Hrv Dragovoljac, NK Osijek, NK Osijek II, NK Dugo Selo

*** Alexander-Arnold - Trent Alexander-Arnold (Trent John Alexander-Arnold) (a) 07/10/1998, Liverpool (England) (b) 1,80 (c) D - right back (d) Liverpool FC (e) -

*** Alexandersson - Kári Daníel Alexandersson (a) 29/09/2003, ¿? (Iceland) (b) - (c) D - central defense (d) - (e) Valur, Grótta, Valur, Njardvík, Valur

*** Alexandersson - Noah Alexandersson (Noah Jonathan Alexandersson) (a) 30/09/2001, Warrington (England) (b) 1,79 (c) F - right winger (d) Moss FK (e) IFK Göteborg, Moss, IFK Göteborg

*** Alexandropoulos - Sotiris Alexandropoulos (Σωτήρης Αλεξανδρόπουλος) (a) 26/11/2001, Marousi (Greece) (b) 1,86 (c) M - central midfielder (d) Olympiakos El Pireo (e) Olympiakos, Sporting Lisboa, Panathinaikos

*** Alexsandro - Alexsandro (Alexsandro Victor de Souza Ribeiro) (a) 09/08/1999, Rio de Janeiro (Brazil) (b) 1,89 (c) D - central defense (d) LOSC Lille Métropole (e) Chaves, Amora FC, Praiense

*** Alfa - Abdullahi Alfa (a) 29/07/1996, Kaduna (Nigeria) (b) 1,76 (c) M - central midfielder (d) Pcimianka Pcim (e) Kalev, Liepaja, JFK Ventspils

*** Alfa Semedo - Alfa Semedo (Alfa Semedo Esteves) (a) 30/08/1997, Bissau (Guinea-Bissau) (b) 1,89 (c) M - pivot (d) Al-Tai FC (e) Vitória Guimarães, Benfica, Reading, Benfica, Nottingham Forest, Benfica, RCD Espanyol, Benfica, Moreirense, Benfica B, Vilafranquense, Benfica B, Fidjus Bideras

*** Alfaiate - Alexandre Alfaiate (Alexandre Correia Alfaiate) (a) 17/08/1995, Peniche (Portugal) (b) 1,85 (c) D - central defense (d) FC Pas de la Casa (e) Penya Encarnada, FC Ordino, AC Escaldes, Penya Encarnada, FC Ordino, Lusitano FCV, Lusitanos, AFC Tubize, Benfica B, Académica Coimbra, Benfica B

*** Alfaro - Alejandro Alfaro (Alejandro Alfaro Cascales) (a) 15/06/2002, Alicante (Spain) (b) 1,83 (c) M - central midfielder (d) Elche Ilicitano (e) -

*** Alfonsi - Oliver Alfonsi (a) 03/06/2003, ¿? (Sweden) (b) - (c) F - right winger (d) Varbergs BoIS (e) -

*** Alfred - Steven Alfred (Steven Alfred) (a) 11/10/1997, ¿? (Nigeria) (b) 1,78 (c) F - center forward (d) Maccabi Herzliya (e) Hapoel Hadera, FK Slutsk, Pyunik Yerevan, Sochi, FC Saxan, Kwara United

*** Al-Ghaddioui - Hamadi Al-Ghaddioui (جاديوى ال هامادى) (a) 22/09/1990, Bonn (Germany) (b) 1,90 (c) F - center forward (d) SC Freiburg II (e) SV Sandhausen, Pafos FC, VfB Stuttgart, Jahn Regensburg, SF Lotte, Borussia Dortmund II, SC Verl, Bayer Leverkusen II, Brüser Berg

*** Algobia - Ángel Algobia (Ángel Algobia Esteves) (a) 23/06/1999, Velilla de San Antonio (Spain) (b) 1,88 (c) M - pivot (d) Levante UD (e) Getafe CF, Getafe CF B, Rayo B

*** Alhadhur - Chaker Alhadhur (a) 04/12/1991, Nantes (France) (b) 1,72 (c) D - left back (d) - (e) AC Ajaccio, LB Châteauroux, SM Caen, LB Châteauroux, SM Caen, FC Nantes, Bayonne, FC Nantes, FC Nantes B

*** Al-Hajj - Rami Al-Hajj (رامي الحاج) (a) 17/09/2001, Beirut (Lebanon) (b) 1,80 (c) M - attacking midfielder (d) Odense Boldklub (e) Heerenveen

*** Al-Hamawi - Amin Al-Hamawi (الحموي أمين) (a) 17/12/2003, ¿? (Irak) (b) - (c) F - center forward (d) Helsingborgs IF (e) Torns IF, Helsingborgs IF

*** Alharaish - Zakaria Alharaish (الهريش زكرياء, Zakaria Elmabruk Alharaish) (a) 23/10/1998, Misrata (Lybia) (b) 1,80 (c) F - right winger (d) - (e) USM Alger, Sutjeska Niksic, Al-Ahli, CS Constantine, Ittihad Tanger, Sutjeska Niksic

*** Alhassan - Baba Alhassan (a) 03/01/2000, Accra (Ghana) (b) - (c) M - central midfielder (d) FC Hermannstadt (e) -

*** Alho - Nikolai Alho (a) 12/03/1993, Helsinki (Finland) (b) 1,72 (c) D - right back (d) Volos NPS (e) MTK Budapest, HJK Helsinki, Halmstads BK, HJK Helsinki, FC Lahti, HJK Helsinki, HJK Klubi 04

*** Ali - Dzhuneyt Ali (Джуниет Али Али) (a) 05/09/1994, Kardzhali (Bulgaria) (b) 1,74 (c) D - right back (d) Krumovgrad (e) Arda Kardzhali, Beroe, Neftochimik, Nesebar, Vereya, B. Galabovo

*** Ali - Hussein Ali (a) 01/03/2002, Malmö (Sweden) (b) 1,80 (c) D - right back (d) SC Heerenveen (e) Örebro SK

*** Ali - Jusif Ali (Jusif Joose Ali) (a) 04/05/2000, Espoo (Finland) (b) 1,74 (c) F - right winger (d) FC Lahti (e) Helsinki IFK, AC Oulu, Ilves, Ilves, HJK Klubi 04

*** Ali - Taha Ali (Taha Abdi Ali) (a) 01/07/1998, Spånga (Sweden) (b) 1,74 (c) F - right winger (d) Malmö FF (e) Helsingborgs IF, Örebro SK, Västerås SK, Örebro SK, Sollentuna FK, IFK Stocksund, Sundbybergs IK

*** Aliaj - Kevin Aliaj (a) 05/08/1999, ¿? (Albania) (b) - (c) F - right winger (d) KS Kastrioti (e) FK Bylis

*** Alibayli - Elton Alibayli (Elton Nəsimi oğlu Əlibəyli) (a) 04/02/2000, ¿? (Azerbaijan) (b) 1,74 (c) D - right back (d) Neftchi 2 Baku (e) Neftchi Baku, FK Sabail, Neftchi Baku, Neftchi 2 Baku

*** Alibec - Denis Alibec (a) 05/01/1991, Mangalia (Romania) (b) 1,87 (c) F - center forward (d) FCV Farul Constanta (e) Kayserispor, Atromitos FC, Kayserispor, CFR Cluj, Kayserispor, Astra Giurgiu, FCSB, Astra Giurgiu, Internazionale Milano, Bologna, Internazionale Milano, FC Viitorul, Internazionale Milano, FC Viitorul, Internazionale Milano, KV Mechelen, Farul Constanta

*** Alibekov - Akhmed Alibekov (Алібеков Ахмед Арсланалійович) (a) 29/05/1998, Zaporizhya (Ukraine) (b) 1,82 (c) M - pivot (d) FC Dinamo de Kiev (e) PFK Lviv, Dinamo Kyïv, Zorya Lugansk, Dinamo Kyïv, Ufa, Dinamo Kyïv, Dinamo Kiev II, Slovan Liberec, Dinamo Kiev II

*** Alic - Adi Alic (Adi Alić) (a) 05/03/2002, Tuzla (Bosnia and Herzegovina) (b) 1,87 (c) F - center forward (d) Achyronas-Onisilos FC (e) Sloboda Tuzla, S. Novi Grad, Sloboda Tuzla

*** Alic - Berin Alic (Berin Alić) (a) 07/01/2000, Konjic (Bosnia and Herzegovina) (b) 1,94 (c) M - pivot (d) FK Gorazde (e) Igman Konjic

*** Alic - Enes Alic (Enes Alić) (a) 03/09/1999, Sarajevo (Bosnia and Herzegovina) (b) 1,75 (c) D - left back (d) Kisvárda FC (e) Domžale, Mladost Kakanj, SK Detmarovice

*** Alic - Ermin Alic (Ermin Alić) (a) 23/02/1992, Pljevlja (Yugoslavia, now in Montenegro) (b) 1,86 (c) D - central defense (d) Jedinstvo Bijelo Polje (e) Drava Ptuj, OFK Titograd, Olimpija, NK Triglav, FK Decic Tuzi, Rudar Pljevlja, Spartak, Villarreal CF B, Rudar Pljevlja, Jedinstvo

*** Alic - Semir Alic (Семир Алић) (a) 27/03/2004, Novi Pazar (Serbia and Montenegro, now in Serbia) (b) 1,87 (c) M - pivot (d) FK Novi Pazar (e) -

*** Alicanov - Elchin Alicanov (Elçin Mübariz oğlu Əlicanov) (a) 15/07/1999, ¿? (Azerbaijan) (b) 1,81 (c) D - central defense (d) Kapaz PFK (e) PFK Zaqatala

*** Alici - Kerim Alici (Kerim Alıcı) (a) 24/06/1997, Izmir (Turkey) (b) 1,83 (c) D - right back (d) Hatayspor (e) Altinordu, Hatayspor, Göztepe, Boluspor, Göztepe, Altinordu

*** Alidema - Festim Alidema (a) 05/10/1997, Gjilan (RF Yugoslavia, now in Kosovo) (b) 1,80 (c) F - right winger (d) - (e) KF Llapi, Slaven Belupo, FC Drita, Slaven Belupo, Hrv Dragovoljac, Slaven Belupo, FC Llapi, KF Vllaznia

*** Alidou - Faride Alidou (a) 18/07/2001, Wilhemsburg, Hamburg (Germany) (b) 1,86 (c) F - left winger (d) Eintracht Frankfurt (e) SV Hamburg, Hamburg II

*** Aliev - Kamran Aliev (Алиев Камран Гурбанович) (a) 15/10/1998, Novoivanovka (Azerbaijan) (b) 1,78 (c) M - attacking midfielder (d) Sumqayit PFK (e) Arsenal Tula, SKA Khabarovsk, Khimki, SKA Khabarovsk, Khimki, Khimki II

*** Alijagic - Denis Alijagic (Denis Alijagić) (a) 10/04/2003, Praha (Czech Rep.) (b) 1,86 (c) F - center forward (d) Olympiakos B (e) NK Maribor, Olympiakos B, Slavia Praha, Slovan Liberec, Slavia Praha, Slavia Praha B, Vlasim, Slavia Praha B

*** Aliji - Burhan Aliji (a) 29/09/1989, Kumanovo (Yugoslavia, now in North Macedonia) (b) 1,76 (c) M - central midfielder (d) - (e) Sileks, Ohrid Lihnidos, KF Vëllaznimi, Euromilk GL, KF Liria, Euromilk GL, Gostivar, Drita Bogovinje, Shkëndija, Teteks Tetovo, FK Milano Kumanovo, Baskimi

*** Aliji - Naser Aliji (Naser Ismail Aliji) (a) 27/12/1993, Kumanovo (North Macedonia) (b) 1,77 (c) D - left back (d) FC Voluntari (e) Honvéd, FC Dinamo, Virtus Entella, 1.FC Kaiserslautern, FC Basel, FC Vaduz, FC Basel

*** Alilovic - Ailan Alilovic (a) 30/11/2004, ¿? (Luxembourg) (b) - (c) G (d) Jeunesse Esch (e) -

*** Alimbarashvili - Giorgi Alimbarashvili (გიორგი ალიმბარაშვილი) (a) 01/09/2001, ¿? (Georgia) (b) - (c) M - central midfielder (d) FC Meshakhte Tkibuli (e) Guria, Gori FC, FC Dila, Chikhura, FC Dila, Gori FC, Dila II

*** Alimi - Armend Alimi (a) 11/12/1987, Kumanovo (Yugoslavia, now in North Macedonia) (b) 1,78 (c) M - central midfielder (d) Besa Dobri Dol (e) Rabotnicki, Shkëndija, Ermis Aradippou, Nea Salamis, Örebro SK, NK Istra, FK Milano Kumanovo, Baskimi

*** Alimi - Isnik Alimi (a) 02/02/1994, Isnik

*** Alioski - Ezgjan Alioski (Езѓан Алиоски) (a) 12/02/1992, Prilep (North Macedonia) (b) 1,71 (c) D - left back (d) Al-Ahli SFC (e) Fenerbahce, Al-Ahli, Leeds Utd., FC Lugano, FC Schaffhausen, FC Lugano, FC Schaffhausen

*** Alip - Nuraly Alip (Әліп Нұралы Пақтұлы) (a) 22/12/1999, Aktau (Kazakhstan) (b) 1,88 (c) D - central defense (d) Zenit de San Petersburgo (e) Kairat Almaty, Zenit, Kairat Almaty, Kairat II

*** Alipour - Ali Alipour (علیپور علی Ali Alipourghara) (a) 11/11/1995, Qaemshahr, Mazandaran (Iran) (b) 1,81 (c) F - center forward (d) Gil Vicente FC (e) Marítimo, Persepolis, Rah Ahan, Sang Ahan, Steel Azin, FC Nassaji M.

*** Alisah - Haris Alisah (HarisAlišah) (a) 03/11/2004, Sarajevo (Bosnia and Herzegovina) (b) 1,88 (c) M - pivot (d) FK Sarajevo (e) -

*** Aliseda - Ignacio Aliseda (Ignacio Santiago Aliseda) (a) 14/03/2000, Buenos Aires (Argentina) (b) 1,68 (c) F - left winger (d) FC Lugano (e) Chicago, Defensa y Justicia, Defensa II

*** Aliseyko - Dmitriy Aliseyko (Алисейко Дмитрий Александрович) (a) 28/08/1992, Bobruisk (Belarus) (b) 1,79 (c) D - right back (d) FK Ostrovets (e) FK Minsk, Torpedo Zhodino, Khimki, Isloch, Dynamo Brest, FK Slutsk, Neman Grodno, FK Slutsk, Neman Grodno, Dinamo Minsk II, Torpedo Zhodino, Dinamo Minsk II

*** Alisson - Alisson (Alisson Ramses Becker) (a) 02/10/1992, Novo Hamburgo (Brazil) (b) 1,93 (c) G (d) Liverpool FC (e) AS Roma, Internacional, Inter B

*** Alisson Taddei - Alisson Taddei (Alisson Fabrício dos Santos Taddei) (a) 10/07/1997, Marília (Brazil) (b) 1,73 (c) M - attacking midfielder (d) Operário Ferroviário Esporte Clube (PR) (e) Siroki Brijeg, São Joseense, Paraná, São Joseense, Ferroviária, XV Piracicaba, Aparecidense, Goiás B, Goiânia, Goiás B, Criciúma EC, Goiás B, Goiânia, Marília

*** Aliti - Fidan Aliti (a) 03/10/1993, Binningen (Switzerland) (b) 1,86 (c) D - central defense (d) Alanyaspor (e) FC Zürich, Kalmar FF, FC Zürich, Kalmar FF, KF Skënderbeu, Slaven Belupo, FC Sheriff, FC Luzern, BSC Old Boys, BSC Old Boys II

*** Aliti - Shefki Aliti (Шефки Алити) (a) 27/07/2003, Bujanovac (Serbia and Montenegro, now in Serbia) (b) 1,77 (c) F - right winger (d) - (e) KF Erzeni, KF 2 Korriku, KF Lugina

*** Aliu - Adonis Aliu (a) 01/03/2001, Prishtinë (RF Yugoslavia, now in Kosovo) (b) 1,82 (c) F - left winger (d) FC Malisheva (e) FC Malisheva, KF Vjosa, FC Prishtina, FC Prishtina, FC Llapi, KF 2 Korriku

*** Aliu - Altin Aliu (a) 11/11/1999, Arbëri, Gjilan (RF Yugoslavia, now in Kosovo) (b) 1,78 (c) F - left winger (d) FC Malisheva (e) KF Flamurtari, KF Liria, FC Malisheva, KF Vllaznia, SC Gjilani

*** Aliu - Armend Aliu (a) 26/04/1996, Kicevo (North Macedonia) (b) 1,80 (c) M - pivot (d) Pobeda Prilep (e) Arsimi, Voska Sport, Korabi Debar, Renova, KF Ferizaj, Vëllazërimi

*** Aliu - Lukuman Aliu (Lukuman Aliu) (a) 25/03/2003, Agege (Nigeria) (b) - (c) M - central midfielder (d) FK Smorgon (e) FK Slutsk, Ifeanyi Ubah

*** Alivoda - Rejan Alivoda (a) 05/06/2003, Shkodër (Albania) (b) 1,83 (c) M - pivot (d) KF Vllaznia (e) -

*** Aliyev - Azer Aliyev (Azər İlqar oğlu Əliyev) (a) 12/05/1994, Bezaglo (Georgia) (b) 1,68 (c) D - left back (d) Neftchi Baku (e) Ufa, Tambov, Ufa, KS Samara, Enisey, Sakhalin, Enisey, Enisey II

*** Aliyev - Ibrahim Aliyev (İbrahim Fariz oğlu Əliyev) (a) 17/07/1999, ¿? (Azerbaijan) (b) 1,85 (c) F - center forward (d) MOIK Baku (e) Sumqayit, PFK Zaqatala, Turan Tovuz, FC Shamakhi 2

*** Aliyev - Nicat Aliyev (Nicat Əliyev) (a) 24/09/2001, ¿? (Azerbaijan) (b) - (c) D - right back (d) FK Qabala 2 (e) Sumqayit 2

*** Aliyev - Qismat Aliyev (Qismət Qardaşxan oğlu Alıyev) (a) 24/10/1996, ¿? (Azerbaijan) (b) 1,78 (c) D - right back (d) Zira FK (e) FK Qabala, FK Qabala 2
*** Aliyev - Rauf Aliyev (Rauf Sehraman oğlu Əliyev) (a) 12/02/1989, Füzuli (Soviet Union, now in Azerbaijan) (b) 1,87 (c) F - center forward (d) - (e) Kapaz PFK, FK Sabail, Neftchi Baku, FK Qabala, FK Kukësi, Keshla, Neftchi Baku, Xäzär Länkäran, FK Baku, Qarabag FK, Premyer Liqa
*** Aliyev - Shahriyar Aliyev (a) 25/12/1992, Baku (Azerbaijan) (b) 1,81 (d) Turan-Tovuz IK (e) Shamakhi, Sumqayit, Kapaz PFK, Qarabag FK, Kapaz PFK, Qarabag FK, FK Baku
*** Aliyev - Zamiq Aliyev (Zamiq Arastun oğlu Əliyev) (a) 05/05/2001, Baku (Azerbaijan) (b) 1,91 (c) D - central defense (d) Araz-Naxcivan Nakchivan (e) Qarabag 2, Kapaz PFK, Qarabag 2
*** Aliyu - Ibrahim Aliyu (a) 16/01/2002, Kano (Nigeria) (b) 1,84 (c) F - center forward (d) Houston Dynamo FC (e) NK Lokomotiva, Footwork FC, Oasis FC
*** Aliyu - Isah Aliyu (a) 08/08/1999, Kaduna (Nigeria) (b) 1,66 (c) M - attacking midfielder (d) Remo Stars FC (e) Ararat Yerevan, FC Urartu, Shoalah, UD Almería B, Lori Vanadzor, Remo Stars FC
*** Alizada - Asim Alizada (Asim Xosrov oğlu Əlizadə) (a) 05/02/2000, ¿? (Azerbaijan) (b) 1,77 (c) M - central midfielder (d) FC Shamakhi (e) Neftchi Baku, Daugavpils, Neftchi Baku, Neftchi 2 Baku
*** Alkan - Erol Alkan (Erol Erdal Alkan) (a) 16/02/1994, Amsterdam (Netherlands) (b) 1,93 (c) D - central defense (d) KFC Esperanza Pelt (e) Finn Harps, Usak Spor, Etar, Türkgücü Münch., Beroe, FC Dordrecht, Hatayspor, Kocaeli Birlik, Elazigspor
*** Alkhasov - Slavik Alkhasov (a) 06/02/1993, Qusar (Azerbaijan) (b) 1,77 (d) Turan-Tovuz IK (e) Zira FK, Sabah FK, Keshla, Sumqayit, Khazar Lankaran, Neftchi Baku, Sumqayit, Neftchi Baku
*** Alkhazov - Aleksandr Alkhazov (Алхазов Александр Николаевич) (a) 27/05/1984, Stepnoy, Krasnodar Region (Soviet Union, now in Russia) (b) 1,84 (c) F - center forward (d) - (e) Khimki 2, Dolgoprudnyi, Olimp Khimki, Fakel Voronezh, Mordovia, Okzhetpes, Volgar, Shinnik Yaroslav, Luch Vladivostok, KS Samara, Alania, KS Samara, KamAZ, Zvezda Irkutsk, KamAZ, Spartak Nizhny Novgorod, Rostov, Torpedo Armavir
*** Alkokin - Roee Alkokin (a) 07/04/2004, ¿? (Israel) (b) - (c) M - central midfielder (d) - (e) Hapoel Tel Aviv
*** Alla - Albi Alla (a) 01/02/1993, Pogradec (Albania) (b) 1,88 (c) D - central defense (d) - (e) KF Laçi, SX Chang'an At., NJ City, SX Chang'an At., ZB Cuju, SX Chang'an At., YB Funde, Flamurtari FC, FK Kukësi, KF Skënderbeu, FK Bylis, KF Skënderbeu, Ergotelis, Panachaiki, Ergotelis, AS Fokikos, Ergotelis
*** Allach - Ayyoub Allach (a) 28/01/1998, Mechelen (Belgium) (b) 1,80 (c) M - attacking midfielder (d) FK Qabala (e) RE Virton, KSK Lierse Kem., Kansas City II, Lierse SK, JMG Lier
*** Allain - Bobby Allain (a) 28/11/1991, Clamart (France) (b) 1,85 (c) G (d) Grenoble Foot 38 (e) Ionikos Nikeas, G. Ajaccio, Dalkurd, Örebro SK, Olympiakos, Dijon, Red Star FC, US Ivry
*** Allan - Allan (Allan Marques Loureiro) (a) 08/01/1991, Rio de Janeiro (Brazil) (b) 1,75 (c) M - pivot (d) Al-Wahda FC Abu Dhabi (e) Everton, Napoli, Udinese, Granada CF, Udinese, Granada CF, Maldonado, Vasco da Gama, Maldonado, Madureira, Vasco da Gama, Madureira
*** Allan - Connor Allan (a) 10/01/2004, ¿? (Scotland) (b) - (c) D - central defense (d) Rangers FC Reserves (e) -

*** Allano - Allano (Allano Brendon de Souza Lima) (a) 24/04/1995, Rio de Janeiro (Brazil) (b) 1,82 (c) F - right winger (d) Goiás EC (e) Santa Clara, Estoril Praia, CSA, Estoril Praia, Ventforet Kofu, Estoril Praia, Bursaspor, Estoril Praia, Cruzeiro, Estoril Praia, Cruzeiro, EC Bahia, Cruzeiro
*** Allansson - Marius Allansson (Marius Árting Allansson) (a) 27/02/2005, ¿? (Faroe Islands) (b) - (c) F - center forward (d) B36 Tórshavn (e) B36 II
*** Allast - Markus Allast (a) 05/09/2000, Tallinn (Estonia) (b) - (c) D - central defense (d) FC Kuressaare (e) Kalev, Paide
*** Allen - Cameron Allen (Cameron Matt Allen) (a) 04/05/2005, ¿? (Wales) (b) - (c) F - center forward (d) Carmarthen Town (e) Aberystwyth
*** Allen - Curtis Allen (a) 22/02/1988, Belfast (Northern Ireland) (b) 1,80 (c) F - center forward (d) Carrick Rangers (e) Coleraine, Glentoran, Coleraine, Glentoran, Inverness Caledonian, Coleraine, Linfield, Lisburn FC, Bournemouth, Leyton Orient, Bournemouth
*** Allen - Harry Allen (a) 01/11/2001, ¿? (England) (b) 1,88 (c) G (d) Farsley Celtic (e) Flint Town
*** Allevinah - Jim Allevinah (Jim Emilien Ngowet Allevinah) (a) 27/02/1995, Agen (France) (b) 1,72 (c) M - right midfielder (d) Clermont Foot 63 (e) Le Puy Foot, Bayonne, FC Marmande 47, SU Agen
*** Alli - Dele Alli (Bamidele Jermaine Alli) (a) 11/04/1996, Milton Keynes (England) (b) 1,88 (c) M - attacking midfielder (d) Everton FC (e) Besiktas, Everton, Tottenham Hotspur, MK Dons, Tottenham Hotspur, MK Dons
*** Alli - Wale Musa Alli (a) 31/12/2000, Lagos (Nigeria) (b) 1,60 (c) F - right winger (d) FC Zbrojovka Brno (e) SKU Amstetten, Kalev
*** Alliku - Rauno Alliku (a) 02/03/1990, Pärnu (Estonia)Soviet Union, now in Estonia) (b) 1,79 (c) F - right winger (d) FC Flora Tallinn (e) JK Viljandi, FC Flora, Pärnu Vaprus
*** Alliu - Olalekan Ibrahim Alliu (a) 11/11/2003, Abeokuta (Nigeria) (b) - (c) M - attacking midfielder (d) - (e) FK Kukësi
*** Allix - Téo Allix (a) 05/07/2004, Montpellier (France) (b) 1,83 (c) D - central defense (d) HSC Montpellier B (e) -
*** Allogho - Dallian Allogho (a) 08/06/1996, ¿? (Gabon) (b) - (c) G (d) - (e) Dinamo-Auto, AS Bouenguidi
*** Alloh - Teddy Alloh (a) 23/01/2002, Paris (France) (b) 1,76 (c) D - left back (d) KAS Eupen (e) Paris Saint-Germain, KAS Eupen, Paris Saint-Germain
*** Allyson - Allyson (Allyson Aires dos Santos) (a) 23/10/1990, São Paulo (Brazil) (b) 1,84 (c) D - central defense (d) Cuiabá Esporte Clube (MT) (e) Ümraniyespor, Bandirmaspor, Bnei Yehuda, Maccabi Haifa, M. Petah Tikva, Independente-SP, Barueri
*** Alm - Marius Alm (Marius Svanberg Alm) (a) 03/12/1997, Moen (Norway) (b) 1,97 (c) D - central defense (d) IL Hødd (e) Kristiansund, KFUM, Raufoss
*** Alm - Rasmus Alm (a) 17/08/1995, Landskrona (Sweden) (b) 1,74 (c) F - right winger (d) St. Louis CITY SC (e) Elfsborg, Degerfors, Brommapojkarna, Landskrona
*** Almada Correia - Lenny Almada Correia (a) 19/09/2002, ¿? (Luxembourg) (b) - (c) D - right back (d) Racing FC Union Luxembourg (e) CS Fola Esch
*** Almadjed - Sumar Almadjed (a) 13/03/1996, Helsingborg (Sweden) (b) - (c) M - central midfielder (d) Helsingborgs IF (e) Landskrona, Hittarps IK, Höganäs BK, Högaborgs BK
*** Almasi - Ladislav Almasi (Ladislav Almási) (a) 06/03/1999, Bratislava (Slovakia) (b) 1,96 (c) F - center forward (d) FC Banik Ostrava (e) Ružomberok,

Akhmat Grozny, Ružomberok, Dunajska Streda, FC Petrzalka, Dunajska Streda, STK Samorin, Dunajska Streda, Dun. Streda B, FK Senica
*** Almássy - Levente Almássy (Almássy Levente András) (a) 28/09/2005, ¿? (Hungary) (b) - (c) D - left back (d) Ferencvárosi TC II (e) -
*** Almeida - André Almeida (André Gomes Magalhães de Almeida) (a) 10/09/1990, Lisboa (Portugal) (b) 1,85 (c) D - right back (d) - (e) Benfica, Leiria, Benfica, Belenenses
*** Almeida - André Almeida (Domingos André Ribeiro Almeida) (a) 30/05/2000, Guimarães (Portugal) (b) 1,76 (c) M - central midfielder (d) Valencia CF (e) Vitória Guimarães, Vitória Guimarães B
*** Almeida - Bruno Almeida (Bruno Filipe Pereira Soares Almeida) (a) 09/09/1996, Porto (Portugal) (b) 1,72 (c) M - attacking midfielder (d) CD Santa Clara (e) Trofense, Santa Clara, Trofense, Anadia FC, Pedras Rubras, Bustelo, Sanjoanense
*** Almeida - Dinis Almeida (Dinis Da Costa Lima Almeida) (a) 28/06/1995, Esposende (Portugal) (b) 1,86 (c) D - central defense (d) Ludogorets Razgrad (e) Royal Antwerp, Lokomotiv Plovdiv, AS Monaco B, AO Xanthi, AS Monaco B, Braga B, AS Monaco B, Belenenses, AS Monaco B, Reus Deportiu
*** Almeida - Gonçalo Almeida (Goncalo Jorge Almeida da Silva) (a) 26/11/1990, Vila Real (Portugal) (b) 1,81 (c) F - left winger (d) Jeunesse Esch (e) Differdange 03, CS Grevenmacher, Echternach
*** Almeida - Leandro Almeida (Leandro Almeida da Silva) (a) 14/03/1987, Belo Horizonte (Brazil) (b) 1,88 (c) D - central defense (d) Zebbug Rangers FC (e) Hibernians FC, Guarani, Paraná, Palmeiras, Paraná, Palmeiras, Londrina-PR, Palmeiras, Figueirense FC, Palmeiras, Internacional, Palmeiras, Coritiba FC, Dinamo Kyïv, At. Mineiro, At. Mineiro B
*** Almeida - Ramilson Almeida (a) 21/08/1999, ¿? (Brazil) (b) 1,87 (c) G (d) Ekenäs IF (e) Helsinki IFK, Nurmijärvi, Helsinki IFK, Atlantis FC, Manaus FC
*** Almeida - Stephano Almeida (Stephano Alves de Almeida) (a) 17/09/1993, São Paulo (Brazil) (b) 1,81 (c) F - right winger (d) Buducnost Podgorica (e) Zlaté Moravce, SILON Taborsko, Académica SF, Gafanha, Oliveira Bairro, Ituano
*** Almeida - Tiago Almeida (Tiago Miguel Monteiro de Almeida) (a) 13/09/1990, Lisboa (Portugal) (b) 1,81 (c) D - right back (d) - (e) Suduva, Feirense, Varzim, Feirense, FC Hermannstadt, Académico Viseu, União Madeira, ACSM Poli Iasi, Moreirense, Belenenses, Chaves, Belenenses, Académico Viseu, Belenenses, Vitória Guimarães B, Belenenses, Pinhalnovense, Belenenses, Tourizense, Belenenses, Mafra, Belenenses
*** Almen - Antonio Almen (a) 07/04/2004, ¿? (Finland) (b) 1,84 (c) M - central midfielder (d) Vaasan Palloseura (e) -
*** Almén - Mikael Almén (a) 08/03/2000, Naantali (Finland) (b) 1,83 (c) D - central defense (d) FC Inter Turku (e) Ilves
*** Almirón - Miguel Almirón (Miguel Ángel Almirón Rejala) (a) 10/02/1994, Asunción (Paraguay) (b) 1,74 (c) F - right winger (d) Newcastle United (e) Atlanta, Lanús, Cerro Porteño
*** Almodóvar - Nando Almodóvar (Hernando Almodóvar Marrufo) (a) 03/11/2003, Jerez de la Frontera (Spain) (b) 1,92 (c) G (d) Cádiz CF Mirandilla (e) -
*** Almog - Eylon Almog (אלמוג אילון) (a) 08/01/1999, Ness Ziona (Israel) (b) 1,81 (c) F - left winger (d) Maccabi Tel Aviv (e) TSV Hartberg, Maccabi Tel Aviv, Hapoel Hadera, Maccabi Tel Aviv, Beitar TA Ramla, Maccabi Tel Aviv
*** Al-Mohaimeed - Samer Al-Mohaimeed (a) 01/04/2001, ¿? (Saudi Arabia) (b) 1,71 (c) M - central midfielder (d) OFI Creta (e) Slavia Praha B, Future Falcons

*** Almqvist - Pontus Almqvist (Pontus Skule Erik Almqvist) (a) 10/07/1999, Nyköping (Sweden) (b) 1,83 (c) F - right winger (d) US Lecce (e) Lecce, Rostov, Pogon Szczecin, Rostov, FC Utrecht, Rostov, Norrköping, Sylvia, Norrköping, Norrby, Norrköping, Varbergs BoIS, Norrköping

*** Al-Musrati - Al-Musrati (المصراتي محمد علي المؤتمة), Almoatasembellah Ali Mohamed Al-Musrati) (a) 06/04/1996, Misurata (Lybia) (b) 1,89 (c) M - pivot (d) SC Braga (e) Vitória Guimarães, Rio Ave, Vitória Guimarães, Vitória Guimarães B, Al-Ittihad

*** Aloe - Kevin Aloe (a) 07/05/1995, Tallinn (Estonia) (b) 1,79 (c) D - left back (d) Pärnu JK Vaprus (e) JK Trans Narva, JK Tammeka, FC Flora, JK Tammeka, FC Flora, FC Flora II, Warrior Valga

*** Alomerovic - Bele Alomerovic (Беле Аломеровиќ) (a) 05/11/2004, Reykjavik (Iceland) (b) 1,84 (c) M - central midfielder (d) KF Aegir (e) Valur, KV Vesturbaejar, Valur

*** Alomerovic - Din Alomerovic (Дин Аломеровиќ) (a) 29/06/1997, Skopje (North Macedonia) (b) 1,74 (c) D - left back (d) Rabotnicki Skopje (e) R. B. Linense, Rabotnicki, CF La Nucía, Salamanca CF, Celta B, Fuenlabrada B, Makedonija, Euromilk GL

*** Alomerovic - Zlatan Alomerovic (Златан Аломериовић) (a) 15/06/1991, Priboj (Yugoslavia, now in Serbia) (b) 1,87 (c) G (d) Jagiellonia Białystok (e) Lechia Gdánsk,   Korona Kielce, 1.FC Kaiserslautern, Borussia Dortmund, Borussia Dortmund II

*** Alonso - Júnior Alonso (Júnior Osmar Ignacio Alonso Mujica) (a) 09/02/1993, Asunción (Paraguay) (b) 1,85 (c) D - central defense (d) FK Krasnodar (e) At. Mineiro, Krasnodar, At. Mineiro, Lille, Boca Juniors, Lille, RC Celta, Lille, Cerro Porteño

*** Alonso - Marcos Alonso (Marcos Alonso Mendoza) (a) 28/12/1990, Madrid (Spain) (b) 1,88 (c) D - left back (d) FC Barcelona (e) Chelsea, Fiorentina, Sunderland, Fiorentina, Bolton Wanderers, RM Castilla

*** Alonso - Rodri Alonso (Rodrigo Alonso Martín) (a) 04/01/2003, Castellón (Spain) (b) 1,72 (c) M - central midfielder (d) Villarreal CF B (e) Albacete, Villarreal CF B, Villarreal CF C

*** Alonso - Víctor Alonso (Víctor Alonso Madueño) (a) 23/12/1994, Barcelona (Spain) (b) 1,83 (c) M - attacking midfielder (d) Atlètic Club d'Escaldes (e) FC Santa Coloma, Sant Andreu, CF Peralada, At. Levante, Sant Andreu

*** Aloy - Gerard Aloy (Gerard Aloy Soler) (a) 17/04/1989, Andorra la Vella (Andorra) (b) - (c) F - right winger (d) UE Santa Coloma (e) FC Andorra

*** Alpens - Markuss Alpens (Markuss Maksimuss Alpēns) (a) 24/01/2004, Liepaja (Latvia) (b) 1,77 (c) M - central midfielder (d) FK RFS II (e) Tukums, RFS, Spartaks

*** Alphonse - Mickaël Alphonse (Mickaël David Alphonse) (a) 12/07/1989, Champigny-sur-Marne (France) (b) 1,82 (c) D - right back (d) AC Ajaccio (e) Maccabi Haifa, Amiens SC, Dijon, FC Sochaux, Bourg-en-Bresse, AS Moulins, FC Rouen 1899, Louhans-Cuiseaux

*** Alpisbaev - Marat Alpisbaev (Алписпаев Марат) (a) 08/04/2002, ¿? (Kazakhstan) (b) 1,75 (c) D - left back (d) - (e) FK Ekibastuz, Tobol II

*** Al-Saed - Danilo Al-Saed (Danilo Andrés Al-Saed Alvarado) (a) 24/02/1999, Bålsta (Sweden) (b) 1,78 (c) F - left winger (d) Sandefjord Fotball (e) Sandvikens IF, Enköpings SK

*** Alshanik - Andrey Alshanik (Альшаник Андрей Денисович) (a) 03/05/1999, Osipovichi (Belarus) (b) 1,73 (c) D - right back (d) BK Maxline Vitebsk (e) Slavia,

Energetik-BGU, Krumkachi, Energetik-BGU, Smolevichi, Energetik-BGU, Naftan, Energetik-BGU, BATE II, Energetik-BGU, BATE II

*** Alshikh - Mohamad Alshikh (a) 01/01/2001, ¿? (Syria) (b) 1,77 (c) M - central midfielder (d) FC Paradiso (e) FC Paradiso, FC Lugano II, Rapperswil-Jona, FC Lugano II, FC Chiasso, FC Lugano II

*** Alshin - Ilnur Alshin (Альшин Ильнур Туфикович) (a) 31/08/1993, Tyumen (Russia) (b) 1,75 (c) F - right winger (d) Fakel Voronezh (e) Baltika, Tambov, Avangard Kursk, Tosno, Avangard Kursk, Tosno, Fakel Voronezh, Spartak Moskva II, Hapa

*** Alston - Blair Alston (a) 23/03/1992, Kirkcaldy (Scotland) (b) 1,81 (c) M - central midfielder (d) Partick Thistle FC (e) Kilmarnock FC, Falkirk FC, St. Johnstone, Falkirk FC

*** Alsultanov - Islam Alsultanov (Альсултанов Ислам Асхабович) (a) 18/08/2001, ¿? (Russia) (b) 1,85 (c) F - center forward (d) Volga Uljanovsk (e) Akhmat Grozny, Akhmat II, Akademia Ramzan

*** Al-Tamari - Mousa Al-Tamari (سليمان موسى محمد موسى) (a) 10/06/1997, Amman (Jordania) (b) 1,78 (c) F - right winger (d) Montpellier HSC (e) OH Leuven, APOEL FC, Shabab Al-Ordon, Al-Jazeera Club, Shabab Al-Ordon

*** Altanov - Dimitar Altanov (a) 07/07/2006, ¿? (Bulgaria) (b) - (c) G (d) Beroe Stara Zagora (e) Beroe Stara Zagora II

*** Altikardes - Taha Altikardes (Taha Altıkardeş) (a) 22/08/2003, Bursa (Turkey) (b) 1,90 (c) D - central defense (d) Göztepe (e) Trabzonspor, Bursaspor

*** Altiparmakovski - Marjan Altiparmakovski (Марјан Алтипармаковски) (a) 18/07/1991, Bitola (Yugoslavia, now in North Macedonia) (b) 1,83 (c) F - center forward (d) - (e) Bregalnica Stip, Struga, Pirin, KF Laçi, FK Sarajevo, Suduva, Inter Zaprešić, Rabotnicki, Paniliakos, Pelister Bitola, Skoda Xanthi, Pelister Bitola

*** Altman - Omri Altman (אלטמן עומרי) (a) 23/03/1994, Ramat Gan (Israel) (b) 1,81 (c) F - attacking midfielder (d) Hapoel Tel Aviv (e) AEK Larnaca, Arouca, Hapoel Tel Aviv, Panathinaikos, Hapoel Tel Aviv, Maccabi Tel Aviv, H. Petah Tikva, Maccabi Tel Aviv

*** Altman - Tomer Altman (אלטמן תומר) (a) 08/02/1998, ¿? (Israel) (b) 1,75 (c) M - central midfielder (d) Hapoel Jerusalem (e) Roda JC, Maccabi Tel Aviv, Hapoel Haifa, Maccabi Tel Aviv, B TLV Bat Yam, Maccabi Tel Aviv

*** Altrovich - Dudu Altrovich (אלטרוביץ דודו) (a) 12/07/1999, ¿? (Israel) (b) - (c) F - right winger (d) - (e) Hapoel Haifa, H. Nof HaGalil, Hapoel Haifa, H. Petah Tikva, Hapoel Haifa

*** Altunashvili - Sandro Altunashvili (სანდრო ალთუნაშვილი) (a) 19/05/1997, Tbilisi (Georgia) (b) 1,69 (c) M - central midfielder (d) Wolfsberger AC (e) Dinamo Batumi, Saburtalo

*** Altynkhan - Ansar Altynkhan (Алтынхан Ансар) (a) 08/11/2003, ¿? (Kazakhstan) (b) 1,65 (c) M - central midfielder (d) Shakhter Karaganda (e) Shakhter-Bulat

*** Alun - Rhys Alun (Rhys Alun Williams) (a) 13/11/1997, ¿? (Wales) (b) - (c) M - attacking midfielder (d) Caernarfon Town (e) Porthmadog, Nantlle Vale, Porthmadog, Nantlle Vale, Llanllyfni

*** Alunni - Alessandro Alunni (a) 19/12/1991, ¿? (Luxembourg) (b) 1,74 (c) M - left midfielder (d) Maurizio Alunni (e) Mondercange, Hamm Benfica, UN Käerjeng 97, CS Fola Esch, Differdange 03, CS Fola Esch, Differdange 03

*** Alvarado - Alejandro Alvarado (Alejandro Alvarado Jr.) (a) 29/07/2003, Los Angeles, California (United States) (b) 1,80 (c) M - central midfielder (d) FC Vizela (e) -

*** Alvarenga - Fabricio Alvarenga (Fabricio Oscar Alvarenga) (a) 17/02/1996, Misiones (Argentina) (b) 1,75 (c) F - right winger (d) Rukh Lviv (e) Olimpik Donetsk, Vélez Sarsfield II, Morón, Vélez Sarsfield II, Coritiba FC, Vélez Sarsfield II

*** Álvarez - Agustín Álvarez (Agustín Álvarez Martínez) (a) 19/05/2001, San Bautista (Uruguay) (b) 1,77 (c) F - center forward (d) US Sassuolo (e) Peñarol

*** Álvarez - Blas Álvarez (Blas Álvarez Cortés) (a) 19/07/1995, La Línea de la Concepción (Spain) (b) 1,84 (c) M - central midfielder (d) Lynx FC (e) Ugento, Los Barrios, Europa FC, Lincoln FC, Gibraltar Utd., Sperre) Gibraltar Phoenix, CD Badajoz, Betis B, Linense B

*** Álvarez - Carlos Álvarez (Carlos Álvarez Rivera) (a) 06/08/2003, Sanlúcar la Mayor (Spain) (b) 1,68 (c) M - attacking midfielder (d) Levante UD (e) Sevilla At.

*** Álvarez - Edson Álvarez (Edson Omar Álvarez Velázquez) (a) 24/10/1997, Tlalnepantla de Baz (Mexico) (b) 1,87 (c) M - pivot (d) West Ham United (e) Ajax, CF América

*** Álvarez - Federico Álvarez (Federico Hernán Álvarez) (a) 07/08/1994, Córdoba (Argentina) (b) 1,83 (c) D - left back (d) Asteras Tripolis (e) Quilmes, Belgrano, Quilmes, Belgrano, Belgrano II

*** Álvarez - Freddy Álvarez (Freddy Antonio Álvarez Rodríguez) (a) 26/04/1995, Nicoya (Costa Rica) (b) 1,70 (c) M - attacking midfielder (d) BG Pathum United (e) FC Shkupi, ADR Jicaral, FC Shkupi, ADR Jicaral, Herediano, ADR Jicaral, Herediano, LD Alajuelense, Dep. Municipal, Saprissa, UCR, Saprissa, CS Uruguay, Saprissa, Gen. Saprissa

*** Álvarez - Gastón Álvarez (Pedro Gastón Álvarez Sosa) (a) 24/03/2000, Melo (Uruguay) (b) 1,84 (c) D - central defense (d) Getafe CF (e) Boston River, Getafe CF, Boston River, Defensor

*** Álvarez - Hugo Álvarez (Hugo Álvarez Antúnez) (a) 02/07/2003, Ourense (Spain) (b) 1,76 (c) F - left winger (d) RC Celta Fortuna (e) -

*** Álvarez - Iker Álvarez (Iker Álvarez de Eulate Molne) (a) 25/07/2001, Andorra la Vella (Andorra) (b) 1,90 (c) G (d) Villarreal CF B (e) Villarreal CF C

*** Álvarez - Julián Álvarez (a) 31/01/2000, Calchín (Argentina) (b) 1,70 (c) F - center forward (d) Manchester City (e) River Plate, Manchester City, River Plate, River Plate II, CA Atalaya

*** Álvarez - Pablo Álvarez (Pablo Álvarez García) (a) 23/04/1997, Langreo (Spain) (b) 1,87 (c) M - central midfielder (d) Cherno More Varna (e) HNK Rijeka, Cherno More, Depor. Alavés B, San Ignacio, Depor. Alavés B, Villarreal CF C

*** Álvarez - Yeray Álvarez (Yeray Álvarez López) (a) 24/01/1995, Barakaldo (Spain) (b) 1,82 (c) D - central defense (d) Athletic Club (e) Bilbao Athletic, CD Basconia

*** Alvarez Saavedra (c) D - central defense (d) Lions Gibraltar FC Reserve (e) - - Hugo Alvarez Saavedra (c) D - central defense (d) Lions Gibraltar FC Reserve (e) -

*** Álvaro - Pedro Álvaro (Pedro Miguel da Costa Álvaro) (a) 02/03/2000, Seia (Portugal) (b) 1,87 (c) D - central defense (d) GD Estoril Praia (e) Benfica B, B SAD, Benfica B

*** Álvaro Djaló - Álvaro Djaló (Álvaro Djaló Dias Fernandes) (a) 16/08/1999, Madrid (Spain) (b) 1,75 (c) F - left winger (d) SC Braga (e) Braga B

*** Álvaro Vieira - Álvaro Vieira (Alvaro Luis Tavares Vieira) (a) 10/03/1995, São Paulo (Brazil) (b) 1,72 (c) M - attacking midfielder (d) - (e) PFK Lviv, São Luiz, PFK Lviv, FC Dila, PFK Lviv, Keshla, PFC Lviv, AA Francana, Monte Azul, União Mogi, Suzano-SP

*** Alverdi - Luca Alverdi (a) 17/10/1999, ¿? (Luxembourg) (b) 1,80 (c) M - attacking midfielder (d) US Hostert (e) Differdange 03, UN Käerjeng 97, Differdange 03, FC Rodange 91

*** Alverdi - Sam Alverdi (a) 23/08/1997, ¿? (Luxembourg) (b) 1,83 (c) M - right midfielder (d) UN Käerjeng 97 (e) FC Rodange 91, FC UNA Strassen, FC Rodange 91

*** Alves - Frederik Alves (Frederik Alves Ibsen) (a) 08/11/1999, Hvidovre (Denmark) (b) 1,95 (c) D - central defense (d) Brøndby IF (e) West Ham Utd., Sunderland, West Ham Utd., Silkeborg IF

*** Alves - Michael Alves (Michael Santos Silva Alves) (a) 16/02/1996, Feira de Santana (Brazil) (b) 1,78 (c) F - right winger (d) Cherno More Varna (e) Praiense, UNIRB

*** Alves - Ricardo Alves (Ricardo Azevedo Alves) (a) 02/12/2001, Genève (Switzerland) (b) 1,77 (c) M - central midfielder (d) Yverdon Sport FC (e) FC St. Gallen, Servette FC

*** Alves - Roberto Alves (Roberto Emanuel Oliveira Alves) (a) 08/06/1997, Wetzikon ZH (Switzerland) (b) 1,80 (c) M - attacking midfielder (d) Radomiak Radom (e) FC Winterthur, Grasshoppers, FC Winterthur, Grasshoppers, FC Wil 1900, Grasshoppers, FC Wil 1900

*** Alves Margato - João Alves Margato (a) 17/12/2005, ¿? (Luxembourg) (b) - (c) G (d) F91 Dudelange (e) -

*** Alves Raposo - Stephane Alves Raposo (a) 07/06/1994, ¿? (Luxembourg) (b) - (c) D (d) UN Käerjeng 97 (e) Sporting Bertrange

*** Alvheim - Leander Alvheim (Leander Næss Alvheim) (a) 15/09/2004, ¿? (Norway) (b) - (c) F - center forward (d) Kristiansund BK (e) Kristiansund II

*** Alvir - Marko Alvir (a) 19/04/1994, Zagreb (Croatia) (b) 1,81 (c) M - attacking midfielder (d) - (e) Viktoria Plzen, NK Maribor, Viktoria Plzen, Ceske Budejovice, Viktoria Plzen, Slavia Praha B, 1.FK Pribram, Slavia Praha B, Slavia Praha, Domžale, Slavia Praha, Domžale, At. Madrid C

*** Alvsaker - Martin Alvsaker (a) 03/02/2005, ¿? (Norway) (b) - (c) M (d) FK Haugesund II (e) -

*** Alyagon - Rom Alyagon (אליגון רום) (a) 24/12/2002, ¿? (Israel) (b) - (c) F - center forward (d) Hapoel Beer Sheva (e) Ramat haSharon, H. Beer Sheva, Hapoel Hadera, H. Beer Sheva

*** Alykulov - Gulzhigit Alykulov (Гулжигит Жаныбекович Алыкулов) (a) 25/11/2000, Bishkek (Kyrgyzstan) (b) 1,69 (c) F - left winger (d) Neman Grodno (e) Kairat Almaty, Neman Grodno, Alga Bishkek, Dordoi

*** Alyshov - Nail Alyshov (Nail Alışov) (a) 30/07/2000, Baku (Azerbaijan) (b) 1,87 (c) G (d) Zira FK (e) FK Zira 2, FK Sabail 2, Qaradag, FK Zira 2

*** Alzate - Steven Alzate (a) 08/09/1998, Camden (England) (b) 1,80 (c) M - central midfielder (d) Brighton & Hove Albion (e) Standard Liège, Brighton & Hove Albion, Swindon Town, Leyton Orient

*** Amade - Alfons Amade (Alfons Antonio Chico Amade) (a) 12/11/1999, Heidelberg (Germany) (b) 1,70 (c) M - pivot (d) KV Oostende (e) Hoffenheim II, Eintracht Braunschweig, Hoffenheim II

*** Amadei - Johnny Amadei (a) 18/07/1992, ¿? (France) (b) - (c) M - attacking midfielder (d) FC Mondercange (e) FCJL Arlon, RUS Ethe, Schifflange 95, ES Clemency

*** Amadou - Ibrahim Amadou (a) 06/04/1993, Douala (Cameroon) (b) 1,83 (c) M - pivot (d) Shanghai Shenhua (e) Angers SCO, FC Metz, Sevilla FC, Angers SCO,

Sevilla FC, CD Leganés, Sevilla FC, Norwich City, Sevilla FC, Lille, AS Nancy, AS Nancy B

*** Amadu - Latif Amadu (Abedel Latif Amadu) (a) 20/08/1993, Accra (Ghana) (b) 1,90 (c) F - center forward (d) - (e) Pietà Hotspurs, KF Llapi, Al-Ansar, Khaleej, SC Kfar Qasem, KF Teuta, Dynamo Brest, Asante Kotoko, Berekum Chelsea

*** Amallah - Selim Amallah (a) 15/11/1996, Hautrage (Belgium) (b) 1,86 (c) M - attacking midfielder (d) Real Valladolid CF (e) Standard Liège, Excelsior Mouscron, AFC Tubize, Excelsior Mouscron

*** Amangali - Islam Amangali (Амангали (Русланулы) Ислам) (a) 09/07/2003, Aktobe (Kazakhstan) (b) 1,73 (c) F - right winger (d) FK Aktobe II (e) -

*** Amani - Lazare Amani (Jean Thierry Lazare Amani) (a) 07/03/1998, Diégonéfla (Ivory Coast) (b) 1,72 (c) M - central midfielder (d) Royale Union Saint Gilloise (e) RSC Charleroi, Union St. Gilloise, RSC Charleroi, Estoril Praia, RSC Charleroi, KAS Eupen, ASPIRE FD

*** Amanovic - Aleksa Amanovic (Алекса Амановић) (a) 24/10/1996, Beograd (RF Yugoslavia, now in Serbia) (b) 1,87 (c) D - central defense (d) FC Astana (e) Tobol Kostanay, Javor-Matis, IMT Beograd, FK Partizan, Teleoptik, FK Partizan

*** Amanzhol - Rauan Amanzhol (Аманжол Рауан) (a) 24/06/2001, ¿? (Kazahstan) (b) - (c) D - right back (d) - (e) Atyrau, FK Turan II, SDYuSShOR-8 Nursultan, Kairat-Zhas

*** Amar - Tomer Amar (עמר תומר) (a) 01/07/2002, ¿? (Israel) (b) - (c) G (d) FC Ashdod (e) Ironi Ashdod, FC Ashdod, Bnei Eilat, FC Ashdod

*** Amaral - João Amaral (Joao Pedro Reis Amaral) (a) 07/09/1991, Vila Nova de Gaia (Portugal) (b) 1,72 (c) M - attacking midfielder (d) Kocaelispor (e) Lech Poznan, Paços Ferreira, Lech Poznan, Benfica, Vitória Setúbal, Benfica, Vitória Setúbal, Pedras Rubras, AD Oliveirense, Pedras Rubras, Mirandela, Padroense, Candal

*** Amaral - Pedro Amaral (Pedro Miguel Gaspar Amaral) (a) 25/08/1997, ¿? (Portugal) (b) 1,78 (c) D - left back (d) Khaleej FC (e) Rio Ave, Benfica B, Panetolikos, Benfica B

*** Amaro - André Amaro (André Fonseca Amaro) (a) 13/08/2002, Coimbra (Portugal) (b) 1,88 (c) D - central defense (d) Al-Rayyan SC (e) Vitória Guimarães, Vitória Guimarães B

*** Amartey - Daniel Amartey (a) 21/12/1994, Accra (Ghana) (b) 1,86 (c) D - central defense (d) Besiktas JK (e) Leicester City, FC København, Djurgården, Inter Allies

*** Amasihohu - James Amasihohu (James Akugbe Amasihohu) (a) 04/07/2000, Kortrijk (Belgium) (b) 1,83 (c) F - left winger (d) SC Dikkelvenne (e) FK Skopje, Pobeda Prilep, Digenis Morfou, Juven. Sexitana

*** Amati - Armando Amati (a) 15/01/1995, ¿? (Italy) (b) 1,78 (c) M - central midfielder (d) La Fiorita 1967 (e) Romagna Centro, Ribelle, Bellaria Igea Marina

*** Amavi - Jordan Amavi (a) 09/03/1994, Toulon (France) (b) 1,76 (d) Olympique Marseille (e) Getafe CF, Ol. Marseille, OGC Nice, Ol. Marseille, Aston Villa, Ol. Marseille, Aston Villa, OGC Nice, OGC Nice B

*** Ambartsumyan - Armen Ambartsumyan (Амбарцумян Армен Гарикович) (a) 11/04/1994, Saratov (Russia) (b) 1,77 (c) M - central midfielder (d) FC Ararat-Armenia (e) Fakel Voronezh, Mordovia, CSKA Moskva II, Torpedo Armavir, CSKA Moskva II, Zenit Penza, CSKA Moskva II

*** Ambri - Steve Ambri (Steve Brahim Joshep Omar Ambri) (a) 12/08/1997, Mont-Saint-Aignan (France) (b) 1,83 (c) M - left midfielder (d) - (e) Nîmes, FC Sheriff, FC Sochaux, Valenciennes FC, Valenciennes B, ESM Gonfreville

*** Ambros - Lukas Ambros (Lukáš Ambros) (a) 05/06/2004, Dolní Němčí (Czech Rep.) (b) 1,82 (c) M - attacking midfielder (d) VfL Wolfsburg (e) -

*** Ambros - Vladimir Ambros (a) 30/12/1993, Hincesti (Moldova) (b) 1,80 (c) F - center forward (d) FC Petrocub Hîncești (e) FC Sheriff, FC Petrocub, Rapid G.
*** Ambrose - Peter Ambrose (a) 10/06/2002, ¿? (Nigeria) (b) - (c) F - center forward (d) Újpest FC (e) Balikesirspor
*** Ambrose - Thierry Ambrose (Thierry Winston Ambrose) (a) 28/03/1997, Sens (France) (b) 1,80 (c) F - center forward (d) KV Oostende (e) FC Metz, RC Lens, NAC Breda
*** Ambrosidze - Giorgi Ambrosidze (გიორგი ამბროსიძე) (a) 23/11/2003, ¿? (Georgia) (b) - (c) M - attacking midfielder (d) FC Saburtalo II (e) -
*** Ambroz - Filip Ambroz (Filip Alexander Ambroz) (a) 01/12/2003, Göteborg (Sweden) (b) - (c) M - central midfielder (d) Ljungskile SK (e) Ljungskile SK, IFK Göteborg, NK Dugopolje, IFK Göteborg
*** Amdouni - Zeki Amdouni (Mohamed Zeki Amdouni) (a) 04/12/2000, Genève (Switzerland) (b) 1,85 (c) F - center forward (d) Burnley FC (e) FC Basel, Lausanne-Sport, FC Basel, Lausanne-Sport, Stade-Lausanne, Etoile Carouge, Etoile Carouge
*** Amehi - Kilian Amehi (a) 14/11/1997, ¿? (France) (b) 1,70 (c) F - left winger (d) US Hostert (e) FC Rodange 91, Pietà Hotspurs, Sliema Wanderers, FC Montceau B.
*** Amenda - Aurèle Amenda (Aurèle Florian Amenda) (a) 31/07/2003, Biel/Bienne (Switzerland) (b) 1,94 (c) D - central defense (d) BSC Young Boys (e) -
*** Amer - Basel Amer (a) 01/11/1998, ¿? (Israel) (b) - (c) M (d) Maccabi Bnei Reineh (e) -
*** Amer - Mohamad Amer (עאמר מוחמד) (a) 01/10/2003, ¿? (Israel) (b) - (c) M (d) Maccabi Haifa (e) FC Ashdod, Maccabi Haifa
*** Ameworlorna - Augustine Ameworlorna (a) 10/06/1999, ¿? (Ghana) (b) - (c) D - central defense (d) KF Trepca 89 (e) -
*** Amey - Wisdom Amey (a) 11/08/2005, Bassano del Grappa (Italy) (b) 1,87 (c) D - central defense (d) Bologna (e) -
*** Ameyaw - Michael Ameyaw (a) 16/09/2000, Łódź (Poland) (b) 1,76 (c) F - right winger (d) Piast Gliwice (e) Widzew Lódz, Bytovia Bytow, Widzew Lódz,
*** Amian - Kelvin Amian (Kelvin Amian Adou) (a) 08/02/1998, Toulouse (France) (b) 1,80 (c) D - right back (d) Spezia (e) Toulouse
*** Amidon - Juri Amidon (a) 30/07/2001, Trier (Germany) (b) - (c) D - central defense (d) FC Victoria Rosport (e) FC Homburg II, Eintracht Trier
*** Amijekori - Joachim Amijekori (Joachim Clydio Amijekori) (a) 14/02/2004, ¿? (France) (b) - (c) D (d) Racing FC Union Luxembourg (e) -
*** Amilton - Amilton (Amilton Minervino da Silva) (a) 12/08/1989, Pernambuco (Brazil) (b) 1,72 (c) F - left winger (d) Genclerbirligi Ankara (e) Çaykur Rizespor, Konyaspor, Antalyaspor, Desportivo Aves, Antalyaspor, Desportivo Aves, 1860 München, Portimonense, União Madeira, Varzim, Valenciano, Ourense, CD Ourense B
*** Amin - Simon Amin (Simon Alexander Amin, أمين سيمون) (a) 13/11/1997, Örebro (Sweden) (b) 1,83 (c) M - central midfielder (d) Sandefjord Fotball (e) Trelleborg, Örebro SK, Karlslunds IF
*** Amine - Amine (أمين, ادريسي اودريري مهدي, Amine Mehdi Oudrhiri Idrissi) (a) 04/11/1992, Ermont (France) (b) 1,84 (c) M - pivot (d) Rio Ave FC (e) Farense, Leixões, Lusitano FCV, FC Nantes B, CS Sedan, FC Nantes B, AC Arles-Avignon, FC Nantes B, Red Star FC, Racing CFF
*** Aminu - Rafiq Aminu (a) 09/09/1999, Kumasi (Ghana) (b) 1,81 (c) F - center forward (d) Friends Club (e) Alcúdia, Samgurali, Saburtalo, FC Shevardeni, Shevardeni II

*** Amione - Bruno Amione (Bruno Agustín Amione) (a) 03/01/2002, Calchaquí (Argentina) (b) 1,87 (c) D - central defense (d) Hellas Verona (e) Sampdoria, Hellas Verona, Reggina, Hellas Verona, Belgrano, Belgrano II

*** Amiri - Dinan Amiri (a) 29/05/2002, ¿? (Algeria) (b) - (c) M (d) Racing FC Union Luxembourg (e) -

*** Amiri - Nadiem Amiri (a) 27/10/1996, Ludwigshafen am Rhein (Germany) (b) 1,80 (c) M - central midfielder (d) Bayer 04 Leverkusen (e) Genoa, Bayer Leverkusen, Hoffenheim

*** Amirkhanov - Maksat Amirkhanov (Әмирханов Максат Айдарханұлы) (a) 10/02/1992, Taraz (Kazakhstan) (b) 1,72 (c) D - right back (d) Zhetysu Taldykorgan (e) Taraz, Irtysh, Taraz, Taraz-Karatau

*** Amirli - Cabir Amirli (Cabir Alim oğlu Әmirli) (a) 06/01/1997, Baku (Azerbaijan) (b) 1,78 (c) D - right back (d) FK Sabail (e) Neftchi Baku, Sumqayit, Neftchi Baku, Keshla, FC Shamakhi 2

*** Amirov - Temirlan Amirov (Әміров Темірлан Нұртазаұлы) (a) 13/04/1997, Kyzemshek, Suzakskiy Region (Kazakhstan) (b) 1,78 (c) F - right winger (d) FC Arys (e) FK Turan, Atyrau, Kyran, Zhas Ulan

*** Amirquliyev - Rahid Amirquliyev (Rahid Әləkbər oğlu Әmirquliyev) (a) 01/09/1989, Qusar (Soviet Union, now in Azerbaijan) (b) 1,75 (c) M - pivot (d) - (e) FK Sabail, Qarabag FK, Xäzär Länkäran, Shahdag FK, Premyer Liqa

*** Amirseitov - Ilyas Amirseitov (Іліяс Ерсейітұлы Әмірсейітов) (a) 22/10/1989, ¿? (Soviet Union, now in Kazakhstan) (b) 1,79 (c) D - right back (d) Zhetysu Taldykorgan (e) Maktaaral, Kaysar, Zhetysu, Kyran, Sp. Semey, Zhetysu-Sunkar, Kairat Almaty, Sunkar Kaskelen

*** Amirzian - Sergej Amirzian (a) 26/12/1999, Siauliai (Lithuania) (b) 1,75 (c) M - right midfielder (d) - (e) FA Siauliai, Dziugas, Suduva, FA Siauliai, Zalgiris B, FA Siauliai

*** Ammitzbøll - Alexander Ammitzbøll (Alexander Ballegaard Ammitzbøll) (a) 17/02/1999, Skanderborg (Denmark) (b) 1,87 (c) F - center forward (d) Aalesunds FK (e) Aarhus GF, Haugesund, Aarhus GF, Skanderborg

*** Amo - Eric Amo (a) 15/06/2003, ¿? (Ghana) (b) - (c) D - left back (d) - (e) Pobeda Prilep

*** Amoah - Joseph Amoah (a) 01/01/2002, Accra (Ghana) (b) 1,78 (c) F - right winger (d) FK Zeljeznicar Sarajevo (e) Accra Lions, Rudar Prijedor, AS Trencin, Accra Lions

*** Amoako - Joseph Amoako (a) 13/09/2002, Kumasi (Ghana) (b) 1,78 (c) F - left winger (d) Asante Kotoko SC (e) Helsingborgs IF, Asante Kotoko

*** Amo-Ameyaw - Samuel Amo-Ameyaw (a) 18/07/2006, ¿? (England) (b) - (c) F - left winger (d) Southampton FC (e) -

*** Amodio - Andrea Amodio (a) 13/07/1997, ¿? (Luxembourg) (b) - (c) G (d) Jeunesse Esch (e) Differdange 03, Union Titus Petange, Belvaux

*** Amofa - Brian Amofa (a) 07/09/1992, Strasbourg (France) (b) 1,84 (c) M - pivot (d) FC Progrès Niederkorn (e) ASM Belfort, Les Herbiers VF, Jura Sud, Hyères FC, Racing Club Strasbourg, Racing Strasbourg B

*** Amofa - Jamal Amofa (a) 25/11/1998, Amsterdam (Netherlands) (b) 1,85 (c) D - central defense (d) Go Ahead Eagles Deventer (e) ADO Den Haag

*** Amoo - Akinkunmi Amoo (Akinkunmi Ayobami Amoo) (a) 07/06/2002, Ibadan (Nigeria) (b) 1,63 (c) F - right winger (d) FC Copenhague (e) Hammarby IF, Sido's FC

*** Amos - Gad Amos (גד עמוס) (a) 24/12/1988, Tiberias (Israel) (b) 1,86 (c) G (d) Maccabi Bnei Reineh (e) Bnei Sakhnin, M. Ahi Nazareth, Kiryat Shmona, M. Ahi

Nazareth, Ironi Nesher, M. Ahi Nazareth, Hapoel Haifa, Maccabi Haifa, M. Ahi Nazareth, Maccabi Haifa, Hapoel Haifa, Maccabi Haifa, Hapoel Acre, Maccabi Haifa
*** Amos - Oliver Amos (Oliver Jay Amos) (a) 16/08/2004, ¿? (Wales) (b) - (c) F - center forward (d) Goytre United (e) Cambrian & C., Pontypridd DVP, Garw
*** Amos - Tom Amos (Tom Shiran Amos) (a) 06/02/1998, Göteborg (Sweden) (b) 1,96 (c) G (d) Hapoel Beer Sheva (e) J-Södra IF, IFK Göteborg, Utsiktens BK, IFK Göteborg
*** Amou - Lionel Amou (Taylan Lionel Amou) (a) 24/02/2005, ¿? (Luxembourg) (b) - (c) D - left back (d) CS Fola Esch (e) -
*** Amougui - Vitus Amougui (a) 15/01/1996, ¿? (Cameroon) (b) 1,83 (c) M - central midfielder (d) FC Milsami Orhei (e) UMS de Loum
*** Amoura - Mohamed Amoura (Mohamed El Amine Amoura محمد الأمين عمورة) (a) 09/05/2000, Tahir (Algeria) (b) 1,70 (c) F - center forward (d) FC Lugano (e) ES Sétif
*** Ampadu - Ethan Ampadu (Ethan Kwame Colm Raymond Ampadu) (a) 14/09/2000, Exeter (England) (b) 1,82 (c) M - pivot (d) Leeds United (e) Chelsea, Spezia, Chelsea, Venezia, Chelsea, Sheffield Utd., Chelsea, RB Leipzig, Chelsea, Exeter City
*** Ampem - Prince Ampem (Prince Obeng Ampem) (a) 13/04/1998, Sunyani (Ghana) (b) 1,69 (c) F - right winger (d) Eyüpspor (e) HNK Rijeka, HNK Sibenik, WAFA SC, HNK Sibenik, WAFA SC
*** Amrabat - Nordin Amrabat (نور الدين المرابط) (a) 31/03/1987, Naarden (Netherlands) (b) 1,79 (c) F - right winger (d) AEK Athína FC (e) Al-Nassr, Watford, CD Leganés, Watford, Málaga CF, Galatasaray, Málaga CF, Galatasaray, Málaga CF, Galatasaray, Kayserispor, PSV Eindhoven, VVV-Venlo, FC Omniworld, SV Huizen
*** Amrabat - Sofyan Amrabat (أمرابط سفيان) (a) 21/08/1996, Huizen (Netherlands) (b) 1,85 (c) M - pivot (d) Fiorentina (e) Hellas Verona, Fiorentina, Hellas Verona, KV Brugge, Hellas Verona, KV Brugge, Feyenoord, FC Utrecht
*** Amraoui - Ayoub Amraoui (a) 14/05/2004, La Seyne (France) (b) 1,86 (c) D - left back (d) OGC Niza (e) OGC Nice B
*** Amundsen - Isak Helstad Amundsen (a) 14/10/1999, Brønnøysund (Norway) (b) 1,90 (c) D - central defense (d) FK Bodø/Glimt (e) Tromsø, Bodø/Glimt, Bodø/Glimt II, Brønnøysund
*** Amuzu - Francis Amuzu (Francis Apelete Amuzu) (a) 23/08/1999, Accra (Ghana) (b) 1,69 (c) F - left winger (d) RSC Anderlecht (e) JMG Lier
*** Amuzu - Joseph Amuzu (a) 18/08/2004, ¿? (Belgium) (b) - (c) F - left winger (d) Helmond Sport (e) Jong KV Mechelen
*** Amzai - Astrit Amzai (a) 04/07/2002, ¿? (RF Yugoslavia, now in Kosovo) (b) 1,84 (c) G (d) Teteks Tetovo (e) Shkëndija, Gostivar, Shkëndija, Teteks Tetovo, Shkëndija
*** Anaba - Michael Anaba (a) 05/12/1993, Kumasi (Ghana) (b) 1,77 (c) M - central midfielder (d) - (e) Kauno Zalgiris, Atzeneta UE, Al-Jahra SC, AFC Eskilstuna, CD Alcoyano, Ontinyent, Sud America, CD Eldense, Elche CF, CD Alcoyano, Elche CF, Elche Ilicitano, Asante Kotoko
*** Anaebonam - Stanley Anaebonam (Stanley Obinna Anaebonam) (a) 14/04/1999, ¿? (England) (b) 1,90 (c) F - center forward (d) FC Hereford (e) Stourbridge, Hednesford, Truro City FC, Shelbourne, Solihull Moors, Redditch Utd., Solihull Moors, Wolverh. Cas.
*** Anagnostopoulos - Panagiotis Anagnostopoulos (Παναγιώτης Αναγνωστόπουλος) (a) 16/05/2003, ¿? (Greece) (b) - (c) M (d) PAS Lamia 1964 (e) Aris Avatou, PAS Lamia

*** Anaku - Sadat Anaku (Sadat Happy Anaku Ada) (a) 09/12/2000, Arua (Uganda) (b) - (c) F - center forward (d) Dundee United FC (e) Kampala CC

*** Anane - Tidjani Anane (a) 29/03/1997, Gangban (Benin) (b) 1,75 (c) F - left winger (d) - (e) Doxa Katokopias, Menemenspor, Esperance, AS Soliman, Esperance, US Ben Guerdane, Esperance, US Monastir, ASPAC FC

*** Anang - Benson Anang (a) 01/05/2000, ¿? (Ghana) (b) 1,72 (c) D - right back (d) Othellos Athienou (e) MSK Zilina, New Life FC

*** Anang - Joseph Anang (Joseph Tetteh Anang) (a) 08/06/2000, Accra (Ghana) (b) 1,90 (c) G (d) West Ham United (e) Derby, St. Patrick's Ath., Stevenage

*** Ananidze - Jano Ananidze (ჯანო ანანიძე) (a) 10/10/1992, Kobuleti (Georgia) (b) 1,71 (c) M - attacking midfielder (d) - (e) Dinamo Batumi, Dinamo Tbilisi, Rotor Volgograd, Anorthosis, Spartak Moskva, KS Samara, Spartak Moskva, Rostov, Spartak Moskva, Spartak Moskva II

*** Anapa - Erkan Anapa (a) 27/01/1998, Giresun (Turkey) (b) 1,87 (c) G (d) Giresunspor (e) BB Erzurumspor, Giresunspor, Payasspor, Giresunspor

*** Anarbekov - Temirlan Anarbekov (Анарбеков Темірлан Анарбекұлы) (a) 14/10/2003, Atyrau (Kazakhstan) (b) 1,89 (c) G (d) Kairat Almaty (e) Kairat-Zhas

*** Anastasi - Mattia Anastasi (a) 19/03/1997, ¿? (Italy) (b) - (c) D - central defense (d) Tropical Coriano (e) Fiorentino

*** Anastasiadis - Efthymios Anastasiadis (Ευθύμιος Αναστασιάδης) (a) 20/08/2003, Limassol (Cyprus) (b) 1,73 (c) F - right winger (d) Apollon Limassol (e) APEA Akrotiri, Apollon Limassol

*** Anastasopoulos - Panagiotis Anastasopoulos (Παναγιώτης Αναστασόπουλος) (a) 24/10/2003, ¿? (Greece) (b) - (c) D - central defense (d) Panetolikos GFS (e) -

*** Anaya - Javi Anaya (Javier Anaya Rojas) (a) 12/07/1995, Algeciras (Spain) (b) 1,80 (c) F - center forward (d) FC College 1975 (e) San Roque Cádiz, St Joseph's FC, FC Olympique, Algeciras CF, Algeciras B, AD Taraguilla

*** Anbo - Magnus Anbo (Magnus Anbo Clausen) (a) 18/09/2000, Risskov (Denmark) (b) 1,85 (c) M - central midfielder (d) - (e) Aarhus GF, Stjarnan, Aarhus GF

*** Andersen - Alexander Juel Andersen (a) 29/01/1991, Viborg (Denmark) (b) 1,90 (c) D - central defense (d) Aalesunds FK (e) Odense BK, Aalesund, Odense BK, Vendsyssel FF, Odense BK, Vendsyssel FF, Aarhus GF, AC Horsens, Viborg FF, Randers FC, Viborg FF

*** Andersen - Benjamin Hellum Andersen (a) 21/06/2005, ¿? (Norway) (b) - (c) M (d) FK Eik Tønsberg 871 (e) Sandefjord II

*** Andersen - Eirik Ulland Andersen (a) 21/09/1992, Randers (Denmark) (b) 1,81 (c) F - right winger (d) Strømsgodset IF (e) Molde, Strømsgodset, Hødd, Vard, Hødd, Vard, Haugesund, Vard, Haugesund, Vard

*** Andersen - Jacob Andersen (a) 26/01/2004, ¿? (Denmark) (b) - (c) D - right back (d) Aarhus GF (e) -

*** Andersen - Jacob Andersen (Jacob Getachew Andersen) (a) 15/09/1993, ¿? (Denmark) (b) 1,76 (c) F - center forward (d) - (e) EB/Streymur, Djerv 1919, VSK Aarhus, SC Weiche 08, Ringköbing IF, Víkingur Ó., Egersund, Ringköbing IF, Hvidovre

*** Andersen - Jeppe Andersen (a) 06/12/1992, ¿? (Denmark) (b) 1,78 (c) M - pivot (d) Sarpsborg 08 FF (e) Hammarby IF, Esbjerg fB, Vejle-Kolding

*** Andersen - Joachim Andersen (Joachim Christian Andersen) (a) 31/05/1996, Frederiksberg (Denmark) (b) 1,92 (c) D - central defense (d) Crystal Palace (e) Olympique Lyon, Fulham, Olympique Lyon, Sampdoria, FC Twente

*** Andersen - Joakim Samuel Andersen (a) 27/05/2003, ¿? (Norway) (b) - (c) D - central defense (d) Alta IF (e) Tromsø IL II, Porsanger IL

*** Andersen - Kristian Andersen (Kristian Mamush Andersen) (a) 01/09/1994, ¿? (Denmark) (b) 1,70 (c) M - left midfielder (d) - (e) Hilleröd F., NSÍ Runavík, Kokkolan PV, Kolding IF, Brage, HB Köge, Brøndby IF, HB Köge, Brøndby IF

*** Andersen - Lucas Andersen (a) 13/09/1994, Aalborg (Denmark) (b) 1,84 (c) F - left winger (d) Aalborg BK (e) Grasshoppers, Aalborg BK, Grasshoppers, Ajax, Willem II, Ajax, Aalborg BK

*** Andersen - Marcus Andersen (Marcus Ellingsen Andersen) (a) 29/05/2001, ¿? (Norway) (b) 1,85 (c) G (d) IL Hødd (e) Bodø/Glimt, Fløya, Bodø/Glimt, Bodø/Glimt II

*** Andersen - Mikkel Andersen (a) 17/12/1988, Herlev (Denmark) (b) 1,95 (c) G (d) BK Fremad Amager (e) Viborg FF, Brann, Midtjylland, Lyngby BK, Midtjylland, Reading, Randers FC, Reading, FC Portsmouth, Reading, Bristol Rovers, Reading, Bristol Rovers, Reading, Brighton & Hove Albion, Reading, Brentford, Reading, Rushden & Diamonds, Reading, Torquay, Reading, Akademisk BK

*** Anderson - Anderson (Anderson de Jesus Santos) (a) 02/03/1995, Lagarto (Brazil) (b) 1,86 (c) D - central defense (d) FC Vizela (e) América-MG, Bahia B, Grêmio Porto Alegre B, Confiança, Grêmio Porto Alegre B, Guarani, Confiança, Guarani-SC, Confiança

*** Anderson - Anderson (Anderson Dos Santos Gomes) (a) 03/01/1998, São Paulo (Brazil) (b) 1,84 (c) D - right back (d) SC Austria Lustenau (e) SCR Altach, FC Dornbirn, SCR Altach, GO Audax, SCR Altach, GO Audax, Osasco FC

*** Anderson - Bruce Anderson (a) 23/09/1998, Banff (Scotland) (b) 1,73 (c) F - center forward (d) Livingston FC (e) Aberdeen FC, Aberdeen FC, Ayr United, Aberdeen FC, Dunfermline A., Aberdeen FC, Elgin City

*** Anderson - Djavan Anderson (Djavan Lorenzo Anderson) (a) 21/04/1995, Amsterdam (Netherlands) (b) 1,78 (c) D - right back (d) - (e) Oxford United, Lazio, PEC Zwolle, Lazio, Cosenza, Lazio, Salernitana, Lazio, Bari, SC Cambuur, AZ Alkmaar

*** Anderson - Elliot Anderson (a) 06/11/2002, Whitley Bay (England) (b) 1,79 (c) M - attacking midfielder (d) Newcastle United (e) Bristol Rovers

*** Anderson - Harry Anderson (a) 01/11/2002, ¿? (Northern Ireland) (b) - (c) F - center forward (d) - (e) Portadown, Armagh City FC, Portadown

*** Anderson - Jonathan Anderson (Jonathan Osazee Anderson Ogbomo) (a) 19/10/2001, Roma (Italy) (b) - (c) D - left back (d) - (e) Caernarfon, Hyde United, Caernarfon

*** Anderson - Kevin Anderson (a) 10/11/1993, Tartu (Estonia) (b) 1,87 (c) D - central defense (d) Jalgpallikool Tammeka (e) Tammeka Tartu, JK Tammeka, Tammeka Tartu, JK Tammeka II

*** Anderson - Lloyd Anderson (a) 09/03/1998, Belfast (Northern Ireland) (b) 1,78 (c) M - attacking midfielder (d) Crusaders FC (e) Carrick Rangers, Crusaders, Carrick Rangers, Crusaders, Knockbreda FC

*** Anderson - Mikael Anderson (Mikael Neville Anderson) (a) 01/07/1998, Reykjavík (Iceland) (b) 1,80 (c) F - left winger (d) Aarhus GF (e) Midtjylland, Excelsior, Midtjylland, Vendsyssel FF, Midtjylland, Aarhus GF II

*** Anderson - Sam Anderson (a) 14/07/2006, Loughgall (Northern Ireland) (b) - (c) F - center forward (d) - (e) Dungannon Swifts

*** Anderson Cordeiro - Anderson Cordeiro (Anderson Cordeiro Costa) (a) 10/10/1998, Bom Despacho (Brazil) (b) 1,76 (c) F - left winger (d) ABC Futebol

Clube (RN) (e) A. Keciörengücü, Casa Pia, Tsarsko Selo, CF Fuenlabrada, Tsarsko Selo, Taubaté
*** Anderson Correia - Anderson Correia (Anderson Correia de Barros) (a) 06/05/1991, São Paulo (Brazil) (b) 1,77 (c) D - left back (d) Anorthosis Famagusta (e) Nea Salamis, Boavista, São Paulo-RS, Paulista, Botafogo-SP, Paulista, Patrocinense-MG, Santo André, Santo André B
*** Anderson Oliveira - Anderson Oliveira (Anderson de Oliveira da Silva) (a) 16/07/1998, Sinop (Brazil) (b) 1,69 (c) F - left winger (d) Goiás EC (e) Portimonense, Londrina-PR
*** Anderson Pico - Anderson Pico (Anderson da Silveira Ribeiro) (a) 04/11/1988, Porto Alegre (Brazil) (b) 1,70 (c) D - left back (d) - (e) Metalist, Cruzeiro-RS, EC São José, FK Metal, Juventus-SC, Kisvárda, São Paulo-RS, Dnipro, Flamengo, Dnipro, Flamengo, Novo Hamburgo, Chapecoense, Grêmio Porto Alegre, EC São José, Grêmio Porto Alegre, Juventude, Grêmio Porto Alegre, Brasiliense, Grêmio Porto Alegre, Figueirense FC, Grêmio Porto Alegre, Grêmio Porto Alegre B
*** Anderson Pinto - Anderson Pinto (Anderson Rene Pinto Nogueira) (a) 11/02/1994, ¿? (Portugal) (b) - (c) M - attacking midfielder (d) Billericay Town (e) Connah's Quay, Billericay, Braintree, Cheshunt, Royston Town, Walton & Hersham FC, Europa Point FC, Glacis United, Banbury, Carshalton Ath., Wingate FC
*** Anderson Silva - Anderson Silva (Anderson Oliveira Silva) (a) 21/11/1997, São Paulo (Brazil) (b) 1,86 (c) F - center forward (d) Alanyaspor (e) Vitória Guimarães, BJ Guoan, Famalicão, Guarani
*** Andersson - Adam Andersson (Carl Adam Andersson) (a) 11/11/1996, ¿? (Sweden) (b) 1,78 (c) D - right back (d) Rosenborg BK (e) Randers FC, Rosenborg, Häcken, Västra Frölunda
*** Andersson - Albin Andersson (a) 28/07/2003, ¿? (Sweden) (b) - (c) M - central midfielder (d) - (e) Mjällby AIF
*** Andersson - Andreas Andersson (a) 27/02/1991, ¿? (Sweden) (b) 1,92 (c) G (d) - (e) GIF Sundsvall, Dalkurd, Östersund, Gefle, Östersund, Gefle, Sirius, Elfsborg, Ljungskile SK, Elfsborg, FC Trollhättan, Elfsborg
*** Andersson - Casper Andersson (a) 24/06/2005, ¿? (Sweden) (b) 1,84 (c) G (d) Kalmar FF (e) -
*** Andersson - Elias Andersson (Nils Erik Elias Andersson) (a) 31/01/1996, Hässleholm (Sweden) (b) 1,78 (c) D - left back (d) Lech Poznan (e) Djurgården, Mjällby AIF, Djurgården, Sirius, Varbergs BoIS, Helsingborgs IF, Varbergs BoIS, Helsingborgs IF
*** Andersson - Erik Andersson (a) 03/05/1997, ¿? (Sweden) (b) 1,79 (c) M - central midfielder (d) GIF Sundsvall (e) Trelleborg, Malmö FF, Trelleborg, Malmö FF, Trelleborg, Malmö FF, Landskrona
*** Andersson - Fredrik Andersson (a) 25/10/1988, Skene (Sweden) (b) 1,96 (c) G (d) Varbergs BoIS (e) Örgryte, Malmö FF, Örgryte, Skene IF
*** Andersson - Hugo Andersson (Per Emil Hugo Andersson) (a) 01/01/1999, Skurup (Sweden) (b) 1,96 (c) D - central defense (d) Randers FC (e) Malmö FF, Värnamo, Malmö FF, Hobro IK, Malmö FF, Trelleborg, Malmö FF
*** Andersson - Joel Andersson (a) 11/11/1996, Göteborg (Sweden) (b) 1,78 (c) D - right back (d) FC Midtjylland (e) Häcken, Västra Frölunda
*** Andersson - Leo Andersson (a) 11/06/2004, ¿? (Finland) (b) 1,85 (c) M - central midfielder (d) IFK Mariehamn (e) -
*** Andersson - Sebastian Andersson (Martin Sebastian Andersson) (a) 15/07/1991, Ängelholm (Sweden) (b) 1,90 (c) F - center forward (d) - (e) 1.FC Köln, Union Berlin, 1.FC Kaiserslautern, Norrköping, Djurgården, Kalmar FF, Ängelholms FF

*** Andersson - Tobias Andersson (a) 18/02/1994, ¿? (Sweden) (b) 1,87 (c) G (d) - (e) Kalmar FF, Östers IF, Värnamo, Ljungby IF, Värnamo, Gnosjö IF, Värnamo
*** Andersson - Victor Andersson (Victor David Goncalves Andersson) (a) 22/10/2004, Danderyd (Sweden) (b) 1,74 (c) M - central midfielder (d) AIK Solna (e) -
*** Andersson - Viktor Andersson (a) 30/03/2004, Malmö (Sweden) (b) 1,89 (c) G (d) Lunds BK (e) Malmö FF
*** Andjelkovic - Jovan Andjelkovic (a) 23/04/2004, Paraćin (Serbia and Montenegro, now in Serbia) (b) - (c) F (d) FK Radnik Surdulica (e) Borac Paracin, Radnik, FK Hajduk Veljko Negotin, Paracin, Borac Paracin
*** Andjelkovic - Nemanja Andjelkovic (Немања Анђелковић) (a) 26/04/1997, Kosovska Mitrovica (RF Yugoslavia, now in Kosovo) (b) 1,88 (c) D - central defense (d) Akron Togliatti (e) Zira FK, Zlatibor, Metalac, Javor-Matis, Zlatibor, Javor-Matis, Zlatibor, CSK Celarevo, Radnik, Zlatibor, Mokra Gora ZP
*** Andjusic - Nemanja Andjusic (Nemanja Anđušić) (a) 17/10/1996, Trebinje (Bosnia and Herzegovina) (b) 1,77 (c) M - attacking midfielder (d) FK Velez Mostar (e) Trabzonspor, Balikesirspor, Trabzonspor, Mladost Kakanj, FK Sarajevo, Celik Zenica, FK Sarajevo, FK Olimpik, FK Sarajevo, Travnik, FK Sarajevo, Leotar Trebinje
*** Andonov - Dimitar Andonov (Димитър Владимиров Андонов) (a) 15/04/2004, Sofia (Bulgaria) (b) - (c) D - central defense (d) Sportist Svoge (e) Levski Sofia II
*** Andonov - Ivan Andonov (Иван Георгиев Андонов) (a) 27/12/2003, Sofia (Bulgaria) (b) 1,90 (c) G (d) Levski Sofia (e) Levski Sofia
*** Andonov - Zoran Andonov (Зоран Андонов) (a) 09/06/2000, Strumica (North Macedonia) (b) 1,82 (c) D - left back (d) Bregalnica Stip (e) Detonit, Pehcevo, Belasica
*** Andonovski - Marko Andonovski (Марко Андоновски) (a) 30/01/2001, Skopje (North Macedonia) (b) 1,78 (c) M - pivot (d) FK Skopje (e) Kadino
*** Andov - Matej Andov (Матеј Андов) (a) 16/11/2001, Skopje (North Macedonia) (b) 1,87 (c) G (d) Sileks Kratovo (e) Osogovo, Kadino, Osogovo, Rabotnicki, Vardar
*** Andrade - Fernando Andrade (Fernando Andrade dos Santos) (a) 08/01/1993, São Caetano do Sul (Brazil) (b) 1,82 (c) F - left winger (d) Casa Pia AC (e) FC Porto, Al-Fayha, FC Porto, Çaykur Rizespor, FC Porto, Sivasspor, FC Porto, Santa Clara, Penafiel, Oriental, Rio Branco-SP, Guarani, São Caetano B, Vissel Kobe, São Caetano B
*** Andrade - Pablo Andrade (Pablo Andrade Plaza da Silva) (a) 15/02/1994, Rio de Janeiro (Brazil) (b) 1,79 (c) D - left back (d) FC Lahti (e) SJK Seinäjoki, Racing, Ourense CF, Rayo Majadahonda, Ourense CF, Recreativo, Ourense CF, Bouzas, Ourense CF, Silva SD, Botafogo, Bangu-RJ, Botafogo
*** Andrade - Patrick Andrade (Erickson Patrick Correia Andrade) (a) 09/02/1993, Praia (Cabo Verde) (b) 1,73 (c) M - central midfielder (d) Qarabağ FK (e) FK Partizan, Qarabag FK, Cherno More, Salgueiros, Moreirense, Salgueiros, Moreirense, Famalicão, Moreirense, GD Ribeirão, GD Joane, GD Ribeirão, Desp. da Praia, Sporting Praia
*** Andrason - Atli Hrafn Andrason (a) 04/01/1999, Reykjavík (Iceland) (b) 1,78 (c) F - attacking midfielder (d) HK Kópavogs (e) ÍBV Vestmannaeyjar, Breidablik, Víkingur, Víkingur, KR Reykjavík
*** Andrason - Viktor Örlygur Andrason (a) 05/02/2000, ¿? (Iceland) (b) 1,78 (c) M - pivot (d) Víkingur Reykjavík (e) -

*** André - André André (André Filipe Brás André) (a) 26/08/1989, Vila do Conde (Portugal) (b) 1,74 (c) M - central midfielder (d) Vitória Guimarães SC (e) Ittihad Club, Vitória Guimarães, FC Porto, Vitória Guimarães, Varzim, Deportivo B, Varzim
*** André - Benjamin André (a) 03/08/1990, Nice (France) (b) 1,80 (c) M - pivot (d) LOSC Lille Métropole (e) Stade Rennes, AC Ajaccio, AC Ajaccio B
*** André Felipe - André Felipe (André Felipe Ribeiro de Souza) (a) 27/09/1990, Cabo Frio (Brazil) (b) 1,84 (c) F - center forward (d) Associação Atlética Ponte Preta SP (e) Torpedo Moskva, Cuiabá-MT, Sport Recife, Gaziantep FK, Grêmio Porto Alegre, Sport Recife, Grêmio Porto Alegre, Sport Recife, Sporting Lisboa, Corinthians, At. Mineiro, Sport Recife, At. Mineiro, Vasco da Gama, At. Mineiro, Santos, At. Mineiro, Dinamo Kyïv, At. Mineiro, Dinamo Kyïv, Girondins Bordeaux, Dinamo Kyïv, Santos
*** André Mensalão - André Mensalão (André Luiz Leão Lima) (a) 21/06/1990, Belém (Brazil) (b) 1,74 (c) M - central midfielder (d) FC West Armenia (e) Ethnikos, Pyunik Yerevan, Shkëndija, FC Sevan, Lori Vanadzor, Ferroviário, Caldense, Maringá, Marcílio Dias, Rio Claro, Cuiabá-MT, Moto Club, Tuna Luso, Guarany Sobral, Glória
*** Andreas - Mike Andreas (a) 31/01/1997, ¿? (Germany) (b) 1,81 (c) M - pivot (d) FC UNA Strassen (e) Swift Hesperange, SC Wiedenbrück, SV Röchling, FSV Mainz 05 II
*** Andreasen - Dávid Andreasen (Dávid Biskopstø Andreasen) (a) 27/06/2004, ¿? (Faroe Islands) (b) 1,83 (c) M - central midfielder (d) KÍ Klaksvík (e) KÍ II
*** Andreasen - Jákup Andreasen (Jákup Biskopstø Andreasen) (a) 31/05/1998, ¿? (Faroe Islands) (b) 1,88 (c) M - pivot (d) KÍ Klaksvík (e) KÍ II
*** Andreev - Petar Andreev (Петър Димитров Андреев) (a) 02/07/2004, Plovdiv (Bulgaria) (b) - (c) M - central midfielder (d) Lokomotiv Plovdiv (e) Lokomotiv Plovdiv II
*** Andreev - Plamen Andreev (Пламен Пламенов Андреев) (a) 15/12/2004, Sofia (Bulgaria) (b) 1,91 (c) G (d) Levski Sofia (e) -
*** Andreev - Yancho Andreev (Янчо Иванов Андреев) (a) 08/01/1990, Dobrich (Bulgaria) (b) 1,77 (c) M - attacking midfielder (d) Dobrudzha Dobrich (e) Spartak Varna, Dob. Dobrich, Botev Ihtiman, Oborishte, Vitosha, Minyor Pernik, Kaliakra, Cherno More, C. Balchik, Cherno More
*** Andrei - Doru Andrei (a) 03/02/2003, Timișoara (Romania) (b) 1,76 (c) M - attacking midfielder (d) FC Voluntari (e) SSU Poli, Comprest Gim
*** Andrejasic - Jan Andrejasic (Jan Andrejašič) (a) 16/09/1995, ¿? (Slovenia) (b) 1,83 (c) D - right back (d) - (e) ND Gorica, Olimpija, NK Celje, Koper
*** Andrejev - Maksim Andrejev (a) 09/06/2004, ¿? (Lithuania) (b) - (c) D - right back (d) FK Banga Gargzdai (e) Banga B, Klaipedos FM, Rosa, Klaipedos FM
*** Andrejic - Aleksa Andrejic (Алекса Андрејић) (a) 24/01/1993, Kruševac (RF Yugoslavia, now in Serbia) (b) 1,75 (c) F - left winger (d) Balzan FC (e) FK Krupa, Tarxien, FK Indjija, Trayal, FK SEKO Louny, FK Most, 1.SC Znojmo, BASK Beograd
*** Andreou - Evangelos Andreou (Ευάγγελος "Άγγελος" Ανδρέου) (a) 24/09/2002, Limassol (Cyprus) (b) 1,73 (c) F - right winger (d) AEL Limassol (e) At. Levante, AEL Limassol
*** Andreou - Stelios Andreou (Στέλιος Ανδρέου) (a) 24/07/2002, Nicosia (Cyprus) (b) 1,87 (c) D - central defense (d) RSC Charleroi (e) Olympiakos N.
*** Andres - Ionut Andres (Ionuț-Vlăduț Andreș) (a) 23/05/2000, Piatra Neamț (Romania) (b) 1,93 (c) D - central defense (d) FC Voluntari (e) Ceahlaul

*** Andrésen - Aske Andrésen (Aske Leth Andrésen) (a) 12/07/2005, Aarhus (Denmark) (b) 1,99 (c) G (d) Silkeborg IF (e) -
*** Andrésson - Benoný Breki Andrésson (a) 03/08/2005, ¿? (Iceland) (b) - (c) F - center forward (d) KR Reykjavík (e) -
*** Andreu - Sascha Andreu (Sascha Fernando Lahrach Andreu) (a) 12/08/1986, Barcelona (Spain) (b) - (c) F - center forward (d) Inter Club d'Escaldes (e) Badalona Futur, Cornellà, UE Costa Brava, Ontinyent, Cornellà, CF Gavà, AE Prat, Montañesa, Gramenet, Castelldefels, Santfeliuenc FC, CE Júpiter, UE Sants
*** Andrew - Andrew (Andrew da Silva Ventura) (a) 01/07/2001, Duque de Caxias (Brazil) (b) 1,89 (c) G (d) Gil Vicente FC (e) Botafogo, Botafogo B, Maranhão, Botafogo B
*** Andrew - Colin Andrew (a) 14/08/2004, Praha (Czech Rep.) (b) - (c) G (d) SK Dynamo Ceske Budejovice B (e) -
*** Andrews - Josh Andrews (Joshua Andrews) (a) 12/06/2004, ¿? (Northern Ireland) (b) - (c) M - central midfielder (d) Carrick Rangers (e) -
*** Andrey Yago - Andrey Yago (Andrey Yago da Silva Mesquita Almeida) (a) 29/12/1997, ¿? (Brazil) (b) 1,78 (c) D - left back (d) Makedonija Gjorce Petrov (e) Laranjeiras-ES, Desportiva-ES, CD Fátima, Colégio Josee
*** Andreychuk - Andriy Andreychuk (Андрейчук Андрій Васильович) (a) 17/02/2003, Nebyliv, Ivano-Frankivsk Oblast (Ukraine) (b) 1,87 (c) F - center forward (d) - (e) Prykarpattya
*** Andrezinho - Andrezinho (André Miguel Pinto Lopes) (a) 01/12/1996, Lisboa (Portugal) (b) 1,74 (c) F - right winger (d) CD Santa Clara (e) Dunajska Streda, Mafra, Alverca, Casa Pia, Alverca
*** Andric - Komnen Andric (Комнен Андрић) (a) 01/07/1995, Novi Pazar (RF Yugoslavia, now in Serbia) (b) 1,89 (c) F - center forward (d) Clermont Foot 63 (e) Dinamo Zagreb, Ufa, Dinamo Zagreb, Inter Zaprešić, Dinamo Zagreb, Inter Zaprešić, B SAD, Inter Zaprešić, Belenenses, Zalgiris, Belenenses, OFK Beograd, Radnicki 1923
*** Andric - Nemanja Andric (Немања Андрић) (a) 13/06/1987, Beograd (Yugoslavia, now in Serbia) (b) 1,71 (c) F - left winger (d) Karcagi SE (e) Vrsac, Kolubara, Kaposvár, ETO FC Győr, Balmazújváros, Újpest FC, ETO FC Győr, Újpest FC, ETO FC Győr, Rad Beograd, FK Obilic
*** Andric - Nikola Andric (Никола Андрић) (a) 23/05/1992, Beograd (Yugoslavia, now in Serbia) (b) 1,83 (c) D - right back (d) FK Novi Pazar (e) Radnicki Niš, Borac Banja Luka, Radnicki 1923, Vojvodina, Mladost, Podbrezova, OFK Mladenovac
*** Andrich - Robert Andrich (a) 22/09/1994, Potsdam (Germany) (b) 1,87 (c) M - central midfielder (d) Bayer 04 Leverkusen (e) Union Berlin, 1.FC Heidenheim, Wehen Wiesbaden, Dynamo Dresden, Hertha BSC II, Hertha Berlin, Hertha BSC II
*** Andriuskevic - Emil Andriuskevic (Emil Andriuškevič) (a) 07/10/2004, ¿? (Lithuania) (b) - (c) M - central midfielder (d) FK Riteriai B (e) -
*** Andriyevskyi - Oleksandr Andriyevskyi (Андрієвський Олександр Петрович) (a) 25/06/1994, Kyiv (Ukraine) (b) 1,79 (c) M - central midfielder (d) FC Dinamo de Kiev (e) Dinamo Kiev II, Zorya Lugansk, Dinamo Kiev II, Chornomorets, Dinamo Kiev II, Metalist II, Girnyk-Sport, Metalist II
*** Andronache - Luca Andronache (Luca Cristian Andronache) (a) 26/07/2003, Bucuresti (Romania) (b) 1,89 (c) F - center forward (d) FCV Farul Constanta (e) FCSB II
*** Andronic - Gheorghe Andronic (a) 25/09/1991, Chişinău (Moldova) (b) 1,72 (c) M - attacking midfielder (d) CF Spartanii Sportul Selemet (e) Zimbru Chisinau, Milsami, FC Buzau, CSF Speranta, Rukh, Astra Giurgiu, Milsami, Zimbru Chisinau,

Degerfors, Värnamo, NK Lokomotiva, HNK Gorica, NK Lokomotiva, Zimbru Chisinau
*** Andronikashvili - Aleksandre Andronikashvili (ალექსანდრე ანდრონიკაშვილი) (a) 09/04/1999, ¿? (Georgia) (b) - (c) M - pivot (d) FC Dila Gori (e) Shukura, FC Locomotive, 35 FS
*** Andronikou - Theodoros Andronikou (Θεόδωρος Ανδρόνικου) (a) 07/07/2001, Limassol (Cyprus) (b) 1,72 (c) M - central midfielder (d) FK Pribram (e) Karmiotissa, Olympiakos N., Karmiotissa, Kouris Erimis, Karmiotissa, Karmiotissa
*** Androutsos - Athanasios Androutsos (Αθανάσιος-Γεώργιος Ανδρούτσος) (a) 06/05/1997, Marousi (Greece) (b) 1,82 (c) D - right back (d) Olympiakos El Pireo (e) Atromitos FC, Olympiakos
*** Andyrmash - Dias Andyrmash (Андырмаш Диас Кайратулы) (a) 28/06/2001, Aktobe (Kazakhstan) (b) 1,72 (c) M - left midfielder (d) FK Aktobe II (e) -
*** Andzouana - Yhoan Andzouana (Yhoan Many Andzouana) (a) 13/12/1996, Brazzaville (Congo) (b) 1,80 (c) F - left winger (d) DAC Dunajska Streda (e) KSV Roeselare, Girona FC, CF Peralada, AS Monaco B
*** Anello - Agustín Anello (Agustín Anello Giaquinta) (a) 22/04/2002, Miami, Florida (United States) (b) 1,82 (c) F - left winger (d) Sparta Rotterdam (e) Lommel SK, Hajduk Split, Lommel SK
*** Anestis - Giannis Anestis (Γιάννης Ανέστης) (a) 09/03/1991, Chalkida (Greece) (b) 1,98 (c) G (d) Karmiotissa Pano Polemidion (e) Panetolikos, IFK Göteborg, H. Beer Sheva, AEK Athína, Panionios
*** Anet - Sagi Anet (Анет Саги Махсутулы) (a) 26/02/2002, Kyzemshek, Suzakskiy Rayon (Kazakhstan) (b) 1,69 (c) M - pivot (d) FK Jetisay (e) Turkistan, Kairat Moskva, Kairat-Zhas
*** Angban - Victorien Angban (Bekanty Victorien Angban) (a) 29/09/1996, Abidjan (Ivory Coast) (b) 1,80 (c) M - central midfielder (d) FK Sochi (e) FC Metz, Waasland-Beveren, Granada CF, Sint-Truiden, Stade d'Abidjan
*** Angeli - Matteo Angeli (a) 30/12/2002, Cuneo (Italy) (b) 1,85 (c) D - central defense (d) AS Cittadella (e) Bologna, Renate, Bologna, Imolese
*** Angeli - Nicola Angeli (a) 28/05/1989, ¿? (Italy) (b) 1,70 (c) F - center forward (d) AC Virtus Acquaviva (e) Gambettola, Classe, Tropical Coriano, Gambettola, Ribelle, Verucchio
*** Angelini - Francesco Angelini (a) 23/01/2003, Rimini (Italy) (b) - (c) M - central midfielder (d) SS San Giovanni (e) Sammaurese
*** Angelini - Luca Angelini (a) 17/09/1989, ¿? (Italy) (b) - (c) D - central defense (d) - (e) San Giovanni, Tre Fiori, Stella
*** Angelini - Nicolò Angelini (a) 15/03/1992, ¿? (San Marino) (b) - (c) F - center forward (d) FC Domagnano (e) Murata, Libertas
*** Angeliño - Angeliño (José Ángel Esmoris Tasende) (a) 04/01/1997, Coristanco (Spain) (b) 1,71 (c) D - left back (d) Galatasaray (e) Galatasaray, RB Leipzig, Hoffenheim, RB Leipzig, Manchester City, RB Leipzig, Manchester City, PSV Eindhoven, NAC Breda, RCD Mallorca, Girona FC, New York City
*** Angelis Angeli - Angelis Angeli (Αγγελής Αγγελή Χαραλάμπους) (a) 31/05/1989, Larnaka (Cyprus) (b) 1,89 (c) D - central defense (d) Karmiotissa Pano Polemidion (e) IFK Mariehamn, EN Paralimniou, Apollon Limassol, Ermis Aradippou, Motherwell FC, Anorthosis
*** Angeloff - David Angeloff (David Alcides Angeloff) (a) 18/02/1991, Corzuela (Argentina) (b) 1,80 (c) D - left back (d) - (e) Jonava, Lamadrid, Sol de Mayo, Cruz del Sur, Sol de Mayo, Lamadrid, Cruz del Sur, Lamadrid, Tristán Suárez, CAD Paraguayo

*** Angelopoulos - Giannis Angelopoulos (Γιάννης Αγγελόπουλος) (a) 03/04/1998, ¿? (Greece) (b) 1,85 (c) G (d) APO Levadiakos (e) APO Levadiakos, Pafos FC

*** Angelov - Angel Angelov (Ангел Григоров Ангелов) (a) 17/11/1999, Varna (Bulgaria) (b) - (c) F - left winger (d) Cherno More Varna (e) C. Balchik, B. Botevgrad

*** Angelov - Ayvan Angelov (Айвън Росенов Ангелов) (a) 10/10/2001, Lovech (Bulgaria) (b) 1,68 (c) M - central midfielder (d) Spartak Varna (e) Spartak Varna, CSKA 1948 II, Belasitsa, Lokomotiv Plovdiv, Belasitsa

*** Angelov - Matej Angelov (Матеј Ангелов) (a) 11/07/2004, Stip (North Macedonia) (b) 1,78 (c) M - pivot (d) Rabotnicki Skopje (e) -

*** Angelov - Viktor Angelov (Виктор Ангелов) (a) 27/03/1994, Dortmund (Germany) (b) 1,75 (c) F - center forward (d) AS FC Buzau (e) AP Brera, FC Voluntari, Siroki Brijeg, FC Shkupi, Újpest FC, Rabotnicki, Újpest FC, Metalurg Skopje, Rabotnicki, Teteks Tetovo, Rabotnicki

*** Angielski - Karol Angielski (a) 20/03/1996, Kielce (Poland) (b) 1,81 (c) F - center forward (d) Atromitos FC (e) Sivasspor, Radomiak, Wisła Płock, Piast Gliwice, Olimpia Grudz., Piast Gliwice, Zawisza, Piast Gliwice, Śląsk Wroclaw, Korona Kielce, Korona Kielce II

*** Angileri - Fabrizio Angileri (Fabrizio Germán Angileri) (a) 15/03/1994, Junín (Argentina) (b) 1,85 (c) D - left back (d) Getafe CF (e) River Plate, Godoy Cruz, River Plate, Godoy Cruz, Godoy Cruz II

*** Angjeleski - Darko Angjeleski (Дарко Анѓелески) (a) 19/07/1999, Prilep (North Macedonia) (b) 1,82 (c) M - pivot (d) Sileks Kratovo (e) Pobeda Prilep, Pelister Bitola

*** Angori - Samuele Angori (a) 07/10/2003, Cortona (Italy) (b) 1,84 (c) D - left back (d) US Città di Pontedera (e) Pontedera, FC Empoli, Perugia

*** Angstmann - Johann Angstmann (a) 16/01/2003, Hollywood, Florida (United States) (b) 1,87 (c) F - center forward (d) FC Lugano II (e) -

*** Anguissa - Frank Anguissa (André-Frank Zambo Anguissa) (a) 16/11/1995, Yaoundé (Cameroon) (b) 1,84 (c) M - central midfielder (d) SSC Nápoles (e) Fulham, Napoli, Fulham, Villarreal CF, Fulham, Ol. Marseille, Ol. Marseille B, Stade Reims B, Coton Sport FC

*** Angulo - Marvin Angulo (Marvin Santiago Angulo Perea) (a) 02/03/2000, ¿? (Colombia) (b) 1,81 (c) F - center forward (d) - (e) Lernayin Artsakh, UD Son Verí, C. Boca Juniors Cali

*** Angulo - Nilson Angulo (Nilson David Angulo Ramírez) (a) 19/06/2003, ¿? (Ecuador) (b) 1,83 (c) M - attacking midfielder (d) RSC Anderlecht (e) LDU Quito, LDU Quito B, Atlético Kin

*** Angulo - Wbeymar Angulo (Վբեյմար Անգուլո - Wbeymar Angulo Mosquera) (a) 06/03/1992, Quibdó (Colombia) (b) 1,81 (c) M - pivot (d) Alashkert Yerevan CF (e) Alashkert CF, Ararat-Armenia, Gandzasar, Murciélagos, Alianza Petrol., Atlético Huila, Bogotá FC, Patriotas

*** Ani - Ifeanyi Ani (Ifeanyi Emmanuel Ani) (a) 29/08/2002, ¿? (Nigeria) (b) 1,78 (c) M - central midfielder (d) Atlantis FC (e) FC Finnkurd, Helsinki IFK, Tiki Taka

*** Anicet - Anicet (Anicet Andrianantenaina Abel) (a) 13/03/1990, Antananarivo (Madagascar) (b) 1,79 (c) M - central midfielder (d) - (e) M. Bnei Reineh, Beroe, Future FC, Ludogorets, Botev Plovdiv, CSKA Sofia, Chern. Burgas, AJ Auxerre B

*** Anicic - Marin Anicic (Marin Aničić) (a) 17/08/1989, Mostar (Yugoslavia, now in Bosnia and Herzegovina) (b) 1,92 (c) D - central defense (d) FK Sarajevo (e) Konyaspor, FC Astana, Zrinjski Mostar

*** Anicic - Petar Anicic (Петар Аничић) (a) 12/07/2004, ¿? (Serbia and Montenegro, now in Montenegro) (b) 1,90 (c) F - right winger (d) FK Sutjeska Niksic (e) Sutjeska II

*** Anier - Hannes Anier (a) 16/01/1993, Tallinn (Estonia) (b) 1,82 (c) F - center forward (d) Henri Anier (e) Kalev, FCI Levadia, Kalev, Thisted FC, FC Flora, Erzgebirge Aue, Odense BK, FC Flora, FC Flora II, Warrior Valga

*** Anier - Henri Anier (a) 17/12/1990, Tallinn (Estonia) (b) 1,83 (c) F - center forward (d) Lee Man (e) Muangthong Utd., Paide, Go Ahead Eagles, Suwon FC, FC Lahti, Inverness Caledonian, Kalmar FF, Dundee United, Hibernian FC, Dundee United, Erzgebirge Aue, Motherwell FC, Viking, Motherwell FC, Viking, Fredrikstad, Viking, FC Flora, Warrior Valga

*** Anikeev - Vladlen Anikeev (Аникеев Владлен Игоревич) (a) 09/02/2004, Vitebsk (Belarus) (b) - (c) F - center forward (d) FK Vitebsk (e) Vitebsk II, RUOR Minsk

*** Anim Cudjoe - Mathew Anim Cudjoe (a) 11/11/2003, Accra (Ghana) (b) 1,63 (c) M - attacking midfielder (d) Dundee United FC (e) Y. Apostles FC, Legon Cities FC, Y. Apostles FC, Asante Kotoko, Y. Apostles FC

*** Animasahun - Mayowa Animasahun (a) 08/08/2003, ¿? (Ireland) (b) - (c) D - central defense (d) Dundalk FC (e) Dungannon, Dundalk FC

*** Anini Jr. - Samuel Anini Jr. (Samuel Anini Junior) (a) 07/09/2002, ¿? (Finland) (b) 1,75 (c) F - left winger (d) IFK Mariehamn (e) IFK Mariehamn, HJK Helsinki, AC Oulu, HJK Helsinki, HJK Klubi 04

*** Anisas - Benas Anisas (a) 29/02/2000, Mazeikiai (Lithuania) (b) 1,81 (c) M - right midfielder (d) FK Atmosfera Mazeikiai (e) Kauno Zalgiris, Banga, Kauno Zalgiris, Dziugas, Atmosfera

*** Anisimov - Artur Anisimov (Анисимов Артур Евгеньевич) (a) 31/12/1992, Naberezhnye Chelny (Russia) (b) 1,86 (c) G (d) KamAZ Naberezhnye Chelny (e) Pari Nizhny Novgórod, KamAZ, KamAZ II

*** Anisorac - Ionut Anisorac (Ionuț Anișorac) (a) 01/01/2005, ¿? (Romania) (b) - (c) D - left back (d) AFC Chindia Targoviste (e) UTA Arad

*** Anita - Vurnon Anita (Vurnon San Benito Anita) (a) 04/04/1989, Willemstad, Curaçao (Netherlands Antilles) (b) 1,69 (c) M - pivot (d) Al-Orobah FC (e) RKC Waalwijk, CSKA-Sofia, Leeds Utd., Willem II, Leeds Utd., Newcastle Utd., Ajax

*** Ankersen - Jakob Ankersen (a) 22/09/1990, Esbjerg (Denmark) (b) 1,79 (c) M - left midfielder (d) AC Horsens (e) Randers FC, EFB Reserves, Esbjerg fB, Aarhus GF, Zulte Waregem, IFK Göteborg, Esbjerg fB

*** Ankersen - Peter Ankersen (Peter Svarrer Ankersen) (a) 22/09/1990, Esbjerg (Denmark) (b) 1,80 (c) D - right back (d) FC Copenhague (e) Genoa, FC København, RB Salzburg, FC København, RB Salzburg, Esbjerg fB, Rosenborg, Vejle-Kolding, Vejle BK, Esbjerg fB

*** Ankotovych - Oleg Ankotovych (a) 11/08/2004, ¿? (Ukraine) (b) - (c) D (d) SS Folgore/Falciano (e) -

*** Ankrah - Ahmed Ankrah (Ahmed Awua Ankrah) (a) 05/01/2002, Drobo (Ghana) (b) 1,84 (c) M - pivot (d) Parma (e) ND Gorica

*** Ankudinov - Danil Ankudinov (Анкудинов Данил) (a) 31/07/2003, Karagandá (Kazakhstan) (b) 1,88 (c) F - center forward (d) FC Dziugas Telsiai (e) Dziugas, FC Sheriff, FC Van, FC Sheriff, Rodina 2 Moskva, F. Marcet

*** Ankudinovas - Lukas Ankudinovas (a) 10/08/1995, Taurage (Lithuania) (b) 1,83 (c) D - central defense (d) FC Dziugas Telsiai (e) Tortolì, Tauras, Tortolì, Lanusei, Tauras

*** Anmanis - Kaspars Anmanis (a) 22/01/2002, ¿? (Latvia) (b) - (c) M - pivot (d) FK Tukums 2000 (e) -

*** Annan - Anthony Annan (Anthony Gildas Kofi Annan) (a) 21/07/1986, Accra (Ghana) (b) 1,75 (c) M - pivot (d) - (e) TPS, FC Inter, B. Jerusalem, HJK Helsinki,

Stabæk, 1860 München, HJK Helsinki, FC Schalke 04, CA Osasuna, FC Schalke 04, Vitesse, FC Schalke 04, Rosenborg, Start, Stabæk, Start, Hearts of Oak, S. Hasaacas, Eleven Wise

*** Annan - Isaac Annan (a) 09/09/2001, ¿? (Ghana) (b) 1,78 (c) D - left back (d) Kristiansund BK (e) -

*** Annell - Oskar Annell (a) 15/02/2005, ¿? (Belgium) (b) 1,90 (c) G (d) KV Mechelen (e) Jong KV Mechelen

*** Annett - Rhys Annett (a) 06/11/2004, Newtownards (Northern Ireland) (b) - (c) F - center forward (d) Linfield FC (e) Dundela FC

*** Anniste - Aivar Anniste (a) 18/02/1980, Põltsamaa (Soviet Union, now in Estonia) (b) 1,81 (c) D - central defense (d) Kalev Tallinn Junior (e) Kalev III, Viimsi JK, Viimsi JK II, FCF Ülikool, Nomme United, FC Flora, TVMK Tallinn, Enköpings SK, Ullensaker/Kisa, Hønefoss, Tammeka Tartu, Ullensaker/Kisa, JK Viljandi, Warrior Valga, FC Flora, Lelle SK

*** Anoff - Blankson Anoff (a) 24/03/2001, Konkonuru (Ghana) (b) 1,73 (c) M - attacking midfielder (d) Swift Hesperange (e) Clermont Foot, Austria Lustenau, Clermont Foot, JMG Abidjan

*** Anomerawani - Andrew Anomerawani (Andrew Vivien Anomerawani Ombenidjouwa) (a) 08/07/2001, ¿? (Gabon) (b) 1,9 (c) D - central defense (d) FK Gomel (e) Dinamo-Auto

*** Anquibou - Emmanuel Anquibou (a) 31/03/1999, ¿? (France) (b) - (c) F (d) FC Mondercange (e) Saint-Pierroise

*** Ansah - Eugene Ansah (a) 16/12/1994, Accra (Ghana) (b) 1,83 (c) F - left winger (d) FC Dallas (e) H. Beer Sheva, Hapoel Raanana, Kiryat Shmona, Hapoel Raanana, Beitar TA Ramla, KSC Lokeren, Lommel United, KSC Lokeren

*** Ansarifard - Karim Ansarifard (انصاريفرد كريم) (a) 03/04/1990, Ardabil (Iran) (b) 1,86 (c) F - attacking midfielder (d) Omonia Nicosia (e) AEK Athína, Al-Sailiya SC, Nottingham Forest, Olympiakos, Panionios, CA Osasuna, Persepolis, Tractor Sazi, Persepolis, Saipa FC, Zob Ahan Ard.

*** Anselm - Tobias Anselm (a) 24/02/2000, ¿? (Austria) (b) 1,86 (c) F - center forward (d) LASK (e) WSG Tirol, LASK, FC Liefering

*** Antal - Liviu Antal (Liviu Ion Antal) (a) 02/06/1989, Şimleu Silvaniei (Romania) (b) 1,78 (c) F - right winger (d) FK Zalgiris Vilnius (e) CS Mioveni, Haladás, Zalaegerszeg, Haladás, UTA Arad, Zalgiris, CFR Cluj, Hapoel Tel Aviv, Pandurii, Hapoel Tel Aviv, Pandurii, Hapoel Tel Aviv, Genclerbirligi, B. Jerusalem, Genclerbirligi, FC Vaslui, Otelul Galati, FCM Targu Mures, Concordia

*** Antalyali - Taylan Antalyali (Taylan Antalyalı) (a) 08/01/1995, Mugla (Turkey) (b) 1,80 (c) M - central midfielder (d) Samsunspor (e) Samsunspor, Galatasaray, Ankaragücü, Galatasaray, BB Erzurumspor, Genclerbirligi, Hacettepe, Genclerbirligi, K. Erciyesspor, Genclerbirligi, Bucaspor

*** Antanavicius - Domantas Antanavicius (Domantas Antanavičius) (a) 18/11/1998, Marijampole (Lithuania) (b) 1,77 (c) M - pivot (d) FK Atyrau (e) NK Celje, Panevezys, NK Celje, NK Triglav, NK Celje, Maardu LM, Stumbras, Suduva, Suduva B

*** Antczak - Jakub Antczak (Jakub Antczak) (a) 29/04/2004, Wrocław (Poland) (b) 1,68 (c) F - left winger (d) Odra Opole (e) Odra Opole, Lech Poznan, Lech Poznan II

*** Anthony - Beji Anthony (Amos Beji Anthony) (a) 04/01/1999, Jos (Nigeria) (b) 1,78 (c) F - left winger (d) - (e) FK Bylis, KF Egnatia, FK Bylis, KF Egnatia

*** Anthony - Jaidon Anthony (a) 01/12/1999, London (England) (b) 1,83 (c) F - left winger (d) AFC Bournemouth (e) Weymouth FC

*** Antic - Dimitrije Antic (Димитрије Антић) (a) 05/05/2003, Subotica (Serbia and Montenegro, now in Serbia) (b) 1,88 (c) F - center forward (d) FK Kolubara Lazarevac (e) FK Zemun, Kolubara

*** Antic - Nikola Antic (Никола Антић) (a) 04/01/1994, Beograd (RF Yugoslavia, now in Serbia) (b) 1,78 (c) D - left back (d) Partizán Beograd (e) Khimki, Soligorsk, Vojvodina, Jagodina, Crvena zvezda, Rad Beograd, FK Palic Koming, Rad Beograd

*** Antilevskiy - Aleksey Antilevskiy (Антилевский Алексей Сергеевич) (a) 02/02/2002, Minsk (Belarus) (b) 1,81 (c) F - center forward (d) Slavia Mozyr (e) Slavia, Torpedo Zhodino, Dynamo Brest II, Rukh, Dynamo Brest II

*** Antilevskiy - Dmitriy Antilevskiy (Антилевский Дмитрий Сергеевич) (a) 12/06/1997, Minsk (Belarus) (b) 1,79 (c) F - attacking midfielder (d) BATE Borisov (e) Dinamo Tbilisi, Torpedo Zhodino, Dinamo Minsk, FK Minsk, BATE II, Dnepr Mogilev, BATE II

*** Antipov - Ivan Antipov (Антипов Иван Александрович) (a) 14/01/1996, Uralsk (Kazakhstan) (b) 1,82 (c) F - right winger (d) FC Turkistan (e) Peresvet, Akzhayik, Atyrau, Zhetysu, Akzhayik, Akzhayik II

*** Antiste - Janis Antiste (a) 18/08/2002, Toulouse (France) (b) 1,83 (c) F - center forward (d) US Sassuolo (e) Amiens SC, Sassuolo, Spezia, Toulouse, Toulouse B

*** Antman - Niv Antman (ניב אנטמן) (a) 02/08/1992, Kiryat Motzkin (Israel) (b) - (c) G (d) Hapoel Haifa (e) Ness Ziona, Hapoel Raanana, Ironi Nesher, FC Dordrecht, H Rishon leZion, Hapoel Haifa

*** Antman - Oliver Antman (a) 15/08/2001, Vantaa (Finland) (b) 1,85 (c) F - right winger (d) FC Nordsjælland (e) FC Groningen, Nordsjælland, IF Gnistan, TiPS

*** Antoche - Marius Antoche (Marius Paul Antoche) (a) 21/06/1992, Vatra Dornei (Romania) (b) 1,84 (c) D - central defense (d) FC Hermannstadt (e) U. Constanta, Petrolul, CS Balotesti, Tarlungeni, CS Balotesti, CS Otopeni, CS Balotesti, CS Otopeni, CS Mioveni

*** Antoine - Carnejy Antoine (a) 27/07/1991, Paris (France) (b) 1,91 (c) F - center forward (d) SC União Torreense (e) Hapoel Haifa, Casa Pia, US Orléans, Saint-Pryvé FC, St-Jean, Mézières, RE Bertrix, Noisy-le-Sec

*** Antolin - Aljaz Antolin (Aljaž Antolin) (a) 02/08/2002, Murska Sobota (Slovenia) (b) 1,78 (c) M - central midfielder (d) NK Maribor (e) Beltinci, NK Maribor, NS Mura

*** Anton - Gheorghe Anton (a) 27/01/1993, Chitcanii Vechi (Moldova) (b) 1,80 (c) M - pivot (d) - (e) Zimbru Chisinau, FC Brasov-SR, FC Buzau, Zira FK, FC Sheriff, Zimbru Chisinau, Divizia Nationala (-2017)

*** Anton - Paul Anton (Paul Viorel Anton) (a) 10/05/1991, Bistrița (Romania) (b) 1,82 (c) M - central midfielder (d) ETO FC Győr (e) UTA Arad, Ponferradina, FC Dinamo, KS Samara, Anzhi, FC Dinamo, Getafe CF, FC Dinamo, Pandurii, Gloria Bistrita, FCM Targu Mures, Gloria Bistrita, Delta Tulcea, Gloria Bistrita

*** Anton - Waldemar Anton (Рипцов-Антон Владимир Александрович) (a) 20/07/1996, Almalyk (Uzbekistan) (b) 1,89 (c) D - central defense (d) VfB Stuttgart (e) Hannover 96

*** Antoniadis - Marios Antoniadis (Μάριος Αντωνιάδης) (a) 14/05/1990, Nicosia (Cyprus) (b) 1,83 (c) D - central defense (d) Doxa Katokopias (e) Anorthosis, AEK Larnaca, Apollon Limassol, AEK Larnaca, Panionios, APOEL FC

*** Antonic - Goran Antonic (Горан Антонић) (a) 03/11/1990, Sremska Mitrovica (Yugoslavia, now in Serbia) (b) 1,85 (c) D - central defense (d) FK TSC Backa Topola (e) Alashkert CF, Elverum, Nea Salamis, Spartak, FK Palic Koming, LSK Lacarak

*** Antonijevic - Filip Antonijevic (Филип Антонијевић) (a) 24/07/2000, Beograd (RF Yugoslavia, now in Serbia) (b) 1,75 (c) D - left back (d) FK Vojvodina Novi Sad (e) Metalac, MTK Budapest, Metalac, Kolubara, Teleoptik

*** Antonio - Bill Antonio (Bill Leeroy Antonio) (a) 03/09/2002, Dzivarasekwa (Zimbabwe) (b) - (c) F - right winger (d) Jong KV Mechelen (e) Dynamos FC

*** Antonio - Michail Antonio (Michail Gregory Antonio) (a) 28/03/1990, Wandsworth, London (England) (b) 1,80 (c) F - center forward (d) West Ham United (e) Nottingham Forest, Sheffield Wednesday, Reading, Sheffield Wednesday, Reading, Colchester Utd., Reading, Southampton, Reading, Cheltenham Town, Reading, Tooting & Mitcham FC, Reading, Tooting & Mitcham FC

*** Antonioli - Joey Antonioli (a) 15/12/2003, Woerden (Netherlands) (b) - (c) M - central midfielder (d) FC Volendam (e) FC Volendam

*** Antoniou - Charalampos Antoniou (Χαράλαμπος "Χάμπος" Αντωνίου) (a) 01/07/2005, Limassol (Cyprus) (b) 1,86 (c) D - left back (d) AEZ Zakakiou (e) Olympiakos N., AEL Limassol

*** Antoniou - Minas Antoniou (Μηνάς Αντωνίου) (a) 22/02/1994, Limassol (Cyprus) (b) 1,85 (c) D - right back (d) Anorthosis Famagusta (e) AEL Limassol, APOEL FC, EN Paralimniou, APOEL FC, Aris Limassol, AEL Limassol, AEZ Zakakiou, AEL Limassol, Nikos & Sokrati, AEL Limassol

*** Antonisse - Jeremy Antonisse (Jeremy Cornelis Jacobus Antonisse) (a) 29/03/2002, Rosmalen (Netherlands) (b) 1,84 (c) F - left winger (d) - (e) FC Emmen

*** Antoniuc - Alexandru Antoniuc (a) 23/05/1989, Chişinău (Soviet Union, now in Moldova) (b) 1,80 (c) F - right winger (d) FC Milsami Orhei (e) FC Veris, Rubin Kazan, Zimbru Chisinau, Rubin Kazán II, KamAZ, Rubin Kazan, Zimbru Chisinau

*** Antonov - Ilian Antonov (Илиан Илианов Антонов) (a) 22/05/2005, Berkovitsa (Bulgaria) (b) 1,75 (c) F - right winger (d) CSKA-Sofia (e) CSKA-Sofia II

*** Antonov - Ilja Antonov (a) 05/12/1992, Tallinn (Estonia) (b) 1,73 (c) M - pivot (d) CS Corvinul 1921 Hunedoara (e) Kalju FC, FCI Levadia, Ararat-Armenia, FC Hermannstadt, Rudar Velenje, SV Horn, Levadia, FC Puuma

*** Antonov - Nemanja Antonov (Немања Антонов) (a) 06/05/1995, Pančevo (RF Yugoslavia, now in Serbia) (b) 1,82 (c) D - left back (d) MTK Budapest (e) Újpest FC, Excelsior Mouscron, Grasshoppers, FK Partizan, Grasshoppers, OFK Beograd

*** Antonov - Preslav Antonov (Преслав Стефчев Антонов) (a) 02/10/1996, Pleven (Bulgaria) (b) 1,85 (c) F - attacking midfielder (d) CSKA 1948 II (e) Spartak Pleven, Vih Slavyanovo, Litex Lovetch, Spartak Pleven, Akademik

*** Antonsen - Kent-Are Antonsen (a) 12/02/1995, Storsteinnes (Norway) (b) 1,72 (c) M - central midfielder (d) Tromsø IL (e) -

*** Antonsson - Marcus Antonsson (a) 08/05/1991, Unnaryd (Sweden) (b) 1,84 (c) F - center forward (d) Western Sydney Wanderers (e) Al-Adalah, Värnamo, Malmö FF, Halmstads BK, Malmö FF, Stabæk, Malmö FF, Leeds Utd., Blackburn, Leeds Utd., Kalmar FF, Halmstads BK

*** Antonsson - Thorsteinn Antonsson (Þorsteinn Aron Antonsson) (a) 13/01/2004, ¿? (Iceland) (b) 1,98 (c) D - central defense (d) UMF Selfoss (e) Stjarnan, Selfoss

*** Antonucci - Francesco Antonucci (a) 20/06/1999, Charleroi (Belgium) (b) 1,71 (c) M - attacking midfielder (d) - (e) Feyenoord, FC Volendam, Feyenoord, FC Volendam, Feyenoord, AS Monaco B, FC Volendam, AS Monaco B

*** Antony - Antony (Antony Alves Santos) (a) 08/09/2001, ¿? (Brazil) (b) 1,85 (c) F - left winger (d) Portland Timbers (e) Arouca, Joinville-SC, Arouca, Joinville-SC

*** Antony - Antony (Antony Matheus dos Santos) (a) 24/02/2000, Osasco (Brazil) (b) 1,72 (c) F - right winger (d) Manchester United (e) Ajax, São Paulo

*** Antoñín - Antoñín (Antonio Cortés Heredia) (a) 16/04/2000, Málaga (Spain) (b) 1,82 (c) F - center forward (d) Granada CF (e) Anorthosis, Granada CF, Vitória Guimarães, Granada CF, Málaga CF, Granada CF, Rayo Vallecano, Granada CF, Málaga CF, At. Malagueño, CD El Palo

*** Antosch - Daniel Antosch (a) 07/03/2000, Wien (Austria) (b) 1,90 (c) G (d) Apollon Limassol (e) Pafos FC, FC Liefering, SV Horn, FC Liefering

*** Antov - Valentin Antov (Валентин Ивайлов Антов) (a) 09/11/2000, Sofia (Bulgaria) (b) 1,87 (c) D - central defense (d) AC Monza (e) CSKA-Sofia, Monza, CSKA-Sofia, Bologna, CSKA-Sofia

*** Antovski - Filip Antovski (Филип Антовски) (a) 24/11/2000, Kumanovo (North Macedonia) (b) 1,74 (c) D - left back (d) MFK Karvina (e) Austria Viena, NK Istra, Austria Viena, Din. Zagreb II, Slavia Sofia, Din. Zagreb II, Vardar

*** Antropov - Kirill Antropov (Антропов Кирилл Кириллович) (a) 22/06/2003, ¿? (Russia) (b) 1,80 (c) D - central defense (d) FC Onor (e) FC Van, Ufa II

*** Antunes - Antunes (Vitorino Gabriel Pacheco Antunes) (a) 01/04/1987, Freamunde (Portugal) (b) 1,75 (c) D - left back (d) FC Paços de Ferreira (e) Sporting Lisboa, Getafe CF, Dinamo Kyïv, Getafe CF, Dinamo Kyïv, Málaga CF, Paços Ferreira, Málaga CF, Paços Ferreira, AS Roma, Panionios, AS Roma, AS Livorno, AS Roma, Leixões, AS Roma, Lecce, AS Roma, Paços Ferreira, AS Roma, Paços Ferreira, Freamunde

*** Antunes - Alexis Antunes (Alexis Antunes Gomez) (a) 31/07/2000, Genève (Switzerland) (b) 1,81 (c) M - attacking midfielder (d) Servette FC (e) FC Chiasso, Servette FC

*** Antunes - Fabien Antunes (a) 19/11/1991, Paris (France) (b) 1,83 (c) M - pivot (d) AE Kifisias (e) Ionikos Nikeas, Panetolikos, KVC Westerlo, Sint-Truiden, KVC Westerlo, Sint-Truiden, KV Oostende, RE Virton, Red Star FC, JA Drancy

*** Antunes - Hugo Antunes (a) 06/01/2004, ¿? (Luxembourg) (b) - (c) M (d) F91 Dudelange II (e) -

*** Antunovic - Mate Antunovic (Mate Antunović) (a) 03/03/2004, Metković (Croatia) (b) - (c) F - center forward (d) - (e) Jadran Luka Ploce

*** Antuzis - Valdas Antuzis (Valdas Antužis) (a) 19/06/2000, Klaipeda (Lithuania) (b) 1,77 (c) D - right back (d) FK Banga Gargzdai (e) -

*** Antwi - Clinton Antwi (a) 06/11/1999, ¿? (Ghana) (b) 1,70 (c) D - left back (d) Kuopion Palloseura (e) Nordsjælland, Esbjerg fB, Nordsjælland, Right to Dream

*** Antwi - Ishmael Kofi Antwi (a) 04/09/1992, Accra (Ghana) (b) 1,70 (c) F - center forward (d) Lynx FC (e) St Joseph's FC, UP Plasencia, Ciudad Real, UP Plasencia, Elche Ilicitano, Inter de Madrid, UD Sanse, Cacereño, At. Madrid C, Hellín, CD Madridejos, Real Ávila, CD Leganés B

*** Antwi - Nana Antwi (Nana Kwame Antwi) (a) 10/08/2000, Accra (Ghana) (b) 1,80 (c) D - right back (d) FC Urartu Yerevan (e) Lori Vanadzor, LOSC Lille B, Lori Vanadzor, Young Wise FC

*** Antwi - Rodney Antwi (a) 03/11/1995, Amsterdam (Netherlands) (b) 1,76 (c) F - left winger (d) - (e) Spartak Varna, Ingulets, Jerv, Ingulets, Wadi Degla, Tsarsko Selo, Wadi Degla, Tsarsko Selo, FC Volendam

*** Antwi-Adjei - Christopher Antwi-Adjei (a) 07/02/1994, Hagen (Germany) (b) 1,74 (c) F - left winger (d) VfL Bochum (e) SC Paderborn, Sprockhövel, Westfalia Herne

*** Antyukh - Denys Antyukh (Антюх Денис Миколайович) (a) 30/07/1997, Okhtyrka, Sumy Oblast (Ukraine) (b) 1,83 (c) F - left winger (d) Zorya Lugansk (e) Dinamo Kyïv, Kolos Kovalivka, Balkany Zorya, Kolos Kovalivka, Naftovyk, Naftovyk II

*** Antzoulas - Georgios Antzoulas (Γεώργιος Αντζουλάς) (a) 04/02/2000, Tripoli (Greece) (b) 1,88 (c) D - central defense (d) Újpest FC (e) Asteras Tripoli, Cosenza, Asteras Tripoli, Asteras Tripoli, PAS Patraikos

*** Anuar - Anuar (تهامي محمد أنور, Anuar Mohamed Tuhami) (a) 15/01/1995, Ceuta (Spain) (b) 1,73 (c) M - central midfielder (d) Real Valladolid CF (e) APOEL FC, Real Valladolid, Panathinaikos, Real Valladolid, R. Valladolid B

*** Anufriev - Aleksandr Anufriev (Ануфриев Александр Сергеевич) (a) 21/07/1995, Novyi Dvor (Belarus) (b) 1,79 (c) M - attacking midfielder (d) FK Gomel (e) Dynamo Brest, Isloch, FK Minsk, Slavia, BATE II, FK Smorgon, BATE II, Smolevichi, BATE II, FK Smorgon, BATE II

*** Anyamele - Nnaemeka Anyamele (a) 16/05/1994, ¿? (Finland) (b) 1,78 (c) D - left back (d) - (e) Ekenäs IF, Helsinki IFK, IF Gnistan, BSV Rehden, Helsinki IFK, FC Honka, HJK Klubi 04

*** Anyembe - Daniel Anyembe (Daniel Francis Anyembe) (a) 22/07/1998, Esbjerg (Denmark) (b) 1,89 (c) D - central defense (d) Viborg FF (e) Esbjerg fB

*** Anyukevich - Aleksandr Anyukevich (Анюкевич Александр Антонович) (a) 10/04/1992, Grodno (Belarus) (b) 1,88 (c) D - left back (d) Neman Grodno (e) FK Slutsk, Neman Grodno, Neman II

*** Anzolin - Matteo Anzolin (a) 11/11/2000, Latisana (Italy) (b) 1,81 (c) D - left back (d) US Triestina (e) Wolfsberger AC, Juve Next Gen

*** Añón - Javier Añón (Javier Añón Estéban) (a) 30/08/1986, Marbella (Spain) (b) 1,80 (c) M - central midfielder (d) CD Atlético de Marbella (e) Lincoln FC, Marbella FC, Unión Estepona, UD San Pedro, Villanovense, UD Marbella, Puerto Real CF, UD San Pedro, Los Barrios, Afición Xerez, Hellín, Marbella FC B

*** Aosman - Aias Aosman (عثمان أياز) (a) 21/10/1994, Kamishli (Siria) (b) 1,75 (c) M - attacking midfielder (d) Pendikspor (e) Ionikos Nikeas, Adana Demirspor, Ionikos Nikeas, FC Hermannstadt, Tuzlaspor, Adana Demirspor, Dynamo Dresden, Jahn Regensburg, 1.FC Köln II, SC Wiedenbrück, Pr. Espelkamp

*** Aouacheria - Bilel Aouacheria (a) 02/04/1994, Saint-Étienne (France) (b) 1,82 (c) F - left winger (d) FK Qabala (e) Gil Vicente, Farense, Moreirense, SC Covilhã, Sporting B, SC Covilhã, Saint-Étienne B

*** Aouar - Houssem Aouar (a) 30/06/1998, Lyon (France) (b) 1,75 (c) M - central midfielder (d) AS Roma (e) Olympique Lyon, Olymp. Lyon B

*** Aouchiche - Adil Aouchiche (a) 15/07/2002, Le Blanc-Mesnil (France) (b) 1,81 (c) M - attacking midfielder (d) FC Lorient (e) St.-Étienne, Paris Saint-Germain

*** Aourir - Ayman Aourir (أورير أيمن) (a) 06/10/2004, Köln (Germany) (b) 1,72 (c) M - attacking midfielder (d) Bayer 04 Leverkusen (e) -

*** Apanasovich - Evgeniy Apanasovich (Апанасович Евгений Анатольевич) (a) 18/07/2002, Luninets (Belarus) (b) 1,80 (c) F - center forward (d) FK Slutsk (e) BK Maxline, FK Slutsk, Lokomotiv Gomel, FK Slutsk, Slutsk II

*** Apap - Ferdinando Apap (a) 29/07/1992, Victoria (Malta) (b) 1,89 (c) D - central defense (d) Hibernians FC (e) Victoria Hotspurs, Ghajnsielem, Victoria Hotspurs, Mosta FC, Xewkija Tigers, Mosta FC, Ghajnsielem

*** Apeh - Emmanuel Apeh (a) 25/10/1996, Kaduna (Nigeria) (b) 1,83 (c) F - center forward (d) Sabah FK (e) CD Tenerife, Alcorcón, CD Tenerife, Celta B, Lorca FC, Lorca FC B, RSD Alcalá, RSD Alcalá B

*** Apekov - Ruslan Apekov (Апеков Руслан Хажисмелович) (a) 08/06/2000, Nalchik (Russia) (b) 1,76 (c) F - left winger (d) Akron Togliatti (e) Krasnodar-2, Akron Togliatti, Krasnodar-2, Krasnodar 3

*** Apezteguia - Joel Apezteguia (Joel Apezteguía Hijuelos) (a) 17/12/1983, La Habana (Cuba) (b) 1,83 (c) F - center forward (d) ACD Torconca Cattolica (e) Santa Veneranda, Cailungo, Virtus, Tre Fiori, Anconitana, Chisola, Gassino, AJ Fano, CD Utiel, Tre Fiori, KF Teuta, Ripollet, Manresa, Nistru Otaci, Manresa, Industriales

*** Apockinas - Orestas Apockinas (a) 23/08/2004, ¿? (Lithuania) (b) - (c) G (d) FA Siauliai B (e) -
*** Aponzá - Wilinton Aponzá (Wilinton Aponzá Carabalí) (a) 29/03/2000, Santiago de Cali (Colombia) (b) 1,93 (c) F - center forward (d) Chungnam Asan (e) Chungnam Asan, Portimonense, SC Covilhã, Portimonense, Berço
*** Apostolachi - Cristian Apostolachi (a) 13/09/2000, Chişinău (Moldova) (b) 1,94 (c) G (d) FC Dinamo-Auto Tiraspol (e) Dinamo-Auto, Petrolul, SCM Gloria Buzau, Milsami, FC Ungheni, Codru
*** Apostolakis - Giannis Apostolakis (Γιάννης Αποστολάκης) (a) 24/09/2004, Rethymno (Greece) (b) - (c) M - central midfielder (d) OFI Creta (e) AO Neos Asteras
*** Apostolakis - Konstantinos Apostolakis (Κωνσταντίνος Αποστολάκης) (a) 28/05/1999, Marousi (Greece) (b) 1,82 (c) D - right back (d) FC Sheriff Tiraspol (e) Panetolikos, APOEL FC, Panathinaikos
*** Appaev - Khyzyr Appaev (Аппаев Хызыр Хакимович) (a) 27/01/1990, Nalchik (Soviet Union, now in Russia) (b) 1,92 (c) F - center forward (d) Fakel Voronezh (e) Tekstilshchik, Tambov, Rotor Volgograd, Avangard Kursk, Riga, Arsenal Tula, Orenburg, Krasnodar, Rotor Volgograd, Krasnodar, KS Samara, KS Samara II, Druzhba Maikop, Zhemchuzhina II
*** Appiah - Arvin Appiah (Arvin Amoakoh Appiah) (a) 05/01/2001, Amsterdam (Netherlands) (b) 1,77 (c) F - right winger (d) UD Almería (e) Málaga CF, UD Almería, CD Tenerife, UD Almería, CD Lugo, UD Almería, Nottingham Forest
*** Appiah - Dennis Appiah (a) 09/06/1992, Toulouse (France) (b) 1,79 (c) D - right back (d) AS Saint-Étienne (e) FC Nantes, RSC Anderlecht, SM Caen, AS Monaco, AS Monaco B
*** Appindangoyé - Aaron Appindangoyé (Aaron Christopher Billy Ondélé Appindangoyé) (a) 20/02/1992, Franceville (Gabon) (b) 1,84 (c) D - central defense (d) Sivasspor (e) Ümraniyespor, Stade Lavallois, CF Mounana, Évian, CF Mounana, Boavista, CF Mounana, FC 105 Libreville
*** Appuah - Stredair Appuah (Stredair Owusu Appuah) (a) 27/06/2004, Sarcelles (France) (b) 1,85 (c) F - left winger (d) FC Nantes (e) -
*** Apridonidze - Shota Apridonidze (a) 05/07/2004, ¿? (Georgia) (b) - (c) G (d) Torpedo Kutaisi Academy (e) -
*** Arab - Samir Arab (a) 25/03/1994, ¿? (Malta) (b) - (c) D - central defense (d) Balzan FC (e) Sperre) Balzan FC, Valletta, Balzan FC, Valletta, Balzan FC, Valletta, Balzan FC, Valletta, Vittoriosa, Valletta, Vittoriosa, Valletta
*** Arab - Siraj Arab (Siraj Eddin Arab) (a) 25/03/1994, ¿? (Malta) (b) - (c) F - right winger (d) Sirens FC (e) Sliema Wanderers, Marsa FC, Floriana, Senglea Ath., Sirens FC, Balzan FC, Tarxien, Balzan FC, Hamrun Spartans, Pembroke, Valletta, Pembroke, Valletta, Pembroke, Valletta, Vittoriosa, Valletta, Vittoriosa, Valletta
*** Arabidze - Giorgi Arabidze (გიორგი არაბიძე) (a) 04/03/1998, Vani (Georgia) (b) 1,73 (c) F - right winger (d) Torpedo Kutaisi (e) Nacional, FC Samtredia, Nacional, Rotor Volgograd, Nacional, Adanaspor, Nacional, Shakhtar II, FC Locomotive
*** Arabyan - Gevorg Arabyan (Գևորգ Արաբյան) (a) 22/06/2002, ¿? (Armenia) (b) 1,70 (c) D - right back (d) - (e) Ararat Yerevan, Shirak Gyumri, Ararat II, Urartu II
*** Arad - Ofri Arad (ארד עופרי) (a) 11/09/1998, haHotrim (Israel) (b) 1,82 (c) D - central defense (d) Kairat Almaty (e) Kairat Almaty, Maccabi Haifa, H. Ramat Gan, Maccabi Haifa
*** Arai - Haruki Arai (新井 晴樹) (a) 12/04/1998, ¿?, Saitama (Japan) (b) 1,68 (c) M - left midfielder (d) Cerezo Osaka (e) Tiamo Hirakata, HNK Sibenik, Tiamo Hirakata, Cerezo Osaka, Tiamo Hirakata, Kokushikan Univ., Shochi HS

*** Arai - Mizuki Arai (新井 瑞樹) (a) 14/04/1997, Ina, Saitama (Japan) (b) 1,70 (c) F - left winger (d) Yokohama FC (e) Tokyo Verdy, Gil Vicente, Tokyo Verdy, Kataller Toyama, Tokyo Verdy, Kataller Toyama, SC Sagamihara, SV Horn

*** Arajuuri - Paulus Arajuuri (a) 15/06/1988, Helsinki (Finland) (b) 1,93 (c) D - central defense (d) Helsinki IFK (e) HJK Helsinki, Anorthosis, Pafos FC, Brøndby IF, Lech Poznan, Kalmar FF, IFK Mariehamn, HJK Helsinki, FC Honka, FC Espoo

*** Arakelyan - Alik Arakelyan (Ալիկ Արայիկի Առաքելյան) (a) 21/05/1996, Spitak (Armenia) (b) 1,73 (c) M - left midfielder (d) Lernayin Artsakh Goris (e) Ararat Yerevan, Pyunik Yerevan, MIKA Aschtarak, Mika Erewan II

*** Aralica - Ante Aralica (a) 23/07/1996, Zagreb (Croatia) (b) 1,90 (c) F - center forward (d) - (e) KF Vllaznia, FC Hermannstadt, Lokomotiv Plovdiv, NK Lokomotiva, NK Rudes, NK Lokomotiva, NK Sesvete, NK Lokomotiva, NK Lucko, NK Lokomotiva, NK Lucko, Spansko

*** Arambarri - Aritz Arambarri (Aritz Arambarri Murua) (a) 31/01/1998, Azkoitia (Spain) (b) 1,86 (c) D - central defense (d) CD Leganés (e) Real Sociedad B, Real Sociedad C

*** Arambarri - Mauro Arambarri (Mauro Wilney Arambarri Rosa) (a) 30/09/1995, Salto (Uruguay) (b) 1,75 (c) M - central midfielder (d) Getafe CF (e) Boston River, Getafe CF, Boston River, Girondins Bordeaux, Defensor

*** Arana - Egoitz Arana (Egoitz Arana Aizpuru) (a) 19/02/2002, Zarautz (Spain) (b) 1,97 (c) G (d) San Fernando CD (e) Real Sociedad B, Real Sociedad C

*** Aránguiz - Charles Aránguiz (Charles Mariano Aránguiz Sandoval) (a) 17/04/1989, Puente Alto (Chile) (b) 1,71 (c) M - central midfielder (d) Sport Club Internacional (e) Bayer Leverkusen, Internacional, Udinese, Internacional, Udinese, U. de Chile, Quilmes, Colo Colo, Cobreloa, Cobresal, Cobreloa

*** Arão - Willian Arão (Willian Souza Arão da Silva) (a) 12/03/1992, São Paulo (Brazil) (b) 1,81 (c) M - pivot (d) Fenerbahce (e) Flamengo, Botafogo, Corinthians, Atlético-GO, Corinthians, Chapecoense, Corinthians, Portuguesa, Corinthians

*** Arapi - Galip Arapi (a) 20/01/2001, Pontedera (Italy) (b) 1,75 (c) M - central midfielder (d) - (e) La Fiorita, FK Partizani, Cenaia, Miniato Basso, AC Fucecchio

*** Arapi - Zajsar Arapi (Zajsar Arjanit Arapi) (a) 20/10/2003, Tiranë (Albania) (b) 1,70 (c) F - left winger (d) KS Kastrioti (e) -

*** Arase - Kelvin Arase (a) 15/01/1999, Benin City (Nigeria) (b) 1,72 (c) F - right winger (d) SV Waldhof Mannheim (e) Karlsruher SC, KV Oostende, Karlsruher SC, Rapid Wien, SV Ried, Rapid Wien, SV Horn, Rapid Wien, Rapid Wien II

*** Araujo - Daniel Araujo (Daniel Silva Araujo) (a) 04/05/1997, ¿? (Brazil) (b) - (c) F - center forward (d) Melita FC (e) Jonava, Barretos-SP

*** Araujo - Miguel Araujo (Miguel Gianpierre Araujo Blanco) (a) 24/10/1994, Lima (Peru) (b) 1,81 (c) D - central defense (d) Portland Timbers (e) FC Emmen, Alianza Lima, Talleres, Alianza Lima, Crvena zvezda, Sport Huancayo, Cobresol, Cobresol II

*** Araujo - Sergio Araujo (Sergio Ezequiel Araujo) (a) 28/01/1992, Buenos Aires (Argentina) (b) 1,80 (c) F - center forward (d) AEK Athína FC (e) UD Las Palmas, AEK Athína, UD Las Palmas, AEK Athína, UD Las Palmas, AEK Athína, UD Las Palmas, Boca Juniors, UD Las Palmas, Boca Juniors, Tigre, Boca Juniors, FC Barcelona B, Boca Juniors

*** Araújo - Brian Araújo (Brian da Rocha Araújo) (a) 29/04/2000, ¿? (Portugal) (b) 1,89 (c) G (d) Gil Vicente FC (e) -

*** Araújo - Henrique Araújo (Henrique Pereira Araújo) (a) 19/01/2002, Funchal (Portugal) (b) 1,82 (c) F - center forward (d) FC Famalicão (e) Famalicão, Benfica, Watford, Benfica, Benfica B

*** Araújo - Ronald Araújo (Ronald Federico Araújo da Silva) (a) 07/03/1999, Rivera (Uruguay) (b) 1,92 (c) D - central defense (d) FC Barcelona (e) FC Barcelona B, Boston River, Rentistas

*** Araújo - Tiago Araújo (Tiago Filipe Alves Araújo) (a) 27/03/2001, Vila do Conde (Portugal) (b) 1,84 (c) D - left back (d) GD Estoril Praia (e) Benfica B, Arouca, Benfica B

*** Araújo - Tomás Araújo (Tomás Lemos Araújo) (a) 16/05/2002, Famalicão (Portugal) (b) 1,87 (c) D - central defense (d) SL Benfica (e) Gil Vicente, Benfica, Benfica B

*** Araz - Musa Araz (a) 17/01/1994, Fribourg (Switzerland) (b) 1,73 (c) M - central midfielder (d) FC Winterthur (e) FC Sion, Neuchâtel Xamax, Konyaspor, Bursaspor, Konyaspor, Afyonspor, Konyaspor, Lausanne-Sport, FC Basel, FC Winterthur, FC Basel, Le Mont LS, FC Basel

*** Arazly - Ayhan Arazly (Ayhan Arazlı) (a) 29/03/2001, ¿? (Azerbaijan) (b) - (c) G (d) Qarabag 2 Agdam (e) -

*** Árbol - Matías Árbol (Matías Árbol González) (a) 12/09/2002, Palomares del Río (Spain) (b) 1,84 (c) G (d) Sevilla Atlético (e) Sevilla FC C

*** Arbuzov - Yaroslav Arbuzov (Арбузов Ярослав Вячеславович) (a) 12/01/2004, Lugansk (Ukraine) (b) 1,76 (c) M - right midfielder (d) CSKA Moskva II (e) -

*** Archel - Tal Archel (טל לארץ') (a) 10/06/2003, ¿? (Israel) (b) 1,87 (c) M - pivot (d) Hapoel Tel Aviv (e) -

*** Archer - Cameron Archer (Cameron Desmond Archer) (a) 09/12/2001, Walsall (England) (b) 1,75 (c) F - center forward (d) Aston Villa (e) Middlesbrough, Aston Villa, Preston North End, Aston Villa, Solihull Moors

*** Archer - Josh Archer (Joshua Archer) (a) 21/07/2003, Belfast (Northern Ireland) (b) - (c) M - central midfielder (d) Linfield FC (e) Portadown, Linfield

*** Arciero - Rodrigo Arciero (Rodrigo Sebastián Arciero) (a) 12/03/1993, Ushuaia (Argentina) (b) 1,81 (c) D - right back (d) FC Inter Turku (e) SJK Seinäjoki, Banfield, Patronato, Independiente Rivadavia, Talleres, All Boys

*** Arconte - Taïryk Arconte (a) 12/11/2003, Les Abymes (Guadaloupe) (b) 1,81 (c) F - right winger (d) Stade Brestois 29 (e) AC Ajaccio

*** Arcus - Carlens Arcus (Carlens Jean Fedlaire Ruby Arcus) (a) 28/06/1996, Port-au-Prince (Haiti) (b) 1,76 (c) D - right back (d) Vitesse Arnhem (e) AJ Auxerre, Cercle Brugge, AJ Auxerre, Cercle Brugge, LOSC Lille B, Troyes, Troyes B, RC Haïtien

*** Arda - Alp Arda (a) 07/06/1995, Istanbul (Turkey) (b) 1,92 (c) G (d) Istanbulspor (e) Isparta 32 Spor, Istanbulspor, Cizre Spor, Istanbulspor, Osmaniyespor FK, Merzifonspor, Beylikdüzü, Yesilköy

*** Ardaiz - Joaquín Ardaiz (Joaquín Matías Ardaiz de los Santos) (a) 11/01/1999, Salto (Uruguay) (b) 1,86 (c) F - center forward (d) Sanliurfaspor (e) Sanliurfaspor, FC Luzern, FC Winterthur, FC Luzern, FC Schaffhausen, FC Lugano, FC Chiasso, Vancouver, FC Chiasso, Frosinone, FC Chiasso, Tanque Sisley, Royal Antwerp, Tanque Sisley, Danubio FC, Tanque Sisley, Danubio FC

*** Ardazishvili - Rati Ardazishvili (რატი არდაზიშვილი) (a) 27/01/1998, ¿? (Georgia) (b) 1,77 (c) M - attacking midfielder (d) Zhetysu Taldykorgan (e) Kaspiy Aktau, FC Telavi, Rukh Lviv, FC Locomotive, Chikhura, FC Locomotive

*** Arel - Gal Arel (גל אראל) (a) 09/07/1989, Kiryat Haim (Israel) (b) 1,82 (c) M - pivot (d) Shay Arel (e) Hapoel Haifa, Hapoel Acre, Hapoel Raanana, Zawisza, Gimnàstic, H. Beer Sheva, H. Petah Tikva, H. Beer Sheva, Hapoel Haifa

*** Arenate - Alexandre Arenate (Alexandre Frédéric Arénate) (a) 20/07/1995, Sarcelles (France) (b) 1,83 (c) F (d) Jeunesse Esch (e) Solières, Patro Eisden, KSV

Roeselare, FCV Dender EH, RE Virton, Red Star FC, FC Chambly Oise, Red Star FC, Stade Rennes B

*** Areola - Alphonse Areola (Alphonse Francis Aréola) (a) 27/02/1993, Paris (France) (b) 1,95 (c) G (d) West Ham United (e) Paris Saint-Germain, West Ham Utd., Paris Saint-Germain, Fulham, Paris Saint-Germain, Real Madrid, Paris Saint-Germain, Villarreal CF, Paris Saint-Germain, SC Bastia, Paris Saint-Germain, RC Lens, Paris Saint-Germain

*** Ares - Adu Ares (Malcom Abdulai Ares Djaló) (a) 12/10/2001, Bilbao (Spain) (b) 1,83 (c) F - left winger (d) Athletic Club (e) Bilbao Athletic, CD Basconia, Santutxu

*** Aretzis - Nicholas Aretzis (a) 22/06/2003, ¿? (Northern Ireland) (b) - (c) D - central defense (d) Larne FC (e) Bangor, Larne FC

*** Arfield - Scott Arfield (Scott Harry Nathaniel Arfield) (a) 01/11/1988, Livingston (Scotland) (b) 1,78 (c) M - central midfielder (d) Charlotte FC (e) Rangers FC, Burnley, Huddersfield Town, Falkirk FC

*** Arge - Ári Arge (a) 02/05/2002, Tórshavn (Faroe Islands) (b) 1,80 (c) D - left back (d) HB Tórshavn II (e) HB Tórshavn, 07 Vestur, HB Tórshavn, EB/Streymur, HB Tórshavn, AB Argir, HB Tórshavn, HB Tórshavn II

*** Argilashki - Georgi Argilashki (Георги Рангелов Аргилашки) (a) 13/06/1991, Plovdiv (Bulgaria) (b) 1,87 (c) G (d) Dobrudzha Dobrich (e) Botev Plovdiv, Beroe, Vereya, Ludogorets, Vereya, Ludogorets, Pirin, Ludogorets, Pirin Razlog, Ludogorets, Brestnik 1948

*** Argyrides - Mike Argyrides (Michael Argyrides) (a) 06/04/1999, Richmond Hill, Ontario (Canada) (b) 1,85 (c) G (d) Glentoran FC (e) HW Welders, Glentoran, Larne FC, Dundela FC, Vaughan Azzurri

*** Argyrou - Sotiris Argyrou (Σωτήρης Αργυρού) (a) 08/01/2005, Larnaca (Cyprus) (b) 1,78 (c) F - center forward (d) Anorthosis Famagusta (e) -

*** Arhipov - Leonid Arhipov (a) 03/12/2002, Tallinn (Estonia) (b) - (c) F - left winger (d) Tallinn JK Legion (e) JK Legion II, FC Flora, JK Legion II

*** Ari Moura - Ari Moura (Ari Moura Vieira Filho) (a) 31/07/1996, Quaraí (Brazil) (b) 1,74 (c) F - left winger (d) Metalist 1925 Kharkiv (e) Metalist 1925, Metropolitano, Ness Ziona, Metropolitano, Bnei Sakhnin, Metropolitano, Paysandu, Metropolitano, Confiança, Metropolitano, Chapecoense, Metropolitano, Brasil Pelotas, Metropolitano, Confiança, Metropolitano, Toledo, Marcílio Dias, São Luiz, Veranópolis

*** Arias - Ramón Arias (Ramón Ginés Arias Quinteros) (a) 27/07/1992, Montevideo (Uruguay) (b) 1,81 (c) D - central defense (d) Muaither SC (e) Giresunspor, Peñarol, U. de Chile, San Lorenzo, Al-Ettifaq, Peñarol, LDU Quito, Defensor, Club Puebla, Defensor

*** Arias - Ulises Jesús Arias (a) 05/08/1996, Colon (Argentina) (b) 1,60 (c) M - attacking midfielder (d) Floriana FC (e) Sarmiento Junín, Comunicaciones, Sarmiento Junín, CA Sarmiento II

*** Aribo - Joe Aribo (Joseph Oluwaseyi Temitope Ayodele-Aribo) (a) 21/07/1996, Camberwell, London (England) (b) 1,83 (c) M - attacking midfielder (d) Southampton FC (e) Rangers FC, Charlton Ath., Staines Town FC

*** Arican - Kagan Arican (Kağan Arıcan) (a) 10/03/2006, Antalya (Turkey) (b) 1,87 (c) G (d) - (e) Antalya Orman

*** Ariely - Amir Ariely (Amir Moshe Ariely - אריאלי משה אמיר) (a) 03/03/2003, ¿? (Israel) (b) 1,86 (c) D - central defense (d) Hapoel Jerusalem (e) H. Jerusalem, H. Beer Sheva

*** Arifi - Doni Arifi (a) 11/04/2002, ¿? (Finland) (b) 1,95 (c) M - pivot (d) Ilves Tampere (e) FC Honka II

*** Arigoni - Allan Arigoni (a) 04/11/1998, Zürich (Switzerland) (b) 1,84 (c) D - central defense (d) FC Lugano (e) Grasshoppers

*** Arikan - Muhammed Eren Arikan (Muhammed Enes Arıkan) (a) 29/01/2005, Yozgat (Turkey) (b) - (c) D - left back (d) Kayserispor (e) -

*** Aripov - Dierzhon Aripov (Арипов Диёржон Расулович) (a) 10/03/1997, Komintern, Turkestan Region (Kazakhstan) (b) 1,74 (c) D - right back (d) FK Maktaaral (e) FK Maktaaral II

*** Aris - Nigel Aris (a) 29/01/2003, London (England) (b) - (c) F - left winger (d) - (e) Newtown, Waterford FC

*** Ariyibi - Gboly Ariyibi (Omogbolahan Gregory Ariyibi) (a) 18/01/1995, Arlington, Virginia (United States) (b) 1,83 (c) F - left winger (d) Ankara Keciörengücü (e) Ankaragücü, Panetolikos, Nottingham Forest, Motherwell FC, Nottingham Forest, Northampton, Nottingham Forest, MK Dons, Nottingham Forest, FC Chesterfield, Leeds Utd., Tranmere Rovers, Leeds Utd.

*** Arizankoski - Andrej Arizankoski (Андреј Аризанкоски) (a) 08/05/2005, Prilep (North Macedonia) (b) 1,78 (c) M - pivot (d) AP Brera (e) Pobeda Prilep

*** Arkhypchuk - Kyrylo Arkhypchuk (Архипчук Кирило Васильович) (a) 13/08/2003, ¿? (Latvia) (b) 1,87 (c) G (d) FK Trostyanets (e) Ingulets, FK Vovchansk

*** Arko-Mensah - Edmund Arko-Mensah (a) 09/09/2001, ¿? (Ghana) (b) 1,72 (c) F - left winger (d) FC Honka (e) Legon Cities FC, Berekum Chelsea, Wa All Stars FC

*** Arlauskis - Davydas Arlauskis (a) 18/11/1986, Telsiai (Soviet Union, now in Lithuania) (b) 1,87 (c) D - central defense (d) FK Atmosfera Mazeikiai (e) Dziugas, Egersund, MRU-TiuMenas, Banga, Kruoja, Atlantas, Tauras, Zalgiris, Banga, Unirea Urziceni, Siauliai

*** Arlauskis - Giedrius Arlauskis (a) 01/12/1987, Telšiai (Soviet Union, now in Lithuania) (b) 1,91 (c) G (d) - (e) CS U Craiova, CFR Cluj, Al-Shabab, CFR Cluj, Watford, RCD Espanyol, Watford, Steaua Bucuresti, Rubin Kazan, Unirea Urziceni, Siauliai, Mastis

*** Armalas - Vilius Armalas (a) 21/07/2000, Kaunas (Lithuania) (b) 1,91 (c) D - central defense (d) FC Hegelmann (e) AO Kavala, Hegelmann, Stumbras, Stumbras B

*** Armanavicius - Vilius Armanavicius (Vilius Armanavičius) (a) 08/05/1995, Kaunas (Lithuania) (b) 1,83 (c) M - central midfielder (d) FK Kauno Zalgiris (e) Kaspiy Aktau, Hegelmann, Atlantas, Jonava, Stumbras

*** Armas - Igor Armas (Igor Armaş) (a) 14/07/1987, Căuşeni (Soviet Union, now in Moldova) (b) 1,94 (c) D - central defense (d) FC Voluntari (e) Anzhi, Kuban Krasnodar, Hammarby IF, Zimbru Chisinau, FC Zimbru-2

*** Armenov - Almas Armenov (Арменов Алмас Нурбергенович) (a) 27/01/1992, Aktau (Kazakhstan) (b) 1,70 (c) F - center forward (d) Kaspiy Aktau (e) Kaspiy Aktau, Okzhetpes, Baikonur, Kaspiy Aktau, Atyrau, Kaspiy Aktau

*** Arminen - Taavi Arminen (a) 23/01/2004, ¿? (Finland) (b) - (c) D - central defense (d) Järvenpään Palloseura (e) HJK Klubi 04

*** Armstrong - Adam Armstrong (Adam James Armstrong) (a) 10/02/1997, West Denton (England) (b) 1,73 (c) F - center forward (d) Southampton FC (e) Blackburn, Newcastle Utd., Blackburn, Newcastle Utd., Bolton Wanderers, Newcastle Utd., Barnsley FC, Newcastle Utd., Coventry City, Newcastle Utd.

*** Armstrong - Danny Armstrong (Daniel Armstrong) (a) 11/10/1997, Taunton (England) (b) 1,75 (c) F - right winger (d) Kilmarnock FC (e) Raith Rovers, Ross County, Raith Rovers, Dunfermline A.

*** Armstrong - Stuart Armstrong (a) 30/03/1992, Inverness (Scotland) (b) 1,83 (c) M - central midfielder (d) Southampton FC (e) Celtic FC, Dundee United
*** Arnaldarson - Bjarki Arnaldarson (a) 27/04/2003, ¿? (Iceland) (b) - (c) G (d) Leiknir Reykjavík (e) -
*** Arnarson - Adam Örn Arnarson (a) 27/08/1995, Akureyri (Iceland) (b) 1,80 (c) D - right back (d) Fram Reykjavík (e) Breidablik, Leiknir, Breidablik, Tromsø, Górnik Zabrze, Aalesund, Nordsjælland, NEC Nijmegen, Breidablik
*** Arnarsson - Alex Bergmann Arnarsson (a) 27/12/1999, ¿? (Iceland) (b) - (c) D - central defense (d) UMF Njardvík (e) Víkingur, ÍR, Víkingur, ÍR, Víkingur, Víkingur Ó., Víkingur, Fram Reykjavík, Njardvík, Fram Reykjavík, Fjardabyggd, Fram Reykjavík, Úlfarnir
*** Arnarsson - Jóhann Aegir Arnarsson (Jóhann Ægir Arnarsson) (a) 09/12/2002, ¿? (Iceland) (b) - (c) D - central defense (d) FH Hafnarfjördur (e) -
*** Arnarsson - Jóhann Thór Arnarsson (Jóhann Þór Arnarsson) (a) 07/05/2002, ¿? (Iceland) (b) - (c) F (d) Thróttur Vogum (e) Keflavík, Vídir, Keflavík, Vídir, Keflavík
*** Arnarsson (c) M (d) FH Hafnarfjördur (e) - - Bjarki Steinsen Arnarsson (c) M (d) FH Hafnarfjördur (e) -
*** Árnason - Árni Elvar Árnason (a) 18/11/1996, ¿? (Iceland) (b) - (c) M - attacking midfielder (d) Leiknir Reykjavík (e) Leiknir, KB
*** Árnason - Ívar Örn Árnason (a) 12/04/1996, ¿? (Iceland) (b) 1,85 (c) D - central defense (d) KA Akureyri (e) Víkingur Ó., KA Akureyri, Magni, KA Akureyri
*** Árnason - Jakob Snaer Árnason (Jakob Snær Árnason) (a) 04/07/1997, ¿? (Iceland) (b) - (c) M - attacking midfielder (d) KA Akureyri (e) Thór, KF Fjallabyggd, Thór
*** Árnason - Pétur Theodór Árnason (a) 04/06/1995, ¿? (Faroe Islands) (b) 1,98 (c) F - center forward (d) ÍF Grótta (e) Breidablik, Grótta, KF Kría, Grótta
*** Árnason - Robert Árnason (Róbert Quental Árnason) (a) 23/05/2005, ¿? (Iceland) (b) - (c) F - right winger (d) Leiknir Reykjavík (e) -
*** Arnautovic - Marko Arnautovic (Marko Arnautović) (a) 19/04/1989, Wien (Austria) (b) 1,90 (c) F - center forward (d) Bologna (e) SH Port, West Ham Utd., Stoke City, Werder Bremen, FC Twente, Internazionale Milano, FC Twente, Floridsdorfer AC
*** Arngrímsson - Hans Jákup Arngrímsson (a) 29/03/2004, ¿? (Faroe Islands) (b) - (c) G (d) Víkingur Gøta (e) -
*** Arngrímsson - Ingi Arngrímsson (a) 17/02/2006, ¿? (Faroe Islands) (b) - (c) D - central defense (d) Víkingur Gøta (e) Víkingur II
*** Arnison - Harry Arnison (a) 03/03/2002, ¿? (England) (b) 1,86 (c) M - central midfielder (d) Blyth Spartans (e) Aberystwyth, SC Wanderers
*** Arnold - Maximilian Arnold (a) 27/05/1994, Riesa (Germany) (b) 1,84 (c) M - central midfielder (d) VfL Wolfsburg (e) -
*** Arnold - Remo Arnold (a) 17/01/1997, Sursee (Switzerland) (b) 1,90 (c) M - pivot (d) FC Winterthur (e) FC Luzern, FC Winterthur, FC Luzern
*** Arnórsson - Aron Bjarni Arnórsson (a) 25/03/2006, ¿? (Iceland) (b) - (c) M (d) KV Vesturbaejar (e) -
*** Arnstad - Kristian Arnstad (Kristian Fredrik Malt Arnstad) (a) 07/09/2003, Oslo (Norway) (b) 1,75 (c) M - central midfielder (d) RSC Anderlecht (e) -
*** Arokodare - Tolu Arokodare (Toluwalase Emmanuel Arokodare) (a) 23/11/2000, Festac (Nigeria) (b) 1,97 (c) F - center forward (d) KRC Genk (e) Amiens SC, Valmiera, Amiens SC, Valmiera, 1.FC Köln, Valmiera
*** Arong - Victor Arong (a) 09/09/2004, Cross River (Nigeria) (b) 1,75 (c) F - center forward (d) Drogheda United FC (e) Athboy FC

*** Arribas - Sergio Arribas (Sergio Arribas Calvo) (a) 30/09/2001, Madrid (Spain) (b) 1,74 (c) M - attacking midfielder (d) UD Almería (e) RM Castilla

*** Arrigoni - Nicholas Arrigoni (a) 09/01/1995, Cesena (Italy) (b) - (c) D - central defense (d) La Fiorita 1967 (e) Pennarossa, Fiorentino, SS Folgore, Murata, Martorano, Sampierana, Romagna Centro

*** Arrizabalaga - Kepa Arrizabalaga (Kepa Arrizabalaga Revuelta) (a) 03/10/1994, Ondarroa (Spain) (b) 1,86 (c) G (d) Real Madrid CF (e) Real Madrid, Chelsea, Athletic, Real Valladolid, Athletic, Ponferradina, Athletic, Bilbao Athletic, CD Basconia

*** Arrocha - Daniel Arrocha (Daniel Michael Rodriguez Arrocha) (a) 09/01/1995, ¿? (Denmark) (b) 1,83 (c) D - central defense (d) Sogndal IL Fotball (e) Mjøndalen, Jerv, Øygarden FK, Nest-Sotra IL, HB Köge

*** Arroyo - Roberto Arroyo (Roberto Arroyo Gregorio) (a) 25/08/2003, Valladolid (Spain) (b) 1,81 (c) F - center forward (d) UD Ibiza (e) Valladolid Promesas

*** Arsalo - Markus Arsalo (a) 21/10/2002, Tampere (Finland) (b) 1,83 (c) M - pivot (d) SJK Seinäjoki (e) FC Inter, FC Jazz, FC Inter

*** Arsan - Naim Arsan (a) 14/12/1993, ¿? (Wales) (b) - (c) D - left back (d) Bala Town (e) Newtown, Cefn Druids, Conwy, Penycae, The New Saints

*** Arsenic - Zoran Arsenic (Zoran Arsenić) (a) 02/06/1994, Osijek (Croatia) (b) 1,88 (c) D - central defense (d) Rakow Czestochowa (e) Jagiellonia, Rakow, Jagiellonia, HNK Rijeka, Jagiellonia, Wisla Kraków, NK Osijek, NK Sesvete, NK Osijek, Segesta Sisak, NK Osijek, NK Visnjevac

*** Arsénio - Arsénio (Arsénio Martins Lafuente Nunes) (a) 30/08/1989, Esposende (Portugal) (b) 1,80 (c) F - left winger (d) União de Leiria (e) Arouca, Al-Fayha, Moreirense, CSKA-Sofia, Litex Lovetch, Moreirense, Belenenses, Moreirense, Belenenses, GD Ribeirão, Marítimo B, Padroense

*** Arshakyan - David Arshakyan (Դավիթ Արշակյան) (a) 16/08/1994, St. Petersburg (Russia) (b) 1,95 (c) F - center forward (d) - (e) BKMA Yerevan, FC Van, FA Siauliai, Irtysh Omsk, Ararat Yerevan, NK Rudes, Fakel Voronezh, HNK Gorica, Vejle BK, Chicago, Trakai, MIKA Aschtarak

*** Arsic - Lazar Arsic (Лазар Арсић) (a) 24/09/1991, Beograd (Yugoslavia, now in Serbia) (b) 1,73 (c) M - attacking midfielder (d) Racing Club Beirut (e) Mladost GAT, Radnicki Niš, Vozdovac, Seoul E-Land, MZ Hakka, Vozdovac, Vojvodina, Radnicki Niš, Radnik, Apollon Smyrnis, Radnicki 1923, Lombard Pápa, Vasas SC, FK Obilic

*** Arslan - Hakan Arslan (a) 18/07/1988, Istanbul (Turkey) (b) 1,86 (c) M - central midfielder (d) Sivasspor (e) Kasimpasa, Sivasspor, Samsunspor, I. Güngörenspor

*** Arslan - Tolgay Arslan (Tolgay Ali Arslan) (a) 16/08/1990, Paderborn (Germany) (b) 1,80 (c) M - central midfielder (d) Melbourne City FC (e) Udinese, Fenerbahce, Besiktas, SV Hamburg, Alemannia Aachen, SV Hamburg

*** Arslantas - Muhammet Arslantas (Muhammet Arslantaş) (a) 27/01/2001, Bayburt (Turkey) (b) 1,88 (c) F - center forward (d) Sanliurfaspor (e) Sanliurfaspor, Basaksehir, Bld Kütahya, Basaksehir, Turgutluspor, Basaksehir, Boluspor, Basaksehir

*** Arsov - Ivan Arsov (Иван Георгиев Арсов) (a) 26/09/2000, Sofia (Bulgaria) (b) 1,96 (c) D - central defense (d) Septemvri Sofia (e) Pirin Razlog, Septemvri Sofia

*** Artan - Ömürcan Artan (a) 27/07/1999, Ankara (Turkey) (b) 1,79 (c) D - right back (d) Gaziantep FK (e) Tuzlaspor, Gaziantep FK, Genclerbirligi, Hacettepe, Genclerbirligi

*** Arteaga - Gerardo Arteaga (Gerardo Daniel Arteaga Zamora) (a) 07/09/1998, Zapopan (Mexico) (b) 1,75 (c) D - left back (d) KRC Genk (e) Santos Laguna

*** Artean - Andrei Artean (a) 14/08/1993, Hunedoara (Romania) (b) 1,83 (d) FCV Farul Constanta (e) ACS Poli, Rm. Valcea, ACS Poli, FC Caransebes, ACS Poli, Poli. Timisoara

*** Artemchuk - Maksim Artemchuk (Артемчук Максим Александрович) (a) 09/08/1999, Kaliningrad (Russia) (b) 1,92 (c) F - center forward (d) - (e) Baltika-BFU, Dynamo Brest, Baltika-BFU, Neftekhimik, Kolomna, Zlatibor, Sochi, Dinamo 2 S-Pb, Proleter, Dinamo 2 S-Pb

*** Arter - Harry Arter (Harry Nicholas Arter) (a) 28/12/1989, Sidcup (England) (b) 1,77 (c) M - central midfielder (d) Nottingham Forest (e) Notts County, Nottingham Forest, Charlton Ath., Nottingham Forest, Bournemouth, Fulham, Bournemouth, Cardiff City, Bournemouth, Carlisle United, Bournemouth, Woking, Charlton Ath., Welling Utd., Charlton Ath., Staines Town FC, Charlton Ath.

*** Artero - Ricard Artero (Ricard Artero Ruiz) (a) 05/02/2003, La Bisbal d'Empordà (Spain) (b) 1,81 (c) M - attacking midfielder (d) Girona FC B (e) -

*** Arthur - James Arthur (a) 17/02/1998, ¿? (Ghana) (b) 1,75 (c) M - central midfielder (d) Gudja United FC (e) Valletta, Fafe, Gil Vicente, ARS Martinho, Charity Stars

*** Arthur - Jude Arthur (Jude Ekow Arthur) (a) 08/06/1999, Accra (Ghana) (b) 1,90 (c) M - pivot (d) FC Samgurali Tskaltubo (e) SJK Seinäjoki, FC Haka, SJK Seinäjoki, Liberty Prof., SJK Seinäjoki, Liberty Prof.

*** Arthur Gomes - Arthur Gomes (Arthur Gomes Lourenço) (a) 03/07/1998, Uberlândia (Brazil) (b) 1,74 (c) F - left winger (d) Cruzeiro Esporte Clube (e) Sporting Lisboa, Estoril Praia, Santos, Atlético-GO, Santos, Chapecoense, Santos

*** Arthur Melo - Arthur Melo (Arthur Henrique Ramos de Oliveira Melo) (a) 12/08/1996, Goiânia (Brazil) (b) 1,72 (c) M - central midfielder (d) Fiorentina (e) Fiorentina, Juventus, Liverpool, Juventus, FC Barcelona, Grêmio Porto Alegre, Grêmio Porto Alegre B

*** Arthur Sales - Arthur Sales (Arthur de Oliveira Sales) (a) 03/07/2002, São Gabriel da Palha (Brazil) (b) 1,84 (c) F - center forward (d) Lommel SK (e) EC Bahia, Lommel SK, Paços Ferreira, Lommel SK, Vasco da Gama

*** Artigas - Gerard Artigas (Gerard Artigas Fonullet) (a) 10/01/1995, Barcelona (Spain) (b) 1,82 (c) F - center forward (d) Inter Club d'Escaldes (e) Nam Dinh FC, IC d'Escaldes, PERSIS, IC d'Escaldes, AE Prat, Lorca FC, Chrobry Glogow, Lorca FC, CD Izarra, Astorga, Cacereño, Quintanar Rey, CD Sariñena, CD Masnou, At. Albacete

*** Artjomovs - Kirils Artjomovs (a) 09/05/2006, ¿? (Latvia) (b) - (c) F (d) - (e) SK Super Nova

*** Artjunin - Artjom Artjunin (a) 24/01/1990, Tallinn (Soviet Union, now in Estonia) (b) 1,90 (c) D - central defense (d) FC Tallinn (e) TJK Legion, Etar, Kalev, FCI Levadia, Miedź Legnica, Levadia, FC Brasov, Levadia, Tammeka Tartu, Levadia, Levadia II

*** Artymatas - Kostakis Artymatas (Κωστάκης Αρτυματάς) (a) 15/04/1993, Paralimni (Cyprus) (b) 1,84 (c) M - pivot (d) Anorthosis Famagusta (e) APOEL FC, AOK Kerkyra, APOEL FC, EN Paralimniou

*** Artymatas - Panagiotis Artymatas (Παναγιώτης Αρτυματάς) (a) 12/11/1998, Famagusta (Cyprus) (b) 1,86 (c) D - central defense (d) Apollon Limassol (e) Anorthosis, AE Kifisias, Anorthosis, EN Paralimniou

*** Artyukh - Martin Artyukh (Артюх Мартин Евгеньевич) (a) 06/05/1996, Volkovysk (Belarus) (b) 1,74 (c) F - center forward (d) Dnepr Mogilev (e) Isloch, FK Baranovichi, Slonim, Gorodeya, Slonim

*** Arubi - Gbemi Arubi (Gbemi Kingslyn Arubi) (a) 26/05/2004, ¿? (Ireland) (b) 1,83 (c) F - center forward (d) Shelbourne FC (e) -
*** Aruci - Armando Aruci (a) 10/07/1989, ¿? (San Marino) (b) - (c) F - attacking midfielder (d) SP Cailungo (e) Libertas, Virtus, Pennarossa
*** Arveladze - Levan Arveladze (Арвеладзе Леван Гівійович, ლევან არველაძე) (a) 06/04/1993, Tbilisi (Georgia) (b) 1,81 (c) M - central midfielder (d) FK Andijon (e) Torpedo Kutaisi, Desna, Zorya Lugansk, Desna, Naftovyk, Agrobiznes TSK, Skala Stryi, Kryvbas II, Dnipro II
*** Arveladze - Vato Arveladze (ვატო არველაძე) (a) 04/03/1998, Homburg (Germany) (b) 1,84 (c) M - attacking midfielder (d) - (e) Neftchi Baku, Karagümrük, FC Locomotive, Korona Kielce, FC Locomotive, 35 FS
*** Arvidsson - Johan Arvidsson (a) 25/02/2000, Kalmar (Sweden) (b) - (c) M - attacking midfielder (d) IK Brage (e) Kalmar FF, Oskarshamns AIK, Kalmar FF, Oskarshamns AIK, Kalmar FF
*** Arvidsson - Nils Arvidsson (Nils Erik Hjalmar Arvidsson) (a) 28/04/2003, ¿? (Sweden) (b) - (c) G (d) Helsingborgs IF (e) Ängelholms FF, Helsingborgs IF, Grimslöv-VTIF
*** Arweiler - Jonas Arweiler (a) 10/04/1997, Püttlingen (Germany) (b) 1,88 (c) F - center forward (d) SK Austria Klagenfurt (e) Almere City, FC Utrecht, ADO Den Haag, FC Utrecht, Borussia Dortmund II
*** Arzamendia - Santiago Arzamendia (Santiago Arzamendia Duarte) (a) 05/05/1998, Wanda, Misiones (Argentina) (b) 1,72 (c) D - left back (d) Club Cerro Porteño (e) Cerro Porteño, Cádiz CF, Cerro Porteño
*** Arzoyan - Vardan Arzoyan (Վարդան Արզոյան) (a) 30/04/1995, Yerevan (Armenia) (b) 1,86 (c) D - left back (d) - (e) Ararat Yerevan, FC Urartu, Shirak Gyumri, Gandzasar, Ararat Yerevan, Ararat II, Pyunik Yerevan B
*** Asadov - Gülaga Asadov (Gülağa Arif oğlu Əsədov) (a) 30/04/2003, ¿? (Azerbaijan) (b) - (c) M - central midfielder (d) - (e) FK Qabala, FK Qabala 2
*** Asamoah - Benjamin Asamoah (Benjamin Akoto Asamoah) (a) 04/01/1994, Accra (Ghana) (b) 1,78 (c) M - central midfielder (d) ENAD Polis Chrysochous (e) Doxa Katokopias, At. Madrid B, CE L'Hospitalet, At. Madrid B, At. Madrid C, Rayo Majadahonda
*** Asamoah - Kwadwo Asamoah (a) 15/07/2002, Accra (Ghana) (b) 1,75 (c) F - right winger (d) FK Panevezys (e) Spartaks, Bechem United
*** Asamoah - Samuel Asamoah (a) 23/03/1994, Accra (Ghana) (b) 1,66 (c) M - pivot (d) FC U Craiova 1948 (e) Sint-Truiden, KAS Eupen, OH Leuven, KAS Eupen
*** Asan - Serkan Asan (a) 28/04/1999, Trabzon (Turkey) (b) 1,70 (c) D - right back (d) Trabzonspor (e) 1461 Trabzon
*** Asani - Jasir Asani (a) 19/05/1995, Skopje (North Macedonia) (b) 1,75 (c) F - right winger (d) Gwangju FC (e) Kisvárda, FK Partizani, AIK, FK Partizani, Pobeda Prilep, Vardar, FC Shkupi, Vardar
*** Asani - Xhelil Asani (a) 12/09/1995, Kicevo (North Macedonia) (b) 1,87 (c) D - left back (d) KF Vllaznia (e) KF Erzeni, Rudar Prijedor, Pittsburgh, SKA Khabarovsk, Mladost Kakanj, Mash'al, Shkëndija, Torpedo Zhodino, Pembroke, Metalurg Skopje, FK Bylis, Vëllazërimi
*** Asano - Takuma Asano (浅野 拓磨) (a) 10/11/1994, Komono, Mie (Japan) (b) 1,73 (c) F - right winger (d) VfL Bochum (e) FK Partizan, Arsenal, Hannover 96, Arsenal, VfB Stuttgart, Arsenal, Sanf. Hiroshima, Yokkaichi CT HS
*** Asante - Ernest Asante (Ernest Kwabena Asante) (a) 06/11/1988, Sunyani (Ghana) (b) 1,71 (c) F - right winger (d) Doxa Katokopias (e) AEK Larnaca, Doxa

Katokopias, Omonia Nicosia, Fujairah SC, Al-Hazem, Al-Jazira, Nordsjælland, Stabæk, Start, Maxbee's FC, KSK Beveren, Feyenoord Ghana
*** Asare - Dirk Asare (Dirk Junior Asare) (a) 04/07/2004, (Mol, Belgium) (b) - (c) M - central midfielder (d) KV Mechelen (e) Jong KV Mechelen
*** Asatiani - Davit Asatiani (დავით ასათიანი) (a) 05/09/2003, ¿? (Georgia) (b) - (c) G (d) Chikhura Sachkhere (e) Merani Martvili, FC Dila, FC Zestafoni, Torpedo Kutaisi
*** Asatiani - Luka Asatiani (ლუკა ასათიანი) (a) 22/04/1999, Tbilisi (Georgia) (b) 1,88 (c) D - central defense (d) Shukura Kobuleti (e) Sioni Bolnisi, FC Samtredia, Samgurali, Rustavi, Jagiellonia II, O. Zambrow, Jagiellonia II, Wigry Suwalki, Jagiellonia II, 35 FS
*** Asatryan - Artak Asatryan (Արտակ Ասատրյան) (a) 25/01/2001, Yerevan (Armenia) (b) 1,80 (c) D - left back (d) FC Syunik (e) Ararat II, Gandzasar, Pyunik Yerevan B, BKMA Yerevan, Pyunik Yerevan B
*** Asatryan - Harutyun Asatryan (Հարություն Ասատրյան) (a) 25/06/2003, ¿? (Armenia) (b) 1,75 (c) M - central midfielder (d) FC Pyunik Yerevan B (e) BKMA Yerevan II, Pyunik Yerevan B
*** Ascacíbar - Santiago Ascacíbar (Santiago Lionel Ascacíbar) (a) 25/02/1997, La Plata (Argentina) (b) 1,68 (c) M - pivot (d) Club Estudiantes de La Plata (e) Hertha Berlin, Estudiantes, Hertha Berlin, Cremonese, Hertha Berlin, VfB Stuttgart, Estudiantes
*** Ascone - Rocco Ascone (a) 12/09/2003, Villeneuve-d'Ascq (France) (b) 1,80 (c) M - central midfielder (d) FC Nordsjælland (e) LOSC Lille B, Nordsjælland, LOSC Lille B
*** Åsen - Gjermund Åsen (a) 22/05/1991, Trondheim (Norway) (b) 1,82 (c) M - central midfielder (d) Lillestrøm SK (e) Rosenborg, Lillestrøm, Rosenborg, Tromsø, Ranheim, Rosenborg, Ranheim, Rosenborg, Ranheim, Rosenborg
*** Asenjo - Sergio Asenjo (Sergio Asenjo Andrés) (a) 28/06/1989, Palencia (Spain) (b) 1,89 (c) G (d) Real Valladolid CF (e) Villarreal CF, Atlético Madrid, Villarreal CF, Atlético Madrid, Málaga CF, Atlético Madrid, Real Valladolid, R. Valladolid B
*** Asensio - Marco Asensio (Marco Asensio Willemsen) (a) 21/01/1996, Palma de Mallorca (Spain) (b) 1,82 (c) F - right winger (d) París Saint-Germain FC (e) Real Madrid, RCD Espanyol, Real Madrid, RCD Mallorca, RCD Mallorca B
*** Asgarov - Vuqar Asgarov (Vüqar Kamal oğlu Əsgərov) (a) 14/05/1985, Sumgayit (Soviet Union, now in Azerbaijan) (b) 1,84 (c) F - center forward (d) FK PPK/Betsafe (e) Super Nova, Daugavpils, Liepaja, Daugavpils, Progress, AFA Olaine, FK 1625 Liepaja, Zira FK, Araz-Naxcivan, Sumqayit, Metalurgs, Varaviksne, FC Jurmala
*** Asgarov - Vusal Asgarov (Vüsal Hikmət oğlu Əsgərov) (a) 23/08/2001, ¿? (Azerbaijan) (b) 1,73 (c) M - attacking midfielder (d) Neftchi Baku (e) Neftchi 2 Baku
*** Ásgrímsson - Haraldur Einar Ásgrímsson (a) 16/06/2000, ¿? (Iceland) (b) - (c) D - left back (d) FH Hafnarfjördur (e) Fram Reykjavík, Álftanes, Fram Reykjavík, Úlfarnir, Fram Reykjavík
*** Ashby - Harrison Ashby (Harrison Charles Ashby) (a) 14/11/2001, Milton Keynes (England) (b) 1,79 (c) D - right back (d) Swansea City (e) Swansea City, Newcastle Utd.
*** Ashimeru - Majeed Ashimeru (a) 10/10/1997, Accra (Ghana) (b) 1,74 (c) M - central midfielder (d) RSC Anderlecht (e) RB Salzburg, RSC Anderlecht, RB Salzburg, FC St. Gallen, RB Salzburg, Wolfsberger AC, RB Salzburg, Austria Lustenau, RB Salzburg, WAFA SC
*** Ashkenazi - Yuval Ashkenazi (אשכנזי יובל) (a) 13/02/1992, Givatayim (Israel) (b) 1,73 (c) M - central midfielder (d) Beitar Jerusalem (e) Bnei Sakhnin, Maccabi

Netanya, Maccabi Haifa, Bnei Yehuda, H. Kfar Shalem, Hapoel Azor, H. Kfar Shalem, Kiryat Malachi, Hapoel Azor

*** Ashkovski - Stefan Ashkovski (Стефан Ашковски) (a) 24/02/1992, Skopje (North Macedonia) (b) 1,79 (c) F (d) - (e) PAS Lamia, Sepsi OSK, FC Botosani, Slavia Sofia, Fortuna Sittard, Gornik Leczna, Fortuna Sittard, K. Erciyesspor, FK Partizan, Novi Pazar, FK Partizan, Shkëndija, FK Partizan, Strømsgodset, FK Partizan, Napredak, FK Partizan, Donji Srem, FK Partizan, Teleoptik

*** Ashortia - Imeda Ashortia (იმედა აშორტია) (a) 30/10/1996, ¿? (Georgia) (b) 1,83 (c) F - center forward (d) FC Telavi (e) Turan Tovuz, FC Telavi, Shukura, Tskhinvali, Kolkheti Poti, FC Dila, Merani Martvili

*** Ashour - Emam Ashour (عاشور إمام) (a) 20/02/1998, ¿? (Egypt) (b) 1,82 (c) M - central midfielder (d) El Ahly Cairo (e) Midtjylland, Zamalek, El Mahalla, Harras Hodoud, El Mahalla

*** Ashworth - MJ Ashworth (Michael-Jay Paul Ashworth) (a) 11/10/2003, ¿? (England) (b) - (c) M - right midfielder (d) Brickfield Rangers (e) -

*** Asimenos - Andreas Asimenos (Ανδρέας Ασημένος) (a) 02/07/2004, Nicosia (Cyprus) (b) 1,76 (c) M - central midfielder (d) Olympiakos Nikosia (e) Omonia Nicosia, MEAP Nisou, Omonia Nicosia

*** Askar - Amin Soleiman Askar (عسكر امين) (a) 01/10/1985, Harer (Ethiopia) (b) 1,76 (c) D - right back (d) Sprint/Jeløy (e) Moss, Kristiansund, Sarpsborg 08, Sanliurfaspor, Brann, Sarpsborg 08, Brann, Fredrikstad, Moss

*** Askham - Hördur Askham (Hørður Heðinsson Askham) (a) 22/09/1994, Tórshavn (Faroe Islands) (b) 1,91 (c) D - central defense (d) Akademisk Boldklub (e) HB Tórshavn, KÍ Klaksvík, B36 Tórshavn, 07 Vestur, B36 Tórshavn

*** Askham - Trygvi Askham (a) 28/03/1988, Sørvágur (Faroe Islands) (b) - (c) G (d) - (e) B36 Tórshavn, EB/Streymur, B36 Tórshavn, IF Føroyar, FC Hoyvík, 07 Vestur

*** Askias - Netanel Askias (אסקיאס נתנאל) (a) 01/05/2001, ¿? (Israel) (b) - (c) F - left winger (d) Hapoel Ramat haSharon (e) Ramat haSharon, H. Beer Sheva, H Rishon leZion, H. Beer Sheva

*** Askildsen - Kristoffer Askildsen (a) 09/01/2001, Oslo (Norway) (b) 1,90 (c) M - central midfielder (d) UC Sampdoria (e) Lecce, Sampdoria, Stabæk, Sampdoria, Stabæk, Stabæk II

*** Aslan - Nurullah Aslan (a) 05/07/1997, Samsun (Turkey) (b) 2,02 (c) G (d) Van Spor FK (e) Samsunspor, Genclerbirligi, Samsunspor, Ankaragücü, Samsunspor, Erbaaspor, Termespor

*** Aslanidis - Kyriakos Aslanidis (Κυριάκος Ασλανίδης) (a) 11/03/2002, Serres (Greece) (b) 1,84 (c) D - central defense (d) Volos NPS (e) Aris Thessaloniki

*** Aslanly - Ibrahim Aslanly (İbrahim Adil oğlu Aslanlı) (a) 01/12/1996, ¿? (Azerbaijan) (b) 1,78 (c) D - right back (d) FC Shamakhi (e) FK Sabail, FK Zira 2

*** Aslanyan - Sevak Aslanyan (Սևակ Ասլանյան) (a) 17/05/1998, Vardenis (Armenia) (b) 1,86 (c) G (d) FC Syunik (e) Alashkert CF, Pyunik Yerevan, Pyunik Yerevan B

*** Asllani - Fisnik Asllani (a) 08/08/2002, Berlin (Germany) (b) 1,88 (c) F - center forward (d) TSG 1899 Hoffenheim (e) Hoffenheim II

*** Asllani - Kristjan Asllani (a) 09/03/2002, Elbasan (Albania) (b) 1,75 (c) M - pivot (d) Internazionale Milano (e) FC Empoli, Internazionale Milano, FC Empoli

*** Ásmundsson - Emil Ásmundsson (a) 08/01/1995, ¿? (Iceland) (b) - (c) M - central midfielder (d) Fylkir Reykjavík (e) KR Reykjavík, Fylkir, KR Reykjavík, Fylkir, Brighton & Hove Albion, Fylkir

*** Asoro - Joel Asoro (Joel Joshoghene Asoro) (a) 27/04/1999, Haninge (Sweden) (b) 1,75 (c) F - right winger (d) Djurgårdens IF (e) Swansea City, Genoa, Swansea City, FC Groningen, Swansea City, Sunderland

*** Asoyan - Hamlet Asoyan (Համլետ Ասոյան) (a) 13/01/1995, Yerevan (Armenia) (b) 1,78 (c) D - central defense (d) FC Van (e) Lernayin Artsakh, Alashkert II, Lernayin Artsakh, FC Sevan, Gandzasar, Artsakh Erewan, Homenetmen, Gandzasar, Alashkert II, Pyunik Yerevan B

*** Aspas - Iago Aspas (Iago Aspas Juncal) (a) 01/08/1987, Moaña (Spain) (b) 1,76 (c) F - center forward (d) RC Celta de Vigo (e) Sevilla FC, Liverpool, Sevilla FC, Liverpool, RC Celta, Celta B, Bouzas

*** Aspegren - Felipe Aspegren (a) 12/02/1994, Cali (Colombia) (b) 1,73 (c) D - right back (d) Ilves Tampere (e) SJK Seinäjoki, KuPS, Ilves, FC KTP, SJK Seinäjoki, TPS, SJK Seinäjoki, FC Inter, HJK Helsinki, HJK Klubi 04

*** Asprilla - Danilo Asprilla (Danilo Moreno Asprilla) (a) 12/01/1989, Chigorodó (Colombia) (b) 1,77 (c) F - right winger (d) CSKA-Sofia (e) B. Jerusalem, H. Beer Sheva, Al-Qadsiah FC, Al-Shabab, Al-Ain FC, Al-Fayha, Al-Ain FC, Litex Lovetch, Patriotas, Indep. Santa Fe, Rampla Juniors, Pereira, Al-Shahania SC, Juventude

*** Asrankulov - Roman Asrankulov (Асранкулов Роман Максимович) (a) 30/07/1999, Kostanay (Kazakhstan) (b) 1,86 (c) D - left back (d) Tobol Kostanay (e) Tobol II

*** Asryan - Sergey Asryan (Սերգեյ Ասրյան) (a) 02/01/1993, Stepanakert (Armenia) (b) - (c) G (d) - (e) Lernayin Artsakh

*** Assayeg - Ravve Assayeg (אסייג רווה) (a) 01/05/2001, Rishon leZion (Israel) (b) 1,86 (c) F - center forward (d) Hapoel Acre (e) Hapoel Tel Aviv, Hapoel Acre, Maccabi Tel Aviv, B TLV Bat Yam, Maccabi Tel Aviv

*** Assehnoun - Jasin Assehnoun (Jasin-Amin Assehnoun) (a) 26/12/1998, Tampere (Finland) (b) 1,75 (c) F - left winger (d) Vejle Boldklub (e) FC Emmen, FC Lahti, FC Espoo

*** Assignon - Lorenz Assignon (a) 22/06/2000, Grasse (France) (b) 1,81 (c) D - right back (d) Stade Rennais FC (e) Stade Rennes B, SC Bastia, Stade Rennes B

*** Assombalonga - Britt Assombalonga (Britoli Curtis Assombalonga) (a) 06/12/1992, Kinshasa (Zaire, now DR Congo) (b) 1,77 (c) F - center forward (d) Antalyaspor (e) Watford, Adana Demirspor, Middlesbrough, Nottingham Forest, Peterborough, Watford, Southend United, Watford, Braintree, Watford

*** Assoubre - Jean Luc Assoubre (Jean Luc Gbayara Assoubre) (a) 08/08/1992, Lakota (Ivory Coast) (b) 1,72 (c) F - right winger (d) Inter Club d'Escaldes (e) Marbella FC, Ethnikos, Sigma Olomouc, AE Larisa, AEK Larnaca, PAS Lamia, AEK Larnaca, Gimnàstic, Pobla de Mafumet CF, Villarreal CF B, Villarreal CF C

*** Assunção - Gustavo Assunção (Gustavo Enrique Giordano Amaro Assunção da Silva) (a) 30/03/2000, São Paulo (Brazil) (b) 1,78 (c) M - pivot (d) FC Famalicão (e) Galatasaray, Famalicão

*** Astakhov - Ernest Astakhov (Астахов Ернест Дмитрович) (a) 21/08/1998, Dnipropetrovsk (Ukraine) (b) 1,78 (c) D - right back (d) FK Livyi Bereg (e) Jonava, FC Continentals, Torpedo Zhodino, Kremin, FK Nikopol

*** Astanov - Elkhan Astanov (Астанов Елхан Астанұлы) (a) 21/05/2000, Shymkent (Kazakhstan) (b) 1,86 (c) F - left winger (d) FC Astana (e) Ordabasy, Ordabasy II

*** Astanov - Sultanbek Astanov (Сұлтанбек Астанұлы Астанов) (a) 23/03/1999, Shymkent (Kazakhstan) (b) 1,79 (c) D - right back (d) Ordabasy Shymkent (e) Kairat Almaty, Ordabasy, Kairat Almaty, Kairat-Zhas, Kairat II

*** Astles - Ryan Astles (a) 01/07/1994, ¿? (England) (b) - (c) D - central defense (d) The New Saints (e) Southport, Chester, Northwich Vic, Rhyl FC
*** Astolfi - Andrea Astolfi (a) 12/08/1980, Rimini (Italy) (b) - (c) G (d) SS Folgore/Falciano (e) Santarcangelo, Castel San P.
*** Astralaga - Ander Astralaga (Ander Astralaga Aranguren) (a) 03/03/2004, Berango (Spain) (b) 1,90 (c) G (d) FC Barcelona Atlètic (e) -
*** Atakayi - Serge Atakayi (a) 30/01/1999, Kinshasa (Congo DR) (b) 1,71 (c) F - right winger (d) Waterford FC (e) Waterford FC, St. Patrick's Ath., SJK Seinäjoki, TPS, SJK Seinäjoki, Rangers II, SJK Seinäjoki, Rangers II, FF Jaro
*** Atakishiyev - Arzu Atakishiyev (a) 05/09/2005, ¿? (Azerbaijan) (b) - (c) D (d) Kapaz 2 Ganja (e) Kapaz PFK
*** Atal - Youcef Atal (a) 17/05/1996, Boghni (Algeria) (b) 1,76 (c) D - right back (d) OGC Niza (e) KV Kortrijk, Paradou AC, KV Kortrijk, Paradou AC, JMG Algier
*** Atanase - Cosmin Atanase (Cosmin Gabriel Atanase) (a) 03/01/2001, Târgoviște (Romania) (b) 1,75 (c) M - central midfielder (d) AFC Unirea 04 Slobozia (e) Chindia
*** Atanaskoski - David Atanaskoski (Давид Атанаскоски) (a) 21/10/1996, Skopje (North Macedonia) (b) 1,76 (c) D - left back (d) FK Partizani (e) Makedonija, Shakhter K., Makedonija, AP Brera, Horizont, Teteks Tetovo
*** Atanasov - Georgi Atanasov (Георги Атанасов Атанасов) (a) 06/03/2004, Toronto (Canada) (b) 1,80 (c) F - right winger (d) - (e) Arda Kardzhali, Sportist Svoge, Arda Kardzhali
*** Atanasov - Jani Atanasov (Јани Атанасов) (a) 31/10/1999, Strumica (North Macedonia) (b) 1,87 (c) M - pivot (d) Cracovia (e) Hajduk Split, Bursaspor, AP Brera
*** Atanasov - Martin Atanasov (Мартин Чавдаров Атанасов) (a) 19/01/2002, Sofia (Bulgaria) (b) 1,76 (c) M - pivot (d) CSKA 1948 II (e) Botev Vratsa, Slavia Sofia, Minyor Pernik
*** Atanasov - Zahari Atanasov (Захари Атанасов Атанасов) (a) 31/01/2005, ¿? (Bulgaria) (b) - (c) M - right midfielder (d) Septemvri Sofia (e) Septemvri Sofia II
*** Atanasov - Zhivko Atanasov (Живко Станиславов Атанасов) (a) 03/02/1991, Dobroplodno, Varna (Bulgaria) (b) 1,87 (c) D - central defense (d) Cherno More Varna (e) Levski Sofia, Catanzaro, Viterbese, Juve Stabia, Slavia Sofia, Cherno More, Levski Sofia
*** Atanda - Sodiq Atanda (Sodiq Ololade Atanda) (a) 26/08/1993, ¿? (Nigeria) (b) 1,82 (c) D - central defense (d) - (e) KF Egnatia, Dhofar Club, FC Prishtina, H. Kfar Saba, FK Partizani, FK Apolonia, 36 Lion FC
*** Atanga - David Atanga (David Dona Atanga) (a) 25/12/1996, Bolgatanga (Ghana) (b) 1,80 (c) F - right winger (d) KV Oostende (e) Holstein Kiel, Admira Wacker, Holstein Kiel, RB Salzburg, Greuther Fürth, RB Salzburg, SKN St. Pölten, RB Salzburg, SV Mattersburg, RB Salzburg, 1.FC Heidenheim, RB Salzburg, FC Liefering, RB Ghana
*** Atangana - Christophe Atangana (Christophe Atangana Assimba) (a) 02/03/2000, Douala (Cameroon) (b) 1,82 (c) G (d) FK Qabala (e) Bilbao Athletic, Arenas Club, Bilbao Athletic, Somorrostro, Bilbao Athletic, SD Leioa, Bilbao Athletic, CD Basconia, SD Leioa, CD Basconia
*** Atangana Edoa - Valentin Atangana Edoa (a) 25/08/2005, Yaoundé (Cameroon) (b) - (c) M - pivot (d) Stade Reims B (e) -
*** Atars - Kristers Atars (a) 21/04/2004, ¿? (Latvia) (b) - (c) D - left back (d) SK Super Nova (e) Spartaks, RFS II
*** Atasayar - Onur Atasayar (a) 01/01/1995, Tavsanli (Turkey) (b) 1,84 (c) D - left back (d) Kocaelispor (e) Ümraniyespor, Bursaspor, Ankaragücü

*** Atemona - Christalino Atemona (a) 26/04/2002, Zwiesel (Germany) (b) 1,87 (c) D - central defense (d) KV Kortrijk (e) Hertha BSC II

*** Atesyakan - Berkay Atesyakan (Berkay Ateşyakan) (a) 31/05/2003, Ankara (Turkey) (b) 1,72 (c) M - attacking midfielder (d) - (e) Etimesgut Belediye

*** Athanasiadis - Georgios Athanasiadis (Γεώργιος Αθανασιάδης) (a) 07/04/1993, Thessaloniki (Greece) (b) 1,91 (c) G (d) AEK Athína FC (e) FC Sheriff, AEK Athína, Asteras Tripoli, Panthrakikos, Ethnikos Sochou

*** Athanasiou - Nikolaos Athanasiou (Νικόλαος Αθανασίου) (a) 16/03/2001, Athen (Greece) (b) 1,77 (c) D - left back (d) Atromitos FC (e) Niki Volou, Atromitos FC

*** Athanasiou - Vasilios Athanasiou (Βασίλειος Αθανασίου) (a) 24/07/1999, Egio (Greece) (b) 1,88 (c) G (d) PAS Giannina (e) Mantova, UC AlbinoLeffe, Panegialios, Thyella Egiou

*** Atherton - Christopher Atherton (a) 19/10/2008, ¿? (Northern Ireland) (b) 1,72 (c) F - right winger (d) - (e) Glenavon

*** Atherton - Daniel Atherton (a) 18/12/1999, Haydock (England) (b) 1,84 (c) G (d) Warrington Town (e) Hyde United, The New Saints, Warrington, Marine FC

*** Ati Zigi - Lawrence Ati Zigi (a) 29/11/1996, Accra (Ghana) (b) 1,88 (c) G (d) FC St. Gallen 1879 (e) FC Sochaux, RB Salzburg, FC Liefering, RB Ghana

*** Atiemwen - Iyayi Atiemwen (Iyayi Believe Atiemwen) (a) 24/01/1996, Ogbe (Nigeria) (b) 1,80 (c) F - left winger (d) FC Sheriff Tiraspol (e) Dinamo Zagreb, HNK Gorica, Dinamo Zagreb, Omonia Nicosia, Dinamo Zagreb, NK Lokomotiva, Dinamo Zagreb, HNK Gorica, Çaykur Rizespor, Manisaspor, Çaykur Rizespor, Sanliurfaspor, Çaykur Rizespor, K. Erciyesspor, Dogan TBSK, Bendel Ins.

*** Atienza - Pichu Atienza (Francisco Javier Atienza Valverde) (a) 18/01/1990, Córdoba (Spain) (b) 1,90 (c) D - central defense (d) Asteras Tripolis (e) Real Zaragoza, CD Numancia, Reus Deportiu, Hércules CF, SD Huesca, Sevilla At., At. Madrid B, At. Madrid C

*** Atkinson - Coby Atkinson (a) 21/05/2000, Kingston (Jamaica) (b) 1,80 (c) M - central midfielder (d) Brabrand IF (e) AB Argir, CSUSB Coyotes, Portland 2

*** Atkinson - Kevaughn Atkinson (Kevaughn St. Michael Atkinson) (a) 11/11/1995, ¿? (Malta) (b) - (c) F - left winger (d) - (e) Gzira Utd., Zebbug Rangers, Gzira Utd., Senglea Ath., Gzira Utd., St. Andrews FC, Austria Lustenau, St. Andrews FC, FK Senica, St. Andrews FC, Mosta FC, Sporting C., ASV Salzburg

*** Atkinson - Nathaniel Atkinson (Nathaniel Caleb Atkinson) (a) 13/06/1999, Launceston, Tasmania (Australia) (b) 1,81 (c) D - right back (d) Heart of Midlothian FC (e) Melbourne City

*** Atlason - Árni Nóa Atlason (a) 15/01/2006, ¿? (Faroe Islands) (b) - (c) M - central midfielder (d) Víkingur Gøta (e) -

*** Atlason - Davíd Örn Atlason (Davíð Örn Atlason) (a) 18/08/1994, ¿? (Iceland) (b) - (c) D - right back (d) Víkingur Reykjavík (e) Breidablik, Víkingur, Dalvík/Reynir, Víkingur, KA Akureyri, Víkingur

*** Atlason - Emil Atlason (a) 22/07/1993, ¿? (Iceland) (b) 1,89 (c) F - center forward (d) Stjarnan Gardabaer (e) HK Kópavogs, Thróttur, KR Reykjavík, Thróttur, KR Reykjavík, Valur, KR Reykjavík, Preussen Münster, KR Reykjavík

*** Atola Meja - Henry Atola Meja (a) 21/12/2001, Kakamega (Kenya) (b) - (c) F - center forward (d) Norrby IF (e) AIK, Tusker FC, Lihrembe A. FC, Vihiga Sportiff, Lihrembe A. FC, Green Commandos

*** Atrashkevich - Stanislav Atrashkevich (Атрашкевич Станислав Сергеевич) (a) 22/10/2002, Minsk (Belarus) (b) 1,81 (c) M - central midfielder (d) FK Smorgon (e) Isloch, Dzerzhinsk, Isloch, Isloch II

*** Átrok - István Átrok (Átrok István Zalán) (a) 06/12/2005, ¿? (Hungary) (b) 1,75 (c) M - attacking midfielder (d) Budapest Honvéd FC (e) Honvéd II

*** Atshimene - Charles Atshimene (a) 05/02/2001, ¿? (Nigeria) (b) 1,88 (c) F - center forward (d) - (e) FK Bylis, Feirense, Leixões, Feirense, Akwa United, Warri Wolves FC

*** Atskureli - Lasha Atskureli (ლაშა აწყურელი) (a) 11/04/2001, ¿? (Georgia) (b) 1,70 (c) D - right back (d) - (e) FC Locomotive, Dinamo II, Chikhura, Dinamo II, Sioni Bolnisi, Dinamo II

*** Atsu - Christian Atsu (Christian Atsu Twasam) (a) 10/01/1992, Ada Foah (Ghana) (b) 1,65 (c) F - left winger (d) --- (e) Al-Raed, Newcastle Utd., Chelsea, Newcastle Utd., Chelsea, Málaga CF, Chelsea, Bournemouth, Chelsea, Everton, Chelsea, Vitesse, Chelsea, FC Porto, Rio Ave, FC Porto, Feyenoord Ghana

*** Attamah - Joseph Attamah (Joseph Larweh Attamah) (a) 22/05/1994, Accra (Ghana) (b) 1,80 (c) M - pivot (d) Kayserispor (e) Basaksehir, Karagümrük, Basaksehir, Çaykur Rizespor, Basaksehir, Adana Demirspor

*** Attard - Ayrton Attard (a) 05/11/2000, ¿? (Malta) (b) 1,78 (c) F - left winger (d) Hibernians FC (e) Marsaxlokk, Hibernians FC, Birkirkara FC

*** Attard - Cain Attard (a) 10/09/1994, ¿? (Malta) (b) 1,77 (c) D - right back (d) CF Os Belenenses (e) Birkirkara FC, Pietà Hotspurs

*** Attard - Jean Paul Attard (a) 28/05/2001, ¿? (Malta) (b) - (c) M - pivot (d) Fgura United FC (e) Gzira Utd., Fgura Utd.

*** Attard - Joseph Attard (a) 14/10/2002, Floriana (Malta) (b) - (c) D (d) Gudja United FC (e) Mqabba FC

*** Attard - Shaisen Attard (a) 29/10/2004, ¿? (Malta) (b) - (c) F (d) Hamrun Spartans (e) Gudja United FC

*** Atubolu - Noah Atubolu (a) 25/05/2002, Freiburg im Breisgau (Germany) (b) 1,90 (c) G (d) SC Freiburg (e) SC Freiburg II

*** Atzili - Omer Atzili (עומר אציל) (a) 27/07/1993, Holon (Israel) (b) 1,77 (c) F - right winger (d) Al-Ain FC (e) Maccabi Haifa, APOEL FC, Maccabi Tel Aviv, Granada CF, B. Jerusalem, H Rishon leZion

*** Auassar - Adil Auassar (a) 06/10/1986, Dordrecht (Netherlands) (b) 1,86 (c) D - central defense (d) Mohammed Auassar (e) Sparta Rotterdam, Roda JC, Excelsior, De Graafschap, Feyenoord, RKC Waalwijk, Feyenoord, VVV-Venlo, FC Dordrecht

*** Aubameyang - Pierre-Emerick Aubameyang (Pierre-Emerick Emiliano François Aubameyang) (a) 18/06/1989, Laval (France) (b) 1,87 (c) F - center forward (d) Olympique Marseille (e) Chelsea, FC Barcelona, Arsenal, Borussia Dortmund, St.-Étienne, AC Milan, St.-Étienne, AC Milan, AS Monaco, AC Milan, Lille, AC Milan, Dijon, AC Milan

*** Audero - Emil Audero (Emil Audero Mulyadi) (a) 18/01/1997, Mataram (Indonesia) (b) 1,92 (c) G (d) Internazionale Milano (e) Internazionale Milano, Sampdoria, Juventus, Sampdoria, Juventus, Venezia, Juventus

*** Audinis - Nojus Audinis (Nojus Vytis Audinis) (a) 15/02/2006, ¿? (Lithuania) (b) 1,93 (c) D - central defense (d) FA Siauliai B (e) -

*** Audoor - Lynnt Audoor (a) 13/10/2003, Merelbeke (Belgium) (b) 1,84 (c) M - pivot (d) KV Kortrijk (e) KV Kortrijk, KV Brugge, Club NXT

*** Audunsson - Steinthór Már Audunsson (Steinþór Már Auðunsson) (a) 23/02/1990, ¿? (Iceland) (b) - (c) G (d) KA Akureyri (e) Magni, Thór, Völsungur ÍF, Thór, Dalvík/Reynir, KA Akureyri, Dalvík/Reynir, KA Akureyri

*** Audunsson - Uggi Jóhann Audunsson (Uggi Jóhann Auðunsson) (a) 04/12/2004, ¿? (Iceland) (b) - (c) G (d) Víkingur Reykjavík (e) -

*** Auer - Jonas Auer (Jonas Antonius Auer) (a) 05/08/2000, Ruprechtshofen (Austria) (b) 1,82 (c) D - left back (d) SK Rapid Wien (e) Mlada Boleslav, Viktoria Zizkov, Mlada Boleslav, Slavia Praha, Viktoria Zizkov, Slavia Praha, Slavia Praha B
*** Augello - Tommaso Augello (a) 30/08/1994, Milano (Italy) (b) 1,80 (c) D - left back (d) Cagliari (e) Sampdoria, Spezia, Sampdoria, Spezia, Giana Erminio, Pontisola, Pol. Cimiano
*** Augoyat - Keanan Augoyat (a) 30/05/2004, ¿? (France) (b) - (c) D (d) CS Fola Esch (e) Aubenas Sud Ardeche
*** Augustijns - Sebbe Augustijns (a) 03/09/1999, Kalmthout (Belgium) (b) 1,79 (c) M - central midfielder (d) SC Telstar (e) RKC Waalwijk
*** Augustin - Jean-Kévin Augustin (a) 16/06/1997, Paris (France) (b) 1,79 (c) F - center forward (d) FC Basel (e) FC Nantes, Leeds Utd., RB Leipzig, Leeds Utd., RB Leipzig, AS Monaco, RB Leipzig, Paris Saint-Germain, Paris Saint Germain B
*** Augustinsson - Jonathan Augustinsson (Hans Oskar Jonathan Augustinsson) (a) 30/03/1996, ¿? (Sweden) (b) 1,85 (c) D - left back (d) Rosenborg BK (e) Djurgården, Brommapojkarna
*** Augustinsson - Ludwig Augustinsson (Hans Carl Ludwig Augustinsson) (a) 21/04/1994, Stockholm (Sweden) (b) 1,81 (c) D - left back (d) Sevilla FC (e) RCD Mallorca, Sevilla FC, Aston Villa, Sevilla FC, Werder Bremen, FC København, IFK Göteborg, Brommapojkarna
*** Augusto - Douglas Augusto (Douglas Augusto Gomes Soares) (a) 13/01/1997, Rio de Janeiro (Brazil) (b) 1,73 (c) M - central midfielder (d) FC Nantes (e) PAOK, Corinthians, EC Bahia, Corinthians, Fluminense
*** Augustyniak - Rafal Augustyniak (Rafał Sylwester Augustyniak) (a) 14/10/1993, Zduńska Wola (Poland) (b) 1,85 (c) D - central defense (d) Legia de Varsovia (e) Ural, Miedź Legnica, Jagiellonia, Miedź Legnica, Jagiellonia, Wigry Suwalki, Jagiellonia, Pogon Siedlce, Jagiellonia, Widzew Lódz, Widzew II, Pogon Siedlce, Widzew II, Pogon Z. W.
*** Auklend - Sondre Auklend (a) 10/06/2003, ¿? (Norway) (b) 1,72 (c) M - attacking midfielder (d) Viking FK (e) Jerv, Viking, Åsane, Viking, Viking FK II
*** Aun - Rudolf Aun (a) 27/01/2005, Viimsi Vald (Estonia) (b) - (c) G (d) Keila JK (e) -
*** Aurélio - Douglas Aurélio (a) 27/03/1999, Teófilo Otoni (MG) (Brazil) (b) 1,83 (c) M - attacking midfielder (d) Riga FC (e) Pafos FC, Riga, Pafos FC
*** Aurier - Serge Aurier (Serge Alain Stephane Aurier) (a) 24/12/1992, Ouragahio (Ivory Coast) (b) 1,76 (c) D - right back (d) Nottingham Forest (e) Villarreal CF, Tottenham Hotspur, Paris Saint-Germain, Toulouse, Paris Saint-Germain, Toulouse, RC Lens, RC Lens B
*** Aursnes - Fredrik Aursnes (a) 10/12/1995, Hareid (Norway) (b) 1,79 (c) M - central midfielder (d) SL Benfica (e) Feyenoord, Molde, Hødd
*** Aurtenetxe - Jon Aurtenetxe (Jon Aurtenetxe Borde) (a) 03/01/1992, Amorebieta-Etxano (Spain) (b) 1,83 (c) D - central defense (d) SD Logroñés (e) Miedź Legnica, Las Rozas CF, At. Baleares, Adelaide Comets, SD Amorebieta, Dundee FC, SD Amorebieta, CD Mirandés, Athletic, CD Tenerife, Athletic, RC Celta, Athletic
*** Aussi - Alan Aussi (Ауссі Алан Гозанович) (a) 30/06/2001, Donetsk (Ukraine) (b) 1,87 (c) D - central defense (d) SD Ponferradina B (e) Dinamo Kiev II, Pyunik Yerevan, Dinamo Kiev II, Veres Rivne, Dinamo Kiev II, Torpedo Zhodino, Dinamo Kiev II, Slovan Liberec B, Dinamo Kiev II, BRW-VIK
*** Austbø - Edvin Austbø (a) 01/05/2005, Stavanger (Norway) (b) 1,72 (c) F - right winger (d) Viking FK (e) Viking FK II

*** Austin - Brandon Austin (Brandon Anthony Austin) (a) 08/01/1999, Hemel Hempstead (England) (b) 1,88 (c) G (d) Tottenham Hotspur (e) Orlando, Viborg FF
*** Austys - Eivydas Austys (a) 16/07/2006, ¿? (Lithuania) (b) - (c) M (d) FC Dziugas Telsiai B (e) -
*** Autret - Mathias Autret (a) 01/03/1991, Saint-Thégonnec (France) (b) 1,79 (c) M - attacking midfielder (d) SM Caen (e) AJ Auxerre, Stade Brestois, RC Lens, FC Lorient, SM Caen, FC Lorient, Brest B
*** Auvinen - Eero-Matti Auvinen (a) 05/03/1996, Janakkala (Finland) (b) 1,88 (c) D - central defense (d) FC Haka (e) Helsinki IFK, VPS, AC Oulu, FC Haka, Hämeenlinna
*** Auzmendi - Xabi Auzmendi (Xabier Auzmendi Arruabarrena) (a) 01/05/1997, Segura (Spain) (b) 1,80 (c) M - left midfielder (d) FK Kauno Zalgiris (e) Suduva, Sestao River, Lori Vanadzor, Real Sociedad C, Calahorra, Real Sociedad C, SD Beasain, Real Sociedad C
*** Auzqui - Carlos Auzqui (Carlos Daniel Auzqui) (a) 16/03/1991, Bernal (Argentina) (b) 1,80 (c) F - right winger (d) CA San Lorenzo de Almagro (e) Ferencváros, River Plate, Talleres, River Plate, Lanús, River Plate, Huracán, River Plate, Estudiantes
*** Avagimyan - Artur Avagimyan (a) 16/01/1997, Mariupol, Donetsk Oblast (Ukraine) (b) 1,72 (d) Chornomorets Odessa (e) Chornomorets, FK Oleksandriya, Chornomorets, FK Oleksandriya, Chornomorets, Alashkert CF, Arsenal Kyiv, FK Mariupol II, Shakhtar II, Illichivets 2, Shakhtar II
*** Avagyan - Arthur Avagyan (Արթուր Ավագյան) (a) 04/07/1987, Yerevan (Soviet Union, now in Armenia) (b) 1,72 (c) D - left back (d) FC Pyunik Yerevan (e) SC Noravank, FC Sevan, Lori Vanadzor, FC Urartu, Alashkert CF, Gandzasar, Sp. Semey, Gandzasar, Ararat Yerevan, Kilikia Yerevan, Gandzasar, Gandzasar II
*** Avagyan - Eduard Avagyan (Էդուարդ Ավագյան) (a) 21/03/1996, Yerevan (Armenia) (b) 1,77 (c) M - left midfielder (d) Lernayin Artsakh Goris (e) FC Syunik, BKMA Yerevan, FC Van, Gandzasar, Alashkert CF, Pyunik Yerevan, FC Noah, Banants II, Banants, Banants II
*** Avagyan - Henri Avagyan (Հենրի Միքայելի Ավագյան) (a) 16/01/1996, Yerevan (Armenia) (b) 1,89 (c) G (d) FC Pyunik Yerevan (e) BKMA Yerevan, SC Noravank, FC Van, Alashkert CF, Banants, MIKA Aschtarak, Mika Erewan II
*** Avanesyan - Artem Avanesyan (Аванесян Артём Арегович) (a) 17/07/1999, Zheleznodorozhnyi, Moskva Region (Russia) (b) 1,77 (c) F - right winger (d) FC Ararat-Armenia (e) Pyunik Yerevan, Ararat-Armenia, Ararat Moskva, CSKA Moskva II
*** Avdijaj - Donis Avdijaj (a) 25/08/1996, Osnabrück (Germany) (b) 1,73 (c) F - left winger (d) FC Zürich (e) TSV Hartberg, FC Zürich, TSV Hartberg, AEL Limassol, FC Emmen, Heart of Midlothian, Trabzonspor, Willem II, FC Schalke 04, Roda JC, FC Schalke 04, Sturm Graz, FC Schalke 04
*** Avdiu - Argel Avdiu (a) 25/09/2002, Tiranë (Albania) (b) - (c) F - right winger (d) KF Vora (e) KF Erzeni, Olimpic Tirana
*** Avdiu - Haris Avdiu (a) 21/10/1997, ¿? (Sweden) (b) 1,84 (c) F - center forward (d) Västra Frölunda IF (e) Västra Frölunda, IF Karlstad, Värnamo, Östersund, Värnamo, Angered BK, Utsiktens BK, Torslanda IK, Gunnilse IS
*** Avdullahu - Leon Avdullahu (a) 23/02/2004, Solothurn (Switzerland) (b) 1,85 (c) M - pivot (d) FC Basel (e) -
*** Avdulli - Qlirim Avdulli (a) 06/06/1999, Kromerizh (Czech Rep.) (b) 1,76 (c) D - left back (d) KF Ferizaj (e) FC Malisheva, KF Ulpiana, KF Drenica, FC Llapi, KF Arbëria, KF Hajvalia

*** Avdusinovic - Kenan Avdusinovic (a) 03/03/1998, Luxembourg (Luxembourg) (b) 1,71 (c) M - right midfielder (d) US Hostert (e) Swift Hesperange, Union Titus Petange, Differdange 03, Union Titus Petange, Swift Hesperange
*** Avdyli - Florent Avdyli (a) 10/07/1993, Prishtinë (RF Yugoslavia, now in Kosovo) (b) 1,86 (c) M - central midfielder (d) - (e) FC Malisheva, KF Drenica, KF Teuta, FC Prishtina, KF Teuta, KF Liria, KF Trepca, KF Feronikeli, KF Fushë Kosova, KF Hajvalia, Ramiz Sadiku, Kek-U Kastriot
*** Avdyli - Ilir Avdyli (a) 20/05/1990, Podujevë (Yugoslavia, now in Kosovo) (b) 1,89 (c) G (d) KF Llapi (e) KF Feronikeli, FK Kukësi, FC Kamza, Shkëndija, FC Llapi, KF Tirana, KF Hajvalia, KF Ferizaj
*** Avdyli (c) D (d) KF Drenica (e) - - Albion Avdyli (c) D (d) KF Drenica (e) -
*** Avellano - Bradley Avellano (Bradley Emile Avellano) (a) 01/11/2002, Gibraltar (Gibraltar) (b) 1,71 (c) G (d) Lynx FC (e) Red Imps Reserves, Lynx FC, Red Imps Reserves
*** Avellano - Leon Avellano (Leon Gerald Avellano) (a) 25/04/2004, Gibraltar (Gibraltar) (b) - (c) D - right back (d) Europa Point FC (e) La Rock FC, Europa Point FC, Lynx Reserve
*** Avenatti - Felipe Avenatti (Felipe Nicolás Avenatti Dovillabichus) (a) 26/04/1993, Montevideo (Uruguay) (b) 1,97 (c) F - center forward (d) KV Kortrijk (e) Standard Liège, Beerschot V.A., Standard Liège, Union St. Gilloise, Standard Liège, Royal Antwerp, Standard Liège, Bologna, KV Kortrijk, Bologna, Luqueño, Bologna, Luqueño, Ternana U., River Plate
*** Aventisian - Aventis Aventisian (Αβέντις Αβεντισιάν) (a) 17/08/2002, Thessaloniki (Greece) (b) 1,72 (c) D - left back (d) Go Ahead Eagles Deventer (e) PAOK B
*** Averhoff - Samuel Averhoff (Samuel Averhoff Alvarez) (a) 19/11/1999, Città di San Marino (San Marino) (b) 1,83 (c) D - right back (d) - (e) Domagnano, ACD Torconca
*** Avetisyan - Mark Avetisyan (Մարկ Ավետիսյան) (a) 24/06/2005, ¿? (Armenia) (b) - (c) D - central defense (d) BKMA Yerevan II (e) Pyunik Yerevan B
*** Avetisyan - Patvakan Avetisyan (Պատվական Արթուրի Ավետիսյան) (a) 24/08/2001, Nor Hachn (Armenia) (b) - (c) M - central midfielder (d) FC Syunik (e) Ararat-Armenia II, FC Noah, Ararat-Armenia II, BKMA Yerevan, Ararat-Armenia II, Ararat-Armenia
*** Avetisyan - Petros Avetisyan (Պետրոս Ավետիսյան) (a) 07/01/1996, Yerevan (Armenia) (b) 1,78 (c) M - attacking midfielder (d) FK Khimki (e) Maktaaral, Akzhayik, Shakhter K., FC Noah, Tobol Kostanay, Ararat-Armenia, Pyunik Yerevan, Banants, Pyunik Yerevan, Banants, Banants II
*** Avgerinos - Panagiotis Avgerinos (Παναγιώτης Αυγερινός) (a) 11/04/2003, ¿? (Greece) (b) 1,97 (c) G (d) Diagoras Rodou (e) Volos NPS, Aittitos Spaton, Triglia Rafinas, Panionios
*** Avgousti - Marios Avgousti (Μάριος Αυγουστή) (a) 28/01/2004, Limassol (Cyprus) (b) 1,77 (c) M - central midfielder (d) Apollon Limassol (e) -
*** Ávila - Chimy Ávila (Luis Ezequiel Ávila) (a) 06/02/1994, Rosario (Argentina) (b) 1,72 (c) F - center forward (d) CA Osasuna (e) San Lorenzo, SD Huesca, San Lorenzo, Tiro Federal
*** Ávila - Gastón Ávila (a) 30/09/2001, Rosario (Argentina) (b) 1,82 (c) D - left back (d) Royal Antwerp FC (e) Boca Juniors, Rosario Central, Boca Juniors, Boca Juniors II, Rosario Central II
*** Avilov - Vladimir Avilov (a) 10/03/1995, Maardu ((b) 1,87 (c) D - central defense (d) Kalju FC (e) FCI Tallinn, Maardu LM

*** Avinel - Cédric Avinel (Cédric Mickael Avinel) (a) 11/09/1986, Paris (France) (b) 1,87 (c) D - central defense (d) AC Ajaccio (e) Clermont Foot, Cannes, FC Gueugnon, Watford, Stafford Rangers, Watford, US Créteil-Lusitanos, US Créteil B
*** Avlonitis - Anastasios Avlonitis (Αναστάσιος Αυλωνίτης) (a) 01/01/1990, Chalkida (Greece) (b) 1,90 (c) D - central defense (d) Panserraikos (e) Apollon Limassol, Ascoli, Sturm Graz, Panathinaikos, Heart of Midlothian, Olympiakos, Sturm Graz, Olympiakos, Panionios, AO Kavala, AO Egaleo, Ilysiakos, AO Egaleo, Chalkineos
*** Avounou - Durel Avounou (a) 25/09/1997, Brazzaville (Congo) (b) 1,79 (c) M - central midfielder (d) CFR Cluj (e) Ümraniyespor, Le Mans FC, SM Caen, US Orléans, SM Caen, SM Caen B
*** Avraam - Andreas Avraam (Ανδρέας Αβρααμ) (a) 06/06/1987, Lárnaca (Cyprus) (b) 1,71 (c) M - left midfielder (d) - (e) Karmiotissa, Anorthosis, AEL Limassol, AE Larisa, Anorthosis, Omonia Nicosia, Apollon Limassol, Omonia Aradippou, Protathlima Cyta
*** Avraham - Aviv Avraham (אברהם אביב) (a) 30/03/1996, Afula (Israel) (b) 1,73 (c) M - attacking midfielder (d) Maccabi Netanya (e) -
*** Avram - Costel Avram (a) 11/06/2002, ¿? (Romania) (b) - (c) D - central defense (d) CSA Steaua (e) Chindia, Dunarea Calarasi, Astra II
*** Avram - Cristian Avram (a) 27/07/1994, Anenii Noi (Moldova) (b) 1,93 (c) G (d) Araz-Naxcivan Nakchivan (e) Petrocub, FC Buzau, Petrocub, Dinamo-Auto, Dacia, Ac. Chisinau
*** Avram - Raul Avram (a) 20/06/1993, Prundu Bârgăului (Romania) (b) 1,95 (c) G (d) FC Metaloglobus Bucharest (e) Minaur, Petrolul, FC Farul 1920, Dacia U. Braila, Petrolul, FC Botosani, Miroslava, FC Botosani, FC Botosani II
*** Avramovski - Daniel Avramovski (Даниел Аврамовски) (a) 20/02/1995, Skopje (North Macedonia) (b) 1,84 (c) M - attacking midfielder (d) FK Sarajevo (e) Kayserispor, Vardar, Olimpija, Vojvodina, Olimpija, Crvena zvezda, OFK Beograd, Crvena zvezda, Rabotnicki, Makedonija, Rabotnicki
*** Avto - Avto (ავთანდილ ებრალიძე, Avtandil Ebralidze) (a) 03/10/1991, Tbilisi (Georgia) (b) 1,76 (c) F - left winger (d) Leixões SC (e) Anorthosis, Doxa Katokopias, Leixões, FC Voluntari, Nacional, Chaves, Académico Viseu, Gil Vicente, Oliveirense, Esp. Lagos
*** Awany - Timothy Dennis Awany (a) 06/08/1996, ¿? (Israel) (b) 1,83 (c) D - central defense (d) FC Ashdod (e) Kampala CC
*** Awaziem - Chidozie Awaziem (Chidozie Collins Awaziem) (a) 01/01/1997, Enugu (Nigeria) (b) 1,89 (c) D - central defense (d) Boavista Porto FC (e) Hajduk Split, Boavista, Alanyaspor, Boavista, FC Porto, Boavista, FC Porto, CD Leganés, FC Porto, Çaykur Rizespor, FC Porto, FC Porto B, FC Nantes, FC Porto B, FC Porto, FC Porto B
*** Awlesu - Christian Awlesu (a) 23/04/2003, ¿? (Ghana) (b) - (c) M (d) - (e) Metta, Zilina Africa
*** Awoniyi - Taiwo Awoniyi (Taiwo Michael Awoniyi) (a) 12/08/1997, Ilorin (Nigeria) (b) 1,83 (c) F - center forward (d) Nottingham Forest (e) Union Berlin, Liverpool, Union Berlin, Liverpool, Mainz 05, Liverpool, Excelsior Mouscron, Liverpool, KAA Gent, Liverpool, Excelsior Mouscron, Liverpool, NEC Nijmegen, Liverpool, FSV Frankfurt, Liverpool
*** Awoudja - Maxime Awoudja (Maxime Aglago Awoudja) (a) 02/02/1998, München (Germany) (b) 1,88 (c) D - central defense (d) - (e) Excelsior, VfB Stuttgart, WSG Tirol, VfB Stuttgart, Türkgücü Münch., VfB Stuttgart, FC Bayern II

*** Awwad - Mohammad Awwad (עואד מוחמד) (a) 09/06/1997, Tamra (Israel) (b) 1,82 (c) F - attacking midfielder (d) - (e) Bnei Sakhnin, Maccabi Haifa, M. Petah Tikva, Maccabi Haifa, Lech Poznan, Maccabi Haifa

*** Axenti - Cristian Axenti (a) 04/01/2004, ¿? (Moldova) (b) 1,82 (c) D - central defense (d) FC Petrocub Hîncești (e) Real Succes

*** Ayad - Liam Ayad (Blie Bi Bah Liam Ayad) (a) 27/06/1998, Vavoua (Ivory Coast) (b) 1,87 (c) M - central midfielder (d) FK Radnicki Niš (e) Santa Lucia FC, Salamanca CF, At. Baleares, Extremadura, CD Ebro, Extremadura, Extremadura B

*** Ayala - Jesús Ayala (Jesús María Ayala Sánchez) (a) 16/11/1993, Algeciras (Spain) (b) - (c) F - left winger (d) Mons Calpe SC (e) Guadiaro, San Roque Cádiz, Los Barrios, Algeciras CF, FC Vilafranca, San Roque Cádiz, Recr. Huelva B, Algeciras CF, Recr. Huelva B

*** Ayankhan - Dunaybek Ayankhan (Аянхан Дунайбек) (a) 08/03/2000, Almaty Region (Kazakhstan) (b) 1,87 (c) F - center forward (d) - (e) Maktaaral, Okzhetpes II

*** Ayari - Taha Ayari (a) 10/05/2005, Solna (Sweden) (b) 1,77 (c) F - left winger (d) AIK Solna (e) -

*** Ayari - Yasin Ayari (Yasin Abbas Ayari) (a) 06/10/2003, Solna (Sweden) (b) 1,72 (c) M - central midfielder (d) Brighton & Hove Albion (e) AIK

*** Ayazbaev - Nurlybek Ayazbaev (Аязбаев Нурлыбек Куанышкерейұлы) (a) 24/01/1991, Aktau (Soviet Union, now in Kazakhstan) (b) 1,83 (c) G (d) Kaspiy Aktau (e) Kaspiy Aktau, Zhetysu, Kaspiy Aktau, Zhetysu, Kaspiy Aktau

*** Aydin - Dijlan Aydin (Abdullah Dijlan Aydın) (a) 16/06/2000, Diyarbakir (Turkey) (b) 1,83 (c) M - central midfielder (d) Amed SK (e) Amed SK, Istanbulspor, Karacabey Belediye, Istanbulspor, Karacabey Belediye, Istanbulspor, Karacabey Belediye, Istanbulspor

*** Aydin - Hakan Aydin (Hakan Aydın) (a) 05/02/2003, Trabzon (Turkey) (b) 1,92 (c) G (d) Sebat Gençlik Spor (e) Sebat Gençlik, Trabzonspor

*** Aydin - Mehmet Aydin (Mehmet Can Aydin) (a) 09/02/2002, Würselen (Germany) (b) 1,80 (c) D - right back (d) Trabzonspor (e) Trabzonspor, FC Schalke 04

*** Aydin - Oguz Aydin (Oğuz Aydın) (a) 27/10/2000, Den Haag (Netherlands) (b) 1,83 (c) F - left winger (d) Alanyaspor (e) Bucaspor 1928, Karacabey Belediye, 1928 Bucaspor, Bucaspor

*** Aydin - Okan Aydin (Okan Aydın) (a) 08/05/1994, Würselen (Germany) (b) 1,72 (c) M - attacking midfielder (d) - (e) Debrecen, TSV Hartberg, FC Wacker, JX Beidamen, Austria Klagenfurt, Viktoria Berlin, Austria Klagenfurt, Viktoria Berlin, Chemnitzer FC, Rot-Weiß Erfurt, Eskisehirspor, Bayer Leverkusen II

*** Aydin - Taylan Utku Aydin (Taylan Utku Aydın) (a) 10/02/2006, Istambul (Turkey) (b) - (c) D - central defense (d) Kasimpasa (e) -

*** Aydogdu - Soner Aydogdu (Soner Aydoğdu) (a) 05/01/1991, Ankara (Turkey) (b) 1,80 (c) M - central midfielder (d) Samsunspor (e) Antalyaspor, Basaksehir, Göztepe, Basaksehir, Akhisarspor, Trabzonspor, Genclerbirligi, Hacettepe, Genclerbirligi

*** Aydogmus - Berkay Aydogmus (Berkay Aydoğmuş) (a) 07/01/2004, Canakkale (Turkey) (b) 1,80 (c) M - central midfielder (d) Basaksehir FK (e) Nazilli Bld.

*** Ayer Boya - Keanin Ayer Boya (a) 21/04/2000, Johannesburg (South Africa) (b) 1,72 (c) M - right midfielder (d) Sandefjord Fotball (e) Varbergs BoIS, Right to Dream

*** Ayew - André Ayew (André Morgan Rami Ayew) (a) 17/12/1989, Seclin (France) (b) 1,75 (c) F - left winger (d) - (e) Nottingham Forest, Al-Sadd SC, Swansea City, Fenerbahce, Swansea City, West Ham Utd., Swansea City, Ol. Marseille, AC Arles-Avignon, Ol. Marseille, FC Lorient, Ol. Marseille, Ol. Marseille B

*** Ayew - Ibrahim Ayew (Ibrahim Abdul Rahim Ayew) (a) 16/04/1988, Tamale (Ghana) (b) 1,78 (c) D - right back (d) Lincoln Red Imps FC (e) Bruno's Magpies, Europa FC, Asante Kotoko, Lierse SK, Zamalek, Eleven Wise, Nania FC

*** Ayew - Jordan Ayew (Jordan Pierre Ayew) (a) 11/09/1991, Marseille (France) (b) 1,82 (c) F - center forward (d) Crystal Palace (e) Swansea City, Crystal Palace, Swansea City, Aston Villa, FC Lorient, Ol. Marseille, FC Sochaux, Ol. Marseille, Ol. Marseille B

*** Aygün - Yavuz Aygün (a) 27/06/1996, Trabzon (Turkey) (b) 1,93 (c) G (d) Alanyaspor (e) Isparta 32 Spor, Karagümrük, Boluspor, Yeni Orduspor, Göztepe, Trabzonspor

*** Ayhan - Kaan Ayhan (a) 10/11/1994, Gelsenkirchen (Germany) (b) 1,85 (c) D - central defense (d) Galatasaray (e) Sassuolo, Galatasaray, Sassuolo, Fortuna Düsseldorf, FC Schalke 04, Eintracht, FC Schalke 04

*** Ayik - Onur Ayik (Onur Ayık) (a) 28/01/1990, Walsrode (Germany) (b) 1,83 (c) F - right winger (d) Ümraniyespor (e) Tuzlaspor, Akhisarspor, Karabükspor, Elazigspor, FC Oberneuland, Werder Bremen, Werder Bremen II

*** Ayina - Loick Ayina (Loick Denis Henry Ayina) (a) 20/04/2003, Brazzaville (Congo) (b) 1,83 (c) D - central defense (d) Huddersfield Town (e) Huddersfield B, Dundee United, Huddersfield B, Boston Utd.

*** Ayinde - James Ayinde (James Gbenga Ayinde) (a) 17/09/2001, ¿? (Nigeria) (b) - (c) F (d) KS Lushnja (e) KF Egnatia, KS Lushnja

*** Ayling - Luke Ayling (Luke David Ayling) (a) 25/08/1991, Lambeth, London (England) (b) 1,83 (c) D - right back (d) Leeds United (e) Bristol City, Yeovil Town, Arsenal Reserves, Yeovil Town, Arsenal Reserves

*** Aymanov - Alen Aymanov (Айманов Ален Кайратович) (a) 02/06/2002, Almaty (Kazakhstan) (b) 1,78 (c) F - left winger (d) Yelimay Semey (e) Yelimay, Kairat Almaty, FK Turan, Kairat Almaty, Kairat Moskva, Kairat Almaty, Kairat-Zhas, Akad. Ontustik

*** Aymanov - Marlen Aymanov (Айманов Марлен Кайратулы) (a) 14/06/1999, Almaty (Kazakhstan) (b) 1,91 (c) F - center forward (d) FC Khan Tengri (e) FK Ekibastuz, Maktaaral, FK Turan, Kairat-Zhas, Kairat II

*** Aymbetov - Abat Aymbetov (Абат Қайратұлы Айымбетов) (a) 07/08/1995, Kyzylorda (Kazakhstan) (b) 1,84 (c) F - center forward (d) FC Astana (e) KS Samara, FC Astana, KS Samara, Kairat Almaty, Aktobe, Aktobe II

*** Ayoub - Yassin Ayoub (أيوب ياسين) (a) 06/03/1994, Al Hoceima (Morocco) (b) 1,74 (c) M - central midfielder (d) Excelsior Rotterdam (e) Panathinaikos, Feyenoord, FC Utrecht

*** Aytbaev - Berik Aytbaev (Айтбаев Берик Ромазанулы) (a) 26/06/1991, Taraz (Soviet Union, now in Kazakhstan) (b) 1,84 (c) D - central defense (d) Yelimay Semey (e) Taraz, Irtysh, Aktobe, Atyrau, Taraz, Atyrau, Taraz, Taraz-Karatau

*** Ayunga - Jonah Ayunga (Jonah Ananias Paul Ayunga) (a) 24/05/1997, Beaminster (England) (b) 1,85 (c) F - center forward (d) St. Mirren FC (e) FC Morecambe, Bristol Rovers, Havant & Waterlooville, Sutton Utd., Havant & Waterlooville, Sutton Utd., Poole Town, Galway United, Sligo Rovers, Burgess Hill, Dorchester

*** Ayunts - Tigran Ayunts (Տիգրան Այունց) (a) 15/03/2000, Yerevan (Armenia) (b) 1,81 (c) M - central midfielder (d) FC Syunik (e) Gandzasar, FC Urartu, Urartu II

*** Ayupov - Timur Ayupov (Аюпов Тимур Ансарович) (a) 26/07/1993, Moskva (Russia) (b) 1,83 (c) M - pivot (d) Ural Ekaterimburgo (e) Orenburg, Nizhny Novgorod, Rubin Kazán II, Rubin 2, LFK Rubin Kazan

*** Ayvazov - Anatoliy Ayvazov (Айвазов Анатолий Ашотович) (a) 08/06/1996, Vladikavkaz (Russia) (b) 1,85 (c) G (d) Alashkert Yerevan CF (e) Chaika Pes., FC Noah, FC Urartu, Shirak Gyumri, Pyunik Yerevan, Strogino Moskva

*** Ayvazyan - Khariton Ayvazyan (Խարիտոն Այվազյան) (a) 08/11/2003, Akhalkalaki (Georgia) (b) 1,81 (c) D - right back (d) BKMA Yerevan (e) BKMA Yerevan, FC Urartu, Urartu II

*** Ayvazyan - Michel Ayvazyan (Միշել Այվազյան) (a) 21/06/2005, ¿? (Armenia) (b) - (c) M - central midfielder (d) FC Ararat-Armenia II (e) -

*** Ayvazyan - Poghos Ayvazyan (Պողոս Այվազյան) (a) 09/06/1995, Vagharshapat (Armenia) (b) 1,86 (c) G (d) Lernayin Artsakh Goris (e) Shirak Gyumri, Ararat Yerevan, Mika Erewan II

*** Ayvazyan - Vahagn Ayvazyan (Վահագն Այվազյան) (a) 16/04/1992, Yerevan (Armenia) (b) 1,81 (c) D - right back (d) - (e) Alashkert CF, FC Van, FC Urartu, Lori Vanadzor, Al-Nasr SC, FC Urartu, Impuls Dilijan, Ararat II

*** Ayzen - Shay Lee Ayzen (איזן לי שי) (a) 27/08/2000, ¿? (Israel) (b) - (c) M - pivot (d) Bnei Yehuda Tel Aviv (e) B. Jerusalem, Hapoel Tel Aviv

*** Azadov - Parviz Azadov (Pərviz Çingiz oğlu Azadov) (a) 19/10/2000, ¿? (Azerbaijan) (b) - (c) M - pivot (d) Zira FK (e) Shamakhi, FC Shamakhi 2

*** Azango - Philip Azango (Philip Azango Elayo) (a) 21/05/1997, Jos Plateau (Nigeria) (b) 1,67 (c) F - left winger (d) Spartak Trnava (e) AS Trencin, KAA Gent, AS Trencin, Plateau United, Nasarawa United

*** Azaria - Dan Azaria (עזריה דן) (a) 29/08/1995, ¿? (Israel) (b) 1,76 (c) M - central midfielder (d) Beitar Jerusalem (e) H. Kfar Saba, Hapoel Tel Aviv, H. Kfar Saba, Ness Ziona, H. Kiryat Ono

*** Azarkan - Marouan Azarkan (a) 08/12/2001, Rotterdam (Netherlands) (b) 1,65 (c) F - right winger (d) FC Utrecht (e) Feyenoord, Excelsior, Feyenoord, NAC Breda

*** Azarovi - Irakli Azarovi (ირაკლი აზაროვი) (a) 21/02/2002, Batumi (Georgia) (b) 1,79 (c) D - left back (d) Crvena zvezda Beograd (e) Dinamo Batumi, Dinamo Tbilisi

*** Azarovs - Timurs Azarovs (a) 23/03/2006, ¿? (Latvia) (b) 1,90 (c) D - central defense (d) - (e) Spartaks

*** Azatov - Arsen Azatov (Азатов Арсен Азатович) (a) 30/08/2003, Taldykorgan (Kazakhstan) (b) 1,80 (c) D - left back (d) Kairat-Zhas (e) -

*** Azatskyi - Oleksandr Azatskyi (Азацький Олександр Олександрович) (a) 13/01/1994, Kharkiv (Ukraine) (b) 1,92 (c) D - central defense (d) Arka Gdynia (e) Dinamo Batumi, Banik Ostrava, Fastav Zlin, Banik Ostrava, Torpedo Kutaisi, Banik Ostrava, Torpedo Kutaisi, Banik Ostrava, Chornomorets, Dinamo Kiev II, Dynamo 2 Kyiv, Metalist II

*** Azemovic - Emir Azemovic (Емир Аземовић) (a) 06/01/1997, Novi Pazar (RF Yugoslavia, now in Serbia) (b) 1,93 (c) D - central defense (d) FK Novi Pazar (e) Kolubara, NK Aluminij, Rakow, FK Zemun, Domžale, Benfica B, Fafe, Benfica B

*** Azevedo - Dyjan Azevedo (Dyjan Carlos de Azevedo) (a) 23/06/1991, Dois Córregos (Brazil) (b) 1,68 (c) F - left winger (d) - (e) Spartak Trnava, Banik Ostrava, Paris FC, Banik Ostrava, Bardejov, Moldava, Honvéd II

*** Azhil - Ayman Azhil (a) 10/04/2001, Düsseldorf (Germany) (b) 1,75 (c) M - pivot (d) Borussia Dortmund II (e) Bayer Leverkusen, RKC Waalwijk, Bayer Leverkusen

*** Azhimov - Alisher Azhimov (Ажимов Алишер Муратович) (a) 29/05/2001, Aktyubinsk (Kazakhstan) (b) 1,78 (c) D - left back (d) FK Aktobe (e) -

*** Aziamale - Christoph Aziamale (Yao Christoph Aziamale) (a) 18/12/1997, ¿? (Germany) (b) 1,83 (c) F - right winger (d) - (e) Bala, Sutton Common, Basildon Utd.,

Sittingbourne FC, Cefn Druids, Market Drayton, Stafford Rangers, Bangor City, Rhyl FC

*** Aziz - Aziz (Abdul-Aziz Yakubu) (a) 10/11/1998, Tamale (Ghana) (b) 1,87 (c) F - center forward (d) Wuhan Three Towns (e) WH Three Towns, Rio Ave, Vitória Guimarães, Rio Ave, Vitória Guimarães, Estoril Praia, Vitória Guimarães, Vizela, Vitória Guimarães B, Vizela, Charity Stars

*** Aziz - Keita Lanzeni Aziz (a) 28/12/1996, ¿? (Ivory Coast) (b) 1,89 (c) M - central midfielder (d) - (e) SC Gjilani, Majees SC

*** Aziz - Serdar Aziz (a) 23/10/1990, Bursa (Turkey) (b) 1,83 (c) D - central defense (d) Fenerbahce (e) Galatasaray, Bursaspor, Merinosspor

*** Aziz Soumah - Abdoul Aziz Soumah (a) 22/01/1993, ¿? (San Marino) (b) - (c) D - central defense (d) SC Faetano (e) Riccione, Libertas

*** Azizli - Rashad Azizli (Rəşad Faiq oğlu Əzizli) (a) 01/01/1994, Baku (Azerbaijan) (b) 1,85 (c) G (d) FK Qabala (e) Shamakhi, Neftchi Baku, FK Sabail, Neftchi Baku, Zira FK, Keshla, Sumqayit, Neftchi Baku, FK Sabail, AZAL, Ravan Baku, Simurq, Neftchi Baku

*** Azizyan - Erik Azizyan (Էրիկ Ազիզյան) (a) 04/03/2000, Yerevan (Armenia) (b) 1,70 (c) M - attacking midfielder (d) FC Ararat Yerevan (e) BKMA Yerevan, Pyunik Yerevan, FC Van, Pyunik Yerevan, Ararat-Armenia II, Ararat-Armenia, Ararat-Armenia

*** Azmoun - Sardar Azmoun (آزمون سردار) (a) 01/01/1995, Gonbad-e Kavus, Golestan (Iran) (b) 1,86 (c) F - center forward (d) Bayer 04 Leverkusen (e) Zenit, Rubin Kazan, Rostov, Rubin Kazan, Rostov, Rubin Kazan, Rostov, Rubin Kazan, Rubin Kazán II

*** Aznar - Victor Aznar (Victor Wehbi Aznar Ussen) (a) 17/10/2002, São Paulo (Brazil) (b) 1,89 (c) G (d) Cádiz CF Mirandilla (e) -

*** Aznar Fernández - Christian Aznar Fernández (a) 10/01/2003, ¿? (Spain) (b) - (c) M - central midfielder (d) St Joseph's FC (e) -

*** Azodo - Robbie Azodo (Robbie Floyd Odimegwu Azodo) (a) 23/04/2001, Vantaa (Finland) (b) 1,76 (c) F - right winger (d) Helsinki IFK (e) AB Argir, HJK Klubi 04, FC Honka II, Pallokerho

*** Azong - Conrad Azong (a) 27/03/1993, Kumba (Cameroon) (b) 1,90 (c) F (d) FC UNA Strassen (e) Progrès Niederkorn, SF Lotte, VfL Oldenburg, VfB Oldenb. II, VfB Oldenburg, Holst. Kiel II, SC Victoria, Hannover 96 II

*** Azoulay - Ethane Azoulay (אזולאי איתן) (a) 26/05/2002, Paris (France) (b) 1,68 (c) M - pivot (d) Maccabi Netanya (e) M. Petah Tikva

*** Azpilicueta - César Azpilicueta (César Azpilicueta Tanco) (a) 28/08/1989, Pamplona (Spain) (b) 1,78 (c) D - right back (d) Atlético de Madrid (e) Chelsea, Ol. Marseille, CA Osasuna, Osasuna Prom.

*** Azrual - Dolev Azrual (אזרואל דולב) (a) 20/02/1998, ¿? (Israel) (b) - (c) D - left back (d) Hapoel Hadera (e) M. Bnei Reineh, Maccabi Herzlya, Hapoel Hadera, Maccabi Herzlya, M. Ata Bialik, M. Kiryat Ata, M. Zur Shalom, Maccabi Tamra, M. Zur Shalom

*** Azubuike - Okechukwu Azubuike (Okechukwu Godson Azubuike) (a) 19/04/1997, Katsina (Nigeria) (b) 1,70 (c) M - pivot (d) Caykur Rizespor (e) Basaksehir, Yeni Malatyaspor, Basaksehir, Sivasspor, Basaksehir, Pyramids FC, Basaksehir, Pyramids FC, Çaykur Rizespor, Pyramids FC, Yeni Malatyaspor, Bayelsa, Niger Tornadoes

*** Azulay - Shlomi Azulay (אזולאי שלומי) (a) 18/10/1989, Tiberias (Israel) (b) 1,86 (c) F - center forward (d) Maccabi Bnei Reineh (e) Hapoel Tel Aviv, Astra Giurgiu, B. Jerusalem, Bnei Sakhnin, Kiryat Shmona, Bnei Sakhnin, Hapoel Tel Aviv,

Maccabi Haifa, B. Jerusalem, Maccabi Haifa, Kiryat Shmona, Maccabi Haifa, H. Kfar Saba
*** Azulay - Shlomi Azulay (אזולאי שלומי) (a) 30/03/1990, Hadera (Israel) (b) 1,86 (c) M - central midfielder (d) FC Ashdod (e) Hapoel Tel Aviv, FC Ashdod, Maccabi Haifa, Hapoel Haifa, Maccabi Haifa, Maccabi Tel Aviv, Kiryat Shmona, Maccabi Tel Aviv, B. Jerusalem, H Rishon leZion, B. Jerusalem, H Rishon leZion, Hapoel Haifa, Maccabi Haifa, Hapoel Herzliya, Maccabi Haifa, H. Petah Tikva, Maccabi Haifa
*** Azzi - Hugo Azzi (Hugo Bernard Louis Ginés Azzi) (a) 23/12/2003, Sète (France) (b) 1,81 (c) D - left back (d) - (e) Botev II, Krumovgrad, Botev II
*** Azzopardi - Ayrton Azzopardi (a) 12/09/1993, ¿? (Malta) (b) 1,81 (c) M - attacking midfielder (d) Gudja United FC (e) San Gwann FC, Floriana, Tarxien, Sliema Wanderers, Tarxien, Sliema Wanderers, Tarxien, Hibernians FC, Pembroke, Hibernians FC, Msida SJ, Hibernians FC
*** Azzopardi - Jake Azzopardi (a) 13/02/2006, ¿? (Malta) (b) - (c) M (d) - (e) Valletta FC
*** Azzopardi - Jamie Azzopardi (a) 01/09/1997, ¿? (Malta) (b) - (c) G (d) Zebbug Rangers FC (e) Gudja United FC, Qormi FC, Gzira Utd., Qormi FC, Gzira Utd., Rabat Ajax
*** Azzopardi - Miguel Azzopardi (a) 24/05/2004, ¿? (Malta) (b) - (c) D - central defense (d) Zabbar St. Patrick FC (e) -
*** Azzopardi - Zeron Azzopardi (a) 09/08/2004, ¿? (Malta) (b) - (c) M (d) Hamrun Spartans (e) -
*** Ba - Abdoulaye Ba (a) 01/01/1991, St. Louis (Senegal) (b) 1,97 (c) D - central defense (d) CD Tondela (e) Sabah FK, Arouca, Moreirense, FC Dinamo, Rayo Vallecano, RC Deportivo, Rayo Vallecano, FC Porto, 1860 München, FC Porto, Alanyaspor, FC Porto, Fenerbahce, FC Porto, Rayo Vallecano, FC Porto, Vitória Guimarães, FC Porto, Académica Coimbra, FC Porto, SC Covilhã, FC Porto
*** Ba - Abou Ba (Abou-Malal Ba) (a) 29/07/1998, Saint-Dié (France) (b) 1,83 (c) M - pivot (d) FC Villefranche-Beaujolais (e) FC Nantes B, RFC Seraing, FC Nantes B, Alessandria, FC Nantes B, Cosenza, FC Nantes B, FC Nantes, Aris Thessaloniki, FC Nantes, AS Nancy, AS Nancy B
*** Ba - El-Hadji Ba (a) 05/03/1993, Paris (France) (b) 1,83 (c) M - pivot (d) - (e) Apollon Limassol, Guingamp, RC Lens, FC Sochaux, Stabæk, Charlton Ath., Sunderland, SC Bastia, Sunderland, Le Havre AC B
*** Ba - Lamine Ba (a) 24/08/1997, Villepinte (France) (b) 1,89 (c) D - central defense (d) NK Varazdin (e) Progrès Niederkorn, Doxa Katokopias, Virtus Entella
*** Ba - Mahamadou Ba (a) 21/09/1999, Bamako (Mali) (b) 1,75 (c) M - pivot (d) Tuzlaspor (e) Adana Demirspor, Istanbulspor, Adana Demirspor, Menemen FK, BB Erzurumspor, Bandirmaspor, BB Erzurumspor
*** Ba - Ousseynou Ba (a) 11/11/1995, Dakar (Senegal) (b) 1,92 (c) D - central defense (d) Olympiakos El Pireo (e) G. Ajaccio, Olympiakos, G. Ajaccio, CNEPS Excel.
*** Ba - Sanoussy Ba (a) 05/01/2004, Hof (Germany) (b) 1,84 (c) D - left back (d) LASK (e) LASK, RB Leipzig
*** Ba - Soulemane Ba (a) 19/08/2003, ¿? (Ivory Coast) (b) - (c) M - central midfielder (d) Glacis United (e) San Jorge
*** Ba Loua - Adriel Ba Loua (Adriel D'Avila Ba Loua) (a) 25/07/1996, Yopougon (Ivory Coast) (b) 1,70 (c) F - right winger (d) Lech Poznan (e) Viktoria Plzen, Karvina, ASEC Mimosas, Karvina, ASEC Mimosas, Vejle BK, ASEC Mimosas, LOSC Lille B, ASEC Mimosas

*** Baak - Florian Baak (a) 18/03/1999, Berlin (Germany) (b) 1,91 (c) D - central defense (d) FC Honka (e) FC Winterthur, Hertha BSC II, Hertha Berlin
*** Baas - Julian Baas (a) 16/04/2002, Dordrecht (Netherlands) (b) - (c) M - central midfielder (d) Excelsior Rotterdam (e) -
*** Baas - Youri Baas (a) 17/03/2003, Oostvoorne (Netherlands) (b) 1,82 (c) D - left back (d) NEC Nijmegen (e) NEC Nijmegen, Ajax, Ajax B
*** Baba - Abdul Rahman Baba (Baba Abdul Rahman) (a) 02/07/1994, Tamale (Ghana) (b) 1,79 (c) D - left back (d) PAOK Thessaloniki (e) Chelsea, Reading, Chelsea, Reading, Chelsea, PAOK, Chelsea, RCD Mallorca, Chelsea, Stade Reims, Chelsea, FC Schalke 04, Chelsea, FC Schalke 04, Chelsea, FC Augsburg, Greuther Fürth, Dreams FC, Asante Kotoko, Dreams FC
*** Baba - Iddrisu Baba (Iddrisu Baba Mohammed) (a) 22/01/1996, Accra (Ghana) (b) 1,82 (c) M - central midfielder (d) UD Almería (e) UD Almería, RCD Mallorca, RCD Mallorca B, Barakaldo CF, RCD Mallorca B, CD Leganés B, RCD Mallorca B
*** Baba - Sudais Ali Baba (a) 25/08/2000, Kano (Nigeria) (b) 1,85 (c) F - center forward (d) Panserraikos (e) Spartak Trnava, Asteras Tripoli, AO Xanthi, Asteras Tripoli
*** Babacan - Alperen Babacan (a) 18/07/1997, Denizli (Turkey) (b) 1,85 (c) D - central defense (d) Genclerbirligi Ankara (e) Ankaragücü, Akhisarspor, Denizlispor, Akhisarspor, Denizlispor, Akhisarspor, Denizlispor
*** Babacan - Volkan Babacan (a) 11/08/1988, Antalya (Turkey) (b) 1,92 (c) G (d) Basaksehir FK (e) Manisaspor, Fenerbahce, Manisaspor, Fenerbahce, Kayserispor, Fenerbahce, Istanbulspor
*** Babacar - Khouma Babacar (Khouma El Hadji Babacar) (a) 17/03/1993, Thiès (Senegal) (b) 1,85 (c) F - center forward (d) FC Copenhague (e) Sassuolo, Alanyaspor, Sassuolo, Lecce, Sassuolo, Fiorentina, Sassuolo, Fiorentina, Modena, Fiorentina, Padova, Fiorentina, Racing, Fiorentina
*** Babacic - Jasmin Babacic (Јасмин Бабациц) (a) 14/06/2003, ¿? (RF Yugoslavia, now in Montenegro) (b) 1,78 (c) M - central midfielder (d) FC Mondercange (e) -
*** Babaev - Ulvi Babaev (Бабаев Ульви Лачын Оглы) (a) 30/03/2004, Khimki, Moskau Oblast (Russia) (b) 1,72 (c) F - left winger (d) Dinamo 2 Moskva (e) Dinamo Moskva II
*** Babakhanov - Dzhurakhon Babakhanov (Бабаханов Джурахон Юлдашович) (a) 31/10/1991, Taraz (Soviet Union, now in Kazakhstan) (b) 1,90 (c) G (d) Qyzyljar Petropavlovsk (e) Taraz, Okzhetpes, Irtysh, Zhetysu, Taraz, Okzhetpes, Taraz, Taraz-Karatau
*** Babaliev - Georgi Babaliev (Георги Николаев Бабалиев) (a) 14/05/2001, Karnobat (Bulgaria) (b) 1,73 (c) M - left midfielder (d) FC Ararat Yerevan (e) Spartak Varna, Lokomotiv Sofia, Sozopol, Vitosha
*** Babati - Benjamin Babati (a) 29/11/1995, Zalaegerszeg (Hungary) (b) 1,76 (c) F - right winger (d) Mezőkövesd Zsóry FC (e) ETO FC Győr, Mezőkövesd, Zalaegerszeg
*** Babatunde - Michel Babatunde (a) 24/12/1992, Lagos (Nigeria) (b) 1,79 (c) M - attacking midfielder (d) KF Laçi (e) Wydad AC, Qatar SC, Raja Casablanca, Dnipro, Volyn Lutsk, Kryvbas, FC Heartland
*** Babayan - Edgar Babayan (Էդգար Բաբայան) (a) 28/10/1995, Berlin (Germany) (b) 1,80 (c) F - left winger (d) Randers FC (e) Vejle BK, Pafos FC, Riga, Hobro IK, Randers FC, Hobro IK, Randers FC
*** Babayev - Hüseyn Babayev (Hüseyn Babayev) (a) 01/01/2003, ¿? (Azerbaijan) (b) 1,80 (c) D - central defense (d) Neftchi 2 Baku (e) -

*** Babboni - Daniele Babboni (a) 09/01/2000, Città di San Marino (San Marino) (b) 1,81 (c) F - center forward (d) FC Domagnano (e) Murata, Tropical Coriano

*** Babec - Hrvoje Babec (a) 28/07/1999, Virovitica (Croatia) (b) 1,87 (c) M - pivot (d) Riga FC (e) HNK Gorica, NK Virovitica

*** Babenko - Ruslan Babenko (Бабенко Руслан Олександрович) (a) 08/07/1992, Dnipropetrovsk (Ukraine) (b) 1,72 (c) M - central midfielder (d) SK Dnipro-1 (e) Metalist, FK Polissya, Olimpik Donetsk, Rakow, Chornomorets, Zorya Lugansk, Bodø/Glimt, Stal D., Dnipro, Volyn Lutsk, Dnipro, Dnipro II

*** Babic - Andro Babic (Andro Babić) (a) 08/09/2004, Rijeka (Croatia) (b) 1,81 (c) M - pivot (d) HSK Posusje (e) HSK Posusje, HNK Rijeka, NK Krk

*** Babic - Anto Babic (Anto Babić) (a) 25/01/2000, Niksic (RF Yugoslavia, Montenegro) (b) 1,85 (c) D - central defense (d) FK Sutjeska Niksic (e) Buducnost Podgorica, OFK Grbalj, Sutjeska Niksic, Sutjeska II

*** Babic - Boris Babic (a) 10/11/1997, Walenstadt (Switzerland) (b) 1,80 (c) F - center forward (d) FC Lugano (e) FC St. Gallen, FC Vaduz, FC St. Gallen, FC Biel-Bienne

*** Babic - Djordje Babic (Ђорђе Бабић) (a) 04/08/2000, Užice (RF Yugoslavia, now in Serbia) (b) 1,76 (c) F - left winger (d) FK Mladost Lucani (e) FK FAP Priboj, Mladost, FK Loznica, Mladost, LFK Mladost, Mladost, Sloboda Užice, Mladost

*** Babic - Dominik Babic (Dominik Babić) (a) 05/09/2006, Bjelovar (Croatia) (b) - (c) F - right winger (d) - (e) NK Pitomaca

*** Babic - Filip Babic (Филип Бабић) (a) 27/05/1995, Uzice (RF Yugoslavia, now in Serbia) (b) 1,87 (c) D - central defense (d) - (e) Mladost, FK Loznica, FK TSC, Vojvodina, Proleter, Sloboda Užice

*** Babic - Ilija Babic (Илија Бабић) (a) 03/08/2002, Novi Sad (Yugoslavia, now in Serbia) (b) 1,85 (c) F - center forward (d) FK Vozdovac (e) Vozdovac, Crvena zvezda, Mladost GAT, Crvena zvezda, Graficar, Kovilj

*** Babic - Matko Babic (Matko Babić) (a) 28/07/1998, Zagreb (Croatia) (b) 1,84 (c) F - center forward (d) - (e) FC Hermannstadt, AEL Limassol, PAEEK Kyrenia, AEL Limassol, HNK Rijeka, Karvina, HNK Rijeka, NK Lokomotiva, NK Rudes

*** Babic - Sinisa Babic (Синиша Бабић) (a) 13/02/1991, Novi Sad (Yugoslavia, now in Serbia) (b) 1,78 (c) M - attacking midfielder (d) FK Napredak Krusevac (e) Al-Nasr Bengh., Radnik, FK Turon, Proleter, FK Krupa, Radnicki Niš, AE Larisa, Vojvodina, Proleter, Vojvodina II, Veternik, Vojvodina II, Slavija S., Vojvodina II, FK Palic Koming, Vojvodina II

*** Babic - Slobodan Babic (Слободан Бабић) (a) 04/03/2000, Niksic (RF Yugoslavia, Montenegro) (b) 1,88 (c) F - center forward (d) OFK Petrovac (e) OFK Grbalj, Backa, Radnicki Srem, Backa, Sloga Kraljevo, Napredak, Smederevo 1924, Napredak, Sloga Kraljevo

*** Babic - Srdjan Babic (Срђан Бабић) (a) 22/04/1996, Banja Luka (Bosnia and Herzegovina) (b) 1,94 (c) D - central defense (d) UD Almería (e) Crvena zvezda, UD Almería, Crvena zvezda, Famalicão, Crvena zvezda, Real Sociedad, Crvena zvezda, Real Sociedad, Reus Deportiu, Real Sociedad B, Vojvodina

*** Babichev - Mikhail Babichev (Бабичев Михаил Анатольевич) (a) 02/02/1995, Postavy (Belarus) (b) 1,91 (c) M - pivot (d) Kalju FC (e) RFS, Neman Grodno, Torpedo Zhodino, Vitebsk, Orsha, Kras Repen, Rubin Kazán II, FK Postavy

*** Babicka - Shavy Babicka (Shavy Warren Babicka) (a) 01/06/2000, Libreville (Gabon) (b) 1,79 (c) F - right winger (d) Aris Limassol (e) Kiyovu Sports, Mangasport

*** Babis - Paris Babis (Πάρης Μπάμπης) (a) 17/07/1999, Athina (Greece) (b) 1,72 (c) M - pivot (d) Athens Kallithea FC (e) PAS Lamia, AEK Athína B, AEK Athína,

Apollon Larisas, AEK Athína, Platanias, AEK Athína, PS Kalamata, AEK Athína, Apollon Pontou, AEK Athína

*** Babit - Brian Babit (a) 21/03/1993, Saint-Avold (France) (b) 1,70 (c) F - attacking midfielder (d) SSEP Hombourg-Haut (e) FC UNA Strassen, Swift Hesperange, RE Virton, Sarreguemines, ASM Belfort, Dijon, Amiens SC, Dijon, Dijon FCO B

*** Babkin - Sergey Babkin (Бабкин Сергей Сергеевич) (a) 25/09/2002, Volgograd (Russia) (b) 1,76 (c) M - central midfielder (d) Krylya Sovetov Samara (e) KS Samara, Lokomotiv Moskva, Loko-Kazanka M., Lokomotiv Moskva II, Anzhi II

*** Babluani - Luka Babluani (ლუკა ბაბლუანი) (a) 04/04/2003, ¿? (Georgia) (b) - (c) M (d) FC Locomotive Tbilisi II (e) -

*** Baboglo - Vladyslav Baboglo (Бабогло Владислав Віталійович) (a) 14/11/1998, Copceac (Moldova) (b) 1,88 (c) D - central defense (d) FK Oleksandriya (e) Oleksandriya II

*** Babos - Bence Babos (a) 12/02/2004, Győr (Hungary) (b) - (c) M - attacking midfielder (d) FC Ajka (e) Fehérvár II

*** Babós - Levente Babós (a) 16/01/2004, Szeged (Hungary) (b) - (c) D - central defense (d) Aqvital FC Csákvár (e) Csákvár, Puskás AFC, Puskás AFC II

*** Babunski - David Babunski (Давид Бабунски) (a) 01/03/1994, Skopje (North Macedonia) (b) 1,78 (c) M - central midfielder (d) Mezőkövesd Zsóry FC (e) Debrecen, FCV Farul, FC Botosani, Omiya Ardija, Yokohama F. M., Crvena zvezda, FC Barcelona B

*** Babunski - Dorian Babunski (Дориан Бабунски Христовски) (a) 29/08/1996, Skopje (North Macedonia) (b) 1,87 (c) F - center forward (d) Debreceni VSC (e) Botev Vratsa, Machida Zelvia, Kagoshima Utd., Machida Zelvia, NK Radomlje, Olimpija, CF Fuenlabrada

*** Baburin - Egor Baburin (Бабурин Егор Константинович) (a) 09/08/1993, Chernigiv (Ukraine) (b) 1,91 (c) G (d) Torpedo Moskva (e) Rostov, Torpedo Moskva, Rostov, Krasnodar, Rostov, Zenit, Rubin Kazan, Zenit, Zenit St. Peterburg II

*** Babuscu - Onurhan Babuscu (Onurhan Babuşcu) (a) 05/09/2003, Baden bei Wien (Austria) (b) 1,76 (c) M - attacking midfielder (d) Gaziantep FK (e) Admira Wacker

*** Bacak - Boris Bacak (Baćak Boris) (a) 17/04/1987, Imotski (Yugoslavia, now in Croatia) (b) - (c) G (d) HSK Posusje (e) Mladost Prolozac, HSK Posusje, NK Dugopolje, Mladost Prolozac, Siroki Brijeg, Branitelj Mostar, Siroki Brijeg, GOSK Gabela, Siroki Brijeg, HNK Capljina, Siroki Brijeg, Damash Doroud, Siroki Brijeg, HSK Posusje

*** Baccay - Josef Brian Baccay (a) 29/04/2001, Kolbotn (Norway) (b) 1,80 (c) D - left back (d) Odds BK (e) Lillestrøm, Kongsvinger, Lillestrøm, Fredrikstad, Lillestrøm, Lillestrøm II

*** Bacchiocchi - Nicolò Bacchiocchi (a) 26/02/1991, Pesaro (Italy) (b) 1,72 (c) M - pivot (d) ACD Torconca Cattolica (e) Domagnano, Cantiano, G. Cattolica, Juvenes-Dogana, Sasso Marconi, Spoleto, Rimini, Vastese, Castelfidardo, Corridonia, Castelfidardo, Sambenedettese, Fermana, Santarcangelo

*** Bacconnier - Kévin Bacconnier (a) 01/05/1993, Marseille (France) (b) 1,87 (c) M - pivot (d) - (e) FC UNA Strassen, Marignane G. FC, Endoume, Rhône Vallées, AC Arles

*** Baccus - Keanu Baccus (Keanu Kole Baccus) (a) 07/06/1998, Durban (South Africa) (b) 1,78 (c) M - pivot (d) St. Mirren FC (e) Western Sydney, West Sydney II, Blacktown City

*** Bachek - Dmitriy Bachek (Бачек Дмитрий) (a) 13/12/2000, Karaganda (Kazakhstan) (b) 1,68 (c) M - attacking midfielder (d) Arsenal Dzerzhinsk (e) FK Aksu, Antequera, UD Poblense, Shakhter K., Shakhter-Bulat

*** Bacher - Felix Bacher (a) 25/10/2000, Lienz (Austria) (b) 1,90 (c) D - central defense (d) WSG Tirol (e) SC Freiburg II, FC Wacker, FC Wacker II

*** Bachev - Martin Bachev (Мартин Станиславов Бачев) (a) 28/06/2004, Blagoevgrad (Bulgaria) (b) - (c) D - central defense (d) Pirin Blagoevgrad (e) -

*** Bachev - Preslav Bachev (Преслав Валериев Бачев) (a) 14/03/2006, Ruse (Bulgaria) (b) 1,87 (c) F - center forward (d) Levski Sofia (e) Levski Sofia II

*** Bachiashvili - Vako Bachiashvili (ვაკო ბაჩიაშვილი) (a) 04/11/1992, Tbilisi (Georgia) (b) 1,79 (c) D - left back (d) - (e) FC Telavi, Merani Tbilisi, JFK Ventspils, FC Telavi, Sioni Bolnisi, FC Samtredia, Kauno Zalgiris, Liepaja, Tskhinvali, FC Dila, Dinamo II

*** Bachirou - Fouad Bachirou (a) 15/04/1990, Valence (France) (b) 1,69 (c) M - pivot (d) Omonia Nicosia (e) Nottingham Forest, Malmö FF, Östersund, Morton, Paris Saint Germain B

*** Bacic - Angelo Bacic (Angelo Bačić) (a) 13/02/2004, Lustenau (Austria) (b) - (c) M (d) VfB Hohenems (e) Austria Lustenau

*** Baciu (c) D - left back (d) Dacia Buiucani (e) - - Denis Baciu (c) D - left back (d) Dacia Buiucani (e) -

*** Backaliden - Gustaf Backaliden (a) 15/09/1997, ¿? (Sweden) (b) 1,86 (c) M - central midfielder (d) FC Rosengård (e) Torns IF, VPS, SJK Seinäjoki, IFK Mariehamn, IFK Malmö, Kvarnby IK

*** Backhaus - Mio Backhaus (a) 16/04/2004, Mönchengladbach (Germany) (b) 1,94 (c) G (d) FC Volendam (e) FC Volendam, Werder Bremen

*** Backman - Victor Backman (a) 16/03/2001, Västerås (Sweden) (b) 1,68 (c) M - central midfielder (d) Örebro SK (e) Kalmar FF, Köping FF

*** Bäckman - Jani Bäckman (a) 20/03/1988, Helsinki (Finland) (b) 1,81 (c) M - central midfielder (d) - (e) Helsinki IFK, PK-35, FC Viikingit, FC Lahti, FF Jaro, HJK Klubi 04, FC Honka, FC Haka, FC Honka, HJK Klubi 04

*** Backovsky - Hugo Jan Backovsky (Hugo Jan Bačkovský) (a) 10/10/1999, ¿? (Czech Rep.) (b) 1,85 (c) G (d) FC Slovan Liberec (e) Sparta Praha, Slovan Liberec, Sparta Praha, Bohemians 1905, Sparta Praha, Vlasim, Sparta Praha, Sparta Praha B, Vlasim, Sparta Praha B

*** Baco - Ondrej Baco (Ondřej Bačo) (a) 25/03/1996, Brumov-Bylnice (Czech Rep.) (b) 1,87 (c) D - central defense (d) Hapoel Jerusalem (e) Gaz Metan, Fastav Zlin, SK Lisen, Fastav Zlin, FC Zlin B

*** Badalassi - Imre Badalassi (a) 08/02/1995, Firenze (Italy) (b) - (c) F - center forward (d) SP Tre Penne (e) SS Folgore, Tre Fiori, Marignanese, Santarcangelo

*** Badalov - Elvin Badalov (Elvin Natiq oğlu Bədəlov) (a) 14/06/1995, St. Petersburg (Russia) (b) 1,84 (c) D - central defense (d) Sumqayit PFK (e) Sabah FK, Mauerwerk, Neftchi Baku, Zenit St. Peterburg II

*** Badamosi - Mohamed Badamosi (a) 27/12/1998, Bundung (Gambia) (b) 1,96 (c) F - center forward (d) FK Čukarički (e) KV Kortrijk, Čukarički, KV Kortrijk, FUS Rabat, Real de Banjul

*** Badash - Guy Badash (בדש גיא) (a) 24/05/1994, Kfar Saba (Israel) (b) 1,81 (c) F - right winger (d) Hapoel Beer Sheva (e) H. Jerusalem, Hapoel Tel Aviv, Ness Ziona, Hapoel Tel Aviv, Beitar TA Ramla, Hapoel Tel Aviv, H. Kfar Saba, Ramat haSharon, H. Kfar Saba

*** Badé - Loïc Badé (a) 11/04/2000, Sèvres (France) (b) 1,91 (c) D - central defense (d) Sevilla FC (e) Stade Rennes, Sevilla FC, Stade Rennes, Nottingham Forest, Stade Rennes, RC Lens, Le Havre AC, Le Havre AC B

*** Badelj - Juraj Badelj (a) 24/08/2003, Zagreb (Croatia) (b) 1,90 (c) D - central defense (d) Universitatea Craiova (e) -

*** Baden Frederiksen - Nikolai Baden Frederiksen (a) 18/05/2000, Odense (Denmark) (b) 1,79 (c) F - center forward (d) Ferencváros TC (e) Ferencváros, Vitesse, WSG Tirol, Fortuna Sittard

*** Badescu - Robert Badescu (Robert Bădescu) (a) 02/04/2005, ¿? (Moldova) (b) - (c) D - central defense (d) - (e) Clinceni II

*** Badía - Édgar Badía (Édgar Badía Guardiola) (a) 12/02/1992, Barcelona (Spain) (b) 1,80 (c) G (d) Elche CF (e) Reus Deportiu, Granada B, RCD Espanyol B

*** Badiashile - Benoît Badiashile (Benoît Badiashile Mukinayi) (a) 26/03/2001, Limoges (France) (b) 1,94 (c) D - central defense (d) Chelsea FC (e) AS Monaco

*** Badibanga - Ziguy Badibanga (a) 26/11/1991, Evere (Belgium) (b) 1,72 (c) F - right winger (d) Chornomorets Odessa (e) Anag. Karditsas, AE Larisa, Shakhter K., Ordabasy, FC Sheriff, Omonia Nicosia, Asteras Tripoli, Ergotelis, RSC Anderlecht, RSC Charleroi, RSC Anderlecht, De Graafschap, RSC Anderlecht

*** Badji - Youssouph Badji (Youssouph Mamadou Badji) (a) 20/12/2001, Ziguinchor (Senegal) (b) 1,92 (c) F - center forward (d) RSC Charleroi (e) KV Brugge, RSC Charleroi, KV Brugge, Stade Brestois, KV Brugge, Casa Sports

*** Badmus - Olaide Badmus (Olaide Muhammed Badmus) (a) 12/03/1999, ¿? (Nigeria) (b) - (c) D - central defense (d) FK Riteriai (e) Valmiera

*** Bado - Julio Bado (Julio Gil Bado) (a) 03/06/1983, Los Barrios (Spain) (b) 1,76 (c) M - pivot (d) Mons Calpe SC (e) Europa Point FC, Boca Gibraltar, Gibraltar Utd., Boca Gibraltar, Mons Calpe, Glacis United, Manchester 62, Lynx FC, Los Cortijillos

*** Badolo - Cedric Badolo (Cédric Badolo) (a) 04/11/1998, Ouagadougou (Burkina Faso) (b) 1,72 (c) M - attacking midfielder (d) FC Sheriff Tiraspol (e) Pohronie, FC Sheriff, Pohronie, Salitas, Kawkab Marrak., Ouagadougou

*** Badoyan - Zaven Badoyan (Զավեն Բադոյան) (a) 22/12/1989, Yerevan (Soviet Union, now in Armenia) (b) 1,72 (c) F - left winger (d) - (e) Akzhayik, FC Van, Ararat Yerevan, Shabab Al-Sahel, Alashkert CF, Gomel, Banants, Pyunik Yerevan, Gomel, BATE Borisov, Impuls Dilijan, Gandzasar, Kilikia Yerevan

*** Badr - Mohamed Badr (Mohamed Badr Hassan حسن بدر محمد) (a) 18/11/1989, Maadi, Kairo (Egypt) (b) 1,85 (c) M - right midfielder (d) FC Manchester 62 (e) Europa FC, Mons Calpe, Europa FC, Lynx FC, Aswan SC, El Shorta

*** Badu - Richmond Badu (a) 03/05/2002, Oostende (Belgium) (b) 1,90 (c) G (d) KV Oostende (e) -

*** Baena - Álex Baena (Alejandro Baena Rodríguez) (a) 20/07/2001, Roquetas de Mar (Spain) (b) 1,74 (c) M - attacking midfielder (d) Villarreal CF (e) Girona FC, Villarreal CF, Villarreal CF B

*** Baertelsen - Anders Baertelsen (Anders Bloch Bærtelsen) (a) 09/05/2000, Støvring (Denmark) (b) 1,90 (c) D - central defense (d) FK Haugesund (e) Vendsyssel FF, Aalborg BK

*** Baeten - William Baeten (William Guido R. Baeten) (a) 07/02/1997, ¿? (Belgium) (b) 1,81 (c) F - right winger (d) FC U Craiova 1948 (e) Patro Eisden, Dessel Sport

*** Báez - Jaime Báez (Jaime Báez Stábile) (a) 25/04/1995, Montevideo (Uruguay) (b) 1,78 (c) F - left winger (d) Frosinone Calcio (e) Cremonese, Cosenza, Fiorentina, Cosenza, Fiorentina, Pescara, Fiorentina, Spezia, Fiorentina, AS Livorno, Fiorentina, Juventud, Defensor, Juventud

*** Baeza - Miguel Baeza (Miguel Baeza Pérez) (a) 27/03/2000, Córdoba (Spain) (b) 1,77 (c) M - attacking midfielder (d) RC Celta de Vigo (e) Rio Ave, RC Celta, Ponferradina, RC Celta, RM Castilla

*** Bafdili - Bilal Bafdili (a) 03/08/2004, ¿? (Belgium) (b) 1,67 (c) M - attacking midfielder (d) KV Mechelen (e) Jong KV Mechelen

*** Baffoni - Filippo Baffoni (Filippo Maria Baffoni) (a) 25/09/1991, ¿? (Italy) (b) - (c) D - right back (d) - (e) Domagnano, Stella, Sant'Ermete, Morciano, San Giovanni, Tropical Coriano

*** Baftiu - Blend Baftiu (a) 17/02/1998, Prishtinë (Yugoslavia, now in Kosovo) (b) 1,82 (c) M - central midfielder (d) FC Drita Gjilan (e) FC Ballkani, FC Prishtina, KF Flamurtari, FC Prishtina, Ramiz Sadiku

*** Baga - Dmitriy Baga (Бага Дмитрий Анатольевич) (a) 04/01/1990, Minsk (Soviet Union, now in Belarus) (b) 1,85 (c) M - central midfielder (d) Dynamo Brest (e) Gomel, Liepaja, BATE Borisov, Atromitos FC, Hapoel Haifa, BATE Borisov, BATE II

*** Bagachanskyi - Maksym Bagachanskyi (Багачанський Максим Михайлович) (a) 05/06/2002, Krasnograd, Kharkiv Oblast (Ukraine) (b) 1,80 (c) M - attacking midfielder (d) Metalist Kharkiv (e) FK Vovchansk, Metalist, Olimpik K

*** Bagalianis - Petros Bagalianis (Πέτρος Μπαγκαλιάνης) (a) 06/02/2001, Kallikratia (Greece) (b) 1,85 (c) D - central defense (d) Olympiakos B (e) PAS Giannina, Olympiakos B, Aris Thessaloniki

*** Bagamaev - Abdulla Bagamaev (Багамаев Абдула Мусаевич) (a) 18/10/2004, Nyagan (Russia) (b) 1,76 (c) F - right winger (d) Fakel Voronezh II (e) Lokomotiv Moskva II

*** Bagaric - Drazen Bagaric (Dražen Bagarić) (a) 12/11/1992, Wien (Austria) (b) 1,93 (c) F - center forward (d) FK Kolubara Lazarevac (e) FC Honka, FK Sarajevo, FC Hermannstadt, Olimpija, Siroki Brijeg, Soligorsk, FC Ashdod, RNK Split, NK Dugopolje, RNK Split, NK Dinara Knin

*** Bagaric - Ilija Bagaric (Ilija Bagarić) (a) 02/07/1999, Tomislavgrad (Bosnia and Herzegovina) (b) 1,76 (c) F - left winger (d) NK Siroki Brijeg (e) NK Dugopolje, Karlovac 1919, NK Rudes, Din. Zagreb II

*** Bagci - Halil Bagci (Halil Bağcı) (a) 04/04/2003, Gaziantep (Turkey) (b) 1,97 (c) G (d) Salon Palloilijat (e) SalPa, HJK Helsinki

*** Bager - Jonas Bager (Jonas Valentin Bager) (a) 18/07/1996, Hadsten (Denmark) (b) 1,82 (c) D - central defense (d) RSC Charleroi (e) Union St. Gilloise, Randers FC

*** Baghramyan - Robert Baghramyan (Ռոբերտ Բաղրամյան) (a) 29/06/2002, Vagharshapat (Armenia) (b) 1,70 (c) M - pivot (d) FC Noah Yerevan (e) FC Urartu, FC Noah, FC Urartu, Urartu II, BKMA Yerevan, Ararat-Armenia II

*** Bagin - Samuel Bagin (Samuel Bagín) (a) 08/02/2004, Ilava (Slovakia) (b) 1,89 (c) D - central defense (d) AS Trencin (e) -

*** Bagirov - Sabayil Bagirov (Səbayıl Məhəmməd oğlu Bağırov) (a) 30/01/1995, ¿? (Azerbaijan) (b) - (c) M - pivot (d) Turan-Tovuz IK (e) Diyarbakir Yol, Siirt IÖI

*** Bagis - Kagan Bagis (Kağan Miray Bağış) (a) 10/04/1998, Kayseri (Turkey) (b) 1,78 (c) F - right winger (d) Istanbulspor (e) Yeni Mersin IY, Istanbulspor, Giresunspor, Manisaspor, BB Bodrumspor

*** Bagnack - Macky Bagnack (Macky Frank Bagnack Mouegni) (a) 07/06/1995, Tobagné (Cameroon) (b) 1,87 (c) D - central defense (d) Kairat Almaty (e) Pari Nizhny Novgórod, Kairat Almaty, FK Partizan, Olimpija, Admira Wacker, Real Zaragoza, FC Nantes B, FC Barcelona B

*** Bagnolini - Nicola Bagnolini (a) 14/03/2004, Cesena (Italy) (b) 1,93 (c) G (d) Bologna (e) -

*** Bagrintsev - Eduard Bagrintsev (Багринцев Эдуард Артурович) (a) 13/01/2003, Sochi, Krasnodar Region (Russia) (b) 1,77 (c) F - right winger (d) FK Krasnodar-2 (e) Dubnica, CSKA Moskva, CSKA Moskva II

*** Baguska - Zygimantas Baguska (Žygimantas Baguška) (a) 09/04/2002, Panevezys (Lithuania) (b) 1,84 (c) M - attacking midfielder (d) FK Panevezys (e) Panevezys B

*** Bah - Alexander Bah (Alexander Hartmann Bah) (a) 09/12/1997, Årslev (Denmark) (b) 1,83 (c) D - right back (d) SL Benfica (e) Slavia Praha, SønderjyskE, HB Köge, Naesby BK

*** Bah - Amadou Djoulde Bah (a) 02/10/2003, Conakry (Guinea) (b) 1,60 (c) M - central midfielder (d) FC Dinamo-Auto Tiraspol (e) -

*** Bah - Mamadou Cellou Bah (a) 26/02/2005, ¿? (Guinea) (b) - (c) F (d) Union Titus Petange (e) Progrès Niederkorn, F91 Dudelange

*** Bah - Mario Charbel Bah (a) 19/12/2001, Lougba (Benin) (b) 1,76 (c) M - pivot (d) - (e) FC Gagra, Sitatunga FC

*** Baha - Regis Baha (Regis Samuel Baha) (a) 21/10/1996, Yaoundé (Cameroon) (b) 1,85 (c) M - pivot (d) FK Mladost Lucani (e) Napredak, AS Marsa, Unisport Bafang

*** Bahadir - Yunus Bahadir (Yunus Bahadır) (a) 07/08/2002, Liège (Belgium) (b) 1,80 (c) D - right back (d) Alanyaspor (e) RSC Charleroi

*** Bahamboula - Dylan Bahamboula (a) 22/05/1995, Grigny (France) (b) 1,92 (c) M - attacking midfielder (d) Livingston FC (e) Oldham Athletic, Tsarsko Selo, CS Constantine, Astra Giurgiu, Dijon, G. Ajaccio, Dijon, AS Monaco, Paris FC, AS Monaco, AS Monaco B, AS Nancy B

*** Bahamboula - Jason Bahamboula (a) 15/06/2001, Caen (France) (b) 1,78 (c) F - right winger (d) Vitória Guimarães SC B (e) SM Caen B

*** Bahanack - Patrick Bahanack (a) 03/08/1997, Yaoundé (Cameroon) (b) 1,85 (c) D - central defense (d) - (e) APO Levadiakos, PAS Lamia, Stade Reims, Ergotelis, Stade Reims, Stade Reims B

*** Bahassa - Yassine Bahassa (a) 21/05/1992, Sauveterre-de-Guyenne (France) (b) 1,87 (c) F - left winger (d) FC U Craiova 1948 (e) Quevilly Rouen, US Avranches, Stade Bordelais, Lège Cap-Ferret, Lormont, FCE MA

*** Bahi - Ismail Bahi (a) 03/11/2001, ¿? (Morocco) (b) - (c) M - central midfielder (d) SS Pennarossa (e) Vignolese 1907, Formigine, Vignolese 1907

*** Bahlouli - Farès Bahlouli (a) 08/04/1995, Lyon (France) (b) 1,82 (c) M - attacking midfielder (d) - (e) Metalist, SK Dnipro-1, Metalist, SC Lyon, LOSC Lille B, Lille, AS Monaco, Standard Liège, AS Monaco, Olympique Lyon, Olymp. Lyon B

*** Bahlouli - Mohamed Bahlouli (Mohamed Rayane Bahlouli) (a) 17/02/2000, Lyon (France) (b) 1,78 (c) M - attacking midfielder (d) - (e) Kauno Zalgiris, Sampdoria, Cosenza

*** Bahoken - Stéphane Bahoken (Stéphane Cédric Bahoken) (a) 28/05/1992, Grasse (France) (b) 1,85 (c) F - center forward (d) Kasimpasa (e) Angers SCO, Racing Club Strasbourg, OGC Nice, St. Mirren, OGC Nice, OGC Nice B

*** Baholli - Endrit Baholli (a) 26/02/2000, Prishtinë (RF Yugoslavia, now in Kosovo) (b) 1,73 (c) M - attacking midfielder (d) FC Prishtina (e) KF Fushë Kosova, FC Prishtina, KF 2 Korriku

*** Bahoui - Nabil Bahoui (a) 05/02/1991, Stockholm (Sweden) (b) 1,88 (c) F - center forward (d) - (e) Qatar SC, AIK, De Graafschap, Grasshoppers, AIK, Grasshoppers, SV Hamburg, Al-Ahli, AIK, Brommapojkarna, Akropolis IF, Brommapojkarna, Gröndals IK, Brommapojkarna, AFC Eskilstuna, Brommapojkarna

*** Bahoya - Jean-Mattéo Bahoya (Jean-Mattéo Bahoya Négoce) (a) 07/05/2005, Montfermeil (France) (b) 1,80 (c) M - attacking midfielder (d) Angers SCO (e) Angers SCO B

*** Bähre - Mike-Steven Bähre (a) 10/08/1995, Garbsen (Germany) (b) 1,79 (c) M - central midfielder (d) SCR Altach (e) SV Meppen, Barnsley FC, Hannover 96, Barnsley FC, Hannover 96, SV Meppen, Hannover 96, Hallescher FC, Hannover 96, Hannover 96 II

*** Bahtiri - Kreshnik Bahtiri (a) 29/07/1992, Lipjan (RF Yugoslavia, now in Kosovo) (b) 1,80 (c) M - pivot (d) - (e) KF Ulpiana, FC Malisheva, FK Kukësi, KF Arbëria, KF Ulpiana

*** Baiaram - Stefan Baiaram (Ștefan Baiaram) (a) 31/12/2002, Craiova (Romania) (b) - (c) M - attacking midfielder (d) Universitatea Craiova (e) -

*** Baic - Mihajlo Baic (Михајло Баић) (a) 21/11/2002, Subotica (RF Yugoslavia, now in Serbia) (b) 1,91 (c) F - center forward (d) FK Radnik Surdulica (e) NK Lokomotiva, NK Osijek II, NS Mura, NK Osijek II, Čukarički

*** Baidoo - Michael Baidoo (a) 14/05/1999, Accra (Ghana) (b) 1,74 (c) M - attacking midfielder (d) IF Elfsborg (e) Sandnes Ulf, Jerv, Midtjylland, Jerv, Midtjylland, Jerv, Midtjylland, FC Fredericia, Midtjylland, Vision FC

*** Baidoo - Samson Baidoo (a) 31/03/2004, Graz (Austria) (b) 1,87 (c) D - central defense (d) Red Bull Salzburg (e) FC Liefering

*** Baier - Viktor Baier (a) 16/01/2005, ¿? (Czech Rep.) (b) - (c) G (d) FC Viktoria Plzen B (e) -

*** Bailey - Leon Bailey (Leon Patrick Bailey Butler) (a) 09/08/1997, Kingston (Jamaica) (b) 1,78 (c) F - left winger (d) Aston Villa (e) Bayer Leverkusen, KRC Genk

*** Baillet - Blaise Baillet (a) 30/12/1999, ¿? (Belgium) (b) 1,80 (c) F - right winger (d) UN Käerjeng 97 (e) FC UNA Strassen, RUS Rebecq, RUS Givry

*** Bailly - Eric Bailly (Eric Bertrand Bailly) (a) 12/04/1994, Bingerville (Ivory Coast) (b) 1,87 (c) D - central defense (d) Manchester United (e) Ol. Marseille, Manchester Utd., Villarreal CF, RCD Espanyol, RCD Espanyol B

*** Bain - Denys Bain (a) 02/07/1993, Paris (France) (b) 1,81 (c) D - central defense (d) - (e) AJ Auxerre, Stade Brestois, Le Havre AC, LB Châteauroux, Châteauroux B

*** Bain - Scott Bain (a) 22/11/1991, Edinburgh (Scotland) (b) 1,83 (c) G (d) Celtic FC (e) Dundee FC, Celtic FC, Dundee FC, Hibernian FC, Dundee FC, Alloa Athletic, Elgin City

*** Bainovic - Filip Bainovic (Филип Баиновић) (a) 23/06/1996, Pozarevac (RF Yugoslavia, now in Serbia) (b) 1,78 (c) M - central midfielder (d) Spartak Trnava (e) AS Trencin, Górnik Zabrze, Radnik, Górnik Zabrze, Rad Beograd, Crvena zvezda, Rad Beograd, Crvena zvezda, Rad Beograd, Zarkovo, Rad Beograd, Zarkovo, Rad Beograd, FK Homoljac

*** Bair - Theo Bair (Thelonius Bair) (a) 27/08/1999, Ottawa, Ontario (Canada) (b) 1,91 (c) F - center forward (d) Motherwell FC (e) St. Johnstone, Vancouver, HamKam, Vancouver, Whitecaps FC 2, Whitecaps Reserves

*** Bairam - Binu Bairam (Robert Bairam Mihalache) (a) 19/11/2000, San Cristóbal de La Laguna (Spain) (b) 1,71 (c) D - right back (d) Hibernians FC (e) Santa Lucia FC, Intercity, Villarreal CF C

*** Baird - Isaac Baird (a) 16/03/2004, ¿? (Northern Ireland) (b) - (c) M - central midfielder (d) Glenavon FC (e) -

*** Baiverlin - Cédric Baiverlin (a) 12/03/2003, ¿? (Luxembourg) (b) - (c) M - pivot (d) FC UNA Strassen (e) -

*** Baixinho - Marco Baixinho (Marco João Costa Baixinho) (a) 11/07/1989, Arruda dos Vinos (Portugal) (b) 1,87 (c) D - central defense (d) União de Leiria (e) Anorthosis, Paços Ferreira, Mafra, Carregado, AD Oeiras

*** Baiye - Brandon Baiye (a) 27/12/2000, Liège (Belgium) (b) 1,77 (c) M - pivot (d) KAS Eupen (e) Clermont Foot, Austria Lustenau, Clermont Foot, Austria Lustenau, Clermont Foot, KV Brugge

*** Baizan - Maximiliano Baizan (a) 23/03/1993, ¿? (San Marino) (b) - (c) D - left back (d) FC Fiorentino (e) Pennarossa, Fiorentino, Tre Fiori

*** Bajcetic - Stefan Bajcetic (Stefan Bajčetić Maquieira) (a) 22/10/2004, Vigo (Spain) (b) 1,85 (c) M - pivot (d) Liverpool FC (e) -

*** Bajde - Gregor Bajde (a) 29/04/1994, ¿? (Slovenia) (b) 1,86 (c) F - center forward (d) NK Celje (e) NK Bravo, NK Maribor, Novara, NK Maribor, NK Celje, NK Interblock, NK Bravo

*** Bajic - Ante Bajic (a) 22/08/1995, ¿? (Austria) (b) 1,83 (c) F - right winger (d) SK Rapid Wien (e) SV Ried, Union Gurten

*** Bajic - Riad Bajic (Riad Bajić) (a) 06/05/1994, Sarajevo (Bosnia and Herzegovina) (b) 1,89 (c) F - center forward (d) MKE Ankaragücü (e) Giresunspor, Udinese, Brescia, Udinese, Ascoli, Udinese, Konyaspor, Udinese, Basaksehir, Udinese, Konyaspor, Zeljeznicar

*** Bajlicz - Nicolas Bajlicz (a) 08/07/2004, Wien (Austria) (b) 1,73 (c) M - pivot (d) SK Rapid Wien (e) Rapid Wien II

*** Bajnoci - Tim Bajnoci (a) 20/05/2004, ¿? (Slovenia) (b) - (c) M - pivot (d) NK Tabor Sezana (e) -

*** Bajović - Andrej Bajović (Андреј Бајовић) (a) 06/06/2003, ¿? (RF Yugoslavia, now in Montenegro) (b) 1,85 (c) M - central midfielder (d) FK Decic Tuzi (e) FK Podgorica, Mladost DG

*** Bajraktari - Danilo Bajraktari (a) 08/07/2004, Tiranë (Albania) (b) - (c) M (d) - (e) KF Tirana

*** Bajraktari - Drin Bajraktari (a) 19/07/2005, ¿? (Serbia and Montenegro, now in Kosovo) (b) - (c) D (d) KF Ferizaj (e) -

*** Bajraktari - Milazim Bajraktari (a) 13/07/2003, Mitrovica (Serbia and Montenegro, now in Kosovo) (b) 1,77 (c) M - attacking midfielder (d) KF Trepca 89 (e) -

*** Bajraktari (c) G (d) KF Ferizaj (e) - - Blend Bajraktari (c) G (d) KF Ferizaj (e) -

*** Bajrami - Medin Bajrami (Медин Бајрами) (a) 27/02/1998, ¿? (Slovenia) (b) 1,90 (c) D - central defense (d) Voska Sport (e) FC Malisheva, Renova, Belasica, NK Maribor, Drava Ptuj, NK Maribor, ND Ilirija, NK Maribor, NK Krsko, ND Ilirija

*** Bajrami - Melos Bajrami (a) 29/09/2001, Resen (North Macedonia) (b) 1,89 (c) D - central defense (d) Makedonija Gjorce Petrov (e) FC Shkupi, KF Skënderbeu, FC Ballkani

*** Bajrami - Nedim Bajrami (a) 28/02/1999, Zürich (Switzerland) (b) 1,79 (c) M - attacking midfielder (d) US Sassuolo (e) FC Empoli, Sassuolo, FC Empoli, Grasshoppers, Empoli, Grasshoppers

*** Bajric - Adin Bajric (Adin Bajrić) (a) 22/07/2003, Livno (Bosnia and Herzegovina) (b) - (c) D - central defense (d) FK Velez Mostar (e) -

*** Bajric - Kenan Bajric (Kenan Bajrić) (a) 20/12/1994, Ljubljana (Slovenia) (b) 1,89 (c) D - central defense (d) Slovan Bratislava (e) Pafos FC, Slovan Bratislava, Olimpija

*** Bajza - Pavol Bajza (a) 04/09/1991, Žilina (Czechoslovakia, now in Slovakia) (b) 1,97 (c) G (d) FC Hradec Kralove (e) Slovácko, Karvina, Slovácko, Olympiakos N., Vejle BK, Iskra Borcice, DNŠ Zavrč, Parma, Crotone, Parma, Dubnica

*** Bak Jensen - Victor Bak Jensen (a) 03/10/2003, ¿? (Denmark) (b) - (c) D - left back (d) CD Mafra (e) Midtjylland, Hobro IK, Midtjylland

*** Bakadimas - Gerasimos Bakadimas (Γεράσιμος Μπακαδήμας) (a) 06/06/2000, Xiromero (Greece) (b) 1,81 (c) D - central defense (d) PAS Giannina (e) Panetolikos, Anag. Karditsas, Panetolikos, AE Mesolongiou, Panetolikos

*** Bakaev - Amirbek Bakaev (Бакаев Амирбек Улугбекович) (a) 23/07/2004, Tashkent (Uzbekistan) (b) - (c) F - center forward (d) Energetik-BGU Minsk (e) -

*** Bakaev - Mikhail Bakaev (Бакаев Михаил Хазбиевич) (a) 05/08/1987, Tsjinvali (Soviet Union, now in Georgia/South Ossetia) (b) 1,75 (c) M - pivot (d) Alania Vladikavkaz (e) FK Aksu, Shakhter K., Shinnik Yaroslav, Orenburg, Anzhi, Kairat Almaty, Alania, Anzhi, Alania, Avtodor Vladikavkaz

*** Bakaev - Zelimkhan Bakaev (Бакаев Зелимхан Джабраилович) (a) 01/07/1996, Nazran (Russia) (b) 1,80 (c) F - right winger (d) Zenit de San Petersburgo (e) Spartak Moskva, Arsenal Tula, Spartak Moskva, Spartak-2, Spartak Moskva II

*** Bakakis - Michalis Bakakis (Μιχάλης Μπακάκης) (a) 18/03/1991, Agrinio (Greece) (b) 1,75 (c) D - right back (d) Panetolikos GFS (e) AEK Athína, Panetolikos, AO Chania, Panetolikos

*** Bakala - Mikulas Bakala (Mikuláš Bakaľa) (a) 04/01/2001, Dolný Kubín (Slovakia) (b) 1,87 (c) D - central defense (d) FK Zeleziarne Podbrezova (e) -

*** Bakalov - Dimo Bakalov (Димо Найденов Бакалов) (a) 19/12/1988, Sliven (Bulgaria) (b) 1,77 (c) F - right winger (d) Etar Veliko Tarnovo (e) Lokomotiv Sofia, Tsarsko Selo, Beroe, Ludogorets, Lokomotiv Plovdiv, Beroe, Ludogorets, Sliven

*** Bakambu - Cédric Bakambu (a) 11/04/1991, Ivry-sur-Seine (France) (b) 1,82 (c) F - center forward (d) Galatasaray (e) Al-Nasr SC, Olympiakos, Ol. Marseille, BJ Guoan, Villarreal CF, Bursaspor, FC Sochaux, FC Sochaux B

*** Bakare - Michael Bakare (Michael Adewale A. Oluwabunmi Bakare) (a) 01/12/1986, London (England) (b) 1,81 (c) F - center forward (d) Enfield Town (e) Helsinki IFK, Arbroath, Leatherhead FC, Fjölnir, Hereford, Connah's Quay, Warrington, Wrexham, Welling Utd., Bury Town, Braintree, Tonbridge, Dover Athletic, Chelmsford, Southport, Droylsden, Southport, Macclesfield, Chelmsford, Bishop's Stortford, Thurrock, Welling Utd., Leyton Orient

*** Bakari - Saïd Bakari (Saïd Riad Bakari) (a) 22/09/1994, La Courneuve (France) (b) 1,78 (c) D - right back (d) Sparta Rotterdam (e) RKC Waalwijk, UR Namur, Bonchamp, KFC Turnhout

*** Bakasetas - Anastasios Bakasetas (Αναστάσιος Μπακασέτας) (a) 28/06/1993, Korinth (Greece) (b) 1,81 (c) M - attacking midfielder (d) Trabzonspor (e) Alanyaspor, AEK Athína, Panionios, Asteras Tripoli, Aris Thessaloniki, Asteras Tripoli, Thrasyvoulos, Asteras Tripoli

*** Bakatukanda - Elias Bakatukanda (Elias-Geoffrey Bakatukanda) (a) 13/04/2004, Köln (Germany) (b) 1,93 (c) D - central defense (d) 1.FC Köln (e) -

*** Bakayoko - Johan Bakayoko (Saint-Cyr Johan Bakayoko) (a) 20/04/2003, Overijse (Belgium) (b) 1,79 (c) F - right winger (d) PSV Eindhoven (e) -

*** Bakayoko - Moussa Bakayoko (Moussa Paul Bakayoko) (a) 27/12/1996, ¿? (Ivory Coast) (b) 1,81 (c) F - attacking midfielder (d) Zhetysu Taldykorgan (e) Shirak Gyumri, ASEC Mimosas, Blansko, Havant & Waterlooville, Dartford, Derry City, Shirak Gyumri, Raja Casablanca, USC Bassam

*** Bakayoko - Tiemoué Bakayoko (a) 17/08/1994, Paris (France) (b) 1,89 (c) M - pivot (d) - (e) Chelsea, AC Milan, Chelsea, Napoli, Chelsea, AS Monaco, Chelsea, AC Milan, Chelsea, AS Monaco, Stade Rennes, Stade Rennes B

*** Baker - Ash Baker (Ashley Thomas Baker) (a) 30/10/1996, Bridgend (Wales) (b) 1,78 (c) D - right back (d) The New Saints (e) Newport County, Sheffield Wednesday

*** Baker - Chris Baker (Christopher Neil Alan Baker) (a) 29/11/1993, Neath (Wales) (b) - (c) M - central midfielder (d) - (e) Cardiff Metropolitan Police, Ynysygerwn

*** Baker - Sam Baker (Sam Frederick Baker) (a) 02/12/2004, ¿? (England) (b) - (c) F - left winger (d) Airbus UK Broughton (e) -

*** Bakhar - Ivan Bakhar (Бахар Иван Васильевич) (a) 10/07/1998, Minsk (Belarus) (b) 1,75 (c) F - left winger (d) Dinamo Minsk (e) Kiryat Shmona, Dinamo Minsk, FK Minsk, FK Minsk II

*** Bakhshaly - Mehrac Bakhshaly (Mehrac Rasif oğlu Baxşalı) (a) 11/06/2003, ¿? (Azerbaijan) (b) 1,81 (c) F - center forward (d) FK Qabala (e) FK Qabala 2

*** Bakhtiyarov - Akmal Bakhtiyarov (Акмал Анварұлы Бақтияров) (a) 02/06/1998, Talgar (Kazakhstan) (b) 1,69 (c) M - right midfielder (d) Ordabasy Shymkent (e) Dolgoprudnyi, Zhetysu, Sochi, Artsakh Erewan, Kairat II

*** Bakic - Danilo Bakic (Данило Бакић) (a) 28/10/1995, ¿? (RF Yugoslavia, now in Montenegro) (b) 1,80 (c) M - central midfielder (d) OFK Petrovac (e) Arsenal Tivat, Mornar Bar, FK Bokelj, OFK Grbalj, FK Lovcen, OFK Grbalj, OFK Beograd, OFK Petrovac, Mogren

*** Bakic - Dusan Bakic (Dušan Bakić) (a) 23/02/1999, Podgorica (RF Yugoslavia, Montenegro) (b) 1,90 (c) F - center forward (d) Dinamo Minsk (e) TJK Legion, Dinamo Minsk, Energetik-BGU, Buducnost Podgorica

*** Bakic - Marko Bakic (Marko Bakić) (a) 01/11/1993, Budva (RF Yugoslavia, now in Montenegro) (b) 1,86 (c) M - central midfielder (d) OFI Creta (e) Buducnost Podgorica, Excelsior Mouscron, SC Braga, Excelsior Mouscron, SC Braga, Belenenses, SC Braga, Alcorcón, SC Braga, Fiorentina, Belenenses, Fiorentina, Spezia, Fiorentina, Torino, Mogren

*** Bakic - Ognjen Bakic (Ognjen Bakić) (a) 06/01/2003, Kotor (RF Yugoslavia, now in Montenegro) (b) - (c) M - central midfielder (d) NK Osijek (e) NK Osijek II

*** Bakic - Vasilije Bakic (Василије Бакић) (a) 24/05/2000, Beograd (RF Yugoslavia, now in Serbia) (b) 1,92 (c) D - central defense (d) FK Radnicki Niš (e) Kolubara, FK Indjija, Vozdovac

*** Bakirov - Shadman Bakirov (a) 23/07/2001, ¿? (Kazakhstan) (b) 1,73 (c) F - left winger (d) Akademia Ontustik Shymkent (e) FC Arys, FK Turan II

*** Bakiz - Younes Bakiz (a) 05/02/1999, ¿? (Denmark) (b) 1,86 (c) F - left winger (d) Aalborg BK (e) Viborg FF, FC Roskilde

*** Bakkali - Zakaria Bakkali (البقالي زكريا) (a) 26/01/1996, Liège (Belgium) (b) 1,68 (c) F - left winger (d) RKC Waalwijk (e) RSC Anderlecht, Beerschot V.A., RSC Anderlecht, Valencia CF, RC Deportivo, Valencia CF, PSV Eindhoven

*** Bakkar - Mohammed Bakkar (a) 28/05/2003, ¿? (Finland) (b) 1,74 (c) F - right winger (d) Atlantis FC II (e) FC Inter

*** Bakke - Johan Bakke (Johan Johanessen Bakke) (a) 01/04/2004, Sogndal (Norway) (b) 1,86 (c) M - central midfielder (d) Molde FK (e) Sogndal, Sogndal IL II

*** Bakker - Justin Bakker (a) 03/03/1998, Amsterdam (Netherlands) (b) 1,89 (c) D - central defense (d) Kuopion Palloseura (e) Go Ahead Eagles

*** Bakker - Mitchel Bakker (a) 20/06/2000, Purmerend (Netherlands) (b) 1,85 (c) D - left back (d) Atalanta de Bérgamo (e) Bayer Leverkusen, Paris Saint-Germain, Ajax B

*** Baklanov - Ivan Baklanov (Бакланов Иван Александрович) (a) 16/03/1995, Aleksin, Tula Region (Russia) (b) 1,76 (c) M - right midfielder (d) Belshina Bobruisk (e) Neman Grodno, Palanga, Ekaterinodar, Afips Afipskiy, Sokol Saratov, Domodedovo, Sokol Saratov, Domodedovo, Rostov II, Arsenal 2 Tula, Rostov II, CSKA Moskva II

*** Baklov - Oleg Baklov (Баклов Олег Юрьевич) (a) 20/10/1994, Istiklol (Tajikistan) (b) 2,01 (c) G (d) FK Ufa (e) Ural, KamAZ, Ural, Syzran-2003, KS Samara II, Syzran-2003

*** Bakowski - Krzysztof Bakowski (Krzysztof Bąkowski) (a) 04/01/2003, Poznań (Poland) (b) 1,90 (c) G (d) Radomiak Radom (e) Radomiak, Lech Poznan, Stal Rzeszow, Lech Poznan, Stomil, Lech Poznan

*** Bakrac - Milos Bakrac (Miloš Bakrač) (a) 25/02/1992, ¿? (Yugoslavia, now in Montenegro) (b) 1,88 (c) D - central defense (d) Rudar Pljevlja (e) FK Iskra, Zira FK, OFK Titograd, Zeljeznicar, Sutjeska Niksic, Travnik, Buducnost Podgorica, FC Sion

*** Bakrar - Monsef Bakrar (a) 13/01/2001, Sétif (Algeria) (b) 1,83 (c) F - center forward (d) New York City FC (e) NK Istra, ES Sétif

*** Bakti - Balázs Bakti (a) 31/12/2004, Budapest (Hungary) (b) 1,71 (c) M - attacking midfielder (d) Vasas FC (e) Vasas FC, Puskás AFC, Budafoki MTE, Puskás AFC

*** Baku - Makana Baku (Makana Nsimba Baku) (a) 08/04/1998, Mainz (Germany) (b) 1,77 (c) M - attacking midfielder (d) Legia de Varsovia (e) Göztepe, Holstein Kiel, Warta Poznań, Holstein Kiel, Sonnenhof-Gr.

*** Baku - Ridle Baku (Bote Nzuzi Baku) (a) 08/04/1998, Mainz (Germany) (b) 1,76 (c) D - right back (d) VfL Wolfsburg (e) Mainz 05, FSV Mainz 05 II

*** Balaj - Bekim Balaj (a) 11/01/1991, Shkodër (Albania) (b) 1,88 (c) F - center forward (d) KF Vllaznia (e) A. Keciörengücü, Boluspor, Nizhny Novgorod, Sturm Graz, Akhmat Grozny, HNK Rijeka, Slavia Praha, Sparta Praha, Jagiellonia, Sparta Praha, KF Tirana, Genclerbirligi, KF Vllaznia

*** Balaj - Dashnor Balaj (a) 24/03/2003, ¿? (Serbia and Montenegro, now in Kosovo) (b) - (c) G (d) - (e) FC Ballkani

*** Balaj - Filip Balaj (a) 02/08/1997, Zlaté Moravce (Slovakia) (b) 1,92 (c) F - center forward (d) Cracovia (e) Trinity Zlin, Cracovia, Zlaté Moravce, MSK Zilina, FC Nitra

*** Balakhonov - Maksim Balakhonov (Балахонов Максим Дмитриевич) (a) 15/01/2005, Kirov (Russia) (b) 1,75 (c) D - left back (d) Dinamo 2 Moskva (e) -

*** Balan - Adrian Balan (Adrian Ionuț Bălan) (a) 14/03/1990, Bucuresti (Romania) (b) 1,81 (c) F - center forward (d) Concordia Chiajna (e) Universitatea Cluj, FC Rapid 1923, FC Hermannstadt, ACSM Poli Iasi, FC Voluntari, Stefanesti, Damila Maciuca, Dinamo II

*** Balan - Claudiu Balan (Claudiu Cristian Bălan) (a) 22/06/1994, Craiova (Romania) (b) 1,86 (c) F - center forward (d) PAS Giannina (e) FC U Craiova, FC Olt Slatina, CS Mioveni, FC U Craiova

*** Balan - Denys Balan (Балан Денис Дмитрович) (a) 18/08/1993, Odesa (Ukraine) (b) 1,76 (c) D - right back (d) NK Veres Rivne (e) Zlaté Moravce, SILON Taborsko, Kryvbas, Ingulets, Chornomorets, Cherk. Dnipro, Real Farma, Dynamo 2 Kyiv, Dinamo Kiev II, Dnipro II, Dinamo Kiev II

*** Balan - Florin Balan (Francis Florin Bălan) (a) 02/01/2002, Huși (Romania) (b) - (c) M - central midfielder (d) Gloria 2018 Bistrita-Nasaud (e) FC Voluntari, CS Afumati, FC Voluntari, FC Farul 1920, FC Voluntari

*** Balan - Rares Balan (Rareş Cristian Bălan) (a) 19/01/2000, Bistrița (Romania) (b) 1,90 (c) D - central defense (d) Gloria 2018 Bistrita-Nasaud (e) Gloria 2018, CFR Cluj II, FC Gl. Bistrita

*** Balanovich - Sergey Balanovich (Баланович Сергей Михайлович) (a) 29/08/1987, Pinsk (Soviet Union, now in Belarus) (b) 1,72 (c) M - left midfielder (d) BK Maxline Vitebsk (e) FK Slutsk, Akron Togliatti, Soligorsk, Amkar Perm, Soligorsk, Volna Pinsk

*** Balanta - Éder Balanta (Éder Fabián Álvarez Balanta) (a) 28/02/1993, Bogotá (Colombia) (b) 1,80 (c) M - pivot (d) KV Brugge (e) FC Schalke 04, KV Brugge, FC Basel, River Plate

*** Balanyuk - Denys Balanyuk (Баланюк Денис Сергійович) (a) 16/01/1997, Odesa (Ukraine) (b) 1,80 (c) F - center forward (d) FC Samgurali Tskaltubo (e) Spartak Varna, IFK Mariehamn, Torpedo Moskva, Olimpik Donetsk, Wisla Kraków, Arsenal Kyiv, Wisla Kraków, Dnipro, Dnipro II

*** Balasa - Mihai Balasa (Mihai Alexandru Bălaşa) (a) 14/01/1995, Târgovişte (Romania) (b) 1,86 (c) D - central defense (d) Sepsi OSK Sf. Gheorghe (e) CS U Craiova, FCSB, AS Roma, Trapani, AS Roma, Crotone, FC Viitorul, Academia Hagi

*** Balashov - Vitaliy Balashov (Балашов Віталій Юрійович) (a) 15/01/1991, Odessa (Soviet Union, now in Ukraine) (b) 1,77 (c) F - left winger (d) Tytan Odessa (e) FK Turan, Aktobe, Shakhter K., Tambov, Olimpik Donetsk, Isloch, Milsami, Wisla Kraków, Chornomorets, Goverla, Chornomorets, Chornomorets II

*** Balastegui - Eric Balastegui (Eric Balastegui Martínez) (a) 29/06/2003, Andorra la Vella (Andorra) (b) - (c) F - center forward (d) CF Atlètic Amèrica (e) Engordany B, ENFAF

*** Balatoni - Maximilian Balatoni (Maximilian Mortensen Balatoni) (a) 16/03/2005, ¿? (Norway) (b) 1,96 (c) D - central defense (d) Lillestrøm SK II (e) -

*** Balaur - Ionut Balaur (Ionuţ Balaur) (a) 06/06/1989, Vaslui (Romania) (b) 1,88 (c) D - central defense (d) ACSC FC Arges (e) CS Mioveni, FC Voluntari, Dunarea Calarasi, FC Voluntari, ASA Tg. Mures, FC Vaslui, CS Otopeni, FC Vaslui, CSM Focsani, FC Vaslui

*** Balaure - Silviu Balaure (Silviu Nicolae Balaure) (a) 06/02/1996, Drobeta-Turnu Severin (Romania) (b) 1,78 (c) F - left winger (d) FC Hermannstadt (e) Astra Giurgiu, Minaur, ACS Poli, Nova Mama Mia, ACS Poli

*** Balauru - Dragos Balauru (Dragoş Balauru) (a) 11/11/1989, Poroschia (Romania) (b) 1,89 (c) G (d) - (e) UTA Arad, SCM Gloria Buzau, APO Levadiakos, Daco-Getica, FC Voluntari, FC Viitorul, Rapid Bucureşti, ASA Tg. Mures, Universitatea Cluj, FCM Targu Mures, FC Snagov

*** Balayev - Emil Balayev (Emil Nazim oğlu Balayev) (a) 17/04/1994, Volgograd (Russia) (b) 1,89 (c) G (d) Neftchi Baku (e) FK Sabail, FK Turan, Qarabag FK, Zira FK, Tobol Kostanay, FK Sabail, Qarabag FK, Eintracht, Neftchi Baku, Araz-Naxcivan, Neftchi Baku, Sumqayit, Neftchi Baku

*** Balaz - Filip Balaz (Filip Baláž) (a) 12/04/2003, ¿? (Slovakia) (b) 1,85 (c) G (d) FK Spisska Nova Ves (e) Banska Bystrica

*** Balazic - Gregor Balazic (Gregor Balažic) (a) 12/02/1988, Murska Sobota (Yugoslavia, now in Slovenia) (b) 1,90 (c) D - central defense (d) Marko Balazic (e) NS Mura, EN Paralimniou, Ural, FK Partizan, Karpaty, ND Gorica, Águilas, NS Mura

*** Balázs - József Balázs (Balázs József Balázs) (a) 02/12/2003, Karcag (Hungary) (b) 1,85 (c) G (d) MTK Budapest II (e) Paksi FC, MTK Budapest, III. Kerület, Szent István

*** Balbarau - Raul Balbarau (Raul Andrei Bălbărău) (a) 07/04/2001, Galaţi (Romania) (b) 1,89 (c) G (d) - (e) Debrecen, FC Noah, Debrecen, Steaua, Slatina

*** Balci - Bünyamin Balci (Bünyamin Balcı) (a) 31/05/2000, Samsun (Turkey) (b) 1,73 (c) D - right back (d) Antalyaspor (e) -

*** Balci - Ethem Balci (Ethem Balcı) (a) 17/06/2003, Kayseri (Turkey) (b) 1,84 (c) F - right winger (d) Kayserispor (e) -

*** Balcombe - Ellery Balcombe (Ellery Ronald Balcombe) (a) 15/10/1999, Bedfordshire (England) (b) 1,90 (c) G (d) Brentford FC (e) Bristol Rovers, Brentford,

Crawley Town, Brentford, Bromley, Brentford, Burton Albion, Brentford, Doncaster Rovers, Brentford, Viborg FF, Brentford, Boreham Wood, Brentford, Brentford B
*** Baldanzi - Tommaso Baldanzi (a) 23/03/2003, Poggibonsi (Italy) (b) 1,70 (c) M - attacking midfielder (d) FC Empoli (e) -
*** Baldazzi - Alberto Baldazzi (a) 08/11/2001, ¿? (San Marino) (b) - (c) M - central midfielder (d) AC Juvenes-Dogana (e) -
*** Balde - Alejandro Balde (Alejandro Balde Martínez) (a) 18/10/2003, Barcelona (Spain) (b) 1,75 (c) D - left back (d) FC Barcelona (e) Barcelona Atlètic
*** Balde - Prince Balde (a) 23/03/1998, Monrovia (Liberia) (b) 1,87 (c) D - central defense (d) - (e) Al-Diwaniya SC, FC Drita, KF Feronikeli, KF Drenica, KF Feronikeli, Club Breweries, Champasak Utd.
*** Baldé - Alberto Baldé (Alberto Baldé Almánzar) (a) 21/03/2002, Madrid (Spain) (b) 1,78 (c) F - center forward (d) Loughgall FC (e) Portadown, Pickering
*** Baldé - Ibrahima Baldé (a) 17/01/2003, Paris (France) (b) 1,85 (c) F - center forward (d) RC Lens (e) FC Annecy, RC Lens, RC Lens B
*** Baldé - Keita Baldé (Keita Baldé Diao) (a) 08/03/1995, Arbùcies (Spain) (b) 1,78 (c) F - center forward (d) FC Spartak de Moscú (e) Cagliari, AS Monaco, Sampdoria, AS Monaco, Internazionale Milano, AS Monaco, Lazio
*** Baldé - Mama Baldé (Mama Samba Baldé) (a) 06/11/1995, Bissau (Guinea-Bissau) (b) 1,76 (c) F - center forward (d) ESTAC Troyes (e) Dijon, Desportivo Aves, Sporting B, Desportivo Aves, Sporting B, Castelo Branco, Sporting B
*** Baldé - Manuel Baldé (Manuel Mama Samba Baldé) (a) 14/11/2002, Albufeira (Portugal) (b) 1,94 (c) G (d) FC Penafiel (e) Vizela
*** Baldé - Rachid Baldé (a) 24/02/2000, ¿? (Guinea-Bissau) (b) 1,74 (c) M - central midfielder (d) MSV Pampow (e) AS Kastoria, Zimbru Chisinau, Somuz Falticeni, Sacavenense, Fátima, UA Povoense, Curzon Ashton
*** Baldé - Thierno Baldé (a) 10/06/2002, Villeneuve-Saint-Georges (France) (b) 1,82 (c) D - right back (d) ESTAC Troyes (e) Paris Saint-Germain, Le Havre AC, Paris Saint-Germain
*** Baldi - Gabriele Baldi (a) 24/08/2004, Roma (Italy) (b) 1,96 (c) G (d) Giugliano Calcio 1928 (e) -
*** Baldini - Matteo Baldini (a) 02/10/1998, ¿? (Italy) (b) - (c) F - center forward (d) Polisportiva Vismara 2008 (e) Murata, Vismara Calcio, Juvenes-Dogana, Fiorentino, Misano, United Riccione, Misano
*** Baldock - Lee Baldock (Lee Anthony Baldock) (a) 19/01/1992, ¿? (Wales) (b) - (c) D - left back (d) Trethomas Bluebirds (e) Pontypridd, Port Talbot, Barry Town
*** Baldursson - Andri Fannar Baldursson (a) 10/01/2002, Kópavogur (Iceland) (b) 1,87 (c) M - central midfielder (d) IF Elfsborg (e) Elfsborg, Bologna, NEC Nijmegen, Bologna, FC København, Bologna, Breidablik, Breidablik
*** Baldursson - Breki Baldursson (a) 11/08/2006, ¿? (Iceland) (b) - (c) M - central midfielder (d) Fram Reykjavík (e) -
*** Baldvinsson - Birgir Baldvinsson (a) 10/01/2001, ¿? (Iceland) (b) - (c) D - left back (d) KA Akureyri (e) Leiknir, KA Akureyri, Afturelding, KA Akureyri, Leiknir, KA Akureyri
*** Baldwin - Jack Baldwin (a) 30/06/1993, London (England) (b) 1,85 (c) D - central defense (d) Ross County FC (e) Bristol Rovers, Sunderland, Salford, Sunderland, Peterborough, Hartlepool Utd., Faversham Town
*** Baldyga - Dawid Baldyga (Dawid Bałdyga) (a) 08/01/2003, Złocieniec (Poland) (b) 1,94 (c) F - center forward (d) Polonia Sroda Wielkopolska (e) Śląsk Wroclaw, Slask Wroclaw II, Siarka T., Blekitni Wronki, FASE Szczecin, AP Pogon

*** Baleba - Carlos Baleba (Carlos Noom Quomah Baleba) (a) 03/01/2004, Douala (Cameroon) (b) 1,79 (c) M - central midfielder (d) LOSC Lille Métropole (e) LOSC Lille B, Brasseries
*** Balenziaga - Mikel Balenziaga (Mikel Balenziaga Oruesagasti) (a) 29/02/1988, Zumarraga (Spain) (b) 1,77 (c) D - left back (d) RC Deportivo de La Coruña (e) Athletic, Real Valladolid, Athletic, CD Numancia, Athletic, Bilbao Athletic, Real Sociedad B
*** Balerdi - Leonardo Balerdi (Leonardo Julián Balerdi Rosa) (a) 26/01/1999, Villa Mercedes (Argentina) (b) 1,87 (c) D - central defense (d) Olympique Marseille (e) Borussia Dortmund, Ol. Marseille, Borussia Dortmund, Boca Juniors, Boca Juniors II
*** Bales (c) F (d) Aberystwyth Town (e) - - Archie Bales (c) F (d) Aberystwyth Town (e) -
*** Balgradean - Cristian Balgradean (Cristian Emanuel Bălgrădean) (a) 21/03/1988, Sânnicolau Mare (Romania) (b) 1,87 (c) G (d) CFR Cluj (e) FCSB, Concordia, CS U Craiova, FC Dinamo, Unirea Urziceni, FC Dinamo, UTA Arad, Liberty Salonta, FC Brasov, Minerul Lupeni, Atletico Arad
*** Balic - Andrija Balic (Andrija Balić) (a) 11/08/1997, Split (Croatia) (b) 1,80 (c) M - central midfielder (d) - (e) Dunajska Streda, Banska Bystrica, Dunajska Streda, Udinese, Dunajska Streda, Udinese, Perugia, Udinese, Fortuna Sittard, Udinese, Hajduk Split
*** Balic - Husein Balic (a) 15/02/1996, Linz (Austria) (b) 1,83 (d) LASK (e) SCR Altach, LASK, SKN St. Pölten, Vorwarts Steyr
*** Balic - Nihad Balic (a) 21/05/2004, ¿? (Serbia and Montenegro, now in Montenegro) (b) - (c) D (d) Jedinstvo Bijelo Polje (e) -
*** Balic - Sasa Balic (Saša Balić) (a) 29/01/1990, Kotor (Yugoslavia, now in Montenegro) (b) 1,85 (c) D - central defense (d) Dinamo Batumi (e) Korona Kielce, Zagłębie, CFR Cluj, FK Sarajevo, ASA Tg. Mures, Metalurg Z., Kryvbas, Inter Zaprešić, OFK Grbalj, OFK Beograd
*** Balikwisha - Michel-Ange Balikwisha (a) 10/05/2001, Gent (Belgium) (b) 1,78 (c) F - left winger (d) Royal Antwerp FC (e) Standard Liège
*** Balikwisha - William Balikwisha (a) 12/05/1999, Brussel (Belgium) (b) 1,73 (c) M - attacking midfielder (d) Standard de Lieja (e) MVV Maastricht, Standard Liège, Cercle Brugge, Standard Liège
*** Balinov - Dimitar Balinov (Димитър Благоев Балинов) (a) 19/01/2001, Sveti Vlas (Bulgaria) (b) 1,73 (c) D - central defense (d) Spartak Plovdiv 1947 (e) Botev II, Botev Plovdiv, Sozopol, Botev Plovdiv, Neftochimik, Botev Plovdiv
*** Baliso - Yanga Baliso (a) 27/03/1997, Cape Town, Western Cape (South Africa) (b) 1,75 (c) M - central midfielder (d) - (e) AC Oulu, IFK Mariehamn, Pargas IF, Orlando P. Reserves, Cape Umoya Utd., Orlando P. Reserves
*** Baliutavicius - Gustas Baliutavicius (Gustas Baliutavičius) (a) 27/08/2000, Siauliai (Lithuania) (b) 1,93 (c) G (d) FA Siauliai (e) Suduva B, FA Siauliai
*** Balk - Remco Balk (a) 02/03/2001, Zuidhorn (Netherlands) (b) - (c) F - right winger (d) SC Cambuur Leeuwarden (e) FC Utrecht, SC Cambuur, FC Utrecht
*** Balker - Radinio Balker (Radinio Roberto Balker) (a) 03/09/1998, Amsterdam (Netherlands) (b) 1,93 (c) D - central defense (d) FC Groningen (e) Almere City
*** Balkovec - Jure Balkovec (a) 09/09/1994, Novo Mesto (Slovenia) (b) 1,85 (c) D - left back (d) Alanyaspor (e) Karagümrük, Hellas Verona, Empoli, Hellas Verona, Bari, Domžale, NK Radomlje, Domžale, NK Krka, Domžale, Bela Krajina
*** Ballantine - Scott Ballantine (Scott Glenn Ballantine) (a) 12/04/1996, Gibraltar (Gibraltar) (b) 1,75 (c) M - central midfielder (d) FC Bruno's Magpies (e) Manchester

62, Bruno's Magpies, Manchester 62, Gibraltar Phoenix, Northumbria, Lincoln FC, Manchester 62

*** Ballantyne - Cammy Ballantyne (Cameron F Ballantyne) (a) 22/04/2000, Armadale (Scotland) (b) 1,87 (c) M - attacking midfielder (d) St. Johnstone FC (e) Montrose, St. Johnstone, Montrose, St. Johnstone, Montrose, St. Johnstone, St. Johnstone B, Montrose, St. Johnstone B, BSC Glasgow, St. Johnstone B

*** Ballard - Dom Ballard (Dominic Ballard) (a) 01/04/2005, ¿? (England) (b) - (c) F - center forward (d) Southampton FC B (e) -

*** Ballester - Jesse Ballester (a) 30/06/1993, Gibraltar (Gibraltar) (b) 1,70 (c) D - left back (d) - (e) Europa Point FC, FC Hound Dogs, Manchester 62, Bruno's Magpies, FC Olympique, Lions Gibraltar, Red Imps FC II

*** Ballester - Mark Ballester (Mark Anthony Ballester) (a) 19/03/1995, Gibraltar (Gibraltar) (b) 1,76 (c) D - right back (d) - (e) Europa Point FC, Europa FC, Europa Point FC, Europa FC, Mons Calpe, Red Imps FC II, Lincoln FC

*** Ballet - Samuel Ballet (Samuel Leo Beat Ballet) (a) 12/03/2001, Bern (Switzerland) (b) 1,84 (c) F - center forward (d) FC Winterthur (e) FC Winterthur, FC Wil 1900

*** Balliu - Iván Balliu (Iván Balliu Campeny) (a) 01/01/1992, Caldes de Malavella (Spain) (b) 1,72 (c) D - right back (d) Rayo Vallecano (e) UD Almería, FC Metz, Arouca, FC Barcelona B

*** Ballo - Thierno Ballo (Thierno Mamadou Lamarana Ballo) (a) 02/01/2002, Abidjan (Ivory Coast) (b) 1,72 (c) M - attacking midfielder (d) Wolfsberger AC (e) Rapid Wien

*** Ballo-Touré - Fodé Ballo-Touré (Fodé Ballo-Touré) (a) 03/01/1997, Conflans-Sainte-Honorine (France) (b) 1,82 (c) D - left back (d) AC Milan (e) AS Monaco, Lille, Paris Saint Germain B

*** Balmer - Kofi Balmer (a) 19/09/2000, Newtownabbey (Northern Ireland) (b) 1,83 (c) D - central defense (d) Port Vale FC (e) Port Vale, Larne FC, Ballymena

*** Balodis - Daniels Balodis (a) 10/06/1998, Riga (Latvia) (b) 1,88 (c) D - central defense (d) Valmiera FC (e) RFS II, Jelgava, RFS II, Daugavpils, RFS II, RTU, Skonto

*** Balodis - Patriks Balodis (a) 03/12/2001, ¿? (Latvia) (b) - (c) G (d) AFA Olaine (e) Super Nova

*** Balogh - Balázs Balogh (a) 11/06/1990, Budapest (Hungary) (b) 1,82 (c) M - central midfielder (d) Paksi FC (e) Puskás AFC, Újpest FC, Lecce, Empoli

*** Balogh - Norbert Balogh (Balogh Norbert Sándor) (a) 21/02/1996, Hajdúböszörmény (Hungary) (b) 1,96 (c) F - center forward (d) Kisvárda FC (e) Kisvárda, Dunajska Streda, Vasas FC, Dunajska Streda, Honvéd, Dunajska Streda, Honvéd, Hull City, Palermo, APOEL FC, US Palermo, Debrecen, Létavértes SC 97

*** Balogiannis - Konstantinos Balogiannis (Κωνσταντίνος Μπαλογιάννης) (a) 08/02/1999, Thessaloniki (Greece) (b) 1,80 (c) D - left back (d) Botev Plovdiv (e) OFI Creta, PAOK, Volos NPS, PAOK

*** Balogun - Folarin Balogun (Folarin Jerry Balogun) (a) 03/07/2001, New York City, New York (United States) (b) 1,78 (c) F - center forward (d) Arsenal FC (e) Stade Reims, Arsenal, Middlesbrough

*** Baloteli - Philip Baloteli (Philip Christopher Baloteli) (a) 15/02/2004, ¿? (Nigeria) (b) - (c) F - center forward (d) Zalaegerszegi TE FC (e) Zalaegerszeg II

*** Balotelli - Mario Balotelli (Mario Barwuah Balotelli) (a) 12/08/1990, Palermo (Italy) (b) 1,89 (c) F - center forward (d) FC Sion (e) Adana Demirspor, Monza, Brescia, Ol. Marseille, OGC Nice, Liverpool, AC Milan, Liverpool, AC Milan, Manchester City, Internazionale Milano, Lumezzane

*** Baloun - Vojtech Baloun (Vojtěch Baloun) (a) 25/10/2002, ¿? (Czech Rep.) (b) 1,87 (c) D (d) FC Hradec Kralove B (e) -

*** Baltaci - Metehan Baltaci (Metehan Baltacı) (a) 03/11/2002, Istanbul (Turkey) (b) 1,89 (c) D - central defense (d) Eyüpspor (e) Eyüpspor, Galatasaray, Manisa FK, Galatasaray, Iskenderunspor, Galatasaray

*** Baltanov - Lachezar Baltanov (Лъчезар Росенов Балтанов) (a) 11/07/1988, Sofia (Bulgaria) (b) 1,80 (c) M - central midfielder (d) Botev Plovdiv (e) Botev II, Botev Plovdiv, Tsarsko Selo, Botev Plovdiv, Levski Sofia, Chern. Burgas, Levski Sofia, Botev Vratsa, Levski Sofia, Kaliakra, Levski Sofia

*** Baltaxa - Matan Baltaxa (בלטקסה מתן) (a) 20/09/1995, Shoham (Israel) (b) 1,85 (c) D - left back (d) FK Austria Viena (e) Maccabi Tel Aviv, Bnei Yehuda, Maccabi Tel Aviv, Bnei Yehuda, Maccabi Tel Aviv, Hapoel Acre, Maccabi Tel Aviv, H. Petah Tikva

*** Baltazar - Baltazar (Baltazar Costa Rodrigues de Oliveira) (a) 06/05/2000, Jaragua (Brazil) (b) 1,78 (c) D - left back (d) FC Sion (e) Vila Nova FC

*** Baltazar - Gee Baltazar (Guilherme Fernandes Mateus Baltazar) (a) 27/11/1999, Lisboa (Portugal) (b) 1,78 (c) M - attacking midfielder (d) - (e) Rapid Brodoc, Mons Calpe, West Allot., Billingham, Benfield FC, Ashington AFC, Jarrow FC, Whitby

*** Baltic - Lazar Baltic (Лазар Балтић) (a) 27/03/2002, ¿? (RF Yugoslavia, now in Montenegro) (b) 1,85 (c) G (d) Rudar Pljevlja (e) Arsenal Tivat, Mornar Bar, Rudar Pljevlja

*** Baltrunas - Zygimantas Baltrunas (Žygimantas Baltrūnas) (a) 11/03/2002, Marijampole (Lithuania) (b) 1,79 (c) D - left back (d) FK Suduva Marijampole (e) USD Breno, Clodiense

*** Baluta - Alexandru Baluta (Alexandru Mihail Băluţă) (a) 13/09/1993, Craiova (Romania) (b) 1,66 (c) M - attacking midfielder (d) FCSB (e) Puskás AFC, Slavia Praha, Slovan Liberec, Slavia Praha, CS U Craiova, FC Viitorul, Chindia, AF Gică Popescu

*** Baluta - Tudor Baluta (Tudor Cristian Băluţă) (a) 27/03/1999, Craiova (Romania) (b) 1,92 (c) M - pivot (d) FCV Farul Constanta (e) Brighton & Hove Albion, Dinamo Kyïv, Brighton & Hove Albion, ADO Den Haag, Brighton & Hove Albion, FC Viitorul, Brighton & Hove Albion, FC Viitorul, Academia Hagi

*** Bamba - Abdoul Kader Bamba (a) 25/04/1994, Sarcelles (France) (b) 1,77 (c) F - right winger (d) FC Nantes (e) St.-Étienne, FC Nantes, Amiens SC, FC Nantes, FC Nantes B, Le Mans FC, Taverny

*** Bamba - Abdoulaye Bamba (a) 25/04/1990, Abidjan (Ivory Coast) (b) 1,82 (c) D - right back (d) Angers SCO (e) Dijon

*** Bamba - Daouda Bamba (Daouda Karamoko Bamba) (a) 05/03/1995, Dabou (Ivory Coast) (b) 1,84 (c) F - center forward (d) Ümraniyespor (e) CSKA-Sofia, Altay SK, Brann, Kristiansund, Sp. Consultant, Kongsvinger, Sp. Consultant

*** Bamba - Ibra Bamba (Ibrahima Kader Ariel Bamba) (a) 22/04/2002, Vercelli (Italy) (b) 1,85 (c) D - central defense (d) Al-Duhail SC (e) Vitória Guimarães, Vitória Guimarães B

*** Bamba - Jonathan Bamba (a) 26/03/1996, Alfortville (France) (b) 1,75 (c) F - left winger (d) RC Celta de Vigo (e) Lille, St.-Étienne, Angers SCO, St.-Étienne, Sint-Truiden, St.-Étienne, Paris FC, St.-Étienne, Saint-Étienne B

*** Bambam - Bambam (Claudivan dos Santos Bezerra) (a) 06/02/1994, Recife (Brazil) (b) 1,83 (c) F - center forward (d) Internacional de Lages (e) Itabaiana, KF Egnatia, Betim Futebol, Taubaté, Jacuipense-BA, Água Santa, Juventude, São Bento (SP), Central, Brusque, Globo, Fluminense-BA, Coruripe, Vera Cruz, Ypiranga-PE, Boa Esporte

*** Bamford - Patrick Bamford (Patrick James Bamford) (a) 05/09/1993, Grantham (England) (b) 1,85 (c) F - center forward (d) Leeds United (e) Middlesbrough, Chelsea, Burnley, Chelsea, Norwich City, Chelsea, Crystal Palace, Chelsea, Middlesbrough, Chelsea, Derby, Chelsea, MK Dons, Chelsea, MK Dons, Chelsea, Nottingham Forest

*** Bamgboye - Funsho Bamgboye (Funsho Ibrahim Bamgboye) (a) 09/01/1999, Ibadan (Nigeria) (b) 1,73 (c) F - right winger (d) FC Rapid 1923 (e) Fehérvár, Haladás

*** Banada - Yevgen Banada (a) 29/02/1992, Nikopol, Dnipropetrovsk Oblast (Ukraine) (b) 1,82 (d) LNZ Cherkasy (e) Kryvbas, Metalist, FK Oleksandriya, Oleksandriya II

*** Banahene - Nasiru Banahene (Nasiru Zakari Banahene) (a) 08/07/2000, ¿? (Ghana) (b) 1,71 (c) M - pivot (d) FC Honka (e) MTK Budapest, FC Honka, MTK Budapest, Liberty Prof.

*** Banai - Dávid Banai (a) 09/05/1994, Budapest (Hungary) (b) 1,90 (c) G (d) Újpest FC (e) Újpest II

*** Bancu - Nicusor Bancu (Nicuşor Silviu Bancu) (a) 18/09/1992, Slatina (Romania) (b) 1,82 (c) D - left back (d) Universitatea Craiova (e) FC Olt Slatina

*** Banda - B.J. Banda (Billy Banda Jr) (a) 01/06/1998, Johannesburg, Gauteng (South Africa) (b) 1,76 (c) F - center forward (d) Finn Harps (e) Larne FC, Ballinamallard, Letterkenny, Finn Harps

*** Banda - Bradley Banda (Bradley James Banda) (a) 20/01/1998, Gibraltar (Gibraltar) (b) 1,83 (c) G (d) St Joseph's FC (e) Europa FC, Lynx FC, Glacis United, Team Solent, Lincoln FC, Manchester 62, Lions Gibraltar

*** Banda - Emmanuel Banda (Emmanuel Justine Rabby Banda) (a) 29/09/1997, Chililabombwe (Zambia) (b) 1,78 (c) M - central midfielder (d) HNK Rijeka (e) Djurgården, KV Oostende, AS Béziers, KV Oostende, Esmoriz, Nchanga Rangers FC

*** Banda - Haris Banda (a) 14/05/1993, ¿? (RF Yugoslavia, now in Montenegro) (b) - (c) D - right back (d) Jedinstvo Bijelo Polje (e) FK Iskra, Jedinstvo, FK Brskovo, Jedinstvo

*** Banda - Lameck Banda (a) 29/01/2001, Lusaka (Zambia) (b) 1,69 (c) F - left winger (d) US Lecce (e) M. Petah Tikva, Arsenal Tula, M. Petah Tikva, Arsenal Tula, Maccabi Netanya, Arsenal Tula, ZESCO United FC, Nkwazi FC

*** Bandeira - Mauro Bandeira (Mauro Gomes Bandeira) (a) 18/11/2003, Loures (Portugal) (b) 1,78 (c) M - central midfielder (d) Colchester United (e) Colchester Utd.

*** Bandinelli - Filippo Bandinelli (a) 29/03/1995, Firenze (Italy) (b) 1,80 (c) M - central midfielder (d) Spezia (e) FC Empoli, Sassuolo, Benevento, Sassuolo, Perugia, Sassuolo, Latina Calcio, Fiorentina, Latina Calcio, Fiorentina

*** Bandura - Oleksandr Bandura (Бандура Олександр Вікторович) (a) 30/05/1986, Gamaliivka, Sumy Oblast (Soviet Union, now in Russia) (b) 1,86 (c) G (d) FK Minaj (e) Rukh Lviv, PFC Lviv, Veres Rivne, Stal Kamyanske, Metalurg Donetsk, Krymteplytsya, SK Tavriya, Krymteplytsya, SK Tavriya, Yavir, Spartak Sumy, Yavir, Spartak Sumy

*** Bandzeladze - Ushangi Bandzeladze (უშანგი ბანძელაძე) (a) 09/02/1993, ¿? (Georgia) (b) 1,82 (c) D - right back (d) - (e) Samgurali, Merani Martvili, Samgurali, FC Sapovnela

*** Bane - Sidi Bane (Sidi Bane) (a) 14/01/2004, Pir-Goureye (Senegal) (b) 1,84 (c) D - central defense (d) BATE Borisov (e) USP Goureye

*** Banel - Jaydon Banel (Jaydon Amauri Banel) (a) 19/10/2004, ¿? (Netherlands) (b) - (c) F - left winger (d) Ajax Amsterdam B (e) -

*** Bánfalvi - Gergő Bánfalvi (a) 14/07/2005, ¿? (Hungary) (b) - (c) G (d) Vasas FC II (e) -

*** Bangsbo - Johan Bangsbo (Mats Johan Edward Bångsbo) (a) 10/02/2003, ¿? (Sweden) (b) - (c) D - central defense (d) IFK Göteborg (e) -

*** Bangura - Alex Bangura (a) 13/07/1999, Mokomre (Sierra Leona) (b) 1,83 (c) D - left back (d) SC Cambuur Leeuwarden (e) -

*** Bangura - Clinton Bangura (a) 22/03/1998, Kumasi (Ghana) (b) 1,84 (c) D - central defense (d) - (e) Pietà Hotspurs, FC Marchfeld, SV Horn, Bruck/L., FAC, SC Neusiedl/See, FAC, Wiener Linien, Wr. Linien II, Simmering II

*** Banic - Ivan Banic (Ivan Banić) (a) 18/07/1994, Sinj (Croatia) (b) 1,87 (c) G (d) HNK Gorica (e) Olimpija, HNK Gorica, NK Rudes, NK Dugopolje, Junak Sinj, RNK Split, Junak Sinj, RNK Split, NK Imotski, RNK Split, NK Imotski, Hajduk Split, Primorac 1929, Hajduk Split, NK Hrvace, Hajduk Split, Primorac 1929, Hajduk Split

*** Baningime - Beni Baningime (Beni Tangama Baningime) (a) 09/09/1998, Kinshasa (Congo DR) (b) 1,78 (c) M - central midfielder (d) Heart of Midlothian FC (e) Everton, Derby, Everton, Wigan Ath., Everton

*** Baniya - Rayyan Baniya (a) 18/02/1999, Bologna (Italy) (b) 1,94 (c) D - central defense (d) Fatih Karagümrük (e) Hellas Verona, Mantova, Hellas Verona, Renate, Hellas Verona, Mantova

*** Banjac - Mihajlo Banjac (Михајло Бањац) (a) 10/11/1999, Novi Sad (Yugoslavia, now in Serbia) (b) 1,86 (c) M - central midfielder (d) FK Krasnodar (e) FK TSC, FK Indjija

*** Banks - Lewis Banks (a) 14/04/1997, Stone (England) (b) 1,83 (c) D - right back (d) Altrincham FC (e) Arbroath, Sligo Rovers, Stafford Rangers

*** Banó-Szabó - Bence Banó-Szabó (Banó-Szabó Bence Zoltán) (a) 25/07/1999, Kecskemét (Hungary) (b) 1,80 (c) M - attacking midfielder (d) Kecskeméti TE (e) Honvéd

*** Banovec - Lovro Banovec (a) 28/10/2001, Zagreb (Croatia) (b) - (c) F - right winger (d) NK Varazdin (e) Inker, NK Ponikve

*** Banozic - Sebastian Banozic (a) 17/07/2003, ¿? (Sweden) (b) 1,91 (c) G (d) BK Häcken (e) -

*** Banse - Sacha Banse (Sacha Jordan Banse) (a) 16/03/2001, ¿? (Belgium) (b) - (c) M - pivot (d) Standard de Lieja (e) SL16 FC, Jong KAA Gent

*** Banu - Luca Banu (Luca Nicolae Banu) (a) 31/01/2005, Constanța (Romania) (b) 1,78 (c) M - pivot (d) FCV Farul Constanta (e) Academia Hagi

*** Banza - Enoch Banza (Bile-Enoch Banza) (a) 04/02/2000, Helsinki (Finland) (b) 1,76 (c) F - right winger (d) Järvenpään Palloseura (e) JäPS, Raufoss, AC Oulu, Raufoss, HJK Helsinki, RoPS, HJK Helsinki, Kokkolan PV, HJK Helsinki, HJK Klubi 04

*** Banza - Simon Banza (Simon Bokoté Banza) (a) 13/08/1996, Creil (France) (b) 1,89 (c) F - center forward (d) SC Braga (e) RC Lens, Famalicão, RC Lens, Union Titus Petange, RC Lens, AS Béziers, RC Lens, RC Lens B

*** Banzaru - Ruslan Banzaru (Ruslan Bânzaru) (a) 18/05/2002, Lăpușna (Moldova) (b) 1,75 (c) F - left winger (d) FC Victoria Chisinau (e) Petrocub

*** Baosic - Jovan Baosic (Jovan Baošić) (a) 07/07/1995, Bijelo Polje (Yugoslavia, now in Montenegro) (b) 1,87 (c) D - central defense (d) FK Mornar Bar (e) Buducnost Podgorica, Újpest FC, Zeta Golubovac, Jedinstvo, Rudar Pljevlja, Jedinstvo, Jagodina, Mogren

*** Baptiste - Shandon Baptiste (Shandon Harkeem Baptiste) (a) 08/04/1998, Reading (England) (b) 1,80 (c) M - central midfielder (d) Brentford FC (e) Oxford United, Hampton & Rich., Oxford United

*** Bara - Karim Abdoul Bara (a) 22/09/1997, Béguédo (Burkina Faso) (b) - (c) F - right winger (d) SP Cailungo (e) Domagnano, BSK Zmaj Blato, Fosso Ghiaia

*** Barac - Mateo Barac (Mateo Barać) (a) 20/07/1994, Sinj (Croatia) (b) 1,94 (c) D - central defense (d) Krylya Sovetov Samara (e) KV Oostende, KS Samara, Sochi, KS Samara, Sochi, Rapid Wien, NK Osijek, HNK Sibenik, Hrv Dragovoljac, FC Wohlen, Junak Sinj

*** Barak - Antonin Barak (Antonín Barák) (a) 03/12/1994, Příbram (Czech Rep.) (b) 1,90 (c) M - attacking midfielder (d) Fiorentina (e) Hellas Verona, Fiorentina, Hellas Verona, Udinese, Hellas Verona, Udinese, Lecce, Udinese, Slavia Praha, 1.FK Pribram, 1.FK Pribram B, Graffin Vlasim, 1.FK Pribram B

*** Baranok - Nikita Baranok (Баранок Никита Андреевич) (a) 31/03/2004, ¿? (Belarus) (b) 1,88 (c) D - central defense (d) Shakhter Soligorsk (e) Vitebsk, Vitebsk II, RUOR Minsk

*** Baranov - Nikita Baranov (a) 19/08/1992, Tallinn (Estonia) (b) 1,84 (c) D - central defense (d) FC Pyunik Yerevan (e) Hamrun Spartans, Karmiotissa, Alashkert CF, Beroe, Sogndal, Kristiansund, FC Flora, FC Flora II, Warrior Valga, FC Ararat

*** Baranov - Pavel Baranov (Баранов Павел Дмитриевич) (a) 16/05/1999, Seltso, Bryansk Region (Russia) (b) 1,78 (c) M - right midfielder (d) FK Sloga Meridian (e) Veles Moskva, Neftekhimik, Dinamo Bryansk, ArsenaL-Dinamo, Dinamo Bryansk, Sokol Seltso

*** Baranovskiy - Aleksey Baranovskiy (Барановский Алексей Тимофеевич) (a) 25/01/2005, St. Petersburg (Russia) (b) 1,84 (c) F - center forward (d) Zenit 2 St. Petersburg (e) Zenit St. Peterburg II

*** Baranovskiy - Mikhail Baranovskiy (Барановский Михаил Викторович) (a) 04/01/1983, Dimitrovgrad, Uljanovsk Region (Soviet Union, now in Russia) (b) 1,83 (c) G (d) - (e) Slavia, Baltika, Sokol Saratov, FK Kaluga, Ufa, Rotor Volgograd, Dinamo Bryansk, Zhemchuzhina, Baltika, Soligorsk, Baltika, Lada Dimitrovgrad

*** Baranovskyi - Artem Baranovskyi (Барановський Артем Миколайович) (a) 17/03/1990, Krasnogorivka, Donetsk Oblast (Soviet Union, now in Ukraine) (b) 1,90 (c) D - central defense (d) Michigan Stars FC (e) Kaspiy Aktau, Akzhayik, Kyzyl-Zhar, FK Buxoro, Shakhter K., Istiqlol, Olimpik Donetsk, Stal Kamyanske, Metalurg Donetsk, Metalurg II

*** Baranowski - Pawel Baranowski (Paweł Baranowski) (a) 11/10/1990, Suwałki (Poland) (b) 1,91 (c) D - central defense (d) Ruch Chorzów (e) Atyrau, Gornik Leczna, Odra Opole, Stomil, Wigry Suwalki, Podbeskidzie, Erzgebirge Aue, GKS Belchatow, Stomil, Podbeskidzie, Stomil, Podbeskidzie, Wigry Suwalki, Podbeskidzie, Wigry Suwalki

*** Bárány - Donát Bárány (a) 04/09/2000, Debrecen (Hungary) (b) 1,79 (c) F - center forward (d) Debreceni VSC (e) Debrecen II, Debreceni EAC, Debrecen II

*** Baranyai - Nimród Baranyai (a) 06/08/2003, Debrecen (Hungary) (b) 1,80 (c) D - right back (d) Debreceni VSC (e) Mezőkövesd, Debrecen, Debrecen II

*** Barasi - Yusuf Barasi (Yusuf Barası) (a) 31/03/2003, Alkmaar (Netherlands) (b) 1,83 (c) F - center forward (d) AZ Alkmaar (e) -

*** Baráth - Botond Baráth (a) 21/04/1992, Budapest (Hungary) (b) 1,88 (c) D - central defense (d) Vasas FC (e) Honvéd, Kansas City, Honvéd, Honvéd II

*** Baráth - Péter Baráth (a) 21/02/2002, Kisvárda (Hungary) (b) 1,85 (c) M - central midfielder (d) Ferencváros TC (e) Debrecen, Ferencváros, Debrecen

*** Baratuipre - Hanson Richmond Baratuipre (a) 01/03/2004, ¿? (Nigeria) (b) - (c) F - left winger (d) Mosta FC (e) Garden City

*** Barauskas - Dominykas Barauskas (a) 18/04/1997, Vilnius (Lithuania) (b) 1,88 (c) D - central defense (d) - (e) Stal Mielec, Riteriai, Suduva, Zalgiris, Stumbras, Zalgiris

*** Baravykas - Rolandas Baravykas (a) 23/08/1995, Siauliai (Lithuania) (b) 1,85 (c) D - right back (d) - (e) FCV Farul, Universitatea Cluj, UTA Arad, FK Kukësi, Nea Salamis, Zalgiris, Atlantas

*** Baraye - Yves Baraye (Bertrand Yves Baraye) (a) 22/06/1992, Dakar (Senegal) (b) 1,77 (c) F - right winger (d) FK Vojvodina Novi Sad (e) B SAD, Gil Vicente, Parma, Gil Vicente, Parma, Padova, Parma, Chievo Verona, Torres, Chievo Verona, Juve Stabia, Lumezzane, Udinese, Lumezzane, Udinese

*** Barbara - Zak Barbara (a) 07/02/2005, ¿? (Malta) (b) - (c) F (d) - (e) Valletta FC,

*** Barbaro - Valerio Barbaro (a) 16/02/1998, Niederkorn (Luxembourg) (b) - (c) F - right winger (d) UN Käerjeng 97 (e) FC Rodange 91, Progrès Niederkorn, FC UNA Strassen, Progrès Niederkorn, Progrès Niederkorn

*** Barberis - Andrea Barberis (a) 11/12/1993, Genoa (Italy) (b) 1,77 (c) M - pivot (d) - (e) Monza, Crotone, Varese, AC Pisa, Varese

*** Barbieri - Tommaso Barbieri (a) 26/08/2002, Magenta (Italy) (b) 1,81 (c) D - right back (d) Pisa Sporting Club (e) Pisa, Juve Next Gen, Novara

*** Barbosa - Bertino Barbosa (Bertino João Cabral Barbosa) (a) 06/05/1992, Oeiras (Portugal) (b) 1,88 (c) F - center forward (d) Al-Fujairah SC (e) Differdange 03, F91 Dudelange, Hamm Benfica, F91 Dudelange, Hamm Benfica, US Rumelange, AD Oeiras, Real SC, Cinfães, GD Ribeirão, Real SC

*** Barbosa - Diogo Barbosa (a) 13/01/1996, ¿? (Portugal) (b) - (c) M - central midfielder (d) Botev Vratsa (e) Darlington, Mt Druitt Town, PO Xylotymbou, Dulwich Hamlet, Marítimo B, Vilafranquense, Torreense

*** Barbosa - Gabriel Barbosa (Gabriel Barbosa Avelino) (a) 17/03/1999, Anápolis (Brazil) (b) 1,95 (c) F - center forward (d) FC Penafiel (e) APO Levadiakos, FK Kukësi, APO Levadiakos, Palmeiras, FC Seoul, Palmeiras, Paysandu, Figueirense FC, Londrina-PR

*** Barbut - Cristi Barbut (Cristi Marian Bărbuţ) (a) 22/04/1995, Timişoara (Romania) (b) 1,66 (c) F - right winger (d) FC Hermannstadt (e) Sepsi OSK, CS U Craiova, ACS Poli

*** Barcia - Sergio Barcia (Sergio Barcia Laranxeira) (a) 31/12/2000, Vigo (Spain) (b) 1,86 (c) D - central defense (d) CD Mirandés (e) Celta Fortuna, Recreativo Granada, Celta B, Ourense CF, Celta B

*** Barcola - Bradley Barcola (a) 02/09/2002, Lyon (France) (b) 1,82 (c) F - right winger (d) Olympique de Lyon (e) Olymp. Lyon B

*** Barcola - Malcolm Barcola (a) 14/05/1999, Lyon (France) (b) 1,95 (c) G (d) - (e) FK Tuzla City, Olympique Lyon, Olymp. Lyon B

*** Bard - Melvin Bard (Melvin Michel Maxence Bard) (a) 06/11/2000, Écully (France) (b) 1,73 (c) D - left back (d) OGC Niza (e) Olympique Lyon, Olymp. Lyon B

*** Bardakci - Abdülkerim Bardakci (Abdülkerim Bardakcı) (a) 07/09/1994, Konya (Turkey) (b) 1,85 (c) D - central defense (d) Galatasaray (e) Konyaspor, Altay SK, Konyaspor, Denizlispor, Konyaspor, Giresunspor, Konyaspor, Samsunspor, Konyaspor, Samsunspor, Konyaspor, Adana Demirspor, Konyaspor, A. Selcukluspor, Konyaspor

*** Bárdarson - Jóhannes Karl Bárdarson (Jóhannes Karl Bárðarson) (a) 24/09/2003, ¿? (Faroe Islands) (b) - (c) D - right back (d) Thróttur Vogum (e) Víkingur, Aegir, Víkingur

*** Bárdarson - Olaf Bárdarson (Olaf Bárðarson) (a) 20/10/2003, ¿? (Faroe Islands) (b) 1,80 (c) M - left midfielder (d) Víkingur Gøta (e) Víkingur II

*** Bardea - Nir Bardea (ניר ברדע) (a) 25/01/1996, Rishon LeZion (Israel) (b) 1,89 (c) D - central defense (d) FK Sabail (e) M. Bnei Reineh, Honvéd, FC Ashdod

*** Bardghji - Roony Bardghji (روني بردغجي) (a) 15/11/2005, Kuwait City (Kuwait) (b) 1,82 (c) F - right winger (d) FC Copenhague (e) -

*** Bardhi - Behar Bardhi (Бехар Барди) (a) 24/03/1993, Skopje (North Macedonia) (b) - (c) D - central defense (d) KF Ferizaj (e) KF Vitia, KF Ferizaj

*** Bardhi - Enis Bardhi (a) 02/07/1995, Blace (North Macedonia) (b) 1,72 (d) Trabzonspor (e) Levante UD, Újpest FC, Prespa Birlik

*** Bardhoku - Tun Bardhoku (a) 12/09/1993, Gjakovë (RF Yugoslavia, now in Kosovo) (b) 1,79 (c) D - right back (d) KF Feronikeli Drenas (e) FC Drita, FC Prishtina, KF Vëllaznimi

*** Bardi - Francesco Bardi (a) 18/01/1992, Livorno (Italy) (b) 1,88 (c) G (d) AC Reggiana 1919 (e) Bologna, Frosinone, Internazionale Milano, Frosinone, Internazionale Milano, RCD Espanyol, Internazionale Milano, Chievo Verona, Internazionale Milano, AS Livorno, Internazionale Milano, Novara, Internazionale Milano, AS Livorno

*** Bardis - Maxim Bardis (a) 16/07/1997, ¿? (Moldova) (b) 1,86 (c) G (d) FC Floresti (e) Sfintul Gheorghe, Dinamo-Auto, FC Sheriff, Sheriff-2

*** Bardy - Pierre Bardy (Pierre Luc Bardy-Alenda) (a) 27/08/1992, Rodez (France) (b) 1,82 (c) D - central defense (d) - (e) Olympiakos N., Rodez AF, Rodez AF B

*** Bare - Keidi Bare (a) 28/08/1997, Fier (Albania) (b) 1,74 (c) M - central midfielder (d) RCD Espanyol (e) Málaga CF, At. Malagueño, At. Madrid B

*** Bareiro - Mariano Bareiro (Lucas Mariano Bareiro) (a) 08/05/1995, Buenos Aires (Argentina) (b) 1,82 (c) M - pivot (d) Hapoel Beer Sheva (e) Racing, H. Beer Sheva, Racing, Huracán, Racing, Defensa y Justicia, Racing

*** Barella - Nicolò Barella (a) 07/02/1997, Cagliari (Italy) (b) 1,75 (c) M - central midfielder (d) Internazionale Milano (e) Cagliari, Internazionale Milano, Cagliari, Como, Cagliari

*** Baresic - Marko Baresic (Marko Barešić) (a) 30/04/1999, Zadar (Croatia) (b) 1,96 (c) G (d) NK Osijek (e) NK Osijek II

*** Barga Ngoba - Anael Barga Ngoba (Anaël Barga Ngoba) (a) 08/10/1998, ¿? (Cameroon) (b) 1,84 (c) F - center forward (d) - (e) Tikves, Al-Akhdar SC, Majees SC, Al-Watani

*** Bargiel - Przemyslaw Bargiel (Przemysław Gabriel Bargiel) (a) 26/03/2000, Ruda Śląska (Poland) (b) 1,79 (c) M - central midfielder (d) Wieczysta Krakow (e) Śląsk Wroclaw, Ruch

*** Bari - Bilal Bari (باري بلال) (a) 19/01/1998, Lens (France) (b) 1,84 (c) F - center forward (d) Levski Sofia (e) Montana, Concordia, RC Lens B, RS Berkane, RC Lens B

*** Bari - Kristian Bari (Kristián Bari) (a) 06/02/2001, Fiľakovo (Slovakia) (b) 1,73 (c) D - left back (d) MSK Zilina (e) MSK Zilina B

*** Baribo - Tai Baribo (תאי בריבו) (a) 15/01/1998, Eilat (Israel) (b) 1,81 (c) F - center forward (d) Philadelphia Union (e) Wolfsberger AC, M. Petah Tikva

*** Barinov - Dmitriy Barinov (Баринов Дмитрий Николаевич) (a) 11/09/1996, Ogudnevo, Moskau Oblast (Russia) (b) 1,81 (c) M - pivot (d) Lokomotiv Moskva (e) Lokomotiv Moskva II, Master-Saturn

*** Baris - Damian Baris (Damián Bariš) (a) 09/12/1994, Trenčín (Slovakia) (b) 1,80 (c) M - central midfielder (d) AS Trencin (e) Podbrezova, Zbrojovka Brno, Zlaté Moravce, Skalica, AS Trencin, Nove Mesto, AS Trencin

*** Barisic - Adrian Leon Barisic (Adrian Leon Barišić) (a) 19/07/2001, Stuttgart (Germany) (b) 1,93 (c) D - central defense (d) NK Osijek (e) Frosinone, NK Osijek, NK Osijek II

*** Barisic - Bartol Barisic (Bartol Barišić) (a) 01/01/2003, Zagreb (Croatia) (b) 1,87 (c) F (d) GNK Dinamo Zagreb (e) Domžale, Dinamo Zagreb, NK Istra, Dinamo Zagreb, Din. Zagreb II

*** Barisic - Borna Barisic (Borna Barišić) (a) 10/11/1992, Osijek (Croatia) (b) 1,86 (c) D - left back (d) Rangers FC (e) NK Osijek, Dinamo Zagreb, NK Lokomotiva, Dinamo Zagreb, NK Osijek, Bijelo Brdo, NK Osijek

*** Barisic - Branimir Barisic (Branimir Barišić) (a) 31/05/1998, Livno (Bosnia and Herzegovina) (b) 1,88 (c) M - pivot (d) NK Siroki Brijeg (e) Inker, Hajduk Split II, HNK Sibenik, Hajduk Split II

*** Barisic - Hrvoje Barisic (Hrvoje Barišić) (a) 03/02/1991, Split (Yugoslavia, now in Croatia) (b) 1,93 (c) D - central defense (d) HSK Zrinjski Mostar (e) FK Tuzla City, Sepsi OSK, Zrinjski Mostar, NK Vitez, Slaven Belupo, NK Vitez, Slaven Belupo, Zrinjski Mostar, NK Dugopolje, RNK Split, NK Dugopolje, HBDNK Mosor

*** Barisic - Maks Barisic (Maks Barišič) (a) 06/03/1995, Ljubljana (Slovenia) (b) 1,87 (c) F - right winger (d) FC Koper (e) Catania, Padova, Catania, Andria, Catania, ACR Messina, Catania, Koper

*** Barja - Kike Barja (Enrique Barja Alfonso) (a) 01/04/1997, Noáin (Spain) (b) 1,79 (c) F - right winger (d) CA Osasuna (e) Osasuna Prom.

*** Barjamaj - Mario Barjamaj (a) 27/06/1998, Tiranë (Albania) (b) - (c) M - attacking midfielder (d) KF Laçi (e) FK Tomori Berat, FK Bylis, FK Partizani B

*** Barkarson - Jón Hrafn Barkarson (a) 14/09/2003, ¿? (Iceland) (b) - (c) M (d) Leiknir Reykjavík (e) -

*** Barkas - Vasilios Barkas (Βασίλειος Μπάρκας) (a) 30/05/1994, Athina (Greece) (b) 1,96 (c) G (d) FC Utrecht (e) Celtic FC, FC Utrecht, Celtic FC, AEK Athína, Atromitos FC

*** Barker - Brandon Barker (Brandon Lee Colin Barker) (a) 04/10/1996, Manchester (England) (b) 1,80 (c) F - left winger (d) - (e) Omonia Nicosia, Reading, Rangers FC, Oxford United, Rangers FC, Preston North End, Hibernian FC, NAC Breda, Rotherham

*** Barkley - Ross Barkley (a) 05/12/1993, Liverpool (England) (b) 1,89 (c) M - central midfielder (d) Luton Town (e) OGC Nice, Chelsea, Aston Villa, Chelsea, Everton, Leeds Utd., Everton, Sheffield Wednesday, Everton

*** Barkok - Aymen Barkok (أيمن بركوك) (a) 21/05/1998, Frankfurt am Main (Germany) (b) 1,89 (c) M - central midfielder (d) 1.FSV Mainz 05 (e) Eintracht, Fortuna Düsseldorf, Eintracht

*** Barkovskiy - German Barkovskiy (Барковский Герман Анатольевич) (a) 25/06/2002, Bobruisk (Belarus) (b) 1,90 (c) F - center forward (d) Energetik-BGU Minsk (e) Isloch, Rukh, Isloch, Rukh, Belshina, Belshina II

*** Barkunov - Pavel Barkunov (Баркунов Павел Александрович) (a) 22/03/1999, Irkutsk Oblast (Russia) (b) 1,86 (c) D - central defense (d) - (e) FK Aksu, FC Zhenis, FK Aksu, FK Ekibastuz, Pavlodar II

*** Barlafante - Federico Barlafante (a) 06/06/2000, Giulianova (Italy) (b) 1,73 (c) F - right winger (d) Chieti FC 1922 (e) Libertas, Juve Stabia, Pineto, Giulianova

*** Barlow - Kailin Barlow (a) 28/06/2003, ¿? (Ireland) (b) - (c) M - attacking midfielder (d) Sligo Rovers (e) -

*** Barmen - Kristoffer Barmen (Kristoffer Ramos Barmen) (a) 19/08/1993, Bergen (Norway) (b) 1,90 (c) M - central midfielder (d) Aalesunds FK (e) Brann

*** Barnabas - Moses Zambrang Barnabas (a) 06/05/2003, Lagos (Nigeria) (b) - (c) M - pivot (d) NK Sesvete (e) NK Sesvete, Tehnicar 1974

*** Barnes - Harvey Barnes (Harvey Lewis Barnes) (a) 09/12/1997, Burnley (England) (b) 1,82 (c) F - left winger (d) Newcastle United (e) Leicester City, West Bromwich Albion, Leicester City, Barnsley FC, MK Dons

*** Barnes - Joselpho Barnes (a) 12/12/2001, Oberhausen (Germany) (b) 1,87 (c) F - center forward (d) Sint-Truidense VV (e) Riga, Schalke 04 II

*** Barnett - Erin Barnett (Erin Anthony Barnett) (a) 02/09/1996, Gibraltar (Gibraltar) (b) 1,85 (c) D - central defense (d) St Joseph's FC (e) Marine FC, Boca Gibraltar, Gibraltar Utd., Lions Gibraltar

*** Baró - Romário Baró (Romário Miguel Silva Baró) (a) 25/01/2000, Bissau (Guinea-Bissau) (b) 1,79 (c) M - central midfielder (d) FC Porto (e) Casa Pia, FC Porto, Estoril Praia, FC Porto, FC Porto B

*** Baroan - Antoine Baroan (a) 24/06/2000, Niort (France) (b) 1,88 (c) F - center forward (d) Botev Plovdiv (e) Chamois Niort, Niort B

*** Baron - Anthony Baron (Anthony Kévin Baron) (a) 29/12/1992, Villepinte (France) (b) 1,80 (c) D - central defense (d) Servette FC (e) Yverdon Sport, Stade Nyonnais, Yverdon Sport, Stade Nyonnais, Saint-Pryvé FC, AS Beauvais, Amiens SC B, FC Chartres, Bourges Foot, Lormont

*** Baron - Dirk Baron (Dirk Jan Baron) (a) 16/08/2002, ¿? (Netherlands) (b) - (c) G (d) FC Groningen (e) ONS Sneek

*** Barone - Gareth Barone (a) 04/07/2001, ¿? (Malta) (b) 1,88 (c) D - central defense (d) Marsaxlokk FC (e) Mqabba FC, Marsaxlokk

*** Barone - Mario Barone (a) 13/06/1984, Napoli (Italy) (b) 1,72 (c) M - pivot (d) AC Libertas (e) Victor SM, Matese, R. Aversa, Flaminia, Albalonga, Massese, Nocerina, Sambenedettese, Lupa Cast Rom, Olbia 1905, Fondi, Sora, FC Mugnano, Puteoli Sport, Savoia, Viribus Somma, Pomigliano, Cavese, Ariano Irpino, Viterbese

*** Barou - Stephane Joel Barou (a) 21/12/2003, Abidjan (Ivory Coast) (b) - (c) M - attacking midfielder (d) AS Denguélé d'Odienné (e) Velez Mostar

*** Baroyan - Narek Baroyan (Նարեկ Բարոյան) (a) 05/05/2005, Vanadzor (Armenia) (b) - (c) F - attacking midfielder (d) FC Pyunik Yerevan B (e) Lori Vanadzor

*** Barr - Brendan Barr (a) 05/05/2001, Derry (Northern Ireland) (b) 1,77 (c) M - pivot (d) University College Dublin (e) Derry City, Dungannon, Derry City, Ballymena, Derry City

*** Barr - Jethren Barr (Jethren Keith Barr) (a) 13/09/1995, Durban (South Africa) (b) 1,84 (c) G (d) - (e) Portadown, Maritzburg Utd., Bidvest Wits FC, Stellenbosch FC, Bidvest Wits FC

*** Barr - Lewis Barr (a) 20/04/2003, Belfast (Northern Ireland) (b) - (c) D - left back (d) Harland & Wolff Welders (e) HW Welders, Crusaders

*** Barrales - Jerónimo Barrales (a) 28/01/1987, Adrogué (Argentina) (b) 1,86 (c) F - center forward (d) PS Kalamata (e) Asteras Tripoli, PAS Lamia, Gimnasia y Esgrima, Sivasspor, Johor DT, Sivasspor, Huracán, Sivasspor, Asteras Tripoli, Huracán, Unión Santa Fe, Banfield, Wanderers, Banfield, Recreativo, Banfield

*** Barreiro - Leandro Barreiro (Leandro Barreiro Martins) (a) 03/01/2000, Erpeldingen (Luxembourg) (b) 1,74 (c) M - central midfielder (d) 1.FSV Mainz 05 (e) Erpeldange

*** Barrela - André Barrela (André Leite Barrela) (a) 22/01/2001, Ettelbrück (Luxembourg) (b) 1,85 (c) G (d) Union Titus Petange (e) Etzella Ettelbrück

*** Barrenechea - Enzo Barrenechea (Enzo Alan Tomás Barrenechea) (a) 22/05/2001, Villa María (Argentina) (b) 1,86 (c) M - pivot (d) Juventus de Turín (e) Juve Next Gen, FC Sion, Newell's II
*** Barrenetxea - Ander Barrenetxea (Ander Barrenetxea Muguruza) (a) 27/12/2001, Donostia-San Sebastián (Spain) (b) 1,75 (c) F - left winger (d) Real Sociedad (e) Real Sociedad B
*** Barreto - Michaël Barreto (a) 18/01/1991, Paris (France) (b) 1,75 (c) M - attacking midfielder (d) AC Ajaccio (e) AJ Auxerre, US Orléans, Troyes, US Avranches, Troyes, Cannes, Troyes, Fréjus-St-Raphaël, Troyes, Troyes B
*** Barrett - Paddy Barrett (Patrick Barrett) (a) 22/07/1993, Waterford (Ireland) (b) 1,82 (c) D - central defense (d) Shelbourne FC (e) St. Patrick's Ath., Svay Rieng, Indy Eleven, Cincinnati, Dundalk FC, Waterford FC, Dundalk FC, Galway United, Waterford Utd., Dundee United, Waterford Utd., Dundee United
*** Barretta - Antonio Barretta (a) 19/09/1995, Napoli (Italy) (b) 1,82 (c) D - central defense (d) SP Tre Penne (e) Libertas, Pennarossa, Tropical Coriano, Isernia, Ghivizzano, Matera, Lucchese
*** Barretta - Domenico Barretta (a) 26/06/2000, ¿? (Italy) (b) - (c) D (d) - (e) Faetano
*** Barri - Diego Barri (Diego Hernández Barriuso) (a) 19/09/1995, Salamanca (Spain) (b) 1,88 (c) M - central midfielder (d) Cultural Leonesa (e) NK Osijek, CD Badajoz, Celta B, CD Badajoz, Albacete, Getafe CF B, CD Móstoles, CD Los Yébenes, RSD Alcalá
*** Barrientos - Jean Barrientos (Jean Pierre Agustín Barrientos Díaz) (a) 16/09/1990, Montevideo (Uruguay) (b) 1,74 (c) M - attacking midfielder (d) Volos NPS (e) AO Xanthi, Racing Club, FBC Melgar, Olimpo, Racing Club, Wisla Kraków, Vitória Guimarães, Racing Club
*** Barrios - Federico Barrios (Federico Barrios Rubio) (a) 05/10/1996, Cali (Colombia) (b) 1,86 (c) G (d) Botev Vratsa (e) Independiente, Dayton Flyers, Dayton Dutch L., Dayton Flyers
*** Barrios - Pablo Barrios (Pablo Barrios Rivas) (a) 15/06/2003, Madrid (Spain) (b) 1,81 (c) M - central midfielder (d) Atlético de Madrid (e) At. Madrid B
*** Barrios - Wilmar Barrios (Wílmar Enrique Barrios Terán) (a) 16/10/1993, Cartagena de Indias (Colombia) (b) 1,78 (c) M - pivot (d) Zenit de San Petersburgo (e) Boca Juniors, Deportes Tolima, Tolima B
*** Barrios - Wilson Barrios (Wilson José Barrios Rondón) (a) 23/08/2000, Mérida, Mérida (Venezuela) (b) 1,73 (c) F - center forward (d) - (e) FC Van, Estudiantes
*** Barron - Connor Barron (a) 29/08/2002, Kintore (Scotland) (b) 1,75 (c) M - central midfielder (d) Aberdeen FC (e) Aberdeen FC B, Kelty Hearts, Aberdeen FC B, Brechin City, Aberdeen FC B
*** Barros - João Barros (João Paulo Rodrigues Barros) (a) 24/06/2001, Funchal (Portugal) (b) 1,86 (c) D - left back (d) Gil Vicente FC (e) Valadares Gaia, Camacha
*** Barros - Lucas Barros (Lucas Barros da Cunha) (a) 21/08/1999, Rio de Janeiro (Brazil) (b) 1,80 (c) D - left back (d) CD Tondela (e) Tondela, Gil Vicente, SC Covilhã, Botafogo, Botafogo B
*** Barroso - Sergio Barroso (Sergio Rivera Barroso) (a) 08/04/2001, Alcalá del Valle (Spain) (b) 1,78 (c) M - attacking midfielder (d) AD Ceuta FC B (e) Europa FC, UD Gran Tarajal, CD Leganés C
*** Barrow - Musa Barrow (a) 14/11/1998, Banjul (Gambia) (b) 1,84 (c) F - left winger (d) Bologna (e) Atalanta, Bologna, Atalanta, Hawks FC
*** Barry - Yacouba Barry (a) 25/11/2002, Gonesse (France) (b) 1,88 (c) D - central defense (d) FC Annecy (e) RC Lens B, US Chantilly

*** Barseghyan - Tigran Barseghyan (Տիգրան Բարսեղյան) (a) 22/09/1993, Yerevan (Armenia) (b) 1,79 (c) F - right winger (d) Slovan Bratislava (e) FC Astana, Kaysar, Vardar, Gandzasar, MIKA Aschtarak, Gandzasar II, Banants II

*** Barsky - Roslan Barsky (ברסקי רוסלן) (a) 03/01/1992, Holon (Israel) (b) 1,78 (c) M - central midfielder (d) FK Borac Banja Luka (e) Hapoel Hadera, M. Bnei Reineh, H. Jerusalem, Maccabi Tel Aviv, Hapoel Haifa, Maccabi Tel Aviv, Hapoel Haifa, Maccabi Tel Aviv, Beitar TA Ramla, Maccabi Tel Aviv, H. Jerusalem, Maccabi Tel Aviv, Kabilio Jaffa, Maccabi Tel Aviv, Bnei Yehuda, Maccabi Tel Aviv

*** Barslund - Kaare Barslund (Kaare Brøckner Barslund) (a) 23/03/2004, ¿? (Denmark) (b) 1,82 (c) D - central defense (d) FC Nordsjælland (e) -

*** Barsov - Maksim Barsov (Барсов Максим Борисович) (a) 29/04/1993, Tver (Russia) (b) 1,77 (c) F - center forward (d) Spartak Kostroma (e) Neftekhimik, Sochi, Baltika, Sochi, Dinamo S-Pb, Solyaris Moskva, KamAZ, Gazovik Orenburg, FK Kaluga, Lokomotiv Moskva II, Volga Uljanovsk, Lokomotiv Moskva II

*** Barsukov - Evgeniy Barsukov (Барсуков Евгений Юрьевич) (a) 05/07/1990, Gomel (Soviet Union, now in Belarus) (b) 1,78 (c) F - right winger (d) Slavia Mozyr (e) Smolevichi, Dnepr Mogilev, Gomel, Gomelzheldor, Rechitsa, Gomel, Rechitsa, Gomel, Vedrich-97, Gomel, Gomel II

*** Barsukov - Mark Barsukov (Барсуков Марк Максимович) (a) 24/05/2001, Minsk (Belarus) (b) - (c) G (d) Polonia Slubice (e) Belshina, Belshina II, BGU Minsk II, Viktoria MG

*** Bartalsstovu - Kaj Leo í Bartalsstovu (a) 23/06/1991, Syðrugøta (Faroe Islands) (b) 1,83 (c) F - left winger (d) UMF Njarðvík (e) Leiknir, ÍA Akranes, Valur, ÍBV Vestmannaeyjar, Hafnarfjörður, FC Dinamo, Levanger, Víkingur

*** Bartek - David Bartek (a) 13/02/1988, Praha (Czechoslovakia, now in Czech Rep.) (b) - (c) M - right midfielder (d) Bohemians Praha 1905 B (e) Bohemians 1905, SK Kladno, Bohemians 1905

*** Bartia - Giorgi Bartia (a) 03/03/2004, ¿? (Georgia) (b) - (c) D - central defense (d) FC Saburtalo II (e) -

*** Bartkowiak - Hugo Bartkowiak (a) 23/07/2000, Koziegłowy (Poland) (b) 1,86 (c) F - center forward (d) FC College 1975 (e) Lynx FC, Silva SD, Afición Xerez, Almagro CF, Rakow II, Kotwica

*** Bartkowski - Jakub Bartkowski (Jakub Bartkowski) (a) 07/11/1991, Łódź (Poland) (b) 1,82 (c) M - right midfielder (d) Warta Poznań (e) Lechia Gdánsk, Pogon Szczecin, Wisla Kraków, Wigry Suwalki, Widzew Lódz, Widzew II

*** Bartkus - Dziugas Bartkus (Džiugas Bartkus) (a) 07/11/1989, Kaunas (Soviet Union, now in Lithuania) (b) 1,91 (c) G (d) Al-Orobah FC (e) Kiryat Shmona, Zalgiris, Valletta, Gornik Leczna, Suduva, FBK Kaunas, Dinamo Brest, FBK Kaunas, Partizan Minsk, FBK Kaunas

*** Bartolec - Karlo Bartolec (a) 20/04/1995, Zagreb (Croatia) (b) 1,78 (c) D - right back (d) Puskás Akadémia FC (e) NK Osijek, FC København, Nordsjælland, NK Lokomotiva

*** Bartoletti - Mattia Bartoletti (a) 09/08/2005, ¿? (Luxembourg) (b) - (c) F - left winger (d) CS Fola Esch (e) -

*** Bartolewski - Mateusz Bartolewski (a) 12/01/1998, Szczecinek (Poland) (b) 1,87 (c) D - left back (d) Ruch Chorzów (e) Zagłębie, Ruch, Pogon II, Stilon, Pogon II

*** Bartolini - Enrico Bartolini (a) 24/11/1981, Forlimpopoli (Italy) (b) 1,84 (c) F - center forward (d) ASD Gabicce Gradara (e) La Fiorita, Colbordolo, Vis Pesaro, Foligno, San Nicolò, Potenza, Fermana, Termoli, AJ Fano, Perugia, AJ Fano, Foligno, Lecco, Foligno, Tolentino, Grottammare, AS Gubbio, Riccione

*** Bartolo - Jaiden Bartolo (Jaiden Kamil Bartolo) (a) 10/02/2006, Slough (England) (b) 1,84 (c) F - center forward (d) FC Manchester 62 (e) Manchester 62

*** Bartolo - Julián Bartolo (a) 15/04/1996, Quilmes (Argentina) (b) 1,66 (c) F - left winger (d) Asteras Tripolis (e) Volos NPS, Acassuso CF, Guillermo Brown, San Miguel, CA San Miguel B

*** Bartolo - Manuel Bartolo (a) 26/08/1983, Pieta (Malta) (b) - (c) G (d) San Gwann FC (e) Gudja United FC, Floriana, Valletta, Hamrun Spartans, San Gwann FC, Mosta FC, Valletta, Zebbug Rangers, Valletta, Balzan FC, Valletta, Msida SJ, Floriana, Msida SJ, Birkirkara FC, Msida SJ, San Gwann FC

*** Bartolo - Travis Bartolo (a) 05/04/1995, ¿? (Malta) (b) - (c) D - right back (d) Zebbug Rangers FC (e) Pietà Hotspurs

*** Bartolomei - Paolo Bartolomei (a) 22/08/1989, Lucca (Italy) (b) 1,83 (c) M - central midfielder (d) AC Perugia Calcio (e) Cremonese, Spezia, Cittadella, Reggiana, Teramo, Pontedera, Massese, Castelnuovo

*** Bartos - Marek Kristian Bartos (Marek Kristián Bartoš) (a) 13/10/1996, Spišská Nová Ves (Slovakia) (b) 1,93 (c) D - central defense (d) FK Zeleziarne Podbrezova (e) Pohronie, Podbrezova, Pohronie, Dunajska Luzna, Puchov

*** Bartos - Richard Bartos (Richard Bartoš) (a) 28/06/1992, ¿? (Czechoslovakia, now in Slovakia) (b) 1,82 (c) F - center forward (d) Tatran Liptovsky Mikulas (e) SKF Sered, Liptovsky Mik., SKF Sered, Lip. Stiavnica, SKF Sered, Dolny Kubin, Ružomberok

*** Bartos - Vojtech Bartos (Vojtěch Bartoš) (a) 14/01/2002, ¿? (Czech Rep.) (b) - (c) D - right back (d) 1.SK Prostejov (e) Slovácko B

*** Bartosak - Lukas Bartosak (Lukáš Bartošák) (a) 03/07/1990, Brumov-Bylnice (Czechoslovakia, now in Czech Rep.) (b) 1,77 (c) D - left back (d) FC Zlin (e) Karvina, Fastav Zlin, Slovan Liberec, Viktoria Zizkov, Karvina, Hlucin, Brumov

*** Bartouche - Teddy Bartouche (Teddy Bartouche-Selbonne) (a) 05/06/1997, Lagny-sur-Marne (France) (b) 1,78 (c) G (d) EA Guingamp (e) FC Lorient, Lorient B, JA Drancy

*** Bartra - Marc Bartra (Marc Bartra Aregall) (a) 15/01/1991, Sant Jaume dels Domenys (Spain) (b) 1,84 (c) D - central defense (d) Real Betis Balompié (e) Trabzonspor, Real Betis, Borussia Dortmund, FC Barcelona, FC Barcelona B

*** Baruca - Luka Baruca (a) 09/01/2003, ¿? (Slovenia) (b) 1,83 (c) M - attacking midfielder (d) ND Gorica (e) Rudar Velenje, ND Gorica

*** Barzegar - Aria Barzegar (آریا برزگر) (a) 10/10/2002, Shiraz, Fars (Iran) (b) 1,89 (c) F - center forward (d) Esteghlal FC (e) Naft M.I.S F.C., Vitebsk, Persepolis, Fajr Sepasi, Persepolis

*** Bas - Luka Bas (Luka Baš) (a) 30/04/2002, Trbovlje (Slovenia) (b) 1,91 (c) G (d) NK Radomlje (e) ND Ilirija

*** Bas - Sadik Bas (Sadık Baş) (a) 11/05/1994, Bursa (Turkey) (b) 1,80 (c) F - right winger (d) Tuzlaspor (e) Hatayspor, Bucaspor 1928, Hatayspor, Eyüpspor, Tuzlaspor, Bursa Nilüfer, Tuzlaspor, Bursa Nilüfer, Mudanyaspor

*** Basa - Edi Basa (Edi Baša) (a) 29/06/1993, Pula (Croatia) (b) 1,80 (c) F - right winger (d) - (e) FK Kukësi, Borec Veles, Ast. Vlachioti, Koper, NK Novigrad, Siroki Brijeg, Cibalia, Jadran Porec, Zeljeznicar, Jadran Porec, NK Istra, Rovinj

*** Basaric - Zeljko Basaric (Жељко Басарић) (a) 08/03/2001, Čačak (RF Yugoslavia, now in Serbia) (b) 1,85 (c) M - pivot (d) FK Javor-Matis Ivanjica (e) Budućnost, Javor-Matis, Budućnost, Javor-Matis, Budućnost, Javor-Matis

*** Baschetti - Gianmarco Baschetti (a) 29/04/1991, ¿? (San Marino) (b) - (c) F - attacking midfielder (d) SS Pennarossa (e) Virtus, Verucchio, Murata, Villa Verucchio, Virtus, Murata, Verucchio, Virtus, Verucchio

*** Baschirotto - Federico Baschirotto (a) 20/09/1996, Isola della Scala (Italy) (b) 1,87 (c) D - central defense (d) US Lecce (e) Ascoli, Viterbese, Cremonese, Vigor Carpaneto, Cremonese, Cuneo, Cremonese, Forlì, Cremonese, Seregno, Legnago
*** Basha - Arber Basha (Arbër Basha) (a) 13/01/1998, Tiranë (Albania) (b) 1,83 (c) M - central midfielder (d) FK Kukësi (e) KS Kastrioti, JK Trans Narva, FC Kamza, KF Vllaznia
*** Basha - Sadik Basha (a) 04/06/2002, Gjirokastër (Albania) (b) - (c) G (d) KF Egnatia (e) Luftëtari, KF Butrinti, FC Luftëtari
*** Basha - Serkan Basha (a) 21/01/2000, Kukës (Albania) (b) 1,73 (c) M - central midfielder (d) - (e) US Hostert, RFC Seraing, KF Tirana
*** Basheleishvili - Mikheil Basheleishvili (მიხეილ ბაშალეიშვილი) (a) 21/06/1997, ¿? (Georgia) (b) 1,79 (c) M - pivot (d) FC Telavi (e) Samgurali, FC Telavi
*** Basheleishvili - Nikoloz Basheleishvili (ნიკოლოზ ბაშელეიშვილი) (a) 21/06/1997, ¿? (Georgia) (b) 1,79 (c) M - attacking midfielder (d) FC Locomotive Tbilisi (e) Shukura, FC Telavi, FC Aragvi, FC Telavi
*** Bashilov - Mikhail Bashilov (Башилов Михаил Сергеевич) (a) 12/01/1993, Tomsk (Russia) (b) 1,80 (c) M - pivot (d) FK Turan (e) SC Noravank, Energetik-BGU, Belshina, Gorodeya, Utenis, Tom-2 Tomsk, Tom Tomsk, Tyumen, Tom Tomsk, Irtysh Omsk, Tom Tomsk, Tom Tomsk II
*** Bashoyan - Levon Bashoyan (Լևոն Բաշոյան) (a) 15/09/2005, ¿? (Armenia) (b) 1,73 (c) M - central midfielder (d) FC Urartu Erewan II (e) -
*** Basic - Adnan Basic (Adnan Bašić) (a) 13/12/1996, Mostar (Bosnia and Herzegovina) (b) 1,85 (c) F - center forward (d) OFK Petrovac (e) Panevezys, OFK Petrovac, Vysehrad, FC UNA Strassen, Union Titus Petange, NK Celje, Drava Ptuj, NK Celje, Drava Ptuj, NK Celje
*** Basic - Ivan Basic (Ivan Bašić) (a) 30/04/2002, Imotski (Croatia) (b) 1,78 (c) M - attacking midfielder (d) FK Orenburg (e) Zrinjski Mostar
*** Basic - Jakov Basic (Jakov Bašić) (a) 25/11/1996, Zagreb (Croatia) (b) 1,90 (c) M - pivot (d) NK Rudes (e) Slaven Belupo, NK Rudes, Hrv Dragovoljac, NK Dugopolje, Hajduk Split II, Boston Bolts, Reading United
*** Basic - Toma Basic (Toma Bašić) (a) 25/11/1996, Zagreb (Croatia) (b) 1,90 (c) M - central midfielder (d) SS Lazio (e) Girondins Bordeaux, Hajduk Split, NK Rudes
*** Basile - Paolo Basile (a) 08/06/1992, ¿? (Italy) (b) - (c) F - attacking midfielder (d) - (e) Cosmos, Riccione, Libertas, Faetano, United Riccione, SS Folgore, United Riccione, Riccione, Tropical Coriano, Riccione
*** Basile - Vincenzo Basile (Vincenzo Giovanni Basile) (a) 04/11/2003, Cosenza (Italy) (b) 1,73 (c) M - attacking midfielder (d) Glacis United (e) -
*** Basit - Khalid Basit (Abdul Khalid Basit) (a) 10/08/1996, Accra (Ghana) (b) 1,87 (c) F - center forward (d) Makedonija Gjorce Petrov (e) Al-Tadamon SC, FC Sheriff, Esperance, Makedonija, KF Teuta, FC Prishtina, Dreams FC
*** Basko - Ralfs Basko (Ralfs Baško) (a) 10/01/2005, ¿? (Latvia) (b) - (c) M - central midfielder (d) BFC Daugavpils (e) -
*** Basmanov - Stanislav Basmanov (Басманов Станислав Игоревич) (a) 24/06/2001, Astana (Kazakhstan) (b) 1,79 (c) F - left winger (d) FC Astana (e) Astana-M, Astana-Zhas
*** Basrak - Milan Basrak (Милан Басрак) (a) 24/12/1994, St. Gallen (Switzerland) (b) 1,82 (c) F - center forward (d) Termoli Calcio 1920 (e) Sloga Meridian, Lavello, Dobanovci, Jagodina, AP Brera, Smederevo 1924, Tatran Presov, Birkirkara FC, Napredak, FK Partizani, Catanzaro, Metalac, FK Rad. Lukavac, Radnik Bijelj., FK Indjija, FK Zemun

*** Basriu - Elton Basriu (a) 03/08/1987, Elbasan (Albania) (b) - (c) D - central defense (d) KF Dukagjini (e) KF Trepca 89, KF Liria, FC Kamza, FK Bylis, KF Elbasani, FK Bylis, KF Gramshi, KF Tërbuni, FK Apolonia, KF Gramshi, KF Elbasani
*** Bassan - Emrah Bassan (Emrah Başsan) (a) 17/04/1992, Gebze (Turkey) (b) 1,77 (c) F - right winger (d) Sivasspor (e) Kayserispor, BB Erzurumspor, Vitória Setúbal, Galatasaray, Fortuna Sittard, Galatasaray, Çaykur Rizespor, Galatasaray, Antalyaspor, Pendikspor
*** Bassene - Boris Bassene (Boris Olivier Tiotio Bassene) (a) 16/09/1993, ¿? (Luxembourg) (b) - (c) G (d) SC Bettembourg (e) SC Bettembourg, RFCU Luxembourg, FC Rodange 91, Union Titus Petange, Muhlenbach, FC Atert Bissen
*** Bassene - Jean Francis Bassene (a) 18/11/1992, ¿? (Senegal) (b) - (c) G (d) AS Colmar-Berg (e) Etzella Ettelbrück, CS&O Blénod PaM, US Hostert, CS&O Blénod PaM
*** Bassett - Cole Bassett (Cole John Bassett) (a) 28/07/2001, Littleton, Colorado (United States) (b) 1,80 (c) M - attacking midfielder (d) Colorado Rapids (e) Fortuna Sittard, Colorado, Feyenoord, Colorado, Colorado Rush
*** Bassey - Calvin Bassey (Calvin Bassey Ughelumba) (a) 31/12/1999, Aosta (Italy) (b) 1,85 (c) D - central defense (d) Fulham FC (e) Ajax, Rangers FC
*** Bassey - Fortune Bassey (Fortune Akpan Bassey) (a) 06/10/1998, Benin City (Nigeria) (b) 1,85 (c) F - center forward (d) Hapoel Petah Tikva (e) H. Petah Tikva, Ferencváros, Degerfors, Ferencváros, Viktoria Plzen, Ferencváros, Ceske Budejovice, Vlasim, Ceske Budejovice, Usti nad Labem, Olympia, Bohemians B, Eagle Wings
*** Bassi - Daniel Bassi (Daniel Joshua Bassi Jakobsen) (a) 31/10/2004, Oslo (Norway) (b) 1,78 (c) M - left midfielder (d) FK Bodø/Glimt (e) Tromsø, Tromsø IL II
*** Bassi - Matteo Bassi (a) 08/01/2004, ¿? (Italy) (b) - (c) M - central midfielder (d) Cjarlins Muzane (e) -
*** Basso - Greyson Basso (a) 13/07/2004, ¿? (United States) (b) - (c) M - attacking midfielder (d) Europa FC Reserve (e) -
*** Basso Ricci - Alberto Basso Ricci (a) 29/06/2004, ¿? (Italy) (b) - (c) F - center forward (d) FC Lumezzane (e) -
*** Bassong - Zorhan Bassong (Zorhan Ludovic Bassong) (a) 07/05/1999, Toronto, Ontario (Canada) (b) 1,79 (c) D - left back (d) FCV Farul Constanta (e) FC Arges, Montréal, Cercle Brugge, LOSC Lille B
*** Bastajic - Nebojsa Bastajic (Небојша Бастајић) (a) 20/08/1990, Beograd (Yugoslavia, now in Serbia) (b) 1,84 (c) F - left winger (d) Al-Bukiryah FC (e) Napredak, Vojvodina, FK Indjija, FK TSC, Dobanovci, Smederevo 1924, Bangkok FC, Smederevo 1924, FK Bezanija, Dobanovci, Vataniakos, Srem Jakovo, Vozdovac, FK Kupinovo
*** Basterrechea - Matías Basterrechea (a) 02/01/1994, La Plata (Argentina) (b) 1,91 (c) G (d) Penya Encarnada d'Andorra (e) FC Ordino, Penya Encarnada, CE Carroi, Amantea, San Luca, Sodupe UC, Sol de Mayo, San Carlos, Defensa y Justicia
*** Basterrechea - Patricio Basterrechea (a) 02/02/1995, La Plata (Argentina) (b) 1,76 (c) D - left back (d) - (e) Penya Encarnada, CD Madridejos, Sodupe UC, CD Puertollano
*** Bastianelli - Tommaso Bastianelli (a) 09/03/2003, ¿? (Italy) (b) - (c) F (d) - (e) Cosmos

*** Bastic - Stasa Bastic (Staša Baštić) (a) 24/12/2001, Banja Luka (Bosnia and Herzegovina) (b) 1,90 (c) M - central midfielder (d) FK Sloga Meridian (e) Zeljeznicar BL

*** Bastida - Álvaro Bastida (Álvaro Bastida Moya) (a) 12/05/2004, Chiclana de la Frontera (Spain) (b) 1,70 (c) M - central midfielder (d) Cádiz CF Mirandilla (e) -

*** Bastl - Libor Bastl (a) 20/12/2003, ¿? (Czech Rep.) (b) - (c) F - left winger (d) SK Dynamo Ceske Budejovice B (e) -

*** Basto - Hugo Basto (a) 14/05/1993, Amarante (Portugal) (b) 1,88 (c) D - central defense (d) AEL Limassol (e) Neftchi Baku, Estoril Praia, Chaves, Arouca, Braga B, Varzim, Amarante Forma.

*** Bastoni - Alessandro Bastoni (a) 13/04/1999, Casalmaggiore (Italy) (b) 1,90 (c) D - central defense (d) Internazionale Milano (e) Parma, Internazionale Milano, Atalanta, Internazionale Milano, Atalanta

*** Bastoni - Simone Bastoni (a) 05/11/1996, La Spezia (Italy) (b) 1,81 (c) M - central midfielder (d) Spezia (e) Novara, Spezia, Trapani, Spezia, Carrarese, Spezia, Robur Siena, Spezia

*** Bastos - Luís Bastos (Luís Pedro Alves Bastos) (a) 10/09/2001, Paços de Ferreira (Portugal) (b) 1,75 (c) D - left back (d) FC Paços de Ferreira (e) Felgueiras

*** Bastos - Yannick Bastos (a) 30/05/1993, Luxembourg (Luxembourg) (b) 1,74 (c) D - right back (d) FC Progrès Niederkorn (e) Differdange 03, Bolton Wanderers, Differdange 03, US Rumelange

*** Bastos Moncalvo - Martin Bastos Moncalvo (a) 19/10/1994, Montevideo (Uruguay) (b) 1,75 (c) M - central midfielder (d) - (e) Libertas, Fabriano, Club Milano, NC Latina, Castelnuovo, Colon FC, Bella Vista

*** Bastunov - Angel Bastunov (Ангел Георгиев Бастунов) (a) 18/05/1999, Razlog (Bulgaria) (b) 1,83 (c) F - left winger (d) Hebar Pazardzhik (e) CSKA 1948, Kariana Erden

*** Batagov - Arseniy Batagov (Батагов Арсеній Павлович) (a) 05/03/2002, Berezivka, Kharkiv Oblast (Ukraine) (b) 1,85 (c) D - central defense (d) Zorya Lugansk (e) SK Dnipro-1, FK Polissya, SK Dnipro-1, Dnipro

*** Bataille - Jelle Bataille (a) 20/05/1999, Oostende (Belgium) (b) 1,80 (c) D - right back (d) Royal Antwerp FC (e) KV Oostende

*** Bates - Alfie Bates (a) 03/05/2001, Coventry (England) (b) 1,70 (c) M - central midfielder (d) Brackley Town (e) SJK Seinäjoki, FC Walsall

*** Bates - David Bates (David Robert Bates) (a) 05/10/1996, Kirkcaldy (Scotland) (b) 1,93 (c) D - central defense (d) KV Mechelen (e) Aberdeen FC, SV Hamburg, Cercle Brugge, SV Hamburg, Sheffield Wednesday, SV Hamburg, Rangers FC, Raith Rovers, Brechin City, Raith Rovers, East Stirlingshire FC, Raith Rovers

*** Bates Andreou - Henry Bates Andreou (Χένρη Μπέιτς Ανδρέου) (a) 02/04/2001, Larnaca (Cyprus) (b) 1,93 (c) D - left back (d) AEK Larnaca (e) Omonia Aradippou, AEK Larnaca

*** Batha - Idriz Batha (a) 28/03/1992, Gjirokastër (Albania) (b) 1,73 (c) M - central midfielder (d) Al-Najma SC (e) UTA Arad, KF Tirana, Flamurtari FC, FK Partizani, KS Besa, KF Teuta, KS Besa, FK Partizani

*** Batik - Bence Batik (a) 08/11/1993, Szeged (Hungary) (b) 1,90 (c) D - central defense (d) Puskás Akadémia FC (e) Honvéd, Ferencváros, MTK Budapest, Ferencváros, Szeged, Kisteleki TE, Hódmezővásárhely FC

*** Batista - Gabriel Batista (Gabriel Batista de Souza) (a) 03/06/1998, São Gonçalo (Brazil) (b) 1,88 (c) G (d) CD Santa Clara (e) Flamengo, Sampaio Corrêa, Flamengo

*** Batista - Ricardo Batista (Ricardo Jorge Cecília Batista) (a) 19/11/1986, Setúbal (Portugal) (b) 1,92 (c) G (d) Casa Pia AC (e) Gaz Metan, C.R.D. Libolo, Vitória

Setúbal, Nacional, Sperre) Sporting Lisboa, Olhanense, Sporting Lisboa, Fulham, Wycombe Wanderers, Fulham, Wycombe Wanderers, Fulham, MK Dons, Fulham
*** Batori - Lorenzo Batori (a) 07/11/1993, ¿? (Italy) (b) - (c) G (d) SS Cosmos (e) -
*** Batrakov - Aleksey Batrakov (Батраков Алексей Андреевич) (a) 09/06/2005, Orekhovo-Zuevo, Moskva Region (Russia) (b) 1,69 (c) M - attacking midfielder (d) Lokomotiv Moskva II (e) -
*** Batshuayi - Michy Batshuayi (Michy Batshuayi-Atunga) (a) 02/10/1993, Bruxelles (Belgium) (b) 1,85 (c) F - center forward (d) Fenerbahce (e) Chelsea, Besiktas, Chelsea, Crystal Palace, Chelsea, Crystal Palace, Chelsea, Valencia CF, Chelsea, Borussia Dortmund, Chelsea, Ol. Marseille, Standard Liège
*** Batsula - Andriy Batsula (Бацула Андрій Сергійович) (a) 06/02/1992, Kremenchuk, Poltava Oblast (Ukraine) (b) 1,84 (c) D - left back (d) Vorskla Poltava (e) Dinamo Minsk, KV Kortrijk, Dinamo Minsk, KV Kortrijk, FK Oleksandriya, Zirka, Vorskla II, Kremin, Vorskla II, Kremin, Vorskla II
*** Battaglia - Rodrigo Battaglia (Rodrigo Andrés Battaglia) (a) 12/07/1991, Morón (Argentina) (b) 1,87 (c) M - pivot (d) Clube Atlético Mineiro (e) RCD Mallorca, Sporting Lisboa, RCD Mallorca, Sporting Lisboa, Alavés, Sporting Lisboa, SC Braga, Chaves, SC Braga, Rosario Central, SC Braga, Moreirense, SC Braga, Racing, Huracán
*** Battiata - Gianvito Battiata (a) 22/10/2003, ¿? (Italy) (b) - (c) D - left back (d) SS Pennarossa (e) -
*** Battison - Bobby Battison (a) 31/01/2004, Málaga (Spain) (b) - (c) M - attacking midfielder (d) Mickleover Sports FC (e) Europa FC, Mickleover
*** Battistini - Andrea Battistini (a) 10/08/2000, Rimini (Italy) (b) 1,81 (c) G (d) AC Virtus Acquaviva (e) Ancona, Santarcangelo
*** Battistini - Manuel Battistini (a) 22/07/1994, Borgo Maggiore (San Marino) (b) - (c) D - right back (d) AC Virtus Acquaviva (e) Juvenes-Dogana, Virtus, Juvenes-Dogana, Tropical Coriano, Juvenes-Dogana, Libertas, Juvenes-Dogana, Tre Penne, Juvenes-Dogana, Tropical Coriano, Sammaurese, Cattolica, San Marino
*** Battistini - Michael Battistini (a) 08/10/1996, ¿? (San Marino) (b) - (c) M - central midfielder (d) SP Tre Penne (e) Libertas, ACD Torconca, Juvenes-Dogana
*** Battistini - Nicolò Battistini (a) 03/07/1999, ¿? (Italy) (b) - (c) G (d) AC Libertas (e) Virtus, Victor SM, YOU, Cesenatico, Tre Fiori, Savignanese
*** Battocchio - Cristian Battocchio (Cristian Damián Battocchio) (a) 10/02/1992, Rosario (Argentina) (b) 1,69 (c) M - central midfielder (d) - (e) Ness Ziona, Volos NPS, Pumas UNAM, Tokushima Vort., Stade Brestois, Maccabi Tel Aviv, Stade Brestois, Watford, Virtus Entella, Watford, Udinese, Watford, Udinese
*** Batubinsika - Dylan Batubinsika (Buduka Dylan Batubinsika) (a) 15/02/1996, Cergy-Pontoise (France) (b) 1,85 (c) D - central defense (d) AS Saint-Étienne (e) Famalicão, Maccabi Haifa, Famalicão, Royal Antwerp, Paris Saint Germain B
*** Batur - Marko Batur (a) 26/06/2004, Zagreb (Croatia) (b) - (c) F (d) NK Lokomotiva Zagreb (e) Hrvat. Leskovac
*** Baturina - Josip Baturina (a) 12/01/2004, Zadar (Croatia) (b) - (c) D (d) - (e) HNK Sibenik
*** Baturina - Martin Baturina (a) 16/02/2003, Split (Croatia) (b) 1,72 (c) M - attacking midfielder (d) GNK Dinamo Zagreb (e) Din. Zagreb II
*** Baturina - Roko Baturina (a) 20/06/2000, Split (Croatia) (b) 1,87 (c) F - center forward (d) Gil Vicente FC (e) Ferencváros, Racing, Ferencváros, NK Maribor, Ferencváros, Lech Poznan, Ferencváros, Din. Zagreb II, NK Bravo, Din. Zagreb II
*** Baturins - Ivans Baturins (a) 25/06/1997, ¿? (Latvia) (b) 1,92 (c) G (d) Harju JK Laagri (e) TJK Legion, Tukums, JFK Ventspils, Ventspils II, Knyazha

*** Batyrev - Amir Batyrev (Батырев Амир Ренатович) (a) 11/03/2002, Toronto (Canada) (b) 1,75 (c) M - attacking midfielder (d) FK Sochi (e) FC Tver

*** Batyshchev - Oleksandr Batyshchev (Батищев Олександр Володимирович) (a) 14/09/1991, Rubizhne, Lugansk Oblast (Ukraine) (b) 1,74 (c) M - pivot (d) Torpedo-BelAZ Zhodino (e) Ordabasy, Gomel, Dnyapro Mogilev, Torpedo Minsk, Gomel, Krumkachi, Belshina, Zorya II, Stal Alchevsk, Zorya II, PFK Sumy, Zorya II, Shakhtar II, Zorya II

*** Batyushyn - Yuriy Batyushyn (Батюшин Юрій Валентинович) (a) 07/12/1992, Alchevsk, Lugansk Oblast (Ukraine) (b) 1,80 (c) M - central midfielder (d) - (e) Neftchi, FC Dila, Metalist 1925, Girnyk-Sport, MFK Mykolaiv, Stal Alchevsk

*** Bätzner - Nick Bätzner (a) 15/03/2000, Ludwigsburg (Germany) (b) 1,76 (c) M - attacking midfielder (d) SV Wehen Wiesbaden (e) KV Oostende, Stuttgart II

*** Bauer - Maximilian Bauer (a) 09/02/2000, Vilshofen (Germany) (b) 1,89 (c) D - central defense (d) FC Augsburg (e) Greuther Fürth, Greuther Fürth II

*** Bauer - Moritz Bauer (a) 25/01/1992, Winterthur (Switzerland) (b) 1,81 (c) D - right back (d) - (e) Servette FC, Ufa, Stoke City, Ufa, Stoke City, Celtic FC, Stoke City, Rubin Kazan, Grasshoppers

*** Bauer - Robert Bauer (a) 09/04/1995, Pforzheim (Germany) (b) 1,83 (c) D - central defense (d) Al-Tai FC (e) Sint-Truiden, Arsenal Tula, Werder Bremen, 1.FC Nürnberg, Werder Bremen, FC Ingolstadt

*** Bauernfeind - Kilian Bauernfeind (a) 23/04/2002, Schwaz (Austria) (b) 1,81 (c) M - central midfielder (d) SV Horn (e) WSG Tirol, FC Dornbirn, WSG Tirol, WSG Tirol II

*** Baumann - Oliver Baumann (a) 02/06/1990, Breisach am Rhein (Germany) (b) 1,87 (c) G (d) TSG 1899 Hoffenheim (e) SC Freiburg

*** Baumgartl - Timo Baumgartl (a) 04/03/1996, Böblingen (Germany) (b) 1,90 (c) D - central defense (d) FC Schalke 04 (e) PSV Eindhoven, Union Berlin, PSV Eindhoven, VfB Stuttgart, Stuttgart II

*** Baumgartlinger - Julian Baumgartlinger (a) 02/01/1988, Salzburg (Austria) (b) 1,84 (c) M - pivot (d) - (e) FC Augsburg, Bayer Leverkusen, Mainz 05, Austria Viena, 1860 München

*** Baumgartner - Christoph Baumgartner (a) 01/08/1999, Horn (Austria) (b) 1,80 (c) M - attacking midfielder (d) RB Leipzig (e) Hoffenheim, Hoffenheim II

*** Baumgartner - Denis Baumgartner (a) 02/02/1998, Skalica (Slovakia) (b) 1,80 (c) M - central midfielder (d) MFK Skalica (e) FK Senica, Sampdoria, Dunajska Streda, Sampdoria, AS Livorno, FK Senica

*** Baumgartner - Dominik Baumgartner (a) 20/07/1996, Horn (Austria) (b) 1,88 (c) D - central defense (d) Wolfsberger AC (e) VfL Bochum, Wolfsberger AC, VfL Bochum, FC Wacker, Grödig, SV Horn

*** Baúque - Clésio Baúque (Clésio Palmirim David Baúque) (a) 11/10/1994, Maputo (Mozambique) (b) 1,74 (c) F - left winger (d) FC Honka (e) Marítimo, Zira FK, FK Qabala, Istanbulspor, Panetolikos, Benfica B, Harrisburg City, Benfica B, Philadelphia, Benfica B, Ferroviário

*** Baurenski - Yoan Baurenski (Йоан Христов Бауренски) (a) 25/10/2001, Montana (Bulgaria) (b) 1,78 (c) M - pivot (d) Spartak Varna (e) Beroe, CSKA-Sofia, Botev Vratsa, CSKA-Sofia, Litex Lovetch, CSKA-Sofia

*** Bauress - Bradley Bauress (Bradley Stephen Bauress) (a) 28/04/1996, Liverpool (England) (b) - (c) M - central midfielder (d) - (e) Bala, Chester, Southport, Barrow, Witton Albion, Colwyn Bay

*** Bauta - Jetmir Bauta (a) 18/02/2004, Struga (North Macedonia) (b) - (c) M (d) Karaorman Struga (e) -

*** Bauthéac - Eric Bauthéac (a) 24/08/1987, Bagnols-sur-Cèze (France) (b) 1,68 (c) F - right winger (d) - (e) Nea Salamis, Omonia Nicosia, Brisbane Roar, Lille, OGC Nice, Dijon, Cannes, Saint-Étienne B

*** Bauti - Bauti (David Alberto Bautista Martos) (a) 27/02/1992, Linares (Spain) (b) - (c) D - central defense (d) St Joseph's FC (e) Lynx FC, St Joseph's FC, Lynx FC, CD Torreperogil, Ontinyent, Mancha Real, R. B. Linense, Linares, Martos CD, Carolinense

*** Bautista - Luke Bautista (a) 09/11/2001, Gibraltar (Gibraltar) (b) - (c) D - left back (d) FC Bruno's Magpies (e) Glacis United, Bruno's Magpies, Glacis United, Europa FC, Glacis United, Europa FC, Europa Reserve, Europa FC, Mons Calpe Reserves

*** Bauza - Juan Bauza (Juan Francisco Bauza) (a) 03/05/1996, Gualeguaychú (Argentina) (b) 1,77 (c) M - attacking midfielder (d) FC U Craiova 1948 (e) Csikszereda, FC U Craiova, Csikszereda, Colón, Górnik Zabrze, Colón, GyE Mendoza, Colón, CA Colón II

*** Baxevanos - Nikolaos Baxevanos (Νικόλαος Μπαξεβάνος) (a) 16/07/1999, Thessaloniki (Greece) (b) 1,87 (c) D - central defense (d) PS Kalamata (e) Spartak, Chindia, Lazio, ACSM Poli Iasi, Lazio, FC Botosani, Lazio, Panionios, Lazio

*** Bayala - Cyrille Bayala (Cyrille Barros Bayala) (a) 24/05/1996, Ouagadougou (Burkina Faso) (b) 1,81 (c) F - right winger (d) AC Ajaccio (e) RC Lens, AC Ajaccio, RC Lens, FC Sochaux, RC Lens, FC Sheriff, El Dakhlia, ASFA Yennenga

*** Bayazit - Bilal Bayazit (Bilal Bayazıt) (a) 08/04/1999, Amsterdam (Netherlands) (b) 1,85 (c) G (d) Kayserispor (e) Vitesse

*** Baybalayev - Vüqar Baybalayev (Vüqar Bəybala oğlu Bəybalayev) (a) 05/08/1993, Sumqayit (Azerbaijan) (b) 1,81 (c) M - central midfielder (d) - (e) Sumqayit, FC Telavi, FK Sabail, Sumqayit, Kapaz PFK, Xäzär Länkäran, Ravan Baku, FK Baku, Turan Tovuz, FK Baku

*** Baybek - Olzhas Baybek (Байбек Олжас Сыдыкалиулы) (a) 11/02/2005, ¿? (Kazakhstan) (b) 1,81 (c) M - pivot (d) Kairat-Zhas (e) -

*** Baydal - Anton Baydal (Байдал Антон Олександрович) (a) 08/02/2000, Mariupol, Donetsk Oblast (Ukraine) (b) 1,82 (c) F - left winger (d) FK Viktoriya Sumy (e) FK Minaj, FK Mariupol II

*** Baydavletov - Toktar Baydavletov (Байдавлетов Токтар) (a) 23/02/2004, ¿? (Kazakhstan) (b) 1,60 (c) M - pivot (d) Tobol Kostanay II (e) -

*** Bayere Junior - Loué Bayere Junior (a) 14/01/2001, Abidjan (Ivory Coast) (b) 1,88 (c) F - center forward (d) FK Javor-Matis Ivanjica (e) Göztepe, Hammarby IF, Göztepe, Hammarby IF, Hammarby TFF, Hammarby IF, Zeleznicar Pancevo, Hammarby IF, IK Frej Täby, Hammarby IF, ASEC Mimosas, Hammarby IF, ASEC Mimosas

*** Bayeye - Brian Bayeye (Brian Jephte Bayeye) (a) 30/06/2000, Paris (France) (b) 1,82 (c) D - right back (d) Torino FC (e) Catanzaro, Carpi, Catanzaro, Troyes B

*** Bayiha - Clément Bayiha (Clément Yvan Landry Bayiha) (a) 08/03/1999, Yaoundé (Cameroon) (b) 1,73 (c) F - right winger (d) York United FC (e) HamKam, Montréal, Ottawa Fury, Montreal, Ottawa Fury

*** Bayindir - Altay Bayindir (Altay Bayındır) (a) 14/04/1998, Bursa (Turkey) (b) 1,98 (c) G (d) Fenerbahce (e) Ankaragücü

*** Bayir - Furkan Bayir (Furkan Bayır) (a) 09/02/2000, Izmir (Turkey) (b) 1,88 (c) D - central defense (d) Alanyaspor (e) Menemenspor, Alanyaspor, Menemenspor

*** Baykadamov - Aslan Baykadamov (Байкадамов Аслан) (a) 28/01/2005, ¿? (Kazakhstan) (b) - (c) G (d) Kyzylzhar SK Petropavlovsk II (e) -

*** Baymagambetov - Sultan Baymagambetov (Баймагамбетов Султан Жамбулович) (a) 02/09/2001, North Kazakhstan Region (Kazakhstan) (b) - (c) D - right back (d) Kyzylzhar SK Petropavlovsk II (e) -
*** Bayo - Mohamed Bayo (Mohamed Lamine Bayo) (a) 04/06/1998, Clermont-Ferrand (France) (b) 1,88 (c) F - center forward (d) LOSC Lille Métropole (e) Clermont Foot, USL Dunkerque, Clermont Foot, Clermont B
*** Bayo - Vakoun Bayo (Vakoun Issouf Bayo) (a) 10/01/1997, Daloa (Ivory Coast) (b) 1,84 (c) F - center forward (d) Watford FC (e) RSC Charleroi, Watford, RSC Charleroi, KAA Gent, RSC Charleroi, KAA Gent, Celtic FC, Toulouse, Celtic FC, Dunajska Streda, ES Sahel, Stade d'Abidjan
*** Bayode - Olatunde Bayode (a) 07/02/1999, ¿? (England) (b) - (c) F - right winger (d) - (e) Bruno's Magpies, Colne, Bamber Bridge, Curzon Ashton
*** Bayrakdar - Gökdeniz Bayrakdar (a) 23/11/2001, Kocaeli (Turkey) (b) 1,81 (c) F - right winger (d) Bodrum FK (e) Antalyaspor, Bodrum FK, Antalyaspor, Kocaelispor
*** Bayram - Emin Bayram (a) 02/04/2003, Istanbul (Turkey) (b) 1,92 (c) D - central defense (d) Galatasaray (e) Boluspor, Galatasaray
*** Bayramly - Tural Bayramly (Tural Mayıl oğlu Bayramlı) (a) 07/01/1998, Sumqayit (Azerbaijan) (b) 1,77 (c) M - attacking midfielder (d) Araz-Naxcivan Nakhchivan (e) FK Sabail 2, FK Sabail, Pierikos, Zira FK, Keshla, Daugavpils
*** Bayramov - Aydin Bayramov (Aydın Elmar oğlu Bayramov) (a) 18/02/1996, ¿? (Azerbaijan) (b) 1,87 (c) G (d) Turan-Tovuz IK (e) Sumqayit, Sabah FK, MOIK
*** Bayramov - Elgün Bayramov (Elgün Rəşad oğlu Bayramov) (a) 04/03/2003, ¿? (Azerbaijan) (b) - (c) G (d) Kapaz PFK (e) MOIK
*** Bayramov - Fuad Bayramov (Fuad Ehtibar oğlu Bayramov) (a) 20/05/1998, ¿? (Azerbaijan) (b) 1,81 (c) D - left back (d) Zira FK (e) Shamakhi, FC Shamakhi 2, Turan Tovuz, Sumqayit 2
*** Bayramov - Kamal Bayramov (Kamal Bəhram oğlu Bayramov) (a) 19/08/1985, Tovuz (Soviet Union, now in Azerbaijan) (b) 1,78 (c) G (d) Turan-Tovuz IK (e) Shamakhi, FK Sabail, Zira FK, AZAL, Araz-Naxcivan, Ravan Baku, Turan Tovuz, Xäzär Länkäran, Turan Tovuz, Mughan, Neftchi Baku
*** Bayramov - Nurlan Bayramov (Nurlan Bayramov) (a) 20/09/2003, ¿? (Azerbaijan) (b) - (c) M (d) Sumqayit 2 (e) -
*** Bayramov - Toral Bayramov (Toral Mais oglu Bayramov) (a) 23/02/2001, Baku (Azerbaijan) (b) 1,85 (c) D - left back (d) Qarabağ FK (e) -
*** Bayramyan - Khoren Bayramyan (Байрамян Хорен Робертович) (a) 07/01/1992, Koti, Tavush Province (Armenia) (b) 1,69 (c) M - attacking midfielder (d) FK Rostov (e) Rubin Kazan, Rostov, Volgar, Rostov, Rotor Volgograd, Rostov, Rostov II, MITOS
*** Bayshik - Kurban Bayshik (Байшык Курбан Дуйсенбайулы) (a) 05/03/2001, Tortkol, Ordabasy Region (Kazakhstan) (b) 1,77 (c) M (d) FK Turan II (e) Ordabasy II
*** Baytalenko - Danila Baytalenko (Байталенко Данила) (a) 11/06/2006, ¿? (Kazakhstan) (b) 1,81 (c) D (d) Tobol Kostanay II (e) -
*** Baytana - Bauyrzhan Baytana (Байтана Бауыржан Нұрланұлы) (a) 06/05/1992, Taraz (Kazakhstan) (b) 1,74 (c) M - attacking midfielder (d) FK Aktobe (e) Taraz, Shakhter K., Taraz, Aktobe, Taraz, Kairat Almaty, Taraz, Tobol Kostanay, Taraz, Sunkar Kaskelen, Taraz, Atyrau, Taraz, Taraz-Karatau
*** Bayzhanov - Nurbek Bayzhanov (Байжанов Нурбек) (a) 04/04/2003, ¿? (Kazakhstan) (b) 1,74 (c) M - central midfielder (d) Tobol Kostanay II (e) -

*** Bazdar - Samed Bazdar (Самед Баждар) (a) 31/01/2004, Novi Pazar (Serbia and Montenegro, now in Serbia) (b) 1,86 (c) F - attacking midfielder (d) Partizán Beograd (e) -

*** Bazea - Nowaf Bazea (בזיע נואף) (a) 16/11/2000, Nazareth (Israel) (b) 1,78 (c) M - attacking midfielder (d) Hapoel Umm al-Fahm (e) H. Jerusalem, M. Ahi Nazareth, FC Ashdod, M. Ahi Nazareth, FC Ashdod, M. Ahi Nazareth

*** Bazoer - Riechedly Bazoer (a) 12/10/1996, Utrecht (Netherlands) (b) 1,84 (c) M - central midfielder (d) AZ Alkmaar (e) Vitesse, VfL Wolfsburg, FC Utrecht, VfL Wolfsburg, FC Porto, VfL Wolfsburg, Ajax, Ajax B

*** Bazunu - Gavin Bazunu (Gavin Okeroghene Bazunu) (a) 20/02/2002, Dublin (Ireland) (b) 1,88 (c) G (d) Southampton FC (e) FC Portsmouth, AFC Rochdale, Shamrock Rovers

*** Bazzoli - Luca Bazzoli (Luca Juliano Bazzoli) (a) 01/11/2000, Bad Homburg (Germany) (b) 1,88 (c) M - pivot (d) Preußen Münster (e) Stuttgart II, FSV Frankfurt

*** Bdarney - Mohammad Bdarney (בדארנה מידו מוחמד) (a) 15/11/1995, ¿? (Israel) (b) 1,83 (c) M - attacking midfielder (d) Ihud Bnei Sakhnin (e) H. Umm al-Fahm, Hapoel Raanana, FC Winterthur, Hapoel Ikhsal, Bnei Sakhnin, H Rishon leZion, Bnei Sakhnin, Hapoel Afula, Bnei Sakhnin

*** Beaka - Yoann Beaka (a) 06/04/2003, ¿? (France) (b) 1,94 (c) F - center forward (d) - (e) Troyes B

*** Beattie - Spencer Beattie (a) 16/01/2002, Belfast (Northern Ireland) (b) 1,84 (c) F - right winger (d) - (e) Ballymena, Dundela FC, Ballymena, Dundela FC, Ballymena

*** Beaumont - Bobby Beaumont (Bobby Beaumont-Broadhead) (a) 25/03/2002, Wrexham (Wales) (b) - (c) D - central defense (d) - (e) Flint Town, Caernarfon

*** Bebé - Bebé (Tiago Manuel Dias Correia) (a) 12/07/1990, Lisboa (Portugal) (b) 1,90 (c) F - left winger (d) Rayo Vallecano (e) Real Zaragoza, Rayo Vallecano, SD Eibar, Rayo Vallecano, SD Eibar, Benfica, Rayo Vallecano, Benfica, Córdoba CF, Benfica, Manchester Utd., Paços Ferreira, Manchester Utd., Rio Ave, Manchester Utd., Besiktas, Manchester Utd., Vitória Guimarães, CF Estrela

*** Bebou - Ihlas Bebou (a) 23/04/1994, Sokodé (Togo) (b) 1,85 (c) F - center forward (d) TSG 1899 Hoffenheim (e) Hannover 96, Fortuna Düsseldorf

*** Beca - Omar Beca (Omar Beća) (a) 01/01/2002, Sarajevo (Bosnia and Herzegovina) (b) 1,86 (c) M - pivot (d) FK Zeljeznicar Sarajevo (e) -

*** Beccari - Simon Beccari (a) 18/11/1998, Bozen (Italy) (b) 1,88 (c) G (d) - (e) WSG Tirol, Wattens II, SV Innsbruck, FC Bolzano 1996

*** Bech - Tobias Bech (Tobias Bech Kristensen) (a) 19/02/2002, Møldrup (Denmark) (b) 1,89 (c) F - right winger (d) Aarhus GF (e) FC Ingolstadt, Viborg FF

*** Bech Sörensen - Mads Bech Sörensen (Mads Bech Sørensen) (a) 07/01/1999, Horsens (Denmark) (b) 1,93 (c) D - central defense (d) Brentford FC (e) FC Groningen, Brentford, OGC Nice, Brentford, AFC Wimbledon, Brentford, Brentford B, AC Horsens

*** Bechtold - Michel Bechtold (a) 01/07/1995, ¿? (Luxembourg) (b) - (c) M - pivot (d) FC Victoria Rosport (e) CS Fola Esch, Victoria Rosport, CS Fola Esch, CS Grevenmacher

*** Becirovic - Edvin Becirovic (a) 29/03/2000, ¿? (Sweden) (b) - (c) F - left winger (d) IFK Värnamo (e) Anderstorps IF

*** Beck - Asker Beck (Asker Beck Jensen) (a) 07/07/2003, ¿? (Denmark) (b) 1,84 (c) M - attacking midfielder (d) Kolding IF (e) -

*** Beck - Julius Beck (Julius Eskelund Beck) (a) 27/04/2005, Haderslev (Denmark) (b) 1,78 (c) M - central midfielder (d) Spezia (e) -

*** Beck - Morten Beck (Morten Beck Guldsmed) (a) 02/01/1988, ¿? (Denmark) (b) 1,91 (c) F - center forward (d) - (e) Skive IK, Hafnarfjördur, ÍA Akranes, Hafnarfjördur, Viborg FF, FC Fredericia, KR Reykjavík, Hobro IK, Silkeborg IF, Skive IK, Aarhus GF, Aarhus GF II

*** Beck - Owen Beck (Owen Michael Beck) (a) 09/08/2002, Wrexham (Wales) (b) 1,77 (c) D - left back (d) Dundee FC (e) Dundee FC, Bolton Wanderers, Famalicão

*** Becker - Finn Ole Becker (a) 08/06/2000, Elmshorn (Germany) (b) 1,77 (c) M - central midfielder (d) TSG 1899 Hoffenheim (e) FC St. Pauli

*** Becker - Sheraldo Becker (Sheraldo Rudi Becker) (a) 09/02/1995, Amsterdam (Netherlands) (b) 1,80 (c) F - attacking midfielder (d) 1.FC Union Berlin (e) ADO Den Haag, Ajax B, PEC Zwolle, Ajax B

*** Bedecs - Imrich Bedecs (a) 12/12/1991, ¿? (Czechoslovakia, now in Slovakia) (b) 1,88 (c) D - central defense (d) Spartak Myjava (e) Liptovsky Mik., Trinec, SK Senec

*** Bedi - Bence Bedi (a) 14/11/1996, Nagykanizsa (Hungary) (b) 1,82 (c) M - central midfielder (d) Zalaegerszegi TE FC (e) -

*** Bedia - Chris Bedia (Chris Vianney Bedia) (a) 05/03/1996, Abidjan (Ivory Coast) (b) 1,90 (c) F - center forward (d) Servette FC (e) RSC Charleroi, FC Sochaux, RSC Charleroi, Troyes, RSC Charleroi, Zulte Waregem, RSC Charleroi, Tours B

*** Bediashvili - Giorgi Bediashvili (გიორგი ბედიაშვილი) (a) 21/06/2005, ¿? (Georgia) (b) - (c) G (d) FC Gagra (e) -

*** Bednar - Martin Bednar (Martin Bednár) (a) 22/04/1999, Prešov (Slovakia) (b) 1,90 (c) D - central defense (d) Zemplin Michalovce (e) Zlaté Moravce, Dunajska Streda, Michalovce, Dunajska Streda, Michalovce

*** Bednar - Samuel Bednar (Samuel Bednár) (a) 30/04/2004, Trenčín (Slovakia) (b) 1,83 (c) M - attacking midfielder (d) FK Teplice B (e) -

*** Bednarek - Filip Bednarek (Filip Bednarek) (a) 26/09/1992, Słupca (Poland) (b) 1,88 (c) G (d) Lech Poznan (e) Heerenveen, De Graafschap, FC Utrecht, FC Twente

*** Bednarek - Jan Bednarek (a) 12/04/1996, SÅ‚upca (Poland) (b) 1,89 (d) Southampton FC (e) Aston Villa, Southampton, Lech Poznan, Gornik Leczna, Lech Poznan, Lech Poznan II, MSP Szamotuly

*** Bedouret - Juan Bedouret (a) 16/08/1998, ¿? (Argentina) (b) 1,84 (c) D - central defense (d) FC Differdange 03 (e) -

*** Beernaert - Martijn Beernaert (a) 03/10/2002, Ieper (Belgium) (b) 1,88 (c) G (d) SC Dikkelvenne (e) Zulte Waregem

*** Begala - Matus Begala (Matúš Begala) (a) 07/04/2001, Stará Ľubovňa (Slovakia) (b) 1,86 (c) M - pivot (d) PAS Giannina (e) Michalovce

*** Began - Razvan Began (Răzvan Cătălin Began) (a) 12/08/1996, Sighetu Marmaţiei (Romania) (b) 1,93 (c) G (d) FC Dinamo 1948 (e) FC Botosani, Sepsi OSK, Dunarea Calarasi, Daco-Getica, ACS Poli, FC Hermannstadt, Foresta Suceava, Luceafarul, Farul Constanta, CSM Sighet

*** Beganovic - Amar Beganovic (Amar Beganović) (a) 25/11/1999, Tuzla (Bosnia and Herzegovina) (b) 1,84 (c) D - right back (d) FK Sarajevo (e) NS Mura, Sloboda Tuzla

*** Beganovic - Belmin Beganovic (Belmin Beganović) (a) 09/09/2004, Bihać (Bosnia and Herzegovina) (b) 1,83 (c) F - left winger (d) SV Ried (e) SV Ried II

*** Beganovic - Dzenis Beganovic (Dženis Beganović) (a) 23/03/1996, Sarajevo (Bosnia and Herzegovina) (b) 1,85 (c) M - central midfielder (d) Istiqlol Dushanbe (e) Zeljeznicar, Sloboda Tuzla, FK Tuzla City, 1.SC Znojmo, Kom Podgorica, Zeljeznicar, NK Jajce, Zeljeznicar

*** Begashvili - Giorgi Begashvili (გიორგი ბეგაშვილი) (a) 12/02/1991, ¿? (Georgia) (b) 1,96 (c) G (d) Dinamo Batumi (e) Merani Martvili, Chikhura, FC Dila,

Dinamo Tbilisi, FC Dila, Dinamo Tbilisi, Merani Martvili, FC Samtredia, Merani Martvili, FC Gagra, Chikhura

*** Begic - Amar Begic (Amar Begić) (a) 07/08/2000, Zenica (Bosnia and Herzegovina) (b) 1,83 (c) M - central midfielder (d) FC Telavi (e) Borac Banja Luka, Mladost Kakanj

*** Begic - Dominik Begic (Dominik Begić) (a) 03/08/1997, Mostar (Bosnia and Herzegovina) (b) - (c) F - center forward (d) HSK Posusje (e) NK Imotski, HSK Posusje, HNK Capljina, HSK Posusje

*** Begic - Luka Begic (Luka Begić) (a) 05/02/1994, Posusje (Bosnia and Herzegovina) (b) - (c) M - attacking midfielder (d) FK Leotar Trebinje (e) HSK Posusje, Croat. Zmijavci, NK Kamen, Croat. Zmijavci, NK Urania BV, NK Imotski, HBDNK Mosor, Mracaj Runovic, NK Imotski, HSK Posusje

*** Begic - Silvije Begic (Silvije Begić) (a) 03/06/1993, Posušje (Bosnia and Herzegovina) (b) 1,97 (c) D - central defense (d) Ural Ekaterimburgo (e) Rubin Kazan, KS Samara, Rubin Kazan, Orenburg, Inter Zaprešić, NK Rudes, NK Kamen, HSK Posusje

*** Begic - Zvonimir Begic (Zvonimir Begić) (a) 22/09/1990, Mostar (Yugoslavia, now in Bosnia and Herzegovina) (b) 1,84 (c) M - pivot (d) HSK Posusje (e) Siroki Brijeg, Croat. Zmijavci, NK Zadar, Croat. Zmijavci, NK Kamen, HSK Posusje, NK Kamen, Mladost Prolozac

*** Beglarishvili - Zakaria Beglarishvili (ზაქარია ბეგლარიშვილი) (a) 30/04/1990, Tbilisi (Soviet Union, now in Georgia) (b) 1,71 (c) M - attacking midfielder (d) FC Gagra (e) FK Turon, FCI Levadia, FC KTP, FC Flora, SJK Seinäjoki, FC Flora, Honvéd, FC Flora, Sioni Bolnisi, FC Flora, FC Locomotive, Metalurgi R.

*** Beglaryan - Arsen Beglaryan (Արսեն Բեգլարյան) (a) 18/02/1993, Krasnodar (Russia) (b) 1,87 (c) G (d) FC Ararat-Armenia (e) FC Urartu, Dnyapro Mogilev, Liepaja, Alashkert CF, MIKA Aschtarak, Ulisses, Shirak Gyumri, Gandzasar, Krasnodar II

*** Begolli - Gentrit Begolli (a) 21/02/1992, Prishtinë (Yugoslavia, now in Kosovo) (b) 1,75 (c) F - left winger (d) Granit Begolli (e) FC Prishtina, FC Llapi, KF Flamurtari, FC Llapi, FC Prishtina

*** Begovic - Asmir Begovic (Asmir Begović) (a) 20/06/1987, Trebinje (Yugoslavia, now in Bosnia and Herzegovina) (b) 1,99 (c) G (d) Queens Park Rangers (e) Everton, Bournemouth, AC Milan, Bournemouth, Qarabag FK, Bournemouth, Chelsea, Stoke City, FC Portsmouth, Ipswich, FC Portsmouth, Yeovil Town, FC Portsmouth, Yeovil Town, FC Portsmouth, Bournemouth, FC Portsmouth, Macclesfield, FC Portsmouth, La Louviere, FC Portsmouth

*** Begraoui - Yanis Begraoui (بگراوي يانيس) (a) 04/07/2001, Étampes (France) (b) 1,79 (c) F - center forward (d) Toulouse FC (e) Pau FC, Toulouse, AJ Auxerre

*** Begun - Dmitriy Begun (Бегун Дмитрий Александрович) (a) 23/04/2003, Vladivostok (Russia) (b) 1,75 (c) D - left back (d) SKA Khabarovsk (e) Dinamo 2, Dinamo Moskva II, CSKA Moskva II, Luch, Luch II

*** Begunov - Roman Begunov (Бегунов Роман Игоревич) (a) 22/03/1993, Minsk (Belarus) (b) 1,81 (c) D - right back (d) Dinamo Minsk (e) Soligorsk, Torpedo Zhodino, Dinamo Minsk, FK Minsk, FK Minsk II

*** Behich - Aziz Behich (Aziz Eraltay Behich) (a) 16/12/1990, Melbourne (Australia) (b) 1,70 (c) D - left back (d) Melbourne City FC (e) Dundee United, Giresunspor, Basaksehir, Kayserispor, Basaksehir, PSV Eindhoven, Bursaspor, Melbourne Heart, Bursaspor, Melbourne Heart, Hume City FC, Green Gully SC

*** Behiratche - Jocelin Behiratche (a) 08/05/2000, ¿? (Ivory Coast) (b) 1,87 (c) D - central defense (d) FC Dinamo (e) KF Tirana, Giorgione

*** Behounek - Raffael Behounek (a) 16/04/1997, Wien (Austria) (b) 1,87 (c) D - central defense (d) Willem II Tilburg (e) WSG Tirol, FC Wacker, SV Mattersburg, Mattersburg II, SV Horn, Mattersburg II, FC Stadlau

*** Behram - Seid Behram (a) 12/07/1998, Mostar (Bosnia and Herzegovina) (b) 1,83 (c) M - attacking midfielder (d) NK Mladost Zdralovi (e) Slaven Belupo, Mlad. Zdralovi, Velez Mostar, RFCU Luxembourg

*** Behrami - Valton Behrami (a) 16/03/2004, Genève (Switzerland) (b) 1,82 (c) D - left back (d) AC Bellinzona (e) Servette FC

*** Behrens - Kevin Behrens (a) 03/02/1991, Bremen (Germany) (b) 1,85 (c) F - center forward (d) 1.FC Union Berlin (e) SV Sandhausen, Saarbrücken, RW Essen, Alemannia Aachen, Hannover 96 II, Wilhelmshaven, Werder Bremen III

*** Bei - Gianluca Bei (a) 17/05/1995, ¿? (Luxembourg) (b) - (c) D - right back (d) FC Differdange 03 (e) Hamm Benfica, US Hostert, Differdange 03, Mondercange

*** Beijmo - Felix Beijmo (Felix Olof Allan Nelson Beijmo) (a) 31/01/1998, Stockholm (Sweden) (b) 1,85 (c) D - right back (d) Aarhus GF (e) Malmö FF, Aarhus GF, Malmö FF, Werder Bremen, Greuther Fürth, Werder Bremen, Malmö FF, Werder Bremen, Djurgården, Brommapojkarna

*** Bejan - Alexandru Bejan (a) 07/05/1996, Chișinău (Moldova) (b) 1,78 (c) M - left midfielder (d) - (e) Petrocub, Zimbru Chisinau, Petrocub, Dinamo-Auto, Dacia

*** Bejan - Florin Bejan (a) 28/03/1991, Mangalia (Romania) (b) 1,86 (c) D - central defense (d) FC Hermannstadt (e) FC Dinamo, Academica Clinceni, FC Dinamo, Astra Giurgiu, Cracovia, Concordia, Cracovia, ASA Tg. Mures, FC Viitorul, FCSB II

*** Bejan - Iulian Bejan (a) 04/03/2004, Chișinău (Moldova) (b) 1,92 (c) M - attacking midfielder (d) FC Zimbru Chisinau (e) Zimbru Chisinau

*** Bejan - Roman Bejan (a) 01/08/2003, ¿? (Moldova) (b) 1,92 (c) D - central defense (d) - (e) Dacia Buiucani

*** Bejarano - Danny Bejarano (Danny Bryan Bejarano Yañez) (a) 03/01/1994, Santa Cruz de la Sierra (Bolivia) (b) 1,82 (c) M - pivot (d) Nea Salamis (e) PAS Lamia, Oriente P., Panetolikos, Sport Boys, Panetolikos, Bolívar, Panetolikos, Oriente P.

*** Bejarano - José Bejarano (José Bejarano Leandro) (a) 10/02/2002, Figueres (Spain) (b) 1,86 (c) G (d) FC Santa Coloma (e) CE Carroi

*** Bejger - Lukasz Bejger (Łukasz Bejger) (a) 11/01/2002, Golub-Dobrzyń (Poland) (b) 1,90 (c) D - central defense (d) Śląsk Wroclaw (e) -

*** Bejta - Azem Bejta (a) 03/08/1990, Skënderaj (RF Yugoslavia, now in Kosovo) (b) - (c) D - central defense (d) KF Vëllaznimi Gjakovë (e) KF Drenica, KF Feronikeli, FC Malisheva, KF Drenica

*** Bejtulai - Egzon Bejtulai (Егзон Бејтулаи) (a) 07/01/1994, Tetovo (North Macedonia) (b) 1,82 (c) D - central defense (d) - (e) Shkëndija, Helsingborgs IF, Shkëndija, Teteks Tetovo

*** Bejzade - Abjel Bejzade (a) 30/10/2001, Tiranë (Albania) (b) - (c) M - central midfielder (d) KS Kastrioti (e) KF Turbina, NK Lokomotiva, KF Turbina, NK Lokomotiva, KF Korabi

*** Beka - Ismajl Beka (Ismajl Isak Beka) (a) 31/10/1999, Frauenfeld (Switzerland) (b) 1,97 (c) D - central defense (d) FC Lucerna (e) FC Wil 1900, Rapperswil-Jona, FC Wil 1900, FC Wil II, FC Wittenbach, FC Wil II

*** Beka (c) D (d) KF Drenica (e) - - Arblert Beka (c) D (d) KF Drenica (e) -

*** Beka Beka - Alexis Beka Beka (Alexis Adelin Beka Beka) (a) 29/03/2001, Paris (France) (b) 1,78 (c) M - pivot (d) OGC Niza (e) Lokomotiv Moskva, SM Caen, SM Caen B

*** Bekaj - Visar Bekaj (a) 24/05/1997, Prishtinë (RF Yugoslavia, now in Kosovo) (b) 1,91 (c) G (d) Hatayspor (e) KF Tirana, FC Prishtina, Ramiz Sadiku

*** Bekale - Eneme Bekale (Christ Junior-Ray Eneme Bekale) (a) 20/03/1999, ¿? (Gabon) (b) 1,80 (c) M - pivot (d) - (e) FC Sheriff, EO Sidi Bouzid, Almahalla Tripoli, US Tataouine, CA Bizertin, ES Metlaoui

*** Bekale Biyoghe - Eric Jospin Bekale Biyoghe (a) 04/03/2000, ¿? (Gabon) (b) - (c) F - center forward (d) - (e) Dinamo-Auto, US Tataouine

*** Bekamenga - Christian Bekamenga (Christian Bekamenga Bekamengo Aymard) (a) 09/05/1986, Yaoundé (Cameroon) (b) 1,85 (c) F - center forward (d) - (e) Sant Julià, Albères Argelès, Real Potosí, Muktijoddha, Genclik Gücü, Elazigspor, BB Erzurumspor, Liaoning FC, Balikesirspor, Troyes, FC Metz, Troyes, RC Lens, Troyes, Stade Lavallois, Troyes, Stade Lavallois, Carquefou, US Orléans, FC Nantes, Skoda Xanthi, FC Nantes, Persib, Negeri Sembilan

*** Bekaroglu - Burak Bekaroglu (Burak Bekaroğlu) (a) 16/04/1997, Sakarya (Turkey) (b) 1,91 (c) D - central defense (d) Hatayspor (e) Karagümrük, Boluspor, Sakaryaspor

*** Bekauri - Temur Bekauri (თემურ ბექაური) (a) 12/02/1994, ¿? (Georgia) (b) - (c) D - central defense (d) Merani Tbilisi (e) Sioni Bolnisi, Spaeri, FC Shevardeni, WIT Georgia, FC Gareji

*** Bekbaev - Almat Bekbaev (Бекбаев Алмат Маратович) (a) 14/07/1984, Kyzylorda (Soviet Union, now in Kazakhstan) (b) 1,94 (c) G (d) - (e) Maktaaral, Qyzyljar, Zhetysu, Irtysh, Ordabasy, Aktobe, Tobol Kostanay, Ordabasy, FK Andijon, Akzhayik, Ordabasy, Kaysar, Ordabasy, Ordabasy II

*** Bekeshov - Madiyar Bekeshov (Бекешов Мадияр Серикбайулы) (a) 10/09/2004, Aktau (Kazakhstan) (b) 1,81 (c) F - left winger (d) Kaspiy Aktau II (e) -

*** Bekhaled - Anasse Bekhaled (a) 30/10/1995, ¿? (France) (b) - (c) M (d) FC Mondercange (e) RSC Habay

*** Bekic - Almir Bekic (Almir Bekić) (a) 01/06/1989, Tuzla (Yugoslavia, now in Bosnia and Herzegovina) (b) 1,81 (c) D - left back (d) - (e) Zrinjski Mostar, Sloboda Tuzla, FK Sarajevo, Sloboda Tuzla, Din. Zagreb II, Dinamo Zagreb, NK Sesvete, Dinamo Zagreb, GOSK Gabela, Dinamo Zagreb, Sloboda Tuzla, Dinamo Zagreb, Sloboda Tuzla, Dinamo Zagreb, NK Lokomotiva, Dinamo Zagreb, Sloboda Tuzla

*** Bekic - Amer Bekic (Amer Bekić) (a) 05/08/1992, Tuzla (Bosnia and Herzegovina) (b) 1,86 (c) F - center forward (d) - (e) Sloboda Tuzla, NK Opatija, Borneo FC, Sloboda Tuzla, Zrinjski Mostar, Sloboda Tuzla, Tobol Kostanay, FK Sarajevo, Zrinjski Mostar, Sloboda Tuzla

*** Bekiroglu - Efkan Bekiroglu (Efkan Bekiroğlu) (a) 14/09/1995, Dachau (Germany) (b) 1,85 (c) M - central midfielder (d) MKE Ankaragücü (e) Alanyaspor, 1860 München, FC Augsburg II, FC Unterföhring, Phönix München

*** Bekkema - Jan Bekkema (a) 09/04/1996, Drachten (Netherlands) (b) 1,86 (c) G (d) SC Heerenveen (e) SV Straelen, Heerenveen

*** Bekkouche - Sofiane Bekkouche (a) 02/05/1996, ¿? (France) (b) 1,85 (c) F - right winger (d) US Mondorf-Les-Bains (e) Schiltigheim, CS Sedan, Saint-Quentin, ASM Belfort, US Mondorf, Racing Strasbourg B, AS Nancy B

*** Bekmyrza - Anuar Bekmyrza (Бекмырза Ануар) (a) 07/05/2001, Aktau (Kazakhstan) (b) 1,75 (c) D - left back (d) Kaspiy Aktau (e) -

*** Bekric - Samir Bekric (Samir Bekrić) (a) 20/10/1984, Tuzla (Yugoslavia, now in Bosnia and Herzegovina) (b) 1,81 (c) M - attacking midfielder (d) - (e) Zeljeznicar, Sloboda Tuzla, Zrinjski Mostar, Zeljeznicar, Bunyodkor, Fajr Sepasi, Mes Kerman, Zeljeznicar, Tobol Kostanay, Incheon Utd., Zeljeznicar, OFK Gradina

*** Beks - Janis Beks (Jānis Beks) (a) 01/11/2002, ¿? (Latvia) (b) 1,88 (c) G (d) FK Metta (e) RFS, Metta, FS Metta II
*** Bekteshi - Leotrim Bekteshi (a) 21/04/1992, Mitrovicë (Yugoslavia, now in Kosovo) (b) 1,85 (c) D - central defense (d) KF Llapi (e) FC Ballkani, Mjøndalen, FC Prishtina, SC Gjilani, Iskra Borcice, FC Besa, KF Trepca 89
*** Bel Hassani - Iliass Bel Hassani (بلحساني إلياس) (a) 16/09/1992, Rotterdam (Netherlands) (b) 1,75 (c) M - attacking midfielder (d) Al-Jabalain FC (e) RKC Waalwijk, Ajman Club, Al-Wakrah SC, PEC Zwolle, AZ Alkmaar, FC Groningen, AZ Alkmaar, Heracles Almelo, Sparta Rotterdam
*** Bela - Jérémie Bela (a) 08/04/1993, Melun (France) (b) 1,73 (c) F - left winger (d) Clermont Foot 63 (e) Birmingham City, Albacete, Dijon, RC Lens, RC Lens B
*** Belahyane - Reda Belahyane (a) 01/06/2004, Aubervilliers (France) (b) 1,69 (c) M - pivot (d) OGC Niza (e) OGC Nice B
*** Belaïli - Youcef Belaïli (بلايلي يوسف محمد) (a) 14/03/1992, Oran (Algeria) (b) 1,82 (c) F - left winger (d) MC Alger (e) AC Ajaccio, Stade Brestois, Qatar SC, Al-Ahli, Esperance, Angers SCO, Sperre) USM Alger, Esperance, MC Orán
*** Belakovic - Nemanja Belakovic (Немања Белаковић) (a) 08/01/1997, Kraljevo (RF Yugoslavia, now in Serbia) (b) 1,83 (c) F - left winger (d) FK Radnicki Niš (e) Liepaja, TSV Hartberg, Spartaks, Čukarički, NK Novigrad, OFK Beograd
*** Belameiri - El Hadi Belameiri (a) 24/04/1991, Florange (France) (b) 1,66 (c) M - attacking midfielder (d) Swift Hesperange (e) US Monastir, CABB Arreridj, Alki Oroklini, CS Constantine, ES Sétif, Amnéville
*** Belanik - Samuel Belanik (Samuel Belaník) (a) 26/08/2003, ¿? (Slovakia) (b) 1,95 (c) G (d) MSK Zilina (e) MSK Zilina B
*** Belay - Naftali Belay (בלאי נפתלי) (a) 28/03/1997, Netanya (Israel) (b) - (c) M - pivot (d) Maccabi Netanya (e) Ramat haSharon, Maccabi Netanya, H. Petah Tikva, Maccabi Netanya, Hapoel Hadera, Maccabi Netanya, Hapoel Acre, Maccabi Netanya
*** Belcar - Leon Belcar (a) 04/01/2002, Varaždin (Croatia) (b) 1,86 (c) M - pivot (d) NK Varazdin (e) -
*** Belec - Vid Belec (a) 06/06/1990, Maribor (Yugoslavia, now in Slovenia) (b) 1,92 (c) G (d) APOEL FC (e) Salernitana, Sampdoria, APOEL FC, Sampdoria, Benevento, Sampdoria, Benevento, Carpi, Internazionale Milano, Konyaspor, Internazionale Milano, Olhanense, Internazionale Milano, Crotone, Internazionale Milano
*** Belen - Arda Belen (a) 14/01/2001, Karabük (Turkey) (b) 1,85 (c) D - right back (d) Istanbulspor (e) Sivas Belediye, Istanbulspor, Karabükspor
*** Belényesi - Csaba Belényesi (a) 03/03/1994, Debrecen (Hungary) (b) 1,93 (c) D - central defense (d) Kecskeméti TE (e) Diósgyőr, Kecskemét, Dorog, Debreceni EAC, Debrecen, Debrecen II, Kazincbarcika, Putnok, Cigánd, Gyulai FC, Puskás AFC II
*** Belesi - Benis Belesi (a) 01/06/1999, Rotterdam (Netherlands) (b) 1,88 (c) D - central defense (d) UN Käerjeng 97 (e) Olym. Charleroi, KSK Ronse
*** Belhadji - Ahmed Belhadji (بلحاج أحمد) (a) 16/11/1997, Alhucemas (Morocco) (b) 1,76 (c) M - central midfielder (d) Aswan SC (e) Zamalek, Aswan SC, IC d'Escaldes, Orihuela CF, Dep. Aragón, R. B. Linense, Dep. Aragón, Cornellà
*** Belhanda - Younès Belhanda (بلهندة يونس) (a) 25/02/1990, Avignon (France) (b) 1,75 (c) M - attacking midfielder (d) Adana Demirspor (e) Galatasaray, Dinamo Kyïv, OGC Nice, Dinamo Kyïv, FC Schalke 04, Dinamo Kyïv, Montpellier
*** Belibi - Ange Belibi (Ange Aboa Belibi) (a) 11/12/2001, ¿? (Cameroon) (b) - (c) M - attacking midfielder (d) - (e) Pietà Hotspurs, Boluspor, Walhain

*** Belic - Kristijan Belic (Кристијан Белић) (a) 25/03/2001, Sint-Truiden (Belgium) (b) 1,77 (c) M - pivot (d) Partizán Beograd (e) Čukarički

*** Belic - Nemanja Belic (Немања Белић) (a) 24/04/1987, Beograd (Yugoslavia, now in Serbia) (b) 1,88 (c) G (d) FK Čukarički (e) Metalac, Donji Srem, Radnicki Obrenovac, OFK Beograd, Radnicki Obrenovac, OFK Beograd, FK Palilulac, OFK Beograd

*** Belica - Egzon Belica (a) 03/09/1990, Struga (Yugoslavia, now in North Macedonia) (b) 1,89 (c) D - central defense (d) Rabotnicki Skopje (e) FC Prishtina, FK Partizani, Riga, FC Inter, Shkëndija, Concordia, Ohrid Lihnidos, Rabotnicki, KS Besa

*** Belikov - Ilya Belikov (Беликов Илья Александрович) (a) 23/05/2003, ¿? (Russia) (b) 1,84 (c) D - left back (d) Lokomotiv Moskva II (e) -

*** Beljo - Dion Beljo (Dion Drena Beljo) (a) 01/03/2002, Zagreb (Croatia) (b) 1,95 (c) F - center forward (d) FC Augsburg (e) NK Osijek, NK Istra, NK Osijek, NK Osijek II, Cibalia

*** Belkebla - Haris Belkebla (a) 28/01/1994, Drancy (France) (b) 1,77 (c) M - central midfielder (d) - (e) Stade Brestois, Tours FC, Valenciennes B, Aubervilliers

*** Belkhdim - Yassin Belkhdim (a) 14/02/2002, Meulan-en-Yvelines (France) (b) 1,75 (c) M - central midfielder (d) Angers SCO (e) Angers SCO B, FC Mantois

*** Belko - Lubomir Belko (Ľubomír Belko) (a) 04/02/2002, Žilina (Slovakia) (b) 1,89 (c) G (d) MSK Zilina (e) -

*** Belko - Marek Belko (a) 18/10/2003, ¿? (Slovakia) (b) - (c) F (d) Banik Kalinovo (e) Podbrezova, Pohronie, Podbrezova

*** Bell - Joe Bell (Joe Zen Robert Bell) (a) 27/04/1999, Bristol (England) (b) 1,82 (c) M - pivot (d) Brøndby IF (e) Viking, Virginia Cavs, W. Phoenix Reserves

*** Bell - Laurie Bell (Laurence Edward John Bell) (a) 01/09/1992, Poynton (England) (b) 1,88 (c) M - central midfielder (d) - (e) Caernarfon, Örebro Syr., BK Forward, Karlslunds IF, Macclesfield, Hyde United, Macclesfield, Karlslunds IF, Roughnecks FC, Milwaukee P., Ventura County, Milwaukee P.

*** Bell - Stefan Bell (a) 24/08/1991, Andernach (Germany) (b) 1,92 (c) D - central defense (d) 1.FSV Mainz 05 (e) Eintracht, Mainz 05, 1860 München, Mainz 05

*** Bellache - Yuliwes Bellache (a) 15/12/2002, Lyon (France) (b) 1,73 (c) M - central midfielder (d) JS Kabylie (e) Clermont Foot, Austria Lustenau, Clermont Foot, Clermont B

*** Bella-Kotchap - Armel Bella-Kotchap (a) 11/12/2001, Paris (France) (b) 1,90 (c) D - central defense (d) Southampton FC (e) VfL Bochum

*** Bellanova - Raoul Bellanova (a) 17/05/2000, Rho (Italy) (b) 1,88 (c) D - right back (d) Torino FC (e) Cagliari, Internazionale Milano, Cagliari, Girondins Bordeaux, Cagliari, Girondins Bordeaux, Atalanta, Pescara, Atalanta, Girondins Bordeaux, Girondins Bordeaux

*** Bellarabi - Karim Bellarabi (بلعربي كريم) (a) 08/04/1990, Berlin (Germany) (b) 1,84 (c) F - right winger (d) - (e) Bayer Leverkusen, Eintracht Braunschweig, Bayer Leverkusen, Eintracht Braunschweig, Eintracht Braunschweig II

*** Bellegarde - Jean-Ricner Bellegarde (a) 27/06/1998, Colombes (France) (b) 1,72 (c) M - central midfielder (d) Racing Club Strasbourg (e) RC Lens, RC Lens B

*** Bellerín - Héctor Bellerín (Héctor Bellerín Moruno) (a) 19/03/1995, Badalona (Spain) (b) 1,78 (c) D - right back (d) Real Betis Balompié (e) Sporting Lisboa, FC Barcelona, Arsenal, Real Betis, Arsenal, Watford

*** Bellingham - Jude Bellingham (Jude Victor William Bellingham) (a) 29/06/2003, Stourbridge (England) (b) 1,86 (c) M - central midfielder (d) Real Madrid CF (e) Borussia Dortmund, Birmingham City

*** Bellman - Henrik Bellman (a) 24/03/1999, ¿? (Sweden) (b) - (c) M - right midfielder (d) RSC Anderlecht Futures (e) Östersund, Levanger, Östersund
*** Bellmunt - Vicente Bellmunt (Vicente Bellmunt García) (a) 28/01/2000, Villarreal (Spain) (b) - (c) G (d) Getafe CF B (e) CD Acero, Villarreal CF C
*** Bellon - Paul Bellon (a) 15/01/2000, Issoire (France) (b) 1,75 (c) M - central midfielder (d) FC Lorient B (e) -
*** Belmenen - Aaron Belmenen (a) 07/01/2003, Mexico City (Mexico) (b) 1,77 (c) D - central defense (d) SC/ESV Parndorf (e) Zlaté Moravce
*** Belmonte - Anthony Belmonte (a) 16/10/1995, Istres (France) (b) 1,85 (c) M - central midfielder (d) APO Levadiakos (e) Grenoble, Levski Sofia, Dijon, FC Istres
*** Belocian - Jeanuël Belocian (a) 17/02/2005, Les Abymes (Guadaloupe) (b) 1,82 (c) D - central defense (d) Stade Rennais FC (e) -
*** Beloko - Nicky Beloko (Nicky Stéphane Medja Beloko) (a) 16/02/2000, Ebolowa (Cameroon) (b) 1,84 (c) M - central midfielder (d) FC Lucerna (e) Neuchâtel Xamax, Neuchâtel Xamax, KAA Gent
*** Belotti - Andrea Belotti (a) 20/12/1993, Calcinate (Italy) (b) 1,81 (c) F - center forward (d) AS Roma (e) Torino, US Palermo, UC AlbinoLeffe, US Palermo, UC AlbinoLeffe
*** Belous - Ilya Belous (Белоус Илья Андреевич) (a) 01/01/1995, Iskitim, Novosibirsk Region (Russia) (b) 1,87 (c) F - center forward (d) Dinamo Bryansk (e) Belshina, Shinnik, Volgar, Chaika Pes., Khimki, Chaika Pes., Khimki, Krasnodar-2, Afips Afipskiy, Krasnodar-2, Milsami, Krasnodar-2, CSKA Moskva II, Lokomotiv 2, CSKA Moskva II, Volga Nizhny Novgorod II, CSKA Moskva II, Olympia G., Hapa
*** Belousov - Alexandr Belousov (a) 14/05/1998, Tiraspol (Moldova) (b) 1,80 (c) D - right back (d) - (e) Spartak Varna, FC Sheriff, Milsami, FC Sheriff, Sfintul Gheorghe, FC Sheriff, Dinamo-Auto, FC Sheriff, Sheriff-2
*** Belov - Mikhail Belov (Белов Михаил Валерьевич) (a) 22/04/1992, Novaya Usmanj, Voronezh Region (Russia) (b) 1,75 (c) M - pivot (d) Spartak Tambov (e) Atom, JK Trans Narva, Lada Dimitrovgrad, Chelyabinsk, Zenit Penza, Chaika Pes., Lokomotiv Liski, Fakel Voronezh, Lokomotiv Liski, Fakel Voronezh, Amkar II, Lokomotiv Liski, Fakel-M
*** Belporo - Malick Belporo (a) 21/10/2004, ¿? (Cameroon) (b) - (c) M (d) FC Wiltz 71 (e) FC Wiltz 71 II
*** Beltrame - Stefano Beltrame (a) 08/02/1993, Biella (Italy) (b) 1,83 (c) F - attacking midfielder (d) CS Marítimo (e) CSKA-Sofia, FC Den Bosch, Go Ahead Eagles, Juventus, FC Den Bosch, Juventus, Pordenone, Juventus, Pro Vercelli, Juventus, Sampdoria, Modena, Sampdoria, Juventus, Bari
*** Beltrán - Fran Beltrán (Francisco José Beltrán Peinado) (a) 03/02/1999, Madrid (Spain) (b) 1,65 (c) M - central midfielder (d) RC Celta de Vigo (e) Rayo Vallecano, Rayo B
*** Belu - Claudiu Belu (Claudiu Belu-Iordache) (a) 07/11/1993, Timişoara (Romania) (b) 1,85 (c) D - right back (d) ACSM Politehnica Iasi (e) FC Rapid 1923, FC Hermannstadt, FCSB, FC Voluntari, FCSB, Astra Giurgiu, ASA Tg. Mures, ACS Poli, Concordia, Poli. Timisoara, P. Timisoara B
*** Beluli - Jashar Beluli (a) 07/06/2004, Aabenraa (Denmark) (b) - (c) F - center forward (d) AC Horsens (e) -
*** Bely - Álvaro Bely (Álvaro Bely Medina) (a) 21/03/1994, Córdoba (Argentina) (b) - (c) D - central defense (d) FC Bălţi (e) Linense, Serrato, Sport Boys, CD Dragón, CA Las Palmas
*** Belyaev - Oleksandr Belyaev (Бєляєв Олександр Андрійович) (a) 04/10/1999, Dnipropetrovsk (Ukraine) (b) 1,74 (c) M - central midfielder (d) FK Oleksandriya (e)

Genclerbirligi, PFK Lviv, Genclerbirligi, SK Dnipro-1, Genclerbirligi, SK Dnipro-1, VPK-Agro, SK Dnipro-1, Saburtalo, SK Dnipro-1, Zirka, SK Dnipro-1
*** Ben Amar - Sami Ben Amar (عمر بن سامي) (a) 02/03/1998, Nice (France) (b) 1,84 (c) F - center forward (d) Lyon - La Duchère (e) US Mondorf, Dundalk FC, Nîmes, Nîmes B, SC Bastia B
*** Ben Harush - Noam Ben Harush (הרוש בן נועם) (a) 13/05/2005, Megadim (Israel) (b) 1,76 (c) D - right back (d) - (e) Hapoel Haifa
*** Ben Harush - Omri Ben Harush (הרוש בן עומרי) (a) 07/03/1990, Netanya (Israel) (b) 1,85 (c) D - left back (d) Hapoel Kfar Saba (e) Ness Ziona, Bnei Sakhnin, FC Ashdod, KSC Lokeren, Maccabi Haifa, Maccabi Tel Aviv, Maccabi Netanya
*** Ben Kacem - Mohamed Ben Kacem (a) 27/02/1994, ¿? (Morocco) (b) - (c) F - center forward (d) SS Cosmos (e) Libertas, Pennarossa, Fiorentino, Riolo Terme, Fratta Terme, Valbidente, Fratta Terme, Valbidente, Cava Ronco
*** Ben Lulu - Guy Ben Lulu (לולו בן גיא) (a) 19/05/2000, ¿? (Israel) (b) 1,76 (c) F - center forward (d) Ironi Kiryat Shmona (e) Hapoel Acre, Kiryat Shmona
*** Ben Ouanes - Mortadha Ben Ouanes (وناس بن مرتضى) (a) 02/07/1994, Sousse (Tunisia) (b) 1,82 (c) D - left back (d) Kasimpasa (e) ES Sahel, CA Bizertin, ES Sahel, US Monastir, ES Sahel
*** Ben Sallam - Samir Ben Sallam (a) 03/06/2001, Amsterdam (Netherlands) (b) 1,85 (c) M - central midfielder (d) Karmiotissa Pano Polemidion (e) FC Volendam
*** Ben Seghir - Eliesse Ben Seghir (a) 16/02/2005, Saint-Tropez (France) (b) 1,78 (c) M - attacking midfielder (d) AS Mónaco (e) -
*** Ben Seghir - Salim Ben Seghir (a) 24/02/2003, Saint-Tropez (France) (b) 1,74 (c) F - left winger (d) Olympique de Marseille B (e) Valenciennes FC, Ol. Marseille B, OGC Nice B
*** Ben Shabat - Itay Ben Shabat (שבת בן איתי) (a) 09/07/2000, ¿? (Israel) (b) 1,90 (c) D - central defense (d) Maccabi Netanya (e) Kiryat Shmona
*** Ben Shimol - Ziv Ben Shimol (שימול בן זיו) (a) 27/01/2004, Ma'ale Adumim (Israel) (b) - (c) M - attacking midfielder (d) Hapoel Afula (e) Maccabi Haifa
*** Ben Shimon - Roei Ben Shimon (שמעון בן רועי) (a) 04/12/2000, Beit Ezra (Israel) (b) 1,85 (c) F - center forward (d) Hapoel Kfar Saba (e) H. Kfar Saba, Bnei Yehuda, FC Ashdod, Bnei Yehuda
*** Ben Yakar - Shahar Ben Yakar (יקר בן שחר) (a) 31/01/2001, ¿? (Israel) (b) - (c) G (d) - (e) Maccabi Netanya, Hapoel Raanana
*** Ben Yedder - Wissam Ben Yedder (a) 12/08/1990, Sarcelles (France) (b) 1,70 (c) F - center forward (d) AS Mónaco (e) Sevilla FC, Toulouse, Toulouse B, Alfortville, Saint-Denis
*** Ben Zaken - Tom Ben Zaken (זקן בן טום) (a) 29/10/1994, Ashdod (Israel) (b) - (c) D - right back (d) FC Ashdod (e) -
*** Benamar - Benaissa Benamar (بنعمر بنعيسى) (a) 08/04/1997, Amsterdam (Netherlands) (b) 1,91 (c) D - central defense (d) FC Volendam (e) FC Utrecht, FC Volendam, FC Utrecht, Telstar, Ittihad Tanger
*** Benamra - Marwane Benamra (a) 09/04/1995, Lyon (France) (b) 1,80 (c) F - center forward (d) US Mondorf-Les-Bains (e) Swift Hesperange, RE Virton, RUS Givry, RE Virton, US Mondorf, UD Horadada, CR Belouizdad, USM El Harrach, FC Villefranche, Thonon Évian B
*** Benassi - Marco Benassi (a) 08/09/1994, Modena (Italy) (b) 1,84 (c) M - central midfielder (d) Fiorentina (e) Cremonese, Fiorentina, FC Empoli, Fiorentina, Hellas Verona, Fiorentina, Torino, Internazionale Milano, AS Livorno, Internazionale Milano

*** Benatelli - Rico Benatelli (a) 17/03/1992, Herdecke (Germany) (b) 1,81 (c) M - central midfielder (d) SK Austria Klagenfurt (e) FC St. Pauli, Dynamo Dresden, Würzb. Kickers, Erzgebirge Aue, Borussia Dortmund II

*** Benbenishti - Ofir Benbenishti (בנבנישטי אופיר) (a) 08/08/2000, ¿? (Israel) (b) 1,94 (c) D - central defense (d) Ironi Kiryat Shmona (e) H. Ramat Gan, Kiryat Shmona, H. Ramat Gan, H. Umm al-Fahm, H. Ramat Gan

*** Benbenisti - Leo Benbenisti (a) 01/07/2004, ¿? (Israel) (b) - (c) D - central defense (d) - (e) Hapoel Tel Aviv

*** Benbouali - Nadhir Benbouali (Ahmed Nadhir Benbouali) (a) 17/04/2000, Chlef (Algeria) (b) 1,90 (c) F - center forward (d) RSC Charleroi (e) Paradou AC

*** Benchaâ - Zakaria Benchaâ (a) 11/01/1997, Oran (Algeria) (b) 1,78 (c) F - center forward (d) - (e) Cherno More, USM Alger, CS Sfaxien, USM Alger, Tours B, MC Orán

*** Benchaib - Amine Benchaib (a) 18/06/1998, Gent (Belgium) (b) 1,81 (c) M - attacking midfielder (d) FCV Farul Constanta (e) CS Mioveni, KV Kortrijk, RSC Charleroi, KSC Lokeren, KSC Lokeren II

*** Benchimol - Benchimol (Gilson Benchimol Tavares) (a) 29/12/2001, Praia (Cabo Verde) (b) 1,87 (c) F - center forward (d) SL Benfica B (e) Benfica B, Estoril Praia, Damaiense

*** Bencze - Antal Bencze (a) 03/06/2002, Budapest (Hungary) (b) 1,90 (c) G (d) Kazincbarcikai SC (e) Vitória Guimarães B

*** Benczenleitner - Barna Benczenleitner (a) 16/09/2003, Szombathely (Hungary) (b) 1,86 (c) D - left back (d) Budapest Honvéd FC (e) Honvéd II, ETO FC Győr, Honvéd II

*** Bender - Josip Bender (a) 01/03/1995, Dubrovnik (Croatia) (b) 1,90 (c) G (d) - (e) Zeljeznicar, NK Solin, NK Zadar, RNK Split, Hajduk Split II, Primorac 1929, Hajduk Split II, Primorac 1929, NK Zupa

*** Benedetti - Gianluca Benedetti (a) 04/11/1995, ¿? (Italy) (b) - (c) F - center forward (d) AC Juvenes-Dogana (e) Cailungo, Misano

*** Benedettini - Elia Benedettini (a) 22/06/1995, Borgo Maggiore (San Marino) (b) 1,89 (c) G (d) AC Libertas (e) Cailungo, Cesena, Novara, Pianese, San Marino

*** Benedettini - Simone Benedettini (a) 21/01/1997, San Marino (San Marino) (b) 1,91 (c) G (d) FC Fiorentino (e) Pennarossa, Murata, Cattolica SM, Sammaurese, Pianese

*** Benedicic - Zan Benedicic (Žan Benedičič) (a) 03/10/1995, Kranj (Slovenia) (b) 1,87 (c) M - pivot (d) NK Rogaska (e) Koper, NK Celje, Olbia, Leyton Orient, Ascoli, Como, AC Milan, Leeds Utd.

*** Benediktsson - Adam Ingi Benediktsson (a) 28/10/2002, Grundarfjörður (Iceland) (b) 1,96 (c) G (d) IFK Göteborg (e) FC Trollhättan, IFK Göteborg, HK Kópavogs

*** Benediktsson - Hafthor Andri Benediktsson (a) ¿?, ¿? (Iceland) (b) - (c) M (d) - (e) Stjarnan Gardabaer

*** Benediktsson (c) M (d) Leiknir Reykjavík (e) - - Egill Ingi Benediktsson (c) M (d) Leiknir Reykjavík (e) -

*** Benes - Vit Benes (Vít Beneš) (a) 12/08/1988, Ústí nad Labem (Czechoslovakia, now in Czech Rep.) (b) 1,92 (c) D - central defense (d) SK Sigma Olomouc (e) Vasas FC, Haladás, Vasas FC, Jablonec, SK Kladno, Kladno B, Usti nad L. Jdg

*** Beneta - Markas Beneta (a) 08/07/1993, Klaipėda (Lithuania) (b) 1,82 (c) D - right back (d) FK Panevezys (e) Suduva, Z. Sosnowiec, JK Trans Narva, Kauno Zalgiris, Atlantas, Zalgiris, Atlantas, Zalgiris, Klaipeda

*** Benga - Alexandru Benga (Alexandru Constantin Benga) (a) 15/06/1989, Brașov (Romania) (b) 1,88 (c) D - central defense (d) UTA Arad (e) Chindia, Septemvri Sofia,

Sandecja, Juventus Bucuresti, Ermis Aradippou, Petrolul, FK Qabala, Botev Plovdiv, Petrolul, Otelul Galati, Petrolul, Otelul Galati, FC Brasov, Petrolul, FC Brasov, Forex Brasov, FC Brasov, FC Sacele, FC Brasov

*** Benga - Denis Benga (Denis Mirel Benga) (a) 24/07/2005, Drobeta Turnu Severin (Romania) (b) - (c) D - left back (d) Universitatea Craiova (e) -

*** Bengo - Renato Bengo (Renato Bengo Bondjale) (a) 25/06/2003, Valencia (Spain) (b) - (c) M - left midfielder (d) - (e) FC Van, Selhurst

*** Bengtsson - Johan Bengtsson (a) 01/01/2004, ¿? (Sweden) (b) 1,78 (c) M - attacking midfielder (d) GIF Sundsvall (e) -

*** Bengtsson - Leo Bengtsson (Erik Martin Leo Bengtsson) (a) 26/05/1998, Ingarö (Sweden) (b) 1,79 (c) F - left winger (d) Aris Limassol (e) Häcken, Hammarby IF, IK Frej Täby, Hammarby IF, Gefle, Hammarby IF

*** Bengtsson - Pierre Bengtsson (Pierre Thomas Robin Bengtsson) (a) 12/04/1988, Kumla (Sweden) (b) 1,77 (c) D - left back (d) Djurgårdens IF (e) FC København, Vejle BK, FC København, Mainz 05, SC Bastia, Mainz 05, FC København, Nordsjælland, AIK

*** Bengtsson - Simon Bengtsson (a) 23/04/2004, ¿? (Sweden) (b) - (c) D - left back (d) Helsingborgs IF (e) -

*** Bengyuzov - Ventsislav Bengyuzov (Венцислав Божидаров Бенгюзов) (a) 22/01/1991, Kresna (Bulgaria) (b) 1,77 (c) M - pivot (d) Pirin Blagoevgrad (e) Slavia Sofia, Arda Kardzhali, Vereya, Pirin, Bansko, Pirin, Litex Lovetch, Vidima-Rakovski, Litex Lovetch, Pirin, Litex Lovetch, Brestnik 1948, Litex Lovetch

*** Benhemine - Ahmed Benhemine (a) 15/01/1987, ¿? (France) (b) - (c) D - central defense (d) US Mondorf-Les-Bains (e) CABB Arreridj, CS&O Blénod PaM, JS Saoura, FC Lunéville

*** Beni - Beni (Benedito Mambuene Mukendi) (a) 21/05/2002, Luanda (Angola) (b) 1,80 (c) M - central midfielder (d) Casa Pia AC (e) Trofense

*** Beni - Golan Beni (בני גולן) (a) 31/10/2000, ¿? (Israel) (b) 1,70 (c) M - central midfielder (d) - (e) H. Jerusalem, Hapoel Raanana

*** Benincasa - Simone Benincasa (a) 25/01/2001, Napoli (Italy) (b) 1,85 (c) F - center forward (d) AC Virtus Acquaviva (e) Savignanese, US Corticella, Imolese

*** Benita - Mimeirhel Benita (Mimeirhel Obispo Benita) (a) 17/11/2003, Spijkenisse (Netherlands) (b) 1,73 (c) D - right back (d) Excelsior Rotterdam (e) Excelsior, Feyenoord

*** Benítez - Álvaro Benítez (Álvaro Benítez Huelva) (a) 20/04/1989, Algeciras (Spain) (b) 1,85 (c) D - central defense (d) - (e) Europa FC, Los Barrios, Algeciras CF, Arcos CF, AD Ceuta, CD Badajoz, Algeciras CF

*** Benítez - Oliver Benítez (Oliver Paz Benítez) (a) 07/06/1991, Puerto Iguazú (Argentina) (b) 1,85 (c) D - central defense (d) Sport Boys Association (e) PAS Lamia, Patronato, San Martín (T), Gimnasia y Esgrima, Palestino, Gimnasia y Esgrima, Tigre, Gimnasia y Esgrima

*** Benítez - Samuel Benítez (Samuel Benítez Fajardo) (a) 13/01/2000, Benalmádena (Spain) (b) - (c) F - center forward (d) FC Manchester 62 (e) Cala Mijas, At. Benamiel, CD Casabermeja, Vélez CF, At. Benamiel

*** Benítez - Walter Benítez (Walter Daniel Benítez) (a) 19/01/1993, General José de San Martín (Argentina) (b) 1,91 (c) G (d) PSV Eindhoven (e) OGC Nice, Quilmes

*** Benito - Benito (Olabiran Blessing Muyiwa) (a) 07/09/1998, Abidjan (Ivory Coast) (b) 1,80 (c) F - right winger (d) FC Dinamo de Kiev (e) HNK Gorica, Dinamo Kyïv, Olimpik Donetsk, Dinamo Kyïv, Tambov, Luch, Lokomotiv Tashkent, FC Saxan

*** Benito - Asier Benito (Asier Benito Sasiain) (a) 11/02/1995, Amurrio (Spain) (b) 1,83 (c) F - center forward (d) Real Unión Club (e) Asteras Tripoli, SD Eibar, CD Numancia, SD Eibar, Ponferradina, SD Eibar, Bilbao Athletic, Depor. Alavés B, Aurrera, Indartsu
*** Benito - Iker Benito (Iker Benito Sánchez) (a) 10/08/2002, Miranda de Ebro (Spain) (b) 1,76 (c) F - right winger (d) FC Andorra (e) FC Andorra, CA Osasuna, Osasuna Prom.
*** Benito - Loris Benito (Loris Benito Souto) (a) 07/01/1992, Aarau (Switzerland) (b) 1,86 (c) D - left back (d) BSC Young Boys (e) FC Sion, Girondins Bordeaux, BSC Young Boys, Benfica, FC Zürich, FC Aarau
*** Benjaminsen - Andri Benjaminsen (a) 12/01/1999, ¿? (Faroe Islands) (b) - (c) F - left winger (d) NSÍ Runavík (e) B68 Toftir, NSÍ Runavík, Skála, NSÍ Runavík, NSÍ II
*** Benkovic - Filip Benkovic (Filip Benković) (a) 13/07/1997, Zagreb (Croatia) (b) 1,94 (c) D - central defense (d) Trabzonspor (e) Trabzonspor, Udinese, Eintracht Braunschweig, Udinese, Leicester City, OH Leuven, Leicester City, Cardiff City, Leicester City, Bristol City, Leicester City, Celtic FC, Leicester City, Dinamo Zagreb
*** Bennacer - Ismaël Bennacer (ناصر بن اسماعيل) (a) 01/12/1997, Arles (France) (b) 1,75 (c) M - pivot (d) AC Milan (e) Empoli, Tours FC, AC Arles
*** Bennett - Leon Bennett (a) 12/12/2004, ¿? (Wales) (b) - (c) D - central defense (d) Connah's Quay Nomads (e) -
*** Benny - Benny (Bernardo Martins de Sousa) (a) 27/03/2000, Treixedo (Portugal) (b) 1,78 (c) F - right winger (d) GD Chaves (e) Sporting B
*** Benny - Benny (Bernardo Oliveira Dias) (a) 04/01/1997, Lisboa (Portugal) (b) 1,77 (c) M - central midfielder (d) SC União Torreense (e) Doxa Katokopias, Chaves, B SAD, Benfica B, B SAD, Belenenses
*** Benónýsson - Sigurdur Grétar Benónýsson (Sigurður Grétar Benónýsson) (a) 27/08/1996, ¿? (Iceland) (b) - (c) F - center forward (d) ÍBV Vestmannaeyjar (e) Framherjar, ÍBV Vestmannaeyjar, Vestri, ÍBV Vestmannaeyjar, High Point, ÍBV Vestmannaeyjar, Framherjar
*** Benrahma - Saïd Benrahma (Mohamed Saïd Benrahma) (a) 10/08/1995, Aïn Témouchent (Algeria) (b) 1,72 (c) F - left winger (d) West Ham United (e) Brentford, West Ham Utd., Brentford, OGC Nice, LB Châteauroux, OGC Nice, G. Ajaccio, OGC Nice, Angers SCO, OGC Nice, OGC Nice B, US Colomiers
*** Benrahou - Yassine Benrahou (بنرحو ياسين) (a) 24/01/1999, Le Blanc-Mesnil (France) (b) 1,72 (c) M - attacking midfielder (d) HNK Hajduk Split (e) Nîmes, Girondins Bordeaux, Nîmes, Girondins Bordeaux, Girondins Bordeaux B
*** Bensebaini - Ramy Bensebaini (سبعيني بن رامي) (a) 16/04/1995, Constantine (Algeria) (b) 1,87 (c) D - left back (d) Borussia Dortmund (e) Borussia Mönchengladbach, Stade Rennes, Paradou AC, Montpellier, Paradou AC, Lierse SK, Paradou AC, JMG Algier
*** Bensi - Stefano Bensi (a) 11/08/1988, Luxembourg (Luxembourg) (b) 1,85 (c) F - center forward (d) Michel Kettenmeyer (e) CS Fola Esch, F91 Dudelange, KMSK Deinze, US Rumelange, Schifflange 95
*** Benson - Manuel Benson (Benson Manuel Hedilazio) (a) 28/03/1997, Lokeren (Belgium) (b) 1,66 (c) F - right winger (d) Burnley FC (e) Royal Antwerp, PEC Zwolle, Royal Antwerp, KRC Genk, Excelsior Mouscron, KRC Genk, Lierse SK
*** Benson - Robbie Benson (Robert Benson) (a) 07/05/1992, Athlone, Westmeath (Ireland) (b) 1,75 (c) M - attacking midfielder (d) Dundalk FC (e) St. Patrick's Ath., Dundalk FC, UCD, Athlone Town

*** Bent - Dan Bent (Daniel Bent) (a) 10/01/1996, ¿? (England) (b) 1,85 (c) M - pivot (d) FC Manchester 62 (e) Bruno's Magpies, Wright State Univ., Reinhardt Eagles, Corinthians-Casuals

*** Bentaleb - Nabil Bentaleb (طالب بن نبيل) (a) 24/11/1994, Lille (France) (b) 1,87 (c) M - central midfielder (d) Angers SCO (e) FC Schalke 04, Newcastle Utd., FC Schalke 04, Tottenham Hotspur, FC Schalke 04, Tottenham Hotspur

*** Bentancur - Rodrigo Bentancur (Rodrigo Bentancur Colmán) (a) 25/06/1997, Nueva Helvecia (Uruguay) (b) 1,87 (c) M - central midfielder (d) Tottenham Hotspur (e) Juventus, Boca Juniors

*** Bentebbal - Hadi Bentebbal (a) 06/07/2001, ¿? (France) (b) 1,85 (c) M - attacking midfielder (d) Racing FC Union Luxemburg II (e) RFCU Luxembourg, Montana, RFCU Luxembourg

*** Bentley - Daniel Bentley (Daniel Ian Bentley) (a) 13/07/1993, Basildon (England) (b) 1,93 (c) G (d) Wolverhampton Wanderers (e) Bristol City, Brentford, Southend United, Braintree, Southend United

*** Benyu - Kundai Benyu (Kundai Leroy Jeremiah Benyu) (a) 12/12/1997, London (England) (b) 1,78 (c) M - central midfielder (d) - (e) ÍBV Vestmannaeyjar, Vestri, Wealdstone, Celtic FC, Helsingborgs IF, Celtic FC, Oldham Athletic, Celtic FC, Aldershot

*** Benz - Leo Benz (a) 18/04/1999, ¿? (Austria) (b) 1,85 (c) D - central defense (d) SGV Freiberg (e) US Hostert, TSV Rain/Lech, 1860 Rosenheim, FC 08 Villingen, SV Zimmern

*** Benzar - Romario Benzar (Romario Sandu Benzar) (a) 26/03/1992, Timişoara (Romania) (b) 1,80 (c) D - right back (d) - (e) UTA Arad, FCV Farul, Lecce, FC Viitorul, Lecce, Perugia, Lecce, FCSB, FC Viitorul, Academia Hagi

*** Benzema - Karim Benzema (زيما بن كريم) (a) 19/12/1987, Lyon (France) (b) 1,85 (c) F - center forward (d) Ittihad Club (e) Real Madrid, Olympique Lyon

*** Benzia - Yassine Benzia (a) 08/09/1994, Saint-Aubin-les-Elbeuf (France) (b) 1,78 (c) M - attacking midfielder (d) Qarabağ FK (e) Dijon, Hatayspor, Dijon, Lille, Olympiakos, Lille, Fenerbahce, Lille, Olympique Lyon

*** Beqaj - Renato Beqaj (a) 22/06/2004, Ballsh (Albania) (b) - (c) G (d) FK Bylis (e) -

*** Beqiraj - Fatos Beqiraj (Фатос Бећирај) (a) 05/05/1988, Peć (Yugoslavia, now in Kosovo) (b) 1,88 (c) F - center forward (d) - (e) Mornar Bar, FK Decic Tuzi, FC Astana, Wisla Kraków, Bnei Yehuda, Wisla Kraków, Maccabi Netanya, KV Mechelen, Dinamo Moskva, Dinamo Minsk, CC Yatai, Dinamo Zagreb, Buducnost Podgorica, FC Besa, KF Shqiponja, SuperSport HNL

*** Beqja - Fabjan Beqja (a) 15/02/1994, Durrës (Albania) (b) 1,76 (c) M - central midfielder (d) Flamurtari FC (e) SC Gjilani, KF Teuta, KS Besa, KF Teuta

*** Beqja - Ledio Beqja (a) 18/06/2001, Castiglione del Lago (Italy) (b) 1,83 (c) M - pivot (d) KF Teuta (e) -

*** Berahino - Saido Berahino (a) 04/08/1993, Bujumbura (Burundi) (b) 1,80 (c) F - center forward (d) AEL Limassol (e) Sheffield Wednesday, Zulte Waregem, RSC Charleroi, Zulte Waregem, Stoke City, West Bromwich Albion, Peterborough, Brentford, West Brom Reserves, Northampton, West Brom Reserves

*** Beran - Michal Beran (a) 22/08/2000, ¿? (Finland) (b) 1,67 (c) M - attacking midfielder (d) Bohemians Praha 1905 (e) Slavia Praha, Pardubice, Slavia Praha, Slovan Liberec, Slavia Praha, Slovan Liberec

*** Beran - Stepan Beran (Štěpán Beran) (a) 10/03/2004, ¿? (Czech Rep.) (b) 1,76 (c) M - attacking midfielder (d) FC Sellier & Bellot Vlasim (e) Vlasim, Slavia Praha, Slavia Praha B

*** Beranek - Marek Beranek (Marek Beránek) (a) 16/05/2003, ¿? (Czech Rep.) (b) 1,80 (c) M (d) FK Teplice B (e) Fotbalova Farma

*** Berardi - Alessandro Berardi (a) 16/01/1991, Roma (Italy) (b) 1,85 (c) G (d) Hellas Verona (e) Bari, ACR Messina, Lazio, ACR Messina, Lazio, Grosseto, Lazio, Salernitana, Lazio, Hellas Verona, Lazio

*** Berardi - Domenico Berardi (a) 01/08/1994, Cariatti (Italy) (b) 1,83 (c) F - right winger (d) US Sassuolo (e) Juventus, Sassuolo, Juventus, Sassuolo

*** Berardi - Federico Berardi (a) 17/09/1997, Cesena (Italy) (b) - (c) M - central midfielder (d) - (e) San Giovanni, Gambettola, Diegaro, Gambettola

*** Berardi - Jacopo Berardi (a) 23/02/2004, ¿? (San Marino) (b) - (c) M (d) La Fiorita 1967 (e) -

*** Berardi - Michele Berardi (a) 30/11/1991, ¿? (San Marino) (b) - (c) G (d) FC Fiorentino (e) -

*** Berber - Oguzhan Berber (Oğuzhan Berber) (a) 10/04/1992, Izmir (Turkey) (b) 1,76 (c) D - right back (d) Manisa FK (e) Istanbulspor, Boluspor, Istanbulspor, Kayserispor, Istanbulspor, Kayserispor, Adana Demirspor, Çaykur Rizespor, Samsunspor, Çaykur Rizespor, Altinordu, Çaykur Rizespor, Adana Demirspor, Çaykur Rizespor, Denizlispor, Denizli Belediye, Denizlispor

*** Berberi - Rayan Berberi (a) 18/03/2004, ¿? (Luxembourg) (b) - (c) M - attacking midfielder (d) Standard de Lieja (e) SL16 FC

*** Berbic - Adnan Berbic (Adnan Berbić) (a) 11/02/2004, Kakanj (Bosnia and Herzegovina) (b) 1,90 (c) F - center forward (d) HSK Zrinjski Mostar (e) -

*** Berbic - Serif Berbic (Serif Berbić) (a) 25/11/2001, Uznach (Switzerland) (b) 1,94 (c) G (d) FC Lugano (e) Rapperswil-Jona

*** Berchiche - Yuri Berchiche (Yuri Berchiche Izeta) (a) 10/02/1990, Zarautz (Spain) (b) 1,81 (c) D - left back (d) Athletic Club (e) Paris Saint-Germain, Real Sociedad, SD Eibar, Real Sociedad, Real Unión, Tottenham Hotspur Reserves, R. Valladolid B, Tottenham Hotspur Reserves, Cheltenham Town, Tottenham Hotspur Reserves

*** Berden - Martijn Berden (a) 29/07/1997, Den Haag (Netherlands) (b) 1,72 (c) F - right winger (d) VVV-Venlo (e) Go Ahead Eagles, VVV-Venlo, Go Ahead Eagles

*** Berdibek - Darkhan Berdibek (Бердибек Дархан Нурлыбекулы) (a) 31/05/2004, Aktau (Kazakhstan) (b) 1,79 (c) M - central midfielder (d) Kaspiy Aktau (e) Kaspiy II

*** Berecz - Zsombor Berecz (a) 13/12/1995, Miskolc (Hungary) (b) 1,80 (c) M - central midfielder (d) Vasas FC (e) Mezőkövesd, Fehérvár, Mezőkövesd, Vidi FC, Vasas FC

*** Berenger - Toussaint Berenger (a) 01/01/2001, Douala (Cameroon) (b) 1,86 (c) M - central midfielder (d) - (e) UE Santa Coloma, Cádiz B, Balón de Cádiz, Cádiz CF B, Union Douala

*** Berenguer - Álex Berenguer (Alejandro Berenguer Remiro) (a) 04/07/1995, Barañain (Spain) (b) 1,75 (c) F - left winger (d) Athletic Club (e) Torino, CA Osasuna, Osasuna Prom.

*** Berenschot - Milan Berenschot (a) 10/11/2004, ¿? (Netherlands) (b) 1,79 (c) F - center forward (d) - (e) avv Columbia

*** Bereszynski - Bartosz Bereszynski (Bartosz Bereszyński) (a) 12/07/1992, Poznań (Poland) (b) 1,83 (c) D - right back (d) UC Sampdoria (e) Napoli, Sampdoria, Legia Warszawa, Lech Poznan, Warta Poznań, Lech Poznan

*** Berezkin - Evgeniy Berezkin (Берёзкин Евгений Сергеевич) (a) 05/07/1996, Vitebsk (Belarus) (b) 1,82 (c) M - central midfielder (d) Qyzyljar Petropavlovsk (e) Torpedo Zhodino, Liepaja, BATE Borisov, Naftan, Naftan II, Vitebsk II

*** Berezun - Ivan Berezun (Березун Иван Олегович) (a) 19/08/1997, Vitebsk (Belarus) (b) 1,82 (c) M - central midfielder (d) FK Orsha (e) Vitebsk II, Orsha, Vitebsk II, Orsha, Vitebsk II, Orsha, Vitebsk II, FK Postavy
*** Berezutskiy - Andrey Berezutskiy (Березуцкий Андрей) (a) 30/01/2004, ¿? (Kazakhstan) (b) 1,90 (c) F - center forward (d) FC Astana-M (e) -
*** Berg - Marcus Berg (Bengt Erik Marcus Berg) (a) 17/08/1986, Torsby (Sweden) (b) 1,84 (c) F - center forward (d) IFK Göteborg (e) Krasnodar, Al-Ain FC, Panathinaikos, SV Hamburg, PSV Eindhoven, SV Hamburg, FC Groningen, IFK Göteborg
*** Berg - Moritz Berg (a) 07/08/2003, Stendal (Germany) (b) - (c) M - central midfielder (d) SK Austria Klagenfurt (e) -
*** Berg - Oliver Berg (a) 28/08/1993, Gjøvik (Norway) (b) 1,78 (c) M - attacking midfielder (d) Djurgårdens IF (e) Kalmar FF, GIF Sundsvall, Dalkurd, Odd, Raufoss
*** Berg - Patrick Berg (a) 24/11/1997, Bodø (Norway) (b) 1,78 (c) M - pivot (d) FK Bodø/Glimt (e) RC Lens, Bodø/Glimt
*** Berg - Teitur Berg (a) 31/07/2003, ¿? (Faroe Islands) (b) - (c) F - right winger (d) AB Argir II (e) HB Tórshavn II
*** Berger - Emil Berger (Henrik Emil Hahne Berger) (a) 23/05/1991, Degerfors (Sweden) (b) 1,71 (c) M - central midfielder (d) HB Tórshavn (e) Leiknir, Dalkurd, Rynninge IK, BK Forward, Kongsvinger, Örebro SK, Fylkir, Örebro SK, Degerfors, Carlstad United, Degerfors, AIK, AFC Eskilstuna, AIK, Degerfors
*** Berger - Sofus Berger (Sofus Berger Brix) (a) 02/06/2003, ¿? (Denmark) (b) 1,75 (c) M - central midfielder (d) FC Fredericia (e) FC Fredericia, Viborg FF
*** Berger - Tobias Berger (a) 02/11/2001, ¿? (Austria) (b) - (c) D - left back (d) SC Austria Lustenau (e) FC Liefering
*** Berger - Tom Berger (Tom Kaspar Berger) (a) 31/07/2001, ¿? (Germany) (b) 1,84 (c) M - central midfielder (d) - (e) Werder Bremen II, Wolfsburg II
*** Berget - Jo Inge Berget (a) 11/09/1990, Oslo (Norway) (b) 1,86 (c) F - right winger (d) - (e) Malmö FF, New York City, Malmö FF, Cardiff City, Celtic FC, Cardiff City, Molde, Strømsgodset, Lyn
*** Berggren - Gustav Berggren (Karl Gustav Vilhelm Berggren) (a) 07/09/1997, ¿? (Sweden) (b) 1,87 (c) M - pivot (d) Rakow Czestochowa (e) Häcken, Varbergs BoIS, Häcken
*** Berghuis - Steven Berghuis (a) 19/12/1991, Apeldoorn (Netherlands) (b) 1,82 (c) M - attacking midfielder (d) Ajax de Ámsterdam (e) Feyenoord, Watford, Feyenoord, Watford, AZ Alkmaar, FC Twente, VVV-Venlo, FC Twente
*** Bergier - Sebastian Bergier (a) 20/12/1999, Wrocław (Poland) (b) 1,85 (c) F - center forward (d) GKS Katowice (e) Śląsk Wroclaw, Wigry Suwalki, Śląsk Wroclaw, Stal Mielec, Śląsk Wroclaw, Slask Wroclaw II
*** Berglie - Fredrik Tobias Berglie (a) 28/12/1996, Halsen (Norway) (b) 1,84 (c) D - central defense (d) Sandefjord Fotball (e) Skeid, Halsen IF
*** Bergman - Alexander Bergman (Alexander Kapitan Bergman) (a) 08/12/2004, Warschau (Poland) (b) - (c) D - central defense (d) FC Nomme United (e) Nomme United, Kalev, Nomme United, Kalev
*** Bergqvist - Douglas Bergqvist (Jan Douglas Bergqvist) (a) 29/03/1993, Stockholm (Sweden) (b) 1,85 (c) D - central defense (d) Degerfors IF (e) Riga, Auda, Riga, Chornomorets, Kalmar FF, Chornomorets, Kalmar FF, Arka Gdynia, Östersund, Haugesund, Östersund, Exeter City, Welling Utd., Exeter City, Aldershot, Farnborough, Aldershot, Dorchester, Aldershot, Thatcham, Aldershot

*** Bergsen - Menno Bergsen (Menno Alexander Bergsen) (a) 26/08/1999, Oud-Beijerland (Netherlands) (b) 1,86 (c) G (d) NK Maribor (e) AS Trencin, FC Eindhoven
*** Bergsma - Leon Bergsma (a) 25/01/1997, Amsterdam (Netherlands) (b) 1,86 (c) D - central defense (d) SC Cambuur Leeuwarden (e) FC Aarau, AZ Alkmaar, FC Den Bosch, AZ Alkmaar, Ajax B
*** Bergström - Emil Bergström (Emil Evert Bergström) (a) 19/05/1993, Stockholm (Sweden) (b) 1,88 (c) D - central defense (d) Panserraikos (e) Górnik Zabrze, FC Utrecht, Willem II, FC Utrecht, FC Basel, FC Utrecht, Rubin Kazan, Grasshoppers, Rubin Kazan, Djurgården
*** Bergström - Jacob Bergström (a) 26/04/1995, ¿? (Sweden) (b) 1,91 (c) F - center forward (d) Mjällby AIF (e) Djurgården, Mjällby AIF, Mjøndalen, Mjällby AIF, Ronneby BK, FK Karlskrona, Karlskrona AIF
*** Bergström - Lucas Bergström (Lucas Carl Edvard Bergström) (a) 05/09/2002, Pargas (Finland) (b) 2,05 (c) G (d) - (e) Peterborough
*** Bergwijn - Steven Bergwijn (Steven Charles Bergwijn) (a) 08/10/1997, Amsterdam (Netherlands) (b) 1,78 (c) F - left winger (d) Ajax de Ámsterdam (e) Tottenham Hotspur, PSV Eindhoven
*** Beriashvili - Ilia Beriashvili (ილია ბერიაშვილი) (a) 09/07/1998, Telavi (Georgia) (b) 1,90 (c) D - central defense (d) Mezőkövesd Zsóry FC (e) FC Telavi, Rotor Volgograd, FC Telavi, FC Alazani
*** Beridze - Giorgi Beridze (გიორგი ბერიძე) (a) 12/05/1997, Mestia (Georgia) (b) 1,74 (c) F - left winger (d) MKE Ankaragücü (e) Újpest FC, KAA Gent, KSC Lokeren, KAA Gent, Újpest FC, AS Trencin, FC Zestafoni, FC Dila
*** Berisbek - Rahmetullah Berisbek (Rahmetullah Berişbek) (a) 22/03/1999, Elmadag (Turkey) (b) 1,71 (c) M - right midfielder (d) Bandirmaspor (e) Giresunspor, Genclerbirligi
*** Berisha - Albin Berisha (a) 14/01/2001, Gjinoc (RF Yugoslavia, now in Kosovo) (b) - (c) F - center forward (d) FC Ballkani (e) FC Malisheva, FC Ballkani, KF Liria, FC Ballkani, FC Besa, KF Laçi
*** Berisha - Albion Berisha (a) 04/08/1999, ¿? (RF Yugoslavia, now in Kosovo) (b) - (c) G (d) FC Phoenix Banjë (e) FC Malisheva
*** Berisha - Bernard Berisha (a) 24/10/1991, Pejë (Yugoslavia, now in Kosovo) (b) 1,65 (c) F - left winger (d) Akhmat Grozny (e) Anzhi, KF Skënderbeu, KS Besa, FC Besa
*** Berisha - Elvi Berisha (a) 02/03/1999, Fier (Albania) (b) 1,84 (c) F - left winger (d) Flamurtari FC (e) KF Tirana, KF Skënderbeu, KF Laçi, CD Leganés B, KF Tirana
*** Berisha - Etrit Berisha (a) 10/03/1989, Prishtinë (Yugoslavia, now in Kosovo) (b) 1,94 (c) G (d) Torino FC (e) SPAL, Torino, SPAL, Atalanta, SPAL, Atalanta, Lazio, Atalanta, Lazio, Kalmar FF, KF 2 Korriku
*** Berisha - Florent Berisha (a) 01/08/2000, Lippstadt (Germany) (b) 1,85 (c) D - central defense (d) - (e) Etzella Ettelbrück, FC Oberneuland, SF Lotte, SV Lippstadt 08
*** Berisha - Florim Berisha (a) 07/12/1988, Kaçanik (Yugoslavia, now in Kosovo) (b) - (c) M - central midfielder (d) - (e) KF Ferizaj, KF Vitia, KF Arbëria, KF Lepenci, KF Ferizaj, FC Drita
*** Berisha - Jakup Berisha (a) 20/02/2000, Skopje (North Macedonia) (b) 1,81 (c) F - right winger (d) - (e) FK Kukësi, Pelister Bitola, FC Shkupi, Shkëndija, Vardar
*** Berisha - Medon Berisha (a) 21/10/2003, Münsingen (Switzerland) (b) 1,86 (c) M - central midfielder (d) US Lecce (e) -

*** Berisha - Mergim Berisha (a) 11/05/1998, Berchtesgaden (Germany) (b) 1,88 (c) F - center forward (d) FC Augsburg (e) Fenerbahce, FC Augsburg, Fenerbahce, RB Salzburg, SCR Altach, RB Salzburg, 1.FC Magdeburg, RB Salzburg, LASK, RB Salzburg, FC Liefering
*** Berisha - Veton Berisha (a) 13/04/1994, Egersund (Norway) (b) 1,75 (c) F - center forward (d) Molde FK (e) Hammarby IF, Viking, Brann, Rapid Wien, Greuther Fürth, Viking
*** Berisha - Vlerson Berisha (a) 28/06/2004, ¿? (Serbia and Montenegro, now in Kosovo) (b) - (c) M - central midfielder (d) KF Dukagjini (e) -
*** Berisha (c) D - right back (d) KF Ferizaj (e) - - Genc Berisha (c) D - right back (d) KF Ferizaj (e) -
*** Berkani - Stan Berkani (a) 13/08/2003, Vichy (France) (b) - (c) M - pivot (d) Clermont Foot 63 B (e) -
*** Berko - Erich Berko (a) 06/09/1994, Ostfildern-Ruit (Germany) (b) 1,81 (c) F - right winger (d) Hallescher FC (e) Maccabi Netanya, SV Sandhausen, Darmstadt 98, Dynamo Dresden, Stuttg. Kickers, Stuttgart II
*** Berkovec - Martin Berkovec (a) 12/02/1989, Mariánské Lázně (Czechoslovakia, now in Czech Rep.) (b) 1,90 (c) G (d) FC Zbrojovka Brno (e) Zalgiris, Karvina, Slavia Praha, Karvina, Slavia Praha, Bohemians 1905, Slavia Praha, Bohemians 1905, Slavia Praha, Sezimovo Usti, Slavia Praha, Slavia Praha B, Hlucin, Slavia Praha B
*** Berkovich - Amir Berkovich (אמיר ברקוביץ') (a) 03/06/2000, Even Yehuda (Israel) (b) 1,72 (c) F - right winger (d) Beitar Jerusalem (e) M. Petah Tikva, Maccabi Netanya, Maccabi Tel Aviv, B TLV Bat Yam, Maccabi Tel Aviv
*** Berkovich - Tom Berkovich (a) 07/01/2002, ¿? (Israel) (b) - (c) M - attacking midfielder (d) Hapoel Kfar Saba (e) Hapoel Hadera, H. Ramat Gan
*** Berkovskiy - Ilya Berkovskiy (Берковский Илья Витальевич) (a) 15/03/2000, Tavricheskoe, Omsk Oblast (Russia) (b) 1,80 (c) M - attacking midfielder (d) FK Khimki (e) Khimki, Lokomotiv Moskva, Pari Nizhny Novgórod, Lokomotiv Moskva, Torpedo Moskva, Irtysh Omsk
*** Berlanga - Domi Berlanga (Domingo Berlanga Ouggouti) (a) 06/05/1995, Tanger (Morocco) (b) 1,80 (c) F - right winger (d) Inter Club d'Escaldes (e) CF Peralada, UE Figueres, T Val Pescara, AE Prat, Terrassa FC, UA Horta, CF Gavà, Rayo Cantabria, Santfeliuenc FC, Sant Andreu, CD Llosetense, RCD Mallorca B
*** Bermingham - Ian Bermingham (a) 16/06/1989, Dublin (Ireland) (b) 1,77 (c) D - left back (d) - (e) St. Patrick's Ath., Shamrock Rovers, UCD
*** Berna - Berna (Bernardo Silva Conceição) (a) 15/09/2003, Porto (Portugal) (b) 1,69 (c) M - attacking midfielder (d) Boavista Porto FC (e) -
*** Bernabéi - Alexandro Bernabéi (Alexandro Ezequiel Bernabéi) (a) 24/09/2000, Cañada de Gómez (Argentina) (b) 1,69 (c) D - left back (d) Celtic FC (e) Lanús
*** Bernacchia - Andrea Bernacchia (a) 06/02/2004, ¿? (San Marino) (b) - (c) D (d) SS San Giovanni (e) -
*** Bernad - Emilio Bernad (Emilio Bernad Sánchez) (a) 22/09/1999, La Vall d'Uixó (Spain) (b) 1,84 (c) G (d) Racing de Ferrol (e) Valencia Mestalla, CE Sabadell, Valencia Mestalla
*** Bernadou - Lucas Bernadou (a) 24/09/2000, Le Chesnay (France) (b) 1,78 (c) M - pivot (d) FC Emmen (e) Paris Saint Germain B
*** Bernaola - Julen Bernaola (Julen Bernaola Cuezva) (a) 29/04/1999, Bilbao (Spain) (b) 1,87 (c) M - pivot (d) Atlètic Club d'Escaldes (e) Urduliz FT, Rayo Cantabria, Bilbao Athletic, CD Basconia

*** Bernard - Bernard (Bernard Anício Caldeira Duarte) (a) 08/09/1992, Belo Horizonte (Brazil) (b) 1,64 (c) F - left winger (d) Panathinaikos FC (e) Sharjah FC, Everton, Shakhtar Donetsk, At. Mineiro, At. Mineiro B, Democrata, At. Mineiro B
*** Bernard - Billy Bernard (a) 09/04/1991, ¿? (Luxembourg) (b) - (c) D - central defense (d) FC The Belval Belvaux (e) Mondercange, CS Fola Esch
*** Bernard - Brice Bernard (Brice Norbert Henri Bernard) (a) 02/01/2000, ¿? (Luxembourg) (b) - (c) D - central defense (d) FC Kehlen (e) CS Fola Esch, US Esch, CS Fola Esch, Schifflange 95, CS Fola Esch
*** Bernard - Gary Bernard (a) 24/10/2000, ¿? (Luxembourg) (b) - (c) F - center forward (d) Jeunesse Esch (e) Jeunesse Canach
*** Bernard - Quentin Bernard (a) 07/07/1989, Poitiers (France) (b) 1,84 (c) D - left back (d) Chamois Niortais FC (e) AJ Auxerre, Stade Brestois, Dijon, Chamois Niort, Niort B
*** Bernardelli - Gauthier Bernardelli (a) 21/08/1992, ¿? (France) (b) 1,79 (c) D - central defense (d) FC UNA Strassen (e) RFCU Luxembourg, RE Bertrix, Amnéville, FC Metz B
*** Bernardes - Renan Bernardes (Renan Bernardes Alt) (a) 21/03/1992, ¿? (Gibraltar) (b) 1,86 (c) D - central defense (d) FC Manchester 62 (e) Mons Calpe, Bruno's Magpies, Mons Calpe, Serrano FC, Glacis United, Mons Calpe, FC Britannia XI
*** Bernardi - Balthazar Bernardi (Yago Balthazar Bernardi Gutierrez) (a) 10/08/2001, Buenos Aires (Argentina) (b) 1,87 (c) D - central defense (d) CA Boca Juniors II (e) Akritas Chlor., Boca Juniors II
*** Bernardi - Marco Bernardi (a) 02/01/1994, Città di San Marino (San Marino) (b) 1,90 (c) F - left winger (d) SS Folgore/Falciano (e) Murata, SS Folgore, Domagnano, SS Folgore, Fiorentino, Juvenes-Dogana, Tropical Coriano, ACD Torconca, Sammaurese
*** Bernardi - Tommaso Bernardi (Tommaso Leon Bernardi) (a) 08/04/2001, Cesena (Italy) (b) 1,82 (c) F - center forward (d) Tre Fiori FC (e) Mezzolara, Cesena, Vastese, Cesena, Savignanese, Cesena, Cattolica SM, Cesena, Santarcangelo
*** Bernardo - Bernardo (Bernardo Fernandes da Silva Junior) (a) 14/05/1995, São Paulo (Brazil) (b) 1,86 (c) D - central defense (d) VfL Bochum (e) RB Salzburg, Brighton & Hove Albion, RB Salzburg, Brighton & Hove Albion, RB Leipzig, RB Salzburg, Ponte Preta, RB Brasil, Ponte Preta, RB Brasil
*** Bernardo - Paulo Bernardo (Paulo Guilherme Gonçalves Bernardo) (a) 24/01/2002, Almada (Portugal) (b) 1,80 (c) M - central midfielder (d) SL Benfica (e) Paços Ferreira, Benfica, Benfica B
*** Bernardoni - Paul Bernardoni (a) 18/04/1997, Évry (France) (b) 1,90 (c) G (d) Konyaspor (e) Angers SCO, St.-Étienne, Angers SCO, Girondins Bordeaux, Nîmes, Girondins Bordeaux, Clermont Foot, Girondins Bordeaux, Troyes, Girondins Bordeaux, Troyes
*** Bernardy - Loris Bernardy (a) 22/01/2001, ¿? (Luxembourg) (b) - (c) D - central defense (d) US Hostert (e) Swift Hesperange, US Hostert, Swift Hesperange
*** Bernat - Hans Christian Bernat (a) 13/11/2000, Morud (Denmark) (b) 1,92 (c) G (d) Odense Boldklub (e) -
*** Bernat - Jan Bernat (Ján Bernát) (a) 10/01/2001, Prešov (Slovakia) (b) 1,80 (c) M - attacking midfielder (d) KVC Westerlo (e) MSK Zilina, KVC Westerlo, MSK Zilina
*** Bernat - Juan Bernat (Juan Bernat Velasco) (a) 01/03/1993, Cullera (Spain) (b) 1,70 (c) D - left back (d) París Saint-Germain FC (e) Bayern München, Valencia CF, Valencia Mestalla

*** Bernat - Víctor Bernat (Víctor Bernat Cuadros) (a) 17/05/1987, Barcelona (Spain) (b) - (c) F - center forward (d) Penya Encarnada d'Andorra (e) UE Engordany, FC Ordino, UE Santa Coloma, UE Engordany

*** Bernatowicz - Bartosz Bernatowicz (Bartosz Bernatowicz) (a) 14/02/2005, Białystok (Poland) (b) 1,83 (c) M - pivot (d) LKS Lomza (e) Jagiellonia, Jagiellonia II

*** Bernede - Antoine Bernede (Antoine Joseph Emmanuel Bernede) (a) 26/05/1999, Paris (France) (b) 1,78 (c) M - central midfielder (d) FC Lausanne-Sport (e) RB Salzburg, Lausanne-Sport, RB Salzburg, Paris Saint-Germain, Paris Saint Germain B

*** Bernhardsson - Alexander Bernhardsson (Alexander Olof Bernhardsson) (a) 08/09/1998, Göteborg (Sweden) (b) 1,85 (c) F - right winger (d) IF Elfsborg (e) Örgryte, Sävedalens IF, Jonsereds IF

*** Bernier - Antoine Bernier (Antoine Rudy Bernier) (a) 10/09/1997, Dinant (Belgium) (b) 1,70 (c) F - left winger (d) RSC Charleroi (e) RFC Seraing, F91 Dudelange, KSK Lierse Kem.

*** Bero - Matus Bero (Matúš Bero) (a) 06/09/1995, Ilava (Slovakia) (b) 1,81 (c) M - central midfielder (d) VfL Bochum (e) Vitesse, Trabzonspor, AS Trencin

*** Berretti - Maicol Berretti (a) 01/05/1989, San Marino (San Marino) (b) - (c) M - pivot (d) SS Pennarossa (e) Libertas, Pennarossa, Castellarano, Real Montecchio, Pennarossa

*** Berrut - Evan Berrut (a) 24/03/2003, Aigle (Switzerland) (b) 1,72 (c) M - pivot (d) FC Sion U21 (e) -

*** Berry - Jack Berry (a) 17/07/2005, Belfast (Northern Ireland) (b) - (c) F - center forward (d) Cliftonville FC (e) -

*** Bertasius - Mantas Bertasius (Mantas Bertašius) (a) 03/05/2000, ¿? (Lithuania) (b) 1,91 (c) G (d) FK Banga Gargzdai (e) Atlantas, Klaipedos FM

*** Bertaud - Dimitry Bertaud (a) 06/06/1998, Montpellier (France) (b) 1,80 (c) G (d) Montpellier HSC (e) Montpellier B

*** Berte - Mohamed Berte (a) 25/03/2002, Brussel (Belgium) (b) 1,75 (c) F - right winger (d) KV Oostende (e) FC Den Bosch

*** Berthomier - Jason Berthomier (a) 06/01/1990, Montluçon (France) (b) 1,77 (c) M - attacking midfielder (d) Valenciennes FC (e) Clermont Foot, Troyes, Stade Brestois, Bourg-en-Bresse, AS Moulins, Domérat, EDS Montluçon

*** Bertilsson - Johan Bertilsson (Karl Johan Walter Bertilsson) (a) 15/02/1988, Hova (Sweden) (b) 1,77 (c) F - attacking midfielder (d) IF Karlstad Fotboll (e) Degerfors, Örebro SK, Dalkurd, Östersund, Gefle, Zagłębie, Kalmar FF, Degerfors, Kalmar FF, J-Södra IF, Kalmar FF, Degerfors, Carlstad United, Hova IF

*** Bertini - Marco Bertini (a) 07/08/2002, Roma (Italy) (b) 1,85 (c) M - pivot (d) SS Lazio (e) -

*** Bertini - Tommaso Bertini (a) 13/01/2004, Lucca (Italy) (b) - (c) G (d) Latina Calcio 1932 (e) Latina Calcio

*** Bertoglio - Facundo Bertoglio (Facundo Daniel Bertoglio) (a) 30/06/1990, San José de la Esquina (Argentina) (b) 1,72 (c) M - attacking midfielder (d) Asteras Tripolis (e) Aris Thessaloniki, Aldosivi, PAS Lamia, Ordabasy, APOEL FC, Dinamo Kyïv, Asteras Tripoli, Dinamo Kyïv, Tigre, Dinamo Kyïv, Évian, Dinamo Kyïv, Grêmio Porto Alegre, Dinamo Kyïv, Colón

*** Bertola - Nicolò Bertola (a) 23/03/2003, Carrara (Italy) (b) 1,92 (c) D - central defense (d) Spezia (e) Montevarchi, Spezia

*** Bertolacci - Andrea Bertolacci (a) 11/01/1991, Roma (Italy) (b) 1,79 (c) M - central midfielder (d) US Cremonese (e) Karagümrük, Kayserispor, Karagümrük, Sampdoria, AC Milan, Genoa, AC Milan, AS Roma, Genoa, AS Roma, Lecce

*** Bertoux - Julien Bertoux (a) 24/01/1993, Paris (France) (b) 1,80 (c) D - right back (d) US Pays de Saint-Omer (e) Jeunesse Esch, Frontignan, FC Sète 34, Andrézieux, FC Sète 34, US Hostert, RFC Seraing, UR La Louvière, CS Avion
*** Bertozzi - Alan Bertozzi (Alan Christopher Bertozzi) (a) 13/07/2003, ¿? (Italy) (b) 1,93 (c) M - left midfielder (d) AC Bellaria Igea Marina (e) Tre Fiori, Cava Ronco, Del Duca Grama, United Riccione, Savignanese
*** Bertrand - Dorian Bertrand (a) 21/05/1993, Saint-Denis (Reunion) (b) 1,76 (c) F - left winger (d) ACSC FC Arges (e) AS Nancy, Angers SCO, AS Béziers, Angers SCO, SO Cholet, Angers SCO B, FC Nantes B
*** Bertrand - Ryan Bertrand (Ryan Dominic Bertrand) (a) 05/08/1989, Southwark, London (England) (b) 1,79 (c) D - left back (d) - (e) Leicester City, Southampton, Chelsea, Southampton, Chelsea, Aston Villa, Chelsea, Nottingham Forest, Chelsea, Reading, Chelsea, Norwich City, Chelsea, Oldham Athletic, Chelsea, Bournemouth
*** Bertuccini - Alessio Bertuccini (a) 04/07/2005, ¿? (Italy) (b) - (c) M (d) SC Faetano (e) -
*** Beruashvili - Papuna Beruashvili (პაპუნა ბერუაშვილი) (a) 21/03/2004, Tbilisi (Georgia) (b) 1,96 (c) G (d) Dinamo Tbilisi II (e) Sporting B, Dinamo II
*** Berzins - Arturs Berzins (Artūrs Bērziņš) (a) 01/12/2003, ¿? (Latvia) (b) - (c) M - pivot (d) FK Smiltene/BJSS (e) Valmiera II
*** Berzonskis - Timuras Berzonskis (Timūras Beržonskis) (a) 26/08/2004, ¿? (Lithuania) (b) 1,91 (c) D - central defense (d) FK Banga Gargzdai B (e) -
*** Besagic - Armin Besagic (Armin Bešagić) (a) 01/10/1998, Travnik (Bosnia and Herzegovina) (b) 1,78 (c) M - pivot (d) FK Igman Konjic (e) J. Bihac, NK Jajce, NK Iskra Bugojno
*** Besara - Nahir Besara (a) 25/02/1991, Västertälje (Sweden) (b) 1,82 (c) M - central midfielder (d) Hammarby IF (e) Örebro SK, Hatta Club, Örebro SK, Pafos FC, Al-Fayha, Örebro SK, Göztepe, Hammarby IF, Assyriska FF
*** Besch - Dennis Besch (a) 02/04/1999, ¿? (Luxembourg) (b) - (c) D - left back (d) Jeunesse Esch (e) Mertert-Wass., CS Grevenmacher, Mertert-Wass.
*** Bese - Barnabás Bese (a) 06/05/1994, Budapest (Hungary) (b) 1,88 (c) D - right back (d) Fehérvár FC (e) OH Leuven, Le Havre AC, MTK Budapest, MTK Budapest II
*** Besedin - Artem Besedin (Бєсєдін Артем Юрійович) (a) 31/03/1996, Kharkiv (Ukraine) (b) 1,85 (c) F - center forward (d) Ordabasy Shymkent (e) Dinamo Kyïv, Omonia Nicosia, Dinamo Kyïv, Dinamo Kiev II, Metalist, Dinamo Kiev II
*** Besic - Muhamed Besic (Muhamed Bešić) (a) 10/09/1992, Berlin (Germany) (b) 1,80 (c) M - pivot (d) Ferencváros TC (e) Everton, Sheffield Utd., Everton, Middlesbrough, Everton, Middlesbrough, Everton, Ferencváros, SV Hamburg
*** Besio - Alessio Besio (a) 18/03/2004, St. Gallen (Switzerland) (b) 1,85 (c) F - center forward (d) SC Freiburg II (e) FC St. Gallen
*** Besir - Zan Besir (Žan Bešir) (a) 17/10/2000, ¿? (Slovenia) (b) - (c) M - attacking midfielder (d) ND Primorje (e) Koper, Tabor Sezana, Koper, ND Gorica, Koper, NK Dekani, Koper
*** Besirovic - Dino Besirovic (Dino Beširović) (a) 31/01/1994, Viseu (Portugal) (b) 1,79 (c) M - attacking midfielder (d) AIK Solna (e) Mezőkövesd, Hajduk Split, Mezőkövesd, Hajduk Split, Radnik Bijelj., Priluk, Académico Viseu, UD Sampedrense, Académico Viseu
*** Beskorovaynyi - Danylo Beskorovaynyi (Бескоровайний Данило Леонідович) (a) 07/02/1999, Kryvyi Rig, Dnipropetrovsk Oblast (Ukraine) (b) 1,94 (c) D - central defense (d) Kryvbas Kryvyi Rig (e) Dunajska Streda, FC Astana, Dunajska Streda,

Michalovce, Dunajska Streda, Atlantas, Volyn Lutsk, Kovel-Volyn, FK Lutsk, UFK Kharkiv

*** Beskorvajni - Aleksa Beskorvajni (Алекса Бескорвајни) (a) 06/06/2003, Vrbas (Serbia and Montenegro, now in Serbia) (b) 1,94 (c) F - center forward (d) FK Trayal Kruševac (e) Trayal, Javor-Matis

*** Beslic - Ivan Beslic (Ivan Bešlić) (a) 03/06/2001, Mostar (Bosnia and Herzegovina) (b) 1,79 (c) F - right winger (d) - (e) HSK Posusje

*** Beslic - Josip Beslic (Josip Bešlić) (a) 13/09/1999, Split (Croatia) (b) - (c) D - right back (d) HSK Posusje (e) HNK Tomislav T., HSK Posusje, Croat. Zmijavci, Siroki Brijeg, Croat. Zmijavci

*** Bessilé - Loïc Bessilé (Loïc Anthony Bessilé) (a) 19/02/1999, Toulouse (France) (b) 1,84 (c) D - central defense (d) RSC Charleroi (e) KAS Eupen, RSC Charleroi, Girondins Bordeaux, Girondins Bordeaux B, Toulouse B

*** Bessmertniy - Stanislav Bessmertniy (Бессмертный Станислав Васильевич) (a) 11/03/2004, Rostov-na-Donu (Russia) (b) 1,80 (c) D - right back (d) Dinamo 2 Moskva (e) -

*** Bessmertnyi - Dmitriy Bessmertnyi (Бессмертный Дмитрий Сергеевич) (a) 03/01/1997, Minsk (Belarus) (b) 1,75 (c) F - right winger (d) FK Aktobe (e) BATE Borisov, FK Minsk, FK Minsk II

*** Besson - Léo Besson (a) 27/10/2002, ¿? (Switzerland) (b) 1,87 (c) G (d) Servette FC (e) -

*** Bestpomostsnov - Andrei Bestpomostsnov (Andrei Bespomoštšnov) (a) 06/05/2001, Tallinn (Estonia) (b) - (c) M - central midfielder (d) Tallinn JK Legion (e) FC Kuressaare II, JK Järve, FC Strommi

*** Besuijen - Vicente Besuijen (Vicente Andrés Felipe Federico Besuijen) (a) 10/04/2001, Bogotá (Colombia) (b) 1,69 (c) F - right winger (d) Aberdeen FC (e) Excelsior, Aberdeen FC, ADO Den Haag

*** Betancor - Jefté Betancor (Jefté Betancor Sánchez) (a) 06/07/1993, Las Palmas de Gran Canaria (Spain) (b) 1,86 (c) F - center forward (d) CFR Cluj (e) Pafos FC, CFR Cluj, FCV Farul, FC Voluntari, SV Ried, SV Mattersburg, Vorwärts Steyr, SV Mattersburg, Stadl-Paura, Unión Viera, Las Palmas At., UD San Fernando, Las Palmas At., Arandina, Las Palmas At., Unión Viera, CD Eldense, CD Tenerife B, Ontinyent, Hércules CF B

*** Beto - Beto (António Alberto Bastos Pimparel) (a) 01/05/1982, Loures (Portugal) (b) 1,82 (c) G (d) - (e) Helsinki IFK, Farense, Leixões, Göztepe, Sporting Lisboa, Sevilla FC, SC Braga, Sevilla FC, SC Braga, FC Porto, CFR Cluj, FC Porto, Leixões, FC Marco, Sporting Lisboa, Chaves, Sporting Lisboa, Casa Pia, Sporting Lisboa, Sporting B

*** Beto - Beto (Norberto Bercique Gomes Betuncal) (a) 31/01/1998, Lisboa (Portugal) (b) 1,94 (c) F - center forward (d) Udinese (e) Portimonense, Udinese, Portimonense, CO Montijo, Tires

*** Betriu - Jordi Betriu (Jordi Betriu Armengol) (a) 29/06/1995, Coll de Nargó (Spain) (b) - (c) F - left winger (d) FC Ordino (e) CF Balaguer, IC d'Escaldes, FC Andorra, IC d'Escaldes, FC Andorra, Lleida Esp. B

*** Bettaieb - Adel Bettaieb (a) 28/01/1997, Villiers-le-Bel (France) (b) 1,84 (c) F - center forward (d) Boluspor (e) Ümraniyespor, F91 Dudelange, UR La Louvière, Angers SCO B

*** Bettinelli - Marcus Bettinelli (a) 24/05/1992, London (England) (b) 1,93 (c) G (d) Chelsea FC (e) Fulham, Middlesbrough, Fulham, Accrington St., Fulham, Dartford, Fulham

*** Bettmer - Gilles Bettmer (a) 31/03/1989, Esch/Alzette (Luxembourg) (b) 1,75 (c) M - central midfielder (d) - (e) UN Käerjeng 97, Differdange 03, Eintracht Trier, SC Freiburg II

*** Beukema - Sam Beukema (a) 17/11/1998, Deventer (Netherlands) (b) 1,88 (c) D - central defense (d) Bologna (e) AZ Alkmaar, Go Ahead Eagles

*** Bevan - Lewis Bevan (a) ¿?,), ¿? (Wales) (b) - (c) D (d) - (e) Airbus UK Broughton

*** Bevan - Owen Bevan (Owen Lucas Bevan) (a) 26/10/2003, Winchester (England) (b) 1,86 (c) D - central defense (d) - (e) Yeovil Town, Truro City FC

*** Bévárdi - Zsombor Bévárdi (a) 30/01/1999, Siófok (Hungary) (b) 1,77 (c) D - right back (d) Debreceni VSC (e) Kaposvár, Debrecen, Vidi FC, Vasas FC, Vidi FC, BFC Siófok, Videoton FC, Videoton II

*** Beveev - Mingiyan Beveev (Бевеев Мингиян Валерьевич) (a) 30/11/1995, Elista (Russia) (b) 1,82 (c) D - right back (d) Ural Ekaterimburgo (e) Enisey, KamAZ, Ural 2, Nosta, Volgar, Nosta, Volgar, MITOS, Volgar, Volgar II

*** Beverland - Howard Beverland (a) 30/03/1990, Ballymoney (Northern Ireland) (b) 1,83 (c) D - central defense (d) Ballyclare Comrades FC (e) Portadown, Ballyclare, Coleraine, Crusaders, Coleraine

*** Bevis - Kilian Bevis (a) 13/02/1998, Villepinte (France) (b) 1,73 (c) F - right winger (d) FK Radnicki 1923 Kragujevac (e) Valletta, Birkirkara FC, FC Messina, Castelvetro

*** Beyaz - Ömer Beyaz (Ömer Faruk Beyaz) (a) 29/08/2003, Istanbul (Turkey) (b) 1,71 (c) M - attacking midfielder (d) Hatayspor (e) Hatayspor, VfB Stuttgart, 1.FC Magdeburg, VfB Stuttgart, Fenerbahce

*** Beyer - Jordan Beyer (Louis Jordan Beyer) (a) 19/05/2000, Kempen (Germany) (b) 1,87 (c) D - central defense (d) Burnley FC (e) Borussia Mönchengladbach, Burnley, Borussia Mönchengladbach, SV Hamburg, Borussia Mönchengladbach

*** Beyhan - Berk Beyhan (Берк Бейхан) (a) 29/10/2004, Varna (Bulgaria) (b) 1,84 (c) F - center forward (d) Cherno More Varna (e) Cherno More II

*** Beysebekov - Abzal Beysebekov (Абзал Талғатұлы Бейсебеков) (a) 30/11/1992, Almaty (Kazakhstan) (b) 1,87 (c) D - right back (d) FC Astana (e) Korona Kielce, FC Astana, Vostok Oskemen, Kairat Almaty, Lokomotiv Astana, Kairat Almaty

*** Bezarashvili - Vakhtang Bezarashvili (ვახტანგ ბეზარაშვილი) (a) 21/02/2002, ¿? (Georgia) (b) 1,82 (c) F - center forward (d) Marijampole City (e) Daugavpils

*** Bezborodko - Denys Bezborodko (Безбородько Денис Олегович) (a) 31/05/1994, Chernigiv (Ukraine) (b) 1,83 (c) F - center forward (d) Kolos Kovalivka (e) Zorya Lugansk, Kolos Kovalivka, Desna, Gyirmót FC, Desna, FK Oleksandriya, Shakhtar II, Desna, Shakhtar II, Zorya Lugansk, Shakhtar II, Illichivets, Shakhtar II, Shakhtar 3

*** Bezkrovnyi - Bogdan Bezkrovnyi (Безкровний Богдан Ігорович) (a) 21/11/1998, Kyiv (Ukraine) (b) 1,85 (c) G (d) - (e) FC Telavi, FC Gareji, FC Telavi, FC Aragvi, FC Telavi, Ol. Donetsk II, RVUFK Kyiv

*** Bezuglyi - Mykyta Bezuglyi (Безуглий Микита Сергійович) (a) 01/08/1995, Volnovakha, Donetsk Oblast (Ukraine) (b) 1,86 (c) D - central defense (d) Metalist 1925 Kharkiv (e) Obolon, Shakhtar II

*** Bezus - Roman Bezus (Безус Роман Анатолійович) (a) 26/09/1990, Kremenchuk, Poltava Oblast (Soviet Union, now in Ukraine) (b) 1,85 (c) M - attacking midfielder (d) Omonia Nicosia (e) KAA Gent, Sint-Truiden, Dnipro, Dinamo Kyïv, Vorskla Poltava, Kremin

*** Bezzina - Johan Bezzina (a) 30/05/1994, ¿? (Malta) (b) 1,80 (c) M - right midfielder (d) Hibernians FC (e) Gudja United FC, Birkirkara FC, Mosta FC, Birkirkara FC, Hibernians FC, Sliema Wanderers, Hibernians FC
*** Bhandari - Kailash Bhandari (a) 07/07/2003, ¿? (Finland) (b) - (c) D - right back (d) PEPO Lappeenranta (e) HJK Klubi 04, Pallokerho, HJK Klubi 04
*** Biagui - Yannick Biagui (a) 21/02/1994, ¿? (Senegal) (b) - (c) D (d) UN Käerjeng 97 (e) Neuves-Maisons
*** Biai - Celton Biai (Celton Anssumane Biai) (a) 13/08/2000, Lisboa (Portugal) (b) 1,88 (c) G (d) Vitória Guimarães SC (e) Vitória Guimarães B
*** Biai - Mimito Biai (Atair Mimito Rocha Biai) (a) 12/12/1997, Bissau (Guinea-Bissau) (b) 1,73 (c) M - central midfielder (d) Alashkert Yerevan CF (e) FC Arges, Cherno More, Académica Coimbra, Vitória Guimarães B, Panetolikos, Vitória Guimarães B
*** Bialek - Bartosz Bialek (Bartosz Białek) (a) 11/11/2001, Brzeg (Poland) (b) 1,91 (c) F - center forward (d) KAS Eupen (e) KAS Eupen, VfL Wolfsburg, Vitesse, VfL Wolfsburg, Zagłębie
*** Bianchetti - Matteo Bianchetti (a) 17/03/1993, Como (Italy) (b) 1,89 (c) D - central defense (d) US Cremonese (e) Hellas Verona, Spezia, Hellas Verona, Empoli, Hellas Verona, Spezia, Hellas Verona, Internazionale Milano, Hellas Verona, Internazionale Milano, Corsico
*** Bianchi - Luca Bianchi (a) 07/01/1990, ¿? (San Marino) (b) - (c) G (d) FC Fiorentino (e) Virtus
*** Bianco - Alessandro Bianco (a) 01/10/2002, Torino (Italy) (b) 1,73 (c) M - central midfielder (d) AC Reggiana 1919 (e) Reggiana, Fiorentina
*** Biancone - Giulian Biancone (a) 31/03/2000, Fréjus (France) (b) 1,87 (c) D - right back (d) Nottingham Forest (e) Troyes, AS Monaco, Cercle Brugge, AS Monaco, Cercle Brugge, AS Monaco
*** Bianda - William Bianda (William Ludovic Brandon Bianda) (a) 30/04/2000, Suresnes (France) (b) 1,85 (c) D - central defense (d) - (e) AS Roma, AS Nancy, AS Roma, Zulte Waregem, AS Roma, RC Lens, RC Lens B
*** Bianor - Bianor (Bianor das Graças Lima da Silva NetoNeto) (a) 28/06/1994, Manaus (Brazil) (b) 1,87 (c) D - central defense (d) Samut Prakan City (e) KF Llapi, FC Shkupi, Makedonija, Fast, Paraná, Rio Negro-AM
*** Biatoumoussoka - Messie Biatoumoussoka (a) 05/06/1998, Saint-Denis (France) (b) 1,89 (c) D - central defense (d) FAR Rabat (e) Botev Vratsa, PO Xylotymbou, CSC Selimbar, PO Xylotymbou, US Avranches, Girondins Bordeaux B
*** Biba - Ortelio Biba (a) 17/09/2004, Tiranë (Albania) (b) - (c) G (d) KF Laçi (e) -
*** Biba (c) M (d) KF Ferizaj (e) - - Laurent Biba (c) M (d) KF Ferizaj (e) -
*** Biber - Edin Biber (a) 06/01/1999, Sarajevo (Bosnia and Herzegovina) (b) 1,80 (c) M - central midfielder (d) FK Zeljeznicar Sarajevo (e) Igman Konjic, Radnik, Mladost Kakanj
*** Bibic - Elvis Bibic (Elvis Bibić) (a) 04/03/1992, Sarajevo (Bosnia and Herzegovina) (b) - (c) F - left winger (d) FK Igman Konjic (e) TOSK Tesanj, FK Olimpik, NK Vitez, NK Jajce, FK Olimpik, GOSK Gabela, Zrinjski Mostar, Bosna Sarajevo
*** Bibishkov - Marsel Bibishkov (Марсел Крумов Бибишков) (a) 11/04/2007, ¿? (Bulgaria) (b) 1,90 (c) F - center forward (d) - (e) DIT Sofia
*** Bibo - Stiven Bibo (a) 26/09/2003, ¿? (Albania) (b) - (c) M - central midfielder (d) KF Laçi (e) -
*** Bic - Ovidiu Bic (Ovidiu Alexandru Bic) (a) 23/02/1994, Abrud (Romania) (b) 1,77 (c) M - central midfielder (d) FC Universitatea Cluj (e) CS U Craiova, Kiryat

Shmona, CS U Craiova, Chindia, CS U Craiova, Gaz Metan, Olimpia SM, Liberty Salonta, Bihor Oradea, Liberty Salonta
*** Bicakcic - Ermin Bicakcic (Ermin Bičakčić) (a) 24/01/1990, Zvornik (Yugoslavia, now in Bosnia and Herzegovina) (b) 1,85 (c) D - central defense (d) - (e) Hoffenheim, Eintracht Braunschweig, VfB Stuttgart, Stuttgart II
*** Biceanu - Ciprian Biceanu (a) 26/02/1994, PiteĒ™ti (Romania) (b) 1,84 (d) FC Hermannstadt (e) Concordia, Astra Giurgiu, CS Mioveni, FC D. Coman
*** Bicfalvi - Eric Bicfalvi (Eric Cosmin Bicfalvi) (a) 05/02/1988, Carei (Romania) (b) 1,87 (c) M - attacking midfielder (d) Ural Ekaterimburgo (e) Tom Tomsk, FC Dinamo, Liaoning FC, Volyn Lutsk, Steaua Bucuresti, AS FC Buzău, Steaua Bucuresti, Jiul Petroşani
*** Bichakhchyan - Vahan Bichakhchyan (Վահան Վարդանի Բիչախչյան) (a) 09/07/1999, Gyumri (Armenia) (b) 1,72 (c) F - right winger (d) Pogon Szczecin (e) MSK Zilina, Shirak Gyumri, Shirak II
*** Bichsel - Joel Bichsel (a) 04/03/2002, Olten (Switzerland) (b) 1,94 (c) D - central defense (d) SC Freiburg II (e) SC Freiburg II, BSC Young Boys
*** Bici - Bujar Bici (a) 24/01/2004, ¿? (Serbia and Montenegro, now in Kosovo) (b) - (c) G (d) Kek-U Kastriot (e) -
*** Bida - Bartosz Bida (Bartosz Bida) (a) 21/02/2001, Rzeszów (Poland) (b) 1,75 (c) F - center forward (d) TS Podbeskidzie Bielsko-Biala (e) Jagiellonia, Wigry Suwalki, Jagiellonia, AP Jagiellonia
*** Bidon - Julian Bidon (a) 22/10/1990, Trier (Germany) (b) 1,74 (c) F - center forward (d) FSG Ehrang/Pfalzel (e) US Hostert, FSV Salmrohr, Etzella Ettelbrück, Eintracht Trier, FSV Salmrohr, Borussia Neunkirchen, Eintracht Trier, Eintr. Trier II
*** Bidounga - Ryan Bidounga (a) 29/04/1997, Rambouillet (France) (b) 1,86 (c) D - central defense (d) CSKA 1948 (e) Lokomotiv Plovdiv, AS Monaco B, AS Nancy, Le Mans FC, AS Nancy, AS Nancy B
*** Bidstrup - Mads Bidstrup (a) 25/02/2001, Køge (Denmark) (b) 1,75 (c) M - central midfielder (d) Red Bull Salzburg (e) Brentford, Nordsjælland, Brentford, Brentford B
*** Bidzinashvili - Irakli Bidzinashvili (ირაკლი ბიძინაშვილი) (a) 27/02/1997, ¿? (Georgia) (b) 1,68 (c) M - attacking midfielder (d) Dinamo Batumi (e) FC Dila, Jelgava, Artsakh Erewan, Saburtalo
*** Bieganski - Jan Bieganski (Jan Biegański) (a) 04/12/2002, Gliwice (Poland) (b) 1,83 (c) M - pivot (d) KS Lechia Gdańsk (e) GKS Tychy, Lechia Gdánsk, GKS Tychy, Lechia Gdánsk, GKS Tychy
*** Biegon - Erik Biegon (a) 29/04/2004, ¿? (Czech Rep.) (b) 1,79 (c) F - center forward (d) FC Sellier & Bellot Vlasim (e) Vlasim, Slavia Praha B
*** Biel - Pep Biel (Pep Biel Mas Jaume) (a) 05/09/1996, Sant Joan (Spain) (b) 1,72 (c) M - attacking midfielder (d) Olympiakos El Pireo (e) FC København, Real Zaragoza, Dep. Aragón, RCD Mallorca B, AD Almudévar, RCD Mallorca B, CD Llosetense, CE Constància
*** Bielak - Lukas Bielak (Lukáš Bielák) (a) 14/12/1986, Ruzomberok (Czechoslovakia, now in Slovakia) (b) 1,84 (c) M - pivot (d) Tatran Liptovsky Mikulas (e) Dolny Kubin, Liptovsky Mik., NKP Podhale, Stal Mielec, GKS Jastrzebie, Stal Mielec, ŁKS, Bytovia Bytow, Gornik Leczna, Ružomberok, Liptovsky Mik., Raca Bratislava
*** Bielica - Daniel Bielica (Daniel Bielica) (a) 30/04/1999, Zabrze (Poland) (b) 1,91 (c) G (d) Górnik Zabrze (e) Warta Poznań, Górnik Zabrze, Sandecja, Górnik Zabrze, Gornik II, Zaborze Zabrze

*** Biereth - Mika Biereth (Mika Miles Biereth) (a) 08/02/2003, London (England) (b) 1,87 (c) F - center forward (d) Motherwell FC (e) Motherwell FC, RKC Waalwijk
*** Bieszczad - Kacper Bieszczad (a) 11/09/2002, Krosno (Poland) (b) 1,92 (c) G (d) Rakow Czestochowa (e) Rakow, Zagłębie, Chrobry Glogow, Zagłębie, AP Zagłębie
*** Bifouma - Thievy Bifouma (Thievy Guivane Bifouma Koulossa) (a) 13/05/1992, Saint Denis (France) (b) - (c) F - right winger (d) OFI Creta (e) Bursaspor, Shenzhen FC, HLJ Ice City, Shenzhen FC, Yeni Malatyaspor, Ankaragücü, Sivasspor, Osmanlispor, SC Bastia, RCD Espanyol, Stade Reims, RCD Espanyol, Granada CF, RCD Espanyol, UD Almería, RCD Espanyol, West Bromwich Albion, RCD Espanyol, UD Las Palmas, RCD Espanyol
*** Bigas - Pedro Bigas (Pedro Bigas Rigo) (a) 15/05/1990, Palma de Mallorca (Spain) (b) 1,81 (c) D - central defense (d) Elche CF (e) SD Eibar, UD Las Palmas, SD Eibar, UD Las Palmas, RCD Mallorca, RCD Mallorca B, At. Baleares, CD Montuiri
*** Biggs - Ranaldo Biggs (a) 11/07/2002, ¿? (Slovenia) (b) - (c) F - center forward (d) NK Domžale (e) Rudar Velenje, Domžale, ND Gorica, Domžale
*** Biglia - Lucas Biglia (Lucas Rodrigo Biglia) (a) 30/01/1986, Mercedes (Argentina) (b) 1,78 (c) M - pivot (d) - (e) Basaksehir, Karagümrük, AC Milan, Lazio, RSC Anderlecht, Independiente, Argentinos Jrs., Argentinos Juniors II
*** Bihorac - Faruk Bihorac (Фарук Бихорац) (a) 12/05/1996, Novi Pazar (RF Yugoslavia, now in Serbia) (b) 1,91 (c) D - central defense (d) FK Tuzla City (e) FC Malisheva, Sileks, AP Brera, Kabel Novi Sad, Velez Mostar, Kabel Novi Sad, Novi Pazar, FK Josanica, Novi Pazar, Zeleznicar Lajkovac, Novi Pazar, FK Josanica, Novi Pazar, Hajduk 1912, Novi Pazar
*** Bijelic - Emir Bijelic (a) 16/01/1998, Luxembourg (Luxembourg) (b) 1,85 (c) M - pivot (d) FC Progrès Niederkorn (e) Union Titus Petange, FC Metz B
*** Bijelovic - Luka Bijelovic (Лука Бијеловић) (a) 11/04/2001, Subotica (RF Yugoslavia, now in Serbia) (b) 1,88 (c) F - right winger (d) FK Spartak Subotica (e) FK Backa, Spartak, FK Backa
*** Bijker - Lucas Bijker (a) 04/03/1993, São Paulo (Brazil) (b) 1,74 (c) D - left back (d) - (e) KV Mechelen, Cádiz CF, Heerenveen, SC Cambuur
*** Bijl - Glenn Bijl (a) 13/07/1995, Stadskanaal (Netherlands) (b) 1,79 (c) D - right back (d) Krylya Sovetov Samara (e) FC Emmen, FC Dordrecht
*** Bijleveld - Teun Bijleveld (a) 27/05/1998, Amstelveen (Netherlands) (b) 1,76 (c) D - left back (d) Roda JC Kerkrade (e) FC Emmen, Heracles Almelo, Ajax B
*** Bijlow - Justin Bijlow (a) 22/01/1998, Rotterdam (Netherlands) (b) 1,88 (c) G (d) Feyenoord Rotterdam (e) -
*** Bijol - Jaka Bijol (a) 05/02/1999, Vuzenica (Slovenia) (b) 1,90 (c) D - central defense (d) Udinese (e) CSKA Moskva, Hannover 96, CSKA Moskva, Rudar Velenje
*** Bikel - Janio Bikel (Janio Bikel Figueiredo da Silva) (a) 28/06/1995, Bissau (Guinea-Bissau) (b) 1,74 (c) M - central midfielder (d) - (e) Khimki, Vancouver, LR Vicenza, Vancouver, CSKA-Sofia, NEC Nijmegen, Heerenveen
*** Bikoro - Federico Bikoro (Fréderic Bikoro Akieme Nchama) (a) 17/03/1996, Douala (Cameroon) (b) 1,88 (c) M - central midfielder (d) Sandefjord Fotball (e) Real Zaragoza, Hércules CF, Real Zaragoza, Badalona, Real Zaragoza, CD Numancia, Real Zaragoza, CD Badajoz, Real Zaragoza, CD Teruel, Lorca FC B, UD Sanse, RSD Alcalá, Sony Ela Nguema, Akonangui FC
*** Bilal - Adonis Bilal (a) 05/08/1999, Banja Luka (Bosnia and Herzegovina) (b) - (c) M - central midfielder (d) FK Zeljeznicar Banja Luka (e) Sloga Meridian, Zeljeznicar BL, FK Krupa, Zeljeznicar BL

*** Bilal Mazhar - Bilal Mazhar (عبدالرحمن مظهر بلال, Bilal Mazhar Abdelrahman) (a) 21/11/2003, Châteauroux (France) (b) 1,82 (c) F - center forward (d) Panathinaikos Athina B (e) -
*** Bilali - Amir Bilali (a) 15/05/1994, Skopje (North Macedonia) (b) 1,89 (c) D - central defense (d) Gostivar (e) Sutjeska Niksic, Akzhayik, Mezőkövesd, Academica Clinceni, FK Partizani, FC Shkupi, KF Teuta, Rabotnicki, FK Bylis, NK Celje
*** Bilali - Ayoub Idrissa Bilali (Ayoub Idrissa Bilali) (a) 27/07/2001, Tanga (Tanzania) (b) - (c) ¿? (d) FK Gorazde (e) Hegelmann B, FK Ibar, A. Keciörengücü, Mtibwa Sugar
*** Bilali - Sabit Bilali (a) 15/08/1997, Pula (Croatia) (b) 1,81 (c) M - central midfielder (d) FK Partizani (e) Shkëndija, FC Shkupi, Makedonija, Gostivar, Shkëndija, FSV Luckenwalde
*** Bilalli - Oltion Bilalli (a) 03/01/2002, Gjilan (RF Yugoslavia, now in Kosovo) (b) 1,76 (c) F - right winger (d) SC Gjilani (e) Balikesirspor
*** Bilaloglu - Mert Can Bilaloglu (Mert Can Bilaloğlu) (a) 12/10/2000, Sakarya (Turkey) (b) 1,83 (c) F - right winger (d) FC Dinamo-Auto Tiraspol (e) Boluspor, Artvin Hopaspor, Boluspor
*** Bilalovic - Kenan Bilalovic (a) 22/06/2005, ¿? (Sweden) (b) - (c) M (d) IFK Värnamo (e) -
*** Bilazer - Hayrullah Bilazer (a) 20/05/1995, Trabzon (Turkey) (b) 1,70 (c) D - right back (d) MKE Ankaragücü (e) Giresunspor, Boluspor, Darica GB, T. Akcaabat, A.Sebatspor
*** Bilbao - Iker Bilbao (Iker Bilbao Mendiguren) (a) 20/03/1996, Bilbao (Spain) (b) 1,82 (c) M - central midfielder (d) PAS Giannina (e) SD Amorebieta, Bilbao Athletic, Gernika, Bilbao Athletic, CD Basconia
*** Bilbija - Nemanja Bilbija (a) 02/11/1990, Banja Luka (Yugoslavia, now in Bosnia and Herzegovina) (b) 1,81 (c) F - center forward (d) HSK Zrinjski Mostar (e) Gangwon FC, Zrinjski Mostar, RNK Split, FK Sarajevo, Vojvodina, Borac Banja Luka, Vojvodina, Borac Banja Luka, Vojvodina, Borac Banja Luka
*** Bilenkyi - Stanislav Bilenkyi (Біленький Станіслав Сергійович) (a) 22/08/1998, Donetsk (Ukraine) (b) 1,82 (c) F - center forward (d) Maccabi Netanya (e) Dinamo Tbilisi, Maccabi Netanya, Dinamo Tbilisi, Dunajska Streda, Dynamo Brest, Dunajska Streda, Rukh Lviv, Dunajska Streda, Z. Sosnowiec, Dunajska Streda, Olimpik Donetsk, Ol. Donetsk II
*** Bilgin - Emre Bilgin (a) 26/02/2004, Istanbul (Turkey) (b) 1,88 (c) G (d) Fatih Karagümrük (e) Karagümrük, Besiktas
*** Bilic - Karlo Bilic (Karlo Bilić) (a) 06/09/1993, Split (Croatia) (b) 1,88 (c) D - central defense (d) Hamrun Spartans (e) Koper, HNK Sibenik, Podbrezova, VSS Kosice, Orkan Dugi Rat, Slavija S., NK Dugopolje
*** Bility - Hosine Bility (a) 10/05/2001, ¿? (Guinea) (b) 1,87 (c) D - central defense (d) - (e) Midtjylland, Fram Reykjavík, Midtjylland, Croydon
*** Bill - Bill (Fabricio Rodrigues da Silva Ferreira) (a) 07/05/1999, Belford Roxo (Brazil) (b) 1,75 (c) F - left winger (d) SK Dnipro-1 (e) Sampaio Corrêa, SK Dnipro-1, Inter Limeira, SK Dnipro-1, RFS, SK Dnipro-1, Sport Recife, SK Dnipro-1, Flamengo, SK Dnipro-1, CRB, Ponte Preta
*** Bille - Eric Bille (Eric Yves Bille) (a) 24/12/2004, ¿? (Ivory Coast) (b) 1,81 (c) F - right winger (d) MSK Zilina B (e) Zilina Africa
*** Billing - Philip Billing (Philip Anyanwu Billing) (a) 11/06/1996, Copenhagen (Denmark) (b) 1,93 (c) M - central midfielder (d) AFC Bournemouth (e) Huddersfield Town

*** Billong - Jean-Claude Billong (a) 28/12/1993, Mantes-la-Jolie (France) (b) 1,92 (c) D - central defense (d) Muangthong United (e) CFR Cluj, Clermont Foot, Benevento, Hatayspor, Benevento, Salernitana, Benevento, Foggia, Benevento, NK Maribor, Rudar Velenje, Leixões, NY Red Bulls II, FC Mantois, US Créteil B

*** Bilonog - Dmytro Bilonog (Білоног Дмитро Іванович) (a) 26/05/1995, Cherkasy (Ukraine) (b) 1,83 (c) F - right winger (d) Nejmeh SC (e) Chrobry Glogow, Riteriai, Metalist, FK Minaj, Metalist, Enisey, IFK Mariehamn, Dinamo Minsk, Zirka, Olimpik Donetsk, Zirka, Ural, Zirka, Ural, Shakhtar II, Shakhtar 3

*** Biloshevskyi - Bogdan Biloshevskyi (Білошевський Богдан Олегович) (a) 12/01/2000, Nizhyn, Chernigiv Oblast (Ukraine) (b) 1,87 (c) M - pivot (d) FK Oleksandriya (e) Dinamo Kyïv, FK Oleksandriya, Dinamo Kyïv, Chornomorets, Dinamo Kyïv, Dinamo Kiev II, Desna, Dinamo Kiev II

*** Bilovar - Kristian Bilovar (Біловар Крістіан Русланович, Bilovar Kristian Ruslanovych) (a) 05/02/2001, Debrecen (Hungary) (b) 1,91 (c) D - central defense (d) FC Dinamo de Kiev (e) AEL Limassol, Dinamo Kyïv, Chornomorets, Dinamo Kyïv, Desna, Dinamo Kyïv, Dinamo Kiev II

*** Bilsel - Ege Bilsel (a) 04/01/2004, Ankara (Turkey) (b) 1,75 (c) F - left winger (d) Antalyaspor (e) -

*** Bilu - Oz Bilu (בילו עוז) (a) 16/01/2001, Rishon LeZion (Israel) (b) 1,78 (c) M - attacking midfielder (d) Maccabi Netanya (e) FC Ashdod, Maccabi Netanya, FC Ashdod

*** Bilyi - Artem Bilyi (Білий Артем Костянтинович) (a) 03/10/1999, Novomoskovsk, Dnipropetrovsk Oblast (Ukraine) (b) 1,82 (c) M - central midfielder (d) NK Aluminij Kidricevo (e) NK Aluminij, NK Celje, Liepaja, FC Van, Metalist, FK Vovchansk, Vorskla II, VPK-Agro, Vorskla II

*** Bilyi - Maksym Bilyi (Білий Максим Ігорович) (a) 21/06/1990, Vasylkivka, Dnipropetrovsk Oblast (Soviet Union, now in Ukraine) (b) 1,87 (c) D - central defense (d) Rukh Lviv (e) Chornomorets, Rukh Lviv, Zorya Lugansk, Rukh Lviv, Zorya Lugansk, FK Mariupol, Anzhi, Hajduk Split, Zorya Lugansk, Shakhtar 3, Stal Alchevsk, Shakhtar 3

*** Bilyk - Oleg Bilyk (Білик Олег Степанович) (a) 11/01/1998, Pidvolochysk, Ternopil Oblast (Ukraine) (b) 1,87 (c) G (d) Chornomorets Odessa (e) Ingulets, FK Oleksandriya, Oleksandriya II, Skala Stryi

*** Binaku - Egzon Binaku (a) 27/08/1995, Åmål (Sweden) (b) 1,82 (c) D - left back (d) GAIS Göteborg (e) Norrköping, Malmö FF, Häcken, Ljungskile SK, Häcken, IFK Åmål

*** Binder - Nicolas Binder (a) 13/01/2002, Wien (Austria) (b) 1,93 (c) F - center forward (d) SK Austria Klagenfurt (e) Rapid Wien II

*** Bingöl - Tayfur Bingöl (a) 11/01/1993, Ankara (Turkey) (b) 1,80 (c) D - right back (d) Alanyaspor (e) Besiktas, Alanyaspor, Bursaspor, Alanyaspor, Göztepe, Genclerbirligi, Alanyaspor, Genclerbirligi, Adana Demirspor, Genclerbirligi, Bandirmaspor, Genclerbirligi, Hacettepe, Genclerbirligi, Hacettepe

*** Bintsouka - Archange Bintsouka (Archange Dieudonne Bintsouka Koxy) (a) 25/10/2002, ¿? (Congo) (b) 1,87 (c) F - center forward (d) - (e) KF Drenica, AS Kondzo

*** Binyamin - Ran Binyamin (בנימין רן) (a) 06/02/2004, ¿? (Israel) (b) 1,80 (c) M - central midfielder (d) Hapoel Tel Aviv (e) -

*** Biordi - Juri Biordi (a) 01/01/1995, ¿? (San Marino) (b) - (c) D - central defense (d) FC Fiorentino (e) Cailungo, Fiorentino, Domagnano, Fiorentino, Tre Fiori, Fiorentino

*** Biraghi - Cristiano Biraghi (a) 01/09/1992, Cernusco sul Naviglio (Italy) (b) 1,85 (c) D - left back (d) Fiorentina (e) Internazionale Milano, Fiorentina, Pescara, Fiorentina, Pescara, Internazionale Milano, Granada CF, Internazionale Milano, Chievo Verona, Internazionale Milano, Cittadella, Catania, Cittadella, Internazionale Milano, Cittadella, Internazionale Milano, Juve Stabia
*** Biraschi - Davide Biraschi (a) 02/07/1994, Roma (Italy) (b) 1,82 (c) D - right back (d) Génova (e) Karagümrük, Genoa, Avellino, Grosseto
*** Bircaj - Luis Bircaj (Luis Birçaj) (a) 19/05/2003, Tiranë (Albania) (b) - (c) M - attacking midfielder (d) FK Partizani (e) -
*** Birgiola - Klaidas Birgiola (a) 18/03/2004, ¿? (Lithuania) (b) 1,86 (c) M - central midfielder (d) FK Banga Gargzdai B (e) -
*** Birgisson - Adolf Dadi Birgisson (Adolf Daði Birgisson) (a) 03/06/2004, ¿? (Iceland) (b) - (c) F - right winger (d) Stjarnan Gardabaer (e) -
*** Birglehner - Philipp Birglehner (a) 23/11/1998, ¿? (Austria) (b) 1,80 (c) D - left back (d) SPG Wels (e) SV Ried, SV Ried II, Vöcklamarkt
*** Birighitti - Mark Birighitti (Mark Romano Birighitti) (a) 17/04/1991, Perth (Australia) (b) 1,88 (c) G (d) Dundee United FC (e) Central Coast, Melbourne City, NAC Breda, Swansea City, Newcastle, Varese, Newcastle, Adelaide United, FFA C. of Excel
*** Birindelli - Samuele Birindelli (a) 19/07/1999, Pisa (Italy) (b) 1,76 (c) D - right back (d) AC Monza (e) Pisa
*** Birka - Emils Birka (Emīls Birka) (a) 25/04/2000, Limbaži (Latvia) (b) 1,79 (c) D - left back (d) Valmiera FC (e) Metta, FS Metta II
*** Birkfeldt - Jon Birkfeldt (Jon Henrik Erik Birkfeldt) (a) 03/06/1996, ¿? (Sweden) (b) 1,83 (c) D - central defense (d) Varbergs BoIS (e) IK Frej Täby, Värnamo, Åtvidabergs FF
*** Birligea - Daniel Birligea (George Daniel Bîrligea) (a) 19/04/2000, Brăila (Romania) (b) 1,84 (c) F - center forward (d) CFR Cluj (e) Teramo
*** Birmancevic - Veljko Birmancevic (Вељко Бирманчевић) (a) 05/03/1998, Šabac (RF Yugoslavia, now in Serbia) (b) 1,79 (c) F - left winger (d) AC Sparta Praga (e) Sparta Praha, Toulouse, Malmö FF, Čukarički, FK Partizan, Čukarički, FK Partizan, Rad Beograd, FK Partizan, Teleoptik, FK Partizan, Teleoptik, FK Partizan
*** Birney - Calum Birney (a) 19/04/1993, Belfast (Northern Ireland) (b) 1,88 (c) D - central defense (d) Glenavon FC (e) Glentoran
*** Biró - Roland Biró (a) 30/05/2003, Nyíregyháza (Hungary) (b) 1,87 (c) M - pivot (d) Kisvárda FC (e) Kisvárda II
*** Birzu - Daniel Birzu (Daniel Bîrzu) (a) 28/05/2002, Constanța (Romania) (b) 1,97 (c) D - central defense (d) CS Mioveni (e) CS Mioveni, FCV Farul, Academia Hagi
*** Bischof - Noah Bischof (a) 07/12/2002, Feldkirch (Austria) (b) 1,85 (c) F - center forward (d) SCR Altach (e) -
*** Bischof - Tom Bischof (a) 28/06/2005, Aschaffenburg (Germany) (b) 1,76 (c) M - attacking midfielder (d) TSG 1899 Hoffenheim (e) -
*** Bisekenov - Mukhametali Bisekenov (Бисекенов Мухаметали Каирбекович) (a) 12/07/2003, ¿?, Tashkent Region (Uzbekistan) (b) - (c) F - left winger (d) Kyzylzhar SK Petropavlovsk II (e) -
*** Biseswar - Diego Biseswar (Diego Marvin Biseswar) (a) 08/03/1988, Amsterdam (Netherlands) (b) 1,76 (c) M - attacking midfielder (d) - (e) PAOK, Apollon Limassol, PAOK, Kayserispor, Feyenoord, De Graafschap, Feyenoord, Heracles Almelo, Feyenoord
*** Bishop - Nathan Bishop (Nathan James Bishop) (a) 15/10/1999, Hillingdon (England) (b) 1,85 (c) G (d) Sunderland AFC (e) Mansfield Town, Southend United

*** Bislimi - Egzon Bislimi (a) 15/01/2000, Prishtinë (RF Yugoslavia, now in Kosovo) (b) 1,92 (c) G (d) KF Shkëndija Hajvali (e) FC Prishtina, Ramiz Sadiku, KF 2 Korriku
*** Bislimi - Uran Bislimi (a) 25/09/1999, Basel (Switzerland) (b) 1,83 (c) M - central midfielder (d) FC Lugano (e) FC Schaffhausen
*** Bisseck - Yann Aurel Bisseck (Yann Aurel Ludger Bisseck) (a) 29/11/2000, Köln (Germany) (b) 1,96 (c) D - central defense (d) Internazionale Milano (e) Aarhus GF, 1.FC Köln, Aarhus GF, 1.FC Köln, Vitória Guimarães B, Vitória Guimarães, 1.FC Köln, Roda JC, 1.FC Köln, Holstein Kiel, 1.FC Köln
*** Bissi - Matheus Bissi (Matheus Bissi da Silva) (a) 19/03/1991, Piracicaba (Brazil) (b) 1,88 (c) D - central defense (d) FK Atyrau (e) Panevezys, Al-Muharraq, Stumbras, Slavia Sofia, Tourizense, Rakow, Birkirkara FC, Banga, Flamengo B, Marcílio Dias, Flamengo B
*** Bissouma - Yves Bissouma (a) 30/08/1996, Issia (Ivory Coast) (b) 1,82 (c) M - central midfielder (d) Tottenham Hotspur (e) Brighton & Hove Albion, Lille, AS Real Bamako, JMG Bamako
*** Bistrovic - Kristijan Bistrovic (Kristijan Bistrović) (a) 09/04/1998, Koprivnica (Croatia) (b) 1,83 (c) M - central midfielder (d) CSKA Moskva (e) Fortuna Sittard, CSKA Moskva, Lecce, CSKA Moskva, Karagümrük, CSKA Moskva, Kasimpasa, CSKA Moskva, Slaven Belupo
*** Bita - Junior Bita (Wibuala Junior Bita Bueto) (a) 08/06/2005, Adzopé (Ivory Coast) (b) 1,82 (c) M - central midfielder (d) Bilbao Athletic (e) CD Basconia
*** Bitekenov - Asan Bitekenov (Битекенов Асан) (a) 07/10/2003, ¿? (Kazakhstan) (b) 1,77 (c) M - pivot (d) Tobol Kostanay II (e) -
*** Bitlan - Vasile Bitlan (Vasile Bîtlan) (a) 31/01/2004, ¿? (Moldova) (b) - (c) M - pivot (d) Dacia Buiucani (e) -
*** Biton - Dan Biton (ביטון דן) (a) 20/07/1995, Beer Sheva (Israel) (b) 1,75 (c) M - attacking midfielder (d) Maccabi Tel Aviv (e) Ludogorets, Maccabi Tel Aviv, Ludogorets, FC Ashdod, H. Beer Sheva, FC Ashdod, H. Beer Sheva
*** Biton - Ofek Biton (ביטון אופק) (a) 27/09/1999, ¿? (Israel) (b) 1,75 (c) M - central midfielder (d) Hapoel Jerusalem (e) Hapoel Tel Aviv, H. Jerusalem, Hapoel Tel Aviv, Ness Ziona
*** Biton - Oren Biton (ביטון אורן) (a) 16/06/1994, Atlit (Israel) (b) 1,84 (c) D - left back (d) Hapoel Haifa (e) B. Jerusalem, H. Beer Sheva, Kiryat Shmona, Hapoel Haifa, H. Nazareth Illit, Hapoel Haifa
*** Bitri - Eneo Bitri (a) 26/08/1996, Berat (Albania) (b) 1,92 (c) D - central defense (d) FC Banik Ostrava (e) FK Partizani, FC Astana, FK Partizani, FC Kamza, FK Partizani, FK Tomori Berat
*** Bitshiabu - El Chadaille Bitshiabu (a) 16/05/2005, Villeneuve-Saint-Georges (France) (b) 1,96 (c) D - central defense (d) RB Leipzig (e) Paris Saint-Germain
*** Bitsindou - Scott Bitsindou (Romcni Scott Bitsindou) (a) 11/05/1996, Brussel (Belgium) (b) 1,94 (c) M - pivot (d) Livingston FC (e) Arbroath, Livingston FC, KSK Lierse Kem., Lommel SK, Javor-Matis, United Zürich
*** Bittencourt - Leonardo Bittencourt (Leonardo Jesus Loureiro Bittencourt) (a) 19/12/1993, Leipzig (Germany) (b) 1,71 (c) M - attacking midfielder (d) SV Werder Bremen (e) Hoffenheim, Werder Bremen, Hoffenheim, 1.FC Köln, Hannover 96, Borussia Dortmund, Energie Cottbus
*** Bitton - Ben Bitton (ביטון בן) (a) 03/01/1991, Bat Yam (Israel) (b) 1,75 (c) D - right back (d) Beitar Jerusalem (e) Hapoel Tel Aviv, H. Beer Sheva, Maccabi Tel Aviv, H. Beer Sheva, Hapoel Tel Aviv, H. Nazareth Illit, Hapoel Tel Aviv, Ness Ziona, Hapoel Tel Aviv

*** Bitton - Nir Bitton (ביטון ניר) (a) 30/10/1991, Ashdod (Israel) (b) 1,96 (c) M - pivot (d) Maccabi Tel Aviv (e) Celtic FC, FC Ashdod

*** Bitumazala - Nathan Bitumazala (a) 10/12/2002, Fontainebleau (France) (b) 1,78 (c) M - attacking midfielder (d) KAS Eupen (e) Paris Saint-Germain

*** Biuk - Stipe Biuk (a) 26/12/2002, Split (Croatia) (b) 1,84 (c) F - left winger (d) Los Ángeles FC (e) Hajduk Split

*** Biver - Ben Biver (a) 31/10/1997, ¿? (Luxemburg) (b) - (c) D - right back (d) FC Wiltz 71 (e) Sporting Mertzig

*** Bivol - Dumitru Bivol (a) 03/10/2001, ¿? (Moldova) (b) - (c) M - central midfielder (d) Dacia Buiucani (e) Dinamo-Auto, Victoria

*** Bizjak - Lovro Bizjak (a) 12/11/1993, Šmartno ob Paki (Slovenia) (b) 1,84 (c) F - center forward (d) NK Celje (e) FC Sheriff, Ufa, Domžale, NK Aluminij, Wildon, NK Smartno 1928, SD Kovinar, NK Smartno 1928

*** Bizot - Marco Bizot (a) 10/03/1991, Hoorn (Netherlands) (b) 1,93 (c) G (d) Stade Brestois 29 (e) AZ Alkmaar, KRC Genk, FC Groningen, Ajax B, SC Cambuur, Ajax B

*** Bizoza - Parfait Bizoza (a) 03/03/1999, Skodje (Norway) (b) 1,87 (c) M - pivot (d) Lyngby BK (e) Vendsyssel FF, Ufa, Aalesund, Raufoss, SK Herd, Aalesund II

*** Bjarnason - Andri Rúnar Bjarnason (a) 12/11/1990, Bolungarvík (Iceland) (b) 1,93 (c) F - center forward (d) Valur Reykjavík (e) ÍBV Vestmannaeyjar, Esbjerg fB, 1.FC Kaiserslautern, Helsingborgs IF, Grindavík, Víkingur, Grindavík, Víkingur, BÍ/Bol

*** Bjarnason - Aron Bjarnason (a) 14/10/1995, ¿? (Iceland) (b) 1,73 (c) F - left winger (d) IK Sirius (e) Újpest FC, Valur, Újpest FC, Breidablik, ÍBV Vestmannaeyjar, Fram Reykjavík, Thróttur

*** Bjarnason - Birkir Bjarnason (a) 27/05/1988, Akureyri (Iceland) (b) 1,84 (c) M - central midfielder (d) Brescia Calcio (e) Viking, Adana Demirspor, Brescia, Al-Arabi SC, Aston Villa, FC Basel, Pescara, Sampdoria, Pescara, Standard Liège, Pescara, Standard Liège, Viking, Bodø/Glimt, Viking

*** Bjarnason - Björgvin Máni Bjarnason (a) 06/05/2004, ¿? (Iceland) (b) - (c) M (d) Völsungur ÍF (e) KA Akureyri, Hamrarnir

*** Bjarnason - Brynjar Ingi Bjarnason (a) 06/12/1999, Akureyri (Iceland) (b) 1,94 (c) D - central defense (d) Hamarkameratene (e) Vålerenga, Lecce, KA Akureyri, Magni, KA Akureyri, Magni, KA Akureyri, Einherji, KA Akureyri

*** Bjarnason - Eidur Snorri Bjarnason (Eiður Snorri Bjarnason) (a) 14/03/2003, ¿? (Iceland) (b) - (c) M - right midfielder (d) KV Vesturbaejar (e) -

*** Bjarnason - Elmar Bjarnason (Theodór Elmar Bjarnason) (a) 04/03/1987, Reykjavík (Iceland) (b) 1,83 (c) M - central midfielder (d) KR Reykjavík (e) PAS Lamia, Akhisarspor, Gaziantep FK, Elazigspor, Aarhus GF, Randers FC, IFK Göteborg, Lyn

*** Bjarnason - Ernir Bjarnason (a) 22/08/1997, ¿? (Iceland) (b) 1,75 (c) M - central midfielder (d) Keflavík ÍF (e) Leiknir, Breidablik, Vestri, Breidablik, Fram Reykjavík, Breidablik

*** Bjärsmyr - Mattias Bjärsmyr (Nils Erik Mattias Bjärsmyr) (a) 03/01/1986, Hestra (Sweden) (b) 1,86 (c) D - central defense (d) Kungsbacka City FC (e) IFK Göteborg, Genclerbirligi, Sivasspor, IFK Göteborg, Panathinaikos, Rosenborg, Panathinaikos, IFK Göteborg, Husqvarna FF

*** Bjartalid - Jóannes Bjartalid (a) 10/07/1996, Tórshavn (Faroe Islands) (b) 1,80 (c) M - attacking midfielder (d) Fredrikstad FK (e) KÍ Klaksvík, KÍ II

*** Bjekovic - Marko Bjekovic (Марко Бјековић) (a) 21/09/2000, Novi Sad (Yugoslavia, now in Serbia) (b) 1,82 (c) D - right back (d) FK Vojvodina Novi Sad (e) Kabel Novi Sad, Vojvodina
*** Bjelica - David Bjelica (a) 02/10/1997, Podgorica (RF Yugoslavia, Montenegro) (b) 1,96 (c) G (d) FK Berane (e) TOSK Tesanj, Mladost, OSK Igalo, FK Bokelj, Mornar Bar, OSK Igalo, FK Bokelj
*** Bjelicic - Ognjen Bjelicic (Огњен Бјеличић) (a) 29/07/1997, Beograd (RF Yugoslavia, now in Serbia) (b) 1,84 (c) M - pivot (d) Hamrun Spartans (e) Radnicki Niš, FK Indjija, Sindjelic Bg, Viktoria Plzen B
*** Bjelland - Andreas Bjelland (a) 11/07/1988, Fredensborg (Denmark) (b) 1,88 (c) D - central defense (d) Lyngby BK (e) FC København, Lyngby BK, FC København, Brentford, FC Twente, Nordsjælland, Lyngby BK
*** Bjelos - Miroslav Bjelos (Мирослав Бјелош) (a) 29/10/1990, Novi Sad (Yugoslavia, now in Serbia) (b) 1,78 (c) M - pivot (d) FK Mladost GAT Novi Sad (e) Újpest FC, Napredak, Backa, Limón FC, Backa, Burlington SC, Backa, Burlington SC, Backa, Radnicki Sid, Backa, Futog
*** Bjerkebo - Isak Bjerkebo (a) 19/01/2003, ¿? (Sweden) (b) 1,72 (c) F - center forward (d) Skövde AIK (e) Kalmar FF
*** Bjørdal - Henrik Bjørdal (Henrik Rørvik Bjørdal) (a) 04/02/1997, Ålesund (Norway) (b) 1,88 (c) M - central midfielder (d) Vålerenga Fotball (e) Zulte Waregem, IFK Göteborg, Aalesund
*** Björgvinsson - Tómas Atli Björgvinsson (a) 14/06/2005, ¿? (Iceland) (b) - (c) M - central midfielder (d) ÍH Hafnarfjördur (e) Hafnarfjördur, ÍH, Hafnarfjördur, KFA Austfjarda, Hafnarfjördur, Fjardabyggd, Hafnarfjördur, Fjardabyggd
*** Björk - Carl Björk (a) 19/01/2000, ¿? (Sweden) (b) 1,88 (c) F - center forward (d) Brøndby IF (e) Norrköping, Trelleborg, Norrköping, Sylvia, Norrköping
*** Bjørkan - Fredrik Bjørkan (Fredrik André Bjørkan) (a) 21/08/1998, Bodø (Norway) (b) 1,80 (c) D - left back (d) FK Bodø/Glimt (e) Hertha Berlin, Feyenoord, Hertha Berlin, Bodø/Glimt
*** Björklund - William Björklund (a) 20/03/2002, ¿? (Sweden) (b) - (c) G (d) United IK Nordic (e) Hammarby TFF, Enskede IK, Hammarby TFF
*** Björkman - Daniel Björkman (Lars Daniel Björkman) (a) 21/02/1993, Falun (Sweden) (b) 1,84 (c) D - central defense (d) BK Forward (e) KÍ Klaksvík, Örebro SK, BK Forward, Brage
*** Björkqvist - Markus Björkqvist (a) 04/09/2003, Malmö (Sweden) (b) 1,81 (c) M - central midfielder (d) Trelleborgs FF (e) Malmö FF, Utsiktens BK, Malmö FF
*** Björkström - Tim Björkström (Tim Denny Björkström) (a) 08/01/1991, ¿? (Sweden) (b) 1,80 (c) D - central defense (d) Fredrikstad FK (e) Sirius, Djurgården, Östersund, Djurgården, Brommapojkarna, Gröndals IK, Brommapojkarna
*** Bjørlo - Morten Bjørlo (a) 04/10/1995, Jørpeland (Norway) (b) 1,76 (c) M - central midfielder (d) Rosenborg BK (e) HamKam, Strømmen, Egersund, Nest-Sotra IL, Egersund, Sola FK, Jørpeland, Staal II
*** Bjørnbak - Martin Bjørnbak (a) 22/03/1992, Mo i Rana (Norway) (b) 1,93 (c) D - central defense (d) Molde FK (e) Bodø/Glimt, Haugesund, Bodø/Glimt
*** Björnsson - Björn Aron Björnsson (a) 11/02/2001, ¿? (Iceland) (b) - (c) D - right back (d) KF Vídir (e) Keflavík, Reynir S., Keflavík, Vídir, Keflavík
*** Björnsson - Elís Rafn Björnsson (a) 13/10/1992, ¿? (Iceland) (b) - (c) D - right back (d) Fylkir Reykjavík (e) Stjarnan, Fjölnir, Stjarnan, Fylkir
*** Björnsson - Halldór Orri Björnsson (a) 02/03/1987, Reykjavík (Iceland) (b) 1,85 (c) M - attacking midfielder (d) - (e) Stjarnan, Hafnarfjördur, Stjarnan, Falkenbergs FF, Stjarnan, SC Pfullendorf, Stjarnan

*** Björnsson - Haraldur Björnsson (a) 11/01/1989, Reykjavík (Iceland) (b) 1,92 (c) G (d) Stjarnan Gardabaer (e) Lillestrøm, Östersund, Sarpsborg 08, Strømmen, Sarpsborg 08, Fredrikstad, Sarpsborg 08, Valur, Thróttur, Valur, Hearts FC II
*** Björnsson - Sigurdur Steinar Björnsson (Sigurður Steinar Björnsson) (a) 15/01/2004, ¿? (Iceland) (b) - (c) F - left winger (d) ÍF Grótta (e) Grótta, Víkingur
*** Björnsson - Sindri Björnsson (a) 29/03/1995, ¿? (Iceland) (b) 1,81 (c) M - central midfielder (d) Leiknir Reykjavík (e) Grindavík, Clemson Tigers, ÍBV Vestmannaeyjar, Clemson Tigers, Valur, Leiknir, Valur, Leiknir
*** Björnsson - Úlfur Ágúst Björnsson (a) 12/06/2003, ¿? (Iceland) (b) - (c) F - center forward (d) FH Hafnarfjördur (e) Njardvík, Hafnarfjördur, ÍH, Hafnarfjördur
*** Björnström - Axel Björnström (Axel Erik Gustaf Björnström) (a) 10/09/1995, Danderyd (Sweden) (b) 1,76 (c) D - left back (d) AIK Solna (e) Arsenal Tula, Sirius, Vasalunds IF
*** Bjørshol - Sondre Bjørshol (Sondre Flem Bjørshol) (a) 30/04/1994, Stavanger (Norway) (b) 1,84 (c) D - right back (d) Viking FK (e) Åsane, Vidar
*** Bjørtuft - Odin Bjørtuft (Odin Lurås Bjørtuft) (a) 19/12/1998, Porsgrunn (Norway) (b) 1,85 (c) D - central defense (d) FK Bodø/Glimt (e) Odd, Odd II, Eidanger IL
*** Bjur - Peter Bjur (a) 02/02/2000, ¿? (Denmark) (b) 1,80 (c) D - left back (d) Aarhus GF (e) Brøndby IF, B.93
*** Black - Conor Black (a) 01/03/2002, Kilmacrennan, Donegal (Ireland) (b) 1,80 (c) M - left midfielder (d) Dergview FC (e) Bonagee United, Finn Harps
*** Black - Johnny Black (John Reid Black) (a) 26/02/1988, Monkstown Ireland (Ireland) (b) 1,75 (c) M - pivot (d) - (e) Airbus UK, Northwich Vic, Crusaders, St. Kilda Celts, Oakleigh Cannon, Portadown, Linfield, Coleraine, Glentoran
*** Black - Stephen Black (a) 11/03/2002, ¿? (Ireland) (b) - (c) D - central defense (d) Dergview FC (e) Bonagee United, Finn Harps
*** Black - Stevie Black (Stephen Luke Black) (a) 19/02/2001, Leytonstone (England) (b) 1,78 (c) F - left winger (d) - (e) Europa Point FC
*** Blackman - César Blackman (César Rodolfo Blackman Camarena) (a) 02/04/1998, Panama City (Panamá) (b) 1,74 (c) D - right back (d) Slovan Bratislava (e) Dunajska Streda, Chorrillo FC
*** Blagaic - Jakov Blagaic (Jakov Blagaić) (a) 08/02/2000, Split (Croatia) (b) 1,73 (c) F - left winger (d) FK Borac Banja Luka (e) Hajduk Split, Siroki Brijeg, Hajduk Split, Hajduk Split II, Hajduk Split, Olimpija, Hajduk Split, Hajduk Split II, Adriatic Split
*** Blagojevic - Dario Blagojevic (Dario Blagojević) (a) 09/11/1989, Foca (Yugoslavia, Bosnia and Herzegovina) (b) - (c) F - center forward (d) FK Gorazde (e) Igman Konjic, HSK Posusje, FK Gorazde, FK Buducnost, FK Gorazde, Sloga Doboj, FK Gorazde, Sutjeska Foca, Jedinstvo Brcko, Mrkonjic, Sutjeska Foca
*** Blagojevic - Jovan Blagojevic (Jovan Blagojević) (a) 15/03/1988, Beograd (Yugoslavia, now in Serbia) (b) - (c) M - pivot (d) - (e) Velez Mostar, Radnik Bijelj., Ankaraspor, Altay SK, Ankaraspor, Zeljeznicar, Velez Mostar, Sindjelic Bg, Sumadija, FK Srem, Čukarički, Sindjelic Bg, Zeleznicar B.
*** Blagojevic - Slavko Blagojevic (Slavko Blagojević) (a) 21/03/1987, Otok (Yugoslavia, now in Croatia) (b) 1,79 (c) M - pivot (d) NK Istra 1961 (e) RFS, Zalgiris, RNK Split, NK Istra, NK Lucko, NK Granicar Zupanja, Cibalia, NK Granicar Zupanja, Cibalia
*** Blagojevic - Uros Blagojevic (Урош Благојевић) (a) 21/03/2002, Beograd (RF Yugoslavia, now in Serbia) (b) 1,93 (c) D - left back (d) Jedinstvo Bijelo Polje (e) Rad Beograd, Radnicki 1923, Novi Pazar, Graficar

*** Blahut - Patrik Blahut (Patrik Blahút) (a) 07/10/1997, Voznica (Slovakia) (b) 1,72 (c) M - right midfielder (d) FK Zeleziarne Podbrezova (e) Pohronie
*** Blair - Marley Blair (a) 05/10/1999, Huddersfield (England) (b) - (c) M - left midfielder (d) Farsley Celtic (e) Keflavík, Keflavík
*** Blakçori - Armend Blakçori (a) 06/08/1990, ¿? (RF Yugoslavia, now in Kosovo) (b) - (c) G (d) KF Feronikeli Drenas (e) KF Istogu, KF Ulpiana, KF Ferizaj, KF Liria, KF Hajvalia, FC Llapi, KF Hysi
*** Blakçori - Ilir Blakçori (a) 01/02/1993, Podujevë (RF Yugoslavia, now in Kosovo) (b) 1,73 (c) D - left back (d) KF Llapi (e) FC Drita, FC Llapi, KF Gjilani, FC Llapi
*** Blanaru - Stefan Blanaru (Ştefan Miluţă Blănaru) (a) 20/02/1989, Moldova Nouă (Romania) (b) 1,78 (c) F - center forward (d) CS Mioveni (e) FC Brasov-SR, CS Mioveni, AFC Turris, Petrolul, FC Hermannstadt, SSU Poli, Mil. Giarmata, Ripensia, FC Olt Slatina, National Sebis, CS Osorhei, Luceafarul, Mil. Giarmata
*** Blanco - Antonio Blanco (Antonio Blanco Conde) (a) 23/07/2000, Montalbán (Spain) (b) 1,76 (c) M - pivot (d) Deportivo Alavés (e) Real Madrid, Alavés, Real Madrid, Cádiz CF, Real Madrid, RM Castilla
*** Blanco - Domingo Blanco (Domingo Felipe Blanco) (a) 22/04/1995, Buenos Aires (Argentina) (b) 1,67 (c) M - central midfielder (d) SK Dnipro-1 (e) Independiente, Defensa y Justicia, Independiente, Olimpo II, Indep'te II, Olimpo II
*** Blanco - Lautaro Blanco (Lautaro Emanuel Blanco) (a) 19/02/1999, Rosario (SFE) (Argentina) (b) 1,76 (c) D - left back (d) Elche CF (e) Rosario Central, Elche CF, Rosario Central, Rosario Central II
*** Blanco - Lluis Blanco (Luis Emilio Blanco Coto) (a) 15/01/1990, Barcelona (Spain) (b) 1,83 (c) M - central midfielder (d) UE Engordany (e) FC Santa Coloma, Sant Julià, FC Santa Coloma, CD Carmelo
*** Blanco - Rubén Blanco (Rubén Blanco Veiga) (a) 25/07/1995, Mos (Spain) (b) 1,88 (c) G (d) Olympique Marseille (e) RC Celta, Ol. Marseille, RC Celta, Celta B
*** Blaney - Jacob Blaney (a) 08/09/2004, Coatbridge (Scotland) (b) 1,86 (c) D - central defense (d) Hibernian FC B (e) Stenhousemuir, Hibernian B
*** Blaney - Shane Blaney (a) 20/01/1999, Letterkenny, Donegal (Ireland) (b) 1,90 (c) D - central defense (d) Motherwell FC (e) Sligo Rovers, Doncaster Rovers, Grantham, Doncaster Rovers, Tamworth, Doncaster Rovers, Finn Harps
*** Blanik - Dawid Blanik (Dawid Błanik) (a) 15/04/1997, Jastrzębie Zdrój (Poland) (b) 1,73 (c) F - left winger (d) Korona Kielce (e) Sandecja, GKS Belchatow, Pogon Szczecin, Odra Opole, Pogon Szczecin, GKS Tychy, GKS Tychy II, AKS Mikolow
*** Blanuta - Vladislav Blanuta (Vladislav Blănuţă) (a) 12/01/2002, Hîncești (Moldova) (b) 1,90 (c) F - center forward (d) FC U Craiova 1948 (e) Pescara, FC U Craiova, Pescara
*** Blas - Ludovic Blas (a) 31/12/1997, Colombes (France) (b) 1,80 (c) M - attacking midfielder (d) Stade Rennais FC (e) FC Nantes, Guingamp, EA Guingamp B
*** Blaschka - Jett Blaschka (a) 16/09/1999, Racine, Wisconsin (United States) (b) 1,88 (c) D - right back (d) FC Manchester 62 (e) Pittsburgh CUFC, Golden Eagles, Bavarian United
*** Blasucci - Noah Blasucci (Noah Matteo Blasucci) (a) 19/06/1999, Aadorf (Switzerland) (b) 1,75 (c) M - attacking midfielder (d) - (e) SC Brühl SG, FC Wil 1900, Rapperswil-Jona, FC Chiasso, FC Sion, FC Vaduz, FC St. Gallen
*** Blaswich - Janis Blaswich (Janis Jonathan Blaswich) (a) 02/05/1991, Willich (Germany) (b) 1,93 (c) G (d) RB Leipzig (e) Heracles Almelo, Borussia Mönchengladbach, Hansa Rostock, Borussia Mönchengladbach, Dynamo Dresden, Borussia Mönchengladbach, Borussia Mönchengladbach II

*** Blauensteiner - Michael Blauensteiner (a) 11/02/1995, Wien (Austria) (b) 1,82 (c) D - right back (d) - (e) Austria Klagenfurt, SKN St. Pölten, Young Violets, Austria Viena, Suduva, Austria Viena, TSV Hartberg, Austria Viena, Austria Wien Reserves
*** Blazek - Filip Blazek (Filip Blažek) (a) 11/03/1998, Skalica (Slovakia) (b) 1,89 (c) D - central defense (d) FC Banik Ostrava (e) Skalica, Brøndby IF, Skalica, Brøndby IF, FK Senica
*** Blazevic - Ante Blazevic (Ante Blažević) (a) 05/05/1996, Split (Croatia) (b) 1,77 (c) D - right back (d) - (e) Levski Sofia, Zeljeznicar, Celik Zenica, NK Brezice 1919, VfV Hildesheim, Junak Sinj, KV Oostende
*** Blazevic - Davor Blazevic (Davor Blažević) (a) 07/02/1993, Falun (Sweden) (b) 1,90 (c) G (d) Hammarby IF (e) GIF Sundsvall, Hammarby IF, Assyriska FF, AFC Eskilstuna, Brommapojkarna, Gröndals IK
*** Blazevski - Martin Blazevski (a) 13/05/1992, Skopje (North Macedonia) (b) 1,80 (c) M - pivot (d) Vardar Skopje (e) FK Skopje, Vardar, FK Skopje, Borec Veles, Makedonija, Pelister Bitola, FC Drita, Teteks Tetovo, Gostivar, Teteks Tetovo, Vardar, Teteks Tetovo, Ohrid Lihnidos, Metalurg Skopje, Lokomotiva, Metalurg Skopje, Vardar
*** Blazic - Miha Blazic (Miha Blažič) (a) 08/05/1993, Koper (Slovenia) (b) 1,85 (c) D - central defense (d) Lech Poznan (e) Angers SCO, Ferencváros, Domžale, Koper
*** Blázquez - Joaquín Blázquez (a) 28/01/2001, Luque (Argentina) (b) 1,93 (c) G (d) CA Platense (e) Platense, Talleres, Stade Brestois, Talleres, Talleres II
*** Blecha - Filip Blecha (a) 16/07/1997, ¿? (Czech Rep.) (b) 1,85 (c) M - central midfielder (d) Slezsky FC Opava (e) Slavia Praha, Zbrojovka Brno, Slavia Praha, Vlasim, Bohemians 1905, Vlasim, Bohemians 1905, FC MAS Taborsko, Bohemians 1905
*** Blesa - Jalen Blesa (Jalen Aleix Miller Blesa) (a) 05/02/2001, Barcelona (Spain) (b) 1,87 (c) F - center forward (d) FC Prishtina (e) KF Rahoveci, KF Istogu, Arlesey Town
*** Bleve - Marco Bleve (a) 18/10/1995, San Cesario di Lecce (Italy) (b) 1,84 (c) G (d) Carrarese Calcio 1908 (e) Carrarese, Lecce, Catanzaro, Lecce, Ternana U., Lecce, Martina Franca, Lecce
*** Blidar - Alexandru Blidar (Alexandru Krisztian Blidar) (a) 19/12/2002, Budapest (Hungary) (b) 1,79 (c) M - right midfielder (d) FC U Craiova 1948 (e) -
*** Blikstad - Eirik Blikstad (Eirik Espelid Blikstad) (a) 16/05/2004, Oslo (Norway) (b) 1,85 (c) D - central defense (d) Strømsgodset IF (e) Strømsgodset II
*** Blin - Alexis Blin (a) 16/09/1996, Le Mans (France) (b) 1,84 (c) M - pivot (d) US Lecce (e) Amiens SC, Toulouse, Amiens SC, Toulouse, Toulouse B, FC Le Mans B
*** Blind - Daley Blind (a) 09/03/1990, Amsterdam (Netherlands) (b) 1,80 (c) D - left back (d) Girona FC (e) Bayern München, Ajax, Manchester Utd., Ajax, FC Groningen, Ajax, Ajax B
*** Bliznichenko - Andriy Bliznichenko (Блізніченко Андрій Валерійович) (a) 24/07/1994, Novograd-Volynskyi, Zhytomyr Oblast (Ukraine) (b) 1,79 (c) F - right winger (d) NK Veres Rivne (e) Ingulets, FC Sheriff, Karabükspor, Dnipro, Dnipro II
*** Bliznichenko - Viktor Bliznichenko (Блізніченко Віктор Валерійович) (a) 29/09/2002, Novograd-Volynskyi, Zhytomyr Oblast (Ukraine) (b) 1,74 (c) F - left winger (d) Kryvbas Kryvyi Rig (e) Kryvbas, Ingulets, Dinamo Kiev II
*** Bllaca - Aridon Bllaca (a) 03/05/2001, ¿? (RF Yugoslavia, now in Kosovo) (b) - (c) G (d) SC Gjilani (e) -
*** Blokhin - Danil Blokhin (Блохин Данил) (a) 26/08/2003, ¿? (Kazakhstan) (b) 1,77 (c) D - left back (d) Shakhter-Bulat (e) -

*** Blokzijl - Thijmen Blokzijl (a) 25/02/2005, Groningen (Netherlands) (b) 1,90 (c) D - central defense (d) FC Groningen (e) -
*** Blom - Jordi Blom (a) 05/06/2002, Amsterdam (Netherlands) (b) - (c) F - right winger (d) Quick Boys (e) FC Volendam
*** Blomme - Xander Blomme (a) 21/06/2002, Eeklo (Belgium) (b) 1,72 (c) M - pivot (d) Go Ahead Eagles Deventer (e) Club NXT
*** Blomqvist - Alexander Blomqvist (Johan Nicklas Alexander Blomqvist) (a) 03/08/1994, Simrishamn (Sweden) (b) 1,85 (c) D - central defense (d) GIF Sundsvall (e) Trelleborg, Malmö FF, Värnamo, Malmö FF
*** Blomqvist - Andreas Blomqvist (a) 05/05/1992, ¿? (Sweden) (b) 1,82 (c) M - central midfielder (d) - (e) Mjällby AIF, Norrköping, Aalborg BK, Mjällby AIF
*** Bloom - James Bloom (a) 11/08/1991, Cardiff (Wales) (b) - (c) M - central midfielder (d) - (e) Pontypridd, Mangotsfield, Cinderford, Newtown, Port Talbot, Gloucester, Falkirk FC, Alloa Athletic, Falkirk FC, Alloa Athletic
*** Blorian - Or Blorian (אור בלוריאן) (a) 07/03/2000, Petah Tikva (Israel) (b) 1,88 (c) D - central defense (d) Hapoel Tel Aviv (e) Hapoel Tel Aviv, H. Beer Sheva, M. Petah Tikva
*** Blotskiy - Arseniy Blotskiy (Блоцкий Арсений Алексеевич) (a) 18/06/2004, Minsk (Belarus) (b) 1,71 (c) M - pivot (d) BATE Borisov II (e) -
*** Blum - Danny Blum (a) 07/01/1991, Frankenthal (Germany) (b) 1,84 (c) F - left winger (d) - (e) 1.FC Nürnberg, APOEL FC, VfL Bochum, Eintracht, UD Las Palmas, Eintracht, 1.FC Nürnberg, SV Sandhausen, Karlsruher SC, SV Sandhausen
*** Blum - Lewin Blum (a) 27/07/2001, Rothrist AG (Switzerland) (b) 1,81 (c) D - right back (d) BSC Young Boys (e) Yverdon Sport, BSC Young Boys
*** Blume - Bror Blume (Bror Emil Blume Jensen) (a) 22/01/1992, Kopenhagen (Denmark) (b) 1,78 (c) M - central midfielder (d) WSG Tirol (e) Aarhus GF, Lyngby BK
*** Blummé - Viggo Blummé (a) 07/10/2004, ¿? (Finland) (b) - (c) D - left back (d) HJK Klubi 04 Helsinki (e) -
*** Bnou Marzouk - Younes Bnou Marzouk (مرزوق بنو يونس) (a) 02/03/1996, Freyming-Merlebach (France) (b) 1,87 (c) F - center forward (d) - (e) FC Rapid 1923, FC Chiasso, FC Lugano, Sliema Wanderers, FC Lugano, Dalkurd, FC Lugano, Juventus, FC Chiasso, Juventus, Angers SCO B, Juventus, KVC Westerlo
*** Bö - Hans Pauli á Bö (a) 29/10/2005, ¿? (Faroe Islands) (b) - (c) M - left midfielder (d) EB/Streymur (e) -
*** Boadu - Myron Boadu (a) 14/01/2001, Amsterdam (Netherlands) (b) 1,81 (c) F - center forward (d) AS Mónaco (e) AZ Alkmaar
*** Boahene - Ernest Boahene (a) 06/03/2000, Accra (Ghana) (b) 1,72 (c) D - right back (d) Strømsgodset IF (e) FC Metz, Rainbow FC, Paris FC, Rainbow FC
*** Boakye - Augustine Boakye (a) 03/11/2000, Bompata (Ghana) (b) 1,78 (c) M - attacking midfielder (d) Wolfsberger AC (e) WAFA SC
*** Boakye - Eric Boakye (a) 19/11/1999, Accra (Ghana) (b) 1,73 (c) D - right back (d) Aris Limassol (e) Olimpija, Asokwa FC, Olimpija, Asokwa FC
*** Boakye - Richmond Boakye (Richmond Yiadom Boakye) (a) 28/01/1993, Accra (Ghana) (b) 1,86 (c) F - center forward (d) Selangor FC (e) Al-Akhdar SC, PAS Lamia, B. Jerusalem, Górnik Zabrze, Crvena zvezda, JS Suning, Crvena zvezda, Latina Calcio, Crvena zvezda, Latina Calcio, Atalanta, Latina Calcio, Atalanta, Roda JC, Atalanta, Juventus, Elche CF, Juventus, Sassuolo, Juventus, Genoa, Sassuolo, Genoa
*** Boakye (c) F - center forward (d) Newtown AFC (e) - - Hanoch Boakye (c) F - center forward (d) Newtown AFC (e) -

*** Boamah - Michael Boamah (a) 16/04/2003, ¿? (Finland) (b) - (c) D - central defense (d) HJK Klubi 04 Helsinki (e) VJS Vantaa, HJK Klubi 04, Imatran PS
*** Boateng - David Boateng (David Lionel Akrobor-Boateng) (a) 08/05/2001, ¿? (England) (b) 1,76 (c) D - right back (d) - (e) Dover Athletic, Queen's Park
*** Boateng - Emmanuel Boateng (a) 17/06/1997, Akwatia (Ghana) (b) - (c) M - central midfielder (d) IF Elfsborg (e) Hapoel Tel Aviv, Aduana Stars, WAFA SC, Feyenoord Ghana
*** Boateng - Emmanuel Boateng (Emmanuel Okyere Boateng) (a) 23/05/1996, Accra (Ghana) (b) 1,75 (c) F - center forward (d) Rio Ave FC (e) Dalian PFC, Levante UD, Moreirense, Rio Ave, Charity Stars
*** Boateng - Jérôme Boateng (Jérôme Agyenim Boateng) (a) 03/09/1988, Berlin (Germany) (b) 1,92 (c) D - central defense (d) - (e) Olympique Lyon, Bayern München, Manchester City, SV Hamburg, Hertha Berlin, Hertha BSC II
*** Boateng - Kelvin Boateng (Kelvin Owusu Boateng) (a) 24/03/2000, Accra (Ghana) (b) 1,84 (c) F - center forward (d) First Vienna FC (e) Spartak Trnava, Karvina, Spartak Trnava, FC Porto B, Right to Dream
*** Boateng - Kennedy Boateng (Kennedy Kofi Boateng) (a) 29/11/1996, ¿? (Ghana) (b) 1,91 (c) D - central defense (d) - (e) Santa Clara, SV Ried, LASK, SV Ried, LASK, WAFA SC
*** Boateng - Kevin-Prince Boateng (a) 06/03/1987, Berlin (Germany) (b) 1,86 (c) M - attacking midfielder (d) Jérôme Boateng (e) Hertha Berlin, Monza, Fiorentina, Besiktas, Fiorentina, Sassuolo, FC Barcelona, Sassuolo, Eintracht, UD Las Palmas, AC Milan, FC Schalke 04, AC Milan, Genoa, AC Milan, Genoa, FC Portsmouth, Tottenham Hotspur, Borussia Dortmund, Tottenham Hotspur, Hertha Berlin, Hertha BSC II
*** Boateng - Nana Boateng (Bismark Adjei-Boateng) (a) 10/05/1994, Accra (Ghana) (b) 1,80 (c) M - pivot (d) Jeonbuk Hyundai Motors (e) CFR Cluj, KuPS, Colorado, Strømsgodset, Right to Dream
*** Boateng Welbeck - Richard Boateng Welbeck (a) 10/07/1992, Accra (Ghana) (b) 1,80 (c) M - central midfielder (d) Hapoel Petah Tikva (e) M. Bnei Reineh, FC Cartagena, Alcorcón, Real Oviedo, Alcorcón, Real Oviedo, UD Melilla, Extremadura, Granada B, San Roque Lepe, Granada B, Cádiz CF, Granada B, Liberty Prof.
*** Bobál - Dávid Bobál (a) 31/08/1995, Pásztó (Hungary) (b) 1,88 (c) D - central defense (d) MTK Budapest (e) Mezőkövesd, MTK Budapest, Mezőkövesd, Zalaegerszeg, Paksi FC, Dukla Praha, Honvéd, Soproni VSE, Honvéd
*** Bobál - Gergely Bobál (a) 31/08/1995, Pásztó (Hungary) (b) 1,88 (c) F - center forward (d) - (e) Vasas FC, Mezőkövesd, Vasas FC, Nacional, Zalaegerszeg, Csákvár, Honvéd, Zalaegerszeg, Honvéd, Wolfsburg II, Honvéd, Gyirmót FC, Honvéd
*** Boban - Gabrijel Boban (a) 23/07/1989, Požega (Yugoslavia, now in Croatia) (b) 1,85 (c) F - left winger (d) HSK Posusje (e) NK Varazdin, FC Sheriff, NK Osijek, NK Zagreb, NK Pomorac, NK Vinogradar, NK Virovitica, Kamen Ingrad
*** Bobcek - Tomas Bobcek (Tomáš Bobček) (a) 08/09/2001, Ružomberok (Slovakia) (b) 1,86 (c) F - center forward (d) MFK Ružomberok (e) Ruzomberok B
*** Bobchenok - Nikita Bobchenok (Бобчёнок Никита Николаевич) (a) 04/09/1999, Mogilev (Belarus) (b) 1,76 (c) M - central midfielder (d) FK Orsha (e) Dnepr Mogilev, Dnyapro II
*** Bobcik - Libor Bobcik (Libor Bobčík) (a) 08/08/2002, ¿? (Czech Rep.) (b) 1,86 (c) F - center forward (d) FC Zlin B (e) Hodonin, FC Zlin B
*** Bober - Ivan Bober (Бобёр Иван Антонович) (a) 07/01/2006, Samara (Russia) (b) 1,79 (c) M - left midfielder (d) Krylya Sovetov Samara II (e) -

*** Bobic - Luka Bobic (Luka Bobić) (a) 08/02/2002, Banja Luka (Bosnia and Herzegovina) (b) 1,86 (c) D - central defense (d) FK Sloboda Mrkonjic Grad (e) Borac Banja Luka, Ljubic Prnjavor, Borac Banja Luka, Ljubic Prnjavor, Borac Banja Luka, Kozara Gradiska, Borac Banja Luka
*** Bobicanec - Luka Bobicanec (Luka Bobičanec) (a) 23/05/1993, Čakovec (Croatia) (b) 1,78 (c) M - attacking midfielder (d) NK Celje (e) NS Mura, NK Polet SMnM, NK Nafta 1903, Heiligenbrunn, Stegersbach, NK Cakovec, Medjimurje
*** Bobichon - Antonin Bobichon (a) 14/09/1995, Bagnols-sur-Cèze (France) (b) 1,78 (c) M - central midfielder (d) Stade Lavallois (e) Angers SCO, AS Nancy, Angers SCO, Nîmes, CA Bastia, Nîmes, Nîmes B
*** Bobjerg - Marcus Bobjerg (Marcus Bobjerg Jakobsen) (a) 26/01/1998, ¿? (Denamrk) (b) - (c) G (d) AC Horsens (e) Skive IK, AC Horsens
*** Bobko - Igor Bobko (Бобко Игорь Анатольевич) (a) 09/09/1985, Osa (Soviet Union, now in Russia) (b) 1,76 (c) M - left midfielder (d) Kronon Stolbtsy (e) FK Baranovichi, FK Slutsk, Gorodeya, FK Postavy, Lokomotiv Minsk, Atlant Kobrin
*** Bobko - Ivan Bobko (Бобко Іван Михайлович) (a) 10/12/1990, Odessa (Soviet Union, now in Ukraine) (b) 1,81 (c) M - attacking midfielder (d) - (e) Chornomorets, Karpaty Lviv, Chornomorets, LNZ Cherkasy, Sfintul Gheorghe, Torpedo Kutaisi, Okzhetpes, AFC Eskilstuna, Chornomorets, Debrecen, Metalist, Chornomorets, Chornomorets II
*** Boboc - Radu Boboc (Radu Ştefăniţă Boboc) (a) 24/04/1999, Craiova (Romania) (b) 1,80 (c) D - right back (d) FC Voluntari (e) FCSB, FCV Farul, Academia Hagi
*** Boboev - Sheriddin Boboev (Шериддин Зоирович Бобоев) (a) 21/04/1999, Dushanbe (Tajikistan) (b) 1,82 (c) F - center forward (d) - (e) Sanat Naft, Maktaaral, Penang, Istiqlol, Barqchi
*** Bobsin - Bobsin (Victor Bobsin Pereira) (a) 12/01/2000, Osório (Brazil) (b) 1,84 (c) M - pivot (d) Daegu FC (e) Daegu FC, Santa Clara, Grêmio Porto Alegre, Grêmio Porto Alegre B
*** Bobzien - Ben Bobzien (a) 29/04/2003, Gießen (Germany) (b) 1,74 (c) F - right winger (d) SC Austria Lustenau (e) Austria Lustenau, Mainz 05, SV Elversberg, Mainz 05, FSV Mainz 05 II
*** Bocat - Eric Junior Bocat (a) 16/07/1999, ¿? (France) (b) 1,82 (c) D - left back (d) Sint-Truidense VV (e) Excelsior Mouscron, LOSC Lille B, Brest B, Dijon FCO B
*** Bocchetti - Christian Bocchetti (a) 24/06/2002, Giugliano in Campania (Italy) (b) 1,85 (c) D - central defense (d) SC Faetano (e) S. Vito Positano, Costa Amalfi, Brindisi
*** Bocharov - Pavel Bocharov (Бочаров Павел Сергеевич) (a) 21/06/2005, ¿? (Russia) (b) 1,81 (c) D - central defense (d) FK Rostov II (e) -
*** Bocherov - Valeriy Bocherov (Бочеров Валерий Юрьевич) (a) 10/08/2000, Minsk (Belarus) (b) 1,82 (c) M - pivot (d) BATE Borisov (e) BATE II, FK Slutsk, BATE II, Smolevichi, BATE II
*** Bochnak - Mateusz Bochnak (Mateusz Bochnak) (a) 11/02/1998, Szczecin (Poland) (b) 1,79 (c) M - right midfielder (d) Cracovia (e) Chrobry Glogow, Blekitni, Pogon Szczecin, Pogon Siedlce, Pogon Szczecin, Pogon II, S. Szczecin, AP Pogon
*** Bochniewicz - Pawel Bochniewicz (Paweł Piotr Bochniewicz) (a) 30/01/1996, Dębica (Poland) (b) 1,94 (c) D - central defense (d) SC Heerenveen (e) Górnik Zabrze, Udinese, Górnik Zabrze, Udinese, Granada B, Reggina
*** Boci - Muco Boci (a) 09/06/2003, Delvinë (Albania) (b) - (c) M - attacking midfielder (d) KF Teuta (e) -
*** Bockaj - Petar Bockaj (Petar Bočkaj) (a) 23/07/1996, Zagreb (Croatia) (b) 1,79 (c) D - left back (d) Pafos FC (e) Pafos FC, Dinamo Zagreb, NK Osijek, NK

Lokomotiva, Inter Zaprešić, NK Maksimir, Inter Zaprešić, NK Maksimir, Inter Zaprešić, NK Maksimir
*** Bockus - Vilius Bockus (Vilius Bočkus) (a) 26/08/2003, ¿? (Lithuania) (b) - (c) D (d) FK Banga Gargzdai B (e) -
*** Bocskay - Bertalan Bocskay (a) 02/03/2002, Budapest (Hungary) (b) 1,85 (c) M - central midfielder (d) Budapest Honvéd FC (e) FK TSC, Honvéd
*** Boda - Martin Boda (Martin Boďa) (a) 02/02/1997, ¿? (Slovakia) (b) 1,94 (c) F - center forward (d) MFK Ružomberok (e) Fomat Martin, Bela-Dulice, Maly Cepcin
*** Bodart - Arnaud Bodart (a) 11/03/1998, Seraing (Belgium) (b) 1,86 (c) G (d) Standard de Lieja (e) -
*** Böde - Dániel Böde (a) 21/10/1986, Szekszárd (Hungary) (b) 1,90 (c) F - center forward (d) Paksi FC (e) Ferencváros, Paksi FC
*** Bódi - Ádám Bódi (a) 18/10/1990, Nyiregyháza (Hungary) (b) 1,73 (c) M - right midfielder (d) Debreceni VSC (e) Vidi FC, Debrecen, Videoton FC, Debrecen, Debrecen II
*** Bodnár - Attila Bodnár (a) 29/01/2005, Eger (Hungary) (b) 1,70 (c) M - attacking midfielder (d) Putnok FC (e) Mezőkövesd, Mezőkövesd II
*** Bodor - Zoltán Bodor (a) 04/03/2003, ¿? (Hungary) (b) - (c) F - center forward (d) Kecskeméti TE (e) Szegedi VSE
*** Bodul - Darko Bodul (a) 11/01/1989, Sarajevo (Yugoslavia, now in Bosnia and Herzegovina) (b) 1,86 (c) F - attacking midfielder (d) FK Igman Konjic (e) FK Sarajevo, Ankaraspor, Soligorsk, Enisey, Amkar Perm, Dundee United, SCR Altach, Odense BK, Sturm Graz, Nacional, Ajax, Sparta Rotterdam, Ajax, Ajax B
*** Bodurov - Nikolay Bodurov (Николай Георгиев Бодуров) (a) 30/05/1986, Blagoevgrad (Bulgaria) (b) 1,82 (c) D - central defense (d) Pirin Blagoevgrad (e) Esteghlal FC, CSKA-Sofia, Fulham, Midtjylland, Fulham, Litex Lovetch, Pirin
*** Boer - Pietro Boer (a) 12/05/2002, Mestre (Italy) (b) 1,93 (c) G (d) AS Roma (e) -
*** Boere - Tom Boere (a) 24/11/1992, Breda (Netherlands) (b) 1,83 (c) F - center forward (d) NAC Breda (e) SC Cambuur, SV Meppen, Türkgücü Münch., KFC Uerdingen, FC Twente, FC Oss, FC Eindhoven, KAA Gent, Hoogstraten VV, KAA Gent, Ajax B
*** Boëtius - Jean-Paul Boëtius (Jean-Paul Patrick Boëtius) (a) 22/03/1994, Rotterdam (Netherlands) (b) 1,78 (c) M - attacking midfielder (d) - (e) Hertha Berlin, Mainz 05, Feyenoord, FC Basel, KRC Genk, FC Basel, Feyenoord
*** Boets - Keo Boets (a) 21/12/2003, ¿? (Belgium) (b) 1,89 (c) G (d) - (e) Sint-Truiden
*** Boev - Velislav Boev (Велислав Петров Боев) (a) 19/12/2003, Varna (Bulgaria) (b) 1,70 (c) D - left back (d) Spartak Varna (e) Spartak Varna
*** Boey - Sacha Boey (a) 13/09/2000, Montreuil (France) (b) 1,78 (c) D - right back (d) Galatasaray (e) Stade Rennes, Dijon, Stade Rennes, Stade Rennes B
*** Boffelli - Valerio Boffelli (a) 04/09/2004, Santa Maria Capua Vetere (Italy) (b) 1,85 (c) G (d) Cavese 1919 (e) Cavese
*** Boffin - Ruud Boffin (Ruud Jorge Boffin) (a) 05/11/1987, Sint-Truiden (Belgium) (b) 1,96 (c) G (d) - (e) Antalyaspor, Eskisehirspor, West Ham Utd., MVV Maastricht, VVV-Venlo, MVV Maastricht, PSV Eindhoven, FC Eindhoven
*** Boga - Jérémie Boga (a) 03/01/1997, Marseille (France) (b) 1,74 (c) F - left winger (d) OGC Niza (e) Atalanta, Sassuolo, Atalanta, Sassuolo, Birmingham City, Granada CF, Stade Rennes
*** Bogaciuc - Victor Bogaciuc (a) 17/10/1999, Rezina (Moldova) (b) 1,85 (c) M - central midfielder (d) FC Petrocub Hîncești (e) Zimbru Chisinau

*** Bogacz - Wiktor Bogacz (a) 14/07/2004, Starachowice (Poland) (b) 1,93 (c) F - center forward (d) Miedź Legnica (e) Miedz Legnica II
*** Bogarde - Lamare Bogarde (Lamare Trenton Chansey Bogarde) (a) 05/01/2004, Rotterdam (Netherlands) (b) 1,85 (c) M - pivot (d) - (e) Bristol Rovers
*** Bogarde - Melayro Bogarde (Melayro Chakewno Jalaino Bogarde) (a) 28/05/2002, Rotterdam (Netherlands) (b) 1,86 (c) M - pivot (d) TSG 1899 Hoffenheim II (e) Hoffenheim, PEC Zwolle, Hoffenheim, FC Groningen, Hoffenheim
*** Bogdán - Ádám Bogdán (a) 27/09/1987, Budapest (Hungary) (b) 1,94 (c) G (d) - (e) Ferencváros, Hibernian FC, Liverpool, Hibernian FC, Liverpool, Wigan Ath., Liverpool, Bolton Wanderers, Crewe Alexandra, Bolton Wanderers, Vasas SC, Vecsés, Vasas SC
*** Bogdanets - Kirill Bogdanets (Богданец Кирилл Викторович) (a) 28/03/2004, Krasnodar (Russia) (b) 1,80 (c) F - right winger (d) FK Krasnodar-2 (e) Krasnodar II
*** Bogdanoski - Aleksandar Bogdanoski (Александар Богданоски) (a) 28/03/2005, Struga (North Macedonia) (b) 1,83 (c) F - center forward (d) Kozuf Gevgelija (e) -
*** Bogdanov - Andriy Bogdanov (Богданов Андрій Євгенович) (a) 21/01/1990, Kyiv (Soviet Union, now in Ukraine) (b) 1,82 (c) M - central midfielder (d) Kolos Kovalivka (e) Desna, Arka Gdynia, Olimpik Donetsk, Volyn Lutsk, FC Saxan, Metalist, Ergotelis, Metalist, Dinamo Kyïv, Arsenal Kyiv, Dinamo Kyïv, Arsenal Kyiv, PFK Oleksandria, Arsenal Kyiv, Arsenal Kyiv II, Dynamo 3 Kyiv
*** Bogdanovic - Pavle Bogdanovic (a) 10/05/2003, Niš (Serbia and Montenegro, now in Serbia) (b) - (c) M (d) FK Radnicki Pirot (e) Radnicki Pirot, Radnicki Niš
*** Bogdanovic - Slavisa Bogdanovic (Slaviša Bogdanović) (a) 11/10/1993, Trebinje (Bosnia and Herzegovina) (b) 1,93 (c) G (d) Al-Qaisumah FC (e) Velez Mostar, Zarkovo, Smederevo 1924, FK BSK Borča, Srem Jakovo, Radnik, Dorcol, Spartak, FK Palic Koming, Spartak, Rad Beograd, Leotar Trebinje
*** Bogdanovic - Vuk Bogdanovic (Вук Богдановић) (a) 03/04/2002, Beograd (RF Yugoslavia, Serbia) (b) 1,90 (c) D - central defense (d) FK Vozdovac (e) Vozdovac, Vojvodina, Crvena zvezda, Rad Beograd, Spartak
*** Bogdanovic - Vukasin Bogdanovic (Вукашин Богдановић) (a) 04/10/2002, Prokuplje (RF Yugoslavia, now in Serbia) (b) 1,84 (c) F - center forward (d) FK Radnik Surdulica (e) Vojvodina, Backa, Vojvodina, Kabel Novi Sad
*** Bogdanovich - Ilya Bogdanovich (Богданович Илья Геннадьевич) (a) 30/01/2004, Baranovichi (Belarus) (b) - (c) D (d) Dynamo Brest (e) -
*** Bogdanovski - Nikola Bogdanovski (Никола Богдановски) (a) 25/01/1999, Pančevo (RF Yugoslavia, now in Serbia) (b) 1,79 (c) F - right winger (d) FK Novi Pazar (e) Radnik, Novi Pazar, Radnik, Zarkovo, Radnik, FK Bezanija, Rad Beograd
*** Bogicevic - Mihailo Bogicevic (Михаило Богићевић) (a) 30/05/1998, Lausanne (Switzerland) (b) 1,91 (c) D - central defense (d) FK Spartak Subotica (e) FK Loznica
*** Bogojevic - Bruno Bogojevic (Bruno Bogojević) (a) 29/06/1998, Koprivnica (Croatia) (b) 1,79 (c) F - right winger (d) HNK Rijeka (e) Slaven Belupo, NK Novigrad, Slaven Belupo
*** Bogomolskiy - Egor Bogomolskiy (Багамольскі Ягор Аляксандравіч) (a) 03/06/2000, Valerianovo (Belarus) (b) 1,86 (c) F - center forward (d) Neftchi Baku (e) FK Minsk, Rukh, FK Minsk, Rukh, Dynamo Brest II, Rukh, Dynamo Brest II, Dinamo Minsk, Dinamo Minsk II
*** Bogosavac - Miroslav Bogosavac (Мирослав Богосавац) (a) 14/10/1996, Sremska Mitrovica (RF Yugoslavia, now in Serbia) (b) 1,76 (c) D - left back (d) Akhmat Grozny (e) Čukarički, Akhmat Grozny, Čukarički, FK Partizan, Teleoptik, FK Partizan, Teleoptik, FK Partizan

*** Bogunov - Yaroslav Bogunov (Богунов Ярослав Геннадійович) (a) 04/09/1993, Lugansk (Ukraine) (b) 1,69 (c) F - left winger (d) Ingulets Petrove (e) PFK Lviv, Dinaz Vyshgorod, Sperre) PFC Lviv, Krumkachi, FK Polissya, Krumkachi, Naftan, Belshina, TSG Neustrelitz, FK Stakhanov, Metalist II
*** Bohar - Damjan Bohar (a) 18/10/1991, Murska Sobota (Slovenia) (b) 1,72 (c) F - left winger (d) Zagłębie Lubin (e) NK Osijek, Zagłębie, NK Maribor, NS Mura
*** Bohinen - Emil Bohinen (a) 12/03/1999, Derby (England) (b) 1,89 (c) M - central midfielder (d) US Salernitana 1919 (e) CSKA Moskva, Salernitana, CSKA Moskva, Stabæk
*** Böhm - Sebastien Böhm (a) 09/08/2000, ¿? (Czech Rep.) (b) 1,94 (c) D - central defense (d) SK Dynamo Ceske Budejovice B (e) FK Nyrsko, Robst. Prestice
*** Bohman - Filip Bohman (a) 24/11/1996, ¿? (Sweden) (b) 1,85 (c) F - center forward (d) Trelleborgs FF (e) Varbergs BoIS, BK Olympic, Lunds BK, BK Olympic, Skurups AIF
*** Bohnert - Florian Bohnert (a) 09/11/1997, Luxembourg (Luxembourg) (b) 1,82 (c) D - right back (d) SC Bastia (e) Progrès Niederkorn, FSV Mainz 05 II, FK Pirmasens, Schalke 04 II
*** Boiciuc - Alexandru Boiciuc (a) 21/08/1997, Chișinău (Moldova) (b) 1,91 (c) F - center forward (d) CSA Steaua (e) FC Buzau, Universitatea Cluj, Turris, Academica Clinceni, Karpaty, Vejle BK, FC Sheriff, Sfintul Gheorghe, FC Sheriff, Vejle BK, Milsami, ASA Tg. Mures, ACSM Poli Iasi, Milsami, ACSM Poli Iasi, Rapid Suceava, CSMS Iași
*** Boico - Vladislav Boico (a) 27/09/2006, Bălți (Moldova) (b) - (c) D - central defense (d) FC Bălți (e) SSS Balti
*** Boilesen - Nicolai Boilesen (Nicolai Møller Boilesen) (a) 16/02/1992, Ballerup (Denmark) (b) 1,86 (c) D - central defense (d) FC Copenhague (e) Ajax, Ajax B
*** Boisgard - Quentin Boisgard (a) 17/03/1997, Toulouse (France) (b) 1,74 (c) M - attacking midfielder (d) FC Lorient (e) Pau FC, FC Lorient, Toulouse, Pau FC, Toulouse, Toulouse B
*** Bojanczyk - Kacper Bojanczyk (Kacper Bojańczyk) (a) 04/01/2005, Piaseczno (Poland) (b) 1,75 (c) M - attacking midfielder (d) Korona Kielce (e) Korona Kielce II
*** Bojang - Momodou Bojang (a) 19/06/2001, Brikama (Gambia) (b) 1,82 (c) F - center forward (d) Kawkab Marrakech (e) Real de Banjul, Rainbow FC, Hibernian FC, Rainbow FC, Casa Sports, Brikama United
*** Bojanic - Darijan Bojanic (Darijan Bojanić) (a) 28/12/1994, Gislaved (Sweden) (b) 1,86 (c) M - central midfielder (d) Ulsan Hyundai (e) Hammarby IF, Helsingborgs IF, Östersund, Helsingborgs IF, IFK Göteborg, Östers IF
*** Bojanic - Nemanja Bojanic (a) 04/02/2006, ¿? (Serbia y Montenero, now in Montenegro) (b) - (c) M (d) - (e) Arsenal Tivat
*** Bojic - Bojan Bojic (Бојан Бојић) (a) 03/03/2000, ¿? (RF Yugoslavia, now in Serbia) (b) 1,74 (c) F - right winger (d) Jedinstvo Bijelo Polje (e) Rad Beograd, Radnik
*** Bojic - Filip Bojic (Filip Bojić) (a) 05/10/1992, Zagreb (Croatia) (b) 1,90 (c) M - central midfielder (d) F91 Dudelange (e) RE Virton, Union Titus Petange, RNK Split, NK Rudes, SV Neuberg, Stinatz, NK Trnje Zagreb, NK Sloga Gredelj Zagreb, NK Trnje Zagreb
*** Bojic - Luka Bojic (Лука Бојић) (c) M (d) FK Lovcen Cetinje (e) Arsenal Tivat, Kom Podgorica, OFK Titograd, Mladost DG
*** Bojku - Besmir Bojku (a) 03/01/1995, Velesta (North Macedonia) (b) - (c) M - pivot (d) Struga Trim & Lum (e) Shkëndija, KF Feronikeli, Shkëndija, FC Shkupi, Shkëndija, Rabotnicki, Makedonija

*** Bojo - Petar Bojo (a) 08/01/1998, Kiseljak (Bosnia and Herzegovina) (b) 1,75 (c) M - pivot (d) FK Igman Konjic (e) Zrinjski Mostar, Igman Konjic, Zrinjski Mostar, Zeljeznicar, Mladost Kakanj, NK Vitez
*** Bojovic - Ivan Bojovic (Иван Бојовић) (a) 20/02/2001, ¿? (RF Yugoslavia, now in Montenegro) (b) 1,89 (c) F - left winger (d) - (e) Rudar Pljevlja, OFK Titograd, Buducnost Podgorica, OFK Titograd, Buducnost Podgorica
*** Bojovic - Marko Bojovic (Марко Бојовић) (a) 15/06/2002, Nikšić (RF Yugoslavia, now in Montenegro) (b) 1,87 (c) F - right winger (d) FK Napredak Krusevac (e) OFK Grbalj, Sutjeska II, OSK Igalo, Sutjeska II
*** Bojovic - Matija Bojovic (Матија Бојовић) (a) 03/05/2004, Nikšić (Serbia and Montenegro, now in Montenegro) (b) 1,84 (c) M - right midfielder (d) FK Sutjeska Niksic II (e) OFK Grbalj, Sutjeska II
*** Bojovic - Milan Bojovic (Милан Бојовић) (a) 13/04/1987, Čačak (Yugoslavia, now in Serbia) (b) 1,87 (c) F - center forward (d) - (e) FK Turon, Mladost, Radnicki Niš, Mladost, Zhetysu, Kaysar, Mladost, AE Larisa, Bnei Sakhnin, Panetolikos, Vojvodina, Jagodina, Čukarički, FK Srem, Teleoptik, FK Srem, Radnicki Klupci
*** Bokadi - Merveille Bokadi (Merveille Bopé Bokadi) (a) 21/05/1996, Kinshasa (Zaire, now DR Congo) (b) 1,86 (c) D - central defense (d) Standard de Lieja (e) TP Mazembe, Standard Liège, TP Mazembe
*** Bokalo - Ivan Bokalo (Бокало Іван Михайлович) (a) 25/04/2006, Lviv (Ukraine) (b) 1,75 (c) M - central midfielder (d) - (e) PFK Lviv
*** Bokov - Danila Bokov (Боков Данила Максимович) (a) 09/08/2002, Moskva (Russia) (b) 1,84 (c) G (d) Chaika Peschanokopskoe (e) Chaika Pes., CSKA Moskva, Salyut Belgorod, CSKA Moskva, CSKA Moskva II
*** Bokov - Denis Bokov (Боков Денис Игоревич) (a) 06/10/2005, ¿? (Russia) (b) 1,74 (c) F - right winger (d) Dinamo 2 Moskva (e) -
*** Bol - Anton Bol (Боль Антон Юрійович) (a) 08/01/2003, Zhytomyr (Ukraine) (b) 1,87 (c) D - central defense (d) Zorya Lugansk (e) Zorya Lugansk, Dinamo Kyїv, Dinamo Kiev II
*** Bolaji - Kazeem Bolaji (Kazeem Bolaji Soliu) (a) 13/12/2002, Oko Ode (Nigeria) (b) 1,73 (c) D - left back (d) Spartak Trnava (e) JK Viljandi, Team360
*** Bolaños - Juan Bolaños (Juan Andrés Bolaños Ramírez) (a) 22/07/1991, Villavicencio (Colombia) (b) 1,89 (c) D - central defense (d) Valletta FC (e) Gudja United FC, Honduras Progr., Gudja United FC, Platense FC, FBC Melgar, Tianjin Quanjian, Godoy Cruz, Academia FC
*** Bolat - Sinan Bolat (a) 03/09/1988, Kayseri (Turkey) (b) 1,86 (c) G (d) KVC Westerlo (e) KAA Gent, Royal Antwerp, FC Porto B, Arouca, FC Porto B, Nacional, FC Porto B, FC Porto, KV Brugge, FC Porto, Galatasaray, FC Porto, Kayserispor, FC Porto, Standard Liège, KRC Genk
*** Bolbat - Sergiy Bolbat (Болбат Сергій Сергійович) (a) 13/06/1993, Volnovakha, Donetsk Oblast (Ukraine) (b) 1,75 (c) F - right winger (d) Kolos Kovalivka (e) Shakhtar Donetsk, Desna, Shakhtar Donetsk, FK Mariupol, Shakhtar Donetsk, KSC Lokeren, Shakhtar Donetsk, Shakhtar II, Metalist, Shakhtar II, Metalurg Donetsk, Shakhtar II, Shakhtar 3
*** Boldini - Christian Boldini (a) 21/07/2004, ¿? (Italy) (b) - (c) D (d) Tre Fiori FC (e) -
*** Boldor - Deian Boldor (a) 03/02/1995, Timişoara (Romania) (b) 1,89 (c) D - central defense (d) - (e) Chindia, FC Arges, Potenza, Hellas Verona, FK Partizani, Hellas Verona, Foggia, Hellas Verona, Bologna, Hellas Verona, Bologna, Montreal, Bologna, Hellas Verona, Bologna, Virtus Lanciano, AS Roma, Pescara, LPS Banatul

*** Boldrini - Francesco Boldrini (a) 09/01/1995, ¿? (Italy) (b) - (c) M - pivot (d) SS San Giovanni (e) Vismara Calcio, Juvenes-Dogana, Morciano

*** Boldysh - Stanislav Boldysh (Болдыш Станислав Дмитриевич) (a) 30/01/2004, Minsk (Belarus) (b) - (c) G (d) FK Minsk II (e) -

*** Bőle - Lukács Bőle (a) 27/03/1990, Marcali (Hungary) (b) 1,71 (c) M - attacking midfielder (d) Paksi FC (e) Honvéd, Ferencváros, Zalaegerszeg, Ferencváros, ACSM Poli Iasi, Kaposvár, Kaposvár II

*** Bolger - Cian Bolger (Cian Thomas Bolger) (a) 12/03/1992, County Kildare (Ireland) (b) 1,93 (c) D - central defense (d) Larne FC (e) Northampton, Lincoln City, Fleetwood, Southend United, Bury, Southend United, Bolton Wanderers, Southend United, Bolton Wanderers, Colchester Utd., Bolton Wanderers, Bristol Rovers, Leicester Reserves

*** Bolger - Greg Bolger (Gregory Bolger) (a) 09/09/1988, Wexford (Ireland) (b) 1,80 (c) M - pivot (d) Sligo Rovers (e) Shamrock Rovers, Cork City, St. Patrick's Ath., Dundalk FC, UCD, Cherry Orchard FC, New Ross

*** Bolha - Klemen Bolha (Klemen Bolha) (a) 19/03/1993, Celje (Slovenia) (b) 1,95 (c) M - pivot (d) 1. FC Leibnitz (e) Napredak, NK Aluminij, Zalgiris, Rudar Velenje, NK Smartno 1928

*** Boli - Franck Boli (Bi Sylvestre Franck Fortune Boli) (a) 07/12/1993, Yamoussoukro (Ivory Coast) (b) 1,80 (c) F - center forward (d) Portland Timbers (e) Ferencváros, Stabæk, Liaoning FC, Aalesund, Liaoning FC, Stabæk, Grassland FC

*** Boli - Kevin Boli (Kévin Gnoher Boli) (a) 21/06/1991, Lens (France) (b) 1,86 (c) D - central defense (d) FCV Farul Constanta (e) FC Botosani, Samsunspor, CFR Cluj, GuiZ FC, CFR Cluj, GZ Hengfeng, CFR Cluj, FC Viitorul, Excelsior Mouscron, CS Sedan, CS Sedan B

*** Bolin - Hugo Bolin (a) 24/07/2003, Borås (Sweden) (b) 1,79 (c) M - central midfielder (d) Malmö FF (e) BK Olympic, Malmö FF

*** Bolingoli - Boli Bolingoli (Boli Bolingoli-Mbombo) (a) 01/07/1995, Kinshasa (Zaire, now DR Congo) (b) 1,81 (c) D - left back (d) KV Mechelen (e) Celtic FC, Ufa, Celtic FC, Basaksehir, Celtic FC, Rapid Wien, KV Brugge, Sint-Truiden, KV Brugge

*** Bolivar - Jorge Bolivar (Jorge Bolívar Cano) (a) 18/07/1997, Maracena (Spain) (b) 1,70 (c) F - left winger (d) - (e) AC Escaldes, UD Maracena, CD Huétor Vega

*** Boljevic - Aleksandar Boljevic (Aleksandar Boljević) (a) 12/12/1995, Podgorica (Yugoslavia, now in Montenegro) (b) 1,85 (c) F - right winger (d) - (e) Hapoel Tel Aviv, Standard Liège, KAS Eupen, Standard Liège, Waasland-Beveren, Zeta Golubovac

*** Boljevic - Dejan Boljevic (Дејан Бољевић) (a) 30/05/1990, Cetinje (Yugoslavia, now in Montenegro) (b) 1,83 (c) D - left back (d) OFK Petrovac (e) Teplice, Alashkert CF, Taraz, Buducnost Podgorica, Luch, Hibernians FC, Vozdovac, Nasaf Qarshi, Čukarički, Novi Pazar, Tatran Presov, Smederevo 1924, Teleoptik, OFK Petrovac, Mogren

*** Boljevic - Vladimir Boljevic (Vladimir Boljević) (a) 17/01/1988, Titograd (now Podgorica) (Yugoslavia, now in Montenegro) (b) 1,75 (c) M - pivot (d) - (e) FK Iskra, FK Podgorica, Doxa Katokopias, AEK Larnaca, Cracovia, Zeta Golubovac

*** Bolla - Bendegúz Bolla (Bolla Bendegúz Bence) (a) 22/11/1999, Székesfehérvár (Hungary) (b) 1,79 (c) D - right back (d) Wolverhampton Wanderers (e) Grasshoppers, Wolverhampton Wanderers, Fehérvár, Zalaegerszeg, Vidi FC, Zalaegerszeg, Vidi FC, BFC Siófok, Vidi FC

*** Boller - Jan Boller (a) 14/03/2000, Siegen (Germany) (b) 1,85 (c) D - central defense (d) - (e) LASK, Juniors OÖ, LASK, Bayer Leverkusen

*** Bolly - Fran Bolly (Francisco Javier Jiménez Benitez) (a) 28/05/2003, Alcalá de los Gazules (Spain) (b) - (c) F - center forward (d) Algeciras CF B (e) Europa FC

*** Bolly - Mathis Bolly (Mathis Gazoa Kippersund Bolly) (a) 14/11/1990, Oslo (Norway) (b) 1,85 (c) F - left winger (d) - (e) Molde, Stabæk, Molde, Greuther Fürth, Fortuna Düsseldorf, Lillestrøm

*** Bolohan - Vadim Bolohan (a) 15/08/1986, Sîngerei (Soviet Union, now in Moldova) (b) 1,86 (c) D - central defense (d) FC Milsami Orhei (e) FC Tiraspol, Milsami, Rapid G., Karpaty, Milsami, FK Sevastopol, Zakarpattia, Zorya Lugansk, Dacia

*** Bolotnikov - Vladislav Bolotnikov (Болотников Владислав Витальевич) (a) 23/01/2004, ¿? (Belarus) (b) - (c) M - right midfielder (d) FK Belshina Bobruisk II (e) -

*** Boltrushevich - Ilya Boltrushevich (Болтрушевич Илья Эдуардович) (a) 30/03/1999, Mogilev (Belarus) (b) 1,94 (c) D - central defense (d) Dnepr Mogilev (e) Isloch, Dnepr Mogilev, FK Smorgon, Belshina, Dnyapro Mogilev, FK Lida, Dnyapro Mogilev, Mogilev II, Soligorsk II, Mogilev II

*** Boly - Willy Boly (Willy-Arnaud Zobo Boly) (a) 03/02/1991, Melun (France) (b) 1,95 (c) D - central defense (d) Nottingham Forest (e) Wolverhampton Wanderers, FC Porto, Wolverhampton Wanderers, FC Porto, SC Braga, AJ Auxerre, AJ Auxerre B

*** Boman - André Boman (a) 15/11/2001, ¿? (Sweden) (b) - (c) M - right midfielder (d) IF Elfsborg (e) Varbergs BoIS, Ullareds IK, Varbergs BoIS, Varbergs GIF, Varbergs BoIS, Varbergs GIF, Varbergs BoIS, Lilla Träslöv

*** Bonanni - Claudio Bonanni (a) 05/03/1997, Genoa (Italy) (b) 1,83 (c) M - pivot (d) Hibernians FC (e) Marsaxlokk, Hebar P., Birkirkara FC, Castellanzese, FC Kamza, Caratese, Varese, Pavia

*** Bonaventura - Giacomo Bonaventura (a) 22/08/1989, San Severino Marche (Italy) (b) 1,80 (c) M - central midfielder (d) Fiorentina (e) AC Milan, Atalanta, Padova, Atalanta, Pergocrema, Atalanta

*** Bonazzoli - Federico Bonazzoli (a) 21/05/1997, Manerbio (Italy) (b) 1,82 (d) Hellas Verona (e) Hellas Verona, Salernitana, Sampdoria, Salernitana, Sampdoria, Torino, Sampdoria, Padova, Sampdoria, SPAL, Sampdoria, Brescia, Sampdoria, Virtus Lanciano, Sampdoria, Internazionale Milano, Sampdoria, Internazionale Milano

*** Bondar - Andrey Bondar (Бондарь Андрей Юрьевич) (a) 07/09/2004, Moskva (Russia) (b) 1,89 (c) G (d) Torpedo Moskva (e) Torpedo 2, TR Moskva

*** Bondar - Valeriy Bondar (Бондар Валерій Юрійович) (a) 27/02/1999, Kharkiv (Ukraine) (b) 1,85 (c) D - central defense (d) Shakhtar Donetsk (e) Shakhtar II

*** Bondarenco - Igor Bondarenco (Бондаренко Игорь) (a) 28/06/1995, ¿? (Moldova) (b) 1,81 (c) D - right back (d) FC Floresti (e) Milsami, Floresti, Sfintul Gheorghe, Sheriff-2, FC Tighina, Sheriff-2, CSF Speranta, Sheriff-2, FC Sheriff

*** Bondarenko - Artem Bondarenko (Бондаренко Артем Юрійович) (a) 21/08/2000, Cherkasy (Ukraine) (b) 1,82 (c) M - attacking midfielder (d) Shakhtar Donetsk (e) FK Mariupol, Shakhtar Donetsk, Shakhtar II

*** Bondarenko - Taras Bondarenko (Бондаренко Тарас Романович) (a) 23/09/1992, Zaporizhya (Ukraine) (b) 1,87 (c) D - central defense (d) AS Trencin (e) Radnik, Kaspiy Aktau, Okzhetpes, Kaspiy Aktau, Radnicki Niš, Metalac, Avangard K., FK Poltava, Zaporizhya II

*** Bondarenko - Valeriy Bondarenko (Бондаренко Валерій Сергійович) (a) 03/02/1994, Kyiv (Ukraine) (b) 1,94 (c) D - central defense (d) Kolos Kovalivka (e) Shakhtar Donetsk, FK Oleksandriya, Shakhtar Donetsk, Vorskla Poltava, Shakhtar

Donetsk, FK Oleksandriya, Shakhtar Donetsk, Vitória Guimarães, Shakhtar Donetsk, FK Oleksandriya, Skala Stryi, Torpedo Kutaisi, Arsenal Kyiv II
*** Bonde - Jakob Bonde (Jakob Bonde Jensen) (a) 29/12/1993, ¿? (Denmark) (b) 1,86 (c) M - central midfielder (d) Viborg FF (e) Nyköbing FC
*** Böndergaard - Asbjörn Böndergaard (Asbjørn Bøndergaard) (a) 05/05/2004, ¿? (Denmark) (b) - (c) F - center forward (d) - (e) Silkeborg
*** Bondin - Kurt Bondin (a) 03/06/2002, ¿? (Malta) (b) - (c) D (d) Zebbug Rangers FC (e) -
*** Bondo - Warren Bondo (Warren Pierre Bondo) (a) 15/09/2003, Évry (France) (b) 1,77 (c) M - central midfielder (d) AC Monza (e) Reggina, Monza, AS Nancy
*** Bone - Sam Bone (Samuel Bone) (a) 06/02/1998, Kuching (Malaysia) (b) 1,87 (c) D - central defense (d) Maidstone United (e) Dundalk FC, St. Patrick's Ath., Waterford FC, Shamrock Rovers
*** Bonello - Henry Bonello (a) 13/10/1988, Pieta (Malta) (b) 1,86 (c) G (d) Hamrun Spartans (e) Valletta, Birkirkara FC, Valletta, Sliema Wanderers, Valletta, Sliema Wanderers, Hibernians FC, Sliema Wanderers, Vittoriosa, Sliema Wanderers
*** Bonet - Donovan Bonet (a) 18/03/1989, ¿? (France) (b) - (c) M - attacking midfielder (d) FC Wiltz 71 (e) US Hostert, Junglinster, Bar-le-Duc, Sainte-Marienne, AS Pagny, CS Grevenmacher, Jeunesse Canach, Bar-le-Duc, Stranraer, Stranraer, Bar-le-Duc
*** Bonev - Biser Bonev (Бисер Бисеров Бонев) (a) 04/06/2003, Ruse (Bulgaria) (b) 1,80 (c) M - central midfielder (d) Krumovgrad (e) Krumovgrad, Botev II, Botev Plovdiv
*** Bonga - Tarsis Bonga (a) 10/01/1997, Neuwied (Germany) (b) 1,97 (c) F - right winger (d) TSV 1860 München (e) Eintracht Braunschweig, VfL Bochum, Chemnitzer FC, FSV Zwickau, Düsseldorf II
*** Bongiovanni - Adrien Bongiovanni (Adrien Ignazio Bongiovanni) (a) 20/09/1999, Seraing (Belgium) (b) 1,73 (c) F - left winger (d) Zébra Élites (e) SL16 FC, Patro Eisden, AS Monaco, FC Den Bosch, AS Monaco, Cercle Brugge, AS Béziers, Cercle Brugge, AS Monaco, AS Monaco B
*** Bongonda - Théo Bongonda (Théo Bongonda Mbul'Ofeko Batombo) (a) 20/11/1995, Charleroi (Belgium) (b) 1,75 (c) F - right winger (d) FC Spartak de Moscú (e) Cádiz CF, KRC Genk, Zulte Waregem, RC Celta, Zulte Waregem, RC Celta, Trabzonspor, RC Celta, Zulte Waregem, JMG Lier
*** Boniface - Christopher Boniface (a) 01/01/2002, Kaduna (Nigeria) (b) 1,80 (c) M - attacking midfielder (d) FC Van (e) Right2Win SA
*** Boniface - Victor Boniface (Victor Okoh Boniface) (a) 23/12/2000, Akure (Nigeria) (b) 1,90 (c) F - center forward (d) Bayer 04 Leverkusen (e) Union St. Gilloise, Bodø/Glimt, Real Sapphire
*** Bonifazi - Kevin Bonifazi (a) 19/05/1996, Bologna (Italy) (b) 1,87 (c) D - central defense (d) Bologna (e) SPAL, Udinese, SPAL, Torino, SPAL, Torino, SPAL, Torino, SPAL, Torino, Casertana, Torino, Benevento, Torino
*** Bonifazi - Luca Bonifazi (a) 12/11/1982, ¿? (San Marino) (b) 1,76 (c) M - central midfielder (d) - (e) La Fiorita, SS Folgore, Virtus, Pennarossa, Tre Fiori, Libertas, Juvenes-Dogana, Domagnano, Libertas
*** Bonini - Giovanni Bonini (a) 05/09/1986, Borgo Maggiore (San Marino) (b) 1,74 (c) D - right back (d) - (e) Domagnano, SS Folgore, Domagnano, Tre Fiori, Libertas, Tre Penne, San Marino, Cailungo, AC Dozzese
*** Bonis - Lee Bonis (a) 03/08/1999, Portadown (Northern Ireland) (b) 1,86 (c) F - center forward (d) Larne FC (e) Portadown, Seagoe FC

*** Bonmann - Hendrik Bonmann (a) 22/01/1994, Essen (Germany) (b) 1,94 (c) G (d) Wolfsberger AC (e) Würzb. Kickers, 1860 München, Borussia Dortmund, Borussia Dortmund II, RW Essen
*** Bonnah - Solomon Bonnah (Solomon Owusu Bonnah) (a) 19/08/2003, Amsterdam (Netherlands) (b) 1,65 (c) D - right back (d) SK Austria Klagenfurt (e) RB Leipzig
*** Bonnevie - Kayne Bonnevie (a) 22/07/2001, Écully (France) (b) 1,91 (c) G (d) Quevilly Rouen Métropole (e) Olympique Lyon, Olymp. Lyon B
*** Bonnici - Duane Bonnici (a) 10/10/1995, ¿? (Malta) (b) - (c) D (d) Marsaxlokk FC (e) Mosta FC, Naxxar Lions FC, Mosta FC, Naxxar Lions FC
*** Bono - Bono (بونو ياسين, Yassine Bounou) (a) 05/04/1991, Montreal, Quebec (Canada) (b) 1,92 (c) G (d) Sevilla FC (e) Girona FC, Sevilla FC, Girona FC, Atlético Madrid, Real Zaragoza, At. Madrid B, Wydad AC, WAC Reserve
*** Bonsu - Derrick Bonsu (Derrick Osei Bonsu) (a) 07/01/2002, ¿? (Ghana) (b) - (c) D - central defense (d) FK Pohronie (e) Podbrezova, Pohronie, Podbrezova, Loja CD
*** Bonte - Nolan Bonte (Nolan Hamidou Bonte) (a) 19/01/2004, Montivilliers (France) (b) 1,75 (c) M - attacking midfielder (d) RC Lens B (e) -
*** Bonte (c) G (d) ZMVV Zeerobben (e) - - Sem Bonte (c) G (d) ZMVV Zeerobben (e) -
*** Bonucci - Leonardo Bonucci (a) 01/05/1987, Viterbo (Italy) (b) 1,90 (c) D - central defense (d) Juventus de Turín (e) Juventus, AC Milan, Juventus, Bari, Genoa, Internazionale Milano, AC Pisa, Internazionale Milano, Treviso, Internazionale Milano
*** Boone - Viktor Boone (Viktor Luc Boone) (a) 25/01/1998, ¿? (Belgium) (b) 1,91 (c) D - central defense (d) Royale Union Saint Gilloise (e) KMSK Deinze, Sparta Petegem
*** Boonen - Indy Boonen (Indy Zeb Boonen) (a) 04/01/1999, Dilsen (Belgium) (b) 1,77 (c) M - attacking midfielder (d) - (e) KV Oostende
*** Boore - Luke Boore (a) 28/03/1999, ¿? (Ireland) (b) 1,85 (c) D - central defense (d) University College Dublin (e) -
*** Booth - Callum Booth (a) 30/05/1991, Stranraer (Scotland) (b) 1,81 (c) D - left back (d) St. Johnstone FC (e) Dundee United, Partick Thistle, Hibernian FC, Partick Thistle, Hibernian FC, Raith Rovers, Hibernian FC, Livingston FC, Hibernian FC, Brechin City, Arbroath
*** Booth - Taylor Booth (Taylor Anthony Booth) (a) 31/05/2001, Eden, Utah (United States) (b) 1,74 (c) M - central midfielder (d) FC Utrecht (e) FC Bayern II, SKN St. Pölten, FC Bayern II
*** Bopesu - Joël Bopesu (Joël Fey d'Or Bopesu) (a) 25/01/1995, Kinshasa (Zaire, now DR Congo) (b) 1,84 (c) D - left back (d) FK Zalgiris Vilnius (e) Canet Rous., PFC Lviv, Riga, Rabotnicki, FK Skopje, RUFC Calais, SAS Epinal, AC Arles B
*** Boranijasevic - Nikola Boranijasevic (Никола Боранијашевић) (a) 19/05/1992, Nova Varos (Yugoslavia, now in Serbia) (b) 1,82 (c) M - right midfielder (d) FC Zürich (e) Lausanne-Sport, Napredak, JFK Ventspils, Borac Cacak, FK Rudar, Borac Cacak
*** Boras - Marco Boras (a) 28/09/2001, Frankfurt am Main (Germany) (b) 1,99 (c) D - central defense (d) Slaven Belupo Koprivnica (e) Hoffenheim II, FC Gießen
*** Borchers - Mads Borchers (a) 18/06/2002, Sønderborg (Denmark) (b) 1,88 (c) F - center forward (d) Varbergs BoIS (e) HB Tórshavn, Esbjerg fB, 07 Vestur, Esbjerg fB, SUB Sönderborg

*** Borchgrevink - Christian Borchgrevink (Christian Dahle Borchgrevink) (a) 11/05/1999, Oslo (Norway) (b) 1,82 (c) D - right back (d) Vålerenga Fotball (e) Notodden, Vålerenga, HamKam, Vålerenga, Vålerenga II

*** Borda - Shane Borda (a) 07/05/2005, ¿? (Gibraltar) (b) 1,74 (c) M - central midfielder (d) Lincoln Red Imps FC Reserve (e) -

*** Bordachev - Maksim Bordachev (Бордачёв Максим Александрович) (a) 18/05/1986, Grodno (Soviet Union, now in Belarus) (b) 1,90 (c) D - left back (d) - (e) BATE Borisov, Torpedo Zhodino, Soligorsk, Torpedo Zhodino, Soligorsk, Tom Tomsk, Orenburg, Tom Tomsk, Rostov, Tom Tomsk, BATE Borisov, Tom Tomsk, BATE Borisov, MTZ-Ripo Minsk, Neman Grodno

*** Bordeianu - Mihai Bordeianu (Mihai Cătălin Bordeianu) (a) 18/11/1991, Flămânzi (Romania) (b) 1,75 (c) M - central midfielder (d) ACSM Politehnica Iasi (e) Universitatea Cluj, CFR Cluj, Al-Qadsiah FC, CFR Cluj, Al-Qadsiah FC, CFR Cluj, FC Botosani, FCM Dorohoi, FC Botosani, Ceahlăul

*** Bordukov - Pavel Bordukov (Бордуков Павел Викторович) (a) 10/04/1993, Mogilev (Belarus) (b) 1,74 (c) M - central midfielder (d) Dnepr Mogilev (e) Belshina, Dnepr Mogilev, Mogilev II

*** Borek - Jiri Borek (Jiří Borek) (a) 23/09/2002, ¿? (Czech Rep.) (b) - (c) G (d) MFK Vyskov (e) Slovácko B

*** Borello - Giuseppe Borello (a) 28/04/1999, Catanzaro (Italy) (b) 1,68 (c) F - right winger (d) SS Monopoli 1966 (e) Újpest FC, Crotone, Cesena, Crotone, Pro Vercelli, Crotone, Cesena, Crotone, Rende, Crotone, Cuneo, Crotone, Catanzarese

*** Borevkovic - Toni Borevkovic (Toni Borevković) (a) 18/06/1997, Slavonski Brod (Croatia) (b) 1,93 (c) D - central defense (d) Vitória Guimarães SC (e) Hajduk Split, Vitória Guimarães, Rio Ave, NK Rudes, NK Rudes, Marsonia 1909

*** Borg - Adrian Borg (a) 20/05/1989, ¿? (Malta) (b) - (c) D - right back (d) FC Mgarr United (e) Sirens FC, St. Andrews FC, Pembroke, Mosta FC, Hamrun Spartans, Mosta FC, Hamrun Spartans, Mosta FC

*** Borg - Andy Borg (a) 27/06/2004, ¿? (Malta) (b) 1,76 (c) M - central midfielder (d) Gzira United FC (e) -

*** Borg - Arziel Borg (a) 27/04/2003, ¿? (Malta) (b) - (c) M (d) - (e) Hibernians Valetta

*** Borg - Brooklyn Borg (a) 08/01/2004, ¿? (Malta) (b) - (c) F - left winger (d) Gzira United FC (e) -

*** Borg - Conor Borg (a) 13/05/1997, ¿? (Malta) (b) 1,85 (c) M - attacking midfielder (d) Marsaxlokk FC (e) Qrendi FC, Marsaxlokk, Sirens FC, Hamrun Spartans, Floriana

*** Borg - Jean Borg (a) 08/01/1998, ¿? (Malta) (b) 1,84 (c) D - central defense (d) Sliema Wanderers (e) Fidelis Andria, Valletta

*** Borg - Krist Borg (a) 28/12/2005, ¿? (Malta) (b) - (c) D (d) - (e) Sirens FC

*** Borg - Leon Borg (a) 27/10/2003, ¿? (Malta) (b) - (c) M (d) - (e) Hamrun Spartans

*** Borg - Neil Borg (a) 30/10/2000, ¿? (Malta) (b) - (c) D (d) SC Mellieha (e) Gzira Utd., FC Swieqi Utd., Gzira Utd., Msida SJ

*** Borg - Oscar Borg (Oscar Francis Borg) (a) 05/09/1997, Sutton (England) (b) 1,79 (c) D - left back (d) Haverfordwest County (e) Haukar, Stjarnan, Arenas Club, Braintree

*** Borg - Sacha Borg (a) 26/04/1993, ¿? (Malta) (b) - (c) D - left back (d) Sirens FC (e) Gzira Utd., Tarxien, Floriana, Gzira Utd., Floriana, Marsaxlokk

*** Borg - Steve Borg (a) 15/05/1988, Mosta (Malta) (b) 1,78 (c) D - central defense (d) Hamrun Spartans (e) Gzira Utd., Valletta, Aris Limassol, Valletta, Mosta FC

*** Borgagni - Andrea Borgagni (a) 21/10/1996, ¿? (San Marino) (b) - (c) M - right midfielder (d) FC Fiorentino (e) San Giovanni, Fiorentino, Murata, Fiorentino

*** Borge - Billy Borge (Billy John Borge) (a) 22/05/1998, ¿? (Wales) (b) 1,78 (c) D - central defense (d) Penybont FC (e) -

*** Borge - Dylan Borge (a) 15/10/2003, Gibraltar (Gibraltar) (b) 1,75 (c) F - center forward (d) St Joseph's FC (e) Europa FC, Red Imps Reserves

*** Borges - Gonçalo Borges (Gonçalo Óscar Albuquerque Borges) (a) 29/03/2001, Lisboa (Portugal) (b) 1,84 (c) F - right winger (d) FC Porto B (e) -

*** Borges - Kady Borges (Kady Iuri Borges Malinowski) (a) 02/05/1996, Curitiba (Brazil) (b) 1,73 (c) M - attacking midfielder (d) FK Krasnodar (e) Qarabag FK, Vilafranquense, Estoril Praia, Coritiba FC, Foz do Iguaçu, Coritiba FC, Londrina-PR, Coritiba FC, Coritiba FC B

*** Borges - Neto Borges (Vivaldo Borges dos Santos Neto) (a) 13/09/1996, Saubara (Brazil) (b) 1,85 (c) D - left back (d) Clermont Foot 63 (e) KRC Genk, Tondela, KRC Genk, Vasco da Gama, KRC Genk, Hammarby IF, Tubarão-SC

*** Borges - Ricky Borges (Ricardo Borges Magalhães) (a) 28/05/1999, ¿? (Luxembourg) (b) - (c) M - attacking midfielder (d) - (e) US Hostert, FC Mamer 32, Progrès Niederkorn, UN Käerjeng 97, Progrès Niederkorn

*** Borges - Zidane Borges (Zidane Borges Monteiro) (a) 02/01/2001, ¿? (Cabo Verde) (b) - (c) M (d) FC Yellow Boys Weiler-La-Tour (e) Weiler, UN Käerjeng 97

*** Borges Sanches - Yvandro Borges Sanches (a) 24/05/2004, Luxembourg (Luxembourg) (b) 1,75 (c) F - left winger (d) Borussia Mönchengladbach (e) -

*** Borghesan - Luca Borghesan (a) 05/01/2004, ¿? (Italy) (b) - (c) M - central midfielder (d) - (e) Montebelluna

*** Borghini - Giacomo Borghini (a) 27/07/2001, ¿? (Italy) (b) - (c) D - left back (d) AC Juvenes-Dogana (e) Spontricciolo

*** Borghini - Gianmaria Borghini (a) 04/03/1997, Rimini (Italy) (b) 1,80 (c) D - right back (d) AC Juvenes-Dogana (e) United Riccione, Tropical Coriano, San Marino

*** Boricic - Balsa Boricic (a) 07/01/1997, ¿? (RF Yugoslavia, now in Montenegro) (b) 1,76 (c) M - attacking midfielder (d) FK Sutjeska Niksic (e) OFK Petrovac, FK Iskra, Buducnost Podgorica, OFK Petrovac, FK Mladost

*** Boricic - Luka Boricic (a) 18/05/2002, ¿? (RF Yugoslavia, now in Montenegro) (b) - (c) D - right back (d) FK Mladost Donja Gorica (e) Rudar Pljevlja, Mladost DG, FK Podgorica

*** Boril - Jan Boril (Jan Bořil) (a) 11/01/1991, Nymburk (Czechoslovakia, now in Czech Rep.) (b) 1,75 (c) D - left back (d) SK Slavia Praga (e) Mlada Boleslav, Viktoria Zizkov, Mlada Boleslav

*** Borini - Fabio Borini (a) 29/03/1991, Bentivoglio (Italy) (b) 1,80 (c) F - left winger (d) UC Sampdoria (e) Karagümrük, Hellas Verona, AC Milan, Sunderland, AC Milan, Sunderland, Liverpool, Sunderland, Liverpool, AS Roma, Parma, AS Roma, Parma, Chelsea, Swansea City, Chelsea

*** Borioni - Nicolò Borioni (a) 31/07/2002, ¿? (Italy) (b) - (c) M - pivot (d) SC Faetano (e) Spontricciolo, Urbino Calcio, Cattolica

*** Boris Enow - Boris Enow (Boris Enow Takang) (a) 30/03/2000, ¿? (Cameroon) (b) 1,75 (c) M - central midfielder (d) Maccabi Netanya (e) RC Lens B, FC Porto B, Brasseries

*** Borisov - Nikola Borisov (Никола Бориславов Борисов) (a) 21/11/2000, Sofia (Bulgaria) (b) 1,85 (c) D - central defense (d) - (e) Spartak Varna, Dunav, Spartak Varna, Dobroslavtsi, Neftochimik, CSKA-Sofia, Litex Lovetch, CSKA-Sofia

*** Borisov - Nikola Borisov (Никола Борисов Борисов) (a) 14/07/2000, Sofia (Bulgaria) (b) 1,85 (c) D - central defense (d) Montana (e) CSKA 1948 II, Strumska Slava, Vitosha

*** Borja - Alexander Borja (Alexander Borja Córdoba) (a) 25/10/1998, Chigorodó (Colombia) (b) 1,81 (c) D - left back (d) Besa Dobri Dol (e) Bregalnica Stip, Renova, Pehcevo, Pelister Bitola, Rabotnicki, Makedonija, Rabotnicki, Lokomotiva, Rabotnicki

*** Borja - Cristián Borja (Cristián Alexis Borja González) (a) 18/02/1993, Quibdó (Colombia) (b) 1,80 (c) D - left back (d) SC Braga (e) Alanyaspor, SC Braga, Sporting Lisboa, Toluca, Cortuluá, Indep. Santa Fe, Cortuluá

*** Borjan - Milan Borjan (Милан Борјан) (a) 23/10/1987, Knin (Yugoslavia, now in Croatia) (b) 1,96 (c) G (d) Slovan Bratislava (e) Slovan Bratislava, Crvena zvezda, Ludogorets, Korona Kielce, Ludogorets, Radnicki Niš, Ludogorets, Sivasspor, FC Vaslui, Sivasspor, Rad Beograd, Quilmes

*** Børkeeiet - Tobias Børkeeiet (Tobias Borchgrevink Børkeeiet) (a) 18/04/1999, Oslo (Norway) (b) 1,88 (c) M - pivot (d) Rosenborg BK (e) Brøndby IF, Stabæk

*** Borkovic - Alexandar Borkovic (Alexandar Borković) (a) 11/06/1999, Wien (Austria) (b) 1,84 (c) D - central defense (d) SK Sturm Graz (e) Hoffenheim II, Sturm Graz, Hoffenheim II, Austria Viena, Austria Wien Reserves

*** Bormanis - Davis Bormanis (a) 01/11/2005, ¿? (Latvia) (b) - (c) M (d) FK Tukums 2000 (e) Tukums II

*** Bornauw - Sebastiaan Bornauw (a) 22/03/1999, Wemmel (Belgium) (b) 1,91 (c) D - central defense (d) VfL Wolfsburg (e) 1.FC Köln, RSC Anderlecht

*** Borne - Théo Borne (a) 15/07/2002, Montbéliard (France) (b) - (c) G (d) Clermont Foot 63 (e) Angers SCO, Angers SCO B

*** Boro - Boro (Salvador Manuel Alegre Delgado) (a) 04/05/1991, Puerto Real (Spain) (b) 1,85 (c) F - center forward (d) St Joseph's FC (e) Almagro CF, Angels FC, Marino Luanco, Arroyo CP, Conil CF, Puerto Real CF

*** Borodin - Dmitriy Borodin (Бородин Дмитрий Анатольевич) (a) 19/07/1999, Gomel (Belarus) (b) 1,94 (c) M - central midfielder (d) Kaysar Kyzylorda (e) Ordabasy, Dinamo Minsk, Gomel, Dinamo Minsk, Chaika Pes., Dinamo Minsk, Isloch, Dinamo Minsk, Smolevichi, Gomel II, Orsha, Gomel II

*** Borodin - Sergey Borodin (Бородин Сергей Алексеевич) (a) 30/01/1999, Lazarevskoe, Krasnodar Region (Russia) (b) 1,87 (c) D - central defense (d) Torpedo Moskva (e) Krasnodar, B. Jerusalem, Krasnodar, Krasnodar-2, Ufa, Krasnodar-2, Krasnodar II

*** Boros - Zsombor Boros (a) 07/02/2005, ¿? (Hungary) (b) - (c) M - pivot (d) Kazincbarcikai SC (e) Zalaegerszeg, NK Nafta 1903, Zalaegerszeg

*** Borovskij - Valdemar Borovskij (a) 02/05/1984, Vilnius (Soviet Union, now in Lithuania) (b) 1,81 (c) D - right back (d) FK Riteriai (e) Jonava, Beroe, Siauliai, Daugava Riga, Suduva, Siauliai, Vetra

*** Borré - Rafael Borré (Rafael Santos Borré Maury) (a) 15/09/1995, Barranquilla (Colombia) (b) 1,74 (c) F - center forward (d) Eintracht Frankfurt (e) River Plate, Atlético Madrid, Villarreal CF, Atlético Madrid, Deportivo Cali, Atlético Madrid, Deportivo Cali, Cali B

*** Bors - Ion Bors (Ion Borş) (a) 25/07/2002, ¿? (Moldova) (b) - (c) D - right back (d) FC Petrocub Hîncești (e) Sfintul Gheorghe, Spartanii, Speranţa D

*** Börset - Anders Rönne Börset (Anders Rønne Børset) (a) 22/02/2006, Hommelvik (Norway) (b) 1,85 (c) D - central defense (d) - (e) Molde, Molde FK II

*** Borta - Florin Borta (Florin Borța) (a) 21/06/1999, Râmnicu Vâlcea (Romania) (b) 1,75 (c) D - right back (d) Universitatea Craiova (e) Petrolul, CS U Craiova, Concordia, CS U Craiova, Petrolul, CS U Craiova

*** Bortagaray - Gerónimo Bortagaray (Gerónimo Bortagaray Derregibus) (a) 05/08/2000, Salto (Uruguay) (b) 1,84 (c) D - central defense (d) PAS Giannina (e) Danubio FC, Wanderers, Villa Española, Wanderers

*** Bortniczuk - Maciej Bortniczuk (a) 06/09/2001, Białystok (Poland) (b) 1,81 (c) F - center forward (d) Wisla Pulawy (e) Jagiellonia, Pogon Grodzisk, Jagiellonia, Korona Kielce, Jagiellonia, O. Zambrow, AP Jagiellonia

*** Boruc - Maksymilian Boruc (Maksymilian Pawel Boruc) (a) 15/11/2002, Warszawa (Poland) (b) 1,95 (c) G (d) Hibernian FC (e) Śląsk Wroclaw, Husqvarna FF

*** Borukov - Preslav Borukov (Преслав Николаев Боруков) (a) 23/04/2000, Sofia (Bulgaria) (b) 1,89 (c) F - center forward (d) Arda Kardzhali (e) Lokomotiv Plovdiv, Zalaegerszeg, Etar

*** Børven - Torgeir Børven (a) 03/12/1991, Øystese (Norway) (b) 1,85 (c) F - center forward (d) Vålerenga Fotball (e) Gaziantep FK, Ankaragücü, Rosenborg, Odd, Brann, FC Twente, Brann, FC Twente, Vålerenga, Odd, Øystese Fotball

*** Boryachuk - Andriy Boryachuk (Борячук Андрій Васильович) (a) 23/04/1996, Vinnytsya (Ukraine) (b) 1,76 (c) F - center forward (d) - (e) Shakhtar Donetsk, Metalist 1925, Shakhtar Donetsk, Rukh Lviv, Shakhtar Donetsk, Mezőkövesd, Shakhtar Donetsk, Çaykur Rizespor, Shakhtar Donetsk, FK Mariupol, Shakhtar Donetsk, Shakhtar II

*** Borys - Karol Borys (a) 28/09/2006, Otmuchów (Poland) (b) 1,74 (c) M - attacking midfielder (d) Śląsk Wroclaw (e) Slask Wroclaw II

*** Borysiuk - Ariel Borysiuk (a) 29/07/1991, Biała Podlaska (Poland) (b) 1,80 (c) M - pivot (d) Chojniczanka Chojnice (e) KF Laçi, Chennaiyin FC, Jagiellonia, FC Sheriff, Lechia Gdánsk, Wisła Płock, Lechia Gdánsk, Queen's Park Rangers, Lechia Gdánsk, Queen's Park Rangers, Legia Warszawa, Lechia Gdánsk, 1.FC Kaiserslautern, Lechia Gdánsk, 1.FC Kaiserslautern, Volga Nizhny Novgorod, 1.FC Kaiserslautern, Legia Warszawa, Legia II

*** Borza - Andrei Borza (Sebastian Andrei Borza) (a) 12/11/2005, Năvodari (Romania) (b) 1,80 (c) D - left back (d) FCV Farul Constanta (e) Academia Hagi

*** Bosancic - Nemanja Bosancic (Немања Босанчић) (a) 01/03/1995, Prishtinë (RF Yugoslavia, now in Kosovo) (b) 1,80 (c) M - central midfielder (d) Dalian Professional (e) FC Lahti, Struga, Kolubara, FK Indjija, FK Berane, Borac Cacak, FK Indjija

*** Bosancic - Petar Bosancic (Petar Bosančić) (a) 19/04/1996, Split (Croatia) (b) 1,90 (c) D - central defense (d) Riga FC (e) Cherno More, Siroki Brijeg, FK Mariupol, NK Istra, Hajduk Split, Hajduk Split II, NK Sesvete, Hajduk Split II, NK Dugopolje, Hajduk Split II

*** Bosano - Owen Bosano (Owen Anthony Bosano) (a) 09/12/2005, Gibraltar (Gibraltar) (b) - (c) G (d) St Joseph's FC Reserve (e) Europa FC, Europa Reserve

*** Boscagli - Olivier Boscagli (a) 18/11/1997, Monaco (Monaco) (b) 1,81 (c) D - central defense (d) PSV Eindhoven (e) OGC Nice, Nîmes, OGC Nice, OGC Nice B

*** Bosch - Pau Bosch (Pau Bosch Hueso) (a) 30/03/1988, Fondarella (Spain) (b) 1,78 (c) D - central defense (d) Inter Club d'Escaldes (e) Racing Ferrol, Llagostera, CD Alcoyano, Kitchee, Lleida Esportiu, UE Lleida, CA Monzón, UE Lleida

*** Boschi - Alessio Boschi (a) 22/11/2005, ¿? (Italy) (b) - (c) M (d) SS Pennarossa (e) -

*** Bosec - Antonio Bosec (a) 28/08/1997, Zagreb (Croatia) (b) 1,78 (c) D - right back (d) Slaven Belupo Koprivnica (e) Inter Zaprešić, NK Tondach
*** Boselli - Juan Manuel Boselli (Juan Manuel Boselli Graff) (a) 09/11/1999, Montevideo (Uruguay) (b) 1,74 (c) F - right winger (d) Gil Vicente FC (e) Tondela, Defensor, Cádiz CF B, Defensor, Athletico-PR, América-MG, Athletico-PR, Defensor, CF Peralada, Defensor
*** Bosheski - Antonio Bosheski (Антонио Бошески) (a) 03/09/1995, Prilep (North Macedonia) (b) 1,68 (c) D - right back (d) - (e) Pobeda Prilep, FK Sasa, Lokomotiva, Euromilk GL
*** Bosheski - David Bosheski (Давид Бошески) (a) 19/02/2003, Skopje (North Macedonia) (b) - (c) D - central defense (d) Detonit Plackovica (e) Sloga 1934, AP Brera, Pehcevo, New Stars
*** Boshnak - Tarek Boshnak (בושאנק טארק) (a) 03/06/1999, Shefaram (Israel) (b) - (c) D - central defense (d) Maccabi Bnei Reineh (e) Hapoel Hadera, M. Ahi Nazareth, M. Zur Shalom, Kiryat Shmona
*** Boshnjaku - Lorik Boshnjaku (a) 07/07/1995, Prishtinë (RF Yugoslavia, now in Kosovo) (b) 1,79 (c) M - pivot (d) KF Vllaznia (e) FC Prishtina, KF 2 Korriku
*** Bosic - Radivoj Bosic (Радивој Босић) (a) 01/12/2000, Beograd (RF Yugoslavia, now in Serbia) (b) 1,83 (c) F - left winger (d) FK Javor-Matis Ivanjica (e) Spartak, Nacional, Olimpija, FC Wil 1900, Graficar
*** Bosio - Jamie Bosio (Jamie Ralph Bosio) (a) 27/03/1991, Gibraltar (Gibraltar) (b) 1,86 (c) D - central defense (d) FC Manchester 62 (e) Europa FC, Lions Gibraltar, FC Olympique, Gibraltar Utd., Manchester 62
*** Boskovic - Blaz Boskovic (Blaž Bošković) (a) 15/12/2001, Mostar (Bosnia and Herzegovina) (b) - (c) M - pivot (d) NK Lokomotiva Zagreb (e) Zrinjski Mostar, GOSK Gabela, Zrinjski Mostar, HSK Posusje, Zrinjski Mostar
*** Boskovski - Filip Boskovski (Филип Бошковски) (a) 28/10/2000, Bitola (North Macedonia) (b) 1,78 (c) D - right back (d) Rabotnicki Skopje (e) Pelister Bitola
*** Bosluk - Arif Bosluk (Arif Boşluk) (a) 06/06/2003, Trabzon (Turkey) (b) 1,84 (c) D - left back (d) Trabzonspor (e) -
*** Bosnjak - Ivan Bosnjak (Ivan Bošnjak) (a) 16/09/1998, Bjelovar (Croatia) (b) - (c) D - central defense (d) - (e) Siroki Brijeg, Mlad. Zdralovi, NK Jarun, Mlad. Zdralovi
*** Bosnjak - Leon Bosnjak (Leon Bošnjak) (a) 23/01/2006, Virovitica (Croatia) (b) - (c) M (d) - (e) Koprivnica, NK Kalinovac, NK Ferdinandovac
*** Bosnjak - Strahinja Bosnjak (Страхиња Бошњак) (a) 18/02/1999, Kraljevo (RF Yugoslavia, now in Serbia) (b) 1,84 (c) D - central defense (d) - (e) FK Krupa, Borac Banja Luka, Kolubara, Vozdovac, Kolubara, Vozdovac, FK Partizan, FK Zemun, FK Partizan, Teleoptik, FK Partizan, Teleoptik
*** Bossi - Paul Bossi (a) 22/07/1991, Niederkorn (Luxembourg) (b) - (c) M - left midfielder (d) FC The Belval Belvaux (e) Mondercange, Union Titus Petange, CS Sanem, Union Titus Petange, Progrès Niederkorn, CS Fola Esch, Progrès Niederkorn
*** Bossut - Sammy Bossut (Sammy Andre Bossut) (a) 11/08/1985, Tielt (Belgium) (b) 1,86 (c) G (d) Racing Harelbeke (e) Zulte Waregem, SWI Harelbeke
*** Bostyn - Louis Bostyn (a) 04/10/1993, Roeselare (Belgium) (b) 1,95 (c) G (d) SV Zulte Waregem (e) KSV Roeselare
*** Bota - Alexandru Bota (Alexandru Cristian Bota) (a) 31/03/2008, Cluj-Napoca (Romania) (b) - (c) M - central midfielder (d) - (e) Universitatea Cluj
*** Bota - Marco Bota (Marco Beniamin Bota) (a) 26/02/2004, Satu Mare (Romania) (b) 1,86 (c) D - left back (d) CSM Olimpia Satu Mare (e) CSM Olimpia SM, UTA Arad

*** Botaka - Jordan Botaka (Jordan Rolly Botaka) (a) 24/06/1993, Kinshasa (Zaire, now DR Congo) (b) 1,84 (c) F - right winger (d) - (e) KAA Gent, H. Jerusalem, KAA Gent, Fortuna Sittard, KAA Gent, RSC Charleroi, KAA Gent, Sint-Truiden, Leeds Utd., Charlton Ath., Leeds Utd., Excelsior, KV Brugge, Belenenses, KV Brugge
*** Botchorishvili - Vakhtang Botchorishvili (ვახტანგ ბოჭორიშვილი) (a) 21/08/2001, ¿? (Georgia) (b) - (c) D - left back (d) FC Samtredia (e) Torpedo Kutaisi, FC Samtredia, Torpedo Kutaisi
*** Botheim - Erik Botheim (a) 10/01/2000, Oslo (Norway) (b) 1,85 (c) F - center forward (d) US Salernitana 1919 (e) Krasnodar, Bodø/Glimt, Rosenborg, Stabæk, Rosenborg, Rosenborg II, Lyn
*** Botic - Zoran Botic (Zoran Botić) (a) 17/10/2005, ¿? (Bosnia and Herzegovina) (b) - (c) D (d) FK Velez Nevesinje (e) -
*** Botis - Nikolaos Botis (Νικόλαος Μπότης) (a) 31/03/2004, Larisa (Greece) (b) 1,96 (c) G (d) - (e) PAOK
*** Botka - Endre Botka (a) 25/08/1994, Budapest (Hungary) (b) 1,78 (c) D - right back (d) Ferencváros TC (e) Honvéd, Kecskeméti TE, Honvéd
*** Botman - Sven Botman (Sven Adriaan Botman) (a) 12/01/2000, Badhoevedorp (Netherlands) (b) 1,95 (c) D - central defense (d) Newcastle United (e) Lille, Ajax B, Heerenveen, Ajax B
*** Botnar - Vitaliy Botnar (Ботнарь Виталий Валерьевич) (a) 19/05/2001, Bălți (Moldova) (b) 1,87 (c) G (d) FC Pari Nizhniy Novgorod (e) Torpedo Moskva, Loko-Kazanka M., Lokomotiv Moskva II, Sokol Moskva
*** Botnari - Ilie Botnari (a) 25/07/2003, ¿? (Moldova) (b) - (c) F - left winger (d) Dacia Buiucani (e) -
*** Boto - Kenji-Van Boto (a) 07/03/1996, Saint-Denis (Reunion) (b) 1,83 (c) D - left back (d) Pau FC (e) AJ Auxerre, Pau FC, AJ Auxerre
*** Botos - Giannis-Fivos Botos (Γιάννης-Φοίβος Μπότος) (a) 20/12/2000, Athina (Greece) (b) 1,73 (c) M - attacking midfielder (d) Helmond Sport (e) AEK Athína, FC Sheriff, AEK Athína, Go Ahead Eagles, AEK Athína
*** Bottani - Mattia Bottani (a) 24/05/1991, Sorengo TI (Switzerland) (b) 1,70 (c) M - attacking midfielder (d) FC Lugano (e) FC Wil 1900, FC Lugano, Genoa, FC Lugano, Genoa, FC Lugano, FC Chiasso
*** Bottoni - Luca Bottoni (a) 12/08/1996, ¿? (Italy) (b) - (c) D - right back (d) FC Fiorentino (e) ACD Torconca
*** Botué - Jean Botué (Kouame Jean Fiacre Botué) (a) 07/08/2002, Marcory (Ivory Coast) (b) 1,84 (c) F - left winger (d) - (e) AC Ajaccio, Ouagadougou
*** Bouanani - Badredine Bouanani (بوعناني الدين بدر) (a) 08/12/2004, Lille (France) (b) 1,77 (c) F - right winger (d) OGC Niza (e) LOSC Lille B
*** Bouaraba - Syphax Bouaraba (a) 15/02/2004, ¿? (France) (b) - (c) M - attacking midfielder (d) Union Titus Petingen II (e) Union Titus Petange
*** Boubane - Jules Boubane (Jules Cesar Boubane) (a) 19/09/2003, ¿? (Senegal) (b) 1,86 (c) D - left back (d) St Joseph's FC (e) Drachtster Boys
*** Bouchalakis - Andreas Bouchalakis (Ανδρέας Μπουχαλάκης) (a) 05/04/1993, Heraklion (Greece) (b) 1,86 (c) M - central midfielder (d) Olympiakos El Pireo (e) Konyaspor, Olympiakos, Nottingham Forest, Olympiakos, Ergotelis, Olympiakos, Ergotelis
*** Bouché - Yan Bouché (a) 19/03/1999, ¿? (Luxembourg) (b) 1,75 (c) F - right winger (d) FC Victoria Rosport (e) Jammerbugt FC, Excelsior Mouscron, RFCU Luxembourg, LOSC Lille B

*** Bouchouari - Mohamed Bouchouari (a) 15/11/2000, ¿? (Belgium) (b) 1,70 (c) D - right back (d) RSC Anderlecht Futures (e) FC Emmen, RSC Anderlecht Futures, F91 Dudelange

*** Boudah - Abdelrahman Boudah (a) 13/08/1999, Göteborg (Sweden) (b) 1,86 (c) F - left winger (d) Hammarby IF (e) Degerfors, Norrby

*** Boudaoui - Hicham Boudaoui (هشام بوداوي) (a) 23/09/1999, Béchar (Algeria) (b) 1,75 (c) M - central midfielder (d) OGC Niza (e) Paradou AC

*** Boudega - Fabrice Boudega (a) 24/07/1998, ¿? (Cameroon) (b) 1,76 (c) M - attacking midfielder (d) - (e) Dzerzhinsk, KF Flamurtari, KF Ulpiana, KF Istogu, FC Ballkani, KF Istogu, FC Ballkani

*** Boudiaf - Mohamed Boudiaf (a) 15/06/2002, ¿? (Ireland) (b) - (c) F - left winger (d) Longford Town FC (e) Glebe North, Newry City, Drogheda United

*** Boudjemaa - Mehdi Boudjemaa (a) 07/04/1998, Cergy (France) (b) 1,82 (c) M - central midfielder (d) Hatayspor (e) Ferencváros, Hatayspor, Guingamp, Stade Lavallois, Guingamp, Quevilly Rouen, Guingamp, EA Guingamp B

*** Bouebari - Franci Bouebari (Franci Clarck Bouebari Kitsamoutse) (a) 12/09/2003, Strasbourg (France) (b) 1,92 (c) D - central defense (d) SC Freiburg II (e) Racing Strasbourg B

*** Bouekou - Natanaël Bouekou (Shurwin Natanaël Bouekou Mahania) (a) 10/05/2002, Paris (France) (b) - (c) M - pivot (d) Chamois Niortais FC (e) AJ Auxerre B

*** Boufal - Sofiane Boufal (بوفال سفيان) (a) 17/09/1993, Paris (France) (b) 1,75 (c) F - left winger (d) Al-Rayyan SC (e) Angers SCO, Southampton, RC Celta, Southampton, Lille, Angers SCO, Angers SCO B

*** Bouhenna - Rachid Bouhenna (بوهنة احمد رشيد) (a) 29/06/1991, Méru (France) (b) 1,91 (c) D - central defense (d) Ionikos Nikeas (e) FCSB, CFR Cluj, Sepsi OSK, Dundee United, MC Alger, CS Constantine, AFC Compiègne, RE Bertrix, Doncaster Rovers, CS Sedan B

*** Boujellab - Nassim Boujellab (a) 20/06/1999, Hagen (Germany) (b) 1,82 (c) M - central midfielder (d) Arminia Bielefeld (e) FC Schalke 04, HJK Helsinki, FC Schalke 04, FC Ingolstadt, HJK Helsinki, FC Ingolstadt, FC Schalke 04, Schalke 04 II

*** Boujir - Youssef Boujir (a) 11/11/2005, ¿? (Morocco) (b) 1,88 (c) G (d) SS Pennarossa (e) Santarcangelo

*** Boukamir - Mehdi Boukamir (a) 26/01/2004, ¿? (Morocco) (b) 1,88 (c) D - central defense (d) RSC Charleroi (e) Zébra Élites

*** Boukassi - Mehdi Boukassi (بوكاسي المهدي محمد) (a) 17/06/1996, Sidi Bel Abbés (Algeria) (b) 1,83 (c) M - attacking midfielder (d) FC Haka (e) FC Haka, Raja Casablanca, Al-Quwa Al-Jaw., Torpedo Kutaisi, Cherno More, Oliveirense, JMG Algier

*** Boukholda - Chahreddine Boukholda (a) 24/05/1996, Marseille (France) (b) 1,84 (c) M - central midfielder (d) Etar Veliko Tarnovo (e) Arda Kardzhali, Mafra, LOSC Lille B, AS Monaco B

*** Boula - Jiri Boula (Jiří Boula) (a) 08/04/1999, Praha (Czech Rep.) (b) 1,83 (c) M - central midfielder (d) FC Banik Ostrava (e) FC MAS Taborsko, Banik Ostrava, FC MAS Taborsko, Mickleover, Uni of Derby, Sparta Praha B

*** Boulbrachène - Redouane Boulbrachène (Redouane Saci Boulbrachène) (a) 25/11/1996, ¿? (France) (b) - (c) F - left winger (d) FC Alisontia Steinsel (e) FC Wiltz 71, Steinsel, Olympique Alès, Steinsel

*** Boulhendi - Teddy Boulhendi (a) 09/04/2001, Martigues (France) (b) 1,85 (c) G (d) OGC Niza (e) OGC Nice B

*** Boultam - Reda Boultam (a) 03/03/1998, Almere (Netherlands) (b) 1,87 (c) M - attacking midfielder (d) US Salernitana 1919 (e) NK Istra, Salernitana, Cosenza, Salernitana, Triestina, Salernitana, Triestina, Cremonese, Ajax B

*** Boumal - Petrus Boumal (Petrus Boumal Mayega) (a) 20/04/1993, Yaoundé (Cameroon) (b) 1,77 (c) M - pivot (d) Al-Bataeh CSC (e) Újpest FC, Nizhny Novgorod, BB Erzurumspor, Ural, CSKA-Sofia, Litex Lovetch, FC Sochaux, FC Sochaux B

*** Boura - Ismaël Boura (a) 14/08/2000, Bandrele (Mayotte) (b) 1,73 (c) D - left back (d) ESTAC Troyes (e) RC Lens, Le Havre AC, RC Lens, RC Lens B

*** Bourabia - Mehdi Bourabia (بوربيعة مهدي) (a) 07/08/1991, Dijon (France) (b) 1,83 (c) M - pivot (d) Spezia (e) Sassuolo, Spezia, Sassuolo, Konyaspor, Levski Sofia, Cherno More, Lokomotiv Plovdiv, LOSC Lille B, Grenoble, Grenoble B

*** Bourard - Samy Bourard (a) 29/03/1996, Liège (Belgium) (b) 1,80 (c) M - attacking midfielder (d) Hapoel Hadera (e) ADO Den Haag, Fehérvár, ADO Den Haag, FC Eindhoven, Sint-Truiden

*** Bourigeaud - Alexis Bourigeaud (a) 02/07/1999, Calais (France) (b) 1,75 (c) M - pivot (d) US Mondorf-Les-Bains (e) Fréjus-St-Raphaël, RC Lens B

*** Bourigeaud - Benjamin Bourigeaud (a) 14/01/1994, Calais (France) (b) 1,78 (c) M - right midfielder (d) Stade Rennais FC (e) RC Lens, RC Lens B

*** Bourtal - Kader Bourtal (a) 08/10/1991, Metz (France) (b) 1,77 (c) M - attacking midfielder (d) FC Mondercange (e) Hombourg-Haut, US Hostert, Steinsel, US Hostert, CR Al Hoceima, US Forbach, FCJL Arlon, US Forbach, RE Bertrix, US Forbach, CS&O Blénod PaM, Mondercange, RS Magny

*** Boury - Alexis Boury (a) 31/10/2001, Metz (France) (b) 1,92 (c) M - central midfielder (d) Jeunesse Esch (e) AS Cherbourg, Jeunesse Esch, RS Magny

*** Boussaid - Othmane Boussaid (a) 07/03/2000, Kortrijk (Belgium) (b) 1,66 (c) F - left winger (d) FC Utrecht (e) NAC Breda, FC Utrecht, Lierse SK

*** Boussong - Tom Boussong (a) 20/08/1998, ¿? (Luxembourg) (b) 1,86 (c) G (d) FC Marisca Mersch (e) Progrès Niederkorn, US Mondorf, Jeunesse Canach, US Mondorf, SC Bettembourg

*** Bouzaiene - Elyas Bouzaiene (a) 08/09/1997, Flemingsberg (Sweden) (b) 1,80 (c) D - right back (d) Degerfors IF (e) Lunds BK, Kristianstad FC, Bromölla, Viby IF

*** Bouzoukis - Giannis Bouzoukis (Γιάννης Μπουζούκης) (a) 27/03/1998, Preveza (Greece) (b) 1,72 (c) M - attacking midfielder (d) Panetolikos GFS (e) OFI Creta, Panathinaikos

*** Bove - Edoardo Bove (a) 16/05/2002, Roma (Italy) (b) 1,81 (c) M - central midfielder (d) AS Roma (e) -

*** Böving - William Böving (William Bøving Wick) (a) 01/03/2003, Copenhagen (Denmark) (b) 1,76 (c) F - center forward (d) SK Sturm Graz (e) FC København

*** Bowden - Ryan Bowden (a) 19/08/2003, Athy, Kildare (Ireland) (b) 1,88 (c) D - central defense (d) University College Dublin (e) Bray Wanderers

*** Bowen - Dan Bowen (a) 11/09/2004, ¿? (Wales) (b) 1,73 (c) F - right winger (d) Caerau Ely (e) Cardiff Metropolitan Police, Caerau Ely

*** Bowen - Jarrod Bowen (a) 20/12/1996, Leominster (England) (b) 1,82 (c) F - right winger (d) West Ham United (e) Hull City, Hereford Utd.

*** Bowler - Josh Bowler (Joshua Luke Bowler) (a) 05/03/1999, Chertsey (England) (b) 1,84 (c) F - right winger (d) Cardiff City (e) Cardiff City, Nottingham Forest, Blackpool, Nottingham Forest, Olympiakos, Nottingham Forest, Blackpool, Hull City

*** Boya - Frank Boya (Frank Thierry Boya) (a) 01/07/1996, Douala (Cameroon) (b) 1,95 (c) M - pivot (d) Royal Antwerp FC (e) Sint-Truiden, Royal Antwerp, Zulte Waregem, Royal Antwerp, Excelsior Mouscron, 1860 München, Apejes FC

*** Boyaci - Hijran Boyaci (Hijran Ali Boyacı) (a) 11/01/2005, Edmonton (Canada) (b) 1,78 (c) M - pivot (d) Adana Demirspor (e) -

*** Boyar - Yavuz Bugra Boyar (Yavuz Buğra Boyar) (a) 10/08/1998, Mersin (Turkey) (b) 1,90 (c) G (d) Hatayspor (e) GMG Kastamonu

*** Boyata - Dedryck Boyata (Anga Dedryck Boyata) (a) 28/11/1990, Brussel (Belgium) (b) 1,88 (c) D - central defense (d) KV Brugge (e) Hertha Berlin, Celtic FC, Manchester City, FC Twente, Manchester City, Bolton Wanderers, Manchester City, Man City Reserves

*** Boyce - Liam Boyce (a) 08/04/1991, Belfast (Northern Ireland) (b) 1,84 (c) F - center forward (d) Heart of Midlothian FC (e) Burton Albion, Ross County, Cliftonville, Werder Bremen II, Cliftonville

*** Boyce - Ronan Boyce (a) 12/05/2001, Ramelton, Donegal (Ireland) (b) 1,80 (c) D - right back (d) Derry City (e) -

*** Boychuk - Bogdan Boychuk (Бойчук Богдан Сергійович) (a) 30/05/1996, Gola Prystan, Kherson Oblast (Ukraine) (b) 1,70 (c) F - right winger (d) Chornomorets Odessa (e) Metalist, Rukh Lviv, Dinamo-Auto, Neftekhimik, Metalist II, Zaria Balti, Metalist II

*** Boyd - Jay Boyd (a) 09/01/2003, Belfast (Northern Ireland) (b) - (c) F - center forward (d) Crusaders FC (e) -

*** Boyd - Leon Boyd (Leon Philip Boyd) (a) 05/12/2005, Belfast (Northern Ireland) (b) 1,80 (c) F - right winger (d) Glentoran FC (e) -

*** Boyd - Sean Boyd (a) 20/06/1998, Swords, Dublin (Ireland) (b) 1,91 (c) F - center forward (d) Shelbourne FC (e) Finn Harps, Longford Town, Shamrock Rovers, Finn Harps, Shamrock Rovers, Malahide

*** Boyd - Tyler Boyd (Tyler Dominic Boyd) (a) 30/12/1994, Tauranga (New Zealand) (b) 1,83 (c) F - left winger (d) Los Ángeles Galaxy (e) Besiktas, Çaykur Rizespor, Besiktas, Sivasspor, Besiktas, Vitória Guimarães, Ankaragücü, Vitória Guimarães, Vitória Guimarães B, Tondela, Vitória Guimarães B, Wellington P., Waikato FC, Melville Utd.

*** Boyd-Munce - Caolan Boyd-Munce (Caolan Stephen Boyd-Munce) (a) 26/01/2000, Belfast (Northern Ireland) (b) 1,83 (c) M - central midfielder (d) St. Mirren FC (e) Middlesbrough, Birmingham City, Redditch Utd.

*** Boyé - Lucas Boyé (a) 28/02/1996, San Gregorio (Argentina) (b) 1,83 (c) F - center forward (d) Elche CF (e) Torino, Elche CF, Torino, Reading, Torino, AEK Athína, Torino, RC Celta, Torino, River Plate, Newell's Old Boys, River Plate

*** Boyes - Morgan Boyes (Morgan Marc Boyes) (a) 22/04/2001, Holywell (Wales) (b) 1,89 (c) D - central defense (d) Livingston FC (e) Fleetwood

*** Boyko - Denys Boyko (Бойко Денис Олександрович) (a) 29/01/1988, Kyiv (Soviet Union, now in Ukraine) (b) 1,97 (c) G (d) FK Polissya Zhytomyr (e) Dinamo Kyïv, Besiktas, Dinamo Kyïv, Besiktas, Málaga CF, Besiktas, Dnipro, Dinamo Kyïv, Dnipro, Dinamo Kyïv, Kryvbas, Dinamo Kyïv, Obolon Kyiv, Dinamo Kyïv, Dynamo 2 Kyiv

*** Boyko - Vitaliy Boyko (Бойко Віталій Володимирович) (a) 03/12/1997, Voznesenske, Cherkasy Oblast (Ukraine) (b) 1,83 (c) M - attacking midfielder (d) LNZ Cherkasy (e) PFK Lviv, Volyn Lutsk, Kremin, FK Minaj, Sant Rafel, Cherkashchyna, FK Umanf. Uman, Zorya Bilozirya

*** Boylan - Gary Boylan (a) 24/04/1996, Belmullet, Mayo (Ireland) (b) - (c) D - right back (d) Sligo Rovers (e) Galway United, Finn Harps, Galway United, Cork City, Sligo Rovers

*** Boyle - Andy Boyle (Andrew Boyle) (a) 07/03/1991, Dublin (Ireland) (b) 1,85 (c) D - central defense (d) Dundalk FC (e) Preston North End, Ross County, Preston

North End, Dundee FC, Preston North End, Doncaster Rovers, Preston North End, Dundalk FC, Shelbourne, UCD, Crumlin United
*** Boyle - Ethan Boyle (a) 04/01/1997, Wexford (Ireland) (b) 1,87 (c) D - right back (d) Wexford FC (e) Finn Harps, Linfield, Shamrock Rovers, Finn Harps, Waterford Utd., North End Utd.
*** Boyle - Martin Boyle (a) 25/04/1993, Aberdeen (Scotland) (b) 1,72 (c) F - right winger (d) Hibernian FC (e) Al-Faisaly FC, Hibernian FC, Dundee FC, Hibernian FC, Dundee FC, Montrose, Dundee FC, Montrose, Lewis Utd.
*** Bozan - Burak Bozan (Mustafa Burak Bozan) (a) 23/08/2000, Mardin (Turkey) (b) 1,90 (c) G (d) Gaziantep FK (e) Tuzlaspor, Gaziantep FK
*** Bozanovic - Matija Bozanovic (Матија Божановић) (a) 13/04/1994, ¿? (RF Yugoslavia, now in Montenegro) (b) 1,88 (c) M - central midfielder (d) FK Mornar Bar (e) FK Decic Tuzi, FK Podgorica, FK Decic Tuzi, OFK Petrovac, FK Decic Tuzi
*** Bozdogan - Can Bozdogan (Can Bozdoğan) (a) 05/04/2001, Köln (Germany) (b) 1,74 (c) M - central midfielder (d) FC Utrecht (e) FC Schalke 04, FC Utrecht, FC Schalke 04, Besiktas, FC Schalke 04
*** Bozenik - Robert Bozenik (Róbert Boženík) (a) 18/11/1999, Terchová (Slovakia) (b) 1,88 (c) F - center forward (d) Boavista Porto FC (e) Feyenoord, Boavista, Feyenoord, Fortuna Düsseldorf, Feyenoord, MSK Zilina, MSK Zilina B
*** Bozhenov - Kirill Bozhenov (Боженов Кирилл Викторович) (a) 07/12/2000, Barnaul (Russia) (b) 1,74 (c) D - right back (d) FK Rostov (e) Dinamo Makhach., Rostov, Khimki, Rostov, Khimki, Rostov, Khimki, Khimki 2, Master-Saturn
*** Bozhev - Aleks Bozhev (Алекс Анастасов Божев) (a) 19/07/2005, Plovdiv (Bulgaria) (b) 1,89 (c) G (d) Litex Lovech (e) CSKA-Sofia
*** Bozhilov - Aleksandar Bozhilov (Александър Ивайлов Божилов) (a) 23/02/2006, ¿? (Bulgaria) (b) - (c) D - left back (d) Levski Sofia (e) Levski Sofia II
*** Bozhin - Sergey Bozhin (Божин Сергей Витальевич) (a) 12/09/1994, Samara (Russia) (b) 1,85 (c) D - central defense (d) Fakel Voronezh (e) KS Samara, Torpedo Moskva, Fakel Voronezh, Syzran-2003, Lada Togliatti, KS Samara, KS Samara II, Yunit Samara, Akron Konoplev
*** Bozhko - Roman Bozhko (Божко Роман Владимирович) (a) 13/08/2002, ¿? (Kazakhstan) (b) 1,90 (c) D - central defense (d) Akzhayik Uralsk (e) Akzhayik II
*** Bozhurkin - Bogomil Bozhurkin (Богомил Костадинов Божуркин) (a) 02/09/2002, Pazardzhik (Bulgaria) (b) - (c) M - attacking midfielder (d) Hebar Pazardzhik (e) Hebar II
*** Bozic - Ivan Bozic (Ivan Božić) (a) 08/06/1997, Vinkovci (Croatia) (b) 1,81 (c) F (d) HNK Sibenik (e) NK Celje, Din. Zagreb II, NK Celje, Din. Zagreb II, NK Rudes, Din. Zagreb II, NK Lokomotiva, Din. Zagreb II
*** Bozic - Marko Bozic (Marko Božić) (a) 14/05/1998, Wien (Austria) (b) 1,83 (c) M - right midfielder (d) NK Maribor (e) Frosinone, NK Maribor, Frosinone, NK Radomlje, Rapid Wien II, FC Stadlau, Rapid Wien II
*** Bozic - Tomislav Bozic (Tomislav Božić) (a) 01/11/1987, Požega (Yugoslavia, now in Croatia) (b) 1,86 (c) D - central defense (d) Slaven Belupo Koprivnica (e) Miedź Legnica, Wisła Płock, Gornik Leczna, Dukla Praha, HNK Gorica, Cibalia, HNK Suhopolje, Siroki Brijeg, Kamen Ingrad
*** Bozickovic - Luka Bozickovic (Luka Božičković) (a) 02/09/2003, ¿? (Slovenia) (b) 1,85 (c) M - central midfielder (d) NK Maribor (e) -
*** Bozinoski - Antonio Bozinoski (Антонио Божиноски) (a) 16/01/2000, Skopje (North Macedonia) (b) 1,77 (c) D - left back (d) FK Skopje (e) Kadino, Sileks, Plackovica, Sileks, Madzari Solidarnost

*** Bozinovski - Daniel Bozinovski (Даниел Божиновски) (a) 08/07/1989, Stip (Yugoslavia, now in North Macedonia) (b) 1,84 (c) G (d) Sileks Kratovo (e) FK Sabail, Rabotnicki, Bregalnica Stip, Sileks

*** Bozok - Umut Bozok (Umut Dilan Bozok) (a) 19/09/1996, Saint-Avold (France) (b) 1,78 (c) F - center forward (d) Trabzonspor (e) FC Lorient, Kasimpasa, FC Lorient, Troyes, FC Lorient, Nîmes, GS Consolat M., FC Metz B

*** Bozovic - Drasko Bozovic (Draško Božović) (a) 30/06/1988, Podgorica (Yugoslavia, now in Montenegro) (b) 1,82 (c) M - pivot (d) FK Decic Tuzi (e) Buducnost Podgorica, FC Prishtina, Rudar Pljevlja, Sutjeska Niksic, Rudar Pljevlja, Sutjeska Niksic, FK Lovcen, Domžale, FK Mladost, H. Beer Sheva, Buducnost Podgorica, Mogren, Buducnost Podgorica

*** Bozovic - Ivan Bozovic (a) 26/05/1990, Kragujevac (Yugoslavia, now in Serbia) (b) 1,85 (c) D - right back (d) Balzan FC (e) Timok Zajecar, Lori Vanadzor, Balzan FC, FK Zemun, Balzan FC, FK Zemun, Jedinstvo Uzice, Donji Srem, Smederevo 1924, OFK Beograd, Radnicki 1923

*** Bozzolan - Andrea Bozzolan (a) 23/02/2004, Desio (Italy) (b) 1,78 (c) D - left back (d) AC Perugia Calcio (e) Perugia

*** Braaf - Jayden Braaf (Jayden Jezairo Braaf) (a) 31/08/2002, Amsterdam (Netherlands) (b) 1,80 (c) F - center forward (d) Hellas Verona (e) Borussia Dortmund II, Hellas Verona, Borussia Dortmund II, Udinese

*** Brabec - Jakub Brabec (Jakub Brabec) (a) 06/08/1992, Praha (Czechoslovakia, now in Czech Rep.) (b) 1,86 (c) D - central defense (d) Aris Thessaloniki (e) Viktoria Plzen, KRC Genk, Viktoria Plzen, KRC Genk, Çaykur Rizespor, KRC Genk, Sparta Praha, Zbrojovka Brno, Sparta Praha, Sparta Praha B, Viktoria Zizkov

*** Bracali - Rafael Bracali (Rafael Wihby Bracali) (a) 05/05/1981, Santos (Brazil) (b) 1,85 (c) G (d) - (e) Boavista, Arouca, Panetolikos, FC Porto, Olhanense, FC Porto, Nacional, Paulista

*** Bracik - Krystian Bracik (a) 18/03/2001, Starachowice (Poland) (b) 1,84 (c) D - central defense (d) Star Starachowice (e) Cracovia, Wisla Pulawy, Cracovia, Cracovia II

*** Bradaric - Domagoj Bradaric (Domagoj Bradarić) (a) 10/12/1999, Split (Croatia) (b) 1,78 (c) D - left back (d) US Salernitana 1919 (e) Lille, Hajduk Split, Hajduk Split II

*** Bradaric - Luka Bradaric (Luka Bradarić) (a) 08/09/2003, Split (Croatia) (b) - (c) D - central defense (d) NK Istra 1961 (e) -

*** Bradford - Louis Bradford (a) 21/02/2002, Wolverhampton (England) (b) 1,88 (c) D - central defense (d) Aberystwyth Town (e) The New Saints, Aberystwyth, The New Saints, Aberystwyth, The New Saints, Aberystwyth, The New Saints, TNS Development

*** Bradley - Eoin Bradley (a) 30/12/1983, Derry (Northern Ireland) (b) 1,83 (c) F - center forward (d) Portadown FC (e) Glenavon, Coleraine, Glenavon, Coleraine, Ballymoney

*** Bradley - Sion Bradley (Sion Alun Bradley) (a) 20/02/1998, Bangor (Wales) (b) - (c) M - attacking midfielder (d) Caernarfon Town (e) Porthmadog, Bangor City

*** Bradley - Steven Bradley (a) 17/03/2002, Glasgow (Scotland) (b) 1,87 (c) F - right winger (d) Livingston FC (e) Hibernian FC, Dundalk FC, Hibernian FC, Ayr United, Hibernian FC, Hibernian B

*** Bradshaw - Adam Bradshaw (a) 31/10/2001, ¿? (Malta) (b) - (c) M (d) Balzan FC (e) -

*** Brady - Niall Brady (a) 02/02/2002, Dundalk (Ireland) (b) - (c) G (d) - (e) Newry City

*** Braem - Stan Braem (a) 25/11/1998, ¿? (Belgium) (b) - (c) F - center forward (d) SV Zulte Waregem (e) Zwevezele, KSV Oostkamp, KFC Varsenare, Dosko St-Kruis

*** Braga - Victor Braga (Victor Cristiano Braga) (a) 18/04/2001, ¿? (Brazil) (b) 1,75 (c) M - pivot (d) FK Maktaaral (e) Ordabasy, Londrina-PR, Santos B, Santa Cruz-RS, Avenida

*** Bragança - Daniel Bragança (Daniel Santos Bragança) (a) 27/05/1999, Almeirim (Portugal) (b) 1,69 (c) M - central midfielder (d) Sporting de Lisboa (e) Estoril Praia, Farense

*** Bragantini - Davide Bragantini (a) 17/08/2003, ¿? (Italy) (b) - (c) F - right winger (d) Mantova 1911 (e) -

*** Bragaru - Maksym Bragaru (Брагару Максим Ігорович) (a) 21/07/2002, Reni, Odesa Oblast (Ukraine) (b) 1,75 (c) F - right winger (d) Chornomorets Odessa (e) Chornomorets 2

*** Bragason - Brynjar Atli Bragason (a) 01/04/2000, ¿? (Iceland) (b) 1,87 (c) G (d) Breidablik Kópavogur (e) Víkingur Ó., Breidablik, Njardvík, Vídir, Njardvík

*** Brahilika - Mikel Brahilika (a) 05/08/1999, Tiranë (Albania) (b) - (c) M - pivot (d) FK Bylis (e) KF Turbina, FC Luftëtari, KF Iliria, FC Kamza

*** Brahimi - Billal Brahimi (a) 14/03/2000, Paris (France) (b) 1,83 (c) F - left winger (d) OGC Niza (e) Angers SCO, Stade Reims, Stade Reims B, Le Mans FC, Stade Reims B

*** Brahimi - Mohamed Brahimi (Mohamed Amine Brahimi محمد أمين براهيمي) (a) 17/09/1998, Lyon (France) (b) 1,81 (c) F - left winger (d) Botev Plovdiv (e) Fakel Voronezh, Botev Plovdiv, Pirin, Neftochimik, Tsarsko Selo, FC Vaulx-en-Vel

*** Braithwaite - Martin Braithwaite (Martin Christensen Braithwaite) (a) 05/06/1991, Esbjerg (Denmark) (b) 1,77 (c) F - center forward (d) RCD Espanyol (e) FC Barcelona, CD Leganés, Middlesbrough, CD Leganés, Middlesbrough, Girondins Bordeaux, Middlesbrough, Toulouse, Esbjerg fB

*** Brajkovic - Roko Brajkovic (Roko Brajković) (a) 03/07/2005, Split (Croatia) (b) 1,76 (c) F - right winger (d) HNK Hajduk Split (e) -

*** Brajlovic - Bakir Brajlovic (Bakir Brajlović) (a) 02/09/2002, Sarajevo (Bosnia and Herzegovina) (b) 1,89 (c) G (d) FK Novi Pazar (e) Sloga Meridian, FK Tuzla City

*** Braletic - Nikola Braletic (Никола Бралетић) (a) 25/02/2004, ¿? (Serbia and Montenegro, now in Montenegro) (b) 1,82 (c) M - central midfielder (d) - (e) OFK Grbalj, FK Bokelj II

*** Bralic - Slavko Bralic (Slavko Bralić) (a) 15/12/1992, Split (Croatia) (b) 1,91 (c) D - central defense (d) NK Osijek (e) HNK Gorica, NK Osijek, Vojvodina, AE Larisa, Neftchi Baku, Siroki Brijeg, NK Osijek, NK Solin, NK Omladinac

*** Brama - Wout Brama (a) 21/08/1986, Almelo (Netherlands) (b) 1,76 (c) M - pivot (d) - (e) FC Twente, Central Coast, FC Utrecht, PEC Zwolle, FC Twente

*** Brambilla - Lukas Brambilla (Lukas Pivetta Brambilla) (a) 04/01/1995, Caxias do Sul (Brazil) (b) 1,80 (c) M - attacking midfielder (d) Othellos Athienou (e) Botev Vratsa, Al-Mesaimeer, Anag. Karditsas, PAE Chania, Doxa Katokopias, Apollon Larisas, AC Kajaani, Krymteplitsa, Guarany Bagé, EC Igrejinha, Náutico B

*** Brancolini - Federico Brancolini (a) 14/07/2001, Modena (Italy) (b) 1,92 (c) G (d) US Lecce (e) Fiorentina, Modena

*** Brandao - Brandao (Ubiratan Brandao de Souza) (a) 01/11/1995, Salvador de Bahía (Brazil) (b) 1,80 (c) F - left winger (d) Jedinstvo Bijelo Polje (e) Prudente-SP, Qyzyljar, Velez Mostar, Araçatuba, Galícia-BA

*** Brandenburger - Eric Brandenburger (a) 08/09/1998, ¿? (Luxembourg) (b) 1,84 (c) D - right back (d) FC Victoria Rosport (e) -

*** Branderhorst - Mattijs Branderhorst (a) 31/12/1993, Tiel (Netherlands) (b) 1,92 (c) G (d) FC Utrecht (e) NEC Nijmegen, Willem II, NEC Nijmegen, Willem II, MVV Maastricht, Willem II

*** Brandhof - Frederik Brandhof (a) 05/07/1996, Skive (Denmark) (b) 1,82 (c) M - central midfielder (d) Aarhus GF (e) Viborg FF, Midtjylland, Skive IK, Midtjylland, Skive IK, Midtjylland, Skive IK

*** Brandner - Patrik Brandner (Patrik Brandner) (a) 04/01/1994, Drozdov (Czech Rep.) (b) 1,80 (c) F - center forward (d) 1.FC Slovácko (e) Ceske Budejovice, Dukla Praha, 1.FK Pribram

*** Brandon - Jamie Brandon (a) 05/02/1998, Glasgow (Scotland) (b) 1,73 (c) D - right back (d) Livingston FC (e) Heart of Midlothian, Morton, Heart of Midlothian

*** Brandt - Julian Brandt (a) 02/05/1996, Bremen (Germany) (b) 1,85 (c) M - attacking midfielder (d) Borussia Dortmund (e) Bayer Leverkusen

*** Branescu - Laurentiu Branescu (Laurențiu Constantin Brănescu) (a) 30/03/1994, Râmnicu Vâlcea (Romania) (b) 1,94 (c) G (d) - (e) Atromitos FC, Universitatea Cluj, FCV Farul, ACSM Poli Iasi, Kilmarnock FC, HNK Gorica, Zalgiris, HNK Gorica, FC Dinamo, Juventus, Omonia Nicosia, Juventus, Haladás, Juventus, Virtus Lanciano, Juventus, Juve Stabia, Juventus, Rm. Valcea

*** Branovets - Ilya Branovets (Брановец Илья Васильевич) (a) 16/04/1990, Slutsk (Soviet Union, now in Belarus) (b) 1,88 (c) G (d) - (e) FK Slutsk, Volna Pinsk, FK Slutsk, Slutsk II

*** Bransteter - Luka Bransteter (Luka Branšteter) (a) 19/06/2002, Slavonski Brod (Croatia) (b) 1,83 (c) F - center forward (d) NK Osijek II (e) Cibalia, NK Osijek II, Slaven Belupo, NK Osijek II, NK Aluminij, NK Osijek II, NK Granicar Zupanja

*** Branthwaite - Jarrad Branthwaite (Jarrad Paul Branthwaite) (a) 27/06/2002, Carlisle (England) (b) 1,95 (c) D - central defense (d) Everton FC (e) PSV Eindhoven, Everton, Blackburn, Everton, Carlisle United

*** Brasanac - Darko Brasanac (Дарко Брашанац) (a) 12/02/1992, Čajetina (Yugoslavia, now in Serbia) (b) 1,78 (c) M - central midfielder (d) CA Osasuna (e) Real Betis, Alavés, Real Betis, CD Leganés, Real Betis, FK Partizan, Smederevo 1924, FK Partizan

*** Brass - Lewis Brass (a) 26/08/1996, Newcastle upon Tyne (England) (b) - (c) G (d) - (e) Haverfordwest, Bangor City, Caernarfon, Connah's Quay, Gateshead, Carlisle United, Workington AFC, Carlisle United

*** Brassier - Lilian Brassier (a) 02/11/1999, Argenteuil (France) (b) 1,86 (c) D - central defense (d) Stade Brestois 29 (e) Stade Rennes, Stade Brestois, Stade Rennes, Stade Rennes B, Valenciennes FC, Stade Rennes B

*** Bratkov - Anton Bratkov (Братков Антон Вікторович) (a) 14/05/1993, Kirovograd (Ukraine) (b) 1,86 (c) D - central defense (d) FC Pyunik Yerevan (e) Metalist 1925, PFC Lviv, M. Petah Tikva, Desna, Zirka, Desna, Veres Rivne, Dynamo 2 Kyiv, Dinamo Kiev II

*** Bratley - Callum Bratley (Callum Anthony Bratley) (a) 12/03/1995, ¿? (Wales) (b) 1,78 (c) M - attacking midfielder (d) Connah's Quay Nomads (e) Flint Town, Christleton FC

*** Brattberg - Johan Brattberg (a) 28/12/1996, ¿? (Sweden) (b) 2,00 (c) G (d) BK Häcken (e) Utsiktens BK, Häcken, Falkenbergs FF, Häcken, Falkenbergs FF, Ullareds IK, Falkenbergs FF, Eskilsminne IF, Falkenbergs FF

*** Bratu - Mario Bratu (Mario George Bratu) (a) 07/06/2002, Ploiești (Romania) (b) - (c) M - right midfielder (d) Petrolul Ploiesti (e) -

*** Bråtveit - Per Kristian Bråtveit (Per Kristian Worre Bråtveit) (a) 15/02/1996, Haugesund (Norway) (b) 1,87 (c) G (d) Odds BK (e) Aarhus GF, Vålerenga, Djurgården, Nîmes, Djurgården, FC Groningen, Djurgården, Haugesund, Djerv 1919
*** Braun - Christopher Braun (a) 15/07/1991, Hamburg (Germany) (b) 1,81 (c) D - right back (d) FC Rapid 1923 (e) CFR Cluj, FC Botosani, OFI Creta, Fortuna Sittard, Wattenscheid 09, VfB Oldenburg, Wilhelmshaven, St. Pauli II
*** Braun - Dominik Braun (a) 03/12/2003, Zagreb (Croatia) (b) - (c) D - central defense (d) GNK Dinamo Zagreb (e) Hrv Dragovoljac, Dinamo Zagreb, NK Lokomotiva, Dinamo Zagreb, Din. Zagreb II
*** Braunöder - Matthias Braunöder (a) 27/03/2002, Eisenstadt (Austria) (b) 1,74 (c) M - central midfielder (d) FK Austria Viena (e) Young Violets
*** Braunovic - Nikola Braunovic (a) 21/07/1997, ¿? (RF Yugoslavia, now in ¿?) (b) - (c) M - central midfielder (d) Balzan FC (e) FK Bokelj, Mosta FC, Senglea Ath., FK Bokelj
*** Braut - Filip Braut (a) 05/06/2002, Rijeka (Croatia) (b) 1,79 (c) M - right midfielder (d) NK Rogaska (e) HNK Rijeka, Hrv Dragovoljac, HNK Rijeka
*** Bravo - Claudio Bravo (Claudio Andrés Bravo Muñoz) (a) 13/04/1983, Viluco (Chile) (b) 1,84 (c) G (d) Real Betis Balompié (e) Manchester City, FC Barcelona, Real Sociedad, Colo Colo
*** Bravo - Juan Bravo (Juan David Bravo Padilla) (a) 01/04/1990, ¿? (Colombia) (b) 1,83 (c) D - right back (d) FC Pyunik Yerevan (e) Ararat Yerevan, Lori Vanadzor, Barracas Bol., Los Andes, Boca Unidos, Deportivo Merlo, Los Andes, Deportivo Merlo
*** Braz - Ivo Braz (Ivo Alexandre Pereira Braz) (a) 25/05/1995, Casa Pia (Portugal) (b) 1,80 (c) M - attacking midfielder (d) KF Aegir (e) Dziugas, Olhanense, Oriental, Sacavenense, Loures, Mirandela, GDR Gafetense, Casa Pia, Operário Lagoa, Casa Pia
*** Brazão - Gabriel Brazão (Gabriel Nascimento Resende Brazão) (a) 05/10/2000, Uberlândia (Brazil) (b) 1,92 (c) G (d) Ternana Calcio (e) Ternana, Internazionale Milano, SPAL, Internazionale Milano, Cruzeiro, Internazionale Milano, Real Oviedo, Internazionale Milano, Albacete, Internazionale Milano, Parma, Cruzeiro
*** Brazhko - Volodymyr Brazhko (Бражко Володимир Володимирович) (a) 23/01/2002, Zaporizhya (Ukraine) (b) 1,84 (c) M - pivot (d) FC Dinamo de Kiev (e) Zorya Lugansk, Dinamo Kyïv, Dinamo Kiev II
*** Brazinskas - Arijus Brazinskas (Arijus Bražinskas) (a) 26/01/2000, Marijampole (Lithuania) (b) 1,95 (c) G (d) FK Kauno Zalgiris (e) DFK Dainava, Montevarchi, Mantova, DFK Dainava
*** Brdarovski - Vladica Brdarovski (Владица Брдаровски) (a) 07/02/1990, Bitola (Yugoslavia, now in North Macedonia) (b) 1,83 (c) D - right back (d) Vardar Skopje (e) FC Shkupi, FC Drita, Vardar, ETO FC Győr, Pelister Bitola, Rabotnicki, Zbrojovka Brno, Pelister Bitola
*** Breakspear - Shea Breakspear (Shea Kevin Luke Breakspear) (a) 22/11/1991, Folkestone (England) (b) - (c) D - right back (d) Lions Gibraltar FC (e) Bruno's Magpies, Lions Gibraltar, Manchester 62, FC Britannia XI, Manchester 62, Lincoln FC
*** Brebels - Sebastiaan Brebels (a) 05/05/1995, Aalst (Belgium) (b) 1,83 (c) M - central midfielder (d) KSK Lierse Kempenzonen (e) KA Akureyri, Lommel SK, Zulte Waregem, Cercle Brugge, Zulte Waregem
*** Brecher - Yanick Brecher (a) 25/05/1993, Zürich (Switzerland) (b) 1,96 (c) G (d) FC Zürich (e) FC Wil 1900, FC Zürich

*** Brecka - Tomas Brecka (Tomáš Břečka) (a) 12/05/1994, Kroměříž (Czech Rep.) (b) 1,85 (c) D - central defense (d) 1.FC Slovácko (e) Kasimpasa, Jablonec, Slovácko
*** Breckmann - Jákup Pauli Breckmann (a) 16/04/1998, ¿? (Faroe Islands) (b) - (c) D - right back (d) AB Argir (e) HB Tórshavn II, TB Tvøroyri, HB Tórshavn II
*** Brecl - Amadej Brecl (a) 06/04/1997, ¿? (Slovenia) (b) 1,74 (c) D - right back (d) NK Domžale (e) NK Celje, NK Bravo, NK Celje, NK Celje
*** Breda - Dominik Breda (a) 27/02/1998, ¿? (Czech Rep.) (b) 1,75 (c) M - attacking midfielder (d) FK Jablonec B (e) Varnsdorf, FK Jablonec B
*** Bredeli - Henrik Bredeli (a) 01/04/1998, Drammen (Norway) (b) 1,91 (c) D - central defense (d) FK Jerv (e) Grorud, SMU Mustangs, Tar Heels, Fram, Strømsgodset, Fredrikstad, Strømsgodset, Strømmen, Strømsgodset
*** Bredlow - Fabian Bredlow (a) 02/03/1995, Berlin (Germany) (b) 1,90 (c) G (d) VfB Stuttgart (e) 1.FC Nürnberg, Hallescher FC, RB Leipzig, RB Salzburg, RB Leipzig
*** Bree - James Bree (James Patrick Bree) (a) 11/12/1997, Wakefield (England) (b) 1,78 (c) D - right back (d) Southampton FC (e) Luton Town, Aston Villa, Luton Town, Aston Villa, Ipswich, Aston Villa, Barnsley FC
*** Breedijk - Luuk Breedijk (Luuk Johannes Christianus Breedijk) (a) 20/02/2004, Locarno (Switzerland) (b) 1,85 (c) F - left winger (d) FC Lucerna (e) -
*** Breen - Declan Breen (a) 24/09/2002, Belfast (Northern Ireland) (b) - (c) G (d) Ballyclare Comrades FC (e) Ballyclare, Cliftonville, Ballyclare, Cliftonville
*** Breen - Garry Breen (a) 13/04/1989, Kilkenny (Ireland) (b) 1,90 (c) D - central defense (d) - (e) Dungannon, Cliftonville, Portadown, Dundalk FC, Galway United, Hereford Utd.
*** Breij - Michael Breij (a) 15/01/1997, Amstelveen (Netherlands) (b) 1,81 (c) F - right winger (d) SC Cambuur Leeuwarden (e) FC Groningen
*** Breite - Radim Breite (Radim Breite) (a) 10/08/1989, Krupka (Czechoslovakia, now in Czech Rep.) (b) 1,75 (c) M - central midfielder (d) SK Sigma Olomouc (e) Slovan Liberec, Teplice, Slovan Liberec, Teplice, Varnsdorf, Caslav, Ceska Lipa, Teplice, Teplice B
*** Breitenmoser - Magnus Breitenmoser (a) 06/08/1998, Wil (Switzerland) (b) 1,83 (c) M - central midfielder (d) AC Oulu (e) FC Thun, AC Oulu, FC Thun, FC Schaffhausen, FC Wil 1900, FC Wil II, FC Tobel
*** Breivik - Emil Breivik (Emil Varhaugvik Breivik) (a) 11/06/2000, Gossen (Norway) (b) 1,80 (c) M - central midfielder (d) Molde FK (e) Raufoss, Molde, Raufoss, Molde, Molde FK II
*** Brekalo - David Brekalo (a) 03/12/1998, Ljubljana (Slovenia) (b) 1,88 (c) D - central defense (d) Viking FK (e) NK Bravo
*** Brekalo - Filip Brekalo (a) 09/06/2002, Mostar (Bosnia and Herzegovina) (b) - (c) D - left back (d) - (e) Zrinjski Mostar, Siroki Brijeg, NK Neretvanac
*** Brekalo - Filip Brekalo (a) 20/01/2003, Zagreb (Croatia) (b) 1,80 (c) D - left back (d) GNK Dinamo Zagreb (e) ND Gorica, Dinamo Zagreb, NK Varazdin, Dinamo Zagreb, Din. Zagreb II
*** Brekalo - Josip Brekalo (a) 23/06/1998, Zagreb (Croatia) (b) 1,75 (c) F - left winger (d) Fiorentina (e) VfL Wolfsburg, Torino, VfL Wolfsburg, VfB Stuttgart, VfL Wolfsburg, Dinamo Zagreb, Din. Zagreb II
*** Bremer - Bremer (Gleison Bremer Silva Nascimento) (a) 18/03/1997, Itapitanga (Brazil) (b) 1,88 (c) D - central defense (d) Juventus de Turín (e) Torino, At. Mineiro
*** Brenden - Erik Brenden (Erik Næsbak Brenden) (a) 07/01/1994, Elverum (Norway) (b) 1,83 (c) M - central midfielder (d) FK Jerv (e) Sandefjord, Lillestrøm, Nybergsund

*** Brendon Lucas - Brendon Lucas (Brendon Lucas da Silva Estevam) (a) 20/05/1995, Brasília (Brazil) (b) 1,88 (c) D - central defense (d) Ho Chi Minh City FC (e) FC Arges, HCMC FC, Portimonense, Leixões, Portimonense, SC Covilhã, Portimonense, Académica Coimbra, Portimonense, Anápolis
*** Brenet - Joshua Brenet (Joshua Benjamin Brenet) (a) 20/03/1994, Kerkrade (Netherlands) (b) 1,81 (c) D - right back (d) FC Twente Enschede (e) Hoffenheim, Vitesse, Hoffenheim, PSV Eindhoven
*** Brenkus - Adam Brenkus (a) 08/01/1999, Dolný Kubín (Slovakia) (b) 1,79 (c) M - attacking midfielder (d) ViOn Zlate Moravce-Vrable (e) Ružomberok, Bardejov, Ružomberok
*** Brennan - Caiolan Brennan (a) 23/11/2001, Coleraine (Northern Ireland) (b) 1,60 (c) F - left winger (d) Limavady United (e) Coleraine, Limavady United, Coleraine, Ballyclare, Coleraine, Limavady United, Coleraine, Limavady United, Coleraine
*** Brennan - Ryan Brennan (a) 11/11/1991, Drogheda, Louth (Ireland) (b) 1,80 (c) M - central midfielder (d) Drogheda United FC (e) Shelbourne, St. Patrick's Ath., Bray Wanderers, Shamrock Rovers, Drogheda United, Monaghan United, Drogheda United
*** Brennan - Sean Brennan (Sean Anthony Brennan) (a) 05/07/2001, Blanchardstown, Dublin (Ireland) (b) - (c) M - attacking midfielder (d) University College Dublin (e) Drogheda United, UCD, Southampton B, Shamrock II, Longford Town, Belvedere FC
*** Breslin - Anto Breslin (Anthony Breslin) (a) 13/02/1997, ¿? (Ireland) (b) 1,73 (c) D - left back (d) St. Patrick's Athletic (e) Bohemians, Longford Town, St. Kevins Boys
*** Bretschneider - Niko Bretschneider (a) 10/08/1999, Berlin (Germany) (b) 1,81 (c) D - left back (d) FK Auda (e) MSV Duisburg, Hertha BSC II
*** Breum - Jakob Breum (Jakob Breum Martinsen) (a) 17/11/2003, Odense (Denmark) (b) 1,78 (c) F - left winger (d) Go Ahead Eagles Deventer (e) Odense BK
*** Breznanik - Michal Breznanik (Michal Breznaník) (a) 16/12/1985, Revúca (Czechoslovakia, now in Slovakia) (b) 1,78 (c) M - left midfielder (d) Banik Kalinovo (e) Podbrezova, Dukla Praha, Sparta Praha, Slovan Liberec, Sparta Praha, Amkar Perm, Slovan Liberec, Slovan Bratislava, Podbrezova
*** Bri - Diego Bri (Diego Vicente Bri Carrazoni) (a) 12/09/2002, Elche (Spain) (b) - (c) F - center forward (d) Atlético de Madrid B (e) Elche Ilicitano
*** Briceag - Marius Briceag (Marius Ionuț Briceag) (a) 06/04/1992, Pitești (Romania) (b) 1,75 (c) D - left back (d) Korona Kielce (e) Universitatea Cluj, FC Voluntari, FCSB, FC Voluntari, FCSB, CS U Craiova, FC Voluntari, CS U Craiova, Rm. Valcea, FC Arges
*** Brics - Edgars Brics (a) 10/04/2003, ¿? (Latvia) (b) - (c) M (d) AFA Olaine (e) Super Nova
*** Briega - Álex Briega (Alejandro Briega de la Cruz) (a) 19/12/2001, Madrid (Spain) (b) 1,78 (c) F - left winger (d) UD Socuéllamos (e) La Unión At., Penya Encarnada, Salamanca CF B, UE Santa Coloma
*** Briffa - Kurt Briffa (a) 22/06/2003, ¿? (Malta) (b) - (c) M (d) - (e) Pietà Hotspurs
*** Briffa - Roderick Briffa (a) 24/08/1981, Valletta (Malta) (b) 1,83 (c) M - right midfielder (d) - (e) Mosta FC, Birkirkara FC, Gzira Utd., Valletta, Sliema Wanderers, Birkirkara FC, Pietà Hotspurs, Birkirkara FC
*** Briffa - Rudi Briffa (a) 21/08/1996, ¿? (Malta) (b) - (c) G (d) Balzan FC (e) Hibernians FC, Tarxien, Hibernians FC
*** Brigant - Tomas Brigant (Tomáš Brigant) (a) 11/10/1994, Považská Bystrica (Slovakia) (b) 1,69 (c) F - right winger (d) FCU Winklarn (e) Skalica, FC Petrzalka,

Skalica, Bardejov, Spartak Trnava, Zbrojovka Brno, FK Senica, Zbrojovka Brno, Spartak Myjava, Zbrojovka Brno, FCZ Brno B, AS Trencin, Dubnica
*** Brighi - Andrea Brighi (a) 29/07/1992, Rimini (Italy) (b) - (c) D - central defense (d) La Fiorita 1967 (e) Sammaurese, Rimini, San Nicolò, Vis Pesaro, Rimini
*** Bright - Harrison Bright (Harrison William Bright) (a) 23/02/2004, Monmouth (Wales) (b) - (c) D - right back (d) Newport County (e) Pontypridd, Newport County
*** Brígido - Rúben Brígido (Rúben Luís Maurício Brígido) (a) 23/06/1991, Leiria (Portugal) (b) 1,72 (c) F - left winger (d) - (e) Kaspiy Aktau, Tobol Kostanay, Ordabasy, Beroe, Nea Salamis, Anagen.Derynias, Othellos Athien, Ermis Aradippou, Otelul Galati, Marítimo, Leiria
*** Brignoli - Alberto Brignoli (a) 19/08/1991, Trescore Balneario (Italy) (b) 1,88 (c) G (d) Panathinaikos FC (e) FC Empoli, Palermo, Juventus, Benevento, Juventus, Perugia, Juventus, CD Leganés, Juventus, Sampdoria, Juventus, Ternana, AC Montichiari, Lumezzane, AC Montichiari, Grumellese, Sarnico
*** Brihon - Yaakov Brihon (בריהון יעקב) (a) 06/07/1993, Rishon LeZion (Israel) (b) 1,75 (c) F - right winger (d) FC Ashdod (e) B. Jerusalem, H Rishon leZion
*** Brik - Yaniv Brik (בריק יניב) (a) 28/05/1995, Zichron Ja'akow (Israel) (b) - (c) M - central midfielder (d) Ironi Tiberias (e) M. Bnei Reineh, Hapoel Ikhsal, Ness Ziona, Maccabi Haifa, Ramat haSharon, Maccabi Haifa, H Rishon leZion, Maccabi Haifa, FC Ashdod, Maccabi Haifa, Maccabi Netanya, Maccabi Haifa, M. Petah Tikva, Maccabi Haifa, Hapoel Acre, Maccabi Haifa, H. Nazareth Illit, Maccabi Haifa
*** Brilhante - Gabriel Brilhante (Gabriel Pereira Brilhante) (a) 03/07/2002, Diadema (SP) (Brazil) (b) 1,87 (c) M - pivot (d) FC Dornbirn (e) Hohenems, Minija, Banga
*** Brima - TJ Brima (Tejan Brima) (a) 28/08/1999, Freetown (Sierra Leona) (b) 1,72 (c) F - left winger (d) Lynx FC (e) Europa Point FC, St Joseph's FC, Europa Point FC, Castuera, UD San Pedro, San Roque Lepe, UD San Pedro
*** Brincat - Zachary Brincat (a) 24/06/1998, ¿? (Malta) (b) - (c) F - left winger (d) Mosta FC (e) -
*** Brinck - Jesper Brinck (a) 22/03/1989, ¿? (Denmark) (b) 1,87 (c) D - central defense (d) Brabrand IF (e) KÍ Klaksvík, Brabrand IF, Varde IF, Esbjerg fB II
*** Brindley-Peagram - Harley Brindley-Peagram (a) 12/11/2005, Wrexham (Wales) (b) - (c) F - center forward (d) Flint Town United (e) -
*** Brink - Mark Brink (Mark Brink Christensen) (a) 15/03/1998, ¿? (Denmark) (b) 1,77 (c) M - pivot (d) Silkeborg IF (e) Esbjerg fB
*** Brinkman - Julian Brinkman (a) 02/01/2003, Gibraltar (Gibraltar) (b) 1,80 (c) M - central midfielder (d) Glacis United (e) -
*** Brinzaniuc - Gheorghe Brinzaniuc (Gheorghe Brînzaniuc) (a) 06/05/2001, Sîngera (Moldova) (b) 1,76 (c) D - right back (d) CF Spartanii Sportul Selemet (e) Dacia Buiucani, Spartanii, Petrocub, Zimbru Chisinau
*** Brinzea - Andres Brinzea (Andres Luciano Brînzea) (a) 15/09/2005, ¿? (Romania) (b) - (c) G (d) AFC Chindia Targoviste (e) -
*** Briski - Mihael Briski (Mihael Briški) (a) 02/01/1999, Varaždin (Croatia) (b) 1,78 (c) D - central defense (d) Sangiuliano City (e) Tabor Sezana, NK Sesvete, Din. Zagreb II, NK Sesvete, Din. Zagreb II
*** Brisola - Felipe Brisola (Felipe Bezerra Brisola) (a) 06/06/1990, Boa Vista (Brazil) (b) 1,70 (c) M - attacking midfielder (d) - (e) Riteriai, Riga, Botev Plovdiv, Atlético-GO, Itumbiara, Atlético-GO, CRAC (GO), Atlético-GO, AA Anapolina, Atlético-GO, Vila Nova FC, Atlético-GO, AA Anapolina
*** Bristric - Admir Bristric (Admir Bristrić) (a) 28/04/2003, Tuzla (Bosnia and Herzegovina) (b) 1,87 (c) F - center forward (d) NK Olimpija Ljubljana (e) HNK Rijeka, Hrv Dragovoljac

*** Brito - Rafael Brito (Rafael Alexandre de Sousa Gancho de Brito) (a) 19/01/2002, Almada (Portugal) (b) 1,83 (c) M - pivot (d) Casa Pia AC (e) Benfica B, Marítimo, Benfica B

*** Brito - Rick Brito (a) 25/11/2000, Luxembourg (Luxembourg) (b) - (c) D - central defense (d) FC Wiltz 71 (e) Jeunesse Esch, FC AS Hosingen, FC Wiltz 71, FC AS Hosingen, FF Norden 02, FC AS Hosingen

*** Britto - Ethan Britto (a) 30/11/2000, Gibraltar (Gibraltar) (b) 1,78 (c) D - left back (d) Lincoln Red Imps FC (e) Mons Calpe, Lincoln FC, Europa Point FC, Lincoln FC

*** Britto - Julian Britto (a) 28/06/2004, Gibraltar (Gibraltar) (b) - (c) D - right back (d) Algeciras CF B (e) Glacis United, Algeciras B, Lincoln FC, Europa Reserve, FC College 1975, Europa Reserve

*** Brkic - Ajdin Brkic (a) 31/01/2004, Zenica (Bosnia and Herzegovina) (b) - (c) G (d) NK Celik Zenica (e) -

*** Brkic - Ivan Brkic (Ivan Brkić) (a) 29/06/1995, Koprivnica (Croatia) (b) 1,94 (c) G (d) Neftchi Baku (e) Riga, Zrinjski Mostar, Cibalia, NK Lokomotiva, NK Imotski, NK Lokomotiva, NK Istra

*** Brkljaca - Marko Brkljaca (Marko Brkljača) (a) 15/07/2004, Zadar (Croatia) (b) 1,76 (c) M - attacking midfielder (d) NK Aluminij Kidricevo (e) NK Aluminij, Dinamo Zagreb, NK Velebit Benkovac

*** Brkovic - Arijan Brkovic (Arijan Brković) (a) 03/02/2001, Vukovar (Croatia) (b) 1,73 (c) M - attacking midfielder (d) HSK Posusje (e) Slaven Belupo, NK Dugopolje, Slaven Belupo, NK Vukovar 1991

*** Brkovic - Dusan Brkovic (Душан Брковић) (a) 20/01/1989, Užice (Yugoslavia, now in Serbia) (b) 1,82 (c) D - central defense (d) KA Akureyri (e) Radnik, Diósgyőr, Riga, Debrecen, Hapoel Haifa, Smederevo 1924, Teleoptik, Hajduk Kula, Teleoptik

*** Brlek - Petar Brlek (a) 29/01/1994, Varaždin (Croatia) (b) 1,80 (c) M - central midfielder (d) NK Osijek (e) Genoa, Ascoli, Genoa, FC Lugano, Genoa, Wisla Kraków, Genoa, Wisla Kraków, Slaven Belupo

*** Brnic - Ivan Brnic (Ivan Brnić) (a) 23/08/2001, Split (Croatia) (b) 1,73 (c) F - left winger (d) NK Maribor (e) NK Dugopolje, Hajduk Split, Hajduk Split II, Zmaj Makarska

*** Brnovic - Marko Brnovic (a) 27/06/2003, Podgorica (Serbia and Montenegro, now in Montenegro) (b) - (c) F - right winger (d) Rudar Pljevlja (e) FK Partizan, Arsenal Tivat, FK Partizan, Teleoptik

*** Brnovic - Milos Brnovic (Miloš Brnović) (a) 26/04/2000, Cetinje (RF Yugoslavia, now in Montenegro) (b) - (c) M - central midfielder (d) Buducnost Podgorica (e) OFK Petrovac, Radnicki 1923, OFK Titograd

*** Brobbel - Ryan Brobbel (a) 05/03/1993, Hartlepool (England) (b) 1,76 (c) M - attacking midfielder (d) The New Saints (e) Whitby, Darlington 1883, Hartlepool Utd., York City

*** Brobbey - Brian Brobbey (Brian Ebenezer Adjei Brobbey) (a) 01/02/2002, Amsterdam (Netherlands) (b) 1,80 (c) F - center forward (d) Ajax de Ámsterdam (e) RB Leipzig, Ajax, RB Leipzig, Ajax B

*** Broccoli - Denis Broccoli (a) 10/08/1988, ¿? (San Marino) (b) - (c) G (d) AC Juvenes-Dogana (e) Faetano, Murata, Tre Fiori, Virtus, Pennarossa, Villa Verucchio, Bellaria Igea Marina, Verucchio

*** Brockbank - Harry Brockbank (Harry William Brockbank) (a) 26/09/1998, Bolton (England) (b) 1,80 (c) D - right back (d) St. Patrick's Athletic (e) El Paso, Bolton Wanderers, Salford

*** Brock-Madsen - Nicolai Brock-Madsen (a) 09/01/1993, Randers (Denmark) (b) 1,91 (c) F - center forward (d) - (e) Randers FC, FC Fredericia, Randers FC, AC

Horsens, Birmingham City, St. Mirren, Birmingham City, Cracovia, Birmingham City, PEC Zwolle, Birmingham City, Randers FC

*** Brodic - Fran Brodic (Fran Brodić) (a) 08/01/1997, Zagreb (Croatia) (b) 1,80 (c) F - center forward (d) NK Varazdin (e) HNK Gorica, NK Varazdin, HNK Gorica, NK Kustosija, Reggiana, Catania, KV Brugge, Catania, KV Brugge, KSV Roeselare, KV Brugge, Royal Antwerp, KV Brugge, Dinamo Zagreb

*** Broetto - Rafael Broetto (Rafael Broetto Henrique) (a) 18/08/1990, Cianorte (Brazil) (b) 1,96 (c) G (d) Vestri Ísafjördur (e) Panevezys, Marítimo, Varzim, Marítimo, Stumbras, Bragantino, Mamoré-MG, Nacional, Mamoré-MG, Santa Helena, Mamoré-MG, Port. Santista, PSTC, Coritiba FC, PSTC

*** Brogno - Loris Brogno (a) 18/09/1992, Charleroi (Belgium) (b) 1,78 (c) F - right winger (d) - (e) Zira FK, Beerschot V.A., Sparta Rotterdam, RAEC Mons, OH Leuven, Lommel United, OH Leuven

*** Broholm - Marius Broholm (Marius Sivertsen Broholm) (a) 26/12/2004, Tiller (Norway) (b) 1,72 (c) M - attacking midfielder (d) Kristiansund BK (e) Kristiansund, Rosenborg, Rosenborg II

*** Broja - Armando Broja (a) 10/09/2001, Slough (England) (b) 1,91 (c) F - center forward (d) Chelsea FC (e) Southampton, Vitesse

*** Broja - Rron Broja (a) 09/04/1996, Mitrovica (Yugoslavia, now in Kosovo) (b) 1,86 (c) M - pivot (d) FC Drita Gjilan (e) FK Partizani, FC Shkupi, KF Trepca 89, KMSK Deinze, KF Trepca 89

*** Brolin - Samuel Brolin (a) 29/09/2000, Lidköping (Sweden) (b) 2,02 (c) G (d) AIK Solna (e) AC Horsens, AIK, Mjällby AIF, AIK, Akropolis IF, AIK, Vasalunds IF, AIK

*** Broll - Kevin Broll (a) 23/08/1995, Mannheim (Germany) (b) 1,85 (c) G (d) SG Dynamo Dresden (e) Górnik Zabrze, Dynamo Dresden, Sonnenhof-Gr., FC 08 Homburg, Waldh. Mannheim

*** Brolli - Cristian Brolli (a) 28/02/1992, Serravalle (San Marino) (b) - (c) D - central defense (d) SS Folgore/Falciano (e) Sammaurese, Cattolica, SS Folgore

*** Brolli - Nicolò Brolli (a) 03/04/2002, ¿? (Italy) (b) - (c) M (d) - (e) Domagnano

*** Broman - Gustav Broman (a) 25/07/2001, ¿? (Sweden) (b) 1,84 (c) D - central defense (d) Skövde AIK (e) Norrby, Elfsborg

*** Bronja - Hamza Bronja (a) 27/08/2004, Novi Pazar (Serbia and Montenegro, now in Serbia) (b) - (c) F - center forward (d) NK Celik Zenica (e) GAK 1902 II

*** Bronkhorst - Ilias Bronkhorst (a) 10/05/1997, Haarlem (Netherlands) (b) 1,85 (c) D - right back (d) - (e) NEC Nijmegen, Telstar, Koninklijke HFC, Kon. HFC 2

*** Bronn - Dylan Bronn (Dylan Daniel Mahmoud Bronn) (a) 19/06/1995, Cannes (France) (b) 1,86 (c) D - central defense (d) US Salernitana 1919 (e) FC Metz, KAA Gent, Chamois Niort, Cannes

*** Brooks - David Brooks (David Robert Brooks) (a) 08/07/1997, Warrington (England) (b) 1,73 (c) F - right winger (d) AFC Bournemouth (e) Sheffield Utd., Halifax Town, Sheffield Utd.

*** Brooks - John Anthony Brooks (a) 28/01/1993, Berlin (Germany) (b) 1,94 (c) D - central defense (d) TSG 1899 Hoffenheim (e) Benfica, VfL Wolfsburg, Hertha Berlin, Hertha BSC II

*** Brophy - Eamonn Brophy (a) 10/03/1996, Cleland (Scotland) (b) 1,75 (c) F - center forward (d) Ross County FC (e) St. Mirren, Ross County, St. Mirren, Kilmarnock FC, St. Mirren, Kilmarnock FC, Dumbarton FC, Queen's Park

*** Brorsson - Franz Brorsson (Franz Denniz Brorsson) (a) 30/01/1996, Trelleborg (Sweden) (b) 1,86 (c) D - central defense (d) Aris Limassol (e) Malmö FF, Esbjerg fB, Malmö FF

*** Broschinski - Moritz Broschinski (a) 23/09/2000, Finsterwalde (Germany) (b) 1,90 (c) F - center forward (d) VfL Bochum (e) Borussia Dortmund II, Energie Cottbus

*** Broukal - David Broukal (a) 16/03/1996, ¿? (Czech Rep.) (b) - (c) D - central defense (d) SK Dynamo Ceske Budejovice (e) Vlasim, Olympia, Slavia Praha B

*** Broun - Samuel Broun (ברואון סמואל) (a) 03/03/1998, Ramat Gan (Israel) (b) - (c) M - central midfielder (d) Hapoel Petah Tikva (e) Kiryat Shmona

*** Brounchtine - Leeor Brounchtine (a) 08/10/2001, ¿? (United States) (b) 1,83 (c) G (d) FC College 1975 (e) LV Legends

*** Brouwer - Patrick Brouwer (a) 19/03/2001, Leiden (Netherlands) (b) 1,76 (c) F - right winger (d) FC Emmen (e) FC Emmen, Sparta Rotterdam

*** Brouwers - Luuk Brouwers (a) 03/05/1998, Helmond (Netherlands) (b) 1,83 (c) M - pivot (d) FC Utrecht (e) Go Ahead Eagles, FC Den Bosch

*** Brown - James Brown (James Dominic Brown) (a) 12/01/1998, Dover (England) (b) 1,86 (c) D - right back (d) St. Johnstone FC (e) Millwall, St. Johnstone, Millwall, Lincoln City, Millwall, Livingston FC, Millwall, Carlisle United, Millwall

*** Brown - Morgan Brown (Morgan Lea Brown) (a) 29/11/1999, Leicester (England) (b) 1,82 (c) M - pivot (d) Aris Limassol (e) Stratford Town, Aberdeen FC B

*** Brown - Rodney Brown (a) 13/08/1995, Kells (Northern Ireland) (b) - (c) D - central defense (d) Coleraine FC (e) Crusaders, Coleraine, Linfield

*** Brown - Rory Brown (Rory Francis Brown) (a) 25/05/2000, Londonderry (Northern Ireland) (b) 1,87 (c) G (d) Glenavon FC (e) Glentoran, Ballinamallard, Glentoran, Institute FC

*** Brown - Sean Brown (Sean Brendan Brown) (a) 01/04/2005, ¿? (Northern Ireland) (b) - (c) D - right back (d) Bangor FC (e) -

*** Browne - David Browne (David Eric Browne) (a) 27/12/1995, Port Moresby (Papua New Guinea) (b) 1,75 (c) F - left winger (d) - (e) HJK Helsinki, Auckland City, Central United

*** Browne - Luke Browne (a) 06/10/2005, ¿? (Ireland) (b) - (c) D - central defense (d) Wexford FC (e) Shelbourne

*** Brozi - Marvin Brozi (a) 07/07/2001, Latisana (Italy) (b) 1,95 (c) G (d) FK Kukësi (e) Este

*** Brozovic - Marcelo Brozovic (Marcelo Brozović) (a) 16/11/1992, Zagreb (Croatia) (b) 1,81 (c) M - pivot (d) Al-Nassr FC (e) Internazionale Milano, Dinamo Zagreb, Internazionale Milano, Dinamo Zagreb, NK Lokomotiva, Hrv Dragovoljac

*** Brruti - Etnik Brruti (a) 04/03/2004, Kaçanik (Serbia and Montenegro, now in Kosovo) (b) 1,80 (c) M - central midfielder (d) FC Malisheva (e) FC Besa

*** Brtan - Marko Brtan (a) 07/04/1991, Zagreb (Yugoslavia, now in Croatia) (b) 1,89 (c) M - pivot (d) Mezőkövesd Zsóry FC (e) Hrv Dragovoljac, Borac Banja Luka, FC Urartu, FK Krupa, Kalju FC, HNK Gorica, NK Lucko, Liepaja, Wigry Suwalki, NK Lucko, HNK Gorica, Hrv Dragovoljac, NK Rudes

*** Brucic - Karlo Brucic (Karlo Bručić) (a) 17/04/1992, Zagreb (Croatia) (b) 1,84 (c) D - left back (d) NK Varazdin (e) CFR Cluj, Koper, Apollon Smyrnis, Dinamo Minsk, Suduva, Sagan Tosu, FC Ashdod, NK Lokomotiva, Dinamo Zagreb, NK Lokomotiva, Dinamo Zagreb, Radnik Sesvete

*** Bruijn - Jordy Bruijn (a) 23/07/1996, Amsterdam (Netherlands) (b) 1,71 (d) Safa Beirut SC (e) NEC Nijmegen, Heerenveen, NEC Nijmegen, Heerenveen, Ajax B

*** Brüll - Maximilian Brüll (a) 26/08/2002, München (Germany) (b) 1,87 (c) G (d) Borussia Mönchengladbach (e) Borussia Mönchengladbach II

*** Brüls - Christian Brüls (a) 30/09/1988, Malmedy (Belgium) (b) 1,79 (c) M - attacking midfielder (d) SV Zulte Waregem (e) Sint-Truiden, KVC Westerlo, Pafos FC, KAS Eupen, Stade Rennes, Standard Liège, Stade Rennes, KAA Gent, OGC Nice, KAA Gent, KVC Westerlo, MVV Maastricht, Trabzonspor, MVV Maastricht, Trabzonspor, KAS Eupen

*** Bruma - Bruma (Armindo Tué Na Bangna) (a) 24/10/1994, Bissau (Guinea-Bissau) (b) 1,73 (c) F - left winger (d) SC Braga (e) Fenerbahce, SC Braga, Fenerbahce, PSV Eindhoven, Fenerbahce, PSV Eindhoven, Olympiakos, PSV Eindhoven, RB Leipzig, Galatasaray, Real Sociedad, Galatasaray, Gaziantepspor, Galatasaray, Sporting Lisboa, Sporting B

*** Bruma - Jeffrey Bruma (Jeffrey Kevin van Homoet Bruma) (a) 13/11/1991, Rotterdam (Netherlands) (b) 1,89 (c) D - central defense (d) RKC Waalwijk (e) Heerenveen, Kasimpasa, VfL Wolfsburg, Mainz 05, VfL Wolfsburg, FC Schalke 04, VfL Wolfsburg, PSV Eindhoven, Chelsea, SV Hamburg, Chelsea, Leicester City, Chelsea

*** Bruma - Mihail Bruma (a) 22/12/1995, ¿? (Romania) (b) - (c) F - center forward (d) SS San Giovanni (e) Murata, Verucchio, CBR Carli Pietracuta, Verucchio

*** Bruna - Gerardo Bruna (Gerardo Alfredo Bruna Blanco) (a) 29/01/1991, Mendoza (Argentina) (b) 1,78 (c) M - central midfielder (d) CD Unión Puerto (e) Dungannon, Shelbourne, Derry City, Ottawa Fury, Accrington St., Whitehawk, Tranmere Rovers, SD Huesca, Blackpool, Liverpool Reserves

*** Bruncevic - Ensar Bruncevic (Енсар Брунчевић) (a) 13/02/1999, Novi Pazar (RF Yugoslavia, now in Serbia) (b) 1,96 (c) D - central defense (d) FK Novi Pazar (e) Balestier Khals, Spartak Moskva II, Spartak, FK Josanica, Spartak

*** Brunes - Jonatan Braut Brunes (a) 07/08/2000, Bryne (Norway) (b) 1,88 (c) F - center forward (d) Oud-Heverlee Leuven (e) Strømsgodset, Lillestrøm, Start, Lillestrøm, Florø SK, Lillestrøm, Florø SK, Bryne, Sola FK, Bryne

*** Brunetti - Mateus Brunetti (Mateus Brunetti Valor) (a) 18/11/1999, São Paulo (Brazil) (b) 1,85 (c) D - central defense (d) DAC Dunajska Streda (e) Figueirense FC

*** Bruninho - Bruninho (Bruno Miguel Carapeto dos Reis) (a) 20/07/1999, Portimão (Portugal) (b) 1,76 (c) M - central midfielder (d) SC Covilhã (e) SC Covilhã, Portimonense

*** Brunner - Cédric Brunner (a) 17/02/1994, Zollikon (Switzerland) (b) 1,81 (c) D - right back (d) FC Schalke 04 (e) Arminia Bielefeld, FC Zürich

*** Brúnni - Signar á Brúnni (a) 19/11/2002, ¿? (Faroe Islands) (b) - (c) D - central defense (d) Víkingur Gøta (e) Víkingur II

*** Bruno - Bruno (Bruno Felipe Souza da Silva) (a) 26/05/1994, Barueri, São Paulo (Brazil) (b) 1,80 (c) F - left winger (d) Pafos FC (e) Omonia Nicosia, FC Sheriff, Aris Thessaloniki, Olympiakos, LASK, Atromitos FC, LASK, Austria Lustenau, Austria Lustenau II

*** Bruno - Gianni Bruno (a) 19/08/1991, Rocourt (Belgium) (b) 1,80 (c) F - center forward (d) Eyüpspor (e) KAA Gent, Sint-Truiden, KAA Gent, Zulte Waregem, Cercle Brugge, Thonon Évian, KS Samara, Évian, FC Lorient, Évian, Lille, SC Bastia, Lille, LOSC Lille B

*** Bruno - Massimo Bruno (a) 17/09/1993, Boussu (Belgium) (b) 1,78 (c) F - right winger (d) KV Kortrijk (e) Bursaspor, RSC Charleroi, RB Leipzig, RSC Anderlecht, RB Leipzig, RB Salzburg, RB Leipzig, RSC Anderlecht

*** Bruno Fuchs - Bruno Fuchs (Bruno de Lara Fuchs) (a) 01/04/1999, Ponta Grossa (Brazil) (b) 1,90 (c) D - central defense (d) Clube Atlético Mineiro (e) At. Mineiro, CSKA Moskva, Internacional

*** Bruno Marques - Bruno Marques (Bruno Henrique Marques Torres) (a) 22/02/1999, Recife (Brazil) (b) 1,94 (c) F - center forward (d) CS Marítimo (e) Marítimo, Santos, Arouca, Santos, Lagarto, Santos, Santos B, Lagarto
*** Bruno Oliveira - Bruno Oliveira (Bruno de Oliveira Souza) (a) 09/06/1996, ¿? (Brazil) (b) 1,86 (c) D - central defense (d) - (e) Siroki Brijeg, São Joseense, EC Lemense, Brasiliense, Central, São Paulo-RS, Portuguesa
*** Bruno Santos - Bruno Santos (Bruno Araújo dos Santos) (a) 07/02/1993, Rio de Janeiro (Brazil) (b) 1,82 (c) D - right back (d) Goiás EC (e) AEL Limassol, Paços Ferreira, Freamunde, Sourense, Alcanenense, Nova Cidade, Mesquita-RJ
*** Bruns - Max Bruns (a) 06/11/2002, Almelo (Netherlands) (b) 1,83 (c) D - central defense (d) FC Twente Enschede (e) -
*** Brunt - Lewis Brunt (a) 06/11/2000, Birmingham (England) (b) 1,87 (c) M - pivot (d) Leicester City (e) Gloucester
*** Bruqi - Agron Bruqi (a) 27/01/1993, Isniq (RF Yugoslavia, now in Kosovo) (b) 1,85 (c) M - central midfielder (d) - (e) FC Malisheva, KF Arbëria, KF Flamurtari, Kek-U Kastriot, KF Istogu, KF 2 Korriku, Decani
*** Brusco - Théo Brusco (a) 20/11/1999, ¿? (France) (b) - (c) D - central defense (d) FC Differdange 03 (e) Villerupt-Thil
*** Bruseth - Heine Gikling Bruseth (a) 06/04/2004, Gjemnes (Norway) (b) 1,77 (c) M - central midfielder (d) Kristiansund BK (e) Levanger, Kristiansund
*** Brush - Richard Brush (a) 26/11/1984, Birmingham (England) (b) 1,86 (c) G (d) Sligo Rovers (e) Cliftonville, Ballinamallard, Finn Harps, Sligo Rovers, Shamrock Rovers, Sligo Rovers, Shamrock Rovers, Sligo Rovers, Shrewsbury, Coventry City, Tamworth, Coventry City
*** Bruun Larsen - Jacob Bruun Larsen (a) 19/09/1998, Lyngby (Denmark) (b) 1,83 (c) F - left winger (d) Burnley FC (e) Burnley, Hoffenheim, RSC Anderlecht, Hoffenheim, Borussia Dortmund, VfB Stuttgart, Borussia Dortmund
*** Bruus - Andreas Bruus (a) 16/01/1999, ¿? (Denmark) (b) 1,83 (c) D - right back (d) ESTAC Troyes (e) Brøndby IF, FC Roskilde, Brøndby IF
*** Bruzzese - Sébastien Bruzzese (Sébastien Nicodemo Bruzzese) (a) 01/03/1989, Liège (Belgium) (b) 1,85 (c) G (d) Cercle Brugge (e) KV Kortrijk, KV Brugge, Sint-Truiden, KV Brugge, Zulte Waregem, KAA Gent, RSC Anderlecht, RFC Liégeois
*** Bryan - Bryan (Bryan Silva Garcia) (a) 28/03/1992, Belo Horizonte (Brazil) (b) 1,77 (c) D - left back (d) FK Aksu (e) FC Astana, Atyrau, Alashkert CF, CRB, Cruzeiro, EC Vitória, Cruzeiro, América-MG, Ponte Preta, América-MG, Portuguesa, América-MG, Benfica B, América-MG
*** Bryan - Joe Bryan (Joseph Edward Bryan) (a) 17/09/1993, Bristol (England) (b) 1,70 (c) D - left back (d) Millwall FC (e) Fulham, OGC Nice, Fulham, Bristol City, Plymouth Argyle, Bristol City, Bath City
*** Bryan Idowu - Bryan Idowu (Bryan Oladapo Idowu) (a) 18/05/1992, St. Petersburg (Russia) (b) 1,79 (c) D - left back (d) - (e) Khimki, Lokomotiv Moskva, Khimki, Lokomotiv Moskva, Amkar Perm, Amkar II, Dinamo SPb, Amkar II, Smena S-Pb
*** Bryde - Björn Berg Bryde (a) 08/07/1992, ¿? (Iceland) (b) - (c) D - central defense (d) Stjarnan Gardabaer (e) HK Kópavogs, Stjarnan, Grindavík, Hafnarfjördur
*** Brym - Charles-Andreas Brym (a) 08/08/1998, Colombes (France) (b) 1,85 (c) F - right winger (d) Sparta Rotterdam (e) FC Eindhoven, Sparta Rotterdam, FC Eindhoven, Excelsior Mouscron, LOSC Lille B
*** Brynhildsen - Ola Brynhildsen (a) 27/04/1999, Bærum (Norway) (b) 1,75 (c) F - center forward (d) Molde FK (e) Stabæk

*** Brynjarsson - Terji Brynjarsson (Terji Þór Brynjarsson) (a) 11/12/1991, ¿? (Faroe Islands) (b) - (c) G (d) B71 Sandoy (e) FC Hoyvík, B68 Toftir, Undrid FF, B71 Sandoy, Undrid FF, B36 II, Undrid FF

*** Bryzgalov - Sergey Bryzgalov (Брызгалов Сергей Владимирович) (a) 15/11/1992, Pavlovo, Nizhniy Novgorod Region (Russia) (b) 1,82 (c) D - central defense (d) Fakel Voronezh (e) Ural, Anzhi, Terek Grozny, Spartak Moskva, Saturn II, Master-Saturn

*** Brzek - Bartosz Brzek (Bartosz Brzęk) (a) 01/12/2005, ¿? (Poland) (b) 1,80 (c) D - right back (d) KS Lechia Gdańsk (e) Lechia II, AP Lechia

*** Bua - Kevin Bua (a) 11/08/1993, Genève (Switzerland) (b) 1,80 (c) F - left winger (d) FC Sion (e) CD Leganés, FC Basel, FC Zürich, Servette FC

*** Bubanja - Vladan Bubanja (Владан Бубања) (a) 21/02/1999, Nikšić (RF Yugoslavia, now in Montenegro) (b) 1,94 (c) M - pivot (d) NK Lokomotiva Zagreb (e) Sutjeska Niksic, Sutjeska II

*** Bucci - Marco Bucci (a) 19/07/1999, ¿? (Italy) (b) 1,86 (c) F - right winger (d) Gioiese 1918 (e) Libertas

*** Bucek - Zan Bucek (a) 26/01/2004, ¿? (Slovenia) (b) - (c) D - left back (d) NS Mura (e) -

*** Buch - Andreas Buch (Andreas Funk) (a) 25/04/1993, Frankenthal (Germany) (b) 1,95 (c) F - center forward (d) Racing FC Union Luxembourg (e) Differdange 03, Pfeddersheim, VfR Grünstadt, SV Horchheim

*** Bucha - Pavel Bucha (Pavel Bucha) (a) 11/03/1998, Mělník (Czech Rep.) (b) 1,77 (c) M - central midfielder (d) FC Viktoria Plzen (e) Mlada Boleslav, Viktoria Plzen, Slavia Praha, Slavia Praha B

*** Buchalik - Michal Buchalik (Michał Buchalik) (a) 03/02/1989, Rybnik (Poland) (b) 1,90 (c) G (d) Ruch Chorzów (e) Lechia Gdánsk, Wisla Kraków, Ruch, Lechia Gdánsk, Odra Wodzislaw, ROW Rybnik

*** Buchanan - Lee Buchanan (Lee David Buchanan) (a) 07/03/2001, Mansfield (England) (b) 1,79 (c) D - left back (d) Birmingham City (e) Werder Bremen, Derby

*** Buchanan - Tajon Buchanan (Tajon Trevor Buchanan) (a) 08/02/1999, Brampton, Ontario (Canada) (b) 1,83 (c) F - right winger (d) KV Brugge (e) New England, Syracuse, Sigma FC, Syracuse, Real Colorado, Mississauga F.

*** Buchanan-Rolleston - Benjamin Buchanan-Rolleston (a) 03/02/2002, Belfast (Northern Ireland) (b) - (c) D - central defense (d) Carrick Rangers (e) -

*** Buchin (c) G (d) CSF Balti-SSS Balti (e) - - Alexandr Buchin (c) G (d) CSF Balti-SSS Balti (e) -

*** Buchkov - Aleksandar Buchkov (Александър Мирославов Бучков) (a) 13/09/2003, Ruse (Bulgaria) (b) 1,80 (c) D - right back (d) Pirin Blagoevgrad (e) Pirin, CSKA-Sofia, Litex Lovetch

*** Buchnev - Stanislav Buchnev (Ստանիսլավ Սերգեևիչ Բուչնև) (a) 17/07/1990, Vladikavkaz (Soviet Union, now in Russia) (b) 1,86 (c) G (d) FC Pyunik Yerevan (e) Fakel Voronezh, Tyumen, Volgar, Angusht Nazran, Mashuk, Neftekhimik, Avtodor Vladikavkaz

*** Buchta - David Buchta (a) 27/06/1999, ¿? (Czech Rep.) (b) 1,84 (c) M - attacking midfielder (d) FC Banik Ostrava (e) Baník Ostrava B

*** Buckley - Garry Buckley (a) 19/08/1993, Cork (Ireland) (b) 1,85 (c) D - central defense (d) Sligo Rovers (e) Cork City

*** Buckley - Keith Buckley (a) 17/06/1992, Dublin (Ireland) (b) 1,80 (c) M - central midfielder (d) Bohemian FC (e) B. Spartans, Bohemians, Bray Wanderers, Bohemians

*** Bucur - Laurentiu Bucur (Laurenţiu Marian Bucur) (a) 08/09/2005, Piteşti (Romania) (b) - (c) G (d) CS Mioveni (e) -

*** Bucur - Raul Bucur (Raul Gabriel Bucur) (a) 24/12/2002, Ploieşti (Romania) (b) - (c) F - center forward (d) Petrolul Ploiesti (e) CSO Plopeni, Sportul Snagov

*** Bucuroiu - Cosmin Bucuroiu (Cosmin Alexandru Bucuroiu) (a) 11/09/2003, Bucuresti (Romania) (b) - (c) F - right winger (d) FC Hermannstadt (e) Unirea Bascov, FC Hermannstadt, Unirea Bascov, FC D. Coman, SCM Piteşti

*** Budachev - Ivan Budachev (Будачёв Иван Сергеевич) (a) 20/07/2001, St. Petersburg (Russia) (b) 1,93 (c) G (d) Dinamo Moskva (e) Leningradets, SShOR Zenit

*** Budescu - Constantin Budescu (Constantin Valentin Budescu) (a) 19/02/1989, Urziceni (Romania) (b) 1,86 (c) M - attacking midfielder (d) FCV Farul Constanta (e) Petrolul, FC Voluntari, FCSB, Damac FC, Astra Giurgiu, Al-Shabab, FCSB, Astra Giurgiu, DL Yifang, Astra Giurgiu, DL Yifang, Astra Giurgiu, Petrolul

*** Budimir - Ante Budimir (a) 22/07/1991, Zenica (Yugoslavia, now in Bosnia and Herzegovina) (b) 1,90 (c) F - center forward (d) CA Osasuna (e) RCD Mallorca, CA Osasuna, RCD Mallorca, Crotone, RCD Mallorca, Crotone, Sampdoria, Crotone, Sampdoria, Crotone, FC St. Pauli, Crotone, FC St. Pauli, NK Lokomotiva, Inter Zaprešić, HNK Gorica, LASK, NK Radnik

*** Budinauckas - Lewis Budinauckas (a) 19/06/2002, ¿? (Scotland) (b) - (c) G (d) Rangers FC Reserves (e) Raith Rovers, Rangers II, Civil Service, Rangers II

*** Budinov - Ilker Budinov (Илкер Илков Будинов) (a) 11/08/2000, Targovishte (Bulgaria) (b) 1,84 (c) D - right back (d) Etar Veliko Tarnovo (e) Etar, Ludogorets II, Pirin, Ludogorets II, Spartak Varna, Ludogorets II, Ludogorets

*** Budinsky - Lukas Budinsky (Lukáš Budínský) (a) 27/03/1992, Praha (Czechoslovakia, now in Czech Rep.) (b) 1,78 (c) M - attacking midfielder (d) MFK Karvina (e) Banik Ostrava, Karvina, Banik Ostrava, Mlada Boleslav, Karvina, Bohemians 1905, Karvina, Bohemians 1905

*** Budinsky - Viktor Budinsky (Viktor Budinský) (a) 09/05/1993, Banská Štiavnica (Slovakia) (b) 1,86 (c) G (d) FK Pardubice (e) Banik Ostrava, Pardubice, Banik Ostrava, Sparta Praha, Bohemians 1905, Sparta Praha, Bohemians 1905, Sparta Praha, Vlasim, Banska Bystrica

*** Budzinski - Marcin Budzinski (Marcin Budziński) (a) 06/07/1990, Giżycko (Poland) (b) 1,84 (c) M - attacking midfielder (d) Hutnik Krakow (e) Cracovia, Cracovia II, Stal Mielec, Cracovia, Radomiak, Arka Gdynia, Cracovia, Melbourne City, Cracovia, Arka Gdynia, Cracovia, Arka Gdynia

*** Buendía - Emiliano Buendía (Emiliano Buendía Stati) (a) 25/12/1996, Mar del Plata (Argentina) (b) 1,72 (c) F - right winger (d) Aston Villa (e) Norwich City, Getafe CF, Cultural Leonesa, Getafe CF, Getafe CF B, Cadetes

*** Bueno - Hugo Bueno (Hugo Bueno López) (a) 18/09/2002, Vigo (Spain) (b) 1,80 (c) D - left back (d) Wolverhampton Wanderers (e) -

*** Bueno - Manu Bueno (Manuel Bueno Sebastián) (a) 27/07/2004, Jerez de la Frontera (Spain) (b) 1,78 (c) M - central midfielder (d) Sevilla Atlético (e) -

*** Bueno - Santiago Bueno (Santiago Ignacio Bueno Sciutto) (a) 09/11/1998, Montevideo (Uruguay) (b) 1,92 (c) D - central defense (d) Girona FC (e) FC Barcelona B, CF Peralada, FC Barcelona B

*** Buess - Roman Buess (a) 21/09/1992, Basel (Switzerland) (b) 1,83 (c) F - center forward (d) FC Winterthur (e) Lausanne-Sport, FC St. Gallen, FC Thun, FC Wohlen, FC Locarno, FC Aarau

*** Buff - Oliver Buff (a) 03/08/1992, Baden (Switzerland) (b) 1,76 (c) M - attacking midfielder (d) FK Zalgiris Vilnius (e) Selangor FC, Grasshoppers, Anorthosis, Real Zaragoza, FC Zürich

*** Buga - Victor Buga (a) 29/06/1994, Anenii Noi (Moldova) (b) 1,80 (c) G (d) CF Spartanii Sportul Selemet (e) Milsami, Viitorul Tîrgu Jiu, Zimbru Chisinau, FC Petrocub, Zimbru Chisinau, FC Petrocub, Zimbru Chisinau

*** Buganim - Itay Buganim (בוגאנים איתי) (a) 29/05/2001, ¿? (Israel) (b) - (c) F - left winger (d) Hapoel Haifa (e) -

*** Bugarin - Marko Bugarin (Марко Бугарин) (a) 16/08/1999, ¿? (RF Yugoslavia, now in Montenegro) (b) 1,98 (c) D - central defense (d) FK Spartak Subotica (e) Jedinstvo, Mornar Bar, FK Bokelj, Mornar Bar, Jedinstvo, OSK Igalo, Jedinstvo

*** Bugay - Vladyslav Bugay (Бугай Владислав Сергійович) (a) 27/10/1997, Kyiv (Ukraine) (b) 1,86 (c) F - center forward (d) Zorya Lugansk (e) PFK Lviv, Chornomorets, FK Mariupol, MFK Mykolaiv, FK Mariupol, FK Mariupol II, Shakhtar II, Bukovyna, Shakhtar II, Lokomotyv Kyiv

*** Bugeja - Jean Claude Bugeja (Jean Claude Aboumehdi Bugeja) (a) 10/02/2004, ¿? (Malta) (b) - (c) F (d) St. Andrews FC (e) Gudja United FC, FC Chiasso

*** Bugeja - Shaun Bugeja (a) 03/08/1995, ¿? (Malta) (b) - (c) D - central defense (d) Zebbug Rangers FC (e) FC Swieqi Utd., Siggiewi FC

*** Bugridze - Irakli Bugridze (ირაკლი ბუგრიძე) (a) 03/01/1998, Tbilisi (Georgia) (b) 1,78 (c) F - left winger (d) Torpedo Kutaisi (e) FC Dila, Dinamo Tbilisi, Beerschot V.A., Chikhura, FC Locomotive

*** Bugriev - Sergey Bugriev (Бугриёв Сергей Сергеевич) (a) 16/03/1998, St. Petersburg (Russia) (b) 1,97 (c) D - central defense (d) Spartak Kostroma (e) Vitebsk, Qyzyljar, Tom Tomsk, Zenit 2 St. Peterburg, Zenit St. Peterburg II, Kosice B, Zenit St. Peterburg II

*** Bugulov - Georgiy Bugulov (Бугулов Георгий Олегович) (a) 17/03/1993, Vladikavkaz (Russia) (b) 1,90 (c) D - central defense (d) Kaspiy Aktau (e) Slavia, KamAZ, Rustavi, CSF Speranta, Druzhba Maikop, Alania, S2V, Beslan-FAUR

*** Buhacianu - Valentin Buhacianu (Valentin Buhăcianu) (a) 28/10/1993, Vatra Dornei (Romania) (b) 1,82 (c) F - center forward (d) ACSC FC Arges (e) FC Hermannstadt, UTA Arad, Aerostar, Miroslava, Atletico Vaslui, Bucovina Poj., Dorna V. Dornei

*** Buhagiar - Bjorn Buhagiar (a) 10/02/2004, ¿? (Malta) (b) - (c) M (d) Zejtun Corinthians FC (e) Zejtun C., Hamrun Spartans

*** Buhagiar - Mark Buhagiar (a) 04/06/1986, ¿? (Malta) (b) - (c) D (d) Xaghra United FC (e) Victoria Hotspurs

*** Buhagiar - Maverick Buhagiar (a) 28/07/1998, ¿? (Malta) (b) - (c) G (d) Valletta FC (e) Mqabba FC, Valletta, Tarxien, Valletta, Tarxien

*** Buhanga - Lamine Buhanga (Lamine Robert Buhanga) (a) 03/10/2001, ¿? (France) (b) 1,88 (c) D - central defense (d) - (e) AJ Auxerre B, EA Guingamp B

*** Buhari - Ibrahim Buhari (a) 08/10/2001, ¿? (Nigeria) (b) 1,90 (c) D - central defense (d) IF Elfsborg (e) Plateau United

*** Buhari - Sani Buhari (a) 10/01/2004, Zaria (Nigeria) (b) 1,73 (c) F - left winger (d) FC Van (e) Right2Win SA

*** Buighlishvili - Beka Buighlishvili (ბეკა ბუიღლიშვილი) (a) 27/09/2000, ¿? (Georgia) (b) - (c) D - central defense (d) - (e) FC Locomotive, FC Gagra, FC Locomotive

*** Buitink - Thomas Buitink (a) 14/06/2000, Nijkerk (Netherlands) (b) - (c) F - center forward (d) Vitesse Arnhem (e) Fortuna Sittard, Vitesse, PEC Zwolle, Vitesse

*** Buiu - Buiu (Deividi Oliveira da Silva) (a) 24/06/2004, ¿? (Brazil) (b) - (c) F - left winger (d) Esporte Clube Noroeste (SP) (e) Ivinhema, Noroeste, FC Urartu, Noroeste

*** Buiucli - Alexandr Buiucli (Alexandr Buiuclî) (a) 01/01/2001, ¿? (Moldova) (b) 1,88 (c) D - central defense (d) FC Dinamo-Auto Tiraspol (e) FC Saksan, Real Succes
*** Bujnacek - Tobias Bujnacek (Tobias Bujňaček) (a) 17/08/2004, Prešov (Slovakia) (b) 1,82 (c) M - attacking midfielder (d) Slavoj Trebisov (e) Slavoj Trebisov, Ružomberok
*** Bujupi - Amrush Bujupi (a) 30/10/1996, Arllat (RF Yugoslavia, now in Kosovo) (b) 1,89 (c) G (d) KF Feronikeli Drenas (e) KF Liria, KF Drenasi, KF Llapi, KF Drenasi, KF Fushë Kosova
*** Bukari - Osman Bukari (a) 13/12/1998, Accra (Ghana) (b) 1,70 (c) F - right winger (d) Crvena zvezda Beograd (e) KAA Gent, FC Nantes, KAA Gent, AS Trencin, Accra Lions, Accra Lions
*** Bukata - Martin Bukata (a) 02/10/1993, Košice (Slovakia) (b) 1,75 (c) M - central midfielder (d) Spartak Trnava (e) Karvina, Benevento, Piast Gliwice, VSS Kosice
*** Bukhaidze - Giorgi Bukhaidze (გიორგი ბუხაიძე) (a) 09/12/1991, ¿? (Georgia) (b) 1,80 (c) F - center forward (d) Kaysar Kyzylorda (e) Marsa FC, FC Gagra, Samgurali, Chikhura, Stade Portelois, Merani Martvili, Tskhinvali, Chikhura, Kolkheti Poti, Saburtalo, FC Sapovnela, Samgurali, Kolkheti Poti, Samgurali
*** Bukhal - Glib Bukhal (Бухал Гліб Геннадійович) (a) 12/11/1995, Kyiv (Ukraine) (b) 1,90 (c) D - central defense (d) Resovia Rzeszów (e) Chojniczanka, Hebar P., Kryvbas, Sigma Olomouc B, Kryvbas, FK Oleksandriya, PFC Lviv, FK Oleksandriya, PFC Lviv, SK Chayka, Metalist 1925, Metalist II, Arsenal Kyiv, Metalist II, Arsenal Kyiv II
*** Bukia - André Bukia (André Watshini Bukia) (a) 03/03/1995, Kinshasa (Zaire, now DR Congo) (b) 1,73 (c) F - right winger (d) FC Arouca (e) Al-Batin, Arouca, Kaysar, Arouca, Boavista, Arouca, Boavista, Vila Real
*** Bukinac - Stefan Bukinac (Стефан Букинац) (a) 08/07/2005, Srbobran (Serbia and Montenegro, now in Serbia) (b) 1,83 (c) D - left back (d) FK Vojvodina Novi Sad (e) -
*** Bukorac - Stefan Bukorac (Стефан Букорац) (a) 15/02/1991, Sremska Mitrovica (Yugoslavia, now in Serbia) (b) 1,93 (c) M - pivot (d) Shakhter Karaganda (e) Kaspiy Aktau, Shakhter K., Kaspiy Aktau, Torpedo Zhodino, Proleter, FK Mladost, EN Paralimniou, Metalac, Dinamo Tbilisi, Donji Srem
*** Bukowski - Adrian Bukowski (a) 18/03/2003, ¿? (Poland) (b) 1,88 (c) M - pivot (d) Śląsk Wroclaw (e) Zaglebie Lubin II, AP Zagłębie
*** Buksa - Adam Buksa (a) 12/07/1996, Kraków (Poland) (b) 1,93 (c) F - center forward (d) Antalyaspor (e) Antalyaspor, RC Lens, New England, Pogon Szczecin, Zagłębie, Pogon Szczecin, Zagłębie, Lechia Gdánsk,
*** Buksa - Aleksander Buksa (a) 15/01/2003, Kraków (Poland) (b) 1,89 (c) F - center forward (d) WSG Tirol (e) WSG Tirol, Genoa, SL16 FC, Genoa, OH Leuven, Genoa, Wisla Kraków, AP Wisla
*** Bukta - Csaba Bukta (a) 25/07/2001, Törökszentmiklós (Hungary) (b) 1,76 (c) F - right winger (d) SCR Altach (e) FC Liefering, SCR Altach, FC Liefering
*** Bukusu - Kevin Bukusu (Kevin Vangu Phambu Bukusu) (a) 27/02/2001, Aachen (Germany) (b) 1,84 (c) D - central defense (d) Wolfsberger AC (e) NEC Nijmegen, Helmond Sport, NEC Nijmegen
*** Bukvic - Domagoj Bukvic (Domagoj Bukvić) (a) 22/02/2004, Osijek (Croatia) (b) 1,74 (c) F - left winger (d) NK Osijek (e) NK Osijek II
*** Bukvic - Semir Bukvic (Semir Bukvić) (a) 21/05/1991, Visoko (Yugoslavia, now in Bosnia and Herzegovina) (b) 1,88 (c) G (d) Araz-Naxcivan Nakchivan (e) Sloboda Tuzla, Mladost Kakanj, Celik Zenica, Warta Poznań, Travnik, Zeljeznicar, FK Olimpik, Bosna Visoko

*** Bulat - Marino Bulat (a) 26/06/1999, Split (Croatia) (b) 1,94 (c) G (d) NK Istra 1961 (e) NK Varazdin, Croat. Zmijavci, Rudar Labin, Zagora Unesic, NK Omladinac, RNK Split

*** Bulat - Marko Bulat (a) 26/09/2001, Šibenik (Croatia) (b) 1,78 (c) M - pivot (d) GNK Dinamo Zagreb (e) HNK Sibenik, Dinamo Zagreb, HNK Sibenik

*** Bulat - Octavian Bulat (a) 23/08/2000, Anenii Noi (Moldova) (b) 1,76 (c) F - left winger (d) - (e) Floresti, Zimbru Chisinau, Dinamo-Auto

*** Bulatovic - Darko Bulatovic (Дарко Булатовић) (a) 05/09/1989, Niksic (Yugoslavia, now in Montenegro) (b) 1,85 (c) D - central defense (d) Qyzyljar Petropavlovsk (e) KF Vllaznia, Sutjeska Niksic, Vozdovac, KA Akureyri, Čukarički, Radnicki Niš, FK Celik Niksic, Miedź Legnica, Czarni Zagan, Miedź Legnica, Sutjeska Niksic

*** Bulatovic - Ivan Bulatovic (Иван Булатовић) (a) 16/02/1996, Mojkovac (RF Yugoslavia, now in Montenegro) (b) 1,90 (c) F - center forward (d) NK Lokomotiva Zagreb (e) Arsenal Tivat, Mornar Bar, FK Podgorica, FK Bokelj, FK Brskovo, FK Gorstak

*** Bulatovic - Uros Bulatovic (Урош Булатовић) (a) 07/12/2004, ¿? (Serbia and Montenegro, now in Montenegro) (b) 1,85 (c) M - attacking midfielder (d) FK Berane (e) Kom Podgorica, Rudar Pljevlja

*** Buletsa - Sergiy Buletsa (Булеца Сергій Анатолійович) (a) 16/02/1999, Korytnyany, Zakarpattya Oblast (Ukraine) (b) 1,72 (c) M - attacking midfielder (d) Zagłębie Lubin (e) Zagłębie, Dinamo Kyїv, Zorya Lugansk, Dinamo Kyїv, SK Dnipro-1, Dinamo Kyїv, Dinamo Kiev II, SK Dnipro-1, Dinamo Kiev II

*** Buleza - Andriy Buleza (Булеза Андрій Михайлович) (a) 25/01/2004, Zarichya, Zakarpattya Oblast (Ukraine) (b) 1,77 (c) D - left back (d) FK Minaj (e) FK Minaj, Shakhtar II

*** Buliskeria - Demetre Buliskeria (დემეტრე ბულისკერია) (a) 09/01/2000, ¿? (Georgia) (b) 1,93 (c) G (d) - (e) FC Dila, FC Didube, Merani Tbilisi, Torpedo Kutaisi, FC Locomotive, Dinamo Tbilisi

*** Buljan - Borna Buljan (a) 05/04/2005, Split (Croatia) (b) 1,95 (c) G (d) HNK Hajduk Split (e) NK Omladinac

*** Buljan - Tvrtko Buljan (a) 26/01/2002, Split (Croatia) (b) 1,85 (c) D - central defense (d) NK Siroki Brijeg (e) Hajduk Split, NK Solin, Hajduk Split, NK Neretvanac, Hajduk Split

*** Buljubasic - Muhamed Buljubasic (Muhamed Buljubašić) (a) 04/07/2004, Gracanica (Bosnia and Herzegovina) (b) 1,80 (c) M - central midfielder (d) FK Sarajevo (e) -

*** Bulka - Marcin Bulka (Marcin Bułka) (a) 04/10/1999, Płock (Poland) (b) 1,99 (c) G (d) OGC Niza (e) Paris Saint-Germain, OGC Nice, Paris Saint-Germain, LB Châteauroux, Paris Saint-Germain, FC Cartagena, Paris Saint-Germain

*** Bullaude - Ezequiel Bullaude (Ezequiel Eduardo Bullaude) (a) 26/10/2000, Maipú (Argentina) (b) 1,84 (c) M - attacking midfielder (d) CA Boca Juniors (e) Feyenoord, Godoy Cruz, Godoy Cruz II

*** Bulliqi (c) G (d) FC Prishtina (e) - - Butrint Bulliqi (c) G (d) FC Prishtina (e) -

*** Bullock - Charlie Bullock (Charles Bullock) (a) 11/12/2003, ¿? (England) (b) 1,71 (c) M - pivot (d) Cardiff Metropolitan University (e) -

*** Bülter - Marius Bülter (a) 29/03/1993, Ibbenbüren (Germany) (b) 1,88 (c) F - left winger (d) TSG 1899 Hoffenheim (e) FC Schalke 04, Union Berlin, 1.FC Magdeburg, Union Berlin, 1.FC Magdeburg, SV Rödinghausen, Neuenkirchen, Eintr. Rheine

*** Buludov - Omar Buludov (Ömər Fuad oğlu Buludov) (a) 15/12/1998, Agstafa (Azerbaijan) (b) 1,76 (c) D - right back (d) Neftchi Baku (e) -

*** Bulut - Onur Bulut (a) 16/04/1994, Werdohl (Germany) (b) 1,79 (c) D - right back (d) Besiktas JK (e) Kayserispor, Alanyaspor, Çaykur Rizespor, Alanyaspor, Eintracht Braunschweig, SC Freiburg, VfL Bochum

*** Bulychev - Aleksandr Bulychev (Булычев Александр Игоревич) (a) 19/11/1999, Vitebsk (Belarus) (b) - (c) M - attacking midfielder (d) Dynamo Brest (e) BK Maxline, Torpedo Vlad., Dynamo Brest, Soligorsk II, Energetik-BGU, Soligorsk II, Vitebsk, Soligorsk II, Gorodeya, Soligorsk II

*** Bumba - Claudiu Bumba (Claudiu Vasile Bumba) (a) 05/01/1994, Baia Mare (Romania) (b) 1,72 (c) M - attacking midfielder (d) ETO FC Győr (e) Fehérvár, Kisvárda, Adanaspor, Concordia, FC Dinamo, Hapoel Tel Aviv, ASA Tg. Mures, FCM Targu Mures, FC Maramures, Minaur

*** Buna - Gábor Buna (a) 24/05/2002, Kaposvár (Hungary) (b) 1,82 (c) D - right back (d) ETO FC Győr (e) Kecskemét, Honvéd II

*** Bunch - Sam Bunch (Sam Carlo E. Bunch) (a) 15/04/2003, Ixelles (Belgium) (b) 1,78 (c) D - left back (d) - (e) Europa Point FC, Paterna B

*** Bunchukov - Denys Bunchukov (Бунчуков Денис Олегович) (a) 20/06/2003, ¿? (Ukraine) (b) - (c) M - central midfielder (d) - (e) Atlet Kyiv

*** Bundgaard - Filip Bundgaard (Filip Bundgaard Kristensen) (a) 03/07/2004, ¿? (Denmark) (b) 1,76 (c) F - left winger (d) Randers FC (e) -

*** Bundgaard - Oliver Bundgaard (Oliver Bundgaard Kristensen) (a) 15/06/2001, Randers (Denmark) (b) 1,82 (c) D - left back (d) Viborg FF (e) Randers FC

*** Bunga - Keinus Bunga (Keinus Bunga N'Kala) (a) 01/08/1997, ¿? (Belgium) (b) - (c) F - left winger (d) - (e) Sfintul Gheorghe, FC Wiltz 71, Pandurii, Erpeldange

*** Buntic - Fabijan Buntic (Fabijan Buntić) (a) 24/02/1997, Stuttgart (Germany) (b) 1,94 (c) G (d) FC Vizela (e) FC Ingolstadt

*** Buonaiuto - Cristian Buonaiuto (a) 29/12/1992, Napoli (Italy) (b) 1,79 (c) F - left winger (d) US Cremonese (e) Perugia, Benevento, Perugia, Latina Calcio, Perugia, Pescara, Maceratese, Pescara, Benevento, Torres, Benevento, Teramo, Benevento, Padova, Benevento, Aprilia

*** Buonanotte - Facundo Buonanotte (Facundo Valentín Buonanotte) (a) 23/12/2004, Pérez (Argentina) (b) 1,74 (c) M - attacking midfielder (d) Brighton & Hove Albion (e) Rosario Central, Rosario Central II

*** Buongiorno - Alessandro Buongiorno (a) 06/06/1999, Torino (Italy) (b) 1,94 (c) D - central defense (d) Torino FC (e) Trapani, Torino, Carpi, Torino

*** Buonocunto - Ivan Buonocunto (a) 24/02/1986, Napoli (Italy) (b) 1,82 (c) M - attacking midfielder (d) AC Virtus Acquaviva (e) Forlì, Vis Pesaro, La Fiorita, Vis Pesaro, San Marino, Lecco, Pergolettese, Alessandria, Pergolettese, Voghera, Rimini, ISM Gradisca, Udinese, Prato, Udinese, Ascoli, Udinese, ASG Nocerina

*** Buqinca - Granit Buqinca (a) 01/06/2002, Drenas (RF Yugoslavia, now in Kosovo) (b) - (c) G (d) KF Dukagjini (e) KF Feronikeli

*** Buraev - Marat Buraev (Бураев Марат Николаевич) (a) 22/10/1995, Vladikavkaz (Russia) (b) 1,64 (c) M - attacking midfielder (d) - (e) Zhetysu, Metallurg Vidn., FK Slutsk, Akzhayik, FK Slutsk, Krymteplitsa, Artsakh Erewan, Pyunik Yerevan, Spartak V., FK Sevastopol, Berkut Armyansk, Krasnodar 3

*** Burakovsky - Samuel Burakovsky (a) 29/12/2002, Malmö (Sweden) (b) 1,86 (c) F - center forward (d) Landskrona BoIS (e) Malmö FF, BK Olympic, Malmö FF, BK Olympic, Malmö FF

*** Buranchiev - Arsen Buranchiev (Буранчиев Арсен Мукашбекович) (a) 12/09/2001, Bishkek (Kyrgyzstan) (b) 1,81 (c) M - pivot (d) Kairat Almaty (e) Kairat-Zhas

*** Burba - Motiejus Burba (a) 10/08/2003, Vilnius (Lithuania) (b) 1,77 (c) F - right winger (d) FC Dziugas Telsiai (e) Dziugas, Zalgiris, Nevezis, Zalgiris, Sevenoaks, Tunbridge Wells, Vilniaus FM
*** Burbano - Fabio Burbano (Fáider Fabio Burbano Castillo) (a) 19/06/1992, Tumaco (Colombia) (b) 1,70 (c) F - left winger (d) - (e) Alashkert CF, CD Águila, Pereira, Once Caldas, Botev Plovdiv, Indep. Santa Fe, Rampla Juniors, Indep. Santa Fe, Águilas Doradas, A. Bucaramanga, Indep. Medellín, Envigado
*** Burca - Andrei Burca (Andrei Andonie Burcă) (a) 15/04/1993, Bacău (Romania) (b) 1,88 (c) D - central defense (d) Al-Okhdood Club (e) CFR Cluj, FC Botosani, SC Bacău, Aerostar, FCM Bacău
*** Burcea - Robert Burcea (a) 14/03/1999, ¿? (Moldova) (b) 1,80 (c) D - right back (d) CS Ocna Mures (e) Zimbru Chisinau, Daesti, FC Kray II, Academia Hagi
*** Burch - Marco Burch (a) 19/10/2000, Sarnen (Switzerland) (b) 1,86 (c) D - central defense (d) FC Lucerna (e) -
*** Burda - Mykyta Burda (Бурда Микита Валерійович) (a) 24/03/1995, Yenakiieve, Donetsk Oblast (Ukraine) (b) 1,87 (c) D - central defense (d) Kolos Kovalivka (e) Dinamo Kyïv, Zorya Lugansk, Dinamo Kyïv, Dinamo Kiev II, RVUFK Kyiv
*** Burdzilauskas - Ernestas Burdzilauskas (a) 22/06/2003, ¿? (Lithuania) (b) 1,89 (c) M - central midfielder (d) FK Suduva Marijampole (e) Suduva B
*** Burdzilauskas - Tautvydas Burdzilauskas (a) 18/05/2005, ¿? (Lithuania) (b) 1,82 (c) D - right back (d) FK Suduva Marijampole B (e) -
*** Burekovic - Dzenan Burekovic (Dženan Bureković) (a) 29/05/1995, Zenica (Bosnia and Herzegovina) (b) 1,78 (c) D - left back (d) Újpest FC (e) Spartak, Újpest FC, Göztepe, Újpest FC, Vojvodina, Celik Zenica, Vojvodina, Celik Zenica
*** Burger - Wouter Burger (a) 16/02/2001, Zuid-Beijerland (Netherlands) (b) 1,91 (c) M - central midfielder (d) FC Basel (e) Feyenoord, Sparta Rotterdam, Feyenoord, Excelsior, Feyenoord
*** Bürger - Niklas Bürger (a) 07/10/1992, ¿? (Germany) (b) - (c) G (d) FC Victoria Rosport (e) -
*** Burgess - Christian Burgess (a) 07/10/1991, London (England) (b) 1,96 (d) Royale Union Saint Gilloise (e) FC Portsmouth, Peterborough, Middlesbrough, Peterborough, Middlesbrough, Hartlepool Utd., Middlesbrough, Bishop's Stortford
*** Burghiu - Stefan Burghiu (Ştefan Burghiu) (a) 28/03/1991, Zăicani (Soviet Union, now in Moldova) (b) 1,91 (c) D - central defense (d) FC Zimbru Chisinau (e) CSF Speranta, CSM Focsani, FC Petrocub, Sfintul Gheorghe, Zhetysu, Zimbru Chisinau, FC Petrocub, Zimbru Chisinau, Nistru Otaci
*** Burgos - Jordi Burgos (Jordi Pérez Burgos) (a) 01/01/1999, Terrassa (Spain) (b) - (c) M (d) UE Engordany (e) UD San Lorenzo, UD Can Trías, UD San Lorenzo
*** Burgstaller - Guido Burgstaller (a) 29/04/1989, Villach (Austria) (b) 1,87 (c) F - center forward (d) SK Rapid Wien (e) FC St. Pauli, FC Schalke 04, 1.FC Nürnberg, Cardiff City, Rapid Wien, Wiener Neustadt, FC Kärnten
*** Burgui - Burgui (Jorge Franco Alviz) (a) 29/10/1993, Burguillos del Cerro (Spain) (b) 1,86 (c) F - left winger (d) - (e) HNK Sibenik, Alavés, Real Zaragoza, Alavés, Real Madrid, Real Sporting, Real Madrid, RCD Espanyol, RM Castilla, Real Madrid C, CD Diocesano
*** Bürgy - Nicolas Bürgy (a) 07/08/1995, Belp (Switzerland) (b) 1,85 (c) D - central defense (d) Viborg FF (e) BSC Young Boys, Viborg FF, BSC Young Boys, SC Paderborn, BSC Young Boys, FC Aarau, BSC Young Boys, FC Thun, BSC Young Boys, FC Wohlen, BSC Young Boys

*** Burgzorg - Delano Burgzorg (a) 07/11/1998, Amsterdam (Netherlands) (b) 1,86 (c) F - left winger (d) 1.FSV Mainz 05 (e) Heracles Almelo, Mainz 05, Heracles Almelo, Spezia, Heracles Almelo, Spezia, De Graafschap

*** Buric - Jasmin Buric (Jasmin Burić) (a) 18/02/1987, Zenica (Yugoslavia, now in Bosnia and Herzegovina) (b) 1,93 (c) G (d) Zagłębie Lubin (e) Hapoel Haifa, Lech Poznan, Celik Zenica

*** Buric - Samir Buric (Samir Burić) (a) 08/06/1998, Tuzla (Bosnia and Herzegovina) (b) - (c) F - left winger (d) - (e) FK Tuzla City, OFK Gradina, Slaven Zivinice, Zvijezda G., FK Tuzla City

*** Burin - Matija Burin (a) 25/03/2001, Izola (Slovenia) (b) 1,81 (c) D - central defense (d) NK Dekani (e) NK Bravo, NK Celje, Hajduk Split II

*** Burjanadze - Shalva Burjanadze (შალვა ბურჯანაძე) (a) 29/10/1998, ¿? (Georgia) (b) 1,86 (c) D - central defense (d) - (e) Samgurali, Torpedo Kutaisi, Merani Martvili, Torpedo Kutaisi, Torpedo Kutaisi II

*** Burkardt - Jonathan Burkardt (Jonathan Michael Burkardt) (a) 11/07/2000, Darmstadt (Germany) (b) 1,83 (c) F - center forward (d) 1.FSV Mainz 05 (e) -

*** Burkart - Nishan Burkart (Nishan Connell Burkart) (a) 31/01/2000, Aarau (Switzerland) (b) 1,74 (c) F - left winger (d) FC Winterthur (e) SC Freiburg, FC Winterthur, SC Freiburg, SC Freiburg II

*** Burke - Graham Burke (Graham Dylan Burke) (a) 21/09/1993, Dublin (Ireland) (b) 1,80 (c) F - left winger (d) Shamrock Rovers (e) Preston North End, Shamrock Rovers, Preston North End, Gillingham FC, Preston North End, Shamrock Rovers, Notts County, Aston Villa, Notts County, Aston Villa, Shrewsbury, Aston Villa, Belvedere FC

*** Burke - Jaheem Burke (a) 19/08/2001, ¿? (Sweden) (b) - (c) F - right winger (d) Västerås SK (e) Varbergs BoIS, Norrby, Varbergs BoIS, Hammarby TFF, Rågsveds IF, Fagersta Södra, Rågsveds IF, UCAM Murcia B, IFK Haninge

*** Burke - Michael Burke (Michael David Burke) (a) 19/10/2002, ¿? (Wales) (b) - (c) F - left winger (d) Prestatyn Town (e) Airbus UK

*** Burke - Nathan Burke (a) 15/09/1995, Liverpool (England) (b) - (c) M - central midfielder (d) Bala Town (e) City of Liverp., FC United, Bala, Warrington

*** Burke - Oliver Burke (Oliver Jasen Burke) (a) 07/04/1997, Kirkcaldy (Scotland) (b) 1,88 (c) F - center forward (d) SV Werder Bremen (e) Millwall, Werder Bremen, Sheffield Utd., Millwall, Sheffield Utd., West Bromwich Albion, Alavés, West Bromwich Albion, Celtic FC, West Bromwich Albion, RB Leipzig, Nottingham Forest, Bradford City

*** Burke - Ryan Burke (Ryan Darren Burke) (a) 23/11/2000, Dublin (Ireland) (b) 1,77 (c) D - left back (d) Waterford FC (e) Bohemians, Mansfield Town, Yeovil Town, St. Josephs Boys

*** Burkic - Dragoslav Burkic (a) 01/07/2000, Wien (Austria) (b) 1,71 (c) M (d) - (e) Tabor Sczana, Mauerwerk, Traiskirchen, Vorwärts Steyr, Bruck/L., Wiener Neustadt, Schwechat II, Vienna II

*** Burkic - Emir Burkic (a) 27/07/1993, ¿? (Slovenia) (b) - (c) M - central midfielder (d) US Feulen (e) FC Wiltz 71, NK Ankaran, FC Wiltz 71, NK Ankaran, NK Izola

*** Burko - Igor Burko (Бурко Игорь Васильевич) (a) 08/09/1988, Berezino (Soviet Union, now in Belarus) (b) 1,76 (c) D - right back (d) Torpedo-BelAZ Zhodino (e) Soligorsk, Torpedo Zhodino, Dynamo Brest, Dynamo Brest II

*** Burko - Maksim Burko (Бурко Максим Александрович) (a) 23/01/2004, Minsk (Belarus) (b) - (c) M - pivot (d) Shakhter Petrikov (e) Soligorsk II, BGU Minsk II, Soligorsk II, BGU Minsk II

*** Burlacu - Andrei Burlacu (a) 12/01/1997, Botoşani (Romania) (b) 1,86 (c) F - left winger (d) CSM Resita (e) FC Botosani, CS Mioveni, FCSB, CS U Craiova, Concordia, CS U Craiova, Chindia, CS U Craiova, ACSM Poli Iasi, CS U Craiova, CS U Craiova II, FC Botosani
*** Burman - Jack Burman (a) 09/11/2004, ¿? (Wales) (b) - (c) M - central midfielder (d) Connah's Quay Nomads (e) -
*** Burman - Marcus Burman (Lars Marcus Burman) (a) 09/08/1996, ¿? (Sweden) (b) 1,80 (c) M - attacking midfielder (d) GIF Sundsvall (e) Akropolis IF, Nyköpings BIS, FC Gute
*** Burmaz - Borisav Burmaz (Борислав Бурмаз) (a) 21/04/2001, Valjevo (RF Yugoslavia, now in Serbia) (b) 1,85 (c) F - center forward (d) FK Vozdovac (e) Graficar, Radnicki 1923, Crvena zvezda, Graficar, Crvena zvezda
*** Burmistrov - Nikita Burmistrov (Бурмистров Никита Александрович) (a) 06/07/1989, Primorsk, Kaliningrad Region (Soviet Union, now in Russia) (b) 1,86 (c) F - right winger (d) FK Sochi (e) Rotor Volgograd, Baltika, Arsenal Tula, Krasnodar, Ural, Krasnodar, Tom Tomsk, Krasnodar, Anzhi, Amkar Perm, Anzhi, Amkar Perm, CSKA Moskva, Shinnik Yaroslav, CSKA Moskva, Luch Vladivostok, CSKA Moskva, CSKA Moskva II
*** Burn - Dan Burn (Daniel Johnson Burn) (a) 09/05/1992, Blyth (England) (b) 2,01 (c) D - left back (d) Newcastle United (e) Brighton & Hove Albion, Wigan Ath., Brighton & Hove Albion, Wigan Ath., Fulham, Birmingham City, Fulham, Yeovil Town, Fulham, Darlington, Blyth Spartans, AFC Blyth, Hartley Juniors
*** Burnadze - Irakli Burnadze (ირაკლი ბურნაძე) (a) 14/06/1998, ¿? (Georgia) (b) - (c) M - central midfielder (d) - (e) Sioni Bolnisi
*** Burnea - Ionut Burnea (Ionuţ Georgian Burnea) (a) 12/08/1992, Câmpulung (Romania) (b) 1,81 (c) D - left back (d) CS Mioveni (e) Tarlungeni, Stefanesti, Chiajna II, FC Costuleni, Stefanesti, Dinamo II
*** Burnet - Djumaney Burnet (Djumaney Kaydon Alfred Burnet) (a) 31/03/2001, ¿? (Netherlands) (b) 1,78 (c) M - central midfielder (d) Lincoln Red Imps FC (e) Glacis United, FC Den Bosch
*** Burnet - Lorenzo Burnet (a) 11/01/1991, Amsterdam (Netherlands) (b) 1,70 (c) D - left back (d) FC Emmen (e) HB Köge, FC Emmen, Excelsior, Slovan Bratislava, NEC Nijmegen, Slovan Bratislava, FC Groningen, Ajax B
*** Burns - Billy Joe Burns (William Joseph Burns) (a) 28/04/1989, Belfast (Northern Ireland) (b) - (c) D - right back (d) Crusaders FC (e) Linfield
*** Burns - Bobby Burns (Robert Burns) (a) 07/10/1999, ¿? (Northern Ireland) (b) 1,75 (c) D - left back (d) Glentoran FC (e) Barrow, Glentoran, Barrow, Heart of Midlothian, Newcastle, Heart of Midlothian, Livingston FC, Heart of Midlothian, Glenavon, Knockbreda FC
*** Burns - Darragh Burns (a) 06/08/2002, Stamullen, Meath (Ireland) (b) 1,76 (c) M - right midfielder (d) Milton Keynes Dons (e) St. Patrick's Ath.
*** Burns - Paddy Burns (Patrick Burns) (a) 09/01/2001, Crumlin (Northern Ireland) (b) 1,80 (c) D - left back (d) Notre Dame Fighting Irish (Uni. of Notre Dame) (e) Glenavon, Knockbreda FC, Glenavon
*** Burns - Ronan Burns (a) 27/04/2005, Rathfriland (Northern Ireland) (b) - (c) G (d) Rathfriland Rangers FC (e) Portadown, Annagh United, Portadown
*** Burov - Kevin Burov (a) 27/04/2004, Tartu (Estonia) (b) - (c) F - right winger (d) Jalgpallikool Tammeka (e) -
*** Bursac - Nikola Bursac (Никола Бурсаћ) (a) 11/09/2001, Toronto (Canada) (b) 1,91 (c) G (d) FC Vizela (e) FK TSC, Spartak, FK TSC, Radnicki Srem, FK TSC, York9 FC

*** Burset - Franco Burset (a) 09/05/2000, Buenos Aires (Argentina) (b) 1,85 (c) M - attacking midfielder (d) - (e) AB Argir, Scarlet Knights

*** Bursik - Josef Bursik (Josef John Bursik) (a) 12/07/2000, Lambeth, London (England) (b) 1,90 (c) G (d) KV Brugge (e) Stoke City, Lincoln City, Stoke City, Peterborough, Stoke City, Doncaster Rovers, Stoke City, Accrington St., Telford Utd., Hednesford

*** Burt - Liam Burt (a) 01/02/1999, Glasgow (Scotland) (b) 1,73 (c) M (d) Shamrock Rovers (e) Bohemians, Celtic Reserves, Rangers II, Alloa Athletic, Rangers II, Dumbarton FC

*** Burta - Jozef Burta (Józef Burta) (a) 20/09/1999, Siedlce (Poland) (b) 1,95 (c) G (d) Odra Opole (e) Śląsk Wroclaw, Piast Zmigrod, Pogon Siedlce, KKS Kalisz, Pogon Siedlce, Victoria Sulejowek

*** Burton - Robbie Burton (Robert Lee Burton) (a) 26/12/1999, Gravesend (England) (b) 1,75 (c) M - central midfielder (d) - (e) Dinamo Zagreb, Sligo Rovers, Dinamo Zagreb, NK Istra, Dinamo Zagreb, Din. Zagreb II

*** Burzanovic - Marko Burzanovic (Marko Burzanović) (a) 13/01/1998, Podgorica (RF Yugoslavia, Montenegro) (b) 1,82 (c) M - central midfielder (d) FK Otrant-Olympic Ulcinj (e) FK Podgorica, Rudar Pljevlja, Zeta Golubovac, OFK Grbalj, Pyunik Yerevan, Inter Zaprešić, Rudar Pljevlja, FK Mladost, Buducnost Podgorica, FK Zabjelo, Buducnost Podgorica

*** Bus - Sergiu Bus (Sergiu Florin Buş) (a) 02/11/1992, Cluj-Napoca (Romania) (b) 1,85 (c) F - center forward (d) ACSM Politehnica Iasi (e) CFR Cluj, Chindia, CFR Cluj, Seongnam FC, FCSB, Gaz Metan, Levski Sofia, Astra Giurgiu, Sheffield Wednesday, Salernitana, Sheffield Wednesday, CSKA Sofia, Corona Brasov, CFR Cluj, Gaz Metan, CFR Cluj, FCM Targu Mures, CFR Cluj, Alba Iulia, CFR Cluj

*** Busanello - Busanello (Gabriel Dal Toé Busanello) (a) 29/10/1998, Frederico Westphalen (Brazil) (b) 1,80 (c) D - left back (d) Malmö FF (e) Chapecoense, SK Dnipro-1, Juventude, SK Dnipro-1, Chapecoense, Pelotas, Hercílio Luz, Frederiquense

*** Busatto - Gustavo Busatto (a) 23/10/1990, Arroio do Tigre (Brazil) (b) 1,90 (c) G (d) CSKA-Sofia (e) Ituano, Sampaio Corrêa, Aparecidense, Náutico, Podbeskidzie, Aparecidense, América-RN, Atlético-GO, América-RN, Grêmio Porto Alegre, Icasa, Grêmio Porto Alegre, ASA, Grêmio Porto Alegre, Grêmio Porto Alegre B

*** Busby - Matthew Busby (a) 07/08/2002, ¿? (Wales) (b) - (c) G (d) Gresford Athletic (e) Airbus UK

*** Busch - Alexander Busch (Alexander Magnus Busch) (a) 25/07/2003, Resenbro (Denmark) (b) 1,90 (c) D - central defense (d) Silkeborg IF (e) -

*** Buschman-Dormond - Carson Buschman-Dormond (Carson Emanuel Buschman-Dormond) (a) 27/10/2002, Vancouver, British Columbia (Canada) (b) 1,88 (c) F - center forward (d) York United FC (e) JK Viljandi, FC Zürich, JK Viljandi

*** Bushara - Badreddine Bushara (a) 04/01/2004, ¿? (Finland) (b) 1,73 (c) F - center forward (d) Ilves Tampere (e) Ilves II

*** Bushchan - Georgiy Bushchan (Бущан Георгій Миколайович) (a) 31/05/1994, Odesa (Ukraine) (b) 1,96 (c) G (d) FC Dinamo de Kiev (e) Dinamo Kiev II, Dinamo Kyïv, Dynamo 2 Kyiv, Dinamo Kiev II

*** Bushelashvili - Revaz Bushelashvili (რევაზ ბუშელაშვილი) (a) 20/01/2004, ¿? (Georgia) (b) - (c) M (d) FC Locomotive Tbilisi (e) -

*** Bushiri - Rocky Bushiri (Rocky Bushiri Kisonga) (a) 30/11/1999, Duffel (Belgium) (b) 1,87 (c) D - central defense (d) Hibernian FC (e) Norwich City, Hibernian FC, Norwich City, KAS Eupen, Norwich City, KV Mechelen, Norwich

City, Sint-Truiden, Norwich City, Blackpool, Norwich City, KV Oostende, KAS Eupen, KV Oostende

*** Bushma - Vladimir Bushma (Бушма Владимир Фомич) (a) 24/11/1983, Minsk (Soviet Union, now in Belarus) (b) 1,90 (c) G (d) Krumkachi Minsk (e) BK Maxline, Torpedo Zhodino, Soligorsk, FK Minsk, Gomel, Torpedo Zhodino, Zhodino II, SKAF Minsk

*** Bushman - Yuriy Bushman (Бушман Юрій Вячеславович) (a) 14/05/1990, Kyiv (Soviet Union, now in Ukraine) (b) 1,78 (c) D - left back (d) Qyzyljar Petropavlovsk (e) Kauno Zalgiris, Arsenal Kyiv, PFK Sumy, Cherk. Dnipro, Arsenal Kyiv, Arsenal Kyiv II, Zirka, Arsenal Kyiv II, Naftovyk, Arsenal Kyiv II, Prykarpattya, Arsenal Kyiv II

*** Bushnak - Jubayer Bushnak (בושנאק בייר'ג) (a) 21/05/2003, ¿? (Israel) (b) - (c) F (d) - (e) Hapoel Haifa,

*** Busi - Maxime Busi (a) 14/10/1999, Liège (Belgium) (b) 1,82 (c) D - right back (d) Stade de Reims (e) Parma, Stade Reims, Parma, RSC Charleroi

*** Busk - Jakob Busk (Jakob Busk Jensen) (a) 12/09/1993, Kopenhagen (Denmark) (b) 1,89 (c) G (d) 1.FC Union Berlin (e) FC København, Sandefjord, FC København, AC Horsens, FC København

*** Busko - Andriy Busko (Бусько Андрій Васильович) (a) 20/05/1997, Cherneve, Lviv Oblast (Ukraine) (b) 1,77 (c) D - right back (d) Metalist Kharkiv (e) PFK Lviv, Karpaty, Karpaty II, Rukh Vynnyky, Karpaty II

*** Busnic - Aleksandar Busnic (Александар Буснић) (a) 04/12/1997, Beograd (RF Yugoslavia, now in Serbia) (b) 1,91 (c) M - pivot (d) FK Vojvodina Novi Sad (e) Rad Beograd, FK Bezanija, Rad Beograd, Zarkovo, Rad Beograd

*** Busnja - Denis Busnja (Denis Bušnja) (a) 14/04/2000, Varaždin (Croatia) (b) 1,73 (c) F - left winger (d) HNK Rijeka (e) NK Bravo, HNK Rijeka, SKF Sered, HNK Rijeka, NK Istra, HNK Rijeka

*** Busquets - Sergio Busquets (Sergio Busquets Burgos) (a) 16/07/1988, Badia del Vallès (Spain) (b) 1,89 (c) M - pivot (d) Inter Miami CF (e) FC Barcelona, Barcelona Atlètic

*** Busquets - Uri Busquets (Oriol Busquets Mas) (a) 20/01/1999, Sant Feliu de Guíxols (Spain) (b) 1,85 (c) M - pivot (d) FC Arouca (e) Clermont Foot, FC Barcelona B, FC Twente, FC Barcelona B

*** Busurmanov - Sultan Busurmanov (Бусурманов Султан Асильханович) (a) 10/05/1996, Almaty (Kazakhstan) (b) 1,86 (c) G (d) Tobol Kostanay (e) Tobol II

*** Busuttil - Jan Busuttil (a) 06/03/1999, ¿? (Malta) (b) 1,71 (c) M - attacking midfielder (d) Floriana FC (e) Pietà Hotspurs

*** Buta - Aurélio Buta (Aurélio Gabriel Ulineia Buta) (a) 10/02/1997, Miconge (Angola) (b) 1,72 (c) D - right back (d) Eintracht Frankfurt (e) Royal Antwerp, Benfica B, Royal Antwerp, Benfica B

*** Buta - Leonardo Buta (Leonardo Daniel Ulineia Buta) (a) 05/06/2002, Águeda (Portugal) (b) 1,82 (c) D - left back (d) Gil Vicente FC (e) Gil Vicente, Udinese, Braga B

*** Butarevich - Aleksey Butarevich (Бутаревич Алексей Станиславович) (a) 12/01/1997, Lida (Belarus) (b) 1,80 (c) M - pivot (d) Zenit 2 St. Petersburg (e) Rotor Volgograd, Dinamo Minsk, FK Slutsk, Dinamo Minsk, Smolevichi, Torpedo Minsk, Smolevichi, Neman II

*** Butcher - Calum Butcher (Calum James Butcher) (a) 26/02/1991, Rochford (England) (b) 1,96 (c) M - pivot (d) Motherwell FC (e) Burton Albion, Dundee United, Mansfield Town, Millwall, Burton Albion, Dundee United, Hayes & Yeading, FC Hjörring, Tottenham Hotspur Reserves, Barnet, Tottenham Hotspur Reserves

*** Butean - Mihai Butean (Mihai Ionuţ Butean) (a) 14/09/1996, Cluj Napoca (Romania) (b) 1,81 (c) D - right back (d) FC Hermannstadt (e) CFR Cluj, Chindia, CFR Cluj, Gaz Metan, CFR Cluj, Gaz Metan, CFR Cluj, Astra Giurgiu, Academica Clinceni, Astra Giurgiu, Universitatea Cluj

*** Butenas - Ivan Butenas (Бутенас Иван Игоревич) (a) 01/12/2000, Borisov (Belarus) (b) - (c) M (d) FK Slutsk II (e) Zhodino II, Belshina, Zhodino II

*** Butez - Jean Butez (a) 08/06/1995, Lille (France) (b) 1,89 (c) G (d) Royal Antwerp FC (e) Excelsior Mouscron, Lille, Excelsior Mouscron, Lille, LOSC Lille B

*** Butko - Bogdan Butko (Бутко Богдан Євгенович) (a) 13/01/1991, Kostyantynivka, Donetsk Oblast (Soviet Union, now in Ukraine) (b) 1,82 (c) D - right back (d) Zorya Lugansk (e) Shakhtar Donetsk, BB Erzurumspor, Shakhtar Donetsk, Lech Poznan, Shakhtar Donetsk, Lech Poznan, Shakhtar Donetsk, Amkar Perm, Shakhtar Donetsk, Shakhtar II, Illichivets, Shakhtar II, Volyn Lutsk, Shakhtar II

*** Butkus - Lukas Butkus (a) 16/07/2005, ¿? (Lithuania) (b) - (c) M (d) FC Dziugas Telsiai B (e) -

*** Butland - Jack Butland (a) 10/03/1993, Bristol (England) (b) 1,96 (c) G (d) Rangers FC (e) Crystal Palace, Manchester Utd., Crystal Palace, Stoke City, Derby, Stoke City, Leeds Utd., Stoke City, Barnsley FC, Stoke City, Birmingham City, Stoke City, Birmingham City, Cheltenham Town, Birmingham City, Cheltenham Town, Birmingham City

*** Butler-Oyedeji - Nathan Butler-Oyedeji (Nathan Jerome Chatoyer Butler-Oyedeji) (a) 04/01/2003, London (England) (b) 1,77 (c) F - center forward (d) - (e) Accrington St.

*** Buttigieg - Shamison Buttigieg (a) 16/06/2003, ¿? (Malta) (b) - (c) F (d) - (e) Zebbug Rangers

*** Butucel - Tudor Butucel (a) 14/08/2003, Chişinău (Moldova) (b) 1,81 (c) M - attacking midfielder (d) FC Petrocub Hînceşti (e) -

*** Butucel - Valeriu Butucel (a) 09/08/2005, ¿? (Moldova) (b) - (c) G (d) - (e) Sfintul Gheorghe

*** Butzke - Adrián Butzke (Adrián Butzke Benavides) (a) 30/03/1999, Monachil (Spain) (b) 1,93 (c) F - center forward (d) Vitória Guimarães SC (e) Granada CF, Paços Ferreira, Granada CF, Paços Ferreira, Granada CF, Recreativo Granada, Haro Deportivo, Recreativo Granada, CD Huétor Vega

*** Buur - Oskar Buur (Oskar Buur Rasmussen) (a) 31/03/1998, Skanderborg (Denmark) (b) 1,80 (c) D - right back (d) FC Volendam (e) Wolverhampton Wanderers, Grasshoppers, Wolverhampton Wanderers, Brabrand IF, Aarhus GF

*** Buurmeester - Zico Buurmeester (a) 07/06/2002, Egmond aan den Hoef (Netherlands) (b) - (c) M - central midfielder (d) PEC Zwolle (e) PEC Zwolle, AZ Alkmaar

*** Buxhelaj - Paulo Buxhelaj (a) 01/05/2003, Kuc, Vlorë (Albania) (b) 1,76 (c) D - left back (d) FK Partizani (e) -

*** Buya Turay - Mohamed Buya Turay (a) 10/01/1995, Freetown (Sierra Leona) (b) 1,80 (c) F - center forward (d) Odense Boldklub (e) Malmö FF, HN FC, HB FC, Sint-Truiden, Djurgården, Sint-Truiden, Dalkurd, AFC Eskilstuna, Västerås SK, Juventus IF, Västerås SK, Juventus IF

*** Buyalskyi - Vitaliy Buyalskyi (Буяльський Віталій Казимирович) (a) 06/01/1993, Kalynivka, Vinnytsya Oblast (Ukraine) (b) 1,75 (c) M - attacking midfielder (d) FC Dinamo de Kiev (e) Dinamo Kiev II, Goverla, Dinamo Kiev II, RVUFK Kyiv

*** Büyüksayar - Mehmet Ali Büyüksayar (a) 08/05/2004, Konya (Turkey) (b) 1,66 (c) F - left winger (d) Konyaspor (e) 1922 Konya

*** Buyvolov - Andrey Buyvolov (Буйволов Андрей Валерьевич) (a) 12/01/1987, Büzmeyin, Asgabat Region (Soviet Union, now in Turkmenistan) (b) 1,86 (c) D - central defense (d) SAtlant-Shakhter Peshelan (e) Shakhter K., Enisey, SKA Khabarovsk, Baltika, Tosno, Volga Nizhny Novgorod,

*** Buzaglo - Almog Buzaglo (בוזגלו אלמוג) (a) 08/12/1992, Karmi'el (Israel) (b) 1,81 (c) F - right winger (d) Bnei Yehuda Tel Aviv (e) Ness Ziona, Bnei Yehuda, Hapoel Haifa, Bnei Yehuda, H. Ramat Gan, Maccabi Amishav, Kabilio Jaffa, Maccabi Amishav

*** Buzas - Titas Buzas (a) 14/06/2004, Mariampole (Lithuania) (b) 1,76 (c) M - attacking midfielder (d) - (e) Jonava, DFK Dainava

*** Buzbuchi - Alexandru Buzbuchi (a) 31/10/1993, Constanța (Romania) (b) 1,87 (c) G (d) FCV Farul Constanta (e) Gaz Metan, FC Viitorul, Academia Hagi

*** Buzek - Alexandr Buzek (Alexandr Bužek) (a) 02/08/2004, ¿? (Slovakia) (b) - (c) M - pivot (d) FC Zlin B (e) -

*** Buziuc - Alexandru Buziuc (Alexandru Daniel Buziuc) (a) 15/03/1994, Suceava (Romania) (b) 1,82 (c) F - center forward (d) CSA Steaua (e) CS Mioveni, FCSB, Academica Clinceni, Gaz Metan, Rapid Suceava, Gaz Metan, FC Vaslui, Sport. Suceava

*** Bwomono - Elvis Bwomono (Elvis Okello Bwomono) (a) 29/11/1998, ¿? (Uganda) (b) 1,75 (c) D - central defense (d) ÍBV Vestmannaeyjar (e) Southend United

*** Byazrov - David Byazrov (Бязров Давид Таймуразович) (a) 12/02/2003, ¿? (Russia) (b) 1,90 (c) G (d) Zenit 2 St. Petersburg (e) Zenit St. Peterburg II

*** Bychek - Kostyantyn Bychek (Бичек Костянтин Романович) (a) 21/04/2000, Bila Tserkva, Kyiv Oblast (Ukraine) (b) 1,80 (c) F - left winger (d) Metalist 1925 Kharkiv (e) Nyva Ternopil, Karpaty, Karpaty II

*** Bye - Bendik Bye (a) 09/03/1990, Steinkjer (Norway) (b) 1,85 (c) F - left winger (d) Ranheim IL (e) Kristiansund, Sogndal, Levanger, Ranheim, Steinkjer FK

*** Bykov - Artem Bykov (Быков Артем Геннадьевич) (a) 19/10/1992, Minsk (Belarus) (b) 1,83 (c) M - central midfielder (d) Dinamo Minsk (e) Dynamo Brest, Dinamo Minsk, FK Minsk, Dinamo Minsk, Dinamo Minsk II, FK Bereza, Dinamo Minsk II, BGU Minsk II

*** Bykov - Oleksiy Bykov (Биков Олексій Олексійович) (a) 29/03/1998, Khartsyzk, Donetsk Oblast (Ukraine) (b) 1,86 (c) D - central defense (d) Zaglebie Sosnowiec (e) FK Mariupol, Z. Sosnowiec, FK Mariupol, KA Akureyri, FK Mariupol, Lokomotiv Plovdiv, FK Mariupol, FK Mariupol II, Oleksandriya II

*** Bykovskiy - Artem Bykovskiy (Быковский Артем Александрович) (a) 15/06/2004, Voronezh (Russia) (b) 1,96 (c) F - center forward (d) Spartak de Moskva II (e) -

*** Bykovskiy - Ilya Bykovskiy (Быковский Илья Валерьевич) (a) 16/02/2001, Lyubertsy, Moskau Oblast (Russia) (b) 1,77 (c) D - left back (d) Arsenal Tula (e) Ural, Ural 2, Ural II, Arsenal Tula II

*** Bylinkin - Nikita Bylinkin (Былинкин Никита Владимирович) (a) 27/01/1999, Slutsk (Belarus) (b) 1,85 (c) D - central defense (d) FK Slutsk (e) Dzerzhinsk, FK Slutsk, Viktoria MG, FK Slutsk, Smolevichi, FK Slutsk, Slutsk II

*** Bynoe-Gittens - Jamie Bynoe-Gittens (Jamie Jermaine Bynoe-Gittens) (a) 08/08/2004, London (England) (b) 1,77 (c) F - left winger (d) Borussia Dortmund (e) -

*** Byrne - Cian Byrne (a) 31/01/2003, Dublin (Ireland) (b) 1,86 (c) D - central defense (d) Bohemian FC (e) Longford Town, Bohemians, St. Kevins Boys

*** Byrne - Conner Byrne (a) 27/03/2003, Portadown (Northern Ireland) (b) 1,92 (c) G (d) Dungannon Swifts (e) Armagh City FC, Dungannon, Armagh City FC, Dungannon
*** Byrne - Jack Byrne (a) 24/04/1996, Dublin (Ireland) (b) 1,71 (c) F - right winger (d) Shamrock Rovers (e) APOEL FC, Shamrock Rovers, Kilmarnock FC, Oldham Athletic, Wigan Ath., Oldham Athletic, Wigan Ath., Blackburn, SC Cambuur
*** Byrne - Luke Byrne (a) 08/07/1993, Dublin (Ireland) (b) 1,83 (c) D - left back (d) Shelbourne FC (e) Shamrock Rovers, Bohemians
*** Byrne - Mark Byrne (a) 12/08/2000, ¿? (Ireland) (b) 1,78 (c) M - pivot (d) Sligo Rovers (e) -
*** Byrne - Mark Byrne (a) 15/09/2000, ¿? (Ireland) (b) - (c) G (d) Dundalk FC (e) Monaghan United, Newry City, Warrenpoint
*** Byrne - Reece Byrne (a) 20/11/2004, ¿? (Ireland) (b) 1,88 (c) G (d) - (e) Bohemians
*** Byskov - Valdemar Byskov (Valdemar Byskov Andreasen) (a) 25/01/2005, Herning (Denmark) (b) - (c) M - attacking midfielder (d) CD Mafra (e) Mafra, Midtjylland
*** Bystrov - Marat Bystrov (Быстров Марат Вячеславович) (a) 19/06/1992, Bolshevik, Kostanay Region (Kazakhstan) (b) 1,81 (c) D - right back (d) Akhmat Grozny (e) Ordabasy, FC Astana, Ordabasy, FC Astana, Tobol Kostanay, FC Astana, Tambov, Chelyabinsk, FK Magnitogorsk
*** Bytyci - Altin Bytyci (Altin Bytyçi) (a) 14/01/2001, Nishor (RF Yugoslavia, now in Kosovo) (b) 1,84 (c) D - central defense (d) FK Kukësi (e) Medjimurje, FC Besa, KF Laçi
*** Bytyqi - Arber Bytyqi (Arbër Bytyqi) (a) 16/10/2003, Prizren (RF Yugoslavia, now in Kosovo) (b) 1,80 (c) D - left back (d) KF Llapi (e) KF Tirana, KF Laçi
*** Bytyqi - Ramiz Bytyqi (a) 10/01/1999, ¿? (RF Yugoslavia, now in Kosovo) (b) - (c) D - right back (d) FC Prishtina (e) FC Ballkani
*** Bytyqi - Zymer Bytyqi (a) 11/09/1996, Sint-Truiden (Belgium) (b) 1,76 (c) F - left winger (d) Antalyaspor (e) Olympiakos, Konyaspor, Viking, RB Salzburg, Sandnes Ulf, RB Salzburg, Sandnes Ulf
*** Cabal - Juan Cabal (Juan David Cabal Murillo) (a) 08/01/2001, Cali (Colombia) (b) 1,86 (c) D - central defense (d) Hellas Verona (e) At. Nacional
*** Caballé - Marc Caballé (Marc Caballé Naranjo) (a) 22/06/1991, L'Hospitalet de Llobregat (Spain) (b) 1,85 (c) M - central midfielder (d) Inter Club d'Escaldes (e) Zamora CF, Linares, Sanluqueño, Rayo Majadahonda, Recreativo, Cornellà, RCD Espanyol B, Cornellà, RCD Espanyol B, CD Lugo, RCD Espanyol B, At. Malagueño, At. Madrid C
*** Caballero - Manu Caballero (Manuel Caballero González) (a) 10/04/1992, Jerez de la Frontera (Spain) (b) - (c) M - attacking midfielder (d) St Joseph's FC (e) Jerez Ind., CD Rota, Jerez Ind., Arcos CF, Xerez Deportivo, CA Antoniano, Arcos CF, Algeciras CF, Balón de Cádiz, Cádiz CF B
*** Caballero - Mauro Caballero (Mauro Andrés Caballero Aguilera) (a) 08/10/1994, Asunción (Paraguay) (b) 1,80 (c) F - center forward (d) Torpedo Kutaisi (e) Académica Coimbra, Arouca, Unión Española, San Luis, FC Porto B, San Luis, FC Porto B, Palestino, FC Porto B, Olimpia, FC Porto B, FC Vaduz, FC Porto B, Desportivo Aves, FC Porto B, Penafiel, FC Porto B, Libertad
*** Caballero - Sergi Caballero (Sergi Caballero Mateo) (a) 08/07/1998, Mataró (Spain) (b) - (c) D - right back (d) UE Vilassar de Mar (e) FC Ordino, Sant Andreu, CF Peralada, Pobla de Mafumet CF, FC Santboià, Palamós CF, CF Gavà

*** Caballero - Willy Caballero (Wilfredo Daniel Caballero Lazcano) (a) 28/09/1981, Santa Elena (Argentina) (b) 1,86 (c) G (d) - (e) Southampton, Chelsea, Manchester City, Málaga CF, Elche CF, Arsenal, Elche CF, Boca Juniors

*** Cabella - Rémy Cabella (Rémy Joseph Cabella) (a) 08/03/1990, Ajaccio (France) (b) 1,72 (c) M - attacking midfielder (d) LOSC Lille Métropole (e) Montpellier, Krasnodar, St.-Étienne, Ol. Marseille, St.-Étienne, Ol. Marseille, Newcastle Utd., Ol. Marseille, Newcastle Utd., Montpellier, AC Arles-Avignon, Montpellier, Montpellier B

*** Cabot - Jimmy Cabot (a) 18/04/1994, Chambéry (France) (b) 1,64 (c) M - right midfielder (d) RC Lens (e) Angers SCO, FC Lorient, Troyes, Troyes B

*** Cabraja - Marijan Cabraja (Marijan Čabraja) (a) 25/02/1997, Pula (Croatia) (b) 1,82 (c) D - left back (d) HNK Rijeka (e) Hibernian FC, Dinamo Zagreb, Olimpija, Dinamo Zagreb, Ferencváros, Dinamo Zagreb, HNK Gorica, Din. Zagreb II, Jadran Porec

*** Cabrajic - Kristijan Cabrajic (Kristijan Čabrajić) (a) 12/06/2004, Zagreb (Croatia) (b) - (c) D - left back (d) NK Lokomotiva Zagreb (e) Hrv Dragovoljac, Spansko

*** Cabral - Arthur Cabral (Arthur Mendonça Cabral) (a) 25/04/1998, Campina Grande (Brazil) (b) 1,86 (c) F - center forward (d) SL Benfica (e) Fiorentina, FC Basel, Palmeiras, FC Basel, Palmeiras, Ceará SC

*** Cabral - Emanuel Cabral (Emanuel Tomas Cabral) (a) 02/08/1996, ¿? (Portugal) (b) 1,87 (c) G (d) CS Fola Esch (e) -

*** Cabral - Euclides Cabral (Euclides da Silva Cabral) (a) 05/01/1999, Lisboa (Portugal) (b) 1,78 (c) D - right back (d) - (e) Apollon Limassol, FC St. Gallen, Grasshoppers

*** Cabral - Jerson Cabral (a) 03/01/1991, Rotterdam (Netherlands) (b) 1,77 (c) F - left winger (d) Ionikos Nikeas (e) Ionikos Nikeas, Pafos FC, Levski Sofia, SC Bastia, Sparta Rotterdam, SC Bastia, FC Twente, Willem II, FC Twente, ADO Den Haag, FC Twente, Feyenoord

*** Cabrera - Aridai Cabrera (Ariday Cabrera Suárez) (a) 26/09/1988, Las Palmas de Gran Canaria (Spain) (b) 1,68 (c) F - right winger (d) Inter Club d'Escaldes (e) Odisha FC, UD Las Palmas, RCD Mallorca, Cultural Leonesa, Valencia Mestalla, Huracán, CE Sabadell, CE L'Hospitalet, Betis B, Girona FC, RCD Mallorca B, Uni. Las Palmas, U. Las Palmas B

*** Cabrera - Enzo Cabrera (Enzo Daniel Cabrera) (a) 20/11/1999, Casilda (Argentina) (b) 1,75 (c) F - center forward (d) Ethnikos Achnas (e) Ethnikos, Newell's Old Boys, Birkirkara FC, Newell's Old Boys, Intercity, Newell's Old Boys, Newell's II

*** Cabrera - George Cabrera (a) 14/12/1988, Gibraltar (Gibraltar) (b) 1,70 (c) F - center forward (d) Mons Calpe SC (e) Lynx FC, Bruno's Magpies, Lincoln FC, Algeciras CF, Sanluqueño B, Atlético Zabal

*** Cabrera - Leandro Cabrera (Leandro Daniel Cabrera Sasía) (a) 17/06/1991, Montevideo (Uruguay) (b) 1,90 (c) D - central defense (d) RCD Espanyol (e) Getafe CF, Crotone, Getafe CF, Crotone, Real Zaragoza, RM Castilla, Atlético Madrid, Hércules CF, Atlético Madrid, CD Numancia, Atlético Madrid, Recreativo, Atlético Madrid, Defensor

*** Cabuz - Catalin Cabuz (Cătălin Vasile Căbuz) (a) 18/06/1996, Avrig (Romania) (b) 1,87 (c) G (d) CFR Cluj (e) Chindia, FCV Farul, FC Hermannstadt, Academia Hagi, Chindia, Academia Hagi, Rm. Valcea, Academia Hagi, FC Cisnadie, Academia Hagi, Voinţa Sibiu

*** Cacace - Liberato Cacace (Liberato Gianpaolo Cacace) (a) 27/09/2000, Wellington (New Zealand) (b) 1,83 (c) D - left back (d) FC Empoli (e) Sint-Truiden, FC Empoli, Sint-Truiden, Wellington P., W. Phoenix Reserves, Island Bay Utd.

*** Caccavo - Luigi Caccavo (a) 03/02/2004, Bari (Italy) (b) 1,92 (c) F - center forward (d) US Pergolettese 1932 (e) Pergolettese

*** Cacciabue - Jerónimo Cacciabue (a) 24/01/1998, Montes de Oca (Argentina) (b) 1,73 (c) M - central midfielder (d) CA Platense (e) Platense, Newell's Old Boys, Miedź Legnica, Newell's Old Boys, Newell's II

*** Cachbach - Mathieu Cachbach (Mathieu Joseph Cachbach) (a) 23/05/2001, Arlon (Belgium) (b) 1,80 (c) M - central midfielder (d) RFC Seraing (e) FC Metz, RFC Seraing, FC Metz, FC Metz B

*** Caci - Anthony Caci (a) 01/07/1997, Forbach (France) (b) 1,84 (c) D - left back (d) 1.FSV Mainz 05 (e) Racing Club Strasbourg, Racing Strasbourg B

*** Caddell - Declan Caddell (a) 13/04/1988, Belfast (Northern Ireland) (b) 1,83 (c) M - central midfielder (d) - (e) Crusaders

*** Cadden - Chris Cadden (Christopher Cadden) (a) 19/09/1996, Bellshill (Scotland) (b) 1,83 (c) D - right back (d) Hibernian FC (e) Columbus, Oxford United, Columbus Crew, Motherwell FC, Albion Rovers

*** Cadete - Kike Cadete (Enrique López Fernández) (a) 24/06/1994, Madrid (Spain) (b) 1,86 (c) D - left back (d) - (e) Melbourne, FC Astana, San Luis, Querétaro FC, San Luis, Unión Adarve, AD Alcorcón B

*** Cádiz - Jhonder Cádiz (Jhonder Leonel Cádiz Fernández) (a) 29/07/1995, Caracas, Distrito Capital (Venezuela) (b) 1,90 (c) F - center forward (d) FC Famalicão (e) Benfica, Nashville, Benfica, Dijon, Benfica, Vitória Setúbal, Monagas SC, Moreirense, Nacional, Caracas FC, União Madeira, Caracas FC, Caracas FC B, Dep. Miranda

*** Cadjenovic - Jovan Cadjenovic (Јован Чађеновић) (a) 13/01/1995, Cetinje (Yugoslavia, now in Montenegro) (b) 1,84 (c) M - pivot (d) FK Panevezys (e) Metalac, Kaysar, Taraz, Suduva, Borac Cacak, FK Zemun, FK Partizan, FK Bezanija, FK Partizan, Teleoptik, FK Partizan, Teleoptik

*** Cadu - Cadu (Carlos Eduardo Lopes Cruz) (a) 08/08/1997, Salvador (Brazil) (b) 1,77 (c) M - right midfielder (d) FC Viktoria Plzen (e) Banik Ostrava, Viktoria Plzen, Pardubice, EC Olímpia

*** Cadwallader - Mark Cadwallader (a) 08/07/1988, ¿? (Wales) (b) - (c) F - center forward (d) Aberystwyth Town (e) Flint Town, Rhyl FC, Airbus UK, Colwyn Bay, Northwich Vic, Airbus UK, Connah's Quay, Bangor City, Chester City

*** Caetano - Jamie Caetano (James Mark Caetano) (a) 27/09/2004, Gibraltar (Gibraltar) (b) - (c) M - left midfielder (d) Europa FC Reserve (e) FC College 1975, St Joseph's FC, St Joseph's Reserves

*** Cafarov - Camal Cafarov (Camal Əli-Abasov oğlu Cəfərov) (a) 25/02/2002, ¿? (Azerbaijan) (b) 1,78 (c) F - right winger (d) Sabah FK (e) Sabah 2, Anzhi II

*** Cafarov - Rza Cafarov (Rza İsa oğlu Cəfərov) (a) 03/07/2003, ¿? (Azerbaijan) (b) 1,90 (c) G (d) Neftchi Baku (e) Neftchi 2 Baku

*** Cafarquliyev - Elvin Cafarquliyev (Elvin Eldar oğlu Cəfərquliyev) (a) 26/10/2000, Baku (Azerbaijan) (b) 1,80 (c) D - left back (d) Qarabağ FK (e) Sumqayit, Qarabag FK

*** Caffrey - Evan Caffrey (a) 27/02/2003, ¿? (Ireland) (b) - (c) M - attacking midfielder (d) Shelbourne FC (e) UCD

*** Cafú - Cafú (Carlos Miguel Ribeiro Dias) (a) 26/02/1993, Guimarães (Portugal) (b) 1,85 (c) M - central midfielder (d) Rotherham United (e) Nottingham Forest,

Olympiakos, Nottingham Forest, Olympiakos, Legia Warszawa, FC Metz, Legia Warszawa, FC Metz, FC Lorient, Vitória Guimarães, Benfica B
*** Cagiran - Musa Cagiran (Musa Çağıran) (a) 17/11/1992, Ilgin (Turkey) (b) 1,85 (c) M - central midfielder (d) Hatayspor (e) Bucaspor 1928, Hatayspor, Konyaspor, Alanyaspor, Osmanlispor, Çaykur Rizespor, Osmanlispor, Karabükspor, Bursaspor, Galatasaray, Konyaspor, Galatasaray, Altay SK, Aliaga Belediye, Altay SK
*** Caglar - Sarper Caglar (Sarper Çağlar) (a) 31/01/2003, Ankara (Turkey) (b) 1,80 (c) F - left winger (d) Zonguldak Kömürspor (e) Z. Kömürspor, Hatayspor, Eyüpspor, Hatayspor, Nigde Anadolu, Turgutluspor
*** Caglayan - Ogulcan Caglayan (Oğulcan Çağlayan) (a) 22/03/1996, Ankara (Turkey) (b) 1,88 (c) F - center forward (d) Galatasaray (e) Pendikspor, Galatasaray, Giresunspor, Galatasaray, Eyüpspor, Galatasaray, Çaykur Rizespor, Gazisehir, Çaykur Rizespor, K. Erciyesspor, Kayserispor, K. Erciyesspor, Gaziantepspor
*** Cahangirov - Ugur Cahangirov (Uğur Höccət oğlu Cahangirov) (a) 22/09/2001, ¿? (Azerbaijan) (b) - (c) F - center forward (d) Sumqayit 2 (e) Shamakhi, FC Shamakhi 2
*** Caia - Federico Caia (a) 21/04/2003, Livorno (Italy) (b) 1,83 (c) F - center forward (d) US Pergolettese 1932 (e) Pergolettese, Livorno
*** Caicedo - Brayan Caicedo (Brayan Caicedo Mosquera) (a) 27/04/1996, ¿? (Colombia) (b) - (c) F - left winger (d) - (e) Conil CF, Penya Encarnada, UE Santa Coloma, CD Masnou, CD Bupolsa, Ter Leede, FC Boshuizen
*** Caicedo - Jordy Caicedo (Jordy Josué Caicedo Medina) (a) 18/11/1997, Machala (Ecuador) (b) 1,87 (c) F - center forward (d) Atlas Guadalajara (e) Atlas, Tigres UANL, Sivasspor, Tigres UANL, CSKA-Sofia, EC Vitória, Uni. Católica, CD El Nacional, Uni. Católica, Uni. Católica B, Norte América, Deportivo Azogues, Norte América
*** Caicedo - Moisés Caicedo (Moisés Isaac Caicedo Corozo) (a) 02/11/2001, Santo Domingo (Ecuador) (b) 1,78 (c) M - pivot (d) Chelsea FC (e) Brighton & Hove Albion, Beerschot V.A., Brighton & Hove Albion, Independiente, Independiente B
*** Cailloce - Killian Cailloce (a) 09/12/2005, Dublin (Ireland) (b) 1,86 (c) F - center forward (d) - (e) Drogheda United
*** Caimacov - Mihail Caimacov (Каймаков Михаил Андреевич) (a) 22/07/1998, Tiraspol (Moldova) (b) 1,84 (c) M - central midfielder (d) Slaven Belupo Koprivnica (e) Torpedo Moskva, Slaven Belupo, NK Osijek II, Koper, NK Osijek II, Olimpija, NK Osijek II, FC Sheriff, Sheriff-2
*** Cain - Jake Cain (Jake Steven Cain) (a) 02/09/2001, Wigan (England) (b) 1,76 (c) M - central midfielder (d) Swindon Town (e) Newport County
*** Caio Henrique - Caio Henrique (Caio Henrique Oliveira Silva) (a) 31/07/1997, Santos (Brazil) (b) 1,78 (c) D - left back (d) AS Mónaco (e) Atlético Madrid, Grêmio Porto Alegre, Atlético Madrid, Fluminense, Atlético Madrid, At. Madrid B, Paraná, At. Madrid B, Santos B
*** Caio Vidal - Caio Vidal (Caio Vidal Rocha) (a) 04/11/2000, Fortaleza (Brazil) (b) 1,74 (c) F - right winger (d) Ludogorets Razgrad (e) Internacional, EC Bahia, Internacional
*** Cairney - Tom Cairney (Thomas Cairney) (a) 20/01/1991, Nottingham (England) (b) 1,85 (c) M - central midfielder (d) Fulham FC (e) Blackburn, Hull City, Blackburn, Hull City
*** Cajic - Aldin Cajic (Aldin Čajić) (a) 11/09/1992, Konjic (Bosnia and Herzegovina) (b) 1,82 (c) M - central midfielder (d) - (e) Istanbulspor, Tuzlaspor, Istanbulspor, Elazigspor, Dukla Praha, Teplice

*** Caju - Caju (Wanderson de Jesus Martins) (a) 17/07/1995, Irecê (Brazil) (b) 1,83 (c) D - left back (d) Aris Limassol (e) SC Braga, Aris Limassol, SC Braga, Goiás, SC Braga, Santos, APOEL FC, Santos
*** Cajuste - Jens Cajuste (Jens-Lys Michel Cajuste) (a) 10/08/1999, Göteborg (Sweden) (b) 1,88 (c) M - central midfielder (d) SSC Nápoles (e) Stade Reims, Midtjylland, Örgryte
*** Cakaj - Gledis Cakaj (a) 26/09/2003, Belfast (Northern Ireland) (b) - (c) F - right winger (d) Lisburn Distillery FC (e) Dollingstown FC
*** Cakar - Abdulkerim Cakar (Abdulkerim Çakar) (a) 14/04/2001, Germersheim (Germany) (b) 1,76 (c) F - right winger (d) Gaziantep FK (e) Hoffenheim II, Académico Viseu, Hoffenheim II
*** Cake - Klisman Cake (a) 02/05/1999, Pogradec (Albania) (b) 1,85 (c) D - central defense (d) Shkëndija Tetovo (e) Struga, KF Tirana
*** Cakir - Ferhat Cakir (a) 07/07/2002, Genk (Belgium) (b) - (c) D - left back (d) - (e) Torre del Mar
*** Cakir - Ugurcan Cakir (Uğurcan Çakır) (a) 05/04/1996, Antalya (Turkey) (b) 1,91 (c) G (d) Trabzonspor (e) 1461 Trabzon, Trabzonspor
*** Cakolli - Enhar Cakolli (a) 26/05/2000, Ferizaj (RF Yugoslavia, now in Kosovo) (b) 1,77 (c) D - right back (d) KF Ferizaj (e) FC Drita, KF Ferizaj, FC Drita, Ramiz Sadiku, KF Ferizaj
*** Cakolli (c) G (d) KF Ferizaj (e) - - Shqiprim Cakolli (c) G (d) KF Ferizaj (e) -
*** Caks - Robert Caks (Robert Čakš) (a) 31/01/2001, Šmarje pri Jelšah (Slovenia) (b) 1,97 (c) F - center forward (d) ND Beltinci (e) Tabor Sezana, Beltinci, Tabor Sezana, ND Primorje, Tabor Sezana, NK Smartno 1928
*** Caktas - Mijo Caktas (Mijo Caktaš) (a) 08/05/1992, Split (Croatia) (b) 1,79 (c) M - attacking midfielder (d) NK Osijek (e) Damac FC, Hajduk Split, Rubin Kazan, Hajduk Split, NK Dugopolje
*** Cala - Juan Cala (Juan Torres Ruiz) (a) 26/11/1989, Lebrija (Spain) (b) 1,86 (c) D - central defense (d) Cádiz CF (e) UD Las Palmas, Henan Jianye, Getafe CF, Granada CF, Cardiff City, Sevilla FC, AEK Athína, Sevilla FC, FC Cartagena, Sevilla FC, Sevilla At., Sevilla FC C
*** Calabresi - Arturo Calabresi (a) 17/03/1996, Roma (Italy) (b) 1,86 (c) D - right back (d) Pisa Sporting Club (e) Lecce, Bologna, Cagliari, Bologna, Amiens SC, Bologna, AS Roma, Foggia, AS Roma, Spezia, AS Roma, Brescia, AS Roma, AS Livorno
*** Calabria - Davide Calabria (a) 06/12/1996, Brescia (Italy) (b) 1,76 (c) D - right back (d) AC Milan (e) -
*** Calafiori - Riccardo Calafiori (a) 19/05/2002, Roma (Italy) (b) 1,88 (c) D - left back (d) FC Basel (e) AS Roma, Genoa, AS Roma
*** Calaidjoglu - Calin Calaidjoglu (Călin Calaidjoglu) (a) 18/01/2001, Chișinău (Moldova) (b) 1,70 (c) M - attacking midfielder (d) FC Petrocub Hîncești (e) Sfintul Gheorghe, AS Béziers, SO Cholet B
*** Calancea - Nicolae Calancea (a) 29/08/1986, Chișinău (Soviet Union, now in Moldova) (b) 1,89 (c) G (d) - (e) Sfintul Gheorghe, Dunarea Calarasi, Academica Clinceni, Dunarea Calarasi, CS U Craiova, FC Voluntari, Ceahlăul, Zimbru Chisinau, KS Samara, Zimbru Chisinau
*** Calcan - Andreias Calcan (a) 09/04/1994, Slatina (Romania) (b) 1,72 (d) FC Universitatea Cluj (e) FC Arges, Mezökövesd, ACSM Poli Iasi, Újpest FC, FC Viitorul, Almere City, Willem II, FC Dordrecht, Willem II, Universitatea Cluj, Rm. Valcea, Universitatea Cluj, U Cluj II

*** Caldara - Mattia Caldara (a) 05/05/1994, Bergamo (Italy) (b) 1,87 (c) D - central defense (d) AC Milan (e) Spezia, AC Milan, Venezia, AC Milan, Atalanta, AC Milan, Juventus, Atalanta, Juventus, Atalanta, Cesena, Atalanta, Trapani
*** Caldirola - Luca Caldirola (a) 01/02/1991, Desio (Italy) (b) 1,86 (c) D - central defense (d) AC Monza (e) Benevento, Werder Bremen, Darmstadt 98, Werder Bremen, Internazionale Milano, Cesena, Brescia, Cesena, Internazionale Milano, Brescia, Internazionale Milano, Vitesse, Internazionale Milano
*** Calero - Fernando Calero (Fernando Calero Villa) (a) 14/09/1995, Boecillo (Valladolid) (Spain) (b) 1,84 (c) D - central defense (d) RCD Espanyol (e) Real Valladolid, R. Valladolid B, At. Malagueño
*** Caleta-Car - Duje Caleta-Car (Duje Ćaleta-Car) (a) 17/09/1996, Šibenik (Croatia) (b) 1,92 (c) D - central defense (d) Olympique de Lyon (e) Olympique Lyon, Southampton, Ol. Marseille, RB Salzburg, FC Liefering, RB Salzburg, FC Pasching, RB Salzburg, HNK Sibenik
*** Calhanoglu - Hakan Calhanoglu (Hakan Çalhanoğlu) (a) 08/02/1994, Mannheim (Germany) (b) 1,78 (c) M - central midfielder (d) Internazionale Milano (e) AC Milan, Bayer Leverkusen, SV Hamburg, Karlsruher SC, SV Hamburg, Karlsruher SC
*** Calhanoglu - Kerim Calhanoglu (Kerim Çalhanoğlu) (a) 26/08/2002, Mannheim (Germany) (b) 1,80 (c) D - left back (d) SpVgg Greuther Fürth (e) FC Schalke 04, SV Sandhausen, FC Schalke 04
*** Caligiuri - Daniel Caligiuri (a) 15/01/1988, Villingen-Schwenningen (Germany) (b) 1,82 (c) F - right winger (d) - (e) FC Augsburg, FC Schalke 04, VfL Wolfsburg, SC Freiburg, SC Freiburg II
*** Calila - Calila (Diogo dos Santos Cabral) (a) 10/10/1998, Seixal (Portugal) (b) 1,80 (c) D - right back (d) CD Santa Clara (e) B SAD, Paços F. B, Belenenses
*** Calin - Alexandru Calin (Alexandru Calîn) (a) 26/06/2005, ¿? (Moldova) (b) 1,70 (c) D - right back (d) Univer Oguzsport (e) Dinamo-Auto, FC Saksan, Umutluc
*** Calisir - André Calisir (Անդրե Քալիշիր) (a) 13/06/1990, Stockholm (Sweden) (b) 1,87 (c) D - central defense (d) IF Brommapojkarna (e) Silkeborg IF, Apollon Smyrnis, IFK Göteborg, J-Södra IF, Djurgården, J-Södra IF, Djurgården, Skellefteå FF
*** Callachan - Ross Callachan (a) 04/09/1993, Edinburgh (Scotland) (b) 1,78 (c) M - central midfielder (d) Ross County FC (e) St. Johnstone, Dundee FC, St. Johnstone, Heart of Midlothian, Raith Rovers, Musselburgh Athletic FC, Raith Rovers
*** Callacher - Jimmy Callacher (a) 11/06/1991, Belfast (Northern Ireland) (b) - (c) D - central defense (d) Crusaders FC (e) Linfield, Glentoran, Dungannon, Glentoran
*** Callegari - Rodrigo Callegari (Rodrigo Callegari Torre) (a) 22/06/1997, Buenos Aires (Argentina) (b) 1,84 (c) D - central defense (d) - (e) Hamrun Spartans, Fasano, Lanusei, San Telmo
*** Callegari Torre - Emiliano Callegari Torre (Emiliano Callegari Torre) (a) 26/02/1996, Buenos Aires (Argentina) (b) 1,86 (c) D - central defense (d) - (e) Floriana, Sirens FC, Insieme Formia, Ducato Spoleto, Borgaro, Imperia
*** Calleja Cremona - Matthew Calleja Cremona (a) 14/09/1994, ¿? (Malta) (b) 1,80 (c) G (d) Santa Lucia FC (e) Hibernians FC, St. Andrews FC, Pembroke, Floriana, Pembroke, Floriana, Pembroke
*** Callens - Alexander Callens (Alexander Martín Marquinho Callens Asín) (a) 04/05/1992, Callao (Peru) (b) 1,85 (c) D - central defense (d) Girona FC (e) New York City, CD Numancia, Real Sociedad B, Sport Boys, Sport Boys II
*** Calu - Madalin Calu (Mădălin Iulian Calu) (a) 14/07/2000, Brăila (Romania) (b) - (c) M - right midfielder (d) FCV Farul Constanta (e) Dunarea Calarasi, FC Buzau,

Dunarea Calarasi, SCM Gloria Buzau, CSM Resita, SCM Gloria Buzau, Dacia U. Braila, Chiajna II, Academica Clinceni, Dacia U. Braila, FC Viitorul

*** Calusic - Ivan Calusic (Ivan Čalušić) (a) 12/09/1999, Split (Croatia) (b) 1,87 (c) M - pivot (d) NK Istra 1961 (e) Hajduk Split, NK Radomlje, Hajduk Split, Hajduk Split II, Croat. Zmijavci, RNK Split

*** Calusic - Josip Calusic (Josip Ćalušić) (a) 11/10/1993, Split (Croatia) (b) 1,87 (c) D - central defense (d) FK TSC Backa Topola (e) NK Celje, Din. Zagreb II, NK Lokomotiva, Dinamo Zagreb, NK Lokomotiva, Dinamo Zagreb, NK Lokomotiva, Radnik Sesvete, NK Lokomotiva, NK Omladinac

*** Calut - Alexandro Calut (a) 22/04/2003, Charleroi (Belgium) (b) 1,80 (c) D - left back (d) Oud-Heverlee Leuven (e) OH Leuven, Standard Liège

*** Calvert-Lewin - Dominic Calvert-Lewin (Dominic Nathaniel Calvert-Lewin) (a) 16/03/1997, Sheffield (England) (b) 1,89 (c) F - center forward (d) Everton FC (e) Sheffield Utd., Northampton, Sheffield Utd., Stalybridge, Sheffield Utd.

*** Calvo - Francisco Calvo (Francisco Javier Calvo Quesada) (a) 08/07/1992, San José (Costa Rica) (b) 1,80 (c) D - central defense (d) Konyaspor (e) San José, Chicago, Minnesota, Saprissa, Herediano, Santos FC, Herediano, Nordsjælland, Pérez Zeledón, Herediano, San Jacinto

*** Calzolari - Pietro Calzolari (a) 28/10/1991, ¿? (San Marino) (b) - (c) M - pivot (d) FC Fiorentino (e) Tre Penne, La Fiorita, Murata, Fiorentino

*** Camacho - Rafael Camacho (Rafael Euclides Soares Camacho) (a) 22/05/2000, Lisboa (Portugal) (b) 1,75 (c) F - right winger (d) Sporting de Lisboa (e) Aris Thessaloniki, Sporting Lisboa, B SAD, Sporting Lisboa, Rio Ave, Sporting Lisboa

*** Camaj - Driton Camaj (Дритон Цамај) (a) 07/03/1997, Podgorica (RF Yugoslavia, Montenegro) (b) 1,82 (c) F - left winger (d) Kisvárda FC (e) FK Iskra, FK Lovcen, Buducnost Podgorica, FK Decic Tuzi

*** Camaj - Ilir Camaj (a) 24/06/1996, ¿? (RF Yugoslavia, now in Montenegro) (b) 1,85 (c) F - center forward (d) FK Decic Tuzi (e) KF Egnatia, Dhofar Club, FK Decic Tuzi, FK Jezero, FK Decic Tuzi

*** Camaj - Romario Camaj (a) 06/06/2005, ¿? (Serbia and Montenegro, now in Kosovo) (b) - (c) D (d) FK Decic Tuzi (e) -

*** Camalov - Elvin Camalov (Elvin Sərkər oğlu Camalov) (a) 04/02/1995, Qakh (Azerbaijan) (b) 1,75 (c) M - pivot (d) Sabah FK (e) Zira FK, FK Qabala, FK Qabala 2

*** Camalov - Famil Camalov (Famil Şahinoviç oğlu Camalov) (a) 08/04/1998, ¿? (Azerbaijan) (b) 1,81 (c) F - center forward (d) Turan 2 Tovuz (e) Turan Tovuz, Neftchi 2 Baku, PFK Zaqatala

*** Camara - Aboubacar Camara (a) 04/01/2002, Dabou (Ivory Coast) (b) 1,70 (c) F - left winger (d) FK Bylis (e) FK Partizani, Volcan Junior

*** Camara - Aguibou Camara (a) 20/05/2001, Matam (Guinea) (b) 1,70 (c) M - attacking midfielder (d) Atromitos FC (e) Atromitos FC, Olympiakos, LOSC Lille B, Eleph. Coléah

*** Camara - Amadou Camara (a) 30/06/2000, Bamako (Mali) (b) 1,87 (c) F - center forward (d) Sarpsborg 08 FF (e) Oslo FA Dakar, Sarpsborg 08, Oslo FA Dakar, AS Real Bamako

*** Camara - Dawda Camara (Dawda Camara Sankharé) (a) 04/11/2002, Banyoles (Spain) (b) - (c) F - center forward (d) Girona FC B (e) -

*** Camara - Idrissa Camara (a) 11/01/2002, ¿? (Finland) (b) - (c) F - center forward (d) Pallokerho Keski-Uusimaa (e) FC Honka II

*** Camara - Mady Camara (Mohamed Mady Camara) (a) 28/02/1997, Matam (Guinea) (b) 1,82 (c) M - central midfielder (d) Olympiakos El Pireo (e) AS Roma, Olympiakos, AC Ajaccio, Santoba FC

*** Camara - Mahdi Camara (a) 30/06/1998, Martigues (France) (b) 1,78 (c) M - central midfielder (d) Stade Brestois 29 (e) St.-Étienne, Stade Brestois, St.-Étienne, Stade Lavallois, St.-Étienne, Saint-Étienne B

*** Camara - Mamadou Camara (a) 15/10/2002, Dakar (Senegal) (b) 1,85 (c) M - central midfielder (d) RC Lens (e) SC Bastia, RC Lens, Sacré-Cœur

*** Camara - Mamadou Harouna Camara (a) 18/02/2001, ¿? (Mali) (b) - (c) F - right winger (d) FC Milsami Orhei (e) Black Stars

*** Camara - Mohamed Camara (a) 06/01/2000, Bamako (Mali) (b) 1,73 (c) M - pivot (d) AS Mónaco (e) RB Salzburg, FC Liefering, TSV Hartberg, FC Liefering, AS Real Bamako

*** Camara - Mohamed Camara (Mohamed Ali Camara) (a) 28/08/1997, Kerouane (Guinea) (b) 1,91 (c) D - central defense (d) BSC Young Boys (e) Hapoel Raanana, Horoya AC, Hafia FC, Horoya AC, Satellite FC

*** Camara - Mohamed Camara (Mohamed Fulake Camara) (a) 14/04/2000, ¿? (Congo RD) (b) - (c) M - pivot (d) CS Fola Esch (e) Red Star Merl, Plantières

*** Camara - Moustapha Camara (a) 05/06/2003, Maka Fall (Senegal) (b) 1,84 (c) F - left winger (d) Ankara Keciörengücü (e) KS Kastrioti, A. Keciörengücü, Jolof OC

*** Camara - Ousmane Camara (a) 03/11/2001, Conakry (Guinea) (b) - (c) F - center forward (d) AJ Auxerre (e) AJ Auxerre B

*** Camara - Ousmane Camara (a) 06/03/2003, Paris (France) (b) 1,97 (c) D - central defense (d) Angers SCO (e) Paris FC, Paris FC B

*** Camara - Ousmane Camara (a) 28/12/1998, Conakry (Guinea) (b) 1,67 (c) F - left winger (d) Dinamo Tbilisi (e) FC Dila, Vålerenga, FC Dila, Vålerenga, AFC Eskilstuna, Eskilstuna City, FC Atouga

*** Camara - Ousoumane Camara (a) 19/12/1998, Pontoise (France) (b) 1,84 (c) M - pivot (d) AJ Auxerre (e) AJ Auxerre B

*** Camara - Samba Camara (a) 14/11/1992, Le Havre (France) (b) 1,90 (c) D - central defense (d) Sivasspor (e) New England, Le Havre AC, Le Havre AC B

*** Camara - Sekou Camara (a) 20/07/1997, Conakry (Guinea) (b) 1,83 (c) F - center forward (d) FC Botosani (e) ACSM Poli Iasi, FC Botosani, Besëlidhja, HJK Helsinki, Besëlidhja, KF Teuta, Besëlidhja, Flamurtari FC, Besëlidhja, KF Luzi United

*** Camara - Sékou Camara (Sékou Amadou Camara) (a) 23/09/1997, Kamsar (Guinea) (b) 1,87 (c) F - center forward (d) Stade Beaucairois 30 (e) Pietà Hotspurs, Paide, FC Wil 1900, Difaâ El Jadida, Horoya AC, Eendracht Aalst, Horoya AC, Satellite FC

*** Camara - Sidiki Camara (a) 23/08/2002, Genève (Switzerland) (b) 1,79 (c) M - central midfielder (d) FC Stade Nyonnais (e) Stade Nyonnais, Servette FC

*** Camara - Yamoussa Camara (Yamoussa Camara) (a) 26/04/2000, Boke (Guinea) (b) 1,70 (c) M - pivot (d) FK Smorgon (e) Energetik-BGU, Isloch, Rukh, BATE Borisov, Rukh, FK Smorgon, Rukh, Ac. SM Dixinn

*** Cámara - Juan Cámara (Juan del Carmen Cámara Mesa) (a) 13/02/1994, Jaén (Spain) (b) 1,84 (c) M - attacking midfielder (d) Zaglebie Sosnowiec (e) Jagiellonia, Sabah FK, Jagiellonia, CS U Craiova, Jagiellonia, FC Dinamo, Jagiellonia, Miedź Legnica, FC Barcelona B, Reus Deportiu, FC Barcelona B, Girona FC, FC Barcelona B, Villarreal CF B, Villarreal CF C

*** Camarasa - Víctor Camarasa (Víctor Camarasa Ferrando) (a) 28/05/1994, Meliana (Spain) (b) 1,83 (c) M - central midfielder (d) Real Oviedo (e) Real Betis,

Alavés, Real Betis, Crystal Palace, Real Betis, Cardiff City, Real Betis, Levante UD, Alavés, Levante UD, At. Levante, CF Cracks

*** Camavinga - Eduardo Camavinga (Eduardo Celmi Camavinga) (a) 10/11/2002, Cabinda (Angola) (b) 1,82 (c) M - central midfielder (d) Real Madrid CF (e) Stade Rennes, Stade Rennes B

*** Cambiaghi - Nicolò Cambiaghi (a) 28/12/2000, Monza (Italy) (b) 1,73 (c) F - left winger (d) Atalanta de Bérgamo (e) FC Empoli, Atalanta, Pordenone, Reggiana

*** Cambiaso - Andrea Cambiaso (a) 20/02/2000, Genoa (Italy) (b) 1,83 (c) D - left back (d) Juventus de Turín (e) Bologna, Juventus, Genoa, Empoli, Genoa, Alessandria, Genoa, Savona, Genoa, Albissola, Genoa

*** Camblan - Axel Camblan (a) 30/08/2003, Brest (France) (b) 1,69 (c) M - left midfielder (d) Stade Brestois 29 (e) Concarneau, Stade Brestois, Brest B

*** Cambura - Nichita Cambura (a) 28/01/2005, ¿? (Moldova) (b) - (c) F - left winger (d) CSF Balti-SSS Balti (e) FC Bălți, SSS Balti

*** Camello - Sergio Camello (Sergio Camello Pérez) (a) 10/02/2001, Madrid (Spain) (b) 1,77 (c) F - center forward (d) Atlético de Madrid (e) Rayo Vallecano, Atlético Madrid, CD Mirandés, Atlético Madrid, At. Madrid B

*** Camenzuli - Ryan Camenzuli (a) 08/09/1994, ¿? (Malta) (b) 1,73 (c) M - left midfielder (d) Hamrun Spartans (e) Floriana, Birkirkara FC, Floriana, Birkirkara FC, Sperre) Birkirkara FC, Floriana, Birkirkara FC

*** Cameron - Innes Cameron (a) 22/08/2000, Oban (Scotland) (b) 1,90 (c) F - center forward (d) Kilmarnock FC (e) Queen of the South, Kilmarnock FC, Queen of the South, Kilmarnock FC, Alloa Athletic, Kilmarnock FC, Ayr United, Kilmarnock FC, Kilmarnock B, Stranraer, Kilmarnock B

*** Camilleri - Adam Camilleri (a) 29/01/2002, ¿? (Malta) (b) - (c) D (d) - (e) Birkirkara

*** Camilleri - Emerson Camilleri (a) 01/05/2002, ¿? (Malta) (b) - (c) M (d) Zurrieq FC (e) Santa Lucia FC

*** Camilleri - Gary Camilleri (a) 05/08/1999, ¿? (Malta) (b) - (c) D - central defense (d) Marsaxlokk FC (e) Balzan FC, Sirens FC, Balzan FC, Tarxien, Balzan FC, Senglea Ath., Balzan FC

*** Camilleri - Luca Camilleri (a) 25/11/2005, ¿? (Malta) (b) 1,87 (c) G (d) Mosta FC (e) -

*** Camilleri - Luciano Camilleri (a) 27/11/2003, ¿? (Malta) (b) 1,86 (c) G (d) - (e) Mosta FC

*** Camilleri - Romario Camilleri (a) 13/05/2000, ¿? (Malta) (b) - (c) D - right back (d) Santa Lucia FC (e) Gzira Utd.

*** Camilleri - Ryan Camilleri (a) 22/05/1988, Pieta (Malta) (b) 1,78 (c) D - right back (d) FC Mgarr United (e) Valletta, Hibernians FC, Pietà Hotspurs

*** Camilo Almeida - Dany Camilo Almeida (a) 12/01/2001, ¿? (Luxembourg) (b) - (c) F - center forward (d) FC Kehlen (e) FC UNA Strassen, US Rumelange

*** Camora - Mário Camora (Mário Jorge Paulino Malico) (a) 10/11/1986, Samora Correia (Portugal) (b) 1,78 (c) D - left back (d) CFR Cluj (e) Naval, Beira-Mar, Avanca, Beira-Mar, Samora Correia, CA Valdevez

*** Campanharo - Campanharo (Gustavo Campanharo) (a) 04/04/1992, Caxias do Sul (Brazil) (b) 1,78 (c) M - pivot (d) Sport Club Internacional (e) Kayserispor, Chapecoense, Ludogorets, Bragantino, Évian, Bragantino, Hellas Verona, Bragantino, Juventude

*** Campbell - Aaron Campbell (a) 19/04/2005, ¿? (Northern Ireland) (b) - (c) D - central defense (d) Daytona State Falcons (e) -

*** Campbell - Chem Campbell (a) 30/12/2002, Birmingham (England) (b) 1,80 (c) M - attacking midfielder (d) - (e) Wycombe Wanderers

*** Campbell - Dean Campbell (Dean Graeme Campbell) (a) 19/03/2001, Bridge of Don (Scotland) (b) 1,81 (c) M - pivot (d) AFC Barrow (e) Aberdeen FC, Stevenage, Aberdeen FC, Kilmarnock FC, Aberdeen FC, Aberdeen FC B

*** Campbell - Josh Campbell (a) 06/05/2000, Edinburgh (Scotland) (b) 1,82 (c) M - central midfielder (d) Hibernian FC (e) Hibernian B, Edinburgh City, Hibernian B, Arbroath, Hibernian B, Airdrieonians, Hibernian B

*** Campbell - Kenroy Campbell (a) 30/05/2002, ¿? (Jamaica) (b) - (c) F - left winger (d) BFC Daugavpils (e) RFS, Cavalier FC, Zimbru Chisinau, Cavalier FC

*** Campbell - Norman Campbell (Norman Odale Campbell) (a) 24/11/1999, Kingston (Jamaica) (b) 1,75 (c) F - right winger (d) FK Javor-Matis Ivanjica (e) Čukarički, Harbour View FC, Graficar, Harbour View FC

*** Campbell - Peter Campbell (a) 16/09/1997, Portadown (Northern Ireland) (b) - (c) F - left winger (d) Glenavon FC (e) Loughgall

*** Campbell - Rhyss Campbell (a) 30/11/1998, ¿? (Northern Ireland) (b) - (c) M - attacking midfielder (d) Dungannon Swifts (e) -

*** Campbell - Sam Campbell (a) 01/09/2004, Falkirk (Scotland) (b) 1,89 (c) D - central defense (d) Annan Athletic FC (e) Annan Athletic FC, Motherwell FC, Motherwell B

*** Campo - Samuele Campo (a) 06/07/1995, Basel (Switzerland) (b) 1,77 (c) M - attacking midfielder (d) FC Lucerna (e) FC Basel, Darmstadt 98, FC Basel, Lausanne-Sport

*** Campos - Diego Campos (Diego de Jesús Campos Ballestero) (a) 01/10/1995, San José (Costa Rica) (b) 1,78 (c) F - left winger (d) Degerfors IF (e) Jerv, Chicago, Indy Eleven, Chicago, Clemson Tigers

*** Campuzano - Jorman Campuzano (Jorman David Campuzano Puentes) (a) 30/04/1996, Tamalameque (Colombia) (b) 1,75 (c) M - pivot (d) CA Boca Juniors (e) Giresunspor, Boca Juniors, At. Nacional, Pereira, At. Nacional, Pereira

*** Can - Emre Can (a) 12/01/1994, Frankfurt am Main (Germany) (b) 1,86 (c) M - pivot (d) Borussia Dortmund (e) Juventus, Borussia Dortmund, Juventus, Liverpool, Bayer Leverkusen, Bayern München, FC Bayern II

*** Can - Mert Can (a) 07/02/2005, Ankara (Turkey) (b) - (c) D - central defense (d) MKE Ankaragücü (e) -

*** Canadi - Marcel Canadi (Marcel Čanadi) (a) 27/10/1997, Wien (Austria) (b) 1,84 (c) M - attacking midfielder (d) - (e) Brisbane Roar, HNK Sibenik, SV Ried, SKU Amstetten, Austria Lustenau, Borussia Mönchengladbach II

*** Canadjija - Dario Canadjija (Dario Čanađija) (a) 17/04/1994, Bjelovar (Croatia) (b) 1,76 (c) M - pivot (d) HSK Zrinjski Mostar (e) HNK Sibenik, Aalesund, Sarpsborg 08, Astra Giurgiu, HNK Gorica, Slaven Belupo, HNK Rijeka, Olimpija, HNK Rijeka, Spezia, HNK Rijeka, Slaven Belupo

*** Canak - Cihan Canak (Cihan Çanak) (a) 24/01/2005, Verviers (Belgium) (b) 1,75 (c) M - attacking midfielder (d) Standard de Lieja (e) SL16 FC

*** Canales - Sergio Canales (Sergio Canales Madrazo) (a) 16/02/1991, Santander (Spain) (b) 1,78 (c) M - attacking midfielder (d) CF Monterrey (e) Real Betis, Real Sociedad, Valencia CF, Real Madrid, Valencia CF, Real Madrid, Racing, Rayo Cantabria

*** Canavan - Jake Canavan (Jake George Canavan) (a) 17/12/2003, Liverpool (England) (b) - (c) M - central midfielder (d) The New Saints (e) Aberystwyth, The New Saints, TNS Development

*** Cancar - Phillip Cancar (Phillip Čančar) (a) 11/05/2001, Wollongong, New South Wales (Australia) (b) 1,86 (c) D - central defense (d) Newcastle United Jets (e) Livingston FC, Western Sydney, Hrv Dragovoljac, Sydney FC II

*** Cancarevic - Ognjen Cancarevic (Огњен Чанчаревић) (a) 25/09/1989, Uzice (Yugoslavia, now in Serbia) (b) 1,87 (c) G (d) Alashkert Yerevan CF (e) Radnik, Mladost, OFK Beograd, Sloboda Užice, Radnicki 1923, Sloboda Užice

*** Cancellieri - Matteo Cancellieri (a) 12/02/2002, Roma (Italy) (b) 1,80 (c) F - right winger (d) SS Lazio (e) Hellas Verona, Lazio, Hellas Verona

*** Cancelo - João Cancelo (João Pedro Cavaco Cancelo) (a) 27/05/1994, Barreiro (Portugal) (b) 1,82 (c) D - right back (d) Manchester City (e) Bayern München, Manchester City, Juventus, Valencia CF, Internazionale Milano, Valencia CF, Benfica, Valencia CF, Benfica, Benfica B

*** Cancola - David Cancola (a) 23/10/1996, Wien (Austria) (b) 1,84 (c) M - pivot (d) - (e) Ross County, Slovan Liberec, TSV Hartberg, Young Violets, Austria Viena, Wiener Neustadt, Austria Viena, Austria Wien Reserves

*** Candeias - Daniel Candeias (Daniel João Santos Candeias) (a) 25/02/1988, Fornos de Algodres (Portugal) (b) 1,77 (c) F - right winger (d) Kocaelispor (e) Alanyaspor, Genclerbirligi, Rangers FC, Benfica, Alanyaspor, Benfica, FC Metz, Benfica, Granada CF, Benfica, 1.FC Nürnberg, Benfica, Nacional, Portimonense, Nacional, FC Porto, Paços Ferreira, FC Porto, Recreativo, FC Porto, Rio Ave, FC Porto, Varzim, FC Porto

*** Candreva - Antonio Candreva (a) 28/02/1987, Roma (Italy) (b) 1,80 (c) M - right midfielder (d) US Salernitana 1919 (e) Sampdoria, Salernitana, Sampdoria, Internazionale Milano, Sampdoria, Internazionale Milano, Lazio, Udinese, Lazio, Udinese, Lazio, Udinese, Cesena, Udinese, Parma, Udinese, Juventus, Udinese, AS Livorno, Udinese, Ternana

*** Cangiano - Gianmarco Cangiano (a) 16/11/2001, Napoli (Italy) (b) 1,76 (c) F - left winger (d) Delfino Pescara 1936 (e) Pescara, Bologna, Fortuna Sittard, Bologna, Bari, Bologna, Crotone, Bologna, Ascoli, Bologna

*** Cangini - Alessio Cangini (a) 05/01/1991, ¿? (Italy) (b) 1,73 (c) M - pivot (d) Riccione (e) Domagnano, SS Folgore, Murata, Domagnano, United Riccione, La Fiorita, Valfoglia, Urbinelli, Forlì, Del Conca

*** Canini - Francesco Canini (a) 08/05/2002, ¿? (Italy) (b) - (c) F - center forward (d) SP Cailungo (e) Tropical Coriano

*** Cankaya - Atakan Cankaya (Atakan Rıdvan Çankaya) (a) 25/06/1998, Konak, Izmir (Turkey) (b) 1,80 (c) D - central defense (d) MKE Ankaragücü (e) Göztepe, Ankaragücü, Ankaraspor, Altay SK

*** Cann - Francis Cann (a) 06/02/1998, Tema (Ghana) (b) 1,75 (c) F - left winger (d) CS Marítimo (e) Vizela, Al-Hazem, Vizela, Mafra, Vizela, Vizela

*** Cannatov - Mehdi Cannatov (a) 26/01/1992, Makhachkala (Russia) (b) - (c) G (d) Sumqayit PFK (e) Zira FK, Sumqayit, Anzhi, Baltika, Anzhi, Anzhi 2, Anzhi II

*** Canning - Aaron Canning (a) 07/03/1992, ¿? (Northern Ireland) (b) 1,76 (c) D - right back (d) - (e) Portadown, Coleraine, Dungannon, Coleraine, Institute FC, Limavady United, Glenavon, Ballinamallard, Glenavon, Loughgall, Coagh United, Coleraine

*** Cannon - Reggie Cannon (Reginald Jacob Cannon) (a) 11/06/1998, Chicago, Illinois (United States) (b) 1,80 (c) D - right back (d) - (e) Boavista, Dallas, UCLA Bruins, Solar SC

*** Cannon - Thomas Cannon (Thomas Christopher Cannon) (a) 28/12/2002, Aintree (England) (b) - (c) F - center forward (d) Everton FC (e) Preston North End

*** Canós - Sergi Canós (Sergi Canós Tenés) (a) 02/02/1997, Nules (Spain) (b) 1,77 (c) F - right winger (d) Brentford FC (e) Olympiakos, Brentford, Norwich City, Brentford
*** Canpolat - Erdem Canpolat (a) 13/04/2001, Duisburg (Germany) (b) 1,94 (c) G (d) Pendikspor (e) Kasimpasa, Schalke 04 II
*** Cantalapiedra - Aitor Cantalapiedra (Aitor Cantalapiedra Fernández) (a) 10/02/1996, Barcelona (Spain) (b) 1,77 (c) F - right winger (d) Panathinaikos FC (e) FC Twente, Sevilla At., Villarreal CF B, FC Barcelona B
*** Canteros - Federico Canteros (Federico Nevel Canteros) (c) M - central midfielder (d) - (e) Europa Point FC, Lynx Reserve
*** Cantwell - Todd Cantwell (Todd Owen Cantwell) (a) 27/02/1998, Dereham (England) (b) 1,80 (c) M - left midfielder (d) Rangers FC (e) Norwich City, Bournemouth, Norwich City, Fortuna Sittard
*** Cañas - José Alberto Cañas (José Alberto Cañas Ruiz Herrera) (a) 27/05/1987, Rota (Spain) (b) 1,78 (c) M - central midfielder (d) Ionikos Nikeas (e) At. Baleares, Crvena zvezda, PAOK, RCD Espanyol, Swansea City, Real Betis, Betis B, Betis C
*** Cañas - Róger Cañas (Róger Cañas Henao) (a) 27/03/1990, Medellín (Colombia) (b) 1,90 (c) M - pivot (d) Shakhter Karaganda (e) Barnechea, Irtysh, Soligorsk, Ordabasy, FC Astana, APOEL FC, FC Astana, Shakhter K., Sibir, Jagiellonia, Sibir, FC Tranzits, Indep. Medellín
*** Cañizares - Lucas Cañizares (Lucas Cañizares Conchello) (a) 10/05/2002, Valencia (Spain) (b) 1,88 (c) G (d) Real Madrid Castilla (e) -
*** Capa - Ander Capa (Ander Capa Rodríguez) (a) 08/02/1992, Portugalete (Spain) (b) 1,75 (c) D - right back (d) - (e) Athletic, SD Eibar, SD Eibar B
*** Capaldo - Nicolás Capaldo (Nicolás Capaldo Taboas) (a) 14/09/1998, Santa Rosa (Argentina) (b) 1,77 (c) M - central midfielder (d) Red Bull Salzburg (e) Boca Juniors, Boca Juniors II
*** Capan - Luka Capan (a) 06/04/1995, Zagreb (Croatia) (b) 1,86 (c) D - central defense (d) AE Kifisias (e) Honvéd, Bursaspor, HNK Rijeka, NK Lokomotiva, Din. Zagreb II, Dinamo Zagreb
*** Capan - Marko Capan (a) 24/02/2004, Bjelovar (Croatia) (b) 1,80 (c) M - pivot (d) NK Siroki Brijeg (e) Siroki Brijeg, Hajduk Split
*** Capatina - Mihai Capatina (Cristian Mihai Căpăţînă) (a) 16/12/1995, Slatina (Romania) (b) 1,83 (c) M - central midfielder (d) Universitatea Craiova (e) FC Voluntari, FC Olt Slatina
*** Capelle - Pierrick Capelle (a) 15/04/1987, Lesquin (France) (b) 1,81 (c) M - central midfielder (d) Angers SCO (e) Clermont Foot, Quevilly, CS Avion, Stade Héninois, L'Aumône
*** Capezzi - Leonardo Capezzi (a) 28/03/1995, Figline Valdarno (Italy) (b) 1,78 (c) M - central midfielder (d) - (e) Perugia, Salernitana, Sampdoria, Salernitana, Sampdoria, Albacete, Sampdoria, Empoli, Sampdoria, Crotone, Sampdoria, Crotone, Fiorentina, Crotone, Fiorentina, Varese, Fiorentina
*** Capicchioni - Lorenzo Capicchioni (a) 19/01/2002, ¿? (San Marino) (b) - (c) M - central midfielder (d) Sammaurese Calcio (e) Cosmos, United Riccione, Rimini
*** Capiga - Kacper Capiga (a) 20/02/2005, ¿? (Poland) (b) 1,84 (c) M - pivot (d) Górnik Zabrze (e) AP Gornik
*** Capilla - Eneko Capilla (Eneko Capilla Gonzalez) (a) 13/06/1995, San Sebastián (Spain) (b) 1,67 (c) M - attacking midfielder (d) Asteras Tripolis (e) Real Sociedad, Cultural Leonesa, Real Sociedad, Real Sociedad B, CD Numancia, Real Sociedad B
*** Capon - Brecht Capon (a) 22/04/1988, Oostende (Belgium) (b) 1,79 (c) D - right back (d) - (e) KV Oostende, KV Kortrijk, KV Brugge, KV Kortrijk, KV Brugge

*** Capoue - Étienne Capoue (a) 11/07/1988, Niort (France) (b) 1,89 (c) M - pivot (d) Villarreal CF (e) Watford, Tottenham Hotspur, Toulouse

*** Cappa - Guillaume Cappa (a) 29/07/1993, ¿? (France) (b) 1,88 (c) G (d) EN Saint-Avold (e) Differdange 03, Swift Hesperange, ASC Biesheim, Sarreguemines, US Forbach, AS Pagny, Tarbes Pyrénées, FC Metz, FC Metz B

*** Cappis - Christian Cappis (Christian Jaeger Cappis) (a) 13/08/1999, Katy, Texas (United States) (b) 1,85 (c) M - central midfielder (d) Brøndby IF (e) Hobro IK, Texans SC

*** Capradossi - Elio Capradossi (a) 11/03/1996, Kampala (Uganda) (b) 1,85 (c) D - central defense (d) Cagliari (e) Spezia, SPAL, Spezia, AS Roma, Spezia, AS Roma, Bari, AS Roma, Bari, AS Roma

*** Caprari - Gianluca Caprari (a) 30/07/1993, Roma (Italy) (b) 1,71 (c) F - attacking midfielder (d) AC Monza (e) Hellas Verona, Monza, Hellas Verona, Sampdoria, Hellas Verona, Sampdoria, Benevento, Sampdoria, Parma, Sampdoria, Internazionale Milano, Pescara, Internazionale Milano, Pescara, AS Roma, Pescara, AS Roma, Pescara, AS Roma

*** Caprescu - Andrei Caprescu (Mateo Andrei Căprescu) (a) 23/10/2004, Câmpulung Muscel (Romania) (b) - (c) F - center forward (d) CS Mioveni (e) -

*** Capusa - Tiberiu Capusa (Tiberiu Ionuț Căpușă) (a) 06/04/1998, Bacău (Romania) (b) 1,83 (c) D - right back (d) - (e) Chindia, FCV Farul, Chindia, FC Viitorul, Universitatea Cluj, FC Viitorul, Academia Hagi

*** Caputo - Francesco Caputo (a) 06/08/1987, Altamura (Italy) (b) 1,81 (c) F - center forward (d) FC Empoli (e) Sampdoria, FC Empoli, Sampdoria, Sassuolo, Sampdoria, Sassuolo, Empoli, Virtus Entella, Bari, Virtus Entella, Bari, AC Siena, Bari, Salernitana, Bari, Noicattaro, Team Altamura, Toritto

*** Caqueret - Maxence Caqueret (a) 15/02/2000, Vénissieux (France) (b) 1,74 (c) M - central midfielder (d) Olympique de Lyon (e) Olymp. Lyon B

*** Cara - Tedi Cara (a) 15/04/2000, Durrës (Albania) (b) 1,75 (c) F - center forward (d) FK Partizani (e) KS Besa

*** Carabajal - Ignacio Carabajal (Ignacio Fabian Carabajal Baldovino) (a) 04/11/1997, San Juan (Argentina) (b) 1,82 (c) D - central defense (d) APD Leonfortese (e) Gela, Faetano, Li Punti, Asseminese, CD Alcalá, Pro Cervignano, Huracán LH, Deportivo Kivon

*** Caraballo - José Caraballo (José Enrique Caraballo Rosal) (a) 21/02/1996, Carúpano, Sucre (Venezuela) (b) 1,68 (c) M - attacking midfielder (d) FC Pyunik Yerevan (e) Pyunik Yerevan, Huachipato, Real Santa Cruz, Huachipato, Deportivo Lara, Huachipato, Club San José, Huachipato, Deportivo Lara, Atlante, Deportivo Lara, Caracas FC, Deportivo Lara, Caracas FC

*** Caracciolo - Julian Caracciolo (Julian Rocco Caracciolo) (a) 20/05/1995, ¿? (France) (b) - (c) D - right back (d) - (e) Mondercange, Trémery, UL Rombas

*** Carapic - Strahinja Carapic (Страхиња Чарапић) (a) 17/10/2002, Beograd (RF Yugoslavia, Serbia) (b) 1,79 (c) M - attacking midfielder (d) FK IMT Belgrad (e) FK TSC, Radnicki Srem, FK TSC, Radnicki Srem, FK TSC, Zarkovo, FK TSC, Sindjelic Bg

*** Carausu - Codrin Carausu (Iulian Codrin Petrişor Cărăuşu) (a) 03/07/2005, Botoşani (Romania) (b) - (c) F - center forward (d) FC Botosani (e) -

*** Carbone - Jamie Carbone (a) 16/08/2002, ¿? (Malta) (b) 1,81 (c) F - left winger (d) Santa Lucia FC (e) -

*** Carboni - Andrea Carboni (a) 04/02/2001, Sorgono (Italy) (b) 1,87 (c) D - central defense (d) AC Monza (e) Venezia, Monza, Cagliari

*** Carboni - Franco Carboni (Franco Ezequiel Carboni) (a) 04/04/2003, Buenos Aires (Argentina) (b) 1,90 (c) D - left back (d) AC Monza (e) Monza, Internazionale Milano, Cagliari, Internazionale Milano
*** Carboni - Valentín Carboni (a) 05/03/2005, Buenos Aires (Argentina) (b) 1,85 (c) M - attacking midfielder (d) AC Monza (e) Monza, Internazionale Milano
*** Carcelén - Iza Carcelén (Isaac Carcelén Valencia) (a) 23/04/1993, El Puerto de Santa María (Spain) (b) 1,70 (c) D - right back (d) Cádiz CF (e) Rayo Majadahonda, Cultural Leonesa, Real Zaragoza, Betis B
*** Cardona - Irvin Cardona (a) 08/08/1997, Nîmes (France) (b) 1,85 (c) F - center forward (d) FC Augsburg (e) Stade Brestois, AS Monaco, Cercle Brugge, AS Monaco, AS Monaco B
*** Cardoso - Alexandre Cardoso (Alexandre Cardoso Garcia) (a) 30/04/1992, Ribeirão Preto (Brazil) (b) 1,82 (c) M - pivot (d) Nagaworld FC (e) UE Santa Coloma, Boeung Ket, Erbil SC, KF Turbina, FK Bylis, KF Turbina, Pedras Rubras, Al-Nahda, Trofense, Damac FC, Al-Nahda, Trofense, Vitória Setúbal, Trofense, Vitória Setúbal, Beira-Mar, Nacional-MG, Vasco-AC
*** Cardoso - André Cardoso (Nuno André Gomes Cardoso) (a) 16/01/2001, Madeira (Portugal) (b) 1,79 (c) M - attacking midfielder (d) CS Marítimo B (e) -
*** Cardoso - Fábio Cardoso (Fábio Rafael Rodrigues Cardoso) (a) 19/04/1994, Águeda (Portugal) (b) 1,87 (c) D - central defense (d) FC Porto (e) Santa Clara, Rangers FC, Vitória Setúbal, Benfica B, Paços Ferreira, Benfica B
*** Cardoso - Gonçalo Cardoso (Gonçalo Bento Soares Cardoso) (a) 21/10/2000, Marco de Canaveses (Portugal) (b) 1,86 (c) D - central defense (d) CS Marítimo B (e) Betis Deportivo, FC Basel, Boavista
*** Cardoso - Miguel Cardoso (Miguel Felipe Nunes Cardoso) (a) 19/06/1994, Lisboa (Portugal) (b) 1,76 (c) F - right winger (d) Kayserispor (e) Dinamo Moskva, B SAD, Dinamo Moskva, Tambov, Dinamo Moskva, Tondela, RC Deportivo, União Madeira, Deportivo B, Real SC
*** Cardoso - Nicolao Cardoso (Nicolao Manuel Dumitru Cardoso) (a) 12/10/1991, Nacka (Sweden) (b) 1,84 (c) F - left winger (d) Buriram United (e) Bnei Sakhnin, UTA Arad, Suwon Bluewings, Gaz Metan, AS Livorno, Gimnàstic, Alcorcón, Napoli, Nottingham Forest, Napoli, Latina Calcio, Napoli, PAE Veria, Napoli, Reggina, Napoli, Cittadella, Napoli, Cittadella, Napoli, Ternana, Napoli, Empoli, Napoli, Empoli
*** Cardoso Monteiro - Dwain Cardoso Monteiro (a) 01/09/1999, ¿? (Luxembourg) (b) - (c) F (d) FC Rodange 91 II (e) Jeunesse Esch, Rodange II
*** Cardozo - Facundo Cardozo (Facundo Omar oğlu Cardozo) (a) 06/04/1995, San Miguel (Argentina) (b) 1,82 (c) D - central defense (d) Arsenal Fútbol Club (e) FK Sabail, Platense, All Boys, Coquimbo, Oaxaca, Arsenal, Vélez Sarsfield II, Mumbai City, Vélez Sarsfield II, Bolívar, Vélez Sarsfield II
*** Carevic - Lazar Carevic (Лазар Царевић) (a) 16/03/1999, Cetinje (RF Yugoslavia, now in Montenegro) (b) 1,95 (c) G (d) FK Vojvodina Novi Sad (e) Barcelona Atlètic, OFK Grbalj
*** Carevic - Nemanja Carevic (Немања Царевић) (a) 08/04/2004, Cetinje (Serbia and Montenegro, now in Montenegro) (b) 1,85 (c) M - central midfielder (d) OFK Petrovac (e) OFK Grbalj, FK Budva
*** Carey - Graham Carey (a) 20/05/1989, Blanchardstown (Ireland) (b) 1,83 (c) F - left winger (d) St. Johnstone FC (e) CSKA-Sofia, Plymouth Argyle, Ross County, St. Mirren, Celtic FC, Huddersfield Town, Celtic FC, St. Mirren, Celtic FC, Bohemians, Celtic FC

*** Carey - Sean Carey (Sean Jones-Carey) (a) 16/01/2004, Clondalkin, South Dublin (Ireland) (b) 1,84 (c) D - right back (d) Shamrock Rovers (e) Glenavon, Shamrock Rovers

*** Carlén - Adam Carlén (a) 27/06/2000, ¿? (Sweden) (b) 1,93 (c) M - central midfielder (d) IFK Göteborg (e) Degerfors

*** Carlgren - Patrik Carlgren (Patrik Ulf Anders Carlgren) (a) 08/01/1992, Falun (Sweden) (b) 1,89 (c) G (d) Randers FC (e) Konyaspor, Nordsjælland, AIK, Brage

*** Carlin - Jamie Carlin (Jamie Payas-Carlin) (a) 27/08/1992, ¿? (Gibraltar) (b) 1,84 (c) G (d) - (e) Mons Calpe, Glacis Utd. Reserves, Mons Calpe Reserves, Leo FC, Boca Gibraltar, Gibraltar Utd., Glacis United

*** Carlin - Sean Carlin (a) 06/11/2004, ¿? (Northern Ireland) (b) - (c) M (d) Institute FC (e) -

*** Carlinhos - Carlinhos (Carlos Vinícius Santos de Jesús) (a) 22/06/1994, Camacan (Brazil) (b) 1,79 (c) M - attacking midfielder (d) Portimonense SC (e) Vasco da Gama, Standard Liège, Vitória Setúbal, Standard Liège, Guarani, Standard Liège, Estoril Praia, Monte Azul, FC Thun, Monte Azul, FC Aarau, Monte Azul, RB Brasil, Monte Azul, Desp. Brasil, Bayer Leverkusen, Jahn Regensburg, Bayer Leverkusen, Desp. Brasil

*** Carlini - Nicola Carlini (a) 07/11/2002, ¿? (San Marino) (b) - (c) D - central defense (d) SS Murata (e) -

*** Carlitos - Carlitos (Carlos Daniel López Huesca) (a) 12/06/1990, Alicante (Spain) (b) 1,76 (c) F - center forward (d) PAS Lamia 1964 (e) Legia Warszawa, Panathinaikos, Al-Wahda FC, Legia Warszawa, Wisla Kraków, Villarreal CF B, CD Eldense, Aris Limassol, Novelda CF, CF Fuenlabrada, Petrotrest, Ontinyent, Torrellano

*** Carlitos - Carlitos (Norberto Carlos Costa Dos Santos) (a) 16/05/1999, Lisboa (Portugal) (b) 1,85 (c) M - central midfielder (d) Nea Salamis (e) PO Xylotymbou, 1º Dezembro, Pinhalnovense

*** Carlius - Ludvig Carlius (a) 14/03/2001, ¿? (Sweden) (b) - (c) M (d) Mjällby AIF (e) IFK Malmö, Mjällby AIF

*** Carlos - Juan Carlos (Juan Carlos Machuca de Lira) (a) 21/11/1993, Guadalajara (Mexico) (b) - (c) F (d) UE Engordany B (e) FC Santa B, CF Amèrica

*** Carlos Augusto - Carlos Augusto (Carlos Augusto Zopolato Neves) (a) 07/01/1999, Campinas (Brazil) (b) 1,84 (c) D - left back (d) AC Monza (e) Corinthians

*** Carlos Dias - Carlos Dias (Carlos Eduardo Oliveira Dias) (a) 23/01/2000, Rio Negro (Brazil) (b) 1,79 (c) M - pivot (d) Al-Fujairah SC (e) Fujairah SC, APOEL FC, PAEEK Kyrenia, APOEL FC, Paraná, Paraná B

*** Carlos Eduardo - Carlos Eduardo (Carlos Eduardo Borges Parente) (a) 10/08/2002, Santa Catarina (Brazil) (b) 1,92 (c) F - center forward (d) CS Marítimo (e) Brusque

*** Carlos Eduardo - Carlos Eduardo (Carlos Eduardo da Silva Cândido) (a) 17/11/1996, ¿? (Brazil) (b) 1,79 (c) D - right back (d) FK Banga Gargzdai (e) Hercílio Luz, Tubarão-SC, Criciúma EC

*** Carlos Eduardo - Carlos Eduardo (Carlos Eduardo Ferreira de Souza) (a) 10/10/1996, Nerópolis (Brazil) (b) 1,73 (c) F - left winger (d) Alanyaspor (e) Palmeiras, Estoril Praia, Palmeiras, RB Bragantino, Palmeiras, Athletico-PR, Palmeiras, Pyramids FC, Goiás

*** Carlos Vinícius - Carlos Vinícius (Carlos Vinicius Alves Morais) (a) 25/03/1995, Bom Jesus das Selvas (Brazil) (b) 1,90 (c) F - center forward (d) Fulham FC (e) Benfica, PSV Eindhoven, Benfica, Tottenham Hotspur, Benfica, Napoli, AS Monaco, Napoli, Rio Ave, Napoli, Real SC, Anápolis, Caldense

*** Carlsson - Tobias Carlsson (a) 28/07/1995, ¿? (Sweden) (b) 1,87 (c) D - central defense (d) BK Häcken (e) Varbergs BoIS, Häcken, Varbergs BoIS, Grebbestads IF
*** Carlstrand - Linus Carlstrand (a) 31/08/2004, Göteborg (Sweden) (b) 1,84 (c) F - center forward (d) IFK Göteborg (e) -
*** Carmo - David Carmo (David Mota Veiga Teixeira Carmo) (a) 19/07/1999, Aveiro (Portugal) (b) 1,96 (c) D - central defense (d) FC Porto (e) SC Braga, Braga B
*** Carmona - David Carmona (David Carmona Sierra) (a) 11/01/1997, Palma del Río (Spain) (b) 1,76 (c) D - right back (d) Asteras Tripolis (e) Betis Deportivo, Cádiz CF, Racing, Cádiz CF, Sevilla At.
*** Carmona - José Ángel Carmona (José Ángel Carmona Navarro) (a) 29/01/2002, El Viso del Alcor (Spain) (b) 1,84 (c) D - right back (d) Getafe CF (e) Getafe CF, Sevilla FC, Elche CF, Sevilla FC, Sevilla At.
*** Carmona - Xavi Carmona (Xavier Carmona Velasco) (a) 21/01/1993, Santa Coloma de Gramanet (Spain) (b) 1,83 (c) D - right back (d) FC Ordino (e) UE Engordany, FC Ordino, Sant Julià, Moralo CP, Atlético Ibañés, Gibraltar Utd., Los Barrios, Unionistas CF, Montañesa, Cádiz CF, Barakaldo CF, Cádiz CF, UD Almería B, R. Valladolid B, Real Madrid C, CD Leganés, Real Madrid C
*** Carnat - Nicolae Carnat (a) 08/04/1998, Alba Iulia (Romania) (b) 1,85 (c) F - right winger (d) FCV Farul Constanta (e) CS Mioveni, CFR Cluj, FC Rapid 1923, CFR Cluj, FC Rapid 1923, Sepsi OSK, Dunarea Calarasi, Esbjerg fB, Academia Hagi
*** Carné - Marcelo Carné (Marcelo Henrique Passos Carné) (a) 06/02/1990, Rio de Janeiro (Brazil) (b) 1,88 (c) G (d) GD Estoril Praia (e) Marítimo, CSA, Juventude, Bonsucesso, Brasília, Audax-RJ, Brasília, América TO-MG, Brasília, Boavista, Nova Iguaçu, Boavista, Tombense, Flamengo, Boavista, Flamengo, Duque de Caxias, Flamengo, Boavista, Flamengo
*** Carnegie - Fraser Carnegie (a) 14/11/2005, ¿? (Gibraltar) (b) - (c) F - right winger (d) FC Manchester 62 Reserve (e) -
*** Carneil - Hussein Carneil (كارنيل حسين) (a) 09/05/2003, Mazar-i-Sharif (Afghanistan) (b) 1,76 (c) M - attacking midfielder (d) IFK Göteborg (e) -
*** Carnesecchi - Marco Carnesecchi (a) 01/07/2000, Rimini (Italy) (b) 1,91 (c) G (d) Atalanta de Bérgamo (e) Cremonese, Atalanta, Cremonese, Atalanta, Trapani, Atalanta, Sant'Ermete
*** Carnevalli - Lucas Carnevalli (Lucas Lima Carnevalli) (a) 29/03/1995, Goiânia (Brazil) (b) 1,84 (c) D - central defense (d) Union Titus Petange (e) Anápolis, Varzim, Union Titus Petange, Silva SD, Unipomezia, Anzio, Goiás B
*** Carniello - Óscar Carniello (Óscar Matías Carniello) (a) 18/09/1988, Vila (Argentina) (b) 1,77 (c) D - central defense (d) Marsaxlokk FC (e) Birkirkara FC, Boca Unidos, Rafaela, San Martín (SJ), Everton, Colón, Rafaela
*** Carole - Lionel Carole (Lionel Jules Carole) (a) 12/04/1991, Montreuil (France) (b) 1,82 (c) D - left back (d) Kayserispor (e) Racing Club Strasbourg, Galatasaray, Sevilla FC, Galatasaray, Troyes, Benfica B, Benfica, CS Sedan, Benfica, FC Nantes, FC Nantes B
*** Carolina - Jurich Carolina (Jurich Christopher Alexander Carolina) (a) 15/07/1998, Willemstad (Netherlands Antilles) (b) 1,82 (c) D - left back (d) Miedź Legnica (e) Stomil, NAC Breda, FC Den Bosch, NAC Breda
*** Carr - Danny Carr (Daniel Clive Carr) (a) 29/05/1994, Lambeth, London (England) (b) 1,80 (c) F - center forward (d) Sevenoaks Town (e) Shelbourne, Welling Utd., Bengaluru U., RoPS, Apollon Limassol, Shamrock Rovers, Karlstad BK, Dulwich Hamlet, Leatherhead FC, Dulwich Hamlet, Cambridge Utd., Woking, Cambridge Utd., Aldershot, Cambridge Utd., Huddersfield Town, FC Dagenham &

Redbridge, Huddersfield Town, Mansfield Town, Huddersfield Town, Fleetwood, Huddersfield Town, Dulwich Hamlet

*** Carraça - Carraça (Rui Filipe Caetano Moura) (a) 01/03/1993, Folgosa (Portugal) (b) 1,77 (c) D - right back (d) FC Porto (e) Gil Vicente, FC Porto, B SAD, FC Porto, Boavista, Santa Clara, Boavista, Tondela, Boavista

*** Carrascal - Jorge Carrascal (Jorge Andrés Carrascal Guardo) (a) 25/05/1998, Cartagena (Colombia) (b) 1,80 (c) M (d) CSKA Moskva (e) River Plate, CSKA Moskva, River Plate, Karpaty, River Plate, Karpaty, Sevilla At., Karpaty, Sevilla At., Millonarios

*** Carrasco - Yannick Carrasco (Yannick Ferreira Carrasco) (a) 04/09/1993, Ixelles (Belgium) (b) 1,81 (c) F - left winger (d) Atlético de Madrid (e) Dalian PFC, Atlético Madrid, Dalian PFC, Atlético Madrid, AS Monaco, AS Monaco B

*** Carratala-Jimenez - Ernesto Carratala-Jimenez (Ernesto José Carratala Jiménez) (a) 10/11/1999, Halle an der Saale (Germany) (b) 1,76 (c) F - right winger (d) FC Victoria Rosport (e) Hennef 05, Viktoria Köln, B. Gladbach 09, Viktoria Köln, Vikt. Köln II

*** Carreazo - Marcelino Carreazo (Marcelino Jr Carreazo Betin) (a) 17/12/1999, El Carmen de Bolívar (Colombia) (b) 1,79 (c) M - central midfielder (d) CSKA-Sofia (e) Once Caldas

*** Carreira - Sergio Carreira (Sergio Carreira Vilariño) (a) 13/10/2000, Vigo (Spain) (b) 1,70 (c) D - right back (d) RC Celta de Vigo (e) Villarreal CF B, RC Celta, CD Mirandés, RC Celta, Celta B

*** Carrillo - Coke Carrillo (Jorge Carrillo Balea) (a) 07/01/2002, Poio (Spain) (b) 1,88 (c) G (d) RC Celta Fortuna (e) Barcelona Atlètic, Celta B, FC Barcelona B

*** Carrillo - Daniel Carrillo (Daniel José Carrillo Montilla) (a) 02/12/1995, Barquisimeto, Lara (Venezuela) (b) 1,75 (c) D - left back (d) Alashkert Yerevan CF (e) KuPS, Deportivo Lara

*** Carrillo - José Carrillo (José Carrillo Mancilla) (a) 04/03/1995, Granada (Spain) (b) 1,85 (c) D - central defense (d) El Paso Locomotive FC (e) Finn Harps, FK Senica, Michalovce, UD Logroñés, Getafe CF B, Zamora CF, RCD Mallorca B

*** Carroll - Jake Carroll (a) 11/08/1991, Dublin (Ireland) (b) 1,84 (c) D - left back (d) - (e) Motherwell FC, Cambridge Utd., Hartlepool Utd., Huddersfield Town, Partick Thistle, Huddersfield Town, Bury, Huddersfield Town, St. Patrick's Ath.

*** Carroll - Jordan Carroll (a) 24/10/2000, ¿? (Ireland) (b) - (c) M - right midfielder (d) Farsley Celtic (e) Flint Town, Radcliffe, Athlone Town

*** Carson - Jak Carson (a) 07/07/2004, ¿? (Wales) (b) - (c) D - right back (d) Taffs Well (e) Penybont

*** Carson - Josh Carson (Joshua Glyn Carson) (a) 03/06/1993, Ballymena (Northern Ireland) (b) 1,75 (c) M - central midfielder (d) Coleraine FC (e) Linfield, York City, Ipswich, York City, Ipswich

*** Carson - Scott Carson (Scott Paul Carson) (a) 03/09/1985, Whitehaven (England) (b) 1,88 (c) G (d) Manchester City (e) Derby, Manchester City, Derby, Wigan Ath., Bursaspor, West Bromwich Albion, Liverpool, Aston Villa, Liverpool, Charlton Ath., Liverpool, Sheffield Wednesday, Liverpool, Leeds Utd.

*** Carson - Trevor Carson (a) 05/03/1988, Downpatrick (Northern Ireland) (b) 1,85 (c) G (d) Dundee FC (e) St. Mirren, Dundee United, FC Morecambe, Dundee United, Motherwell FC, Hartlepool Utd., Cheltenham Town, Bury, FC Portsmouth, Bury, Sunderland, Bury, Sunderland, Hull City, Sunderland, Bury, Sunderland, Brentford, Sunderland, Lincoln City, Sunderland, FC Chesterfield, Sunderland

*** Carstensen - Frederik Carstensen (a) 09/04/2002, ¿? (Denmark) (b) 1,79 (c) F - right winger (d) Silkeborg IF (e) FC Fredericia, Silkeborg IF

*** Carstensen - Rasmus Carstensen (a) 10/11/2000, Virklund (Denmark) (b) 1,83 (c) D - right back (d) 1.FC Köln (e) 1.FC Köln, KRC Genk, Silkeborg IF

*** Carström - Jesper Carström (a) 18/05/2002, ¿? (Sweden) (b) 1,78 (c) M - central midfielder (d) GIF Sundsvall (e) Gefle, GIF Sundsvall

*** Carter-Vickers - Cameron Carter-Vickers (Cameron Robert Carter-Vickers) (a) 31/12/1997, Southend (England) (b) 1,83 (c) D - central defense (d) Celtic FC (e) Tottenham Hotspur, Celtic FC, Tottenham Hotspur, Bournemouth, Tottenham Hotspur, Luton Town, Tottenham Hotspur, Stoke City, Tottenham Hotspur, Swansea City, Tottenham Hotspur, Ipswich, Tottenham Hotspur, Sheffield Utd., Tottenham Hotspur

*** Cartwright - Iwan Cartwright (a) 09/08/1996, Wrexham (Wales) (b) - (c) M - central midfielder (d) Caernarfon Town (e) Cefn Druids, Newtown, Nuneaton, Hednesford, Nuneaton, Wrexham

*** Caruana - Tristan Caruana (a) 15/09/1991, ¿? (Malta) (b) 1,84 (c) M - pivot (d) Balzan FC (e) Valletta, Hamrun Spartans, Tarxien, Hibernians FC, Qormi FC, Hibernians FC, Qormi FC, Hibernians FC

*** Caruntu - Marin Caruntu (Marin Căruntu) (a) 28/11/1997, ¿? (Moldova) (b) 1,78 (c) F - center forward (d) FC Zimbru Chisinau (e) Sfintul Gheorghe, Dinamo-Auto, Dacia Buiucani, Dinamo-Auto, Sheriff-2

*** Caruso - Samuele Caruso (a) 05/04/1995, ¿? (Italy) (b) - (c) F (d) SC Mallare (e) -

*** Carvajal - Daniel Carvajal (Daniel Carvajal Ramos) (a) 11/01/1992, Leganés (Spain) (b) 1,73 (c) D - right back (d) Real Madrid CF (e) Bayer Leverkusen, RM Castilla

*** Carvalho - Anderson Carvalho (Anderson Carvalho Santos) (a) 20/05/1990, Cubatão (Brazil) (b) 1,74 (c) M - central midfielder (d) - (e) Santa Clara, Tosno, Boavista, Santos, Penapolense, Santos, Vissel Kobe, Santos, Barueri-SP, Santos, Santos B

*** Carvalho - Duarte Carvalho (Duarte Barros Mariano de Carvalho) (a) 30/05/2002, ¿? (Portugal) (b) 1,78 (c) M - central midfielder (d) - (e) Torreense, Sporting B

*** Carvalho - Fábio Carvalho (Fábio Leandro Freitas Gouveia Carvalho) (a) 30/08/2002, Torres Vedras (Portugal) (b) 1,70 (c) M - attacking midfielder (d) RB Leipzig (e) RB Leipzig, Liverpool, Fulham

*** Carvalho - João Carvalho (João António Antunes Carvalho) (a) 09/03/1997, Castanheira De Pêra (Portugal) (b) 1,72 (c) M - attacking midfielder (d) Olympiakos El Pireo (e) Estoril Praia, Olympiakos, Nottingham Forest, UD Almería, Nottingham Forest, Benfica, Benfica B, Vitória Setúbal, Benfica B

*** Carvalho - Matis Carvalho (a) 28/04/1999, Nantes (France) (b) 1,86 (c) G (d) - (e) Montpellier, Toulouse B

*** Carvalho - Vitor Carvalho (Vitor Carvalho Vieira) (a) 27/05/1997, Palmas (Brazil) (b) 1,83 (c) M - pivot (d) SC Braga (e) Gil Vicente, Coritiba FC, Gil Vicente, Coritiba FC

*** Carvalho - Vítor Carvalho (Vítor Francisco dos Santos de Carvalho) (a) 17/02/1993, São José do Rio Preto (Brazil) (b) 1,92 (c) D - central defense (d) KF Oriku (e) Sioni Bolnisi, SC Covilhã, Capital-DF, CE União, Anápolis, Itabaiana, Galícia-BA, SC Covilhã, Galícia-BA, Catanduvense

*** Carvalho - William Carvalho (William Silva de Carvalho) (a) 07/04/1992, Luanda (Angola) (b) 1,87 (c) M - pivot (d) Real Betis Balompié (e) Sporting Lisboa, Cercle Brugge, Sporting Lisboa, CD Fátima, Sporting Lisboa

*** Carville - Declan Carville (a) 13/12/1989, Newry (Northern Ireland) (b) - (c) M - central midfielder (d) Annagh United FC (e) Newry City, Ballymena, Newry City, Rathfriland, Newry City

*** Casadesús - Víctor Casadesús (Víctor Casadesús Castaño) (a) 28/02/1985, Algaida (Spain) (b) 1,80 (c) F - center forward (d) Atlètic Club d'Escaldes (e) IC d'Escaldes, FC Andorra, Alcorcón, CD Tenerife, Levante UD, RCD Mallorca, Gimnàstic, RCD Mallorca, Real Sociedad, RCD Mallorca, RCD Mallorca B

*** Casadó - Marc Casadó (Marc Casadó Torras) (a) 14/09/2003, Sant Pere de Vilamajor (Spain) (b) 1,72 (c) M - pivot (d) FC Barcelona Atlètic (e) -

*** Casalboni - Marco Casalboni (a) 04/12/1982, Cesena (Italy) (b) - (c) G (d) SC Faetano (e) Delfini Rimini, Cosmos, Tre Fiori, Meldola, Pennarossa, Faetano, Virtus, Misano, Riccione, Rimini, S. Arcangiolese

*** Casale - Nicolò Casale (a) 14/02/1998, Negran (Italy) (b) 1,91 (c) D - central defense (d) SS Lazio (e) Hellas Verona, Empoli, Hellas Verona, Venezia, Hellas Verona, Südtirol, Hellas Verona, Prato, Hellas Verona, Perugia, Hellas Verona

*** Casali - Giacomo Casali (a) 14/02/2004, ¿? (San Marino) (b) - (c) D - left back (d) SC Faetano (e) -

*** Casali - Tino Casali (a) 14/11/1995, Villach (Austria) (b) 1,92 (c) G (d) Eintracht Braunschweig (e) SCR Altach, SV Mattersburg, Austria Viena, FAC, Austria Viena, Austria Wien Reserves

*** Casanova - Fernando Casanova (Fernando del Carmen Casanova) (a) 17/05/1998, ¿? (Spain) (b) - (c) D - central defense (d) UE Engordany B (e) FC Rànger's, Sporting Club

*** Casap - Carlo Casap (Carlo Roberto Casap) (a) 29/12/1998, Timişoara (Romania) (b) 1,78 (c) M - central midfielder (d) - (e) FCV Farul, Concordia, FCV Farul, Academia Hagi

*** Casares - Javi Casares (Francisco Javier Casares García) (a) 13/06/1984, Jerez de la Frontera (Spain) (b) 1,70 (c) F - right winger (d) - (e) Bruno's Magpies, CD Rota, Xerez Deportivo, San Fernando CD, Lleida Esportiu, At. Baleares, Hércules CF, SD Amorebieta, Salamanca AC, Real Oviedo, Alavés, Granada CF, San Fernando CD, Arcos CF, RSD Alcalá, Sanluqueño, Sanluqueño B, 2ª B - Grupo II

*** Casas - Ismael Casas (Ismael Casas Casado) (a) 07/03/2001, Linares (Spain) (b) 1,74 (c) D - right back (d) AEK Larnaca (e) Málaga CF, At. Malagueño

*** Cascardo - Gustavo Cascardo (Gustavo Cascardo de Assis) (a) 24/03/1997, Mogi das Cruzes (SP) (Brazil) (b) 1,74 (c) D - right back (d) Beroe Stara Zagora (e) Campinense-PB, Confiança, Botafogo, Athletico-PR, FK Senica, Athletico-PR, Vitória Setúbal, Athletico-PR, Portuguesa

*** Casciaro - Kyle Casciaro (a) 02/12/1987, Gibraltar (Gibraltar) (b) 1,75 (c) F - left winger (d) FC Bruno's Magpies (e) Lincoln FC, St Joseph's FC, Lincoln FC, FC Olympique, Lincoln FC

*** Casciaro - Lee Casciaro (Lee Henry Casciaro) (a) 29/09/1981, Gibraltar (Gibraltar) (b) 1,78 (c) F - center forward (d) Lincoln Red Imps FC (e) -

*** Casciato - Alessandro Casciato (a) 30/05/2000, Uznach (Switzerland) (b) 1,87 (c) F - center forward (d) SC YF Juventus Zürich (e) FC Lugano, Rapperswil-Jona, FC Lugano, Rapperswil-Jona, FC Schaffhausen, Rapperswil-Jona, FC Schaffhausen, Rapperswil II

*** Cascini - Bautista Cascini (Juan Bautista Cascini) (a) 04/06/1997, La Plata (Argentina) (b) 1,71 (c) M - central midfielder (d) Slaven Belupo Koprivnica (e) UTA Arad, The Strongest, Academica Clinceni, FC Botosani, Estudiantes, APOEL FC, Estudiantes, Estudiantes II

*** Casemiro - Casemiro (Carlos Henrique Casimiro)

*** Cáseres - Augusto Cáseres (Augusto René Cáseres) (a) 21/11/1997, ¿? (Malta) (b) - (c) F - center forward (d) Marsa FC (e) Floriana, Marsaxlokk, Floriana, Santa Lucia FC, Floriana, Gudja United FC, Floriana, Senglea Ath., Senglea Ath., Viareggio
*** Cáseres - Facundo Cáseres (Facundo Agustín Cáseres) (a) 28/05/2001, Arteaga (Argentina) (b) 1,78 (c) M - central midfielder (d) CA Vélez Sarsfield (e) NK Istra, Vélez Sarsfield, Vélez Sarsfield II
*** Cases - Nacho Cases (Ignacio Cases Mora) (a) 22/12/1987, Gijón (Spain) (b) 1,75 (c) M - central midfielder (d) - (e) Marino Luanco, Ermis Aradippou, Anagen.Derynias, Suduva, AEK Larnaca, Volos NPS, AEK Larnaca, Real Sporting, Sporting B
*** Casey - Dan Casey (a) 29/10/1997, Dublin (Ireland) (b) 1,86 (c) D - central defense (d) Motherwell FC (e) Sacramento FC, Bohemians, Cork City, Bohemians, St. Josephs Boys
*** Casey - Odhran Casey (a) 09/04/2002, ¿? (Northern Ireland) (b) 1,86 (c) M - pivot (d) Cliftonville FC (e) Newry City, Cliftonville
*** Cash - Matty Cash (Matthew Stuart Cash) (a) 07/08/1997, Slough (England) (b) 1,85 (c) D - right back (d) Aston Villa (e) Nottingham Forest, FC Dagenham & Redbridge
*** Casilla - Kiko Casilla (Francisco Casilla Cortés) (a) 02/10/1986, Alcover (Spain) (b) 1,90 (c) G (d) - (e) Getafe CF, Leeds Utd., Elche CF, Leeds Utd., Real Madrid, RCD Espanyol, FC Cartagena, RCD Espanyol, Cádiz CF, RCD Espanyol, RCD Espanyol B, RM Castilla, Real Madrid C
*** Cassamá - Moreto Cassamá (Moreto Moro Cassamá) (a) 16/02/1998, Bissau (Guinea-Bissau) (b) 1,65 (c) M - central midfielder (d) Omonia Nicosia (e) Stade Reims, FC Porto B
*** Cassandro - Tommaso Cassandro (a) 09/01/2000, Dolo (Italy) (b) 1,85 (c) D - right back (d) Como 1907 (e) Lecce, Cittadella, Bologna, Novara
*** Cassano - Claudio Cassano (a) 22/07/2003, Trani (Italy) (b) - (c) F - right winger (d) AS Cittadella (e) -
*** Cassar - Andrea Cassar (a) 19/12/1992, ¿? (Malta) (b) 1,77 (c) G (d) Sirens FC (e) Marsa FC, Floriana, Tarxien, Pembroke, Hamrun Spartans
*** Cassar - David Cassar (a) 24/11/1987, ¿? (Malta) (b) 1,71 (c) G (d) Gzira United FC (e) Sliema Wanderers, Sirens FC, Qormi FC, Birkirkara FC, Hamrun Spartans, Tarxien, Pietà Hotspurs, Tarxien, Pietà Hotspurs, Tarxien, Hibernians FC
*** Cassar - Neil Cassar (a) 12/03/2004, ¿? (Malta) (b) - (c) M (d) - (e) Floriana FC
*** Cassar - Stefan Cassar (a) 29/10/1997, ¿? (Malta) (b) - (c) M - left midfielder (d) Nadur Youngsters FC (e) Hamrun Spartans, Nadur Y., Sliema Wanderers, Nadur Y., Ghajnsielem
*** Cassar - Zachary Cassar (a) 02/11/1998, ¿? (Malta) (b) 1,73 (c) D - left back (d) Floriana FC (e) Birkirkara FC, Senglea Ath., Birkirkara FC, Gudja United FC, Birkirkara FC, Senglea Ath., Birkirkara FC
*** Cassaro - Gianni Cassaro (Ian Cassaro Usart) (a) 10/04/1992, Lloret de Mar (Spain) (b) 1,92 (c) G (d) - (e) Villarreal CF B, Yeclano, UCAM Murcia, CF Talavera, CF Peralada, UE Olot, CE Europa, UE Olot, CF Lloret
*** Cassiano - Cassiano (Cassiano Dias Moreira) (a) 16/06/1989, Porto Alegre (Brazil) (b) 1,84 (c) F - center forward (d) GD Estoril Praia (e) Al-Faisaly FC, Vizela, Boavista, CSA, HLJ Lava Spring, Paysandu, Brasil Pelotas, Internacional, Aktobe, Internacional, Goiás, Internacional, Gwangju FC, Internacional, Fortaleza, Internacional, Santa Cruz, Internacional, Criciúma EC, Internacional, EC São José, Inter B, EC São José, Nea Salamis, EC São José

*** Cassidy - Ryan Cassidy (Ryan McClean Cassidy) (a) 02/03/2001, Dublin (Ireland) (b) 1,73 (c) F - center forward (d) Tolka Rovers (e) Hayes & Yeading, Bohemians, Accrington St., St. Kevins Boys

*** Cassierra - Mateo Cassierra (Zander Mateo Cassierra Cabezas) (a) 13/04/1997, Barbacoas (Colombia) (b) 1,86 (c) F - center forward (d) Zenit de San Petersburgo (e) Sochi, B SAD, Ajax, Racing, Ajax, FC Groningen, Ajax, Deportivo Cali

*** Castagne - Timothy Castagne (a) 05/12/1995, Arlon (Belgium) (b) 1,85 (c) D - right back (d) Leicester City (e) Atalanta, KRC Genk

*** Castagnetti - Michele Castagnetti (a) 27/12/1989, Montecchio Emilia (Italy) (b) 1,80 (c) M - pivot (d) US Cremonese (e) SPAL, Empoli, SPAL, Carrarese, Nuova Cosenza, Feralpisalò, Crociati Noceto

*** Castagnoli - Alex Castagnoli (a) 13/04/1989, ¿? (Italy) (b) - (c) G (d) Tre Fiori FC (e) Gambettola, Gatteo FC, Fosso Ghiaia, Polisp. Sala, Gatteo FC, Sant'Ermete, Gatteo FC

*** Castanheira - Telmo Castanheira (Telmo Ferreira Castanheira) (a) 13/04/1992, Porto (Portugal) (b) 1,85 (c) M - central midfielder (d) Sabah FC (e) ÍBV Vestmannaeyjar, Trofense, Gondomar, Leixões, Santa Clara, Gondomar, Felgueiras, Vitória Guimarães B, Freamunde, Tourizense

*** Castañé - Adrià Castañé (Adrià Torres Castañé) (a) 21/03/1999, Terrassa (Spain) (b) - (c) M (d) UE Engordany (e) -

*** Castañeda - Frank Castañeda (Frank Andersson Castañeda Vélez) (a) 17/07/1994, Santiago de Cali (Colombia) (b) 1,72 (c) F - left winger (d) Radomiak Radom (e) Buriram Utd., Warta Poznań, FC Sheriff, FK Senica, Orsomarso SC, FK Senica, Orsomarso SC, Caracas FC

*** Castaño - Pepe Castaño (José Castaño Muñoz) (a) 10/12/1998, Arcos de la Frontera (Spain) (b) 1,85 (c) D - central defense (d) Asteras Tripolis (e) Villarreal CF B, Villarreal CF C, Cádiz CF B

*** Casteels - Koen Casteels (a) 25/06/1992, Bonheiden (Belgium) (b) 1,97 (c) G (d) VfL Wolfsburg (e) Werder Bremen, VfL Wolfsburg, Hoffenheim, KRC Genk

*** Castegren - Henrik Castegren (Sven Henrik Olof Castegren) (a) 28/03/1996, Norrköping (Sweden) (b) 1,86 (c) D - central defense (d) IK Sirius (e) Lechia Gdánsk, Norrköping, Degerfors, Norrköping, Sylvia, Norrköping, Sylvia, Norrköping, Sylvia

*** Castellanos - Taty Castellanos (Valentín Mariano José Castellanos Giménez) (a) 03/10/1998, Mendoza (Argentina) (b) 1,78 (c) F - center forward (d) SS Lazio (e) New York City, Girona FC, New York City, CA Torque, New York City, CA Torque, U. de Chile, CA Torque, U. de Chile

*** Castellazzi - Fabrizio Castellazzi (a) 29/07/1984, ¿? (Italy) (b) 1,85 (c) F - center forward (d) La Fiorita 1967 (e) Fiorentino, La Fiorita, Cernusco Merate, Borgomanero, Accad. Pavese, Cavenago, Fiorenzuola, Solbiatese Arno Calcio, Casteggio, AC Merate, Casteggio, Saronno

*** Castelletto - Jean-Charles Castelletto (Jean-Charles Victor Castelletto) (a) 26/01/1995, Clamart (France) (b) 1,86 (c) D - central defense (d) FC Nantes (e) Stade Brestois, KV Brugge, Red Star FC, KV Brugge, Excelsior Mouscron, KV Brugge, AJ Auxerre, AJ Auxerre B

*** Castiglioni - Nicolò Castiglioni (a) 16/07/1996, ¿? (Italy) (b) - (c) D - left back (d) AC Virtus Acquaviva (e) Sant'Ermete

*** Castillejo - Samu Castillejo (Samuel Castillejo Azuaga) (a) 18/01/1995, Málaga (Spain) (b) 1,82 (c) F - right winger (d) Valencia CF (e) AC Milan, Villarreal CF, Málaga CF, At. Malagueño

*** Castle - Kivan Castle (Kivan Francharles Castle) (a) 21/02/1990, Gibraltar (Gibraltar) (b) 1,81 (c) D - central defense (d) FC College 1975 (e) Europa Point FC,

Glacis United, Mons Calpe, Glacis United, St Joseph's FC, Europa Point FC, St Joseph's FC, Europa Point FC, Glacis United
*** Castro - Castro (André de Castro Pereira) (a) 02/04/1988, Gondomar (Portugal) (b) 1,81 (c) M - central midfielder (d) SC Braga (e) Göztepe, Kasimpasa, FC Porto, Kasimpasa, FC Porto, Real Sporting, FC Porto, Olhanense, FC Porto
*** Castro - Carlos Castro (Carlos Castro García) (a) 01/06/1995, Mieres (Spain) (b) 1,77 (c) F - center forward (d) - (e) Racing, Dinamo Tbilisi, RCD Mallorca, CD Lugo, RCD Mallorca, Elche CF, RCD Mallorca, Real Sporting, Sporting B
*** Castro - Érico Castro (Érico Roberto Mendes Alves Castro) (a) 21/09/1992, Oeiras (Portugal) (b) 1,85 (c) F - center forward (d) FC Differdange 03 (e) Petro Luanda, Louletano, Felgueiras, Casa Pia, Sintrense, Real SC, Aljustrelense, CD Fátima, Tires, AD Oeiras, Tires
*** Castro - Gabriel Castro (Gabriel Venceslau Fernandes Castro) (a) 15/11/2000, Lisboa (Portugal) (b) 1,82 (c) D - right back (d) SU 1º Dezembro (e) GIF Sundsvall, Sintrense
*** Castro - Maximiliano Castro (Maximiliano Do Sacramento Castro) (a) 23/02/2002, Amsterdam (Netherlands) (b) 1,83 (c) M - pivot (d) FC Floresti (e) Zimbru Chisinau, Werder Bremen III, 4ThePlayers
*** Castro - Nicolás Castro (Nicolás Federico Castro) (a) 01/11/2000, Rafaela (Argentina) (b) 1,82 (c) M - attacking midfielder (d) Elche CF (e) Elche CF, KRC Genk, Newell's Old Boys, Newell's II, 9 de Julio
*** Castro-Montes - Alessio Castro-Montes (Alessio Daniel Castro-Montes) (a) 17/05/1997, Sint-Truiden (Belgium) (b) 1,75 (c) M - right midfielder (d) KAA Gent (e) KAS Eupen
*** Castrovilli - Gaetano Castrovilli (a) 17/02/1997, Canosa di Puglia (Italy) (b) 1,87 (c) M - central midfielder (d) Fiorentina (e) Cremonese, Fiorentina, Bari
*** Catakovic - Hamza Catakovic (Hamza Ćataković) (a) 15/01/1997, Cazin (Bosnia and Herzegovina) (b) 1,86 (c) F - center forward (d) FK Sarajevo (e) CSKA-Sofia, AS Trencin, FK Sarajevo, AS Trencin, FK Sarajevo
*** Cataldi - Danilo Cataldi (a) 06/08/1994, Roma (Italy) (b) 1,80 (c) M - pivot (d) SS Lazio (e) Benevento, Lazio, Genoa, Lazio, Crotone, Lazio
*** Catamo - Geny Catamo (Geny Cipriano Catamo) (a) 26/01/2001, Maputo (Mozambique) (b) 1,74 (c) F - left winger (d) Sporting de Lisboa (e) Sporting B, Marítimo, Sporting B, Vitória Guimarães, Sporting B, Amora FC
*** Catania - Kaydon Catania (a) 01/12/2005, ¿? (Malta) (b) - (c) D (d) - (e) Pietà Hotspurs
*** Catena - Alejandro Catena (Alejandro Catena Marugán) (a) 28/10/1994, Móstoles (Spain) (b) 1,94 (c) D - central defense (d) CA Osasuna (e) Rayo Vallecano, Reus Deportiu, Marbella FC, Navalcarnero, CD Móstoles
*** Cathline - Yoann Cathline (a) 22/07/2002, Champigny-sur-Marne (France) (b) 1,76 (c) F - left winger (d) FC Lorient (e) Guingamp
*** Caufriez - Maximiliano Caufriez (a) 16/02/1997, Saint-Ghislain (Belgium) (b) 1,89 (c) D - central defense (d) Clermont Foot 63 (e) Spartak Moskva, Clermont Foot, Spartak Moskva, Sint-Truiden, Waasland-Beveren
*** Caulker - Steven Caulker (Steven Roy Caulker) (a) 29/12/1991, Feltham (England) (b) 1,91 (c) D - central defense (d) - (e) Wigan Ath., Karagümrük, Fenerbahce, Gaziantep FK, Fenerbahce, Alanyaspor, Dundee FC, Queen's Park Rangers, Liverpool, Queen's Park Rangers, Southampton, Queen's Park Rangers, Cardiff City, Tottenham Hotspur, Swansea City, Tottenham Hotspur, Bristol City, Tottenham Hotspur, Yeovil Town, Tottenham Hotspur

*** Caull - Kegan Caull (Kegan Montgomery Caull) (a) 20/03/2004, Vieux Fort (Saint Lucia) (b) 1,78 (c) F - center forward (d) - (e) NK Tolmin, Europa Point FC, VSADC, Europa Point FC, VSADC

*** Cauly - Cauly (Cauly Oliveira Souza) (a) 15/09/1995, Porto Seguro (Brazil) (b) 1,75 (c) M - attacking midfielder (d) Esporte Clube Bahia (e) Ludogorets, SC Paderborn, MSV Duisburg, Fortuna Köln

*** Caushaj - Alesio Caushaj (a) 31/08/2003, Tiranë (Albania) (b) - (c) F - left winger (d) FC Mauerwerk (e) Europa FC, St. Johann, Amora B, FC Term

*** Cauterucci - Piero Cauterucci (a) 06/04/1999, Belvedere Marittimo (Italy) (b) - (c) D - left back (d) ASD Vastese Calcio 1902 (e) Tre Penne, Grosseto, Tre Penne, Vastese, Bangor City, Rimini, Scandicci, Pistoiese, Scandicci, Pistoiese

*** Cavaleiro - Ivan Cavaleiro (Ivan Ricardo Neves Abreu Cavaleiro) (a) 18/10/1993, Vila Franca de Xira (Portugal) (b) 1,75 (c) F - left winger (d) LOSC Lille Métropole (e) Fulham, Alanyaspor, Fulham, Wolverhampton Wanderers, Fulham, Wolverhampton Wanderers, AS Monaco, Benfica, RC Deportivo, Benfica, Benfica B

*** Cavalli - Alex Cavalli (a) 26/02/1992, ¿? (San Marino) (b) - (c) D - right back (d) SS Folgore/Falciano (e) Juvenes-Dogana, Cosmos, Faetano, Cosmos

*** Cavani - Edinson Cavani (Édinson Roberto Cavani Gómez) (a) 14/02/1987, Salto (Uruguay) (b) 1,84 (c) F - center forward (d) CA Boca Juniors (e) Valencia CF, Manchester Utd., Paris Saint-Germain, Napoli, US Palermo, Napoli, US Palermo, Danubio FC

*** Cavar - Marijan Cavar (Marijan Ćavar) (a) 02/02/1998, Rama Prozor (Bosnia and Herzegovina) (b) 1,84 (c) M - central midfielder (d) NK Siroki Brijeg (e) Greuther Fürth, Eintracht, NK Osijek, Eintracht, Zrinjski Mostar, Branitelj M.

*** Cavaré - Dimitri Cavaré (Dimitri Kevin Cavaré) (a) 05/02/1995, Pointe-à-Pitre (Guadaloupe) (b) 1,84 (c) D - central defense (d) - (e) FC Sion, Barnsley FC, Stade Rennes, RC Lens, Stade Rennes, RC Lens, RC Lens B

*** Cavegn - Fabrizio Cavegn (a) 28/08/2002, Ilanz/Glion (Switzerland) (b) 1,78 (c) F - center forward (d) FC Vaduz (e) Chur 97, US Schluein I.

*** Cavic - David Cavic (David Čavić) (a) 21/11/2002, Banja Luka (Bosnia and Herzegovina) (b) - (c) F - right winger (d) FK Borac Banja Luka (e) Leotar Trebinje, Borac Banja Luka

*** Cavion - Michele Cavion (a) 08/12/1994, Schio (Italy) (b) 1,80 (c) M - central midfielder (d) LR Vicenza (e) Salernitana, LR Vicenza, Salernitana, Brescia, Salernitana, Ascoli, Cremonese, Juventus, Cremonese, Juventus, Carrarese, Juventus, Feralpisalò, Juventus, Reggiana

*** Cavlina - Nikola Cavlina (Nikola Čavlina) (a) 02/06/2002, Zagreb (Croatia) (b) 1,92 (c) G (d) NK Lokomotiva Zagreb (e) Din. Zagreb II

*** Cavor - Marko Cavor (Марко Чавор) (a) 05/07/1999, ¿? (RF Yugoslavia, now in Montenegro) (b) 1,77 (c) D - left back (d) Arsenal Tivat (e) Rudar Pljevlja, FK Podgorica, Mladost DG, FK Podgorica, FK Bokelj

*** Cavos - Patrik Cavos (Patrik Čavoš) (a) 07/01/1995, Praha (Czech Rep.) (b) 1,80 (c) M - pivot (d) - (e) Ceske Budejovice, Sparta Praha B, Ceske Budejovice, Sparta Praha B, FK Kolin, Sparta Praha B

*** Cavric - Aleksandar Cavric (Александар Чаврић) (a) 18/05/1994, Vukovar (Croatia) (b) 1,86 (c) F - right winger (d) Slovan Bratislava (e) KRC Genk, Aarhus GF, KRC Genk, OFK Beograd, Banat Zrenjanin

*** Cawley - David Cawley (a) 17/09/1991, Ballina, Mayo (Ireland) (b) 1,78 (c) M - pivot (d) Sligo Rovers (e) Galway United, St. Patrick's Ath., Sligo Rovers

*** Cawthorn - Finlay Cawthorn (Finlay James Cawthorn) (a) 15/03/2004, Gibraltar (Gibraltar) (b) 1,80 (c) F - center forward (d) Lincoln Red Imps FC Reserve (e) FC College 1975, Red Imps Reserves

*** Cayarga - Berto Cayarga (Alberto Cayarga Fernández) (a) 17/09/1996, Avilés (Spain) (b) 1,70 (c) F - right winger (d) Radomiak Radom (e) FC Cartagena, Racing, Sporting B, UP Langreo

*** Ceballos - Cristian Ceballos (Cristian Ceballos Prieto) (a) 03/12/1992, Santander (Spain) (b) 1,73 (c) M - attacking midfielder (d) Sabah FK (e) Qatar SC, Al-Wakrah SC, Sint-Truiden, Charlton Ath., Sint-Truiden, Charlton Ath., Tottenham Hotspur, Arouca, Tottenham Hotspur

*** Ceballos - Dani Ceballos (Daniel Ceballos Fernández) (a) 07/08/1996, Utrera (Spain) (b) 1,79 (c) M - central midfielder (d) Real Madrid CF (e) Arsenal, Real Madrid, Real Betis, Betis B

*** Cebeci - Süleyman Cebeci (a) 05/01/2003, Trabzon (Turkey) (b) 1,79 (c) M - attacking midfielder (d) - (e) Trabzonspor

*** Cebotari - Nicolae Cebotari (a) 24/05/1997, Chişinău (Moldova) (b) 1,85 (c) G (d) - (e) Petrocub, Petrolul, Sfintul Gheorghe, FC Sheriff, Sfintul Gheorghe, FC Sheriff, SSC Farul, Sfintul Gheorghe, Botev Vratsa, Leiria

*** Cebotaru - Eugeniu Cebotaru (Чеботарь Евгений Сергеевич) (a) 16/10/1984, Chişinău (Soviet Union, now in Moldova) (b) 1,75 (c) M - central midfielder (d) - (e) Petrolul, Academica Clinceni, Sibir, Spartak Nalchik, Ceahlăul, Zimbru Chisinau

*** Cebula - Marcin Cebula (Marcin Cebula) (a) 06/12/1995, Staszów (Poland) (b) 1,77 (c) M - attacking midfielder (d) Rakow Czestochowa (e) Korona Kielce, Korona Kielce II, AP Korona

*** Cecaric - Bojan Cecaric (Бојан Чечарић) (a) 10/10/1993, Nova Pazova (RF Yugoslavia, now in Serbia) (b) 1,90 (c) F - center forward (d) - (e) Napredak, Novi Pazar, Napredak, Cracovia, Korona Kielce, Cracovia, Spartak, Mladost, Novi Pazar, Mladost, Javor-Matis, Pazova

*** Ceccaroli - Luca Ceccaroli (a) 05/07/1995, Serravalle (San Marino) (b) - (c) F - left winger (d) SP Tre Penne (e) Domagnano, Tre Penne, Domagnano, Misano, Cattolica

*** Ceccaroli - Mattia Ceccaroli (a) 03/02/1999, ¿? (San Marino) (b) - (c) M - attacking midfielder (d) FC Domagnano (e) San Marino

*** Ceccaroni - Pietro Ceccaroni (a) 21/12/1995, Sarzana (Italy) (b) 1,88 (c) D - central defense (d) Palermo FC (e) Venezia, Lecce, Venezia, Spezia, Venezia, Spezia, Padova, Spezia, SPAL, Spezia

*** Ceccherini - Federico Ceccherini (a) 11/05/1992, Livorno (Italy) (b) 1,87 (c) D - central defense (d) Hellas Verona (e) Fiorentina, Hellas Verona, Fiorentina, Crotone, AS Livorno, Pistoiese, Livorno

*** Cecchetti - Luca Cecchetti (a) 03/07/2000, ¿? (San Marino) (b) - (c) M - attacking midfielder (d) SP Tre Penne (e) Pennarossa, Cailungo, United Riccione

*** Cecen - Kemal Cecen (a) 01/01/2003, ¿? (France) (b) - (c) M - central midfielder (d) - (e) Penya Encarnada

*** Cech - Frantisek Cech (František Čech) (a) 12/06/1998, ¿? (Czech Rep.) (b) 1,79 (c) D - central defense (d) FC Hradec Kralove (e) Usti nad Orlici, Hradec Kralove

*** Cedidla - Martin Cedidla (a) 22/11/2001, ¿? (Czech Rep.) (b) 1,85 (c) D - right back (d) FC Zlin (e) -

*** Ceesay - Assan Ceesay (Assan Torrez Ceesay) (a) 17/03/1994, Banjul (Gambia) (b) 1,88 (c) F - center forward (d) US Lecce (e) FC Zürich, VfL Osnabrück, FC Zürich, FC Lugano, FC Chiasso, FC Lugano, Casa Sports, Gamtel FC

*** Ceesay - Jesper Ceesay (Jesper Ismaila Ceesay) (a) 20/10/2001, Solna (Sweden) (b) 1,92 (c) M - pivot (d) IFK Norrköping (e) AIK, Brommapojkarna
*** Ceesay - Joseph Ceesay (Lars Joseph Ceesay) (a) 03/06/1998, Stockholm (Sweden) (b) 1,84 (c) D - right back (d) Malmö FF (e) Lechia Gdánsk, Helsingborgs IF, Djurgården, Dalkurd, Djurgården, Brage, Djurgården, IK Frej Täby, Djurgården
*** Ceide - Emil Konradsen Ceide (a) 03/09/2001, Finnsnes (Norway) (b) 1,75 (c) F - left winger (d) US Sassuolo (e) Rosenborg, Sassuolo, Rosenborg
*** Ceide - Mikkel Konradsen Ceide (Mikkel Konradsen Ceïde) (a) 03/09/2001, Finnsnes (Norway) (b) 1,90 (c) M - pivot (d) Kristiansund BK (e) Kristiansund, Rosenborg, Tromsø, Rosenborg, Utsiktens BK, Rosenborg, Ranheim, Rosenborg, Rosenborg II
*** Cejku - Alban Cejku (Alban Çejku) (a) 23/07/2001, Tiranë (Albania) (b) - (c) M - central midfielder (d) - (e) KF Teuta
*** Cekici - Endri Cekici (Endri Çekiçi) (a) 23/11/1996, Pogradec (Albania) (b) 1,78 (c) M - attacking midfielder (d) - (e) Konyaspor, Ankaragücü, Olimpija, Din. Zagreb II, Dinamo Zagreb, NK Lokomotiva, Dinamo Zagreb, Din. Zagreb II, KF Teuta
*** Ceklic - Zvonko Ceklic (a) 11/04/1999, Podgorica (RF Yugoslavia, Montenegro) (b) 1,90 (c) D - central defense (d) Buducnost Podgorica (e) Michalovce, FK Turan, FK Bokelj, Zeta Golubovac, FK Bratstvo
*** Cela - Joan Cela (Joan Çela) (a) 06/01/2000, Tiranë (Albania) (b) 1,80 (c) F - left winger (d) KS Kastrioti (e) KF Skënderbeu, FC Luftëtari
*** Celaj - Endri Celaj (Endri Çelaj) (a) 23/01/2004, Tiranë (Albania) (b) 1,70 (c) F - center forward (d) FK Partizani (e) -
*** Celani - Fatjon Celani (a) 14/01/1992, München (Germany) (b) 1,82 (c) F - center forward (d) - (e) FC Malisheva, SSU Poli, Etzella Ettelbrück, FC Memmingen, TSV Steinbach, TSG Neustrelitz, TuS Koblenz, VfR Mannheim, FC Unterföhring, FC Augsburg II, Burghausen II
*** Celar - Zan Celar (Žan Celar) (a) 14/03/1999, Kranj (Slovenia) (b) 1,86 (c) F - center forward (d) FC Lugano (e) AS Roma, Cremonese, AS Roma, Cittadella, NK Maribor
*** Cele - Thabo Cele (a) 15/01/1997, KwaMashu, KwaZulu-Natal (South Africa) (b) 1,78 (c) M - pivot (d) Radomiak Radom (e) Cova Piedade, Benfica B, Real SC, Benfica B, Real SC
*** Celea - Daniel Celea (Daniel Marinel Celea) (a) 06/07/1995, Braloştiţa (Romania) (b) 1,87 (c) D - central defense (d) Nea Salamis (e) Chindia, ŁKS, Sepsi OSK, CS Mioveni, Pandurii, UTA BD, Pandurii II, ACSO Filiasi, Sp. Rosiori, ACSO Filiasi
*** Celeadnic - Dumitru Celeadnic (a) 23/04/1992, Straseni (Moldova) (b) 1,95 (c) G (d) ACSM Politehnica Iasi (e) FC Sheriff, FC Petrocub, Dacia, Dinamo-Auto, Dacia, FC Speranta, Dacia, FC Speranta, Dacia Buiucani
*** Celebic - Nikola Celebic (a) 04/07/1989, ¿? (Yugoslavia, now in ¿Montenegro?) (b) - (c) D - central defense (d) Arsenal Tivat (e) FK Podgorica, OFK Grbalj, Radnik Bijelj., FK Bokelj, Buducnost Podgorica, OFK Petrovac, FK BSK Borča, Kom Podgorica
*** Celecia - Aidan Celecia (Aidan Mark Celecia) (c) G (d) FC College 1975 Reserve (e) -
*** Célestine - Enzo Célestine (a) 24/07/1997, Paris (France) (b) 1,91 (c) F - center forward (d) - (e) FC Arges, FC Sète 34, Hyères 83, Giugliano, AFC Tubize, URSL Visé, Walhain, CA Pontarlier, Neuweg, FC Martigues
*** Çelhaka - Jurgen Çelhaka (a) 06/12/2000, Tiranë (Albania) (b) 1,83 (c) M - pivot (d) Legia de Varsovia (e) KF Tirana

*** Celic - Maks Celic (Maks Juraj Ćelić) (a) 08/03/1996, Zagreb (Croatia) (b) 1,91 (c) D - central defense (d) FK Borac Banja Luka (e) Beroe, ACR Messina, NK Varazdin, PFC Lviv, HNK Gorica, NK Varazdin, HASK Zagreb

*** Celic - Nemanja Celic (Nemanja Čelić) (a) 26/04/1999, Linz (Austria) (b) 1,85 (c) M - pivot (d) SV Darmstadt 98 (e) LASK, Darmstadt 98, WSG Tirol, Juniors OÖ, LASK, Juniors OÖ

*** Celik - Batuhan Celik (Batuhan Çelik) (a) 12/01/2005, Istanbul (Turkey) (b) 1,87 (c) F - center forward (d) Basaksehir FK (e) -

*** Celik - Mert Celik (Mert Çelik) (a) 10/06/2000, Istanbul (Turkey) (b) 1,86 (c) D - central defense (d) Bandirmaspor (e) Bandirmaspor, Basaksehir, Neftchi Baku, Basaksehir, Kirsehir Belediye

*** Celik - Zeki Celik (Mehmet Zeki Çelik) (a) 17/02/1997, Yildirim (Turkey) (b) 1,80 (c) D - right back (d) AS Roma (e) Lille, Istanbulspor, Bursaspor, Bursa Nilüfer, Bursaspor

*** Celikovic - Jasmin Celikovic (Jasmin Čeliković) (a) 07/01/1999, Bihać (Bosnia and Herzegovina) (b) 1,88 (c) D - central defense (d) Akhmat Grozny (e) Akhmat Grozny, FK Tuzla City, HNK Rijeka, Zeljeznicar, HNK Rijeka, SKF Sered, HNK Rijeka, Zrinjski Mostar, HNK Rijeka, Inter Zaprešić, NK Vrapce

*** Celina - Bersant Celina (a) 09/09/1996, Prizren (Yugoslavia, now in Kosovo) (b) 1,81 (c) M - attacking midfielder (d) Dijon FCO (e) Stoke City, Dijon, Kasimpasa, Dijon, Ipswich, Dijon, Swansea City, Manchester City, Ipswich, Manchester City, FC Twente, Manchester City

*** Celli - Alberto Celli (a) 24/06/1985, ¿? (San Marino) (b) 1,75 (c) D - left back (d) SS Cosmos (e) SS Folgore, Pennarossa, Libertas, Murata, Cosmos, Murata, Tre Penne, Murata, Domagnano, Sant'Ermete, Domagnano

*** Celli - Andrea Celli (a) 27/11/1996, ¿? (Italy) (b) - (c) M (d) SS San Giovanni (e) Bellariva

*** Celso Raposo - Celso Raposo (Celso Daniel Caeiro Raposo) (a) 03/04/1996, Barreiro (Portugal) (b) 1,80 (c) D - right back (d) PS Kalamata (e) Lokomotiv Sofia, Vestri, Pinhalnovense, Cova Piedade, Praiense, Almancilense, Fabril Barreiro, Quintanar Rey, At. Tomelloso, Alginet

*** Celustka - Ondrej Celustka (Ondřej Čelůstka) (a) 18/06/1989, Zlín (Czechoslovakia, Czech Rep.) (b) 1,87 (c) D - central defense (d) Bodrum FK (e) Sparta Praha, Antalyaspor, 1.FC Nürnberg, Trabzonspor, Sunderland, Trabzonspor, Slavia Praha, US Palermo, Slavia Praha, Tescoma Zlin

*** Celustka - Tomas Celustka (Tomáš Čelůstka) (a) 19/07/1991, Zlín (Czechoslovakia, Czech Rep.) (b) 1,81 (c) D - left back (d) FC Zlin (e) Karmiotissa, Pardubice, SFC Opava, Pardubice, SFC Opava, Bohemians 1905, SFC Opava, Bohemians 1905, Roudnice n. L., Bohemians 1905, Graffin Vlasim, Bohemians 1905, FC Zlin B, FK Kunice, FC Zlin B, FS Napajedla, Zlin B

*** Ceman - Aldin Ceman (Aldin Ćeman) (a) 05/01/1995, Sarajevo (Bosnia and Herzegovina) (b) 1,91 (c) G (d) FK Igman Konjic (e) Br. Gracanica, NK Jajce, Zeljeznicar, Igman Konjic, Zeljeznicar, NK Iskra Bugojno, Zeljeznicar, FK Gorazde, Zeljeznicar

*** Censoni - Luca Censoni (a) 18/07/1996, ¿? (San Marino) (b) - (c) M - pivot (d) Tre Fiori FC (e) United Riccione, Tre Penne

*** Censoni - Mattia Censoni (a) 31/03/1996, ¿? (San Marino) (b) - (c) D - central defense (d) SP Cailungo (e) Domagnano

*** Centelles - Álex Centelles (Alejandro Centelles Plaza) (a) 30/08/1999, Valencia (Spain) (b) 1,85 (c) D - left back (d) UD Almería (e) Valencia CF, Famalicão, Valencia CF, Valencia Mestalla

*** Centis - Alberto Centis (a) 13/02/2004, Latisana (Italy) (b) - (c) M - attacking midfielder (d) FC Arzignano Valchiampo (e) -

*** Centonze - Fabien Centonze (a) 16/01/1996, Voiron (France) (b) 1,82 (c) D - right back (d) FC Nantes (e) FC Metz, RC Lens, Clermont Foot, Thonon Évian, Thonon Évian B

*** Cephas - Renaldo Cephas (Renaldo Showayne Cephas) (a) 08/12/1999, Kingston (Jamaica) (b) 1,79 (c) F - left winger (d) MKE Ankaragücü (e) FC Shkupi, Arnett Gardens, Allman/Woodford

*** Cepic - Arsenije Cepic (Arsenije Čepić) (c) M (d) Rudar Pljevlja (e) -

*** Cepkauskas - Lukas Cepkauskas (Lukas Čepkauskas) (a) 15/03/1997, ¿? (Lithuania) (b) - (c) D - right back (d) FK Garliava (e) Jonava, Lietava, Stumbras

*** Cerar - Luka Cerar (a) 26/05/1993, ¿? (Slovenia) (b) 1,71 (c) F - right winger (d) NK Radomlje (e) NK Krka, NK Radomlje

*** Cerepkai - Roman Cerepkai (Roman Čerepkai) (a) 06/04/2002, Bratislava (Slovakia) (b) 1,90 (c) F - center forward (d) ViOn Zlate Moravce-Vrable (e) Zlaté Moravce, Teplice, Zlaté Moravce, Teplice, Slovan Bratislava

*** Cerkauskas - Lukas Cerkauskas (Lukas Čerkauskas) (a) 12/03/1994, Panevėžys (Lithuania) (b) 1,79 (c) D - right back (d) FC Hegelmann (e) Panevezys, Stumbras, DFK Dainava, Stumbras, Ekranas

*** Cerkini - Dardan Cerkini (Dardan Qerkini) (a) 27/09/1991, Brod (Yugoslavia, now in Serbia) (b) - (c) D - left back (d) KF Ferizaj (e) KF Vitia, KF Ferizaj, KF Trepca 89, Flamurtari FC, FC Drita, KF Ferizaj

*** Cermak - Ales Cermak (Aleš Čermák) (a) 01/10/1994, Prague (Czech Rep.) (b) 1,81 (c) M - attacking midfielder (d) DAC Dunajska Streda (e) Viktoria Plzen, Bohemians 1905, Viktoria Plzen, Sparta Praha, Mlada Boleslav, Sparta Praha, Hradec Kralove, Sparta Praha, Lokomotiv Vltavin, Sparta Praha

*** Cermak - Marcel Cermak (Marcel Čermák) (a) 25/11/1998, Praha (Czech Rep.) (b) 1,78 (c) M - attacking midfielder (d) SK Dynamo Ceske Budejovice (e) Viagem Pribram, NK Aluminij, Slavia Praha B, Viktoria Zizkov, Slavia Praha B

*** Cernak - Michal Cernak (Michal Černák) (a) 01/09/2003, ¿? (Czech Rep.) (b) - (c) F - right winger (d) FK Jablonec (e) FK Jablonec B

*** Cërnavërni - Mergim Cërnavërni (a) 20/11/2005, Podujevë (Serbia and Montenegro, now in Kosovo) (b) 1,85 (c) F - center forward (d) - (e) KF Llapi

*** Cernek - Martin Cernek (Martin Černek) (a) 30/12/1994, Skalica (Slovakia) (b) 1,80 (c) D (d) MFK Skalica (e) Druz. Radimov, Skalica, Druz. Radimov, Oreske, Skalica

*** Cerniauskas - Vytautas Cerniauskas (Vytautas Gediminas Černiauskas) (a) 12/03/1989, Panevezys (Soviet Union, now in Lithuania) (b) 1,90 (c) G (d) FK Panevezys (e) RFS, CSKA-Sofia, FC Dinamo, Ermis Aradippou, FC Dinamo, Korona Kielce, FC Vaslui, Ekranas

*** Cernicky - Radim Cernicky (Radim Černický) (a) 18/02/2001, ¿? (Czech Rep.) (b) 1,90 (c) M - pivot (d) FC Slovan Liberec B (e) SILON Taborsko, Slovan Liberec B, Al-Dhaid, Slovan Liberec B

*** Cernomordijs - Antonijs Cernomordijs (Antonijs Černomordijs) (a) 26/09/1996, Daugavpils (Latvia) (b) 1,90 (c) D - central defense (d) Riga FC (e) Pafos FC, Riga, Daugavpils, Lech Poznan II, Daugavpils

*** Cernovs - Kristians Sergejs Cernovs (a) 27/06/2006, ¿? (Latvia) (b) - (c) F (d) SK Super Nova (e) -

*** Cerny - Pavel Cerny (Pavel Černý) (a) 28/01/1985, Hradec Králové (Czechoslovakia, now in Czech Rep.) (b) 1,85 (c) F - center forward (d) FK Pardubice

(e) Hradec Kralove, Ordabasy, Akzhayik, Hradec Kralove, FK Jablonec, Hradec Kralove, Hradec Kralove B

*** Cerny - Vaclav Cerny (a) 17/10/1997, PÅ™íbram (Czech Rep.) (b) 1,82 (d) VfL Wolfsburg (e) FC Twente, FC Utrecht, FC Twente, FC Utrecht, Ajax, Ajax B

*** Černych - Fedor Černych (Черных Фёдор Иванович) (a) 21/05/1991, Moskva (Soviet Union, now in Russia) (b) 1,83 (c) F - left winger (d) AEL Limassol (e) Jagiellonia, Dinamo Moskva, Orenburg, Dinamo Moskva, Jagiellonia, Gornik Leczna, Dnepr Mogilev, Naftan, Dnepr Mogilev, Granitas

*** Cerofolini - Michele Cerofolini (a) 04/01/1999, Arezzo (Italy) (b) 1,88 (c) G (d) Frosinone Calcio (e) Fiorentina, Alessandria, Fiorentina, Reggiana, Fiorentina, Casertana, Fiorentina, Bisceglie, Fiorentina, Cosenza, Fiorentina

*** Cerovec - Denis Cerovec (a) 24/04/1991, Krapina (Yugoslavia, Croatia) (b) - (c) D - central defense (d) ND Gorica (e) Koper, NK Zagorec, NK Krka, BV Cloppenburg, NK Zagorec, HNK Gorica, NK Lokomotiva, Radnik Sesvete, NK Lokomotiva

*** Cerqueira - Daniel Cerqueira (Daniel Miguel Cerqueira Carvalho) (a) 05/01/2003, Montalegre (Portugal) (b) - (c) M - central midfielder (d) UE Engordany B (e) ENFAF

*** Cerqueira - Fabio Cerqueira (Fabio Cerqueira Martins) (a) 08/01/2003, ¿? (Luxembourg) (b) - (c) D - central defense (d) CS Fola Esch (e) Union Titus Petange, CS Fola Esch

*** Cerqueira - Mauro Cerqueira (Mauro Rafael Geral Cerqueira) (a) 20/08/1992, Lisboa (Portugal) (b) 1,78 (c) D - left back (d) - (e) AD Ceuta, Hebar P., Újpest FC, Académica Coimbra, Nacional, Moura, Naval, Eléctrico

*** Cerquetti - Alan Cerquetti (a) 01/08/1989, ¿? (San Marino) (b) - (c) M (d) SS Folgore/Falciano (e) -

*** Cerv - Lukas Cerv (Lukáš Červ) (a) 10/04/2001, ¿? (Czech Rep.) (b) 1,82 (c) M - central midfielder (d) FC Slovan Liberec (e) Slavia Praha, Pardubice, Slavia Praha, Jihlava, Slavia Praha, Slavia Praha B

*** Cervellera - Yannick Cervellera (a) 04/04/2001, ¿? (Luxembourg) (b) - (c) M (d) US Mondorf-Les-Bains (e) Progrès Niederkorn, US Hostert, Progrès Niederkorn, Differdange 03, Progrès Niederkorn

*** Cervellini - Michele Cervellini (a) 14/04/1988, ¿? (San Marino) (b) 1,80 (c) M - pivot (d) FC Domagnano (e) Cailungo, Cosmos, Libertas, Juvenes-Dogana, Sant'Ermete

*** Cerven - Adam Cerven (Adam Červeň) (a) 20/08/2003, ¿? (Slovakia) (b) - (c) D - central defense (d) MFK Vyskov (e) Banska Bystrica

*** Cervenka - Marek Cervenka (Marek Červenka) (a) 17/12/1992, Praha (Czechoslovakia, now in Czech Rep.) (b) 1,82 (c) F - center forward (d) FK Dukla Praga (e) Pardubice, Dukla Praha, Vlasim, Banik Sokolov, Teplice, Linfield, Teplice, Slavia Praha, Banik Ostrava, Slavia Praha, Slavia Praha B, Banik Sokolov, Slavia Praha B, Viktoria Zizkov, Slavia Praha B, Graffin Vlasim, Slavia Praha B

*** Cervi - Franco Cervi (Franco Emanuel Cervi) (a) 26/05/1994, San Lorenzo (Argentina) (b) 1,66 (c) F - left winger (d) RC Celta de Vigo (e) Benfica, Rosario Central, Rosario Central II

*** Cesar - Julio Cesar (Júlio César Basílio da Silva) (a) 06/12/1996, Mogi das Cruzes (Brazil) (b) 1,92 (c) D - central defense (d) NK Veres Rivne (e) Veres Rivne, Borneo FC, Vitebsk, FC Vilafranca, América-RN

*** César - César (César Bernardo Dutra) (a) 27/01/1992, Rio de Janeiro (Brazil) (b) 1,92 (c) G (d) Boavista Porto FC (e) EC Bahia, Flamengo, Ferroviária, Flamengo, Ponte Preta, Flamengo

*** Cesarini - Davide Cesarini (a) 16/02/1995, Città di San Marino (San Marino) (b) - (c) D - right back (d) SP Tre Penne (e) CBR Carli Pietracuta, Tre Penne, Riccione
*** Cespedes - Boris Cespedes (a) 19/06/1995, Santa Cruz de la Sierra (Bolivia) (b) 1,81 (c) M - pivot (d) Yverdon Sport FC (e) Servette FC, Etoile Carouge, Servette FC, Etoile Carouge, Servette FC
*** Cestor - Mike Cestor (Mike Cestor Botuli) (a) 30/04/1992, Paris (France) (b) 1,83 (c) D - central defense (d) Radomiak Radom (e) FC Arges, CFR Cluj, Astra Giurgiu, SAS Epinal, Woking, Leyton Orient, Woking, Leyton Orient, Woking, Leyton Orient, Boreham Wood, Leyton Orient, AC Pisa
*** Cetin - Ertugrul Cetin (Osman Ertuğrul Çetin) (a) 21/04/2003, Istanbul (Turkey) (b) 1,88 (c) G (d) Genclerbirligi Ankara (e) Genclerbirligi, Fenerbahce, Altinordu
*** Cetin - Mert Cetin (Yıldırım Mert Çetin) (a) 01/01/1997, Ankara (Turkey) (b) 1,89 (c) D - central defense (d) MKE Ankaragücü (e) Ankaragücü, Hellas Verona, Adana Demirspor, Hellas Verona, Lecce, Hellas Verona, Kayserispor, Hellas Verona, AS Roma, Hellas Verona, AS Roma, Genclerbirligi, Hacettepe, Hacettepe
*** Cetin - Sahverdi Cetin (Şahverdi Çetin) (a) 28/09/2000, Mainz (Germany) (b) 1,74 (c) M - central midfielder (d) Ankara Keciörengücü (e) FC Dordrecht, Ankaragücü, Eintracht
*** Cetinkaya - Erdem Cetinkaya (Erdem Çetinkaya) (a) 29/03/2001, Ankara (Turkey) (b) 1,77 (c) F - center forward (d) Kasimpasa (e) Bodrum FK, Kasimpasa, Ankaraspor, Bodrum FK, Ankaraspor
*** Cetkovic - Aleksa Cetkovic (a) 13/02/2004, Podgorica (Serbia and Montenegro, now in Montenegro) (b) 1,87 (c) M - central midfielder (d) Buducnost Podgorica (e) Arsenal Tivat, Buducnost Podgorica
*** Cetkovic - Dragan Cetkovic (a) 16/08/2004, ¿? (Serbia and Montenegro, now in Montenegro) (b) - (c) G (d) Arsenal Tivat (e) OFK Grbalj
*** Cetkovic - Marko Cetkovic (Marko Ćetković) (a) 10/07/1986, Podgorica (Yugoslavia, now in Montenegro) (b) 1,70 (c) M - attacking midfielder (d) FK Mornar Bar (e) Sutjeska Niksic, FK Mladost, FK Partizani, FK Sarajevo, KF Laçi, Buducnost Podgorica, Jagiellonia, Podbeskidzie, Jagiellonia, Buriram Utd., Jagiellonia, Mogren, FK Partizan, Zeta Golubovac, FK Mladost
*** Cetkovic - Nikola Cetkovic (Nikola Ćetković) (a) 06/02/2002, Banja Luka (Bosnia and Herzegovina) (b) 1,90 (c) G (d) FK Borac Banja Luka (e) Zeljeznicar BL
*** Cevers - Leonards Cevers (Leonards Čevers) (a) 17/05/2005, ¿? (Latvia) (b) 1,90 (c) G (d) FK Tukums 2000 (e) Tukums II
*** Cevoli - Michele Cevoli (a) 22/07/1998, Borgo Maggiore (San Marino) (b) 1,94 (c) D - central defense (d) AC Juvenes-Dogana (e) Pennarossa, Cattolica SM, Savignanese
*** Ceylan - Furkan Ceylan (a) 01/01/2003, Kirikkale (Turkey) (b) 1,79 (c) F - center forward (d) Fethiyespor (e) Ankaragücü
*** Ceylan - Oguz Ceylan (Oğuz Ceylan) (a) 15/12/1990, Canakkale (Turkey) (b) 1,74 (c) D - right back (d) Kocaelispor (e) Çaykur Rizespor, Ankaragücü, Gaziantep FK, Ümraniyespor, Kartalspor, Bugsas Spor, K.Maras BB, Siirtspor
*** Chabbi - Seifedin Chabbi (a) 04/07/1993, Bludenz (Austria) (b) 1,87 (c) F - center forward (d) FC Vaduz (e) SV Ried, TSV Hartberg, Gaziantep FK, St. Mirren, Gaziantep FK, SV Ried, Sturm Graz, FC St. Gallen, Austria Lustenau, Hoffenheim II
*** Chabo - Emanuel Chabo (a) 27/09/2002, ¿? (Sweden) (b) - (c) F - center forward (d) Åtvidabergs FF (e) Norrköping, Sylvia, Norrköping
*** Chabot - Julian Chabot (Julian Jeffrey Gaston Chabot) (a) 12/02/1998, Hanau (Germany) (b) 1,95 (c) D - central defense (d) 1.FC Köln (e) Sampdoria, 1.FC Köln, Sampdoria, Spezia, Sampdoria, FC Groningen, Sparta Rotterdam

*** Chabradze - Grigol Chabradze (გრიგოლ ჩაბრაძე) (a) 20/04/1996, Tbilisi (Georgia) (b) 1,76 (c) D - right back (d) Dinamo Batumi (e) Saburtalo, FC Telavi, Saburtalo

*** Chabrolle - Florian Chabrolle (a) 07/04/1998, Montmorency (France) (b) 1,71 (c) M - attacking midfielder (d) - (e) AC Ajaccio, Ol. Marseille, Ol. Marseille B

*** Chaby - Filipe Chaby (Carlos Filipe Fonseca Chaby) (a) 22/01/1994, Setúbal (Portugal) (b) 1,74 (c) M - attacking midfielder (d) CF Os Belenenses (e) Sumqayit, Sporting B, Nacional, Sporting B, Académica Coimbra, Sporting B, Sporting Lisboa, Académica Coimbra, Sporting Lisboa, Estoril Praia, Sporting Lisboa, B SAD, Belenenses, Sporting B, SC Covilhã, Sporting B, União Madeira, Sporting B

*** Chachua - Roman Chachua (რომან ჩაჩუა) (a) 01/11/1997, ¿? (Georgia) (b) 1,82 (c) D - right back (d) FC Locomotive Tbilisi (e) Shukura, Saburtalo, Shukura, Sioni Bolnisi, Sepidrood, FC Samtredia, Shukura

*** Chadala - Filip Chadala (Filip Chadała) (a) 06/06/2004, Kędzierzyn-Koźle (Poland) (b) 1,92 (c) G (d) Miedź Legnica (e) Miedz Legnica II, SMS Lodz

*** Chader - Sofyan Chader (a) 12/05/2000, Lyon (France) (b) 1,78 (c) F - left winger (d) FC Lucerna (e) Clermont Foot, Stade-Lausanne, Clermont Foot, Clermont B, FC Vaulx-en-Vel

*** Chadli - Nacer Chadli (الشادلي ناصر) (a) 02/08/1989, Liège (Belgium) (b) 1,87 (c) F - left winger (d) Basaksehir FK (e) KVC Westerlo, Basaksehir, AS Monaco, RSC Anderlecht, AS Monaco, West Bromwich Albion, Tottenham Hotspur, FC Twente, AGOVV

*** Chaduneli - Gia Chaduneli (გია ჩადუნელი) (a) 15/05/1994, Poti (Georgia) (b) 1,91 (c) D - central defense (d) FC Saburtalo (e) FC Gagra, FC Dila, Dinamo Tbilisi, Shukura, Guria, Kolkheti Poti, Kolkheti II

*** Chaganava - Luka Chaganava (ლუკა ჩაგანავა) (a) 09/11/2004, ¿? (Georgia) (b) - (c) F - right winger (d) FC Gagra (e) Sioni Bolnisi, Locomotive II

*** Chagas - Caique Chagas (Caique Augusto Correia Chagas) (a) 26/04/1994, Barueri (Brazil) (b) 1,84 (c) M - central midfielder (d) FK Decic Tuzi (e) OFK Petrovac, Sutjeska Niksic, FK Bokelj, Zvijezda 09, Arsenal Tivat, Stade Bordelais, Taubaté

*** Chagovets - Yevgeniy Chagovets (Чаговець Євгеній Вячеславович) (a) 24/03/1998, Andriivka, Kharkiv Oblast (Ukraine) (b) 1,92 (c) D - central defense (d) - (e) Ordabasy, Rukh, FK Minsk, Shakhtar II, UFK Kharkiv

*** Chaib - Youssef Chaib (a) 12/08/1996, ¿? (Norway) (b) 1,81 (c) F - right winger (d) Sandefjord Fotball (e) Strømmen, Kvik Halden, Fredrikstad, Moss, Trosvik IF

*** Chaïbi - Farès Chaïbi (a) 28/11/2002, Lyon (France) (b) 1,83 (c) F - left winger (d) Toulouse FC (e) Toulouse B

*** Chaïbi - Ilyes Chaïbi (Mohamed Ilyes Chaïbi) (a) 12/10/1996, Bron (France) (b) 1,76 (c) F - center forward (d) Thonon Évian Grand Genève FC (e) Thonon Évian, MC Alger, AS Monaco B, FC Wacker, AS Monaco B, AC Ajaccio, AS Monaco B

*** Chaiwa - Miguel Chaiwa (Miguel Changa Chaiwa) (a) 07/06/2004, Luanshya (Zambia) (b) 1,79 (c) M - pivot (d) BSC Young Boys (e) Shamuel FC, Atletico Lusaka, Shamuel FC

*** Chajani - Sufjan Chajani (a) 24/12/2004, Skopje (North Macedonia) (b) 1,72 (c) D - left back (d) - (e) Pobeda Prilep

*** Chakla - Soufiane Chakla (Soufiane Chakla Mrioued) (a) 02/09/1993, Kenitra (Morocco) (b) 1,88 (c) D - central defense (d) Sabah FK (e) Ponferradina, OH Leuven, Villarreal CF, Getafe CF, Villarreal CF, Villarreal CF B, UD Melilla, UD Almería B, CP El Ejido, La Roda CF, Videoton FC, Betis B, At. Malagueño

*** Chakvetadze - Aliko Chakvetadze (ალიკო ჩაკვეტაძე) (a) 28/03/1995, Tbilisi (Georgia) (b) 1,92 (c) D - central defense (d) Shukura Kobuleti (e) Torpedo Kutaisi, FC Samtredia, WIT Georgia, Kolkheti Poti, Torpedo Kutaisi, Dila II
*** Chakvetadze - Giorgi Chakvetadze (გიორგი ჩაკვეტაძე) (a) 29/08/1999, Tbilisi (Georgia) (b) 1,83 (c) M - attacking midfielder (d) Watford FC (e) Watford, KAA Gent, Slovan Bratislava, KAA Gent, SV Hamburg, KAA Gent, Dinamo Tbilisi
*** Chaladze - Lasha Chaladze (ლაშა ჩალაძე) (a) 11/05/1987, ¿? (Georgia) (b) 1,79 (c) M (d) FC Margveti 2006 (e) Merani Martvili, Torpedo Kutaisi, Dinamo Batumi, Merani Martvili, Shukura, FC Samtredia, Guria, Kolkheti Poti, Merani Martvili, Tskhinvali, FC Samtredia, Tskhinvali
*** Challouk - Youssef Challouk (a) 28/08/1995, Boom (Belgium) (b) 1,73 (c) M - attacking midfielder (d) KV Kortrijk (e) RWDM, KV Kortrijk, KMSK Deinze, KSK Heist, Rupel Boom
*** Chalmers - Logan Chalmers (a) 24/03/2000, Dundee (Scotland) (b) 1,75 (c) F - left winger (d) Dundee United FC (e) Tranmere Rovers, Dundee United, Ayr United, Dundee United, Inverness Caledonian, Dundee United, Arbroath, Dundee United, Dundee Utd. B
*** Chalobah - Nathaniel Chalobah (Nathaniel Nyakie Chalobah) (a) 12/12/1994, Freetown (Sierra Leona) (b) 1,85 (c) M - pivot (d) West Bromwich Albion (e) Fulham, Watford, Chelsea, Napoli, Chelsea, Reading, Chelsea, Burnley, Chelsea, Middlesbrough, Chelsea, Nottingham Forest, Chelsea, Watford, Chelsea
*** Chalobah - Trevoh Chalobah (Trevoh Thomas Chalobah) (a) 05/07/1999, Freetown (Sierra Leona) (b) 1,92 (c) D - central defense (d) Chelsea FC (e) FC Lorient, Huddersfield Town, Ipswich
*** Chaloupek - Stepan Chaloupek (Štěpán Chaloupek) (a) 08/03/2003, ¿? (Czech Rep.) (b) 1,88 (c) D - central defense (d) FK Teplice (e) -
*** Chalov - Fedor Chalov (Чалов Фёдор Николаевич) (a) 10/04/1998, Moskva (Russia) (b) 1,81 (c) F - center forward (d) CSKA Moskva (e) FC Basel, CSKA Moskva, CSKA Moskva II
*** Chalus - Matej Chalus (Matěj Chaluš) (a) 02/02/1998, Praha (Czech Rep.) (b) 1,90 (c) D - central defense (d) FC Slovan Liberec (e) Slovan Liberec, Malmö FF, FC Groningen, Malmö FF, Slovan Liberec, Slavia Praha, 1.FK Pribram, Slavia Praha, Mlada Boleslav, Slavia Praha, 1.FK Pribram
*** Cham - Babou Cham (a) 03/03/1999, Banjul (Gambia) (b) 1,70 (c) M - attacking midfielder (d) FC Nomme United (e) Nomme United, Paide, Ararat Yerevan, SC Noravank, FC Sevan, Real de Banjul
*** Chambaere - Vic Chambaere (a) 10/01/2003, Roeselare (Belgium) (b) 1,93 (c) G (d) KRC Genk (e) -
*** Chambers - Calum Chambers (a) 20/01/1995, Petersfield (England) (b) 1,82 (c) D - right back (d) Aston Villa (e) Arsenal, Fulham, Arsenal, Middlesbrough, Arsenal, Southampton
*** Chambers - Jack Chambers (Maurice Jack Chambers) (a) 12/07/2000, Banbridge (Northern Ireland) (b) 1,73 (c) M - central midfielder (d) Rathfriland Rangers FC (e) Carrick Rangers, Hednesford
*** Chambers - Luke Chambers (a) 24/06/2004, Preston (England) (b) 1,81 (c) D - left back (d) - (e) Kilmarnock FC
*** Chamed - Nasser Chamed (a) 04/10/1993, Lyon (France) (b) 1,74 (c) F - right winger (d) AFC Chindia Targoviste (e) Gaz Metan, Nîmes, LB Châteauroux, Châteauroux B

*** Chanba - Daur Chanba (Чанба Даур Асланович) (a) 07/07/2000, Sokhumi (Georgia) (b) 1,83 (c) D - right back (d) - (e) FC Van, Krasnodar 3, Backa, Teleoptik
*** Chandarov - Asen Chandarov (Асен Руменов Чандъров) (a) 13/11/1998, Sofia (Bulgaria) (b) 1,89 (c) M - pivot (d) Levski Sofia (e) Septemvri Sofia, Academica Clinceni, Septemvri Sofia, Levski Sofia, Septemvri Sofia, Botev Plovdiv, Septemvri Sofia, Pirin Razlog, Septemvri Sofia, DIT Sofia
*** Chandler - Timothy Chandler (a) 29/03/1990, Frankfurt am Main (Germany) (b) 1,86 (c) D - right back (d) Eintracht Frankfurt (e) 1.FC Nürnberg, Nurernberg II, Eintracht II
*** Chantakias - Dimitrios Chantakias (Δημήτριος Χαντάκιας) (a) 04/01/1995, Agrinio (Greece) (b) 1,84 (c) D - central defense (d) Zira FK (e) Cherno More, Panetolikos, AOK Kerkyra, Panetolikos, AS Fokikos, Panetolikos
*** Chanturia - Nika Chanturia (ნიკა ჭანტურია) (a) 19/01/1995, Zugdidi (Georgia) (b) 1,81 (c) D - central defense (d) FC Locomotive Tbilisi (e) FC Gagra, Shukura, FC Locomotive, Dinamo Tbilisi, FC Locomotive, Torpedo Kutaisi, FC Locomotive
*** Chanturishvili - Vakhtang Chanturishvili (ვახტანგ ჭანტურიშვილი) (a) 05/08/1993, Ozurgeti (Georgia) (b) 1,73 (c) M - left midfielder (d) FK Jablonec (e) Zlin, Spartak Trnava, FK Oleksandriya, Dinamo Tbilisi, FC Zestafoni, Zestafoni II, Merani Tbilisi, FC Sasco
*** Chapman - Lee Chapman (a) 09/11/1994, Belfast (Northern Ireland) (b) - (c) D - right back (d) Portadown FC (e) Dundela FC, Ballymena, Carrick Rangers, Glentoran, Carrick Rangers, Lisburn FC
*** Charalampous - Charalampos Charalampous (Χαράλαμπος "Χάμπος" Χαραλάμπους) (a) 04/04/2002, Larnaca (Cyprus) (b) 1,75 (c) M - central midfielder (d) Omonia Nicosia (e) -
*** Charalampous - Pavlos Charalampous (Παύλος Χαραλάμπους) (a) 09/02/2004, Limassol (Cyprus) (b) 1,87 (c) D - central defense (d) AEK Larnaca (e) Akritas Chlor.
*** Charalampous - Stavros Charalampous (Σταύρος Χαραλάμπους) (a) 23/02/2005, Latsia (Cyprus) (b) 1,78 (c) M - central midfielder (d) California Baptist Lancers (Cali. Baptist Uni.) (e) APOEL FC
*** Charalampous - Stefanos Charalampous (Στέφανος Χαραλάμπους) (a) 03/09/1999, Paphos (Cyprus) (b) 1,75 (c) M - attacking midfielder (d) Anorthosis Famagusta (e) Olympiakos N., Doxa Katokopias, Digenis Morfou, Doxa Katokopias, PAEEK Kyrenia, Doxa Katokopias, Akritas Chlor.
*** Charbonnier - Gaëtan Charbonnier (a) 27/12/1988, Saint-Mandé (France) (b) 1,88 (c) F - center forward (d) AS Saint-Étienne (e) AJ Auxerre, Stade Brestois, Stade Reims, Montpellier, Angers SCO, Paris Saint Germain B, Châtellerault
*** Chardonnet - Brendan Chardonnet (a) 22/12/1994, Saint-Renan (France) (b) 1,84 (c) D - central defense (d) Stade Brestois 29 (e) SAS Epinal, Stade Brestois, Brest B
*** Chargeishvili - Vano Chargeishvili (a) 15/05/2001, ¿? (Georgia) (b) - (c) F - center forward (d) FC Samtredia (e) Torpedo Kutaisi, Torpedo Kutaisi II
*** Charisis - Charilaos Charisis (Χαρίλαος Χαρίσης) (a) 12/01/1995, Ioannina (Greece) (b) 1,77 (c) M - central midfielder (d) Sivasspor (e) Atromitos FC, PAOK, KV Kortrijk, PAOK, Sint-Truiden, PAOK, PAS Giannina
*** Charles - Charles (Charles Marcelo da Silva) (a) 04/02/1994, Belo Horizonte (Brazil) (b) 1,86 (c) G (d) Vitória Guimarães SC (e) Olympiakos N., Vizela, Marítimo, Vasco da Gama
*** Charles - Charles (Charles Rigon Matos) (a) 19/06/1996, Santiago (Brazil) (b) 1,87 (c) M - central midfielder (d) FC Midtjylland (e) Ceará SC, Internacional, Sport Recife, Internacional, Inter B

*** Charles - Bismark Charles (Bismark Charles Kwarena Sie) (a) 26/05/2001, Berekum (Ghana) (b) 1,83 (c) F - center forward (d) Pirin Blagoevgrad (e) Pirin, CSKA-Sofia, KF Trepca 89, KF Vushtrria, B. Chelsea II

*** Charles - Shea Charles (Shea Emmanuel Charles) (a) 05/11/2003, Manchester (England) (b) 1,89 (c) M - pivot (d) Southampton FC (e) -

*** Charles - Uba Charles (Uba Charles Nwokoma) (a) 10/10/2002, Owerri (Nigeria) (b) 1,76 (c) M - central midfielder (d) Lillestrøm SK (e) Ljungskile SK, Linköping City

*** Charles-Cook - Regan Charles-Cook (Regan Evans Charles-Cook) (a) 14/02/1997, Lewisham-London (England) (b) 1,74 (c) F - left winger (d) KAS Eupen (e) Ross County, Gillingham FC, Woking, Woking, Solihull Moors

*** Charleston - Charleston (Charleston Silva dos Santos) (a) 23/09/1996, ¿? (North Macedonia) (b) 1,95 (c) D - central defense (d) FK Maktaaral (e) Debrecen, Sfintul Gheorghe, Makedonija, Vardar, Tsarsko Selo, Porto-PE

*** Chatziantoni - Theodoros Chatziantoni (Θεόδωρος Χατζηαντώνη) (a) 30/11/2003, Larnaca (Cyprus) (b) - (c) F (d) Nea Salamis (e) ASIL Lysi, Nea Salamis

*** Chatzidiakos - Pantelis Chatzidiakos (Παντελής Χατζηδιάκος) (a) 18/01/1997, Rhodos (Greece) (b) 1,85 (c) D - central defense (d) AZ Alkmaar (e) -

*** Chatziemmanouil - Vasilios Chatziemmanouil (Βασίλειος Χατζηεμμανουήλ) (a) 09/08/1999, Nea Makri (Greece) (b) 1,87 (c) G (d) PAS Lamia 1964 (e) PAS Lamia, AEK Athína B, AEK Athína, Fostiras, AEK Athína, Ag. Anargyroi, AEK Athína

*** Chatzigiovanis - Anastasios Chatzigiovanis (Αναστάσιος Χατζηγιοβάνης) (a) 31/05/1997, Mytilini (Greece) (b) 1,77 (c) F - right winger (d) MKE Ankaragücü (e) Panathinaikos

*** Chatziioannou - Christos Chatziioannou (Χρήστος Χατζηϊωάννου) (a) 10/01/2004, ¿? (Greece) (b) - (c) F - center forward (d) Panathinaikos Athina B (e) Aris Thessaloniki

*** Chatziisaias - Dimitrios Chatziisaias (Δημήτριος Χατζηησαΐας) (a) 21/09/1992, Thessaloniki (Greece) (b) 1,93 (c) D - central defense (d) - (e) Atromitos FC, Çaykur Rizespor, Cercle Brugge, Çaykur Rizespor, PAOK, Atromitos FC, PAOK, Panionios, AO Chania, AO Glyfadas, Vataniakos, O. Stavroupolis

*** Chatzimitsis - Nikolas Chatzimitsis (Νικόλας Χατζημιτσής) (a) 10/09/2003, Yeroskipou (Cyprus) (b) 1,83 (c) D - right back (d) Lafayette Leopards (Lafayette College) (e) Olympiakos N., Anorthosis, D. Oroklinis

*** Chatzitheodoridis - Ilias Chatzitheodoridis (Ηλίας Χατζηθεοδωρίδης) (a) 05/11/1997, Katerini (Greece) (b) 1,71 (c) D - left back (d) Panetolikos GFS (e) Panathinaikos, Brentford, Cheltenham Town, Brentford, Brentford B

*** Chatzivasili - Ioannis Chatzivasili (Ιωάννης Χατζηβασίλη) (a) 26/04/1990, Páfos (Cyprus) (b) 1,85 (c) F - left winger (d) AEZ Zakakiou (e) Karmiotissa, Anorthosis, Doxa Katokopias, Apollon Limassol, Ethnikos, Omonia Nicosia, Aris Limassol, Omonia Nicosia, A. Geroskipou, AE Pafos

*** Chavalerin - Xavier Chavalerin (a) 07/03/1991, Villeurbanne (France) (b) 1,79 (c) M - central midfielder (d) ESTAC Troyes (e) Stade Reims, Red Star FC, Tours FC, Olymp. Lyon B

*** Chavarría - Pep Chavarría (Josep María Chavarría Pérez) (a) 10/04/1998, Figueres (Spain) (b) 1,74 (c) D - left back (d) Rayo Vallecano (e) Real Zaragoza, UE Olot, UE Figueres

*** Chavez Borelli - Antonío Chavez Borelli (Antonío Joseph Chavez Borelli) (a) 23/11/1998, Valley Village, California (United States) (b) 1,85 (c) G (d) AB Argir (e) Boston Eagles, Ventura County, Boston Eagles

*** Chavorski - Todor Chavorski (Тодор Костадинов Чаворски) (a) 30/03/1993, Sofia (Bulgaria) (b) 1,86 (c) F - center forward (d) Chernomorets 1919 Burgas (e) Yantra, Hebar II, Hebar P., Lokomotiv Sofia, Botev Vratsa, Lokomotiv Mezdra, Dob. Dobrich, Levski Sofia, Pirin Razlog, Levski Sofia

*** Chaykovskyi - Igor Chaykovskyi (Чайковський Ігор Геннадійович) (a) 07/10/1991, Chernivtsi (Soviet Union, now in Ukraine) (b) 1,75 (c) M - pivot (d) Bukovyna Chernivtsi (e) Metalist, Bukovyna, FK Polissya, Ingulets, Zorya Lugansk, Anzhi, Zorya Lugansk, Illichivets, Zorya Lugansk, Illichivets, Shakhtar II, Illichivets, Shakhtar II, Zorya Lugansk, Shakhtar II

*** Che - Justin Che (Justin Isiah Che) (a) 18/11/2003, Richardson, Texas (United States) (b) 1,85 (c) D - right back (d) Brøndby IF (e) Dallas, Hoffenheim, Hoffenheim II, Hoffenheim, Dallas, North Texas SC, Dallas, North Texas SC

*** Chebake - Issam Chebake (عصام شباك) (a) 12/10/1989, Agadir (Morocco) (b) 1,75 (c) D - right back (d) APOEL FC (e) Yeni Malatyaspor, Le Havre AC, Rodez AF, US Sarre-Union, US Forbach, Stade Rennes B, SG Marienau

*** Cheberko - Yevgen Cheberko (Чеберко Євген Ігорович) (a) 23/01/1998, Melitopol (Ukraine) (b) 1,84 (c) D - central defense (d) Columbus Crew (e) NK Osijek, LASK, NK Osijek, LASK, Zorya Lugansk, Dnipro, Dnipro II

*** Checa - Checa (José Carlos Caballero Vargas) (a) 09/05/1998, Alcalá del Valle (Spain) (b) 1,87 (c) D - central defense (d) CD Utrera (e) UE Santa Coloma, CP El Ejido, Arenas Club, At. Baleares, Sevilla At., Sevilla FC C

*** Chegra - Ivane Chegra (a) 03/03/2004, ¿? (Algeria) (b) - (c) F - right winger (d) AC Ajaccio (e) AC Ajaccio B

*** Cheikh - Pape Cheikh (Pape Cheikh Diop Gueye) (a) 08/08/1997, Guédiawaye (Senegal) (b) 1,80 (c) M - central midfielder (d) - (e) Elche CF, Aris Thessaloniki, Olympique Lyon, Dijon, Olympique Lyon, RC Celta, Olympique Lyon, RC Celta, Celta B

*** Chekh - Maksym Chekh (Чех Максим Сергійович) (a) 03/01/1999, Krasna Polyana, Donetsk Oblast (Ukraine) (b) 1,75 (c) M - pivot (d) Karpaty Lviv (e) Shakhtar Donetsk, FK Sabail, Shakhtar Donetsk, Shakhtar II, FK Mariupol, Shakhtar II

*** Chelari - Ruslan Chelari (a) 27/02/1999, ¿? (Moldova) (b) 1,81 (c) M - pivot (d) FC Bălți (e) Sfintul Gheorghe, FC Bălți, Foresta Suceava, CSF Speranta, Real Succes

*** Chelidze - Georgi Chelidze (Челидзе Георгий Кахаберович) (a) 20/01/2000, Moskva (Russia) (b) 1,81 (c) M - attacking midfielder (d) - (e) Samgurali, Zenit 2 St. Peterburg, Ararat Yerevan, AFC Tubize, Dinamo Moskva II

*** Chelyadin - Artem Chelyadin (Челядін Артем Геннадійович) (a) 29/12/1999, Novograd-Volynskyi, Zhytomyr Oblast (Ukraine) (b) 1,84 (c) M - pivot (d) Vorskla Poltava (e) Vorskla II, Skala Stryi

*** Chenbay - Sergiy Chenbay (Ченбай Сергій Дмитрович) (a) 06/11/1992, Kyiv (Ukraine) (b) 1,85 (c) D - left back (d) Ingulets Petrove (e) Metalist 1925, Kremin, Girnyk-Sport, Kremin, Vorskla II

*** Cheng - Chun-Hin Ryan Cheng (鄭浚軒) (a) 11/06/2003, ¿? (Malta) (b) 1,70 (c) M - pivot (d) Zejtun Corinthians FC (e) Valletta

*** Cherchesov - Stanislav Cherchesov (Черчесов Станислав Станиславович) (a) 26/09/1994, Dresden (Germany) (b) 1,86 (c) G (d) - (e) Khimki 2, Dolgoprudnyi, Olimp Khimki, Baltika, Chernomorets N., Dinamo Moskva, Dinamo Moskva II, Amkar II, FC Wacker II, SV Innsbruck

*** Cherchez - Cristian Cherchez (Cristian Georgian Cherchez) (a) 01/02/1991, Târgoviște (Romania) (b) 1,83 (c) M - attacking midfielder (d) - (e) Chindia, FCM Targoviste

*** Cheredinov - Artem Cheredinov (Черединов Артем Сергеевич) (a) 17/07/1998, Medvezhka (Kazakhstan) (b) 1,82 (c) F - center forward (d) FC Zhenis Astana (e) Qyzyljar, FC Zhenis, Qyzyljar

*** Cherki - Rayan Cherki (Mathis Rayan Cherki) (a) 17/08/2003, Lyon (France) (b) 1,77 (c) M - attacking midfielder (d) Olympique de Lyon (e) Olymp. Lyon B

*** Chermiti - Chermiti (Youssef Ramalho Chermiti) (a) 24/05/2004, Santa Maria, Açores (Portugal) (b) 1,92 (c) F - center forward (d) Everton FC (e) Sporting Lisboa, Sporting B

*** Chernenko - Ruslan Chernenko (Черненко Руслан Сергійович) (a) 29/09/1992, Kyiv (Ukraine) (b) 1,78 (c) M - central midfielder (d) Obolon Kyiv (e) Spartak Varna, Agrobiznes V., Marek Dupnitsa, Agrobiznes V., Arsenal Kyiv, SK Chayka, RVUFK Kyiv, Arsenal Kyiv II, Desna, Arsenal Kyiv II

*** Chernev - Atanas Chernev (Атанас Атанасов Чернев) (a) 25/03/2002, Plovdiv (Bulgaria) (b) 1,95 (c) D - central defense (d) Botev Plovdiv (e) Botev Plovdiv

*** Chernik - Sergey Chernik (Черник Сергей Викторович) (a) 20/07/1988, Grodno (Soviet Union, now in Belarus) (b) 1,87 (c) G (d) Shakhter Soligorsk (e) Gorodeya, Irtysh, BATE Borisov, AS Nancy, BATE Borisov, Neman Grodno, Neman II

*** Chernikov - Aleksandr Chernikov (Черников Александр Евгеньевич) (a) 01/02/2000, Vyselki, Krasnodar Region (Russia) (b) 1,84 (c) M - pivot (d) FK Krasnodar (e) Krasnodar-2, Krasnodar II

*** Chernook - Kirill Chernook (Черноок Кирилл Игоревич) (a) 02/01/2003, Verkhnedvinsk (Belarus) (b) 1,77 (c) M - attacking midfielder (d) BATE Borisov (e) FK Minsk, Rukh, Dynamo Brest II

*** Chernov - Evgeniy Chernov (Чернов Евгений Александрович) (a) 23/10/1992, Tomsk (Russia) (b) 1,80 (c) D - left back (d) FK Rostov (e) Krasnodar, Rostov, Krasnodar, Rostov, Zenit, Tosno, Zenit, Zenit 2 St. Peterburg, Tom Tomsk, Enisey, Tom Tomsk, Khimik, Tom Tomsk, Gazovik Orenburg, Tom Tomsk, Tom Tomsk II

*** Chernov - Nikita Chernov (Чернов Никита Александрович) (a) 14/01/1996, Volzhskiy, Volgograd Oblast (Russia) (b) 1,88 (c) D - central defense (d) FC Spartak de Moscú (e) KS Samara, CSKA Moskva, CSKA Moskva II, Ural, CSKA Moskva II, Enisey, CSKA Moskva II, Baltika, CSKA Moskva II

*** Chernyak - Ilya Chernyak (Черняк Илья Игоревич) (a) 19/05/2002, Eremino, Gomel Region (Belarus) (b) 1,84 (c) F - attacking midfielder (d) Kaspiy Aktau (e) Akhmat Grozny, Soligorsk, Soligorsk II, Din. Zagreb II, Soligorsk II, Gomel II

*** Chernyakov - Daniil Chernyakov (Черняков Даниил Романович) (a) 07/01/2001, Davydovo, Moscow Region (Russia) (b) 1,78 (c) M - central midfielder (d) Metallurg Lipetsk (e) M. Lipetsk, Fakel Voronezh, Loko-Kazanka M., Lokomotiv Moskva II

*** Chernyavskiy - Mikhail Chernyavskiy (Чернявский Михаил Владимирович) (a) 05/01/2002, Mogilev (Belarus) (b) 1,78 (c) D - left back (d) Luban Maniowy (e) Dnepr Mogilev, Dnyapro II, Mogilev II

*** Chernyi - Artur Chernyi (Чёрный Артур Гариевич) (a) 11/12/2000, Vladikavkaz (Russia) (b) 1,84 (c) D - central defense (d) Zenit 2 St. Petersburg (e) Zenit 2 St. Peterburg, Khimki, Lokomotiv Moskva, Loko-Kazanka M., Lokomotiv Moskva II

*** Cherov - Vasiliy Cherov (Черов Василий Сергеевич) (a) 13/01/1996, Slavyansk-na-Kubani, Krasnodar Region (Russia) (b) 1,85 (c) D - right back (d) Fakel Voronezh (e) Kuban, Chernomorets N., Druzhba Maikop, Afips Afipskiy, Krasnodar-2, Khimki, Krasnodar-2, Krasnodar II

*** Cherrie - Peter Cherrie (a) 01/10/1983, Bellshill (Scotland) (b) 1,88 (c) G (d) Dundalk FC (e) Derry City, Cork City, Bray Wanderers, Cliftonville, Dundalk FC, Clyde FC, Ayr United, Kilsyth, Airdrie United

*** Cherry - Kyle Cherry (a) 13/05/1993, Belfast (Northern Ireland) (b) - (c) M - central midfielder (d) Carrick Rangers (e) Ards FC, Carrick Rangers, Glentoran, Dundela FC, Glentoran, Glenavon, Glentoran

*** Chertkoev - Inal Chertkoev (Черткоєв Інал Володимирович) (a) 08/10/1999, Kharkiv (Ukraine) (b) 1,73 (c) M - right midfielder (d) Girnyk-Sport Gorishni Plavni (e) Chornomorets, Vorskla II, UFK Kharkiv

*** Chervyakov - Zakhar Chervyakov (Червяков Захар Александрович) (a) 30/08/2002, Vitebsk (Belarus) (b) - (c) F - center forward (d) FK Vitebsk (e) Vitebsk II

*** Chery - Tjaronn Chery (Tjaronn Inteff Chefren Chery) (a) 04/06/1988, Den Haag (Netherlands) (b) 1,71 (c) M - attacking midfielder (d) Maccabi Haifa (e) GZ Hengfeng, Kayserispor, GZ Hengfeng, Queen's Park Rangers, FC Groningen, ADO Den Haag, FC Groningen, ADO Den Haag, FC Emmen, RBC Roosendaal, Cambuur L.

*** Cheshmedjiev - Konstantin Cheshmedjiev (Константин Чешмеџиев) (a) 29/01/1996, Skopje (North Macedonia) (b) 1,85 (c) D - central defense (d) KF Vllaznia (e) Septemvri Sofia, Slavia Sofia, FC Shkupi, Velez Mostar, Shkëndija, AP Brera, Makedonija, Ljubanci, Pelister Bitola

*** Chesnakov - Volodymyr Chesnakov (Чеснаков Володимир Геннадійович) (a) 12/02/1988, Globyne, Poltava Oblast (Soviet Union, now in Ukraine) (b) 1,84 (c) D - central defense (d) Vorskla Poltava (e) Vorskla II

*** Chesnokov - Islam Chesnokov (Чесноков Ислам Хусиевич) (a) 21/11/1999, Ustj-Kamenogorsk (Kazakhstan) (b) 1,82 (c) F - right winger (d) Tobol Kostanay (e) Belshina, FK Altay, FK Altay II, FK Altay, FK Altay II

*** Chesnovskiy - Pavel Chesnovskiy (Чесновский Павел Геннадиевич) (a) 04/03/1986, Minsk (Soviet Union, now in Belarus) (b) 1,93 (c) G (d) - (e) Soligorsk, FK Minsk, Gorodeya, Torpedo Zhodino, BATE Borisov, JFK Ventspils, FC Tranzits, JFK Ventspils, Vitebsk, MTZ-Ripo Minsk, Partizan II, BATE II, Smena Minsk

*** Chesters - Dan Chesters (Daniel Peter Chesters) (a) 04/04/2002, Hitchin (England) (b) - (c) M - right midfielder (d) - (e) Colchester Utd.

*** Chesters - John Chesters (a) 14/07/2006, ¿? (Wales) (b) - (c) G (d) Haverfordwest County (e) -

*** Chetcuti - Miguel Chetcuti (a) 26/01/2000, ¿? (Malta) (b) - (c) G (d) Zebbug Rangers FC (e) Pietà Hotspurs

*** Chete - Chete (Cristian González López) (a) 12/05/1995, Albacete (Spain) (b) - (c) D - central defense (d) Inter Club d'Escaldes (e) Lorca Deportiva, Orihuela CF, Socuéllamos, Zamora CF, Astorga, Calahorra, Quintanar Rey, At. Albacete

*** Chetti - Ilyes Chetti (شتي إلياس) (a) 22/01/1995, Annaba (Algeria) (b) 1,76 (c) D - left back (d) Wydad Casablanca (e) Angers SCO, Esperance, JS Kabylie, US Chaouia, USM Annaba

*** Cheukoua - Michael Cheukoua (a) 13/01/1997, ¿? (Austria) (b) 1,81 (c) F - right winger (d) Grazer AK 1902 (e) Austria Lustenau, SV Horn, SCR Altach, Wiener Neustadt, SCR Altach, Canon Yaoundé

*** Chevalier - Lucas Chevalier (a) 06/11/2001, Calais (France) (b) 1,89 (c) G (d) LOSC Lille Métropole (e) Valenciennes FC, Lille, LOSC Lille B

*** Chezhia - Irakliy Chezhia (Чежия Ираклий Робертович) (a) 22/05/1992, Gali (Georgia) (b) 1,88 (c) D - central defense (d) FK Khimki (e) Khimki 2, Dolgoprudnyi, Olimp Khimki, Olimp 2, Olimp Khimki, Shukura, Armavir, Ulisses, Arsenal 2 Tula, FK Kaluga, Khimik, Spartak Moskva II

*** Chiabrishvili - Irakli Chiabrishvili (ირაკლი ჭიაბრიშვილი) (a) 02/09/2001, ¿? (Georgia) (b) - (c) F - right winger (d) FC Gareji (e) FC Locomotive

*** Chiacig - Matteo Chiacig (Matteo Pierre Chiacig) (a) 22/08/2003, Liège (Belgium) (b) 1,92 (c) G (d) Zébra Élites (e) RSC Charleroi

*** Chiappetta - Carmine Chiappetta (Carmine Soel Chiappetta) (a) 09/03/2003, Wetzikon ZH (Switzerland) (b) 1,75 (c) M - left midfielder (d) FC Winterthur (e) FC Winterthur

*** Chiarodia - Fabio Chiarodia (Fabio Cristian Chiarodia) (a) 05/06/2005, Oldenburg (Germany) (b) 1,86 (c) D - central defense (d) Borussia Mönchengladbach (e) Werder Bremen

*** Chibsah - Raman Chibsah (Yussif Raman Chibsah) (a) 10/03/1993, Accra (Ghana) (b) 1,77 (c) M - central midfielder (d) Ionikos Nikeas (e) Apollon Smyrnis, VfL Bochum, Gaziantep FK, Frosinone, Benevento, Frosinone, Benevento, Sassuolo, Benevento, Sassuolo, Frosinone, Sassuolo, Parma, Sassuolo, Parma, Bechem United

*** Chibueze - Odi Chibueze (Odi Henry Chibueze) (a) 15/11/1992, ¿? (RF Yugoslavia, now in Kosovo) (b) - (c) F - center forward (d) KF Vushtrria (e) KF Dukagjini, KF Vëllaznimi, KF Trepca 89, KF Vëllaznimi, KF Trepca 89, Esentepe SK, KF Trepca 89, KF Liria

*** Chichinadze - Anri Chichinadze (ანრი ჭიჭინაძე) (a) 05/10/1997, Kutaisi (Georgia) (b) 1,89 (c) D - central defense (d) Torpedo Kutaisi (e) FK Turon, FC Dila, Saburtalo, Torpedo Kutaisi, Torpedo Kutaisi II

*** Chichkan - Anton Chichkan (a) 10/07/1995, Minsk (Belarus) (b) 1,88 (c) G (d) Dinamo Batumi (e) Dinamo Tbilisi, Ufa, BATE Borisov, BATE II, Smolevichi, BATE II

*** Chichon - Mark Chichon (Mark Joseph Chichon) (a) 24/12/1994, Gibraltar (Gibraltar) (b) 1,65 (c) F - center forward (d) Europa Point FC (e) Mons Calpe, Europa Point FC, Manchester 62, Leeds Beckett, Lynx FC

*** Chico Banza - Chico Banza (Francisco Gonçalves Sacalumbo) (a) 17/12/1998, Mungo, Huambo (Angola) (b) 1,82 (c) F - left winger (d) Anorthosis Famagusta (e) Nea Salamis, PO Xylotymbou, Nea Salamis, PO Xylotymbou, Nea Salamis, Marítimo B, Leixões B, Real Sambila

*** Chico Geraldes - Chico Geraldes (Francisco de Oliveira Geraldes) (a) 18/04/1995, Lisboa (Portugal) (b) 1,75 (c) M - attacking midfielder (d) FC Baniyas (e) Estoril Praia, Rio Ave, Sporting Lisboa, AEK Athína, Sporting Lisboa, Eintracht, Sporting Lisboa, Rio Ave, Sporting Lisboa, Sporting B, Moreirense, Sporting B

*** Chidomere - Aleks Chidomere (Чідомере Алекс) (a) 12/08/2002, Kyiv (Ukraine) (b) 1,86 (c) M - attacking midfielder (d) Metalist Kharkiv (e) Obolon, FK Obolon-2

*** Chierighini - Alfredo Chierighini (a) 07/02/1966, ¿? (San Marino) (b) - (c) G (d) SP Tre Penne (e) -

*** Chiesa - Federico Chiesa (a) 25/10/1997, Genoa (Italy) (b) 1,75 (c) F - left winger (d) Juventus de Turín (e) Fiorentina, Juventus, Fiorentina

*** Chiesa - Mattia Chiesa (a) 16/07/2000, Rovereto (Italy) (b) 1,90 (c) G (d) Hellas Verona (e) Mantova, Hellas Verona, Trento, Hellas Verona, Virtus Verona, Hellas Verona, Ambrosiana, Ambrosiana

*** Chikanchi - Maksim Chikanchi (Чиканчи Максим Евгеньевич) (a) 29/08/1998, Bender (Moldova) (b) 1,84 (c) F - center forward (d) Qyzyljar Petropavlovsk (e) Krasava, Dolgoprudnyi, Kuban Holding, Dolgoprudnyi, Loko-Kazanka M., Lokomotiv Moskva II

*** Chikhladze - Demur Chikhladze (დემურ ჩიხლაძე) (a) 23/09/1996, ¿? (Georgia) (b) 1,80 (c) M - central midfielder (d) FC Samgurali Tskaltubo (e) Chikhura, Samgurali, FC Locomotive, Dinamo II

*** Chikhradze - Lado Chikhradze (ლადო ჩიხრაძე) (a) 03/09/2001, Tbilisi (Georgia) (b) 1,85 (c) F - center forward (d) FC Samgurali Tskaltubo (e) Extremadura, Extremadura B, At. Onubense

*** Chikhradze - Lasha Chikhradze (ლაშა ჩიხრაძე) (a) 24/09/2002, ¿? (Georgia) (b) - (c) M - central midfielder (d) FC Gagra (e) Merani Tbilisi, FC Gagra

*** Chikida - Pavel Chikida (Чикида Павел Иванович) (a) 21/06/1995, Smolevichi (Belarus) (b) 1,78 (c) D - right back (d) Slavia Mozyr (e) Maktaaral, Gomel, Dnyapro Mogilev, Smolevichi, Krumkachi, Smolevichi, Zhodino II

*** Chiles-Cowell - James Chiles-Cowell (James William Chiles-Cowell) (a) 14/02/2003, Gibraltar (Gibraltar) (b) - (c) D - central defense (d) Härnösand FC United (e) Glacis United, Lions Gibraltar Reserves, Europa Point FC, Boca Gibraltar

*** Chilili - Alexandru Chilili (Alexandru Constantin Chilili) (a) 01/08/2002, ¿? (Romania) (b) - (c) D - central defense (d) FC Voluntari (e) -

*** Chilingaryan - Ararat Chilingaryan (Արարատ Չիլինգարյան) (a) 08/08/2000, Stepanakert (Armenia) (b) 1,71 (c) M - central midfielder (d) Lernayin Artsakh Goris (e) Ararat II, Erebuni Erewan

*** Chiloyan - Vrezh Chiloyan (Վրեժ Չիլոյան) (a) 06/04/2002, ¿? (Armenia) (b) - (c) F - left winger (d) FC Van (e) Pyunik Yerevan, Pyunik Yerevan B, Gandzasar, Pyunik Yerevan B

*** Chilufya - Edward Chilufya (a) 17/09/1999, Kasama (Zambia) (b) 1,71 (c) F - right winger (d) FC Midtjylland (e) Djurgården

*** Chilwell - Ben Chilwell (Benjamin James Chilwell) (a) 21/12/1996, Milton Keynes (England) (b) 1,80 (c) D - left back (d) Chelsea FC (e) Leicester City, Huddersfield Town, Leicester City

*** China - China (Fábio Diogo Agrela Ferreira) (a) 07/07/1992, Estreito da Calheta (Portugal) (b) 1,79 (c) D - left back (d) CS Marítimo (e) Marítimo B, Estrela Calheta

*** China - China (Rogerio Alves dos Santos) (a) 02/08/1996, São Paulo (Brazil) (b) 1,79 (c) F - right winger (d) FK Aktobe (e) Dibba Fujairah, PFK Lviv, Aktobe, PFK Lviv, Karpaty II, Juventus-SP

*** Chindris - Andrei Chindris (Andrei Chindriş) (a) 12/01/1999, Cluj-Napoca (Romania) (b) 1,91 (c) D - central defense (d) KS Lechia Gdańsk (e) UTA Arad, Santa Clara, FC Botosani, Miroslava, FC Botosani, Academica Clinceni, FC Botosani

*** Chipciu - Alexandru Chipciu (Alexandru Mihăiţă Chipciu) (a) 18/05/1989, Brăila (Romania) (b) 1,76 (c) F - right winger (d) FC Universitatea Cluj (e) CFR Cluj, RSC Anderlecht, Sparta Praha, RSC Anderlecht, Steaua Bucuresti, FC Brasov, CF Braila, FC Brasov, Forex Brasov, FC Brasov

*** Chipev - Hristian Chipev (Християн Цветомиров Чипев) (a) 23/07/2001, ¿? (Bulgaria) (b) 1,83 (c) F - left winger (d) - (e) Lokomotiv Sofia, Yantra, Lokomotiv Sofia, Tsarsko Selo

*** Chipolina - Joseph Chipolina (Joseph Louis Chipolina) (a) 14/12/1987, Gibraltar (Gibraltar) (b) 1,78 (c) D - left back (d) FC Bruno's Magpies (e) Lincoln FC, Glacis United, Lincoln FC, St Joseph's FC, Real Colorado, R. B. Linense, San Roque Lepe, R. B. Linense

*** Chipolina - Kenneth Chipolina (Kenneth George Chipolina) (a) 08/04/1994, Gibraltar (Gibraltar) (b) - (c) D - left back (d) Mons Calpe SC (e) Manchester 62, Europa FC, St Joseph's FC, Lincoln FC, Lynx FC, Lincoln FC, Lions Gibraltar, Lincoln FC, Red Imps FC II, Lincoln FC, Gibraltar Utd., Lincoln FC, Gibraltar Utd., Lions Pilots, St Joseph's FC, Gibraltar Utd., St Joseph's FC

*** Chipolina - Lee Chipolina (Lee Martin Chipolina) (a) 27/02/2006, ¿? (Gibraltar) (b) - (c) M - attacking midfielder (d) Lincoln Red Imps FC (e) -

*** Chipolina - Michael Chipolina (Michael Ryan Chipolina) (a) 06/09/2000, ¿? (Gibraltar) (b) 1,75 (c) M - central midfielder (d) FC Manchester 62 (e) Manchester 62 Reserves, Manchester 62
*** Chipolina - Roy Chipolina (Roy Alan Chipolina) (a) 20/01/1983, Enfield (England) (b) 1,77 (c) D - central defense (d) Lincoln Red Imps FC (e) Lynx FC
*** Chipperfield - Liam Chipperfield (Liam Scott Chipperfield) (a) 14/02/2004, Basel (Switzerland) (b) 1,78 (c) M - central midfielder (d) FC Sion (e) FC Basel
*** Chiquinho - Chiquinho (Francisco Jorge Tavares Oliveira) (a) 05/02/2000, Cascais (Portugal) (b) 1,79 (c) F - left winger (d) Stoke City (e) Stoke City, Wolverhampton Wanderers, Estoril Praia
*** Chiquinho - Chiquinho (Francisco Leonel Lima Silva Machado) (a) 19/07/1995, Santo Tirso (Portugal) (b) 1,75 (c) M - central midfielder (d) SL Benfica (e) Giresunspor, Benfica, SC Braga, Benfica, Moreirense, Benfica, Académica Coimbra, NK Lokomotiva, Académica Coimbra, NK Lokomotiva, Leixões, Gondomar, Leixões
*** Chiriches - Vlad Chiriches (Vlad Iulian Chiricheş) (a) 14/11/1989, Bacău (Romania) (b) 1,84 (c) D - central defense (d) FCSB (e) Cremonese, Sassuolo, Napoli, Sassuolo, Napoli, Tottenham Hotspur, Steaua Bucuresti, Pandurii, Curtea de Arges, FC Ardealul
*** Chirinciuc - Anatol Chirinciuc (a) 04/02/1989, Nisporeni (Soviet Union, now in Moldova) (b) 1,85 (c) G (d) FC Zimbru Chisinau (e) CSF Speranta, Milsami, CSF Speranta, FC Saxan, Zimbru Chisinau, Dunarea Galati, Zimbru Chisinau
*** Chirinos - Michaell Chirinos (Michaell Anthony Chirinos Cortez) (a) 17/06/1995, Tegucigalpa (Honduras) (b) 1,67 (c) F - right winger (d) Deportivo Saprissa (e) Volos NPS, CD Olimpia, Vancouver, CD Olimpia, Lobos BUAP, CD Olimpia, Olimpia Reserves
*** Chirivella - Pedro Chirivella (a) 23/05/1997, Valencia (Spain) (b) 1,78 (d) FC Nantes (e) Extremadura, Willem II, Go Ahead Eagles
*** Chistyakov - Dmitriy Chistyakov (Чистяков Дмитрий Юрьевич) (a) 13/01/1994, Pikaliovo (Russia) (b) 1,85 (c) D - central defense (d) Zenit de San Petersburgo (e) Rostov, Zenit, Rostov, Tambov, Shinnik Yaroslav, Zenit 2 St. Peterburg, MIKA Aschtarak, Zenit 2 St. Peterburg, Zenit St. Peterburg II, Rostov II, SShOR Zenit
*** Chitanu - Laur Chitanu (Laur Chiţanu) (a) 01/09/2000, Chişinău (Moldova) (b) 1,87 (c) F - center forward (d) - (e) Dacia Buiucani, Chieti FC, Spartak Varna, Floresti, Scandicci, Marinhense
*** Chiteishvili - Revaz Chiteishvili (რევაზ ჩიტეიშვილი) (a) 30/01/1994, ¿? (Georgia) (b) 1,78 (c) D - right back (d) FC Dila Gori (e) Chikhura, FC Locomotive, Torpedo Kutaisi, FC Locomotive
*** Chitu - Aurelian Chitu (Aurelian Ionuţ Chiţu) (a) 25/03/1991, Ţăndărei (Romania) (b) 1,83 (c) F - center forward (d) FC U Craiova 1948 (e) FCV Farul, Daejeon Hana C., FC Viitorul, Astra Giurgiu, Valenciennes FC, PAS Giannina, Valenciennes FC, FC Viitorul, Unirea Slobozia
*** Chiurato - Alessandro Chiurato (a) 16/01/1983, Carpi (Italy) (b) - (c) F - center forward (d) - (e) Tre Penne, La Fiorita, Lentigione, Correggese, Südtirol, Sambenedettese, Fiorenzuola
*** Chiwisa - Mannah Chiwisa (Mannah Chiwisa Mwewa) (a) 12/12/2003, ¿? (Zambia) (b) - (c) M - pivot (d) - (e) Sammaurese
*** Chizh - Aleksandr Chizh (Чиж Александр Викторович) (a) 10/02/1997, Beryoza (Belarus) (b) 1,85 (c) D - central defense (d) Torpedo-BelAZ Zhodino (e)

Dinamo Minsk, FK Turan, Dinamo Minsk, Dinamo Minsk II, Naftan, Dinamo Minsk II

*** Chizh - Nazar Chizh (Чиж Назар Андреевич) (a) 20/04/2006, ¿? (Belarus) (b) - (c) G (d) Torpedo-BelAZ Zhodino II (e) -

*** Chkhetiani - Giorgi Chkhetiani (გიორგი ჩხეტიანი) (a) 20/02/2003, Tbilisi (Georgia) (b) 1,71 (c) D - left back (d) Dinamo Tbilisi II (e) Dinamo II

*** Chlumecky - Martin Chlumecky (Martin Chlumecký) (a) 11/01/1997, ¿? (Czech Rep.) (b) 1,88 (c) D - central defense (d) TS Podbeskidzie Bielsko-Biala (e) Banik Ostrava, Pardubice, Banik Ostrava, Teplice, Dukla Praha, Jihlava, Dukla Praha, Slovan Liberec, Varnsdorf, Slovan Liberec, Slovan Liberec B

*** Chmyrikov - Oleg Chmyrikov (Чмыриков Олег Александрович) (a) 08/02/1996, Mogilev (Belarus) (b) 1,82 (c) D - left back (d) Sperre (e) Dnepr Mogilev, Svetlogorsk, FK Slutsk, Gomel, Dnepr Mogilev, Gomel, Belshina, Gomel, Gomel II

*** Cho - Mohamed-Ali Cho (a) 19/01/2004, Stains (France) (b) 1,81 (c) F - center forward (d) Real Sociedad (e) Angers SCO

*** Chobanov - Ruslan Chobanov (Чобанов Руслан Заурович) (a) 30/03/2004, ¿? (Russia) (b) 1,80 (c) M - pivot (d) FK Krasnodar-2 (e) Krasnodar II

*** Chobotenko - Sergiy Chobotenko (a) 16/01/1997, Zaporizhya (Ukraine) (b) 1,93 (d) FK Polissya Zhytomyr (e) Kolos Kovalivka, FK Mariupol, Shakhtar II, FK Mariupol, Shakhtar II, Dinamo Kiev II

*** Chochev - Ivaylo Chochev (Ивайло Людмилов Чочев) (a) 18/02/1993, Tranchovitsa, Pleven (Bulgaria) (b) 1,90 (c) M - central midfielder (d) CSKA 1948 (e) Pescara, Palermo, CSKA Sofia, Chavdar

*** Chochishvili - Giorgi Chochishvili (გიორგი ჩოჩიშვილი) (a) 07/05/1998, Tbilisi (Georgia) (b) 1,95 (c) G (d) - (e) Sioni Bolnisi, Merani Tbilisi, FC Telavi, FC Dila, FC Shevardeni, Sioni Bolnisi, Slavia Praha B, Zlaté Moravce, Slavia Praha B, Saburtalo, FC Shevardeni, Saburtalo

*** Choco - Choco (Guilherme de Souza) (a) 18/01/1990, São Paulo (Brazil) (b) 1,73 (c) D - right back (d) Ipatinga FC (e) Riteriai, Kauno Zalgiris, Ludogorets II, Lokomotiv Sofia, Ituano, Juventude, Suduva, Lokomotiv Plovdiv, Montana, Itabaiana, Sampaio Corrêa, APOEL FC, Ludogorets, Santos, RB Brasil, Santos

*** Chodyna - Kacper Chodyna (a) 24/05/1999, Drawsko Pomorskie (Poland) (b) 1,76 (c) F - right winger (d) Zagłębie Lubin (e) Zaglebie Lubin II, Bytovia Bytow, Zaglebie Lubin II, Swiatowid Lobez

*** Chogadze - Temur Chogadze (თემურ ჩოგაძე) (a) 05/05/1998, Batumi (Georgia) (b) 1,77 (c) F - right winger (d) Shakhter Karaganda (e) FC Gagra, FC Telavi, Ingulets, Olimpik Donetsk, Rustavi, Torpedo Kutaisi, Rustavi, Dinamo Batumi, Saburtalo

*** Cholewiak - Mateusz Cholewiak (Mateusz Cholewiak) (a) 05/02/1990, Krosno (Poland) (b) 1,84 (c) F - center forward (d) Puszcza Niepolomice (e) Górnik Zabrze, Legia Warszawa, Śląsk Wroclaw, Stal Mielec, P. Niepolomice, SMS Lodz, UKS SMS Balucz

*** Chopart - Kennie Chopart (Kennie Knak Chopart) (a) 01/06/1990, ¿? (Denmark) (b) - (c) D - right back (d) KR Reykjavík (e) Fjölnir, Arendal, Stjarnan, Varde IF, Esbjerg fB

*** Chorbadzhiyski - Bozhidar Chorbadzhiyski (Божидар Чорбаджийски) (a) 08/08/1995, Sofia (Bulgaria) (b) 1,95 (c) D - central defense (d) Diósgyőri VTK (e) Widzew Lódz, Stal Mielec, CSKA-Sofia, FCSB, CSKA-Sofia

*** Chornomorets - Oleksandr Chornomorets (Чорноморець Олександр Сергійович) (a) 05/04/1993, Zelenodolsk, Dnipropetrovsk Oblast (Ukraine) (b) 1,82

(c) D - left back (d) Kolos Kovalivka (e) Volyn Lutsk, Desna, Dynamo 2 Kyiv, Dinamo Kiev II, Skala Morshyn, BRW-VIK
*** Chory - Tomas Chory (Tomáš Chorý) (a) 26/01/1995, Olomouc (Czech Rep.) (b) 1,99 (c) F - center forward (d) FC Viktoria Plzen (e) Zulte Waregem, Viktoria Plzen, Sigma Olomouc
*** Chotard - Joris Chotard (a) 24/09/2001, Orange (France) (b) 1,79 (c) M - pivot (d) Montpellier HSC (e) Montpellier B
*** Chouaib - Faysal Chouaib (Faysal Chouaib Hassany) (a) 07/01/2000, Barcelona (Spain) (b) - (c) F - left winger (d) UE Santa Coloma (e) Sant Rafel, UE Santa Coloma, CD Badajoz B, AE Prat
*** Chouaref - Ilyas Chouaref (a) 12/12/2000, Châteauroux (France) (b) 1,84 (c) F - left winger (d) FC Sion (e) LB Châteauroux
*** Chouchoumis - Diamantis Chouchoumis (Διαμαντής Χουχούμης) (a) 17/07/1994, Aliveri (Greece) (b) 1,83 (c) D - left back (d) Asteras Tripolis (e) Panetolikos, Apollon Smyrnis, Vojvodina, Slovan Bratislava, Panathinaikos
*** Choudhury - Hamza Choudhury (Hamza Dewan Choudhury) (a) 01/10/1997, Loughborough (England) (b) 1,78 (c) M - pivot (d) Leicester City (e) Watford, Leicester City, Burton Albion, Burton Albion
*** Chouiar - Mounir Chouiar (a) 23/01/1999, Liévin (France) (b) 1,77 (c) F - left winger (d) - (e) Basaksehir, Kasimpasa, Basaksehir, Dijon, Yeni Malatyaspor, Dijon, RC Lens, RC Lens B
*** Choupo-Moting - Eric Maxim Choupo-Moting (Jean-Eric Maxim Choupo-Moting) (a) 23/03/1989, Hamburg (Germany) (b) 1,91 (c) F - center forward (d) Bayern München (e) Paris Saint-Germain, Stoke City, FC Schalke 04, Mainz 05, SV Hamburg, 1.FC Nürnberg, SV Hamburg
*** Choutesiotis - Lefteris Choutesiotis (Λευτέρης Χουτεσιώτης) (a) 20/07/1994, Makrychori (Greece) (b) 1,92 (c) G (d) Aris Thessaloniki (e) Ionikos Nikeas, PAS Giannina, Olympiakos
*** Chovan - Adrian Chovan (Adrián Chovan) (a) 08/10/1995, Partizánske (Slovakia) (b) 1,92 (c) G (d) Panserraikos (e) Slovan Bratislava, Zlaté Moravce, AS Trencin, Zlaté Moravce, AS Trencin, Nove Mesto, AS Trencin, Kanianka
*** Chramosta - Jan Chramosta (Jan Chramosta) (a) 12/10/1990, Praha (Czechoslovakia, now in Czech Rep.) (b) 1,81 (c) F - center forward (d) FK Jablonec (e) Bohemians 1905, Jablonec, Mlada Boleslav, Viktoria Plzen, Mlada Boleslav
*** Chrapek - Michal Chrapek (Michał Łukasz Chrapek) (a) 03/04/1992, Jaworzno (Poland) (b) 1,75 (c) M - attacking midfielder (d) Piast Gliwice (e) Śląsk Wroclaw, Lechia Gdánsk, Catania, Wisla Kraków, Kolejarz Stróże, Wisla Kraków
*** Chrien - Martin Chrien (a) 08/09/1995, Banská Bystrica (Slovakia) (b) 1,91 (c) M - central midfielder (d) MFK Ružomberok (e) Pohronie, Mezőkövesd, Benfica B, Santa Clara, Benfica B, Benfica, Viktoria Plzen, Ružomberok, Viktoria Plzen, Zbrojovka Brno, Viktoria Plzen, Ceske Budejovice, Viktoria Plzen, Banska Bystrica
*** Chrisantus - Macauley Chrisantus (a) 20/08/1990, Abuja (Nigeria) (b) 1,83 (c) F - center forward (d) Lynx FC (e) Aprilia, UD Tamaraceite, FF Jaro, Hetten FC, Zob Ahan, UB Conquense, HJK Helsinki, Real Murcia, PAS Lamia, Reus Deportiu, AEK Athína, Sivasspor, UD Las Palmas, SV Hamburg, FSV Frankfurt, SV Hamburg, Karlsruher SC, SV Hamburg, Hearts of Abuja
*** Chrisene - Ben Chrisene (Benjamin Joshua Chrisene) (a) 12/01/2004, Exeter (England) (b) 1,83 (c) D - left back (d) - (e) Kilmarnock FC
*** Chriso - Chriso (Banhourin Chris Emmanuel Kouakou) (a) 15/12/1999, ¿? (Ivory Coast) (b) 1,75 (c) M - central midfielder (d) CD Mafra (e) Midtjylland, CS Sfaxien

*** Christaki - Antonis Christaki (Αντώνης Χριστάκη) (a) 04/06/2004, Larnaca (Cyprus) (b) - (c) F (d) AEK Larnaca (e) -
*** Christensen - Andreas Christensen (Andreas Bødtker Christensen) (a) 10/04/1996, Lillerød (Denmark) (b) 1,87 (c) D - central defense (d) FC Barcelona (e) Chelsea, Borussia Mönchengladbach, Chelsea, Bröndby IF II
*** Christensen - Gustav Christensen (Gustav Ørsøe Christensen) (a) 07/09/2004, Ikast (Denmark) (b) 1,78 (c) F - left winger (d) Hertha Berlín (e) -
*** Christensen - Jacob Christensen (Jacob Steen Christensen) (a) 25/06/2001, Copenhagen (Denmark) (b) 1,80 (c) M - pivot (d) 1.FC Köln (e) Nordsjælland
*** Christensen - Magnus Christensen (a) 20/08/1997, Frederikshavn (Denmark) (b) 1,82 (c) M - central midfielder (d) FK Haugesund (e) Aalborg BK
*** Christensen - Oliver Christensen (a) 22/03/1999, Kerteminde (Denmark) (b) 1,90 (c) G (d) Fiorentina (e) Hertha Berlin, Odense BK
*** Christensen - Tobias Christensen (a) 11/05/2000, Kristiansand (Norway) (b) 1,79 (c) M - pivot (d) Fehérvár FC (e) Vålerenga, Molde, Start, IK Start II, FK Vigør
*** Christian - Christian (Christian da Silva Fiel) (a) 14/06/1989, Belém do Pará (Brazil) (b) 1,82 (c) M - central midfielder (d) Sabah FK (e) Académica Coimbra, Casa Pia, Feirense, Paços Ferreira, Nacional, Paços Ferreira, CFR Cluj, Nacional, CFR Cluj, Anápolis, APOEL FC, Anápolis, Queimados FC, Castanhal, ASEEV, Goiatuba, Tuna Luso, Carajás, Tuna Luso
*** Christian Joel - Christian Joel (Christian Joel Sánchez Leal) (a) 09/07/1999, La Habana (Cuba) (b) 1,93 (c) G (d) Real Sporting de Gijón (e) Celta B, Real Sporting, AEK Larnaca, Real Sporting, Sporting B
*** Christiansen - Anders Christiansen (Anders Bleg Christiansen) (a) 08/06/1990, Kopenhagen (Denmark) (b) 1,74 (c) M - central midfielder (d) Malmö FF (e) KAA Gent, Malmö FF, Chievo Verona, Nordsjælland, Lyngby BK
*** Christiansen - Rasmus Christiansen (Rasmus Steenberg Christiansen) (a) 06/10/1989, Gribskov (Denmark) (b) 1,85 (c) D - central defense (d) UMF Afturelding (e) Valur, Fjölnir, Valur, KR Reykjavík, Ullensaker/Kisa, ÍBV Vestmannaeyjar, Lyngby BK, ÍBV Vestmannaeyjar, Lyngby BK
*** Christiansen - Sander Christiansen (Sander Johan Christiansen) (a) 29/04/2001, Bergen (Norway) (b) 1,85 (c) M - central midfielder (d) Sarpsborg 08 FF (e) Borussia Mönchengladbach II
*** Christie - Ryan Christie (a) 22/02/1995, Inverness (Scotland) (b) 1,78 (c) M - attacking midfielder (d) AFC Bournemouth (e) Celtic FC, Aberdeen FC, Celtic FC, Aberdeen FC, Celtic FC, Inverness Caledonian, Celtic FC, Inverness Caledonian
*** Christie-Davies - Isaac Christie-Davies (Isaac David Christie-Davies) (a) 18/10/1997, Brighton (England) (b) 1,88 (c) M - attacking midfielder (d) KAS Eupen (e) Barnsley FC, Dunajska Streda, Barnsley FC, Cercle Brugge
*** Christodoulidis - Michalis Christodoulidis (Μιχάλης Χριστοδουλίδης) (a) 09/07/2004, Nicosia (Cyprus) (b) - (c) G (d) UB Purple Knights (University of Bridgeport) (e) -
*** Christodoulis - Georgios Christodoulis (Γεώργιος Χριστοδουλής) (a) 04/01/2001, Katerini (Greece) (b) 1,91 (c) G (d) Ionikos Nikeas (e) Iraklis, Pierikos, Eth. Keramidiou, Pierikos
*** Christodoulopoulos - Lazaros Christodoulopoulos (Λάζαρος Χριστοδουλόπουλος) (a) 19/12/1986, Thessaloniki (Greece) (b) 1,83 (c) M - attacking midfielder (d) Aris Thessaloniki (e) Anorthosis, Atromitos FC, Olympiakos, Hellas Verona, AEK Athína, Hellas Verona, Sampdoria, Hellas Verona, Bologna, Panathinaikos, PAOK

*** Christodoulou - Andreas Christodoulou (Ανδρέας Νικόλας Χριστοδούλου) (a) 26/03/1997, New Jersey (United States) (b) 1,88 (c) G (d) APOEL FC (e) Ethnikos, AEK Larnaca, Omonia Nicosia, Olympiakos N., Orfeas
*** Christodoulou - Michalis Christodoulou (Μιχάλης Χριστοδούλου) (a) 06/03/2000, Agios Athanasios (Cyprus) (b) 1,80 (c) D - left back (d) Nea Salamis (e) Olympiakos N., Akritas Chlor., PAEEK Kyrenia, Akritas Chlor.
*** Christodoulou - Savvas Christodoulou (a) 02/01/2005, ¿? (Cyprus) (b) - (c) M (d) - (e) AEL Limassol
*** Christofi - Alkiviadis Christofi (Αλκιβιάδης "Άλκης" Χριστοφή) (a) 20/01/1992, Limassol (Cyprus) (b) 1,78 (c) D - right back (d) AEZ Zakakiou (e) Karmiotissa, Nea Salamis, Karmiotissa
*** Christofi - Andreas Christofi (Ανδρεάς Χριστοφή) (a) 31/10/1998, Aradippou (Cyprus) (b) 1,82 (c) D - central defense (d) Enosis Neon Paralimniou (e) Omonia Aradippou
*** Christofi - Dimitrios Christofi (Δημήτριος Χριστοφή) (a) 28/09/1988, Sotira (Cyprus) (b) 1,75 (c) F - right winger (d) Ethnikos Achnas (e) Anorthosis, Omonia Nicosia, FC Sion, Omonia Nicosia, EN Paralimniou, Onisillos Sotira
*** Christofi - Martinos Christofi (Μαρτίνος Χριστοφή) (a) 26/07/1993, Limassol (Cyprus) (b) 1,87 (c) D - central defense (d) Olympiakos Nikosia (e) KF Llapi, FC Lahti, Doxa Katokopias, Alki Oroklini, Karmiotissa, Ermis Aradippou, Alki Larnaca, AEL Limassol, Parekklisia, AEL Limassol
*** Christoforou - Giorgos Christoforou (Γιώργος Χριστοφόρου) (a) 05/02/2004, Nicosia (Cyprus) (b) - (c) G (d) - (e) Olympiakos N.
*** Christoforou - Kypros Christoforou (Κύπρος Χριστοφόρου) (a) 24/04/1993, Limassol (Cyprus) (b) 1,80 (c) D - right back (d) Karmiotissa Pano Polemidion (e) AEK Larnaca, Nea Salamis, APOEL FC, Nea Salamis, APOEL FC, Aris Limassol, APOEL FC, Aris Limassol, APOEL FC, Aris Limassol
*** Christogeorgos - Nikolaos Christogeorgos (Νικόλαος Χριστογεώργος) (a) 03/01/2000, Marousi (Greece) (b) 1,93 (c) G (d) OFI Creta (e) Panathinaikos B, Panathinaikos
*** Christopoulos - Efthymios Christopoulos (Ευθύμιος Χριστόπουλος) (a) 20/09/2000, Athina (Greece) (b) 1,81 (c) F - left winger (d) - (e) AEK Athína B, AEK Athína
*** Christopoulos - Giannis Christopoulos (Γιάννης Χριστόπουλος) (a) 22/06/2000, Patra (Greece) (b) 1,91 (c) D - central defense (d) Asteras Tripolis (e) Slaven Belupo, Asteras Tripoli, Doxa Paralias
*** Christopoulos - Ilias Christopoulos (Ηλίας Χριστόπουλος) (a) 02/02/2003, ¿? (Greece) (b) 1,73 (c) D - left back (d) Asteras Tripolis (e) -
*** Christou - Andreas Christou (Ανδρέας Χρίστου) (a) 12/03/1994, Limassol (Cyprus) (b) 1,81 (c) M - pivot (d) AEZ Zakakiou (e) Achyronas FC, Karmiotissa, AEZ Zakakiou, Agia Napa, AEZ Zakakiou, Parekklisia, APEP Pitsilia
*** Chropovsky - Matus Chropovsky (Matúš Chropovský) (a) 03/06/2002, Skalica (Slovakia) (b) 1,93 (c) G (d) ViOn Zlate Moravce-Vrable (e) FK Senica
*** Chrupalla - Pawel Chrupalla (Paweł Chrupałła) (a) 16/03/2003, Szprotawa (Poland) (b) 1,84 (c) D - right back (d) Wisła Płock (e) Rosenborg, Kristiansund, Rosenborg, Rosenborg II, Stjørdals-Blink, Rosenborg II, AP Śląsk
*** Chrysostomou - Andreas Chrysostomou (Ανδρέας Χρυσοστόμου) (a) 14/01/2001, Nicosia (Cyprus) (b) 1,80 (c) M - central midfielder (d) Anorthosis Famagusta (e) -
*** Chrysostomou - Konstantinos Chrysostomou (Κωνσταντίνος Χρυσοστόμου) (a) 07/01/2003, Limassol (Cyprus) (b) 1,82 (c) G (d) Aris Limassol (e) Karmiotissa

*** Chrzanowski - Adam Chrzanowski (Adam Jan Chrzanowski) (a) 31/03/1999, Warszawa (Poland) (b) 1,86 (c) D - central defense (d) Wisła Płock (e) Pordenone, Wisła Płock, Pordenone, Lechia Gdánsk, Miedź Legnica, Lechia Gdánsk, Wigry Suwalki, Lechia Gdánsk, Lechia Gdánsk, Znicz Pruszkow

*** Chubb - Matt Chubb (Matthew Chubb) (a) 31/08/1998, ¿? (Wales) (b) 1,90 (c) D - right back (d) Cardiff Metropolitan University (e) -

*** Chuca - Chuca (Víctor Moya Martínez) (a) 10/06/1997, Jacarilla (Spain) (b) 1,81 (c) M - central midfielder (d) Racing de Ferrol (e) Racing Ferrol, Miedź Legnica, Wisla Kraków, Villarreal CF B, Elche CF, Villarreal CF B, Villarreal CF C

*** Chuev - Bogdan Chuev (Чуєв Богдан Янович) (a) 23/02/2000, Zaporizhya (Ukraine) (b) 1,84 (c) D - central defense (d) FK Minaj (e) Vorskla II, Girnyk-Sport, Vorskla II

*** Chukalov - Georgi Chukalov (Георги Йорданов Чукалов) (a) 25/02/1998, Plovdiv (Bulgaria) (b) 1,83 (c) F - left winger (d) Gigant Saedinenie (e) Spartak Varna, Ludogorets II, Pomorie, Arda Kardzhali, Lokomotiv GO, Lokomotiv Plovdiv

*** Chukhley - Andrey Chukhley (Чухлей Андрей Владимирович) (a) 02/10/1987, Minsk (Soviet Union, now in Belarus) (b) 1,73 (c) M - attacking midfielder (d) FK Ostrovets (e) Slavia, Ararat Yerevan, Dnepr Mogilev, Smolevichi, Jonava, Kauno Zalgiris, Neman Grodno, Vitebsk, FK Minsk, Tyumen, Ural, Dinamo Minsk, Dinamo Minsk II, Darida, Dinamo Minsk II

*** Chukunyere - Isaiah Chukunyere (a) 28/04/2005, ¿? (Malta) (b) - (c) F - right winger (d) - (e) Hibernians FC Valletta,

*** Chukwuani - Tochi Chukwuani (Tochi Phil Chukwuani) (a) 24/03/2003, Hvidovre (Denmark) (b) 1,87 (c) M - central midfielder (d) Lyngby BK (e) Nordsjælland

*** Chukwudi - Samuel Chukwudi (Samuel Johansen Chukwudi) (a) 25/06/2003, ¿? (Faroe Islands) (b) 1,95 (c) D - central defense (d) HB Tórshavn (e) HB Tórshavn II

*** Chukwudi Ndukwe - Samuel Chukwudi Ndukwe (a) 18/04/2002, ¿? (Nigeria) (b) 1,81 (c) F - center forward (d) FC Dinamo-Auto Tiraspol (e) -

*** Chukwuemeka - Carney Chukwuemeka (Carney Chibueze Chukwuemeka) (a) 20/10/2003, Eisenstadt (Austria) (b) 1,87 (c) M - central midfielder (d) Chelsea FC (e) Aston Villa

*** Chukwueze - Samuel Chukwueze (Samuel Chimerenka Chukwueze) (a) 22/05/1999, Umahaia (Nigeria) (b) 1,72 (c) F - right winger (d) AC Milan (e) Villarreal CF, Villarreal CF B

*** Chukwurah - Raphael Chukwurah (Ukwubile Raphael Chukwurah) (a) 17/05/1992, Enugu (Nigeria) (b) 1,77 (c) D - left back (d) Marijampole City (e) FC Telavi, Sioni Bolnisi, Dinamo Batumi, FC Telavi, Dinamo Batumi, FC Telavi, Torpedo Kutaisi, Merani Tbilisi, Rustavi, Merani Tbilisi, Merani Martvili, FK Zugdidi, Chkherimela, FC Alazani, Chkherimela, Merani Martvili, Chkherimela

*** Chul - Danila Chul (Чуль Данила Александрович) (a) 14/02/2005, Pogost-Zagorodskiy (Belarus) (b) - (c) F - center forward (d) Energetik-BGU Minsk II (e) -

*** Chumi - Chumi (Juan Brandáriz Movilla) (a) 02/03/1999, Laracha (Spain) (b) 1,85 (c) D - central defense (d) UD Almería (e) FC Barcelona B

*** Chuperka - Valeriy Chuperka (Чуперка Валерий Николаевич) (a) 12/06/1992, Tiraspol (Moldova) (b) 1,77 (c) M - central midfielder (d) Kuban Krasnodar (e) Rubin Kazan, Kuban, FC Astana, Tambov, Rostov, Baltika, Anzhi, Tom Tomsk, Anzhi, Spartak Nalchik, Krasnodar-2, Krasnodar II, Ac. Chisinau, Krasnodar II, Enisey, Krasnodar II, Ac. Chisinau

*** Churko - Vyacheslav Churko (Чурко Вячеслав Вячеславович, ung. Csurko Vjacseszlav) (a) 10/05/1993, Uzhgorod (Ukraine) (b) 1,80 (c) F - right winger (d)

Zorya Lugansk (e) Kolos Kovalivka, Mezőkövesd, Kolos Kovalivka, Shakhtar Donetsk, Kolos Kovalivka, Shakhtar Donetsk, FK Mariupol, Shakhtar Donetsk, Frosinone, Shakhtar Donetsk, Shakhtar II, Puskás AFC, Shakhtar II, Metalist, Shakhtar II, Illichivets, Shakhtar II, Goverla II, Shakhtar II

*** Churlinov - Darko Churlinov (Дарко Чурлинов) (a) 11/07/2000, Skopje (North Macedonia) (b) 1,80 (c) F - left winger (d) Burnley FC (e) VfB Stuttgart, FC Schalke 04, VfB Stuttgart, 1.FC Köln

*** Churlinov - Kristijan Churlinov (Кристијан Чурлинов) (a) 23/02/2001, Skopje (North Macedonia) (b) 1,73 (c) D - right back (d) Sileks Kratovo (e) FK Skopje

*** Chust - Víctor Chust (Víctor Chust García) (a) 05/03/2000, Valencia (Spain) (b) 1,84 (c) D - central defense (d) Cádiz CF (e) Real Madrid, Cádiz CF, Real Madrid, RM Castilla

*** Chvatal - Juraj Chvatal (Juraj Chvátal) (a) 13/07/1996, Malacky (Slovakia) (b) 1,77 (c) D - right back (d) SK Sigma Olomouc (e) Podbrezova, Sigma Olomouc, Sparta Praha, MSK Zilina, Sparta Praha, Slovácko, Sparta Praha, Slovácko, Sparta Praha, FK Senica

*** Chveja - Ondrej Chveja (Ondřej Chvěja) (a) 17/07/1998, Hlučín (Czech Rep.) (b) 1,85 (c) F - attacking midfielder (d) FC Banik Ostrava (e) 1.SK Prostejov, Banik Ostrava, Pardubice, Banik Ostrava, Karvina, Banik Ostrava, Pohronie, Banik Ostrava, Vitkovice, Banik Ostrava, Frydek-Mistek, Banik Ostrava

*** Chygrynskyi - Dmytro Chygrynskyi (Чигринський Дмитро Анатолійович) (a) 07/11/1986, Iziaslav, Khmelnytskyi Oblast (Soviet Union, now in Ukraine) (b) 1,89 (c) D - central defense (d) Shakhtar Donetsk (e) Ionikos Nikeas, AEK Athína, Dnipro, Shakhtar Donetsk, FC Barcelona, Shakhtar Donetsk, Shakhtar 2, Metalurg Z., Shakhtar 2, UFK Lviv

*** Chyruk - Andriy Chyruk (Чирук Андрій Юрійович) (a) 08/01/2001, Rivne (Ukraine) (b) 1,84 (c) F - center forward (d) Metalist 1925 Kharkiv (e) Shakhtar II

*** Chytil - Mojmir Chytil (Mojmír Chytil) (a) 29/04/1999, Skalka (Czech Rep.) (b) 1,87 (c) F - center forward (d) SK Slavia Praga (e) Sigma Olomouc, Pardubice, Sigma Olomouc, Sigma Olomouc B

*** Ciacci - Elia Ciacci (a) 13/11/2001, ¿? (San Marino) (b) - (c) M - central midfielder (d) AC Virtus Acquaviva (e) -

*** Ciappara - Dylan Ciappara (a) 12/07/2002, ¿? (Malta) (b) 1,81 (c) G (d) Santa Lucia FC (e) Mosta FC

*** Cibelli - Enrico Cibelli (a) 14/07/1987, ¿? (San Marino) (b) 1,78 (c) M - right midfielder (d) SP Tre Penne (e) Libertas, Tre Penne, San Marino

*** Cibi - Fabiano Cibi (Fabiano Duarte Cibi) (a) 22/03/2005, Timişoara (Romania) (b) 1,86 (c) M - pivot (d) CSC Dumbravita (e) Dumbravita, UTA Arad, LPS Banatul

*** Cicaldau - Alexandru Cicaldau (Alexandru Cicâldău) (a) 08/07/1997, Medgidia (Romania) (b) 1,78 (c) M - central midfielder (d) Konyaspor (e) Konyaspor, Galatasaray, Ittihad Kalba, Galatasaray, CS U Craiova, FC Viitorul, Academia Hagi

*** Ciccarelli - Gabriele Ciccarelli (Gabriele Aniello Ciccarelli) (a) 23/02/1994, ¿? (Italy) (b) - (c) M - pivot (d) AC Juvenes-Dogana (e) Verucchio, Sant'Ermete, Miramare

*** Ciccione - Federico Ciccione (a) 03/01/2001, ¿? (Italy) (b) - (c) F - right winger (d) Tre Fiori FC (e) -

*** Cicek - Ibrahim Yilmaz Cicek (İbrahim Yılmaz Çiçek) (a) 17/09/2006, Sanliurfa (Turkey) (b) - (c) M - central midfielder (d) - (e) MKE Ankaragücü

*** Cichocki - Mateusz Cichocki (a) 31/01/1992, Warszawa (Poland) (b) 1,87 (c) D - central defense (d) Radomiak Radom (e) Z. Sosnowiec, Ruch, Legia Warszawa,

Dolcan Zabki, Legia Warszawa, Arka Gdynia, Legia Warszawa, Dolcan Zabki, Legia Warszawa, Legia II

*** Cicinho - Cicinho (Neuciano de Jesus Gusmão) (a) 26/12/1988, Belém (Brazil) (b) 1,68 (c) D - right back (d) Esporte Clube Bahia (e) Ludogorets, Santos, Ponte Preta, Brasiliense, Juventude, Remo

*** Cicovsky - Adam Cicovsky (Adam Čičovský) (a) 08/12/2002, Ústí nad Labem (Czech Rep.) (b) 1,70 (c) M - attacking midfielder (d) FK Viagem Usti nad Labem (e) Teplice, Usti nad Labem, Usti nad L. Jdg

*** Cielemecki - Radoslaw Cielemecki (Radosław Cielemęcki) (a) 19/02/2003, Świebodzice (Poland) (b) 1,73 (c) M - attacking midfielder (d) Wisła Płock (e) Legia II

*** Ciepiela - Bartlomiej Ciepiela (Bartłomiej Ciepiela) (a) 24/05/2001, Tarnów (Poland) (b) 1,82 (c) M - attacking midfielder (d) Resovia Rzeszów (e) Resovia, Legia Warszawa, Stal Mielec, Legia Warszawa, Legia II, Stalowa Wola, Legia II

*** Cierpka - Adrian Cierpka (a) 06/01/1995, Ostrów Wielkopolski (Poland) (b) 1,84 (c) M - central midfielder (d) KKS 1925 Kalisz (e) Concordia, CS Mioveni, Gornik Leczna, Warta Poznań, Miedź Legnica, Wisla Pulawy, Miedź Legnica, Lech Poznan II

*** Cieslewicz - Adrian Cieslewicz (Adrian Cieślewicz) (a) 16/11/1990, Gniezno (Poland) (b) 1,77 (c) F - right winger (d) The New Saints (e) B36 Tórshavn, Kidderminster Harriers, Wrexham

*** Cieslewicz - Lukasz Cieslewicz (Łukasz Cieślewicz) (a) 15/11/1987, Gniezno (Poland) (b) 1,82 (c) M - attacking midfielder (d) Adrian Cieslewicz (e) B68 Toftir, Víkingur, B36 Tórshavn, Hvidovre, Bröndby IF II, Hvidovre, Bröndby IF II

*** Ciezkowski - Dorian Ciezkowski (Dorian Jerzy Ciężkowski) (a) 22/03/2001, Kraków (Poland) (b) 1,92 (c) G (d) - (e) Cremonese, Taranto

*** Cifci - Dogac Cifci (Mehmet Doğaç Çifçi) (a) 24/02/2003, Giresun (Turkey) (b) 1,86 (c) G (d) Giresunspor (e) -

*** Ciftci - Ugur Ciftci (Uğur Çiftçi) (a) 04/05/1992, Sivas (Turkey) (b) 1,79 (c) D - left back (d) Sivasspor (e) Genclerbirligi, Hacettepe

*** Ciftpinar - Sadik Ciftpinar (Sadık Çiftpınar) (a) 01/01/1993, Adana (Turkey) (b) 1,83 (c) D - central defense (d) Kasimpasa (e) Yeni Malatyaspor, Fenerbahce, Yeni Malatyaspor, T. Akcaabat

*** Cifuentes - Daniel Cifuentes (Juan Daniel Cifuentes Vergara) (a) 21/04/1999, Yumbo (Colombia) (b) 1,80 (c) D - central defense (d) FC Van (e) Racing Club

*** Ciganiks - Andrejs Ciganiks (Andrejs Cigaņiks) (a) 12/04/1997, Riga (Latvia) (b) 1,73 (c) D - left back (d) RTS Widzew Łódź (e) Dunajska Streda, Zorya Lugansk, RFS, SC Cambuur, Schalke 04 II, Bayer Leverkusen, Viktoria Köln, Bayer Leverkusen, Skonto II

*** Cigerci - Tolga Cigerci (Tolga Ciğerci) (a) 23/03/1992, Nordenham (Germany) (b) 1,85 (c) M - pivot (d) MKE Ankaragücü (e) Hertha Berlin, Ankaragücü, Basaksehir, Fenerbahce, Galatasaray, Hertha Berlin, VfL Wolfsburg, Hertha Berlin, VfL Wolfsburg, Borussia Mönchengladbach, VfL Wolfsburg

*** Cihak - Adam Cihak (Adam Čihák) (a) 13/04/1995, ¿? (Czech Rep.) (b) - (c) D - central defense (d) FC Viktoria Plzen B (e) Banik Sokolov, Viktoria Plzen B, Banik Sokolov, Viktoria Plzen B, FC Rokycany, Viktoria Plzen B, SK Doubravka

*** Cihak - Filip Cihak (Filip Čihák) (a) 10/07/1999, Plzeň (Czech Rep.) (b) 1,90 (c) D - central defense (d) FC Viktoria Plzen (e) Hradec Kralove, Viktoria Plzen, Pardubice, Viktoria Plzen B, Pardubice, Viktoria Plzen B, Domazlice, Viktoria Plzen B

*** Cihan - Mirza Cihan (a) 26/10/2000, Denizli (Turkey) (b) 1,75 (c) F - left winger (d) Gaziantep FK (e) Istanbulspor, Gaziantep FK

*** Cijntje - Jeremy Cijntje (a) 08/01/1998, Dordrecht (Netherlands) (b) 1,83 (c) F - left winger (d) FK Jerv (e) Heracles Almelo, FC Den Bosch, Heracles Almelo, Roda JC, Heracles Almelo, Waasland-Beveren, Heracles Almelo, FC Dordrecht

*** Cikalleshi - Sokol Cikalleshi (Sokol Çikalleshi) (a) 27/07/1990, Kavajë (Albania) (b) 1,87 (c) F - center forward (d) Konyaspor (e) Khaleej, Konyaspor, Akhisarspor, Osmanlispor, Göztepe, Osmanlispor, Basaksehir, Akhisar Belediye, Basaksehir, RNK Split, FK Kukësi, KS Besa, Incheon Utd., KS Besa, KF Tirana, KS Besa, KF Skënderbeu, KS Besa

*** Cikani - Dionis Cikani (a) 10/03/1999, Athina (Greece) (b) 1,75 (c) F - center forward (d) - (e) KF Drenica, KS Besa, KF Tirana B, Torre Levante, Int. Tiranë, O. Tirana

*** Cikarski - Mite Cikarski (Мите Цикарски) (a) 06/01/1993, Strumica (North Macedonia) (b) 1,75 (c) D - left back (d) - (e) AP Brera, Botev Plovdiv, AP Brera, Gaz Metan, PAS Giannina, Ethnikos, Rabotnicki, Vardar

*** Cillessen - Jasper Cillessen (Jacobus Antonius Peter Cillessen) (a) 22/04/1989, Nijmegen (Netherlands) (b) 1,87 (c) G (d) NEC Nijmegen (e) Valencia CF, FC Barcelona, Ajax, NEC Nijmegen

*** Cimignani - Yanis Cimignani (a) 22/01/2002, Lyon (France) (b) 1,76 (c) M - left midfielder (d) FC Lugano (e) AC Ajaccio, AC Ajaccio B

*** Cimirot - Gojko Cimirot (a) 19/12/1992, Trebinje (Bosnia and Herzegovina) (b) 1,78 (c) M - pivot (d) Al-Fayha FC (e) Standard Liège, PAOK, FK Sarajevo, Leotar Trebinje

*** Cimpanu - George Cimpanu (George Alexandru Cîmpanu) (a) 08/10/2000, Bucuresti (Romania) (b) 1,78 (c) F - right winger (d) Universitatea Craiova (e) FC Botosani

*** Cinajevs - Daniils Cinajevs (Daņiils Čiņajevs) (a) 03/07/2003, ¿? (Latvia) (b) - (c) M - central midfielder (d) FK Metta (e) Skanste

*** Cinar - Anil Yigit Cinar (Anıl Yiğit Çınar) (a) 10/07/2003, Istanbul (Turkey) (b) 1,93 (c) D - central defense (d) Giresunspor (e) Eynesil Belediye, Giresunspor

*** Cinari - Eraldo Cinari (Eraldo Çinari) (a) 11/10/1996, Shkodër (Albania) (b) 1,82 (c) F - right winger (d) Shkëndija Tetovo (e) Samsunspor, FK Partizani, KF Vllaznia

*** Cini - Alex Cini (a) 28/10/1991, ¿? (Malta) (b) 1,79 (c) D - right back (d) Sirens FC (e) Floriana, Mosta FC, Floriana, Mosta FC, Pembroke, Mosta FC, Tarxien, Mosta FC

*** Cini - Reeves Cini (a) 14/01/2002, ¿? (Malta) (b) - (c) G (d) Valletta FC (e) Pietà Hotspurs, Valletta, Sirens FC, Valletta

*** Cinkaya - Kaan Cinkaya (Kaan Çinkaya) (a) 06/01/2004, Amasya (Turkey) (b) 1,90 (c) G (d) - (e) Ankaragücü

*** Cinotti - Francesco Cinotti (a) 14/04/1986, Fano (Italy) (b) - (c) F - center forward (d) ASD K-Sport Montecchio (e) Gabicce Gradara, FC Senigallia, Atletico Alma, Mondolfo, Pergolese, Tolentino, Fossombrone, Pergolese, Fano

*** Cintas - Antonio Cintas (Antonio Cintas Sánchez) (a) 11/05/1995, San Roque (Spain) (b) - (c) M - attacking midfielder (d) Lions Gibraltar FC (e) Lions Gibraltar, San Roque Cádiz, Cádiz CF B, San Roque Cádiz

*** Cintas - Marc Cintas (Marc Cintas Sánchez) (a) 07/04/2002, Terrassa (Spain) (b) 1,70 (c) M - attacking midfielder (d) - (e) FC Santa Coloma, UE Santa Coloma

*** Cioban - Mihail Cioban (a) 03/02/2001, ¿? (Moldova) (b) 1,88 (c) G (d) FC Milsami Orhei (e) Sheriff-2

*** Ciobanu - Andrei Ciobanu (Andrei Virgil Ciobanu) (a) 18/01/1998, Bârlad (Romania) (b) 1,76 (c) M - central midfielder (d) ACSM Politehnica Iasi (e) ACSM Poli Iasi, FC Rapid 1923, FCV Farul, Academia Hagi
*** Ciobanu - Luca Ciobanu (a) 01/01/2006, ¿? (Romania) (b) 1,83 (c) D - central defense (d) FCSB II (e) -
*** Ciobanu-Vanghele - Marius Ciobanu-Vanghele (Marius Florian Ciobanu-Vanghele) (a) 31/03/2003, Bucuresti (Romania) (b) - (c) F - right winger (d) FC U Craiova 1948 (e) Unirea Slobozia, Universitatea Cluj, Academica Clinceni, Unirea Slobozia, Academica Clinceni, FCSB II
*** Ciobotariu - Denis Ciobotariu (a) 10/06/1998, Bucuresti (Romania) (b) 1,85 (c) D - central defense (d) Sepsi OSK Sf. Gheorghe (e) CFR Cluj, FC Voluntari, CFR Cluj, FC Dinamo, Chindia, Dinamo II
*** Ciofani - Daniel Ciofani (a) 31/07/1985, Avezzano (Italy) (b) 1,91 (c) F - center forward (d) US Cremonese (e) Frosinone, Parma, Perugia, Parma, AS Gubbio, Parma, Atletico Roma, Gela, Pescara, Celano, Pescara
*** Cioiu - Marius Cioiu (Marius Iulian Cioiu) (a) 01/11/1999, Târgu Jiu (Romania) (b) - (c) F - right winger (d) FC Botosani (e) Petrolul, Academica Clinceni, Viitorul Tîrgu Jiu, Luceafarul, Şirineasa, Pandurii
*** Ciolacu - Andrei Ciolacu (Andrei Cosmin Ciolacu) (a) 09/08/1992, Bucuresti (Romania) (b) 1,85 (c) F - center forward (d) Birkirkara FC (e) Floriana, FC U Craiova, Avezzano, Tskhinvali, Metaloglobus, Daco-Getica, Warriors FC, ASA Tg. Mures, Slask Wroclaw II, Śląsk Wroclaw, Rapid Bucureşti, CS Otopeni, Rapid Bucureşti, Rapid 1923 II
*** Ciopa - Alexei Ciopa (a) 27/10/1998, Chişinău (Moldova) (b) 1,88 (c) D - central defense (d) - (e) Zimbru Chisinau, FC Noah, Zimbru Chisinau
*** Cipetic - Branimir Cipetic (Branimir Cipetić) (a) 24/05/1995, Split (Croatia) (b) 1,84 (c) D - right back (d) Kisvárda FC (e) NK Lokomotiva, Siroki Brijeg, CD Vitoria, Elche Ilicitano, CD Torrevieja
*** Cipf - Dominik Cipf (a) 31/01/2001, Kisvárda (Hungary) (b) 1,80 (c) F - left winger (d) Tiszakécskei LC (e) Vasas FC, BFC Siófok, Honvéd, BFC Siófok, Honvéd
*** Cipot - Kai Cipot (a) 28/04/2001, Murska Sobota (Slovenia) (b) 1,87 (c) D - central defense (d) NS Mura (e) -
*** Cipot - Tio Cipot (a) 20/04/2003, Murska Sobota (Slovenia) (b) 1,84 (c) M - central midfielder (d) Spezia (e) NS Mura
*** Cipri - Cipri (José Antonio Ojeda Delgado) (a) 01/01/2000, San Roque (Spain) (b) - (c) F - right winger (d) Europa FC (e) Linense B, Guadiaro, Guadiaro
*** Cipriott - Sean Cipriott (a) 10/09/1997, ¿? (Malta) (b) - (c) M - central midfielder (d) Gudja United FC (e) Sirens FC, Balzan FC, Senglea Ath., Balzan FC, Tarxien, Balzan FC
*** Ciranni - Alessandro Ciranni (a) 28/06/1996, Genk (Belgium) (b) 1,72 (c) D - right back (d) SV Zulte Waregem (e) Excelsior Mouscron, Fortuna Sittard, MVV Maastricht, MVV Maastricht
*** Ciriaco - Alex Ciriaco (Alex Manuel Ciriaco Somero) (a) 21/03/2004, ¿? (Dominican Rep.) (b) 1,80 (c) D - central defense (d) Ilves Tampere II (e) -
*** Cirjak - Frane Cirjak (Frane Čirjak) (a) 23/06/1995, Zadar (Croatia) (b) 1,80 (c) M - central midfielder (d) FK Novi Pazar (e) FK Sarajevo, Lokomotiv Sofia, PFK Lviv, Zrinjski Mostar, NK Zagreb, FC Luzern, NK Zadar
*** Cirjan - Catalin Cirjan (Cătălin Ionuţ Cîrjan) (a) 01/12/2002, Domneşti (Romania) (b) - (c) M - central midfielder (d) FC Rapid 1923 (e) FC Rapid 1923, V. Domnesti

*** Cirkovic - Aleksandar Cirkovic (Александар Ђирковић) (a) 21/09/2001, Smederevska Palanka (RF Yugoslavia, now in Serbia) (b) 1,80 (c) F - left winger (d) FK TSC Backa Topola (e) FK TSC, KS Samara, Vozdovac, Gimnàstic, Admira Wacker, Macva, Admira Wacker, FC Admira II
*** Cirkovic - Lazar Cirkovic (Лазар Ђирковић) (a) 22/08/1992, Niš (RF Yugoslavia, now in Serbia) (b) 1,92 (c) D - central defense (d) - (e) Honvéd, Kisvárda, Maccabi Netanya, FC Luzern, FK Partizan, Rad Beograd, FK Palic Koming, Rad Beograd
*** Cirkovic - Nikola Cirkovic (Никола Ђирковић) (a) 04/12/1991, Priboj (Yugoslavia, now in Serbia) (b) 1,88 (c) D - right back (d) FK Mladost Lucani (e) SC Kfar Qasem, Bnei Sakhnin, Čukarički, Vozdovac, FK Minsk, Metalac, Borac Cacak
*** Cirulis - Jegors Cirulis (Jegors Cīrulis) (a) 31/07/2003, ¿? (Latvia) (b) - (c) D - left back (d) SK Super Nova (e) AFA Olaine, Super Nova
*** Ciss - Amadou Ciss (a) 10/04/1999, Guédiawaye (Senegal) (b) 1,86 (c) F - left winger (d) Amiens SC (e) AEL Limassol, Amiens SC, Adanaspor, Amiens SC, Fortuna Sittard, Pau FC, Teungueth FC
*** Ciss - Pathé Ciss (Pathé Ismaël Ciss) (a) 16/03/1994, Dakar (Senegal) (b) 1,86 (c) M - central midfielder (d) Rayo Vallecano (e) CF Fuenlabrada, União Madeira, CF Fuenlabrada, União Madeira, Famalicão, União Madeira, Diambars FC
*** Cisse - Namory Cisse (Namory Noel Cisse) (a) 05/01/2003, ¿? (Austria) (b) 1,92 (c) F - center forward (d) SC Austria Lustenau (e) -
*** Cisse - Vally Cisse (a) 15/05/1999, Divo (Ivory Coast) (b) 1,79 (c) F - center forward (d) Shirak Gyumri C.F. (e) Xerez CD, L'Entregu CF, Pobla de Mafumet CF, LFA
*** Cissé - Ibrahim Cissé (a) 06/12/2003, ¿? (Ivory Coast) (b) - (c) D - central defense (d) SJK Seinäjoki II (e) Lillestrøm
*** Cissé - Ibrahima Cissé (a) 15/02/2001, Dreux (France) (b) 1,96 (c) D - central defense (d) FC Schalke 04 (e) Jong KAA Gent, Châteauroux B
*** Cissé - Ibrahima Cissé (a) 28/02/1994, Liège (Belgium) (b) 1,84 (c) M - pivot (d) Ural Ekaterimburgo (e) RFC Seraing, Fulham, Standard Liège, KV Mechelen, Standard Liège
*** Cissé - Jonathan Cissé (a) 18/05/1997, Divo (Ivory Coast) (b) 1,95 (c) D - central defense (d) - (e) Hapoel Hadera, AS Monaco B
*** Cissé - Pape Abou Cissé (a) 14/09/1995, Pikine (Senegal) (b) 1,98 (c) D - central defense (d) Olympiakos El Pireo (e) St.-Étienne, Olympiakos, AC Ajaccio, AS Pikine
*** Cissé - Salif Cissé (a) 12/07/1992, Dreux (France) (b) 1,87 (c) F - center forward (d) - (e) Kapaz PFK, Hegelmann, Botev Plovdiv, Tsarsko Selo, US Granville, Athl. Marseille, ASM Belfort, DC Motema Pembe, Luçon VF, Limoges FC, FC Le Mans B
*** Cissé - Souleymane Cissé (a) 08/08/2002, ¿? (France) (b) 1,90 (c) D - central defense (d) Dijon FCO (e) Clermont Foot, RC Lens B
*** Cissoko - Ibrahim Cissoko (a) 26/03/2003, Nijmegen (Netherlands) (b) - (c) F - left winger (d) Toulouse FC (e) NEC Nijmegen
*** Cissoko - Ibrahima Cissoko (a) 18/04/2003, Leona-Thiaroye (Senegal) (b) 1,78 (c) M - central midfielder (d) US Gorée (e) Haugesund, US Gorée
*** Cisteró - Aleix Cisteró (Aleix Cisteró Serna) (a) 25/06/1994, Lleida (Spain) (b) - (c) D - left back (d) Atlètic Club d'Escaldes (e) FC Santa Coloma, FC Andorra
*** Ciuciulete - Radu Ciuciulete (Radu Andrei Ciuciulete) (a) 09/12/2003, Bucuresti (Romania) (b) 1,89 (c) D - central defense (d) - (e) FC D. Coman, FC D. Coman, FC D. Coman, FC D. Coman

*** Ciucka - Jan Ciucka (Jan Ciućka) (a) 19/06/2003, Żywiec (Poland) (b) 1,81 (c) F - center forward (d) Skra Czestochowa (e) Skra Czestochowa, Górnik Zabrze, Gornik Polk., Górnik Zabrze, Rekord B-B

*** Ciurria - Patrick Ciurria (a) 09/02/1995, Sassuolo (Italy) (b) 1,78 (c) F - right winger (d) AC Monza (e) Pordenone, Spezia, Robur Siena, Spezia, Südtirol, Spezia, Castellarano

*** Civelek - Ramazan Civelek (a) 22/01/1996, Istanbul (Turkey) (b) 1,71 (c) F - right winger (d) Kayserispor (e) Karagümrük, Sakaryaspor, Gaziantep BB

*** Civic - Eldar Civic (Eldar Ćivić) (a) 28/05/1996, Tuzla (Bosnia and Herzegovina) (b) 1,82 (c) D - left back (d) Ferencváros TC (e) Sparta Praha, Spartak Trnava, Sparta Praha, Slovácko

*** Civic - Muharem Civic (Čivić Muharem) (a) 04/01/1993, Tuzla (Bosnia and Herzegovina) (b) 1,85 (c) D - left back (d) FK Sloboda Tuzla (e) FK Krupa, Velez Mostar, Sloboda Tuzla, Zvijezda G., Travnik, Sloga Tojsici, Travnik, Taborsko B, FC MAS Taborsko, Sloboda Tuzla

*** Ciz - Adam Ciz (Adam Číž) (a) 16/05/2003, ¿? (Czech Rep.) (b) - (c) M (d) FC Zlin B (e) -

*** Claesson - Viktor Claesson (Viktor Johan Anton Claesson) (a) 02/01/1992, Värnamo (Sweden) (b) 1,83 (c) M - central midfielder (d) FC Copenhague (e) Krasnodar, Elfsborg, Värnamo

*** Clancy - Éanna Clancy (a) 26/02/2004, Glenfarne, Leitrim (Ireland) (b) 1,85 (c) D - central defense (d) University College Dublin (e) Sligo Rovers

*** Clark - Ben Clark (a) 14/10/2000, Chester (England) (b) - (c) M - central midfielder (d) The New Saints (e) Caernarfon, The New Saints, Llandudno, The New Saints, TNS Development

*** Clark - Caden Clark (Caden Christopher Clark) (a) 27/05/2003, Medina, Minnesota (United States) (b) 1,80 (c) M - attacking midfielder (d) RB Leipzig (e) New York, RB Leipzig, New York, RB Leipzig, New York, NY Red Bulls II, Minnesota Thunder

*** Clark - Ciaran Clark (a) 26/09/1989, Harrow (England) (b) 1,85 (c) D - central defense (d) - (e) Newcastle Utd., Sheffield Utd., Newcastle Utd., Aston Villa, Aston Villa Reserves

*** Clark - Dan Clark (a) 11/02/2004, ¿? (England) (b) - (c) G (d) - (e) Bala

*** Clark - Nicky Clark (Nicholas Clark) (a) 03/06/1991, Bellshill (Scotland) (b) 1,78 (c) F - center forward (d) St. Johnstone FC (e) Dundee United, Dunfermline A., Bury, Rangers FC, Queen of the South, Peterhead FC

*** Clark - Zander Clark (a) 26/06/1992, Glasgow (Scotland) (b) 1,91 (c) G (d) Heart of Midlothian FC (e) St. Johnstone, Queen of the South, St. Johnstone, Queen of the South, St. Johnstone, Elgin City, St. Johnstone

*** Clarke - Andrew Clarke (a) 12/12/2002, ¿? (Northern Ireland) (b) 1,88 (c) M - central midfielder (d) Linfield FC (e) -

*** Clarke - Brendan Clarke (a) 17/09/1985, Dublin (Ireland) (b) 1,85 (c) G (d) Galway United FC (e) Shelbourne, St. Patrick's Ath., Limerick FC, St. Patrick's Ath., Sligo Rovers, Sporting Fingal, St. Patrick's Ath., Sporting Fingal, St. Patrick's Ath., Cherry Orchard FC

*** Clarke - James Clarke (a) 28/01/2001, ¿? (Ireland) (b) 1,86 (c) M - central midfielder (d) Bohemian FC (e) Drogheda United

*** Clarke - Jamie Clarke (a) 18/06/1989, ¿? (Northern Ireland) (b) - (c) F - left winger (d) - (e) Newry City, Crossmaglen

*** Clarke - Matthew Clarke (a) 03/03/1994, Castlederg (Northern Ireland) (b) - (c) D - left back (d) Linfield FC (e) -

*** Clarke - Nathan Clarke (a) 04/03/2002, ¿? (Northern Ireland) (b) - (c) D (d) Newington FC (e) -

*** Clarke - Ross Clarke (a) 17/05/1993, Kircubbin (Northern Ireland) (b) - (c) F - right winger (d) Crusaders FC (e) Linfield, Ards FC, Linfield

*** Clarke - Zack Clarke (a) 25/01/2003, ¿? (Wales) (b) - (c) F - center forward (d) Caernarfon Town (e) Chester, Flint Town, Chester, Runcorn Linnets, Caernarfon, Chester, Atherton Collieries, Chester, Atherton Collieries, Chester, Clitheroe, Chester, Leek Town FC, Chester

*** Clarkson - Leighton Clarkson (Leighton Owen Clarkson) (a) 19/10/2001, Clitheroe (England) (b) - (c) M - pivot (d) Aberdeen FC (e) Aberdeen FC, Blackburn

*** Clasie - Jordy Clasie (a) 27/06/1991, Haarlem (Netherlands) (b) 1,69 (c) M - pivot (d) AZ Alkmaar (e) Southampton, Feyenoord, Southampton, KV Brugge, Southampton, Feyenoord, Excelsior, Feyenoord

*** Claude-Maurice - Alexis Claude-Maurice (a) 06/06/1998, Noisy-le-Grand (France) (b) 1,75 (c) M - attacking midfielder (d) OGC Niza (e) RC Lens, OGC Nice, FC Lorient, Lorient B

*** Claudemir - Claudemir (Claudemir Domingues de Souza) (a) 27/03/1988, Macaúbas (Brazil) (b) 1,85 (c) M - pivot (d) - (e) Vizela, Sivasspor, SC Braga, Al-Ahli, KV Brugge, FC København, Vitesse

*** Claudinho - Claudinho (Cláudio Luiz Rodrigues Parise Leonel) (a) 28/01/1997, Guarulhos (Brazil) (b) 1,70 (c) M - attacking midfielder (d) Zenit de San Petersburgo (e) RB Bragantino, Ponte Preta, RB Bragantino, Ponte Preta, RB Brasil, Ponte Preta, Oeste, Ponte Preta, RB Brasil, Ponte Preta, Corinthians B, Corinthians, Bragantino, Corinthians, Corinthians B

*** Cláudio Murici - Cláudio Murici (Cláudio Henrique da Silva Barboza) (a) 13/05/1998, Murici (AL) (Brazil) (b) 1,64 (c) F - right winger (d) Hamrun Spartans (e) Ghajnsielem, Zejtun C., América-RN, Treze, América-RN, Força e Luz, América-RN, Globo, América-RN

*** Clauss - Jonathan Clauss (a) 25/09/1992, Strasbourg (France) (b) 1,78 (c) D - right back (d) Olympique Marseille (e) RC Lens, Arminia Bielefeld, Quevilly Rouen, US Avranches, US Raon-l'Étape, SV Linx, Vauban S.

*** Clayton - Clayton (Clayton Fernandes Silva) (a) 11/01/1999, Belo Horizonte (Brazil) (b) 1,84 (c) F - center forward (d) Casa Pia AC (e) Vila Nova FC, Coritiba FC, Vila Nova FC, Globo, Guarany Sobral, EC Juventude B

*** Cleary - Dan Cleary (Daniel Cleary) (a) 09/03/1996, Dublin (Ireland) (b) 1,82 (c) D - central defense (d) Shamrock Rovers (e) St. Johnstone, Dundalk FC, Solihull Moors

*** Clem - William Clem (a) 20/06/2004, Vedbæk (Denmark) (b) - (c) M - pivot (d) FC Copenhague (e) -

*** Clemens - Christian Clemens (a) 04/08/1991, Köln (Germany) (b) 1,80 (c) F - right winger (d) 1.FC Düren (e) Lechia Gdánsk, Darmstadt 98, 1.FC Köln, Mainz 05, FC Schalke 04, Mainz 05, FC Schalke 04, 1.FC Köln, 1.FC Köln II

*** Clement - Pelle Clement (a) 19/05/1996, Amsterdam (Netherlands) (b) 1,77 (c) M - central midfielder (d) Sparta Rotterdam (e) RKC Waalwijk, PEC Zwolle, Reading, Ajax B

*** Clemente - Eneko Clemente (Eneko Agegnehu Clemente Galíndez) (a) 24/09/2003, Addis Abeba (Ethiopia) (b) 1,71 (c) F - left winger (d) Casalarreina CF (e) Penya Encarnada, Oregon State

*** Clemente - Ludovic Clemente (a) 09/06/1987, Andorra la Vella (Andorra) (b) 1,71 (d) UE Santa Coloma (e) IC d'Escaldes, FC Andorra, Manresa, FC Andorra

*** Clemente - Matheus Clemente (Matheus dos Santos Clemente) (a) 10/06/1998, Fronteira (Brazil) (b) 1,82 (c) M - central midfielder (d) FK Auda (e) Akritas Chlor., Cherno More, Felgueiras, Olhanense, ARS Martinho, Paços F. B
*** Clementsen - Esmar Clementsen (Esmar Petur Clementsen) (a) 29/09/1996, ¿? (Faroe Islands) (b) - (c) M - right midfielder (d) B68 Toftir II (e) B68 Toftir, B68 Toftir II
*** Clementsen - Karstin Clementsen (a) 12/09/2001, ¿? (Faroe Islands) (b) - (c) M - right midfielder (d) B68 Toftir (e) -
*** Clenahan - Matt Clenahan (Matthew David Clenahan) (a) 11/02/1996, Barnstaple (England) (b) 1,98 (c) D - central defense (d) FC Manchester 62 (e) Leo FC, Buckland
*** Cleonise - Denilho Cleonise (Denilson Edilson Cleonise Denliho) (a) 08/12/2001, Amsterdam (Netherlands) (b) 1,79 (c) F - right winger (d) RKC Waalwijk (e) FC Twente
*** Clerc - Carlos Clerc (Carlos Clerc Martínez) (a) 21/02/1992, Badalona (Spain) (b) 1,81 (c) D - left back (d) Elche CF (e) Levante UD, CA Osasuna, RCD Espanyol, Girona FC, RCD Espanyol, CE Sabadell, RCD Espanyol, CE Sabadell, RCD Espanyol B
*** Clescenco - Nicky Clescenco (Nicky Serghei Cleşcenco) (a) 23/07/2001, Dublin (Ireland) (b) 1,78 (c) F - left winger (d) FC Petrocub Hîncești (e) Petrocub, Leiria
*** Clichy - Gaël Clichy (Gaël Dimitri Clichy) (a) 26/07/1985, Toulouse (France) (b) 1,76 (c) D - left back (d) - (e) Servette FC, Basaksehir, Manchester City, Arsenal, Cannes
*** Clinton - Kyle Clinton (a) 18/03/2004, Gibraltar (Gibraltar) (b) - (c) M - left midfielder (d) Lincoln Red Imps FC (e) Red Imps Reserves
*** Clinton - Leon Clinton (a) 19/07/1998, Gibraltar (Gibraltar) (b) 1,70 (c) M - attacking midfielder (d) Mons Calpe SC (e) Glacis United, Europa FC, Boca Gibraltar, St Joseph's FC, Lincoln FC, Lynx FC, Lincoln FC
*** Clucas - Seanan Clucas (Martin Seanan Clucas) (a) 08/11/1992, Dungannon (Northern Ireland) (b) 1,78 (c) M - central midfielder (d) Glentoran FC (e) Dungannon, Derry City, Linfield, Bristol Rovers, Preston North End, Burton Albion, Preston North End
*** Clutton - Lewis Clutton (Lewis David Clutton) (a) 31/08/2001, ¿? (Wales) (b) 1,72 (c) M - central midfielder (d) Loyola Greyhounds (Loyola University Maryland) (e) Penybont, Salisbury
*** Clyne - Nathaniel Clyne (Nathaniel Edwin Clyne) (a) 05/04/1991, Stockwell, London (England) (b) 1,75 (c) D - right back (d) Crystal Palace (e) Liverpool, Bournemouth, Liverpool, Southampton, Crystal Palace
*** Cmelik - Lukas Cmelik (Lukáš Čmelík) (a) 13/04/1996, Žilina (Slovakia) (b) 1,84 (c) F - right winger (d) SK Dynamo Ceske Budejovice (e) Karvina, Ceske Budejovice, Karvina, Dunajska Streda, MSK Zilina, Piast Gliwice, MSK Zilina
*** Cmiljanic - Boris Cmiljanic (Boris Cmiljanić) (a) 17/03/1996, Podgorica (Yugoslavia, now in Montenegro) (b) 1,93 (c) F - center forward (d) Qyzyljar Petropavlovsk (e) FK Decic Tuzi, FK Sarajevo, Slovan Bratislava, Zlaté Moravce, Slovan Bratislava, Admira Wacker, Slovan Bratislava, SD Huesca, At. Levante, SD Huesca, Buducnost Podgorica
*** Cmiljanovic - Mihailo Cmiljanovic (Михаило Цмиљановић) (a) 15/06/1994, Prijepolje (RF Yugoslavia, now in Serbia) (b) 1,80 (c) D - left back (d) FK Leotar Trebinje (e) Bardejov, 1.FK Pribram, Tatran Presov, Kolubara, Vikt. Griesheim, FK Polimlje, Alem. Haibach, Sloga Kraljevo, FK Polimlje, Sloga Kraljevo

*** Coady - Conor Coady (Conor David Coady) (a) 25/02/1993, Liverpool (England) (b) 1,85 (c) D - central defense (d) Leicester City (e) Wolverhampton Wanderers, Everton, Wolverhampton Wanderers, Huddersfield Town, Sheffield Utd.

*** Coates - Colin Coates (a) 26/10/1985, Belfast (Northern Ireland) (b) 1,85 (c) D - central defense (d) Ballymena United (e) Cliftonville, Glenavon, Crusaders

*** Coba - Mehdi Coba (Mehdi Çoba) (a) 09/03/2000, Shkodër (Albania) (b) 1,82 (c) F - left winger (d) KF Vllaznia (e) Sabah 2

*** Cobet - Andrei Cobet (Andrei Cobeț) (a) 03/01/1997, Tiraspol (Moldova) (b) 1,86 (c) F - center forward (d) Slavia Mozyr (e) Floresti, Dinamo-Auto, FC Sheriff

*** Cobnan - Moses David Cobnan (a) 10/09/2002, ¿? (Nigeria) (b) 1,78 (c) F - right winger (d) FK Krasnodar (e) Podbrezova, SKF Sered, Duslo Sala, SKF Sered, Obazz FC

*** Coca - Jesús Coca (Jesús Coca Noguerol) (a) 22/05/1989, Almodóvar del Río (Spain) (b) 1,89 (c) G (d) UE Engordany (e) IC d'Escaldes, UE Engordany, Lusitanos, Sant Julià, Lucena, Córdoba CF, Real Madrid C

*** Cocalic - Edin Cocalic (Edin Cocalić) (a) 05/12/1987, Visegrad (Yugoslavia, now in Bosnia and Herzegovina) (b) 1,90 (c) D - central defense (d) FK Zeljeznicar Sarajevo (e) Panetolikos, Altay SK, Akhisarspor, KV Mechelen, Maccabi Haifa, Panionios, Zeljeznicar

*** Cocca - Manuel Cocca (Manuel Martín Cocca) (a) 08/11/2002, Buenos Aires (Argentina) (b) 1,82 (c) D - central defense (d) SD Tarazona (e) Elche Ilicitano

*** Cocetta - Nicolò Cocetta (a) 19/12/2003, San Daniele del Friuli (Italy) (b) - (c) D - central defense (d) SS Turris Calcio (e) -

*** Cochrane - Alex Cochrane (Alexander William Cochrane) (a) 21/04/2000, Brighton (England) (b) 1,73 (c) D - left back (d) Heart of Midlothian FC (e) Heart of Midlothian, Union St. Gilloise, East Grinstead

*** Cociuc - Eugeniu Cociuc (a) 11/05/1993, Chișinău (Moldova) (b) 1,82 (c) M - central midfielder (d) FC Pyunik Yerevan (e) Zimbru Chisinau, Shamakhi, Sabah FK, FK Sabail, MSK Zilina, FK Sabail, MSK Zilina, Dacia, Dacia Buiucani

*** Cockram (c) M (d) Cardiff Metropolitan Police Reserves (e) - - William Cockram (c) M (d) Cardiff Metropolitan Police Reserves (e) -

*** Coco - Marcus Coco (Marcus Regis Coco) (a) 24/06/1996, Les Abymes (Guadaloupe) (b) 1,84 (c) F - right winger (d) FC Nantes (e) Guingamp, EA Guingamp B

*** Codali - Matthew Codali (Matthew Joseph Codali) (a) 02/07/2005, ¿? (Gibraltar) (b) - (c) M - attacking midfielder (d) FC College 1975 (e) Europa Point FC, Europa Reserve

*** Coeff - Alexandre Coeff (Alexandre Serge Coeff) (a) 20/02/1992, Brest (France) (b) 1,85 (c) D - central defense (d) SM Caen (e) Brescia, AJ Auxerre, G. Ajaccio, AE Larisa, Udinese, Stade Brestois, Udinese, G. Ajaccio, Udinese, Excelsior Mouscron, Udinese, RCD Mallorca, Udinese, Granada CF, Udinese, RC Lens, RC Lens B

*** Coelho - Diogo Coelho (a) 08/07/1992, Oeiras (Portugal) (b) 1,75 (d) SU 1Âº Dezembro (e) Suduva, Vestri, Gandzasar, Lori Vanadzor, Ã• BV, Real SC, Santa Clara, UniÃ£o Madeira, Farense, UniÃ£o Madeira, Braga B, UniÃ£o Madeira, Braga B, Real SC, Trofense, Real SC, GD RibeirÃ£o, Real SC

*** Cofie - Isaac Cofie (a) 20/09/1991, Accra (Ghana) (b) 1,84 (c) M - pivot (d) - (e) Sivasspor, Real Sporting, Genoa, Carpi, Genoa, Chievo Verona, Genoa, Chievo Verona, Genoa, Sassuolo, Genoa, Piacenza, Genoa, Torino, Genoa

*** Cögley - Peter Cögley (Peter Čögley) (a) 11/08/1988, Trenčín (Czechoslovakia, now in Slovakia) (b) 1,74 (c) D - right back (d) - (e) Skalica, Zlaté Moravce, AS Trencin, Spartak Trnava, Bohemians 1905, AS Trencin

*** Cognat - Timothé Cognat (a) 25/01/1998, Arnas (France) (b) 1,73 (c) M - central midfielder (d) Servette FC (e) Olympique Lyon, Servette FC, Olympique Lyon, Olymp. Lyon B

*** Cohen - Amit Cohen (כהן עמית) (a) 21/11/1998, ¿? (Israel) (b) 1,84 (c) D - right back (d) - (e) B. Jerusalem, Bnei Yehuda, B. Jerusalem, Bnei Yehuda, Hapoel Raanana, Bnei Yehuda, Hapoel Raanana, Hapoel Hadera, Hapoel Raanana

*** Cohen - Ariel Cohen (כהן אריאל) (a) 12/08/2003, ¿? (Israel) (b) - (c) M - central midfielder (d) Hapoel Tel Aviv (e) -

*** Cohen - Avishai Cohen (כהן אבישי) (a) 19/06/1995, Jerusalem (Israel) (b) 1,81 (c) D - right back (d) - (e) B. Jerusalem, Bnei Yehuda, B. Jerusalem, Hapoel Katamon, B. Jerusalem, Beitar TA Ramla, B. Jerusalem

*** Cohen - Bar Cohen (כהן בר) (a) 10/03/2001, Lod (Israel) (b) - (c) M - attacking midfielder (d) Maccabi Netanya (e) Maccabi Tel Aviv, B. Jerusalem, Maccabi Tel Aviv, H. NofHaGalil, Maccabi Tel Aviv, B TLV Bat Yam, Maccabi Tel Aviv, Hapoel Haifa, Maccabi Tel Aviv, B TLV Bat Yam, Maccabi Tel Aviv

*** Cohen - Gil Cohen (כהן גיל) (a) 08/11/2000, Ashdod (Israel) (b) 1,80 (c) D - central defense (d) FC Ashdod (e) -

*** Cohen - Josh Cohen (Joshua Cohen) (a) 18/08/1992, Mountain View, California (United States) (b) 1,86 (c) G (d) - (e) Maccabi Haifa, Sacramento FC, Phoenix Rising, Orange County, Burlingame

*** Cohen - Noam Cohen (כהן נעם) (a) 06/01/1999, ¿? (Israel) (b) 1,82 (c) D - right back (d) Maccabi Tel Aviv (e) Kiryat Shmona, Maccabi Tel Aviv, Hapoel Haifa, Maccabi Tel Aviv, Hapoel Hadera, Maccabi Tel Aviv, Ness Ziona, Maccabi Tel Aviv, Beitar TA Ramla, Maccabi Tel Aviv

*** Cohen - Yonatan Cohen (כהן יונתן) (a) 29/06/1996, Tel Aviv (Israel) (b) 1,86 (c) F - left winger (d) Maccabi Tel Aviv (e) Pisa, Maccabi Tel Aviv, Pisa, Maccabi Tel Aviv, Bnei Yehuda, Maccabi Tel Aviv, Bnei Yehuda, Maccabi Tel Aviv, Beitar TA Ramla, Maccabi Tel Aviv

*** Cohen - Yuval Cohen (a) 01/02/2005, ¿? (Israel) (b) - (c) M (d) - (e) Hapoel Tel-Aviv

*** Cojocari - Andrei Cojocari (a) 21/01/1987, Chișinău (Soviet Union, now in Moldova) (b) 1,82 (c) M - pivot (d) Speranis Nisporeni (e) Sfintul Gheorghe, Dinamo-Auto, Zimbru Chisinau, Petrocub, CSF Speranta, FC Petrocub, Zimbru Chisinau, Milsami, Lokomotiv Tashkent, Zimbru Chisinau, Dacia, Rapid G., Metalurgs, Zimbru Chisinau

*** Cojocari - Serafim Cojocari (a) 07/01/2001, Chișinău (Moldova) (b) 1,81 (c) M - left midfielder (d) AFC Unirea 04 Slobozia (e) FC Sheriff, FC Bălți, FC Sheriff, Sheriff-2

*** Cojocaru - Ionut Cojocaru (Ionuț Sebastian Cojocaru) (a) 28/07/2003, ¿? (Romania) (b) 1,83 (c) F - center forward (d) Petrolul Ploiesti (e) FCV Farul

*** Cojocaru - Maxim Cojocaru (a) 13/01/1998, Cahul (Moldova) (b) 1,77 (c) F - right winger (d) AFC Chindia Targoviste (e) Petrocub, FC Sheriff, FC Petrocub, JFK Ventspils, Dacia

*** Cojocaru - Maxim Cojocaru (a) 29/10/1999, Chișinău (Moldova) (b) 1,88 (c) D - central defense (d) - (e) Dacia Buiucani, Zimbru Chisinau, Dacia Buiucani, Oțelul Galați, Ceahlaul, KF Vllaznia, Codru

*** Cojocaru - Valentin Cojocaru (Valentin Alexandru Cojocaru) (a) 01/10/1995, Bucharest (Romania) (b) 1,95 (c) G (d) Oud-Heverlee Leuven (e) SK Dnipro-1, Feyenoord, SK Dnipro-1, FCV Farul, FC Voluntari, FC Viitorul, Apollon Limassol, FCSB, Crotone, Frosinone, Crotone, Steaua Bucuresti

*** Cokaj - Enis Cokaj (Enis Çokaj) (a) 23/02/1999, Koplik (Albania) (b) 1,82 (c) M - pivot (d) Panathinaikos FC (e) NK Lokomotiva, KF Laçi, NK Lokomotiva
*** Cokcalis - Ismail Cokcalis (İsmail Çokçalış) (a) 21/06/2000, Osmangazi (Turkey) (b) 1,75 (c) D - right back (d) Adana Demirspor (e) Bursaspor, Karacabey Belediye
*** Cola - Claudio Cola (a) 24/04/1986, Cesena (Italy) (b) 1,86 (c) D - central defense (d) - (e) Domagnano, Pennarossa, Savignanese, Cattolica SM, RC Cesena, Rimini, Forlì, Santarcangelo, Modena, Bellaria Igea Marina, Forlì, Riccione
*** Colagiovanni - Matias Colagiovanni (a) 16/01/1993, ¿? (Argentina) (b) 1,82 (c) M - central midfielder (d) FC Fiorentino (e) Pennarossa, Villa S. Martino, Pennarossa, Pennarossa
*** Colak - Antonio Colak (Antonio-Mirko Čolak) (a) 17/09/1993, Ludwigsburg (Germany) (b) 1,88 (c) F - center forward (d) Parma (e) Rangers FC, PAOK, Malmö FF, PAOK, HNK Rijeka, Hoffenheim, HNK Rijeka, Hoffenheim, FC Ingolstadt, Hoffenheim, Darmstadt 98, Hoffenheim, 1.FC Kaiserslautern, Hoffenheim, 1.FC Nürnberg, Lechia Gdánsk, 1.FC Nürnberg, Nurernberg II
*** Colas - Erwan Colas (a) 22/04/1997, Chartres (France) (b) 1,79 (c) M - left midfielder (d) Le Mans FC (e) Lorient B, C'Chartres, Chartres Horiz.
*** Colassin - Antoine Colassin (Antoine Benjamin Colassin) (a) 26/02/2001, Charleroi (Belgium) (b) 1,86 (c) F - center forward (d) RSC Anderlecht (e) Heerenveen, RSC Anderlecht, Zulte Waregem, RSC Anderlecht
*** Colback - Jack Colback (Jack Raymond Colback) (a) 24/10/1989, Killingworth (England) (b) 1,77 (c) M - pivot (d) Queens Park Rangers (e) Nottingham Forest, Newcastle Utd., Nottingham Forest, Newcastle Utd., Nottingham Forest, Newcastle Utd., Sunderland, Ipswich, Sunderland, Ipswich, Sunderland, Sunderland Reserves
*** Cole - Darren Cole (a) 03/01/1992, Edinburgh (Scotland) (b) 1,89 (c) D - central defense (d) Coleraine FC (e) Glentoran, Dungannon, Glentoran, Derry City, Broxburn FC, Livingston FC, Morton, Rangers FC, Partick Thistle, Rangers FC
*** Cole - Larnell Cole (Larnell James Cole) (a) 09/03/1993, Manchester (England) (b) 1,68 (c) M - right midfielder (d) Warrington Town (e) Flint Town, Radcliffe, FC United, Tranmere Rovers, Fulham, Inverness Caledonian, Fulham, Shrewsbury, Fulham, MK Dons, Fulham
*** Coleing - Dayle Coleing (Dayle Edward Coleing) (a) 23/10/1996, Gibraltar (Gibraltar) (b) 1,94 (c) G (d) Lincoln Red Imps FC (e) Glentoran, Lincoln FC, Glentoran, Europa FC, Gibraltar Phoenix, Leeds Trinity, Liversedge, Manchester 62, Thackley, Manchester 62, Lincoln FC
*** Coleman - Luke Coleman (a) 02/01/2002, ¿? (England) (b) - (c) F - center forward (d) - (e) Manchester 62, P. Targowiska, Tamworth
*** Coleman - Seamus Coleman (Séamus Coleman) (a) 11/10/1988, Donegal (Ireland) (b) 1,77 (c) D - right back (d) Everton FC (e) Blackpool, Everton, Sligo Rovers, St. Catherines
*** Coleman (c) M (d) Cardiff Metropolitan Police Reserves (e) - - Kyle Coleman (c) M (d) Cardiff Metropolitan Police Reserves (e) -
*** Colic - Benjamin Colic (Benjamin Čolić) (a) 23/07/1991, Sarajevo (Yugoslavia, now in Bosnia and Herzegovina) (b) 1,82 (c) D - right back (d) - (e) Ceske Budejovice, Karvina, FK Olimpik, Zrinjski Mostar, Celik Zenica, Zeljeznicar
*** Colic - David Colic (David Čolić) (a) 12/04/2000, Banja Luka (Bosnia and Herzegovina) (b) 1,77 (c) D - right back (d) FK Zeljeznicar Banja Luka (e) Sloga Meridian, Leotar Trebinje, Zeljeznicar BL
*** Colic - Nikola Colic (Никола Чолић) (a) 17/08/2002, Beograd (RF Yugoslavia, now in Serbia) (b) 1,75 (c) F - right winger (d) RFK Novi Sad 1921 (e) RFK Novi Sad, FK TSC, Čukarički, FK Partizan, Teleoptik

*** Colina - David Colina (David Čolina) (a) 19/07/2000, Zagreb (Croatia) (b) 1,74 (c) D - left back (d) FC Augsburg (e) Hajduk Split

*** Coll - Ciarán Coll (a) 19/08/1991, Letterkenny, Donegal (Ireland) (b) 1,78 (c) D - left back (d) Derry City (e) Finn Harps

*** Coll - Israel Coll (Israel Emanuel Coll) (a) 22/07/1993, Córdoba (Argentina) (b) 1,76 (c) M - central midfielder (d) Apollon Limassol (e) Apollon Smyrnis, Panachaiki, Central Córdoba, Ferro, Central Córdoba, Ferro, Sarmiento Junín, Ferro, Ferro II

*** Collado - Álex Collado (Álex Collado Gutiérrez) (a) 22/04/1999, Sabadell (Spain) (b) 1,77 (c) F - right winger (d) Al-Okhdood Club (e) Al-Okhdood, Real Betis, FC Barcelona, Elche CF, FC Barcelona, Granada CF, FC Barcelona, FC Barcelona B

*** Collado - Diego Collado (Diego Collado Raya) (a) 09/01/2001, Granada (Spain) (b) 1,83 (c) F - left winger (d) Villarreal CF B (e) Granada 74 FB

*** Collander - Dennis Collander (a) 09/05/2002, Västerås (Sweden) (b) - (c) M - central midfielder (d) Hammarby IF (e) Örebro SK, Skiljebo SK

*** Collao - Gonzalo Collao (Gonzalo Antonio Collao Villegas) (a) 09/09/1997, Coquimbo (Chile) (b) 1,91 (c) G (d) - (e) Palestino, NK Istra, Extremadura B, U. de Chile, Cobreloa, U. de Chile

*** Collard - Dylan Collard (Dylan João Raymond Collard) (a) 16/04/2000, Sydney (Australia) (b) 2,00 (c) D - central defense (d) CS Marítimo (e) Marítimo B, Stal Rzeszow, Lusitano FCV

*** Collet - Adrià Collet (Adrià Collet Sallares) (a) 21/10/1999, Barcelona (Spain) (b) 1,78 (c) G (d) FC Santa Coloma (e) Lleida Esp. B, Calahorra, CE Sabadell, Girona FC B

*** Colley - Ebrima Colley (a) 01/02/2000, Serrekunda (Gambia) (b) 1,80 (c) F - right winger (d) Atalanta de Bérgamo (e) Karagümrük, Atalanta, Spezia, Atalanta, Hellas Verona, Atalanta

*** Colley - Joseph Colley (a) 13/04/1999, Kanifing (Gambia) (b) 1,87 (c) D - central defense (d) Wisla Cracovia (e) Chievo Verona, Sirius, Chievo Verona

*** Colley - Lamin Colley (a) 05/07/1993, ¿? (Gambia) (b) 1,95 (c) F - center forward (d) Puskás Akadémia FC (e) Koper, ND Gorica, La Louvière, Stalybridge, Boston Utd., Scarborough Athletic, Boston Utd., Bradford PA, Stockport, Bradford PA, Harrogate R., Farsley

*** Colley - Omar Colley (a) 24/10/1992, Lamin (Gambia) (b) 1,91 (c) D - central defense (d) Besiktas JK (e) Sampdoria, KRC Genk, Djurgården, KuPS, Real de Banjul, Wallidan

*** Collin - Elias Collin (a) 12/09/2003, ¿? (Finland) (b) 1,77 (c) D - left back (d) AC Oulu (e) FC Haka, Käpylän Pallo

*** Collings - Niall Collings (a) 08/11/2005, ¿? (Wales) (b) - (c) G (d) Flint Town United (e) -

*** Collins - Darren Collins (a) 29/09/2000, ¿? (Ireland) (b) 1,74 (c) F - center forward (d) - (e) Treaty United, Sligo Rovers

*** Collins - Nathan Collins (Nathan Michael Collins) (a) 30/04/2001, Leixlip (Ireland) (b) 1,93 (c) D - central defense (d) Brentford FC (e) Wolverhampton Wanderers, Burnley, Stoke City, Cherry Orchard FC

*** Colombatto - Santiago Colombatto (a) 17/01/1997, Ucacha (Argentina) (b) 1,80 (c) M - pivot (d) Club León FC (e) Famalicão, León, Sint-Truiden, León, Sint-Truiden, Cagliari, Hellas Verona, Cagliari, Perugia, Cagliari, Trapani, Cagliari, AC Pisa

*** Colombo - Lorenzo Colombo (a) 08/03/2002, Vimercate (Italy) (b) 1,83 (c) F - center forward (d) AC Milan (e) Lecce, AC Milan, SPAL, AC Milan, Cremonese, AC Milan

*** Colonato - Diego Colonato (a) 31/01/2005, ¿? (Luxembourg) (b) - (c) M (d) CS Fola Esch (e) -

*** Colonna - Davide Colonna (a) 10/11/2000, Borgo Maggiore (San Marino) (b) - (c) G (d) FC Domagnano (e) USD Bobbiese, Marignanese, V. Francavilla, Riccione, V. Francavilla, Forlì, V. Francavilla

*** Colonna - Riccardo Colonna (a) 10/04/1999, ¿? (San Marino) (b) - (c) M - central midfielder (d) AC Juvenes-Dogana (e) Novafeltria Calcio, Fiorentino, Riccione, Virtus, Pennarossa

*** Colorado - Andrés Colorado (Andrés Felipe Colorado Sánchez) (a) 01/12/1998, El Cerrito (Colombia) (b) 1,93 (c) M - pivot (d) Club Necaxa (e) Cortuluá, FK Partizan, Cortuluá, São Paulo, Cortuluá, Deportivo Cali, Cortuluá

*** Colovic - Stefan Colovic (Стефан Чоловић) (a) 16/04/1994, Beograd (RF Yugoslavia, now in Serbia) (b) 1,75 (c) F - right winger (d) FK Radnicki 1923 Kragujevac (e) Čukarički, Dundalk FC, Proleter, Radnicki Pirot, Jagodina, Drina Zvornik, Sloboda Tuzla, Drina Zvornik, Rad Beograd

*** Colpani - Andrea Colpani (a) 11/05/1999, Brescia (Italy) (b) 1,84 (c) M - central midfielder (d) AC Monza (e) Atalanta, Monza, Atalanta, Trapani

*** Colton - Jayme Colton (Jayme Francis Colton) (a) 29/08/2005, ¿? (Gibraltar) (b) - (c) M - pivot (d) Glacis United Reserve (e) Red Imps Reserves

*** Colwill - Levi Colwill (Levi Lemar Samuel Colwill) (a) 26/02/2003, Southampton (England) (b) 1,87 (c) D - central defense (d) Chelsea FC (e) Brighton & Hove Albion, Huddersfield Town

*** Coly - Aliou Coly (a) 10/12/1992, Bila (Senegal) (b) 1,86 (c) D - central defense (d) - (e) Kristiansund, Molde, Kristiansund, Molde, Casa Sports

*** Coman - Florinel Coman (Florinel Teodor Coman) (a) 10/04/1998, Brăila (Romania) (b) 1,82 (c) F - left winger (d) FCSB (e) FC Viitorul, Academia Hagi, Luceafarul BR

*** Coman - Kingsley Coman (a) 13/06/1996, Paris (France) (b) 1,81 (d) Bayern München (e) Juventus, Bayern München, Juventus, Paris Saint-Germain

*** Comanducci - Martin Comanducci (a) 01/10/2000, ¿? (Italy) (b) - (c) D - central defense (d) SS Cosmos (e) United Riccione

*** Comara - Evgheni Comara (a) 27/08/1990, ¿? (Moldova) (b) - (c) G (d) FC Dinamo-Auto Tiraspol (e) -

*** Comas - Arnau Comas (Arnau Comas Freixas) (a) 11/04/2000, Cassà de la Selva (Spain) (b) 1,91 (c) D - central defense (d) FC Basel (e) Barcelona Atlètic, UE Olot, FC Barcelona B

*** Cömert - Eray Cömert (Eray Ervin Cömert) (a) 04/02/1998, Rheinfelden (Switzerland) (b) 1,83 (c) D - central defense (d) Valencia CF (e) FC Basel, FC Sion, FC Basel, FC Lugano, FC Basel

*** Comesaña - Santi Comesaña (Santiago Comesaña Veiga) (a) 05/10/1996, Vigo (Spain) (b) 1,88 (c) M - central midfielder (d) Villarreal CF (e) Rayo Vallecano, Coruxo FC

*** Compagno - Andrea Compagno (a) 22/04/1996, Palermo (Italy) (b) 1,95 (c) F - center forward (d) FCSB (e) FC U Craiova, Tre Fiori, Nuorese, Borgosesia, Argentina, Pinerolo, Due Torri

*** Compagnon - Mattia Compagnon (a) 06/11/2001, Remanzacco (Italy) (b) 1,71 (c) F - right winger (d) Feralpisalò (e) Feralpisalò, Juve Next Gen, Udinese, Potenza

*** Compaoré - Moubarack Compaoré (a) 24/09/2002, ¿? (Burkina Faso) (b) 1,78 (c) F - right winger (d) Hobro IK (e) Sarpsborg 08, Oslo FA Dakar

*** Composto - Luciano Composto (a) 28/01/2003, Buenos Aires (Argentina) (b) 1,79 (c) M - central midfielder (d) SC Faetano (e) Nueva Chicago

*** Comuniello - Andrea Comuniello (a) 27/04/1995, ¿? (Italy) (b) - (c) F - left winger (d) Santarcangelo Calcio (e) Murata, San Giovanni, Gatteo FC

*** Conaty - Oisin Conaty (a) 17/02/2003, ¿? (Northern Ireland) (b) - (c) F - center forward (d) Portadown FC (e) -

*** Conceição - Francisco Conceição (Francisco Fernandes da Conceição) (a) 14/12/2002, Coimbra (Portugal) (b) 1,70 (c) F - right winger (d) Ajax de Ámsterdam (e) FC Porto, FC Porto B, Belenenses

*** Conceição - Rodrigo Conceição (Rodrigo Fernandes da Conceição) (a) 02/01/2000, Lisboa (Portugal) (b) 1,75 (c) D - right back (d) - (e) FC Porto, FC Porto B, Moreirense, FC Porto B, Benfica B, Belenenses

*** Conceição - Sérgio Conceição (Sérgio Emanuel Fernandes da Conceição) (a) 12/11/1996, Porto (Portugal) (b) 1,77 (c) D - right back (d) CD Feirense (e) Portimonense, RFC Seraing, CF Estrela, Académica Coimbra, Chaves B, Cesarense, Espinho, Oliveira Bairro, Sobrado, Felgueiras

*** Concha - David Concha (David Concha Salas) (a) 20/11/1996, Santander (Spain) (b) 1,79 (c) F - right winger (d) Gimnàstic de Tarragona (e) Hammarby IF, CD Badajoz, Real Sociedad, Gamba Osaka, Real Sociedad, FC Barcelona B, Real Sociedad, CD Numancia, Real Sociedad, Racing

*** Conde - Abdoulaye Conde (a) 01/02/2002, Conakry (Guinea) (b) 1,87 (c) M - pivot (d) Dibba Al-Fujairah Club (e) Isloch, FC Atouga

*** Conde - Cheick Conde (Cheick Oumar Conde) (a) 26/07/2000, Conakry (Guinea) (b) 1,85 (c) M - pivot (d) FC Zürich (e) Trinity Zlin, FC MAS Taborsko, FC Sequence

*** Conde - Diego Conde (Diego José Conde Alcoado) (a) 28/10/1998, Madrid (Spain) (b) 1,88 (c) G (d) CD Leganés (e) Getafe CF, At. Madrid B, CD Leganés, At. Madrid B, Navalcarnero, At. Madrid B

*** Conde - Martín Conde (Martín Conde Gómez) (a) 25/03/2003, Ourense (Spain) (b) - (c) D - left back (d) RC Celta Fortuna (e) -

*** Conde - Pedro Conde (Pedro Pérez Conde) (a) 26/07/1988, Villafranca de Córdoba (Spain) (b) 1,81 (c) F - center forward (d) PAS Giannina (e) Shabab Al-Ahli, Al-Dhafra FC, Shabab Al-Ahli, FC Baniyas, PAS Giannina, Mérida AD, UD Melilla, CD Alcoyano, Granada B, CD Pozoblanco, Real Jaén CF, At. Madrid C, Córdoba CF B

*** Condric - Josip Condric (Josip Čondrić) (a) 27/08/1993, Zagreb (Croatia) (b) 1,94 (c) G (d) FC Astana (e) Zrinjski Mostar, Rotor Volgograd, NK Istra, NK Rudes, NK Zagreb, NK Bistra, NK Zagreb, NK Tresnjevka, NK Zagreb, HASK Zagreb

*** Conk - Matyas Conk (Matyáš Coňk) (a) 03/07/2002, Praha (Czech Rep.) (b) 1,84 (c) D - central defense (d) FK Mlada Boleslav B (e) -

*** Conka - Matus Conka (Matúš Čonka) (a) 15/10/1990, Košice (Czechoslovakia, now in Slovakia) (b) 1,75 (c) D - left back (d) ViOn Zlate Moravce-Vrable (e) Karvina, Spartak Trnava, Slavia Praha, Ružomberok, Slavia Praha, MFK Košice, Kosice B

*** Connell - Kyle Connell (a) 19/12/2001, Glasgow (Scotland) (b) 1,86 (c) F - center forward (d) Cove Rangers FC (e) East Kilbride, Kilmarnock FC, Raith Rovers, Kilmarnock FC, East Fife, Kilmarnock FC, Airdrieonians, Kilmarnock FC, Kilmarnock B

*** Connelly - Matty Connelly (Matthew Connelly) (a) 02/03/2003, Wishaw (Scotland) (b) 1,79 (c) G (d) Motherwell FC (e) Stranraer, Motherwell FC, Motherwell B, Gretna, Motherwell B, Falkirk FC, Motherwell B

*** Connolly - Aaron Connolly (Aaron Anthony Connolly) (a) 28/01/2000, Galway (Ireland) (b) 1,74 (c) F - center forward (d) Hull City (e) Brighton & Hove Albion,

Hull City, Brighton & Hove Albion, Venezia, Brighton & Hove Albion, Middlesbrough, Brighton & Hove Albion, Luton Town

*** Connolly - Mark Connolly (Mark Gerard Connolly) (a) 16/12/1991, Clones, Monaghan (Ireland) (b) 1,85 (c) D - central defense (d) Derry City (e) Dundee United, Dundalk FC, Dundee United, Dunfermline A., Dundee United, Crawley Town, Kilmarnock FC, Crawley Town, Bolton Wanderers, Macclesfield, Bolton Wanderers, St. Johnstone, Bolton Wanderers

*** Connolly - Ryan Connolly (Ryan Michael Connolly) (a) 13/01/1992, Castlebar, Mayo (Ireland) (b) 1,77 (c) M - central midfielder (d) Ballyglass FC (e) Treaty United, Finn Harps, Ballyglass, Galway United, Shamrock Rovers, Galway United, Sligo Rovers, Longford Town, Sligo Rovers, Derby, Ayr United, Derby

*** Conraad - Tyrone Conraad (a) 07/04/1997, Rotterdam (Netherlands) (b) 1,81 (c) F - center forward (d) Meizhou Hakka (e) Sutjeska Niksic, Ergotelis, Kozakken Boys, SC Cambuur

*** Conrado - Conrado (Conrado Buchanelli Holz) (a) 03/04/1997, Ajuricaba (Brazil) (b) 1,74 (c) D - left back (d) KS Lechia Gdańsk (e) Figueirense FC, Oeste, Grêmio Porto Alegre B

*** Considine - Andy Considine (Andrew MacLaren Considine) (a) 01/04/1987, Banchory (Scotland) (b) 1,83 (c) D - central defense (d) St. Johnstone FC (e) Aberdeen FC

*** Consigli - Andrea Consigli (a) 27/01/1987, Milano (Italy) (b) 1,89 (c) G (d) US Sassuolo (e) Atalanta, Rimini, Atalanta, Sambenedettese, Atalanta

*** Consigliero - Jayce Consigliero (Jayce Nicholas Consigliero) (a) 03/08/1997, Gibraltar (Gibraltar) (b) 1,70 (c) M - pivot (d) Glacis United (e) Bruno's Magpies, Boca Gibraltar, Gibraltar Phoenix, Lions Gibraltar, Red Imps FC II

*** Constantin - Marius Constantin (Marius Marcel Constantin) (a) 25/10/1984, Braşov (Romania) (b) 1,85 (c) D - central defense (d) - (e) FC Arges, CS U Craiova, Gaz Metan, FC Viitorul, ASA Tg. Mures, JS Suning, ASA Tg. Mures, FC Brasov, Rapid Bucureşti, FC Vaslui, Rapid 1923 II, Rapid Bucureşti, FC Brasov

*** Contadini - Lorenzo Contadini (a) 05/10/1994, ¿? (Italy) (b) - (c) M - pivot (d) SS San Giovanni (e) Virtus, Sant'Ermete, Bellaria Igea Marina, Misano

*** Conte - Antoine Conte (Antoine Conté) (a) 29/01/1994, Paris (France) (b) 1,87 (c) D - central defense (d) - (e) Hapoel Tel Aviv, CS U Craiova, B. Jerusalem, Stade Reims, B. Jerusalem, Stade Reims, Paris Saint-Germain, Stade Reims, Paris Saint-Germain, Paris Saint Germain B

*** Conté - Abdu Conté (Abdu Cadri Conté) (a) 24/03/1998, Bissau (Guinea-Bissau) (b) 1,83 (c) D - left back (d) ESTAC Troyes (e) Moreirense, Sporting B

*** Conté - Ibrahima Conté (Ibrahima Sory Conté) (a) 03/04/1991, Conakry (Guinea) (b) 1,74 (c) M - attacking midfielder (d) Maccabi Kabilio Jaffa (e) Bnei Sakhnin, Beroe, KV Oostende, Waasland-Beveren, KV Oostende, RSC Anderlecht, Zulte Waregem, KAA Gent, Zulte Waregem, KAA Gent, FS Labé

*** Conteh - Alpha Conteh (Alpha Bedor Conteh) (a) 01/05/2000, ¿? (Sierra Leona) (b) - (c) F - left winger (d) Lokomotiv Plovdiv (e) H Rishon leZion, H. Umm al-Fahm, Central Parade

*** Conti - Alessandro Conti (a) 07/01/1998, ¿? (Italy) (b) 1,80 (c) M - central midfielder (d) SS Pennarossa (e) Cattolica SM, Avezzano, San Marino

*** Conti - Andrea Conti (a) 02/03/1994, Lecco (Italy) (b) 1,84 (c) D - right back (d) UC Sampdoria (e) AC Milan, Parma, AC Milan, Atalanta, Virtus Lanciano, Atalanta, Perugia

*** Conti - Andrea Conti (a) 26/08/2002, ¿? (San Marino) (b) - (c) G (d) SS San Giovanni (e) Tropical Coriano

*** Conti - Daniele Conti (a) 06/06/1990, ¿? (San Marino) (b) 1,80 (c) D - left back (d) Monte Grimano Terme (e) Pennarossa

*** Conti - Germán Conti (Germán Andrés Conti) (a) 03/06/1994, Santa Fe (Argentina) (b) 1,93 (c) D - central defense (d) Lokomotiv Moskva (e) Benfica, América-MG, Benfica, EC Bahia, Benfica, Atlas, Benfica, Colón

*** Conti - Giacomo Conti (a) 21/07/1999, ¿? (San Marino) (b) - (c) D - central defense (d) SS San Giovanni (e) Tropical Coriano, San Marino

*** Conti - Mathias Conti (a) 05/03/2004, ¿? (Malta) (b) - (c) F (d) - (e) Birkirkara FC

*** Conti - Tommaso Conti (a) 18/06/1992, ¿? (Italy) (b) - (c) M - central midfielder (d) ACD Torconca Cattolica (e) Cailungo, Riccione, Faetano, Pennarossa

*** Continella - Vittorio Continella (a) 31/12/2002, Torino (Italy) (b) - (c) M - central midfielder (d) AEL Limassol (e) Casale

*** Contini - Nikita Contini (Nikita Contini Baranovskiy, Нікіта Контіні-Барановський) (a) 21/05/1996, Cherkasy (Ukraine) (b) 1,90 (c) G (d) SSC Nápoles (e) Reggina, Napoli, Sampdoria, Napoli, Crotone, LR Vicenza, Crotone, Napoli, Virtus Entella, Napoli, Robur Siena, Napoli, Pontedera, Napoli, Taranto, Napoli, Carrarese, Napoli, SPAL, Napoli

*** Convie - James Convie (a) 01/07/2002, ¿? (Northern Ireland) (b) - (c) M - attacking midfielder (d) Dungannon Swifts (e) Armagh City FC, Dungannon

*** Cook - Lewis Cook (Lewis John Cook) (a) 03/02/1997, York (England) (b) 1,75 (c) M - central midfielder (d) AFC Bournemouth (e) Leeds Utd.

*** Cook - Steve Cook (Steve Anthony Cook) (a) 19/04/1991, Hastings (England) (b) 1,85 (c) D - central defense (d) Queens Park Rangers (e) Nottingham Forest, Bournemouth, Brighton & Hove Albion, Bournemouth, Brighton & Hove Albion, Mansfield Town, Brighton & Hove Albion, Eastbourne, Brighton & Hove Albion, Eastleigh, Brighton & Hove Albion, Havant & Waterlooville, Brighton & Hove Albion

*** Cooke - Kaiden Cooke (Kaiden Anthony Cooke) (c) F - center forward (d) Airbus UK Broughton (e) -

*** Cools - Dion Cools (Dion-Johan Chai Cools) (a) 04/06/1996, Kuching (Malaysia) (b) 1,85 (c) D - central defense (d) Buriram United (e) Jablonec, Midtjylland, Zulte Waregem, Midtjylland, KV Brugge, OH Leuven

*** Coombes - Jamie Coombes (James Timothy Barry Coombes) (a) 27/05/1996, Gibraltar (Gibraltar) (b) 1,72 (c) M - attacking midfielder (d) FC Bruno's Magpies (e) Lincoln FC, West Didsbury, Lincoln FC, Undy, Lincoln FC, Undy, Manchester 62, Europa FC

*** Coombes - Lee Coombes (a) 20/06/1996, Gibraltar (Gibraltar) (b) 1,88 (c) D - left back (d) FC Bruno's Magpies (e) Boca Gibraltar, Lions Gibraltar, City of Liverp., LJMU, ES Pennoise, Manchester 62, Europa FC, St Joseph's FC

*** Cooper - Godberg Cooper (Godberg Barry Cooper) (a) 20/08/1997, Bergamo (Italy) (b) 1,90 (c) F - center forward (d) UTA Arad (e) Chindia, Makedonija, Lavello, FK Kukësi, FC Schaffhausen, Arouca, Vianense, Arouca, Espinho, Arouca, Condeixa, Aurora Seriate, Verdello, Aurora Seriate, Scanzorosciate, Aurora Seriate

*** Cooper - Joel Cooper (a) 29/02/1996, Ballyclare (Northern Ireland) (b) 1,80 (c) M - left midfielder (d) Linfield FC (e) Oxford United, Port Vale, Oxford United, Linfield, Oxford United, Linfield, Glenavon, Ballyclare

*** Cooper - Liam Cooper (Liam David Ian Cooper) (a) 30/08/1991, Kingston upon Hull (England) (b) 1,86 (c) D - central defense (d) Leeds United (e) FC Chesterfield, Hull City, FC Chesterfield, Hull City, Huddersfield Town, Hull City, Carlisle United, Hull City

*** Cooper-Love - Jack Cooper-Love (a) 25/12/2001, Aneby (Sweden) (b) 1,84 (c) F - center forward (d) Halmstads BK (e) Elfsborg, Skövde AIK, Elfsborg, Örgryte, Elfsborg, Aneby SK

*** Coosemans - Colin Coosemans (Colin Maurice Coosemans) (a) 03/08/1992, Gent (Belgium) (b) 1,84 (c) G (d) RSC Anderlecht (e) KAA Gent, KV Mechelen, Waasland-Beveren, KV Brugge, Waasland-Beveren, KV Brugge

*** Coote - Ali Coote (Alistair Coote) (a) 11/06/1998, Bedford (England) (b) 1,70 (c) F - left winger (d) Bohemian FC (e) Waterford FC, Brentford B, Dundee United, East Fife

*** Cop - Duje Cop (Duje Čop) (a) 01/02/1990, Vinkovci (Yugoslavia, now in Croatia) (b) 1,84 (c) F - center forward (d) GNK Dinamo Zagreb (e) HNK Sibenik, Dinamo Zagreb, NK Celje, Dinamo Zagreb, Standard Liège, Real Valladolid, Standard Liège, Cagliari, Real Sporting, Cagliari, Málaga CF, Cagliari, Dinamo Zagreb, Cagliari, Dinamo Zagreb, RNK Split, Hajduk Split, Nacional, Hajduk Split

*** Copete - José Copete (José Manuel Arias Copete) (a) 10/10/1999, Écija (Spain) (b) 1,90 (c) D - central defense (d) RCD Mallorca (e) Ponferradina, Villarreal CF B, Penya Deportiva, Villarreal CF B, Villarreal CF C, Córdoba CF B, Écija Balompié

*** Coppens - Jo Coppens (a) 21/12/1990, Heusden-Zolder (Belgium) (b) 1,90 (c) G (d) Sint-Truidense VV (e) MSV Duisburg, Unterhaching, Lillestrøm, Carl Zeiss Jena, KSV Roeselare, MVV Maastricht, Cercle Brugge

*** Coppola - Alessandro Coppola (a) 13/03/2000, Torino (Italy) (b) 2,02 (c) D - central defense (d) Birkirkara FC (e) Birkirkara FC, Triestina, Tsarsko Selo, Triestina, Olhanense, AS Livorno, Livorno, Sondrio, Ercolanese

*** Coppola - Diego Coppola (a) 28/12/2003, Verona (Italy) (b) 1,92 (c) D - central defense (d) Hellas Verona (e) -

*** Coppola - Raffaele Alessandro Coppola (a) 16/09/2003, ¿? (Italy) (b) - (c) M (d) - (e) Tre Penne

*** Coquelin - Francis Coquelin (a) 13/05/1991, Laval (France) (b) 1,77 (c) M - pivot (d) Villarreal CF (e) Valencia CF, Arsenal, Charlton Ath., Arsenal, SC Freiburg, Arsenal, Arsenal Reserves, FC Lorient, Arsenal Reserves

*** Corbalan - Juan Corbalan (a) 03/03/1997, ¿? (Malta) (b) 1,69 (c) F - right winger (d) Hamrun Spartans (e) Gzira Utd., Balzan FC

*** Corbally - Kian Corbally (a) 31/12/2003, Dublin (Ireland) (b) 1,73 (c) M - central midfielder (d) Wexford FC (e) St. Patrick's Ath., Longford Town, St. Patrick's Ath.

*** Corbanie - Kobe Corbanie (a) 10/05/2005, ¿? (Belgium) (b) - (c) D - right back (d) Royal Antwerp FC (e) Young Reds

*** Corbaz - Thibault Corbaz (a) 07/01/1994, Morges (Switzerland) (b) 1,80 (c) M - pivot (d) FC Winterthur (e) Neuchâtel Xamax, FC Biel-Bienne

*** Corbett - Jake Corbett (a) 28/07/2001, Dromore (Northern Ireland) (b) 1,78 (c) M - pivot (d) Dundela FC (e) Ballymena, Dundela FC, Ballymena, Linfield, HW Welders, Linfield, Ards FC, Linfield, Ards FC, Linfield

*** Corbu - Marius Corbu (Marius Dumitru Corbu) (a) 07/05/2002, Cădăreşti (Romania) (b) 1,76 (c) M - attacking midfielder (d) Puskás Akadémia FC (e) Puskás AFC II, Csikszereda

*** Corchia - Sébastien Corchia (a) 01/11/1990, Noisy-le-Sec (France) (b) 1,76 (c) D - right back (d) Amiens SC (e) FC Nantes, Sevilla FC, RCD Espanyol, Sevilla FC, Benfica, Sevilla FC, Lille, FC Sochaux, Le Mans FC, Le Mans UC 72 B

*** Cordaz - Alex Cordaz (a) 01/01/1983, Vittorio Veneto (Italy) (b) 1,88 (c) G (d) - (e) Internazionale Milano, Crotone, Parma, Crotone, Parma, ND Gorica, Parma, Cittadella, FC Lugano, Treviso, AS Pizzighettone, Acireale, Internazionale Milano, Spezia, Internazionale Milano, Spezia

*** Cordea - Andrei Cordea (Andrei Ioan Cordea) (a) 24/06/1999, Aiud (Romania) (b) 1,80 (c) F - right winger (d) FCSB (e) Academica Clinceni, Novara, FC Hermannstadt, Novara, FC Ardealul
*** Córdoba - Iñigo Córdoba (Iñigo Córdoba Querejeta) (a) 13/03/1997, Bilbao (Spain) (b) 1,80 (c) F - left winger (d) Fortuna Sittard (e) Athletic, Go Ahead Eagles, Athletic, Alavés, Athletic, Bilbao Athletic, CD Basconia
*** Córdoba - Jhon Córdoba (Jhon Andrés Córdoba Copete) (a) 11/05/1993, Istmina (Colombia) (b) 1,88 (c) F - center forward (d) FK Krasnodar (e) Hertha Berlin, 1.FC Köln, Mainz 05, Granada CF, Mainz 05, Granada CF, Chiapas FC, RCD Espanyol, Chiapas FC, Envigado
*** Córdoba - José Córdoba (José Ángel Córdoba Chambers) (a) 03/06/2001, Panama City (Panamá) (b) 1,87 (c) D - central defense (d) Levski Sofia (e) Independiente, Levski Sofia, Independiente, Etar, Independiente
*** Córekci - Kamil Ahmet Córekci (Kamil Ahmet Çörekçi) (a) 01/02/1992, London (England) (b) 1,73 (c) D - right back (d) Hatayspor (e) Trabzonspor, Eskisehirspor, Kayserispor, Adana Demirspor, Kayserispor, Bucaspor
*** Coremans - Tim Coremans (a) 10/04/1991, Breda (Netherlands) (b) 1,86 (c) G (d) - (e) Sparta Rotterdam, ADO Den Haag, FC Dordrecht, ADO Den Haag, SC Cambuur, NAC Breda
*** Coric - Ante Coric (Ante Ćorić) (a) 14/04/1997, Zagreb (Croatia) (b) 1,76 (c) M - attacking midfielder (d) - (e) AS Roma, FC Zürich, AS Roma, Olimpija, AS Roma, VVV-Venlo, AS Roma, UD Almería, AS Roma, Dinamo Zagreb
*** Coric - Dino Coric (Dino Ćorić) (a) 30/06/1990, Siroki Brijeg (Yugoslavia, now in Bosnia and Herzegovina) (b) - (c) D - right back (d) FK Tuzla City (e) Borac Banja Luka, Siroki Brijeg, HSK Posusje
*** Coric - Marijan Coric (Marijan Ćorić) (a) 06/02/1995, Čapljina (Bosnia and Herzegovina) (b) 2,04 (c) G (d) NK Istra 1961 (e) NK Opatija, KF Llapi, TEC, NK Uljanik, Palanga, NK Kustosija, NK Istra, Parma, Spezia, Parma, NK Vodnjan
*** Corinti - Andrea Corinti (a) 23/11/1998, Viterbo (Italy) (b) - (c) M - central midfielder (d) - (e) San Giovanni, Tre Fiori, CF Sóller, Montefiascone, Viterbese, Rieti, Arzachena, Rieti, Jolly & Montemurlo
*** Corinus - Jérémy Corinus (Jérémy Jimmy Théophile Corinus) (a) 16/03/1997, Évry (France) (b) 1,84 (c) M - pivot (d) Othellos Athienou (e) Chindia, FCV Farul, Academica Clinceni, Fermana, AC Ajaccio, AC Ajaccio B, Gozzano, Amiens SC B, Girondins Bordeaux B
*** Corish - Aaron Corish (a) ¿?, ¿? (Ireland) (b) - (c) M (d) - (e) University College Dublin
*** Corkovic - Ivan Corkovic (Иван Ћорковић) (a) 10/05/2001, Beograd (RF Yugoslavia, now in Serbia) (b) 1,82 (c) D - left back (d) FK Smederevo 1924 (e) Kolubara, Vozdovac, Teleoptik
*** Corlu - Rezan Corlu (a) 07/08/1997, Glostrup (Denmark) (b) 1,71 (c) M - attacking midfielder (d) Lyngby BK (e) Brøndby IF, Lyngby BK, Brøndby IF, Lyngby BK, Brøndby IF
*** Corluka - Josip Corluka (Josip Ćorluka) (a) 03/03/1995, Grude (Bosnia and Herzegovina) (b) 1,84 (c) D - right back (d) HSK Zrinjski Mostar (e) Domžale, Siroki Brijeg
*** Cornago - Roberto Cornago (Roberto Cornago Lázaro) (a) 08/03/2003, Madrid (Spain) (b) 1,70 (c) F - right winger (d) AD Cartaya (e) FC Santa Coloma
*** Cornelisse - Enzo Cornelisse (a) 29/06/2002, Arnhem (Netherlands) (b) - (c) D - central defense (d) Vitesse Arnhem (e) -

*** Cornelius - Andreas Cornelius (Andreas Evald Cornelius) (a) 16/03/1993, Copenhagen (Denmark) (b) 1,93 (c) F - center forward (d) FC Copenhague (e) Trabzonspor, Parma, Atalanta, Parma, Atalanta, Girondins Bordeaux, Atalanta, FC København, Cardiff City, FC København
*** Cornelius - Dean Cornelius (a) 11/04/2001, Bellshill (Scotland) (b) 1,76 (c) M - central midfielder (d) Harrogate Town (e) Motherwell FC, Motherwell B
*** Cornelius - Derek Cornelius (Derek Austin Cornelius) (a) 25/11/1997, Ajax, Ontario (Canada) (b) 1,88 (c) D - central defense (d) Malmö FF (e) Vancouver, Panetolikos, Vancouver, Javor-Matis, VfR Neumünster, VfB Lübeck, Unionville, Spartacus SC
*** Cornet - Maxwel Cornet (Gnaly Maxwel Cornet) (a) 27/09/1996, Bregbo (Ivory Coast) (b) 1,79 (c) F - left winger (d) West Ham United (e) Burnley, Olympique Lyon, FC Metz
*** Cornic - Leo Cornic (Leo Erik Jean Cornic) (a) 02/01/2001, Oslo (Norway) (b) 1,78 (c) M - right midfielder (d) Rosenborg BK (e) Djurgården, Grorud, Vålerenga, Bærum, Vålerenga
*** Cornish - Beau Cornish (a) 05/11/2001, ¿? (Wales) (b) - (c) M - central midfielder (d) Aberystwyth Town (e) The New Saints, Airbus UK, The New Saints, Airbus UK, The New Saints
*** Cornud - Pierre Cornud (a) 12/12/1996, Avignon (France) (b) 1,77 (c) D - left back (d) Maccabi Haifa (e) Real Oviedo, Maccabi Haifa, Real Oviedo, CE Sabadell, RCD Mallorca, UD Ibiza, RCD Mallorca, Oviedo Vetusta, RCD Mallorca, R. B. Linense, RCD Mallorca, RCD Mallorca B, Dijon FCO B, Montpellier B
*** Cornwall - Robert Cornwall (a) 16/10/1994, Drumcondra, Dublin (Ireland) (b) 1,83 (c) D - central defense (d) Northern Colorado Hailstorm FC (e) Bohemians, Shamrock Rovers, Derry City, Shamrock Rovers, Shelbourne
*** Corominas - David Corominas (David Corominas Saura) (a) 29/09/1985, Vilassar de Mar (Spain) (b) 1,68 (c) F - right winger (d) Penya Encarnada d'Andorra (e) FC Ordino, UE Santa Coloma, Terrassa FC, CF Peralada, CE L'Hospitalet, FC Imabari, UE Olot, CE L'Hospitalet, Badalona, Uni. Las Palmas, CE Mataró
*** Corona - Joe Corona (Joe Benny Corona Crespín) (a) 09/07/1990, Los Angeles, California (United States) (b) 1,76 (c) M - central midfielder (d) San Diego Loyal SC (e) Houston, GIF Sundsvall, Houston, Austin, Los Ángeles, Club Tijuana, CF América, Club Tijuana, Dorados Sinaloa, Club Tijuana, Dorados Sinaloa, Club Tijuana, Tiburones Rojos, Club Tijuana, San Diego State, Nomads SC
*** Corral - Adrián Corral (Adrián Corral Alciturri) (a) 05/01/2003, Santander (Spain) (b) 1,83 (c) D - left back (d) Atlético de Madrid B (e) -
*** Corral - Ken Corral (Ken Corral Garcia) (a) 08/05/1992, Luxembourg (Luxembourg) (b) 1,81 (c) F - right winger (d) Swift Hesperange (e) CS Fola Esch, Jeunesse Esch, UN Käerjeng 97
*** Corral - Roberto Corral (Roberto Corral García) (a) 14/09/1997, Valladolid (Spain) (b) 1,82 (c) D - left back (d) - (e) Metalist, Korona Kielce, Real Valladolid, CD Numancia, Real Valladolid, Valladolid Promesas
*** Correa - Alvaro Correa (a) 08/11/1996, Ponferrada (Spain) (b) 1,88 (c) M - central midfielder (d) UE Sant Julia (e) Manresa
*** Correa - Ángel Correa (Ángel Martín Correa Martínez) (a) 09/03/1995, Rosario (Argentina) (b) 1,71 (c) F - right winger (d) Atlético de Madrid (e) San Lorenzo, San Lorenzo II
*** Correa - Joaquín Correa (Carlos Joaquín Correa) (a) 13/08/1994, Tucumán (Argentina) (b) 1,88 (c) F - attacking midfielder (d) Internazionale Milano (e) Lazio, Internazionale Milano, Lazio, Sevilla FC, Sampdoria, Estudiantes

*** Correa - Pavlos Correa (Παύλος Κορρέα) (a) 14/07/1998, Pafos (Cyprus) (b) 1,86 (c) D - central defense (d) Anorthosis Famagusta (e) Ethnikos, Anorthosis, Aris Limassol, Anorthosis, Akritas Chlor.

*** Correa - Ricardo Correa (Ricardo Calixto Correa Duarte) (a) 20/07/1994, Montevideo (Uruguay) (b) 1,70 (c) M - attacking midfielder (d) Gzira United FC (e) Sirens FC, Gzira Utd., Balzan FC, Sliema Wanderers, Gzira Utd., Club Oriental, Miramar

*** Corréa - Mohamet Corréa (Mohamet Lamine Corréa) (a) 30/08/2001, Guédiawaye (Senegal) (b) 1,93 (c) F - left winger (d) FK Metta (e) AS Pikine

*** Correia - Félix Correia (Félix Alexandre Andrade Sanches Correia) (a) 22/01/2001, Lisboa (Portugal) (b) 1,78 (c) F - left winger (d) Juventus Next Gen (e) Marítimo, Juve Next Gen, Parma

*** Correia - João Correia (João Pedro Araújo Correia) (a) 05/09/1996, Setúbal (Portugal) (b) 1,75 (c) D - right back (d) GD Chaves (e) Vitória Guimarães, Chaves, Vitória Guimarães, Vitória Guimarães B, Pinhalnovense

*** Correia - Lucas Correia (a) 18/04/2002, ¿? (Luxembourg) (b) 1,65 (c) M - left midfielder (d) Swift Hesperange (e) CS Fola Esch

*** Correia - Omar Correia (a) 10/04/2000, Evreux (France) (b) 1,87 (c) M - pivot (d) FC Koper (e) Paris Saint Germain B, FC Versailles, Entente SSG, Le Havre AC B

*** Correia - Ruben Correia (Ruben Machado Correia) (a) 06/01/2000, Lausanne (Switzerland) (b) 1,82 (c) D - left back (d) CD Teruel (e) CD Eldense

*** Correia - Rui Correia (Rui Daniel Ribeiro Correia) (a) 16/02/2002, Guimarães (Portugal) (b) 1,82 (c) D - central defense (d) Vitória Guimarães SC B (e) -

*** Correia - Thierry Correia (Thierry Rendall Correia) (a) 09/03/1999, Amadora (Portugal) (b) 1,76 (c) D - right back (d) Valencia CF (e) Sporting Lisboa

*** Corryn - Milan Corryn (a) 04/04/1999, Aalst (Belgium) (b) 1,80 (c) M - attacking midfielder (d) Almere City FC (e) Warta Poznań, AS Trencin

*** Corsby - Charlie Corsby (Charles Corsby) (a) 14/10/1991, ¿? (Wales) (b) - (c) M - central midfielder (d) Cardiff Metropolitan University (e) Brockenhurst

*** Cortaberría - José Cortaberría (José Carlos Cortaberría Gasso) (a) 30/08/1990, Santa Lucía (Uruguay) (b) 1,91 (c) G (d) Wanderers A.C. de Santa Lucía (e) UE Engordany, CE Carroi, Cerro Largo, CA Atenas, Rocha FC, CA Torque, Racing Club

*** Cortés - Germán Cortés (Germán Cortés Narváez) (a) 03/02/1994, La Linea de la Concepcion (Spain) (b) 1,86 (c) F - center forward (d) FC College 1975 (e) Lions Gibraltar, Boca Gibraltar, Gibraltar Phoenix, Sperre) Gibraltar Utd., Gibraltar Phoenix, Glacis United, San Roqueno

*** Cortinovis - Alessandro Cortinovis (a) 25/01/2001, Bergamo (Italy) (b) 1,80 (c) M - attacking midfielder (d) - (e) Hellas Verona, Cosenza, Hellas Verona, Atalanta, Reggina, Atalanta

*** Cosano - Fernando Cosano (Fernando Cosano Diaz) (a) 20/07/1999, Algeciras (Spain) (b) - (c) F - right winger (d) Mons Calpe SC (e) Algeciras B

*** Coselev - Alexei Coselev (Alexei Vasilievitsj Koşelev, Кошелев Алексей Васильевич) (a) 19/11/1993, Chişinău (Moldova) (b) 2,00 (c) G (d) PAS Lamia 1964 (e) Júbilo Iwata, Fortuna Sittard, ACSM Poli Iasi, FC Sheriff, FC Tiraspol, FC Saxan, Kuban Krasnodar, Dacia Buiucani, Sfintul Gheorghe, Dacia Buiucani, Gagauzia Comrat

*** Cosereanu - Valentin Cosereanu (Valentin Coşereanu) (a) 17/07/1991, Scorniceşti (Romania) (b) 1,87 (c) M - right midfielder (d) CS Mioveni (e) Gaz Metan, SCM Piteşti, CSMS Iaşi, Concordia, CS Mioveni

*** Cosgrove - Tomas Cosgrove (a) 11/12/1992, Ardoyne (Northern Ireland) (b) 1,78 (c) D - right back (d) Larne FC (e) Cliftonville

*** Cosgun - Denizcan Cosgun (a) 16/02/2002, Salzburg (Austria) (b) 1,77 (c) M - attacking midfielder (d) - (e) SV Ried, FC Wacker, SV Horn, FC Wacker

*** Cosic - Anis Cosic (Anis Ćosić) (a) 27/05/2004, ¿? (Bosnia and Herzegovina) (b) - (c) D - central defense (d) OFK Gradina Srebrenik (e) -

*** Cosic - Djordje Cosic (Đorđe Ćosić) (a) 11/09/1995, Sarajevo (Bosnia and Herzegovina) (b) 1,87 (c) D - central defense (d) FK Mladost GAT Novi Sad (e) Shakhter K., Borac Banja Luka, Zrinjski Mostar, NK Vitez, Zrinjski Mostar, Drina Zvornik, Zvijezda 09

*** Cosic - Marko Cosic (Marko Ćosić) (a) 02/03/1994, Zagreb (Croatia) (b) 1,91 (c) D - central defense (d) Gzira United FC (e) Hrv Dragovoljac, NK Rudes, Hapoel Afula, Rudar Velenje, Haugesund, Inter Zaprešić, Hajduk Split, Inter Zaprešić

*** Cosic - Mehmed Cosic (Mehmed Ćosić) (a) 25/06/1997, Tuzla (Bosnia and Herzegovina) (b) 1,77 (c) D - right back (d) FK Zeljeznicar Sarajevo (e) Kolubara, Velez Mostar, FK Rad. Lukavac

*** Cosic - Robert Cosic (Robert Ćosić) (a) 08/07/1997, Zagreb (Croatia) (b) 1,84 (c) D - central defense (d) HNK Sibenik (e) HNK Gorica, NK Rudes, NK Osijek II, NK Rudes, NK Osijek II, HNK Sibenik, NK Osijek II, NK Libertas

*** Cossou - Cédric Cossou (a) 20/04/1997, ¿? (France) (b) - (c) D - left back (d) US Rumelange (e) FC UNA Strassen, US Rumelange, Livry-Gargan

*** Costa - Bruno Costa (Bruno Xavier Almeida Costa) (a) 19/04/1997, Oliveira de Azeméis (Portugal) (b) 1,74 (c) M - central midfielder (d) FC Porto B (e) FC Porto, Portimonense, Paços Ferreira, Portimonense, FC Porto, FC Porto B

*** Costa - David Costa (David Pereira da Costa) (a) 05/01/2001, Almada (Portugal) (b) 1,68 (c) M - attacking midfielder (d) RC Lens (e) RC Lens B

*** Costa - Diogo Costa (Diogo Meireles da Costa) (a) 19/09/1999, Rothrist (Switzerland) (b) 1,86 (c) G (d) FC Porto (e) FC Porto B

*** Costa - Edgar Costa (José Edgar Andrade da Costa) (a) 14/04/1987, Câmara de Lobos (Portugal) (b) 1,77 (c) F - right winger (d) CS Marítimo (e) Nacional, Moreirense, Nacional, União Madeira

*** Costa - Ewandro Costa (Ewandro Felipe de Lima Costa) (a) 15/03/1996, Recife (Brazil) (b) 1,76 (c) F - center forward (d) Lokomotiv Plovdiv (e) Spartak Varna, Lokomotiv Plovdiv, Náutico, CRB, Udinese, Sport Recife, EC Vitória, Sport Recife, Udinese, Fluminense, Udinese, Austria Viena, Udinese, Estoril Praia, Udinese, São Paulo, Atlético-PR, São Paulo

*** Costa - Gilson Costa (Gilson Sequeira da Costa) (a) 24/09/1996, São Tomé (Sao Tome & Principe) (b) 1,85 (c) M - pivot (d) Nejmeh SC (e) FK Aksu, Al-Nahda, Doxa Katokopias, Estoril Praia, Boavista, Benfica B, Arouca, Benfica B

*** Costa - Gonçalo Costa (Gonçalo Faria Costa) (a) 18/02/2000, Setúbal (Portugal) (b) 1,79 (c) D - left back (d) Portimonense SC (e) Sporting B

*** Costa - Jaume Costa (Jaume Vincent Costa Jordá) (a) 18/03/1988, Valencia (Spain) (b) 1,71 (c) D - left back (d) RCD Mallorca (e) Villarreal CF, Valencia CF, Villarreal CF, Villarreal CF B, Valencia Mestalla, Cádiz CF, Valencia Mestalla

*** Costa - Logan Costa (a) 01/04/2001, Saint-Denis (France) (b) 1,90 (c) D - central defense (d) Toulouse FC (e) Stade Reims, Le Mans FC, Stade Reims, Stade Reims B

*** Costa - Lorenzo Costa (a) 01/03/1992, ¿? (Italy) (b) - (c) D - left back (d) La Fiorita 1967 (e) Libertas, Tre Penne, Gabicce Gradara, Marignanese, Misano

*** Costa - Matheus Costa (Matheus de Mello Costa) (a) 26/01/1995, Minas Gerais (Brazil) (b) 1,88 (c) D - central defense (d) CS Marítimo (e) Vizela, Leixões, Real SC, Democrata GV

*** Costa - Rui Costa (Rui Jorge Costa de Sousa) (a) 26/12/2002, ¿? (Luxembourg) (b) - (c) F (d) CS Fola Esch (e) -

*** Costa - Rui Costa (Rui Pedro da Silva Costa) (a) 20/02/1996, Vila Nova de Famalicão (Portugal) (b) 1,79 (c) F - attacking midfielder (d) SC Farense (e) Santa Clara, RC Deportivo, FC Porto B, Alcorcón, FC Porto B, Portimonense, Famalicão, Portimonense, Varzim, Varzim SC B

*** Costa - Samú Costa (Samuel de Almeida Costa) (a) 27/11/2000, Aveiro (Portugal) (b) 1,85 (c) M - pivot (d) RCD Mallorca (e) UD Almería, SC Braga, UD Almería, SC Braga

*** Costa - Vítor Costa (Vítor Costa de Brito) (a) 01/07/1994, Valente (Brazil) (b) 1,82 (c) D - left back (d) CS Marítimo (e) Inter de Lages, CSA, Inter de Lages, RC Lens, Inter de Lages, Desportivo Aves, Inter de Lages, Arouca, Inter de Lages, Avaí FC, Inter de Lages, EC Bahia

*** Costa Tavares - Humberto Alexandre Costa Tavares (a) 01/01/1999, Andorra la Vella (Andorra) (b) - (c) M - central midfielder (d) UE Engordany B (e) FC Rànger's, FC Santa B

*** Costache - Valentin Costache (Valentin Ionuț Costache) (a) 02/08/1998, Videle (Romania) (b) 1,78 (c) F - left winger (d) FC Rapid 1923 (e) CFR Cluj, FC Dinamo, CS Afumati, FC Dinamo, Dinamo II

*** Costantini - Mattia Costantini (a) 24/07/1989, ¿? (Italy) (b) - (c) D - central defense (d) FC Fiorentino (e) Murata, Tropical Coriano, Tre Fiori

*** Costanza - Fernando Costanza (Fernando Peixoto Costanza) (a) 29/11/1998, Rio de Janeiro (Brazil) (b) 1,82 (c) D - right back (d) Krylya Sovetov Samara (e) FC Sheriff, Botafogo, LOSC Lille B, Botafogo

*** Costil - Benoît Costil (a) 03/07/1987, Caen (France) (b) 1,88 (c) G (d) US Salernitana 1919 (e) Lille, AJ Auxerre, Girondins Bordeaux, Stade Rennes, CS Sedan, SM Caen, Vannes, SM Caen

*** Costin - Cristian Costin (Cristian Ionuț Costin) (a) 17/06/1998, Beclean (Romania) (b) 1,78 (c) D - right back (d) FC Dinamo 1948 (e) FC Voluntari, UTA Arad, Scolar Resita, UTA Arad

*** Costinha - Costinha (João José Pereira da Costa) (a) 25/08/1992, Coimbra (Portugal) (b) 1,70 (c) M - attacking midfielder (d) CD Tondela (e) Santa Clara, Chaves, Vitória Setúbal, Lusitano FCV, FC Fredericia, UD Tocha, Sertanense

*** Costinha - Costinha (João Pedro Loureiro da Costa) (a) 26/03/2000, Póvoa de Varzim (Portugal) (b) 1,81 (c) D - right back (d) Rio Ave FC (e) -

*** Costinha - Costinha (Pedro Miguel Neves da Costa) (a) 11/03/1994, Abrantes (Portugal) (b) 1,87 (c) D - central defense (d) US Mondorf-Les-Bains (e) Hamm Benfica, CS Grevenmacher, Louletano, Trofense, Naval

*** Costrov - Igor Costrov (Костров Игорь Викторович) (a) 03/08/1987, Bender (Soviet Union, now in Moldova) (b) 1,76 (c) M - central midfielder (d) Slavia Mozyr (e) Gomel, Slavia, Dinamo-Auto, Kyzyl-Zhar, FC Veris, FC Costuleni, Slavia, Dacia, FC Tiraspol, Iskra-Stali, Kansas City, Maccabi Herzlya, H. Beer Sheva, Dinamo Bendery

*** Coto - Carles Coto (Carles Coto Pagès) (a) 11/02/1988, Figueres (Spain) (b) 1,73 (c) F - left winger (d) CD Roda (e) FC Santa Coloma, UE Figueres, Volos NPS, Rayo Majadahonda, Ermis Aradippou, Doxa Katokopias, Ethnikos, San Marino, Bunyodkor, Dinamo Minsk, Dinamo Tbilisi, Anorthosis, Benidorm, Sevilla At., Barcelona Atlètic, Excelsior Mouscron, FC Barcelona B

*** Cotogoi - Corneliu Cotogoi (a) 23/06/2001, Chișinău (Moldova) (b) 1,77 (c) M - central midfielder (d) FC Petrocub Hîncești (e) Dacia Buiucani

*** Cotter - Barry Cotter (Barry Noel Cotter) (a) 04/12/1998, Ennis, Clare (Ireland) (b) 1,84 (c) D - right back (d) Barnsley FC (e) Shamrock Rovers, St. Patrick's Ath., Shamrock Rovers, Ipswich, Chelmsford, Ipswich, Chelmsford, Ipswich, Limerick FC

*** Cottrell - Max Cottrell (Michael Maximillian Philip Cottrell) (a) 15/09/1999, ¿? (Gibraltar) (b) 1,80 (c) M - pivot (d) FC Manchester 62 Reserve (e) Glacis United, St Joseph's FC, Boca Gibraltar, Brymbo, Mons Calpe, LJMU, Gibraltar Utd., Mons Calpe

*** Coubis - Andrei Coubis (Andrei Coubiş) (a) 29/09/2003, Milano (Italy) (b) 1,89 (c) D - central defense (d) - (e) Lombardia uno

*** Coubronne - Jean-Christophe Coubronne (Jean-Christophe Sébastien Coubronne) (a) 30/07/1989, Lyon (France) (b) 1,80 (c) D - right back (d) IFK Mariehamn (e) FC Lahti, FC KTP, Olhanense, Novara, FC Sochaux B

*** Coucke - Gaëtan Coucke (a) 03/11/1998, Tongeren (Belgium) (b) 1,87 (c) G (d) KV Mechelen (e) KRC Genk, Lommel SK, KRC Genk

*** Coudek - Ondrej Coudek (Ondřej Čoudek) (a) 25/10/2004, ¿? (Georgia) (b) - (c) D - central defense (d) SK Dynamo Ceske Budejovice (e) -

*** Coudert - Grégoire Coudert (a) 03/04/1999, Rodez (France) (b) 1,88 (c) G (d) Stade Brestois 29 (e) Amiens SC, Amiens SC B, Tours FC, Tours B

*** Coufal - Vladimir Coufal (Vladimír Coufal) (a) 22/08/1992, Ostrava (Czechoslovakia, now in Czech Rep.) (b) 1,74 (c) D - right back (d) West Ham United (e) Slavia Praha, Slovan Liberec, SFC Opava, Hlucin, SSK Bilovec

*** Coughlan - Ronan Coughlan (Ronan Liam Coughlin) (a) 02/10/1996, Limerick (Ireland) (b) 1,78 (c) F - center forward (d) Waterford FC (e) St. Patrick's Ath., Sligo Rovers, Cork City, Bray Wanderers

*** Coulibaly - Amadou Coulibaly (a) 05/05/1997, Bamako (Mali) (b) 1,81 (c) F - center forward (d) Angoulême Charente FC (e) FK Tuzla City, Le Puy Foot, FC Nantes B, Yeelen

*** Coulibaly - Kalifa Coulibaly (a) 21/08/1991, Bamako (Mali) (b) 1,97 (c) F - center forward (d) - (e) Crvena zvezda, FC Nantes, KAA Gent, RSC Charleroi, Paris Saint Germain B, AS Real Bamako

*** Coulibaly - Lassana Coulibaly (a) 10/04/1996, Bamako (Mali) (b) 1,83 (c) M - central midfielder (d) US Salernitana 1919 (e) Angers SCO, Cercle Brugge, Angers SCO, Rangers FC, Angers SCO, SC Bastia, SC Bastia B

*** Coulibaly - Lasso Coulibaly (a) 19/10/2002, ¿? (Ivory Coast) (b) 1,86 (c) M - central midfielder (d) FC Nordsjælland (e) Right to Dream

*** Coulibaly - Sékou Coulibaly (a) 03/06/1994, ¿? (France) (b) 1,89 (c) D - central defense (d) US Forbach (e) US Hostert, Junglinster, US Forbach, JA Drancy

*** Coulibaly - Souleymane Coulibaly (a) 26/12/1994, Anguededou Songon (Ivory Coast) (b) 1,72 (c) F - center forward (d) Karmiotissa Pano Polemidion (e) ES Sahel, Partick Thistle, El Ahly, Kilmarnock FC, Peterborough, Newport County, Peterborough, Bari, Pistoiese, Bari, Grosseto

*** Coulibaly - Soumaïla Coulibaly (a) 14/10/2003, Montfermeil (France) (b) 1,91 (c) D - central defense (d) Royal Antwerp FC (e) Royal Antwerp, Borussia Dortmund

*** Coulibaly - Tanguy Coulibaly (a) 18/02/2001, Sèvres (France) (b) 1,78 (c) F - right winger (d) - (e) VfB Stuttgart

*** Coulson - Hayden Coulson (Hayden Ross Coulson) (a) 17/06/1998, Gateshead (England) (b) 1,72 (c) D - left back (d) Middlesbrough FC (e) Aberdeen FC, Middlesbrough, Peterborough, Middlesbrough, Ipswich, Middlesbrough, Cambridge Utd., St. Mirren

*** Coupland - Antoine Coupland (Antoine Ryan Coupland) (a) 12/12/2003, Chelsea, Quebec (Canada) (b) 1,74 (c) M - central midfielder (d) Vancouver Whitecaps FC 2 (e) HNK Rijeka, At. Ottawa, Ottawa Fury

*** Coureur - Mathias Coureur (a) 22/03/1988, Fort-de-France (Martinica) (b) 1,77 (c) F - left winger (d) Stade Poitevin FC (e) AC Escaldes, Golden Lion, Cherno More, NorthEast Utd., Samsunspor, Cherno More, Seongnam FC, Kaysar, Lokomotiv GO, Dinamo Tbilisi, Cherno More, Huracán, Golden Lion, At. Baleares, Orihuela CF, Golden Lion, FC Nantes, FC Gueugnon, FC Nantes, AS Beauvais, US Créteil B, Le Havre AC B

*** Courtet - Gaëtan Courtet (a) 22/02/1989, Lorient (France) (b) 1,80 (c) F - center forward (d) EA Guingamp (e) AC Ajaccio, FC Lorient, AC Ajaccio, FC Lorient, AJ Auxerre, Stade Reims, Stade Brestois, Stade Reims, Lorient B

*** Courtois - Thibaut Courtois (Thibaut Nicolas Marc Courtois) (a) 11/05/1992, Bree (Belgium) (b) 2,00 (c) G (d) Real Madrid CF (e) Chelsea, Atlético Madrid, Chelsea, KRC Genk

*** Coutadeur - Mathieu Coutadeur (a) 20/03/1986, Le Mans (France) (b) 1,69 (c) M - central midfielder (d) Le Mans FC (e) AC Ajaccio, Stade Lavallois, AEL Limassol, FC Lorient, AS Monaco, Le Mans UC 72, Le Mans UC 72 B

*** Coutinho - Philippe Coutinho (Philippe Coutinho Correia) (a) 12/06/1992, Rio de Janeiro (Brazil) (b) 1,72 (c) F - left winger (d) Aston Villa (e) FC Barcelona, Aston Villa, FC Barcelona, Bayern München, FC Barcelona, Liverpool, Internazionale Milano, RCD Espanyol, Internazionale Milano, Vasco da Gama, Internazionale Milano

*** Couto - Yan Couto (Yan Bueno Couto) (a) 03/06/2002, Curitiba (Brazil) (b) 1,68 (c) D - right back (d) Girona FC (e) Girona FC, Manchester City, SC Braga, Manchester City, Girona FC, Manchester City, Coritiba FC

*** Couto Pinto - Ricardo Couto Pinto (a) 14/01/1996, Luxembourg (Luxembourg) (b) - (c) M - right midfielder (d) SC Bettembourg (e) US Mondorf, F91 Dudelange, Differdange 03, F91 Dudelange, FSV Salmrohr

*** Couturier - Clément Couturier (a) 13/09/1993, Chaumont (France) (b) 1,83 (c) M - central midfielder (d) Swift Hesperange (e) Bastia-Borgo, RE Virton, F91 Dudelange, Les Herbiers VF, FC Chambly Oise, ASM Belfort, FC Montceau B., Dijon FCO B

*** Covaci - Razvan Covaci (Horaţiu Răzvan Covaci) (a) 10/10/2003, Ludus (Romania) (b) 1,69 (c) M - central midfielder (d) ACS Medias 2022 (e) FC Arges, Jiul Petrosani, FC Arges, Gaz Metan

*** Covali - Nichita Covali (a) 07/09/2002, ¿? (Moldova) (b) 1,77 (c) F - left winger (d) FC Floresti (e) Floresti, FC Sheriff, Sheriff-2

*** Coventry - Conor Coventry (a) 25/03/2000, Waltham Forest (England) (b) 1,77 (c) M - pivot (d) West Ham United (e) Rotherham, West Ham Utd., MK Dons, West Ham Utd., Peterborough, West Ham Utd., Lincoln City

*** Covic - Ivan Covic (Ivan Čović) (a) 17/09/1990, Zagreb (Yugoslavia, now in Croatia) (b) 1,95 (c) G (d) Slaven Belupo Koprivnica (e) HNK Gorica, Sepsi OSK, Apollon Smyrnis, Inter Zaprešić, Hrv Dragovoljac, Inter Zaprešić

*** Cowan - Keith Cowan (a) 23/08/1985, Ramelton, Donegal (Ireland) (b) 1,88 (c) D - central defense (d) Dergview FC (e) Finn Harps, Drogheda United, Dungannon, Glentoran, Finn Harps, Swilly Rovers, Finn Harps, Swilly Rovers

*** Cowan - Zach Cowan (a) 20/09/2005, ¿? (Northern Ireland) (b) - (c) M - central midfielder (d) Dollingstown FC (e) Portadown

*** Cowans - Henry Cowans (Henry Gordon Mander Cowans) (a) 02/10/1996, Birmingham (England) (b) 1,75 (c) M - central midfielder (d) Newtown AFC (e) Telford Utd., Stevenage

*** Cowderoy - Richard Cowderoy (Richard Charles William Cowderoy) (a) 01/04/1983, ¿? (England) (b) - (c) G (d) Marine FC (e) Llandudno, Connah's Quay, Prestatyn

*** Cox - Colm Cox (a) 13/02/2001, Ashbourne, Meath (Ireland) (b) 1,87 (c) G (d) Drogheda United FC (e) Wexford FC, Longford Town, Shelbourne

*** Cox - George Cox (George Frederick Cox) (a) 14/01/1998, Worthing (England) (b) 1,71 (c) D - left back (d) - (e) Fortuna Sittard, Fortuna Sittard, Northampton

*** Cox - Matthew Cox (a) 02/05/2003, ¿? (England) (b) 1,83 (c) G (d) Bristol Rovers (e) Brentford, Brentford B, AFC Wimbledon

*** Coxi - Salomão Coxi (Salomão Ludy Luvunga Coxi) (a) 24/07/2002, Luanda (Angola) (b) 1,82 (c) M - pivot (d) UE Santa Coloma (e) Cartaxo, Hatta Club, Wahda Reserve

*** Coyle - Caolin Coyle (a) 23/04/2000, Magherafelt (Northern Ireland) (b) - (c) D - right back (d) Portadown FC (e) Dungannon, Carrick Rangers, Dungannon

*** Coyle - Mark Coyle (a) 13/02/1997, Burt, Donegal (Ireland) (b) 1,78 (c) M - central midfielder (d) Shelbourne FC (e) Finn Harps, Cockhill Celtic

*** Cózar - Nando Cózar (Fernando Cózar Torres) (a) 02/03/1991, Cádiz (Spain) (b) 1,88 (c) M - central midfielder (d) ASD Sambiase 2023 (e) St Joseph's FC, Xerez CD, Mons Calpe, UD Lanzarote, PEPO, Øygarden FK, Angkor Tiger, Helsinki IFK, Kokkolan PV, FC Legirus, Los Barrios, Arcos CF, Chiclana CF, Los Barrios, Betis B, Cádiz CF B

*** Cozari - Mihai Cozari (a) 07/02/2004, Chişinău (Moldova) (b) 1,85 (c) F - center forward (d) FC Zimbru-2 Chisinau (e) Zimbru Chisinau

*** Cozza - Nicolas Cozza (Nicolas Louis Marcel Cozza) (a) 08/01/1999, Ganges (France) (b) 1,78 (c) D - left back (d) VfL Wolfsburg (e) Montpellier

*** Cozzella - Vincenzo Cozzella (a) 21/12/2001, Bitonto (Italy) (b) 1,90 (c) G (d) - (e) AJ Auxerre, AJ Auxerre B, Casale, Montpellier B

*** Cragno - Alessio Cragno (a) 28/06/1994, Fiesole (Italy) (b) 1,84 (c) G (d) US Sassuolo (e) Sassuolo, Monza, Cagliari, Monza, Cagliari, Benevento, Cagliari, Virtus Lanciano, Cagliari, Brescia

*** Crama - Tristan Crama (a) 08/11/2001, Béziers (France) (b) 1,92 (c) D - central defense (d) Bristol Rovers (e) Bristol Rovers, Brentford B, AS Béziers, Béziers B

*** Craninx - Álex Craninx (Alexandro Marco Craninx Joostens) (a) 21/10/1995, Málaga (Spain) (b) 1,97 (c) G (d) CF Fuenlabrada (e) Molde, RFC Seraing, Molde, Lillestrøm, Molde, FC Cartagena, Sparta Rotterdam, RM Castilla, Real Madrid C

*** Crankshaw - Oliver Crankshaw (Oliver Samuel Crankshaw) (a) 12/08/1998, Preston (England) (b) 1,82 (c) F - right winger (d) Stockport County (e) Motherwell FC, Stockport, Bradford City, Wigan Ath., Dundee FC, Curzon Ashton, Curzon Ashton, Colne, Clitheroe, Ramsbottom

*** Cravcescu - Vadim Cravcescu (a) 07/03/1985, Chişinău (Soviet Union, now in Moldova) (b) 1,75 (c) D - central defense (d) FC Victoria Chisinau (e) Dacia Buiucani, Codru, CSF Speranta, FK Buxoro, FC Saxan, Rapid G., Zimbru Chisinau, Milsami

*** Craven - CJ Craven (Christopher Jack Craven) (a) 03/10/2000, Wrexham (Wales) (b) 1,74 (c) D - central defense (d) Cardiff Metropolitan University (e) The New Saints

*** Crawford - Ali Crawford (Alistair Crawford) (a) 30/07/1991, Lanark (Scotland) (b) 1,79 (c) M - central midfielder (d) St. Johnstone FC (e) Morton, St. Johnstone, Bolton Wanderers, St. Johnstone, Bolton Wanderers, Tranmere Rovers, Bolton Wanderers, Doncaster Rovers, Bo'ness United

*** Creciun (c) D - central defense (d) FC Bălți (e) SSS Balti, FC Bălți, SSS Balti - Sebastian Creciun (c) D - central defense (d) FC Bălți (e) SSS Balti, FC Bălți, SSS Balti

*** Cremona - Llywelyn Cremona (a) 07/05/1995, Pieta (Malta) (b) - (c) F - attacking midfielder (d) Valletta FC (e) Gudja United FC, Birkirkara FC, Gudja United FC, Birkirkara FC, Gudja United FC, Birkirkara FC, Sperre) Birkirkara FC, Valletta

*** Crepulja - Ljuban Crepulja (a) 02/09/1993, Čapljina (Bosnia and Herzegovina) (b) 1,78 (c) M - pivot (d) FC Voluntari (e) FC Rapid 1923, Astra Giurgiu, FK Sarajevo, KV Mechelen, Soligorsk, KV Mechelen, Slaven Belupo, Hrv Dragovoljac, Segesta Sisak

*** Crescentini - Lorenzo Crescentini (a) 20/10/2004, ¿? (San Marino) (b) - (c) M - central midfielder (d) - (e) Domagnano

*** Crespi - Gian Marco Crespi (a) 28/06/2001, Udine (Italy) (b) 1,89 (c) G (d) FC Crotone (e) Juve Next Gen, Crotone, Picerno, Crotone, Pistoiese, Crotone, Renate, Crotone, Gozzano, Crotone, Gozzano

*** Crespo - David Crespo (David Crespo Zurita) (a) 26/08/1995, Palma de Mallorca (Spain) (b) - (c) D - right back (d) FC Santa Coloma (e) Badalona Futur, UD Llanera, Penya Deportiva, Llagostera, Formentera, CD Llosetense, Ferriolense

*** Crespo - José Crespo (José Ángel Crespo Rincón) (a) 09/02/1987, Lora del Río (Spain) (b) 1,85 (c) D - central defense (d) APOEL FC (e) PAOK, Aston Villa, Rayo Vallecano, Aston Villa, Córdoba CF, Bologna, Córdoba CF, Bologna, Hellas Verona, Bologna, Padova, Sevilla FC, Racing, Sevilla FC, Sevilla At., Sevilla FC C

*** Crespo - Miguel Crespo (Miguel Crespo da Silva) (a) 11/09/1996, Lyon (France) (b) 1,86 (c) M - central midfielder (d) Fenerbahce (e) Estoril Praia, Braga B, Merelinense, Neves FC

*** Crespo - Sergio Crespo (Sergio Crespo Alonso) (a) 29/09/1992, Andorra la Vella (Andorra) (b) - (c) M - central midfielder (d) Penya Encarnada d'Andorra (e) UE Santa Coloma, UE Santa B

*** Cresswell - Aaron Cresswell (a) 15/12/1989, Liverpool (England) (b) - (c) D - left back (d) West Ham United (e) Ipswich, Tranmere Rovers

*** Cresswell - Charlie Cresswell (Charlie Richard Cresswell) (a) 17/08/2002, Preston (England) (b) 1,90 (c) D - central defense (d) Leeds United (e) Millwall, Leeds Utd.

*** Cretu - Alexandru Cretu (Alexandru Crețu) (a) 24/04/1992, Pașcani (Romania) (b) 1,89 (c) M - pivot (d) Universitatea Craiova (e) FCSB, NK Maribor, Olimpija, ACSM Poli Iasi, FC Hunedoara, CSMS Iași

*** Cretu - Geani Cretu (Geani Mihai Crețu) (a) 12/01/2000, Piatra Neamț (Romania) (b) 1,77 (c) M - central midfielder (d) FC Dinamo 1948 (e) FC Arges, FC Dinamo, FC Rapid 1923, FC Dinamo

*** Cretu - Valentin Cretu (Valentin Iulian Crețu) (a) 02/01/1989, Buzău (Romania) (b) 1,76 (c) D - right back (d) FCSB (e) Gaz Metan, ACS Poli, Gaz Metan, Energie Cottbus, Gaz Metan, Concordia, Sageata Navodar, Beroe, Concordia, Rapid București, Concordia, AS FC Buzău, Râmnicu Sarat, AS FC Buzău, Râmnicu Sarat

*** Cricimari - Vadim Cricimari (Кричмарь Вадим Викторович) (a) 22/08/1988, Tiraspol (Soviet Union, now in Moldova) (b) 1,78 (c) F - center forward (d) FC Victoria Chisinau (e) Dacia Buiucani, Oțelul Galați, Dacia Buiucani, Floresti, CSF Speranta, Ac. Chisinau, Dinamo-Auto, Ac. Chisinau, Tosno, SKA-Energia, Tosno, FC Speranta, Tosno, Zimbru Chisinau, FC Speranta, Rapid G.

*** Crillon - Judicaël Crillon (a) 21/11/1988, Nancy (France) (b) 1,79 (c) D - left back (d) APM Metz (e) RFCU Luxembourg, FC Chambly Oise, Pau FC, LB Châteauroux, SR Colmar, SAS Epinal, US Raon-l'Étape, AS Nancy B

*** Crinacoba - Henry Crinacoba (Henry Cipriano Mendes Crinacoba) (a) 17/05/2004, ¿? (Portugal) (b) - (c) F - center forward (d) - (e) NK Tabor Sezana

*** Cristante - Bryan Cristante (a) 03/03/1995, San Vito al Tagliamento (Italy) (b) 1,86 (c) M - pivot (d) AS Roma (e) Atalanta, AS Roma, Atalanta, Benfica, Atalanta, Benfica, Pescara, Benfica, US Palermo, Benfica, AC Milan

*** Cristea - Iulian Cristea (Iulian Lucian Cristea) (a) 17/07/1994, Mediaş (Romania) (b) 1,84 (c) D - central defense (d) FC Rapid 1923 (e) FCSB, Gaz Metan, Metalurg. Cugir, Gaz Metan

*** Cristian - Cristian (Cristian Daniel Dal Bello Fagundes) (a) 13/12/1999, Pelotas (Brazil) (b) 1,78 (c) F - right winger (d) FK Mladost GAT Novi Sad (e) Zorya Lugansk, Caxias-RS, Zorya Lugansk, Brasil Pelotas, Botafogo-PB, Brasil Pelotas

*** Cristiano Ronaldo - Cristiano Ronaldo (Cristiano Ronaldo dos Santos Aveiro) (a) 05/02/1985, Funchal (Portugal) (b) 1,87 (c) F - center forward (d) Al-Nassr FC (e) Manchester Utd., Juventus, Real Madrid, Manchester Utd., Sporting Lisboa

*** Crivac - Alexandru Crivac (Alexandru Mihail Crivac) (a) 06/05/2002, ¿? (Romania) (b) 1,79 (c) M - pivot (d) FC Rapid 1923 (e) FC Arges, FCV Farul, FC D. Coman

*** Crivelli - Enzo Crivelli (Enzo Vito Gabriel Crivelli) (a) 06/02/1995, Rouen (France) (b) 1,83 (c) F - center forward (d) Servette FC (e) Basaksehir, St.-Étienne, Basaksehir, Antalyaspor, Basaksehir, SM Caen, Angers SCO, SM Caen, Angers SCO, Girondins Bordeaux, SC Bastia, Girondins Bordeaux, Girondins Bordeaux B

*** Crnac - Ante Crnac (a) 17/12/2003, Sisak (Croatia) (b) 1,89 (c) F - right winger (d) Slaven Belupo Koprivnica (e) Din. Zagreb II

*** Crncevic - Mate Crncevic (Mate Crnčević) (a) 20/03/1995, Metković (Croatia) (b) 1,85 (c) M - pivot (d) NK Bjelovar (e) Aktobe, Akzhayik, Aktobe, Zeljeznicar, Din. Zagreb II, Din. Zagreb II, Hrv Dragovoljac, Neretva Metkovic, Cibalia, Neretva Metkovic

*** Crnigoj - Domen Crnigoj (Domen Črnigoj) (a) 18/11/1995, Koper (Slovenia) (b) 1,88 (c) M - central midfielder (d) Venezia FC (e) Salernitana, Venezia, FC Lugano, Koper

*** Crnomarkovic - Djordje Crnomarkovic (Ђорђе Црномарковић) (a) 10/09/1993, Beograd (RF Yugoslavia, now in Serbia) (b) 1,88 (c) D - central defense (d) FK Vojvodina Novi Sad (e) Olimpija, Lech Poznan, Zagłębie, Lech Poznan, Radnicki Niš, Javor-Matis, Čukarički, Olimpija, Javor-Matis, Donji Srem, Sumadija, FK Beograd

*** Crociata - Giovanni Crociata (a) 11/08/1997, Palermo (Italy) (b) 1,74 (c) M - central midfielder (d) FC Empoli (e) Cittadella, FC Empoli, Südtirol, FC Empoli, SPAL, FC Empoli, Crotone, Empoli, Crotone, Carpi, Crotone, AC Milan, Brescia

*** Croitoru - David Croitoru (David Marian Croitoru) (a) 09/08/2003, Bacău (Romania) (b) 1,77 (c) M - central midfielder (d) CSC Dumbravita (e) FC Arges, FC U Craiova, FC Botosani

*** Croitoru - Flavius Croitoru (Flavius Dănuţ Croitoru) (a) 13/07/1992, Piteşti (Romania) (b) 1,86 (c) G (d) CS Mioveni (e) FC Arges, CS Mioveni, FC Arges

*** Croizet - Yohan Croizet (a) 15/02/1992, Sarrebourg (France) (b) 1,80 (c) M - attacking midfielder (d) Újpest FC II (e) OH Leuven, Kansas City, KV Mechelen, OH Leuven, RE Virton, FC Metz, FC Metz B

*** Crona - Edvin Crona (a) 25/01/2000, ¿? (Sweden) (b) - (c) F (d) Oskarshamns AIK (e) Oskarshamns AIK, Kalmar FF, Åtvidabergs FF, Kalmar FF, Oskarshamns AIK, Kalmar FF, Värnamo, Kalmar FF

*** Cross - Nathan Cross (a) 01/09/2004, ¿? (Malta) (b) - (c) F - center forward (d) - (e) Birkirkara

*** Crowe - Joe Crowe (a) 20/04/1998, Belfast (Northern Ireland) (b) - (c) M - pivot (d) Carrick Rangers (e) Glentoran, Linfield, Limerick FC, Plunkett FC
*** Crowther - Jamie Crowther (a) 10/02/1992, Wrexham (Wales) (b) - (c) M - central midfielder (d) - (e) Airbus UK, Caernarfon, Airbus UK, Caernarfon, Airbus UK, Aberystwyth, Bala, Connah's Quay, Barrow
*** Crowther - Sam Crowther (a) 03/04/2000, Groningen (Netherlands) (b) 1,94 (c) F - center forward (d) DVS '33 Ermelo (e) Victoria Rosport, Go Ahead Eagles, ONS Sneek
*** Cruise - Kieran Cruise (a) 03/01/2004, ¿? (Ireland) (b) - (c) D - left back (d) Shamrock Rovers (e) -
*** Cruz - Andrew Cruz (Andrew Viñas Cruz) (a) 11/02/2005, Gibraltar (Gibraltar) (b) - (c) M - attacking midfielder (d) - (e) Europa Point FC, Red Imps Reserves, Europa Reserve
*** Cruz - Juan Cruz (Juan Cruz Díaz Espósito) (a) 25/04/2000, Quilmes (Argentina) (b) 1,80 (c) F - right winger (d) Real Betis Balompié (e) Betis Deportivo, At. Malagueño
*** Cruz - Juan Cruz (Juan-Cruz Álvaro Armada) (a) 28/07/1992, Madrid (Spain) (b) 1,82 (c) D - left back (d) CA Osasuna (e) Elche CF, Rayo Majadahonda, UD Sanse, Pistoiese, San Marino, Bologna, Carrarese, Bologna
*** Cruz - Sandro Cruz (Sandro Plínio Rosa da Cruz) (a) 12/05/2001, Braga (Portugal) (b) 1,82 (c) D - left back (d) GD Chaves (e) Benfica, Chaves, Benfica, Benfica B
*** Cruz - Stélvio Cruz (Stélvio Rosa da Cruz) (a) 24/01/1989, Luanda (Angola) (b) 1,87 (c) M - pivot (d) FC Mondercange (e) Jeunesse Esch, RWDM, RE Virton, F91 Dudelange, Alki Larnaca, Caála, SC Braga, C.R.D. Libolo, SC Braga, 1° de Agosto, SC Braga, Leiria, SC Braga
*** Cseke - Benjámin Cseke (a) 22/07/1994, Budapest (Hungary) (b) 1,84 (c) M - central midfielder (d) Mezőkövesd Zsóry FC (e) Diósgyőr, Mezőkövesd, MTK Budapest, Paksi FC, MTK Budapest, Paksi FC, Újpest FC, MTK Budapest, Újpest FC, MTK Budapest, Vasas FC
*** Cseri - Tamás Cseri (a) 15/01/1988, Győr (Hungary) (b) 1,74 (c) M - attacking midfielder (d) Mezőkövesd Zsóry FC (e) Kisvárda, Gyirmót FC, BKV Előre, Pécsi MFC, BKV Előre, Pécsi MFC, ETO FC Győr, Mosonmagyaróvár
*** Csoboth - Kevin Csoboth (a) 20/06/2000, Pécs (Hungary) (b) 1,74 (c) F - right winger (d) Újpest FC (e) Fehérvár, Szeged, Fehérvár, Benfica B
*** Csóka - Dániel Csóka (a) 04/04/2000, Zalaegerszeg (Hungary) (b) 1,88 (c) D - central defense (d) Zalaegerszegi TE FC (e) AFC Wimbledon, Dunajska Streda
*** Csóka - Dominik Csóka (a) 29/03/2004, Zalaegerszeg (Hungary) (b) - (c) M (d) Zalaegerszegi TE FC (e) Zalaegerszeg II
*** Csongvai - Áron Csongvai (a) 31/10/2000, Budapest (Hungary) (b) 1,86 (c) M - central midfielder (d) Fehérvár FC (e) Újpest FC, Újpest II
*** Cuadrado - Juan Cuadrado (Juan Guillermo Cuadrado Bello) (a) 26/05/1988, Necoclí (Colombia) (b) 1,76 (c) M - right midfielder (d) Internazionale Milano (e) Juventus, Chelsea, Juventus, Chelsea, Juventus, Chelsea, Fiorentina, Udinese, Fiorentina, Udinese, Lecce, Udinese, Indep. Medellín
*** Cubara - Almir Cubara (a) 21/11/1997, Sarajevo (Bosnia and Herzegovina) (b) 1,93 (c) D - central defense (d) Tikves Kavadarci (e) Igman Konjic, TOSK Tesanj, Celik Zenica, Zeljeznicar, Bosna Visoko, Zeljeznicar, Bosna Visoko, FK Olimpik
*** Cubelic - Ivan Cubelic (Ivan Ćubelić) (a) 02/06/2003, Split (Croatia) (b) 1,84 (c) M - attacking midfielder (d) HNK Hajduk Split (e) NK Varazdin, Hajduk Split, NK Dugopolje, Hajduk Split, Hajduk Split II, Adriatic Split

*** Cubrilo - Marko Cubrilo (Marko Čubrilo) (a) 03/05/1998, Novi Sad (Yugoslavia, now in Serbia) (b) 1,73 (c) D - left back (d) FK Igman Konjic (e) Leotar Trebinje, Mladost GAT, Dinamo Vranje, Dobanovci, Zarkovo, Domžale, Radnik, Teleoptik, Teleoptik

*** Cuca - Cuca (Carlos Miguel Pereira Fernandes) (a) 09/01/1991, Lisboa (Portugal) (b) 1,77 (c) M - pivot (d) - (e) Casa Pia, Mafra, Felgueiras, Omonia Aradippou, 1º Dezembro, AD Oeiras

*** Cucchi - Alessandro Cucchi (a) 18/03/2000, ¿? (Italy) (b) - (c) D - left back (d) SS Cosmos (e) Diegaro, Bra, Nuorese

*** Cucin - Luka Cucin (Лука Цуцин) (a) 24/11/1998, Beograd (RF Yugoslavia, Serbia) (b) 1,82 (c) D - right back (d) FK Kolubara Lazarevac (e) RFK Novi Sad, KF Laçi, Borac Banja Luka, Vojvodina, FK Partizan, FK Indjija, FK Partizan, Spartak, FK Partizan, Teleoptik

*** Cuckic - Nikola Cuckic (Никола Цуцкић) (a) 11/04/1997, Gnjilane (RF Yugoslavia, now in Kosovo) (b) 1,75 (c) M - central midfielder (d) Zhetysu Taldykorgan (e) Kaspiy Aktau, Aktobe, Javor-Matis, FK Zemun, Mladost, OFK Beograd

*** Cucos - Catalin Cucos (Cătălin Cucoş) (a) 29/09/2003, Chişinău (Moldova) (b) 1,90 (c) D - central defense (d) Kolos Kovalivka (e) Zimbru Chisinau, FC Zimbru-2

*** Cuculi - Ardian Cuculi (a) 19/07/1987, ¿? (Yugoslavia, now in North Macedonia) (b) 1,84 (c) D - central defense (d) - (e) Shkëndija, FC Drita, FK Kukësi, Shkëndija, FK Partizani, Shkëndija, FK Milano Kumanovo, Pobeda Prilep, Shkëndija, Vëllazërimi

*** Cucurella - Marc Cucurella (Marc Cucurella Saseta) (a) 22/07/1998, Alella (Spain) (b) 1,73 (c) D - left back (d) Chelsea FC (e) Brighton & Hove Albion, Getafe CF, FC Barcelona, Getafe CF, FC Barcelona, SD Eibar, FC Barcelona, SD Eibar, FC Barcelona, FC Barcelona B

*** Cucurs - Davis Cucurs (a) 19/03/2000, Riga (Latvia) (b) - (c) D - right back (d) BFC Daugavpils (e) -

*** Cudars - Kristers Cudars (Kristers Čudars) (a) 03/09/1999, Rīga (Latvia) (b) 1,85 (c) M - pivot (d) Valmiera FC (e) Metta, Liepaja, Riga II

*** Cuéllar - Iván Cuéllar (Iván Cuéllar Rivera) (a) 01/01/2003, ¿? (Spain) (b) - (c) F - center forward (d) UDC Txantrea (e) AC Escaldes

*** Cuéllar - Ronald Cuéllar (Ronald Cuéllar Ortiz) (a) 09/06/1997, ¿? (Bolivia) (b) - (c) F - left winger (d) Blooming Santa Cruz (e) Alashkert CF, Nacional Potosí, Atlántico, Blooming

*** Cuenca - Jorge Cuenca (Jorge Cuenca Barreno) (a) 17/11/1999, Madrid (Spain) (b) 1,90 (c) D - central defense (d) Villarreal CF (e) Getafe CF, Villarreal CF, UD Almería, Villarreal CF, FC Barcelona B, AD Alcorcón B

*** Cuesta - Carlos Cuesta (Carlos Eccehomo Cuesta Figueroa) (a) 09/03/1999, Quibdó (Colombia) (b) 1,79 (c) D - central defense (d) KRC Genk (e) At. Nacional

*** Cuesta - Julián Cuesta (Julián Cuesta Díaz) (a) 28/03/1991, Campotéjar (Spain) (b) 1,96 (c) G (d) Aris Thessaloniki (e) Wisla Kraków, UD Almería, Sevilla FC, UD Almería, Sevilla FC, Sevilla At., Sevilla FC C

*** Cufré - Braian Cufré (Braian Ezequiel Cufré) (a) 15/12/1996, Mar de Plata (Argentina) (b) 1,78 (c) D - left back (d) New York City FC (e) New York City, RCD Mallorca, Málaga CF, RCD Mallorca, Vélez Sarsfield

*** Cugunovs - Svetoslavs Cugunovs (a) 10/01/2002, ¿? (Latvia) (b) 1,90 (c) F - center forward (d) SK Super Nova (e) Riga II, Auda, Riga II

*** Cuic - Filip Cuic (Filip Čuić) (a) 22/02/2003, Split (Croatia) (b) 1,80 (c) F - center forward (d) HNK Hajduk Split (e) NK Radomlje, Hajduk Split

*** Cuic - Mario Cuic (Mario Čuić) (a) 22/04/2001, Split (Croatia) (b) 1,84 (c) M - central midfielder (d) NK Istra 1961 (e) Hajduk Split, NK Radomlje, Hajduk Split, Hajduk Split II, HNK Tomislav T.

*** Cuic - Petar Cuic (Petar Čuić) (a) 02/06/1999, Zagreb (Croatia) (b) 1,85 (c) M - pivot (d) - (e) Septemvri Sofia, Tulsa, Kansas City II, Din. Zagreb II

*** Cuisance - Michaël Cuisance (Michaël Bruno Dominique Cuisance) (a) 16/08/1999, Strasbourg (France) (b) 1,81 (c) M - central midfielder (d) Venezia FC (e) Sampdoria, Venezia, Bayern München, Ol. Marseille, Bayern München, Borussia Mönchengladbach

*** Cukici - Denis Cukici (a) 10/02/2003, ¿? (Finland) (b) - (c) M - pivot (d) SJK Seinäjoki II (e) HJK Klubi 04

*** Cukon - Marko Cukon (a) 01/04/2005, Pula (Croatia) (b) 1,78 (c) F - left winger (d) - (e) NK Veli Vrh

*** Cukovic - Igor Cukovic (Igor Ćuković) (a) 06/06/1993, Nikšić (RF Yugoslavia, now in Montenegro) (b) 1,91 (c) D - central defense (d) - (e) FK Decic Tuzi, Buducnost Podgorica, Rudar Pljevlja, 1.SC Znojmo, FC Kamza, Elverum, FK Iskra, Sutjeska Niksic

*** Cukovic - Mitar Cukovic (Mitar Ćuković) (a) 06/04/1995, Nikšić (RF Yugoslavia, now in Montenegro) (b) 1,78 (c) D - left back (d) FK Riteriai (e) Velez Mostar, Panevezys, Napredak, Proleter, FK Lovcen, OFK Petrovac, OSK Igalo

*** Culen - Tobias Culen

*** Cumic - Luka Cumic (Лука Чумић) (a) 25/05/2001, Beograd (RF Yugoslavia, now in Serbia) (b) 1,90 (c) F - center forward (d) FK Radnik Surdulica (e) Zlatibor, Novi Pazar, Rabotnicki, Metalac, FK Vrčin

*** Cumic - Nikola Cumic (Никола Чумић) (a) 20/11/1998, Užice (RF Yugoslavia, now in Serbia) (b) 1,78 (c) F - right winger (d) FK Vojvodina Novi Sad (e) Olympiakos, FC Luzern, Olympiakos, Real Sporting, Olympiakos, Radnicki Niš, Olympiakos, Radnicki Niš, Metalac, Sloboda Užice

*** Cummings - Luke Cummings (Luke Owen Cummings) (a) 25/10/1991, Merthyr Tydfil (Wales) (b) - (c) D - right back (d) Pontypridd United (e) Barry Town, Merthyr Town, Barry Town, Carmarthen, Bath City, Neath, Cardiff City,

*** Cumur - Ebrar Cumur (Tayyip Ebrar Cumur) (a) 19/11/1999, Trabzon (Turkey) (b) 1,76 (c) M - attacking midfielder (d) - (e) Trabzonspor, Istanbulspor, Trabzonspor, Trabzonspor

*** Cundle - Luke Cundle (Luke James Cundle) (a) 26/04/2002, Warrington (England) (b) 1,71 (c) M - central midfielder (d) Plymouth Argyle (e) Plymouth Argyle, Wolverhampton Wanderers, Swansea City, Wolverhampton Wanderers

*** Cunha - Gonçalo Cunha (Gonçalo Ferreira da Cunha) (a) 24/05/2002, Guimarães (Portugal) (b) 1,89 (c) D - central defense (d) Anadia FC (e) Pedras Salgadas, Moreirense Yout

*** Cunha - Matheus Cunha (Matheus Santos Carneiro da Cunha) (a) 27/05/1999, João Pessoa (Brazil) (b) 1,83 (c) F - center forward (d) Wolverhampton Wanderers (e) Atlético Madrid, Wolverhampton Wanderers, Atlético Madrid, Hertha Berlin, RB Leipzig, FC Sion

*** Cuperman - David Cuperman (David Cuperman Coifman) (a) 08/11/1996, Bogotá (Colombia) (b) 1,81 (c) D - left back (d) FC Ashdod (e) Fortaleza CEIF, Alianza Petrol., Fortaleza CEIF, Averett Univ.

*** Curatolo - Dennis Curatolo (a) 03/04/2004, Como (Italy) (b) - (c) F - center forward (d) Fermana FC (e) Fermana

*** Curic - Emro Curic (a) 25/07/2000, ¿? (Germany) (b) 1,88 (c) F - center forward (d) - (e) Etzella Ettelbrück, HSC Hannover, SC Paderborn II

*** Curic - Mario Curic (Mario Ćurić) (a) 28/09/1998, Split (Croatia) (b) 1,82 (c) M - pivot (d) Torpedo Moskva (e) HNK Sibenik, NK Solin, Hajduk Split II

*** Curma - Matej Curma (Matej Čurma) (a) 27/03/1996, Pliešovce (Slovakia) (b) 1,81 (c) D - right back (d) MFK Karvina (e) Spartak Trnava, Ružomberok, Ruzomberok B, MFK Zvolen, Ruzomberok B, Liptovsky Mik.

*** Curmi - Anthony Curmi (a) 20/11/1982, Valletta (Malta) (b) - (c) G (d) Hamrun Spartans (e) Senglea Ath., Gzira Utd., Tarxien, Gzira Utd., Tarxien, Gzira Utd., Tarxien, Gzira Utd., Tarxien, Gzira Utd., Tarxien, Sliema Wanderers, Hamrun Spartans, Sliema Wanderers, Tarxien, Sliema Wanderers

*** Curos - Marius Curos (Marius Curoș) (a) 30/10/2003, ¿? (Moldova) (b) 1,70 (c) M - central midfielder (d) - (e) Zimbru Chisinau, FC Zimbru-2, Zimbru Chisinau

*** Curran - Chris Curran (Christopher Patrick Curran) (a) 05/01/1991, ¿? (Northern Ireland) (b) 1,76 (c) M - central midfielder (d) Cliftonville FC (e) Ballinamallard, Portadown

*** Curran - Conall Curran (a) 22/03/2004, ¿? (Northern Ireland) (b) - (c) F - center forward (d) Dundela FC (e) Larne FC, Ballyclare, Larne FC

*** Curran - Craig Curran (Craig Carl Curran) (a) 23/08/1989, Liverpool (England) (b) 1,75 (c) F - center forward (d) - (e) Airbus UK, Marine FC, Airbus UK, Connah's Quay, Dundee FC, Dundee United, Ross County, Nuneaton, Limerick FC, AFC Rochdale, Limerick FC, AFC Rochdale, Chester, AFC Rochdale, Carlisle United, FC Morecambe, Carlisle United, Tranmere Rovers

*** Curran - Ryan Curran (a) 13/10/1993, Derry (Northern Ireland) (b) - (c) F - center forward (d) Cliftonville FC (e) Ballinamallard, Finn Harps, Derry City

*** Curry - Dean Curry (a) 11/12/1994, ¿? (Northern Ireland) (b) - (c) D - central defense (d) Dungannon Swifts (e) Ballinamallard, Institute FC, Newbuildings

*** Curtis - Ben Curtis (a) 27/03/2004, Navan, Meath (Ireland) (b) 1,86 (c) D - central defense (d) Sam Curtis (e) Drogheda United, St. Patrick's Ath.

*** Curtis - Sam Curtis (a) 01/12/2005, Navan (Ireland) (b) 1,85 (c) D - right back (d) St. Patrick's Athletic (e) -

*** Cushley - David Cushley (a) 22/07/1989, Belfast (Northern Ireland) (b) - (c) M - central midfielder (d) Carrick Rangers (e) Crusaders, Ballymena, Lisburn FC, Ballymena, Shankill

*** Cushnie - Ben Cushnie (a) 07/08/2001, Hillsborough (Northern Ireland) (b) 1,76 (c) F - center forward (d) Bangor FC (e) Bangor, Glentoran, Dungannon, Glentoran, Ards FC

*** Cuypers - Hugo Cuypers (Hugo Jean-Marc Cuypers) (a) 07/02/1997, Liège (Belgium) (b) 1,85 (c) F - center forward (d) KAA Gent (e) KV Mechelen, Olympiakos, AC Ajaccio, Olympiakos, Ergotelis, Standard Liège, RFC Seraing, Standard Liège

*** Cuze - Mario Cuze (Mario Ćuže) (a) 24/04/1999, Metković (Croatia) (b) 1,88 (c) F - left winger (d) HSK Zrinjski Mostar (e) Dinamo Zagreb, Zrinjski Mostar, Dinamo Zagreb, SK Dnipro-1, Dinamo Zagreb, SK Dnipro-1, Dinamo Zagreb, NK Lokomotiva, Dinamo Zagreb, NK Istra, Din. Zagreb II, Neretva Metkovic

*** Cvancara - Tomas Cvancara (Tomáš Čvančara) (a) 13/08/2000, Neratovice (Czech Rep.) (b) 1,90 (c) F - center forward (d) Borussia Mönchengladbach (e) Sparta Praha, Jablonec, SFC Opava, Jablonec, Vysehrad, Jablonec, Jablonec

*** Cvek - Lovro Cvek (a) 06/07/1995, Varaždin (Croatia) (b) 1,83 (c) M - pivot (d) CFR Cluj (e) Zorya Lugansk, FK Senica, NK Celje, NK Aluminij, DNŠ Zavrč, NK Varazdin

*** Cvetanoski - Dejan Cvetanoski (Дejaн Цветаноски) (a) 15/05/1990, Kicevo (Yugoslavia, now in North Macedonia) (b) 1,83 (c) F - center forward (d) Vardar

Skopje (e) Sileks, Struga, Renova, Pobeda Prilep, Pelister Bitola, Carev Dvor, Teteks Tetovo, Horizont, Napredok Kicevo

*** Cvetanoski - Matej Cvetanoski (Матеј Цветаноски) (a) 18/08/1997, Skopje (North Macedonia) (b) 1,79 (c) F - left winger (d) - (e) AP Brera, FK Partizani, Gyirmót FC, FC Shkupi, Vardar, Pelister Bitola, Makedonija

*** Cvetinovic - Dusan Cvetinovic (Душан Цветиновић) (a) 24/12/1988, Šabac (Yugoslavia, now in Serbia) (b) 1,86 (c) D - central defense (d) FK TSC Backa Topola (e) Radnicki 1923, Tokushima Vort., Yokohama F. M., RC Lens, Haugesund, RC Lens, Haugesund, FC Vaduz, FC Wohlen, Grasshoppers, FC Wohlen, Dinamo Vranje

*** Cvetko - Christopher Cvetko (Christopher Brian Cvetko) (a) 02/04/1997, Klagenfurt (Austria) (b) 1,82 (c) M - central midfielder (d) SK Austria Klagenfurt (e) Juniors OÖ, Blau Weiss Linz

*** Cvetkovic - Milos Cvetkovic (Милош Цветковић) (a) 06/01/1990, Beograd (Yugoslavia, now in Serbia) (b) 1,75 (c) D - right back (d) FK TSC Backa Topola (e) Mladost, Levski Sofia, Napredak, Crvena zvezda, Napredak, Hajduk 1912, Rad Beograd, FK Palic Koming, Rad Beograd, FK Zemun

*** Cvetkovic - Nemanja Cvetkovic (Немања Цветковић) (a) 03/01/1996, Užice (RF Yugoslavia, now in Serbia) (b) 1,88 (c) D - central defense (d) FK Radnicki Sremska Mitrovica (e) Leotar Trebinje, Vozdovac, Kolubara, Jedinstvo Uzice, Čukarički, BASK Beograd, Čukarički, Sloboda Užice

*** Cvetkovic - Nenad Cvetkovic (Ненад Цветковић) (a) 06/01/1996, Užice (RF Yugoslavia, now in Serbia) (b) 1,95 (c) D - central defense (d) SK Rapid Wien (e) FC Ashdod, Vozdovac, FK Zemun, Crvena zvezda, Rad Beograd, Crvena zvezda, Rakovica, Crvena zvezda

*** Cvetkovic - Stefan Cvetkovic (Стефан Цветковић) (a) 12/01/1998, Leskovac (RF Yugoslavia, now in Serbia) (b) 1,84 (c) F - left winger (d) FK Radnicki Niš (e) RFS, Metalac, Graficar, Čukarički, Crvena zvezda Beograd II, Graficar, Crvena zvezda Beograd II, Backa, Crvena zvezda Beograd II, Graficar

*** Cvetojevic - Igor Cvetojevic (Игор Цветојевић) (a) 01/07/2001, Beograd (RF Yugoslavia, now in Serbia) (b) 1,88 (c) D - central defense (d) FK Teleoptik Zemun (e) FK Partizan, Novi Banovci, Kolubara, Budućnost, Kolubara, Stara Pazova, Kolubara, FK Loznica, Batajnica

*** Cvijanovic - Ivan Cvijanovic (Ivan Cvijanović) (a) 09/10/2003, Zagreb (Croatia) (b) 1,85 (c) D - left back (d) HNK Sibenik (e) NK Osijek, NK Osijek II, NK Naftas - IG

*** Cvijanovic - Obren Cvijanovic (Obren Cvijanović) (a) 30/08/1994, Banja Luka (Bosnia and Herzegovina) (b) 1,85 (c) F - right winger (d) - (e) Borac Banja Luka, Velez Mostar, Zvijezda G., FK Krupa

*** Cvijovic - Andrej Cvijovic (Андреј Цвијовић) (a) 11/12/2001, ¿? (RF Yugoslavia, now in Montenegro) (b) 1,80 (c) D - right back (d) Jedinstvo Bijelo Polje (e) Mornar Bar, Jedinstvo

*** Cvijovic - Djordjije Cvijovic (a) 01/01/2000, Bijelo Polje (RF Yugoslavia, now in Montenegro) (b) - (c) D - left back (d) Jedinstvo Bijelo Polje (e) -

*** Cvijovic (c) D - left back (d) Jedinstvo Bijelo Polje (e) - - Nikola Cvijovic (c) D - left back (d) Jedinstvo Bijelo Polje (e) -

*** Cyprian - Matthew Cyprian (a) 01/10/1994, Abuja (Nigeria) (b) 1,88 (c) G (d) - (e) NK Bravo, NK Dubrava ZG, Junak Sinj

*** Cyprien - Wylan Cyprien (Wylan Jean-Claude Cyprien) (a) 28/01/1995, Les Abymes (Guadaloupe) (b) 1,80 (c) M - central midfielder (d) Parma (e) FC Sion, Parma, FC Nantes, Parma, OGC Nice, Parma, OGC Nice, RC Lens

*** Cyrbja - Arber Cyrbja (Arbër Çyrbja) (a) 18/09/1993, Shijak (Albania) (b) 1,78 (c) M - right midfielder (d) KF Teuta (e) KF Erzeni, KF Egnatia, SC Gjilani, KF Teuta, FK Kukësi, KF Teuta, KF Elbasani, KF Erzeni, KF Teuta
*** Czekala - Maksym Czekala (Maksym Czekała) (a) 05/03/2004, ¿? (Poland) (b) 1,83 (c) M - attacking midfielder (d) Lech Poznan (e) Lech Poznan II
*** Czekanowicz - Youn Czekanowicz (a) 08/08/2000, Wiltz (Luxembourg) (b) 1,91 (c) G (d) Swift Hesperange (e) Progrès Niederkorn, FC UNA Strassen, Progrès Niederkorn, Etzella Ettelbrück
*** Czerech - Patryk Czerech (Patryk Czerech) (a) 06/04/2001, Białystok (Poland) (b) 1,90 (c) D - central defense (d) Jagiellonia Białystok (e) Jagiellonia II
*** Czérna - Erik Czérna (Czérna Erik Gábor) (a) 07/05/2003, Kisvárda (Hungary) (b) 1,71 (c) M - attacking midfielder (d) Kisvárda FC (e) Kisvárda II
*** Czerwinski - Alan Czerwinski (Alan Czerwiński) (a) 02/02/1993, Olkusz (Poland) (b) 1,81 (c) D - right back (d) Lech Poznan (e) Zagłębie, GKS Katowice, Rekord B-B, Bolesław B.
*** Czerwinski - Jakub Czerwinski (Jakub Czerwiński) (a) 06/08/1991, Krynica Zdrój (Poland) (b) 1,83 (c) D - central defense (d) Piast Gliwice (e) Legia Warszawa, Piast Gliwice, Legia Warszawa, Pogon Szczecin, Nieciecza, OKS Brzesko, Promien Opalenica, Poprad Muszyna
*** Czyz - Szymon Czyz (Szymon Czyż) (a) 08/07/2001, Gdynia (Poland) (b) 1,76 (c) M - pivot (d) Rakow Czestochowa (e) Warta Poznań, SI Arka Gdynia
*** da Costa - Coba da Costa (Coba Gomes da Costa) (a) 26/07/2002, La Mojonera (Spain) (b) - (c) F - left winger (d) UB Conquense (e) Tabor Sezana, Berja CF, UD Maracena
*** da Costa - Danny da Costa (Danny Vieira da Costa) (a) 13/07/1993, Neuss (Germany) (b) 1,87 (c) D - right back (d) 1.FSV Mainz 05 (e) Eintracht, Mainz 05, Eintracht, Bayer Leverkusen, FC Ingolstadt, Bayer Leverkusen, FC Ingolstadt, Bayer Leverkusen
*** da Costa - Evan da Costa (Evan da Costa e Sousa) (a) 07/05/2003, ¿? (Luxembourg) (b) 1,90 (c) G (d) CS Fola Esch (e) -
*** da Costa - Manuel da Costa (Manuel Marouan da Costa Trindade Senoussi) (a) 06/05/1986, Saint-Max (France) (b) 1,91 (c) D - central defense (d) - (e) F91 Dudelange, SK Beveren, BB Erzurumspor, Trabzonspor, Ittihad Club, Basaksehir, Olympiakos, Sivasspor, Lokomotiv Moskva, Nacional, Lokomotiv Moskva, West Ham Utd., Fiorentina, Sampdoria, Fiorentina, PSV Eindhoven, AS Nancy, AS Nancy B
*** Da Costa - Nuno Da Costa (Nuno Miguel da Costa Jóia) (a) 10/02/1991, Praïa (Cabo Verde) (b) 1,82 (c) F - center forward (d) AJ Auxerre (e) Nottingham Forest, SM Caen, Nottingham Forest, Excelsior Mouscron, Nottingham Forest, Racing Club Strasbourg, Valenciennes FC, Aubagne
*** Da Cruz - Alessio Da Cruz (Alessio Sergio Fernando Da Cruz) (a) 18/01/1997, Almere (Netherlands) (b) 1,86 (c) M - attacking midfielder (d) Feralpisalò (e) KV Mechelen, Parma, LR Vicenza, Parma, Santos Laguna, Parma, FC Groningen, Parma, Sheffield Wednesday, Parma, Ascoli, Parma, Spezia, Parma, Novara, FC Dordrecht, FC Twente
*** Da Cruz - Caio Da Cruz (Caio Da Cruz Oliveira Queiroz) (a) 13/03/2002, Serra (Brazil) (b) - (c) F - center forward (d) HNK Gorica (e) NK Dugopolje, HNK Gorica, NK Kurilovec
*** Da Graca - Cosimo Marco Da Graca (a) 01/05/2002, Palermo (Italy) (b) 1,85 (c) F - center forward (d) Juventus Next Gen (e) Calcio Sicilia

*** Da Graca - Kristopher Da Graca (Kristopher Santos Da Graca) (a) 16/01/1998, Göteborg (Sweden) (b) 1,90 (c) D - central defense (d) HJK Helsinki (e) HJK Helsinki, Sirius, VVV-Venlo, IFK Göteborg

*** da Luz - Nélson da Luz (Nélson Conceição da Luz) (a) 04/02/1998, Luanda (Angola) (b) 1,83 (c) F - left winger (d) Vitória Guimarães SC (e) Vitória Guimarães B, 1º de Agosto

*** da Mota - Daniel da Mota (Daniel Alves da Mota) (a) 11/09/1985, Ettelbrück (Luxembourg) (b) 1,77 (c) F - left winger (d) FC Atert Bissen (e) Etzella Ettelbrück, Differdange 03, Desenzano, Sona, RFCU Luxembourg, F91 Dudelange, Etzella Ettelbrück

*** da Rocha - Joel Marques da Rocha (a) 19/11/1984, Canedo - Lobão (Portugal) (b) - (c) M (d) Penya Encarnada d'Andorra (e) Penya Encarnada, FC Ordino, Lusitanos, Penya Encarnada, UE Engordany, FC Encamp

*** Da Silva - Damien Da Silva (a) 17/05/1988, Talence (France) (b) 1,84 (c) D - central defense (d) Melbourne Victory (e) Olympique Lyon, Stade Rennes, SM Caen, Clermont Foot, FC Rouen 1899, LB Châteauroux, FC Rouen 1899, LB Châteauroux, Chamois Niort, Niort B

*** da Silva - Edgar da Silva (Edgar Antonio da Silva) (a) 14/02/1998, ¿? (Luxembourg) (b) - (c) F (d) - (e) Etzella Ettelbrück, Erpeldange, Etzella Ettelbrück, Erpeldange, Sporting Mertzig, Erpeldange, Sporting Mertzig

*** Da Silva - Patrick Da Silva (a) 23/10/1994, Kalundborg (Denmark) (b) 1,76 (c) D - left back (d) KÍ Klaksvík (e) Taarnby FF, Lyngby BK, FC Roskilde, Nordsjælland, Brøndby IF, Randers FC, Brøndby IF

*** da Silva - Teddy da Silva (a) 01/06/1995, ¿? (France) (b) - (c) G (d) FC Mondercange (e) Amnéville

*** da Silva Kiala - Joel da Silva Kiala (Joel Miguel da Silva Kiala) (a) 21/01/2004, Berlin (Germany) (b) 1,89 (c) D - central defense (d) Hertha BSC II (e) -

*** Da Sylva - Jean-Pierre Da Sylva (a) 03/01/1997, ¿? (Bulgaria) (b) 1,80 (c) F - left winger (d) Botev Vratsa (e) Septemvri Simitli, Neftochimik

*** Dabbagh - Oday Dabbagh (الدباغ محمد ابراهيم عدي) (a) 03/12/1998, Al-Quds (Palestine) (b) 1,83 (c) F - center forward (d) RSC Charleroi (e) Arouca, Al-Arabi SC, Qadsia SC, Al-Salmiya SC, Hilal Al-Quds

*** Dabbur - Munas Dabbur (דאבור מואנס) (a) 14/05/1992, Nazareth (Israel) (b) 1,82 (c) F - center forward (d) FC Shabab Al-Ahli Dubai (e) Hoffenheim, Sevilla FC, RB Salzburg, Grasshoppers, RB Salzburg, Grasshoppers, Maccabi Tel Aviv, M. Ahi Nazareth

*** Dabic - Mihajlo Dabic (Mihajlo Dabić) (a) 24/03/2002, Vlasenica (Bosnia and Herzegovina) (b) 1,93 (c) G (d) FK Sutjeska Foca (e) Zvijezda G., Sloga Meridian, Ljubic Prnjavor

*** Dabiqaj - Albert Dabiqaj (a) 10/07/1996, Deçan (RF Yugoslavia, now in Kosovo) (b) 1,85 (c) M - pivot (d) FC Drita Gjilan (e) SC Gjilani, KF Feronikeli, FC Besa

*** Dabo - Abdoulaye Dabo (a) 04/03/2001, Nantes (France) (b) 1,81 (c) M - attacking midfielder (d) Olympiakos B (e) APO Levadiakos, Olympiakos B, FC Nantes B, FC Nantes B, Bell. Nantes

*** Dabo - Augusto Dabo (Augusto Júlio Dabó) (a) 13/03/2004, Bissau (Guinea-Bissau) (b) 1,86 (c) D - left back (d) Boavista Porto FC (e) -

*** Dabo - Bagaliy Dabo (a) 27/07/1988, Clichy (France) (b) 1,80 (c) F - center forward (d) - (e) Apollon Limassol, Neftchi Baku, FK Qabala, US Créteil-Lusitanos, FC Istres, US Créteil-Lusitanos, US Ivry, Lorient B

*** Dabo - Boubacar Sidik Dabo (a) 10/10/1997, Kandiounkou (Senegal) (b) 1,76 (c) F - left winger (d) - (e) B68 Toftir, CD Manacor, Cabecense, CA Antoniano, CD Llosetense, CD Felanitx, CD Llosetense

*** Dabo - Bryan Dabo (Bryan Boulaye Kevin Dabo) (a) 18/02/1992, Marseille (France) (b) 1,87 (c) M - central midfielder (d) - (e) Aris Thessaloniki, Çaykur Rizespor, Benevento, Fiorentina, SPAL, Fiorentina, St.-Étienne, Montpellier, Blackburn, Montpellier, Montpellier B

*** Dabo - Mamudo Dabo (a) 10/11/1997, ¿? (Guinea-Bissau) (b) 1,98 (c) F - center forward (d) Prescot Cables FC (e) Airbus UK, Alsager Town FC, Ruthin, Flint Town, Nomads, Flint Town, Ashton Town, Skelmersdale, AFC Liverpool, Weirside Rang.

*** Dabrowski - Damian Dabrowski (Damian Dąbrowski) (a) 27/08/1992, Kamienna Góra (Poland) (b) 1,78 (c) M - pivot (d) Zagłębie Lubin (e) Pogon Szczecin, Cracovia, Zagłębie, Cracovia, Zagłębie, Gornik Polk., Zagłębie, Zaglebie Lubin II

*** Dabrowski - Maciej Dabrowski (Maciej Kevin Dąbrowski) (a) 09/06/1998, Poznań (Poland) (b) 1,97 (c) G (d) Raith Rovers FC (e) Hibernian FC, Queen of the South, Hibernian FC, Dumbarton FC, Hibernian FC, Hibernian B, Cowdenbeath FC, Hibernian B, Civil Service, Hibernian B, Berwick Rangers FC, Hibernian B, Lech Poznan II, Lech Poznan II, Międzychód, Lech Poznan II

*** Dabuzinskas - Nedas Dabuzinskas (a) 28/11/2003, ¿? (Lithuania) (b) - (c) M (d) Marijampole City (e) Hegelmann B

*** Daci - Besmir Daci (a) 29/09/2004, Skopje (North Macedonia) (b) 1,77 (c) F - right winger (d) FK Skopje (e) Lokomotiva

*** Daci - Erdon Daci (Ердон Даци) (a) 04/07/1998, Skopje (North Macedonia) (b) 1,87 (c) F - center forward (d) KVC Westerlo (e) Konyaspor

*** Daci - Klejdi Daci (a) 22/04/1999, Tiranë (Albania) (b) 1,86 (c) F - center forward (d) KF Teuta (e) FK Kukësi, KF Teuta, FK Kukësi, KS Kastrioti, FK Partizani B

*** Dacic - Sead Dacic (a) 10/11/1997, ¿? (RF Yugoslavia, now in Montenegro) (b) 1,87 (c) M - pivot (d) Jedinstvo Bijelo Polje (e) FK Ibar, Otrant-Olympic, FK Iskra, FK Ibar

*** Dacourt - Andrea Dacourt (a) 30/07/2005, Paris (France) (b) 1,70 (c) M - attacking midfielder (d) - (e) OGC Nice

*** Dacu - Dacu (Adrian da Cunha Costa Gomes) (a) 16/05/2001, Andorra la Vella (Andorra) (b) - (c) D - left back (d) UE Santa Coloma (e) FC Ordino, FC Andorra B, ENFAF

*** Dadaev - Ibragim Dadaev (Дадаев Ибрагим Русланович) (a) 11/06/2002, Almaty (Kazakhstan) (b) 1,78 (c) M - central midfielder (d) FC Khan Tengri (e) Shakhter K., Kairat-Zhas, Shakhter K., Kairat-Zhas

*** Dadakdeniz - Ataberk Dadakdeniz (Mehmet Ataberk Dadakdeniz) (a) 05/08/1999, Izmir (Turkey) (b) 1,86 (c) G (d) Antalyaspor (e) Bursaspor

*** Dadashov - Renat Dadashov (Renat Oleq Oğlu Dadaşov) (a) 17/05/1999, Rüdesheim (Germany) (b) 1,88 (c) F - center forward (d) Grasshopper Club Zürich (e) Wolverhampton Wanderers, Tondela, Wolverhampton Wanderers, Grasshoppers, Wolverhampton Wanderers, Paços Ferreira, Wolverhampton Wanderers, Estoril Praia, Eintracht

*** D'Addario - Alessandro D'Addario (a) 09/09/1997, San Marino (San Marino) (b) 1,79 (c) D - right back (d) SS Cosmos (e) Tre Fiori, Cattolica SM, La Fiorita, Rimini, Pianese, San Marino

*** D'Addario - Nicola D'Addario (a) 21/12/2003, ¿? (San Marino) (b) - (c) M - right midfielder (d) FC Fiorentino (e) -

*** Dadet - Amos Dadet (a) 30/11/1999, Kaduna (Nigeria) (b) 1,80 (c) M - central midfielder (d) - (e) Pobeda Prilep, NK Krsko

*** Dadia - Or Dadia (אור דדיה) (a) 12/07/1997, Be'er Sheva (Israel) (b) 1,84 (c) D - right back (d) Aberdeen FC (e) Aberdeen FC, H. Beer Sheva, Hapoel Bnei Lod, H. Beer Sheva

*** Dadic - Franko Dadic (Franko Dadić) (a) 02/12/2000, Tesanj (Bosnia and Herzegovina) (b) 1,87 (c) D - left back (d) FK Sloga Meridian (e) Zeljeznicar BL, NK Usora

*** Dadic - Tomislav Dadic (Tomislav Dadić) (a) 15/12/1997, Split (Croatia) (b) 1,85 (c) D - left back (d) NK Siroki Brijeg (e) HSK Posusje, HSK Posusje, NK Solin, NK Dugopolje, NK Hrvace, NK Osijek II, NK Dugopolje, NK Hrvace, NK Dugopolje

*** Dadok - Robert Dadok (Robert Dadok) (a) 24/12/1996, Cieszyn (Poland) (b) 1,84 (c) M - attacking midfielder (d) Górnik Zabrze (e) Stal Mielec, Stalowa Wola, Wigry Suwalki, Stadion Slaski Chorzow, Pniowek P., Stadion Slaski Chorzow, GKS Belchatow, Stadion Slaski Chorzow

*** Daffé - Arfang Daffé (Arfang Boubacar Daffé) (a) 24/06/1991, Sali (Senegal) (b) 1,78 (c) F - left winger (d) - (e) FC Gagra, Al-Shabab, Dinamo Tbilisi, FC Samtredia, Dinamo Tbilisi, Merani Tbilisi, Dinamo Tbilisi, FC Nassaji M., Torpedo Kutaisi, Paykan FC, Kolkheti Poti, Diambars FC, At. Madrid B, Diambars FC

*** Dafydd - Gwion Dafydd (Gwion Dafydd Jones) (a) 11/03/2005, ¿? (Wales) (b) - (c) F - center forward (d) The New Saints (e) Caernarfon

*** Dagba - Colin Dagba (a) 09/09/1998, Béthune (France) (b) 1,70 (c) D - right back (d) París Saint-Germain FC (e) Racing Club Strasbourg, Paris Saint-Germain, Paris Saint Germain B, Boulogne B

*** Dagerstal - Filip Dagerstal (Per Filip Dagerstål) (a) 01/02/1997, Norrköping (Sweden) (b) 1,89 (c) D - central defense (d) Lech Poznan (e) Khimki, Lech Poznan, Khimki, Norrköping, Khimki, Norrköping

*** Daghim - Adam Daghim (a) 28/09/2005, ¿? (Denmark) (b) - (c) F - left winger (d) Aarhus GF (e) -

*** Dago - Nadrey Dago (Nadrey Ange Stephane Dago) (a) 07/05/1997, Attecoube (Ivory Coast) (b) 1,75 (c) F - left winger (d) APO Levadiakos (e) Panetolikos, FC Sheriff, NK Osijek II, NK Dugopolje, NK Osijek II, NK Sesvete, Ivoire Academie

*** D'Agostino - Nick D'Agostino (Nicholas D'Agostino) (a) 25/02/1998, Gold Coast (Australia) (b) 1,75 (c) F - center forward (d) Viking FK (e) Melbourne, Perth Glory, Brisbane Roar

*** Dagrou - Armand Dagrou (Armand Dagrou Djédjé) (a) 30/06/2000, ¿? (Ivory Coast) (b) 1,69 (c) F - right winger (d) - (e) Ararat Yerevan, RC Abidjan, Williamsville

*** Dagsson - Sigurdur Dagsson (Sigurður Dagsson) (a) 07/08/2002, ¿? (Iceland) (b) - (c) M (d) KH Hlídarendi (e) Valur, ÍR, Valur, ÍR, Valur, KH, Valur, KH

*** Dahan - Guy Dahan (גיא דהן) (a) 08/03/2000, ¿? (Israel) (b) 1,84 (c) F - center forward (d) SC Kfar Qasem (e) M. Petah Tikva, SCR Altach, Maccabi Haifa, H. Umm al-Fahm, Maccabi Haifa, FC Ashdod, Maccabi Haifa, Hapoel Afula, Maccabi Haifa, H. Nof HaGalil, Maccabi Haifa

*** Dahan - Ori Dahan (אורי דהן) (a) 07/12/1999, Hatzor HaGlilit (Israel) (b) 1,92 (c) D - central defense (d) Maccabi Haifa (e) B. Jerusalem, Maccabi Haifa, Kiryat Shmona

*** Dahl - Anders Dahl (a) 01/05/2002, ¿? (Denmark) (b) 1,76 (c) M - central midfielder (d) Silkeborg IF (e) -

*** Dahl - Gustav Dahl (Gustav Bonde Dahl) (a) 20/03/2004, ¿? (Denmark) (b) 1,78 (c) M - central midfielder (d) Vendsyssel FF (e) -

*** Dahl - Gustav Dahl (Gustav Klitgaard Dahl) (a) 21/01/1996, ¿? (Denmark) (b) 1,81 (c) D - left back (d) - (e) Silkeborg IF

*** Dahl - Mikkel Dahl (a) 22/06/1993, ¿? (Denmark) (b) 1,84 (c) F - center forward (d) HB Tórshavn (e) Leiknir, HB Tórshavn, Nyköbing FC, Hvidovre, Avarta

*** Dahl - Tobias Solheim Dahl (a) 12/01/2005, ¿? (Norway) (b) - (c) M - central midfielder (d) Rosenborg BK II (e) -

*** Dahlberg - Pontus Dahlberg (Pontus Jacob Ragne Dahlberg) (a) 21/01/1999, Älvängen (Sweden) (b) 1,94 (c) G (d) IFK Göteborg (e) Watford, Gillingham FC, Watford, Doncaster Rovers, Watford, Häcken, Watford, FC Emmen, Watford, IFK Göteborg, Watford, IFK Göteborg, Älvängens IK

*** Dahlin - Johan Dahlin (Johan Helge Dahlin) (a) 08/09/1986, Trollhättan (Sweden) (b) 1,91 (c) G (d) Malmö FF (e) Midtjylland, Genclerbirligi, Malmö FF, Lyn, Trelleborg, Lyn, Åsebro IF

*** Dahl-Olsen - Gutti Dahl-Olsen (a) 19/01/2002, ¿? (Faroe Islands) (b) 1,80 (c) F - center forward (d) EB/Streymur (e) EB/S II

*** Dahlqvist - Isak Dahlqvist (a) 25/09/2001, Öckerö (Sweden) (b) 1,73 (c) F - right winger (d) Örgryte IS (e) IFK Göteborg

*** Dahlström - Niklas Dahlström (a) 28/05/1997, ¿? (Sweden) (b) 1,93 (c) D - right back (d) Varbergs BoIS (e) J-Södra IF, GIF Sundsvall, Hudiksvalls FF

*** Dahlström - Sebastian Dahlström (a) 05/11/1996, Helsinki (Finland) (b) 1,83 (c) M - central midfielder (d) Kuopion Palloseura (e) HJK Helsinki, FC Sheriff, HJK Helsinki, HJK Klubi 04

*** Dahmen - Finn Dahmen (Finn Gilbert Dahmen) (a) 27/03/1998, Wiesbaden (Germany) (b) 1,88 (c) G (d) FC Augsburg (e) Mainz 05, FSV Mainz 05 II

*** Dahoud - Mahmoud Dahoud (a) 01/01/1996, Amûdê (Siria) (b) 1,78 (c) M - central midfielder (d) Brighton & Hove Albion (e) Borussia Dortmund, Borussia Mönchengladbach

*** Dairov - Nurlan Dairov (Нұрлан Дәіров) (a) 26/06/1995, Almaty (Kazakhstan) (b) 1,81 (c) D - central defense (d) FK Maktaaral (e) Taraz, Qyzyljar, FK Turan, Kairat Almaty, Okzhetpes, Kairat Almaty, Okzhetpes, Kairat Almaty, Kairat II

*** Dajaku - Leon Dajaku (a) 12/04/2001, Waiblingen (Germany) (b) 1,80 (c) F - attacking midfielder (d) HNK Hajduk Split (e) Sunderland, FC St. Gallen, Sunderland, Union Berlin, Sunderland, Union Berlin, FC Bayern II, Union Berlin, FC Bayern II, VfB Stuttgart

*** Dajcar - Matevz Dajcar (Matevž Dajčar) (a) 05/02/2002, ¿? (Slovenia) (b) 1,90 (c) G (d) - (e) ND Gorica

*** Dajko - Ajdi Dajko (a) 28/10/2002, ¿? (Albania) (b) 1,88 (c) D - central defense (d) AEK Athína B (e) Asteras Tripoli

*** Dajsinani - Mario Dajsinani (a) 23/12/1998, Durrës (Albania) (b) 1,93 (c) G (d) KF Laçi (e) KF Skënderbeu, KF Erzeni, KF Skënderbeu, FK Partizani, KS Besa

*** Daka - Patson Daka (a) 09/10/1998, Chingola (Zambia) (b) 1,83 (c) F - center forward (d) Leicester City (e) RB Salzburg, Kafue Celtic FC, FC Liefering, Kafue Celtic FC, Power Dynamos FC, Kafue Celtic FC, Green Buffaloes, Nchanga Rangers FC

*** Dakaj - Arlind Dakaj (a) 13/10/2001, Muri AG (Switzerland) (b) 1,76 (c) M - pivot (d) Cherno More Varna (e) FC Winterthur

*** Dakhnovskyi - Vitaliy Dakhnovskyi (Дахновський Віталій Олегович) (a) 10/02/1999, Pyatnytsya, Lviv Oblast (Ukraine) (b) 1,75 (c) M - right midfielder (d) NK Veres Rivne (e) Wisla Sand., C. Nowotaniec, PFK Lviv II, Veres Rivne II, PFC Lviv

*** Dakic - Damjan Dakic (a) 28/04/2004, ¿? (Serbia and Montenegro, now in Montenegro) (b) - (c) D - central defense (d) Buducnost Podgorica (e) -

*** Daku - Mirlind Daku (a) 01/01/1998, Gjilan (RF Yugoslavia, now in Kosovo) (b) 1,92 (c) F - center forward (d) Rubin Kazan (e) NK Osijek, NS Mura, NK Osijek, NK Osijek II, FC Ballkani, NK Osijek II, FK Kukësi, NK Osijek II, FC Llapi, KF Hajvalia
*** Dala - Martin Dala (a) 26/04/2004, Székesfehérvár (Hungary) (b) 1,90 (c) G (d) Nyíregyháza Spartacus (e) Nyíregyháza, Fehérvár, Fehérvár II
*** Dalamitras - Panagiotis Dalamitras (Παναγιώτης Δαλαμήτρας) (a) 13/04/2003, ¿? (Greece) (b) - (c) F - center forward (d) Atromitos FC (e) PAO Rouf, Atromitos FC
*** Daland - Jesper Daland (Jesper Norman Daland) (a) 06/01/2000, Kristiansand (Norway) (b) 1,91 (c) D - central defense (d) Cercle Brugge (e) Start, Stabæk II, FK Vigør
*** Dalberson - Dalberson (Dalberson Ferreira do Amaral) (a) 13/01/1997, Belo Horizonte (Brazil) (b) 1,91 (c) G (d) Centro Sportivo Alagoano (AL) (e) Famalicão, Brusque, Joinville-SC, Boa Esporte
*** Dalbert - Dalbert (Dalbert Henrique Chagas Estevão) (a) 08/09/1993, Barra Mansa (Brazil) (b) 1,81 (c) D - left back (d) - (e) Internazionale Milano, Cagliari, Internazionale Milano, Stade Rennes, Internazionale Milano, Fiorentina, Internazionale Milano, OGC Nice, Vitória Guimarães, Académico Viseu, Flamengo, Barra Mansa, Fluminense, Barra Mansa
*** D'Alberto - Anthony D'Alberto (a) 13/10/1994, Lubumbashi (Zaire, now DR Congo) (b) 1,78 (c) D - right back (d) SC União Torreense (e) Aarhus GF, Moreirense, Braga B, RSC Charleroi, Braga B
*** Dalbúd - Össur Dalbúd (Øssur Meinhardtsson Dalbúð) (a) 28/03/1989, ¿? (Faroe Islands) (b) 1,90 (c) F - center forward (d) - (e) HB Tórshavn, NSÍ Runavík, HB Tórshavn, BK Frem, HB Tórshavn, Fremad Amager, ÍF Fuglafjördur, B1908 Amager, Hvidovre, NSÍ Runavík
*** Dálcio - Dálcio (Euciodalcio Gomes) (a) 22/05/1996, Almada (Portugal) (b) 1,86 (c) M - central midfielder (d) APOEL FC (e) Ionikos Nikeas, Panetolikos, Benfica B, B SAD, Benfica B, Rangers FC, Benfica B, Belenenses, Benfica B, Belenenses
*** d'Alessandro - Fabio d'Alessandro (a) 28/06/1996, ¿? (Luxembourg) (b) - (c) M - central midfielder (d) US Mondorf-Les-Bains (e) Mondercange, US Mondorf-Les-Bains II, US Mondorf, F91 Dudelange II
*** D'Alessandro - Marco D'Alessandro (a) 17/02/1991, Roma (Italy) (b) 1,73 (c) F - right winger (d) Pisa Sporting Club (e) Pisa, Monza, SPAL, Atalanta, SPAL, Atalanta, Udinese, Atalanta, Benevento, Atalanta, AS Roma, Cesena, AS Roma, Cesena, AS Roma, Hellas Verona, AS Roma, AS Livorno, AS Roma, Bari, AS Roma, Grosseto
*** Daley - Cristojaye Daley (Cristojaye Damarrio Daley) (a) 23/08/2002, ¿? (Jamaica) (b) 1,73 (c) F - right winger (d) Rabotnicki Skopje (e) Harbour View FC, Koper, Harbour View FC
*** Dallas - Stuart Dallas (Stuart Alan Dallas) (a) 19/04/1991, Cookstown (Northern Ireland) (b) 1,83 (c) D - right back (d) Leeds United (e) Brentford, Northampton, Brentford, Crusaders
*** Dalli - Cameron Dalli (a) 18/12/2002, ¿? (Malta) (b) 1,79 (c) D - right back (d) Sirens FC (e) -
*** Dallinga - Thijs Dallinga (a) 03/08/2000, Groningen (Netherlands) (b) 1,90 (c) F - center forward (d) Toulouse FC (e) Excelsior, FC Groningen
*** Dallku - Ardin Dallku (a) 01/11/1994, Vushtrri (RF Yugoslava, now in Kosovo) (b) 1,84 (c) D - central defense (d) KF Dukagjini (e) SC Gjilani, Shkëndija, Vorskla Poltava, Vorskla II

*** Dall'Oca - Dall'Oca (Diego Pires Dall'Oca) (a) 13/09/1995, ¿? (Malta) (b) - (c) M - pivot (d) Marsaxlokk FC (e) Birkirkara FC, Iguaçu, PSTC

*** Dalot - Diogo Dalot (José Diogo Dalot Teixeira) (a) 18/03/1999, Braga (Portugal) (b) 1,83 (c) D - right back (d) Manchester United (e) AC Milan, Manchester Utd., FC Porto, FC Porto B

*** Daloya - Netanel Daloya (דלויה נתנאל) (a) 14/07/1998, ¿? (Israel) (b) 1,90 (c) G (d) Beitar Jerusalem (e) M. Zur Shalom, B. Jerusalem, M. Zur Shalom

*** Dalsgaard - Henrik Dalsgaard (a) 27/07/1989, Roum (Denmark) (b) 1,92 (c) D - right back (d) FC Midtjylland (e) Brentford, Zulte Waregem, Aalborg BK, Møldrup/Tostr.

*** Dalsgard - Jóhannes Dalsgard (Jóhannes Dalsgarð) (a) 11/12/2000, ¿? (Faroe Islands) (b) - (c) M - central midfielder (d) AB Argir II (e) AB Argir, AB Argir II

*** Dalton - Oliver Dalton (Oliver James Dalton) (a) 12/05/1990, ¿? (Wales) (b) 1,88 (c) D - central defense (d) - (e) Pontypridd, Penybont, Goytre United, Barry Town, Goytre United, Rhoose, Dinas Powys

*** Dalügge - Zean Dalügge (Zean Peetz Dalügge) (a) 11/07/2003, Tønder (Denmark) (b) 1,85 (c) F - center forward (d) Lyngby BK (e) HB Köge, Lyngby BK, Leiknir, Lyngby BK

*** Dam - Ási Dam (Ási Pálsson Dam) (a) 18/12/2002, ¿? (Faroe Islands) (b) - (c) M - left midfielder (d) 07 Vestur (e) HB Tórshavn, EB/Streymur III, HB Tórshavn, HB Tórshavn II

*** Damadayev - Süleyman Damadayev (Süleyman Osman oğlu Damadayev) (a) 01/03/2003, Zakatala (Azerbaijan) (b) 1,82 (c) D - left back (d) FK Qabala 2 (e) -

*** Damar - Muhammed Damar (Muhammed Mehmet Damar) (a) 09/04/2004, Berlin (Germany) (b) 1,85 (c) M - attacking midfielder (d) TSG 1899 Hoffenheim (e) -

*** Damascan - Ilie Damascan (Ilie Damaşcan) (a) 12/10/1995, Soroca (Moldova) (b) 1,72 (c) F - left winger (d) FC Zimbru Chisinau (e) Sfintul Gheorghe, U. Constanta, AFC Turris, Petrocub, FC Urartu, Zimbru Chisinau

*** Damascan - Vitalie Damascan (Vitalie Damaşcan) (a) 24/01/1999, Soroca (Moldova) (b) 1,80 (c) F - center forward (d) Sepsi OSK Sf. Gheorghe (e) FC Voluntari, Sepsi OSK, Torino, RKC Waalwijk, Torino, Fortuna Sittard, Torino, FC Sheriff, Torino, FC Sheriff, Zimbru Chisinau

*** D'Ambrosio - Danilo D'Ambrosio (a) 09/09/1988, Napoli (Italy) (b) 1,80 (c) D - central defense (d) AC Monza (e) Internazionale Milano, Torino, Juve Stabia, Potenza SC, Fiorentina

*** Damcevski - Aleksandar Damcevski (Александар Дамчевски) (a) 21/11/1992, Strasbourg (France) (b) 1,94 (c) D - central defense (d) Kitchee (e) FK Bylis, FK Partizani, Ararat-Armenia, Ermis Aradippou, Mezőkövesd, Atyrau, NAC Breda, Chern. Burgas, SC Kriens, Toulouse Font.

*** Damergy - Elias Damergy (الدمرجي الياس) (a) 17/10/2002, Mantes-la-Jolie (France) (b) 1,86 (c) G (d) - (e) Stade Rennes, Stade Rennes B

*** Damjanoski - Blaze Damjanoski (Блаже Дамјаноски) (a) 18/11/2004, Kavadarci (North Macedonia) (b) 1,81 (c) G (d) Tikves Kavadarci (e) -

*** Damjanovic - Filip Damjanovic (Филип Дамјановић) (a) 02/07/1998, Beograd (RF Yugoslavia, now in Serbia) (b) - (c) D - central defense (d) FK Vozdovac (e) IMT Beograd, Vozdovac, IMT Beograd, Vozdovac, IMT Beograd, Vozdovac

*** Damjanovic - Slavko Damjanovic (Славко Дамјановић) (a) 02/11/1992, Niksic (Yugoslavia, now in Montenegro) (b) 1,89 (c) D - central defense (d) Bengaluru FC (e) Mohun Bagan SG, Novi Pazar, Chennaiyin FC, FK TSC, Lokomotiv Tashkent, Buducnost Podgorica, Bidvest Wits FC, Sutjeska Niksic, Békéscsaba, FK Backa, Spartak, Mornar Bar

*** Damjanović - Bojan Damjanović (Бојан Дамјановић) (a) 06/06/2006, ¿? (Montenegro) (b) - (c) D (d) FK Sutjeska Niksic II (e) -

*** Dammers - Wessel Dammers (a) 01/03/1995, Ouderkerk aan den IJssel (Netherlands) (b) 1,85 (c) D - central defense (d) Randers FC (e) Willem II, FC Groningen, Willem II, FC Groningen, Fortuna Sittard, Feyenoord, SC Cambuur, Feyenoord

*** Damsgaard - Mikkel Damsgaard (Mikkel Krogh Damsgaard) (a) 03/07/2000, Jyllinge (Denmark) (b) 1,80 (c) F - left winger (d) Brentford FC (e) Sampdoria, Nordsjælland

*** Damus - Ronaldo Damus (a) 12/09/1999, Hinche (Haiti) (b) 1,80 (c) F - center forward (d) San Diego Loyal SC (e) San Diego Loyal, GIF Sundsvall, Orange County, North Texas SC

*** Damyanov - Damyan Damyanov (Дамян Валерий Дамянов) (a) 29/06/2000, Sofia (Bulgaria) (b) 1,88 (c) G (d) Dunav Ruse (e) Lokomotiv Sofia, Ludogorets II, Levski Lom, Ludogorets II, Botev Vratsa, Ludogorets II

*** Dancak - Samuel Dancak (Samuel Dancák) (a) 06/03/1998, ¿? (Czech Rep.) (b) 1,82 (c) M - central midfielder (d) FC Hradec Kralove (e) Hradec Kralove, Mlada Boleslav, Dukla Praha, Dukla B, Olympia, Dukla B

*** Danchenko - Oleg Danchenko (Данченко Олег Сергійович) (a) 01/08/1994, Zaporizhya (Ukraine) (b) 1,79 (c) D - right back (d) Zorya Lugansk (e) Zorya Lugansk, AEK Athína, Rubin Kazan, Ufa, Rubin Kazan, Shakhtar Donetsk, Enisey, Shakhtar Donetsk, Anzhi, Shakhtar Donetsk, Chornomorets, Shakhtar Donetsk, Chornomorets, Shakhtar Donetsk, Chornomorets, Chornomorets II, Dyn. Khmeln.

*** Danciu - Marian Danciu (a) 24/04/2002, Târgu Cărbuneşti (Romania) (b) - (c) F - left winger (d) Universitatea Craiova (e) Slatina, CS U Craiova, CS U Craiova II

*** D'Andrea - Luca D'Andrea (a) 06/09/2004, Ponticelli (Italy) (b) 1,73 (c) F - right winger (d) US Catanzaro (e) Catanzaro, Sassuolo

*** Daneels - Lennerd Daneels (a) 10/04/1998, Gierle (Belgium) (b) 1,72 (c) F - left winger (d) Roda JC Kerkrade (e) RKC Waalwijk

*** Danek - Adrian Danek (a) 01/08/1994, Nowy Sącz (Poland) (b) 1,80 (c) M - right midfielder (d) GKS Katowice (e) Korona Kielce, Sandecja, Cracovia, Sandecja, Kolejarz Stróże, Sandecja, Sandecja II

*** Danek - Krystof Danek (Kryštof Daněk) (a) 05/01/2003, ¿? (Czech Rep.) (b) 1,82 (c) M - attacking midfielder (d) AC Sparta Praga (e) Sigma Olomouc, Sigma Olomouc B

*** Danfa - Mamadou Danfa (Mamadou Lamine Danfa) (a) 06/03/2001, Ziguinchor (Senegal) (b) 1,90 (c) F - right winger (d) - (e) FC Shkupi, Kolos Kovalivka, Casa Sports

*** D'Angeli - Eric D'Angeli (a) 04/05/2000, Rimini (Italy) (b) 1,85 (c) F - right winger (d) SS San Giovanni (e) Juvenes-Dogana, Pavia, Cattolica, Afro Napoli, Tre Fiori, Sammaurese, Savoia, Forlì, Savoia, Savignanese

*** Dani - Fikri Dani (a) 25/12/2002, Struga (North Macedonia) (b) - (c) M (d) Karaorman Struga (e) Struga, Veleshta

*** Dani - Mrgim Dani (a) 16/04/1994, Kicevo (North Macedonia) (b) 1,82 (c) M - central midfielder (d) FK Skopje (e) Voska Sport, Korabi Debar

*** Dani Figueira - Dani Figueira (Daniel Alexis Leite Figueira) (a) 20/07/1998, Vizela (Portugal) (b) 1,89 (c) G (d) GD Estoril Praia (e) Vitória Guimarães B

*** Dani Silva - Dani Silva (Daniel Filipe Bandeira e Silva) (a) 11/04/2000, Beja (Portugal) (b) 1,80 (c) M - central midfielder (d) Vitória Guimarães SC (e) Vitória Guimarães B

*** Danicek - Vlastimil Danicek (Vlastimil Daníček) (a) 15/07/1991, Zlín (Czechoslovakia, Czech Rep.) (b) 1,87 (c) M - pivot (d) 1.FC Slovácko (e) Karvina, Slovácko

*** Danicic - Damjan Danicic (Дамјан Даничић) (a) 24/01/2000, Zagreb (Croatia) (b) 1,86 (c) D - left back (d) FK Vozdovac (e) Sumqayit, Din. Zagreb II, NK Istra, Din. Zagreb II, Dinamo Zagreb, NK Varazdin, Dinamo Zagreb, Din. Zagreb II, Vozdovac, Graficar

*** Daniel - Erik Daniel (a) 04/02/1992, Bratislava (Czechoslovakia, now in Slovakia) (b) 1,78 (c) F - right winger (d) Spartak Trnava (e) Slovan Bratislava, Zagłębie, Slovan Bratislava, Ružomberok, Spartak Myjava, Slovan Liberec, Slovan Liberec B

*** Danielak - Karol Danielak (a) 29/09/1991, Jarocin (Poland) (b) 1,70 (c) F - right winger (d) Wieczysta Krakow (e) Widzew Lódz, Podbeskidzie, Arka Gdynia, Chrobry Glogow, Pogon Szczecin, Zawisza, Pogon Szczecin, Chrobry Glogow, Jarota Jarocin

*** Daniels - Joshua Daniels (a) 22/02/1996, Derry (Northern Ireland) (b) 1,75 (c) F - right winger (d) The New Saints (e) Shrewsbury, Glenavon, Derry City

*** Danielsen - Dánial Danielsen (a) 25/04/2002, ¿? (Faroe Islands) (b) - (c) G (d) FC Hoyvík (e) NSÍ Runavík, NSÍ II

*** Danielsen - Dánjal Danielsen (a) 05/07/2004, ¿? (Faroe Islands) (b) - (c) D - central defense (d) AB Argir (e) -

*** Danielsen - Jóannes Danielsen (Jóannes Kalsø Danielsen) (a) 10/09/1997, ¿? (Faroe Islands) (b) 1,71 (c) D - right back (d) KÍ Klaksvík (e) Naestved BK, KÍ Klaksvík, KÍ II

*** Danielsen - Niels Pauli Danielsen (Niels Pauli Bjartalíð Danielsen) (a) 18/01/1989, ¿? (Faroe Islands) (b) - (c) M - central midfielder (d) EB/Streymur (e) Skála, ÍF Fuglafjördur, KÍ Klaksvík, EB/Streymur, KÍ Klaksvík

*** Danielsen - Ragnar Danielsen (Ragnar Bjartalíð Danielsen) (a) 24/04/1992, Klaksvík (Faroe Islands) (b) - (c) D - right back (d) EB/Streymur II (e) EB/Streymur, KÍ II, KÍ III, KÍ II

*** Danielsen - Svend Danielsen (a) 24/10/2005, ¿? (Faroe Islands) (b) - (c) G (d) B68 Toftir (e) -

*** Danielson - Marcus Danielson (Marcus Andreas Danielsson) (a) 08/04/1989, Eskilstuna (Sweden) (b) 1,92 (c) D - central defense (d) Djurgårdens IF (e) Dalian PFC, Djurgården, GIF Sundsvall, Västerås SK, IFK Eskilstuna

*** Danielyan - Artur Danielyan (Danielyan Artur Gegamovych) (a) 09/02/1998, Taverivka, Poltava Region (Ukraine) (b) 1,82 (c) D - right back (d) FC Noah Yerevan (e) Panserraikos, FC Sevan, Ararat Yerevan, Ararat-Armenia, Stal Kamyanske, PFK Stal II

*** Danilin - Maksim Danilin (Данилин Максим Николаевич) (a) 26/05/2001, Novomoskovsk (Russia) (b) 1,86 (c) F - center forward (d) Torpedo Moskva (e) Dinamo 2, Torpedo 2, Dinamo 2, Neftekhimik, Dinamo 2, Dinamo Bryansk, Dinamo 2, Dinamo Moskva II, Khimik 2

*** Daniliuc - Flavius Daniliuc (Flavius David Daniliuc) (a) 27/04/2001, Wien (Austria) (b) 1,88 (c) D - central defense (d) US Salernitana 1919 (e) OGC Nice, DFI Bad Aibl.

*** Danilkin - Egor Danilkin (Данилкин Егор Романович) (a) 01/08/1995, Vladimir (Russia) (b) 1,85 (c) D - central defense (d) Akron Togliatti (e) Volga Uljanovsk, Khimki, Dinamo 2, Dinamo Moskva II

*** Danilo - Danilo (Danilo dos Santos de Oliveira) (a) 29/04/2001, Salvador de Bahia (Brazil) (b) 1,77 (c) M - pivot (d) Nottingham Forest (e) Palmeiras, PFC Cajazeiras

*** Danilo - Danilo (Danilo Luiz da Silva) (a) 15/07/1991, Bicas (Brazil) (b) 1,84 (c) D - central defense (d) Juventus de Turín (e) Manchester City, Real Madrid, FC Porto, Santos, FC Porto, Santos, América-MG

*** Danilo - Danilo (Danilo Pereira da Silva) (a) 07/04/1999, São Paulo (Brazil) (b) 1,74 (c) F - center forward (d) Rangers FC (e) Feyenoord, Ajax, Ajax B, FC Twente, Ajax B

*** Danjuma - Arnaut Danjuma (Arnaut Danjuma Adam Groeneveld) (a) 31/01/1997, Lagos (Nigeria) (b) 1,78 (c) F - left winger (d) Everton FC (e) Everton, Villarreal CF, Tottenham Hotspur, Villarreal CF, Bournemouth, KV Brugge, NEC Nijmegen

*** Dankerlui - Damil Dankerlui (Damil Serena Dankerlui Wadilie) (a) 24/08/1996, Amsterdam (Netherlands) (b) 1,72 (c) D - right back (d) Panserraikos (e) FC Groningen, Willem II, Ajax B

*** Danko - Adam Danko (a) 27/06/2003, ¿? (Slovakia) (b) 1,86 (c) G (d) FK Zeleziarne Podbrezova (e) Pohronie, Podbrezova

*** Danladi - Abu Danladi (a) 18/10/1995, Takoradi (Ghana) (b) 1,78 (c) F - center forward (d) - (e) FK Bylis, Minnesota, Nashville, Minnesota, Forward Madison, Minnesota, UCLA Bruins, Ventura County, UCLA Bruins, Santa Barbara, Right to Dream

*** Danny Henriques - Danny Henriques (Danny Agostinho Henriques) (a) 29/07/1997, Rotterdam (Netherlands) (b) 1,85 (c) D - central defense (d) FC U Craiova 1948 (e) B SAD, Vilafranquense

*** Danny Namaso - Danny Namaso (Daniel Namaso Edi-Mesumbe Loader) (a) 28/08/2000, Reading (England) (b) 1,82 (c) F - center forward (d) FC Porto (e) FC Porto B, Reading

*** Danois - Kévin Danois (a) 28/06/2004, Basse-Terre (Guadaloupe) (b) - (c) M - attacking midfielder (d) AJ Auxerre (e) AJ Auxerre B

*** Danoski - Zoran Danoski (Зоран Даноски) (a) 20/10/1990, Prilep (Yugoslavia, now in North Macedonia) (b) 1,73 (c) F - left winger (d) FK Zvijezda 09 (e) Radnik, Novi Pazar, Mladost, Proleter, Radnik, Pobeda Prilep, 1.FK Pribram, Tikves, Inter Zaprešić, Pobeda Prilep, Metalurg Skopje, 1.FK Pribram, FK Most, 1.FK Pribram, FK Most, FC Chomutov, FK Most, Kozuf

*** Danso - Emmanuel Danso (a) 10/11/2000, Accra (Ghana) (b) 1,75 (c) M - central midfielder (d) Strømsgodset IF (e) Olymp. Lyon B, SC Accra, Olymp. Lyon B, SC Accra

*** Danso - Kevin Danso (a) 19/09/1998, Voitsberg (Austria) (b) 1,90 (c) D - central defense (d) RC Lens (e) FC Augsburg, Fortuna Düsseldorf, FC Augsburg, Southampton, FC Augsburg

*** Dansu - Sunday Dansu (Sunday Abiodun Dansu) (a) 09/04/2003, ¿? (Nigeria) (b) 1,76 (c) F - center forward (d) - (e) Helsinki IFK

*** Dantas - Tiago Dantas (Tiago Filipe Oliveira Dantas) (a) 24/12/2000, Lisboa (Portugal) (b) 1,70 (c) M - central midfielder (d) AZ Alkmaar (e) AZ Alkmaar, Benfica, PAOK, Benfica, Tondela, Benfica, Bayern München, Benfica, Benfica B

*** Dantas Fernandes - Rúben Dantas Fernandes (a) 19/05/2003, Luzern (Switzerland) (b) 1,80 (c) D - left back (d) FC Wil 1900 (e) FC Wil 1900, FC Luzern

*** Dante - Dante (Dante Bonfim Costa Santos) (a) 18/10/1983, Salvador da Bahia (Brazil) (b) 1,88 (c) D - central defense (d) OGC Niza (e) VfL Wolfsburg, Bayern München, Borussia Mönchengladbach, Standard Liège, RSC Charleroi, Lille, RSC Charleroi, Lille, Juventude, Capivariano

*** Dante - Amadou Dante (a) 07/10/2000, ¿? (Mali) (b) 1,79 (c) D - left back (d) SK Sturm Graz (e) TSV Hartberg, Sturm Graz, Yeelen

*** Danté - Abdoul Karim Danté (a) 29/10/1998, Bamako (Mali) (b) 1,82 (c) D - central defense (d) Swift Hesperange (e) RWDM, RSC Anderlecht, RE Virton, RSC Anderlecht, Jeanne d'Arc FC

*** Danu - Daniel Danu (a) 26/08/2002, Bălți (Moldova) (b) 1,77 (c) M - attacking midfielder (d) FC Bălți (e) Zaria Balti

*** Danuleasa - Gabriel Danuleasa (Gabriel Leonard Dănuleasă) (a) 08/05/2003, ¿? (Romania) (b) 1,87 (c) D - central defense (d) FCV Farul Constanta (e) Academia Hagi

*** Danylyuk - Artem Danylyuk (Данилюк Артем Юрійович) (a) 06/07/2001, Rivne (Ukraine) (b) 1,77 (c) D - left back (d) Bukovyna Chernivtsi (e) Veres Rivne, Bukovyna, Veres Rivne, Karpaty II, UFK Lviv

*** Danzaki - Riku Danzaki (檀崎 竜孔) (a) 31/05/2000, Natori, Miyagi (Japan) (b) 1,74 (c) M - attacking midfielder (d) Western United FC (e) Motherwell FC, H. C. Sapporo, Brisbane Roar, H. C. Sapporo, JEF Utd. Chiba, H. C. Sapporo, Brisbane Roar, H. C. Sapporo, Aomori Yama. HS

*** d'Anzico - Kevin d'Anzico (a) 14/08/2000, Niederkorn (Luxembourg) (b) - (c) D - central defense (d) FC Differdange 03 (e) UN Käerjeng 97

*** Dao - Ben Aziz Dao (Ben Aziz Dao) (a) 08/07/1999, ¿? (Burkina Faso) (b) 1,80 (c) D - left back (d) - (e) Turan Tovuz, FK Smorgon, FK Slutsk, AS Douanes, Kaloum, Accra Lions, Santos FC, Salitas

*** Daou - Raimane Daou (a) 20/11/2004, ¿? (Comores) (b) 1,82 (c) M - pivot (d) Olympique de Marseille B (e) -

*** Dapkus - Martynas Dapkus (a) 16/02/1993, Tauragė (Lithuania) (b) 1,85 (c) D - central defense (d) FK Kauno Zalgiris (e) Jonava, Silas, Trakai, Stumbras, H. Nazareth Illit

*** Dapo - Jan Dapo (Jan Đapo) (a) 17/09/2002, Brezice (Slovenia) (b) 1,85 (c) D - left back (d) NK Domžale (e) NS Mura, NK Krka, NS Mura, NK Krka, NS Mura, NK Krka

*** Daprelà - Fabio Daprelà (a) 19/02/1991, Zürich (Switzerland) (b) 1,83 (c) D - central defense (d) FC Zürich (e) FC Lugano, Chievo Verona, Bari, Chievo Verona, Carpi, US Palermo, Brescia, West Ham Utd., Grasshoppers

*** Darabaev - Aslan Darabaev (Дарабаев Аслан Кайратович) (a) 21/01/1989, Karagaily, Karaganda Region (Soviet Union, now in Kazakhstan) (b) 1,79 (c) M - central midfielder (d) FC Astana (e) Kaspiy Aktau, Zhetysu, Irtysh, Tobol Kostanay, Irtysh, Kairat Almaty, Shakhter K., Atyrau, Aktobe, Shakhter K., Shakhter-Bulat

*** Daramy - Mohamed Daramy (a) 07/01/2002, Hvidovre (Denmark) (b) 1,80 (c) F - left winger (d) Stade de Reims (e) Ajax, FC København, Ajax, FC København

*** Darbinyan - Levon Darbinyan (Լեւոն Դարբինյան) (a) 24/01/2002, Gyumri (Armenia) (b) 1,72 (c) M - central midfielder (d) Shirak Gyumri C.F. (e) BKMA Yerevan, Shirak Gyumri, Shirak II

*** Darbinyan - Robert Darbinyan (Дарбинян Роберт Меликович) (a) 04/10/1995, Togliatti, Samara Region (Russia) (b) 1,71 (c) D - right back (d) Shirak Gyumri C.F. (e) Ararat Yerevan, Pyunik Yerevan, FC Urartu, Ararat-Armenia, Shirak Gyumri, KS Samara II, Shirak Gyumri, KS Samara II, Akad. Togliatti, Akron Konoplev

*** Darboe - Dembo Darboe (Dembo Darboe) (a) 17/08/1998, Brikama (Gambia) (b) 1,87 (c) F - center forward (d) FC Astana (e) FC Astana, Al-Nasr SC, Soligorsk, FC Shkupi, ASAC Ndiambour, Real de Banjul

*** Darboe - Ebrima Darboe (a) 06/06/2001, Bakoteh (Gambia) (b) 1,79 (c) M - pivot (d) LASK (e) LASK, AS Roma

*** Darboe - Foday Darboe (a) 09/03/2003, Gunjur (Gambia) (b) - (c) M - pivot (d) Paide Linnameeskond (e) Paide, Real de Banjul

*** Dárdai - Márton Dárdai (a) 12/02/2002, Berlin (Germany) (b) 1,88 (c) M - pivot (d) Hertha Berlín (e) Hertha BSC II

*** Dárdai - Palkó Dárdai (Dárdai Pál) (a) 24/04/1999, Berlin (Germany) (b) 1,80 (c) F - right winger (d) Hertha Berlín (e) Fehérvár, Hertha BSC II, Hertha Berlin

*** Darder - Sergi Darder (Sergi Darder Moll) (a) 22/12/1993, Artà (Spain) (b) 1,80 (c) M - central midfielder (d) RCD Mallorca (e) RCD Espanyol, Olympique Lyon, RCD Espanyol, Olympique Lyon, Málaga CF, At. Malagueño, RCD Espanyol B

*** Darfalou - Oussama Darfalou (a) 29/09/1993, Menaâ (Algeria) (b) 1,87 (c) F - center forward (d) CR Belouizdad (e) FC Emmen, MAS Fes, Vitesse, PEC Zwolle, Vitesse, VVV-Venlo, Vitesse, USM Alger, RC Arbaa, USM Alger, RC Arbaa, USM Alger

*** Darge - Arron Darge (a) 26/04/2003, ¿? (Scotland) (b) - (c) D - central defense (d) Cove Rangers FC (e) Hearts FC II, Kelty Hearts, Hearts FC II, Gala Fairydean, Hearts FC II

*** Dari - Achraf Dari (داري أشرف) (a) 06/05/1999, Casablanca (Morocco) (b) 1,88 (c) D - central defense (d) Stade Brestois 29 (e) Wydad AC, WAC Reserve

*** Darida - Vladimir Darida (Vladimír Darida) (a) 08/08/1990, Pilsen (Czechoslovakia, now in Czech Rep.) (b) 1,72 (c) M - central midfielder (d) Aris Thessaloniki (e) Hertha Berlin, SC Freiburg, Viktoria Plzen, Banik Sokolov, Viktoria Plzen, Viktoria Plzen B

*** Darlington - Alex Darlington (Alexander Darlington) (a) 26/12/1988, Wrexham (Wales) (b) 1,80 (c) F - center forward (d) Aberystwyth Town (e) Cefn Druids, Airbus UK, Mosta FC, Bangor City, The New Saints

*** Darlow - Karl Darlow (a) 08/10/1990, Northampton (England) (b) 1,90 (c) G (d) Leeds United (e) Newcastle Utd., Hull City, Newcastle Utd., Nottingham Forest, Newcastle Utd., Nottingham Forest, FC Walsall, Nottingham Forest, FC Walsall, Nottingham Forest, Newport County, Nottingham Forest

*** Darmian - Matteo Darmian (a) 02/12/1989, Legnano (Italy) (b) 1,83 (c) D - right back (d) Internazionale Milano (e) Parma, Internazionale Milano, Parma, Manchester Utd., Torino, US Palermo, Torino, US Palermo, AC Milan, Padova, AC Milan

*** Darmovzal - Denis Darmovzal (a) 17/07/2000, ¿? (Czech Rep.) (b) 1,84 (c) M - attacking midfielder (d) FK Pardubice (e) Mlada Boleslav, Pardubice, Mlada Boleslav, SFC Opava, SFC Opava B, Petrkovice, SFC Opava B

*** D'Arpino - Maxime D'Arpino (Maxime Vincent D'Arpino) (a) 17/06/1996, Villeurbanne (France) (b) 1,75 (c) M - central midfielder (d) KV Oostende (e) US Orléans, Olymp. Lyon B, US Orléans, Olymp. Lyon B

*** Darri - Brahim Darri (a) 14/09/1994, Amersfoort (Netherlands) (b) 1,75 (c) F - left winger (d) Fatih Karagümrük (e) Al-Mesaimeer, Samsunspor, Denizlispor, Samsunspor, BB Erzurumspor, Karagümrük, NEC Nijmegen, FC Den Bosch, NEC Nijmegen, Heracles Almelo, Vitesse, De Graafschap, Vitesse

*** Dartsmelia - Beka Dartsmelia (ბექა დარცმელია) (a) 21/03/2000, ¿? (Georgia) (b) 1,77 (c) M - central midfielder (d) FC Samgurali Tskaltubo (e) Saburtalo, Newcastle, FC Locomotive, Dinamo Tbilisi, FC Locomotive, Dinamo Tbilisi

*** Darwish - Ovadia Darwish (דרויש עובדיה) (a) 24/09/1998, Ramat Gan (Israel) (b) - (c) D - right back (d) Ihud Bnei Sakhnin (e) H. Ramat Gan, Ramat haSharon, H. Ramat Gan, H Rishon leZion, H. Ramat Gan, Hakoah Amidar, H. Ramat Gan

*** Darwish - Walid Darwish (דרויש וליד) (a) 31/05/1996, ¿? (Israel) (b) 1,79 (c) F - center forward (d) Hapoel Nof HaGalil (e) Bnei Sakhnin, H. Kfar Saba, Ness Ziona, M. Ata Bialik, B TLV Bat Yam, Hapoel Ikhsal, H Migdal haEmek

*** Dasa - Eli Dasa (דסה אלי) (a) 03/12/1992, Netanya (Israel) (b) 1,77 (c) D - right back (d) Dinamo Moskva (e) Vitesse, Maccabi Tel Aviv, B. Jerusalem

*** Dashaev - Aslan Dashaev (Дашаев Аслан Абдусалаевич) (a) 19/02/1989, Grozny (Soviet Union, now in Russia) (b) 1,80 (c) D - central defense (d) Volga Uljanovsk (e) Fakel Voronezh, Avangard Kursk, Spartak Nalchik, Sperre) Angusht Nazran, Terek II

*** Dashdamirov - Rahman Dashdamirov (Rəhman Nazim oğlu Daşdəmirov) (a) 20/10/1999, ¿? (Azerbaijan) (b) 1,78 (c) D - central defense (d) Sabah FK (e) Shamakhi, FC Shamakhi 2, MOIK

*** Dashyan - Artak Dashyan (Արտակ Դաշյան) (a) 20/11/1989, Yerevan (Soviet Union, now in Armenia) (b) 1,81 (c) M - central midfielder (d) FC Pyunik Yerevan (e) Atyrau, FC Urartu, Alashkert CF, Vardar, Gandzasar, Al-Muharraq, Gandzasar, Banants, Metalurg Donetsk, Banants, Banants II

*** Dašić - Jovan Dašić (a) 29/03/2003, ¿? (RF Yugoslavia, now in Montenegro) (b) - (c) M - central midfielder (d) Buducnost Podgorica (e) Arsenal Tivat

*** Dasilva - Josh Dasilva (Pelenda Joshua Tunga Dasilva) (a) 23/10/1998, Ilford, London (England) (b) 1,84 (c) M - central midfielder (d) Brentford FC (e) -

*** Daskalov - Reyan Daskalov (Реян Стилиянов Даскалов) (a) 10/02/1995, Ruse (Bulgaria) (b) 1,80 (c) D - central defense (d) CSKA 1948 (e) Beroe, Tsarsko Selo, CSKA-Sofia II, Litex II, Chern. Burgas, Litex II

*** Daskalytsya - Valeriy Daskalytsya (Даскалиця Валерій Вікторович) (a) 17/01/2002, ¿? (Ukraine) (b) 1,91 (c) G (d) Tytan Odessa (e) Chornomorets 2, Real Farma, Chornomorets 2

*** Daskevics - Eduards Daskevics (Eduards Daškevičs) (a) 12/07/2002, Daugavpils (Latvia) (b) 1,71 (c) M - left midfielder (d) Riga FC (e) HamKam, BFC Daugavpils

*** Dat - Emanuel Dat (Emanuel Andrei Dat) (a) 18/01/2001, Fâşca (Romania) (b) 1,71 (c) M - left midfielder (d) CSM Sighetu Marmaţiei (e) CS Mioveni, CSM Resita, Dunarea Calarasi

*** Datko - Samuel Datko (Samuel Ďatko) (a) 24/06/2001, Brezno (Slovakia) (b) - (c) M - right midfielder (d) FK Zeleziarne Podbrezova (e) -

*** Datkovic - Niko Datkovic (Niko Datković) (a) 21/04/1993, Rijeka (Croatia) (b) 1,90 (c) D - central defense (d) Nea Salamis (e) CD Mirandés, Admira Wacker, Kisvárda, Cracovia, Spezia, CS U Craiova, Spezia, HNK Rijeka, FC Lugano, HNK Rijeka, Spezia, HNK Rijeka

*** Daushvili - Murtaz Daushvili (მურთაზ დაუშვილი) (a) 01/05/1989, Tbilisi (Soviet Union, now in Georgia) (b) 1,77 (c) M - pivot (d) - (e) APOEL FC, Anorthosis, Haladás, FC Samtredia, Diósgyőr, Karpaty, PFC Lviv, Karpaty, PFC Lviv, FC Zestafoni, Dinamo II

*** Davas - Dogan Can Davas (Doğan Can Davas) (a) 22/08/1997, Edirne (Turkey) (b) 1,70 (c) M - attacking midfielder (d) Bandirmaspor (e) Giresunspor, Bandirmaspor, Galatasaray, Bandirmaspor, Galatasaray, Corum Belediye, Erbaaspor

*** Davey - Alex Davey (Alexander James Davey) (a) 24/11/1994, Welwyn Garden City (England) (b) 1,91 (c) D - central defense (d) ÍA Akranes (e) TB Rowdies, Hartford, FC Dagenham & Redbridge, Boreham Wood, Cheltenham Town, Torquay, Cheltenham Town, Crawley Town, Stabæk, Peterborough, Scunthorpe Utd.

*** Davi Araújo - Davi Araújo (Davi Machado dos Santos Araújo) (a) 20/03/1999, Paracatu (Brazil) (b) 1,79 (c) M - attacking midfielder (d) Ituano Futebol Clube (SP) (e) Ituano, Real Brasília, Akritas Chlor., Real Brasília, Athletico-PR B, Real Brasília, Botafogo, Real Brasília, Unaí, Mamoré-MG

*** David - Dean David (דוד דין) (a) 14/03/1996, Nehora (Israel) (b) 1,84 (c) F - center forward (d) Maccabi Haifa (e) FC Ashdod

*** David - Emmanuel David (a) 07/07/2001, ¿? (Denmark) (b) 1,73 (c) F - right winger (d) Harras El Hodoud (e) Fremad Amager, Kauno Zalgiris, Fremad Amager
*** David - Gabriel David (Gabriel Eugen David) (a) 11/02/2003, ¿? (Romania) (b) - (c) M - central midfielder (d) FC Botosani (e) -
*** David - Joel David (Joel David Rodriguez Macias) (a) 10/06/1999, San Roque (Spain) (b) - (c) D - right back (d) Lions Gibraltar FC (e) CD San Bernardo
*** David - Jonathan David (Jonathan Christian David) (a) 14/01/2000, Brooklyn, New York (United States) (b) 1,75 (c) F - center forward (d) LOSC Lille Métropole (e) KAA Gent, Ottawa ISC
*** David - Promise David (Promise Oluwatobi Emmanuel David) (a) 03/07/2001, Brampton, Ontario (Canada) (b) 1,95 (c) F - center forward (d) Kalju FC (e) Sirens FC, Valletta, Tulsa, NK Trnje Zagreb, Vaughan Azzurri
*** David (c) D - central defense (d) FC Dinamo-Auto Tiraspol (e) - - Etomba Samba David (c) D - central defense (d) FC Dinamo-Auto Tiraspol (e) -
*** David Alonso - David Alonso (David Alonso Sierra Morales) (a) 07/05/2002, Madrid (Spain) (b) - (c) M - attacking midfielder (d) CS Fola Esch (e) Racing Lermeño
*** David Neres - David Neres (David Neres Campos) (a) 03/03/1997, São Paulo (Brazil) (b) 1,76 (c) F - right winger (d) SL Benfica (e) Shakhtar Donetsk, Ajax, São Paulo
*** David Sousa - David Sousa (David Sousa Albino) (a) 04/07/2001, Rio de Janeiro (Brazil) (b) 1,92 (c) D - central defense (d) Botafogo de Futebol e Regatas (e) Cercle Brugge, Botafogo
*** Davida - Osher Davida (דויד אושר) (a) 18/02/2001, Ashdod (Israel) (b) - (c) M - attacking midfielder (d) Standard de Lieja (e) Hapoel Tel Aviv
*** Davidenkovs - Aleksejs Davidenkovs (a) 27/06/1998, Riga (Latvia) (b) 1,82 (c) F - right winger (d) Mārupes SC Futbols (e) Tukums, Auda, Super Nova, Jelgava, Montefiascone, Riga II, Babite, RFS, FS Jelgava II, Skonto II
*** Davidovich - Artem Davidovich (Давидович Артем Алексеевич) (a) 17/01/2005, Minsk (Belarus) (b) 1,78 (c) F - center forward (d) Isloch Minsk Region II (e) -
*** Davidsen - Hans Marius Davidsen (a) 12/05/1998, ¿? (Faroe Islands) (b) - (c) D - central defense (d) NSÍ Runavík II (e) NSÍ Runavík, NSÍ II
*** Davidsen - Jóannes Davidsen (Jóannes Eyðfinnsson Davidsen) (a) 19/09/2002, ¿? (Faroe Islands) (b) - (c) G (d) EB/Streymur (e) EB/S II
*** Davidsen - Jóhan Troest Davidsen (a) 31/01/1988, ¿? (Faroe Islands) (b) 1,78 (c) D - central defense (d) NSÍ Runavík III (e) NSÍ Runavík, HB Tórshavn, Aarhus Fremad, NSÍ Runavík, Skála, NSÍ Runavík
*** Davidsen - Viljormur Davidsen (Viljormur í Heiðunum Davidsen) (a) 19/07/1991, Runavík (Faroe Islands) (b) 1,77 (c) D - left back (d) HB Tórshavn (e) Helsingborgs IF, Vejle BK, FC Fredericia, Jerv, NSÍ Runavík, Odense BK, FC Fyn, Odense BK, NSÍ II
*** Davidson - Jason Davidson (Jason Alan Davidson) (a) 29/06/1991, Melbourne (Australia) (b) 1,82 (c) D - left back (d) KAS Eupen (e) Melbourne, Ulsan Hyundai, Perth Glory, HNK Rijeka, Olimpija, HNK Rijeka, Huddersfield Town, FC Groningen, Huddersfield Town, West Bromwich Albion, Heracles Almelo, Paços Ferreira, SC Covilhã, Paços Ferreira, Hume City FC, Seiritsu HS
*** Davidson - Murray Davidson (a) 07/03/1988, Edinburgh (Scotland) (b) 1,80 (c) M - central midfielder (d) - (e) St. Johnstone, Livingston FC, Cowdenbeath FC, Livingston FC

*** Davidyan - David Davidyan (Դավիթ Ռուդիկի Դավոյան - Давидян Давид Рудикович) (a) 14/12/1997, Nizhniy Novgorod (Russia) (b) 1,73 (c) M - right midfielder (d) FC Pyunik Yerevan (e) Khimki, Pyunik Yerevan, Khimki, Alashkert CF, Ararat Yerevan, Ararat-Armenia, Ararat Moskva, Nosta, Olimpiets 2
*** Davidzada - Ofir Davidzada (דוידזאדה אופיר) (a) 05/05/1991, Be'er Sheva (Israel) (b) 1,78 (c) D - left back (d) Maccabi Tel Aviv (e) KAA Gent, Maccabi Tel Aviv, KAA Gent, H. Beer Sheva
*** Davies - Adam Davies (a) 13/10/1996, Shrewsbury (England) (b) - (c) F - center forward (d) Caernarfon Town (e) Airbus UK, Aberystwyth, Guilsfield FC, Ellesmere Rang, Welshpool, FC Haughmond
*** Davies - Alphonso Davies (Alphonso Boyle Davies) (a) 02/11/2000, Buduburam (Ghana) (b) 1,85 (c) D - left back (d) Bayern München (e) Vancouver, Whitecaps FC 2, Whitecaps Reserves
*** Davies - Ben Davies (Benjamin Keith Davies) (a) 11/08/1995, Barrow-in-Furness (England) (b) 1,85 (c) D - central defense (d) Rangers FC (e) Liverpool, Sheffield Utd., Liverpool, Preston North End, Fleetwood, Preston North End, Newport County, Preston North End, Southport, Preston North End, Tranmere Rovers, Preston North End, York City, Preston North End
*** Davies - Ben Davies (Benjamin Thomas Davies) (a) 24/04/1993, Neath (Wales) (b) 1,81 (c) D - left back (d) Tottenham Hotspur (e) Swansea City
*** Davies - Craig Davies (Thomas Craig Davies) (a) 18/10/2000, ¿? (Wales) (b) - (c) M - attacking midfielder (d) Ammanford AFC (e) Cardiff Metropolitan Police
*** Davies - Danny Davies (Daniel James Davies) (a) 28/06/1995, ¿? (Wales) (b) - (c) D - right back (d) The New Saints (e) Connah's Quay, Prestatyn
*** Davies - Harvey Davies (a) 03/09/2003, Liverpool (England) (b) 1,90 (c) G (d) Crewe Alexandra (e) -
*** Davies - Jac Davies (Jac Tomos Davies) (a) 28/02/2001, ¿? (Wales) (b) - (c) D - left back (d) Caerau Ely (e) Cardiff Metropolitan Police, Taffs Well
*** Davies - James Davies (James Rhys Davies) (a) 02/10/1993, ¿? (Wales) (b) - (c) F - right winger (d) - (e) Bala, Newtown, Cefn Druids, Llanfair United, Airbus UK
*** Davies - Jordan Davies (Jordan Levi Davies) (a) 16/11/1995, ¿? (Wales) (b) - (c) F - center forward (d) Connah's Quay Nomads (e) Haverfordwest, Connah's Quay, Haverfordwest, Connah's Quay, King's Lynn, Telford Utd., Prestatyn, Nantwich Town, Prestatyn, Brickfield R.
*** Davies - Keston Davies (Keston Ellis Davies) (a) 02/10/1996, Swansea (Wales) (b) 1,88 (c) D - central defense (d) Pontypridd United (e) The New Saints, Notts County, Yeovil Town
*** Davies - Lucas Davies (a) 12/02/2005, ¿? (Wales) (b) - (c) D - central defense (d) Haverfordwest County (e) -
*** Davies - Mael Davies (Mael Daniel Davies) (a) 10/10/1998, ¿? (Wales) (b) - (c) D - right back (d) Penybont FC (e) Cardiff Metropolitan Police, Carmarthen
*** Davies - Morgan Davies (Morgan Rhys Davies) (a) 15/04/1998, ¿? (Wales) (b) - (c) G (d) Cambrian & Clydach Vale (e) Pontypridd, AFC Porth
*** Davies - Steff Davies (Steffan Ioan Davies) (a) 14/07/1989, Carmarthen (Wales) (b) 1,78 (c) F - center forward (d) Aberystwyth Town (e) Penrhyncoch, Haverfordwest, Bow Street, Dinas Powys, Newcastle Emlyn, Carmarthen, Pontardawe
*** Davies - Tom Davies (Thomas Alfred Davies) (a) 11/11/2003, ¿? (Wales) (b) - (c) D - left back (d) Kilmarnock FC (e) Pontypridd
*** Davies - Tom Davies (Thomas Davies) (a) 30/06/1998, Liverpool (England) (b) 1,80 (c) M - central midfielder (d) - (e) Everton

*** Davis - Aaron Davis (a) 23/08/2002, ¿? (Ireland) (b) - (c) G (d) - (e) Drogheda United

*** Davis - Éric Davis (Éric Javier Davis Grajales) (a) 31/03/1991, Colón (Panamá) (b) 1,80 (c) D - left back (d) D.C. United (e) Dunajska Streda, Árabe Unido, San Miguelito, CA Fénix, Árabe Unido, CA Fénix, Árabe Unido

*** Davis - Keinan Davis (Keinan Vincent Joseph Davis) (a) 13/02/1998, Stevenage (England) (b) 1,89 (c) F - center forward (d) Aston Villa (e) Watford, Aston Villa, Nottingham Forest, Aston Villa, Biggleswade Town

*** Davis - Martin Davis (Martin George Edward Davis) (a) 11/10/1996, Kingston (Jamaica) (b) 1,65 (c) M - attacking midfielder (d) Gzira United FC (e) Sliema Wanderers, Gzira Utd., St. Andrews FC, Harbour View FC, St. Andrews FC, Harbour View FC, Toronto FC II, Harbour View FC

*** Davis - Sammi Davis (Ralph Sammi Emanuel Davis) (a) 11/05/2005, ¿? (Sweden) (b) - (c) D - central defense (d) - (e) Härnösands FF

*** Davis - Steven Davis (a) 01/01/1985, Ballymena (Northern Ireland) (b) 1,72 (c) M - central midfielder (d) Rangers FC (e) Southampton, Rangers FC, Southampton, Rangers FC, Fulham, Rangers FC, Fulham, Aston Villa, St. Andrews BC

*** Davitashvili - Zuriko Davitashvili (ზურიკო დავითაშვილი) (a) 15/02/2001, Tbilisi (Georgia) (b) 1,75 (c) F - right winger (d) FC Girondins de Burdeos (e) Dinamo Batumi, Girondins Bordeaux, Dinamo Batumi, Arsenal Tula, Rubin Kazan, Rotor Volgograd, Rubin Kazan, FC Locomotive, Dinamo Tbilisi

*** Davkov - Martin Davkov (Мартин Давков) (a) 18/12/1998, Stip (North Macedonia) (b) 1,87 (c) G (d) Bregalnica Stip (e) Tikves, Pehcevo, Bregalnica Stip

*** Davo - Davo (Antonio David Álvarez Rey) (a) 18/12/1994, Luarca (Spain) (b) 1,78 (c) F - left winger (d) RC Deportivo de La Coruña (e) RC Deportivo, KAS Eupen, Wisła Płock, UD Ibiza, UP Langreo, Zamora CF, CCD Cerceda, Bouzas, Oviedo Vetusta, Zamora CF, Caudal, UP Langreo, Oviedo Vetusta, Real Avilés B

*** Davydov - Denis Davydov (Давыдов Денис Алексеевич) (a) 22/03/1995, Moskva (Russia) (b) 1,77 (c) F - center forward (d) - (e) Khimki 2, Znamya Truda OZ, Tom Tomsk, CSKA-Sofia, Nizhny Novgorod, Spartak-2, Spartaks, Spartak-2, Spartak Moskva, Mlada Boleslav, Spartak Moskva, Spartak Moskva II

*** Davydov - Vladislav Davydov (Давыдов Владислав Витальевич) (a) 18/06/1999, Oblivskaya, Rostov Region (Russia) (b) 1,80 (c) M - attacking midfielder (d) FK Vitebsk (e) Murom, Smolensk, O. Volgograd

*** Davyskiba - Roman Davyskiba (Давыскиба Роман Сергеевич) (a) 31/03/2001, Zhlobin (Belarus) (b) 1,80 (c) F - left winger (d) Naftan Novopolotsk (e) Dinamo Minsk II, Dinamo Minsk, Soligorsk, Dinamo Minsk, Dinamo Minsk II

*** Dawa - Joyskim Dawa (Joyskim Aurélien Dawa Tchakonte) (a) 09/04/1996, Colombes (France) (b) 1,94 (c) D - central defense (d) FCSB (e) FC Botosani, Valmiera, FK Mariupol, Gil Vicente, AS Monaco B, US Avranches

*** Dawid - Ignacy Dawid (a) 15/01/2003, Łódź (Poland) (b) 1,69 (c) M - pivot (d) RTS Widzew Łódź (e) Widzew II

*** Dawidowicz - Pawel Dawidowicz (Paweł Marek Dawidowicz) (a) 20/05/1995, Olsztyn (Poland) (b) 1,89 (c) D - central defense (d) Hellas Verona (e) Benfica, Hellas Verona, Benfica, US Palermo, Benfica B, VfL Bochum, Benfica B, Lechia Gdánsk, Lechia II

*** Dawson - Craig Dawson (a) 06/05/1990, Rochdale (England) (b) 1,88 (c) D - central defense (d) Wolverhampton Wanderers (e) West Ham Utd., Watford, West Ham Utd., Watford, West Bromwich Albion, Bolton Wanderers, West Bromwich Albion, AFC Rochdale, West Bromwich Albion, AFC Rochdale, Radcliffe, AFC Rochdale, Radcliffe

*** Dé - Dé (Cledson Carvalho da Silva) (a) 06/02/1998, ¿? (Brazil) (b) 1,86 (c) F - center forward (d) IFK Mariehamn (e) Águia de Marabá

*** de Almeida - Mayron de Almeida (a) 22/11/1995, Virton (Belgium) (b) 1,77 (c) F - center forward (d) FC Progrès Niederkorn (e) Red Star FC, Progrès Niederkorn, Tours FC, RE Virton

*** De Angelis - Mirco De Angelis (a) 03/03/2000, Città di San Marino (San Marino) (b) 1,95 (c) G (d) SS San Giovanni (e) Tre Fiori, Rimini, Tropical Coriano, Rimini, La Fiorita

*** de Arruabarrena - Ignacio de Arruabarrena (Ignacio de Arruabarrena Fernández) (a) 16/01/1997, Montevideo (Uruguay) (b) 1,85 (c) G (d) FC Arouca (e) Wanderers, Tacuarembó, Wanderers

*** De Biagi - Alex De Biagi (a) 02/01/2000, ¿? (San Marino) (b) - (c) D - right back (d) SS San Giovanni (e) Domagnano, San Giovanni, Domagnano, Faetano, Virtus, Tropical Coriano

*** De Biagi - Manuel De Biagi (a) 07/03/2002, ¿? (San Marino) (b) - (c) D - right back (d) SS Pennarossa (e) -

*** De Bock - Laurens De Bock (Laurens Henry Cristine De Bock) (a) 07/11/1992, Dendermonde (Belgium) (b) 1,79 (c) D - left back (d) Atromitos FC (e) Zulte Waregem, Leeds Utd., Zulte Waregem, Leeds Utd., ADO Den Haag, Leeds Utd., Sunderland, Leeds Utd., KV Oostende, Leeds Utd., KV Brugge, KSC Lokeren

*** de Boer - Jan de Boer (a) 20/05/2000, Sneek (Netherlands) (b) 2,02 (c) G (d) VVV-Venlo (e) FC Groningen

*** de Brauwer - Octavi de Brauwer (Octavi de Brauwer López) (a) 27/11/2002, Ordino (Andorra) (b) - (c) G (d) UE Engordany B (e) Sant Julia B, Engordany B, UE Engordany

*** De Bruyn - Alexandre De Bruyn (Alexandre Jospeh De Bruyn) (a) 04/06/1994, ¿? (Belgium) (b) 1,77 (c) M - attacking midfielder (d) KSK Lierse Kempenzonen (e) KV Kortrijk, FCV Dender EH, KV Kortrijk, KAA Gent, Sint-Truiden, Lommel SK

*** De Bruyne - Kevin De Bruyne (a) 28/06/1991, Drongen (Belgium) (b) 1,81 (c) M - attacking midfielder (d) Manchester City (e) VfL Wolfsburg, Chelsea, Werder Bremen, Chelsea, KRC Genk, Chelsea, KRC Genk

*** De Buyser - Wout De Buyser (Wout Didier De Buyser) (a) 29/06/2001, Sint-Niklaas (Belgium) (b) 1,83 (c) D - left back (d) SV Zulte Waregem (e) Club NXT

*** de Carvalho - Filipe de Carvalho (Filipe de Carvalho Ferreira) (a) 01/12/2003, Zürich (Switzerland) (b) 1,76 (c) F - left winger (d) Grasshopper Club Zürich (e) -

*** de Cillia - Max de Cillia (a) 14/03/2003, ¿? (Luxembourg) (b) - (c) G (d) US Mondorf-Les-Bains (e) -

*** de Cillia - Tom de Cillia (a) 14/03/2003, ¿? (Luxembourg) (b) - (c) M (d) US Mondorf-Les-Bains II (e) -

*** De Cordova-Reid - Bobby De Cordova-Reid (Bobby Armani De Cordova-Reid) (a) 02/02/1993, Bristol (England) (b) 1,70 (c) M - attacking midfielder (d) Fulham FC (e) Cardiff City, Fulham, Cardiff City, Bristol City, Plymouth Argyle, Bristol City, Plymouth Argyle, Bristol City, Plymouth Argyle, Bristol City, Oldham Athletic, Bristol City, Cheltenham Town, Bristol City

*** De Cuyper - Maxim De Cuyper (a) 22/12/2000, Knokke-Heist (Belgium) (b) 1,82 (c) D - left back (d) KV Brugge (e) KVC Westerlo, KV Brugge

*** De Donno - Jonathan De Donno (a) 16/02/2002, Bern (Switzerland) (b) 1,93 (c) F - center forward (d) FC Biel-Bienne 1896 (e) -

*** De Falco - Andrea De Falco (a) 19/06/1986, Ancona (Italy) (b) 1,79 (c) M - central midfielder (d) - (e) Tre Fiori, Nereto, Siena, Viterbese, Reggina, LR Vicenza, Benevento, Matera, Benevento, Bari, Juve Stabia, Bari, Chievo Verona, Bari, Chievo

Verona, Sassuolo, Chievo Verona, Ancona, Chievo Verona, Taranto, Chievo Verona, Pescara, AC Pisa

*** de França - Gustavo de França (Gustavo Moreno de França) (a) 20/07/1996, ¿? (Brazil) (b) - (c) D - central defense (d) - (e) FK Sabail, Leixões, Nacional-SP

*** de Gea - David de Gea (David de Gea Quintana) (a) 07/11/1990, Madrid (Spain) (b) 1,89 (c) G (d) - (e) Manchester Utd., Atlético Madrid, At. Madrid B

*** de Graaff - Tom de Graaff (Tom Gerard de Graaff) (a) 10/12/2004, Amsterdam (Netherlands) (b) 1,93 (c) G (d) Ajax Amsterdam B (e) -

*** De Grazia - Lorenzo De Grazia (a) 01/04/1995, Ascoli Piceno (Italy) (b) 1,76 (c) M - central midfielder (d) Floriana FC (e) Teramo, Piacenza, Ravenna, Modena, Teramo, Ascoli, Maceratese, Ascoli, Maceratese

*** de Guzmán - Jonathan de Guzmán (Jonathan Alexander de Guzmán) (a) 13/09/1987, Toronto, Ontario (Canada) (b) 1,73 (c) M - pivot (d) Sparta Rotterdam (e) OFI Creta, Eintracht, Napoli, Chievo Verona, Napoli, Carpi, Napoli, Villarreal CF, Swansea City, Villarreal CF, RCD Mallorca, Feyenoord

*** de Haas - Justin de Haas (a) 01/02/2000, Zaandam (Netherlands) (b) 1,94 (c) D - central defense (d) FC Famalicão (e) NK Lokomotiva, Din. Zagreb II

*** De Haro - Evan De Haro (Evan Francis De Haro) (a) 28/09/2002, ¿? (Gibraltar) (b) 1,77 (c) M - pivot (d) FC Bruno's Magpies (e) Lancaster City, Bruno's Magpies, Lancaster City, Europa FC, Bruno's Magpies, Europa FC, Red Imps Reserves

*** De Jesus Sousa - Michel De Jesus Sousa (Michel De Jesus Sousa Da Cruz) (a) 22/03/2001, Sorengo TI (Switzerland) (b) 1,76 (c) M - right midfielder (d) FC Lugano II (e) FC Chiasso, FC Lugano II

*** de Jong - Fedde de Jong (a) 13/06/2003, Uitgeest (Netherlands) (b) 1,85 (c) M - attacking midfielder (d) SC Cambuur Leeuwarden (e) -

*** de Jong - Frenkie de Jong (Frenkie de Jong) (a) 12/05/1997, Arkel (Netherlands) (b) 1,81 (c) M - central midfielder (d) FC Barcelona (e) Ajax, Ajax B, Willem II, Ajax B, Willem II

*** de Jong - Luuk de Jong (a) 27/08/1990, Aigle (Switzerland) (b) 1,88 (c) F - center forward (d) PSV Eindhoven (e) Sevilla FC, FC Barcelona, Sevilla FC, PSV Eindhoven, Borussia Mönchengladbach, Newcastle Utd., Borussia Mönchengladbach, FC Twente, De Graafschap

*** de Kamps - Joeri de Kamps (a) 10/02/1992, Amsterdam (Netherlands) (b) 1,76 (c) M - pivot (d) IK Sirius (e) Lechia Gdánsk, Slovan Bratislava, Sparta Rotterdam, Slovan Bratislava, NAC Breda, Ajax B, Heerenveen, Ajax B

*** de Keijzer - Fabian de Keijzer (a) 10/05/2000, Leusden (Netherlands) (b) 1,93 (c) G (d) Heracles Almelo (e) FC Utrecht

*** De Ketelaere - Charles De Ketelaere (a) 10/03/2001, Brugge (Belgium) (b) 1,92 (c) M - attacking midfielder (d) AC Milan (e) KV Brugge

*** De La Flor - Fernando De La Flor (Fernando De La Flor Armario) (a) 24/04/1998, Sevilla (Spain) (b) 1,84 (c) D - central defense (d) - (e) Glacis United, Podlasie, UD Rinconada, CMD San Juan

*** de la Fuente - Adrián de la Fuente (Adrián de la Fuente Barquilla) (a) 26/02/1999, El Escorial (Spain) (b) 1,79 (c) D - central defense (d) Levante UD (e) Villarreal CF B, RM Castilla, Unión Collado

*** de la Fuente - Ángel de la Fuente (Ángel de la Fuente Fernández) (a) 29/12/1997, ¿? (Spain) (b) - (c) G (d) FC Andorra B (e) AC Escaldes, FC Andorra B, FC Encamp, FC Encamp B

*** de la Fuente - Hernán de la Fuente (a) 07/01/1997, Buenos Aires (Argentina) (b) 1,78 (c) D - right back (d) Club Atlético Tucumán (e) At. Tucumán, Famalicão, Vélez Sarsfield, Vélez Sarsfield II

*** de la Fuente - Konrad de la Fuente (a) 16/07/2001, Miami, Florida (United States) (b) 1,76 (c) F - left winger (d) SD Eibar (e) SD Eibar, Ol. Marseille, Olympiakos, Ol. Marseille, FC Barcelona B

*** de la Hoz - César de la Hoz (César de la Hoz López) (a) 30/03/1992, Orejo (Spain) (b) 1,79 (c) M - central midfielder (d) Real Valladolid CF (e) UD Almería, Betis Deportivo, Albacete, Betis Deportivo, Barakaldo CF, Rayo Cantabria

*** de la Rosa - José Antonio de la Rosa (José Antonio de la Rosa Garrido) (a) 28/07/2004, Huelva (Spain) (b) 1,74 (c) F - left winger (d) Cádiz CF Mirandilla (e) -

*** de la Sousa - Raphael de la Sousa (סוזה לה דה רפאל) (a) 16/11/1996, ¿? (Israel) (b) 1,88 (c) F - center forward (d) - (e) M. Ahi Nazareth, Sioni Bolnisi, H. Ashkelon, Hapoel Ikhsal, H. Ashkelon, Rustavi, Hapoel Ikhsal, Sporting TA, M. Ahi Nazareth, Ihud Kfar Qara

*** De la Torre - Ángel De la Torre (Ángel Pérez de la Torre) (a) 04/11/1994, Terrassa (Spain) (b) - (c) F - right winger (d) Inter Club d'Escaldes (e) Vilassar de Mar, FC Vilafranca, Cerdanyola FC, CE Europa, CE Júpiter, Terrassa FC, Badalona

*** de la Torre - Luca de la Torre (a) 23/05/1998, San Diego, California (United States) (b) 1,77 (c) M - central midfielder (d) RC Celta de Vigo (e) Heracles Almelo, Fulham, San Diego Surf, S. Diego Nomads

*** De Laet - Ritchie De Laet (Ritchie Ria Alfons De Laet) (a) 28/11/1988, Antwerpen (Belgium) (b) 1,84 (c) D - right back (d) Royal Antwerp FC (e) Aston Villa, Melbourne City, Aston Villa, Royal Antwerp, Aston Villa, Leicester City, Middlesbrough, Leicester City, Manchester Utd., Norwich City, Manchester Utd., FC Portsmouth, Manchester Utd., Preston North End, Manchester Utd., Sheffield Utd., Manchester Utd., Stoke City, Wrexham, Stoke City, Royal Antwerp

*** de Lange - Jeffrey de Lange (a) 01/04/1998, Amstelveen (Netherlands) (b) 1,90 (c) G (d) Go Ahead Eagles Deventer (e) FC Twente

*** de Lanlay - Yann-Erik de Lanlay (Yann-Erik Randa Bahezre de Lanlay) (a) 14/05/1992, Stavanger (Norway) (b) 1,80 (c) M - central midfielder (d) Viking FK (e) Rosenborg, Viking

*** de Ligt - Matthijs de Ligt (a) 12/08/1999, Leiderdorp (Netherlands) (b) 1,89 (c) D - central defense (d) Bayern München (e) Juventus, Ajax, Ajax B

*** De Lorenzis - Cristiano De Lorenzis (a) 01/08/2004, ¿? (Italy) (b) - (c) M (d) - (e) Fiorentino

*** De Los Santos - Dylan De Los Santos (a) 27/06/2002, Gibraltar (Gibraltar) (b) 1,64 (c) M - central midfielder (d) Mons Calpe SC (e) Manchester 62

*** De Luca - Manuel De Luca (a) 17/07/1998, Bolzano (Italy) (b) 1,92 (c) F - center forward (d) UC Sampdoria (e) Perugia, Sampdoria, Chievo Verona, Torino, Virtus Entella, Torino, Alessandria, Torino, Renate, Torino

*** de Lucas - Luiyi de Lucas (Luiyi Ramón de Lucas Pérez) (a) 31/08/1994, Galván (Dominican Rep.) (b) 1,94 (c) D - central defense (d) Livingston FC (e) FC Haka, CD Izarra, CD Lealtad, Caudal, Cibao FC, La Roda CF, At. Barcelona, CD Azuqueca, Marchamalo, CD Azuqueca, Alameda Osuna, CD Guada. B

*** De Lucia - Umberto De Lucia (a) 07/01/1992, Mugnano di Napoli (Italy) (b) 1,81 (c) D - central defense (d) Tre Fiori FC (e) Correggese, Pianese, Jesina, FC Messina, Montegiorgio, Castrovillari, Palmese, Agropoli, San Marino, Lecco, Martina, Teramo, Cesenatico, Fossombrone

*** De Luigi - Dario De Luigi (a) 19/03/1990, Cesena (Italy) (b) - (c) D - central defense (d) Riccione (e) SS Folgore, Tropical Coriano, Domagnano, United Riccione, Rimini

*** de Luis - Mario de Luis (Mario de Luis Jiménez) (a) 06/05/2002, Madrid (Spain) (b) 1,85 (c) G (d) Real Madrid Castilla (e) Xerez Deportivo, RM Castilla, Real Avilés, RM Castilla

*** De Marco - Vernon De Marco (Vernon De Marco Morlacchi) (a) 18/11/1992, Cordoba (Argentina) (b) 1,86 (c) D - central defense (d) Hatta Club (e) Slovan Bratislava, Lech Poznan, Slovan Bratislava, Michalovce, Slovan Bratislava, Michalovce, CE Constància

*** de Marcos - Óscar de Marcos (Óscar de Marcos Arana) (a) 14/04/1989, Laguardia (Spain) (b) 1,82 (c) D - right back (d) Athletic Club (e) Alavés, Depor. Alavés B

*** De Matteis - Jacopo De Matteis (a) 28/12/2002, Roma (Italy) (b) 1,86 (c) G (d) US Salernitana 1919 (e) Fermana, Salernitana, Trastevere, Savio, Massiminiana

*** de Mol - Nils de Mol (a) 03/05/2001, Muttenz (Switzerland) (b) 1,83 (c) G (d) FC Basel (e) FC Wil 1900, FC Wil 1900

*** De Neve - Dion De Neve (a) 12/06/2001, Aalst (Belgium) (b) 1,80 (c) M - left midfielder (d) KV Kortrijk (e) Zulte Waregem

*** De Nipoti - Tommaso De Nipoti (a) 23/07/2003, Udine (Italy) (b) 1,80 (c) F - attacking midfielder (d) - (e) Atalanta

*** De Nitti - Gianni De Nitti (a) 09/04/2003, Zürich (Switzerland) (b) 1,86 (c) G (d) FC Schaffhausen (e) FC Schaffhausen, FC Zürich

*** de Nooijer - Bradley de Nooijer (a) 07/11/1997, Oost-Souburg (Netherlands) (b) 1,80 (c) D - left back (d) CSKA-Sofia (e) FCV Farul, Vorskla Poltava, FC Viitorul, FC Dordrecht

*** de Nooijer - Yanilio de Nooijer (a) 02/05/2003, Vlissingen (Netherlands) (b) 1,86 (c) D - left back (d) Karmiotissa Pano Polemidion (e) AEP Polemidion, Karmiotissa

*** De Norre - Casper De Norre (a) 07/02/1997, Hasselt (Belgium) (b) 1,75 (c) M - central midfielder (d) Millwall FC (e) OH Leuven, KRC Genk, OH Leuven, KRC Genk, Sint-Truiden, ASV Geel, Sint-Truiden

*** De Nova - Iván De Nova (Iván De Nova Ruiz) (a) 22/09/1996, Tarragona (Spain) (b) - (c) D - central defense (d) - (e) IC d'Escaldes, UA Horta, CF Igualada, Villanovense, Pobla de Mafumet CF, FC Ascó

*** de Oliveira - Jeoffrey de Oliveira (Jeoffrey de Oliveira Ramos Correia) (a) 25/11/1999, Luxembourg (Luxembourg) (b) - (c) F - center forward (d) FC Blo-Wäiss Medernach (e) UN Käerjeng 97, Medernach, Steinsel, Swift Hesperange

*** de Pablos - Eric de Pablos (Eric de Pablos Sola) (a) 08/03/1999, Andorra la Vella (Andorra) (b) - (c) D - right back (d) UE Santa Coloma (e) FC Santa Coloma, UE Santa Coloma, FC Ordino, FC Andorra

*** de Palmas - Lilian de Palmas (a) 02/02/2002, ¿? (Spain) (b) - (c) D - left back (d) CyD Leonesa Júpiter Leonés B (e) Penya Encarnada, FC Cartagena B, Elche Ilicitano

*** de Paul - Rodrigo de Paul (Rodrigo Javier de Paul) (a) 24/05/1994, Sarandí (Argentina) (b) 1,80 (c) M - central midfielder (d) Atlético de Madrid (e) Udinese, Valencia CF, Racing, Valencia CF, Racing

*** De Percin - Théo De Percin (Théo Franck Mathias De Percin) (a) 02/02/2001, Tarbes (France) (b) 1,85 (c) G (d) AJ Auxerre (e) AJ Auxerre B

*** De Queiroz - Noah De Queiroz (Noah De Queiroz Pacheco) (a) 10/12/2002, Sorengo (Switzerland) (b) 1,82 (c) D - central defense (d) FC Lugano II (e) FC Chiasso, FC Lugano II

*** de Regt - Gyan de Regt (a) 14/08/2002, Papendrecht (Netherlands) (b) 1,76 (c) F - left winger (d) Vitesse Arnhem (e) -

*** De Ridder - Noah De Ridder (a) 08/10/2003, ¿? (Belgium) (b) - (c) M - right midfielder (d) Jong KAA Gent (e) -

*** De Roeve - Denzel De Roeve (a) 10/08/2004, ¿? (Belgium) (b) - (c) D - right back (d) Club NXT (e) -
*** de Roon - Marten de Roon (Marten Elco de Roon) (a) 29/03/1991, Zwijndrecht (Netherlands) (b) 1,85 (c) M - pivot (d) Atalanta de Bérgamo (e) Middlesbrough, Atalanta, Heerenveen, Sparta Rotterdam
*** De Rosa - Giovanni De Rosa (a) 12/06/2002, Napoli (Italy) (b) 1,89 (c) D - central defense (d) FC Fiorentino (e) Roccella
*** de Santis - Jeriel de Santis (Jeriel Nicolás de Santis Córdova) (a) 18/06/2002, El Callao (Venezuela) (b) 1,90 (c) F - center forward (d) Boavista Porto FC (e) FC Cartagena B, Boavista, Caracas FC
*** De Sart - Julien De Sart (a) 23/12/1994, Waremme (Belgium) (b) 1,87 (c) M - pivot (d) KAA Gent (e) KV Kortrijk, Middlesbrough, Zulte Waregem, Middlesbrough, Derby, Middlesbrough, Standard Liège
*** De Schrevel - Célestin De Schrevel (Célestin Eric De Schrevel) (a) 08/05/2002, ¿? (Belgium) (b) - (c) G (d) KAA Gent (e) Jong KAA Gent
*** De Sciglio - Mattia De Sciglio (a) 20/10/1992, Milano (Italy) (b) 1,83 (c) D - right back (d) Juventus de Turín (e) Olympique Lyon, Juventus, AC Milan
*** De Silvestri - Lorenzo De Silvestri (a) 23/05/1988, Roma (Italy) (b) 1,86 (c) D - right back (d) Bologna (e) Torino, Sampdoria, Fiorentina, Sampdoria, Fiorentina, Lazio
*** De Smet - Thibault De Smet (a) 05/06/1998, Brugge (Belgium) (b) 1,83 (c) D - left back (d) Stade de Reims (e) Beerschot V.A., Stade Reims, Sint-Truiden, KAA Gent
*** de Sousa - Alex de Sousa (a) 18/09/2003, ¿? (Luxembourg) (b) - (c) M (d) Jeunesse Esch (e) -
*** de Sousa - Clayton de Sousa (Clayton de Sousa Moreira) (a) 24/02/1988, Luxemburg-Stadt (Luxembourg) (b) - (c) D - right back (d) - (e) Mondercange, Jeunesse Esch, F91 Dudelange, Jeunesse Esch
*** de Sousa - Dany de Sousa (Dany de Sousa Xavier) (a) 08/11/2000, ¿? (Luxembourg) (b) - (c) M (d) US Mondorf-Les-Bains (e) Mondercange, Jeunesse Esch
*** de Sousa - Raphael de Sousa (a) 05/03/1993, ¿? (Luxembourg) (b) 1,76 (c) M - pivot (d) FC Lorentzweiler (e) Etzella Ettelbrück, Hamm Benfica, Jeunesse Esch, F91 Dudelange, Victoria Rosport, F91 Dudelange, Alemannia Aachen II
*** de Souza - Murilo de Souza (Murilo de Souza Costa) (a) 31/10/1994, São José do Norte (Brazil) (b) 1,76 (c) F - right winger (d) Gil Vicente FC (e) SC Braga, RCD Mallorca, SC Braga, Real Sporting, SC Braga, Barra FC, Nacional, Barra FC, Juventude, Barra FC, Joinville-SC, Barra FC, Lajeadense, Barra FC, Macaé, Barra FC, Botafogo, Barra FC, Inter B, Barra FC, SER Caxias B, Barra FC
*** De Taddeo - Maxime De Taddeo (a) 11/07/1994, Metz (France) (b) 1,93 (c) D - central defense (d) US Thionville Lusitanos (e) Differdange 03, Jeunesse Esch, Differdange 03, US Créteil-Lusitanos, Panionios, CS Sedan, SM Caen B, Amiens SC B
*** de Tomás - Raúl de Tomás (Raúl de Tomás Gómez) (a) 17/10/1994, Madrid (Spain) (b) 1,80 (c) F - center forward (d) Rayo Vallecano (e) RCD Espanyol, Benfica, Real Madrid, Rayo Vallecano, Real Madrid, RM Castilla, Rayo Vallecano, RM Castilla, Real Valladolid, RM Castilla, Córdoba CF, RM Castilla, Real Madrid C
*** De Torres - Carl De Torres (a) 26/02/2005, ¿? (Gibraltar) (b) - (c) M - pivot (d) FC Manchester 62 (e) -
*** De Vincenti - Tomás De Vincenti (Tomás Sebastián De Vincenti) (a) 09/02/1989, Buenos Aires (Argentina) (b) 1,78 (c) M - attacking midfielder (d) PAS Lamia 1964

(e) APOEL FC, Shabab Al-Ahli, Al-Shabab, APOEL FC, Olympiakos, APOEL FC, Olympiakos, PAS Giannina, Olympiakos, PAS Giannina, PS Kalamata, PAS Giannina, Excursionistas

*** de Vries - Francis de Vries (a) 28/11/1994, Christchurch (New Zealand) (b) 1,88 (c) D - left back (d) Eastern Suburbs AFC (e) Värnamo, Nyköpings BIS, Canterbury Utd., Whitecaps FC 2, Vancouver, Saint Francis U, Canterbury Utd.

*** De Vries - Ryan De Vries (Ryan Keith De Vries) (a) 14/09/1991, Cape Town, Western Cape (South Africa) (b) 1,82 (c) F - center forward (d) Auckland City FC (e) Sligo Rovers, FC Gifu, Auckland City, Bentleigh, Waitakere Utd., Bentleigh, Waitakere Utd., Bentleigh, Waitakere Utd.

*** de Vrij - Stefan de Vrij (a) 05/02/1992, Ouderkerk aan den IJssel (Netherlands) (b) 1,89 (c) D - central defense (d) Internazionale Milano (e) Lazio, Feyenoord

*** De Winter - Koni De Winter (a) 12/06/2002, Antwerpen (Belgium) (b) 1,91 (c) D - central defense (d) Génova (e) Genoa, Juventus, FC Empoli, Juve Next Gen

*** de Wit - Dani de Wit (a) 28/01/1998, Hoorn (Netherlands) (b) 1,84 (c) M - attacking midfielder (d) AZ Alkmaar (e) Ajax, Ajax B

*** de Wit - Kas de Wit (a) 26/07/2003, Nijmegen (Netherlands) (b) - (c) M - attacking midfielder (d) NEC Nijmegen (e) -

*** de Wit - Mees de Wit (a) 17/04/1998, Amsterdam (Netherlands) (b) 1,81 (c) D - left back (d) AZ Alkmaar (e) PEC Zwolle, Sporting B, Orihuela CF, Ajax B

*** De Wolf - Mathias De Wolf (Mathias Marcel De Wolf) (a) 21/02/2002, Leuven (Belgium) (b) 1,87 (c) M - central midfielder (d) - (e) NEC Nijmegen, Club NXT

*** De Wolf - Ortwin De Wolf (a) 23/04/1997, ¿? (Belgium) (b) 1,90 (c) G (d) Royal Antwerp FC (e) KAS Eupen, Royal Antwerp, KAS Eupen, KSC Lokeren, KSC Lokeren II

*** Deac - Ciprian Deac (Ciprian Ioan Deac) (a) 16/02/1986, Bistriţa (Romania) (b) 1,77 (c) F - right winger (d) CFR Cluj (e) Tobol Kostanay, Aktobe, CFR Cluj, FC Schalke 04, Rapid Bucureşti, FC Schalke 04, CFR Cluj, Otelul Galati, CFR Cluj, Unirea Dej

*** Deaconu - Ronaldo Deaconu (Ronaldo Octavian Andrei Deaconu) (a) 13/05/1997, Bucuresti (Romania) (b) 1,82 (c) M - attacking midfielder (d) Korona Kielce (e) SX Chang'an At., Gaz Metan, Sepsi OSK, HNK Gorica, Concordia, ASA Tg. Mures, Academia Hagi

*** Dean - Lloyd Dean (a) 17/07/1988, ¿? (England) (b) - (c) F - center forward (d) - (e) Airbus UK

*** Dean - Ryan Dean (Ryan John Dean) (a) 18/07/1998, ¿? (Gibraltar) (b) 1,80 (c) D - central defense (d) Mons Calpe SC (e) Manchester 62, Manchester 62 Reserves, Lynx FC, Lynx Reserve, Lynx FC

*** Deana - Steven Deana (a) 04/03/1990, Schaffhausen (Switzerland) (b) 1,90 (c) G (d) FC Lugano (e) Servette FC, MSV Duisburg, FC Aarau, FC Wil 1900, FC Sion, FC Aarau, FC Sion, FC Vaduz

*** Deane - Gareth Deane (a) 14/06/1994, Lisburn (Northern Ireland) (b) - (c) G (d) Coleraine FC (e) Linfield, Coleraine, Linfield, Carrick Rangers, Linfield

*** Debarliev - Petar Debarliev (Петър Дебърлиев) (a) 19/06/1991, Plovdiv (Bulgaria) (b) - (c) G (d) Hebar Pazardzhik (e) Septemvri Sofia, Pirin Razlog, Saedinenie, Oborishte, B. Galabovo, Lyubimets

*** Debast - Zeno Debast (Zeno Koen Debast) (a) 24/10/2003, Halle (Belgium) (b) 1,91 (c) D - central defense (d) RSC Anderlecht (e) -

*** Debeljuh - Gabriel Debeljuh (a) 28/09/1996, Pula (Croatia) (b) 1,88 (c) F - center forward (d) Sepsi OSK Sf. Gheorghe (e) CFR Cluj, FC Hermannstadt, Este, Mantova, Piacenza, Rovinj

*** Debelko - Roman Debelko (Дебелко Роман Миколайович) (a) 08/08/1993, Sopiv, Ivano-Frankivsk Oblast (Ukraine) (b) 1,87 (c) F - center forward (d) Kryvbas Kryvyi Rig (e) Soligorsk, Riga, Karpaty, FCI Levadia, Karpaty, Stal Kamyanske, Metalurg II, Banants, Metalurg II

*** Debijadji - Jan Paolo Debijadji (Jan Paolo Debijađi) (a) 16/04/2000, Zagreb (Croatia) (b) 1,91 (c) G (d) HNK Gorica (e) NK Dubrava ZG, HNK Gorica, NK Lucko, HNK Gorica, NK Kurilovec, HNK Gorica, NK Kurilovec

*** Debinski - Adam Debinski (Adam Dębiński) (a) 07/07/2004, Łódź (Poland) (b) 1,82 (c) D - central defense (d) KKS 1925 Kalisz (e) Widzew Lódz, Widzew II

*** Deblé - Serges Deblé (a) 01/10/1989, Anyama (Ivory Coast) (b) 1,71 (c) F - center forward (d) Tobol Kostanay (e) Pyunik Yerevan, Ararat Yerevan, Viborg FF, R&F, MZ Hakka, Viborg FF, Shirak Gyumri, Khimki, SKA-Energia, Khimki, Charlton Ath., FC Nantes, Charlton Ath., Angers SCO, Charlton Ath., ASEC Mimosas

*** Debono - Jonathan Debono (a) 17/07/1985, ¿? (Malta) (b) - (c) G (d) Hibernians FC (e) Balzan FC, Sirens FC, Hibernians FC, Hamrun Spartans, Gudja United FC, Mqabba FC, Tarxien, Mqabba FC, Mosta FC, Marsa FC, St. Andrews FC, Mqabba FC, Birkirkara FC

*** Debono - Matthias Debono (a) 11/02/2002, ¿? (Malta) (b) - (c) G (d) Hamrun Spartans (e) Tarxien, Hamrun Spartans

*** Debreceni - Zalán Debreceni (a) 06/07/2002, Szekszárd (Hungary) (b) 1,88 (c) D - central defense (d) Paksi FC (e) Haladás, Nyíregyháza, Haladás

*** Debreshlioski - David Debreshlioski (Давид Дебрешлиоски) (a) 24/08/2004, Prilep (North Macedonia) (b) 1,81 (c) F - center forward (d) - (e) Pobeda Prilep

*** Decker - Vincent Decker (a) 30/04/1993, Strasbourg (France) (b) 1,86 (c) D - central defense (d) F91 Dudelange (e) Canet Rous., Saint-Pryvé FC, Schiltigheim, SR Colmar, Racing Strasbourg B

*** Decoene - Massimo Decoene (Massimo Stephane Decoene) (a) 11/02/2004, ¿? (Belgium) (b) - (c) M - central midfielder (d) KV Kortrijk (e) -

*** Decostere - Robbe Decostere (a) 08/05/1998, Roeselare (Belgium) (b) 1,78 (c) D - right back (d) Cercle Brugge (e) AFC Tubize, Cercle Brugge

*** Dedechko - Denys Dedechko (Дедечко Денис Михайлович) (a) 02/07/1987, Kyiv (Soviet Union, now in Ukraine) (b) 1,88 (c) M - pivot (d) FC Zimbru Chisinau (e) JK Trans Narva, FC Noah, Ararat Yerevan, FK Oleksandriya, SKA Khabarovsk, FK Mariupol, SKA Khabarovsk, FK Oleksandriya, FC Astana, Vorskla Poltava, Kryvbas, Luch Vladivostok, Krasnodar, Amkar Perm, Dynamo 2 Kyiv, Luch Vladivostok, Dynamo 2 Kyiv, Naftovyk, Dynamo 2 Kyiv

*** Dede-Lhomme - Yanis Dede-Lhomme (a) 13/06/2002, ¿? (Sarcelles, France) (b) 1,84 (c) D - central defense (d) AEZ Zakakiou (e) Aris Limassol, Achyronas FC, Aris Limassol, Stade Rennes B

*** Dédenon - Noah Dédenon (a) 08/01/2001, ¿? (Luxembourg) (b) 1,81 (c) D - central defense (d) US Hostert (e) FC Rodange 91

*** Dedia - Valon Dedia (a) 31/08/2000, Mitrovice (RF Yugoslavia, now in Kosovo) (b) - (c) D - left back (d) FC Phoenix Banjë (e) KF Trepca 89

*** Dedic - Amar Dedic (Amar Dedić) (a) 18/08/2002, Zell am See (Austria) (b) 1,80 (c) D - right back (d) Red Bull Salzburg (e) Wolfsberger AC, RB Salzburg, FC Liefering

*** Dedic - Rene Dedic (René Dedič) (a) 07/08/1993, ¿? (Czechoslovakia, now in Slovakia) (b) 1,93 (c) F - center forward (d) FK Trinec (e) Liptovsky Mik., Trinec, Viktoria Plzen, Trinec, 1.FK Pribram, SFC Opava, Fotbal Trinec, MSK Zilina B, STK Samorin, MSK Zilina B

*** Dedov - Alexandru Dedov (a) 26/07/1989, Chişinău (Soviet Union, now in Moldova) (b) 1,75 (c) F - left winger (d) FC Zimbru Chisinau (e) Milsami, CSF Speranta, FC Petrocub, Zira FK, Milsami, ASA Tg. Mures, Zimbru Chisinau, Ac. Chisinau, FC Sheriff, Dacia, JFK Ventspils
*** Dedura - Matas Dedura (a) 17/05/2002, Moskva (Russia) (b) 1,88 (c) D - central defense (d) BE1 National Football Academy (e) Nevezis, Hegelmann, Kauno Zalgiris, Kauno FM
*** Deegan - Gary Deegan (Gary Richard Deegan) (a) 28/09/1987, Coolock, Dublin (Ireland) (b) 1,75 (c) M - pivot (d) Drogheda United FC (e) Shelbourne, Cambridge Utd., Shrewsbury, Southend United, Northampton, Hibernian FC, Coventry City, Bohemians, Galway United, Longford Town, Shelbourne, Kilkenny City, Shelbourne
*** Defrel - Grégoire Defrel (Grégoire André Defrel) (a) 17/06/1991, Meudon (France) (b) 1,79 (c) F - center forward (d) US Sassuolo (e) AS Roma, Sassuolo, AS Roma, Sampdoria, AS Roma, Sassuolo, AS Roma, Sassuolo, Cesena, Parma, Foggia
*** Degabriele - Jurgen Degabriele (a) 10/10/1996, Pietà (Malta) (b) 1,75 (c) F - left winger (d) Hibernians FC (e) -
*** Degli Innocenti - Duccio Degli Innocenti (a) 28/04/2003, Montevarchi (Italy) (b) 1,80 (c) M - pivot (d) Calcio Lecco 1912 (e) Lecco, FC Empoli
*** Degtyarov - Maksym Degtyarov (Дегтярьов Максим Сергійович) (a) 30/05/1993, Kirovsk, Lugansk Oblast (Ukraine) (b) 1,85 (c) F - center forward (d) FK Atyrau (e) Taraz, Desna, Olimpik Donetsk, Desna, Olimpik Donetsk, FK Poltava, Avangard K., Metalurg Donetsk, Stal Alchevsk, Metalurg Donetsk, Metalurg II, Stal Alchevsk, Metalurg II, Stal Alchevsk
*** Dehl - Laurenz Dehl (a) 12/12/2001, Berlin (Germany) (b) 1,80 (c) M - right midfielder (d) 1.FC Union Berlin (e) Viktoria Berlin, Union Berlin, Bohemians, Union Berlin, Hallescher FC, Union Berlin
*** Deidda - Andrea Deidda (a) 15/12/1993, ¿? (Luxembourg) (b) - (c) F - attacking midfielder (d) Jeunesse Esch (e) -
*** Deijl - Mats Deijl (a) 15/07/1997, Vlaardingen (Netherlands) (b) 1,81 (c) D - right back (d) Go Ahead Eagles Deventer (e) FC Den Bosch
*** Deja - Adam Deja (a) 24/06/1993, Olesno (Poland) (b) 1,85 (c) M - pivot (d) Gornik Leczna (e) Korona Kielce, Arka Gdynia, Cracovia, Podbeskidzie, MKS Kluczbork, Podbeskidzie, MKS Kluczbork, OKS Olesno
*** Dejaegere - Brecht Dejaegere (Brecht Emiel Dejaegere) (a) 29/05/1991, Oostende (Belgium) (b) 1,73 (c) M - central midfielder (d) Charlotte FC (e) Toulouse, KAA Gent, Toulouse, KAA Gent, KV Kortrijk
*** Dejanovic - Alen Dejanovic (Alen Dejanović) (a) 19/01/2000, Sarajevo (Bosnia and Herzegovina) (b) - (c) F - right winger (d) SK Dynamo Ceske Budejovice (e) Velez Mostar, Mladost Kakanj, Din. Zagreb II, Cibalia
*** Dekker - Maxim Dekker (a) 21/04/2004, Rijsenhout (Netherlands) (b) - (c) D - central defense (d) AZ Alkmaar (e) -
*** Del Bello - Jacopo Del Bello (a) 25/09/2004, Castel Ritaldi (Italy) (b) 1,87 (c) G (d) US Vibonese (e) -
*** Del Castillo - Romain Del Castillo (a) 29/03/1996, Lyon (France) (b) 1,72 (c) M - right midfielder (d) Stade Brestois 29 (e) Stade Rennes, Olympique Lyon, Nîmes, Olympique Lyon, Bourg-en-Bresse, Olympique Lyon, Olymp. Lyon B
*** Del Lungo - Tommaso Del Lungo (a) 21/11/2003, ¿? (Italy) (b) - (c) D - central defense (d) - (e) Grassina
*** del Moral - Alberto del Moral (Alberto del Moral Saclices) (a) 20/07/2000, Villacañas (Spain) (b) 1,85 (c) M - central midfielder (d) Villarreal CF B (e) Córdoba CF, Córdoba CF B

*** Del Pozo - Cristian Del Pozo (Cristian Del Pozo Morenilla) (a) 12/08/1999, Olot (Spain) (b) 1,78 (c) F - left winger (d) - (e) UE Santa Coloma, UA Horta, UA Horta, CF Peralada, CE Banyoles

*** Del Rio - Julian Del Rio (a) 15/02/2002, Málaga (Spain) (b) - (c) F - center forward (d) FC Bruno's Magpies (e) Córdoba CF B, Lincoln FC, Red Imps Reserves

*** Del Valle - Yonathan Del Valle (Yonathan Alexander del Valle Rodríguez) (a) 28/05/1990, Guacara (Venezuela) (b) 1,73 (c) F - left winger (d) Sakaryaspor (e) Eyüpspor, Ümraniyespor, Bandirmaspor, Giresunspor, Gaziantep FK, Rio Ave, Bursaspor, Rio Ave, Kasimpasa, Rio Ave, Paços Ferreira, Rio Ave, AJ Auxerre, Rio Ave, AJ Auxerre, Táchira, Funda UAM

*** Delac - Matej Delac (Matej Delač) (a) 20/08/1992, Gornji Vakuf-Uskoplje (Bosnia and Herzegovina) (b) 1,90 (c) G (d) AC Horsens (e) Chelsea, Excelsior Mouscron, Chelsea, FK Sarajevo, Chelsea, FK Sarajevo, Chelsea, AC Arles-Avignon, Chelsea, FK Sarajevo, Chelsea, Vojvodina, Chelsea, Inter Zaprešić, Chelsea, Vitória Guimarães, Chelsea, Ceske Budejovice, Chelsea, Vitesse, Chelsea, Inter Zaprešić

*** Delaine - Thomas Delaine (a) 24/03/1992, Lens (France) (b) 1,80 (c) D - left back (d) Racing Club Strasbourg (e) FC Metz, Paris FC, RC Lens B

*** Delaj - Antonio Delaj (a) 06/09/2003, Shkodër (Albania) (b) 1,74 (c) M - left midfielder (d) KF Vllaznia (e) -

*** Delaney - Thomas Delaney (Thomas Joseph Delaney) (a) 03/09/1991, Frederiksberg (Denmark) (b) 1,82 (c) M - central midfielder (d) Sevilla FC (e) Hoffenheim, Sevilla FC, Borussia Dortmund, Werder Bremen, FC København

*** Delap - Liam Delap (Liam Rory Delap) (a) 08/02/2003, Winchester (England) (b) 1,86 (c) F - center forward (d) Hull City (e) Hull City, Preston North End, Stoke City

*** Delarge - Dzon Delarge (a) 24/06/1990, Brazzaville (Congo DR) (b) 1,73 (c) F - right winger (d) - (e) KF Egnatia, Akhisarspor, Boluspor, Ceske Budejovice, Qarabag FK, Bursaspor, Admira Wacker, Osmanlispor, Admira Wacker, Slovan Liberec, Dunajska Streda, Union Douala, Coton Sport FC, Kadji Sports

*** Delavallée - Martin Delavallée (a) 18/03/2004, ¿? (Belgium) (b) - (c) G (d) RSC Charleroi (e) Excelsior Mouscron

*** Delaye - Sacha Delaye (a) 23/04/2002, Rennes (France) (b) 1,71 (c) M - attacking midfielder (d) Montpellier HSC (e) Le Puy Foot, Montpellier, Montpellier B

*** Delcroix - Hannes Delcroix (a) 28/02/1999, Grande Hatte (Haiti) (b) 1,83 (c) D - central defense (d) RSC Anderlecht (e) RKC Waalwijk, RSC Anderlecht

*** Dele - Dele (Bamidele Isa Yusuf) (a) 22/02/2001, Lagos (Nigeria) (b) 1,80 (c) F - left winger (d) GD Estoril Praia (e) Spartak Trnava, Obazz FC

*** Deletic - Milos Deletic (Милош Делетић) (a) 14/10/1993, Beograd (RF Yugoslavia, now in Serbia) (b) 1,79 (c) F - right winger (d) Volos NPS (e) AEK Athína, Anorthosis, AEK Athína, PAS Lamia, AEK Athína, Asteras Tripoli, AEK Athína, AE Larisa, Radnik, Jagodina, Academica Clinceni, Sageata Navodar, Napredak, Vojvodina, OFK Mladenovac

*** Delev - Spas Delev (Спас Бориславов Делев) (a) 22/09/1989, Klyuch (Bulgaria) (b) 1,69 (c) F - left winger (d) Ludogorets Razgrad (e) Arda Kardzhali, Pogon Szczecin, Beroe, Lokomotiv Plovdiv, UD Las Palmas, CSKA Sofia, Mersin IY, CSKA Sofia, Pirin, CSKA Sofia, Pirin

*** Delevic - Milan Delevic (Милан Делевић) (a) 23/02/1998, Duisburg (Germany) (b) 1,86 (c) D - central defense (d) FK IMT Belgrad (e) Kolubara, FK Loznica, Kolubara, Zarkovo, Zvezdara, FC Kray

*** Delferriere - Allan Delferriere (Allan Michaël Delferriere) (a) 03/03/2002, Liège (Belgium) (b) 1,83 (c) M - pivot (d) Hibernian FC (e) Hibernian B, FC Edinburgh, Hibernian B, Standard Liège, MVV Maastricht, Standard Liège
*** Delgado - Fran Delgado (Francisco Javier Delgado Rojano) (a) 11/07/2001, Écija (Spain) (b) 1,81 (c) D - right back (d) SC Farense (e) Betis Deportivo
*** Delgado - Gilson Delgado (Gilson Delgado Freitas) (a) 19/10/1992, Ettelbrück (Luxembourg) (b) 1,89 (c) D - central defense (d) FC Progrès Niederkorn (e) CS Fola Esch, FC Wiltz 71, CS Fola Esch, FC UNA Strassen, Etzella Ettelbrück, FC UNA Strassen, Etzella Ettelbrück
*** Delgado - Juan Delgado (Juan Antonio Delgado Baeza) (a) 05/03/1993, Santiago de Chile (Chile) (b) 1,76 (c) F - right winger (d) Sheffield Wednesday (e) Paços Ferreira, Necaxa, Gimnàstic, Tondela, Gimnàstic, Colo Colo
*** Delgado - Kevin Delgado (Kevin Alexandre Delgado Martins) (a) 13/03/2002, ¿? (Luxembourg) (b) - (c) F (d) FC Green Boys 77 Harlange-Tarchamps (e) Kehlen, FC Wiltz 71, Kehlen, SC Celoricense, Marinhais
*** Delgado - Ricardo Delgado (Ricardo Aleixo Delgado) (a) 22/02/1994, Sao Francisco Xavier (Portugal) (b) 1,91 (c) D - central defense (d) Swift Hesperange (e) F91 Dudelange, Jeunesse Esch
*** Deli - Simon Deli (Simon Désiré Sylvanus Deli) (a) 27/10/1991, Abidjan (Ivory Coast) (b) 1,92 (c) D - central defense (d) - (e) Adana Demirspor, Istanbulspor, Adana Demirspor, KV Brugge, Slavia Praha, KV Brugge, Slavia Praha, Sparta Praha B, 1.FK Pribram, Sparta Praha B, Ceske Budejovice, Sparta Praha B, Africa Sports
*** Delibas - Emirhan Delibas (Emirhan Delibaş) (a) 01/01/2003, Istanbul (Turkey) (b) - (c) F - right winger (d) Besiktas JK (e) Göztepe, Besiktas
*** Delibasic - Vasilije Delibasic (Василије Делибашић) (a) 14/03/2003, ¿? (Serbia and Montenegro, now in Serbia) (b) 1,94 (c) F - center forward (d) FK Rad Belgrado (e) Pobeda Prilep, Rad Beograd, Dobanovci, Rad Beograd
*** Delic - Ivan Delic (Ivan Delić) (a) 29/09/1998, Split (Croatia) (b) 1,86 (c) F - center forward (d) HNK Sibenik (e) Cosenza, HNK Sibenik, Slaven Belupo, Hajduk Split, NK Varazdin, Hajduk Split, NK Istra, Hajduk Split, Hajduk Split II
*** Delic - Kenan Delic (Kenan Delić) (a) 02/05/1999, Tešanj (Bosnia and Herzegovina) (b) 1,77 (c) M - attacking midfielder (d) FK Sloboda Tuzla (e) TOSK Tesanj, Radnik Bijelj., TOSK Tesanj, Radnik Bijelj., NK Dugopolje
*** Delimedjac - Mirza Delimedjac (Мирза Делимеђац) (a) 24/10/1999, Novi Pazar (RF Yugoslavia, now in Serbia) (b) 1,79 (c) M - pivot (d) FK Tuzla City (e) FK Kukësi, Septemvri Sofia, Novi Pazar, Tampines Rovers, FK Josanica
*** Deliu - Ardit Deliu (a) 26/10/1997, Durrës (Albania) (b) 1,73 (c) M - pivot (d) KF Tirana (e) Liepaja, KF Laçi, Hajduk Split II, RNK Split
*** Deljanin - Aleksandar Deljanin (Александар Дељанин) (a) 05/10/2002, ¿? (Serbia and Montenegro, now in Serbia) (b) 1,86 (c) F - left winger (d) FK Mesevo Gornji Stepoš (e) Javor-Matis, BASK Beograd, Javor-Matis, Rad Beograd
*** Delkus - Joris Delkus (a) 29/07/2002, ¿? (Lithuania) (b) - (c) D (d) Top Kickers (e) FK TransINVEST, Riteriai B
*** Della Croce - Gabriele Della Croce (a) 20/06/2000, ¿? (Italy) (b) - (c) M - right midfielder (d) ASD Colonnella Rimini (e) San Giovanni, ASD Colonnella, Cailungo, Cosmos
*** Della Valle - Alex Della Valle (a) 13/06/1990, ¿? (San Marino) (b) - (c) D - central defense (d) SC Faetano (e) Sanvitese
*** Della Valle - Nicola Della Valle (a) 19/05/1997, ¿? (San Marino) (b) - (c) D - right back (d) Tre Fiori FC (e) -

*** Delle - Joris Delle (a) 29/03/1990, Briey (France) (b) 1,89 (c) G (d) - (e) KV Kortrijk, Orlando Pirates, Feyenoord, NEC Nijmegen, RC Lens, OGC Nice, Cercle Brugge, OGC Nice, FC Metz

*** Dellkrans - Edwin Dellkrans (a) 17/04/2003, ¿? (Sweden) (b) 1,75 (c) M - central midfielder (d) GIF Sundsvall (e) Täfteå IK

*** Dellova - Lumbardh Dellova (a) 01/01/1999, Krushë e Madhe (RF Yugoslavia, now in Kosovo) (b) 1,87 (c) D - central defense (d) FC Ballkani (e) Hajduk Split, FC Prishtina, Hajduk Split, Hajduk Split II, KF Liria, Slovan Ljublj, KF Liria

*** Delmiro - Delmiro (Delmiro Évora Nascimento) (a) 29/08/1988, Mindelo (Cabo Verde) (b) 1,90 (c) D - central defense (d) AEZ Zakakiou (e) Aris Limassol, Farense, Arenas Club, Varzim, Farense, Progresso, União Madeira, Castelo Branco, Lusitano FCV, Madalena, Batuque, Mindelo

*** Delort - Andy Delort (ديلور أندي) (a) 09/10/1991, Sète (France) (b) 1,81 (c) F - center forward (d) Umm Salal SC (e) FC Nantes, OGC Nice, FC Nantes, OGC Nice, Montpellier, Toulouse, Montpellier, Toulouse, Tigres UANL, SM Caen, Wigan Ath., Tours FC, Wigan Ath., Tours FC, AC Ajaccio, FC Metz, AC Ajaccio, Nîmes, AC Ajaccio B

*** Delos - Shaquil Delos (a) 16/06/1999, Les Lilas (France) (b) 1,83 (c) D - right back (d) AS Nancy-Lorraine (e) Estoril Praia, AS Nancy, FC Chambly Oise, FC Chambly B

*** Delov - Metodija Delov (Методија Делов) (a) 02/06/1993, Kavadarci (North Macedonia) (b) 1,90 (c) D - central defense (d) Slovan Duslo Sala (e) Pobeda Prilep, Tikves, Kariana Erden, Kozuf, Vardar Negotino

*** Delva - Judler Delva (a) 10/12/2002, Saint-Louis-du-Nord (Haiti) (b) 1,91 (c) G (d) FC Manchester 62 (e) Pittsburgh CUFC, Violette AC

*** Dema - Endri Dema (a) 17/07/2004, Durrës (Albania) (b) - (c) G (d) KF Teuta (e) -

*** Demaku - Vesel Demaku (a) 05/02/2000, Baden (Austria) (b) 1,80 (c) M - pivot (d) SK Sturm Graz (e) Austria Klagenfurt, Sturm Graz, Austria Viena

*** Deman - Maxim Deman (a) 23/10/2001, ¿? (Belgium) (b) 1,94 (c) G (d) SK Beveren (e) KV Kortrijk

*** Deman - Olivier Deman (a) 06/04/2000, Antwerpen (Belgium) (b) 1,81 (c) M - left midfielder (d) Cercle Brugge (e) -

*** Dembélé - Karamoko Dembélé (Karamoko Kader Dembélé) (a) 22/02/2003, London (England) (b) 1,67 (c) F - right winger (d) Stade Brestois 29 (e) Celtic FC, Celtic Reserves

*** Dembélé - Mahamadou Dembélé (a) 10/04/1999, Brétigny-sur-Orge (France) (b) 1,86 (c) D - central defense (d) RFC Seraing (e) Troyes, Pau FC, Troyes, Pau FC, Troyes, RB Salzburg, Fortuna Sittard, RB Salzburg, FC Liefering, RB Salzburg

*** Dembélé - Moussa Dembélé (a) 12/07/1996, Pontoise (France) (b) 1,87 (c) F - center forward (d) Al-Ettifaq FC (e) Olympique Lyon, Atlético Madrid, Olympique Lyon, Celtic FC, Fulham

*** Dembélé - Ousmane Dembélé (Masour Ousmane Dembélé) (a) 15/05/1997, Vernon (France) (b) 1,78 (c) F - right winger (d) París Saint-Germain FC (e) FC Barcelona, Borussia Dortmund, Stade Rennes, Stade Rennes B

*** Dembélé - Siriki Dembélé (Ben Siriki Dembélé) (a) 07/09/1996, Ouragahio (Ivory Coast) (b) 1,73 (c) F - left winger (d) Birmingham City (e) Bournemouth, AJ Auxerre, Bournemouth, Peterborough, Grimsby Town

*** Demchenko - Nikita Demchenko (Демченко Никита Юрьевич) (a) 06/09/2002, Minsk (Belarus) (b) 1,80 (c) M - attacking midfielder (d) Dinamo Minsk (e) Dinamo Minsk II, Smolevichi, Dinamo Minsk II

*** Demchenko - Oleksandr Demchenko (Демченко Олександр Вікторович) (a) 13/02/1996, Vinnytsya (Ukraine) (b) 1,81 (c) M - pivot (d) Kolos Kovalivka (e) Chornomorets, FK Oleksandriya, Kremin, Nyva Ternopil, Nyva Vinnytsya, Metalist 1925, Nyva Vinnytsya, ASD Portuense, Abano, FK Vinnytsya, UFK Lviv
*** Demchenko - Yegor Demchenko (Демченко Єгор Васильович) (a) 25/07/1997, Stepnogirsk, Zaporizhya Oblast (Ukraine) (b) 1,81 (c) M - central midfielder (d) Karpaty Lviv (e) Metalist, Avangard K., Kolos Kovalivka, Avangard K., Olimpik Donetsk, Bukovyna, Zorya II, Metalurg Z., Zaporizhya II
*** Demhasaj - Shkelqim Demhasaj (a) 19/04/1996, Schaffhausen (Switzerland) (b) 1,91 (c) F - center forward (d) FC Aarau (e) Grasshoppers, FC Winterthur, Grasshoppers, FC Luzern, FC Schaffhausen
*** Demian - Dumitru Demian (a) 08/02/1999, Chişinău (Moldova) (b) 1,84 (c) F - right winger (d) FC Petrocub Hînceşti (e) Dacia Buiucani, Oţelul Galaţi, Dacia Buiucani, Legnago, Levico Terme, Virtus Verona
*** Demian - Gabriel Demian (a) 04/12/2004, Levice (Slovakia) (b) 1,78 (c) M - central midfielder (d) MFK Dukla Banska Bystrica (e) -
*** Demidchik - Pavel Demidchik (Демидчик Павел Дмитриевич) (a) 30/01/1996, Minsk (Belarus) (b) - (c) F - center forward (d) - (e) Dzerzhinsk, Oshmyany-BDUFK, Yerevan CF, FK Smorgon, FK Smorgon, Soligorsk II, FK Slutsk, Soligorsk II
*** Demidov - Jevgeni Demidov (a) 11/02/2000, Tallinn (Estonia) (b) - (c) F - right winger (d) FC Nomme United (e) JK Trans Narva, JK Viljandi, Kalju FC
*** Demir - Anil Demir (Anıl Demir) (a) 04/11/1996, Istanbul (Turkey) (b) 1,90 (c) G (d) Fethiyespor (e) Ümraniyespor, Tarsus IY
*** Demir - Muhammet Demir (a) 10/01/1992, Trabzon (Turkey) (b) 1,80 (c) F - center forward (d) Konyaspor (e) Gaziantep FK, Basaksehir, Gaziantep FK, Basaksehir, Sivasspor, Trabzonspor, Gaziantepspor, Trabzonspor, Gaziantepspor, Bursaspor
*** Demir - Yigit Efe Demir (Yiğit Efe Demir) (a) 02/08/2004, Istanbul (Turkey) (b) 1,93 (c) D - central defense (d) Fenerbahce (e) -
*** Demir - Yusuf Demir (a) 02/06/2003, Wien (Austria) (b) 1,73 (c) F - right winger (d) Galatasaray (e) Rapid Wien, FC Barcelona, Rapid Wien
*** Demiral - Merih Demiral (a) 05/03/1998, Karamürsel (Turkey) (b) 1,90 (c) D - central defense (d) Atalanta de Bérgamo (e) Juventus, Atalanta, Juventus, Sassuolo, Alanyaspor, Sassuolo, Alanyaspor, Sporting Lisboa, Alanyaspor, Sporting Lisboa, Sporting B, Alcanenense, Sporting B, Alcanenense
*** Demirbag - Adil Demirbag (Adil Demirbağ) (a) 10/12/1997, Elazig (Turkey) (b) 1,85 (c) D - central defense (d) Konyaspor (e) Adana Demirspor, Karagümrük, Adana Demirspor, Bucaspor
*** Demirbay - Kerem Demirbay (a) 03/07/1993, Herten (Germany) (b) 1,83 (c) M - central midfielder (d) Galatasaray (e) Bayer Leverkusen, Hoffenheim, SV Hamburg, Fortuna Düsseldorf, SV Hamburg, 1.FC Kaiserslautern, SV Hamburg, Borussia Dortmund II
*** Demircan - Berke Demircan (Bahattin Berke Demircan) (a) 25/11/2002, Istanbul (Turkey) (b) 1,83 (c) F - center forward (d) Van Spor FK (e) Karagümrük, Isparta 32 Spor, Karagümrük
*** Demirci - Mehmet Demirci (a) 18/03/2002, Istanbul (Turkey) (b) 1,93 (c) G (d) Fatih Karagümrük (e) -
*** Demirci - Oguzhan Demirci (Muhammed Oğuzhan Demirci) (a) 15/06/1999, Ludwigshafen am Rhein (Germany) (b) 1,83 (c) M - attacking midfielder (d) - (e) Tabor Sezana, Zvijezda G., Amed SK, Bayrampasa, NK Radomlje

*** Demirel - Ali Demirel (Ali Sühan Demirel) (a) 02/01/2003, Lünen (Germany) (b) - (c) F - center forward (d) Kasimpasa (e) -

*** Demiri - Adem Demiri (Адем Демири) (a) 08/03/1999, Bern (Switzerland) (b) 1,87 (c) F - center forward (d) FK Decic Tuzi (e) FC Besa Biel, FC Prishtina BE, FC Bern, FC Prishtina BE

*** Demiri - Besir Demiri (a) 01/08/1994, Skopje (North Macedonia) (b) 1,78 (c) D - left back (d) - (e) FC Shkupi, FC Dinamo, FK Kukësi, MSK Zilina, FK Mariupol, Vardar, Shkëndija, FC Shkupi

*** Demirol - Alper Demirol (a) 01/10/2002, Stockholm (Sweden) (b) 1,84 (c) M - central midfielder (d) Hammarby IF (e) Hammarby TFF, Hammarby IF

*** Demirovic - Ermedin Demirovic (Ermedin Demirović) (a) 25/03/1998, Hamburg (Germany) (b) 1,85 (c) F - center forward (d) FC Augsburg (e) SC Freiburg, Alavés, FC St. Gallen, Alavés, UD Almería, Alavés, FC Sochaux, Alavés, Depor. Alavés B

*** Demirtas - Kahraman Demirtas (Kahraman Demirtaş) (a) 01/05/1994, Mardin (Turkey) (b) 1,84 (c) D - central defense (d) Konyaspor (e) Göztepe, Altinordu, Nigde Anadolu, Altinordu, FC Den Bosch, Roda JC, RCS Verviers

*** Demitra - Lucas Demitra (a) 09/04/2003, St. Louis, Missouri (United States) (b) 1,84 (c) F - right winger (d) AS Trencin (e) Zlaté Moravce, AS Trencin

*** Demjén - Patrik Demjén (a) 22/03/1998, Esztergom (Hungary) (b) 1,86 (c) G (d) MTK Budapest (e) Zalaegerszeg, MTK Budapest, Budaörs, MTK Budapest, Budaörs, MTK Budapest, Dorog, MTK Budapest

*** Demme - Diego Demme (a) 21/11/1991, Herford (Germany) (b) 1,70 (c) M - pivot (d) SSC Nápoles (e) RB Leipzig, SC Paderborn, Arminia Bielefeld

*** Demolli - Amar Demolli (a) 16/07/2006, Prishtinë (Kosovo) (b) - (c) D (d) FC Prishtina (e) KF Kurda

*** Demuynck - Dylan Demuynck (a) 06/05/2004, ¿? (Belgium) (b) - (c) F - left winger (d) Jong Essevee (e) -

*** Demydenko - Ivan Demydenko (Демиденко Іван Михайлович) (a) 11/06/2003, ¿? (Ukraine) (b) 1,93 (c) F - center forward (d) FK Minaj (e) Asteras Tripoli, Minija, Ol. Donetsk II, Cherkashchyna

*** Dendoncker - Leander Dendoncker (a) 15/04/1995, Passendale (Belgium) (b) 1,88 (c) M - pivot (d) Aston Villa (e) Wolverhampton Wanderers, RSC Anderlecht, Wolverhampton Wanderers, RSC Anderlecht

*** Denholm - Aidan Denholm (a) 09/11/2003, East Calder (Scotland) (b) - (c) M - central midfielder (d) Heart of Midlothian FC (e) Hearts FC II, East Fife, Hearts FC II, Berwick Rangers FC, Hearts FC II

*** Deni Júnior - Deni Júnior (Denílson Pereira Júnior) (a) 18/07/1995, Rio de Janeiro (Brazil) (b) 1,88 (c) F - center forward (d) Avaí FC (e) Famalicão, Hatta Club, Paços Ferreira, At. Mineiro, Al-Dhafra FC, At. Mineiro, Paços Ferreira, At. Mineiro, Tondela, At. Mineiro, Al-Faisaly FC, At. Mineiro, Recreativo Granada, EC Vitória, Recreativo Granada, São Paulo, Granada B, Recreativo Granada, Avaí FC, Granada B, Neftchi Baku

*** Denic - Djordje Denic (a) 01/04/1996, Beograd (RF Yugoslavia, now in Serbia) (b) 1,82 (d) Henan FC (e) Mladost GAT, Apollon Limassol, Atromitos FC, Apollon Limassol, Rosenborg, Apollon Limassol, Rosenborg, Rad Beograd

*** Denis Ribeiro - Denis Ribeiro (Denis Custodio Ribeiro) (a) 09/09/1998, Cambuquira (Brazil) (b) 1,78 (c) F - right winger (d) Birkirkara FC (e) Icasa, Juazeirense

*** Denisenko - Artem Denisenko (Денисенко Артём Вячеславович) (a) 12/04/1999, Brest (Belarus) (b) 1,88 (c) G (d) Isloch Minsk Region (e) Belshina, Dynamo Brest, Rukh, Dynamo Brest II, Rukh, Dynamo Brest II

*** Denisenko - Dmitriy Denisenko (Денисенко Дмитрий Павлович) (a) 23/02/2004, Osipovichi (Belarus) (b) - (c) M - attacking midfielder (d) Belshina Bobruisk (e) Belshina II

*** Denisov - Daniil Denisov (Денисов Даниил Сергеевич) (a) 21/10/2002, St.Petersburg (Russia) (b) 1,85 (c) D - right back (d) FC Spartak de Moscú (e) Spartak-2, Spartak Moskva II, SShOR Zenit

*** Denkey - Kévin Denkey (Steeve Kévin Denkey Ahoueke) (a) 30/11/2000, Lomé (Togo) (b) 1,81 (c) F - center forward (d) Cercle Brugge (e) Nîmes, AS Béziers, Nîmes, Nîmes B

*** Denkovic - Stefan Denkovic (Стефан Денковић) (a) 16/06/1991, Beograd (Yugoslavia, now in Serbia) (b) 1,84 (c) F - left winger (d) FK Igman Konjic (e) FK Decic Tuzi, Dinamo Batumi, Kaysar, Spartak, Sutjeska Niksic, FK Bokelj, FK Zemun, Zawisza, Puskás AFC, Vojvodina, Hapoel Haifa, Crvena zvezda, Sopot, Crvena zvezda

*** Denkovski - David Denkovski (Давид Денковски) (a) 17/08/2000, Kumanovo (North Macedonia) (b) 2,02 (c) G (d) FC Shkupi (e) Bregalnica Stip, Pehcevo, AP Brera

*** Dennis - Emmanuel Dennis (Emmanuel Bonaventure Dennis) (a) 15/11/1997, Abuja (Nigeria) (b) 1,75 (c) F - center forward (d) Nottingham Forest (e) Watford, KV Brugge, 1.FC Köln, KV Brugge, Zorya Lugansk, Abuja College

*** Dennis - Will Dennis (William Jonathan Dennis) (a) 10/07/2000, ¿? (England) (b) 1,88 (c) G (d) Kilmarnock FC (e) Kilmarnock FC, Bournemouth, Slough, Bournemouth, Wealdstone, Bournemouth, Weymouth FC, FC Guernsey

*** Denswil - Stefano Denswil (Stefano Wilfred Denswil) (a) 07/05/1993, Zaandam (Netherlands) (b) 1,88 (c) D - central defense (d) Trabzonspor (e) Bologna, Trabzonspor, Bologna, KV Brugge, Bologna, KV Brugge, Ajax

*** Dentakis - Antonis Dentakis (Αντώνης Ντεντάκης) (a) 13/03/1995, Chania (Greece) (b) 1,79 (c) D - right back (d) APO Levadiakos (e) Apollon Smyrnis, Volos NPS, AEEK SYNKA, Platanias, PGS Kissamikos, Platanias, PGS Kissamikos

*** Deocleciano - Emerson Deocleciano (Emerson Santana Deocleciano) (a) 27/07/1999, Itamaraju (Brazil) (b) 1,74 (c) F - left winger (d) RFS (e) NK Lokomotiva, RFS, NK Lokomotiva, Vila Nova, NK Lokomotiva

*** Déom - Jérôme Déom (a) 19/04/1999, Libramont-Chevigny (Belgium) (b) 1,75 (c) M - central midfielder (d) KAS Eupen (e) MVV Maastricht, Standard Liège, MVV Maastricht, Standard Liège

*** Depaoli - Fabio Depaoli (a) 24/04/1997, Riva del Garda (Italy) (b) 1,82 (c) D - right back (d) UC Sampdoria (e) Hellas Verona, Sampdoria, Hellas Verona, Sampdoria, Benevento, Sampdoria, Atalanta, Sampdoria, Chievo Verona

*** Depay - Memphis Depay (a) 13/02/1994, Moordrecht (Netherlands) (b) 1,78 (c) F - center forward (d) Atlético de Madrid (e) FC Barcelona, Olympique Lyon, Manchester Utd., PSV Eindhoven

*** Depetris - David Depetris (David Alberto Depetris) (a) 11/11/1988, San Jorge (Argentina) (b) 1,85 (c) F - center forward (d) MFK Dukla Banska Bystrica (e) Savoia, AS Trencin, Spartak Trnava, Huracán, Sarmiento Junín, Huracán, Olimpo, Huracán, Spartak Trnava, Monarcas Morelia, Çaykur Rizespor, Sigma Olomouc, Çaykur Rizespor, AS Trencin, FC Omniworld, AS Trencin, Rafaela

*** Depoitre - Laurent Depoitre (a) 07/12/1988, Tournai (Belgium) (b) 1,91 (c) F - center forward (d) KAA Gent (e) Huddersfield Town, FC Porto, KAA Gent, KV Oostende, Eendracht Aalst, RRC Péruwelz, RFC Tournai

*** Depú - Depú (Laurindo Dilson M. Aurélio) (a) 08/01/2000, Lobito (Angola) (b) 1,87 (c) F - center forward (d) Gil Vicente FC (e) Petro Luanda, Sagrada, Caála, Académica Lobito

*** Derdiyok - Eren Derdiyok (a) 12/06/1988, Basel (Switzerland) (b) 1,91 (c) F - center forward (d) FC Schaffhausen (e) Ankaragücü, Pakhtakor, Göztepe, Galatasaray, Kasimpasa, Hoffenheim, Bayer Leverkusen, Hoffenheim, Bayer Leverkusen, FC Basel, BSC Old Boys

*** Dergachev - Vyacheslav Dergachev (Дергачев Вячеслав Анатольевич) (a) 01/07/2001, Minsk (Belarus) (b) 1,85 (c) G (d) BATE Borisov (e) BATE II

*** Derijck - Timothy Derijck (a) 25/05/1987, Dendermonde (Belgium) (b) 1,85 (c) D - central defense (d) SV Zulte Waregem (e) KV Kortrijk, KAA Gent, Zulte Waregem, ADO Den Haag, PSV Eindhoven, FC Utrecht, PSV Eindhoven, ADO Den Haag, Feyenoord, FCV Dender EH, Feyenoord, NAC Breda, Feyenoord

*** Dermaku - Kastriot Dermaku (a) 15/01/1992, Scandiano (Italy) (b) 1,94 (c) D - central defense (d) US Lecce (e) Parma, Lecce, Parma, Cosenza, Empoli, Lucchese, Empoli, Pavia, Empoli, Melfi

*** Deruffe - Maxime Deruffe (a) 13/05/1988, Saint-Dizier (France) (b) 1,75 (c) F - center forward (d) Jeunesse Esch (e) Hamm Benfica, Differdange 03, RC Epernay, SA Sézanne, Saint-Dizier

*** Dervin - Aodh Dervin (a) 21/07/1999, Longford (Ireland) (b) - (c) M - central midfielder (d) Galway United FC (e) Shelbourne, Longford Town, Shelbourne, Longford Town

*** Dervisevic - Aldin Dervisevic (a) 19/08/1989, Titograd (now Podgorica) (Yugoslavia, now in Montenegro) (b) 1,91 (c) M - pivot (d) FC Jeunesse Canach (e) Jeunesse Esch, Weiler, Jeunesse Esch, US Hostert, Jeunesse Canach, CS Pétange, US Hostert, CS Pétange, Jeunesse Canach

*** Dervishaj - Besfort Dervishaj (a) 24/09/1998, Skenderaj (RF Yugoslavia, now in Kosovo) (b) - (c) M - pivot (d) KF Vëllaznimi Gjakovë (e) KF Drenica, KF Vushtrria, KF Drenica

*** Dervisoglu - Halil Dervisoglu (Halil İbrahim Dervişoğlu) (a) 08/12/1999, Rotterdam (Netherlands) (b) 1,83 (c) F - center forward (d) Galatasaray (e) Brentford, Burnley, Brentford, Galatasaray, Brentford, Galatasaray, Brentford, FC Twente, Brentford, Sparta Rotterdam

*** Descamps - Rémy Descamps (a) 25/06/1996, Marcq-en-Barœul (France) (b) 1,96 (c) G (d) FC Nantes (e) RSC Charleroi, Paris Saint-Germain, Clermont Foot, Paris Saint-Germain, Tours FC, Paris Saint-Germain, Paris Saint Germain B

*** Descotte - Anthony Descotte (Anthony Kevin N. Descotte) (a) 03/08/2003, Gosselies (Belgium) (b) 1,80 (c) F - center forward (d) FC Utrecht (e) FC Utrecht, RSC Charleroi

*** Desira - Kurt Desira (a) 05/03/2002, ¿? (Malta) (b) - (c) M - left midfielder (d) Qormi FC (e) Valletta, Gzira Utd., Pietà Hotspurs, Gzira Utd.

*** Desira - Timothy Tabone Desira (a) 15/07/1995, ¿? (Malta) (b) - (c) D - right back (d) Zabbar St. Patrick FC (e) Marsaxlokk, Sirens FC, Hibernians FC, Santa Lucia FC, Hibernians FC, Tarxien, Hibernians FC

*** Désiré - Jonel Désiré (a) 12/02/1997, Mirebalais (Haiti) (b) 1,80 (c) F - center forward (d) FC Telavi (e) Olympiakos N., Pyunik Yerevan, Olympiakos N., FC Urartu, Lori Vanadzor, Mirebalais, Lori Vanadzor, Mirebalais, AS Capoise, Real Monarchs, Mirebalais, AS Capoise, Mirebalais

*** Deslandes - Sylvain Deslandes (Sylvain Boris Nabil Deslandes) (a) 25/04/1997, Kouoptamo (Cameroon) (b) 1,90 (c) D - central defense (d) - (e) Debrecen, FC Arges,

Wolverhampton Wanderers, Jumilla, Wolverhampton Wanderers, FC Portsmouth, Wolverhampton Wanderers, Bury, Wolverhampton Wanderers, SM Caen B
*** Desler - Mikkel Desler (a) 19/02/1995, Assens (Denmark) (b) 1,84 (c) D - right back (d) Toulouse FC (e) Haugesund, Odense BK
*** Despa - Alexandru Despa (a) 31/03/2002, Bucuresti (Romania) (b) - (c) F - center forward (d) CS Tunari (e) FC Rapid 1923, Progresul Sp., FC Rapid 1923
*** Despodov - Kiril Despodov (Кирил Деспοдов) (a) 11/11/1996, Kresna (Bulgaria) (b) 1,80 (c) F - right winger (d) Ludogorets Razgrad (e) Cagliari, Ludogorets, Cagliari, Sturm Graz, Cagliari, CSKA-Sofia, Litex Lovetch
*** Despotovski - Stefan Despotovski (Стефан Деспотовски) (a) 23/01/2003, Skopje (North Macedonia) (b) 1,84 (c) D - central defense (d) Rabotnicki Skopje (e) Graficar
*** Dessers - Cyriel Dessers (Cyriel Kolawole Dessers) (a) 08/12/1994, Leuven (Belgium) (b) 1,85 (c) F - center forward (d) Rangers FC (e) Cremonese, KRC Genk, Feyenoord, KRC Genk, Heracles Almelo, FC Utrecht, NAC Breda, KSC Lokeren, OH Leuven
*** Dessoleil - Dorian Dessoleil (a) 07/08/1992, Charleroi (Belgium) (b) 1,88 (c) D - central defense (d) Royal Antwerp FC (e) KV Kortrijk, Royal Antwerp, RSC Charleroi, RE Virton, Sint-Truiden, RSC Charleroi
*** Dest - Sergiño Dest (Sergiño Gianni Dest) (a) 03/11/2000, Almere (Netherlands) (b) 1,71 (c) D - right back (d) FC Barcelona (e) AC Milan, FC Barcelona, Ajax, Ajax B
*** Desta - Shalev Desta (דסתה שלו) (a) 07/08/2001, Afula (Israel) (b) - (c) F - right winger (d) Hapoel Afula (e) Hapoel Afula, Kiryat Shmona
*** Destan - Enis Destan (a) 15/06/2002, Izmir(Turkey) (b) 1,85 (c) F - center forward (d) Trabzonspor (e) Warta Poznań, Trabzonspor, Altinordu
*** Destanoglu - Ersin Destanoglu (Ersin Destanoğlu) (a) 01/01/2001, Gaziosmanpasa (Turkey) (b) 1,95 (c) G (d) Besiktas JK (e) -
*** Destro - Mattia Destro (a) 20/03/1991, Ascoli Piceno (Italy) (b) 1,82 (c) F - center forward (d) - (e) FC Empoli, Genoa, Bologna, Genoa, Bologna, AS Roma, AC Milan, AS Roma, Genoa, AS Roma, Genoa, AC Siena, Genoa, AC Siena, Genoa, Internazionale Milano, Genoa
*** Deulofeu - Gerard Deulofeu (Gerard Deulofeu Lázaro) (a) 13/03/1994, Riudarenes (Spain) (b) 1,77 (c) F - center forward (d) Udinese (e) Watford, Udinese, Watford, FC Barcelona, Watford, FC Barcelona, Everton, AC Milan, Everton, FC Barcelona, Sevilla FC, FC Barcelona, Everton, FC Barcelona, FC Barcelona B
*** Deutsch - László Deutsch (a) 09/03/1999, Budapest (Hungary) (b) 1,82 (c) D - left back (d) Vasas FC (e) Puskás AFC, Puskás AFC II, Csákvár, Puskás AFC II, Csákvár, Puskás AFC II
*** Devalckeneer - Niels Devalckeneer (a) 17/05/2004, ¿? (Belgium) (b) 1,93 (c) G (d) Royal Antwerp FC (e) Young Reds
*** Devdariani - Andria Devdariani (ანდრია დევდარიანი) (a) 09/09/2002, ¿? (Georgia) (b) 1,72 (c) M - central midfielder (d) Sioni Bolnisi (e) Samgurali, FC Saburtalo II, Torpedo Kutaisi II
*** Devedzic - Kenin Devedzic (Kenin Devedžić) (a) 01/01/2000, Gracanica (Bosnia and Herzegovina) (b) 1,90 (c) D - central defense (d) Achyronas-Onisilos FC (e) Sloboda Tuzla, HNK Orasje, Sloboda Tuzla
*** Devers - Jesse Devers (Jesse James Devers) (a) 11/01/1997, Ballina, Mayo (Ireland) (b) 1,74 (c) F - center forward (d) Geelong Soccer Club (e) Magni, Finn Harps, Ballina Town, Sligo Rovers, Finn Harps, Manulla, Galway United, Manulla

*** Devid - Devid (Devid De Santana Silva) (a) 28/03/1996, ¿? (Brazil) (b) 1,90 (c) F - center forward (d) Kelantan United (e) KF Tirana, SC Covilhã, KS Kastrioti, Londrina-PR, Foz do Iguaçu, Londrina-PR, Avaí FC B

*** Deville - Maurice Deville (Maurice John Deville) (a) 31/07/1992, Sulingen (Germany) (b) 1,94 (c) F - right winger (d) Swift Hesperange (e) SV Sandhausen, Saarbrücken, Waldh. Mannheim, 1.FC Kaiserslautern, FSV Frankfurt, 1.FC Kaiserslautern, Kaiserslautern II, Saarbrücken II, Saarbrücken, SV Elversberg

*** Devine - Adam Devine (Adam Gary Devine) (a) 25/03/2003, Glasgow (Scotland) (b) 1,90 (c) D - right back (d) Rangers FC (e) Rangers II, Brechin City, Rangers II, Partick Thistle, Rangers II

*** Devine - David Devine (a) 20/06/2001, Wishaw (Scotland) (b) 1,90 (c) D - central defense (d) Alloa Athletic FC (e) Motherwell FC, Alloa Athletic, Motherwell FC, East Fife, Motherwell FC, Motherwell B, Queen of the South, Motherwell B

*** Devine - Ethan Devine (a) 08/02/2001, Belfast (Northern Ireland) (b) - (c) F - center forward (d) Dungannon Swifts (e) Dungannon, Linfield, Knockbreda FC, Cliftonville, Newington FC

*** Devine - Senan Devine (a) 12/01/2007, ¿? (Northern Ireland) (b) - (c) M - attacking midfielder (d) - (e) Coleraine FC

*** Devlin - Cammy Devlin (Cameron Peter Devlin) (a) 07/06/1998, Sydney (Australia) (b) 1,69 (c) M - pivot (d) Heart of Midlothian FC (e) Newcastle, Wellington P., Sydney FC, Sydney FC II, West Sydney II

*** Devlin - Mikey Devlin (Michael James Devlin) (a) 03/10/1993, Motherwell (Scotland) (b) 1,88 (c) D - central defense (d) Livingston FC (e) Hibernian FC, Fleetwood, Aberdeen FC, Stenhousemuir

*** Devlin - Nicky Devlin (a) 17/10/1993, Glasgow (Scotland) (b) - (c) D - right back (d) Aberdeen FC (e) Livingston FC, FC Walsall, Ayr United, Stenhousemuir, Dumbarton FC, Stenhousemuir, Dumbarton FC, Drumchapel

*** Devlin - Terry Devlin (a) 06/11/2003, Cookstown (Northern Ireland) (b) - (c) M - central midfielder (d) FC Portsmouth (e) Glentoran, Dungannon

*** Devoy - Dawson Devoy (a) 20/11/2001, Dublin (Ireland) (b) 1,77 (c) M - attacking midfielder (d) Milton Keynes Dons (e) Bohemians

*** Dewaele - Gilles Dewaele (Gilles Henri Dewaele) (a) 13/02/1996, Knokke (Belgium) (b) 1,82 (c) D - right back (d) Standard de Lieja (e) KV Kortrijk, KVC Westerlo, Cercle Brugge

*** Dewaele - Sieben Dewaele (a) 02/02/1999, Kortrijk (Belgium) (b) 1,80 (c) M - pivot (d) KV Oostende (e) AS Nancy, KV Oostende, RSC Anderlecht, Heerenveen, RSC Anderlecht

*** Dewaest - Sébastien Dewaest (Sébastien Tony Dewaest) (a) 27/05/1991, Poperinge (Belgium) (b) 1,88 (c) D - central defense (d) AEL Limassol (e) KRC Genk, OH Leuven, KRC Genk, Toulouse, KRC Genk, RSC Charleroi, KSV Roeselare, LOSC Lille B

*** Dewalque - Lohan Dewalque (Lohan Pascal Dewalque) (a) 28/02/2004, ¿? (Belgium) (b) - (c) M - central midfielder (d) Racing FC Union Luxembourg (e) -

*** Dewsbury-Hall - Kiernan Dewsbury-Hall (Kiernan Frank Dewsbury-Hall) (a) 06/09/1998, Shepshed (England) (b) 1,78 (c) M - central midfielder (d) Leicester City (e) Luton Town, Blackpool

*** Dgani - Orel Dgani (דגני אוראל) (a) 08/01/1989, Pardes Hanna-Karkur (Israel) (b) 1,80 (c) D - central defense (d) Beitar Jerusalem (e) Hapoel Tel Aviv, Maccabi Haifa, Hapoel Tel Aviv, Maccabi Haifa, Maccabi Netanya

*** D'Haene - Kristof D'Haene (a) 06/06/1990, Kortrijk (Belgium) (b) 1,68 (c) D - left back (d) SK Roeselare-Daisel (e) KV Kortrijk, Cercle Brugge

*** D'Haese - Robbie D'Haese (a) 25/02/1999, ¿? (Belgium) (b) 1,80 (c) D - right back (d) KV Oostende (e) -

*** Dhanda - Yan Dhanda (a) 14/12/1998, Dudley (England) (b) 1,73 (c) M - attacking midfielder (d) Ross County FC (e) Swansea City

*** Dhimitri - Ernis Dhimitri (a) 19/07/2003, Tiranë (Albania) (b) - (c) D - central defense (d) - (e) KF Drenica

*** Di Carmine - Samuel Di Carmine (a) 29/09/1988, Firenze (Italy) (b) 1,87 (c) F - center forward (d) - (e) Perugia, Cremonese, Hellas Verona, Crotone, Hellas Verona, Perugia, Hellas Verona, Perugia, Virtus Entella, Perugia, Juve Stabia, Cittadella, Frosinone, Fiorentina, Gallipoli, Fiorentina, Queen's Park Rangers, Fiorentina

*** Di Francesco - Federico Di Francesco (a) 14/06/1994, Pisa (Italy) (b) 1,71 (c) F - left winger (d) US Lecce (e) SPAL, FC Empoli, SPAL, Sassuolo, SPAL, Sassuolo, Bologna, Virtus Lanciano, Parma, Cremonese, Parma, Pescara, AS Gubbio, Pescara

*** Di Giusto - Matteo Di Giusto (Matteo Emilio Di Giusto) (a) 18/08/2000, Wetzikon (Switzerland) (b) 1,68 (c) M - attacking midfielder (d) FC Winterthur (e) FC Vaduz

*** Di Gregorio - Michele Di Gregorio (a) 27/07/1997, Milano (Italy) (b) 1,87 (c) G (d) AC Monza (e) Internazionale Milano, Monza, Internazionale Milano, Pordenone, Internazionale Milano, Novara, Internazionale Milano, Avellino, Internazionale Milano, Renate

*** Di Lorenzo - Giovanni Di Lorenzo (a) 04/08/1993, Castelnuovo di Garfagnana (Italy) (b) 1,83 (c) D - right back (d) SSC Nápoles (e) Empoli, Matera, Reggio Calabria, Cuneo

*** Di Lorenzo - Juan Di Lorenzo (Juan Antonio Di Lorenzo) (a) 06/07/1998, Quilmes (Argentina) (b) 1,82 (c) D - central defense (d) - (e) KF Llapi, OF Ierapetras, Indep'te II, Socuéllamos, Indep'te II

*** Di Maio - Roberto Di Maio (a) 21/09/1982, Napoli (Italy) (b) 1,85 (c) D - central defense (d) SS Cosmos (e) La Fiorita, San Marino, Correggese, Matelica, AS Gubbio, Rimini, Torres, L'Aquila, Lecce, ASG Nocerina, Catanzaro, San Marino, Versilia 1998, Venturina, Castelnuovo, Virtus Castelfr.

*** Di María - Ángel Di María (Ángel Fabián Di María) (a) 14/02/1988, Rosario (Argentina) (b) 1,80 (c) F - right winger (d) SL Benfica (e) Juventus, Paris Saint-Germain, Manchester Utd., Real Madrid, Benfica, Rosario Central, Rosario Central II

*** Di Mariano - Francesco Di Mariano (a) 20/04/1996, Palermo (Italy) (b) 1,77 (c) F - left winger (d) Palermo FC (e) Lecce, Venezia, Juve Stabia, Venezia, Novara, AS Roma, Monopoli, AS Roma, Ancona, Lecce

*** Di Marzio - Marco Di Marzio (a) 16/07/2000, ¿? (Italy) (b) - (c) F - center forward (d) SS Folgore/Falciano (e) Riccione

*** Di Meo - Nicholas Di Meo (a) 01/04/2002, Rivoli (Italy) (b) 1,89 (c) D - central defense (d) AC Libertas (e) Volpiano, Nereto, La Fiorita, Pontedera, Venaria Reale, Bruinese

*** Di Piedi - Francesco Di Piedi (a) 17/06/2003, San Fili (Italy) (b) - (c) F - center forward (d) Glacis United (e) Crema, Glacis United

*** Dia - Boulaye Dia (a) 16/11/1996, Oyonnax (France) (b) 1,80 (c) F - center forward (d) US Salernitana 1919 (e) Villarreal CF, Salernitana, Villarreal CF, Stade Reims, Jura Sud, Pl.Vallée

*** Diabaté - Bassekou Diabaté (a) 15/04/2000, Bamako (Mali) (b) 1,84 (c) F - right winger (d) FK Jerv (e) Lechia Gdánsk, Yeelen, Lechia Gdánsk, Yeelen

*** Diabaté - Fousseni Diabaté (a) 18/10/1995, Aubervilliers (France) (b) 1,75 (c) F - right winger (d) Partizán Beograd (e) Trabzonspor, Giresunspor, Trabzonspor,

Göztepe, Trabzonspor, Leicester City, Amiens SC, Leicester City, Sivasspor, Leicester City, G. Ajaccio, EA Guingamp B, Stade Reims B

*** Diaby - Abdoulaye Diaby (a) 04/07/2000, Bamako (Mali) (b) 1,98 (c) D - central defense (d) FC St. Gallen 1879 (e) Újpest FC, KSC Lokeren, Djoliba AC

*** Diaby - Alassane Diaby (Alassane-Méba Diaby) (a) 06/01/1995, Saint-Denis (France) (b) 1,85 (c) M - pivot (d) AS Nancy-Lorraine (e) FK Tuzla City, Quevilly Rouen, Pau FC, Septemvri Sofia, Osmanlispor, Lierse SK, AS Monaco B

*** Diaby - Moussa Diaby (a) 07/07/1999, Paris (France) (b) 1,71 (c) F - right winger (d) Aston Villa (e) Bayer Leverkusen, Paris Saint-Germain, Paris Saint Germain B, Crotone, Paris Saint Germain B

*** Diaby - Souleymane Diaby (a) 08/10/1999, Divo (Ivory Coast) (b) 1,73 (c) D - left back (d) FC Winterthur (e) SC Gagnoa, AS Denguélé, ES Bingerville

*** Diaby - Yadaly Diaby (a) 09/08/2000, Saint-Étienne (France) (b) - (c) F - left winger (d) SC Austria Lustenau (e) Austria Lustenau, Clermont Foot, Clermont B, Andrézieux

*** Diack - Lamine Diack (a) 15/11/2000, Dakar (Senegal) (b) 1,86 (c) M - pivot (d) FC Nantes (e) Ankaragücü, FC Nantes, Ankaragücü, Fenerbahce, Tuzlaspor, FC Shkupi, Oslo FA Dakar

*** Diagne - Mbaye Diagne (a) 28/10/1991, Dakar (Senegal) (b) 1,91 (c) F - center forward (d) Al-Qadsiah FC (e) Karagümrük, Galatasaray, West Bromwich Albion, Galatasaray, KV Brugge, Galatasaray, Kasimpasa, Tianjin Teda, Újpest FC, Juventus, KVC Westerlo, Juventus, Al-Shabab, Juventus, Lierse SK, Juventus, AC Ajaccio, Juventus, Bra

*** Diakhaby - Adama Diakhaby (a) 05/07/1996, Ajaccio (France) (b) 1,84 (c) F - right winger (d) Qarabağ FK (e) Amiens SC, Huddersfield Town, Nottingham Forest, Huddersfield Town, AS Monaco, Stade Rennes, Stade Rennes B, SM Caen B

*** Diakhaby - Mouctar Diakhaby (a) 19/12/1996, Vendôme (France) (b) 1,92 (c) D - central defense (d) Valencia CF (e) Olympique Lyon, Olymp. Lyon B

*** Diakhate - Abdoulaye Diakhate (a) 16/01/1988, Guédiawaye (Senegal) (b) 1,81 (c) M - pivot (d) - (e) Kaspiy Aktau, FK Turan, Ordabasy, Atyrau, Ordabasy, Taraz, Sakaryaspor, Çaykur Rizespor, Sakaryaspor, Kartalspor

*** Diakhate - Ousmane Diakhate (a) 01/06/2003, ¿? (Senegal) (b) 1,90 (c) M - central midfielder (d) - (e) Botev II

*** Diakhon - Mamadou Diakhon (a) 22/09/2005, ¿? (France) (b) - (c) F - left winger (d) Stade Reims B (e) -

*** Diakite - Abdelaye Diakite (Abdelaye Diakité) (a) 08/01/1990, Les Mureaux (France) (b) 1,90 (c) D - central defense (d) Nea Salamis (e) FC U Craiova, ACSM Poli Iasi, Menemenspor, Al-Ahli, Alki Oroklini, Siracusa, FK Bylis, Parma, Teramo, Parma, ND Gorica, Parma, Aprilia, Le Havre AC B

*** Diakité - Ali Diakité (a) 03/03/1993, Béoumi (Ivory Coast) (b) 1,80 (c) M - central midfielder (d) Hibernians FC (e) Socuéllamos, CD Alcoyano, Villanovense, Lorca Deportiva, CD Badajoz, UD Melilla, CD Guadalajara, SD Leioa, UB Conquense, Pobla de Mafumet CF

*** Diakité - Bafodé Diakité (a) 06/01/2001, Toulouse (France) (b) 1,85 (c) D - right back (d) LOSC Lille Métropole (e) Toulouse

*** Diakité - Ibrahim Diakité (a) 31/10/2003, ¿? (Guinea) (b) 1,78 (c) D - right back (d) Stade de Reims (e) KAS Eupen, Stade Reims, Stade Reims B

*** Diakité - Moussa Diakité (a) 04/11/2003, ¿? (Mali) (b) 1,89 (c) M - central midfielder (d) Cádiz CF Mirandilla (e) Etoiles Mandé

*** Diakité - Oumar Diakité (a) 20/12/2003, Bingerville (Ivory Coast) (b) 1,82 (c) F - center forward (d) Stade de Reims (e) RB Salzburg, FC Liefering, RB Salzburg, ASEC Mimosas

*** Diakité - Ousmane Diakité (a) 25/07/2000, ¿? (Mali) (b) 1,89 (c) M - pivot (d) TSV Hartberg (e) RB Salzburg, FC St. Gallen, RB Salzburg, SCR Altach, RB Salzburg, FC Liefering, RB Salzburg, Yeelen

*** Diallo - Abdou Diallo (Abdou-Lakhad Diallo) (a) 04/05/1996, Tours (France) (b) 1,87 (c) D - central defense (d) París Saint-Germain FC (e) RB Leipzig, Paris Saint-Germain, Borussia Dortmund, Mainz 05, AS Monaco, Zulte Waregem, AS Monaco, AS Monaco B

*** Diallo - Adama Diallo (Adama Mamadou Diallo) (a) 31/10/1997, Conakry (Guinea) (b) 1,79 (c) F - center forward (d) FK Turan (e) Energetik-BGU, Kaysar, Energetik-BGU, Eleph. Coléah

*** Diallo - Amad Diallo (Amad Diallo Traoré) (a) 11/07/2002, Abidjan (Ivory Coast) (b) 1,73 (c) F - right winger (d) Manchester United (e) Sunderland, Manchester Utd., Rangers FC, Manchester Utd., Atalanta, Boca Barco

*** Diallo - Amadou Diallo (Amadou Tidiane Diallo) (a) 21/06/1994, Paris (France) (b) 1,79 (c) F - right winger (d) - (e) CS Mioveni, Jerv, Teplice, Sabah FK, Red Star FC, Cercle Brugge, White Star, UR Namur, AS Monaco B

*** Diallo - Baïla Diallo (a) 24/06/2001, Toulouse (France) (b) 1,76 (c) D - left back (d) SC Austria Lustenau (e) Clermont Foot, US Orléans, Clermont Foot, Clermont B

*** Diallo - Bradley Diallo (a) 20/07/1990, Marseille (France) (b) 1,83 (c) D - central defense (d) FC Metaloglobus Bucharest (e) FC Brasov-SR, SJK Seinäjoki, FC U Craiova, Chindia, ACSM Poli Iasi, Gaz Metan, Los Ángeles, LA Galaxy II, Los Ángeles, LA Galaxy II, White Star, Oldham Athletic, Ol. Marseille B

*** Diallo - Habib Diallo (Habibou Mouhamadou Diallo) (a) 18/06/1995, Thiès (Senegal) (b) 1,86 (c) F - center forward (d) Al-Shabab FC (e) Racing Club Strasbourg, FC Metz, Stade Brestois, FC Metz, Stade Brestois, FC Metz, FC Metz B, Génération Foot

*** Diallo - Ibrahima Diallo (a) 08/03/1999, Tours (France) (b) 1,79 (c) M - pivot (d) Al-Duhail SC (e) Southampton, Stade Brestois, AS Monaco, Stade Brestois, AS Monaco, AS Monaco B

*** Diallo - Ismaël Diallo (Ismaël Jean Chester Diallo) (a) 29/01/1997, Séguéla (Ivory Coast) (b) 1,78 (c) D - left back (d) HNK Hajduk Split (e) AC Ajaccio, SC Bastia, SC Bastia B, ES Bingerville

*** Diallo - Ismaila Diallo (a) 12/12/2001, Brighton (England) (b) 1,77 (c) F - left winger (d) FK Buducnost Banovici (e) UE Santa Coloma, Hastings United, FC Lancing

*** Diallo - Jules Diallo (a) 08/03/1993, ¿? (France) (b) - (c) F - center forward (d) CS Fola Esch (e) US Rumelange, Amnéville, FC Metz B

*** Diallo - Moussa Diallo (a) 27/01/1997, Corbeil-Essonnes (France) (b) 1,84 (c) D - right back (d) Servette FC (e) SO Cholet, AJ Auxerre, AJ Auxerre B

*** Diallo - Sadou Diallo (a) 10/06/1999, ¿? (England) (b) 1,88 (c) M - pivot (d) Derry City (e) Forest Green Rovers, Accrington St.

*** Diallo - Samba Diallo (a) 05/01/2003, Dakar (Senegal) (b) 1,68 (c) F - left winger (d) FC Dinamo de Kiev (e) AF Darou Salam

*** Diallo - Ulysse Diallo (a) 26/10/1992, Bamako (Mali) (b) 1,82 (c) F - center forward (d) Rahmatganj MFS (e) Panevezys, Mezőkövesd, Sabah FK, MTK Budapest, Puskás AFC, Mezőkövesd, Marítimo, Académica Coimbra, Arouca, Ferencváros, Shabab Al-Sahel, Djoliba AC

*** Diamanti - Gersi Diamanti (a) 15/10/1999, Gjorm (Albania) (b) - (c) F - left winger (d) - (e) KF Egnatia, Flamurtari FC

*** Diamantis - Apostolos Diamantis (Απόστολος Διαμαντής) (a) 20/05/2000, Serres (Greece) (b) 1,87 (c) D - central defense (d) Istanbulspor (e) OFI Creta, PAOK, Volos NPS, PAOK

*** Diambou - Mamady Diambou (a) 11/11/2002, Bamako (Mali) (b) 1,76 (c) M - pivot (d) Red Bull Salzburg (e) FC Luzern, RB Salzburg, FC Liefering, RB Salzburg, Guidars FC

*** Diarra - Boubakary Diarra (a) 30/08/1993, Villepinte (France) (b) 1,87 (c) M - pivot (d) PSIS Semarang (e) Mosta FC, Kazma SC, Varzim, Cova Piedade, Rieti, Tondela, SC Covilhã, Kruoja, Torino, Bra

*** Diarra - Habib Diarra (Mouhamadou Habib Diarra) (a) 03/01/2004, Guédiawaye (Senegal) (b) 1,79 (c) M - pivot (d) Racing Club Strasbourg (e) -

*** Diarra - Mamady Diarra (a) 26/06/2000, Bamako (Mali) (b) 1,80 (c) F - right winger (d) ETO FC Győr (e) Cádiz B, Yeelen

*** Diarra - Moussa Diarra (a) 10/11/2000, Stains (France) (b) 1,85 (c) D - central defense (d) Toulouse FC (e) Toulouse B

*** Diarra - Sory Ibrahim Diarra (Sory Ibrahim Diarra) (a) 28/02/2000, Segou (Mali) (b) 1,87 (c) F - center forward (d) FK Haugesund (e) Petrolul, Unirea Slobozia, Petrolul, Ceahlaul, Etoiles Mandé

*** Diarra - Stéphane Diarra (Stéphane Imad Diarra) (a) 09/12/1998, Abidjan (Ivory Coast) (b) 1,73 (c) F - right winger (d) FC Lorient (e) Le Mans FC, Stade Rennes B, Le Mans FC, Stade Rennes B, Thonon Évian

*** Diarra - Youba Diarra (Hamaciré Youba Diarra) (a) 24/03/1998, Bamako (Mali) (b) 1,78 (c) M - central midfielder (d) Cádiz CF (e) RB Salzburg, TSV Hartberg, RB Salzburg, New York, RB Salzburg, FC St. Pauli, RB Salzburg, TSV Hartberg, RB Salzburg, Wiener Neustadt, RB Salzburg, Yeelen

*** Dias - Gil Dias (Gil Bastião Dias) (a) 28/09/1996, Gafanha da Nazaré (Portugal) (b) 1,86 (c) F - right winger (d) VfB Stuttgart (e) Benfica, AS Monaco, Famalicão, AS Monaco, Granada CF, AS Monaco, Olympiakos, AS Monaco, Nottingham Forest, AS Monaco, Fiorentina, AS Monaco, Rio Ave, AS Monaco, Varzim, AS Monaco, Braga B, Braga B

*** Dias - Rúben Dias (Rúben Santos Gato Alves Dias) (a) 14/05/1997, Amadora (Portugal) (b) 1,87 (c) D - central defense (d) Manchester City (e) Benfica, Benfica B

*** Diasamidze - Giorgi Diasamidze (გიორგი დიასამიძე) (a) 08/05/1992, Tbilisi (Georgia) (b) 1,82 (c) M - attacking midfielder (d) - (e) FC Locomotive, Soligorsk, Saburtalo, FC Locomotive, FC Sasco, Dinamo II, FC Dila, FC Sasco, Aarhus GF, Merani Tbilisi

*** Diatta - Krépin Diatta (a) 25/02/1999, Dakar (Senegal) (b) 1,75 (c) F - right winger (d) AS Mónaco (e) KV Brugge, Sarpsborg 08, Oslo FA Dakar

*** Diau - Brandon Diau (Berti Brandon Diau) (a) 02/06/1993, Bonn (Germany) (b) 1,96 (c) D - central defense (d) - (e) Flint Town, Víkingur Ó., Pandurii, Kidderminster Harriers, Great Wakering Rovers, Truro City FC, Tunbridge Wells, Burgess Hill, Billericay, SVN Zweibrücken, Hapoel Afula, TSC Euskirchen, Hilal Bergheim, HSV III

*** Diaw - Elhadji Pape Diaw (Elhadji Pape Djibril Diaw) (a) 31/12/1994, Dakar (Senegal) (b) 1,91 (c) D - central defense (d) Stade Lavallois (e) Stade Lavallois, Rukh Lviv, Arka Gdynia, Rukh Lviv, Zalgiris, Angers SCO, SM Caen, Angers SCO, Korona Kielce, ASV Geel, Port Autonme, ASC Yeggo, Jeanne d'Arc

*** Diaw - Mamadou Diaw (a) 02/01/2001, ¿? (Norway) (b) 1,76 (c) F - left winger (d) Sandnes Ulf (e) Aalesund, Bryne, Aalesund, Bryne, Aalesund, Excellence F.A.

*** Diaw - Mory Diaw (a) 22/06/1993, Poissy (France) (b) 1,95 (c) G (d) Clermont Foot 63 (e) Lausanne-Sport, United Zürich, Lokomotiv Plovdiv, Mafra, Paris Saint-Germain, Paris Saint Germain B
*** Diawara - Amadou Diawara (a) 17/07/1997, Conakry (Guinea) (b) 1,83 (c) M - pivot (d) RSC Anderlecht (e) AS Roma, Napoli, Bologna, San Marino, FC Sequence
*** Diawara - Ismael Diawara (Ismael Diarra Diawara) (a) 11/11/1994, Örebro (Sweden) (b) 1,94 (c) G (d) Malmö FF (e) Degerfors, Motala AIF, Landskrona, Gjøvik-Lyn, BK Forward, Rynninge IK
*** Diawara - Kandet Diawara (a) 10/02/2000, Lille (France) (b) 1,80 (c) F - left winger (d) Le Havre AC (e) APOEL FC, EN Paralimniou, APOEL FC, PO Xylotymbou, RC Lens B
*** Diawusie - Agyemang Diawusie (a) 12/02/1998, Berlin (Germany) (b) 1,80 (c) F - right winger (d) SSV Jahn Regensburg (e) SpVgg Bayreuth, SV Ried, Dynamo Dresden, FC Ingolstadt, Wehen Wiesbaden, FC Ingolstadt, RB Leipzig, Wehen Wiesbaden, RB Leipzig
*** Diaz - Michel Diaz (Michel Junior Diaz) (a) 23/07/2003, Saint-Herblain (France) (b) 1,93 (c) D - central defense (d) FC Nantes B (e) -
*** Diaz - Sebastian Diaz (Sebastián Díaz Bedoya) (a) 30/04/2001, ¿? (Colombia) (b) 1,83 (c) M - left midfielder (d) Lernayin Artsakh Goris (e) -
*** Díaz - Bladimir Díaz (Bladimir Yovany Díaz Saavedra) (a) 10/07/1992, Buenaventura (Colombia) (b) 1,83 (c) F - center forward (d) Sekzia Ness Ziona (e) Al-Diraiyah FC, Alashkert CF, FAS, Chalatenango, Cobán Imperial, Comunicaciones, Alianza FC, Comunicaciones, Alianza FC, Nongbua FC, Alianza FC, Chalatenango, Once Lobos, El Roble, Alianza Petrol., Real Santander, Casanare
*** Díaz - Brahim Díaz (Brahim Abdelkader Díaz) (a) 03/08/1999, Málaga (Spain) (b) 1,70 (c) M - attacking midfielder (d) Real Madrid CF (e) AC Milan, Real Madrid, AC Milan, Real Madrid, Manchester City
*** Díaz - Iván Díaz (Iván Santiago Díaz) (a) 23/01/1993, San Fernando (Argentina) (b) 1,80 (c) M - pivot (d) - (e) GS Ilioupolis, Ararat Yerevan, SKF Sered, MSK Zilina B, Viktoria Plzen, MSK Zilina, Estudiantes II, River Plate II, AS Trencin
*** Díaz - Jorge Díaz (Jorge Luis Díaz Gutiérrez) (a) 28/06/1989, Montevideo (Uruguay) (b) 1,69 (c) F - right winger (d) - (e) Panetolikos, Real Zaragoza, Reus Deportiu, Real Zaragoza, CD Numancia, Real Zaragoza, Albacete, RCD Espanyol B, Reus Deportiu
*** Díaz - Luis Díaz (Luis Fernando Díaz Marulanda) (a) 13/01/1997, Barrancas (Colombia) (b) 1,80 (c) F - left winger (d) Liverpool FC (e) FC Porto, Junior FC, Barranquilla FC
*** Díaz - Marcos Díaz (Marcos Guillermo Díaz) (a) 05/02/1986, Santa Fe (Argentina) (b) 1,87 (c) G (d) CD Santa Clara (e) Huracán, Talleres, Boca Juniors, Huracán, Colón, CA Colón II
*** Díaz - Mariano Díaz (Mariano Díaz Mejía) (a) 01/08/1993, Premià de Mar (Spain) (b) 1,80 (c) F - center forward (d) - (e) Real Madrid, Olympique Lyon, Real Madrid, RM Castilla, Real Madrid C
*** Díaz - Rubén Díaz (Rubén Díaz Menacho) (a) 10/06/1989, Cádiz (Spain) (b) 1,83 (c) D - central defense (d) FC Bruno's Magpies (e) Conil CF, Arcos CF, Los Barrios, Conil CF, CD Rivera, Cádiz CF B, San Roque Lepe, Recr. Huelva B, Cádiz CF B, Balón de Cádiz
*** Dib - Djibrail Dib (a) 03/07/2002, Lyon (France) (b) 1,72 (c) F - right winger (d) Olympique Lyon B (e) -
*** Diba - Samba Diba (Samba Lélé Diba) (a) 24/12/2003, Louga (Senegal) (b) 1,92 (c) M - pivot (d) Servette FC (e) ASAC Ndiambour

*** Dibango - Yvan Dibango (Junior Yvan Nyabeye Dibango) (a) 10/03/2002, Yaoundé (Cameroon) (b) 1,84 (c) D - left back (d) Kryvbas Kryvyi Rig (e) Kryvbas, FCI Levadia, Isloch, Dragon Club
*** Dibirov - Ismail Dibirov (Дибиров Исмаил Шейхмагомедович) (a) 15/07/2004, ¿? (Russia) (b) 1,75 (c) M - attacking midfielder (d) FK Khimki 2 (e) -
*** Dibon - Christopher Dibon (a) 02/11/1990, Schwechat (Austria) (b) 1,83 (c) D - central defense (d) SK Rapid Wien II (e) Rapid Wien, RB Salzburg, Rapid Wien, RB Salzburg, Admira Wacker, ASK Schwadorf, Admira Wacker
*** Dibusz - Dénes Dibusz (a) 16/11/1990, Pécs (Hungary) (b) 1,88 (c) G (d) Ferencváros TC (e) Pécsi MFC, Barcs, Pécsi MFC
*** Dican - Victor Dican (Victor Robert Dican) (a) 11/10/2000, Râmnicu Vâlcea (Romania) (b) 1,92 (c) M - pivot (d) FC Botosani (e) Universitatea Cluj, Metalurg. Cugir
*** Dichev - Martin Dichev (Мартин Данаилов Дичев) (a) 22/08/2000, Varna (Bulgaria) (b) 1,77 (c) D - left back (d) Cherno More Varna (e) Dob. Dobrich, Cherno More
*** Dichevski - Ivan Dichevski (Иван Марианов Дичевски) (a) 24/04/2001, Varna (Bulgaria) (b) 1,87 (c) G (d) Arda Kardzhali (e) Spartak Varna, Cherno More
*** Dickman - Jesper Dickman (a) 10/04/2001, ¿? (Sweden) (b) - (c) F - right winger (d) Trelleborgs FF (e) Värnamo, Nordsjælland
*** Dicko - Nouha Dicko (a) 14/05/1992, Saint-Maurice (Val-de-Marne) (France) (b) 1,73 (c) F - center forward (d) OFI Creta (e) Yeni Malatyaspor, Gaziantep FK, Hull City, Vitesse, Hull City, Wolverhampton Wanderers, Wigan Ath., Rotherham, Wigan Ath., Wolverhampton Wanderers, Wigan Ath., Blackpool, Wigan Ath., Blackpool, Wigan Ath., Racing Strasbourg B
*** Dida - Bekim Dida (a) 27/08/1997, Kukës (Albania) (b) - (c) D - central defense (d) KS Kastrioti (e) KF Korabi, KS Besa, FK Kukësi B
*** Didden - Matisse Didden (a) 08/10/2001, As (Belgium) (b) 1,98 (c) D - central defense (d) Roda JC Kerkrade (e) KRC Genk, Jong Genk, Patro Eisden
*** Didiba - Joss Didiba (Joss Didiba Moudoumbou) (a) 11/11/1997, Douala (Cameroon) (b) 1,85 (c) M - pivot (d) FC Zlin (e) SFC Opava, FK Senica, SFC Opava, FK Senica, Troina, Perugia, Matera, Perugia, Perugia
*** Didillon - Thomas Didillon (a) 28/11/1995, Séclin (France) (b) 1,93 (c) G (d) Cercle Brugge (e) AS Monaco, Cercle Brugge, RSC Anderlecht, KRC Genk, RSC Anderlecht, FC Metz, Seraing United, FC Metz, FC Metz B
*** Didyk - Roman Didyk (Дідик Роман Ігорович) (a) 02/12/2002, Lviv (Ukraine) (b) 1,85 (c) D - central defense (d) Rukh Lviv (e) Agrobiznes V.
*** Diédhiou - Famara Diédhiou (a) 15/12/1992, Saint-Louis (Senegal) (b) 1,89 (c) F - center forward (d) Granada CF (e) Alanyaspor, Granada CF, Alanyaspor, Bristol City, Angers SCO, Clermont Foot, FC Sochaux, Clermont Foot, FC Sochaux, FC Sochaux B, G. Ajaccio, FC Sochaux B, SAS Epinal, FC Sochaux B, ASM Belfort, FC Sochaux B
*** Diego - Diego (Diego Fracarolli Pacheco) (a) 23/09/1998, Santo Antonio Da Plat, PR (Brazil) (b) 1,84 (c) D - central defense (d) Santa Lucia FC (e) Laranja (PR), Bardejov, Itararé, Almirante Barr., Apucarana
*** Diego Alves - Diego Alves (Diego Alves Carreira) (a) 24/06/1985, Rio de Janeiro (Brazil) (b) 1,87 (c) G (d) - (e) RC Celta, Flamengo, Valencia CF, UD Almería, At. Mineiro, At. Mineiro B
*** Diego Callai - Diego Callai (Diego Callai Silva) (a) 18/07/2004, Caxias do Sul (Brazil) (b) 1,92 (c) G (d) Sporting CP B (e) -

*** Diego Carioca - Diego Carioca (Diego Santos Carioca) (a) 06/02/1998, Niterói (Brazil) (b) 1,77 (c) F - left winger (d) Kolos Kovalivka (e) Sumqayit, Kolos Kovalivka, Zalaegerszeg, Kolos Kovalivka, Jagiellonia, Kolos Kovalivka, Vitebsk, Soligorsk, Vitebsk, Lajeadense, Aimoré
*** Diego Carlos - Diego Carlos (Diego Carlos Santos Silva) (a) 15/03/1993, Barra Bonita (SP) (Brazil) (b) 1,85 (c) D - central defense (d) Aston Villa (e) Sevilla FC, FC Nantes, Estoril Praia, FC Porto B, Estoril Praia, Madureira, Paulista
*** Diego Castaneda - Diego Castaneda (Diego Andres Castaneda Martinez) (a) 22/05/2003, ¿? (Colombia) (b) - (c) M (d) Lernayin Artsakh II (e) -
*** Diego Costa - Diego Costa (Diego da Silva Costa) (a) 07/10/1988, Lagarto (Brazil) (b) 1,86 (c) F - center forward (d) Botafogo de Futebol e Regatas (e) Wolverhampton Wanderers, At. Mineiro, Atlético Madrid, Chelsea, Atlético Madrid, Rayo Vallecano, Atlético Madrid, Real Valladolid, Atlético Madrid, Albacete, Atlético Madrid, RC Celta, Atlético Madrid, SC Braga, Atlético Madrid, SC Braga, Penafiel, SC Braga, Barcelona EC
*** Diego Fumaça - Diego Fumaça (Diego César de Oliveira) (a) 18/12/1994, Barbacena (Brazil) (b) 1,76 (c) M - pivot (d) Amazonas FC (e) Amazonas, Athletic, EC Vitória, Athletic, Helsingborgs IF, Athletic, Pouso Alegre, Athletic, Académica Coimbra, Athletic, Villa Nova, Athletic, Goiânia, Marcílio Dias, Atlético-GO, Goiânia, Ipatinga, Patrocinense, Valeriodoce-MG, Araxá, Figueirense-MG
*** Diego Rosa - Diego Rosa (Diego Gabriel Silva Rosa) (a) 12/10/2002, Salvador de Bahía (Brazil) (b) 1,82 (c) M - central midfielder (d) Esporte Clube Bahia (e) Manchester City, Vizela, Manchester City, Lommel SK, Manchester City, Grêmio Porto Alegre
*** Diehl - Justin Diehl (a) 27/11/2004, Köln (Germany) (b) 1,74 (c) F - attacking midfielder (d) 1.FC 1.FC Köln II (e) -
*** Diemers - Mark Diemers (a) 11/10/1993, Leeuwarden (Netherlands) (b) 1,75 (c) M - attacking midfielder (d) - (e) Feyenoord, FC Emmen, Feyenoord, Hannover 96, Feyenoord, Fortuna Sittard, De Graafschap, FC Utrecht, De Graafschap, FC Utrecht, SC Cambuur, FC Utrecht
*** Diène - Albert Diène (Albert Lamane Diène) (a) 12/02/1998, Pikine (Senegal) (b) 1,80 (c) M - pivot (d) FC Shkupi (e) ASC Jaraaf
*** Dieng - Bamba Dieng (Cheikh Ahmadou Bamba Mbacké Dieng) (a) 23/03/2000, Pikine (Senegal) (b) 1,78 (c) F - center forward (d) FC Lorient (e) Ol. Marseille, Diambars FC, Ol. Marseille B, Diambars FC
*** Dieng - Cheikhou Dieng (a) 23/11/1993, Thiès (Senegal) (b) 1,80 (c) F - center forward (d) - (e) Zagłębie, Wolfsberger AC, Basaksehir, FC Wacker, Basaksehir, Spartak, Basaksehir, Ankaragücü, Basaksehir, SKN St. Pölten, Basaksehir, SKN St. Pölten, Sandefjord
*** Dier - Eric Dier (Eric Jeremy Edgar Dier) (a) 15/01/1994, Cheltenham (England) (b) 1,88 (c) D - central defense (d) Tottenham Hotspur (e) Sporting Lisboa
*** Dierckx - Tuur Dierckx (a) 09/05/1995, Broechem (Belgium) (b) 1,71 (c) F - right winger (d) Atromitos FC (e) KVC Westerlo, Waasland-Beveren, Royal Antwerp, KV Brugge, KV Kortrijk, KV Brugge
*** Dietrich - Tim-Justin Dietrich (a) 08/11/2002, Seehausen (Germany) (b) 1,90 (c) D - central defense (d) Hallescher FC (e) Werder Bremen II
*** Dietsch - Guillaume Dietsch (Guillaume Laurent Dietsch) (a) 17/04/2001, Forbach (France) (b) 1,84 (c) G (d) FC Metz (e) RFC Seraing, FC Metz
*** Dietz - Florian Dietz (a) 03/08/1998, Bad Neustadt an der Saale (Germany) (b) 1,90 (c) F - center forward (d) 1.FC Köln (e) 1.FC Köln II, Unterhaching, 1.FC Köln II, Unterhaching, Werder Bremen II, Carl Zeiss Jena

*** Dieye - Matar Dieye (a) 10/01/1998, Mbédiène (Senegal) (b) 1,90 (c) F - center forward (d) AC Bellinzona (e) Debrecen, KuPS, Debrecen, HNK Gorica, Olimpik Donetsk, Karpaty, Olimpik Donetsk, Este, Tarxien

*** Diez - Sergio Diez (Sergio Diez Roldán) (a) 28/07/2003, Madrid (Spain) (b) 1,78 (c) D - right back (d) Recreativo de Huelva (e) Recreativo, At. Madrid B

*** Digana - Tomas Digana (Tomáš Digaňa) (a) 14/05/1997, ¿? (Czech Rep.) (b) 1,89 (c) G (d) SK Sigma Olomouc (e) SFC Opava, Dubnica

*** Dignam - Mark Dignam (a) 17/04/1999, ¿? (Ireland) (b) 1,81 (c) M - right midfielder (d) University College Dublin (e) Cabinteely

*** Digne - Lucas Digne (a) 20/07/1993, Meaux (France) (b) 1,78 (c) D - left back (d) Aston Villa (e) Everton, FC Barcelona, Paris Saint-Germain, AS Roma, Paris Saint-Germain, Lille, LOSC Lille B, Crepy en Valois

*** Digtyar - Kyrylo Digtyar (Дігтярь Кирило Сергійович) (a) 25/11/2007, ¿? (Ukraine) (b) 1,82 (c) D - central defense (d) Metalist Kharkiv (e) -

*** Diguiny - Nicolas Diguiny (Nicolas Jean Pierre Diguiny) (a) 31/05/1988, Saint-Germain-en-Laye (France) (b) 1,79 (c) F - attacking midfielder (d) Apollon Limassol (e) Aris Thessaloniki, Atromitos FC, Panthrakikos, Poiré-sur-Vie, Vannes

*** Dijakovic - Marko Dijakovic (a) 18/03/2002, Wien (Austria) (b) 1,85 (c) D - central defense (d) GKS Tychy (e) Rapid Wien, Rapid Wien II

*** Dijinari - Vadim Dijinari (a) 01/04/1999, Bender (Moldova) (b) 1,88 (c) D - left back (d) FC Milsami Orhei (e) FC Sheriff, Milsami, FC Sheriff, Dinamo-Auto, FC Sheriff

*** Dijks - Mitchell Dijks (Mitchell Clement Dijks) (a) 09/02/1993, Purmerend (Netherlands) (b) 1,94 (c) D - left back (d) Fortuna Sittard (e) Vitesse, Bologna, Ajax, Norwich City, Ajax, Willem II, Ajax, Heerenveen, Ajax

*** Dik - Sahin Dik (Şahin Dik) (a) 07/02/2004, Giresun (Turkey) (b) - (c) D - left back (d) Giresunspor (e) -

*** Dikajev - Emir Dikajev (a) 27/03/2005, Tallinn (Estonia) (b) - (c) F - center forward (d) - (e) Kalju FC

*** Dikmen - Soner Dikmen (a) 01/09/1993, Ankara (Turkey) (b) 1,79 (c) M - central midfielder (d) Konyaspor (e) Genclerbirligi, Kastamonu 1966, Genclerbirligi, Hacettepe, Genclerbirligi, Hacettepe, Göztepe, Hacettepe

*** Dikov - Svetoslav Dikov (Светослав Димитров Диков) (a) 18/04/1992, Sofia (Bulgaria) (b) 1,96 (c) F - center forward (d) CSKA 1948 II (e) Sportist Svoge, Sandecja, Lokomotiv Sofia, Tsarsko Selo, Tabor Sezana, CSKA 1948, Tsarsko Selo, Vereya, Sl. Geroy, Marek Dupnitsa, Sl. Geroy, Akademik Sofia, Sliven

*** Diks - Kevin Diks (Kevin Diks Bakarbessy) (a) 06/10/1996, Apeldoorn (Netherlands) (b) 1,82 (c) D - right back (d) FC Copenhague (e) Fiorentina, Aarhus GF, Fiorentina, Empoli, Fiorentina, Feyenoord, Fiorentina, Vitesse, Fiorentina, Vitesse

*** Dilaver - Emir Dilaver (a) 07/05/1991, Tomislavgrad (Yugoslavia, now in Bosnia and Herzegovina) (b) 1,84 (c) D - central defense (d) HNK Rijeka (e) Dinamo Zagreb, Çaykur Rizespor, Dinamo Zagreb, Lech Poznan, Ferencváros, Austria Viena, Austria Wien Reserves, Wienerberg

*** Dilli - Selim Dilli (a) 26/05/1998, Trabzon (Turkey) (b) 1,77 (c) M - central midfielder (d) Kasimpasa (e) Karaman FK, Kasimpasa, Artvin Hopaspor, Konyaspor, 1922 Konya, Konyaspor, Usak Spor, Fatsa Belediye, Y. Corumspor

*** Dilmen - Deniz Dilmen (a) 05/06/2005, Istanbul (Turkey) (b) 2,00 (c) G (d) Basaksehir FK (e) -

*** Dilrosun - Javairô Dilrosun (Javairô Joreno Faustino Dilrosun) (a) 22/06/1998, Amsterdam (Netherlands) (b) 1,75 (c) F - right winger (d) Feyenoord Rotterdam (e) Hertha Berlin, Girondins Bordeaux, Hertha Berlin

*** Dima - Constantin Dima (a) 21/07/1999, Bucuresti (Romania) (b) - (c) D - central defense (d) FC Metaloglobus Bucharest (e) Chindia, UTA Arad, Desna, Astra Giurgiu, FC Viitorul, FC Dinamo, Dinamo II, Sepsi OSK, Dinamo II, Metalul Resita, Dinamo II

*** Dimarco - Federico Dimarco (a) 10/11/1997, Milano (Italy) (b) 1,75 (c) D - left back (d) Internazionale Milano (e) Hellas Verona, Internazionale Milano, Parma, Internazionale Milano, FC Sion, Internazionale Milano, Empoli, Internazionale Milano, Ascoli, Internazionale Milano

*** Dimata - Landry Dimata (Nany Landry Dimata) (a) 01/09/1997, Mbuji-Mayi (Congo DR) (b) 1,85 (c) F - center forward (d) RCD Espanyol (e) NEC Nijmegen, RCD Espanyol, RSC Anderlecht, RCD Espanyol, RSC Anderlecht, VfL Wolfsburg, RSC Anderlecht, VfL Wolfsburg, KV Oostende

*** Dimech - Kaylon Dimech (a) 08/10/2004, ¿? (Malta) (b) - (c) M (d) - (e) Marsaxlokk

*** Dimech - Shaun Dimech (a) 08/08/2001, ¿? (Malta) (b) 1,82 (c) M - central midfielder (d) Valletta FC (e) -

*** Dimeji - Awosanya Oluwatobiloba Dimeji (a) 15/01/2003, ¿? (Nigeria) (b) - (c) F - left winger (d) Balzan FC (e) Domžale

*** Dimic - Stefan Dimic (Стефан Димић) (a) 01/05/1993, Istok (RF Yugoslavia, now in Kosovo) (b) 1,84 (c) F - right winger (d) FC Telavi (e) Radnicki Niš, Novi Pazar, Balzan FC, Mladost, FK Zemun, Čukarički, Sindjelic Bg, Čukarički, Rad Beograd, FK Palic Koming

*** Dimitrievski - Dimitrij Dimitrievski (Димитриј Димитриевски) (a) 11/07/2002, Veles (North Macedonia) (b) 1,75 (c) F - left winger (d) Bregalnica Stip (e) Pehcevo, Makedonija, New Stars

*** Dimitrievski - Mihail Dimitrievski (Михаил Димитриевски) (a) 11/07/2002, Veles (North Macedonia) (b) 1,80 (c) D - right back (d) Bregalnica Stip (e) Pehcevo, Lokomotiva, New Stars

*** Dimitrievski - Stole Dimitrievski (Столе Димитриевски) (a) 25/12/1993, Kumanovo (North Macedonia) (b) 1,88 (c) G (d) Rayo Vallecano (e) Gimnàstic, Rayo Vallecano, Gimnàstic, Granada B, Cádiz CF B, Rabotnicki

*** Dimitrijevic - Vuk Oskar Dimitrijevic (a) 28/02/2001, ¿? (Iceland) (b) - (c) F - left winger (d) FH Hafnarfjördur (e) Leiknir, Hafnarfjördur, Leiknir

*** Dimitriou - Andreas Dimitriou (Αντρέας Δημητρίου) (a) 08/10/2003, Limassol (Cyprus) (b) 1,73 (c) D - left back (d) Aris Limassol (e) Karmiotissa

*** Dimitriou - Dimitris Dimitriou (Δημήτρης Δημητρίου) (a) 15/01/1999, Nicosia (Cyprus) (b) 1,93 (c) G (d) Apollon Limassol (e) Anorthosis

*** Dimitriou - Marinos Dimitriou (Μαρίνος Δημητρίου) (a) 20/11/2004, Nicosia (Cyprus) (b) 1,81 (c) F - left winger (d) Olympiakos Nikosia (e) -

*** Dimitriou - Marios Dimitriou (Μάριος Δημητρίου) (a) 25/12/1992, Nicosia (Cyprus) (b) 1,72 (c) D - right back (d) Pafos FC (e) PAEEK Kyrenia, Nea Salamis, Omonia Nicosia, Ermis Aradippou, Omonia Nicosia, Alki Larnaca, Omonia Nicosia

*** Dimitrov - Andrian Dimitrov (Андриян Димитров Димитров) (a) 03/10/1999, Pleven (Bulgaria) (b) 1,82 (c) F - center forward (d) Spartak Varna (e) Dob. Dobrich, Spartak Varna, Dob. Dobrich, Spartak Pleven, Ludogorets II

*** Dimitrov - Iliya Dimitrov (Илия Асенов Димитров) (a) 10/07/1996, Dupnitsa (Bulgaria) (b) 1,87 (c) F - center forward (d) SC Otelul Galati (e) Lokomotiv Sofia,

Levski Sofia, Vitosha, Levski Sofia, Septemvri Sofia, Levski Sofia, Lokomotiv Sofia, Levski Sofia, Pirin, Levski Sofia, Neftochimik, Levski Sofia

*** Dimitrov - Ivaylo Dimitrov (Ивайло Емилов Димитров) (a) 26/03/1989, Sofia (Bulgaria) (b) 1,86 (c) F - center forward (d) Etar Veliko Tarnovo (e) Lokomotiv Plovdiv, Minyor Pernik, Slavia Sofia, Arda Kardzhali, Etar, Arda Kardzhali, Ararat-Armenia, Zhetysu, Ararat-Armenia, Slavia Sofia, Dob. Dobrich, Nesebar, Etar, Akademik Sofia, CSKA Sofia, Sportist Svoge, CSKA Sofia

*** Dimitrov - Kristian Dimitrov (Кристиян Трайчев Димитров) (a) 27/02/1997, Plovdiv (Bulgaria) (b) 1,93 (c) D - central defense (d) Levski Sofia (e) Hajduk Split, CFR Cluj, Hajduk Split, Botev Plovdiv, Montana, Botev Plovdiv

*** Dimitrov - Radoslav Dimitrov (Радослав Бончев Димитров) (a) 12/08/1988, Lovech (Bulgaria) (b) 1,75 (c) D - right back (d) FC Universitatea Cluj (e) Sepsi OSK, CS U Craiova, FC Botosani, Lokomotiv Plovdiv, Levski Sofia, Slavia Sofia, Montana, Slavia Sofia, Litex Lovetch, Sportist Svoge, Litex Lovetch, Montana

*** Dimitrov - Srdjan Dimitrov (Срђан Димитров) (a) 28/07/1992, Novi Sad (Yugoslavia, now in Serbia) (b) 1,75 (c) M - attacking midfielder (d) Okzhetpes Kokshetau (e) Mladost GAT, MTK Budapest, FK Indjija, Ubon United, Birkirkara FC, RFS, Birkirkara FC, FK Indjija, Napredak, FK Indjija

*** Dimitrov - Tihomir Dimitrov (Тихомир Тихомиров Димитров) (a) 04/02/2000, Sofia (Bulgaria) (b) 1,76 (c) D - central defense (d) Sportist Svoge (e) Ludogorets II, Spartak Varna, Ludogorets II

*** Dimitrov - Yordan Dimitrov (Йордан Димитров) (a) 29/11/2003, ¿? (Bulgaria) (b) - (c) G (d) - (e) Pirin II

*** Dimitrov - Zdravko Dimitrov (Здравко Минчев Димитров) (a) 24/08/1998, Bankya (Bulgaria) (b) 1,80 (c) F - left winger (d) Septemvri Sofia (e) Septemvri Sofia, Levski Sofia, Sakaryaspor, Levski Sofia, Spartak Varna, Levski Sofia, Septemvri Sofia, Lokomotiv Sofia, Botev Vratsa, Septemvri Sofia

*** Dimoski - Bojan Dimoski (Бојан Димоски) (a) 23/11/2001, Prilep (North Macedonia) (b) 1,76 (c) D - left back (d) Akron Togliatti (e) AP Brera, Vardar

*** Dimosthenous - Vasilis Dimosthenous (Βασίλης Δημοσθένους) (a) 27/03/2000, Limassol (Cyprus) (b) 1,73 (c) M - attacking midfielder (d) Enosis Neon Paralimniou (e) Akritas Chlor., Omonia Aradippou, Nea Salamis, Doxa Katokopias, Olympia, Aris Limassol

*** Dimov - Daniel Dimov (Даниел Димов) (a) 21/01/1989, Shabla (Bulgaria) (b) 1,88 (c) D - central defense (d) Cherno More Varna (e) Boluspor, Cherno More, Manisaspor, Denizlispor, M. Petah Tikva, Levski Sofia, Cherno More

*** Dimov - Dime Dimov (Диме Димов) (a) 25/07/1994, Skopje (North Macedonia) (b) 1,84 (c) D - central defense (d) Lokomotiv Sofia (e) AP Brera, Horizont, Gostivar, Kozuf Miravci, Metalurg Skopje

*** Dimov - Diyan Dimov (Диян Бориславов Димов) (a) 02/10/2002, Plovdiv (Bulgaria) (b) 1,93 (c) G (d) Hebar Pazardzhik II (e) Sokol Markovo

*** Dimov - Hristijan Dimov (Христијан Димов) (a) 23/03/2000, Skopje (North Macedonia) (b) 1,85 (c) D - central defense (d) - (e) FK Skopje, FK Sasa

*** Dimov - Plamen Dimov (Пламен Диянов Димов) (a) 29/10/1990, Burgas (Bulgaria) (b) 1,87 (c) D - central defense (d) Etar Veliko Tarnovo (e) Spartak Varna, Riteriai, FK Andijon, Okzhetpes, Cherno More, Botev Plovdiv, FK Altay, Shakhter K., Kaysar, Levski Sofia, Chern. Burgas, Pomorie

*** Dimovski - Stojan Dimovski (Стојан Димовски) (a) 19/09/1982, Skopje (Yugoslavia, now in North Macedonia) (b) - (c) G (d) Tikves Kavadarci (e) Makedonija, Borec Veles, Horizont, Teteks Tetovo, Metalurg Skopje, Horizont, Madzari Solidarnost

*** Dimun - Milan Dimun (a) 19/09/1996, Košice (Slovakia) (b) 1,88 (c) M - pivot (d) DAC Dunajska Streda (e) Cracovia, VSS Kosice

*** Dina Ebimbe - Junior Dina Ebimbe (Éric Junior Dina Ebimbe) (a) 21/11/2000, Stains (France) (b) 1,84 (c) M - central midfielder (d) Eintracht Frankfurt (e) Paris Saint-Germain, Eintracht, Paris Saint-Germain, Dijon, Paris Saint-Germain, Le Havre AC, Paris Saint-Germain, Paris Saint Germain B

*** Dinev - David Dinev (Давид Динев) (a) 18/01/2002, Stip (North Macedonia) (b) 1,76 (c) M - pivot (d) FK Skopje (e) Osogovo

*** Dinev - Denis Dinev (Денис Стефанов Динев) (a) 18/02/2004, Sofia (Bulgaria) (b) 1,86 (c) D - central defense (d) Montana (e) Levski Sofia II, Dob. Dobrich, Levski Sofia II, Yantra

*** Dinga - Dominik Dinga (Доминик Динга) (a) 07/04/1998, Novi Sad (Yugoslavia, now in Serbia) (b) 1,86 (c) D - central defense (d) - (e) Soligorsk, Ordabasy, Ural, Dinamo Minsk, Ural, FK Partizan, Ural, Vojvodina

*** Dingomé - Tristan Dingomé (a) 17/02/1991, Les Ulis (France) (b) 1,74 (c) M - central midfielder (d) - (e) Al-Fateh, Troyes, Stade Reims, Troyes, Excelsior Mouscron, AS Monaco, Le Havre AC, AS Monaco, AS Monaco B

*** Diniyev - Coshqun Diniyev (Coşqun Şahin oğlu Diniyev) (a) 13/09/1995, Baku (Azerbaijan) (b) 1,69 (c) M - pivot (d) Ümraniyespor (e) Zira FK, Sabah FK, Qarabag FK, Inter Baku

*** Dinkci - Eren Dinkci (Eren Sami Dinkçi) (a) 13/12/2001, Bremen (Germany) (b) 1,88 (c) F - center forward (d) 1.FC Heidenheim 1846 (e) 1.FC Heidenheim, Werder Bremen, Werder Bremen II

*** Dinkov - Georgi Dinkov (Георги Иванов Динков) (a) 20/05/1991, Stara Zagora (Bulgaria) (b) 1,86 (c) D - left back (d) Septemvri Sofia (e) Beroe, Spartak Varna, Dunav, Beroe, Sliven, Beroe, Spartak Varna, Beroe, Beroe Stara Zagora II

*** Dinosha - Egzon Dinosha (a) 18/01/2001, Detroit (United States) (b) 1,73 (c) F - left winger (d) FK Decic Tuzi (e) FK Cetinje, Mladost DG, FK Jezero, FK Ibar, FK Jezero, Mornar Bar, Otrant-Olympic, OFK Titograd, FK Decic Tuzi, OFK Titograd, FK Decic Tuzi

*** Dinu - Cornel Dinu (a) 09/06/1989, Târgoviște (Romania) (b) 1,75 (c) D - left back (d) AFC Chindia Targoviste (e) FCM Targoviste

*** Diogo Jota - Diogo Jota (Diogo José Teixeira da Silva) (a) 04/12/1996, Porto (Portugal) (b) 1,78 (c) F - left winger (d) Liverpool FC (e) Wolverhampton Wanderers, Atlético Madrid, Wolverhampton Wanderers, Atlético Madrid, FC Porto, Atlético Madrid, Paços Ferreira

*** Diomande - Adama Diomande (Valentin Adama Diomande) (a) 14/02/1990, Oslo (Norway) (b) 1,83 (c) F - center forward (d) Toronto FC (e) Odd, Al-Arabi SC, Al-Sailiya SC, CZ Mighty Lions, LAFC, Hull City, Stabæk, Dubai CSC, Dinamo Minsk, Strømsgodset, Hødd, Skeid, Lyn, Lyn FK II

*** Diomande - Gontie Junior Diomande (a) 20/05/2003, ¿? (Ivory Coast) (b) 1,69 (c) M - attacking midfielder (d) SV Ried (e) SKU Amstetten, SV Ried, SV Ried II, SC Accra

*** Diomande - Ismael Diomande (Ismaël Diomandé) (a) 07/12/2003, ¿? (Ivory Coast) (b) - (c) F - right winger (d) RFS (e) Daugavpils, RFS, Pohronie, RFS, AFAD Djékanou

*** Diomande - Ismael Diomande (Tiémoko Ismaël Diomandé) (a) 28/08/1992, Bingerville (Ivory Coast) (b) 1,83 (c) M - pivot (d) Petrolul Ploiesti (e) Samsunspor, Konyaspor, Çaykur Rizespor, SM Caen, St.-Étienne, SM Caen, St.-Étienne, Saint-Étienne B

*** Diomande - Mohamed Diomande (Mohamed Baba Diomandé) (a) 30/10/2001, Yopougon (Ivory Coast) (b) 1,83 (c) M - central midfielder (d) FC Nordsjælland (e) Right to Dream
*** Diomande - Ousmane Diomande (a) 04/12/2003, Abidjan (Ivory Coast) (b) 1,90 (c) D - central defense (d) Sporting de Lisboa (e) Midtjylland, Mafra, Midtjylland, OS Abobo
*** Diomandé - Sinaly Diomandé (a) 09/04/2001, Yopougon (Ivory Coast) (b) 1,84 (c) D - central defense (d) Olympique de Lyon (e) Olymp. Lyon B, Guidars FC
*** Dione - Babacar Dione (a) 22/03/1997, Mbayard (Senegal) (b) 1,67 (c) F - right winger (d) Lokomotiv Plovdiv (e) Excelsior Mouscron
*** Diony - Loïs Diony (a) 20/12/1992, Mont-de-Marsan (France) (b) 1,83 (c) F - center forward (d) Angers SCO (e) Crvena zvezda, Angers SCO, St.-Étienne, Bristol City, St.-Étienne, Dijon, Mont-de-Marsan, FC Nantes B, Girondins Bordeaux B
*** Diop - Amidou Diop (a) 25/02/1992, Missirah (Senegal) (b) 1,96 (c) M - central midfielder (d) Aalesunds FK (e) Kristiansund, Adanaspor, Kristiansund, Molde, Kristiansund, Molde, Mjøndalen, Molde, Diambars FC
*** Diop - Dame Diop (a) 15/02/1993, Louga (Senegal) (b) 1,83 (c) F - center forward (d) - (e) Pyunik Yerevan, Ceske Budejovice, Hatayspor, Banik Ostrava, Fastav Zlin, Slavia Praha, Shirak Gyumri, Khimki, Shirak Gyumri, Khimki, Touré Kunda
*** Diop - Djibril Diop (Djibril Thialaw Diop) (a) 06/01/1999, Thiès (Senegal) (b) 1,88 (c) D - central defense (d) Viking FK (e) Hassania, Génération Foot
*** Diop - Edan Diop (a) 28/08/2004, Tours (France) (b) 1,73 (c) M - central midfielder (d) AS Mónaco (e) -
*** Diop - Issa Diop (Issa Laye Lucas Jean Diop) (a) 09/01/1997, Toulouse (France) (b) 1,94 (c) D - central defense (d) Fulham FC (e) West Ham Utd., Toulouse
*** Diop - Meïssa Diop (a) 02/02/2003, Dakar (Senegal) (b) 1,80 (c) M - right midfielder (d) Valmiera FC (e) Valmiera
*** Diop - Mouhamed Diop (a) 30/09/2000, Thiaroye (Senegal) (b) 1,82 (c) M - attacking midfielder (d) ESTAC Troyes (e) Kocaelispor, FC Sheriff, Kocaelispor, Sacré-Cœur
*** Diop - Pape Diop (Pape Demba Diop) (a) 04/09/2003, Ouakam (Senegal) (b) 1,82 (c) M - central midfielder (d) SV Zulte Waregem (e) Diambars FC
*** Diop - Sofiane Diop (a) 09/06/2000, Tours (France) (b) 1,75 (c) F - left winger (d) OGC Niza (e) AS Monaco, FC Sochaux, AS Monaco, Stade Rennes B
*** Dioudis - Sokratis Dioudis (Σωκράτης Διούδης) (a) 03/02/1993, Thessaloniki (Greece) (b) 1,89 (c) G (d) Zagłębie Lubin (e) Panathinaikos, Aris Thessaloniki, KV Brugge, Panionios, KV Brugge, Aris Thessaloniki
*** Diouf - Andy Diouf (Andy Alune Diouf) (a) 17/05/2003, Neuilly-sur-Seine (France) (b) 1,87 (c) M - central midfielder (d) RC Lens (e) FC Basel, Stade Rennes, FC Basel, Stade Rennes, Stade Rennes B
*** Diouf - El Hadji Malick Diouf (a) 28/12/2004, ¿? (Senegal) (b) - (c) D - left back (d) Tromsø IL (e) Academy Mawade Wade
*** Diouf - Gora Diouf (a) 20/09/2003, ¿? (Senegal) (b) 1,85 (c) D - central defense (d) FC Sion (e) Lusitana
*** Diouf - Jules Diouf (a) 05/03/1992, Neuilly-sur-Seine (France) (b) 1,86 (c) D - central defense (d) F91 Dudelange (e) Union Titus Petange, Penafiel, Mafra, CR Al Hoceima, Angoulême CFC, Boulogne B, Toulouse B
*** Diouf - Mame Diouf (Mame Biram Diouf) (a) 16/12/1987, Dakar (Senegal) (b) 1,85 (c) F - center forward (d) Göztepe (e) Konyaspor, Hatayspor, Stoke City, Hannover 96, Manchester Utd., Blackburn, Manchester Utd., Molde, Manchester Utd., Molde, ASC Jaraaf

*** Diouf - Papa Diouf (Papa Alioune Diouf) (a) 22/06/1989, Dakar (Senegal) (b) 1,80 (c) F - center forward (d) Oskarshamns AIK (e) Brindisi, Kalmar FF, Ermis Aradippou, Boluspor, Istanbulspor, Kalmar FF, Dakar UC, Litex Lovetch, Dakar UC
*** Diouf - Yehvann Diouf (a) 16/11/1999, Montreuil-sous-Bois (France) (b) 1,84 (c) G (d) Stade de Reims (e) Troyes
*** Dioussé - Assane Dioussé (Assane Dioussé El Hadji) (a) 20/09/1997, Dakar (Senegal) (b) 1,75 (c) M - pivot (d) AJ Auxerre (e) OFI Creta, St.-Étienne, Ankaragücü, St.-Étienne, Chievo Verona, St.-Étienne, Empoli
*** Dirks Riis - Kristian Dirks Riis (a) 17/02/1997, Haderslev (Denmark) (b) 1,89 (c) D - central defense (d) Stjarnan Gardabaer (e) Lyngby BK, Midtjylland, Esbjerg fB, Midtjylland, Vendsyssel FF, Midtjylland
*** Dirksen - Julius Dirksen (a) 02/02/2003, Amersfoort (Netherlands) (b) 1,85 (c) D - central defense (d) FC Emmen (e) Ajax B
*** Disasi - Axel Disasi (a) 11/03/1998, Gonesse (France) (b) 1,90 (c) D - central defense (d) Chelsea FC (e) AS Monaco, Stade Reims, Stade Reims B, Paris FC B
*** Diskerud - Mix Diskerud (Mikkel Morgenstar Pålssønn Diskerud) (a) 02/10/1990, Oslo (Norway) (b) 1,84 (c) M - central midfielder (d) - (e) Omonia Nicosia, Denizlispor, Helsingborgs IF, Ulsan Hyundai, IFK Göteborg, New York City, IFK Göteborg, New York City, Rosenborg, Stabæk, KAA Gent, Stabæk
*** Disney - John Disney (John James Disney) (a) 15/05/1992, Truro (England) (b) - (c) D - central defense (d) Connah's Quay Nomads (e) Bala, Altrincham, Connah's Quay, Hednesford, Telford Utd., Chester, Hednesford, Northwich Vic, Stockport
*** Distefano - Filippo Distefano (a) 28/08/2003, Camaiore (Italy) (b) - (c) F - attacking midfielder (d) Ternana Calcio (e) Ternana
*** Dita - Bruno Dita (a) 18/02/1993, Tiranë (Albania) (b) 1,85 (c) M - pivot (d) Shkëndija Tetovo (e) KF Skënderbeu, KF Teuta, KS Besa
*** Dithmer - Andreas Dithmer (Andreas Frederik Dithmer) (a) 01/08/2005, Copenhagen (Denmark) (b) 1,98 (c) G (d) FC Copenhague (e) -
*** Divanovic - Zaim Divanovic (Заим Дивановић) (a) 09/12/2000, ¿? (RF Yugoslavia, now in Montenegro) (b) 1,79 (c) M - central midfielder (d) Akhmat Grozny (e) Soligorsk, OFK Petrovac, OFK Titograd, Otrant-Olympic
*** Diveev - Igor Diveev (Дивеев Игорь Сергеевич) (a) 27/09/1999, Ufa (Russia) (b) 1,94 (c) D - central defense (d) CSKA Moskva (e) Ufa, CSKA Moskva, Ufa, Ufa II
*** Divis - Tobias Divis (Tobiáš Diviš) (a) 02/12/2003, Ružomberok (Slovakia) (b) 1,78 (c) D - right back (d) Tatran Liptovsky Mikulas (e) -
*** Divisek - Josef Divisek (Josef Divíšek) (a) 24/09/1990, Praha (Czechoslovakia, now in Czech Rep.) (b) 1,86 (c) D - left back (d) FC Zbrojovka Brno (e) Slovácko, 1.FK Pribram, FC MAS Taborsko, 1.FK Pribram, Sparta Praha B, 1.FK Pribram, Sparta Praha B
*** Divkovic - Marko Divkovic (Marko Divković) (a) 11/06/1999, Vinkovci (Croatia) (b) 1,81 (c) F - center forward (d) Brøndby IF (e) Dunajska Streda, Brøndby IF, Dunajska Streda, NK Otok
*** Dizdarevic - Alen Dizdarevic (Alen Dizdarević) (a) 22/01/2004, Zagreb (Croatia) (b) 1,86 (c) M - attacking midfielder (d) NK Dekani (e) NK Dekani, NK Maribor
*** Dizdarevic - Belmin Dizdarevic (Belmin Dizdarević) (a) 09/08/2001, Zenica (Bosnia and Herzegovina) (b) - (c) G (d) Montpellier HSC (e) FK Sarajevo, Mladost Kakanj, FK Sarajevo
*** Djabi Embalo - Abdulai Djabi Embalo (a) 30/06/2005, ¿? (Luxembourg) (b) - (c) M (d) - (e) CS Fola Esch

*** Djajic - Darko Djajic (Darko Đajić) (a) 30/08/1992, Berane (RF Yugoslavia, now in Montenegro) (b) 1,93 (c) D - central defense (d) FK Leotar Trebinje (e) FK Podgorica, GOSK Gabela, Leotar Trebinje, Borac Banja Luka, Leotar Trebinje, GOSK Dubrovnik, Leotar Trebinje, Vojvodina II
*** Djakovac - Ifet Djakovac (Ифет Ђаковац) (a) 05/12/1997, Sjenica (RF Yugoslavia, now in Serbia) (b) 1,80 (c) M - central midfielder (d) FK TSC Backa Topola (e) Zlatibor, FK Tutin, Zlatibor
*** Djakovic - Antonio Djakovic (Antonio Đaković) (a) 12/06/2001, Šibenik (Croatia) (b) 1,90 (c) G (d) HNK Sibenik (e) Cibalia, HNK Sibenik, Zagora Unesic
*** Djalma Silva - Djalma Silva (Djalma Antônio da Silva Filho) (a) 19/09/1994, Recife (Brazil) (b) 1,80 (c) D - left back (d) AEL Limassol (e) EC Bahia, Operário-PR, At. Pernamb., Confiança, At. Pernamb., Treze, At. Pernamb., Treze, At. Pernamb., UR Trabalhadore, At. Pernamb., Treze, Nacional Patos
*** Djaló - Bubacar Djaló (Bubacar Boi Djaló) (a) 02/02/1997, Bissau (Guinea-Bissau) (b) 1,88 (c) M - pivot (d) FC Lahti (e) Rochester NY, HJK Helsinki, Sporting B
*** Djaló - Matchoi Djaló (Matchoi Bobó Djaló) (a) 10/04/2003, Bissau (Guinea-Bissau) (b) 1,80 (c) M - central midfielder (d) FC Paços de Ferreira (e) -
*** Djaló - Tiago Djaló (Tiago Emanuel Embaló Djaló) (a) 09/04/2000, Amadora (Portugal) (b) 1,90 (c) D - central defense (d) LOSC Lille Métropole (e) -
*** Djamas - David Djamas (Ντέιβιντ Τζιάμας) (a) 21/04/2004, Mammari (Cyprus) (b) 1,82 (c) D - left back (d) APOEL FC (e) -
*** Djaniny - Djaniny (Jorge Djaniny Tavares Semedo) (a) 21/03/1991, Santa Cruz (Cabo Verde) (b) 1,90 (c) F - center forward (d) Trabzonspor (e) Sharjah FC, Trabzonspor, Al-Ahli, Santos Laguna, Nacional, Benfica, Olhanense, Benfica, Leiria, Velense
*** Djattit - Billal Djattit (Billal Amar Djattit) (a) 16/11/1999, Marseille (France) (b) 1,80 (c) G (d) UE Sant Julia (e) CD Leganés C, CS Sedan B, Athl. Mars. B
*** Djattit - Celyan Djattit (Celyan Belaid Djattit) (a) 05/01/2003, ¿? (France) (b) 1,73 (c) M - attacking midfielder (d) UE Sant Julia (e) -
*** Djave - Floriss Djave (a) 29/07/2003, Lambaréné (Gabon) (b) 1,71 (c) F - left winger (d) RFS (e) Aris Limassol, EN Paralimniou, Aris Limassol, Djoliba AC, AS Bouenguidi
*** Djekovic - Nemanja Djekovic (Немања Ђековић) (a) 09/05/2003, ¿? (Serbia and Montenegro, now in Serbia) (b) 1,95 (c) D - central defense (d) FK Napredak Krusevac (e) Paracin
*** Djembe - Nelson Djembe (a) 11/03/2002, ¿? (Cameroon) (b) 1,75 (c) F - right winger (d) AS Pagny-sur-Moselle (e) FC St-Jean B, Dziugas, Brasseries
*** Djené - Djené (Dakonam Ortega Djené) (a) 31/12/1991, Lome Dapaong (Togo) (b) 1,78 (c) D - central defense (d) Getafe CF (e) Sint-Truiden, Alcorcón, Coton Sport FC, Tonnerre, Etoile Filante
*** Djenepo - Moussa Djenepo (a) 15/06/1998, Bamako (Mali) (b) 1,77 (c) F - left winger (d) Southampton FC (e) Standard Liège, Yeelen, Standard Liège, Yeelen
*** Djerkovic - Vasilije Djerkovic (Василије Ђерковић) (a) 15/04/2003, ¿? (Serbia and Montenegro, now in Serbia) (b) - (c) M - pivot (d) FK Real Podunavci (e) Mladost, FK FAP Priboj, Mladost
*** Djerlek - Armin Djerlek (Армин Ђерлек) (a) 15/07/2000, Novi Pazar (RF Yugoslavia, now in Serbia) (b) 1,73 (c) M - attacking midfielder (d) Sivasspor (e) NK Aluminij, Sivasspor, NK Aluminij, Sivasspor, FK Partizan

*** Djibrilla - Issa Djibrilla (Issa Ibrahim Djibrilla) (a) 01/01/1996, Niamey (Niger) (b) 1,75 (c) D - left back (d) Zira FK (e) A. Keciörengücü, Sahel SC, Rahimo FC, Sahel SC

*** Djidji - Koffi Djidji (Lévy Koffi Djidji) (a) 30/11/1992, Bagnolet (France) (b) 1,84 (c) D - central defense (d) Torino FC (e) Crotone, Torino, FC Nantes, Torino, FC Nantes, FC Nantes B

*** Djiga - Nasser Djiga (a) 15/11/2002, Bobo-Dioulasso (Burkina Faso) (b) 1,87 (c) D - central defense (d) FC Basel (e) Nîmes, FC Basel, Vitesse FC

*** Djiku - Alexander Djiku (Alexander Kwabena Baidoo Djiku) (a) 09/08/1994, Montpellier (France) (b) 1,82 (c) D - central defense (d) Fenerbahce (e) Racing Club Strasbourg, SM Caen, SC Bastia, SC Bastia B

*** Djilobodji - Papy Djilobodji (El Hadji Papy Mison Djilobodji) (a) 01/12/1988, Kaolack (Senegal) (b) 1,93 (c) D - central defense (d) Gaziantep FK (e) Kasimpasa, Gaziantep FK, Guingamp, Sunderland, Dijon, Sunderland, Chelsea, Werder Bremen, Chelsea, FC Nantes, Sénart-Moissy, ASC Saloum

*** Djimsiti - Berat Djimsiti (Berat Ridvan Gjimshiti) (a) 19/02/1993, Zürich (Switzerland) (b) 1,90 (c) D - central defense (d) Atalanta de Bérgamo (e) Benevento, Atalanta, Avellino, Atalanta, FC Zürich

*** Djinovic - Ognjen Djinovic (Ognjen Đinović) (a) 12/09/2003, ¿? (Sserbia and Montenegro, now in Montenegro) (b) 1,71 (c) D - left back (d) FK Sutjeska Niksic (e) Zeta Golubovac

*** Djira - Marko Djira (Marko Đira) (a) 05/05/1999, Šibenik (Croatia) (b) 1,71 (c) M - pivot (d) HNK Sibenik (e) Dinamo Zagreb, Koper, Dinamo Zagreb, NK Lokomotiva, Dinamo Zagreb, Din. Zagreb II

*** Djitté - Moussa Djitté (Moussa Kalilou Djitté) (a) 04/10/1999, Diattouma (Senegal) (b) 1,80 (c) F - center forward (d) Bandirmaspor (e) Bandirmaspor, Austin, AC Ajaccio, Austin, Grenoble, FC Sion, Niarry Tally

*** Djoco - Ouparine Djoco (a) 22/04/1998, Juvisy-sur-Orge (France) (b) 1,89 (c) G (d) Royal Francs Borains (e) Francs Borains, Clermont Foot, Clermont B, FC Fleury 91

*** Djokanovic - Andrej Djokanovic (Andrej Đokanović) (a) 01/03/2001, Kasindo (Bosnia and Herzegovina) (b) 1,80 (c) M - pivot (d) MKE Ankaragücü (e) FK Sarajevo

*** Djokic - Milan Djokic (Милан Ђокић) (a) 12/09/1997, Leskovac (RF Yugoslavia, now in Serbia) (b) 1,86 (c) F - center forward (d) FK Dubocica Leskovac (e) Bregalnica Stip, FK TSC, Zlatibor, Moravac, Spartak, FK Backa, Spartak, FK TSC, Spartak, CSK Celarevo, Spartak, FK TSC, Spartak

*** Djokic - Milos Djokic (Милош Ђокић) (a) 06/09/1991, Užice (Yugoslavia, now in Serbia) (b) 1,82 (c) F - right winger (d) FK Kolubara Lazarevac (e) Novi Pazar, FK Tutin, Tatran Presov, Sloboda Užice, Sloga Požega, Sloboda Užice

*** Djokovic - Damjan Djokovic (Damjan Đoković) (a) 18/04/1990, Zagreb (Yugoslavia, now in Croatia) (b) 1,90 (c) M - central midfielder (d) FCSB (e) Al-Raed, Çaykur Rizespor, Adana Demirspor, Çaykur Rizespor, CFR Cluj, HNK Rijeka, Spezia, Greuther Fürth, G. Ajaccio, Bologna, AS Livorno, Bologna, CFR Cluj, Bologna, Cesena, Monza, Spartak Trnava

*** Djokovic (c) G (d) FK Decic Tuzi (e) OFK Titograd, FK Decic Tuzi - Hamza Djokovic (c) G (d) FK Decic Tuzi (e) OFK Titograd, FK Decic Tuzi

*** Djolonga - Niko Djolonga (Niko Đolonga) (a) 24/05/2004, Split (Croatia) (b) - (c) D - right back (d) HNK Hajduk Split (e) -

*** Djordjevic - Boban Djordjevic (Бобан Ђорђевић) (a) 20/02/1997, Herceg Novi (RF Yugoslavia, Montenegro) (b) 1,88 (c) F - center forward (d) Arsenal Tivat (e)

OSK Igalo, Mornar Bar, Aktobe, OFK Grbalj, Arsenal Tivat, OSK Igalo, FK Dobrovice, OSK Igalo, Teplice B

*** Djordjevic - Filip Djordjevic (Филип Ђорђевић) (a) 07/03/1994, ¿? (RF Yugoslavia, now in Serbia) (b) 1,74 (c) F - attacking midfielder (d) EB/Streymur (e) TB Tvøroyri, ÍF Fuglafjördur, Víkingur, KÍ Klaksvík

*** Djordjevic - Lazar Djordjevic (Лазар Ђорђевић) (a) 14/07/1992, Vranje (RF Yugoslavia, now in Serbia) (b) 1,87 (c) D - central defense (d) - (e) Radnicki Niš, Al-Khaldiya FC, Zira FK, Radnicki Niš, Karvina, Vojvodina, Podbrezova, VSS Kosice, Sileks, FK Palilulac

*** Djordjevic - Luka Djordjevic (Лука Ђорђевић) (a) 09/07/1994, Budva (RF Yugoslavia, now in Montenegro) (b) 1,85 (c) F - center forward (d) FK Sochi (e) Vejle BK, Lokomotiv Moskva, Arsenal Tula, Lokomotiv Moskva, Zenit, Arsenal Tula, Zenit, Ponferradina, Zenit, Sampdoria, Zenit, FC Twente, Zenit, Mogren

*** Djordjevic - Luka Djordjevic (Лука Ђорђевић) (a) 05/05/2001, Beograd (RF Yugoslavia, now in Serbia) (b) 1,75 (c) F - left winger (d) FK Indjija (e) Jedinstvo, Budućnost, Stara Pazova, Batajnica

*** Djordjevic - Mateja Djordjevic (Матеја Ђорђевић) (a) 17/01/2003, Beograd (RF Yugoslavia, now in Serbia) (b) 1,91 (c) D - central defense (d) FK TSC Backa Topola (e) Vozdovac, FK Partizan

*** Djordjevic - Stefan Djordjevic (Стефан Ђорђевић) (a) 13/03/1991, Novi Sad (Yugoslavia, now in Serbia) (b) 1,87 (c) D - left back (d) FK Vojvodina Novi Sad (e) Radnicki Niš, Potenza, Catania, Borac Cacak, Crvena zvezda, Vozdovac, Banat Zrenjanin, Spartak, Proleter

*** Djoric - Ivan Djoric (Иван Ђорић) (a) 07/07/1995, Niš (RF Yugoslavia, now in Serbia) (b) 1,83 (c) M - pivot (d) FK Igman Konjic (e) Sloga Meridian, Radnik Bijelj., Mosta FC, FK Iskra, Vozdovac, Napredak, Backa, Radnik, FC Sion, Radnik, FC Sion, Stade Nyonnais, FC Sion, JFK Ventspils

*** Djoric - Nikola Djoric (Никола Ђорић) (a) 03/03/2000, Beograd (RF Yugoslavia, now in Serbia) (b) 1,92 (c) D - central defense (d) SK Austria Klagenfurt (e) HNK Sibenik, Austria Klagenfurt, Rad Beograd, Sindjelic Bg, Rad Beograd, Zeleznicar Pancevo, Rad Beograd

*** Djouahra - Näis Djouahra (a) 23/11/1999, Bourgoin-Jallieu (France) (b) 1,72 (c) F - left winger (d) HNK Rijeka (e) Real Sociedad B, CD Mirandés, Real Sociedad B

*** Djoum - Arnaud Djoum (Arnaud Gilles Sutchuin Djoum) (a) 02/05/1989, Yaoundé (Cameroon) (b) 1,83 (c) M - central midfielder (d) - (e) Dundee United, Apollon Limassol, Al-Raed, Heart of Midlothian, Lech Poznan, Akhisar Belediye, Roda JC, RSC Anderlecht, FC Brüssel

*** Djú - Mésaque Djú (Mésaque Geremias Djú) (a) 18/03/1999, Bissau (Guinea-Bissau) (b) 1,78 (c) F - right winger (d) CD Mafra (e) OFI Creta, Benfica B

*** Djuderija - Ammar Djuderija (Ammar Ђuderija) (a) 06/08/2002, Sarajevo (Bosnia and Herzegovina) (b) 1,76 (c) F - right winger (d) FK Leotar Trebinje (e) FK Gorazde

*** Djukanovic - Viktor Djukanovic (Viktor Djukanović) (a) 29/01/2004, ¿? (Serbia and Montenegro, now in Montenegro) (b) 1,84 (c) F - left winger (d) Hammarby IF (e) Buducnost Podgorica, Sutjeska II

*** Djukic - Bratislav Djukic (Братислав Ђукић) (a) 29/09/1999, Troyes (France) (b) - (c) D - central defense (d) FC Telavi (e) Javor-Matis, Le Touquet ACF, CS Sedan, FCM Troyes, Troyes B

*** Djulcic - Danilo Djulcic (Данило Ђулчић) (a) 02/10/1998, Novi Pazar (RF Yugoslavia, now in Serbia) (b) 1,93 (c) G (d) RFK Novi Sad 1921 (e) FK Loznica, Sloga Meridian, HNK Orasje, Novi Pazar, Vrsac, Lokomotiva, FK Josanica

*** Djulovic - Damir Mustafa Djulovic (a) 24/12/2004, Amsterdam (Netherlands) (b) 1,84 (c) F - center forward (d) Rudar Pljevlja (e) -
*** Djurak - David Djurak (David Đurak) (a) 09/03/2000, Zagreb (Croatia) (b) 1,81 (c) M - attacking midfielder (d) - (e) NK Radomlje, Beltinci, NK Radomlje, NK Krsko, Doxa Dramas, NS Mura, Medjimurje, St. Kevins Boys, St. Josephs Boys
*** Djuranovic - Uros Djuranovic (Урош Ђурановић) (a) 01/02/1994, Budva (RF Yugoslavia, now in Montenegro) (b) 1,84 (c) F - center forward (d) Hamrun Spartans (e) Kolubara, Kecskemét, Kolubara, ACSM Poli Iasi, Radnicki Niš, Korona Kielce, Dukla Praha, FK Decic Tuzi, FK Iskra, Mogren
*** Djurasek - Neven Djurasek (Neven Đurasek) (a) 15/08/1998, Varaždin (Croatia) (b) 1,73 (c) M - pivot (d) Aris Thessaloniki (e) Shakhtar Donetsk, Din. Zagreb II, Olimpija, Din. Zagreb II, SK Dnipro-1, Din. Zagreb II, NK Varazdin, Din. Zagreb II, NK Lokomotiva, Din. Zagreb II
*** Djurasovic - Aleksa Djurasovic (Алекса Ђурасовић) (a) 21/04/2004, Podgorica (Serbia and Montenegro, now in Montenegro) (b) - (c) D - central defense (d) FK Spartak Subotica (e) -
*** Djurasovic - Aleksa Djurasovic (Алекса Ђурасовић) (a) 23/12/2002, Subotica (RF Yugoslavia, now in Serbia) (b) 1,88 (c) M - central midfielder (d) FK Spartak Subotica (e) -
*** Djurdjevic - Fahrudin Djurdjevic (Фахрудин Ѓурѓевиќ) (a) 17/02/1992, Skopje (North Macedonia) (b) 1,78 (c) F - center forward (d) Gostivar (e) Makedonija, KF Vllaznia, Rabotnicki, Hradec Kralove, Varnsdorf, Makedonija, Zvijezda G., Spartak, Vardar, Makedonija
*** Djurdjevic - Vukasin Djurdjevic (Вукашин Ђуровић) (a) 24/01/2004, ¿? (Serbia and Montenegro, now in Serbia) (b) 1,84 (c) D - central defense (d) FK Vozdovac (e) Rad Beograd
*** Djurdjic - Nikola Djurdjic (Никола Ђурђић) (a) 01/04/1986, Pirot (Yugoslavia, now in Serbia) (b) 1,86 (c) F - center forward (d) Degerfors IF (e) Chengdu Rongcheng, Zhejiang FC, Chengdu Rongcheng, Hammarby IF, Randers FC, FK Partizan, FC Augsburg, Fortuna Düsseldorf, FC Augsburg, Malmö FF, FC Augsburg, Greuther Fürth, Haugesund, Helsingborgs IF, Haugesund, Vozdovac, Radnicki Pirot
*** Djurhuus - Páll Eirik Djurhuus (a) 16/11/2003, ¿? (Faroe Islands) (b) - (c) M - central midfielder (d) Víkingur Gøta (e) Víkingur III
*** Djuric - Andrej Djuric (Andrej Đurić) (a) 21/07/1998, Trebinje (Bosnia and Herzegovina) (b) 1,90 (c) D - central defense (d) FK Leotar Trebinje (e) Zvijezda 09, Leotar Trebinje, HNK Capljina, Igman Konjic, Radnik Bijelj., Po-dri-nje
*** Djuric - Andrej Djuric (Андреј Ђурић) (a) 21/09/2003, Beograd (Serbia and Montenegro, now in Serbia) (b) 1,92 (c) D - central defense (d) NK Domžale (e) Crvena zvezda, Domžale, Crvena zvezda, Graficar
*** Djuric - Danijel Djuric (Danijel Dejan Djuric) (a) 05/01/2003, Varna (Bulgaria) (b) 1,74 (c) M - central midfielder (d) Víkingur Reykjavík (e) -
*** Djuric - Dejan Djuric (Дејан Ђурић) (a) 27/10/1998, Loznica (RF Yugoslavia, now in Serbia) (b) 1,87 (c) D - central defense (d) - (e) Rabotnicki, Radnicki Srem, FK Brodarac, Zarkovo, FK Brodarac
*** Djuric - Milan Djuric (Milan Đurić) (a) 03/10/1987, Beograd (Yugoslavia, now in Serbia) (b) 1,88 (c) M - attacking midfielder (d) FK Javor-Matis Ivanjica (e) Balzan FC, Rad Beograd, Central Coast, Vojvodina, Zira FK, NK Istra, Jagodina, Radnik Bijelj., Sandecja, Metalurg Skopje, FK Beograd
*** Djuric - Milan Djuric (Milan Đurić) (a) 22/05/1990, Tuzla (Yugoslavia, now in Bosnia and Herzegovina) (b) 1,99 (c) F - center forward (d) Hellas Verona (e)

Salernitana, Bristol City, Cesena, Cittadella, Cesena, Trapani, Cesena, Cremonese, Cesena, Parma, Crotone, Parma, Ascoli, Parma, Cesena

*** Djuric - Vasilije Djuric (Василије Ђурић) (a) 18/07/1998, Subotica (RF Yugoslavia, now in Serbia) (b) 1,76 (c) M - attacking midfielder (d) FK Radnicki 1923 Kragujevac (e) Metalac, FK TSC, FK Indjija, FK TSC, Sindjelic Bg, OFK Beograd

*** Djuricic - Filip Djuricic (Филип Ђуричић) (a) 30/01/1992, Obrenovac (Yugoslavia, now in Serbia) (b) 1,81 (c) M - attacking midfielder (d) Panathinaikos FC (e) Sampdoria, Sassuolo, Sampdoria, Benevento, Sampdoria, Benfica, Sampdoria, Benfica, RSC Anderlecht, Benfica, Southampton, Benfica, Mainz 05, Benfica, Heerenveen, Radnicki Obrenovac

*** Djuricic - Nikola Djuricic (Никола Ђурић) (a) 12/12/1999, Beograd (RF Yugoslavia, now in Serbia) (b) 1,80 (c) D - left back (d) FK Vozdovac (e) Rad Beograd, Smederevo 1924, Rad Beograd

*** Djuricin - Marco Djuricin (Marco Djuričin) (a) 12/12/1992, Wien (Austria) (b) 1,82 (c) F - center forward (d) Spartak Trnava (e) Spartak Trnava, HNK Rijeka, Austria Viena, Karlsruher SC, Grasshoppers, RB Salzburg, Grasshoppers, RB Salzburg, Ferencváros, RB Salzburg, Brentford, RB Salzburg, Sturm Graz, Hertha Berlin, Jahn Regensburg, Hertha Berlin

*** Djurickovic - Miomir Djurickovic (a) 26/07/1997, ¿? (RF Yugoslavia, now in Montenegro) (b) 1,91 (c) M - pivot (d) Buducnost Podgorica (e) OFK Grbalj, FK Iskra, Rudar Pljevlja, SO Cholet

*** Djurickovic - Petar Djurickovic (Петар Ђуричковић) (a) 20/06/1991, Prishtinë (Yugoslavia, now in Kosovo) (b) 1,78 (c) M - attacking midfielder (d) - (e) Novi Pazar, Kolubara, Napredak, Radnicki Niš, AO Xanthi, FK Partizan, Radnicki Niš, Crvena zvezda, Radnicki Niš, Crvena zvezda, Radnicki 1923, Crvena zvezda, Sopot

*** Djurisic - Marko Djurisic (Марко Ђуришић) (a) 17/07/1997, Novi Sad (Yugoslavia, now in Serbia) (b) 1,82 (c) M - pivot (d) FK Radnicki Niš (e) Vozdovac, Riga, Vojvodina, Dinamo Vranje, Macva, Vojvodina, Proleter, Vojvodina, Proleter, Vojvodina

*** Djurkovic - Nikola Djurkovic (Никола Ђурковић) (a) 15/04/2003, ¿? (Serbia and Montenegro, now in Montenegro) (b) - (c) M (d) FK Sutjeska Niksic (e) Sutjeska II, FK Bokelj, Sutjeska II

*** Djurkovic - Ognjen Djurkovic (Огњен Ђурковић) (a) 11/12/2001, Beograd (RF Yugoslavia, now in Serbia) (b) 1,88 (c) D - central defense (d) - (e) Pobeda Prilep, Dobanovci, Zarkovo, Teleoptik

*** Dlugosz - Wiktor Dlugosz (Wiktor Długosz) (a) 01/07/2000, Kielce (Poland) (b) 1,83 (c) F - right winger (d) Ruch Chorzów (e) Ruch, Rakow, Korona Kielce, Warta Poznań, Korona Kielce, Korona Kielce II, AP Korona

*** Dmitrenko - Viktor Dmitrenko (Дмитренко Виктор Николаевич) (a) 04/04/1991, Primorsko-Akhtarsk, Krasnodar Region (Soviet Union, now in Russia) (b) 1,90 (c) D - central defense (d) Shakhter Karaganda (e) Kaspiy Aktau, Atyrau, Ordabasy, Tobol Kostanay, Shakhter K., Tobol Kostanay, Aktobe, FC Astana, Kuban Krasnodar, Torpedo Armavir, Kuban Krasnodar, Zimbru Chisinau, Kuban Krasnodar, Kuban II

*** Dmitriev - Oleg Dmitriev (Дмитриев Олег Сергеевич) (a) 18/11/1995, Vyazma, Smolensk Region (Russia) (b) 1,80 (c) M - attacking midfielder (d) Rodina Moscow (e) Fakel Voronezh, Urozhay, Baltika, Spartaks, Baltika, Atlantas, Orel, Krasniy-SGAFKST

*** Dmitrijev - Aleksandr Dmitrijev (a) 18/02/1982, Tallinn (Soviet Union, now in Estonia) (b) ¿? (c) M - pivot (d) Tallinna FC Pocarr (e) TJK Legion, JK Legion II, JK

Retro, FC Flora, FCI Tallinn, Hønefoss, FCI Tallinn, Levadia, Levadia, Gomel, Neman Grodno, Ural, Hønefoss, Levadia, M.C. Tallinn, Levadia, HÜJK Emmaste, TVMK Tallinn

*** Dmitrović - Marko Dmitrović (Марко Дмитровић) (a) 24/01/1992, Subotica (Yugoslavia, now in Serbia) (b) 1,89 (c) G (d) Sevilla FC (e) SD Eibar, Alcorcón, Charlton Ath., Alcorcón, Charlton Ath., Újpest FC, Crvena zvezda

*** Dmytrenko - Vladyslav Dmytrenko (Дмитренко Владислав Миколайович) (a) 24/05/2000, Lutsk, Volyn Oblast (Ukraine) (b) 1,70 (c) F - left winger (d) Metalist 1925 Kharkiv (e) Volyn Lutsk, Volyn Lutsk II

*** Dmytruk - Taras Dmytruk (Дмитрук Тарас Валерійович) (a) 09/03/2000, Novovolynsk, Volyn Oblast (Ukraine) (b) 1,71 (c) D - right back (d) FK Minaj (e) Vorskla II, Girnyk-Sport, Vorskla II, Dinamo Kiev II

*** Do Marcolino - Alan Do Marcolino (Fabrice-Alan Do Marcolino) (a) 19/03/2002, Libreville (Gabon) (b) - (c) F - center forward (d) Quevilly Rouen Métropole (e) Quevilly Rouen, Stade Rennes, Stade Rennes B

*** Doan - Ritsu Doan (堂安 律) (a) 16/06/1998, Amagasaki, Hyogo (Japan) (b) 1,72 (c) F - right winger (d) SC Freiburg (e) PSV Eindhoven, Arminia Bielefeld, PSV Eindhoven, FC Groningen, Gamba Osaka, FC Groningen, Gamba Osaka

*** Dobay - Adilkhan Dobay (Добай Адильхан) (a) 02/06/2002, Shymkent (Kazakhstan) (b) 1,83 (c) M - right midfielder (d) FK Maktaaral (e) Ordabasy, Ordabasy II, Akad. Ontustik

*** Dobozi - Krisztian Dobozi (a) 29/11/2004, Târgu Secuiesc (Romania) (b) - (c) D - central defense (d) Sepsi OSK Sf. Gheorghe (e) Sepsi OSK II, KSE Tîrgu Secuiesc, Sepsi OSK II

*** Dobra - Luan Dobra (a) 20/01/2005, Landsberg am Lech (Germany) (b) 1,83 (c) M - central midfielder (d) KF Drenica (e) -

*** Dobre - Alexandru Dobre (Mihai-Alexandru Dobre) (a) 30/08/1998, Bucharest (Romania) (b) 1,85 (c) F - left winger (d) FC Famalicão (e) Dijon, Famalicão, Dijon, Wigan Ath., Yeovil Town, AFC Rochdale, Bury, VMG Cluj

*** Dobrescu - Mihai Dobrescu (a) 12/09/1992, Otopeni (Romania) (b) 1,73 (c) D - left back (d) CSA Steaua (e) UTA Arad, Universitatea Cluj, Gaz Metan, Academica Clinceni, V. Domnesti, CS Balotesti, Chindia, Ceahlăul, CS Otopeni, Ceahlăul

*** Dobrodey - Georgiy Dobrodey (Добродей Георгий Владимирович) (a) 09/01/2004, ¿? (Belarus) (b) - (c) G (d) Niva Dolbizno (e) Dynamo Brest II

*** Dobrosavlevici - Alin Dobrosavlevici (a) 24/10/1994, Moldova Nouă (Romania) (b) 1,87 (c) D - central defense (d) AS FC Buzau (e) FC Arges, FCV Farul, FC Hermannstadt, Concordia, Dunarea Calarasi, Concordia, ASA Tg. Mures, Academica Clinceni, ACS Berceni, Avicola Buzias, AFC Fortuna PC, Avicola Buzias, ACS Poli, Avicola Buzias, Dinamo II, Avicola Buzias

*** Dobrovoljc - Gaber Dobrovoljc (a) 27/01/1993, Ljubljana (Slovenia) (b) 1,85 (c) D - central defense (d) NS Mura (e) NK Radomlje, KA Akureyri, Domžale, Karagümrük, Domžale

*** Dobrovolski - Daniil Dobrovolski (a) 31/01/2004, Narva (Estonia) (b) - (c) G (d) - (e) JK Trans Narva

*** Docente - Emilio Docente (Emilio Benito Docente) (a) 11/12/1983, Comiso (Italy) (b) 1,78 (c) F - center forward (d) Cattolica Calcio 1923 (e) Cosmos, SS Folgore, Cattolica, Urbino Calcio, United Riccione, Miramare, La Fiorita, Delta Rovigo, Forlì, Trapani, Ternana, Gela, Rimini, Perugia, Rimini, Ancona, Rimini, Sambenedetese, Rimini, Avellino, Rimini, Messina Peloro, Gela

*** Docic - Marko Docic (Марко Доцић) (a) 21/04/1993, Beograd (RF Yugoslavia, now in Serbia) (b) 1,76 (c) M - pivot (d) FK Čukarički (e) Javor-Matis, Srem Jakovo, Radnicki Obrenovac, Radnicki (O)

*** Dodev - Darko Dodev (Дарко Додев) (a) 16/01/1998, ¿? (RF Yugoslavia, now in North Macedonia) (b) 1,76 (c) F - left winger (d) KF Vllaznia (e) Bregalnica Stip, Sileks, Tikves, Sileks, Metalurg Skopje

*** Dodic - Dusan Dodic (Душан Додић) (a) 09/03/2004, Vranje (Serbia and Montenegro, now in Serbia) (b) - (c) F - center forward (d) FK Vozdovac (e) -

*** Dodo - Dodo (Ailton Jorge dos Santos Soares) (a) 06/12/1990, ¿? (Cabo Verde) (b) 1,78 (c) F - right winger (d) Al-Ain FC (e) Hamrun Spartans, Afro Napoli, Procida, Batuque

*** Dodô - Dodô (Domilson Cordeiro dos Santos) (a) 17/11/1998, Taubaté (Brazil) (b) 1,66 (c) D - right back (d) Fiorentina (e) Shakhtar Donetsk, Vitória Guimarães, Shakhtar Donetsk, Coritiba FC

*** Dodô - Dodô (Luiz Paulo Hilario) (a) 16/10/1987, Rio de Janeiro (Brazil) (b) 1,74 (c) F - center forward (d) FK Liepaja (e) Penapolense, AE Larisa, Joinville-SC, FK Qabala, Dinamo Zagreb, NK Lokomotiva, Dinamo Zagreb, Inter Zaprešić, Juventus-RJ

*** Dodon - Victor Dodon (a) 01/03/2004, ¿? (Moldova) (b) 1,86 (c) G (d) Dacia Buiucani (e) -

*** Doekhi - Danilho Doekhi (Danilho Raimundo Doekhi) (a) 30/06/1998, Rotterdam (Netherlands) (b) 1,90 (c) D - central defense (d) 1.FC Union Berlin (e) Vitesse, Ajax B

*** Doffo - Agustín Doffo (a) Oliva (Argentina) (b) 1,79 (c) M - pivot (d) NK Olimpija Ljubljana (e) FK Tuzla City, Colón, O'Higgins, Chapecoense, Vélez Sarsfield II, Villarreal CF B, Vélez Sarsfield II, Vélez Sarsfield

*** Doga - Roy Doga (דוגה רוי) (a) 23/07/2002, ¿? (Israel) (b) 1,80 (c) F - center forward (d) SC Kfar Qasem (e) B. Jerusalem, SC Kfar Qasem, B. Jerusalem

*** Dogjani - Uran Dogjani (a) 23/06/2004, Kukës (Albania) (b) - (c) G (d) - (e) Brians

*** Doherty - Ben Doherty (a) 24/03/1997, Derry (Northern Ireland) (b) 1,75 (c) M - left midfielder (d) Derry City (e) Larne FC, Coleraine, Derry City, Glenavon, Derry City

*** Doherty - Gerard Doherty (a) 24/08/1981, Derry (Northern Ireland) (b) 1,88 (c) G (d) - (e) Cliftonville, Finn Harps, Crusaders, Derry City, The New Saints, Barry, TNS, Derby, Derry City

*** Doherty - Jordan Doherty (a) 29/08/2000, Balbriggan, North Dublin (Ireland) (b) 1,80 (c) D - central defense (d) Tampa Bay Rowdies (e) Bohemians, TB Rowdies, TB Rowdies

*** Doherty - Matt Doherty (Matthew James Doherty) (a) 16/01/1992, Dublin (Ireland) (b) 1,85 (c) D - right back (d) Wolverhampton Wanderers (e) Atlético Madrid, Tottenham Hotspur, Wolverhampton Wanderers, Bury, Wolverhampton Wanderers, Hibernian FC, Wolverhampton Wanderers, Bohemians, Belvedere FC

*** Doherty - Michael Doherty (a) 19/10/1983, Derry (Northern Ireland) (b) - (c) G (d) - (e) Coleraine, Institute FC, Coleraine, Limavady United

*** Doherty - Ronan Doherty (a) 10/01/1996, Buncrana (Northern Ireland) (b) 1,85 (c) M - central midfielder (d) Cliftonville FC (e) Institute FC, Cockhill Celtic

*** Doi - Tomoyuki Doi (土井 智之) (a) 24/09/1997, ¿?, Hyogo (Japan) (b) 1,79 (c) F - center forward (d) - (e) FK Bylis, Fujieda MYFC, Hougang Utd., Albirex N. (S), Tokoha Univ. Ha

*** Doidge - Christian Doidge (Christian Rhys Doidge) (a) 25/08/1992, Newport (Wales) (b) 1,88 (c) F - center forward (d) Hibernian FC (e) Kilmarnock FC, Hibernian FC, Forest Green Rovers, Bolton Wanderers, Forest Green Rovers, FC Dagenham & Redbridge, Dartford, FC Dagenham & Redbridge, Carmarthen, Barry, Croesyceiliog, Cwmbran Celtic

*** Doig - Josh Doig (Josh Thomas Doig) (a) 18/05/2002, Edinburgh (Scotland) (b) 1,89 (c) D - left back (d) Hellas Verona (e) Hibernian FC, Hibernian B, Queen's Park, Hibernian B

*** Dojcinovic - Sergej Dojcinovic (Sergej Dojčinović) (a) 14/04/2000, Banja Luka (Bosnia and Herzegovina) (b) - (c) D - right back (d) FK Laktasi (e) Borac Banja Luka, FK Laktasi, Rudar Prijedor, S. Novi Grad, Rudar Prijedor, S. Novi Grad, Rudar Prijedor

*** Doka - Albi Doka (a) 26/06/1997, Tirana (Albania) (b) 1,81 (c) D - right back (d) KF Tirana (e) Honvéd, HNK Gorica, Honvéd, HNK Gorica, KF Tirana, KF Tirana B

*** Doké - Josué Doké (Josué Yayra Doké) (a) 20/04/2004, Lomé (Togo) (b) 1,78 (c) F - center forward (d) BE1 National Football Academy (e) Planète Foot, Zébra Élites, Planète Foot, WAFA SC

*** Doksani - Elis Doksani (a) 05/07/1998, Fier (Albania) (b) 1,88 (c) D - central defense (d) KS Lushnja (e) KF Erzeni, KF Turbina, KF Egnatia, FK Bylis, FC Dinamo, FK Partizani, FK Bylis

*** Doku - Jérémy Doku (a) 27/05/2002, Borgerhout (Belgium) (b) 1,73 (c) F - right winger (d) Stade Rennais FC (e) RSC Anderlecht

*** Dolberg - Kasper Dolberg (Kasper Dolberg Rasmussen) (a) 06/10/1997, Silkeborg (Denmark) (b) 1,87 (c) F - center forward (d) RSC Anderlecht (e) OGC Nice, Hoffenheim, OGC Nice, Sevilla FC, OGC Nice, Ajax

*** Dolcek - Ivan Dolcek (Ivan Dolček) (a) 24/04/2000, Koprivnica (Croatia) (b) 1,81 (c) F - left winger (d) HNK Hajduk Split (e) HNK Sibenik, Hajduk Split, Famalicão, Hajduk Split, Slaven Belupo, NK Granicar Djurdjevac

*** Dolcini - Andrea Dolcini (a) 14/04/2003, ¿? (San Marino) (b) - (c) M - pivot (d) FC Fiorentino (e) -

*** Dolcini - Federico Dolcini (a) 22/03/2000, ¿? (San Marino) (b) - (c) M - attacking midfielder (d) Tre Fiori FC (e) -

*** Dolente - Simone Dolente (a) 31/12/2000, ¿? (Italy) (b) - (c) M - right midfielder (d) AC Libertas (e) Cosmos, Roccella, Bisaccese

*** Dolezal - David Dolezal (David Doležal) (a) 05/01/2000, ¿? (Czech Rep.) (b) 1,77 (c) M - right midfielder (d) FK Chlumec nad Cidlinou (e) Chlumec n/Cidl., Hradec Kralove

*** Dolezal - Martin Dolezal (Martin Doležal) (a) 03/05/1990, Valašské Meziříčí (Czechoslovakia, now in Czech Rep.) (b) 1,89 (c) F - center forward (d) MFK Karvina (e) Zagłębie, Jablonec, Sigma Olomouc, Zbrojovka Brno, Sigma Olomouc, Fotbal Trinec, Sigma Olomouc

*** Dolgov - Aleksandr Dolgov (Долгов Александр Владимирович) (a) 24/09/1998, Voronezh (Russia) (b) 1,83 (c) F - center forward (d) Fakel Voronezh (e) Khimki, Rostov, Khimki, Rostov, Loko-Kazanka M., Lokomotiv Moskva II, LFK Lokomotiv 2

*** Dolgov - Pavel Dolgov (Долгов Павел Владимирович) (a) 16/08/1996, Mamonovo, Kaliningrad Region (Russia) (b) 1,85 (c) F - center forward (d) Chaika Peschanokopskoe (e) Atyrau, M. Lipetsk, Zenit 2 St. Peterburg, Amkar Perm, Zenit 2 St. Peterburg, Tom Tomsk, Enisey, Anzhi, Torpedo Zhodino, Anzhi, Zenit 2 St. Peterburg, Zenit St. Peterburg II

*** Dolidze - Grigol Dolidze (გრიგოლ დოლიძე) (a) 25/10/1982, Lanchkhuti (Soviet Union, now in Georgia) (b) 1,80 (c) F - right winger (d) - (e) Samgurali, Torpedo Kutaisi, FC Dila, Shukura, FC Samtredia, FC Zestafoni, FC Dila, Torpedo Kutaisi, Baia Zugdidi, Metalurgi R., Dinamo Tbilisi, Simurq, Ameri, Sioni Bolnisi, Spartaki, Mertskhali, Guria

*** Dolmagic - Dino Dolmagic (Дино Долмагић) (a) 26/02/1994, Nova Varos (Yugoslavia, now in Serbia) (b) 1,75 (c) F - right winger (d) FK Javor-Matis Ivanjica (e) FK TSC, Javor-Matis, Breidablik, FK Indjija, Sloboda Užice, FK Zemun

*** Dolznikov - Artur Dolznikov (Artūr Dolžnikov) (a) 06/06/2000, ¿? (Lithuania) (b) 1,76 (c) F - right winger (d) FK Kauno Zalgiris (e) Riteriai, Vytis Vilnius, Riteriai, Riteriai B, Zalgiris B, Vilniaus FM

*** Dom - Joren Dom (a) 29/11/1989, Antwerpen (Belgium) (b) 1,78 (c) D - right back (d) Oud-Heverlee Leuven (e) Beerschot V.A., Royal Antwerp, FCV Dender EH, KV Mechelen, Rupel Boom, KV Mechelen

*** Domanico - Giuseppe Domanico (a) 25/05/2002, Cosenza (Italy) (b) - (c) F - center forward (d) - (e) Glacis United, Rende

*** Domanski - Maciej Domanski (Maciej Domański) (a) 05/09/1990, Rzeszów (Poland) (b) 1,67 (c) M - attacking midfielder (d) Stal Mielec (e) Rakow, P. Niepolomice, Siarka T., Stal Mielec, Radomiak, Stal Mielec, Polonia II, Stal Mielec

*** Domazetovic - Filip Domazetovic (a) 31/03/2004, ¿? (Serbia and Montenegro, now in Montenegro) (b) - (c) G (d) - (e) Mladost DG

*** Dombó - Dávid Dombó (a) 26/02/1993, Pápa (Hungary) (b) 1,87 (c) G (d) - (e) Vasas FC, Kisvárda, Mezőkövesd, Haladás, SV Lafnitz, Haladás, Haladás II, Vác, Haladás II

*** Dombrauskis - Tomas Dombrauskis (a) 24/09/1996, Plunge (Lithuania) (b) - (c) M - central midfielder (d) FK Riteriai (e) Palanga, Dziugas, Utenis

*** Doménech - Jaume Doménech (Jaume Doménech Sánchez) (a) 05/11/1990, Almenara (Spain) (b) 1,85 (c) G (d) Valencia CF (e) Valencia Mestalla, Huracán, CD El Palo, Villarreal CF B, Villarreal CF C, Onda, Villarreal CF C

*** Domgjoni - Toni Domgjoni (a) 04/09/1998, Koprivnica (Croatia) (b) 1,79 (c) M - central midfielder (d) Vitesse Arnhem (e) FC Zürich, Koprivnica

*** Domi - Fluturim Domi (a) 14/10/2000, ¿? (Albania) (b) 1,83 (c) F - left winger (d) FK Kukësi (e) -

*** Domic - Sasa Domic (Saša Domić) (a) 18/02/1998, Sombor (RF Yugoslavia, now in Serbia) (b) 1,86 (c) D - central defense (d) FK Velez Mostar (e) NK Dugo Selo, NK Dubrava ZG, NK Krsko, Lokomotiv Sofia, NK Brezice 1919, Zarkovo, FK Dunav

*** Domingo - Domingo (José Domingo Utrera García) (a) 26/10/1988, La Linea de la Concepción (Spain) (b) - (c) M - pivot (d) - (e) FC College 1975, CD San Bernardo, Europa FC, UD Tesorillo, Los Barrios, San Roque Cádiz, Los Barrios, San Roque Cádiz, Atlético Zabal

*** Domingos - Hugo Domingos (Hugo Antonio Monteiro Domingos) (a) 28/04/2002, ¿? (Luxembourg) (b) 1,80 (c) D - right back (d) FC Jeunesse Canach (e) CS Fola Esch

*** Domingos - Tomás Domingos (Tomás Caldas Januário Carvalho Domingos) (a) 01/05/1999, Oeiras (Portugal) (b) 1,75 (c) D - right back (d) CS Marítimo (e) Santa Clara, Mafra

*** Dominguès - Brandon Dominguès (a) 06/06/2000, Grenoble (France) (b) 1,72 (c) M - attacking midfielder (d) Debreceni VSC (e) Honvéd, Troyes, Troyes B

*** Dominguez - Mario Dominguez (Mario Dominguez Franco) (a) 10/02/2004, Granada (Spain) (b) 1,75 (c) F - center forward (d) Valencia Mestalla (e) -

*** Dominguez - Maxime Dominguez (a) 01/02/1996, Genève (Switzerland) (b) 1,73 (c) M - pivot (d) Gil Vicente FC (e) Rakow, Miedź Legnica, Neuchâtel Xamax, Lausanne-Sport, FC Zürich, Servette FC
*** Domínguez - Carlos Domínguez (Carlos Domínguez Cáceres) (a) 11/02/2001, Vigo (Spain) (b) 1,87 (c) D - central defense (d) RC Celta de Vigo (e) Celta B
*** Domínguez - Javi Domínguez (Javier Domínguez Arribas) (a) 26/03/2001, Madrid (Spain) (b) 1,95 (c) D - central defense (d) RC Celta Fortuna (e) CF Talavera, RM Castilla, CF Talavera, RM Castilla
*** Domínguez - Juan Domínguez (Juan Domínguez Lamas) (a) 08/01/1990, Pontedeume (Spain) (b) 1,81 (c) M - pivot (d) - (e) Asteras Tripoli, PAS Giannina, Sturm Graz, Reus Deportiu, RC Deportivo, RCD Mallorca, RC Deportivo, Deportivo B, Narón Balompié
*** Domínguez - Nicolás Domínguez (Nicolás Martín Domínguez) (a) 28/06/1998, Haedo (Argentina) (b) 1,79 (c) M - central midfielder (d) Bologna (e) Vélez Sarsfield, Bologna, Vélez Sarsfield, Vélez Sarsfield II
*** Dominic - Ivan Dominic (Ivan Dominić) (a) 07/01/2003, Čakovec (Croatia) (b) 1,82 (c) D - left back (d) HNK Hajduk Split (e) KuPS, Hajduk Split
*** Domjan - Jaka Domjan (a) 05/05/2004, ¿? (Slovenia) (b) - (c) M - attacking midfielder (d) NS Mura (e) -
*** Domjanic - Niko Domjanic (Niko Domjanić) (a) 19/02/2003, Stuttgart (Germany) (b) - (c) F - center forward (d) NK Varazdin (e) -
*** Domonkos - Kristof Domonkos (Kristóf Domonkos) (a) 17/08/1998, Galanta (Slovakia) (b) 1,73 (c) M - attacking midfielder (d) MFK Ružomberok (e) Komarno, ETO FC Győr, Komarno, ETO FC Győr, Dunajska Streda, Komarno, Dunajska Streda
*** Domov - Pavel Domov (Pavel Dõmov) (a) 31/12/1993, Tallinn (Estonia) (b) 1,74 (c) M - central midfielder (d) FC Kuressaare (e) TJK Legion, FC Flora, Kalev, FC Flora, FCI Levadia, Paide, FCI Levadia, FCI Tallinn, TJK Legion, FC Flora, FC Strommi
*** Dompé - Jean-Luc Dompé (Jean-Luc Mamadou Diarra Dompé) (a) 12/08/1995, Arpajon (France) (b) 1,70 (c) F - left winger (d) Hamburgo SV (e) Zulte Waregem, KAA Gent, Standard Liège, Amiens SC, Standard Liège, KAS Eupen, Standard Liège, Sint-Truiden, Valenciennes FC, Valenciennes B
*** Domulevs - Normunds Domulevs (a) 09/03/2005, ¿? (Latvia) (b) - (c) D (d) BFC Daugavpils II (e) -
*** Don - Cédric Franck Don (Cédric Franck Emmanuel Don) (a) 03/05/2004, Man (Ivory Coast) (b) 1,67 (c) F - attacking midfielder (d) Hapoel Jerusalem (e) JC Abidjan
*** Donald - John Donald (John Chetauya Nwankwo Donald Okeh) (a) 25/09/2000, Murcia (Spain) (b) 1,82 (c) D - central defense (d) Elche CF (e) Elche Ilicitano, Villarreal CF C
*** Donat - Denis Donat (Denis Donát) (a) 14/09/2001, ¿? (Czech Rep.) (b) 1,89 (c) D - central defense (d) FK Pardubice (e) Pardubice, Mlada Boleslav, Hradec Kralove, Chrudim, Hradec Kralove
*** Donati - Giulio Donati (a) 05/02/1990, Pietrasanta (Italy) (b) 1,78 (c) D - right back (d) - (e) Monza, Lecce, Mainz 05, Bayer Leverkusen, Internazionale Milano, Grosseto, Internazionale Milano, Padova, Internazionale Milano, Lecce, Internazionale Milano
*** Donchev - Asen Donchev (Асен Петров Дончев) (a) 22/10/2001, Blagoevgrad (Bulgaria) (b) 1,76 (c) D - right back (d) CSKA-Sofia (e) -
*** Donchev - Gligor Donchev (Глигор Дончев) (a) 04/05/1998, Strumica (North Macedonia) (b) 1,78 (c) D - left back (d) Tikves Kavadarci (e) Ohrid Lihnidos, FK Sasa, Osogovo, AP Brera, Horizont, AP Brera

*** Donelon - Regan Donelon (a) 17/04/1996, Manchester (England) (b) 1,71 (c) D - left back (d) Galway United FC (e) Finn Harps, Sligo Rovers, Finn Harps, Sligo Rovers

*** Dong - Kyliane Dong (a) 27/09/2004, Évry-Courcouronnes (France) (b) - (c) F - left winger (d) ESTAC Troyes B (e) -

*** Dongmo - Danel Dongmo (Danel Jordan Dongmo) (a) 31/01/2001, Douala (Cameroon) (b) 1,82 (c) M - central midfielder (d) ESTAC Troyes B (e) Brasseries

*** Dongou - Jean Marie Dongou (Jean Marie Dongou Tsafack) (a) 22/04/1995, Douala (Cameroon) (b) 1,75 (c) F - center forward (d) FC Osaka (e) Anag. Karditsas, Zamora CF, FC Honka, CD Lugo, Lleida Esportiu, CD Lugo, Gimnàstic, Real Zaragoza, FC Barcelona B

*** Donis - Anastasios Donis (a) 29/08/1996, Blackburn (England) (b) 1,78 (d) APOEL FC (e) Stade Reims, APOEL FC, Stade Reims, VVV-Venlo, Stade Reims, VfB Stuttgart, Stade Reims, VfB Stuttgart, Juventus, OGC Nice, Juventus, FC Lugano, Juventus, Sassuolo, Juventus

*** Donis - Christos Donis (Χρήστος Δώνης) (a) 09/10/1994, Athen (Greece) (b) 1,84 (c) M - pivot (d) Radomiak Radom (e) Ascoli, VVV-Venlo, Ascoli, Panathinaikos, Iraklis, Panathinaikos, PAS Giannina, Panathinaikos, FC Lugano, Panathinaikos

*** Donisa - Julio Donisa (Julio Kenny Donisa) (a) 15/01/1994, L'Haÿ-les-Roses (France) (b) 1,84 (c) F - center forward (d) - (e) FC Arges, Le Mans FC, Clermont Foot, Red Star FC, AS Lyon-Duchère, Red Star FC, Concarneau, AS Pagny, Fondi, Battipagliese, FC Rouen B

*** Donk - Ryan Donk (Ryan Henk Donk) (a) 30/03/1986, Amsterdam (Netherlands) (b) 1,92 (c) D - central defense (d) - (e) Kasimpasa, Galatasaray, Real Betis, Galatasaray, Kasimpasa, KV Brugge, AZ Alkmaar, West Bromwich Albion, AZ Alkmaar, RKC Waalwijk

*** Donkor - Jacky Donkor (a) 12/11/1998, Gent (Belgium) (b) 1,76 (c) F - left winger (d) Excelsior Rotterdam (e) FC Dordrecht, Fortuna Sittard, FC Eindhoven, Fortuna Sittard, KSC Lokeren II

*** Donnarumma - Gianluigi Donnarumma (a) 25/02/1999, Castellammare di Stabia (Italy) (b) 1,96 (c) G (d) París Saint-Germain FC (e) AC Milan, Castellammare

*** Donnellan - Leo Donnellan (a) 07/07/1998, London (England) (b) 1,81 (c) M - central midfielder (d) Hendon FC (e) Portadown, Harrow Borough, Finn Harps, Maidstone, FC Dagenham & Redbridge

*** Donnelly - Aaron Donnelly (a) 22/03/2000, ¿? (Northern Ireland) (b) 1,80 (c) D - central defense (d) Larne FC (e) Cliftonville

*** Donnelly - Aaron Donnelly (Aaron Martin Donnelly) (a) 08/06/2003, Magherafelt (Northern Ireland) (b) 1,85 (c) D - left back (d) Dundee FC (e) Dundee FC, Port Vale

*** Donnelly - Caolan Donnelly (a) 14/01/2005, ¿? (Northern Ireland) (b) - (c) M - central midfielder (d) Larne FC (e) -

*** Donnelly - Jay Donnelly (a) 10/04/1995, Belfast (Northern Ireland) (b) 1,81 (c) F - center forward (d) Glentoran FC (e) Belfast Celtic, Sperre) Cliftonville

*** Donnelly - Liam Donnelly (Liam Francis Peadar Donnelly) (a) 07/03/1996, Dungannon (Northern Ireland) (b) 1,81 (c) M - pivot (d) Kilmarnock FC (e) Motherwell FC, Hartlepool Utd., Crawley Town

*** Donnelly - Lorcan Donnelly (Lorcán Donnelly) (a) 23/01/2006, Belfast (Northern Ireland) (b) - (c) G (d) Glentoran FC (e) -

*** Donnelly - Orann Donnelly (a) 23/01/2005, ¿? (Northern Ireland) (b) - (c) G (d) Cliftonville FC (e) -

*** Donnelly - Philip Donnelly (a) 29/04/1992, Monaghan (Ireland) (b) - (c) M - right midfielder (d) Newry City AFC (e) Warrenpoint, Lurgan Celtic, Dungannon, Monaghan United

*** Donnelly - Rory Donnelly (Ruaridhri Donnelly) (a) 18/02/1992, Belfast (Northern Ireland) (b) 1,88 (c) F - center forward (d) Glentoran FC (e) Cliftonville, Gillingham FC, Swansea City, Tranmere Rovers, Swansea City, Coventry City, Swansea City, Cliftonville

*** Dönnum - Aron Dönnum (Aron Leonard Dønnum) (a) 20/04/1998, Eidsvoll (Norway) (b) 1,78 (c) M - left midfielder (d) Standard de Lieja (e) Vålerenga, Standard Liège, Vålerenga, HamKam, Vålerenga

*** D'Onofrio - Francesco D'Onofrio (a) 06/10/1990, Liège (Belgium) (b) 1,80 (c) D - right back (d) Dominique D'Onofrio (e) RFC Seraing, KSK Lierse Kem., Penafiel, RFC Seraing, Olhanense

*** Donohue - Dion Donohue (Dion James Donohue) (a) 26/08/1993, Bodedern (Wales) (b) 1,80 (c) D - central defense (d) Caernarfon Town (e) Barrow, Swindon Town, Swindon Town, Mansfield Town, FC Portsmouth, FC Chesterfield, Sutton C., Caernarfon, Holyhead H., Porthmadog

*** Donov - Ilija Donov (Илија Донов) (a) 31/08/2001, Negotino (North Macedonia) (b) 1,76 (c) M - pivot (d) AP Brera (e) FK Sasa, AP Brera, FK Sasa, AP Brera, Vardar Negotino

*** Dony - Arnaud Dony (Arnaud Pierre Dony) (a) 08/05/2004, ¿? (Belgium) (b) 1,70 (c) D - left back (d) Royale Union Saint Gilloise (e) -

*** Donyoh - Godsway Donyoh (a) 14/10/1994, Accra (Ghana) (b) 1,79 (c) F - center forward (d) Apollon Limassol (e) Neftchi Baku, Maccabi Haifa, Nordsjælland, Dynamo Dresden, Nordsjælland, Falkenbergs FF, Djurgården, Right to Dream

*** Doobi - Ramin Doobi (a) 21/12/2001, Accra (Ghana) (b) 1,84 (c) F - center forward (d) - (e) Sioni Bolnisi, FK Qabala 2, FC Shevardeni, FC Samtredia

*** Dopater - Michal Dopater (a) 26/02/2001, ¿? (Slovakia) (b) 1,79 (c) M - attacking midfielder (d) Tatran Oravske Vesele (e) Ružomberok, Humenne, Ružomberok, Bardejov, Ružomberok, FC Petrzalka, Ružomberok, Ruzomberok B

*** Doran - Aaron Doran (a) 23/05/2003, Portlaoise, Laois (Ireland) (b) - (c) M - central midfielder (d) Wexford FC (e) Bohemians

*** Doran - Jamie Doran (a) 11/02/2004, Newry (Northern Ireland) (b) - (c) M - central midfielder (d) Glenavon FC (e) -

*** Doré - Férébory Doré (a) 21/01/1989, Brazzaville (Congo DR) (b) 1,93 (c) F - center forward (d) Mosta FC (e) USM Saran, Beaucouzé, Botev Plovdiv, Angers SCO, Clermont Foot, Angers SCO, Botev Plovdiv, CFR Cluj, Botev Plovdiv, Petrolul, Angers SCO, Angers SCO B, AS Kondzo

*** Dorgeles - Mario Dorgeles (Maho Yepie Dorgeles Guy-Mario Bocha) (a) 07/08/2004, Andokoi (Ivory Coast) (b) 1,77 (c) M - central midfielder (d) FC Nordsjælland (e) Right to Dream

*** Doriev - Ljupco Doriev (Љупчо Дориев) (a) 13/09/1995, Strumica (North Macedonia) (b) 1,86 (c) F - left winger (d) Sogdiana Jizzakh (e) Shkëndija, AP Brera, Horizont, AP Brera

*** Dormi - Lorenzo Dormi (a) 11/02/1995, ¿? (Italy) (b) - (c) F - attacking midfielder (d) SP Tre Penne (e) SS Folgore, Cosmos, SS Folgore, Rimini, Savignanese, Rimini

*** Dorn - Pius Dorn (a) 24/09/1996, Freiburg im Breisgau (Germany) (b) 1,79 (c) M - right midfielder (d) FC Lucerna (e) FC Thun, FC Vaduz, Austria Lustenau, SC Freiburg II

*** Dorovskikh - Vyacheslav Dorovskikh (Доровских Вячеслав Сергеевич) (a) 14/09/2003, ¿? (Russia) (b) 1,97 (c) G (d) Fakel Voronezh (e) Fakel II, Fakel-M

*** Dorph - Oliver Dorph (Oliver Friis Dorph) (a) 06/01/2004, ¿? (Denmark) (b) - (c) D - central defense (d) Skive IK (e) -

*** Dorregaray - Diego Dorregaray (Diego Fernando Dorregaray) (a) 09/05/1992, Campana, Buenos Aires (Argentina) (b) 1,87 (c) F - center forward (d) Nea Salamis (e) Ismaily, Dep. Cuenca, Técnico U., Def. Belgrano, Guayaquil City, Atlanta, Barracas Bol.

*** Dorsch - Niklas Dorsch (Niklas Bernd Dorsch) (a) 15/01/1998, Lichtenfels (Germany) (b) 1,78 (c) M - pivot (d) FC Augsburg (e) KAA Gent, 1.FC Heidenheim, Bayern München, FC Bayern II, D-CZ FB-Schule

*** Dorsett - Jeriel Dorsett (Abraham Jeriel Richard Dorsett) (a) 04/05/2002, Enfield (England) (b) 1,85 (c) D - central defense (d) FC Reading (e) Kilmarnock FC, AFC Rochdale

*** dos Santos - Andre dos Santos (André Luiz Dos Santos) (a) 19/02/1992, Petrópolis (Brazil) (b) 1,73 (c) D - right back (d) FC Bruno's Magpies (e) Mons Calpe, Lincoln FC, Mons Calpe, FC Britannia XI, Atlantis FC, Petrópolis, Serrano FC

*** dos Santos - Dabney dos Santos (a) 21/07/1996, Amsterdam (Netherlands) (b) 1,73 (d) AS Trencin (e) FC Sheriff, Heracles Almelo, AZ Alkmaar, Sparta Rotterdam, AZ Alkmaar

*** dos Santos - Luís dos Santos (Luís Miguel Castelo dos Santos) (a) 20/01/2000, Entroncamento (Portugal) (b) 1,76 (c) F - right winger (d) Boavista Porto FC (e) Trofense, Boavista

*** dos Santos Silva Cardoso - Kevin dos Santos Silva Cardoso (a) 05/04/2002, ¿? (Portugal) (b) - (c) F (d) Jeunesse Esch II (e) -

*** Dosa - Deou Dosa (Deou Dosa Olatunji) (a) 29/07/1998, Lagos (Nigeria) (b) 1,83 (c) D - left back (d) FC Van (e) Lernayin Artsakh, Alashkert CF, FC Van, Lori Vanadzor, FC Van, Lori Vanadzor

*** Dosca - Daniel Dosca (a) 20/02/2003, ¿? (Moldova) (b) - (c) F - center forward (d) Dacia Buiucani (e) -

*** Dosis - Nikolaos Dosis (Νικόλαος Δόσης) (a) 25/01/2001, ¿? (Greece) (b) 1,82 (c) M - pivot (d) - (e) Olympiakos N., Östersund

*** Doski - Merchas Doski (دوسكي ميرخاس) (a) 07/12/1999, Hannover (Germany) (b) 1,73 (c) D - left back (d) 1.FC Slovácko (e) FC Wacker, FC Wacker II, MTVE Celle, Heeßeler SV, Egestorf/L. II

*** Dosljak - Boris Dosljak (Boris Došljak) (a) 04/06/1989, Titograd (now Podgorica) (Yugoslavia, now in Montenegro) (b) 1,77 (c) F - right winger (d) FK Mladost Donja Gorica (e) Arsenal Tivat, KÍ Klaksvík, FK Iskra, Sloboda Užice, FK Lovcen, FK Bokelj, Sloboda Užice, Widzew Lódz, Zeta Golubovac, FK Zabjelo

*** Dosmagambetov - Timur Dosmagambetov (Досмагамбетов Тимур Талгатович) (a) 01/05/1989, Kokshetau (Soviet Union, now in Kazakhstan) (b) 1,72 (c) D - left back (d) FC Astana (e) Shakhter K., Taraz, Ordabasy, Okzhetpes, Tobol Kostanay, Taraz, Vostok Oskemen, Okzhetpes, Aktobe, Okzhetpes

*** Dosso - Abou Dosso (a) 26/03/1996, ¿? (Ivory Coast) (b) - (c) D - left back (d) - (e) Bnei Sakhnin, Hapoel Tel Aviv, H Rishon leZion, SO Armée

*** Dossou - Jodel Dossou (a) 17/03/1992, Dassa-Zoumé (Benin) (b) 1,71 (c) F - right winger (d) FC Sochaux-Montbéliard (e) Clermont Foot, TSV Hartberg, FC Vaduz, Austria Lustenau, FC Liefering, RB Salzburg, Cub Africain, Tonnerre, CIFAS

*** Dost - Bas Dost (Bas Leon Dost) (a) 31/05/1989, Deventer (Netherlands) (b) 1,96 (c) F - center forward (d) - (e) FC Utrecht, KV Brugge, Eintracht, Sporting Lisboa, VfL Wolfsburg, Heerenveen, Heracles Almelo, FC Emmen

*** Dostal - Martin Dostal (Martin Dostál) (a) 23/09/1989, Praha (Czechoslovakia, now in Czech Rep.) (b) 1,77 (c) D - right back (d) Bohemians Praha 1905 (e) Slavia Praha, Banik Ostrava, Slavia Praha, Celakovice

*** Dostal - Stanislav Dostal (Stanislav Dostál) (a) 20/06/1991, Zlín (Czechoslovakia, Czech Rep.) (b) 1,85 (c) G (d) FC Zlin (e) -

*** Dostanic - Damjan Dostanic (Дамјан Достанић) (a) 03/12/2001, Rotterdam (Netherlands) (b) 1,85 (c) F - center forward (d) BATE Borisov (e) FK TSC, Zarkovo, FK TSC

*** Dotor - Carlos Dotor (Carlos Dotor Gonzalez) (a) 15/03/2001, Madrid (Spain) (b) 1,80 (c) M - central midfielder (d) RC Celta de Vigo (e) RM Castilla

*** Doua - Seniko Doua (Seniko Romeo Doua) (a) 01/11/2001, Attecoube Abidjan (Ivory Coast) (b) 1,78 (c) D - right back (d) Petrolul Ploiesti (e) SO Armée

*** Douah - Bilal Douah (Bilal Douhan) (a) 25/07/2003, Kenitra (Morocco) (b) 1,91 (c) M - central midfielder (d) Lynx FC (e) FC College 1975, Mons Calpe, Europa FC, Europa Reserve

*** Doucet - Lohann Doucet (a) 14/09/2002, Nantes (France) (b) 1,80 (c) M - pivot (d) Paris FC (e) Paris FC, FC Nantes, FC Nantes B

*** Doucouré - Abdoulaye Doucouré (a) 01/01/1993, Meulan-en-Yvelines (France) (b) 1,83 (c) M - central midfielder (d) Everton FC (e) Watford, Granada CF, Watford, Stade Rennes, Stade Rennes B

*** Doucouré - Boubacari Doucouré (a) 19/03/1999, Beaumont-sur-Oise (France) (b) 1,92 (c) M - pivot (d) FK Javor-Matis Ivanjica (e) FK TSC, FC Chambly Oise, Javor-Matis, FC Chambly Oise, FC Chambly B

*** Doucouré - Cheick Doucouré (Cheick Oumar Doucouré) (a) 08/01/2000, Bamako (Mali) (b) 1,80 (c) M - pivot (d) Crystal Palace (e) RC Lens, RC Lens B, AS Real Bamako, JMG Bamako

*** Doucouré - Mamadou Doucouré (a) 21/05/1998, Dakar (Senegal) (b) 1,83 (c) D - central defense (d) Borussia Mönchengladbach (e) Paris Saint Germain B

*** Doucouré - Siriné Doucouré (Siriné Ckene Doucouré) (a) 08/04/2002, Nogent-sur-Marne (France) (b) 1,93 (c) F - center forward (d) FC Lorient (e) LB Châteauroux, Châteauroux B

*** Doudera - David Doudera (David Douděra) (a) 31/05/1998, Brandýs nad Labem-Stará Boleslav (Czech Rep.) (b) 1,75 (c) D - right back (d) SK Slavia Praga (e) Mlada Boleslav, Dukla Praha, Dukla B

*** Doué - Désiré Doué (a) 03/06/2005, Angers (France) (b) 1,81 (c) M - attacking midfielder (d) Stade Rennais FC (e) -

*** Doué - Guéla Doué (a) 17/10/2002, Angers (France) (b) 1,86 (c) D - right back (d) Stade Rennais FC (e) Stade Rennes B

*** Douglas - Barry Douglas (Barry James Douglas) (a) 04/09/1989, Glasgow (Scotland) (b) 1,76 (c) D - left back (d) Lech Poznan (e) Leeds Utd., Blackburn, Leeds Utd., Wolverhampton Wanderers, Konyaspor, Lech Poznan, Dundee United, Queen's Park

*** Douglas Luiz - Douglas Luiz (Douglas Luiz Soares de Paulo) (a) 09/05/1998, Rio de Janeiro (Brazil) (b) 1,77 (c) M - central midfielder (d) Aston Villa (e) Manchester City, Girona FC, Manchester City, Vasco da Gama

*** Douiri - Achraf Douiri (a) 27/11/1999, Amsterdam (Netherlands) (b) 1,80 (c) D - right back (d) FC Volendam (e) IJsselm.vogels, IFK Eskilstuna, Zuidoost Utd., HFC EDO O19

*** Doukouo - Lorougnon Doukouo (Lorougnon Henri Joel Doukouo) (a) 16/11/2002, ¿? (Ivory Coast) (b) 1,81 (c) F - center forward (d) KF Egnatia (e) Al-Yarmouk

*** Doukoure - Kevin Doukoure (Kevin Doukoure Grobry) (a) 30/03/1999, Seguela (Ivory Coast) (b) 1,78 (c) M - central midfielder (d) FCV Farul Constanta (e) Tabor Sezana, AFAD Djékanou

*** Doukouré - Cheick Doukouré (a) 11/09/1992, Abidjan (Ivory Coast) (b) 1,80 (c) M - pivot (d) Aris Thessaloniki (e) CD Leganés, Levante UD, SD Huesca, Levante UD, FC Metz, FC Lorient, SAS Epinal, FC Lorient, Lorient B

*** Doukouré - Ismaël Doukouré (a) 24/07/2003, Lille (France) (b) 1,83 (c) D - central defense (d) Racing Club Strasbourg (e) Valenciennes FC

*** Douline - David Douline (David Marc Michel Douline) (a) 28/05/1993, Grenoble (France) (b) 1,82 (c) M - pivot (d) Servette FC (e) Rodez AF, Clermont Foot, Rodez AF, Clermont Foot, Le Puy Foot, MDA Chasselay, Thonon Évian B, Saint-Étienne B

*** Doumbia - Abdoul Aziz Doumbia (a) 17/12/2000, Bouaké (Ivory Coast) (b) 1,77 (c) M - pivot (d) Shukura Kobuleti (e) Sioni Bolnisi, Dinamo II, Tbilisi City, FC Aragvi, Tbilisi City

*** Doumbia - Aboubacar Doumbia (Aboubacar Junior Doumbia) (a) 12/11/1999, Attecoube (Ivory Coast) (b) 1,72 (c) F - right winger (d) Karmiotissa Pano Polemidion (e) Maccabi Netanya, Karmiotissa, Maccabi Netanya, M. Petah Tikva, Maccabi Netanya, Kokkolan PV, SO Armée

*** Doumbia - Allasana Doumbia (a) 28/12/2002, ¿? (Ivory Coast) (b) - (c) F - left winger (d) - (e) Shirak Gyumri, M. Petah Tikva

*** Doumbia - Idrissa Doumbia (a) 14/04/1998, Yamoussoukro (Ivory Coast) (b) 1,87 (c) M - pivot (d) Al-Ahli SC (e) Sporting Lisboa, Alanyaspor, Sporting Lisboa, Zulte Waregem, Sporting Lisboa, SD Huesca, Sporting Lisboa, Akhmat Grozny, RSC Anderlecht, Zulte Waregem, RSC Anderlecht, ES Bingerville

*** Doumbia - Kamory Doumbia (a) 18/02/2003, Bamako (Mali) (b) 1,70 (c) M - attacking midfielder (d) Stade de Reims (e) Stade Reims B, JMG Bamako

*** Doumbia - Mahamadou Doumbia (a) 15/05/2004, ¿? (Mali) (b) - (c) M - central midfielder (d) JMG Academy Bamako (e) Nordsjælland, JMG Bamako

*** Doumbia - Mohamed Doumbia (a) 25/12/1998, Abidjan (Ivory Coast) (b) 1,74 (c) M - central midfielder (d) FC Slovan Liberec (e) Dukla Praha, Ekenäs IF

*** Doumbia - Ousmane Doumbia (a) 21/05/1992, Adjamé (Ivory Coast) (b) 1,74 (c) M - pivot (d) Chicago Fire FC (e) Chicago, FC Lugano, FC Zürich, FC Winterthur, Yverdon Sport, Servette FC, Athletic Adjamé, Servette FC, Athletic Adjamé

*** Doumbia - Sekou Doumbia (a) 13/06/1994, Adzopé (Ivory Coast) (b) 1,84 (c) M - central midfielder (d) Maccabi Herzliya (e) Maktaaral, Ordabasy, Hapoel Hadera, Armavir, Tambov, FK Slutsk, FC Saxan, Zaria Balti, FC Saxan

*** Doumbia - Souleyman Doumbia (a) 24/09/1996, Paris (France) (b) 1,83 (c) D - left back (d) - (e) Angers SCO, Stade Rennes, Angers SCO, Stade Rennes, Grasshoppers, Bari, Grasshoppers, Bari, Vicenza, Bari, Paris Saint Germain B

*** Doumbouya - Amadou Doumbouya (a) 12/10/2002, Kindia (Guinea) (b) 1,72 (c) F - right winger (d) Botev Plovdiv (e) Djurgården

*** Doumtsios - Konstantinos Doumtsios (Κωνσταντίνος Δούμτσιος) (a) 20/09/1997, Serres (Greece) (b) 1,85 (c) F - center forward (d) TOP Oss (e) APO Levadiakos, AE Karaiskakis, Panionios, Doxa Dramas, Eginiakos, Panserraikos, Iraklis, PS Serres

*** Douvikas - Anastasios Douvikas (Αναστάσιος Δουβίκας) (a) 02/08/1999, Athina (Greece) (b) 1,86 (c) F - center forward (d) FC Utrecht (e) Volos NPS, Asteras Tripoli

*** Doval - David Doval (David Pérez Doval) (a) 12/02/2002, Sarria (Spain) (b) 1,70 (c) M - attacking midfielder (d) - (e) Sant Julià, FC Santa Coloma, AD Ceuta B, SD Sarriana

*** Dovbetskyi - Denys Dovbetskyi (Довбецький Денис Романович) (a) 27/01/2004, Radekhiv, Lviv Oblast (Ukraine) (b) 1,73 (c) F - right winger (d) - (e) PFK Lviv

*** Dovbnya - Aleksandr Dovbnya (Довбня Александр Вячеславович) (a) 10/04/1987, Moskva (Soviet Union, now in Russia) (b) 1,93 (c) G (d) Shinnik Yaroslavl (e) Torpedo Moskva, Rotor Volgograd, Orenburg, SKA Khabarovsk, CRFSO Smolensk, Luch Vladivostok, Torpedo Moskva, Luch Vladivostok, Torpedo Moskva, FK Podolje, FK Novgorod, Sibir, FC Haka, Rosich, Znamya Truda OZ, Spartak 2

*** Dovbnya - Aleksandr Dovbnya (Довбня Александр Евгеньевич) (a) 14/02/1996, Moskva (Russia) (b) 1,89 (c) D - central defense (d) - (e) Amkal Moskva, Qyzyljar, Arsenal Tula, Rotor Volgograd, Arsenal Tula, Pafos FC, Ethnikos, Lokomotiv Moskva II

*** Dovbyk - Artem Dovbyk (Довбик Артем Олександрович) (a) 21/06/1997, Cherkasy (Ukraine) (b) 1,89 (c) F - center forward (d) Girona FC (e) SK Dnipro-1, Midtjylland, SønderjyskE, Midtjylland, Dnipro, Zaria Balti, Dnipro, Cherk. Dnipro

*** Dovedan - Nikola Dovedan (a) 06/07/1994, Tulln (Austria) (b) 1,72 (c) F - attacking midfielder (d) 1.FC Heidenheim 1846 (e) Austria Viena, 1.FC Nürnberg, 1.FC Heidenheim, SCR Altach, LASK, SCR Altach, LASK, FC Liefering

*** Dovgyi - Oleksiy Dovgyi (Довгий Олексій Володимирович) (a) 02/11/1989, Kyiv (Soviet Union, now in Ukraine) (b) 1,86 (c) M - pivot (d) Rukh Lviv (e) PFK Lviv, FK Oleksandriya, Stal Kamyanske, Vorskla Poltava, Metalist, Illichivets, PFK Oleksandria, Dynamo 2 Kyiv, PFK Oleksandria, Dynamo 2 Kyiv, Volyn Lutsk, Dynamo 2 Kyiv, CSKA Kyiv, Dynamo 2 Kyiv, Lokomotyv Kyiv

*** Dovin - Oliver Dovin (Oliver Lukas Dozae Nnonyelu Dovin) (a) 11/07/2002, London (England) (b) 1,88 (c) G (d) Hammarby IF (e) IK Frej Täby, Hammarby IF, IK Frej Täby

*** Dovydaitis - Deividas Dovydaitis (a) 26/01/2003, Siauliai (Lithuania) (b) 1,72 (c) M - right midfielder (d) FA Siauliai (e) Banga, FA Siauliai

*** Downes - Flynn Downes (a) 20/01/1999, Brentwood (England) (b) 1,78 (c) M - central midfielder (d) West Ham United (e) Swansea City, Ipswich, Luton Town, Ipswich

*** Downs - Damion Downs (Damion Lamar Downs) (a) 06/07/2004, Werneck (Germany) (b) - (c) F - center forward (d) 1.FC 1.FC Köln II (e) -

*** Downs - Dylan Downs (a) 07/01/2002, ¿? (England) (b) 1,8 (c) M - pivot (d) Newtown AFC (e) -

*** Doyle - Andrew Doyle (a) 28/10/1990, Newtonabbey (Northern Ireland) (b) - (c) D - central defense (d) Rathcoole FC (e) Glenavon, Carrick Rangers, Ballyclare, Nortel FC

*** Doyle - Brandon Doyle (a) 20/08/1998, Newtownabbey (Northern Ireland) (b) 1,82 (c) F - center forward (d) - (e) Crusaders, Linfield, Warrenpoint, Linfield, Warrenpoint, Linfield

*** Doyle - Eoin Doyle (a) 12/03/1988, Dublin (Ireland) (b) 1,82 (c) F - center forward (d) David Webster (e) St. Patrick's Ath., Bolton Wanderers, Swindon Town, Bradford City, Swindon Town, Bradford City, Preston North End, Oldham Athletic, Preston North End, Oldham Athletic, Preston North End, FC Portsmouth, Preston North End, Cardiff City, Preston North End, Cardiff City, FC Chesterfield, Hibernian FC, Sligo Rovers, Shamrock Rovers, Crumlin United, Cherry Orchard FC

*** Doyle - Jonathan Doyle (a) 13/02/2003, Belfast (Northern Ireland) (b) - (c) F - center forward (d) Lisburn Distillery FC (e) Carrick Rangers

*** Doyle - Josh Doyle (a) 19/06/2002, Ballyfermot (Ireland) (b) - (c) F - center forward (d) Bluebell United AFC (e) Glenavon, Bluebell United
*** Doyle - Mark Doyle (a) 19/11/1998, ¿? (Ireland) (b) 1,83 (c) F - left winger (d) St. Patrick's Athletic (e) Drogheda United
*** Doyle - Paul Doyle (a) 10/04/1998, Westport, Co. Mayo (Ireland) (b) 1,77 (c) M - central midfielder (d) Dundalk FC (e) UCD
*** Doyle-Hayes - Jake Doyle-Hayes (Jake Billy Doyle-Hayes) (a) 30/12/1998, Ballyjamesduff (Ireland) (b) 1,75 (c) M - central midfielder (d) Hibernian FC (e) St. Mirren, Cheltenham Town, Cambridge Utd.
*** Drabinko - Deniss Drabinko (a) 07/05/2002, Tallinn (Estonia) (b) - (c) F - left winger (d) - (e) TJK Legion, Harju JK II
*** Drabinko - Filipp Drabinko (a) 07/05/2002, Tallinn (Estonia) (b) - (c) F - center forward (d) - (e) TJK Legion, Harju JK II
*** Drachal - Dawid Drachal (a) 31/01/2005, Radom (Poland) (b) 1,82 (c) M - attacking midfielder (d) Rakow Czestochowa (e) Miedź Legnica
*** Drachmann - Janus Drachmann (a) 11/05/1988, Frederikssund (Denmark) (b) 1,79 (c) M - pivot (d) - (e) AC Horsens, Odense BK, Midtjylland, SønderjyskE, AC Horsens, Grenaa IF
*** Dragaj - Klevis Dragaj (a) 22/03/2003, Shkodër (Albania) (b) 1,86 (c) F - center forward (d) NK Lokomotiva Zagreb (e) FK Partizani
*** Dräger - Mohamed Dräger (a) 25/06/1996, Freiburg (Germany) (b) 1,81 (c) D - right back (d) Nottingham Forest (e) FC Luzern, Nottingham Forest, Olympiakos, SC Freiburg, SC Paderborn, SC Freiburg, SC Freiburg II
*** Draghia - Virgil Draghia (Virgil Drăghia) (a) 31/07/1990, Bucuresti (Romania) (b) 1,91 (c) G (d) FC Rapid 1923 (e) FC Voluntari, Daco-Getica, Concordia, Academia Rapid, Juventus Bucuresti, Rapid Bucureşti, Rapid 1923 II
*** Dragicevic - Danilo Dragicevic (Данило Драгићевић) (a) 31/08/2004, Niksic (Serbia and Montenegro, now in Montenegro) (b) 1,83 (c) M - central midfielder (d) OFK Grbalj (e) FK Budva
*** Dragićević - Marko Dragićević (Марко Драгићевић) (a) 01/06/2003, ¿? (Serbia and Montenegro, now in Montenegro) (b) 1,88 (c) D - central defense (d) FK Internacional (e) Arsenal Tivat, OSK Igalo
*** Dragojevic - Miloš Dragojevic (Miloš Dragojević) (a) 03/02/1989, Podgorica (Yugoslavia, now in Montenegro) (b) 1,90 (c) G (d) Buducnost Podgorica (e) OFK Petrovac, Pelister Bitola, OFK Beograd, FK Mladost, Widzew Lódz, Buducnost Podgorica, FK Bratstvo, Buducnost Podgorica, FK Mladost
*** Dragomir - George Dragomir (George Ionuţ Dragomir) (a) 06/08/2003, Făurei (Romania) (b) 1,79 (c) M - attacking midfielder (d) ACSM Politehnica Iasi (e) FC Botosani, Sepsi OSK, CS Faurei, Academia Hagi
*** Dragomir - Vlad Dragomir (Vlad Mihai Dragomir) (a) 24/04/1999, Timişoara (Romania) (b) 1,78 (c) M - central midfielder (d) Pafos FC (e) Virtus Entella, Perugia, ACS Poli
*** Dragoshi - Redon Dragoshi (a) 18/03/2000, Tiranë (Albania) (b) 1,82 (c) D - right back (d) KF Vllaznia (e) FK Kukësi, FC Luftëtari, KF Erzeni
*** Dragovic - Aleksandar Dragovic (Aleksandar Dragović) (a) 06/03/1991, Wien (Austria) (b) 1,86 (c) D - central defense (d) Crvena zvezda Beograd (e) Bayer Leverkusen, Leicester City, Bayer Leverkusen, Dinamo Kyïv, FC Basel, Austria Viena, Austria Wien Reserves
*** Dragovic - Nenad Dragovic (a) 04/06/1994, ¿? (Luxembourg) (b) - (c) M - central midfielder (d) US Rumelange (e) CS Fola Esch, US Rumelange, CS Fola Esch, US

Rumelange, CS Fola Esch, US Rumelange, RFCU Luxembourg, Jeunesse Esch, RFCU Luxembourg, Racing FC II

*** Dragowski - Bartlomiej Dragowski (Bartłomiej Drągowski) (a) 19/08/1997, Białystok (Poland) (b) 1,91 (c) G (d) Spezia (e) Fiorentina, Empoli, Fiorentina, Jagiellonia, Jagiellonia II

*** Dragsnes - Vetle Dragsnes (Vetle Winger Dragsnes) (a) 06/02/1994, Rælingen (Norway) (b) 1,87 (c) D - left back (d) Lillestrøm SK (e) Mjøndalen, Ullensaker/Kisa, Strømmen

*** Dragu - Andrei Dragu (Andrei Fernando Dragu) (a) 07/10/1999, Târgu Jiu (Romania) (b) 1,71 (c) F - right winger (d) FC Botosani (e) Viitorul Tîrgu Jiu, Luceafarul

*** Dragun - Stanislav Dragun (Драгун Станислав Эдуардович) (a) 04/06/1988, Minsk (Soviet Union, now in Belarus) (b) 1,82 (c) M - central midfielder (d) - (e) BATE Borisov, Orenburg, Dinamo Moskva, KS Samara, Dinamo Minsk, SKVICH, Gomel, Lokomotiv Minsk, SKVICH Minsk II

*** Dragus - Denis Dragus (Denis-Mihai Drăguș) (a) 06/07/1999, Bucuresti (Romania) (b) 1,85 (c) F - center forward (d) Standard de Lieja (e) Genoa, Standard Liège, Crotone, Standard Liège, FC Viitorul, Academia Hagi

*** Drakpe - Augustin Drakpe (a) 08/12/2001, Dordrecht (Netherlands) (b) 1,85 (c) D - central defense (d) - (e) Sparta Rotterdam

*** Drambayev - Oleksandr Drambayev (Драмбаєв Олександр Олександрович) (a) 21/04/2001, Zaporizhya (Ukraine) (b) 1,85 (c) D - left back (d) NK Osijek (e) NK Osijek, Shakhtar Donetsk, Zulte Waregem, Shakhtar Donetsk, FK Mariupol, Shakhtar Donetsk, Shakhtar II

*** Dramé - Hadji Dramé (a) 10/09/2000, Bamako (Mali) (b) 1,68 (c) F - right winger (d) - (e) FC Dila, Paide, Yeelen

*** Dramé - Hamed Dramé (Hamed Karamoko Dramé) (a) 13/06/2001, Vitry-sur-Seine (France) (b) 1,93 (c) D - central defense (d) AC Oulu (e) Francs Borains, Akritas Chlor., Rubikon, Quevilly B, Montrouge FC

*** Dramé - Ibrahima Dramé (a) 06/10/2001, Sedhiou (Senegal) (b) 1,67 (c) F - right winger (d) Bandirmaspor (e) Austria Viena, Young Violets, LASK, Juniors OÖ, LASK, Diambars FC

*** Dramé - Ismaël Dramé (a) 27/05/2001, Laval (France) (b) 1,86 (c) D - central defense (d) SO Cholet (e) Angers SCO B

*** Dramé - Soufiane Dramé (Soufiane Dramé) (a) 27/02/1996, ¿? (Slovakia) (b) 1,90 (c) D - central defense (d) FK Teplice (e) Karvina, 1.FK Pribram, Karvina, Slovácko, Vitkovice, Slovácko B

*** Dramé - Youba Dramé (Youba Dramé) (a) 16/01/1998, Béziers (France) (b) 1,85 (c) F - right winger (d) FC Zlin (e) Usti nad Labem, RCO Agde

*** Drameh - Cody Drameh (Cody Callum Pierre Drameh) (a) 08/12/2001, Dulwich, London (England) (b) 1,75 (c) D - right back (d) Leeds United (e) Luton Town, Leeds Utd., Cardiff City, Leeds Utd.

*** Drangastein - Jobin Drangastein (a) 01/11/1990, ¿? (Faroe Islands) (b) - (c) M - attacking midfielder (d) AB Argir II (e) AB Argir, AB Argir II, AB Argir, Víkingur, AB Argir

*** Drapeza - Vladislav Drapeza (Драпеза Владислав Леонидович) (a) 31/08/2001, Gomel (Belarus) (b) - (c) M - left midfielder (d) Lokomotiv Gomel (e) Lokomotiv Gomel, Gomel, Gomel II, Lokomotiv Gomel, Gomel II, Bumprom, Gomel II

*** Drapinski - Igor Drapinski (Igor Drapiński) (a) 31/05/2004, Koło (Poland) (b) 1,86 (c) D - central defense (d) Wisła Płock (e) -

*** Draxler - Julian Draxler (a) 20/09/1993, Gladbeck (Germany) (b) 1,85 (c) F - left winger (d) París Saint-Germain FC (e) Benfica, Paris Saint-Germain, VfL Wolfsburg, FC Schalke 04

*** Drazdauskas - Harvey Drazdauskas (a) 11/04/2006, ¿? (Wales) (b) - (c) M (d) Flint Town United (e) -

*** Drazdzewski - Karol Drazdzewski (Karol Drażdzewski) (a) 02/02/2002, ¿? (Poland) (b) 1,98 (c) G (d) - (e) Lech Poznan II, Wda Swiecie, Lech Poznan II, Jarota Jarocin, Lech Poznan II, Wda Swiecie

*** Drazic - Dejan Drazic (Дејан Дражић) (a) 26/09/1995, Sombor (RF Yugoslavia, now in Serbia) (b) 1,78 (c) F - left winger (d) Ethnikos Achnas (e) Radnik, Bodrum FK, Slovan Bratislava, Honvéd, Slovan Bratislava, Zagłębie, Slovan Bratislava, Zagłębie, Slovan Bratislava, Celta B, RC Celta, Real Valladolid, RC Celta, OFK Beograd, Teleoptik

*** Drazic - Stefan Drazic (Стефан Дражић) (a) 12/11/2001, ¿? (Serbia an Montenegro, now in Serbia) (b) 1,95 (c) G (d) FK Mladost GAT Novi Sad (e) -

*** Drazic - Stefan Drazic (Стефан Дражић) (a) 14/08/1992, Beograd (RF Yugoslavia, now in Serbia) (b) 1,87 (c) F - center forward (d) Mezőkövesd Zsóry FC (e) Diósgyőr, CC Yatai, Mezőkövesd, KV Mechelen, Vozdovac, Javor-Matis, Radnicki Obrenovac

*** Drchal - Vaclav Drchal (Václav Drchal) (a) 25/07/1999, České Budějovice (Czech Rep.) (b) 1,87 (c) F - center forward (d) FK Jablonec (e) Sparta Praha, Bohemians 1905, Sparta Praha, Dynamo Dresden, Sparta Praha, Mlada Boleslav, Sparta Praha

*** Dreksa - Pavel Dreksa (a) 17/09/1989, Prostějov (Czechoslovakia, now in Czech Rep.) (b) 1,85 (c) D - central defense (d) Enosis Neon Paralimniou (e) Zbrojovka Brno, Karvina, Neftchi Baku, Karvina, 1.SC Znojmo, Sigma Olomouc, Banik Ostrava, Sigma Olomouc, Usti nad Labem, Sigma Olomouc, Sigma Olomouc B

*** Dresaj - Jonathan Dresaj (Џонатан Дрешај) (a) 15/03/2000, ¿? (RF Yugoslavia, now in Montenegro) (b) - (c) D - right back (d) FK Decic Tuzi (e) -

*** Dresevic - Ibrahim Dresevic (Ibrahim Dreshaj) (a) 24/01/1997, Fuxerna (Sweden) (b) 1,86 (c) D - central defense (d) Fatih Karagümrük (e) Heerenveen, Elfsborg

*** Dreskovic - Meldin Dreskovic (Мелдин Дрешковић) (a) 26/03/1998, Plav (RF Yugoslavia, now in Montenegro) (b) 1,91 (c) D - central defense (d) Debreceni VSC (e) Sutjeska Niksic, FK Jezero, Mladost Ljes, FK Jezero

*** Drexler - Dominick Drexler (a) 26/05/1990, Bonn (Germany) (b) 1,83 (c) M - attacking midfielder (d) FC Schalke 04 (e) 1.FC Köln, Midtjylland, Holstein Kiel, VfR Aalen, Greuther Fürth, Rot-Weiß Erfurt, Bayer Leverkusen II

*** Dreyer - Anders Dreyer (Anders Laustrup Dreyer) (a) 02/05/1998, Bramming (Denmark) (b) 1,74 (c) F - right winger (d) RSC Anderlecht (e) Midtjylland, Rubin Kazan, Midtjylland, Rubin Kazan, Midtjylland, Brighton & Hove Albion, Heerenveen, Brighton & Hove Albion, St. Mirren, Brighton & Hove Albion, Esbjerg fB

*** Drezgic - Uros Drezgic (Урош Дрезгић) (a) 04/10/2002, Šabac (RF Yugoslavia, now in Serbia) (b) 1,90 (c) D - central defense (d) FK Čukarički (e) -

*** Drif - Achraf Drif (a) 22/03/1992, Nancy (France) (b) 1,78 (c) F - left winger (d) Jeunesse Esch (e) Swift Hesperange, CS Fola Esch, US Hostert, FC Lunéville, Jarville JF, AS Nancy B

*** Drina - Ajdin Drina (a) 22/03/2004, Sarajevo (Bosnia and Herzegovina) (b) - (c) M - central midfielder (d) FK Radnik Hadzici (e) Radnik Hadzici, Velez Mostar, J. Bihac

*** Drina - Amar Drina (a) 30/05/2002, Sarajevo (Bosnia and Herzegovina) (b) 1,86 (c) D - central defense (d) FK Zeljeznicar Sarajevo (e) -

*** Drincic - Milos Drincic (Miloš Drinčić) (a) 14/02/1999, ¿? (RF Yugoslavia, now in Montenegro) (b) 1,95 (c) D - central defense (d) Kerala Blasters FC (e) Soligorsk, Sutjeska Niksic, FK Iskra

*** Driomovas - Ignas Driomovas (a) 27/04/1997, Gargzdai (Lithuania) (b) 1,91 (c) G (d) FK Panevezys (e) Banga, Egersund, Banga, Egersund, Stumbras, Banga, Banga B, SK Taskas Gargzdai

*** Driouech - Couhaib Driouech (a) 17/04/2002, Haarlem (Netherlands) (b) 1,75 (c) F - left winger (d) Excelsior Rotterdam (e) -

*** Drkusic - Vanja Drkusic (Vanja Drkušić) (a) 30/10/1999, Novo mesto (Slovenia) (b) 1,88 (c) D - central defense (d) FK Sochi (e) NK Bravo, Rende, Heerenveen

*** Drljevic - Amer Drljevic (Amer Drljević) (a) 18/05/1994, Goražde (Bosnia and Herzegovina) (b) 1,90 (c) M - central midfielder (d) FK Igman Konjic (e) Slavija S., FK Olimpik, Igman Konjic, FK Gorazde, FK Olimpik, FK Gorazde

*** Drljo - Andrija Drljo (a) 06/09/2002, Mostar (Bosnia and Herzegovina) (b) 1,81 (c) F - right winger (d) FK Zeljeznicar Sarajevo (e) Zrinjski Mostar, MTK Budapest II, Szentlőrinc SE, MTK Budapest II

*** Drmic - Josip Drmic (Josip Drmić) (a) 08/08/1992, Lachen (Switzerland) (b) 1,84 (c) F - center forward (d) GNK Dinamo Zagreb (e) Norwich City, HNK Rijeka, Norwich City, Borussia Mönchengladbach, SV Hamburg, Borussia Mönchengladbach, Bayer Leverkusen, 1.FC Nürnberg, FC Zürich

*** Drobarov - Vlatko Drobarov (Влатко Дробаров) (a) 02/11/1992, Skopje (North Macedonia) (b) 1,87 (c) D - central defense (d) Cherno More Varna (e) FK Sarajevo, Cherno More, Kerala Blasters, Belasica, Ohod Club, Aris Limassol, Banants, Teteks Tetovo, Murciélagos, Teteks Tetovo, Napredok Kicevo, FK Skopje, Vardar

*** Drobnjak - Marko Drobnjak (Марко Дробњак) (a) 17/05/1995, Čačak (RF Yugoslavia, now in Serbia) (b) 1,96 (c) G (d) Marsaxlokk FC (e) Radnicki Niš, FC Sevan, Novi Pazar, FK Josanica, Zlatibor, Podbrezova, Polet Ljubic, Borac Cacak, Polet Ljubic, Borac Cacak, Radnicki 1923, Borac Cacak, Polet Ljubic, Borac Cacak

*** Drobysh - Maksim Drobysh (Дробыш Максим Андреевич) (a) 30/01/2001, Vitebsk (Belarus) (b) - (c) M - central midfielder (d) FK Vitebsk (e) Vitebsk II

*** Drommel - Joël Drommel (a) 16/11/1996, Bussum (Netherlands) (b) 1,92 (c) G (d) PSV Eindhoven (e) FC Twente

*** Dronov - Nikita Dronov (a) 25/04/2002, Tallinn (Estonia) (b) - (c) F - center forward (d) - (e) Kalev, Maardu II

*** Droppa - Lukas Droppa (Lukáš Droppa) (a) 22/04/1989, Uherské Hradiště (Czechoslovakia, now in Czech Rep.) (b) 1,83 (c) M - pivot (d) FC Voluntari (e) Gaz Metan, Shakhter K., Slovan Bratislava, Bandirmaspor, Tom Tomsk, Pandurii, Śląsk Wroclaw, Banik Ostrava, Sparta Praha B, Graffin Vlasim, Sparta Praha B

*** Drori - Nir David Drori (דרורי דוד ניר) (a) 25/12/2001, ¿? (Israel) (b) 1,79 (c) D - left back (d) Ironi Kiryat Shmona (e) -

*** Dros - Cristian Dros (a) 15/04/1998, Bălți (Moldova) (b) 1,85 (c) M - pivot (d) Slavia Mozyr (e) Spartaks, Slavia, Spartaks, SSU Poli, Zaria Balti

*** Droste - Wout Droste (a) 20/05/1989, Oldenzaal (Netherlands) (b) 1,80 (c) D - right back (d) - (e) ÍA Akranes, Go Ahead Eagles, Heracles Almelo, SC Cambuur, Go Ahead Eagles

*** Drozdek - Domagoj Drozdek (Domagoj Drožđek) (a) 20/03/1996, Varaždin (Croatia) (b) 1,80 (c) F - left winger (d) NK Varazdin (e) Busan IPark, NK Lokomotiva, NK Varazdin, NK Lokomotiva, NK Varazdin, Borussia Dortmund II

*** Druijf - Ferdy Druijf (a) 12/02/1998, Uitgeest (Netherlands) (b) 1,90 (c) F - center forward (d) PEC Zwolle (e) PEC Zwolle, Rapid Wien, AZ Alkmaar, Rapid Wien, AZ Alkmaar, KV Mechelen, AZ Alkmaar, NEC Nijmegen

*** Drygas - Kamil Drygas (Kamil Drygas) (a) 07/09/1991, Kępno (Poland) (b) 1,84 (c) M - pivot (d) Miedź Legnica (e) Pogon Szczecin, Zawisza, Lech Poznan, Zawisza, Lech Poznan, Lech Poznan II

*** Dryselius - Viktor Dryselius (a) 11/09/2003, ¿? (Sweden) (b) 1,80 (c) G (d) Varbergs BoIS (e) Vinbergs IF, Varbergs BoIS, Varbergs GIF, Varbergs BoIS, Vinbergs IF, Varbergs BoIS, Tvååkers IF, Varbergs BoIS

*** Dryshlyuk - Kyrylo Dryshlyuk (Дришлюк Кирило Павлович) (a) 16/09/1999, Boryspil, Kyiv Oblast (Ukraine) (b) 1,85 (c) M - central midfielder (d) Zorya Lugansk (e) FK Oleksandriya, Spartaks, FK Oleksandriya, Zirka, Zirka II

*** D'Sena - Ryley D'Sena (a) 31/01/2003, Sydney (Australia) (b) - (c) D - central defense (d) - (e) Larne FC, Bangor, Larne FC

*** Duarte - Alexis Duarte (Alexis David Duarte Pereira) (a) 12/03/2000, Itauguá (Paraguay) (b) 1,85 (c) D - central defense (d) FC Spartak de Moscú (e) Cerro Porteño

*** Duarte - André Duarte (André Lourenço Duarte) (a) 12/09/1997, Sacavém (Portugal) (b) 1,95 (c) D - central defense (d) AC Reggiana 1919 (e) FC U Craiova, CF Estrela, Praiense, Alverca, Sacavenense

*** Duarte - Deroy Duarte (a) 04/07/1999, Rotterdam (Netherlands) (b) 1,77 (c) M - central midfielder (d) Fortuna Sittard (e) Sparta Rotterdam

*** Duarte - Domingos Duarte (Domingos de Sousa Coutinho Meneses Duarte) (a) 10/03/1995, Cascais (Portugal) (b) 1,92 (c) D - central defense (d) Getafe CF (e) Granada CF, Sporting Lisboa, RC Deportivo, Sporting Lisboa, Chaves, Sporting Lisboa, Sporting B, Belenenses, Sporting B

*** Duarte - Frederico Duarte (Frederico Fonseca Pires de Almeida Duarte) (a) 30/03/1999, Lisboa (Portugal) (b) 1,75 (c) F - left winger (d) Panetolikos GFS (e) Vilafranquense, Panetolikos, Vilafranquense, Sacavenense

*** Duarte - John-Paul Duarte (a) 13/12/1986, Gibraltar (Gibraltar) (b) 1,73 (c) F - center forward (d) Mons Calpe SC (e) Bruno's Magpies, St Joseph's FC, Manchester 62, Lincoln FC

*** Duarte - Jonathan Duarte (Jonathan Alexander Duarte Durán) (a) 29/05/1997, Socorro (Colombia) (b) - (c) F - right winger (d) FC Ararat-Armenia (e) Orsomarso SC, Real Santander

*** Duarte - Laros Duarte (Laros d'Encarnação Duarte) (a) 28/02/1997, Rotterdam (Netherlands) (b) 1,80 (c) M - pivot (d) FC Groningen (e) Sparta Rotterdam

*** Duarte - Léo Duarte (Leonardo Campos Duarte Da Silva) (a) 17/07/1996, Mococa (Brazil) (b) 1,83 (c) D - central defense (d) Basaksehir FK (e) AC Milan, Basaksehir, AC Milan, Flamengo, Flamengo B

*** Dubek - Tomas Dubek (Tomáš Ďubek) (a) 22/01/1987, Zvolen (Czechoslovakia, now in Slovakia) (b) 1,78 (c) M - attacking midfielder (d) ViOn Zlate Moravce-Vrable (e) Zalaegerszeg, Ružomberok, Slovan Liberec, Ružomberok

*** Dubickas - Augustas Dubickas (a) 17/03/2001, ¿? (Lithuania) (b) - (c) D - central defense (d) FK Suduva Marijampole (e) Marijampole C., FC Brandenburg, Suduva B, Marijampoles FM

*** Dubinchak - Vladyslav Dubinchak (Дубінчак Владислав Юрійович) (a) 01/07/1998, Tomashpil, Vinnytsya Oblast (Ukraine) (b) 1,73 (c) D - left back (d) FC Dinamo de Kiev (e) SK Dnipro-1, Dinamo Kyïv, Dinamo Kiev II, SK Dnipro-1, Dinamo Kiev II, Karpaty, Dinamo Kiev II, Arsenal Kyiv, Dinamo Kiev II

*** Dubljanic - Miso Dubljanic (Mišo Dubljanić) (a) 20/12/1999, Nikšić (RF Yugoslavia, now in Montenegro) (b) 2,03 (c) G (d) - (e) Spartak, Ceske Budejovice B, Sutjeska II

*** Dubljevic - Balsa Dubljevic (Балша Дубљевић) (a) 02/12/2001, ¿? (RF Yugoslavia, now in Montenegro) (b) 1,77 (c) M - central midfielder (d) FK Mornar Bar (e) OFK Petrovac, OSK Igalo, Sutjeska Niksic, Sutjeska II

*** Dubljevic - Rados Dubljevic (Радош Дубљевић) (a) 22/04/2002, ¿? (RF Yugoslavia, now in Montenegro) (b) 1,90 (c) G (d) FK Sutjeska Niksic (e) FK Ibar, Sutjeska Niksic, FK Bokelj, Sutjeska Niksic, Sutjeska II, FK Bokelj, Sutjeska II

*** Dubois - Léo Dubois (Léo Michel Joseph Claude Dubois) (a) 14/09/1994, Segré (France) (b) 1,78 (c) D - right back (d) Galatasaray (e) Olympique Lyon, FC Nantes, FC Nantes B

*** Dubov - Nikita Dubov (Дубов Никита Романович) (a) 15/08/2000, Hastings (England) (b) 1,73 (c) D - right back (d) Akritas Chlorakas (e) Pafos FC, Akritas Chlor., Pafos FC, Pegia 2014, Pafos FC

*** Dubova - Muhamed Dubova (a) 14/06/2001, ¿? (RF Yugoslavia, now in Kosovo) (b) - (c) M - attacking midfielder (d) FC Prishtina (e) Dubnica, SC Gjilani, KF Vitia, SC Gjilani

*** Dubra - Kaspars Dubra (a) 20/12/1990, Riga (Soviet Union, now in Latvia) (b) 1,90 (c) D (d) FK Panevezys (e) RFS, FK Oleksandriya, Irtysh, RFS, BATE Borisov, JFK Ventspils, Polonia Bytom, Skonto, Olimps Riga, Skonto, Olimps Riga

*** Dúbravka - Martin Dúbravka (a) 15/01/1989, Žilina (Czechoslovakia, now in Slovakia) (b) 1,91 (c) G (d) Newcastle United (e) Manchester Utd., Newcastle Utd., Sparta Praha, Newcastle Utd., Sparta Praha, Slovan Liberec, Esbjerg fB, MSK Zilina

*** Dubrovin - Daniil Dubrovin (Дубровин Даниил) (a) 11/07/2002, ¿? (Kazakhstan) (b) 1,77 (c) F - right winger (d) Tobol Kostanay II (e) -

*** Ducan - Razvan Ducan (Răzvan Cristian Ducan) (a) 09/02/2001, Videle (Romania) (b) 1,92 (c) G (d) FC Botosani (e) FCSB, CS Mioveni, FCSB, AFC Turris, FCSB, FC Arges, FCSB

*** Ducksch - Marvin Ducksch (a) 07/03/1994, Dortmund (Germany) (b) 1,88 (c) F - center forward (d) SV Werder Bremen (e) Hannover 96, Fortuna Düsseldorf, FC St. Pauli, Holstein Kiel, FC St. Pauli, Borussia Dortmund II, Borussia Dortmund, SC Paderborn, Borussia Dortmund, Borussia Dortmund II

*** Duda - Ondrej Duda (a) 05/12/1994, Snina (Slovakia) (b) 1,81 (c) M - attacking midfielder (d) Hellas Verona (e) 1.FC Köln, Hellas Verona, 1.FC Köln, Hertha Berlin, Norwich City, Hertha Berlin, Legia Warszawa, MFK Košice

*** Dudar - Dmitriy Dudar (Дударь Дмитрий Николаевич) (a) 08/11/1991, Grodno (Soviet Union, now in Belarus) (b) 1,97 (c) G (d) Torpedo-BelAZ Zhodino (e) Neman Grodno, Gomel, FK Slutsk, Granit, Dynamo Brest, Svetlogorsk, Neman-Belkard, Dinamo Minsk II

*** Dudek - Mateusz Dudek (a) 14/12/2002, Kolbuszowa (Poland) (b) 1,86 (c) G (d) Stal Mielec (e) Olimpia Elblag, Stal Mielec, Stal Mielec II

*** Dudik - Artem Dudik (Дудік Артем Ростиславович) (a) 02/01/1997, Kamin-Kashyrskyi, Volyn Oblast (Ukraine) (b) 1,73 (c) F - right winger (d) Barycz Sułów (e) Metalist 1925, VPK-Agro, Agrobiznes V., Sandecja, Shakhtar II, FK Mariupol, Shakhtar II, FK Slutsk, Shakhtar II, Volyn Lutsk, Volyn Lutsk II

*** Dudu - Dudu (Eduardo dos Santos Haesler) (a) 10/02/1999, Duisburg (Germany) (b) 1,96 (c) G (d) SV Werder Bremen (e) Nordsjælland, Werder Bremen, Werder Bremen II

*** Dudziak - Jeremy Dudziak (Jeremy Calvin Dudziak) (a) 28/08/1995, Hamburg (Germany) (b) 1,76 (c) D - left back (d) Hertha Berlín (e) Greuther Fürth, Hatayspor,

Greuther Fürth, SV Hamburg, FC St. Pauli, Borussia Dortmund, Borussia Dortmund II

*** Duelund - Mikkel Duelund (Mikkel Duelund Poulsen) (a) 29/06/1997, Aarhus (Denmark) (b) 1,78 (c) F - left winger (d) Aarhus GF (e) Aarhus GF, Dinamo Kyïv, NEC Nijmegen, Dinamo Kyïv, Midtjylland, Aarhus GF II

*** Duesund - Eskil Topland Duesund (a) 20/08/2006, Grimstad (Norway) (b) - (c) F (d) FK Jerv (e) FK Jerv II

*** Dufek - Ladislav Dufek (a) 23/12/2002, ¿? (Czech Rep.) (b) - (c) F - left winger (d) FK Varnsdorf (e) Varnsdorf, Mlada Boleslav B, Pardubice, Mlada Boleslav B, SK Benesov

*** Duffy - Damian Duffy (a) 12/11/2002, Gleneely, Donegal (Ireland) (b) 1,73 (c) M - central midfielder (d) Finn Harps (e) -

*** Duffy - Dylan Duffy (a) 28/11/2002, ¿? (Ireland) (b) 1,89 (c) M - left midfielder (d) Lincoln City (e) UCD, Shamrock Rovers

*** Duffy - Flynn Duffy (Flynn Alistair Duffy) (a) 13/08/2003, Dundee (Scotland) (b) 1,74 (c) D - left back (d) Dundee United FC (e) Stirling Albion, Dundee United, Peterhead FC, Dundee United

*** Duffy - Michael Duffy (a) 28/07/1994, Derry (Northern Ireland) (b) - (c) F - left winger (d) Derry City (e) Dundalk FC, Celtic FC, Dundee FC, Celtic FC, Alloa Athletic, Celtic FC, Derry City

*** Duffy - Shane Duffy (Shane Patrick Michael Duffy) (a) 01/01/1992, Derry (Northern Ireland) (b) 1,93 (c) D - central defense (d) Norwich City (e) Fulham, Brighton & Hove Albion, Fulham, Brighton & Hove Albion, Celtic FC, Brighton & Hove Albion, Blackburn, Everton, Yeovil Town, Everton, Scunthorpe Utd., Everton, Burnley, Everton, Foyle Harps

*** Duga - Denis Duga (a) 05/09/1994, Myjava (Slovakia) (b) 1,76 (c) M - central midfielder (d) ViOn Zlate Moravce-Vrable (e) FK Senica, Vlasim, Spartak Myjava

*** Dugalic - Rade Dugalic (Раде Дугалић) (a) 05/11/1992, Niš (RF Yugoslavia, now in Serbia) (b) 1,94 (c) D - central defense (d) Meizhou Hakka (e) Kairat Almaty, Enisey, Tosno, Armavir, Ulisses, Radnicki Niš, Car Konstantin, Radnicki Niš, FK Olimpik, Radnicki Niš

*** Dugan - Elliott Dugan (a) 18/09/2000, Bath (England) (b) 1,83 (c) F - center forward (d) - (e) Haverfordwest, Portadown, Kouris Erimis, APEA Akrotiri, Ytterhogdals IK

*** Dugandzic - Marko Dugandzic (Marko Dugandžić) (a) 07/04/1994, Osijek (Croatia) (b) 1,90 (c) F - center forward (d) FC Rapid 1923 (e) CFR Cluj, Sochi, FC Botosani, NK Osijek, Matera, Ternana U., NK Osijek, Ternana, NK Osijek

*** Duggan - Jamie Duggan (a) 20/09/2004, ¿? (Ireland) (b) 1,85 (c) D - right back (d) University College Dublin (e) -

*** Dugimont - Rémy Dugimont (a) 01/07/1986, Saint-Cloud (France) (b) 1,82 (c) F - left winger (d) JS Saint-Pierroise (e) AJ Auxerre, Clermont Foot, FC Rouen 1899, AS Poissy, Levallois SC

*** Duhaney - Demeaco Duhaney (Demeaco D'Vaughn Duhaney) (a) 13/10/1998, Manchester (England) (b) 1,80 (c) D - right back (d) Istanbulspor (e) Stoke City, Istanbulspor, Stoke City, Huddersfield Town, Boston Utd.

*** Duin - Jelle Duin (a) 27/01/1999, Heemstede (Netherlands) (b) 1,86 (c) F - center forward (d) AZ Alkmaar (e) Aarhus GF, AZ Alkmaar, MVV Maastricht, FC Volendam

*** Dujmovic - Duje Dujmovic (Duje Dujmović) (a) 15/12/2003, Split (Croatia) (b) 1,88 (c) D - central defense (d) HNK Sibenik (e) HNK Sibenik, HNK Rijeka, NK Solin, Uskok

*** Dujmovic - Filip Dujmovic (Filip Dujmović) (a) 04/08/2001, Zagreb (Croatia) (b) 1,73 (c) F - left winger (d) NK Kustosija Zagreb (e) HNK Rijeka, NK Jarun, NK Maksimir, HASK Zagreb

*** Dujmovic - Filip Dujmovic (Filip Dujmović) (a) 12/03/1999, Livno (Bosnia and Herzegovina) (b) 1,91 (c) G (d) FC Dinamo 1948 (e) Radnicki Niš, Spartak, Mladost Kakanj, Spartak, Mladost Kakanj

*** Dujovski - Vladimir Dujovski (Владимир Дуjовски) (a) 30/06/1996, Stip (North Macedonia) (b) 1,76 (c) M - pivot (d) Pobeda Prilep (e) FK Sasa, Bregalnica Stip, Pehcevo

*** Duk - Duk (Luís Henrique Barros Lopes) (a) 16/02/2000, Lisboa (Portugal) (b) 1,82 (c) F - center forward (d) Aberdeen FC (e) Benfica B

*** Duka - Amer Duka (a) 21/01/1999, Shijak (Albania) (b) 1,83 (c) D - central defense (d) KF Erzeni (e) KF Tërbuni, KF Korabi, KF Dukagjini, KS Kastrioti, KF Skënderbeu, FC Luftëtari, KF Teuta, KF Erzeni, KF Teuta, KF Laçi

*** Duka - Anxhelo Duka (a) 06/03/2002, Shijak (Albania) (b) - (c) F - center forward (d) - (e) KF Korabi

*** Duka - Nikolin Duka (a) 05/01/2000, Devoll (Albania) (b) - (c) D - right back (d) KF Laçi (e) KF Korabi, KF Devolli, Lorca FC

*** Duka - Tomislav Duka (a) 07/09/1992, Split (Croatia) (b) 1,91 (c) G (d) FK Zalgiris Vilnius (e) Zagora Unesic, NK Istra, Hajduk Split, CFR Cluj, RNK Split, NK Imotski, RNK Split, Zagora Unesic, RNK Split, NK Kamen, RNK Split

*** Dulaev - Dzhambulat Dulaev (Дулаев Джамбулат Олегович) (a) 18/10/1998, ¿? (Russia) (b) 1,79 (c) F - center forward (d) - (e) Khimki 2, Dolgoprudnyi, Mashuk, Olimp Khimki, Olimp 2, Rostov II, Alania

*** Dulanto - Gustavo Dulanto (Gustavo Alfonso Dulanto Sanguinetti) (a) 09/05/1995, Lima (Peru) (b) 1,96 (c) D - central defense (d) Riga FC (e) FC Sheriff, Boavista, Cusco FC, UTC, Universitario, Rosario Central II

*** Dulca - Marco Dulca (Marco Alexandru Dulca) (a) 11/05/1999, Pohang, Gyeongbuk (South Korea) (b) 1,84 (c) M - pivot (d) - (e) Chindia, FCSB, Chindia, FCV Farul, Chindia, FC Viitorul

*** Dulcetti - Mario Dulcetti (a) 18/03/2004, ¿? (Italy) (b) - (c) F (d) - (e) Murata

*** Dulovic - Momcilo Dulovic (a) 25/05/1992, ¿? (RF Yugoslavia, now in Montenegro) (b) 1,95 (c) D - central defense (d) Jedinstvo Bijelo Polje (e) FK Berane, Prespa Birlik, FK Podgorica, Jagodina, Jedinstvo, FK Berane, Jedinstvo, Čukarički, Rudar Pljevlja

*** Dumani - Gentrit Dumani (a) 13/07/1993, ¿? (RF Yugoslavia, now in Kosovo) (b) - (c) D - left back (d) KF Trepca 89 (e) KF Trepca 89, FC Prishtina, FC Malisheva, KF Drenica, KF Flamurtari, FC Prishtina, KF Flamurtari, FC Prishtina, KF Fushë Kosova

*** Dumbrava - Vitalie Dumbrava (a) 23/04/2004, ¿? (Moldova) (b) - (c) D - left back (d) Dacia Buiucani (e) -

*** Dumbravanu - Daniel Dumbravanu (Daniel Dumbrăvanu) (a) 22/07/2001, Bălţi (Moldova) (b) 1,92 (c) D - central defense (d) SPAL (e) APOEL FC, SPAL, Genoa, Siena, Genoa, Lucchese, Zaria Balti

*** Dumenco - Roman Dumenco (a) 30/07/2004, ¿? (Moldava) (b) 1,85 (c) G (d) FC Sheriff-2 Tiraspol (e) -

*** Dumfries - Denzel Dumfries (Denzel Justus Morris Dumfries) (a) 18/04/1996, Rotterdam (Netherlands) (b) 1,88 (c) M - right midfielder (d) Internazionale Milano (e) PSV Eindhoven, Heerenveen, Sparta Rotterdam

*** Dumiter - Andrei Dumiter (Ioan Andrei Vasile Dumiter) (a) 10/04/1999, Timişoara (Romania) (b) 1,84 (c) F - center forward (d) FC Voluntari (e) FCSB, Sepsi

OSK, Chindia, Sepsi OSK, Ripensia, LPS Banatul, Ripensia, LPS Banatul, Nova Mama Mia, LPS Banatul

*** Dumitrache - Valentin Dumitrache (Valentin-Laurențiu Dumitrache) (a) 29/03/2003, Buzău (Romania) (b) - (c) F - center forward (d) AS FC Buzau (e) FC Buzau, FCV Farul, FCV Farul II, Academica Clinceni, LPS Buzău

*** Dumitrascu - Denis Dumitrascu (Denis Constantin Dumitrașcu) (a) 27/04/1995, Râmnicu Vâlcea (Romania) (b) 1,82 (c) M - left midfielder (d) UTA Arad (e) Chindia, FC Arges, Chindia, Rm. Valcea

*** Dumitrescu - Andres Dumitrescu (Andres Mihai Dumitrescu) (a) 11/03/2001, Slatina (Romania) (b) - (c) D - left back (d) Sepsi OSK Sf. Gheorghe (e) -

*** Dumitriu - Lucian Dumitriu (Lucian Mihai Dumitriu) (a) 21/09/1992, Bârlad (Romania) (b) 1,80 (c) M - central midfielder (d) Petrolul Ploiesti (e) CS Mioveni, Academica Clinceni, FC Hermannstadt, Foresta Suceava, SC Bacău

*** Dumitru - Cristian Dumitru (Cristian Cosmin Dumitru) (a) 13/12/2001, Buzău (Romania) (b) 1,73 (c) F - left winger (d) AS FC Buzau (e) FC Voluntari, FCSB, CS Mioveni, FCSB, FC Arges, FCSB, FC Arges, FCSB, Academica Clinceni, FCSB, Academica Clinceni, FCSB, FCSB II, Academica Clinceni, FCSB II

*** Dummett - Paul Dummett (a) 26/09/1991, Newcastle upon Tyne (England) (b) 1,83 (c) D - left back (d) Newcastle United (e) St. Mirren, Newcastle Utd., St. Mirren, Newcastle Utd., Gateshead, Newcastle Reserves

*** Dummigan - Cameron Dummigan (a) 02/06/1996, Lurgan (Northern Ireland) (b) 1,80 (c) D - right back (d) Derry City (e) Dundalk FC, Crusaders, Dundalk FC, Oldham Athletic

*** Dumont - Olivier Dumont (a) 06/03/2002, Visé (Belgium) (b) 1,82 (c) M - central midfielder (d) Sint-Truidense VV (e) SL16 FC

*** Dumrath - Bela Dumrath (a) 18/11/2003, Hamburg (Germany) (b) 1,98 (c) G (d) FC St. Gallen 1879 (e) Chur 97

*** Dunachie - Logan Dunachie (a) 03/02/2004, Cumbernauld (Scotland) (b) 2,00 (c) D - central defense (d) Clyde FC (e) Motherwell B, Forfar Athletic, Motherwell B, East Kilbride, Motherwell B

*** Dunaev - Aleksey Dunaev (Дунаев Алексей Валерьевич) (a) 11/09/2004, Donetsk (Ukraine) (b) - (c) D - central defense (d) Dnepr Mogilev (e) Dnepr-Yuni Mogilev

*** Duncan - Alfred Duncan (Joseph Alfred Duncan) (a) 10/03/1993, Accra (Ghana) (b) 1,78 (c) M - central midfielder (d) Fiorentina (e) Cagliari, Fiorentina, Sassuolo, Fiorentina, Sassuolo, Sampdoria, Sassuolo, Sampdoria, Internazionale Milano, Sampdoria, Internazionale Milano, AS Livorno, Internazionale Milano, AS Livorno, Internazionale Milano

*** Duncan - Dylan Duncan (a) 25/01/1999, London (England) (b) 1,78 (c) M - central midfielder (d) - (e) Finn Harps, Dunfermline A.

*** Duncan - Ryan Duncan (Ryan Andrew Duncan) (a) 18/01/2004, Keig (Scotland) (b) - (c) F - left winger (d) Aberdeen FC (e) Aberdeen FC B, Peterhead FC, Aberdeen FC B

*** Duncan - Zachary Duncan (a) 31/05/2000, Sydney (Australia) (b) 1,83 (c) M - central midfielder (d) Aarhus GF (e) Perth Glory, Aarhus GF

*** Dundjerski - David Dundjerski (Давид Дунђерски) (a) 28/10/1999, Bergamo (Italy) (b) 1,83 (c) D - right back (d) FK Spartak Subotica (e) Mladost, Proleter, Spartak

*** Dundua - Tornike Dundua (თორნიკე დუნდუა) (a) 01/10/2003, ¿? (Georgia) (b) 1,90 (c) D - central defense (d) - (e) FC Telavi, Dinamo II

*** Dungel - Peter Dungel (Peter Ďungel) (a) 06/09/1993, Nededza (Slovakia) (b) 1,88 (c) F - center forward (d) Fomat Martin (e) Povazska Byst., Liptovsky Mik., Ružomberok, Stal Mielec, Ružomberok, Stal Mielec, Pohronie, FK Senica, Pohronie, MSK Zilina B, Pohronie, MSK Zilina B, Fomat Martin, MSK Zilina B, Liptovsky Mik., MSK Zilina B

*** Dunk - Lewis Dunk (Lewis Carl Dunk) (a) 21/11/1991, Brighton (England) (b) 1,92 (c) D - central defense (d) Brighton & Hove Albion (e) Bristol City, Brighton & Hove Albion

*** Dunn - Julian Dunn (Julian Fletcher Dunn-Johnson) (a) 11/07/2000, Toronto, Ontario (Canada) (b) 1,91 (c) D - central defense (d) Hamarkameratene (e) Toronto, Toronto FC II, Toronto, Valour FC, Toronto, Toronto FC II, Toronto FC II

*** Dunne - Alex Dunne (a) 05/08/2002, ¿? (Ireland) (b) 1,72 (c) D - right back (d) University College Dublin (e) Shamrock Rovers

*** Dunne - Charles Dunne (a) 13/02/1993, London (England) (b) 1,88 (c) D - left back (d) St. Mirren FC (e) Motherwell FC, Oldham Athletic, Blackpool, Crawley Town, Blackpool, Wycombe Wanderers, Blackpool, Wycombe Wanderers, Staines Town FC

*** Dunne - Declan Dunne (a) 31/03/2000, Belfast (Northern Ireland) (b) 1,92 (c) G (d) Dungannon Swifts (e) Cliftonville, Portadown, Cliftonville

*** Dunsby - Jakob Dunsby (Jakob Maslø Dunsby) (a) 13/03/2000, Nøtterøy (Norway) (b) 1,74 (c) F - right winger (d) Sandefjord Fotball (e) Egersund, Fram, Egersund, Fram, Sandefjord, Helsinki IFK, Sandefjord, Sandefjord II

*** Dunwoody - Jake Dunwoody (a) 28/09/1998, Glossop (England) (b) 1,80 (c) M - central midfielder (d) SJK Seinäjoki (e) Helsinki IFK, Derry City, Curzon Ashton, Leek Town FC

*** Dunzurov - Makhmud Dunzurov (Дунзуров Махмуд) (a) 22/03/2001, ¿? (Kazakhstan) (b) 1,75 (c) F - right winger (d) SD Family Nur-Sultan (e) Astana-M

*** Duo - Dylan Duo (a) 17/01/2006, Gibraltar (Gibraltar) (b) 1,70 (c) M - pivot (d) St Joseph's FC Reserve (e) -

*** Duparchy - Florent Duparchy (a) 20/06/2000, Lyon (France) (b) 1,87 (c) G (d) EA Guingamp (e) Stade Reims B, Olymp. Lyon B, AJ Auxerre B

*** Dupé - Maxime Dupé (a) 04/03/1993, Malestroit (France) (b) 1,88 (c) G (d) RSC Anderlecht (e) Toulouse, FC Nantes, Clermont Foot, FC Nantes, FC Nantes B

*** Dupire - Geordan Dupire (a) 28/09/1993, Valenciennes (France) (b) 1,93 (c) G (d) Swift Hesperange (e) US Hostert, RE Virton, US Boulogne, UR Namur, RAEC Mons, Lorient B

*** Dupovac - Amer Dupovac (a) 29/05/1991, Sarajevo (Yugoslavia, now in Bosnia and Herzegovina) (b) 1,88 (c) D - central defense (d) FK Igman Konjic (e) FK Sarajevo, Igman Konjic, FK Sarajevo, Borac Cacak, RNK Split, FC Sheriff, FK Sarajevo

*** Dupree - Jamal Dupree (a) 11/08/1997, Belfast (Northern Ireland) (b) 1,78 (c) M - attacking midfielder (d) Ards FC (e) Carrick Rangers, Derriaghy, Portadown, Waterford FC, Evergreen Hawks, Queen's Uni, Derriaghy

*** Duracak - Amar Duracak (Amar Duračak) (a) 17/06/1992, Rijeka (Croatia) (b) 1,87 (c) D - central defense (d) RUS Ethe Belmont (e) US Hostert, RUS Ethe, FC Mamer 32, FCJL Arlon, NK Krk, NK Pomorac, NK Krk

*** Durak - Abdullah Durak (a) 01/04/1987, Nigde (Turkey) (b) 1,81 (c) M - central midfielder (d) Genclerbirligi Ankara (e) Ankaragücü, Çaykur Rizespor, Kasimpasa, Kayserispor, Kastamonuspor

*** Durakovic - Elvir Durakovic (a) 07/02/2000, Bugojno (Bosnia and Herzegovina) (b) - (c) D - left back (d) FK Sarajevo (e) Igman Konjic, Mladost Kakanj, FK Tuzla City, Br. Gracanica

*** Durán - Jhon Durán (Jhon Jader Durán Palacio) (a) 13/12/2003, Medellín (Colombia) (b) 1,85 (c) F - center forward (d) Aston Villa (e) Chicago, Envigado

*** Durán - Pablo Durán (Pablo Durán Fernández) (a) 25/05/2001, Tomiño (Spain) (b) 1,76 (c) F - center forward (d) RC Celta Fortuna (e) SD Compostela, Porriño FC

*** Duranski - Filip Duranski (Филип Дурански) (a) 17/07/1991, Skopje (Yugoslavia, now in North Macedonia) (b) 1,74 (c) M - central midfielder (d) FK Skopje (e) Olympiakos N., KF Egnatia, FC Sevan, Sileks, SKF Sered, Sileks, Rabotnicki, Sileks, Rabotnicki, FK Skopje, Horizont, Slavia Praha B, Mlada Boleslav, Slavia Praha B

*** Duranville - Julien Duranville (a) 05/05/2006, Uccle (Belgium) (b) 1,70 (c) F - right winger (d) Borussia Dortmund (e) RSC Anderlecht

*** Durdov - Ivan Durdov (a) 17/07/2000, Split (Croatia) (b) 1,94 (c) F - center forward (d) KV Oostende (e) Domžale, NK Orijent 1919, NK Solin, NK Rudes, NK Osijek II, NK Solin, NK Osijek II, Adriatic Split

*** Duriatti - Luca Duriatti (a) 11/02/1998, ¿? (Luxembourg) (b) 1,66 (c) F - left winger (d) Racing FC Union Luxembourg (e) Union Titus Petange, Jeunesse Esch, Union Titus Petange, Jeunesse Esch, Swift Hesperange

*** Duris - David Duris (Dávid Ďuriš) (a) 22/03/1999, Žilina (Slovakia) (b) 1,86 (c) F - left winger (d) MSK Zilina (e) MSK Zilina B

*** Duris - Michal Duris (Michal Ďuriš) (a) 01/06/1988, Uherské Hradiště (Czechoslovakia, now in Czech Rep.) (b) 1,83 (c) F - center forward (d) Othellos Athienou (e) Karmiotissa, Ethnikos, Omonia Nicosia, Anorthosis, Orenburg, Anorthosis, Orenburg, Viktoria Plzen, Mlada Boleslav, Viktoria Plzen, Banska Bystrica

*** Duriska - Lukas Duriska (Lukáš Ďuriška) (a) 16/08/1992, Trenčín (Czechoslovakia, now in Slovakia) (b) 1,91 (c) D - central defense (d) - (e) AS Trencin, Z. Sosnowiec, Olimpia Grudz., Rakow, Ruch, Rakow, Frydek-Mistek, AS Trencin, Mosta FC, AS Trencin, AGOVV, AS Trencin

*** Durmaz - Jimmy Durmaz (Jakup Jimmy Durmaz) (a) 22/03/1989, Örebro (Sweden) (b) 1,80 (c) M - central midfielder (d) AIK Solna (e) Karagümrük, Galatasaray, Karagümrük, Galatasaray, Toulouse, Olympiakos, Genclerbirligi, Malmö FF, BK Forward

*** Durmishaj - Fiorin Durmishaj (Φιορίν Ντουρμισάι) (a) 14/11/1996, Avlona (Greece) (b) 1,87 (c) F - center forward (d) Nea Salamis (e) OFI Creta, Olympiakos N., OFI Creta, Olympiakos, AE Larisa, Olympiakos, Aris Thessaloniki, Olympiakos, Waasland-Beveren, Olympiakos, Panionios, PAS Lamia, Panionios, GS Kallithea, Panionios, GS Kallithea, Panionios

*** Durmus - Ilkay Durmus (İlkay Durmuş) (a) 01/05/1994, Stuttgart (Germany) (b) 1,80 (c) F - right winger (d) - (e) Lechia Gdánsk, St. Mirren, FC Wacker, SV Ried, Austria Lustenau, FAC, Antalyaspor, Genclerbirligi

*** Duro - Hugo Duro (Hugo Duro Perales) (a) 10/11/1999, Getafe (Spain) (b) 1,82 (c) F - center forward (d) Valencia CF (e) Getafe CF, Valencia CF, Getafe CF, RM Castilla, Getafe CF, Getafe CF B

*** Duronjic - Borko Duronjic (Борко Дуроњић) (a) 24/09/1997, Banja Luka (Bosnia and Herzegovina) (b) 1,73 (c) F - left winger (d) FK Radnik Surdulica (e) Radnicki Niš, FK TSC, Vozdovac, OFK Beograd

*** Durosinmi - Rafiu Durosinmi (Rafiu Adekunle Durosinmi) (a) 01/01/2003, Lagos (Nigeria) (b) 1,92 (c) F - center forward (d) FC Viktoria Plzen (e) Karvina, Viktoria Plzen, Karvina, Box2Box FC

*** Durrans - Matthew Durrans (Matthew Richard Wordsworth Durrans) (a) 10/12/1998, Vancouver, British Columbia (Canada) (b) 1,83 (c) F - center forward (d) - (e) Austria Klagenfurt, Klagenfurt II, FC Pipinsried, FC Edmonton, 1860 München, 1860 München II, VfR Garching

*** Durrer - Adrian Durrer (a) 13/07/2001, Basel (Switzerland) (b) 1,88 (c) M - pivot (d) FC Lugano (e) AC Bellinzona, FC Lugano

*** Dursun - Abdurrahim Dursun (a) 01/12/1998, Bayburt (Turkey) (b) 1,76 (c) D - left back (d) Adana Demirspor (e) Trabzonspor, Boluspor, Trabzonspor, Bandirmaspor, Trabzonspor, 1461 Trabzon, Trabzonspor, Kirklarelispor, Trabzonspor

*** Dursun - Mert Dursun (Muhammed Mert Dursun) (a) 30/11/2004, Ankara (Turkey) (b) 1,82 (c) F - left winger (d) Sivasspor (e) -

*** Dursun - Salih Dursun (a) 12/07/1991, Sakarya (Turkey) (b) 1,88 (c) D - right back (d) Fatih Karagümrük (e) Genclerbirligi, Antalyaspor, Galatasaray, Antalyaspor, Galatasaray, Trabzonspor, Galatasaray, Kayserispor, Sakaryaspor

*** Dursun - Serdar Dursun (a) 19/10/1991, Hamburg (Germany) (b) 1,90 (c) F - center forward (d) Fenerbahce (e) Darmstadt 98, Greuther Fürth, Karagümrük, Eskisehirspor, Denizlispor, Eskisehirspor, Sanliurfaspor, Eskisehirspor, Hannover 96 II

*** Dusalijevs - Niks Dusalijevs (a) 17/01/2001, ¿? (Latvia) (b) 1,86 (c) F - right winger (d) Valmiera FC (e) JFK Ventspils, Ventspils II

*** Dusanic - Aleksa Dusanic (Алекса Душанић) (a) 05/02/2003, Niš (Serbia and Montenegro, now in Serbia) (b) - (c) F - right winger (d) FK Radnicki Niš (e) Car Konstantin, Radnicki Niš

*** Dushevskiy - Daniil Dushevskiy (Душевский Даниил Дмитриевич) (a) 01/03/2004, Minsk (Belarus) (b) 1,85 (c) M - pivot (d) FK Minsk (e) FK Minsk II

*** Dushi - Erdin Dushi (a) 07/10/2002, Vushtrri (RF Yugoslavia, now in Kosovo) (b) 1,77 (c) D - right back (d) KF Trepca 89 (e) KF Drenica, FC Prishtina

*** Dusinszki - Szabolcs Dusinszki (a) 06/08/2005, Odorheiu Secuiesc (Romania) (b) - (c) M - attacking midfielder (d) Puskás Akadémia FC (e) Puskás AFC II, O. Secuiesc

*** Dussaut - Damien Dussaut (Damien Dylan Dussaut) (a) 08/11/1994, Créteil (France) (b) 1,82 (c) D - right back (d) FCV Farul Constanta (e) FC Rapid 1923, FCV Farul, FC Dinamo, Sint-Truiden, Standard Liège, Valenciennes B

*** Dussenne - Noë Dussenne (Noë Georges Dussenne) (a) 07/04/1992, Mons (Belgium) (b) 1,92 (c) D - central defense (d) FC Lausanne-Sport (e) Standard Liège, Excelsior Mouscron, Crotone, KAA Gent, Crotone, Excelsior Mouscron, Cercle Brugge, RAEC Mons, AFC Tubize, RAEC Mons

*** Duta - Bogdan Duta (Bogdan Gabriel Duță) (a) 01/01/2005, ¿? (Romania) (b) - (c) F - left winger (d) FC U Craiova 1948 (e) -

*** Duta - Lucian Duta (Lucian Mihai Duță) (a) 01/01/2005, ¿? (Romania) (b) - (c) M - central midfielder (d) FC U Craiova 1948 (e) -

*** Dutton - Lewis Dutton (a) 03/06/2001, Wrexham (Wales) (b) 1,88 (c) G (d) Airbus UK Broughton (e) Chorley, Whitchurch, Chorley, The New Saints, TNS Development

*** Dutu - Stefan Dutu (a) 16/02/2004, ¿? (Romania) (b) - (c) D - central defense (d) FCV Farul Constanta II (e) -

*** Duverne - Jean-Kévin Duverne (a) 12/07/1997, Paris (France) (b) 1,86 (c) D - left back (d) - (e) Stade Brestois, RC Lens, RC Lens B

*** Duvnjak - Tomislav Duvnjak (a) 05/02/2003, Zagreb (Croatia) (b) - (c) M - pivot (d) NK Sesvete (e) NK Sesvete, NK Istra, Din. Zagreb II

*** Duysenbekuly - Kuanysh Duysenbekuly (a) 14/08/2003, ¿? (Kazakhstan) (b) - (c) M - right midfielder (d) FK Turan II (e) Akad. Ontustik

*** Duyseshov - Sultanbek Duyseshov (Дуйсешов Султанбек Гарифоллаулы) (a) 06/08/2001, Atyrau (Kazakhstan) (b) 1,82 (c) F - center forward (d) FK Maktaaral (e) FK Maktaaral II, Atyrau II

*** Dúzs - Gellért Dúzs (a) 24/02/2002, Salgótarján (Hungary) (b) 1,90 (c) G (d) Budapest Honvéd FC (e) Honvéd II

*** Dvali - Lasha Dvali (ლაშა დვალი) (a) 14/05/1995, Tbilisi (Georgia) (b) 1,91 (c) D - central defense (d) APOEL FC (e) Ferencváros, Pogon Szczecin, Śląsk Wroclaw, Irtysh, Śląsk Wroclaw, MSV Duisburg, Reading, Kasimpasa, Reading, Skonto, Reading, Skonto, Saburtalo

*** Dvorak - Adam Dvorak (Adam Dvořák) (a) 28/07/2004, ¿? (Czech Rep.) (b) 1,89 (c) G (d) SK Slavia Praga B (e) -

*** Dvorak - Pavel Dvorak (Pavel Dvořák) (a) 19/02/1989, Vysoké Mýto (Czechoslovakia, now in Czech Rep.) (b) 1,87 (c) F - center forward (d) - (e) Hradec Kralove, Sigma Olomouc, Slovácko, Sigma Olomouc, Jihlava, Hradec Kralove

*** Dwamena - Raphael Dwamena (a) 12/09/1995, Nkawkaw, Eastern Region (Ghana) (b) 1,86 (c) F - center forward (d) KF Egnatia (e) BSC Old Boys, Blau Weiss Linz, Vejle BK, Levante UD, Real Zaragoza, Levante UD, FC Zürich, Austria Lustenau, FC Liefering, RB Ghana, Ul. Soccer A.

*** Dwomoh - Pierre Dwomoh (Pierre Junior Dwomoh) (a) 21/06/2004, ¿? (Belgium) (b) 1,88 (c) M - central midfielder (d) RWD Molenbeek (e) Royal Antwerp, KV Oostende, Royal Antwerp, Braga B, Royal Antwerp, KRC Genk

*** Dyachkov - Aleksandr Dyachkov (Дьячков Александр Евгеньевич) (a) 06/06/2003, Moskva (Russia) (b) 1,87 (c) G (d) Salyut Belgorod (e) Salyut Belgorod, Rostov II, Din. Stavropol, Rostov II

*** Dyachuk - Maksym Dyachuk (Дячук Максим Ростиславович) (a) 21/07/2003, Yasinya, Zakarpattya Oblast (Ukraine) (b) 1,85 (c) D - central defense (d) FC Dinamo de Kiev (e) FK Oleksandriya, Dinamo Kyïv

*** Dybala - Paulo Dybala (Paulo Bruno Exequiel Dybala) (a) 15/11/1993, Laguna Larga (Argentina) (b) 1,77 (c) F - attacking midfielder (d) AS Roma (e) Juventus, US Palermo, Instituto

*** Dygun - Aleksandr Dygun (Дыгун Александр Михайлович) (a) 21/08/2001, Mozyr (Belarus) (b) - (c) M (d) Slavia Mozyr II (e) Lokomotiv Gomel, Slavia Mozyr II

*** Dyhr - Nikolas Dyhr (Nikolas Langberg Dyhr) (a) 18/06/2001, Horsens (Denmark) (b) 1,79 (c) D - left back (d) FC Midtjylland (e) KV Kortrijk, Midtjylland, AC Horsens, Midtjylland

*** Dylevskiy - Artem Dylevskiy (Дылевский Артём Владимирович) (a) 20/02/1997, Kuntsevshchina (Belarus) (b) 1,86 (c) D - central defense (d) FK Molodechno (e) FK Smorgon, Kaysar, Belshina, FK Lida, Belshina, FK Minsk, FK Minsk II

*** Dyngeland - Mathias Dyngeland (Mathias Lønne Dyngeland) (a) 07/10/1995, Bergen (Norway) (b) 1,87 (c) G (d) SK Brann (e) Elfsborg, Vålerenga, Elfsborg, Sogndal, Fana IL, Sogndal, Fana IL

*** Dytyatyev - Oleksiy Dytyatyev (a) 07/11/1988, Nova Kakhovka, Kherson Oblast (Soviet Union, now in Ukraine) (b) 1,96 (d) - (e) PFK Lviv, FK Aksu, Cracovia II,

Cracovia, P. Niepolomice, Cracovia, Karpaty, Vorskla Poltava, Olimpik Donetsk, Bukovyna, Krymteplytsya, Energiya NK

*** Dyulgerov - Aleksandar Dyulgerov (Александър Антониев Дюлгеров) (a) 19/04/1990, Blagoevgrad (Bulgaria) (b) 1,84 (c) D - right back (d) Pirin Blagoevgrad (e) Etar, Septemvri Sofia, CSKA-Sofia, Pirin, Concordia, Slavia Sofia, Lokomotiv Sofia, CSKA Sofia, Montana, CSKA Sofia, Pirin

*** Dyulgerov - Ivan Dyulgerov (Иван Василев Дюлгеров) (a) 15/07/1999, Varna (Bulgaria) (b) 1,88 (c) G (d) Cherno More Varna (e) -

*** Dyulgerov - Stanislav Dyulgerov (Станислав Петков Дюлгеров) (a) 23/08/2003, ¿? (Bulgaria) (b) 1,71 (c) M - pivot (d) Arda Kardzhali (e) Apollon Larisas

*** Dzafic - Adnan Dzafic (Adnan Džafić) (a) 10/05/1990, Visoko (Yugoslavia, now in Bosnia and Herzegovina) (b) 1,86 (c) F - left winger (d) FK Velez Mostar (e) FK Sarajevo, FK Tuzla City, Fastav Zlin, Mlada Boleslav, Fastav Zlin, FC MAS Taborsko, Caslav, Bosna Visoko

*** Dzalto - Patrik Dzalto (Patrik Džalto) (a) 19/02/1997, Reutlingen (Germany) (b) 1,75 (c) M - attacking midfielder (d) Bregalnica Stip (e) NK Vukovar 1991, Austria Klagenfurt, FC Memmingen, TuS Koblenz, Jahn Regensburg, Bayer Leverkusen, Jahn Regensburg, Bayer Leverkusen

*** Dzankovic - Arman Dzankovic (Arman Džanković) (a) 24/03/2002, Stavanger (Norway) (b) 1,84 (c) F - left winger (d) - (e) Pohronie, Velez Mostar, Ålgård FK, Sandnes Ulf II

*** Dzaria - Irakli Dzaria (ირაკლი ძარია) (a) 01/12/1988, Poti (Soviet Union, now in Georgia) (b) 1,73 (c) M - pivot (d) - (e) Torpedo Kutaisi, Valletta, FK Kukësi, FC Dila, Sioni Bolnisi, FC Dila, Dinamo Tbilisi, FC Zestafoni, Tskhinvali, FC Zestafoni, Kolkheti Poti

*** Dzebniauri - Tornike Dzebniauri (თორნიკე ძებნიაური) (a) 27/11/1999, ¿? (Georgia) (b) - (c) M - pivot (d) - (e) FC Zhenis, FC Locomotive, Saburtalo, FC Locomotive, Locomotive II

*** Dzeko - Edin Dzeko (Edin Džeko) (a) 17/03/1986, Sarajevo (Yugoslavia, now in Bosnia and Herzegovina) (b) 1,93 (c) F - center forward (d) Fenerbahce (e) Internazionale Milano, AS Roma, Manchester City, AS Roma, Manchester City, VfL Wolfsburg, Teplice, Usti nad Labem, Teplice, Zeljeznicar

*** Dzelili - Flamur Dzelili (a) 09/09/1999, ¿? (Sweden) (b) 1,83 (c) F - right winger (d) Jönköpings Södra IF (e) Varbergs BoIS, Oskarshamns AIK, Högsby IK, Oskarshamns AIK, Kalmar AIK

*** Dzemaili - Blerim Dzemaili (Блерим Цемаили) (a) 12/04/1986, Tetovo (Yugoslavia, now in North Macedonia) (b) 1,80 (c) M - central midfielder (d) - (e) FC Zürich, Shenzhen FC, Bologna, Montreal, Bologna, Galatasaray, Genoa, Galatasaray, Napoli, Parma, Torino, Parma, Torino, Bolton Wanderers, Torino, Bolton Wanderers, FC Zürich

*** Dzenyagha - Saagi Dzenyagha (Saagi Mmmbi Avah Mmbi Dzenyagha) (a) 12/12/2001, Yaounde (Cameroon) (b) - (c) F - center forward (d) FK Minsk (e) Stade Renard, RC Bafoussam

*** Dzhabaev - Damirkhan Dzhabaev (Джабаев Дамирхан) (a) 25/02/2003, ¿? (Kazakhstan) (b) 1,90 (c) D - central defense (d) Shakhter-Bulat (e) -

*** Dzhanaev - Soslan Dzhanaev (Джанаев Сослан Тотразович) (a) 13/03/1987, Vladikavkaz (Soviet Union, now in Russia) (b) 1,88 (c) G (d) - (e) Sochi, Miedź Legnica, Rubin Kazan, Rostov, Spartak Moskva, Alania, Spartak Moskva, Terek Grozny, Spartak Moskva, KamAZ, CSKA Moskva II

*** Dzhebov - Abdullo Dzhebov (Джебов Абдулло Давлакадамович) (a) 29/05/2004, ¿? (Russia) (b) 1,72 (c) M - central midfielder (d) FK Rostov II (e) -

*** Dzhigero - Aleksandr Dzhigero (Джигеро Александр Владимирович) (a) 15/04/1996, Machesk, Minskaya Oblast (Belarus) (b) 1,73 (c) M - left midfielder (d) Slavia Mozyr (e) Okzhetpes, FK Minsk, Neman Grodno, Smolevichi, Torpedo Minsk, BATE Borisov, Luch, BATE Borisov, Dnepr Mogilev, BATE Borisov, BATE II, Zvezda-BGU, BATE II

*** Dzhikiya - Georgiy Dzhikiya (Джикия Георгий Тамазович) (a) 21/11/1993, Moskva (Russia) (b) 1,88 (c) D - central defense (d) FC Spartak de Moscú (e) Amkar Perm, Khimik, Spartak Nalchik, Lokomotiv 2, LFK Lokomotiv 2

*** Dzhikiya - Temur Dzhikiya (Джикия Темур Тенгизович) (a) 08/05/1998, Moskva (Russia) (b) 1,86 (c) F - center forward (d) FC Urartu Yerevan (e) FC Urartu, Volga Uljanovsk, Veles Moskva, Volga Uljanovsk, Kolomna, Zorkiy, Ararat Moskva, Khimki 2, Domodedovo, Spartak 2

*** Dzhikov - Georgi Dzhikov (Георги Кирилов Джиков) (a) 05/01/2005, ¿? (Bulgaria) (b) - (c) F - center forward (d) Septemvri Sofia (e) -

*** Dzhumatov - Rinat Dzhumatov (Джуматов Ринат Женисбайулы) (a) 13/10/1997, Atyrau (Kazakhstan) (b) 1,74 (c) M - central midfielder (d) FK Atyrau (e) Maktaaral, Atyrau, Atyrau II

*** Dziczek - Patryk Dziczek (a) 25/03/1998, Gliwice (Poland) (b) 1,82 (c) M - pivot (d) Piast Gliwice (e) Lazio, Salernitana, Lazio, Piast Gliwice

*** Dziedzic - Adrian Dziedzic (a) 22/03/2003, Kraków (Poland) (b) 1,85 (c) M - pivot (d) Gornik Zabrze II (e) Górnik Zabrze, Garbarnia, Górnik Zabrze, Gornik II

*** Dziekonski - Xavier Dziekonski (Xavier Dziekoński) (a) 06/10/2003, Grajewo (Poland) (b) 1,88 (c) G (d) Korona Kielce (e) Korona Kielce, Rakow, Garbarnia, Rakow, Jagiellonia, Jagiellonia II

*** Dzinga - Eimantas Dzinga (a) 03/02/2003, Marijampole (Lithuania) (b) 1,82 (c) M - central midfielder (d) FK Panevezys (e) Panevezys B

*** Dzombic - Rade Dzombic (Rade Džombić) (a) 27/11/1997, Banja Luka (Bosnia and Herzegovina) (b) - (c) D - right back (d) FK Laktasi (e) Ljubic Prnjavor, Sloga Meridian, Zeljeznicar BL, EG El Palmar CF, Kozara Gradiska

*** Dzotsenidze - Tornike Dzotsenidze (თორნიკე ძოწენიძე) (a) 07/11/1999, Tbilisi (Georgia) (b) 1,87 (c) D - central defense (d) FC Dila Gori (e) FC Telavi, FC Telavi, Dinamo Tbilisi

*** Dzsudzsák - Balázs Dzsudzsák (a) 23/12/1986, Nyírlugos (Hungary) (b) 1,79 (c) M - attacking midfielder (d) Debreceni VSC (e) Al-Ain FC, Ittihad Kalba, Al-Wahda FC, Bursaspor, Dinamo Moskva, Anzhi, PSV Eindhoven, Debrecen

*** Dzugurdic - Milos Dzugurdic (Милош Џугурдић) (a) 02/12/1992, Krusevac (Yugoslavia, now in Serbia) (b) 1,79 (c) F - center forward (d) FK Indjija (e) Napredak, FK Mesevo, Jagodina, Graficar, OFK Grbalj, Borac Cacak, FK Skopje, FK Olimpik, FK BSK Borča, Mladost, Vozdovac, Spartak, Teleoptik

*** Dzumadil - Alger Dzumadil (Alger Džumadil) (a) 29/07/1996, Keila ((b) 1,72 (c) D - left back (d) FC Eston Villa (e) Kalev, Maardu LM, Kalev, FCI Levadia, Paide, Levadia, Levadia II

*** Dzyuba - Artem Dzyuba (Дзюба Артём Сергеевич) (a) 22/08/1988, Moskva (Soviet Union, now in Russia) (b) 1,97 (c) F - center forward (d) Lokomotiv Moskva (e) Adana Demirspor, Zenit, Arsenal Tula, Zenit, Spartak Moskva, Rostov, Spartak Moskva, Rostov, Spartak Moskva, Tom Tomsk, Spartak Moskva, Tom Tomsk, Spartak Moskva, Spartak Moskva II

*** Eacock - Adrian Alexandre Eacock (a) 22/03/1992, ¿? (England) (b) - (c) D (d) - (e) Juvenes-Dogana

*** Eardley - Neal Eardley (Neal James Eardley) (a) 06/11/1988, Llandudno (Wales) (b) 1,80 (c) D - right back (d) Sean Eardley (e) Connah's Quay, Burton Albion, Barrow, Burton Albion, Lincoln City, Northampton, Hibernian FC, Birmingham City, Leyton Orient, Birmingham City, Blackpool, Oldham Athletic

*** Eastwood - Jake Eastwood (a) 03/10/1996, Rotherham (England) (b) 1,93 (c) G (d) Grimsby Town (e) Sheffield Utd., AFC Rochdale, Sheffield Utd., Ross County, Sheffield Utd., FC Portsmouth, Sheffield Utd., Grimsby Town, Sheffield Utd., Kilmarnock FC, Sheffield Utd., Scunthorpe Utd., Sheffield Utd., FC Chesterfield, Sheffield Utd., Mickleover, Gainsborough, Sheffield FC

*** Ebbe - Dean Ebbe (a) 16/07/1994, Dublin (Ireland) (b) - (c) F - center forward (d) FC Manchester 62 (e) Crusaders, The New Saints, Bala, The New Saints, Bluebell United, Inverness Caledonian, Bluebell United, Cabinteely, Collinstown, Athlone Town, Shamrock Rovers, Longford Town, Shamrock Rovers

*** Ebenezer - Okezie Prince Ebenezer (a) 28/02/2001, Umuahia (Nigeria) (b) 1,79 (c) D - left back (d) Arda Kardzhali (e) FC Noah, Zimbru Chisinau, Right2Win SA

*** Ebert - Ebert (Ebert Cardoso da Silva) (a) 25/05/1993, Nortelândia, Mato Grosso (Brazil) (b) 1,82 (c) D - central defense (d) - (e) FK Kukësi, SC Noravank, Metalist, FC Van, FC Urartu, Botev Plovdiv, Stal Kamyanske, Macaé, Internacional

*** Ebert - Patrick Ebert (a) 17/03/1987, Potsdam (East Germany, now in Germany) (b) 1,75 (c) F - right winger (d) - (e) Istanbulspor, AO Kavala, AO Xanthi, Dynamo Dresden, FC Ingolstadt, Rayo Vallecano, Spartak Moskva, Real Valladolid, Hertha Berlin, Hertha BSC II

*** Ebiowei - Malcolm Ebiowei (Malcolm Perewari Ebiowei) (a) 04/09/2003, London (England) (b) 1,85 (c) F - right winger (d) Crystal Palace (e) Hull City, Crystal Palace, Derby

*** Ebiye - Moses Ebiye (a) 28/04/1997, Warri (Nigeria) (b) 1,85 (c) F - center forward (d) Aalesunds FK (e) Tromsø, HamKam, Lillestrøm, Strømmen, Lillestrøm, Akwa United

*** Eboli - Ciro Eboli (a) 04/09/2000, ¿? (Italy) (b) - (c) D - right back (d) SC Faetano (e) Mondaino, Faetano

*** Ebong - Maks Ebong (Африд Макс Эбонг Нгоме) (a) 26/08/1999, Vitebsk (Belarus) (b) 1,80 (c) M - central midfielder (d) FC Astana (e) Soligorsk, Soligorsk II

*** Ebosele - Festy Ebosele (Festy Oseiwe Ebosele) (a) 02/08/2002, Enniscorthy, Wexford (Ireland) (b) 1,80 (c) D - right back (d) Udinese (e) Derby

*** Ebosse - Enzo Ebosse (Enzo Jacques Rodolphe Ebosse) (a) 11/03/1999, Amiens (France) (b) 1,85 (c) D - central defense (d) Udinese (e) Angers SCO, Le Mans FC, RC Lens B

*** Ebuehi - Tyronne Ebuehi (Tyronne Efe Ebuehi) (a) 16/12/1995, Haarlem (Netherlands) (b) 1,87 (c) D - right back (d) FC Empoli (e) Benfica B, Venezia, Benfica B, FC Twente, Benfica B, Benfica, ADO Den Haag, HFC EDO O19

*** Eckert Ayensa - Dennis Eckert Ayensa (Dennis-Yerai Eckert Ayensa) (a) 09/01/1997, Bonn (Germany) (b) 1,83 (c) F - center forward (d) Royale Union Saint Gilloise (e) FC Ingolstadt, RC Celta, Excelsior, RC Celta, Celta B, Borussia Mönchengladbach II

*** Eckl - Patrik Eckl (a) 21/09/2001, ¿? (Hungary) (b) 1,87 (c) D - central defense (d) KFC Komarno (e) Újpest FC, Újpest II, Főnix FC

*** Edera - Simone Edera (a) 09/01/1997, Torino (Italy) (b) 1,74 (c) F - right winger (d) - (e) Pordenone, Torino, Reggina, Torino, Bologna, Torino, Parma, Torino, Venezia, Torino

*** Ederson - Ederson (Ederson Bruno Domingos) (a) 21/08/1989, Jacarezinho (Brazil) (b) 1,78 (c) F - right winger (d) Hamrun Spartans (e) Nadur Y., América-RN,

Aimoré, ABC FC, Caxias-RS, São Luiz, Ypiranga-RS, Luverdense, Lajeadense, Canoas, Brasil Pelotas, Novo Hamburgo, Veranópolis, Ferroviário, Canoas, Ypiranga-RS, Yokohama FC, Internacional, Yokohama FC, Internacional, Inter B
*** Ederson - Ederson (Ederson Santana de Moraes) (a) 17/08/1993, Osasco (SP) (Brazil) (b) 1,88 (c) G (d) Manchester City (e) Benfica, Rio Ave, GD Ribeirão
*** Éderson - Éderson (Éderson José dos Santos Lourenço da Silva) (a) 07/07/1999, Campo Grande (Brazil) (b) 1,83 (c) M - central midfielder (d) Atalanta de Bérgamo (e) Salernitana, Corinthians, Fortaleza, Corinthians, Cruzeiro, Desp. Brasil
*** Edery - Yaniv Edery (a) 23/06/2003, Marseille (France) (b) 1,80 (c) D - left back (d) - (e) Sfintul Gheorghe, Zorya Lugansk, FC Nitra, R. B. Linense
*** Edet - Emmanuel Edet (Emmanuel Edet Ibok) (a) 22/08/1989, Abuja (Nigeria) (b) 1,88 (c) D - central defense (d) UE Rapitenca (e) Calvo Sotelo, Europa FC, CD Gerena, Lorca Deportiva, Xerez Deportivo, UP Plasencia, Mosta FC, UP Plasencia, Desportivo Aves, Naxxar Lions FC, Floriana, At. Baleares
*** Edgar - André Edgar (André Edgar Antonio) (a) 28/06/1999, Sion (Switzerland) (b) 1,85 (c) M - central midfielder (d) FC Sion (e) AC Bellinzona, FC Sion, Neuchâtel Xamax, FC Sion, FC Conthey
*** Edge - Charley Edge (Charley Joseph Edge) (a) 14/05/1997, Aberystwyth (Wales) (b) - (c) M - attacking midfielder (d) Gresford Athletic (e) Aberystwyth, Cefn Druids, Marine FC, Needham Market, Leamington, Maldon/Tiptree
*** Edh - Eskil Edh (Eskil Smidesang Edh) (a) 04/08/2002, ¿? (Norway) (b) 1,81 (c) M - right midfielder (d) Lillestrøm SK (e) Lillestrøm II
*** Edjouma - Malcom Edjouma (Malcom Sylas Edjouma Laouari) (a) 08/10/1996, Toulouse (France) (b) 1,91 (c) M - central midfielder (d) FCSB (e) FC Botosani, KSV Roeselare, FC Viitorul, FC Lorient, FC Chambly Oise, FC Lorient, Red Star FC, FC Lorient, Concarneau, FC Lorient, Concarneau, ASM Belfort, Châteauroux B, SC Balma
*** Edmundsson - Hákun Edmundsson (a) 21/03/1996, ¿? (Faroe Islands) (b) - (c) M - pivot (d) - (e) 07 Vestur, B36 Tórshavn, ÍF Fuglafjördur, KÍ Klaksvík, Skála, Vendsyssel FF, Skála, Vendsyssel FF, B68 Toftir, NSÍ Runavík, B68 Toftir
*** Edomwonyi - Bright Edomwonyi (Bright Osagie Edomwonyi) (a) 24/07/1994, Benin City (Nigeria) (b) 1,86 (c) F - center forward (d) Diósgyőri VTK (e) Koper, Young Violets, Austria Viena, Atromitos FC, Austria Viena, Çaykur Rizespor, Sturm Graz, Çaykur Rizespor, Sturm Graz, FC Liefering, TSV Hartberg, FC Liefering, FC Wacker, FC Liefering, RB Salzburg
*** Edouard - Odsonne Edouard (Odsonne Édouard) (a) 16/01/1998, Kourou (Guayana Francesa) (b) 1,87 (c) F - center forward (d) Crystal Palace (e) Celtic FC, Paris Saint-Germain, Celtic FC, Paris Saint-Germain, Toulouse, Paris Saint-Germain
*** Edozie - Samuel Edozie (Samuel Ikechukwu Edozie) (a) 28/01/2003, Lewisham, London (England) (b) 1,81 (c) F - left winger (d) Southampton FC (e) -
*** Edson Fernando - Edson Fernando (Edson Fernando da Silva Gomes) (a) 24/04/1998, Natal (Brazil) (b) 1,78 (c) M - pivot (d) Rukh Lviv (e) Atlético-GO, Rukh Lviv, EC Bahia, Bahia B
*** Edu - Edu (Eduardo Salvador Rosa de Oliveira Borges) (a) 27/05/2002, Chaves (Portugal) (b) 1,85 (c) D - central defense (d) GD Chaves (e) Pedras Salgadas, Chaves, Pedras Salgadas, Chaves B
*** Eduardo - Wilson Eduardo (Wilson Bruno Naval Costa Eduardo) (a) 08/07/1990, Massarelos (Portugal) (b) 1,79 (c) F - left winger (d) APOEL FC (e) Alanyaspor, Al-Ain FC, SC Braga, Sporting Lisboa, ADO Den Haag, Sporting Lisboa, Dinamo Zagreb, Sporting Lisboa, Académica Coimbra, Sporting Lisboa, Olhanense, Sporting Lisboa, Beira-Mar, Sporting Lisboa, Portimonense, Sporting Lisboa, Real SC

*** Eduardo Henrique - Eduardo Henrique (Eduardo Henrique da Silva) (a) 17/05/1995, Limeira (Brazil) (b) 1,86 (c) M - pivot (d) Sporting de Lisboa (e) Al-Raed, Sporting Lisboa, Crotone, Sporting Lisboa, Internacional, B SAD, Internacional, Atlético-PR, Internacional, Académica Coimbra, At. Mineiro, Académica Coimbra, Guarani

*** Eduardo Kau - Eduardo Kau (Eduardo de Sousa Santos) (a) 17/01/1999, Brasília (Brazil) (b) 1,90 (c) D - central defense (d) - (e) Sfintul Gheorghe, B SAD, Avaí FC

*** Eduardo Santos - Eduardo Santos (Eduardo Gonzaga Mendes Santos) (a) 28/11/1997, São Paulo (Brazil) (b) 1,96 (c) D - central defense (d) Red Bull Bragantino (e) RB Bragantino, Slavia Praha, Karvina, Viktoria Plzen, Karvina, Capivariano, Karvina, Capivariano, São Bento (SP), Famalicão, Real SC

*** Eduok - Samuel Eduok (Samuel Emem Eduok) (a) 31/01/1994, Itu (Nigeria) (b) 1,76 (c) F - right winger (d) - (e) Hajduk Split, Konyaspor, Hajduk Split, BB Erzurumspor, Kasimpasa, Esperance, Kasimpasa, Esperance, Dolphin FC, Akwa United

*** Edvardsen - Oliver Valaker Edvardsen (a) 19/03/1999, Bærum (Norway) (b) - (c) F - left winger (d) Go Ahead Eagles Deventer (e) Stabæk, Grorud, Vålerenga II, Drøbak-Frogn

*** Edvardsen - Victor Edvardsen (Victor Kaj Edvardsen) (a) 14/01/1996, Göteborg (Sweden) (b) 1,85 (c) F - center forward (d) Go Ahead Eagles Deventer (e) Djurgården, Degerfors, Karlstad BK, IK Oddevold, Stenungsund IF, Elverum, Utsiktens BK

*** Edvardsson - David Edvardsson (David Mikael Edvardsson) (a) 05/03/2002, Grebbestad (Sweden) (b) 1,74 (c) M - central midfielder (d) Landskrona BoIS (e) Landskrona, Malmö FF, Värnamo, Malmö FF, Jammerbugt FC, Malmö FF, Grebbestads IF, Grebbestads IF, Grebbestad 2

*** Edwards - Aaran Edwards (a) 17/02/2003, ¿? (England) (b) - (c) M - central midfielder (d) - (e) Airbus UK

*** Edwards - Aeron Edwards (a) 16/02/1988, Wrexham (Wales) (b) 1,80 (c) M - central midfielder (d) Bala Town (e) Connah's Quay, The New Saints, Caersws

*** Edwards - David Edwards (David Alexander Edwards) (a) 03/02/1986, Pontesbury (England) (b) 1,80 (c) M - central midfielder (d) - (e) Bala, Shrewsbury, Reading, Wolverhampton Wanderers, Luton Town, Shrewsbury

*** Edwards - Diamond Edwards (Milan Diamond Lazane Edwards) (a) 18/09/2003, ¿? (England) (b) - (c) M - attacking midfielder (d) Southampton FC B (e) -

*** Edwards - Gareth Edwards (a) 20/07/1983, ¿? (Wales) (b) - (c) D - central defense (d) - (e) Airbus UK, Caernarfon, Cefn Druids, Buckley

*** Edwards - Gwion Edwards (Gwion Dafydd Rhys Edwards) (a) 01/03/1993, Lampeter (Wales) (b) 1,75 (c) F - right winger (d) - (e) Wigan Ath., Ross County, Wigan Ath., Ipswich, Peterborough, Crawley Town, St. Johnstone

*** Edwards - Jack Edwards (Jack David Edwards) (a) 04/08/2005, ¿? (England) (b) - (c) G (d) The New Saints (e) -

*** Edwards - Marcus Edwards (a) 03/12/1998, London (England) (b) 1,68 (c) F - right winger (d) Sporting de Lisboa (e) Vitória Guimarães, Excelsior, Norwich City

*** Edwards - Noah Edwards (a) 30/05/1996, St. Asaph (Wales) (b) - (c) M - central midfielder (d) Connah's Quay Nomads (e) Caernarfon, Connah's Quay, Prestatyn

*** Edwards - Owura Edwards (Owura Nsiah Edwards) (a) 10/04/2001, Bristol (England) (b) 1,73 (c) F - right winger (d) - (e) Ross County, Colchester Utd., Exeter City, Grimsby Town, Bath City

*** Edwards - Ryan Edwards (Ryan Christopher Edwards) (a) 07/10/1993, Liverpool (England) (b) 1,95 (c) D - central defense (d) - (e) Dundee United, Blackpool,

Plymouth Argyle, FC Morecambe, Blackburn, FC Morecambe, Blackburn, Tranmere Rovers, Blackburn, FC Chesterfield, Blackburn, Fleetwood, Blackburn, AFC Rochdale, Blackburn

*** Edwards - Ryan Edwards (Ryan Raymond Edwards) (a) 22/06/1988, ¿? (Wales) (b) - (c) M - central midfielder (d) Airbus UK Broughton (e) Bangor City, Airbus UK, Halkyn United

*** Edzes - Mark Edzes (Mark Anthony Edzes) (a) 14/08/1991, ¿? (England) (b) 1,80 (c) D - central defense (d) FC Manchester 62 (e) Darlington R., St Helens

*** Eerdhuijzen - Mike Eerdhuijzen (a) 13/07/2000, Volendam (Netherlands) (b) 1,94 (c) D - central defense (d) Sparta Rotterdam (e) FC Volendam

*** Effaghe - Rody Junior Effaghe (a) 11/04/2004, ¿? (Gabon) (b) 1,85 (c) F - center forward (d) FK Gomel (e) Dinamo-Auto

*** Effiong - Alfred Effiong (a) 29/11/1984, Lagos (Nigeria) (b) 1,82 (c) F - center forward (d) - (e) Marsaxlokk, Sirens FC, Balzan FC, Qormi FC, Gzira Utd., Valletta, Marsaxlokk, Qormi FC, Hamrun Spartans, St. George's FC, Kercem Ajax FC, Negeri Sembilan, Shooting Stars

*** Efford - Joseph Efford (Joseph Isiah Efford) (a) 29/08/1996, Gwinnett County, Georgia (United States) (b) 1,76 (c) F - center forward (d) Motherwell FC (e) Waasland-Beveren, Ergotelis, RCD Mallorca, FC Botosani

*** Efrat - Itamar Efrat (אפרת איתמר) (a) 02/10/2001, ¿? (Israel) (b) - (c) M (d) Hapoel Tel Aviv (e) Yermiahu Holon, Hapoel Tel Aviv, Shimshon TLV, Hapoel Tel Aviv, H. Kfar Shalem, Hapoel Tel Aviv

*** Efrem - Georgios Efrem (Γεώργιος Εφραίμ) (a) 05/07/1989, Limassol (Cyprus) (b) 1,71 (c) F - left winger (d) APOEL FC (e) Omonia Nicosia, Rangers FC, Dundee FC, Rangers FC, Arsenal Reserves

*** Efremov - Andreja Efremov (Андреја Ефремов) (a) 02/09/1992, Sveti Nikole (North Macedonia) (b) 1,89 (c) G (d) FC Shkupi (e) FK Skopje, Borec Veles, KF Vllaznia, Sileks, Lokomotiv Sofia, Famalicão, Renova, Rabotnicki, Metalurg Skopje

*** Efros - Stefan Efros (Ştefan Efros) (a) 08/05/1990, Măgdăceşti (Soviet Union, now in Moldova) (b) 1,95 (c) D - central defense (d) Dacia Buiucani (e) Milsami, Petrocub, CS Mioveni, CSF Speranta, Real Succes

*** Efthymiou - Efthymios Efthymiou (a) 03/11/2006, ¿? (Cyprus) (b) - (c) M (d) - (e) Nea Salamis

*** Eftichidis - Filippos Eftichidis (Φίλιππος Ευτυχίδης) (a) 26/02/2002, Nicosia (Cyprus) (b) 1,77 (c) M - central midfielder (d) Olympiakos Nikosia (e) -

*** Eftimov - Kristijan Eftimov (Кристијан Ефтимов) (a) 01/09/1999, Skopje (North Macedonia) (b) 1,77 (c) D - left back (d) Sileks Kratovo (e) Borec Veles, Rabotnicki

*** Egan-Riley - CJ Egan-Riley (Conrad Jaden Egan-Riley) (a) 02/01/2003, Manchester (England) (b) 1,83 (c) D - central defense (d) Burnley FC (e) Hibernian FC, Burnley

*** Egeli - Vetle Walle Egeli (a) 23/06/2004, Larvik (Norway) (b) 1,78 (c) D - left back (d) Sandefjord Fotball (e) -

*** Egell-Johnsen - Kevin Egell-Johnsen (a) 13/05/2000, ¿? (Norway) (b) - (c) D - right back (d) Arendal Fotball (e) Odd, Kongsvinger, Odd, Odd II

*** Eggestein - Maximilian Eggestein (a) 08/12/1996, Hannover (Germany) (b) 1,81 (c) M - central midfielder (d) SC Freiburg (e) Werder Bremen, Werder Bremen II

*** Egho - Marvin Egho (a) 09/05/1994, Wien (Austria) (b) 1,88 (c) F - center forward (d) Randers FC (e) Spartak Trnava, SV Ried, Admira Wacker, Wiener Neustadt, Admira Wacker, Rapid Wien II, SR Donaufeld

*** Egilsson - Búi Egilsson (a) 04/01/1996, ¿? (Faroe Islands) (b) - (c) M - attacking midfielder (d) NSÍ Runavík (e) TB/FCS/Royn, FC Suduroy

*** Egilsson - Magnus Egilsson (a) 19/03/1994, ¿? (Faroe Islands) (b) 1,80 (c) D - left back (d) B36 Tórshavn (e) Valur, HB Tórshavn, B36 II, HB Tórshavn, AB Argir, HB Tórshavn

*** Egilsson - Sölvi Egilsson (Sølvi Egilsson) (a) 24/01/1995, ¿? (Faroe Islands) (b) 1,85 (c) D - left back (d) 07 Vestur (e) 07 Vestur, 07 Vestur II

*** Egilstoft - Rógvi Egilstoft (a) 07/12/1992, ¿? (Faroe Islands) (b) - (c) M - central midfielder (d) EB/Streymur (e) EB/S II, NSÍ Runavík, EB/Streymur, Skála, EB/Streymur, 07 Vestur

*** Egloff - Lilian Egloff (Lilian Niclas Egloff) (a) 20/08/2002, Heilbronn (Germany) (b) 1,82 (c) M - attacking midfielder (d) VfB Stuttgart (e) -

*** Egorychev - Andrey Egorychev (Егорычев Андрей Сергеевич) (a) 14/02/1993, Voronezh (Russia) (b) 1,83 (c) M - central midfielder (d) Ural Ekaterimburgo (e) Nosta, Atom, MITOS, Vybor-Kurbatovo

*** Egribayat - Irfan Can Egribayat (İrfan Can Eğribayat) (a) 30/06/1998, Adana (Turkey) (b) 1,93 (c) G (d) Fenerbahce (e) Göztepe, Fenerbahce, Göztepe, Adanaspor

*** Eguaras - Iñigo Eguaras (Iñigo Eguaras Álvarez) (a) 07/03/1992, Antsoain (Spain) (b) 1,81 (c) M - pivot (d) UD Almería (e) Real Zaragoza, CD Mirandés, CE Sabadell, Bilbao Athletic, CD Basconia

*** Ehizibue - Kingsley Ehizibue (Kingsley Osezele Ehizibue) (a) 25/05/1995, München (Germany) (b) 1,89 (c) D - right back (d) Udinese (e) 1.FC Köln, PEC Zwolle

*** Ehmann - Fabian Ehmann (a) 28/08/1998, Graz (Austria) (b) 1,89 (c) G (d) TSV Hartberg (e) SV Horn, Vendsyssel FF, Aris Thessaloniki, Sturm Graz, SV Kapfenberg, Sturm Graz, Sturm Graz II

*** Ehmann - Marco Ehmann (a) 03/08/2000, Spaichingen (Germany) (b) 1,89 (c) D - central defense (d) Stal Mielec (e) EN Paralimniou, FC Dinamo, CSM Resita, FC Dinamo, FC Farul 1920, FC Dinamo

*** Eid - Daniel Eid (Daniel Fritz Eid) (a) 14/10/1998, Ulsteinvik (Norway) (b) 1,83 (c) D - right back (d) IFK Norrköping (e) Sogndal, Hødd

*** Eijgenraam - Joshua Eijgenraam (a) 18/02/2002, Berkel en Rodenrijs (Netherlands) (b) - (c) M - pivot (d) TOP Oss (e) TOP Oss, Excelsior

*** Eikrem - Magnus Wolff Eikrem (a) 08/08/1990, Molde (Norway) (b) 1,73 (c) M - attacking midfielder (d) Molde FK (e) Seattle, Malmö FF, Cardiff City, Heerenveen, Molde, Manchester Utd. Reserves

*** Eile - Noah Eile (a) 19/07/2002, Lund (Sweden) (b) 1,95 (c) D - central defense (d) Mjällby AIF (e) Mjällby AIF, Malmö FF, Mjällby AIF, Malmö FF

*** Eiloz - Or Eiloz (אילוז אור) (a) 12/01/1996, Hadera (Israel) (b) - (c) M - central midfielder (d) - (e) Ness Ziona, Yermiahu Holon, Maccabi Haifa, Kabilio Jaffa, Maccabi Haifa, Bikat haYarden, Maccabi Haifa, Kabilio Jaffa, Maccabi Haifa, Hapoel Hadera, Maccabi Haifa, Hapoel Bnei Lod, Maccabi Haifa, Hapoel Herzliya, Maccabi Haifa, H. Petah Tikva, Maccabi Haifa, Hapoel Raanana, Maccabi Haifa

*** Einarsson - Anton Ari Einarsson (a) 25/08/1994, ¿? (Iceland) (b) - (c) G (d) Breidablik Kópavogur (e) Valur, Grindavík, Valur, Tindastóll, Valur, Afturelding

*** Einarsson - Árni Marinó Einarsson (a) 18/02/2002, ¿? (Iceland) (b) - (c) G (d) ÍA Akranes (e) Skallagrímur

*** Einarsson - Viktor Karl Einarsson (a) 30/01/1997, Kópavogur (Iceland) (b) 1,76 (c) M - central midfielder (d) Breidablik Kópavogur (e) Värnamo

*** Einbinder - Dan Einbinder (דן איינבינדר) (a) 16/02/1989, Jerusalem (Israel) (b) 1,84 (c) M - central midfielder (d) Hapoel Tel Aviv (e) B. Jerusalem, H. Beer Sheva, B. Jerusalem, Maccabi Tel Aviv, Kiryat Shmona, B. Jerusalem
*** Einer - Matrix Einer (a) 25/08/2003, Paide (Estonia) (b) - (c) M - attacking midfielder (d) - (e) Paide
*** Eino - Raimond Eino (a) 15/02/2000, Keila ((c) F - left winger (d) Pärnu JK Vaprus (e) Saku Sporting, Paide, Nomme United
*** Eiríksson - Loftur Páll Eiríksson (a) 11/12/1992, ¿? (Iceland) (b) - (c) D - right back (d) Leiknir Reykjavík (e) Thór, Tindastóll
*** Eiting - Carel Eiting (Carel Willem Eiting) (a) 11/02/1998, Amsterdam (Netherlands) (b) 1,79 (c) M - central midfielder (d) FC Volendam (e) Huddersfield Town, KRC Genk, Ajax, Huddersfield Town, Ajax, Ajax B
*** Eitschberger - Julian Eitschberger (a) 05/03/2004, Hohen Neuendorf (Germany) (b) 1,79 (c) D - right back (d) Hertha Berlín (e) -
*** Eixler - Benoît Eixler (a) 06/02/2003, ¿? (Luxembourg) (b) - (c) D (d) US Hostert II (e) US Hostert
*** Eizenchart - Bartłomiej Eizenchart (Bartłomiej Eizenchart) (a) 23/08/2001, Łęczyca (Poland) (b) 1,82 (c) F - left winger (d) Resovia Rzeszów (e) Górnik Zabrze, Resovia, Górnik Zabrze, GKS Belchatow, Górnik Zabrze, P. Niepolomice, Górnik Zabrze
*** Ejdum - Max Ejdum (Max Isaac Ejdum) (a) 15/10/2004, ¿? (Denmark) (b) - (c) M - central midfielder (d) Odense Boldklub (e) -
*** Ejuke - Chidera Ejuke (a) 02/01/1998, Zaria (Nigeria) (b) 1,76 (c) F - left winger (d) Royal Antwerp FC (e) CSKA Moskva, Hertha Berlin, CSKA Moskva, Heerenveen, Vålerenga, Gombe United, Supreme Court
*** Ejupi - Albert Ejupi (a) 28/08/1992, Stockholm (Sweden) (b) 1,91 (c) M - central midfielder (d) AC Horsens (e) Hapoel Hadera, TSV Hartberg, Helsingborgs IF, Varbergs BoIS, Kristianstad FC, Mjällby AIF, Kristianstad FC, Sölvesborg, Kristianstad FF
*** Ekdal - Albin Ekdal (a) 28/07/1989, Stockholm (Sweden) (b) 1,86 (c) M - pivot (d) Spezia (e) Sampdoria, SV Hamburg, Cagliari, Juventus, Bologna, Juventus, AC Siena, Juventus, Brommapojkarna
*** Ekdal - Hjalmar Ekdal (a) 21/10/1998, Stockholm (Sweden) (b) 1,87 (c) D - central defense (d) Burnley FC (e) Djurgården, Hammarby IF, Sirius, Hammarby IF, IK Frej Täby, Hammarby IF, IK Frej Täby, Assyriska FF, IK Frej Täby, UNC Wilmington, Brommapojkarna
*** Ekeberg - Oskar Ekeberg (a) 29/03/2002, ¿? (United States) (b) - (c) F (d) CS Fola Esch (e) Sandefjord II
*** Ekelik - Mevlüthan Ekelik (a) 16/12/2004, Antalya (Turkey) (b) 1,82 (c) M - central midfielder (d) Antalyaspor (e) Antalyaspor
*** Ekitiké - Hugo Ekitiké (a) 20/06/2002, Reims (France) (b) 1,89 (c) F - center forward (d) París Saint-Germain FC (e) Stade Reims, Paris Saint-Germain, Stade Reims, Stade Reims B, Vejle BK, Stade Reims B
*** Ekkelenkamp - Jurgen Ekkelenkamp (a) 05/04/2000, Zeist (Netherlands) (b) 1,88 (c) M - central midfielder (d) Royal Antwerp FC (e) Hertha Berlin, Ajax, Ajax B
*** Ekofo - Négo Ekofo (a) 17/05/1997, ¿? (France) (b) 1,80 (c) M - right midfielder (d) Swift Hesperange (e) Blois Foot 41, AS Poissy, MDA Chasselay, Avranches B, US Avranches, US Ivry
*** Ekong - Emmanuel Ekong (a) 25/06/2002, Reggio Emilia (Italy) (b) 1,76 (c) F - center forward (d) FC Empoli (e) Perugia, FC Empoli

*** Ekpai - Ubong Ekpai (Ubong Moses Ekpai) (a) 17/10/1995, Uyo (Nigeria) (b) 1,76 (c) F - right winger (d) SK Slavia Praga (e) Mlada Boleslav, Slavia Praha, Banik Ostrava, Slavia Praha, Viktoria Plzen, Ceske Budejovice, Viktoria Plzen, Ceske Budejovice, Viktoria Plzen, Fastav Zlin, Maccabi Haifa, Slovan Liberec, Maccabi Haifa, Akwa United, Kano Pillars

*** Ekpolo - Godswill Ekpolo (Elohor Godswill Ekpolo Egbulu) (a) 14/05/1995, Benin City (Nigeria) (b) 1,81 (c) D - right back (d) Apollon Limassol (e) Norrköping, Häcken, Mérida AD, Fleetwood, FC Barcelona B

*** Ekrene - Andreas Nordentoft Ekrene (a) 04/01/2005, ¿? (Norway) (b) - (c) D - central defense (d) FK Haugesund II (e) -

*** Ekroth - Oliver Ekroth (Peter Oliver Ekroth) (a) 18/01/1992, ¿? (Sweden) (b) 1,87 (c) D - central defense (d) Víkingur Reykjavík (e) Degerfors, Kristianstad FC, Västerås SK, Brattvåg, Västerås SK, Sandvikens IF, Oskarshamns AIK

*** Ektov - Aleksandr Ektov (Эктов Александр Юрьевич) (a) 30/01/1996, Volokolamsk, Moskau Oblast (Russia) (b) 1,73 (c) D - right back (d) FK Krasnodar (e) Orenburg, Shinnik Yaroslav, FK Dolgoprudnyi, CSKA Moskva II, Master-Saturn

*** Ekwah - Pierre Ekwah (Pierre-Emmanuel Ekwah Elimby) (a) 15/01/2002, Massy (France) (b) 1,89 (c) M - pivot (d) Sunderland AFC (e) -

*** Ekwe - David Ekwe (a) 23/10/2002, Kribi (Cameroon) (b) 1,78 (c) D - right back (d) - (e) Kairat Almaty, OFTA Kribi

*** El Aabchi - Selim El Aabchi (a) 23/03/1993, Rabat (Morocco) (b) - (c) F - center forward (d) - (e) Kalev, Kalev III

*** El Afghani - Boucif El Afghani (a) 20/08/1997, Clermont-Ferrand (France) (b) - (c) F - center forward (d) - (e) Tabor Sezana, Côte Bleue

*** El Alami - Issam El Alami (a) 14/10/2003, Luxembourg (Luxembourg) (b) 1,76 (c) F (d) CS Fola Esch (e) -

*** El Allouchi - Mounir El Allouchi (a) 27/09/1994, Roosendaal (Netherlands) (b) 1,72 (c) M - attacking midfielder (d) - (e) Karmiotissa, FAR Rabat, NAC Breda, Helmond Sport, NAC Breda

*** El Amri - Soulayman El Amri (a) 11/05/1998, Verona (Italy) (b) - (c) M - attacking midfielder (d) Ruthin Town (e) Flint Town, Bala, FC Paradiso, A.C. Garda

*** El Anabi - Sami El Anabi (a) 21/06/2000, Lüttich (Belgium) (b) 1,90 (c) D - central defense (d) Wydad Casablanca (e) Spartak Varna, Cherno More, Real Avilés

*** El Andaloussi - Naoufal El Andaloussi (a) 07/03/1991, Gibraltar (Gibraltar) (b) - (c) M - attacking midfielder (d) Glacis United (e) Europa Point FC, Mons Calpe, Glacis United, Mons Calpe, Gibraltar Utd., Manchester 62

*** El Arabi - Youssef El Arabi (العربي يوسف) (a) 03/02/1987, Caen (France) (b) 1,83 (c) F - center forward (d) Olympiakos El Pireo (e) Al-Duhail SC, Granada CF, Al-Hilal, SM Caen, SM Caen B, Mondeville

*** El Arouch - Mohamed El Arouch (a) 06/04/2004, Orange (France) (b) 1,66 (c) M - central midfielder (d) Olympique de Lyon (e) Olymp. Lyon B

*** El Azzouzi - Oussama El Azzouzi (a) 29/05/2001, Veenendaal (Netherlands) (b) 1,89 (c) M - pivot (d) Bologna (e) Union St. Gilloise, FC Emmen

*** El Fardou Ben - El Fardou Ben (El Fardou Mohamed Ben Nabouhane) (a) 10/06/1989, Passamainty (Mayotte) (b) 1,74 (c) F - attacking midfielder (d) APOEL FC (e) Crvena zvezda, Olympiakos, Panionios, Olympiakos, APO Levadiakos, Olympiakos, PAE Veria, Vannes, Le Havre AC, Vannes, Le Havre AC, Le Havre AC B, Saint-Pierroise

*** El Ghazi - Anwar El Ghazi (Anwar El-Ghazi) (a) 03/05/1995, Barendrecht (Netherlands) (b) 1,89 (c) F - right winger (d) PSV Eindhoven (e) Aston Villa, Everton, Aston Villa, Lille, Aston Villa, Lille, Ajax

*** El Ghazoui - Youssef El Ghazoui (Youssef El Ghazoui Darir) (a) 25/10/2000, Tarragona (Spain) (b) 1,84 (c) M - central midfielder (d) Dubai City FC (e) UE Santa Coloma, Elche Ilicitano, Rayo Cantabria, CD Tenerife B

*** el Guerrab - Ayoub el Guerrab (a) 01/04/1992, ¿? (France) (b) - (c) F - center forward (d) FC Mondercange (e) Vandœuvre, FC Rodange 91, Neuves-Maisons, Vandœuvre

*** El Hari - Ilias El Hari (a) 06/07/2005, ¿? (Belgium) (b) - (c) F - right winger (d) KVC Westerlo (e) -

*** El Hasni - Oualid El Hasni (وليد الحسني) (a) 09/08/1993, Cannes (France) (b) 1,92 (c) D - central defense (d) Floriana FC (e) Stade Tunisien, UTA Arad, Triestina, ES Sahel, Vicenza, Monza, Vicenza

*** El Hilali - Omar El Hilali (عمر الهلالي) (a) 12/09/2003, L'Hospitalet de Llobregat (Spain) (b) 1,83 (c) D - right back (d) RCD Espanyol (e) RCD Espanyol B

*** El Hmidi - Ayoub El Hmidi (a) 30/09/2000, Gibraltar (Gibraltar) (b) 1,82 (c) F - left winger (d) CD Torrijos (e) St Joseph's FC, Europa FC, Mons Calpe, Lions Gibraltar

*** El Idrissy - Mounaïm El Idrissy (منعم الإدريسي) (a) 10/02/1999, Martigues (France) (b) 1,81 (c) F - center forward (d) AC Ajaccio (e) AC Ajaccio B

*** El Jebari - Salim El Jebari (ساليم الجباري) (a) 05/02/2004, Madrid (Spain) (b) 1,78 (c) F - left winger (d) Atlético de Madrid B (e) -

*** El Jemili - Jawad El Jemili (جواد الجميلي ستيجواد الجميلي ستي) (a) 04/09/2002, Barcelona (Spain) (b) 1,79 (c) F - left winger (d) Levski Sofia (e) Akritas Chlor.

*** El Kaabi - Ayoub El Kaabi (أيوب الكعبي) (a) 25/06/1993, Casablanca (Morocco) (b) 1,82 (c) F - center forward (d) Olympiakos El Pireo (e) Al-Sadd SC, Hatayspor, Wydad AC, HB FC, Wydad AC, HB CFFC, RS Berkane, RAC Casablanca

*** El Kabbou - Imad El Kabbou (Imad El Kabbou Elazz, عماد القبو العاز) (a) 02/04/2000, Lakrakcha (Morocco) (b) 1,72 (c) F - left winger (d) - (e) Aswan SC, UE Santa Coloma, FC Ascó, Palencia CF, Ponte S. Pietro, Fasano

*** El Kaddouri - Omar El Kaddouri (عمر القادوري) (a) 21/08/1990, Brussel (Belgium) (b) 1,85 (c) M - attacking midfielder (d) - (e) PAOK, Empoli, Napoli, Torino, Napoli, Torino, Napoli, Brescia, Südtirol

*** El Kadiri - Ibrahim El Kadiri (a) 23/01/2002, Amsterdam (Netherlands) (b) 1,70 (c) F - left winger (d) FC Volendam (e) -

*** El Karouani - Souffian El Karouani (a) 19/10/2000, 's-Hertogenbosch (Netherlands) (b) 1,78 (c) D - left back (d) FC Utrecht (e) NEC Nijmegen

*** El Khannouss - Bilal El Khannouss (بلال الخنوص) (a) 10/05/2004, Strombeek-Bever (Belgium) (b) 1,80 (c) M - attacking midfielder (d) KRC Genk (e) Jong Genk

*** El Maach - Issam El Maach (عصام المعاش) (a) 01/02/2000, Heerlen (Netherlands) (b) 1,87 (c) G (d) FC Twente Enschede (e) RKC Waalwijk, Ajax B

*** El Melali - Farid El Melali (a) 13/07/1997, Blida (Algeria) (b) 1,68 (c) F - left winger (d) Angers SCO (e) Pau FC, Angers SCO, Paradou AC

*** El Messaoudi - Ahmed El Messaoudi (a) 03/08/1995, Brussel (Belgium) (b) 1,82 (c) M - pivot (d) FC Emmen (e) Gaziantep FK, FC Groningen, KV Mechelen, Fortuna Sittard, KV Mechelen, Lierse SK, KV Mechelen, Lierse SK, Standard Liège, Lierse SK, JMG Lier

*** El Morabet - Soufiane El Morabet (a) 19/01/2006, ¿? (Gibraltar) (b) - (c) G (d) St Joseph's FC Reserve (e) -

*** El Moustage - Elias El Moustage (Elias El Moustage Gilston) (a) 30/05/2001, København (Denmark) (b) 1,85 (c) M - pivot (d) EB/Streymur (e) Thisted FC

*** El Ouahabi - Ilyas El Ouahabi (a) 20/06/1999, ¿? (Morocco) (b) - (c) M - central midfielder (d) FC Hound Dogs (e) Europa Point FC, Mons Calpe Reserves, Gibraltar Utd.

*** El Shaarawy - Stephan El Shaarawy (Stephan Kareem El Shaarawy) (a) 27/10/1992, Savona (Italy) (b) 1,78 (c) F - left winger (d) AS Roma (e) SH Shenhua, AS Roma, AC Milan, AS Roma, AC Milan, AS Monaco, AC Milan, Genoa, Padova, Genoa

*** El Sheiwi - Ziad El Sheiwi (a) 11/03/2004, ¿? (Austria) (b) 1,80 (c) D - left back (d) FK Austria Viena (e) Young Violets

*** El Yaakoubi - Redouan El Yaakoubi (a) 25/01/1996, Utrecht (Netherlands) (b) 1,83 (c) D - central defense (d) Excelsior Rotterdam (e) Telstar, De Meern

*** El Yamiq - Jawad El Yamiq (اليميق جواد) (a) 29/02/1992, Khouribga (Morocco) (b) 1,93 (c) D - central defense (d) Real Valladolid CF (e) Genoa, Real Zaragoza, Genoa, Perugia, Genoa, Raja Casablanca, O. Khouribga, Khouribga Reserves

*** El Yettefti - Omar El Yettefti (a) 23/11/2002, ¿? (Gibraltar) (b) 1,77 (c) M - central midfielder (d) - (e) Europa Point FC, FC College 1975, Europa Point FC, Manchester 62

*** Elabdellaoui - Omar Elabdellaoui (a) 05/12/1991, Oslo (Norway) (b) 1,79 (c) D - right back (d) FK Bodø/Glimt (e) Galatasaray, Olympiakos, Hull City, Olympiakos, Eintracht Braunschweig, Feyenoord, Strømsgodset, Man City Reserves

*** El-Abdellaoui - Jones El-Abdellaoui (اللاوي عبد يونس) (a) 12/01/2006, ¿? (Norway) (b) 1,84 (c) F - center forward (d) KFUM-Kameratene Oslo (e) Vålerenga

*** El-Amraoui - Bilal El-Amraoui (a) 01/01/1997, ¿? (France) (b) - (c) M - pivot (d) FC Mondercange (e) -

*** Elanga - Anthony Elanga (Anthony David Junior Elanga) (a) 27/04/2002, Hyllie (Sweden) (b) 1,78 (c) F - left winger (d) Nottingham Forest (e) Manchester Utd.

*** Elbakidze - Luka Elbakidze (ლუკა ელბაქიძე) (a) 16/03/2004, ¿? (Georgia) (b) - (c) M - central midfielder (d) Merani Martvili (e) Merani Martvili, Torpedo Kutaisi II

*** Elbouzedi - Zack Elbouzedi (Zachary Elbouzedi) (a) 05/04/1998, Dublin (Ireland) (b) 1,85 (c) F - right winger (d) AIK Solna (e) Lincoln City, Bolton Wanderers, Lincoln City, Waterford FC, Inverness Caledonian, Elgin City, Inverness Caledonian, Malahide

*** Electeur - Maxime Electeur (a) 22/10/1996, ¿? (Belgium) (b) - (c) M - pivot (d) KFC Houtvenne (e) Swift Hesperange, RE Virton, Swift Hesperange, RWDM, RFC Liégeois, Jet Wavre

*** Eleev - Maksim Eleev (Елеев Максим Игоревич) (a) 03/03/2001, ¿? (Russia) (b) 1,82 (c) D - right back (d) Metallurg Lipetsk (e) CSKA Moskva, CSKA Moskva II, Amkar Perm, CSKA Moskva II, Enisey, CSKA Moskva II, Akron Togliatti, CSKA Moskva II

*** Eleferenko - Vlad Eleferenko (Елеференко Влад Алексеевич) (a) 20/12/2000, Enakievo, Donetsk Oblast (Ukraine) (b) 1,88 (c) G (d) - (e) Krasava, Valmiera, Saturn Ramenskoe, Spartak Moskva II

*** Eleftheriadis - Christos Eleftheriadis (Χρήστος Ελευθεριάδης) (a) 30/09/1991, Kavala (Greece) (b) 1,73 (c) F - left winger (d) PAE Chania (e) Ionikos Nikeas, PAS Lamia, PAS Giannina, Panachaiki, Niki Volou, PS Serres, Almopos, Pierikos, AO Kavala, Almopos

*** Eleouet - Allan Eleouet (a) 29/07/1994, Paris (France) (b) 1,74 (c) F - right winger (d) Etoile Carouge FC (e) FK Tuzla City, Yverdon Sport, Stade-Lausanne, Yverdon Sport, FC Bavois, FC Baulmes

*** Elez - Josip Elez (a) 25/04/1994, Split (Croatia) (b) 1,89 (c) D - central defense (d) HNK Hajduk Split (e) Hannover 96, HNK Rijeka, Hannover 96, HNK Rijeka, Lazio, HNK Rijeka, Lazio, Aarhus GF, Lazio, Honvéd, Lazio, Grosseto, Lazio
*** Elezaj - Granit Elezaj (a) 03/08/1996, Pejë (RF Yugoslavia, now in Kosovo) (b) 1,77 (c) F - left winger (d) KF Dukagjini (e) -
*** Elezi - Agon Elezi (Агон Елъези) (a) 01/03/2001, Skopje (North Macedonia) (b) 1,78 (c) M - pivot (d) NK Varazdin (e) KF Skënderbeu, Vëllazërimi
*** Elezi - Dashmir Elezi (a) 21/11/2004, Tetovo (North Macedonia) (b) 1,74 (c) F - center forward (d) Shkëndija Tetovo (e) -
*** Elhi - Trevor Elhi (a) 11/04/1993, Tallinn (Estonia) (b) 1,77 (c) D - left back (d) FC Zenit Tallinn (e) Kalju FC, FCI Levadia, SJK Seinäjoki, Botev Vratsa, Kalju FC, Levadia, FC Infonet, Levadia, Levadia II
*** Elia - Meschack Elia (Meschack Elia Lina) (a) 06/08/1997, Kinshasa (Congo DR) (b) 1,73 (c) F - attacking midfielder (d) BSC Young Boys (e) TP Mazembe, CS Don Bosco
*** Elias - Shai Elias (שי אליאס) (a) 25/02/1999, Herzliya (Israel) (b) 1,85 (c) M - pivot (d) Hapoel Beer Sheva (e) Hapoel Tel Aviv, Ness Ziona, Hapoel Tel Aviv
*** Eliasi - Niv Eliasi (ניב אליאסי) (a) 21/02/2002, ¿? (Israel) (b) - (c) G (d) Hapoel Beer Sheva (e) Ramat haSharon, H. Beer Sheva
*** Eliasson - Niclas Eliasson (Niclas Eliasson Santana) (a) 07/12/1995, Varberg (Sweden) (b) 1,78 (c) M - right midfielder (d) AEK Athína FC (e) Nîmes, Bristol City, Norrköping, AIK, Norrköping, AIK, Falkenbergs FF
*** Elíasson - Jón Kristinn Elíasson (a) 20/03/2001, ¿? (Iceland) (b) - (c) G (d) ÍBV Vestmannaeyjar (e) Framherjar, ÍBV Vestmannaeyjar, Framherjar, ÍBV Vestmannaeyjar, Framherjar, ÍBV Vestmannaeyjar
*** Eliomar - Eliomar (Eliomar Correia Silva) (a) 16/03/1988, Cardoso Moreira (Brazil) (b) 1,75 (c) F - left winger (d) FK Javor-Matis Ivanjica (e) Zlatibor, FK Indjija, Mladost, Siroki Brijeg, Javor-Matis, FK Partizan, Javor-Matis, FK Partizan, AE Larisa, FK Partizan, Pierikos, FK Partizan, Kecskeméti TE, FK Partizan, Javor-Matis, Cardoso Moreira
*** Eliosius - Tadas Eliosius (Tadas Eliošius) (a) 01/03/1990, Ukmerge (Soviet Union, now in Lithuania) (b) 1,83 (c) M - left midfielder (d) FK Jonava (e) Palanga, Panevezys, Nevezis, Jonava, Kruoja, Siauliai, Atlantas, Suduva, Kruoja, Vetra
*** Eliosius - Tautvydas Eliosius (Tautvydas Eliošius) (a) 03/11/1991, Ukmergė (Lithuania) (b) 1,72 (c) M - central midfielder (d) FK Panevezys (e) Jonava, Zalgiris, Jonava, Zalgiris, Kruoja, Siauliai
*** Elis - Alberth Elis (Alberth Josué Elis Martínez) (a) 12/02/1996, San Pedro Sula (Honduras) (b) 1,85 (c) F - right winger (d) FC Girondins de Burdeos (e) Stade Brestois, Girondins Bordeaux, Boavista, Girondins Bordeaux, Boavista, Houston, Monterrey, Houston, Monterrey, CD Olimpia, Olimpia Reserves
*** Elisor - Simon Elisor (Simon Tom Elisor) (a) 22/07/1999, Périgueux (France) (b) 1,86 (c) F - center forward (d) FC Metz (e) RFC Seraing, Stade Lavallois, RFC Seraing, AC Ajaccio, FC Villefranche, AC Ajaccio, FC Sète 34, AC Ajaccio, AC Ajaccio B, Istres FC
*** Elísson - Alex Freyr Elísson (a) 09/10/1997, ¿? (Iceland) (b) - (c) D - right back (d) KA Akureyri (e) KA Akureyri, Breidablik, Fram Reykjavík
*** Elivelto - Elivelto (Elivelton Ribeiro Dantas) (a) 02/01/1992, Holambra (Brazil) (b) 1,70 (c) F - left winger (d) Anagennisi Karditsas (e) Panevezys, Sogdiana, Taraz, RFS, M. Petah Tikva, Zalgiris, Ekranas, Imperial-RJ
*** Eliyahu - Osher Eliyahu (אליהו אושר) (a) 15/01/2003, Ramla (Israel) (b) - (c) F - attacking midfielder (d) - (e) Maccabi Netanya

*** Eliyahu - Yinon Eliyahu (יינון אליהו) (a) 01/11/1993, Jerusalem (Israel) (b) - (c) D - right back (d) Hapoel Haifa (e) Maccabi Haifa, M. Petah Tikva, H. Ramat Gan, Hapoel Acre, Hapoel Katamon, Maccabi Herzlya, Kiryat Malachi, Ironi Modiin
*** Ellahi - Mohammad Hossein Ellahi (a) 25/10/1996, Tehran (Iran) (b) 1,75 (c) F - center forward (d) FC Ulaanbaatar (e) Glacis United, Stadl-Paura, Holzheimer SG, FC Vaulx-en-Vel, Albion W. Eagles, Corrimal RFC, Hanauer SC 1960, Sounders Reserves
*** Ellborg - Melker Ellborg (a) 22/05/2003, Kalmar (Sweden) (b) 1,91 (c) G (d) Ariana FC (e) Ariana FC, Malmö FF, IFK Malmö, Malmö FF, IFK Berga
*** Ellertsson - Mikael Egill Ellertsson (a) 11/03/2002, Reykjavík (Iceland) (b) 1,82 (c) M - central midfielder (d) Venezia FC (e) Spezia, SPAL, Spezia, Fram Reykjavík
*** Ellingsgaard - Ari Ellingsgaard (Ari Ólavsson Ellingsgaard) (a) 03/02/1993, ¿? (Faroe Islands) (b) 1,72 (c) M - attacking midfielder (d) Skála IF (e) ÍF Fuglafjördur, EB/Streymur, ÍF Fuglafjördur, NSÍ Runavík, ÍF Fuglafjördur
*** Ellingsgaard - Aron Ellingsgaard (Aron Jarnskor Ellingsgaard) (a) 16/09/2002, ¿? (Faroe Islands) (b) - (c) M - central midfielder (d) Víkingur Gøta (e) Víkingur II
*** Elliott - Harvey Elliott (Harvey Scott Elliott) (a) 04/04/2003, Chertsey (England) (b) 1,70 (c) M - attacking midfielder (d) Liverpool FC (e) Blackburn
*** Ellis - Gruff Ellis (Gruffydd Rees Ellis) (a) 16/08/2004, ¿? (Wales) (b) - (c) D - central defense (d) CPD Porthmadog (e) -
*** Ellis - Liam Ellis (Liam David Ellis) (a) 16/04/2003, ¿? (Wales) (b) - (c) M - central midfielder (d) Llandudno FC (e) Ruthin, Flint Town, Ruthin, Flint Town
*** Ellul - Matthew Ellul (a) 23/05/2002, ¿? (Malta) (b) 1,79 (c) D - central defense (d) Hibernians FC (e) -
*** Elm - Rasmus Elm (Rasmus Christoffer Elm) (a) 17/03/1988, Kalmar (Sweden) (b) 1,84 (c) M - central midfielder (d) Viktor Elm (e) Kalmar FF, CSKA Moskva, AZ Alkmaar, Kalmar FF, Emmaboda IS
*** Elmali - Eren Elmali (Evren Eren Elmalı) (a) 07/07/2000, Istanbul (Turkey) (b) 1,80 (c) D - left back (d) Trabzonspor (e) Kasimpasa, Silivrispor, Kasimpasa
*** Elmas - Eljif Elmas (Елиф Елмас) (a) 24/09/1999, Skopje (North Macedonia) (b) 1,82 (c) M - central midfielder (d) SSC Nápoles (e) Fenerbahce, Rabotnicki
*** Elmaz - Bartug Elmaz (Bartuğ Elmaz) (a) 19/02/2003, Tekirdag (Turkey) (b) 1,79 (c) M - pivot (d) Fenerbahce (e) Ol. Marseille B, Galatasaray
*** Elneny - Mohamed Elneny (Mohamed Naser Elsayed Elneny, محمد النني) (a) 11/07/1992, Mahalla (Egypt) (b) 1,79 (c) M - pivot (d) Arsenal FC (e) Besiktas, Arsenal, FC Basel, El Mokawloon, FC Basel, El Mokawloon
*** Elo - Dor Elo (דור אלו) (a) 26/09/1993, Petah Tikva (Israel) (b) 1,79 (c) D - right back (d) Maccabi Bnei Reineh (e) Hapoel Tel Aviv, M. Petah Tikva, Kiryat Shmona, H. Beer Sheva, Bnei Yehuda, H. Beer Sheva, M. Petah Tikva
*** Eloyan - Arayik Eloyan (Արայիկ Էլոյան) (a) 16/03/2004, ¿? (Armenia) (b) 1,88 (c) F - center forward (d) BKMA Yerevan (e) BKMA Yerevan II, Ararat-Armenia II, Urartu II
*** Elsnik - Timi Max Elsnik (Timi Max Elšnik) (a) 29/04/1998, Zlatoličje (Slovenia) (b) 1,82 (c) M - central midfielder (d) NK Olimpija Ljubljana (e) Northampton, Mansfield Town, Swindon Town
*** Élton Calé - Élton Calé (Élton Pereira Gomes) (a) 12/07/1988, Barro Duro (Piauí) (Brazil) (b) 1,69 (c) F - left winger (d) SC Gjilani (e) KF Tirana, Flamurtari FC, FK Kukësi, Ergotelis, OFI Creta, Ergotelis, União Madeira, Tondela, Leixões, Gazovik Orenburg, Belenenses, Desp. Brasil, Estoril Praia, Desp. Brasil, São Bento (SP), Desp. Brasil, Ituano, Desp. Brasil, Avaí FC B, Desp. Brasil

*** Elustondo - Aritz Elustondo (Aritz Elustondo Irribarria) (a) 28/03/1994, Beasain (Spain) (b) 1,82 (c) D - central defense (d) Real Sociedad (e) Real Sociedad B, SD Beasain

*** Elvarsson - Frans Elvarsson (a) 14/08/1990, ¿? (Iceland) (b) - (c) M - pivot (d) Keflavík ÍF (e) Njardvík, Keflavík, Njardvík, Sindri

*** Elvedi - Nico Elvedi (a) 30/09/1996, Zürich (Switzerland) (b) 1,89 (c) D - central defense (d) Borussia Mönchengladbach (e) FC Zürich

*** Ely - Rodrigo Ely (a) 03/11/1993, Lajeado (Brazil) (b) 1,88 (c) D - central defense (d) Grêmio Foot-Ball Porto Alegrense (e) UD Almería, Nottingham Forest, Alavés, AC Milan, Alavés, AC Milan, Avellino, AC Milan, Varese, AC Milan, Reggina

*** Elyounoussi - Mohamed Elyounoussi (a) 04/08/1994, Al-Hoceima (Morocco) (b) 1,78 (c) F - left winger (d) FC Copenhague (e) Southampton, Celtic FC, Southampton, FC Basel, Molde, Sarpsborg 08

*** Elysée - Elysée (Bi Sehi Elysée Irie) (a) 13/09/1989, Yopougon (Ivory Coast) (b) 1,84 (c) M - pivot (d) JK Trans Narva (e) Narva United FC, Johvi Lokomotiv, JK Trans Narva, Mordovia, ES Bingerville

*** Elzbergas - Dovas Elzbergas (a) 29/03/2005, ¿? (Lithuania) (b) 1,87 (c) G (d) FK Zalgiris Vilnius B (e) Zalgiris C

*** Emakhu - Aidomo Emakhu (a) 26/10/2003, Clondalkin, Dublin (Ireland) (b) 1,80 (c) F - left winger (d) Millwall FC (e) Shamrock Rovers

*** Emanuel - Emanuel (Emanuel Leone Moura) (a) 01/11/1999, São Paulo (Brazil) (b) 1,85 (c) D - central defense (d) - (e) Spartak Varna, Grêmio Porto Alegre B, EC São José, Grêmio Porto Alegre B, Inter Limeira, Grêmio Porto Alegre B

*** Emanuel - Emanuel (José Emanuel Carvalho Teixeira) (a) 10/11/2001, Andorra la Vella (Andorra) (b) - (c) G (d) CF Esperança d'Andorra (e) UE Santa Coloma, UE Santa B

*** Embaló - Sandro Embaló (Sandro Sene Aníbal Embaló) (a) 01/05/1996, Lisboa (Portugal) (b) 1,90 (c) D - central defense (d) Al-Qaisumah FC (e) Al-Naft SC, AC Oulu, Oly. Lympion, Dulwich Hamlet, CD Fátima, Ermis Aradippou, Kalev, Genoa

*** Embaló - Úmaro Embaló (a) 06/05/2001, Bissau (Guinea-Bissau) (b) 1,70 (c) F - right winger (d) Fortuna Sittard (e) Benfica B

*** Embarba - Adrián Embarba (Adrián Embarba Blazquez) (a) 07/05/1992, Madrid (Spain) (b) 1,73 (c) F - right winger (d) UD Almería (e) RCD Espanyol, Rayo Vallecano, Rayo B, Carabanchel, Marchamalo

*** Embolo - Breel Embolo (Breel Donald Embolo) (a) 14/02/1997, Yaoundé (Cameroon) (b) 1,87 (c) F - center forward (d) AS Mónaco (e) Borussia Mönchengladbach, FC Schalke 04, FC Basel

*** Emegha - Emanuel Emegha (Emmanuel Esseh Emegha) (a) 03/02/2003, Den Haag (Netherlands) (b) 1,95 (c) F - center forward (d) Racing Club Strasbourg (e) Sturm Graz, Royal Antwerp, Sparta Rotterdam

*** Emeka - Chinonso Emeka (a) 30/08/2001, ¿? (Nigeria) (b) 1,97 (c) F - center forward (d) AS Trencin (e) KAA Gent, Water FC

*** Emeljanov - Dmitriy Emeljanov (Емельянов Дмитрий Павлович) (a) 02/06/2004, ¿? (Belarus) (b) - (c) M - attacking midfielder (d) FK Gomel II (e) -

*** Emeljanov - Roman Emeljanov (Емельянов Роман Павлович) (a) 08/05/1992, Pavlovo, Nizhniy Novgorod Region (Russia) (b) 1,89 (c) M - pivot (d) Shinnik Yaroslavl (e) Shinnik, Ural, Shakhtar Donetsk, Ural, Shakhtar II, Rostov, Shakhtar II, Illichivets, Shakhtar II, Rostov, Shakhtar II, Zorya Lugansk, Shakhtar II, Akad. Togliatti, Akron Konoplev

*** Ememe - Evo Christ Ememe (a) 30/04/2001, ¿? (Nigeria) (b) 1,77 (c) F - left winger (d) Ironi Kiryat Shmona (e) Mosta FC

*** Ementa - Anosike Ementa (Anosike Victor Ementa) (a) 03/05/2002, Annisse (Denmark) (b) 2,02 (c) F - center forward (d) Viborg FF (e) Aalborg BK
*** Emërllahu - Lindon Emërllahu (a) 07/12/2002, Mushtishtë (RF Yugoslavia, now in Kosovo) (b) 1,75 (c) M - pivot (d) FC Ballkani (e) -
*** Emerson - Emerson (Emerson Marcelina) (a) 24/02/1991, ¿? (Brazil) (b) 1,90 (c) M - pivot (d) Hamrun Spartans (e) Nadur Y., Floriana, Birkirkara FC, Tarxien, Birkirkara FC, Floriana, Birkirkara FC, Floriana, FC Viitorul, Imbituba-SC, Jabaquara-SP
*** Émerson - Émerson (Іллой-Айєт Владіс-Еммерсон) (a) 07/10/1995, Odessa (Ukraine) (b) 1,95 (c) D - central defense (d) Ural Ekaterimburgo (e) SKA Khabarovsk, Vejle BK, Armavir, Vejle BK, R&F, Vejle BK, Olimpik Donetsk, Karpaty, Nyva Ternopil, Karpaty, Chornomorets II
*** Emerson Brito - Emerson Brito (Emerson Rodrigues Brito) (a) 06/05/2002, Santa Cruz do Sul (Brazil) (b) 1,75 (c) F - left winger (d) Pouso Alegre FC (e) Javor-Matis, Grêmio Porto Alegre B, Esportivo, Grêmio Porto Alegre B, Esportivo
*** Emerson Palmieri - Emerson Palmieri (Emerson Palmieri dos Santos) (a) 03/08/1994, Santos (Brazil) (b) 1,76 (c) D - left back (d) West Ham United (e) Chelsea, Olympique Lyon, Chelsea, AS Roma, Santos, AS Roma, Santos, US Palermo, Santos, Santos B
*** Emerson Royal - Emerson Royal (Emerson Aparecido Leite de Souza Júnior) (a) 14/01/1999, São Paulo (Brazil) (b) 1,83 (c) D - right back (d) Tottenham Hotspur (e) FC Barcelona, Real Betis, FC Barcelona, At. Mineiro, Ponte Preta
*** Emilsen - Mathias Emilsen (Mathias Johnsrud Emilsen) (a) 08/06/2003, Oslo (Norway) (b) 1,86 (c) M - pivot (d) Ranheim IL (e) Vålerenga, Sandnes Ulf, Vålerenga, Vålerenga II
*** Emini - Benjamin Emini (a) 20/07/1992, Podujevë (RF Yugoslavia, now in Kosovo) (b) 1,80 (c) D - right back (d) KF Llapi (e) FC Llapi
*** Emini - Gentian Emini (a) 03/08/1997, ¿? (RF Yugoslavia, now in Kosovo) (b) - (c) D - left back (d) - (e) KF Ferizaj, KF Ulpiana, KF Arbëria, KF Ulpiana
*** Emini - Lorik Emini (a) 29/08/1999, Zug (Switzerland) (b) 1,76 (c) M - central midfielder (d) FC Vaduz (e) FC Luzern
*** Emini - Sefer Emini (Сефер Емини) (a) 15/07/2000, Skopje (North Macedonia) (b) 1,74 (c) M - pivot (d) SønderjyskE (e) Makedonija, Akron Togliatti, Makedonija, Akron Togliatti, Makedonija
*** Emini - Serxhio Emini (a) 03/12/2002, Sarandë (Albania) (b) 1,75 (c) F - right winger (d) FK Bylis (e) FK Tomori Berat, FK Bylis
*** Emirov - Rustam Emirov (Эмиров Рустам Русланович) (a) 14/09/2000, Tashkensaz, Almaty Oblast (Kazakhstan) (b) 1,80 (c) M - pivot (d) FC Khan Tengri (e) Khan Tengri, Kairat Almaty, Kairat Moskva, Kairat-Zhas
*** Emmanuel - Umeh Emmanuel (a) 31/08/2004, ¿? (Nigeria) (b) 1,75 (c) F - center forward (d) Botev Plovdiv (e) FDC Vista
*** Emmer - Jakub Emmer (a) 30/03/2001, Teplice (Czech Rep.) (b) 1,75 (c) M - central midfielder (d) FK Teplice B (e) Usti nad Labem, Teplice B
*** Emmers - Xian Emmers (Xian Ghislaine Emmers) (a) 20/07/1999, Lugano (Switzerland) (b) 1,78 (c) M - attacking midfielder (d) FC Rapid 1923 (e) Roda JC, Internazionale Milano, Almere City, Internazionale Milano, Waasland-Beveren, Internazionale Milano, Cremonese, Internazionale Milano
*** Emond - Renaud Emond (Renaud Thierry Emond) (a) 05/12/1991, Virton (Belgium) (b) 1,85 (c) F - center forward (d) Standard de Lieja (e) FC Nantes, Standard Liège, Waasland-Beveren, RE Virton

*** Emreli - Mahir Emreli (Mahir Mahir oğlu Emreli) (a) 01/07/1997, Tver (Azerbaijan) (b) 1,87 (c) F - center forward (d) GNK Dinamo Zagreb (e) Konyaspor, Dinamo Zagreb, Legia Warszawa, Qarabag FK

*** Emsis - Aivars Emsis (a) 01/04/1998, ¿? (Latvia) (b) 1,92 (c) F - center forward (d) FK Suduva Marijampole (e) Lavello, Dziugas, AO Kavala, Dziugas, Bischofswerda, Spartaks, Jelgava, JDFS Alberts, FS Metta II, JDFS Alberts

*** Emsis - Eduards Emsis (a) 23/02/1996, ¿? (Latvia) (b) - (c) M - pivot (d) Raufoss IL (e) KF Egnatia, FC Lahti, FC Noah, Jelgava, Metta, FS Metta II, Skonto II

*** Emurli - Amar Emurli (a) 04/01/2003, Tetovo (North Macedonia) (b) 1,80 (c) F - right winger (d) Arsimi (e) Sileks, Renova

*** Enache - Gabriel Enache (Gabriel Nicolae Enache) (a) 18/08/1990, Piteşti (Romania) (b) 1,74 (c) D - right back (d) - (e) FC U Craiova, Zhetysu, FCSB, Kyzyl-Zhar, Astra Giurgiu, FK Partizan, Dunarea Calarasi, FK Partizan, Rubin Kazan, FCSB, Astra Giurgiu, CS Mioveni

*** Enciso - Julio Enciso (Julio César Enciso) (a) 23/01/2004, Caaguazú (Paraguay) (b) 1,73 (c) F - attacking midfielder (d) Brighton & Hove Albion (e) Libertad

*** Enck - Enck (Enck Pablo Oliveira de Souza) (a) 13/01/2000, Camaçari (Brazil) (b) - (c) D - central defense (d) Zakho SC (e) KF Erzeni, Maruinense

*** Endeladze - Avto Endeladze (ავთო ენდელაძე) (a) 17/09/1994, Kutaisi (Georgia) (b) 1,76 (c) D - left back (d) - (e) Zugdidi, FC Samtredia, Sioni Bolnisi, Rustavi, FC Samtredia, Rustavi, FC Meshakhte, Kolkheti Poti, Torpedo Kutaisi, FC Samtredia, FK Zugdidi, FC Zestafoni, Baia, Baia Zugdidi, Baia

*** Endl - Lukas Endl (Lukáš Endl) (a) 17/06/2003, Brno (Czech Rep.) (b) 1,91 (c) D - central defense (d) FC Zbrojovka Brno (e) -

*** Endo - Wataru Endo (遠藤 航) (a) 09/02/1993, Yokohama, Kanagawa (Japan) (b) 1,78 (c) M - pivot (d) VfB Stuttgart (e) Sint-Truiden, VfB Stuttgart, Sint-Truiden, Urawa Reds, Shonan Bellmare

*** Ene - Cornel Ene (Cornel Alexandru Ene) (a) 21/07/1993, Satu Mare (Romania) (b) 1,87 (c) D - central defense (d) - (e) FC Hermannstadt, CS Mioveni, Gyirmót FC, Kisvárda, Daco-Getica, ASA Tg. Mures, Pandurii, CFR Cluj, Olimpia SM, CFR Cluj, UTA Arad, CFR Cluj, Olimpia SM

*** Ene - Robert Ene (Robert Andrei Ene) (a) 20/01/2005, Piteşti (Romania) (b) - (c) M - central midfielder (d) - (e) FC D. Coman, FC D. Coman, AS Metropolitan

*** Eneme - Santiago Eneme (Santiago Eneme Bocari) (a) 29/09/2000, Malabo (Equatorial Guinea) (b) 1,83 (c) F - left winger (d) MFK Vyskov (e) FC Nantes B, Cano Sport

*** Eneme-Ella - Ulrick Eneme-Ella (Ulrick Brad Eneme-Ella) (a) 22/05/2001, Sens (France) (b) 1,84 (c) F - center forward (d) Angers SCO B (e) Amiens SC, FC Liefering, FC Sens

*** Enersen - Ole Enersen (Ole Kristian Bergcm Enersen) (a) 06/09/2002, ¿? (Norway) (b) 1,81 (c) F - left winger (d) Strømsgodset IF (e) Strømsgodset II

*** Enevoldsen - Lukas Enevoldsen (Lukas Schmedes Enevoldsen) (a) 24/05/1993, ¿? (Denmark) (b) 1,92 (c) D - central defense (d) Brabrand IF (e) B36 Tórshavn, FC Fredericia, Brabrand IF, Thisted FC, Brabrand IF, Kjellerup IF

*** Eng - Jacob Dicko Eng (Jacob Emile Dicko Eng) (a) 14/09/2004, ¿? (Norway) (b) 1,80 (c) F - left winger (d) Vålerenga Fotball (e) Vålerenga II

*** Engblom - Pontus Engblom (a) 03/11/1991, Sundsvall (Sweden) (b) 1,83 (c) F - center forward (d) GIF Sundsvall (e) Sandefjord, Strømsgodset, Sandnes Ulf, Haugesund, GIF Sundsvall, Haugesund, AIK, GIF Sundsvall, AIK, Västerås SK, AIK, AFC Eskilstuna, IFK Sundsvall, AIK

*** Engdahl - Ben Engdahl (a) 17/09/2003, Stockholm (Sweden) (b) - (c) D - right back (d) Jönköpings Södra IF (e) J-Södra IF, Nordsjælland, Hammarby IF, Hammarby TFF, Hammarby IF
*** Engdahl - Martin Engdahl (Martin Rolando Maccallun-Coffiny Engdahl) (a) 04/06/2003, ¿? (Norway) (b) - (c) F (d) Sandefjord Fotball II (e) -
*** Engel - Lukas Engel (Lukas Ahlefeld Engel) (a) 14/12/1998, Kastrup (Denmark) (b) 1,78 (c) D - left back (d) Silkeborg IF (e) Vejle BK, Silkeborg IF, Vejle BK, Fremad Amager, Kastrup BK
*** Engels - Arne Engels (a) 08/09/2003, ¿? (Belgium) (b) 1,85 (c) M - central midfielder (d) FC Augsburg (e) Club NXT
*** Engels - Björn Engels (Björn Lionel Engels) (a) 15/09/1994, Kaprijke (Belgium) (b) 1,95 (c) D - central defense (d) Royal Antwerp FC (e) Aston Villa, Stade Reims, Olympiakos, Stade Reims, Olympiakos, KV Brugge
*** Engels - Mario Engels (a) 22/10/1993, Troisdorf (Germany) (b) 1,84 (c) F - center forward (d) Heracles Almelo (e) Tokyo Verdy, Sparta Rotterdam, SV Sandhausen, Roda JC, Śląsk Wroclaw, FSV Frankfurt, 1.FC Köln II
*** Enggaard - Mads Enggaard (Mads Enggård) (a) 20/01/2004, Silkeborg (Denmark) (b) 1,80 (c) M - central midfielder (d) Randers FC (e) -
*** Engin - Ahmet Engin (Ahmet Emin Engin) (a) 09/08/1996, Moers (Germany) (b) 1,80 (c) F - left winger (d) Volos NPS (e) Kasimpasa, MSV Duisburg
*** Englaro - Ivan Englaro (a) 12/11/2004, ¿? (Luxembourg) (b) 1,75 (c) M - central midfielder (d) F91 Dudelange (e) Swift Hesperange
*** Englaro - Sergio Englaro (a) 03/02/2002, Luxembourg (Luxembourg) (b) - (c) G (d) FC Etzella Ettelbruck (e) Pevidém
*** Englezou - Nikolas Englezou (Νικόλας Εγγλέζου) (a) 11/07/1993, Limassol (Cyprus) (b) 1,72 (c) D - left back (d) AEK Larnaca (e) Doxa Katokopias, Anorthosis, AEK Larnaca, Aris Limassol, AEK Larnaca, Nea Salamis, AEK Larnaca, AEK Athína, Nea Salamis, AEK Athína
*** Engolo - François Engolo (François Xavier Engolo) (a) 27/11/2002, ¿? (Belgium) (b) - (c) F - center forward (d) FC Mondercange (e) Olym. Charleroi
*** Engström - Jesper Engström (a) 24/04/1992, Vöyri (Finland) (b) 1,73 (c) D - left back (d) Vaasan Palloseura (e) FC Inter, VPS, FC YPA, VPS, Vaasa IFK, Norrvalla FF
*** Engvall - Gustav Engvall (Gustav Per Fredrik Engvall) (a) 29/04/1996, Kalmar (Sweden) (b) 1,85 (c) F - center forward (d) IFK Värnamo (e) KV Mechelen, Sarpsborg 08, KV Mechelen, Bristol City, IFK Göteborg, Bristol City, Djurgården, Bristol City, Djurgården, Bristol City, IFK Göteborg
*** Enin - Ivan Enin (Енин Иван Владимирович) (a) 06/02/1994, Kherson (Ukraine) (b) 1,83 (c) M - pivot (d) Torpedo Moskva (e) Zrinjski Mostar, Siroki Brijeg, Riga, Vityaz Podolsk, Riga, Vityaz Podolsk, Vityaz P. II
*** Enkerud - Jonas Enkerud (a) 25/04/1990, Åsnes (Norway) (b) 1,90 (c) F - center forward (d) Hamarkameratene (e) Elverum, Eidsvold Turn, Nybergsund
*** En-Nesyri - Youssef En-Nesyri (a) 01/06/1997, Fès (Morocco) (b) 1,92 (c) F - center forward (d) Sevilla FC (e) CD Leganés, Málaga CF, At. Malagueño, AM Football
*** Ennin - Richlord Ennin (Richlord Ennin) (a) 17/09/1998, Toronto, Ontario (Canada) (b) 1,83 (c) F - center forward (d) FK Spartaks Jurmala (e) Honvéd, Spartaks, Nizhny Novgorod, Spartaks, Tom Tomsk, Spartaks, Zalgiris, Tom Tomsk, Zalgiris, Spartaks, Castrovillari, Capo Rizzuto, Toronto FC II
*** Enobakhare - Bright Enobakhare (a) 08/02/1998, Benin City (Nigeria) (b) 1,80 (c) F - center forward (d) - (e) Rukh Lviv, H. Jerusalem, Coventry City, SC East

Bengal, AEK Athína, Wolverhampton Wanderers, Wigan Ath., Wolverhampton Wanderers, Coventry City, Wolverhampton Wanderers, Kilmarnock FC, Wolverhampton Wanderers
*** Enoh - Lewis Enoh (Lewis Mbah Enoh) (a) 23/10/1992, Bamenda (Cameroon) (b) 1,89 (c) F - right winger (d) O Elvas CAD (e) Olympiakos N., PAEEK Kyrenia, SC Covilhã, Leixões, Casa Pia, Leixões, ACSM Poli Iasi, KSC Lokeren, Sporting B, Leixões, Sporting B, Sourense, Alcanenense
*** Enriles - Aidan Enriles (Aidan Nicholas Enriles) (a) 22/02/2001, ¿? (Gibraltar) (b) - (c) M - central midfielder (d) - (e) FC College 1975, Red Imps Reserves
*** Entrena - Juanan Entrena (Juan Antonio Entrena Gálvez) (a) 19/05/1996, Huétor Tájar (Spain) (b) 1,83 (c) F - left winger (d) CD Huétor Tájar (e) UE Santa Coloma, Helsinki IFK, UD Melilla, Orihuela CF, UD Melilla, Omonia Nicosia, Alavés, NK Rudes, Alavés, Recreativo Granada, RCD Espanyol B
*** Eördögh - András Eördögh (a) 09/03/2002, Budapest (Hungary) (b) 1,87 (c) M - attacking midfielder (d) Budapest Honvéd FC (e) Honvéd II, BFC Siófok, Honvéd II
*** Ephestion - Thomas Ephestion (a) 09/06/1995, Sucy-en-Brie (France) (b) 1,89 (c) M - central midfielder (d) - (e) Mezőkövesd, RWDM, KVC Westerlo, RWDM, KVC Westerlo, RWDM, KVC Westerlo, US Orléans, RC Lens, AS Béziers, Ol. Marseille B
*** Epolo - Matthieu Epolo (Matthieu Luka Epolo) (a) 15/01/2005, ¿? (Belgium) (b) 1,85 (c) G (d) Standard de Lieja (e) -
*** Epureanu - Alexandru Epureanu (Alexandru Ion Epureanu) (a) 27/09/1986, Chisinau (Soviet Union, now in Moldova) (b) 1,89 (c) D - central defense (d) - (e) Ümraniyespor, Basaksehir, Anzhi, Dinamo Moskva, Anzhi, Dinamo Moskva, KS Samara, Dinamo Moskva, FC Moskva, FC Sheriff, Zimbru Chisinau
*** Erabi - Jusef Erabi (a) 08/06/2003, Stockholm (Sweden) (b) - (c) F - center forward (d) Hammarby IF (e) Hammarby TFF, Hammarby IF, Hammarby TFF, IK Frej Täby
*** Erakovic - Novica Erakovic (Novica Eraković) (a) 12/11/1999, Nikšić (RF Yugoslavia, now in Montenegro) (b) 1,87 (c) M - central midfielder (d) Omonia Nicosia (e) Sutjeska Niksic, FK Lovcen, Sutjeska Niksic, Sutjeska II
*** Erakovic - Strahinja Erakovic (Страхиња Ераковић) (a) 22/01/2001, Batajnica (RF yugoslavia, now in Serbia) (b) 1,88 (c) D - central defense (d) Zenit de San Petersburgo (e) Crvena zvezda, Graficar
*** Eraso - Javi Eraso (Javier Eraso Goñi) (a) 22/03/1990, Pamplona (Spain) (b) 1,80 (c) M - central midfielder (d) SD Amorebieta (e) Akritas Chlor., CD Leganés, Athletic, CD Leganés, Bilbao Athletic, CD Basconia
*** Erataman - Yagiz Efe Erataman (Yağız Efe Erataman) (a) 18/08/2005, Istanbul (Turkey) (b) 1,94 (c) G (d) - (e) Basaksehir
*** Erceg - Ante Erceg (a) 12/12/1989, Split (Yugoslavia, now in Croatia) (b) 1,80 (c) F - center forward (d) NK Istra 1961 (e) Debrecen, Brøndby IF, NK Osijek, Brøndby IF, Esbjerg fB, Brøndby IF, Shabab Al-Ahli, Hajduk Split, Balikesirspor, RNK Split, Junak Sinj, RNK Split
*** Erciyas - Cagan Erciyas (Çağan Kayra Erciyas) (a) 04/02/2003, Hatay (Turkey) (b) - (c) D - right back (d) Fethiyespor (e) Fethiyespor, Alanyaspor
*** Erdal - Ziya Erdal (a) 05/01/1988, Sivas (Turkey) (b) 1,73 (c) D - left back (d) Sivasspor (e) A. Üsküdar 1908, Kirsehirspor
*** Erdélyi - Benedek Erdélyi (Erdélyi Benedek Miklós) (a) 28/09/2005, Debrecen (Hungary) (b) 1,90 (c) G (d) Debreceni VSC (e) Debrecen II
*** Erdilman - Mustafa Erdilman (a) 01/01/2004, Burdur (Turkey) (b) - (c) M - central midfielder (d) Antalyaspor (e) -

*** Erdogan - Bugra Erdogan (Osman Buğra Erdoğan) (a) 16/07/2004, Istanbul (Turkey) (b) 1,86 (c) F - center forward (d) - (e) Ümraniyespor

*** Erdogan - Dogan Erdogan (Doğan Erdoğan) (a) 22/08/1996, Samsun (Turkey) (b) 1,82 (c) M - pivot (d) - (e) Fortuna Sittard, Gaziantep FK, Çaykur Rizespor, Trabzonspor, LASK, Juniors OÖ, LASK, Samsunspor

*** Erdogan - Mehmet Erdogan (Mehmet Erdoğan) (a) 04/07/2004, ¿? (Turkey) (b) 1,93 (c) G (d) Konyaspor (e) -

*** Erdogan - Okan Erdogan (Okan Erdoğan) (a) 29/09/1998, Bremen (Germany) (b) 1,85 (c) D - central defense (d) Istanbulspor (e) Preussen Münster, VfB Oldenburg

*** Erdogan - Yusuf Erdogan (Yusuf Erdoğan) (a) 07/08/1992, Isparta (Turkey) (b) 1,71 (c) F - left winger (d) Adana Demirspor (e) Trabzonspor, Kasimpasa, Bursaspor, Trabzonspor, 1461 Trabzon, Trabzonspor, 1461 Trabzon, Araklispor

*** Eremenko - Roman Eremenko (Ерёменко Роман Алексеевич) (a) 19/03/1987, Moskva (Soviet Union, now in Russia) (b) 1,86 (c) M - attacking midfielder (d) FC Honka (e) Helsinki IFK, Rostov, Spartak Moskva, Sperre) CSKA Moskva, Rubin Kazan, Dinamo Kyïv, Udinese, Dinamo Kyïv, Udinese, AC Siena, Udinese, FF Jaro

*** Eremenko - Sergey Eremenko (Ерёменко Сергей Алексеевич) (a) 06/01/1999, Jakobstad (Finland) (b) 1,82 (c) M - central midfielder (d) FF Jaro (e) Spartaks, Helsinki IFK, Spartaks, AC Oulu, Spartaks, Orenburg, Spartaks, SJK Seinäjoki, Spartaks, Spartak-2, Spartaks, FF Jaro

*** Ereminok - Nikita Ereminok (Ереминок Никита Валентинович) (a) 25/01/2002, Minsk (Belarus) (b) 1,77 (c) M - central midfielder (d) FK Molodechno (e) FK Lida, Isloch II, Dzerzhinsk, Isloch II

*** Eren - Fatih Eren (a) 17/01/1995, Thann (France) (b) 1,84 (c) D - central defense (d) Racing FC Union Luxembourg (e) US Mondorf, Differdange 03, US Mondorf, Ankara Adliye

*** Erentürk - Erhan Erentürk (a) 30/05/1995, Izmir (Turkey) (b) 1,90 (c) G (d) Sivasspor (e) Konyaspor, Bursaspor, Altinordu, Karsiyaka

*** Ergelas - Mitar Ergelas (Митар Ергелаш) (a) 05/08/2002, Ruma (RF Yugoslavia, now in Serbia) (b) 1,78 (c) M - attacking midfielder (d) FK Novi Pazar (e) Čukarički, Novi Pazar, Čukarički

*** Ergemlidze - Mikheil Ergemlidze (მიხეილ ერგემლიძე) (a) 28/09/1999, Tbilisi (Georgia) (b) 1,92 (c) F - center forward (d) - (e) AP Brera, Kapaz PFK, Sabah FK, Dinamo Tbilisi, Adana Demirspor, Dinamo Tbilisi, FC Gagra, Dinamo Tbilisi, Chikhura, Dinamo Tbilisi

*** Ergin - Muhammed Ergin (Muhammed Emin Ergin) (a) 24/04/2001, Kayseri (Turkey) (b) - (c) F - right winger (d) Iskenderunspor (e) Iskenderunspor, Sivasspor, Sapanca Genclik, Sivasspor, Iskenderunspor, Sivasspor

*** Ergün - Onur Ergün (a) 15/11/1992, Bingöl (Turkey) (b) 1,85 (c) M - pivot (d) - (e) Hatayspor, Istanbulspor, Hatayspor, Istanbulspor, Tire 1922 Spor, Cigli Belediye, Menemen Belediye

*** Erhahon - Ethan Erhahon (a) 09/05/2001, Glasgow (Scotland) (b) 1,76 (c) M - central midfielder (d) Lincoln City (e) St. Mirren, St. Mirren, St. Mirren B

*** Erhardt - Philipp Erhardt (a) 10/09/1993, ¿? (Austria) (b) 1,85 (c) M - pivot (d) ASV Draßburg (e) TSV Hartberg, Türkgücü Münch., SV Mattersburg, Mattersburg II

*** Eric - Filip Eric (Филип Ерић) (a) 10/10/1994, Loznica (RF Yugoslavia, now in Serbia) (b) 1,96 (c) G (d) - (e) Sloboda Tuzla, Zeljeznicar, Zvijezda 09, Sloboda Tuzla, Drina Zvornik, Rad Beograd, Drina Zvornik, Vozdovac, Sumadija, Vozdovac

*** Erick Brendon - Erick Brendon (Erick Brendon Pinheiro da Silva) (a) 23/05/1995, Rio de Janeiro (Brazil) (b) 1,73 (c) M - central midfielder (d) Östersunds FK (e)

Värnamo, Goytacaz-RJ, CA Barra, Central, Portuguesa-RJ, Botafogo, América-RJ, Botafogo, Botafogo B

*** Erickson - Ben Erickson (Benjamin James Erickson) (a) 04/12/2000, ¿? (Wales) (b) - (c) D - central defense (d) Carmarthen Town (e) Aberystwyth

*** Erico - Erico (Erico Constantino da Silva) (a) 20/07/1989, Juazeiro (Brazil) (b) 1,86 (c) D - central defense (d) - (e) UTA Arad, FK Sabail, Astra Giurgiu, Pandurii, Guaratinguetá, Universitatea Cluj

*** Eriksen - Andrias Eriksen (a) 22/02/1994, ¿? (Faroe Islands) (b) 1,80 (d) B36 Tórshavn (e) B36 II

*** Eriksen - Christian Eriksen (Christian Dannemann Eriksen) (a) 14/02/1992, Middelfart (Denmark) (b) 1,82 (c) M - central midfielder (d) Manchester United (e) Brentford, Internazionale Milano, Tottenham Hotspur, Ajax

*** Eriksen - Kristian Eriksen (a) 18/07/1995, Hamar (Norway) (b) 1,77 (c) M - attacking midfielder (d) Molde FK (e) HamKam, Elverum, Brumunddal Fotball, HamKam

*** Erikson Carlos - Erikson Carlos (Erikson Carlos Batista dos Santos) (a) 26/02/1995, Belo Horizonte (Brazil) (b) 1,69 (c) F - center forward (d) Helsinki IFK (e) HJK Klubi 04, Helsinki IFK, FC KTP, Helsinki IFK, Rio Branco-ES, SC Sagamihara, Rio Branco-ES, Rio Branco VN, Athletic, FC Betinense

*** Eriksson - Anton Eriksson (Anton Mikael Eriksson) (a) 05/03/2000, ¿? (Sweden) (b) 1,88 (c) D - central defense (d) IFK Norrköping (e) GIF Sundsvall, Umeå FC

*** Eriksson - Carljohan Eriksson (Carljohan Daniel Viktor Eriksson) (a) 25/04/1995, Helsinki (Finland) (b) 1,91 (c) G (d) FC Nordsjælland (e) Dundee United, Nordsjælland, Dundee United, Mjällby AIF, J-Södra IF, Helsinki IFK, HJK Helsinki, PK-35, HJK Helsinki

*** Eriksson - Felix Eriksson (a) 21/05/2004, ¿? (Sweden) (b) 1,77 (c) D - right back (d) IFK Göteborg (e) -

*** Eriksson - Filip Eriksson (Filip Kim Oscar Eriksson) (a) 25/08/1998, Värnamo (Sweden) (b) 1,84 (c) G (d) Piteå IF (e) Värnamo

*** Eriksson - Magnus Eriksson (Magnus Lennart Eriksson) (a) 08/04/1990, Solna (Sweden) (b) 1,79 (c) M - central midfielder (d) Djurgårdens IF (e) San José, Djurgården, Brøndby IF, BJ Renhe, Malmö FF, KAA Gent, Åtvidabergs FF, AFC Eskilstuna

*** Eriksson - Sebastian Eriksson (Sebastian Anders Fredrik Eriksson) (a) 31/01/1989, Brålanda (Sweden) (b) 1,84 (c) M - central midfielder (d) IFK Göteborg (e) Genoa, IFK Göteborg, Panetolikos, IFK Göteborg, Cagliari, IFK Göteborg, Cagliari, IFK Göteborg, Cagliari, IFK Göteborg

*** Eriksson - Victor Eriksson (a) 17/09/2000, Värnamo (Finland) (b) - (c) D - central defense (d) IFK Värnamo (e) -

*** Erison - Erison (Erison Danilo de Souza) (a) 13/04/1999, Campinas (Brazil) (b) 1,80 (c) F - center forward (d) São Paulo FC (e) São Paulo, Botafogo, Estoril Praia, Botafogo, XV Piracicaba, Brasil Pelotas, XV Piracicaba, Figueirense FC, XV Piracicaba

*** Eristavi - Giorgi Eristavi (გიორგი ერისთავი) (a) 04/02/1994, Samtredia (Georgia) (b) 1,66 (c) F - left winger (d) - (e) Saburtalo, JFK Ventspils, FC Telavi, FC Samtredia, Liepaja, FC Dila, Dinamo II, FC Gagra, FC Samtredia, FC Gagra, Gagra II

*** Erkin - Caner Erkin (a) 04/10/1988, Balikesir (Turkey) (b) 1,81 (c) D - left back (d) Eyüpspor (e) Basaksehir, Karagümrük, Fenerbahce, Besiktas, Internazionale Milano, Besiktas, Internazionale Milano, Fenerbahce, CSKA Moskva, Galatasaray, CSKA Moskva, Manisaspor

*** Erkinov - Khozhimat Erkinov (Хожимат Ботир оглы Эркинов) (a) 29/05/2001, Tashkent (Uzbekistan) (b) 1,73 (c) F - left winger (d) Pakhtakor Tashkent (e) Pakhtakor, Torpedo Moskva, Pakhtakor, AGMK Olmaliq, Pakhtakor, Kokand 1912
*** Erkip - Hayrullah Erkip (a) 20/06/2003, Kayseri (Turkey) (b) 1,75 (c) F - left winger (d) Kayserispor (e) Genclerbirligi, Kayserispor
*** Erlanov - Temirlan Erlanov (Ерланов Темірлан Ерланұлы) (a) 09/07/1993, Oskemen (Kazakhstan) (b) 1,90 (c) D - central defense (d) Ordabasy Shymkent (e) Aktobe, Ordabasy, Tobol Kostanay, Ordabasy, Vostok Oskemen, Vostok II, Sunkar II, Zhetysu II
*** Erlic - Martin Erlic (Martin Erlić) (a) 24/01/1998, Zadar (Croatia) (b) 1,93 (c) D - central defense (d) US Sassuolo (e) Spezia, Spezia, Sassuolo, Sassuolo, Spezia, Sassuolo, Südtirol
*** Erlien - Vegard Erlien (Vegard Østraat Erlien) (a) 07/01/1998, Trondheim (Norway) (b) 1,83 (c) F - center forward (d) Tromsø IL (e) Ranheim, Sandnes Ulf, Rosenborg II
*** Erlingmark - August Erlingmark (Jan August Erlingmark) (a) 22/04/1998, Göteborg (Sweden) (b) 1,89 (c) M - pivot (d) Atromitos FC (e) IFK Göteborg
*** Erlingsson - Elmar Erlingsson (a) 16/05/2004, ¿? (Iceland) (b) - (c) M (d) KF Framherjar-Smástund (e) -
*** Ermakov - Nikita Ermakov (Ермаков Никита Владленович) (a) 19/01/2003, Syzran, Samara Region (Russia) (b) 1,83 (c) M - attacking midfielder (d) CSKA Moskva (e) CSKA Moskva II
*** Ermakov - Vsevolod Ermakov (Ермаков Всеволод Викторович) (a) 06/01/1996, St. Petersburg (Russia) (b) 1,86 (c) G (d) FC Ararat-Armenia (e) Ararat Yerevan, Shirak Gyumri, Ararat Yerevan, Shirak Gyumri, Zenit Izhevsk, Shirak Gyumri, Armavir, Shirak Gyumri, Krasnodar II, Shirak Gyumri, Krasnodar II
*** Ermakovich - Kirill Ermakovich (Ермакович Кирилл Александрович) (a) 11/01/1999, Minsk (Belarus) (b) 1,81 (c) F - left winger (d) FK Gomel (e) Vitebsk, Krumkachi, Gomel, BATE II, Belshina, BATE II
*** Ermekbaev - Bekzat Ermekbaev (Ермекбаев Бекзат) (a) 06/12/2001, ¿? (Kazakhstan) (b) 1,73 (c) F - right winger (d) Tobol Kostanay II (e) -
*** Ernec - Kristijan Ernec (a) 19/01/2003, ¿? (Serbia and Montenegro, now in Montenegro) (b) - (c) F - right winger (d) Rudar Pljevlja (e) FK Pljevlja, Rudar Pljevlja
*** Ernest Antwi - Ernest Antwi (Ernest Nyarko Antwi) (a) 09/09/1995, Accra (Ghana) (b) 1,78 (c) F - left winger (d) Doxa Katokopias (e) Aktobe, PFK Lviv, Najran SC, PFK Lviv, Rukh Lviv, Leiria, Desportivo Aves, Tudu Mighty Jet, Oliv. Hospital, Tudu Mighty Jet
*** Ernst - Tjark Ernst (a) 15/03/2003, Stuttgart (Germany) (b) 1,93 (c) G (d) Hertha Berlín (e) -
*** Erokhin - Aleksandr Erokhin (Ерохин Александр Юрьевич) (a) 13/10/1989, Barnaul (Soviet Union, now in Russia) (b) 1,95 (c) M - attacking midfielder (d) Zenit de San Petersburgo (e) Rostov, Ural, SKA-Energia, Ural, SKA-Energia, Krasnodar, SKA-Energia, Krasnodar, FC Sheriff
*** Erramuspe - Rodrigo Erramuspe (Rodrigo Nahuel Erramuspe) (a) 03/05/1990, Mar del Plata (Argentina) (b) 1,91 (c) D - central defense (d) PAS Giannina (e) Belgrano, Blooming, Nacional, Indep. Medellín, Unión Santa Fe, Lanús, Tigre, Lanús, LDU Quito, Lanús, Huracán, Lanús, Rafaela, Lanús, Huracán, Lanús, Unión Santa Fe, Lanús

*** Errico - Simone Errico (a) 30/04/1992, Mesagne (Italy) (b) 1,80 (c) M - central midfielder (d) SS Cosmos (e) La Fiorita, Jesina, Sammaurese, Trestina, San Marino, Sammaurese, Albalonga, Cynthia, Ragusa, Sarnese, Sora, Boville Ernica, Cynthia
*** Ershov - Nikita Ershov (Ершов Никита Владимирович) (a) 17/09/2002, Shebekino, Belgorod Oblast (Russia) (b) 1,78 (c) F - left winger (d) Irtysh Omsk (e) Irtysh Omsk, Fakel II, Fakel-M, Salyut Belgorod, AF Shebekino
*** Ersoy - Ertugrul Ersoy (Ertuğrul Ersoy) (a) 13/02/1997, Kocaeli (Turkey) (b) 1,87 (c) D - central defense (d) Gaziantep FK (e) Istanbulspor, Gaziantep FK, Le Havre AC, Gaziantep FK, Le Havre AC, Bursaspor, Çaykur Rizespor, Bursaspor, Yesil Bursa
*** Ersu - Erten Ersu (a) 21/04/1994, Istanbul (Turkey) (b) 1,95 (c) G (d) Gaziantep FK (e) Konyaspor, Fenerbahce, Gaziantepspor, Fenerbahce
*** Ertas - Deniz Ertas (Deniz Ertaş) (a) 20/03/2005, Izmir (Turkey) (b) - (c) G (d) Konyaspor (e) -
*** Ertlthaler - Julius Ertlthaler (a) 25/04/1997, ¿? (Austria) (b) 1,69 (c) M - attacking midfielder (d) WSG Tirol (e) TSV Hartberg, SV Mattersburg, Mattersburg II
*** Ervin - Jim Ervin (James Ervin) (a) 05/06/1985, Belfast (Northern Ireland) (b) 1,73 (c) D - central defense (d) - (e) Carrick Rangers, Ballymena, Linfield
*** Erwin - Lee Erwin (Lee Harry Erwin) (a) 19/03/1994, Bellshill (Scotland) (b) 1,88 (c) F - center forward (d) Al-Ahed (e) FC Haka, St. Mirren, Ross County, Tractor, Kilmarnock FC, Leeds Utd., Oldham Athletic, Leeds Utd., Bury, Leeds Utd., Motherwell FC, Arbroath, Motherwell FC
*** Erzhigit - Zhasulan Erzhigit (Ержигит Жасулан Абайұлы) (a) 21/01/2002, Aktobe (Kazakhstan) (b) 1,73 (c) D - right back (d) Kyran Shymkent (e) FK Turan II, Ontustik II
*** Esanu - Mihai Esanu (Mihai Alexandru Eşanu) (a) 25/07/1998, Bucuresti (Romania) (b) 1,88 (c) G (d) Petrolul Ploiesti (e) Chindia, FC Dinamo, FC Farul 1920, FC Dinamo, Daco-Getica, FC Dinamo, Dinamo II, CS Balotesti, Dinamo II
*** Escalante - Gonzalo Escalante (a) 27/03/1993, Bella Vista (Argentina) (b) 1,82 (c) M - central midfielder (d) Cádiz CF (e) Lazio, Cádiz CF, Lazio, Cremonese, Lazio, Alavés, Lazio, SD Eibar, Catania, SD Eibar, Catania, Boca Juniors, Catania, Boca Juniors
*** Escartin - Josué Escartin (a) 21/03/2003, Fleury-les-Aubrais (France) (b) 1,93 (c) D - central defense (d) Stade Brestois 29 (e) Borgo, Stade Brestois, Brest B
*** Escoval - Rodrigo Escoval (João Rodrigo Pereira Escoval) (a) 08/05/1997, Lisboa (Portugal) (b) 1,88 (c) D - central defense (d) FC Vizela (e) Volos NPS, Anorthosis, HNK Rijeka, NK Istra, Benfica B, Sacavenense F.
*** Escriba - César Escriba (César Escriba Recuero) (a) 26/03/2001, Madrid (Spain) (b) 1,78 (c) M - central midfielder (d) Olivenza FC (e) Penya Encarnada, Villaverde CF, CD El Álamo, DAV Santa Ana, CD Canillas
*** Escudero - Sergio Escudero (Sergio Escudero Palomo) (a) 02/09/1989, Valladolid (Spain) (b) 1,76 (c) D - left back (d) Real Valladolid CF (e) Granada CF, Sevilla FC, Getafe CF, FC Schalke 04, Getafe CF, FC Schalke 04, Real Murcia
*** Eseola - Aderinsola Habib Eseola (Есеола Адерінсола Хабіб) (a) 28/06/1991, Zhytomyr (Soviet Union, now in Ukraine) (b) 1,88 (c) F - center forward (d) Shturm Ivankiv (e) PFK Lviv, Hebar P., Vorskla Poltava, Kairat Almaty, Zirka, Akzhayik, Zirka, Arsenal Kyiv, Zirka, Arsenal Kyiv, FK Oleksandriya, Desna, Capo Rizzuto, Vibonese, HinterReggio, Dinamo Kiev II
*** Eser - Mustafa Eser (a) 29/08/2001, Istanbul (Turkey) (b) 1,85 (c) D - central defense (d) Ümraniyespor (e) -

*** Esgaio - Ricardo Esgaio (Ricardo Sousa Esgaio) (a) 16/05/1993, Nazaré (Portugal) (b) 1,72 (c) D - right back (d) Sporting de Lisboa (e) SC Braga, Sporting Lisboa, Académica Coimbra, Sporting Lisboa, Sporting B
*** Esgaio - Tiago Esgaio (Tiago Alexandre de Sousa Esgaio) (a) 01/08/1995, Nazaré (Portugal) (b) 1,75 (c) D - right back (d) FC Arouca (e) Arouca, SC Braga, B SAD, Torreense, Caldas
*** Eshata - Awaka Eshata (אשטה אווקה) (a) 05/09/1999, Ethiopia (Ethiopia) (b) - (c) M - central midfielder (d) Hapoel Jerusalem (e) -
*** Esimov - Ruslan Esimov (Есимов Руслан Жумабекович) (a) 28/04/1990, ¿? (Kazakhstan) (b) 1,82 (c) D - right back (d) FK Aksu (e) Qyzyljar, FK Ekibastuz, Irtysh, Kaspiy Aktau, FK Ekibastuz
*** Esin - Vladimir Esin (Есин Владимир Александрович) (a) 11/01/1995, St. Petersburg (Russia) (b) 1,84 (c) D - left back (d) FK Smorgon (e) Slavia, Salyut Belgorod, 1.SC Znojmo, Aluston-YBK, FC Luftëtari, Din. Stavropol, Kyzyltash, FK Kaluga, Zenit Penza, Dinamo SPb, Petrotrest
*** Esiti - Anderson Esiti (a) 24/05/1994, Warri (Nigeria) (b) 1,89 (d) Ferencváros TC (e) PAOK, Göztepe, PAOK, KAA Gent, Estoril Praia, Leixoes
*** Eskesen - Julius Eskesen (Julius Eskesen) (a) 16/03/1999, Odense (Denmark) (b) 1,75 (c) M - central midfielder (d) FK Haugesund (e) SønderjyskE, Odense BK
*** Eskic - Nikola Eskic (Nikola Eskić, Никола Ескић) (a) 19/12/1997, Milići (Bosnia and Herzegovina) (b) 1,82 (c) M - central midfielder (d) FK Aksu (e) Riteriai, Bregalnica Stip, Backa, Napredak, Zvijezda 09, FK Vlasenica
*** Eskihellac - Mustafa Eskihellac (Mustafa Eskihellaç) (a) 05/05/1997, Trabzon (Turkey) (b) 1,75 (c) F - right winger (d) Gaziantep FK (e) Kasimpasa, Gaziantep FK, Yeni Malatyaspor, Boluspor, Yeni Malatyaspor, Elazigspor, Yeni Malatyaspor, Düzyurtspor
*** Eskin - Berat Eskin (a) 13/10/2004, Kayseri (Turkey) (b) - (c) M - pivot (d) - (e) Kayserispor
*** Eskinja - Gabriel Eskinja (a) 29/08/2003, Graz (Austria) (b) 1,91 (c) D - central defense (d) Slaven Belupo Koprivnica (e) SC Kalsdorf, Kalsdorf II, Gratkorn II
*** Espejord - Runar Espejord (a) 26/02/1996, Tromsø (Norway) (b) 1,89 (c) F - center forward (d) FK Bodø/Glimt (e) Heerenveen, Tromsø, Heerenveen, Tromsø
*** Espino - Alfonso Espino (Luis Alfonso Espino García) (a) 05/01/1992, San Jacinto (Uruguay) (b) 1,72 (c) D - left back (d) Rayo Vallecano (e) Cádiz CF, Nacional, Nacional B
*** Espinosa - Bernardo Espinosa (Bernardo José Espinosa Zúñiga) (a) 11/07/1989, Santiago de Cali (Colombia) (b) 1,92 (c) D - central defense (d) Girona FC (e) RCD Espanyol, Girona FC, Middlesbrough, Real Sporting, Sevilla FC, Real Sporting, Sevilla FC, Racing, Sevilla FC, Sevilla At.
*** Espinosa - Byron Espinosa (Byron Manuel Espinosa) (a) 15/03/1999, Gibraltar (Gibraltar) (b) - (c) F - right winger (d) Lions Gibraltar FC (e) Europa Reserve, Lions Gibraltar, Europa Point FC, Gibraltar Phoenix, Lions Gibraltar, Gibraltar Utd., Lions Gibraltar
*** Espinoza - Jhon Espinoza (Jhon Jairo Espinoza Izquierdo) (a) 24/02/1999, Guayaquil (Ecuador) (b) 1,80 (c) D - right back (d) FC Lugano (e) Chicago, SD Aucas, Dep. Cuenca, SD Aucas, Dep. Cuenca, Cuenca B, San Antonio FC, San Antonio FC, San Antonio FC
*** Esposito - Salvatore Esposito (a) 07/10/2000, Castellammare di Stabia (Italy) (b) 1,78 (c) M - pivot (d) Spezia (e) SPAL, Spezia, SPAL, Chievo Verona, SPAL, Ravenna, SPAL, Castellammare

*** Esposito - Sebastiano Esposito (a) 02/07/2002, Castellammare di Stabia (Italy) (b) 1,83 (c) F - center forward (d) Internazionale Milano (e) Bari, Internazionale Milano, RSC Anderlecht, Internazionale Milano, FC Basel, Internazionale Milano, Venezia, Internazionale Milano, SPAL, Internazionale Milano, Castellammare
*** Esquerdinha - Esquerdinha (Sanaido Pereira da Silva) (a) 21/05/1991, Manaus (Brazil) (b) 1,74 (c) M - attacking midfielder (d) Floresta Esporte Clube (CE) (e) FK Bylis, Botafogo-PB, Ferroviário, Brasiliense, Sampaio Corrêa, Bragantino, Sampaio Corrêa, Altos, Mamoré-MG, Uberlândia, Santa Helena
*** Esquivel - Diego Esquivel (Diego José Esquivel McGann) (a) 04/01/2005, Belfast (Northern Ireland) (b) - (c) M - central midfielder (d) Linfield FC Reserves (e) -
*** Esselink - Bert Esselink (Bert Johan Esselink) (a) 16/08/1999, Arnhem (Netherlands) (b) 1,91 (c) D - central defense (d) Stal Mielec (e) APOEL FC, Olympiakos N., APOEL FC, PAEEK Kyrenia
*** Esser - Michael Esser (a) 22/11/1987, Castrop-Rauxel (Germany) (b) 1,98 (c) G (d) VfL Bochum (e) Hannover 96, Hoffenheim, Hannover 96, Darmstadt 98, Sturm Graz, VfL Bochum, VfL Bochum II, SV Sodingen, Wacker Castrop, VfB Habinghorst
*** Essiam - Emmanuel Essiam (a) 19/12/2003, Accra (Ghana) (b) 1,83 (c) M - central midfielder (d) FC Basel (e) Berekum Chelsea, B. Chelsea II
*** Essien - Harold Essien (a) 22/12/2001, Manchester (England) (b) - (c) D - right back (d) - (e) Caernarfon, Stockport Town
*** Essogo - Emmanuel Essogo (Emmanuel Romess Ovono Essogo) (a) 26/03/2001, Libreville (Gabon) (b) 1,84 (c) F - center forward (d) Torpedo-BelAZ Zhodino (e) Slavia, AS Bouenguidi
*** Essomba - Loic Essomba (Antoine Loic Essomba Bikoula) (a) 01/12/2003, ¿? (Cameroon) (b) 1,77 (c) F - left winger (d) MSK Zilina B (e) Gambinos Stars, MSK Zilina B, Gambinos Stars
*** Essono - Stane Essono (a) 28/05/1998, ¿? (Gabon) (b) - (c) D - right back (d) FC Dinamo-Auto Tiraspol (e) -
*** Essugo - Dário Essugo (Dário Cassia Luís Essugo) (a) 14/03/2005, Lisboa (Portugal) (b) 1,78 (c) M - pivot (d) Sporting de Lisboa (e) Sporting B
*** Esteban - Esteban (Juan Esteban Gómez Michellod) (a) 01/10/1997, San Sebastián (Spain) (b) 1,86 (c) D - central defense (d) - (e) FC Ordino, CD Sant Jordi, CF Gavà, Irún B, UD San Pedro
*** Estève - Maxime Estève (a) 26/05/2002, Montpellier (France) (b) 1,93 (c) D - central defense (d) Montpellier HSC (e) Montpellier B
*** Esteves - Gonçalo Esteves (Gonçalo do Lago Pontes Esteves) (a) 27/02/2004, Arcos de Valdevez (Portugal) (b) 1,71 (c) D - right back (d) Sporting de Lisboa (e) Estoril Praia, Sporting Lisboa
*** Estevez Fernandez - Leif Estevez Fernandez (a) 04/04/1997, ¿? (Germany) (b) 1,75 (c) M - attacking midfielder (d) FC Hegelmann (e) FV Illertissen, Winthrop Eagles, Pfullendorf II
*** Estiven - Estiven (Estiven Morente Vélez) (a) 16/02/1991, La Linea de la Concepción (Spain) (b) 1,78 (c) M - attacking midfielder (d) Lions Gibraltar FC (e) Lions Gibraltar, Lynx FC, Lions Gibraltar, Manchester 62, Los Barrios, R. B. Linense, Betis C, Poli Ejido, Balón de Cádiz
*** Estrada - Johnatan Estrada (Johnatan Estrada Campillo) (a) 27/01/1983, Medellín (Colombia) (b) 1,82 (c) M - attacking midfielder (d) - (e) FC Ordino, CE Carroi, CE Jenlai, Envigado, A. Bucaramanga, Junior FC, Millonarios, Deportes Tolima, Patriotas, Indep. Medellín, Avaí FC, Millonarios, Real Sociedad, Millonarios, Envigado

*** Estrada - Pascal Estrada (Pascal Juan Estrada) (a) 12/03/2002, Linz (Austria) (b) 1,87 (c) D - central defense (d) NK Olimpija Ljubljana (e) -

*** Estrela - Paulo Estrela (Paulo Estrela Moreira Alves) (a) 20/02/1999, Paços de Ferreira (Portugal) (b) 1,71 (c) M - central midfielder (d) Portimonense SC (e) FC Porto B

*** Estupiñán - Pervis Estupiñán (Pervis Josué Estupiñán Tenorio) (a) 21/01/1998, Esmeraldas (Ecuador) (b) 1,75 (c) D - left back (d) Brighton & Hove Albion (e) Villarreal CF, Watford, CA Osasuna, Watford, RCD Mallorca, Watford, UD Almería, Watford, Udinese, Granada B, Udinese, LDU Quito, LDU Quito B

*** Etebo - Peter Etebo (Oghenekaro Peter Etebo) (a) 09/11/1995, Warri (Nigeria) (b) 1,74 (c) M - central midfielder (d) Stoke City (e) Aris Thessaloniki, Stoke City, Watford, Stoke City, Galatasaray, Stoke City, Getafe CF, Stoke City, Feirense, UD Las Palmas, Feirense, Warri Wolves FC

*** Eteki - Yan Eteki (Yan Brice Eteki) (a) 26/08/1997, Yaoundé (Cameroon) (b) 1,82 (c) M - pivot (d) AD Alcorcón (e) Casa Pia, FC Cartagena, Casa Pia, Granada CF, Sevilla FC, UD Almería, Sevilla At., Sevilla FC C

*** Ethemi - Valon Ethemi (Валон Етеми) (a) 03/10/1997, Palatica (North Macedonia) (b) 1,79 (c) F - left winger (d) Istanbulspor (e) FK Kukësi, KF Adriatiku

*** Etim - Etim (Friday Ubi Etim) (a) 21/05/2002, Lagos (Nigeria) (b) 1,86 (c) F - center forward (d) CD Mafra (e) Vizela

*** Etongou - Thierry Etongou (Amougou Ignace Thierry Etongou) (a) 22/09/1999, Yaounde (Cameroon) (b) - (c) D - central defense (d) FK Radnicki Niš (e) Fortuna du Mfou

*** Eto'o - James Eto'o (James Armel Eto'o Eyenga) (a) 19/11/2000, ¿? (Cameroon) (b) 1,76 (c) M - pivot (d) Botev Plovdiv (e) US Boulogne, FC Nantes B

*** Etou - Ramaric Etou (Ramaric Presley Etou Thomaso) (a) 25/01/1995, ¿? (Congo) (b) 1,74 (c) D - central defense (d) FC Dila Gori (e) Ness Ziona, B TLV Bat Yam, FC Dila, Beitar TA Ramla, AC Léopards

*** Etoundi - Franck Etoundi (Franck M'bia Etoundi) (a) 30/08/1990, Douala (Cameroon) (b) 1,85 (c) F - center forward (d) - (e) UN Käerjeng 97, AS Vitré, Slaven Belupo, FC Sochaux, Boluspor, Kasimpasa, FC Zürich, FC St. Gallen, Neuchâtel Xamax, FC Biel-Bienne, Xamax, Dragon Club

*** Etta Eyong - Etta Eyong (Karl Edouard Blaise Etta Eyong) (a) 14/10/2003, ¿? (Cameroon) (b) - (c) M - central midfielder (d) Cádiz CF Mirandilla (e) -

*** Euller - Euller (Elosman Euller Silva Cavalcanti) (a) 04/01/1995, São Paulo (Brazil) (b) 1,75 (c) D - left back (d) GD Chaves (e) AEL Limassol, Ferroviária, CSA, Al-Shabab, Avispa Fukuoka, EC Vitória, Vitória B

*** Europaeus - Joel Europaeus (a) 22/11/2001, Vantaa (Finland) (b) 1,88 (c) D - central defense (d) - (e) PK-35, VJS Vantaa, AC Oulu, IF Gnistan, US Hostert, FC Honka II

*** Eustaquio - Stephen Eustaquio (Stephen Antunes Eustaquio) (a) 21/12/1996, Leamington, Ontario (Canada) (b) 1,77 (c) M - central midfielder (d) FC Porto (e) Paços Ferreira, FC Porto, Paços Ferreira, Cruz Azul, Paços Ferreira, Cruz Azul, Chaves, Leixões, Torreense

*** Eva - Rooney Eva (Rooney Eva Wankewai) (a) 25/12/1996, Kelleng (Cameroon) (b) 1,85 (c) F - center forward (d) CSKA 1948 (e) Turan Tovuz, A. Keciörengücü, Apollon Pontou, AE Karaiskakis, MC Alger, AS Aïn M'lila, MC Alger, Aittitos Spaton, AO Trikala, Asteras Tripoli, PAE Veria, AO Chania, Apejes FC

*** Evaldo Netinho - Evaldo Netinho (Evaldo Nascimento Lamaur Neto) (a) 05/04/1994, Curitiba (Brazil) (b) 1,71 (c) D - right back (d) IFK Värnamo (e) Brasil

Pelotas, ABC FC, Paysandu, GAIS, Värnamo, Anápolis, JMalucelli, Trindade, Coritiba FC B, Paraná, Paraná B

*** Evander - Evander (Evander da Silva Ferreira) (a) 09/06/1998, Rio de Janeiro (Brazil) (b) 1,80 (c) M - central midfielder (d) Portland Timbers (e) Midtjylland, Vasco da Gama, Midtjylland, Vasco da Gama

*** Evandro - Evandro (Evandro da Silva) (a) 14/01/1997, Messias (Brazil) (b) 1,74 (c) F - left winger (d) ABC Futebol Clube (RN) (e) Radnicki 1923, Fehérvár, Proleter, Fehérvár, CSKA-Sofia, Coritiba FC, RB Brasil, Coritiba FC

*** Evangelou - Stefanos Evangelou (Στέφανος Ευαγγέλου) (a) 12/05/1998, Athina (Greece) (b) 1,85 (c) D - central defense (d) NK Osijek (e) FC Sheriff, Górnik Zabrze, Olympiakos, Panionios, Olympiakos, PAS Giannina, Olympiakos, Panathinaikos, Panionios

*** Evanilson - Evanilson (Francisco Evanilson de Lima Barbosa) (a) 06/10/1999, Fortaleza (Brazil) (b) 1,83 (c) F - center forward (d) FC Porto (e) Tombense, Fluminense, Tombense, Fluminense, STK Samorin

*** Evans - Ashley Evans (a) 18/07/1989, Church Village (Wales) (b) 1,75 (c) M - central midfielder (d) Penybont FC (e) Merthyr Town, Port Talbot, Llanelli, Neath

*** Evans - Caio Evans (Caio Steffan Evans) (a) 18/12/2004, ¿? (Wales) (b) - (c) M - central midfielder (d) CPD Porthmadog (e) -

*** Evans - Cameron Evans (Cameron James Evans) (a) 23/02/2001, ¿? (Ireland) (b) 1,82 (c) D - central defense (d) Taunton Town (e) Sligo Rovers, Waterford FC

*** Evans - Eliot Evans (a) 26/11/1991, ¿? (Wales) (b) 1,85 (c) F - right winger (d) Cardiff Metropolitan University (e) Monmouth

*** Evans - Ioan Evans (Ioan Langdon Evans) (a) 22/09/2001, ¿? (Wales) (b) - (c) M - central midfielder (d) - (e) Haverfordwest, Cefn Druids, Pontardawe, Carmarthen

*** Evans - Jack Evans (a) 08/08/2000, Portadown (Northern Ireland) (b) - (c) F (d) Annagh United FC (e) Portadown, Bourneview Mill, Lurgan

*** Evans - Joe Evans (Joseph Evans) (a) 26/11/1997, ¿? (Wales) (b) - (c) D - central defense (d) Cardiff Metropolitan University (e) Cardiff Metropolitan Police, Pontypridd, Cardiff Metropolitan Police, Cambrian & C.

*** Evans - Jonathan Evans (David Jonathan Evans) (a) 10/03/1993, ¿? (Wales) (b) - (c) M - attacking midfielder (d) Penrhyncoch FC (e) Aberystwyth, Penrhyncoch, Aberystwyth, Penrhyncoch, Aberystwyth

*** Evans - Jonny Evans (Jonathan Grant Evans) (a) 03/01/1988, Belfast (Northern Ireland) (b) 1,88 (c) D - central defense (d) Manchester United (e) Leicester City, West Bromwich Albion, Manchester Utd., Sunderland, Manchester Utd., Sunderland, Manchester Utd., Royal Antwerp, Manchester Utd.

*** Evans - Osian Evans (Osian Wyn Evans) (a) 13/07/2006, ¿? (Wales) (b) - (c) F - center forward (d) Caernarfon Town (e) -

*** Evdokimov - Andrey Evdokimov (Евдокимов Андрей Владимирович) (a) 09/03/1999, Georgiyevsk, Stavropol Region (Russia) (b) 1,92 (c) D - central defense (d) Sokol Saratov (e) Torpedo Moskva, Khimki 2, Master-Saturn

*** Evdokimov - Oleg Evdokimov (Евдокимов Олег Григорьевич) (a) 25/02/1994, Minsk (Belarus) (b) 1,77 (c) M - central midfielder (d) Neman Grodno (e) Dinamo Minsk, FK Turan, FK Minsk, Neman Grodno, FK Minsk, Minsk-2, FK Minsk, FK Minsk II

*** Everink - Luca Everink (a) 09/02/2001, Diepenveen (Netherlands) (b) 1,79 (c) D - right back (d) Go Ahead Eagles Deventer (e) TOP Oss, FC Twente

*** Éverson Bispo - Éverson Bispo (Éverson Bispo Pereira) (a) 24/07/1997, Salvador de Bahía (Brazil) (b) 1,89 (c) D - central defense (d) - (e) Santa Cruz, FC Urartu, Goiás, Bahia B, Paraná, Bahia B, Portimonense, EC Bahia

*** Evgenjev - Roman Evgenjev (Евгеньев Роман Алексеевич) (a) 23/02/1999, Spasskoe, Primorje Region (Russia) (b) 1,93 (c) D - central defense (d) Krylya Sovetov Samara (e) Dinamo Moskva, Dinamo Moskva II, Dinamo 2, Dinamo Moskva II
*** Evjen - Håkon Evjen (a) 14/02/2000, Narvik (Norway) (b) 1,83 (c) M - central midfielder (d) Brøndby IF (e) AZ Alkmaar, Bodø/Glimt, Mjølner
*** Evseev - Aleksey Evseev (Евсеев Алексей Витальевич) (a) 30/03/1994, St. Petersburg (Russia) (b) 1,84 (c) M - central midfielder (d) Tekstilshchik Ivanovo (e) Ural, Ufa, Ural, Rotor Volgograd, Fakel Voronezh, Rotor Volgograd, Khimki, Ural, Zenit 2 St. Peterburg, Zenit St. Peterburg II
*** Evtimov - Dimitar Evtimov (Димитър Иванов Евтимов) (a) 07/09/1993, Shumen (Bulgaria) (b) 1,90 (c) G (d) CSKA-Sofia (e) Accrington St., Burton Albion, Nottingham Forest, Port Vale, Nottingham Forest, Olhanense, Nottingham Forest, Mansfield Town, Nottingham Forest, Nuneaton, Nottingham Forest, Gainsborough, Nottingham Forest, Ilkeston Town, Nottingham Forest, Chavdar
*** Ewan - Connall Ewan (a) 11/03/2006, Inverness (Scotland) (b) - (c) D - central defense (d) Elgin City FC (e) Elgin City, Ross County, Forres, Ross County
*** Ewert - Noé Ewert (a) 24/02/1997, ¿? (Luxembourg) (b) 1,77 (c) D - right back (d) UN Käerjeng 97 (e) F91 Dudelange, UN Käerjeng 97
*** Ewert - Tim Ewert (a) 25/10/1995, ¿? (Luxembourg) (b) 1,71 (c) M (d) UN Käerjeng 97 (e) US Hostert, UN Käerjeng 97
*** Ewerton - Ewerton (Ewerton da Silva Pereira) (a) 01/12/1992, São Paulo (Brazil) (b) 1,81 (c) M - central midfielder (d) Vegalta Sendai (e) Vegalta Sendai, Portimonense, FC Porto, Portimonense, FC Porto, Urawa Reds, FC Porto, Portimonense, FC Porto, Portimonense, Madureira, Paulista, Desp. Brasil, América-RN, Desp. Brasil
*** Ewerton - Ewerton (Ewerton Paixão da Silva) (a) 28/12/1996, Amapá (Brazil) (b) 1,75 (c) F - left winger (d) FC Banik Ostrava (e) Banik Ostrava, Slavia Praha, Mlada Boleslav, Pardubice, Mlada Boleslav, Zlaté Moravce, EC São Bernardo
*** Ewertton - Ewertton (Ewertton José Costa Silva) (a) 10/08/1997, ¿? (Brazil) (b) 1,64 (c) M - attacking midfielder (d) Gzira United FC (e) Fgura Utd., AA Anapolina, Santos
*** Expósito - Edu Expósito (Eduardo Expósito Jaén) (a) 01/08/1996, Barcelona (Spain) (b) 1,78 (c) M - central midfielder (d) RCD Espanyol (e) SD Eibar, RC Deportivo, Depor Fabril
*** Expósito - Erik Expósito (Erik Alexander Expósito Hernández) (a) 23/06/1996, Santa Cruz de Tenerife (Spain) (b) 1,90 (c) F - center forward (d) Śląsk Wroclaw (e) Las Palmas At., Córdoba CF, Las Palmas At., Rayo Cantabria, At. Malagueño
*** Eydsteinsson - Silas Eydsteinsson (Silas Eyðsteinsson) (a) 13/02/1998, ¿? (Faroe Islands) (b) 1,88 (c) G (d) B36 Tórshavn (e) 07 Vestur, AB Argir, HB Tórshavn, AB Argir, 07 Vestur, 07 Vestur II
*** Eyibil - Erkan Eyibil (a) 15/06/2001, Kassel (Germany) (b) 1,75 (c) D - left back (d) Antalyaspor (e) Genclerbirligi, Antalyaspor, Stuttgart II, Antalyaspor, FSV Mainz 05 II, Go Ahead Eagles, FSV Mainz 05 II
*** Eyjólfsson - Gísli Eyjólfsson (a) 31/05/1994, ¿? (Iceland) (b) 1,80 (c) M - central midfielder (d) Breidablik Kópavogur (e) Mjällby AIF, Breidablik, Víkingur Ó., Breidablik, Haukar, Breidablik, Augnablik, Breidablik, Augnablik
*** Eyjólfsson - Hólmar Örn Eyjólfsson (a) 06/08/1990, Saudarkrókur (Iceland) (b) 1,90 (c) D - central defense (d) Valur Reykjavík (e) Rosenborg, Levski Sofia, Maccabi Haifa, Levski Sofia, Maccabi Haifa, Rosenborg, VfL Bochum, West Ham Reserves,

KSV Roeselare, West Ham Reserves, Cheltenham Town, West Ham Reserves, HK Kópavogs
*** Eyongo - Raphaël Eyongo (a) 21/05/2003, Breda (Netherlands) (b) - (c) F - center forward (d) Excelsior Rotterdam (e) -
*** Eyre - Jake Eyre (a) 02/11/1995, Chester (England) (b) - (c) F - center forward (d) Airbus UK Broughton (e) Gresford, Denbigh, Gresford, Rhyl FC, Airbus UK
*** Eysseric - Valentin Eysseric (a) 25/03/1992, Aix-en-Provence (France) (b) 1,81 (c) M - attacking midfielder (d) - (e) Kasimpasa, Fiorentina, Hellas Verona, Fiorentina, FC Nantes, Fiorentina, OGC Nice, St.-Étienne, OGC Nice, AS Monaco, OGC Nice, AS Monaco, AS Monaco B
*** Eysteinsson - Róbert Aron Eysteinsson (a) 17/06/1999, Vestmannaeyjar (Iceland) (b) - (c) M - central midfielder (d) KF Framherjar-Smástund (e) ÍBV Vestmannaeyjar, Framherjar, ÍBV Vestmannaeyjar
*** Eza - Wilfried Eza (Wilfried Kwassi Eza) (a) 28/12/1996, Abidjan (Ivory Coast) (b) 1,81 (c) F - center forward (d) FC Ararat-Armenia (e) FC Van, FC Noah, Gomel, FC Saxan
*** Eze - Eberechi Eze (Eberechi Oluchi Eze) (a) 29/06/1998, Greenwich (England) (b) 1,78 (c) M - attacking midfielder (d) Crystal Palace (e) Queen's Park Rangers, Wycombe Wanderers, Queen's Park Rangers
*** Eze - Emeka Eze (Emeka Friday Eze) (a) 26/09/1996, Lagos (Nigeria) (b) 1,87 (c) F - center forward (d) Pendikspor (e) Eyüpspor, Istanbulspor, Eyüpspor, A. Keciörengücü, Sturm Graz, Adanaspor, Sturm Graz, RoPS, AR Menoua
*** Eze - Joshua Eze (Joshua Chima Eze) (a) 20/03/2003, Leverkusen (Germany) (b) 1,83 (c) M - pivot (d) SC Fortuna Köln (e) Bayer Leverkusen
*** Ezekwem - Kimberly Ezekwem (Kimberly Chiwetalu Akwaeze Ezekwem) (a) 19/06/2001, München (Germany) (b) 1,87 (c) D - left back (d) SC Paderborn 07 (e) SC Paderborn, SC Freiburg, SC Freiburg II
*** Ezequiel Teixeira - Fabio Ezequiel Teixeira (a) 13/05/2004, ¿? (Luxembourg) (b) - (c) D (d) Union Titus Petange (e) -
*** Ezhov - Roman Ezhov (Ежов Роман Владимирович) (a) 02/09/1997, Nizhnekamsk, Tatarstan Republic (Russia) (b) 1,81 (c) F - right winger (d) Krylya Sovetov Samara (e) Chertanovo
*** Ezzalzouli - Abde Ezzalzouli (عبد الصمد الزلزولي ; Abdessamad Ezzalzouli) (a) 17/12/2001, Beni Melal (Morocco) (b) 1,77 (c) F - left winger (d) FC Barcelona (e) CA Osasuna, FC Barcelona, Barcelona Atlètic, Hércules CF, Hércules CF B
*** Fábiánkovits - István Fábiánkovits (a) 30/04/2005, Sopron (Hungary) (b) 1,86 (c) F - center forward (d) Szeged-Csanád - GA (e) Honvéd II
*** Fabiano - Fabiano (Fabiano Leismann) (a) 18/11/1991, São José do Oeste (Brazil) (b) 1,88 (c) D - central defense (d) Aris Thessaloniki (e) Denizlispor, Palmeiras, Boavista, Palmeiras, Internacional, Palmeiras, Cruzeiro, Palmeiras, Cruzeiro, Chapecoense
*** Fabiano - Fabiano (Fabiano Ribeiro de Freitas) (a) 29/02/1988, Munod Novo (Brazil) (b) 1,97 (c) G (d) Omonia Nicosia (e) FC Porto, Fenerbahce, FC Porto, Olhanense, São Paulo, América-RN, São Paulo, Santo André, São Paulo, Toledo, São Paulo
*** Fabiano Souza - Fabiano Souza (Fabiano Josué de Souza Silva) (a) 14/03/2000, Presidente Prudente (Brazil) (b) 1,75 (c) D - right back (d) Moreirense FC (e) SC Braga, Kasimpasa, SC Braga, Braga B, Académica Coimbra, Braga B, Linense, Penapolense
*** Fabianski - Lukasz Fabianski (Łukasz Marek Fabiański) (a) 18/04/1985, Kostrzyn nad Odrą (Poland) (b) 1,90 (c) G (d) West Ham United (e) Swansea City,

Arsenal, Legia Warszawa, Lech Poznan, Mieszko Gniezno, Sparta Brodnica, Lubuszanin Drezdenko, MSP Szamotuly

*** Fabinho - Fabinho (Fábio Alexandre Cruz Martins) (a) 10/02/1996, Lisboa (Portugal) (b) 1,81 (c) M - central midfielder (d) Penya Encarnada d'Andorra (e) Karmiotissa, Oly. Lympion, Fafe, AO Episkopi, Alverca, AO Episkopi, Estoril Praia, Cherno More, Sporting B, SC Covilhã, Sporting B

*** Fabinho - Fabinho (Fabio Henrique Tavares) (a) 23/10/1993, Campinas (Brazil) (b) 1,88 (c) M - pivot (d) Ittihad Club (e) Liverpool, AS Monaco, Rio Ave, AS Monaco, Rio Ave, RM Castilla, Rio Ave, Paulínia Futebol Clube (SP)

*** Fabinho - Fabinho (Fábio Pereira Baptista) (a) 29/03/2001, Lisboa (Portugal) (b) 1,81 (c) D - right back (d) Leixões SC (e) Sint-Truiden, Benfica B

*** Fábio - Fábio (Fábio Pereira da Silva) (a) 09/07/1990, Petrópolis (Brazil) (b) 1,72 (c) D - right back (d) Grêmio Foot-Ball Porto Alegrense (e) FC Nantes, Middlesbrough, Cardiff City, Manchester Utd., Queen's Park Rangers, Manchester Utd., Fluminense

*** Fábio Gomes - Fábio Gomes (Fábio Roberto Gomes Netto) (a) 25/05/1997, São Paulo (Brazil) (b) 1,92 (c) F - center forward (d) Esporte Clube Juventude (e) Juventude, At. Mineiro, Paços Ferreira, At. Mineiro, Vasco da Gama, At. Mineiro, Oeste, New York, Oeste, Albirex Niigata, Oeste, CAC Renaux, Oeste, GO Audax

*** Fabis - Lukas Fabis (Lukáš Fabiš) (a) 05/05/1998, Nitra (Slovakia) (b) 1,85 (c) D - right back (d) FC Kosice (e) Ružomberok, FC Nitra

*** Fabre - Giles Fabre (Giles Albert Fabre) (c) M (d) FC College 1975 Reserve (e) Europa Point FC

*** Fabrice Kah - Fabrice Kah (Fabrice Kah Nkwoh) (a) 09/03/1996, Yaoundé (Cameroon) (b) 1,70 (c) F - right winger (d) - (e) Olympiakos N., Leiria, Penelense, Saint-Liguaire, Brasseries

*** Fabrício Oya - Fabrício Oya (Fabrício Keiske Rodrigues Oya) (a) 23/07/1999, Campinas (Brazil) (b) 1,74 (c) M - attacking midfielder (d) SER Caxias do Sul (RS) (e) Caxias-RS, Azuriz, Torpedo Zhodino, Azuriz, Torpedo Zhodino, Corinthians B, Oeste, Corinthians B, São Bento (SP), Corinthians B

*** Fabry - Andrej Fabry (Andrej Fábry) (a) 01/03/1997, Topoľčany (Slovakia) (b) 1,77 (c) M - attacking midfielder (d) UTA Arad (e) Skalica, Dunajska Streda, SKF Sered, Dunajska Streda, SKF Sered, Dunajska Streda, Jablonec, Dunajska Streda, Jablonec, FC Nitra

*** Facchinetti - Mickaël Facchinetti (a) 15/02/1991, Neuchâtel (Switzerland) (b) 1,83 (c) D - left back (d) - (e) FC Lugano, FC Sion, APOEL FC, FC Thun, Neuchâtel Xamax, FC St. Gallen, Lausanne-Sport, FC Lugano, Chievo Verona, FC Lugano, Neuchâtel Xamax

*** Fadairo - David Fadairo (David Adeniyi Fadairo) (a) 07/11/2000, Lagos (Nigeria) (b) 1,77 (c) F - right winger (d) FC Banik Ostrava (e) Banik Ostrava, Lagos Islanders, Rimavska Sobota, Liptovsky Mik., Rimavska Sobota, Alki Oroklini, SV Stripfing, Rimavska Sobota, Lagos Islanders, Podbrezova, Lagos Islanders

*** Fadera - Alieu Fadera (a) 03/11/2001, Bakau (Gambia) (b) 1,82 (c) F - left winger (d) KRC Genk (e) Zulte Waregem, Pohronie, Real de Banjul

*** Fadida - Mor Fadida (פדידה מור) (a) 26/01/1997, ¿? (Israel) (b) - (c) F - center forward (d) Maccabi Bnei Reineh (e) Ness Ziona, SC Kfar Qasem, H. Kfar Shalem, Ramat haSharon, H Rishon leZion

*** Fadida - Saar Fadida (פדידה סער) (a) 04/01/1997, Haifa (Israel) (b) 1,82 (c) M - attacking midfielder (d) NK Olimpija Ljubljana (e) Hapoel Hadera, Hapoel Haifa, H Rishon leZion, Hapoel Haifa

*** Fadiga - Bandiougou Fadiga (a) 15/01/2001, Paris (France) (b) 1,78 (c) M - attacking midfielder (d) Olympiakos El Pireo (e) Ionikos Nikeas, Olympiakos, Paris Saint Germain B, Paris Saint-Germain, Stade Brestois, Paris Saint-Germain
*** Fadiga - Noah Fadiga (a) 03/12/1999, Brugge (Belgium) (b) 1,87 (c) D - right back (d) KAA Gent (e) Stade Brestois, Heracles Almelo, Club NXT, FC Volendam
*** Fadinger - Lukas Fadinger (a) 27/09/2000, Weiz (Austria) (b) 1,76 (c) M - attacking midfielder (d) SCR Altach (e) TSV Hartberg, SV Lafnitz, TSV Hartberg, Sturm Graz, SV Lafnitz, Sturm Graz, Sturm Graz II
*** Faerö - Odmar Faerö (Odmar Færø) (a) 01/11/1989, Tórshavn (Faroe Islands) (b) 1,85 (c) D - central defense (d) KÍ Klaksvík (e) HamKam, B36 Tórshavn, Forfar Athletic, B36 Tórshavn, Keith FC, B36 Tórshavn, Bröndby IF II, B36 Tórshavn, Keith FC, Dyce Juniors FC
*** Faerron - Fernán Faerron (Fernán José Faerron Tristán) (a) 22/08/2000, San Rafael de Escazú (Costa Rica) (b) 1,88 (c) D - central defense (d) CS Herediano (e) Fútbol Cons., HamKam, Fútbol Cons., LD Alajuelense, Fútbol Cons., Santos FC, Fútbol Cons.
*** Faes - Wout Faes (a) 03/04/1998, Mol (Belgium) (b) 1,87 (c) D - central defense (d) Leicester City (e) Stade Reims, KV Oostende, Stade Reims, KV Oostende, RSC Anderlecht, Excelsior, RSC Anderlecht, Heerenveen, RSC Anderlecht
*** Faetanini - Angelo Faetanini (a) 17/01/1993, ¿? (San Marino) (b) - (c) D - central defense (d) FC Domagnano (e) Murata, Cailungo
*** Fage - Ryan Fage (a) 31/10/2003, Ivry-sur-Seine (France) (b) - (c) M - attacking midfielder (d) US Avranches (e) US Avranches, Troyes B
*** Fagerberg - Hugo Fagerberg (a) 04/05/2004, ¿? (Sweden) (b) - (c) G (d) Mjällby AIF (e) -
*** Fagerström - Tobias Fagerström (Tobias Allan Diego Fagerström) (a) 12/07/2000, ¿? (Finland) (b) - (c) F - center forward (d) Ekenäs IF (e) FC Inter, Teutonia 05, Hamburg II
*** Faghir - Wahid Faghir (Wahidullah Faghir) (a) 29/07/2003, Vejle (Denmark) (b) 1,86 (c) F - center forward (d) SV 07 Elversberg (e) SV Elversberg, VfB Stuttgart, Nordsjælland, VfB Stuttgart, Vejle BK
*** Fagioli - Nicolò Fagioli (a) 12/02/2001, Piacenza (Italy) (b) 1,78 (c) M - central midfielder (d) Juventus de Turín (e) Cremonese, Juventus
*** Fagrá - Elias Fagrá (a) 13/05/1996, ¿? (Faroe Islands) (b) - (c) G (d) Víkingur Göta III (e) Víkingur, ÍF Fuglafjördur, Víkingur, Víkingur II
*** Fährmann - Ralf Fährmann (Ralf Sebastian Fährmann) (a) 27/09/1988, Karl-Marx-Stadt (East Germany, now in Germany) (b) 1,97 (c) G (d) FC Schalke 04 (e) Brann, FC Schalke 04, Norwich City, FC Schalke 04, Eintracht, FC Schalke 04
*** Failla - Clayton Failla (a) 08/01/1986, Żabbar (Malta) (b) 1,75 (c) M - attacking midfielder (d) Mosta FC (e) Hamrun Spartans, Birkirkara FC, Floriana, Hibernians FC, Sperre) Hibernians FC, Sliema Wanderers, Hibernians FC, Zabbar SP
*** Faist - Florian Faist (a) 10/04/1989, Hartberg (Austria) (b) 1,84 (c) G (d) TSV Hartberg II (e) TSV Hartberg, Anger, Hartberg Umgebung, TSV Pöllau, Anger, Greinbach, Hartberg Umgebung
*** Faivre - Romain Faivre (a) 14/07/1998, Asnières-sur-Seine (France) (b) 1,80 (c) M - right midfielder (d) FC Lorient (e) FC Lorient, Bournemouth, Olympique Lyon, FC Lorient, Olympique Lyon, Stade Brestois, AS Monaco B
*** Falcao - Radamel Falcao (Radamel Falcao García Zárate) (a) 10/02/1986, Santa Marta (Colombia) (b) 1,77 (c) F - center forward (d) Rayo Vallecano (e) Galatasaray, AS Monaco, Chelsea, AS Monaco, Manchester Utd., AS Monaco, Atlético Madrid, FC Porto, River Plate, River Plate II

*** Falchou - Rayyane Falchou (a) 09/10/2004, ¿? (Morocco) (b) - (c) G (d) Jong KV Mechelen (e) KV Mechelen, Jong KV Mechelen

*** Falcone - Federico Falcone (Federico Matías Falcone) (a) 21/02/1990, Rosario (Argentina) (b) 1,85 (c) F - center forward (d) Valletta FC (e) Birkirkara FC, Boavista, Desportivo Aves, Terengganu FC, Valletta, Rangers, Barnechea, Huachipato, Newell's Old Boys, La Serena, Newell's II

*** Falcone - Wladimiro Falcone (a) 12/04/1995, Roma (Italy) (b) 1,95 (c) G (d) US Lecce (e) Sampdoria, Lecce, Sampdoria, Cosenza, Sampdoria, Lucchese, Sampdoria, Gavorrano, Sampdoria, Bassano, Sampdoria, AS Livorno, Sampdoria, Savona, Sampdoria, Como, Sampdoria, Vigor Perconti

*** Falette - Simon Falette (Simon Augustin Falette) (a) 19/02/1992, Le Mans (France) (b) 1,85 (c) D - central defense (d) - (e) Hatayspor, Hannover 96, Eintracht, Fenerbahce, Eintracht, FC Metz, Stade Brestois, FC Lorient, Stade Brestois, FC Lorient, Stade Lavallois, FC Lorient, Lorient B

*** Fali - Fali (Rafael Jiménez Jarque) (a) 12/08/1993, Valencia (Spain) (b) 1,86 (c) D - central defense (d) Cádiz CF (e) Gimnàstic, Cádiz CF, Gimnàstic, FC Barcelona B, Gimnàstic, Huracán, Levante B, Catarroja CF

*** Falk - Rasmus Falk (Rasmus Falk Jensen) (a) 15/01/1992, Middelfart (Denmark) (b) 1,77 (c) M - central midfielder (d) FC Copenhague (e) Odense BK

*** Falkeborn - Martin Falkeborn (Martin Filip Falkeborn) (a) 08/01/1993, Ekerö (Sweden) (b) 1,82 (c) D - right back (d) Europa Point FC (e) Brommapojkarna, Akropolis IF, Syrianska FC, Lillestrøm, IK Frej Täby, Lillestrøm, Ullensaker/Kisa, Lillestrøm, Egersund, Brommapojkarna, Akropolis IF

*** Fall - Assane Fall (a) 26/02/1994, ¿? (Senegal) (b) - (c) M - pivot (d) SC Faetano (e) Murata

*** Fall - Babacar Fall (a) 01/01/2001, Dakar (Senegal) (b) 1,91 (c) F - center forward (d) FK Bylis (e) FC Dinamo, FK Bylis, Mlad. Petrinja, FK Bylis

*** Fall - Fallou Fall (a) 15/04/2004, ¿? (Senegal) (b) 1,92 (c) D - central defense (d) Stade Reims B (e) Graficar

*** Fall - Lamine Fall (a) 22/02/1994, ¿? (France) (b) 1,84 (c) D - left back (d) FC Mondercange (e) Swift Hesperange, RE Virton, Les Herbiers VF, Chamois Niort, SM Caen B

*** Fall - Mamadou Fall (a) 31/12/1991, Dakar (Senegal) (b) 1,84 (c) F - right winger (d) Kasimpasa (e) RSC Charleroi, KAS Eupen, RSC Charleroi, White Star, RSC Charleroi, Port Autonme

*** Fall - Mamadou Fall (Mamadou Ibra Mbacke Fall) (a) 21/11/2002, Rufisque (Senegal) (b) 1,89 (c) D - central defense (d) Los Ángeles FC (e) Villarreal CF B, LAFC

*** Fall - Pape Fall (Pape Yare Fall) (a) 09/09/2000, ¿? (Senegal) (b) 1,82 (c) D - left back (d) Valmiera FC (e) AS Douanes

*** Fallatah - Rayan Edrees Fallatah (a) 06/10/2003, ¿? (Saudi Arabia) (b) - (c) F - center forward (d) OFI Creta (e) -

*** Fällman - David Fällman (David Thomas Fällman) (a) 04/02/1990, Stockholm (Sweden) (b) 1,87 (c) D - central defense (d) Aalesunds FK (e) Hammarby IF, DL Transcen., Gefle, AFC Eskilstuna, Eskilstuna City, Triangelns IK

*** Fallmann - Pascal Fallmann (Pascal Armando Fallmann) (a) 07/11/2003, ¿? (Austria) (b) 1,87 (c) D - right back (d) SC Freiburg II (e) SC Freiburg II, Rapid Wien, Rapid Wien II

*** Fallon - Stephen Fallon (a) 03/03/1997, Belfast (Northern Ireland) (b) - (c) M - right midfielder (d) Linfield FC (e) Linfield, De La Salle

*** Falta - Simon Falta (Šimon Falta) (a) 23/04/1993, Dolní Dobrouč (Czech Rep.) (b) 1,83 (c) M - left midfielder (d) - (e) Viktoria Plzen, Zbrojovka Brno, Viktoria Plzen, Banik Ostrava, Viktoria Plzen, Sigma Olomouc

*** Faltsetas - Alexander Faltsetas (Alexander Daniel Faltsetas) (a) 04/07/1987, Göteborg (Sweden) (b) 1,81 (c) M - pivot (d) Utsiktens BK (e) Häcken, Helsingborgs IF, Häcken, Djurgården, Gefle, IFK Göteborg, Brage, IFK Göteborg, FC Trollhättan, Västra Frölunda

*** Falzetta - Lorenzo Falzetta (a) 28/03/2000, Cosenza (Italy) (b) 1,83 (c) M - right midfielder (d) Tre Fiori FC (e) Nereto, Brindisi, Roccella, Rende, Francavilla

*** Fandiño - Sebastián Fandiño (Sebastián Roa Fandiño) (a) 11/07/2003, Bogotá (Colombia) (b) 1,87 (c) D - central defense (d) FC Ordino (e) -

*** Fangaj - Abdurraman Fangaj (a) 12/10/1997, Shkodër (Albania) (b) 1,82 (c) D - right back (d) KF Egnatia (e) KF Vllaznia, KF Laçi, KF Vllaznia, KF Tërbuni, KF Vllaznia

*** Fanimo - Matthias Fanimo (Matthias Olubori Ayodluwa Fanimo) (a) 28/01/1994, Lambeth, London (England) (b) 1,75 (c) F - right winger (d) Ebbsfleet United (e) Koper, Slaven Belupo, FK Sarajevo, Mladost Kakanj, Drava Ptuj, Margate FC, Eastleigh, Bishop's Stortford, Tranmere Rovers

*** Fantis - Antonin Fantis (Antonín Fantiš) (a) 15/04/1992, Praha (Czechoslovakia, now in Czech Rep.) (b) 1,75 (c) M - attacking midfielder (d) FC Zlin (e) 1.FK Pribram, Fastav Zlin, 1.FK Pribram, Fastav Zlin, Jablonec, Fastav Zlin, Jablonec, Banik Ostrava, 1.FK Pribram

*** Fantoni - Gian Marco Fantoni (a) 24/01/2004, Bagno a Ripoli (Italy) (b) - (c) G (d) Nocerina 1910 (e) -

*** Faqa - Ahmad Faqa (فقا احمد) (a) 10/01/2003, Qamishli (Siria) (b) - (c) D - central defense (d) HK Kópavogs (e) HK Kópavogs, AIK, Sandvikens IF, AIK, Västerås SK, AIK

*** Faraas - Benjamin Thoresen Faraas (a) 08/09/2005, Flisa (Norway) (b) 1,80 (c) M - central midfielder (d) Hamarkameratene (e) -

*** Faraci - Nihat Faraci (Nihat Fərəci) (a) 30/03/2003, ¿? (Azerbaijan) (b) - (c) F - left winger (d) Kapaz 2 Ganja (e) -

*** Farada - Ayano Farada (פרדה איינאו) (a) 29/04/2002, ¿? (Israel) (b) - (c) M - pivot (d) Hapoel Jerusalem (e) -

*** Faragau - Alexandru Faragau (Alexandru Florin Fărăgău) (a) 25/04/2005, Cluj Napoca (Romania) (b) - (c) D - right back (d) CSM Ceahlaul Piatra Neamt (e) Ceahlaul, CS U Craiova II

*** Faraj - Imad Faraj (a) 11/02/1999, Croix (France) (b) 1,77 (c) F - right winger (d) AEK Larnaca (e) Excelsior Mouscron, LOSC Lille B, B SAD, LOSC Lille B, Lille, LOSC Lille B

*** Faraj - Omar Faraj (فرج عمر) (a) 09/03/2002, Stockholm (Sweden) (b) 1,82 (c) F - center forward (d) AIK Solna (e) At. Levante, Degerfors, At. Levante, Brommapojkarna

*** Faraoni - Davide Faraoni (Marco Davide Faraoni) (a) 25/10/1991, Bracciano (Italy) (b) 1,80 (c) D - right back (d) Hellas Verona (e) Crotone, Hellas Verona, Crotone, Udinese, Novara, Udinese, Perugia, Udinese, Watford, Udinese, Internazionale Milano

*** Fares - Mohamed Fares (Mohamed Salim Fares) (a) 15/02/1996, Aubervilliers (France) (b) 1,83 (c) D - left back (d) SS Lazio (e) Torino, Lazio, Genoa, Lazio, SPAL, Hellas Verona, SPAL, Hellas Verona

*** Farinha - André Farinha (André de Oliveira Silva Farinha) (a) 06/04/1998, Évora (Portugal) (b) 1,75 (c) D - right back (d) Juventude Évora SC (e) Lusitano Évora,

Helsinki IFK, ASIL Lysi, PO Xylotymbou, Académica Coimbra, ARC Oleiros, Gibraltar Utd., Lusitano Évora

*** Fariñez - Wuilker Fariñez (Wuilker Fariñez Aray) (a) 15/02/1998, Caracas, Distrito Capital (Venezuela) (b) 1,80 (c) G (d) RC Lens (e) Millonarios, RC Lens, Millonarios, Caracas FC, Caracas FC B

*** Farji - Marko Farji (Marko Lawk Farji - فرجي لاوك ماركو) (a) 16/03/2004, Grimstad (Norway) (b) 1,84 (c) F - left winger (d) Strømsgodset IF (e) Strømsgodset II, Jerv

*** Farkas - Patrick Farkas (a) 09/09/1992, Oberwart (Austria) (b) 1,79 (c) D - right back (d) SV Oberwart (e) TSV Hartberg, FC Luzern, RB Salzburg, SV Mattersburg, Mattersburg II

*** Farkas - Tamás Farkas (a) 14/07/2003, Debrecen (Hungary) (b) 1,77 (c) M - attacking midfielder (d) Debreceni VSC (e) Debrecen II

*** Farley - Ben Farley (a) 12/09/2004, ¿? (Wales) (b) - (c) F - center forward (d) Connah's Quay Nomads (e) -

*** Farmer - Tom Farmer (a) 11/12/1996, ¿? (Wales) (b) 1,83 (c) D - left back (d) FC Manchester 62 (e) Pontypridd

*** Farquhar - Craig Farquhar (a) 09/05/2003, Ballymena (Northern Ireland) (b) - (c) D - central defense (d) Larne FC (e) Ballymena, Dundela FC, Ballymena

*** Farrell - Eoin Farrell (a) 27/03/2002, Athy, Kildare (Ireland) (b) - (c) D - right back (d) Hofstra Pride (Hofstra University) (e) Bray Wanderers, Wexford FC, UCD

*** Farrell - Shane Farrell (a) 26/06/2000, Dublin (Ireland) (b) - (c) F - right winger (d) Shelbourne FC (e) Finglas

*** Farren - Kieran Farren (a) 21/11/2000, Carndonagh (Ireland) (b) 1,88 (c) D - central defense (d) Coleraine FC (e) Dergview, Finn Harps

*** Farrés - Biel Farrés (Biel Farrés del Castillo) (a) 01/05/2002, Vic (Spain) (b) - (c) D - central defense (d) CE Sabadell FC (e) CE Sabadell, Girona FC B

*** Farrugia - Gabriel Diego Farrugia (a) 14/06/2004, ¿? (Malta) (b) - (c) F (d) - (e) Balzan FC

*** Farrugia - Ivin Farrugia (a) 02/06/2005, ¿? (Malta) (b) - (c) D - central defense (d) - (e) Pietà Hotspurs,

*** Farrugia - Jake Farrugia (a) 07/03/2004, ¿? (Malta) (b) - (c) G (d) - (e) Pietà Hotspurs

*** Farrugia - Jean Paul Farrugia (a) 21/03/1992, ¿? (Malta) (b) 1,84 (c) F - center forward (d) Sliema Wanderers (e) Birkirkara FC, Sliema Wanderers, FC Chiasso, Sliema Wanderers, Hibernians FC, Sliema Wanderers, Hibernians FC, Spartak Trnava, Hibernians FC, Marsaxlokk, Hibernians FC

*** Farrugia - Kayden Farrugia (a) 02/04/2006, ¿? (Malta) (b) - (c) D (d) - (e) Valletta FC

*** Farrugia - Matthew Farrugia (a) 17/03/1985, ¿? (Malta) (b) 1,78 (c) G (d) Gudja United FC (e) Tarxien, Senglea Ath., Hamrun Spartans, Pembroke, Qormi FC

*** Farrugia - Neil Farrugia (a) 19/05/1999, ¿? (Ireland) (b) 1,85 (c) D - right back (d) Shamrock Rovers (e) UCD, Belvedere FC

*** Farrugia - Tyron Farrugia (a) 22/02/1989, ¿? (Malta) (b) - (c) D - central defense (d) Msida St. Joseph FC (e) Mosta FC, Sirens FC, Mosta FC, Floriana, Msida SJ

*** Farrugia Cross - Nikolai Farrugia Cross (a) 08/10/2002, ¿? (Malta) (b) 1,70 (c) D - left back (d) Mqabba FC (e) -

*** Faryna - Maryan Faryna (Фарина Мар'ян Іванович) (a) 28/08/2003, Kamyane, Lviv Oblast (Ukraine) (b) 1,80 (c) D - central defense (d) Shakhtar Donetsk (e) -

*** Farzullayev - Khayal Farzullayev (a) 14/06/2005, ¿? (Azerbaijan) (b) - (c) G (d) Sumqayit 2 (e) -

*** Fase - Anton Fase (a) 06/02/2000, Haarlem (Netherlands) (b) 1,85 (c) F - left winger (d) FK Kauno Zalgiris (e) Botev Vratsa, NEC Nijmegen

*** Fasko - Michal Fasko (Michal Faško) (a) 24/08/1994, Brezno (Slovakia) (b) 1,83 (c) M - central midfielder (d) FC Kosice (e) Banska Bystrica, Slovan Liberec, FC Nitra, Grasshoppers, Karvina, Grasshoppers, Eintracht Braunschweig, Grasshoppers, Ružomberok, Banska Bystrica

*** Fasko - Simon Fasko (Šimon Faško) (a) 09/04/2006, Brezno (Slovakia) (b) - (c) M - central midfielder (d) FK Zeleziarne Podbrezova (e) -

*** Fasouliotis - Marios Fasouliotis (Μάριος Φασουλιώτης) (a) 26/05/2005, Nicosia (Cyprus) (b) 1,72 (c) F - left winger (d) ASIL Lysi (e) Doxa Katokopias

*** Fassnacht - Christian Fassnacht (a) 11/11/1993, Zürich (Switzerland) (b) 1,85 (c) M - right midfielder (d) Norwich City (e) BSC Young Boys, FC Thun, FC Winterthur, FC Thalwil, FC Tuggen, FC Thalwil, Red Star ZH

*** Fasson - Lucas Fasson (Lucas Fasson dos Santos) (a) 30/05/2001, Santo André (Brazil) (b) 1,85 (c) D - central defense (d) Lokomotiv Moskva (e) Athletico-PR, La Serena

*** Fastov - Artem Fastov (Фастов Артем Олексійович) (a) 23/07/2003, ¿? (Georgia) (b) 1,94 (c) G (d) FC Kolkheti-1913 Poti (e) Jonava, Sumy

*** Fatah - Amar Fatah (Amar Abdirahman Ahmed Fatah) (a) 19/02/2004, Solna (Sweden) (b) 1,80 (c) F - left winger (d) Lommel SK (e) Troyes, AIK

*** Fatai - Kehinde Fatai (Kehinde Abdul Feyi Fatai) (a) 19/02/1990, Abuja (Nigeria) (b) 1,80 (c) F - center forward (d) SC Otelul Galati (e) FK Turan, FC Arges, Astra Giurgiu, Dinamo Minsk, Ufa, Sparta Praha, Astra Giurgiu, KV Brugge, Astra Giurgiu, Farul Constanta, JUTH FC

*** Fatau - Mohammed Fatau (a) 24/12/1992, Accra (Ghana) (b) 1,78 (c) M - pivot (d) FC Van (e) Spartak Varna, Zakho SC, Mohammedan, Al-Qadsiah FC, Kuwait SC, Al-Qadsiah FC, Gaziantepspor, Granada CF, UD Almería, Granada CF, Rayo Vallecano, Granada B, San Roque Lepe, Granada B, Cádiz CF B, Granada B

*** Fatawu - Issahaku Fatawu (Issahaku Abdul Fatawu) (a) 08/03/2004, Tamale (Ghana) (b) 1,77 (c) F - right winger (d) Sporting de Lisboa (e) Steadfast FC, Dreams FC, Steadfast FC, TUFA

*** Fati - Ansu Fati (Anssumane Fati Vieira) (a) 31/10/2002, Bissau (Guinea-Bissau) (b) 1,78 (c) F - left winger (d) FC Barcelona (e) FC Barcelona B

*** Fati - Babacar Fati (a) 01/02/2000, ¿? (Finland) (b) 1,77 (c) D - left back (d) SJK Seinäjoki II (e) SJK Seinäjoki, Sporting B

*** Fati - Jeff Fati (a) 13/04/1999, Luton (England) (b) 1,75 (c) M - attacking midfielder (d) Glacis United (e) Sollentuna FK

*** Fatica - Lorenzo Fatica (a) 31/08/1988, Fano (Italy) (b) 1,95 (c) D - central defense (d) La Fiorita 1967 (e) Faetano, Urbino Calcio, Jesina, AJ Fano, Atletico Alma, Cattolica

*** Fatty - Madi Karamo Fatty (a) 11/12/1999, Serekunda (Gambia) (b) 1,84 (c) F - center forward (d) KF Trepca 89 (e) FC Phoenix, West United

*** Fauriel - Loïs Fauriel (Loïs Sylvain Fauriel) (a) 17/07/2002, Guilherand-Granges (France) (b) 1,84 (c) D - left back (d) - (e) Akritas Chlor., Ol. Marseille B

*** Faust - Rodrigo Faust (Rodrigo Emilio Faust) (a) 14/09/1995, Villa Madero (Argentina) (b) 1,86 (c) F - center forward (d) Olancho FC (e) OFK Petrovac, FK Jezero, Excursionistas, Paraná, San Miguel, UAI Urquiza

*** Fausto - André Fausto (André Fausto Prates Rodrigues Júnior) (a) 02/05/1994, Porto Alegre (Brazil) (b) 1,80 (c) D - central defense (d) Balzan FC (e) Gudja United FC, Santa Lucia FC, Avenida, Barra

*** Faux - Joe Faux (Josef Eugene Faux) (a) 06/08/1996, ¿? (Wales) (b) 1,73 (c) M - left midfielder (d) Connah's Quay Nomads (e) Caernarfon, Cefn Druids, Caernarfon, Cefn Druids, Prescot Cables, West Didsbury

*** Favasuli - Costantino Favasuli (a) 26/04/2004, ¿? (Italy) (b) - (c) M - left midfielder (d) Ternana Calcio (e) -

*** Favorov - Artem Favorov (Фаворов Артем Володимирович) (a) 19/03/1994, Kyiv (Ukraine) (b) 1,85 (c) M - central midfielder (d) Puskás Akadémia FC (e) Zalaegerszeg, Puskás AFC, Desna, Zirka, Vejle BK, Zirka, Obolon-Brovar, Dynamo 2 Kyiv

*** Fawakhri - Saleem Fawakhri (פיאחרי סלים) (a) 04/04/1999, Mazra'a (Israel) (b) 1,80 (c) M - attacking midfielder (d) - (e) Pobeda Prilep, M. Neve Shaanan, Ahva Reineh, Maccabi Tamra, T. Kfar Kana, H. Robi Shapira, H. Kfar Kana, M. Neve Shaanan, FC Daburiyya, Hapoel Ikhsal, Nachlat Yehuda, M. Neve Shaanan

*** Fawcett - Ben Fawcett (Ben Thomas Fawcett) (a) 07/09/2000, ¿? (Wales) (b) 1,76 (c) F - center forward (d) Haverfordwest County (e) -

*** Fawzi - Yahaya Fawzi (Yahaya Mohammad Fawzi) (a) 28/11/2001, ¿? (Nigeria) (b) 1,80 (c) D - right back (d) FK Neptunas Klaipeda (e) Jonava, Real Farma

*** Fay - Ross Fay (a) 22/01/2003, ¿? (Ireland) (b) - (c) M - central midfielder (d) Longford Town FC (e) St. Patrick's Ath.

*** Fayad - Khalil Fayad (a) 09/06/2004, Montpellier (France) (b) 1,76 (c) M - central midfielder (d) Montpellier HSC (e) Montpellier B

*** Faye - Alasan Faye (a) 28/09/2003, ¿? (Gambia) (b) 1,85 (c) M - pivot (d) FC Ararat Yerevan (e) Casa Sports, Fortune FC, BK Milan FC, Marimoo

*** Faye - Serigne Faye (a) 05/04/2004, Dakar (Senegal) (b) 1,86 (c) F - center forward (d) HSC Montpellier B (e) -

*** Fayulu - Timothy Fayulu (Timothy Bruce Fayulu) (a) 24/07/1999, Genève (Switzerland) (b) 1,92 (c) G (d) FC Sion (e) FC Winterthur, FC Sion, Olymp. Genève, Olymp. Genève, Olymp. Genève, Etoile Carouge FC II

*** Fazio - Federico Fazio (Federico Julián Fazio) (a) 17/03/1987, Buenos Aires (Argentina) (b) 1,95 (c) D - central defense (d) US Salernitana 1919 (e) AS Roma, Tottenham Hotspur, AS Roma, Tottenham Hotspur, Sevilla FC, Tottenham Hotspur, Sevilla FC, Ferro, Ferro II

*** Fazlagic - Enis Fazlagic (Енис Фазлагиќ) (a) 27/03/2000, Veles (North Macedonia) (b) 1,88 (c) M - pivot (d) Wisla Cracovia (e) Dunajska Streda, Wisla Kraków, MSK Zilina, Shkëndija, FK Skopje

*** Fazli - Samir Fazli (a) 22/04/1991, Skopje (Yugoslavia, now in North Macedonia) (b) 1,85 (c) F - center forward (d) Makedonija Gjorce Petrov (e) FK Turan, Makedonija, FK Turan, Makedonija, Shkëndija, NK Rudes, FC Wil 1900, Heerenveen, Helmond Sport, Heerenveen, Makedonija

*** Fazlic - Elmedin Fazlic (a) 18/07/2002, Liestal BL (Switzerland) (b) 1,88 (c) D - central defense (d) NK Domžale (e) FC Linth 04

*** Fazlija - Shpresim Fazlija (a) 08/03/1997, Genève (Switzerland) (b) - (c) M - left midfielder (d) - (e) Etzella Ettelbrück, FC Echallens, FC Echichens, KF Liria, Plan-les-Ouates, Etoile Carouge, Etoile Carouge FC II

*** Fazliu - Astrit Fazliu (a) 28/10/1987, Ferizaj (Yugoslavia, now in Kosovo) (b) 1,75 (c) M - attacking midfielder (d) KF Vjosa (e) KF Ferizaj, FC Drita, KF Feronikeli, FC Drita, Flamurtari FC, FK Partizani, Shkëndija, KF Ferizaj, FC Prishtina, KF Ferizaj, KF Ulpiana, KF Ferizaj

*** Fazliu - Drilon Fazliu (a) 17/11/2000, Vushtrri (RF Yugoslavia, now in Kosovo) (b) 1,77 (c) F - center forward (d) KF Vushtrria (e) KF Llapi, KF Vushtrria

*** Fazliu - Egzon Fazliu (a) 30/05/2003, Skenderaj (Serbia and Montenegro, now in Kosovo) (b) 1,76 (c) F - center forward (d) KF Trepca 89 (e) KF Drenica, KF Kurda
*** Fazzini - Jacopo Fazzini (a) 16/03/2003, Massa (Italy) (b) 1,78 (c) M - central midfielder (d) FC Empoli (e) Capezzano
*** Feargod - Ibe Joseph Feargod (a) 01/03/2004, ¿? (Nigeria) (b) - (c) D - central defense (d) Mosta FC (e) Garden City
*** Feczesin - Róbert Feczesin (a) 22/02/1986, Dabas (Hungary) (b) 1,87 (c) F - center forward (d) - (e) Vasas FC, Újpest FC, Adanaspor, Jeonnam Dragons, Videoton FC, Padova, Ascoli, Brescia, Ascoli, Brescia, Debrecen, Brescia, FC Sopron, Újpest FC
*** Feddal - Zouhair Feddal (Zouhair Feddal Agharbi) (a) 23/12/1989, Tétouan (Morocco) (b) 1,91 (c) D - central defense (d) - (e) Alanyaspor, Real Valladolid, Sporting Lisboa, Real Betis, Alavés, Levante UD, Parma, US Palermo, Parma, AC Siena, Parma, FUS Rabat, RCD Espanyol B, San Roque Lepe, CD Teruel, Terrassa FC, Vilajuïga, CE Mataró
*** Fedele - Matteo Fedele (a) 20/07/1992, Lausanne (Switzerland) (b) 1,85 (c) M - central midfielder (d) AFC Chindia Targoviste (e) Birkirkara FC, Hamrun Spartans, CS U Craiova, Valenciennes FC, Foggia, CS U Craiova, Foggia, Cesena, Foggia, Carpi, Bari, Carpi, FC Sion, Carpi, FC Sion, Grasshoppers, FC Sion
*** Fedeli - Eric Fedeli (a) 13/01/1992, ¿? (Italy) (b) - (c) F - center forward (d) Tre Fiori FC (e) Domagnano, SS Folgore, Murata, Faetano, ACD Torconca, Cesenatico, ACD Torconca
*** Fedin - Maksim Fedin (Федин Максим Сергеевич) (a) 08/06/1996, Ekibastuz (Kazakhstan) (b) 1,75 (c) F - right winger (d) Ordabasy Shymkent (e) FK Turan, Aktobe, Tobol Kostanay, Kaysar, Tobol Kostanay, Okzhetpes, Atyrau, Spartak, FC Bayterek
*** Fedorchuk - Valeriy Fedorchuk (Федорчук Валерій Юрійович) (a) 05/10/1988, Netishyn, Khmelnytskyi Oblast (Soviet Union, now in Ukraine) (b) 1,78 (c) M - central midfielder (d) - (e) Rukh Lviv, FK Mariupol, Riga, Veres Rivne, Dinamo Kyïv, Dnipro, Volyn Lutsk, Dnipro, Karpaty, Dnipro, Kryvbas, Dnipro, Kryvbas, Dnipro, Kryvbas, Dnipro, PFC Lviv, Kryvbas II
*** Fedoriv - Vitaliy Fedoriv (Федорів Віталій Миколайович) (a) 21/10/1987, Mezhyrichya, Lviv Oblast (Soviet Union, now in Ukraine) (b) 1,81 (c) D - central defense (d) SK Dnipro-1 (e) Metalist, SK Dnipro-1, Metalist, Nizhny Novgorod, Olimpik Donetsk, Goverla, Spartaks, Kryvbas, Amkar Perm, Dinamo Kyïv, Amkar Perm, Dinamo Kyïv, Dinamo Kiev II, Dynamo 2 Kyiv, Dynamo 3 Kyiv, RVUFK Kyiv
*** Fedorov - Artem Fedorov (Федоров Артем Віталійович) (a) 18/09/1998, Bilgorod-Dnistrovskyi, Odesa Oblast (Ukraine) (b) 1,72 (c) F - left winger (d) FK Suduva Marijampole (e) Petrocub, Dinamo-Auto, Pakruojis
*** Fedorovics - Daniels Fedorovics (Daniels Fedorovičs) (a) 07/10/2001, Riga (Latvia) (b) 1,86 (c) D - central defense (d) Dinamo Riga (e) HS Kromeriz, Metta, FS Metta II
*** Fedotov - Daniel Fedotov (a) 16/08/2001, Tallinn (Estonia) (b) - (c) F - center forward (d) Tallinn JK Legion (e) -
*** Fedyanin - Artem Fedyanin (Федянин Артём Александрович) (a) 25/04/1994, Gomel (Belarus) (b) 1,74 (c) M - pivot (d) Bumprom Gomel (e) Dnepr Mogilev, DYuSSh-2 Rechitsa, Smolevichi, Osipovichi, Svetlogorsk, Gomel, Gomel II, Rechitsa, Gomel II
*** Feely - Rory Feely (a) 03/01/1997, ¿? (Ireland) (b) 1,91 (c) D - right back (d) AFC Barrow (e) Bohemians, St. Patrick's Ath., Waterford FC, St. Patrick's Ath.

*** Feghouli - Sofiane Feghouli (سفيان فاغولي) (a) 26/12/1989, Levallois-Perret (France) (b) 1,77 (c) F - right winger (d) Fatih Karagümrük (e) Galatasaray, West Ham Utd., Valencia CF, UD Almería, Valencia CF, Grenoble

*** Fegrouch - Karim Fegrouch (كريم فكروش) (a) 14/02/1982, Fès (Morocco) (b) 1,85 (c) G (d) - (e) Sirius, FAR Rabat, AEL Limassol, PAS Giannina, Wydad AC, MAS Fes, Marruecos

*** Feher - Raul Feher (Raul Mihai Feher) (a) 12/03/1997, Zalău (Romania) (b) 1,90 (c) D - central defense (d) Inter Club d'Escaldes (e) CD Ibiza, FC Andorra, CD Ibiza, FC Andorra, IC d'Escaldes, FC Andorra, Lleida Esp. B, CF Balaguer

*** Fehér - Csanád Fehér (Fehér Csanád Levente) (a) 13/06/2002, Szeged (Hungary) (b) 1,87 (c) D - central defense (d) Újpest FC (e) Újpest II, Kecskeméti TE

*** Fein - Adrian Fein (Adrian Markus Fein) (a) 18/03/1999, München (Germany) (b) 1,87 (c) M - pivot (d) Excelsior Rotterdam (e) Bayern München, Dynamo Dresden, Bayern München, Greuther Fürth, Bayern München, PSV Eindhoven, Bayern München, SV Hamburg, Bayern München, FC Bayern II, Jahn Regensburg, FC Bayern II

*** Fejsa - Ljubomir Fejsa (Љубомир Фејса) (a) 14/08/1988, Kula (Yugoslavia, now in Serbia) (b) 1,83 (c) M - pivot (d) - (e) FK Partizan, Al-Ahli, Benfica, Alavés, Benfica, Olympiakos, FK Partizan, Hajduk Kula

*** Fejzic - Nevres Fejzic (Nevres Fejzić) (a) 04/11/1990, Zvornik (Yugoslavia, now in Bosnia and Herzegovina) (b) 1,85 (c) G (d) FK Tuzla City (e) FK Krupa, NK Jajce, Travnik, Radnik Hadzici

*** Fejzulla - Devid Fejzulla (a) 13/02/2003, ¿? (Albania) (b) 1,78 (c) M - attacking midfielder (d) - (e) FC Dinamo, KF Teuta, FC Dinamo

*** Fekir - Nabil Fekir (a) 18/07/1993, Lyon (France) (b) 1,73 (c) M - attacking midfielder (d) Real Betis Balompié (e) Olympique Lyon, Olymp. Lyon B, AS Saint-Priest, FC Vaulx-en-Vel, Caluire, FC Vaulx-en-Vel, Villeurbanne EL

*** Fekoua - Junah Fekoua (Junah Cyrille Fekoua) (c) D - left back (d) - (e) Penya Encarnada

*** Felek - Cem Felek (Cem Fələk) (a) 12/05/1996, Buchen (Germany) (b) 1,80 (c) M - attacking midfielder (d) Delay Sports Berlin II (e) JK Trans Narva, VfB Ginsheim, SG Dersim/VfR, RW Darmstadt, KuPS, Aris Limassol, KuPS, FCI Levadia, TSV Steinbach, RoPS, Karagümrük

*** Felida - Kevin Felida (Kevin Antonio Felida) (a) 11/11/1999, Spijkenisse (Netherlands) (b) 1,74 (c) M - pivot (d) RKC Waalwijk (e) FC Den Bosch

*** Feliks - Michal Feliks (Michał Feliks) (a) 19/03/1999, Kraków (Poland) (b) 1,86 (c) F - center forward (d) Ruch Chorzów (e) Ruch, Radomiak, Garbarnia, Garbarnia II, AP Wisla

*** Felipe - Felipe (Felipe Augusto de Almeida Monteiro) (a) 16/05/1989, Mogi das Cruzes (Brazil) (b) 1,90 (c) D - central defense (d) Nottingham Forest (e) Atlético Madrid, FC Porto, Corinthians, Académica Coimbra, Corinthians, Académica Coimbra, Bragantino, Académica Coimbra, Bragantino, União Mogi

*** Felipe - Felipe (Luis Felipe Queiroz dos Santos) (a) 15/09/2000, ¿? (Brazil) (b) 1,78 (c) F - left winger (d) - (e) IFK Mariehamn, Ekenäs IF, IFK Mariehamn, Tapajós

*** Felipe Anderson - Felipe Anderson (Felipe Anderson Pereira Gomes) (a) 15/04/1993, Brasília (Brazil) (b) 1,75 (c) F - right winger (d) SS Lazio (e) West Ham Utd., FC Porto, West Ham Utd., Lazio, Santos

*** Felipe Vizeu - Felipe Vizeu (Felipe dos Reis Pereira Vizeu do Carmo) (a) 12/03/1997, Três Rios (Brazil) (b) 1,85 (c) F - center forward (d) Criciúma Esporte Clube (e) Atlético-GO, FC Sheriff, Udinese, Yokohama FC, Udinese, Ceará SC, Udinese, Akhmat Grozny, Udinese, Grêmio Porto Alegre, Udinese, Flamengo

*** Felippe Cardoso - Felippe Cardoso (Wanderson Felippe Cardoso dos Santos) (a) 04/10/1998, São Paulo (Brazil) (b) 1,87 (c) F - center forward (d) Casa Pia AC (e) Santos, Vegalta Sendai, Santos, Fluminense, Santos, Ceará SC, Santos, Ponte Preta, Santos, Ponte Preta, Osvaldo-SP

*** Felix - Felix (João Victor Felix Alves) (a) 02/01/2002, Rio de Janeiro (Brazil) (b) 1,85 (c) D - central defense (d) Ypiranga-RS FC (e) -

*** Felix - Joel Felix (Joel Rasmus Felix) (a) 13/01/1998, St. Marteen (Saint Lucia) (b) 1,90 (c) D - central defense (d) Silkeborg IF (e) Naestved BK

*** Feltes - Gilles Feltes (a) 06/12/1995, ¿? (Luxembourg) (b) - (c) D - central defense (d) FC Victoria Rosport (e) CS Grevenmacher

*** Feltham - Harris Feltham (a) 15/06/2003, ¿? (Wales) (b) - (c) M - central midfielder (d) Cardiff Metropolitan University (e) Eastleigh

*** Femenía - Kiko Femenía (Francisco Femenía Far) (a) 02/02/1991, Sanet y Negrals (Spain) (b) 1,71 (c) D - right back (d) Villarreal CF (e) Watford, Alavés, Alcorcón, RM Castilla, FC Barcelona B, Hércules CF, Hércules CF B

*** Femic - Filip Femic (a) 25/02/2003, Bijelo Polje (Serbia and Montenegro, now in Montenegro) (b) - (c) F (d) Arsenal Tivat (e) OFK Petrovac

*** Fendrich - Vilem Fendrich (Vilém Fendrich) (a) 22/01/1991, ¿? (Czechoslovakia, now in Czech Rep.) (b) 1,93 (c) G (d) FK Jablonec (e) Sigma Olomouc, Hradec Kralove, SFC Opava, Viktorie Jirny, Jablonec, Graffin Vlasim, FK Jablonec, Varnsdorf, FK Jablonec, FK Jablonec B, FK Jablonec, Usti nad Labem, FK Jablonec

*** Fenech - Kieran Fenech (Kieran Paul Fenech) (a) 07/11/2002, ¿? (Malta) (b) - (c) M (d) Zejtun Corinthians FC (e) Valletta, Marsa FC

*** Fenech - Paul Fenech (a) 20/12/1986, Naxxar (Malta) (b) 1,65 (c) M - left midfielder (d) Balzan FC (e) Birkirkara FC, Balzan FC, Birkirkara FC, Msida SJ

*** Fenger - Mads Fenger (Mads Fenger Nielsen) (a) 10/09/1990, ¿? (Denmark) (b) 1,85 (c) D - central defense (d) Hammarby IF (e) Randers FC

*** Fenger - Max Fenger (Max Johannes Whitta Fenger) (a) 07/08/2001, Roskilde (Denmark) (b) 1,85 (c) F - center forward (d) Mjällby AIF (e) Mjällby AIF, Odense BK

*** Fer - Leroy Fer (Leroy Johan Fer) (a) 05/01/1990, Zoetermeer (Netherlands) (b) 1,88 (c) M - pivot (d) Alanyaspor (e) Feyenoord, Swansea City, Queen's Park Rangers, Swansea City, Queen's Park Rangers, Norwich City, FC Twente, Feyenoord

*** Ferahyan - Felix Ferahyan (Felix Nikolas Antti Matias Ferahyan) (a) 29/11/1998, Göppingen (Germany) (b) 1,93 (c) G (d) Pallokerho-35 (e) Helsinki IFK, K. Offenbach, Ekenäs IF, FC Honka, KuPS

*** Ferati - Arianit Ferati (a) 07/09/1997, Stuttgart (Germany) (b) 1,68 (c) M - attacking midfielder (d) Fortuna Sittard (e) Waldh. Mannheim, SV Hamburg, Hamburg II, SV Hamburg, Erzgebirge Aue, SV Hamburg, Fortuna Düsseldorf, SV Hamburg, VfB Stuttgart

*** Ferati - Besnik Ferati (a) 19/04/2000, Skopje (North Macedonia) (b) 1,86 (c) M - pivot (d) FC Malisheva (e) Pobeda Prilep, FC Shkupi, AP Brera, FK Partizani, FK Partizani B

*** Fercec - Anej Fercec (Anej Ferčec) (a) 26/08/2004, ¿? (Slovenia) (b) - (c) D - right back (d) NK Maribor (e) -

*** Fereira - Eduardo Fereira (Eduardo Enrique Fereira Peñaranda) (a) 29/09/2000, Valencia, Carabobo (Venezuela) (b) 1,69 (c) D - right back (d) Academia Puerto Cabello (e) Puerto Cabello, Casa Pia, Caracas FC

*** Ferenc - Maros Ferenc (Maroš Ferenc) (a) 19/02/1981, Prešov (Czechoslovakia, now in Slovakia) (b) 1,84 (c) G (d) - (e) OFK Raslavice, Tatran Presov, Lok. Kosice, Tatran Presov, Rozvoj Pusovce, Tatran Presov, MEAP Nisou, FC Eindhoven,

Michalovce, Slavoj Trebisov, MEAP Nisou, Tatran Presov, AS Trencin, Tatran Presov

*** Ferenczi - János Ferenczi (a) 03/04/1991, Debrecen (Hungary) (b) 1,80 (c) D - left back (d) Debreceni VSC (e) Debrecen II, Létavértes SC 97

*** Ferguson - Alex Ferguson (Alexander Ferguson) (a) 10/09/2003, ¿? (Scotland) (b) - (c) M - central midfielder (d) St. Johnstone FC (e) East Fife, St. Johnstone B, Cowdenbeath FC, St. Johnstone B, Edinburgh City, St. Johnstone B

*** Ferguson - Evan Ferguson (a) 19/10/2004, Bettystown, Meath (Ireland) (b) 1,83 (c) F - center forward (d) Brighton & Hove Albion (e) Bohemians

*** Ferguson - Lewis Ferguson (a) 24/08/1999, Hamilton (Scotland) (b) 1,81 (c) M - central midfielder (d) Bologna (e) Aberdeen FC

*** Ferguson - Nathan Ferguson (Nathan Kirk-Patrick Ferguson) (a) 06/10/2000, Birmingham (England) (b) 1,84 (c) D - central defense (d) Crystal Palace (e) West Bromwich Albion

*** Ferguson - Rohan Ferguson (a) 06/12/1997, Bathgate (Scotland) (b) - (c) G (d) Larne FC (e) Queen of the South, Motherwell FC, Linfield, Motherwell FC, Airdrieonians, Motherwell FC, Airdrieonians

*** Ferhat - Zinedine Ferhat (a) 01/03/1993, Bordj Menaïel (Algeria) (b) 1,80 (c) F - right winger (d) Alanyaspor (e) Nîmes, Le Havre AC, USM Alger, Academie FAF

*** Ferigra - Erick Ferigra (Erick Steven Ferigra Burnham) (a) 07/02/1999, Guayaquil (Ecuador) (b) 1,80 (c) D - central defense (d) FC Paços de Ferreira (e) UD Las Palmas, Torino, Ascoli, Torino

*** Ferizaj - Justin Ferizaj (a) 13/01/2005, ¿? (Ireland) (b) - (c) M - central midfielder (d) Shamrock Rovers (e) -

*** Fernandes - Alex Fernandes (Alex Nascimento Fernandes) (a) 03/06/2002, ¿? (Brazil) (b) - (c) M - attacking midfielder (d) Cherno More Varna (e) -

*** Fernandes - Bruno Fernandes (Bruno Miguel Borges Fernandes) (a) 08/09/1994, Maia (Portugal) (b) 1,79 (c) M - attacking midfielder (d) Manchester United (e) Sporting Lisboa, Sampdoria, Udinese, Sampdoria, Udinese, Novara

*** Fernandes - Daniel Fernandes (Daniel Márcio Fernandes) (a) 25/09/1983, Edmonton (Canada) (b) 1,95 (c) G (d) - (e) Gudja United FC, Birkirkara FC, Tarxien, Farense, Lillestrøm, Rayo OKC, San Antonio, FC Twente, Panthrakikos, FC Twente, OFI Creta, FC Twente, CFR Cluj, VfL Bochum, Panserraikos, VfL Bochum, Panathinaikos, VfL Bochum, Iraklis, VfL Bochum, PAOK, Regensburg II, Celta B, FC Porto B

*** Fernandes - Dany Fernandes (Dany Fernandes Ventura Goncalves) (a) 09/05/1994, Wiltz (Luxembourg) (b) 1,74 (c) M - left midfielder (d) US Hostert (e) FC Wiltz 71, Sporting Mertzig, FC Wiltz 71, Etzella Ettelbrück

*** Fernandes - Edimilson Fernandes (Edimilson Fernandes Ribeiro) (a) 15/04/1996, Sion (Switzerland) (b) 1,90 (c) D - central defense (d) 1.FSV Mainz 05 (e) BSC Young Boys, Mainz 05, Arminia Bielefeld, Mainz 05, West Ham Utd., Fiorentina, West Ham Utd., FC Sion

*** Fernandes - Ely Fernandes (Ely Ernesto Lopes Fernandes) (a) 04/11/1990, Tarrafal (Cabo Verde) (b) 1,87 (c) F - left winger (d) FC Universitatea Cluj (e) FCV Farul, Gaz Metan, Pinhalnovense, Vilafranquense, Gil Vicente, Santa Clara, Gil Vicente, Oliveirense, Gil Vicente, CD Fátima, Infesta, Marinhense, Marinha

*** Fernandes - Gedson Fernandes (Gedson Carvalho Fernandes) (a) 09/01/1999, São Tomé (Sao Tome & Principe) (b) 1,83 (c) M - central midfielder (d) Besiktas JK (e) Benfica, Çaykur Rizespor, Benfica, Galatasaray, Benfica, Tottenham Hotspur, Benfica, Benfica B

*** Fernandes - Ivanildo Fernandes (Ivanildo Jorge Mendes Fernandes) (a) 26/03/1996, Amadora (Portugal) (b) 1,94 (c) D - central defense (d) Ittihad Kalba FC (e) Vizela, Sporting Lisboa, UD Almería, Sporting Lisboa, Çaykur Rizespor, Trabzonspor, Moreirense, Sporting B

*** Fernandes - Joelson Fernandes (Joelson Augusto Mendes Mango Fernandes) (a) 28/02/2003, Bissau (Guinea-Bissau) (b) 1,72 (c) F - left winger (d) Hatayspor (e) Sporting B, FC Basel, Sporting B

*** Fernandes - Jorge Fernandes (Jorge Filipe Oliveira Fernandes) (a) 02/04/1997, Braga (Portugal) (b) 1,91 (c) D - central defense (d) Vitória Guimarães SC (e) FC Porto, Kasimpasa, FC Porto, Tondela, FC Porto, FC Porto B

*** Fernandes - Leandro Fernandes (Leandro Fernandes Da Cunha) (a) 25/12/1999, Nijmegen (Netherlands) (b) 1,76 (c) M - central midfielder (d) FK Jerv (e) PEC Zwolle, Pescara, Fortuna Sittard

*** Fernandes - Mateus Fernandes (Mateus Gonçalo Espanha Fernandes) (a) 10/07/2004, Olhão (Portugal) (b) 1,78 (c) M - attacking midfielder (d) Sporting de Lisboa (e) Sporting B

*** Fernandes - Nicolas Fernandes (a) 07/01/1988, Metz (France) (b) 1,86 (c) D - central defense (d) - (e) UN Käerjeng 97, F91 Dudelange, RFCU Luxembourg, F91 Dudelange, Amnéville, SV Elversberg, Eintracht Trier, Dijon FCO B, FC Metz B, Ehrenpromotion

*** Fernandes - Noah Fernandes (a) 19/10/2005, ¿? (Luxembourg) (b) - (c) M - central midfielder (d) FC Etzella Ettelbruck (e) -

*** Fernandes - Paolo Fernandes (Paolo Fernandes Cantin) (a) 09/08/1998, Zaragoza (Spain) (b) 1,67 (c) F - right winger (d) AEK Athína FC (e) Volos NPS, AEK Athína, Volos NPS, CD Castellón, Perugia, NAC Breda

*** Fernandes - Rafael Fernandes (Rafael Tavares Gomes Fernandes) (a) 28/06/2002, Setúbal (Portugal) (b) 1,91 (c) D - central defense (d) FC Arouca (e) Sporting B

*** Fernandes - Rashaan Fernandes (a) 29/07/1998, Rotterdam (Netherlands) (b) 1,70 (c) F - right winger (d) Go Ahead Eagles Deventer (e) Telstar

*** Fernandes - Ricardo Fernandes (Ricardo José da Silva Fernandes) (a) 28/10/1994, Oliveira do Bairro (Portugal) (b) 1,93 (c) G (d) SC União Torreense (e) Santa Clara, Académico Viseu, Famalicão, Belenenses, Fafe, Belenenses, Anadia FC, Belenenses, AD Oliveirense, Belenenses, Eléctrico, Belenenses, Torreense, Belenenses

*** Fernandes - Rúben Fernandes (Rúben Miguel Marques dos Santos Fernandes) (a) 06/05/1986, Portimão (Portugal) (b) 1,87 (c) D - central defense (d) Gil Vicente FC (e) Portimonense, Sint-Truiden, Estoril Praia, Portimonense, Varzim, Portimonense, Portimonense

*** Fernandes - Stanley Fernandes (Stanley Mendes Fernandes) (a) 30/05/2002, ¿? (France) (b) 1,77 (c) D - right back (d) FC Ordino (e) Ordino B

*** Fernandes - Vasco Fernandes (Vasco Herculano Salgado da Cunha Mango Fernandes) (a) 12/11/1986, Olhão (Portugal) (b) 1,82 (c) D - central defense (d) Casa Pia AC (e) Chaves, Ümraniyespor, Vitória Setúbal, Pandurii, Aris Thessaloniki, Platanias, Olhanense, Beira-Mar, Elche CF, Leixões, RC Celta, Leixões, UD Salamanca, Olhanense, Girondins Bordeaux, Olhanense

*** Fernandes Lopes - Diogo Fernandes Lopes (a) 30/06/2002, ¿? (France) (b) - (c) F - center forward (d) US Mondorf-Les-Bains (e) Differdange 03, FC Metz B

*** Fernandez - Álvaro Fernandez (Álvaro Fernández Carreras) (a) 23/03/2003, Ferrol (Spain) (b) 1,86 (c) D - left back (d) Manchester United (e) Preston North End, Manchester Utd.

*** Fernandez - Nehemiah Fernandez (Nehemiah Fernandez Veliz) (a) 11/12/2004, Stains (France) (b) 1,84 (c) D - central defense (d) París Saint-Germain FC B (e) -

*** Fernández - Aitor Fernández (Aitor Fernández Abarisketa) (a) 03/05/1991, Arrasate (Spain) (b) 1,82 (c) G (d) CA Osasuna (e) Levante UD, CD Numancia, Villarreal CF B, Bilbao Athletic, Barakaldo CF, Bilbao Athletic, CD Basconia

*** Fernández - Álex Fernández (Alejandro Fernández Iglesias) (a) 15/10/1992, Alcalá de Henares (Spain) (b) 1,83 (c) M - attacking midfielder (d) Cádiz CF (e) Elche CF, RCD Espanyol, Reading, RCD Espanyol, HNK Rijeka, RCD Espanyol, RM Castilla

*** Fernández - Álvaro Fernández (Álvaro Fernández Llorente) (a) 13/04/1998, Arnedo (Spain) (b) 1,86 (c) G (d) SD Huesca (e) RCD Espanyol, SD Huesca, Brentford, SD Huesca, AS Monaco B, Extremadura, AS Monaco B, Osasuna Prom.

*** Fernández - Carlos Fernández (Carlos Fernández Luna) (a) 22/05/1996, Castilleja de Guzmán (Spain) (b) 1,85 (c) F - center forward (d) Real Sociedad (e) Sevilla FC, Granada CF, Sevilla FC, RC Deportivo, Sevilla FC, Sevilla At.

*** Fernández - Enzo Fernández (Enzo Jeremías Fernández) (a) 17/01/2001, San Martín (Argentina) (b) 1,78 (c) M - pivot (d) Chelsea FC (e) Benfica, River Plate, River Plate II, Defensa y Justicia, River Plate II

*** Fernández - Federico Fernández (a) 21/02/1989, Tres Algarrobos (Argentina) (b) 1,90 (c) D - central defense (d) - (e) Al-Duhail SC, Elche CF, Newcastle Utd., Swansea City, Napoli, Getafe CF, Napoli, Estudiantes, Estudiantes II

*** Fernández - Jesús Fernández (Jesús Fernández Collado) (a) 11/06/1988, Madrid (Spain) (b) 1,90 (c) G (d) FC Voluntari (e) Hércules CF, Sepsi OSK, CFR Cluj, Panetolikos, CFR Cluj, Cultural Leonesa, Cádiz CF, Granada CF, Levante UD, Real Madrid, RM Castilla, CD Numancia, CD Numancia B

*** Fernández - Joaquín Fernández (Joaquín Fernández Moreno) (a) 31/05/1996, Huercal de Almería (Spain) (b) 1,90 (c) D - central defense (d) Trabzonspor (e) Real Valladolid, UD Almería, UD Almería B

*** Fernández - Julián Fernández (a) 18/07/1989, El Arañado (Argentina) (b) 1,90 (c) D - central defense (d) UE Engordany (e) Sant Julià, Boca Unidos, CD Acero, FC Messina, Indep. Alicante, LDU de Loja, GyE Mendoza, Sport. Belgrano, San Telmo, Real España, Chacarita Jrs., Talleres, Rafaela, La Serena, Argentinos Jrs., Rafaela, Argentinos Jrs., Rafaela

*** Fernández - Marcos Fernández (Marcos Fernández Cózar) (a) 17/07/2003, Andratx (Spain) (b) - (c) D - left back (d) RCD Mallorca B (e) -

*** Fernández - Nacho Fernández (José Ignacio Fernández Iglesias) (a) 18/01/1990, Madrid (Spain) (b) 1,80 (c) D - central defense (d) Real Madrid CF (e) RM Castilla, Real Madrid C

*** Fernández - Nacho Fernández (Luis Ignacio Fernández Ríos) (a) 28/01/1988, La Linea de la Concepción (Spain) (b) 1,80 (c) M - central midfielder (d) Glacis United (e) Bruno's Magpies, Glacis United, San Roque Lepe, Los Barrios, San Roque Cádiz, Algeciras CF, CD Alcalá, R. B. Linense, Real Madrid C

*** Fernández - Quique Fernández (Enrique Fernández López) (a) 16/09/2003, Trebujena (Spain) (b) 1,77 (c) M - pivot (d) Betis Deportivo Balompié (e) -

*** Fernández - Roberto Fernández (Roberto Fernández Urbieta) (a) 07/06/2000, Concepción (Paraguay) (b) 1,88 (c) D - central defense (d) Dinamo Moskva (e) Guaraní

*** Fernández - Santiago Fernández (Santiago Antonio Fernández Alves) (a) 19/06/2000, Caracas, Venezuela (Venezuela) (b) 1,76 (c) D - left back (d) - (e) FC Santa Coloma, CD Benavente, CD Pontellas, Los Barrios, Metropolitanos

*** Fernández - Valery Fernández (Valery Fernández Estrada) (a) 23/11/1999, L'Escala (Spain) (b) 1,82 (c) F - right winger (d) Girona FC (e) CF Peralada, L'Escala

*** Fernández - Víctor Fernández (Víctor Fernández Satue) (a) 02/05/1998, Barcelona (Spain) (b) 1,74 (c) F - left winger (d) Nea Salamis (e) EN Paralimniou, Volos NPS, Cornellà, FC Botosani, FC Viitorul

*** Fernández Mercau - Nicolás Fernández Mercau (Nicolás Ezequiel Fernández Mercau) (a) 11/01/2000, Buenos Aires (Argentina) (b) 1,72 (c) D - left back (d) Elche CF (e) San Lorenzo, San Lorenzo II

*** Fernandez-Pardo - Matias Fernandez-Pardo (a) 03/02/2005, ¿? (Belgium) (b) 1,83 (c) F - left winger (d) KAA Gent (e) Jong KAA Gent

*** Fernandinho - Fernandinho (Fernando Augusto Rodrigues de Araujo) (a) 25/07/1993, Araxá (Brazil) (b) 1,73 (c) D - left back (d) - (e) KF Llapi, Uberaba, FK Partizani, Makedonija, Moto Club, Rio Preto EC, Caldense, Pelister Bitola, UR Trabalhadore, Juazeirense, Caldense

*** Fernando - Fernando (Fernando dos Santos Pedro) (a) 01/03/1999, Belo Horizonte (Brazil) (b) 1,76 (c) F - center forward (d) Red Bull Salzburg (e) Shakhtar Donetsk, Sporting Lisboa, Shakhtar Donetsk, Palmeiras

*** Fernando - Fernando (Fernando Francisco Reges) (a) 25/07/1987, Brasília (Brazil) (b) 1,83 (c) M - pivot (d) Sevilla FC (e) Galatasaray, Manchester City, FC Porto, CF Estrela, FC Porto, Vila Nova FC

*** Fernando - Fernando (Fernando Lucas Martins) (a) 03/03/1992, Erechim (Brazil) (b) 1,75 (c) M - pivot (d) Al-Jazira (Abu Dhabi) (e) Antalyaspor, BJ Guoan, Spartak Moskva, BJ Guoan, Spartak Moskva, Sampdoria, Shakhtar Donetsk, Grêmio Porto Alegre, Grêmio Porto Alegre B

*** Ferraresso - Diego Ferraresso (Diego Gustavo Ferraresso) (a) 21/05/1992, Serra Negra, Sao Paulo (Brazil) (b) 1,71 (c) D - right back (d) AS FC Buzau (e) Botev Vratsa, Cracovia, Slavia Sofia, Lokomotiv Plovdiv, Litex Lovetch, Chavdar, Litex Lovetch

*** Ferrari - Alex Ferrari (a) 01/07/1994, Modena (Italy) (b) 1,91 (c) D - central defense (d) UC Sampdoria (e) Cremonese, Sampdoria, Bologna, Sampdoria, Bologna, Hellas Verona, Bologna, Crotone, Bologna

*** Ferrari - Franco Ferrari (Franco Ariel Ferrari) (a) 09/05/1992, Buenos Aires (Argentina) (b) 1,67 (c) D - left back (d) Aris Thessaloniki (e) APOEL FC, Volos NPS, CA Mitre, Santamarina, Tiro Federal

*** Ferrari - Gian Marco Ferrari (a) 15/05/1992, Parma (Italy) (b) 1,89 (c) D - central defense (d) US Sassuolo (e) Sampdoria, Sassuolo, Crotone, Sassuolo, Crotone, Parma, Crotone, Parma, AS Gubbio, Renate, Fiorenzuola, Crociati Noceto, Ter. Monticelli

*** Ferrari - Matteo Ferrari (a) 23/02/1994, Rimini (Italy) (b) 1,81 (c) D - right back (d) SP Cailungo (e) Cosmos, Domagnano, Diegaro, Romagna Centro, Sammaurese, Ribelle, Rimini

*** Ferrarini - Gabriele Ferrarini (a) 09/04/2000, La Spezia (Italy) (b) 1,80 (c) D - right back (d) Feralpisalò (e) Feralpisalò, Fiorentina, Monza, Modena, Monza, Fiorentina, Perugia, Fiorentina, Venezia, Fiorentina, Pistoiese

*** Ferrario - Gianluca Ferrario (a) 16/08/1996, ¿? (Italy) (b) - (c) F - center forward (d) SC Faetano (e) Moliterno

*** Ferraris - Andrea Ferraris (a) 22/02/2003, Torino (Italy) (b) - (c) F - left winger (d) - (e) Juve Next Gen

*** Ferraris - Santiago Ferraris (a) 26/02/1999, ¿? (Malta) (b) - (c) M - attacking midfielder (d) Marsaxlokk FC (e) -

*** Ferraro - Luciano Ferraro (Luciano Nicolas Ferraro) (a) 04/04/1994, Buenos Aires (Argentina) (b) 1,79 (c) D - central defense (d) - (e) Domagnano, Marsala, Governolo, San Lazzaro, San Teodoro, Bellaria Igea Marina, San Teodoro

*** Ferraro - Nicolas Ferraro (a) 17/08/1995, ¿? (Italy) (b) - (c) F - center forward (d) SS Murata (e) Polisp. Sala, Roncofreddo, Sammaurese

*** Ferré - Marc Ferré (Marc Ferré Nazzaro) (a) 11/01/1994, Andorra la Vella (Andorra) (b) 1,75 (c) M - central midfielder (d) Penya Encarnada d'Andorra (e) Sant Julià, FC Ordino, UE Santa Coloma, UE Engordany, FC Andorra

*** Ferreira - Albert Ferreira (a) 14/02/2005, ¿? (Luxembourg) (b) 1,87 (c) D - left back (d) FC Victoria Rosport (e) -

*** Ferreira - Aldaír Ferreira (Aldaír Caputa Ferreira) (a) 26/03/1998, Luanda (Angola) (b) 1,75 (c) M - attacking midfielder (d) FC Dziugas Telsiai (e) Ast. Vlachioti, AS Rodos, Etar, Vilaverdense, AD Oliveirense

*** Ferreira - André Ferreira (André Miguel da Silva Ferreira) (a) 16/05/1996, Castro Daire (Portugal) (b) 1,73 (c) D - right back (d) CS Fola Esch (e) US Esch, US Mondorf, US Esch, CS Fola Esch, US Esch, CS Fola Esch, Hamm Benfica, CS Fola Esch, Mondercange, CS Fola Esch

*** Ferreira - Diogo Ferreira (Diogo Miguel Faria Ferreira) (a) 09/09/2001, ¿? (Portugal) (b) 1,76 (c) F - right winger (d) Vitória Guimarães SC B (e) Sacavenense

*** Ferreira - Filipe Ferreira (Filipe Miguel Neves Ferreira) (a) 27/09/1990, Lisboa (Portugal) (b) 1,78 (c) D - left back (d) Boavista Porto FC (e) Tondela, Sturm Graz, Nacional, Sturm Graz, Paços Ferreira, Belenenses, Atlético CP

*** Ferreira - João Ferreira (João Diogo Fonseca Ferreira) (a) 22/03/2001, Vila do Conde (Portugal) (b) 1,85 (c) D - right back (d) Udinese (e) Udinese, Watford, Benfica B, Rio Ave, Benfica B, Vitória Guimarães, Benfica B

*** Ferreira - Pedro Ferreira (Pedro Miguel Dinis Ferreira) (a) 05/01/1998, Marinha Grande (Portugal) (b) 1,83 (c) M - pivot (d) Aalborg BK (e) Varzim, Mafra, Sporting B

*** Ferreira - Raul Ferreira (a) 18/11/2002, ¿? (Luxembourg) (b) - (c) F (d) Daring-Club Echternach (e) Victoria Rosport, Echternach, Victoria Rosport, Echternach, Victoria Rosport

*** Ferreira - Ricardo Ferreira (Ricardo Abel Barbosa Ferreira) (a) 03/12/1989, Braga (Portugal) (b) 1,86 (c) G (d) - (e) Dunajska Streda, Portimonense, Marítimo, Marítimo B, Olhanense, SC Braga, Olhanense, SC Braga

*** Ferreira - Tiago Ferreira (Tiago Emanuel Canelas Almeida Ferreira) (a) 10/07/1993, Porto (Portugal) (b) 1,85 (c) D - central defense (d) União de Leiria (e) Trofense, FK Kukësi, Tractor, MTK Budapest, CS U Craiova, União Madeira, Zulte Waregem, FC Porto B

*** Ferreira - Yann Ferreira (a) 16/01/2004, ¿? (Luxembourg) (b) - (c) F (d) US Hostert (e) -

*** Ferreiro - Luis Ferreiro (Luis Ángel Ferreiro) (a) 28/10/1988, Ituzaingó (Argentina) (b) - (c) G (d) FC Pas de la Casa (e) FC Ordino, CDyS Juventud Unida (San Miguel), Ituzaingó

*** Ferrer - Adri Ferrer (Adrián Ferrer Pérez) (a) 12/02/2001, Melilla (Spain) (b) 1,86 (c) F - left winger (d) FC La Unión Atlético (e) FC Cubillas, Penya Encarnada, At. Porcuna, Los Barrios, Churriana

*** Ferrer - Domingo Ferrer (Domingo Jesús Ferrer López) (a) 10/04/1989, Málaga (Spain) (b) 1,68 (c) F - right winger (d) - (e) CD Estepona FS, St Joseph's FC, Los Barrios, UD San Pedro, Marbella FC, Unión Estepona, R. B. Linense

*** Ferrer - Salva Ferrer (Salvador Ferrer Canals) (a) 21/01/1998, Martorell (Spain) (b) 1,84 (c) D - right back (d) Spezia (e) Gimnàstic, Pobla de Mafumet CF, Martorell

*** Ferreyra - Fernando Dario Ferreyra (a) 19/01/1997, Buenos Aires (Argentina) (b) 1,68 (c) D - left back (d) - (e) FK Tuzla City, Velez Mostar, Boca Juniors II

*** Ferri - Jordan Ferri (a) 12/03/1992, Cavaillon (France) (b) 1,73 (c) M - central midfielder (d) Montpellier HSC (e) Olympique Lyon, Nîmes, Olympique Lyon, Olymp. Lyon B
*** Ferri - Mario Ferri (Mario Ferri Falco) (a) 13/04/1987, ¿? (Italy) (b) 1,75 (c) M - right midfielder (d) ASD Castel di Sangro (e) Tre Fiori, United SC, Castel di Sangro, Tre Fiori, Audax Herajon, Côte d'Or FC, Alto Casertano, Al-Faisaly SC, Venafro, Castel di Sangro
*** Ferrie - Mark Ferrie (a) 02/12/2005, Wishaw (Scotland) (b) 1,80 (c) F - center forward (d) Motherwell FC B (e) -
*** Ferro - Ferro (Francisco Reis Ferreira) (a) 26/03/1997, Oliveira de Azeméis (Portugal) (b) 1,91 (c) D - central defense (d) HNK Hajduk Split (e) Benfica, Vitesse, Benfica, Hajduk Split, Benfica, Valencia CF, Benfica, Benfica B
*** Fesyuk - Davyd Fesyuk (a) 24/04/2005, ¿? (Ukraine) (b) 1,85 (c) G (d) - (e) Jupie FSMH
*** Fesyun - Kiril Fesyun (Фесюн Кіріл Вадимович) (a) 07/08/2002, Chernigiv (Ukraine) (b) 1,91 (c) G (d) Kolos Kovalivka (e) Kolos II, Vorskla II
*** Fet - Sondre Brunstad Fet (a) 17/01/1997, Aure (Norway) (b) 1,78 (c) M - central midfielder (d) FK Bodø/Glimt (e) Aalesund, Bodø/Glimt, Aalesund
*** Fetai - Feta Fetai (a) 11/05/2005, Skopje (North Macedonia) (b) 1,72 (c) M - attacking midfielder (d) - (e) Rabotnicki
*** Fewster - Billy Fewster (William Charles Storm Fewster) (a) 31/07/2003, Scarborough (England) (b) 1,78 (c) M - central midfielder (d) Alfreton Town (e) Scunthorpe Utd.
*** Fiabema - Bryan Fiabema (Bryan Solhaug Fiabema) (a) 16/02/2003, Tromsø (Norway) (b) 1,83 (c) F - center forward (d) Real Sociedad B (e) Forest Green Rovers, Rosenborg, Tromsø IL II
*** Fiakas - Sotiris Fiakas (Σωτήρης Φιάκας) (a) 08/09/1998, Larnaca (Cyprus) (b) 1,73 (c) M - pivot (d) Ethnikos Achnas (e) Nea Salamis, Othellos Athien, Nea Salamis, Alki Oroklini, Othellos Athien, Omonia Nicosia, Chalkanoras, Omonia Nicosia
*** Fica - Alin Fica (Alin Razvan Fica) (a) 14/06/2001, Cluj-Napoca (Romania) (b) 1,81 (c) M - central midfielder (d) CFR Cluj (e) Comuna Recea, CFR Cluj, FC Rapid 1923, CFR Cluj
*** Fickentscher - Kevin Fickentscher (a) 06/07/1988, Nyon (Switzerland) (b) 1,81 (c) G (d) - (e) FC Sion, Lausanne-Sport, FC Sion, Chaux-de-Fonds, Werder Bremen II, FC Rolle
*** Fidel - Fidel (Fidel Chaves de la Torre) (a) 27/10/1989, Minas de Riotinto (Spain) (b) 1,80 (c) F - left winger (d) Elche CF (e) UD Las Palmas, UD Almería, Córdoba CF, Elche CF, Córdoba CF, Elche CF, Recreativo, Recr. Huelva B
*** Field - Angel Field (Angel Allen Field) (a) 19/08/2002, Gibraltar (Gibraltar) (b) - (c) D - right back (d) FC College 1975 (e) College Reserve, Lions Gibraltar Reserves
*** Figueira - Walter Figueira (Walter Capango Figueira) (a) 17/03/1995, London (England) (b) 1,82 (c) F - center forward (d) Bognor Regis Town (e) Carshalton Ath., Kingstonian FC, Sligo Rovers, Derry City, Waterford FC, Merstham, Dulwich Hamlet, Merstham, Dulwich Hamlet, Moura, Wingate FC, Bognor Regis, Platanias, Acharnaikos, Platanias, Hayes & Yeading
*** Figueiredo - Cristiano Figueiredo (Cristiano Pereira Figueiredo) (a) 29/11/1990, München (Germany) (b) 1,95 (c) G (d) - (e) Spartak Varna, FC Dinamo, CFR Cluj, FC Hermannstadt, Vitória Setúbal, Belenenses, Panetolikos, SC Braga, Académica Coimbra, SC Braga, Valencia Mestalla, SC Braga, Vizela, SC Braga

*** Figueiredo - João Figueiredo (João Vitor Brandão Figueiredo) (a) 27/05/1996, São Paulo (Brazil) (b) 1,80 (c) F - center forward (d) Basaksehir FK (e) Gaziantep FK, Al-Wasl, Gaziantep FK, Al-Wasl, OFI Creta, Kauno Zalgiris, At. Mineiro B, Democrata GV, At. Mineiro B

*** Figueiredo - Lucas Figueiredo (Lucas Ferreira Figueiredo) (a) 14/05/2003, ¿? (Luxembourg) (b) 1,74 (c) M - central midfielder (d) FC Progrès Niederkorn (e) Etzella Ettelbrück

*** Figueredo - Hugo Figueredo (a) 18/05/1992, São Paulo (Brazil) (b) 1,82 (c) D - left back (d) FC Hegelmann (e) Panevezys, Rio Branco-SP, Glória, ABC FC, Boa Esporte, River-PI, Cerâmica, CRAC (GO), CS Esportiva

*** Fijuljanin - Ibrahim Fijuljanin (Ибрахим Фијуљанин) (a) 08/02/2004, Novi Pazar (Serbia and Montenegro, now in Serbia) (b) 1,78 (c) F - left winger (d) - (e) FK Novi Pazar

*** Fiksdal - Jesper Fiksdal (a) 26/05/2004, Sandnes (Norway) (b) - (c) F - center forward (d) Viking FK II (e) -

*** Fila - Daniel Fila (a) 21/08/2002, Brno (Czech Rep.) (b) 1,90 (c) F - center forward (d) FK Teplice (e) Teplice, Slavia Praha, Mlada Boleslav, Zbrojovka Brno

*** Fila - Karol Fila (a) 13/06/1998, Gdańsk (Poland) (b) 1,83 (c) D - right back (d) Racing Club Strasbourg (e) Zulte Waregem, Racing Club Strasbourg, Lechia Gdánsk, Chojniczanka, Lechia Gdánsk, AP Lechia, Zulawy

*** Filet - Elias Filet (a) 06/03/2002, Paris (France) (b) 1,86 (c) F - center forward (d) - (e) FC Sochaux, Progrès Niederkorn, FC Sochaux, FC Sochaux B

*** Filev - Kliment Filev (Климент Филев) (a) 11/04/2004, ¿? (North Macedonia) (b) 1,89 (c) D - central defense (d) Karaorman Struga (e) New Stars

*** Fili - Realdo Fili (a) 14/05/1996, Fier (Albania) (b) 1,76 (c) F - left winger (d) KF Teuta (e) Chornomorets, FC Botosani, FC Luftëtari, KF Skënderbeu, FC Kamza, FK Partizani, FK Partizani B, FK Apolonia

*** Filin - Aleksandr Filin (Филин Александр Васильевич) (a) 25/06/1996, Simferopol, Krym (Ukraine) (b) 1,85 (c) D - central defense (d) KAS Eupen (e) Khimki, Tambov, Khimki, Nizhny Novgorod, Ufa, Shakhtar 3

*** Filinsky - David Filinsky (Dávid Filinský) (a) 18/01/1999, Spišska Nová Ves (Slovakia) (b) 1,85 (c) M - pivot (d) - (e) Liptovsky Mik., Ružomberok

*** Filip - Ioan Filip (Ioan Constantin Filip) (a) 20/05/1989, Ștei (Romania) (b) 1,87 (c) M - pivot (d) FC Universitatea Cluj (e) Gaz Metan, Universitatea Cluj, FC Dinamo, Debrecen, FC Viitorul, Petrolul, Otelul Galati, Bihor Oradea

*** Filip - Robert Filip (Robert Costantin Filip) (a) 02/03/2002, Piatra Neamț (Romania) (b) 1,80 (c) M - central midfielder (d) CFR Cluj (e) Alessandria, Derthona, Alessandria, PDHA, Alessandria

*** Filip - Steliano Filip (a) 15/05/1994, Buzău (Romania) (b) 1,79 (c) D - left back (d) Mezőkövesd Zsóry FC (e) FC Dinamo, AE Larisa, FC Viitorul, Dunarea Calarasi, Hajduk Split, FC Dinamo, Avicola Buzias, FC Maramures, Avicola Buzias, LPS Banatul

*** Filipavicius - Rokas Filipavicius (Rokas Filipavičius) (a) 22/12/1999, Klaipeda (Lithuania) (b) 1,81 (c) M - attacking midfielder (d) FK Riteriai (e) Atlantas

*** Filipenko - Egor Filipenko (Филипенко Егор Всеволодович) (a) 10/04/1988, Minsk (Soviet Union, now in Belarus) (b) 1,90 (c) D - central defense (d) Ural Ekaterimburgo (e) Soligorsk, BATE Borisov, Maccabi Tel Aviv, FC Ashdod, Maccabi Tel Aviv, Málaga CF, BATE Borisov, Spartak Moskva, BATE Borisov, Spartak Moskva, Sibir, Spartak Moskva, Tom Tomsk, Spartak Moskva, BATE Borisov, BATE II

*** Filipovic - Aleksandar Filipovic (Александар Филиповић) (a) 20/12/1994, Leskovac (Yugoslavia, now in Serbia) (b) 1,84 (c) D - right back (d) Partizán Beograd (e) BATE Borisov, Vozdovac, Jagodina

*** Filipovic - Andrija Filipovic (Andrija Filipović) (a) 18/04/1997, Rijeka (Croatia) (b) 1,81 (c) F - right winger (d) FK Aktobe (e) Atyrau, FK Partizani, NS Mura, NAC Breda, ND Gorica, Robur Siena, HNK Rijeka II, NK Crikvenica

*** Filipovic - Jakov Filipovic (Jakov Filipović) (a) 17/10/1992, Pećnik (Bosnia and Herzegovina) (b) 1,91 (c) D - central defense (d) SK Beveren (e) BATE Borisov, KSC Lokeren, Inter Zaprešić, Cibalia, Bijelo Brdo

*** Filipovic - Josip Filipovic (Josip Filipović) (a) 08/05/1996, Zagreb (Croatia) (b) 1,84 (c) D - right back (d) NK Jarun (e) Hrv Dragovoljac, Mjällby AIF, Rudar Velenje, NK Rudes, Cibalia, Austria Klagenfurt, RNK Split, DNŠ Zavrč, Inter Zaprešić

*** Filipovic - Milos Filipovic (Милош Филиповић) (a) 09/05/1990, Kosovska Mitrovica (Yugoslavia, now in Kosovo) (b) 1,78 (c) F - left winger (d) FK Kolubara Lazarevac (e) Novi Pazar, Kolubara, Zrinjski Mostar, AE Larisa, Zrinjski Mostar, Drina Zvornik, Vozdovac, FK BSK Borča, Vozdovac, Timok Zajecar, OFK Beograd, Kolubara, OFK Beograd, Mladost Apatin, OFK Beograd

*** Filipovic - Nenad Filipovic (Ненад Филиповић) (a) 24/04/1987, Užice (Yugoslavia, now in Serbia) (b) 1,91 (c) G (d) FK Čukarički (e) FK TSC, Macva, Rad Beograd, Radnicki Niš, Etar, Teleoptik, Rad Beograd, Videoton FC, MTK Budapest, Videoton FC, Banat Zrenjanin, Bečej

*** Filipovic - Petar Filipovic (Petar Filipović) (a) 14/09/1990, Hamburg (Germany) (b) 1,88 (c) D - central defense (d) AEL Limassol (e) LASK, Konyaspor, Austria Viena, SV Ried, Slaven Belupo, Cibalia, FC St. Pauli, St. Pauli II

*** Filipovic - Stefan Filipovic (Стефан Филиповић) (a) 21/06/1994, Beograd (RF Yugoslavia, now in Serbia) (b) 1,86 (c) D - central defense (d) FK Riteriai (e) Spartak, Radnicki 1923, Buducnost Podgorica, FK Bezanija, IMT Beograd, Zarkovo, Srem Jakovo, BASK Beograd

*** Filippi - Luca Filippi (a) 27/09/1988, ¿? (Italy) (b) - (c) D - central defense (d) Mondaino (e) Fiorentino, Faetano, Tre Fiori, Riccione, Misano, Rivazzurra

*** Filippov - Oleksandr Filippov (Філіппов Олександр Олександрович) (a) 23/10/1992, Avdiivka, Donetsk Oblast (Ukraine) (b) 1,83 (c) F - center forward (d) SK Dnipro-1 (e) Sint-Truiden, Riga, Sint-Truiden, Desna, Avangard K., Nikopol-NPGU, Illichivets, Arsenal Kyiv, Arsenal Kyiv II

*** Fillion - Yann Fillion (Yann-Alexandre Fillion) (a) 14/02/1996, Ottawa, Ontario (Canada) (b) 1,93 (c) G (d) HFX Wanderers FC (e) IFK Mariehamn, AC Oulu, Ekenäs IF, FC Zürich, Toronto FC II, FC Zürich, FC Aarau, FC Zürich, Nest-Sotra IL, FC Zürich, Umeå FC, FC Zürich, FC Montréal

*** Fillo - Martin Fillo (Martin Fillo) (a) 07/02/1986, Planá (Czechoslovakia, now in Czech Rep.) (b) 1,79 (c) M - right midfielder (d) Tianjin Jiskra Domazlice (e) Zlin, Banik Ostrava, Teplice, Viktoria Plzen, 1.FK Pribram, Viktoria Plzen, Brentford, Viktoria Plzen, Mlada Boleslav, Viktoria Plzen, Mlada Boleslav, Viktoria Plzen, Viking, Viktoria Plzen

*** Filosa (c) F - center forward (d) - (e) FC Ordino, CD Benicarló - Agustín Filosa (c) F - center forward (d) - (e) FC Ordino, CD Benicarló

*** Fink - Bradley Fink (Bradley Thomas Fink) (a) 17/04/2003, Cham (Switzerland) (b) 1,92 (c) F - center forward (d) Grasshopper Club Zürich (e) Grasshoppers, FC Basel, Borussia Dortmund II

*** Finlayson - Danny Finlayson (Daniel Finlayson) (a) 19/01/2001, Glasgow (Scotland) (b) 1,91 (c) D - right back (d) Linfield FC (e) St. Mirren, Linfield, St.

Mirren, Kelty Hearts, St. Mirren, Rangers II, St. Mirren, Rangers II, Orange County, Rangers II
*** Finn - John Joe Patrick Finn (John Joe Patrick Finn Benoa) (a) 24/10/2003, Madrid (Spain) (b) 1,92 (c) M - central midfielder (d) Getafe CF B (e) -
*** Finn - Ronan Finn (Ronan Michael Finn) (a) 21/12/1987, Dublin (Ireland) (b) 1,85 (c) D - right back (d) Shamrock Rovers (e) Dundalk FC, Shamrock Rovers, Sporting Fingal, UCD
*** Finnbogason - Alfred Finnbogason (Alfreð Finnbogason) (a) 01/02/1989, Reykjavík (Iceland) (b) 1,84 (c) F - center forward (d) Lyngby BK (e) FC Augsburg, Real Sociedad, FC Augsburg, Real Sociedad, Olympiakos, Real Sociedad, Heerenveen, KSC Lokeren, Helsingborgs IF, KSC Lokeren, Breidablik, Augnablik, Breidablik
*** Finnbogason - Ármann Ingi Finnbogason (a) 16/06/2004, ¿? (Iceland) (b) - (c) M (d) ÍA Akranes (e) Kári
*** Finnbogason - Kjartan Finnbogason (Kjartan Henrý Finnbogason) (a) 09/07/1986, Reykjavík (Iceland) (b) 1,88 (c) F - center forward (d) FH Hafnarfjördur (e) KR Reykjavík, Esbjerg fB, AC Horsens, Vejle BK, Ferencváros, AC Horsens, KR Reykjavík, Sandefjord, Falkirk FC, Sandefjord, Åtvidabergs FF, KR Reykjavík
*** Finnbogason - Kristján Flóki Finnbogason (a) 12/01/1995, Hafnarfjörður (Iceland) (b) 1,90 (c) F - center forward (d) KR Reykjavík (e) Start, Brommapojkarna, Start, Hafnarfjördur
*** Finndell - Hampus Finndell (a) 06/06/2000, Västerås (Sweden) (b) 1,77 (c) M - central midfielder (d) Djurgårdens IF (e) Dalkurd, Djurgården
*** Finnerty - James Finnerty (James John Finnerty) (a) 01/02/1999, Skryne, Meath (Ireland) (b) 1,83 (c) D - central defense (d) Sligo Rovers (e) Bohemians, Galway United, Bohemians, AFC Rochdale, Belvedere FC
*** Finnigan - Ryan Finnigan (Ryan James Finnigan) (a) 23/09/2003, ¿? (England) (b) - (c) M - central midfielder (d) Southampton FC B (e) Crewe Alexandra, Southampton B
*** Finnsson - Kolbeinn Finnsson (a) 25/08/1999, Reykjavík (Iceland) (b) 1,81 (c) D - left back (d) Lyngby BK (e) Borussia Dortmund II, Brentford B, Fylkir, Brentford B, Fylkir
*** Finsen - Ólafur Karl Finsen (a) 30/03/1992, ¿? (Iceland) (b) 1,80 (c) M - attacking midfielder (d) Fylkir Reykjavík (e) Stjarnan, Valur, Hafnarfjördur, Valur, Stjarnan, Sandnes Ulf, Stjarnan, Selfoss, Stjarnan
*** Fiola - Attila Fiola (a) 17/02/1990, Szekszárd (Hungary) (b) 1,83 (c) D - right back (d) Fehérvár FC (e) Puskás AFC, Paksi FC
*** Fiolic - Ivan Fiolic (Ivan Fiolić) (a) 29/04/1996, Zagreb (Croatia) (b) 1,76 (c) M - attacking midfielder (d) NK Osijek (e) KRC Genk, Cracovia, KRC Genk, AEK Larnaca, KRC Genk, Dinamo Zagreb, NK Lokomotiva, Dinamo Zagreb, NK Lokomotiva, Din. Zagreb II
*** Fiorenza - Matteo Fiorenza (a) 15/06/2003, ¿? (Italy) (b) 1,95 (c) G (d) Torino FC (e) -
*** Fiorillo - Vincenzo Fiorillo (a) 13/01/1990, Genoa (Italy) (b) 1,90 (c) G (d) US Salernitana 1919 (e) Pescara, Juventus, Pescara, Juventus, Sampdoria, AS Livorno, Sampdoria, Spezia, Sampdoria, Reggina, Sampdoria
*** Firmino - Alef Firmino (Alef Firmino Dos Anjos) (a) 16/03/1998, Sao Paulo (Brazil) (b) 1,86 (c) F - center forward (d) KF Llapi (e) NK Dubrava ZG, NK Nasice, Union Douala
*** Firmino - Hugo Firmino (Hugo Filipe Pinto Servulo Firmino) (a) 22/12/1988, Lisboa (Portugal) (b) 1,85 (c) F - left winger (d) FC Penafiel (e) Ararat-Armenia,

Pyunik Yerevan, Cova Piedade, Doxa Katokopias, Estoril Praia, Universitatea Cluj, Cova Piedade, Gil Vicente, União Madeira, AEL Limassol, Oriental, Kabuscorp SC, Caála, GD Interclube, Torreense, Moura, Portosantense, Odivelas, Encarnacense, Torreense
*** Firpo - Junior Firpo (Héctor Junior Firpo Adamés) (a) 22/08/1996, Santo Domingo de Guzmán (Dominican Rep.) (b) 1,84 (c) D - left back (d) Leeds United (e) FC Barcelona, Real Betis, Betis Deportivo, At. Benamiel
*** Firsov - Aleksey Firsov (Фирсов Алексей Сергеевич) (a) 07/02/2002, Smolevichi (Belarus) (b) 1,82 (c) D - right back (d) Naftan Novopolotsk (e) Naftan, Dinamo Minsk II, Dynamo Brest, Dinamo Minsk II, Dnepr Mogilev, Dinamo Minsk II
*** Firth - Andy Firth (Andrew Firth) (a) 26/09/1996, Ripon (England) (b) 1,83 (c) G (d) Connah's Quay Nomads (e) Rangers FC, Partick Thistle, Rangers FC, Barrow, Chester, Witton Albion
*** Fischer - Kilian Fischer (a) 12/10/2000, Miltenberg (Germany) (b) 1,82 (c) D - right back (d) VfL Wolfsburg (e) 1.FC Nürnberg, Türkgücü Münch.
*** Fischer - Manfred Fischer (a) 06/08/1995, ¿? (Austria) (b) 1,79 (c) M - attacking midfielder (d) FK Austria Viena (e) SCR Altach, TSV Hartberg, Wiener Neustadt, SC Kalsdorf, DSV Leoben, DSV II
*** Fischer - Mikkel Fischer (Mikkel Rosleff Fischer) (a) 23/03/2004, ¿? (Denmark) (b) - (c) D - central defense (d) FC Fredericia (e) Midtjylland
*** Fischer - Viktor Fischer (Viktor Gorridsen Fischer) (a) 09/06/1994, Aarhus (Denmark) (b) 1,81 (c) F - left winger (d) Poul Pedersen (e) Royal Antwerp, AIK, Royal Antwerp, FC København, Mainz 05, Middlesbrough, Ajax, Aarhus GF II
*** Fish - Will Fish (a) 17/02/2003, Manchester (England) (b) 1,85 (c) D - central defense (d) Hibernian FC (e) Hibernian FC, Stockport
*** Fitz - Dominik Fitz (a) 16/06/1999, Wien (Austria) (b) 1,74 (c) M - attacking midfielder (d) FK Austria Viena (e) Austria Wien Reserves
*** Fitzgerald - Will Fitzgerald (a) 19/05/1999, Limerick (Ireland) (b) 1,87 (c) F - left winger (d) Sligo Rovers (e) Derry City, Waterford FC, Limerick FC
*** Fitz-Jim - Kian Fitz-Jim (a) 05/07/2003, Amsterdam (Netherlands) (b) 1,74 (c) M - central midfielder (d) Ajax de Ámsterdam (e) Ajax B
*** Fitzpatrick - Matthew Fitzpatrick (a) 02/09/1994, Belfast (Northern Ireland) (b) - (c) F - center forward (d) Linfield FC (e) Glenavon, Coleraine, Belfast Celtic, Immaculata
*** Fitzsimons - Ross Fitzsimons (Ross Alan Richard Frank Fitzsimons) (a) 28/05/1994, London (England) (b) 1,85 (c) G (d) Scunthorpe United (e) FC Chesterfield, St Joseph's FC, Weymouth FC, Stockport, Boston Utd., Notts County, FC Chesterfield, Notts County, Chelmsford, Braintree, Bishop's Stortford, Farnborough, Hendon, Havant & Waterlooville, Harrow Borough
*** Fitzwater - Jack Fitzwater (Jackson Joseph Fitzwater) (a) 23/09/1997, Birmingham (England) (b) 1,88 (c) D - central defense (d) - (e) Livingston FC, FC Walsall, FC Walsall, FC Walsall, Forest Green Rovers, Hednesford, FC Chesterfield
*** Fixelles - Mathias Fixelles (Mathias Frédéric Fixelles) (a) 11/08/1996, Soignies (Belgium) (b) 1,83 (c) M - pivot (d) KVC Westerlo (e) KV Kortrijk, Union St. Gilloise, KVW Zaventem
*** Fjodorovs - Maksims Fjodorovs (a) 24/09/2003, ¿? (Latvia) (b) - (c) M - pivot (d) Grobinas SC/LFS (e) Liepaja, Tukums, Auda, Liepaja II
*** Fjodorovs - Vladislavs Fjodorovs (a) 27/09/1996, Daugavpils (Latvia) (b) 1,87 (c) D - right back (d) FK Metta (e) RFS, Riga, Metta, Daugavpils, Lech Poznan II, Daugavpils, Ventspils II

*** Fjóluson - Jon Gudni Fjóluson (Jón Guðni Fjóluson) (a) 10/04/1989, Þorlákshöfn (Iceland) (b) 1,92 (c) D - central defense (d) Hammarby IF (e) Brann, Krasnodar, Norrköping, GIF Sundsvall, Beerschot AC, Fram Reykjavík

*** Flakus Bosilj - David Flakus Bosilj (a) 01/02/2002, Maribor (Slovenia) (b) 1,85 (c) F - center forward (d) De Graafschap Doetinchem (e) De Graafschap, NK Bravo, NK Aluminij

*** Flamarion - Flamarion (ფლამარიონ ჯოვინო ფილიუ)

*** Flamingo - Ryan Flamingo (a) 31/12/2002, Blaricum (Netherlands) (b) 1,86 (c) D - central defense (d) US Sassuolo (e) Vitesse, Sassuolo

*** Flauss - Sebastien Flauss (a) 19/08/1989, ¿? (France) (b) 1,86 (c) G (d) FC Progrès Niederkorn (e) Borussia Neunkirchen, SF Köllerbach, Elversberg II, SV Elversberg, Saarbrücken II, US Forbach

*** Flávio Carioca - Flávio Carioca (Flávio dos Santos da Silva Cheveresan) (a) 11/12/1988, ¿? (Brazil) (b) 1,88 (c) F - center forward (d) East Riffa Club (e) Valletta, Al-Muharraq, Floriana, Sirens FC, Campinense-PB, AA Anapolina, Nova Iguaçu, Cuiabá-MT, América-RN, Taubaté, Água Santa, Velo Clube

*** Flecker - Florian Flecker (a) 29/10/1995, Voitsberg (Austria) (b) 1,77 (c) M - right midfielder (d) LASK (e) TSV Hartberg, Würzb. Kickers, Union Berlin, TSV Hartberg, Wolfsberger AC, SV Kapfenberg, Kapfenberg II, Rapid/KSV III, AKA Kapfenberg

*** Fleisman - Jiri Fleisman (Jiří Fleišman) (a) 02/10/1984, Most (Czechoslovakia, now in Czech Rep.) (b) 1,83 (c) D - left back (d) FC Banik Ostrava (e) Mlada Boleslav, Slovan Liberec, FK Most, Banik Sokolov, FK Most, FK Most B, Chmel Blsany, FK Most B, Brandov, Banik Sous

*** Flekken - Mark Flekken (a) 13/06/1993, Bocholtz (Netherlands) (b) 1,95 (c) G (d) Brentford FC (e) SC Freiburg, MSV Duisburg, Greuther Fürth, Alemannia Aachen

*** Flemmings - Junior Flemmings (a) 16/01/1996, Kingston (Jamaica) (b) 1,80 (c) F - left winger (d) Toulouse FC (e) Chamois Niort, Toulouse, Legion FC, Phoenix Rising, TB Rowdies, NY Red Bulls II, Tivoli Gardens FC

*** Fletcher - Steven Fletcher (Steven Kenneth Fletcher) (a) 26/03/1987, Shrewsbury (England) (b) 1,85 (c) F - center forward (d) - (e) Dundee United, Stoke City, Sheffield Wednesday, Sunderland, Ol. Marseille, Sunderland, Wolverhampton Wanderers, Burnley, Hibernian FC

*** Fletcher (c) F - center forward (d) - (e) Bala - Alex Fletcher (c) F - center forward (d) - (e) Bala

*** Flick - Florian Flick (a) 01/05/2000, Mannheim (Germany) (b) 1,88 (c) M - pivot (d) 1.FC Nürnberg (e) FC Schalke 04, 1.FC Nürnberg, FC Schalke 04, Schalke 04 II, Waldh. Mannheim

*** Flint - Josh Flint (Joshua Hughson Flint) (a) 13/10/2000, Waterlooville (England) (b) - (c) D - central defense (d) FC Volendam (e) Bognor Regis

*** Flint - Niall Flint (Niall Daniel Flint) (a) 15/08/1997 (c) F - right winger (d) Stourbridge FC (e) Aberystwyth, Cefn Druids, Newtown, Matlock, Scarborough Athletic, Telford Utd., Shrewsbury

*** Flips - Alexis Flips (a) 18/01/2000, Villeneuve-d'Ascq (France) (b) 1,73 (c) F - left winger (d) RSC Anderlecht (e) Stade Reims, Stade Reims B, LOSC Lille B, AC Ajaccio, LOSC Lille B

*** Flis - Marcin Flis (a) 10/02/1994, Bychawa (Poland) (b) 1,85 (c) D - central defense (d) ŁKS Łódź (e) Stal Mielec, Sandecja, Gornik Leczna, Piast Gliwice, GKS Katowice, Piast Gliwice, GKS Belchatow, Belchatow II

*** Flis - Zan Flis (Žan Flis) (a) 30/07/1997, ¿? (Slovenia) (b) 1,87 (c) D - left back (d) NK Rogaska (e) NK Celje, NK Fuzinar, NK Celje, NK Triglav, NK Celje, Drava Ptuj, NK Maribor B
*** Flo - Fredrik Flo (a) 10/10/1996, ¿? (Norway) (b) 1,91 (c) D - central defense (d) Skeid Oslo (e) Sandefjord, Øygarden FK, Sotra, Sogndal, Fana IL, Sogndal, Bryne, Sogndal, Fana IL, Sogndal
*** Floranus - Sherel Floranus (Sherel Constancio Floranus) (a) 23/08/1998, Rotterdam (Netherlands) (b) 1,81 (c) D - right back (d) Almere City FC (e) Antalyaspor, Heerenveen, Sparta Rotterdam
*** Florea - Daniel Florea (Daniel Constantin Florea) (a) 17/04/1988, Târgoviște (Romania) (b) 1,75 (c) F - center forward (d) FC Voluntari (e) Chindia, UTA Arad, Astra Giurgiu, Concordia, Delta Tulcea, Callatis, Farul Constanta
*** Florentín - Gabriel Florentín (César Gabriel Florentín) (a) 13/03/1999, Gregorio de Laferrere (Argentina) (b) 1,73 (c) M - attacking midfielder (d) FK Orenburg (e) Argentinos Jrs., Argentinos Juniors II
*** Florentino - Florentino (Florentino Ibrain Morris Luís) (a) 19/08/1999, Lobito (Angola) (b) 1,84 (c) M - pivot (d) SL Benfica (e) Getafe CF, Benfica, AS Monaco, Benfica, Benfica B
*** Florenzi - Alessandro Florenzi (a) 11/03/1991, Roma (Italy) (b) 1,73 (c) D - right back (d) AC Milan (e) AS Roma, AC Milan, AS Roma, Paris Saint-Germain, AS Roma, Valencia CF, AS Roma, Crotone
*** Flores - Alberto Flores (Alberto Flores López) (a) 10/11/2003, Fuentes de Andalucía (Spain) (b) 1,87 (c) G (d) Sevilla Atlético (e) -
*** Flores - Deybi Flores (Deybi Aldair Flores Flores) (a) 16/06/1996, San Pedro Sula (Honduras) (b) 1,80 (c) M - pivot (d) Fehérvár FC (e) Panetolikos, CD Olimpia, Vancouver, FC Motagua, Vancouver, FC Motagua, Vancouver, FC Motagua, Vancouver, FC Motagua
*** Flores - Jordan Flores (Jordan Michael Flores) (a) 04/10/1995, Wigan (England) (b) 1,80 (c) M - central midfielder (d) Bohemian FC (e) Northampton, Hull City, Northampton, Hull City, Dundalk FC, Wigan Ath., Östersund, Wigan Ath., Fylde, Wigan Ath., FC Chesterfield, Wigan Ath., Blackpool, Wigan Ath.
*** Florescu - Alexandru Florescu (Andrei Alexandru Florescu) (a) 24/07/2001, Câmpulung Muscel (Romania) (b) - (c) F - center forward (d) Gloria 2018 Bistrita-Nasaud (e) FC Arges, V. Colonesti, FC Arges, FC Argeş II, Unirea Bascov
*** Florescu - Eduard Florescu (Eduard Marian Florescu) (a) 27/06/1997, Piteşti (Romania) (b) 1,83 (c) M - attacking midfielder (d) FC Botosani (e) CS U Craiova, FC Botosani, FC Arges, FC Botosani, FC Viitorul, CS Mioveni, FC Arges
*** Floriani Mussolini - Romano Floriani Mussolini (a) 27/01/2003, Roma (Italy) (b) 1,88 (c) D - right back (d) Delfino Pescara 1936 (e) Pescara, Vigor Perconti
*** Floro - Rafael Floro (Rafael da Silva Floro) (a) 19/01/1994, Quarteira (Portugal) (b) 1,75 (c) D - left back (d) FK Novi Pazar (e) AC Oulu, Panevezys, Olhanense, Felgueiras, Stumbras, Cova Piedade, Gil Vicente, Louletano, Belenenses, Almancilense, Belenenses, Casa Pia, Belenenses, Sheffield Wednesday
*** Florucz - Raul Florucz (Raul Alexander Florucz) (a) 10/06/2001, Vöcklabruck (Austria) (b) 1,82 (c) F - right winger (d) NK Olimpija Ljubljana (e) NK Lokomotiva, NK Jarun, NK Lokomotiva, Hrv Dragovoljac, NK Lokomotiva, NK Sesvete, NK Lokomotiva
*** Flosason - Hallur Flosason (a) 01/05/1993, ¿? (Iceland) (b) - (c) D - right back (d) - (e) ÍA Akranes, Afturelding, ÍA Akranes
*** Flouris - Dimitris Flouris (Δημήτρης Φλουρής) (a) 23/07/2002, Paralimni (Cyprus) (b) 1,81 (c) F - right winger (d) Enosis Neon Paralimniou (e) -

*** Flouris - Dimitris Flouris (Δημήτρης Φλουρίς) (a) 12/11/2001, Limassol (Cyprus) (b) - (c) F (d) - (e) Agiou Tychona

*** Flowers - Marquis Flowers (Marquis McKinley Flowers-Gamboa) (a) 27/12/1996, Pittsburgh, Pennsylvania (United States) (b) - (c) D - left back (d) FC Manchester 62 (e) Pittsburgh CUFC

*** Flynn - Ryan Flynn (a) 04/09/1988, Edinburgh (Scotland) (b) 1,71 (c) M - right midfielder (d) St. Mirren FC (e) Oldham Athletic, Sheffield Utd., Falkirk FC, Liverpool Reserves, Wrexham, Liverpool Reserves, Hereford Utd., Liverpool Reserves

*** Flyuk - Shyngys Flyuk (Флюк Шынгыс Бауржанулы) (a) 28/12/2001, Karaganda (Kazakhstan) (b) 1,78 (c) F - center forward (d) Shakhter Karaganda (e) Shakhter-Bulat

*** Focsa - Maxim Focsa (Maxim Focşa) (a) 21/04/1992, Edinet (Moldova) (b) 1,86 (c) D - central defense (d) Afif FC (e) SCM Zalau, Dacia Buiucani, Dordoi Bishkek, FK Slutsk, Sfintul Gheorghe, Ma'an SC, Sfintul Gheorghe, Pembroke, Zaria Balti, FC Petrocub, Valletta, Balzan FC, Valletta, Dinamo-Auto, Ac. Chisinau, FC Sheriff, Ac. Chisinau, FC Sheriff

*** Foden - Phil Foden (Philip Walter Foden) (a) 28/05/2000, Stockport (England) (b) 1,71 (c) F - left winger (d) Manchester City (e) -

*** Fofana - Boubacar Fofana (a) 07/09/1998, Paris (France) (b) 1,83 (c) F - left winger (d) Servette FC (e) Olymp. Lyon B, G. Ajaccio, AS Saint-Priest, SAS Epinal

*** Fofana - David Datro Fofana (a) 22/12/2002, Ouragahio (Ivory Coast) (b) 1,82 (c) F - center forward (d) 1.FC Union Berlin (e) Union Berlin, Chelsea, Molde, Abidjan City FC, AFAD Djékanou, Abidjan City FC

*** Fofana - Fodé Fofana (a) 26/10/2002, Groningen (Netherlands) (b) 1,87 (c) F - center forward (d) - (e) PSV Eindhoven

*** Fofana - Habib Omar Fofana (Habib Omar Fofana) (a) 16/11/1998, ¿? (Ivory Coast) (b) 1,92 (c) D - central defense (d) Belshina Bobruisk (e) Dinamo-Auto, Entente II

*** Fofana - Ismaël Fofana (Ismaël Béko Fofana) (a) 08/09/1988, Abidjan (Ivory Coast) (b) 1,82 (c) F - center forward (d) - (e) Alashkert CF, IMT Beograd, Zira FK, Alki Oroklini, Vojvodina, Čukarički, Irtysh, Čukarički, FK Partizan, QD Jonoon, FK Partizan, Shirak Gyumri, Zob Ahan, Shirak Gyumri, FC Saint-Lô, Charlton Ath., AS Cherbourg, Charlton Ath., Fredrikstad, Charlton Ath., ASEC Mimosas

*** Fofana - Malick Fofana (Malick Martin Fofana) (a) 31/03/2005, Aalst (Belgium) (b) 1,69 (c) F - right winger (d) KAA Gent (e) Jong KAA Gent

*** Fofana - Manssour Fofana (Mohamed Manssour Fofana) (a) 10/07/2002, Abobo (Ivory Coast) (b) 1,75 (c) F - left winger (d) PAS Giannina (e) Veria NPS, Cannara

*** Fofana - Seko Fofana (Seko Mohamed Fofana) (a) 07/05/1995, Paris (France) (b) 1,85 (c) M - central midfielder (d) Al-Nassr FC (e) RC Lens, Udinese, SC Bastia, Fulham, Lorient B

*** Fofana - Souleymane Fofana (a) 20/01/2002, ¿? (France) (b) 1,94 (c) D - central defense (d) Akritas Chlorakas (e) Rostocker FC

*** Fofana - Wesley Fofana (a) 17/12/2000, Marseille (France) (b) 1,86 (c) D - central defense (d) Chelsea FC (e) Leicester City, St.-Étienne, Saint-Étienne B

*** Fofana - Yahia Fofana (a) 21/08/2000, Paris (France) (b) 1,94 (c) G (d) Angers SCO (e) Le Havre AC, Le Havre AC B

*** Fofana - Yaya Fofana (Yaya Kader Fofana) (a) 12/06/2004, Abidjan (Ivory Coast) (b) 1,80 (c) M - central midfielder (d) Stade Reims B (e) RC Lens B, Afrique Football Elite

*** Fofana - Youssouf Fofana (a) 10/01/1999, Paris (France) (b) 1,85 (c) M - central midfielder (d) AS Mónaco (e) Racing Club Strasbourg, Racing Strasbourg B
*** Foix - Josep Foix (Josep Maria Cabanes Foix) (a) 02/04/1996, Andorra la Vella (Angola) (b) 1,71 (c) D - central defense (d) Inter Club d'Escaldes (e) IC d'Escaldes
*** Foket - Thomas Foket (a) 25/09/1994, Brussel (Belgium) (b) 1,77 (c) D - right back (d) Stade de Reims (e) KAA Gent, KV Oostende, KAA Gent, Dilbeek Sport
*** Folan (c) G (d) Shelbourne FC (e) - - Dáithí Folan (c) G (d) Shelbourne FC (e) -
*** Foley - Adam Foley (a) 11/12/1989, Balbriggan, Dublin (Ireland) (b) 1,88 (c) M - right midfielder (d) Drogheda United FC (e) Finn Harps, Newry City, Glebe North, Glenavon, Portadown, Tolka Rovers, Glenavon, Glebe North
*** Folha - Bernardo Folha (Bernardo Pereira Folha) (a) 23/03/2002, Porto (Portugal) (b) 1,80 (c) M - central midfielder (d) FC Porto (e) FC Porto B
*** Folmer - Kirill Folmer (Фольмер Кирилл Алексеевич) (a) 25/02/2000, Engels, Saratov Oblast (Russia) (b) 1,78 (c) M - central midfielder (d) Volgar Astrakhan (e) Rostov, Baltika, Rostov, Akhmat Grozny, Rostov, Ufa, Spartak-2, Spartak Moskva II
*** Fomba - Bourama Fomba (a) 10/07/1999, Bamako (Mali) (b) 1,86 (c) D - central defense (d) FCI Levadia (e) FK Minsk, FK Oleksandriya, Chindia, Ceahlaul, ACSM Poli Iasi, Ceahlaul, FC Rustavi II, Etoiles Mandé
*** Fomin - Daniil Fomin (Фомин Даниил Дмитриевич) (a) 02/03/1997, Tikhoretsk, Krasnodar Region (Russia) (b) 1,87 (c) M - pivot (d) Dinamo Moskva (e) Ufa, Krasnodar-2, Nizhny Novgorod, Krasnodar-2, Krasnodar II
*** Fonrose - Fabien Fonrose (a) 03/04/1998, ¿? (France) (b) - (c) D (d) FC UNA Strassen (e) FC O. Tourangeau
*** Fonseca - Diogo Fonseca (Diogo Fernandes Fonseca) (a) 10/04/2002, Viseu (Portugal) (b) 1,91 (c) D - central defense (d) SC Braga B (e) -
*** Fonseca - Fábio Fonseca (Fábio Pinheiro da Fonseca) (a) 28/01/1997, Póvoa de Varzim (Portugal) (b) 1,95 (c) M - central midfielder (d) CDC Montalegre (e) Salamanca CF, UE Santa Coloma, FC Ordino, Berço, Varzim, AD Oliveirense, Varzim, Varzim
*** Fonseca - Fernando Fonseca (Fernando Manuel Ferreira Fonseca) (a) 14/03/1997, Porto (Portugal) (b) 1,83 (c) D - right back (d) Avs Futebol SAD (e) Paços Ferreira, Gil Vicente, FC Porto B, Estoril Praia, FC Porto B
*** Fonseca - Lorenzo Fonseca (Lorenzo Soares Fonseca) (a) 17/01/1998, Rotterdam (Netherlands) (b) 1,89 (c) D - central defense (d) CSM Ceahlaul Piatra Neamt (e) Hibernians FC, Santa Lucia FC, Hibernians FC, Santa Lucia FC, Académica Coimbra, FC Den Bosch, Sparta Rotterdam, Sparta Rotterdam
*** Fonseca - Théo Fonseca (Théo Luís Fonseca) (a) 11/06/2000, Ermonit (France) (b) 1,78 (c) F - right winger (d) FC Famalicão (e) Felgueiras
*** Fonsell - Michael Fonsell (a) 26/07/2003, ¿? (Finland) (b) 1,87 (c) M - pivot (d) IFK Mariehamn (e) -
*** Fontaine - Thomas Fontaine (a) 08/05/1991, Saint-Pierre (Reunion) (b) 1,85 (c) D - central defense (d) Genclerbirligi Ankara (e) Beroe, AS Nancy, FC Lorient, Stade Reims, Clermont Foot, AJ Auxerre, Tours FC, Olymp. Lyon B
*** Fontán - José Fontán (José Manuel Fontán Mondragón) (a) 11/02/2000, Vilagarcía de Arousa (Spain) (b) 1,82 (c) D - central defense (d) RC Celta de Vigo (e) Go Ahead Eagles, RC Celta, Celta B
*** Fontanarosa - Alessandro Fontanarosa (a) 07/02/2003, San Gennaro Vesuviano (Italy) (b) 1,85 (c) D - central defense (d) Cosenza Calcio (e) Cosenza, Internazionale Milano
*** Fonte - José Fonte (José Miguel da Rocha Fonte) (a) 22/12/1983, Penafiel (Portugal) (b) 1,87 (c) D - central defense (d) SC Braga (e) Lille, DL Yifang, West

Ham Utd., Southampton, Crystal Palace, Benfica, CF Estrela, Benfica, Paços Ferreira, Benfica, Vitória Setúbal, Felgueiras, Sporting B
*** Fonte - Rui Fonte (Rui Pedro da Rocha Fonte) (a) 23/04/1990, Lisboa (Portugal) (b) 1,80 (c) F - center forward (d) FC Paços de Ferreira (e) Famalicão, Estoril Praia, SC Braga, Fulham, Lille, Fulham, SC Braga, Benfica, SC Braga, Benfica B, Belenenses, Benfica B, RCD Espanyol, Sporting Lisboa, RCD Espanyol B, Sporting Lisboa, Vitória Setúbal, Sporting Lisboa, Arsenal Reserves, Crystal Palace, Arsenal Reserves, Sacavenense F.
*** Foor - Navarone Foor (Navarone Chesney Kai Foor) (a) 04/02/1992, Opheusden (Netherlands) (b) 1,70 (c) M - attacking midfielder (d) - (e) SC Cambuur, Riga, Pafos FC, Ittihad Kalba, Vitesse, NEC Nijmegen
*** Forde - Lorcan Forde (a) 07/11/1999, Newry (Northern Ireland) (b) - (c) M - right midfielder (d) Newry City AFC (e) Loughgall, Dungannon, Linfield, Warrenpoint, Linfield, Warrenpoint
*** Forenc - Konrad Forenc (a) 17/07/1992, Oława (Poland) (b) 1,91 (c) G (d) Korona Kielce (e) Zagłębie, Calisia, Zagłębie, F. Świnoujście, Zagłębie, Kolejarz Stróże, Zagłębie, MKS Olawa
*** Formosa - Cain Formosa (a) 26/11/2000, San Gwann (Malta) (b) - (c) G (d) Valletta FC (e) San Gwann FC, Gharghur FC, Mdina Knights, San Gwann FC
*** Formosa - Duncan Formosa (a) 30/06/2000, ¿? (Malta) (b) - (c) G (d) Floriana FC (e) Gudja United FC, St. Andrews FC
*** Fornalczyk - Mariusz Fornalczyk (Mariusz Fornalczyk) (a) 15/01/2003, Bytom (Poland) (b) 1,72 (c) F - left winger (d) Pogon Szczecin (e) Nieciecza, Pogon Szczecin, Polonia Bytom
*** Fornals - Pablo Fornals (Pablo Fornals Malla) (a) 22/02/1996, Castelló de la Plana (Spain) (b) 1,78 (c) M - attacking midfielder (d) West Ham United (e) Villarreal CF, Málaga CF, At. Malagueño
*** Forrest - Alan Forrest (a) 09/09/1996, Irvine (Scotland) (b) 1,75 (c) M - left midfielder (d) Heart of Midlothian FC (e) Livingston FC, Ayr United
*** Forrest - James Forrest (a) 07/07/1991, Prestwick (Scotland) (b) 1,75 (c) F - right winger (d) Celtic FC (e) -
*** Forrester - Chris Forrester (Christopher Forrester) (a) 17/12/1992, Dublin (Ireland) (b) 1,80 (c) M - central midfielder (d) St. Patrick's Athletic (e) Aberdeen FC, Peterborough, St. Patrick's Ath., Bohemians
*** Forsberg - Emil Forsberg (Emil Peter Forsberg) (a) 23/10/1991, Sundsvall (Sweden) (b) 1,77 (c) M - attacking midfielder (d) RB Leipzig (e) Malmö FF, GIF Sundsvall, Medskogsbron, GIF Sundsvall
*** Forsell - Petteri Forsell (Jani Petteri Forsell) (a) 16/10/1990, Kokkola (Finland) (b) 1,70 (c) M - attacking midfielder (d) FC Inter Turku (e) Stal Mielec, Korona Kielce, Miedź Legnica, HJK Helsinki, Miedź Legnica, Örebro SK, Miedź Legnica, IFK Mariehamn, Bursaspor, IFK Mariehamn, Bursaspor, IFK Mariehamn, VPS, Virkiä, VPS, Kokkolan PV
*** Forshaw - Adam Forshaw (Adam John Forshaw) (a) 08/10/1991, Liverpool (England) (b) 1,75 (c) M - central midfielder (d) - (e) Leeds Utd., Middlesbrough, Wigan Ath., Brentford, Everton Reserves
*** Forsman - Oskari Forsman (a) 28/01/1988, Oulu (Finland) (b) 1,87 (c) G (d) Kalev Tallinn (e) VPS, IFK Mariehamn, FC Lahti, Kemi City, TPS, RoPS, FC Jazz, FC KTP, OPS, FC KTP, FC Inter, VG-62
*** Forson - Amankwah Forson (a) 31/12/2002, ¿? (Austria) (b) 1,73 (c) M - attacking midfielder (d) Red Bull Salzburg (e) SCR Altach, RB Salzburg, FC Liefering, RB Salzburg, WAFA SC

*** Forst - Justin Forst (a) 21/02/2003, Innsbruck (Austria) (b) - (c) F - center forward (d) WSG Tirol (e) -

*** Forster - Fraser Forster (Fraser Gerard Forster) (a) 17/03/1988, Hexham (England) (b) 2,01 (c) G (d) Tottenham Hotspur (e) Southampton, Celtic FC, Southampton, Celtic FC, Newcastle Utd., Celtic FC, Newcastle Utd., Celtic FC, Newcastle Utd., Norwich City, Newcastle Utd., Bristol Rovers, Newcastle Utd., Stockport, Newcastle Utd.

*** Förster - Philipp Förster (a) 04/02/1995, Bretten (Germany) (b) 1,88 (c) M - attacking midfielder (d) VfL Bochum (e) VfB Stuttgart, SV Sandhausen, 1.FC Nürnberg, Waldh. Mannheim

*** Forsythe - Jordan Forsythe (a) 11/02/1991, Belfast (Northern Ireland) (b) 1,88 (c) M - central midfielder (d) Crusaders FC (e) Bangor, Lisburn FC

*** Forsythe - Kurtis Forsythe (a) 28/09/2002, Carrickfergus (Northern Ireland) (b) - (c) D - right back (d) Carrick Rangers (e) Carrick Rangers

*** Fortelny - Jan Fortelny (Jan Fortelný) (a) 19/01/1999, Praha (Czech Rep.) (b) 1,74 (c) M - attacking midfielder (d) SK Sigma Olomouc (e) Sigma Olomouc, Sparta Praha, Teplice, Sparta Praha, Teplice, Sparta Praha, Teplice, Sparta Praha, Jihlava, Sparta Praha, Vlasim, Sparta Praha

*** Fortes - Adilson Fortes (Adilson Fortes Neves) (a) 19/12/2005, ¿? (Luxembourg) (b) - (c) D (d) FC Etzella Ettelbruck (e) -

*** Fortes - Amancio Fortes (Amâncio José Pinto Fortes) (a) 18/04/1990, Luanda (Angola) (b) 1,70 (c) M - attacking midfielder (d) CS Unirea Ungheni (e) Zimbru Chisinau, Jeunesse Esch, Radomiak, Águeda, Liepaja, JFK Ventspils, Dacia, Casa Pia, Zimbru Chisinau, Coruchense, Zimbru Chisinau, CSKA Sofia, CD Fátima, Semarang United, GD Interclube, C.R.D. Libolo

*** Fortes - Steven Fortes (a) 17/04/1992, Marseille (France) (b) 1,92 (c) D - central defense (d) - (e) RC Lens, KV Oostende, RC Lens, Toulouse, RC Lens, Toulouse, Le Havre AC, AC Arles-Avignon, AC Arles B, La Cayolle

*** Forti - Matteo Forti (a) 03/03/2001, Savignano sul Rubicone (Italy) (b) 1,82 (c) G (d) CBR Carli Pietracuta (e) Victor SM, Chieti FC, Lanciano, Santarcangelo

*** Fortin - Louis Fortin (a) 12/01/2002, ¿? (Belgium) (b) 1,93 (c) G (d) KAA Gent (e) -

*** Fortounis - Konstantinos Fortounis (Κωνσταντίνος Φορτούνης) (a) 16/10/1992, Trikala (Greece) (b) 1,83 (c) M - attacking midfielder (d) Olympiakos El Pireo (e) 1.FC Kaiserslautern, Asteras Tripoli, AO Trikala

*** Fortuna - Nick Fortuna (Nicholas Keith Fortuna) (a) 22/06/2001, ¿? (Gibraltar) (b) - (c) D (d) FC College 1975 Reserve (e) Europa Reserve

*** Fortuna - Núrio Fortuna (Núrio Domingos Matias Fortuna) (a) 24/03/1995, Luanda (Angola) (b) 1,77 (c) D - left back (d) KAA Gent (e) RSC Charleroi, Braga B, AEL Limassol, Braga B

*** Fortune - Dre Fortune (Andre Sherman Fortune II) (a) 03/07/1996, Raleigh, North Carolina (United States) (b) 1,80 (c) M - attacking midfielder (d) Kalju FC (e) Memphis 901, North Carolina, Rochester, RailHawks

*** Fortuné - Yassin Fortuné (Yassin Enzo Fortuné) (a) 30/01/1999, Aubervilliers (France) (b) 1,86 (c) F - right winger (d) FC Sion (e) SO Cholet, FC Sion, Angers SCO, FC Sion

*** Fortuño - Ángel Fortuño (Ángel Fortuño Viñas) (a) 05/10/2001, Barcelona (Spain) (b) 1,83 (c) G (d) RCD Espanyol B (e) -

*** Foss - Sander Moen Foss (a) 31/12/1998, Barkåker (Norway) (b) 1,90 (c) D - central defense (d) Sandefjord Fotball (e) Sandefjord, Sandefjord II, Tønsberg, Sandefjord II, Eik-Tønsberg

*** Fossati - Marco Fossati (Marco Ezio Fossati) (a) 05/10/1992, Monza (Italy) (b) 1,80 (c) M - pivot (d) - (e) Hajduk Split, Monza, Hajduk Split, Monza, Hellas Verona, Cagliari, Hellas Verona, Cagliari, AC Milan, Perugia, AC Milan, Bari, AC Milan, Ascoli, AC Milan, Latina Calcio

*** Fossey - Marlon Fossey (Marlon Joseph Fossey) (a) 09/09/1998, Los Angeles, California (United States) (b) 1,79 (c) D - right back (d) Standard de Lieja (e) Bolton Wanderers, Shrewsbury

*** Fossum - Iver Fossum (Iver Tobias Rørvik Fossum) (a) 15/07/1996, Drammen (Norway) (b) 1,80 (c) M - central midfielder (d) FC Midtjylland (e) Aalborg BK, Hannover 96, Strømsgodset

*** Foster - Lyle Foster (Lyle Brent Foster) (a) 03/09/2000, Soweto (South Africa) (b) 1,85 (c) F - center forward (d) Burnley FC (e) KVC Westerlo, Vitória Guimarães B, KVC Westerlo, Vitória Guimarães B, Vitória Guimarães, AS Monaco, Cercle Brugge, AS Monaco, Orlando Pirates, O. Pirates YD

*** Foster - Seanna Foster (Seanan Foster) (a) 29/01/1997, Belfast (Northern Ireland) (b) 1,70 (c) D - right back (d) Cliftonville FC (e) Bangor, Cliftonville, Warrenpoint, Carrick Rangers, Plunkett FC

*** Fostier - Julien Fostier (a) 27/08/1990, ¿? (France) (b) 1,76 (c) M - left midfielder (d) UN Käerjeng 97 (e) US Rumelange, FC Villefranche, RE Virton, FC Metz B

*** Fosu - Tariqe Fosu (Tariqe Kumahl Malachi Akwesi Fosu-Henry) (a) 05/11/1995, London (England) (b) 1,80 (c) F - left winger (d) - (e) Brentford, Rotherham, Brentford, Stoke City, Brentford, Oxford United, Charlton Ath., Colchester Utd., Accrington St., Fleetwood

*** Fosu-Mensah - Timothy Fosu-Mensah (Timothy Evans Fosu-Mensah) (a) 02/01/1998, Amsterdam (Netherlands) (b) 1,85 (c) D - right back (d) Bayer 04 Leverkusen (e) Manchester Utd., Fulham, Manchester Utd., Crystal Palace, Manchester Utd.

*** Fotheringham - Kai Fotheringham (a) 18/04/2003, Larbert (Scotland) (b) 1,69 (c) F (d) Dundee United FC (e) Stirling Albion, Dundee United, Cove Rangers FC, Dundee United, Raith Rovers, Dundee United, Falkirk FC, Dundee United

*** Foti - Sotiris Foti (Σωτήρης Φώτη) (a) 12/06/2004, Limassol (Cyprus) (b) 1,70 (c) M - pivot (d) Apollon Limassol (e) Kouris Erimis

*** Foubert - Luca Foubert (a) 25/04/2004, Kortrijk (Belgium) (b) 1,84 (c) M - attacking midfielder (d) KSK Lierse Kempenzonen (e) -

*** Foufoué - Sulayman Foufoué (a) 09/10/2001, Orsay (France) (b) - (c) D - right back (d) US Mondorf-Les-Bains (e) S. Maria Cilento, Bitonto, AS Nancy B

*** Foulquier - Dimitri Foulquier (a) 23/03/1993, Sarcelles (France) (b) 1,83 (c) D - right back (d) Valencia CF (e) Granada CF, Watford, Granada CF, Watford, Getafe CF, Watford, Racing Club Strasbourg, Watford, Granada CF, Stade Rennes, Granada CF, Stade Rennes, Stade Rennes B, Club Amical

*** Fousek - Adam Fousek (a) 08/03/1994, Pardubice (Czech Rep.) (b) 1,85 (c) M - left midfielder (d) FC Zbrojovka Brno (e) Pardubice, Mlada Boleslav, Pardubice

*** Fox - Lucas Fox (a) 02/10/2000, ¿? (Luxembourg) (b) 1,93 (c) G (d) 1.FC Bocholt (e) F91 Dudelange, Jeunesse Esch

*** Fox - Scott Fox (a) 28/06/1987, Bellshill (Scotland) (b) 1,82 (c) G (d) - (e) Cove Rangers FC, Motherwell FC, Queen of the South, Motherwell FC, Morton, Motherwell FC, Partick Thistle, Ross County, Partick Thistle, Dundee FC, Queen of the South, Celtic Reserves, Ayr United, Celtic Reserves, East Fife, Celtic Reserves

*** Foyth - Juan Foyth (Juan Marcos Foyth) (a) 12/01/1998, La Plata (Argentina) (b) 1,87 (c) D - right back (d) Villarreal CF (e) Tottenham Hotspur, Villarreal CF, Tottenham Hotspur, Estudiantes, Estudiantes II

*** Frabotta - Gianluca Frabotta (a) 24/06/1999, Roma (Italy) (b) 1,87 (c) D - left back (d) Juventus de Turín (e) Lecce, Frosinone, Lecce, Juventus, Hellas Verona, Juventus, Pordenone, Renate, Savio

*** Fraczczak - Adam Fraczczak (Adam Frączczak) (a) 07/08/1987, Kołobrzeg (Poland) (b) 1,82 (c) F - center forward (d) Pogon Szczecin II (e) Kotwica, Korona Kielce, Pogon Szczecin, Kotwica, Legia Warszawa, Dolcan Zabki, Legia Warszawa, Legia II, Rega Trzebiatow, Zaki Kolobrzeg

*** Fraiz - Christian Fraiz (Christian Hernán Fraiz García) (a) 22/02/1988, Buenos Aires (Argentina) (b) 1,79 (c) G (d) Mons Calpe SC (e) Lynx FC, Somozas, SD Compostela, CA Kimberley

*** Framberger - Raphael Framberger (a) 06/09/1995, Augsburg (Germany) (b) 1,79 (c) D - right back (d) FC Augsburg (e) SV Sandhausen, FC Augsburg

*** Fran Pereira - Fran Pereira (Francisco João Rodrigues Baptista Monteiro) (a) 06/02/2002, Vila Nova de Gaia (Portugal) (b) 1,85 (c) M - pivot (d) GD Estoril Praia (e) Boavista

*** França - França (Carlos Henrique França Freires) (a) 09/02/1995, Brasília (Brazil) (b) 1,73 (c) F - right winger (d) Lokomotiv Sofia (e) Brasil Pelotas, Cianorte, Brasil Pelotas, Caxias-RS, Cianorte, Caxias-RS, Cianorte, Santa Cruz, Cianorte, EC São José, Cianorte, Mirassol-SP, Cianorte, América-MG, Cianorte

*** Franchelli - Luciano Baltazar Franchelli (a) 28/07/2003, ¿? (Argentina) (b) - (c) F - attacking midfielder (d) ASD Supergiovane Castelbuono (e) Pennarossa

*** Francioni - Adriano Francioni (a) 16/05/1991, Città di San Marino (San Marino) (b) - (c) D - central defense (d) - (e) Domagnano

*** Francioni - Giacomo Francioni (a) 25/10/2000, San Marino (San Marino) (b) - (c) D - right back (d) SS Folgore/Falciano (e) -

*** Francis - Abu Francis (a) 27/04/2001, Accra (Ghana) (b) 1,82 (c) M - central midfielder (d) Cercle Brugge (e) Nordsjælland, Right to Dream

*** Francis - Chris Francis (a) 15/11/2002, ¿? (England) (b) - (c) D - central defense (d) - (e) Weymouth FC, North Leigh

*** Francis - Daniel Francis (a) 27/09/2003, ¿? (Nigeria) (b) 1,76 (c) M - central midfielder (d) FC Wacker Innsbruck (e) FC Bayern II, Austria Klagenfurt, FC Bayern II, Hearts of Abuja

*** Francis - Lewis Francis (a) 15/04/2004, ¿? (Northern Ireland) (b) - (c) D - central defense (d) Bangor FC (e) Dungannon

*** Franco - André Franco (André Filipe Russo Franco) (a) 12/04/1998, Lisboa (Portugal) (b) 1,77 (c) M - attacking midfielder (d) FC Porto (e) Estoril Praia

*** Franco - Bruno Franco (Bruno Alexandre Franco) (a) 10/04/1998, Araraquara (Brazil) (b) - (c) D - left back (d) Lokomotiv Sofia (e) Spartak Pleven, Matonense, Rio Branco-PR, AD Guarulhos, Batatais, Mogi Mirim

*** Franco - Kaylan Franco (Kaylan Edward Franco) (a) 13/08/2001, Gibraltar (Gibraltar) (b) - (c) M - central midfielder (d) FC College 1975 (e) -

*** Franco - Nahuel Franco (Nahuel Ismael Franco) (a) 12/09/2001, San Lorenzo (Argentina) (b) 1,77 (c) D - left back (d) AP Brera (e) Rosario Central II, Boca Unidos, Rosario Central II

*** Francois - Tyrese Francois (Tyrese Jay Francois) (a) 16/07/2000, Campbelltown (Australia) (b) 1,73 (c) M - central midfielder (d) Fulham FC (e) HNK Gorica, Fulham

*** François - Guillaume François (a) 03/06/1990, Libramont (Belgium) (b) 1,74 (c) D - right back (d) Royale Union Saint Gilloise (e) RE Virton, KFCO Beerschot, RSC Charleroi, Beerschot AC, Excelsior Mouscron

*** Francoise - Emmanuel Francoise (Emmanuel Françoise) (a) 08/06/1987, Metz (France) (b) 1,76 (c) F - left winger (d) - (e) RFCU Luxembourg, Swift Hesperange,

Progrès Niederkorn, CS Fola Esch, Cremonese, CS Visé, F91 Dudelange, Kaiserslautern II, FC Metz B, FC Metz
*** Françoise - Noah Françoise (a) 05/07/2003, Rennes (France) (b) 1,77 (c) M - pivot (d) CS Marítimo (e) Stade Rennes, US Avranches, Stade Rennes, Stade Rennes B
*** Franeta - Marko Franeta (a) ¿?, ¿? (Montenegro) (b) - (c) D (d) - (e) OFK Petrovac,
*** Frangeski - Michalis Frangeski (Μιχάλης Φραγκέσκη) (a) 24/12/2005, Nicosia (Cyprus) (b) - (c) G (d) - (e) Chalkanoras
*** Frangos - Andreas Frangos (Ανδρέας Φράγκος) (a) 19/01/1997, Limassol (Cyprus) (b) 1,80 (c) M - central midfielder (d) - (e) Nea Salamis, Aris Limassol, AEL Limassol, Aris Limassol, AEL Limassol, Karmiotissa, AEL Limassol, EN Paralimniou, AEL Limassol, Aris Limassol, AEL Limassol, Apollon Limassol
*** Franjic - Bartol Franjic (Bartol Franjić) (a) 14/01/2000, Zagreb (Croatia) (b) 1,88 (c) M - pivot (d) VfL Wolfsburg (e) Dinamo Zagreb, Din. Zagreb II
*** Franklin - Harry Franklin (a) 02/12/1999, ¿? (Wales) (b) 1,82 (c) M - attacking midfielder (d) Connah's Quay Nomads (e) Aberystwyth, Evesham, Redditch Utd., Hereford, Merthyr Town
*** Franko - Matej Franko (a) 14/02/2001, Galanta (Slovakia) (b) 1,92 (c) F - center forward (d) MFK Karvina (e) Banska Bystrica, FC Nitra, Banska Bystrica, FC Nitra
*** Frankowski - Przemyslaw Frankowski (Przemysław Frankowski) (a) 12/04/1995, Gdańsk (Poland) (b) 1,75 (c) M - right midfielder (d) RC Lens (e) Chicago, Jagiellonia, Lechia Gdánsk, Lechia II
*** Fransson - Alexander Fransson (Alexander Martin Fransson) (a) 02/04/1994, Norrköping (Sweden) (b) 1,83 (c) M - central midfielder (d) - (e) AEK Athína, Norrköping, FC Basel, Lausanne-Sport, FC Basel, Norrköping
*** Frantsuzov - Aleksandr Frantsuzov (Французов Александр Владимирович) (a) 19/05/2004, Polotsk (Belarus) (b) 1,79 (c) F - center forward (d) BATE Borisov II (e) -
*** Frantzis - Christoforos Frantzis (Χριστόφορος Φραντζής) (a) 25/02/2001, Limassol (Cyprus) (b) 1,83 (c) D - right back (d) AEL Limassol (e) Kouris Erimis, AEL Limassol
*** Franzoni - Geoffrey Franzoni (a) 18/02/1991, ¿? (France) (b) - (c) D - right back (d) FC Differdange 03 (e) ES Clemency
*** Fraser - Marcus Fraser (a) 23/06/1994, Glasgow (Scotland) (b) 1,82 (c) D - right back (d) St. Mirren FC (e) Ross County, Celtic FC, Cowdenbeath FC, Celtic FC
*** Fraser - Robbie Fraser (a) 02/04/2003, Glasgow (Scotland) (b) 1,82 (c) D - left back (d) Rangers FC Reserves (e) -
*** Fraser - Ryan Fraser (a) 24/02/1994, Aberdeen (Scotland) (b) 1,63 (c) F - left winger (d) Newcastle United (e) Bournemouth, Ipswich, Bournemouth, Aberdeen FC
*** Frashëri - Stivi Frashëri (a) 29/08/1990, Korçë (Albania) (b) 1,91 (c) G (d) - (e) FC Ballkani, KF Teuta, FK Kukësi, Flamurtari FC, FK Bylis, KF Tirana, FK Bylis, Aris Thessaloniki
*** Frattesi - Davide Frattesi (a) 22/09/1999, Roma (Italy) (b) 1,78 (c) M - central midfielder (d) Internazionale Milano (e) Internazionale Milano, Sassuolo, Monza, Sassuolo, Empoli, Sassuolo, Ascoli, Sassuolo, AS Roma
*** Fraulo - Gustav Fraulo (Gustav Leone Fraulo) (a) 23/04/2005, Odense (Denmark) (b) 1,83 (c) M - central midfielder (d) CD Mafra (e) Mafra, Midtjylland
*** Fraulo - Oscar Fraulo (Oscar Luigi Fraulo) (a) 06/12/2003, Odense (Denmark) (b) 1,80 (c) M - central midfielder (d) Borussia Mönchengladbach (e) Midtjylland

*** Fred - Fred (Frederico Rodrigues de Paula Santos) (a) 05/03/1993, Belo Horizonte (Brazil) (b) 1,69 (c) M - central midfielder (d) Fenerbahce (e) Manchester Utd., Shakhtar Donetsk, Internacional, Inter B
*** Fred Saraiva - Fred Saraiva (Frederico Bello Saraiva) (a) 15/08/1996 (b) 1,72 (c) F - left winger (d) Fram Reykjavík (e) São Paulo-RS, Operário-PR
*** Fredericks - Ryan Fredericks (Ryan Marlowe Fredericks) (a) 10/10/1992, Hammersmith (England) (b) 1,81 (c) D - right back (d) AFC Bournemouth (e) West Ham Utd., Fulham, Bristol City, Tottenham Hotspur, Middlesbrough, Tottenham Hotspur, Millwall, Tottenham Hotspur, Brentford, Tottenham Hotspur
*** Frederiksberg - Árni Frederiksberg (a) 13/06/1992, ¿? (Faroe Islands) (b) 1,80 (c) F - right winger (d) KÍ Klaksvík (e) B36 Tórshavn, NSÍ Runavík, NSÍ II
*** Frederiksberg - Jákup Pauli Frederiksberg (a) 03/04/2004, ¿? (Faroe Islands) (b) - (c) D (d) Skála IF (e) -
*** Fredriksen - Ulrik Fredriksen (Ulrik Tillung Fredriksen) (a) 17/06/1999, Bergen (Norway) (b) 1,89 (c) D - central defense (d) FK Haugesund (e) Sogndal, Sogndal IL II, Fyllingsdalen
*** Fredy - Fredy (Alfredo Kulembe Ribeiro) (a) 27/03/1990, Luanda (Angola) (b) 1,70 (c) M - attacking midfielder (d) Antalyaspor (e) B SAD, Belenenses, Excelsior, C.R.D. Libolo, Belenenses, C.R.D. Libolo, Belenenses
*** Freeman - Kieran Freeman (Kieran Ewan Freeman) (a) 30/03/2000, Aberdeen (Scotland) (b) 1,78 (c) D - right back (d) Dundee United FC (e) Peterhead FC, Dundee United, Peterhead FC, Dundee United
*** Frei - Fabian Frei (a) 08/01/1989, Frauenfeld (Switzerland) (b) 1,83 (c) M - pivot (d) FC Basel (e) Mainz 05, FC Basel, FC St. Gallen, FC Basel
*** Frei - Filip Frei (a) 07/01/2001, Kilchberg ZH (Switzerland) (b) 1,75 (c) D - left back (d) FK Radnicki Niš (e) FC Zürich, FC Wil 1900, FC Zürich
*** Frei - Kerim Frei (Kerim Frei Koyunlu) (a) 19/11/1993, Feldkirch (Austria) (b) 1,71 (c) F - left winger (d) Manisa FK (e) Karagümrük, FC Emmen, Basaksehir, FC Emmen, Basaksehir, Maccabi Haifa, Basaksehir, Birmingham City, Besiktas, Fulham, Cardiff City, Fulham
*** Freire - Bruno Freire (Bruno Adelino Freire Fernandes) (a) 27/03/1999, ¿? (Portugal) (b) 1,83 (c) M - pivot (d) F91 Dudelange (e) CS Fola Esch
*** Freitas - Afonso Freitas (Afonso Manuel Abreu de Freitas) (a) 07/04/2000, Guimarães (Portugal) (b) 1,81 (c) D - left back (d) Vitória Guimarães SC (e) Vitória Guimarães B
*** Freitas - Dani Freitas (Daniel Filipe) (a) 18/02/2005, ¿? (France) (b) - (c) M (d) CS Fola Esch (e) -
*** Frelih - Ziga Frelih (Žiga Frelih) (a) 06/02/1998, Ljubljana (Slovenia) (b) 1,97 (c) G (d) - (e) CD Mirandés, Gil Vicente, Chaves, Gil Vicente, Olimpija, Inter Zaprešić, NK Krsko
*** French - Tyler French (Tyler Frederick French) (a) 14/10/1996, Bangor (Wales) (b) 1,88 (c) G (d) Holywell Town (e) Conwy, Caernarfon, Llangefni, Holywell, Penrhyndeu, Barmouth & Dyff, Porthmadog, Penrhyndeu, Barmouth & Dyff
*** Frendo - Neil Frendo (a) 04/01/1999, ¿? (Malta) (b) 1,78 (c) M - central midfielder (d) Sliema Wanderers (e) Balzan FC, Sliema Wanderers, Balzan FC, Pembroke, Balzan FC, Pembroke, Balzan FC, Balzan FC
*** Frese - Martin Frese (Martin Sønder Frese) (a) 04/01/1998, Rødovre (Denmark) (b) 1,79 (c) D - left back (d) FC Nordsjælland (e) -
*** Fresneda - Iván Fresneda (Iván Fresneda Corraliza) (a) 28/09/2004, Madrid (Spain) (b) 1,82 (c) D - right back (d) Real Valladolid CF (e) Valladolid Promesas

*** Freuler - Remo Freuler (Remo Marco Freuler) (a) 15/04/1992, Ennenda (Switzerland) (b) 1,80 (c) M - central midfielder (d) Nottingham Forest (e) Atalanta, FC Luzern, FC Winterthur, Grasshoppers, FC Winterthur, Grasshoppers
*** Frey - Michael Frey (a) 19/07/1994, Münsingen (Switzerland) (b) 1,88 (c) F - center forward (d) Royal Antwerp FC (e) FC Schalke 04, Royal Antwerp, Fenerbahce, Waasland-Beveren, Fenerbahce, 1.FC Nürnberg, Fenerbahce, FC Zürich, BSC Young Boys, Lille, FC Luzern, Lille, BSC Young Boys
*** Friberg - Erik Friberg (John Erik Gunnar Friberg) (a) 10/02/1986, Lindome (Sweden) (b) 1,80 (c) M - pivot (d) - (e) Häcken, Seattle, Esbjerg fB, Bologna, Malmö FF, Seattle, Häcken, Västra Frölunda
*** Friberg - Niklas Friberg (a) 14/03/1996, Halikko (Finland) (b) 1,86 (c) D - central defense (d) FC Haka (e) TPS, SalPa
*** Frick - Jérémy Frick (a) 08/03/1993, Genève (Switzerland) (b) 1,92 (c) G (d) Servette FC (e) FC Biel-Bienne, Olympique Lyon, Servette FC, Olympique Lyon, Olymp. Lyon B
*** Frick - Per Frick (Per Samuel Frick) (a) 14/04/1992, Kil (Sweden) (b) 1,82 (c) F - center forward (d) IF Elfsborg (e) Falkenbergs FF, Elfsborg, FBK Karlstad
*** Friday - Adams Friday (a) 23/11/2002, ¿? (Nigeria) (b) 1,72 (c) M - right midfielder (d) FC Botosani (e) FC Noah, FDC Vista
*** Friday - Fred Friday (Frederick Friday Imoh) (a) 22/05/1995, Port Harcourt (Nigeria) (b) 1,87 (c) F - center forward (d) Beitar Jerusalem (e) Strømsgodset, AZ Alkmaar, FC Twente, AZ Alkmaar, Sparta Rotterdam, AZ Alkmaar, Lillestrøm, Bujoc FC, Gabros International FC, Calabar Rovers
*** Fridjónsson - Hólmbert Aron Fridjónsson (Hólmbert Aron Briem Friðjónsson) (a) 19/04/1993, Reykjavík (Iceland) (b) 1,95 (c) F - center forward (d) Holstein Kiel (e) Lillestrøm, Holstein Kiel, Brescia, Aalesund, Stjarnan, KR Reykjavík, Stjarnan, KR Reykjavík, Celtic FC, Brøndby IF, Celtic FC, Fram Reykjavík, HK Kópavogs
*** Fridjónsson - Samúel Fridjónsson (Samúel Kári Friðjónsson) (a) 22/02/1996, Reykjanesbær (Iceland) (b) 1,86 (c) M - central midfielder (d) Atromitos FC (e) Viking, SC Paderborn, Vålerenga, Viking, Vålerenga, Keflavík
*** Fridrikas - Lukas Fridrikas (a) 30/12/1997, ¿? (Austria) (b) 1,80 (c) F - center forward (d) SC Austria Lustenau (e) Austria Klagenfurt, FC Wacker, FC Dornbirn, Wiener Neustadt, SC/ESV Parndorf, Wiener Neustadt, Seekirchen, USK Anif
*** Fridrikas - Mantas Fridrikas (a) 13/09/1988, Kaunas (Soviet Union, now in Lithuania) (b) 1,92 (c) D - central defense (d) - (e) Marijampole C., Hegelmann, Panevezys, Atlantas, DFK Dainava, Kauno Zalgiris, Utenis, Zalgiris, Siauliai, FBK Kaunas, FC Fyn, FBK Kaunas, Atletas
*** Fridriksson - Aron Snaer Fridriksson (Aron Snær Friðriksson) (a) 29/01/1997, ¿? (Iceland) (b) - (c) G (d) KR Reykjavík (e) Fylkir, Breidablik, Vestri, Breidablik, Tindastóll, Breidablik
*** Fridriksson - Felix Örn Fridriksson (Felix Örn Friðriksson) (a) 16/03/1999, Vestmannaeyjar (Iceland) (b) - (c) D - left back (d) ÍBV Vestmannaeyjar (e) Vejle BK, ÍBV Vestmannaeyjar
*** Fridriksson - Hlynur Már Fridriksson (Hlynur Már Friðriksson) (a) 09/03/2003, ¿? (Iceland) (b) - (c) M (d) KFG Gardabaer (e) -
*** Fridriksson - Stefán Jón Fridriksson (a) 12/02/2004, ¿? (Iceland) (b) - (c) M - right midfielder (d) Thróttur Vogum (e) Keflavík
*** Fridriksson - Valgeir Lunddal Fridriksson (Valgeir Lunddal Friðriksson) (a) 24/09/2001, ¿? (Iceland) (b) 1,91 (c) D - right back (d) BK Häcken (e) Valur, Fjölnir

*** Friedl - Marco Friedl (a) 16/03/1998, Kirchbichl (Austria) (b) 1,87 (c) D - central defense (d) SV Werder Bremen (e) Bayern München, Werder Bremen, Bayern München

*** Friedrich - Christian Friedrich (a) 15/02/2003, ¿? (Denmark) (b) 1,87 (c) D - right back (d) Naestved Boldklub (e) Brøndby IF, Fremad Amager, Brøndby IF

*** Friedrich - Marvin Friedrich (a) 13/12/1995, Kassel (Germany) (b) 1,93 (c) D - central defense (d) Borussia Mönchengladbach (e) Union Berlin, FC Augsburg, Union Berlin, FC Augsburg, FC Schalke 04

*** Friedrich - Ricardo Friedrich (Ricardo Henrique Schuck Friedrich) (a) 18/02/1993, Candelária (Brazil) (b) 1,88 (c) G (d) Kalmar FF (e) Ankaragücü, Bodø/Glimt, RoPS, Esportivo, Ituano

*** Friel - Cathair Friel (a) 25/05/1993, Limavady (Northern Ireland) (b) 1,78 (c) F - center forward (d) - (e) Coleraine, Portadown, Coleraine, Institute FC, Coleraine, Dungannon, Coleraine, Carrick Rangers, Ballymena, Limavady United, Portstewart FC, Coleraine, Limavady United

*** Friesenbichler - Kevin Friesenbichler (a) 06/05/1994, Weiz (Austria) (b) 1,85 (c) F - center forward (d) DSV Leoben (e) Lechia Gdánsk, RFS, Sturm Graz, VfL Osnabrück, Austria Viena, Wolfsberger AC, Austria Viena, Benfica B, Austria Viena, Benfica B, Austria Viena, Benfica B, Lechia Gdánsk, Benfica B, FC Bayern II

*** Frieser - Dominik Frieser (a) 09/09/1993, Graz (Austria) (b) 1,76 (c) F - right winger (d) TSV Hartberg (e) Cesena, Barnsley FC, LASK, Wolfsberger AC, SV Kapfenberg, TSV Hartberg, SC Kalsdorf, TSV Hartberg, Fürstenfeld, Seiersberg, Kumberg, Seiersberg

*** Frigan - Matija Frigan (a) 11/02/2003, Rijeka (Croatia) (b) 1,85 (c) F - center forward (d) KVC Westerlo (e) HNK Rijeka, Hrv Dragovoljac, NK Orijent 1919

*** Friggieri - Aidan Friggieri (Aidan Jake Friggieri) (a) 28/04/1998, ¿? (Malta) (b) 1,72 (c) F - right winger (d) Sliema Wanderers (e) Balzan FC, Gudja United FC, St. Andrews FC, Sliema Wanderers

*** Frimpong - Abraham Frimpong (Abraham Akwasi Frimpong) (a) 06/04/1993, Accra (Ghana) (b) 1,84 (c) D - central defense (d) - (e) Dinamo Batumi, Al-Ain FC, Ferencváros, Crvena zvezda, Napredak, Vojvodina

*** Frimpong - Jeremie Frimpong (Jeremie Agyekum Frimpong) (a) 10/12/2000, Amsterdam (Netherlands) (b) 1,71 (c) D - right back (d) Bayer 04 Leverkusen (e) Celtic FC

*** Frising - Joé Frising (a) 13/01/1994, ¿? (Luxembourg) (b) - (c) G (d) UN Käerjeng 97 (e) Jeunesse Canach, F91 Dudelange, FC Rodange 91, F91 Dudelange, FC Rodange 91, CS Fola Esch, FC Rodange 91, CS Fola Esch, FC Rodange 91

*** Fródason - Eiler Fródason (Eiler Fróðason) (a) 24/04/2003, ¿? (Faroe Islands) (b) 1,93 (c) D - central defense (d) 07 Vestur (e) -

*** Frökjaer-Jensen - Mads Frökjaer-Jensen (Mads Frøkjær-Jensen) (a) 29/07/1999, Kopenhagen (Denmark) (b) 1,86 (c) M - attacking midfielder (d) Preston North End (e) Odense BK

*** Frolov - Andre Frolov (a) 18/04/1988, Hiiumaa, Emmaste (Soviet Union, now in Estonia) (b) 1,75 (c) M - central midfielder (d) Paide Linnameeskond (e) FC Flora, JK Viljandi, FC Flora II, Warrior Valga, Tervis Pärnu, FC Lelle

*** Frolov - Evgeniy Frolov (Фролов Евгений Константинович) (a) 05/02/1988, Krasnoyarsk-26, Krasnoyarsk Region (Soviet Union, now in Russia) (b) 1,94 (c) G (d) Krylya Sovetov Samara (e) Sochi, Orenburg, Baltika, Kuban Krasnodar, Dinamo Moskva, Sakhalin, Dinamo Moskva, Mordovia, Torpedo Moskva, Mordovia, Znamya Truda OZ, Mordovia, MCPUFP Mordovia

*** Frroku - Leandro Frroku (a) 03/09/2003, Vari (Greece) (b) 1,79 (c) M - pivot (d) Panathinaikos FC (e) Panathinaikos B
*** Früchtl - Christian Früchtl (a) 28/01/2000, Bischofsmais (Germany) (b) 1,93 (c) G (d) FK Austria Viena (e) Bayern München, 1.FC Nürnberg, Bayern München
*** Fruhwald - Tomas Fruhwald (a) 23/09/2002, ¿? (Slovakia) (b) 1,93 (c) G (d) MFK Ružomberok (e) -
*** Fruk - Toni Fruk (a) 09/03/2001, Našice (Croatia) (b) 1,78 (c) M - attacking midfielder (d) HNK Rijeka (e) Fiorentina, HNK Gorica, Fiorentina, NK Dubrava ZG, NK Nasice
*** Frydek - Christian Frydek (Christian Frýdek) (a) 01/02/1999, Leverkusen (Germany) (b) 1,71 (c) M - attacking midfielder (d) FC Slovan Liberec (e) Sparta Praha B, Hradec Kralove, Sparta Praha B, FC MAS Taborsko, Sparta Praha B, Vlasim, Sparta Praha B
*** Frydek - Martin Frydek (Martin Frýdek) (a) 24/03/1992, Hradec Králové (Czechoslovakia, now in Czech Rep.) (b) 1,79 (c) D - left back (d) FC Lucerna (e) Sparta Praha, Slovan Liberec, Sparta Praha, FK Senica, Sparta Praha, Sparta Praha B
*** Frydrych - Michal Frydrych (Michal Frydrych) (a) 27/02/1990, Hustopeče nad Bečvou (Czechoslovakia, now in Czech Rep.) (b) 1,88 (c) D - central defense (d) FC Banik Ostrava (e) Wisla Kraków, Slavia Praha, Banik Ostrava
*** Frye - Louis Frye (a) 22/09/1997, Osnabrück (Germany) (b) 1,78 (c) F - right winger (d) FC SW Kalkriese (e) Europa Point FC, FC SW Kalkriese, SF Lotte II, SF Lechtingen, Dodesheide II, SF Lotte II, TuS Haste 01 II, Dodesheide II, SC Kosmos
*** Frystak - Tomas Frystak (Tomáš Fryšták) (a) 18/08/1987, Uherské Hradiště (Czechoslovakia, now in Czech Rep.) (b) 1,93 (c) G (d) 1.FC Slovácko (e) AS Trencin, FK Senica, Bohemians 1905, Banik Sokolov, Bohemians 1905, Slovácko B, Ceske Budejovice, Slovácko B, FC MAS Taborsko, Slovácko B, Caslav, Slovácko B
*** Fucak - Kristian Fucak (Kristian Fućak) (a) 14/11/1998, Rijeka (Croatia) (b) 1,93 (c) F - left winger (d) NK Osijek (e) HNK Gorica, NK Osijek, NK Orijent 1919, NK Grobnican, NK Varazdin, NK Orijent 1919, NK Varazdin, NK Grobnican
*** Fuchs - Alexander Fuchs (a) 05/01/1997, München (Germany) (b) 1,86 (c) M - central midfielder (d) SV Sandhausen (e) Austria Klagenfurt, Unterhaching, 1.FC Nürnberg, 1860 München II
*** Fucs - Roee Fucs (פוקס רועי) (a) 14/12/1998, ¿? (Israel) (b) - (c) G (d) Maccabi Haifa (e) H. Nof HaGalil, Maccabi Haifa, H Rishon leZion, Maccabi Haifa
*** Führich - Chris Führich (a) 09/01/1998, Castrop-Rauxel (Germany) (b) 1,81 (c) F - attacking midfielder (d) VfB Stuttgart (e) SC Paderborn, Borussia Dortmund II, SC Paderborn, Borussia Dortmund II, 1.FC Köln
*** Fuidias - Toni Fuidias (Toni Fuidias Ribera) (a) 15/04/2001, Berga (Spain) (b) 1,95 (c) G (d) Girona FC (e) RM Castilla
*** Fujimoto - Kanya Fujimoto (藤本 寛也) (a) 01/07/1999, ¿?, Yamanashi (Japan) (b) 1,76 (c) M - attacking midfielder (d) Gil Vicente FC (e) Tokyo Verdy, Gil Vicente, Tokyo Verdy
*** Fukala - Michal Fukala (a) 22/10/2000, Frýdek-Místek (Czech Rep.) (b) 1,80 (c) D - right back (d) FC Slovan Liberec (e) Frydek-Mistek
*** Fukra - Mohamad Fukra (a) 01/06/2002, ¿? (Iceland) (b) - (c) M (d) Ihud Bnei Shefaram (e) -
*** Fulgini - Angelo Fulgini (a) 20/08/1996, Abidjan (Ivory Coast) (b) 1,82 (c) M - attacking midfielder (d) RC Lens (e) Mainz 05, RC Lens, Mainz 05, Angers SCO, Valenciennes FC, Valenciennes B

*** Füllkrug - Niclas Füllkrug (a) 09/02/1993, Hannover (Germany) (b) 1,89 (c) F - center forward (d) SV Werder Bremen (e) Hannover 96, 1.FC Nürnberg, Werder Bremen, Greuther Fürth, Werder Bremen, Werder Bremen II

*** Fulnek - Jakub Fulnek (a) 26/04/1994, ¿? (Czech Rep.) (b) 1,72 (c) F - left winger (d) FK Mlada Boleslav (e) Bohemians 1905, Mlada Boleslav, Jihlava, FC MAS Taborsko, Jihlava, Jihlava B

*** Fülöp - Lóránd Fülöp (Fülöp Lóránd Levente) (a) 24/07/1997, Târgu Mureş (Romania) (b) 1,80 (c) M - central midfielder (d) - (e) Universitatea Cluj, FC Voluntari, Puskás AFC, Sepsi OSK, Puskás AFC, FC Botosani, Sepsi OSK, FC Ardealul, ACS Kinder

*** Fuoli - Diego Fuoli (Diego Licinio Lázaro Fuoli) (a) 20/10/1997, Zaragoza (Spain) (b) 1,88 (c) G (d) San Fernando CD (e) UD Almería, UD Almería B, CE Sabadell, Villarreal CF B, Villarreal CF C

*** Furlan - Jacopo Furlan (a) 22/02/1993, San Daniele del Friuli (Italy) (b) 1,89 (c) G (d) AC Perugia Calcio (e) FC Empoli, Catania, Catanzaro, Bari, Trapani, Bari, Monopoli, Bari, Lumezzane, Viareggio, Empoli

*** Furlan - Marko Furlan (a) 09/08/2004, ¿? (Slovenia) (b) - (c) D - central defense (d) NK Tabor Sezana (e) -

*** Furlong - James Furlong (Walter James Byrne Furlong) (a) 07/06/2002, Dublin (Ireland) (b) 1,78 (c) D - left back (d) - (e) Motherwell FC, Shamrock II

*** Furman - Dominik Furman (Dominik Grzegorz Furman) (a) 06/07/1992, Szydłowiec (Poland) (b) 1,83 (c) M - central midfielder (d) - (e) Wisła Płock, Genclerbirligi, Wisła Płock, Toulouse, Wisła Płock, Toulouse, Hellas Verona, Toulouse, Legia Warszawa, Toulouse, Legia Warszawa, Legia II

*** Furtado - Steeve Furtado (a) 22/11/1994, Creil (France) (b) 1,75 (c) D - right back (d) CSKA 1948 II (e) CSKA 1948, Beroe, Albacete, US Orléans, US Créteil-Lusitanos, SM Caen B, Stade Rennes B

*** Furtado - Willis Furtado (Luis Willis Alves Furtado) (a) 04/09/1997, Ivry-sur-Seine (France) (b) 1,82 (c) F - right winger (d) FC KTP (e) Jerv, FC Masr, Raith Rovers, Airdrieonians, Stenhousemuir, US Ivry

*** Furtuna - Denis Furtuna (Denis Furtună) (a) 13/10/1999, Făleşti (Moldova) (b) 1,89 (c) D - central defense (d) FC Zimbru Chisinau (e) FC Bălţi, Dacia Buiucani, Zimbru Chisinau

*** Furuhashi - Kyogo Furuhashi (古橋 亨梧) (a) 20/01/1995, Ikoma, Nara (Japan) (b) 1,70 (c) F - center forward (d) Celtic FC (e) Vissel Kobe, FC Gifu, Chuo University, Kokoku HS

*** Furuholm - Timo Furuholm (a) 11/10/1987, Pori (Finland) (b) 1,85 (c) F - center forward (d) - (e) FC Inter, Hallescher FC, Fortuna Düsseldorf, Hallescher FC, Fortuna Düsseldorf, FC Inter, MuSa, FC Jazz

*** Fuseini - Mohammed Fuseini (Mohammed Gadafi Fuseini) (a) 16/05/2002, ¿? (Ghana) (b) 1,69 (c) F - right winger (d) SK Sturm Graz (e) Sturm Graz II, Right to Dream

*** Fyfe - Eamon Fyfe (a) 01/04/1998, Cargan (Northern Ireland) (b) - (c) F - center forward (d) Portadown FC (e) Portadown, Coleraine, Dundela FC, All Saints O B, Queen's Uni

*** Fylaktou - Gerasimos Fylaktou (Γεράσιμος Φυλακτού) (a) 24/07/1991, Nikosia (Cyprus) (b) 1,74 (c) M - central midfielder (d) ENAD Polis Chrysochous (e) Pafos FC, Ermis Aradippou, Omonia Nicosia, Pafos FC, Oinonia Nicosia, Alki Larnaca, Digenis Morfou

*** Gaaei - Anton Gaaei (a) 19/11/2002, ¿? (Denmark) (b) 1,83 (c) D - right back (d) Viborg FF (e) -

*** Gaard - Silas Gaard (Silas Ólavsson Gaard) (a) 22/05/2004, ¿? (Faroe Islands) (b) 1,76 (c) F - right winger (d) KÍ Klaksvík (e) KÍ II

*** Gaari - Juriën Gaari (Juriën Godfried Juan Gaari) (a) 23/12/1993, Kerkrade (Netherlands) (b) 1,83 (c) D - central defense (d) RKC Waalwijk (e) Kozakken Boys, Smitshoek

*** Gaba - Josue Gaba (a) 12/01/2002, Abidjan (Ivory Coast) (b) 1,83 (c) D - right back (d) FC Van (e) -

*** Gabadze - Giorgi Gabadze (გიორგი გაბაძე) (a) 02/03/1995, ¿? (Georgia) (b) 1,88 (c) D - central defense (d) FC Locomotive Tbilisi (e) Torpedo Kutaisi, FC Locomotive

*** Gabbia - Matteo Gabbia (a) 21/10/1999, Busto Arsizio (Italy) (b) 1,85 (c) D - central defense (d) Villarreal CF (e) Villarreal CF, AC Milan, Lucchese, AC Milan

*** Gabbiadini - Manolo Gabbiadini (a) 26/11/1991, Calcinate (Italy) (b) 1,86 (c) F - center forward (d) Al-Nasr SC (UAE) (e) Sampdoria, Southampton, Napoli, Sampdoria, Juventus, Bologna, Juventus, Atalanta, Cittadella

*** Gabedava - Giorgi Gabedava (გიორგი გაბედავა) (a) 03/10/1989, Tbilisi (Soviet Union, now in Georgia) (b) 1,82 (c) F - center forward (d) Hapoel Acre (e) Dinamo Tbilisi, Saburtalo, Z. Sosnowiec, Chikhura, Dinamo Batumi, FC Samtredia, Chikhura, FK Zugdidi, Baia Zugdidi, FC Gagra, Illichivets, FC Gagra

*** Gabelli - Leonardo Gabelli (a) 30/04/2002, ¿? (Italy) (b) - (c) D - left back (d) - (e) Pergolettese, Levanto, Rivasamba

*** Gabelok - Artem Gabelok (Габелок Артем Юрійович) (a) 02/01/1995, Dnipropetrovsk (Ukraine) (b) 1,77 (c) M - central midfielder (d) Metalist 1925 Kharkiv (e) Pyunik Yerevan, Vorskla Poltava, Spartaks, Shakhtar II, Shakhtar 3

*** Gabi - Gabi (João Gabriel Carvalho Castro) (a) 19/11/2001, ¿? (Portugal) (b) 1,84 (c) F - center forward (d) - (e) UE Santa Coloma, Bragança, Fafe

*** Gabovda - Yuriy Gabovda (Габовда Юрій Вікторович) (a) 06/05/1989, Mukacheve, Zakarpattia Region (Soviet Union, now in Ukraine) (b) 1,81 (c) M - right midfielder (d) Janos Gabovda (e) Sokol Hostoun, Dukla Praha, Torpedo Zhodino, Debrecen, Haladás, Balmazújváros, Rukh Vynnyky, Dinamo Minsk, Granit, Karpaty, SK Tavriya, Kryvbas, Karpaty, Karpaty II

*** Gabriel - Adam Gabriel (a) 28/05/2001, ¿? (Czech Rep.) (b) 1,90 (c) D - right back (d) FC Hradec Kralove (e) Sparta Praha B

*** Gabriel - Zevai Gabriel (a) ¿?, ¿? (England) (b) - (c) M (d) - (e) Newtown AFC

*** Gabriel Bispo - Gabriel Bispo (Gabriel Bispo dos Santos) (a) 05/03/1997, Porto Seguro (Brazil) (b) 1,77 (c) M - central midfielder (d) Kuopion Palloseura (e) EC Vitória, Juventude, EC Vitória, AD Bahia-BA, EC Vitória, AD Bahia-BA

*** Gabriel Gomes - Gabriel Gomes (Gabriel Gomes Ferreira) (a) 23/08/1999, São Gonçalo (Brazil) (b) 1,86 (c) D - central defense (d) Metalist Kharkiv (e) Inter de Minas, SK Dnipro-1, Inter de Minas, Brasil Pelotas, Inter de Minas, América-MG, Inter de Minas, Bangu-RJ, AD Itaboraí-RJ

*** Gabriel Jesus - Gabriel Jesus (Gabriel Fernando de Jesus) (a) 03/04/1997, São Paulo (Brazil) (b) 1,75 (c) F - center forward (d) Arsenal FC (e) Manchester City, Palmeiras

*** Gabriel Nazário - Gabriel Nazário (Gabriel da Rosa Nazário) (a) 06/04/2002, Braço do Norte (Brazil) (b) 1,89 (c) D - central defense (d) Caravaggio Futebol Clube (SC) (e) Vorskla Poltava, União São João

*** Gabriel Paulista - Gabriel Paulista (Gabriel Armando de Abreu) (a) 26/11/1990, São Paulo (Brazil) (b) 1,87 (c) D - central defense (d) Valencia CF (e) Arsenal, Villarreal CF, EC Vitória, Vitória B, Taboão Serra

*** Gabriel Pereira - Gabriel Pereira (Gabriel Pereira Magalhães dos Santos) (a) 07/05/2000, Volta Redonda (Brazil) (b) 1,88 (c) D - central defense (d) Gil Vicente FC (e) Vilafranquense, Volta Redonda, Vilafranquense, Volta Redonda

*** Gabriel Ramos - Gabriel Ramos (Gabriel Ramos da Penha) (a) 20/03/1996, Rio de Janeiro (Brazil) (b) 1,84 (c) F - left winger (d) Bucheon FC 1995 (e) Riga, Londrina-PR, Riga, Torpedo Zhodino, Dinamo Batumi, Cuiabá-MT

*** Gabriel Silva - Gabriel Silva (Gabriel Silva Vieira) (a) 22/03/2002, Ribeirão Preto (Brazil) (b) 1,77 (c) F - right winger (d) SE Palmeiras (e) Santa Clara, Palmeiras

*** Gabriel Veron - Gabriel Veron (Gabriel Veron Fonseca de Souza) (a) 03/09/2002, Assu (Brazil) (b) 1,76 (c) F - right winger (d) FC Porto (e) Palmeiras

*** Gabrielsen - Ruben Gabrielsen (Lunan Ruben Gabrielsen) (a) 10/03/1992, Lena (Norway) (b) 1,86 (c) D - central defense (d) Lillestrøm SK (e) Austin, Toulouse, FC København, Toulouse, Molde, Lillestrøm

*** Gaby - Gaby (Gabriel Marcel Leighton Mateos) (a) 16/10/2000, Nîmes (France) (b) - (c) F - right winger (d) UE Engordany (e) FS La Massana, Penya Encarnada, CE Carroi, Penya Encarnada, IC d'Escaldes, FC Rànger's, CE Carroi

*** Gabyshev - Mikhail Gabyshev (a) 02/01/1990, Oskemen (Soviet Union, now in Kazakhstan) (b) 1,85 (c) D - right back (d) FC Astana (e) Shakhter K., Kaspiy Aktau, Atyrau, Kaspiy Aktau, Shakhter K., Vostok Oskemen

*** Gacinovic - Mijat Gacinovic (Мијат Гаћиновић) (a) 08/02/1995, Novi Sad (Yugoslavia, now in Serbia) (b) 1,75 (c) M - left midfielder (d) AEK Athína FC (e) Hoffenheim, Panathinaikos, Hoffenheim, Eintracht, Apollon Limassol, Vojvodina, Vojvodina II

*** Gadegaard Andersen - Daniel Gadegaard Andersen (a) 31/05/2001, ¿? (Denmark) (b) 1,91 (c) G (d) Esbjerg fB (e) Aarhus GF

*** Gadrani - Giorgi Gadrani (გიორგი გადრანი) (a) 30/09/1994, Tbilisi (Georgia) (b) 1,92 (c) D - central defense (d) FC Spaeri Tbilisi (e) Sioni Bolnisi, FC Samtredia, VPK-Agro, Shukura, Torpedo Kutaisi, Dinamo Batumi, FC Dila, Desna, Dinamo Tbilisi, Chornomorets, FC Gagra

*** Gadrani - Luka Gadrani (ლუკა გადრანი) (a) 12/04/1997, Tbilisi (Georgia) (b) 1,85 (c) D - central defense (d) FK Aktobe (e) Taraz, Valmiera, Shahin Bushehr, Rustavi, Tskhinvali, Depor. Alavés B, Dinamo II, WIT Georgia II

*** Gadze - Richard Gadze (a) 23/08/1994, Accra (Ghana) (b) 1,73 (c) F - center forward (d) - (e) Sumqayit, Sheikh Russel, Bnei Sakhnin, FC Sheriff, Zira FK, FC Voluntari, Zira FK, Delhi Dynamos, Zira FK, Delhi Dynamos, HJK Helsinki, Delhi Dynamos, Ebusua Dwarfs

*** Gadzhibekov - Ali Gadzhibekov (Гаджибеков Али Амрахович) (a) 06/08/1989, Makhachkala (Soviet Union, now in Russia) (b) 1,85 (c) D - central defense (d) - (e) FK Aksu, Legion-Dinamo, Chaika Pes., KS Samara, Nizhny Novgorod, KS Samara, Enisey, KS Samara, Anzhi

*** Gadzhimuradov - Ramazan Gadzhimuradov (Гаджимурадов Рамазан Ирбайханович) (a) 09/01/1998, Khasavyurt, Dagestan Republic (Russia) (b) 1,78 (c) F - right winger (d) Rotor Volgograd (e) Rotor Volgograd, Ural, Dinamo Makhach., Ural, SKA Khabarovsk, Veles Moskva, Veles 2, FShM

*** Gaetano - Gianluca Gaetano (a) 05/05/2000, Cimitile (Italy) (b) 1,83 (c) M - attacking midfielder (d) SSC Nápoles (e) Cremonese, Napoli, Cremonese, Napoli

*** Gaevoy - Maksim Gaevoy (Гаевой Максим Артемович) (a) 27/05/2002, Grodno (Belarus) (b) 1,78 (c) M - central midfielder (d) FK Smorgon (e) FK Smorgon, BATE II, Dzerzhinsk, BATE II

*** Gaffney - Rory Gaffney (Rory Nicholas Gaffney) (a) 23/10/1989, Tuam, Galway (Ireland) (b) 1,84 (c) F - center forward (d) Shamrock Rovers (e) Salford, FC Walsall,

Salford, Bristol Rovers, Cambridge Utd., Bristol Rovers, Cambridge Utd., Limerick FC, Mervue United

*** Gaggi - Enzo Gaggi (a) 14/01/1998, Rafaela (Argentina) (b) 1,74 (c) M - right midfielder (d) - (e) Volos NPS, Chaco For Ever, Def. Belgrano, Central Norte, Rafaela II, Central Norte, Rafaela II

*** Gagliardini - Roberto Gagliardini (a) 07/04/1994, Bergamo (Italy) (b) 1,88 (c) M - central midfielder (d) AC Monza (e) Internazionale Milano, Atalanta, Internazionale Milano, Atalanta, Vicenza, Atalanta, Spezia, Atalanta, Cesena, Atalanta

*** Gagnidze - Luka Gagnidze (ლუკა გაგნიძე) (a) 28/02/2003, Kutaisi (Georgia) (b) 1,75 (c) M - central midfielder (d) Dinamo Moskva (e) Rakow, Dinamo Moskva, Ural, Dinamo Moskva, Dinamo Tbilisi

*** Gagnidze - Nika Gagnidze (ნიკა გაგნიძე) (a) 20/03/2001, Gori (Georgia) (b) 1,80 (c) M - central midfielder (d) FC Dila Gori (e) Ümraniyespor, FC Dila, Dila II

*** Gagoshidze - Malkhaz Gagoshidze (მალხაზ გაგოშიძე) (a) 20/02/1993, ¿? (Georgia) (b) 1,81 (c) D - central defense (d) - (e) FC Dila, Merani Martvili, Dinamo Batumi, FC Dila, Samgurali, FK Zugdidi, Samgurali, FC Zestafoni, Zestafoni II

*** Gagun - Roman Gagun (Гагун Роман Валентинович) (a) 16/07/1993, Shepetivka, Khmelnytskyi Oblast (Ukraine) (b) 1,70 (c) D - right back (d) NK Veres Rivne (e) Rukh Lviv, Agrobiznes V., FC Odishi, Goverla II, Temp Shepetivka

*** Gai - Nicola Gai (a) 06/12/1987, Sansepolcro (Italy) (b) 1,82 (c) M - attacking midfielder (d) SP Tre Penne (e) Paganese, Martina Franca, Castel Rigone, Montevarchi, US Sansovino

*** Gaiani - Matteo Gaiani (a) 02/01/1995, ¿? (Italy) (b) 1,74 (c) M - central midfielder (d) SS Murata (e) Domagnano, Libertas, ASD San Pietro, Sammaurese, Ribelle

*** Gaich - Adolfo Gaich (Adolfo Julián Gaich) (a) 26/02/1999, Córdoba (Argentina) (b) 1,90 (c) F - center forward (d) CSKA Moskva (e) Hellas Verona, CSKA Moskva, SD Huesca, CSKA Moskva, Benevento, CSKA Moskva, San Lorenzo, San Lorenzo II

*** Gailius - Benediktas Gailius (a) 15/06/2002, ¿? (Lithuania) (b) - (c) M (d) FK Banga Gargzdai B (e) -

*** Gaiu - Valeriu Gaiu (a) 06/02/2001, ¿? (Moldova) (b) 1,73 (c) D - right back (d) FC Zimbru Chisinau (e) Zimbru Chisinau, FC Sheriff, FC Bălți, FC Sheriff, Dinamo-Auto, FC Sheriff, Sheriff-2, Real Succes

*** Gaivizo - Charles Gaivizo (John Charles Gaivizo) (a) 27/07/1993, ¿? (Gibraltar) (b) - (c) M - central midfielder (d) Lions Gibraltar FC (e) Lions Gibraltar Reserves

*** Gajdos - Artur Gajdos (Artur Gajdoš) (a) 20/01/2004, Ilava (Slovakia) (b) 1,70 (c) M - attacking midfielder (d) AS Trencin (e) -

*** Gajgier - Aleksander Gajgier (a) 10/08/2003, Otwock (Poland) (b) 1,93 (c) D - central defense (d) Pogon Grodzisk Mazowiecki (e) Pogon Grodzisk, Radomiak, Pogon Grodzisk, Radomiak

*** Gajic - Marko Gajic (Марко Гајић) (a) 10/03/1992, Beograd (Yugoslavia, now in Serbia) (b) 1,90 (c) D - central defense (d) - (e) Čukarički, Borac Banja Luka, Radnicki 1923, FC U Craiova, Vozdovac, Olimpija, Vozdovac, Javor-Matis, OFK Beograd, Pazova

*** Gajic - Milan Gajic (a) 28/01/1996, Vukovar (Croatia) (b) 1,78 (d) CSKA Moskva (e) Crvena zvezda, Girondins Bordeaux, OFK Beograd

*** Gajic - Zoran Gajic (Зоран Гајић) (a) 18/05/1990, Beograd (Yugoslavia, now in Serbia) (b) 1,87 (c) D - central defense (d) FK Kolubara Lazarevac (e) Pyunik

Yerevan, Zbrojovka Brno, Arda Kardzhali, Fastav Zlin, Bohemians 1905, FK BSK Borča, OFK Mladenovac

*** Gajos - Maciej Gajos (a) 19/03/1991, Blachownia (Poland) (b) 1,74 (c) M - attacking midfielder (d) Persija Jakarta (e) Lechia Gdánsk, Lech Poznan, Jagiellonia, Rakow

*** Gajzler - Niko Gajzler (a) 21/12/2004, Rijeka (Croatia) (b) 1,76 (c) F - center forward (d) HNK Rijeka (e) NK Krk

*** Gakou - Maka Gakou (a) 17/03/2000, Montivilliers (France) (b) 1,88 (c) D - left back (d) FK Radnicki Niš (e) Jura Dolois, CMS Oissel, Le Havre AC B

*** Gakpo - Cody Gakpo (Cody Mathès Gakpo) (a) 07/05/1999, Eindhoven (Netherlands) (b) 1,93 (c) F - left winger (d) Liverpool FC (e) PSV Eindhoven

*** Gal - Jeff Gal (Jeffrey Joseph Gal) (a) 06/04/1993, Chicago, Illinois (United States) (b) 1,87 (c) G (d) Chicago Fire FC (e) Degerfors, Skövde AIK, BK Forward, Lidköpings FK, Bridges FC, Virginia Cavs, CU Bluejays, Chicago Inferno, CU Bluejays, Sockers FC

*** Gal - Rares Gal (Rareş Florian Gal) (a) 25/01/2001, Cluj-Napoca (Romania) (b) 1,86 (c) G (d) CSU Alba Iulia (e) CFR Cluj, CSC Selimbar

*** Gala - Antonio Gala (a) 07/06/2004, Napoli (Italy) (b) 1,75 (c) M - central midfielder (d) USD Sestri Levante 1919 (e) Sestri Levante, Internapoli

*** Galabov - Plamen Galabov (Пламен Йорданов Гълъбов) (a) 02/11/1995, Shumen (Bulgaria) (b) 1,91 (c) D - central defense (d) Maccabi Netanya (e) CSKA-Sofia, Etar, CSKA-Sofia, Etar, CSKA-Sofia, Litex Lovetch

*** Galán - Francisco Galán (Francisco Javier Denches Galán) (a) 03/06/2000, Pinto (Spain) (b) 1,84 (c) D - central defense (d) FC Ordino (e) Penya Encarnada

*** Galán - Javi Galán (Javier Galán Gil) (a) 19/11/1994, Badajoz (Spain) (b) 1,72 (c) D - left back (d) Atlético de Madrid (e) RC Celta, SD Huesca, Córdoba CF, Córdoba CF B, CD Badajoz, Flecha Negra

*** Galán - Jose Galán (Jose Antonio Pedrosa Galán) (a) 02/02/1986, León (Spain) (b) 1,77 (c) M - central midfielder (d) FC Bruno's Magpies (e) Valour FC, CP Villarrobledo, Valour FC, Al-Jabalain, Al-Shamal SC, Dreams, FC Santa Coloma, CE L'Hospitalet, RoPS, Persela, Ceahlăul, Aris Limassol, Shabab Al-Ordon, SKN St. Pölten, Pro Duta, Chainat FC, Cultural Leonesa, Níjar, Astorga, UD Almería B, CD Toledo, At. Madrid B

*** Galanopoulos - Konstantinos Galanopoulos (Κωνσταντίνος Γαλανόπουλος) (a) 28/12/1997, Athen (Greece) (b) 1,72 (c) M - central midfielder (d) AEK Athína FC (e) -

*** Galarza - Matías Galarza (Matías Alejandro Galarza) (a) 04/03/2002, San Isidro (Argentina) (b) 1,80 (c) M - central midfielder (d) KRC Genk (e) Argentinos Jrs., Argentinos Juniors II

*** Galchev - Patrik-Gabriel Galchev (Патрик-Габриел Галчев) (a) 14/04/2001, Zaragoza (Spain) (b) 1,78 (c) D - right back (d) Levski Sofia (e) -

*** Galcik - Roland Galcik (Roland Galčík) (a) 30/07/2001, Námestovo (Slovakia) (b) 1,73 (c) F - right winger (d) FK Zeleziarne Podbrezova (e) MSK Zilina, Podbrezova, MSK Zilina, Podbrezova

*** Galdames - Pablo Galdames (Pablo Ignacio Galdames Millán) (a) 30/12/1996, Santiago de Chile (Chile) (b) 1,76 (c) M - central midfielder (d) Génova (e) Cremonese, Genoa, Vélez Sarsfield, Unión Española, Unión Española B

*** Gale - Thierry Gale (Thierry Mikael Gale) (a) 01/05/2002, Bridgetown (Barbados) (b) 1,68 (c) F - left winger (d) FC Dila Gori (e) Honvéd, Notre Dame SC

*** Galea - Emanuel Galea (a) 17/12/1999, Mtarfa (Malta) (b) - (c) G (d) Gudja United FC (e) -

*** Galea - Jake Galea (a) 15/04/1996, ¿? (Malta) (b) 1,80 (c) G (d) Valletta FC (e) Etzella Ettelbrück, Balzan FC, Sliema Wanderers, Hamrun Spartans, St. Andrews FC
*** Galea - Lee Galea (a) 14/02/1988, ¿? (Malta) (b) 1,79 (c) D - central defense (d) Pietà Hotspurs FC (e) Senglea Ath., Zebbug Rangers, Santa Lucia FC, Zebbug Rangers, Santa Lucia FC, Zebbug Rangers, Gharghur FC, Zebbug Rangers, Tarxien
*** Galea - Paul Galea (a) 16/11/2002, ¿? (Malta) (b) - (c) D (d) Zebbug Rangers FC (e) -
*** Galeno - Galeno (Wenderson Rodrigues do Nascimento Galeno) (a) 22/10/1997, Barra da Corda (Brazil) (b) 1,79 (c) F - left winger (d) FC Porto (e) SC Braga, FC Porto, Rio Ave, FC Porto, Portimonense, FC Porto, FC Porto B, Anápolis, FC Porto B, Anápolis, Trindade
*** Galesic - Antonio Galesic (Antonio Galešić) (a) 15/04/2003, Zadar (Croatia) (b) 1,85 (c) M - attacking midfielder (d) HNK Rijeka (e) -
*** Galesic - Niko Galesic (Niko Galešić) (a) 26/03/2001, Berlin (Germany) (b) 1,87 (c) D - central defense (d) HNK Rijeka (e) Hrv Dragovoljac, HNK Rijeka
*** Galevski - Ivan Galevski (Иван Галевски) (a) 15/11/1996, Skopje (North Macedonia) (b) 1,84 (c) F - right winger (d) AP Brera (e) Pobeda Prilep, Struga, Sileks, Lusitano SAD, Pehcevo, Euromilk GL
*** Galic - Marin Galic (Marin Galić) (a) 21/09/1995, Kiseljak (Bosnia and Herzegovina) (b) 1,81 (c) D - right back (d) FK Zeljeznicar Sarajevo (e) Z. Sosnowiec, FK Krupa, Borac Banja Luka, Inter Zaprešić, Zrinjski Mostar, Mladost Kakanj, Branitelj Mostar, Zrinjski Mostar
*** Galic - Marko Galic (Marko Galić) (a) 13/02/1999, Imotski (Croatia) (b) - (c) G (d) HSK Posusje (e) HNK Tomislav T., HSK Posusje
*** Galilea - Einar Galilea (Einar Galilea Azaceta) (a) 22/05/1994, Vitoria-Gasteiz (Spain) (b) 1,85 (c) D - central defense (d) Málaga CF (e) NK Istra, Depor. Alavés B, NK Istra, Depor. Alavés B, FC Sochaux, Depor. Alavés B, NK Rudes, Depor. Alavés B
*** Galjé - Timothy Galjé (a) 05/06/2001, Duffel (Belgium) (b) 1,80 (c) G (d) RFC Seraing (e) -
*** Galkin - Andrey Galkin (Галкин Андрей) (a) 01/01/2005, ¿? (Kazakhstan) (b) 1,82 (c) F - center forward (d) Kyzylzhar SK Petropavlovsk II (e) -
*** Galkin - Maksim Galkin (Галкин Максим Евгеньевич) (a) 12/07/1999, Karaganda (Kazakhstan) (b) 1,73 (c) F - right winger (d) Shakhter Karaganda (e) Shakhter-Bulat, Shakhter K., Shakhter-Bulat, Bolat, Shakhter-Bulat
*** Galkin - Vladislav Galkin (Галкин Владислав Иванович) (a) 03/04/2002, Krasnogorsk (Russia) (b) 1,79 (c) M - attacking midfielder (d) Akron Togliatti (e) Akron Togliatti, Dinamo 2, RFS, Dinamo 2, Dinamo Moskva II
*** Gall - Romain Gall (a) 31/01/1995, Paris (France) (b) 1,76 (d) - (e) Mladost GAT, Malmö FF, Örebro SK, Malmö FF, Örebro SK, Malmö FF, StabÃ¦k, Malmö FF, GIF Sundsvall, Nyköpings BIS, Columbus Crew, Austin Aztex, Columbus Crew
*** Gallacher - Tony Gallacher (a) 23/07/1999, Glasgow (Scotland) (b) 1,73 (c) D - left back (d) St. Johnstone FC (e) Toronto, Falkirk FC
*** Gallagher - Ben Gallagher (a) 30/03/2002, ¿? (Northern Ireland) (b) - (c) F - left winger (d) Dungannon Swifts (e) Dergview, Dungannon
*** Gallagher - Chris Gallagher (Christopher Gallagher) (a) 30/03/1999, Belfast (Northern Ireland) (b) 1,75 (c) M - pivot (d) Cliftonville FC (e) Glentoran, Shrewsbury, Stourbridge, Shrewsbury, Stalybridge, Shrewsbury
*** Gallagher - Conor Gallagher (a) 06/02/2000, Epsom (England) (b) 1,82 (c) M - central midfielder (d) Chelsea FC (e) Crystal Palace, West Bromwich Albion, Swansea City, Charlton Ath.

*** Gallagher - Declan Gallagher (Declan Patrick Gallagher) (a) 13/02/1991, Rutherglen (Scotland) (b) 1,96 (c) D - central defense (d) Dundee United FC (e) St. Mirren, Aberdeen FC, Motherwell FC, Livingston FC, Dundee FC, Clyde FC, Stranraer

*** Gallagher - Marty Gallagher (Martin Gallagher) (a) 26/10/1990, Londonderry (Northern Ireland) (b) 1,78 (c) G (d) Coleraine FC (e) Institute FC, Derry City

*** Gallagher - Michael Gallagher (a) 09/07/2000, Letterkenny, Donegal (Ireland) (b) 1,78 (c) D - right back (d) University College Dublin (e) -

*** Gallapeni - Dion Gallapeni (a) 22/12/2004, ¿? (Serbia and Montenegro, now in Kosovo) (b) 1,76 (c) D - left back (d) FC Prishtina (e) -

*** Gallardo - Dani Gallardo (Daniel Gallardo Aragón) (a) 26/07/1990, La Línea de la Concepción (Spain) (b) 1,69 (c) D - left back (d) Lynx FC (e) Guadiaro, Cacereño, Burgos Promesas, Algeciras CF, AD Ceuta, Algeciras CF, San Roque Cádiz, R. B. Linense, Los Barrios, Atlético Zabal

*** Gallardo - David Gallardo (David Paul Gallardo) (a) 04/05/1991, Belfast (Northern Ireland) (b) - (c) D - central defense (d) Lions Gibraltar FC (e) Mons Calpe, Lions Gibraltar, Gibraltar Phoenix, Gibraltar Phoenix, Gibraltar Utd.

*** Gallardo - Luis Manuel Gallardo (Luis Manuel Gallardo Monje) (a) 20/07/1992, Algeciras (Spain) (b) 1,81 (c) F (d) Mons Calpe SC (e) Lions Gibraltar, FC College 1975, San Roque Cádiz, Los Barrios, San Roque Cádiz, Lions Gibraltar, San Roque Cádiz, Los Barrios, Algeciras B, Los Barrios, AD Taraguilla

*** Gallego - Adrià Gallego (Adrià Gallego Arias) (a) 09/04/1990, Lleida (Spain) (b) 1,84 (c) D - right back (d) Inter Club d'Escaldes (e) ACSM Poli Iasi, At. Saguntino, Ciudad de Ibiza, Storm FC, FC Ascó, Portugalete, CD Castellón, CD Binéfar, Deportivo B, UE Lleida

*** Gallo - Antonino Gallo (a) 05/01/2000, Palermo (Italy) (b) 1,83 (c) D - left back (d) US Lecce (e) V. Francavilla, Lecce, Palermo

*** Gallon - Gauthier Gallon (a) 23/04/1993, Nice (France) (b) 1,86 (c) G (d) Stade Rennais FC (e) Troyes, US Orléans, Nîmes, Nîmes B

*** Galovic - Nino Galovic (Nino Galović) (a) 06/07/1992, Supetar (Croatia) (b) 1,84 (c) D - central defense (d) FC Arouca (e) HNK Rijeka, Sagan Tosu, Dinamo Minsk, Sagan Tosu, Dinamo Minsk, FC Ashdod, RNK Split, Slaven Belupo, RNK Split

*** Galstyan - Arsen Galstyan (Արսեն Գալստյան) (a) 01/05/2002, Goris (Armenia) (b) 1,70 (c) D - left back (d) FC Ararat Yerevan (e) FC Noah, BKMA Yerevan, Ararat-Armenia II

*** Galstyan - Eduard Galstyan (Էդուարդ Գալստյան) (a) 01/05/2004, ¿? (Armenia) (b) 1,77 (c) M - pivot (d) FC Ararat Yerevan II (e) -

*** Galstyan - Serob Galstyan (Սերոբ Գալստյան) (a) 23/09/2002, Masis (Armenia) (b) 1,72 (c) M - right midfielder (d) FC Ararat Yerevan (e) BKMA Yerevan, Ararat II, Torpedo, FC Ani

*** Galushko - Arseniy Galushko (Галушко Арсений Викторович) (a) 09/06/2003, ¿? (Belarus) (b) - (c) F - left winger (d) Torpedo-BelAZ Zhodino II (e) RUOR Minsk

*** Gálvez - Lucas Gálvez (Lucas Emanuel Gálvez) (a) 05/04/1992, Rio Gallegos (Argentina) (b) - (c) F - right winger (d) - (e) FC Ordino, FS La Massana, Penya Encarnada, FS La Massana

*** Galym - Beybit Galym (Ғалым Бейбит) (a) 25/10/2004, ¿? (Kazakhstan) (b) 1,75 (c) M - attacking midfielder (d) Tobol Kostanay (e) Tobol II

*** Gama - Bruno Gama (Bruno Alexandre Vilela Gama) (a) 15/11/1987, Vila Verde (Portugal) (b) 1,75 (c) F - left winger (d) AEK Larnaca (e) Aris Thessaloniki, Alcorcón, RC Deportivo, Dnipro, RC Deportivo, Rio Ave, FC Porto, Vitória Setúbal, FC Porto, SC Braga, FC Porto B

*** Gamakov - Milen Gamakov (Милен Георгиев Гамаков) (a) 12/04/1994, Burgas (Bulgaria) (b) 1,89 (c) M - pivot (d) Dobrudzha Dobrich (e) Sozopol, Taraz, Zalgiris, Slavia Sofia, Lechia Gdánsk, Stomil, Lechia Gdánsk, Ruch, Lechia Gdánsk, Botev Plovdiv, Chern. Burgas, Neftochimik, Chern. Burgas

*** Gaman - Valerica Gaman (Marius Valerică Găman) (a) 25/02/1989, Băileşti (Romania) (b) 1,91 (c) D - central defense (d) FC Hermannstadt (e) CS U Craiova, Astra Giurgiu, Al-Shabab, FCSB, Karabükspor, Astra Giurgiu, FC Dinamo, FC U Craiova

*** Gambin - Matteo Gambin (a) 04/05/2004, ¿? (Malta) (b) 1,82 (c) M - attacking midfielder (d) - (e) Zabbar SP

*** Gamboa - Cristian Gamboa (Cristian Esteban Gamboa Luna) (a) 24/10/1989, Liberia (Costa Rica) (b) 1,75 (c) D - right back (d) VfL Bochum (e) Celtic FC, West Bromwich Albion, Rosenborg, FC København, Rosenborg, FC København, Fredrikstad, Águilas, Mpl. Liberia II

*** Gamboa - João Gamboa (João Pedro da Costa Gamboa) (a) 31/08/1996, Póvoa de Varzim (Portugal) (b) 1,87 (c) M - pivot (d) Pogon Szczecin (e) OH Leuven, Estoril Praia, OH Leuven, Estoril Praia, Marítimo, Chaves, Marítimo, SC Braga, Braga B

*** Gameiro - Kévin Gameiro (a) 09/05/1987, Senlis (France) (b) 1,72 (c) F - center forward (d) Racing Club Strasbourg (e) Valencia CF, Atlético Madrid, Sevilla FC, Paris Saint-Germain, FC Lorient, Racing Club Strasbourg, Racing Strasbourg B

*** Gammelby - Jens Martin Gammelby (a) 05/02/1995, Ikast (Denmark) (b) 1,92 (c) D - right back (d) Hamarkameratene (e) Brøndby IF, Miedź Legnica, Brøndby IF, Lyngby BK, Brøndby IF, Silkeborg IF

*** Gamonal - José Luis Gamonal (José Luis Gamonal Ruiz) (a) 09/10/1989, Temuco (Chile) (b) 1,80 (c) G (d) Marsaxlokk FC (e) Fernández Vial, Cobresal, Deportes Temuco

*** Ganago - Ignatius Ganago (Ignatius Kpene Ganago) (a) 16/02/1999, Douala (Cameroon) (b) 1,76 (c) F - center forward (d) FC Nantes (e) RC Lens, OGC Nice, OGC Nice B, Brasseries

*** Ganah - Amir Ganah (גנאח אמיר) (a) 07/09/2004, ¿? (Israel) (b) - (c) M - attacking midfielder (d) Hapoel Beer Sheva (e) -

*** Ganayem - Ihab Ganayem (גנאים איהאב) (a) 11/06/1996, Sakhnin (Israel) (b) 1,87 (c) M - pivot (d) FK Aktobe (e) Bnei Sakhnin

*** Ganchas - Pedro Ganchas (Pedro Luís Machado Ganchas) (a) 31/05/2000, Lisboa (Portugal) (b) 1,90 (c) D - central defense (d) FC Paços de Ferreira (e) Benfica B, Sacavenense

*** Ganchev - Aleksandar Ganchev (Александър Пламенов Ганчев) (a) 09/07/2001, Sofia (Bulgaria) (b) 1,85 (c) D - central defense (d) Ludogorets Razgrad II (e) -

*** Gandelman - Omri Gandelman (גנדלמן עמרי) (a) 16/05/2000, Hod haSharon (Israel) (b) 1,88 (c) M - central midfielder (d) Maccabi Netanya (e) -

*** Gando - Marcelin Gando (Aimé Marcelin Gando Biala) (a) 27/02/1997, Loum (Cameroon) (b) 1,74 (c) F - left winger (d) Rabotnicki Skopje (e) Petrojet, EN Paralimniou, FCI Levadia, Apejes FC, New Star FC, Les Astres FC, Unisport Bafang

*** Ganea - Cristian Ganea (Cristian George Ganea) (a) 24/05/1992, Bistriţa (Romania) (b) 1,76 (c) D - left back (d) Panathinaikos FC (e) Aris Thessaloniki, Athletic, FC Viitorul, Athletic, CD Numancia, Athletic, FC Viitorul, FC Brasov, Sageata Navodar, CS U Craiova, ASA Tg. Mures, RCD Mallorca B, CD Santanyi, RCD Mallorca B

*** Ganea - George Ganea (George Dănuţ Ganea) (a) 26/05/1999, Bucharest (Romania) (b) 1,80 (c) F - center forward (d) Újpest FC (e) FC U Craiova, FCV Farul, FC Arges, FCV Farul, CFR Cluj, Academia Rapid

*** Ganev - Gennadiy Ganev (Ганєв Геннадій Юрійович) (a) 15/05/1990, Kamchik, Odessa Oblast (Soviet Union, now in Ukraine) (b) 1,86 (c) G (d) CSKA 1948 (e) Beroe, Dunav, Vereya, Ingulets, Zirka, Girnyk KR, Stal Alchevsk, Nyva Vinnytsia, Chornomorets 2, Chornomorets II

*** Ganev - Petko Ganev (Петко Танев Ганев) (a) 17/09/1996, Haskovo (Bulgaria) (b) 1,83 (c) D - central defense (d) Botev Vratsa (e) Montana, Arda Kardzhali, Litex Lovetch, Arda Kardzhali, Litex Lovetch, Botev Vratsa, Litex Lovetch, Sozopol, Vereya

*** Ganiou - Ismaëlo Ganiou (Pierre-Ismaëlo Ganiou) (a) 14/03/2005, ¿? (France) (b) 1,91 (c) D - central defense (d) RC Lens B (e) -

*** Gannon - Sean Gannon (Seán Gannon) (a) 11/07/1991, ¿? (Ireland) (b) 1,83 (c) D - right back (d) Shamrock Rovers (e) Dundalk FC, St. Patrick's Ath., Shamrock Rovers

*** Gano - Zinho Gano (a) 13/10/1993, St.-Katelijne-Waver (Belgium) (b) 1,98 (c) F - center forward (d) SV Zulte Waregem (e) KRC Genk, KV Kortrijk, KRC Genk, Royal Antwerp, KRC Genk, KV Oostende, Waasland-Beveren, KV Brugge, Excelsior Mouscron, KV Brugge, Lommel United, KV Brugge

*** Gantenbein - Adrian Gantenbein (Adrian Tobias Gantenbein) (a) 18/04/2001, Winterthur (Switzerland) (b) 1,83 (c) D - right back (d) FC Winterthur (e) -

*** Gantus - Maroun Gantus (גנטוס מארון) (a) 15/06/1996, Sakhnin (Israel) (b) - (c) D - central defense (d) Ihud Bnei Sakhnin (e) -

*** Ganusauskas - Marius Ganusauskas (a) 13/05/1994, Jonava (Lithuania) (b) 1,84 (c) F - center forward (d) FK Jonava (e) Snaefell, Jonava

*** Ganvoula - Silvère Ganvoula (Silvère Ganvoula M'boussy) (a) 29/06/1996, Brazzaville (Congo) (b) 1,91 (c) F - center forward (d) BSC Young Boys (e) VfL Bochum, Cercle Brugge, VfL Bochum, RSC Anderlecht, VfL Bochum, RSC Anderlecht, KV Mechelen, RSC Anderlecht, KVC Westerlo, RSC Anderlecht, KVC Westerlo, Elazigspor, Raja Casablanca, Sainte Anne

*** Gaponov - Ilya Gaponov (Гапонов Илья Сергеевич) (a) 25/10/1997, Orel (Russia) (b) 1,85 (c) D - central defense (d) Krylya Sovetov Samara (e) Spartak Moskva, KS Samara, Spartak Moskva, Spartak-2, Strogino Moskva, Strogino II, Master-Saturn

*** Gaprindashvili - Aleksandre Gaprindashvili (ალექსანდრე გაფრინდაშვილი) (a) 16/07/2004, ¿? (Georgia) (b) - (c) D (d) FC Saburtalo II (e) FC Dila

*** Gaprindashvili - Giorgi Gaprindashvili (გიორგი გაფრინდაშვილი) (a) 06/05/1995, ¿? (Georgia) (b) 1,69 (c) D - right back (d) FC Dila Gori (e) Shukura, Merani Tbilisi, WIT Georgia, FC Gagra, Sioni Bolnisi, Rustavi, Sioni Bolnisi, FC Dila

*** Gaprindashvili - Tornike Gaprindashvili (თორნიკე გაფრინდაშვილი) (a) 20/07/1997, Tbilisi (Georgia) (b) 1,71 (c) F - right winger (d) Zagłębie Lubin (e) Dinamo Batumi, FC Gagra, FC Sasco

*** Garananga - Munashe Garananga (Munashe Garananga) (a) 18/01/2001, Harare (Zimbabwe) (b) 1,86 (c) D - central defense (d) FC Sheriff Tiraspol (e) Dynamo Brest

*** Garavelis - Athanasios Garavelis (Αθανάσιος Γκαραβέλης) (a) 06/08/1992, Kozani (Greece) (b) 1,90 (c) G (d) Niki Volou (e) PAS Lamia, Volos NPS, AO Xanthi, Panegialios, AO Xanthi, Panthrakikos, AO Xanthi, FS Kozani

*** Garay - Benjamín Garay (a) 19/04/2000, Rosario (Argentina) (b) 1,83 (c) D - central defense (d) Pontevedra CF (e) RCD Mallorca B, Mérida AD, Zamora CF, Unionistas CF, RM Castilla, UD Melilla, RM Castilla

*** Garbett - Matthew Garbett (Matthew Jimmy David Garbett) (a) 13/04/2002, London (England) (b) 1,88 (c) M - central midfielder (d) NAC Breda (e) Torino, NAC Breda, Torino, Falkenbergs FF

*** Garcia - Christian Garcia (Christian Garcia Gonzalez) (a) 04/02/1999, Andorra la Vella (Andorra) (b) - (c) D - central defense (d) - (e) UE Santa Coloma, Marchamalo, SD Tarazona, AD Alcorcón B, UE Santa Coloma, FC Ordino, FC Andorra

*** Garcia - Emili Garcia (Emili Josep Garcia Miramontes) (a) 11/01/1989, Andorra la Vella (Andorra) (b) 1,88 (c) D - central defense (d) UE Santa Coloma (e) IC d'Escaldes, FC Andorra, Le Pontet, ES Pennoise, Racing Lermeño, FC Andorra

*** Garcia - Jean-Carlos Garcia (Jean-Carlos Anthony Garcia) (a) 05/07/1992, Gibraltar (Gibraltar) (b) 1,76 (c) D - right back (d) Lynx FC (e) Glacis United, Bruno's Magpies, Gibraltar Utd., Lincoln FC, Gibraltar Phoenix, Lincoln FC, R. B. Linense, Atlético Zabal, R. B. Linense

*** Garcia - Kieron Garcia (Kieron Joseph Garcia) (a) 04/08/1998, Gibraltar (Gibraltar) (b) 1,70 (c) M - central midfielder (d) FC Manchester 62 (e) Bruno's Magpies, Manchester 62

*** Garcia - Ulisses Garcia (Ulisses Alexandre Garcia Lopes) (a) 11/01/1996, Almada (Portugal) (b) 1,83 (c) D - left back (d) BSC Young Boys (e) Werder Bremen, 1.FC Nürnberg, Werder Bremen, Grasshoppers

*** Garcia - William Edoardo Garcia (a) 13/05/2002, ¿? (Italy) (b) - (c) F - right winger (d) SS Folgore/Falciano (e) -

*** García - Aleix García (Aleix García Serrano) (a) 28/06/1997, Ulldecona (Spain) (b) 1,73 (c) M - central midfielder (d) Girona FC (e) SD Eibar, FC Dinamo, Manchester City, Excelsior Mouscron, Manchester City, Girona FC, Manchester City, Villarreal CF B, Villarreal CF C

*** García - Álvaro García (Álvaro García Rivera) (a) 27/10/1992, Utrera (Spain) (b) 1,67 (c) F - left winger (d) Rayo Vallecano (e) Cádiz CF, Granada CF, Cádiz CF, Granada CF, Racing, Granada B, San Fernando CD, Utrera

*** García - Ángel García (Ángel García Cabezali) (a) 03/02/1993, Madrid (Spain) (b) 1,85 (c) D - left back (d) AEK Larnaca (e) Wisła Płock, Cultural Leonesa, Real Valladolid, R. Valladolid B, Real Madrid C

*** García - Borja García (Borja García Freire) (a) 02/11/1990, Torremocha de Jarama (Spain) (b) 1,75 (c) M - attacking midfielder (d) Girona FC (e) SD Huesca, Girona FC, RM Castilla, Córdoba CF, RM Castilla, Córdoba CF, Rayo Vallecano, Rayo B, Villaverde CF

*** García - Carlo García (Carlo Adriano García Prades) (a) 12/02/2001, Villarreal (Spain) (b) 1,82 (c) M - attacking midfielder (d) Villarreal CF B (e) Villarreal CF C

*** García - Carlos García (Carlos García-Die Sánchez) (a) 07/07/2000, Barcelona (Spain) (b) 1,88 (c) D - central defense (d) Cádiz CF Mirandilla (e) Cornellà, Terrassa FC, Cornellà

*** García - Dani García (Daniel García Carrillo) (a) 24/05/1990, Zumarraga (Spain) (b) 1,79 (c) M - central midfielder (d) Athletic Club (e) SD Eibar, Real Sociedad B, SD Eibar, Real Sociedad B, SD Eibar, Real Sociedad B, Getafe CF B, Alicante

*** García - David García (David García Zubiria) (a) 14/02/1994, Pamplona (Spain) (b) 1,86 (c) D - central defense (d) CA Osasuna (e) Cultural Leonesa, CA Osasuna, Osasuna Prom.

*** García - Eric García (Eric García Martret) (a) 09/01/2001, Barcelona (Spain) (b) 1,82 (c) D - central defense (d) FC Barcelona (e) Manchester City

*** García - Ernesto García (Ernesto García Gallego) (a) 23/01/1986, Palma de Mallorca (Spain) (b) 1,76 (c) M - central midfielder (d) - (e) Lynx FC, Santa Catalina, CE Andratx, AD Llerenense, Penya Deportiva, CD Gerena, Somozas, Algeciras CF, AD Ceuta, CD Binissalem, Racing Ferrol, At. Baleares, Mazarrón FC
*** García - Fran García (Francisco José García Torres) (a) 14/08/1999, Bolaños de Calatrava (Spain) (b) 1,69 (c) D - left back (d) Real Madrid CF (e) Rayo Vallecano, RM Castilla, Rayo Vallecano, RM Castilla
*** García - Germán García (Germán García Fernández) (a) 01/02/2004, Alcalá de Guadaíra (Spain) (b) - (c) G (d) Real Betis Balompié C (e) -
*** García - Germán García (Germán García) (a) 18/02/1996, ¿? (Argentina) (b) 1,74 (c) M - attacking midfielder (d) - (e) Europa Point FC, ACyD Altos Hornos Zapla, Lynx FC
*** García - Joan García (Joan García Pons) (a) 04/05/2001, Sallent de Llobregat (Spain) (b) 1,91 (c) G (d) RCD Espanyol (e) RCD Espanyol B
*** García - Kike García (Enrique García Martínez) (a) 25/11/1989, Motilla de Palancar (Spain) (b) 1,86 (c) F - center forward (d) Deportivo Alavés (e) CA Osasuna, SD Eibar, Middlesbrough, Real Murcia, Murcia Imperial, Quintanar Rey
*** García - Levi García (Levi Samuel García) (a) 20/11/1997, Santa Flora (Trinidad and Tobago) (b) 1,82 (c) F - center forward (d) AEK Athína FC (e) B. Jerusalem, Kiryat Shmona, AZ Alkmaar, Excelsior, AZ Alkmaar, Central FC, T&TEC SC
*** García - Manu García (Manuel García Alonso) (a) 02/01/1998, Oviedo (Spain) (b) 1,69 (c) M - attacking midfielder (d) Aris Thessaloniki (e) Real Sporting, Alavés, Real Sporting, Manchester City, Toulouse, Manchester City, NAC Breda, Depor. Alavés B
*** García - Marc García (Marc García Renom) (a) 21/03/1988, Andorra la Vella (Andorra) (b) 1,74 (c) D - left back (d) UE Engordany (e) Sant Andreu, Montañesa, Granollers, UE Rubí, Llagostera, Palamós CF, Llagostera, CA Monzón, UD Fraga, AEC Manlleu
*** García - Mateo García (Mateo Ezequiel García) (a) 10/09/1996, Córdoba (Argentina) (b) 1,72 (c) F - right winger (d) Atlas Guadalajara (e) Aris Thessaloniki, Crvena zvezda, UD Las Palmas, Aris Thessaloniki, UD Las Palmas, Alcorcón, UD Las Palmas, CA Osasuna, UD Las Palmas, Instituto
*** García - Matías García (Matías Nicolás García) (a) 22/07/1996, La Banda (Argentina) (b) - (c) M - pivot (d) Floriana FC (e) Senglea Ath., Belgrano II, Senglea Ath., Belgrano II
*** García - Nacho García (Ignacio García Antuña) (a) 01/01/2001, Pola de Siero (Spain) (b) - (c) D - left back (d) - (e) Penya Encarnada, Luarca CF, Urraca CF, CD Praviano
*** García - Nauzet García (Nauzet García Santana) (a) 08/04/1994, Santa Cruz de Tenerife (Spain) (b) 1,84 (c) G (d) Lincoln Red Imps FC (e) Mensajero, UD Tamaraceite, Chennai City, Real Ávila, Rayo Cantabria, Recreativo Granada, CF Fuenlabrada, Pobla de Mafumet CF, CD Tenerife B
*** García - Pere García (Pere Joan García Bauzà) (a) 22/03/2002, Ca'n Picafort (Spain) (b) 1,93 (c) G (d) RCD Mallorca B (e) -
*** García - Raúl García (Raúl García Escudero) (a) 11/07/1986, Zizur Mayor (Spain) (b) 1,84 (c) F - center forward (d) Athletic Club (e) Atlético Madrid, CA Osasuna, Atlético Madrid, CA Osasuna, Osasuna Prom.
*** García - Raúl García (Raúl García González) (a) 27/01/2000, León (Spain) (b) 1,88 (c) G (d) RC Celta Fortuna (c) Unionistas CF, Celta B, Astorga, Celta B

*** García - Rubén García (Rubén García Canales) (a) 23/10/1998, Elche (Spain) (b) 1,80 (c) D - right back (d) Asteras Tripolis (e) At. Levante, CD Castellón, Elche Ilicitano

*** García - Rubén García (Rubén García Santos) (a) 14/07/1993, Xàtiva (Spain) (b) 1,71 (c) F - left winger (d) CA Osasuna (e) Levante UD, CA Osasuna, Levante UD, Real Sporting, Levante UD, Levante B

*** García - Santi García (Santiago García González) (a) 29/08/2001, Madrid (Spain) (b) 1,84 (c) M - attacking midfielder (d) Getafe CF B (e) Trival Vald. B

*** García - Unai García (Unai García Lugea) (a) 03/02/1992, Esquiroz (Spain) (b) 1,86 (c) D - central defense (d) CA Osasuna (e) Osasuna Prom., CD Tudelano, Osasuna Prom.

*** García - Víctor García (Víctor Garcia Marín) (a) 31/05/1994, Requena (Spain) (b) 1,80 (c) D - left back (d) Málaga CF (e) Śląsk Wroclaw, CD Castellón, CD Ebro, UCAM Murcia, Badalona, CD Tenerife, Pobla de Mafumet CF, CD Tenerife, AE Prat

*** Garcia Tsotidis - Alexandros Garcia Tsotidis (Alexandros Elias Garcia Tsotidis) (a) 19/07/2004, Tyresö (Sweden) (b) 1,78 (c) F - center forward (d) - (e) Djurgardens IF

*** Gardarsson (c) M (d) Kári Akranes (e) - - Hektor Bergmann Gardarsson (c) M (d) Kári Akranes (e) -

*** Gardawski - Michael Gardawski (Michał Gardawski) (a) 25/09/1990, Köln (Germany) (b) 1,77 (c) M - left midfielder (d) - (e) Asteras Tripoli, PAS Giannina, Cracovia, Korona Kielce, Hansa Rostock, MSV Duisburg, Viktoria Köln, VfL Osnabrück, 1.FC Köln, Stuttgart II, 1.FC Köln, Carl Zeiss Jena, 1.FC Köln

*** Gareginyan - Yuri Gareginyan (Յուրի Գարեգինյան) (a) 03/02/1994, Yerevan (Armenia) (b) 1,80 (c) M - pivot (d) Alashkert Yerevan CF (e) Pyunik Yerevan, FC Noah, Ararat Yerevan, Ararat II, Pyunik Yerevan B

*** Gargalatzidis - Alexandros Gargalatzidis (Αλέξανδρος Γκαργκαλατζίδης) (a) 12/04/2000, Thessaloniki (Greece) (b) 1,81 (c) F - center forward (d) - (e) Proodeftiki, OFI Creta, Olympiakos Volou, OFI Creta, Suduva, OFI Creta, PAOK, AO Xanthi, PAOK

*** Garganciuc - Rostislav Garganciuc (a) 16/04/2003, ¿? (Moldova) (b) 1,75 (c) F - right winger (d) FC Zimbru-2 Chisinau (e) Codru

*** Garita - Arnold Garita (Paul Arnold Garita) (a) 18/06/1995, Douala (Cameroon) (b) 1,86 (c) F - center forward (d) Al-Faisaly FC (e) FC Arges, Bourg-en-Bresse, RSC Charleroi, FC Villefranche, RSC Charleroi, US Boulogne, RSC Charleroi, USL Dunkerque, RSC Charleroi, Bristol City, Plymouth Argyle, Bristol City, LB Châteauroux, Châteauroux B

*** Garmash - Denys Garmash (Гармаш Денис Вікторович) (a) 19/04/1990, Milove, Lugansk Oblast (Soviet Union, now in Ukraine) (b) 1,86 (c) M - attacking midfielder (d) FC Dinamo de Kiev (e) Çaykur Rizespor, Dinamo Kyïv, Dinamo Kiev II, Dynamo 2 Kyiv, RVUFK Kyiv

*** Garnacho - Alejandro Garnacho (Alejandro Garnacho Ferreyra) (a) 01/07/2004, Madrid (Spain) (b) 1,80 (c) F - left winger (d) Manchester United (e) -

*** Garnås - Espen Garnås (Espen Bjørnsen Garnås) (a) 31/12/1994, Nesbyen (Norway) (b) 1,90 (c) D - central defense (d) Lillestrøm SK (e) Ullensaker/Kisa, Kjelsås, Hallingdal FK

*** Garner - James Garner (James David Garner) (a) 13/03/2001, Birkenhead (England) (b) 1,82 (c) M - pivot (d) Everton FC (e) Manchester Utd., Nottingham Forest, Manchester Utd., Nottingham Forest, Manchester Utd., Watford, Manchester Utd.

*** Garofani - Giovanni Garofani (Giovanni Gabriele Garofani) (a) 20/10/2002, Roma (Italy) (b) 1,88 (c) G (d) Juventus Next Gen (e) -

*** Garos - Mickael Garos (a) 10/05/1988, Rouen (France) (b) 1,81 (c) M - central midfielder (d) FC Schifflange 95 (e) RFCU Luxembourg, Swift Hesperange, F91 Dudelange, Differdange 03, F91 Dudelange, Progrès Niederkorn, Neuweg, SR Saint-Dié

*** Garratt - Tyler Garratt (Tyler John Garratt) (a) 26/10/1996, Lincoln (England) (b) 1,82 (c) D - left back (d) Europa Point FC (e) Flint Town, Spennymoor Town, Flint Town, Northwich Vic, Cefn Druids, Bangor City, Chorley, Stockport, Wrexham, Stockport, Doncaster Rovers, AFC Wimbledon, Doncaster Rovers, Eastleigh, Doncaster Rovers

*** Garré - Benjamín Garré (Benjamín Antonio Garré) (a) 11/07/2000, Buenos Aires (Argentina) (b) 1,72 (c) F - left winger (d) Krylya Sovetov Samara (e) Racing, Huracán, Racing

*** Garreta - Félix Garreta (Félix Martí Garreta) (a) 21/04/2004, Palau-solità i Plegamans (Spain) (b) 1,83 (c) D - central defense (d) SD Amorebieta (e) SD Amorebieta, Real Betis, Betis Deportivo

*** Garrett - Robert Garrett (a) 05/05/1988, Belfast (Northern Ireland) (b) 1,70 (c) M - central midfielder (d) Glenavon FC (e) Linfield, Portadown, Linfield, FC Edmonton, Linfield, Stoke City, Wrexham, Stoke City, Wrexham, Stoke City

*** Garrido - Aleix Garrido (Aleix Garrido Cañizares) (a) 22/02/2004, Ripoll (Spain) (b) 1,70 (c) M - central midfielder (d) FC Barcelona Atlètic (e) -

*** Garrido - Enzo Garrido (a) 26/07/2003, Toulouse (France) (b) 1,82 (c) G (d) - (e) OGC Nice B

*** Garrido - Iván Garrido (Iván Garrido Ciaurriz) (a) 01/11/1994, Calahorra (Spain) (b) 1,74 (c) F - left winger (d) FC Santa Coloma (e) Bergantiños FC, AC Escaldes, Haro Deportivo, Unionistas CF, CD Izarra, CD Lealtad, CD Izarra, Calahorra, CD Alfaro, CD Berceo, UD Logroñés B

*** Garrido - Jon Ander Garrido (Jon Ander Garrido Moracia) (a) 09/10/1989, Bilbao (Spain) (b) 1,85 (c) M - pivot (d) - (e) Cádiz CF, CD Mirandés, Cádiz CF, Racing Ferrol, Cádiz CF, Granada CF, Cádiz CF, Granada CF, Barakaldo CF, CD Getxo

*** Garro - Sykes Garro (Sykes Al Garro) (a) 26/02/1993, Gibraltar (Gibraltar) (b) 1,80 (c) M - left midfielder (d) Mons Calpe SC (e) Lions Gibraltar, St Joseph's FC, Lincoln FC, Europa FC, Lions Gibraltar, Lions Pilots

*** Gartenmann - Stefan Gartenmann (a) 02/02/1997, Roskilde (Denmark) (b) 1,87 (d) FC Midtjylland (e) SönderjyskE, Heerenveen

*** Gartland - Brian Gartland (a) 04/11/1986, Dublin (Ireland) (b) 1,80 (c) D - central defense (d) - (e) Dundalk FC, Portadown, Monaghan United, Shelbourne, Bray Wanderers

*** Gartler - Paul Gartler (a) 10/03/1997, Gleisdorf (Austria) (b) 1,87 (c) G (d) SK Rapid Wien (e) SV Kapfenberg, Rapid Wien, Rapid Wien II

*** Gartside - Nathan Gartside (a) 08/03/1998, Maydown (Northern Ireland) (b) - (c) G (d) Cliftonville FC (e) Derry City, Chelmsford, Institute FC

*** Garuch - Marcin Garuch (a) 14/09/1988, Legnica (Poland) (b) 1,54 (c) M - right midfielder (d) Miedz Legnica II (e) GKS Belchatow, OFK Grbalj, Miedź Legnica, Chojniczanka, Miedź Legnica

*** Garutti - Guilherme Garutti (Guilherme Gomes Garutti) (a) 08/03/1994, ¿? (Brazil) (b) 1,94 (c) D - central defense (d) Petrolul Ploiesti (e) CS Mioveni, Sertãozinho, Aparecidense, Portuguesa, Boa Esporte, São Caetano, AA Anapolina, Oeste

*** Garzia - Alejandro Garzia (a) 21/03/2002, ¿? (Malta) (b) 1,80 (c) D - central defense (d) Floriana FC (e) -
*** Garziano - Giuseppe Garziano (a) 11/12/2001, ¿? (Italy) (b) 1,71 (c) F - attacking midfielder (d) - (e) Murata, Marsala
*** Gasal - Hamza Gasal (a) 16/12/2002, Travnik (Bosnia and Herzegovina) (b) 1,70 (c) F - left winger (d) FK Zeljeznicar Sarajevo (e) -
*** Gasc - Valentín Gasc (Valentín Román Gasc) (a) 09/10/2000, Temperley (Argentina) (b) 1,72 (c) M - central midfielder (d) SJK Seinäjoki (e) SJK II
*** Gasevic - Ognjen Gasevic (Огњен Гашевић) (a) 02/04/2002, ¿? (RF Yugoslavia, now in Montenegro) (b) 1,81 (c) F - left winger (d) Buducnost Podgorica (e) Rudar Pljevlja, OFK Titograd
*** Gashi - Armend Gashi (a) 29/01/2001, Prishtinë (RF Yugoslavia, now in Kosovo) (b) - (c) F - left winger (d) KF Trepca 89 (e) FC Prishtina, KF Vëllaznimi, FC Prishtina
*** Gashi - Eliot Gashi (a) 15/04/1995, Pejë (Yugoslavia, now in Kosovo) (b) - (c) F - right winger (d) Racing FC Union Luxembourg (e) F91 Dudelange, US Hostert, F91 Dudelange, Union Titus Petange, UT Petingen II, Remich-Bous, Lamadelaine, Progrès Niederkorn, Lamadelaine
*** Gashi - Fatlum Gashi (a) 12/11/1995, ¿? (RF Yugoslavia, now in Kosovo) (b) 1,63 (c) M - central midfielder (d) KF Drenica (e) KF Dukagjini, FC Besa, KF Istogu, FC Besa, KF Istogu
*** Gashi - Flamur Gashi (a) 06/06/2000, ¿? (RF Yugoslavia, now in Kosovo) (b) 1,88 (c) G (d) FC Malisheva (e) FC Ballkani, KF Liria
*** Gashi - Kushtrim Gashi (a) 15/11/1992, ¿? (Yugoslavia, now in Kosovo) (b) - (c) M - central midfielder (d) FC Prishtina (e) FC Ballkani, KF Vëllaznimi, KF Istogu, FC Besa
*** Gasiunas - Emilis Gasiunas (Emilis Gasiūnas) (a) 12/06/2003, ¿? (Lithuania) (b) 1,87 (c) M - central midfielder (d) FA Siauliai (e) -
*** Gaspar - Bruno Gaspar (Bruno Miguel Boialvo Gaspar) (a) 21/04/1993, Évora (Portugal) (b) 1,80 (c) D - right back (d) Vitória Guimarães SC (e) Sporting Lisboa, Vancouver, Sporting Lisboa, Olympiakos, Sporting Lisboa, Fiorentina, Vitória Guimarães, Benfica B, Vitória Guimarães, Benfica B
*** Gaspar - Gabriel Gaspar (Gabriel Gaspar Pereira) (a) 20/07/1990, Coimbra (Portugal) (b) 1,83 (c) M - pivot (d) Kevin Marques (e) Victoria Rosport, CS Grevenmacher, Victoria Rosport, CS Grevenmacher, Victoria Rosport
*** Gaspar - Ramon Gaspar (Dobrin Ramon Gaşpar) (a) 02/02/2003, Mediaş (Romania) (b) 1,80 (c) M - attacking midfielder (d) Jiul Petrosani (e) CSM Focsani, FC Arges, Gaz Metan
*** Gasparovic - Lukas Gasparovic (Lukáš Gašparovič) (a) 17/02/1993, Bratislava (Slovakia) (b) 1,75 (c) M - central midfielder (d) FC Petrzalka (e) Banska Bystrica, FC Petrzalka, SV Stripfing, Svaty Jur, Slovan B, Iskra Borcice, Slovan B
*** Gasperoni - Alex Gasperoni (a) 30/06/1984, Città di San Marino (San Marino) (b) 1,80 (c) M - central midfielder (d) AC Libertas (e) Tre Penne, United Riccione, Tre Penne, Murata, San Marino
*** Gasperoni - Lorenzo Gasperoni (a) 03/01/1990, ¿? (San Marino) (b) - (c) M - central midfielder (d) AC Libertas (e) Juvenes-Dogana
*** Gasperoni - Marco Gasperoni (a) 18/02/1992, Rimini (Italy) (b) - (c) D - right back (d) La Fiorita 1967 (e) Bellaria Igea Marina, Rimini
*** Gaspuitis - Vytas Gaspuitis (Vytas Gašpuitis) (a) 04/03/1994, Šiauliai (Lithuania) (b) 1,97 (c) D - central defense (d) - (e) SLNA FC, FA Siauliai, Dunfermline A., Panevezys, Atlantas, Siauliai, Venta

*** Gassama - Djeidi Gassama (a) 10/09/2003, Nieleba Haouisse (Mauritania) (b) 1,77 (c) F - left winger (d) París Saint-Germain FC B (e) KAS Eupen, Paris Saint Germain B

*** Gassama - Sekou Gassama (Sekou Gassama Cissokho) (a) 06/05/1995, Granollers (Spain) (b) 1,89 (c) F - center forward (d) Anorthosis Famagusta (e) Real Valladolid, Racing, Real Valladolid, Málaga CF, Real Valladolid, CF Fuenlabrada, Real Valladolid, CF Fuenlabrada, Real Valladolid, UD Almería, Valencia Mestalla, UD Almería, UD Almería B, Sant Andreu, Badalona, Bergantiños FC, Rayo B, R. Valladolid B, UD Almería B

*** Gastien - Johan Gastien (a) 25/01/1988, Niort (France) (b) 1,79 (c) M - pivot (d) Clermont Foot 63 (e) Stade Brestois, Dijon, Chamois Niort, Niort B

*** Gaston - Alfie Gaston (a) 11/10/2007, ¿? (Northern Ireland) (b) - (c) M (d) - (e) Coleraine FC

*** Gaszczyk - Pavel Gaszczyk (a) 17/02/2005, ¿? (Czech Rep.) (b) 1,79 (c) D - left back (d) FC Zbrojovka Brno (e) Viktoria Plzen B

*** Gatt - Kyle Gatt (a) 12/06/1996, ¿? (Malta) (b) - (c) D - central defense (d) Mosta FC (e) Tarxien, Mosta FC, San Gwann FC, Mosta FC, San Gwann FC, Dingli Swallows

*** Gatt - Luca Gatt (a) 21/12/1999, ¿? (Malta) (b) - (c) M (d) Pietà Hotspurs FC (e) -

*** Gattei Colonna - Alex Gattei Colonna (Alex Gattei Colonna) (a) 16/07/1988, ¿? (Italy) (b) - (c) D - central defense (d) Polisportiva Stella Rimini (e) SS Folgore, Sant'Ermete, Juvenes-Dogana, Tre Penne, Juvenes-Dogana

*** Gatti - Federico Gatti (a) 24/06/1998, Rivoli (Italy) (b) 1,90 (c) D - central defense (d) Juventus de Turín (e) Frosinone, Juventus, Frosinone, Pro Patria, Verbania, Pavarolo, Pavarolo, Saluzzo, Pavarolo

*** Gatti - Tommaso Gatti (a) 14/07/2003, ¿? (San Marino) (b) - (c) F - center forward (d) SC Faetano (e) -

*** Gau - Alexandru Gau (Alexandru Gău) (a) 27/01/2004, ¿? (Moldova) (b) 1,81 (c) D - left back (d) CS Stiinta Miroslava (e) ACSM Poli Iasi, V. Darabani, ACSM Poli Iasi, V. Darabani, Zimbru Chisinau

*** Gauci - Christian Gauci (a) 26/12/2001, ¿? (Malta) (b) - (c) D - central defense (d) Valletta FC (e) San Gwann FC

*** Gauci - Clive Gauci (a) 24/04/1996, ¿? (Malta) (b) - (c) M - attacking midfielder (d) Gzira United FC (e) Naxxar Lions FC, Gzira Utd., Zebbug Rangers, Pietà Hotspurs, Sirens FC, Pietà Hotspurs

*** Gauci - Matthew Gauci (Matthew Robert Gauci) (a) 02/09/1991, ¿? (Malta) (b) - (c) D - left back (d) Zejtun Corinthians FC (e) Qrendi FC, Gzira Utd., Marsa FC, Hamrun Spartans, St. Andrews FC, Zebbug Rangers, Fgura Utd., Zebbug Rangers, Hibernians FC, Qormi FC, Hibernians FC, Hamrun Spartans, Hibernians FC

*** Gaudiesius - Vykintas Gaudiesius (Vykintas Gaudiešius) (a) 19/07/2006, ¿? (Lithuania) (b) 1,88 (c) G (d) BE1 National Football Academy (e) Dziugas B

*** Gaustad - Dennis Bakke Gaustad (a) 01/05/2004, Trondheim (Norway) (b) 1,67 (c) F - left winger (d) Ranheim IL (e) Rosenborg II

*** Gautason - Kári Gautason (a) 11/12/2003, ¿? (Iceland) (b) - (c) M (d) Dalvík/Reynir (e) KA Akureyri, Magni, KA Akureyri

*** Gautason - Viktor Elmar Gautason (a) 09/10/2003, ¿? (Iceland) (b) - (c) M (d) Augnablik Kópavogur (e) Breidablik, Thróttur, Breidablik

*** Gavashelishvili - Mamia Gavashelishvili (მამია გავაშელიშვილი) (a) 08/01/1995, Oni (Georgia) (b) 1,77 (c) F - center forward (d) FC Kolkheti-1913 Poti (e) Samgurali, FC Locomotive, Torpedo Kutaisi II

*** Gavazaj - Alush Gavazaj (a) 24/03/1995, Prizren (RF Yugoslavia, now in Kosovo) (b) 1,87 (c) M - pivot (d) FC Malisheva (e) KF Vëllaznimi, FK Bylis, Renova, KF Vushtrria, KF Feronikeli, KF Liria, KF Korabi, KF Tirana, KF Tërbuni, KF Tirana, FK Bylis, KF Tirana
*** Gavazaj - Enis Gavazaj (a) 21/03/1995, Prizren (Yugoslavia, now in Kosovo) (b) 1,77 (c) F - left winger (d) - (e) Struga, FC Dinamo, FC Prishtina, FK Kukësi, KF Skënderbeu, Dinamo Minsk, KF Skënderbeu, Enisey, KF Skënderbeu, KAA Gent, KSV Roeselare, KAA Gent, FC Prishtina
*** Gavazaj - Zenel Gavazaj (a) 02/05/2000, Prizren (RF Yugoslavia, now in Kosovo) (b) 1,72 (c) F - right winger (d) KF Drenica (e) FK Kukësi, KF Skënderbeu, KF Liria
*** Gavi - Gavi (Pablo Martín Páez Gavira) (a) 05/08/2004, Los Palacios y Villafranca (Spain) (b) 1,73 (c) M - central midfielder (d) FC Barcelona (e) -
*** Gavim - Bruno Marcelo Gavim (a) 09/04/1999, ¿? (Brazil) (b) 1,79 (c) F - center forward (d) - (e) UE Santa Coloma, AO Ypatou, Boa Esporte, CF União B, Juventus-SP
*** Gavranovic - Mario Gavranovic (Mario Gavranović) (a) 24/11/1989, Lugano (Switzerland) (b) 1,75 (c) F - center forward (d) - (e) Kayserispor, Dinamo Zagreb, HNK Rijeka, FC Zürich, FC Schalke 04, Mainz 05, FC Schalke 04, Yverdon Sport, Xamax, Yverdon Sport, FC Lugano
*** Gavric - Nebojsa Gavric (Небојша Гаврић) (a) 27/08/1991, Zrenjanin (Yugoslavia, now in Serbia) (b) 1,87 (c) M - central midfielder (d) FK Zvijezda 09 (e) FK Tuzla City, FK Olimpik, Backa, FK Sarajevo, Backa, Vozdovac, Mladost, Borac Cacak, FK Rudar Ugljevik, Borac Cacak, FK Rudar Ugljevik, Borac Cacak
*** Gavric - Nemanja Gavric (Nemanja Gavrić) (a) 20/10/2003, ¿? (Slovenia) (b) 1,92 (c) M - pivot (d) NK Olimpija Ljubljana (e) NK Krsko
*** Gavric - Nenad Gavric (Ненад Гаврић) (a) 12/12/1991, Šabac (Yugoslavia, now in Serbia) (b) 1,76 (c) F - left winger (d) - (e) Novi Pazar, AO Xanthi, Kaspiy Aktau, Radnicki Niš, Napredak, Macva, Mladost, Vojvodina, Crvena zvezda, Napredak, Macva
*** Gavric - Zeljko Gavric (Жељко Гаврић) (a) 05/12/2000, Ugljevik (Bosnia and Herzegovina) (b) 1,81 (c) F - left winger (d) DAC Dunajska Streda (e) Ferencváros, Dunajska Streda, Ferencváros, Crvena zvezda, Graficar
*** Gavriel - Pantelis Gavriel (Παντελής Γαβριήλ) (a) 07/01/2004, Paralimni (Cyprus) (b) 1,73 (c) F - left winger (d) South Carolina Gamecocks (University of SC) (e) EN Paralimniou
*** Gavriel - Stavros Gavriel (Σταύρος Γαβριήλ) (a) 29/01/2002, Nicosia (Cyprus) (b) 1,78 (c) F - right winger (d) APOEL FC (e) Akritas Chlor., APOEL FC
*** Gavrilov - Stefan Gavrilov (Стефан Емилов Гаврилов) (a) 09/07/2000, Sofia (Bulgaria) (b) 1,78 (c) M - central midfielder (d) Beroe Stara Zagora (e) Botev Vratsa, Septemvri Sofia, Septemvri YL
*** Gavrilov - Yoan Gavrilov (Йоан Цветанов Гаврилов) (a) 25/01/1999, ¿? (Bulgaria) (b) 1,75 (c) M - central midfielder (d) Septemvri Sofia (e) Botev Ihtiman
*** Gavrylyuk - Nazariy Gavrylyuk (Гаврилюк Назарій Ігорович) (a) 07/02/2003, Kolomyya, Ivano-Frankivsk Oblast (Ukraine) (b) 1,75 (c) D - right back (d) Tarpa SC (e) Zlaté Moravce
*** Gawne - Alex Gawne (Alexander Gawne) (a) 22/05/2001, Coleraine (Northern Ireland) (b) 1,71 (c) F - right winger (d) Ballymena United (e) Coleraine, Carrick Rangers, Coleraine, Carrick Rangers, Coleraine, Carrick Rangers, Coleraine, Carrick Rangers, Coleraine

*** Gaya - Yacine Gaya (a) 15/11/2004, Bondy (France) (b) 1,84 (c) D - central defense (d) Angers SCO (e) Angers SCO B

*** Gayá - Josep Gayá (Josep Antoni Gayá Martínez) (a) 07/07/2000, Palma de Mallorca (Spain) (b) - (c) D - central defense (d) RCD Mallorca (e) RCD Mallorca B

*** Gayà - José Gayà (José Luis Gayà Peña) (a) 25/05/1995, Pedreguer (Spain) (b) 1,72 (c) D - left back (d) Valencia CF (e) Valencia Mestalla

*** Gayduchyk - Mykola Gayduchyk (Гайдучик Микола Михайлович) (a) 30/12/1999, Zdolbuniv, Rivne Oblast (Ukraine) (b) 1,88 (c) F - center forward (d) NK Veres Rivne (e) FK Uzhgorod, Veres Rivne, ODEK Orzhiv, FK Malynsk, Veres Rivne II

*** Gaye - Baboucarr Gaye (a) 24/02/1998, Bielefeld (Germany) (b) 1,96 (c) G (d) Lokomotiv Sofia (e) SV Rödinghausen, RW Koblenz, Stuttgart II, Wattenscheid 09, Arminia Bielefeld

*** Gaye - Mor Talla Gaye (a) 07/01/1999, Guinaw Rails (Senegal) (b) 1,64 (c) D - left back (d) Riga FC (e) Riga, Auda, Diambars FC

*** Gazdanov - Artur Gazdanov (Газданов Артур Сосланович) (a) 26/07/1992, Vladikavkaz (Russia) (b) 1,80 (c) F - right winger (d) Rodina Media Moskau (e) Akzhayik, Akron Togliatti, Tyumen, KamAZ, Avangard 2, Avangard Kursk, KamAZ, Volgar, Alania-D Vladik., Alania II

*** Gazdeliani - Gaga Gazdeliani (გაგა გაზდელიანი) (a) 13/10/1997, ¿? (Georgia) (b) 1,76 (c) D - left back (d) Shukura Kobuleti (e) Rustavi, Shukura, Samgurali, FC Gagra, Samgurali, FC Meshakhte, Merani Martvili

*** Gazi - Adam Gazi (Adam Gaži) (a) 01/03/2003, Dubnica nad Váhom (Slovakia) (b) 1,70 (c) F - right winger (d) AS Trencin (e) Liptovsky Mik., AS Trencin

*** Gazibegovic - Jusuf Gazibegovic (Jusuf Gazibegović) (a) 11/03/2000, Salzburg (Austria) (b) 1,74 (c) D - right back (d) SK Sturm Graz (e) FC Liefering

*** Gazinskiy - Yuriy Gazinskiy (Газинский Юрий Александрович) (a) 20/07/1989, Komsomoljsk-na-Amure, Khabarovsk Region (Soviet Union, now in Russia) (b) 1,84 (c) M - central midfielder (d) Ural Ekaterimburgo (e) Krasnodar, Torpedo Moskva, Luch Vladivostok, Smena

*** Gazivoda - Savo Gazivoda (Саво Газивода) (a) 18/07/1994, ¿? (RF Yugoslavia, now in Montenegro) (b) 1,80 (c) M - right midfielder (d) FK Mornar Bar (e) FK Iskra, OFK Petrovac, Mornar Bar, Rad Beograd, Mornar Bar, Kom Podgorica, FK Bokelj, FK Iskra, Radnicki Niš, Radnik, Extremadura, CSK Celarevo, Buducnost Podgorica

*** Gaztañaga - Jon Gaztañaga (Jon Gaztañaga Arrospide) (a) 28/06/1991, Andoain (Spain) (b) 1,81 (c) M - central midfielder (d) Barakaldo CF (e) Karmiotissa, NorthEast Utd., Cultural Leonesa, FCV Farul, AEL Limassol, Gimnàstic, Real Sociedad, CD Numancia, Real Sociedad, Ponferradina, Real Sociedad, Real Sociedad B

*** Gazzaniga - Paulo Gazzaniga (Paulo Dino Gazzaniga Farias) (a) 02/01/1992, Murphy (Argentina) (b) 1,95 (c) G (d) Girona FC (e) Fulham, Girona FC, Fulham, Tottenham Hotspur, Elche CF, Tottenham Hotspur, Southampton, Rayo Vallecano, Southampton, Gillingham FC

*** Gazzetta - Karim Gazzetta (Karim Emilio Roberto Gazzetta) (a) 01/04/1995, Genève (Switzerland) (b) 1,80 (c) M - attacking midfielder (d) --- (e) Neuchâtel Xamax, Stade-Lausanne, FC Winterthur, Servette FC, FC Winterthur, Servette FC, Etoile Carouge, Servette FC

*** Gbamblé - Bi Néné Junior Gbamblé (a) 09/05/2002, ¿? (Ivory Coast) (b) 1,73 (c) F - right winger (d) Akhmat Grozny (e) NK Celje, Olimpik Donetsk, Rubikon

*** Gbamin - Jean-Philippe Gbamin (a) 25/09/1995, San-Pédro (Ivory Coast) (b) 1,86 (c) M - pivot (d) Everton FC (e) Trabzonspor, Everton, CSKA Moskva, Everton, Mainz 05, RC Lens, RC Lens B

*** Gbane - Mory Gbane (Roman Mory Diaman Gbane) (a) 25/12/2000, Tontonou Toumodi (Ivory Coast) (b) 1,88 (c) M - pivot (d) Gil Vicente FC (e) Gil Vicente, Khimki, Bijelo Brdo, Khimki, Bijelo Brdo, Stade d'Abidjan

*** Gbe - Vigori Gbe (a) 10/02/2002, Man (Ivory Coast) (b) 1,70 (c) D - right back (d) - (e) FC Haka, Ilves, Williamsville

*** Gbegnon - Simon Gbegnon (Simon Gbegnon Amoussou) (a) 27/10/1992, Nantes (France) (b) 1,90 (c) D - central defense (d) - (e) SO Cholet, Dinamo Tbilisi, CD Mirandés, AS Béziers, SAS Epinal, Carquefou, AC Chapelain

*** Gboho - Yann Gboho (Gnantin Yann Gboho) (a) 14/01/2001, Man (Ivory Coast) (b) 1,78 (c) M - attacking midfielder (d) Cercle Brugge (e) Stade Rennes, Vitesse, Stade Rennes, Stade Rennes B

*** Geana - Mario Geana (Mario Kostantin Geană) (a) 30/04/2005, Bucuresti (Romania) (b) 1,73 (c) D - right back (d) Unirea Dej (e) Unirea Dej

*** Gebauer - Thomas Gebauer (a) 30/06/1982, Augsburg (Germany) (b) 1,91 (c) G (d) - (e) LASK, SV Ried, SpVgg Bayreuth, 1860 München II, TSV Aindling, TSV Meitingen

*** Gebre Selassie - Theodor Gebre Selassie (a) 24/12/1986, Třebíč (Czechoslovakia, now in Czech Rep.) (b) 1,82 (c) D - right back (d) - (e) Slovan Liberec, Werder Bremen, Slovan Liberec, Slavia Praha, Jihlava, Velke Mezirici, Jihlava

*** Gebreyesus - Esey Gebreyesus (a) 23/01/2004, Zürich (Switzerland) (b) 1,82 (c) M - right midfielder (d) FC Aarau (e) Ol. Marseille B

*** Gebuhr - Dario Gebuhr (Dario Ndubuisi Gebuhr) (a) 06/05/2003, Wiesbaden (Germany) (b) 1,88 (c) D - central defense (d) Eintracht Frankfurt (e) E. Frankfurt II

*** Gecaj - Danilo Gecaj (a) 21/07/2000, Durrës (Albania) (b) - (c) M (d) KF Erzeni (e) Besëlidhja, KF Erzeni, KF Teuta, KF Erzeni

*** Gechter - Linus Gechter (Linus Jasper Gechter) (a) 27/02/2004, Berlin (Germany) (b) 1,91 (c) D - central defense (d) Hertha Berlín (e) Eintracht Braunschweig, Hertha Berlin

*** Geci - Diart Geci (a) 21/03/2003, ¿? (Serbia and Montenegro, now in Kosovo) (b) - (c) M - central midfielder (d) KF Drenica (e) -

*** Geci - Segerso Geci (a) 16/08/2001, Tiranë (Albania) (b) - (c) F - right winger (d) KF Laçi (e) KF Korabi, KF Vora

*** Gedikli - Emrehan Gedikli (a) 25/04/2003, Oberhausen (Germany) (b) 1,87 (c) F - center forward (d) Trabzonspor (e) Austria Lustenau, Trabzonspor, Bayer Leverkusen

*** Gedo - Hunor Gedo (Hunor Botond Gedő) (a) 16/01/2004, Odorheiu Secuiesc (Romania) (b) - (c) G (d) Sepsi OSK Sf. Gheorghe (e) -

*** Geertruida - Lutsharel Geertruida (a) 18/07/2000, Rotterdam (Netherlands) (b) 1,84 (c) D - central defense (d) Feyenoord Rotterdam (e) -

*** Geferson - Geferson (Geferson Cerqueira Teles) (a) 13/05/1994, Lauro de Freitas (BA) (Brazil) (b) 1,82 (c) M - pivot (d) - (e) CSKA-Sofia, Internacional, EC Vitória, Internacional, Inter B

*** Gega - Xhulio Gega (a) 17/02/1995, ¿? (Albania) (b) - (c) D - left back (d) SS Murata (e) Gambettola, Cailungo, Virtus

*** Gegedosh - Robert Gegedosh (Гегедош Роберт Володимирович) (a) 02/05/1993, Svalyava, Zakarpattya Oblast (Ukraine) (b) 1,80 (c) F - center forward (d) Keflavík ÍF (e) Santa Lucia FC, Pyunik Yerevan, Gornik Polk., Peremoga Dnipro, Veres Rivne, Metalist 1925, FK Minaj, SK Sacurov, Slavoj Secovce, FK Uzhgorod,

FK Polyana, Goverla II, FK Polyana, Kremin, Metalist II, FK Polyana, Goverla II, RVUFK Kyiv

*** Gegetchkori - Levan Gegetchkori (ლევან გეგეჭკორი) (a) 05/06/1994, Martvili (Georgia) (b) 1,83 (c) D - right back (d) - (e) Torpedo Kutaisi, Dinamo Batumi, Torpedo Kutaisi, Rustavi, Dinamo Tbilisi, Chikhura, Dinamo Batumi, Shukura, Merani Martvili, Merani II

*** Geguchadze - Gegi Geguchadze (გეგი გეგუჩაძე) (a) 30/12/2003, ¿? (Georgia) (b) - (c) M - central midfielder (d) FC Locomotive Tbilisi (e) Saburtalo, FC Saburtalo II

*** Geiger - Dennis Geiger (a) 10/06/1998, Mosbach (Germany) (b) 1,73 (c) M - central midfielder (d) TSG 1899 Hoffenheim (e) -

*** Geirdal - Jóhannes Dagur Geirdal (a) 08/06/2004, ¿? (Iceland) (b) - (c) M (d) Víkingur Reykjavík (e) -

*** Geirsson - Halldór Páll Geirsson (a) 21/07/1994, ¿? (Iceland) (b) - (c) G (d) KF Framherjar-Smástund (e) ÍBV Vestmannaeyjar, Framherjar, ÍBV Vestmannaeyjar, Framherjar, ÍBV Vestmannaeyjar, Framherjar, ÍBV Vestmannaeyjar, Framherjar, ÍBV Vestmannaeyjar, Framherjar

*** Geirsson - Stefán Árni Geirsson (a) 06/11/2000, ¿? (Iceland) (b) - (c) F - left winger (d) KR Reykjavík (e) Leiknir, KR Reykjavík

*** Geirsson - Tryggvi Snaer Geirsson (Tryggvi Snær Geirsson) (a) 11/06/2000, ¿? (Iceland) (b) - (c) M - right midfielder (d) Fram Reykjavík (e) KR Reykjavík, KV Vesturbaejar, KR Reykjavík

*** Gelashvili - Iva Gelashvili (ივა გელაშვილი) (a) 08/04/2001, Tbilisi (Georgia) (b) 1,91 (c) D - central defense (d) Dinamo Batumi (e) Saburtalo, Dinamo Batumi, Sioni Bolnisi, Dinamo Batumi, Sparta Praha B

*** Gelesh - Yaroslav Gelesh (Гелеш Ярослав Євгенович) (a) 20/07/2004, ¿? (Ukraine) (b) - (c) F - center forward (d) Kisvárda FC (e) Kisvárda II

*** Gelhardt - Joe Gelhardt (Joseph Paul Gelhardt) (a) 04/05/2002, Liverpool (England) (b) 1,79 (c) F - center forward (d) Leeds United (e) Sunderland, Leeds Utd., Wigan Ath.

*** Gelin - Nikola Gelin (Никола Любенов Гелин) (a) 06/04/2004, Plovdiv (Bulgaria) (b) 1,81 (c) F - center forward (d) Botev Plovdiv II (e) -

*** Geljic - Mihovil Geljic (Mihovil Geljić) (a) 25/02/1992, Zagreb (Croatia) (b) 1,87 (c) F - center forward (d) NK Sesvete (e) NK Kustosija, NK Jarun, NK Sesvete, RFS, NK Sesvete, Stadtallendorf, Pischelsdorf, RNK Split, Pischelsdorf, NK Trnje Zagreb

*** Gelmi - Roy Gelmi (a) 01/03/1995, Bülach (Switzerland) (b) 1,88 (c) D - central defense (d) FC Winterthur (e) VVV-Venlo, FC Thun, VVV-Venlo, FC Thun, FC St. Gallen

*** Gemello - Luca Gemello (a) 03/07/2000, Savigliano (Italy) (b) 1,90 (c) G (d) Torino FC (e) Renate, Torino, Fermana, Torino, Fossano, Fossano

*** Gemicibasi - Turgay Gemicibasi (Turgay Philipp Gemicibaşi) (a) 23/04/1996, Riesa (Germany) (b) 1,80 (c) M - pivot (d) SK Austria Klagenfurt (e) Kasimpasa, Austria Klagenfurt, Blau Weiss Linz, Mauerwerk, FC Gütersloh, Spfr. Siegen

*** Gemmer - Jonas Gemmer (Jonas Skjøtt Gemmer) (a) 31/01/1996, ¿? (Denmark) (b) 1,79 (c) M - central midfielder (d) Hvidovre IF (e) AC Horsens, Kolding IF, AC Horsens, Fremad Amager, Midtjylland, AC Horsens, Midtjylland, AC Horsens, Midtjylland

*** Genc - Faruk Can Genc (Faruk Can Genç) (a) 16/02/2000, Trabzon (Turkey) (b) 1,80 (c) D - left back (d) Giresunspor (e) Trabzonspor, A. Keciörengücü, Trabzonspor, Ümraniyespor, Trabzonspor

*** Gendrey - Valentin Gendrey (Valentin André Stanislas Gendrey) (a) 21/06/2000, La Garenne-Colombes (France) (b) 1,79 (c) D - right back (d) US Lecce (e) Amiens SC, Amiens SC B

*** Generalov - Egor Generalov (Генералов Егор Дмитриевич) (a) 24/01/1993, Smorgon (Belarus) (b) 1,89 (c) G (d) Dnepr Mogilev (e) Isloch, FK Minsk, Khimki, SKA Khabarovsk, Dinamo S-Pb, Dinamo Moskva II, Dinamo SPb, Dinamo Moskva II, Saturn Ramenskoe, Dinamo Moskva II, Lokomotiv Moskva II

*** Genesini - Brooklyn Genesini (Brooklyn David Anthony Genesini) (a) 12/12/2001, Yeovil (England) (b) - (c) D - right back (d) Swindon Town (e) Naestved BK, Poole Town

*** Genev - Viktor Genev (Виктор Викторов Генев) (a) 27/10/1988, Sofia (Bulgaria) (b) 1,88 (c) D - central defense (d) Slavia Sofia (e) Botev Plovdiv, Beroe, Cherno More, FC Ashdod, Botev Plovdiv, Levski Sofia, Dinamo Minsk, Petrolul, St. Mirren, Sp. Semey, Slavia Sofia, PFK Oleksandria, Slavia Sofia, KS Samara, Slavia Sofia, Levski Sofia

*** Genis - Sagi Genis (גניס שגיא) (a) 10/01/2004, ¿? (Israel) (b) 1,78 (c) F - left winger (d) Hapoel Tel Aviv (e) -

*** Genov - Daniel Genov (Даниел Недялков Генов) (a) 19/05/1989, Sofia (Bulgaria) (b) 1,82 (c) F - right winger (d) Botev Vratsa (e) Beroe, Botev Vratsa, EN Paralimniou, Montana, Pirin, Botev Plovdiv, Lokomotiv Sofia, Inter Baku, Simurq, Inter Baku, Kom Berkovitsa, M. Radnevo

*** Genreau - Denis Genreau (a) 21/05/1999, Paris (France) (b) 1,75 (c) M - attacking midfielder (d) Toulouse FC (e) Macarthur, Melbourne City, PEC Zwolle, Melbourne City

*** Gentilini - Fabio Gentilini (a) 09/09/1984, ¿? (Italy) (b) - (c) G (d) AC Juvenes-Dogana (e) Libertas, Tre Fiori, Marignanese, Vallesavio, Forlimpopoli, Meldola, Sampierana, Classe, Castrocaro, Savignanese, Sampierana, Cattolica, Cervia

*** Gentner - Christian Gentner (a) 14/08/1985, Nürtingen (Germany) (b) 1,89 (c) M - central midfielder (d) Michael Gentner (e) FC Luzern, Union Berlin, VfB Stuttgart, VfL Wolfsburg, VfB Stuttgart, VfL Wolfsburg, VfB Stuttgart, Stuttgart II

*** Geoffrey - Chinedu Geoffrey (Chinedu Charles Geoffrey) (a) 01/10/1997, Lagos (Nigeria) (b) 1,92 (c) F - center forward (d) FK Radnicki 1923 Kragujevac (e) FC Lahti, Olimpik Donetsk, FC Lahti, Olimpik Donetsk, JK Trans Narva, Olimpik Donetsk, AFC Turris, KF Skënderbeu B, Rabotnicki, KF Skënderbeu B, KS Besa, KF Skënderbeu B, Teplice B, KF Skënderbeu B, Dogan TBSK

*** George - Ryan George (a) 27/11/2001, ¿? (Wales) (b) 1,73 (c) D - right back (d) Briton Ferry Llansawel (e) Haverfordwest, Redditch Utd., Walton Casuals

*** George - Shamal George (a) 06/01/1998, Wirral (England) (b) 1,98 (c) G (d) Livingston FC (e) Colchester Utd., Marine FC, Tranmere Rovers, Carlisle United

*** Georgiev - Aleksandar Georgiev (Александър Веселинов Георгиев) (a) 10/11/1997, Targovishte (Bulgaria) (b) 1,76 (c) D - left back (d) Krumovgrad (e) Arda Kardzhali, CSKA-Sofia, Etar, CSKA-Sofia, Septemvri Sofia, CSKA-Sofia, Litex Lovetch

*** Georgiev - Aleksandar Georgiev (Александър Йорданов Георгиев) (a) 28/05/2003, ¿? (Bulgaria) (b) 1,86 (c) D - central defense (d) Lokomotiv Plovdiv (e) B. Botevgrad, CSKA 1948 II, Strumska Slava

*** Georgiev - Antonio Georgiev (Антонио Георгиев Георгиев) (a) 26/10/1997, Yambol (Bulgaria) (b) 1,80 (c) M - pivot (d) AS FC Buzau (e) Botev Vratsa, Tsarsko Selo, B. Galabovo, Ludogorets II

*** Georgiev - Asen Georgiev (Асен Кирилов Георгиев) (a) 09/07/1993, Sofia (Bulgaria) (b) 1,86 (c) D - central defense (d) Septemvri Sofia (e) Hebar P., Lokomotiv Plovdiv, Beroe, NK Istra, Montana, Lokomotiv Plovdiv, Botev Vratsa

*** Georgiev - Boban Georgiev (Бобан Георгиев) (a) 26/01/1997, Stip (North Macedonia) (b) 1,74 (c) F - left winger (d) Voska Sport (e) Leotar Trebinje, Bregalnica Stip, Borac Banja Luka, Radnik, Sileks, Bregalnica Stip

*** Georgiev - Georgi Georgiev (Георги Николаев Георгиев) (a) 12/10/1988, Shumen (Bulgaria) (b) 1,89 (c) G (d) Spartak Varna (e) Cherno More, Levski Sofia, Slavia Sofia, Vereya, Pirin, Dacia, Botev Plovdiv, FC Sheriff, Gostaresh FC, FC Sheriff, Naft M.I.S F.C., FC Sheriff, FC Tiraspol, FC Sheriff, FC Tiraspol, Sliven, M. Radnevo, Lokomotiv Mezdra, Svilengrad 1921

*** Georgiev - Miroslav Georgiev (Мирослав Петков Георгиев) (a) 19/10/2005, Barcelona (Spain) (b) 1,92 (c) D - central defense (d) Chernomorets 1919 Burgas (e) Chern. Burgas, Botev II

*** Georgiev - Petar Georgiev (Петър Росенов Георгиев) (a) 10/05/2002, ¿? (Bulgaria) (b) 1,79 (c) M - attacking midfielder (d) Ludogorets Razgrad II (e) -

*** Georgiev - Spas Georgiev (Спас Иванов Георгиев) (a) 21/06/1992, Stara Zagora (Bulgaria) (b) 1,76 (c) F - right winger (d) Botev Vratsa (e) Beroe, Pirin, Septemvri Sofia, CSKA 1948, Botev Vratsa, Dunav, Livingston FC, Albion Rovers, Livingston FC, Dob. Dobrich, Slavia Sofia, Montana, Slavia Sofia

*** Georgiev - Yanko Georgiev (Янко Иванов Георгиев) (a) 22/10/1988, Burgas (Bulgaria) (b) 1,86 (c) G (d) Krumovgrad (e) Pirin, Tsarsko Selo, Botev Plovdiv, Septemvri Sofia, Neftochimik, Pomorie, Chern. Burgas, Burgas, Chern. Burgas, Pomorie, Neftochimik, Chern. Burgas, Pomorie

*** Georgievski - Hristijan Georgievski (Христијан Георгиевски) (a) 12/04/2003, Skopje (North Macedonia) (b) 1,88 (c) M - central midfielder (d) - (e) Sileks, FK Skopje, MTK Budapest II

*** Georgievsky - Kostya Georgievsky (a) 28/06/1996, Newry (Northern Ireland) (b) - (c) F - right winger (d) - (e) Penybont, Carmarthen, Penybont, Port Talbot, Port Talbot

*** Georgijevic - Dejan Georgijevic (Дејан Георгијевић) (a) 19/01/1994, Zemun (RF Yugoslavia, now in Serbia) (b) 1,87 (c) F - center forward (d) OFK Beograd (e) HSK Posusje, Simba SC, Domžale, Velez Mostar, Ferencváros, Irtysh, Ferencváros, FK Partizan, Ferencváros, Vozdovac, FK Indjija, Spartak, Teleoptik, FK Zemun

*** Georgiou - Stavros Georgiou (Σταύρος Γεωργίου) (a) 19/10/2004, Mammari, Nicosia (Cyprus) (b) 1,88 (c) F - attacking midfielder (d) APOEL FC (e) -

*** Gerafi - Yoav Gerafi (גראפי יואב) (a) 29/08/1993, Tel Mond (Israel) (b) 1,85 (c) G (d) Hapoel Haifa (e) FC Ashdod, Hapoel Tel Aviv, FC Ashdod, Hapoel Raanana, FC Ashdod, H. Kfar Saba

*** Geraldes - André Geraldes (André Geraldes de Barros) (a) 02/05/1991, Maia (Portugal) (b) 1,81 (c) D - right back (d) Casa Pia AC (e) Maccabi Tel Aviv, APOEL FC, Sporting B, Sporting Lisboa, Maccabi Tel Aviv, Sporting Lisboa, Real Sporting, Sporting Lisboa, Belenenses, Sporting Lisboa, Sporting B, Vitória Setúbal, Sporting B, Belenenses, Sporting B, Basaksehir, Belenenses, Istanbul BBSK, Rio Ave, Desportivo Aves, Rio Ave, Chaves, Rio Ave, Maia Lidador

*** Geraldo - Geraldo (Hermenegildo da Costa Paulo Bartolomeu) (a) 23/11/1991, Luanda (Angola) (b) 1,70 (c) F - right winger (d) Corum FK (e) Ümraniyespor, Ankaragücü, El Ahly, 1º de Agosto, Atlético-GO, RB Brasil, Coritiba FC, Paraná, Coritiba FC, Coritiba FC B

*** Gerasimov - Aleksey Gerasimov (Герасимов Алексей Алексеевич) (a) 15/04/1993, Borisoglebsk, Voronezh Region (Russia) (b) 1,94 (c) D - central defense

(d) Neftekhimik Nizhnekamsk (e) Neftekhimik, Ural, KamAZ, Ural, Ural 2, Ural II, Tom Tomsk, Ural II, Belshina, Ural II, Volga-Olimpiets, Ural II, Zhetysu, Ural II, SKA-Energia, Ural II, Tobol Kurgan

*** Gerat - Tomas Gerat (Tomáš Gerát) (a) 15/06/1993, ¿? (Czechoslovakia, now in Slovakia) (b) 1,79 (c) M - central midfielder (d) Tatran Liptovsky Mikulas (e) Podbrezova B, Ružomberok, Rimavska Sobota, Ružomberok, Namestovo, Ružomberok, Dunajska Streda, Ružomberok

*** Gerbowski - Fryderyk Gerbowski (a) 17/01/2003, Warszawa (Poland) (b) 1,81 (c) M - attacking midfielder (d) Wisła Płock (e) Stal Mielec, Wisła Płock

*** Gerec - Stefan Gerec (Štefan Gerec) (a) 10/11/1992, Ľubochňa (Czechoslovakia, now in Slovakia) (b) 1,76 (c) F - center forward (d) MFK Ružomberok (e) Liptovsky Mik., Ružomberok, Podbrezova, Ružomberok, Dunajska Streda, Ružomberok

*** Géresi - Krisztián Géresi (a) 14/06/1994, Székesfehérvár (Hungary) (b) 1,82 (c) F - left winger (d) Nyíregyháza Spartacus (e) Szeged, Szeged, Vasas FC, Fehérvár, Puskás AFC, Fehérvár, Videoton II

*** Gereta - Yuriy-Volodymyr Gereta (Герета Юрій-Володимир Остапович) (a) 30/01/2004, Lviv (Ukraine) (b) 1,89 (c) G (d) Rukh Lviv (e) Karpaty

*** Gergely - Botond Gergely (a) 11/01/2003, Gheorgheni (Romania) (b) - (c) D - central defense (d) AFK Csikszereda Miercurea Ciuc (e) Csikszereda, Zalaegerszeg, NK Nafta 1903, Zalaegerszeg, Csikszereda

*** Gergely - Roland Gergely (a) 06/04/2005, ¿? (Hungary) (b) 1,90 (c) G (d) Fehérvár FC (e) Fehérvár II

*** Gergényi - Bence Gergényi (a) 16/03/1998, Budapest (Hungary) (b) 1,87 (c) D - left back (d) Zalaegerszegi TE FC (e) NK Nafta 1903, Zalaegerszeg, Honvéd II, Zalaegerszeg, Honvéd II, Szeged, Honvéd II

*** Gerhardt - Yannick Gerhardt (a) 13/03/1994, Würselen (Germany) (b) 1,84 (c) M - central midfielder (d) VfL Wolfsburg (e) 1.FC Köln

*** Geris - Thomas Geris (a) 16/10/2002, Innsbruck (Austria) (b) - (c) F - right winger (d) WSG Tirol (e) WSG Tirol II, FC Wacker II

*** Gerkens - Pieter Gerkens (a) 17/02/1995, Bilzen (Belgium) (b) 1,79 (c) M - central midfielder (d) KAA Gent (e) Royal Antwerp, RSC Anderlecht, Sint-Truiden, KRC Genk

*** Germain - Valère Germain (a) 17/04/1990, Marseille (France) (b) 1,81 (c) F - center forward (d) Macarthur FC (e) Montpellier, Ol. Marseille, AS Monaco, OGC Nice, AS Monaco, AS Monaco B

*** Germanov - Simeon Germanov (Симеон Антонов Германов) (a) 01/01/2005, ¿? (Bulgaria) (b) - (c) D - central defense (d) Beroe Stara Zagora II (e) -

*** Gershon - Rami Gershon (גרשון רמי) (a) 12/08/1988, Rishon Lezion (Israel) (b) 1,89 (c) D - central defense (d) Maccabi Haifa (e) KAA Gent, Waasland-Beveren, Standard Liège, Celtic FC, Standard Liège, KV Kortrijk, Standard Liège, H Rishon leZion, Standard Liège, H Rishon leZion

*** Gersi - Denis Gersi (Denis Gerši) (a) 05/03/2001, Topoľčany (Slovakia) (b) - (c) M (d) FC Zlate Moravce-Vrable B (e) Kovarce, Oponice

*** Gerson - Gerson (Gerson Santos da Silva) (a) 20/05/1997, Belford Roxo (Brazil) (b) 1,84 (c) M - central midfielder (d) CR Flamengo (e) Ol. Marseille, Flamengo, AS Roma, Fiorentina, AS Roma, Fluminense

*** Gerstenstein - Lukasz Gerstenstein (a) 06/10/2004, Kowary (Poland) (b) 1,75 (c) M - right midfielder (d) Stal Mielec (e) Stal Mielec, Śląsk Wroclaw, Slask Wroclaw II

*** Gertmonas - Edvinas Gertmonas (a) 01/06/1996, Šilalė (Lithuania) (b) 1,92 (c) G (d) FK Zalgiris Vilnius (e) Stade Rennes, Atlantas, Stade Rennes, Atlantas, Tauras

*** Gertsen - Guus Gertsen (a) 16/04/2003, Bemmel (Netherlands) (b) 1,89 (c) D - central defense (d) TOP Oss (e) TOP Oss

*** Gervinho - Gervinho (Gervais Lombe Yao Kouassi) (a) 27/05/1987, Anyama (Ivory Coast) (b) 1,79 (c) F - left winger (d) - (e) Aris Thessaloniki, Trabzonspor, Parma, HB CFFC, HB FC Reserves, HB CFFC, AS Roma, Arsenal, Lille, Le Mans UC 72, KSK Beveren, JMG Abidjan

*** Gerxhaliu - Amar Gerxhaliu (Amar Gërxhaliu) (a) 26/04/2002, Vushtrri (RF Yugoslavia, now in Kosovo) (b) 1,93 (c) D - central defense (d) Antalyaspor (e) KF Vushtrria

*** Gerych - Vladyslav Gerych (Герич Владислав Володимирович) (a) 07/11/2005, ¿? (Ukraine) (b) 1,80 (c) F - center forward (d) - (e) PFK Lviv

*** Gestsson - Teitur Gestsson (Teitur Matras Gestsson) (a) 19/08/1992, Tórshavn (Faroe Islands) (b) 1,90 (c) G (d) HB Tórshavn (e) HB Tórshavn II

*** Gesualdi - Joseph Gaetano Gesualdi (a) 15/02/1992, ¿? (Malta) (b) - (c) D (d) Zebbug Rangers FC (e) Sirens FC, Qormi FC, Mqabba FC, St. George's FC, Tarxien, Inter Leipzig, Weißenfels, Inter Leipzig, Valletta, Rabat Ajax, Valletta, Qormi FC

*** Getinger - Krystian Getinger (a) 29/08/1988, Mielec (Poland) (b) 1,88 (c) M - left midfielder (d) Stal Mielec (e) Stalowa Wola, Zagłębie, Stal Mielec, Zagłębie, Zaglebie Lubin II, Stal Mielec

*** Geubbels - Willem Geubbels (Willem Davnis Louis Didier Geubbels) (a) 16/08/2001, Villeurbanne (France) (b) 1,85 (c) F - left winger (d) FC St. Gallen 1879 (e) AS Monaco, FC Nantes, AS Monaco, Olympique Lyon

*** Geusens - Jay-Dee Geusens (a) 05/03/2002, Genk (Belgium) (b) - (c) M - attacking midfielder (d) SK Beveren (e) KRC Genk

*** Gévay - Zsolt Gévay (a) 19/11/1987, Dunaújváros (Hungary) (b) 1,87 (c) D - central defense (d) Paksi FC (e) Mezőkövesd, Gyirmót FC, Paksi FC, Makói FC, Alba Regia FC, Makói FC, Alba Regia FC

*** Gevorgyan - Hovhannes Gevorgyan (Հովհաննես Գևորգյան) (a) 17/06/2003, ¿? (Armenia) (b) - (c) D - central defense (d) Shirak Gyumri C.F. (e) BKMA Yerevan II, Shirak II

*** Gevorgyan - Levon Gevorgyan (Լևոն Գևորգյան) (a) 01/01/2003, ¿? (Armenia) (b) - (c) M - pivot (d) Shirak Gyumri C.F. (e) Shirak II

*** Gevorkyan - Artem Gevorkyan (Геворкян Артём Сейранович) (a) 21/05/1993, Chaltyr, Rostov Region (Russia) (b) 1,75 (c) F - attacking midfielder (d) FC West Armenia (e) Shirak Gyumri, Chaika Pes., Afips Afipskiy, SKA Rostov, Torpedo Armavir, Kuban II

*** Gey - Viktor Gey (Гей Віктор Вікторович) (a) 02/02/1996, Nyzhniy Koropets, Zakarpattya Oblast (Ukraine) (b) 1,83 (c) D - right back (d) MTK Budapest (e) Kisvárda, Goverla

*** Geyrhofer - Niklas Geyrhofer (a) 11/02/2000, Graz (Austria) (b) 1,88 (c) D - central defense (d) SK Sturm Graz (c) Sturm Graz II

*** Geyti - Meinhard Geyti (Meinhard Debes Geyti) (a) 03/05/2001, ¿? (Faroe Islands) (b) - (c) D - central defense (d) NSÍ Runavík (e) NSÍ II

*** Gezek - Baran Gezek (Baran Ali Gezek) (a) 26/08/2005, Mersin (Turkey) (b) 1,82 (c) M - central midfielder (d) Kayserispor (e) -

*** Gezos - Kosmas Gezos (Κοσμάς Γκέζος) (a) 15/08/1992, Athen (Greece) (b) 1,82 (c) M - pivot (d) SK Austria Klagenfurt (e) Akropolis IF, Panionios, AO Glyfadas, Panionios, Acharnaikos, Panionios

*** Ghacha - Houssam Ghacha (Houssam Eddine Ghacha) (a) 25/10/1995, Ouled Djellal (Algeria) (b) 1,70 (c) F - left winger (d) Esperance Tunis (e) Antalyaspor, ES Sétif, USM Blida, A Bou Saâda, Ain Djasser

*** Ghaghanidze - Konsantine Ghaghanidze (კონსტანტინე დალანიძე) (a) 03/02/1994, ¿? (Georgia) (b) 1,85 (c) D - central defense (d) - (e) FC Telavi, FC Bakhmaro, FC Gardabani, FC Locomotive, Guria, Dila II, Metallurgist II
*** Ghali - Ahmad Ghali (Ahmad Ghali Abubakar) (a) 23/06/2000, Kano (Nigeria) (b) 1,70 (c) F - left winger (d) FC Slovan Liberec (e) AS Trencin, MFM FC
*** Ghalidi - Brahim Ghalidi (a) 31/01/2005, ¿? (Belgium) (b) 1,74 (c) F - left winger (d) Standard Lieja 16 FC (e) Standard Liège, SL16 FC
*** Ghambarashvili - Nika Ghambarashvili (ნიკა ღამბარაშვილი) (a) 02/04/2003, ¿? (Georgia) (b) - (c) M - attacking midfielder (d) Sioni Bolnisi (e) -
*** Ghanem - Qays Ghanem (גאנם קייס) (a) 31/12/1997, Zemer (Israel) (b) 1,90 (c) F - center forward (d) Maccabi Bnei Reineh (e) Hapoel Tel Aviv, H. Beer Sheva, Hapoel Haifa, H. Beer Sheva, Hapoel Raanana, Ramat haSharon, Hapoel Raanana, Ramat haSharon
*** Gharbi - Ismaël Gharbi (Ismaël Gharbi Álvarez) (a) 10/04/2004, Paris (France) (b) 1,73 (c) M - attacking midfielder (d) París Saint-Germain FC (e) -
*** Ghasem - Alai Ghasem (علي الاي فاضل ~ Alai Fadel Ali Hussain Ghasem) (a) 16/02/2003, Göteborg (Sweden) (b) 1,78 (c) D - right back (d) Utsiktens BK (e) IFK Göteborg
*** Ghazaryan - Arman Ghazaryan (Արման Ղազարյան) (a) 24/07/2001, Yerevan (Armenia) (b) 1,91 (c) D - central defense (d) FC Urartu Yerevan (e) BKMA Yerevan, Banants III
*** Ghazaryan - Gevorg Ghazaryan (Գևորգ Ղազարյան) (a) 05/04/1988, Yerevan (Soviet Union, now in Armenia) (b) 1,80 (c) F - left winger (d) FC Ararat-Armenia (e) Pyunik Yerevan, AEL Limassol, PAS Lamia, AEL Limassol, Chaves, Marítimo, AOK Kerkyra, Olympiakos, Metalurg Donetsk, Shakhter K., Metalurg Donetsk, Pyunik Yerevan, Banants, Pyunik Yerevan, Pyunik Yerevan B
*** Ghazaryan - Hayk Ghazaryan (Հայկ Ղազարյան) (a) 19/09/2006, ¿? (Armenia) (b) - (c) G (d) FC Urartu Erewan II (e) -
*** Ghazaryan - Norayr Ghazaryan (Նորայր Ղազարյան) (a) 22/01/2002, Yerevan (Armenia) (b) 1,74 (c) M - left midfielder (d) FC Syunik (e) Ararat II, Ararat-Armenia II, Pyunik Yerevan B
*** Ghecev - Mihail Ghecev (a) 05/11/1997, Leova (Moldova) (b) 1,78 (c) M - left midfielder (d) FK Minaj (e) Zimbru Chisinau, Veres Rivne, Sfintul Gheorghe, Veres Rivne, Sfintul Gheorghe, Noah Jurmala, FC Sheriff, Sfintul Gheorghe, FC Sheriff, FC Petrocub, Sfintul Gheorghe
*** Gheorghe - Gabriel Gheorghe (a) 25/11/2006, ¿? (Romania) (b) - (c) M - attacking midfielder (d) - (e) FC Juniorul
*** Gheorghe - Ion Gheorghe (a) 08/10/1999, Bucuresti (Romania) (b) 1,74 (c) M - attacking midfielder (d) Sepsi OSK Sf. Gheorghe (e) FC Voluntari, FC Dinamo, Dinamo II
*** Gheorghe - Valentin Gheorghe (a) 14/02/1997, Ploieşti (Romania) (b) 1,75 (c) F - left winger (d) FCSB (e) Ümraniyespor, FCSB, Astra Giurgiu, Astra II, CS Afumati, Astra II
*** Ghevondyan - Hayk Ghevondyan (Հայկ Ղևոնդյան) (a) 01/07/2001, Vagharshapat (Armenia) (b) 1,71 (c) M - left midfielder (d) FC Noah Yerevan (e) FC Noah, FC Urartu, Urartu II, BKMA Yerevan, Banants III
*** Ghezzal - Rachid Ghezzal (غزال رشيد) (a) 09/05/1992, Décines-Charpieu (France) (b) 1,82 (c) F - right winger (d) Besiktas JK (e) Leicester City, Besiktas, Leicester City, Fiorentina, Leicester City, AS Monaco, Olympique Lyon, Olymp. Lyon B
*** Ghiasyan - David Ghiasyan (Դավիթ Ղիասյան) (a) 21/04/2006, ¿? (Armenia) (b) - (c) M - central midfielder (d) FC Urartu Erewan II (e) -

*** Ghiglione - Paolo Ghiglione (a) 02/02/1997, Voghera (Italy) (b) 1,91 (c) D - right back (d) US Cremonese (e) Genoa, Frosinone, Genoa, Pro Vercelli, Genoa, SPAL, Genoa
*** Ghimp - Ion Ghimp (a) 11/09/1996, ¿? (Moldova) (b) - (c) D - left back (d) CF Spartanii Sportul Selemet (e) Dacia Buiucani, Milsami, CSF Speranta, CSM Pascani, Foresta Suceava, Sfintul Gheorghe, FC Ungheni
*** Ghinaitis - Vladimir Ghinaitis (a) 30/03/1995, ¿? (Moldova) (b) 1,80 (c) D - right back (d) Kaysar Kyzylorda (e) Aktobe, Floresti, Sfintul Gheorghe, FC Ungheni, Zaria Balti, FC Saxan, Zaria Balti
*** Ghio - Jake Ghio (a) 08/09/2001, ¿? (Malta) (b) - (c) M - pivot (d) Marsaxlokk FC (e) Pietà Hotspurs
*** Ghita - Virgil Ghita (Virgil Eugen Ghiţă) (a) 04/06/1998, Piteşti (Romania) (b) 1,86 (c) D - central defense (d) Cracovia (e) FCV Farul, Academia Hagi
*** Ghoddos - Saman Ghoddos (سامان قدوس) (a) 06/09/1993, Malmö (Sweden) (b) 1,75 (c) M - attacking midfielder (d) - (e) Brentford, Amiens SC, Brentford, Amiens SC, Östersund, Syrianska FC, Trelleborg, Bunkeflo
*** Gholizadeh - Ali Gholizadeh (علی زاده قلی) (a) 10/03/1996, Tehran (Iran) (b) 1,75 (c) F - right winger (d) Lech Poznan (e) RSC Charleroi, Kasimpasa, RSC Charleroi, Saipa FC
*** Ghoulam - Faouzi Ghoulam (غلام فوزي) (a) 01/02/1991, Saint-Priest-en-Jarez (France) (b) 1,84 (c) D - left back (d) - (e) Angers SCO, Napoli, St.-Étienne, Saint-Étienne B
*** Ghubasaryan - Erjanik Ghubasaryan (Երջանիկ Խաչատուրի Ղուբասարյան) (a) 21/02/2001, Hamburg (Germany) (b) 1,85 (c) D - central defense (d) FC Noah Yerevan (e) BKMA Yerevan, LSK Hansa
*** Ghukasyan - Samvel Ghukasyan (Սամվել Ղուկասյան) (a) 19/05/2002, ¿? (Armenia) (b) - (c) M - pivot (d) Shirak Gyumri C.F. (e) Shirak II
*** Giacomoni - Aron Giacomoni (a) 22/08/1987, Lugo (Italy) (b) 1,80 (c) D - central defense (d) AC Virtus Acquaviva (e) Alfonsine, Tre Penne, Sasso Marconi, Trento, Ravenna, Chieri, Inveruno, Bra, Borgosesia, Asti, AC Mezzocorona
*** Giadas - Joel Giadas (Joel Rodríguez Giadas) (a) 11/06/2005, Escaldes-Engordany (Andorra) (b) - (c) D (d) CF Atlètic Amèrica (e) Sant Julià, Sant Julia B, ENFAF
*** Giakoumakis - Georgios Giakoumakis (Γεώργιος Γιακουμάκης) (a) 09/12/1994, Heraklion (Greece) (b) 1,85 (c) F - center forward (d) Atlanta United FC (e) Celtic FC, VVV-Venlo, AEK Athína, Górnik Zabrze, AEK Athína, OFI Creta, AEK Athína, Platanias, AO Episkopi, Platanias, PO Atsaleniou
*** Giakoumakis - Petros Giakoumakis (Πέτρος Γιακουμάκης) (a) 03/07/1992, Heraklion (Greece) (b) 1,79 (c) F - attacking midfielder (d) PAS Lamia 1964 (e) Olympiakos N., PAS Lamia, Veria NPS, Atromitos FC, APO Levadiakos, PO Atsaleniou, Chersonisos
*** Giambalvo - Alessandro Giambalvo (a) 23/04/2003, ¿? (San Marino) (b) - (c) D - central defense (d) - (e) San Giovanni
*** Giampaoli - Ignacio Giampaoli (a) 19/02/1992, Tucuman (Argentina) (b) 1,70 (c) M - attacking midfielder (d) Stallion Laguna FC (e) Mons Calpe, Fagersta Södra, Cefn Druids, Aris Archang., Hamilton W., Devonport, Golden State, Weston Bears, Pisek, IMG Soccer, Iztapa, San Martin II
*** Giampaoli - Renzo Giampaoli (a) 07/01/2000, Bombal (Argentina) (b) 1,87 (c) D - central defense (d) Quilmes Atlético Club (e) Quilmes, Boca Juniors II, Rosenborg, Boca Juniors II

*** Giangrandi - Alessandro Giangrandi (a) 09/12/1996, ¿? (Italy) (b) 1,70 (c) M - central midfielder (d) SP Cailungo (e) Juvenes-Dogana, Fiorentino, Meldola, Valbidente, Meldola

*** Giannakopoulos - Nikolaos Giannakopoulos (a) 19/02/1993, Tripoli (Greece) (b) 1,93 (c) G (d) - (e) Zimbru Chisinau, Apollon Smyrnis, Panetolikos, AOK Kerkyra, Panathinaikos, Aris Limassol, Panathinaikos, Panionios

*** Giannakou - Konstantinos Giannakou (Κωνσταντίνος Γιαννακού) (a) 25/04/2005, Nicosia (Cyprus) (b) 1,93 (c) D - central defense (d) APOEL FC (e) -

*** Giannikoglou - Makis Giannikoglou (a) 25/03/1993, Kavala (Greece) (b) 1,89 (c) G (d) PS Kalamata (e) Panserraikos, Suduva, PAS Giannina, AEK Athína, PAS Giannina, Iraklis, AS Fokikos, AO Kavala, Omonia Nicosia

*** Giannini - Daniel Giannini (a) 25/11/2002, ¿? (San Marino) (b) - (c) M (d) Monte Grimano Terme (e) Cailungo, SS Folgore

*** Gianniotas - Giannis Gianniotas (Γιάννης Γιαννιώτας) (a) 29/04/1993, Neochori, Chalkidiki (Greece) (b) 1,74 (c) F - right winger (d) APO Levadiakos (e) Apollon Smyrnis, Apollon Limassol, AEK Athína, Olympiakos, Real Valladolid, Olympiakos, APOEL FC, Olympiakos, APOEL FC, Olympiakos, Fortuna Düsseldorf, Asteras Tripoli, Fortuna Düsseldorf, Aris Thessaloniki

*** Gianniotis - Andreas Gianniotis (Ανδρέας Γιαννιώτης) (a) 18/12/1992, Serres (Greece) (b) 1,90 (c) G (d) Kasimpasa (e) Atromitos FC, Maccabi Tel Aviv, Atromitos FC, Maccabi Tel Aviv, Olympiakos, Atromitos FC, Olympiakos, Panionios, Olympiakos, PAS Giannina, Olympiakos, Fostiras, Olympiakos, Ethn. Gazoros, Thrakikos

*** Giannoulis - Konstantinos Giannoulis (Κωνσταντίνος Γιαννούλης) (a) 09/12/1987, Katerini (Greece) (b) 1,84 (c) D - central defense (d) OFI Creta (e) Pafos FC, Asteras Tripoli, Olympiakos, Atromitos FC, 1.FC Köln, Atromitos FC, 1.FC Köln, Iraklis, Panionios, Pierikos, Panionios, Fostiras, Panionios, Vataniakos

*** Giardi - Matteo Giardi (a) 14/04/1997, ¿? (San Marino) (b) - (c) F - left winger (d) SS Folgore/Falciano (e) Virtus, Murata, SS Folgore, Cosmos

*** Giardi - Mattia Giardi (a) 15/12/1991, ¿? (San Marino) (b) - (c) M - attacking midfielder (d) SC Faetano (e) SS Folgore, Tropical Coriano, Tre Fiori, Faetano

*** Giargiana - Randy Giargiana (a) 22/11/1995, ¿? (Belgium) (b) 1,79 (c) D - right back (d) Stade Verviétois (e) FC Wiltz 71, RFC Liégeois, RFC Seraing, Sprimont

*** Gibbs - Joey Gibbs (Joseph Arthur Gibbs) (a) 13/06/1992, Gosford (Australia) (b) 1,84 (c) F - center forward (d) Stjarnan Gardabaer (e) Keflavík, Blacktown City, Tai Po, Newcastle, Western Sydney, Marc. Stallions, Sydney FC II, Manly United, ROC Charleroi-M., Manly United, Sydney FC II, Manly United

*** Gibbs-White - Morgan Gibbs-White (Morgan Anthony Gibbs-White) (a) 27/01/2000, Stafford (England) (b) 1,78 (c) M - attacking midfielder (d) Nottingham Forest (e) Wolverhampton Wanderers, Sheffield Utd., Wolverhampton Wanderers, Swansea City, Wolverhampton Wanderers

*** Gíber - Attila Gíber (a) 19/01/2001, ¿? (Hungary) (b) - (c) F (d) Eger SE (e) Mezőkövesd II

*** Gibson - Jordan Gibson (a) 23/06/1995, Donaghcloney (Northern Ireland) (b) - (c) F - center forward (d) Ballymena United (e) Carrick Rangers, Loughgall, Lurgan Celtic, Dollingstown FC

*** Gibson - Jordan Gibson (Jordan Lewis Gibson) (a) 26/02/1998, Birmingham (England) (b) 1,78 (c) M (d) Carlisle United (e) Sligo Rovers, St. Patrick's Ath., Bradford City, Stevenage, Bradford City, Alvechurch, Bromsgrove Spo

*** Gibson - Mitch Gibson (Mitchell Dean Gibson) (a) 08/10/2001, Gibraltar (Gibraltar) (b) 1,70 (c) M - attacking midfielder (d) Europa FC (e) Glacis United, Europa FC, Europa Reserve
*** Gichev - Daniel Gichev (Даниел Петров Гичев) (a) 21/11/2004, Plovdiv (Bulgaria) (b) 1,73 (c) M - central midfielder (d) Botev Plovdiv II (e) -
*** Gidea - Adrian Gidea (Adrian Mihai Gîdea) (a) 13/03/2000, Drobeta-Turnu Severin (Romania) (b) 1,80 (c) M - central midfielder (d) CSM Alexandria (e) CFR Cluj, SSU Poli, CFR Cluj
*** Gidi - Samuel Gidi (a) 15/04/2004, ¿? (Ghana) (b) 1,78 (c) M - attacking midfielder (d) MSK Zilina (e) Zilina Africa
*** Gierlach - Szymon Gierlach (a) 18/01/2006, ¿? (Poland) (b) - (c) M - pivot (d) Stal Mielec II (e) -
*** Gießelmann - Niko Gießelmann (a) 26/09/1991, Hannover (Germany) (b) 1,82 (c) D - left back (d) - (e) Union Berlin, Fortuna Düsseldorf, Greuther Fürth, Hannover 96, Hannover 96 II
*** Giessing - Lukas Giessing (Lukas Grenaa Giessing) (a) 09/05/2000, ¿? (Faroe Islands) (b) 1,75 (c) M - right midfielder (d) B36 Tórshavn (e) NSÍ Runavík, Nyköbing FC, HB Tórshavn, Akademisk BK, AB Argir
*** Gigashvili - Zurab Gigashvili (ზურაბ გიგაშვილი) (a) 20/11/2001, Tbilisi (Georgia) (b) 1,89 (c) D - central defense (d) FK Mladost Donja Gorica (e) FC Telavi, Kryvbas, Tambov, Armavir
*** Gigauri - Archil Gigauri (a) 08/04/2002, ¿? (Georgia) (b) - (c) M (d) Gori FC (e) Dila II
*** Gigauri - Merab Gigauri (მერაბ გიგაური) (a) 05/06/1993, Tbilisi (Georgia) (b) 1,82 (c) M - pivot (d) Torpedo Kutaisi (e) Shamakhi, FK Qabala, Torpedo Kutaisi, Rustavi, Kolkheti Poti, Tskhinvali, Kolkheti Poti, Tskhinvali, Metalurgi R., Torpedo Kutaisi, Jagiellonia, Torpedo Kutaisi, Avaza Tbilisi
*** Gigic - Petar Gigic (Петар Гигић) (a) 07/03/1997, Prishtinë (RF Yugoslavia, now in Kosovo) (b) 1,86 (c) F - center forward (d) FK Javor-Matis Ivanjica (e) Zeleznicar Pancevo, Macva, FK Partizan, Novi Pazar, FK Partizan, Újpest FC, FK Partizan, Macva, FK Partizan, Macva, OFK Beograd
*** Gigot - Samuel Gigot (Samuel Florent Thomas Gigot) (a) 12/10/1993, Avignon (France) (b) 1,87 (c) D - central defense (d) Olympique Marseille (e) Spartak Moskva, Ol. Marseille, Spartak Moskva, KAA Gent, KV Kortrijk, AC Arles, AC Arles B
*** Gigovic - Armin Gigovic (Armin Gigović) (a) 06/04/2002, Lund (Sweden) (b) 1,87 (c) M - central midfielder (d) FC Midtjylland (e) Rostov, Odense BK, Rostov, Helsingborgs IF, Rostov, Helsingborgs IF
*** Gigovic - Ervin Gigovic (a) 16/09/2003, ¿? (Sweden) (b) - (c) M - pivot (d) Helsingborgs IF (e) -
*** Gikiewicz - Rafal Gikiewicz (Rafał Gikiewicz) (a) 26/10/1987, Olsztyn (Poland) (b) 1,90 (c) G (d) MKE Ankaragücü (e) FC Augsburg, Union Berlin, SC Freiburg, Eintracht Braunschweig, Śląsk Wroclaw, Jagiellonia, Stomil, Jagiellonia, Wigry Suwalki, Drweca NML, Sokol Ostroda, Dobre Miasto
*** Gil - Bryan Gil (Bryan Gil Salvatierra) (a) 11/02/2001, Barbate (Cádiz) (Spain) (b) 1,75 (c) F - left winger (d) Tottenham Hotspur (e) Sevilla FC, Tottenham Hotspur, Valencia CF, Tottenham Hotspur, Sevilla FC, SD Eibar, Sevilla FC, CD Leganés, Sevilla FC, Sevilla At., Barbate CF
*** Gil - David Gil (David Gil Mohedano) (a) 11/01/1994, Getafe (Spain) (b) 1,86 (c) G (d) Cádiz CF (e) Cádiz CF B, Getafe CF B, At. Madrid B, At. Madrid C
*** Gil - Jagoba Gil (Jagoba Gil Roz) (a) 09/04/1998, Erandio (Spain) (b) 1'76 (c) M - central midfielder (d) Atlético Bembibre (e) Sant Julià

*** Gil - Óscar Gil (Óscar Gil Regaño) (a) 26/04/1998, Elche (Spain) (b) 1,75 (c) D - right back (d) RCD Espanyol (e) Elche CF, Elche Ilicitano

*** Gil - Pablo Gil (Pablo Gil González) (a) 22/01/2003, Marbella (Spain) (b) 1,79 (c) F - center forward (d) UD San Pedro (e) UE Santa Coloma

*** Gila - Eloy Gila (Eloy Gila Marín) (a) 21/06/1988, Sabadell (Spain) (b) 1,75 (c) M - attacking midfielder (d) FC Santa Coloma (e) Cornellà, Albacete, CD Mirandés, Albacete, Llagostera, CE Sabadell, Llagostera, Gimnàstic, Betis B, Gimnàstic, Gramenet, Gramenet B

*** Gila - Mario Gila (Mario Gila Fuentes) (a) 29/08/2000, Barcelona (Spain) (b) 1,85 (c) D - central defense (d) SS Lazio (e) RM Castilla

*** Gilbert - Alex Gilbert (Alexander George Henry Gilbert) (a) 28/12/2001, Birmingham (England) (b) 1,83 (c) F - left winger (d) Middlesbrough FC (e) Brentford B, Swindon Town, Brentford B

*** Gilbert - Sean Gilbert (Sean Alexander Gilbert) (a) 14/11/1992, Gibraltar (Gibraltar) (b) - (c) M - right midfielder (d) Glacis United (e) Boca Gibraltar, Europa Reserve, Europa FC, Gibraltar Utd.

*** Gilberto - Gilberto (Gilberto Moraes Júnior) (a) 07/03/1993, Rio de Janeiro (Brazil) (b) 1,81 (c) D - right back (d) Esporte Clube Bahia (e) Benfica, Fluminense, Fiorentina, Fluminense, Fiorentina, Vasco da Gama, Fiorentina, Latina Calcio, Fiorentina, Hellas Verona, Fiorentina, Botafogo, Internacional, Botafogo, Botafogo B

*** Gilis - Jo Gilis (a) 05/02/2000, Geel (Belgium) (b) 1,73 (c) M - attacking midfielder (d) - (e) KSK Heist, KSK Lierse Kem., OH Leuven, Eendracht Aalst, OH Leuven

*** Giljen - Vladan Giljen (a) 07/12/1989, Niksic (Yugoslavia, now in Montenegro) (b) - (c) G (d) FK Sutjeska Niksic (e) KS Kastrioti, KF Tërbuni, FK Celik Niksic, OFK Beograd, Nacional, Sutjeska Niksic

*** Gill - Lennon Gill (a) 24/08/2004, ¿? (Ireland) (b) - (c) F - center forward (d) University College Dublin (e) -

*** Gillekens - Nick Gillekens (Nick José Gillekens) (a) 05/07/1995, Leuven (Belgium) (b) 1,86 (c) G (d) KVC Westerlo (e) Excelsior Mouscron, OH Leuven

*** Gillen - Aodhán Gillen (a) 03/03/2001, Belfast (Northern Ireland) (b) - (c) F - left winger (d) death (Dundela FC) (e) Carrick Rangers, Newington FC

*** Gillespie - Mark Gillespie (Mark Joseph Gillespie) (a) 27/03/1992, Newcastle upon Tyne (England) (b) 1,91 (c) G (d) Newcastle United (e) Motherwell FC, FC Walsall, Carlisle United, Blyth Spartans, Carlisle United

*** Gilmartin - Aiden Gilmartin (a) 02/06/2005, Greenock (Scotland) (b) - (c) F - center forward (d) East Kilbride FC (e) East Kilbride, St. Mirren B, Cowdenbeath FC

*** Gilmore - Luqman Gilmore (a) 10/05/1996, Iwo (Nigeria) (b) 1,78 (c) M - pivot (d) FK Liepaja (e) Samgurali, Zugdidi, Dinamo Tbilisi, FC Imereti

*** Gilmour - Billy Gilmour (Billy Clifford Gilmour) (a) 11/06/2001, Irvine (Scotland) (b) 1,70 (c) M - central midfielder (d) Brighton & Hove Albion (e) Chelsea, Norwich City, Chelsea

*** Gilmour - Charlie Gilmour (Charlie Ian Gilmour) (a) 11/02/1999, Brighton (England) (b) 1,87 (c) M - pivot (d) Inverness Caledonian Thistle FC (e) St. Johnstone, Cove Rangers FC, St. Johnstone, Alloa Athletic, St. Johnstone, Telstar

*** Gimenez - Santiago Gimenez (Santiago Tomás Giménez) (a) 18/04/2001, Buenos Aires (Argentina) (b) 1,82 (c) F - center forward (d) Feyenoord Rotterdam (e) Cruz Azul

*** Giménez - Álvaro Giménez (Álvaro Giménez Candela) (a) 19/05/1991, Elche (Spain) (b) 1,83 (c) F - center forward (d) Racing de Ferrol (e) Cádiz CF, Real

Zaragoza, Cádiz CF, RCD Mallorca, Cádiz CF, Birmingham City, Cádiz CF, Birmingham City, UD Almería, Alcorcón, Elche CF, Elche Ilicitano, RCD Mallorca B, Torrellano, Elche Ilicitano

*** Giménez - Gonzalo Giménez (Gonzalo Giménez Munzón) (a) 24/12/2000, Elda (Spain) (b) 1,76 (c) M - central midfielder (d) Europa FC (e) Lynx FC, CD Almoradí, Redován, Crevillente

*** Giménez - José María Giménez (José María Giménez de Vargas) (a) 20/01/1995, Toledo (Uruguay) (b) 1,85 (c) D - central defense (d) Atlético de Madrid (e) Danubio FC

*** Gimsay - Manji Moses Gimsay (a) 29/09/1999, ¿? (Nigeria) (b) - (c) F - right winger (d) - (e) Tabor Sezana, NK Dubrava ZG

*** Ginat - Alon Ginat (גינת אלון) (a) 26/04/2002, ¿? (Israel) (b) - (c) D - central defense (d) Hapoel Ramat haSharon (e) Maccabi Netanya, H. Nof HaGalil, Maccabi Netanya, M. Bnei Reineh, Maccabi Netanya

*** Gineitis - Gvidas Gineitis (a) 15/04/2004, Mazeikiai (Lithuania) (b) 1,87 (c) M - central midfielder (d) Torino FC (e) Atmosfera

*** Ginnelly - Josh Ginnelly (Joshua Lloyd Ginnelly) (a) 24/03/1997, Coventry (England) (b) 1,75 (c) F - left winger (d) Swansea City (e) Heart of Midlothian, Preston North End, Heart of Midlothian, Preston North End, Bristol Rovers, Preston North End, FC Walsall, Tranmere Rovers, Lincoln City, Lincoln City, FC Walsall, Altrincham

*** Gino - Federico Gino (Federico Gino Acevedo Fagúndez) (a) 26/02/1993, Melo (Uruguay) (b) 1,76 (c) M - central midfielder (d) PAS Giannina (e) Platense, Aldosivi, San Luis, Aldosivi, All Boys, Santa Cruz, Cruzeiro, Defensor, Carpi, Defensor

*** Ginsari - Radu Ginsari (Radu Gînsari) (a) 10/12/1991, Chişinău (Moldova) (b) 1,79 (c) M - attacking midfielder (d) FC Milsami Orhei (e) AO Xanthi, Milsami, KS Samara, Kiryat Shmona, KS Samara, Hapoel Haifa, FC Sheriff, Zimbru Chisinau, Ac. Chisinau, Buiucani

*** Ginter - Matthias Ginter (Matthias Lukas Ginter) (a) 19/01/1994, Freiburg im Breisgau (Germany) (b) 1,91 (c) D - central defense (d) SC Freiburg (e) Borussia Mönchengladbach, Borussia Dortmund, SC Freiburg

*** Ginzburg - Yossi Ginzburg (גינזבורג יוסי) (a) 11/10/1991, ¿? (Israel) (b) - (c) G (d) Ihud Bnei Shefaram (e) Ness Ziona, Hapoel Afula, M. Petah Tikva, Kabilio Jaffa, Hakoah Amidar, Maccabi Tel Aviv, Ness Ziona, Maccabi Tel Aviv, Hapoel Herzliya, Maccabi Tel Aviv

*** Giorbelidze - Guram Giorbelidze (გურამ გიორბელიძე) (a) 25/02/1996, Bolnisi (Georgia) (b) 1,74 (c) D - left back (d) FK Vojvodina Novi Sad (e) Zagłębie, Dinamo Batumi, Zagłębie, Wolfsberger AC, Dynamo Dresden, Wolfsberger AC, FC Dila, Sioni Bolnisi

*** Giordano - Carmine Pietro Giordano (a) 12/07/2003, ¿? (Italy) (b) - (c) M - left midfielder (d) SS Pennarossa (e) -

*** Giorgadze - Andro Giorgadze (ანდრო გიორგაძე) (a) 03/05/1996, Tbilisi (Georgia) (b) 1,97 (c) D - central defense (d) Mash'al Mubarek (e) FC Locomotive, FC Samtredia, Torpedo Kutaisi, Karpaty, Fastav Zlin, Vorskla Poltava, Merani Martvili, Merani II

*** Giorgeschi - Simone Giorgeschi (a) 28/06/2004, Genoa (Italy) (b) - (c) D - central defense (d) Pro Sesto 1913 (e) Pro Sesto

*** Giorgini - Matteo Giorgini (a) 08/04/1998, ¿? (San Marino) (b) - (c) D - central defense (d) AC Libertas (e) Libertas, Juvenes-Dogana

*** Giousis - Christos Giousis (Χρήστος Γιούσης) (a) 08/02/1999, Volos (Greece) (b) 1,77 (c) F - left winger (d) SC Telstar (e) AEK Athína B, AEK Athína, Panachaiki, AEK Athína, Platanias, AEK Athína

*** Giovagnoli - Fabio Giovagnoli (a) 10/06/1992, ¿? (Italy) (b) - (c) M - central midfielder (d) SP Tre Penne (e) Libertas, Cosmos, Villa Verucchio

*** Giovanardi - Matisse Giovanardi (Matisse Leonardo Giovanardi) (a) 28/04/2005, ¿? (Belgium) (b) - (c) G (d) Union Titus Petange (e) -

*** Giovanny - Giovanny (Giovanny Bariani Marques) (a) 19/09/1997, São Paulo (Brazil) (b) 1,75 (c) F - left winger (d) Lokomotiv Plovdiv (e) Tombense, Santo André, Tombense, Náutico, Tombense, Guarani, Tombense, Athletico-PR B, Goiás, Athletico-PR B, Paraná, Atlético-PR B, Guaratinguetá, Guaratinguetá, Guaratinguetá

*** Girdvainis - Edvinas Girdvainis (a) 17/01/1993, Klaipeda (Lithuania) (b) 1,89 (c) D - central defense (d) FK Kauno Zalgiris (e) KFC Uerdingen, RFS, Keshla, Hapoel Tel Aviv, Piast Gliwice, Tom Tomsk, Piast Gliwice, Marbella FC, Ekranas

*** Girdvainis - Gvidas Girdvainis (a) 14/04/2006, ¿? (Lithuania) (b) - (c) M (d) FC Dziugas Telsiai B (e) -

*** Girmai Netabay - Nahom Girmai Netabay (a) 28/08/1994, Kristianstad (Sweden) (b) 1,72 (c) M - central midfielder (d) Kalmar FF (e) Sirius, Varbergs BoIS, Kristianstad FC

*** Girotto - Andrei Girotto (a) 17/02/1992, Bento Gonçalves (Brazil) (b) 1,86 (c) D - central defense (d) Al-Taawoun FC (e) FC Nantes, Tombense, Chapecoense, Tombense, Kyoto Sanga, Tombense, Palmeiras, Tombense, América-MG, Tombense, Metropolitano, Hercílio Luz, Metropolitano

*** Giroud - Olivier Giroud (Olivier Jonathan Giroud) (a) 30/09/1986, Chambéry (France) (b) 1,92 (c) F - center forward (d) AC Milan (e) Chelsea, Arsenal, Montpellier, Tours FC, Grenoble, FC Istres, Grenoble, Grenoble B

*** Girs - Dmitriy Girs (Гирс Дмитрий Фёдорович) (a) 11/06/1997, Chashniki (Belarus) (b) 1,80 (c) M - right midfielder (d) FK Slutsk (e) Energetik-BGU, BGU Minsk II, Granit, BGU Minsk II

*** Gíslason - Arnar Númi Gíslason (a) 15/12/2004, Reykjavík (Iceland) (b) - (c) D - left back (d) ÍF Grótta (e) Breidablik, Fjölnir, Breidablik, Haukar

*** Gíslason - Jón Gísli Eyland Gíslason (a) 25/02/2002, ¿? (Iceland) (b) - (c) D - right back (d) ÍA Akranes (e) Tindastóll

*** Gismera - Aitor Gismera (Aitor Gismera Monge) (a) 21/02/2004, Getafe (Spain) (b) - (c) M - central midfielder (d) Atlético de Madrid B (e) -

*** Gissurarson - Rúnar Gissurarson (a) 23/11/1986, ¿? (Iceland) (b) - (c) G (d) Thróttur Vogum (e) Keflavík, Reynir S., Njardvík, Reynir S., Vídir

*** Giuliani - Christopher Giuliani (a) 07/05/1999, Graz (Austria) (b) 1,87 (c) G (d) First Vienna FC (e) SV Kapfenberg, Sturm Graz, SV Kapfenberg, Sturm Graz, Sturm Graz II

*** Giuliano - Alex Giuliano (a) 05/01/1999, ¿? (Italy) (b) - (c) D - left back (d) - (e) San Giovanni, Verucchio, Stella, Verucchio, Rivazzurra, Stella

*** Giunashvili - Akaki Giunashvili (აკაკი გიუნაშვილი) (a) 01/03/2005, ¿? (Georgia) (b) - (c) D - central defense (d) FC Kolkheti-1913 Poti (e) FC Dila

*** Giurgi - Josh Giurgi (Joshua Alexander Harsani Giurgi) (a) 18/06/2002, Dublin (Ireland) (b) 1,76 (c) D - right back (d) Longford Town FC (e) Shelbourne

*** Gjelaj - Robert Gjelaj (a) 23/09/2002, Podgorica (RF Yugoslavia, Montenegro) (b) 1,85 (c) D - left back (d) FK Decic Tuzi (e) -

*** Gjengaar - Dennis Gjengaar (a) 24/02/2004, Horten (Norway) (b) 1,76 (c) F - right winger (d) Odds BK (e) Odd II, Ørn Horten

*** Gjertsen - Torgil Gjertsen (a) 12/03/1992, Melhus (Norway) (b) - (c) F - left winger (d) Kristiansund BK (e) Wisła Płock, Kristiansund, Ranheim, Strindheim IL, Ranheim, Strindheim IL

*** Gjesdal - Henrik Gjesdal (Henrik Solheim Gjesdal) (a) 19/07/1993, Bergen (Norway) (b) 1,92 (c) D - central defense (d) Moss FK (e) Start, Kristiansund, Start, Kristiansund, Tromsø, Brann, Nest-Sotra IL, Brann

*** Gjeta - Stuart Gjeta (a) 15/12/2000, Leicester (England) (b) 1,70 (c) F - attacking midfielder (d) KS Kastrioti (e) -

*** Gjinollari - David Gjinollari (a) 17/04/1999, Tiranë (Albania) (b) 1,79 (c) D - left back (d) KF Teuta (e) KS Burreli, KF Vora, Hradec Kralove B

*** Gjokaj - Altin Gjokaj (a) 11/11/2005, ¿? (Serbia and Montenegro, now in Kosovo) (b) - (c) G (d) KF Drenica (e) FC Besa

*** Gjolaj - Mario Gjolaj (a) 06/04/2002, ¿? (RF Yugoslavia, now in Montenegro) (b) - (c) M - left midfielder (d) FK Decic Tuzi (e) FK Iskra, FK Decic Tuzi, Zeta Golubovac, FK Decic Tuzi

*** Gjone - Martin Gjone (a) 29/05/2005, ¿? (Norway) (b) - (c) M (d) Sandefjord Fotball II (e) -

*** Gjorcheski - Boban Gjorcheski (Бобан Ѓорчески) (a) 09/10/2004, Prilep (North Macedonia) (b) 1,78 (c) D - right back (d) - (e) Pobeda Prilep

*** Gjorgiev - Pepi Gjorgiev (Пепи Ѓоргиев) (a) 04/10/1994, Gevgelija (North Macedonia) (b) 1,84 (c) F - center forward (d) Gostivar (e) FC Shkupi, AP Brera, KF Teuta, Sileks, Bregalnica Stip, Belasica, Kozuf

*** Gjorgievski - Martin Gjorgievski (Мартин Ѓоргиевски) (a) 28/02/2005, Ohrid (North Macedonia) (b) 1,79 (c) M - central midfielder (d) AP Brera (e) -

*** Gjorgjieski - Aleksandar Gjorgjieski (Александар Ѓорѓиески) (a) 24/07/2000, Ohrid (North Macedonia) (b) 1,92 (c) M - pivot (d) Voska Sport (e) Makedonija, Ohrid Lihnidos, Makedonija, Borec Veles, Ohrid Lihnidos, Vardar

*** Gjorgjiev - Gjorgji Gjorgjiev (Ѓорѓи Ѓорѓиев) (a) 18/06/1996, Veles (North Macedonia) (b) 1,80 (c) F - right winger (d) Bregalnica Stip (e) Borec Veles, Ljubanci

*** Gjorgjievski - Marko Gjorgjievski (Марко Ѓорѓиевски) (a) 18/04/2000, Skopje (North Macedonia) (b) 1,86 (c) F - center forward (d) Sileks Kratovo (e) AP Brera, Vozdovac, FC Shkupi, Vozdovac, Radnicki Pirot, Vozdovac, Borec Veles

*** Gjorretaj - Samel Gjorretaj (a) 04/01/2002, ¿? (Albania) (b) - (c) M - central midfielder (d) SS Murata (e) Cosmos

*** Gjumsi - Aldi Gjumsi (a) 15/03/2002, ¿? (Albania) (b) 1,76 (c) F - right winger (d) KF Teuta (e) KF Tirana, KF Tirana B

*** Gjurchinoski - Bojan Gjurchinoski (Бојан Ѓурчиноски) (a) 13/04/1994, Struga (North Macedonia) (b) - (c) F - attacking midfielder (d) ASD Ilvamaddalena 1903 (e) Tre Fiori, Po-dri-nje, Tre Fiori, Guglionesi, NK Funtana, Pazinka Pazin, Rovinj, NK Funtana

*** Gjurkovski - Aleksandar Gjurkovski (Александар Ѓурковски) (a) 11/02/2002, Skopje (North Macedonia) (b) 1,84 (c) D - central defense (d) Tikves Kavadarci (e) FC Shkupi, Tikves, FC Shkupi, Vardar

*** Glackin - Jamie Glackin (a) 16/02/1995, Omagh (Northern Ireland) (b) 1,86 (c) M - left midfielder (d) Coleraine FC (e) Crusaders, Dungannon

*** Gladkyi - Oleksandr Gladkyi (Гладкий Олександр Миколайович) (a) 24/08/1987, Lozova, Kharkiv Oblast (Soviet Union, now in Ukraine) (b) 1,88 (c) F - center forward (d) - (e) Chornomorets, Zorya Lugansk, Adana Demirspor, Çaykur Rizespor, Chornomorets, Karpaty, Dinamo Kyïv, Karpaty, Dinamo Kyïv, Shakhtar Donetsk, Dnipro, Karpaty, Dnipro, Shakhtar Donetsk, FK Kharkiv, Arsenal Kharkiv, Metalist Kharkiv, UFK Kharkiv

*** Gladon - Paul Gladon (a) 18/03/1992, Haarlem (Netherlands) (b) 1,88 (c) F - center forward (d) Fortuna Sittard (e) FC Emmen, Willem II, FC Groningen, Wolverhampton Wanderers, Sint-Truiden, Wolverhampton Wanderers, Heracles Almelo, Wolverhampton Wanderers, Heracles Almelo, Sparta Rotterdam, FC Dordrecht, Sparta Rotterdam

*** Gladyshev - Yaroslav Gladyshev (Гладышев Ярослав Вадимович) (a) 05/05/2003, Kirov (Russia) (b) 1,81 (c) F - center forward (d) Dinamo Moskva (e) Dinamo 2, Dinamo Moskva II

*** Glamour - Eziefula Chibueze Glamour (a) 15/02/2003, ¿? (Nigeria) (b) - (c) M - pivot (d) Mosta FC (e) Garden City

*** Glamuzina - Kresimir Glamuzina (a) 14/02/2006, ¿? (Croatia) (b) - (c) D (d) Racing FC Union Luxembourg (e) -

*** Glass - Declan Glass (a) 07/06/2000, Edinburgh (Scotland) (b) 1,72 (c) M - attacking midfielder (d) Dundee United FC (e) Cove Rangers FC, Dundee United, Derry City, Dundee United, Kilmarnock FC, Dundee United, Dundee Utd. B, Cove Rangers FC, Dundee Utd. B, Airdrieonians, Dundee Utd. B, Hutchison Vale BC

*** Glaus - Nicolas Glaus (Nicolas Roger Glaus) (a) 10/05/2002, Binningen BL (Switzerland) (b) 1,87 (c) G (d) Grasshopper Club Zürich (e) Stuttgart II

*** Glavcic - Nemanja Glavcic (Немања Главчић) (a) 19/02/1997, Kraljevo (RF Yugoslavia, now in Serbia) (b) 1,70 (c) M - central midfielder (d) Volos NPS (e) Khimki, Slaven Belupo, Spartak, FK Partizan, Spartak, FK Partizan, Teleoptik, FK Partizan, Teleoptik

*** Glazer - Amit Glazer (גלזר עמית) (a) 30/05/2000, Tel Aviv (Israel) (b) 1,84 (c) D - central defense (d) Hapoel Jerusalem (e) H. Jerusalem, Maccabi Tel Aviv, Bnei Yehuda, Maccabi Tel Aviv, B TLV Bat Yam, Maccabi Tel Aviv

*** Glazer - Dan Glazer (גלזר דן) (a) 20/09/1996, ¿? (Israel) (b) 1,78 (c) M - pivot (d) Maccabi Tel Aviv (e) Maccabi Netanya, Maccabi Tel Aviv, Beitar TA Ramla, Maccabi Tel Aviv, Bnei Yehuda, Maccabi Tel Aviv, Beitar TA Ramla, Maccabi Tel Aviv

*** Glazer - Omri Glazer (גלזר עמרי) (a) 11/03/1996, Tel Aviv (Israel) (b) 1,90 (c) G (d) Crvena zvezda Beograd (e) H. Beer Sheva, Maccabi Haifa, Ness Ziona, Maccabi Haifa, Hapoel Raanana

*** Glazer - Tamir Glazer (גלזר תמיר) (a) 30/05/2000, Tel Aviv (Israel) (b) 1,89 (c) M - pivot (d) Hapoel Hadera (e) Hapoel Hadera, Maccabi Tel Aviv, Hapoel Haifa, Maccabi Tel Aviv, Hapoel Hadera, Maccabi Tel Aviv, B TLV Bat Yam, Maccabi Tel Aviv

*** Glazunov - Saveliy Glazunov (Глазунов Савелий Эдуардович) (a) 13/11/2000, Almaty (Kazakhstan) (b) 1,71 (c) F - right winger (d) Zhas Kyran Almaty (e) Akzhayik, Zhas-Kyran, Belshina, Akad. Ontustik

*** Glebko - Sergey Glebko (Глебко Сергей Александрович) (a) 23/08/1992, Minsk (Belarus) (b) 1,80 (c) M - central midfielder (d) FK Slutsk (e) Belshina, Gomel, Torpedo Minsk, Bardejov, Torpedo Minsk, Gorodeya, FK Slutsk, BATE II, FK Slutsk, BATE II, FK Slutsk, BATE II

*** Glebov - Danil Glebov (Глебов Данил Александрович) (a) 03/11/1999, Tomsk (Russia) (b) 1,78 (c) M - pivot (d) FK Rostov (e) Anzhi, Anzhi II

*** Glebov - Kirill Glebov (Глебов Кирилл Артёмович) (a) 10/11/2005, Chelyabinsk (Russia) (b) 1,74 (c) F - right winger (d) CSKA Moskva II (e) Signal

*** Glendinning - Reece Glendinning (a) 09/06/1995, Belfast (Northern Ireland) (b) - (c) D - central defense (d) Carrick Rangers (e) Ballymena, Linfield, Ards FC, Linfield

*** Glendinning - Ross Glendinning (a) 18/05/1993, Newtownabbey (Northern Ireland) (b) 1,88 (c) G (d) Carrick Rangers (e) Glentoran, Ballymena, Linfield, Ballyclare, Linfield

*** Glenna - Casper Glenna (Casper Glenna Andersen) (a) 07/02/2005, ¿? (Norway) (b) - (c) D - right back (d) Odds BK (e) Odd II

*** Glenny - Adam Glenny (a) 30/05/2002, Portadown (Northern Ireland) (b) 1,81 (c) D - left back (d) Dungannon Swifts (e) Annagh United, Dungannon

*** Gliga - Eugeniu Gliga (a) 12/05/2001, ¿? (Moldova) (b) 1,71 (c) M - attacking midfielder (d) FC Milsami Orhei (e) Milsami, FC Sheriff

*** Gligorov - Filip Gligorov (Филип Глигоров) (a) 31/07/1993, Skopje (North Macedonia) (b) 1,81 (c) D - right back (d) KF Ferizaj (e) Shakhter K., FK Kukësi, FK Partizani, FC Shkupi, KF Vllaznia, Dunarea Calarasi, Sileks, FC Shkupi, FK Olimpik, Euromilk GL, STK Samorin, Banik Ruzina, Rabotnicki

*** Gliklich - Lior Gliklich (גליקליך ליאור) (a) 02/01/2003, ¿? (Israel) (b) 1,84 (c) G (d) Hapoel Rishon leZion (e) Hapoel Tel Aviv

*** Glinskiy - Vladislav Glinskiy (Глинский Владислав Витальевич) (a) 29/05/2000, Polotsk (Belarus) (b) 1,78 (c) M - central midfielder (d) FK Vitebsk (e) Isloch, Vitebsk, Isloch, BATE II, Torpedo Minsk, RUOR Minsk

*** Glisic - Aleksandar Glisic (Aleksandar Glišić) (a) 03/09/1992, Banjaluka (Bosnia and Herzegovina) (b) 1,83 (c) F - center forward (d) FC Noah Yerevan (e) Ararat Yerevan, Dinamo, Alashkert CF, FC Urartu, Radnik Bijelj., Zvijezda G., Radnik Bijelj., Tekstilac, FK Crvena Zemlja Nova Ves

*** Gllogu - Pëllumb Gllogu (a) 07/05/2005, Prishtinë (Serbia and Montenegro, now in Kosovo) (b) - (c) M - pivot (d) FC Prishtina (e) -

*** Gloukh - Oscar Gloukh (גלוך אוסקר) (a) 01/04/2004, Rehovot (Israel) (b) 1,70 (c) M - attacking midfielder (d) Red Bull Salzburg (e) Maccabi Tel Aviv

*** Gloydman - Nikita Gloydman (Глойдман Никита Игоревич) (a) 10/01/2002, Moskva (Russia) (b) 1,89 (c) D - central defense (d) Torpedo 2 Moskau (e) Arsenal 2 Tula, Arsenal Tula II

*** Glumac - Tomislav Glumac (a) 14/05/1991, Dubrovnik (Yugoslavia, now in Croatia) (b) 1,94 (c) D - central defense (d) Ümraniyespor (e) Balikesirspor, RNK Split, Balikesirspor, RNK Split, Hajduk Split, NK Zadar, GOSK Dubrovnik

*** Glushach - Yegor Glushach (Глушач Єгор Олександрович) (a) 21/11/2002, Yevpatoriya, Krym (Ukraine) (b) 1,83 (c) M - central midfielder (d) FK Hodonin (e) Jonava, 1.SC Znojmo, Real Farma

*** Glushakov - Denis Glushakov (Глушаков Денис Борисович) (a) 27/01/1987, Millerovo, Rostov Oblast (Soviet Union, now in Russia) (b) 1,81 (c) M - central midfielder (d) - (e) Pari Nizhny Novgórod, Khimki, Akhmat Grozny, Spartak Moskva, Lokomotiv Moskva, Lokomotiv Moskva II, Zvezda Irkutsk, Lokomotiv Moskva II, SKA Rostov, Lokomotiv Moskva II, Nika Moskva

*** Glushchenkov - Kirill Glushchenkov (Глущенков Кирилл Юрьевич) (a) 05/02/2000, Stavropol (Russia) (b) 1,91 (c) D - central defense (d) Torpedo-BelAZ Zhodino (e) Isloch, Fakel Voronezh, Dinamo Moskva II

*** Glushenkov - Maksim Glushenkov (Глушенков Максим Александрович) (a) 28/07/1999, Smolensk (Russia) (b) 1,79 (c) F - center forward (d) Lokomotiv Moskva (e) KS Samara, Spartak Moskva, KS Samara, Spartak Moskva, Khimki, Spartak Moskva, KS Samara, Spartak Moskva, Chertanovo

*** Glynn - Kaydan Glynn (Kaydan Charles Glynn) (a) 16/05/2005, Gibraltar (Gibraltar) (b) - (c) M - central midfielder (d) St Joseph's FC Reserve (e) Red Imps Reserves

*** Glynn - Micheál Glynn (a) 12/03/2002, Derrygonnelly, Fermanagh (Northern Ireland) (b) 1,82 (c) D - left back (d) Larne FC (e) Derry City, Glenavon, Derry City, Dungannon, Derry City, Ballinamallard

*** Gmeiner - Fabian Gmeiner (a) 27/01/1997, Dornbirn (Austria) (b) 1,77 (c) D - right back (d) SC Austria Lustenau (e) SF Lotte, Hamburg II, NEC Nijmegen

*** Gnabouyou - Guy Gnabouyou (Guy Kassa Gnabouyou) (a) 01/12/1989, ¿? (France) (b) 1,83 (c) F - center forward (d) - (e) Sioni Bolnisi, FC Gareji, Sabah, Petrolul, Iraklis, ÍBV Vestmannaeyjar, Torquay, FC Inter, Sliema Wanderers, AEL Kalloni, FC Inter, Paris FC, US Orléans 45, Ol. Marseille, Ol. Marseille B

*** Gnabry - Serge Gnabry (Serge David Gnabry) (a) 14/07/1995, Stuttgart (Germany) (b) 1,76 (c) F - right winger (d) Bayern München (e) Hoffenheim, Bayern München, Werder Bremen, Arsenal, West Bromwich Albion, Arsenal

*** Gnapi - Angenor Gnapi (Angenor Bosco Gnapi) (a) 18/12/1998, ¿? (Ivory Coast) (b) 1,81 (c) M - pivot (d) FC Dinamo-Auto Tiraspol (e) AS Denguélé, AS Tanda, CO Bouaflé

*** Gnezda Cerin - Adam Gnezda Cerin (Adam Gnezda Čerin) (a) 16/07/1999, Postojna (Slovenia) (b) 1,80 (c) M - central midfielder (d) Panathinaikos FC (e) 1.FC Nürnberg, HNK Rijeka, 1.FC Nürnberg, Domžale

*** Gning - Abdallah Gning (a) 29/09/1998, ¿? (Senegal) (b) 1,84 (c) F - center forward (d) FK Teplice (e) Vlasim, Stade de Mbour

*** Gnjatic - Ognjen Gnjatic (Ognjen Gnjatić) (a) 16/10/1991, Bugojno (Yugoslavia, now in Bosnia and Herzegovina) (b) 1,90 (c) M - pivot (d) NK Radomlje (e) Erzgebirge Aue, Korona Kielce, Roda JC, Platanias, Rad Beograd, Kozara Gradiska

*** Gnonto - Wilfried Gnonto (Degnand Wilfried Gnonto) (a) 05/11/2003, Verbania (Italy) (b) 1,70 (c) F - left winger (d) Leeds United (e) FC Zürich

*** Goba Zakpa - Goba Zakpa (Elysée Goba Zakpa) (a) 17/08/1992, Abidjan (Ivory Coast) (b) 1,85 (c) F - center forward (d) - (e) FK Sabail, Ethnikos, Lus. Lourosa, Felgueiras, Gil Vicente, Santa Maria, Gil Vicente, SAS Epinal, Valenciano, SAS Epinal, Rio Ave, Gondomar, Rio Ave

*** Gobbi - Jose Gobbi (Jose Maria Gobbi) (a) 08/10/1992, ¿? (Malta) (b) 1,83 (c) G (d) - (e) Marsaxlokk, Calangianus, Sarmiento de Leones

*** Gobeljic - Marko Gobeljic (Марко Гобељић) (a) 13/09/1992, Kraljevo (RF Yugoslavia, now in Serbia) (b) 1,85 (c) D - right back (d) Crvena zvezda Beograd (e) Napredak, Sloga Kraljevo

*** Gocholeishvili - Giorgi Gocholeishvili (გიორგი გოჩოლეიშვილი) (a) 14/02/2001, Kutaisi (Georgia) (b) 1,78 (c) D - right back (d) Shakhtar Donetsk (e) Saburtalo

*** Goda - Bruno Goda (a) 17/04/1998, Vinkovci (Croatia) (b) 1,82 (c) D - left back (d) HNK Rijeka (e) Slaven Belupo, NK Granicar Zupanja

*** Godal - Boris Godal (Boris Godál) (a) 27/05/1987, Trenčín (Czechoslovakia, now in Slovakia) (b) 1,88 (c) D - central defense (d) MFK Dukla Banska Bystrica (e) Podbrezova, Al-Adalah, Podbrezova, AEL Limassol, Spartak Trnava, Zagłębie, AS Trencin

*** Godeau - Bruno Godeau (a) 10/05/1992, Brussel (Belgium) (b) 1,90 (c) D - central defense (d) Sint-Truidense VV (e) KAA Gent, Excelsior Mouscron, KV Oostende, Zulte Waregem, KVC Westerlo, Zulte Waregem

*** Godfrey - Ben Godfrey (Benjamin Matthew Godfrey) (a) 15/01/1998, York (England) (b) 1,84 (c) D - central defense (d) Everton FC (e) Norwich City, Shrewsbury, Norwich City, York City

*** Godinho - Marcus Godinho (Marcus Valdez Pereira Godinho) (a) 28/06/1997, Toronto, Ontario (Canada) (b) 1,78 (c) D - right back (d) Korona Kielce (e)

Vancouver, FSV Zwickau, Heart of Midlothian, Berwick Rangers FC, Heart of Midlothian, Vaughan Azzurri, Toronto FC II
*** Godins - Kristians Godins (Kristians Godiņš) (a) 20/05/2004, ¿? (Latvia) (b) - (c) M (d) SK Super Nova (e) Spartaks
*** Godo - Martial Godo (Becket Fabrice-Martial Godo) (a) 14/03/2003, ¿? (England) (b) - (c) F - left winger (d) - (e) Margate FC
*** Godtfred - Dánjal Godtfred (a) 07/03/1996, Tórshavn (Faroe Islands) (b) 1,83 (c) M - pivot (d) EB/Streymur (e) TB Tvøroyri, TB/FCS/Royn, FC Suduroy
*** Godts - Mika Godts (Mika Marcel Godts) (a) 07/06/2005, Leuven (Belgium) (b) 1,76 (c) F - left winger (d) Ajax Amsterdam B (e) Jong Genk
*** Godwin - Joseph Godwin (Joseph Enziwanne Godwin) (a) 15/07/2003, ¿? (Nigeria) (b) 2,03 (c) F - center forward (d) CSM Resita (e) UTA Arad, FC Buzau, UTA Arad
*** Godwin - Saviour Godwin (Saviour Amunde Godwin) (a) 22/08/1996, Jos (Nigeria) (b) 1,73 (c) F - left winger (d) Casa Pia AC (e) KSV Roeselare, KV Oostende
*** Godya - Dmytro Godya (Годя Дмитро Васильович) (a) 10/03/2005, ¿? (Ukraine) (b) 1,70 (c) M - attacking midfielder (d) - (e) NK Veres Rivne
*** Goes - Wouter Goes (a) 10/06/2004, Amsterdam (Netherlands) (b) 1,87 (c) D - central defense (d) AZ Alkmaar (e) -
*** Goga - Ergi Goga (a) 25/10/2002, Tiranë (Albania) (b) - (c) D - left back (d) KF Luzi United (e) KF Erzeni
*** Gogescu - George Gogescu (George Cristian Gogescu) (a) 27/08/2005, Bucharest (Romania) (b) 1,76 (c) D - central defense (d) - (e) ACS Prosport
*** Gogia - Akaki Gogia (a) 18/01/1992, Rustavi (Georgia) (b) 1,78 (c) F - right winger (d) VSG Altglienicke (e) Dynamo Dresden, FC Zürich, Union Berlin, Dynamo Dresden, Brentford, Dynamo Dresden, Brentford, Hallescher FC, VfL Wolfsburg, FC St. Pauli, VfL Wolfsburg, FC Augsburg, VfL Wolfsburg, Wolfsburg II
*** Gogic - Alex Gogic (Αλέξανδρος Γκόγκιτς) (a) 13/04/1994, Nicosia (Cyprus) (b) 1,85 (c) M - pivot (d) St. Mirren FC (e) Hibernian FC, St. Mirren, Hibernian FC
*** Goglichidze - Leo Goglichidze (Гогличидзе Лео Зурабович) (a) 29/04/1997, Rostov-na-Donu (Russia) (b) 1,82 (c) D - left back (d) FK Orenburg (e) Orenburg, Ural, Krasnodar, Ural, Krasnodar, Nizhny Novgorod, Krasnodar, Chaika Pes., Krasnodar-2, Chaika Pes., Krasnodar-2, Nizhny Novgorod, Krasnodar-2, Krasnodar II
*** Goglichidze - Saba Goglichidze (a) 25/06/2004, ¿? (Georgia) (b) - (c) D - central defense (d) Torpedo Kutaisi (e) Torpedo Kutaisi II
*** Gogolashvili - Giorgi Gogolashvili (გიორგი გოგოლაშვილი) (a) 02/08/1997, Signagi (Georgia) (b) 1,87 (c) F - center forward (d) Shukura Kobuleti (e) Gomel, FC Shevardeni, Merani Tbilisi, Kolkheti Poti, Super Nova, RTU, Härnösands FF, Jelenia Gora, WIT Georgia, WIT Georgia II
*** Gogua - Gogita Gogua (გოგიტა გოგუა) (a) 04/10/1983, Chkhorotsku (Soviet Union, now in Georgia) (b) 1,70 (c) M - pivot (d) FC Samegrelo Chkhorotsku (e) Kolkheti Poti, Sioni Bolnisi, FC Shevardeni, FC Samtredia, FC Dila, Kyzyl-Zhar, Okzhetpes, Ordabasy, Irtysh, FC Dila, SKA-Energia, FC Dila, Dinamo Tbilisi, Volga Nizhny Novgorod, Spartak Nalchik, Terek Grozny, Spartak Nalchik, Saturn Ramenskoe, Spartak Nalchik, Khimki, FC Tbilisi, Dinamo Tbilisi, FC Tbilisi, Merani, Dinamo Tbilisi, Guria, FC Guria II
*** Goh - Massimo Goh (Massimo Virou N'Ccde Goh) (a) 01/02/1999, ¿? (Italy) (b) 1,93 (c) F - center forward (d) - (e) Tre Fiori, FC Clivense SM, Fanfulla, CSC Selimbar, Cattolica, Crema, Cavese, Virtus Verona, Arsenal Kyiv II, Virtus Verona

*** Gohou - Gerard Gohou (Gerard Bi Goua Gohou) (a) 29/12/1988, Soubré (Ivory Coast) (b) 1,84 (c) F - center forward (d) - (e) Aktobe, Kasimpasa, BJ BSU, Kairat Almaty, Krasnodar, K. Erciyesspor, Denizlispor, Neuchâtel Xamax, Hassania, JC Abidjan

*** Goiginger - Thomas Goiginger (a) 15/03/1993, Salzburg (Austria) (b) 1,81 (c) F - right winger (d) LASK (e) Blau Weiss Linz, Grödig, Neumarkt, Vöcklamarkt, Eugendorf, Köstendorf

*** Gojak - Amer Gojak (a) 13/02/1997, Sarajevo (Bosnia and Herzegovina) (b) 1,84 (c) M - attacking midfielder (d) Ferencváros TC (e) Dinamo Zagreb, Torino, Dinamo Zagreb, FK Olimpik

*** Gojani - Robert Gojani (a) 19/10/1992, Kalix (Sweden) (b) 1,74 (c) M - central midfielder (d) Kalmar FF (e) Silkeborg IF, Elfsborg, J-Södra IF

*** Gojkovic - Luka Gojkovic (Лука Гојковић) (a) 28/11/1999, Beograd (RF Yugoslavia, now in Serbia) (b) 1,76 (c) M - attacking midfielder (d) FK Javor-Matis Ivanjica (e) Rad Beograd, IMT Beograd, Backa, FK BSK Borča

*** Gojkovic - Renato Gojkovic (Renato Gojković) (a) 10/09/1995, Tuzla (Bosnia and Herzegovina) (b) 1,95 (c) D - central defense (d) FK Orenburg (e) Zrinjski Mostar, FK Partizani, NK Istra, Celik Zenica, Sloboda Tuzla

*** Gökay - Emre Gökay (a) 18/02/2006, Kayseri (Turkey) (b) 1,81 (c) F - right winger (d) Sivasspor (e) Erkiletspor

*** Göksu - Serkan Göksu (a) 19/05/1993, Istanbul (Turkey) (b) 1,82 (c) M - central midfielder (d) Ümraniyespor (e) Altinordu, Yeni Malatyaspor, Bayrampasa

*** Göktas - Yusuf Eren Göktas (Yusuf Eren Göktaş) (a) 23/06/2004, Ankara (Turkey) (b) - (c) D - central defense (d) MKE Ankaragücü (e) Ankaragücü

*** Golan - Shahar Golan (a) 01/07/2003, ¿? (Slovenia) (b) - (c) G (d) - (e) NK Celje

*** Golasa - Eyal Golasa (איל גולסה) (a) 07/10/1991, Netanya (Israel) (b) 1,78 (c) M - central midfielder (d) Maccabi Tel Aviv (e) PAOK, Maccabi Haifa

*** Golban - David Golban (a) 12/11/2004, ¿? (Moldova) (b) - (c) D - central defense (d) Dacia Buiucani (e) -

*** Goldberg - Shon Goldberg (שון גולדברג) (a) 13/06/1995, Tel Aviv (Israel) (b) 1,79 (c) D - central defense (d) Maccabi Haifa (e) H. Beer Sheva, Hapoel Haifa, Maccabi Tel Aviv, B. Jerusalem, Maccabi Tel Aviv, Bnei Yehuda, Maccabi Tel Aviv, Hapoel Tel Aviv, Maccabi Tel Aviv

*** Goldenberg - Hagai Goldenberg (חגי גולדנברג) (a) 15/09/1990, Oranit (Israel) (b) 1,84 (c) D - right back (d) Hapoel Nof HaGalil (e) B. Jerusalem, H. Nof HaGalil, Bnei Sakhnin, Hapoel Hadera, Kiryat Shmona, Maccabi Netanya, M. Petah Tikva

*** Goldson - Connor Goldson (Connor Lambert Goldson) (a) 18/12/1992, Wolverhampton (England) (b) 1,91 (c) D - central defense (d) Rangers FC (e) Brighton & Hove Albion, Shrewsbury, Cheltenham Town, Shrewsbury

*** Golebiowski - Radoslaw Golebiowski (Radosław Gołębiowski) (a) 24/11/2001, Częstochowa (Poland) (b) 1,78 (c) M - left midfielder (d) Sandecja Nowy Sącz (e) Widzew Lódz, Skra Czestochowa, Widzew Lódz, Skra Czestochowa

*** Golenkov - Egor Golenkov (Голенков Егор Дмитриевич) (a) 07/07/1999, Samara (Russia) (b) 1,89 (c) F - center forward (d) FK Rostov (e) Sigma Olomouc, KS Samara, KS Samara II, KS Samara II, Akron Konoplev

*** Gölgeli - Bahadir Gölgeli (Bahadır Gölgeli) (a) 01/07/2003, Gaziantep (Turkey) (b) - (c) M - pivot (d) Gaziantep FK (e) -

*** Golinucci - Alessandro Golinucci (a) 10/10/1994, San Marino (San Marino) (b) - (c) M - central midfielder (d) AC Virtus Acquaviva (e) CBR Carli Pietracuta, Tropical Coriano, Sammaurese

*** Golinucci - Enrico Golinucci (a) 16/07/1991, ¿? (San Marino) (b) - (c) M - central midfielder (d) - (e) SS Folgore, Libertas, Domagnano

*** Goljan - Adam Goljan (a) 15/04/2001, Žilina (Slovakia) (b) 1,85 (c) F - left winger (d) AC Sparta Praha B (e) MSK Zilina, MSK Zilina B

*** Golla - Wojciech Golla (a) 12/01/1992, Złotów (Poland) (b) 1,86 (c) D - central defense (d) Puskás Akadémia FC (e) Śląsk Wroclaw, NEC Nijmegen, Pogon Szczecin, Lech Poznan, Lech Poznan II

*** Goller - Benjamin Goller (a) 01/01/1999, Reutlingen (Germany) (b) 1,80 (c) F - right winger (d) 1.FC Nürnberg (e) Werder Bremen, Karlsruher SC, Werder Bremen, Darmstadt 98, Werder Bremen, Karlsruher SC, Werder Bremen, FC Schalke 04

*** Golliard - Théo Golliard (a) 27/09/2002, Riaz (Switzerland) (b) 1,74 (c) M - attacking midfielder (d) FC Vaduz (e) FC Vaduz, BSC Young Boys

*** Gollini - Pierluigi Gollini (a) 18/03/1995, Bologna (Italy) (b) 1,94 (d) SSC Nápoles (e) Napoli, Atalanta, Fiorentina, Atalanta, Tottenham Hotspur, Atalanta, Aston Villa, Atalanta, Aston Villa, Hellas Verona

*** Gollner - Manfred Gollner (a) 22/12/1990, Judenburg (Austria) (b) 1,84 (c) D - central defense (d) TSV Hartberg (e) Wolfsberger AC, TSV Hartberg, SV Kapfenberg, Kapfenberg II, Rapid/KSV III, AKA Kapfenberg

*** Golofca - Catalin Golofca (a) 21/04/1990, Suceava (Romania) (b) 1,69 (d) AFC Chindia Targoviste (e) FC Botosani, Sepsi OSK, CFR Cluj, Sepsi OSK, CFR Cluj, FC Botosani, FCSB, FC Botosani, Rapid Suceava, FC Botosani, Rapid Suceava, Cetatea Suceava

*** Golovatyuk - Kyrylo Golovatyuk (Головатюк Кирило) (a) 03/02/2003, ¿? (Ukraine) (b) - (c) G (d) - (e) Juvenes-Dogana, Spontricciolo

*** Golovenko - Pavel Golovenko (Головенко Павел Викторович) (a) 12/01/1997, Minsk (Belarus) (b) 1,82 (c) G (d) Zyrardowianka Zyrardow (e) ZY Zhodino, Dzerzhinsk, FK Lida, FK Minsk, FK Minsk II

*** Golovin - Aleksandr Golovin (Головин Александр Сергеевич) (a) 30/05/1996, Kaltan, Kemerovo Oblast (Russia) (b) 1,78 (c) M - attacking midfielder (d) AS Mónaco (e) CSKA Moskva, CSKA Moskva II

*** Golovkin - Ivan Golovkin (Головкін Іван Миколайович) (a) 24/05/2000, Donetsk (Ukraine) (b) 1,78 (c) F - right winger (d) Zorya Lugansk (e) Ingulets, Krystal Kherson, Volyn Lutsk II, FK Mariupol II, Krystal Kherson

*** Golovljov - Eduard Golovljov (a) 25/01/1997, Tallinn (Estonia) (b) 1,78 (c) F - center forward (d) FC Tallinn (e) JK Trans Narva, Kalev, JK Trans Narva, FCI Levadia, JK Trans Narva, FCI Levadia, FCI Tallinn

*** Golub - Danylo Golub (Голуб Данило Олегович) (a) 03/07/2003, Vugledar, Donetsk Oblast (Ukraine) (b) 1,76 (c) F - right winger (d) FK Minaj (e) -

*** Golubickas - Paulius Golubickas (a) 19/08/1999, Ignalina (Lithuania) (b) 1,73 (c) M - attacking midfielder (d) FK Zalgiris Vilnius (e) HNK Gorica, DFK Dainava, HNK Gorica, DFK Dainava, HNK Gorica, DFK Dainava, Suduva, DFK Dainava

*** Golubnichiy - Mikhail Golubnichiy (Голубничий Михаил Валерьевич) (a) 31/01/1995, Pavlodar (Kazakhstan) (b) 1,88 (c) G (d) FK Aksu (e) Zhetysu, FK Aksu, Atyrau, FK Aksu, Okzhetpes II, FC Astana, Kyzyl-Zhar, FC Astana, Pavlodar II, FC Bayterek, Pavlodar II

*** Golubovic - Adnan Golubovic (Adnan Golubović) (a) 22/07/1995, Ljubljana (Slovenia) (b) 1,86 (c) G (d) FC Dinamo 1948 (e) Koper, Sloboda Tuzla, Vis Pesaro, Sloboda Tuzla, Vis Pesaro, Catanzaro, Matera, Domžale, NK Triglav

*** Golubovic - Aleksa Golubovic (a) 19/11/2002, ¿? (RF Yugoslavia, now in Montenegro) (b) - (c) M - attacking midfielder (d) Rudar Pljevlja (e) -

*** Golubovic - Petar Golubovic (Петар Голубовић) (a) 13/07/1994, Beograd (RF Yugoslavia, now in Serbia) (b) 1,86 (c) D - right back (d) FK Khimki (e) Aalesund, KV Kortrijk, Novara, AS Roma, AC Pisa, AS Roma, Pistoiese, AS Roma, Novara, AS Roma, OFK Beograd

*** Golubović - Stefan Golubović (Стефан Голубовић) (a) 02/09/2005, ¿? (Serbia and Montenegro, now in Montenegro) (b) 1,90 (c) F - center forward (d) Rudar Pljevlja (e) -

*** Gomanov - Kirill Gomanov (Гоманов Кирилл Александрович) (a) 17/02/2005, Vitebsk (Belarus) (b) 1,86 (c) M - attacking midfielder (d) Isloch Minsk Region (e) -

*** Gome - Wangu Gome (Wangu Baptista Gome) (a) 13/02/1993, Windhoek (Namibia) (b) 1,58 (c) M - pivot (d) - (e) Alashkert CF, Civics FC, Cape Umoya Utd., Civics FC, Bidvest Wits FC, Civics FC, Bidvest Wits FC, Civics FC

*** Gomelko - Artem Gomelko (Гомелько Артём Викторович) (a) 08/12/1989, Zhodino (Soviet Union, now in Belarus) (b) 1,92 (c) G (d) Sparta Kazimierza Wielka (e) FK Slutsk, Lori Vanadzor, Smolevichi, Slonim, Gorodeya, Slonim, Granit, Lokomotiv Moskva II, Torpedo Zhodino, Lokomotiv Moskva II, Naftan, Lokomotiv Moskva II, Torpedo Zhodino

*** Gomelt - Tomislav Gomelt (a) 07/01/1995, Sisak (Croatia) (b) 1,85 (c) M - central midfielder (d) - (e) NK Rudes, Suduva, ADO Den Haag, Crotone, FC Dinamo, HNK Rijeka, Lorca FC, HNK Rijeka, Bari, CFR Cluj, Bari, CFR Cluj, Bari, Tottenham Hotspur, Bari, Tottenham Hotspur, Royal Antwerp, Tottenham Hotspur, RCD Espanyol B

*** Gomes - André Gomes (André Filipe Tavares Gomes) (a) 30/07/1993, Grijó (Portugal) (b) 1,88 (c) M - central midfielder (d) Everton FC (e) Lille, Everton, FC Barcelona, Everton, FC Barcelona, Valencia CF, Benfica, Valencia CF, Benfica

*** Gomes - André Gomes (André Nogueira Gomes) (a) 20/10/2004, Ponte de Lima (Portugal) (b) 1,82 (c) G (d) SL Benfica B (e) -

*** Gomes - Angel Gomes (Angel Almeida Gomés) (a) 31/08/2000, London (England) (b) 1,68 (c) M - central midfielder (d) LOSC Lille Métropole (e) Boavista, Lille, Manchester Utd.

*** Gomes - António Gomes (António Pedro Pina Gomes) (a) 29/08/2000, Lisboa (Portugal) (b) 1,76 (c) F - right winger (d) Union Titus Petange (e) Oliveirense, FC Rodange 91

*** Gomes - Claudio Gomes (a) 23/07/2000, Argenteuil (France) (b) 1,80 (c) M - pivot (d) Palermo FC (e) Barnsley FC, Paris Saint Germain B

*** Gomes - Francisco Gomes (Francisco Tomás Aguiar Gomes) (a) 14/04/2004, Funchal (Portugal) (b) 1,75 (c) F - right winger (d) CS Marítimo (e) -

*** Gomes - Henrique Gomes (Henrique Martins Gomes) (a) 30/11/1995, Barcelos (Portugal) (b) 1,85 (c) D - left back (d) Académico Viseu FC (e) Gil Vicente, SC Covilhã, Vilaverdense, Gil Vicente, Vilaverdense, Gil Vicente, Santa Maria

*** Gomes - João Gomes (João Victor Gomes da Silva) (a) 12/02/2001, Rio de Janeiro (Brazil) (b) 1,76 (c) M - central midfielder (d) Wolverhampton Wanderers (e) Flamengo

*** Gomes - Josep Gomes (Josep Antoni Gomes Moreira) (a) 03/12/1985, La Massana (Andorra) (b) 1,81 (c) G (d) FC Santa Coloma (e) IC d'Escaldes, UE Santa Coloma, Villaverde CF, CD Illescas, ES Pennoise, CD Fortuna, Carabanchel, Sant Rafel, Ciudad Vicar, Ibiza-Eivissa, FC Andorra

*** Gomes - Ricardo Gomes (Ricardo Jorge Pires Gomes) (a) 18/12/1991, Praia (Cabo Verde) (b) 1,87 (c) F - center forward (d) Al-Shamal SC (e) FK Partizan, Sharjah FC, BB Erzurumspor, Sharjah FC, Ittihad Kalba, Sharjah FC, FK Partizan,

Nacional, Vitória Guimarães, Nacional, Vitória Guimarães, Vitória Guimarães B, Vizela, Batuque

*** Gomes - Roberto Gomes (Roberto Carlos Gomes Rebelo) (a) 21/10/1999, ¿? (Andorra) (b) - (c) F - left winger (d) FC Pas de la Casa (e) UE Santa Coloma, Lleida Esp. B, UD Fraga, UE Santa Coloma, Inter Escald. B

*** Gomes - Rodrigo Gomes (Rodrigo Martins Gomes) (a) 07/07/2003, Póvoa de Varzim (Portugal) (b) 1,75 (c) F - right winger (d) GD Estoril Praia (e) Estoril Praia, SC Braga, Braga B, SC Braga

*** Gomes - Rui Gomes (Rui Pedro Ribeiro Fernandes Duarte Gomes) (a) 04/09/1997, Braga (Portugal) (b) 1,75 (c) F - left winger (d) CD Tondela (e) Tondela, Portimonense, SC Covilhã, Legia Warszawa, Legia II, Leiria, Mafra, Gil Vicente, Vitória Guimarães B, Merelinense Fr.

*** Gomes - Samuel Gomes (Samuel Gomes da Mata) (a) 20/08/1999, ¿? (Brazil) (b) 1,80 (c) F - right winger (d) Sliema Wanderers (e) Gudja United FC, FC Cascavel, Goiás, Aparecidense, Goiás, Londrina-PR, Goiás

*** Gomes - Toni Gomes (Toni Correia Gomes) (a) 16/11/1998, Bissau (Guinea-Bissau) (b) 1,82 (c) F - left winger (d) Zira FK (e) Tuzlaspor, Menemen FK, Gaish, Harras Hodoud, Arouca, Forest Green Rovers

*** Gomes - Vítor Gomes (Vítor Hugo Gomes da Silva) (a) 25/12/1987, Vila do Conde (Portugal) (b) 1,82 (c) M - pivot (d) Rio Ave FC (e) Omonia Nicosia, Desportivo Aves, Belenenses, Moreirense, Balikesirspor, Moreirense, Videoton FC, Rio Ave, Videoton FC, Rio Ave, Cagliari, Rio Ave

*** Gomes Rodrigues - Marleigh Gomes Rodrigues (a) 14/12/2002, ¿? (Luxembourg) (b) - (c) D (d) Racing FC Union Luxemburg II (e) -

*** Gomez - James Gomez (a) 14/11/2001, Bakary Sambouya (Gambia) (b) 1,89 (c) D - central defense (d) AC Sparta Praga (e) AC Horsens, Real de Banjul, AC Horsens, Real de Banjul, AC Horsens, Real de Banjul

*** Gomez - Joe Gomez (Joseph Dave Gomez) (a) 23/05/1997, Catford (England) (b) 1,88 (c) D - central defense (d) Liverpool FC (e) Charlton Ath.

*** Gómez - Dani Gómez (Daniel Gómez Alcón) (a) 30/07/1998, Alcorcón (Spain) (b) 1,78 (c) F - center forward (d) Levante UD (e) RCD Espanyol, Levante UD, Real Madrid, CD Tenerife, Real Madrid, RM Castilla

*** Gómez - Gerard Gómez (Gerard Gómez Gómez) (a) 02/08/2002, Barcelona (Spain) (b) 1,80 (c) D - central defense (d) FC Santa Coloma (e) Rayo B

*** Gómez - Jonathan Gómez (Jonathan Germán Gómez Mendoza) (a) 01/09/2003, North Richland Hills, Texas (United States) (b) 1,78 (c) D - left back (d) CD Mirandés (e) CD Mirandés, Real Sociedad B, Louisville City, North Texas SC, Solar SC

*** Gómez - Kike Gómez (Enrique Gómez Bernal) (a) 04/05/1994, Sevilla (Spain) (b) 1,70 (c) F - center forward (d) Lincoln Red Imps FC (e) R. B. Linense, Europa FC, Coria CF, UD Pilas

*** Gómez - Maxi Gómez (Maximiliano Gómez González) (a) 14/08/1996, Paysandú (Uruguay) (b) 1,86 (c) F - center forward (d) Trabzonspor (e) Valencia CF, RC Celta, Defensor

*** Gómez - Moi Gómez (Moisés Gómez Bordonado) (a) 23/06/1994, Rojales (Spain) (b) 1,76 (c) F - left winger (d) CA Osasuna (e) Villarreal CF, Real Sporting, SD Huesca, Real Sporting, Villarreal CF, Getafe CF, Villarreal CF, Villarreal CF B, Villarreal CF C

*** Gómez - Sebastián Gómez (Sebastián Gómez Pérez) (a) 01/11/1983, Murcia (Spain) (b) 1,76 (c) F - left winger (d) CF Atlètic Amèrica (e) UE Engordany, FC Andorra, Sant Julià, FC Rànger's, CE Principat, FC Rànger's, FC Santa Coloma, CE Principat

*** Gómez - Sergi Gómez (Sergi Gómez Solà) (a) 28/03/1992, Arenys de Mar (Spain) (b) 1,85 (c) D - central defense (d) RCD Espanyol (e) Sevilla FC, RC Celta, FC Barcelona B, CE Mataró

*** Gómez - Sergio Gómez (Sergio Gómez Martín) (a) 04/09/2000, Badalona (Spain) (b) 1,71 (c) D - left back (d) Manchester City (e) RSC Anderlecht, Borussia Dortmund, SD Huesca, Borussia Dortmund

*** Gómez - Unai Gómez (Unai Gómez Etxebarria) (a) 25/05/2003, Bermeo (Spain) (b) 1,83 (c) M - attacking midfielder (d) Bilbao Athletic (e) CD Basconia

*** Gómez - Víctor Gómez (Víctor Gómez Perea) (a) 01/04/2000, Olesa de Montserrat (Spain) (b) 1,69 (c) D - right back (d) SC Braga (e) RCD Espanyol, SC Braga, RCD Espanyol, Málaga CF, RCD Espanyol, CD Mirandés, RCD Espanyol, RCD Espanyol B

*** Gomi - Ikuto Gomi (五味 郁登) (a) 09/05/2002, ¿?, Hyogo (Japan) (b) 1,77 (c) F - right winger (d) FS Jelgava (e) DFK Dainava, Tukums, Metta

*** Gomis - Antonio Gomis (Antonio Gomis Alemañ) (a) 20/05/2003, Elche (Spain) (b) - (c) G (d) Atlético de Madrid B (e) -

*** Gomis - Bafétimbi Gomis (Bafétimbi Fredius Gomis) (a) 06/08/1985, La Seyne-sur-Mer (France) (b) 1,84 (c) F - center forward (d) Kawasaki Frontale (e) Galatasaray, Al-Hilal, Galatasaray, Swansea City, Ol. Marseille, Swansea City, Olympique Lyon, St.-Étienne, Troyes, St.-Étienne, Saint-Étienne B

*** Gomis - Christian Gomis (a) 25/08/1998, Dakar (Senegal) (b) 2,02 (c) M - pivot (d) - (e) Honvéd, Lokomotiv Plovdiv, Paris Saint Germain B, EF Bastia, Pacy Ménilles

*** Gomis - David Gomis (David Cafimipon Gomis) (a) 21/12/1992, Toulon (France) (b) 1,73 (c) F - left winger (d) FK Sabail (e) Pau FC, Clermont Foot, G. Ajaccio, SC Toulon, Toulon Le Las, Fréjus-St-Raphaël, Sp. Toulon Var

*** Gomis - Honore Gomis (Honoré Gomis) (a) 27/02/1996, Leona Thiaroye (Senegal) (b) 1,72 (c) F - right winger (d) FC Dila Gori (e) Menemenspor, Ümraniyespor, Hatayspor, Sacré-Cœur, Guédiawaye FC

*** Gomis - Mechini Gomis (a) 14/12/2001, ¿? (Senegal) (b) 1,85 (c) F - center forward (d) Al-Sailiya SC (e) Paide, Wallidan, Cayor Foot

*** Gomis - Yannick Gomis (Yannick Arthur Gomis) (a) 03/02/1992, Dakar (Senegal) (b) 1,80 (c) F - center forward (d) Aris Limassol (e) Guingamp, RC Lens, US Orléans, Ngor

*** Gomza - Dmitriy Gomza (Гомза Дмитрий Владимирович) (a) 03/05/1987, Baranovichi (Soviet Union, now in Belarus) (b) 1,76 (c) F - center forward (d) Sperre (e) Bumprom, Belshina, Gomel, Smolevichi, Belshina, Gomel, Gomelzheldor, Vitebsk, Gorodeya, Torpedo Zhodino, Gomel, Vitebsk, Gomel, Beltransgaz, FK Baranovichi, FK Bereza, FK Baranovichi, Gorodeya

*** Gonalons - Maxime Gonalons (a) 10/03/1989, Vénissieux (France) (b) 1,87 (c) M - pivot (d) Clermont Foot 63 (e) Granada CF, AS Roma, Granada CF, AS Roma, Sevilla FC, AS Roma, Olympique Lyon, Olymp. Lyon B

*** Gonçalves - Claude Gonçalves (Joaquim Claude Gonçalves Araújo) (a) 09/04/1994, Propriano (France) (b) 1,74 (c) M - pivot (d) Ludogorets Razgrad (e) Gil Vicente, Troyes, Tondela, AC Ajaccio, AC Ajaccio B

*** Gonçalves - Diogo Gonçalves (Diogo António Cupido Gonçalves) (a) 06/02/1997, Almodôvar (Portugal) (b) 1,78 (c) F - left winger (d) FC Copenhague (e) Benfica, Famalicão, Benfica, Nottingham Forest, Benfica, Benfica B

*** Gonçalves - Esmaël Gonçalves (Esmaël Ruti Tavares Cruz da Silva Gonçalves) (a) 25/06/1991, Bissau (Guinea-Bissau) (b) 1,84 (c) F - center forward (d) Livingston FC (e) Raith Rovers, Livingston FC, Sheikh Russel, Chennaiyin FC, Matsumoto

Yama., Esteghlal FC, Pakhtakor, Heart of Midlothian, Anorthosis, Al-Ettifaq, Anorthosis, Rio Ave, Anorthosis, Rio Ave, PAE Veria, Rio Ave, APOEL FC, Rio Ave, St. Mirren, Rio Ave, OGC Nice, OGC Nice B

*** Gonçalves - João Gonçalves (João Pedro Oliveira Gonçalves) (a) 05/11/2000, Matosinhos (Portugal) (b) 1,88 (c) G (d) Boavista Porto FC (e) Boavista

*** Gonçalves - Michael Gonçalves (Michael Jose Barroso Gonçalves) (a) 10/03/1995, Basel (Switzerland) (b) 1,74 (c) D - right back (d) FC Winterthur (e) Servette FC, FC Wil 1900, Neuchâtel Xamax, FC Wil 1900

*** Gonçalves - Pedro Gonçalves (Pedro António Pereira Gonçalves) (a) 28/06/1998, Vidago (Portugal) (b) 1,73 (c) F - left winger (d) Sporting de Lisboa (e) Famalicão

*** Gonçalves - Tiago Gonçalves (Tiago André das Dores Gonçalves) (a) 26/04/2003, Vinhais (Portugal) (b) 1,97 (c) G (d) Vitória Guimarães SC B (e) -

*** Gonçalves - Vagner Gonçalves (Vagner Goncalves Nogueira de Souza) (a) 27/04/1996, Porto Alegre (Brazil) (b) 1,74 (c) F - right winger (d) FC Pyunik Yerevan (e) Pyunik Yerevan, Dinamo Tbilisi, Shkëndija, FC Dila, SK Dnipro-1, Kryvbas, SK Dnipro-1, Dinamo Batumi, Saburtalo, Cercle Brugge, Saburtalo, SC Bastia B

*** Goncalves Matheus - Ruben Goncalves Matheus (Rúben Gonçalves Matheus) (a) 03/02/2003, Luxembourg (Luxembourg) (b) 1,72 (c) F - center forward (d) Union Titus Petange (e) -

*** Gonchar - Igor Gonchar (Гончар Ігор Вікторович) (a) 10/01/1993, Chernivtsi (Ukraine) (b) 1,80 (c) D - right back (d) FK Suduva Marijampole (e) FK Minaj, Pyunik Yerevan, Alashkert CF, PFC Lviv, Vorskla Poltava, Girnyk-Sport, Vorskla Poltava, FK Senica, Shakhtar II, Goverla, Shakhtar II, Shakhtar 3, Obolon Kyiv II, Dyn. Khmeln., Obolon Kyiv II, RVUFK Kyiv

*** Goncharenko - Roman Goncharenko (Гончаренко Роман Олександрович) (a) 16/11/1993, Potash, Cherkasy Oblast (Ukraine) (b) 1,84 (c) D - central defense (d) Kolos Kovalivka (e) Veres Rivne, Kremin, FK Polissya, Ingulets, Cherk. Dnipro

*** Gönen - Cenk Gönen (a) 21/02/1988, Izmir (Turkey) (b) 1,90 (c) G (d) - (e) Kayserispor, Denizlispor, Alanyaspor, Málaga CF, Galatasaray, Besiktas, Denizlispor, Altay SK, Denizlispor, Göztepe

*** Gong - Hilary Gong (Hilary Chukwah Gong) (a) 10/10/1998, Zawan (Nigeria) (b) 1,69 (c) F - right winger (d) AS Trencin (e) Ararat-Armenia, Haugesund, Vitesse, AS Trencin

*** Gongadze - Georgiy Gongadze (Гонгадзе Георгий Михайлович) (a) 20/03/1996, Moskva (Russia) (b) 1,86 (c) F - center forward (d) Torpedo Moskva (e) Fakel Voronezh, SKA Khabarovsk, Torpedo Moskva, SKA Rostov, Olimp Khimki, Mashuk, Din. Stavropol, FK Dolgoprudnyi, Aventa-2000, Yunost Moskvy Torpedo,

*** Gono - Miroslav Gono (a) 01/11/2000, Piešťany (Slovakia) (b) 1,81 (c) M - attacking midfielder (d) ViOn Zlate Moravce-Vrable (e) MSK Zilina, Wisła Płock, MSK Zilina, MSK Zilina B

*** Gonsevich - Oleg Gonsevich (a) 13/05/2005, Narva (Estonia) (b) - (c) D - central defense (d) JK Trans Narva (e) -

*** Gonstad - Julian Bakkeli Gonstad (a) 29/06/2006, ¿? (Norway) (b) 1,73 (c) F (d) Hamarkameratene (e) -

*** Gonzalez - Jesse Gonzalez (a) 16/11/2005, Gibraltar (Gibraltar) (b) 1,80 (c) G (d) Europa Point FC (e) -

*** Gonzalez - Kayden Gonzalez (Kayden Lee Gonzalez) (a) 14/11/2006, Gibraltar (Gibraltar) (b) - (c) F - left winger (d) St Joseph's FC Reserve (e) -

*** Gonzalez - Kevan Gonzalez (a) 19/10/2005, Gibraltar (Gibraltar) (b) - (c) F - center forward (d) FC Manchester 62 (e) Manchester 62 Reserves

*** González - Abraham González (Abraham González Casanova) (a) 16/07/1985, Barcelona (Spain) (b) 1,75 (c) M - central midfielder (d) Akritas Chlorakas (e) Ethnikos, AEK Larnaca, Tiburones Rojos, Lobos BUAP, Pumas UNAM, RCD Espanyol, Alcorcón, Gimnàstic, Ponferradina, Gimnàstic, Cádiz CF, Barcelona Atlètic, Terrassa FC

*** González - Alexander González (Alexander David González Sibulo) (a) 13/09/1992, Caracas (Venezuela) (b) 1,77 (c) D - right back (d) Caracas FC (e) Pyunik Yerevan, Málaga CF, FC Dinamo, CD Mirandés, Elche CF, SD Huesca, BSC Young Boys, FC Thun, BSC Young Boys, FC Aarau, BSC Young Boys, Caracas FC, Caracas FC B

*** González - Antonio González (Antonio González García) (a) 06/05/1996, La Línea de la Concepión (Spain) (b) 1,77 (c) M - central midfielder (d) Lynx FC (e) Boca Gibraltar, San Roque Cádiz, Linense B, UD Tesorillo, Linense B

*** González - Christopher González (a) 18/08/1996, Luxembourg (Luxembourg) (b) 1,86 (c) G (d) Cibao FC (e) FC UNA Strassen, Weiler, FC UNA Strassen, Weiler, Weiler, Sandweiler, Sandweiler, FC Red Black, Sandweiler, Sandweiler

*** González - Diego González (Diego González Polanco) (a) 28/01/1995, Chiclana de la Frontera (Cádiz) (Spain) (b) 1,85 (c) D - central defense (d) Elche CF (e) Málaga CF, Sevilla At., Cádiz CF, Granada B, Cádiz CF B

*** González - Diego González (Diego Luis González Alcaraz) (a) 07/01/2003, Alto Paraná (Paraguay) (b) 1,77 (c) F - left winger (d) SS Lazio (e) Celaya, Potros del Este, U. San Martín, Potros del Este, Ciudad del Este II

*** González - Eder González (Eder González Tortella) (a) 07/01/1997, Palma de Mallorca (Spain) (b) 1,70 (c) M - pivot (d) Atromitos FC (e) Sepsi OSK, Csikszereda, Terrassa FC, RCD Mallorca B, Cornellà

*** González - Edgar González (Edgar González Estrada) (a) 01/04/1997, Sant Joan Despí (Spain) (b) 1,93 (c) D - central defense (d) UD Almería (e) Real Betis, Real Oviedo, Real Betis, Betis Deportivo, RCD Espanyol B, Cornellà, RCD Espanyol B, Cornellà, RCD Espanyol B

*** González - Giovanni González (Giovanni Alessandro González Apud) (a) 20/09/1994, Montevideo (Uruguay) (b) 1,78 (c) D - right back (d) RCD Mallorca (e) Peñarol, River Plate

*** González - Joan González (Joan González Cañellas) (a) 01/02/2002, Barcelona (Spain) (b) 1,90 (c) M - central midfielder (d) US Lecce (e) -

*** González - José González (José Gonzalez Morales) (a) 09/10/1994, La Linea de la Concepción (Spain) (b) - (c) M - central midfielder (d) - (e) Lynx FC, UD Tesorillo, San Roque Cádiz, Linense B, UD Tesorillo

*** González - Mario González (Mario González Gutiérrez) (a) 25/02/1996, Villarcayo (Spain) (b) 1,83 (c) F - center forward (d) Los Ángeles FC (e) SC Braga, OH Leuven, SC Braga, CD Tenerife, SC Braga, Villarreal CF, Tondela, Villarreal CF, Clermont Foot, Villarreal CF B, Villarreal CF C

*** González - Mikel González (Mikel González de Martín Martínez) (a) 24/09/1985, Mondragón (Spain) (b) 1,90 (c) D - central defense (d) - (e) AEK Larnaca, Real Zaragoza, Real Sociedad, Real Sociedad B

*** González - Nico González (Nicolás González Iglesias) (a) 03/01/2002, A Coruña (Spain) (b) 1,88 (c) M - central midfielder (d) FC Porto (e) FC Barcelona, Valencia CF, FC Barcelona, FC Barcelona B

*** González - Nicolás González (Nicolás Iván González) (a) 06/04/1998, Belén de Escobar (Argentina) (b) 1,80 (c) F - left winger (d) Fiorentina (e) VfB Stuttgart, Argentinos Jrs.

*** González - Olmo González (Olmo González Casado) (a) 15/06/1987, La Línea de la Concepción (Spain) (b) 1,78 (c) D - central defense (d) FC Bruno's Magpies (e) Europa FC, R. B. Linense, CP Villarrobledo, Daimiel CF, Rayo Majadahonda, Cádiz CF B

*** González - Oumar González (a) 25/02/1998, Douala (Cameroon) (b) 1,86 (c) D - central defense (d) AC Ajaccio (e) FC Chambly Oise, FC Metz, FC Villefranche, FC Metz, Rodez AF, FC Metz, SAS Epinal, FC Metz, FC Metz B

*** González - Pablo González (Pablo González Juárez) (a) 12/05/1993, Almuñécar (Spain) (b) 1,73 (c) M - attacking midfielder (d) Hapoel Tel Aviv (e) Sigma Olomouc, Dukla Praha, Salamanca CF, Recreativo Granada, CD Toledo, SD Huesca, CD Toledo, SD Huesca, Villarreal CF B, Villarreal CF C

*** González - Rober González (Roberto González Bayón) (a) 08/01/2001, Mérida (Spain) (b) 1,69 (c) F - right winger (d) NEC Nijmegen (e) NEC Nijmegen, Real Betis, Alavés, Real Betis, UD Las Palmas, Real Betis, UD Las Palmas, Real Betis, Betis Deportivo

*** González - Urko González (Urko González de Zárate Quirós) (a) 20/03/2001, Vitoria-Gasteiz (Spain) (b) 1,89 (c) D - central defense (d) Real Sociedad B (e) Real Sociedad C

*** González - Walter González (Walter Rodrigo González Sosa) (a) 21/05/1995, Juan León Mallorquín (Paraguay) (b) 1,85 (c) F - center forward (d) Club Olimpia Asunción (e) Santa Clara, Olimpia, Pachuca, Everton, Pachuca, León, Pachuca, Olimpia, Pachuca, Olimpia, Arouca, Olimpia

*** González - Yony González (Yony Alexander González Copete) (a) 11/07/1994, Medellín (Colombia) (b) 1,84 (c) F - right winger (d) Fluminense FC (e) Portimonense, Benfica, Deportivo Cali, Benfica, Ceará SC, Benfica, Los Ángeles, Benfica, Corinthians, Benfica, Fluminense, Junior FC, Envigado

*** González Zapico - Andres González Zapico (Andrés Cristobal González Zapico) (a) 26/02/2001, ¿? (Argentina) (b) 1,83 (c) D - left back (d) CD Huracán de Balazote (e) Lynx FC, La Garrovilla, GCE Villaralbo, Palm Beach, Defensores II

*** Goode - Charlie Goode (Charles James Goode) (a) 03/08/1995, Watford (England) (b) 1,96 (c) D - central defense (d) Brentford FC (e) Blackpool, Brentford, Sheffield Utd., Brentford, Northampton, Scunthorpe Utd., Northampton, Scunthorpe Utd., Hendon, AFC Hayes

*** Goodman - Owen Goodman (Owen Olamidayo Goodman) (a) 27/11/2003, Romford, Essex (England) (b) 1,93 (c) G (d) Colchester United (e) Colchester Utd.

*** Gooijer - Tristan Gooijer (a) 02/09/2004, Blaricum (Netherlands) (b) 1,85 (c) D - central defense (d) Ajax Amsterdam B (e) -

*** Goralski - Jacek Goralski (Jacek Góralski) (a) 21/09/1992, Bydgoszcz (Poland) (b) 1,72 (c) M - pivot (d) - (e) VfL Bochum, Kairat Almaty, Ludogorets, Jagiellonia, Wisła Płock, Blekitni Gabin, Victoria Koronowo, Zawisza II

*** Goranov - Ivan Goranov (Иван Горанов) (a) 10/06/1992, Velingrad (Bulgaria) (b) 1,78 (c) D - left back (d) - (e) Universitatea Cluj, PAS Lamia, RSC Charleroi, Levski Sofia, RSC Charleroi, Levski Sofia, Lokomotiv Plovdiv, Litex Lovetch, Beroe

*** Göransson - Victor Göransson (a) 28/04/2001, ¿? (Sweden) (b) - (c) M - central midfielder (d) Ängelholms FF (e) Ängelholms FF, Helsingborgs IF, Ängelholms FF, Helsingborgs IF

*** Gorbachik - Valeriy Gorbachik (Горбачик Валерий Сергеевич) (a) 19/01/1995, Pukhovichi (Belarus) (b) 1,83 (c) F - center forward (d) Torpedo-BelAZ Zhodino (e) Isloch, Torpedo Zhodino, Liepaja, Torpedo Zhodino, Smolevichi, Dinamo Minsk II, FK Bereza, Dinamo Minsk II

*** Gorbunov - Igor Gorbunov (Горбунов Игорь Владимирович) (a) 20/09/1994, Nikitino, Tambov Region (Russia) (b) 1,72 (c) M - left midfielder (d) Torpedo Moskva (e) Rubin Kazan, Pari Nizhny Novgórod, Armavir, Rotor Volgograd, Sochi, Nizhny Novgorod, Dinamo SPb, Dinamo Moskva II

*** Gorbunov - Sergiy Gorbunov (Горбунов Сергій Олегович) (a) 14/03/1994, Mariupol, Donetsk Oblast (Ukraine) (b) 1,81 (c) D - left back (d) SK Dnipro-1 (e) Karpaty Lviv, SK Dnipro-1, Metalist, FK Mariupol, Shakhtar II, Dnipro II

*** Gorby - Gorby (Jean-Baptiste Gorby) (a) 25/07/2002, Mayotte (France) (b) 1,83 (c) M - pivot (d) FC Paços de Ferreira (e) Paços Ferreira, SC Braga, Braga B

*** Gorcea - Andrei Gorcea (Andrei Cristian Gorcea) (a) 02/08/2001, Cluj-Napoca (Romania) (b) - (c) G (d) FC Universitatea Cluj (e) -

*** Gordana - Roei Gordana (גורדנה רועי) (a) 06/07/1990, Tel Aviv (Israel) (b) 1,76 (c) M - central midfielder (d) Hapoel Beer Sheva (e) FC Ashdod, Slaven Belupo, Bnei Yehuda, H. Beer Sheva, M. Petah Tikva, H. Beer Sheva, Hapoel Tel Aviv, H. Petah Tikva, Hapoel Tel Aviv

*** Gordeychuk - Mikhail Gordeychuk (Гордейчук Михаил Николаевич) (a) 23/10/1989, Saran (Soviet Union, now in Kazakhstan) (b) 1,76 (c) F - right winger (d) Dynamo Brest (e) Liepaja, Dynamo Brest, Tobol Kostanay, BATE Borisov, Belshina, BATE Borisov, Belshina, BATE Borisov, Naftan, Volna Pinsk, Shakhter-Bulat

*** Gordeziani - Vasilios Gordeziani (Βασίλειος Γκορντεζιάνι) (a) 29/01/2002, Thessaloniki (Greece) (b) 1,85 (c) F - center forward (d) PAOK Thessaloniki B (e) -

*** Gordic - Djordje Gordic (Ђорђе Гордић) (a) 05/11/2004, Priboj (Serbia and Montenegro, now in Serbia) (b) - (c) M - central midfielder (d) Lommel SK (e) Mladost

*** Gordic - Milos Gordic (Милош Гордић) (a) 05/03/2000, Beograd (RF Yugoslavia, now in Serbia) (b) 1,93 (c) G (d) FK IMT Belgrad (e) IMT Beograd, Crvena zvezda, AEK Larnaca, Crvena zvezda, Macva, Crvena zvezda, GSP Polet, Crvena zvezda

*** Gordon - Anthony Gordon (Anthony Michael Gordon) (a) 24/02/2001, Liverpool (England) (b) 1,82 (c) F - left winger (d) Newcastle United (e) Everton, Preston North End, Everton

*** Gordon - Craig Gordon (a) 31/12/1982, Edinburgh (Scotland) (b) 1,93 (c) G (d) Heart of Midlothian FC (e) Celtic FC, Sunderland, Heart of Midlothian, Cowdenbeath FC, Heart of Midlothian

*** Gordon - John-Kymani Gordon (John-Kymani Linton Michael Gordon) (a) 13/02/2003, London (England) (b) 1,81 (c) F - center forward (d) - (e) Carlisle United

*** Gordon - Liam Gordon (Liam Craig Gordon) (a) 26/01/1996, Perth (Scotland) (b) 1,83 (c) D - central defense (d) St. Johnstone FC (e) Peterhead FC, St. Johnstone, Elgin City, Arbroath

*** Gordon - Shea Gordon (Shea Martin Gordon) (a) 16/05/1998, Larne (Northern Ireland) (b) 1,79 (c) M - central midfielder (d) Larne FC (e) Partick Thistle, Queen of the South, Partick Thistle, Motherwell B, Partick Thistle, Motherwell B

*** Gordon - Steven Gordon (a) 27/07/1993, Newtownards (Northern Ireland) (b) 1,83 (c) D - central defense (d) Carrick Rangers (e) Glentoran, Carrick Rangers, Glentoran, Ards FC, Glentoran, Lisburn FC, Glentoran, Glenavon

*** Gordulava - Lasha Gordulava (ლაშა გორდულავა) (a) 10/05/1998, ¿? (Georgia) (b) 1,96 (c) G (d) FC Aragvi Dusheti (e) Dinamo Batumi, Merani Martvili, FC Bakhmaro, Guria, FC Dila, FC Odishi

*** Gorelov - Pavel Gorelov (Горелов Павел Вартанович) (a) 22/01/2003, Rostov-on-Don (Russia) (b) 1,80 (c) M - pivot (d) KamAZ Naberezhnye Chelny (e) Rostov II, FC Van, Rostov II

*** Gorenak - Gal Gorenak (a) 24/10/2003, Dravinja (Slovenia) (b) 1,80 (c) M - central midfielder (d) NK Aluminij Kidricevo (e) NK Maribor, NK Aluminij, NK Maribor, ND Ilirija

*** Gorenc - Jan Gorenc (a) 26/07/1999, Brezice (Slovenia) (b) 1,92 (c) D - central defense (d) KAS Eupen (e) NS Mura, Olimpija, NK Krsko, Trbovlje

*** Gorenc Stankovic - Jon Gorenc Stankovic (a) 14/01/1996, Ljubljana (Slovenia) (b) 1,90 (d) SK Sturm Graz (e) Huddersfield Town, Borussia Dortmund II, Domzale

*** Gorenko - Roman Gorenko (Горенко Роман Олександрович) (a) 20/10/2006, ¿? (Ukraine) (b) 1,64 (c) M - pivot (d) Metalist Kharkiv (e) -

*** Goretzka - Leon Goretzka (Leon Christoph Goretzka) (a) 06/02/1995, Bochum (Germany) (b) 1,89 (c) M - central midfielder (d) Bayern München (e) FC Schalke 04, VfL Bochum

*** Gorgiashvili - Tornike Gorgiashvili (თორნიკე გორგიაშვილი) (a) 27/04/1988, Tbilisi (Soviet Union, now in Georgia) (b) 1,84 (c) M - attacking midfielder (d) - (e) Sioni Bolnisi, FC Dila, Saburtalo, Chikhura, FC Samtredia, Tskhinvali, FC Samtredia, Dinamo Tbilisi, FC Zestafoni, FC Tbilisi

*** Gorgon - Alexander Gorgon (Alexander Gorgon) (a) 28/10/1988, Wien (Austria) (b) 1,85 (c) M - attacking midfielder (d) Pogon Szczecin (e) HNK Rijeka, Austria Viena, Austria Wien Reserves

*** Gori - Nicola Gori (a) 08/05/1997, ¿? (Italy) (b) - (c) D - central defense (d) AC Virtus Acquaviva (e) Savignanese, Virtus, Savignanese, Tropical Coriano, Savignanese

*** Gorican - Silvio Gorican (Silvio Goričan) (a) 27/02/2000, Zabok (Croatia) (b) 1,76 (c) F - left winger (d) NK Lokomotiva Zagreb (e) Inter Zaprešić, NK Lokomotiva, NK Jarun, NK Lokomotiva, NK Rudes

*** Gorin - Oleg Gorin (Горін Олег Андрійович) (a) 02/02/2000, Lviv (Ukraine) (b) 1,88 (c) D - central defense (d) SK Dnipro-1 (e) FK Minaj, Jagiellonia, PFK Lviv II

*** Gorino Jorge - Yannick Gorino Jorge (Yannick Gorino Jorge) (a) 13/10/1993, ¿? (Luxembourg) (b) - (c) G (d) - (e) UN Käerjeng 97, FC Izeg, UN Käerjeng 97, FC Stengefort, Jeunesse II, Jeunesse Esch, SC Bettembourg, SC Steinfort, SC Bettembourg, F91 Dudelange, SC Bettembourg, Coupe de Luxembourg

*** Gormley - Joe Gormley (Joseph Anthony Gormley) (a) 26/11/1989, Belfast (Northern Ireland) (b) 1,83 (c) F - center forward (d) Cliftonville FC (e) Peterborough, St. Johnstone, Peterborough, Cliftonville, Crumlin Star, Cliftonville

*** Gorobsov - Nicolás Gorobsov (Nicolás Martín Gorobsov) (a) 25/11/1989, San Pedro (Argentina) (b) 1,79 (c) M - pivot (d) FK Zalgiris Vilnius (e) Suduva, Concordia, FC Voluntari, Concordia, Miami United, Paraná, ASA Tg. Mures, Hapoel Tel Aviv, ASA Tg. Mures, Torino, ACS Poli, Torino, ASG Nocerina, Torino, Poli. Timisoara, Torino, Cesena, Torino, Vicenza

*** Gorodovoy - Alekscy Gorodovoy (Городовой Алексей Владимирович) (a) 10/08/1993, Stavropol (Russia) (b) 1,92 (c) G (d) Rodina Moscow (e) Fakel Voronezh, Rubin Kazan, SKA Khabarovsk, Rubin Kazan, Veles Moskva, Rubin Kazan, Zenit 2 St. Peterburg, Rubin Kazan, Kongsvinger, Spartak Nalchik, Yakutia Yakutsk, Sakhalin, Stavropol, Stavropol II

*** Gorokh - Valentyn Gorokh (Горох Валентин Вікторович) (a) 14/02/2001, Slavuta, Khmelnytskyi Oblast (Ukraine) (b) 1,87 (c) G (d) Kolos Kovalivka (e) FK Oleksandriya, Karpaty, Karpaty II, UFK Lviv

*** Gorosabel - Andoni Gorosabel (Andoni Gorosabel Espinosa) (a) 04/08/1996, Arrasate (Spain) (b) 1,74 (c) D - right back (d) Deportivo Alavés (e) Real Sociedad, Real Sociedad B, Real Unión, Real Sociedad B, Real Sociedad C, SD Beasain, Berio

*** Gorosito - Nicolas Gorosito (Nicolás Ezequiel Gorosito) (a) 17/08/1988, Rafaela (Argentina) (b) 1,85 (c) D - central defense (d) Spartak Trnava (e) Banska Bystrica, Alcorcón, Albacete, Getafe CF, Slovan Bratislava, FK Senica, Sport. Belgrano, Independiente, Ben Hur, Independiente

*** Gorré - Kenji Gorré (Kenji Joel Gorré) (a) 29/09/1994, Spijkenisse (Netherlands) (b) 1,78 (c) F - left winger (d) Umm Salal SC (e) Boavista, Nacional, Estoril Praia, Nacional, Swansea City, Northampton, Swansea City, ADO Den Haag, Swansea City

*** Gorshkov - Sergey Gorshkov (Горшков Сергей Алексеевич) (a) 29/11/1999, Moskva (Russia) (b) 1,83 (c) D - right back (d) FK Khimki 2 (e) Dolgoprudnyi-2, Olimp Khimki

*** Gorshkov - Yuriy Gorshkov (Горшков Юрий Александрович) (a) 13/03/1999, Kondapoga, Karelia Republic (Russia) (b) 1,74 (c) D - left back (d) Krylya Sovetov Samara (e) Chertanovo

*** Gorter - Jay Gorter (a) 30/05/2000, Amsterdam (Netherlands) (b) 1,90 (c) G (d) Ajax de Ámsterdam (e) Aberdeen FC, Ajax, Go Ahead Eagles

*** Görtler - Lukas Görtler (a) 15/06/1994, Bamberg (Germany) (b) 1,86 (c) M - right midfielder (d) FC St. Gallen 1879 (e) FC Utrecht, 1.FC Kaiserslautern, FC Bayern II, Eintr. Bamberg

*** Gorupec - Toni Gorupec (a) 04/07/1993, Zagreb (Croatia) (b) 1,78 (c) D - right back (d) - (e) Olympiakos N., Ethnikos, NK Rudes, Hrv Dragovoljac, NK Kurilovec, Vitória Setúbal, Santa Clara, Vitória Setúbal, Astra Giurgiu, NK Lokomotiva, Dinamo Zagreb, Radnik Sesvete, Sava Zagreb

*** Goryainov - Oleksiy Goryainov (Горяінов Олексій Олександрович) (a) 22/08/2003, Kharkiv (Ukraine) (b) 1,82 (c) M - central midfielder (d) Metalist Kharkiv (e) FK Kvadro, Metalist, Olimpik K

*** Gosens - Robin Gosens (Robin Everardus Gosens) (a) 05/07/1994, Emmerich (Germany) (b) 1,83 (c) M - left midfielder (d) Internazionale Milano (e) Atalanta, Internazionale Milano, Atalanta, Heracles Almelo, FC Dordrecht

*** Goshadze - Oto Goshadze (ოთო გოშაძე) (a) 13/10/1997, Tbilisi (Georgia) (b) 1,88 (c) G (d) Torpedo Kutaisi (e) FC Locomotive, Saburtalo, FC Telavi, Sioni Bolnisi, Dinamo Batumi, Saburtalo, Dinamo Tbilisi, Saburtalo

*** Goshev - Evgeniy Goshev (Гошев Евгений Николаевич) (a) 17/06/1997, Nizhnevartovsk (Russia) (b) 1,97 (c) G (d) Dinamo Makhachkala (e) Orenburg, Shinnik Yaroslav, Rostov II

*** Goshev - Ivan Goshev (Иван Христов Гошев) (a) 17/06/2000, ¿? (Bulgaria) (b) 1,92 (c) G (d) Sportist Svoge (e) Beroe, Yantra, Beroe

*** Goshteliani - Guram Goshteliani (გურამ გოშთელიანი) (a) 05/01/1997, Tbilisi (Georgia) (b) 1,74 (c) F - center forward (d) FC Telavi (e) Saburtalo, FC Telavi, Pirin, Saburtalo, FC Dila, Saburtalo

*** Gospodinov - Anatoli Gospodinov (Анатоли Енчев Господинов) (a) 21/03/1994, Sliven (Bulgaria) (b) 1,89 (c) G (d) Arda Kardzhali (e) Etar, Chrobry Glogow, CSKA-Sofia, Vitosha, Sliven

*** Goss - Sean Goss (Sean Richard Goss) (a) 01/10/1995, Wegberg (Germany) (b) 1,91 (c) M - central midfielder (d) - (e) Motherwell FC, Shrewsbury, Queen's Park Rangers, St. Johnstone, Queen's Park Rangers, Rangers FC, Queen's Park Rangers

*** Gosset - Danny Gosset (Daniel Gosset) (a) 30/09/1994, Bangor (Wales) (b) 1,80 (c) M - central midfielder (d) Caernarfon Town (e) Bala, Cefn Druids, Bala, Bangor City, Rhyl FC, The New Saints, Rhyl FC, Oldham Athletic, Stockport, Oldham Athletic

*** Gotlieb - Adi Gotlieb (אדי גוטליב - Готлиб Эдуард Эдуардович) (a) 16/08/1992, Karmiel (Israel) (b) 1,87 (c) D - central defense (d) Beitar Jerusalem (e) Hapoel Tel Aviv, Orenburg, Hapoel Tel Aviv, Hapoel Acre

*** Gotlieb - Niv Gotlieb (ניב גוטליב) (a) 29/10/2002, ¿? (Israel) (b) - (c) M - attacking midfielder (d) Hapoel Hadera (e) Hapoel Raanana

*** Gotra - Mykhaylo Gotra (Готра Михайло Іванович) (a) 20/04/2000, ¿? (Ukraine) (b) 1,90 (c) G (d) Kisvárda FC (e) FK Uzhgorod, Karpaty II

*** Gotsuk - Kirill Gotsuk (Гоцук Кирилл Вадимович) (a) 10/09/1992, Yelets, Lipetsk Region (Russia) (b) 1,94 (c) D - central defense (d) FC Pari Nizhniy Novgorod (e) KS Samara, Avangard Kursk, KS Samara, Shinnik Yaroslav, M. Lipetsk, FK Yelets

*** Gotter - Hervé Mattia Gotter (a) 08/11/2004, ¿? (Italy) (b) - (c) F - center forward (d) - (e) Sistiana

*** Götze - Felix Götze (a) 11/02/1998, Dortmund (Germany) (b) 1,85 (c) M - central midfielder (d) Rot-Weiss Essen (e) FC Augsburg, RW Essen, FC Augsburg, 1.FC Kaiserslautern, FC Augsburg, Bayern München

*** Götze - Mario Götze (a) 03/06/1992, Memmingen (Germany) (b) 1,76 (c) M - attacking midfielder (d) Eintracht Frankfurt (e) PSV Eindhoven, Borussia Dortmund, Bayern München, Borussia Dortmund

*** Goudmijn - Kenzo Goudmijn (a) 18/12/2001, Hoorn (Netherlands) (b) 1,73 (c) M - attacking midfielder (d) AZ Alkmaar (e) Excelsior, AZ Alkmaar, Sparta Rotterdam, AZ Alkmaar

*** Gouiri - Amine Gouiri (Amine Ferid Gouiri) (a) 16/02/2000, Bourgoin-Jallieu (France) (b) 1,81 (c) F - center forward (d) Stade Rennais FC (e) OGC Nice, Olympique Lyon, Olymp. Lyon B

*** Gouré - Fernand Gouré (Fernand Gouré Bi Irié) (a) 12/04/2002, Yamoussoukro (Ivory Coast) (b) 1,89 (c) F - center forward (d) KVC Westerlo (e) Újpest FC, KVC Westerlo, Maccabi Netanya, AS Denguélé

*** Gourna-Douath - Lucas Gourna-Douath (a) 05/08/2003, Villeneuve-Saint-Georges (France) (b) 1,85 (c) M - pivot (d) Red Bull Salzburg (e) St.-Étienne, Saint-Étienne B

*** Goutas - Dimitrios Goutas (Δημήτριος Γούτας) (a) 04/04/1994, Kavala (Greece) (b) 1,89 (c) D - central defense (d) Cardiff City (e) Sivasspor, Atromitos FC, Olympiakos, Lech Poznan, Olympiakos, Sint-Truiden, Olympiakos, KV Kortrijk, Olympiakos, Skoda Xanthi, Olympiakos, Skoda Xanthi

*** Gouveia - Tiago Gouveia (Tiago Maria Antunes Gouveia) (a) 18/06/2001, Cascais (Portugal) (b) 1,76 (c) F - left winger (d) SL Benfica (e) Estoril Praia, Benfica, Benfica B

*** Gouweleeuw - Jeffrey Gouweleeuw (a) 10/07/1991, Heemskerk (Netherlands) (b) 1,87 (c) D - central defense (d) FC Augsburg (e) FC Augsburg, AZ Alkmaar, Heerenveen, H'veen/Emmen B

*** Govaers - Milan Govaers (a) 23/03/2004, Wilrijk (Belgium) (b) 1,87 (c) D - right back (d) FC Slovan Liberec B (e) -

*** Govea - Omar Govea (Omar Nicolás Govea García) (a) 18/01/1996, San Luis Potosí (Mexico) (b) 1,76 (c) M - pivot (d) CF Monterrey (e) Monterrey, FC Voluntari, Zulte Waregem, FC Porto B, Royal Antwerp, FC Porto B, Excelsior Mouscron, FC Porto B, Min. Zacatecas

*** Goxha - Jurgen Goxha (a) 29/12/1992, Durrës (Albania) (b) 1,83 (c) D - central defense (d) KF Egnatia (e) KF Teuta, KF Egnatia, FK Sabail, FK Qabala, FK Bylis, KF Tirana, KF Erzeni, FC Shënkolli, Besëlidhja, KF Erzeni, KF Iliria, FK Sukthi

*** Goylo - Nikita Goylo (Гойло Никита Сергеевич) (a) 10/08/1998, St. Petersburg (Russia) (b) 1,89 (c) G (d) FK Sochi (e) Sochi, Zenit, Pari Nizhny Novgórod, Zenit 2 St. Peterburg, Pari Nizhny Novgórod, Zenit 2 St. Peterburg, Akron Togliatti, Zenit 2 St. Peterburg, Zenit St. Peterburg II, SShOR Zenit

*** Gozlan - Shoval Gozlan (גוזלן שובל) (a) 25/04/1994, Tiberias (Israel) (b) 1,77 (c) F - center forward (d) Hapoel Haifa (e) Hapoel Hadera, Maccabi Netanya, FC Ashdod, Maccabi Netanya, EN Paralimniou, Maccabi Netanya, Kiryat Shmona, Maccabi Haifa, Kiryat Shmona, Maccabi Haifa, Hapoel Raanana, Maccabi Haifa, Hapoel Tel Aviv, Maccabi Haifa

*** Grabanica - Diar Grabanica (a) 17/03/2004, Mitrovica (Serbia and Montenegro, now in Kosovo) (b) - (c) M - central midfielder (d) KF Trepca 89 (e) -

*** Grabanica - Mhill Grabanica (a) 17/04/1996, ¿? (RF Yugoslavia, in Kosovo) (b) - (c) M - central midfielder (d) KF Dukagjini (e) KF Rahoveci, KF Dukagjini

*** Grabara - Kamil Grabara (Kamil Mieczysław Grabara) (a) 08/01/1999, Ruda Śląska (Poland) (b) 1,95 (c) G (d) FC Copenhague (e) Aarhus GF, Huddersfield Town, Aarhus GF, AP Ruch

*** Grabez - Srdjan Grabez (Срђан Грабеж) (a) 02/04/1991, Apatin (Yugoslavia, now in Serbia) (b) 1,86 (c) D - left back (d) FK Sloga Meridian (e) Mladost GAT, Javor-Matis, FK TSC, Backa, FK Elan, FK Feniks, Spartak Trnava, Dubnica, Mladost Apatin

*** Grabher - Pius Grabher (a) 11/08/1993, ¿? (Austria) (b) 1,70 (c) M - central midfielder (d) SC Austria Lustenau (e) SV Ried, Austria Lustenau, Austria Lustenau II

*** Graça - João Graça (João Salazar da Graça) (a) 18/06/1995, Matosinhos (Portugal) (b) 1,77 (c) M - central midfielder (d) Rio Ave FC (e) Mafra, Leixões, Oliveirense, Feirense, Arouca, Feirense, FC Porto B

*** Grace - Lee Grace (a) 01/12/1992, Tipperary (Ireland) (b) 1,85 (c) D - central defense (d) Shamrock Rovers (e) Galway United, Wexford FC, Carrick United

*** Gracia - Adam Gracia (Adam Charles Gracia) (a) 28/05/2001, Gibraltar (Gibraltar) (b) - (c) F - center forward (d) St Joseph's FC (e) FC College 1975, Europa FC, FC College 1975, Europa FC, Europa Reserve, Red Imps Reserves

*** Gracia - Saúl Gracia (Saúl Gracia Campillos) (a) 11/04/2000, Saragossa (Spain) (b) 1,86 (c) G (d) Atlètic Club d'Escaldes (e) SD Logroñés, CD Brea, CD Belchite 97, CA Monzón

*** Gradecki - Bartlomiej Gradecki (Bartłomiej Gradecki) (a) 26/12/1999, Płock (Poland) (b) 1,94 (c) G (d) Wisła Płock (e) Wisla Pulawy, Wisła Płock, Znicz Pruszkow, Wisła Płock, Wisla Plock II

*** Gradel - Max Gradel (Max-Alain Gradel) (a) 30/11/1987, Abidjan (Ivory Coast) (b) 1,75 (c) F - left winger (d) Gaziantep FK (e) Sivasspor, Toulouse, Bournemouth, Toulouse, Bournemouth, St.-Étienne, Leeds Utd., Leicester City, Bournemouth, Leicester City

*** Gradinaru - Razvan Gradinaru (Răzvan Toni Augustin Grădinaru) (a) 23/08/1995, Zimnicea (Romania) (b) 1,80 (c) M - left midfielder (d) Karmiotissa Pano Polemidion (e) FC Dinamo, Gaz Metan, FCV Farul, FC Voluntari, ACSM Poli Iasi, Concordia, Steaua Bucuresti, Concordia, Steaua Bucuresti, Otelul Galati, Steaua Bucuresti

*** Gradit - Jonathan Gradit (a) 24/11/1992, Talence (France) (b) 1,80 (c) D - central defense (d) RC Lens (e) SM Caen, Tours FC, Tours B, Bayonne, Girondins Bordeaux B

*** Graf - André Graf (a) 22/03/2000, ¿? (Luxembourg) (b) - (c) F - right winger (d) FC Etzella Ettelbruck (e) Charn. Caparica, GD Alfarim, Moura, Medernach

*** Graf - Ivan Graf (a) 17/06/1987, Zagreb (Yugoslavia, now in Croatia) (b) 1,94 (c) D - central defense (d) Qyzyljar Petropavlovsk (e) Shakhter K., Kaysar, Irtysh, NK Istra, NK Zagreb, NK Lucko, SK Tavriya, ND Primorje, NK Vrapce
*** Gragera - José Gragera (José Gragera Amado) (a) 14/05/2000, Gijón (Spain) (b) 1,86 (c) M - central midfielder (d) RCD Espanyol (e) Real Sporting, Sporting B
*** Gragger - Matthias Gragger (a) 03/11/2001, Bad Ischl (Austria) (b) 1,88 (c) D - right back (d) SV Ried (e) SV Ried II
*** Graham - Braiden Graham (a) 07/11/2007, ¿? (Northern Ireland) (b) - (c) F - center forward (d) - (e) Linfield FC
*** Graham - Ross Graham (a) 20/02/2001, Blairgowrie (Scotland) (b) - (c) D - central defense (d) Dundee United FC (e) Dunfermline A., Dundee United, Cove Rangers FC, Dundee United, Cove Rangers FC, Dundee United, Dundee Utd. B, Elgin City, Dundee Utd. B
*** Graham - Scott Graham (a) 27/08/2004, ¿? (Northern Ireland) (b) - (c) M - central midfielder (d) Carrick Rangers (e) -
*** Graham - Sean Graham (a) 20/11/2000, Belfast (Northern Ireland) (b) 1,73 (c) M - pivot (d) Ballymena United (e) Loyola Greyh., Ballymena, Blackpool, Larne FC, Blackpool
*** Grahl - Jens Grahl (a) 22/09/1988, Stuttgart (Germany) (b) 1,92 (c) G (d) Eintracht Frankfurt (e) VfB Stuttgart, Hoffenheim, SC Paderborn, Hoffenheim, Greuther Fürth, Greuther Fürth II
*** Grahv - Georg Grahv (a) 17/10/2001, Pärnu (Estonia) (b) - (c) D - right back (d) - (e) Pärnu Vaprus, Pärnu JK II
*** Grajfoner - Lovro Grajfoner (a) 25/01/2000, Maribor (Slovenia) (b) 1,86 (c) M - pivot (d) ND Dravinja Kostroj (e) NK Aluminij, FK Minaj, Akritas Chlor., NK Maribor, NK Aluminij, NK Maribor, Drava Ptuj
*** Grameni - Constantin Grameni (a) 23/10/2002, Constanța (Romania) (b) 1,79 (c) M - central midfielder (d) FCV Farul Constanta (e) FC Viitorul II, Academia Hagi
*** Grammatikakis - Nikolaos Grammatikakis (Νικόλαος Γραμματικάκης) (a) 26/05/2003, ¿? (Greece) (b) - (c) G (d) Asteras Tripolis (e) -
*** Granath - Gustav Granath (Gustav Frans Vallentin Granath) (a) 15/02/1997, Timmersdala (Sweden) (b) 1,91 (c) D - central defense (d) Degerfors IF (e) Skövde AIK
*** Granchov - Angel Granchov (Ангел Симеонов Грънчов) (a) 16/10/1992, Elin Pelin (Bulgaria) (b) 1,85 (c) D - central defense (d) Spartak Varna (e) CSKA 1948 II, Maritsa, Septemvri Sofia, AP Brera, KF Flamurtari, Minyor Pernik, Spartak Pleven, Stal Mielec, Neftochimik, CSKA-Sofia, Slavia Sofia, Lokomotiv Plovdiv, CSKA Sofia, CSKA-Sofia II
*** Grandoni - Andrea Grandoni (a) 23/03/1997, Città di San Marino (San Marino) (b) - (c) D - left back (d) La Fiorita 1967 (e) Marignanese Catt, San Marino, Marignanese, Ravenna, Juvenes-Dogana
*** Granecny - Denis Granecny (Denis Granečný) (a) 07/09/1998, Ostrava (Czech Rep.) (b) 1,80 (c) D - left back (d) FC Zbrojovka Brno (e) Banik Ostrava, Mezőkövesd, Banik Ostrava, FC Emmen, Banik Ostrava, Ceske Budejovice, Banik Ostrava
*** Grani - Eros Grani (a) 17/02/1999, Genoa (Italy) (b) 1,84 (c) D - left back (d) Angelo Baiardo (e) Tre Fiori, Ligorna, Savona, Savona, OltrepòVoghera
*** Grankin - Nikita Grankin (a) 29/08/2000, Tallinn (Estonia) (b) - (c) M - right midfielder (d) - (e) FCI Tallinn, TJK Legion, FCI Tallinn, FCI Tallinn III

*** Granli - Daniel Granli (Daniel Fredrik Granli) (a) 01/05/1994, Sandvika (Norway) (b) 1,90 (c) D - central defense (d) ADO Den Haag (e) Aalborg BK, AIK, Aalborg BK, AIK, Stabæk, Stabæk II

*** Granlund - Albin Granlund (Eddie Albin Alexander Granlund) (a) 01/09/1989, Parainen (Finland) (b) 1,79 (c) D - right back (d) IFK Mariehamn (e) Stal Mielec, Örebro SK, IFK Mariehamn, RoPS, Åbo IFK, Pargas IF

*** Grant - Jorge Grant (Jorge Edward Grant) (a) 19/12/1994, Oxford (England) (b) 1,75 (c) M - central midfielder (d) Heart of Midlothian FC (e) Peterborough, Lincoln City, Nottingham Forest, Mansfield Town, Nottingham Forest, Luton Town, Nottingham Forest, Notts County, Nottingham Forest, Notts County, Nottingham Forest

*** Grant - Kilian Grant (Kilian Grant Carvalheira) (a) 18/05/1994, Figueres (Spain) (b) 1,80 (c) F - left winger (d) Inter Club d'Escaldes (e) FC Santa Coloma, Real Avilés, UE Olot, UCAM Murcia, SD Huesca, AD Almudévar, Dep. Aragón, RCD Espanyol B, UE Olot, RCD Espanyol B

*** Graovac - Daniel Graovac (Daniel Graovac) (a) 08/08/1993, Bosanski Novi (Bosnia and Herzegovina) (b) 1,85 (c) D - central defense (d) Manisa FK (e) Kasimpasa, CFR Cluj, Astra Giurgiu, Vojvodina, Excelsior Mouscron, Zeljeznicar, Excelsior Mouscron, Zrinjski Mostar, Excelsior Mouscron, Zrinjski Mostar, Novi Grad

*** Grassi - Alberto Grassi (Alberto Grassi) (a) 07/03/1995, Lumezzane(Italy) (b) 1,83 (c) M - pivot (d) FC Empoli (e) Parma, FC Empoli, Parma, Cagliari, Parma, Napoli, Parma, Napoli, SPAL, Napoli, Atalanta, Napoli, Atalanta

*** Grassi - Andrea Grassi (a) 30/09/1993, Cattolica (Italy) (b) - (c) M - central midfielder (d) La Fiorita 1967 (e) Gabicce Gradara, Libertas, Gabicce Gradara, United Riccione, Misano

*** Grassi - Mathias Grassi (a) 23/03/2004, ¿? (San Marino) (b) - (c) F (d) - (e) Domagnano

*** Graterol - Joel Graterol (Joel David Graterol Nader) (a) 15/05/1997, Valencia (Venezuela) (b) 1,82 (c) G (d) Panetolikos GFS (e) CD América, Zamora FC, Carabobo FC

*** Grauds - Daniels Grauds (a) 27/07/2003, ¿? (Latvia) (b) 1,85 (c) D - right back (d) FK Tukums 2000 (e) Jelgava, Spartaks, Jelgava

*** Graur - Alexandru Graur (a) 11/02/2001, Chişinău (Moldova) (b) 1,89 (c) M - central midfielder (d) Germania Leer (e) Spartanii, Petrocub, Spartanii, Petrocub, Zimbru Chisinau

*** Graur - Dinu Graur (a) 27/12/1994, Chisinau (Moldova) (b) 1,78 (c) D - right back (d) FC Milsami Orhei (e) AE Larisa, Astra Giurgiu, Milsami, Zimbru Chisinau

*** Grave - Paul Grave (a) 10/04/2001, Borken (Germany) (b) 1,93 (c) G (d) Wuppertaler SV (e) Wuppertaler SV, VfL Bochum

*** Gravenberch - Danzell Gravenberch (Danzell Orlando Marcelino Gravenberch) (a) 13/02/1994, Amsterdam (Netherlands) (b) 1,86 (c) F - center forward (d) Karmiotissa Pano Polemidion (e) De Graafschap, Sparta Rotterdam, FC Dordrecht, TOP Oss, Reading, KSV Roeselare, Reading, FC Dordrecht, Universitatea Cluj, Ajax B, NEC Nijmegen, Ajax B

*** Gravenberch - Ryan Gravenberch (Ryan Jiro Gravenberch) (a) 16/05/2002, Amsterdam (Netherlands) (b) 1,90 (c) M - central midfielder (d) Bayern München (e) Ajax, Ajax B

*** Graves - Simon Graves (Simon Graves Jensen) (a) 22/05/1999, ¿? (Denmark) (b) 1,91 (c) D - central defense (d) Palermo FC (e) Randers FC

*** Gravillon - Andreaw Gravillon (Andreaw Rayan Gravillon) (a) 08/02/1998, Pointe-à-Pitre (Guadaloupe) (b) 1,88 (c) D - central defense (d) Adana Demirspor (e) Stade Reims, Torino, Stade Reims, Internazionale Milano, Stade Reims, Internazionale Milano, FC Lorient, Internazionale Milano, Sassuolo, Ascoli, Sassuolo, Internazionale Milano, Pescara, Internazionale Milano, Pescara, Benevento, Internazionale Milano, ASM Gargeoise
*** Gravius - Christos Gravius (Christos Emil Gravius) (a) 14/10/1997, Kungsängen (Sweden) (b) 1,81 (c) M - central midfielder (d) Degerfors IF (e) AIK, Degerfors, AIK, Degerfors, AIK, J-Södra IF, AIK, Vasalunds IF, AIK
*** Gray - Andre Gray (Andre Anthony Gray) (a) 26/06/1991, Wolverhampton (England) (b) 1,78 (c) F - center forward (d) Aris Thessaloniki (e) Watford, Queen's Park Rangers, Watford, Burnley, Brentford, Luton Town, Hinckley United, Luton Town, Hinckley United, Shrewsbury, Hinckley United, Shrewsbury, Telford Utd., Shrewsbury
*** Gray - Archie Gray (a) 12/03/2006, ¿? (England) (b) - (c) M - central midfielder (d) Leeds United (e) -
*** Gray - Demarai Gray (Demarai Ramelle Gray) (a) 28/06/1996, Birmingham (England) (b) 1,83 (c) F - left winger (d) Everton FC (e) Bayer Leverkusen, Leicester City, Birmingham City
*** Gray - Ross Gray (a) 12/09/1994, Dumfries (Scotland) (b) 1,91 (c) D - left back (d) FC Manchester 62 (e) Manchester 62, Bruno's Magpies, Threave Rovers
*** Graydon - Ryan Graydon (a) 11/04/1999, ¿? (Ireland) (b) - (c) F - left winger (d) Fleetwood Town (e) Derry City, Longford Town, Bray Wanderers, Bohemians
*** Grazis - Algirdas Grazis (a) 12/06/2003, ¿? (Latvia) (b) - (c) F - center forward (d) - (e) Super Nova, Spartaks, Riga II
*** Grazziani - Rodolfo Grazziani (Rodolfo Rafael Grazziani González) (a) 06/10/2002, Barranquilla (Colombia) (b) 1,75 (c) F - right winger (d) - (e) Daugavpils
*** Grbic - Adrian Grbic (a) 04/08/1996, Wien (Austria) (b) 1,88 (c) F - center forward (d) FC Lorient (e) Valenciennes FC, FC Lorient, Vitesse, FC Lorient, Clermont Foot, SCR Altach, FAC, Stuttgart II
*** Grbic - Ivo Grbic (Ivo Grbić) (a) 18/01/1996, Split (Croatia) (b) 1,95 (c) G (d) Atlético de Madrid (e) Lille, Atlético Madrid, NK Lokomotiva, Hajduk Split, Hajduk Split II
*** Grbic - Petar Grbic (a) 07/08/1988, Titograd (now Podgorica) (Yugoslavia, now in Montenegro) (b) - (c) F - left winger (d) Buducnost Podgorica (e) Mornar Bar, Buducnost Podgorica, Radnicki Niš, Buducnost Podgorica, Akhisarspor, Adana Demirspor, Akhisar Belediye, FK Partizan, Olympiakos, FK Partizan, Olympiakos, OFK Beograd, Olympiakos, H. Beer Sheva, Olympiakos, APO Levadiakos, Olympiakos, Mogren, FK Mladost
*** Grdic - Doni Grdic (Doni Grdić) (a) 22/01/2002, Šibenik (Croatia) (b) 1,90 (c) D - central defense (d) Western Sydney Wanderers (e) HNK Sibenik, Bijelo Brdo, HNK Sibenik
*** Grdzelidze - Levan Grdzelidze (ლევან გრძელიძე) (a) 18/08/2000, Tbilisi (Georgia) (b) - (c) F - right winger (d) - (e) FC Telavi, FC Samtredia, Samgurali, Dinamo II, FC Samtredia, Dep. Aragón
*** Greab - Alexandru Greab (Alexandru Doru Greab) (a) 26/05/1992, Bistrița (Romania) (b) 1,98 (c) G (d) AS FC Buzau (e) CS Mioveni, FC Arges, Sepsi OSK, Concordia, Gaz Metan, Gloria Bistrita
*** Grealish - Jack Grealish (Jack Peter Grealish) (a) 10/09/1995, Birmingham (England) (b) 1,80 (c) F - left winger (d) Manchester City (e) Aston Villa, Notts County, Aston Villa

*** Greca - Bedri Greca (a) 23/10/1990, Tiranë (Albania) (b) 1,83 (c) F - left winger (d) AF Elbasani (e) KS Kastrioti, KF Feronikeli, KF Laçi, SC Gjilani, KF Tirana, FC Luftëtari, FK Kukësi, Flamurtari FC, KF Tërbuni, KF Skrapari

*** Grech - Jake Grech (a) 06/03/2004, ¿? (Malta) (b) - (c) M - central midfielder (d) Balzan FC (e) -

*** Grech - Jake Grech (a) 18/11/1997, Pieta (Malta) (b) 1,83 (c) M - central midfielder (d) Balzan FC (e) Hibernians FC, Birkirkara FC, Hamrun Spartans

*** Grech - Luke Grech (a) 06/01/1994, ¿? (Malta) (b) - (c) D - central defense (d) Gudja United FC (e) FC Mgarr United, Marsa FC, Sirens FC, Hamrun Spartans, Tarxien, Hamrun Spartans, Tarxien, Hamrun Spartans, St. George's FC, Hamrun Spartans

*** Grech - Matthew Grech (a) 19/02/1996, ¿? (Malta) (b) - (c) G (d) Zabbar St. Patrick FC (e) Sirens FC, Pembroke, Zebbug Rangers, Floriana, San Gwann FC, Senglea Ath., Pietà Hotspurs

*** Grech - Zachary Grech (Zachary Karl Grech) (a) 25/08/2000, ¿? (Malta) (b) - (c) D - right back (d) Hibernians FC (e) Balzan FC, Pembroke, Balzan FC

*** Grech - Zak Grech (a) 21/07/1999, ¿? (Malta) (b) - (c) D - left back (d) Balzan FC (e) -

*** Grechikho - Denis Grechikho (Гречихо Денис Викторович) (a) 22/05/1999, Mogilev (Belarus) (b) 1,85 (c) M - central midfielder (d) BATE Borisov (e) Dinamo Minsk, Rukh, Dnyapro Mogilev, Rukh, Dnyapro Mogilev, Dnepr Mogilev, Mogilev II

*** Grechishko - Pavel Grechishko (Гречишко Павел Юрьевич) (a) 23/03/1989, Minsk (Soviet Union, now in Belarus) (b) 1,84 (c) D - central defense (d) FK Slutsk (e) Krumkachi, Energetik-BGU, Belshina, Slavia, Gomel, Slavia, Gomel, Smolevichi, Zvezda-BGU, FK Most, Zvezda-BGU

*** Grechkin - Maksim Grechkin (מקסים גרצ'קין) (a) 04/03/1996, Kyiv (Ukraine) (b) 1,82 (c) D - left back (d) Hapoel Jerusalem (e) B. Jerusalem, Hapoel Hadera, B. Jerusalem, Zorya Lugansk, B. Jerusalem, Maccabi Tel Aviv, Hapoel Hadera, Maccabi Tel Aviv, Ramat haSharon, Maccabi Tel Aviv, Beitar TA Ramla, Maccabi Tel Aviv, Ramat haSharon, Maccabi Tel Aviv

*** Greco - Giulio Greco (a) 20/02/2001, ¿? (Italy) (b) - (c) G (d) Tre Fiori FC (e) -

*** Greco - Nicola Greco (a) 30/06/2000, Rimini (Italy) (b) 1,80 (c) D - left back (d) AC Libertas (e) La Fiorita, Victor SM, Cattolica, Savignanese, Atletico Lazio, Marignanese Catt, Santarcangelo

*** Gréczi - Márton Gréczi (Gréczi Márton Péter) (a) 10/07/2000, Szeged (Hungary) (b) 1,75 (c) F - right winger (d) Hódmezővásárhely FC (e) Kecskemét, Szeged, Békéscsaba, MTK Budapest II, Tiszakécske, MTK Budapest II

*** Green - Andre Green (Andre Jay Green) (a) 26/07/1998, Solihull (England) (b) 1,80 (c) F - left winger (d) Rotherham United (e) Slovan Bratislava, Sheffield Wednesday, Aston Villa, Charlton Ath., Aston Villa, Preston North End, Aston Villa, FC Portsmouth, Aston Villa

*** Green - Clayton Green (a) 27/02/1994, ¿? (Wales) (b) 1,77 (c) M - central midfielder (d) Pontypridd United (e) Barry Town, Carmarthen, Barry Town, Frome Town, Carmarthen, Cinderford

*** Green - Evan Green (Evan James Green) (a) 13/03/1993, Eastbourne (England) (b) - (c) F - left winger (d) Lions Gibraltar FC (e) Boca Gibraltar, St Joseph's FC, Boca Gibraltar, St Joseph's FC, Chertsey, Kingstonian FC, Gibraltar Utd., Lions Gibraltar, Gibraltar Utd., Lions Gibraltar

*** Greene - Aaron Greene (a) 02/01/1990, Tallaght, Dublin (Ireland) (b) 1,81 (c) F - center forward (d) Shamrock Rovers (e) Bray Wanderers, Limerick FC, St. Patrick's Ath., Sligo Rovers, Shamrock Rovers, Sligo Rovers, Bohemians, Galway United

*** Greenwood - Ben Greenwood (a) 20/02/2003, Frimley (England) (b) - (c) D - left back (d) AFC Bournemouth (e) Weymouth FC, Wimborne

*** Greenwood - Mason Greenwood (Mason Will John Greenwood) (a) 01/10/2001, Wibsey, Bradford (England) (b) 1,81 (c) F - right winger (d) Manchester United (e) -

*** Greenwood - Sam Greenwood (a) 26/01/2002, Sunderland (England) (b) 1,80 (c) M - attacking midfielder (d) Leeds United (e) -

*** Greer - Max Greer (a) 15/04/2004, Belfast (Northern Ireland) (b) - (c) D - right back (d) Ards FC (e) Larne FC, Knockbreda FC, Larne FC, Knockbreda FC, Larne FC

*** Gregersen - Atli Gregersen (a) 15/06/1982, Tórshavn (Faroe Islands) (b) 1,94 (c) D - central defense (d) Víkingur Gøta (e) Ross County, Víkingur, GI Gota, BK Frem, IFS Birkeröd, GI Gota, Lyngby BK, Randers FC

*** Gregersen - Bergur Gregersen (a) 11/09/1994, ¿? (Faroe Islands) (b) 1,85 (c) D - left back (d) - (e) Víkingur, Víkingur II, B68 Toftir, Víkingur II

*** Gregersen - Stian Gregersen (Stian Rode Gregersen) (a) 17/05/1995, Kristiansund (Norway) (b) 1,91 (c) D - central defense (d) FC Girondins de Burdeos (e) Molde, Elfsborg, Molde, Kristiansund, Molde

*** Gregor - Pascal Gregor (a) 18/02/1994, ¿? (Denmark) (b) 1,89 (c) D - central defense (d) Lyngby BK (e) FC Helsingör, Haugesund, FC Helsingör, Nordsjælland

*** Gregori - Emanuele Gregori (a) 12/07/1995, Cesena (Italy) (b) 1,74 (c) M - attacking midfielder (d) ASD Calcio Del Duca Grama (e) CBR Carli Pietracuta, La Fiorita, Due Emme, Faetano, Due Emme, Sampierana, Vallesavio, Sampierana, Vallesavio

*** Grégorini - Damien Grégorini (a) 02/03/1979, Nice (France) (b) 1,94 (c) G (d) - (e) Mondercange, AS Nancy, OGC Nice, Ol. Marseille, OGC Nice, Ol. Marseille, OGC Nice, OGC Nice B

*** Gregorio - Angelo Gregorio (a) 11/04/1991, Forlimpopoli (Italy) (b) - (c) D - central defense (d) AC Libertas (e) Tre Fiori, Sammaurese, Franciacorta, Team Altamura, Savignanese, Tuttocuoio, Bra, Romagna Centro, Bologna, Teramo, Bologna, Cesena, Pontedera, Cesena, Santarcangelo

*** Gregoritsch - Michael Gregoritsch (a) 18/04/1994, Graz (Austria) (b) 1,93 (c) F - center forward (d) SC Freiburg (e) FC Augsburg, FC Schalke 04, FC Augsburg, SV Hamburg, VfL Bochum, Hoffenheim, VfL Bochum, Hoffenheim, FC St. Pauli, Hoffenheim, SV Kapfenberg, Hoffenheim, SV Kapfenberg, Kapfenberg II, AKA Kapfenberg

*** Grehan - Sean Grehan (a) 08/01/2004, ¿? (Ireland) (b) - (c) D - central defense (d) - (e) Bohemians

*** Greif - Dominik Greif (a) 06/04/1997, Bratislava (Slovakia) (b) 1,97 (c) G (d) RCD Mallorca (e) Slovan Bratislava

*** Greil - Patrick Greil (a) 08/09/1996, Salzburg (Austria) (b) 1,84 (c) M - central midfielder (d) SK Rapid Wien (e) Austria Klagenfurt, USK Anif, USK Anif II

*** Greiml - Leo Greiml (a) 03/07/2001, Horn (Austria) (b) 1,87 (c) D - central defense (d) FC Schalke 04 (e) Rapid Wien, Rapid Wien II

*** Greive - Alex Greive (a) 13/05/1999, Auckland (New Zealand) (b) 1,78 (c) F - center forward (d) St. Mirren FC (e) Birkenhead, Waitakere Utd., NKU Norse

*** Grekovich - Vladislav Grekovich (Грекович Владислав Александрович) (a) 01/06/2005, ¿? (Belarus) (b) 1,89 (c) D - central defense (d) FK Minsk II (e) -

*** Gremsl - Armin Gremsl (a) 13/08/1994, ¿? (Austria) (b) 1,90 (c) G (d) First Vienna FC (e) Arminia Bielefeld, SCR Altach, FC U Craiova, SKN St. Pölten, Doxa Katokopias, SV Horn, FAC, Pasching/LASK, TSV Hartberg, Hartberg II
*** Grendel - Erik Grendel (a) 13/10/1988, Handlová (Czechoslovakia, now in Slovakia) (b) 1,76 (c) M - pivot (d) - (e) Pohronie, Podbrezova, Spartak Trnava, Górnik Zabrze, Slovan Bratislava, Dubnica
*** Grenier - Clément Grenier (a) 07/01/1991, Annonay (France) (b) 1,86 (c) M - central midfielder (d) RCD Mallorca (e) Stade Rennes, Guingamp, Olympique Lyon, AS Roma, Olympique Lyon, Olymp. Lyon B
*** Greppi - Simone Greppi (a) 03/09/2001, ¿? (Italy) (b) - (c) F - center forward (d) ASD Gatteo FC (e) San Giovanni, Tropical Coriano, Sammaurese, Stella
*** Gresak - Matej Gresak (Matej Grešák) (a) 31/05/1999, Tulčík (Slovakia) (b) 1,75 (c) D - central defense (d) FK Zeleziarne Podbrezova (e) FK Poprad, Tatran Presov
*** Gressak - Lukas Gressak (Lukáš Greššák) (a) 23/01/1989, Trstena (Czechoslovakia, now in Slovakia) (b) 1,83 (c) M - pivot (d) FC Kosice (e) Sigma Olomouc, Z. Sosnowiec, Spartak Trnava, Ružomberok
*** Grétarsson - Daníel Leó Grétarsson (Daníel Leó Grétarsson Schmidt) (a) 02/10/1995, Grindavík (Iceland) (b) 1,85 (c) D - central defense (d) SønderjyskE (e) Śląsk Wroclaw, Blackpool, Aalesund, Grindavík
*** Greve - Mathias Greve (a) 11/02/1995, Langeskov (Denmark) (b) 1,86 (c) M - central midfielder (d) Brøndby IF (e) Randers FC, Odense BK
*** Grezda - Eros Grezda (Eros Genc Grezda) (a) 15/04/1995, Gjakovë (RF Yugoslavia, now in Kosovo) (b) 1,82 (c) F - right winger (d) FK Partizani (e) Zalaegerszeg, Manisa FK, HNK Sibenik, NK Osijek, Zalaegerszeg, NK Osijek, Rangers FC, NK Osijek, NK Lokomotiva, DNŠ Zavrč, NK Aluminij, GAK 1902 II
*** Grgic - Alen Grgic (Alen Grgić) (a) 10/08/1994, Nova Gradiška (Croatia) (b) 1,87 (c) D - right back (d) HNK Rijeka (e) NK Osijek, Slaven Belupo, NK Osijek, Diósgyőr, NK Osijek, NK Sesvete, NK Osijek, Mladost Cernik
*** Grgic - Anto Grgic (Anto Grgić) (a) 28/11/1996, Schlieren (Switzerland) (b) 1,89 (c) M - central midfielder (d) FC Lugano (e) FC Sion, VfB Stuttgart, FC Sion, VfB Stuttgart, FC Zürich
*** Grgic - Ivan Grgic (Ivan Grgić) (a) 02/02/2003, Sarajevo (Bosnia and Herzegovina) (b) 1,84 (c) M - pivot (d) - (e) Borac Banja Luka, Siroki Brijeg
*** Grgic - Leon Grgic (Leon Grgić) (a) 22/01/2006, Bruck an der Mur (Austria) (b) 1,89 (c) F - center forward (d) SK Sturm Graz (e) Sturm Graz II, NWM KSV
*** Grgic - Lukas Grgic (Lukas Grgić) (a) 17/08/1995, Wels (Austria) (b) 1,83 (c) M - pivot (d) SK Rapid Wien (e) Hajduk Split, LASK, WSG Tirol, SV Ried, LASK, SV Ried, LASK, SV Wallern, WSC Hertha Wels, FC Wels
*** Gribov - Nikita Gribov (Грибов Никита Витальевич) (a) 25/05/2002, Brest (Belarus) (b) - (c) D - central defense (d) Belshina Bobruisk (e) Dynamo Brest II, FK Malorita, Rukh II, Dynamo Brest II
*** Gribovskiy - Roman Gribovskiy (Роман Андреевич Грибовский) (a) 17/07/1995, Mogilev (Belarus) (b) 1,82 (c) F - center forward (d) Neman Grodno (e) FK Minsk, Dnyapro Mogilev, Luch, FK Lida, Dnepr Mogilev, Belshina, Belshina II
*** Gric - Jakub Gric (Jakub Grič) (a) 05/07/1996, Prešov (Slovakia) (b) 1,80 (c) M - pivot (d) Wisła Płock (e) Ceske Budejovice, Spartak Trnava, Michalovce, Sandecja, Michalovce
*** Grieco - Cristian Grieco (a) 27/10/1998, ¿? (San Marino) (b) - (c) D - central defense (d) SS Murata (e) Cailungo, San Giovanni
*** Griezmann - Antoine Griezmann (Antoine Griezmann) (a) 21/03/1991, Mâcon (France) (b) 1,76 (c) F - attacking midfielder (d) Atlético de Madrid (e) FC Barcelona,

Atlético Madrid, FC Barcelona, Atlético Madrid, Real Sociedad, Real Sociedad B, Berio, UF Mâcon
*** Griffin - Luke Griffin (a) 26/12/2002, ¿? (Wales) (b) - (c) M - attacking midfielder (d) Cefn Albion (e) -
*** Griffin - Shane Griffin (a) 08/09/1994, Cork (Ireland) (b) 1,78 (d) Shelbourne FC (e) St. Patrick's Ath., Cork City, Reading, Carrigaline
*** Griffith - Cai Griffith (Cai Morgan Griffith) (a) 17/07/2005, ¿? (Wales) (b) - (c) D - left back (d) - (e) Caernarfon Town
*** Griffiths - Rhys Griffiths (a) 01/03/1980, Cardiff (Wales) (b) 1,91 (c) F - center forward (d) Penybont FC (e) Aberystwyth, Port Talbot, Newport County, Plymouth Argyle, Port Talbot, Llanelli, Port Talbot, Carmarthen, Haverfordwest, Cwmbran
*** Grifo - Vincenzo Grifo (a) 07/04/1993, Pforzheim (Germany) (b) 1,80 (c) F - left winger (d) SC Freiburg (e) Hoffenheim, SC Freiburg, Hoffenheim, Borussia Mönchengladbach, SC Freiburg, Hoffenheim, FSV Frankfurt, Hoffenheim, Dynamo Dresden, Hoffenheim, Hoffenheim II
*** Grigalashvili - Nikoloz Grigalashvili (ნიკოლოზ გრიგალაშვილი) (a) 22/07/2004, ¿? (Georgia) (b) - (c) D - right back (d) FC Locomotive Tbilisi (e) Locomotive II
*** Grigalashvili - Tedore Grigalashvili (თედორე გრიგალაშვილი) (a) 12/05/1993, Tbilisi (Georgia) (b) 1,85 (c) D - central defense (d) - (e) Torpedo Kutaisi, Saburtalo, Terek Grozny, FC Samtredia, FC Zestafoni
*** Grigar - Tomas Grigar (Tomáš Grigar) (a) 01/02/1983, Opava (Czechoslovakia, now in Czech Rep.) (b) 1,92 (c) G (d) FK Teplice (e) Sparta Praha B, Sparta Praha, Vitkovice
*** Grigaravicius - Mindaugas Grigaravicius (Mindaugas Grigaravičius) (a) 15/07/1992, ¿? (Latvia) (b) 1,72 (c) F - left winger (d) FK Riteriai (e) Jelgava, Jonava, Jelgava, Metta, Stumbras, Utenis, Suduva, Jelgava, Klaipeda, MIKA Aschtarak, Klaipeda
*** Grigore - Dragos Grigore (Dragoş Grigore) (a) 07/09/1986, Vaslui (Romania) (b) 1,85 (c) D - central defense (d) FC Rapid 1923 (e) Ludogorets, Al-Sailiya SC, Toulouse, Al-Sailiya SC, Toulouse, FC Dinamo, Dinamo II, CFR Timisoara, FCM Husi (ext.)
*** Grigore - Iustin Grigore (a) 09/09/2004, ¿? (Romania) (b) - (c) F - center forward (d) Sepsi OSK Sf. Gheorghe (e) -
*** Grigore - Ricardo Grigore (Ricardo Florin Grigore) (a) 07/04/1999, Bucuresti (Romania) (b) 1,92 (c) D - central defense (d) FC Dinamo 1948 (e) Petrolul, FC Dinamo, FC U Craiova, FC Dinamo, Dinamo II
*** Grigorjev - Aleksandr Grigorjev (Григорьев Александр) (a) 27/05/2004, ¿? (Russia) (b) 1,93 (c) G (d) Tekstilshchik Ivanovo (e) Rostov II, SShOR Zenit
*** Grigorov - Galin Grigorov (Галин Веселинов Григоров) (a) 31/10/2003, Varna (Bulgaria) (b) - (c) G (d) Chernomorets Balchik (e) C. Balchik, Cherno More II
*** Grigoryan - Artak Grigoryan (Արտակ Գրիգորյան) (a) 19/10/1987, Abovyan (Soviet Union, now in Armenia) (b) 1,82 (c) M - pivot (d) FC Pyunik Yerevan (e) Alashkert CF, MIKA Aschtarak, Gandzasar, Ulisses, Ararat Yerevan, Ararat II, FC Kotayk
*** Grigoryan - Artur Grigoryan (Արթուր Գրիգորյան) (a) 10/07/1993, Yerevan (Armenia) (b) 1,71 (c) M - central midfielder (d) BKMA Yerevan (e) BKMA Yerevan, Pyunik Yerevan, Gandzasar, FC Noah, Alashkert II, MIKA Aschtarak, Ulisses, Pyunik Yerevan, Pyunik Yerevan B

*** Grigoryan - Edgar Grigoryan (Էդգար Գրիգորյան) (a) 25/08/1998, ¿? (Armenia) (b) 1,80 (c) D - left back (d) FC Ararat-Armenia (e) FC Urartu, FC Noah, FC Urartu, Urartu II

*** Grigoryan - Garnik Grigoryan (Գառնիկ Գրիգորյան) (a) 01/11/2004, ¿? (Armenia) (b) 1,81 (c) G (d) FC Ararat Yerevan II (e) -

*** Grigoryan - Narek Grigoryan (Նարեկ Գրիգորյան) (a) 17/06/2001, Yerevan (Armenia) (b) 1,80 (c) F - right winger (d) FC Urartu Yerevan (e) Jagiellonia, FC Urartu, BKMA Yerevan, FC Urartu

*** Grigoryan - Serob Grigoryan (Григорян Сероб Давидович) (a) 04/02/1995, Vladikavkaz (Russia) (b) 1,75 (c) D - left back (d) Alashkert Yerevan CF (e) BKMA Yerevan, Pyunik Yerevan, KS Samara II, Zenit Penza, KS Samara II, Shirak Gyumri, KS Samara II, Akad. Togliatti, Akron Konoplev

*** Grigoryan - Vyacheslav Grigoryan (Григорян Вячеслав Вадимович) (a) 23/04/1999, Moskva (Russia) (b) 1,93 (c) G (d) Sakhalinets Moscow (e) Lernayin Artsakh, SKA Rostov, Khimki, Ararat Moskva, Khimki, Strogino Moskva, Strogino II

*** Grigs - Jurgis Grigs (a) 09/09/2003, ¿? (Latvia) (b) - (c) G (d) FK Tukums 2000 II (e) -

*** Grill - Lennart Grill (Hannes Lennart Grill) (a) 25/01/1999, Idar-Oberstein (Germany) (b) 1,92 (c) G (d) VfL Osnabrück (e) VfL Osnabrück, Union Berlin, Bayer Leverkusen, Union Berlin, Bayer Leverkusen, Brann, Bayer Leverkusen, 1.FC Kaiserslautern

*** Grillitsch - Florian Grillitsch (a) 07/08/1995, Neunkirchen (Austria) (b) 1,87 (c) M - pivot (d) TSG 1899 Hoffenheim (e) Ajax, Hoffenheim, Werder Bremen, Werder Bremen II

*** Grillo - Danny Grillo (a) 04/09/1998, Messina (Italy) (b) - (c) M - pivot (d) - (e) San Giovanni, Tre Penne, Igea Virtus, Mosta FC, Cotronei 1994, ACR Messina, FC Chiasso

*** Grima - Marcus Grima (a) 22/07/2000, ¿? (Malta) (b) 1,78 (c) M - attacking midfielder (d) Balzan FC (e) St. Andrews FC

*** Grimaldo - Alejandro Grimaldo (Alejandro Grimaldo García) (a) 20/09/1995, Valencia (Spain) (b) 1,71 (c) D - left back (d) Bayer 04 Leverkusen (e) Benfica, FC Barcelona B

*** Grimci - Fjorest Grimci (a) 19/12/2002, Laç (Albania) (b) - (c) M (d) KS Kastrioti (e) -

*** Grimes - Dylan Grimes (a) 10/03/1998, ¿? (Ireland) (b) - (c) M - right midfielder (d) Drogheda United FC (e) Longford Town, Sheriff YC, Shelbourne, Home Farm

*** Grinbergs - Janis Grinbergs (Jānis Grīnbergs) (a) 28/02/1999, Riga (Latvia) (b) 1,79 (c) D - right back (d) FK Liepaja (e) Metta, Albatroz/Jelgava, Schalke 04 II, RFS, Skonto

*** Gripshi - Nazmi Gripshi (a) 05/07/1997, Durrës (Albania) (b) 1,76 (c) M - attacking midfielder (d) FC Ballkani (e) KF Skënderbeu, KF Teuta

*** Grishchenko - Ilya Grishchenko (Грищенко Илья Алексеевич) (a) 18/12/2000, Balakovo (Russia) (b) 1,79 (c) F - center forward (d) - (e) Energetik-BGU, FK Malorita, Orsha, Sokol Saratov, Zenit St. Peterburg II

*** Grishin - Valentin Grishin (Гришин Валентин Владимирович) (a) 14/02/2003, Krasnodar (Russia) (b) 1,85 (c) G (d) FK Krasnodar-2 (e) Krasnodar II

*** Grivas - Frixos Grivas (Φροίξος Γρίβας) (a) 23/09/2000, Livadia (Greece) (b) 1,78 (c) F - left winger (d) PS Kalamata (e) PS Kalamata, OFI Creta, PS Kalamata, OFI Creta, Panionios, AO Glyfadas

*** Grivić - Dragan Grivić (a) 12/02/1996, Kotor (RF Yugoslavia, now in Montenegro) (b) 1,77 (c) D - right back (d) FK Sutjeska Niksic (e) OFK Grbalj
*** Grivosti - Tom Grivosti (a) 15/06/1999, Liverpool (England) (b) 1,85 (c) D - central defense (d) St. Patrick's Athletic (e) Ross County, Elgin City, Ross County, Skelmersdale
*** Grjaznovs - Aleksejs Grjaznovs (a) 01/10/1997, Riga (Latvia) (b) 1,79 (c) M - pivot (d) FK Liepaja (e) FC Noah, Slovan Velvary, Sokol Brozany, Noah Jurmala, Albatroz/Jelgava, Valmiera, RTU, RFS, Babite, RFS
*** Grobelny - Jedrzej Grobelny (Jędrzej Grobelny) (a) 28/06/2001, Poznań (Poland) (b) 1,90 (c) G (d) Warta Poznań (e) Pogon Szczecin, Miedź Legnica, Pogon Szczecin, Pogon II
*** Grødem - Magnus Grødem (Magnus Retsius Grødem) (a) 14/08/1998, Bryne (Norway) (b) 1,92 (c) M - attacking midfielder (d) Molde FK (e) Sandnes Ulf, Vejle BK, Sandnes Ulf, Vejle BK, Vålerenga, Ullensaker/Kisa, Vålerenga, Ullensaker/Kisa, Vålerenga, Bryne
*** Gróf - Dávid Gróf (Gróf Dávid Attila) (a) 17/04/1989, Budapest (Hungary) (b) 1,93 (c) G (d) APO Levadiakos (e) Debrecen, Ferencváros, Debrecen, Ferencváros, Honvéd, Csákvár, Notts County, Berliner AK, Goslarer SC, FC Walsall, Notts County, Mansfield Town, Notts County, Hibernian FC
*** Grøgaard - Thomas Grøgaard (a) 08/02/1994, Arendal (Norway) (b) 1,80 (c) D - left back (d) Strømsgodset IF (e) Brann, Odd
*** Grogan - Nick Grogan (Nicholas Arthur Jonathon Grogan) (a) 23/02/2004, ¿? (Wales) (b) - (c) D - central defense (d) - (e) Cefn Druids, Llandudno
*** Gröger - Denis Gröger (a) 17/02/1999, Šternberk (Czech Rep.) (b) 1,92 (c) G (d) FC Zlinsko (e) Liptovsky Mik., Skalica, Sigma Olomouc B, Otrokovice, Sigma Olomouc B, SFK Vrchovina, Sigma Olomouc B
*** Gromov - Artem Gromov (Громов Артем Ігорович) (a) 14/01/1990, Stryi, Lviv Oblast (Soviet Union, now in Ukraine) (b) 1,78 (c) F - left winger (d) - (e) AEK Larnaca, SK Dnipro-1, Zorya Lugansk, KS Samara, Dinamo Kyïv, Vorskla Poltava, Vorskla II
*** Gromyko - Valeriy Gromyko (Громыко Валерий Игоревич) (a) 23/01/1997, Minsk (Belarus) (b) 1,77 (c) M - attacking midfielder (d) BATE Borisov (e) Arsenal Tula, BATE Borisov, Arsenal Tula, Soligorsk, FK Minsk
*** Grønbæk - Albert Grønbæk (Albert Grønbæk Erlykke) (a) 23/05/2001, Risskov (Denmark) (b) 1,76 (c) M - central midfielder (d) FK Bodø/Glimt (e) Aarhus GF
*** Grönning - Jeppe Grönning (Jeppe Nørregaard Grønning) (a) 24/05/1991, ¿? (Denmark) (b) 1,80 (c) M - pivot (d) Viborg FF (e) Hobro IK, Viborg FF, FC Fyn
*** Grönning - Sebastian Grönning (Sebastian Grønning Andersen) (a) 03/02/1997, Aalborg (Denmark) (b) 1,88 (c) F - center forward (d) - (e) OFI Creta, Aarhus GF, Suwon Bluewings, Viborg FF, Skive IK, Hobro IK, Aalborg BK
*** Groogan - Adam Groogan (a) 21/05/2003, ¿? (Northern Ireland) (b) - (c) G (d) Dergview FC (e) Dungannon
*** Groothusen - Terence Groothusen (Terence Clyde Leon Groothusen) (a) 16/09/1996, Amsterdam (Netherlands) (b) 1,92 (c) F - center forward (d) Sportlust '46 (e) AO Porou, Sliema Wanderers, Hibernians FC, Rot Weiss Ahlen, Alemannia Aachen, SV Straelen, Kozakken Boys, Hibernians FC, FC Dordrecht, EDO, HFC EDO O19
*** Gropper - Denny Gropper (גרופר דני) (a) 16/03/1999, Haifa (Israel) (b) - (c) D - left back (d) Ludogorets Razgrad (e) Hapoel Tel Aviv, Hapoel Afula, Ironi Nesher
*** Grosicki - Kamil Grosicki (Kamil Grosicki) (a) 08/06/1988, Szczecin (Poland) (b) 1,80 (c) F - left winger (d) Pogon Szczecin (e) West Bromwich Albion, Hull City,

Stade Rennes, Sivasspor, Jagiellonia, Legia Warszawa, Jagiellonia, Legia Warszawa, FC Sion, Legia Warszawa, Pogon Szczecin, Pogon II
*** Groß - Christian Groß (a) 08/02/1989, Bremen (Germany) (b) 1,82 (c) M - pivot (d) SV Werder Bremen (e) Werder Bremen II, VfL Osnabrück, SF Lotte, Babelsberg 03, Hamburg II, SV Hamburg, Hamburg II
*** Gross - Jake Gross (Jake Lewis Gross) (a) 30/03/2001, ¿? (Faroe Islands) (b) 1,93 (c) D - central defense (d) - (e) AB Argir
*** Groß - Pascal Groß (a) 15/06/1991, Mannheim (Germany) (b) 1,81 (c) M - central midfielder (d) Brighton & Hove Albion (e) FC Ingolstadt, Karlsruher SC, Hoffenheim II
*** Grosu - Arsen Grosu (Гросу Арсен Дмитрович) (a) 13/04/2001, Kolomyya, Ivano-Frankivsk Oblast (Ukraine) (b) 1,75 (c) M - attacking midfielder (d) Stal Rzeszow II (e) Górnik Zabrze, Gornik II, C. Nowotaniec, Pokuttya Kolom.
*** Grosu - Darius Grosu (Darius Constantin Grosu) (a) 07/06/2002, ¿? (Romania) (b) 1,73 (c) D - right back (d) FCV Farul Constanta (e) Metaloglobus, FC Viitorul, Academia Hagi
*** Grot - Jay-Roy Grot (Jay-Roy Jornell Grot) (a) 13/03/1998, Arnhem (Netherlands) (b) 1,93 (c) F - center forward (d) Kashiwa Reysol (e) Viborg FF, VfL Osnabrück, Leeds Utd., Vitesse, Leeds Utd., VVV-Venlo, Leeds Utd., NEC Nijmegen
*** Grozav - Gheorghe Grozav (Gheorghe Teodor Grozav) (a) 29/09/1990, Alba Iulia (Romania) (b) 1,82 (c) F - left winger (d) Petrolul Ploiesti (e) MTK Budapest, Diósgyőr, Kisvárda, FC Dinamo, Bursaspor, Karabükspor, Akhmat Grozny, FC Dinamo, Terek Grozny, Petrolul, Standard Liège, Universitatea Cluj, Standard Liège, Alba Iulia
*** Grozdanovski - Tomce Grozdanovski (Томче Грозданоски) (a) 14/03/2000, Skopje (North Macedonia) (b) 1,80 (c) M - pivot (d) Rabotnicki Skopje (e) Zlaté Moravce, NK Dugopolje, Zlaté Moravce, Kozuf
*** Groznica - Gabriel Groznica (a) 12/03/2002, Zagreb (Croatia) (b) - (c) M - attacking midfielder (d) FC Koper (e) Koper, NK Lokomotiva, NK Jarun, NK Lokomotiva
*** Grozurek - Lukas Grozurek (a) 22/12/1991, Wien (Austria) (b) 1,89 (c) F - center forward (d) ASV Siegendorf (e) First Vienna FC, Dinamo Batumi, SKN St. Pölten, Sturm Graz, Karlsruher SC, Sturm Graz, Admira Wacker, Rapid Wien, Rapid Wien II, Wiener Sportklub, Wiener SC II
*** Grub - Sebastian Grub (a) 18/10/1987, Zweibrücken (Germany) (b) 1,92 (c) G (d) FC Berdenia Berbourg (e) US Hostert, FSV Salmrohr, Etzella Ettelbrück, SC Hauenstein, FSV Salmrohr, Borussia Neunkirchen, Hoffenheim II, SF Köllerbach, FC 08 Homburg, FK Pirmasens
*** Grubac - Sergej Grubac (Сергеj Грубач, Σεργκέι Γκρούμπατς) (a) 29/05/2000, Beograd (RF Yugoslavia, now in Serbia) (b) 1,90 (c) F - center forward (d) - (e) Chindia, FC Botosani, Chievo Verona, APOEL FC, Digenis Morfou
*** Grubbe - Gustav Grubbe (Gustav Grubbe Madsen) (a) 27/01/2003, Odense (Denmark) (b) 1,81 (c) D - right back (d) Odense Boldklub (e) -
*** Gruber - Andreas Gruber (a) 29/06/1995, Mürzzuschlag (Austria) (b) 1,74 (c) F - right winger (d) FK Austria Viena (e) LASK, SV Mattersburg, Sturm Graz, Sturm Graz II
*** Gruber - Zsombor Gruber (a) 07/09/2004, Győr (Hungary) (b) 1,80 (c) F - center forward (d) Puskás Akadémia FC (e) Puskás AFC, Puskás AFC II
*** Gruda - Brajan Gruda (a) 31/05/2004, Speyer (Germany) (b) 1,78 (c) F - right winger (d) 1.FSV Mainz 05 (e) -

*** Gruda - Ildi Gruda (a) 13/12/1999, Lezhë (Albania) (b) 1,75 (c) F - center forward (d) KF Vllaznia (e) KF Teuta, FC Shënkolli, Valletta

*** Gruev - Ilia Gruev (Илия Илиев Груев) (a) 06/05/2000, Sofia (Bulgaria) (b) 1,85 (c) M - pivot (d) SV Werder Bremen (e) -

*** Gruezo - Carlos Gruezo (Carlos Armando Gruezo Arboleda) (a) 19/04/1995, Santo Domingo (Ecuador) (b) 1,72 (c) M - pivot (d) San José Earthquakes (e) FC Augsburg, Dallas, VfB Stuttgart, Barcelona SC, Independiente, Independiente B

*** Grujcic - Darijo Grujcic (a) 19/05/1999, Lustenau (Austria) (b) 1,88 (c) D - central defense (d) SC Austria Lustenau (e) FC Wacker, Austria Lustenau, FC Dornbirn

*** Grujic - Marko Grujic (Марко Грујић) (a) 13/04/1996, Beograd (RF Yugoslavia, now in Serbia) (b) 1,91 (c) M - pivot (d) FC Porto (e) Liverpool, FC Porto, Liverpool, FC Porto, Liverpool, Hertha Berlin, Liverpool, Hertha Berlin, Liverpool, Cardiff City, Liverpool, Crvena zvezda, Liverpool, Crvena zvezda, Kolubara, Crvena zvezda

*** Grulev - Vyacheslav Grulev (Грулёв Вячеслав Дмитриевич) (a) 23/03/1999, Kemerovo (Russia) (b) 1,90 (c) F - left winger (d) Dinamo Moskva (e) Nizhny Novgorod, Dinamo Moskva, Dinamo Moskva II, Dinamo 2, Dinamo Moskva II, Akron Konoplev

*** Grüll - Marco Grüll (a) 06/07/1998, Schwarzach im Pongau (Austria) (b) 1,82 (c) F - left winger (d) SK Rapid Wien (e) SV Ried, St. Johann, Pfarrwerfen

*** Grun - Allan Grun (a) 22/01/1998, Forbach (France) (b) 1,90 (c) M - pivot (d) US Hostert (e) Chaux-de-Fonds

*** Grünvald - Attila Grünvald (Grünvald Attila László) (a) 26/07/1991, Szeged (Hungary) (b) 1,84 (c) D - left back (d) Kecskeméti TE (e) SZEOL

*** Grünvald - Evert Grünvald (a) 06/04/2001, Tallinn (Estonia) (b) - (c) G (d) FC Flora Tallinn (e) JK Tabasalu

*** Gruzhevskiy - Denis Gruzhevskiy (Гружевский Денис Викторович) (a) 10/03/2000, Smorgon (Belarus) (b) 1,85 (c) D - left back (d) Shakhter Soligorsk (e) Torpedo Zhodino, Sputnik, FK Smorgon, FK Minsk II, RUOR Minsk

*** Gryglak - Filip Gryglak (a) 02/09/2004, Zgorzelec (Poland) (b) 1,80 (c) M - pivot (d) Slask Wroclaw II (e) Slask Wroclaw II

*** Gryn - Sergiy Gryn (Гринь Сергій Віталійович) (a) 06/06/1994, Volnovaja (Ukraine) (b) 1,78 (c) F - left winger (d) Epicentr Kamyanets-Podilskyi (e) FK Oleksandriya, Zorya Lugansk, Vejle BK, Shakhtar Donetsk, Arsenal Kyiv, Shakhtar Donetsk, Veres Rivne, Shakhtar Donetsk, Olimpik Donetsk, Shakhtar Donetsk, Illichivets, Shakhtar Donetsk, Shakhtar II, Illichivets, Shakhtar II

*** Grysyo - Maksym Grysyo (Грисьо Максим Йосипович) (a) 14/05/1996, Chyshky, Lviv Oblast (Ukraine) (b) 1,72 (c) M - right midfielder (d) Chornomorets Odessa (e) PFK Lviv, Cherkashchyna, Karpaty, Rukh Vynnyky, Karpaty, Karpaty II, UFK Lviv

*** Gryszkiewicz - Adrian Gryszkiewicz (a) 13/12/1999, Bytom (Poland) (b) 1,85 (c) D - central defense (d) Rakow Czestochowa (e) SC Paderborn, Górnik Zabrze

*** Grytebust - Sten Grytebust (Sten Michael Grytebust) (a) 25/10/1989, Ålesund (Norway) (b) 1,87 (c) G (d) Aalesunds FK (e) FC København, Vejle BK, FC København, Odense BK, Aalesund

*** Grytsenko - Yevgen Grytsenko (Гриценко Євген Олександрович) (a) 05/02/1995, Donetsk (Ukraine) (b) 1,91 (c) G (d) Ravshan Kulob (e) FC Van, Shakhtar Donetsk, Shakhtar II, FK Mariupol, Shakhtar II

*** Grzan - Sime Grzan (Šime Gržan) (a) 06/04/1994, Zadar (Croatia) (b) 1,72 (c) D - right back (d) NK Osijek (e) Zalaegerszeg, NK Osijek, NK Istra, GOSK Gabela, Zrinjski Mostar, NK Istra, NK Lokomotiva, NK Zadar

*** Grzelczak - Piotr Grzelczak (a) 02/03/1988, Łódź (Poland) (b) 1,86 (c) F - center forward (d) Barycz Sułów (e) Atyrau, Chojniczanka, Platanias, Gornik Leczna, Jagiellonia, Lechia Gdánsk, Polonia, Lechia Gdánsk, Widzew Lódz, Pelikan Lowicz, Widzew Lódz, KKS Koluszki, Widzew Lódz,

*** Grzesiak - Jakub Grzesiak (a) 22/02/2003, Bydgoszcz (Poland) (b) 1,94 (c) G (d) ORU Golden Eagles (Oral Roberts Uni.) (e) Górnik Zabrze, Stomil, Górnik Zabrze, MKS Kluczbork, Górnik Zabrze, Gornik II

*** Grzesik - Jan Grzesik (Jan Grzesik) (a) 21/10/1994, Olesno (Poland) (b) 1,78 (c) D - right back (d) Radomiak Radom (e) Warta Poznań, ŁKS, Siarka T., Nadwislan Gora, Legia II, Pogon Siedlce, Legia II, Z. Sosnowiec, Legia II

*** Grzybek - Mateusz Grzybek (a) 30/03/1996, Tychy (Poland) (b) 1,78 (d) Zagglbie Lubin (e) Radomiak, Nieciecza, GKS Tychy

*** Guaita - Vicente Guaita (Vicente Guaita Panadero) (a) 10/01/1987, Torrente (Spain) (b) 1,90 (c) G (d) Crystal Palace (e) Getafe CF, Valencia CF, Recreativo, Valencia CF, Valencia Mestalla

*** Gual - Marc Gual (Marc Gual Huguet) (a) 13/03/1996, Badalona (Spain) (b) 1,86 (c) F - center forward (d) Legia de Varsovia (e) SK Dnipro-1, Jagiellonia, SK Dnipro-1, Alcorcón, Sevilla FC, RM Castilla, Sevilla FC, Girona FC, Sevilla FC, Real Zaragoza, Sevilla FC, Sevilla At., RCD Espanyol B

*** Guardado - Andrés Guardado (José Andrés Guardado Hernández) (a) 28/09/1986, Guadalajara (Mexico) (b) 1,67 (c) M - central midfielder (d) Real Betis Balompié (e) PSV Eindhoven, Valencia CF, PSV Eindhoven, Valencia CF, Bayer Leverkusen, Valencia CF, RC Deportivo, Atlas

*** Guardiola - Sergi Guardiola (Sergio Guardiola Navarro) (a) 29/05/1991, Manacor (Spain) (b) 1,85 (c) F - center forward (d) Cádiz CF (e) Real Valladolid, Cádiz CF, Real Valladolid, Rayo Vallecano, Real Valladolid, Córdoba CF, Getafe CF, Córdoba CF, Recreativo Granada, Real Murcia, Granada B, Adelaide United, Granada B, Alcorcón, CD Eldense, Novelda CF, Getafe CF B, Ontinyent, CF La Nucía, Jumilla CF, LD Olímpico

*** Guarino - Gabriele Guarino (a) 14/04/2004, Molfetta (Italy) (b) 1,86 (c) D - central defense (d) FC Empoli (e) -

*** Guarnone - Alessandro Guarnone (a) 27/03/1999, ¿? (Italy) (b) 1,89 (c) G (d) - (e) Valletta, Birkirkara FC, FC Chiasso, FC Chiasso II, Matera

*** Gubenko - Ilya Gubenko (Губенко Илья) (a) 25/09/2002, ¿? (Kazakhstan) (b) 1,81 (c) G (d) Shakhter-Bulat (e) -

*** Guca - Konrad Guca (a) 18/08/2003, Tarnobrzeg (Poland) (b) - (c) G (d) Czarni Polaniec (e) Czarni Polaniec, Stal Mielec, Stal Mielec II

*** Gucek - Luka Gucek (Luka Guček) (a) 29/01/1999, Brežice (Slovenia) (b) 1,89 (c) D - central defense (d) Chornomorets Odessa (e) NK Radomlje, Domžale, NK Dob, Domžale

*** Guchmazov - Ilya Guchmazov (Гучмазов Тимурович Илья) (a) 14/04/2001, Vidnoe, Moskva Oblast (Russia) (b) 1,88 (c) G (d) FK Sloga Meridian (e) Po-dri-nje, Zvijezda 09, Internacional

*** Güçlü - Metehan Güçlü (Metehan Güçlü) (a) 02/04/1999, Montfermeil (France) (b) 1,82 (c) F - center forward (d) - (e) FC Emmen, Stade Rennes, FC Emmen, Stade Rennes, Valenciennes FC, Stade Rennes, Paris Saint Germain B

*** Gudbjargarson - Sölvi Snaer Gudbjargarson (Sölvi Snær Guðbjargarson) (a) 25/07/2001, ¿? (Iceland) (b) - (c) M - right midfielder (d) Breidablik Kópavogur (e) Stjarnan

*** Gudbrandsson - Gyrdir Hrafn Gudbrandsson (Gyrðir Hrafn Guðbrandsson) (a) 30/03/1999, ¿? (Iceland) (b) - (c) D - central defense (d) FH Hafnarfjördur (e) Leiknir

*** Gudelj - Nemanja Gudelj (Немања Гудељ) (a) 16/11/1991, Beograd (Yugoslavia, now in Serbia) (b) 1,87 (c) M - pivot (d) Sevilla FC (e) GZ Evergrande, Sporting Lisboa, GZ Evergrande, Tianjin Teda, Ajax, AZ Alkmaar, NAC Breda
*** Gudiev - Vitaliy Gudiev (Гудиев Виталий Казимирович) (a) 22/04/1995, Vladikavkaz (Russia) (b) 1,92 (c) G (d) Fakel Voronezh (e) Khimki, Akhmat Grozny, Alania
*** Gudjohnsen - Andri Gudjohnsen (Andri Lucas Guðjohnsen) (a) 29/01/2002, London (England) (b) 1,88 (c) F - center forward (d) IFK Norrköping (e) RM Castilla
*** Gudjohnsen - Arnór Borg Gudjohnsen (Arnór Borg Guðjohnsen) (a) 16/09/2000, ¿? (Iceland) (b) - (c) F - center forward (d) FH Hafnarfjördur (e) Hafnarfjördur, Víkingur, Fylkir
*** Gudjohnsen - Sveinn Aron Gudjohnsen (Sveinn Aron Guðjohnsen) (a) 12/05/1998, Reykjavík (Iceland) (b) 1,89 (c) F - center forward (d) IF Elfsborg (e) Spezia, Odense BK, Spezia, Ravenna, Spezia, Breidablik, Valur, HK Kópavogs
*** Gudjónsson - Brynjar Gauti Gudjónsson (Brynjar Gauti Guðjónsson) (a) 27/02/1992, ¿? (Iceland) (b) - (c) D - central defense (d) Fram Reykjavík (e) Stjarnan, ÍBV Vestmannaeyjar, Víkingur Ó.
*** Gudjónsson - Helgi Gudjónsson (Helgi Guðjónsson) (a) 04/08/1999, ¿? (Iceland) (b) 1,80 (c) F - attacking midfielder (d) Víkingur Reykjavík (e) Fram Reykjavík
*** Gudjónsson - Thórir Gudjónsson (Þórir Guðjónsson) (a) 07/04/1991, ¿? (Iceland) (b) 1,89 (c) D - central defense (d) Fram Reykjavík (e) Breidablik, Fjölnir, Valur, Fjölnir, Valur, Leiknir, Valur
*** Gudlaugsson - Baldur Logi Gudlaugsson (Baldur Logi Guðlaugsson) (a) 21/01/2002, ¿? (Iceland) (b) - (c) M - central midfielder (d) Stjarnan Gardabaer (e) Hafnarfjördur
*** Gudmundsson - Ari Steinn Gudmundsson (Ari Steinn Guðmundsson) (a) 31/12/1996, ¿? (Iceland) (b) - (c) F - left winger (d) KF Vídir (e) Keflavík, Vídir, Keflavík, Vídir, Keflavík, Vídir, Keflavík, Vídir, Keflavík, Njardvík, Keflavík, Njardvík, Keflavík
*** Gudmundsson - Arngrímur Bjartur Gudmundsson (Arngrímur Bjartur Guðmundsson) (a) 14/03/2005, ¿? (Iceland) (b) - (c) D (d) KF Aegir (e) Aegir, Hafnarfjördur
*** Gudmundsson - Atli Gunnar Gudmundsson (Atli Gunnar Guðmundsson) (a) 08/10/1993, ¿? (Iceland) (b) - (c) G (d) KFK Kópavogur (e) Hafnarfjördur, Fjölnir, Fram Reykjavík, ÍF Huginn, Tindastóll
*** Gudmundsson - Eggert Aron Gudmundsson (Eggert Aron Guðmundsson) (a) 08/02/2004, ¿? (Iceland) (b) - (c) M - attacking midfielder (d) Stjarnan Gardabaer (e) -
*** Gudmundsson - Elvar Máni Gudmundsson (Elvar Máni Guðmundsson) (a) 26/01/2006, ¿? (Iceland) (b) - (c) F (d) Stjarnan Gardabaer (e) KA Akureyri
*** Gudmundsson - Gabriel Gudmundsson (a) 29/04/1999, Malmö (Sweden) (b) 1,80 (c) D - left back (d) LOSC Lille Métropole (e) FC Groningen, Halmstads BK
*** Gudmundsson - Galdur Gudmundsson (Ásgeir Galdur Guðmundsson) (a) 14/04/2006, ¿? (Iceland) (b) 1,86 (c) F - right winger (d) - (e) Breidablik
*** Gudmundsson - Ólafur Gudmundsson (Ólafur Guðmundsson) (a) 18/03/2002, Kópavogur (Iceland) (b) 1,88 (c) D - left back (d) FH Hafnarfjördur (e) Breidablik, Grindavík, Breidablik, Keflavík, Breidablik, Augnablik, Breidablik
*** Gudmundsson - Óttar Bjarni Gudmundsson (Óttar Bjarni Guðmundsson) (a) 15/04/1990, ¿? (Iceland) (b) - (c) D - central defense (d) Leiknir Reykjavík (e) ÍA Akranes, Stjarnan, Leiknir, KB, Leiknir

*** Gudmundsson - Sigfús Árni Gudmundsson (Sigfús Árni Guðmundsson) (a) 13/04/2004, ¿? (Iceland) (b) - (c) M (d) Fram Reykjavík (e) -

*** Gudmundsson - Sindri Thór Gudmundsson (Sindri Þór Guðmundsson) (a) 11/08/1997, ¿? (Iceland) (b) - (c) D - right back (d) Keflavík ÍF (e) -

*** Gudmundsson - Tómas Gudmundsson (Tómas Guðmundsson) (a) 10/02/1992, ¿? (Iceland) (b) - (c) D - central defense (d) - (e) Víkingur

*** Gudnason - Erlendur Gudnason (a) 25/02/2004, ¿? (Iceland) (b) - (c) D (d) - (e) Hamrarnir

*** Gudnason - Ingimundur Aron Gudnason (Ingimundur Aron Guðnason) (a) 29/03/1999, ¿? (Iceland) (b) - (c) M - pivot (d) Keflavík ÍF (e) -

*** Gudushauri - Paata Gudushauri (პაატა გუდუშაური) (a) 07/06/1997, Tbilisi (Georgia) (b) 1,79 (c) F - right winger (d) Dinamo Batumi (e) FC Dila, WIT Georgia

*** Gudzulic - Marko Gudzulic (Марко Гуџулић) (a) 05/07/2002, Kruševac (RF Yugoslavia, now in Serbia) (b) - (c) G (d) FK Kolubara Lazarevac (e) Dobanovci, Dobanovci, FK Zemun

*** Gué - Gué (Ricardo Gué Rosa Cardoso) (a) 23/09/2001, ¿? (Finland) (b) 1,71 (c) F - left winger (d) Skellefteå FF (e) HJK Klubi 04, Kajaanin Haka

*** Guedes - Alexandre Guedes (Alexandre Xavier Pereira Guedes) (a) 11/02/1994, Arcozelo (Portugal) (b) 1,85 (c) F - center forward (d) CA Petróleos Luanda (e) Paços Ferreira, Albirex Niigata, Rakow, Famalicão, Vitória Guimarães, Vegalta Sendai, Vitória Guimarães, Desportivo Aves, Reus Deportiu, Sporting B

*** Guedes - Gonçalo Guedes (Gonçalo Manuel Ganchinho Guedes) (a) 29/11/1996, Benavente (Portugal) (b) 1,79 (c) F - left winger (d) Wolverhampton Wanderers (e) Benfica, Wolverhampton Wanderers, Valencia CF, Paris Saint-Germain, Valencia CF, Paris Saint-Germain, Benfica, Benfica B

*** Guedes - Gui Guedes (Guilherme Borges Guedes) (a) 17/04/2002, Santa Marta de Penaguião (Portugal) (b) 1,84 (c) M - central midfielder (d) UD Almería (e) CD Lugo, UD Almería, Vitória Guimarães

*** Guedes - Luizinho Guedes (Luiz Enrique Guedes) (a) 22/05/1999, ¿? (Brazil) (b) 1,80 (c) F - center forward (d) FK Aksu (e) Ordabasy, XV de Jaú, Grêmio Sorriso, XV de Jaú, Oeste Paulista Esporte Clube (SP), Itapirense, Oeste Paulista Esporte Clube (SP)

*** Gueguin - Axel Gueguin (a) 24/03/2005, Montpellier (France) (b) 1,70 (c) F - right winger (d) HSC Montpellier B (e) Montpellier For

*** Guéhi - Marc Guéhi (Addji Keaninkin Marc-Israel Guéhi) (a) 13/07/2000, Abidjan (Ivory Coast) (b) 1,82 (c) D - central defense (d) Crystal Palace (e) Chelsea, Swansea City, Chelsea, Swansea City, Chelsea

*** Guendouzi - Mattéo Guendouzi (Matteo Elias Kenzo Guendouzi Olié) (a) 14/04/1999, Poissy (France) (b) 1,85 (c) M - central midfielder (d) Olympique Marseille (e) Arsenal, Ol. Marseille, Arsenal, Hertha Berlin, Arsenal, FC Lorient, Lorient B

*** Guenouche - Hakim Guenouche (a) 30/05/2000, Nancy (France) (b) 1,72 (c) D - left back (d) FK Austria Viena (e) Austria Lustenau, KFC Uerdingen, FC Zürich

*** Guererro - Dani Guererro (Daniel Guerrero Heredia) (a) 08/07/1983, Los Barrios (Spain) (b) 1,85 (c) D - central defense (d) Glacis United (e) FC College 1975, CD San Bernardo, Los Barrios, St Joseph's FC, Glacis United, Los Barrios, UD Pastores, UD Tesorillo, Manilva Sabini

*** Guermouche - Yanis Guermouche (قرموش يانيس) (a) 15/04/2001, Neuilly-sur-Seine (France) (b) 1,92 (c) F - center forward (d) Montpellier HSC (e) LB Châteauroux, Montpellier, Montpellier B

*** Guerra - Alberto Guerra (a) 13/01/2004, San Marino (San Marino) (b) - (c) D - right back (d) CBR Carli Pietracuta (e) Cosmos, Victor SM

*** Guerra - Javi Guerra (Javier Guerra Moreno) (a) 13/05/2003, Valencia (Spain) (b) 1,87 (c) M - central midfielder (d) Valencia CF (e) Valencia Mestalla

*** Guerreiro - Raphaël Guerreiro (Raphaël Adelino José Guerreiro) (a) 22/12/1993, Le Blanc-Mesnil (France) (b) 1,70 (c) D - left back (d) Bayern München (e) Borussia Dortmund, FC Lorient, SM Caen, SM Caen B

*** Guerrero - Adrián Guerrero (Adrián Guerrero Aguilar) (a) 28/01/1998, Blanes (Spain) (b) 1,74 (c) M - left midfielder (d) FC Zürich (e) Valencia Mestalla, FC Lugano, Valencia Mestalla, Reus Deportiu, Reus B

*** Guerrero - Eduardo Guerrero (Eduardo Antonio Guerrero Locano) (a) 21/02/2000, Panama City (Panamá) (b) 1,80 (c) F - center forward (d) Zorya Lugansk (e) Maccabi Tel Aviv, Zorya Lugansk, Maccabi Tel Aviv, B. Jerusalem, Maccabi Tel Aviv, H. Jerusalem, Maccabi Tel Aviv, B TLV Bat Yam, Maccabi Tel Aviv, Universitario, Universitario

*** Guerrero - Jorge Guerrero (Jorge David Guerrero Guio) (a) ¿?, Bogotá (Colombia) (b) - (c) D - right back (d) - (e) FC Ordino, CE Carroi

*** Guerrero - Miguel Ángel Guerrero (Miguel Ángel Guerrero Martín) (a) 12/07/1990, Toledo (Spain) (b) 1,80 (c) F - attacking midfielder (d) Anorthosis Famagusta (e) OFI Creta, UD Ibiza, Rayo Vallecano, Nottingham Forest, Olympiakos, CD Leganés, Olympiakos, CD Leganés, Real Sporting, Sporting B, At. Albacete

*** Guerrico - Ignacio Guerrico (a) 09/07/1998, La Plata (Argentina) (b) 1,75 (c) D - left back (d) NK Maribor (e) Tabor Sezana, NK Maribor, San Carlos, ADIP

*** Guerrier - Wilde-Donald Guerrier (a) 31/03/1989, Port-à-Piment (Haiti) (b) 1,80 (c) D - left back (d) - (e) Zira FK, Olympiakos N., Wieczysta, Apollon Limassol, Qarabag FK, Neftchi Baku, Qarabag FK, Alanyaspor, Wisla Kraków, América, Violette AC

*** Guessand - Axel Guessand (Axel Thurel Sahuye Guessand) (a) 06/11/2004, Schiltigheim (France) (b) 1,84 (c) D - central defense (d) Udinese (e) AS Nancy B

*** Guessand - Evann Guessand (a) 01/07/2001, Ajaccio (France) (b) 1,87 (c) F - center forward (d) OGC Niza (e) FC Nantes, OGC Nice, Lausanne-Sport, OGC Nice, OGC Nice B

*** Guest - Ben Guest (Benjamin Alan Guest) (a) 22/05/2003, ¿? (England) (b) - (c) M - central midfielder (d) Guilsfield FC (e) -

*** Guett Guett - Alex Guett Guett (Alex Angelin Guett Guett) (a) 26/11/2002, Ngaoundéré (Cameroon) (b) 1,80 (c) D - right back (d) FC Progrès Niederkorn (e) Progrès Niederkorn, FC Sochaux, FC Sochaux B

*** Guevara - Ander Guevara (Ander Guevara Lajo) (a) 07/07/1997, Vitoria-Gasteiz (Spain) (b) 1,80 (c) M - central midfielder (d) Deportivo Alavés (e) Real Sociedad, Real Sociedad B, Real Sociedad C

*** Gueye - Djibril Gueye (a) 19/11/1996, Ngor (Senegal) (b) 1,85 (c) F - center forward (d) Valmiera FC (e) AS Douanes, US Ouakam, Ngor

*** Gueye - Idrissa Gueye (Idrissa Gana Gueye) (a) 26/09/1989, Dakar (Senegal) (b) 1,74 (c) M - central midfielder (d) Everton FC (e) Paris Saint-Germain, Everton, Aston Villa, Lille, LOSC Lille B, Diambars FC

*** Gueye - Maguette Gueye (a) 30/12/2002, Sakal (Senegal) (b) 1,83 (c) M - attacking midfielder (d) FK Partizani (e) -

*** Gueye - Makhtar Gueye (a) 04/12/1997, Dakar (Senegal) (b) 1,95 (c) F - center forward (d) RWD Molenbeek (e) KV Oostende, Real Zaragoza, KV Oostende, St.-Étienne, AS Nancy, St.-Étienne, Saint-Étienne B, US Gorée

*** Gueye - Moussa Gueye (a) 31/12/1995, ¿? (Senegal) (b) - (c) G (d) - (e) Murata, Pennarossa, SS Folgore, Riccione
*** Gueye - Pape Gueye (Pape Alassane Gueye) (a) 24/01/1999, Montreuil (France) (b) 1,89 (c) M - pivot (d) Olympique Marseille (e) Sevilla FC, Ol. Marseille, Le Havre AC, Le Havre AC B
*** Gueye - Pape Habib Gueye (a) 20/09/1999, ¿? (Senegal) (b) 1,88 (c) F - center forward (d) KV Kortrijk (e) Aalesund
*** Guga - Guga (Gonçalo Rosa Gonçalves Pereira Rodrigues) (a) 18/07/1997, Faro (Portugal) (b) 1,68 (c) M - attacking midfielder (d) Rio Ave FC (e) Famalicão, Benfica B, Panetolikos, Benfica B
*** Gugeshashvili - Luka Gugeshashvili (ლუკა გუგეშაშვილი) (a) 29/04/1999, Tbilisi (Georgia) (b) 1,96 (c) G (d) Qarabağ FK (e) Jagiellonia, Qarabag FK, Jagiellonia, FC Dila, Jagiellonia, Recreativo Granada, Jagiellonia, FC Dila, Jagiellonia, Podlasie B.P., Dinamo Tbilisi
*** Gugganig - David Gugganig (a) 10/02/1997, Spittal an der Drau (Austria) (b) 1,92 (c) D - central defense (d) WSG Tirol (e) Wolfsberger AC, WSG Tirol, FC Liefering, WSG Wattens, FC Liefering
*** Gugganig - Lukas Gugganig (Lukas Josef Gugganig) (a) 14/02/1995, Spittal an der Drau (Austria) (b) 1,91 (c) D - central defense (d) SCR Altach (e) VfL Osnabrück, Greuther Fürth, FSV Frankfurt, FC Liefering
*** Guglielmi - Filippo Guglielmi (a) 16/03/2001, Rimini (Italy) (b) 1,80 (c) D - central defense (d) AC Libertas (e) Victor SM, Correggese, Vastogirardi, Cattolica SM, Santarcangelo
*** Guiagon - Parfait Guiagon (a) 22/02/2001, ¿? (Israel) (b) 1,69 (c) M - attacking midfielder (d) Maccabi Tel Aviv (e) Maccabi Netanya, Maccabi Tel Aviv, B TLV Bat Yam, Maccabi Tel Aviv, Africa Sports
*** Guidetti - John Guidetti (John Alberto Fernando Andres Luigi Olof Guidetti) (a) 15/04/1992, Stockholm (Sweden) (b) 1,85 (c) F - center forward (d) AIK Solna (e) Alavés, Hannover 96, Alavés, RC Celta, Alavés, RC Celta, Manchester City, Celtic FC, Manchester City, Stoke City, Manchester City, Feyenoord, Manchester City, Burnley, Manchester City, Brommapojkarna, Manchester City
*** Guidi - Simone Guidi (a) 14/06/2000, ¿? (San Marino) (b) - (c) G (d) - (e) Domagnano, Juvenes-Dogana, Faetano
*** Guidi - Tommaso Guidi (a) 21/10/1998, ¿? (San Marino) (b) - (c) F - left winger (d) La Fiorita 1967 (e) Cosmos, La Fiorita, Fiorentino, Santarcangelo, San Marino, Tre Penne, Tre Penne
*** Guidotti - Stefano Guidotti (Stefano Alessandro Guidotti) (a) 16/06/1999, Locarno (Switzerland) (b) 1,85 (c) M - central midfielder (d) FC St. Gallen 1879 (e) FC Lugano, FC Chiasso, FC Lugano
*** Guilavogui - Josuha Guilavogui (a) 19/09/1990, Toulon (France) (b) 1,88 (c) M - pivot (d) - (e) VfL Wolfsburg, Girondins Bordeaux, VfL Wolfsburg, Atlético Madrid, VfL Wolfsburg, Atlético Madrid, St.-Étienne, Atlético Madrid, St.-Étienne, Saint-Étienne B
*** Guilbert - Frédéric Guilbert (a) 24/12/1994, Valognes (France) (b) 1,78 (c) D - right back (d) Racing Club Strasbourg (e) Aston Villa, Racing Club Strasbourg, Aston Villa, Racing Club Strasbourg, Aston Villa, SM Caen, Aston Villa, SM Caen, Girondins Bordeaux, SM Caen, Girondins Bordeaux, Girondins Bordeaux B, AS Cherbourg, SM Caen B
*** Guilherme - Guilherme (Guilherme Alvim Marinato) (a) 12/12/1985, Cataguases (Brazil) (b) 1,97 (c) G (d) Lokomotiv Moskva (e) Atlético-PR, PSTC

*** Guilherme - Guilherme (Guilherme Haubert Sityá) (a) 01/04/1990, Porto Alegre (Brazil) (b) 1,80 (c) D - left back (d) Konyaspor (e) Jagiellonia, Nieciecza, Steaua Bucuresti, Petrolul, Greuther Fürth, Petrolul, Concordia, Caxias-RS, Porto Alegre
*** Guilherme - Guilherme (Guilherme Silva Souza) (a) 12/06/2001, ¿? (Brazil) (b) 1,92 (c) D - central defense (d) - (e) PFK Lviv, Gil Vicente
*** Guilherme - Guilherme (Guilherme Willian da Silva) (a) 21/10/2000, ¿? (Brazil) (b) 1,91 (c) D - central defense (d) SC União Torreense (e) Chaves, Vianense, Mirandela, Monção
*** Guilherme Pato - Guilherme Pato (Guilherme Nunes Rodrigues) (a) 17/02/2001, Quaraí (Brazil) (b) 1,60 (c) F - left winger (d) Figueirense Futebol Clube (e) Neftchi Baku, Internacional, Cuiabá-MT, Internacional, Ponte Preta, Internacional
*** Guillamón - Hugo Guillamón (Hugo Guillamón Sanmartín) (a) 31/01/2000, Donostia-San Sebastián (Spain) (b) 1,78 (c) M - pivot (d) Valencia CF (e) Valencia Mestalla
*** Guillaume - Valentin Guillaume (a) 17/04/2001, Arlon (Belgium) (b) 1,81 (c) M - central midfielder (d) RFC Seraing (e) RE Virton
*** Guillaumier - Matthew Guillaumier (a) 09/04/1998, Sliema (Malta) (b) 1,83 (c) M - pivot (d) Stal Mielec (e) Hamrun Spartans, Siena, Hamrun Spartans, Birkirkara FC, St. Andrews FC
*** Guillemenot - Jérémy Guillemenot (Jérémy Bruno Guillemenot) (a) 06/01/1998, Genève (Switzerland) (b) 1,84 (c) F - center forward (d) Servette FC (e) FC St. Gallen, Rapid Wien, FC Barcelona B, CE Sabadell, FC Barcelona B, Servette FC
*** Guima - Guima (Ricardo Martins Guimarães) (a) 14/11/1995, Aveiro (Portugal) (b) 1,81 (c) M - pivot (d) GD Chaves (e) ŁKS, Académica Coimbra, ŁKS, Académica Coimbra, Sporting B, Académica Coimbra, Sporting B, Oliveirense
*** Guimarães - Bruno Guimarães (Bruno Guimarães Rodrigues Moura) (a) 16/11/1997, Rio de Janeiro (Brazil) (b) 1,82 (c) M - pivot (d) Newcastle United (e) Olympique Lyon, Athletico-PR, GO Audax
*** Guinari - Peter Guinari (a) 02/06/2001, Bangui (Centroafrican Rep.) (b) 1,90 (c) D - central defense (d) - (e) FC Wiltz 71, FC Pipinsried, 1860 München II
*** Guindo - Daouda Guindo (a) 14/10/2002, ¿? (Austria) (b) 1,83 (c) D - left back (d) Red Bull Salzburg (e) FC St. Gallen, RB Salzburg, FC Liefering, RB Salzburg, Guidars FC
*** Guindo - Saliou Guindo (a) 12/09/1996, Ségou (Mali) (b) 1,84 (c) F - center forward (d) Maccabi Petah Tikva (e) Dibba Fujairah, KF Laçi, Dibba Fujairah, KF Laçi, G. Kerala B, Gokulam FC, A. Keciörengücü, FK Bylis, KF Skënderbeu, FK Bylis, KF Skënderbeu, Al-Ahli Club, ASEC Mimosas, AS Bamako, Jeanne d'Arc FC
*** Guirassy - Serhou Guirassy (Serhou Yadaly Guirassy) (a) 12/03/1996, Arles (France) (b) 1,87 (c) F - center forward (d) VfB Stuttgart (e) Stade Rennes, VfB Stuttgart, Stade Rennes, Amiens SC, 1.FC Köln, Amiens SC, 1.FC Köln, Lille, AJ Auxerre, Lille, Stade Lavallois, Stade Laval B
*** Guitane - Rafik Guitane (a) 26/05/1999, Évreux (France) (b) 1,70 (c) M - attacking midfielder (d) GD Estoril Praia (e) Stade Reims, Estoril Praia, Stade Reims, Marítimo, Stade Reims, Stade Rennes, Marítimo, Stade Rennes, Le Havre AC, Stade Rennes, Le Havre AC
*** Guiu - Sebastian Guiu (Sebastian Andrei Guiu) (a) 14/05/2006, ¿? (Romania) (b) - (c) F - center forward (d) Petrolul Ploiesti (e) -
*** Guk - Igor Guk (Гук Ігор Олегович) (a) 11/06/2002, ¿? (Ukraine) (b) 1,81 (c) D - central defense (d) PFK Zvyagel (e) Veres Rivne, PFK Zvyagel, Veres Rivne

*** Gül - Gökhan Gül (a) 17/07/1998, Castrop-Rauxel (Germany) (b) 1,83 (c) D - central defense (d) Kasimpasa (e) Genclerbirligi, Fortuna Düsseldorf, Wehen Wiesbaden, Fortuna Düsseldorf, VfL Bochum
*** Gulácsi - Péter Gulácsi (a) 06/05/1990, Budapest (Hungary) (b) 1,90 (c) G (d) RB Leipzig (e) RB Salzburg, Liverpool, Hull City, Liverpool, Tranmere Rovers, Liverpool, Tranmere Rovers, Liverpool, Hereford Utd., Liverpool
*** Gülay - Ahmet Gülay (a) 13/01/2003, Trabzon (Turkey) (b) 1,74 (c) D - left back (d) Aliaga FK (e) Aliaga FK, Besiktas, Alanyaspor, Besiktas
*** Gulbrandsen - Fredrik Gulbrandsen (Fredrik Aasmundrud Gulbrandsen) (a) 10/09/1992, Lillestrøm (Norway) (b) 1,75 (c) F - center forward (d) - (e) Adana Demirspor, Basaksehir, RB Salzburg, New York, RB Salzburg, Molde, Lillestrøm, Lyn, Lillestrøm
*** Gulceac - Vadim Gulceac (a) 06/08/1998, Bălți (Moldova) (b) 1,84 (c) F - center forward (d) - (e) Kalkara FC, FC Bălți, Unirea Slobozia, Petrocub, Zaria Balti
*** Gulde - Manuel Gulde (a) 12/02/1991, Mannheim (Germany) (b) 1,84 (c) D - central defense (d) SC Freiburg (e) Karlsruher SC, SC Paderborn, Hoffenheim
*** Gülen - Levent Gülen (a) 24/02/1994, Zürich (Switzerland) (b) 1,86 (c) D - central defense (d) - (e) Miedź Legnica, Volos NPS, Ankaraspor, Kayserispor, Grasshoppers, FC Vaduz, Grasshoppers, Kayserispor, Grasshoppers
*** Güler - Arda Güler (a) 25/02/2005, Altindag (Turkey) (b) 1,75 (c) M - attacking midfielder (d) Real Madrid CF (e) Fenerbahce
*** Güler - Semih Güler (a) 30/11/1994, Castrop-Rauxel (Germany) (b) 1,84 (c) D - central defense (d) Adana Demirspor (e) Eskisehirspor, Eyüpspor, Eskisehirspor, Eyüpspor, Eskisehirspor, Westfalia Herne
*** Guletskiy - Evgeniy Guletskiy (Гулецкий Евгений Александрович) (a) 15/01/2001, Molodechno (Belarus) (b) 1,76 (c) D - left back (d) FK Vitebsk (e) Isloch II, Dzerzhinsk, Rukh, Dzerzhinsk, Rukh, Dzerzhinsk, BATE II, Dzerzhinsk, BATE II, Energetik-BGU
*** Guliashvili - Giorgi Guliashvili (გიორგი გულიაშვილი) (a) 05/09/2001, Tbilisi (Georgia) (b) 1,75 (c) F - right winger (d) FK Velez Mostar (e) Velez Mostar, FK Sarajevo, Saburtalo
*** Guliev - Ayaz Guliev (Гулиев Аяз Бахтиярович) (a) 27/11/1996, Moskva (Russia) (b) 1,72 (c) M - central midfielder (d) FK Khimki (e) Arsenal Tula, Spartak Moskva, Rostov, Spartak-2, Rostov, Spartak-2, Anzhi, Spartak-2, Spartak Moskva II
*** Gulko - Ilya Gulko (Гулько Iлля Сергійович) (a) 17/11/2002, Lugansk (Ukraine) (b) 1,83 (c) M - pivot (d) Zorya Lugansk (e) FK Mariupol
*** Gullfoss - Jógvan Gullfoss (a) 25/05/2004, ¿? (Faroe Islands) (b) - (c) M - central midfielder (d) B36 Tórshavn III (e) B36 Tórshavn
*** Gullick - Luke Gullick (a) 24/10/1986, ¿? (England) (b) - (c) F - center forward (d) Pontypridd United (e) Chippenham, SJ Jabloteh, Chippenham
*** Gulliksen - Tobias Gulliksen (Tobias Fjeld Gulliksen) (a) 09/07/2003, Drammen (Norway) (b) 1,77 (c) F - left winger (d) FK Bodø/Glimt (e) Strømsgodset
*** Gullit - Maxim Gullit (a) 20/05/2001, Zaanstad (Netherlands) (b) 1,91 (c) D - left back (d) - (e) SC Cambuur, AZ Alkmaar
*** Gulluni - Kilian Gulluni (a) 20/04/1999, ¿? (France) (b) 1,75 (c) M - pivot (d) SSEP Hombourg-Haut (e) Differdange 03, US Forbach
*** Gülstorff - Andreas Gülstorff (Andreas Gülstorff Pedersen) (a) 26/01/2003, Farum (Denmark) (b) 1,81 (c) G (d) FC Nordsjælland (e) -
*** Gültekin - Emir Kaan Gültekin (a) 02/10/2000, Mersin (Turkey) (b) 1,81 (c) F - center forward (d) Istanbulspor (e) Isparta 32 Spor, Istanbulspor, Tarsus IY, Mersin IY

*** Gumbaravicius - Gustas Gumbaravicius (Gustas Gumbaravičius) (a) 21/02/2000, ¿? (Lithuania) (b) 1,79 (c) D - right back (d) FK Riteriai B (e) Minija, Banga, Atlantas, Minija, Atlantas

*** Gumbau - Gerard Gumbau (Gerard Gumbau Garriga) (a) 18/12/1994, Campllong (Spain) (b) 1,88 (c) M - pivot (d) Granada CF (e) Elche CF, Girona FC, CD Leganés, FC Barcelona B, Girona FC B

*** Gumny - Robert Gumny (a) 04/06/1998, Poznań (Poland) (b) 1,82 (c) D - right back (d) FC Augsburg (e) Lech Poznan, Podbeskidzie, Lech Poznan

*** Gümüs - Ömer Gümüs (Ömer Faruk Gümüş) (a) 07/07/2003, Istanbul (Turkey) (b) 1,75 (c) M - central midfielder (d) Karaman FK (e) Karagümrük, Van Spor FK, Karagümrük

*** Gümüs - Sinan Gümüs (Sinan Gümüş) (a) 15/01/1994, Pfullendorf (Germany) (b) 1,79 (c) F - right winger (d) Antalyaspor (e) Fenerbahce, Genoa, Antalyaspor, Genoa, Galatasaray, Stuttgart II

*** Gümüskaya - Muhammed Gümüskaya (Muhammed Gümüşkaya) (a) 01/01/2001, Istanbul (Turkey) (b) 1,77 (c) M - central midfielder (d) KVC Westerlo (e) Fenerbahce, Giresunspor, Fenerbahce, Boluspor, Fenerbahce

*** Gundersen - Jostein Gundersen (Jostein Maurstad Gundersen) (a) 02/04/1996, ¿? (Norway) (b) 1,86 (c) D - central defense (d) Tromsø IL (e) -

*** Gündogan - Ilkay Gündogan (İlkay Gündoğan) (a) 24/10/1990, Gelsenkirchen (Germany) (b) 1,80 (c) M - central midfielder (d) FC Barcelona (e) Manchester City, Borussia Dortmund, 1.FC Nürnberg

*** Güneren - Ali Kaan Güneren (a) 08/04/2000, Amasya (Turkey) (b) 1,83 (c) M - central midfielder (d) MKE Ankaragücü (e) Samsunspor, Ankaragücü, Akhisarspor, Yeni Amasya

*** Günes - Umut Günes (Umut Güneş) (a) 16/03/2000, Albstadt (Germany) (b) 1,77 (c) M - central midfielder (d) Alanyaspor (e) Stuttgart II

*** Güney - Gökay Güney (a) 19/05/1999, Istanbul (Turkey) (b) 1,80 (c) D - central defense (d) Kirsehir Futbol Spor Kulübü (e) Galatasaray, Bandirmaspor, Galatasaray, Bandirmaspor, Galatasaray, Galatasaray

*** Güngördü - Bahadir Güngördü (Bahadır Han Güngördü) (a) 16/01/1996, Corum (Turkey) (b) 1,90 (c) G (d) MKE Ankaragücü (e) Ankara Demir, Boluspor, Trabzonspor, 1461 Trabzon, Trabzonspor, Ankara Demir, Trabzonspor, Karabükspor

*** Gunichev - Yegor Gunichev (Гунічев Єгор Максимович) (a) 31/12/2003, Slovyansk, Donetsk Oblast (Ukraine) (b) 1,80 (c) F - center forward (d) FK Minaj (e) FK Minaj, FK Oleksandriya, FK Kramatorsk

*** Gunnarsson - Arnar Breki Gunnarsson (a) 23/05/2002, Vestmannaeyjar (Iceland) (b) - (c) F - center forward (d) ÍBV Vestmannaeyjar (e) Framherjar, ÍBV Vestmannaeyjar, Framherjar

*** Gunnarsson - Bjarki Björn Gunnarsson (a) 06/06/2000, ¿? (Iceland) (b) 1,71 (c) M - central midfielder (d) ÍBV Vestmannaeyjar (e) Víkingur, Kórdrengir, Víkingur, Thróttur Vogum, Víkingur, Haukar, Víkingur

*** Gunnarsson - Grétar Snaer Gunnarsson (Grétar Snær Gunnarsson) (a) 08/01/1997, ¿? (Iceland) (b) - (c) D - central defense (d) FH Hafnarfjördur (e) KR Reykjavík, Fjölnir, Víkingur Ó., Hafnarfjördur, HB Tórshavn, Hafnarfjördur, HK Kópavogs, Hafnarfjördur, Haukar

*** Gunnarsson - Gunnar Gunnarsson (a) 22/09/1993, ¿? (Iceland) (b) - (c) D - central defense (d) Fram Reykjavík (e) Thróttur, Haukar, Valur, Haukar, Valur, Grótta

*** Gunnarsson - Gunnar Magnús Gunnarsson (a) 10/02/2006, ¿? (Iceland) (b) - (c) M (d) KV Vesturbaejar (e) KR Reykjavík

*** Gunnarsson - Hördur Ingi Gunnarsson (Hörður Ingi Gunnarsson) (a) 14/08/1998, Reykjavík (Iceland) (b) 1,84 (c) D - right back (d) FH Hafnarfjördur (e) Sogndal, Hafnarfjördur, ÍA Akranes, Hafnarfjördur, HK Kópavogs, Hafnarfjördur, Víkingur Ó., Hafnarfjördur
*** Gunnarsson - Jóhann Árni Gunnarsson (a) 06/04/2001, ¿? (Iceland) (b) - (c) M - central midfielder (d) Stjarnan Gardabaer (e) Fjölnir
*** Gunnarsson - Karl Fridleifur Gunnarsson (Karl Friðleifur Gunnarsson) (a) 06/07/2001, ¿? (Iceland) (b) 1,86 (c) D - right back (d) Víkingur Reykjavík (e) Breidablik, Víkingur, Breidablik, Grótta, Breidablik
*** Gunnarsson - Niklas Gunnarsson (a) 27/04/1991, Tønsberg (Norway) (b) 1,88 (c) D - central defense (d) IFK Norrköping (e) Strømsgodset, Sarpsborg 08, Palermo, Djurgården, Vålerenga, Hibernian FC, Vålerenga, Elfsborg, Vålerenga, Odd, Pors Fotball
*** Gunnarsson - Orri Gunnarsson (a) 05/04/1992, ¿? (Iceland) (b) - (c) D - right back (d) Fram Reykjavík (e) -
*** Gunnarsson - Patrik Gunnarsson (Patrik Sigurður Gunnarsson) (a) 15/11/2000, Kópavogur (Iceland) (b) 1,90 (c) G (d) Viking FK (e) Brentford, Viking, Brentford, Silkeborg IF, Brentford, Viborg FF, Brentford, Southend United, Brentford, Breidablik, ÍR, Breidablik
*** Gunnarsson - Rúrik Gunnarsson (a) 09/03/2005, ¿? (Iceland) (b) - (c) D - right back (d) KR Reykjavík (e) KV Vesturbaejar, KR Reykjavík
*** Gunneröd - Julian Lerato Gunneröd (a) 15/09/2004, ¿? (Norway) (b) - (c) D (d) Sandefjord Fotball II (e) -
*** Gunnlaugsson - Gardar Gunnlaugsson (Garðar Bergmann Gunnlaugsson) (a) 25/04/1983, Akranes (Iceland) (b) 1,83 (c) F - center forward (d) Arnar Gunnlaugsson (e) ÍA Akranes, Kári, Valur, ÍA Akranes, Unterhaching, LASK, CSKA Sofia, Norrköping, Valur, Dunfermline A., Valur, ÍA Akranes
*** Gunnlaugsson - Höskuldur Gunnlaugsson (a) 26/09/1994, Reykjavík (Iceland) (b) 1,73 (c) D - right back (d) Breidablik Kópavogur (e) Halmstads BK, Breidablik, Halmstads BK, Breidablik, Augnablik, Breidablik, Augnablik, Breidablik
*** Günok - Mert Günok (Fehmi Mert Günok) (a) 01/03/1989, Karabük (Turkey) (b) 1,96 (c) G (d) Besiktas JK (e) Basaksehir, Bursaspor, Fenerbahce
*** Günter - Christian Günter (a) 28/02/1993, Villingen-Schwenningen (Germany) (b) 1,84 (c) D - left back (d) SC Freiburg (e) -
*** Günter - Koray Günter (a) 16/08/1994, Höxter (Germany) (b) 1,86 (c) D - central defense (d) Hellas Verona (e) Sampdoria, Hellas Verona, Genoa, Hellas Verona, Genoa, Galatasaray, Borussia Dortmund
*** Gurau - Ionut Gurau (Ion Cristian Gurău) (a) 27/03/1999, ¿? (Romania) (b) 1,98 (c) G (d) FC U Craiova 1948 (e) Unirea Slobozia, Academia Hagi, Daco-Getica, Academia Hagi, SCM Gloria Buzau, Academia Hagi, SSC Farul, Academia Hagi
*** Gurban - Gleb Gurban (Гурбан Глеб Витальевич) (a) 15/05/2001, Minsk (Belarus) (b) 1,77 (c) D - right back (d) FK Minsk (e) Rukh, Orsha, Rukh, FK Minsk, Smolevichi, FK Minsk, FK Minsk II
*** Gürbulak - Oguz Gürbulak (Oğuz Gürbulak) (a) 10/08/1992, Erzincan (Turkey) (b) 1,78 (c) M - central midfielder (d) Manisa FK (e) Ümraniyespor, Samsunspor, A. Selcukspor, Manavgatspor, Sarayönü Belediye, Konya Sekerspor
*** Gürbüz - Berke Gürbüz (a) 27/01/2003, Ankara (Turkey) (b) 1,72 (c) M - attacking midfielder (d) Gaziantep FK (e) Etimesgut Belediye, Gaziantep FK, Sloboda Tuzla, Gaziantep FK, Ankaragücü, Etimesgut Belediye

*** Güreler - Yasin Güreler (a) 02/07/1991, Izmir (Turkey) (b) 1,87 (c) D - left back (d) Genclerbirligi Ankara (e) Ankaragücü, Tuzlaspor, Hatayspor, Menemen Belediye, Yesilovaspor

*** Gurenko - Artem Gurenko (Гуренко Артём Сергеевич) (a) 18/06/1994, Grodno (Belarus) (b) 1,71 (c) F - right winger (d) FK Ufa (e) Belshina, FK Turan, Belshina, Isloch, Vitebsk, Riteriai, Dinamo Minsk, FK Slutsk, Suduva, Trakai, Minsk-2, FK Minsk II

*** Gureshidze - Aleksandre Gureshidze (ალექსანდრე გურეშიძე) (a) 23/04/1995, Tbilisi (Georgia) (b) 1,88 (c) D - central defense (d) - (e) Saburtalo, FC Locomotive, Sioni Bolnisi, Kolkheti Poti, Sioni Bolnisi, Dinamo II, FC Locomotive, Dinamo II

*** Gurfinkel - Yahav Gurfinkel (גורפינקל יהב) (a) 27/06/1998, Haifa (Israel) (b) 1,71 (c) D - left back (d) Hapoel Tel Aviv (e) Norrköping, Maccabi Haifa, Hapoel Haifa, Maccabi Haifa, Hapoel Hadera, Maccabi Haifa, H. Nazareth Illit, Maccabi Haifa

*** Gurgul - Michal Gurgul (Michał Gurgul) (a) 30/01/2006, Poznań (Poland) (b) 1,81 (c) D - central defense (d) Lech Poznan (e) -

*** Guri - Arianit Guri (a) 21/05/2003, ¿? (Serbia and Montenegro, now in Kosovo) (b) - (c) M - right midfielder (d) KF Ferizaj (e) KF Vjosa, KF Ferizaj

*** Guri - Sidrit Guri (a) 23/10/1993, Shkodër (Albania) (b) 1,89 (c) F - center forward (d) - (e) Istanbulspor, Shkëndija, KV Oostende, FK Kukësi, KF Korabi, KF Vllaznia, KS Kastrioti, KF Vllaznia, KS Besa, KF Vllaznia, KF Shkodra

*** Gurishta - Erdenis Gurishta (a) 24/04/1995, Shkodër (Albania) (b) 1,79 (c) D - right back (d) CSKA 1948 (e) KF Vllaznia, FK Veleçiku

*** Gürler - Serdar Gürler (a) 14/09/1991, Haguenau (France) (b) 1,75 (c) F - right winger (d) Basaksehir FK (e) Konyaspor, Antalyaspor, SD Huesca, Göztepe, SD Huesca, Osmanlispor, Genclerbirligi, Trabzonspor, K. Erciyesspor, Trabzonspor, Elazigspor, FC Sochaux, FC Sochaux B

*** Gurlica - Jakov Gurlica (a) 10/01/2004, Zadar (Croatia) (b) - (c) D - central defense (d) NK Bravo (e) Dinamo Zagreb

*** Gurman - Mark Gurman (Гурман Марк Михайлович) (a) 09/02/1989, Almaty (Soviet Union, now in Kazakhstan) (b) 1,79 (c) D - central defense (d) - (e) Qyzyljar, FC Astana, Kaysar, Tobol Kostanay, FC Astana, Kairat Almaty, Samsunspor, FC Astana, Kairat Almaty, FC Astana, M. Ahi Nazareth, H. Petah Tikva, Beitar Netanya

*** Gürpüz - Göktan Gürpüz (a) 22/01/2003, Duisburg (Germany) (b) 1,76 (c) M - attacking midfielder (d) Trabzonspor (e) Borussia Dortmund II

*** Gurtsiev - Batraz Gurtsiev (Гурциев Батраз Олегович) (a) 12/12/1998, Vladikavkaz (Russia) (b) 1,81 (c) M - right midfielder (d) Alania Vladikavkaz (e) Alania Vl., Orenburg, Alania Vl., Chaika Pes., Alania Vl., Chaika Pes., Spartak V., Krasnodar II

*** Guruzeta - Gorka Guruzeta (Gorka Guruzeta Rodríguez) (a) 12/09/1996, Donostia-San Sebastián (Spain) (b) 1,88 (c) F - center forward (d) Athletic Club (e) SD Amorebieta, CE Sabadell, Bilbao Athletic, CD Basconia

*** Gusev - Kirill Gusev (Гусев Кирилл Игоревич) (a) 06/04/1999, Mogilev (Belarus) (b) 1,92 (c) F - center forward (d) FK Orsha (e) Orsha, Dnepr Mogilev, Slonim, Dnepr Mogilev, Dnyapro II, Mogilev II

*** Guseynov - Aykhan Guseynov (Гусейнов Айхан Илхамович) (a) 03/09/1999, St. Peterburg (Russia) (b) 1,81 (c) M - attacking midfielder (d) Turan-Tovuz IK (e) Khimki 2, Dolgoprudnyi, Ural 2, Nizhny Novgorod, Leningradets, SShOR Zenit

*** Guseynov - Rinat Guseynov (Гусейнов Ринат Алиага Оглы (az. Rinat Əliağa oğlu Hüseynov)) (a) 29/01/1997, Perm (Russia) (b) 1,92 (c) D - central defense (d) - (e) Kapaz PFK, Zvezda Perm, Amkar II

*** Gushchenko - Dmitriy Gushchenko (Гущенко Дмитрий Викторович) (a) 12/05/1988, Vitebsk (Soviet Union, now in Belarus) (b) 1,87 (c) G (d) FK Vitebsk (e) Belshina, Dinamo Minsk, Belshina, Dinamo Minsk, Vitebsk, Slavia, Vitebsk, Myaso. Vitebs, Vitebsk, Vitebsk II
*** Gusman - Tensior Gusman (a) 24/01/1997, ¿? (Malta) (b) 1,79 (c) F - center forward (d) Gudja United FC (e) Qormi FC
*** Gusol - Artem Gusol (Гусол Артем Валерійович) (a) 05/01/2006, Boryspil, Kyiv Oblast (Ukraine) (b) 1,84 (c) F - right winger (d) - (e) Camisano
*** Gussev - Maksim Gussev (a) 20/07/1994, Narva (Estonia) (b) 1,73 (c) F - left winger (d) Kalju FC (e) TJK Legion, FC Flora, MyPa, FC Flora, Kokkolan PV, FC Flora, TJK Legion
*** Gussiås - Sivert Gussiås (Sivert Stenseth Gussiås) (a) 18/08/1999, Molde (Norway) (b) 1,83 (c) F - center forward (d) KÍ Klaksvík (e) Sandefjord, Molde FK II, Strømmen, Molde FK II
*** Gustafson - Samuel Gustafson (a) 11/01/1995, Mölndal (Sweden) (b) 1,87 (c) M - pivot (d) BK Häcken (e) Cremonese, Torino, Hellas Verona, Torino, Perugia, Torino, Häcken, Fässbergs IF
*** Gustafson - Simon Gustafson (a) 11/01/1995, Mölndal (Sweden) (b) 1,85 (c) M - central midfielder (d) BK Häcken (e) FC Utrecht, Feyenoord, Roda JC, Feyenoord, Häcken, Fässbergs IF
*** Gustafson - Viktor Gustafson (a) 22/03/1995, ¿? (Sweden) (b) - (c) M - pivot (d) Mjällby AIF (e) FK Karlskrona, Asarums IF
*** Gustafsson - Carl Gustafsson (a) 18/03/2000, ¿? (Sweden) (b) 1,80 (c) M - central midfielder (d) Kalmar FF (e) -
*** Gustafsson - Hampus Gustafsson (a) 20/06/2001, ¿? (Sweden) (b) - (c) G (d) Norrby IF (e) Norrby, Värnamo, Åtvidabergs FF, Värnamo, Åtvidabergs FF, Värnamo
*** Gustavo - Gustavo (Gustavo Alexandre Hemkemeier) (a) 19/06/1997, Toledo (Brazil) (b) 1,78 (c) M - attacking midfielder (d) Swift Hesperange (e) Etzella Ettelbrück, Toledo, Guarani-SC, Toledo, Brusque, Toledo, Próspera, Toledo
*** Gustavo - Gustavo (Gustavo Di Mauro Vagenin) (a) 14/11/1991, Sao Paulo (Brazil) (b) 1,74 (c) M - attacking midfielder (d) Tractor FC (e) CS U Craiova, Ajman Club, CS U Craiova, Liaoning FC, CS U Craiova, ACR Messina, Novara, Lecce, Novara, Salernitana, GO Audax
*** Gustavo - Diego Gustavo (Diego Gustavo Rodrigues de Lima) (a) 19/06/2004, ¿? (Brazil) (b) - (c) M - attacking midfielder (d) FC Volendam (e) Laranja (PR)
*** Gustavo Henrique - Gustavo Henrique (Gustavo Henrique Vernes) (a) 24/03/1993, São Paulo (Brazil) (b) 1,96 (c) D - central defense (d) Fenerbahce (e) Flamengo, Fenerbahce, Flamengo, Santos, Santos B
*** Gustavo Marins - Gustavo Marins (Gustavo Henrique Marins Silva) (a) 11/02/2002, Goiânia (Brazil) (b) - (c) D - central defense (d) FCV Farul Constanta (e) São Luiz
*** Gustavo Marmentini - Gustavo Marmentini (Gustavo Marmentini dos Santos) (a) 08/03/1994, Cascavel (Brazil) (b) 1,79 (c) F (d) - (e) PAS Lamia, M. Bnei Reineh, PAS Lamia, Hapoel Hadera, H. Beer Sheva, Hapoel Hadera, Athletico-PR B, Alashkert CF, Athletico-PR B, Ittihad Kalba, Atlético-PR B, GO Audax, Atlético-PR B, Sampaio Corrêa, Atlético-PR B, Luverdense, Atlético-PR B, Delhi Dynamos, Atlético-PR B, Delhi Dynamos, Atlético-PR B
*** Gustavsson - Jesper Gustavsson (a) 29/10/1994, ¿? (Sweden) (b) 1,74 (c) M - pivot (d) Mjällby AIF (e) Mjølner, Mjällby AIF

*** Gusto - Malo Gusto (a) 19/05/2003, Décines-Charpieu (France) (b) 1,78 (c) D - right back (d) Chelsea FC (e) Olympique Lyon, Chelsea, Olympique Lyon, Olymp. Lyon B

*** Gutea - Remus Gutea (Remus Gabriel Guțea) (a) 18/04/2005, Videle (Romania) (b) - (c) M - left midfielder (d) CS Mioveni (e) -

*** Guth - Rodrigo Guth (a) 10/11/2000, Curitiba (Brazil) (b) 1,91 (c) D - central defense (d) Fortuna Sittard (e) Atalanta, NEC Nijmegen, Atalanta, Pescara

*** Guthrie - Kurtis Guthrie (Kurtis Owen Guthrie) (a) 21/04/1993, Jersey (Jersey) (b) 1,91 (c) F - center forward (d) Livingston FC (e) Punjab FC, Port Vale, Bradford City, Stevenage, Colchester Utd., Forest Green Rovers, Welling Utd., Bath City, Accrington St., Southport, Accrington St., Trinity, SC St. Clement

*** Guti - Raúl Guti (José Raúl Gutiérrez Parejo) (a) 30/12/1996, Zaragoza (Spain) (b) 1,78 (c) M - central midfielder (d) Elche CF (e) Real Zaragoza, Dep. Aragón

*** Gutiérrez - Érick Gutiérrez (Érick Gabriel Gutiérrez Galaviz) (a) 15/06/1995, Los Mochis (Mexico) (b) 1,81 (c) M - central midfielder (d) CD Guadalajara (e) PSV Eindhoven, Pachuca

*** Gutiérrez - Jordan Gutiérrez (Jordan Gutiérrez Nsang) (a) 08/07/1998, Barcelona (Spain) (b) 1,69 (c) F - right winger (d) - (e) UE Santa Coloma, AE Prat, Ciudad Real, Granollers, CD Leganés B, Penya Deportiva, UA Horta, RCD Espanyol B, AD Alcorcón B, RCD Espanyol B

*** Gutiérrez - Juan Diego Gutiérrez (Juan Diego Gutiérrez de las Casas) (a) 28/04/1992, Lima (Peru) (b) 1,74 (c) F - left winger (d) Unión Huaral (e) Dep. Garcilaso, Sant Julià, Sololá FC, Unión Comercio, Carlos Stein, Oriente P., HFX Wanderers, Rosario FC, Sport Boys, Vejle BK, Gefle, Vejle BK, Universitario, Vejle BK, Universitario, U. San Martín

*** Gutiérrez - Miguel Gutiérrez (Miguel Gutiérrez Ortega) (a) 27/07/2001, Madrid (Spain) (b) 1,80 (c) D - left back (d) Girona FC (e) Real Madrid, RM Castilla

*** Gutiérrez - Silvio Gutiérrez (Silvio Patricio Gutiérrez Álvarez) (a) 28/02/1993, Cuenca (Ecuador) (b) 1,75 (c) D - left back (d) Deportivo Cuenca (e) FC Van, Estudiantes, CD América, Delfín SC, Gualaceo SC, Dep. Cuenca, Cuenca B

*** Gutium - Alexandru Gutium (a) 15/07/2003, ¿? (Moldova) (b) 1,81 (c) D - right back (d) Dacia Buiucani (e) -

*** Gutkovskis - Vladislavs Gutkovskis (a) 02/04/1995, Riga (Latvia) (b) 1,87 (c) F - center forward (d) Daejeon Hana Citizen (e) Rakow, Nieciecza, Skonto, Skonto II, Olimps Riga

*** Gütlbauer - Lukas Gütlbauer (a) 06/12/2000, Kirchdorf an der Krems (Austria) (b) 1,92 (c) G (d) Wolfsberger AC (e) SV Ried, FAC, SV Ried, SV Ried II

*** Gutor - Aleksandr Gutor (Гутор Александр Петрович) (a) 18/04/1989, Minsk (Soviet Union, now in Belarus) (b) 1,90 (c) G (d) - (e) FK Aksu, Soligorsk, Dynamo Brest, Chornomorets, Tosno, Orenburg, Dinamo Minsk, BATE Borisov, BATE II

*** Gutsulyak - Oleksiy Gutsulyak (Гуцуляк Олексій Олександрович) (a) 25/12/1997, Krasyliv, Khmelnytskyi Oblast (Ukraine) (b) 1,84 (c) M - left midfielder (d) SK Dnipro-1 (e) Desna, Karpaty, Villarreal CF C, Karpaty, UFK Lviv

*** Guttesen - Leivur Guttesen (Leivur Fossdal Guttesen) (a) 17/01/2002, Tórshavn (Faroe Islands) (b) 1,89 (c) F - right winger (d) HB Tórshavn (e) HB Tórshavn II, AB Argir, HB Tórshavn II

*** Gutu - Vitalie Gutu (Vitalie Guțu) (a) 28/08/2005, ¿? (Moldova) (b) - (c) M - central midfielder (d) - (e) Sfintul Gheorghe

*** Güvenc - Günay Güvenc (Günay Güvenç) (a) 25/06/1991, Neu-Ulm (Germany) (b) 1,87 (c) G (d) Galatasaray (e) Gaziantep FK, Kasimpasa, Gaziantep FK, Göztepe, Besiktas, Mersin IY, Besiktas, Adanaspor, Besiktas, Stuttg. Kickers, St. Kickers II

*** Güventürk - Günes Güventürk (a) 18/07/2005, ¿? (Turkey) (b) - (c) F - center forward (d) - (e) Ümraniyerspor

*** Guz - Aleksandr Guz (Гуз Александр Васильевич) (a) 22/05/2004, Rechitsa (Belarus) (b) 1,87 (c) M - pivot (d) Isloch Minsk Region (e) Isloch II

*** Guzina - Bosko Guzina (Boško Guzina) (a) 30/04/1996, Nikšić (RF Yugoslavia, now in Montenegro) (b) 1,81 (c) F - center forward (d) - (e) OSK Igalo, Mornar Bar, FK Bokelj, NK Lukavec, Telcoptik, Rad Beograd, FK Bezanija, Rad Beograd, Zarkovo

*** Guzov - Ioann Guzov (Гузов Иоанн Олегович) (a) 07/04/2004, ¿? (Belarus) (b) - (c) F - center forward (d) FK Belshina Bobruisk II (e) Belshina 2 B.

*** Guzzo - Ramon Guzzo (Ramon Francesco Guzzo) (a) 05/07/2004, Baden (Switzerland) (b) 1,76 (c) D - central defense (d) FC Zürich (e) -

*** Guzzo - Raphael Guzzo (Raphael Gregório Guzzo) (a) 06/01/1995, São Paulo (Brazil) (b) 1,78 (c) M - central midfielder (d) Goiás EC (e) Vizela, Chaves, Reus Deportiu, Famalicão, Reus Deportiu, Benfica B, Tondela, Benfica B, Chaves, Benfica B

*** Gvaradze - Beka Gvaradze (ბექა გვარაძე) (a) 11/08/1997, ¿? (Georgia) (b) 1,80 (c) M - left midfielder (d) FC Saburtalo (e) Energetik-BGU, FC Shevardeni, Saburtalo, Rustavi, Saburtalo, Sioni Bolnisi, Saburtalo

*** Gvardiol - Josko Gvardiol (Joško Gvardiol) (a) 23/01/2002, Zagreb (Croatia) (b) 1,85 (c) D - central defense (d) Manchester City (e) RB Leipzig, Dinamo Zagreb, NK Tresnjevka

*** Gvazava - Shota Gvazava (შოთა გვაზავა) (a) 26/10/1992, Tbilisi (Georgia) (b) 1,85 (c) M - pivot (d) Mash'al Mubarek (e) FC Van, FK Slutsk, Chikhura, Vereya, FC Gagra, FC Odishi, Merani Martvili, FK Zugdidi, STU, Dinamo II, STU

*** Gvilia - Valeriane Gvilia (ვალერიან გვილია) (a) 24/05/1994, Zugdidi (Georgia) (b) 1,82 (c) M - central midfielder (d) - (e) Rakow, Legia Warszawa, FC Luzern, Górnik Zabrze, FC Luzern, BATE Borisov, FK Minsk, Metalurg Z., Zaporizhya II

*** Gvishiani - Giorgi Gvishiani (გიორგი გვიშიანი) (a) 19/11/2003, ¿? (Georgia) (b) - (c) D - right back (d) FC Samtredia (e) Dinamo Tbilisi, FC Gagra, Dinamo Tbilisi, Dinamo II, FC Gagra, Dinamo II

*** Gwargis - Peter Gwargis (a) 04/09/2000, Sydney (Australia) (b) 1,81 (c) F - right winger (d) Degerfors IF (e) Degerfors, Malmö FF, J-Södra IF, Malmö FF, J-Södra IF, Husqvarna FF, IFK Öxnehaga

*** Gyabi - Darko Gyabi (Darko Boateng Gyabi) (a) 18/02/2004, London (England) (b) 1,96 (c) M - central midfielder (d) Leeds United (e) -

*** Gyasi - Edwin Gyasi (Edwin Oppong Anane-Gyasi) (a) 01/07/1991, Amsterdam (Netherlands) (b) 1,85 (c) F - right winger (d) - (e) FK Kukësi, B. Jerusalem, Samsunspor, Boluspor, Samsunspor, CSKA-Sofia, Dallas, CSKA-Sofia, Aalesund, Roda JC, Heracles Almelo, De Graafschap, Telstar

*** Gyasi - Emmanuel Gyasi (Emanuel Quartsin Gyasi) (a) 11/01/1994, Palermo (Italy) (b) 1,81 (c) F - left winger (d) FC Empoli (e) Spezia, Südtirol, Spezia, Pistoiese, Spezia, Pistoiese, Torino, Carrarese, Torino, Mantova, Torino, AC Pisa

*** Gyau - Joe Gyau (Joseph-Claude Agyeman Gyau) (a) 16/09/1992, Tampa, Florida (United States) (b) 1,75 (c) F - left winger (d) Degerfors IF (e) Cincinnati, MSV Duisburg, Sonnenhof-Gr., Borussia Dortmund II, Hoffenheim, FC St. Pauli, Hoffenheim, Hoffenheim II, Bethesda Roadr.

*** Gyetván - Márk Gyetván (a) 01/02/2005, ¿? (Hungary) (b) - (c) G (d) Budapest Honvéd FC (e) Honvéd II

*** Gyomber - Norbert Gyomber (Norbert Gyömbér) (a) 03/07/1992, Revúca (Czechoslovakia, now in Czech Rep.) (b) 1,89 (c) D - central defense (d) US Salernitana 1919 (e) Perugia, AS Roma, Bari, AS Roma, Terek Grozny, AS Roma, Pescara, AS Roma, Catania, AS Roma, Catania, Banska Bystrica
*** Győri - Ábel Győri (Győri Ábel Zsolt) (a) 16/03/2004, ¿? (Hungary) (b) - (c) D - right back (d) Karcagi SE (e) Kecskemét
*** Győri - Benjámin Győri (a) 16/03/2003, ¿? (Hungary) (b) - (c) F - right winger (d) Karcagi SE (e) Kecskemét
*** Gytkjaer - Christian Gytkjaer (Christian Lund Gytkjær) (a) 06/05/1990, Roskilde (Denmark) (b) 1,85 (c) F - center forward (d) Venezia FC (e) Monza, Lech Poznan, 1860 München, Rosenborg, Haugesund, Nordsjælland, Sandnes Ulf, Nordsjælland, Akademisk BK, Nordsjælland, Lyngby BK
*** Gytkjaer - Frederik Gytkjaer (Frederik Lund Gytkjær) (a) 16/03/1993, Roskilde (Denmark) (b) 1,80 (c) F - center forward (d) Lyngby BK (e) Haugesund, Lyngby BK
*** Gyurcsó - Ádám Gyurcsó (a) 06/03/1991, Tatabánya (Hungary) (b) 1,81 (c) F - left winger (d) AEK Larnaca (e) NK Osijek, Hajduk Split, Puskás AFC, Hajduk Split, Pogon Szczecin, Hajduk Split, Pogon Szczecin, Videoton FC, Videoton II, Kecskeméti TE, Videoton II
*** Gyurján - Márton Gyurján (Gyurján Márton László) (a) 01/05/1995, Nyíregyháza (Hungary) (b) 1,86 (c) G (d) Zalaegerszegi TE FC (e) Haladás
*** Gyurkits - Gergő Gyurkits (a) 05/06/2002, Baja (Hungary) (b) 1,84 (c) M - central midfielder (d) Pécsi MFC (e) Paksi FC, Paksi FC II
*** Haakenstad - Mats Haakenstad (a) 14/11/1993, Horten (Norway) (b) 1,83 (c) D - right back (d) Kongsvinger IL (e) Sandefjord, KuPS, Lillestrøm, Fram, Sandefjord, Fram
*** Haaland - Erling Haaland (Erling Braut Håland) (a) 21/07/2000, Leeds (England) (b) 1,95 (c) F - center forward (d) Manchester City (e) Borussia Dortmund, RB Salzburg, Molde, Bryne
*** Haarala - Santeri Haarala (a) 17/12/1999, Tampere (Finland) (b) 1,80 (c) F - right winger (d) Ilves Tampere (e) KuPS, TPS, Ilves II, RoPS, Ilves
*** Haarup - Mathias Haarup (a) 10/02/1996, ¿? (Denmark) (b) 1,80 (c) D - right back (d) Vendsyssel FF (e) Hobro IK, Jerv, Hobro IK, Brabrand IF, Freja (RFC II)
*** Haas - Nicolas Haas (Nicolas Thibault Haas) (a) 23/01/1996, Sursee (Switzerland) (b) 1,78 (c) M - central midfielder (d) FC Empoli (e) Atalanta, Empoli, Atalanta, Frosinone, Atalanta, US Palermo, Atalanta, FC Luzern
*** Habbas - Ryad Habbas (a) 16/07/1997, Roubaix (France) (b) 1,73 (c) F - center forward (d) Swift Hesperange II (e) Swift Hesperange, Progrès Niederkorn, US Hostert, Progrès Niederkorn, US Créteil-Lusitanos, IC de Croix, LOSC Lille B
*** Haber - Justin Haber (a) 09/06/1981, Floriana (Malta) (b) 1,80 (c) G (d) Hibernians FC (e) Santa Lucia FC, Gzira Utd., Floriana, Hibernians FC, Birkirkara FC, Mosta FC, AO Kerkyra, Ferencváros, Sheffield Utd., AO Chaidariou, Marsaxlokk, RE Virton, Quevilly, Birkirkara FC, Floriana, Dob. Dobrich, Floriana
*** Haberer - Janik Haberer (a) 02/04/1994, Wangen im Allgäu (Germany) (b) 1,86 (c) M - central midfielder (d) 1.FC Union Berlin (e) SC Freiburg, Hoffenheim, VfL Bochum, Hoffenheim, Unterhaching
*** Habibovic - Enes Habibovic (Енес Хабибовић) (a) 28/06/2003, ¿? (Serbia and Montenegro, now in Montenegro) (b) 1,80 (c) F - right winger (d) - (e) Mornar Bar, FK Podgorica
*** Habimana - Glen Habimana (a) 13/11/2001, ¿? (Rwanda) (b) - (c) F - center forward (d) - (e) Victoria Rosport, U. Fürstenwalde

*** Habran - Romain Habran (a) 14/06/1994, Villeneuve-la-Garenne (France) (b) 1,78 (c) F - right winger (d) Hapoel Afula (e) Suduva, Gimnàstic, UD Melilla, Gimnàstic, FC Ashdod, Royal Antwerp, Paris Saint Germain B, US Boulogne, Paris Saint Germain B, Stade Lavallois, Paris Saint Germain B, FC Sochaux, Paris Saint Germain B

*** Habshi - Ayid Habshi (חבשי עאיד) (a) 10/05/1995, Iksal (Israel) (b) 1,84 (c) D - central defense (d) Ironi Kiryat Shmona (e) Maccabi Haifa, Bnei Yehuda, Maccabi Haifa, Hapoel Raanana, Maccabi Haifa, Bnei Sakhnin, Maccabi Haifa

*** Hacimustafaoglu - Tahsin Hacimustafaoglu (Tahsin Hacımustafaoğlu) (a) 14/11/1997, Istanbul (Turkey) (b) 1,80 (c) F - right winger (d) Erbaaspor (e) 68 Aksaray Belediye, Ümraniyespor, Batman Petrol, Ümraniyespor, Sile Yildizspor, Kartalspor

*** Haciyev - Faiq Haciyev (Faiq Fərman oğlu Hacıyev) (a) 22/05/1999, ¿? (Azerbaijan) (b) 1,79 (c) D - right back (d) Turan-Tovuz IK (e) FK Qabala, MOIK, FK Qabala, FK Qabala 2

*** Haciyev - Mehman Haciyev (Mehman Sadiq oğlu Hacıyev) (a) 28/01/1995, Tovuz (Azerbaijan) (b) 1,83 (c) G (d) Turan-Tovuz IK (e) Turan 2 Tovuz

*** Haciyev - Rahman Haciyev (Rəhman Xudayət oğlu Hacıyev) (a) 25/07/1993, Tovuz (Azerbaijan) (b) 1,71 (c) M - attacking midfielder (d) Neftchi Baku (e) Shamakhi, Neftchi Baku, Keshla, Neftchi Baku, Gaziantep BB, Sumqayit, FK Baku, Altay SK, FK Baku

*** Haciyev - Ruslan Haciyev (Ruslan Ramiz oğlu Hacıyev) (a) 26/03/1998, Baku (Azerbaijan) (b) 1,80 (c) F - right winger (d) - (e) Qarabag FK, FK Sabail, Qarabag FK, FK Sabail, Qarabag FK, FK Sabail, Qarabag FK, FK Sabail, Qarabag FK, FK Sabail 2

*** Hack - Alexander Hack (a) 08/09/1993, Memmingen (Germany) (b) 1,93 (c) D - central defense (d) Al-Qadsiah FC (e) Mainz 05, FSV Mainz 05 II, Unterhaching, FC Memmingen

*** Hackman - Emmanuel Hackman (a) 14/05/1995, Accra (Ghana) (b) 1,87 (c) D - central defense (d) - (e) Mladost GAT, Gil Vicente, Portimonense, Boavista, Desportivo Aves, Boavista, Vila Real

*** Hacyly - Hacyaga Hacyly (Hacıağa Habil oğlu Hacılı) (a) 30/01/1998, Agdam (Azerbaijan) (b) 1,83 (c) M - pivot (d) Zira FK (e) Qarabag FK, Zira FK, Qarabag FK, FK Qabala, Qarabag FK, FK Qabala

*** Hadaró - Valentin Hadaró (a) 08/06/1995, Kaposvár (Hungary) (b) 1,86 (c) D - left back (d) Pécsi MFC (e) Kecskemét, Pécsi MFC, Kecskemét, Kaposvár, Kisvárda, Kaposvár

*** Hadas - Matej Hadas (Matěj Hadaš) (a) 25/11/2003, ¿? (Czech Rep.) (b) - (c) F - center forward (d) SK Sigma Olomouc B (e) -

*** Haddock - Evan Haddock (Evan Thomas Haddock) (a) 07/07/2005, Duleek, Meath (Ireland) (b) 1,90 (c) D - central defense (d) Drogheda United FC (e) -

*** Hadergjonaj - Florent Hadergjonaj (a) 31/07/1994, Langnau im Emmental (Switzerland) (b) 1,82 (c) D - right back (d) Alanyaspor (e) Kasimpasa, Huddersfield Town, Kasimpasa, Huddersfield Town, FC Ingolstadt, Huddersfield Town, FC Ingolstadt, BSC Young Boys

*** Hadida - Guy Hadida (חדידה גיא) (a) 23/07/1995, Arad (Israel) (b) 1,77 (c) M - attacking midfielder (d) Chornomorets Odessa (e) Sakaryaspor, M. Bnei Reineh, H. Jerusalem, M. Petah Tikva, Hapoel Haifa, Beitar TA Ramla, H. Kfar Saba, Maccabi Yavne, Ramat haSharon

*** Hadj Mahmoud - Hadj Mahmoud (محمود بلحاج محمد, Mohamed Belhadj Mahmoud) (a) 24/04/2000, Susa (Tunisia) (b) 1,79 (c) M - pivot (d) FC Lugano (e) ES Sahel

*** Hadjam - Jaouen Hadjam (حجام جوين) (a) 26/03/2003, Paris (France) (b) 1,84 (c) D - left back (d) FC Nantes (e) Paris FC
*** Hadji - Kassim Hadji (a) 23/03/2000, ¿? (Comores) (b) 1,82 (c) M - right midfielder (d) FC Ararat Yerevan (e) Stade Nyonnais, Ain Sud
*** Hadji - Samir Hadji (a) 12/09/1989, Creutzwald (France) (b) 1,90 (c) F - center forward (d) F91 Dudelange (e) RE Virton, CS Fola Esch, Hassania, Racing Club Strasbourg, AS Nancy B, Saarbrücken, SR Creutzwald
*** Hadroj - Andi Hadroj (a) 22/02/1999, Pukë (Albania) (b) 1,78 (c) D - right back (d) FK Partizani (e) FK Bylis, KF Laçi
*** Hadzanovic - Adis Hadzanovic (Adis Hadžanović) (a) 02/01/1993, Sarajevo (Bosnia and Herzegovina) (b) 1,75 (c) M - pivot (d) - (e) Bregalnica Stip, AP Brera, FK Olimpik, FK Tuzla City, Sloboda Tuzla, NK Vitez, FK Iskra, NK Brezice 1919, Segesta Sisak, NK Istra, JK Nomme Kalju, Al-Ahli Club, JK Nomme Kalju, FK Famos, FK Olimpik
*** Hadzhiev - Kamen Hadzhiev (Камен Гълъбов Хаджиев) (a) 22/09/1991, Kochan (Bulgaria) (b) 1,88 (c) D - central defense (d) SSV Jeddeloh II (e) Hebar P., Lokomotiv Sofia, Pakhtakor, Beroe, Puskás AFC, Beroe, Fortuna Sittard, VfB Oldenburg, Lokomotiv Sofia, Doxa Petrousas, Minyor Pernik, Chepinets, Pirin GD
*** Hadziahmetovic - Amir Hadziahmetovic (Amir Hadžiahmetović) (a) 08/03/1997, Nexø (Denmark) (b) 1,79 (c) M - pivot (d) Besiktas JK (e) Konyaspor, Zeljeznicar
*** Hadzibeganovic - Harun Hadzibeganovic (Harun Hadžibeganović) (a) 05/01/2002, Tuzla (Bosnia and Herzegovina) (b) - (c) D - right back (d) FK Sloboda Tuzla (e) Simm-Bau
*** Hadzic - Irfan Hadzic (Irfan Hadžić) (a) 15/06/1993, Prozor-Rama (Bosnia and Herzegovina) (b) 1,92 (c) F - center forward (d) FK Tuzla City (e) Zrinjski Mostar, NK Lokomotiva, Akhisarspor, Zrinjski Mostar, Radnik Bijelj., NK Celje, Royal Antwerp, VW Hamme, Royal Antwerp, Zlaté Moravce, Inter Zaprešić, Zulte Waregem
*** Hadzic - Nedim Hadzic (Nedim Hadžić) (a) 19/03/1999, Sarajevo (Bosnia and Herzegovina) (b) 1,84 (c) F - center forward (d) - (e) Velez Mostar, NK Radomlje, Slaven Belupo, Sloboda Tuzla, Slaven Belupo, Mladost Kakanj, FK Sarajevo
*** Hadzikadunic - Dennis Hadzikadunic (Dennis Hadžikadunić) (a) 09/07/1998, Malmö (Sweden) (b) 1,91 (c) D - central defense (d) Hamburgo SV (e) SV Hamburg, Rostov, RCD Mallorca, Rostov, Malmö FF, Rostov, Malmö FF, Trelleborg, Malmö FF
*** Hadzikic - Osman Hadzikic (Osman Hadžikić) (a) 12/03/1996, Klosterneuburg (Austria) (b) 1,86 (c) G (d) FK Velez Mostar (e) Admira Wacker, FC Zürich, Inter Zaprešić, FC Zürich, Austria Viena, Austria Wien Reserves
*** Hafstad - Didrik Hafstad (a) 26/12/2003, ¿? (Norway) (b) 1,85 (c) F - center forward (d) Tromsdalen UIL (e) Tromsø IL II
*** Hafstad - Tobias Hafstad (a) 01/06/2002, ¿? (Norway) (b) 1,78 (c) M - central midfielder (d) Egersunds IK (e) Tromsø, Arendal, Tromsø, Arendal, Tromsø, Tromsø IL II
*** Hafsteinsson - Albert Hafsteinsson (a) 05/06/1996, ¿? (Iceland) (b) - (c) M - central midfielder (d) ÍA Akranes (e) Fram Reykjavík, ÍA Akranes, Kári, ÍA Akranes
*** Hafsteinsson - Daníel Hafsteinsson (a) 12/11/1999, Akureyri (Iceland) (b) 1,83 (c) M - central midfielder (d) KA Akureyri (e) Helsingborgs IF, Hafnarfjördur, Helsingborgs IF, KA Akureyri, Dalvík/Reynir
*** Hagelskjaer - Anders Hagelskjaer (Anders Hagelskjær) (a) 16/02/1997, Herning (Denmark) (b) 1,92 (c) D - central defense (d) Molde FK (e) Aalborg BK, Sarpsborg 08, Aalborg BK, Silkeborg IF, Skive IK, IfS (FCM II), Skive IK, IfS (FCM II)

*** Hagen - Elias Hagen (Elias Kristoffersen Hagen) (a) 20/01/2000, Oslo (Norway) (b) 1,88 (c) M - pivot (d) Vålerenga Fotball (e) IFK Göteborg, Bodø/Glimt, Grorud, Lillestrøm II

*** Hagen - Iver Krogh Hagen (a) 08/05/2004, ¿? (Norway) (b) 1,79 (c) D - right back (d) Aalesunds FK II (e) -

*** Hagen - Marius Hagen (a) 23/07/1992, Nordfjordeid (Norway) (b) 1,83 (c) M - central midfielder (d) Notodden FK (e) Moss, 07 Vestur, Strømmen, 07 Vestur, Fredrikstad, Hødd, Elverum, HamKam, Kristiansund, Husqvarna FF, Nest-Sotra IL, Notodden, Stryn IL, Volda TI, Eid IL

*** Hagen - Nicholas Hagen (Nicholas George Hagen Godoy) (a) 02/08/1996, Nueva Guatemala de la Asunción (Guatemala) (b) 1,93 (c) G (d) Ihud Bnei Sakhnin (e) HamKam, FK Sabail, CSD Municipal

*** Hagen - Steffen Hagen (a) 08/03/1986, Kristiansand (Norway) (b) 1,85 (c) D - central defense (d) Odds BK (e) Mandalskameratene, FK Vigør

*** Hägg Johansson - Lucas Hägg Johansson (a) 11/07/1994, ¿? (Sweden) (b) 1,89 (c) G (d) IF Brommapojkarna (e) Vejle BK, Kalmar FF, Oskarshamns AIK, Kalmar FF, Oskarshamns AIK, Kalmar FF, FC Rosengård

*** Häggström - Oscar Häggström (a) 24/04/2004, ¿? (Finland) (b) - (c) D - right back (d) HJK Klubi 04 Helsinki (e) Käpylän Pallo

*** Hagi - Ianis Hagi (a) 22/10/1998, Istanbul (Turkey) (b) 1,82 (c) M - attacking midfielder (d) Rangers FC (e) KRC Genk, Rangers FC, KRC Genk, FC Viitorul, Fiorentina, FC Viitorul, Academia Hagi

*** Hahn - André Hahn (a) 13/08/1990, Otterndorf (Germany) (b) 1,85 (c) F - right winger (d) - (e) FC Augsburg, SV Hamburg, Borussia Mönchengladbach, FC Augsburg, K. Offenbach, TuS Koblenz, FC Oberneuland, Hamburg II

*** Hahn - János Hahn (Hahn János Csaba) (a) 15/03/1995, Szekszárd (Hungary) (b) 1,83 (c) F - center forward (d) Paksi FC (e) Dunajska Streda, Paksi FC, Puskás AFC, Paksi FC

*** Hahn - Warner Hahn (Warner Lloyd Hahn) (a) 15/06/1992, Rotterdam (Netherlands) (b) 1,90 (c) G (d) Kyoto Sanga (e) IFK Göteborg, Go Ahead Eagles, RSC Anderlecht, Heerenveen, Feyenoord, Excelsior, Feyenoord, PEC Zwolle, Feyenoord, FC Dordrecht, Ajax B

*** Haidara - Amadou Haidara (a) 31/01/1998, Bamako (Mali) (b) 1,75 (c) M - central midfielder (d) RB Leipzig (e) RB Salzburg, FC Liefering, RB Salzburg, JMG Bamako

*** Haidara - Massadio Haidara (Massadio Haïdara) (a) 02/12/1992, Trappes (France) (b) 1,79 (c) D - left back (d) RC Lens (e) Newcastle Utd., AS Nancy, AS Nancy B

*** Haikin - Nikita Haikin (Хайкин Никита Ильич) (a) 11/07/1995, Netanya (Israel) (b) 1,85 (c) G (d) FK Bodø/Glimt (e) Bristol City, Bodø/Glimt, H. Kfar Saba, Bnei Yehuda, Kuban 2, Kuban II, Mordovia II, Marbella FC

*** Haile-Selassie - Maren Haile-Selassie (a) 13/03/1999, Zürich (Switzerland) (b) 1,76 (c) M - left midfielder (d) Chicago Fire FC (e) Chicago, FC Lugano, Neuchâtel Xamax, FC Zürich, FC Wil 1900, FC Zürich, Neuchâtel Xamax, FC Zürich, Rapperswil-Jona, FC Zürich

*** Hairemans - Geoffry Hairemans (a) 21/10/1991, Wilrijk (Belgium) (b) 1,83 (c) F - right winger (d) KV Mechelen (e) Royal Antwerp, Dessel Sport, KSK Heist, Lierse SK, KV Turnhout, Lierse SK, De Graafschap, Royal Antwerp

*** Hais - Daniel Hais (a) 02/06/2003, ¿? (Czech Rep.) (b) - (c) F - center forward (d) SK Dynamo Ceske Budejovice (e) -

*** Haist - John Haist (a) 05/12/1995, Wantage (England) (b) 1,88 (c) F - center forward (d) University College Dublin (e) Colorado SM, Wantage, Hungerford

*** Haita - Florian Haita (Florian Nichita Haită) (a) 29/10/2000, ¿? (Romania) (b) 1,81 (c) F - right winger (d) ACSC FC Arges (e) FCV Farul, Universitatea Cluj, FCV Farul, AFC Turris, Sport Team Buc.

*** Hajdarevic - Haris Hajdarevic (Haris Hajdarević) (a) 07/10/1998, Sarajevo (Bosnia and Herzegovina) (b) 1,81 (c) M - pivot (d) FK Radnik Surdulica (e) Zeljeznicar, Boluspor, Zeljeznicar, Sloboda Tuzla, Zeljeznicar

*** Hajdari - Albian Hajdari (a) 18/05/2003, Binningen (Switzerland) (b) 1,89 (c) D - central defense (d) FC Lugano (e) Juve Next Gen, FC Lugano, Juve Next Gen, FC Basel

*** Hajdari - Bujar Hajdari (a) 23/08/2002, Skopje (North Macedonia) (b) 1,92 (c) F - center forward (d) - (e) KF Vllaznia, FK Skopje, Rabotnicki, FC Vernier

*** Hajdari - Fiton Hajdari (a) 19/09/1991, ¿? (Yugoslavia, now in Kosovo) (b) - (c) F - left winger (d) - (e) FC Malisheva, SC Gjilani, FC Llapi, KF Trepca 89, KF Trepca, FC Llapi, KF Hysi

*** Hajdin - Stefan Hajdin (Стефан Хајдин) (a) 15/04/1994, Glina (Croatia) (b) 1,88 (c) D - left back (d) Zeleznicar Pancevo (e) Vozdovac, Crvena zvezda, Vozdovac, Crvena zvezda, Spartak, Pazova, Stari Banovci, FK Zemun, BASK Beograd, FK Zemun

*** Hajdini - Florent Hajdini (a) 02/09/2006, ¿? (Austria) (b) - (c) M - pivot (d) Wolfsberger AC II (e) -

*** Hajek - Lukas Hajek (Lukáš Hájek) (a) 11/06/2002, ¿? (Czech Rep.) (b) - (c) F (d) MFK Chrudim (e) Chrudim, Hradec Kralove B

*** Hajek - Tomas Hajek (Tomáš Hájek) (a) 01/12/1991, Zlín (Czechoslovakia, Czech Rep.) (b) 1,87 (c) D - central defense (d) Panserraikos (e) Vitesse, Viktoria Plzen, Mlada Boleslav, Viktoria Plzen, Fastav Zlin, Hradec Kralove, Fastav Zlin

*** Hajiagha - Amirhossein Hajiagha (حاجیآقا امیرحسین) (a) 19/02/2001, ¿? (Iran) (b) 1,88 (c) G (d) - (e) Makedonija

*** Hajradinovic - Haris Hajradinovic (Haris Hajradinović) (a) 18/02/1994, Prilep (North Macedonia) (b) 1,78 (c) M - attacking midfielder (d) Kasimpasa (e) NK Osijek, Haugesund, KAA Gent, AS Trencin, Inter Zaprešić, FK Olimpik

*** Hajrizi - Kreshnik Hajrizi (a) 28/05/1999, Sierre (Switzerland) (b) 1,85 (c) D - central defense (d) FC Lugano (e) FC Chiasso

*** Hajrovic - Izet Hajrovic (IzetHajrović) (a) 04/08/1991, Brugg (Switzerland) (b) 1,77 (c) F - right winger (d) Aris Thessaloniki (e) Dinamo Zagreb, Werder Bremen, SD Eibar, Werder Bremen, Galatasaray, Grasshoppers

*** Hajrovic - Orhan Hajrovic (Орхан Хајровић) (a) 16/05/1996, ¿? (RF Yugoslavia, now in Montenegro) (b) - (c) M - right midfielder (d) Jedinstvo Bijelo Polje (e) Rudar Pljevlja, Jedinstvo, FK Iskra, Jedinstvo, FK Iskra, Jedinstvo, BW Königsdorf

*** Hajsafi - Ehsan Hajsafi (احسان حاجصفی) (a) 25/02/1990, Kashan, Isfahan (Iran) (b) 1,78 (c) D - left back (d) AEK Athína FC (e) Sepahan, Tractor, Olympiakos, Panionios, Sepahan, FSV Frankfurt, Sepahan, Tractor Sazi, Sepahan

*** Hakaj - Esin Hakaj (a) 06/12/1996, Shkodër (Albania) (b) 1,76 (c) D - left back (d) KF Vllaznia (e) Samsunspor, FK Partizani, KF Teuta, FK Partizani, KF Vllaznia

*** Hakala - Aatu Hakala (a) 28/07/2000, Vantaa (Finland) (b) 1,84 (c) G (d) FC Haka (e) IF Gnistan, TiPS

*** Håkans - Daniel Håkans (Daniel Noel Mikael Håkans) (a) 26/10/2000, Vaasa (Finland) (b) 1,78 (c) F - right winger (d) Vålerenga Fotball (e) Jerv, SJK Seinäjoki, Jerv, SJK Seinäjoki, Vaasa IFK

*** Hakiki - Jad Hakiki (a) 23/06/2004, ¿? (Ireland) (b) - (c) F - center forward (d) Shelbourne FC (e) -

*** Hakim - Luqman Hakim (Luqman Hakim Bin Shamsudin) (a) 05/03/2002, Kota Bharu, Kelantan (Malaysia) (b) 1,70 (c) F - center forward (d) UMF Njardvík (e) Njardvík, KV Kortrijk, Selangor FC, NFDP Malaysia

*** Hakimi - Achraf Hakimi (Achraf Hakimi Mouh) (a) 04/11/1998, Madrid (Spain) (b) 1,81 (c) D - right back (d) París Saint-Germain FC (e) Internazionale Milano, Real Madrid, Borussia Dortmund, Real Madrid, RM Castilla

*** Hakmon - Shaked Hakmon (חכמון שלמה שקד) (a) 15/06/2002, ¿? (Israel) (b) - (c) D - central defense (d) FC Ashdod (e) -

*** Hakobyan - Davit Hakobyan (Դավիթ Հակոբյան) (a) 09/08/2005, ¿? (Armenia) (b) 1,80 (c) F - left winger (d) BKMA Yerevan (e) BKMA Yerevan II

*** Hakobyan - Hakob Hakobyan (Հակոբ Հակոբյան) (a) 29/03/1997, Akhalkalaki (Georgia) (b) 1,79 (c) D - left back (d) FC Ararat-Armenia (e) FC Urartu, Banants III

*** Hakobyan - Misak Hakobyan (Միսակ Հակոբյան) (a) 11/06/2004, ¿? (Armenia) (b) 1,79 (c) F - center forward (d) BKMA Yerevan (e) Ararat-Armenia, Ararat-Armenia II

*** Hakobyan - Razmik Hakobyan (Ռազմիկ Հակոբյան) (a) 09/02/1996, Mrgashat (Armenia) (b) 1,75 (c) F - center forward (d) FC Ararat Yerevan (e) Alashkert CF, Pyunik Yerevan, Pyunik Yerevan B

*** Hakobyan - Robert Hakobyan (Ռոբերտ Հակոբյան) (a) 22/10/1996, Yerevan (Armenia) (b) 1,75 (c) D - right back (d) - (e) Shirak Gyumri, Ararat Yerevan, Shirak Gyumri, Pyunik Yerevan, Pyunik Yerevan B

*** Hakobyan - Samvel Hakobyan (Սամվել Հակոբյան) (a) 30/04/2003, ¿? (Armenia) (b) 1,81 (c) F - center forward (d) BKMA Yerevan (e) FC Noah, Urartu II, FC Urartu, Urartu II

*** Hákonarson - Stefán Orri Hákonarson (a) 19/07/2005, ¿? (Iceland) (b) - (c) M (d) KR Reykjavík (e) Fram Reykjavík, KV Vesturbaejar, Fram Reykjavík

*** Hákonarson - Valur Thór Hákonarson (Valur Þór Hákonarson) (a) 20/01/2004, ¿? (Iceland) (b) - (c) M (d) Keflavík ÍF (e) Thróttur Vogum, Keflavík

*** Hakšabanović - Sead Hakšabanović (Сеад Хакшабановић) (a) 04/05/1999, Hyltebruk (Sweden) (b) 1,74 (c) F - left winger (d) Celtic FC (e) Rubin Kazan, Djurgården, Rubin Kazan, Norrköping, West Ham Utd., Norrköping, West Ham Utd., Málaga CF, West Ham Utd., Halmstads BK

*** Hala - Martin Hala (Martin Hála) (a) 24/03/1992, Olomouc (Czechoslovakia, now in Czech Rep.) (b) 1,77 (c) M - right midfielder (d) Bohemians Praha 1905 (e) Sigma Olomouc, Ceske Budejovice, Sigma Olomouc, FC Nitra, Sigma Olomouc, Slovácko, Sigma Olomouc

*** Halabaku - Kevin Halabaku (a) 29/11/2001, Sion (Switzerland) (b) 1,81 (c) F - left winger (d) FC Sion (e) -

*** Halabrin - Gabriel Halabrin (Gabriel Halabrín) (a) 21/04/2003, Brodské (Slovakia) (b) 1,70 (c) M - central midfielder (d) Spartak Myjava (e) Spartak Myjava, Ružomberok, FK Senica

*** Halaf - Loai Halaf (חלף לואי) (a) 08/08/2000, ¿? (Israel) (b) 1,85 (c) F - attacking midfielder (d) Maccabi Bnei Reineh (e) Ironi Nesher, Hapoel Acre, Ironi Nesher

*** Halasz - Jan Halasz (Jan Halász) (a) 28/02/2001, Kladno (Czech Rep.) (b) - (c) D - right back (d) FK Pardubice (e) Chrudim, Pardubice, Viktoria Plzen B

*** Hale - Ronan Hale (Ronan Aiden Connolly Shea Chapman Hale) (a) 08/09/1998, Belfast (Northern Ireland) (b) 1,76 (c) F - center forward (d) Cliftonville FC (e) Larne FC, St. Patrick's Ath., Crusaders, Derry City

*** Hale - Rory Hale (Rory Danny Hale) (a) 27/11/1996, Belfast (Northern Ireland) (b) 1,75 (c) M - central midfielder (d) Cliftonville FC (e) Crusaders, Derry City, Galway United

*** Haley - Joe Haley (a) 29/09/2003, ¿? (Wales) (b) - (c) D - right back (d) Buckley Town (e) Connah's Quay

*** Halhal - Redouane Halhal (a) 05/03/2003, Montpellier (France) (b) 1,87 (c) D - central defense (d) HSC Montpellier B (e) Montpellier For

*** Halilaj - Arseld Halilaj (a) 11/01/2004, Tiranë (Albania) (b) - (c) M - attacking midfielder (d) KF Teuta (e) -

*** Halili - Armend Halili (a) 22/06/1997, ¿? (RF Yugoslavia, now in Kosovo) (b) - (c) D - left back (d) KF Feronikeli Drenas (e) SC Gjilani

*** Halili - Diar Halili (a) 02/07/2003, Prishtinë (Serbia and Montenegro, now in Kosovo) (b) 1,93 (c) D - central defense (d) FC Prishtina (e) FC Besa, KF 2 Korriku

*** Halili - Gentrit Halili (a) 14/12/2001, ¿? (RF Yugoslavia, now in Kosovo) (b) 1,90 (c) D - central defense (d) FC Ballkani (e) KF Ferizaj

*** Halilovic - Alen Halilovic (Alen Halilović) (a) 18/06/1996, Dubrovnik (Croatia) (b) 1,69 (c) M (d) Fortuna Sittard (e) HNK Rijeka, Reading, Birmingham City, AC Milan, Heerenveen, AC Milan, Standard Liège, AC Milan, SV Hamburg, UD Las Palmas, SV Hamburg, FC Barcelona, Real Sporting, FC Barcelona, FC Barcelona B, Dinamo Zagreb

*** Halilovic - Dino Halilovic (Dino Halilović) (a) 08/02/1998, Zagreb (Croatia) (b) 1,81 (c) M - pivot (d) - (e) Tabor Sezana, FC Den Bosch, Esbjerg fB, NK Istra, NK Lokomotiva, NK Rudes, NK Lokomotiva, NK Istra

*** Halilovic - Emir Halilovic (Emir Halilović) (a) 04/11/1989, Zvornik (Yugoslavia, now in Bosnia and Herzegovina) (b) 1,79 (c) M - attacking midfielder (d) FK Velez Mostar (e) Zalaegerszeg, Bandirmaspor, Boluspor, Spartak Trnava, FK Sarajevo, Blau Weiss Linz, Spartak Trnava, Hradec Kralove, SK Prevysov, Hradec Kralove, Zvijezda G., FK Buducnost

*** Halilovic - Tibor Halilovic (Tibor Halilović) (a) 18/03/1995, Zagreb (Croatia) (b) 1,76 (c) M - attacking midfielder (d) SC Heerenveen (e) HNK Rijeka, Wisla Kraków, NK Lokomotiva, Din. Zagreb II

*** Halimi - Besar Halimi (a) 12/12/1994, Frankfurt am Main (Germany) (b) 1,69 (c) M - attacking midfielder (d) Hallescher FC (e) Apollon Smyrnis, Riga, SV Sandhausen, Brøndby IF, Mainz 05, Brøndby IF, Mainz 05, FSV Frankfurt, Mainz 05, Stuttg. Kickers, Stuttgart II, Nurernberg II

*** Halimi - Betim Halimi (a) 28/02/1996, Pozheran (RF Yugoslavia, now in Kosovo) (b) 2,04 (c) G (d) - (e) FK Kukësi, FC Prishtina, Olimpik Donetsk, JK Trans Narva, FC Drita, KF Hajvalia, FC Drita, KF Vllaznia

*** Haliti - Ahmet Haliti (a) 01/10/1988, Podujevë (Yugoslavia, now in Kosovo) (b) 1,88 (c) D - central defense (d) KF Feronikeli Drenas (e) KF Trepca 89, FC Prishtina, FC Llapi, FC Prishtina, KF Feronikeli, FK Bylis, FC Prishtina, KS Besa, KF Hysi

*** Haliti - Jetmir Haliti (a) 14/09/1996, Växjö (Sweden) (b) 1,88 (c) D - central defense (d) AIK Solna (e) Mjällby AIF, AIK, J-Södra IF, FC Rosengård, Landskrona, FC Rosengård, Prespa Birlik, BK Olympic

*** Halkett - Craig Halkett (a) 29/05/1995, Campsie (Scotland) (b) 1,83 (c) D - central defense (d) Heart of Midlothian FC (e) Livingston FC, Rangers FC, Berwick Rangers FC, Rangers FC, Clyde FC

*** Hall - Andy Hall (Andrew Hall) (a) 19/09/1989, Belfast (Northern Ireland) (b) - (c) M - right midfielder (d) Dundela FC (e) Glenavon, Bangor, Lisburn FC, Glentoran

*** Hall - Ben Hall (a) 16/01/1997, Enniskillen (Northern Ireland) (b) 1,85 (c) D - central defense (d) Linfield FC (e) Falkirk FC, Partick Thistle, Notts County

*** Hall - Lewis Hall (a) 08/09/2004, Slough (England) (b) 1,79 (c) D - left back (d) Chelsea FC (e) -
*** Hall - Tim Hall (a) 15/04/1997, Esch/Alzette (Luxembourg) (b) 1,90 (c) D - central defense (d) Újpest FC (e) Ethnikos, Wisla Kraków, Gil Vicente, Karpaty, Progrès Niederkorn, Lierse SK, SV Elversberg, Elversberg II
*** Hallaert - Lennert Hallaert (Lennert Willy Hallaert) (a) 17/04/2003, ¿? (Belgium) (b) 1,87 (c) F - center forward (d) SV Zulte Waregem (e) Jong Essevee, Club NXT
*** Hallberg - Melker Hallberg (Charles Melker Otto Hallberg) (a) 20/10/1995, Ljungbyholm (Sweden) (b) 1,80 (c) M - central midfielder (d) Kalmar FF (e) St. Johnstone, Hibernian FC, Vejle BK, Udinese, Kalmar FF, Udinese, Ascoli, Udinese, Hammarby IF, Udinese, Vålerenga, Udinese, Kalmar FF
*** Halldórsson - Dadi Baerings Halldórsson (Daði Bærings Halldórsson) (a) 08/04/1997, ¿? (Iceland) (b) 1,75 (c) M - central midfielder (d) Leiknir Reykjavík (e) -
*** Halldórsson - Hannes Thór Halldórsson (Hannes Þór Halldórsson) (a) 27/04/1984, Reykjavík (Iceland) (b) 1,94 (c) G (d) - (e) Víkingur, Valur, Qarabag FK, Randers FC, NEC Nijmegen, Bodø/Glimt, NEC Nijmegen, Sandnes Ulf, KR Reykjavík, Brann, KR Reykjavík, Fram Reykjavík, Stjarnan, Afturelding, Leiknir
*** Halldórsson - Hilmar Árni Halldórsson (a) 14/02/1992, Reykjavík (Iceland) (b) 1,80 (c) M - attacking midfielder (d) Stjarnan Gardabaer (e) Leiknir
*** Halldórsson - Torfi Geir Halldórsson (a) 06/01/2004, ¿? (Iceland) (b) - (c) G (d) Haukar Hafnarfjördur (e) Breidablik, Valur
*** Halldórsson - Ýmir Halldórsson (a) 02/05/2002, ¿? (Iceland) (b) - (c) M (d) Smári 2020 (e) Breidablik, Afturelding, Breidablik, Afturelding, Breidablik, Augnablik
*** Haller - Sébastien Haller (Sébastien Romain Teddy Haller) (a) 22/06/1994, Ris-Orangis (France) (b) 1,91 (c) F - center forward (d) Borussia Dortmund (e) Ajax, West Ham Utd., Eintracht, FC Utrecht, AJ Auxerre, FC Utrecht, AJ Auxerre
*** Hallgrimsson - Anton Hrafn Hallgrimsson (a) 30/10/2002, ¿? (Iceland) (b) - (c) M (d) Fram Reykjavík (e) ÍR, Fram Reykjavík, Úlfarnir, Fram Reykjavík, Úlfarnir
*** Hallgrímsson - Sveinn Svavar Hallgrímsson (a) ¿?/¿?/2006, ¿? (Iceland) (b) - (c) D - right back (d) Kári Akranes (e) -
*** Halliday - Andy Halliday (Andrew Halliday) (a) 11/10/1991, Glasgow (Scotland) (b) 1,81 (c) M - pivot (d) Heart of Midlothian FC (e) Rangers FC, FK Qabala, Rangers FC, Bradford City, Middlesbrough, Bradford City, Middlesbrough, Blackpool, Middlesbrough, FC Walsall, Middlesbrough, Livingston FC
*** Hallsson - Sigurdur Bjartur Hallsson (Sigurður Bjartur Hallsson) (a) 01/09/1999, ¿? (Iceland) (b) - (c) F - center forward (d) KR Reykjavík (e) Grindavík, GG Grindavik, Grindavík
*** Halme - Aapo Halme (Aapo Ilmari Halme) (a) 22/05/1998, Helsinki (Finland) (b) 1,96 (c) D - central defense (d) HJK Helsinki (e) Barnsley FC, Leeds Utd., HJK Helsinki, HJK Klubi 04
*** Halme - Jukka Halme (a) 29/05/1985, Helsinki (Finland) (b) 1,80 (c) M - central midfielder (d) - (e) Helsinki IFK, PK-35, Helsinki IFK, PK-35
*** Halpenny - Shane Halpenny (a) 07/01/2004, Ardee, Louth (Ireland) (b) - (c) G (d) - (e) Newry City
*** Halstenberg - Marcel Halstenberg (a) 27/09/1991, Laatzen (Germany) (b) 1,88 (c) D - left back (d) Hannover 96 (e) RB Leipzig, FC St. Pauli, Borussia Dortmund II, Hannover 96 II
*** Halsti - Markus Halsti (Markus Olof Halsti) (a) 19/03/1984, Helsinki (Finland) (b) 1,85 (c) D - central defense (d) SexyPöxyt (e) HJK Helsinki, Esbjerg fB, Midtjylland, D.C. United, Malmö FF, GAIS, HJK Helsinki

*** Halvorsen - Ole Jörgen Halvorsen (Ole Jørgen Halvorsen) (a) 02/10/1987, Sarpsborg (Norway) (b) 1,78 (c) F - right winger (d) Borgen IL (e) Sarpsborg 08, Odd, Bodø/Glimt, Odd, Fredrikstad, Sogndal, Sarpsborg 08, FK Sparta, Notodden, FK Sparta
*** Halwachs - Julian Halwachs (a) 25/01/2003, ¿? (Austria) (b) 1,88 (c) M - pivot (d) TSV Hartberg (e) FC Liefering
*** Hamache - Yanis Hamache (a) 13/07/1999, Marseille (France) (b) 1,77 (c) D - left back (d) SK Dnipro-1 (e) Boavista, OGC Nice, OGC Nice B, Red Star FC, OGC Nice B
*** Hamalainen - Brian Hamalainen (Brian Tømming Hämäläinen) (a) 29/05/1989, Allerød (Denmark) (b) 1,76 (c) D - left back (d) Lyngby BK (e) Dynamo Dresden, Zulte Waregem, KRC Genk, Zulte Waregem, Lyngby BK
*** Hämäläinen - Juuso Hämäläinen (a) 08/12/1993, Raisio (Finland) (b) 1,85 (c) D - central defense (d) FC Inter Turku (e) RoPS, FC Inter
*** Hämäläinen - Taneli Hämäläinen (a) 16/04/2001, Kuopio (Finland) (b) 1,84 (c) D - central defense (d) Kuopion Palloseura (e) -
*** Hambardzumyan - Hovhannes Hambardzumyan (Հովհաննես Համբարձումյան) (a) 04/10/1990, Yerevan (Soviet Union, now in Armenia) (b) 1,80 (c) D - right back (d) Anorthosis Famagusta (e) EN Paralimniou, Vardar, Banants, Banants II
*** Hambo - Vahid Hambo (a) 03/02/1995, Helsinki (Finland) (b) 1,93 (c) F - center forward (d) - (e) IFK Mariehamn, FC Lahti, Suduva, Astra Giurgiu, RoPS, SJK Seinäjoki, FC Inter, Ilves, HJK Klubi 04
*** Hamdaoui - Mohamed Hamdaoui (a) 10/06/1993, Amsterdam (Netherlands) (b) 1,70 (c) M - attacking midfielder (d) - (e) Zira FK, De Graafschap, FC Twente, De Graafschap, Telstar, Go Ahead Eagles, FC Dordrecht
*** Hamdi - Mathis Hamdi (a) 18/10/2003, ¿? (France) (b) 1,80 (c) D - left back (d) ESTAC Troyes (e) Troyes B
*** Hamdiev - Oktay Hamdiev (Октай Ахмедов Хамдиев) (a) 24/07/2000, Shumen (Bulgaria) (b) 1,80 (c) F - right winger (d) Hebar Pazardzhik (e) Septemvri Sofia
*** Hameed - Abdullah Hameed (Abdullah Talal Hameed, حميد طلال عبدالله) (a) 20/11/1995, ¿? (Irak) (b) - (c) F - left winger (d) Zalaegerszegi TE FC II (e) Tabor Sezana, SC Neusiedl/See, MTE SE, Kungsbacka IF, Kristianstad FC, Qviding FIF, IFK Ölme, Carlstad United, Inter CDF, Al-Quwa Al-Jaw., IFK Hässleholm
*** Hamidi - Walid Hamidi (حميدي وليد) (a) 16/10/1996, Oran (Algeria) (b) 1,81 (c) F - right winger (d) FC Ballkani (e) FC Shkupi, JSM Skikda, ASM Oran, MC Orán
*** Hamilton - Gary Hamilton (a) 06/10/1980, Banbridge (Northern Ireland) (b) 1,76 (c) F - center forward (d) Glenavon FC (e) Glentoran, Glenavon, Glentoran, Portadown, Blackburn, AFC Rochdale, Blackburn
*** Hamilton - Jack Hamilton (a) 22/03/1994, Denny (Scotland) (b) 1,90 (c) G (d) Livingston FC (e) Morton, Dundee FC, Heart of Midlothian, Stenhousemuir, Heart of Midlothian, East Fife, Heart of Midlothian, Forfar Athletic
*** Hamilton - Jack Hamilton (a) 30/06/2000, Coldingham (Scotland) (b) 1,87 (c) F - center forward (d) Raith Rovers FC (e) Livingston FC, Hartlepool Utd., Livingston FC, Arbroath, Livingston FC, Arbroath, Livingston FC, East Fife, Livingston FC, Livingston B, Queen of the South, Livingston B, Alloa Athletic, Livingston B, Berwick Rangers FC, Penicuik
*** Hamilton - Jordan Hamilton (Jordan Patrick Dear Hamilton) (a) 17/03/1996, Scarborough, Ontario (Canada) (b) 1,85 (c) F - center forward (d) Forge FC (e) Sligo Rovers, Indy Eleven, Columbus, Toronto, Toronto FC II, Toronto, Toronto FC II, Toronto, Toronto FC II, Toronto, Trofense, Toronto

*** Hamiti - Genc Hamiti (a) 21/09/1993, Skënderaj (RF Yugoslavia, now in Kosovo) (b) 1,77 (c) M - attacking midfielder (d) FC Prishtina (e) KF Drenica, KF Ferizaj, KF Drenica, FC Prishtina, KF Hajvalia

*** Hammar - Fredrik Hammar (a) 26/02/2001, ¿? (Sweden) (b) - (c) M - central midfielder (d) Hammarby IF (e) Hammarby TFF, Hammarby IF, Akropolis IF, Brentford B, Akropolis IF

*** Hammar - Johan Hammar (Per Johan Gustav Hammar) (a) 22/02/1994, Malmö (Sweden) (b) 1,97 (c) D - central defense (d) BK Häcken (e) Örgryte, Malmö FF, Fredrikstad, Malmö FF, Stockport

*** Hammel - Justin Hammel (Justin Pete Hammel) (a) 02/12/2000, Basel (Switzerland) (b) 1,85 (c) G (d) Grasshopper Club Zürich (e) Stade-Lausanne

*** Hammer - Pascal Hammer (a) 20/01/2004, Zollikon (Switzerland) (b) 1,84 (c) D - central defense (d) - (e) FC Winterthur, FC Biel-Bienne, FC Winterthur

*** Hammershöy-Mistrati - Vito Hammershöy-Mistrati (Vito Hammershøy-Mistrati) (a) 15/06/1992, Kopenhagen (Denmark) (b) 1,77 (c) M - central midfielder (d) IFK Norrköping (e) CFR Cluj, Randers FC, Hobro IK, FC Helsingör, Lyngby BK, HB Köge, Naestved BK

*** Hammond - Dion Hammond (Dion William Hammond) (a) 18/08/1994, Gibraltar (Gibraltar) (b) - (c) D - central defense (d) - (e) Europa Point FC, Europa Point FC, FC College 1975, Manchester 62, Europa Point FC, Mons Calpe, Gibraltar Phoenix, Gibraltar Utd., Glacis United, Manchester 62

*** Hammond - Oliver Hammond (Oliver Jack Hammond) (a) 13/11/2002, ¿? (England) (b) 1,79 (c) M - central midfielder (d) Cheltenham Town (e) Cheltenham Town

*** Hammond - Stephen Hammond (Stephen Kwabena Hammond) (a) 06/08/1996, Accra (Ghana) (b) 1,70 (c) M - central midfielder (d) APO Levadiakos (e) Doxa Dramas, RCD Mallorca B, CD Leganés B, RCD Mallorca B, CD Leganés B

*** Hámori - Tamás Hámori (Hámori Tamás Risto) (a) 21/09/2002, Lahti (Finland) (b) 1,93 (c) G (d) Újpest FC (e) Újpest II

*** Hamouma - Romain Hamouma (a) 29/03/1987, Montbéliard (France) (b) 1,79 (c) F - center forward (d) - (e) AC Ajaccio, St.-Étienne, SM Caen, Stade Lavallois, Besançon RC, FC Sochaux B

*** Hampson - Jake Hampson (Jake Robert Hughes Hampson) (a) 09/04/2002, ¿? (Wales) (b) 1,73 (c) F - right winger (d) Ruthin Town (e) Holywell United, Flint Town, Cefn Druids, Flint Town, Vauxhall Motors, Flint Town

*** Hamsik - Marek Hamsik (Marek Hamšík) (a) 27/07/1987, Banská Bystrica (Czechoslovakia, now in Czech Rep.) (b) 1,83 (c) M - central midfielder (d) Raymundo Hamsik (e) Trabzonspor, IFK Göteborg, Dalian PFC, Napoli, Brescia, Slovan Bratislava, Jupie FSMH

*** Hamulic - Said Hamulic (Said Hamulić) (a) 12/11/2000, Leiderdorp (Netherlands) (b) 1,88 (c) F - center forward (d) Vitesse Arnhem (e) Vitesse, Toulouse, Stal Mielec, DFK Dainava, Stal Mielec, DFK Dainava, Suduva, DFK Dainava, Botev Plovdiv, DFK Dainava

*** Hamza - Memetriza Hamza (a) 09/02/2004, ¿? (North Macedonia) (b) - (c) M (d) Besa Dobri Dol (e) -

*** Hamzic - Dino Hamzic (Dino Hamzić) (a) 22/01/1988, Sarajevo (Yugoslavia, now in Bosnia and Herzegovina) (b) 1,89 (c) G (d) FK Igman Konjic (e) Torpedo Kutaisi, FK Olimpik, Chikhura, FK Olimpik, Widzew Lódz, FK Olimpik, FK Sarajevo

*** Han - Jeong-woo Han (한정우) (a) 26/12/1998, ¿? (South Korea) (b) 1,69 (c) F - right winger (d) Veroskronos Tsuno (e) Gimpo FC, Dundalk FC, Suwon FC, Kairat Almaty, Gyeongnam FC, Soongsil Univ.

*** Hana - Guri Hana (a) 27/08/2001, London (England) (b) 1,87 (c) D - central defense (d) KF Shkëndija Hajvali (e) KF Trepca 89, Ramiz Sadiku, FC Besa, LSK Hansa, KF 2 Korriku

*** Hanca - Sergiu Hanca (Sergiu Cătălin Hanca) (a) 04/04/1992, Târgu Mureş (Romania) (b) 1,82 (c) F - right winger (d) Petrolul Ploiesti (e) CS U Craiova, Cracovia, FC Dinamo, ASA Tg. Mures, Bihor Oradea, FC Snagov

*** Hanche-Olsen - Andreas Hanche-Olsen (Andreas Schjølberg Hanche-Olsen) (a) 17/01/1997, Bodø (Norway) (b) 1,85 (c) D - central defense (d) 1.FSV Mainz 05 (e) KAA Gent, Stabæk

*** Hancko - David Hancko (Dávid Hancko) (a) 13/12/1997, Prievidza (Slovakia) (b) 1,88 (c) D - central defense (d) Feyenoord Rotterdam (e) Sparta Praha, Fiorentina, Sparta Praha, Fiorentina, MSK Zilina

*** Hancock - Ashton Hancock (a) 05/10/2006, ¿? (Gibraltar) (b) - (c) F - left winger (d) Mons Calpe SC (e) St Joseph's Reserves

*** Hancock - Mason Hancock (Mason Colin Hancock) (a) 10/02/2003, Surrey (England) (b) - (c) D - central defense (d) Airdrieonians FC (e) Aberdeen FC B, Arbroath, Aberdeen FC B, Stirling Albion, Aberdeen FC B

*** Handanovic - Samir Handanovic (Samir Handanovič) (a) 14/07/1984, Ljubljana (Yugoslavia, now in Slovenia) (b) 1,93 (c) G (d) - (e) Internazionale Milano, Udinese, Rimini, Udinese, Lazio, Udinese, Treviso, Udinese, Domžale

*** Händel - Tomás Händel (Tomás Romano Pereira dos Santos Händel) (a) 27/11/2000, Guimarães (Portugal) (b) 1,80 (c) M - pivot (d) Vitória Guimarães SC (e) Vitória Guimarães B, Moreirense Yout

*** Handl - Johannes Handl (a) 07/05/1998, Graz (Austria) (b) 1,96 (c) D - central defense (d) FK Austria Viena (e) FC Wacker II, SV Lafnitz, Sturm Graz II

*** Handzic - Haris Handzic (Haris Handžić) (a) 20/06/1990, Sarajevo (Yugoslavia, now in Bosnia and Herzegovina) (b) 1,91 (c) F - center forward (d) FK Riteriai (e) Leotar Trebinje, Radnik Bijelj., Al-Ahed, FK Sarajevo, Zrinjski Mostar, Debrecen, HNK Rijeka, Ufa, Borac Banja Luka, FC Vaduz, Rudar Prijedor, Velez Mostar, FK Sarajevo, Lech Poznan, FK Sarajevo, Lech Poznan, FK Sarajevo

*** Hanes - Adam Hanes (a) 17/06/2002, ¿? (Slovakia) (b) - (c) M - attacking midfielder (d) MFK Dukla Banska Bystrica (e) -

*** Hanglin - Aaram Hanglin (Aaram William Marcial Hanglin) (a) 18/08/2005, Gibraltar (Gibraltar) (b) - (c) M - central midfielder (d) Lions Gibraltar FC Reserve (e) -

*** Hangya - Szilveszter Hangya (a) 02/01/1994, Baja (Hungary) (b) 1,76 (c) D - left back (d) Fehérvár FC (e) Vasas FC, MTK Budapest II, Vasas FC, MTK Budapest II, Dunaújváros, MTK Budapest II

*** Hani - Agon Hani (a) 06/04/1998, ¿? (RF Yugoslavia, now in North Macedonia) (b) 1,83 (c) D - left back (d) Voska Sport (e) Pobeda Prilep, Struga, Vysehrad, FK Jablonec B, Slovácko B, Carev Dvor, AP Brera

*** Hani - Omar Hani (عمر هاني اسماعيل الزبدية) (a) 27/06/1999, Zarqa (Jordania) (b) 1,68 (c) F - left winger (d) FK Qabala (e) APOEL FC, Olympiakos N., APOEL FC, Al-Faisaly SC

*** Hankić - Hidajet Hankić (a) 29/06/1994, Schwarzach im Pongau (Austria) (b) 1,87 (c) G (d) Botev Plovdiv (e) FC Botosani, FC Wacker, Blau Weiss Linz, Austria Salzburg, Mlada Boleslav

*** Hankins - Jaylan Hankins (Jaylan Ernest Hankins) (a) 17/11/2000, Gibraltar (Gibraltar) (b) 1,86 (c) G (d) Lincoln Red Imps FC (e) Bruno's Magpies, Lincoln FC, Córdoba CF, Córdoba CF B, Córdoba CF, Extremadura, Córdoba CF, UD Las Palmas C, Lincoln FC, Europa Point FC
*** Hanlon - Paul Hanlon (a) 20/01/1990, Edinburgh (Scotland) (b) 1,80 (c) D - central defense (d) Hibernian FC (e) St. Johnstone, Hibernian FC
*** Hanne - Boubacar Hanne (Boubacar Rafael Neto Hanne) (a) 26/02/1999, Paços de Ferreira (Portugal) (b) 1,75 (c) F - right winger (d) - (e) FC Arges, Gil Vicente, Jumilla
*** Hannesbo - Marcus Hannesbo (Marcus Serup Hannesbo) (a) 11/05/2002, Aalborg (Denmark) (b) 1,85 (c) M - left midfielder (d) Vendsyssel FF (e) Aalborg BK, AC Horsens, Aalborg BK, FC Fredericia, Aalborg BK
*** Hannesson - Stefán Thór Hannesson (Stefán Þór Hannesson) (a) 02/03/1996, ¿? (Iceland) (b) - (c) G (d) KF Aegir (e) Fram Reykjavík, Hamar
*** Hannibal - Hannibal (حنبعل المجبري, Hannibal Mejbri) (a) 21/01/2003, Ivry-sur-Seine (France) (b) 1,83 (c) M - attacking midfielder (d) Manchester United (e) Birmingham City, Manchester Utd.
*** Hänninen - Onni Hänninen (a) 29/04/2005, ¿? (Finland) (b) 1,82 (c) F - center forward (d) FC Lahti (e) -
*** Hänninen - Vertti Hänninen (a) 01/06/2002, Kajaani (Finland) (b) 1,78 (c) M - central midfielder (d) FC Dziugas Telsiai (e) Dziugas, SJK Seinäjoki, RoPS, RoPS II
*** Hannola - Pyry Hannola (Pyry Petteri Hannola) (a) 21/10/2001, Rovaniemi (Finland) (b) 1,85 (c) M - central midfielder (d) SJK Seinäjoki (e) HJK Helsinki, SJK Seinäjoki, HJK Helsinki, RoPS
*** Hannula - Otto Hannula (a) 29/09/2005, ¿? (Finland) (b) - (c) M - attacking midfielder (d) HJK Klubi 04 Helsinki (e) VJS/Akatemia
*** Hanousek - Marek Hanousek (Marek Hanousek) (a) 06/08/1991, Dolní Kralovice (Czechoslovakia, now in Czech Rep.) (b) 1,86 (c) M - pivot (d) RTS Widzew Łódź (e) Karvina, Dukla Praha, Viktoria Plzen, Dukla Praha, Viktoria Plzen, Dukla Praha, Viktoria Plzen, Dukla Praha
*** Hanousek - Matej Hanousek (Matěj Hanousek) (a) 02/06/1993, Praha (Czech Rep.) (b) 1,82 (c) D - left back (d) MKE Ankaragücü (e) Sparta Praha, Ankaragücü, Sparta Praha, Gaziantep FK, Sparta Praha, Wisla Kraków, Sparta Praha, Jablonec, Dukla Praha, Dukla B
*** Hanratty - Mark Hanratty (a) 19/07/2002, ¿? (Ireland) (b) - (c) M - attacking midfielder (d) Wexford FC (e) Longford Town, Dundalk FC, Home Farm
*** Hansen - André Hansen (a) 17/12/1989, Oslo (Norway) (b) - (c) G (d) Rosenborg BK (e) Odd, Lillestrøm, KR Reykjavík, Lillestrøm, Skeid, Lillestrøm, Skeid, Kjelsås, Skeid
*** Hansen - Andreas Hansen (a) 11/08/1995, Brøndbyøster (Denmark) (b) 1,86 (c) G (d) FC Nordsjælland (e) Aalborg BK, Nordsjælland, Aalborg BK, HB Köge, Brøndby IF
*** Hansen - Aron Reinert Hansen (a) 04/10/2004, ¿? (Faroe Islands) (b) - (c) D - central defense (d) B68 Toftir (e) B68 Toftir II
*** Hansen - Bárdur Hansen (Bárður Jógvanson Hansen) (a) 13/03/1992, Tórshavn (Faroe Islands) (b) 1,67 (c) D - right back (d) - (e) Víkingur, NSÍ Runavík, Fremad Amager, Víkingur
*** Hansen - Betuel Hansen (a) 14/03/1997, ¿? (Faroe Islands) (b) - (c) M - central midfielder (d) NSÍ Runavík (e) NSÍ II
*** Hansen - Hedin Hansen (Heðin Hansen) (a) 30/07/1993, ¿? (Faroe Islands) (b) 1,92 (c) M - pivot (d) HB Tórshavn (e) Víkingur, HB Tórshavn, Víkingur

*** Hansen - Jan Hansen (Jan Ingason Hansen) (a) 08/10/1997, ¿? (Faroe Islands) (b) - (c) F - attacking midfielder (d) Skála IF (e) Skála IF II, Skála
*** Hansen - Jesper Hansen (a) 31/03/1985, Slangerup (Denmark) (b) 1,88 (c) G (d) Aarhus GF (e) Midtjylland, Lyngby BK, SC Bastia, Évian, Nordsjælland, Ölstykke FC, Nordsjælland
*** Hansen - Karstin Hansen (a) 05/10/1997, ¿? (Faroe Islands) (b) 1,80 (c) G (d) Skála IF (e) NSÍ Runavík, Skála, NSÍ Runavík, NSÍ II
*** Hansen - Kian Hansen (a) 03/03/1989, Grindsted (Denmark) (b) 1,84 (c) D - central defense (d) FC Nordsjælland (e) Midtjylland, FC Nantes, Esbjerg fB, FC Nantes, Esbjerg fB
*** Hansen - Kristoffer Hansen (Kristoffer Normann Hansen) (a) 12/08/1994, Larvik (Norway) (b) 1,80 (c) M - attacking midfielder (d) RTS Widzew Łódź (e) Sandefjord, Ullensaker/Kisa, Sarpsborg 08, Sandefjord, Fram, Sandefjord, Fram, Sandefjord, Larvik Turn
*** Hansen - Mads Hansen (Mads Kristian Hansen) (a) 28/07/2002, Ikast (Denmark) (b) 1,88 (c) F - right winger (d) FC Nordsjælland (e) Midtjylland
*** Hansen - Magnus Hansen (Magnus Hardahl Hansen) (a) 26/03/2001, ¿? (Luxembourg) (b) - (c) M - attacking midfielder (d) US Mondorf-Les-Bains (e) F91 Dudelange, US Mondorf, F91 Dudelange
*** Hansen - Martin Hansen (a) 15/06/1990, Glostrup (Denmark) (b) 1,88 (c) G (d) Odense Boldklub (e) Hannover 96, Strømsgodset, FC Basel, FC Ingolstadt, Heerenveen, FC Ingolstadt, ADO Den Haag, Nordsjælland, Viborg FF, Liverpool Reserves, Bradford City, Liverpool Reserves
*** Hansen - Nikolaj Hansen (Nikolaj Andreas Hansen) (a) 15/03/1993, Benløse (Denmark) (b) 1,92 (c) F - center forward (d) Víkingur Reykjavík (e) Valur, Vestsjaelland, HB Köge, Vestsjaelland, Ringsted IF
*** Hansen - Olaf Hansen (Olaf Karstensson Hansen) (a) 20/02/2002, ¿? (Faroe Islands) (b) 1,84 (c) F - right winger (d) KÍ Klaksvík (e) KÍ II
*** Hansen - Rani Hansen (a) 27/11/2000, ¿? (Faroe Islands) (b) - (c) F - center forward (d) EB/Streymur (e) Víkingur II
*** Hansen - Sabil Hansen (Sabil Osman Hansen) (a) 14/11/2005, ¿? (Denmark) (b) - (c) D - central defense (d) Randers FC (e) -
*** Hansen - Súni Hansen (a) 21/01/2003, ¿? (Faroe Islands) (b) - (c) M - central midfielder (d) NSÍ Runavík II (e) -
*** Hansen - Tobias Hansen (a) 28/06/2005, ¿? (Faroe Islands) (b) - (c) F - right winger (d) B36 Tórshavn II (e) -
*** Hansen-Taylor - Charlie Hansen-Taylor (a) 22/04/2003, ¿? (Wales) (b) - (c) D - central defense (d) Llantwit Major (e) -
*** Hanson - Henri Hanson (a) 18/04/1995, Pärnu (Estonia) (b) 1,85 (c) M - attacking midfielder (d) JK Tervis Pärnu (e) Pärnu Vaprus, Paide, Pärnu, Pärnu II
*** Hanson - Mait-Markus Hanson (a) 18/09/2003, Rakvere ((c) G (d) Paide Linnameeskond III (e) Paide IV
*** Hanssen - Sondre Fosnaess Hanssen (Sondre Fosnæss Hanssen) (a) 25/05/2001, ¿? (Norway) (b) 1,86 (c) D - central defense (d) Strømsgodset IF (e) Strømsgodset II
*** Hansson - Hallur Hansson (a) 08/07/1992, Tórshavn (Faroe Islands) (b) 1,82 (c) M - central midfielder (d) KÍ Klaksvík (e) KR Reykjavík, Vejle BK, AC Horsens, Vendsyssel FF, Víkingur, Aalborg BK, HB Tórshavn, Aalborg BK, HB Tórshavn
*** Hansson - Noel Hansson (a) 06/09/2003, ¿? (Sweden) (b) 1,95 (c) D - central defense (d) - (e) Sirius, Sunnersta AIF

*** Hanuljak - Marko Hanuljak (a) 31/01/2000, Đakovo (Croatia) (b) 1,81 (c) M - pivot (d) NK Lokomotiva Zagreb (e) HSK Posusje, NK Osijek, NK Osijek II, Djakovo Croatia

*** Hanus - Jan Hanus (Jan Hanuš) (a) 28/04/1988, Chlumec nad Cidlinou (Czechoslovakia, now in Czech Rep.) (b) 1,88 (c) G (d) FK Jablonec (e) Jihlava, Slavia Praha, Jihlava, Slavia Praha, Graffin Vlasim, Slavia Praha, Hradec Kralove, Slavia Praha, Hlucin, Slavia Praha, Slavia Praha B, SK Sparta Krc, Slavia Praha B

*** Hanuszczak - Jedrzej Hanuszczak (Jędrzej Hanuszczak) (a) 23/03/2008, Poznań (Poland) (b) 1,76 (c) M - central midfielder (d) Warta Poznań (e) -

*** Hanzis - Ronen Hanzis (רונן חנציס) (a) 28/02/2002, Nir Israel (Israel) (b) 1,85 (c) F - left winger (d) Maccabi Kabilio Jaffa (e) Kabilio Jaffa, Maccabi Tel Aviv, H Rishon leZion, Maccabi Tel Aviv, B. Jerusalem, Maccabi Tel Aviv, H. Nof HaGalil, Maccabi Tel Aviv, B TLV Bat Yam, Maccabi Tel Aviv

*** Hanzu - Benjamin Hanzu (a) 14/09/2002, Cisnădie (Romania) (b) - (c) D - central defense (d) ACS Medias 2022 (e) FC Hermannstadt, CS Tunari, FC Hermannstadt, Hermannstadt II

*** Haqverdi - Höccət Haqverdi (Höccət Haqverdi) (a) 03/02/1993, Mashhad, Razavi Khorasan (Iran) (b) 1,85 (c) D - central defense (d) Neftchi Baku (e) Sumqayit, Tractor, Sumqayit, Paykan FC, Zob Ahan, FC Aboomoslem

*** Hara - Taichi Hara (原 大智) (a) 05/05/1999, Hino, Tokyo (Japan) (b) 1,92 (c) F - center forward (d) Kyoto Sanga (e) Alavés, Sint-Truiden, Alavés, Sint-Truiden, Alavés, NK Istra, FC Tokyo

*** Hara - Teruki Hara (原 輝綺) (a) 30/07/1998, ¿?, Saitama (Japan) (b) 1,80 (c) D - right back (d) Shimizu S-Pulse (e) Grasshoppers, Shimizu S-Pulse, Sagan Tosu, Albirex Niigata, Ichifuna HS

*** Harabi - Aziz Harabi (a) 11/12/2002, ¿? (Sweden) (b) - (c) F - right winger (d) United IK Nordic (e) US Monastir, Hammarby TFF

*** Haracic - Dzenan Haracic (Dženan Haračić) (a) 30/07/1994, Bugojno (Bosnia and Herzegovina) (b) 1,85 (c) F - center forward (d) FK Zeljeznicar Sarajevo (e) GOSK Gabela, J. Bihac, NK Jajce, HNK Capljina, NK Neretvanac, Koprivnica, Zvijezda G., Slaven Belupo, Segesta Sisak, Slaven Belupo, Koprivnica, Slaven Belupo, NK Iskra Bugojno

*** Harada - Hiroki Harada (原田 拓季) (a) 23/05/1998, ¿? (Japan) (b) 1,72 (c) M - central midfielder (d) FK Otrant-Olympic Ulcinj (e) Rudar Pljevlja, Mladost DG, Chukyo Univ., Chukyo Univ. I, Chukyo Univ.

*** Haraguchi - Genki Haraguchi (原口 元気) (a) 09/05/1991, Kumagaya, Saitama (Japan) (b) 1,78 (c) M - attacking midfielder (d) VfB Stuttgart (e) Union Berlin, Hannover 96, Hertha Berlin, Fortuna Düsseldorf, Hertha Berlin, Urawa Reds

*** Haraldsson - Hákon Arnar Haraldsson (a) 10/04/2003, Raufoss (Norway) (b) 1,80 (c) M - attacking midfielder (d) LOSC Lille Métropole (e) FC København, ÍA Akranes

*** Haraldsson - Haukur Andri Haraldsson (a) 24/08/2005, Akranes (Iceland) (b) - (c) M - central midfielder (d) - (e) ÍA Akranes

*** Haraldsson - Tryggvi Hrafn Haraldsson (a) 30/09/1996, ¿? (Iceland) (b) 1,82 (c) F - left winger (d) Valur Reykjavík (e) Lillestrøm, ÍA Akranes, Halmstads BK, ÍA Akranes, Kári, ÍA Akranes

*** Harambasic - Ivan Harambasic (Ivan Harambašić) (a) 09/12/2000, Osijek (Croatia) (b) 1,94 (c) D - central defense (d) - (e) Metta, SC Kriens, Stade-Lausanne, FC Köniz, Stade-Lausanne, FC Köniz, BSC Old Boys, FC Wangen b. O.

*** Haraslin - Lukas Haraslin (Lukáš Haraslín) (a) 26/05/1996, Bratislava (Slovakia) (b) 1,82 (c) F - left winger (d) AC Sparta Praga (e) Sassuolo, Sparta Praha, Sassuolo, Lechia Gdánsk, Sassuolo, Lechia Gdánsk,

*** Haraszti - Zsolt Haraszti (a) 04/11/1991, Budapest (Hungary) (b) 1,81 (c) F - right winger (d) Paksi FC (e) MTK Budapest, Paksi FC, Videoton FC, Ferencváros, Paksi FC, Videoton FC, Puskás AFC, Videoton FC, Paksi FC, BFC Siófok, Paksi FC

*** Harazim - Stepan Harazim (Štěpán Harazim) (a) 13/07/2000, ¿? (Czech Rep.) (b) 1,83 (c) D - right back (d) FC Hradec Kralove (e) SFC Opava, SFC Opava B

*** Hardarson - Axel Freyr Hardarson (Axel Freyr Harðarson) (a) 22/10/1999, ¿? (Iceland) (b) - (c) F - right winger (d) Fjölnir Reykjavík (e) Kórdrengir, Víkingur, Kórdrengir, Víkingur, Grótta, Fram Reykjavík

*** Hardarson - Einar Örn Hardarson (Einar Örn Harðarson) (a) 04/04/2001, ¿? (Iceland) (b) - (c) D - central defense (d) Thróttur Vogum (e) ÍH, Hafnarfjördur, Fjölnir, Hafnarfjördur

*** Hardén - Kaius Hardén (a) 10/06/2004, ¿? (Finland) (b) - (c) F - center forward (d) HJK Klubi 04 Helsinki (e) -

*** Hardeveld - Jeff Hardeveld (a) 27/02/1995, Delft (Netherlands) (b) 1,84 (c) D - left back (d) FC Emmen (e) Heracles Almelo, FC Utrecht

*** Hardiman - Charlie Hardiman (a) 24/07/2003, Banbury (England) (b) 1,74 (c) M - right midfielder (d) Europa Point FC (e) -

*** Harding - Samuel Harding (Samuel Cleall-Harding) (a) 26/03/2006, Dundee (Scotland) (b) 1,88 (c) D - central defense (d) - (e) Dundee Utd. Ju.

*** Harel - Roy Harel (הראל רוי) (a) 02/12/2003, ¿? (Israel) (b) - (c) M - right midfielder (d) Ironi Kiryat Shmona (e) -

*** Haremi - Oltjan Haremi (a) 02/09/1992, Lushnjë (Albania) (b) - (c) G (d) KS Lushnja (e) FK Bylis, FK Tomori Berat, KS Lushnja, KF Egnatia, KS Lushnja, KF Egnatia, KS Lushnja

*** Harinck - Arthur Harinck (a) 11/12/2004, ¿? (Belgium) (b) - (c) D - right back (d) SV Zulte Waregem (e) Jong Essevee

*** Haring - Peter Haring (a) 02/06/1993, Eisenstadt (Austria) (b) 1,87 (c) M - pivot (d) Heart of Midlothian FC (e) SV Ried, Austria Lustenau, Rapid Wien II, Baumgarten, Schattendorf, Siegendorf

*** Haris - Attila Haris (Haris Attila Mihály) (a) 23/01/1997, Szolnok (Hungary) (b) 1,77 (c) M - central midfielder (d) Szeged-Csanád - GA (e) Paksi FC, Soroksár, Debrecen, Balmazújváros, Ferencváros, Soroksár, Ferencváros, Soroksár, Ferencváros

*** Harit - Amine Harit (أمين حاريث) (a) 18/06/1997, Pontoise (France) (b) 1,80 (c) M - attacking midfielder (d) Olympique Marseille (e) FC Schalke 04, Ol. Marseille, FC Schalke 04, Ol. Marseille, FC Schalke 04, FC Nantes, FC Nantes B

*** Harkes - Ian Harkes (Ian Andrew Harkes) (a) 30/03/1995, Derby (England) (b) 1,80 (c) M - central midfielder (d) New England Revolution (e) Dundee United, D.C. United, Demon Deacons

*** Harkin - Aaron Harkin (a) 03/03/1993, ¿? (Ireland) (b) - (c) M - central midfielder (d) Ballinamallard United (e) Portadown, Maiden City, Derry City, Cliftonville, Institute FC, Finn Harps

*** Harkin - Ciaron Harkin (a) 15/01/1996, Derry (Northern Ireland) (b) 1,80 (c) M - central midfielder (d) Derry City (e) Coleraine, Institute FC

*** Harling - Lewis Harling (Lewis John Harling) (a) 11/06/1992, Cardiff (Wales) (b) - (c) M - central midfielder (d) Pcnybont FC (e) Carmarthen, Port Talbot, Grange Albion

*** Harmon - George Harmon (a) 08/12/2000, Birmingham (England) (b) 1,63 (c) D - left back (d) Ross County FC (e) Oxford City

*** Harmon - Van-Dave Harmon (Van-Dave Gbowea Harmon) (a) 22/09/1995, Gbalatuah (Liberia) (b) 1,82 (c) F - center forward (d) - (e) FC Ballkani, JS Saoura, KF Laçi, KF Feronikeli, KF Drenica, 1.SC Znojmo, Metta, Barrack YC, Diambars FC, Barrack YC

*** Haro - David Haro (David Haro Iniesta) (a) 17/07/1990, Ametlla del Vallès (Spain) (b) 1,68 (c) F - right winger (d) - (e) FC Inter, UE Costa Brava, At. Baleares, GIF Sundsvall, Reus Deportiu, CE L'Hospitalet, Gimnàstic, CE L'Hospitalet, AE Prat, UE Sants

*** Haroun - Faris Haroun (Faris Dominguere Jenny Haroun) (a) 22/09/1985, Brussel (Belgium) (b) 1,87 (c) M - central midfielder (d) Nadjim Haroun (e) Royal Antwerp, Cercle Brugge, Blackpool, Middlesbrough, Beerschot AC, KRC Genk

*** Haroyan - Varazdat Haroyan (Վարազդատ Հարոյան) (a) 24/08/1992, Yerevan (Armenia) (b) 1,85 (c) D - central defense (d) FC Astana (e) Anorthosis, Cádiz CF, FC Astana, Tambov, Ural, Padideh, Pyunik Yerevan, Pyunik Yerevan B, Patani

*** Harrington - Ryan Harrington (a) 03/10/1998, Wrexham (Wales) (b) - (c) D - right back (d) Connah's Quay Nomads (e) The New Saints, Aberdeen FC B, Montrose, Aberdeen FC B

*** Harris - Luke Harris (Luke Bernard Harris) (a) 04/03/2005, Jersey (Jersey) (b) 1,77 (c) M - attacking midfielder (d) Fulham FC (e) -

*** Harrison - Danny Harrison (Daniel Robert Harrison) (a) 04/11/1982, Liverpool (England) (b) 1,80 (c) M - central midfielder (d) Flint Town United (e) Connah's Quay, Chester, Tranmere Rovers, Rotherham, Tranmere Rovers

*** Harrison - Jack Harrison (Jack David Harrison) (a) 20/11/1996, Stoke-on-Trent (England) (b) 1,75 (c) F - left winger (d) Everton FC (e) Everton, Leeds Utd., Manchester City, Leeds Utd., Manchester City, Middlesbrough, Manchester City, New York City, Chicago, Demon Deacons, Manhattan, Black Rock FC

*** Harroui - Abdou Harroui (Abderrahman Harroui) (a) 13/01/1998, Leiden (Netherlands) (b) 1,82 (c) M - central midfielder (d) Frosinone Calcio (e) Sassuolo, Sparta Rotterdam, Sassuolo, Sparta Rotterdam

*** Hart - Joe Hart (Charles Joseph John Hart) (a) 19/04/1987, Shrewsbury (England) (b) 1,96 (c) G (d) Celtic FC (e) Tottenham Hotspur, Burnley, Manchester City, West Ham Utd., Manchester City, Torino, Manchester City, Birmingham City, Manchester City, Blackpool, Manchester City, Tranmere Rovers, Manchester City, Shrewsbury

*** Hartenyan - Hovhannes Hartenyan (Հովհաննես Հարթենյան) (a) 17/03/2004, ¿? (Armenia) (b) - (c) M - pivot (d) FC Shirak Gyumri II (e) -

*** Hartherz - Florian Hartherz (a) 29/05/1993, Offenbach am Main (Germany) (b) 1,87 (c) D - left back (d) Miedź Legnica (e) Podbeskidzie, Maccabi Netanya, Fortuna Düsseldorf, Arminia Bielefeld, SC Paderborn, Werder Bremen, Wolfsburg II

*** Hartman - Quilindschy Hartman (a) 14/11/2001, Zwijndrecht (Netherlands) (b) 1,83 (c) D - left back (d) Feyenoord Rotterdam (e) -

*** Harush - Ariel Harush (הרוש אריאל) (a) 08/02/1988, Jerusalem (Israel) (b) 1,91 (c) G (d) FC Ashdod (e) H. Beer Sheva, Heerenveen, FC Nitra, H. Beer Sheva, Sparta Rotterdam, H. Beer Sheva, Anorthosis, Hapoel Tel Aviv, Maccabi Netanya, B. Jerusalem

*** Harush - Shalev Harush (הראש שלו) (a) 08/05/2002, ¿? (Israel) (b) - (c) M - central midfielder (d) FC Ashdod (e) -

*** Harut - Denis Harut (Denis Grațian Haruț) (a) 25/02/1999, Timișoara (Romania) (b) 1,81 (c) D - central defense (d) FCSB (e) FC Botosani, FCSB, FC Botosani, ACS Poli

*** Harutyunyan - Arman Harutyunyan (Արման Հարությունյան) (a) 05/03/2002, Stepanaker (Armenia) (b) 1,84 (c) G (d) FC Ararat Yerevan (e) Lernayin Artsakh, Torpedo
*** Harutyunyan - Gegham Harutyunyan (Գեղամ Հարությունյան) (a) 23/08/1990, Yerevan (Soviet Union, now in Armenia) (b) 1,85 (c) F - center forward (d) - (e) FC Van, FC Noah, Gandzasar, Shakhter K., Gandzasar, Ulisses, FC Shengavit, Moldava, FC Shengavit
*** Harutyunyan - Georgiy Harutyunyan (Арутюнян Георгий Эдуардович) (a) 09/08/2004, Balakovo (Russia) (b) 1,89 (c) D - central defense (d) FK Krasnodar (e) Krasnodar-2, Krasnodar II
*** Harutyunyan - Hayk Harutyunyan (Հայկ Հարությունյան) (c) G (d) Lernayin Artsakh Goris (e) Artsakh II
*** Harutyunyan - Hovhannes Harutyunyan (Հովhաննես Հարությունյան) (a) 25/05/1999, Yerevan (Armenia) (b) 1,75 (c) M - central midfielder (d) FC Pyunik Yerevan (e) Ararat-Armenia, Michalovce, Ararat-Armenia, Pyunik Yerevan
*** Harvey - Liam Harvey (a) 20/01/2005, Elgin (Scotland) (b) - (c) F - center forward (d) Elgin City FC (e) Elgin City, Aberdeen FC B
*** Hasa - Noel Hasa (a) 06/02/2003, ¿? (Finland) (b) 1,80 (c) M - central midfielder (d) Ilves Tampere (e) -
*** Hasa - Roman Hasa (Roman Haša) (a) 15/02/1993, Staré Město (Czech Rep.) (b) 1,78 (c) F - center forward (d) MFK Skalica (e) SKF Sered, Karvina, Skalica, Komarno, Slovácko, HS Kromeriz, Slovácko, MFK Vyskov, Slovácko, Fotbal Trinec, Slovácko, Slovácko B
*** Hasaj - Francesko Hasaj (Françesko Hasaj) (a) 22/07/2001, Tiranë (Albania) (b) 1,78 (c) M - attacking midfielder (d) FK Kukësi (e) KF Turbina
*** Hasan - Dzhaner Hasan (a) 23/01/2005, ¿? (Bulgaria) (b) - (c) M (d) Arda Kardzhali II (e) -
*** Hasanaj - Donat Hasanaj (a) 18/09/1998, Prishtinë (RF Yugoslavia, now in Kosovo) (b) 1,83 (c) D - right back (d) FC Suhareka (e) KF Liria, KF Feronikeli, KF Ferizaj, KF Dukagjini, FC Prishtina, KF Flamurtari, FC Drita, FC Prishtina, Kek-U Kastriot, FC Prishtina
*** Hasanalizada - Bakhtiyar Hasanalizada (Bəxtiyar Bəyqulu oğlu Həsənalizadə) (a) 29/12/1992, Baku (Azerbaijan) (b) 1,87 (c) D - central defense (d) Tuzlaspor (e) Sabah FK, Zira FK, Sumqayit
*** Hasanbegovic - Eldin Hasanbegovic (Eldin Hasanbegović) (a) 17/09/2000, Tuzla (Bosnia and Herzegovina) (b) 1,88 (c) D - central defense (d) FK Sloboda Tuzla (e) FK Tuzla City, Sloga Meridian, FK Tuzla City, OFK Gradina, FK Tuzla City
*** Hasanbegovic - Mirza Hasanbegovic (Mirza Hasanbegović) (a) 19/07/2001, Stockholm (Sweden) (b) 1,93 (c) F - center forward (d) NK Domžale (e) Venezia, GS Kallithea, Venezia, ND Gorica, Venezia, Lokomotiv Plovdiv
*** Hasanbelli - Klevis Hasanbelli (a) 30/06/1997, Lushnjë (Albania) (b) 1,91 (c) G (d) KF Erzeni (e) KF Egnatia, KF Pogradeci, KF Egnatia, KF Laçi, KF Turbina, KF Laçi, KF Turbina, FK Kukësi B
*** Hasani - Ardian Hasani (a) 03/12/2003, Mitrovica (Serbia and Montenegro, now in Kosovo) (b) - (c) F - center forward (d) KF Trepca 89 (e) -
*** Hasani - Arianit Hasani (a) 24/02/2004, Podujevë (Serbia and Montenegro, now in Kosovo) (b) 1,70 (c) M - attacking midfielder (d) KF Llapi (e) -
*** Hasani - Edon Hasani (a) 09/01/1992, Shkodër (Albania) (b) 1,81 (c) M - central midfielder (d) ΛF Elbasani (e) KS Kastrioti, FK Partizani B, KF Tirana, Sepahan, KF Vllaznia, FK Kukësi, ACS Poli, Ceahlăul, Litex Lovetch, KF Vllaznia

*** Hasani - Ferhan Hasani (a) 18/06/1990, Tetovo (Yugoslavia, now in North Macedonia) (b) 1,88 (c) M - attacking midfielder (d) FC Helsingör (e) Shkëndija, FK Partizani, HJK Helsinki, Al-Raed, Shkëndija, Brøndby IF, VfL Wolfsburg, Shkëndija
*** Hasani - Florent Hasani (a) 30/03/1997, Vushtrri (RF Yugoslavia, now in Kosovo) (b) 1,83 (c) F - right winger (d) KF Tirana (e) Gyirmót FC, H. Kfar Saba, Diósgyőr, KF Trepca 89, KF Vushtrria
*** Hasani - Nderim Hasani (a) 05/01/2002, Podujevë (RF Yugoslavia, now in Kosovo) (b) 1,75 (c) F - left winger (d) KF Llapi (e) KF Feronikeli, KF Llapi, KF Liria, FC Llapi
*** Hasanov - Mahir Hasanov (Mahir Elçin oğlu Həsənov) (a) 12/01/2002, ¿? (Azerbaijan) (b) - (c) M - pivot (d) Kapaz PFK (e) Kapaz 2
*** Hasanov - Sahib Hasanov (Sahib İlham oğlu Həsənov) (a) 26/10/2004, ¿? (Azerbaijan) (b) - (c) G (d) FC Shamakhi (e) FC Shamakhi 2
*** Hasanov - Samir Hasanov (Samir Həsənov) (a) 10/04/2003, ¿? (Azerbaijan) (b) - (c) M (d) Neftchi 2 Baku (e) -
*** Hasanov - Vüqar Hasanov (Vüqar Razi oğlu Həsənov) (a) 05/12/1997, Lankaran (Azerbaijan) (b) - (c) D - central defense (d) FK Sabail (e) Kapaz PFK, Neftchi 2 Baku, FC Shamakhi 2
*** Hasanovic - Dino Hasanovic (Dino Hasanović) (a) 21/01/1996, Sarajevo (Bosnia and Herzegovina) (b) 1,78 (c) M - pivot (d) FK Velez Mostar (e) GOSK Gabela, Zeljeznicar, Celik Zenica, Zeljeznicar
*** Hasanovic - Haris Hasanovic (Haris Hasanović) (a) 20/03/2004, Tuzla (Bosnia and Herzegovina) (b) - (c) M - central midfielder (d) FK Sloboda Tuzla (e) -
*** Hasanzada - Nazim Hasanzada (Nazim Həsənzadə) (a) 27/07/2002, ¿? (Azerbaijan) (b) 1,78 (c) M - central midfielder (d) FK Zira 2 (e) Daugavpils, Turan 2 Tovuz, Sabah 2
*** Hasebe - Makoto Hasebe (長谷部 誠) (a) 18/01/1984, Fujieda, Shizuoka (Japan) (b) 1,80 (c) D - central defense (d) Eintracht Frankfurt (e) 1.FC Nürnberg, VfL Wolfsburg, Urawa Reds, Fujieda Higashi High School
*** Hasek - Martin Hasek (Martin Hašek) (a) 03/10/1995, Liberec (Czech Rep.) (b) 1,81 (c) M - central midfielder (d) - (e) Wisła Płock, Erzurumspor FK, Würzb. Kickers, Sparta Praha, Bohemians 1905, Sparta Praha B, Bohemians 1905, Sparta Praha B, Vlasim, Sparta Praha B, Viktoria Zizkov, Sparta Praha B, Pardubice, Sparta Praha B
*** Hasek - Pavel Hasek (Pavel Hašek) (a) 22/01/2005, ¿? (Czech Rep.) (b) - (c) F (d) FC Viktoria Plzen B (e) -
*** Hasenhüttl - Patrick Hasenhüttl (a) 20/05/1997, Bonheiden (Belgium) (b) 1,90 (c) F - center forward (d) SK Austria Klagenfurt (e) VfB Oldenburg, Austria Klagenfurt, Unterhaching, Türkgücü Münch., Ingolstadt II
*** Hashimov - Salim Hashimov (a) 09/10/2006, ¿? (Azerbaijan) (b) - (c) G (d) FK Zira 2 (e) -
*** Hashioka - Daiki Hashioka (橋岡 大樹) (a) 17/05/1999, Urawa, Saitama (Japan) (b) 1,84 (c) D - right back (d) Sint-Truidense VV (e) Urawa Reds, Sint-Truiden, Urawa Reds
*** Hasic - Ajdin Hasic (Ajdin Hasić) (a) 07/10/2001, Tuzla (Bosnia and Herzegovina) (b) 1,77 (c) F - right winger (d) Besiktas JK (e) Göztepe, Besiktas, Ümraniyespor, Besiktas, Ümraniyespor, Besiktas, Din. Zagreb II
*** Hasin - Or Hasin (a) 09/03/2002, ¿? (Israel) (b) - (c) D - central defense (d) Ironi Kiryat Shmona (e) -
*** Haskic - Nermin Haskic (Nermin Haskić) (a) 27/06/1989, Banovići (Yugoslavia, now in Bosnia and Hercegovina) (b) 1,87 (c) F - center forward (d) FK Velez Mostar

(e) Omiya Ardija, Radnicki Niš, Ružomberok, MSK Zilina, Podbeskidzie, MSK Zilina, VSS Kosice, Vozdovac, FK Sarajevo, FK Buducnost

*** Haspolat - Dogucan Haspolat (Doğucan Haspolat) (a) 11/02/2000, Rotterdam (Netherlands) (b) 1,77 (c) M - pivot (d) Trabzonspor (e) Kasimpasa, Excelsior

*** Hassan - Haissem Hassan (Haissem Hassan) (a) 08/02/2002, Bagnolet (France) (b) 1,75 (c) F - left winger (d) Real Sporting de Gijón (e) Real Sporting, Villarreal CF B, CD Mirandés, Villarreal CF B, LB Châteauroux, Châteauroux B

*** Hassan - Mohcine Hassan (Mohcine Hassan Nader) (a) 30/09/1994, Faro (Portugal) (b) 1,83 (c) F - center forward (d) FC Alverca (e) F91 Dudelange, Olhanense, Vitória Setúbal, Olhanense, Vitória Setúbal, Freamunde, Vitória Setúbal, Pinhalnovense, Vitória Setúbal, Casa Pia, Vitória Setúbal

*** Hassan - Moshe Hassan (Moshe Shalom Hassan) (a) ¿?, ¿? (Gibraltar) (b) - (c) M (d) - (e) Mons Calpe SC

*** Hassan - Rilwan Hassan (Rilwan Olanrewaju Hassan) (a) 09/02/1991, Lagos (Nigeria) (b) 1,72 (c) F - right winger (d) Sreenidi Deccan FC (e) HamKam, SønderjyskE, Midtjylland, FC Ebedei

*** Hasson - Nir Hasson (ניר חסון) (a) 19/12/2001, ¿? (Israel) (b) - (c) M - central midfielder (d) Hapoel Ramat Gan (e) H. Ramat Gan, FC Ashdod, AS Ashdod, FC Ashdod

*** Hasson - Sahar Hasson (סהר חסון) (a) 24/04/1996, ¿? (Israel) (b) - (c) G (d) FC Ashdod (e) Ramat haSharon, Maccabi Tel Aviv, Ramat haSharon, Maccabi Tel Aviv, Beitar TA Ramla, Maccabi Tel Aviv

*** Hastings - Thomas Hastings (a) 23/09/1992, Gibraltar (Gibraltar) (b) 1,85 (c) M - pivot (d) Lions Gibraltar FC (e) Europa Reserve, Europa Point FC, Europa Reserve, Lions Gibraltar, Red Imps FC II, FC Britannia XI, Red Imps FC II

*** Hatakka - Dani Hatakka (a) 12/03/1994, Espoo (Finland) (b) 1,87 (c) D - central defense (d) FH Hafnarfjördur (e) Keflavík, FC Honka, SJK Seinäjoki, Brann, SJK Seinäjoki, Brann, Hødd, Brann, KuPS, FC Honka, AC Oulu, FC Honka, FC Honka II

*** Hatate - Reo Hatate (旗手 怜央) (a) 21/11/1997, Suzuka, Mie (Japan) (b) 1,72 (c) M - central midfielder (d) Celtic FC (e) Kawasaki Front., Juntendo Univ., Kawasaki Front., Juntendo Univ., Kawasaki Front., Juntendo Univ., Shizugaku HS

*** Hateboer - Hans Hateboer (a) 09/01/1994, Beerta (Netherlands) (b) 1,85 (c) D - right back (d) Atalanta de Bérgamo (e) FC Groningen, Gron./Cambuur B

*** Hateley - Tom Hateley (Thomas Nathan Hateley) (a) 12/09/1989, Monte Carlo (Monaco) (b) 1,81 (c) M - pivot (d) Piast Gliwice (e) AEK Larnaca, Piast Gliwice, Dundee FC, Śląsk Wroclaw, Tranmere Rovers, Motherwell FC, Basingstoke

*** Hatlehol - Jørgen Hatlehol (a) 18/06/1997, ¿? (Norway) (b) 1,85 (c) M - right midfielder (d) Bryne FK (e) Aalesund

*** Hatman - Adrian Hatman (Adrian Hătman) (a) 05/01/2003, ¿? (Moldova) (b) 1,78 (c) M - central midfielder (d) FC Sheriff Tiraspol (e) Real Succes

*** Hato - Jorrel Hato (a) 07/03/2006, ¿? (Netherlands) (b) 1,82 (c) D - central defense (d) Ajax de Ámsterdam (e) Ajax B

*** Hatuel - Rotem Hatuel (רותם חטואל) (a) 12/04/1998, Hazor Haglilit (Israel) (b) - (c) F - left winger (d) Hapoel Beer Sheva (e) M. Ahi Nazareth, H. Umm al-Fahm, Ramat haSharon, Kiryat Shmona, Hapoel Acre, Kiryat Shmona

*** Haudum - Stefan Haudum (a) 27/11/1994, Eferding (Austria) (b) 1,88 (c) M - pivot (d) FC Blau-Weiss Linz (e) SCR Altach, LASK, Blau Weiss Linz

*** Haug - Elias Haug (Elias Kringberg Haug) (a) 18/02/2006, Askim (Norway) (b) 1,85 (c) D - central defense (d) Sarpsborg 08 FF (e) -

*** Haug - Kjetil Haug (Christian Kjetil Haug) (a) 12/06/1998, Fredrikstad (Norway) (b) 1,91 (c) G (d) Toulouse FC (e) Vålerenga, Sogndal, Vålerenga, Sogndal, Elverum, Sogndal, CF Peralada

*** Haugaard - Jakob Haugaard (Jakob Let Haugaard) (a) 01/05/1992, Sundby (Denmark) (b) 1,99 (c) G (d) Tromsø IL (e) AIK, Tromsø, AIK, Stoke City, Wigan Ath., Stoke City, Midtjylland, Akademisk BK

*** Haugan - Eirik Haugan (a) 27/08/1997, Molde (Norway) (b) 1,80 (c) D - central defense (d) Molde FK (e) Östersund, Hødd, Ol. Marseille B, Molde FK II

*** Hauge - Jens Petter Hauge (a) 12/10/1999, Bodø (Norway) (b) 1,84 (c) F - left winger (d) Eintracht Frankfurt (e) KAA Gent, Eintracht, AC Milan, Eintracht, AC Milan, Bodø/Glimt, Aalesund, Bodø/Glimt

*** Hauge - Runar Hauge (a) 01/09/2001, Bodø (Norway) (b) 1,75 (c) F - left winger (d) FK Jerv (e) Hibernian B, Dundalk FC, Hibernian B, Bodø/Glimt, Stjørdals-Blink, Bodø/Glimt, Grorud, Bodø/Glimt, Bodø/Glimt II

*** Haugen - Fredrik Haugen (a) 13/06/1992, Bergen (Norway) (b) 1,82 (c) M - central midfielder (d) Stabæk Fotball (e) Aalesund, Stabæk, AEK Larnaca, Brann, Løv-Ham

*** Haugen - Herman Haugen (Herman Johan Haugen) (a) 25/04/2000, ¿? (Norway) (b) 1,82 (c) D - right back (d) Viking FK (e) Raufoss, Viking, Raufoss, Viking, Ullensaker/Kisa, Viking, Viking FK II, Vidar, Viking FK II

*** Haugen - Kristoffer Haugen (a) 21/02/1994, Stavanger (Norway) (b) 1,88 (c) D - left back (d) Molde FK (e) Viking

*** Haugen - Sigurd Haugen (Sigurd Hauso Haugen) (a) 17/07/1997, Haugesund (Norway) (b) 1,87 (c) F - center forward (d) Aarhus GF (e) Aalesund, Union St. Gilloise, Sogndal, Odd

*** Haughey - Mark Haughey (a) 23/01/1991, Newry (Northern Ireland) (b) - (c) D - central defense (d) Glenavon FC (e) Linfield, Glenavon

*** Haukioja - Martti Haukioja (Martti Mikael Haukioja) (a) 06/10/1999, Kuorevesi (Finland) (b) 1,88 (c) D - central defense (d) SJK Seinäjoki (e) FC Inter, VPS, Ilves, Ilves, FC Jazz, Ilves

*** Hauksson - Óskar Örn Hauksson (a) 22/08/1984, Reykjanesbær (Iceland) (b) 1,75 (c) M - attacking midfielder (d) UMF Grindavík (e) Stjarnan, KR Reykjavík, FC Edmonton, KR Reykjavík, Sandnes Ulf, KR Reykjavík, Grindavík, Sogndal, Njardvík

*** Hauksson - Róbert Hauksson (a) 01/10/2001, ¿? (Iceland) (b) - (c) F - center forward (d) Leiknir Reykjavík (e) Thróttur

*** Hauksson - Sveinn Margeir Hauksson (a) 02/11/2001, ¿? (Iceland) (b) 1,88 (c) M - attacking midfielder (d) KA Akureyri (e) Dalvík/Reynir, KA Akureyri, Dalvík/Reynir

*** Haurits - Oliver Haurits (a) 12/12/2000, Viborg (Denmark) (b) 1,87 (c) F - center forward (d) HK Kópavogs (e) Stjarnan, Skive IK, Naestved BK

*** Hause - Kortney Hause (Kortney Paul Duncan Hause) (a) 16/07/1995, Redbridge (England) (b) 1,91 (c) D - central defense (d) Aston Villa (e) Watford, Aston Villa, Wolverhampton Wanderers, Aston Villa, Wolverhampton Wanderers, Gillingham FC, Wolverhampton Wanderers, Wycombe Wanderers

*** Hausner - Sebastian Hausner (a) 11/04/2000, Horsens (Denmark) (b) 1,88 (c) D - central defense (d) IFK Göteborg (e) Aarhus GF

*** Hautamo - Otto Hautamo (a) 07/03/2002, ¿? (Finland) (b) 1,87 (c) G (d) IFK Mariehamn (e) Mikkelin, HJK Klubi 04

*** Hautekiet - Ibe Hautekiet (Ibe Tom Hautekiet) (a) 13/04/2002, Kortrijk (Belgium) (b) 1,88 (c) D - central defense (d) Standard de Lieja (e) KV Brugge, Club NXT

*** Havel - Lukas Havel (Lukáš Havel) (a) 06/06/1996, České Budějovice (Czech Rep.) (b) 1,87 (c) D - central defense (d) SK Dynamo Ceske Budejovice (e) TJM Roudne, Ceske Budejovice, Pisek, Ceske Budejovice
*** Havel - Milan Havel (Milan Havel) (a) 07/08/1994, Benešov (Czech Rep.) (b) 1,83 (c) D - right back (d) FC Viktoria Plzen (e) Bohemians 1905, Viktoria Plzen, Bohemians 1905, Bohemians B
*** Havertz - Kai Havertz (Kai Lukas Havertz) (a) 11/06/1999, Aachen (Germany) (b) 1,93 (c) M - attacking midfielder (d) Arsenal FC (e) Chelsea, Bayer Leverkusen
*** Havier - Mark Havier (Mark Antonio Havier) (a) 23/08/2004, Tallinn (Estonia) (b) - (c) D - central defense (d) Tallinn JK Legion (e) -
*** Havlik - Marek Havlik (Marek Havlík) (a) 08/07/1995, Lubná (Czech Rep.) (b) 1,76 (c) M - central midfielder (d) 1.FC Slovácko (e) HS Kromeriz, Slovácko B, HS Kromeriz
*** Hawkins - Daniel Hawkins (Daniel Thomas Hawkins) (a) 22/04/2001, Cardiff (Wales) (b) - (c) F - center forward (d) Haverfordwest County (e) Shelbourne, Finn Harps, Stafford Rangers, Marine FC
*** Haxhihamza - Kenan Haxhihamza (a) 28/12/1996, Rahovec (RF Yugoslavia, now in Kosovo) (b) - (c) G (d) KF Dukagjini (e) FC Ballkani, SC Gjilani, KF Rahoveci
*** Haxhimusa - Betim Haxhimusa (a) 14/04/1992, Ferizaj (Yugoslavia, now in Kosovo) (b) 1,83 (c) F - center forward (d) KF Ferizaj (e) FC Drita, SC Gjilani, FC Prishtina, KF Ferizaj
*** Haxhiu - Rimal Haxhiu (a) 04/03/1999, Krujë (Albania) (b) 1,81 (c) M - right midfielder (d) KF Tirana (e) FK Apolonia, FK Kukësi, FK Apolonia, FC Dinamo, FK Apolonia, FC Luftëtari, KF Iliria, Bremer SV, Blumenthaler SV, FK Partizani B
*** Hayashi - Daichi Hayashi (林 大地) (a) 23/05/1997, ¿?, Osaka (Japan) (b) 1,78 (c) F - center forward (d) 1.FC Nürnberg (e) 1.FC Nürnberg, Sint-Truiden, Sagan Tosu, Osaka Uni H&SS, Sagan Tosu, Osaka Uni H&SS, Riseisha HS
*** Hayden - Isaac Hayden (Isaac Scott Hayden) (a) 22/03/1995, Chelmsford (England) (b) 1,87 (c) M - pivot (d) Newcastle United (e) Norwich City, Newcastle Utd., Hull City
*** Haye - Thom Haye (Thom Jan Marinus Haye) (a) 09/02/1995, Amsterdam (Netherlands) (b) 1,87 (c) M - pivot (d) SC Heerenveen (e) NAC Breda, ADO Den Haag, NAC Breda, ADO Den Haag, Lecce, Willem II, AZ Alkmaar
*** Hayes - Dylan Hayes (a) 14/04/2004, ¿? (Finland) (b) - (c) F - left winger (d) HJK Klubi 04 Helsinki (e) -
*** Hayes - Jonny Hayes (Jonathan Hayes) (a) 09/07/1987, Dublin (Ireland) (b) 1,68 (c) M - right midfielder (d) Aberdeen FC (e) Celtic FC, Aberdeen FC, Inverness Caledonian, Leicester City, Cheltenham Town, Leicester City, Northampton, Leicester City, Reading, MK Dons, Reading, Forest Green Rovers, Reading
*** Hayes - Mike Hayes (Michael Peter Hayes) (a) 21/11/1987, Chester (England) (b) 1,82 (c) F - center forward (d) Flint Mountain (e) Connah's Quay, Caernarfon, Bala, Connah's Quay, Airbus UK, Connah's Quay, Airbus UK, Bala, Connah's Quay
*** Haygarth - Max Haygarth (Maxwell James Haygarth) (a) 21/01/2002, Manchester (England) (b) 1,75 (c) F - left winger (d) Linfield FC (e) Brentford B
*** Hayiryan - Vadim Hayiryan (Վադիմ Հայիրյան) (a) 06/04/1997, Shushi)) (c) D - right back (d) - (e) Lernayin Artsakh, Artsakh Erewan
*** Hayner - Hayner (Hayner Willian Monjardim Cordeiro) (a) 02/10/1995, Salvador (Brazil) (b) 1,78 (c) D - right back (d) Coritiba Foot Ball Club (e) Coritiba FC, Azuriz, SK Dnipro-1, Azuriz, Atlético-GO, Azuriz, Sport Recife, Azuriz, Cuiabá-MT, Louletano, Novorizontino, EC Bahia, Paysandu, EC Bahia, Náutico, EC Bahia, Rio Branco-ES

*** Hayrapetyan - Aram Hayrapetyan (Արամ Հայրապետյան) (a) 22/11/1986, Adler, Krasnodar Region (Soviet Union, now in Russia) (b) 1,92 (c) G (d) FK Maktaaral (e) Atyrau, Paykan FC, FC Urartu, Ararat Yerevan, Banants, Smena, Kuzbass, FK Adler, Sochi-04

*** Hayrapetyan - Arsen Hayrapetyan (Айрапетян Арсен Мгерович) (a) 16/02/1997, Yaroslavl (Russia) (b) 1,79 (c) M - attacking midfielder (d) Tekstilshchik Ivanovo (e) Rodina Moskva, FC Noah, Rodina Moskva, Shinnik Yaroslav, Murom, Shinnik Yaroslav, Znamya Truda OZ, Shinnik Yaroslav, Ararat Moskva, Shinnik Yaroslav, Shinnik Yaroslav

*** Hayrapetyan - Vahagn Hayrapetyan (Վահագն Հայրապետյան) (a) 14/06/1997, Kapan (Armenia) (b) 1,65 (c) M - pivot (d) Akzhayik Uralsk (e) FC Noah, Kairat Moskva, Alashkert CF, Pyunik Yerevan, Pyunik Yerevan B

*** Hazard - Conor Hazard (a) 05/03/1998, Downpatrick (Northern Ireland) (b) 1,98 (c) G (d) Plymouth Argyle (e) Celtic FC, HJK Helsinki, Celtic FC, Celtic Reserves, Dundee FC, Celtic Reserves, Dundee FC, Celtic Reserves, Partick Thistle, Celtic Reserves, Falkirk FC

*** Hazard - Eden Hazard (Eden Michael Hazard) (a) 07/01/1991, La Louvière (Belgium) (b) 1,75 (c) F - left winger (d) - (e) Real Madrid, Chelsea, Lille

*** Hazard - Thorgan Hazard (Thorgan Ganael Francis Hazard) (a) 29/03/1993, La Louvière (Belgium) (b) 1,75 (c) F - left winger (d) Borussia Dortmund (e) PSV Eindhoven, Borussia Dortmund, Borussia Mönchengladbach, Chelsea, Borussia Mönchengladbach, Chelsea, Zulte Waregem, Chelsea, RC Lens, RC Lens B

*** Haziri - Lirinis Haziri (a) 04/03/1999, ¿? (Finland) (b) - (c) F - right winger (d) FC Reipas Lahti (e) FC Kuusysi

*** Haziyev - Bahadur Haziyev (Bahadur Məmməd oğlu Həziyev) (a) 26/03/1999, Baku (Azerbaijan) (b) 1,77 (c) M - attacking midfielder (d) FK Sabail (e) FK Sabail, Shamakhi, FK Sabail, FK Sabail 2, MOIK

*** Haziza - Dolev Haziza (חזיזה דולב) (a) 05/07/1995, Rehovot (Israel) (b) 1,78 (c) F - left winger (d) Maccabi Haifa (e) Bnei Yehuda, H. Ramat Gan, Bnei Yehuda, Ness Ziona

*** Hazrollaj - Drilon Hazrollaj (a) 19/02/2004, Banjë (Serbia and Montenegro, now in Kosovo) (b) 1,78 (c) F - right winger (d) FC Malisheva (e) Ramiz Sadiku

*** Hazut - Itay Hazut (חזות איתי) (a) 20/09/2006, Beer Sheva (Israel) (b) 1,70 (c) M - attacking midfielder (d) - (e) Hapoel Beer Sheva

*** Healey - Rhys Healey (Rhys Evitt-Healey) (a) 06/12/1994, Manchester (England) (b) 1,80 (c) F - center forward (d) Watford FC (e) Toulouse, MK Dons, Cardiff City, MK Dons, Cardiff City, Torquay, Cardiff City, Newport County, Cardiff City, Dundee FC, Cardiff City, Colchester Utd., Cardiff City, Connah's Quay

*** Healy - Brian Healy (a) 24/08/2004, Belfast (Northern Ireland) (b) - (c) F - right winger (d) Newry City AFC (e) Plunkett FC

*** Healy - Lorcan Healy (a) 23/05/2000, ¿? (Ireland) (b) - (c) G (d) University College Dublin (e) -

*** Healy - Noel Healy (a) 27/07/1999, Belfast (Northern Ireland) (b) - (c) D - left back (d) Newry City AFC (e) Donegal Celtic

*** Heaney - Cillian Heaney (a) 18/04/2002, Westport, Mayo (Ireland) (b) - (c) F - center forward (d) - (e) Sligo Rovers

*** Heatley - Paul Heatley (a) 30/06/1987, Belfast (Northern Ireland) (b) 1,71 (c) F - left winger (d) Crusaders FC (e) Carrick Rangers, Brantwood FC

*** Heaton - Tom Heaton (Thomas David Heaton) (a) 15/04/1986, Chester (England) (b) 1,88 (c) G (d) Manchester United (e) Aston Villa, Burnley, Bristol City, Cardiff City, Manchester Utd., Wycombe Wanderers, Manchester Utd., AFC Rochdale,

Manchester Utd., Queen's Park Rangers, Manchester Utd., Cardiff City, Manchester Utd., Royal Antwerp, Manchester Utd., Swindon Town, Manchester Utd.

*** Hebaj - Rubin Hebaj (a) 30/07/1998, Shkodër (Albania) (b) 1,87 (c) F - center forward (d) FK Andijon (e) KF Teuta, Shkëndija, KF Teuta, Vorskla Poltava, Domžale, FK Partizani, Domžale, KF Vllaznia

*** Hebibovic - Anel Hebibovic (Anel Hebibović) (a) 07/07/1990, Konjic (Yugoslavia, Bosnia and Herzegovina) (b) 1,75 (c) F - right winger (d) FK Igman Konjic (e) FK Sarajevo, FK Olimpik, FK Sarajevo, Velez Mostar, Igman Konjic, GOSK Gabela, Igman Konjic

*** Hebibovic - Kenan Hebibovic (Kenan Hebibović) (a) 14/06/2001, Konjic (Bosnia and Herzegovina) (b) - (c) D - right back (d) FK Igman Konjic (e) FK Klis, Igman Konjic

*** Heca - Milan Heca (Milan Heča) (a) 21/03/1991, Krumvíř (Czechoslovakia, now in Czech Rep.) (b) 1,87 (c) G (d) 1.FC Slovácko (e) Sparta Praha, Slovácko

*** Hecko - Richard Hecko (Richard Hečko) (a) 01/10/2003, Bratislava (Slovakia) (b) 1,90 (c) D - central defense (d) FC Petrzalka (e) FC Petrzalka, Podbrezova

*** Hector - Jonas Hector (a) 27/05/1990, Saarbrücken (Germany) (b) 1,85 (c) D - left back (d) Lucas Hector (e) 1.FC Köln, 1.FC Köln II, Auersmacher

*** Hedenstad - Mads Hedenstad (Mads Hedenstad Christiansen) (a) 21/10/2000, Fetsund (Norway) (b) 1,86 (c) G (d) Lillestrøm SK (e) Lillestrøm II

*** Hedenstad - Vegar Hedenstad (Vegar Eggen Hedenstad) (a) 26/06/1991, Elverum (Norway) (b) - (c) D - right back (d) Vålerenga Fotball (e) Karagümrük, Rosenborg, FC St. Pauli, SC Freiburg, Eintracht Braunschweig, SC Freiburg, Stabæk, Elverum

*** Hedinsson - Asbjörn Hedinsson (Asbjørn Heðinsson) (a) 19/12/2000, ¿? (Faroe Islands) (b) - (c) D - left back (d) - (e) 07 Vestur, AB Argir, 07 Vestur, B36 II, 07 Vestur

*** Hédinsson - Eyjólfur Hédinsson (Eyjólfur Héðinsson) (a) 01/01/1985, Reykjavík (Iceland) (b) 1,85 (c) M - pivot (d) ÍR Reykjavík (e) Stjarnan, Midtjylland, SønderjyskE, GAIS, Fylkir, ÍR

*** Hedl - Niklas Hedl (a) 17/03/2001, Wien (Austria) (b) 1,88 (c) G (d) SK Rapid Wien (e) Rapid Wien II

*** Hedlund - Simon Hedlund (Simon Fredrik Hedlund) (a) 11/03/1993, Trollhättan (Sweden) (b) 1,73 (c) F - center forward (d) Brøndby IF (e) Union Berlin, Elfsborg

*** Hedvall - Oscar Hedvall (Oscar Thore Hedvall) (a) 09/08/1998, ¿? (Denmark) (b) 1,96 (c) G (d) FC Midtjylland (e) Silkeborg IF, FC Fredericia, Silkeborg IF

*** Heekeren - Justin Heekeren (a) 27/11/2000, Xanten (Germany) (b) 1,96 (c) G (d) FC Schalke 04 (e) RW Oberhausen

*** Heeney - Luke Heeney (a) 06/02/1999, Duleek, Meath (Ireland) (b) 1,75 (c) D - right back (d) Drogheda United FC (e) -

*** Hegarty - Chris Hegarty (Christopher Hegarty) (a) 13/08/1992, Dungannon (Northern Ireland) (b) 1,80 (c) D - central defense (d) Dungannon Swifts (e) Crusaders, Dungannon, Linfield, Rangers FC

*** Hegedűs - János Hegedűs (Hegedűs János Krisztián) (a) 04/10/1996, Budapest (Hungary) (b) 1,89 (c) D - central defense (d) Paksi FC (e) Vasas FC, Diósgyőr, Puskás AFC, Haladás, Haladás II, Budaörs, Haladás II

*** Heggheim - Henrik Heggheim (a) 22/04/2001, Stavanger (Norway) (b) 1,89 (c) D - central defense (d) Brøndby IF (e) Vålerenga, Brøndby IF, Viking, Viking FK II

*** Hegyi - Krisztián Hegyi (a) 24/09/2002, Budapest (Hungary) (b) 1,93 (c) G (d) FC Stevenage (e) Stevenage

*** Heidarsson - Oliver Heidarsson (Oliver Heiðarsson) (a) 23/02/2001, ¿? (Iceland) (b) - (c) F - right winger (d) ÍBV Vestmannaeyjar (e) Hafnarfjördur, Thróttur, SR

*** Heidenreich - David Heidenreich (a) 24/06/2000, Ústí nad Labem (Czech Rep.) (b) 1,91 (c) D - central defense (d) FC Hradec Kralove (e) Atalanta, Jablonec, Atalanta, SPAL, Atalanta, Teplice

*** Heikkilä - Aapo Heikkilä (a) 13/04/1994, Haukipudas (Finland) (b) 1,73 (c) F - right winger (d) - (e) AC Oulu, RoPS, AC Oulu

*** Heikkilä - Tapio Heikkilä (a) 08/04/1990, Espoo (Finland) (b) 1,86 (c) D - central defense (d) - (e) FC Honka, Sandnes Ulf, Start, SJK Seinäjoki, HJK Helsinki, FC Honka, FC Honka II

*** Heikkinen - Benjamin Heikkinen (a) 16/12/2002, ¿? (Finland) (b) - (c) F - left winger (d) Kokkolan Pallo-Veikot (e) FC Honka II, Pargas IF, FC Honka II, Käpylän Pallo

*** Heikkinen - Daniel Heikkinen (a) 16/12/2002, ¿? (Finland) (b) 1,76 (c) M - attacking midfielder (d) Käpylän Pallo (e) AC Oulu, FC Honka II, PEPO, FC Honka II, Käpylän Pallo

*** Heil - Jürgen Heil (a) 04/04/1997, ¿? (Austria) (b) 1,76 (c) D - right back (d) TSV Hartberg (e) Anger

*** Heil - Sascha Heil (a) 04/05/1999, Gießen (Germany) (b) 1,84 (c) D - central defense (d) Union Titus Petange (e) FC Gießen, SC Paderborn

*** Heimisson - Árni Salvar Heimisson (a) 10/03/2003, ¿? (Iceland) (b) - (c) M - central midfielder (d) ÍA Akranes (e) Kári, ÍA Akranes

*** Heimisson - Birkir Heimisson (a) 12/02/2000, ¿? (Iceland) (b) - (c) M - central midfielder (d) Valur Reykjavík (e) Thór

*** Hein - Gauthier Hein (a) 07/08/1996, Thionville (France) (b) 1,70 (c) F - right winger (d) AJ Auxerre (e) FC Metz, Valenciennes FC, FC Metz, Tours FC, FC Metz, FC Metz B

*** Hein - Karl Hein (Karl Jakob Hein) (a) 13/04/2002, Põlva ((b) 1,93 (c) G (d) Arsenal FC (e) Reading, Nomme United

*** Heinesen - Benjamin Heinesen (a) 26/03/1996,) (d) B36 Tórshavn (e) -

*** Heinesen - Brandur Heinesen (a) 15/04/2002, ¿? (Faroe Islands) (b) - (c) M (d) 07 Vestur II (e) HB Tórshavn II, 07 Vestur II, 07 Vestur

*** Heino - Aleksi Heino (Aleksi Peter Heino) (a) 25/07/2004, Turku (Finland) (b) - (c) F - center forward (d) SJK Seinäjoki II (e) -

*** Heinonen - Arttu Heinonen (a) 22/04/1999, Oulu (Finland) (b) 1,84 (c) M - attacking midfielder (d) Kuopion Palloseura (e) FC Lahti, KuPS, KuFu-98, Pallo-Kerho 37

*** Heintz - Dominique Heintz (a) 15/08/1993, Neustadt an der Weinstraße (Germany) (b) 1,88 (c) D - central defense (d) 1.FC Union Berlin (e) VfL Bochum, Union Berlin, SC Freiburg, 1.FC Köln, 1.FC Kaiserslautern

*** Heintz - Tobias Heintz (a) 13/07/1998, Moss (Norway) (b) 1,74 (c) F - left winger (d) CSKA-Sofia (e) Häcken, Sarpsborg 08, Häcken, Kasimpasa, Sarpsborg 08, Kasimpasa, Sarpsborg 08, Sprint/Jeløy

*** Heiselberg - Frederik Heiselberg (a) 11/02/2003, Lyne (Denmark) (b) 1,90 (c) F - center forward (d) AC Horsens (e) AC Horsens, Midtjylland, FC Fredericia, Midtjylland

*** Heiskanen - Saku Heiskanen (a) 29/09/2001, Espoo (Finland) (b) 1,71 (c) M - central midfielder (d) UCF Knights (University of Central Florida) (e) FC Honka, HJK Klubi 04, FC Honka, HJK Klubi 04

*** Heiskanen - Taneli Heiskanen (a) 28/05/2000, ¿? (Finland) (b) - (c) F - left winger (d) Kuopion Elo (e) KuPS

*** Heister - Marcel Heister (a) 29/07/1992, Albstadt-Ebingen (Germany) (b) 1,82 (c) D - left back (d) Ludogorets Razgrad (e) Fehérvár, Ferencváros, B. Jerusalem, NK Istra, NK Zadar, Hoffenheim II

*** Heitor - Heitor (Heitor Rodrigues da Fonseca) (a) 05/11/2000, Pelotas (Brazil) (b) 1,74 (c) D - right back (d) Mirassol Futebol Clube (SP) (e) Internacional, Ferroviária, Internacional, Cercle Brugge, Internacional

*** Hejda - Lukas Hejda (Lukáš Hejda) (a) 09/03/1990, Bílovec (Czechoslovakia, now in Czech Rep.) (b) 1,89 (c) D - central defense (d) FC Viktoria Plzen (e) Sparta Praha, 1.FK Pribram, Sparta Praha, FK Jablonec, Sparta Praha, Sparta Praha B

*** Helac - Ammar Helac (a) 13/06/1998, Linz (Austria) (b) 1,90 (c) G (d) SC Austria Lustenau (e) Austria Viena, Blau Weiss Linz, ASKÖ Donau Linz, Donau Linz II

*** Helander - Filip Helander (Filip Viktor Helander) (a) 22/04/1993, Malmö (Sweden) (b) 1,92 (c) D - central defense (d) - (e) Rangers FC, Bologna, Hellas Verona, Bologna, Hellas Verona, Malmö FF

*** Hélder Ferreira - Hélder Ferreira (Hélder José Castro Ferreira) (a) 05/04/1997, Fafe (Portugal) (b) 1,79 (c) F - right winger (d) Anorthosis Famagusta (e) Paços Ferreira, Vitória Guimarães B, Vitória Guimarães, Vitória Guimarães B

*** Hélder Lopes - Hélder Lopes (Hélder Filipe Oliveira Lopes) (a) 04/01/1989, Vila Nova de Gaia (Portugal) (b) 1,79 (c) D - left back (d) Hapoel Beer Sheva (e) AEK Athína, UD Las Palmas, Paços Ferreira, Beira-Mar, Tondela, Espinho, Oliveira Douro, Mirandela

*** Helenius - Nicklas Helenius (Nicklas Helenius Jensen) (a) 08/05/1991, Svenstrup (Denmark) (b) 1,96 (c) F - center forward (d) Aalborg BK (e) Silkeborg IF, Aarhus GF, Odense BK, Aalborg BK, Silkeborg IF, Aalborg BK, SC Paderborn, Aalborg BK, Aston Villa, Aalborg BK, Aston Villa, Aalborg BK

*** Helesic - Matej Helesic (Matěj Helešic) (a) 12/11/1996, ¿? (Czech Rep.) (b) 1,73 (c) D - left back (d) FK Pardubice (e) SFC Opava, Banik Ostrava, SFC Opava, Banik Ostrava, Ceske Budejovice, Banik Ostrava, Ceske Budejovice, Banik Ostrava, Ceske Budejovice, Banik Ostrava

*** Helgason - Baldur Kári Helgason (a) 08/02/2005, ¿? (Iceland) (b) - (c) M (d) FH Hafnarfjördur (e) ÍH, Hafnarfjördur

*** Helgason - Elfar Freyr Helgason (a) 27/07/1989, Reykjavík (Iceland) (b) 1,91 (c) D - central defense (d) Valur Reykjavík (e) Breidablik, AC Horsens, Breidablik, Randers FC, Stabæk, AEK Athína, Breidablik, Augnablik, Breidablik

*** Helgason - Thórir Jóhann Helgason (Þórir Jóhann Helgason) (a) 28/09/2000, Hafnarfjörður (Iceland) (b) 1,87 (c) M - central midfielder (d) US Lecce (e) Hafnarfjörður, Haukar

*** Helgeland - Eivind Helgeland (a) 01/12/2003, ¿? (Norway) (b) - (c) D - left back (d) FK Haugesund (e) Vard, Haugesund, FK Haugesund II

*** Helistano Manga - Helistano Manga (Helistano Ciro Manga) (a) 20/05/1999, ¿? (Guinea-Bissau) (b) 1,84 (c) M - pivot (d) - (e) FC Jazz, KF Ferizaj, Olympiakos Volou, AS Rodos, FC Noah, Leiria

*** Héliton - Héliton (Héliton Jorge Tito dos Santos) (a) 13/11/1995, ¿? (Brazil) (b) 1,95 (c) D - central defense (d) CSKA 1948 (e) SC Covilhã, ABC FC, Santo André, Figueirense FC, Santo André

*** Helland - Pal André Helland (Pål André Helland) (a) 04/01/1990, Orkanger (Norway) (b) 1,86 (c) F - right winger (d) Løvenstad FK (e) Lillestrøm, Rosenborg, Hødd, Byåsen, Rosenborg, Ranheim, Rosenborg, Ranheim, Rosenborg

*** Hellborg - Adam Hellborg (Carl Adam Jonathan Hellborg) (a) 30/07/1998, ¿? (Sweden) (b) 1,88 (c) M - pivot (d) Helsingborgs IF (e) Sirius, Kalmar FF, Oskarshamns AIK, Kalmar FF, Emmaboda IS

*** Hellebrand - Jan Hellebrand (a) 02/03/2002, Zlín (Czech Rep.) (b) 1,77 (c) M - pivot (d) FC Zlin B (e) -

*** Hellebrand - Patrik Hellebrand (a) 16/05/1999, Opava (Czech Rep.) (b) 1,80 (c) M - attacking midfielder (d) SK Dynamo Ceske Budejovice (e) Slavia Praha, Ceske Budejovice, Slavia Praha, SFC Opava, Slavia Praha, Slovácko, Slavia Praha, Slovácko

*** Heller - Diego Heller (a) 20/11/2004, ¿? (Switzerland) (b) 1,80 (c) G (d) FC Lucerna (e) -

*** Hellichius - Fritiof Hellichius (a) 03/08/2003, Trelleborg (Sweden) (b) 1,84 (c) M - central midfielder (d) IFK Norrköping (e) Sylvia, Norrköping, Sylvia

*** Hellisá - Mikkjal Hellisá (Mikkjal Samuelsen Hellisá) (a) 18/02/2002, ¿? (Faroe Islands) (b) 1,85 (c) D - central defense (d) EB/Streymur (e) EB/S II

*** Hellisdal - Markus Hellisdal (a) 11/10/2002, ¿? (Faroe Islands) (b) - (c) D - central defense (d) EB/Streymur (e) B36 Tórshavn, B36 II

*** Hellisdal - Mattias Hellisdal (Mattias Johnnyson Hellisdal) (a) 21/01/2006, ¿? (Faroe Islands) (b) - (c) M - central midfielder (d) B36 Tórshavn (e) -

*** Hellman - Emil Hellman (a) 20/04/2001, ¿? (Sweden) (b) - (c) D - left back (d) Helsingborgs IF (e) Ängelholms FF, Helsingborgs IF

*** Hemed - Tomer Hemed (תומר חמד) (a) 02/05/1987, Kiryat Tiv'on (Israel) (b) 1,82 (c) F - center forward (d) Hapoel Beer Sheva (e) Western Sydney, Wellington P., Charlton Ath., Brighton & Hove Albion, Queen's Park Rangers, Brighton & Hove Albion, UD Almería, RCD Mallorca, Maccabi Haifa, M. Ahi Nazareth, Maccabi Haifa, Bnei Yehuda, Maccabi Haifa, Maccabi Herzlya, Maccabi Haifa

*** Hemming - Zach Hemming (Zachary Hemming) (a) 07/03/2000, Bishop Auckland (England) (b) - (c) G (d) St. Mirren FC (e) St. Mirren, Kilmarnock FC, Kilmarnock FC, Blyth Spartans, Hartlepool Utd., Darlington

*** Hen - Eyal Hen (אייל חן) (a) 14/03/2000, ¿? (Iceland) (b) - (c) F - left winger (d) Bnei Yehuda Tel Aviv (e) Bnei Yehuda, Maccabi Tel Aviv, Hapoel Hadera, Maccabi Tel Aviv, B TLV Bat Yam, Maccabi Tel Aviv

*** Hend - Bilal Hend (a) 18/01/2000, ¿? (France) (b) - (c) F - left winger (d) FC Versailles 78 (e) Progrès Niederkorn, Amnéville, US Sarre-Union

*** Henderson - Alex Henderson (a) 21/08/2004, Limavady (Northern Ireland) (b) - (c) G (d) Dundela FC (e) Dundela FC, Glentoran, Airdrieonians

*** Henderson - Cohen Henderson (a) 29/07/2006, Lurgan (Northern Ireland) (b) - (c) F - center forward (d) Glenavon FC (e) -

*** Henderson - Dean Henderson (Dean Bradley Henderson) (a) 12/03/1997, Whitehaven (England) (b) 1,88 (c) G (d) Manchester United (e) Nottingham Forest, Manchester Utd., Sheffield Utd., Shrewsbury, Grimsby Town, Stockport

*** Henderson - Euan Henderson (a) 29/06/2000, Edinburgh (Scotland) (b) 1,75 (c) F - left winger (d) Hamilton Academical FC (e) Heart of Midlothian, Queen's Park, Heart of Midlothian, Alloa Athletic, Heart of Midlothian, Alloa Athletic, Heart of Midlothian, Hearts FC II, Montrose, Hearts FC II, Hutchison Vale BC

*** Henderson - Ewan Henderson (a) 27/03/2000, Edinburgh (Scotland) (b) 1,86 (c) M - attacking midfielder (d) Hibernian FC (e) Celtic FC, Hibernian FC, Celtic FC, Dunfermline A., Celtic FC, Celtic Reserves, Ross County, Celtic Reserves

*** Henderson - Jack Henderson (Jack Henderson) (a) 17/06/2000, Belfast (Northern Ireland) (b) 1,85 (c) M - pivot (d) Bangor FC (e) Ballymena, Bangor, Crusaders, Glentoran

*** Henderson - Jay Henderson (a) 07/03/2002, Irvine (Scotland) (b) 1,68 (c) M - right midfielder (d) Ross County FC (e) St. Mirren, Inverness Caledonian, St. Mirren, Clyde FC, St. Mirren, St. Mirren B

*** Henderson - Jordan Henderson (Jordan Brian Henderson) (a) 17/06/1990, Sunderland (England) (b) 1,87 (c) M - central midfielder (d) Al-Ettifaq FC (e) Liverpool, Sunderland, Coventry City, Sunderland

*** Henderson - Liam Henderson (a) 25/04/1996, Livingston (Scotland) (b) 1,83 (c) M (d) FC Empoli (e) Lecce, Hellas Verona, Empoli, Hellas Verona, Bari, Celtic FC, Hibernian FC, Celtic FC, Rosenborg, Celtic FC

*** Hendija - Krunoslav Hendija (a) 19/03/1989, Zagreb (Yugoslavia, now in Croatia) (b) 1,94 (c) G (d) NK Lokomotiva Zagreb (e) NK Rudes, Stuben, NK Lucko, NK Gaj (M), HASK Zagreb, NK ZET 1927, NK Lokomotiva, NK Maksimir, NK Lokomotiva

*** Hendrick - Jeff Hendrick (Jeffrey Patrick Hendrick) (a) 31/01/1992, Dublin (Ireland) (b) 1,85 (c) M - central midfielder (d) Newcastle United (e) Reading, Newcastle Utd., Queen's Park Rangers, Newcastle Utd., Burnley, Derby, St. Kevins Boys

*** Hendriks - Ramon Hendriks (a) 18/07/2001, Dordrecht (Netherlands) (b) 1,89 (c) D - central defense (d) Feyenoord Rotterdam (e) FC Utrecht, Feyenoord, NAC Breda

*** Hendriks - Sam Hendriks (a) 25/01/1995, Doetinchem (Netherlands) (b) 1,80 (c) F - center forward (d) - (e) Olympiakos N., SC Cambuur, De Graafschap, SC Cambuur, Go Ahead Eagles, OH Leuven, SC Cambuur, OH Leuven, SC Cambuur, OH Leuven, Go Ahead Eagles, Ajax B, De Graafschap

*** Hendriks - Tom Hendriks (a) 14/05/2002, Heerlen (Netherlands) (b) 1,86 (c) G (d) Fortuna Sittard (e) -

*** Hendrikson - Oskar Hendrikson (a) 19/09/2004, Tallinn (Estonia) (b) - (c) G (d) - (e) FC Kose

*** Hendrix - Jorrit Hendrix (Jorrit Petrus Carolina Hendrix) (a) 06/02/1995, Panningen (Netherlands) (b) 1,81 (c) M - pivot (d) - (e) Fortuna Düsseldorf, Spartak Moskva, Feyenoord, Spartak Moskva, PSV Eindhoven

*** Hendry - Jack Hendry (Jack William Hendry) (a) 07/05/1995, Glasgow (Scotland) (b) 1,92 (c) D - central defense (d) Al-Ettifaq FC (e) KV Brugge, Cremonese, KV Brugge, KV Oostende, Celtic FC, KV Oostende, Celtic FC, Melbourne City, Celtic FC, Dundee FC, Wigan Ath., MK Dons, Wigan Ath., Shrewsbury, Wigan Ath., Partick Thistle

*** Henen - David Henen (David Boris Philippe Henen) (a) 19/04/1996, Libramont-Chevigny (Belgium) (b) 1,86 (c) F - left winger (d) KV Kortrijk (e) Grenoble, RSC Charleroi, Fleetwood, Olympiakos, AS Monaco B

*** Henkinet - Laurent Henkinet (Laurent Claude Henkinet) (a) 14/09/1992, Rocourt (Belgium) (b) 1,88 (c) G (d) Standard de Lieja (e) OH Leuven, Waasland-Beveren, KV Kortrijk, Standard Liège, Dessel Sport, Standard Liège, Sint-Truiden, Standard Liège, Dessel Sport, Standard Liège, Sint-Truiden

*** Hennessey - Wayne Hennessey (Wayne Robert Hennessey) (a) 24/01/1987, Beaumaris (Wales) (b) 1,98 (c) G (d) Nottingham Forest (e) Burnley, Crystal Palace, Wolverhampton Wanderers, Yeovil Town, Wolverhampton Wanderers, Stockport, Wolverhampton Wanderers, Bristol City, Wolverhampton Wanderers

*** Hennetier - Jonathan Hennetier (a) 06/11/1991, ¿? (France) (b) - (c) D - right back (d) FC Schifflange 95 (e) RFCU Luxembourg, Amnéville

*** Henrichs - Benjamin Henrichs (a) 23/02/1997, Bocholt (Germany) (b) 1,85 (c) D - right back (d) RB Leipzig (e) AS Monaco, RB Leipzig, AS Monaco, Bayer Leverkusen

*** Henriksen - Markus Henriksen (a) 25/07/1992, Trondheim (Norway) (b) 1,87 (c) D - central defense (d) Rosenborg BK (e) Hull City, Bristol City, Hull City, AZ Alkmaar, Hull City, AZ Alkmaar, Rosenborg

*** Henriksrud - Oliver Henriksrud (Oliver Odde Henriksrud) (a) 08/08/2005, Skedsmo (Norway) (b) - (c) F - center forward (d) Lillestrøm SK II (e) -
*** Henriksson - Elmo Henriksson (a) 10/03/2003, ¿? (Finland) (b) 1,99 (c) G (d) IFK Mariehamn (e) HJK Helsinki, HJK Klubi 04
*** Henriksson - Gustav Henriksson (Gustav Niklas Henriksson) (a) 03/02/1998, Grebbestad (Sweden) (b) 1,90 (c) D - central defense (d) IF Elfsborg (e) Wolfsberger AC, Elfsborg, Grebbestads IF
*** Henrique - Henrique (Henrique Roberto Rafael) (a) 23/08/1993, Santa Rita do Sapucaí (Brazil) (b) 1,78 (c) F - left winger (d) Sampaio Corrêa Futebol Clube (MA) (e) CSKA 1948, Marítimo, CSKA-Sofia, At. Mineiro, CSKA-Sofia, At. Mineiro, Novorizontino, At. Mineiro, Paraná, At. Mineiro, EC Bahia, At. Mineiro, At. Mineiro B, Paraná, At. Mineiro B, XV Piracicaba, At. Mineiro B
*** Henrique - Alan Henrique (Alan Henrique Ferreira Bastos Soares) (a) 19/06/1991, Belo Horizonte (Brazil) (b) 1,89 (c) D - central defense (d) IFK Mariehamn (e) Santa Lucía C., FC Lahti, IFK Mariehamn, FK Bylis, Varzim, Sriwijaya FC, FC Inter, Umm Salal SC, Nacional, EC Vitória, Beira-Mar, EC Vitória, Duque de Caxias, EC Vitória, Botafogo-BA, EC Vitória, Boa Esporte, EC Vitória, Vitória B
*** Henrique - Paulo Henrique (Paulo Henrique Rodrigues Cabral) (a) 23/10/1996, Fenais da Luz (Portugal) (b) 1,82 (c) D - left back (d) CD Santa Clara (e) Penafiel, Paços Ferreira, SC Covilhã, Paços Ferreira, Santa Clara
*** Henrique Motta - Henrique Motta (Henrique Marcelino Motta) (a) 10/01/1991, Cravinhos (Brazil) (b) 1,88 (c) D - central defense (d) Zebbug Rangers FC (e) Zejtun C., Sirens FC, Persipura, Zejtun C., Penapolense, Portuguesa, UR Trabalhadores, Portuguesa, Olímpia-SP, HAGL FC, Mogi Mirim, São Bento (SP), Mogi Mirim, Rio Branco-SP, Duque de Caxias, Comercial-SP, Votoraty-SP
*** Henríquez - Ángelo Henríquez (Ángelo José Henríquez Iturra) (a) 13/04/1994, La Reina (Chile) (b) 1,75 (c) F - center forward (d) Baltika Kaliningrad (e) Miedź Legnica, Fortaleza, U. de Chile, Atlas, Dinamo Zagreb, Manchester Utd., Dinamo Zagreb, Manchester Utd., Real Zaragoza, Manchester Utd., Wigan Ath., Manchester Utd., U. de Chile
*** Henry - Loris Henry (a) 09/05/2002, ¿? (Belgium) (b) 1,90 (c) D - central defense (d) Jong KAA Gent (e) Excelsior Mouscron
*** Henry - Rico Henry (Rico Antonio Henry) (a) 08/07/1997, Birmingham (England) (b) 1,70 (c) D - left back (d) Brentford FC (e) FC Walsall
*** Henry - Thomas Henry (a) 20/09/1994, Argenteuil (France) (b) 1,91 (c) F - center forward (d) Hellas Verona (e) Venezia, OH Leuven, AFC Tubize, FC Chambly Oise, FC Nantes B, Fréjus-St-Raphaël, AS Beauvais
*** Henty - Ezekiel Henty (a) 13/05/1993, Lagos (Nigeria) (b) 1,85 (d) AEL Limassol (e) Slovan Bratislava, Apollon Limassol, Slovan Bratislava, Al-Hazem, Slovan Bratislava, Puskás AFC, NK Osijek, Puskás AFC, Vidi FC, Puskás AFC, Videoton FC, Lokomotiv Moskva, FC Baniyas, Lokomotiv Moskva, Olimpija, AC Milan, Olimpija, AC Milan, ND Gorica, AC Milan, Perugia, AC Milan, Spezia, Flying Sports
*** Hentze - Mikkjal Hentze (a) 08/12/1986, ¿? (Faroe Islands) (b) - (c) M - pivot (d) - (e) AB Argir II, AB Argir, AB Argir II, AB Argir, Giza/Hoyvík, AB Argir, B71 Sandoy
*** Hentze - Paetur Hentze (Pætur Hentze) (a) 06/11/1999, ¿? (Faroe Islands) (b) - (c) D - right back (d) NSÍ Runavík (e) NSÍ II
*** Hentze - Rói Hentze (Rói Mørk Hentze) (a) 22/09/1999, Tórshavn (Faroe Islands) (b) 1,86 (c) G (d) KÍ Klaksvík (e) B68 Toftir, B36 Tórshavn, HB Tórshavn, B36 II, B36 Tórshavn, B36 II

*** Heras - Nacho Heras (Ignacio Heras Anglada) (a) 27/08/1991, Madrid (Spain) (b) 1,82 (c) D - central defense (d) Keflavík ÍF (e) Leiknir, Víkingur Ó., UP Plasencia, Tatabánya, RCD Espanyol B, At. Madrid C

*** Herbert - Anthony Herbert (Anthony Dwight Herbert) (a) 18/04/1998, Brooklyn (United States) (b) 1,93 (c) D - central defense (d) FC Haka (e) Red Storm, FD Knights

*** Herc - Christian Herc (Christián Herc) (a) 30/09/1998, Levice (Slovakia) (b) 1,85 (c) M - central midfielder (d) DAC Dunajska Streda (e) Grasshoppers, Karvina, Viktoria Plzen, Dunajska Streda

*** Herceg - Karlo Herceg (a) 17/09/2005, Zagreb (Croatia) (b) - (c) M (d) - (e) NK Sesvetski Kraljevec

*** Heredia - Manu Heredia (Manuel Heredia Montoya) (a) 12/01/1995, Jerez de la Frontera (Spain) (b) - (c) F - left winger (d) Europa FC (e) Conil CF, CD Rota, Conil CF, Xerez Deportivo, Sanluqueño, Arcos CF, Xerez CD

*** Hérelle - Christophe Hérelle (a) 22/08/1992, Nizza (France) (b) 1,88 (c) D - central defense (d) Stade Brestois 29 (e) OGC Nice, Troyes, US Créteil-Lusitanos, SR Colmar, FC Sochaux, SR Colmar, FC Sochaux, FC Sochaux B

*** Heric - Elvedin Heric (Elvedin Herić) (a) 09/02/1997, Augsburg (Germany) (b) 1,78 (c) M - central midfielder (d) - (e) KF Vllaznia, SV Kapfenberg, Sloboda Tuzla, NK Triglav, SV Kapfenberg, FK Sarajevo

*** Herman - Guy Herman (גיא הרמן) (a) 19/06/2000, ¿? (Israel) (b) - (c) G (d) Hapoel Hadera (e) AS Ashdod, Maccabi Haifa, Ironi Or Yehuda, Maccabi Haifa

*** Herman - Roy Herman (רועי הרמן) (a) 21/06/2000, ¿? (Israel) (b) 1,87 (c) D - right back (d) Botev Plovdiv (e) Hapoel Raanana, B. Jerusalem, Hapoel Raanana

*** Hermandung - Till Hermandung (a) 10/10/1997, Nastätten (Germany) (b) 1,78 (c) M - pivot (d) - (e) Etzella Ettelbrück, Drochtersen/A., SV Elversberg, Eintracht Trier

*** Hermannsson - Breki Thór Hermannsson (Breki Þór Hermannsson) (a) 20/03/2003, ¿? (Iceland) (b) - (c) M - right midfielder (d) ÍA Akranes (e) Kári

*** Hermannsson - Heidar Máni Hermannsson (Heiður Máni Hermannsson) (a) 12/10/2005, ¿? (Iceland) (b) 1,94 (c) G (d) FH Hafnarfjördur (e) -

*** Hermansen - Andreas Hermansen (Andreas Kampp Kiilerich Hermansen) (a) 01/05/2004, ¿? (Denmark) (b) - (c) G (d) AC Horsens (e) -

*** Hermansen - Mads Hermansen (a) 11/07/2000, Odense (Denmark) (b) 1,87 (c) G (d) Leicester City (e) Brøndby IF

*** Hermoso - Mario Hermoso (Mario Hermoso Canseco) (a) 18/06/1995, Madrid (Spain) (b) 1,84 (c) D - central defense (d) Atlético de Madrid (e) RCD Espanyol, RM Castilla, Real Valladolid, RM Castilla, Real Madrid C

*** Hernandez - Andrew Hernandez (Andrew Albert Hernandez) (a) 10/01/1999, Gibraltar (Gibraltar) (b) 1,74 (c) M - pivot (d) Europa FC (e) St Joseph's FC, Lincoln FC, Uni Notting, Gibraltar Utd.

*** Hernandez - Anthony Hernandez (Anthony Alland Hernandez) (a) 03/02/1995, Gibraltar (Gibraltar) (b) 1,82 (c) M - attacking midfielder (d) FC Bruno's Magpies (e) Europa FC, Lincoln FC, Gibraltar Utd., Manchester 62, Cádiz CF B

*** Hernández - Aldayr Hernández (Aldayr Hernández Basanta) (a) 04/08/1995, Magangué (Colombia) (b) 1,85 (c) D - central defense (d) FC Honka (e) Helsinki IFK, TPS, Bekaa SC, Rocha FC, Bogotá FC

*** Hernández - Aridane Hernández (Aridane Hernández Umpiérrez) (a) 23/03/1989, Tuineje (Spain) (b) 1,88 (c) D - central defense (d) Rayo Vallecano (c) CA Osasuna, Cádiz CF, Granada CF, Cádiz CF, Granada CF, CD Eldense, CD Corralejo, Alavés, Atlético Ceuta, R. Valladolid B

*** Hernández - Héctor Hernández (Héctor José Hernández Marrero) (a) 14/09/1995, Las Palmas de Gran Canaria (Spain) (b) 1,80 (c) F - center forward (d) GD Chaves (e) Rayo Majadahonda, Cultural Leonesa, CF Fuenlabrada, Atlético Madrid, Rayo Majadahonda, Atlético Madrid, Málaga CF, Atlético Madrid, Albacete, Atlético Madrid, Albacete, Atlético Madrid, Elche CF, Atlético Madrid, At. Madrid B
*** Hernández - Javi Hernández (Javier Hernández Carrera) (a) 02/05/1998, Jerez de la Frontera (Spain) (b) 1,85 (c) D - left back (d) Cádiz CF (e) Cádiz CF, CD Leganés, Girona FC, CD Leganés, RM Castilla, Real Oviedo, RM Castilla, CP El Ejido, RM Castilla
*** Hernández - Jorge Hernández (Jorge Hernández Zapién) (a) 08/11/2000, Sahuayo de Morelos (Mexico) (b) 1,70 (c) M - attacking midfielder (d) San Antonio FC (e) KV Mechelen, Chornomorets, LA Galaxy II, UC Irvine, LA Galaxy II, LA Galaxy II, LA Galaxy II
*** Hernández - Lucas Hernández (Lucas François Bernard Hernández Pi) (a) 14/02/1996, Marseille (France) (b) 1,84 (c) D - central defense (d) París Saint-Germain FC (e) Bayern München, Atlético Madrid, At. Madrid B
*** Hernández - Luis Hernández (Luis Hernández Rodríguez) (a) 14/04/1989, Madrid (Spain) (b) 1,82 (c) D - central defense (d) Cádiz CF (e) Maccabi Tel Aviv, Málaga CF, Leicester City, Real Sporting, Sporting B, RM Castilla, Real Madrid C
*** Hernández - Mario Hernández (Mario Hernández Fernández) (a) 25/01/1999, Madrid (Spain) (b) 1,77 (c) D - right back (d) Real Oviedo (e) Rayo Vallecano, UD Sanse, Rayo Vallecano, UD Melilla, Rayo Vallecano, Rayo B, At. Onubense, Rayo B
*** Hernández - Theo Hernández (Theo Bernard François Hernández) (a) 06/10/1997, Marseille (France) (b) 1,84 (c) D - left back (d) AC Milan (e) Real Madrid, Real Sociedad, Real Madrid, Atlético Madrid, Alavés, Atlético Madrid, At. Madrid B
*** Hernández - Unai Hernández (Unai Hernández Lorenzo) (a) 14/12/2004, Badalona (Spain) (b) 1,71 (c) M - central midfielder (d) FC Barcelona Atlètic (e) -
*** Hernandez Martínez - Jose Gines Hernandez Martínez (José Ginés Hernández Martínez) (a) 28/02/1996, Orihuela (Spain) (b) 1,73 (c) F - left winger (d) UE Sant Julia (e) Ordino B, Orihuela Dep.
*** Hernández-Foster - Kobe Hernández-Foster (Kobe André Hernández-Foster) (a) 26/06/2002, Los Angeles, California (United States) (b) 1,73 (c) M - pivot (d) Hamarkameratene (e) LA Galaxy II
*** Hernâni - Hernâni (Hernâni Infande Tchuda da Silva) (a) 03/04/2001, Bissau (Guinea-Bissau) (b) 1,78 (c) F - right winger (d) SC Braga (e) Paços Ferreira, SC Braga
*** Hernâni - Hernâni (Hernâni Jorge Santos Fortes) (a) 20/08/1991, Lisboa (Portugal) (b) 1,80 (c) F - right winger (d) Rio Ave FC (e) UD Las Palmas, Levante UD, Al-Wehda, Levante UD, FC Porto, Vitória Guimarães, FC Porto, Olympiakos, FC Porto, Vitória Guimarães, Vitória Guimarães B, Atlético CP, Mirandela, Atlético CP
*** Herold - David Herold (a) 20/02/2003, Mindelheim (Germany) (b) 1,85 (c) D - left back (d) Karlsruher SC (e) Karlsruher SC, FC Bayern II, SCR Altach, FC Bayern II
*** Heron - Heron (Heron Crespo da Silva) (a) 17/08/2000, Rio de Janeiro (Brazil) (b) 1,86 (c) D - central defense (d) Atlético Clube Goianiense (e) Goiás, FC Sheriff, Goiás, Vejle BK, Goiás, Osvaldo-SP
*** Herr - Téo Herr (a) 12/02/2001, ¿? (France) (b) 1,85 (c) F (d) FC Schifflange 95 (e) Etzella Ettelbrück, Saarbrücken

*** Herrando - Jorge Herrando (Jorge Herrando Oroz) (a) 28/02/2001, Pamplona (Spain) (b) 1,92 (c) D - central defense (d) CA Osasuna (e) Osasuna Prom., UD Logroñés, Osasuna Prom.

*** Herrera - Ander Herrera (Ander Herrera Agüera) (a) 14/08/1989, Bilbao (Spain) (b) 1,82 (c) M - central midfielder (d) Athletic Club (e) Paris Saint-Germain, Athletic, Paris Saint-Germain, Manchester Utd., Athletic, Real Zaragoza, Real Zaragoza B

*** Herrera - Andris Herrera (Andris Jesus Herrera Salgado) (a) 20/10/1996, Caracas, Distrito Capital (Venezuela) (b) 1,75 (c) F - attacking midfielder (d) NK Varazdin (e) Yaracuyanos, Estudiantes, Caracas FC B, Portuguesa FC, Caracas FC B

*** Herrera - Eduardo Herrera (Eduardo Andres Mangles Herrera) (a) 01/11/2004, ¿? (Netherlands) (b) - (c) F (d) - (e) Hibernians FC Valletta

*** Herrera - Sebastián Herrera (Sebastián Herrera Cardona) (a) 23/01/1995, Bello, Antioquia (Colombia) (b) 1,78 (c) D - left back (d) FK Borac Banja Luka (e) Doxa Katokopias, Bregalnica Stip, MTK Budapest, Rabotnicki, Pereira

*** Herrera - Sergio Herrera (Sergio Herrera Pirón) (a) 05/06/1993, Miranda de Ebro (Spain) (b) 1,92 (c) G (d) CA Osasuna (e) SD Huesca, SD Amorebieta, Depor. Alavés B, CD Laudio, Depor. Alavés B

*** Herrera - Yangel Herrera (Yangel Clemente Herrera Ravelo) (a) 07/01/1998, La Guaira, Vargas (Venezuela) (b) 1,84 (c) M - central midfielder (d) Girona FC (e) Manchester City, Girona FC, Manchester City, RCD Espanyol, Manchester City, Granada CF, Manchester City, SD Huesca, Manchester City, New York City, Manchester City, At. Venezuela, Monagas SC, At. Venez. B

*** Herrerín - Iago Herrerín (Iago Herrerín Buisán) (a) 25/01/1988, Bilbao (Spain) (b) 1,87 (c) G (d) AEK Larnaca (e) Valencia CF, Al-Raed, Athletic, CD Leganés, Athletic, CD Numancia, Athletic, At. Madrid B, Bilbao Athletic, CD Basconia, Barakaldo CF, CD Basconia

*** Herrington - Diesel Herrington (a) 04/08/2004, ¿? (Australia) (b) - (c) D - central defense (d) Aarhus GF (e) -

*** Herrmann - Patrick Herrmann (a) 12/02/1991, Uchtelfangen (Germany) (b) 1,79 (c) F - right winger (d) Borussia Mönchengladbach (e) -

*** Herron - John Herron (a) 01/02/1994, Coatbridge (Scotland) (b) 1,80 (c) M - central midfielder (d) FC Manchester 62 (e) Dandenong City, Larne FC, Glentoran, Raith Rovers, Blackpool, Dunfermline A., Blackpool, Celtic FC, Cowdenbeath FC, Celtic FC

*** Hershkovitz - Eden Hershkovitz (הרשקוביץ עדן) (a) 23/08/1997, ¿? (Israel) (b) 1,81 (c) F - attacking midfielder (d) Sekzia Ness Ziona (e) SC Kfar Qasem, Floriana, Hapoel Tel Aviv, B TLV Bat Yam, Hapoel Tel Aviv, H. Ramat Gan, Hapoel Tel Aviv, Karmiotissa, Hapoel Tel Aviv, H. Ramat Gan, Hapoel Tel Aviv

*** Hertsi - Loorents Hertsi (a) 13/11/1992, Helsinki (Finland) (b) 1,69 (c) M - right midfielder (d) FC Lahti (e) AC Oulu, FC Lahti, VPS, FC Lahti, Hämeenlinna, FC Lahti

*** Héry - Bastien Héry (Bastien Charles Patrick Hery) (a) 23/03/1992, Brou-sur-Chantereine (France) (b) 1,75 (c) M - central midfielder (d) Longford Town FC (e) Finn Harps, Galway United, Finn Harps, Bohemians, Derry City, Bohemians, Linfield, Waterford FC, Limerick FC, Accrington St., Carlisle United, AFC Rochdale, Sheffield Wednesday, Paris Saint Germain B

*** Herzig - Marius Herzig (a) 17/12/1999, Waldkirchen (Germany) (b) 1,88 (c) G (d) - (e) Sevilla FC C, Wacker Burghausen, 1860 Rosenheim

*** Hesden - Rhys Hesden (a) 20/10/2002, ¿? (Wales) (b) - (c) F - right winger (d) Caersws FC (e) Newtown, Llanidloes, Newtown

*** Hestad - Eirik Hestad (a) 26/06/1995, Aureosen (Norway) (b) 1,83 (c) F - right winger (d) Molde FK (e) Pafos FC, Molde
*** Hetemaj - Mehdi Hetemaj (a) 07/05/1997, St. Pölten (Austria) (b) 1,89 (c) D - central defense (d) - (e) AC Oulu, Mosta FC, FK Kukësi, Wiener Neustadt, SV Horn
*** Hetemaj - Mehmet Hetemaj (a) 08/12/1987, Skenderaj (Yugoslavia, now in Kosovo) (b) 1,86 (c) M - pivot (d) Perparim Hetemaj (e) SJK Seinäjoki, Monza, UC AlbinoLeffe, FC Honka, UC AlbinoLeffe, Reggina, UC AlbinoLeffe, Panionios, UC AlbinoLeffe, Panionios, Thrasyvoulos, Panionios, HJK Helsinki, FC Viikingit, HJK Helsinki
*** Hetemaj - Perparim Hetemaj (Përparim Hetemaj) (a) 12/12/1986, Skënderaj (Yugoslavia, now in Kosovo) (b) 1,79 (c) M - central midfielder (d) HJK Helsinki (e) Reggina, Benevento, Chievo Verona, Brescia, FC Twente, AEK Athína, Apol. Kalamarias, AEK Athína, HJK Helsinki, HJK Klubi 04
*** Hey - Lucas Hey (Lucas Boel Hey) (a) 13/04/2003, ¿? (Denmark) (b) 1,89 (c) D - central defense (d) FC Nordsjælland (e) Lyngby BK
*** Heylen - Michaël Heylen (a) 03/01/1994, Wommelgem (Belgium) (b) 1,87 (c) D - central defense (d) FC Emmen (e) Sparta Rotterdam, FC Emmen, Zulte Waregem, RSC Anderlecht, KVC Westerlo, RSC Anderlecht, KV Kortrijk, RSC Anderlecht
*** Heymans - Daan Heymans (a) 15/06/1999, Turnhout (Belgium) (b) 1,89 (c) M - attacking midfielder (d) RSC Charleroi (e) Venezia, RSC Charleroi, Venezia, Waasland-Beveren, Lommel SK, Waasland-Beveren, KVC Westerlo
*** Heynen - Bryan Heynen (a) 06/02/1997, Bree (Belgium) (b) 1,83 (c) M - central midfielder (d) KRC Genk (e) -
*** Hibbert - Ellis Hibbert (a) 14/06/2004, ¿? (Wales) (b) - (c) M - attacking midfielder (d) Treowen Stars (e) Cambrian & C., Pontypridd
*** Hickey - Aaron Hickey (Aaron Buchanan Hickey) (a) 10/06/2002, Glasgow (Scotland) (b) 1,85 (c) D - right back (d) Brentford FC (e) Bologna, Heart of Midlothian
*** Hidi - Patrik Hidi (a) 27/11/1990, Györ (Hungary) (b) 1,86 (c) M - pivot (d) Budapesti VSC - Zugló (e) Vasas FC, Honvéd, Irtysh, Honvéd, Real Oviedo, Honvéd
*** Hidi M. - Sándor Hidi M. (a) 20/02/2001, Velyka Dobron (Ukraine) (b) 1,80 (c) M - pivot (d) Vasas FC (e) ETO FC Györ
*** Hien - Isak Hien (Isak Malcolm Kwaku Hien) (a) 13/01/1999, Kista (Sweden) (b) 1,91 (c) D - central defense (d) Hellas Verona (e) Djurgården, Vasalunds IF, Djurgården, Vasalunds IF
*** Hierländer - Stefan Hierländer (a) 03/02/1991, Villach (Austria) (b) 1,80 (c) M - right midfielder (d) SK Sturm Graz (e) RB Leipzig, RB Salzburg, Austria Kärnten
*** Higgins - Donal Higgins (a) 10/09/2001, ¿? (Ireland) (b) - (c) M - central midfielder (d) University College Dublin (e) Galway United
*** Higor Gabriel - Higor Gabriel (Higor Gabriel Fernandes Alves) (a) 28/04/1999, Jaguariúna (Brazil) (b) 1,88 (c) D - central defense (d) Sabah FK (e) PFK Lviv, Sabah FK, Dinamo Minsk, Sabah FK
*** Hila - Ardit Hila (a) 06/01/1993, Elbasan (Albania) (b) 1,85 (c) M - pivot (d) KF Tirana (e) FK Kukësi, SC Gjilani, FC Prishtina, FK Partizani, KF Teuta, KF Elbasani
*** Hilander - Mika Hilander (a) 17/08/1983, Tampere (Finland) (b) 1,93 (c) G (d) - (e) FC Haka, Ilves, KuPS, Tampere United, TPV, Tampere United, PP-70, Tampere United, Ilves
*** Hilgers - Mees Hilgers (a) 13/05/2001, Amersfoort (Netherlands) (b) 1,85 (c) D - central defense (d) FC Twente Enschede (e) -
*** Hili - Benjamin Hili (a) 16/02/2004, ¿? (Malta) (b) - (c) M - attacking midfielder (d) Balzan FC (e) -

*** Hill - James Hill (James Clayton Hill) (a) 10/01/2002, Bristol (England) (b) 1,84 (c) D - central defense (d) AFC Bournemouth (e) Heart of Midlothian, Bournemouth, Fleetwood

*** Hillier - Aaron Hillier (Aaron Jack Hillier) (a) 23/10/2003, ¿? (Wales) (b) - (c) F - left winger (d) Trefelin Boys & Girls Club (e) Briton Ferry, Pontypridd DVP

*** Hillson - James Hillson (James Andrew Hillson) (a) 14/01/2001, ¿? (England) (b) - (c) G (d) - (e) Salisbury

*** Hilmarsson - Alex Freyr Hilmarsson (a) 26/07/1993, ¿? (Iceland) (b) 1,80 (c) M - central midfielder (d) ÍBV Vestmannaeyjar (e) KR Reykjavík, Kórdrengir, KR Reykjavík, Víkingur, Grindavík, Sindri

*** Hilmarsson - Dagur Austmann Hilmarsson (a) 02/06/1998, ¿? (Iceland) (b) - (c) D - central defense (d) UMF Grindavík (e) Leiknir, Thróttur, ÍBV Vestmannaeyjar, Stjarnan, Afturelding, Stjarnan

*** Hilmarsson - Henrik Máni B. Hilmarsson (a) 16/02/2003, ¿? (Iceland) (b) - (c) M (d) Stjarnan Gardabaer (e) KFG Gardabaer

*** Hilmarsson - Hilmar Starri Hilmarsson (a) 27/07/2004, ¿? (Iceland) (b) 2,00 (c) D - central defense (d) Valur Reykjavík (e) -

*** Hilmarsson - Máni Hilmarsson (Máni Austmann Hilmarsson) (a) 02/06/1998, Garðabær (Iceland) (b) 1,83 (c) F - center forward (d) Fjölnir Reykjavík (e) Hafnarfjördur, Leiknir, HK Kópavogs, Akron Zips, HK Kópavogs, Stjarnan, ÍR, Stjarnan

*** Hilo - Hassan Hilo (חילו חסן) (a) 25/11/1999, ¿? (Israel) (b) - (c) D - central defense (d) Ihud Bnei Sakhnin (e) M. Bnei Reineh, Bnei Sakhnin

*** Himeur - Thomas Himeur (a) 17/01/2001, Toulouse (France) (b) 1,92 (c) G (d) Toulouse FC (e) Toulouse B

*** Hincapié - Piero Hincapié (Piero Martín Hincapié Reyna) (a) 09/01/2002, Esmeraldas (Ecuador) (b) 1,84 (c) D - central defense (d) Bayer 04 Leverkusen (e) Talleres, Independiente, Independiente B

*** Hinchy - Jack Hinchy (a) 30/01/2003, ¿? (England) (b) - (c) M - central midfielder (d) - (e) Stockport

*** Hindle - Jack Hindle (Jack Raymond Hindle) (a) 29/10/1993, Warrington (England) (b) 1,83 (c) F - center forward (d) Warrington Rylands (e) Flint Town, Radcliffe, Matlock, Kelantan FC, Barrow, South Shields, Barrow, Gateshead, Barrow, Colwyn Bay, Radcliffe

*** Hindrich - Otto Hindrich (a) 05/08/2002, Cluj-Napoca (Romania) (b) 1,93 (c) G (d) CFR Cluj (e) Kisvárda, CFR Cluj, SSU Poli, CFR Cluj

*** Hing-Glover - Macario Hing-Glover (Macario Darwin Yen Hing-Glover; 晏新力) (a) 04/04/1995, Phoenix, Arizona (United States) (b) 1,84 (c) D - right back (d) Shanghai Shenhua (e) SJK Seinäjoki, Helsinki IFK, Spartak Trnava, NK Krsko, NK Istra, Blue Devils, Burlingame, Blue Devils

*** Hinojosa - Roberto Hinojosa (Roberto Carlos Hinojosa Marín) (a) 02/07/1999, Santa Marta (Colombia) (b) 1,70 (c) F - right winger (d) AD Union Magdalena (e) Portimonense, Union Magdalena

*** Hinokio - Koki Hinokio (檜尾 昂樹) (a) 26/02/2001, Osaka (Japan) (b) 1,65 (c) M - attacking midfielder (d) Stal Mielec (e) Zagłębie, Stal Mielec, Zagłębie, Stomil, Kumiyama HS

*** Hinora - Kristóf Hinora (a) 05/02/1998, Mór (Hungary) (b) 1,80 (c) D - right back (d) Vasas FC (e) MTK Budapest II, Vasas FC, MTK Budapest II, Nyíregyháza, MTK Budapest II

*** Hiros - Amer Hiros (Amer Hiroš) (a) 10/06/1996, Sarajevo (Bosnia and Herzegovina) (b) 1,82 (c) F - left winger (d) NK Osijek (e) HNK Sibenik, NK Osijek,

Mladost Kakanj, FK Olimpik, Mladost Kakanj, FK Gorazde, Zeljeznicar, FK Gorazde, Zeljeznicar

*** Hirsch - Adolfo Hirsch (Adolfo José Hirsch) (a) 31/01/1986, Guerrico (Argentina) (b) 1,75 (c) F - left winger (d) FC Fiorentino (e) SS Folgore, Pennarossa, La Fiorita, SS Folgore, Cosmos, Virtus, Juve Pergamino

*** Hirst - George Hirst (George David Eric Hirst) (a) 15/02/1999, Sheffield (England) (b) 1,91 (c) F - center forward (d) Ipswich Town (e) Leicester City, Ipswich, Leicester City, Blackburn, Leicester City, FC Portsmouth, Leicester City, Rotherham, Leicester City, OH Leuven

*** Hiszpanski - Fabian Hiszpanski (Fabian Hiszpański) (a) 26/10/1993, Płock (Poland) (b) 1,72 (c) D - left back (d) Wisła Płock (e) Stal Mielec, Arka Gdynia, KKS Kalisz, Bytovia Bytow, Wisla Plock II, Wisla Pulawy, Podbeskidzie, Wisła Płock, Podbeskidzie, Wisła Płock

*** Hitz - Marwin Hitz (a) 18/09/1987, St. Gallen (Switzerland) (b) 1,94 (c) G (d) FC Basel (e) Borussia Dortmund, FC Augsburg, VfL Wolfsburg

*** Hiwula - Jordy Hiwula (Jordy Hiwula-Mayifuila) (a) 21/09/1994, Manchester (England) (b) 1,78 (c) F - center forward (d) Ross County FC (e) Doncaster Rovers, FC Portsmouth, Coventry City, Huddersfield Town, Fleetwood, Huddersfield Town, Bradford City, Huddersfield Town, FC Walsall, Huddersfield Town, Wigan Ath., Huddersfield Town, FC Walsall, Yeovil Town

*** Hjaltason - Jón Jökull Hjaltason (a) 09/04/2001, ¿? (Iceland) (b) - (c) M - central midfielder (d) ÍBV Vestmannaeyjar (e) Framherjar, ÍBV Vestmannaeyjar, Thróttur Vogum, ÍBV Vestmannaeyjar

*** Hjaltested - Sverrir Páll Hjaltested (a) 27/06/2000, ¿? (Iceland) (b) 1,81 (c) F - center forward (d) ÍBV Vestmannaeyjar (e) Valur, Kórdrengir, Valur, Völsungur ÍF, Valur, KH

*** Hjelde - Leo Fuhr Hjelde (a) 26/08/2003, Nottingham (England) (b) 1,90 (c) D - left back (d) Leeds United (e) Rotherham, Leeds Utd., Celtic Reserves, Ross County, Celtic Reserves

*** Hjertø-Dahl - Jens Hjertø-Dahl (a) 31/10/2005, ¿? (Norway) (b) 1,93 (c) M - central midfielder (d) Tromsø IL (e) -

*** Hjulmand - Morten Hjulmand (Morten Blom Due Hjulmand) (a) 25/06/1999, Kastrup (Denmark) (b) 1,85 (c) M - pivot (d) Sporting de Lisboa (e) Lecce, Admira Wacker

*** Hjulsager - Andrew Hjulsager (a) 15/01/1995, Amager (Denmark) (b) 1,75 (c) M - attacking midfielder (d) KAA Gent (e) KV Oostende, RC Celta, Granada CF, RC Celta, Brøndby IF

*** Hladik - Jan Hladik (Jan Hladík) (a) 21/09/1993, Znojmo (Czech Rep.) (b) 1,84 (c) F - right winger (d) FC Zbrojovka Brno (e) SK Lisen, Otrokovice, Sigma Olomouc, Otrokovice, Sigma Olomouc, Unicov, Sigma Olomouc, 1.SC Znojmo, Sigma Olomouc, 1.SK Prostejov, Sigma Olomouc, Sigma Olomouc B

*** Hladun - Dominik Hladun (Dominik Hładun) (a) 17/09/1995, Lubin (Poland) (b) 1,90 (c) G (d) Legia de Varsovia (e) Zagłębie, Chojniczanka, Zagłębie, Zaglebie Lubin II

*** Hlavac - Martin Hlavac (Martin Hlaváč) (a) 22/08/2002, ¿? (Czech Rep.) (b) - (c) D - central defense (d) FC Hradec Kralove B (e) Nachod, Hradec Kralove B

*** Hlavaty - Michal Hlavaty (Michal Hlavatý) (a) 17/06/1998, Hořovice (Czech Rep.) (b) 1,72 (c) M - central midfielder (d) FK Pardubice (e) Viktoria Plzen, Mlada Boleslav, Viktoria Plzen, Pardubice, Viktoria Plzen, Banik Sokolov, Viktoria Plzen, Viktoria Plzen B

*** Hlavica - Jan Hlavica (a) 17/07/1994, Kelč (Czech Rep.) (b) 1,86 (c) D - central defense (d) TS Podbeskidzie Bielsko-Biala (e) Zbrojovka Brno, SK Lisen, MFK Vyskov, Sigma Olomouc B, Vitkovice, Sigma Olomouc B, 1.HFK Olomouc, Sigma Olomouc B, SK SULKO Zabreh, Sigma Olomouc B
*** Hlevnjak - Filip Hlevnjak (a) 05/08/2000, Koprivnica (Croatia) (b) 1,86 (c) D - central defense (d) Slaven Belupo Koprivnica (e) NK Sesvete, Slaven Belupo
*** Hlinason (c) M (d) Kári Akranes (e) - - Kristófer Áki Hlinason (c) M (d) Kári Akranes (e) -
*** Hlinka - Marek Hlinka (a) 04/10/1990, Banska Bystrica (Czechoslovakia, now in Slovakia) (b) 1,82 (c) M - central midfielder (d) MFK Dukla Banska Bystrica (e) Zlin, Torpedo Kutaisi, Banik Ostrava, Dukla Praha, Skalica, Dukla Praha, Spartak Trnava, Dukla Praha, Banska Bystrica
*** Hlistei - Catalin Hlistei (Cătălin Florin Hlistei) (a) 24/08/1994, Arad (Romania) (b) 1,78 (c) M - left midfielder (d) ACSM Politehnica Iasi (e) Universitatea Cluj, FC Rapid 1923, Sportul Snagov, UTA Arad, Pandurii, UTA BD
*** Hlödvers - Brynjar Hlödvers (Brynjar Hlöðvers) (a) 03/04/1989, ¿? (Iceland) (b) - (c) M - pivot (d) Leiknir Reykjavík (e) HB Tórshavn, Leiknir
*** Hlousek - Adam Hlousek (Adam Hloušek) (a) 20/12/1988, Turnov (Czechoslovakia, now in Czech Rep.) (b) 1,87 (c) D - left back (d) - (e) Zlin, Nieciecza, Viktoria Plzen, 1.FC Kaiserslautern, Viktoria Plzen, Legia Warszawa, VfB Stuttgart, 1.FC Nürnberg, FK Jablonec, Slavia Praha, FK Jablonec, Slavia Praha, 1.FC Kaiserslautern, Slavia Praha, FK Jablonec
*** Hlozek - Adam Hlozek (Adam Hložek) (a) 25/07/2002, Ivančice (Czech Rep.) (b) 1,88 (c) F - center forward (d) Bayer 04 Leverkusen (e) Sparta Praha
*** Hlynsson - Ágúst Hlynsson (Ágúst Eðvald Hlynsson) (a) 28/03/2000, Akureyri (Iceland) (b) 1,74 (c) M - attacking midfielder (d) Breidablik Kópavogur (e) AC Horsens, Valur, AC Horsens, Hafnarfjördur, AC Horsens, Víkingur, Breidablik
*** Hlynsson - Kristian Hlynsson (Kristian Nökkvi Hlynsson) (a) 23/01/2004, Odense (Denmark) (b) - (c) M - attacking midfielder (d) Ajax Amsterdam B (e) -
*** Hoare - Sean Hoare (Seán Hoare) (a) 15/03/1994, Dublin (Ireland) (b) 1,82 (c) D - central defense (d) Shamrock Rovers (e) Dundalk FC, St. Patrick's Ath.
*** Hoban - Ovidiu Hoban (Ovidiu Ştefan Hoban) (a) 27/12/1982, Baia Mare (Romania) (b) 1,82 (c) M - pivot (d) - (e) CFR Cluj, H. Beer Sheva, Petrolul, Universitatea Cluj, Gaz Metan, Bihor Oradea, U. Craiova, FK Clausen
*** Hoban - Patrick Hoban (Patrick Jefferson Hoban) (a) 28/07/1991, Galway (Ireland) (b) 1,80 (c) F - center forward (d) Dundalk FC (e) Mansfield Town, Oxford United, Grimsby Town, Oxford United, Stevenage, Oxford United, Dundalk FC, Mervue United, Bristol City, Clevedon Town FC, Bristol City, Mervue United
*** Hočko - Deni Hočko (Дени Хочко) (a) 22/04/1994, Cetinje (RF Yugoslavia, now in Montenegro) (b) 1,75 (c) M - pivot (d) - (e) Pafos FC, Excelsior Mouscron, Famalicão, Buducnost Podgorica, FK Lovcen, Lovcen II
*** Hodge - Joe Hodge (Joseph Shaun Hodge) (a) 14/09/2002, Manchester (England) (b) 1,72 (c) M - pivot (d) Wolverhampton Wanderers (e) Derry City
*** Hodgins - Gavin Hodgins (a) 06/06/2005, Darndale, Dublin (Ireland) (b) - (c) M (d) Shelbourne FC (e) -
*** Hodo - Ergi Hodo (a) 24/07/2004, Tiranë (Albania) (b) - (c) F (d) FK Bylis (e) -
*** Hodo - Xhafer Hodo (a) 03/05/2003, Ersekë (Albania) (b) - (c) M - attacking midfielder (d) FK Partizani (e) -
*** Hodson - Lee Hodson (Lee James Stephen Hodson) (a) 02/10/1991, Borehamwood (England) (b) 1,80 (c) D - right back (d) Eastleigh FC (e) Kilmarnock FC, Partick Thistle, Kilmarnock FC, Gillingham FC, St. Mirren, Gillingham FC,

Rangers FC, St. Mirren, Rangers FC, MK Dons, Kilmarnock FC, MK Dons, Watford, Brentford, Watford
*** Hodza - Selmin Hodza (Selmin Hodža) (a) 24/05/2003, Uster (Switzerland) (b) 1,78 (c) M - right midfielder (d) FC Zürich (e) -
*** Hodza - Veldin Hodza (Veldin Hodža) (a) 15/10/2002, Rijeka (Croatia) (b) 1,83 (c) M - pivot (d) HNK Rijeka (e) Hrv Dragovoljac, HNK Rijeka, NK Orijent 1919
*** Hodzic - Armin Hodzic (Armin Hodžić) (a) 17/11/1994, Sarajevo (Bosnia and Herzegovina) (b) 1,82 (c) F - center forward (d) FC Shkupi (e) Zeljeznicar, Fehérvár, Kasimpasa, Fehérvár, Dinamo Zagreb, Zeljeznicar
*** Hodzic - Armin Hodzic (Armin Hodžić) (a) 29/02/2000, Tuzla (Bosnia and Herzegovina) (b) 1,88 (c) M - central midfielder (d) Hatayspor (e) Zeljeznicar, Alcorcón, Sloboda Tuzla
*** Hodzic - Dusan Hodzic (Dušan Hodžić) (a) 31/10/1993, Majdanpek (Yugoslavia, now in Serbia) (b) 1,75 (c) D - right back (d) FK Tuzla City (e) Radnik, FK Sarajevo, Celik Zenica, FK Sarajevo, Radnik Bijelj., Mladost Obarska, Velez Mostar, Mladost Obarska, BASK Beograd, FK Palic Koming
*** Hodzic - Kadir Hodzic (a) 05/08/1994, Srebrenica (Bosnia and Herzegovina) (b) 1,79 (c) D - left back (d) BK Häcken (e) Mjällby AIF, Dalkurd, AFC Eskilstuna, Norrby, Motala AIF, Norrby, Motala AIF, Kinna IF, Skene IF
*** Hodzic - Nermin Hodzic (Nermin Hodžić) (a) 13/07/1994, Treuchtlingen (Germany) (b) 1,79 (c) M - central midfielder (d) NK Domžale (e) Rudar Prijedor, Domžale, FK Tuzla City, Adana Demirspor, Balikesirspor, Adana Demirspor, Domžale, Koper, NK Lucko, HNK Gorica, NK Lucko, NK Podgrmec, Rudar Prijedor, NK Podgrmec, Rudar Prijedor
*** Hoedemakers - Mees Hoedemakers (a) 18/02/1998, Zaandam (Netherlands) (b) 1,81 (c) M - pivot (d) NEC Nijmegen (e) SC Cambuur, AZ Alkmaar, SC Cambuur, AZ Alkmaar
*** Hoedt - Wesley Hoedt (Wesley Theodorus Hoedt) (a) 06/03/1994, Alkmaar (Netherlands) (b) 1,93 (c) D - central defense (d) Watford FC (e) RSC Anderlecht, Southampton, Lazio, Southampton, Royal Antwerp, Southampton, RC Celta, Southampton, Lazio, AZ Alkmaar
*** Höegh - Daniel Höegh (Daniel Mathias Høegh) (a) 06/01/1991, Odense (Denmark) (b) 1,90 (c) D - central defense (d) Randers FC (e) Midtjylland, Heerenveen, FC Basel, Odense BK
*** Hoekstra - Jan Hoekstra (a) 04/08/1998, Eexterveen (Netherlands) (b) 2,00 (c) G (d) FC Emmen (e) FC Groningen, PEC Zwolle, FC Groningen, Roda JC, FC Groningen
*** Hoesen - Danny Hoesen (Daniel Hoesen) (a) 15/01/1991, Heerlen (Netherlands) (b) 1,86 (c) F - center forward (d) - (e) FC Emmen, Austin, San José, FC Groningen, San José, FC Groningen, Ajax, PAOK, Ajax, Ajax B, Fulham, Fortuna Sittard, Fulham Reserves, HJK Helsinki, Fulham Reserves, Fortuna Sittard, MLS
*** Hoever - Ki-Jana Hoever (Ki-Jana Delano Hoever) (a) 18/01/2002, Amsterdam (Netherlands) (b) 1,83 (c) D - right back (d) Stoke City (e) Stoke City, Wolverhampton Wanderers, Stoke City, Wolverhampton Wanderers, PSV Eindhoven, Wolverhampton Wanderers
*** Hoff - Vebjørn Hoff (Vebjørn Alvestad Hoff) (a) 13/02/1996, Ålesund (Norway) (b) 1,81 (c) M - central midfielder (d) Lillestrøm SK (e) Rosenborg, Odd, Rosenborg, Odd, Aalesund, Spjelkavik IL
*** Hoffman - Dilivio Hoffman (a) 11/06/1997, Rotterdam (Netherlands) (b) 1,78 (c) F - left winger (d) Kozakken Boys (e) Hoogstraten VV, FC Ballkani, TEC, De Treffers, XerxesDZB

*** Hoffmann - Yann Hoffmann (a) 02/02/2002, ¿? (Luxembourg) (b) - (c) F - center forward (d) US Hostert (e) Jeunesse Esch, US Rumelange

*** Höfler - Nicolas Höfler (a) 09/03/1990, Überlingen (Germany) (b) 1,81 (c) M - pivot (d) SC Freiburg (e) Erzgebirge Aue, SC Freiburg, SC Freiburg II

*** Hofman - Albert Hofman (a) 10/04/2003, Câmpulung Moldovenesc (Romania) (b) - (c) F - center forward (d) FC Universitatea Cluj (e) -

*** Hofmann - Jonas Hofmann (a) 14/07/1992, Heidelberg (Germany) (b) 1,76 (c) F - right winger (d) Bayer 04 Leverkusen (e) Borussia Mönchengladbach, Borussia Dortmund, Mainz 05, Borussia Dortmund, Borussia Dortmund II

*** Hofmann - Maximilian Hofmann (a) 07/08/1993, Wien (Austria) (b) 1,83 (c) D - central defense (d) SK Rapid Wien (e) Rapid Wien II

*** Hofmann - Philipp Hofmann (a) 30/03/1993, Arnsberg (Germany) (b) 1,95 (c) F - center forward (d) VfL Bochum (e) Karlsruher SC, Eintracht Braunschweig, Greuther Fürth, Brentford, 1.FC Kaiserslautern, FC Schalke 04, FC Ingolstadt, FC Schalke 04, SC Paderborn, FC Schalke 04, Schalke 04 II

*** Hofmann - Stanislav Hofmann (Stanislav Hofmann) (a) 17/06/1990, ¿? (Czechoslovakia, now in Czech Rep.) (b) 1,91 (c) D - central defense (d) 1.FC Slovácko (e) Banik Sokolov, Slovácko, Banik Sokolov, Slovácko, FK Most

*** Hofmayster - Yoav Hofmayster (הופמייסטר יואב) (a) 25/12/2000, Hod HaSharon (Israel) (b) 1,82 (c) M - pivot (d) Korona Kielce (e) Kiryat Shmona, LASK, M. Petah Tikva, LASK, Hapoel Tel Aviv, LASK, Kiryat Shmona, LASK, Ramat haSharon, Maccabi Tel Aviv, B TLV Bat Yam, Maccabi Tel Aviv

*** Hogan - Luca Hogan (Luca Daniel Hogan) (a) 14/08/2005, ¿? (Wales) (b) - (c) F - center forward (d) Connah's Quay Nomads (e) -

*** Hogg - Aaron Hogg (a) 14/01/1988, Belfast (Northern Ireland) (b) 1,90 (c) G (d) Portadown FC (e) Carrick Rangers, Ards FC, Glentoran, Portadown, Crusaders

*** Högh - Christian Högh (Christian Høgh Sørensen) (a) 05/01/1995, ¿? (Denmark) (b) - (c) F - center forward (d) - (e) Skála, Aalborg BK II, Jammerbugt FC, HIK II

*** Høgh - Kasper Høgh (Kasper Waarts Thenza Høgh) (a) 06/12/2000, Randers (Denmark) (b) 1,86 (c) F - center forward (d) Stabæk Fotball (e) Aalborg BK, Stabæk, Aalborg BK, Hobro IK, Randers FC, Valur, Randers FC, Vorup FB

*** Högsberg - Lucas Högsberg (Lucas Høgsberg) (a) 23/06/2006, ¿? (Denmark) (b) - (c) D - right back (d) FC Nordsjælland (e) -

*** Höholt - Thor Höholt (Thor Høholt) (a) 19/03/2001, ¿? (Denmark) (b) 1,88 (c) D - central defense (d) Nyköbing FC (e) Lyngby BK, Nyköbing FC, Lyngby BK, B36 Tórshavn, Lyngby BK

*** Höibraten - Marius Höibraten (Marius Christopher Høibråten) (a) 23/01/1995, Oslo (Norway) (b) 1,84 (c) D - central defense (d) Urawa Red Diamonds (e) Bodø/Glimt, Sandefjord, Strømsgodset, Lillestrøm, Strømmen, Lillestrøm

*** Höj - Aron Höj (a) 12/01/2002, ¿? (Faroe Islands) (b) - (c) D - right back (d) NSÍ Runavík (e) NSÍ II, Skála IF II

*** Höjbjerg - Pierre-Emile Höjbjerg (Pierre-Emile Kordt Højbjerg) (a) 05/08/1995, København (Denmark) (b) 1,85 (c) M - central midfielder (d) Tottenham Hotspur (e) Southampton, Bayern München, FC Schalke 04, Bayern München, FC Augsburg, Bayern München, FC Bayern II, Bröndby IF II

*** Höjer - Casper Höjer (Casper Michael Højer Nielsen) (a) 20/11/1994, Copenhagen (Denmark) (b) 1,83 (c) D - left back (d) AC Sparta Praga (e) Aarhus GF, Lyngby BK, Brönshöj BK

*** Höjgaard - Hanus Höjgaard (a) 03/12/2005, ¿? (Faroe Islands) (b) - (c) F - left winger (d) B68 Toftir (e) -

*** Höjgaard - Jógvan Höjgaard (Jógvan Højgaard) (a) 14/12/2000, ¿? (Faroe Islands) (b) - (c) M - central midfielder (d) NSÍ Runavík (e) NSÍ II
*** Höjgaard - Oddur Höjgaard (a) 12/09/1989, ¿? (Faroe Islands) (b) - (c) D - central defense (d) NSÍ Runavík (e) EB/Streymur, B68 Toftir, B1908 Amager, B68 Toftir
*** Höjgaard - Sonni Höjgaard (Sonni Højgaard) (a) 02/02/1997, ¿? (Faroe Islands) (b) - (c) G (d) NSÍ Runavík III (e) B36 Tórshavn, Víkingur, Skála
*** Höjholt - Malthe Höjholt (Malthe Højholt) (a) 16/04/2001, Hjörring (Denmark) (b) 1,82 (c) M - central midfielder (d) Aalborg BK (e) -
*** Højlund - Rasmus Højlund (Rasmus Winther Højlund) (a) 04/02/2003, København (Denmark) (b) 1,91 (c) F - center forward (d) Manchester United (e) Atalanta, Sturm Graz, FC København
*** Holan - Dominik Holan (Dominik Holaň) (a) 01/07/2002, ¿? (Czech Rep.) (b) - (c) M (d) FC Banik Ostrava B (e) -
*** Holasek - Daniel Holasek (Daniel Holásek) (a) 22/04/2004, Brno (Czech Rep.) (b) 1,85 (c) D (d) 1.FC Slovácko B (e) -
*** Holban - Gabriel Holban (a) 24/10/2003, ¿? (Moldova) (b) - (c) D - central defense (d) - (e) Milsami, Dacia Buiucani
*** Holden - Louis Holden (a) 06/09/2004, Warrington (England) (b) 1,88 (c) D - central defense (d) Newcastle Town FC (e) Runcorn Linnets
*** Holder - Nathan Holder (Nathan Christopher Adam Holder) (a) 02/05/2002, Amsterdam (Netherlands) (b) - (c) M - pivot (d) Levski Sofia (e) Spartak Varna, Levski Sofia
*** Holding - Rob Holding (Robert Samuel Holding) (a) 20/09/1995, Stalybridge (England) (b) 1,89 (c) D - central defense (d) Arsenal FC (e) Bolton Wanderers, Bury
*** Holec - Dominik Holec (a) 28/07/1994, České Budějovice (Czech Rep.) (b) 1,91 (c) G (d) - (e) Sparta Praha, Lech Poznan, Sparta Praha, Rakow, Sparta Praha, MSK Zilina, FK Senica, MSK Zilina, Zlaté Moravce, MSK Zilina, Pohronie, MSK Zilina B, Teplicka nad V., MSK Zilina B
*** Holender - Filip Holender (Филип Холендер) (a) 27/07/1994, Kragujevac (RF Yugoslavia, now in Montenegro) (b) 1,80 (c) F - left winger (d) Vasas FC (e) FK Partizan, FC Lugano, FK Partizan, FC Lugano, Honvéd
*** Holenstein - Noe Holenstein (a) 25/03/2004, ¿? (Switzerland) (b) 1,79 (c) M - left midfielder (d) FC Winterthur (e) -
*** Höler - Lucas Höler (a) 10/07/1994, Achim (Germany) (b) 1,84 (c) F - center forward (d) SC Freiburg (e) SV Sandhausen, FSV Mainz 05 II, VfB Oldenburg
*** Holes - Tomas Holes (Tomáš Holeš) (a) 31/03/1993, Hradec Králové (Czech Rep.) (b) 1,80 (c) D - central defense (d) SK Slavia Praga (e) Jablonec, Hradec Kralove, Jablonec, Hradec Kralove
*** Holgado - Zane Holgado (Zane Charles Holgado) (a) 16/10/1995, ¿? (Gibraltar) (b) - (c) M - attacking midfielder (d) Europa Point FC (e) FC Hound Dogs, Mons Calpe Reserves, FC College 1975, Mons Calpe Reserves, Mons Calpe, Glacis United, Bruno's Magpies, FC Hound Dogs, Mons Calpe
*** Holgate - Mason Holgate (Mason Anthony Holgate) (a) 22/10/1996, Doncaster (England) (b) 1,87 (c) D - central defense (d) Everton FC (e) West Bromwich Albion, Everton, Barnsley FC
*** Holik - Libor Holik (Libor Holík) (a) 12/05/1998, ¿? (Czech Rep.) (b) 1,81 (c) D - right back (d) FC Viktoria Plzen (e) Jablonec, Viktoria Plzen, Jablonec, Fastav Zlin, Jihlava, Fastav Zlin, Slavia Praha, Karvina, Slavia Praha, Slavia Praha B
*** Holland - James Holland (James Robert Holland) (a) 15/05/1989, Sydney (Australia) (b) 1,82 (c) M - pivot (d) FK Austria Viena (e) LASK, Liaoning FC,

Adelaide United, MSV Duisburg, Austria Viena, AZ Alkmaar, Sparta Rotterdam, AZ Alkmaar, Newcastle, FFA C. of Excel, NSWIS
*** Holly - Dominik Holly (Dominik Hollý) (a) 11/11/2003, Bánovce nad Bebravou (Slovakia) (b) 1,81 (c) M - central midfielder (d) AS Trencin (e) -
*** Holly - Mario Holly (Mário Hollý) (a) 25/04/2000, ¿? (Slovakia) (b) 1,85 (c) M - central midfielder (d) MFK Skalica (e) -
*** Holm - Emil Holm (a) 13/05/2000, Göteborg (Sweden) (b) 1,91 (c) D - right back (d) Spezia (e) SønderjyskE, Spezia, SønderjyskE, IFK Göteborg
*** Holm - Noah Jean Holm (Noah Emmanuel Jean Holm) (a) 23/05/2001, Drammen (Norway) (b) 1,86 (c) F - center forward (d) Rosenborg BK (e) Stade Reims, Rosenborg, Vitória Guimarães
*** Holm - Odin Thiago Holm (a) 18/01/2003, Trondheim (Norway) (b) 1,75 (c) M - central midfielder (d) Celtic FC (e) Vålerenga, Tiller IL, Vålerenga
*** Holm Pedersen - Niclas Holm Pedersen (a) 15/03/2002, Engesvang (Denmark) (b) 1,80 (c) M - attacking midfielder (d) Silkeborg IF (e) -
*** Holman - Dávid Holman (a) 17/03/1993, Budapest (Hungary) (b) 1,88 (c) M - attacking midfielder (d) Budapest Honvéd FC (e) Slovan Bratislava, Debrecen, Ferencváros, Lech Poznan, Ferencváros, Ferencváros II, Ersekvadkerti
*** Holmberg - Kalle Holmberg (Karl Holmberg) (a) 03/03/1993, Örebro (Sweden) (b) 1,81 (c) F - center forward (d) Örebro SK (e) Hamrun Spartans, Djurgården, Norrköping, Örebro SK, Karlslunds IF
*** Holmé - Fredrik Holmé (a) 23/07/2001, Oslo (Norway) (b) 1,90 (c) D - central defense (d) Kongsvinger IL (e) Vålerenga, Ullensaker/Kisa, Vålerenga, Vålerenga II
*** Holmén - Kevin Holmén (a) 13/12/2001, ¿? (Sweden) (b) - (c) M - central midfielder (d) Örgryte IS (e) Örgryte, Elfsborg, Skövde AIK, Elfsborg
*** Holmén - Samuel Holmén (Samuel Tobias Holmén) (a) 28/06/1984, Annelund (Sweden) (b) 1,78 (c) M - central midfielder (d) Annelunds IF (e) Elfsborg, Basaksehir, Fenerbahce, Konyaspor, Fenerbahce, Bursaspor, Fenerbahce, Istanbul BBSK, Brøndby IF, Elfsborg, Annelunds IF
*** Holmén - Sebastian Holmén (Rasmus Sebastian Holmén) (a) 29/04/1992, Borås (Sweden) (b) 1,88 (c) D - central defense (d) IF Elfsborg (e) Çaykur Rizespor, Willem II, Dinamo Moskva, Elfsborg
*** Holmes - Danny Holmes (Daniel Holmes) (a) 06/01/1989, Birkenhead (England) (b) 1,75 (c) D - right back (d) Colwyn Bay (e) Connah's Quay, Bangor City, York City, Fylde, Newport County, Tranmere Rovers, Fleetwood, Tranmere Rovers, The New Saints, Tranmere Rovers, Southport, Tranmere Rovers
*** Holmquist Vecchia - Stefano Holmquist Vecchia (Stefano Giuseppe Arne Holmquist Vecchia) (a) 23/01/1995, Stockholm (Sweden) (b) 1,82 (c) F - left winger (d) Malmö FF (e) Rosenborg, Sirius, Brommapojkarna
*** Holp - Jaroslav Holp (a) 23/06/2004, Humenné (Slovakia) (b) 1,82 (c) D - left back (d) Zemplin Michalovce (e) -
*** Holse - Carlo Holse (Carl Johan Holse Justesen) (a) 02/06/1999, Kopenhagen (Denmark) (b) 1,77 (c) M - attacking midfielder (d) Rosenborg BK (e) FC København, Esbjerg fB, FC København
*** Holsgrove - Jordan Holsgrove (Jordan William Holsgrove) (a) 10/09/1999, Edinburgh (Scotland) (b) 1,80 (c) M - central midfielder (d) GD Estoril Praia (e) Estoril Praia, Olympiakos, Paços Ferreira, Celta B, Reading, At. Baleares, Reading
*** Holst - Frederik Holst (Frederik Lucas Holst) (a) 24/09/1994, Vanløse (Denmark) (b) 1,76 (c) M - central midfielder (d) UTA Arad (e) Helsingborgs IF, Lillestrøm, Elfsborg, Sparta Rotterdam, Brøndby IF, Bröndby IF II

*** Holst-Larsen - Fabian Holst-Larsen (a) 30/12/2004, ¿? (Norway) (b) 1,83 (c) D - right back (d) Strømsgodset IF (e) Fram, Strømsgodset

*** Holt - Jason Holt (a) 19/02/1993, Edinburgh (Scotland) (b) 1,68 (c) M - central midfielder (d) Livingston FC (e) Rangers FC, St. Johnstone, Rangers FC, Fleetwood, Rangers FC, Heart of Midlothian, Sheffield Utd., Heart of Midlothian, Raith Rovers

*** Holtan - Joacim Holtan (Joacim Emil Godhei Holtan) (a) 08/08/1998, Øvrebø (Norway) (b) 1,75 (c) F - center forward (d) Kongsvinger IL (e) Haugesund, Kongsvinger, Haugesund, Start, Haugesund, Bryne, Mandalskameratene, Torridal IL, IK Start II

*** Holte - Magnus Holte (a) 27/03/2006, Ler (Norway) (b) 1,93 (c) F - center forward (d) Rosenborg BK II (e) -

*** Holte - Stian Aarønes Holte (a) 15/04/2003, ¿? (Norway) (b) 1,98 (c) D - central defense (d) Aalesunds FK (e) Brattvåg, Aalesund

*** Holter - Dwayn Holter (a) 15/06/1995, Luxembourg (Luxembourg) (b) 1,83 (c) M - pivot (d) US Mondorf-Les-Bains (e) RFCU Luxembourg, RE Virton, Differdange 03, Greuther Fürth, CS Fola Esch, Greuther Fürth, VfR Aalen, Greuther Fürth

*** Holtmann - Gerrit Holtmann (Gerrit Stephan Holtmann) (a) 25/03/1995, Bremerhaven (Germany) (b) 1,85 (c) F - left winger (d) Antalyaspor (e) Antalyaspor, VfL Bochum, Mainz 05, SC Paderborn, Mainz 05, Eintracht Braunschweig, Eintracht Braunschweig II

*** Holtz - Kevin Holtz (a) 06/03/1993, ¿? (Luxembourg) (b) 1,73 (c) M - attacking midfielder (d) FC Sporting Mertzig (e) Progrès Niederkorn, FC Atert Bissen, Progrès Niederkorn, Etzella Ettelbrück, Erpeldange, Etzella Ettelbrück

*** Holubek - Jakub Holubek (Jakub Holúbek) (a) 12/01/1991, Trenčín (Czechoslovakia, now in Slovakia) (b) 1,80 (c) D - left back (d) Piast Gliwice (e) MSK Zilina, AS Trencin

*** Holvad - Anders Holvad (Anders Bak Holvad) (a) 24/06/1990, ¿? (Denmark) (b) 1,87 (c) F - right winger (d) FC Fredericia (e) KÍ Klaksvík, FC Fredericia, Hobro IK, Brabrand IF, Kjellerup IF, Viborg FF II

*** Holzer - Daniel Holzer (Daniel Holzer) (a) 18/08/1995, Ostrava (Czech Rep.) (b) 1,77 (c) M - left midfielder (d) 1.FC Slovácko (e) Banik Ostrava, Sparta Praha, Fastav Zlin, Sparta Praha, Banik Ostrava

*** Holzhauser - Raphael Holzhauser (a) 16/02/1993, Wiener Neustadt (Austria) (b) 1,93 (c) M - attacking midfielder (d) Oud-Heverlee Leuven (e) 1860 München, OH Leuven, Beerschot V.A., Grasshoppers, Austria Viena, VfB Stuttgart, FC Augsburg, VfB Stuttgart, Stuttgart II

*** Homma - Shion Homma (本間 至恩) (a) 09/08/2000, Murakami, Niigata (Japan) (b) 1,64 (c) M - left midfielder (d) KV Brugge (e) Club NXT, Albirex Niigata

*** Hong - Hyun-seok Hong (홍현석) (a) 16/06/1999, Seoul (South Korea) (b) 1,77 (c) M - central midfielder (d) KAA Gent (e) LASK, Juniors OÖ, Ulsan Hyundai, Juniors OÖ, Ulsan Hyundai, Unterhaching, Ulsan Hyundai, Sinjeong ES

*** Hongla - Martin Hongla (Martin Hongla Yma II) (a) 16/03/1998, Yaoundé (Cameroon) (b) 1,81 (c) M - pivot (d) Hellas Verona (e) Real Valladolid, Hellas Verona, Royal Antwerp, Hellas Verona, Royal Antwerp, Recreativo Granada, Karpaty, Recreativo Granada, Granada CF, FC Barcelona B, Granada CF, Granada B

*** Honkola - Eemeli Honkola (a) 28/01/2005, ¿? (Finland) (b) - (c) F - center forward (d) SJK Seinäjoki II (e) -

*** Honorat - Franck Honorat (a) 11/08/1996, Toulon (France) (b) 1,80 (c) F - right winger (d) Borussia Mönchengladbach (e) Stade Brestois, St.-Étienne, Clermont Foot, St.-Étienne, Clermont Foot, OGC Nice, FC Sochaux, OGC Nice, OGC Nice B

*** Hooper - Gary Hooper (a) 26/01/1988, Loughton (England) (b) 1,77 (c) F - center forward (d) Gulf United FC (e) Omonia Nicosia, Wellington P., Kerala Blasters, Wellington P., Sheffield Wednesday, Norwich City, Sheffield Wednesday, Norwich City, Celtic FC, Scunthorpe Utd., Southend United, Hereford Utd., Southend United, Leyton Orient, Southend United, Grays Athletic FC

*** Hopcutt - Jamie Hopcutt (Jamie Ryan Hopcutt) (a) 23/06/1992, York (England) (b) 1,80 (c) M - attacking midfielder (d) IFK Mariehamn (e) Oldham Athletic, H. Kfar Saba, GIF Sundsvall, Östersund, Tadcaster

*** Hope - Mikkel Hope (Mikkel Kalvenes Hope) (a) 08/08/2006, ¿? (Norway) (b) - (c) D - right back (d) FK Haugesund (e) -

*** Hopland - Nikolai Hopland (Nikolai Søyset Hopland) (a) 24/07/2004, ¿? (Norway) (b) 1,86 (c) D - central defense (d) Aalesunds FK (e) Kristiansund, Aalesund

*** Hopmark - Andreas Hopmark (Andreas Eines Hopmark) (a) 06/07/1991, Kristiansund (Norway) (b) 1,92 (c) D - central defense (d) Kristiansund BK (e) -

*** Hoppe - Matthew Hoppe (Matthew Timothy Hoppe) (a) 13/03/2001, Yorba Linda, California (United States) (b) 1,91 (c) F - center forward (d) San José Earthquakes (e) San José, Middlesbrough, Hibernian FC, Middlesbrough, RCD Mallorca, FC Schalke 04, Schalke 04 II

*** Hoppe - Mattis Hoppe (a) 23/07/2003, Bad Cannstatt (Germany) (b) 1,79 (c) D - right back (d) VfB Stuttgart II (e) -

*** Hora - Ioan Hora (Adrian Ioan Hora) (a) 21/08/1988, Oradea (Romania) (b) 1,82 (c) F - center forward (d) CS Lotus Baile Felix (e) FC Hermannstadt, UTA Arad, Gaz Metan, FCSB, Akhisarspor, Elazigspor, Akhisarspor, Konyaspor, Pandurii, ASA Tg. Mures, CFR Cluj, ASA Tg. Mures, CFR Cluj, Gloria Bistrita, UTA Arad

*** Hora - Jakub Hora (a) 08/03/2001, ¿? (Czech Rep.) (b) - (c) D - right back (d) FK Teplice (e) Teplice B, SG Spergau

*** Hora - Jakub Hora (Jakub Hora) (a) 23/02/1991, Most (Czechoslovakia, now in Czech Rep.) (b) 1,76 (c) M - attacking midfielder (d) SK Dynamo Ceske Budejovice (e) Teplice, Podbeskidzie, Teplice, Riga, Teplice, Slavia Praha, Teplice, Viktoria Plzen, Ceske Budejovice, Viktoria Plzen, Bohemians 1905, Viktoria Plzen, Ceske Budejovice, Viktoria Plzen, FK Most, Slavia Praha, FK Most

*** Hora - Vojtech Hora (Vojtěch Hora) (a) 05/05/2004, ¿? (Czech Rep.) (b) - (c) F - center forward (d) SK Dynamo Ceske Budejovice B (e) -

*** Horak - Daniel Horak (Daniel Horák) (a) 10/05/2000, ¿? (Czech Rep.) (b) 1,84 (c) D - left back (d) FC Hradec Kralove (e) Sparta Praha B, Pohronie, Sparta Praha B, Jihlava, Sparta Praha B

*** Horak - Tomas Horak (Tomáš Horák) (a) 03/08/1998, ¿? (Slovakia) (b) 1,84 (c) F - center forward (d) Slovan Galanta (e) Zlaté Moravce, Slovan Galanta, SK Bab, FC-31 Jarok

*** Horan - George Horan (a) 18/02/1982, Chester (England) (b) 1,88 (c) D - central defense (d) Connah's Quay Nomads (e) Chester, Rhyl FC, Connah's Quay, Bangor City

*** Horemans - Siebe Horemans (a) 02/06/1998, Gent (Belgium) (b) 1,86 (c) D - right back (d) Excelsior Rotterdam (e) KAA Gent, Excelsior, KAA Gent, OH Leuven, KAA Gent

*** Horgan - Colm Horgan (a) 02/07/1994, Galway (Ireland) (b) 1,72 (c) D - right back (d) Galway United FC (e) Sligo Rovers, Derry City, Cork City, Galway United, Salthill Devon

*** Horic - Kenan Horic (Kenan Horić) (a) 13/09/1990, Zenica (Yugoslavia, now in Bosnia and Herzegovina) (b) 1,90 (c) D - central defense (d) NK Celik Zenica (e)

HSK Posusje, FK Olimpik, FK Kukësi, Celik Zenica, Mladost Kakanj, Antalyaspor, Pafos FC, Antalyaspor, Domžale, Celik Zenica
*** Horj - Razvan Horj (Răzvan Horj) (a) 17/12/1995, Moisei (Romania) (b) 1,89 (c) D - central defense (d) - (e) Minaur, Petrolul, Gaz Metan, Universitatea Cluj, CFR Cluj, Újpest FC, FC Viitorul, FC Voluntari, FC Viitorul, CFR Cluj, Pandurii II, Minaur
*** Horkas - Dinko Horkas (Dinko Horkaš) (a) 10/03/1999, Sisak (Croatia) (b) 1,89 (c) G (d) Lokomotiv Plovdiv (e) Dinamo Zagreb, HSK Posusje, Dinamo Zagreb, NK Varazdin, Dinamo Zagreb, Zrinjski Mostar, Dinamo Zagreb, Din. Zagreb II
*** Hormigo - Diego Hormigo (Diego Hormigo Iturralde) (a) 16/04/2003, Sevilla (Spain) (b) 1,82 (c) D - left back (d) Sevilla Atlético (e) Sevilla FC C
*** Horn - Jannes Horn (Jannes-Kilian Horn) (a) 06/02/1997, Braunschweig (Germany) (b) 1,86 (c) D - left back (d) 1.FC Nürnberg (e) VfL Bochum, 1.FC Nürnberg, VfL Bochum, 1.FC Köln, Hannover 96, 1.FC Köln, VfL Wolfsburg
*** Horn - Jörgen Horn (Jørgen Horn) (a) 07/06/1987, Oslo (Norway) (b) 1,88 (c) D - central defense (d) Gamle Oslo FK (e) Sarpsborg 08, Elfsborg, Strømsgodset, Fredrikstad, Viking, Vålerenga, Viking, Vålerenga, Moss, Vålerenga, Kjelsås
*** Horn - Timo Horn (a) 12/05/1993, Köln (Germany) (b) 1,92 (c) G (d) - (e) 1.FC Köln, 1.FC Köln II
*** Hornby - Fraser Hornby (a) 13/09/1999, Northampton (England) (b) 1,95 (c) F - center forward (d) SV Darmstadt 98 (e) Stade Reims, KV Oostende, Stade Reims, Aberdeen FC, Stade Reims, KV Kortrijk
*** Hornicek - Lukas Hornicek (Lukáš Horníček) (a) 13/07/2002, Vysoké Mýto (Czech Rep.) (b) 1,94 (c) G (d) SC Braga (e) Braga B, Pardubice
*** Hornschuh - Marc Hornschuh (a) 02/03/1991, Dortmund (Germany) (b) 1,88 (c) D - central defense (d) FC Zürich (e) Hamburg II, FC St. Pauli, FSV Frankfurt, Borussia Dortmund II, Borussia Dortmund, FC Ingolstadt, Borussia Dortmund
*** Hornyak - Gabriel Hornyak (Gabriel Hornyák) (a) 10/01/2002, Bratislava (Slovakia) (b) 1,80 (c) M - central midfielder (d) - (e) FK Senica
*** Horrocks - Jack Horrocks (a) 26/05/1993, Liverpool (England) (b) 1,83 (c) D - left back (d) FC Bruno's Magpies Reserve (e) Heswall FC, Warrington, Vauxhall Motors, AFC Liverpool
*** Horsia - Ovidiu Horsia (Ovidiu Horşia) (a) 30/10/2000, Târgu Mureş (Romania) (b) 1,72 (c) F - right winger (d) CSM Alexandria (e) FCSB, Universitatea Cluj, FCSB, U. Constanta, FCSB, Gaz Metan, FCSB, ACSM Poli Iasi, Academica Clinceni, ACS Kinder
*** Horta - André Horta (André Filipe Luz Horta) (a) 07/11/1996, Almada (Portugal) (b) 1,75 (c) M - central midfielder (d) SC Braga (e) LAFC, Benfica, SC Braga, Benfica, Vitória Setúbal
*** Horta - Ricardo Horta (Ricardo Jorge Luz Horta) (a) 15/09/1994, Almada (Portugal) (b) 1,73 (c) F - left winger (d) SC Braga (e) Málaga CF, SC Braga, Málaga CF, Vitória Setúbal
*** Horton - Grant Horton (Grant Dean Horton) (a) 13/09/2001, Colchester (England) (b) 1,92 (c) D - central defense (d) Cheltenham Town (e) Bohemians, Cheltenham Town, Bohemians, Cheltenham Town, Bath City, Cheltenham Town, Chippenham, Yate Town, Bromsgrove Spo, Worcester City
*** Horvat - Adam Horvat (a) 18/02/2004, ¿? (Slovakia) (b) - (c) F - left winger (d) FK Pohronie (e) -
*** Horvat - Brin Horvat (a) 05/03/2004, ¿? (Slovenia) (b) - (c) M - pivot (d) NK Maribor (e) -

*** Horvat - Matija Horvat (a) 07/05/1999, Čakovec (Croatia) (b) 1,80 (c) M - pivot (d) DSV Leoben (e) TSV Hartberg, SV Kapfenberg, Kapfenberg II, Rapid/KSV III, KSV IV, AKA Kapfenberg

*** Horvat - Tomi Horvat (a) 24/03/1999, Murska Sobota (Slovenia) (b) 1,76 (c) M - attacking midfielder (d) SK Sturm Graz (e) NS Mura

*** Horvath - Sascha Horvath (a) 22/08/1996, Wien (Austria) (b) 1,68 (c) M - attacking midfielder (d) LASK (e) TSV Hartberg, Dynamo Dresden, FC Wacker, Dynamo Dresden, Sturm Graz, Austria Viena, Austria Wien Reserves, Austria Viena, Austria Wien Reserves

*** Horváth - Kevin Horváth (a) 02/03/2005, ¿? (Hungary) (b) - (c) F - center forward (d) Paksi FC (e) Paksi FC II

*** Horváth - Krisztofer Horváth (Horváth Krisztofer György) (a) 08/01/2002, Hévíz (Hungary) (b) 1,85 (c) M - attacking midfielder (d) Kecskeméti TE (e) Kecskemét, Torino, Kecskemét, Torino, Debrecen, Torino, Szeged, Zalaegerszeg

*** Horváth - Milán Horváth (Horváth Milán Gábor) (a) 30/01/2002, Kistarcsa (Hungary) (b) 1,93 (c) D - central defense (d) Budapest Honvéd FC (e) BFC Siófok, Honvéd, Mezőkövesd, Honvéd, BFC Siófok, Honvéd, BFC Siófok, Honvéd, Honvéd II

*** Horwood - Harri Horwood (Harri William Horwood) (a) 24/04/2000, ¿? (Wales) (b) - (c) D - left back (d) Penrhyncoch FC (e) Aberystwyth, Penrhyncoch, Aberystwyth, Briton Ferry, Cardiff Metropolitan Police, Aberystwyth

*** Horz - Jannik Horz (Jannik Reiner Horz) (a) 14/04/2003, Offenbach am Main (Germany) (b) 1,93 (c) G (d) SG Barockstadt Fulda-Lehnerz (e) E. Frankfurt II

*** Hoskonen - Arttu Hoskonen (a) 16/04/1997, Kaarina (Finland) (b) 1,88 (c) D - central defense (d) Cracovia (e) HJK Helsinki, FC Inter

*** Hosseini - Majid Hosseini (حسینی مجید) (a) 20/06/1996, Tehran (Iran) (b) 1,87 (c) D - central defense (d) Kayserispor (e) Trabzonspor, Esteghlal FC, Rah Ahan, Esteghlal FC

*** Hosseinzadeh - Amirhossein Hosseinzadeh (زاده حسین امیرحسین) (a) 30/10/2000, Tehran (Iran) (b) 1,78 (c) M - attacking midfielder (d) Tractor FC (e) RSC Charleroi, Esteghlal FC, Saipa FC

*** Hostikka - Santeri Hostikka (a) 30/09/1997, Järvenpää (Finland) (b) 1,83 (c) F - left winger (d) HJK Helsinki (e) Pogon Szczecin, FC Lahti, Pallokerho

*** Hoti - Andi Hoti (a) 22/12/2003, ¿? (Iceland) (b) - (c) M (d) Leiknir Reykjavík (e) Afturelding, Leiknir, Thróttur, Leiknir

*** Hoti - Ardian Hoti (a) 14/09/1996, ¿? (RF Yugoslavia, now in Kosovo) (b) 1,82 (c) D - central defense (d) KF Drenica (e) FC Malisheva, KF Liria, FC Llapi, KF Dardana, FC Llapi, Kek-U Kastriot

*** Hoti - Art Hoti (a) 09/06/2004, ¿? (Serbia and Montenegro, in Kosovo) (b) 1,91 (c) G (d) KF Llapi (e) -

*** Hoti - Engjell Hoti (Engjëll Hoti) (a) 26/02/1997, Stuttgart (Germany) (b) 1,87 (c) M - attacking midfielder (d) ŁKS Łódź (e) FK Partizani, KF Tirana, FC Llapi, KF Trepca 89, TSG Backnang, Rot Weiss Ahlen, Eintracht Braunschweig II

*** Hoti - Mendurim Hoti (a) 23/02/1996, Malishevë (RF Yugoslavia, now in Kosovo) (b) - (c) F - left winger (d) FC Malisheva (e) FC Prishtina, KF Feronikeli, KF Teuta, KF 2 Korriku

*** Hoti (c) M (d) SC Gjilani (e) KF Liria - Ukshin Hoti (c) M (d) SC Gjilani (e) KF Liria

*** Hotic - Dino Hotic (Dino Hotić) (a) 26/07/1995, Ljubljana (Slovenia) (b) 1,68 (c) F - right winger (d) Lech Poznan (e) Cercle Brugge, NK Maribor, NK Krsko, NK Maribor, Verzej, NK Maribor

*** Houja - David Houja (חוגה דוד) (a) 27/04/2001, ¿? (Israel) (b) 1,90 (c) D - central defense (d) Beitar Jerusalem (e) AS Ashdod, B. Jerusalem

*** Hountondji - Cédric Hountondji (a) 19/01/1994, Toulouse (France) (b) 1,94 (c) D - central defense (d) Angers SCO (e) Clermont Foot, Levski Sofia, New York City, G. Ajaccio, Stade Rennes, AJ Auxerre, Stade Rennes, LB Châteauroux, Stade Rennes, Stade Rennes B

*** Houri - Lyes Houri (Lyes Hafid Houri) (a) 19/01/1996, Lomme (France) (b) 1,69 (c) M - attacking midfielder (d) Fehérvár FC (e) CS U Craiova, Fehérvár, FC Viitorul, RC Lens B, SC Bastia, Roda JC, SC Bastia, ASM Belfort, SC Bastia, Valenciennes B

*** Houska - David Houska (a) 29/06/1993, ¿? (Czechoslovakia, now in Czech Rep.) (b) 1,75 (c) M - central midfielder (d) FK Jablonec (e) Sigma Olomouc

*** Housni - Ilyes Housni (حسني إلياس) (a) 14/05/2005, Créteil (France) (b) 1,72 (c) F - center forward (d) - (e) Paris Saint-Germain

*** Houwen - Jeroen Houwen (a) 18/02/1996, Oirlo (Netherlands) (b) 1,88 (c) G (d) RKC Waalwijk (e) Vitesse, Go Ahead Eagles, Vitesse, Telstar, Vitesse

*** Hovakimyan - Erik Hovakimyan (Էրիկ Հովակիմյան) (a) 24/10/2004, Yerevan (Armenia) (b) 1,83 (c) D - central defense (d) BKMA Yerevan II (e) -

*** Høvdanum - Tróndur á Høvdanum (Tróndur Jóannesson á Høvdanum) (a) 19/08/1995, ¿? (Faroe Islands) (b) - (c) D - central defense (d) AB Argir (e) Víkingur II

*** Hove - Johan Hove (a) 07/09/2000, Sogndal (Norway) (b) 1,77 (c) M - central midfielder (d) FC Groningen (e) Strømsgodset, Sogndal

*** Hovhannisyan - Alexander Hovhannisyan (Оганисян Олександр Андранікович) (a) 20/07/1996, Ashtarak (Armenia) (b) 1,84 (c) D - central defense (d) - (e) FC Van, Gandzasar, Banants, Banants II, Ulisses

*** Hovhannisyan - Arman Hovhannisyan (Արման Հովհաննիսյան) (a) 07/07/1993, Yerevan (Armenia) (b) 1,84 (c) D - left back (d) FC Pyunik Yerevan (e) Ararat Yerevan, Ararat-Armenia, Pyunik Yerevan, Tobol Kostanay, Gandzasar, Ararat-Armenia, Zirka, Shirak Gyumri, Alashkert CF, Pyunik Yerevan, Pyunik Yerevan B

*** Hovhannisyan - Armen Hovhannisyan (Արմեն Հովհաննիսյան) (a) 07/03/2000, Yerevan (Armenia) (b) 1,89 (c) F - center forward (d) Hibernians FC (e) AO Episkopi, Pietà Hotspurs, AO Episkopi, Zimbru Chisinau, Ararat-Armenia, Gandzasar, Ararat-Armenia, FC Nitra, Michalovce, Ararat-Armenia

*** Hovhannisyan - Arsen Hovhannisyan (Արսեն Հովհաննիսյան) (a) 01/03/1996, ¿? (Armenia) (b) 1,72 (c) M - left midfielder (d) - (e) West Armenia, Lernayin Artsakh, West Armenia, Lokomotiv, Artsakh Erewan, Gandzasar II, Ararat II, Ararat Yerevan, Ararat II

*** Hovhannisyan - Benik Hovhannisyan (Բենիկ Հովհաննիսյան) (a) 01/05/1993, Yerevan (Armenia) (b) 1,76 (c) M - pivot (d) FC Van (e) Alashkert CF, FC Van, FC Noah, Alashkert II, Alashkert CF, Ararat Yerevan, Alashkert II, Banants, Banants II

*** Hovhannisyan - Kamo Hovhannisyan (Կամո Հովհաննիսյան) (a) 05/10/1992, Yerevan (Armenia) (b) 1,76 (c) D - right back (d) FC Astana (e) Kairat Almaty, Zhetysu, Alashkert CF, Torpedo Zhodino, Pyunik Yerevan, Pyunik Yerevan B

*** Hovhannisyan - Karlen Hovhannisyan (Կառլեն Հովհաննիսյան) (a) 26/04/2005, Ashtarak (Armenia) (b) 1,64 (c) M - attacking midfielder (d) BKMA Yerevan (e) BKMA Yerevan, Pyunik Yerevan, Pyunik Yerevan B

*** Hovhannisyan - Narek Hovhannisyan (Նարեկ Հովհաննիսյան) (a) 11/06/2002, ¿? (Armenia) (b) - (c) M - central midfielder (d) FC Van (e) Ararat-Armenia II, Ararat II, Pyunik Yerevan B

*** Hovhannisyan - Sokrat Hovhannisyan (Սոկրատ Հովհաննիսյան) (a) 05/04/1996, Artik (Armenia) (b) 1,88 (c) G (d) Shirak Gyumri C.F. (e) Shirak II
*** Hovland - Even Hovland (a) 14/02/1989, Vadheim (Norway) (b) 1,91 (c) D - central defense (d) BK Häcken (e) Rosenborg, Sogndal, 1.FC Nürnberg, Molde, Sogndal
*** Hovsepyan - Ruben Hovsepyan (Ռուբեն Հովսեփյան) (a) 06/11/1999, Yerevan (Armenia) (b) 1,84 (c) D - left back (d) FC Ararat Yerevan II (e) FC Noah, Ararat-Armenia II, Ararat II, Pyunik Yerevan B
*** Hovsepyan - Rumyan Hovsepyan (Ռումյան Հովսեփյան) (a) 13/11/1991, Yerevan (Armenia) (b) 1,86 (c) M - central midfielder (d) FC Noah Yerevan (e) FC Van, Alashkert CF, Floriana, Alashkert CF, Arda Kardzhali, Pyunik Yerevan, Banants, Shirak Gyumri, Stal D., Pyunik Yerevan, Metalurg Donetsk, Banants, Impuls Dilijan, Pyunik Yerevan B
*** Howland - Thomas Howland (a) 01/09/2005, ¿? (Malta) (b) - (c) D (d) - (e) Pietà Hotspurs
*** Hoxha - Alban Hoxha (Alban Bekim Hoxha) (a) 23/11/1987, Cërrik (Albania) (b) 1,88 (c) G (d) FK Partizani (e) KS Besa, KS Kastrioti, FC Dinamo, FK Apolonia, FC Dinamo, KF Turbina, FC Dinamo
*** Hoxha - Arbër Hoxha (a) 06/10/1998, Heidelberg (Germany) (b) 1,85 (c) F - left winger (d) Slaven Belupo Koprivnica (e) NK Lokomotiva, FC Ballkani, FC Prishtina, FC Besa, FC Prishtina, KF Istogu
*** Hoxha - Atiljo Hoxha (a) 21/12/2004, ¿? (Albania) (b) - (c) M (d) La Fiorita 1967 (e) -
*** Hoxha - Florian Hoxha (a) 22/02/2001, Bülach (Switzerland) (b) 1,77 (c) D - left back (d) Grasshopper Club Zürich (e) -
*** Hoxha - Klaid Hoxha (a) 14/08/2001, Pakisht (Albania) (b) - (c) D (d) KF Teuta (e) KF Naftëtari
*** Hoxha - Rinor Hoxha (a) 28/02/2000, Viti (RF Yugoslavia, now in Kosovo) (b) 1,90 (c) F - center forward (d) - (e) KF Llapi, KF Vllaznia
*** Hoxha - Rustem Hoxha (a) 04/07/1991, Durrës (Albania) (b) 1,88 (c) D - central defense (d) FC Dinamo (e) FC Ballkani, KF Teuta, FC Luftëtari, FK Kukësi, KF Teuta, KS Luftëtari, KF Teuta
*** Hoxha - Uheid Hoxha (a) 01/08/2000, Shkodër (Albania) (b) - (c) M - attacking midfielder (d) - (e) KF Teuta, KF Vllaznia, KS Besa
*** Hoxha - Yll Hoxha (a) 26/12/1987, Prishtinë (Yugoslavia, now in Kosovo) (b) 1,83 (c) D - left back (d) FC Suhareka (e) SC Gjilani, KF Feronikeli, KF Vllaznia, Flamurtari FC, FK Kukësi, KF Hysi, TPS, FC Prishtina
*** Hoxhaj - Ardit Hoxhaj (a) 10/07/1994, Vlorë (Albania) (b) 1,81 (c) F - left winger (d) AF Elbasani (e) KF Vllaznia, Flamurtari FC, FC Luftëtari, KF Skënderbeu, KF Ferizaj, KF Skënderbeu, Flamurtari FC, KF Skënderbeu, KF Korabi, KF Skënderbeu, FK Bylis, KF Himara, Flamurtari FC
*** Hoxhallari - Erion Hoxhallari (a) 15/10/1995, Korçë (Albania) (b) 1,83 (c) D - central defense (d) KF Tirana (e) UTA Arad, KF Tirana, KF Laçi, KF Tirana, KF Teuta, KF Tirana, GAK 1902 II
*** Høyland - Martin Høyland (a) 17/09/1995, Kristiansand (Norway) (b) 1,85 (c) M - pivot (d) Sarpsborg 08 FF (e) Stabæk, Grorud, FK Vigør, Vindbjart FK, FK Vigør, Våg FK
*** Hozez - Matan Hozez (מתן חוזז) (a) 12/08/1996, Tel Aviv (Israel) (b) 1,75 (c) F - right winger (d) Hapoel Jerusalem (e) H. Jerusalem, Maccabi Tel Aviv, Hapoel Haifa, Maccabi Tel Aviv, Bnei Yehuda, Maccabi Tel Aviv, H. Ashkelon, Maccabi Tel Aviv, Beitar TA Ramla, Maccabi Tel Aviv

*** Hrabina - Alex Hrabina (a) 05/04/1995, Nyíregyháza (Hungary) (b) 1,90 (c) G (d) - (e) Nyíregyháza, Debrecen, Cigánd, Szolnok, Békéscsaba, Gyirmót FC, Cigánd, Szolnok, Nyíregyháza, Budaörs

*** Hrabina - Matej Hrabina (Matěj Hrabina) (a) 29/04/1993, Opava (Czech Rep.) (b) 1,79 (c) D - right back (d) - (e) Zbrojovka Brno, SFC Opava

*** Hradecky - Lukas Hradecky (Lukáš Hrádecký) (a) 24/11/1989, Bratislava (Czechoslovakia, now in Slovakia) (b) 1,92 (c) G (d) Bayer 04 Leverkusen (e) Eintracht, Brøndby IF, Esbjerg fB, TPS, Åbo IFK, TPS

*** Hradecky - Matej Hradecky (Matej Hrádecký) (a) 17/04/1995, Turku (Finland) (b) 1,96 (c) D - central defense (d) SJK Seinäjoki (e) Helsinki IFK, SJK Seinäjoki, TPS, SJK Seinäjoki, TPS

*** Hrafnkelsson - Gudjón Ernir Hrafnkelsson (Guðjón Ernir Hrafnkelsson) (a) 19/08/2001, ¿? (Iceland) (b) - (c) D - right back (d) ÍBV Vestmannaeyjar (e) Höttur

*** Hranac - Robin Hranac (Robin Hranáč) (a) 29/01/2000, Plzeň (Czech Rep.) (b) 1,90 (c) D - central defense (d) FC Viktoria Plzen (e) Pardubice, Viktoria Plzen, Viktoria Plzen B, Pardubice, Viktoria Plzen B, Liptovsky Mik., Viktoria Plzen B

*** Hrdina - Adam Hrdina (a) 12/02/2004, Nová Baňa (Slovakia) (b) 1,94 (c) G (d) Slovan Bratislava (e) -

*** Hrdlicka - Lukas Hrdlicka (Lukáš Hrdlička) (a) 03/04/2001, ¿? (Czech Rep.) (b) 1,8 (c) M - attacking midfielder (d) FC Zlin B (e) Trinec, FC Zlin B

*** Hrelja - Damir Hrelja (a) 13/10/2001, Gorazde (Bosnia and Herzegovina) (b) 1,91 (c) F - right winger (d) FK Borac Banja Luka (e) Igman Konjic, Zeljeznicar, FK Gorazde, Zeljeznicar, FK Gorazde

*** Hreljic - Kenan Hreljic (Kenan Hreljić) (a) 01/12/1997, Sarajevo (Bosnia and Herzegovina) (b) 1,90 (c) D - central defense (d) SV Straelen (e) Liepaja, Igman Konjic, HNK Capljina, KF Teuta, Mladost Kakanj, NK Jajce, MTK Budapest II

*** Hrgovic - Simun Hrgovic (Šimun Hrgović) (a) 20/03/2004, Vukovar (Croatia) (b) - (c) D - left back (d) HNK Hajduk Split (e) Radn. Vukovar

*** Hristov - Damyan Hristov (Дамян Христов Христов) (a) 10/11/2002, ¿? (Bulgaria) (b) 1,88 (c) G (d) Etar Veliko Tarnovo (e) Ludogorets II

*** Hristov - Hristiyan Hristov (Християн Живков Христов) (a) 09/04/1995, Varna (Bulgaria) (b) 1,90 (c) G (d) FC Fratria (e) Dob. Dobrich, Spartak Varna, CSKA 1948 II, Lokomotiv GO, C. Balchik, Inter Dobrich, Cherno More

*** Hristov - Martin Hristov (Мартин Христов Христов) (a) 02/10/2003, Pazardzhik (Bulgaria) (b) 1,97 (c) D - central defense (d) Botev Vratsa (e) Botev Vratsa, Botev II

*** Hristov - Nikolay Hristov (a) 01/08/1989, Dolni Dabnik (Bulgaria) (b) 1,77 (c) M - pivot (d) - (e) Tikves, Levski Lom, Spartak Pleven, CSKA 1948, Litex Lovetch, Lokomotiv GO, Bregalnica Stip, Pelister Bitola, Botev Vratsa, Belasitsa

*** Hristov - Petko Hristov (Петко Росенов Христов) (a) 01/03/1999, Sofia (Bulgaria) (b) 1,91 (c) D - central defense (d) Spezia (e) Venezia, Spezia, Fiorentina, Pro Vercelli, Fiorentina, Bisceglie, Fiorentina, Ternana, Fiorentina, Slavia Sofia

*** Hristov - Ventsislav Hristov (Венцислав Димитров Христов) (a) 09/11/1988, Sofia (Bulgaria) (b) 1,85 (c) F - center forward (d) Nesebar (e) Botev Vratsa, Tsarsko Selo, Sozopol, Neftochimik, Slavia Sofia, Concordia, Tsarsko Selo, Arda Kardzhali, Vereya, SKA Khabarovsk, Neftochimik, Levski Sofia, HNK Rijeka, KF Skënderbeu, HNK Rijeka, Beroe, Metalurg Donetsk, Beroe, Chern. Burgas, Montana, Nesebar, Sportist Svoge, Lokomotiv Sofia

*** Hristovski - Gordijan Hristovski (Гордијан Христовски) (a) 21/04/2003, ¿? (North Macedonia) (b) 1,84 (c) D - left back (d) Detonit Plackovica (e) Gostivar, FK Skopje, Sileks, Teteks Tetovo, Kadino

*** Hrka - Darko Hrka (a) 20/11/1999, ¿? (Slovenia) (b) 1,87 (c) M - pivot (d) ND Gorica (e) NK Krka

*** Hrkac - Ante Hrkac (Ante Hrkač) (a) 11/03/1992, Mostar (Bosnia and Herzegovina) (b) 1,93 (c) D - central defense (d) FK Velez Mostar (e) FK Tuzla City, Mladost, Novara, Siroki Brijeg, Al-Qaisumah FC, KF Teuta, NK Lokomotiva, Celik Zenica, NK Lokomotiva, NK Lucko, NK Lokomotiva, Segesta Sisak, NK Vitez, Mayrhofen, Branitelj Mostar, GOSK Gabela

*** Hrncar - David Hrncar (David Hrnčár) (a) 10/12/1997, Žilina (Slovakia) (b) 1,87 (c) F - right winger (d) SK Beveren (e) Slovan Bratislava, SK Beveren, Slovan Bratislava, Zlaté Moravce, Slovan Bratislava, Pohronie, Slovan Bratislava, Slovan B, MSK Zilina B, Slovan B

*** Hromada - Jakub Hromada (a) 25/05/1996, Košice (Slovakia) (b) 1,80 (c) M - pivot (d) SK Slavia Praga (e) Slovan Liberec, Slavia Praha, Slovan Liberec, Slavia Praha, Sampdoria, Viktoria Plzen, Sampdoria, FK Senica, Sampdoria, Pro Vercelli, KAC Kosice

*** Hronek - Petr Hronek (Petr Hronek) (a) 04/07/1993, ¿? (Czech Rep.) (b) 1,82 (c) M - central midfielder (d) SK Slavia Praga (e) Bohemians 1905, Fastav Zlin, Bohemians 1905, Fastav Zlin, Jihlava, Vlasim, Jablonec, 1.FK Pribram, FK Jablonec, Graffin Vlasim, FK Jablonec, FK Jablonec B, Sparta Praha B

*** Hrosovsky - Patrik Hrosovsky (Patrik Hrošovský) (a) 22/04/1992, Bojnice (Czechoslovakia, now in Slovakia) (b) 1,73 (c) M - central midfielder (d) KRC Genk (e) Viktoria Plzen, Viktoria Plzen B, 1.SC Znojmo, Viktoria Plzen B, Usti nad Labem, Viktoria Plzen B, Banik Sokolov, Viktoria Plzen B

*** Hrosso - Lukas Hrosso (Lukáš Hroššo) (a) 19/04/1987, Nitra (Czechoslovakia, now in Slovakia) (b) 1,95 (c) G (d) Cracovia (e) Z. Sosnowiec, FC Nitra, Dukla Praha, Slovan Liberec, FC Nitra, Slovan Bratislava, FC Nitra

*** Hrstic - Srdjan Hrstic (Срђан Хрстић) (a) 18/07/2003, Sombor (Serbia and Montenegro, now in Serbia) (b) 1,92 (c) F - center forward (d) BK Häcken (e) Spartak

*** Hruby - Martin Hruby (Martin Hrubý) (a) 22/03/2004, ¿? (Czech Rep.) (b) 1,92 (c) G (d) FC Banik Ostrava B (e) -

*** Hruby - Robert Hruby (Robert Hrubý) (a) 27/04/1994, Praha (Czech Rep.) (b) 1,84 (c) M - central midfielder (d) Bohemians Praha 1905 (e) Zlin, Banik Ostrava, Jablonec, Banik Ostrava, Slavia Praha, Teplice, Slavia Praha, Banik Ostrava, Slavia Praha

*** Hruby - Vlastimil Hruby (Vlastimil Hrubý) (a) 21/02/1985, Znojmo (Czechoslovakia, now in Czech Rep.) (b) 1,85 (c) G (d) FC Zbrojovka Brno (e) Jablonec, 1.SC Znojmo, FCZ Brno B, 1.SC Znojmo, FCZ Brno B, Dosta Bystrc, FCZ Brno B, SC Xaverov, FCZ Brno B

*** Hruska - Matus Hruska (Matúš Hruška) (a) 17/09/1994, Žilina (Slovakia) (b) 1,88 (c) G (d) MFK Dukla Banska Bystrica (e) Dukla Praha, Spartak Myjava, Puchov

*** Hrustic - Ajdin Hrustic (a) 05/07/1996, Melbourne (Australia) (b) 1,80 (c) M - attacking midfielder (d) Hellas Verona (e) Eintracht, FC Groningen

*** Hrvoj - Tin Hrvoj (a) 06/06/2001, Zagreb (Croatia) (b) 1,80 (c) D - right back (d) NK Radomlje (e) Din. Zagreb II, Hrv Dragovoljac, Din. Zagreb II, Dinamo Zagreb, NK Varazdin, Dinamo Zagreb, Din. Zagreb II

*** Hryniewicki - Patryk Hryniewicki (a) 21/05/2000, Stare Juchy (Poland) (b) 1,95 (c) D - central defense (d) Leiknir Reykjavík (e) KV Vesturbaejar, Leiknir, KV Vesturbaejar, Leiknir, Aegir, Leiknir, KB, Leiknir

*** Hubchev - Hristofor Hubchev (Христофор Христофоров Хубчев) (a) 24/11/1995, Sofia (Bulgaria) (b) 1,81 (c) D - left back (d) Spartak Varna (e) Pirin, Levski Sofia, Etar, AE Larisa, Dunav, Beroe, Montana

*** Hübers - Timo Hübers (Timo Bernd Hübers) (a) 20/07/1996, Hildesheim (Germany) (b) 1,90 (c) D - central defense (d) 1.FC Köln (e) Hannover 96, 1.FC Köln II

*** Hubert - David Hubert (a) 12/02/1988, Uccle (Belgium) (b) 1,84 (c) M - pivot (d) - (e) RSC Anderlecht Futures, Zulte Waregem, OH Leuven, KAA Gent, Excelsior Mouscron, KAA Gent, Waasland-Beveren, KAA Gent, H. Beer Sheva, KAA Gent, KRC Genk, KAA Gent, KRC Genk

*** Hubert - Guillaume Hubert (Guillaume Yvon Hubert) (a) 11/01/1994, Charleroi (Belgium) (b) 1,98 (c) G (d) RWD Molenbeek (e) KV Oostende, KV Brugge, Cercle Brugge, KV Brugge, Standard Liège, Sint-Truiden, Standard Liège, Valenciennes B

*** Hübner - Benjamin Hübner (a) 04/07/1989, Wiesbaden (Germany) (b) 1,93 (c) D - central defense (d) - (e) Hoffenheim, FC Ingolstadt, VfR Aalen, Wehen Wiesbaden, SV Wehen II

*** Hubocan - Tomas Hubocan (Tomáš Hubočan) (a) 17/09/1985, Žilina (Czechoslovakia, now in Slovakia) (b) 1,84 (c) D - central defense (d) Karmiotissa Pano Polemidion (e) Omonia Nicosia, Ol. Marseille, Trabzonspor, Ol. Marseille, Dinamo Moskva, Zenit, MSK Zilina, Zlaté Moravce, MSK Zilina

*** Hübschman - Tomas Hübschman (Tomáš Hübschman) (a) 04/09/1981, Praha (Czechoslovakia, now in Czech Rep.) (b) 1,80 (c) M - pivot (d) FK Jablonec (e) Shakhtar Donetsk, Sparta Praha, FK Jablonec, Sparta Praha

*** Hudd - Roni Hudd (a) 20/01/2005, ¿? (Finland) (b) 1,74 (c) F - attacking midfielder (d) Vaasan Palloseura (e) -

*** Hudson - Blaine Hudson (a) 28/10/1991, Gorleston (England) (b) 1,96 (c) D - central defense (d) The New Saints (e) Chester, Wrexham, Cambridge Utd., Welling Utd., Cambridge Utd., Billericay, Cambridge Utd., Cambridge City, Cambridge Utd.

*** Hudson-Odoi - Callum Hudson-Odoi (Callum James Hudson-Odoi) (a) 07/11/2000, Wansworth, London (England) (b) 1,78 (c) F - left winger (d) Chelsea FC (e) Bayer Leverkusen, Chelsea

*** Huerta - Alejandro Huerta (Alfonso Alejandro Huerta) (a) 19/11/1990, San Pedro Garza García (Mexico) (b) - (c) M - central midfielder (d) FC Pas de la Casa (e) Sant Julià, CE Carroi

*** Huf - David Huf (a) 23/01/1999, ¿? (Czech Rep.) (b) 1,87 (c) F - center forward (d) MFK Chrudim (e) Chrudim, Pardubice, Dukla Praha, Pardubice

*** Hughes - Ben Hughes (Ben Daniel Hughes) (a) 12/10/2004, ¿? (Wales) (b) - (c) M - central midfielder (d) Flint Town United (e) -

*** Hughes - Daniel Hughes (a) 03/05/1992, Newry (Northern Ireland) (b) - (c) F - center forward (d) Newry City AFC (e) Dungannon, Cliftonville, Warrenpoint, Newry City

*** Hughes - George Hughes (a) 23/03/1999, ¿? (England) (b) 1,76 (c) M - central midfielder (d) Newtown AFC (e) Airbus UK, Shrewsbury, Newtown, Shrewsbury, Stalybridge, Shrewsbury, Clitheroe, Shrewsbury, Colwyn Bay, Shrewsbury

*** Hughes - Jeff Hughes (Jeffrey Edward Hughes) (a) 29/05/1985, Larne (Northern Ireland) (b) 1,83 (c) M - central midfielder (d) - (e) Larne FC, Tranmere Rovers, Cambridge Utd., Tranmere Rovers, Cambridge Utd., Fleetwood, Notts County, Bristol Rovers, Crystal Palace, Peterborough, Crystal Palace, Lincoln City, Larne FC, Ballymena

*** Hughes - Mark Hughes (a) 28/04/1993, Athy, Kildare (Ireland) (b) 1,80 (c) M - central midfielder (d) - (e) Drogheda United, Shelbourne, Longford Town, Drogheda United, Athlone Town, Scunthorpe Utd., Belvedere FC

*** Hughes - Nazim Hughes (a) 08/10/1992, Gibraltar (Gibraltar) (b) - (c) M - pivot (d) - (e) Europa Point FC, College Reserve, FC College 1975

*** Hughes - Rob Hughes (Robert Derek Ronald Hughes) (a) 22/04/1992, St. Asaph)) (c) M - attacking midfielder (d) Caernarfon Town (e) Flint Town, Prestatyn, Connah's Quay, Rhyl FC, Prestatyn

*** Hughes - Will Hughes (William James Hughes) (a) 17/04/1995, Weybridge (England) (b) 1,85 (c) M - central midfielder (d) Crystal Palace (e) Watford, Derby

*** Hugi - Dor Hugi (חוגי דור) (a) 10/07/1995, Bnei Brak (Israel) (b) 1,80 (c) F - left winger (d) Ihud Bnei Sakhnin (e) Wisla Kraków, Bnei Sakhnin, Wisla Kraków, SKN St. Pölten, M. Petah Tikva, H. Ramat Gan, Hapoel Tel Aviv, Hapoel Raanana, Maccabi Haifa, M. Petah Tikva, Maccabi Haifa, H. Petah Tikva, Maccabi Haifa

*** Hugo Félix - Hugo Félix (Hugo Félix Sequeira) (a) 03/03/2004, Viseu (Portugal) (b) 1,70 (c) M - attacking midfielder (d) - (e) CB Viseu

*** Hugonet - Jean Hugonet (a) 24/11/1999, Paris (France) (b) 1,86 (c) D - central defense (d) 1.FC Magdeburg (e) Austria Lustenau, US Saint-Malo, Paris FC, Paris FC B

*** Huhtala - Jesse Huhtala (a) 21/06/2000, Tampere (Finland) (b) 1,83 (c) F - center forward (d) Salon Palloilijat (e) PEPO, FC Haka, HJS, FC Haka, HJS, Ilves, PEPO, Ilves

*** Huisman - Daan Huisman (a) 26/07/2002, Arnhem (Netherlands) (b) 1,89 (c) M - attacking midfielder (d) Vitesse Arnhem (e) VVV-Venlo, Vitesse

*** Huja - Marian Huja (Marian Fernando Huja) (a) 05/08/1999, Cacém (Portugal) (b) 1,91 (c) D - central defense (d) Petrolul Ploiesti (e) HB Köge, Belenenses

*** Hujber - Luka Hujber (a) 16/06/1999, Nova Gradiška (Croatia) (b) 1,80 (c) D - right back (d) NK Istra 1961 (e) NK Lokomotiva, Din. Zagreb II, NK Lokomotiva, Mladost Cernik

*** Huk - Tomas Huk (Tomáš Huk) (a) 22/12/1994, Košice (Slovakia) (b) 1,84 (c) D - central defense (d) Piast Gliwice (e) Dunajska Streda, VSS Kosice

*** Hulka - Lukas Hulka (Lukáš Hůlka) (a) 31/03/1995, Mladá Boleslav (Czech Rep.) (b) 1,82 (c) D - central defense (d) Bohemians Praha 1905 (e) Mlada Boleslav, Bohemians 1905, Mlada Boleslav, Hradec Kralove, Mlada Boleslav

*** Hult - Niklas Hult (Bo Niklas Hult) (a) 13/02/1990, Värnamo (Sweden) (b) 1,73 (c) D - left back (d) IF Elfsborg (e) Hannover 96, AEK Athína, Panathinaikos, OGC Nice, Elfsborg, Värnamo

*** Humblet - Damien Humblet (a) 21/09/1996, ¿? (Luxembourg) (b) - (c) D - central defense (d) FC Wiltz 71 (e) Solières, FC Wiltz 71

*** Hummeland - Högni Hummeland (Høgni Hummeland) (a) 14/07/1996, ¿? (Faroe Islands) (b) - (c) D - right back (d) EB/Streymur II (e) EB/Streymur, EB/S II, EB/Streymur, EB/S II

*** Hummeland - Jákup Hummeland (a) 10/12/2003, ¿? (Faroe Islands) (b) - (c) M - central midfielder (d) EB/Streymur (e) EB/S II

*** Hummels - Mats Hummels (Mats Julian Hummels) (a) 16/12/1988, Bergisch Gladbach (Germany) (b) 1,91 (c) D - central defense (d) Borussia Dortmund (e) Bayern München, Borussia Dortmund, Bayern München, Borussia Dortmund, Bayern München, FC Bayern II

*** Humphreys - Bashir Humphreys (a) 15/03/2003, Exeter (England) (b) 1,86 (c) D - central defense (d) - (e) SC Paderborn

*** Humphreys - Iori Humphreys (Iori Thomas Humphreys) (a) 22/09/2003, ¿? (Wales) (b) - (c) D - central defense (d) Haverfordwest County (e) -

*** Humphries - Elliot Humphries (a) 28/06/2005, ¿? (Wales) (b) - (c) F - center forward (d) Cardiff Metropolitan University (e) Cardiff Metropolitan Police Reserves

*** Humphrys - Stephen Humphrys (Stephen Peter Humphrys) (a) 15/09/1997, Oldham (England) (b) 1,84 (c) F - center forward (d) Wigan Athletic (e) Heart of

Midlothian, Wigan Ath., AFC Rochdale, Southend United, Scunthorpe Utd., AFC Rochdale, Shrewsbury
*** Hunou - Adrien Hunou (a) 19/01/1994, Évry (France) (b) 1,79 (c) F - center forward (d) Angers SCO (e) Minnesota, Stade Rennes, Clermont Foot, Stade Rennes, Clermont Foot, Stade Rennes, Stade Rennes B
*** Hunt - Joe Hunt (a) 18/11/1999, ¿? (Wales) (b) 1,71 (c) M - left midfielder (d) - (e) Pontypridd, Briton Ferry, Llanelli, Merthyr Town
*** Hunziker - Andrin Hunziker (a) 21/02/2003, Basel (Switzerland) (b) 1,92 (c) F - center forward (d) FC Basel (e) FC Aarau, FC Basel
*** Huovila - Vilho Huovila (a) 10/07/2006, ¿? (Finland) (b) 1,84 (c) F - left winger (d) FC Lahti (e) -
*** Hurtado - Haiderson Hurtado (Haiderson Hurtado Palomino) (a) 25/11/1995, ¿? (Colombia) (b) 1,85 (c) D - central defense (d) FK Jablonec (e) Skalica, Azuriz, SKF Sered, Paraná
*** Husbauer - Josef Husbauer (Josef Hušbauer) (a) 16/03/1990, Praha (Czechoslovakia, now in Czech Rep.) (b) 1,82 (c) M - central midfielder (d) FK Pribram (e) Ypsonas FC, Karmiotissa, Anorthosis, Slavia Praha, Dynamo Dresden, Slavia Praha, Sparta Praha, Cagliari, Sparta Praha, Banik Ostrava, Viktoria Zizkov, 1.FK Pribram, Viktoria Zizkov, Jihlava
*** Huseinbasic - Denis Huseinbasic (Denis Huseinbašić) (a) 03/07/2001, Erbach (Odenwald) (Germany) (b) 1,84 (c) M - central midfielder (d) 1.FC Köln (e) K. Offenbach
*** Husejinovic - Said Husejinovic (Said Husejinović) (a) 17/05/1988, Zvornik (Yugoslavia, now in Bosnia and Herzegovina) (b) - (c) F - left winger (d) FK Sloboda Tuzla (e) FK Tuzla City, Sloboda Tuzla, FK Sarajevo, Dinamo Zagreb, NK Lokomotiva, Dinamo Zagreb, FK Sarajevo, Werder Bremen, 1.FC Kaiserslautern, Werder Bremen, Sloboda Tuzla
*** Hüseynli - Rauf Hüseynli (Rauf Elxan oğlu Hüseynli) (a) 25/01/2000, Baku (Azerbaijan) (b) 1,80 (c) D - right back (d) FK Qabala (e) Shamakhi, Qarabag 2, Zira FK, Qarabag 2, Zira FK, Qarabag 2
*** Hüseynov - Abbas Hüseynov (Abbas İsrafil oğlu Hüseynov) (a) 13/06/1995, Ganja (Azerbaijan) (b) 1,79 (c) D - right back (d) Qarabağ FK (e) Keshla, FC Shamakhi 2
*** Hüseynov - Badavi Hüseynov (Bədavi Ruslan oğlu Hüseynov) (a) 11/07/1991, Kaspiysk (Soviet Union, now in Russia) (b) 1,85 (c) D - central defense (d) Qarabağ FK (e) Sumqayit, Anzhi II, Dagdiesel
*** Hüseynov - Calal Hüseynov (Cəlal Hakim oğlu Hüseynov) (a) 02/01/2003, ¿? (Azerbaijan) (b) 1,83 (c) D - central defense (d) Arda Kardzhali (e) Zira FK, Shamakhi, Zira FK
*** Hüseynov - Hüseyn Hüseynov (Hüseyn Hüseynov) (a) 25/07/2006, ¿? (Azerbaijan) (b) - (c) D (d) Turan 2 Tovuz (e) -
*** Hüseynov - Vurgun Hüseynov (Vurğun Tofiq oğlu Hüseynov) (a) 25/04/1988, Baku (Soviet Union, now in Azerbaijan) (b) 1,82 (c) D - central defense (d) Kapaz PFK (e) Sumqayit, FK Qabala, Turan Tovuz, FK Qabala, Turan Tovuz
*** Huska - David Huska (Dávid Húska) (a) 30/09/2003, ¿? (Slovakia) (b) - (c) G (d) Tatran Liptovsky Mikulas (e) -
*** Huskic - Asim Huskic (a) 01/03/2004, ¿? (Luxembourg) (b) 1,82 (c) M (d) FC Differdange 03 (e) -
*** Huskovic - Muharem Huskovic (Muharem Husković) (a) 05/03/2003, ¿? (Austria) (b) 1,80 (c) F - center forward (d) FK Austria Viena (e) Young Violets

*** Husmani - Zeni Husmani (a) 28/11/1990, Gostivar (Yugoslavia, now in North Macedonia) (b) 1,74 (c) M - pivot (d) NK Domžale (e) Shkëndija, Giresunspor, Domžale, HNK Sibenik, NK Dinara Knin

*** Husovic - Dzemil Husovic (a) 18/05/2003, ¿? (Luxembourg) (b) - (c) G (d) FC Mondercange (e) Mertert-Wass.

*** Hussain - Etzaz Hussain (Etzaz Muzafar Hussain) (a) 27/01/1993, Oslo (Norway) (b) 1,76 (c) M - central midfielder (d) Apollon Limassol (e) Molde, Odd, Molde, NK Rudes, Sivasspor, Molde, Fredrikstad, Vålerenga

*** Hussar - Kristo Hussar (a) 28/06/2002, Tallinn (Estonia) (b) - (c) D - right back (d) FC Flora Tallinn (e) JK Tabasalu, FC Flora, JK Tabasalu

*** Hussein - Bilal Hussein (a) 22/04/2000, Stockholm (Sweden) (b) 1,83 (c) M - central midfielder (d) AIK Solna (e) Vasalunds IF, AIK

*** Hussein - Lukman Hussein (Lukman Olayemi Hussein) (a) 28/08/1996, Lagos (Nigeria) (b) 1,83 (c) D - central defense (d) KF Drenica (e) KF Tirana, KS Kastrioti, KS Burreli, 36 Lion FC

*** Hustad - Erlend Hustad (a) 03/01/1997, ¿? (Norway) (b) 1,92 (c) F - center forward (d) FK Jerv (e) Brann, Sandnes Ulf, Brann, Nest-Sotra IL, Brann, Notodden

*** Huszti - András Huszti (a) 29/01/2001, Pécs (Hungary) (b) 1,84 (c) D - right back (d) Zalaegerszegi TE FC (e) Puskás AFC, Zalaegerszeg, Puskás AFC, Budafoki MTE, Puskás AFC, Tiszakécske

*** Hutba - Iyad Hutba (ויטבא'ח איאד) (a) 20/11/1987, Reineh (Israel) (b) 1,77 (c) D - right back (d) Maccabi Bnei Reineh (e) M. Ahi Nazareth, Hapoel Tel Aviv, H. Petah Tikva, M. Kfar Kana

*** Hutchinson - Adam Hutchinson (Adam Stewart-Hutchinson) (a) 15/02/2003, Alva (Scotland) (b) 1,89 (c) D - central defense (d) Forfar Athletic FC (e) Dundee United, Forfar Athletic, Dundee United, Montrose, Dundee United, Dumbarton FC, Dundee United, Stirling Uni, Dundee United, Dundee Utd. Ju.

*** Hutchinson - Atiba Hutchinson (a) 08/02/1983, Brampton, Ontario (Canada) (b) 1,87 (c) M - pivot (d) - (e) Besiktas, PSV Eindhoven, FC København, Helsingborgs IF, Östers IF, Toronto Lynx, Vaughan Sun Dev.

*** Hutchinson - Omari Hutchinson (Omari Elijah Giraud-Hutchinson) (a) 29/10/2003, Redhill (England) (b) 1,74 (c) M - attacking midfielder (d) Ipswich Town (e) Ipswich

*** Hutchison - Max Hutchison (a) 16/01/2001, ¿? (England) (b) - (c) M - central midfielder (d) Finn Harps (e) Larne FC, Waterford FC

*** Huuhtanen - Eetu Huuhtanen (a) 31/01/2003, ¿? (Finland) (b) 1,87 (c) G (d) FC Inter Turku (e) Ilves

*** Huuhtanen - Otto Huuhtanen (a) 28/02/2000, Espoo (Finland) (b) 1,91 (c) G (d) SJK Seinäjoki (e) Mikkelin, FC Honka, JIPPO, FC Honka, Helsinki IFK, Ilves

*** Huxley - Calum Huxley (a) 07/10/2001, Chester (England) (b) - (c) F - left winger (d) Aberystwyth Town (e) Flint Town, Witton Albion, Nantwich Town, Eccleshall FC, Nantwich Town, Caernarfon, Wrexham

*** Huyghebaert - Jérémy Huyghebaert (a) 07/01/1989, Mouscron (Belgium) (b) 1,80 (c) D - left back (d) - (e) FC U Craiova, Excelsior Mouscron, Neuchâtel Xamax, Excelsior Mouscron, White Star, Excelsior Mouscron, KV Mechelen, KSV Roeselare, KV Mechelen, AJ Auxerre, KSV Roeselare, AJ Auxerre, Excelsior Mouscron

*** Hvalic - Klemen Hvalic (Klemen Hvalič) (a) 18/04/2002, Nova Gorica (Slovenia) (b) 1,95 (c) G (d) FC Koper (e) -

*** Hvidt - Benjamin Hvidt (Benjamin Steenfeldt Hvidt) (a) 12/03/2000, Aarhus (Denmark) (b) 1,84 (c) M - central midfielder (d) Aarhus GF (e) -

*** Hvoinickis - Daniils Hvoinickis (Daņiils Hvoiņickis) (a) 08/04/1998, Liepaja (Latvia) (b) 1,74 (c) F - left winger (d) FK Beitar (e) Spartaks, Liepaja, Albatroz/Jelgava, RFS, Super Nova, RFS, AFA Olaine, FK Salaspils, Liepaja, FHK Liepajas Metalurgs II

*** Hwang - Hee-chan Hwang (황희찬) (a) 26/01/1996, Chuncheon, Gangwon (South Korea) (b) 1,77 (c) F - center forward (d) Wolverhampton Wanderers (e) RB Leipzig, Wolverhampton Wanderers, RB Leipzig, RB Salzburg, SV Hamburg, RB Salzburg, FC Liefering

*** Hwang - In-beom Hwang (황인범) (a) 20/09/1996, Daejeon (South Korea) (b) 1,77 (c) M - central midfielder (d) Olympiakos El Pireo (e) Rubin Kazan, FC Seoul, Rubin Kazan, FC Seoul, Rubin Kazan, Vancouver, Daejeon Citizen, Asan Mugunghwa, Daejeon Citizen, D. Moonhwa ES

*** Hwang - Ui-jo Hwang (황의조) (a) 28/08/1992, Seongnam, Gyeonggi (South Korea) (b) 1,85 (c) F - center forward (d) Nottingham Forest (e) FC Seoul, Nottingham Forest, Olympiakos, Nottingham Forest, Girondins Bordeaux, Gamba Osaka, Seongnam FC, Yonsei Univ.

*** Hybs - Matej Hybs (Matěj Hybš) (a) 03/01/1993, Praha (Czech Rep.) (b) 1,83 (c) D - left back (d) Bohemians Praha 1905 (e) Viktoria Plzen, Teplice, Viktoria Plzen, Nieciecza, Viktoria Plzen, Slovan Liberec, Sparta Praha, Jablonec, Sparta Praha, Jihlava, Sparta Praha

*** Hycka - Alois Hycka (Alois Hyčka) (a) 22/07/1990, Cheb (Czechoslovakia, now in Czech Rep.) (b) 1,69 (c) D - right back (d) FK Viagem Usti nad Labem (e) Teplice, Zbrojovka Brno, Usti nad Labem, Zbrojovka Brno, Usti nad Labem

*** Hyde - Josh Hyde (a) 07/12/2004, ¿? (England) (b) - (c) G (d) Market Drayton Town (e) Newtown, FC Haughmond

*** Hyjek - Javier Hyjek (Javier Ajenjo Hyjek) (a) 12/01/2001, Madrid (Spain) (b) 1,78 (c) M - central midfielder (d) Slask Wroclaw II (e) Recreativo, Śląsk Wroclaw, Piast Gliwice

*** Hyla - Oliwier Hyla (a) 24/08/2004, Kraków (Poland) (b) 1,82 (c) D - right back (d) Cracovia (e) Cracovia, AP Cracovia

*** Hysaj - Elseid Hysaj (Elseid Gëzim Hysaj) (a) 02/02/1994, Shkodër (Albania) (b) 1,82 (c) D - right back (d) SS Lazio (e) Napoli, Empoli

*** Hyseni - Erald Hyseni (a) 12/11/1999, Berat (Albania) (b) 1,83 (c) M - central midfielder (d) FK Tomori Berat (e) KF Skënderbeu, KF Egnatia, KS Besa, FK Tomori Berat, FC Luftëtari, FK Tomori Berat

*** Hyseni - Ergon Hyseni (a) 18/01/1994, Gjilan (RF Yugoslavia, now in Kosovo) (b) 1,90 (c) D - central defense (d) KF Ferizaj (e) KF Arbëria, KF Ferizaj, KF Vitia, SC Gjilani

*** Hyseni - Erzen Hyseni (a) 18/06/2004, ¿? (Serbia and Montenegro, now in Kosovo) (b) - (c) F (d) SC Gjilani (e) -

*** Hyseni - Hasan Hyseni (a) 14/04/1997, Mitrovicë (RF Yugoslavia, now in Kosovo) (b) 1,75 (c) M - left midfielder (d) FC Prishtina (e) FC Malisheva, FC A&N, KF Drenica, KF Trepca 89

*** Hytönen - Teemu Hytönen (a) 15/08/2002 (b) 1,94 (c) F - center forward (d) Vaasan Palloseura (e) VPS II, Ilves II

*** Hyvärinen - Juho Hyvärinen (a) 27/03/2000, ¿? (Finland) (b) 1,78 (c) D - right back (d) FC Inter Turku (e) RoPS

*** í Horni Nielsen - Jón í Horni Nielsen (a) 22/04/2005, ¿? (Faroe Islands) (b) 1,74 (c) M - pivot (d) 07 Vestur (e) 07 Vestur II

*** Iacob - Alexandru Iacob (a) 14/04/1989, Hunedoara (Romania) (b) 1,86 (c) D - central defense (d) FC Metaloglobus Bucharest (e) Minaur, CS Mioveni, FC Rapid 1923, Pafos FC, Ethnikos, Rapid Bucureşti, Delta Tulcea, FC Viitorul, Otelul Galati, Steaua Bucuresti, Vic. Branesti, Steaua Bucuresti, FCSB II, Steaua Bucuresti, AS FC Buzău, Steaua Bucuresti, Corvinul 2005

*** Iacob - Florin Iacob (a) 16/08/1993, Braşov (Romania) (b) 1,80 (c) G (d) UTA Arad (e) Metaloglobus, Sportul Snagov, ASA Tg. Mures, Concordia, FC Brasov, Concordia, FC Brasov, Concordia, FC Brasov, Tarlungeni, FC Brasov, Tarlungeni, FC Brasov, FC Brasov II

*** Iacob - Paul Iacob (Paul Alexandru Iacob) (a) 21/06/1996, Constanţa (Romania) (b) 1,85 (c) D - central defense (d) FC Rapid 1923 (e) Chindia, FCV Farul, Chindia, FC Viitorul, Dunarea Calarasi, FC Viitorul, ASA Tg. Mures, FC Viitorul, FC Brasov, FC Viitorul, Gaz Metan, FC Viitorul

*** Iacovitti - Alex Iacovitti (Alexander Iacovitti) (a) 02/09/1997, Nottingham (England) (b) 1,93 (c) D - central defense (d) Port Vale FC (e) Ross County, Oldham Athletic, Forest Green Rovers, Mansfield Town

*** Iadze - Koba Iadze (კობა იაძე) (a) 27/01/2003, ¿? (Georgia) (b) - (c) D - central defense (d) FC Gagra (e) -

*** Iago - Iago (Iago Amaral Borduchi) (a) 23/03/1997, Monte Azul Paulista (Brazil) (b) 1,81 (c) D - left back (d) FC Augsburg (e) Internacional

*** Iakobidze - Giorgi Iakobidze (გიორგი იაკობიძე) (a) 27/02/2001, ¿? (Georgia) (b) - (c) F - attacking midfielder (d) - (e) FC Locomotive

*** Iakobidze - Irakli Iakobidze (ირაკლი იაკობიძე) (a) 25/01/2002, Tbilisi (Georgia) (b) 1,94 (c) D - central defense (d) Dinamo Tbilisi II (e) -

*** Ialanji - Alexandr Ialanji (a) 14/12/2005, ¿? (Moldova) (b) 1,65 (c) F - right winger (d) FC Dinamo-Auto Tiraspol (e) -

*** Iancu - Dragos Iancu (Dragoş Petru Iancu) (a) 29/09/2002, Huedin (Romania) (b) 1,87 (c) M - central midfielder (d) FC Hermannstadt (e) Gaz Metan

*** Iancu - Gabriel Iancu (Gabriel Cristian Iancu) (a) 15/04/1994, Bucuresti (Romania) (b) 1,86 (c) F - left winger (d) FC Hermannstadt (e) Akhmat Grozny, FC Hermannstadt, Akhmat Grozny, FC U Craiova, Akhmat Grozny, FCV Farul, Akhmat Grozny, FC Viitorul, Dunarea Calarasi, FC Voluntari, Nieciecza, FC Viitorul, Steaua Bucuresti, Karabükspor, Steaua Bucuresti, FC Viitorul, Academia Hagi

*** Iapichino - Dennis Iapichino (a) 27/07/1990, Frauenfeld (Switzerland) (b) 1,82 (c) D - left back (d) - (e) FC Sion, Servette FC, AS Livorno, Servette FC, AS Livorno, Robur Siena, FC Winterthur, D.C. United, Montreal, FC Lugano, FC Biel-Bienne

*** Iashvili - Nodar Iashvili (ნოდარ იაშვილი) (a) 24/01/1993, Tbilisi (Georgia) (b) 1,75 (c) D - right back (d) FC Gonio (e) FC Locomotive, Saburtalo, Dinamo Tbilisi, Saburtalo

*** Ibáñez - Pablo Ibáñez (Pablo Ibáñez Lumbreras) (a) 20/09/1998, Pamplona (Spain) (b) 1,79 (c) M - central midfielder (d) CA Osasuna (e) Osasuna Prom., UD Mutilvera, AD San Juan

*** Ibertsberger - Lukas Ibertsberger (a) 06/08/2003, ¿? (Austria) (b) 1,81 (c) D - left back (d) Wolfsberger AC (e) Wolfsberger AC, RB Salzburg, FC Liefering

*** Ibishev - Turpal-Ali Ibishev (Ибишев Турпал-Али Сайд-Эминович) (a) 18/02/2002, ¿? (Russia) (b) 1,91 (c) D - central defense (d) Druzhba Maikop (e) Akhmat Grozny, Akhmat II, Akademia Ramzan

*** Ibragimov - Ravil Ibragimov (Ибрагимов Равиль Зильфикарович) (a) 25/12/2000, Talgar (Kazakhstan) (b) 1,86 (c) D - central defense (d) FC Arys (e) Atyrau, Kairat-Zhas, Kairat Moskva, Kairat-Zhas, Astana-Zhas

*** Ibrahim - Abbas Ibrahim (a) 02/01/1998, Idah (Nigeria) (b) 1,71 (c) M - pivot (d) Zira FK (e) Paços Ferreira, Arouca, Paços Ferreira, Paredes, Paços Ferreira, Paços F. B, Kwara United
*** Ibrahim - Djibrilla Ibrahim (Djibrilla Ibrahim Mossi) (a) 02/03/2002, Niamey (Niger) (b) 1,94 (c) D - central defense (d) HNK Rijeka (e) NK Orijent 1919, Al Hilal United, NSFC Iyane, Cheetah FC, AS Douanes
*** Ibrahim - Fard Ibrahim (Fard Ibrahim) (a) 07/01/2000, Accra (Ghana) (b) 1,83 (c) D - left back (d) Isloch Minsk Region (e) Verum Ipsum, Inter Allies
*** Ibrahim - Harun Ibrahim (Harun Mohammed Ademnur Ibrahim) (a) 26/02/2003, Göteborg (Sweden) (b) 1,85 (c) M - central midfielder (d) Molde FK (e) GAIS, Angered BK, Angered MBIK
*** Ibrahim - Jibril Ibrahim (a) 01/12/2002, ¿? (Romania) (b) 1,84 (c) F - center forward (d) FC U Craiova 1948 (e) Sfintul Gheorghe, Abuja FC
*** Ibrahim - Omar Ibrahim (Omar Hassan Ibrahim) (a) 04/07/2000, ¿? (England) (b) - (c) M - left midfielder (d) - (e) Flint Town, Radcliffe
*** Ibrahim - Rahim Ibrahim (Rash Rahim Ibrahim) (a) 10/06/2001, Salaga (Ghana) (b) 1,85 (c) M - central midfielder (d) AS Trencin (e) Accra Lions
*** Ibrahima - Ibrahima (Ibrahima Camará) (a) 25/01/1999, Conakry (Guinea) (b) 1,90 (c) M - pivot (d) Boavista Porto FC (e) Moreirense, Braga B
*** Ibrahimaj - Ylldren Ibrahimaj (a) 24/12/1995, Arendal (Norway) (b) 1,78 (c) F - right winger (d) Lillestrøm SK (e) Ural, Viking, Mjøndalen, Arendal
*** Ibrahimi - Yll Ibrahimi (a) 29/07/2003, Gjilan (Serbia and Montenegro, now in Kosovo) (b) 1,78 (c) D - left back (d) FC Drita Gjilan (e) -
*** Ibrahimli - Ismayil Ibrahimli (Ismayıl Khalid oğlu İbrahimli) (a) 13/02/1998, Baku (Azerbaijan) (b) 1,78 (c) M - central midfielder (d) Zira FK (e) Zira FK, Qarabag FK, MOIK
*** Ibrahimov - Kamran Ibrahimov (Kamran Tahir oğlu İbrahimov) (a) 07/06/1999, ¿? (Azerbaijan) (b) 1,89 (c) G (d) Kapaz PFK (e) Kapaz 2, Kapaz PFK, Neftchi Baku
*** Ibrahimovic - Arijon Ibrahimovic (Arijon Ibrahimović) (a) 11/12/2005, Nürnberg (Germany) (b) 1,76 (c) M - attacking midfielder (d) Bayern München (e) -
*** Ibrahimović - Zlatan Ibrahimović (a) 03/10/1981, Malmö (Sweden) (b) 1,95 (c) F - center forward (d) Maximilian Ibrahimović (e) AC Milan, Los Ángeles, Manchester Utd., Paris Saint-Germain, AC Milan, FC Barcelona, AC Milan, FC Barcelona, Internazionale Milano, Juventus, Ajax, Malmö FF, FBK Balkan, Malmö ABI
*** Ibraimi - Besart Ibraimi (a) 17/12/1986, Kicevo (Yugoslavia, now in North Macedonia) (b) 1,82 (c) F - center forward (d) Struga Trim & Lum (e) AO Xanthi, Shkëndija, Ermis Aradippou, EN Paralimniou, FK Sevastopol, Metalurg Z., FK Sevastopol, SK Tavriya, FK Sevastopol, Schalke 04 II, FC Schalke 04, Renova, Napredok Kicevo, Vëllazërimi
*** Ibryam - Ibryam Ibryam (Ибрям Ибрахим Ибрям) (a) 12/01/2001, Silistra (Bulgaria) (b) 1,90 (c) D - central defense (d) FC Fratria (e) Dob. Dobrich, Spartak Varna
*** Ibsen - Frederik Ibsen (a) 28/03/1997, ¿? (Denmark) (b) 1,90 (c) G (d) FC Helsingör (e) Lyngby BK, Kolding IF, FC København, Vendsyssel FF
*** Icardi - Mauro Icardi (Mauro Emanuel Icardi Rivero) (a) 19/02/1993, Rosario (Argentina) (b) 1,81 (c) F - center forward (d) Galatasaray (e) Paris Saint-Germain, Galatasaray, Paris Saint-Germain, Internazionale Milano, Paris Saint-Germain, Internazionale Milano, Sampdoria

*** Icha - Marek Icha (a) 14/03/2002, ¿? (Czech Rep.) (b) 1,87 (c) M - central midfielder (d) FK Pardubice (e) Slavia Praha, Vlasim, Slavia Praha, FC MAS Taborsko

*** Idasiak - Hubert Idasiak (Hubert Dawid Idasiak) (a) 03/02/2002, Slawno (Poland) (b) 1,88 (c) G (d) SSC Nápoles (e) AP Pogon

*** Ideguchi - Yosuke Ideguchi (井手口 陽介) (a) 23/08/1996, Fukuoka, Fukuoka (Japan) (b) 1,71 (c) M - central midfielder (d) Avispa Fukuoka (e) Avispa Fukuoka, Celtic FC, Gamba Osaka, Leeds Utd., Greuther Fürth, Leeds Utd., Cultural Leonesa, Leeds Utd., Gamba Osaka

*** Idowu - David Idowu (David Akintola Idowu) (a) 23/06/2000, ¿? (Nigeria) (b) 1,82 (c) D - central defense (d) - (e) Daugavpils, Real Sapphire

*** Idris - Nuradeen Idris (Nuradeen Idris) (a) 15/01/2002, Kaduna (Nigeria) (b) 1,75 (c) F - center forward (d) FK Smorgon (e) FK Smorgon, BATE II, Dzerzhinsk, BATE II, FK Smorgon, BATE II

*** Idrissi - Oussama Idrissi (a) 26/02/1996, Bergen op Zoom (Netherlands) (b) 1,83 (d) Sevilla FC (e) Feyenoord, Sevilla FC, Cádiz CF, Sevilla FC, Ajax, Sevilla FC, AZ Alkmaar, FC Groningen

*** Idrissou - Ramzi Toure Idrissou (a) 31/07/1996, Oslo (Norway) (b) 1,95 (c) D - central defense (d) AB Argir (e) NK Fuzinar, Hødd, Levanger, Hødd, Atlanta SC, Tampa Spartans, Tropics, Tampa Spartans, Tropics, Tampa Spartans

*** Idrizaj - Hektor Idrizaj (a) 15/04/1989, Vlorë (Albania) (b) 1,74 (c) D - right back (d) AF Elbasani (e) KF Skënderbeu, KF Teuta, FK Partizani, FC Kamza, KF Skënderbeu, Flamurtari FC, FK Bylis, KF Teuta, FK Bylis

*** Idrizi - Blendi Idrizi (a) 02/05/1998, Bonn (Germany) (b) 1,76 (c) M - attacking midfielder (d) FC Schalke 04 (e) Jahn Regensburg, FC Schalke 04, Schalke 04 II, Fortuna Köln, Alemannia Aachen, BW Friesdorf

*** Idrizi - Bujar Idrizi (a) 11/12/1991, ¿? (RF Yugoslavia, now in Kosovo) (b) 1,89 (c) D - right back (d) FC Kosova Düsseldorf (e) KF Llapi, FC Prishtina, FC Llapi, FK Kukësi, FC Llapi, KF Trepca 89, FC Llapi, KF Hysi

*** Idrizi (c) M (d) KF Drenica (e) - - Erion Idrizi (c) M (d) KF Drenica (e) -

*** Idrizović - Mirza Idrizović (a) 10/12/1997, ¿? (RF Yugoslavia, now in Montenegro) (b) 1,82 (c) M - central midfielder (d) Jedinstvo Bijelo Polje (e) Mornar Bar, Jedinstvo

*** Idumbo-Muzambo - Franck Idumbo-Muzambo (a) 23/06/2002, ¿? (Belgium) (b) - (c) F - center forward (d) - (e) Jong KV Mechelen

*** Idzes - Jay Idzes (a) 02/06/2000, Mierlo (Netherlands) (b) 1,90 (c) D - central defense (d) Venezia FC (e) Go Ahead Eagles, FC Eindhoven

*** Idzi - Lee Idzi (a) 08/02/1988, ¿? (Wales) (b) - (c) G (d) Carmarthen Town (e) Haverfordwest, Barry Town, Carmarthen, Bangor City, Neath, Haverfordwest, Hereford Utd.

*** Ié - Edgar Ié (Edgar Miguel Ié) (a) 01/05/1994, Bissau (Guinea-Bissau) (b) 1,82 (c) D - central defense (d) Basaksehir FK (e) Trabzonspor, Feyenoord, Trabzonspor, Lille, FC Nantes, Lille, Belenenses, Villarreal CF B, FC Barcelona B

*** Iervolino - Antonio Pio Iervolino (a) 23/05/2003, San Gennaro Vesuviano (Italy) (b) - (c) M - central midfielder (d) US Salernitana 1919 (e) -

*** Ieseanu - Dinis Ieseanu (Dinis Ieşeanu) (a) 18/02/2000, Lisboa (Portugal) (b) 1,89 (c) D - central defense (d) FC Zimbru Chisinau (e) 1º Dezembro

*** Ifoni - Ejaita Ifoni (a) 13/02/2000, ¿? (Nigeria) (b) 1,87 (c) F - center forward (d) RFC Seraing (e) Black Bulls, FC Porto B, Black Bulls, CD Costa do Sol, Black Bulls, Chibuto, Black Bulls, Chibuto

*** Ifrah - Nehoray Ifrah (יפרח נהוראי) (a) 07/05/2003, Tiberias (Israel) (b) - (c) F - right winger (d) Hapoel Afula (e) Hapoel Afula, Maccabi Haifa, Ironi Tiberias, Maccabi Haifa, Hapoel Hadera, Maccabi Haifa, Hapoel Afula, Maccabi Haifa
*** Igbokwe - Goodnews Igbokwe (a) 26/02/2003, Aba (Nigeria) (b) 1,85 (c) F - center forward (d) Hapoel Ramat Gan (e) H. Ramat Gan, FC Noah, FC Van, Right2Win SA
*** Igiehon - Benny Igiehon (a) 03/11/1993, Leeds (England) (b) 1,93 (c) F - center forward (d) - (e) Portadown, Dundela FC, Ards FC, Dergview, Finn Harps, Larne FC, Boston Utd., Sligo Rovers, Scarborough Athletic, Sheffield FC, Alfreton, Bradford PA, Alfreton, FC Langenthal, FC Solothurn
*** Iglesias - Álex Iglesias (Alejandro Iglesias Rodríguez) (a) 07/04/1997, Murcia (Spain) (b) 1,86 (c) G (d) Atlètic Club d'Escaldes (e) IC d'Escaldes, Sant Julià, UD Caravaca, Elche Ilicitano, Young Harris, Mississippi, Young Harris, Palm Beach Utd., Young Harris, Marym. Mariners
*** Iglesias - Borja Iglesias (Borja Iglesias Quintas) (a) 17/01/1993, Santiago de Compostela (Spain) (b) 1,87 (c) F - center forward (d) Real Betis Balompié (e) RCD Espanyol, RC Celta, Celta B, Real Zaragoza, Celta B, Villarreal CF C
*** Iglesias - Juan Iglesias (Juan Antonio Iglesias Sánchez) (a) 03/07/1998, Valladolid (Spain) (b) 1,87 (c) D - right back (d) Getafe CF (e) Getafe CF B, UD Logroñés, Logroñés Prom.
*** Iglesias - Matias Iglesias (Walter Matías Iglesias) (a) 18/04/1985, Rosario (Argentina) (b) 1,90 (c) M - pivot (d) Ionikos Nikeas (e) Asteras Tripoli, CC Yatai, Atromitos FC, AE Larisa, At. Madrid B, CD Toledo, At. Madrid B
*** Ignat - Cristian Ignat (a) 29/01/2003, Chişinău (Moldova) (b) 1,94 (c) D - central defense (d) CS Mioveni (e) CS Mioveni, FC Rapid 1923, U. Constanta, FC Rapid 1923, Rapid 1923 II, FC Juniorul
*** Ignatenko - Dmitriy Ignatenko (Игнатенко Дмитрий Александрович) (a) 01/02/1995, Gomel (Belarus) (b) 1,89 (c) D - central defense (d) - (e) Slavia, Gorodeya, Gomel, Belshina, Gomel, Gomel II
*** Ignatjev - Ivan Ignatjev (Игнатьев Иван Александрович) (a) 06/01/1999, Achinsk, Krasnoyarsk Region (Russia) (b) 1,80 (c) F - center forward (d) FK Sochi (e) Lokomotiv Moskva, Rubin Kazan, KS Samara, Rubin Kazan, Krasnodar, Krasnodar II
*** Ignatjev - Vladislav Ignatjev (Игнатьев Владислав Николаевич) (a) 13/02/2003, Minsk (Belarus) (b) 1,93 (c) G (d) FK Gomel (e) Gomel, BATE II, Ostrovets, BATE II
*** Ignatov - Danila Ignatov (a) 19/06/2001, ¿? (Moldova) (b) 1,92 (c) D - central defense (d) FC Floresti (e) FC Sheriff, Sheriff-2
*** Ignatov - Kerimdzhan Ignatov (Керимджан Евгениев Игнатов) (a) 15/02/2005, ¿? (Bulgaria) (b) - (c) M - pivot (d) Arda Kardzhali (e) Arda II
*** Ignatov - Leonid Ignatov (Леонид Игнатов) (a) 04/01/2002, Skopje (North Macedonia) (b) 1,77 (c) F - right winger (d) Sileks Kratovo (e) FK Skopje, Vardar
*** Ignatov - Mikhail Ignatov (Игнатов Михаил Александрович) (a) 04/05/2000, Moskva (Russia) (b) 1,87 (c) M - attacking midfielder (d) FC Spartak de Moscú (e) Spartak-2, Spartak Moskva, Spartak-2, Spartak Moskva II
*** Ignatovich - Andrey Ignatovich (Игнатович Андрей Сергеевич) (a) 02/05/2003, ¿? (Belarus) (b) - (c) G (d) Dnepr Mogilev (e) Mogilev II, Dnepr-2, RUOR Minsk
*** Ignatovich - Sergey Ignatovich (Игнатович Сергей Сергеевич) (a) 29/06/1992, Mogilev (Belarus) (b) 1,92 (c) G (d) Shakhter Soligorsk (e) Isloch, FK Minsk, Dynamo Brest, Dinamo Minsk, FK Bereza, Dinamo Minsk, Dinamo Minsk II, FK Bereza, Dinamo Minsk II

*** Ignjatovic - Nikola Ignjatovic (Никола Игњатовић) (a) 02/02/1998, Smederevska Palanka (RF Yugoslavia, now in Serbia) (b) 1,86 (c) D - central defense (d) Diagoras Rodou (e) Radnicki Srem, Radnik, Zarkovo, OFK Beograd
*** Ignjatovic - Uros Ignjatovic (a) 18/02/2001, Raška (RF Yugoslavia, now in Serbia) (b) 1,71 (c) D - right back (d) Buducnost Podgorica (e) FK Indjija, Čukarički, Sindjelic Bg, Čukarički
*** Igonen - Matvei Igonen (a) 02/10/1996, Tallinn (Estonia) (b) 1,88 (c) G (d) Hebar Pazardzhik (e) Podbeskidzie, FC Flora, Lillestrøm, FC Flora, Lillestrøm, FCI Tallinn
*** Igor - Igor (Igor Julio dos Santos de Paulo) (a) 07/02/1998, Bom Sucesso (Brazil) (b) 1,85 (c) D - central defense (d) Brighton & Hove Albion (e) Fiorentina, SPAL, Fiorentina, SPAL, RB Salzburg, Austria Viena, RB Salzburg, Wolfsberger AC, RB Salzburg, FC Liefering
*** Igor Henrique - Igor Henrique (Igor Henrique da Silva Nogueira) (a) 17/02/2004, Alterosa (Brazil) (b) 1,72 (c) F - left winger (d) Metalist 1925 Kharkiv (e) Metalist 1925
*** Igor Thiago - Igor Thiago (Igor Thiago Nascimento Rodrigues) (a) 26/06/2001, Tucuruí (Brazil) (b) 1,88 (c) F - center forward (d) KV Brugge (e) Ludogorets, Cruzeiro
*** Igubaev - Timur Igubaev (Игубаев Тимур) (a) 27/09/2003, ¿? (Kazakhstan) (b) 1,80 (c) M (d) Tobol Kostanay II (e) -
*** Ihattaren - Mohamed Ihattaren (Mohamed Amine Ihattaren) (a) 12/02/2002, Utrecht (Netherlands) (b) 1,83 (c) M - attacking midfielder (d) - (e) Juventus, Ajax, Juventus, Sampdoria, Juventus, PSV Eindhoven
*** Iheanacho - Kelechi Iheanacho (Kelechi Promise Iheanacho) (a) 03/10/1996, Imo (Nigeria) (b) 1,85 (c) F - center forward (d) Leicester City (e) Manchester City
*** İhekuna - Maxmillian İhekuna (Maxmillian Ugochukwu İhekuna) (a) 15/09/2001, Owerri (Nigeria) (b) 1,74 (c) M - central midfielder (d) - (e) Sfintul Gheorghe, Codru, Olympic Hybrid
*** Ihler - Frederik Ihler (Frederik Dahl Ihler) (a) 25/06/2003, ¿? (Denmark) (b) 1,81 (c) F - center forward (d) Landskrona BoIS (e) Aarhus GF, Skive IK, Aarhus GF, Valur, Aarhus GF
*** Ihrig-Farkas - Sebestyén Ihrig-Farkas (a) 28/01/1994, Budapest (Hungary) (b) 1,88 (c) M - attacking midfielder (d) Vasas FC (e) Budafoki MTE, Békéscsaba, Kozármisleny, Honvéd, Parma, ND Gorica, Honvéd II
*** Ikaunieks - Davis Ikaunieks (Dāvis Ikaunieks) (a) 07/01/1994, Kuldiga (Latvia) (b) 1,85 (c) F - center forward (d) FK Jablonec (e) Liepaja, Jablonec, Mlada Boleslav, Jablonec, Fastav Zlin, Jablonec, RFS, Jablonec, Jihlava, Liepaja, Jihlava, Liepaja, Metalurgs, FHK Liepajas Metalurgs II
*** Ikaunieks - Janis Ikaunieks (Jānis Ikaunieks) (a) 16/02/1995, Kuldīga (Latvia) (b) 1,84 (c) F - right winger (d) RFS (e) KuPS, RFS, Strømsgodset, Liepaja, FC Metz, Liepaja, FC Metz, AE Larisa, FC Metz, Liepaja, Metalurgs, FHK Liepajas Metalurgs II
*** Ikene - Farid Ikene (a) 15/12/2000, ¿? (Luxembourg) (b) 1,73 (c) M - pivot (d) Racing FC Union Luxembourg (e) Jammerbugt FC, RFCU Luxembourg, Progrès Niederkorn, Differdange 03
*** Ikene - Sofiane Ikene (a) 27/02/2005, Esch-Alzette (Luxembourg) (b) 1,81 (c) D - central defense (d) 1.FC Nuremberg II (e) Progrès Niederkorn, F91 Dudelange
*** Ikic - Frane Ikic (Frane Ikić) (a) 19/06/1994, Zadar (Croatia) (b) 1,94 (c) D - central defense (d) FC Buxoro (e) Velez Mostar, Gyirmót FC, Zeljeznicar, NK Fuzinar, NK Zadar, Cibalia, Koper, HNK Rijeka, NK Zadar

*** Ikic - Ivan Ikic (Ivan Ikić) (a) 13/09/1999, Đakovo (Croatia) (b) 1,80 (c) F - right winger (d) FK Sarajevo (e) Genclerbirligi, FK Sarajevo, Siroki Brijeg, Medjimurje, NK Osijek II, Medjimurje, NK Osijek II, NK Lucko, NK Osijek II

*** Ikoba - Eduvie Ikoba (a) 26/10/1997, Bettendorf, Iowa (United States) (b) 1,93 (c) F - center forward (d) Zalaegerszegi TE FC (e) AS Trencin, Zalaegerszeg, Dartmouth Col., Black Rock FC, Dartmouth Col.

*** Ikoko - Jordan Ikoko (a) 03/02/1994, Montereau (France) (b) 1,78 (c) D - right back (d) Pafos FC (e) Ludogorets, Guingamp, Paris Saint Germain B, RC Lens, Paris Saint Germain B, Le Havre AC, Paris Saint Germain B, US Créteil-Lusitanos, Paris Saint Germain B

*** Ikoné - Jonathan Ikoné (Nanitamo Jonathan Ikoné) (a) 02/05/1998, Bondy (France) (b) 1,75 (c) F - right winger (d) Fiorentina (e) Lille, Paris Saint-Germain, Montpellier, Paris Saint-Germain, Montpellier, Paris Saint-Germain

*** Ikonomidis - Georgios Ikonomidis (Γιώργος Οικονομίδης) (a) 10/04/1990, Nikosia (Cyprus) (b) 1,80 (c) M - central midfielder (d) Olympiakos Nikosia (e) Karmiotissa, Doxa Katokopias, Olympiakos N., Anorthosis, Omonia Nicosia, Doxa Katokopias, PAEEK Kyrenia, Barnet, APOEL FC, Digenis Morfou, APOEL FC

*** Ikonomidis - Giannis Ikonomidis (Γιάννης Οικονομίδης) (a) 03/01/1998, ¿? (Greece) (b) 1,81 (c) M - central midfielder (d) Ionikos Nikeas (e) Atromitos FC, AE Kifisias, Atromitos FC, Panionios

*** Ikonomopoulos - Antonis Ikonomopoulos (Αντώνης Οικονομόπουλος) (a) 09/05/1998, Athen (Greece) (b) 1,79 (c) D - right back (d) Volos NPS (e) PAS Giannina, Apollon Smyrnis, Panathinaikos, AE Sparti, Panathinaikos

*** Ikonomou - Marios Ikonomou (Μάριος Οικονόμου) (a) 06/10/1992, Ioannina (Greece) (b) 1,89 (c) D - central defense (d) Panetolikos GFS (e) Sampdoria, FC København, AEK Athína, Bologna, AEK Athína, Bologna, Bari, Bologna, SPAL, Bologna, Cagliari, PAS Giannina

*** Ikpeazu - Uche Ikpeazu (a) 28/02/1995, London (England) (b) 1,90 (c) F - center forward (d) Konyaspor (e) Middlesbrough, Cardiff City, Middlesbrough, Wycombe Wanderers, Heart of Midlothian, Cambridge Utd., Watford, Blackpool, Watford, Port Vale, Watford, Crewe Alexandra, Watford, Doncaster Rovers, Watford, Crewe Alexandra, Watford, Crewe Alexandra, Watford, Didcot

*** Ikstens - Kaspars Ikstens (a) 05/06/1988, Riga (Soviet Union, now in Latvia) (b) 1,86 (c) G (d) - (e) Leevon, Liepaja, Leevon, Noah Jurmala, RFS, Jelgava, Víkingur Ó., Daugavpils, Skonto, Olimps Riga

*** Ikugar - Kenneth Ikugar (Kenneth Tig-Ishor Ikugar) (a) 27/10/2000, Calabar (Nigeria) (b) 1,93 (c) F - center forward (d) Spartak Trnava (e) Zlaté Moravce, Spartak Trnava, Slavoj Trebisov, Spartak Trnava, Usti nad Labem, FootyFanz, Pythagorean FC

*** Ikwuemesi - Chukwubuikem Ikwuemesi (a) 05/08/2001, ¿? (Nigeria) (b) 1,95 (c) F - center forward (d) NK Celje (e) NK Krsko, Giant Brillars, Vorwärts Steyr, Giant Brillars

*** Ilaimaharitra - Marco Ilaimaharitra (a) 26/07/1995, Mulhouse (France) (b) 1,78 (c) M - pivot (d) RSC Charleroi (e) FC Sochaux, FC Sochaux B

*** Ilas - Narcis Ilas (Narcis Cosmin Ilaş) (a) 27/03/2007, Botoşani (Romania) (b) - (c) D - right back (d) FC Botosani (e) -

*** Ilenic - Mitja Ilenic (Mitja Ilenič) (a) 26/12/2004, ¿? (Slovenia) (b) 1,80 (c) D - right back (d) New York City FC (e) Domžale

*** Ilia - Marios Ilia (Μάριος Ηλία) (a) 19/05/1996, Xylotymbou (Cyprus) (b) 1,86 (c) F - attacking midfielder (d) Ethnikos Achnas (e) APOEL FC, Ethnikos, AEL Limassol, Alki Oroklini, AEL Limassol, Ethnikos

*** Iliadis - Ilias Iliadis (Ηλίας Ηλιάδης) (a) 21/03/2001, Toronto, Ontario (Canada) (b) 1,81 (c) M - pivot (d) Atlético Ottawa (e) At. Ottawa, Montréal, Panathinaikos B

*** Ilic - Andrej Ilic (Андреj Илић) (a) 03/04/2000, Beograd (RF Yugoslavia, Serbia) (b) 1,89 (c) F - center forward (d) RFS (e) Javor-Matis, Napredak

*** Ilic - Christian Ilic (Christian Ilić) (a) 22/07/1996, Friesach (Austria) (b) 1,85 (c) M - central midfielder (d) FC Dinamo 1948 (e) Doxa Katokopias, Kryvbas, Lokomotiv Plovdiv, Motherwell FC, TSV Hartberg, St. Lambrecht, SC Weiz II, St. Lambrecht

*** Ilic - Hrvoje Ilic (Hrvoje Ilić) (a) 14/04/1999, Slavonski Brod (Croatia) (b) 1,76 (c) M - attacking midfielder (d) Kryvbas Kryvyi Rig (e) Hapoel Tel Aviv, Bijelo Brdo, Hrv Dragovoljac, NK Osijek II, Bijelo Brdo, NK Osijek II, NK Dugopolje, NK Osijek II

*** Ilic - Ivan Ilic (Иван Илић) (a) 17/03/2001, Niš (RF Yugoslavia, now in Serbia) (b) 1,85 (c) M - central midfielder (d) Torino FC (e) Hellas Verona, Torino, Hellas Verona, Hellas Verona, NAC Breda, FK Zemun

*** Ilic - Luka Ilic (Лука Илић) (a) 02/07/1999, Niš (RF Yugoslavia, now in Serbia) (b) 1,82 (c) M - attacking midfielder (d) ESTAC Troyes (e) FK TSC, Troyes, Manchester City, FC Twente, Manchester City, NAC Breda, Manchester City, Crvena zvezda, Manchester City, Crvena zvezda

*** Ilic - Marko Ilic (Марко Илић) (a) 03/02/1998, Novi Sad (Yugoslavia, now in Serbia) (b) 1,91 (c) G (d) Colorado Rapids (e) KV Kortrijk, Colorado, KV Kortrijk, Vozdovac, Vojvodina, Proleter, Vojvodina

*** Ilic - Mihajlo Ilic (Михаjло Илић) (a) 04/06/2003, Jagodina (Serbia and Montenegro, now in Serbia) (b) 1,92 (c) D - central defense (d) Partizán Beograd (e) -

*** Ilic - Milan Ilic (Милан Илић) (a) 07/02/2000, Beograd (RF Yugoslavia, now in Serbia) (b) 1,80 (c) D - right back (d) FK Javor-Matis Ivanjica (e) Crvena zvezda, Graficar, Crvena zvezda, FK Loznica, Crvena zvezda, FK Loznica, IMT Beograd, Teleoptik, GSP Polet

*** Ilic - Milijan Ilic (Милиjан Илић) (a) 23/05/1993, Sombor (RF Yugoslavia, now in Serbia) (b) 1,80 (c) D - left back (d) FK Mladost GAT Novi Sad (e) FCI Levadia, FK Indjija, Javor-Matis, Rakovica, FK Zemun, GSP Polet, FK Zemun, Rakovica, BASK Beograd

*** Ilic - Vanja Ilic (Вања Илић) (a) 03/01/1999, Beograd (RF Yugoslavia, now in Serbia) (b) 1,78 (c) F - right winger (d) FK Radnicki Niš (e) Kolubara, Zarkovo, Radnicki Niš, Zarkovo, Rad Beograd

*** Ilic - Veljko Ilic (Вељко Илић) (a) 20/10/2005, Beograd (Serbia and Montenegro, now in Serbia) (b) - (c) F - left winger (d) FK Brodarac Belgrad (e) Kolubara, RFK Novi Sad, Proleter

*** Ilic - Veljko Ilic (Вељко Илић) (a) 21/07/2003, Beograd (Serbia and Montenegro, now in Serbia) (b) 1,95 (c) G (d) FK TSC Backa Topola (e) -

*** Ilicic - Josip Ilicic (Josip Iličić) (a) 29/01/1988, Prijedor (Yugoslavia, now in Bosnia and Herzegovina) (b) 1,90 (c) M - attacking midfielder (d) NK Maribor (e) Atalanta, Fiorentina, US Palermo, NK Maribor, NK Interblock, NK Bonifika, Britof

*** Ilicic - Miroslav Ilicic (Miroslav Iličić) (a) 17/04/1998, Rijeka (Croatia) (b) 1,87 (c) F - center forward (d) - (e) ND Gorica, NK Celje, NK Istra, Slaven Belupo, NK Orijent 1919, HNK Rijeka II, NK Grobnican

*** Ilie - Alexandru Ilie (Alexandru Mihai Ilie) (a) 19/01/2000, Zărneşti (Romania) (b) 1,65 (c) M - central midfielder (d) Olimpic Zarnesti (e) FC Voluntari, CS Afumati, FC Voluntari, Daco-Getica, FC Ardealul

*** Ilie - Florin Ilie (Florin Ionuţ Ilie) (a) 18/06/1992, Alba Iulia (Romania) (b) 1,88 (c) D - central defense (d) ACSM Politehnica Iasi (e) Universitatea Cluj, UTA Arad, Sportul Snagov, CS Mioveni, ASA Tg. Mures, Pandurii, Luceafarul, Minaur, Concordia, Gaz Metan, Corona Brasov, Concordia, Poli. Timisoara, P. Timisoara B, Alba Iulia

*** Ilie - Rares Ilie (Rareş Ilie) (a) 19/04/2003, Bucharest (Romania) (b) 1,85 (c) F - left winger (d) FC Lausanne-Sport (e) Lausanne-Sport, OGC Nice, Maccabi Tel Aviv, OGC Nice, FC Rapid 1923, Metaloglobus

*** Ilieski - Antonio Ilieski (Антонио Илиески) (a) 23/07/1996, Gostivar (North Macedonia) (b) 1,87 (c) D - central defense (d) Flamurtari FC (e) FK Kukësi, Renova, Korabi Debar, Tikves, Gostivar, Makedonija, Euromilk GL, Gostivar

*** Ilieski - Darko Ilieski (Дарко Илиески) (a) 14/10/1995, Prilep (North Macedonia) (b) 1,90 (c) D - central defense (d) FC Shkupi (e) Struga, Koper, Pelister Bitola, FC Shkupi, Borec Veles, Tikves, Shirak Gyumri, Pobeda Prilep, Metalurg Skopje, 11 Oktomvri

*** Iliev - Atanas Iliev (Атанас Петров Илиев) (a) 09/10/1994, Dobrich (Bulgaria) (b) 1,89 (c) F - center forward (d) Cherno More Varna (e) Ascoli, Botev Plovdiv, Montana, Dob. Dobrich, Cherno More

*** Iliev - Dimitar Iliev (Димитър Емилов Илиев) (a) 22/07/1999, ¿? (Bulgaria) (b) 1,77 (c) D - left back (d) Ludogorets Razgrad II (e) Botev Vratsa, CSKA 1948, Ludogorets II

*** Iliev - Dimitar Iliev (Димитър Красимиров Илиев) (a) 25/09/1988, Plovdiv (Bulgaria) (b) 1,85 (c) F - center forward (d) Lokomotiv Plovdiv (e) Podbeskidzie, Wisła Płock, Lokomotiv Sofia, Montana, CSKA Sofia, Pirin, CSKA Sofia, Minyor Pernik, CSKA Sofia, Lokomotiv Plovdiv

*** Iliev - Ilian Iliev (Илиан Илианов Илиев) (a) 20/08/1999, Funchal (Portugal) (b) 1,73 (c) M - central midfielder (d) Apollon Limassol (e) Cherno More

*** Iliev - Plamen Iliev (Пламен Илиев) (a) 30/11/1991, Botevgrad (Bulgaria) (b) 1,82 (c) G (d) FC Universitatea Cluj (e) FC Hermannstadt, FC Dinamo, Ludogorets, Astra Giurgiu, FC Botosani, Levski Sofia, Vidima-Rakovski

*** Iliev - Tomislav Iliev (Томислав Илиев) (a) 02/12/1993, Turnovo (North Macedonia) (b) 1,78 (c) D - right back (d) - (e) AP Brera, Rabotnicki, Horizont

*** Iliev - Tsvetan Iliev (Цветан Мирославов Илиев) (a) 29/04/1990, Targovishte (Bulgaria) (b) 1,79 (c) M - attacking midfielder (d) Chernomorets Balchik (e) Spartak Varna, Dob. Dobrich, C. Balchik, Svetkavitsa, Neftochimik, Svetkavitsa

*** Ilievski - Bojan Ilievski (Бојан Илиевски) (a) 01/09/1999, Bitola (North Macedonia) (b) 1,82 (c) D - right back (d) Makedonija Gjorce Petrov (e) Rabotnicki, Pelister Bitola

*** Ilievski - Mario Ilievski (Марио Илиевски) (a) 24/04/2002, Skopje (North Macedonia) (b) 1,84 (c) F - center forward (d) Kisvárda FC (e) Septemvri Sofia, Tikves, Septemvri Sofia, Vardar Negotino

*** Ilijoski Kiseski - Teofan Ilijoski Kiseski (Теофан Илијоски Кисески) (a) 19/03/1998, Prilep (North Macedonia) (b) 1,82 (c) D - right back (d) Pobeda Prilep (e) Osogovo

*** Ilikj - Filip Ilikj (Филип Илиќ) (a) 26/01/1997, Skopje (North Macedonia) (b) 1,93 (c) G (d) Rabotnicki Skopje (e) Vardar, Gandzasar, Metalurg Skopje

*** Iling Junior - Samuel Iling Junior (a) 04/10/2003, Islington (England) (b) 1,82 (c) F - left winger (d) Juventus de Turín (e) Juve Next Gen

*** Ilinkovic - Silvio Ilinkovic (Silvio Ilinković) (a) 05/10/2002, Nova Bila (Bosnia and Herzegovina) (b) - (c) M - central midfielder (d) HNK Rijeka (e) Zrinjski Mostar, HNK Rijeka, HSK Posusje, HNK Rijeka

*** Iljazi - Ardit Iljazi (a) 16/06/2000, Gostivar (North Macedonia) (b) 1,85 (c) D - central defense (d) KF Teuta (e) KF Erzeni, FC Shkupi, Gostivar

*** Iljazi - Artan Iljazi (a) 24/02/1999, ¿? (North Macedonia) (b) 1,86 (c) G (d) FC Shkupi (e) Shkëndija, Gostivar, Shkëndija

*** Iljin - Aleksander Iljin (a) 05/09/2002, Tartu (Estonia) (b) 1,77 (c) M - central midfielder (d) FC Kuressaare (e) Kuressaare, Merkuur-Juunior, Merkuur-Juunior, Merkuur-Juunior

*** Iljin - Vladimir Iljin (Ильин Владимир Дмитриевич) (a) 20/05/1992, St. Petersburg (Russia) (b) 1,87 (c) F - center forward (d) Akhmat Grozny (e) Krasnodar, Akhmat Grozny, Ural, Kuban Krasnodar, Tosno, Khimik, Tosno, FK Kaluga, Tosno, Dinamo SPb, FK Piter, Rusj S-Pb, Admiralteets

*** Iljins - Kirils Iljins (Kirils Iļjins) (a) 03/05/2001, ¿? (Latvia) (b) - (c) D - left back (d) Riga FC (e) Daugavpils

*** Ilkhan - Emirhan Ilkhan (Emirhan İlkhan) (a) 01/06/2004, Istanbul (Turkey) (b) 1,75 (c) M - central midfielder (d) Torino FC (e) Sampdoria, Torino, Besiktas

*** Ilko - Patrik Ilko (Patrik Iľko) (a) 16/02/2001, Bardejov (Slovakia) (b) 1,80 (c) F - left winger (d) MSK Zilina (e) MSK Zilina B

*** Illarramendi - Asier Illarramendi (Asier Illarramendi Andonegi) (a) 08/03/1990, Mutriku (Spain) (b) 1,79 (c) M - pivot (d) FC Dallas (e) Real Sociedad, Real Madrid, Real Sociedad, Real Sociedad B

*** Ilondelo - Serge Ilondelo (a) 17/05/2003, ¿? (Sweden) (b) - (c) D - right back (d) Lynx FC (e) BKV Norrtälje, Flemingsberg

*** Ilori - Tiago Ilori (Tiago Abiola Delfim Almeida Ilori) (a) 26/02/1993, Hampstead, London (England) (b) 1,90 (c) D - central defense (d) - (e) Sporting Lisboa, Paços Ferreira, Sporting Lisboa, Boavista, Sporting Lisboa, FC Lorient, Sporting Lisboa, Reading, Liverpool, Aston Villa, Liverpool, Girondins Bordeaux, Liverpool, Granada CF, Liverpool, Sporting Lisboa, Sporting B

*** Ilves - Rasmus Ilves (a) 04/03/1999, Pärnu (Estonia) (b) - (c) D - left back (d) - (e) Pärnu Vaprus, Esiliiga

*** Ilyin - Oleg Ilyin (Ільїн Олег Андрійович) (a) 08/06/1997, Odessa (Ukraine) (b) 1,75 (c) M - right midfielder (d) Kolos Kovalivka (e) Dnipro, Dnipro II

*** Ilyushchenkov - Oleksandr Ilyushchenkov (Ільющенков Олександр Андрійович) (a) 23/03/1990, Ternopil (Soviet Union, now in Ukraine) (b) 1,87 (c) G (d) Karpaty Lviv (e) PFK Lviv, Rukh Lviv, Veres Rivne, Sioni Bolnisi, Metalist, FC Tiraspol, Karpaty, Energetyk, Nyva Ternopil

*** Imangazeev - Bekzat Imangazeev (Имангазеев Бекзат Азаматович) (a) 18/02/2001, West Kazakhstan Region (Kazakhstan) (b) 1,73 (c) F - right winger (d) Akzhayik Uralsk (e) Okzhetpes, Akad. Ontustik

*** Imanov - Yusif Imanov (Yusif Bəhruz oğlu İmanov) (a) 27/09/2002, ¿? (Azerbaijan) (b) 1,92 (c) G (d) Sabah FK (e) Sabah 2

*** Imaz - Jesús Imaz (Jesús Imaz Ballesté) (a) 26/09/1990, Lleida (Spain) (b) 1,74 (c) M - attacking midfielder (d) Jagiellonia Białystok (e) Wisla Kraków, Cádiz CF, UCAM Murcia, Llagostera, Lleida Esportiu, UE Lleida

*** Imbrechts - Joachim Imbrechts (Joachim Lasse Imbrechts) (a) 09/10/2001, ¿? (Sweden) (b) 1,83 (c) G (d) Royale Union Saint Gilloise (e) -

*** Imdat - Sitki Ferdi Imdat (Sıtkı Ferdi İmdat) (a) 05/10/2001, Altindag (Turkey) (b) - (c) F - center forward (d) - (e) Ankaragücü, Igdir FK, Ankaragücü, Altindag Spor

*** Imerekov - Maksym Imerekov (Імереков Максим Ігорович) (a) 23/01/1991, Makiivka, Donetsk Oblast (Soviet Union, now in Ukraine) (b) 1,86 (c) D - central defense (d) Atromitos FC (e) Zorya Lugansk, Desna, Ermis Aradippou, Torpedo Zhodino, FK Oleksandriya, Belshina, Metalurg Z., Shakhtar II

*** Imeri - Demir Imeri (Демир Имери) (a) 27/10/1995, Kicevo (North Macedonia) (b) 1,75 (c) M - attacking midfielder (d) FK Atyrau (e) KF Egnatia, KF Vllaznia, Olimpik Donetsk, Mosta FC, Kemi City, FC Kamza, Shkëndija, Renova, Shkëndija, Horizont, Shkëndija, Rabotnicki, Vëllazërimi

*** Imeri - Gentian Imeri (a) 23/10/1993, ¿? (Austria) (b) - (c) G (d) SV Sigmaringen (e) Pfullendorf II

*** Imeri - Kastriot Imeri (a) 27/06/2000, Genève (Switzerland) (b) 1,78 (c) M - left midfielder (d) BSC Young Boys (e) Servette FC

*** Imeri (c) F - center forward (d) KF Drenica (e) - - Gentian Imeri (c) F - center forward (d) KF Drenica (e) -

*** Immobile - Ciro Immobile (a) 20/02/1990, Torre Annunziata (Italy) (b) 1,85 (c) F - center forward (d) SS Lazio (e) Sevilla FC, Torino, Sevilla FC, Borussia Dortmund, Sevilla FC, Borussia Dortmund, Torino, Juventus, Genoa, Juventus, Pescara, Juventus, Grosseto, Juventus, AC Siena

*** Immonen - Joonas Immonen (a) 05/09/1997, Janakkala (Finland) (b) 1,90 (c) G (d) Hämeenlinnan Jalkapalloseura (e) VPS, HJS, FC Haka, MuSa, FC Haka

*** Imnadze - Luka Imnadze (ლუკა იმნაძე) (a) 26/08/1997, ¿? (Georgia) (b) 1,84 (c) F - left winger (d) Qyzyljar Petropavlovsk (e) Akzhayik, FK Sabail, FC Samtredia, Rustavi, Kolkheti Poti, Saburtalo, Guria

*** Imøy - Eskil August Rønning Imøy (a) 29/05/2003, Bodø (Norway) (b) 1,84 (c) D - central defense (d) Hulløy Bodø (e) Bodø/Glimt II

*** Inácio - Gonçalo Inácio (Gonçalo Bernardo Inácio) (a) 25/08/2001, Almada (Portugal) (b) 1,85 (c) D - central defense (d) Sporting de Lisboa (e) -

*** Inácio Miguel - Inácio Miguel (Inácio Miguel Ferreira Santos) (a) 12/12/1995, Torres Vedras (Portugal) (b) 1,85 (c) D - central defense (d) CA Petróleos Luanda (e) Liepaja, Mafra, Universitatea Cluj, Braga B, Felgueiras, Vila Real

*** Inalkaev - Abubakar Inalkaev (Иналкаев Абубакар Асламбекович) (a) 31/07/2004, ¿? (Russia) (b) 1,85 (c) M - pivot (d) Akhmat Grozny II (e) Akademia Ramzan

*** Inbrum - Or Inbrum (אינברום אור) (a) 12/01/1996, Kiryat Gat (Israel) (b) 1,80 (c) F - left winger (d) Sekzia Ness Ziona (e) H. Umm al-Fahm, FC Ashdod, M. Petah Tikva, FC Ashdod, M. Petah Tikva, KAA Gent, M. Petah Tikva, KAA Gent, Hapoel Tel Aviv, KAA Gent, B. Jerusalem, KAA Gent, FC Ashdod, KAA Gent, NK Maribor, KAA Gent, FC Ashdod

*** Inch - Caio Inch (a) 15/03/2005, ¿? (Wales) (b) - (c) M - central midfielder (d) Nantlle Vale (e) -

*** Indrans - Davis Indrans (Dāvis Indrāns) (a) 06/06/1995, Riga (Latvia) (b) 1,81 (c) M - attacking midfielder (d) JDFS Alberts Riga (e) Super Nova, JDFS Alberts, JFK Ventspils, Valmiera, Albatroz/Jelgava, RFS, Metta, Skonto, Ventspils II

*** Ingason - Aron Snaer Ingason (Aron Snær Ingason) (a) 26/10/2001, ¿? (Iceland) (b) - (c) F - right winger (d) Fram Reykjavík (e) Thróttur, Fram Reykjavík, Thróttur, Fram Reykjavík, Njardvík, Fram Reykjavík, Úlfarnir

*** Ingason - Birnir Snaer Ingason (Birnir Snær Ingason) (a) 04/12/1996, ¿? (Iceland) (b) - (c) F - left winger (d) Víkingur Reykjavík (e) HK Kópavogs, Valur, Fjölnir

*** Ingason - Gudmundur Thor Ingason (Guðmundur Thor Ingason) (c) D (d) KFG Gardabaer (e) -

*** Ingason - Helgi Frodi Ingason (Helgi Fróði Ingason) (a) 06/12/2005, ¿? (Iceland) (b) - (c) M (d) Stjarnan Gardabaer (e) -

*** Ingason - Jón Ingason (a) 21/09/1995, Reykjavík (Iceland) (b) 1,86 (c) D - central defense (d) ÍBV Vestmannaeyjar (e) Grindavík, Virginia Tech, Grindavík, ÍBV Vestmannaeyjar

*** Ingason - Kristall Máni Ingason (a) 18/01/2002, Reykjavík (Iceland) (b) 1,78 (c) F - attacking midfielder (d) SønderjyskE (e) Rosenborg, Víkingur, Víkingur

*** Ingason - Sverrir Ingi Ingason (a) 05/08/1993, Kópavogur (Iceland) (b) 1,88 (c) D - central defense (d) FC Midtjylland (e) PAOK, Rostov, Granada CF, KSC Lokeren, Viking, Breidablik

*** Ingason - Thórdur Ingason (Þórður Ingason) (a) 30/03/1988, ¿? (Iceland) (b) 1,89 (c) G (d) Víkingur Reykjavík (e) Fjölnir, BÍ/Bol, Fjölnir, KR Reykjavík, Fjölnir, Everton Reserves, Fjölnir

*** Ingebrigtsen - Mikael Ingebrigtsen (Mikael Norø Ingebrigtsen) (a) 21/07/1996, Tromsø (Norway) (b) 1,70 (c) F - right winger (d) Odds BK (e) Tromsø, IFK Göteborg, Tromsø

*** Ingimarsson - Sindri Thór Ingimarsson (Sindri Þór Ingimarsson) (a) 24/11/1998, Kópavogur (Iceland) (b) 1,90 (c) D - central defense (d) Stjarnan Gardabaer (e) Augnablik, Breidablik, Augnablik, Breidablik, Augnablik, Breidablik, Augnablik, Breidablik

*** Ingimarsson (c) G (d) Reynir Sandgerdi (e) Keflavík - Sigurdur Orri Ingimarsson (c) G (d) Reynir Sandgerdi (e) Keflavík

*** Ingólfsson - Tristan Freyr Ingólfsson (a) 07/04/1999, ¿? (Iceland) (b) - (c) D - left back (d) Stjarnan Gardabaer (e) Keflavík, Stjarnan, KFG Gardabaer, Stjarnan

*** Ingolitsch - Sandro Ingolitsch (a) 18/04/1997, Schwarzach im Pongau (Austria) (b) 1,79 (c) D - right back (d) SCR Altach (e) Sturm Graz, SKN St. Pölten, FC Liefering

*** Ings - Danny Ings (Daniel William John Ings) (a) 23/07/1992, Winchester (England) (b) 1,77 (c) F - center forward (d) West Ham United (e) Aston Villa, Southampton, Liverpool, Southampton, Liverpool, Burnley, Bournemouth, Dorchester, Bournemouth

*** Ingvarsson - Davíd Ingvarsson (Davíð Ingvarsson) (a) 25/04/1999, ¿? (Iceland) (b) 1,76 (c) D - left back (d) Breidablik Kópavogur (e) Haukar, Breidablik

*** Ingvarsson - Einar Karl Ingvarsson (a) 08/10/1993, ¿? (Iceland) (b) - (c) M - central midfielder (d) UMF Grindavík (e) Stjarnan, Valur, Grindavík, Valur, Hafnarfjördur, Fjölnir, Hafnarfjördur

*** Ingvartsen - Marcus Ingvartsen (Marcus Højriis Ingvartsen) (a) 04/01/1996, Farum (Denmark) (b) 1,87 (c) F - center forward (d) FC Nordsjælland (e) Mainz 05, Union Berlin, Mainz 05, Union Berlin, KRC Genk, Nordsjælland

*** Injgia - Revaz Injgia (რევაზ ინჯგია) (a) 31/12/2000, Tbilisi (Georgia) (b) 1,87 (c) F - right winger (d) FC Samtredia (e) Apollon Limassol, Doxa Katokopias, Apollon Limassol, FC Telavi, Radnicki Srem, FC Locomotive

*** Inkeroinen - Valtteri Inkeroinen (a) 01/04/2003, ¿? (Finland) (b) - (c) G (d) FC Inter Turku II (e) -

*** Inkoom - Samuel Inkoom (Samuel Inkoom) (a) 01/06/1989, Sekondi-Takoradi (Ghana) (b) 1,79 (c) D - right back (d) Hearts of Oak (e) Torpedo Kutaisi, FC Samtredia, Dunav, Vereya, Antalyaspor, Boavista, D.C. United, Dnipro, Platanias, Dnipro II, Dnipro, SC Bastia, Dnipro, FC Basel, Asante Kotoko, S. Hasaacas

*** Inler - Gökhan Inler (Gökhan İnler) (a) 27/06/1984, Olten (Switzerland) (b) 1,83 (c) M - pivot (d) - (e) Adana Demirspor, Basaksehir, Besiktas, Leicester City, Napoli, Udinese, FC Zürich, FC Aarau, Solothurn II

*** Innocent - Bonke Innocent (a) 20/01/1996, Kaduna (Nigeria) (b) 1,78 (c) M - pivot (d) FC Lorient (e) Malmö FF, Lillestrøm, Moderate Stars, Bujoc FC

*** Innocent - Garissone Innocent (a) 16/04/2000, Ivry-sur-Seine (France) (b) 1,92 (c) G (d) KAS Eupen (e) Paris Saint-Germain, Vannes, Paris Saint-Germain, SM Caen, Paris Saint-Germain

*** Innvær - Sander Håvik Innvær (a) 11/10/2004, ¿? (Norway) (b) - (c) M (d) FK Haugesund II (e) -
*** Inqilably - Idris Inqilably (İdris Samad oglu İnqilablı) (a) 06/10/2001, ¿? (Azerbaijan) (b) 1,75 (c) M - pivot (d) Sabah FK (e) Kapaz PFK, Sabah FK, FK Qabala, Sabah FK, FK Qabala
*** Intilla - Cristian Intilla (a) 04/09/2001, ¿? (Italy) (b) - (c) F - right winger (d) - (e) Cailungo, Gabicce Gradara
*** Ioannidis - Christos Ioannidis (Χρήστος Ιωαννίδης) (a) 28/07/2004, Katerini (Greece) (b) - (c) M - pivot (d) Ionikos Nikeas (e) AO Trikala, PAO Koufalion
*** Ioannidis - Fotis Ioannidis (Φώτης Ιωαννίδης) (a) 10/01/2000, Athen (Greece) (b) 1,87 (c) F - center forward (d) Panathinaikos FC (e) APO Levadiakos, Oly. Chalkidas
*** Ioannidis - Nikolaos Ioannidis (Νικόλαος Ιωαννίδης) (a) 26/04/1994, Remscheid (Germany) (b) 1,88 (c) F - center forward (d) Athens Kallithea FC (e) Ionikos Nikeas, Apollon Smyrnis, Doxa Dramas, Marítimo, Diósgyőr, Asteras Tripoli, Olympiakos, Borussia Dortmund II, Olympiakos, PEC Zwolle, Olympiakos, Hansa Rostock, Olympiakos
*** Ioannou - Andreas Ioannou (Ανδρέας Ιωάννου) (a) 23/03/2005, Limassol (Cyprus) (b) 1,88 (c) D - central defense (d) - (e) AEL Limassol
*** Ioannou - Michalis Ioannou (Μιχάλης Ιωάννου) (a) 30/06/2000, Limassol (Cyprus) (b) 1,81 (c) M - central midfielder (d) Anorthosis Famagusta (e) Roda JC, Anorthosis, Nikos & Sokrati
*** Ioannou - Thomas Ioannou (Θωμάς Ιωάννου) (a) 19/07/1995, Pafos (Cyprus) (b) 1,83 (c) D - left back (d) - (e) Olympiakos N., Ethnikos, AEK Larnaca, Doxa Katokopias, AEK Larnaca, Pafos FC, AE Pafos
*** Iobashvili - Jaduli Iobashvili (ჯადული იობაშვილი) (a) 01/01/2004, Tbilisi (Georgia) (b) 1,92 (c) F - center forward (d) Dinamo Tbilisi II (e) -
*** Ion - Robert Ion (Robert Andrei Ion) (a) 05/09/2000, Bucuresti (Romania) (b) 1,80 (c) M - attacking midfielder (d) ACSM Politehnica Iasi (e) FCV Farul, FCSB, Academica Clinceni, FCSB, FC Voluntari, FCSB, Academica Clinceni, AS Metropolitan
*** Ionanidze - Davit Ionanidze (დავით იონანიძე) (a) 05/08/1998, ¿? (Georgia) (b) - (c) F - center forward (d) Kolkheti Khobi (e) FC Zestafoni, FC Samtredia, FC Gagra, Torpedo Kutaisi, Chikhura, Torpedo Kutaisi II
*** Ionita - Adrian Ionita (Adrian Mihai Ioniță) (a) 11/03/2000, Buzău (Romania) (b) 1,78 (c) D - left back (d) AFC Chindia Targoviste (e) -
*** Ionita - Mario Ionita (Mario Alexandru Ioniță) (a) 17/03/2007, ¿? (Romania) (b) - (c) M - central midfielder (d) CSM Cetatea Turnu Magurele (e) -
*** Ionita II - Alexandru Ionita II (Alexandru Ioniță) (a) 14/12/1994, Bucuresti (Romania) (b) 1,78 (c) M - attacking midfielder (d) FC Rapid 1923 (e) CFR Cluj, Astra Giurgiu, CFR Cluj, CS U Craiova, CFR Cluj, Astra Giurgiu, Rapid Bucureşti
*** Ionov - Aleksey Ionov (Ионов Алексей Сергеевич) (a) 18/02/1989, Kingisepp, Leningrad Oblast (Soviet Union, now in Russia) (b) 1,77 (c) F - right winger (d) FK Rostov (e) Krasnodar, Rostov, Dinamo Moskva, CSKA Moskva, Dinamo Moskva, Anzhi, Kuban Krasnodar, Zenit, Zenit St. Peterburg II, SShOR Zenit
*** Iordache - David Iordache (a) 03/11/2004, ¿? (Romania) (b) - (c) M - attacking midfielder (d) CSM Cetatea Turnu Magurele (e) FC Rapid 1923
*** Iorga - Razvan Iorga (Răzvan Ioan Iorga) (a) 12/08/2003, ¿? (Romania) (b) - (c) M - central midfielder (d) FCV Farul Constanta (e) FC Brasov-SR

*** Iorio Forestero - Osvaldo Iorio Forestero (a) 02/08/2000, Montevideo (Uruguay) (b) 1,83 (c) D - right back (d) Birkirkara FC (e) Insieme Formia, CA Atenas, Insieme Formia, Latina Calcio

*** Iosifidis - Theodoros Iosifidis (Θεόδωρος Ιωσηφίδης) (a) 17/01/1997, Limassol (Cyprus) (b) 1,78 (c) F - attacking midfielder (d) AEZ Zakakiou (e) Aris Limassol, Omonia 29 Maiou, Aris Limassol, Doxa Katokopias, Aris Limassol, Sant Rafel, SD Ejea, Extremadura B, CD Móstoles, Apollon Limassol, Fuenlabrada B, Apollon Limassol, EN Paralimniou, Apollon Limassol

*** Iosipoi - Marius Iosipoi (a) 28/04/2000, Ialoveni (Moldova) (b) 1,81 (c) F - left winger (d) FC Petrocub Hîncești (e) Dacia Buiucani, Veles Moskva, Dacia Buiucani, ACSM Poli Iasi

*** Iovino - Antonio Iovino (a) 25/07/2002, ¿? (Italy) (b) - (c) F (d) AC Libertas (e) -

*** Iovu - Iurie Iovu (a) 06/07/2002, Chisinau (Moldova) (b) 1,96 (c) D - central defense (d) NK Istra 1961 (e) Venezia, NK Istra, Venezia

*** Ipalibo - Jack Ipalibo (a) 06/04/1998, ¿? (Nigeria) (b) 1,87 (c) M - pivot (d) AE Kifisias (e) Strømsgodset, Villarreal CF B, Strømsgodset, Villarreal CF B, Villarreal CF C

*** Ipole - Philip Ipole (Philip Orite Ipole) (a) 06/06/2001, Otukpo (Nigeria) (b) 1,87 (c) D - central defense (d) Hapoel Hadera (e) Sochi, Hapoel Hadera, Sochi, Dolgoprudnyi, Sochi, FK Sochi II, Zhetysu, FK Sochi II, NUB Kaduna

*** Iqbal - Zidane Iqbal (a) 27/04/2003, Manchester (England) (b) 1,81 (c) M - central midfielder (d) FC Utrecht (e) Manchester Utd.

*** Iran Júnior - Iran Júnior (Iran da Conceição Gonçalves Júnior) (a) 10/10/1995, São Paulo (Brazil) (b) 1,76 (c) M - attacking midfielder (d) KF Dukagjini (e) FC Drita, KF Ulpiana, KF Teuta, KS Besa, Barretos-SP, AA Francana, América TO-MG, América-PE, Ponte Nova, Nacional-MG, Ponte Nova

*** Irandust - Daleho Irandust (a) 04/06/1998, Göteborg (Sweden) (b) 1,85 (c) M - attacking midfielder (d) FC Groningen (e) Häcken

*** Iranzo - Rubén Iranzo (Rubén Iranzo Lendínez) (a) 14/03/2003, Picanya (Spain) (b) 1,82 (c) D - central defense (d) Valencia Mestalla (e) -

*** Irazábal - Jon Irazábal (Jon Irazábal Iraurgui) (a) 28/11/1996, Bilbao (Spain) (b) 1,87 (c) D - central defense (d) Sabah FK (e) SD Amorebieta, SD Leioa, CD Mirandés, CD Vitoria, CD Mirandés, CD Vitoria

*** Irobiso - Christian Irobiso (Okechukwu Christian Irobiso) (a) 28/05/1993, Lagos (Nigeria) (b) 1,90 (c) F - center forward (d) Petrolul Ploiesti (e) FC Dinamo, Gaz Metan, Varzim, Farense, Cova Piedade, Farense, Jihlava, FK Senica, Paços Ferreira, União Madeira, Paços Ferreira

*** Iroegbunam - Tim Iroegbunam (Timothy Emeka Iroegbunam) (a) 30/06/2003, Birmingham (England) (b) 1,83 (c) M - central midfielder (d) Aston Villa (e) Queen's Park Rangers, Aston Villa

*** Iru - Ander Iru (Ander Iruarrizaga Díez) (a) 22/08/1998, Igorre (Spain) (b) 1,88 (c) G (d) SD Logroñés (e) Athletic, Bilbao Athletic, CD Basconia

*** Irving - Andy Irving (Andrew Irving) (a) 13/05/2000, Edinburgh (Scotland) (b) 1,90 (c) M - central midfielder (d) SK Austria Klagenfurt (e) Türkgücü Münch., Heart of Midlothian, Hearts FC II, Falkirk FC, Hearts FC II, Berwick Rangers FC

*** Irving - Harry Irving (a) 05/07/2002, ¿? (Wales) (b) 1,91 (c) G (d) Trethomas Bluebirds (e) Pontypridd, Trethomas, Pontypridd, Trethomas, Pontypridd

*** Isaac - Isaac (Isaac Bernardo Neto Monteiro) (a) 04/03/2004, ¿? (Portugal) (b) 1,93 (c) D - central defense (d) Casa Pia AC (e) Belenenses

*** Isaac - Barry Isaac (Isaac Barry Ojumah) (a) 28/08/2001, Benin City (Nigeria) (b) 1,90 (c) D - central defense (d) FC Urartu Yerevan (e) Urartu II, Right2Win SA

*** Isaac - Carlos Isaac (Carlos Isaac Muñoz Obejero) (a) 30/04/1998, Navalmoral de la Mata (Spain) (b) 1,84 (c) D - right back (d) Albacete Balompié (e) Vizela, Alavés, Real Oviedo, Alavés, Albacete, Alavés, At. Madrid B

*** Isac - Damian Isac (a) 31/01/2001, Caransebeş (Romania) (b) 1,78 (c) M - central midfielder (d) UTA Arad (e) -

*** Isaenko - Oleg Isaenko (Исаенко Олег Игоревич) (a) 31/01/2000, Kaliningrad (Russia) (b) 1,69 (c) D - left back (d) FK Khimki (e) Krasnodar, Krasnodar-2, Krasnodar 3, Krasnodar II

*** Isaenko - Yevgeniy Isaenko (Ісаєнко Євгеній Юрійович) (a) 07/08/2000, Vinnytsya (Ukraine) (b) 1,69 (c) F - center forward (d) FC Dinamo de Kiev (e) Kolos Kovalivka, Dinamo Kyïv, Chornomorets, Dinamo Kyïv, Dinamo Kiev II, Kolos Kovalivka, Dinamo Kiev II

*** Isaev - Ramazan Isaev (Исаев Рамазан Шамилович) (a) 17/01/1998, Makhachkala (Russia) (b) 1,73 (c) F - center forward (d) Naftan Novopolotsk (e) Belshina, Lada Dimitrovgrad, Legion-Dinamo, Ararat Yerevan, Yerevan CF, Artsakh Erewan, Radnicki Niš, Dynamo Brest, Torpedo Armavir, Yunost Moskvy Torpedo,

*** Isaevski - Aleksandar Isaevski (Александар Исаевски) (a) 19/05/1995, Skopje (North Macedonia) (b) 1,78 (c) D - left back (d) - (e) Milsami, Makedonija, FC Dinamo, KF Vllaznia, Dunav, Pobeda Prilep, Makedonija, Detroit City

*** Isah - Musa Isah (Musa Isah) (a) 04/01/2002, ¿? (Nigeria) (b) - (c) M - central midfielder (d) Lleida Esportiu (e) Belshina, Gomel, FC Saksan

*** Isah - Mustapha Isah (Mustapha Isah Ubandoma) (a) 23/07/2004, ¿? (Nigeria) (b) - (c) F - left winger (d) Randers FC (e) HB Abuja

*** Isaiah - Ahmed Isaiah (a) 10/10/1995, Lagos (Nigeria) (b) 1,76 (c) M - central midfielder (d) FK Qabala (e) Kapaz PFK, Zira FK, SC Covilhã, Gil Vicente, Varzim, Gil Vicente, Vilaverdense, AD Oliveirense, GD Ribeirão

*** Isajevs - Ilja Isajevs (a) 05/12/2000, Riga (Latvia) (b) 1,90 (c) G (d) JFK Ventspils (e) Riga II, Spartaks, Riga II, Auda, Riga II, Tukums

*** Isajevs - Vjaceslavs Isajevs (Vjačeslavs Isajevs) (a) 27/08/1993, Riga (Latvia) (b) 1,87 (c) D - central defense (d) FK Auda (e) Liepaja, RFS, Skonto, Olimps Riga

*** Isak - Alexander Isak (a) 21/09/1999, Solna (Sweden) (b) 1,92 (c) F - center forward (d) Newcastle United (e) Real Sociedad, Borussia Dortmund, Willem II, Borussia Dortmund, AIK

*** Isaki - Fisnik Isaki (Фисник Исаки) (a) 27/04/2003, ¿? (North Macedonia) (b) - (c) F - right winger (d) Boldklubben af 1893 (e) -

*** Isaksen - Elias Isaksen (a) 18/01/2004, ¿? (Faroe Islands) (b) - (c) D - right back (d) EB/Streymur II (e) Víkingur II

*** Isaksen - Gustav Isaksen (Gustav Tang Isaksen) (a) 19/04/2001, Hjerk (Denmark) (b) 1,81 (c) F - right winger (d) SS Lazio (e) Midtjylland

*** Isaksen - Jesper Isaksen (Jesper Strand Isaksen) (a) 13/10/1999, Bærum (Norway) (b) 1,83 (c) M - central midfielder (d) Kristiansund BK (e) Stabæk, Fredrikstad, Stabæk, Jerv, Stabæk, Kristiansund

*** Isaksson - Keaton Isaksson (a) 21/04/1994, Helsinki (Finland) (b) 1,84 (c) M - attacking midfielder (d) FS Kozani (e) Helsinki IFK, SJK Seinäjoki, IFK Mariehamn, Kemi City, IFK Luleå, Ekenäs IF, Helsinki IFK, IF Gnistan, FC Viikingit, Pallokerho

*** Isaraj - Anxhelo Isaraj (a) 25/12/1991, Tiranë (Albania) (b) - (c) M - central midfielder (d) SS Pennarossa (e) KF Luzi United, Shkumbini Peqin, KF Tërbuni, KF Vora, Pennarossa, FC Shënkolli, KF Vora, KF Turbina, KF Gramshi, KF Turbina

*** Isayev - Aleksey Isayev (Aleksey Aleksandr oğlu İsayev) (a) 09/11/1995, Krasnoyarsk (Russia) (b) 1,77 (c) M - central midfielder (d) Sabah FK (e) Sumqayit, Sumqayit, Zenit 2 St. Peterburg, Enisey, Zenit 2 St. Peterburg, Enisey, Enisey II
*** Isayev - Maqsad Isayev (Məqsəd Müzəffər oğlu İsayev) (a) 07/06/1994, Baku (Azerbaijan) (b) 1,68 (c) D - left back (d) Zira FK (e) FK Qabala, FK Sabail, Sabah FK, Keshla, Neftchi Baku
*** Iscaye - Zacharie Iscaye (a) 02/10/2000, ¿? (France) (b) 1,83 (c) D - right back (d) Union Namur (e) Tabor Sezana, FC Rousset, Brest B, Ol. Marseille B
*** Isco - Isco (Francisco Román Alarcón Suárez) (a) 21/04/1992, Benalmádena (Spain) (b) 1,76 (c) M - attacking midfielder (d) Real Betis Balompié (e) Sevilla FC, Real Madrid, Málaga CF, Valencia Mestalla
*** Iseni - Besar Iseni (a) 18/01/1997, Skopje (North Macedonia) (b) 1,82 (c) M - central midfielder (d) Voska Sport (e) KF Ferizaj, KF Egnatia, FC Shkupi, Vardar, FC Shkupi
*** Iseni - Besir Iseni (a) 02/05/2000, Skopje (North Macedonia) (b) 1,88 (c) D - central defense (d) KF Dukagjini (e) KF Tirana, Struga, Vëllazërimi
*** Isenko - Pavlo Isenko (Ісенко Павло Андрійович) (a) 21/07/2003, Poltava (Ukraine) (b) 1,95 (c) G (d) Vorskla Poltava (e) -
*** Isfan - Alexandru Isfan (Alexandru Mihai Işfan) (a) 31/01/2000, Mioveni (Romania) (b) 1,88 (c) F - right winger (d) Universitatea Craiova (e) FC Arges, CS Mioveni, Unirea Bascov, FC D. Coman -
*** Isgandarli - Vüsal Isgandarli (Vüsal Mahmud oğlu İsgəndərli) (a) 03/11/1995, Fuzuli (Azerbaijan) (b) 1,80 (c) F - center forward (d) KF Egnatia (e) Sumqayit, A. Keciörengücü, Shamakhi, Zira FK, Simurq, Ravan Baku
*** Isgandarov - Farid Isgandarov (a) 16/03/2001, ¿? (Azerbaijan) (b) - (c) F - center forward (d) FK Qabala 2 (e) Neftchi 2 Baku
*** Isgandarov - Ülvi Isgandarov (Ülvi Hümbət oğlu İsgəndərov) (a) 24/10/1997, ¿? (Azerbaijan) (b) 1,76 (c) F - center forward (d) FK Qabala (e) Sumqayit, FK Qabala
*** Ishak - Mikael Ishak (a) 31/03/1993, Stockholm (Sweden) (b) 1,85 (c) F - center forward (d) Lech Poznan (e) 1.FC Nürnberg, Randers FC, Parma, Crotone, Parma, 1.FC Köln, FC St. Gallen, 1.FC Köln, Assyriska FF
*** Ishkhanyan - Hayk Ishkhanyan (Հայկ Իշխանյան) (a) 24/06/1989, Yerevan (Soviet Union, now in Armenia) (b) 1,81 (c) D - central defense (d) BKMA Yerevan (e) Ararat Yerevan, BKMA Yerevan, Pyunik Yerevan, Shirak Gyumri, Gandzasar, Alashkert CF, Zhetysu, Alashkert CF, Lori Vanadzor, Gandzasar, Alashkert CF, MIKA Aschtarak, Impuls Dilijan, MIKA Aschtarak, Shirak Gyumri, Shirak II, Dinamo
*** Ishkov - Ilya Ishkov (Ишков Илья Игоревич) (a) 25/05/2005, Ekaterinburg (Russia) (b) 1,75 (c) M - attacking midfielder (d) Ural 2 Ekaterinburg (e) Ural II
*** Isiani - Levan Isiani (ლევან ისიანი) (a) 30/04/1998, Tbilisi (Georgia) (b) 1,89 (c) G (d) Sioni Bolnisi (e) FC Gagra, Dinamo Tbilisi, Dinamo II
*** Isic - Tarik Isic (Tarik Isić) (a) 08/10/1994, Kiseljak (Bosnia and Herzegovina) (b) 1,92 (c) D - central defense (d) Sogdiana Jizzakh (e) FK Kukësi, Velez Mostar, FK Olimpik, Perak, Celik Zenica, Radnik Bijelj., GOSK Gabela, HNK Capljina, FK Olimpik, HNK Capljina, Radnik Hadzici
*** Isidor - Wilson Isidor (a) 27/08/2000, Rennes (France) (b) 1,86 (c) F - center forward (d) Lokomotiv Moskva (e) AS Monaco, Bastia-Borgo, AS Monaco, Stade Lavallois, AS Monaco, AS Monaco B
*** Isimat-Mirin - Nicolas Isimat-Mirin (Nicolas Johnny Isimat-Mirin) (a) 15/11/1991, Meudon (France) (b) 1,87 (c) D - central defense (d) Vitesse Arnhem (e)

Kansas City, Besiktas, Toulouse, Besiktas, PSV Eindhoven, AS Monaco, PSV Eindhoven, AS Monaco, Valenciennes FC
*** Islami - Drilon Islami (a) 18/07/2000, ¿? (RF Yugoslavia, now in Kosovo) (b) 1,77 (c) M - pivot (d) KF Ferizaj (e) FC Drita, KF Ferizaj
*** Islami - Perparim Islami (Përparim Islami) (a) 01/05/1993, Podujevë (RF Yugoslavia, now in Kosovo) (b) 1,71 (c) D - right back (d) SC Gjilani (e) FC Drita, KF Feronikeli, KF Trepca 89, FC Prishtina, KF Hajvalia, KF Hysi
*** Islamkulov - Marsel Islamkulov (Исламкулов Марсель) (a) 18/04/1994, Kant (Kyrgyzstan) (b) 1,88 (c) G (d) FK Abdish-Ata Kant (e) FK Aksu, Kaysar, Baikonur, Astana-1964, Abdish-Ata Kant
*** Islamovic - Dino Islamovic (Dino Islamović) (a) 23/01/2001, Sarajevo (Bosnia and Herzegovina) (b) 1,75 (c) D - left back (d) FK Igman Konjic (e) TOSK Tesanj, FK Sarajevo
*** Islamovic - Sead Islamovic (Сеад Исламовић) (a) 24/09/1999, Novi Pazar (RF Yugoslavia, now in Serbia) (b) 1,83 (c) M - central midfielder (d) BATE Borisov (e) Novi Pazar, Radnik, Novi Pazar, Radnik, Novi Pazar, FK Josanica
*** Islamović - Dino Islamović (Дино Исламовић) (a) 17/01/1994, Hudiksvall (Sweden) (b) 1,90 (c) F - center forward (d) - (e) Gangwon FC, Rosenborg, Östersund, Trelleborg, FC Groningen
*** Islic - Luka Islic (Luka Išlić) (a) 27/01/2003, Samobor (Croatia) (b) 1,80 (c) M - pivot (d) NK Kustosija Zagreb (e) NK Kustosija, NK Lokomotiva, Hrv Dragovoljac, NK Lokomotiva, NK Samobor
*** Islomov - Tabrez Islomov (Исломов Табрез) (a) 06/06/1998, Dushanbe (Tajikistan) (b) 1,78 (c) D - left back (d) Istiqlol Dushanbe (e) JK Trans Narva, Istiqlol, Barqchi
*** Ismaheel - Taofeek Ismaheel (Taofeek Ajibade Ismaheel) (a) 16/07/2000, ¿? (Nigeria) (b) 1,70 (c) F - left winger (d) SK Beveren (e) FC Lorient, Vålerenga, FC Lorient, Fredrikstad, Skeid
*** Ismail - Zeli Ismail (a) 12/12/1993, Kukës (Albania) (b) 1,74 (c) F - right winger (d) Newtown AFC (e) Hereford, Bradford City, FC Walsall, Bury, FC Walsall, Bury, Wolverhampton Wanderers, Cambridge Utd., Wolverhampton Wanderers, Oxford United, Wolverhampton Wanderers, Burton Albion, Wolverhampton Wanderers, Notts County, Wolverhampton Wanderers, Burton Albion, Wolverhampton Wanderers, MK Dons, Wolverhampton Wanderers
*** Ismaila - Origbaajo Ismaila (a) 04/08/1998, Ilorin (Nigeria) (b) 1,88 (c) F - center forward (d) Tochigi SC (e) Tochigi SC, Kyoto Sanga, FC Sheriff, Kyoto Sanga, Fukushima Utd., C. de Joachim, Gateway FC
*** Ismaili - Benet Ismaili (a) 13/03/2002, Prishtinë (RF Yugoslavia, now in Kosovo) (b) - (c) D - right back (d) RNK Split (e) NK Vodice, Ramiz Sadiku, FC Prishtina
*** Ismaili - Fati Ismaili (a) 29/08/1997, Skopje (North Macedonia) (b) 1,86 (c) D - central defense (d) Voska Sport (e) Rabotnicki, FC Shkupi, Gostivar, FC Shkupi
*** Ismaili - Redon Ismaili (a) 23/10/2002, ¿? (RF Yugoslavia, now in Kosovo) (b) 1,81 (c) M - central midfielder (d) SC Gjilani (e) KF Vllaznia, SC Gjilani
*** Ismaily - Ismaily (Ismaily Gonçalves dos Santos) (a) 11/01/1990, Ivinhema (Brazil) (b) 1,77 (c) D - left back (d) LOSC Lille Métropole (e) Shakhtar Donetsk, SC Braga, Olhanense, Desp. Brasil, Estoril Praia, Desp. Brasil, São Bento (SP), Desp. Brasil
*** Ismajlgeci - Marsel Ismajlgeci (a) 14/03/2000, Tiranë (Albania) (b) 1,76 (c) D - left back (d) HSK Zrinjski Mostar (e) KF Tirana

*** Ismajli - Ardian Ismajli (a) 30/09/1996, Majac, Besianë (RF Yugoslavia, now in Kosovo) (b) 1,85 (c) D - central defense (d) FC Empoli (e) Spezia, Hajduk Split, Hajduk Split II, KF 2 Korriku, FC Prishtina, KF 2 Korriku
*** Ismayilov - Afran Ismayilov (Əfran Amid oğlu İsmayılov) (a) 08/10/1988, Baku (Soviet Union, now in Azerbaijan) (b) 1,83 (c) F - left winger (d) - (e) Kapaz PFK, FK Sabail, Keshla, Sumqayit, Qarabag FK, Inter Baku, Xäzär Länkäran, FK Baku, Qarabag FK, Turan Tovuz, Qarabag FK, Premyer Liqa
*** Ispas - Denis Ispas (Denis Florentin Ispas) (a) 05/09/1993, Târgoviște (Romania) (b) 1,86 (c) D - central defense (d) Concordia Chiajna (e) Universitatea Cluj, FC U Craiova, AFC Turris, FC Farul 1920, Dunarea Calarasi, Energeticianul, Chindia
*** Ispas - Rares Ispas (Rareș Sebastian Ispas) (a) 26/08/2000, Cluj Napoca (Romania) (b) - (c) D - left back (d) ACSM Politehnica Iasi (e) Sepsi OSK, CFR Cluj, Sepsi OSK, CFR Cluj, Comuna Recea, CFR Cluj, CSM Resita, CFR Cluj
*** Ispizua - Ibon Ispizua (Ibon Ispizua Helguera) (a) 08/04/2003, Mundaka (Spain) (b) 1,85 (c) G (d) CD Vitoria (e) Bilbao Athletic, Gernika, Bilbao Athletic, CD Basconia
*** Israel - Dele Israel (Dele Ola Israel) (a) 27/10/2001, ¿? (Nigeria) (b) 1,78 (c) M - central midfielder (d) SK Sigma Olomouc (e) Daugavpils, Liepaja, Daugavpils, Liepaja
*** Israel - Franco Israel (Franco Israel Wibmer) (a) 22/04/2000, Nueva Helvecia (Uruguay) (b) 1,90 (c) G (d) Sporting de Lisboa (e) Juve Next Gen
*** Israeli - Itamar Israeli (ישראלי איתמר) (a) 22/03/1992, Holon (Israel) (b) 1,85 (c) G (d) - (e) B. Jerusalem, Maccabi Haifa, H. Kfar Saba, Bnei Yehuda, Hapoel Marmorek, Bnei Yehuda, H Rishon leZion, Bnei Yehuda, Hapoel Morasha, Bnei Yehuda, H. Nazareth Illit, Bnei Yehuda, Hapoel Herzliya, Bnei Yehuda
*** Israeli - Stav Israeli (ישראלי סתיו) (a) 11/12/1998, ¿? (Israel) (b) - (c) D - central defense (d) Bnei Yehuda Tel Aviv (e) Ness Ziona, H. Ramat Gan, Ness Ziona, H. Ramat Gan, AS Ashdod, H. Ramat Gan, Hakoah Amidar, H. Ramat Gan
*** Israelov - Or Israelov (ישראלוב אלון אור) (a) 02/09/2004, Shoham (Israel) (b) 1,87 (c) D - central defense (d) Hapoel Tel Aviv (e) -
*** Israelsson - Erik Israelsson (Erik Gustav Roger Israelsson) (a) 25/02/1989, Kalmar (Sweden) (b) 1,81 (c) M - central midfielder (d) - (e) Kalmar FF, Vålerenga, PEC Zwolle, Vålerenga, PEC Zwolle, Hammarby IF, Kalmar FF, Lindsdals IF
*** Israelyan - Artur Israelyan (Արթուր Իսրայելյան) (a) 16/01/2004, ¿? (Armenia) (b) 1,72 (c) F - right winger (d) FC Urartu Erewan II (e) -
*** Israfilov - Eddy Israfilov (Eddy Silvestre Pascual Israfilov) (a) 02/08/1992, Roquetas de Mar (Spain) (b) 1,91 (c) M - central midfielder (d) Neftchi Baku (e) Albacete, Alcorcón, Gimnàstic, Cádiz CF, Real Murcia, Córdoba CF, Real Murcia, SD Eibar, Real Murcia, Granada CF, Real Murcia, Murcia Imperial
*** Issa - Ismail Issa (Исмаил Иса Мустафа) (a) 26/06/1989, Targovishte (Bulgaria) (b) 1,83 (c) F - center forward (d) Cherno More Varna (e) Cherno More, Dunav, Vereya, Dacia, Beroe, FC Sheriff, Litex Lovetch, Karabükspor, Elazigspor, Karabükspor, Levski Sofia, Lokomotiv Mezdra, Levski Sofia, Sliven, Levski Sofia, Haskovo, Svetkavitsa
*** Issah - Saeed Issah (Seydou Saeed Issah) (a) 11/01/2000, Accra (Ghana) (b) 1,88 (c) D - left back (d) FC Metaloglobus Bucharest (e) Metaloglobus, FC Hermannstadt
*** Issawi - Moatasem Issawi (עיסאוי מועתסם) (a) 24/07/2003, ¿? (Israel) (b) - (c) M (d) Hapoel Beer Sheva (e) H. Nof HaGalil, H. Beer Sheva
*** Isse - Ahmed Isse (Ahmed Abdikarim Isse) (a) 03/02/2001, ¿? (England) (b) 1,86 (c) D - central defense (d) Glacis United (e) San Jorge, Andover Town FC

*** Istatkov - Zharko Istatkov (Жарко Истатков) (a) 23/03/2003, Dimitrovgrad (Serbia and Montenegro, now in Serbia) (b) 1,86 (c) G (d) Lokomotiv Sofia (e) -
*** Isteri - Edi Isteri (a) 22/02/2004, Durres (Albania) (b) - (c) F (d) KF Erzeni (e) -
*** Istrati - Sergiu Istrati (a) 07/08/1988, ¿? (Soviet Union, now in Moldova) (b) 1,74 (c) F - center forward (d) - (e) Milsami, CSM Focsani, Sfintul Gheorghe, FC Brasov, Ac. Chisinau, FC Saxan, Spicul, FC Saxan, Ac. Chisinau, Milsami, Sfintul Gheorghe, Rapid G.
*** Istsenko - Vladimir Istsenko (Vladimir Ištšenko) (a) 23/04/2001, Tallinn (Estonia) (b) - (c) D - left back (d) Tallinn JK Legion (e) FCI Tallinn, TJK Legion, FCI Tallinn, FCI Tallinn III
*** Isuf - Arhan Isuf (Архан Гюнай Исуф) (a) 25/01/1999, Harmanli (Bulgaria) (b) 1,77 (c) D - right back (d) Hebar Pazardzhik (e) CSKA 1948, Spartak Varna, Pirin, Lokomotiv Plovdiv, Spartak Varna, Lokomotiv Plovdiv, Arda Kardzhali, Lokomotiv Plovdiv
*** Isufi - Eron Isufi (a) 05/08/2004, Gjilan (Serbia and Montenegro, now in Kosovo) (b) 1,92 (c) G (d) FC Drita Gjilan (e) -
*** Itaitinga - Itaitinga (Cleilton Monteiro da Costa) (a) 04/10/1998, Itaitinga (Brazil) (b) 1,81 (c) F - right winger (d) FC Sion (e) Pau FC, FC Sion, Fortaleza B
*** Itakura - Ko Itakura (板倉 滉) (a) 27/01/1997, Yokohama, Kanagawa (Japan) (b) 1,88 (c) D - central defense (d) Borussia Mönchengladbach (e) Manchester City, FC Schalke 04, Manchester City, FC Groningen, Manchester City, FC Groningen, Manchester City, Kawasaki Front., Vegalta Sendai, Kawasaki Front.
*** Ítalo - Ítalo (Ítalo Fernando Assis Gonçalves) (a) 18/02/2002, Salvador de Bahia (Brazil) (b) 1,95 (c) D - central defense (d) Ural Ekaterimburgo (e) Santa Clara, São Bernardo, Figueirense FC
*** Ito - Hiroki Ito (伊藤 洋輝) (a) 12/05/1999, Hamamatsu, Shizuoka (Japan) (b) 1,88 (c) D - central defense (d) VfB Stuttgart (e) Júbilo Iwata, VfB Stuttgart, Júbilo Iwata, Nagoya Grampus, Júbilo Iwata
*** Ito - Junya Ito (伊東 純也) (a) 09/03/1993, Yokosuka, Kanagawa (Japan) (b) 1,76 (c) F - right winger (d) Stade de Reims (e) KRC Genk, Kashiwa Reysol, KRC Genk, Kashiwa Reysol, Ventforet Kofu, Kanagawa Uni
*** Ito - Yasukaze Ito (伊藤 涼風) (a) 10/11/1998, ¿?, Hiroshima (Japan) (b) 1,76 (c) M - pivot (d) SRC Hiroshima (e) Pietà Hotspurs, Qrendi FC, Gudja United FC, Kansai UIS
*** Itten - Cedric Itten (a) 27/12/1996, Basel (Switzerland) (b) 1,90 (d) BSC Young Boys (e) Rangers FC, Greuther FÃ¼rth, Rangers FC, FC St. Gallen, FC Basel, FC St. Gallen, FC Basel, FC Luzern, FC Basel
*** Itu - Catalin Itu (Cătălin Mihai Itu) (a) 26/10/1999, Dej (Romania) (b) 1,87 (c) M - central midfielder (d) ACSM Politehnica Iasi (e) CFR Cluj, ACSM Poli Iasi, CFR Cluj, FC Dinamo, CFR Cluj, Academia Hagi
*** Iturbe - Alejandro Iturbe (Alejandro Iturbe Encabo) (a) 02/09/2003, Madrid (Spain) (b) 1,86 (c) G (d) Atlético de Madrid B (e) -
*** Iturbe - Juan Iturbe (Juan Manuel Iturbe Arévalos) (a) 04/06/1993, Buenos Aires (Argentina) (b) 1,73 (c) F - left winger (d) Grêmio Foot-Ball Porto Alegrense (e) Aris Thessaloniki, Pumas UNAM, Pachuca, Pumas UNAM, Club Tijuana, AS Roma, Club Tijuana, AS Roma, Torino, AS Roma, Bournemouth, AS Roma, Hellas Verona, FC Porto, Hellas Verona, FC Porto, River Plate, FC Porto, Cerro Porteño, Trinidense
*** Itzhak - Gil Itzhak (גיל יצחק) (a) 29/06/1993, Tel Aviv (Israel) (b) - (c) F - center forward (d) Maccabi Kabilio Jaffa (e) H. Umm al-Fahm, Maccabi Netanya, H. Kfar

Saba, Hapoel Tel Aviv, Maccabi Haifa, H Rishon leZion, Maccabi Haifa, M. Shaaraim, H Rishon leZion, M. Shaaraim, Bnei Yehuda

*** Iurasco - Nichita Iurasco (Nichita Iuraşco) (a) 17/05/1999, ¿? (Moldova) (b) 1,83 (c) F - left winger (d) - (e) Spartanii, Milsami, Zimbru Chisinau, Milsami, Zimbru Chisinau

*** Iuzzolino - Manuel Iuzzolino (a) 05/05/1990, ¿? (San Marino) (b) - (c) D - central defense (d) SP Cailungo (e) SS Folgore, Cailungo

*** Ivakhnov - Matvey Ivakhnov (Ивахнов Матвей Андреевич) (a) 21/07/2003, Volgograd (Russia) (b) 1,88 (c) F - center forward (d) Fakel Voronezh (e) Krasava, Super Nova

*** Ivan - Ivan (Ivan Quaresma da Silva) (a) 02/07/1997, Rio das Pedras (Brazil) (b) 1,96 (c) G (d) Clube de Regatas Vasco da Gama (e) Vasco da Gama, Corinthians, Zenit, Corinthians, Ponte Preta

*** Ivan - Alex Ivan (Alex Iván) (a) 26/03/1997, Dunajská Streda (Slovakia) (b) 1,84 (c) F - right winger (d) - (e) Spartak Trnava, SKF Sered, Dun. Streda B, FC Petrzalka, Dun. Streda B, Komarno

*** Ivan - Andreas Ivan (Andreas Ionuț Ivan) (a) 10/01/1995, Pitești (Romania) (b) 1,80 (c) F - left winger (d) FC Schalke 04 II (e) Rot Weiss Ahlen, Sonnenhof-Gr., VfR Aalen, New York, Waldh. Mannheim, Wuppertaler SV, RW Essen, Stuttg. Kickers

*** Ivan - Andrei Ivan (Andrei Virgil Ivan) (a) 04/01/1997, Moreni (Romania) (b) 1,85 (c) F - left winger (d) Universitatea Craiova (e) Krasnodar, Rapid Wien, Krasnodar, CS U Craiova

*** Ivan - David Ivan (David Ivan) (a) 26/02/1995, Bratislava (Slovakia) (b) 1,76 (c) M - central midfielder (d) FC Dinamo (e) Dynamo Brest, Chievo Verona, Dynamo Brest, Chievo Verona, Sampdoria, Vis Pesaro, Sampdoria, Pro Vercelli, Sampdoria, Bari, Sampdoria

*** Iván Cédric - Iván Cédric (Iván Cédric Bikoue Embolo) (a) 22/12/2001, Madrid (Spain) (b) 1,87 (c) F - center forward (d) Real Valladolid Promesas (e) Alcorcón, CD Toledo, Alcorcón, AD Alcorcón B, CD Los Yébenes

*** Iván Jaime - Iván Jaime (Iván Jaime Pajuelo) (a) 26/09/2000, Málaga (Spain) (b) 1,80 (c) F - left winger (d) FC Famalicão (e) At. Malagueño

*** Ivancevic - Mihajlo Ivancevic (Михајло Иванчевић) (a) 07/04/1999, Bačka Topola (RF Yugoslavia, now in Serbia) (b) 1,90 (c) D - central defense (d) Odense Boldklub (e) Spartak, Proleter, FK Brodarac, Proleter, FK Brodarac

*** Ivancic - Antonio Ivancic (Antonio Ivančić) (a) 25/05/1995, Zagreb (Croatia) (b) 1,82 (c) M - attacking midfielder (d) HSK Zrinjski Mostar (e) NK Istra, NK Rudes, NK Trnje Zagreb

*** Ivandic - Antonijo Ivandic (Antonijo Ivandić) (a) 28/03/2002, Slavonski Brod (Croatia) (b) - (c) M - pivot (d) NK Marsonia 1909 (e) NK Osijek II

*** Ivanenko - Evgeniy Ivanenko (Иваненко Евгений Владимирович) (a) 22/12/1995, Mozyr (Belarus) (b) 1,84 (c) G (d) Slavia Mozyr (e) Gomel, Slavia, Gomel, Slavia, Granit, Slavia, Svetlogorsk, Slavia, Slavia Mozyr II

*** Ivaniadze - Giorgi Ivaniadze (გიორგი ივანიაძე) (a) 27/01/2000, ¿? (Georgia) (b) 1,75 (c) F - left winger (d) - (e) FK Tuzla City, Qyzyljar, FC Dila, Sioni Bolnisi, Merani Tbilisi, FC Gagra, FC Samtredia, FC Shevardeni, FC Gagra, Shukura

*** Ivanic - Mirko Ivanic (Мирко Иванић) (a) 13/09/1993, Backi Jarak (Yugoslavia, now in Serbia) (b) 1,83 (c) M - attacking midfielder (d) Crvena zvezda Beograd (e) BATE Borisov, Vojvodina, Proleter, Vojvodina

*** Ivanic - Nenad Ivanic (Ненад Иванић) (a) 11/03/2000, Beograd (RF Yugoslavia, now in Serbia) (b) 1,71 (c) M - central midfielder (d) Radnicki Obrenovac (e) Napredak, Trayal, Napredak, Smederevo 1924, Radnicki Obrenovac, Radnicki (O)

*** Ivanilson - Ivanilson (Ivanilson Joaquim Monteiro Magalhães) (a) 04/04/1999, Lisboa (Portugal) (b) 1,76 (c) D - left back (d) - (e) Zimbru Chisinau, Canelas 2010, Leiria

*** Ivanisenya - Dmytro Ivanisenya (Іванісеня Дмитро Олександрович) (a) 11/01/1994, Kryvyi Rig, Dnipropetrovsk Oblast (Ukraine) (b) 1,87 (c) M - pivot (d) Krylya Sovetov Samara (e) Zorya Lugansk, Dinamo Tbilisi, FK Mariupol, Shakhtar II, Illichivets, Shakhtar II, Shakhtar 3

*** Ivankov - Mikhail Ivankov (Иваньков Михаил Алексеевич) (a) 17/06/2001, ¿? (Russia) (b) 1,96 (c) D - central defense (d) Lokomotiv Moskva II (e) Loko-Kazanka M., Lokomotiv Moskva II

*** Ivannikov - Dmitriy Ivannikov (Иванников Дмитрий Сергеевич) (a) 26/02/2005, Moskva (Russia) (b) 1,79 (c) D - left back (d) Spartak de Moskva II (e) -

*** Ivanov - Aleksey Ivanov (Иванов Алексей Дмитриевич) (a) 19/02/1997, Minsk (Belarus) (b) 1,82 (c) D - left back (d) Slavia Mozyr (e) Torpedo Zhodino, Gomel, FK Minsk, Dynamo Brest, Luch, Dynamo Brest, FK Minsk II, Dynamo Brest, FK Minsk II

*** Ivanov - Antoni Ivanov (Антони Иванов) (a) 11/09/1995, Sofia (Bulgaria) (b) 1,70 (c) M - central midfielder (d) - (e) FC Botosani, FC Dinamo, CS U Craiova, FC Voluntari, CS U Craiova, Gaz Metan, Septemvri Sofia, Montana, Sozopol, Spartak Pleven, Ludogorets II, Akademik, Ludogorets II

*** Ivanov - Bojan Ivanov (Бојан Иванов) (a) 07/10/1994, Stip (North Macedonia) (b) 1,75 (c) M - attacking midfielder (d) Kozuf Gevgelija (e) Rabotnicki, Sloga 1934, FK Sasa, Bregalnica Stip, Plackovica, AP Brera, Ovce Pole, Borec Veles, Makedonija

*** Ivanov - Daniel Ivanov (Даниел Иванов Иванов) (a) 22/02/2002, Vratsa (Bulgaria) (b) 1,86 (c) F - right winger (d) Chernomorets 1919 Burgas (e) Sozopol, Pirin, CSKA-Sofia, Neftochimik, CSKA-Sofia, Litex Lovetch, CSKA-Sofia, Neftochimik, CSKA-Sofia, Litex Lovetch, CSKA-Sofia

*** Ivanov - Hristo Ivanov (Христо Бисеров Иванов) (a) 05/12/2000, Sofia (Bulgaria) (b) 1,87 (c) M - attacking midfielder (d) Septemvri Sofia (e) Litex Lovetch, Lokomotiv Plovdiv, Lokomotiv Sofia, Septemvri Simitli, Slavia Sofia, Sportist Svoge, Slavia Sofia, Spartak Varna

*** Ivanov - Hristo Ivanov (Христо Янков Иванов) (a) 16/12/2000, Yambol (Bulgaria) (b) 1,86 (c) M - central midfielder (d) Lokomotiv Plovdiv (e) Arda Kardzhali, Novara, Vitosha

*** Ivanov - Ivan Ivanov (Иван Петров Иванов) (a) 01/03/2004, Plovdiv (Bulgaria) (b) 1,86 (c) D - central defense (d) Botev Plovdiv II (e) -

*** Ivanov - Luka Ivanov (Лука Иванов) (a) 31/12/2003, Sofia (Bulgaria) (b) 1,85 (c) D - central defense (d) Lokomotiv Sofia (e) -

*** Ivanov - Nikita Ivanov (a) 16/08/2003, Narva (Estonia) (b) - (c) M - central midfielder (d) Kalju FC (e) Kalju FC, TJK Legion, NK Rogaska, TJK Legion, JK Legion II

*** Ivanov - Nikolay Ivanov (Иванов Николай Владимирович) (a) 02/01/2000, Minsk (Belarus) (b) 1,89 (c) M - central midfielder (d) BK Maxline Vitebsk (e) Dinamo Minsk II, FK Minsk, Dinamo Minsk II, Naftan, Dinamo Minsk II, Isloch, Dinamo Minsk II, Gomel, Dinamo Minsk II

*** Ivanov - Nikolay Ivanov (Николай Йорданов Иванов) (a) 28/04/1995, Varna (Bulgaria) (b) 1,78 (c) M - pivot (d) Septemvri 98 Tervel (e) Spartak Varna, C. Balchik

*** Ivanov - Robert Ivanov (a) 19/09/1994, Helsinki (Finland) (b) 1,97 (c) D - central defense (d) Eintracht Braunschweig (e) Warta Poznań, FC Honka, FC Viikingit, FC Myllypuro
*** Ivanov - Sergey Ivanov (Иванов Сергей Алексеевич) (a) 07/01/1997, St. Petersburg (Russia) (b) 1,71 (c) M - right midfielder (d) Alashkert Yerevan CF (e) Zenit 2 St. Peterburg, Michalovce, Zenit 2 St. Peterburg, KS Samara, Zenit 2 St. Peterburg, Zenit St. Peterburg II, VSS Kosice, Zenit St. Peterburg II, SShOR Zenit
*** Ivanov - Stanislav Ivanov (Станислав Ивайлов Иванов) (a) 16/04/1999, Gabrovo (Bulgaria) (b) 1,77 (c) F - right winger (d) Arda Kardzhali (e) Chicago, Levski Sofia
*** Ivanov - Teodor Ivanov (Теодор Иванов) (a) 04/05/2004, Sofia (Bulgaria) (b) - (c) M - central midfielder (d) Lokomotiv Sofia (e) -
*** Ivanov - Vladimir Ivanov (Владимир Антонов Иванов) (a) 01/01/2004, ¿? (Bulgaria) (b) - (c) G (d) Septemvri Sofia II (e) -
*** Ivanovic - Djordje Ivanovic (Ђорђе Ивановић) (a) 20/11/1995, Vukovar (Croatia) (b) 1,79 (c) F - left winger (d) FK Čukarički (e) Soligorsk, NK Maribor, Soligorsk, Olimpija, FK Partizan, Spartak, FK Senta, Spartak, FK Palic Koming, Spartak, FK Backa, Spartak
*** Ivanovic - Filip Ivanovic (Филип Ивановић) (a) 13/02/1992, Arandjelovac (Yugoslavia, now in Serbia) (b) 1,89 (c) D - central defense (d) Navbahor Namangan (e) Radnicki 1923, KF Teuta, Sabah FK, Radnik, FK Indjija, Sloga 33, FK Bezanija, Lokomotiva, Zvezdara, FK Hajduk, Zvezdara, FK Hajduk, Zvezdara, FK Hajduk
*** Ivanovic - Igor Ivanovic (Igor Ivanović) (a) 09/09/1990, ¿? (Yugoslavia, now in Montenegro) (b) - (c) F - right winger (d) Bunyodkor Tashkent (e) FK Decic Tuzi, Buducnost Podgorica, Sutjeska Niksic, Zira FK, Rudar Pljevlja, OFK Beograd, Rudar Pljevlja, Kom Podgorica
*** Ivanovic - Igor Ivanovic (Игор Ивановић) (a) 28/07/1997, Jagodina (RF Yugoslavia, now in Serbia) (b) 1,75 (c) F - right winger (d) Tobol Kostanay (e) FC Astana, Soligorsk, Napredak, Jagodina
*** Ivanovic - Mihailo Ivanovic (Михаило Ивановић) (a) 29/11/2004, Novi Sad (Serbia and Montenegro, now in Serbia) (b) - (c) F - center forward (d) FK Vojvodina Novi Sad (e) -
*** Ivanovs - Edgars Ivanovs (a) 07/10/2001, ¿? (Latvia) (b) - (c) M - central midfielder (d) BFC Daugavpils (e) -
*** Ivanovski - Ivan Ivanovski (Иван Ивановски) (a) 27/06/1995, ¿? (North Macedonia) (b) 1,81 (c) F - right winger (d) Tikves Kavadarci (e) Sileks, Tikves, Zvijezda G.
*** Ivanovski - Mirko Ivanovski (Мирко Ивановски) (a) 31/10/1989, Bitola (Yugoslavia, now in North Macedonia) (b) 1,82 (c) F - center forward (d) Concordia Chiajna (e) Petrolul, FC Dinamo, Diósgyőr, Hajduk Split, Slaven Belupo, Boluspor, Videoton FC, CFR Cluj, Astra Giurgiu, Arka Gdynia, Makedonija, Slavia Praha, Makedonija, Pelister Bitola
*** Ivanovski - Zoran Ivanovski (Зоран Ивановски) (a) 07/05/2000, Strumica (North Macedonia) (b) 1,77 (c) D - right back (d) AP Brera (e) Belasica, AP Brera
*** Ivanusec - Luka Ivanusec (Luka Ivanušec) (a) 26/11/1998, Varaždin (Croatia) (b) 1,75 (c) F - left winger (d) GNK Dinamo Zagreb (e) NK Lokomotiva
*** Ivanyushin - Aleksandr Ivanyushin (Александр Иванюшин) (a) 07/09/1995, Kohtla-Järve ((b) 1,74 (c) D - right back (d) Harju JK Laagri (e) Kalju FC, JK Trans Narva, Kalju FC, JK Järve, Sillamäe Kalev, JK Järve, JK Järve II, JK Alko
*** Ívarsson - Ísak Ívarsson (Ísak Daði Ívarsson) (a) 03/07/2004, ¿? (Iceland) (b) 1,78 (c) D - left back (d) Keflavík ÍF (e) Víkingur

*** Ivaylov - Chavdar Ivaylov (Чавдар Желев Ивайлов) (a) 09/07/1996, Teteven (Bulgaria) (b) 1,74 (c) M - attacking midfielder (d) Botev Vratsa (e) CSKA 1948, Etar, Litex II

*** Ivelja - Pavle Ivelja (Павле Ивеља) (a) 20/01/1998, Beograd (RF Yugoslavia, now in Serbia) (b) 1,93 (c) F - center forward (d) FK Radnicki Niš (e) Graficar, Javor-Matis, FK Sremčica, Tek Sloga, Hajduk 1912

*** Iversen - Daniel Iversen (Daniel Lønne Iversen) (a) 19/07/1997, Gørding (Denmark) (b) 1,91 (c) G (d) Leicester City (e) Preston North End, Leicester City, Preston North End, Leicester City, OH Leuven, Leicester City, Rotherham, Oldham Athletic

*** Ives - Levi Ives (a) 28/07/1997, Belfast (Northern Ireland) (b) 1,73 (c) D - left back (d) Larne FC (e) Cliftonville, Torquay

*** Ivetic - Janko Ivetic (Janko Ivetić) (a) 23/02/2001, ¿? (Slovenia) (b) 1,84 (c) D - left back (d) NK Triglav Kranj (e) NK Radomlje, NK Triglav

*** Ivey - Romeesh Ivey (Romeesh Nathaniel Ivey Belgrave) (a) 14/07/1994, Arraiján (Panamá) (b) 1,67 (c) F - left winger (d) Spartak Varna (e) Independiente, Etar, Independiente, Etar, Alianza Petrol., Deportivo Pasto, Independiente, Alianza FC

*** Ivezic - Marko Ivezic (Марко Ивезић) (a) 02/12/2001, ¿? (Serbia and Montenegro, now in Serbia) (b) 1,91 (c) M - pivot (d) Holstein Kiel (e) Vozdovac

*** Ivkovic - Djordje Ivkovic (Ђорђе Ивковић) (a) 06/03/1996, Lazarevac (RF Yugoslavia, now in Serbia) (b) 1,91 (c) F - center forward (d) FK Radnicki Sremska Mitrovica (e) KF Laçi, Akzhayik, IMT Beograd, Zlatibor, Radnicki Srem, Zeleznicar Pancevo, Sindjelic Bg, FK Usce, Teleoptik, NK Ankaran, Spartak 1924, Kolubara, Sloboda Užice, FK Bezanija, Jedinstvo Ub, FK Turbina, Kolubara

*** Ivusic - Ivica Ivusic (Ivica Ivušić) (a) 01/02/1995, Rijeka (Croatia) (b) 1,95 (c) G (d) Pafos FC (e) NK Osijek, Olympiakos, NK Istra, Internazionale Milano, Prato, Seregno

*** Iwata - Tomoki Iwata (岩田 智輝) (a) 07/04/1997, Usa, Oita (Japan) (b) 1,78 (c) M - pivot (d) Celtic FC (e) Yokohama F. M., Celtic FC, Yokohama F. M., Oita Trinita

*** Iwobi - Alex Iwobi (a) 03/05/1996, Lagos (Nigeria) (b) 1,83 (d) Everton FC (e) Arsenal

*** Iwu - Ugochukwu Iwu (Ուգոչուկվու Քրիստուու Իվու) (a) 28/10/1999, Jos (Nigeria) (b) 1,77 (c) M - pivot (d) Rubin Kazan (e) FC Urartu, Lori Vanadzor, Pyunik Yerevan, Lori Vanadzor, Elkanemi

*** Iyede - Samson Iyede (Samson Iyede Onomigho) (a) 28/01/1998, Orogun (Nigeria) (b) 1,81 (c) F - center forward (d) Chornomorets Odessa (e) Chornomorets, AC Horsens, FC Fredericia, Fremad Amager, Lommel SK, Fremad Amager, Paide, FC Ebedei

*** Iyinbor - Patrick Iyinbor (Iyinbor Patrick Osagie) (a) 07/01/2002, ¿? (Hungary) (b) 1,88 (c) D - central defense (d) Kecskeméti TE (e) Kecskemét, Ferencváros II, Vasas FC, Ferencváros II, Vasas FC, Ferencváros II

*** Iyobosa Edokpolor - Nosa Iyobosa Edokpolor (a) 22/09/1996, Benin City (Nigeria) (b) 1,78 (c) D - left back (d) SCR Altach (e) Blau Weiss Linz, SV Horn, Wolfsberg II, Alpe Adria

*** Izbasarov - Nurdaulet Izbasarov (Избасаров Нурдаулет) (a) 17/03/2002, Taraz (Kazakhstan) (b) 1,75 (c) M - pivot (d) FK Aktobe II (e) -

*** Izmaylov - Almas Izmaylov (Измайлов Алмас Жаслanович) (a) 30/01/2002, North Kazakhstan Region (Kazakhstan) (b) 1,79 (c) F - left winger (d) Kyzylzhar SK Petropavlovsk II (e) FK Ekibastuz, Kyzylzhar II

*** Izquier - Gabri Izquier (Gabriel Izquier Artiles) (a) 29/04/1993, Las Palmas de Gran Canaria (Spain) (b) 1,72 (c) D - left back (d) Hibernians FC (e) CD Teruel, Villa Santa Brígida, CD Badajoz, Barakaldo CF, At. Levante, Barakaldo CF, RCD Mallorca B

*** Izzo - Armando Izzo (a) 02/03/1992, Napoli (Italy) (b) 1,83 (c) D - central defense (d) AC Monza (e) Torino, Monza, Torino, Genoa, AS Avellino, Napoli, Triestina

*** Jääskä - Riku Jääskä (a) 04/02/1998, ¿? (Finland) (b) 1,82 (c) F - center forward (d) Vaasan Palloseura (e) FC Kiisto, Vaasa IFK, FC Kiisto

*** Jabarin - Abed Elrauf Jabarin (באריג'ג אלראוף עבד) (a) 22/01/2002, ¿? (Israel) (b) - (c) M - central midfielder (d) Hapoel Haifa (e) H. Umm al-Fahm, Hapoel Haifa

*** Jaber - Abdallah Jaber (جابر عبدالله) (a) 17/02/1993, Tayyibe (Israel) (b) 1,75 (c) D - left back (d) Maccabi Bnei Reineh (e) Bnei Sakhnin, Hapoel Hadera, Hilal Al-Quds, Ahli Al-Khaleel, Hilal Al-Quds, Ramat haSharon

*** Jaber - Ataa Jaber (جابر عطاء) (עטאא גאבר) (a) 03/10/1994, Majd al-Krum (Israel) (b) 1,76 (c) M - pivot (d) Neftchi Baku (e) FC Ashdod, Bnei Sakhnin, Maccabi Haifa, Bnei Sakhnin, Maccabi Haifa

*** Jaber - Karem Jaber (גאבר כראם) (a) 31/10/2000, Jaljulia (Israel) (b) 1,80 (c) D - right back (d) Maccabi Netanya (e) -

*** Jaber - Mahmoud Jaber (אבר'ג מחמוד) (a) 05/10/1999, Tayibe (Israel) (b) 1,78 (c) M - central midfielder (d) Maccabi Haifa (e) H. Nof HaGalil, Maccabi Haifa

*** Jablonsky - David Jablonsky (David Jablonský) (a) 08/10/1991, Sokolov (Czechoslovakia, now in Czech Rep.) (b) 1,90 (c) D - central defense (d) Cracovia (e) Levski Sofia, Tom Tomsk, Teplice, Banik Sokolov, Teplice, Usti nad Labem, Teplice, Caslav, Teplice

*** Jach - Jaroslaw Jach (Jarosław Przemysław Jach) (a) 17/02/1994, Bielawa (Poland) (b) 1,92 (c) D - central defense (d) Zagłębie Lubin (e) Crystal Palace, Rakow, Crystal Palace, Fortuna Sittard, Crystal Palace, Rakow, Crystal Palace, FC Sheriff, Crystal Palace, Çaykur Rizespor, Crystal Palace, Zagłębie, L. Dzierzoniow

*** Jack - Ryan Jack (a) 27/02/1992, Aberdeen (Scotland) (b) 1,82 (c) M - central midfielder (d) Rangers FC (e) Aberdeen FC

*** Jackers - Nordin Jackers (a) 05/09/1997, Veldwezelt (Belgium) (b) 1,87 (c) G (d) KV Brugge (e) KV Brugge, OH Leuven, SK Beveren, KRC Genk, Waasland-Beveren, KRC Genk

*** Jackson - Jackson (Jackson Kenio Santos Laurentino) (a) 24/04/1999, Santana do Ipanema (Brazil) (b) 1,78 (c) F - left winger (d) Istanbulspor (e) KF Egnatia, Murici, Vorwärts Steyr, Ypiranga-BA, ABC FC

*** Jackson - Kemmu Degran Jackson (a) 11/07/1995, ¿? (Malta) (b) - (c) M (d) Sirens FC (e) St. Andrews FC, Mosta FC, Constant Spring

*** Jackson - Nicolas Jackson (a) 20/06/2001, Banjul (Gambia) (b) 1,88 (c) F - center forward (d) Chelsea FC (e) Villarreal CF, Villarreal CF B, CD Mirandés, Villarreal CF B, Casa Sports

*** Jackuliak - David Jackuliak (a) 02/08/2003, ¿? (Slovakia) (b) - (c) F - center forward (d) MFK Ružomberok (e) Banska Bystrica

*** Jacob - Eddie Jacob (a) 18/12/2001, ¿? (Liberia) (b) 1,73 (c) F - right winger (d) FC Dinamo-Auto Tiraspol (e) -

*** Jacobs - Jamie Jacobs (a) 03/12/1997, Purmerend (Netherlands) (b) 1,82 (c) M - central midfielder (d) - (e) SC Cambuur

*** Jacobsen - Anders Jacobsen (Anders Kvindebjerg Jacobsen) (a) 27/10/1989, ¿? (Denmark) (b) 1,81 (c) F - center forward (d) AC Horsens (e) SønderjyskE, Odense BK, Aalborg BK, FC Fredericia, Naesby BK, Naestved BK, Odense BK, Vejle BK, Odense BK

*** Jacobsen - Andreas Jacobsen (Andreas Egebjerg Jacobsen) (a) 25/11/1999, ¿? (Faroe Islands) (b) - (c) F - center forward (d) Skála IF (e) -
*** Jacobsen - Jacob Buus Jacobsen (a) 07/03/1997, ¿? (Denmark) (b) 1,77 (c) D - right back (d) AC Horsens (e) SK Beveren, AC Horsens, FC Fredericia, Odense BK
*** Jacobsen - Jóel Jacobsen (a) 04/11/2002, ¿? (Faroe Islands) (b) - (c) F - center forward (d) NSÍ Runavík II (e) -
*** Jacobsen - Kristian Martin Jacobsen (a) 10/04/1996, ¿? (Faroe Islands) (b) - (c) D - central defense (d) Skála IF (e) Skála IF II
*** Jacobsen - Magnus Jacobsen (Magnus Holm Jacobsen) (a) 23/05/2000, Hoyvík (Faroe Islands) (b) 1,80 (c) M - pivot (d) Chrobry Glogow (e) 07 Vestur, B36 Tórshavn, B36 Tórshavn, B36 II
*** Jacobsen - Paetur Dam Jacobsen (Pætur Dam Jacobsen) (a) 05/12/1982, ¿? (Faroe Islands) (b) 1,74 (c) M - pivot (d) - (e) Skála, EB/Streymur, Skála
*** Jacovic - David Jacovic (a) 05/02/2001, St. Gallen (Switzerland) (b) 1,87 (c) M - pivot (d) FC Wil 1900 (e) FC St. Gallen
*** Jacquet - Jérémy Jacquet (a) 13/07/2005, Bondy (France) (b) - (c) D - central defense (d) Stade Rennais FC B (e) -
*** Jaeckel - Paul Jaeckel (a) 22/07/1998, Eisenhüttenstadt (Germany) (b) 1,86 (c) D - central defense (d) 1.FC Union Berlin (e) Greuther Fürth, VfL Wolfsburg, Wolfsburg II
*** Jaganjac - Hamza Jaganjac (a) 27/02/2004, Sarajevo (Bosnia and Herzegovina) (b) 1,92 (c) F - center forward (d) Adana Demirspor (e) -
*** Jäger - Lukas Jäger (a) 12/02/1994, Alberschwende (Austria) (b) 1,84 (c) M - pivot (d) SCR Altach (e) Sturm Graz, 1.FC Nürnberg, SCR Altach, Altach Juniors
*** Jagodinskis - Rikardo Jagodinskis (a) 07/03/2005, ¿? (Latvia) (b) - (c) M - pivot (d) SK Super Nova (e) Spartaks
*** Jagodinskis - Vitalijs Jagodinskis (Vitālijs Jagodinskis) (a) 28/02/1992, Riga (Latvia) (b) 1,91 (c) D - central defense (d) RFS (e) Valmiera, RFS, JFK Ventspils, ACSM Poli Iasi, Diósgyőr, Dynamo 2 Kyiv, Goverla, Dynamo 2 Kyiv, Dinamo Kiev II, Daugava Riga
*** Jah - Mustapha Jah (a) 27/01/2004, ¿? (Gambia) (b) 1,90 (c) F - center forward (d) CFR Cluj (e) CFR Cluj II, Real de Banjul
*** Jahanbakhsh - Alireza Jahanbakhsh (علیرضا جهانبخش) (a) 11/08/1993, Jirandeh, Gilan (Iran) (b) 1,81 (c) F - right winger (d) Feyenoord Rotterdam (e) Brighton & Hove Albion, AZ Alkmaar, NEC Nijmegen, Damash Gilan, Damash Teh
*** Jahja - Abdulhadi Jahja (a) 03/06/1999, Ohrid (North Macedonia) (b) 1,80 (c) F - left winger (d) Struga Trim & Lum (e) FC Shkupi, Euromilk GL
*** Jahmurataj - Rinor Jahmurataj (a) 17/02/2004, ¿? (Kosovo) (b) 1,73 (c) F - center forward (d) FC Besa Pejë (e) -
*** Jair - Jair (Jair Tavares da Silva) (a) 03/08/1994, Barra de Santo Antônio (Brazil) (b) 1,74 (c) M - central midfielder (d) Petrolul Ploiesti (e) HJK Helsinki, Ilves, AC Oulu, Ituano, AC Oulu, Ituano
*** Jairo - Jairo (Jairo de Macedo da Silva) (a) 06/05/1992, Rio de Janeiro (Brazil) (b) 1,81 (c) F - attacking midfielder (d) Pafos FC (e) Hajduk Split, PAOK, FC Sheriff, PAOK, PAS Giannina, PAOK, AS Trencin, Botafogo, AS Trencin, Botafogo, Madureira, Botafogo
*** Jaiteh - Bakary Jaiteh (a) 30/11/1999, Njaba (Gambia) (b) 1,88 (c) M - central midfielder (d) - (e) FC Wiltz 71, Pandurii, Schiltigheim
*** Jajá - Jajá (Jair Diego Alves de Brito) (a) 15/04/2001, Catanduva (Brazil) (b) 1,77 (c) F - left winger (d) Casa Pia AC (e) Casa Pia, Athletico-PR, Torpedo Moskva, Athletico-PR, Cruzeiro, Athletico-PR B, CRB, Athletico-PR B

*** Jajalo - Kristijan Jajalo (a) 04/03/1993, Široki Brijeg (Bosnia and Herzegovina) (b) - (c) G (d) KA Akureyri (e) Grindavík, Zrinjski Mostar, Din. Zagreb II, Inter Zaprešić, Dinamo Zagreb, NK Sesvete, Dinamo Zagreb, NK Lucko, Dinamo Zagreb, NK Stupnik, Dinamo Zagreb, Radnik Sesvete
*** Jajalo - Mato Jajalo (a) 25/05/1988, Jajce (Yugoslavia, now in Bosnia and Herzegovina) (b) 1,82 (c) M - pivot (d) Venezia FC (e) Udinese, Palermo, HNK Rijeka, 1.FC Köln, FK Sarajevo, 1.FC Köln, AC Siena, 1.FC Köln, AC Siena, Slaven Belupo
*** Jakic - Kristijan Jakic (Kristijan Jakić) (a) 14/05/1997, Split (Croatia) (b) 1,81 (c) M - pivot (d) Eintracht Frankfurt (e) Dinamo Zagreb, Eintracht, Dinamo Zagreb, NK Lokomotiva, NK Istra, NK Lokomotiva, RNK Split
*** Jakimovski - Stefan Jakimovski (Стефан Јакимовски) (a) 28/05/2000, Skopje (North Macedonia) (b) 1,93 (c) G (d) Makedonija Gjorce Petrov (e) FC Shkupi, Almopos, Borec Veles, Kadino, Lokomotiva, New Stars, Euromilk GL
*** Jakobi - Luis Jakobi (a) 15/12/2001, Lautzenhausen (Germany) (b) 1,77 (c) M - pivot (d) Újpest FC II (e) Türkgücü Münch., Greuther Fürth II
*** Jakobowski - Michal Jakobowski (Michał Jakóbowski) (a) 08/09/1992, Radziejów (Poland) (b) 1,70 (c) M - attacking midfielder (d) - (e) Chojniczanka, Warta Poznań, Bytovia Bytow, Chojniczanka, Bytovia Bytow, Lech Poznan II, Warta Poznań, Lech Poznan II
*** Jakobs - Ismail Jakobs (a) 17/08/1999, Köln (Germany) (b) 1,84 (c) D - left back (d) AS Mónaco (e) 1.FC Köln, 1.FC Köln II
*** Jakobsen - Brian Jakobsen (a) 04/11/1991, ¿? (Faroe Islands) (b) - (c) F - center forward (d) AB Argir (e) B36 Tórshavn, Skála, Skála IF II
*** Jakobsen - Hilmar Leon Jakobsen (a) 02/08/1997, ¿? (Faroe Islands) (b) 1,90 (c) F - center forward (d) - (e) HB Tórshavn, HB Tórshavn II
*** Jakobsen - Jákup Jakobsen (a) 22/11/1992, ¿? (Faroe Islands) (b) - (c) D - central defense (d) Skála IF (e) NSÍ Runavík, Skála
*** Jakobsen - Mikkel Jakobsen (Mikkel Elbæk Jakobsen) (a) 23/05/1999, ¿? (Denmark) (b) 1,76 (c) M - left midfielder (d) Vestri Ísafjördur (e) Leiknir, NSÍ Runavík, Kolding IF, Ringköbing IF
*** Jakobsson - Grímur Ingi Jakobsson (a) 26/06/2003, ¿? (Iceland) (b) - (c) M - attacking midfielder (d) ÍF Grótta (e) KR Reykjavík, KV Vesturbaejar, KR Reykjavík, Grótta
*** Jakobsson - Wille Jakobsson (a) 07/01/2002, Arboga (Sweden) (b) 1,89 (c) G (d) IFK Norrköping (e) Sylvia, Norrköping, AFC Eskilstuna, Eskilstuna City
*** Jakolis - Antonio Jakolis (Antonio Jakoliš) (a) 28/02/1992, Varaždin (Croatia) (b) 1,75 (c) F - right winger (d) Fakel Voronezh (e) FC Arges, HNK Sibenik, Panetolikos, APOEL FC, FCSB, Apollon Limassol, FCSB, CFR Cluj, NK Zadar, Excelsior Mouscron, Hajduk Split, Kryvbas, Dnipro, Kryvbas, Dnipro, HNK Sibenik
*** Jakolis - Marin Jakolis (Marin Jakoliš) (a) 26/12/1996, Šibenik (Croatia) (b) 1,82 (c) F - left winger (d) Melbourne City FC (e) Melbourne City, Angers SCO, AEK Larnaca, Angers SCO, Hajduk Split, HNK Sibenik, Hajduk Split, Admira Wacker, KSV Roeselare, Excelsior Mouscron, RE Virton, Excelsior Mouscron, HNK Sibenik
*** Jakopetrevski - Mihail Jakopetrevski (Михаил Јакопетревски) (a) 09/11/2003, Prilep (North Macedonia) (b) 1,79 (c) M - attacking midfielder (d) Pobeda Prilep (e) -
*** Jakovljevic - Slobodan Jakovljevic (Слободан Јаковљевић) (a) 26/05/1989, Prishtinë (Yugoslavia, now in Kosovo) (b) 1,86 (c) D - central defense (d) HSK Zrinjski Mostar (e) Radnik Bijelj., Spartak, Radnik, SZTK, FK Indjija, Novi Pazar, RFK Novi Sad, Mladost Apatin

*** Jaksic - Nemanja Jaksic (Nemanja Jakšić) (a) 11/07/1995, Prishtinë (RF Yugoslavia, now in Kosovo) (b) 1,85 (c) D - central defense (d) - (e) NK Bravo, NK Aluminij, DNŠ Zavrč, Zeta Golubovac, Zeleznik Belgr.
*** Jakubech - Adam Jakubech (a) 02/01/1997, Prešov (Slovakia) (b) 1,88 (c) G (d) LOSC Lille Métropole (e) KV Kortrijk, Lille, Spartak Trnava, Tatran Presov
*** Jakubiak - Sebastian Jakubiak (a) 21/06/1993, Lübeck (Germany) (b) 1,75 (c) M - central midfielder (d) - (e) Septemvri Sofia, 1.FC Magdeburg, Heracles Almelo, SV Rödinghausen, St. Pauli II, VfB Lübeck, VfB Lübeck II
*** Jakubik - Damian Jakubik (a) 25/03/1990, Otwock (Poland) (b) 1,83 (c) D - right back (d) Radomiak Radom (e) Znicz Pruszkow, Podbeskidzie, Gornik Leczna, Dolcan Zabki, Mazur Karczew, Dolcan Zabki, Mazur Karczew
*** Jakubowski - Filip Jakubowski (a) 14/09/2004, Poznań (Poland) (b) - (c) D - central defense (d) Warta Poznań (e) -
*** Jakupi - Blend Jakupi (a) 07/02/2001, Gjilan (RF Yugoslavia, now in Kosovo) (b) - (c) M (d) SC Gjilani (e) -
*** Jakupovic - Arnel Jakupovic (Arnel Jakupović) (a) 29/05/1998, ¿? (Austria) (b) 1,88 (c) F - center forward (d) NK Maribor (e) Domžale, Empoli, Domžale, Empoli, Sturm Graz, Empoli, Austria Wien Reserves
*** Jakupovic - Demir Jakupovic (Demir Jakupović) (a) 16/02/1996, Kitzingen (Germany) (b) 1,73 (c) F (d) NK Podgrmec Sanski Most (e) Igman Konjic, Rudar Prijedor, Borac Banja Luka, Rudar Prijedor, NK Jajce, Rudar Prijedor, Borac Banja Luka, NK Podgrmec
*** Jakupovic - Eldin Jakupovic (Eldin Jakupović) (a) 02/10/1984, Kozarac (Yugoslavia, now in Bosnia and Herzegovina) (b) 1,91 (c) G (d) Los Ángeles FC (e) Everton, Leicester City, Hull City, Leyton Orient, Hull City, Leyton Orient, Hull City, Aris Thessaloniki, Olympiakos Volou, Lokomotiv Moskva, Grasshoppers, Lokomotiv Moskva, Grasshoppers, FC Thun, Grasshoppers
*** Jakupsson - Brandur Jakupsson (a) 27/11/1999, ¿? (Faroe Islands) (b) - (c) D - central defense (d) AB Argir II (e) AB Argir, AB Argir II
*** Jallow - Alexander Jallow (Alexander Jallow) (a) 03/03/1998, Huddinge (Sweden) (b) 1,85 (c) D - right back (d) Brescia Calcio (e) IFK Göteborg, J-Södra IF, Brage, Avesta AIK, Brage, Avesta AIK
*** Jaloliddinov - Jasurbek Jaloliddinov (Жасурбек Жалолиддинов) (a) 15/05/2002, Navoi (Uzbekistan) (b) 1,71 (c) M - attacking midfielder (d) FC Olympic (e) FC Olympic, Lokomotiv Tashkent, Kairat Almaty, Lokomotiv Tashkent, FK Andijon, Lokomotiv Moskva, Tambov, Lokomotiv Moskva, Bunyodkor, Bunyodkor-Farm
*** Jalu - Suleiman Jalu (a) 20/03/2000, ¿? (Malta) (b) 1,79 (c) F - center forward (d) - (e) Qrendi FC, Balzan FC
*** Jaman - Ianus Jaman (Ianuş Jaman) (a) 16/05/2004, ¿? (Moldova) (b) - (c) D - central defense (d) FC Petrocub Hînceşti (e) Atletic S.
*** Jambor - David Jambor (a) 31/01/2003, Nové Město na Moravě (Czech Rep.) (b) 1,80 (c) M - pivot (d) FC Zbrojovka Brno (e) MFK Vyskov, Zbrojovka Brno, MFK Vyskov, Zbrojovka Brno
*** Jambor - Nikola Jambor (a) 25/09/1995, Koprivnica (Croatia) (b) 1,84 (c) M - pivot (d) Hajer Club (e) Slaven Belupo, Moreirense, Rio Ave, KSC Lokeren, NK Osijek, KSC Lokeren, Slaven Belupo, Koprivnica
*** Jambor - Timotej Jambor (a) 04/04/2003, Svit (Slovakia) (b) 1,83 (c) F - center forward (d) MSK Zilina (e) -
*** James - James (James Santos das Neves) (a) 15/07/1995, Foz de Iguaçu (Brazil) (b) 1,73 (c) D - left back (d) FC Pyunik Yerevan (e) Alashkert CF, FC Urartu, Ararat Yerevan, Campinense-PB, Sampaio Corrêa, Bragantino, Inter de Lages

*** James - Daniel James (a) 24/10/2004, ¿? (Wales) (b) - (c) F - center forward (d) Goodwick United (e) Haverfordwest, Goodwick Utd.
*** James - Daniel James (Daniel Owen James) (a) 10/11/1997, Beverley (England) (b) 1,71 (c) F - right winger (d) Leeds United (e) Fulham, Leeds Utd., Manchester Utd., Swansea City, Shrewsbury
*** James - Dean James (Dean Ruben James) (a) 30/04/2000, Leiden (Netherlands) (b) - (c) D - left back (d) Go Ahead Eagles Deventer (e) FC Volendam
*** James - Leke James (Leke Samson James) (a) 01/11/1992, Kaduna (Nigeria) (b) 1,88 (c) F - center forward (d) - (e) Sivasspor, Al-Qadsiah FC, Molde, BJ Enterprises, Aalesund, Bridge FC
*** James - Manjrekar James (a) 05/08/1993, Roseau (Dominica) (b) 1,93 (c) D - central defense (d) Forge FC (e) Chornomorets, Vejle BK, Chornomorets, Vejle BK, Midtjylland, PAS Lamia, Midtjylland, FC Fredericia, Midtjylland, Vasas FC, Diósgyőr, Pécsi MFC, Pécsi MFC II
*** James - Reece James (a) 08/12/1999, Redbridge (England) (b) 1,80 (c) D - right back (d) Chelsea FC (e) Wigan Ath.
*** Jamieson - Lewis Jamieson (a) 17/04/2002, Glasgow (Scotland) (b) 1,69 (c) F - center forward (d) St. Mirren FC (e) Airdrieonians, St. Mirren, Clyde FC, St. Mirren, Inverness Caledonian, St. Mirren, Clyde FC, St. Mirren, St. Mirren B
*** Jan - Dor Jan (אור ג׳אן) (a) 16/12/1994, ¿? (Israel) (b) 1,78 (c) F - center forward (d) Hapoel Hadera (e) H. Jerusalem, FC Ashdod, Paços Ferreira, M. Petah Tikva, Paços Ferreira, Bnei Yehuda, Maccabi Tel Aviv, FC Ashdod, Maccabi Tel Aviv, Beitar TA Ramla, Maccabi Tel Aviv, Hapoel Acre, Maccabi Tel Aviv, H. Petah Tikva, Maccabi Tel Aviv, Kiryat Shmona, Maccabi Tel Aviv
*** Janacek - Martin Janacek (Martin Janáček) (a) 22/09/2000, Cehnice (Czech Rep.) (b) 1,97 (c) G (d) SK Dynamo Ceske Budejovice (e) Ceske Budejovice B, FC MAS Taborsko, Ceske Budejovice B, Sparta Praha B, Motorlet Praha, Sparta Praha B
*** Janakievski - Ivo Janakievski (Иво Јанакиевски) (a) 09/06/1993, Skopje (North Macedonia) (b) 1,78 (c) M - pivot (d) - (e) Rabotnicki, FK Skopje, Teteks Tetovo, Sileks, Teteks Tetovo, Metalurg Skopje, Tikves, Ljubanci, Makedonija, Borec Veles, Makedonija
*** Janasik - Patryk Janasik (a) 25/08/1997, Pniewy (Poland) (b) 1,78 (c) D - left back (d) Śląsk Wroclaw (e) Odra Opole, Blekitni Wronki, Odra Opole, Blekitni Wronki, GKS Belchatow, Blekitni Wronki, Lech Poznan II, Blekitni Wronki, Pniewy
*** Janelidze - Giorgi Janelidze (გიორგი ჯანელიძე) (a) 25/09/1989, Tbilisi (Soviet Union, now in Georgia) (b) 1,77 (c) M - central midfielder (d) Shukura Kobuleti (e) FC Telavi, Torpedo Kutaisi, Dinamo Batumi, Kolkheti Poti, Sioni Bolnisi, Dinamo Tbilisi, WIT Georgia, Neftekhimik, WIT Georgia
*** Janelt - Vitaly Janelt (a) 10/05/1998, Hamburg (Germany) (b) 1,84 (c) M - pivot (d) Brentford FC (e) VfL Bochum, RB Leipzig, VfL Bochum, RB Leipzig
*** Janetzky - Jakub Janetzky (Jakub Janetzký) (a) 12/06/1997, ¿? (Czech Rep.) (b) 1,82 (c) M - attacking midfielder (d) FC Zlin (e) Jablonec, SFC Opava, Jablonec, SFC Opava, Jablonec, SFC Opava
*** Janevski - Igor Janevski (Игор Јаневски) (a) 09/02/2004, Skopje (North Macedonia) (b) 1,79 (c) M - pivot (d) Sileks Kratovo (e) New Stars
*** Jang - Seung-cheol Jang (a) 20/12/1998, Seoul (South Korea) (b) - (c) M (d) UE Sant Julia (e) UD Montijo, CD La Granja
*** Janga - Rangelo Janga (Rangelo Maria Janga) (a) 16/04/1992, Rotterdam (Netherlands) (b) 1,92 (c) F - center forward (d) CFR Cluj (e) Apollon Limassol, FC Astana, Apollon Limassol, FC Astana, NEC Nijmegen, FC Astana, FC Lugano, FC

Astana, KAA Gent, AS Trencin, FC Dordrecht, Omonia Aradippou, Excelsior, Willem II, Excelsior, Willem II, Willem II/RKC-19

*** Jangidze - Tornike Jangidze (თორნიკე ჯანგიძე) (a) 08/01/2001, ¿? (Georgia) (b) - (c) D - central defense (d) FC Gagra (e) Dinamo II, Sioni Bolnisi

*** Janicki - Rafal Janicki (Rafał Janicki) (a) 05/07/1992, Szczecin (Poland) (b) 1,88 (c) D - central defense (d) Górnik Zabrze (e) Podbeskidzie, Wisla Kraków, Lechia Gdánsk, Lech Poznan, Lechia Gdánsk, Chemik Police

*** Jänisch - Mathias Jänisch (a) 27/08/1990, Riedlingen (Germany) (b) 1,82 (c) D - left back (d) UN Käerjeng 97 (e) Progrès Niederkorn, Differdange 03, US Hostert, CS Grevenmacher, US Hostert

*** Janitzek - Justin Janitzek (a) 10/02/2004, ¿? (Switzerland) (b) 1,92 (c) D - central defense (d) FC St. Gallen 1879 (e) FC Bayern II

*** Janjic - Kosta Janjic (Коста Јањић) (a) 22/05/2000, Užice (RF Yugoslavia, now in Serbia) (b) 1,76 (c) D - left back (d) FK FAP Priboj (e) Javor-Matis, FK FAP Priboj, Javor-Matis, Sloga Požega

*** Janjic - Nikola Janjic (Nikola Janjić) (a) 14/07/2002, Niksic (RF Yugoslavia, Montenegro) (b) - (c) F - right winger (d) NK Bravo (e) NK Osijek, Sutjeska Niksic, Sutjeska II

*** Janjic - Stefan Janjic (Stefan Janjić) (a) 11/02/1996, Novi Sad (Yugoslavia, now in Serbia) (b) - (c) D - central defense (d) - (e) Zvijezda 09, Rudar Pljevlja, Sloga Meridian, HNK Orasje, Radnik Bijelj., Po-dri-nje, Zvijezda G., Po-dri-nje, OFK Sloga, Po-dri-nje, Mladost Obarska, Backa, Zvijezda 09, Mladost Obarska

*** Janjic - Vasilije Janjic (Василије Јањић) (a) 25/01/1995, Uzice (Yugoslavia, now in Serbia) (b) 1,77 (c) F - left winger (d) FK Indjija (e) Zlatibor, Radnik, Zlatibor, FK Indjija, FK Zemun, Vozdovac, Sindjelic Bg, Vozdovac, OFK Beograd, Teleoptik, FK Zemun, Teleoptik

*** Janjicic - Vasilije Janjicic (Vasilije Janičić) (a) 02/11/1998, Zürich (Switzerland) (b) 1,80 (c) M - central midfielder (d) FC Thun (e) NK Celje, FC Zürich, SV Hamburg, Hamburg II, FC Zürich

*** Jankauskas - Algis Jankauskas (a) 27/09/1982, Vilnius (Soviet Union, now in Lithuania) (b) 1,85 (c) D - central defense (d) Saulius Jankauskas (e) FA Siauliai, Suduva, Zalgiris, Vetra, Amkar II, Zalgiris

*** Jankauskas - Eligijus Jankauskas (a) 22/06/1998, Siauliai (Lithuania) (b) 1,77 (c) F - right winger (d) FA Siauliai (e) Panevezys, Suduva, SFC Opava, MSK Zilina, Michalovce, MSK Zilina, Suduva, Utenis, Siauliai, FA Siauliai

*** Jankauskas - Jurgis Jankauskas (a) 05/02/2003, ¿? (Lithuania) (b) - (c) D - central defense (d) FC Dziugas Telsiai (e) Dziugas B, FA Siauliai B

*** Janketic - Velizar Janketic (Велизар Јанкетић) (a) 15/11/1996, Podgorica (RF Yugoslavia, now in Montenegro) (b) 1,77 (c) M - attacking midfielder (d) FK Igman Konjic (e) Rudar Pljevlja, FK Decic Tuzi, Buducnost Podgorica, Rudar Pljevlja, OFK Petrovac, Rudar Pljevlja, Kom Podgorica, Buducnost Podgorica, FK Graficar, Buducnost Podgorica

*** Jankevicius - Domas Jankevicius (Domas Jankevičius) (a) 14/09/2006, ¿? (Lithuania) (b) - (c) M (d) FC Dziugas Telsiai B (e) -

*** Jankewitz - Alexandre Jankewitz (Alexandre Tounde Dimitri Jankewitz) (a) 25/12/2001, Vevey (Switzerland) (b) 1,85 (c) M - central midfielder (d) FC Winterthur (e) FC Winterthur, BSC Young Boys, FC Thun, BSC Young Boys, FC St. Gallen, BSC Young Boys, Southampton B

*** Janko - Saidy Janko (a) 22/10/1995, Zürich (Switzerland) (b) 1,81 (c) D - right back (d) BSC Young Boys (e) Real Valladolid, VfL Bochum, Real Valladolid, FC

Porto, BSC Young Boys, FC Porto, Nottingham Forest, FC Porto, St.-Étienne, Celtic FC, Barnsley FC, Celtic FC, Bolton Wanderers
*** Jankov - Risto Jankov (Ристо Јанков) (a) 05/09/1998, Skopje (North Macedonia) (b) 1,90 (c) G (d) ACSM Politehnica Iasi (e) Kaspiy Aktau, Rabotnicki, Lokomotiva, Rabotnicki
*** Jankovic - Aleksa Jankovic (Алекса Јанковић) (a) 12/04/2000, Požarevac (RF Yugoslavia, now in Serbia) (b) 1,83 (c) F - left winger (d) FK Čukarički (e) Vozdovac, FK Partizan, Teleoptik, FK Partizan
*** Jankovic - Branislav Jankovic (Бранислав Јанковић) (a) 08/02/1992, Tivat (Montenegro) (b) 1,82 (c) M - central midfielder (d) OFK Grbalj (e) FK Iskra, Buducnost Podgorica, FK Turan, Sutjeska Niksic, Rudar Pljevlja, Čukarički, OFK Grbalj
*** Jankovic - Leo Jankovic (Leo Janković) (a) 04/09/2000, Split (Croatia) (b) - (c) F - right winger (d) NK GOSK Gabela (e) Sloga Meridian, HSK Posusje, HNK Tomislav T., Sloga Uskoplje, GOSK Gabela, Sloga Uskoplje
*** Jankovic - Marko Jankovic (Марко Јанковић) (a) 09/07/1995, Cetinje (Yugoslavia, now in Montenegro) (b) 1,72 (c) M - central midfielder (d) Qarabağ FK (e) Hapoel Tel Aviv, B. Jerusalem, SPAL, Crotone, SPAL, FK Partizan, Olympiakos, FK Partizan, Olympiakos, NK Maribor, Olympiakos, OFK Beograd, Olympiakos, Teleoptik
*** Jankovic - Marko Jankovic (Марко Јанковић) (a) 29/08/2000, Beograd (RF Yugoslavia, now in Serbia) (b) 1,81 (c) D - right back (d) GFK Sloboda Užice (e) Rad Beograd, Radnicki 1923, Proleter, Radnicki 1923, Proleter, Zarkovo, FK Brodarac
*** Jankovic - Niko Jankovic (Niko Janković) (a) 25/08/2001, Zagreb (Croatia) (b) 1,86 (c) M - attacking midfielder (d) HNK Rijeka (e) Dinamo Zagreb, HNK Rijeka, Dinamo Zagreb, Zrinjski Mostar, Din. Zagreb II, HNK Gorica, Din. Zagreb II, Slaven Belupo, Din. Zagreb II, NK Trnje Zagreb
*** Jankovic - Nikola Jankovic (Никола Јанковић) (a) 07/06/1993, Lazarevac (RF Yugoslavia, now in Serbia) (b) 1,79 (c) D - right back (d) - (e) Mladost GAT, Kolubara, Zvijezda 09, FK Indjija, Jablonec, NK Krsko, Jablonec, NK Krsko, Čukarički, Kolubara
*** Jankovic - Stefan Jankovic (Stefan Janković) (a) 25/06/1997, Zrenjanin (RF Yugoslavia, now in Serbia) (b) 1,78 (c) M - attacking midfielder (d) Zebbug Rangers FC (e) Pembroke, Central Coast, OFK Beograd, FK BSK Borča, OFK Beograd, Borac Cacak, FK BSK Borča, OFK Beograd
*** Jankovic - Vall Jankovic (Vall Janković) (a) 29/03/2004, ¿? (Slovenia) (b) 1,82 (c) D - left back (d) NK Olimpija Ljubljana (e) -
*** Jankto - Jakub Jankto (a) 19/01/1996, Praha (Czech Rep.) (b) 1,84 (c) M - left midfielder (d) Cagliari (e) Getafe CF, Sparta Praha, Getafe CF, Sampdoria, Udinese, Sampdoria, Udinese, Ascoli, Udinese
*** Janku - Stivian Janku (a) 23/06/1997, Ioannina (Greece) (b) 1,91 (c) D - central defense (d) KF Egnatia (e) FK Bylis, FC Luftëtari, FK Bylis, FC Luftëtari, FK Partizani, FK Partizani B, KF Delvina
*** Jankulov - Georgije Jankulov (Георгије Јанкулов) (a) 25/11/2001, Skopje (North Macedonia) (b) 1,81 (c) D - right back (d) AP Brera (e) Sileks, Borec Veles, Zeleznicar Pancevo
*** Janos - Adam Janos (Adam Jánoš) (a) 20/07/1992, Uherské Hradiště (Czechoslovakia, now in Czech Rep.) (b) 1,73 (c) M - pivot (d) Bohemians Praha 1905 (e) Banik Ostrava, Karvina, Banik Ostrava, Mlada Boleslav, Sparta Praha, Jihlava, Sparta Praha, Jihlava, Sparta Praha B

*** Janosek - Dominik Janosek (Dominik Janošek) (a) 13/06/1998, ¿? (Czech Rep.) (b) 1,83 (c) M - central midfielder (d) NAC Breda (e) Pardubice, Viktoria Plzen, Banik Ostrava, Viktoria Plzen, Fastav Zlin, Viktoria Plzen, Mlada Boleslav, Viktoria Plzen, Slovácko, Viktoria Plzen, Slovácko, Zbrojovka Brno

*** Janosevic - Budimir Janosevic (Будимир Јаношевић) (a) 21/10/1989, Beograd (Yugoslavia, now in Serbia) (b) 1,90 (c) G (d) AIK Solna (e) Brommapojkarna, Spartak, Adana Demirspor, Spartak, Teleoptik, Rad Beograd, Vojvodina, Jagodina, Čukarički

*** Janosik - Lukas Janosik (Lukáš Jánošík) (a) 05/03/1994, Hôrky (Slovakia) (b) 1,78 (c) F - right winger (d) Zemplin Michalovce (e) MSK Zilina, Ceske Budejovice, MSK Zilina, MSK Zilina B, Liptovsky Mik., MSK Zilina B, Rimavska Sobota, MSK Zilina B

*** Janoyan - Narek Janoyan (Նարեկ Ջանոյան) (a) 28/10/2005, ¿? (Armenia) (b) - (c) M - central midfielder (d) Shirak Gyumri C.F. (e) Shirak II

*** Janse - Rijk Janse (a) 16/04/2002, Breda (Netherlands) (b) 1,89 (c) G (d) NEC Nijmegen (e) -

*** Jansen - Kevin Jansen (Kevin Johnny Jansen) (a) 08/04/1992, Hoogvliet (Netherlands) (b) 1,83 (c) M - central midfielder (d) FC Honka (e) PAEEK Kyrenia, FC Dordrecht, Quick Boys, Gol Gohar, SC Cambuur, NEC Nijmegen, ADO Den Haag, Excelsior, Rijnmond HS Ju.

*** Jansen - Quint Jansen (a) 10/09/1990, Zaandam (Netherlands) (b) 1,93 (c) D - central defense (d) Othellos Athienou (e) Mjøndalen, Sandefjord, Aalesund, Mjøndalen, Finnsnes IL, Junkeren, Hellas Sport

*** Jansen - Sven Jansen (a) 23/10/2004, Deventer (Netherlands) (b) 1,92 (c) G (d) Go Ahead Eagles Deventer (e) -

*** Jansen - Thijs Jansen (a) 29/11/2001, Rotterdam (Netherlands) (b) 1,92 (c) G (d) De Graafschap Doetinchem (e) De Graafschap, Feyenoord, TOP Oss, Feyenoord

*** Jansonas - Dovydas Jansonas (a) 27/08/2002, Siauliai (Lithuania) (b) 1,72 (c) D - left back (d) FK Atmosfera Mazeikiai (e) FA Siauliai B

*** Jansons - Kristaps Jansons (a) 26/11/2004, ¿? (Latvia) (b) - (c) D - central defense (d) FK Tukums 2000 II (e) -

*** Janssen - Roel Janssen (a) 16/06/1990, Venlo (Netherlands) (b) 1,79 (c) D - central defense (d) VVV-Venlo (e) Fortuna Sittard, VVV-Venlo, Fortuna Sittard, VVV-Venlo

*** Janssen - Vincent Janssen (Vincent Petrus Anna Sebastiaan Janssen) (a) 15/06/1994, Heesch (Netherlands) (b) 1,85 (c) F - center forward (d) Royal Antwerp FC (e) Monterrey, Tottenham Hotspur, Fenerbahce, Tottenham Hotspur, AZ Alkmaar, Almere City

*** Janssens - Wolke Janssens (Wolke Johannes Janssens) (a) 11/01/1995, Peer (Belgium) (b) 1,85 (c) D - central defense (d) Sint-Truidense VV (e) Lierse SK, Sint-Truiden, Dessel Sport

*** Jansson - Isak Jansson (a) 31/01/2002, ¿? (Sweden) (b) 1,75 (c) F - center forward (d) FC Cartagena (e) Kalmar FF, Skene IF

*** Jansson - Oscar Jansson (Oscar Erik Jansson) (a) 23/12/1990, Örebro (Sweden) (b) 1,88 (c) G (d) IFK Norrköping (e) Örebro SK, Shamrock Rovers, Tottenham Hotspur, Shamrock Rovers, Tottenham Hotspur, Bradford City, Tottenham Hotspur, Northampton, Tottenham Hotspur, Exeter City, Tottenham Hotspur

*** Jansson - Pontus Jansson (Pontus Sven Gustav Jansson) (a) 13/02/1991, Arlöv (Sweden) (b) 1,96 (c) D - central defense (d) Malmö FF (e) Brentford, Leeds Utd., Torino, Leeds Utd., Torino, Malmö FF, IFK Malmö, Malmö FF

*** Jantscher - Jakob Jantscher (a) 08/01/1989, Graz (Austria) (b) 1,81 (c) F - center forward (d) SK Sturm Graz (e) Çaykur Rizespor, FC Luzern, NEC Nijmegen, RB Salzburg, Dinamo Moskva, RB Salzburg, Sturm Graz, Sturm Graz II
*** Jantschke - Tony Jantschke (a) 07/04/1990, Hoyerswerda (East Germany, now in Germany) (b) 1,77 (c) D - central defense (d) Borussia Mönchengladbach (e) -
*** Jäntti - Teemu Jäntti (a) 02/03/2000, Tuusula (Finland) (b) 1,78 (c) M - central midfielder (d) Pallokerho Keski-Uusimaa (e) Ilves, FC Lahti, Pallokerho
*** Jantunen - Jaaso Jantunen (a) 31/01/2005, Helsinki (Finland) (b) 1,96 (c) G (d) SC Freiburg II (e) HJK Klubi 04
*** Janus - Krzysztof Janus (Krzysztof Janus) (a) 25/03/1986, Brzeg Dolny (Poland) (b) 1,76 (c) F - left winger (d) Wisła Płock (e) Wisla Plock II, Odra Opole, Arka Gdynia, Zagłębie, Wisła Płock, Cracovia, Gornik Polk., Cracovia, GKS Belchatow, Gawin
*** Janusarson - Meinhard Janusarson (Meinhard Fríðálvur Janusarson) (a) 30/08/2002, ¿? (Faroe Islands) (b) - (c) F - right winger (d) Skála IF (e) NSÍ Runavík, NSÍ II
*** Janusauskas - Paulius Janusauskas (Paulius Janušauskas) (a) 28/02/1989, Panevezys (Soviet Union, now in Lithuania) (b) 1,82 (c) M - attacking midfielder (d) - (e) Panevezys, Suduva, Zalgiris, Siauliai, Ekranas, Optibet A Lyga
*** Janusevskis - Justinas Janusevskis (Justinas Januševskis) (a) 26/03/1994, Trakai (Lithuania) (b) 1,93 (c) D - central defense (d) FK Banga Gargzdai (e) Suduva, Panevezys, Riteriai, Riteriai B
*** Januzaj - Adnan Januzaj (a) 05/02/1995, Brussel (Belgium) (b) 1,86 (c) F - right winger (d) Sevilla FC (e) Basaksehir, Sevilla FC, Real Sociedad, Manchester Utd., Sunderland, Manchester Utd., Borussia Dortmund, Manchester Utd.
*** Januzi - Ahmed Januzi (a) 08/07/1988, ¿? (Yugoslavia, now in Kosovo) (b) 1,84 (c) F - center forward (d) - (e) KF Dukagjini, FC Llapi, FC Prishtina, FC Llapi, FC Prishtina, Vorskla Poltava, KS Besa, KF Vushtrria
*** Januzi - Mal Januzi (a) 05/05/2004, Kumanovo (North Macedonia) (b) 1,79 (c) M - central midfielder (d) FK Partizani (e) -
*** Janvier - Nicolas Janvier (a) 11/08/1998, Saint-Malo (France) (b) 1,72 (c) M - central midfielder (d) Alanyaspor (e) Vitória Guimarães, Vitória Guimarães B, Stade Rennes
*** Janza - Erik Janza (Erik Janža) (a) 21/06/1993, Murska Sobota (Slovenia) (b) 1,75 (c) D - left back (d) Górnik Zabrze (e) NK Osijek, Viktoria Plzen, Pafos FC, Viktoria Plzen, NK Maribor, Domžale, NS Mura
*** Japaridze - Luka Japaridze (ლუკა ჯაფარიძე) (a) 22/12/2000, ¿? (Georgia) (b) - (c) D - right back (d) FC Irao Tbilisi (e) FC Locomotive, Locomotive II, FC Gagra, FC Locomotive, Locomotive II
*** Japiashvili - Zurab Japiashvili (ზურაბ ჯაფიაშვილი) (a) 26/05/1996, Tbilisi (Georgia) (b) 1,84 (c) D - central defense (d) FC Kolkheti-1913 Poti (e) Sioni Bolnisi, Chikhura, FC Gagra, Sioni Bolnisi, Rustavi, FC Aragvi, Sioni Bolnisi, Dinamo Tbilisi, Sioni Bolnisi, Dinamo Tbilisi
*** Jaquenoud - Luca Jaquenoud (a) 21/05/2002, Pompaples (Switzerland) (b) 1,81 (c) D - right back (d) Yverdon Sport FC (e) Yverdon Sport
*** Jaquez - Luca Jaquez (Luca Antony Jaquez) (a) 02/06/2003, Luzern (Switzerland) (b) 1,87 (c) D - central defense (d) FC Lucerna (e) -
*** Jara - Lautaro Jara (Lautaro Ruben Jara) (a) 14/01/1994, Santa Fè (Argentina) (b) 1,80 (c) D - central defense (d) - (e) Tre Fiori, Alto Casertano, Nereto, Idolo, Terracina, GE Ciudadela

*** Jaradat - Mohamad Jaradat (a) 01/01/2002, ¿? (Israel) (b) - (c) M (d) Hapoel Haifa (e) Tzeirei Tamra, Hapoel Haifa, Bnei Fureidis, Hapoel Haifa

*** Jardan - Ion Jardan (a) 10/01/1990, Corneşti (Soviet Union, now in Moldova) (b) 1,82 (c) D - right back (d) FC Petrocub Hînceşti (e) Zimbru Chisinau, FC Sheriff, Zimbru Chisinau, Arsenal Kyiv, Rapid G.

*** Jaritz - Florian Jaritz (a) 18/10/1997, Klagenfurt (Austria) (b) 1,80 (c) F - left winger (d) SK Austria Klagenfurt (e) Klagenfurt II

*** Jarju - Ebrima Jarju (a) 16/03/1998, Sinchu Baliya (Gambia) (b) - (c) G (d) Paide Linnameeskond (e) Real de Banjul, Paide, Real de Banjul

*** Jarjue - Maudo Jarjue (Maudo Lamine Jarjué) (a) 30/09/1997, Serrekunda (Gambia) (b) 1,89 (c) D - central defense (d) IF Elfsborg (e) Slovan Bratislava, Elfsborg, Austria Viena, Elfsborg, Austria Viena, FK Sabail, Gil Vicente

*** Jarl - Sebastian Jarl (a) 11/01/2000, ¿? (Norway) (b) 1,88 (c) D - central defense (d) Kristiansund BK (e) Sarpsborg 08, KFUM, Sarpsborg 08, Kjelsås

*** Järlesand - Filip Järlesand (a) 29/03/2004, ¿? (Sweden) (b) - (c) G (d) Degerfors IF (e) Strömtorps IK, Degerfors, IFK Mariestad

*** Jaron - Petr Jaron (Petr Jaroň) (a) 30/08/2001, ¿? (Czech Rep.) (b) 1,78 (c) F - right winger (d) 1.SK Prostejov (e) Banik Ostrava, Baník Ostrava B, SK Detmarovice

*** Jaroszynski - Pawel Jaroszynski (Paweł Kamil Jaroszyński) (a) 02/10/1994, Lublin (Poland) (b) 1,84 (c) M - left midfielder (d) Cracovia (e) Salernitana, Cracovia, Salernitana, Genoa, Salernitana, Genoa, Pescara, Salernitana, Pescara, Genoa, Salernitana, Genoa, Chievo Verona, Cracovia, Cracovia II

*** Jarovic - Senad Jarovic (a) 20/01/1998, Langenfeld (Rheinland) (Germany) (b) 1,97 (c) F - center forward (d) Struga Trim & Lum (e) Minaur, Sloboda Tuzla, Petrolul, NK Radomlje, SKF Sered, SønderjyskE, Zlaté Moravce, SønderjyskE, Spartak Trnava, Domžale, NK Dob, Domžale

*** Jarstein - Rune Jarstein (Rune Almenning Jarstein) (a) 29/09/1984, Porsgrunn (Norway) (b) 1,92 (c) G (d) - (e) Hertha Berlin, Viking, Rosenborg, Odd Grenland

*** Jarusevicius - Gustas Jarusevicius (Gustas Jarusevičius) (a) 23/05/2003, Alytus (Lithuania) (b) 1,76 (c) M - right midfielder (d) FK Zalgiris Vilnius B (e) Zalgiris, Zalgiris B, DFK Dainava

*** Järve - Andres Järve (a) 21/05/2002, Tallinn (Estonia) (b) - (c) D - right back (d) Harju JK Laagri (e) -

*** Jarvelaid - Henri Jarvelaid (a) 11/12/1998, Tallinn (Estonia) (d) FCI Levadia (e) Kalju FC, Sogndal, Vendsyssel FF, FC Flora, JK Tammeka, FC Flora, FC Flora II, Nomme United

*** Järvenpää - Lassi Järvenpää (a) 28/10/1996, Helsinki (Finland) (b) 1,84 (c) D - right back (d) FC Lahti (e) FC Inter, IFK Mariehamn, RoPS, HJK Helsinki, RoPS, HJK Helsinki, HJK Klubi 04

*** Järvinen - Iiro Järvinen (a) 03/11/1996, Jyväskylä (Finland) (b) 1,72 (c) M - attacking midfielder (d) FC Inter Turku (e) KuPS, Ilves, JJK Jyväskylä

*** Jarvis - Aaron Jarvis (a) 10/05/1997, Londonderry (Northern Ireland) (b) 1,84 (c) M - central midfielder (d) Coleraine FC (e) Institute FC

*** Jarvis - Dean Jarvis (a) 01/06/1992, Derry (Northern Ireland) (b) 1,80 (c) D - left back (d) Coleraine FC (e) Larne FC, Dundalk FC, Derry City, Institute FC, Derry City

*** Järviste - Mihkel Järviste (a) 28/05/2000, Tartu (Estonia) (b) - (c) M - central midfielder (d) FC Flora Tallinn (e) JK Tammeka

*** Jasaragic - Anis Jasaragic (Anis Jašaragič) (a) 09/08/1999, ¿? (Slovenia) (b) 1,78 (c) F - left winger (d) FK Tuzla City (e) Koper, ND Ilirija, NK Krka, NK Triglav, NK Bravo

*** Jasarevic - Irfan Jasarevic (Irfan Jašarević) (a) 24/08/1995, Vitez (Bosnia and Herzegovina) (b) 1,78 (c) D - left back (d) FK Zeljeznicar Sarajevo (e) BK Olympic, Dalkurd, FK Krupa, Travnik, Vitez
*** Jasarevic - Mirza Jasarevic (Mirza Jašarević) (a) 12/12/1999, Tuzla (Bosnia and Herzegovina) (b) 1,69 (c) F - right winger (d) FC Wiltz 71 (e) Slav Pleternica, Marsonia 1909, NK Oriolik
*** Jasarevic - Tarik Jasarevic (Tarik Jašarević) (a) 25/12/2004, Doboj (Bosnia and Herzegovina) (b) - (c) F (d) NK Sesvete (e) -
*** Jaseliunas - Grantas Jaseliunas (Grantas Jaseliūnas) (a) 07/01/2003, ¿? (Lithuania) (b) 1,84 (c) M - central midfielder (d) FA Siauliai (e) -
*** Jashanica - Bajram Jashanica (a) 25/09/1990, Vranidoll, Prishtinë (Yugoslavia, now in Kosovo) (b) 1,90 (c) D - central defense (d) FC Ballkani (e) KF Skënderbeu, KS Besa, KF Skënderbeu, KF Hysi
*** Jashanica - Labinot Jashanica (a) 16/04/1997, Kreuzberg (Germany) (b) 1,85 (c) M - central midfielder (d) - (e) KF Dukagjini, KF Feronikeli, KF Dukagjini, FC Malisheva, FC Llapi, KF Dukagjini, KF Feronikeli, KF Fushë Kosova
*** Jashari - Ardon Jashari (a) 30/07/2002, Cham (Switzerland) (b) 1,81 (c) M - pivot (d) FC Lucerna (e) -
*** Jashari - Granit Jashari (a) 20/08/1998, Skënderaj (RF Yugoslavia, now in Kosovo) (b) 1,80 (c) D - central defense (d) KF Llapi (e) SC Gjilani, KF Drenica, KF Ferizaj, FC Prishtina, KF 2 Korriku, FC Prishtina
*** Jashari - Igball Jashari (a) 14/07/2005, Prekaz (Serbia and Montenegro, now in Kosovo) (b) - (c) F - right winger (d) FC Prishtina (e) KF Kurda
*** Jashari - Muharrem Jashari (a) 21/02/1998, Mitrovica (RF Yugoslavia, now in Kosovo) (b) 1,82 (c) M - attacking midfielder (d) FC Drita Gjilan (e) KF Trepca 89, FC Prishtina, KF Trepca 89
*** Jasic - Adis Jasic (Adis Jašić) (a) 12/02/2003, St. Veit an der Glan (Austria) (b) 1,78 (c) D - right back (d) Wolfsberger AC (e) Wolfsberg II
*** Jastrzembski - Dennis Jastrzembski (a) 20/02/2000, Rendsburg (Germany) (b) 1,80 (c) F - left winger (d) Śląsk Wroclaw (e) Hertha Berlin, Waldh. Mannheim, Hertha Berlin, SC Paderborn, Hertha Berlin
*** Jatta - Alassana Jatta (a) 12/01/1999, Sukuta (Gambia) (b) 1,92 (c) F - center forward (d) Viborg FF (e) Paide, Real de Banjul
*** Jatta - Alfusainey Jatta (a) 05/08/1999, Abuko (Gambia) (b) 1,88 (c) M - pivot (d) RFS (e) Saalfelden, MFK Vyskov, North Texas SC, MFK Vyskov, Fortune FC
*** Jatta - Seedy Jatta (a) 18/03/2003, ¿? (Norway) (b) 1,82 (c) F - center forward (d) Vålerenga Fotball (e) Vålerenga II
*** Jaukovic - Leo Jaukovic (Лео Јауковић) (a) 01/04/2003, ¿? (Serbia and Montenegro, now in Montenegro) (b) 1,87 (c) F - right winger (d) FK Iskra Danilovgrad (e) Zeta Golubovac, FK Iskra
*** Jaunarajs-Janvaris - Roberts Jaunarajs-Janvaris (Roberts Krists Jaunarājs-Janvāris) (a) 23/03/2000, ¿? (Latvia) (b) - (c) D - central defense (d) FK PPK/Betsafe (e) Super Nova, Auda, Tukums, Liepaja, Liepaja II
*** Jaunegg - David Jaunegg (a) 28/02/2003, Hall in Tirol (Austria) (b) 1,89 (c) D - right back (d) WSG Tirol (e) WSG Tirol II, Juniors OÖ, WSG Tirol II
*** Jaunzems - Alvis Jaunzems (a) 16/06/1999, ¿? (Latvia) (b) 1,79 (c) D - right back (d) Valmiera FC (e) Bebri
*** Jaupi - Enea Jaupi (a) 06/10/1993, Gramsh (Albania) (b) 1,83 (c) F - center forward (d) - (e) La Fiorita, Fiorentino, Domagnano, Fiorentino, Domagnano, Fiorentino, Saludecio, Riccione

*** Javashvili - Otar Javashvili (ოთარ ჯავახიშვილი) (a) 17/08/1993, Zugdidi (Georgia) (b) 1,81 (c) D - left back (d) Mash'al Mubarek (e) Sioni Bolnisi, Rustavi, Chikhura, FC Gagra, Florø SK, Gomel, Slavia, FK Zugdidi, WIT Georgia, WIT Georgia II

*** Javito - Javito (David Sebastián Cortez Lillo) (a) 01/01/1993, ¿? (Argentina) (b) - (c) M - pivot (d) - (e) FC Encamp, FC Ordino, FC Encamp, Penya Encarnada, FC Andorra B, Lusitanos, AC Escaldes, Lusitanos, Sant Julià, FC Ordino, CE Principat

*** Javorcek - Dominik Javorcek (Dominik Javorček) (a) 02/11/2002, Bojnice (Slovakia) (b) 1,83 (c) D - left back (d) MSK Zilina (e) -

*** Javorcic - Duje Javorcic (Duje Javorčić) (a) 25/11/1999, Split (Croatia) (b) 1,83 (c) M - central midfielder (d) - (e) Rudar Pljevlja, NK Dugopolje, FC Nitra, Amiens SC B

*** Jawo - Lamin Jawo (a) 15/03/1995, Banjoul (Gambia) (b) 1,91 (c) F - center forward (d) FK Mlada Boleslav (e) Trinity Zlin, Jihlava, Agnonese, Sanremese, Carpi, Feralpisalò, Carpi, Robur Siena, Carpi, Finale, Vado

*** Jazbec - Rok Jazbec (a) 23/09/1995, ¿? (Slovenia) (b) 1,87 (c) D - central defense (d) NK Radomlje (e) NK Celje, NK Radomlje

*** Jazxhi - Artan Jazxhi (a) 06/07/2001, Durrës (Albania) (b) 1,93 (c) D - central defense (d) KF Teuta (e) -

*** Jeahze - Mohanad Jeahze (Mohanad Abdulkadhim Qasim Al-Jebur, عبدالكاظم مهند قاسم الجبر) (a) 10/04/1997, Linköping (Sweden) (b) 1,79 (c) D - left back (d) D.C. United (e) Hammarby IF, Mjällby AIF, Brommapojkarna, Norrköping, Syrianska FC, Norrköping, Degerfors, Norrköping

*** Jean - Dany Jean (a) 28/11/2002, Port-au-Prince (Haiti) (b) - (c) M - left midfielder (d) US Avranches (e) US Avranches, Racing Club Strasbourg, Racing Strasbourg B, Arcahaie FC, Aigle Noir

*** Jean Carlos - Jean Carlos (Jean Carlos de Brito) (a) 09/06/1995, Goiânia (Brazil) (b) 1,84 (c) M - left midfielder (d) AC Horsens (e) AC Horsens, Norrköping, Varbergs BoIS, Hammarby IF, TPS, Hammarby IF, IK Frej Täby, Hammarby IF, Tubarão-SC, Sport Recife, Tubarão-SC, Paysandu

*** Jean Lucas - Jean Lucas (Jean Lucas de Souza Oliveira) (a) 22/06/1998, Rio de Janeiro (Brazil) (b) 1,79 (c) M - central midfielder (d) Santos FC (e) AS Monaco, Olympique Lyon, Stade Brestois, Olympique Lyon, Flamengo, Santos, Flamengo

*** Jean Victor - Jean Victor (Jean Victor Gonçalves) (a) 21/03/1995, ¿? (Portugal) (b) 1,74 (c) M - central midfielder (d) FC Dila Gori (e) KF Skënderbeu, Santarém, Casa Pia, CO Montijo, Angra-RJ, Barcelona EC

*** Jeanvier - Julian Jeanvier (Julian Marc Jeanvier) (a) 31/03/1992, Clichy (France) (b) 1,83 (c) D - central defense (d) - (e) AJ Auxerre, Brentford, Kasimpasa, Brentford, Stade Reims, Lille, Red Star FC, Lille, Excelsior Mouscron, Lille, AS Nancy, AS Nancy B

*** Jebali - Issam Jebali (a) 25/12/1991, Majaz al Bab (Tunisia) (b) 1,86 (c) F - center forward (d) Gamba Osaka (e) Odense BK, Al-Wehda, Rosenborg, Elfsborg, Värnamo, ES Sahel, ES Zarzis, ES Sahel

*** Jebali - Omar Jebali (الجبالي عمر) (a) 19/02/2000, ¿? (Tunisia) (b) - (c) D - central defense (d) Vendsyssel FF (e) ES Zarzis, Odense BK, ES Zarzis

*** Jebor - William Jebor (a) 10/11/1991, Monrovia (Liberia) (b) 1,83 (c) F - center forward (d) - (e) Valletta, Kalju FC, Fujairah SC, Wydad AC, Al-Nassr, Rio Ave, Wydad AC, Rio Ave, Ponferradina, Rio Ave, Gaish, Al-Ahli, Gaish, Sharkia Dokhan, Tersana, Taliya SC, Oilers Monrovia

*** Jedlicka - Martin Jedlicka (Martin Jedlička) (a) 24/01/1998, Příbram (Czech Rep.) (b) 1,87 (c) G (d) FC Viktoria Plzen (e) Bohemians 1905, Viktoria Plzen, Dunajska Streda, Mlada Boleslav, Dunajska Streda, Mlada Boleslav
*** Jedrasik - Jakub Jedrasik (a) 07/04/2005, Łódź (Poland) (b) 1,76 (c) M - attacking midfielder (d) Legia de Varsovia (e) Legia II
*** Jedrzejczyk - Artur Jedrzejczyk (Artur Jędrzejczyk) (a) 04/11/1987, Dębica (Poland) (b) 1,89 (c) D - central defense (d) Legia de Varsovia (e) Krasnodar, Legia Warszawa, Krasnodar, Legia Warszawa, Korona Kielce, Legia Warszawa, Dolcan Zabki, Legia Warszawa, GKS Jastrzebie, Legia Warszawa, Igloopol Debica
*** Jedvaj - Tin Jedvaj (a) 28/11/1995, Zagreb (Croatia) (b) 1,85 (c) D - central defense (d) Panathinaikos FC (e) Panathinaikos, Lokomotiv Moskva, Al-Ain FC, Lokomotiv Moskva, Bayer Leverkusen, FC Augsburg, Bayer Leverkusen, AS Roma, Bayer Leverkusen, AS Roma, Dinamo Zagreb
*** Jeferson Mendes - Jeferson Mendes (Jeferson Mendes da Silva) (a) 25/12/2001, ¿? (Brazil) (b) - (c) M - central midfielder (d) - (e) Globo, Marsaxlokk, ABC FC
*** Jefferies - Dan Jefferies (Daniel Rhys Jefferies) (a) 30/01/1999, Bridgend (Wales) (b) 1,88 (c) D - central defense (d) Penybont FC (e) Dundee Reserves, Partick Thistle, Dundee Reserves
*** Jefferson - Jefferson (Jefferson Mateus de Assis Estácio) (a) 21/10/1994, Porto Alegre (Brazil) (b) 1,85 (c) F - center forward (d) Bali United FC (e) Gzira Utd., Fujairah SC, Gzira Utd., Sliema Wanderers, Nadur Y., Sliema Wanderers, São José-SP, Coritiba FC, Andraus-PR, Coritiba FC, UA Barbarense, GO Audax, Novo Hamburgo
*** Jefferson - Jefferson (Jefferson Nogueira Junior) (a) 22/01/1994, Campinas (Brazil) (b) 1,80 (c) M - central midfielder (d) Petrolul Ploiesti (e) Moreirense, Gaziantep FK, Figueirense FC, Fortaleza, Figueirense FC
*** Jefferson - Jefferson (Jefferson Reis de Jesus) (a) 08/11/1995, ¿? (Brazil) (b) 1,81 (c) F - left winger (d) GD Interclube Luanda (e) Operário-MS, Banga, Dziugas, Operário-MS, ASA, Machine Sazi, Alashkert CF, Operário-MS, Maringá
*** Jefferson Vinicius - Jefferson Vinicius (Jefferson Vinicius Vitor da Silva) (a) 03/05/2000, Natal (Brazil) (b) - (c) D - left back (d) - (e) Rukh Lviv, Grêmio Porto Alegre B, ABC FC
*** Jeffinho - Jeffinho (Jefferson Ruan Pereira dos Santos) (a) Volta Redonda (Brazil) (b) 1,76 (c) F - left winger (d) Olympique de Lyon (e) Botafogo, Resende, Botafogo, Resende
*** Jefinho - Jefinho (Jeferson Geraldo de Almeida) (a) 23/02/1989, Petrópolis (Brazil) (b) 1,85 (c) M - attacking midfielder (d) FC Telavi (e) Samgurali, Shukura, Merani Martvili, Shukura, Ethnikos, Real Estelí FC, UA Barbarense, ABC FC, Duque de Caxias, Tigres
*** Jeggo - James Jeggo (James Alexander Jeggo) (a) 12/02/1992, Wien (Austria) (b) 1,78 (c) M - pivot (d) Hibernian FC (e) KAS Eupen, Aris Thessaloniki, Austria Viena, Sturm Graz, Adelaide United, Melbourne, VIS, Green Gully SC
*** Jegorov - Vladislav Jegorov (a) 27/09/2004, Kohtla-Järve ((c) D - central defense (d) - (e) TJK Legion
*** Jehezkel - Sagiv Jehezkel (יחזקאל שלום שגיב) (a) 21/03/1995, Rishon Lezion (Israel) (b) 1,84 (c) D - right back (d) Hapoel Beer Sheva (e) FC Ashdod, Maccabi Tel Aviv, FC Ashdod, Maccabi Tel Aviv, Bnei Yehuda, Maccabi Tel Aviv, Kiryat Shmona, Maccabi Tel Aviv, Hapoel Tel Aviv
*** Jeimes - Jeimes (Jeimes Menezes de Almeida) (a) 28/04/2001, Brasília (Brazil) (b) 1,88 (c) G (d) FC Paços de Ferreira (e) Montalegre, Paços Ferreira, Montalegre, Paços Ferreira

*** Jelenic - Luka Jelenic (Luka Jelenić) (a) 24/05/2000, Zagreb (Croatia) (b) 1,87 (c) D - central defense (d) NK Varazdin (e) Inker, Din. Zagreb II, Spansko

*** Jelenkovic - Veljko Jelenkovic (a) 05/06/2003, Lovech (Bulgaria) (b) 1,87 (c) D - central defense (d) Slavia Sofia (e) Vojvodina, Kabel Novi Sad, Becej 1918

*** Jelert - Elias Jelert (Elias Jelert Kristensen) (a) 12/06/2003, Virum (Denmark) (b) 1,78 (c) D - right back (d) FC Copenhague (e) -

*** Jelic Balta - Ivan Borna Jelic Balta (Ivan Borna Jelić Balta) (a) 17/09/1992, Zagreb (Croatia) (b) - (c) M - pivot (d) FK Sarajevo (e) Wisla Kraków, FK Sarajevo, Wisla Kraków, Koper, Arsenal Kyiv, NK Varazdin, NK Rudes, Mlad. Zdralovi, St. Kickers II, SV Hellas 94, Mlad. Zdralovi

*** Jelicic - Igor Jelicic (Игор Јеличић) (a) 28/02/2000, ¿? (RF Yugoslavia, now in Serbia) (b) 1,90 (c) D - central defense (d) FK Vojvodina Novi Sad (e) Kabel Novi Sad, Vojvodina

*** Jelonek - Bartlomiej Jelonek (Bartłomiej Jelonek) (a) 22/12/2001, Bytom (Poland) (b) 1,88 (c) G (d) Piast Gliwice (e) Piast Gliwice II

*** Jelovac - Milan Jelovac (Milan Jelovac) (a) 06/08/1993, Pljevlja (RF Yugoslavia, now in Montenegro) (b) 1,90 (c) G (d) FK Zvijezda 09 (e) OFK Petrovac, Spartak, FK Loznica, Club Eagles, Radnicki Srem, OFK Grbalj, Metalac, FK Ibar, Rudar Pljevlja, FK Ibar, Rudar Pljevlja, FK Pljevlja

*** Jemelka - Vaclav Jemelka (Václav Jemelka) (a) 23/06/1995, Uničov (Czech Rep.) (b) 1,87 (c) D - central defense (d) FC Viktoria Plzen (e) Sigma Olomouc, OH Leuven, Sigma Olomouc, Sigma Olomouc B

*** Jendal - Lars Jendal (Lars Larsson Jendal) (a) 24/04/1999, Oslo (Norway) (b) 1,93 (c) G (d) Hamarkameratene (e) Arendal, HamKam, Asker, HamKam, Nybergsund, HamKam

*** Jendrisek - Erik Jendrisek (Erik Jendrišek) (a) 26/10/1986, Trstená (Czechoslovakia, now in Slovakia) (b) 1,76 (c) F - center forward (d) Tatran Liptovsky Mikulas (e) AS Trencin, FC Nitra, Volos NPS, AO Xanthi, Cracovia, Spartak Trnava, Energie Cottbus, SC Freiburg, FC Schalke 04, 1.FC Kaiserslautern, Ružomberok, Hannover 96, Ružomberok

*** Jenkins - Callum Jenkins (a) 13/11/2002, ¿? (Wales) (b) - (c) M (d) Cardiff Metropolitan Police Reserves (e) -

*** Jenkins - Corey Jenkins (Corey Lee Jenkins) (a) 14/02/1991, Newport (Wales) (b) 1,88 (c) F - right winger (d) Pontypridd United (e) Merthyr Town, Carmarthen, Goytre United, Llanelli, Goytre United, Fleur de Lys, Caersws

*** Jenkins - Jordan Jenkins (a) 28/02/2000, Belfast (Northern Ireland) (b) 1,83 (c) F - center forward (d) Glentoran FC (e) Dungannon, Glentoran, Portadown, Glentoran, Glenavon, Carrick Rangers, Glenavon

*** Jenkins - Lee Jenkins (Lee Thomas Jenkins) (a) 30/08/2001, ¿? (Wales) (b) - (c) D - central defense (d) Haverfordwest County (e) Aberystwyth

*** Jenkins - Leigh Jenkins (a) 16/10/1991, Aberystwyth (Wales) (b) - (c) G (d) Penrhyncoch FC (e) Aberystwyth, Penrhyncoch, Aberystwyth, Penrhyncoch

*** Jensen - Aleksandur Jensen (Aleksandur Ólavsson Jensen) (a) 07/05/2001, ¿? (Faroe Islands) (b) - (c) D - central defense (d) B68 Toftir (e) -

*** Jensen - Bárdur Jensen (Bárður Ólavsson Jensen) (a) 07/05/2001, ¿? (Faroe Islands) (b) - (c) M - central midfielder (d) B68 Toftir (e) B68 Toftir II

*** Jensen - Christian Tue Jensen (a) 09/03/2000, ¿? (Denmark) (b) 1,77 (c) M - attacking midfielder (d) - (e) KuPS, Midtjylland, FC Fredericia, Midtjylland, Brentford B, Midtjylland

*** Jensen - David Jensen (David Raagaard Jensen) (a) 25/03/1992, Hillerød (Denmark) (b) 1,95 (c) G (d) Istanbulspor (e) New York, KVC Westerlo, New York,

FC Utrecht, Nordsjælland, Akademisk BK, Nordsjælland, FC Fredericia, Nordsjælland
*** Jensen - Fredrik Jensen (Hans Fredrik Jensen) (a) 09/09/1997, Porvoo (Finland) (b) 1,83 (c) M - attacking midfielder (d) FC Augsburg (e) FC Twente
*** Jensen - Fredrik Oldrup Jensen (a) 18/05/1993, Skien (Norway) (b) 1,86 (c) M - pivot (d) Vålerenga Fotball (e) Zulte Waregem, Odd, Zulte Waregem, IFK Göteborg, Zulte Waregem, Odd
*** Jensen - Kevin Jensen (a) 15/06/2001, ¿? (Sweden) (b) 1,73 (c) F - left winger (d) Kalmar FF (e) Landskrona
*** Jensen - Magnus Jensen (Magnus Riisgaard Jensen) (a) 27/10/1996, Viborg (Denmark) (b) 1,96 (c) D - central defense (d) Lyngby BK (e) AC Horsens, Skive IK, Viborg FF II
*** Jensen - Markus Jensen (Markus Gustav Jensen) (a) 15/07/2005, ¿? (Denmark) (b) - (c) F - left winger (d) Odense Boldklub (e) -
*** Jensen - Mathias Jensen (a) 01/01/1996, Jerslev, West Zealand (Denmark) (b) 1,80 (c) M - central midfielder (d) Brentford FC (e) RC Celta, Nordsjælland
*** Jensen - Niels Jensen (a) 20/10/1994, ¿? (Denmark) (b) 1,79 (c) M - right midfielder (d) Odense KS (e) B68 Toftir, Odense KS, Vatnaliljur, B1913 Odense, Vojens BI, FC Sydvest, Kolding BK
*** Jensen - Oliver Jensen (Oliver Bjerrum Jensen) (a) 30/04/2002, Sunds (Denmark) (b) - (c) M - central midfielder (d) UMF Afturelding (e) Randers FC
*** Jensen - Richard Jensen (Richard Olav Jensen) (a) 17/03/1996, Porvoo (Finland) (b) 1,85 (c) D - central defense (d) Górnik Zabrze (e) Roda JC, FC Twente
*** Jensen - Tróndur Jensen (a) 06/02/1993, ¿? (Faroe Islands) (b) 1,77 (c) M - pivot (d) HB Tórshavn (e) NSÍ Runavík, HB Tórshavn, AB Argir, HB Tórshavn
*** Jensen - Victor Jensen (Victor Christoffer Jensen) (a) 08/02/2000, København (Denmark) (b) 1,75 (c) M - attacking midfielder (d) FC Utrecht (e) Ajax B, Rosenborg, Ajax B, Nordsjælland, Ajax B
*** Jensen-Abbew - Jonas Jensen-Abbew (a) 20/04/2002, Herlev (Denmark) (b) 1,87 (c) D - central defense (d) FC Nordsjælland (e) HB Köge, Nordsjælland
*** Jenssen - Anders Jenssen (Anders Finjord Jenssen) (a) 10/10/1993, Harstad (Norway) (b) 1,85 (c) D - central defense (d) Tromsø IL (e) Tromsdalen, Finnsnes IL, Harstad IL
*** Jenssen - Ruben Yttergård Jenssen (a) 04/05/1988, Tromsø (Norway) (b) 1,73 (c) M - central midfielder (d) Tromsø IL (e) Brann, FC Groningen, 1.FC Kaiserslautern, FC Groningen, 1.FC Kaiserslautern, Tromsø
*** Jenssen - Ulrik Yttergård Jenssen (a) 17/07/1996, Tromsø (Norway) (b) 1,86 (c) D - central defense (d) Rosenborg BK (e) Nordsjælland, Willem II, Nordsjælland, Tromsø, Olymp. Lyon B
*** Jenz - Moritz Jenz (a) 30/04/1999, Berlin (Germany) (b) 1,90 (c) D - central defense (d) VfL Wolfsburg (e) FC Lorient, FC Schalke 04, FC Lorient, Celtic FC, FC Lorient, Lausanne-Sport
*** Jeong - Sang-bin Jeong (정상빈) (a) 01/04/2002, Cheonan, Chungnam (South Korea) (b) 1,75 (c) F - center forward (d) Minnesota United FC (e) Wolverhampton Wanderers, Grasshoppers, Wolverhampton Wanderers, Suwon Bluewings, S. Blue. Juven., Daejeon J ES
*** Jeong - Woo-yeong Jeong (정우영) (a) 20/09/1999, Ulsan (South Korea) (b) 1,79 (c) M - attacking midfielder (d) VfB Stuttgart (e) SC Freiburg, FC Bayern II, SC Freiburg, FC Bayern II, Incheon Utd.

*** Jepsen-Jacob - Rasmus Jepsen-Jacob (a) 27/05/2000, ¿? (Denamrk) (b) - (c) G
(d) Middelfart Boldklub (e) IF Lyseng, AB Argir, Kjellerup IF, Skanderborg
*** Jerabek - Jan Jerabek (Jan Jeřábek) (a) 12/02/1984, Prachovice (Czechoslovakia,
now in Czech Rep.) (b) 1,83 (c) M - pivot (d) FC Hlinsko (e) Pardubice, Tesla
Pardubice, SK Prachovice
*** Jerabek - Michal Jerabek (Michal Jeřábek) (a) 10/09/1993, Praha (Czech Rep.)
(b) 1,91 (c) D - central defense (d) - (e) Zlin, Michalovce, Aktobe, Jablonec, Teplice,
Dukla Praha, Dukla B
*** Jercalau - Andrei Jercalau (Andrei Cristian Jercălău) (a) 10/03/2005, Ploieşti
(Romania) (b) - (c) G (d) CSM Cetatea Turnu Magurele (e) Cetatea Tr. M., Petrolul
*** Jeremejeff - Alexander Jeremejeff (Alexander Thomas Jeremejeff) (a)
12/10/1993, Kungsbacka (Sweden) (b) 1,92 (c) F - center forward (d) Panathinaikos
FC (e) APO Levadiakos, Panathinaikos, Häcken, Dynamo Dresden, FC Twente,
Dynamo Dresden, Häcken, Malmö FF, Häcken, Qviding FIF, Örgryte
*** Jeremic - Predrag Jeremic (Предраг Јеремић) (a) 22/11/1987, Šabac
(Yugoslavia, now in Serbia) (b) 1,79 (c) F - left winger (d) 07 Vestur II (e) Macva,
Sloboda Užice, Radnik, Napredak, Banat Zrenjanin, Dinamo Vranje, Sindjelic,
Napredak, Sindjelic
*** Jeridi - Ilyess Jeridi (الجريدي إلياس) (a) 27/02/1997, ¿? (Tunisia) (b) - (c) M - central
midfielder (d) CS Fola Esch (e) Ain Sud, Stade Tunisien, Swift Hesperange, Stade
Tunisien, Tadcaster
*** Jermatsenko - Artjom Jermatsenko (Artjom Jermatšenko) (a) 14/11/2001, Tallinn
(Estonia) (b) - (c) M - attacking midfielder (d) FC Kuressaare (e) Kuressaare
*** Jervis - Jake Jervis (Jake Mario Jervis) (a) 17/09/1991, Wolverhampton (England)
(b) 1,91 (c) F - right winger (d) Kuopion Palloseura (e) East Bengal FC, SJK
Seinäjoki, Luton Town, Salford, Luton Town, AFC Wimbledon, Luton Town,
Plymouth Argyle, Ross County, FC Portsmouth, Elazigspor, Birmingham City, FC
Portsmouth, Birmingham City, Tranmere Rovers, Birmingham City, Carlisle United,
Birmingham City, Preston North End, Birmingham City, Swindon Town,
Birmingham City, Hereford Utd., Birmingham City, Notts County, Birmingham City,
Hereford Utd., Birmingham City
*** Jesé - Jesé (Jesé Rodríguez Ruiz) (a) 26/02/1993, Las Palmas de Gran Canaria
(Spain) (b) 1,78 (c) F - left winger (d) - (e) Sampdoria, Ankaragücü, UD Las Palmas,
Paris Saint-Germain, Sporting Lisboa, Paris Saint-Germain, Real Betis, Paris Saint-
Germain, Stoke City, Paris Saint-Germain, UD Las Palmas, Paris Saint-Germain,
Real Madrid, RM Castilla
*** Jesic - Aleksandar Jesic (Александар Јешић) (a) 13/09/1994, Gornji Milanovac
(RF Yugoslavia, now in Serbia) (b) 1,77 (c) M - attacking midfielder (d) Zhetysu
Taldykorgan (e) Mladost, Neftchi, Mladost, Metalac, Vozdovac, OFK Beograd,
Borac Cacak
*** Jevremovic - Janko Jevremovic (Јанко Јевремовић) (a) 14/07/2004, Kraljevo
(Serbia and Montenegro, now in Serbia) (b) 1,81 (c) F - right winger (d) Partizán
Beograd (e) -
*** Jevremovic - Marko Jevremovic (Марко Јевремовић) (a) 23/02/1996, Beograd
(RF Yugoslavia, now in Serbia) (b) 1,85 (c) D - left back (d) - (e) EN Paralimniou,
Javor-Matis, Mladost, Sloga Požega, Mladost, Radnicki Obrenovac
*** Jevtoski - Stefan Jevtoski (Стефан Јефтоски) (a) 02/09/1997, Skopje (North
Macedonia) (b) 1,80 (c) M - pivot (d) Újpest FC (e) Rabotnicki, Arsenal Kyiv, NK
Varazdin, Lokomotiv Plovdiv, Metalurg Skopje

*** Jevtovic - Marko Jevtovic (Марко Јевтовић) (a) 24/07/1993, Beograd (RF Yugoslavia, now in Serbia) (b) 1,94 (c) M - pivot (d) Gaziantep FK (e) FK Partizan, Al-Ahli SC, Konyaspor, FK Partizan, Novi Pazar, Hajduk 1912, Sopot, Srem Jakovo
*** Jevtovic - Milan Jevtovic (Милан Јевтовић) (a) 13/06/1993, Cacak (Yugoslavia, now in Serbia) (b) 1,84 (c) F - left winger (d) Ha Noi FC (e) Odd, Aarhus GF, Crvena zvezda, APOEL FC, Crvena zvezda, Antalyaspor, Rosenborg, Antalyaspor, Bodø/Glimt, Borac Cacak
*** Jezdimirovic - Milan Jezdimirovic (Милан Јездимировић) (a) 05/09/1996, Užice (RF Yugoslavia, now in Serbia) (b) 1,80 (c) D - right back (d) FC Dziugas Telsiai (e) Radnik, Spartak, Zlatibor, Sloboda Užice, Jedinstvo Uzice, Zlatibor, Jedinstvo Uzice, Zlatibor, Jedinstvo Uzice
*** Jezdovic - Filip Jezdovic (Филип Јездовић) (a) 09/11/1998, Zemun (RF Yugoslavia, now in Serbia) (b) 1,88 (c) D - right back (d) FK Mladost GAT Novi Sad (e) Arsenal Tivat, Odzaci, Rad Beograd, Dinamo Vranje, Rad Beograd
*** Jgerenaia - Giorgi Jgerenaia (გიორგი ჯგერენაია) (a) 28/12/1993, Tbilisi (Georgia) (b) 1,90 (c) D - central defense (d) FC Saburtalo (e) FC Samtredia, Merani Tbilisi, FC Gagra, Dynamo 2 Kyiv, FC Gagra, MFK Mykolaiv, FC Gagra, Illichivets, FC Gagra
*** Jhonatan - Jhonatan (Jhonatan Luiz da Siqueira) (a) 08/05/1991, São Miguel do Oeste (Brazil) (b) 1,90 (c) G (d) Rio Ave FC (e) Vitória Guimarães, Rio Ave, Vitória Guimarães, Moreirense, Joinville-SC, Operário-PR, Joinville-SC, Joinville EC B
*** Jiang - Bobby Jiang (a) 08/05/1999, ¿? (Luxembourg) (b) - (c) G (d) FC Victoria Rosport (e) Berbourg, CS Grevenmacher
*** Jibril - Taofiq Jibril (a) 23/04/1998, Kaduna (Nigeria) (b) 1,81 (c) F - center forward (d) FC Pyunik Yerevan (e) Ararat-Armenia, MSK Zilina, Zlaté Moravce, MSK Zilina, Valadares Gaia, Vila Real
*** Jie - Zvi Jie (a) 17/03/2002, ¿? (Netherlands) (b) 1,78 (c) D - left back (d) Santa Lucia FC (e) Thesprotos
*** Jigauri - Jaba Jigauri (ჯაბა ჯიღაური) (a) 08/07/1992, Tbilisi (Georgia) (b) 1,75 (c) M - attacking midfielder (d) Nasaf Qarshi (e) Kaspiy Aktau, Dinamo Batumi, Grenoble, Aktobe, Ordabasy, Aktobe, Vardar, Dinamo Tbilisi, Chikhura, Dinamo Tbilisi, Chikhura, Dinamo Tbilisi, Dinamo II
*** Jijavadze - Erekle Jijavadze (ერეკლე ჯიჯავაძე) (a) 24/11/2000, ¿? (Georgia) (b) - (c) M - central midfielder (d) FC Kolkheti-1913 Poti (e) Dinamo Batumi, Rustavi, Dinamo Batumi, Dinamo B. II
*** Jikia - Mirian Jikia (მირიან ჯიქია) (a) 14/10/1990, Senaki (Soviet Union, now in Georgia) (b) 1,82 (c) D - left back (d) FC Telavi (e) FC Liakhvi, FC Liakhvi
*** Jiménez - Raúl Jiménez (Raúl Alonso Jiménez Rodríguez) (a) 05/05/1991, Tepeji del Río de Ocampo (Mexico) (b) 1,87 (c) F - center forward (d) Fulham FC (e) Wolverhampton Wanderers, Benfica, Wolverhampton Wanderers, Benfica, Atlético Madrid, CF América, América Coapa
*** Jimoh - Sherif Jimoh (Sherif Olatunde Jimoh) (a) 04/05/1996, Abidjan (Ivory Coast) (b) 1,79 (c) D - left back (d) BATE Borisov (e) Neman Grodno, FC San Pedro, Athletic Adjamé
*** Jindoyan - Akhmed Jindoyan (Ախմեդ Ջինդոյան) (a) 02/10/1997, Yerevan (Armenia) (b) 1,88 (c) F - attacking midfielder (d) Lernayin Artsakh Goris (e) Alashkert II, BKMA Yerevan, FC Van, FC Sevan, West Armenia, Alashkert II, Mika Erewan II
*** Jindrisek - Josef Jindrisek (Josef Jindřišek) (a) 14/02/1981, Plavy (Czechoslovakia, now in Czech Rep.) (b) 1,78 (c) M - pivot (d) Bohemians Praha

1905 (e) Fotbal Fulnek, Sigma Olomouc, FK Jablonec, FK Jablonec B, FK Velke Hamry, FK Jablonec B, Dukla Praha, FK Jablonec B

*** Jinjolava - Jemali-Giorgi Jinjolava (ჯემალ-გიორგი ჯინჯოლავა) (a) 28/06/2000, Tbilisi (Georgia) (b) 1,81 (c) D - left back (d) FC Saburtalo (e) Cádiz CF B, Saburtalo, FC Locomotive, Saburtalo, F. Benidorm CD, Saburtalo

*** Jipa - Alexandru Jipa (Alexandru Daniel Jipa) (a) 14/08/2002, Târgoviște (Romania) (b) - (c) M - right midfielder (d) FC Hermannstadt (e) Chindia, Sport Team Buc.

*** Jirka - Erik Jirka (Erik Jirka) (a) 19/09/1997, Trnava (Slovakia) (b) 1,83 (c) F - right winger (d) FC Viktoria Plzen (e) Real Oviedo, Crvena zvezda, CD Mirandés, Crvena zvezda, Górnik Zabrze, Crvena zvezda, Radnicki Niš, Crvena zvezda, Spartak Trnava

*** Jô - Jô (Joarlem Batista Santos) (a) 01/05/1995, Teófilo Otoni (Brazil) (b) 1,92 (c) F - center forward (d) GD Chaves (e) SC Covilhã, Juventus-SC, Linense, Mito HollyHock, Linense, Capivariano, Mogi Mirim

*** Jô Santos - Jô Santos (Joálisson Santos Oliveira) (a) 31/03/1991, Campina Grande (Brazil) (b) 1,74 (c) F - right winger (d) - (e) FK Bylis, FK Turan, Radomiak, Al-Riffa SC, FCV Farul, FC Hermannstadt, JFK Ventspils, FC Sheriff, ACSM Poli Iasi, FC Sheriff, Zimbru Chisinau, Freamunde, Tondela, São Bernardo, Rio Preto EC, Campinense-PB

*** João Afonso - João Afonso (João Afonso Crispim) (a) 09/02/1995, Rio de Janeiro (Brazil) (b) 1,81 (c) M - pivot (d) Grêmio Novorizontino (e) Marítimo, Gil Vicente, Goiás, Internacional, Brasil Pelotas, Internacional, Criciúma EC, Internacional, Chapecoense, Internacional

*** João Basso - João Basso (João Othávio Basso) (a) 13/01/1997, Curitiba (Brazil) (b) 1,87 (c) D - central defense (d) Santos FC (e) Arouca, Estoril Praia, Real SC, Estoril Praia, Paraná

*** João Batxi - João Batxi (João Pedro Fortes Bachiessa) (a) 01/05/1998, Sintra (Portugal) (b) 1,74 (c) F - left winger (d) FK Krasnodar (e) Chaves, Chaves B

*** João Carlos - João Carlos (João Carlos Cardoso Santo) (a) 01/03/1995, Coaraci (Brazil) (b) 1,87 (c) F - center forward (d) GD Estoril Praia (e) Académica Coimbra, Estoril Praia, Sampaio-RJ, CRB, Sampaio-RJ, Ponte Preta, Sampaio-RJ, Fluminense, Sampaio-RJ, Portimonense, Sampaio-RJ, Fluminense, Sampaio-RJ, Cabofriense, Sampaio-RJ, Macaé, Sampaio-RJ, Boa Esporte, Sampaio-RJ, Bonsucesso, Sampaio-RJ

*** João Félix - João Félix (João Félix Sequeira) (a) 10/11/1999, Viseu (Portugal) (b) 1,81 (c) F - attacking midfielder (d) Atlético de Madrid (e) Chelsea, Atlético Madrid, Benfica, Benfica B

*** João Magno - João Magno (João Victo Magno de Souza Machado) (a) 15/02/1997, Bahia (Brazil) (b) 1,95 (c) F - center forward (d) Goiás EC (e) F91 Dudelange, Paços Ferreira, Anápolis, Canelas 2010, Anápolis, Real SC, Anápolis, Braga B, Real SC, Braga B, Anápolis

*** João Marcelo - João Marcelo (João Marcelo Messias Ferreira) (a) 13/06/2000, Rio de Janeiro (Brazil) (b) 1,89 (c) D - central defense (d) Cruzeiro Esporte Clube (e) Cruzeiro, FC Porto B, Tombense, FC Porto B, Tombense

*** João Mário - João Mário (João Mário Naval da Costa Eduardo) (a) 19/01/1993, Porto (Portugal) (b) 1,79 (c) M - central midfielder (d) SL Benfica (e) Internazionale Milano, Sporting Lisboa, Internazionale Milano, Lokomotiv Moskva, Internazionale Milano, West Ham Utd., Internazionale Milano, Sporting Lisboa, Sporting B, Vitória Setúbal, Sporting B

*** João Mário - João Mário (João Mário Neto Lopes) (a) 03/01/2000, São João da Madeira (Portugal) (b) 1,78 (c) D - right back (d) FC Porto (e) FC Porto B
*** João Mário - João Mário (João Mário Nunes Fernandes) (a) 11/10/1993, Bissau (Guinea-Bissau) (b) 1,85 (c) F - left winger (d) - (e) Spartak Varna, Vilafranquense, Académica Coimbra, Académico Viseu, Chaves, Atlético CP, Benfica B, Lusitana
*** João Paulo - João Paulo (João Paulo da Silva Araújo) (a) 02/06/1988, Natal (Brazil) (b) 1,70 (c) F - center forward (d) Kairat Almaty (e) Ordabasy, Ludogorets, Ordabasy, Ludogorets, Botev Plovdiv, Ludogorets, Botev Plovdiv, Ferroviária, ABC FC, Botafogo-PB, ABC FC, Incheon Utd., Gwangju FC, Daejeon Citizen, Gwangju FC, ABC FC, Gwangju FC, ABC FC, Botafogo-PB, ABC FC, ABC
*** Joao Pedro - Joao Pedro (Joao Pedro Sacramento da Silva) (a) 18/01/2003, ¿? (Brazil) (b) 1,69 (c) M - left midfielder (d) - (e) Suduva
*** João Pedro - João Pedro (João Pedro Almeida Machado) (a) 03/04/1993, Vermil (Portugal) (b) 1,77 (c) M - central midfielder (d) GD Chaves (e) Tondela, Los Ángeles, Tondela, Los Ángeles, Apollon Smyrnis, Los Ángeles, Vitória Guimarães, Vitória Guimarães B
*** João Pedro - João Pedro (João Pedro de Moura Siembarski) (a) 08/02/2002, São Miguel Arcanjo (Brazil) (b) 1,70 (c) M - attacking midfielder (d) FCI Levadia (e) Athletico-PR B, Pafos FC
*** João Pedro - João Pedro (João Pedro Geraldino dos Santos Galvão) (a) 09/03/1992, Ipatinga (Brazil) (b) 1,84 (c) F - center forward (d) Grêmio Foot-Ball Porto Alegrense (e) Grêmio Porto Alegre, Fenerbahce, Cagliari, Estoril Praia, Desp. Brasil, Estoril Praia, Desp. Brasil, Santos, Desp. Brasil, US Palermo, Peñarol, US Palermo, Vitória Guimarães, US Palermo, At. Mineiro, At. Mineiro B
*** João Pedro - João Pedro (João Pedro Sousa Silva) (a) 13/11/1996, São Miguel (Portugal) (b) 1,85 (c) F - center forward (d) Panetolikos GFS (e) Bursaspor, Paços Ferreira, Vitória Guimarães, Vitória Guimarães B, Trofense, Gil Vicente, Santa Clara, Micaelense
*** João Tomé - João Tomé (João Tomé Esteves Baptista) (a) 12/02/2003, Barreiro (Portugal) (b) 1,85 (c) D - right back (d) SL Benfica B (e) -
*** João Victor - João Victor (João Victor Barbosa Ferreira) (a) 23/10/2000, ¿? (Brazil) (b) 1,91 (c) G (d) - (e) Ituano
*** João Victor - João Victor (João Victor Da Silva Marcelino) (a) 17/07/1998, Bauru (Brazil) (b) 1,87 (c) D - central defense (d) SL Benfica (e) FC Nantes, Benfica, Corinthians, Atlético-GO, Corinthians, Inter Limeira, Corinthians, Corinthians B
*** João Victor - João Victor (João Victor Donna Bravim) (a) 03/05/1998, Venda Nova do Imigrante (Brazil) (b) 1,92 (c) G (d) CD Santa Clara (e) Casa Pia, Alverca, Casa Pia, Alverca
*** Joãozinho - Joãozinho (João Carlos Reis Graça) (a) 02/07/1989, Lisboa (Portugal) (b) 1,85 (c) D - left back (d) SC União Torreense (e) Estoril Praia, APOEL FC, Tondela, KV Kortrijk, SC Braga, União Madeira, SC Braga, Astra Giurgiu, SC Braga, FC Sheriff, SC Braga, Beira-Mar, Sporting Lisboa, Beira-Mar, Mafra, Beira-Mar, Mafra, Moscavide
*** Joãozinho - Joãozinho (João Natailton Ramos dos Santos) (a) 25/12/1988, Umbauba (Brazil) (b) 1,65 (c) F - left winger (d) Grêmio Novorizontino (e) Sochi, Dinamo Moskva, Krasnodar, Levski Sofia, Portuguesa, Portuguesa B
*** Joaquín - Joaquín (Joaquín Sánchez Rodríguez) (a) 21/07/1981, El Puerto de Santa María (Spain) (b) 1,81 (c) F - right winger (d) - (e) Real Betis, Fiorentina, Málaga CF, Valencia CF, Real Betis, Betis B

*** Jobe - Pa Omar Jobe (Pa Omar Jobe) (a) 26/12/1998, Yundum (Gambia) (b) 1,86 (c) F - center forward (d) FC Zhenis Astana (e) Neman Grodno, Shkëndija, Struga, Shkëndija, Sheikh Jamal, ASAC Ndiambour, Real de Banjul

*** Jobello - Wesley Jobello (Wesley Georges Jobello) (a) 23/01/1994, Gennevilliers (France) (b) 1,80 (c) F - left winger (d) - (e) FC Arges, UTA Arad, US Boulogne, Coventry City, G. Ajaccio, Clermont Foot, Ol. Marseille B

*** Joca - Joca (Jorge Samuel Figueiredo Fernandes) (a) 30/01/1996, Braga (Portugal) (b) 1,68 (c) F - right winger (d) Rio Ave FC (e) Leixões, Leixões, Rio Ave, SC Braga, Tondela, SC Braga, Braga B

*** Jocic - Bogdan Jocic (Богдан Јочић) (a) 11/01/2001, Beograd (RF Yugoslavia, Serbia) (b) 1,84 (c) M - attacking midfielder (d) FK Vozdovac (e) Hellas Verona, Pro Vercelli, Hellas Verona, Metalac, Hellas Verona, Graficar

*** Jocic - Branimir Jocic (Бранимир Јочић) (a) 30/11/1994, Sombor (RF Yugoslavia, now in Serbia) (b) 1,82 (c) M - pivot (d) FK Mladost GAT Novi Sad (e) Rudar Pljevlja, Spartak, FK Senta, Spartak, FK Palic Koming, Spartak

*** Jocú - Henrique Jocú (a) 09/09/2001, Bissau (Guinea-Bissau) (b) 1,77 (c) M - pivot (d) CD Feirense (e) Portimonense

*** Jodlowski - Kacper Jodlowski (Kacper Jodłowski) (a) 30/05/1999, Kraków (Poland) (b) 1,87 (c) M - pivot (d) Cracovia (e) Cracovia II, Hutnik Krakow, Hutnik II, Othellos Athien, Gornik Leczna, Sokol Ostroda, AP Profi

*** Joe - Joe (José Manuel Martínez Oliver) (a) 06/02/1991, La Línea de la Concepción (Spain) (b) 1,83 (c) M - pivot (d) FC Bruno's Magpies (e) SD Tarazona, SD Ejea, R. B. Linense, Linense B

*** Joe Mendes - Joe Mendes (Josafat Wooding Mendes) (a) 31/12/2002, Solna (Sweden) (b) 1,77 (c) D - right back (d) SC Braga (e) AIK, Hammarby IF, Hammarby TFF, Hammarby IF, Hammarby TFF

*** Joelinton - Joelinton (Joelinton Cassio Apolinário de Lira) (a) 14/08/1996, Aliança (Brazil) (b) 1,86 (c) M - central midfielder (d) Newcastle United (e) Hoffenheim, Rapid Wien, Hoffenheim, Sport Recife

*** Joelsson - Kalle Joelsson (Julius Kalle Joelsson) (a) 21/03/1998, ¿? (Sweden) (b) 1,89 (c) G (d) Helsingborgs IF (e) Ängelholms FF, Helsingborgs IF

*** Joensen - Emil Joensen (Emil Weihe Joensen) (a) 19/11/2003, ¿? (Faroe Islands) (b) 1,85 (c) M - central midfielder (d) B36 Tórshavn (e) Skála, ÍF Fuglafjördur, B36 II

*** Joensen - Ingi Joensen (a) 29/06/2002, ¿? (Faroe Islands) (b) - (c) F (d) 07 Vestur II (e) 07 Vestur

*** Joensen - Jákup Joensen (a) 27/02/2000, ¿? (Faroe Islands) (b) - (c) M - central midfielder (d) Skála IF (e) Skála IF II, EB/S II, Skála

*** Joensen - Jóhann Joensen (Jóhann Hansson Joensen) (a) 17/08/2001, ¿? (Faroe Islands) (b) 1,85 (c) F - left winger (d) 07 Vestur (e) EB/Streymur, B36 Tórshavn, B36 II, B36 II

*** Joensen - Kristian Joensen (a) 21/12/1992, Runavík (Faroe Islands) (b) 1,90 (c) G (d) NSÍ Runavík (e) EB/Streymur, KÍ Klaksvík, EB/Streymur, KÍ Klaksvík, 07 Vestur, Lyngby BK, NSÍ Runavík, B68 Toftir, NSÍ Runavík, 07 Vestur, NSÍ Runavík

*** Joensen - Mattias Joensen (Mattias Weihe Joensen) (a) 15/02/2003, ¿? (Faroe Islands) (b) - (c) D - central defense (d) B36 Tórshavn (e) EB/Streymur, B36 Tórshavn, B36 II

*** Joensen - Meinhardt Joensen (Meinhardt Pállsson Joensen) (a) 27/11/1979, Runavík (Faroe Islands) (b) 1,86 (c) G (d) - (e) KÍ Klaksvík, B68 Toftir, KÍ Klaksvík, TB Tvøroyri, KÍ Klaksvík, TB Tvøroyri, KÍ Klaksvík, TB Tvøroyri, KÍ Klaksvík, B36 Tórshavn, NSÍ Runavík, B36 Tórshavn, KÍ Klaksvík, GI Gota, B68 Toftir

*** Joensen - René Joensen (René Shaki Joensen) (a) 08/02/1993, ¿? (Faroe Islands) (b) 1,80 (c) M - central midfielder (d) KÍ Klaksvík (e) HB Tórshavn, Grindavík, Vendsyssel FF, HB Tórshavn, Brøndby IF, HB Tórshavn, Brøndby IF
*** Joensen - Teitur Joensen (Teitur Reinert Joensen) (a) 10/11/1986, ¿? (Faroe Islands) (b) 1,76 (c) D - central defense (d) - (e) Skála
*** Jogi - Martin Jogi (Martin Jõgi) (a) 05/01/1995, Tartu (Estonia) (b) 1,84 (c) F - center forward (d) Tartu JK Welco (e) JK Tammeka, Tammeka Tartu, JK Tammeka, Tammeka Tartu
*** Johannesen - Áki Johannesen (a) 11/11/2002, ¿? (Faroe Islands) (b) - (c) M - central midfielder (d) B68 Toftir (e) NSÍ II
*** Johannesen - Albert Róin Johannesen (a) 29/03/1995, ¿? (Faroe Islands) (b) - (c) D - central defense (d) NSÍ Runavík II (e) NSÍ Runavík, NSÍ III, B68 Toftir, NSÍ II
*** Johannesen - Ari Johannesen (a) 07/06/1996, ¿? (Faroe Islands) (b) - (c) D - left back (d) B68 Toftir (e) -
*** Johannesen - Bergur Johannesen (a) 03/05/1999, ¿? (Faroe Islands) (b) - (c) M - central midfielder (d) NSÍ Runavík II (e) B68 Toftir, NSÍ II, Undrid FF, B68 Toftir II
*** Johannesen - Jonn Johannesen (a) 30/12/2001, ¿? (Faroe Islands) (b) 1,76 (c) F - left winger (d) KÍ Klaksvík (e) KÍ II
*** Johannesen - Patrik Johannesen (a) 07/09/1995, Tvøroyri (Faroe Islands) (b) 1,86 (c) M - attacking midfielder (d) Breidablik Kópavogur (e) Keflavík, Egersund, KÍ Klaksvík, Florø SK, B36 Tórshavn, AB Argir, TB Tvøroyri, FC Sudoroy, TB Tvøroyri
*** Johannesen - Tóki Johannesen (Tóki Hammershaimb Johannesen) (a) 17/03/1997, ¿? (Faroe Islands) (b) - (c) M - central midfielder (d) EB/Streymur (e) EB/S II, EB/Streymur, EB/S II
*** Jóhannesson - Axel Ingi Jóhannesson (a) 02/06/2004, ¿? (Iceland) (b) - (c) D (d) Keflavík ÍF (e) -
*** Jóhannesson - Daniel Ingi Jóhannesson (a) 03/04/2007, ¿? (Iceland) (b) - (c) M (d) - (e) ÍA Akranes
*** Jóhannesson - Ísak Bergmann Jóhannesson (a) 23/03/2003, Sutton Coldfield (England) (b) 1,84 (c) M - central midfielder (d) Fortuna Düsseldorf (e) Fortuna Düsseldorf, FC København, Norrköping, ÍA Akranes
*** Jóhannesson - Sveinn Sigurdur Jóhannesson (Sveinn Sigurður Jóhannesson) (a) 22/01/1995, ¿? (Iceland) (b) - (c) G (d) Valur Reykjavík (e) Stjarnan, Fjardabyggd, Stjarnan
*** Jóhannsson - Aron Jóhannsson (a) 10/11/1990, Mobile, Alabama (United States) (b) 1,84 (c) F - center forward (d) Valur Reykjavík (e) Lech Poznan, Hammarby IF, Werder Bremen, AZ Alkmaar, Aarhus GF, Fjölnir, IMG Bradenton
*** Jóhannsson - Davíd Snaer Jóhannsson (Davíð Snær Jóhannsson) (a) 15/06/2002, Oslo (Norway) (b) - (c) M - attacking midfielder (d) FH Hafnarfjördur (e) Keflavík
*** Jóhannsson - Ómar Jóhannsson (a) 02/03/1981, ¿? (Iceland) (b) - (c) G (d) - (e) Keflavík, Njardvík, Keflavík, Bunkcflo, Keflavík, Bunkeflo, Islandia
*** Johansen - Andrass Johansen (a) 16/11/2001, Tórshavn (Faroe Islands) (b) 1,85 (c) F - left winger (d) B36 Tórshavn (e) B36 II
*** Johansen - Daniel Johansen (a) 09/07/1998, ¿? (Faroe Islands) (b) 1,79 (c) D - left back (d) Thisted FC (e) HB Tórshavn, FC Fredericia, HB Tórshavn, HB Tórshavn II
*** Johansen - Dávid Johansen (a) 08/02/1997, ¿? (Faroe Islands) (b) - (c) M - attacking midfielder (d) Skála IF (e) Skála IF II
*** Johansen - Filip Johansen (Filip Kruse Johansen) (a) 21/07/2003, ¿? (Faroe Islands) (b) - (c) D - central defense (d) EB/Streymur (e) EB/S II

*** Johansen - Hjarnar Johansen (Hjarnar Jákupsson Johansen) (a) 13/04/2004, ¿? (Faroe Islands) (b) - (c) F (d) B68 Toftir (e) -

*** Johansen - Jákup Johansen (a) 27/04/1993, ¿? (Faroe Islands) (b) 1,82 (c) M - left midfielder (d) Víkingur Gøta (e) Skála, ÍF Fuglafjördur, Skála

*** Johansen - Jesper Johansen (Jesper Sørum Johansen) (a) 14/10/1991, ¿? (Norway) (b) - (c) D (d) Furnes Fotball (e) Brumunddal Fotball

*** Johansen - Karl Martin Johansen (a) 17/08/1999, ¿? (Faroe Islands) (b) - (c) D - central defense (d) Skála IF (e) -

*** Johansen - Martin Johansen (a) 08/12/2003, ¿? (Faroe Islands) (b) - (c) M - right midfielder (d) Skála IF (e) Skála IF II

*** Johansson - Alexander Johansson (Eric Alexander Johansson) (a) 30/10/1995, ¿? (Sweden) (b) 1,89 (c) F - center forward (d) Mjällby AIF (e) Varbergs BoIS, Brage, Varbergs BoIS, Sandnes Ulf, Varbergs BoIS, Tvååkers IF, Ullareds IK, Stafsinge IF, Vinbergs IF

*** Johansson - Carl Johansson (Carl Anders Lorentz Johansson) (a) 23/05/1994, Lund (Sweden) (b) 1,94 (c) D - central defense (d) Holstein Kiel (e) IFK Göteborg, Randers FC, IFK Göteborg, Falkenbergs FF, Helsingborgs IF

*** Johansson - Herman Johansson (a) 16/10/1997, ¿? (Sweden) (b) 1,90 (c) M - right midfielder (d) Mjällby AIF (e) Sandvikens IF, Friska Viljor

*** Johansson - Marko Johansson (a) 25/08/1998, Malmö (Sweden) (b) 1,94 (c) G (d) Halmstads BK (e) Halmstads BK, SV Hamburg, VfL Bochum, SV Hamburg, Malmö FF, Mjällby AIF, Malmö FF, GAIS, Malmö FF, Trelleborg, Malmö FF

*** Johansson - Mattias Johansson (Mattias Erik Johansson) (a) 16/02/1992, Jönköping (Sweden) (b) 1,74 (c) M - right midfielder (d) - (e) Legia Warszawa, Genclerbirligi, Panathinaikos, AZ Alkmaar, Kalmar FF

*** Johansson - Oliver Johansson (Oliver Stefan Johansson) (a) 13/07/2002, ¿? (Sweden) (b) 1,72 (c) M - central midfielder (d) - (e) Europa Point FC, IFK Österåker

*** Johansson - Oscar Johansson (Oscar Nils Per Johansson) (a) 06/05/1995, ¿? (Sweden) (b) 1,78 (c) M - central midfielder (d) IFK Värnamo (e) Trelleborg, Värnamo, Gnosjö IF

*** Johansson - Piotr Johansson (a) 28/02/1995, Gorlice (Poland) (b) 1,85 (c) D - right back (d) Djurgårdens IF (e) Kalmar FF, Gefle, Malmö FF, Östersund, Malmö FF, Ängelholms FF, Malmö FF

*** Jóhansson - Gutti Jóhansson (Gutti við Streym Jóhansson) (a) 18/08/2004, ¿? (Faroe Islands) (b) - (c) M - central midfielder (d) EB/Streymur (e) EB/S II

*** John - Dan John (Daniel Ryan John) (a) 04/04/2006, ¿? (Wales) (b) - (c) M - central midfielder (d) Haverfordwest County (e) -

*** John - Gruff John (Gruffydd John Williams) (a) 22/06/1994, ¿? (Wales) (b) - (c) D - central defense (d) Caernarfon Town (e) Porthmadog, Llanrug United

*** John - Harri John (a) 04/04/2006, ¿? (Wales) (b) - (c) M - central midfielder (d) Haverfordwest County (e) -

*** John - Jonathan John (Jonathan John) (a) 09/05/2001, Kaduna (Nigeria) (b) 1,79 (c) D - central defense (d) FK Gomel (e) FK Slutsk, FC Saksan

*** John - Kelvin John (Kelvin Pius John) (a) 10/06/2003, Morogoro (Tanzania) (b) 1,75 (c) F - right winger (d) Jong Genk (e) KRC Genk

*** John - Michael John (a) 28/07/2002, ¿? (Finland) (b) 1,98 (c) D - central defense (d) Salon Palloilijat (e) Helsinki IFK, Tiki Taka

*** John - Oto John (John Oto John) (a) 25/01/1998, Akwa Ibom (Nigeria) (b) 1,80 (c) F - center forward (d) Turan-Tovuz IK (e) KF Dukagjini, FC Prishtina, KF Skënderbeu, KF Trepca 89, KF Skënderbeu, 36 Lion FC

*** John Murkin - Derry John Murkin (a) 27/07/1999, Colchester (England) (b) 1,83 (c) D - left back (d) FC Volendam (e) -

*** Johnathan - Johnathan (Johnathan Carlos Pereira) (a) 04/04/1995, Goiânia (Brazil) (b) 1,76 (c) D - right back (d) CSKA 1948 (e) Beroe, Botev Plovdiv, Stal Kamyanske, Goiás B, Tupi, Goiás B

*** Johns - Chris Johns (Christopher Patrick Adam Johns) (a) 13/05/1995, Belfast (Northern Ireland) (b) 1,83 (c) G (d) Linfield FC (e) Coleraine, Bangor

*** Johnsen - Björn Johnsen (Bjørn Maars Johnsen) (a) 06/11/1991, New York City, New York (United States) (b) 1,95 (c) F - center forward (d) FC Seoul (e) SC Cambuur, Montréal, Ulsan Hyundai, AZ Alkmaar, Rosenborg, AZ Alkmaar, ADO Den Haag, Heart of Midlothian, Litex Lovetch, Atlético CP, Louletano, At. Baleares, Antequera, Tønsberg

*** Johnsen - Gabríel Rómeó Johnsen (Gabríel Rómeó Rögnvaldsson Johnsen) (a) 04/09/2003, ¿? (Iceland) (b) - (c) F (d) KFK Kópavogur (e) KH

*** Johnsen - Lasse Berg Johnsen (a) 18/08/1999, Stavanger (Norway) (b) 1,79 (c) M - central midfielder (d) Malmö FF (e) Randers FC, Raufoss, Viking, Tromsdalen, Viking, Viking FK II

*** Johnson - Aidan Johnson (a) 07/03/2005, ¿? (Wales) (b) - (c) G (d) - (e) Flint Town

*** Johnson - Ben Johnson (Benjamin Anthony Johnson) (a) 24/01/2000, Waltham Forest (England) (b) 1,84 (c) D - right back (d) West Ham United (e) -

*** Johnson - Brennan Johnson (Brennan Price Johnson) (a) 23/05/2001, Nottingham (England) (b) 1,79 (c) M - attacking midfielder (d) Nottingham Forest (e) Lincoln City, Nottingham Forest

*** Johnson - Callum Johnson (Callum Charles Johnson) (a) 23/10/1996, Yarm (England) (b) 1,88 (c) D - right back (d) Mansfield Town (e) Ross County, FC Portsmouth, Fleetwood, FC Portsmouth, Accrington St., Accrington St.

*** Johnson - Darius Johnson (a) 15/03/2000, London (England) (b) 1,82 (c) F - left winger (d) FC Volendam (e) FC Kensington, Rising Ballers

*** Johnson - Michael Johnson (a) 11/05/1994, ¿? (Malta) (b) 1,91 (c) D - central defense (d) Santa Lucia FC (e) Balzan FC, St. Andrews FC

*** Johnson - Murray Johnson (a) 13/11/2004, Edinburgh (Scotland) (b) 1,89 (c) G (d) Queen of the South FC (e) Queen of the South, Hibernian B, Airdrieonians, Hibernian B, Airdrieonians, Hibernian B

*** Johnson - Quinn Johnson (a) 09/07/2001, ¿? (Netherlands) (b) - (c) G (d) - (e) Glacis United, San Jorge, Melton Town

*** Johnson - Sam Johnson (Sam Garyahzon Johnson) (a) 06/05/1993, Monrovia (Liberia) (b) 1,80 (c) F - center forward (d) Bodens BK (e) Vasalunds IF, FK Aksu, Mjällby AIF, Sabah, Salt Lake, Vålerenga, WH Yangtze Reserves, WH Zall, Djurgården, IK Frej Täby, Härnösands FF, Juventus IF, Assyriska IF, Dalkurd, Nimba Kwado FC

*** Johnsplass - Brynjar Johnsplass (a) 30/12/2003, ¿? (Norway) (b) 1,78 (c) D - right back (d) Junkeren IK (e) Bodø/Glimt II

*** Johnsson - Karl-Johan Johnsson (a) 28/01/1990, Ränneslöv (Sweden) (b) 1,88 (c) G (d) - (e) FC København, Guingamp, Randers FC, NEC Nijmegen, Halmstads BK

*** Johnston - Alistair Johnston (Alistair William Johnston) (a) 08/10/1998, Vancouver, British Columbia (Canada) (b) 1,80 (c) D - right back (d) Celtic FC (e) Montréal, Nashville, Demon Deacons, Vaughan Azzurri, Demon Deacons, Red Storm, Vaughan Azzurri, Red Storm, Vaughan Azzurri, Red Storm, Vaughan Azzurri, Red Storm, Vaughan Azzurri, ANB Futbol, Aurora FC, Lakeshore SC

*** Johnston - Max Johnston (a) 26/12/2003, Middlesbrough (England) (b) 1,85 (c) D - right back (d) SK Sturm Graz (e) Motherwell FC, Cove Rangers FC, Motherwell FC, Queen of the South, Motherwell FC, Motherwell B

*** Johnston - Mikey Johnston (Michael Andrew Johnston) (a) 19/04/1999, Glasgow (Scotland) (b) 1,76 (c) F - left winger (d) Celtic FC (e) Vitória Guimarães, Celtic FC, Celtic Reserves

*** Johnston - Sam Johnston (Samuel Johnston) (a) 26/03/1996, Belfast (Northern Ireland) (b) - (c) G (d) Ballymena United (e) HW Welders, Ballymena, HW Welders, Ballymena, Dungannon, Ards FC, HW Welders

*** Johnstone - Sam Johnstone (Samuel Luke Johnstone) (a) 25/03/1993, Preston (England) (b) 1,93 (c) G (d) Crystal Palace (e) West Bromwich Albion, Manchester Utd., Aston Villa, Manchester Utd., Aston Villa, Manchester Utd., Preston North End, Manchester Utd., Preston North End, Manchester Utd., Doncaster Rovers, Manchester Utd., Doncaster Rovers, Manchester Utd., Yeovil Town, Manchester Utd., FC Walsall, Manchester Utd., Scunthorpe Utd., Manchester Utd., Oldham Athletic, Manchester Utd.

*** Jojic - Nikola Jojic (Никола Јојић) (a) 15/09/2003, Čačak (Serbia and Montenegro, now in Serbia) (b) 1,83 (c) F - right winger (d) FK Mladost Lucani (e) -

*** Jokela - Ville Jokela (a) 14/10/2000, ¿? (Finland) (b) - (c) D (d) FC Reipas Lahti (e) -

*** Jokelainen - Niklas Jokelainen (a) 30/03/2000, Oulu (Finland) (b) 1,81 (c) M - attacking midfielder (d) AC Oulu (e) RoPS, Ilves, AC Oulu

*** Jokic - Milan Jokic (Милан Јокић) (a) 21/03/1995, Arandjelovac (RF Yugoslavia, now in Serbia) (b) 1,79 (c) M - pivot (d) FK Mladost GAT Novi Sad (e) RFK Novi Sad, Suduva, Novi Pazar, Tsarsko Selo, Metalac, Zlatibor, FK Bezanija, FK BSK Borča, Spartak, Borac Cacak, Vozdovac, Crvena zvezda, Kolubara, Crvena zvezda, FK BSK Borča, Crvena zvezda

*** Jokic - Ranko Jokic (Ранко Јокић) (a) 22/04/1999, Subotica (RF Yugoslavia, now in Serbia) (b) 1,86 (c) D - central defense (d) FK Borac Banja Luka (e) Radnik, FK Backa, Graficar

*** Jokiranta - Viljami Jokiranta (a) 23/07/2006, ¿? (Finland) (b) 1,78 (c) M - central midfielder (d) FC Lahti (e) -

*** Jokovic - Dusan Jokovic (Душан Јоковић) (a) 04/07/1999, Kraljevo (RF Yugoslavia, now in Serbia) (b) 1,87 (c) D - central defense (d) SK Lisen (e) Vozdovac, AP Brera, Proleter, Metalac, Proleter, NK Lokomotiva, NK Sesvete, NK Lokomotiva, LASK, NK Sesvete, LASK

*** Joksimovic - Milan Joksimovic (Милан Јоксимовић) (a) 09/02/1990, Uzice (Yugoslavia, now in Serbia) (b) 1,84 (c) D - central defense (d) FK Mladost Lucani (e) Novi Pazar, Liepaja, Gorodeya, KA Akureyri, Gorodeya, Sloboda Užice, Jedinstvo Uzice, Metalac, Jedinstvo Uzice, Spartak, FK Indjija, Sloboda Užice

*** Joksimovic - Sergej Joksimovic (a) 16/08/2002, ¿? (RF Yugoslavia, now in Montenegro) (b) 1,87 (c) G (d) Jedinstvo Bijelo Polje (e) OFK Petrovac, OFK Titograd

*** Jolley - Ethan Jolley (Ethan Terence Jolley) (a) 29/03/1997, Gibraltar (Gibraltar) (b) 1,78 (c) D - right back (d) St Joseph's FC (e) Europa FC, Mons Calpe, Lincoln FC, Lynx FC, Lincoln FC, Europa FC, Atlético Zabal

*** Joly - Paul Joly (a) 07/06/2000, Orléans (France) (b) 1,82 (c) D - right back (d) AJ Auxerre (e) Dijon, AJ Auxerre, AJ Auxerre B, Amiens SC B

*** Jonas Toró - Jonas Toró (Jonas Gabriel da Silva Nunes) (a) 30/05/1999, Belém de São Francisco (Brazil) (b) 1,77 (c) F - left winger (d) Botafogo FC (e) Botafogo-

SP, Panathinaikos, APO Levadiakos, Panathinaikos, São Paulo, Atlético-GO, São Paulo, Sport Recife, São Paulo, Primavera

*** Jónasson - Aegir Jarl Jónasson (Ægir Jarl Jónasson) (a) 08/03/1998, ¿? (Iceland) (b) - (c) M - attacking midfielder (d) KR Reykjavík (e) Fjölnir

*** Jónasson - Atli Jónasson (a) 12/03/1988, ¿? (Iceland) (b) - (c) G (d) Leiknir Reykjavík (e) Tindastóll, Smári, KFG Gardabaer, KV Vesturbaejar, KR Reykjavík, Hvöt, KR Reykjavík, Våg FK, KR Reykjavík, Haukar, KR Reykjavík, Reynir S., KR Reykjavík

*** Jónasson - Hallgrímur Jónasson (a) 04/05/1986, ¿? (Iceland) (b) 1,84 (c) D - central defense (d) - (e) KA Akureyri, Lyngby BK, Odense BK, SønderjyskE, GAIS, SønderjyskE, GAIS, Keflavík, Thór, Völsungur ÍF

*** Jónasson (c) M (d) Vaengir Júpiters (e) Fjölnir, ÍBV Vestmannaeyjar, Fjölnir - Óskar Dagur Jónasson (c) M (d) Vaengir Júpiters (e) Fjölnir, ÍBV Vestmannaeyjar, Fjölnir

*** Jonathans - Miliano Jonathans (a) 05/04/2004, Arnhem (Netherlands) (b) - (c) F - right winger (d) Vitesse Arnhem (e) -

*** Jones - Alaric Jones (Alaric Anthony Lloyd Jones) (a) 09/02/2001, ¿? (Wales) (b) - (c) D - central defense (d) Cardiff Metropolitan University (e) Haverfordwest, Carmarthen, Haverfordwest

*** Jones - Curtis Jones (a) 30/01/2001, Liverpool (England) (b) 1,85 (c) M - central midfielder (d) Liverpool FC (e) -

*** Jones - Dave Jones (David Edward Jones) (a) 03/02/1990, ¿? (Wales) (b) - (c) G (d) Aberystwyth Town (e) Newtown, Caersws, Welshpool, Newtown

*** Jones - Ethan Jones (a) 16/10/2004, ¿? (Wales) (b) - (c) M - central midfielder (d) - (e) Bala

*** Jones - Gruffydd Jones (Gruffydd Michael Wyn Jones) (a) 31/01/2005, ¿? (Wales) (b) - (c) F - center forward (d) - (e) Caernarfon Town

*** Jones - Henry Jones (Henry Lloyd Jones) (a) 18/09/1993, ¿? (Wales) (b) 1,83 (c) M - attacking midfielder (d) Penybont FC (e) Haverfordwest, Bala, Fylde, Bangor City

*** Jones - Jamie Jones (Jamie Owen Jones) (a) 16/01/2004, ¿? (Wales) (b) - (c) D - left back (d) Caersws FC (e) Aberystwyth, Penrhyncoch, Aberystwyth

*** Jones - Jordan Jones (Jordan Lewis Jones) (a) 24/10/1994, Redcar (England) (b) 1,74 (c) F - left winger (d) Wigan Athletic (e) Kilmarnock FC, Wigan Ath., St. Mirren, Wigan Ath., Rangers FC, Sunderland, Rangers FC, Kilmarnock FC, Cambridge Utd., Hartlepool Utd.

*** Jones - Mathew Jones (Mathew George Jones) (a) 14/07/1999, ¿? (Wales) (b) - (c) D - left back (d) Newtown AFC (e) Aberystwyth

*** Jones - Mike Jones (a) 16/06/1993, ¿? (Wales) (b) - (c) G (d) Gresford Athletic (e) Colwyn Bay, Airbus UK, Guilsfield FC, Holywell, Gresford, Oswestry, Caernarfon, Cefn Druids, Prestatyn, Denbigh, Flint Town

*** Jones - Owain Jones (Owain Rhys Jones) (a) 01/10/1996, Ammanford (Wales) (b) 1,84 (c) F - right winger (d) Pontypridd United (e) Aberystwyth, Merthyr Town, Nuneaton, Merthyr Town, Yeovil Town

*** Jones - Phil Jones (Philip Anthony Jones) (a) 21/02/1992, Preston (England) (b) 1,85 (c) D - central defense (d) - (e) Manchester Utd., Blackburn, Blackburn Reserves

*** Jones - Robert Jones (a) 22/09/1995, Bothwell (Scotland) (b) 1,98 (c) F - center forward (d) - (e) Finn Harps, Clyde FC, Dumbarton FC, Stranraer, Albion Rovers, East Fife, BSC Glasgow

*** Jones - Sam Jones (a) 08/12/1998, ¿? (Wales) (b) - (c) F - center forward (d) Cardiff Metropolitan University (e) Cambrian & C., Barry Town, Cambrian & C.

*** Jones - Shay Jones (a) 24/02/2002, Gibraltar (Gibraltar) (b) 1,80 (c) M - left midfielder (d) FC Bruno's Magpies (e) Glacis United, Bruno's Magpies, LJMU, Red Imps Reserves, Bruno's Magpies, Red Imps Reserves

*** Jones - Zac Jones (Zac Maxwell Jones) (a) 27/11/2000, Wellington (New Zealand) (b) 1,85 (c) G (d) Haverfordwest County (e) Miramar Rangers, Team Wellington, Wellington P., W. Phoenix Reserves, Wellington Ol.

*** Jones - Zyen Jones (Zyen Thyfearious Jones) (a) 25/08/2000, Clarkston, Georgia (United States) (b) 1,81 (c) F (d) Kalju FC (e) Ferencváros II, Tromsø, Ferencváros II, Spartak Trnava, Ferencváros II, Charlotte Ind., Georgia United

*** Jonhardsson - Ingi Jonhardsson (a) 11/09/2001, ¿? (Faroe Islands) (b) - (c) M - left midfielder (d) Víkingur Gøta (e) Víkingur II

*** Jonny - Jonny (Jonny Robert do Nascimento Torres) (a) 18/05/1998, ¿? (Brazil) (b) - (c) F - left winger (d) Hamrun Spartans (e) Zumbi EC, Cruzeiro-AL, Central, Tocantins, Coruripe

*** Jonny Arriba - Jonny Arriba (Jonny Arriba Monroy) (a) 01/11/2001, La Vall d'Uixó (Spain) (b) 1,76 (c) F - right winger (d) Villarreal CF B (e) Chaves, Villarreal CF B, Villarreal CF C, CD Roda

*** Jonsson - Leo Jonsson (a) 16/04/2004, ¿? (Sweden) (b) - (c) M (d) IF Sylvia (e) -

*** Jonsson - Melker Jonsson (a) 10/07/2002, ¿? (Sweden) (b) 1,86 (c) D - central defense (d) Landskrona BoIS (e) Djurgården, Landskrona, Djurgården

*** Jonsson - Oscar Jonsson (Olov Oscar Joel Jonsson) (a) 24/01/1997, ¿? (Sweden) (b) 1,86 (c) G (d) GIF Sundsvall (e) IF Karlstad, Karlstad BK, Djurgården, IK Frej Täby, Djurgården, Enskede IK, Djurgården, Håbo FF, Djurgården, Huddinge IF

*** Jónsson - Ári Mohr Jónsson (a) 22/07/1994, Tórshavn (Faroe Islands) (b) 1,83 (c) D - left back (d) HB Tórshavn (e) Sandnes Ulf, HB Tórshavn, Silkeborg IF

*** Jónsson - Benjamín Jónsson (a) 03/10/2003, ¿? (Iceland) (b) 1,85 (c) G (d) Fram Reykjavík (e) -

*** Jónsson - Davíd Júlían Jónsson (Davíð Júlían Jónsson) (a) 26/06/2004, ¿? (Iceland) (b) - (c) M (d) Leiknir Reykjavík (e) Thróttur Vogum, Leiknir

*** Jónsson - Eggert Gunnthór Jónsson (Eggert Gunnþór Jónsson) (a) 18/08/1988, Reykjavík (Iceland) (b) 1,88 (c) M - pivot (d) FH Hafnarfjördur (e) SønderjyskE, Fleetwood, Vestsjaelland, Belenenses, Wolverhampton Wanderers, Charlton Ath., Wolverhampton Wanderers, Heart of Midlothian, Fjardabyggd

*** Jónsson - Hákon Ingi Jónsson (a) 10/11/1995, ¿? (Iceland) (b) - (c) F - center forward (d) Fjölnir Reykjavík (e) ÍA Akranes, Fylkir, HK Kópavogs, Fylkir

*** Jónsson - Helgi Thór Jónsson (Helgi Þór Jónsson) (a) 25/10/1994, Garður (Iceland) (b) 1,82 (c) F - left winger (d) KF Vídir (e) Vídir, Keflavík, Vídir, Keflavík, Njardvík, Vídir

*** Jónsson - Hlynur Saevar Jónsson (Hlynur Sævar Jónsson) (a) 29/03/1999, ¿? (Iceland) (b) - (c) D - central defense (d) ÍA Akranes (e) Víkingur Ó., ÍA Akranes, Kári

*** Jónsson - Ingvar Jónsson (a) 18/10/1989, Keflavík (Iceland) (b) 1,86 (c) G (d) Víkingur Reykjavík (e) Viborg FF, Sandefjord, Start, Sandnes Ulf, Start, Stjarnan, Njardvík

*** Jónsson - Jónatan Ingi Jónsson (Jónatan Ingi Jónsson) (a) 15/03/1999, Kópavogur (Iceland) (b) 1,71 (c) F - right winger (d) Sogndal IL Fotball (e) Hafnarfjördur

*** Jónsson - Kristinn Jónsson (a) 04/08/1990, Kópavogur (Iceland) (b) 1,74 (c) D - left back (d) KR Reykjavík (e) Breidablik, Sogndal, Sarpsborg 08, Breidablik, Brommapojkarna, Breidablik

*** Jónsson - Kristján Logi Jónsson (a) 17/01/2007, ¿? (Iceland) (b) - (c) G (d) KF Framherjar-Smástund (e) -

*** Jónsson - Óskar Jónsson (a) 28/01/1997, ¿? (Iceland) (b) 1,79 (c) M - pivot (d) Fram Reykjavík (e) Grótta, Breidablik, Thróttur, Breidablik, ÍR, Breidablik, ÍR, Breidablik, Thór, Breidablik
*** Jónsson - Róbert Logi Jónsson (a) 25/07/2003, ¿? (Iceland) (b) - (c) M (d) KV Vesturbaejar (e) -
*** Jónsson - Sámal Jónsson (a) 10/05/2003, ¿? (Faroe Islands) (b) - (c) M - left midfielder (d) - (e) EB/Streymur, EB/Streymur II
*** Jónsson - Sigurdur Steinar Jónsson (a) 02/06/1993, ¿? (Iceland) (b) - (c) M (d) KF Kría (e) Grótta
*** Jónsson - Thorvaldur Dadi Jónsson (Þorvaldur Daði Jónsson) (a) 13/06/2002, ¿? (Iceland) (b) 1,86 (c) D - right back (d) Dalvík/Reynir (e) KA Akureyri, KF Fjallabyggd, KA Akureyri, Dalvík/Reynir, KA Akureyri, Dalvík/Reynir
*** Jónsson - Tómas Bjarki Jónsson (a) 01/09/2003, ¿? (Iceland) (b) - (c) M (d) UMF Njardvík (e) Augnablik, Breidablik
*** Jónsson - Vidar Ari Jónsson (Viðar Ari Jónsson) (a) 10/03/1994, Reykjavík (Iceland) (b) 1,84 (c) F - right winger (d) FH Hafnarfjördur (e) Honvéd, Sandefjord, Brann, Hafnarfjördur, Brann, Fjölnir
*** Jónsson - Viktor Jónsson (a) 23/06/1994, ¿? (Iceland) (b) 1,85 (c) F - center forward (d) ÍA Akranes (e) Thróttur, Víkingur, Thróttur, Víkingur
*** Jónsson - Virgar Jónsson (a) 13/06/2006, ¿? (Faroe Islands) (b) - (c) D - left back (d) EB/Streymur (e) EB/S II
*** Jönsson - Jens Jönsson (Jens Jønsson) (a) 10/01/1993, Aarhus (Denmark) (b) 1,82 (c) M - pivot (d) AEK Athína FC (e) Cádiz CF, Konyaspor, Aarhus GF, Aarhus GF II
*** Jönsson - Rasmus Jönsson (a) 27/01/1990, Viken (Sweden) (b) 1,92 (c) F - center forward (d) Helsingborgs IF (e) Buriram Utd., Helsingborgs IF, Odense BK, Aalborg BK, VfL Wolfsburg, Aalborg BK, VfL Wolfsburg, FSV Frankfurt, VfL Wolfsburg, Helsingborgs IF
*** Jonuzi - Fjoart Jonuzi (a) 09/07/1996, Kukës (Albania) (b) 1,80 (c) M - pivot (d) KF Tirana (e) KF Vllaznia, SC Gjilani, KF Laçi, FK Kukësi
*** Joosten - Patrick Joosten (Patrick Ofori Joosten) (a) 14/04/1996, Nijmegen (Netherlands) (b) 1,85 (c) F - left winger (d) Willem II Tilburg (e) Apollon Limassol, FC Groningen, SC Cambuur, FC Groningen, FC Utrecht, Sparta Rotterdam, FC Utrecht, VVV-Venlo, FC Utrecht
*** Jordan - Jordan (Theoson-Jordan Siebatcheu) (a) 26/04/1996, Washington, D. C. (United States) (b) 1,91 (c) F - center forward (d) 1.FC Union Berlin (e) BSC Young Boys, Stade Rennes, BSC Young Boys, Stade Rennes, Stade Reims, LB Châteauroux, Stade Reims, Stade Reims B
*** Jordan - Reece Jordan (a) 06/03/2005, ¿? (Northern Ireland) (b) - (c) D - left back (d) Portadown FC (e) -
*** Jordán - Joan Jordán (Joan Jordán Moreno) (a) 06/07/1994, Regencós (Spain) (b) 1,85 (c) M - central midfielder (d) Sevilla FC (e) SD Eibar, RCD Espanyol, Real Valladolid, RCD Espanyol, RCD Espanyol B, UD Poblense
*** Jordania - Levan Jordania (ლევან ჯორდანია) (a) 01/01/1997, Tbilisi (Georgia) (b) 1,95 (c) M - attacking midfielder (d) FC Gagra (e) Sioni Bolnisi, Young Violets, FC Locomotive, FC Den Bosch, FC Eindhoven
*** Jordanov - Edisson Jordanov (Edisson Latchezar Jordanov) (a) 08/06/1993, Rostock (Germany) (b) 1,72 (c) D - right back (d) KVC Westerlo (e) Union St. Gilloise, RE Virton, F91 Dudelange, Preussen Münster, Stuttg. Kickers, Borussia Dortmund II, Hansa Rostock

*** Jordão - Bruno Jordão (Bruno André Cavaco Jordão) (a) 12/10/1998, Marinha Grande (Portugal) (b) 1,80 (c) M - central midfielder (d) Wolverhampton Wanderers (e) Santa Clara, Wolverhampton Wanderers, Grasshoppers, Wolverhampton Wanderers, Famalicão, Wolverhampton Wanderers, Lazio, SC Braga, Lazio, SC Braga, Braga B, Leiria

*** Jordi - Jordi (Jordi Martins Almeida) (a) 03/09/1993, Rio de Janeiro (Brazil) (b) 1,92 (c) G (d) Grêmio Novorizontino (e) Paços Ferreira, Vasco da Gama, CSA, Vasco da Gama, Tractor Sazi, Vasco da Gama

*** Jorge Eduardo - Jorge Eduardo (Jorge Eduardo Pedro Junior) (a) 08/09/1994, São Paulo (Brazil) (b) 1,79 (c) F - left winger (d) Visakha FC (e) Dziugas, GO Audax, Juventus-SP, Ferroviária, Portuguesa, Ferroviária, ABC FC, Ferroviária, GO Audax, Grêmio Osasco, GO Audax, Santos, GO Audax

*** Jorge Elias - Jorge Elias (Jorge Elias dos Santos) (a) 05/06/1991, ¿? (Brazil) (b) 1,80 (c) F - center forward (d) - (e) Taraz, Panevezys, Inter Limeira, Hibernians FC, SV Kapfenberg, Chornomorets, SV Kapfenberg, Mogi Mirim, Arapongas, Mogi Mirim, Icasa, Mogi Mirim

*** Jorge Félix - Jorge Félix (Jorge Félix Muñoz García) (a) 22/08/1991, Madrid (Spain) (b) 1,75 (c) F - left winger (d) Piast Gliwice (e) Sivasspor, Piast Gliwice, Lleida Esportiu, Rayo Majadahonda, Trival Valderas, AD Alcorcón B, Getafe CF B, Moscardó, At. Madrid C

*** Jörgensen - Filip Jörgensen (Filip Jørgensen) (a) 16/04/2002, Lomma (Sweden) (b) 1,90 (c) G (d) Villarreal CF (e) Villarreal CF B, Villarreal CF C

*** Jörgensen - Hans Jörgensen (Hans Jørgensen) (a) 13/08/1990, ¿? (Faroe Islands) (b) 1,84 (c) G (d) B36 Tórshavn (e) B36 II, B68 Toftir, AB Argir, HB Tórshavn, EB/Streymur, HB Tórshavn, B68 Toftir, 07 Vestur, Herfölge BK, Herfölge BK II, FC Amager, Fremad Amager, Skála

*** Jörgensen - Kasper Jörgensen (Kasper Poul Mølgaard Jørgensen) (a) 07/11/1999, ¿? (Denmark) (b) 1,85 (c) D - right back (d) Aalborg BK (e) Lyngby BK, Aalesund, Lyngby BK

*** Jörgensen - Sebastian Jörgensen (Sebastian Vinther Jørgensen) (a) 08/06/2000, Silkeborg (Denmark) (b) 1,83 (c) F - right winger (d) Malmö FF (e) Silkeborg IF

*** Jörgensen - Filip Jörgensen (Filip Rønningen Jørgensen) (a) 27/05/2002, Kragerø (Norway) (b) 1,83 (c) M - central midfielder (d) Odds BK (e) Odd II

*** Jorgic - Nemanja Jorgic (Немања Јоргић) (a) 07/04/1988, Novi Sad (Serbia) (b) 1,86 (c) G (d) FK TSC Backa Topola (e) Beocin, Radnicki Sombor, Sloga Temerin, Spartak, FK Palic Koming, Sloga Temerin

*** Jorginho - Jorginho (Jorge Fernando Barbosa Intima) (a) 21/09/1995, Bissau (Guinea-Bissau) (b) 1,71 (c) F - left winger (d) Ordabasy Shymkent (e) Ludogorets, Wisła Płock, Ludogorets, Wadi Degla, Ludogorets, St.-Étienne, CSKA-Sofia, St.-Étienne, Chaves, St.-Étienne, Arouca, St.-Étienne, Arouca

*** Jorginho - Jorginho (Jorge Luiz Frello Filho) (a) 20/12/1991, Imbituba (Brazil) (b) 1,78 (c) M - pivot (d) Arsenal FC (e) Chelsea, Napoli, Hellas Verona, Sambonifacese, Hellas Verona

*** Jorrín - Juan Jorrín (Juan Cruz Jorrín) (a) 13/02/1995, Buenos Aires (Argentina) (b) - (c) F - center forward (d) - (e) Jonava, Calpe, CF Benidorm, CD Jávea, Alcúdia, CD Tarancón, San Roque Lepe, CD Madridejos, UD Almansa, CD Eldense

*** Jörundsson - Sigurbergur Áki Jörundsson (a) 16/03/2004, ¿? (Iceland) (b) - (c) M - central midfielder (d) HK Kópavogs (e) Stjarnan, Grótta, Stjarnan

*** Josan - Josan (José Antonio Ferrández Pomares) (a) 03/12/1989, Crevillente (Spain) (b) 1,76 (c) F - right winger (d) Elche CF (e) Albacete, UCAM Murcia,

Alcorcón, UCAM Murcia, Alcorcón, Granada CF, SD Huesca, Granada CF, La Hoya Lorca, Crevillente, Villajoyosa CF, UD Horadada
*** José Mari - José Mari (José María Martín Bejarano-Serrano) (a) 06/12/1987, Rota (Cádiz) (Spain) (b) 1,82 (c) M - pivot (d) Cádiz CF (e) Levante UD, Colorado, Real Zaragoza, Real Zaragoza B, Real Jaén CF, Murcia Imperial, Sanluqueño, UD Roteña
*** Josele - Josele (José Antonio Aguilar Gómez) (a) 11/10/1989, Terrassa (Spain) (b) 1,77 (c) F - center forward (d) FS La Massana (e) UE Engordany, CF Esperança, Penya Encarnada, FC Ordino, Sant Julià, IC d'Escaldes, Lusitanos, Terrassa FC
*** Joselito - Joselito (Jose Antonio Gómez Márquez) (a) 09/02/2004, Huelva (Spain) (b) 1,84 (c) M - pivot (d) - (e) Coria CF
*** Joselu - Joselu (José Luis Mato Sanmartín) (a) 27/03/1990, Stuttgart (Germany) (b) 1,91 (c) F - center forward (d) Real Madrid CF (e) Real Madrid, RCD Espanyol, Alavés, Newcastle Utd., Stoke City, RC Deportivo, Stoke City, Hannover 96, Hoffenheim, Eintracht, Hoffenheim, RM Castilla, RC Celta, RM Castilla, RC Celta, Celta B
*** Joseph - Mateo Joseph (Mateo Joseph Fernández Regatillo) (a) 19/10/2003, Santander (Spain) (b) 1,80 (c) F - center forward (d) Leeds United (e) -
*** Jósepsson - Aron Bjarki Jósepsson (a) 21/11/1989, ¿? (Iceland) (b) - (c) D - central defense (d) ÍF Grótta (e) ÍA Akranes, KR Reykjavík, Völsungur ÍF, KR Reykjavík, Völsungur ÍF, KR Reykjavík, Völsungur ÍF
*** Josifoski - Hristijan Josifoski (Христијан Јосифоски) (a) 07/01/2003, Prilep (North Macedonia) (b) 1,83 (c) M - central midfielder (d) ND Slovan Ljubljana (e) Pobeda Prilep
*** Josipovic - Renato Josipovic (Renato Josipović) (a) 12/06/2001, Šibenik (Croatia) (b) - (c) G (d) Pafos FC (e) Siroki Brijeg, Din. Zagreb II, NK Bravo, Din. Zagreb II
*** Josipovic - Zoran Josipovic (Zoran Josipović) (a) 25/08/1995, Mendrisio (Switzerland) (b) 1,91 (c) F - center forward (d) NK Istra 1961 (e) Dinamo Minsk, FC Lugano II, Celta B, Beroe, FC Chiasso, FC Aarau, Juventus, FC Aarau, Juventus, FC Lugano, Juventus, Novara
*** Josué - Josué (Josué Filipe Soares Pesqueira) (a) 17/09/1990, Valongo (Portugal) (b) 1,74 (c) M - attacking midfielder (d) Legia de Varsovia (e) H. Beer Sheva, Akhisarspor, Osmanlispor, FC Porto, Galatasaray, FC Porto, SC Braga, FC Porto, Bursaspor, FC Porto, Bursaspor, FC Porto, Paços Ferreira, FC Porto, VVV-Venlo, FC Porto, Penafiel, FC Porto, SC Covilhã, FC Porto
*** Josviaki - Rodrigo Josviaki (Rodrigo Martins Josviaki) (a) 16/02/1995, Ponta Grossa, Paraná (Brazil) (b) 1,95 (c) G (d) FC Hegelmann (e) Remo, Vilafranquense, Stumbras, Operário-PR, Tupi
*** Jota - Jota (João Paulo dos Santos Pereira) (a) 22/07/2002, Guimarães (Portugal) (b) 1,76 (c) F - left winger (d) Vitória Guimarães SC (e) Vitória Guimarães B
*** Jota - Jota (João Pedro Neves Filipe) (a) 30/03/1999, Lisboa (Portugal) (b) 1,75 (c) F - left winger (d) Ittihad Club (e) Celtic FC, Benfica, Celtic FC, Benfica, Real Valladolid, Benfica, Benfica B
*** Jota Oliveira - Jota Oliveira (João Pedro Espírito Santo Oliveira) (a) 18/09/2002, Lisboa (Portugal) (b) 1,85 (c) G (d) União de Leiria (e) Estoril Praia
*** Jota Silva - Jota Silva (João Pedro Ferreira Silva) (a) 01/08/1999, Gondomar (Portugal) (b) 1,79 (c) F - left winger (d) Vitória Guimarães SC (e) Casa Pia, Leixões, Espinho, Sousense
*** Joubert - Jonathan Joubert (a) 12/09/1979, Metz (France) (b) 1,88 (c) G (d) David Hatstadt (e) F91 Dudelange, Swift Hesperange, F91 Dudelange, CS Grevenmacher, FC Metz B

*** Joury - Gaby Joury (גורי גבי) (a) 16/10/2000, ¿? (Israel) (b) - (c) M - central midfielder (d) Ihud Bnei Sakhnin (e) Hapoel Kaukab, Drava Ptuj, M. Kiryat Ata

*** Jova - Levente Jova (a) 30/01/1992, Orosháza (Hungary) (b) 1,86 (c) G (d) Vasas FC (e) Nyíregyháza, Ferencváros, Soroksár, Ferencváros, Ferencváros II

*** Jovancic - Dusan Jovancic (Душан Јованчић) (a) 19/10/1990, Beograd (Yugoslavia, now in Serbia) (b) 1,86 (c) M - pivot (d) FC Astana (e) Tobol Kostanay, Çaykur Rizespor, Tobol Kostanay, Çaykur Rizespor, Crvena zvezda, Vojvodina, Borac Cacak, FK Zemun, Sumadija, Slavija Beograd

*** Jovane - Jovane (Jovane Eduardo Borges Cabral) (a) 14/06/1998, Assomada (Cabo Verde) (b) 1,74 (c) F - left winger (d) Sporting de Lisboa (e) Lazio, Sporting Lisboa, Sporting B, Nhagar

*** Jovanoski - Gjorgji Jovanoski (Ѓорѓи Јовановски) (a) 07/12/1995, Prilep (North Macedonia) (b) 1,80 (c) G (d) Sloga 1934 (e) Pobeda Prilep, Sloga 1934, Osogovo, Pobeda Prilep

*** Jovanov - Vane Jovanov (Ване Јованов) (a) 28/12/1998, Stip (North Macedonia) (b) 1,77 (c) D - right back (d) Bregalnica Stip (e) Pobeda Prilep, FK Sasa, Vardar, AP Brera, Bregalnica Stip, AP Brera

*** Jovanovic - Aleksandar Jovanovic (Александар Јовановић) (a) 06/12/1992, Niš (RF Yugoslavia, now in Serbia) (b) 1,91 (c) G (d) Partizán Beograd (e) Apollon Limassol, SD Huesca, RC Deportivo, SD Huesca, Aarhus GF, SD Huesca, Aarhus GF, Radnicki Niš, Donji Srem, Rad Beograd, FK Palic Koming, Rad Beograd, FK Palilulac

*** Jovanovic - Djordje Jovanovic (Ђорђе Јовановић) (a) 09/03/2003, Kragujevac (Serbia and Montenegro, now in Serbia) (b) 1,87 (c) F - left winger (d) FK Radnicki 1923 Kragujevac (e) -

*** Jovanovic - Djordje Jovanovic (Ђорђе Јовановић) (a) 15/02/1999, Leposavić (RF Yugoslavia, now in Kosovo) (b) 1,87 (c) F - center forward (d) Maccabi Tel Aviv (e) Čukarički, Cádiz CF, FC Cartagena, Cádiz CF, KSC Lokeren, FK Partizan

*** Jovanovic - Djordje Jovanovic (Ђорђе Јовановић) (a) 17/08/2001, Užice (RF Yugoslavia, now in Serbia) (b) 1,74 (c) F - right winger (d) FK Napredak Krusevac (e) Sloga Požega

*** Jovanovic - Igor Jovanovic (Igor Jovanović) (a) 03/05/1989, Zagreb (Yugoslavia, now in Croatia) (b) 1,86 (c) D - central defense (d) - (e) FC Brasov-SR, FC Dinamo, Suduva, Astra Giurgiu, Seongnam FC, Panetolikos, Sepsi OSK, FC Lahti, Bnei Sakhnin, Miedź Legnica, TPS, FF Jaro, Rot-Weiß Erfurt, Babelsberg 03, TPS, 1.FC Kleve, Wacker Burghausen

*** Jovanovic - Lazar Jovanovic (Лазар Јовановић) (a) 13/07/1993, Užice (RF Yugoslavia, now in Serbia) (b) 1,82 (c) F - right winger (d) - (e) M. Bnei Reineh, Radnicki Niš, Pyunik Yerevan, Mladost, Borac Cacak, Mladost, Sloboda Užice

*** Jovanovic - Sasa Jovanovic (Саша Јовановић) (a) 15/12/1991, Lazarevac (Yugoslavia, now in Serbia) (b) 1,76 (c) F - right winger (d) FK TSC Backa Topola (e) Mladost, Al-Fateh, RC Deportivo, Al-Fateh, Córdoba CF, Mladost, Smederevo 1924, Kolubara

*** Jovanovic - Sasa Jovanovic (Саша Јовановић) (a) 30/08/1993, Beograd (RF Yugoslavia, now in Serbia) (b) 1,84 (c) F - left winger (d) FK Novi Pazar (e) Radnicki Niš, Radnicki 1923, Rad Beograd, FK Indjija, Wolfsberger AC, Čukarički, FK Bezanija, Mladost, Vozdovac, Rad Beograd, BASK Beograd, Rad Beograd, FK Palic Koming, Rad Beograd, Teleoptik

*** Jovanovic - Stefan Jovanovic (Стефан Јовановић) (a) 07/04/1994, Kraljevo (RF Yugoslavia, now in Serbia) (b) 1,78 (c) D - right back (d) FK Napredak Krusevac (e)

Backa, Proleter, Backa, Mladost, FK Zemun, Radnicki Pirot, Zeleznicar Lajkovac, FK Zvizd, FK Bane Raska

*** Jovanovic - Veljko Jovanovic (Вељко Јовановић) (a) 02/07/2001, Jagodina (RF Yugoslavia, now in Serbia) (b) 1,92 (c) F - center forward (d) FK Rad Belgrado (e) Radnik, Studentski Grad, FK Pomoravlje, Jagodina

*** Jovanovic - Vukasin Jovanovic (Вукашин Јовановић) (a) 17/05/1996, Beograd (RF Yugoslavia, now in Serbia) (b) 1,88 (c) D - central defense (d) FK Čukarički (e) Apollon Limassol, Girondins Bordeaux, SD Eibar, Girondins Bordeaux, Zenit, Girondins Bordeaux, Zenit, Crvena zvezda

*** Jovanović - Andjelko Jovanović (Анђелко Јовановић) (a) 18/11/1999, Tuzi (RF Yugoslavia, Montenegro) (b) 1,77 (c) M - central midfielder (d) FK Podgorica (e) FK Decic Tuzi, Mornar Bar, FK Decic Tuzi, FK Podgorica, FK Decic Tuzi

*** Jovanovikj - Martin Jovanovikj (Мартин Јовановиќ) (a) 04/03/2006, Kumanovo (North Macedonia) (b) 1,75 (c) M - pivot (d) - (e) Makedonija Gjorce Petrov

*** Jovanovski - Marko Jovanovski (Марко Јовановски) (a) 24/07/1988, Skopje (Yugoslavia, now in North Macedonia) (b) 1,86 (c) G (d) KF Ferizaj (e) AP Brera, Gostivar, Makedonija, Sepsi OSK, Pelister Bitola, Shkëndija, Ethnikos, Shkëndija, Teteks Tetovo, Vardar, Rabotnicki

*** Jovetic - Stevan Jovetic (Стеван Јоветић) (a) 02/11/1989, Titograd (now Podgorica) (Yugoslavia, now in Montenegro) (b) 1,83 (c) F - center forward (d) - (e) Hertha Berlin, AS Monaco, Internazionale Milano, Sevilla FC, Internazionale Milano, Manchester City, Internazionale Milano, Manchester City, Fiorentina, FK Partizan

*** Jovic - Filip Jovic (Филип Јовић) (a) 27/02/2000, Leskovac (RF Yugoslavia, now in Serbia) (b) 1,82 (c) D - left back (d) - (e) Novi Pazar, Spartak, Zeleznicar Pancevo, Spartak, Smederevo 1924, Spartak

*** Jovic - Luka Jovic (Лука Јовић) (a) 23/12/1997, Bijeljina (Bosnia and Herzegovina) (b) 1,82 (c) F - center forward (d) Fiorentina (e) Real Madrid, Eintracht, Real Madrid, Eintracht, Benfica, Eintracht, Benfica, Apollon Limassol, Crvena zvezda

*** Jovic - Nemanja Jovic (Немања Јовић) (a) 08/08/2002, Zvornik (Bosnia and Herzegovina) (b) 1,78 (c) F - left winger (d) Partizán Beograd (e) Teleoptik

*** Jovic - Toni Jovic (Toni Jović) (a) 02/09/1992, Nova Gradiška (Croatia) (b) 1,78 (c) F - right winger (d) - (e) HSK Posusje, Borac Banja Luka, Águilas FC, FK Krupa, Siroki Brijeg, SF Lotte, Zrinjski Mostar, Borac Banja Luka, HNK Rijeka, NK Krk, HNK Rijeka, NK Grobnican, HNK Rijeka, NK Pomorac, HNK Rijeka, NK Krk, Mladost Cernik, Sloga NG

*** Jovicevic - Nikola Jovicevic (Nikola Jovićević) (a) 30/09/2003, ¿? (Slovenia) (b) 1,85 (c) M - attacking midfielder (d) NS Mura (e) Domžale

*** Jovicic - Aleksandar Jovicic (Aleksandar Jovičić) (a) 18/07/1995, Banja Luka (Bosnia and Herzegovina) (b) 1,89 (c) D - central defense (d) Kisvárda FC (e) HNK Gorica, Slaven Belupo, NK Istra, Slaven Belupo, Rudar Prijedor, Borac Banja Luka, FK Krupa, Borac Banja Luka, Rudar Prijedor

*** Jovicic - Branko Jovicic (Бранко Јовичић) (a) 18/03/1993, Raska (Yugoslavia, now in Serbia) (b) 1,79 (c) M - pivot (d) LASK (e) Ural, Crvena zvezda, Amkar Perm, LASK, Amkar Perm, LASK, Borac Cacak

*** Jovicic - Marko Jovicic (Марко Јовичић) (a) 02/02/1995, Beograd (RF Yugoslavia, now in Serbia) (b) 1,87 (c) G (d) - (e) Hibernians FC, Velez Mostar, Mosta FC, FK Indjija, FK Partizan, Hibernians FC, FK Partizan, Teleoptik, Zarkovo

*** Jovicic - Nemanja Jovicic (Немања Јовичић) (a) 13/04/2000, Čačak (RF Yugoslavia, now in Serbia) (b) - (c) D - left back (d) FK Metalac Gornji Milanovac (e) Radnicki Niš, Car Konstantin, Radnicki Niš, Takovo Milanova

*** Jovkovic - Vukasin Jovkovic (Букашин Јовковић) (a) 12/01/2001, Kruševac (RF Yugoslavia, now in Serbia) (b) - (c) Г - center forward (d) Radnicki Obrenovac (e) Makedonija, Olympiakos N., Zeleznicar Pancevo, Vrsac, Zeleznicar Pancevo, Vrsac, Zeleznicar Pancevo, Internacional
*** Jovovic - Vladimir Jovovic (Владимир Јововић) (a) 26/10/1994, Niksic (Yugoslavia, now in Montenegro) (b) 1,73 (c) F - left winger (d) FK Jablonec (e) Sutjeska Niksic, Jablonec, Crvena zvezda, Spartak, Crvena zvezda, Napredak, Crvena zvezda, OFK Beograd, Crvena zvezda, Sutjeska Niksic
*** Jozefzoon - Florian Jozefzoon (Florian Marc Jozefzoon) (a) 09/02/1991, Saint-Laurent-du-Maroni (Guayana Francesa) (b) 1,73 (c) F - right winger (d) Bandirmaspor (e) RKC Waalwijk, Quevilly Rouen, Derby, Rotherham, Derby, Brentford, PSV Eindhoven, RKC Waalwijk, Ajax, NAC Breda, Ajax, Ajax B
*** Jradi - Bassel Jradi (Bassel Zakaria Jradi) (a) 06/07/1993, København (Denmark) (b) 1,87 (c) M - attacking midfielder (d) True Bangkok United (e) Apollon Limassol, Hajduk Split, Strømsgodset, Lillestrøm, Strømsgodset, Nordsjælland, Akademisk BK
*** Juampe - Juampe (Juan Pedro Rico Domínguez) (a) 24/05/1984, Tarifa (Spain) (b) 1,64 (c) F - right winger (d) Lincoln Red Imps FC (e) Europa FC, R. B. Linense, Los Barrios, Algeciras CF, Algeciras B, UD Tarifa, Atlético Zabal
*** Juan Carlos - Juan Carlos (Juan Carlos Martín Corral) (a) 20/01/1988, Guadalajara (Spain) (b) 1,87 (c) G (d) Girona FC (e) CD Lugo, Elche CF, Rayo Vallecano, Córdoba CF, Hércules CF, Rayo Vallecano, Rayo B
*** Juan Felipe - Juan Felipe (Juan Felipe Alves Ribeiro) (a) 05/12/1987, São Vicente (Brazil) (b) 1,75 (c) M - attacking midfielder (d) - (e) Nea Salamis, EN Paralimniou, Bangu-RJ, Shkëndija, Vardar, Kairat Almaty, Vardar, CSKA Sofia, São Carlos, Oriente P., RB Brasil, Santo André
*** Juan Jesus - Juan Jesus (Juan Guilherme Nunes Jesus) (a) 10/06/1991, Belo Horizonte (Brazil) (b) 1,85 (c) D - central defense (d) SSC Nápoles (e) AS Roma, Internazionale Milano, AS Roma, Internazionale Milano, Internacional, Inter B
*** Juanfri - Juanfri (Juan Francisco García Peña) (a) 01/10/1989, Fuengirola (Spain) (b) 1,80 (c) F - center forward (d) Lincoln Red Imps FC (e) St Joseph's FC, Antequera, Saburtalo, Lincoln FC, Marbella FC, UD San Pedro, Écija Balompié, SC de Goa, Écija Balompié, At. Malagueño, Unión Estepona, Fuengirola
*** Juankar - Juankar (Juan Carlos Pérez López) (a) 30/03/1990, Boadilla del Monte (Spain) (b) 1,79 (c) D - left back (d) Panathinaikos FC (e) Málaga CF, SC Braga, Málaga CF, SC Braga, Granada CF, SC Braga, Real Betis, SC Braga, Real Zaragoza, SC Braga, RM Castilla, Real Madrid C
*** Juanma - Juanma (Juan Manuel Gonzáles Pérez) (a) 02/05/1991, ¿? (Spain) (b) 1,87 (c) M - attacking midfielder (d) St Joseph's FC (e) Los Barrios, Glacis United, C. Elblag, San Roque Cádiz, Cádiz CF B
*** Juanmi - Juanmi (Juan Miguel Jiménez López) (a) 20/05/1993, Coín (Spain) (b) 1,72 (c) F - left winger (d) Real Betis Balompié (e) Real Sociedad, Southampton, Málaga CF, Racing, Málaga CF, At. Malagueño
*** Juanpe - Juanpe (Juan Pedro Ramírez López) (a) 30/04/1991, Las Palmas de Gran Canaria (Spain) (b) 1,90 (c) D - central defense (d) Girona FC (e) Granada CF, Real Valladolid, Granada CF, Racing, Granada B, Racing, UD Las Palmas, Las Palmas At.
*** Juanpi - Juanpi (Juan Pablo Añor Acosta) (a) 24/01/1994, Caracas (Venezuela) (b) 1,76 (c) M - attacking midfielder (d) Panetolikos GFS (e) Caracas FC, Al-Ain FC, Málaga CF, SD Huesca, Málaga CF, At. Malagueño
*** Juárez - Fernando Juárez (Fernando Ezequiel Juárez) (a) 23/08/1998, Santiago del Estero (SES) (Argentina) (b) 1,77 (c) M - central midfielder (d) Audax Italiano (e) Audax Italiano, Talleres, Floriana, Talleres, Talleres II, Agropecuario, Talleres II

*** Jubal - Jubal (Jubal Rocha Mendes Júnior) (a) 29/08/1993, Inhumas (Brazil) (b) 1,90 (c) D - central defense (d) AJ Auxerre (e) Vitória Setúbal, Arouca, Boavista, Arouca, Portimonense, Arouca, Vitória Guimarães, Arouca, Santos, Avaí FC, Santos, Vila Nova FC, Santos, Vila Nova FC
*** Juberg-Hovland - Leon-Robin Juberg-Hovland (a) 09/05/2004, Molde (Norway) (b) - (c) M (d) Molde FK II (e) -
*** Juelsgaard - Jesper Juelsgaard (Jesper Lindorff Juelsgård) (a) 26/01/1989, Spjald (Denmark) (b) 1,82 (c) D - central defense (d) FC Fredericia (e) Valur, Aarhus GF, Brøndby IF, Évian, Midtjylland, Skive IK, Midtjylland
*** Jug - Azbe Jug (Ažbe Jug) (a) 03/03/1992, Maribor (Slovenia) (b) 1,92 (c) G (d) NK Maribor (e) Fortuna Sittard, Sporting Lisboa, Girondins Bordeaux, NK Interblock
*** Jug - Patrik Jug (a) 04/02/2002, Zagreb (Croatia) (b) 1,82 (c) M - pivot (d) ND Ilirija 1911 (e) HNK Gorica
*** Jugas - Jakub Jugas (Jakub Jugas) (a) 05/05/1992, Zlín (Czechoslovakia, Czech Rep.) (b) 1,88 (c) D - central defense (d) Cracovia (e) Slavia Praha, Slovan Liberec, Slavia Praha, Jablonec, Slavia Praha, Mlada Boleslav, Slavia Praha, Fastav Zlin, Zbrojovka Brno, Fastav Zlin, 1.FK Pribram, Fastav Zlin
*** Jugovic - Vedran Jugovic (Vedran Jugović) (a) 31/07/1989, Osijek (Yugoslavia, now in Croatia) (b) 1,78 (c) M - central midfielder (d) NK Osijek (e) Jeonnam Dragons, HNK Rijeka, Jeonnam Dragons, HNK Rijeka, NK Osijek, NK Olimpija Osijek
*** Juhkam - Gerdo Juhkam (a) 19/06/1994, Paide (Estonia) (b) 1,89 (c) D - central defense (d) Paide Linnameeskond (e) JK Tammeka, JK Viljandi, Paide, JK Viljandi, FC Flora, FC Flora II, JK Viljandi
*** Juhl - Mikkel Juhl (Mikkel Juhl Aagaard Andersen) (a) 29/01/2000, Præstø (Denmark) (b) 1,78 (c) D - right back (d) FC Fredericia (e) FC Fredericia, Lyngby BK, Nyköbing FC
*** Jukic - Aleksandar Jukic (Aleksandar Jukić) (a) 26/07/2000, Wien (Austria) (b) 1,83 (c) M - central midfielder (d) FK Austria Viena (e) Young Violets
*** Jukic - Ivan Jukic (Ivan Jukić) (a) 21/06/1996, Split (Croatia) (b) 1,76 (c) F - left winger (d) HSK Zrinjski Mostar (e) FK Sarajevo, Korona Kielce, RNK Split, NK Imotski, RNK Split, Orkan Dugi Rat
*** Jukic - Matej Jukic (Matej Jukić) (a) 07/04/1997, Split (Croatia) (b) 1,84 (c) M - attacking midfielder (d) - (e) ND Gorica, NK Solin, Croat. Zmijavci, Slaven Belupo, NK Dugopolje, NK Rudes, SC Freiburg II, RNK Split
*** Jukkola - Oiva Jukkola (a) 21/05/2002, ¿? (Finland) (b) 1,85 (c) F - right winger (d) Ilves Tampere (e) Ilves II
*** Jukl - Robert Jukl (a) 28/10/1998, ¿? (Slovakia) (b) 1,81 (c) M - central midfielder (d) FK Teplice (e) Hradec Kralove, Teplice, Hradec Kralove
*** Juklerød - Simen Juklerød (Simen Kristiansen Juklerød) (a) 18/05/1994, Bærum (Norway) (b) 1,87 (c) D - left back (d) Vålerenga Fotball (e) KRC Genk, Royal Antwerp, Vålerenga, Bærum
*** Julardzija - Edin Julardzija (Edin Julardžija) (a) 21/01/2001, Zagreb (Croatia) (b) 1,73 (c) M - attacking midfielder (d) NK Domžale (e) HNK Gorica, Din. Zagreb II, HNK Sibenik, Din. Zagreb II, HNK Sibenik, Din. Zagreb II, Slaven Belupo, Din. Zagreb II
*** Julerson - Julerson (Julerson Dias de Oliveira da Silva) (a) 06/08/1996, Santa Rita do Sapucaí (Brazil) (b) 1,75 (c) M - attacking midfielder (d) Glacis United (e) Järpens IF, Portimonense B, Castrense, Moimenta Beira, Tupynambás
*** Jules - Jean Jules (Jean Jules Sepp Mvondo) (a) 23/04/1998, Yaoundé (Cameroon) (b) 1,77 (c) M - pivot (d) Aris Thessaloniki (e) Górnik Zabrze, Albacete,

Górnik Zabrze, Albacete, Rayo Majadahonda, Albacete, UCAM Murcia, Albacete, Rayo B

*** Julião - Igor Julião (Igor de Carvalho Julião) (a) 23/08/1994, Leopoldina (Brazil) (b) 1,75 (c) D - right back (d) CS Marítimo (e) Vizela, Fluminense, STK Samorin, Fluminense, Kansas City, Fluminense, Ferroviária, Fluminense, Macaé, Fluminense, ABC FC, Fluminense, Kansas City, Fluminense

*** Julien - Keston Julien (Keston Anthony Julien) (a) 26/10/1998, Port of Spain (Trinidad and Tobago) (b) 1,81 (c) D - left back (d) - (e) FC Sheriff, AS Trencin, SJ Jabloteh, W Connection

*** Julio - Junior Julio (José Junior Julio Bueno) (a) 03/09/1996, Riohacha (Colombia) (b) 1,90 (c) D - central defense (d) FC Ararat-Armenia (e) Once Caldas, Def. Belgrano

*** Júlio Vinícius - Júlio Vinícius (Júlio Vinícius da Fonseca Souza) (a) 04/02/2002, Brasília (Brazil) (b) 1,72 (c) F - left winger (d) - (e) Saburtalo, Dinamo Batumi

*** Julis - Lukas Julis (Lukáš Juliš) (a) 02/12/1994, Chrudim (Czech Rep.) (b) 1,88 (c) F - center forward (d) SK Sigma Olomouc (e) Sparta Praha, UD Ibiza, Sparta Praha, Sigma Olomouc, Sparta Praha, Bohemians 1905, Sparta Praha, Sparta Praha B

*** Jullien - Christopher Jullien (a) 22/03/1993, Lagny-sur-Marne (France) (b) 1,96 (c) D - central defense (d) Montpellier HSC (e) Celtic FC, Toulouse, SC Freiburg, Dijon, SC Freiburg, SC Freiburg II, SC Freiburg, AJ Auxerre, AJ Auxerre B

*** Jumakulov - Abbosbek Jumakulov (Жумакулов Аббосбек Фахриддин Угли) (a) 01/06/1999, ¿? (Uzbekistan) (b) - (c) M - left midfielder (d) Bunyodkor-Farm Tashkent (e) Energetik-BGU, Bunyodkor-Farm, FK Buxoro

*** Junas - Martin Junas (a) 09/03/1996, Skalica (Slovakia) (b) 1,87 (c) G (d) MFK Skalica (e) MSK Breclav, FK Senica, Topolcany, FK Senica

*** Juncaj - Steven Juncaj (Steven George Juncaj) (a) 08/03/1998, Sterling Heights, Michigan (United States) (b) 1,88 (c) M - left midfielder (d) - (e) ND Gorica, Michigan Stars

*** Jung - Anthony Jung (a) 03/11/1991, Villajoyosa (Spain) (b) 1,86 (c) D - left back (d) SV Werder Bremen (e) Brøndby IF, RB Leipzig, Brøndby IF, RB Leipzig, FC Ingolstadt, RB Leipzig, FSV Frankfurt, Eintracht II

*** Jungdal - Andreas Jungdal (Andreas Kristoffer Jungdal) (a) 22/02/2002, Singapore (Singapore) (b) 1,95 (c) G (d) US Cremonese (e) AC Milan, SCR Altach, AC Milan

*** Junge - Thomas Junge (a) 20/12/2002, Filskov (Denmark) (b) - (c) F - center forward (d) - (e) AB Argir, Hobro IK

*** Jungwirth - Lukas Jungwirth (a) 30/04/2004, ¿? (Austria) (b) 1,93 (c) G (d) LASK (e) Amateure OÖ

*** Juninho - Juninho (Carlos Jamisson Teles dos Santos Junior) (a) 29/07/1995, ¿? (Brazil) (b) 1,77 (c) D - left back (d) FC Pyunik Yerevan (e) Paraná, Itabaiana, Freipaulistano, Confiança, AD Bahia-BA, Flamengo-SP

*** Juninho - Juninho (José Carlos Ferreira Júnior) (a) 01/02/1995, Londrina (Brazil) (b) 1,87 (c) D - central defense (d) FC Midtjylland (e) Palmeiras, EC Bahia, Palmeiras, EC Bahia, Palmeiras, At. Mineiro, Palmeiras, Coritiba FC

*** Juninho - Juninho (Leovigildo Júnior Reis Rodrigues) (a) 26/12/1995, Cataguases (Brazil) (b) 1,75 (c) D - left back (d) - (e) Pafos FC, Zorya Lugansk, Vardar, Makedonija, Salgueiro, Tupi, Metropolitano

*** Juninho - Juninho (Olávio Vieira dos Santos Júnior) (a) 21/11/1996, Pitangui (Brazil) (b) 1,79 (c) F - right winger (d) Qarabağ FK (e) Chaves, Athletico-PR B, Estoril Praia, Athletico-PR B, Vila Nova FC, Athletico-PR B, Figueirense FC,

Atlético-PR B, Novorizontino, Atlético-PR B, Brasil Pelotas, Atlético-PR B, Portimonense, Atlético-PR B

*** Juninho Carpina - Juninho Carpina (Jose Roberto da Silva Lima Junior) (a) 09/03/2000, Recife (Brazil) (b) 1,72 (c) F - left winger (d) CE Operário Várzea-Grandense (e) Akritas Chlor., Náutico, América-PE

*** Junior - Junior (Jorge Vicente Camargo) (a) 18/10/2002, Elche (Spain) (b) - (c) M - central midfielder (d) Penya Encarnada d'Andorra (e) FC Ordino, IC d'Escaldes, FC Andorra B

*** Júnior - Eliton Júnior (Eliton Pardinho Toreta Júnior) (a) 26/01/1998, São Mateus (Brazil) (b) 1,81 (c) M - attacking midfielder (d) Kuopion Palloseura (e) KuPS, Varbergs BoIS, RB Brasil, Lokomotiv Plovdiv

*** Júnior - Francisco Júnior (Francisco Santos da Silva Júnior) (a) 18/01/1992, Bissau (Guinea-Bissau) (b) 1,72 (c) M - central midfielder (d) Sepsi OSK Sf. Gheorghe (e) Gaz Metan, Hapoel Haifa, Vendsyssel FF, Strømsgodset, Everton, Wigan Ath., Everton, Port Vale, Everton, Strømsgodset, Everton, Vitesse, Everton, Benfica de Biss

*** Júnior - Lago Júnior (Junior Waka Lible Lago) (a) 31/12/1990, Yamoussoukro (Ivory Coast) (b) 1,80 (c) F - left winger (d) Real Racing Club (e) Málaga CF, RCD Mallorca, SD Huesca, RCD Mallorca, CD Mirandés, Gimnàstic, CD Numancia, SD Eibar, CD Numancia, Issia Wazi FC

*** Júnior Brumado - Júnior Brumado (José Francisco dos Santos Júnior) (a) 15/05/1999, Brumado (Brazil) (b) 1,90 (c) F - center forward (d) FC Midtjylland (e) Silkeborg IF, Midtjylland, EC Bahia, Bahia B

*** Júnior Caiçara - Júnior Caiçara (Uilson de Souza Paula Júnior) (a) 27/04/1989, São Paulo (Brazil) (b) 1,73 (c) D - right back (d) - (e) Basaksehir, FC Schalke 04, Ludogorets, Santo André, Gil Vicente, Santo André, América-SP, Santo André, CSA, Santo André, CSA, Santo André, Santo André B

*** Júnior Morais - Júnior Morais (Iraneuton Sousa Morais Júnior) (a) 22/07/1986, São Luís (Brazil) (b) 1,76 (c) D - left back (d) FC Rapid 1923 (e) Gaziantep FK, FCSB, Astra Giurgiu, Freamunde, São Cristóvão

*** Júnior Palmares - Júnior Palmares (José Ederaldo da Silva Júnior) (a) 14/04/1997, Palmares-PE (Brazil) (b) 1,75 (c) M - attacking midfielder (d) - (e) Arda Kardzhali, Manaus FC, São Bernardo, Linense, XV de Jaú, Penapolense, Central

*** Juranovic - Dragan Juranovic (Dragan Juranović) (a) 10/02/1994, Zagreb (Croatia) (b) 1,78 (c) F - left winger (d) NK Dubrava Tim kabel (e) Zrinjski Mostar, NK Dubrava ZG, NK Osijek II, NK Rudes, NK Osijek II, NK Dubrava ZG

*** Juranovic - Josip Juranovic (Josip Juranović) (a) 16/08/1995, Zagreb (Croatia) (b) 1,73 (c) D - right back (d) 1.FC Union Berlin (e) Celtic FC, Legia Warszawa, Hajduk Split, NK Dubrava ZG

*** Jurasek - Matej Jurasek (Matěj Jurásek) (a) 30/08/2003, ¿? (Czech Rep.) (b) 1,81 (c) F - right winger (d) SK Slavia Praga (e) Slavia Praha B, Vlasim, Slavia Praha B, Karvina, Slavia Praha B, Vlasim, Slavia Praha B

*** Jurásek - David Jurásek (a) 07/08/2000, Dolní Němčí (Czech Rep.) (b) 1,83 (c) D - left back (d) SL Benfica (e) Slavia Praha, Mlada Boleslav, 1.SK Prostejov, Zbrojovka Brno, FCZ Brno B

*** Jurca - Alen Jurca (a) 15/01/2001, ¿? (Slovenia) (b) 1,84 (c) G (d) ND Gorica (e) Tabor Sezana, NK Dekani

*** Jurcec - Jan Jurcec (Jan Jurčec) (a) 27/11/2000, Zagreb (Croatia) (b) 1,77 (c) M - right midfielder (d) SCR Altach (e) NK Kustosija

*** Jurcec - Jurica Jurcec (Jurica Jurčec) (a) 04/04/2002, Zabok (Croatia) (b) 1,76 (c) F - right winger (d) SCR Altach (e) NK Jarun, NK Krsko, NK Tondach

*** Jurcenko - David Jurcenko (David Jurčenko) (a) 28/01/2004, ¿? (Czech Rep.) (b) 1,81 (c) F - center forward (d) MFK Chrudim (e) Hradec Kralove B

*** Jurcevic - Mario Jurcevic (a) 01/06/1995, Ljubljana (Slovenia) (b) 1,86 (c) D - left back (d) Apollon Limassol (e) NK Osijek, Olimpija, NK Aluminij, Olimpija, NK Radomlje

*** Jurecka - Vaclav Jurecka (Václav Jurečka) (a) 26/06/1994, ¿? (Czech Rep.) (b) 1,82 (c) F - center forward (d) SK Slavia Praga (e) Slovácko, SFC Opava, FK Kolin, SFC Opava

*** Jurgelevicius - Darius Jurgelevicius (a) 24/02/2003, ¿? (Lithuania) (b) - (c) M (d) FK Neptunas Klaipeda (e) Panevezys B

*** Jurgelis - Evaldas Jurgelis (a) 21/01/2002, ¿? (Lithuania) (b) 1,93 (c) G (d) - (e) FA Siauliai

*** Jürgenson - Markus Jürgenson (a) 09/09/1987, Tartu (Soviet Union, now in Estonia) (b) 1,80 (c) D - right back (d) - (e) FCI Levadia, VPS, FC Flora, TVMK Tallinn, Tammeka Tartu, JK Tammeka II

*** Jurhar - Metod Jurhar (a) 07/12/1997, ¿? (Slovenia) (b) 1,88 (c) G (d) NK Celje (e) -

*** Juric - Ante Matej Juric (Ante Matej Jurić) (a) 26/11/2002, Osijek (Croatia) (b) - (c) F - center forward (d) HNK Gorica (e) NK Belisce, NK Cepin, Elektra Osijek

*** Juric - Deni Juric (Deni Jurić) (a) 03/09/1997, Kogarah (Australia) (b) 1,89 (c) F - center forward (d) GNK Dinamo Zagreb (e) HNK Rijeka, Dinamo Zagreb, HNK Gorica, Dinamo Zagreb, HNK Sibenik, Dinamo Zagreb, HNK Sibenik, NK Rudes, NK Solin, NK Triglav, Hajduk Split II, NK Solin, Hajduk Split II, Croat. Prigorje

*** Juric - Marko Juric (Marko Jurić) (a) 07/10/1994, Dubrovnik (Croatia) (b) 1,87 (c) D - central defense (d) KF Vllaznia (e) Siroki Brijeg, NK Lokomotiva, Siroki Brijeg, NK Lokomotiva, NK Dugopolje, NK Lokomotiva, NK Dugopolje, GOSK-Dubrovnik, HNK Sibenik, Segesta Sisak, FC Zlin B, Adriatic Split, NK Val

*** Juricic - Luka Juricic (Luka Juričić) (a) 25/11/1996, Neustadt an der Aisch (Germany) (b) 1,90 (c) F - center forward (d) FC Pyunik Yerevan (e) Gimpo FC, Zeljeznicar, HNK Sibenik, Neretva Metkovic, NK Neretvanac, Siroki Brijeg, NK Neretvanac

*** Jurilj - Alen Jurilj (a) 07/03/1996, Zagreb (Croatia) (b) 1,87 (c) F - left winger (d) FK Borac Banja Luka (e) Domžale, Siroki Brijeg, Din. Zagreb II, NK Kustosija, Din. Zagreb II, NK Zagreb

*** Jurina - Marin Jurina (a) 26/11/1993, Livno (Bosnia and Herzegovina) (b) 1,88 (c) F - center forward (d) Diósgyőri VTK (e) Al-Faisaly FC, Mezőkövesd, Celik Zenica, FC Shkupi, Celik Zenica, NK Krsko, Koper, NK Ankaran, Koper, HNK Capljina, Etzella Ettelbrück, NK Zadar, Zrinjski Mostar, Hajduk Split, Primorac 1929, Hajduk Split, Sloga Uskoplje

*** Jurisic - Roko Jurisic (Roko Jurišić) (a) 28/09/2001, Zagreb (Croatia) (b) 1,73 (c) D - left back (d) NS Mura (e) SV Ried, HNK Rijeka, Hrv Dragovoljac, HNK Rijeka, Din. Zagreb II, NK Samobor

*** Jürisoo - Taavi Jürisoo (a) 23/05/2005, Tallinn (Estonia) (b) - (c) F - right winger (d) Kalev Tallinn (e) -

*** Jurkovskis - Raivis Jurkovskis (Raivis Andris Jurkovskis) (a) 09/12/1996, Liepaja (Latvia) (b) 1,87 (c) D - right back (d) Riga FC (e) Dundalk FC, Liepaja, RFS, Liepaja, FHK Liepajas Metalurgs II

*** Juroska - Jan Juroska (Jan Juroška) (a) 02/03/1993, Valašské Meziříčí (Czech Rep.) (b) 1,80 (c) D - right back (d) FC Banik Ostrava (e) Slovácko, Dukla Praha, FC MAS Taborsko, Dukla Praha, Varnsdorf, Dukla Praha, Dukla B

*** Juroska - Pavel Juroska (Pavel Juroška) (a) 07/07/2001, ¿? (Czech Rep.) (b) - (c) M - right midfielder (d) 1.FC Slovácko (e) Slovácko B

*** Jürs - Joakim Jürs (a) 15/12/1996, ¿? (Denmark) (b) 2,00 (c) G (d) Skála IF (e) B68 Toftir, IF Bjaeverkov

*** Jusic - Emir Jusic (Emir Jusić) (a) 13/06/1986, Zenica (Yugoslavia, now in Bosnia and Herzegovina) (b) 1,87 (c) D - central defense (d) - (e) Sloboda Tuzla, FK Olimpik, Celik Zenica, Akzhayik, Celik Zenica, FK Buducnost, Celik Zenica, FK Rudar Kakanj, Celik Zenica

*** Just - Elijah Just (Elijah Henry Just) (a) 01/05/2000, Palmerston North (New Zealand) (b) 1,74 (c) F - right winger (d) AC Horsens (e) FC Helsingör, Eastern Suburbs

*** Justin - James Justin (James Michael Justin) (a) 23/02/1998, Luton (England) (b) 1,83 (c) D - right back (d) Leicester City (e) Luton Town

*** Justin - Klemen Justin (a) 12/06/2002, ¿? (Slovenia) (b) - (c) F - left winger (d) NK Roltek Dob (e) NK Radomlje, NK Dob

*** Justinek - Domen Justinek (a) 18/03/2004, ¿? (Slovenia) (b) - (c) F (d) - (e) NK Celje

*** Justiniano - Pedro Justiniano (Pedro Justiniano Almeida Gomes) (a) 18/04/2000, Vicenza (Italy) (b) 1,90 (c) D - central defense (d) Petrolul Ploiesti (e) Petrolul, Radomiak, Académica Coimbra, FC Porto B

*** Justinussen - Adrian Justinussen (Adrian Rúnason Justinussen) (a) 21/07/1998, Tórshavn (Faroe Islands) (b) 1,80 (c) F - center forward (d) HB Tórshavn (e) HB Tórshavn II

*** Justinussen - Finnur Justinussen (a) 30/03/1989, Tórshavn (Faroe Islands) (b) 1,83 (c) F - center forward (d) Víkingur Gøta (e) FC Roskilde, IF Føroyar, Naestved BK, Fremad Amager, Naestved BK, Fremad Amager, Víkingur, Fremad Amager, Víkingur, J-Södra IF, Víkingur

*** Jusuf - Alpaj Jusuf (a) 26/03/1998, Kumanovo (North Macedonia) (b) 1,77 (c) M - pivot (d) Baskimi (e) Detonit, FK Skopje, Pelister Bitola, Kadino, Pehcevo, Sileks, Lokomotiva

*** Jusuf - Mustafa Jusuf (a) 01/04/2000, Skopje (North Macedonia) (b) 1,72 (c) F - right winger (d) Teteks Tetovo (e) FK Skopje

*** Jusufi - Fatjon Jusufi (a) 17/12/1995, Tetovo (North Macedonia) (b) 1,79 (c) F - attacking midfielder (d) Gostivar (e) Struga, Renova, FC Shkupi, Shirak Gyumri, FK Partizani, Renova

*** Jutglà - Ferran Jutglà (Ferran Jutglà Blanch) (a) 01/02/1999, Sant Julià de Vilatorta (Spain) (b) 1,75 (c) F - center forward (d) KV Brugge (e) Barcelona Atlètic, RCD Espanyol B, Sant Andreu, RCD Espanyol B, Vic Riuprimer

*** Juwara - Musa Juwara (a) 26/12/2001, Tujereng (Gambia) (b) 1,70 (c) F - left winger (d) Vejle Boldklub (e) Bologna, Odense BK, Bologna, Crotone, Bologna, Boavista, Bologna

*** Jyry - Tommi Jyry (a) 16/08/1999, Helsinki (Finland) (b) 1,70 (c) M - central midfielder (d) FC Inter Turku (e) KuPS, Helsinki IFK

*** Kaalund - Mads Kaalund (Mads Kaalund Larsen) (a) 16/08/1996, Kopenhagen (Denmark) (b) 1,82 (c) M - central midfielder (d) Hvidovre IF (e) Silkeborg IF, Nyköbing FC, Lyngby BK

*** Kaasa - Markus André Kaasa (a) 15/07/1997, ¿? (Norway) (b) 1,75 (c) M - central midfielder (d) Molde FK (e) Odd, Odd II, Hei IL

*** Kaastrup - Magnus Kaastrup (Magnus Kaastrup Refstrup Lauritsen) (a) 28/12/2000, ¿? (Denmark) (b) 1,76 (c) F - left winger (d) Lyngby BK (e) Sirius, Lyngby BK, Aarhus GF, Viborg FF, Aarhus GF, Borussia Dortmund II, Aarhus GF

*** Kaastrup - William Kaastrup (William Elgaard Kaastrup) (a) 21/03/2004, Kokkedal (Denmark) (b) - (c) D - left back (d) Randers FC (e) -

*** Kaba - Jusuf Kaba (a) 04/02/2004, Struga (North Macedonia) (b) 1,73 (c) M - central midfielder (d) Struga Trim & Lum (e) -

*** Kaba - Sékouba Kaba (a) 12/02/1992, Perpignan (France) (b) 1,85 (c) D - central defense (d) UE Sant Julia (e) FC Shevardeni, Sp. Rosiori, Saint-Nazaire, Trégunc, UA Cognac, FC Marmande 47, Southall, L'Aumône

*** Kaba - Sory Kaba (a) 28/07/1995, Conakry (Guinea) (b) 1,90 (c) F - center forward (d) FC Midtjylland (e) Cardiff City, Midtjylland, OH Leuven, Midtjylland, Dijon, Elche CF, Elche Ilicitano, Alcobendas CF

*** Kabaev - Vladyslav Kabaev (Кабаєв Владислав Олександрович) (a) 01/09/1995, Odesa (Ukraine) (b) 1,77 (c) M - attacking midfielder (d) FC Dinamo de Kiev (e) Zorya Lugansk, Chornomorets, Chornomorets II

*** Kabak - Adem Eren Kabak (a) 12/12/2000, Konya (Turkey) (b) 1,85 (c) M - pivot (d) Sanliurfaspor (e) Sanliurfaspor, Konyaspor, Bucaspor 1928, Konyaspor, 1922 Konya, Konyaspor, 1922 Konya

*** Kabak - Ozan Kabak (Ozan Muhammed Kabak) (a) 25/03/2000, Ankara (Turkey) (b) 1,87 (c) D - central defense (d) TSG 1899 Hoffenheim (e) FC Schalke 04, Norwich City, FC Schalke 04, Liverpool, FC Schalke 04, VfB Stuttgart, Galatasaray

*** Kabananga - Junior Kabananga (Junior Kabananga Kalonji) (a) 04/04/1989, Kinshasa (Zaire, now DR Congo) (b) 1,90 (c) F - center forward (d) - (e) Maktaaral, CS Mioveni, SZ Dongwu, Soligorsk, Qatar SC, Al-Nassr, FC Astana, Al-Nassr, FC Astana, Karabükspor, FC Astana, Cercle Brugge, KSV Roeselare, RSC Anderlecht, Germ. Beerschot, RSC Anderlecht, MK Etanchéité, AS Vita Club

*** Kabar - Hytem Kabar (a) 23/07/2003, ¿? (Malta) (b) - (c) F - center forward (d) Gzira United FC (e) -

*** Kabasakal - Melih Kabasakal (a) 18/02/1996, Sinop (Turkey) (b) 1,78 (c) M - pivot (d) Eyüpspor (e) Istanbulspor, E. Erokspor, Trabzonspor, 1461 Trabzon, Trabzonspor, Sariyer, Trabzonspor

*** Kabashi - Arian Kabashi (a) 14/03/1997, ¿? (Sweden) (b) 1,80 (c) F - center forward (d) Helsingborgs IF (e) Dalkurd, Elfsborg, Dalkurd, Elfsborg, GAIS, Elfsborg

*** Kabashi - Arian Kabashi (a) 26/09/1996, Sierre (Switzerland) (b) 1,82 (c) D - central defense (d) FC Lahti (e) FC Sion, Martigny-Sports, FC Sierre

*** Kabashi - Armend Kabashi (a) 04/12/1995, Bad Saulgau (Germany) (b) 1,83 (c) M - pivot (d) IF Gnistan (e) AC Oulu, IF Gnistan, Kokkolan PV, FC Honka, TuS Erndtebrück, Eintracht Braunschweig II, FC Honka, FC Viikingit, FC Honka, FC Honka II

*** Kabashi - Veton Kabashi (a) 16/11/1992, ¿? (RF Yugoslavia, now in Kosovo) (b) - (c) D - central defense (d) - (e) KF Drenica, KF Istogu, KF Flamurtari

*** Kabha - Marwan Kabha (קבהא מרואן) (a) 23/02/1991, Ein As-Sahala (Israel) (b) 1,81 (c) M - pivot (d) Maccabi Bnei Reineh (e) Bnei Sakhnin, H. Beer Sheva, NK Maribor, M. Petah Tikva

*** Kabia - Jaze Kabia (a) 07/08/2000, Cork (Ireland) (b) - (c) F - right winger (d) Cork City FC (e) Livingston FC, Queen of the South, Livingston FC, Morton, Livingston FC, Falkirk FC, Livingston FC, Shelbourne, Cobh Ramblers

*** Kabic - Uros Kabic (Урош Кабић) (a) 01/01/2004, Novi Sad (Serbia and Montenegro, now in Serbia) (b) 1,83 (c) F - right winger (d) Crvena zvezda Beograd (e) Vojvodina

*** Kabilo - Omer Kabilo (a) 04/06/2003, ¿? (Israel) (b) - (c) G (d) Maccabi Herzliya (e) H. Jerusalem

*** Kablan - Cem Kablan (Muzaffer Cem Kablan) (a) 01/01/2000, Trabzon (Turkey) (b) 1,92 (c) G (d) Fatih Karagümrük (e) Trabzonspor

*** Käblik - Henri Käblik (a) 19/04/2005, Tartu (Estonia) (b) 1,79 (c) F - center forward (d) FCI Levadia (e) -

*** Kabongo - Christophe Kabongo (a) 27/08/2003, ¿? (Czech Rep.) (b) 1,88 (c) M - attacking midfielder (d) FK Zeleziarne Podbrezova (e) Podbrezova, Lommel SK

*** Kabongo - Dixon Kabongo (a) 21/11/2003, ¿? (Wales) (b) - (c) M - central midfielder (d) Cardiff Metropolitan University (e) -

*** Kaboré - Issa Kaboré (a) 12/05/2001, Bobo-Dioulasso (Burkina Faso) (b) 1,80 (c) D - right back (d) Luton Town (e) Luton Town, Manchester City, Ol. Marseille, Manchester City, Troyes, Manchester City, KV Mechelen, Manchester City, KV Mechelen, Rahimo FC

*** Kabosius - Airidas Kabosius (a) 16/08/2004, ¿? (Lithuania) (b) - (c) D (d) FK Jonava (e) -

*** Kabov - Atanas Kabov (Атанас Василев Кабов) (a) 11/04/1999, Plovdiv (Bulgaria) (b) 1,74 (c) F - right winger (d) Hebar Pazardzhik (e) Septemvri Sofia, Slavia Sofia, Levski Sofia, Vitosha, Levski Sofia, Tsarsko Selo, Levski Sofia, Botev Vratsa, Levski Sofia

*** Kabran - Kevin Kabran (Kevin Alexander Kabran) (a) 22/11/1993, Stockholm (Sweden) (b) 1,85 (c) F - right winger (d) Stabæk Fotball (e) Viking, Start, Elfsborg, Start, Brommapojkarna, Vasalunds IF, FC Den Bosch, Vasalunds IF

*** Kabylan - Bekzat Kabylan (Бекзат Кабылан) (a) 03/03/1996, ¿? (Kazakhstan) (b) 1,62 (c) F - left winger (d) Kaspiy Aktau (e) FK Turan, Kaspiy Aktau

*** Kabyshev - Andrey Kabyshev (Кабышев Андрей Геннадьевич) (a) 28/05/2003, Mogilev (Belarus) (b) 1,80 (c) M - attacking midfielder (d) Shakhter Soligorsk (e) Shakhter P., Soligorsk, Dnepr Mogilev

*** Kabyshev - Vladislav Kabyshev (Кабышев Владислав Геннадьевич) (a) 28/10/2001, ¿? (Belarus) (b) 1,84 (c) M - attacking midfielder (d) Shakhter Soligorsk (e) Shakhter P., Soligorsk II, Dnepr Mogilev, Dnyapro II

*** Kacaniklic - Alexander Kacaniklic (Alexander Kačaniklić) (a) 13/08/1991, Helsingborg (Sweden) (b) 1,81 (c) F - right winger (d) AEL Limassol (e) Hajduk Split, Hammarby IF, FC Nantes, Fulham, FC København, Fulham, Burnley, Fulham, Watford, Fulham, Fulham Reserves, Liverpool Reserves

*** Kacavenda - Lukas Kacavenda (Lukas Kačavenda) (a) 02/03/2003, Zagreb (Croatia) (b) 1,74 (c) M - attacking midfielder (d) NK Lokomotiva Zagreb (e) -

*** Kacbufi - Alessandro Kacbufi (a) 13/05/2001, Pavia (Italy) (b) 1,90 (c) D - central defense (d) - (e) KF Egnatia, KS Besa

*** Kaçe - Ergys Kaçe (Ergys Kaçe) (a) 08/07/1993, Korçë (Albania) (b) 1,71 (c) M - pivot (d) Volos NPS (e) Panevezys, Veria NPS, FK Partizani, Aris Thessaloniki, PAOK, AE Larisa, PAOK, Panathinaikos, PAOK, Viktoria Plzen, PAOK, Anag.Epanomis, PAOK

*** Kacer - Miroslav Kacer (Miroslav Káčer) (a) 02/02/1996, Žilina (Slovakia) (b) 1,70 (c) M - central midfielder (d) DAC Dunajska Streda (e) Viktoria Plzen, Dunajska Streda, Viktoria Plzen, MSK Zilina

*** Kacerik - Adrian Kacerik (Adrián Káčerik) (a) 02/08/1997, ¿? (Slovakia) (b) 1,74 (c) F - left winger (d) MFK Dukla Banska Bystrica (e) Liptovsky Mik., Podbrezova, Liptovsky Mik., Podbrezova, Podbrezova B

*** Kacharaba - Taras Kacharaba (Качараба Тарас Іванович) (a) 07/01/1995, Zhydachiv, Lviv Oblast (Ukraine) (b) 1,89 (c) D - central defense (d) SK Slavia Praga (e) Slovan Liberec, Slavia Praha, Slovan Liberec, Shakhtar II, Slovan Liberec, Shakhtar II, Zirka, Shakhtar II, Goverla, Shakhtar II, Shakhtar 3, UFK Lviv

*** Kachut - Damian Kachut (Damián Kachút) (a) 09/06/2004, Bratislava (Slovakia) (b) 1,81 (c) D - right back (d) STK 1914 Samorin (e) Dunajska Streda
*** Kacić - Benjamin Kacić (a) 28/06/1991, Bar (Yugoslavia, now in Montenegro) (b) 1,83 (c) F - right winger (d) FK Mornar Bar (e) OFK Grbalj, OFK Petrovac, Mornar Bar, OFK Petrovac, Mornar Bar, OFK Petrovac, Mornar Bar
*** Kacinari - Aaron Kacinari (a) 18/08/2001, Izola (Slovenia) (b) 1,86 (c) M - attacking midfielder (d) US Triestina (e) Venezia, KS Kastrioti, Venezia, Tabor Sezana, ND Gorica, Drava Ptuj, NK Ankaran
*** Kaçiu - Donat Kaçiu (a) 20/09/1993, Prishtinë (RF Yugoslavia, now in Kosovo) (b) 1,92 (c) G (d) KF Trepca 89 (e) KF Arbëria, KF Ferizaj, SC Gjilani, KF 2 Korriku
*** Kack - Adrien Kack (a) 11/02/2002, ¿? (France) (b) - (c) D - central defense (d) Jeunesse Esch (e) RC Epernay
*** Käck - Elliot Käck (Carl Elliot Leifson Käck) (a) 18/09/1989, Stockholm (Sweden) (b) 1,74 (c) D - left back (d) Djurgårdens IF (e) Start, Djurgården, Sirius, Hammarby TFF, Värmdö IF, Värtans IK
*** Kacoli - Jetmir Kacoli (a) 09/02/1998, Gjakovë (RF Yugoslavia, now in Kosovo) (b) - (c) D - right back (d) FC Malisheva (e) -
*** Kacorri - Luis Kacorri (a) 24/02/1998, Ronciglione (Italy) (b) 1,94 (c) F - center forward (d) FC Dinamo (e) FK Bylis, Arzachena, Savoia, Correggese, Cittanovese, Ligorna, Fiorenzuola, Fermana, Carpi, Igea Virtus, Jolly & Montemurlo
*** Kacuri - Dion Kacuri (a) 11/02/2004, Baden (Switzerland) (b) 1,88 (c) M - attacking midfielder (d) Grasshopper Club Zürich (e) -
*** Kada - Joakim Kada (Joakim Jean-Philippe Kada) (a) 29/01/2001, Arles (France) (b) 1,89 (c) D - central defense (d) - (e) RFCU Luxembourg, Ol. Marseille B
*** Kadak - Jakub Kadak (Jakub Kadák) (a) 14/12/2000, Trenčín (Slovakia) (b) 1,77 (c) M - attacking midfielder (d) FC Lucerna (e) AS Trencin
*** Kádár - Tamás Kádár (a) 14/03/1990, Veszprém (Hungary) (b) 1,88 (c) D - central defense (d) MTK Budapest (e) Paksi FC, Újpest FC, SD Taishan, Tianjin Jinmen Tiger, SD Taishan, Dinamo Kyïv, Lech Poznan, Diósgyőr, Roda JC, Diósgyőr, Roda JC, Newcastle Utd., Huddersfield Town, Newcastle Utd., Zalaegerszeg
*** Kade - Anton Kade (a) 17/01/2004, Berlin (Germany) (b) 1,85 (c) F - left winger (d) FC Basel (e) Hertha Berlin
*** Kaderabek - Pavel Kaderabek (Pavel Kadeřábek) (a) 25/04/1992, Praha (Czechoslovakia, now in Czech Rep.) (b) 1,82 (c) D - right back (d) TSG 1899 Hoffenheim (e) Sparta Praha, Viktoria Zizkov, Sparta Praha
*** Kadewere - Tino Kadewere (Philana Tinotenda Kadewere) (a) 05/01/1996, Harare (Zimbabwe) (b) 1,83 (c) F - center forward (d) Olympique de Lyon (e) RCD Mallorca, Olympique Lyon, Le Havre AC, Olympique Lyon, Le Havre AC, Djurgården, Harare City, Djurgården, Harare City
*** Kadile - Junior Kadile (Junior Morau Kadile) (a) 16/12/2002, Rennes (France) (b) 1,82 (c) F - right winger (d) Stade Lavallois (e) Stade Rennes, Famalicão, Stade Rennes, Stade Rennes B, Famalicão, Stade Rennes B
*** Kadimyan - Gegam Kadimyan (Գեղամ Կադիմյան) (a) 19/10/1992, Artashat (Armenia) (b) 1,84 (c) F - left winger (d) - (e) FC Van, Neman Grodno, Kaysar, Neman Grodno, Alashkert CF, Arsenal Kyiv, Vorskla Poltava, Zorya Lugansk, Karpaty, Olimpik Donetsk, Goverla, PFK Sumy, Tytan Armyansk, Arsenal Kharkiv
*** Kadio - Didier Kadio (Didier Boris Kadio) (a) 05/04/1990, Man (Ivory Coast) (b) 1,78 (c) D - central defense (d) Zhetysu Taldykorgan (e) Alashkert CF, Al-Hilal, SJK Seinäjoki, Pyunik Yerevan, Shakhter K., Kerala Blasters, Zhetysu, FF Jaro, Shirak Gyumri, Zhetysu, Shirak Gyumri, SO Armée, ASEC Mimosas

*** Kadioglu - Ferdi Kadioglu (Ferdi Erenay Kadıoğlu) (a) 07/10/1999, Arnhem (Netherlands) (b) 1,74 (c) D - right back (d) Fenerbahce (e) NEC Nijmegen
*** Kadlec - Adam Kadlec (a) 06/07/2003, ¿? (Czech Rep.) (b) - (c) D - central defense (d) Bohemians Praha 1905 (e) Bohemians B
*** Kadlec - Michal Kadlec (a) 13/12/1984, Vyškov (Czechoslovakia, now in Czech Rep.) (b) 1,85 (c) D - central defense (d) 1.FC Slovácko (e) Sparta Praha, Fenerbahce, Bayer Leverkusen, Sparta Praha, Bayer Leverkusen, Sparta Praha, Slovácko
*** Kadlec - Vaclav Kadlec (Václav Kadlec) (a) 20/05/1992, Praha (Czechoslovakia, now in Czech Rep.) (b) 1,81 (c) F - center forward (d) Tianjin Ligmet Milin (e) Viktoria Zizkov, Jablonec, Mlada Boleslav, Cerv. Janovice, Sparta Praha, Midtjylland, Eintracht, Sparta Praha, Eintracht, Sparta Praha
*** Kadoch - Ran Kadoch (קדוש רן) (a) 04/10/1985, Maale Adumim (Israel) (b) 1,88 (c) G (d) - (e) Hapoel Haifa, Bnei Yehuda, Hapoel Haifa, H. Kfar Saba, Bnei Sakhnin, Betar Kfar Saba, Kiryat Malachi, Ness Ziona, H. Asi Gilboa, Hapoel Haifa, Bnei Yehuda, Barnet, H Rishon leZion, Ness Ziona, H Rishon leZion, Hakoah Amidar, H Rishon leZion, Hapoel Bnei Lod, H Rishon leZion, Hapoel Raanana, H Rishon leZion
*** Kadri - Abdelkahar Kadri (قادري عبد القهار) (a) 24/06/2000, Hammamet (Algeria) (b) 1,70 (c) M - attacking midfielder (d) KV Kortrijk (e) Paradou AC
*** Kadric - Faris Kadric (Faris Kadrić) (a) 13/03/2005, Sarajevo (Bosnia and Herzegovina) (b) - (c) M (d) - (e) Baton Sarajevo
*** Kadric - Haris Kadric (Haris Kadrić) (a) 16/03/2000, Velenje (Slovenia) (b) 1,88 (c) F - center forward (d) TS Podbeskidzie Bielsko-Biala (e) Vozdovac, Kolubara, NK Aluminij, Olimpija, NK Triglav, Olimpija, Rudar Velenje, Olimpija, NK Bravo
*** Kadrii - Bashkim Kadrii (a) 09/07/1991, Copenhagen (Denmark) (b) 1,77 (c) F - center forward (d) Odense Boldklub (e) Al-Fateh, Odense BK, FC København, Randers FC, FC København, Minnesota, FC København, Odense BK, B.93
*** Kadriu - Andi Kadriu (a) 29/01/2004, Mitrovica (Serbia and Montenegro, now in Kosovo) (b) - (c) D - central defense (d) KF Trepca 89 (e) -
*** Kadriu - Florijan Kadriu (a) 30/09/1995, Tetovo (North Macedonia) (b) 1,69 (c) F - left winger (d) FK Atyrau (e) KF Erzeni, Struga, FK Sabail, Renova, Rabotnicki, FC Shkupi, KF Tirana, KF Teuta, KF Tirana, Vëllazërimi
*** Kadu - Kadu (Carlos Eduardo de Sousa Leopoldo) (a) 03/03/2002, Colombo-PR (Brazil) (b) 1,78 (c) F - left winger (d) - (e) Siroki Brijeg, São Joseense
*** Kadu - Kadu (Kadu Ribeiro Durval) (a) 09/02/1997, ¿? (Brazil) (b) 1,90 (c) D - central defense (d) - (e) Lokomotiv Sofia, Criciúma EC, Hercílio Luz, Luverdense, Prudente-SP, Macaé, Americano
*** Kadusic - Advan Kadusic (Advan Kadušić) (a) 14/10/1997, Zenica (Bosnia and Herzegovina) (b) 1,78 (c) D - right back (d) NK Istra 1961 (e) NK Celje, Zrinjski Mostar, FK Sarajevo
*** Kadyrbaev - Erlan Kadyrbaev (Ерлан Кадырбаев) (a) 05/10/1991, Turkmenbashi (Soviet Union, now in Turkmenistan) (b) 1,81 (c) D - central defense (d) Kaspiy Aktau (e) Kaspiy II, Kaspiy Aktau
*** Kadyrov - Abubakar Kadyrov (Кадыров Абубакар Хамидович) (a) 26/08/1996, Tsentoroy, Chechnya Republic (Russia) (b) 1,80 (c) F - center forward (d) Khalid Kadyrov (e) Akhmat Grozny, Akhmat II
*** Kadyrov - Khalid Kadyrov (Кадыров Халид Хож-Баудиевич) (a) 19/04/1994, Tsentaroy, Chechnya Republic (Russia) (b) 1,64 (c) F - right winger (d) Abubakar Kadyrov (e) Akhmat Grozny, Terek II
*** Kadzior - Damian Kadzior (Damian Kądzior) (a) 16/06/1992, Białystok (Poland) (b) 1,74 (c) F - right winger (d) Piast Gliwice (e) SD Eibar, Alanyaspor, SD Eibar,

Dinamo Zagreb, Górnik Zabrze, Wigry Suwalki, Jagiellonia, Wigry Suwalki, Jagiellonia, Dolcan Zabki, Jagiellonia, Motor Lublin, Jagiellonia, Jagiellonia II
*** Kagawa - Shinji Kagawa (香川 真司) (a) 17/03/1989, Kobe, Hyogo (Japan) (b) 1,75 (c) M - attacking midfielder (d) Cerezo Osaka (e) Sint-Truiden, PAOK, Real Zaragoza, Borussia Dortmund, Besiktas, Borussia Dortmund, Manchester Utd., Borussia Dortmund, Cerezo Osaka
*** Kagawa - Shogo Kagawa (a) 04/10/1998, ¿? (Japan) (b) - (c) D - central defense (d) Lernayin Artsakh Goris (e) -
*** Kagayama - Taiki Kagayama (加賀山 泰毅) (a) 14/05/1996, ¿? (Georgia) (b) 1,68 (c) F - left winger (d) FC Samgurali Tskaltubo (e) Sabah, FC Inter, Kokkolan PV, MuSa, Kansai Univ.
*** Kahfi - Bagus Kahfi (Amiruddin Bagus Kahfi Alfikri) (a) 16/01/2002, Magelang (Indonesia) (b) 1,69 (c) F - center forward (d) PS Barito Putera (e) Asteras Tripoli, Barito Putera, Garuda Select, PSSA Asahan, Frenz United
*** Kahila - Tal Kahila (כחילה טל) (a) 26/06/1992, Jerusalem (Israel) (b) 1,85 (c) D - central defense (d) Hapoel Afula (e) Ness Ziona, Hapoel Hadera, Atromitos FC, B. Jerusalem, Bnei Yehuda, B. Jerusalem
*** Kahl - Eric Kahl (Eric Andre Kahl) (a) 27/09/2001, Solna (Sweden) (b) 1,81 (c) D - left back (d) Aarhus GF (e) AIK
*** Kahnberg - Melvin Kahnberg (a) 26/11/2003, ¿? (Finland) (b) - (c) D - right back (d) - (e) IFK Mariehamn
*** Kahraman - Bedirhan Kahraman (a) 01/01/2003, Sanliurfa(Turkey) (b) - (c) M - pivot (d) Anamur Belediyespor (e) Alanyaspor, Darica GB, Alanyaspor
*** Kahrimanovic - Almin Kahrimanovic (Алмин Кахримановић) (a) 03/10/2003, Novi Pazar (Serbia and Montenegro, now in Serbia) (b) 1,95 (c) G (d) FK Josanica (e) Novi Pazar
*** Kahrimanovic - Amir Kahrimanovic (Amir Kahrimanović) (a) 28/04/1999, Zagreb (Croatia) (b) 1,80 (c) M - attacking midfielder (d) KF Erzeni (e) Renova, Drava Ptuj, ATSV Wolfsberg, Deutschlandsbg., NK Dubrava ZG, Studentski Grad
*** Kahveci - Irfan Can Kahveci (İrfan Can Kahveci) (a) 15/07/1995, Corum (Turkey) (b) 1,76 (c) F - right winger (d) Fenerbahce (e) Basaksehir, Genclerbirligi, Hacettepe
*** Kaiafas - Alexandros Kaiafas (Αλέξανδρος Καϊάφας) (a) 09/02/2004, Nicosia (Cyprus) (b) 1,86 (c) D - central defense (d) MEAP Pera Choriou Nisou (e) Omonia Nicosia, MEAP Nisou
*** Kaiafas - Sotiris Kaiafas (Σωτήρης Καϊάφας) (a) 27/10/2004, Nicosia (Cyprus) (b) 1,83 (c) D - central defense (d) Olympiakos Nikosia (e) -
*** Kaib - Rami Kaib (a) 08/05/1997, Nyköping (Sweden) (b) 1,78 (c) D - left back (d) Djurgårdens IF (e) Heerenveen, Elfsborg
*** Kaied - Adam Kaied (Adam Hamza Kaied, كايد حمزة آدم) (a) 02/03/2002, ¿? (Sweden) (b) 1,77 (c) F - left winger (d) NAC Breda (e) Helsingborgs IF, Stabæk, Helsingborgs IF
*** Kaikkonen - Nuutti Kaikkonen (a) 10/04/2003, ¿? (Finland) (b) 1,98 (c) G (d) AC Oulu (e) JIPPO
*** Kaiky - Kaiky (Kaiky Fernandes Melo) (a) 12/01/2004, Santos (Brazil) (b) 1,81 (c) D - central defense (d) UD Almería (e) Santos
*** Kaina - Kaina (Kainã Nunes da Silva Amarante) (a) 31/05/1997, ¿? (Brazil) (b) 1,96 (c) F - center forward (d) KF Tirana (e) KF Vllaznia, KS Kastrioti, KF Vllaznia, KS Besa, Marco 09, Moura, Olhanense, Felgueiras, CF União B
*** Kainz - Florian Kainz (a) 24/10/1992, Graz (Austria) (b) 1,76 (c) F - left winger (d) 1.FC Köln (e) Werder Bremen, Rapid Wien, Sturm Graz, Sturm Graz II

*** Kainz - Tobias Kainz (a) 31/10/1992, Feldbach (Austria) (b) 1,74 (c) M - pivot (d) TSV Hartberg (e) SV Kapfenberg, Limerick FC, Grödig, Wiener Neustadt, Sturm Graz, Heerenveen, H'veen/Emmen B

*** Kaio - Kaio (Kaio Fernando da Silva Pantaleão) (a) 18/09/1995, Araraquara (SP) (Brazil) (b) 1,86 (c) D - central defense (d) FK Krasnodar (e) Santa Clara, Ferroviária, Santa Clara, Ferroviária

*** Kaio Jorge - Kaio Jorge (Kaio Jorge Pinto Ramos) (a) 24/01/2002, Olinda (Brazil) (b) 1,82 (c) F - center forward (d) Juventus de Turín (e) Santos

*** Kairinen - Kaan Kairinen (Kasper Kaan Kairinen) (a) 22/12/1998, Kaarina (Finland) (b) 1,85 (c) M - central midfielder (d) AC Sparta Praga (e) Lillestrøm, Midtjylland, Lillestrøm, Midtjylland, HJK Helsinki, Midtjylland, FC Inter, Midtjylland, Skive IK, Midtjylland, FC Inter

*** Kairkenov - Zhaslan Kairkenov (Каиркенов Жаслан Жанатович) (a) 27/03/2000, Pavlodar (Kazakhstan) (b) 1,75 (c) M - central midfielder (d) FC Zhenis Astana (e) FK Aksu, FC Astana, FK Aksu, FC Astana, Atyrau, FC Astana, Atyrau, FC Astana, Astana-Zhas

*** Kairov - Bagdat Kairov (Каиров Багдат Санатулы) (a) 27/04/1993, Aktobe (Kazakhstan) (b) 1,78 (c) D - right back (d) Tobol Kostanay (e) Ordabasy, Kaysar, Aktobe, Kaspiy Aktau, Aktobe II

*** Käit - Kristofer Käit (a) 04/04/2005, Tallinn (Estonia) (b) - (c) M - pivot (d) - (e) Kalev

*** Käit - Mattias Käit (a) 29/06/1998, Tallinn (Estonia) (b) 1,87 (c) M - central midfielder (d) FC Rapid 1923 (e) Bodø/Glimt, Domžale, Ross County

*** Kaiuf - Sharif Kaiuf (כיוף שריף) (a) 25/06/2001, Isfiya (Israel) (b) 1,87 (c) G (d) Maccabi Haifa (e) Hapoel Afula, Maccabi Haifa, Hapoel Afula, Maccabi Haifa, H. Kfar Shalem, Maccabi Haifa

*** Kaján - Norbert Kaján (Kaján Norbert Gábor) (a) 11/09/2004, Budapest (Hungary) (b) - (c) D - right back (d) Ferencvárosi TC II (e) -

*** Kajevic - Asmir Kajevic (Асмир Кајевић) (a) 15/02/1990, Rožaje (Yugoslavia, now in Montenegro) (b) 1,87 (c) M - attacking midfielder (d) FK Vojvodina Novi Sad (e) WH Yangtze, Čukarički, HNK Rijeka, FC Zürich, FK BSK Borča

*** Kajevic - Demir Kajevic (Демир Кајевић) (a) 20/04/1989, ¿? (Yugoslavia, now in Montenegro) (b) 1,81 (c) D - left back (d) - (e) Mornar Bar, OFK Petrovac, FK Ibar, OFK Petrovac, Mornar Bar, FK Ibar, OFK Grbalj, Jedinstvo, Rad Beograd

*** Kajtazi - Erion Kajtazi (a) 15/11/2005, Mitrovica (Serbia and Montenegro, now in Kosovo) (b) - (c) M - central midfielder (d) --- (e) -

*** Kakabadze - Otar Kakabadze (ოთარ კაკაბაძე) (a) 27/06/1995, Tbilisi (Georgia) (b) 1,86 (c) M - right midfielder (d) Cracovia (e) CD Tenerife, FC Luzern, Gimnàstic, Esbjerg fB, Gimnàstic, Dinamo Tbilisi

*** Kakhabrishvili - Kakha Kakhabrishvili (კახა კახაბრიშვილი) (a) 08/07/1993, ¿? (Georgia) (b) 1,84 (c) F - left winger (d) FC Gonio (e) FC Locomotive, FC Van, FC Locomotive, Chikhura, Sioni Bolnisi, Tskhinvali, Chikhura, WIT Georgia, STU

*** Kakiashvili - Rati Kakiashvili (რატი კაკიაშვილი) (a) 15/08/1997, Tbilisi (Georgia) (b) 1,84 (c) M - pivot (d) Merani Tbilisi (e) FC Gagra, FC Telavi, FC Gagra, Merani Tbilisi

*** Kakimov - Aslanbek Kakimov (Какимов Асланбек Сыдыкулы) (a) 02/10/1993, Aktobe (Kazakhstan) (b) 1,77 (c) F - left winger (d) FK Aksu (e) FK Turan, FK Aksu, FK Ekibastuz, Shakhter K., Aktobe, Tobol Kostanay, Aktobe, Aktobe II

*** Kakkoev - Nikita Kakkoev (Каккоев Никита Игоревич) (a) 22/08/1999, St. Petersburg (Russia) (b) 1,84 (c) M - pivot (d) FC Pari Nizhniy Novgorod (e) Zenit 2 St. Peterburg, Tom Tomsk, Zenit 2 St. Peterburg, Zenit St. Peterburg II
*** Kakoullis - Andronikos Kakoullis (Ανδρόνικος Κακουλλής) (a) 03/05/2001, Lythrodountas (Cyprus) (b) 1,80 (c) F - center forward (d) Omonia Nicosia (e) -
*** Kakubava - Levan Kakubava (ლევან კაკუბავა) (a) 15/10/1990, Zugdidi (Soviet Union, now in Georgia) (b) 1,84 (c) D - central defense (d) FC Gagra (e) Saburtalo, Chikhura, Tskhinvali, FC Samtredia, Omonia Nicosia, Tskhinvali, Metalurgi R., Dinamo Tbilisi
*** Kakuta - Gaël Kakuta (Gaël Romeo Kakuta Mambenga) (a) 21/06/1991, Lille (France) (b) 1,73 (c) M - attacking midfielder (d) Amiens SC (e) RC Lens, Amiens SC, RC Lens, Amiens SC, Rayo Vallecano, HB CFFC, Amiens SC, HB CFFC, RC Deportivo, HB CFFC, Sevilla FC, Chelsea, Rayo Vallecano, Chelsea, Lazio, Chelsea, Vitesse, Chelsea, Dijon, Chelsea, Bolton Wanderers, Chelsea, Fulham, Chelsea
*** Kalabiska - Jan Kalabiska (Jan Kalabiška) (a) 22/12/1986, Mělník (Czechoslovakia, now in Czech Rep.) (b) 1,88 (c) D - left back (d) 1.FC Slovácko (e) Karvina, Mlada Boleslav, Karvina, Mlada Boleslav, FK Senica, Zbrojovka Brno, Graffin Vlasim, 1.FK Pribram, Sokol Libis
*** Kalachev - Ilya Kalachev (Калачёв Илья Андреевич) (a) 18/01/2000, Samara (Russia) (b) 1,86 (c) D - central defense (d) Isloch Minsk Region (e) Dolgoprudnyi, Dinamo 2, Neftekhimik, Dinamo 2, Tom Tomsk, Dinamo 2, Dinamo Moskva II
*** Kalaica - Branimir Kalaica (a) 01/06/1998, Zagreb (Croatia) (b) 1,92 (c) D - central defense (d) NK Lokomotiva Zagreb (e) Benfica B
*** Kalajdzic - Sasa Kalajdzic (Saša Kalajdžić) (a) 07/07/1997, Wien (Austria) (b) 2,00 (c) F - center forward (d) Wolverhampton Wanderers (e) VfB Stuttgart, Admira Wacker, FC Admira II, SR Donaufeld
*** Kalandadze - Aleksandre Kalandadze (ალექსანდრე კალანდაძე) (a) 09/05/2001, Tbilisi (Georgia) (b) 1,85 (c) D - central defense (d) Dinamo Tbilisi (e) Diósgyőr
*** Kalandadze - Lasha Kalandadze (ლაშა კალანდაძე) (a) 08/05/2004, ¿? (Georgia) (b) - (c) F - left winger (d) FC Locomotive Tbilisi (e) Locomotive II
*** Kalandarishvili - Nika Kalandarishvili (ნიკა კალანდარიშვილი) (a) 09/09/1998, ¿? (Georgia) (b) 1,82 (c) D - left back (d) FC Samgurali Tskaltubo (e) Athlone Town, Cabinteely, Athlone Town, Dila II
*** Kalanidis - Giannis Kalanidis (Γιάννης Καλανίδης) (a) 12/05/2006, Larnaca (Cyprus) (b) 1,84 (c) G (d) - (e) Nea Salamis
*** Kalanoski - Antonio Kalanoski (Антонио Каланоски) (a) 25/04/1994, Ohrid (North Macedonia) (b) 1,83 (c) F - center forward (d) Sileks Kratovo (e) Gostivar, FC Shkupi, Sileks, Belasica, Pobeda Prilep, Struga, Borec Veles, Sileks, Carev Dvor, Euromilk GL, Metalurg Skopje, Napredok Kicevo, Metalurg Skopje, Lokomotiva, Metalurg Skopje, Ohrid Lihnidos
*** Kaldirim - Hasan Ali Kaldirim (Hasan Ali Kaldırım) (a) 09/12/1989, Neuwied (Germany) (b) 1,83 (c) D - left back (d) MKE Ankaragücü (e) Basaksehir, Fenerbahce, Kayserispor, FSV Mainz 05 II, Kaiserslautern II
*** Kaldunski - Bartlomiej Kaldunski (Bartłomiej Kałduński) (a) 16/04/2005, ¿? (Poland) (b) 1,90 (c) G (d) KS Lechia Gdańsk (e) -
*** Kaldybekov - Ersultan Kaldybekov (Калдыбеков Ерсултан Бахытжанулы) (a) 12/01/2002, Taraz (Kazakhstan) (b) 1,85 (c) M - central midfielder (d) FK Atyrau (e) Taraz, Taraz-Karatau

*** Kaleba - Thadée Kaleba (a) 20/04/1999, ¿? (France) (b) 1,86 (c) D - central defense (d) - (e) Tabor Sezana, Solières, Molfetta, Amiens SC B

*** Kalemi - Arneld Kalemi (a) 03/03/2001, ¿? (Albania) (b) - (c) M - attacking midfielder (d) Mondaino (e) Faetano, K-Sport, Colbordolo

*** Kalenchuk - Maksym Kalenchuk (Каленчук Максим Миколайович) (a) 05/12/1989, Donetsk (Soviet Union, now in Ukraine) (b) 1,83 (c) M - pivot (d) - (e) Akzhayik, LNZ Cherkasy, Vitebsk, Rukh Lviv, PFC Lviv, Veres Rivne, FK Oleksandriya, Stal Kamyanske, Zirka

*** Kalenga - Christian Kalenga (Christian Kalenga Ka Mpuluka) (a) 30/01/2001, ¿? (Belgium) (b) - (c) F (d) Jeunesse Esch II (e) Jeunesse Esch, Jeunesse II

*** Kalenik - Oskar Kalenik (a) 15/11/2000, Łuków (Poland) (b) 1,79 (c) M - attacking midfielder (d) KKS 1925 Kalisz (e) Pogon Szczecin, Pogon II, Olimpia Grudz., Pogon Szczecin, Pogon II

*** Kalenkovich - Vitaliy Kalenkovich (Каленкович Виталий Олегович) (a) 03/03/1993, Kaliningrad (Russia) (b) 1,79 (c) D - left back (d) - (e) Kyzyltash, Salyut Belgorod, JK Trans Narva, Tom Tomsk, Baltika, KS Samara, Baltika, Baltika 2

*** Kalermo - Akseli Kalermo (Akseli Matias Kalermo) (a) 17/03/1997, Kannus (Finland) (b) 1,90 (c) D - central defense (d) Thór Akureyri (e) Riteriai, Brattvåg, VPS, AC Kajaani, VPS, AC Oulu, RoPS, AC Oulu, RoPS

*** Kalezic - Milos Kalezic (Miloš Kalezić) (a) 09/08/1993, ¿? (RF Yugoslavia, now in Montenegro) (b) 1,83 (c) M - central midfielder (d) FK Iskra Danilovgrad (e) Sutjeska Niksic, Novi Pazar, KF Vllaznia, OFK Titograd, OFK Petrovac, Sloboda Tuzla, FK Iskra, STK Samorin, OFK Grbalj, Mogren, Buducnost Podgorica

*** Kalik - Anthony Kalik (a) 05/11/1997, St. Leonards (Australia) (b) 1,80 (c) M - attacking midfielder (d) HNK Hajduk Split (e) HNK Gorica, Hajduk Split, NK Rudes, Hajduk Split, Sydney FC, Hajduk Split, Central Coast, Hajduk Split, Central Coast, FFA C. of Excel

*** Kalimuendo - Arnaud Kalimuendo (Arnaud Kalimuendo Muinga) (a) 20/01/2002, Suresnes (France) (b) 1,75 (c) F - center forward (d) Stade Rennais FC (e) Paris Saint-Germain, RC Lens, Paris Saint-Germain, RC Lens, Paris Saint-Germain

*** Kalin - Danila Kalin (Калин Данила Игоревич) (a) 29/06/2002, ¿? (Russia) (b) 1,85 (c) D - central defense (d) Tekstilshchik Ivanovo (e) Krasnoe Znamya, Khimki 2, Khimki II, Khimki 2

*** Kalinic - Lovre Kalinic (Lovre Kalinić) (a) 03/04/1990, Split (Yugoslavia, now in Croatia) (b) 2,01 (c) G (d) HNK Hajduk Split (e) Aston Villa, Hajduk Split, Aston Villa, Toulouse, Aston Villa, KAA Gent, Hajduk Split, Karlovac 1919, Hajduk Split, NK Novalja, Hajduk Split, Junak Sinj

*** Kalinic - Nikola Kalinic (Nikola Kalinić) (a) 05/01/1988, Solin (Yugoslavia, now in Croatia) (b) 1,87 (c) F - center forward (d) - (e) Hajduk Split, Hellas Verona, Atlético Madrid, AS Roma, Atlético Madrid, AC Milan, Fiorentina, AC Milan, Fiorentina, Dnipro, Blackburn, Hajduk Split, HNK Sibenik, Hajduk Split, NK Istra, Hajduk Split

*** Kalinin - Igor Kalinin (Калинин Игорь Олегович) (a) 11/11/1995, Kerch, Krym (Ukraine) (b) 1,85 (c) D - left back (d) Fakel Voronezh (e) Fakel Voronezh, Rostov, Ural, Dinamo Moskva, Ural, Dinamo Moskva, Rubin Kazan, Krasnodar, Volgar, Zirka, Zorya Lugansk, Illichivets, Illichivets II

*** Kalinin - Vladislav Kalinin (Калинин Владислав Геннадьевич) (a) 14/01/2002, Chashniki (Belarus) (b) 1,85 (c) D - central defense (d) Dinamo Minsk (e) Dinamo Minsk II

*** Kalinskiy - Nikolay Kalinskiy (Калинский Николай Николаевич) (a) 22/09/1993, Moskva (Russia) (b) 1,80 (c) M - pivot (d) FC Pari Nizhniy Novgorod (e) Tom Tomsk, SKA Khabarovsk, FK Kaluga, Lokomotiv Moskva II
*** Kalisa - Sven Kalisa (a) 14/03/1997, ¿? (Luxembourg) (b) - (c) M - central midfielder (d) FC Etzella Ettelbruck (e) FC Atert Bissen, Etzella Ettelbrück, US Mondorf, Etzella Ettelbrück, US Mondorf, F91 Dudelange
*** Kalitvintsev - Vladyslav Kalitvintsev (Калітвінцев Владислав Юрійович) (a) 04/01/1993, Moskva (Russia) (b) 1,78 (c) M - right midfielder (d) FK Oleksandriya (e) Desna, Arsenal Kyiv, Dinamo Kyïv, Zorya Lugansk, Dinamo Kyïv, Chornomorets, Dinamo Kyïv, Chornomorets, Dinamo Kyïv, Dinamo Kiev II, Slovan Liberec, Dinamo Kiev II, Dynamo 2 Kyiv
*** Kaljevic - Bojan Kaljevic (a) 25/01/1986, Niksic (Yugoslavia, now in Montenegro) (b) 1,90 (c) F - center forward (d) Tarxien Rainbows (e) Balzan FC, Mosta FC, Valletta, Balzan FC, Mosta FC, FK Mladost, Bunyodkor, Metallurg Bk., Rabotnicki
*** Kaljumäe - Marek Kaljumäe (a) 18/02/1991, Tallinn (Estonia) (b) 1,85 (c) M - central midfielder (d) Kalev Tallinn (e) Pärnu Vaprus, Kalev, FCI Levadia, Kemi City, Levadia, JK Trans Narva, Levadia, Telstar, SC Real
*** Kalkan - Berat Kalkan (Берат Калкан) (a) 02/03/2003, Istanbul (Turkey) (b) 1,71 (c) F - left winger (d) Kasimpasa (e) Kasimpasa, Karacabey Belediye, Kasimpasa
*** Kalla - Ali Kalla (a) 23/04/1998, Paris (France) (b) 1,72 (c) D - right back (d) - (e) Angers SCO, Angers SCO B
*** Kalla - Ronan Kalla (a) 08/03/2003, Belfast (Northern Ireland) (b) - (c) M - central midfielder (d) Knockbreda FC (e) Knockbreda FC, Carrick Rangers
*** Kállai - Kevin Kállai (a) 14/01/2002, Miskolc (Hungary) (b) 1,78 (c) D - right back (d) Mezőkövesd Zsóry FC (e) Haladás
*** Kállai - Zalán Kállai (a) 21/02/2004, Miskolc (Hungary) (b) 1,83 (c) F - left winger (d) Mezőkövesd Zsóry FC (e) -
*** Kallaku - Sherif Kallaku (a) 01/03/1998, Fushë-Krujë (Albania) (b) 1,81 (c) M - central midfielder (d) Sepsi OSK Sf. Gheorghe (e) KF Teuta, KF Tirana, NK Lokomotiva, FK Partizani, NK Lokomotiva, KF Teuta, NK Lokomotiva, KF Teuta, KF Laçi
*** Kallas - Rasmus Kallas (a) 18/11/2003, Paide (Estonia) (b) - (c) D - central defense (d) Jalgpallikool Tammeka (e) Paide
*** Kallaste - Ken Kallaste (a) 31/08/1988, Tallinn (Soviet Union, now in Estonia) (b) 1,82 (c) D - left back (d) FC Flora Tallinn (e) GKS Tychy, Korona Kielce, Górnik Zabrze, Kalju FC, FC Flora, JK Viljandi, FC Flora II, Tervis Pärnu
*** Kallesöe - Mikkel Kallesöe (Mikkel Kallesøe Andreasen) (a) 20/04/1997, Lemvig (Denmark) (b) 1,93 (c) D - right back (d) Randers FC (e) Viborg FF, Randers FC
*** Kallevåg - Torbjørn Kallevåg (a) 21/08/1993, ¿? (Norway) (b) 1,78 (c) F - right winger (d) IL Hødd (e) Aalesund, Lillestrøm, Haugesund, Hødd, Vard
*** Kalley - Yahya Kalley (a) 20/03/2001, Oxie (Sweden) (b) 1,85 (c) D - left back (d) IFK Norrköping (e) FC Groningen, Norrköping, FC Groningen, IFK Göteborg
*** Kallinen - Jere Kallinen (a) 10/01/2002, ¿? (Finland) (b) 1,78 (c) M - central midfielder (d) AC Oulu (e) -
*** Kallio - Milo Kallio (a) 11/04/2002, ¿? (Finland) (b) - (c) G (d) VG-62 Naantali (e) Pargas IF, PIF II, VG-62, PIF II
*** Källman - Benjamin Källman (Benjamin Källman) (a) 17/06/1998, Tammisaari (Finland) (b) 1,82 (c) F - center forward (d) Cracovia (e) FC Inter, Haugesund, FC Inter, Viking, FC Inter, Vendsyssel FF, FC Inter, Dundee FC, FC Inter, Ekenäs IF

*** Kallon - Yayah Kallon (a) 30/06/2001, Koydu-Sefadu (Sierra Leona) (b) 1,75 (c)
F - right winger (d) Hellas Verona (e) Genoa, Hellas Verona, Genoa, Savona
*** Kallsberg - Poul Kallsberg (a) 04/02/2003, ¿? (Faroe Islands) (b) 1,83 (c) F - right
winger (d) Víkingur Gøta (e) Skála, Skála IF II
*** Kalludra - Liridon Kalludra (a) 05/11/1991, Kosovska Mitrovica (Yugoslavia,
now in Kosovo) (b) 1,70 (c) M - attacking midfielder (d) IK Oddevold (e)
Kristiansund, Sarpsborg 08, Kristiansund, Ljungskile SK
*** Kalmakhambet - Zhasasyn Kalmakhambet (Қалмахамбет Жасасын) (a)
21/02/2001, ¿? (Kazakhstan) (b) 1,86 (c) F - left winger (d) - (e) Astana-M
*** Kalmár - Zsolt Kalmár (a) 09/06/1995, Győr (Hungary) (b) 1,85 (c) M - central
midfielder (d) Fehérvár FC (e) Dunajska Streda, RB Leipzig, Dunajska Streda, RB
Leipzig, Brøndby IF, RB Leipzig, FSV Frankfurt, RB Leipzig, ETO FC Győr
*** Kalmuratov - Kuanysh Kalmuratov (Қалмұратов Қуаныш Мұратұлы) (a)
27/08/1996, Atyrau (Kazakhstan) (b) 1,78 (c) D - left back (d) Kaysar Kyzylorda (e)
Taraz, Atyrau, FK Turan, Atyrau, Kaysar, Atyrau, Kaysar, Atyrau, Atyrau II, Astana-
1964, Atyrau II
*** Kalmykov - Amur Kalmykov (Калмыков Амур Арсенович) (a) 29/05/1994,
Islamey, Kabardino-Balkaria Republic (Russia) (b) 1,91 (c) F - center forward (d)
Rodina Moscow (e) Torpedo Moskva, Tambov, Armavir, Anzhi, Ekaterinodar,
Anzhi, Afips Afipskiy, KK Shevchenko
*** Kalmyrza - Meyrambek Kalmyrza (Мейрамбек Қалмырза) (a) 15/12/2002, ¿?
(Kazakhstan) (b) 1,84 (c) M - pivot (d) Okzhetpes Kokshetau (e) Okzhetpes, FC
Astana, Astana-Zhas
*** Kálnoki-Kis - Dávid Kálnoki-Kis (a) 06/08/1991, Budapest (Hungary) (b) 1,87
(c) D - central defense (d) Budapest Honvéd FC (e) Zalaegerszeg, Honvéd, Újpest
FC, MTK Budapest, Oldham Athletic
*** Kaloc - Filip Kaloc (Filip Kaloč) (a) 27/02/2000, ¿? (Czech Rep.) (b) 1,90 (c) M
- central midfielder (d) FC Banik Ostrava (e) Vitkovice, Banik Ostrava
*** Kaloga - Issa Kaloga (a) 27/02/2004, ¿? (Switzerland) (b) 1,82 (c) D - right back
(d) Servette FC (e) -
*** Kalogeropoulos - Alexios Kalogeropoulos (Αλέξιος Καλογερόπουλος) (a)
26/07/2004, Andravida (Greece) (b) 1,87 (c) D - central defense (d) - (e) Olympiakos
B, Olympiakos
*** Kalogirou - Loukas Kalogirou (Λούκας Καλογήρου) (a) 21/02/2002, Nicosia
(Cyprus) (b) 1,86 (c) D - central defense (d) Enosis Neon Paralimniou (e) Nea
Salamis, Ethnikos, Nea Salamis, APOEL FC
*** Kaloshkin - Ivan Kaloshkin (Калошкин Иван Владимирович) (a) 22/04/2001,
Vitebsk (Belarus) (b) 1,82 (c) F - right winger (d) Traktor Minsk (e) Ostrovets,
Krumkachi, Vitebsk II, BATE II
*** Kalpacki - David Kalpacki (Давид Калпачки) (a) 01/06/2000, Berovo (North
Macedonia) (b) 1,76 (c) M - central midfielder (d) Bregalnica Stip (e) FK Skopje, NK
Krka, Belasica
*** Kalsö - Símun Kalsö (Símun Kalsø) (a) 24/02/2003, ¿? (Faroe Islands) (b) 1,85
(c) D - central defense (d) KÍ Klaksvík (e) KÍ II
*** Kaltsas - Nikolaos Kaltsas (Νικόλαος Καλτσάς) (a) 03/05/1990, Veria (Greece)
(b) 1,72 (c) M - right midfielder (d) Asteras Tripolis (e) Karmiotissa, Anorthosis,
Asteras Tripoli, Panathinaikos, PAE Veria
*** Kalu - Chibuike Kalu (Chibuike Ogbonnaya Kalu) (a) 17/01/2003, ¿? (Nigeria)
(b) 1,65 (c) D - right back (d) FC Dinamo-Auto Tiraspol (e) -
*** Kaludjerovic - Andrija Kaludjerovic (Андрија Калуђеровић) (a) 29/10/1993,
Cetinje (RF Yugoslavia, now in Montenegro) (b) 1,75 (c) M - pivot (d) FK Mornar

Bar (e) FK Podgorica, Kom Podgorica, FK Lovcen, OFK Grbalj, FK Mladost, Rudar Pljevlja, Hønefoss, Rudar Pljevlja, FK Jezero, Rudar Pljevlja

*** Kalulu - Gédéon Kalulu (Gédéon Kalulu Kyatengwa) (a) 29/08/1997, Lyon (France) (b) 1,79 (c) D - right back (d) FC Lorient (e) AC Ajaccio, Olymp. Lyon B, Bourg-en-Bresse, Olymp. Lyon B

*** Kalulu - Pierre Kalulu (Pierre Kazeye Rommel Kalulu Kyatengwa) (a) 05/06/2000, Lyon (France) (b) 1,82 (c) D - central defense (d) AC Milan (e) Olymp. Lyon B

*** Kalumba - Justin-Noël Kalumba (Justin-Noël Kalumba Mwana Ngongo) (a) 25/12/2004, Roubaix (France) (b) 1,82 (c) F - right winger (d) Angers SCO (e) Angers SCO B

*** Kaluzinski - Jakub Kaluzinski (Jakub Kałuziński) (a) 31/10/2002, Gdańsk (Poland) (b) 1,84 (c) M - pivot (d) Antalyaspor (e) Lechia Gdánsk, AP Lechia

*** Kalvach - Lukas Kalvach (Lukáš Kalvach) (a) 19/07/1995, ¿? (Czech Rep.) (b) 1,81 (c) M - pivot (d) FC Viktoria Plzen (e) Sigma Olomouc, Sigma Olomouc B, FC MAS Taborsko, Sigma Olomouc B

*** Kalybaev - Dias Kalybaev (Калыбаев Диас Нурланович) (a) 25/08/1999, Almaty (Kazakhstan) (b) 1,85 (c) F - center forward (d) FC Khan Tengri (e) SV Deutz 05, Atyrau, Zhetysu, Atyrau, Zhetysu, Zhetysu B, FC Pesch, DFI Bad Aibling

*** Kalyuzhnyi - Ivan Kalyuzhnyi (Калюжний Іван Володимирович) (a) 21/01/1998, Dovzhyk, Kharkiv Oblast (Ukraine) (b) 1,89 (c) M - central midfielder (d) FK Oleksandriya (e) Kerala Blasters, FK Oleksandriya, Keflavík, FK Oleksandriya, Dinamo Kiev II, Rukh Lviv, Dinamo Kiev II, Metalist 1925, Dinamo Kiev II

*** Kamada - Daichi Kamada (鎌田 大地) (a) 05/08/1996, Iyo, Ehime (Japan) (b) 1,84 (c) M - attacking midfielder (d) SS Lazio (e) Eintracht, Sint-Truiden, Eintracht, Sagan Tosu, Higashiyama HS

*** Kamaheni - Montari Kamaheni (a) 01/02/2000, Tamale (Ghana) (b) 1,74 (c) D - left back (d) FC Ashdod (e) Dreams FC, FC Ashdod, Dreams FC

*** Kamano - François Kamano (a) 02/05/1996, Conakry (Guinea) (b) 1,75 (c) F - left winger (d) Abha Club (e) Lokomotiv Moskva, Girondins Bordeaux, SC Bastia, SC Bastia B, Satellite FC

*** Kamanzi - Warren Kamanzi (Warren Håkon Christofer Kamanzi) (a) 11/11/2000, Namsos (Norway) (b) 1,77 (c) D - right back (d) Toulouse FC (e) Tromsø, Rosenborg, Ranheim, Rosenborg, Rosenborg II

*** Kamara - Abdoulaye Kamara (a) 06/11/2004, Conakry (Guinea) (b) 1,85 (c) M - pivot (d) Borussia Dortmund II (e) -

*** Kamara - Aboubakar Kamara (a) 07/03/1995, Gonesse (France) (b) 1,77 (c) F - center forward (d) Olympiakos El Pireo (e) Aris Thessaloniki, Olympiakos, Aris Thessaloniki, Fulham, Dijon, Fulham, Yeni Malatyaspor, Fulham, Amiens SC, KV Kortrijk, AS Monaco B

*** Kamara - Alhaji Kamara (a) 16/04/1994, Freetown (Sierra Leona) (b) 1,80 (c) F - center forward (d) Randers FC (e) Vendsyssel FF, FC Sheriff, Al-Taawoun, D.C. United, Richmond, D.C. United, Norrköping, Johor DT, Norrköping, Kallon FC, Värnamo, Kallon FC, IK Frej Täby, Kallon FC, Djurgården, Kallon FC

*** Kamara - Bingourou Kamara (a) 21/10/1996, Longjumeau (France) (b) 1,95 (c) G (d) Pau FC (e) Montpellier, Racing Club Strasbourg, RSC Charleroi, Racing Club Strasbourg, Tours FC

*** Kamara - Boubacar Kamara (Boubacar Bernard Kamara) (a) 23/11/1999, Marseille (France) (b) 1,84 (c) M - pivot (d) Aston Villa (e) Ol. Marseille, Ol. Marseille B

*** Kamara - Glen Kamara (a) 28/10/1995, Tampere (Finland) (b) 1,83 (d) Rangers FC (e) Dundee FC, Colchester Utd., Southend United
*** Kamara - Mohammed Kamara (Mohammed Kesselly Kamara) (a) 31/10/1997, Sinkor (Liberia) (b) 1,84 (c) F - right winger (d) Hapoel Haifa (e) Hatayspor, FC Astana, Hatayspor, Menemenspor, LA Galaxy II, SC Paderborn, UCLA Bruins, Apache
*** Kamara - Moussa Kamara (a) 03/04/1999, Paris (France) (b) 1,90 (c) D - central defense (d) Al-Naft SC (e) KF Ferizaj, Jammerbugt FC, Balzan FC, Real Avilés, Toulouse B
*** Kamau - Bruce Kamau (a) 28/03/1995, Nairobi (Kenya) (b) 1,75 (c) F - right winger (d) - (e) OFI Creta, Melbourne, OFI Creta, Western Sydney, Melbourne City, Adelaide United, Adelaide Olym.
*** Kamavuaka - Wilson Kamavuaka (a) 29/03/1990, Düren (Germany) (b) 1,88 (c) M - pivot (d) - (e) Helsinki IFK, MSV Duisburg, GKS Tychy, Darmstadt 98, Panetolikos, Sturm Graz, KV Mechelen, 1.FC Nürnberg, Jahn Regensburg, 1.FC Nürnberg, Hoffenheim II
*** Kamber - Robin Kamber (Robin Roger Kamber) (a) 15/02/1996, Basel (Switzerland) (b) 1,87 (c) M - pivot (d) FC Schaffhausen (e) Górnik Zabrze, Stade-Lausanne, FC Wil 1900, FC Schönenwerd, Slaven Belupo, Grasshoppers, FC Vaduz, FC Winterthur, FC Vaduz, Servette FC
*** Kamberi - Florian Kamberi (a) 08/03/1995, Lachen SZ (Switzerland) (b) 1,89 (c) F - center forward (d) - (e) Huddersfield Town, FC Winterthur, FC St. Gallen, Sheffield Wednesday, FC St. Gallen, Aberdeen FC, FC St. Gallen, Hibernian FC, Rangers FC, Hibernian FC, Grasshoppers, Hibernian FC, Grasshoppers, Karlsruher SC, Grasshoppers, Rapperswil-Jona
*** Kamberi - Lindrit Kamberi (a) 07/10/1999, Zürich (Switzerland) (b) 1,83 (c) D - central defense (d) FC Zürich (e) FC Winterthur, FC Zürich, FC Wil 1900, FC Zürich
*** Kambic - Luka Kambic (Luka Kambič) (a) 20/12/1998, ¿? (Slovenia) (b) 1,70 (c) D - right back (d) FC Koper (e) NK Krka
*** Kambolov - Ruslan Kambolov (Камболов Руслан Александрович) (a) 01/01/1990, Vladikavkaz (Soviet Union, now in Russia) (b) 1,80 (c) M - pivot (d) - (e) Aktobe, Arsenal Tula, Krasnodar, Rubin Kazan, Neftekhimik, Volgar, FK Novgorod, Lokomotiv Moskva II
*** Kamdem - Bradley Kamdem (Bradley Sheede Kamdem Fewo) (a) 18/08/1994, Paris (France) (b) 1,84 (c) D - left back (d) Cavalry FC (e) Valletta, ATL UTD 2, St. Louis FC, Fresno, Rochester, Colorado, UNLV Rebels, Calgary, UNLV Rebels
*** Kamdem - Oliver Kamdem (Wabo Oliver Kamdem) (a) 15/10/2002, Marseille (France) (b) - (c) D - right back (d) - (e) Clermont Foot, Clermont B
*** Kamenar - Karlo Kamenar (a) 15/03/1994, Zagreb (Croatia) (b) 1,75 (c) M - central midfielder (d) HSK Posusje (e) Zrinjski Mostar, Mezőkövesd, NK Osijek, Zalgiris, NK Osijek, NK Rudes, NK Stupnik
*** Kamenar - Lubos Kamenar (Ľuboš Kamenár) (a) 17/06/1987, Trnava (Czechoslovakia, now in Slovakia) (b) 1,93 (c) G (d) Spartak Trnava (e) FC Petrzalka, Mlada Boleslav, Vasas FC, Śląsk Wroclaw, Spartak Trnava, ETO FC Győr, FC Nantes, Celtic FC, FC Nantes, Spartak Trnava, FC Nantes, Sparta Praha, FC Nantes, Sivasspor, FC Nantes, Petrzalka, Spartak Trnava
*** Kameni - Carlos Kameni (Idriss Carlos Kameni) (a) 18/02/1984, Douala (Cameroon) (b) 1,86 (c) G (d) - (e) UE Santa Coloma, AS Arta/Solar7, Fenerbahce, Málaga CF, RCD Espanyol, Le Havre AC, St.-Étienne, Le Havre AC, Kadji Sports

*** Kamenovic - Dimitrije Kamenovic (Димитрије Каменовић) (a) 16/07/2000, Pirot (RF Yugoslavia, now in Serbia) (b) 1,88 (c) D - left back (d) SS Lazio (e) Sparta Praha, Lazio, Čukarički

*** Kameraj - Çendrim Kameraj (Çendrim Kameraj) (a) 13/03/1999, Luzern (Switzerland) (b) 1,80 (c) D - right back (d) KF Dukagjini (e) SC Kriens, FC Lugano

*** Kameri - Dijon Kameri (a) 20/04/2004, Salzburg (Austria) (b) 1,81 (c) M - attacking midfielder (d) Red Bull Salzburg (e) FC Liefering

*** Kamess - Vladimirs Kamess (Vladimirs Kamešs) (a) 28/10/1988, Liepaja (Soviet Union, now in Latvia) (b) 1,81 (c) F - left winger (d) Elverum Fotball (e) Riga, Chaika Pes., Riga, SKA Khabarovsk, Liepaja, Enisey, Liepaja, Pogon Szczecin, Amkar Perm, Neftekhimik, Amkar Perm, Metalurgs, FB Gulbene-2005, Metalurgs

*** Kamilov - Vladislav Kamilov (Камилов Владислав Георгиевич) (a) 29/08/1995, Kalmanka, Altay Region (Russia) (b) 1,83 (c) M - central midfielder (d) Akhmat Grozny (e) Ufa, SKA Khabarovsk, Shinnik Yaroslav, Volgar, Nosta, Dinamo Barnaul, Nosta, Dinamo Barnaul, Din. Barnaul II, Rostov II, Dinamo Barnaul, Akron Konoplev

*** Kaminski - Jakub Kaminski (Jakub Kamiński) (a) 05/06/2002, Ruda Śląska (Poland) (b) 1,79 (c) F - left winger (d) VfL Wolfsburg (e) Lech Poznan, Szombierki B.

*** Kaminski - Krzysztof Kaminski (Krzysztof Kamiński) (a) 26/11/1990, Nowy Dwor Mazowiecki (Poland) (b) 1,91 (c) G (d) Wisła Płock (e) Júbilo Iwata, Ruch, Wisła Płock, Pogon Siedlce, Narew Ostroleka

*** Kaminski - Marcin Kaminski (Marcin Kamiński) (a) 15/01/1992, Konin (Poland) (b) 1,92 (c) D - central defense (d) FC Schalke 04 (e) VfB Stuttgart, Fortuna Düsseldorf, VfB Stuttgart, Lech Poznan, Aluminium Konin

*** Kaminski - Wiktor Kaminski (Wiktor Kamiński) (a) 23/02/2004, Ostrowiec Świętokrzyski (Poland) (b) 1,82 (c) F - center forward (d) Warta Poznań (e) Legia Warszawa, Legia II

*** Kamlashev - Daniil Kamlashev (Камлашев Даниил Вячеславович) (a) 11/09/2002, Moskva (Russia) (b) 1,80 (c) M - left midfielder (d) Rotor Volgograd (e) Strogino Moskva, Volga Uljanovsk, Strogino Moskva, Khimki 2, Strogino Moskva, Strogino II

*** Kampetsis - Argyris Kampetsis (Αργύρης Καμπετσής) (a) 06/05/1999, Athina (Greece) (b) 1,86 (c) F - center forward (d) Diósgyőri VTK (e) Panathinaikos, Willem II, Panathinaikos, Borussia Dortmund II

*** Kampl - Kevin Kampl (a) 09/10/1990, Solingen (Germany) (b) 1,78 (c) M - central midfielder (d) RB Leipzig (e) Bayer Leverkusen, Borussia Dortmund, RB Salzburg, VfR Aalen, VfL Osnabrück, Bayer Leverkusen, Greuther Fürth, Bayer Leverkusen, Bayer Leverkusen II

*** Kamyshev - Ilya Kamyshev (Камышев Илья Владиславович) (a) 13/07/1997, Novotroitsk, Orenburg Region (Russia) (b) 1,86 (c) M - pivot (d) Rodina Moscow (e) Khimki, Chertanovo, Khimki, Chertanovo, Zenit 2 St. Peterburg, Chertanovo

*** Kana - Marco Kana (a) 08/08/2002, Kinshasa (Congo DR) (b) 1,82 (c) M - pivot (d) RSC Anderlecht (e) -

*** Kanaan - Mohamad Kanaan (כנעאן מוחמד) (a) 14/01/2000, Majd al-Krum (Israel) (b) - (c) M - attacking midfielder (d) FC Ashdod (e) -

*** Kanak - Kaan Kanak (a) 06/10/1990, Yozgat (Turkey) (b) 1,80 (c) D - left back (d) Manisa FK (e) Hatayspor, Adana Demirspor, BB Erzurumspor, Alanyaspor, Adana Demirspor, Alanyaspor, Eskisehirspor, Ankaragücü, Inegölspor, Hatayspor, Bugsas Spor

*** Kanatkali - Dias Kanatkali (Қанатқали Диас) (a) 14/02/2001, ¿? (Kazakhstan) (b) 1,75 (c) D - left back (d) SD Family Nur-Sultan (e) Astana-M

*** Kancepolsky - El Yam Kancepolsky (קנצפולסקי ים אל) (a) 22/12/2003, Hawaii (United States) (b) 1,81 (c) M - pivot (d) Hapoel Tel Aviv (e) -

*** Kandil - Maor Kandil (קנדיל מאור) (a) 27/11/1993, Tel Aviv (Israel) (b) 1,78 (c) D - right back (d) Maccabi Haifa (e) Maccabi Tel Aviv, Bnei Yehuda, Ramat haSharon, Bnei Yehuda, Kabilio Jaffa, Bnei Yehuda

*** Kandil - Nordine Kandil (قنديل الدين نور) (a) 31/10/2001, Strasbourg (France) (b) 1,65 (c) M - attacking midfielder (d) FC Annecy (e) FC Annecy, Racing Club Strasbourg, Racing Strasbourg B

*** Kandji - Macoumba Kandji (a) 02/08/1985, Dakar (Senegal) (b) 1,93 (c) F - center forward (d) - (e) FC Lahti, FC Honka, Sanat Naft, FC Honka, FC Inter, HJK Helsinki, Al-Faisaly FC, HJK Helsinki, APO Levadiakos, AEL Kalloni, Houston, Colorado, New York, Silverbacks, New York, Silverbacks

*** Kandouss - Ismaël Kandouss (a) 12/11/1997, Lille (France) (b) 1,92 (c) D - central defense (d) KAA Gent (e) Union St. Gilloise, USL Dunkerque, Dunkerque B

*** Kane - Chris Kane (Christopher Kane) (a) 05/09/1994, Edinburgh (Scotland) (b) 1,74 (c) F - center forward (d) St. Johnstone FC (e) Queen of the South, St. Johnstone, Dumbarton FC, St. Johnstone, Dumbarton FC

*** Kane - Conor Kane (a) 05/11/1998, ¿? (Ireland) (b) 1,78 (c) D - left back (d) Drogheda United FC (e) Shelbourne, Drogheda United

*** Kane - Danny Kane (a) 23/04/1997, Dublin (Ireland) (b) 1,88 (c) D - central defense (d) Cashmere Technical FC (e) Sligo Rovers, Cork City, Fylde, Cork City

*** Kane - Harry Kane (Harry Edward Kane) (a) 28/07/1993, Walthamstow (England) (b) 1,88 (c) F - center forward (d) Bayern München (e) Tottenham Hotspur, Leicester City, Tottenham Hotspur, Norwich City, Tottenham Hotspur, Millwall, Tottenham Hotspur, Leyton Orient, Tottenham Hotspur

*** Kane - Ibrahim Kane (a) 23/06/2000, ¿? (Mali) (b) 1,75 (c) M - left midfielder (d) Vorskla Poltava (e) QD Hainiu, Vorskla Poltava, Duguwolofila, Vorskla Poltava, Duguwolofila, AS Bakaridjan

*** Kane - Kenny Kane (Kenneth Kane) (a) 13/08/1999, Ballymoney (Northern Ireland) (b) 1,85 (c) F - center forward (d) Ballymena United (e) Dervock FC

*** Kane - Lyndon Kane (a) 15/02/1997, Coleraine (Northern Ireland) (b) - (c) D - right back (d) Coleraine FC (e) -

*** Kane - Marcus Kane (a) 08/12/1991, Belfast (Northern Ireland) (b) - (c) D - left back (d) Glentoran FC (e) Linfield, Carrick Rangers, Linfield

*** Kané - Mamadou Kané (Mamadou Kané) (a) 22/01/1997, Conakry (Guinea) (b) 1,73 (c) M - pivot (d) Pafos FC (e) Olympiakos, Pafos FC, Olympiakos, Neftchi Baku, Olympiakos, Neftchi Baku, Kaloum, Gangan FC, Kaloum, Satellite FC

*** Kanellopoulos - Georgios Kanellopoulos (Γεώργιος Κανελλόπουλος) (a) 29/01/2000, ¿? (Greece) (b) 1,85 (c) M - central midfielder (d) HJK Helsinki (e) Asteras Tripoli

*** Kanevtsev - Danylo Kanevtsev (Каневцев Данило Дмитрович) (a) 26/07/1996, Kharkiv (Ukraine) (b) 1,87 (c) G (d) - (e) FC Dila, Metalist, Vorskla Poltava, Metalist 1925, Vorskla Poltava, Metalist 1925, Chornomorets, Metalist II

*** Kanga - Guélor Kanga (Guélor Kanga Kaku) (a) 01/09/1990, Oyem (Gabon) (b) 1,67 (c) M - attacking midfielder (d) Crvena zvezda Beograd (e) Sparta Praha, Crvena zvezda, Rostov, CF Mounana, Missile FC, Mangasport

*** Kanga - Wilfried Kanga (Wilfried Kanga Aka) (a) 21/02/1998, Montreuil-sous-Bois (France) (b) 1,89 (c) F - center forward (d) Standard de Lieja (e) Standard Liège, Hertha Berlin, BSC Young Boys, Kayserispor, Angers SCO, US Créteil-Lusitanos

*** Kangasaho - Tino Kangasaho (a) 09/03/2006, ¿? (Finland) (b) 1,88 (c) G (d) Pargas IF (e) FC Inter

*** Kangaslahti - Oliver Kangaslahti (a) 01/05/2000, ¿? (Finland) (b) 1,88 (c) D - central defense (d) FC Inter Turku II (e) Helsinki IFK, Mikkelin, AC Kajaani, FC Inter II

*** Kangwa - Kings Kangwa (a) 06/04/1999, Kasama (Zambia) (b) 1,70 (c) M - central midfielder (d) Crvena zvezda Beograd (e) Arsenal Tula, Buildicon FC

*** Kanichowsky - Gabi Kanichowsky (קניקובסקי גלעד גבריאל - Gavriel Kanichowsky) (a) 24/08/1997, Ra'anana (Israel) (b) 1,65 (c) M - attacking midfielder (d) Maccabi Tel Aviv (e) Maccabi Netanya, Hapoel Acre, Maccabi Tel Aviv, Hapoel Acre, Maccabi Tel Aviv, H. Petah Tikva, Maccabi Tel Aviv

*** Kankaanpää - Saku Kankaanpää (a) 15/06/2004, ¿? (Finland) (b) - (c) G (d) SJK Seinäjoki II (e) -

*** Kankanyan - Mher Kankanyan (Մհեր Քանքանյան) (a) 19/03/2004, ¿? (Armenia) (b) - (c) D - left back (d) BKMA Yerevan II (e) -

*** Kankava - Jaba Kankava (ჯაბა კანკავა) (a) 18/03/1986, Tbilisi (Soviet Union, now in Georgia) (b) 1,76 (c) M - pivot (d) Slovan Bratislava (e) Valenciennes FC, Tobol Kostanay, Stade Reims, Dnipro, Kryvbas, Dnipro, Arsenal Kyiv, Alania, Dinamo Tbilisi

*** Kannadil - Mahmoud Kannadil (קנאדלי מחמוד) (a) 11/08/1988, Makr (Israel) (b) 1,85 (c) G (d) - (e) Bnei Sakhnin

*** Kanon - Wilfried Kanon (Serge Wilfried Kanon) (a) 06/07/1993, Taabo (Ivory Coast) (b) 1,90 (c) D - central defense (d) Al-Jahra SC (e) Helsinki IFK, Pyramids FC, Al-Gharafa SC, Pyramids FC, ADO Den Haag, Corona Brasov, Gloria Bistrita

*** Kantaria - Giorgi Kantaria (გიორგი ქანთარია) (a) 27/04/1997, Zugdidi (Georgia) (b) 1,84 (c) M - pivot (d) FC Telavi (e) Kapaz PFK, FC Telavi, Neman Grodno, FK Zugdidi

*** Kanté - José Kanté (José Kanté Martínez) (a) 27/09/1990, Sabadell (Spain) (b) 1,84 (c) F - center forward (d) Urawa Red Diamonds (e) CZ Mighty Lions, Kairat Almaty, Legia Warszawa, Gimnàstic, Legia Warszawa, Wisła Płock, Górnik Zabrze, AEK Larnaca, AE Prat, At. Malagueño, AE Prat, UE Rubí, Manresa

*** Kanté - Mohamed Kanté (Mohamed Kefing Kanté) (a) 13/04/2004, ¿? (Guinea) (b) 1,80 (c) F - center forward (d) CS Sfaxien (e) Hafia FC, Odense BK, Hafia FC

*** Kanté - N'Golo Kanté (a) 29/03/1991, Paris (France) (b) 1,71 (c) M - pivot (d) Ittihad Club (e) Chelsea, Leicester City, SM Caen, US Boulogne, Boulogne B, Suresnes

*** Kantola - Roope Kantola (a) 01/04/2002, ¿? (Finland) (b) 1,81 (c) M - central midfielder (d) Salon Palloilijat (e) FC Inter, Pargas IF, FC Inter, Mikkelin, FC Inter

*** Kanu - Stanley Kanu (Stanley Guzorochi Kanu) (a) 17/01/1999, Lagos (Nigeria) (b) 1,81 (c) F - right winger (d) CS Marítimo B (e) Vilar Perdizes, Caçadores, Portosantense

*** Kanu - Wisdom Kanu (Wisdom Uda Kanu) (a) 27/03/1994, Lagos (Nigeria) (b) 1,75 (c) M - attacking midfielder (d) - (e) Michalovce, Slavoj Trebisov, FK Poprad, Vranov, Inter Bratislava, Zlaté Moravce, Inter Bratislava, Spisska N. Ves, Lagos Islanders

*** Kanuric - Adnan Kanuric (Adnan Kanurić) (a) 08/08/2000, Linz (Austria) (b) 1,94 (c) G (d) - (e) Nottingham Forest, Oxford City, Nottingham Forest, FK Sarajevo, SKF Sered

*** Kanyuk - Gidi Kanyuk (קאניוק גידי) (a) 11/02/1993, Ramat Gan (Israel) (b) 1,79 (c) M - attacking midfielder (d) Beitar Jerusalem (e) Hapoel Haifa, Chonburi FC, Swat

Cat, Buriram Utd., Hapoel Haifa, Pakhtakor, M. Petah Tikva, Pakhtakor, Maccabi Tel Aviv, Pakhtakor, M. Petah Tikva

*** Käos - Martin Käos (a) 18/06/1998, Tallinn (Estonia) (b) 1,78 (c) D - right back (d) Pärnu JK Vaprus (e) JK Trans Narva, FCI Levadia, JK Trans Narva, FCI Levadia, Levadia II

*** Kapacak - Burak Kapacak (a) 08/12/1999, Bursa (Turkey) (b) 1,80 (c) F - right winger (d) Fenerbahce (e) Karagümrük, Fenerbahce, Bursaspor

*** Kapanadze - Tornike Kapanadze (თორნიკე კაპანაძე) (a) 04/06/1992, Kutaisi (Georgia) (b) 1,68 (c) F - attacking midfielder (d) Dinamo Batumi (e) FC Dila, Dinamo Tbilisi, Torpedo Kutaisi, FC Samtredia, FC Zestafoni, Torpedo Kutaisi, Samgurali, Torpedo Kutaisi II, FC Samtredia II

*** Kapanadze - Tsotne Kapanadze (ცოტნე კაპანაძე) (a) 30/08/2001, Tbilisi (Georgia) (b) - (c) D - right back (d) FC Saburtalo (e) FC Telavi, FC Locomotive, Rustavi

*** Kapanga - Colet Kapanga (a) 15/04/2000, Kinshasa (Congo DR) (b) 1,87 (c) D - left back (d) FC Hlinsko (e) Pardubice B, Hlinsko, Paris FC B, Noisy-le-Grand, Villemomble, Olympique Alès

*** Kapartis - Chrysovalantis Kapartis (Χρυσοβαλάντης Καπαρτής) (a) 26/10/1991, Nicosia (Cyprus) (b) 1,84 (c) F - center forward (d) ASIL Lysi (e) Olympiakos N., PAEEK Kyrenia, Karmiotissa, Ethnikos, ASIL Lysi, Ethnikos, Olympiakos N., PAEEK Kyrenia, THOI Lakatamias, Chalkanoras, Olympiakos N., Chalkanoras, Olympiakos N.

*** Kapek - Przemyslaw Kapek (Przemysław Kapek) (a) 07/05/2003, Tarnów (Poland) (b) 1,77 (c) M - attacking midfielder (d) Wieczysta Krakow (e) Cracovia

*** Kapetanovic - Tarik Kapetanovic (Tarik Kapetanović) (a) 06/06/2003, Tuzla (Bosnia and Herzegovina) (b) 1,84 (c) D - left back (d) FK Sarajevo (e) Sloboda Tuzla

*** Kapi - Mustafa Kapi (Mustafa Kapı) (a) 08/08/2002, Denizli (Turkey) (b) 1,75 (c) M - central midfielder (d) Tuzlaspor (e) Tuzlaspor, Adana Demirspor, LOSC Lille B

*** Kapianidze - Luka Kapianidze (ლუკა კაპიანიძე) (a) 10/01/1999, ¿? (Georgia) (b) 1,89 (c) D - central defense (d) Dinamo Batumi (e) Torpedo Kutaisi, Tskhinvali, Dinamo Tbilisi

*** Kapic - Rifet Kapic (Rifet Kapić) (a) 03/07/1995, Cazin (Bosnia and Herzegovina) (b) 1,81 (c) M - central midfielder (d) KS Lechia Gdańsk (e) Lechia Gdánsk, Valmiera, Kryvbas, FK Sarajevo, SC Paderborn, FC Sheriff, SC Paderborn, Grasshoppers, FK Sarajevo, Grasshoppers, FC Sheriff, Grasshoppers, ND Gorica, Varnsdorf, Istra 1961 II

*** Kapiloto - Nisso Kapiloto (קפילוטו ניסו) (a) 01/10/1989, Bat Yam (Israel) (b) 1,83 (c) D - central defense (d) Sekzia Ness Ziona (e) Hapoel Haifa, B. Jerusalem, FC St. Gallen, B. Jerusalem, Alki Larnaca, Maccabi Tel Aviv, Hapoel Acre, Maccabi Tel Aviv, FC Ashdod, Maccabi Tel Aviv

*** Kapino - Stefanos Kapino (Στέφανος Καπίνο) (a) 18/03/1994, Piraeus (Greece) (b) 1,96 (c) G (d) Panetolikos GFS (e) Miedź Legnica, Arminia Bielefeld, Werder Bremen, SV Sandhausen, Werder Bremen, Nottingham Forest, Olympiakos, Mainz 05, Panathinaikos

*** Kapinus - Dmytro Kapinus (Капінус Дмитро Іванович) (a) 28/04/2003, Cherkasy (Ukraine) (b) 1,79 (c) D - right back (d) Metalist 1925 Kharkiv (e) Metalist 1925, Shakhtar Donetsk, Shakhtar II

*** Kapitanovic - Dino Kapitanovic (Dino Kapitanović) (a) 16/03/2000, Zadar (Croatia) (b) - (c) F - center forward (d) NK Solin (e) NK Krka, NK Istra, Din. Zagreb II, NK Dubrava ZG, Din. Zagreb II
*** Kaplan - Ahmetcan Kaplan (a) 16/01/2003, Trabzon (Turkey) (b) 1,89 (c) D - central defense (d) Ajax de Ámsterdam (e) Trabzonspor
*** Kaplan - Ferhat Kaplan (a) 07/01/1989, Izmir (Turkey) (b) 1,90 (c) G (d) - (e) Giresunspor, Adana Demirspor, Antalyaspor, Genclerbirligi, Dardanelspor
*** Kaplenko - Kirill Kaplenko (Капленко Кирилл Дмитриевич) (a) 15/06/1999, Minsk (Belarus) (b) 1,87 (c) M - pivot (d) FK Orenburg (e) Zenit 2 St. Peterburg, Orenburg, Zenit 2 St. Peterburg
*** Kapliyenko - Oleksandr Kapliyenko (Каплієнко Олександр Максимович) (a) 07/03/1996, Zaporizhya (Ukraine) (b) 1,79 (c) D - left back (d) SK Dnipro-1 (e) SK Dnipro-1, Metalist, Auda, Torpedo Moskva, Tambov, Dinamo Tbilisi, MFK Metalurg, Smolevichi, Chornomorets, Alanyaspor, Metalist, Metalurg Z., Zaporizhya II
*** Kapllani - Dejvid Kapllani (a) 03/06/2001, Durrës (Albania) (b) 1,84 (c) F - center forward (d) - (e) KF Erzeni, KF Teuta
*** Kaplunov - Dmitriy Kaplunov (Каплунов Дмитрий Викторович) (a) 21/04/1994, Baranovichi (Belarus) (b) 1,78 (c) D - left back (d) Lokomotiv Gomel (e) Dzerzhinsk, Gomel, Dnyapro Mogilev, Granit, Dnyapro Mogilev, Luch, FK Baranovichi, FK Baranovichi Reserves
*** Kapnidis - Antonis Kapnidis (Αντώνης Λούκαρης-Καπνίδης) (a) 15/08/1992, Thessaloniki (Greece) (b) 1,86 (c) F - center forward (d) - (e) Proodeftiki, PAE Chania, Veria NPS, Panevezys, AO Xanthi, Digenis Morfou, Ergotelis, Doxa Dramas, Aris Thessaloniki, AO Kavala, An. Giannitson, Doxa Dramas, Agrotikos
*** Kapornai - Bertalan Kapornai (a) 06/08/2002, Budapest (Hungary) (b) 1,78 (c) M - central midfielder (d) Vasas FC (e) -
*** Kapov - Krasimir Kapov (Капов Красимир Евгеньевич) (a) 14/07/1999, Mogilev (Belarus) (b) 1,81 (c) F - right winger (d) Dnepr Mogilev (e) Dzerzhinsk, Dinamo Minsk II, Underdog, Dinamo Minsk II
*** Kapper - Sander Kapper (a) 08/12/1994, Viljandi (Estonia) (b) 1,75 (c) F - right winger (d) Pärnu JK Vaprus (e) JK Tammeka, JK Viljandi, JK Tammeka, JK Viljandi, JK Tammeka, JK Viljandi, FC Myllypuro
*** Kapra - Albin Kapra (a) 07/06/2000, Prishtinë (Yugoslavia, now in Kosovo) (b) 1,87 (c) D - left back (d) FC Ballkani (e) KF Drenica, FC Ballkani, KF Trepca 89, FC Ballkani, KF 2 Korriku
*** Kapralik - Adrian Kapralik (Adrián Kaprálik) (a) 10/06/2002, Dolný Kubín (Slovakia) (b) 1,78 (c) F - right winger (d) Górnik Zabrze (e) -
*** Kapsarov - Kostadin Kapsarov (Костадин Капсаров) (a) 21/05/2005, Skopje (North Macedonia) (b) 1,77 (c) F - right winger (d) - (e) AP Brera
*** Kapsis - Andreas Kapsis (Ανδρέας Καψής) (a) 21/09/2005, Larnaca (Cyprus) (b) - (c) D - central defense (d) AEK Larnaca (e) -
*** Kaptilovich - Dmitriy Kaptilovich (Каптилович Дмитрий Андреевич) (a) 22/02/2003, ¿? (Russia) (b) 1,86 (c) D - central defense (d) Zvezda St. Petersburg (e) CSKA Moskva, CSKA Moskva II
*** Kapuadi - Steve Kapuadi (a) 30/04/1998, Le Mans (France) (b) 1,96 (c) D - central defense (d) Wisła Płock (e) AS Trencin, Inter Bratislava
*** Kapulica - Luka Kapulica (a) 18/01/2005, Split (Croatia) (b) - (c) M - attacking midfielder (d) HNK Gorica (e) -
*** Kapun - Nik Kapun (a) 09/01/1994, Ljubljana (Slovenia) (b) 1,84 (c) M - central midfielder (d) - (e) Liepaja, Olimpija

*** Kapustka - Bartosz Kapustka (Bartosz Kapustka) (a) 23/12/1996, Tarnów (Poland) (b) 1,79 (c) M - central midfielder (d) Legia de Varsovia (e) Leicester City, OH Leuven, Leicester City, SC Freiburg, Leicester City, Cracovia
*** Kapustyanskiy - Danil Kapustyanskiy (Капустянский Данил Евгеньевич) (a) 30/10/2004, Orenburg (Russia) (b) 1,76 (c) M - attacking midfielder (d) FK Orenburg (e) Orenburg II
*** Kaput - Michal Kaput (Michał Kaput) (a) 18/02/1998, Wyszków (Poland) (b) 1,85 (c) M - pivot (d) Radomiak Radom (e) Radomiak, Piast Gliwice, Radomiak, LKS Lomza
*** Kara - Aytac Kara (Aytaç Kara) (a) 23/03/1993, Bornova (Turkey) (b) 1,88 (c) M - pivot (d) Kasimpasa (e) Galatasaray, Göztepe, Galatasaray, Kasimpasa, Bursaspor, Trabzonspor, Yeni Malatyaspor, Trabzonspor, Eskisehirspor, Altay SK
*** Karababa - Ata Berk Karababa (a) 26/03/2005, Aydin (Turkey) (b) - (c) F - right winger (d) Konyaspor (e) -
*** Karabatic - Jakov Karabatic (Jakov Karabatić) (a) 23/03/2000, Split (Croatia) (b) 1,97 (c) D - central defense (d) NK Varazdin (e) Cibalia, NK Kurilovec, NK Brezice 1919
*** Karabay - Yasir Karabay (Muhammed Yasir Karabay) (a) 26/01/1999, Zaanstad (Netherlands) (b) - (c) F - right winger (d) MKE Ankaragücü (e) Ankara Demir, Ankaragücü, Z. Kömürspor, Ankaragücü, Altindag Belediye
*** Karabec - Adam Karabec (a) 02/07/2003, Praha (Czech Rep.) (b) 1,87 (c) M - attacking midfielder (d) AC Sparta Praga (e) Sparta Praha B
*** Karabeci - Erando Karabeci (a) 06/09/1988, Tiranë (Albania) (b) 1,73 (c) M - central midfielder (d) KF Teuta (e) FC Prishtina, KF Teuta, KF Tirana, FK Kukësi, KF Tirana, FK Partizani
*** Karabelyov - Yanis Karabelyov (Янис Карабельов) (a) 23/01/1996, Sofia (Bulgaria) (b) 1,83 (c) M - pivot (d) Botev Plovdiv (e) Kisvárda, Slavia Sofia, Tsarsko Selo, Slavia Sofia
*** Karabin - Yaroslav Karabin (Карабін Ярослав Миронович) (a) 19/11/2002, Lviv (Ukraine) (b) 1,82 (c) F - center forward (d) Rukh Lviv (e) Rukh Lviv II, Karpaty, Karpaty II
*** Karac - Zoran Karac (Zoran Karać) (a) 30/06/1995, Novi Sad (Yugoslavia, now in Serbia) (b) 1,80 (c) F - left winger (d) FK Sloga Meridian (e) Zlatibor, Mladost GAT, Kabel Novi Sad, CSK Celarevo, Proleter, Sloga Temerin, CSK Celarevo, Beocin, CSK Celarevo, Beocin
*** Karaca - Efecan Karaca (a) 16/11/1989, Istanbul (Turkey) (b) 1,69 (c) F - right winger (d) Alanyaspor (e) Kartalspor, Sariyer, Adana Demirspor, Adanaspor, Kartalspor, Gaziantep BB
*** Karachalios - Zisis Karachalios (Ζήσης Καραχάλιος) (a) 10/01/1996, Karditsa (Greece) (b) 1,81 (c) M - pivot (d) PAS Giannina (e) APO Levadiakos, Anag. Karditsas, Ifestos Kardits
*** Karacic - Goran Karacic (a) 18/08/1996, Mostar (Bosnia and Herzegovina) (b) 1,96 (d) Adana Demirspor (e) Adanaspor, SV Sandhausen, Adanaspor, Zrinjski Mostar
*** Karademir - Ahmet Karademir (a) 02/04/2004, Konya (Turkey) (b) 1,73 (c) F - left winger (d) Karaman FK (e) Konyaspor, Karaman FK, Konyaspor
*** Karadogan - Jack Karadogan (Jack Can Karadogan) (a) 04/02/2004, Newport (Wales) (b) 1,77 (c) M - central midfielder (d) - (e) Newport County, Pontypridd, Newport County

*** Karadzhov - Ivan Karadzhov (Иван Милчов Караджов) (a) 12/07/1989, Kresna (Bulgaria) (b) 1,86 (c) G (d) - (e) Beroe, CSKA 1948, Arda Kardzhali, Soligorsk, Vereya, Beroe, Lokomotiv Plovdiv, CSKA Sofia, Rilski Sportist
*** Karaev - David Karaev (Караев Давид Сосланович) (a) 10/03/1995, Vladikavkaz (Russia) (b) 1,79 (c) F - center forward (d) Alania Vladikavkaz (e) Torpedo Moskva, SKA Khabarovsk, Ural, Kaspiy Aktau, Ural, KamAZ, Olimp Khimki, Khimki, SKA Rostov, Spartak V., Armavir, Neftekhimik, TSK-Tavriya, SKA-Energia, Gubkin, Yunost VKZ
*** Karafiat - Ondrej Karafiat (Ondřej Karafiát) (a) 01/12/1994, Praha (Czech Rep.) (b) 1,82 (c) D - central defense (d) FK Mlada Boleslav (e) Slavia Praha, Mlada Boleslav, Slavia Praha, Slovan Liberec, Slavia Praha, Slovan Liberec, Sparta Praha B, Ceske Budejovice, Sparta Praha B, Viktoria Zizkov, Sparta Praha B
*** Karagaren - Birsent Karagaren (Бирсент Хамди Карагарен) (a) 06/12/1992, Asenovgrad (Bulgaria) (b) 1,79 (c) F - right winger (d) CSKA 1948 (e) Lokomotiv Plovdiv, Dunav, Lokomotiv Plovdiv, Vereya, Etar, Shumen 2010
*** Karagiannis - Konstantinos Karagiannis (Κωνσταντίνος Καραγιάννης) (a) 02/04/2000, Nicosia (Cyprus) (b) 1,76 (c) D - left back (d) Volos NPS (e) Akritas Chlor., Olympiakos N., PAEEK Kyrenia, Olympiakos N., APOEL FC, Alki Oroklini, APOEL FC
*** Karagounis - Vasilios Karagounis (Βασίλειος Καραγκούνης) (a) 18/01/1994, Lamia (Greece) (b) 1,76 (c) M - pivot (d) PS Kalamata (e) Torpedo Kutaisi, Ermis Aradippou, Platanias, Iraklis, AEL Limassol, Olympiakos, Reggina, Olympiakos, Aris Thessaloniki, Olympiakos
*** Karagöz - Mustafa Can Karagöz (a) 13/05/2002, Istambul (Turkey) (b) 1,71 (c) M - central midfielder (d) Ümraniyespor (e) Edirnespor, Ümraniyespor, Amasyaspor FK, Ümraniyespor
*** Karagöz - Yusuf Karagöz (a) 05/10/1999, Hatay (Turkey) (b) 1,95 (c) G (d) Alanyaspor (e) Edirne Belediye, Alanyaspor, Batman Petrol, Alanyaspor, Erzin Spor, Alanyaspor
*** Karagulyan - Ruben Karagulyan (Карагулян Рубен Хачатурович) (a) 15/05/2003, ¿? (Armenia) (b) 1,94 (c) D - central defense (d) FC Syunik (e) Lernayin Artsakh, Stavropol II
*** Karajbic - Ermin Karajbic (Ermin Karajbić) (a) 18/03/2002, ¿? (Slovenia) (b) 1,90 (c) G (d) NK Vrhnika (e) Ivancna Gorica, Koper, NK Brezice 1919, Koper
*** Karakaci - Abaz Karakaci (Abaz Karakaçi) (a) 25/08/1992, Shkodër (Albania) (b) 1,84 (c) M - pivot (d) AF Elbasani (e) KS Kastrioti, KF Egnatia, KS Kastrioti, Besëlidhja, KS Kastrioti, KF Tërbuni, FK Apolonia, KS Luftëtari, KF Butrinti, KF Vllaznia, KF Ada Velipojë, KF Vllaznia, FK Partizani, KF Vllaznia
*** Karakamisev - Riste Karakamisev (a) 16/06/1995, Valandovo (North Macedonia) (b) 1,93 (d) - (e) FK Bylis, Tikves, Sileks, Kozuf, FK Skopje, Kozuf Miravci
*** Karakashev - Georgi Karakashev (Георги Иванов Каракашев) (a) 08/02/1999, Razlog (Bulgaria) (b) 1,84 (c) M - central midfielder (d) Lokomotiv Plovdiv (e) Hebar P., Pirin Razlog, Hebar P., Pirin Razlog
*** Karakasidis - Georgios Karakasidis (Γεώργιος Καρακασίδης) (a) 31/01/2005, ¿? (Greece) (b) - (c) G (d) Panathinaikos Athina B (e) Aris Thessaloniki
*** Karakaya - Ali Karakaya (a) 01/01/2002, Isparta (Turkey) (b) 1,80 (c) M - pivot (d) Konyaspor (e) 1922 Konya, Konyaspor, 1922 Konya, Konyaspor
*** Karakus - Vedat Karakus (Vedat Karakuş) (a) 28/02/1998, Sanliurfa (Turkey) (b) 1,85 (c) G (d) Adana Demirspor (e) Modafen, Kayserispor, Lüleburgazspor

*** Karaman - Dinmukhamed Karaman (Қараман Дінмұхамед Рахымұлы) (a) 26/06/2000, Taraz (Kazakhstan) (b) 1,78 (c) F - right winger (d) FK Aksu (e) FK Aksu, Taraz, Taraz-Karatau

*** Karaman - Kenan Karaman (a) 05/03/1994, Stuttgart (Germany) (b) 1,89 (c) F - right winger (d) FC Schalke 04 (e) Besiktas, Fortuna Düsseldorf, Hannover 96, Hoffenheim, Hoffenheim II

*** Karamanaga - Edin Karamanaga (Един Караманага) (a) 06/02/2004, ¿? (Serbia and Montenegro, now in Serbia) (b) 1,80 (c) F - left winger (d) FK Otrant-Olympic Ulcinj (e) Mornar Bar, Otrant-Olympic

*** Karamanolis - Andreas Karamanolis (Ανδρέας Καραμανώλης) (a) 02/09/2001, Xylofagou (Cyprus) (b) 1,83 (c) D - central defense (d) APOEL FC (e) APOEL FC, Doxa Katokopias, Agia Napa

*** Karamanos - Anastasios Karamanos (Αναστάσιος Καραμάνος) (a) 21/09/1990, Aspropyrgos (Greece) (b) 1,86 (c) F - center forward (d) - (e) PAS Lamia, Olympiakos, Feirense, Olympiakos, Rio Ave, Olympiakos, Feirense, Olympiakos, Panionios, Olympiakos, Atromitos FC, Olympiakos, Atromitos FC, Ast. Magoulas, Aspropyrgos

*** Karamarko - Marin Karamarko (a) 14/04/1998, Pula (Croatia) (b) 1,91 (c) D - central defense (d) TSV Hartberg (e) NS Mura, GOSK Gabela, RNK Split, NK Val, NK OSK Otok

*** Karamarko - Marko Karamarko (a) 27/03/1993, Witten (Germany) (b) 1,77 (c) D - right back (d) - (e) Velez Mostar, Croat. Zmijavci, Zalgiris, Slaven Belupo, Cibalia, NK Osijek, NK Sesvete, NK Osijek, Wegberg-Beeck, Patro Eisden, Wattenscheid 09, SF Lotte, Preussen Münster

*** Karamatic - Mateo Karamatic (Mateo Karamatić) (a) 28/09/2001, Ehenbichl (Austria) (b) 1,87 (c) D - central defense (d) NK Olimpija Ljubljana (e) NK Osijek II, USK Anif

*** Karamoh - Yann Karamoh (Yann Dorgelès Isaac Karamoh) (a) 08/07/1998, Abidjan (Ivory Coast) (b) 1,85 (c) F - left winger (d) Torino FC (e) Parma, Karagümrük, Parma, Internazionale Milano, Parma, Internazionale Milano, Girondins Bordeaux, Internazionale Milano, SM Caen, Internazionale Milano, SM Caen, SM Caen B

*** Karamoko - Aboubakar Karamoko (a) 15/10/1999, Abidjan (Ivory Coast) (b) 1,72 (c) D - right back (d) Riga FC (e) Riga, Auda, Ermis Aradippou, Doxa Katokopias, Digenis Morfou, Doxa Katokopias, Septemvri Sofia, At. Malagueño

*** Karamoko - Ben Karamoko (Benjamin Kantie Karamoko) (a) 17/05/1995, Paris (France) (b) 1,95 (c) D - central defense (d) - (e) Spartak Varna, RSC Charleroi, Sarpsborg 08, Haugesund, Aalesund, Haugesund, Saint-Étienne B, US Créteil-Lusitanos, Saint-Étienne B

*** Karamoko - Hamadou Karamoko (a) 31/10/1995, Paris (France) (b) 1,94 (c) D - central defense (d) FC Progrès Niederkorn (e) Paris 13 At., FC Chambly Oise, Red Star FC, US Lusitanos, FC Nantes B, FC Lorient, Lorient B

*** Karamoko - Mamoudou Karamoko (a) 08/06/1999, Paris (France) (b) 1,88 (c) F - center forward (d) Fehérvár FC (e) Fehérvár, FC København, LASK, Wolfsburg II, Racing Strasbourg B

*** Karanikas - Nikolaos Karanikas (Νικόλαος Καρανίκας) (a) 04/03/1992, Larisa (Greece) (b) 1,76 (c) D - right back (d) - (e) AO Trikala, Zimbru Chisinau, Anag. Karditsas, AE Larisa, PAS Giannina, AE Larisa

*** Karanikolas - Kyriakos Karanikolas (Κυριάκος Καρανικόλας) (a) 08/07/2003, Limassol (Cyprus) (b) - (c) D - central defense (d) Aris Limassol (e) -

*** Karapetyan - Aleksandr Karapetyan (Ալեքսանդր Կարապետյան) (a) 23/12/1987, Tbilisi (Soviet Union, now in Georgia) (b) 1,84 (c) F - center forward (d) - (e) Pyunik Yerevan, Alashkert CF, FC Noah, Ararat-Armenia, Tambov, Sochi, Progrès Niederkorn, Victoria Rosport, F91 Dudelange, CS Grevenmacher, F91 Dudelange, FC 08 Homburg, SV Elversberg, FC Oberneuland, SV Wehen II, SV Gonsenheim
*** Karapetyan - Aris Karapetyan (Արիս Կարապետյան) (a) 24/05/2005, ¿? (Armenia) (b) - (c) F - center forward (d) BKMA Yerevan II (e) Pyunik Yerevan B
*** Karapetyan - Lyova Karapetyan (Լյովա Կարապետյան) (a) 01/03/2001, Gyumri (Armenia) (b) - (c) G (d) Shirak Gyumri C.F. (e) Shirak II
*** Karapetyan - Marat Karapetyan (Մարատ Կարապետյան) (a) 17/05/1991, ¿? (Armenia) (b) - (c) M - right midfielder (d) Lernayin Artsakh Goris (e) -
*** Karapuzov - Vladislav Karapuzov (Карапузов Владислав Александрович) (a) 06/01/2000, Norilsk (Russia) (b) 1,80 (c) F - right winger (d) FC Pari Nizhniy Novgorod (e) Pari Nizhny Novgórod, Dinamo Moskva, Akhmat Grozny, Dinamo Moskva, Akhmat Grozny, Dinamo Moskva, Tambov, Dinamo Moskva, Dinamo Moskva II, Loko-Kazanka M., Lokomotiv Moskva II
*** Karasausks - Arturs Karasausks (Artūrs Karašausks) (a) 29/01/1992, Riga (Latvia) (b) 1,78 (c) F - center forward (d) Krasava Ypsona FC (e) Liepaja, Ethnikos, Liepaja, Riga, Pafos FC, RFS, Akzhayik, Liepaja, FC Wil 1900, Skonto, Piast Gliwice, Skonto, Rubin Kazan, Skonto, FB Gulbene-2005, Skonto, Dnipro, Skonto, Olimps Riga
*** Karasev - Pavel Karasev (Карасёв Павел Сергеевич) (a) 10/07/1992, Drezna, Moskau Oblast (Russia) (b) 1,75 (c) M - pivot (d) Veles Moscú (e) Rotor Volgograd, Pari Nizhny Novgórod, BATE Borisov, Tambov, Anzhi, SKA Khabarovsk, Anzhi, SKA Khabarovsk, Khimik, Loko-Kazanka M., LFK Lokomotiv 2
*** Karashima - Yukiyoshi Karashima (辛島 侑烈) (a) 15/01/1997, Fukushima, Fukushima (Japan) (b) 1,75 (c) M - pivot (d) FK Zalgiris Vilnius (e) Hegelmann, Dinamo Riga, FC Hürth, Biwako Seikei, Toin Gakuen
*** Kárason - Styrmir Máni Kárason (a) 09/08/2004, ¿? (Iceland) (b) - (c) F (d) Haukar Hafnarfjördur (e) KR Reykjavík, KV Vesturbaejar, KR Reykjavík
*** Karasyuk - Roman Karasyuk (Карасюк Роман Іванович) (a) 27/03/1991, Volodymyr-Volynskyi, Volyn Oblast (Soviet Union, now in Ukraine) (b) 1,82 (c) M - pivot (d) Zemplin Michalovce (e) Pyunik Yerevan, Rukh Lviv, Kisvárda, Veres Rivne, Stal Kamyanske, Volyn Lutsk, Volyn Lutsk II, Stal Alchevsk, Volyn Lutsk II, BRW-VIK
*** Karatas - Kazimcan Karatas (Kazımcan Karataş) (a) 16/01/2003, Izmir (Turkey) (b) 1,82 (c) D - left back (d) Galatasaray (e) Altay SK
*** Karavaev - Ilya Karavaev (Караваев Илья Николаевич) (a) 04/05/1995, Almaty (Kazakhstan) (b) 1,86 (c) G (d) FK Atyrau (e) Akzhayik, Kairat-Zhas, Kairat II, FK Altay, Kairat II, ZSKA Almaty, Kairat II
*** Karavaev - Oleksandr Karavaev (Караваєв Олександр Олександрович) (a) 02/06/1992, Kherson (Ukraine) (b) 1,75 (c) D - right back (d) FC Dinamo de Kiev (e) Zorya Lugansk, Shakhtar Donetsk, Fenerbahce, Shakhtar Donetsk, Zorya Lugansk, Shakhtar Donetsk, Shakhtar II, Zorya Lugansk, Shakhtar II, FK Sevastopol, Shakhtar II
*** Karavaev - Vyacheslav Karavaev (Караваев Вячеслав Сергеевич) (a) 20/05/1995, Moskva (Russia) (b) 1,75 (c) D - right back (d) Zenit de San Petersburgo (e) Vitesse, Sparta Praha, CSKA Moskva, Jablonec, CSKA Moskva, Dukla Praha, CSKA Moskva, CSKA Moskva II

*** Karayel - Cebrail Karayel (a) 15/08/1994, Corum (Turkey) (b) 1,76 (c) D - right back (d) Konyaspor (e) Altay SK, Ankaragücü, Sanliurfaspor, BAK FK, Osmanlispor, Bugsas Spor, Ankara Adliye, Polatli Bugsas

*** Karayer - Metin Karayer (a) 18/05/1992, Sarreguemines (France) (b) 1,83 (c) D - central defense (d) FC Progrès Niederkorn (e) Sarreguemines

*** Karazor - Atakan Karazor (a) 13/10/1996, Essen (Germany) (b) 1,91 (c) M - pivot (d) VfB Stuttgart (e) Holstein Kiel, Borussia Dortmund II

*** Karceski - Daniel Karceski (Даниел Карчески) (a) 07/03/1992, Prilep (North Macedonia) (b) 1,79 (c) D - left back (d) Tikves Kavadarci (e) Pobeda Prilep, Sileks, Pobeda Prilep

*** Kardava - Bakar Kardava (ბაქარ ქარდავა) (a) 04/10/1994, Tbilisi (Georgia) (b) 1,85 (c) M - central midfielder (d) FC Saburtalo (e) Dinamo Tbilisi, Tskhinvali, FC Gagra, FC Sasco

*** Kardava - Soso Kardava (სოსო ქარდავა) (a) 08/12/1997, Rustavi (Georgia) (b) 1,90 (c) G (d) Marijampole City (e) Sioni Bolnisi, FC Gareji, Rustavi, FK Zugdidi, Rustavi, Shukura, Rustavi, FC Gardabani, Rustavi, Metalurgi R.

*** Kardesler - Erce Kardesler (Erce Kardeşler) (a) 14/03/1994, Canakkale (Turkey) (b) 1,84 (c) G (d) Hatayspor (e) Trabzonspor, Altinordu, Aliaga FK, Altinordu, Yesil Bursa

*** Kardum - Ivan Kardum (a) 18/07/1987, Osijek (Yugoslavia, now in Croatia) (b) 1,87 (c) G (d) SC Ritzing (e) Traiskirchen, Suduva, Slaven Belupo, Austria Viena, NK Osijek, Graficar V., NK Osijek, Vukovar '91, NK Osijek

*** Kardys - Krystian Kardys (Krystian Kardyś) (a) 03/08/2002, ¿? (Poland) (b) 1,79 (c) M - right midfielder (d) Stal Mielec (e) Czarni Polaniec, Stal Mielec, Stal Mielec II

*** Karelis - Nikolaos Karelis (Νικόλαος Καρέλης) (a) 24/02/1992, Heraklion (Greece) (b) 1,73 (c) F - center forward (d) Panetolikos GFS (e) ADO Den Haag, Brentford, KRC Genk, PAOK, KRC Genk, Panathinaikos, Amkar Perm, Ergotelis

*** Kargas - Giannis Kargas (a) 09/12/1994, Kilkis (Greece) (b) 1,88 (d) Anorthosis Famagusta (e) PAOK, PAS Giannina, Levski Sofia, PAS Giannina, Dynamo Brest, Panionios, Platanias, Panachaiki, Fostiras, AO Kavala

*** Kargbo Jr. - Ibrahim Kargbo Jr. (Ibrahim Kargbo Junior) (a) 03/01/2000, Freetown (Sierra Leona) (b) 1,90 (c) F (d) NK Solin (e) NK Celje, Dinamo Kyïv, Doxa Katokopias, Dinamo Kyïv, NK Celje, Dinamo Kyïv, Olimpik Donetsk, Dinamo Kyïv, KSV Roeselare, KSK Lierse Kem., KSV Roeselare

*** Karginov - Georgiy Karginov (Каргинов Георгий Аланович) (a) 29/01/2001, Vladikavkaz (Russia) (b) 1,76 (c) M - attacking midfielder (d) FK Astrakhan (e) Khimki 2, Zenit 2 St. Peterburg, Zenit St. Peterburg II, Spartak V.

*** Karhan - Patrick Karhan (a) 19/06/2003, Wolfsburg (Germany) (b) 1,85 (c) M - central midfielder (d) Dynamo Malzenice (e) Dyn. Malzenice, Spartak Trnava

*** Kari - Ayman Kari (a) 19/11/2004, Ivry-sur-Seine (France) (b) 1,76 (c) M - central midfielder (d) FC Lorient (e) FC Lorient, Paris Saint-Germain

*** Kari - Soudeysse Kari (a) 07/02/2002, Marseille (France) (b) 1,70 (c) M - central midfielder (d) - (e) OGC Nice B

*** Karic - Harun Karic (Karić Harun) (a) 30/11/2002, Tuzla (Bosnia and Herzegovina) (b) - (c) M - central midfielder (d) NK Lokomotiva Zagreb (e) FK Tuzla City, OFK Gradina, Zvijezda 09

*** Karic - Mahir Karic (Karić Mahir) (a) 05/03/1992, Sarajevo (Bosnia and Herzegovina) (b) - (c) M - attacking midfielder (d) FK Slavija Sarajevo (e) Leotar Trebinje, FK Gorazde, FK Olimpik, Happy Valley, Borac Banja Luka, FK Olimpik,

NK Vitez, FK Olimpik, Slavija S., FK Most, Travnik, Rudar Prijedor, Slovan Liberec B

*** Karic - Sven Karic (Sven Šoštarič Karič) (a) 07/03/1998, ¿? (Slovenia) (b) 1,86 (c) D - central defense (d) NK Maribor (e) Domžale

*** Karic - Tarik Karic (a) 19/09/2005, Sarajevo (Bosnia and Herzegovina) (b) - (c) G (d) SV Kapfenberg (e) -

*** Karimi - Ali Karimi (علی کریمی) (a) 11/02/1994, Isfahan (Iran) (b) 1,85 (c) M - central midfielder (d) Kayserispor (e) Qatar SC, Al-Duhail SC, Qatar SC, Esteghlal FC, Sepahan, Dinamo Zagreb, NK Lokomotiva, Dinamo Zagreb, Sepahan

*** Karimov - Cavad Karimov (a) 16/07/2004, ¿? (Azerbaijan) (b) - (c) F - right winger (d) Kapaz 2 Ganja (e) -

*** Karimov - Mekhrubon Karimov (Каримов Мехрубон) (a) 19/01/2004, ¿? (Tajikistan) (b) 1,90 (c) D - central defense (d) FC Samgurali Tskaltubo (e) Dinamo-Auto, Dynamo Dushanbe

*** Karimov - Ramazan Karimov (Рамазан Кәрімов) (a) 05/07/1999, Astana (Kazakhstan) (b) 1,90 (c) F - center forward (d) FK Maktaaral (e) FC Astana, Kaspiy Aktau, FC Astana, Kaspiy Aktau, FC Astana, Astana-Zhas

*** Karius - Loris Karius (Loris Sven Karius) (a) 22/06/1993, Biberach an der Riß (Germany) (b) 1,91 (c) G (d) Newcastle United (e) Liverpool, Union Berlin, Liverpool, Besiktas, Liverpool, Mainz 05, Man City Reserves, Mainz 05, Man City Reserves

*** Karjalainen - Rasmus Karjalainen (Rasmus Joonatan Karjalainen) (a) 04/04/1996, Oulu (Finland) (b) 1,85 (c) F - center forward (d) AC Oulu (e) Helsingborgs IF, Fortuna Sittard, Örebro SK, Fortuna Sittard, KuPS, Kemi Kings, AC Oulu, SJK II, OLS

*** Karjasevic - Huso Karjasevic (Huso Karjašević) (a) 10/07/1997, Schwelm (Germany) (b) 1,77 (c) M - pivot (d) FK Tuzla City (e) Po-dri-nje, F. Regensburg, Po-dri-nje

*** Karklins - Kriss Karklins (Krišs Kārkliņš) (a) 31/01/1996, Riga (Latvia) (b) 1,78 (c) D - right back (d) - (e) Liepaja, Valmiera, Riga, Liepaja, FHK Liepajas Metalurgs II

*** Karlen - Gaëtan Karlen (a) 07/06/1993, Sion (Switzerland) (b) 1,86 (c) F - center forward (d) - (e) FC Sion, Neuchâtel Xamax, FC Biel-Bienne, FC Thun, FC Sion, FC Biel-Bienne, FC Sion

*** Karlen - Grégory Karlen (a) 30/01/1995, Sion (Switzerland) (b) 1,87 (c) M - attacking midfielder (d) FC St. Gallen 1879 (e) FC Thun, FC Sion, FC Thun, FC Sion

*** Karlsbakk - Daniel Karlsbakk (Daniel Seland Karlsbakk) (a) 07/04/2003, Kristiansand (Norway) (b) 1,86 (c) F - center forward (d) SC Heerenveen (e) Viking, Bryne, Bryne FK II

*** Karlsson - Jesper Karlsson (Karl Jesper Karlsson) (a) 25/07/1998, Falkenberg (Sweden) (b) 1,79 (c) F - left winger (d) AZ Alkmaar (e) Elfsborg, Falkenbergs FF

*** Karlsson - Johan Karlsson (a) 20/06/2001, Uppsala (Sweden) (b) 1,72 (c) M - central midfielder (d) Kalmar FF (e) Sirius

*** Karlsson - Per Karlsson (a) 02/01/1986, Stockholm (Sweden) (b) 1,84 (c) D - central defense (d) - (e) AIK, Åtvidabergs FF, AIK, AFC Eskilstuna, AIK

*** Karlsson - Victor Karlsson (a) 18/05/2001, ¿? (Sweden) (b) - (c) M - central midfielder (d) Varbergs BoIS (e) Norrby, Varbergs BoIS, Onsala BK

*** Karlsson Adjei - Simon Karlsson Adjei (Simon Emanuel Karlsson Adjei) (a) 10/11/1993, ¿? (Sweden) (b) 1,92 (c) F - center forward (d) - (e) AFC Eskilstuna, Varbergs BoIS, Assyriska IK, York9 FC, Assyriska IK, Aurora FC, Husqvarna FF, Tenhults IF, Husqvarna FF, Råslätts SK, Husqvarna FF

*** Karlsson Lagemyr - Patrik Karlsson Lagemyr (a) 18/12/1996, Göteborg (Sweden) (b) 1,67 (c) M - attacking midfielder (d) IK Sirius (e) IFK Göteborg

*** Karlström - Jesper Karlström (Jesper Karlström) (a) 21/06/1995, Stockholm (Sweden) (b) 1,85 (c) M - pivot (d) Lech Poznan (e) Djurgården, Brommapojkarna, Djurgården, Brommapojkarna

*** Karlstrøm - Jacob Karlstrøm (a) 09/01/1997, Tromsø (Norway) (b) 2,00 (c) G (d) Molde FK (e) Tromsø, Tromsø IL II

*** Karmi - Raz Karmi (רז כרמי) (a) 27/01/1996, Shoham (Israel) (b) 1,88 (c) G (d) Maccabi Netanya (e) Hapoel Bnei Lod

*** Karnicnik - Zan Karnicnik (Žan Karničnik) (a) 18/09/1994, Slovenj Gradec (Slovenia) (b) 1,84 (c) D - right back (d) NK Celje (e) NK Celje, Ludogorets, NS Mura, NK Maribor B, Radlje, NK Dravograd

*** Karnitskiy - Aleksandr Karnitskiy (Карницкий Александр Иванович) (a) 14/02/1989, Stolbtsy (Soviet Union, now in Belarus) (b) 1,87 (c) M - pivot (d) Mezőkövesd Zsóry FC (e) Sepsi OSK, Tosno, Gomel, Hapoel Raanana, BATE Borisov, Gomel, Granit, Polotsk, FK Baranovichi

*** Karnitskiy - Valeri Karnitskiy (Карницкий Валерий Иванович) (a) 20/08/1991, Stolbtsy (Soviet Union, now in Belarus) (b) 1,80 (c) D - left back (d) Kronon Stolbtsy (e) Dzerzhinsk, Neman Stolbtsy, Smolevichi, Dynamo Brest, Belshina, Dynamo Brest, FK Baranovichi, Smolevichi

*** Karo - Andreas Karo (Ανδρέας Καρώ) (a) 09/09/1996, Nicosia (Cyprus) (b) 1,90 (c) D - central defense (d) OFI Creta (e) APOEL FC, Lazio, Marítimo, Lazio, Salernitana, Lazio, Apollon Limassol, Pafos FC, Apollon Limassol, Nea Salamis, Apollon Limassol, Nottingham Forest

*** Karofeld - Magnus Karofeld (a) 20/08/1996, Rakvere ((b) 1,87 (c) G (d) FC Kuressaare (e) FC Flora, Kuressaare, FC Flora, Paide, FC Flora, FC Flora II

*** Karpenko - Igor Karpenko (Карпенко Ігор Олегович) (a) 24/09/1997, Lviv (Ukraine) (b) 1,83 (c) F - center forward (d) Podillya Khmelnytskyi (e) JK Trans Narva, Odra Wodzislaw, Akzhayik, Podillya Kh., Karpaty, Volyn Lutsk, Karpaty, Karpaty II, Volyn Lutsk, Karpaty II

*** Karpikov - Danila Karpikov (Карпиков Данила) (a) 15/10/2003, Semey (Kazakhstan) (b) 1,93 (c) G (d) Shakhter Karaganda (e) Shakhter-Bulat, FK Altay

*** Karpitskiy - Egor Karpitskiy (Карпицкий Егор Александрович) (a) 27/11/2003, Vitebsk (Belarus) (b) 1,88 (c) F - center forward (d) Krylya Sovetov Samara (e) Soligorsk, Soligorsk II, Shakhter P., Soligorsk II

*** Karpov - Danil Karpov (Карпов Данил Александрович) (a) 28/06/1999, Tyumen (Russia) (b) 1,79 (c) F - center forward (d) FK Krasnodar-2 (e) Tyumen

*** Karpov - Vadim Karpov (Карпов Вадим Юрьевич) (a) 14/07/2002, Kotlas, Arkhangelsk Region (Russia) (b) 1,91 (c) D - central defense (d) CSKA Moskva (e) Tekstilshchik, CSKA Moskva, CSKA Moskva II, SShOR Zenit

*** Karpovich - Sergey Karpovich (Карпович Сергей Александрович) (a) 29/03/1994, Petrishki (Belarus) (b) 1,82 (c) D - right back (d) Neman Grodno (e) Baltika, Kaysar, Isloch, Torpedo Zhodino, Dinamo Minsk, Gorodeya, Dinamo Minsk, FK Minsk, Dinamo Minsk, Naftan, Dinamo Minsk, Dinamo Minsk II, FK Bereza, Dinamo Minsk II

*** Karpukas - Artem Karpukas (Карпукас Артем Михайлович) (a) 13/06/2002, Biysk, Altai Region (Russia) (b) 1,84 (c) M - pivot (d) Lokomotiv Moskva (e) Loko-Kazanka M., Lokomotiv Moskva II

*** Karpus - Zakhar Karpus (Карпусь Захар Вікторович) (a) 07/04/2005, ¿? (Ukraine) (b) 1,82 (c) M - right midfielder (d) Kryvbas Kryvyi Rig (e) -

*** Karrica - Bernard Karrica (a) 07/01/2001, Gjakovë (RF Yugoslavia, now in Kosovo) (b) 1,84 (c) F - left winger (d) HNK Rijeka (e) ND Gorica, HNK Rijeka, Hrv Dragovoljac, HNK Rijeka, SKF Sered, HNK Rijeka, Din. Zagreb II, KF Gjakova

*** Karrikaburu - Jon Karrikaburu (Jon Karrikaburu Jaimerena) (a) 19/09/2002, Elizondo (Spain) (b) 1,83 (c) F - center forward (d) Real Sociedad (e) CD Leganés, Real Sociedad, Real Sociedad B, Real Sociedad C

*** Karsdorp - Rick Karsdorp (a) 11/02/1995, Schoonhoven (Netherlands) (b) 1,84 (c) D - right back (d) AS Roma (e) Feyenoord, AS Roma, Feyenoord

*** Karse - Karse (ჯორჯ ქარსელაძე, Jorge Karseladze) (a) 18/03/2005, Vila do Conde (Portugal) (b) 1,75 (c) D - right back (d) Rio Ave FC (e) -

*** Karshakevich - Valeriy Karshakevich (Каршакевич Валерий Юрьевич) (a) 15/02/1988, Marina Gorka (Soviet Union, now in Belarus) (b) 1,93 (c) D - central defense (d) Yelimay Semey (e) Qyzyljar, Taraz, Mordovia, Dnyapro Mogilev, Smolevichi, Gomel, FK Slutsk, Torpedo Zhodino, Granit, Belshina, Dynamo Brest, Torpedo Zhodino, Naftan II, Soligorsk II, FK Molodechno

*** Karssies - Sam Karssies (a) 26/02/2003, Enschede (Netherlands) (b) 1,86 (c) G (d) FC Twente Enschede (e) -

*** Kartal - Nemanja Kartal (a) 17/07/1994, Pljevlja (RF Yugoslavia, now in Montenegro) (b) 1,96 (c) D - central defense (d) TuS Bövinghausen (e) Rudar Pljevlja, Maziya S&RC, Rudar Pljevlja, OFK Grbalj, Rudar Pljevlja, FK Krupa, Radnicki Niš, Slavija S., PAOK, An. Giannitson, PAOK, Anag.Epanomis, PAOK, Rudar Pljevlja

*** Kartalis - Alexandros Kartalis (Αλέξανδρος Καρτάλης) (a) 29/01/1995, Nürnberg (Germany) (b) 1,80 (c) M - central midfielder (d) Volos NPS (e) Atromitos FC, PAS Giannina, FSV Zwickau, Greuther Fürth II, Greuther Fürth, VfR Aalen, Greuther Fürth

*** Kartashyan - Artur Kartashyan (Արթուր Քարթաշյան) (a) 08/01/1997, Yerevan (Armenia) (b) 1,88 (c) D - central defense (d) Istiqlol Dushanbe (e) FC Van, Olympiakos N., FC Noah, FC Sevan, Pyunik Yerevan, Pyunik Yerevan B

*** Kartelev - Bogdan Kartelev (Картелев Богдан Константинович) (a) 22/10/2004, ¿? (Belarus) (b) - (c) M (d) Dnepr Mogilev II (e) Dnepr-Yuni Mogilev

*** Kartum - Sander Erik Kartum (a) 03/10/1995, Stjørdal (Norway) (b) 1,80 (c) M - attacking midfielder (d) SK Brann (e) Kristiansund, Stjørdals-Blink, Lånke IL

*** Kartushov - Yegor Kartushov (Картушов Єгор Олександрович) (a) 05/01/1991, Saky, Krym (Soviet Union, now in Ukraine/Crimea) (b) 1,82 (c) M - left midfielder (d) Karpaty Lviv (e) Metalist, Desna, Zorya Lugansk, Shakhtar II, Illichivets, Shakhtar II, Zorya Lugansk, Shakhtar II, Shakhtar 3

*** Karweina - Sinan Karweina (a) 29/03/1999, Gummersbach (Germany) (b) 1,73 (c) F - right winger (d) SK Austria Klagenfurt (e) Türkgücü Münch., MSV Duisburg, SF Lotte

*** Karzev - Eden Karzev (עדן קארצב, Карцев Эден Вадимович) (a) 11/04/2000, Afula (Israel) (b) 1,86 (c) M - pivot (d) Basaksehir FK (e) Maccabi Netanya, Dinamo Moskva, Maccabi Netanya, Maccabi Tel Aviv, Kiryat Shmona, Maccabi Tel Aviv, Hapoel Hadera, Maccabi Tel Aviv, Beitar TA Ramla

*** Kasa - Filip Kasa (Filip Kaša) (a) 01/01/1994, Ostrava (Czech Rep.) (b) 1,91 (c) D - central defense (d) DAC Dunajska Streda (e) Viktoria Plzen, MSK Zilina, Banik Ostrava, Baník Ostrava B

*** Kasa - Lior Kasa (קאסה ליאור) (a) 01/05/2005, ¿? (Israel) (b) - (c) M - pivot (d) - (e) Hapoel Jerusalem

*** Kasa - Redi Kasa (a) 01/09/2001, Parma (Italy) (b) 1,85 (c) F - center forward (d) KF Egnatia (e) Septemvri Sofia, Tsarsko Selo, Septemvri Sofia, Parma, Fermana

*** Kasabulat - Damir Kasabulat (Касабулат Дамир Кайратулы) (a) 29/08/2002, Almaty (Kazakhstan) (b) 1,81 (c) D - central defense (d) Kairat Almaty (e) Kairat Moskva, Kairat-Zhas
*** Kasalica - Ognjen Kasalica (a) 16/10/2002, ¿? (RF Yugoslavia, now in Montenegro) (b) - (c) D - left back (d) Rudar Pljevlja (e) FK Pljevlja, Rudar Pljevlja
*** Kasalo - Niko Kasalo (a) 31/12/2005, ¿? (Slovenia) (b) 1,75 (c) M - attacking midfielder (d) NS Mura (e) -
*** Kasami - Ard Kasami (a) 03/01/1998, Tetovo (North Macedonia) (b) 1,75 (c) M - pivot (d) Struga Trim & Lum (e) -
*** Kasami - Pajtim Kasami (a) 02/06/1992, Andelfingen (Switzerland) (b) 1,88 (c) M - central midfielder (d) - (e) Olympiakos, FC Basel, FC Sion, Olympiakos, Nottingham Forest, Olympiakos, Fulham, FC Luzern, Fulham, US Palermo, AC Bellinzona
*** Kasanwirjo - Neraysho Kasanwirjo (Neraysho Meritchio Kasanwirjo) (a) 18/02/2002, Amsterdam (Netherlands) (b) 1,85 (c) D - central defense (d) Feyenoord Rotterdam (e) FC Groningen, Ajax B
*** Kasarab - Maksim Kasarab (Касараб Максим Дмитриевич) (a) 10/06/2003, Minsk (Belarus) (b) 1,84 (c) D - central defense (d) FK Minsk (e) FK Minsk II
*** Kascelan - Predrag Kascelan (Предраг Кашћелан) (a) 30/06/1990, Cetinje (Yugoslavia, now in Montenegro) (b) 1,84 (c) D - central defense (d) SCM Zalau (e) FK Decic Tuzi, Rudar Pljevlja, OFK Grbalj, FK Bokelj, Vasalunds IF, Arsenal Tula, Khimik, Arsenal Tula, FK Mladost, Doxa Dramas, FK Bokelj, Spartak
*** Kase - Jan Erik Kase (a) 30/04/2004, Tallinn (Estonia) (b) - (c) G (d) FC Flora Tallinn IV (e) JK Loo
*** Kase - Martin Kase (a) 02/09/1993, Tallinn (Estonia) (b) 1,91 (c) D - central defense (d) Saku Sporting (e) Pärnu Vaprus, Paide, FC Flora, JK Viljandi, FC Flora, FC Flora II, FC Flora, Kalev, Kalev Tallinn II
*** Kashchuk - Oleksiy Kashchuk (Кащук Олексій Миколайович) (a) 29/06/2000, Novograd-Volynskyi, Zhytomyr Oblast (Ukraine) (b) 1,80 (c) F - right winger (d) Shakhtar Donetsk (e) Sabah FK, Shakhtar Donetsk, Sabah FK, Shakhtar Donetsk, FK Mariupol, Shakhtar Donetsk, Shakhtar II
*** Kashia - Guram Kashia (გურამ კაშია) (a) 04/07/1987, Tbilisi (Soviet Union, now in Georgia) (b) 1,85 (c) D - central defense (d) Slovan Bratislava (e) FC Locomotive, San José, Vitesse, Dinamo Tbilisi
*** Kashken - Dinmukhammed Kashken (Кашкен Динмухаммед Болатович) (a) 04/01/2000, Almaty (Kazakhstan) (b) 1,87 (c) D - central defense (d) - (e) Zalgiris, Shakhter K., Aktobe, FC Astana, Kaysar, FC Astana, Astana-Zhas, Zhetysu B, Astana-Zhas
*** Kashtanjeva - Qlirim Kashtanjeva (a) 04/02/1999, Hagen (Germany) (b) 1,84 (c) M - right midfielder (d) - (e) KF Ferizaj, KF Arbëria
*** Kashtanov - Aleksey Kashtanov (Каштанов Алексей Дмитриевич) (a) 13/03/1996, Dyatjkovo, Bryansk Region (Russia) (b) 1,93 (c) F - center forward (d) Ural Ekaterimburgo (e) Rodina Moskva, Ural, Rodina Moskva, Volga Uljanovsk, Rodina Moskva, Rosich, Kyzyltash, Kvant Obninsk, FK Kaluga, SShOR Bronnitsy
*** Kasic - Senad Kasic (Senad Kašić) (a) 04/04/1995, Konjic (Bosnia and Herzegovina) (b) 1,70 (c) M - left midfielder (d) Germania Klein-Krotzenburg (e) Igman Konjic, GOSK Gabela, Igman Konjic, Zeljeznicar
*** Kasimov - Dmytro Kasimov (Касімов Дмитро Дмитрович) (a) 14/08/1999, Dnipropetrovsk (Ukraine) (b) 1,78 (c) M - right midfielder (d) Kremin Kremenchuk (e) FK Minaj, Obolon, FK Obolon-2, Yarud Mariupol, Zirka, Zirka II

*** Kasius - Denso Kasius (a) 06/10/2002, Delft (Netherlands) (b) 1,83 (c) D - right back (d) AZ Alkmaar (e) Bologna, Rapid Wien, Bologna, FC Volendam
*** Kask - Kristjan Kask (a) 05/07/1999, Tallinn (Estonia) (b) - (c) M - attacking midfielder (d) Pärnu JK Vaprus (e) JK Viljandi, JK Viljandi, FC Flora III
*** Kasmi - Faysel Kasmi (a) 31/10/1995, ¿? (Belgium) (b) 1,68 (c) M - central midfielder (d) KFC Dessel Sport (e) Bregalnica Stip, Dhofar Club, Cherno More, URSL Visé, ASV Geel, KFCO Beerschot, Waterford FC, Lierse SK, Omonia Nicosia, Lierse SK, Standard Liège, Lierse SK, JMG Lier
*** Kasperkiewicz - Arkadiusz Kasperkiewicz (a) 29/09/1994, Łódź (Poland) (b) 1,87 (c) D - central defense (d) Bruk-Bet Termalica Nieciecza (e) Stal Mielec, Arka Gdynia, Rakow, Gornik Leczna, Olimpia Grudz., Widzew Lódz, Widzew II, MSP Szamotuly
*** Kastanaras - Thomas Kastanaras (Θωμάς Καστανάρας) (a) 09/01/2003, Stuttgart (Germany) (b) 1,86 (c) F - center forward (d) VfB Stuttgart (e) -
*** Kastanek - Daniel Kastanek (Daniel Kaštánek) (a) 12/03/2003, ¿? (Czech Rep.) (b) 1,95 (c) M - central midfielder (d) AC Sparta Praha B (e) -
*** Kastanos - Grigoris Kastanos (Γρηγόρης Κάστανος) (a) 30/01/1998, Sotira (Cyprus) (b) 1,79 (c) M - central midfielder (d) US Salernitana 1919 (e) Juve Next Gen, Salernitana, Frosinone, Pescara, Zulte Waregem, Pescara, Onisillos Sotira
*** Kastrati - Bleart Kastrati (a) 17/02/2003, Karaçevë e Epërme (Serbia and Montenegro, now in Kosovo) (b) - (c) D - left back (d) FK Bylis (e) KF Drenica, FK Bylis, FC A&N, FK Bylis, Ramiz Sadiku
*** Kastrati - Drilon Kastrati (a) 23/10/2001, Zürich (Switzerland) (b) 1,74 (c) M - central midfielder (d) - (e) Ararat Yerevan, FC Schaffhausen, FC Schaffhausen
*** Kastrati - Flamur Kastrati (a) 14/11/1991, Oslo (Norway) (b) 1,80 (c) F - center forward (d) Fitim Kastrati (e) Odd, Kristiansund, Sandefjord, Aalesund, Strømsgodset, Erzgebirge Aue, MSV Duisburg, VfL Osnabrück
*** Kastrati - Lirim Kastrati (a) 02/02/1999, Ogoste (RF Yugoslavia, Kosovo) (b) 1,78 (c) D - right back (d) Újpest FC (e) S. P. Padova
*** Kastrati - Lirim Kastrati (Lirim Kastrati) (a) 16/01/1999, Ogošte / Hogosht (RF Yugoslavia, now in Kosovo) (b) 1,74 (c) F - right winger (d) Fehérvár FC (e) Legia Warszawa, Dinamo Zagreb, NK Lokomotiva, Dinamo Zagreb, NK Lokomotiva
*** Kasym - Alibek Kasym (Касым Алибек Бекбайулы) (a) 27/05/1998, Iliyskiy Rayon (Kazakhstan) (b) 1,93 (c) D - central defense (d) FK Aktobe (e) Qyzyljar, Kairat Almaty, Kyzyl-Zhar, Kairat Almaty, Kyran, Kairat Almaty, Kairat II
*** Kasymbek - Dauren Kasymbek (Касымбек Даурен Толешұлы) (a) 23/01/2001, Arys (Kazakhstan) (b) 1,79 (c) M (d) FK Turan II (e) Ordabasy II
*** Katai - Aleksandar Katai (Александар Катаи) (a) 06/02/1991, Srbobran (Yugoslavia, now in Serbia) (b) 1,82 (c) F - left winger (d) Crvena zvezda Beograd (e) Los Ángeles, Chicago, Alavés, Chicago, Alavés, Crvena zvezda, Olympiakos, Crvena zvezda, Olympiakos, Platanias, Olympiakos, Vojvodina, Olympiakos, OFI Creta, Olympiakos, Vojvodina, FK Palic Koming
*** Katajamäki - Pauli Katajamäki (a) 04/01/2002, ¿? (Finland) (b) 1,76 (c) F - right winger (d) Salon Palloilijat (e) SalPa, FC Honka, FC Honka II
*** Katan - Afik Katan (קטן אפיק) (a) 30/08/2000, ¿? (Israel) (b) 1,83 (c) M - right midfielder (d) - (e) Hapoel Hadera, Hapoel Haifa, Maccabi Herzlya, Hapoel Haifa
*** Katanec - Matija Katanec (a) 04/05/1990, Varaždin (Yugoslavia, now in Croatia) (b) 1,86 (c) D - central defense (d) ACSM Politehnica Iasi (e) NK Varazdin, Mezőkövesd, Zalaegerszeg, Mezőkövesd, Zrinjski Mostar, HNK Gorica, Spezia, Zrinjski Mostar, Radnik Bijelj., OFK Gradina, NK Varazdin, NK Podravina, Baumgarten, NK Varazdin, ND Gorica, Croatia Sesvete

*** Katanic - Aleksandar Katanic (Александар Катанић) (a) 15/08/1995, Loznica (RF Yugoslavia, now in Serbia) (b) 1,85 (c) F - center forward (d) - (e) Sileks, Mladost GAT, FC Honka, Mladost, Metalac, FK Bezanija, Backa, Stari Banovci, Teleoptik, Stari Banovci, FK Loznica, Radnicki Klupci

*** Katavic - Josip Katavic (Josip Katavić) (a) 20/01/2000, Metković (Croatia) (b) - (c) D - central defense (d) - (e) HSK Posusje, Neretva Metkovic, HNK Capljina, Jadran Luka Ploce

*** Katelaris - Fanos Katelaris (Φάνος Κατελάρης) (a) 26/08/1996, Nicosia (Cyprus) (b) 1,85 (c) D - central defense (d) AEK Larnaca (e) KV Oostende, Apollon Limassol, Omonia Nicosia, Zalaegerszeg, Omonia Nicosia, Olympiakos N., Omonia Nicosia, Alki Larnaca, Omonia Nicosia

*** Katic - Andrija Katic (Андрија Катић) (a) 17/02/2002, Kruševac (RF Yugoslavia, now in Serbia) (b) 1,95 (c) G (d) FK Vozdovac (e) IMT Beograd, Dobanovci

*** Katic - Daniel Katic (Daniel Katić) (a) 26/04/2003, ¿? (Slovenia) (b) 1,85 (c) D - central defense (d) NS Mura (e) FC Augsburg II

*** Katic - Nikola Katic (Nikola Katić) (a) 10/10/1996, Ljubuški (Bosnia and Herzegovina) (b) 1,94 (c) D - central defense (d) FC Zürich (e) Rangers FC, Hajduk Split, Rangers FC, Slaven Belupo, NK Neretvanac, Stolac

*** Katinic - Maro Katinic (Maro Katinić) (a) 13/04/2004, Rijeka (Croatia) (b) 1,86 (c) D - central defense (d) NK Bravo (e) NK Bravo, Dinamo Zagreb, Din. Zagreb II

*** Katoh - Haggai Katoh (a) 30/12/1998, ¿? (Nigeria) (b) - (c) M - central midfielder (d) FC Noah Yerevan (e) Plateau United, Nasarawa United, Akwa United

*** Katona - Bálint Katona (Katona Bálint Lajos) (a) 07/09/2002, Budapest (Hungary) (b) 1,78 (c) M - attacking midfielder (d) Ferencváros TC (e) Ferencváros II, Kecskemét, Ferencváros II, Kecskemét, Ferencváros II

*** Katona - Máté Katona (a) 22/06/1997, Sopron (Hungary) (b) 1,76 (c) M - central midfielder (d) Soroksár SC (e) Ferencváros, Kecskemét, Ferencváros, Soroksár, Ferencváros, Soroksár, Ferencváros, MTK Budapest, MTK Budapest II

*** Katona - Mátyás Katona (a) 30/12/1999, Budapest (Hungary) (b) 1,73 (c) M - attacking midfielder (d) Fehérvár FC (e) Újpest FC, Újpest II, II. ker. UFC

*** Katranis - Alexandros Katranis (Αλέξανδρος Κατράνης) (a) 04/05/1998, Volos (Greece) (b) 1,74 (c) D - left back (d) Piast Gliwice (e) St.-Étienne, Hatayspor, St.-Étienne, Atromitos FC, St.-Étienne, Excelsior Mouscron, St.-Étienne, Atromitos FC

*** Katrich - Anatoliy Katrich (Катрич Анатолий Николаевич) (a) 09/07/1994, Primorsko-Akhtarsk, Krasnodar Region (Russia) (b) 1,82 (c) F - right winger (d) Amkal Moskau (e) Atyrau, Tekstilshchik, Krasnodar-2, Luch, Ural, Krasnodar, Dinamo Moskva, Dinamo Moskva II

*** Kats - Artur Kats (Кац Артур Юрьевич) (a) 26/12/1994, Minsk (Belarus) (b) 1,75 (c) D - left back (d) FK Molodechno (e) Naftan, Belshina, Vitebsk, Dnyapro Mogilev, Luch, Gorodeya, BATE II, Smolevichi, BATE II, Gorodeya, BATE II

*** Katsarov - Bozhidar Katsarov (Божидар Иванов Кацаров) (a) 30/12/1993, Stara Zagora (Bulgaria) (b) 1,90 (c) M - pivot (d) Krumovgrad (e) Lokomotiv Sofia, Etar, Tsarsko Selo, Septemvri Sofia, Pirin Razlog, Zagorets

*** Katsiaris - Antonis Katsiaris (Αντώνης Κατσιαρής) (a) 14/10/1996, Famagusta (Cyprus) (b) 1,80 (c) M - central midfielder (d) Nea Salamis (e) EN Paralimniou, Onisilos Sotira

*** Katsikas - Georgios Katsikas (Γεώργιος Κατσικάς) (a) 14/06/1990, Thessaloniki (Greece) (b) 1,87 (c) D - central defense (d) APO Levadiakos (e) Nea Salamis, Lokomotiv Sofia, Dynamo Brest, FC Dinamo, Esbjerg fB, FC Twente, PAOK, Iraklis, Olympiakos Volou, Iraklis

*** Katterbach - Noah Katterbach (a) 13/04/2001, Simmerath (Germany) (b) 1,80 (c) D - left back (d) 1.FC Köln (e) SV Hamburg, 1.FC Köln, FC Basel, 1.FC Köln
*** Katz - Kalle Katz (a) 04/01/2000, Helsinki (Finland) (b) 1,85 (c) D - central defense (d) Ilves Tampere (e) HJK Helsinki, RoPS, HJK Helsinki, RoPS, HJK Helsinki, HJK Klubi 04
*** Kauber - Kevin Kauber (a) 23/03/1995, Tallinn (Estonia) (b) 1,77 (c) F - center forward (d) Pärnu JK Vaprus (e) Paide, Ekenäs IF, The New Saints, Jelgava, Levadia, Jelgava, NK Krka, NK Tolmin, NK Krka, TPS, NK Krka, TPS, FC Puuma, SC Real
*** Kaufmann - Lucas Kaufmann (a) 26/03/1991, Porto Alegre (Brazil) (b) 1,70 (d) Ekenas IF (e) FC Honka, HJK Helsinki, Ekenas IF, PK-35, Ekenas IF, Al-Shabab SC, Pallokerho, PK-35, Pallokerho, Mafra, CerÃ¢mica
*** Kaukua - Tuomas Kaukua (a) 13/10/2000, Rovaniemi (Finland) (b) 1,76 (c) F - right winger (d) SJK Seinäjoki (e) RoPS
*** Kaulfus - Denis Kaulfus (a) 03/06/2004, ¿? (Czech Rep.) (b) 1,71 (c) M - pivot (d) FK Mlada Boleslav B (e) -
*** Kaulinis - Andrius Kaulinis (a) 01/12/2000, ¿? (Lithuania) (b) - (c) F (d) FK Riteriai B (e) -
*** Kaulins - Ricards Kaulins (Ričards Kauliņš) (a) 04/05/2003, ¿? (Latvia) (b) - (c) F - center forward (d) AFA Olaine (e) Super Nova
*** Kauselis - Kristians Kauselis (Kristiāns Kaušelis) (a) 14/03/2003, ¿? (Latvia) (b) - (c) F - center forward (d) FK Tukums 2000 (e) Valmiera, Super Nova, Valmiera, Tukums, Valmiera, Daugavpils, BFC Daugavpils
*** Kausinis - Esmilis Kausinis (Esmilis Kaušinis) (a) 31/05/2004, Vilnius (Lithuania) (b) 1,85 (c) F - left winger (d) FC Hegelmann (e) Riteriai B, Vilniaus FM
*** Kavanagh - Brandon Kavanagh (a) 21/09/2000, ¿? (Ireland) (b) 1,72 (c) M - left midfielder (d) Derry City (e) Shamrock Rovers, Bray Wanderers, Shamrock Rovers
*** Kavanagh - Cian Kavanagh (a) 03/01/2003, Dublin (Ireland) (b) 1,76 (c) F - center forward (d) Derry City (e) Waterford FC, Cowdenbeath FC
*** Kavanagh - Rhys Kavanagh (a) 29/09/1998, ¿? (Wales) (b) 1,8 (c) F - right winger (d) Flint Town United (e) Penybont, Barry Town, Bristol Rovers, Hungerford, Bristol Rovers, Gloucester, Bristol Rovers, Bath City, Barry Town
*** Kavanagh - Sean Kavanagh (a) 20/01/1994, Dublin (Ireland) (b) 1,74 (c) D - left back (d) Shamrock Rovers (e) Fulham, Hartlepool Utd., Fulham, Mansfield Town, Fulham, Belvedere FC
*** Kavcic - Matija Kavcic (Matija Kavčič) (a) 11/07/1997, ¿? (Slovenia) (b) 1,84 (c) D - left back (d) NK Bravo (e) ND Gorica, NK Brda, ND Gorica, NK Brda, ND Gorica, NK Brda, ND Gorica
*** Kavdanski - Martin Kavdanski (Мартин Николаев Кавдански) (a) 13/02/1987, Dupnitsa (Bulgaria) (b) 1,87 (c) D - central defense (d) Botev Vratsa (e) Tsarsko Selo, Botev Vratsa, Clermont Foot, Lokomotiv GO, Lokomotiv Plovdiv, KF Tirana, Marek Dupnitsa, Shkëndija, Chern. Burgas, Lokomotiv Plovdiv, Beroe, Lokomotiv Plovdiv, Slavia Sofia, Lokomotiv Mezdra, Slavia Sofia, FC Metz B
*** Kavelashvili - Guram Kavelashvili (გურამ ყაველაშვილი) (a) 18/08/2001, Zürich (Switzerland) (b) 1,92 (c) F - center forward (d) - (e) FC Telavi, Rustavi, Tskhinvali
*** Kavlinov - Denis Kavlinov (Кавлинов Денис Юрьевич) (a) 10/01/1995, Elista (Russia) (b) 1,91 (c) G (d) Yelimay Semey (e) Taraz, Zhetysu, Kaspiy Aktau, Gomel, Khimki, Rotor Volgograd, Kuban Krasnodar, Krasnodar-2, Dinamo SPb, Krasnodar-2, Krasnodar II
*** Kavrazli - Salih Kavrazli (Salih Kavrazlı) (a) 16/03/2002, Agri (Turkey) (b) 1,78 (c) F - right winger (d) Adana Demirspor (e) Trabzonspor, Hekimoglu, Trabzonspor

*** Kavtaradze - Beka Kavtaradze (ბექა ქავთარაძე) (a) 15/06/1999, Dusheti (Georgia) (b) 1,85 (c) F - center forward (d) Yelimay Semey (e) FC Telavi, Rotor Volgograd, Nizhny Novgorod, Saburtalo, Rustavi, Dinamo Tbilisi
*** Kavtaradze - Nika Kavtaradze (ნიკა ქავთარაძე) (a) 17/06/1998, ¿? (Georgia) (b) 1,89 (c) G (d) FC Gagra (e) WIT Georgia, Chikhura
*** Kavtaradze - Nodar Kavtaradze (ნოდარ ქავთარაძე) (a) 02/01/1993, Moskva (Russia) (b) 1,68 (c) F - left winger (d) FK Andijon (e) Torpedo Kutaisi, Dinamo Tbilisi, Saburtalo, Dinamo Tbilisi, Mezőkövesd, Dinamo Tbilisi, Torpedo Kutaisi, FC Dila, FC Locomotive, Druzhba Maikop, Volga Tver, Tyumen, Loko-Kazanka M., LFK Lokomotiv 2
*** Kawabe - Hayao Kawabe (川辺 駿) (a) 08/09/1995, Hiroshima, Hiroshima (Japan) (b) 1,78 (c) M - central midfielder (d) Standard de Lieja (e) Wolverhampton Wanderers, Grasshoppers, Wolverhampton Wanderers, Grasshoppers, Sanf. Hiroshima, Júbilo Iwata, Sanf. Hiroshima
*** Kawachi - Yoichi Kawachi (川内 陽一) (a) 02/08/1998, Ureshino, Saga (Japan) (b) 1,70 (c) F - attacking midfielder (d) FK TransINVEST (e) Jonava, V. Ichihara Vert, Tokyo Int Univ., Saga Higashi HS
*** Kawashima - Eiji Kawashima (川島 永嗣) (a) 20/03/1983, Yono, Saitama (Japan) (b) 1,85 (c) G (d) - (e) Racing Club Strasbourg, FC Metz, Dundee United, Standard Liège, Lierse SK, Kawasaki Front., Nagoya Grampus, Omiya Ardija
*** Kay - Antony Kay (Antony Roland Kay) (a) 21/10/1982, Barnsley (England) (b) 1,80 (c) M - pivot (d) Runcorn Linnets (e) Bala, Chorley, Port Vale, Bury, MK Dons, Huddersfield Town, Tranmere Rovers, Barnsley FC
*** Kaya - Dogukan Kaya (Doğukan Kaya) (a) 16/01/2000, Kocaeli (Turkey) (b) 1,91 (c) G (d) MKE Ankaragücü (e) Kocaelispor
*** Kaya - Eren Kaya (a) 27/03/2004, Sivas (Turkey) (b) 1,79 (c) M - attacking midfielder (d) Sivasspor (e) -
*** Kaya - Fatih Kaya (a) 13/11/1999, Gießen (Germany) (b) 1,83 (c) F - center forward (d) Sint-Truidense VV (e) FC Ingolstadt
*** Kayal - Beram Kayal (כיאל בירם) (a) 02/05/1988, Jadeidi (Israel) (b) 1,78 (c) M - central midfielder (d) Ihud Bnei Sakhnin (e) Brighton & Hove Albion, Charlton Ath., Brighton & Hove Albion, Celtic FC, Maccabi Haifa
*** Kaydalov - Danylo Kaydalov (Кайдалов Данило Олександрович) (a) 02/02/2006, ¿? (Ukraine) (b) 1,75 (c) F - left winger (d) Metalist Kharkiv (e) -
*** Kayembe - Joris Kayembe (Joris Kayembe Ditu) (a) 08/08/1994, Brussel (Belgium) (b) 1,80 (c) D - left back (d) KRC Genk (e) RSC Charleroi, FC Nantes, FC Porto B, Rio Ave, FC Porto B, Arouca, FC Porto B
*** Kaygisiz - Ayberk Kaygisiz (Ayberk Kaygısız) (a) 11/08/2004, Balikesir (Turkey) (b) - (c) D - right back (d) Isparta 32 Spor (e) Isparta 32 Spor, Basaksehir, Balikesirspor
*** Kayky - Kayky (Kayky da Silva Chagas) (a) 11/06/2003, Rio de Janeiro (Brazil) (b) 1,72 (c) F - right winger (d) Esporte Clube Bahia (e) EC Bahia, Paços Ferreira, Fluminense
*** Kaylesiz - Oguzhan Kaylesiz (Oğuzhan Kaylesız) (a) 06/02/1998, Istanbul (Turkey) (b) 1,84 (c) F - center forward (d) FC Mondercange (e) Bergama Belediye, Weiler, Waremme, Sancaktepe FK, RFCU Kelmis
*** Kayode - Michael Kayode (Michael Olabode Kayode) (a) 10/07/2004, Borgomanero (Italy) (b) 1,79 (c) D - right back (d) - (e) Gozzano
*** Kayode - Olarenwaju Kayode (Tobi Olarenwaju Ayobami Kayode) (a) 08/05/1993, Ibadan (Nigeria) (b) 1,76 (c) F - center forward (d) - (e) Shakhtar

Donetsk, Ümraniyespor, Shakhtar Donetsk, Sivasspor, Shakhtar Donetsk, Gaziantep FK, Shakhtar Donetsk, Manchester City, Shakhtar Donetsk, Manchester City, Girona FC, Manchester City, Austria Viena, Maccabi Netanya, ASEC Mimosas, Maccabi Netanya, ASEC Mimosas, FC Heartland, ASEC Mimosas, FC Luzern, ASEC Mimosas, AFAD Djékanou, ASEC Mimosas, Marvellous
*** Kayode - Oyinlola Kayode (Olaoluwa Oyinlola Kayode) (a) 29/11/2002, ¿? (Lithuania) (b) - (c) F - right winger (d) FK Suduva Marijampole (e) Kauno Zalgiris
*** Kazakov - Maksym Kazakov (Казаков Максим Ігорович) (a) 06/02/1996, Kyiv (Ukraine) (b) 1,78 (c) M - central midfielder (d) Druzhba Myrivka (e) Zorya Lugansk, Dinamo Kiev II
*** Kazantsev - Danil Kazantsev (Казанцев Данил Антонович) (a) 05/01/2001, Syzran (Russia) (b) 1,87 (c) M - pivot (d) Sokol Saratov (e) Khimki 2, Master-Saturn
*** Kazim-Richards - Colin Kazim-Richards (Colin Kazım-Richards) (a) 26/08/1986, Leytonstone, London (England) (b) 1,87 (c) F - center forward (d) - (e) Karagümrük, Derby, Pachuca, Tiburones Rojos, Lobos BUAP, Corinthians, Coritiba FC, Celtic FC, Feyenoord, Bursaspor, Feyenoord, Bursaspor, Galatasaray, Blackburn, Galatasaray, Olympiakos, Galatasaray, Fenerbahce, Toulouse, Fenerbahce, Sheffield Utd., Brighton & Hove Albion, Bury
*** Kazlauskas - Donatas Kazlauskas (a) 31/03/1994, Kretinga (Lithuania) (b) 1,75 (c) M - left midfielder (d) FK Zalgiris Vilnius (e) Academica Clinceni, PFK Lviv, Riteriai, Atlantas, Lechia Gdánsk, Atlantas, Lechia Gdánsk, Olimpia Grudz., Lechia Gdánsk, Atlantas, Zalgiris
*** Kazukolovas - Kipras Kazukolovas (Kipras Kažukolovas) (a) 20/11/2000, Kuršėnai (Lithuania) (b) 1,91 (c) D - central defense (d) FK Zalgiris Vilnius (e) -
*** Kean - Moise Kean (Moise Bioty Kean) (a) 28/02/2000, Vercelli (Italy) (b) 1,83 (c) F - center forward (d) Juventus de Turín (e) Everton, Juventus, Everton, Paris Saint-Germain, Everton, Juventus, Hellas Verona, Juventus
*** Keane - Dara Keane (a) 24/12/1998, ¿? (Ireland) (b) 1,78 (c) M - central midfielder (d) University College Dublin (e) Evergreen FC
*** Keane - Michael Keane (Michael Vincent Keane) (a) 11/01/1993, Stockport (England) (b) 1,88 (c) D - central defense (d) Everton FC (e) Burnley, Blackburn, Derby, Leicester City
*** Keaney - Jack Keaney (a) 18/01/1999, Donegal (Ireland) (b) 1,88 (c) D - central defense (d) University College Dublin (e) Sligo Rovers
*** Kearney - Shea Kearney (a) 26/03/2004, Lurgan (Northern Ireland) (b) - (c) D - right back (d) Cliftonville FC (e) -
*** Kearns - Danny Kearns (Daniel Anthony Kearns) (a) 26/08/1991, Belfast (Northern Ireland) (b) 1,78 (c) M - right midfielder (d) Larne FC (e) Cliftonville, Linfield, Limerick FC, Sligo Rovers, Glenavon, Carlisle United, Peterborough, FC Chesterfield, Peterborough, Rotherham, Peterborough, York City, Peterborough, Dundalk FC, West Ham Utd.
*** Kebano - Neeskens Kebano (a) 10/03/1992, Montereau (France) (b) 1,70 (c) F - left winger (d) Al-Jazira (Abu Dhabi) (e) Fulham, Middlesbrough, Fulham, KRC Genk, RSC Charleroi, Paris Saint-Germain, SM Caen, Paris Saint-Germain
*** Kébé - Ibrahima Kébé (a) 01/08/2000, Bamako (Mali) (b) 1,80 (c) M - pivot (d) Girona FC (e) Girona FC B, FC Danaya
*** Keben - Kévin Keben (Kévin Keben Biakolo) (a) 26/01/2004, Bertoua (Cameroon) (b) - (c) D - central defense (d) Toulouse FC (e) -
*** Kechrida - Wajdi Kechrida (كشريدة وجدي) (a) 05/11/1995, Nice (France) (b) 1,84 (c) D - right back (d) Atromitos FC (e) Salernitana, ES Sahel

*** Kecskés - Ákos Kecskés (a) 04/01/1996, Hódmezővásárhely (Hungary) (b) 1,90 (c) D - central defense (d) LASK (e) Pari Nizhny Novgórod, FC Lugano, Atalanta, Korona Kielce, Atalanta, Nieciecza, Atalanta, Újpest FC, Atalanta

*** Keddari - Simo Keddari (Wassim Keddari Boulif) (a) 03/02/2005, Terrassa (Spain) (b) 1,83 (c) D - central defense (d) Al-Arabi SC (e) RCD Espanyol, RCD Espanyol B

*** Kedziora - Tomasz Kedziora (Tomasz Kędziora) (a) 11/06/1994, Sulechów (Poland) (b) 1,84 (c) D - right back (d) PAOK Thessaloniki (e) PAOK, Dinamo Kyïv, Lech Poznan, Dinamo Kyïv, Lech Poznan, Lech Poznan II

*** Keeley - Conor Keeley (a) 13/12/1997, Dunboyne, Meath (Ireland) (b) 2,00 (c) D - central defense (d) Drogheda United FC (e) Ballymena, Cabinteely, Shelbourne

*** Keeley - Josh Keeley (a) 17/05/2003, Dunboyne, Meath (Ireland) (b) 1,91 (c) G (d) - (e) St. Patrick's Ath.

*** Keena - Aidan Keena (a) 25/04/1999, Mullingar (Ireland) (b) 1,81 (c) F - center forward (d) Cheltenham Town (e) Sligo Rovers, Falkirk FC, Hartlepool Utd., Hearts FC II, Dunfermline A., Hearts FC II, Queen's Park, St. Patrick's Ath.

*** Kehat - Roi Kehat (קהת רועי) (a) 12/05/1992, Rehovot (Israel) (b) 1,80 (c) M - central midfielder (d) Sumqayit PFK (e) Kiryat Shmona, Maccabi Netanya, Maccabi Haifa, Austria Viena, Kiryat Shmona, Maccabi Yavne, Maccabi Tel Aviv, H. Beer Sheva, Maccabi Tel Aviv

*** Kehinde - Tosin Kehinde (Kehinde Oluwatosin) (a) 18/06/1998, Lagos (Nigeria) (b) 1,78 (c) F - left winger (d) Ferencváros TC (e) Randers FC

*** Kehli - Samy Kehli (Samy Loïs Kehli) (a) 27/01/1991, Saint-Avold (France) (b) 1,91 (c) M - attacking midfielder (d) APM Metz (e) RFCU Luxembourg, OH Leuven, KSC Lokeren, OH Leuven, KSC Lokeren, KSV Roeselare, FC Metz, Seraing United, FC Metz, RE Virton, FC Metz, FC Metz B

*** Kehrer - Emilio Kehrer (Emilio Giuseppe Kehrer) (a) 20/03/2002, ¿? (Germany) (b) 1,77 (c) F - center forward (d) Cercle Brugge (e) SC Freiburg II

*** Kehrer - Thilo Kehrer (Jan Thilo Kehrer) (a) 21/09/1996, Tübingen (Germany) (b) 1,86 (c) D - central defense (d) West Ham United (e) Paris Saint-Germain, FC Schalke 04

*** Keiler - Sergey Keiler (Кейлер Сергей Валерьевич) (a) 08/11/1994, Almaty (Kazakhstan) (b) 1,80 (c) D - left back (d) Kairat Almaty (e) Akzhayik, Kairat Almaty, Okzhetpes, Kairat Almaty, Kaysar, Kairat Almaty, Kyzyl-Zhar, Kairat Almaty, Kairat II, Tsesna

*** Keita - Aboubakar Keita (a) 05/11/1997, Abidjan (Ivory Coast) (b) 1,88 (c) M - pivot (d) AIK Solna (e) RSC Charleroi, Ness Ziona, RSC Charleroi, RWDM, RSC Charleroi, OH Leuven, FC København, OH Leuven, FC København, Stabæk, FC København, Halmstads BK, FC København

*** Keita - Alhassane Keita (a) 16/04/1992, Conakry (Guinea) (b) 1,83 (c) F - center forward (d) US Mondorf-Les-Bains (e) B SAD, Al-Riffa SC, B SAD, Marítimo, Maccabi Netanya, Marítimo, SKN St. Pölten, Ermis Aradippou, FC Metz, Lierse SK, FC Metz, US Boulogne, FC Metz, FC Metz B

*** Keita - Amadou Keita (a) 28/10/2001, Conakry (Guinea) (b) 1,70 (c) M - central midfielder (d) KAS Eupen (e) -

*** Keita - Cheick Keita (a) 02/04/2003, Champigny-sur-Marne (France) (b) 1,85 (c) D - central defense (d) Stade de Reims (e) Stade Reims B

*** Keita - Cheick Keita (a) 16/04/1996, Paris (France) (b) 1,80 (c) D - left back (d) HNK Gorica (e) Birmingham City, KAS Eupen, Birmingham City, Bologna, Birmingham City, Virtus Entella

*** Keita - Kader Keita (Abdul Kader Keita) (a) 06/11/2000, ¿? (Ivory Coast) (b) 1,78 (c) M - pivot (d) Sivasspor (e) KVC Westerlo, FC Sion, KVC Westerlo, LOSC Lille B
*** Keita - Mandela Keita (Lamine Mandela Keita) (a) 10/05/2002, Leuven (Belgium) (b) 1,80 (c) M - pivot (d) Royal Antwerp FC (e) Royal Antwerp, OH Leuven, Royal Antwerp, OH Leuven
*** Keita - Seydina Keita (Seydina Aboubakr Lamine Keita) (a) 28/12/1992, Pikine (Senegal) (b) 1,76 (c) D - central defense (d) FK Panevezys (e) Liepaja, Diambars FC, Molde, Diambars FC
*** Keita - Sibiry Keita (a) 30/01/2001, ¿? (Mali) (b) 1,73 (c) M - left midfielder (d) Slavia Sofia (e) KAS Eupen, ASPIRE FD
*** Keïta - Habib Keïta (Habib Ali Keita) (a) 05/02/2002, Bamako (Mali) (b) 1,82 (c) M - central midfielder (d) Clermont Foot 63 (e) Olympique Lyon, KV Kortrijk, Olympique Lyon, Olymp. Lyon B, JMG Bamako
*** Keïta - Naby Keïta (Naby Laye Keïta) (a) 10/02/1995, Conakry (Guinea) (b) 1,72 (c) M - central midfielder (d) SV Werder Bremen (e) Liverpool, RB Leipzig, RB Salzburg, FC Istres, Horoya AC
*** Keitel - Yannik Keitel (a) 15/02/2000, Breisach am Rhein (Germany) (b) 1,86 (c) M - pivot (d) SC Freiburg (e) SC Freiburg II
*** Kekelidze - Luka Kekelidze (ლუკა კეკელიძე) (a) 07/01/2003, ¿? (Georgia) (b) - (c) M - central midfielder (d) FC Locomotive Tbilisi (e) -
*** Kekoh - Felix Kekoh (Felix Kekoh Ndifor II) (a) 02/03/2001, Yaounde (Cameroon) (b) 1,68 (c) M - right midfielder (d) - (e) Kauno Zalgiris, Marsonia 1909, FC Admira II, FAC, FC Admira II, Admira Wacker, Gambinos Stars, Apejes FC
*** Kekonen - Nestori Kekonen (a) 02/02/2003, ¿? (Finland) (b) 1,75 (c) M - central midfielder (d) AC Oulu (e) -
*** Kelaart - Oliver Kelaart (Oliver James Kelaart Torres) (a) 16/04/1998, ¿? (Australia) (b) 1,78 (c) F - right winger (d) UMF Njardvík (e) Thróttur Vogum, Keflavík, Hvöt, CD Calamonte, Orihuela CF
*** Kelder - Silver Alex Kelder (a) 22/10/1995, Tallinn (Estonia) (b) - (c) M - central midfielder (d) Paide Linnameeskond (e) Kuressaare, Kalev, FC Ararat, SC Real
*** Kelemen - Marko Kelemen (a) 29/04/2000, Rožňava (Slovakia) (b) 1,87 (c) F - center forward (d) Szombathelyi Haladás (e) Haladás, Ružomberok, FC Petrzalka, Kazincbarcika, Putnok, Kazincbarcika, Spartak Trnava, Zlaté Moravce, Spartak Trnava
*** Kelement - Marten Kelement (Marten Henrik Kelement) (a) 24/10/2003, Tallinn (Estonia) (b) - (c) M - attacking midfielder (d) Paide Linnameeskond (e) Keila JK
*** Keles - Can Keles (a) 02/09/2001, ¿? (Austria) (b) 1,80 (c) F - left winger (d) Fatih Karagümrük (e) Karagümrük, Austria Viena, Young Violets
*** Kelleher - Caoimhín Kelleher (Caoimhín Odhran Kelleher) (a) 23/11/1998, Cork (Ireland) (b) 1,88 (c) G (d) Liverpool FC (e) Ringmahon
*** Keller - Marvin Keller (a) 03/07/2002, London (England) (b) 1,89 (c) G (d) BSC Young Boys (e) FC Wil 1900, Grasshoppers
*** Keller - Rotem Keller (קלר רותם) (a) 09/11/2002, Hadera (Israel) (b) 1,83 (c) D - left back (d) Maccabi Netanya (e) Hapoel Hadera, Maccabi Netanya, Diósgyőr, Maccabi Netanya
*** Kelly - Bradley Kelly (a) 24/10/2003, ¿? (England) (b) - (c) G (d) AFC Rochdale (e) Airbus UK, AFC Rochdale, Mossley AFC
*** Kelly - Ciaran Kelly (Ciarán Kelly) (a) 04/07/1998, Lucan, Dublin (Ireland) (b) 1,91 (c) D - central defense (d) Bradford City (e) Bohemians, Ballymena, Bohemians, St. Patrick's Ath., Drogheda United, St. Patrick's Ath.

*** Kelly - Daniel Kelly (a) 06/01/1993, Belfast (Northern Ireland) (b) 1,91 (c) M - pivot (d) - (e) Carrick Rangers, Carrick Rangers, Glentoran, Carrick Rangers
*** Kelly - Daniel Kelly (a) 21/05/1996, Ringsend (Ireland) (b) - (c) F - right winger (d) Dundalk FC (e) Bohemians, Bray Wanderers, St. Patrick's CYFC
*** Kelly - Georgie Kelly (George Martin Kelly) (a) 12/11/1996, Donegal (Ireland) (b) 1,87 (c) F - center forward (d) Rotherham United (e) Bohemians, Dundalk FC, St. Patrick's Ath., Dundalk FC, UCD
*** Kelly - Graham Kelly (a) 16/10/1997, Dublin (Ireland) (b) 1,83 (c) D - central defense (d) Coleraine FC (e) Larne FC, Port Vale, Southport, Port Vale, Bradford PA, Port Vale, Sheffield Utd., Stalybridge, Sheffield Utd., St. Josephs Boys
*** Kelly - Jordan Kelly (a) 21/09/2002, ¿? (Malta) (b) - (c) M (d) Sirens FC (e) -
*** Kelly - Josh Kelly (Joshua Kelly) (a) 08/03/1999, Comber (Northern Ireland) (b) 1,85 (c) M - central midfielder (d) Glentoran FC (e) Ballymena, Ards FC
*** Kelly - Liam Kelly (Liam Patrick Kelly) (a) 23/01/1996, Glasgow (Scotland) (b) 1,84 (c) G (d) Motherwell FC (e) Queen's Park Rangers, Motherwell FC, Queen's Park Rangers, Livingston FC, Rangers FC, Livingston FC, Rangers FC, East Fife, Rangers FC
*** Kelly - Lloyd Kelly (a) 06/10/1998, Bristol (England) (b) 1,90 (c) D - central defense (d) AFC Bournemouth (e) Bristol City
*** Kelly - Sean Kelly (a) 01/11/1993, Glasgow (Scotland) (b) 1,88 (c) D - left back (d) Livingston FC (e) Falkirk FC, Ross County, AFC Wimbledon, St. Mirren, East Stirlingshire FC, St. Mirren
*** Kelly - Stephen Kelly (a) 13/04/2000, Port Glasgow (Scotland) (b) 1,76 (c) M - central midfielder (d) Livingston FC (e) Rangers FC, Salford, Rangers FC, Rangers II, Ross County, Rangers II, Ayr United, Rangers II
*** Kelmendi - Shend Kelmendi (a) 21/09/1994, Prishtinë (RF Yugoslavia, now in Kosovo) (b) 1,87 (c) F - right winger (d) SC Gjilani (e) KF Flamurtari, FC Llapi, KF Skënderbeu, KF Trepca 89, KF Skënderbeu, KF Trepca 89, FC Prishtina
*** Kelmendi (c) M (d) KF Trepca 89 (e) FC Phoenix, KF Trepca 89 - Engjell Kelmendi (c) M (d) KF Trepca 89 (e) FC Phoenix, KF Trepca 89
*** Kelsy - Kevin Kelsy (Kevin Jesús Kelsy Genez) (a) 27/07/2004, Valencia (Venezuela) (b) 1,93 (c) F - center forward (d) Shakhtar Donetsk (e) Boston River, Mineros
*** Keltjens - David Keltjens (קלטינס דוד) (a) 11/06/1995, Mevaseret Zion (Israel) (b) 1,81 (c) M - pivot (d) Hapoel Tel Aviv (e) H. Beer Sheva, B. Jerusalem
*** Kelyovluev - Hyusein Kelyovluev (Хюсеин Хюсеинов Кельовлуев) (a) 11/05/2000, Razgrad (Bulgaria) (b) 1,78 (c) F - center forward (d) Ludogorets Razgrad II (e) Ludogorets
*** Kemen - Olivier Kemen (a) 20/07/1996, Douala (Cameroon) (b) 1,75 (d) Kayserispor (e) Chamois Niort, Olympique Lyon, G. Ajaccio, Olympique Lyon, G. Ajaccio, Olympique Lyon
*** Kemendi - Taha Veysel Kemendi (a) 10/05/2003, Istanbul (Turkey) (b) - (c) D - central defense (d) - (e) M. Arguvan SK
*** Kemkin - Oleksandr Kemkin (Кемкін Олександр Олегович) (a) 05/08/2002, Melitopol, Zaporizhya Oblast (Ukraine) (b) 1,87 (c) G (d) FK Minaj (e) Shakhtar II
*** Kemlein - Aljoscha Kemlein (a) 02/08/2004, Berlin (Germany) (b) 1,85 (c) M - pivot (d) 1.FC Union Berlin (e) -
*** Kempf - Marc Oliver Kempf (a) 28/01/1995, Lich (Germany) (b) 1,86 (c) D - central defense (d) Hertha Berlín (e) VfB Stuttgart, SC Freiburg, Eintracht
*** Kempski - Mateusz Kempski (a) 21/03/2003, Radomsko (Poland) (b) 1,92 (c) F - center forward (d) RTS Widzew Łódź (e) Widzew II, Belchatow II, Belchatow II

*** Kempter - Michael Kempter (a) 12/01/1995, Schlieren (Switzerland) (b) 1,81 (c) D - left back (d) Grasshopper Club Zürich (e) FC St. Gallen, Neuchâtel Xamax, FC Zürich

*** Kendysh - Yuriy Kendysh (Кендыш Юрий Игоревич) (a) 10/06/1990, Minsk (Soviet Union, now in Belarus) (b) 1,87 (c) M - central midfielder (d) FK Zalgiris Vilnius (e) Riga, Soligorsk, FC Sheriff, BATE Borisov, FC Sheriff, BATE Borisov, Zalgiris, Trakai, Dynamo Brest, Slavia, Torpedo Zhodino, Partizan Minsk, Partizan II

*** Kenedy - Kenedy (Robert Kenedy Nunes do Nascimento) (a) 08/02/1996, Santa Rita do Sapucaí (Brazil) (b) 1,82 (c) F - left winger (d) Real Valladolid CF (e) Chelsea, Flamengo, Chelsea, Granada CF, Chelsea, Getafe CF, Chelsea, Newcastle Utd., Chelsea, Watford, Chelsea, Fluminense

*** Kenesbek - Adilet Kenesbek (Кенесбек Адилет Нурмашулы) (a) 05/01/1996, Taraz (Kazakhstan) (b) 1,80 (c) D - right back (d) Kaysar Kyzylorda (e) Taraz, FK Altay, Taraz, Taraz-Karatau

*** Kenesov - Arman Kenesov (Кенесов Арман Серикович) (a) 04/09/2000, Pavlodar (Kazakhstan) (b) 1,72 (c) M - attacking midfielder (d) FK Aktobe (e) SKA Khabarovsk, Kaysar, SKA Khabarovsk, Irtysh, Pavlodar II

*** Kenndal - William Kenndal (a) 04/04/1996, ¿? (Sweden) (b) - (c) M - pivot (d) IFK Värnamo (e) Lindome GIF, Utsiktens BK, Sollentuna FK, Qviding FIF

*** Kennedy - Ben Kennedy (Ben James Kennedy) (a) 12/01/1997, Lisburn (Northern Ireland) (b) 1,78 (c) F - center forward (d) Crusaders FC (e) Stevenage, Newport County, Stevenage

*** Kennedy - Matty Kennedy (Matthew Kennedy) (a) 01/11/1994, Belfast (Northern Ireland) (b) 1,75 (c) F - left winger (d) Kilmarnock FC (e) Aberdeen FC, St. Johnstone, Cardiff City, FC Portsmouth, Cardiff City, Plymouth Argyle, Cardiff City, Port Vale, Cardiff City, Everton, Hibernian FC, Everton, MK Dons, Everton, Tranmere Rovers, Everton, Kilmarnock FC

*** Kenneh - Nohan Kenneh (a) 10/01/2003, Zwedru (Liberia) (b) 1,90 (c) M - pivot (d) Shrewsbury Town (e) Shrewsbury, Hibernian FC, Ross County, Hibernian FC

*** Kenny - Gillan Kenny (Gillan Lea Peden Kenny) (a) 03/05/1993, Gibraltar (Gibraltar) (b) - (c) D - left back (d) FC College 1975 (e) -

*** Kenny - Jack Kenny (a) 14/10/1991, ¿? (Wales) (b) - (c) F - center forward (d) Connah's Quay Nomads (e) Ashton United, Flint Town, Caernarfon, Prestatyn, Cefn Druids, Connah's Quay, Prestatyn, Rhyl FC, Leigh Genesis FC

*** Kenny - Johnny Kenny (a) 06/06/2003, Riverstown (Ireland) (b) 1,77 (c) F - center forward (d) Shamrock Rovers (e) Celtic FC, Queen's Park, Celtic FC, Sligo Rovers

*** Kenny - Jonjoe Kenny (a) 15/03/1997, Liverpool (England) (b) 1,76 (c) D - right back (d) Hertha Berlín (e) Everton, Celtic FC, Everton, FC Schalke 04, Everton, Oxford United, Wigan Ath.

*** Kenny - Luke Kenny (a) 28/09/2003, Glasgow (Scotland) (b) - (c) D - central defense (d) St. Mirren FC B (e) East Kilbride, St. Mirren B, East Kilbride, St. Mirren B, East Kilbride, St. Mirren B

*** Kent - Ryan Kent (a) 11/11/1996, Oldham (England) (b) 1,76 (c) F - left winger (d) Fenerbahce (e) Rangers FC, Liverpool, Rangers FC, Liverpool, Bristol City, SC Freiburg, Barnsley FC, Coventry City

*** Keny - Philippe Keny (Philippe Paulin Kény) (a) 18/05/1999, Tivaouane (Senegal) (b) 1,90 (c) F - center forward (d) Basaksehir FK (e) Bandirmaspor, LB Châteauroux, Tours B, UMS Montélimar

*** Kenyaykin - Aleksey Kenyaykin (Кеняйкин Алексей Николаевич) (a) 23/08/1998, Samara (Russia) (b) 1,99 (c) G (d) FK Orenburg (e) Torpedo Moskva, Orenburg, Orenburg II, Orenburg-2, Orenburg II
*** Kenzhebek - Galymzhan Kenzhebek (Кенжебек Галымжан Рахимжанулы) (a) 12/02/2003, Taraz (Kazakhstan) (b) 1,77 (c) F - left winger (d) Kairat Almaty (e) Kairat-Zhas, Maktaaral, Kairat-Zhas
*** Keogh - Seamas Keogh (a) 28/02/2002, Sligo (Ireland) (b) - (c) D - right back (d) Finn Harps (e) Sligo Rovers, Southampton B
*** Kepov - Petar Kepov (Петър Петров Кепов) (a) 22/11/2002, ¿? (Bulgaria) (b) 1,75 (c) D - right back (d) Botev Vratsa (e) Septemvri Simitli, Pirin GD
*** Keqi - Kristian Keqi (a) 28/07/1996, Firenze (Italy) (b) 1,78 (c) F - attacking midfielder (d) - (e) Marsaxlokk, Floriana, Arezzo, Sangiovannese, Scandicci, Monterosi, Foligno, Potenza, Scandicci, Scandicci
*** Keravnos - Andreas Keravnos (Ανδρέας Κεραυνός) (a) 05/05/1999, Limassol (Cyprus) (b) 1,90 (c) G (d) Anorthosis Famagusta (e) AEZ Zakakiou, AEL Limassol, AEZ Zakakiou, AEL Limassol
*** Kerbache - Heythem Kerbache (a) 01/07/2000, Mila (Algeria) (b) 1,84 (c) F - left winger (d) FK Spartaks Jurmala (e) Siena, Spartaks, Troyes B
*** Kerdzevadze - Shota Kerdzevadze (შოთა კერძევაძე) (a) 20/03/1993, ¿? (Georgia) (b) 1,87 (c) D - central defense (d) - (e) FC Gagra, FC Shevardeni, FC Samtredia, Kolkheti Poti, FC Samtredia, Merani Martvili, Merani II, FC Samtredia, FC Samtredia II
*** Kereselidze - Davit Kereselidze (დავით კერესელიძე) (a) 19/08/1999, ¿? (Georgia) (b) 1,91 (c) G (d) Dinamo Tbilisi (e) FC Gagra, Tskhinvali
*** Keresztes - Noel Keresztes (a) 16/09/2004, Pécs (Hungary) (b) 1,84 (c) M - attacking midfielder (d) Budapest Honvéd FC (e) Honvéd II
*** Kerezovic - Tom Kerezovic (Kerezovič Tom) (a) 04/08/2004, ¿? (Slovenia) (b) - (c) M - central midfielder (d) NK Celje (e) -
*** Kerezsi - Zalán Kerezsi (Kerezsi Zalán Márk) (a) 17/07/2003, Mátészalka (Hungary) (b) 1,80 (c) F - left winger (d) Budapest Honvéd FC (e) Honvéd II
*** Kerger - Kevin Kerger (a) 17/11/1994, Luxembourg (Luxembourg) (b) 1,80 (c) M - left midfielder (d) Racing FC Union Luxembourg (e) Union Titus Petange, FC UNA Strassen, Union Titus Petange, Progrès Niederkorn, Union Titus Petange, Progrès Niederkorn, FC UNA Strassen, FC Mamer 32, ES Clemency, Koerich
*** Kerimzhanov - Olzhas Kerimzhanov (Керімжанов Олжас Бақытжанұлы) (a) 16/05/1989, Asa (Soviet Union, now in Kazakhstan) (b) 1,89 (c) D - central defense (d) FK Atyrau (e) FK Turan, Zhetysu, Kaysar, Bolat, Kyran, Okzhetpes, Ak-Bulak, Okzhetpes, Astana-M, Ile-Saulet
*** Kerin - Luka Kerin (a) 23/03/1999, Brezice (Slovenia) (b) 1,79 (c) F - left winger (d) NK Bravo (e) NK Celje, NK Krsko
*** Kerk - Gyrano Kerk (Gyrano Emilio Kerk) (a) 02/12/1995, Amsterdam (Netherlands) (b) 1,83 (c) F - right winger (d) Royal Antwerp FC (e) Royal Antwerp, Lokomotiv Moskva, FC Utrecht, Helmond Sport
*** Kerkez - Dejan Kerkez (Дејан Керкез) (a) 20/01/1996, Novi Sad (Yugoslavia, now in Serbia) (b) 1,90 (c) D - central defense (d) FK Spartak Subotica (e) Napredak, Marítimo, Mafra, Marítimo, Spartak, CSK Celarevo, Spartak, CSK Celarevo
*** Kerkez - Milos Kerkez (Милош Керкез) (a) 07/11/2003, Vrbas (Serbia and Montenegro, now in Serbia) (b) 1,80 (c) D - left back (d) AFC Bournemouth (e) AZ Alkmaar, ETO FC Győr

*** Kerkez - Strahinja Kerkez (Στραχίνια Κέρκεζ - Страхиња Керкез) (a) 13/12/2002, Beograd (RF Yugoslavia, now in Serbia) (b) 1,86 (c) D - central defense (d) AS Trencin (e) LASK, AEL Limassol
*** Kerla - Semir Kerla (a) 26/09/1987, Rogatica (Yugoslavia, now in Bosnia and Herzegovina) (b) 1,91 (c) D - central defense (d) - (e) Doxa Katokopias, Suduva, Zeljeznicar, Irtysh, Zalgiris, Zeljeznicar, MSK Zilina, Panserraikos, Zeljeznicar
*** Kern - Martin Kern (a) 23/03/2006, Szeged (Hungary) (b) 1,76 (c) M - central midfielder (d) Puskás Akadémia FC (e) Puskás AFC II
*** Kerpe - Justas Kerpe (Justas Kerpė) (a) 16/08/2003, ¿? (Lithuania) (b) 1,90 (c) M - central midfielder (d) FK Banga Gargzdai B (e) -
*** Kerr - Conor Kerr (a) 07/06/1999, Middletown (Northern Ireland) (b) 1,85 (c) D - right back (d) Glenavon FC (e) Loughgall, Armagh City FC
*** Kerr - Josh Kerr (a) 24/02/1998, Coatbridge (Scotland) (b) 1,83 (c) D - central defense (d) Cove Rangers FC (e) Bohemians, Airdrieonians, Derry City, East Kilbride
*** Kerrebijn - Ralph Kerrebijn (Ralph Max Alexander Kerrebijn) (a) 16/05/1999, Dordrecht (Netherlands) (b) 1,84 (c) M - attacking midfielder (d) NK Tolmin (e) PASA Irodotos, Mons Calpe, ODIN '59, Dobanovci, Zarkovo, Oakville BD
*** Kerrigan - Liam Kerrigan (a) 09/05/2000, Sligo (Ireland) (b) 1,71 (c) F - right winger (d) Como 1907 (e) UCD, Sligo Rovers
*** Kersák - Roland Kersák (Kersák Roland Attila) (a) 31/07/1997, Budapest (Hungary) (b) 1,91 (c) G (d) Kecskeméti TE (e) FC Dabas, Rákosmente, Soroksár, STC Salgótarján, Ferencváros II, Soroksár
*** Kerschbaum - Roman Kerschbaum (a) 19/01/1994, Neunkirchen (Austria) (b) 1,80 (c) M - central midfielder (d) SK Rapid Wien (e) Admira Wacker, FC Wacker, Grödig, Nurernberg II
*** Kerschbaumer - Konstantin Kerschbaumer (a) 01/07/1992, Tulln (Austria) (b) 1,79 (c) M - central midfielder (d) Wolfsberger AC (e) 1.FC Heidenheim, FC Ingolstadt, Brentford, Arminia Bielefeld, Brentford, Admira Wacker, SKN St. Pölten, Rapid Wien II, SKN St. Pölten, Rapid Wien II, First Vienna FC, Rapid Wien II
*** Kerstenne - Jordan Kerstenne (a) 23/04/1997, ¿? (Belgium) (b) - (c) D - central defense (d) - (e) Mondercange, Aittitos Spaton, RFC Liégeois, FCV Dender EH, Rupel Boom, Spouwen-Moper, RFC Seraing
*** Kersys - Kristupas Kersys (Kristupas Keršys) (a) 06/09/2003, ¿? (Latvia) (b) 1,96 (c) D - central defense (d) FK Metta (e) -
*** Kerzhakov - Mikhail Kerzhakov (Кержаков Михаил Анатольевич) (a) 28/01/1987, Kingisepp, St. Petersburg Region (Soviet Union, now in Russia) (b) 1,90 (c) G (d) Zenit de San Petersburgo (e) Orenburg, Zenit, Anzhi, Volga Nizhny Novgorod, Zenit St. Peterburg II, Alania, Zenit St. Peterburg II, Volgar-Gazprom, Zenit St. Peterburg II, Volga Uljanovsk, Zenit St. Peterburg II, SShOR Zenit
*** Keseru - Claudiu Keseru (Claudiu Andrei Keşerü) (a) 02/12/1986, Oradea (Romania) (b) 1,79 (c) F - center forward (d) - (e) UTA Arad, FCSB, Ludogorets, Al-Gharafa SC, Steaua Bucuresti, SC Bastia, Angers SCO, FC Nantes, Angers SCO, FC Nantes, Tours FC, FC Nantes, Libourne-St.-Seurin, FC Nantes, Bihor Oradea
*** Kesgin - Kerem Atakan Kesgin (a) 05/11/2000, Tokat (Turkey) (b) 1,76 (c) M - central midfielder (d) Besiktas JK (e) Sivasspor, Göztepe, Bucaspor
*** Keshavarz - Peyman Keshavarz (پیمان کشاورز) (a) 03/03/1996, Shabestar, East Azerbaijan (Iran) (b) 1,88 (c) D - central defense (d) - (e) Kapaz PFK, Tractor, FK Sabail, Sumqayit, Jaalan, Gostaresh FC, Machine Sazi, Esteghlal Ahvaz, Machine Sazi, Tractor Sazi

*** Kessié - Franck Kessié (Franck Yannick Kessié) (a) 19/12/1996, Ouragahio (Ivory Coast) (b) 1,83 (c) M - central midfielder (d) Al-Ahli SFC (e) FC Barcelona, AC Milan, Atalanta, AC Milan, Atalanta, Cesena, Atalanta, Stella Club
*** Kesting - Joey Kesting (a) 07/03/2001, Woubrugge (Netherlands) (b) - (c) G (d) RKC Waalwijk (e) -
*** Keto - Hugo Keto (Hugo Oliver Keto) (a) 09/02/1998, Helsinki (Finland) (b) 1,92 (c) G (d) Sandefjord Fotball (e) HJK Helsinki, Waterford FC
*** Ketting - Rick Ketting (a) 15/01/1996, Nieuwerkerk aan den IJssel (Netherlands) (b) 1,88 (c) D - central defense (d) VVV-Venlo (e) FC Inter, IFK Mariehamn, Go Ahead Eagles, Sparta Rotterdam
*** Keyamo - Nick Keyamo (Nicholas Keyamo) (a) 16/02/1996, London (England) (b) 1,86 (c) F - center forward (d) - (e) Manchester 62, IFK Österåker, Molesey FC, Ilford, FC South Park, Lansing United, Daven. Panthers, EOSC, Hampton & Rich.
*** Keyta - Hamidou Keyta (a) 17/12/1994, Montivilliers (France) (b) 1,86 (c) F - left winger (d) Qarabağ FK (e) Zira FK, Santa Clara, FC Botosani, FC Viitorul, Dunarea Calarasi, FC Chambly Oise, Saint-Étienne B, Trélissac FC, Le Havre AC B, AJ Auxerre B
*** Khabelashvili - Ivane Khabelashvili (ივანე ხაბელაშვილი) (a) 04/09/1993, Tbilisi (Georgia) (b) 1,75 (c) F - right winger (d) Sioni Bolnisi (e) FC Gagra, Merani Tbilisi, FC Gagra, Sioni Bolnisi, Merani Martvili, WIT Georgia, FC Zestafoni, Metalurgi R.
*** Khabuliani - Giorgi Khabuliani (გიორგი ხაბულიანი) (a) 25/03/2004, Tbilisi (Georgia) (b) 1,93 (c) F - attacking midfielder (d) Atlético Levante UD (e) Adana Demirspor, FC Telavi, Merani Tbilisi, F. Marcet
*** Khachatryan - Arman Khachatryan (Արման Խաչատրյան) (a) 09/06/1997, Yerevan (Armenia) (b) 1,84 (c) D - right back (d) Alashkert Yerevan CF (e) FC Noah, SC Noravank, FC Van, Ararat-Armenia II, FC Van, Ararat-Armenia II, Banants II, Banants III
*** Khachatryan - Artur Khachatryan (Արթուր Խաչատրյան) (a) 09/04/1999, Aparan (Armenia) (b) 1,60 (c) D - left back (d) Lernayin Artsakh Goris (e) West Armenia, Urartu II
*** Khachatryan - Hayk Khachatryan (Հայկ Խաչատրյան) (a) 27/01/2005, ¿? (Armenia) (b) - (c) G (d) BKMA Yerevan (e) Ararat-Armenia, Ararat-Armenia II
*** Khachatryan - Narek Khachatryan (Նարեկ Խաչատրյան) (a) 28/01/2004, ¿? (Armenia) (b) - (c) F - center forward (d) Shirak Gyumri C.F. (e) Shirak II
*** Khachaturyan - Andrey Khachaturyan (Хачатурян Андрей Владимирович) (a) 02/09/1987, Minsk (Soviet Union, now in Belarus) (b) 1,75 (c) M - pivot (d) Torpedo-BelAZ Zhodino II (e) Torpedo Zhodino, Belshina, Torpedo Zhodino, Neman Grodno, Soligorsk, Zhemchuzhina, FK Minsk, Zhemchuzhina, FK Minsk
*** Khachayev - Murad Khachayev (Murad Şamil oğlu Xaçayev) (a) 14/04/1998, Lugansk (Ukraine) (b) 1,80 (c) D - central defense (d) Sumqayit PFK (e) Shakhtar II, Sumqayit, Shakhtar II
*** Khachumyan - Albert Khachumyan (Ալբերտ Խաչումյան) (a) 23/06/1999, Yerevan (Armenia) (b) 1,84 (c) D - central defense (d) BKMA Yerevan (e) BKMA Yerevan, Ararat-Armenia, Ararat-Armenia II, Ararat-Armenia, Pyunik Yerevan B
*** Khadarkevich - Ruslan Khadarkevich (Хадаркевич Руслан Исаакович) (a) 18/06/1993, Minsk (Belarus) (b) 1,87 (c) D - central defense (d) BATE Borisov (e) Dinamo Minsk, Soligorsk, Slavia, Smolevichi, Slavia, FK Bereza
*** Khadzhiev - Asludin Khadzhiev (Хаджиев Аслудин Бахтиярулы) (a) 24/10/2000, Tolebiyskiy Rayon (Kazakhstan) (b) 1,66 (c) M - right midfielder (d) FK Turan (e) Ordabasy, Akad. Ontustik, Ordabasy, Ordabasy II

*** Khairov - Ruslan Khairov (Хаиров Руслан Казбекович) (a) 18/01/1990, Uralsk (Soviet Union, now in Russia) (b) 1,74 (c) D - right back (d) Akzhayik Uralsk (e) FK Altay, Kyzyl-Zhar, Akzhayik, Akzhayik II

*** Khakhlyov - Oleksiy Khakhlyov (Хахльов Олексій Олексійович) (a) 06/02/1999, Ostrog, Rivne Oblast (Ukraine) (b) 1,79 (c) M - central midfielder (d) Zorya Lugansk (e) FK Minaj, Karpaty, Depor. Alavés B, San Ignacio, Depor. Alavés B

*** Khalaila - Osama Khalaila (חליילה אוסמה) (a) 06/04/1998, Sakhnin (Israel) (b) 1,88 (c) F - center forward (d) FK Qabala (e) Maccabi Tel Aviv, M. Bnei Reineh, Maccabi Tel Aviv, Bnei Sakhnin

*** Khalaili - Anan Khalaili (חלאילי ענאן) (a) 03/09/2004, Haifa (Israel) (b) 1,83 (c) F - center forward (d) Maccabi Haifa (e) -

*** Khali - Nabil Khali (a) 05/04/1998, Villeneuve St George (France) (b) 1,81 (c) F - right winger (d) - (e) Tabor Sezana, Saint-Nazaire

*** Khalili - Abdul Khalili (عبد الرحمن خليلي) (a) 07/06/1992, Raus, Helsingborg (Sweden) (b) 1,80 (c) M - central midfielder (d) - (e) Olympiakos N., Helsingborgs IF, Hammarby IF, Kasimpasa, Genclerbirligi, Mersin IY, Helsingborgs IF, Värnamo, Helsingborgs IF, Värnamo, Helsingborgs IF

*** Khalilzada - Tamkin Khalilzada (Təmkin Şaiq oğlu Xəlilzadə) (a) 06/08/1993, Baku (Azerbaijan) (b) 1,73 (c) D - left back (d) - (e) Zira FK, Sabah FK, FK Qabala, Zira FK, Qarabag FK, AZAL, Qarabag FK

*** Khalimonchik - Nikita Khalimonchik (Халимончик Никита Александрович) (a) 03/01/2000, Minsk (Belarus) (b) 1,73 (c) D - right back (d) Arsenal Dzerzhinsk (e) Dinamo Minsk, FK Minsk, Dinamo Minsk, Dinamo Minsk II, Neman Grodno, Dinamo Minsk II, Smolevichi, Dinamo Minsk II

*** Khalmatov - Murodzhon Khalmatov (Халматов Муроджон Айбекович) (a) 20/07/2003, Karabulak (Kazakhstan) (b) 1,79 (c) M - central midfielder (d) FK Turan (e) Ordabasy, Ordabasy II

*** Khalnazarov - Rustam Khalnazarov (Халназаров Рустам Абдурашитович) (a) 20/07/2000, Novosibirsk (Russia) (b) 1,76 (c) F - left winger (d) Arsenal Tula (e) Krasnodar-2, Krasnodar 3, Krasnodar II

*** Khamelyuk - Vladyslav Khamelyuk (Хамелюк Владислав Русланович) (a) 04/05/1998, Kamyanets-Podilskyi, Khmelnytskyi Oblast (Ukraine) (b) 1,78 (c) M - central midfielder (d) LNZ Cherkasy (e) Dynamo Brest, Jonava, Dynamo Brest, PFK Lviv, Olimpik Donetsk, Chornomorets, Chornomorets II

*** Khammas - Amine Khammas (a) 06/04/1999, Reet (Belgium) (b) 1,74 (c) D - left back (d) Apollon Limassol (e) Waasland-Beveren, KRC Genk, Lommel SK, KRC Genk, FC Den Bosch, KRC Genk, JMG Lier

*** Khamoyan - Aram Khamoyan (Արամ Խամոյան) (a) 10/01/2000, Verin Bazmaberd (Armenia) (b) 1,78 (c) M - pivot (d) BKMA Yerevan (e) Ararat-Armenia, Ararat-Armenia II, Lokomotiv, Banants II

*** Khaoui - Saîf-Eddine Khaoui (سيف الدين خاوي) (a) 27/04/1995, Paris (France) (b) 1,80 (c) M - attacking midfielder (d) Khor Fakkan (e) Clermont Foot, Ol. Marseille, SM Caen, Ol. Marseille, Troyes, Ol. Marseille, Tours FC, Tours B

*** Kharabadze - Levan Kharabadze (ლევან ხარაბაძე) (a) 26/01/2000, Kutaisi (Georgia) (b) 1,85 (c) D - left back (d) Dinamo Batumi (e) Pafos FC, Dinamo Tbilisi, FC Zürich, Dinamo Tbilisi

*** Kharaishvili - Beka Kharaishvili (ბექა ხარაიშვილი) (a) 27/10/2001, ¿? (Georgia) (b) 1,86 (c) D - central defense (d) FC Locomotive Tbilisi (e) FC Saburtalo II

*** Kharaishvili - Giorgi Kharaishvili (გიორგი ხარაიშვილი) (a) 29/07/1996, Marneuli (Georgia) (b) 1,83 (c) M - attacking midfielder (d) Dinamo Tbilisi (e) Dinamo Tbilisi, Ferencváros, IFK Göteborg, Saburtalo, IFK Göteborg, Saburtalo

*** Kharatin - Igor Kharatin (Харатін Ігор Ігорович) (a) 02/02/1995, Mukacheve, Zakarpattya Oblast (Ukraine) (b) 1,88 (c) M - pivot (d) Legia de Varsovia (e) Ferencváros, Zorya Lugansk, Dinamo Kiev II, Metalist, Dinamo Kiev II, Dynamo 2 Kyiv

*** Kharatishvili - Luka Kharatishvili (ლუკა ხარატიშვილი) (a) 11/01/2003, ¿? (Georgia) (b) - (c) G (d) FC Samtredia (e) Dinamo Batumi, Shukura, Dinamo Batumi, Dinamo B. II

*** Kharatyan - Vladimir Kharatyan (Харатян Владимир Самвелович) (a) 14/07/1996, Moskva (Russia) (b) 1,74 (c) D - right back (d) FC West Armenia (e) Lernayin Artsakh, West Armenia, Kolomna, Solyaris II, Sportacademclub, LFK Lokomotiv 2, Spartak 2

*** Kharchouch - Reda Kharchouch (a) 27/08/1995, Amsterdam (Netherlands) (b) 1,92 (c) F - center forward (d) Al-Bukiryah FC (e) Excelsior, Sparta Rotterdam, FC Emmen, Sparta Rotterdam, Telstar, OFC Oostzaan, Quick Boys, Ajax Amateurs, Spartaan

*** Kharin - Evgeniy Kharin (Харин Евгений Валерьевич) (a) 11/06/1995, Tallinn (Estonia) (b) 1,85 (c) M - left midfielder (d) Akhmat Grozny (e) FCI Levadia, FCI Tallinn

*** Kharitonov - Dmitriy Kharitonov (Харитонов Дмитрий) (a) 12/04/1997, Vitebsk (Belarus) (b) 1,86 (c) G (d) FK Vitebsk (e) FK Slutsk, Sperre) Vitebsk II, Orsha, Vitebsk II, Naftan, Vitebsk II, Orsha, Vitebsk II

*** Kharitonovich - Aleksey Kharitonovich (Харитонович Алексей Александрович) (a) 30/04/1995, Minsk (Belarus) (b) 1,85 (c) G (d) Belshina Bobruisk (e) Energetik-BGU, Dinamo Minsk II, FK Bereza, Dinamo Minsk II

*** Kharshiladze - Luka Kharshiladze (ლუკა ხარშილაძე) (a) 18/02/2002, ¿? (Georgia) (b) - (c) G (d) FC Kolkheti-1913 Poti (e) CE Sabadell B, Dinamo II

*** Khasa - Jared Khasa (a) 04/11/1997, Kinshasa (Congo DR) (b) 1,89 (c) F - right winger (d) Maccabi Petah Tikva (e) AEL Limassol, FC Sion, Pau FC, FC Sion, FC Fribourg, Le Havre AC B

*** Khasan - Alisher Khasan (Хасан Алишер) (a) 13/03/2003, ¿? (Kazakhstan) (b) 1,83 (c) F (d) Kyzylzhar SK Petropavlovsk II (e) -

*** Khatib - Mohamed Khatib (חטיב מוחמד) (a) 24/11/1995, ¿? (Israel) (b) 1,88 (c) F - center forward (d) Ironi Kiryat Shmona (e) Hapoel Hadera, H. Umm al-Fahm, Hapoel Hadera, SC Kfar Qasem, M. Ahi Nazareth, SC Kfar Qasem, M. Ahi Nazareth, Ramat haSharon, M. Ahi Nazareth

*** Khatkevich - Egor Khatkevich (Хаткевич Егор Тадеушевич) (a) 09/07/1988, Minsk (Soviet Union, now in Belarus) (b) 1,96 (c) G (d) FK Atyrau (e) Dinamo Minsk, Isloch, Torpedo Zhodino, Naftan, Gomel, Vedrich-97, Vitebsk, Partizan II, Junsele IF, Partizan II, BATE II

*** Khatri - Dipak Khatri (a) 06/07/2005, ¿? (Luxembourg) (b) - (c) M (d) - (e) CS Fola Esch

*** Khattab - Obeida Khattab (עוביידה חטאב) (a) 14/07/1992, Nazareth (Israel) (b) - (c) D - central defense (d) FC Ashdod (e) Bnei Yehuda, Hapoel Hadera, Sperre) FC Ashdod, Bnei Sakhnin, M. Petah Tikva, Hapoel Katamon, Hapoel Acre, Bnei Sakhnin, Hakoah Amidar, Hapoel Tel Aviv, Hakoah Amidar, Hapoel Haifa, Hakoah Amidar

*** Khayat - Sofiane Khayat (a) 05/05/1999, Marseille (France) (b) 1,73 (c) F - right winger (d) FC Mondercange (e) Stade Tunisien, AS Nancy B

*** Khaybulaev - Abdulakh Khaybulaev (Abdulax Tilovur oğlu Xaybulayev) (a) 19/08/2001, Khasavyurt, Dagestan Republic (Russia) (b) 1,78 (c) M - central midfielder (d) FC Samtredia (e) FC Samtredia, Sabah FK, Sabah 2, Anzhi II

*** Khaymanov - Igor Khaymanov (Хайманов Игорь Анатольевич) (a) 26/03/1994, Vladikavkaz (Russia) (b) 1,88 (c) D - central defense (d) Guria Lanchkhuti (e) Dzerzhinsk, Druzhba Maikop, Dinamo Bryansk, Fakel Voronezh, KamAZ, Tyumen, Fakel Voronezh, Afips Afipskiy, Spartak V., Avangard Kursk, Lokomotiv Liski, Stroitel, Alania, Alania II, Alania-D Vladik.

*** Khazeni - Kristoffer Khazeni (خازنى كريستوفر) (a) 25/06/1995, ¿? (Sweden) (b) 1,85 (c) M - attacking midfielder (d) IFK Norrköping (e) Sylvia, IFK Stocksund, Enebybergs IF

*** Khazri - Wahbi Khazri (خزري وهبي) (a) 08/02/1991, Ajaccio (France) (b) 1,76 (c) F - center forward (d) Montpellier HSC (e) St.-Étienne, Sunderland, Stade Rennes, Sunderland, Girondins Bordeaux, SC Bastia, SC Bastia B

*** Khedira - Rani Khedira (a) 27/01/1994, Stuttgart (Germany) (b) 1,89 (c) M - pivot (d) 1.FC Union Berlin (e) FC Augsburg, RB Leipzig, VfB Stuttgart, Stuttgart II

*** Khelifa - Anthony Khelifa (a) 20/09/2005, Marseille (France) (b) - (c) D - central defense (d) - (e) Ajaccio

*** Khetsuriani - Givi Khetsuriani (გივი ხეცურიანი) (a) 02/07/1999, ¿? (Georgia) (b) 1,84 (c) D - central defense (d) - (e) Sioni Bolnisi, Tbilisi City, Sioni Bolnisi, Sioni II

*** Khinchiashvili - Revaz Khinchiashvili (რევაზ ხინჩიაშვილი) (a) 19/11/2000, ¿? (Georgia) (b) 1,86 (c) M - pivot (d) FC Locomotive Tbilisi (e) Locomotive II, Dinamo II

*** Khizhnichenko - Sergey Khizhnichenko (Хижниченко Сергей Александрович) (a) 17/07/1991, Ust-Kamenogorsk (Soviet Union, now in Kazakhstan) (b) 1,87 (c) F - center forward (d) - (e) FK Aksu, Ordabasy, FC Astana, Ordabasy, Shakhter K., Soligorsk, Tobol Kostanay, Aktobe, Korona Kielce, Shakhter K., Atyrau, Lokomotiv Astana, Vostok Oskemen, Vostok II

*** Khlan - Maksym Khlan (Хлань Максим Сергійович) (a) 27/01/2003, Zhytomyr (Ukraine) (b) 1,70 (c) M - attacking midfielder (d) - (e) Zorya Lugansk, Karpaty, UFK Lviv

*** Khlebosolov - Miroslav Khlebosolov (Хлебосолов Мирослав Андреевич) (a) 18/01/1999, Baranovichi (Belarus) (b) 1,85 (c) M - attacking midfielder (d) Ocean Kerch (e) Energetik-BGU, Shakhter P., FK Lida, Volna Pinsk, Smolevichi, FK Baranovichi, FK Baranovichi Reserves

*** Khlusevich - Daniil Khlusevich (Хлусевич Даниил Андреевич) (a) 26/02/2001, Simferopol (Ukraine) (b) 1,86 (c) D - left back (d) FC Spartak de Moscú (e) Arsenal Tula, Arsenal Tula II, Krasnolesje

*** Khlusov - Nikita Khlusov (Хлусов Никита Николаевич) (a) 16/01/2000, St. Petersburg (Russia) (b) 1,84 (c) F - center forward (d) Dnepr Mogilev (e) Dnepr Mogilev, KS Samara, Leningradets, SShOR Zenit

*** Khlyobas - Dmytro Khlyobas (Хльобас Дмитро Вікторович) (a) 09/05/1994, Lokhvytsya, Poltava Oblast (Ukraine) (b) 1,78 (c) F - center forward (d) Qyzyljar Petropavlovsk (e) FC Urartu, Ordabasy, Kolos Kovalivka, Desna, Dinamo Kyïv, Dinamo Minsk, Dinamo Kyïv, Vorskla Poltava, Dinamo Kyïv, Dynamo 2 Kyiv, Goverla, Dynamo 2 Kyiv, Dinamo Kiev II

*** Khoblenko - Oleksiy Khoblenko (Хобленко Олексій Сергійович) (a) 04/04/1994, Ekaterinburg (Russia) (b) 1,85 (c) F - center forward (d) Kryvbas Kryvyi

Rig (e) Karpaty Lviv, Kryvbas, FCI Levadia, Kryvbas, SK Dnipro-1, Kryvbas, SK Dnipro-1, Stabæk, SK Dnipro-1, Dynamo Brest, Chornomorets, Lech Poznan, Chornomorets, Dynamo 2 Kyiv, Chornomorets, Dynamo 2 Kyiv, Goverla, Dynamo 2 Kyiv, FK Poltava, Dynamo 2 Kyiv

*** Khocholava - Davit Khocholava (დავით ხოჭოლავა) (a) 08/02/1993, Tbilisi (Georgia) (b) 1,92 (c) D - central defense (d) FC Copenhague (e) Shakhtar Donetsk, Chornomorets, Shukura, Kolkheti Poti, Dinamo Tbilisi, Dinamo II, Saburtalo, Sioni II, Saburtalo

*** Khodanovich - Andrey Khodanovich (Ходанович Андрей Александрович) (a) 08/09/2004, ¿? (Russia) (b) 1,95 (c) G (d) FK Orenburg-2 (e) -

*** Kholmetskyi - Yevgeniy Kholmetskyi (Холмецький Євгеній Олександрович) (a) 07/04/2004, Kyiv)) (c) F - right winger (d) Mārupes SC Futbols (e) AB Argir

*** Kholod - Maksim Kholod (Холод Максим) (a) 20/05/2005, ¿? (Kazakhstan) (b) 1,77 (c) M - central midfielder (d) Shakhter-Bulat (e) -

*** Kholod - Vitaliy Kholod (Холод Віталій Русланович) (a) 15/01/2004, ¿? (Ukraine) (b) 1,83 (c) D - central defense (d) Rukh Lviv (e) -

*** Khoma - Bogdan Khoma (Хома Богдан Артурович) (a) 02/04/2003, Dnipropetrovsk (Ukraine) (b) 1,96 (c) G (d) Kryvbas Kryvyi Rig (e) FK Nikopol

*** Khomchenovskyi - Dmytro Khomchenovskyi (Хомченовський Дмитро Геннадійович) (a) 16/04/1990, Ugledar, Donetsk Oblast (Soviet Union, now in Ukraine) (b) 1,82 (c) M - attacking midfielder (d) Kryvbas Kryvyi Rig (e) Zorya Lugansk, Ural, Jagiellonia, Ponferradina, Zorya Lugansk, Olimpik Donetsk, Kryvbas, Olimpik Donetsk

*** Khomutov - Vladyslav Khomutov (Хомутов Владислав Денисович) (a) 04/06/1998, Donetsk (Ukraine) (b) 1,87 (c) M - attacking midfielder (d) FC Gagra (e) KF Dukagjini, STK Samorin, Kalju FC, Zlaté Moravce, Chornomorets, Olimpik Donetsk, Ol. Donetsk II

*** Khondak - Danyil Khondak (Хондак Даниїл Дмитрович) (a) 19/04/2001, Kharkiv (Ukraine) (b) 1,88 (c) D - central defense (d) NK Veres Rivne (e) Girnyk-Sport, Nyva Buzova, Dinamo Kiev II

*** Khorava - Luka Khorava (ლუკა ხორავა) (a) 12/02/2002, ¿? (Georgia) (b) - (c) D - left back (d) - (e) FC Locomotive, Locomotive II

*** Khorkheli - Luka Khorkheli (ლუკა ხორხელი) (a) 31/01/2000, ¿? (Georgia) (b) - (c) M - attacking midfielder (d) FC Samgurali Tskaltubo (e) Sioni Bolnisi, Spaeri, Gori FC, FC Iberia

*** Khorkheli - Nika Khorkheli (ნიკა ხორხელი) (a) 09/09/2001, ¿? (Georgia) (b) 1,76 (c) F - right winger (d) FC Samgurali Tskaltubo (e) Sioni Bolnisi, Spaeri, Dinamo II

*** Khositashvili - Vasil Khositashvili (ვასილ ხოსიტაშვილი) (a) 11/05/1996, ¿? (Georgia) (b) 1,77 (c) D - right back (d) FC Gagra (e) FC Meshakhte, FC Gagra

*** Khotulev - Danila Khotulev (Хотулёв Данила Дмитриевич) (a) 01/10/2002, Orenburg (Russia) (b) 1,87 (c) D - central defense (d) FK Orenburg (e) Zenit 2 St. Peterburg, Orenburg, Zenit 2 St. Peterburg, Zenit St. Peterburg II, Akron Konoplev

*** Khovalko - Ivan Khovalko (Ховалко Иван) (a) 09/06/2003, Borisov (Belarus) (b) 1,76 (c) M - pivot (d) Dinamo Minsk II (e) -

*** Khozin - Vladimir Khozin (Хозин Владимир Вячеславович) (a) 03/07/1989, Rostov-na-Donu (Soviet Union, now in Russia) (b) 1,85 (c) D - central defense (d) Enisey Krasnoyarsk (e) SKA Rostov, Enisey, Shakhter K., Chaika Pes., Nizhny Novgorod, Ural, Ararat-Armenia, Ural, Alania, Torpedo Moskva, KS Samara, FC Moskva II, Rostov II

*** Khrypchuk - Daniil Khrypchuk (Хрипчук Даніїл Сергійович) (a) 09/12/2003, Kharkiv (Ukraine) (b) 1,92 (c) D - central defense (d) Vorskla Poltava (e) Vorskla II
*** Khubulov - Vladimir Khubulov (Хубулов Владимир Алексеевич) (a) 02/03/2001, Vladikavkaz (Russia) (b) 1,79 (c) F - left winger (d) Krylya Sovetov Samara (e) Khimki, KS Samara, Alania Vl., Akhmat II, Zenit St. Peterburg II, Akhmat II, Akademia Ramzan
*** Khudoydodzoda - Abdulfattokh Khudoydodzoda (Худойдодзода Абдулфаттох) (a) 15/07/2004, Dushanbe (Tajikistan) (b) - (c) F - center forward (d) Ravshan Kulob (e) Dynamo Dushanbe, Dynamo Brest
*** Khudyakov - Daniil Khudyakov (Худяков Даниил Дмитриевич) (a) 09/01/2004, Moskva (Russia) (b) 1,94 (c) G (d) Lokomotiv Moskva (e) Loko-Kazanka M.
*** Khuri - Baseel Khuri (ורי'ח בסיל) (a) 01/12/2003, Arraba (Israel) (b) 1,75 (c) F - center forward (d) - (e) Ihud Bnei Sakhnin
*** Khurtsidze - David Khurtsidze (Хурцидзе Давид Хвичаевич) (a) 04/07/1993, Kutaisi (Georgia) (b) 1,85 (c) M - attacking midfielder (d) Alashkert Yerevan CF (e) FC Urartu, Alashkert CF, Ararat Yerevan, Ararat Moskva, Torpedo Kutaisi, Amkar Perm, Amkar-Junior, Torpedo Armavir, Ulisses, CSKA Moskva II, Torpedo Kutaisi, CSKA Moskva II, Zenit Penza, CSKA Moskva II
*** Khusanov - Abdukodir Khusanov (Abdukodir Khusanov) (a) 29/02/2004, Tashkent (Uzbekistan) (b) 1,86 (c) D - central defense (d) RC Lens (e) Energetik-BGU
*** Khutsishvili - Gabriel Khutsishvili (გაბრიელ ხუციშვილი) (a) 13/02/2002, Tbilisi (Georgia) (b) 1,81 (c) M - central midfielder (d) FC Locomotive Tbilisi (e) Locomotive II
*** Khutsishvili - Nika Khutsishvili (ნიკა ხუციშვილი) (a) 13/02/2002, ¿? (Georgia) (b) - (c) F (d) FC Locomotive Tbilisi (e) Locomotive II
*** Khvadagiani - Saba Khvadagiani (საბა ხვადაგიანი) (a) 30/01/2003, Tbilisi (Georgia) (b) 1,86 (c) D - central defense (d) Dinamo Tbilisi (e) -
*** Khvalko - Egor Khvalko (Хвалько Ягор Аляксандравіч) (a) 18/02/1997, Baranovichi (Belarus) (b) 1,81 (c) D - central defense (d) Kapaz PFK (e) Dzerzhinsk, Neman Grodno, Dnyapro Mogilev, Neman Grodno, Neman II, FK Lida, Neman II
*** Khvashchinskiy - Vladimir Khvashchinskiy (Хващинский Владимир Александрович) (a) 10/05/1990, Bobruisk (Soviet Union, now in Belarus) (b) 1,79 (c) F - center forward (d) Dinamo Minsk (e) FK Minsk, Dinamo Minsk, Kaspiy Aktau, Dinamo Minsk, Soligorsk, FK Minsk, Soligorsk, Dinamo Minsk, FK Minsk, Dinamo Minsk, FK Minsk, Dinamo Minsk, Dynamo Brest, Dynamo Brest II
*** Kiakos - Giannis Kiakos (Γιάννης Κιακός) (a) 14/02/1998, Bamberg (Germany) (b) 1,80 (c) D - left back (d) PAS Giannina (e) Ionikos Nikeas, Volos NPS, Panionios, AS Meteora, SpVgg Bayreuth, Würzburg Kickers II
*** Kichun - Yevgeniy Kichun (Кічун Євгеній Віталійович) (a) 16/09/2004, Uzhgorod (Ukraine) (b) - (c) F - left winger (d) Gyirmót FC Győr (e) Puskás AFC, Gyirmót FC, Puskás AFC, Puskás AFC II
*** Kiebre - Abdoul Kader Junior Kiebre (a) 24/06/2003, ¿? (Cameroon) (b) 1,74 (c) M - attacking midfielder (d) - (e) ND Gorica
*** Kieftenbeld - Maikel Kieftenbeld (a) 26/06/1990, Lemelerveld (Netherlands) (b) 1,79 (c) M - pivot (d) FC Emmen (e) Millwall, Birmingham City, FC Groningen, Go Ahead Eagles
*** Kielb - Jacek Kielb (Jacek Kiełb) (a) 10/01/1988, Siedlce (Poland) (b) 1,83 (c) F - right winger (d) - (e) Korona Kielce, Nieciecza, Korona Kielce, Śląsk Wroclaw,

Korona Kielce, Lech Poznan, Polonia, Lech Poznan, Korona Kielce, Lech Poznan, Korona Kielce, Pogon Siedlce

*** Kielb - Jakub Kielb (Jakub Kiełb) (a) 15/07/1993, Jarocin (Poland) (b) 1,76 (c) M - left midfielder (d) Warta Poznań (e) Jarota Jarocin, Nieciecza, Chrobry Glogow, Nieciecza, Tur Turek, ŁKS, Tur Turek, SMS Lodz

*** Kieliba - Bartosz Kieliba (Bartosz Kieliba) (a) 01/08/1990, Krotoszyn (Poland) (b) 1,88 (c) D - central defense (d) KKS 1925 Kalisz (e) Warta Poznań, Jarota Jarocin

*** Kiese Thelin - Isaac Kiese Thelin (a) 24/06/1992, Örebro (Sweden) (b) 1,89 (c) F - center forward (d) Malmö FF (e) FC Baniyas, RSC Anderlecht, Kasimpasa, RSC Anderlecht, Malmö FF, RSC Anderlecht, Bayer Leverkusen, RSC Anderlecht, Waasland-Beveren, RSC Anderlecht, Girondins Bordeaux, RSC Anderlecht, Girondins Bordeaux, Malmö FF, Norrköping, Karlslunds IF, Norrköping, Karlslunds IF

*** Kigurs - Martins Kigurs (Mārtiņš Kigurs) (a) 31/03/1997, ¿? (Latvia) (b) 1,83 (c) M - attacking midfielder (d) - (e) Liepaja, Liepaja II

*** Kiidjärv - Carl Kiidjärv (Carl Kaiser Kiidjärv) (a) 05/12/2001, Tartu (Estonia) (b) - (c) G (d) Jalgpallikool Tammeka (e) Nomme United, JK Tammeka

*** Kiilerich - Kasper Kiilerich (Kasper Hartly Kiilerich) (a) 22/11/2005, Viborg (Denmark) (b) 1,98 (c) G (d) Viborg FF (e) -

*** Kiilerich - Malte Kiilerich (Malte Kiilerich Hansen) (a) 16/10/1995, ¿? (Denmark) (b) 1,88 (c) D - central defense (d) AC Horsens (e) Hvidovre, Brönshöj BK

*** Kiivit - Andreas Kiivit (a) 05/07/2003, Tartu (Estonia) (b) - (c) F - center forward (d) Kalev Tallinn (e) FC Flora, Pärnu Vaprus, FC Flora, FC Elva II, FC Elva II

*** Kikabidze - Luka Kikabidze (ლუკა კიკაბიძე) (a) 21/01/1995, Tbilisi (Georgia) (b) 1,80 (c) F - left winger (d) - (e) Merani Tbilisi, Merani Martvili, FC Gagra, Chikhura, FC Locomotive, SC Bastia, CA Bastia, SC Bastia, FC Locomotive

*** Kikabidze - Tedo Kikabidze (თედო კიკაბიძე) (a) 27/04/1996, Gali (Georgia) (b) 1,81 (c) D - right back (d) FC Samgurali Tskaltubo (e) FK Zugdidi, Anzio, Ostiamare

*** Kikalishvili - Davit Kikalishvili (დავით კიკალიშვილი) (a) 19/03/1999, ¿? (Georgia) (b) 1,77 (c) D - right back (d) DFK Dainava Alytus (e) Sioni Bolnisi, FC Saburtalo II, WIT Georgia, FC Gagra, Dinamo Batumi, FC Locomotive

*** Kiki - Kiki (Christian Neiva Afonso) (a) 10/12/1994, Esposende (Portugal) (b) 1,81 (c) D - left back (d) Ural Ekaterimburgo (e) Vizela, B SAD, Feirense, Felgueiras, Feirense, Olhanense, Gil Vicente, Atlético CP, FC Dagenham & Redbridge, Rio Ave

*** Kiki - Kiki (Francisco Pedro Tiago Silva) (a) 14/02/1998, Sintra (Portugal) (b) 1,72 (c) F - right winger (d) Casa Pia AC (e) Leixões, Braga B

*** Kiki - David Kiki (David Enagnon Kiki) (a) 25/11/1993, Vakaon (Benin) (b) 1,80 (c) D - left back (d) FCV Farul Constanta (e) Arda Kardzhali, Montana, Stade Brestois, Red Star FC, Stade Brestois, Chamois Niort, ASM Belfort

*** Kiki - Gaby Kiki (Gaby Kiki Junior) (a) 15/02/1995, Yaoundé (Cameroon) (b) 1,94 (c) D - central defense (d) FC Sheriff Tiraspol (e) Rukh, Dynamo Brest, Dnepr Mogilev, Eding Sport FC

*** Kikín - Kikín (José Antonio Ángel García) (a) 20/01/2003, Trebujena (Spain) (b) - (c) D - right back (d) Cádiz CF Mirandilla (e) -

*** Kikkenborg - Mads Kikkenborg (Mads Juhl Kikkenborg) (a) 07/10/1999, ¿? (Denmark) (b) 1,97 (c) G (d) Lyngby BK (e) Esbjerg fB, FC Sydvest, Esbjerg fB

*** Kiknadze - Saba-Amiko Kiknadze (საბა-ამიკო კიკნაძე) (a) 10/04/2001, ¿? (Georgia) (b) - (c) F - center forward (d) FC Locomotive Tbilisi (e) Locomotive II

*** Kiko - Kiko (Francisco Manuel Geraldo Rosa) (a) 20/01/1993, Alcacer do Sal (Portugal) (b) 1,80 (c) D - left back (d) Anorthosis Famagusta (e) Omonia Nicosia, Olympiakos N., Arouca, Doxa Katokopias, Académico Viseu, Port Vale, Vitória Setúbal, Académico Viseu, Vitória Setúbal

*** Kiko Bondoso - Kiko Bondoso (Francisco Miguel Ribeiro Tomé Tavares Bondoso) (a) 17/11/1995, Moimenta da Beira (Portugal) (b) 1,69 (c) F - left winger (d) FC Vizela (e) Lusitano FCV, Ferreira Aves, Moimenta Beira

*** Kikovic - Danko Kikovic (Данко Киковић) (a) 21/09/1994, Beograd (RF Yugoslavia, now in Serbia) (b) 1,87 (c) M - attacking midfielder (d) FK Kolubara Lazarevac (e) Novi Pazar, Zarkovo, Mladost, Zarkovo, Mladost, FK Indjija, Mladost, Javor-Matis, FK BSK Borča, IMT Beograd, FK Indjija, Lokomotiva, Srem Jakovo

*** Kikushima - Makoto Kikushima (菊島 誠人) (a) 22/06/1999, ¿? (Japan) (b) 1,90 (c) G (d) Santa Lucia FC (e) Amateur (JP), Tokyo UoA, Seiritsu HS

*** Kilasonia - Elguja Kilasonia (ელგუჯა კილასონია) (a) 03/02/2004, ¿? (Georgia) (b) 1,87 (c) G (d) FC Gagra II (e) -

*** Kilasonia - Varlam Kilasonia (ვარლამ კილასონია) (a) 09/01/1993, ¿? (Georgia) (b) 1,81 (c) D - central defense (d) FC Samtredia (e) Sioni Bolnisi, FC Samtredia, Rustavi, FC Shevardeni, Kolkheti Poti, Rustavi, Sioni Bolnisi, Tskhinvali, Metalurgi R., Tskhinvali

*** Kilian - Luca Kilian (Luca Jannis Kilian) (a) 01/09/1999, Witten (Germany) (b) 1,92 (c) D - central defense (d) 1.FC Köln (e) Mainz 05, 1.FC Köln, Mainz 05, SC Paderborn, Borussia Dortmund II

*** Kilic - Arda Kilic (Arda Kılıç) (a) 21/01/2005, ¿? (Turkey) (b) - (c) D - central defense (d) Giresunspor (e) Giresunspor

*** Kilicsoy - Semih Kilicsoy (Semih Kılıçsoy) (a) 15/08/2005, Uyruk (Turkey) (b) 1,78 (c) F - center forward (d) Besiktas JK (e) -

*** Kilinc - Emre Kilinc (Emre Kılınç) (a) 23/08/1994, Sakarya (Turkey) (b) 1,74 (c) F - left winger (d) Samsunspor (e) Galatasaray, Ankaragücü, Galatasaray, Sivasspor, Boluspor

*** Kilkenny - Gavin Kilkenny (a) 01/02/2000, Dublin (Ireland) (b) 1,75 (c) M - central midfielder (d) AFC Bournemouth (e) Charlton Ath., Bournemouth, Stoke City, Bournemouth, St. Kevins Boys

*** Kilman - Max Kilman (Maximilian William Kilman) (a) 23/05/1997, London (England) (b) 1,94 (c) D - central defense (d) Wolverhampton Wanderers (e) Maidenhead Utd., Marlow, Maidenhead Utd.

*** Kilota - Gérald Kilota (Gérald Valentin Kilota) (a) 02/01/1994, Saint-Denis (France) (b) 1,71 (c) D - left back (d) - (e) RFC Seraing, Clermont Foot, SM Caen B

*** Kilov - Atanas Kilov (Атанас Василев Килов) (a) 27/07/2005, Pazardzhik (Bulgaria) (b) - (c) D - left back (d) Hebar Pazardzhik II (e) Levski Sofia II

*** Kiltie - Greg Kiltie (a) 18/01/1997, Irvine (Scotland) (b) 1,73 (d) St. Mirren FC (e) Kilmarnock FC, Dunfermline A., Kilmarnock FC, Morton, Kilmarnock FC, Queen of the South, Kilmarnock FC

*** Kiltmaa - Kairo Kiltmaa (a) 22/02/2003, Pärnu (Estonia) (b) - (c) D - right back (d) - (e) Pärnu Vaprus, Pärnu JK II

*** Kim - Evgeniy Kim (Ким Евгений Эдуардович) (a) 17/05/2003, Almaty (Kazakhstan) (b) 1,81 (c) M - attacking midfielder (d) Zenit 2 St. Petersburg (e) Zenit St. Peterburg II

*** Kim - Min-jae Kim (김민재) (a) 15/11/1996, Tongyeong, Gyeongnam (South Korea) (b) 1,90 (c) D - central defense (d) Bayern München (e) Napoli, Fenerbahce,

BJ Guoan, Jeonbuk Hyundai, Gyeongju KHNP, Yonsei Univ., Suwon THS, Yeoncho MS, Nam. Haesung MS, Gimhae Gaya ES, Dooryong ES

*** Kim - Seung-bin Kim (김승빈) (a) 28/12/2000, ¿? (South Korea) (b) 1,73 (c) M - attacking midfielder (d) 1.FC Slovácko (e) Dukla Praha, Dukla B, Eonnam HS, Mokdong MS

*** Kim - Yeon-seung Kim (김연승) (a) 15/07/1999, ¿? (South Korea) (b) 1,80 (c) M - attacking midfielder (d) - (e) FC Noah, SC St. Tönis, Hannam Univ., Suseong MS (Gy)

*** Kim - Yong-hak Kim (김용학) (a) 20/05/2003, Gwangmyeong, Gyeonggi (South Korea) (b) 1,72 (c) F - right winger (d) Portimonense SC (e) Pohang Steelers, Portimonense, Pohang Steelers

*** Kimadze - Giorgi Kimadze (გიორგი ქიმაძე) (a) 11/02/1992, Kutaisi (Georgia) (b) 1,70 (c) F - left winger (d) - (e) Torpedo Kutaisi, Dinamo Tbilisi, Torpedo Kutaisi, Chikhura

*** Kimishima - Katsuyoshi Kimishima (君島 克佳) (a) 08/09/1998, Miura, Kanagawa (Japan) (b) 1,67 (c) M - attacking midfielder (d) FC Adelaide City (e) Bhayangkara, Jonava, UCA Bears, Laredo Heat, UCA Bears, Toin Gakuen

*** Kimmich - Joshua Kimmich (Joshua Walter Kimmich) (a) 08/02/1995, Rottweil (Germany) (b) 1,77 (c) M - pivot (d) Bayern München (e) VfB Stuttgart, RB Leipzig

*** Kimpembe - Presnel Kimpembe (a) 13/08/1995, Beaumont-sur-Oise (France) (b) 1,83 (c) D - central defense (d) París Saint-Germain FC (e) Paris Saint Germain B

*** Kimpioka - Benjamin Kimpioka (Benjamin Mbunga Kimpioka) (a) 21/02/2000, Knivsta (Sweden) (b) 1,83 (c) F - center forward (d) AIK Solna (e) FC Luzern, AIK, Sunderland, Southend United, Sunderland, Torquay, Sunderland

*** Kinareykin - Yakiv Kinareykin (Кінарейкін Яків Дмитрович) (a) 22/10/2003, ¿? (Ukraine) (b) 1,90 (c) G (d) SK Dnipro-1 (e) -

*** Kindberg - Jakob Kindberg (a) 07/02/1994, ¿? (Sweden) (b) 1,84 (c) G (d) Kalmar FF (e) Örebro Syr., Karlslunds IF, IFK Kumla, IK Sturehov

*** King - Billy King (a) 12/05/1994, Edinburgh (Scotland) (b) 1,78 (c) F - left winger (d) Northern Colorado Hailstorm FC (e) St. Patrick's Ath., Morton, Dundee United, Gillingham FC, Dundee United, Heart of Midlothian, Inverness Caledonian, Heart of Midlothian, Rangers FC, Heart of Midlothian

*** King - Darren King (a) 16/10/1985, ¿? (Northern Ireland) (b) - (c) D - right back (d) Newry City AFC (e) Warrenpoint, Newry City, Midway United

*** King - Dylan King (a) 27/08/1998, Strabane (Northern Ireland) (b) - (c) D - central defense (d) Institute FC (e) Dungannon, Institute FC, Dungannon, Coleraine, Glenavon

*** King - Joel King (Joel Bruce King) (a) 30/10/2000, Figtree, NSW (Australia) (b) 1,79 (c) D - left back (d) Sydney FC (e) Odense BK, Sydney FC, Odense BK, Sydney FC, Sydney FC II, FFA C. of Excel

*** King - Joshua King (Joshua Christian Kojo King) (a) 15/01/1992, Oslo (Norway) (b) 1,87 (c) F - center forward (d) Fenerbahce (e) Watford, Everton, Bournemouth, Blackburn, Hull City, Manchester Utd. Reserves, Borussia Mönchengladbach, Manchester Utd. Reserves, Preston North End, Manchester Utd. Reserves

*** King - Leon King (Leon Thomson King) (a) 14/01/2004, Glasgow (Scotland) (b) 1,83 (c) D - central defense (d) Rangers FC (e) Rangers II

*** Kings - Peter Kings (Peter Ngozi Kings) (a) 04/04/2001, Abakaliki (Nigeria) (b) 1,75 (c) M - attacking midfielder (d) FC Dinamo-Auto Tiraspol (e) FK Slutsk, GB Owerri

*** Kingsley - Stephen Kingsley (a) 23/07/1994, Stirling (Scotland) (b) 1,78 (c) D - left back (d) Heart of Midlothian FC (e) Hull City, Swansea City, Crewe Alexandra, Swansea City, Yeovil Town, Swansea City, Falkirk FC
*** Kingue - Steve Kingue (a) 23/01/2000, Yaoundé (Cameroon) (b) 1,85 (c) D - central defense (d) Mosta FC (e) 1.FK Pribram, Union II, Kalev
*** Kinsey-Wellings - Maxwell Kinsey-Wellings (a) 02/02/2005, ¿? (England) (b) - (c) D - central defense (d) - (e) Gosport Borough, Wimborne
*** Kinyik - Ákos Kinyik (a) 12/05/1993, Debrecen (Hungary) (b) 1,87 (c) D - central defense (d) Paksi FC (e) Debrecen, Budaörs, Debrecen, Debrecen II, Létavértes SC 97
*** Kiomourtzoglou - Orestis Kiomourtzoglou (a) 07/05/1998, München (Germany) (b) 1,88 (c) M - pivot (d) SpVgg Greuther Fürth (e) Heart of Midlothian, Heracles Almelo, Unterhaching
*** Kiqina - Sokol Kiqina (a) 23/03/2002, Skenderaj (RF Yugoslavia, now in Kosovo) (b) 1,85 (c) F - center forward (d) KF Erzeni (e) KF Llapi, KF Feronikeli
*** Király - Marcell Király (a) 17/10/2005, ¿? (Hungary) (b) - (c) D (d) Zalaegerszegi TE FC II (e) -
*** Kirch - Mehdi Kirch (a) 27/01/1990, ¿? (France) (b) 1,72 (c) D - left back (d) FC Schifflange 95 (e) F91 Dudelange, CS Fola Esch, FC Bleid-Gaume, Schiltigheim, Racing Strasbourg B
*** Kireenko - Pavel Kireenko (Киреенко Павел Николаевич) (a) 14/06/1994, St. Petersburg (Russia) (b) 1,75 (c) F - left winger (d) Tobol Kostanay (e) Kaspiy Aktau, FC Noah, Tom Tomsk, Sibir, Dinamo S-Pb, Palanga, Tosno, Palanga, Zenit 2 St. Peterburg, Zenit St. Peterburg II
*** Kirejczyk - Gabriel Kirejczyk (a) 12/02/2003, Oświęcim (Poland) (b) 1,97 (c) F - center forward (d) Piast Gliwice (e) AP Profi
*** Kirev - Mario Kirev (Марио Илиянов Кирев) (a) 15/08/1989, Dupnitsa (Bulgaria) (b) 1,93 (c) G (d) Pirin Blagoevgrad (e) Montana, Kyustendil, Olympiakos N., FC Drita, FC Kamza, Nea Salamis, Slavia Sofia, FC Olt Slatina, ACS Poli, Juventus, Poli. Timisoara, Juventus, FC Thun, Juventus, Grasshoppers, Juventus, Slavia Sofia
*** Kirgetov - Ruslan Kirgetov (Киргетов Руслан) (a) 07/07/2002, ¿? (Kazakhstan) (b) 1,74 (c) F - left winger (d) FC Astana-M (e) -
*** Kiri - Tomas Kiri (a) 02/01/2005, Shkodër (Albania) (b) 1,83 (c) G (d) KF Tirana (e) -
*** Kirilenko - Kirill Kirilenko (Кириленко Кирилл Олегович) (a) 08/10/2000, Minsk (Belarus) (b) 1,80 (c) F - left winger (d) Naftan Novopolotsk (e) FC Brasov-SR, Torpedo Zhodino, Olimpik Donetsk, Karpaty, BATE II, Dynamo Brest, Dynamo Brest II
*** Kirilov - Radoslav Kirilov (Радослав Кирилов Кирилов) (a) 29/06/1992, Simitli (Bulgaria) (b) 1,70 (c) F - left winger (d) CSKA 1948 (e) Slavia Sofia, Chievo Verona, Vis Pesaro, Chievo Verona, Pirin, Chievo Verona, Beroe, Chievo Verona, Südtirol, Chievo Verona, Cremonese, Chievo Verona, Unione Venezia, Chievo Verona, Carpi, Chievo Verona, Lumezzane
*** Kirintili - Serkan Kirintili (Serkan Kırıntılı) (a) 15/02/1985, Adana (Turkey) (b) 1,86 (c) G (d) - (e) Ümraniyespor, Alanyaspor, Konyaspor, Çaykur Rizespor, Fenerbahce, Ankaragücü, Adanaspor
*** Kirk - Paddy Kirk (a) 02/06/1998, ¿? (Ireland) (b) 1,75 (c) D - left back (d) Bohemian FC (e) Sligo Rovers, Longford Town, Bohemians

*** Kirkevold - Pål Alexander Kirkevold (a) 10/11/1990, Re (Norway) (b) 1,85 (c) F - center forward (d) Hamarkameratene (e) Stabæk, Hobro IK, Sarpsborg 08, Hobro IK, Sandefjord, Mjøndalen, HamKam

*** Kirkils - Gabriels Kirkils (a) 24/05/2001, ¿? (Latvia) (b) 1,85 (c) D - right back (d) FK Metta (e) FS Metta II

*** Kirkitadze - Davit Kirkitadze (დავით კირკიტაძე) (a) 03/09/1992, Samtredia (Georgia) (b) 1,62 (c) F - right winger (d) FC Samtredia (e) Samgurali, FC Locomotive, Sioni Bolnisi, FC Samtredia, FC Dila, Guria, Chikhura, Torpedo Kutaisi, Ironi Tiberias, FK Zugdidi, Metalurgi R., Chikhura, Torpedo Kutaisi, FC Samtredia

*** Kirkitadze - Tornike Kirkitadze (თორნიკე კირკიტაძე) (a) 23/07/1996, Tbilisi (Georgia) (b) 1,82 (c) F - right winger (d) Dinamo Tbilisi (e) FC Locomotive, Rustavi, Sioni Bolnisi, Dinamo Tbilisi, Chikhura

*** Kirkman - Billy Kirkman (Billy Naylor Kirkman) (a) 26/02/2004, Blackburn (England) (b) - (c) D - left back (d) Aberystwyth Town (e) The New Saints, Aberystwyth, The New Saints

*** Kirovski - Andrej Kirovski (Андреј Кировски) (a) 11/02/1999, Skopje (North Macedonia) (b) 1,84 (c) D - central defense (d) Gostivar (e) Rabotnicki, Sileks, FK Sasa, NK Sesvete

*** Kirovski - Hristijan Kirovski (Христијан Кировски) (a) 12/10/1985, Skopje (Yugoslavia, now in North Macedonia) (b) 1,89 (c) F - center forward (d) Teteks Tetovo (e) FK Skopje, Gostivar, Struga, Makedonija, Rabotnicki, Chiangmai FC, Prachuap FC, Shkëndija, GKS Belchatow, CSKA Sofia, Iraklis, Ramat haSharon, Apollon Limassol, FK Skopje, Vardar, FC Vaslui, Rabotnicki, Vorskla Poltava, Karpaty, Vardar, Luch Vladivostok, Ethnikos, Makedonija, OFK Beograd, Metalurg Z., OFK Beograd, Vardar

*** Kirsch - Ilya Kirsch (Кирш Илья Евгеньевич) (a) 21/09/2004, ¿? (Russia) (b) 1,92 (c) D - central defense (d) Zenit 2 St. Petersburg (e) Zenit St. Peterburg II

*** Kirss - Raivis Kirss (Raivis Ķiršs) (a) 15/01/2000, ¿? (Latvia) (b) - (c) F - right winger (d) FK Tukums 2000 (e) Auda, Riga, Daugavpils, Riga, Daugavpils, Super Nova, RFS II

*** Kirss - Robert Kirss (a) 03/09/1994, Pärnu (Estonia) (b) 1,84 (c) F - center forward (d) FCI Levadia (e) Sandecja, FCI Levadia, Kalju FC, Pärnu, JK Nomme Kalju, Pärnu, Pärnu Vaprus

*** Kirt - Aron Kirt (a) 26/02/2006, Tallinn (Estonia) (b) - (c) D - left back (d) Kalev Tallinn (e) -

*** Kis - Patrik Kis (Patrik Vilmos Kis) (a) 02/02/2005, Cluj-Napoca (Romania) (b) - (c) G (d) ACS Tg. Mures-Marosvásárhely SE (e) ACS Tg. Mures, Universitatea Cluj

*** Kis - Tomislav Kis (Tomislav Kiš) (a) 04/04/1994, Zagreb (Croatia) (b) 1,81 (c) F - center forward (d) HSK Zrinjski Mostar (e) Mezőkövesd, Zalgiris, Seongnam FC, Zalgiris, NK Dugopolje, Soligorsk, KV Kortrijk, Cercle Brugge, KV Kortrijk, Hajduk Split, DNŠ Zavrč, Hajduk Split, HNK Gorica, Hajduk Split, NK Dugopolje, Hajduk Split

*** Kisiel - Jakub Kisiel (Jakub Kisiel) (a) 05/02/2003, Wyszków (Poland) (b) 1,84 (c) M - pivot (d) TS Podbeskidzie Bielsko-Biala (e) Podbeskidzie, Legia Warszawa, Stomil, Legia Warszawa, Legia II

*** Kislyak - Matvey Kislyak (Кисляк Матвей Алексеевич) (a) 26/07/2005, ¿? (Russia) (b) 1,80 (c) M - attacking midfielder (d) CSKA Moskva II (e) -

*** Kislyak - Sergey Kislyak (Кисляк Сергей Викторович) (a) 06/08/1987, Kamenets (Soviet Union, now in Ukraine) (b) 1,85 (c) M - pivot (d) Dynamo Brest (e) Dinamo Minsk, Dynamo Brest, Irtysh, Gaziantepspor, Rubin Kazan, Krasnodar, Rubin Kazan, Dinamo Minsk, Dinamo Minsk II

*** Kiss - Tamás Kiss (a) 24/11/2000, Győr (Hungary) (b) 1,67 (c) F - left winger (d) Újpest FC (e) Puskás AFC, SC Cambuur, Puskás AFC, Diósgyőr, Puskás AFC, Haladás
*** Kissas - Anastasios Kissas (Αναστάσιος "Τάσος" Κίσσας) (a) 18/01/1988, Nicosia (Cyprus) (b) 1,82 (c) G (d) Nea Salamis (e) Apollon Limassol, APOEL FC
*** Kitanov - Georgi Kitanov (Георги Китанов) (a) 06/03/1995, Blagoevgrad (Bulgaria) (b) 1,88 (c) G (d) Floriana FC (e) Petrolul, Astra Giurgiu, CSKA-Sofia, Cherno More, CSKA-Sofia, Cherno More
*** Kitanovic - Uros Kitanovic (Урош Китановић) (a) 11/04/2004, Niš (Serbia and Montenegro, now in Serbia) (b) 1,85 (c) G (d) FK Radnicki Niš (e) -
*** Kitanovski - Kristijan Kitanovski (Кристијан Китановски) (a) 03/10/2002, Bitola (North Macedonia) (b) 1,83 (c) G (d) Struga Trim & Lum (e) Novaci, Bregalnica Stip
*** Kiteishvili - Otar Kiteishvili (ოთარ კიტეიშვილი) (a) 26/03/1996, Rustavi (Georgia) (b) 1,73 (c) M - attacking midfielder (d) SK Sturm Graz (e) Dinamo Tbilisi, Metalurgi R.
*** Kitela - Andriy Kitela (Кітела Андрій Юрійович) (a) 13/12/2004, Stryi, Lviv Oblast (Ukraine) (b) 1,78 (c) D - right back (d) Rukh Lviv (e) -
*** Kitolano - Eric Kitolano (Eric Bugale Kitolano) (a) 02/09/1997, Uvira (Congo DR) (b) 1,75 (c) M - attacking midfielder (d) Molde FK (e) Tromsø, Ullensaker/Kisa, Notodden, Odd, Gulset
*** Kitolano - John Kitolano (John Shuguto Kitolano) (a) 18/10/1999, Uvira (Congo DR) (b) 1,74 (c) D - left back (d) Aalesunds FK (e) Odd, Odd, Molde, Odd, Odd II
*** Kitolano - Joshua Kitolano (Joshua Gaston Kitolano) (a) 03/08/2001, ¿? (Malawi) (b) 1,70 (c) M - central midfielder (d) Sparta Rotterdam (e) Odd, Odd II, Gulset
*** Kitsiou - Stelios Kitsiou (Στέλιος Κίτσιου) (a) 28/09/1993, Thessaloniki (Greece) (b) 1,75 (c) D - right back (d) MKE Ankaragücü (e) Gaziantep FK, Ankaragücü, PAOK, Ankaragücü, PAOK, Sint-Truiden, PAOK
*** Kitsos - Fotis Kitsos (Φώτης Κίτσος) (a) 31/03/2003, Athen (Greece) (b) 1,74 (c) D - left back (d) Volos NPS (e) Olympiakos, Omonia Nicosia, Olympiakos, Olympiakos B
*** Kittilä - Eetu Kittilä (a) 19/01/2004, ¿? (Finland) (b) - (c) F - center forward (d) FC Haka II (e) -
*** Kittos - Stefanos Kittos (Στέφανος Κίττος) (a) 23/02/2002, Limassol (Cyprus) (b) 1,86 (c) G (d) APOEL FC (e) PO Xylotymbou, APOEL FC, Karmiotissa, APEA Akrotiri, Karmiotissa, Nikos & Sokrati
*** Kivanc - Ahmet Kivanc (Ahmet Said Kivanç) (a) 29/04/1998, Istanbul (Turkey) (b) 1,89 (c) G (d) Adanaspor (e) Istanbulspor, Adanaspor, Basaksehir, Bandirmaspor, Basaksehir
*** Kivi - Andero Kivi (a) 07/11/2003, Kuressaare ((c) F - center forward (d) FC Kuressaare (e) FC Kuressaare II
*** Kivrakidis - Kyriakos Kivrakidis (a) 21/07/1992, Berlin (Germany) (b) 1,70 (d) Atromitos FC (e) Eginiakos, Iraklis, Eginiakos, Iraklis, Pont. Katerini, Ethn. Vaterou
*** Kiwior - Jakub Kiwior (Jakub Piotr Kiwior) (a) 15/02/2000, Tychy (Poland) (b) 1,89 (c) D - central defense (d) Arsenal FC (e) Spezia, MSK Zilina, Podbrezova, GKS Tychy
*** Kiyine - Sofian Kiyine (كيان سفيان) (a) 02/10/1997, Verviers (Belgium) (b) 1,82 (c) M - left midfielder (d) Oud-Heverlee Leuven (e) Lazio, Venezia, Lazio, Salernitana, Lazio, Salernitana, Lazio, Chievo Verona, Salernitana, Chievo Verona, JMG Lier

*** Kiyko - Artem Kiyko (Кийко Артем Сергеевич) (a) 13/01/1996, Marina Gorka (Belarus) (b) 1,84 (c) F - right winger (d) FK Gomel (e) Dzerzhinsk, Luch, Dinamo Minsk, Gorodeya, Dinamo Minsk, Dinamo Minsk II, FK Bereza, Dinamo Minsk II
*** Kizildag - Arda Kizildag (Arda Kızıldağ) (a) 15/10/1998, Ankara (Turkey) (b) 1,87 (c) D - central defense (d) Gaziantep FK (e) Ankaragücü, Gaziantep FK, Genclerbirligi, Hacettepe, Genclerbirligi, Hacettepe, Genclerbirligi
*** Kizito - Kizito (Luwagga William Kizito) (a) 20/12/1993, Kisubi (Uganda) (b) 1,80 (c) F - center forward (d) - (e) FK Sabail, H. Nof HaGalil, H. Kfar Saba, ACSM Poli Iasi, Shakhter K., ACSM Poli Iasi, BATE Borisov, ACSM Poli Iasi, Rio Ave, Feirense, Rio Ave, SC Covilhã, Leixões, Vipers SC
*** Kizza - Mustafa Kizza (a) 03/09/1999, Kibuli (Uganda) (b) 1,85 (c) D - left back (d) - (e) Kampala CC, Arouca, Montréal, Kampala CC, Montréal, Kampala CC
*** Kjaer - Jeppe Kjaer (Jeppe Kjær Jensen) (a) 01/03/2004, Horsens (Denmark) (b) 1,74 (c) M - attacking midfielder (d) FK Bodø/Glimt (e) Ajax B, AC Horsens
*** Kjaer - Simon Kjaer (Simon Thorup Kjær) (a) 26/03/1989, Horsens (Denmark) (b) 1,91 (c) D - central defense (d) AC Milan (e) Sevilla FC, AC Milan, Sevilla FC, Atalanta, Sevilla FC, Fenerbahce, Lille, VfL Wolfsburg, AS Roma, VfL Wolfsburg, US Palermo, Midtjylland
*** Kjaergaard - Maurits Kjaergaard (Maurits Kjærgaard) (a) 26/06/2003, Herlev (Denmark) (b) 1,92 (c) M - central midfielder (d) Red Bull Salzburg (e) FC Liefering, RB Salzburg
*** Kjartansson - Eythór Dadi Kjartansson (Eyþór Daði Kjartansson) (a) 20/06/2000, Vestmannaeyjar (Iceland) (b) - (c) M - right midfielder (d) ÍBV Vestmannaeyjar (e) Framherjar, ÍBV Vestmannaeyjar, Framherjar, ÍBV Vestmannaeyjar, Framherjar, ÍBV Vestmannaeyjar, Framherjar, ÍBV Vestmannaeyjar, Framherjar, ÍBV Vestmannaeyjar, Framherjar, ÍBV Vestmannaeyjar
*** Kjartansson - Kjartan Már Kjartansson (a) 14/07/2006, ¿? (Iceland) (b) - (c) F (d) Stjarnan Gardabaer (e) -
*** Kjartansson - Orri Hrafn Kjartansson (a) 05/02/2002, ¿? (Iceland) (b) - (c) M - attacking midfielder (d) Valur Reykjavík (e) Fylkir
*** Kjartansson - Vidar Örn Kjartansson (Viðar Örn Kjartansson) (a) 11/03/1990, Selfoss (Iceland) (b) 1,87 (c) F - center forward (d) CSKA 1948 (e) Atromitos FC, Vålerenga, Rostov, Yeni Malatyaspor, Rostov, Rubin Kazan, Rostov, Hammarby IF, Rostov, Maccabi Tel Aviv, Malmö FF, JS Suning, Vålerenga, Fylkir, Selfoss, ÍBV Vestmannaeyjar, Selfoss
*** Kjeld Cardoso - Kristófer André Kjeld Cardoso (a) 04/03/2002, Reykjavík (Iceland) (b) 1,82 (c) M - attacking midfielder (d) KH Hlídarendi (e) Valur
*** Kjeldsen - Gustav Kjeldsen (a) 03/07/1999, Fårup (Denmark) (b) 1,93 (c) D - central defense (d) Vestri Ísafjördur (e) HB Tórshavn, Skive IK, Nyköbing FC
*** Kjelsen - Aleksander Hammer Kjelsen (a) 03/01/2006, ¿? (Norway) (b) 1,85 (c) D - central defense (d) Vålerenga Fotball (e) Bærums Verk
*** Kjerrumgaard - Luca Kjerrumgaard (Luca Tange Kjerrumgaard) (a) 09/02/2003, Odense (Denmark) (b) 1,90 (c) F - center forward (d) Odense Boldklub (e) Nyköbing FC, Odense BK
*** Kjölö - Mathias Kjölö (Mathias Ullereng Kjølø) (a) 27/06/2001, Oslo (Norway) (b) 1,74 (c) M - central midfielder (d) FC Twente Enschede (e) -
*** Kjørsvik - Martin Tornes Kjørsvik (a) 17/01/2003, ¿? (Norway) (b) 1,80 (c) F - center forward (d) SK Træff (e) Molde FK II, Elnesvagen & O.
*** Kjosevski - Vedran Kjosevski (Ведран Ќосевски) (a) 22/05/1995, Veles (North Macedonia) (b) 1,87 (c) G (d) Struga Trim & Lum (e) Velez Mostar, Zeljeznicar

*** Klaassen - Davy Klaassen (a) 21/02/1993, Hilversum (Netherlands) (b) 1,79 (c) M - attacking midfielder (d) Ajax de Ámsterdam (e) Werder Bremen, Everton, Ajax
*** Klaesson - Kristoffer Klaesson (Kristoffer-August Sundquist Klaesson) (a) 27/11/2000, Oslo (Norway) (b) 1,89 (c) G (d) Leeds United (e) Vålerenga, Vålerenga II
*** Klaiber - Sean Klaiber (Sean Desmond Klaiber) (a) 31/07/1994, Nieuwegein (Netherlands) (b) 1,84 (c) D - right back (d) FC Utrecht (e) Ajax, FC Utrecht, FC Dordrecht, FC Utrecht
*** Klaidher Macedo - Klaidher Macedo (Klaidher Vittorio Bravin Macedo) (a) 18/01/1999, Maringá (Brazil) (b) 1,89 (c) D - central defense (d) Krumovgrad (e) Beroe, Anápolis, São José-SP, VOCEM, Bandeirante, Desp. Brasil
*** Klapatauskas - Mantas Klapatauskas (a) 30/12/2006, ¿? (Lithuania) (b) - (c) M (d) FK Jonava (e) -
*** Klapp - Ryan Klapp (a) 10/01/1993, ¿? (Luxembourg) (b) - (c) F - right winger (d) FC Mondercange (e) Progrès Niederkorn, F91 Dudelange, CS Fola Esch, RFCU Luxembourg
*** Klassen - Leon Klassen (Классен Леон Сергеевич) (a) 29/05/2000, Bad Neuenahr-Ahrweiler (Germany) (b) 1,76 (c) D - left back (d) FC Spartak de Moscú (e) WSG Tirol, 1860 München, 1860 München II
*** Klausen - Peder Nygaard Klausen (a) 09/05/2003, ¿? (Norway) (b) 1,91 (c) G (d) Odds BK (e) Odd II
*** Klausz - Milán Klausz (Klausz Milán Gábor) (a) 24/02/2005, ¿? (Hungary) (b) 1,88 (c) F - center forward (d) Zalaegerszegi TE FC (e) -
*** Klavan - Ragnar Klavan (a) 30/10/1985, Viljandi (Soviet Union, now in Estonia) (b) 1,87 (c) D - central defense (d) Kalev Tallinn (e) Paide, Cagliari, Liverpool, FC Augsburg, AZ Alkmaar, Heracles Almelo, AZ Alkmaar, Heracles Almelo, FC Flora, Vålerenga, FC Flora, JK Viljandi, FC Elva
*** Klebaniuk - Bartosz Klebaniuk (Bartosz Klebaniuk) (a) 03/04/2002, Biała Podlaska (Poland) (b) 1,93 (c) G (d) Pogon Szczecin (e) Pogon Siedlce, Pogon Szczecin, Pogon Siedlce, Orleta R.P.
*** Klein - Daniel Klein (a) 13/03/2001, Heidelberg (Germany) (b) 1,93 (c) G (d) SV Sandhausen (e) SV Sandhausen, FC Augsburg, Hoffenheim II
*** Klein - Julien Klein (a) 07/04/1988, ¿? (France) (b) 1,80 (c) D - central defense (d) CS Fola Esch (e) Thionville
*** Klein - Martin Klein (Martin Klein Joensen) (a) 26/12/1999, ¿? (Faroe Islands) (b) 1,75 (c) F - center forward (d) Víkingur Gøta (e) Víkingur II
*** Klein - Peeter Klein (a) 28/01/1997, Tallinn (Estonia) (b) 1,91 (c) F - center forward (d) JK Tabasalu (e) Kuressaare, Kalju FC, Kalju Nõmme II, Nomme United
*** Kleinheisler - László Kleinheisler (a) 08/04/1994, Kazincbarcika (Hungary) (b) 1,73 (c) M - attacking midfielder (d) Panathinaikos FC (e) NK Osijek, FC Astana, Werder Bremen, FC Astana, Werder Bremen, Ferencváros, Werder Bremen, Darmstadt 98, Werder Bremen, Videoton FC, Puskás AFC, Videoton FC, Puskás AFC, Videoton FC
*** Klem - Christian Klem (a) 21/04/1991, Graz (Austria) (b) 1,72 (c) D - left back (d) - (e) TSV Hartberg, FC Wacker, SV Lafnitz, Wolfsberger AC, Sturm Graz, Sturm Graz II
*** Klemencic - Tilen Klemencic (Tilen Klemenčič) (a) 21/08/1995, Kranj (Slovenia) (b) 1,80 (c) D - central defense (d) NK Domžale (e) NK Celje, NK Triglav
*** Klemens - Pascal Klemens (a) 23/02/2005, Berlin (Germany) (b) 1,86 (c) D - central defense (d) Hertha Berlín (e) -

*** Klemenz - Lukas Klemenz (a) 24/09/1995, Neu-Ulm (Germany) (b) 1,91 (c) D - central defense (d) Gornik Leczna (e) Honvéd, Wisla Kraków, Jagiellonia, GKS Katowice, Olimpia Grudz., GKS Belchatow, Valenciennes B, Korona Kielce, Valenciennes B, Odra Opole

*** Klenye - Pavel Klenye (Кленьё Павел Владимирович) (a) 28/04/1999, Minsk (Belarus) (b) 1,79 (c) F - center forward (d) BK Maxline Vitebsk (e) FK Minsk, Torpedo Zhodino, Lokomotiv Gomel, Gomel, Torpedo Minsk, Neman Stolbtsy

*** Klepac - Mihael Klepac (Mihael Klepač) (a) 19/09/1997, Našice (Croatia) (b) 1,84 (c) F - left winger (d) Yverdon Sport FC (e) NS Mura, NK Aluminij, NK Osijek II, Zeljeznicar, NK Osijek II, NK Rudes, NK Osijek II, NK Varazdin, NK Osijek II, NK Dugopolje, NK Osijek II, Papuk Orahovica

*** Kleshchenko - Aleksandr Kleshchenko (Клещенко Александр Александрович) (a) 02/11/1995, Vladikavkaz (Russia) (b) 1,87 (c) D - central defense (d) Rodina Moscow (e) FK Turan, Ordabasy, Enisey, Tobol Kostanay, Tom Tomsk, Kuban Krasnodar, Kuban II, S2V, Alania II

*** Kleshchuk - Stanislav Kleshchuk (Клещук Станислав Вячеславович) (a) 11/04/2000, Minsk (Belarus) (b) 1,88 (c) G (d) Energetik-BGU Minsk (e) Dinamo Minsk II, Energetik-BGU, Dinamo Minsk II, Krumkachi, Dinamo Minsk II, Smolevichi, Dinamo Minsk II, Underdog, Dinamo Minsk II

*** Klettskard - Páll Klettskard (Páll Andrasson Klettskarð) (a) 17/05/1990, ¿? (Faroe Islands) (b) 1,85 (c) F - center forward (d) KÍ Klaksvík (e) USD Breno, KÍ Klaksvík, Víkingur, Vanlöse IF, FC Amager, Fremad Amager, KÍ Klaksvík

*** Kleyman - Boris Kleyman (קליימן בוריס) (a) 26/10/1990, Vinnytsia (Soviet Union, now in Ukraine) (b) 1,85 (c) G (d) PAS Giannina (e) Volos NPS, EN Paralimniou, B. Jerusalem, Hapoel Tel Aviv, H. Kfar Saba, Hapoel Tel Aviv, Maccabi Herzlya, Hapoel Tel Aviv

*** Klica - Almir Klica (a) 10/11/1998, ¿? (RF Yugoslavia, now in Montenegro) (b) - (c) D - left back (d) Jeunesse Esch (e) Olympiakos B, Jeunesse Esch, F91 Dudelange, Jeunesse Esch, F91 Dudelange

*** Klich - Mateusz Klich (Mateusz Andrzej Klich) (a) 13/06/1990, Tarnów (Poland) (b) 1,83 (c) M - central midfielder (d) D.C. United (e) Leeds Utd., FC Utrecht, Leeds Utd., FC Twente, 1.FC Kaiserslautern, VfL Wolfsburg, PEC Zwolle, VfL Wolfsburg, PEC Zwolle, VfL Wolfsburg, Cracovia

*** Klidjé - Thibault Klidjé (a) 10/07/2001, Hahotoe-Vo (Togo) (b) 1,70 (c) F - center forward (d) FC Lucerna (e) Girondins Bordeaux B, Gomido FC, Espoir FC

*** Klima - Jakub Klima (Jakub Klíma) (a) 28/08/1998, Nymburk (Czech Rep.) (b) 1,83 (c) D - central defense (d) FC Hradec Kralove (e) Mlada Boleslav, Hradec Kralove, Mlada Boleslav, Pardubice, Mlada Boleslav, Mlada Boleslav B

*** Klima - Jiri Klima (Jiří Klíma) (a) 05/01/1997, ¿? (Czech Rep.) (b) 1,89 (c) F - center forward (d) FC Banik Ostrava (e) Mlada Boleslav, Jihlava, 1.SC Znojmo, Jihlava

*** Klimala - Patryk Klimala (a) 05/08/1998, Świdnica (Poland) (b) 1,83 (c) F - center forward (d) Hapoel Beer Sheva (e) New York, Celtic FC, Jagiellonia, Wigry Suwalki, Jagiellonia

*** Klimas - Laurynas Klimas (a) 22/03/2001, ¿? (Lithuania) (b) 1,87 (c) G (d) FC Hegelmann (e) -

*** Klimavicius - Augustinas Klimavicius (Augustinas Klimavičius) (a) 27/04/2001, Kaunas (Lithuania) (b) 1,91 (c) F - center forward (d) FC Hegelmann (e) Sesto Giovanili

*** Klimavicius - Linas Klimavicius (Linas Klimavičius) (a) 10/04/1989, Panevėžys (Soviet Union, now in Lithuania) (b) 1,90 (c) D - central defense (d) FK Panevezys

(e) DFK Dainava, Suduva, ACSM Poli Iasi, FC Dinamo, Zalgiris, Trakai, Daugava Riga, Dnipro II, Dnipro, Kryvbas, Dnipro, Suduva, Ekranas
*** Kliment - Jan Kliment (a) 01/09/1993, Jihlava (Czech Rep.) (b) 1,85 (c) F - center forward (d) FC Viktoria Plzen (e) Wisla Kraków, Slovácko, Stuttgart II, VfB Stuttgart, Brøndby IF, VfB Stuttgart, Jihlava, Jihlava B, Banska Bystrica, Jihlava B
*** Klimentov - Ivaylo Klimentov (Ивайло Георгиев Климентов) (a) 03/02/1998, Batak (Bulgaria) (b) 1,80 (c) M - pivot (d) - (e) Spartak Varna, CSKA 1948, Ludogorets II, Vitosha, Ludogorets II
*** Klimovich - Dmitriy Klimovich (Климович Дмитрий Ромуальдович) (a) 09/02/1984, Minsk (Soviet Union, now in Belarus) (b) 1,82 (c) D - left back (d) - (e) Dzerzhinsk, FK Minsk, Torpedo Zhodino, Krumkachi, Granit, Zimbru Chisinau, Belshina, Gomel, FK Minsk, Torpedo Zhodino, BATE Borisov, BATE II, Torpedo Zhodino, BATE II
*** Klimovich - Vladislav Klimovich (Климович Владислав Тадеушевич) (a) 12/06/1996, Minsk (Belarus) (b) 1,87 (c) M - central midfielder (d) Diósgyőri VTK (e) Nea Salamis, Gyirmót FC, Dinamo Minsk, Torpedo Zhodino, BATE Borisov, Neman Grodno, BATE Borisov, Jelgava, BATE Borisov, Isloch, BATE Borisov, BATE II
*** Klimowicz - Mateo Klimowicz (a) 06/07/2000, Buenos Aires (Argentina) (b) 1,81 (c) M - attacking midfielder (d) Atlético de San Luis (e) San Luis, VfB Stuttgart, Arminia Bielefeld, VfB Stuttgart, Instituto, Bergfeld/P./T.
*** Klimpl - Oliver Klimpl (a) 20/09/2004, ¿? (Slovakia) (b) - (c) M (d) MFK Dukla Banska Bystrica (e) -
*** Klinar - Denis Klinar (a) 21/02/1992, ¿? (Yugoslavia, now in Slovenia) (b) 1,85 (c) D - central defense (d) NK Fuzinar (e) ND Gorica, Cultural Leonesa, NK Maribor, Puskás AFC, Olimpija, Rudar Velenje
*** Klinga - Matti Klinga (a) 10/12/1994, Helsinki (Finland) (b) 1,73 (c) M - central midfielder (d) FC Lahti (e) SJK Seinäjoki, HJK Helsinki, FC Lahti
*** Klinge - Marcus Klinge (a) 17/10/2002, ¿? (Denmark) (b) - (c) M (d) FC UNA Strassen II (e) FC UNA Strassen
*** Klinger - Niklas Klinger (a) 13/10/1995, Wolfsburg (Germany) (b) 1,87 (c) G (d) VfL Wolfsburg (e) Wolfsburg II
*** Klinkenberg - Daan Klinkenberg (a) 12/01/1996, Beinsdorp (Netherlands) (b) 1,86 (c) D - central defense (d) FC KTP (e) Helsinki IFK, Mjällby AIF, Aalesund, FC Inter, FC Volendam
*** Klishchuk - Andriy Klishchuk (Кліщук Андрій Андрійович) (a) 03/07/1992, Izmail, Odesa Oblast (Ukraine) (b) 1,90 (c) G (d) Kryvbas Kryvyi Rig (e) Ingulets, Girnyk-Sport, Krystal Kherson, SK Dnipro-1, Naftovyk, Nyva Vinnytsya, PFK Sumy, Girnyk-Sport, Chornomorets 2, Chornomorets II
*** Klismahn - Klismahn (Gustavo Klismahn Dimaraes Miranda) (a) 23/11/1999, Santana do Araguaia (PA) (Brazil) (b) 1,79 (c) M - central midfielder (d) CD Santa Clara (e) Santa Clara, Portimonense, Alverca
*** Klitten - Lukas Klitten (Lukas Sparre Klitten) (a) 01/05/2000, ¿? (Denmark) (b) 1,84 (c) D - left back (d) Frosinone Calcio (e) Silkeborg IF, Frosinone, Aalborg BK
*** Kljajic - Filip Kljajic (Филип Кљајић) (a) 16/08/1990, Beograd (Yugoslavia, now in Serbia) (b) 1,97 (c) G (d) Torpedo Kutaisi (e) Novi Pazar, Omiya Ardija, FK Partizan, Platanias, FK Partizan, Teleoptik, FK Partizan, Rad Beograd, Metalac, Sumadija, FK Hajduk
*** Kljajic - Obren Kljajic (a) 18/09/2003, Brisbane (Australia) (b) 1,87 (c) F - right winger (d) Peninsula Power FC (e) Vozdovac

*** Kljun - Tom Kljun (a) 29/01/2004, ¿? (Slovenia) (b) 1,78 (c) F - left winger (d) - (e) Tabor Sezana, NK Celje

*** Klochkov - Yuriy Klochkov (Клочков Юрий Вячеславович) (a) 03/10/1998, Slavyansk-na-Kubani, Krasnodar Region (Russia) (b) 1,78 (c) M - attacking midfielder (d) Dnepr Mogilev (e) FK Slutsk, Aluston-YBK, Chernomorets N., Sp. Rayevskaya

*** Klomp - Flip Klomp (a) 18/10/2001, ¿? (Netherlands) (b) 1,85 (c) M - central midfielder (d) FC Volendam (e) VCU Rams, Ajax Zaterdag 2, Sport. Martinus

*** Klon - Oskar Klon (a) 05/02/2005, Bydgoszcz (Poland) (b) 1,89 (c) G (d) Wisła Płock (e) Chemik Bydgoszcz

*** Klonaridis - Viktor Klonaridis (Βίκτωρ Κλωναρίδης) (a) 28/07/1992, Seraing (Belgium) (b) 1,79 (c) F - right winger (d) Ümraniyespor (e) Atromitos FC, APOEL FC, AEK Athína, RC Lens, Panathinaikos, RC Lens, Panathinaikos, Lille, Excelsior Mouscron, Lille, AEK Athína

*** Kloniunas - Edvinas Kloniunas (Edvinas Kloniūnas) (a) 28/06/1998, Kaunas (Lithuania) (b) 1,86 (c) M - pivot (d) FK Kauno Zalgiris (e) FC Sevan, Bijelo Brdo, Kauno Zalgiris, FA Siauliai

*** Klostermann - Lukas Klostermann (Lukas Manuel Klostermann) (a) 03/06/1996, Gevelsberg (Germany) (b) 1,89 (c) D - right back (d) RB Leipzig (e) VfL Bochum

*** Kludka - Bartlomiej Kludka (Bartłomiej Kłudka) (a) 14/05/2002, Lubin (Poland) (b) 1,86 (c) D - right back (d) Zagłębie Lubin (e) Zaglebie Lubin II, AP Zagłębie

*** Kluivert - Justin Kluivert (Justin Dean Kluivert) (a) 05/05/1999, Zaandam (Netherlands) (b) 1,72 (c) F - left winger (d) AFC Bournemouth (e) AS Roma, Valencia CF, AS Roma, OGC Nice, AS Roma, RB Leipzig, AS Roma, Ajax

*** Kluivert - Ruben Kluivert (a) 21/05/2001, Amsterdam (Netherlands) (b) 1,87 (c) D - central defense (d) FC Utrecht (e) -

*** Kluskins - Glebs Kluskins (Gļebs Kļuškins) (a) 01/10/1992, Riga (Latvia) (b) 1,85 (c) M - central midfielder (d) FK Liepaja (e) Metta, Noah Jurmala, Suduva, RFS, Jelgava, Daugava Riga, RFS, Daugava Riga

*** Klymchuk - Yuriy Klymchuk (Климчук Юрій Сергійович) (a) 05/05/1997, Rogachi, Zhytomyr Oblast (Ukraine) (b) 1,78 (c) F - left winger (d) Rukh Lviv (e) Stal Kamyanske, PFK Stal II

*** Klymenchuk - Yegor Klymenchuk (Клименчук Єгор Олександрович) (a) 11/11/1997, Zaporizhya (Ukraine) (b) 1,84 (c) D - left back (d) Metalist Kharkiv (e) Ararat-Armenia, PFC Lviv, Olimpik Donetsk, Avangard K., Kolos Kovalivka, Naftan, FK Minsk, Metalurg Z., Zaporizhya II

*** Klymenko - Vladyslav Klymenko (Клименко Владислав Сергійович) (a) 19/06/1994, Odesa (Ukraine) (b) 1,75 (c) M - central midfielder (d) Karpaty Lviv (e) Ingulets, FK Mariupol, Chornomorets, Ingulets, Skala Stryi, Real Farma, Kryvbas II, Real Farm Yuzhne

*** Klynge - Anders Klynge (Anders Ferslev Klynge) (a) 14/10/2000, Odense (Denmark) (b) 1,75 (c) M - central midfielder (d) Silkeborg IF (e) -

*** Klyots - Dmytro Klyots (Кльоц Дмитро Віталійович) (a) 15/04/1996, Rivne (Ukraine) (b) 1,74 (c) M - central midfielder (d) NK Veres Rivne (e) Sabah FK, Keshla, Karpaty, Karpaty II, UFK Lviv

*** Klysner - Tobias Klysner (Tobias Klysner Breuner) (a) 03/07/2001, ¿? (Denmark) (b) 1,83 (c) F - right winger (d) Randers FC (e) -

*** Klyushkin - Igor Klyushkin (Клюшкин Игорь Вячеславович) (a) 29/01/2003, Chelyabinsk (Russia) (b) 1,83 (c) D - right back (d) FK Turan (e) Ordabasy, Arsenal Tula II

*** Klyushnev - Roman Klyushnev (Клюшнев Роман Вячеславович) (a) 05/05/2000, Temirtau (Kazakhstan) (b) 1,84 (c) G (d) Shakhter-Bulat (e) -
*** Kmet - Matus Kmet (Matúš Kmet) (a) 27/06/2000, Ružomberok (Slovakia) (b) 1,73 (c) M - right midfielder (d) AS Trencin (e) Ružomberok
*** Knaller - Marco Knaller (a) 26/03/1987, Villach (Austria) (b) 1,92 (c) G (d) SK Austria Klagenfurt (e) FC Wacker, FC Ingolstadt, SV Sandhausen, Wolfsberger AC, 1.FC Kaiserslautern, Kaiserslautern II, FC Lustenau, Admira Wacker, FC Admira II
*** Knap - Karol Knap (Karol Knap) (a) 12/09/2001, Krosno (Poland) (b) 1,80 (c) M - pivot (d) Cracovia (e) P. Niepolomice, Karpaty Krosno
*** Knapik - Jan Knapik (Jan Knapík) (a) 11/12/2000, ¿? (Czech Rep.) (b) 1,93 (c) D - central defense (d) FK Teplice (e) -
*** Knasmüllner - Christoph Knasmüllner (a) 30/04/1992, Wien (Austria) (b) 1,81 (c) M - attacking midfielder (d) - (e) Rapid Wien, Barnsley FC, Admira Wacker, FC Ingolstadt, FC Bayern II
*** Knauff - Ansgar Knauff (a) 10/01/2002, Göttingen (Germany) (b) 1,80 (c) M - right midfielder (d) Eintracht Frankfurt (e) Borussia Dortmund, Eintracht, Borussia Dortmund, Borussia Dortmund II
*** Knezevic - Bojan Knezevic (Bojan Knežević) (a) 28/01/1997, Bjelovar (Croatia) (b) 1,81 (c) M - pivot (d) - (e) Termoli, Hebar P., ND Gorica, NK Opatija, Dinamo Zagreb, Koper, Dinamo Zagreb, Olimpija, Dinamo Zagreb, NK Lokomotiva, Dinamo Zagreb, NK Lokomotiva, Dinamo Zagreb, Din. Zagreb II, Prva NL
*** Knezevic - Branislav Knezevic (Бранислав Кнежевић) (a) 21/07/2002, Šabac (RF Yugoslavia, now in Serbia) (b) 1,88 (c) M - central midfielder (d) Zeleznicar Pancevo (e) Elche Ilicitano, Macva
*** Knezevic - Filip Knezevic (Филип Кнежевић) (a) 08/11/1991, Raška (Yugoslavia, now in Serbia) (b) 1,82 (c) F - right winger (d) - (e) Buducnost Podgorica, Sutjeska Niksic, Da Nang FC, Proleter, Radnicki Niš, FC Ashdod, Borac Cacak, Vojvodina, Čukarički, FK Partizan, Borac Cacak, FK Partizan, Vitória Guimarães B, FK Partizan, Radnicki 1923, FK Partizan, Borac Cacak
*** Knezevic - Josip Knezevic (Josip Knežević) (a) 03/10/1988, Osijek (Yugoslavia, now in Croatia) (b) 1,86 (c) M - attacking midfielder (d) NK BSK Bijelo Brdo (e) HNK Sibenik, Al-Arabi SC, Puskás AFC, NK Osijek, Kaysar, Kairat Almaty, Amkar Perm, Kairat Almaty, Amkar Perm, NK Osijek
*** Knezevic - Lovre Knezevic (Lovre Knežević) (a) 22/07/1998, Zadar (Croatia) (b) 1,86 (c) F - left winger (d) NK Istra 1961 (e) Etar, Arda Kardzhali, NS Mura, Beltinci, NS Mura, NK Zadar, FC Kufstein, Kirchbichl, Hrv Dragovoljac, NK Lucko
*** Knezevic - Luka Knezevic (Luka Knežević) (a) 14/03/1999, Livno (Bosnia and Herzegovina) (b) - (c) M - right midfielder (d) FK Leotar Trebinje (e) Croat. Zmijavci, Cibalia, Siroki Brijeg, Croat. Zmijavci, Siroki Brijeg, GOSK Gabela, Siroki Brijeg, Croat. Zmijavci
*** Knezevic - Marko Knezevic (Марко Кнежевић) (a) 29/03/1989, Beograd (Yugoslavia, now in Serbia) (b) 1,86 (c) G (d) FK Mladost GAT Novi Sad (e) Zeleznicar Pancevo, FK Indjija, Radnicki Niš, Vozdovac, Smederevo 1924, Javor-Matis, FK Bezanija, Vozdovac, Radnicki 1923, Banat Zrenjanin, Borac Banja Luka, Kolubara, Teleoptik, Metalac, Teleoptik
*** Knezevic - Nikola Knezevic (Никола Кнежевић) (a) 10/03/2003, Zemun (Serbia and Montenegro, now in Serbia) (b) 1,80 (c) M - central midfielder (d) Crvena zvezda Beograd (e) Napredak, Crvena zvezda, Graficar, Crvena zvezda, Graficar
*** Knezevic - Stefan Knezevic (a) 30/10/1996, Luzern (Switzerland) (b) 1,87 (c) D - central defense (d) RSC Charleroi (e) FC Luzern, SC Buochs

*** Knezevic - Stefan Knezevic (Stefan Knežević) (a) 28/03/2000, ¿? (RF Yugoslavia, now in Montenegro) (b) - (c) D - right back (d) FK Iskra Danilovgrad (e) Drina Zvornik, FK Sremčica

*** Knezevic - Tomislav Knezevic (Tomislav Knežević) (a) 07/01/1999, Zagreb (Croatia) (b) 1,91 (c) M - attacking midfielder (d) - (e) Siroki Brijeg, Rudar Prijedor, AS Trencin, NK Rudes, AS Trencin, Din. Zagreb II

*** Knight - Ben Knight (Benjamin Leo Knight) (a) 14/06/2002, Cambridge (England) (b) 1,70 (c) F - right winger (d) - (e) Crewe Alexandra

*** Knight - Brad Knight (Bradley James Knight) (a) 30/08/2004, ¿? (England) (b) - (c) F - center forward (d) Airbus UK Broughton (e) -

*** Knobloch - Milan Knobloch (a) 23/08/1992, Městec Králové (Czechoslovakia, now in Czech Rep.) (b) 1,92 (c) G (d) - (e) Karmiotissa, Slovan Liberec, Pardubice, Zivanice, Lounovice, Viktoria Zizkov, Mlada Boleslav B

*** Knoche - Robin Knoche (a) 22/05/1992, Braunschweig (Germany) (b) 1,89 (c) D - central defense (d) 1.FC Union Berlin (e) VfL Wolfsburg, Wolfsburg II

*** Knockaert - Anthony Knockaert (Anthony Patrick Knockaert) (a) 20/11/1991, Roubaix (France) (b) 1,72 (c) F - right winger (d) Fulham FC (e) Huddersfield Town, Fulham, Volos NPS, Fulham, Nottingham Forest, Fulham, Brighton & Hove Albion, Fulham, Brighton & Hove Albion, Standard Liège, Leicester City, Guingamp, EA Guingamp B

*** Knoester - Mats Knoester (a) 19/11/1998, Alphen aan den Rijn (Netherlands) (b) 1,88 (c) D - central defense (d) Ferencváros TC (e) Heracles Almelo, Feyenoord

*** Knollmüller - Jakob Knollmüller (a) 26/07/2003, Baden (Austria) (b) 1,77 (c) F - center forward (d) SV Lafnitz (e) TSV Hartberg, SV Lafnitz, TSV Hartberg

*** Knott - Jordan Knott (a) 13/09/1993, Newport (England) (b) - (c) D - central defense (d) Pontypridd United (e) Taffs Well, Carmarthen, Goytre United

*** Knowles - James Knowles (a) 06/04/1993, Lisburn (Northern Ireland) (b) - (c) M - pivot (d) Dungannon Swifts (e) Ballymena, Glentoran, Cliftonville, Linfield, Ards FC, Linfield, Cliftonville

*** Knudsen - Aron Knudsen (a) 05/11/1999, ¿? (Faroe Islands) (b) - (c) M - left midfielder (d) B36 Tórshavn (e) NSÍ Runavík, NSÍ II

*** Knudsen - Jonas Knudsen (Jonas Hjort Knudsen) (a) 16/09/1992, Esbjerg (Denmark) (b) 1,85 (c) D - left back (d) Malmö FF (e) Ipswich, Esbjerg fB

*** Knudsen - Magnus Knudsen (Magnus Nordengen Knudsen) (a) 15/06/2001, Oslo (Norway) (b) 1,86 (c) M - central midfielder (d) Aarhus GF (e) Aarhus GF, Rostov, Lillestrøm, Rostov, Lillestrøm, Ullensaker/Kisa, Lillestrøm, Lillestrøm II

*** Knudsen - Petur Knudsen (a) 21/04/1998, ¿? (Faroe Islands) (b) 1,80 (c) F - center forward (d) - (e) Lyngby BK, NSÍ Runavík, NSÍ II

*** Knudsen - Rasmus Knudsen (Rasmus Juel Knudsen) (a) 02/10/2002, ¿? (Denamrk) (b) 1,84 (c) D - left back (d) Dalum IF (e) 07 Vestur, Naesby BK

*** Knudtzon - Erling Knudtzon (a) 15/12/1988, Oslo (Norway) (b) 1,78 (c) M - right midfielder (d) Molde FK (e) Lillestrøm, Lyn, Ullern

*** Knysh - Danylo Knysh (Книш Данило Сергійович) (a) 03/03/1996, Artsyz, Odesa Oblast (Ukraine) (b) 1,76 (c) F - right winger (d) Nyva Buzova (e) Metalist, Karpaty Lviv, Metalist, FK Minaj, FK Kalush, Stal Kamyanske, PFK Stal II, Dinamo Kiev II

*** Kobacki - Olaf Kobacki (a) 10/07/2001, Poznań (Poland) (b) 1,78 (c) M - attacking midfielder (d) Arka Gdynia (e) Miedź Legnica, Arka Gdynia, Atalanta, Arka Gdynia

*** Kobakhidze - Mamuka Kobakhidze (მამუკა კობახიძე) (a) 23/08/1992, Tbilisi (Georgia) (b) 1,89 (c) D - central defense (d) Dinamo Batumi (e) Torpedo Kutaisi,

Rustavi, FC Locomotive, Rubin Kazan, Neftekhimik, Rubin Kazan, Mordovia, Rubin Kazan, FC Dila, FC Zestafoni, Alania, FC Zestafoni
*** Kobakhidze - Otar Kobakhidze (ოთარ კობახიძე) (a) 29/02/1996, ¿? (Georgia) (b) 1,75 (c) F - right winger (d) Marijampole City (e) Sioni Bolnisi, FC Samtredia, Torpedo Kutaisi, FC Locomotive, FC Shevardeni, Sioni Bolnisi, Sioni Bolnisi
*** Kobasevic - Ajdin Kobasevic (Ajdin Kobašević) (a) 24/06/2004, Sarajevo (Bosnia and Herzegovina) (b) - (c) D - central defense (d) FK Radnik Hadzici (e) -
*** Kobayashi - Yuki Kobayashi (小林 友希) (a) 18/07/2000, Kobe, Hyogo (Japan) (b) 1,85 (c) D - central defense (d) Celtic FC (e) Vissel Kobe, Yokohama FC, Vissel Kobe, Machida Zelvia, Vissel Kobe
*** Köbbing - Matthias Köbbing (a) 28/05/1997, Koblenz (Germany) (b) 1,96 (c) G (d) 1.FC Köln (e) 1.FC Köln II, FC 08 Homburg, 1.FC Heidenheim, Hoffenheim II
*** Kobeev - Miras Kobeev (Кобеев Мирас Бауржанулы) (a) 09/06/2004, Astana (Kazakhstan) (b) 1,71 (c) M - pivot (d) Kairat Almaty (e) Kairat-Zhas, Astana-Zhas
*** Kobel - Gregor Kobel (a) 06/12/1997, Zürich (Switzerland) (b) 1,94 (c) G (d) Borussia Dortmund (e) VfB Stuttgart, Hoffenheim, VfB Stuttgart, Hoffenheim, FC Augsburg, Hoffenheim
*** Koberidze - Luka Koberidze (ლუკა კობერიძე) (a) 09/09/1994, Tbilisi (Georgia) (b) 1,80 (c) M - pivot (d) Marijampole City (e) Riteriai, Sioni Bolnisi, VPK-Agro, FC Shevardeni, Torpedo Kutaisi, Metalist 1925, Desna, Guria, FK Zugdidi, Baia
*** Kobesov - David Kobesov (Кобесов Давид Бидзинаевич) (a) 06/01/2000, Vladikavkaz (Russia) (b) 1,84 (c) M - pivot (d) Alania Vladikavkaz (e) Alania Vl., Pari Nizhny Novgórod, Khimki, Pari Nizhny Novgórod, Alania Vl., Spartak V.
*** Kobiljar - Rijad Kobiljar (a) 08/04/1996, Sarajevo (Bosnia and Herzegovina) (b) 1,70 (c) M - attacking midfielder (d) FK Tuzla City (e) FK Sarajevo, KFC Uerdingen, Rudar Velenje, Olimpija, Zrinjski Mostar, GOSK Gabela, Zrinjski Mostar, FK Olimpik, FK Sarajevo, Travnik, FK Sarajevo, Jacksonville Dolphins
*** Kobouri - Davit Kobouri (დავით კობოური) (a) 24/01/1998, Telavi (Georgia) (b) 1,88 (c) D - left back (d) Dinamo Tbilisi (e) Karvina, Dinamo Tbilisi, Dinamo II
*** Kobuladze - Giorgi Kobuladze (გიორგი ქობულაძე) (a) 26/02/1997, ¿? (Georgia) (b) - (c) D - left back (d) Torpedo Kutaisi (e) FC Gagra, Ingulets, Ingulets 2, Ingulets 3, Ingulets 2, L-Georgia Kyiv, FC Sasco
*** Kobusinski - Szymon Kobusinski (Szymon Kobusiński) (a) 04/05/1998, Słubice (Poland) (b) 1,83 (c) F - center forward (d) KSP Polonia Warszawa (e) Polonia, Zagłębie, Ruch, Zagłębie, P. Niepolomice, Zielona Gora, Stal Rzeszow, Garbarnia, Zielona Góra
*** Kobylak - Gabriel Kobylak (a) 20/02/2002, Brzozów (Poland) (b) 1,91 (c) G (d) Legia de Varsovia (e) Radomiak, Legia Warszawa, Legia II, P. Niepolomice, Legia II, Karpaty Krosno
*** Kobzar - Bogdan Kobzar (Кобзар Богдан Михайлович) (a) 22/04/2002, Rozhyshche, Volyn Oblast (Ukraine) (b) 1,84 (c) F - center forward (d) FK Oleksandriya (e) Volyn Lutsk, Volyn 2 Lutsk, Volyn Lutsk II
*** Kobzar - Evgeniy Kobzar (Кобзарь Евгений Васильевич) (a) 09/08/1992, Stavropol (Russia) (b) 1,72 (c) F - left winger (d) FK Aksu (e) Akzhayik, Shakhter K., SC Noravank, FC Urartu, Spartaks, FCI Levadia, Zenit Izhevsk, Sakhalin, Loko-Kazanka M., CSKA Moskva II, Khimki, CSKA Moskva II
*** Koc - Musa Koc (Musa Koç) (a) 07/09/2004, Antalya (Turkey) (b) 1,90 (c) G (d) Karaman FK (e) Alanyaspor

*** Koca - Rijad Koca (Ријад Коца) (a) 17/08/2003, Novi Pazar (Serbia and Montenegro, now in Serbia) (b) - (c) D - central defense (d) - (e) OFK Beograd, Novi Pazar

*** Kocaba - Filip Kocaba (a) 13/11/2004, ¿? (Poland) (b) 1,83 (c) M - pivot (d) Zagłębie Lubin (e) Zaglebie Lubin II

*** Kocaman - Arif Kocaman (a) 14/09/2003, Kütahya (Turkey) (b) 1,86 (c) D - central defense (d) Kayserispor (e) Sakaryaspor

*** Kocan - Alis Kocan (a) 03/06/2004, ¿? (Luxembourg) (b) - (c) D (d) FC Differdange 03 (e) -

*** Kocatürk - Yusuf Kocatürk (a) 27/07/2004, Istanbul (Turkey) (b) - (c) M - pivot (d) Fenerbahce (e) -

*** Kocev - Hristijan Kocev (Христијан Коцев) (a) 30/03/2000, Skopje (North Macedonia) (b) 1,74 (c) D - left back (d) - (e) Panargiakos, Pobeda Prilep, Makedonija, Kadino, Osogovo, Korabi Debar, Madzari Solidarnost, Lokomotiva

*** Kocev - Robert Kocev (Роберт Коцев) (a) 14/06/1994, Stip (North Macedonia) (b) 1,76 (c) M - pivot (d) FC Uzwil II (e) Sileks, Tikves, Borec Veles, Plackovica

*** Kocev - Stefan Kocev (Стефан Коцев) (a) 23/02/1994, Stip (North Macedonia) (b) 1,78 (c) D - right back (d) Kaspiy Aktau (e) Bregalnica Stip, FC A&N, Aspropyrgos, Sileks, KF Liria, Bregalnica Stip

*** Koch - Menno Koch (a) 02/07/1994, Heeze (Netherlands) (b) 1,95 (c) D - central defense (d) CSKA-Sofia (e) KAS Eupen, NAC Breda, PSV Eindhoven, FC Utrecht, PSV Eindhoven, NAC Breda, PSV Eindhoven

*** Koch - Robin Koch (Robin Leon Koch) (a) 17/07/1996, Kaiserslautern (Germany) (b) 1,91 (c) D - central defense (d) Eintracht Frankfurt (e) Eintracht, Leeds Utd., SC Freiburg, 1.FC Kaiserslautern, Kaiserslautern II, Eintracht Trier, Eintr. Trier II

*** Koch - Sebastian Koch (a) 11/10/1996, ¿? (Denmark) (b) 1,86 (c) F - right winger (d) SønderjyskE (e) Lyngby BK, Nyköbing FC, B.93, Nyköbing FC

*** Kochakidze - Mikheil Kochakidze (მიხეილ ქოჩაკიძე) (a) 15/10/2002, ¿? (Georgia) (b) - (c) F - center forward (d) Sioni Bolnisi (e) Rustavi, Dinamo II

*** Kochalski - Mateusz Kochalski (a) 25/07/2000, Świdnik (Poland) (b) 1,90 (c) G (d) Stal Mielec (e) Legia Warszawa, Radomiak, Legia Warszawa, Radomiak, Legia Warszawa, Legia II, Radomiak, Legia II, Legionovia, Legia II, BKS Lublin Młod

*** Kochan - Matej Kochan (a) 21/11/1992, Brezno (Czechoslovakia, now in Slovakia) (b) 1,87 (c) M - central midfielder (d) MFK Ružomberok (e) Podbrezova

*** Kocharyan - Aram Kocharyan (Արամ Քոչարյան) (a) 05/03/1996, Kasagh (Armenia) (b) 1,74 (c) M - pivot (d) Alashkert Yerevan CF (e) Vitebsk, SC Noravank, Pyunik Yerevan, Lori Vanadzor, Gandzasar, Lori Vanadzor, Lokomotiv, Ararat Yerevan, Banants II

*** Kocharyan - Ashot Kocharyan (Աշոտ Քոչարյան) (a) 13/07/1999, Yerevan (Armenia) (b) 1,72 (c) F - left winger (d) FC Noah Erewan II (e) West Armenia, Ararat II, Lernayin Artsakh, Alashkert CF, Gandzasar, Pyunik Yerevan B

*** Kochav - Dor Kochav (כוכב דור) (a) 06/05/1993, ¿? (Israel) (b) - (c) M - attacking midfielder (d) Bnei Yehuda Tel Aviv (e) Ness Ziona, Hapoel Afula, Ness Ziona, Bnei Yehuda, Hapoel Afula, Ramat haSharon, Hapoel Afula, Ironi Nesher, Maccabi Haifa, Hapoel Acre, Maccabi Haifa, H. Petah Tikva, Maccabi Haifa, Hapoel Afula, Maccabi Haifa

*** Kochergin - Vladyslav Kochergin (Кочергін Владислав Сергійович) (a) 30/04/1996, Odesa (Ukraine) (b) 1,78 (c) M - attacking midfielder (d) Rakow Czestochowa (e) Zorya Lugansk, Dnipro, Dnipro II

*** Kochetkov - Evgeniy Kochetkov (Кочетков Евгений) (a) 29/01/2004, Kostanay (Kazakhstan) (b) 1,77 (c) D - central defense (d) Tobol Kostanay II (e) -

*** Kochladze - Lasha Kochladze (ლაშა ქოჩლაძე) (a) 22/08/1995, ¿? (Georgia) (b) 1,86 (c) M - attacking midfielder (d) Merani Tbilisi (e) FC Telavi, Sioni Bolnisi, FC Samtredia, Rustavi, Dinamo Tbilisi, Tskhinvali, Dinamo Tbilisi, Tskhinvali, Metallurgist II

*** Kocic - Milan Kocic (Milan Kocić) (a) 16/02/1990, ¿? (Yugoslavia, now in Slovenia) (b) 1,77 (c) D - left back (d) FC Clivense SM (e) Tabor Sezana, Chindia, FC Voluntari, Panionios, Bohemians 1905, NK Aluminij, Rudar Velenje, TSV Hartberg, Shumen 1929, Triestina

*** Kocic - Srdjan Kocic (Срђан Коčић) (a) 16/02/1999, Sombor (RF Yugoslavia, now in Serbia) (b) 1,76 (c) F - left winger (d) FK Kolubara Lazarevac (e) Napredak, Kolubara

*** Kocijan - Mateo Kocijan (a) 27/03/1995, Hlebine (Croatia) (b) 1,88 (c) M - pivot (d) FK Partizani (e) Slaven Belupo, Tehnicar 1974, Mladost Sigetec, Borac Imbriovec, Mladost Sigetec

*** Kockelmann - Cédric Kockelmann (a) 09/09/1998, Luxembourg (Luxembourg) (b) 1,86 (c) M - central midfielder (d) UN Käerjeng 97 (e) Swift Hesperange

*** Kocoski - Dimitri Kocoski (Димитри Кочоски) (a) 20/10/2004, Prilep (North Macedonia) (b) 1,77 (c) M - pivot (d) - (e) Pobeda Prilep

*** Kocoski - Valentin Kocoski (Валентин Кочоски) (a) 01/03/1997, ¿? (RF Yugoslavia, now in North Macedonia) (b) 1,81 (c) M - attacking midfielder (d) Struga Trim & Lum (e) Pelister Bitola, Struga, FC Shkupi, Belasica, Horizont, AP Brera, Horizont, AP Brera

*** Kocovic - Nenad Kocovic (Ненад Кочовић) (a) 20/02/1995, Kragujevac (RF Yugoslavia, now in Montenegro) (b) 1,83 (c) D - left back (d) FK Kolubara Lazarevac (e) Kabel Novi Sad, FK Indjija, Proleter, FK Loznica, Borac Cacak, Proleter, Vojvodina, CSK Celarevo, Vojvodina

*** Kocsis - Bence Kocsis (Kocsis Bence Máté) (a) 23/04/2001, Târgu Mureș (Romania) (b) 1,80 (c) M - attacking midfielder (d) Budafoki MTE (e) Budafoki MTE, Paksi FC, Pécsi MFC, Paksi FC, MTK Budapest, Puskás AFC II, Csákvár, Puskás AFC II, Csákvár, Puskás AFC II

*** Kocsis - Dominik Kocsis (a) 01/08/2002, Nagykanizsa (Hungary) (b) 1,69 (c) F - right winger (d) Budapest Honvéd FC (e) Diósgyőr, Honvéd, Honvéd II

*** Kocsis - Gergely Kocsis (Kocsis Gergely Péter) (a) 20/03/2005, ¿? (Hungary) (b) - (c) M - pivot (d) Budapest Honvéd FC (e) Honvéd II

*** Kocsis - Norbert Kocsis (a) 03/10/2004, Targu Secuiesc (Romania) (b) - (c) F - center forward (d) - (e) KSE Tîrgu Secuiesc

*** Kocuk - Okan Kocuk (a) 27/07/1995, Bursa (Turkey) (b) 1,87 (c) G (d) Samsunspor (e) Galatasaray, Giresunspor, Galatasaray, Bursaspor, Istanbulspor, Bursaspor, Bandirmaspor, Bursaspor

*** Kocyla - Dawid Kocyla (Dawid Kocyła) (a) 23/07/2002, Bełchatów (Poland) (b) 1,80 (c) M - attacking midfielder (d) Wisła Płock (e) Nieciecza, Wisła Płock, GKS Belchatow

*** Kodad - Ladislav Kodad (a) 23/04/1998, ¿? (Czech Rep.) (b) 1,80 (c) M - right midfielder (d) FK Mlada Boleslav (e) Teplice, Teplice B, Litomericko, Teplice B, Reichensachsen

*** Koderman - Vid Koderman (a) 18/04/2003, Ptuj (Slovenia) (b) 1,77 (c) D - left back (d) NK Celje (e) Koper, NK Maribor, Tabor Sezana, NK Maribor

*** Kodes - Petr Kodes (Petr Kodeš) (a) 31/01/1996, Krupka (Czech Rep.) (b) 1,85 (c) M - pivot (d) FC Hradec Kralove (e) Teplice, Hradec Kralove, Teplice, Varnsdorf, Teplice, Viktoria Zizkov, Teplice
*** Kodia - Donald Alvine Kodia (a) 01/01/2003, ¿? (Ivory Coast) (b) - (c) F - left winger (d) Shirak Gyumri C.F. (e) Ness Ziona
*** Kodra - Eneid Kodra (a) 04/11/1999, Tiranë (Albania) (b) 1,84 (c) D - right back (d) KS Kastrioti (e) FK Partizani
*** Kodro - Kenan Kodro (a) 19/08/1993, Donostia-San Sebastián (Spain) (b) 1,88 (c) F - center forward (d) Fehérvár FC (e) Athletic, Real Valladolid, Athletic, FC København, Mainz 05, Grasshoppers, Mainz 05, CA Osasuna, Real Sociedad B, CD Lagun Onak, Real Sociedad B
*** Koeberlé - Samuel Koeberlé (a) 26/11/2004, Reims (France) (b) - (c) M - pivot (d) Stade Reims B (e) -
*** Koffi - Koffi (Emmanuel Amankwaa Akurugu) (a) 20/11/2001, Accra (Ghana) (b) - (c) D - left back (d) UE Cornellà (e) Getafe CF B
*** Koffi - Hervé Koffi (Hervé Koffi Kouakou) (a) 16/10/1996, Bobo-Dioulasso (Burkina Faso) (b) 1,86 (c) G (d) RSC Charleroi (e) Lille, Excelsior Mouscron, Lille, B SAD, Lille, ASEC Mimosas, RC Bobo Diou., Rahimo FC
*** Koffi - N'Dri Koffi (N'Dri Philippe Koffi) (a) 09/03/2002, Abidjan (Ivory Coast) (b) 1,87 (c) F - center forward (d) Stade de Reims (e) Le Mans FC, Stade Reims, Paços Ferreira, Stade Reims, Paços Ferreira, Stade Reims, Stade Reims B
*** Kofilovski - Leonid Kofilovski (Леонид Кофиловски) (a) 24/10/2004, Prilep (North Macedonia) (b) 1,86 (c) D - central defense (d) Pobeda Prilep (e) -
*** Kofler - Thomas Kofler (a) 07/07/1998, ¿? (Austria) (b) - (c) D - left back (d) SC Imst (e) TSV Hartberg, FC Wacker, FC Wacker II
*** Kogut - Bogdan Kogut (Когут Богдан Ігорович) (a) 10/10/1987, Lviv (Soviet Union, now in Ukraine) (b) 1,90 (c) G (d) NK Veres Rivne (e) ODEK Orzhiv, Volyn Lutsk, Veres Rivne, Desna, Zaria Balti, Bukovyna, FK Sevastopol, Obolon Kyiv, Karpaty II, PFC Lviv, Karpaty II, S. Szarowola, Karpaty II, Karpaty 2
*** Kogut - Igor Kogut (Когут Ігор Романович) (a) 07/03/1996, Dnipropetrovsk (Ukraine) (b) 1,83 (c) M - central midfielder (d) SK Dnipro-1 (e) Dnipro, Dnipro II
*** Köhler - Christian Köhler (Christian Thobo Køhler) (a) 10/04/1996, ¿? (Denmark) (b) 1,76 (c) M - central midfielder (d) BK Fremad Amager (e) ÍA Akranes, Valur, Esbjerg fB, Trelleborg, FC Helsingör, Nordsjælland
*** Köhlert - Mats Köhlert (a) 02/05/1998, Hamburg (Germany) (b) 1,69 (c) D - left back (d) SC Heerenveen (e) Willem II, Hamburg II, SV Hamburg
*** Köhn - Philipp Köhn (Philipp François Köhn) (a) 02/04/1998, Dinslaken (Germany) (b) 1,90 (c) G (d) AS Mónaco (e) RB Salzburg, FC Wil 1900, RB Salzburg, RB Leipzig
*** Kohon - Rudy Kohon (a) 23/05/2004, Paris (France) (b) 1,87 (c) D - central defense (d) ESTAC Troyes B (e) -
*** Kohoutek - Ota Kohoutek (a) 23/05/2003, Brno (Czech Rep.) (b) 1,72 (c) M - central midfielder (d) FC Zbrojovka Brno (e) 1.SK Prostejov, Zbrojovka Brno
*** Kohr - Dominik Kohr (a) 31/01/1994, Trier (Germany) (b) 1,83 (c) M - pivot (d) 1.FSV Mainz 05 (e) Eintracht, Mainz 05, Eintracht, Bayer Leverkusen, FC Augsburg, Bayer Leverkusen, FC Augsburg, Bayer Leverkusen
*** Kohut - Michal Kohut (Michal Kohút) (a) 04/06/2000, ¿? (Czech Rep.) (b) - (c) M - right midfielder (d) 1.FC Slovácko (e) Pardubice, Slovácko
*** Koike - Yudai Koike (小池 雄大) (a) 05/11/1995, ¿?, Aichi (Japan) (b) 1,70 (c) F - right winger (d) Dinamo Samarqand (e) Dziugas, Kupiskis, DFK Dainava, Kupiskis, DFK Dainava, Kanagawa Uni

*** Koindredi - Koba Koindredi (Koba Leïn Koindredi) (a) 27/10/2001, Djibouti (Djibouti) (b) 1,84 (c) M - central midfielder (d) GD Estoril Praia (e) Estoril Praia, Valencia CF, Real Oviedo, Valencia CF, Valencia Mestalla
*** Koistinen - Samu Koistinen (a) 15/04/2002, ¿? (Finland) (b) - (c) M (d) Kuopion Palloseura II (e) AC Barca
*** Koita - Aboubakary Koita (Aboubakary Yeli Koita) (a) 20/09/1998, Pikine (Senegal) (b) 1,75 (c) F - left winger (d) Sint-Truidense VV (e) Waasland-Beveren, KAA Gent, KV Kortrijk, KAA Gent, ASV Geel
*** Koita - Fodé Koita (Bengali-Fodé Koita) (a) 21/10/1990, Paris (France) (b) 1,86 (c) F - center forward (d) Trabzonspor (e) Kasimpasa, Trabzonspor, Kasimpasa, Blackburn, SM Caen, Montpellier, Le Havre AC, Montpellier, RC Lens, Montpellier, Montpellier B
*** Koita - Sekou Koita (Sékou Koïta) (a) 28/11/1999, Kita (Mali) (b) 1,73 (c) F - center forward (d) Red Bull Salzburg (e) FC Liefering, Wolfsberger AC, FC Liefering, USC Kita, AS Bakaridjan, USC Kita, AS Bakaridjan
*** Kojasevic - Damir Kojasevic (Дамир Којашевић) (a) 03/06/1987, Podgorica (Yugoslavia, now in Montenegro) (b) 1,72 (c) M - attacking midfielder (d) Arsenal Tivat (e) FK Jezero, FK Iskra, FK Decic Tuzi, KF Feronikeli, Sutjeska Niksic, Radnicki Niš, Shakhter K., Vojvodina, Vardar, FK Mladost, FC Astana, Lokomotiv Tashkent, FC Astana, Buducnost Podgorica, FC Astana, Buducnost Podgorica, FK Sarajevo, Zeta Golubovac, Jagiellonia, Gornik Leczna, Jagiellonia, FK Decic Tuzi
*** Kojcic - Nemanja Kojcic (Немања Којчић) (a) 22/08/1997, Čačak (RF Yugoslavia, now in Serbia) (b) 1,92 (c) D - central defense (d) Al-Bukiryah FC (e) Napredak, Novi Pazar, Kabel Novi Sad, Hajduk 1912, Beocin, FK Novi Sad, Proleter, FK Novi Sad, Proleter
*** Kojic - Adnan Kojic (a) 28/10/1995, ¿? (Sweden) (b) 1,85 (c) D - right back (d) - (e) Kalmar FF, Sylvia, Varbergs BoIS, AFC Eskilstuna, Halmstads BK, Norrköping, Sylvia
*** Kojnok - Zsolt Kojnok (a) 15/02/2001, Mór (Hungary) (b) 1,82 (c) D - right back (d) Mezőkövesd Zsóry FC (e) Fehérvár, Budaörs, Fehérvár, Fehérvár II
*** Kokaev - Zaurbek Kokaev (Кокаев Заурбек Батразович) (a) 12/04/2000, Vladikavkaz (Russia) (b) 1,87 (c) D - central defense (d) - (e) Energetik-BGU, Metallurg Vidn., Spartak V., Fabus Br., Olimp Khimki, SSh-75 Moskva
*** Kokarev - Nikita Kokarev (Кокарев Никита Евгеньевич) (a) 08/01/2003, ¿? (Russia) (b) 1,87 (c) G (d) Arsenal Tula (e) Krasnodar-2, Rotor Volgograd, Krasnodar-2, Krasnodar II
*** Kokaritis - Robins Kokaritis (Robins Kokarītis) (a) 21/10/1999, ¿? (Latvia) (b) 1,76 (c) D - right back (d) - (e) Tukums, JFK Ventspils, Ventspils II
*** Kökcü - Orkun Kökcü (Orkun Kökçü) (a) 29/12/2000, Haarlem (Netherlands) (b) 1,75 (c) M - central midfielder (d) SL Benfica (e) Feyenoord
*** Koke - Koke (Jorge Resurrección Merodio) (a) 08/01/1992, Madrid (Spain) (b) 1,76 (c) M - central midfielder (d) Atlético de Madrid (e) At. Madrid B
*** Kokhreidze - Giorgi Kokhreidze (გიორგი კოხრეიძე) (a) 18/11/1998, Tbilisi (Georgia) (b) 1,67 (c) F - attacking midfielder (d) FC Saburtalo (e) Grenoble, Saburtalo
*** Kokhreidze - Lasha Kokhreidze (ლაშა კოხრეიძე) (a) 18/11/1998, ¿? (Georgia) (b) 1,88 (c) F - center forward (d) FC Kolkheti-1913 Poti (e) FC Telavi, Saburtalo, FC Telavi, Saburtalo
*** Kokkinis - Sotirios Kokkinis (Σωτήριος Κοκκίνης) (a) 11/07/2000, Preveza (Greece) (b) 1,77 (c) F - left winger (d) - (e) PAE Chania, Ionikos Nikeas, Ergotelis

*** Kokla - Joel Kokla (a) 20/06/2001, Tallinn (Estonia) (b) - (c) M - pivot (d) JK Tabasalu (e) Paide

*** Kokoev - David Kokoev (Кокоев Давид Сосланович) (a) 29/08/2002, Vladikavkaz (Russia) (b) 1,80 (c) M - central midfielder (d) Neftekhimik Nizhnekamsk (e) Neftekhimik, Krasnodar-2, Krasnodar II

*** Kokollari - Rrezart Kokollari (a) 03/02/2003, Morges (Switzerland) (b) 1,83 (c) M - attacking midfielder (d) - (e) FK Kukësi, San Luca, Azzurri LS

*** Kokonov - Ivan Kokonov (Иван Стоянов Коконов) (a) 17/08/1991, Sliven (Bulgaria) (b) 1,80 (c) F - left winger (d) Arda Kardzhali (e) Dunav, Montana, Cherno More, Montana, Beroe, Cherno More, Slavia Sofia, Botev Vratsa, Slavia Sofia, Botev Vratsa, Slavia Sofia, Sliven

*** Kokorin - Aleksandr Kokorin (Кокорин Александр Александрович) (a) 19/03/1991, Valuyki, Belgorod Oblast (Soviet Union, now in Russia) (b) 1,84 (c) F - attacking midfielder (d) Fiorentina (e) Aris Limassol, Fiorentina, Spartak Moskva, Zenit, Sochi, Zenit, Dinamo Moskva, Anzhi, Dinamo Moskva, Dinamo Moskva II

*** Kokosadze - Luka Kokosadze (ლუკა კოკოსაძე) (a) 30/07/2001, ¿? (Georgia) (b) - (c) F - center forward (d) Sioni Bolnisi (e) FC Saburtalo II, FC Aragvi

*** Koksharov - Aleksandr Koksharov (Кокшаров Александр Эдуардович) (a) 20/12/2004, ¿? (Russia) (b) 1,90 (c) F - center forward (d) FK Krasnodar-2 (e) -

*** Kola - Jocelyn Kola (Jocelyn Aimeric Kola) (a) 10/03/1994, Paris (France) (b) 1,80 (c) M - central midfielder (d) CP Villarrobledo (e) Europa FC, Lorca Deportiva, UP Plasencia, Moralo CP, Coria CF, Xerez Deportivo, San Roque Lepe, Algarve CF, Linas-Montlhéry, Châteauroux B

*** Kola - Marjus Kola (a) 18/05/2001, Tiranë (Albania) (b) - (c) F - right winger (d) KS Burreli (e) -

*** Kolaj - Agron Kolaj (a) 19/03/2001, Gjakovë (RF Yugoslavia, now in Kosovo) (b) 1,93 (c) G (d) FC Prishtina (e) KF Llapi, FC Besa, KF Gjakova

*** Kolak - Filip Kolak (a) 30/12/2004, ¿? (Bosnia and Herzegovina) (b) - (c) F - right winger (d) FK Leotar Trebinje (e) -

*** Kolan - Jakub Kolan (a) 03/08/2004, Prudnik (Poland) (b) 1,77 (c) D - right back (d) Zagłębie Lubin (e) Zaglebie Lubin II, AP Zagłębie

*** Kolanko - Krzysztof Kolanko (Krzysztof Kolanko) (a) 03/08/2006, ¿? (Poland) (b) 1,63 (c) F - right winger (d) Górnik Zabrze (e) Gornik II, AP Gornik

*** Kolar - Anze Kolar (a) 28/11/2003, ¿? (Slovenia) (b) - (c) D - right back (d) NK Triglav Kranj (e) NK Radomlje, SD Sencur, NK Radomlje

*** Kolar - Jakub Kolar (Jakub Kolář) (a) 16/01/2000, ¿? (Czech Rep.) (b) 1,88 (c) D - central defense (d) FC Zlin (e) FC Zlin B

*** Kolar - Marko Kolar (a) 31/05/1995, Zabok (Croatia) (b) 1,78 (c) F - center forward (d) NK Maribor (e) Wisła Płock, FC Emmen, Wisla Kraków, NK Lokomotiva, Inter Zaprešić, NK Lokomotiva, Dinamo Zagreb, NK Lokomotiva, Dinamo Zagreb, NK Sesvete, Dinamo Zagreb

*** Kolar - Ondrej Kolar (Ondřej Kolář) (a) 17/10/1994, Liberec (Czech Rep.) (b) 1,93 (c) G (d) SK Slavia Praga (e) Slovan Liberec, Varnsdorf, Slovan Liberec, Slovan Liberec B, Varnsdorf, Slovan Liberec B, Slovan Liberec

*** Kolaric - Matija Kolaric (Matija Kolarić) (a) 14/04/1996, Varaždin (Croatia) (b) 1,70 (c) D - right back (d) NK Varazdin (e) Medjimurje, NK Varazdin

*** Kolasa - Jozef Kolasa (Józef Kolasa) (a) 29/08/2004, ¿? (Poland) (b) 1,78 (c) M - pivot (d) Radomiak Radom (e) Radomiak II

*** Kolasinac - Sead Kolasinac (Sead Kolašinac) (a) 20/06/1993, Karlsruhe (Germany) (b) 1,83 (c) D - left back (d) Atalanta de Bérgamo (e) Ol. Marseille, Arsenal, FC Schalke 04, Arsenal, FC Schalke 04

*** Kolb - Jakob Kolb (a) 04/08/2002, ¿? (Austria) (b) 1,90 (c) F - center forward (d) SK Vorwärts Steyr (e) TSV Hartberg, Hartberg II, Hartberg Umgebung, Hartberg II
*** Kolec - Bartlomiej Kolec (Bartłomiej Kolec) (a) 02/03/2004, ¿? (Poland) (b) 1,76 (c) M - pivot (d) Cracovia (e) -
*** Kolega - Toni Kolega (a) 10/10/1998, Zadar (Croatia) (b) 1,75 (c) F - left winger (d) HNK Sibenik (e) Gzira Utd., Siroki Brijeg, NK Rudes, NK Osijek II, NK Rudes, NK Osijek II, NK Kustosija, NK Lokomotiva, NK Sesvete
*** Kolenda - Petar Kolenda (a) 25/09/2004, Travnik (Bosnia and Herzegovina) (b) 1,77 (c) M - attacking midfielder (d) NK Romari (e) -
*** Koleosho - Luca Koleosho (Luca Warrick Daeovie Koleosho) (a) 15/09/2004, Norwalk, Connecticut (United States) (b) 1,75 (c) F - right winger (d) Burnley FC (e) RCD Espanyol B
*** Kolesar - Peter Kolesar (Peter Kolesár) (a) 09/07/1998, Trebišov (Slovakia) (b) 1,70 (c) M - left midfielder (d) Chojniczanka Chojnice (e) Spartak Trnava, Slavoj Trebisov, Spartak Trnava, Zlaté Moravce, Spartak Trnava, Michalovce
*** Kolesnyk - Danylo Kolesnyk (Колесник Данило Ігорович) (a) 22/09/2001, ¿? (France) (b) 1,88 (c) F - center forward (d) FK Minaj (e) VPK-Agro, Kolos II, MSM
*** Kolev - Aleksandar Kolev (Александър Любомиров Колев) (a) 08/12/1992, Sofia (Bulgaria) (b) 1,91 (c) F - center forward (d) Krumovgrad (e) CSKA 1948, Stal Mielec, Kaysar, Rakow, Arka Gdynia, Sandecja, Stal Mielec, Beroe, ASV Geel, Botev Plovdiv, ASV Geel, Dessel Sport
*** Kolev - Ivan Kolev (Иван Веселинов Колев) (a) 15/10/1995, Kazanlak (Bulgaria) (b) 1,82 (c) F - center forward (d) Dunav Ruse (e) Sirens FC, Spartak Varna, Septemvri Sofia, Sozopol, Neftochimik, Botev Vratsa, Lokomotiv GO, Botev Vratsa, Lokomotiv Plovdiv, Nesebar, Lokomotiv Plovdiv, Pomorie, Lokomotiv Plovdiv, Oborishte, Rozova Dolina
*** Kolev - Krasian Kolev (Красиан Божидаров Колев) (a) 18/01/2004, Razgrad (Bulgaria) (b) 1,83 (c) M - central midfielder (d) Botev Plovdiv (e) Septemvri Sofia
*** Kolev - Petar Kolev (Петар Колев) (a) 28/06/2005, Stip (North Macedonia) (b) - (c) M (d) - (e) Bregalnica Stips
*** Kolf - Divaio Kolf (Divaio Irisio Kolf) (a) 19/07/2003, Purmerend (Netherlands) (b) 1,80 (c) F - center forward (d) Gudja United FC (e) Hellerup IK II
*** Kolias - Michalis Kolias (Μιχάλης Γεωργίου Κολιάς) (a) 02/08/2004, Limassol (Cyprus) (b) 1,82 (c) F - left winger (d) AEL Limassol (e) -
*** Kolic - Saban Kolic (Šaban Kolić) (a) 18/01/2004, Bijelo Polje (Serbia and Montenegro, now in Montenegro) (b) 1,87 (c) G (d) OSK Igalo (e) Jedinstvo
*** Kolic (c) M - attacking midfielder (d) Jedinstvo Bijelo Polje (e) - - Danis Kolic (c) M - attacking midfielder (d) Jedinstvo Bijelo Polje (e) -
*** Koliçi - Enea Koliçi (Enea Koliçi) (a) 13/02/1986, Pogradec (Albania) (b) 1,90 (c) G (d) FC Ballkani (e) SC Gjilani, KF Skënderbeu, Flamurtari FC, FK Kukësi, Olympiakos Volou, Iraklis, Flamurtari FC, Panserraikos, Odysseas Kordeliou, Olympiakos Volou, Iraklis, Olympiakos Volou, Iraklis
*** Kolinger - Denis Kolinger (a) 14/01/1994, Malsch (Germany) (b) 1,99 (c) D - central defense (d) Vejle Boldklub (e) CFR Cluj, Vejle BK, NK Lokomotiva, NK Zagreb
*** Kolinko - Nikita Kolinko (Ņikita Koliņko) (a) 10/06/2000, ¿? (Latvia) (b) 1,82 (c) D - left back (d) - (e) Super Nova, Spartaks, Dinamo Riga, Super Nova, RFS II
*** Koljic - Elvir Koljic (Elvir Koljić) (a) 08/07/1995, Valladolid (Spain) (b) 1,94 (c) F - center forward (d) Universitatea Craiova (e) FK Krupa, Lech Poznan, FK Krupa, Borac Banja Luka, FK Krupa, NK Triglav, NK Kljuc

*** Kolmakov - Maksim Kolmakov (Колмаков Максим Евгеньевич) (a) 05/01/2003, Tikhoretsk, Krasnodar Region (Russia) (b) 1,76 (c) F - left winger (d) Neftekhimik Nizhnekamsk (e) Sochi, Chaika Pes., Sochi, FK Sochi II, Dynamo Brest, FK Sochi II, Kuban Holding, Ekaterinodar
*** Kolo Muani - Randal Kolo Muani (a) 05/12/1998, Bondy (France) (b) 1,87 (c) F - center forward (d) Eintracht Frankfurt (e) FC Nantes, US Boulogne, FC Nantes, FC Nantes B
*** Kolobaric - Dario Kolobaric (Dario Kolobarić) (a) 06/02/2000, Teslić (Bosnia and Herzegovina) (b) 1,84 (c) F (d) - (e) ND Gorica, Koper, Soligorsk, Domžale, NK Dob, Domžale
*** Kolobov - Mihhail Kolobov (a) 02/03/2005, Tallinn (Estonia) (b) - (c) D - central defense (d) FC Flora Tallinn (e) TJK Legion
*** Kolodziejczak - Timothée Kolodziejczak (Timothée Christian Kolodziejczak) (a) 01/10/1991, Avion (France) (b) 1,83 (c) D - central defense (d) - (e) FC Schalke 04, St.-Étienne, Tigres UANL, St.-Étienne, Tigres UANL, Borussia Mönchengladbach, Sevilla FC, OGC Nice, Olympique Lyon, RC Lens, Olympique Lyon, RC Lens
*** Kolomoets - Yuriy Kolomoets (Коломоєць Юрій Миколайович) (a) 22/03/1990, Kryvyi Rig, Dnipropetrovsk Oblast (Soviet Union, now in Ukraine) (b) 1,90 (c) F - center forward (d) - (e) FK Minaj, FK Polissya, Volyn Lutsk, Istiqlol, FCI Levadia, Vorskla Poltava, MTK Budapest, Vorskla Poltava, FK Oleksandriya, Girnyk KR, Kryvbas II, Naftovyk, Kryvbas II
*** Kolonias - Konstantinos Kolonias (Κωνσταντίνος Κολώνιας) (a) 20/01/2004, Larissa (Greece) (b) - (c) M - central midfielder (d) Enosis Neon Paralimniou (e) -
*** Kolovetsios - Dimitrios Kolovetsios (Δημήτριος Κολοβέτσιος) (a) 16/10/1991, Larisa (Greece) (b) 1,83 (c) D - central defense (d) Kayserispor (e) Panathinaikos, AEK Athína, PAS Giannina, AE Larisa, Tyrnavos 2005
*** Kolovos - Dimitrios Kolovos (Δημήτριος Κολοβός) (a) 27/04/1993, Athina (Greece) (b) 1,84 (c) M - attacking midfielder (d) Dewa United FC (e) Panetolikos, Kocaelispor, FC Sheriff, Panathinaikos, FC Sheriff, Panathinaikos, Omonia Nicosia, KV Mechelen, Omonia Nicosia, KV Mechelen, Willem II, KV Mechelen, Olympiakos, KV Mechelen, Olympiakos, Panionios, Olympiakos, Panionios, Olympiakos, Panionios, PAS Oropos
*** Kolpachuk - Ilya Kolpachuk (Колпачук Илья Федорович) (a) 09/10/1990, Beryosa (Soviet Union, now in Belarus) (b) 1,84 (c) D - left back (d) Dynamo Brest (e) Zhetysu, Rukh, Kauno Zalgiris, Atlantas, Gorodeya, Gomel, Granit, Gomel, Volna Pinsk, Dinamo Brest, Dynamo Brest II, Dinamo Minsk II
*** Kolskogen - Ole Martin Kolskogen (Ole Martin Lekven Kolskogen) (a) 20/01/2001, Osøyro (Norway) (b) 1,87 (c) D - central defense (d) Åsane Fotball (e) Åsane, Aalesund, Brann, Jerv, Brann, Åsane, Os Turn
*** Koltygin - Aleksey Koltygin (Колтыгин Алексей Максимович) (a) 27/07/2000, Minsk (Belarus) (b) 1,80 (c) G (d) Volna Pinsk (e) Krumkachi, FK Slutsk, Krumkachi, Sputnik, Belshina II, FK Uzda, BATE II
*** Kolundzic - Andrija Kolundzic (Andrija Kolundžić) (a) 23/09/2002, Podgorica (RF Yugoslavia, Montenegro) (b) 1,80 (c) F - right winger (d) FK Mornar Bar (e) FK Iskra, Dinamo Zagreb, Din. Zagreb II, FK Iskra, FK Iskra II
*** Kolve - Eivind Kolve (Eivind Strømsheim Kolve) (a) 22/10/2004, ¿? (Norway) (b) 1,74 (c) M - central midfielder (d) Aalesunds FK II (e) -
*** Kolyadko - Mikhail Kolyadko (Колядко Михаил Владимирович) (a) 21/11/1988, Minsk (Soviet Union, now in Belarus) (b) 1,82 (c) M - central midfielder (d) Belshina Bobruisk (e) Krumkachi, Slavia, Kauno Zalgiris, Atlantas, Gorodeya,

Rechitsa, Dynamo Brest, Olimpia Elblag, Gorodeya, Gomel, FK Minsk, FK Baranovichi, FK Minsk, Коммунальник, FK Minsk, Minsk-2

*** Komáromi - György Komáromi (a) 19/01/2002, Szolnok (Hungary) (b) 1,77 (c) F - left winger (d) Puskás Akadémia FC (e) Puskás ΛFC II

*** Komarov - Ivan Komarov (Комаров Иван Сергеевич) (a) 15/04/2003, Slavyansk-na-Kubani (Russia) (b) 1,77 (c) M - right midfielder (d) FK Rostov (e) Rostov II

*** Komazec - Nikola Komazec (Никола Комазец) (a) 15/11/1987, Vrbas (Yugoslavia, now in Serbia) (b) 1,89 (c) F - center forward (d) FK Rudar Prijedor (e) Sloboda Tuzla, Ayutthaya Utd., Kasetsart FC, Kosice, Kitchee, Southern, Bhayangkara, Pegasus, Salam Zgharta, Smouha, South China, Dinamo Batumi, Haugesund, Pattaya United, Haugesund, Busan IPark, FK Sarajevo, Suphanburi FC, NK Maribor, Petrolul, Hajduk Kula

*** Komisarov - Eitan Komisarov (קומיסרוב איתן) (a) 16/01/2001, ¿? (Israel) (b) - (c) D - central defense (d) Sekzia Ness Ziona (e) Bikat haYarden, Ness Ziona

*** Komissarov - Nikita Komissarov (a) 25/04/2000, Tallinn (Estonia) (b) - (c) M - central midfielder (d) Kalju FC (e) JK Viljandi, Kuressaare, TJK Legion

*** Komlichenko - Nikolay Komlichenko (Комличенко Николай Николаевич) (a) 29/06/1995, Plastunovskaya, Krasnodar Region (Russia) (b) 1,90 (c) F - center forward (d) FK Rostov (e) Dinamo Moskva, Rostov, Dinamo Moskva, Mlada Boleslav, Krasnodar, Mlada Boleslav, Krasnodar, Krasnodar-2, Slovan Liberec, Krasnodar-2, Chernomorets N., Krasnodar-2, Krasnodar II

*** Komlov - Artjom Komlov (a) 09/09/2002, Narva (Estonia) (b) - (c) M - attacking midfielder (d) - (e) FCI Levadia

*** Kompan Breznik - Miha Kompan Breznik (a) 05/10/2003, Maribor (Slovenia) (b) 1,87 (c) D - left back (d) Spartak Trnava (e) NS Mura, Tabor Sezana, NS Mura, Olimpija

*** Kompare - Matic Kompare (a) 01/01/2003, ¿? (Slovenia) (b) - (c) M - central midfielder (d) NK Tabor Sezana (e) -

*** Komposch - Paul Komposch (a) 13/05/2001, ¿? (Austria) (b) 1,87 (c) D - central defense (d) TSV Hartberg (e) Sturm Graz, Sturm Graz II

*** Kömür - Mert Kömür (a) 17/07/2005, Dachau (Germany) (b) 1,83 (c) M - attacking midfielder (d) FC Augsburg (e) -

*** Konate - Pa Konate (Pa Momodou Konate) (a) 25/04/1994, Malmö (Sweden) (b) 1,78 (c) D - left back (d) - (e) Botev Plovdiv, Rosenborg, J-Södra IF, GIF Sundsvall, SPAL, Cincinnati, SPAL, Malmö FF, Östers IF, Malmö FF

*** Konaté - Cheick Oumar Konaté (a) 02/04/2004, Bamoko (Mali) (b) 1,73 (c) D - central defense (d) Clermont Foot 63 (e) Clermont B, JMG Bamako

*** Konaté - Ibrahima Konaté (a) 25/05/1999, Paris (France) (b) 1,94 (c) D - central defense (d) Liverpool FC (e) RB Leipzig, FC Sochaux, FC Sochaux B

*** Konaté - Karim Konaté (a) 21/03/2004, Koumassi (Ivory Coast) (b) 1,78 (c) F - center forward (d) Red Bull Salzburg (e) FC Liefering, RB Salzburg, ASEC Mimosas

*** Konaté - Mohamed Konaté (a) 12/12/1997, Odienné (Ivory Coast) (b) 1,91 (c) F - center forward (d) Akhmat Grozny (e) Khimki, Tambov, Pyunik Yerevan, Gomel, Kairat Almaty, Babite, Ural, FC Saxan, AS Denguélé

*** Konaté - Mory Konaté (a) 15/11/1993, Conakry (Guinea) (b) 1,91 (c) M - pivot (d) KV Mechelen (e) Sint-Truiden, Borussia Dortmund II, TuS Erndtebrück, VfL Alfter, VfL Alfter II

*** Konczkowski - Martin Konczkowski (a) 14/09/1993, Ruda Śląska (Poland) (b) 1,81 (c) D - right back (d) Śląsk Wroclaw (e) Piast Gliwice, Ruch, Ruch Chorzow II

*** Konda - Ishaku Konda (a) 11/09/1999, ¿? (Ghana) (b) 1,90 (c) D - central defense (d) FK Jablonec (e) Asokwa FC, Ceske Budejovice, Asokwa FC, Paide, Asokwa FC, Juniors OÖ, Wa All Stars FC
*** Kondogbia - Geoffrey Kondogbia (Geoffrey Edwin Kondogbia) (a) 15/02/1993, Nemours (France) (b) 1,88 (c) M - pivot (d) Olympique Marseille (e) Atlético Madrid, Valencia CF, Internazionale Milano, Valencia CF, Internazionale Milano, AS Monaco, Sevilla FC, RC Lens, RC Lens B
*** Kondrakov - Daniil Kondrakov (Кондраков Даніїл Сергійович) (a) 19/01/1998, Lugansk (Ukraine) (b) 1,82 (c) F - center forward (d) Pirin Blagoevgrad (e) Suduva, Rukh Lviv, Zirka, Zirka II, Metalurg Z.
*** Kondratenko - Evgeniy Kondratenko (Кондратенко Евгений Геннадьевич) (a) 03/04/1999, Gomel (Belarus) (b) 1,90 (c) G (d) - (e) FK Slutsk, Lokomotiv Gomel, FK Slutsk, Orsha, Osipovichi, Lokomotiv Gomel, Osipovichi
*** Kondratski - Nikita Kondratski (a) 07/05/2004, Tallinn (Estonia) (b) - (c) F - center forward (d) - (e) TJK Legion
*** Kondrattsev - Sergei Kondrattsev (a) 23/09/2001, Narva (Estonia) (b) - (c) D - central defense (d) JK Trans Narva (e) -
*** Kondylis - Giorgos Kondylis (Γιώργος Κονδύλης) (a) 04/03/2005, Limassol (Cyprus) (b) 1,81 (c) M - pivot (d) Memphis Tigers (University of Memphis) (e) Akritas Chlor.
*** Kone - Ibrahim Pekegnon Kone (a) 21/01/2002, Abobo, Abidjan (Ivory Coast) (b) 1,85 (c) M - pivot (d) FK Auda (e) Akritas Chlor., M. Petah Tikva, AS Ashdod, M. Petah Tikva
*** Kone - Mohamed Kone (Mohamed Lamine Kone) (a) 07/08/2003, Abidjan (Ivory Coast) (b) 1,77 (c) F - left winger (d) FC Ararat Yerevan (e) Stade-Lausanne
*** Kone - Mory Kone (a) 13/07/1995, San Pedro (Ivory Coast) (b) 1,78 (c) F - center forward (d) - (e) Tuzlaspor, Újpest FC, Ararat Yerevan, Shirak Gyumri, Daugavpils, FC San Pedro
*** Kone - Seydou Kone (a) 04/11/2002, ¿? (Mali) (b) 1,73 (c) F - right winger (d) - (e) FK Skopje, AS Performance, Jammerbugt FC, AS Performance
*** Koné - Abdul Samir Koné (a) 15/05/2000, ¿? (Ivory Coast) (b) - (c) F - center forward (d) Shirak Gyumri C.F. (e) -
*** Koné - Dramane Koné (a) 10/11/1989, Apprompron-Afêwa (Ivory Coast) (b) 1,83 (c) D - central defense (d) FK Maktaaral (e) Kaspiy Aktau, Astana-1964, Akzhayik
*** Koné - Ibrahim Koné (a) 05/12/1989, Abidjan (Ivory Coast) (b) 1,90 (c) G (d) Hibernians FC (e) Zejtun C., Stade Bordelais, Pau FC, Tarbes Pyrénées, US Boulogne, AS Denguélé, CF Excellence
*** Koné - Ibrahima Koné (a) 16/06/1999, Bamako (Mali) (b) 1,90 (c) F - center forward (d) FC Lorient (e) Sarpsborg 08, Haugesund, Adana Demirspor, Haugesund, CO Bamako
*** Koné - Manu Koné (Kouadio Manu Koné) (a) 17/05/2001, Colombes (France) (b) 1,85 (c) M - central midfielder (d) Borussia Mönchengladbach (e) Toulouse, Borussia Mönchengladbach, Toulouse, Toulouse B
*** Koné - Moussa Koné (Moussa Saib Kone) (a) 12/02/1990, Anyama (Ivory Coast) (b) 1,82 (c) M - pivot (d) - (e) Qyzyljar, BB Erzurumspor, Frosinone, Cesena, Atalanta, AS Avellino, Atalanta, Varese, Atalanta, Pescara, Atalanta, Foggia, Atalanta
*** Koné - Youssouf Koné (a) 05/07/1995, Bamako (Mali) (b) 1,74 (c) D - left back (d) Olympique de Lyon (e) AC Ajaccio, Olympique Lyon, Troyes, Olympique Lyon,

Hatayspor, Olympique Lyon, Elche CF, Olympique Lyon, Lille, Stade Reims, Lille, LOSC Lille B, AS Bakaridjan, JMG Bamako
*** Konecny - Mikulas Konecny (Mikuláš Konečný) (a) 02/06/2006, ¿? (Czech Rep.) (b) 1,86 (c) D - central defense (d) SK Slavia Praga B (e) -
*** Kongsro - Vegard Kongsro (a) 07/08/1998, Herøya (Norway) (b) 1,87 (c) D - left back (d) Hamarkameratene (e) Bodø/Glimt, Ullensaker/Kisa, Pors Fotball, Odd II, Pors Fotball, Odd II
*** Konicanin - Kemal Konicanin (Кемал Коничанин) (a) 07/06/2005, Novi Pazar (Serbia and Montenegro, now in Serbia) (b) - (c) M - pivot (d) - (e) FK Novi Pazar
*** Könkkölä - Marius Könkkölä (a) 31/10/2003, Espoo (Finland) (b) 1,72 (c) M - attacking midfielder (d) FC Lahti (e) AC Oulu
*** Konlimkos - Bakdaulet Konlimkos (Конлимкос Бакдаулет) (a) 05/12/2000, ¿? (Kazakhstan) (b) 1,70 (c) F - right winger (d) Akzhayik Uralsk (e) Kaspiy Aktau, Kaspiy II
*** Kononov - Mykyta Kononov (Кононов Микита Валентинович) (a) 22/01/2003, Dnipropetrovsk (Ukraine) (b) 1,79 (c) D - right back (d) FK UCSA Tarasivka (e) FK UCSA, SK Dnipro-1, SK Dnipro-1 II
*** Konoplya - Yukhym Konoplya (Конопля Юхим Дмитрович) (a) 26/08/1999, Donetsk (Ukraine) (b) 1,80 (c) D - right back (d) Shakhtar Donetsk (e) Desna, Shakhtar Donetsk, Shakhtar II
*** Konoplyanka - Yevgen Konoplyanka (Коноплянка Євген Олегович) (a) 29/09/1989, Kirovograd (Soviet Union, now in Russia) (b) 1,76 (c) M - attacking midfielder (d) CFR Cluj (e) Cracovia, Shakhtar Donetsk, FC Schalke 04, Sevilla FC, FC Schalke 04, Sevilla FC, Dnipro, Dnipro II
*** Konovalov - Igor Konovalov (Коновалов Игорь Олегович) (a) 08/07/1996, Belorechensk, Krasnodar Region (Russia) (b) 1,85 (c) M - central midfielder (d) Rubin Kazan (e) Ural, Rubin Kazan, Akhmat Grozny, Rubin Kazan, Arsenal Tula, Rubin Kazan, Kuban Krasnodar, Kuban II, Spartak Moskva II
*** Konovalov - Ivan Konovalov (Коновалов Иван Андреевич) (a) 18/08/1994, Balashikha, Moskau Oblast (Russia) (b) 1,91 (c) G (d) Tobol Kostanay (e) Livingston FC, Rubin Kazan, Ural, Rubin Kazan, Torpedo Zhodino, Backa, Radnicki Niš, Astrakhan, FK Sevastopol, Amkar II, Spartak Moskva II
*** Konradsen - Anders Konradsen (Anders Ågnes Konradsen) (a) 18/07/1990, Bodø (Norway) (b) 1,83 (c) M - pivot (d) - (e) Bodø/Glimt, Rosenborg, Stade Rennes, Strømsgodset, Bodø/Glimt
*** Konradsen - Morten Konradsen (Morten Ågnes Konradsen) (a) 03/05/1996, Bodø (Norway) (b) 1,76 (c) M - central midfielder (d) FK Bodø/Glimt (e) Rosenborg, Bodø/Glimt
*** Konrádsson - Kristófer Konrádsson (Kristófer Konráðsson) (a) 31/03/1998, ¿? (Iceland) (b) 1,75 (c) D - left back (d) UMF Grindavík (e) Stjarnan, Leiknir, Stjarnan, Boston Eagles, Stjarnan, Boston Eagles, Stjarnan, Boston Eagles, KFG Gardabaer, Boston Eagles, Thróttur, Stjarnan
*** Konsa - Ezri Konsa (Ezri Konsa Ngoyo) (a) 23/10/1997, Newham (England) (b) 1,83 (c) D - central defense (d) Aston Villa (e) Brentford, Charlton Ath.
*** Konstantelias - Giannis Konstantelias (Γιάννης Κωνσταντέλιας) (a) 05/03/2003, Volos (Greece) (b) 1,78 (c) M - attacking midfielder (d) PAOK Thessaloniki (e) KAS Eupen, PAOK
*** Konstanti - Lampros Michail Konstanti (Λάμπρος Μιχαήλ Κωνσταντή) (a) 17/07/2005, Larnaca (Cyprus) (b) 1,81 (c) F - attacking midfielder (d) AEK Larnaca (e) -

*** Konstantin - Shay Konstantin (קונסטטיני שי) (a) 27/06/1996, Holon (Israel) (b) 1,85 (c) D - right back (d) Ironi Tiberias (e) Maccabi Netanya, B. Jerusalem, Bnei Yehuda, H. Nazareth Illit, Bnei Yehuda

*** Konstantinidis - Dimitrios Konstantinidis (Δημήτριος Κωνσταντινίδης) (a) 02/06/1994, Korinos (Greece) (b) 1,73 (c) D - right back (d) APO Levadiakos (e) Ionikos Nikeas, Olympiakos N., Spartak Trnava, Michalovce, Aris Thessaloniki, Brescia, PAOK, Omonia Nicosia, PAOK, Eginiakos, PAOK

*** Konstantinou - Konstantinos Konstantinou (Κωνσταντίνος "Νίνος" Κωνσταντίνου) (a) 08/10/1999, Larnaca (Cyprus) (b) 1,80 (c) M - right midfielder (d) Doxa Katokopias (e) EN Paralimniou, AEK Larnaca, EN Paralimniou, AEK Larnaca, Ethnikos, AEK Larnaca

*** Konstantinou - Konstantinos Konstantinou (Κωνσταντίνος Κωνσταντίνου) (a) 07/09/2005, Larnaca (Cyprus) (b) - (c) M (d) - (e) Anorthosis

*** Konstantinou - Theodoros Konstantinou (Θεόδωρος Κωνσταντίνου) (a) 05/09/1998, Nicosia (Cyprus) (b) 1,86 (c) G (d) APONA Anagyias (e) Doxa Katokopias, APONA Anagyias, Oly. Lympion, Alki Oroklini, Ethnikos Assias, Élitei Project, Nea Salamis, Ethnikos Assias

*** Konstantyn - Jakub Konstantyn (a) 26/06/2002, Kraków (Poland) (b) 1,75 (c) F - left winger (d) Korona Kielce (e) Korona Kielce II

*** Konte - Amdy Konte (Amdy Lamine Konte) (a) 13/07/1997, ¿? (Senegal) (b) - (c) D (d) FC Mondercange (e) RFCU Luxembourg, Thonon Évian, Génération Foot

*** Konté - Boubacar Konté (Aboubacar Dit Boubou Konté) (a) 02/03/2001, ¿? (Mali) (b) 1,75 (c) F - left winger (d) Fredrikstad FK (e) Sarpsborg 08, Nacional, Sarpsborg 08, Jerv, Sarpsborg 08, Nordsjælland, Sarpsborg 08, Etoiles Mandé

*** Kontogiannis - Vangelis Kontogiannis (Βαγγέλης Κοντογιάννης) (a) 09/01/2002, ¿? (Greece) (b) 1,88 (c) G (d) Panetolikos GFS (e) Panagriniakos, Panetolikos, Diagoras, Panetolikos

*** Kontonikos - Vasilios Kontonikos (Βασίλειος Κοντονίκος) (a) 11/10/2005, ¿? (Greece) (b) - (c) F - center forward (d) PAS Lamia 1964 (e) -

*** Kontsedailov - Arseniy Kontsedailov (Концедайлов Арсений Владимирович) (a) 15/07/1997, Kaliningrad (Russia) (b) 1,73 (c) M - attacking midfielder (d) Arsenal Dzerzhinsk (e) Dynamo Brest, FK Slutsk, DYuSSh-2 Rechitsa, Oshmyany-BDUFK, Energetik-BGU, Oshmyany-BDUFK, FK Minsk, FK Minsk II

*** Kontsevoy - Artem Kontsevoy (Концевой Артём Александрович) (a) 26/08/1999, Mogilev (Belarus) (b) 1,82 (c) F - left winger (d) BATE Borisov (e) Dinamo Minsk, Rukh, Banik Ostrava, Rukh, Dnyapro Mogilev, Mezőkövesd, Dnyapro Mogilev, Dnepr Mogilev, Mogilev II

*** Kontsevoy - Sergey Kontsevoy (Концевой Сергей Владимирович) (a) 21/06/1986, Gomel (Soviet Union, now in Belarus) (b) 1,90 (c) D - central defense (d) Artem Kontsevoy (e) Dzerzhinsk, Naftan, FK Minsk, Isloch, Torpedo Zhodino, Gomel, Neftchi, Dinamo Minsk, Belshina, Dinamo Minsk, Gomel, Tobol Kostanay, Gomel, Torpedo Zhodino, Dinamo Minsk II, Savit, Dinamo Minsk II, Gomel, Dinamo Minsk II

*** Kontz - Jeff Kontz (a) 15/07/2006, ¿? (Luxembourg) (b) - (c) D - central defense (d) FC Blo-Wäiss Medernach (e) -

*** Konyrov - Rysbek Konyrov (a) 22/07/2002, ¿? (Russia) (b) 1,86 (c) F - left winger (d) Akzhayik Uralsk (e) Akzhayik II

*** Koomson - Gilbert Koomson (a) 09/09/1994, Accra (Ghana) (b) 1,80 (c) F - right winger (d) Sandefjord Fotball (e) Bodø/Glimt, Aalesund, Bodø/Glimt, Kasimpasa, Brann, Sogndal, BEC Tero Sasana, Sogndal, BEC Tero Sasana, Samutsongkhram, BEC Tero Sasana

*** Koopmeiners - Peer Koopmeiners (a) 04/05/2000, Amsterdam (Netherlands) (b) 1,86 (c) M - pivot (d) Almere City FC (e) Almere City, AZ Alkmaar, Excelsior, AZ Alkmaar

*** Koopmeiners - Teun Koopmeiners (a) 28/02/1998, Castricum (Netherlands) (b) 1,83 (c) M - pivot (d) Atalanta de Bérgamo (e) AZ Alkmaar

*** Koorevaar - Joey Koorevaar (a) 22/02/2001, ¿? (Netherlands) (b) - (c) G (d) - (e) FC Dordrecht

*** Kopacek - Jakub Kopacek (Jakub Kopáček) (a) 23/01/2002, ¿? (Czech Rep.) (b) 1,73 (c) M - central midfielder (d) SK Slavia Praga B (e) -

*** Kopacz - Bartosz Kopacz (a) 21/05/1992, Jastrzębie Zdrój (Poland) (b) 1,88 (c) D - central defense (d) Zagłębie Lubin (e) Lechia Gdánsk, Zagłębie, Górnik Zabrze, Nieciecza, Górnik Zabrze, Zawisza, Górnik Zabrze, Ruch Radzionków, Górnik Zabrze, GKS Jastrzebie

*** Kopaliani - Soso Kopaliani (სოსო კოპალიანი) (a) 07/07/2006, Kutaisi (Georgia) (b) 1,91 (c) G (d) FC Locomotive Tbilisi (e) -

*** Kopas - Adam Kopas (a) 16/08/1999, Žilina (Slovakia) (b) 1,90 (c) D - central defense (d) MSK Zilina (e) MSK Zilina B

*** Kopasek - Samuel Kopasek (Samuel Kopásek) (a) 22/05/2003, Čadca (Slovakia) (b) 1,75 (c) D - right back (d) MSK Zilina B (e) -

*** Kopczynski - Michal Kopczynski (Michał Kopczyński) (a) 15/06/1992, Zamość (Poland) (b) 1,80 (c) M - pivot (d) Warta Poznań (e) Arka Gdynia, Legia Warszawa, Wellington P., Legia Warszawa, Wigry Suwalki, Legia Warszawa, Legia II

*** Koperski - Filip Koperski (a) 24/02/2004, Gdańsk (Poland) (b) 1,87 (c) D - right back (d) KS Lechia Gdańsk (e) Lechia II

*** Kopic - Jan Kopic (Jan Kopic) (a) 04/06/1990, Humpolec (Czechoslovakia, now in Czech Rep.) (b) 1,80 (c) M - left midfielder (d) FC Viktoria Plzen (e) Jablonec, Jihlava, Caslav, Jihlava

*** Kopitovic - Boris Kopitovic (Борис Копитовић) (a) 17/09/1994, Podgorica (RF Yugoslavia, Montenegro) (b) 1,85 (c) D - central defense (d) FK Javor-Matis Ivanjica (e) Vojvodina, BATE Borisov, Čukarički, FK Mladost, Hapoel Acre, Buducnost Podgorica

*** Kopljar - Kristijan Kopljar (a) 07/07/2001, Zagreb (Croatia) (b) - (c) F - left winger (d) NK Sesvete (e) NK Istra, NK Vrapce, Hrv Dragovoljac, NK Ponikve

*** Kopp - Florian Kopp (a) 15/05/2001, ¿? (Austria) (b) 1,86 (c) D - central defense (d) SV Stripfing (e) SV Stripfing, Austria Viena, Young Violets, FC Wacker, FC Wacker II

*** Kopplin - Björn Kopplin (a) 07/01/1989, Berlin (East Germany, now in Germany) (b) 1,84 (c) D - right back (d) Randers FC (e) Brøndby IF, Hobro IK, Preussen Münster, Union Berlin, VfL Bochum, FC Bayern II

*** Koprivec - Jan Koprivec (a) 15/07/1988, Koper (Yugoslavia, now in Slovenia) (b) 1,87 (c) G (d) FC Koper (e) Tabor Sezana, Kilmarnock FC, Pafos FC, Anorthosis, Perugia, Udinese, Bari, Udinese, Gallipoli, Udinese, Cagliari, Koper

*** Koprivnik - Nace Koprivnik (a) 27/06/1999, Celje (Slovenia) (b) 1,83 (c) F - right winger (d) NK Dekani (e) HNK Sibenik, Rudar Velenje

*** Kopyna - Yuriy Kopyna (Копина Юрій Ярославович) (a) 04/07/1996, Pustomyty, Lviv Oblast (Ukraine) (b) 1,81 (c) M - pivot (d) FK Oleksandriya (e) Rukh Lviv, PFC Lviv, Metalist II

*** Korablin - Tymur Korablin (Кораблін Тимур Михайлович) (a) 02/01/2002, Zaporizhya (Ukraine) (b) 1,74 (c) M - right midfielder (d) FK Minaj (e) Kryvbas, OSDYuSShOR Zaporizhya, MFK Metalurg 2

*** Korac - Seid Korac (Seid Korač) (a) 20/10/2001, Niederkorn (Luxembourg) (b) 1,91 (c) D - central defense (d) Degerfors IF (e) Esbjerg fB, Akritas Chlor., Esbjerg fB, Nurernberg II, FC Rodange 91

*** Korac - Zarko Korac (Жарко Кораћ) (a) 11/06/1987, Bijelo Polje (Yugoslavia, now in Montenegro) (b) 1,87 (c) F - center forward (d) Jedinstvo Bijelo Polje (e) Hapoel Afula, UiTM FC, Sisaket FC, Kuantan FA, OFK Grbalj, Hapoel Haifa, B. Jerusalem, Zeta Golubovac, Hapoel Haifa, Zeta Golubovac, FC Sheriff, Zeta Golubovac, Vojvodina, Zeta Golubovac

*** Koran - David Koran (David Kořán) (a) 22/05/2003, ¿? (Czech Rep.) (b) - (c) G (d) FK Mlada Boleslav B (e) FK Zbuzany

*** Korca - Amet Korca (Amet Ylber Korça) (a) 16/09/2000, Arlington, Texas (United States) (b) 1,91 (c) D - central defense (d) FC Dallas (e) HNK Gorica, NK Dubrava ZG, Din. Zagreb II, NK Dubrava ZG, Solar SC

*** Kordic - Marko Kordic (Marko Kordić) (a) 22/02/1995, Kotor (RF Yugoslavia, now in Montenegro) (b) 1,90 (c) G (d) OFK Petrovac (e) FK Iskra, Napredak, FK Bokelj, OFK Grbalj, Vojvodina, Backa, Vojvodina

*** Kordic - Saleta Kordic (Šaleta Kordić) (a) 19/04/1993, Kotor (RF Yugoslavia, now in Montenegro) (b) 1,90 (c) F - center forward (d) - (e) Zeleznicar Pancevo, Leotar Trebinje, Akzhayik, Buducnost Podgorica, Chaika Pes., FK Podgorica, Sutjeska Niksic, OFK Grbalj, Zeta Golubovac, Vojvodina, Sutjeska Niksic, Vojvodina, FK BSK Borča, Euromilk GL, OFK Grbalj, Vojvodina, RFK Novi Sad, Vojvodina, FK Mladost, Vojvodina, Vojvodina II

*** Kordic - Stefan Kordic (a) 14/02/2005, ¿? (Austria) (b) - (c) F - center forward (d) SV Ried II (e) SV Kapfenberg

*** Korenica - Meriton Korenica (a) 15/12/1996, Rahovec (RF Yugoslavia, now in Kosovo) (b) 1,75 (c) F - right winger (d) FC Ballkani (e) FC Prishtina, KF Liria, Metalurg Skopje

*** Korine - Roy Korine (קורין רוי) (a) 10/09/2002, Herzliya (Israel) (b) 1,62 (c) F - right winger (d) Maccabi Netanya (e) H. Ramat Gan, Maccabi Netanya

*** Koripadze - Giorgi Koripadze (გიორგი კორიფაძე) (a) 03/10/1989, ¿? (Georgia) (b) 1,80 (c) D - right back (d) Sioni Bolnisi (e) FC Samtredia, Sioni Bolnisi, Chikhura, FC Dila, Chikhura, WIT Georgia

*** Korkishko - Dmytro Korkishko (Коркішко Дмитро Юрійович) (a) 04/05/1990, Cherkasy (Soviet Union, now in Ukraine) (b) 1,75 (c) F - left winger (d) - (e) Metalist, Aktobe, Chornomorets, SK Dnipro-1, Hatayspor, Giresunspor, Chornomorets, FK Poltava, FK Minsk, Dynamo 2 Kyiv, Dinamo Kiev II, Arsenal Kyiv, Dinamo Kiev II, Dynamo 2 Kyiv

*** Korkmaz - Nurettin Korkmaz (a) 27/06/2002, Kayseri (Turkey) (b) 1,78 (c) F - left winger (d) Kayserispor (e) Trofense, Kayserispor

*** Korkodym - Arseniy Korkodym (Коркодим Арсеній Юрійович) (a) 03/10/2002, Kyiv (Ukraine) (b) 1,94 (c) G (d) NK Veres Rivne (e) Volyn Lutsk, Volyn 2 Lutsk

*** Kornev - Nikita Kornev (Корнев Никита) (a) 21/02/2002, ¿? (Kazakhstan) (b) 1,88 (c) G (d) SD Family Nur-Sultan (e) Astana-M

*** Kornezos - Georgios Kornezos (Γεώργιος Κορνέζος) (a) 23/02/1998, Athen (Greece) (b) 1,91 (c) D - central defense (d) PAS Lamia 1964 (e) AEK Athína B, AEK Athína, Ast. Vlachioti, AEK Athína, Ionikos Nikeas, AEK Athína, Volos NPS, AEK Athína, Ethnikos Pireo, Ionikos Nikeas, AE Sparti, Ast. Vlachioti

*** Kornienko - Viktor Kornienko (Корнієнко Віктор Валерійович) (a) 14/02/1999, Poltava (Ukraine) (b) 1,75 (c) D - left back (d) Shakhtar Donetsk (e) Shakhtar II, FK Mariupol, Shakhtar II

*** Kornvig - Emil Kornvig (Emil Nestved Kornvig) (a) 28/04/2000, Søborg (Denmark) (b) 1,87 (c) M - central midfielder (d) AS Cittadella (e) Spezia, Cosenza, Spezia, SønderjyskE, Spezia, Lyngby BK

*** Kornyushin - Daniil Kornyushin (Корнюшин Даниил Александрович) (a) 08/10/2001, Stavropol (Russia) (b) 1,87 (c) D - right back (d) FC Pari Nizhniy Novgorod (e) Krasnodar-2, Krasnodar 3, Volgar, Krasnodar 3, Krasnodar II

*** Korobenko - Andriy Korobenko (Коробенко Андрій Вячеславович) (a) 28/05/1997, Chernigiv (Ukraine) (b) 1,84 (c) M - central midfielder (d) Valmiera FC (e) Ingulets, Rukh Lviv, Shakhtar II, FK Mariupol, Shakhtar II, Chornomorets II, Shakhtar II

*** Korolev - Georgiy Korolev (Королёв Георгий Михайлович) (a) 22/08/2003, ¿? (Russia) (b) 1,96 (c) G (d) Zenit 2 St. Petersburg (e) -

*** Koroljov - Daniil Koroljov (a) 11/12/1999, Tallinn (Estonia) (b) 1,83 (c) G (d) - (e) Kalev, Kalev III, Kalev Tallinn II

*** Koroma - Osman Koroma (a) 18/07/2002, Freetown (Sierra Leona) (b) 1,90 (c) F - center forward (d) Aris Limassol (e) Olympiakos N., Aris Limassol, Omonia Psevda

*** Koroma - Raphael Koroma (a) 21/09/2000, ¿? (Sierra Leona) (b) 1,90 (c) D - central defense (d) - (e) FK Turan, FC Saksan, FC Johansen

*** Koromias - Konstantinos Koromias (Κωνσταντίνος Κορομίας) (a) 31/03/2004, Nicosia (Cyprus) (b) 1,80 (c) D - central defense (d) - (e) APOEL FC,

*** Körös - Matus Körös (Matúš Köröš) (a) 17/11/2003, ¿? (Slovakia) (b) - (c) M (d) MFK Dukla Banska Bystrica (e) -

*** Korosec - Alen Korosec (Alen Korošec) (a) 17/11/2001, ¿? (Slovenia) (b) 1,82 (c) M - central midfielder (d) NK Rogaska (e) Tabor Sezana, NK Nafta 1903

*** Korotkovs - Ilja Korotkovs (Iļja Korotkovs) (a) 24/05/2000, Riga (Latvia) (b) 1,92 (c) D - central defense (d) FK Auda (e) Riga, Auda, Riga, Metta, FS Metta II

*** Korre - Uku Korre (Uku Kõrre) (a) 19/04/2000, Tartu (Estonia) (b) - (c) D - central defense (d) Pärnu JK Vaprus (e) Pärnu JK

*** Korsia - Omer Korsia (Omer Yoel Corsia Ben Ami - עמי בן ליין יואל עומר) (a) 07/10/2002, Holon (Israel) (b) 1,81 (c) D - central defense (d) Beitar Jerusalem (e) EN Paralimniou, H. Petah Tikva, Ramat haSharon

*** Korun - Uros Korun (Uroš Korun) (a) 25/05/1987, Celje (Yugoslavia, now in Slovenia) (b) 1,88 (c) D - central defense (d) NK Radomlje (e) Olimpija, Piast Gliwice, Domžale, Rudar Velenje, Publikum Celje, ND Dravinja, Publikum Celje

*** Korytskyi - Yegor Korytskyi (Корицький Єгор Сергійович) (a) 09/01/2001, Krasnyi Lyman, Donetsk Oblast (Ukraine) (b) 1,75 (c) F - right winger (d) NSÍ Runavík (e) FSK Mariupol

*** Korzeniecki - Nikolas Korzeniecki (a) 26/09/2001, Vancouver (Canada) (b) 1,86 (c) M - pivot (d) Chrobry Glogow (e) Warta Poznań, Radomiak, Z. Sosnowiec, Sosnowiec II, Chrobry II, AP Śląsk

*** Korzun - Nikita Korzun (a) 06/03/1995, Babiy Les (Belarus) (b) 1,74 (d) Shakhter Soligorsk (e) Dinamo Kyïv, Vilafranquense, Dinamo Kyïv, Al-Fateh, Dinamo Kyïv, Dinamo Minsk, Dinamo Kyïv, Dinamo Minsk, Dinamo Minsk II

*** Kos - Mirko Kos (a) 12/04/1997, Mürzzuschlag (Austria) (b) 1,83 (c) G (d) FK Austria Viena (e) Austria Wien Reserves, NWM KSV

*** Kos - Nemanja Kos (Немања Кос) (a) 30/11/2002, Smederevo (RF Yugoslavia, now in Serbia) (b) 1,85 (c) F - right winger (d) FK Mladost Lucani (e) Mihajlovac, Mladost, Pozarevac, Mladost

*** Kosa - Sebastian Kosa (Sebastián Kóša) (a) 13/09/2003, Nové Zámky (Slovakia) (b) 1,91 (c) D - central defense (d) Spartak Trnava (e) -

*** Kosar - Jakub Kosar (Jakub Kosař) (a) 20/07/2001, ¿? (Czech Rep.) (b) - (c) M (d) FC Hradec Kralove B (e) -

*** Koscelnik - Martin Koscelnik (Martin Koscelník) (a) 02/03/1995, Vranov nad Topľou (Slovakia) (b) 1,80 (c) D - right back (d) SK Rapid Wien (e) Slovan Liberec, Michalovce

*** Koscielny - Kamil Koscielny (Kamil Kościelny) (a) 04/08/1991, Mielec (Poland) (b) 1,85 (c) D - central defense (d) Stal Rzeszow (e) Warta Poznań, P. Niepolomice, Stal Mielec, Rakow, Wigry Suwalki, Radomiak, Siarka T., Stal Mielec, Resovia, Stal Mielec

*** Köse - Berat Köse (a) 26/10/1999, ¿? (Finland) (b) 1,76 (c) M - attacking midfielder (d) Järvenpään Palloseura (e) FC Lahti, JäPS, FC Lahti, Reipas Lahti

*** Köse - Onuray Köse (a) 11/02/1996, Kotka (Finland) (b) 1,72 (c) M - central midfielder (d) FC Reipas Lahti (e) Darica GB, Reipas Lahti, Mikkelin, Yesil Bursa, FC Kuusysi, FC Lahti, Mikkelin, FC Lahti

*** Kosidis - Michalis Kosidis (Μιχάλης Κοσίδης) (a) 09/02/2002, Thessaloniki (Greece) (b) 1,91 (c) F - center forward (d) VVV-Venlo (e) VVV-Venlo, AEK Athína B, AEK Athína

*** Koskela - Miika Koskela (a) 12/07/2003, Oulu (Finland) (b) 1,95 (c) D - central defense (d) Tromsø IL (e) AC Oulu, OLS

*** Koski - Ville Koski (a) 27/01/2002, Tuusula (Finland) (b) 1,85 (c) D - central defense (d) FC Honka (e) FC Honka II, Pallokerho

*** Koskinen - Otso Koskinen (a) 01/01/2003, ¿? (Finland) (b) 1,77 (c) M - attacking midfielder (d) FC Honka (e) VJS/Akatemia

*** Koskipalo - Daniel Koskipalo (a) 03/05/2003, Hartola (Finland) (b) 1,77 (c) D - right back (d) FC Lahti (e) -

*** Koskor - Tristan Koskor (a) 28/11/1995, Tartu (Estonia) (b) 1,91 (c) F - center forward (d) JK Trans Narva (e) Pegia 2014, FC Flora, JK Tammeka, Fylkir, JK Tammeka, Paide, JK Tammeka, JK Luunja, JK Tammeka II, JK Luunja, JK Tammeka II

*** Kosmas - Loizos Kosmas (Λοΐζος Κοσμάς) (a) 25/01/1995, Famagusta (Cyprus) (b) 1,77 (c) M - central midfielder (d) Enosis Neon Paralimniou (e) -

*** Kosoric - Aleksandar Kosoric (Aleksandar Kosorić) (a) 30/01/1987, Pale (Yugoslavia, now in Bosnia and Herzegovina) (b) 1,91 (c) D - central defense (d) FK Zeljeznicar Sarajevo (e) Balzan FC, Spartaks, Radnik Bijelj., Zeljeznicar, Radnicki Niš, Erbil SC, Radnicki 1923, Rad Beograd, FK Partizan, Slavija S.

*** Kosovic - Nebojsa Kosovic (Небојша Косовић ; Nebojša Kosović) (a) 24/02/1995, Nikšić (RF Yugoslavia, now in Montenegro) (b) 1,77 (c) M - central midfielder (d) Meizhou Hakka (e) Kairat Almaty, FK Partizan, Standard Liège, Újpest FC, Standard Liège, Újpest FC, Standard Liège, Vojvodina

*** Kosovshchuk - Oleksandr Kosovshchuk (a) 07/03/2005, ¿? (Ukraine) (b) 1,75 (c) F - right winger (d) Budapest Honvéd II-MFA (e) Zalaegerszeg II

*** Kossounou - Odilon Kossounou (Odilon Kossounou Kouakou) (a) 04/01/2001, Abidjan (Ivory Coast) (b) 1,91 (c) D - central defense (d) Bayer 04 Leverkusen (e) KV Brugge, Hammarby IF, ASEC Mimosas

*** Kostadinov - Dimitar Kostadinov (Димитър Мирославов Костадинов) (a) 14/08/1999, Burgas (Bulgaria) (b) 1,80 (c) M - attacking midfielder (d) Septemvri Sofia (e) Levski Sofia, Septemvri Sofia, Tsarsko Selo, Septemvri Sofia, Neftochimik, Septemvri Sofia, DIT Sofia

*** Kostadinov - Georgi Kostadinov (Георги Георгиев Костадинов) (a) 07/09/1990, Tsarevo (Bulgaria) (b) 1,84 (c) M - pivot (d) APOEL FC (e) Arsenal Tula, Maccabi Haifa, Levski Sofia, Beroe, Ludogorets, Pomorie, Neftochimik

*** Kostadinov - Neven Kostadinov (Невен Костадинов) (a) 16/04/2006, Kavadarci (North Macedonia) (b) 1,87 (c) M - pivot (d) Tikves Kavadarci (e) -
*** Kostadinov - Tihomir Kostadinov (Тихомир Костадинов) (a) 04/03/1996, Valandovo (North Macedonia) (b) 1,79 (c) M - attacking midfielder (d) Piast Gliwice (e) Ružomberok, Zlaté Moravce, Banska Bystrica, Teteks Tetovo, Moravac
*** Kostadinovic - Zivko Kostadinovic (Živko Kostadinović) (a) 10/04/1992, Modriča (Bosnia and Herzegovina) (b) 1,96 (c) G (d) FC Zürich (e) FC Wil 1900, Le Mont LS, FC Schaffhausen, SC YF Juventus, FC Schaffhausen, FC Vaduz, Stade Nyonnais
*** Kostal - Martin Kostal (Martin Košťál) (a) 23/02/1996, Nové Zámky (Slovakia) (b) 1,79 (c) F - left winger (d) - (e) Sandecja, Sigma Olomouc, SKF Sered, Jagiellonia, FK Senica, Jagiellonia, Wisla Kraków, Spartak Trnava
*** Kostandyan - Aram Kostandyan (Արամ Կոստանդյան) (a) 20/06/1989, ¿? (Armenia) (b) - (c) D - central defense (d) Lernayin Artsakh Goris (e) -
*** Kosteas - Georgios Kosteas (Γεώργιος Κωστέας) (a) 16/04/2003, ¿? (Greece) (b) - (c) F - center forward (d) Asteras Tripolis (e) -
*** Köstenbauer - Marcel Köstenbauer (a) 26/08/2001, ¿? (Austria) (b) 1,89 (c) G (d) SK Austria Klagenfurt (e) Viktoria Berlin, Austria Klagenfurt, FC Admira II, Admira Wacker, Juniors OÖ
*** Kostevych - Volodymyr Kostevych (Костевич Володимир Євгенович) (a) 23/10/1992, Derevnya, Lviv Oblast (Ukraine) (b) 1,74 (c) M - left midfielder (d) Warta Poznań (e) Dinamo Kyїv, Rukh Lviv, Dinamo Kyїv, Lech Poznan, Karpaty, Karpaty II, Karpaty 2, UFK Lviv
*** Kostic - Filip Kostic (Филип Костић) (a) 01/11/1992, Kragujevac (Yugoslavia, now in Serbia) (b) 1,84 (c) M - left midfielder (d) Juventus de Turín (e) Eintracht, SV Hamburg, Eintracht, SV Hamburg, VfB Stuttgart, FC Groningen, Radnicki 1923
*** Kostic - Ivan Kostic (Иван Костић) (a) 24/10/1995, Knjaževac (RF Yugoslavia, now in Serbia) (b) 1,91 (c) G (d) Volos NPS (e) EN Paralimniou, Mladost, Radnik, Metalac, Radnicki Pirot, FK Timocanin
*** Kostis - Ilias Kostis (Ηλίας Κωστής) (a) 27/02/2003, Thessaloniki (Greece) (b) 1,88 (c) D - central defense (d) Atlético de Madrid B (e) -
*** Kostka - Dominik Kostka (a) 04/05/1996, ¿? (Czech Rep.) (b) 1,77 (c) M - right midfielder (d) FK Mlada Boleslav (e) Pardubice, Slovácko B, Gmünd, FK Zbuzany, Motorlet Praha, FK Dobrovice, Bohemians B
*** Kostka - Michael Kostka (Michał Kostka) (a) 13/12/2003, Hannover (Germany) (b) 1,83 (c) D - right back (d) Miedź Legnica (e) -
*** Köstl - Daniel Köstl (Daniel Köstl) (a) 23/05/1998, Praha (Czech Rep.) (b) 1,89 (c) D - central defense (d) Bohemians Praha 1905 (e) Sparta Praha B, Slovan Liberec, Sparta Praha B
*** Kostomarov - Nikita Kostomarov (Костомаров Никита Павлович) (a) 29/06/1999, Vitebsk (Belarus) (b) - (c) D - central defense (d) FK Vitebsk (e) Naftan, Vitebsk, Vitebsk II, Orsha, Vitebsk II, Naftan, Vitebsk II
*** Kostorz - Kacper Kostorz (Kacper Kostorz) (a) 21/08/1999, Cieszyn (Poland) (b) 1,91 (c) F - center forward (d) FC Den Bosch (e) FC Den Bosch, Pogon Szczecin, Korona Kielce, Pogon Szczecin, Legia Warszawa, Miedź Legnica, Legia Warszawa, Podbeskidzie, Legia Warszawa, Podbeskidzie, Podbeskidzie II, Piast Cieszyn
*** Kostov - Ilian Kostov (Илиан Илиев Костов) (a) 27/02/2005, Sandanski (Bulgaria) (b) 1,77 (c) D - central defense (d) Pirin Blagoevgrad (e) -
*** Kostov - Krasimir Kostov (Красимир Иванов Костов) (a) 11/02/1995, Petrich (Bulgaria) (b) 1,86 (c) G (d) Botev Vratsa (e) Pirin, Pirin Razlog

*** Kostov - Stanislav Kostov (Станислав Йорданов Костов) (a) 02/10/1991, Blagoevgrad (Bulgaria) (b) 1,83 (c) F - center forward (d) Pirin Blagoevgrad (e) Lokomotiv Sofia, Pirin, Olympiakos N., Levski Sofia, Pirin, Beroe, Botev Plovdiv, CSKA Sofia, Pirin

*** Kostov - Stefan Kostov (Стефан Костов) (a) 31/10/1996, Stip (North Macedonia) (b) 1,87 (c) D - central defense (d) Pelister Bitola (e) Tikves, AP Brera, Renova, Bregalnica Stip

*** Kostrna - Kristian Kostrna (Kristián Koštrna) (a) 15/12/1993, Trnava (Slovakia) (b) 1,78 (c) D - right back (d) Spartak Trnava (e) FC Dinamo, Dunajska Streda, Pirin, SC/ESV Parndorf, Slavoj Boleraz

*** Kostusev - Yaroslav Kostusev (Костусев Ярослав Сергеевич) (a) 21/03/2004, ¿? (Belarus) (b) - (c) D - left back (d) FK Ostrovets (e) Mogilev II, Dnepr-Yuni Mogilev

*** Kostyk - Orest Kostyk (Костик Орест Михайлович) (a) 16/04/1999, Zarvanytsya, Lviv Oblast (Ukraine) (b) 1,89 (c) G (d) DFK Dainava Alytus (e) Metalist, PFK Lviv, Jonava, PFK Lviv, PFK Lviv II, Nyva Ternopil, Veres Rivne II, Sokil Zolochiv, Opir Lviv

*** Kostyshyn - Denys Kostyshyn (Костишин Денис Русланович) (a) 31/08/1997, Khmelnytskyi (Ukraine) (b) 1,79 (c) M - attacking midfielder (d) El Paso Locomotive FC (e) FK Oleksandriya, Kolos Kovalivka, Dnipro, Dnipro II

*** Koszta - Márk Koszta (a) 26/09/1996, Miskolc (Hungary) (b) 1,86 (c) F - center forward (d) Maccabi Bnei Reineh (e) M. Bnei Reineh, Torpedo Moskva, Ulsan Hyundai, Zalaegerszeg, Újpest FC, Mezőkövesd, Honvéd, Honvéd II, Kisvárda, Honvéd II

*** Kotarski - Dominik Kotarski (a) 10/02/2000, Zabok (Croatia) (b) 1,89 (c) G (d) PAOK Thessaloniki (e) HNK Gorica, Ajax, HNK Gorica, Ajax, Ajax B, NK Tondach

*** Kote - Kristi Kote (a) 26/09/1998, Korçë (Albania) (b) 1,74 (c) M - pivot (d) - (e) FK Bylis, FK Kukësi, FK Partizani, KF Liria

*** Kotenko - Artur Kotenko (a) 20/08/1981, Tallinn (Soviet Union, now in Estonia) (b) 1,86 (c) G (d) FC Zenit Tallinn (e) FCI Levadia, JK Trans Narva, Soligorsk, Dnepr Mogilev, FF Jaro, Ravan Baku, AE Pafos, Viking, Sandnes Ulf, Levadia, Maardu LM, Kaujahoen Karhu, Lantana, KSK Vigri

*** Kotev - Lachezar Kotev (Лъчезар Христов Котев) (a) 05/01/1998, Sofia (Bulgaria) (b) 1,85 (c) M - pivot (d) Arda Kardzhali (e) Arda Kardzhali, Khimki, Arda Kardzhali, Vitosha, Oborishte, Vitosha, Septemvri Sofia

*** Kotevski - Daniel Kotevski (Даниел Котевски) (a) 16/08/1999, Prilep (North Macedonia) (b) 1,85 (c) G (d) Pobeda Prilep (e) Ohrid Lihnidos, Pobeda Prilep

*** Kotlajic - Djordje Kotlajic (Ђорђе Котлајић) (a) 13/01/2004, ¿? (Serbia and Montenegro, now in Serbia) (b) - (c) F - left winger (d) FK Napredak Krusevac (e) -

*** Kotnik - Andrej Kotnik (a) 04/08/1995, Nova Gorica (Slovenia) (b) 1,89 (c) M - attacking midfielder (d) Meizhou Hakka (e) Koper, NK Maribor, ND Gorica, Formentera, ND Gorica, Crotone, ND Gorica

*** Kotnik - Matic Kotnik (a) 23/07/1990, Slovenj Gradec (Yugoslavia, now in Slovenia) (b) 1,90 (c) G (d) - (e) Volos NPS, Brescia, Panionios, NK Celje, ND Dravinja, Publikum Celje, NK Dravograd

*** Kotobelli - Blerim Kotobelli (a) 10/08/1992, Skrapar (Albania) (b) 1,78 (c) D - left back (d) KF Teuta (e) FK Kukësi, Flamurtari FC, FK Partizani, KF Teuta, KF Tirana, O. Tirana, AE Larisa

*** Kotora - Ivan Kotora (a) 27/06/1991, Tlmače (Czechoslovakia, now in Slovakia) (b) 1,78 (c) M - right midfielder (d) Tatran Liptovsky Mikulas (e) Oravske Ves., Liptovsky Mik., Oravske Ves., Liptovsky Mik., L. Hradok, Michalovce, Ružomberok

*** Kotov - Konstantin Kotov (Котов Константин Сергеевич) (a) 25/06/1998, St. Petersburg (Russia) (b) 1,75 (c) M - pivot (d) FK Slutsk (e) FK Ryazan, Smolevichi, Nosta, Energia V. Luki, Zenit St. Peterburg II

*** Kotsiras - Giannis Kotsiras (Γιάννης Κώτσιρας) (a) 16/12/1992, Megalopoli (Greece) (b) 1,83 (c) D - right back (d) Panathinaikos FC (e) Asteras Tripoli, Panarkadikos, AO Falesias, D. Megalopolis

*** Kotsonis - Fotis Kotsonis (Φώτης Κοτσώνης) (a) 10/02/2003, Deryneia (Cyprus) (b) 1,78 (c) D - right back (d) Enosis Neon Paralimniou (e) -

*** Kotsopoulos - Konstantinos Kotsopoulos (Κωνσταντίνος Κωτσόπουλος) (a) 17/02/1997, Veria (Greece) (b) 1,77 (c) F - center forward (d) IFK Mariehamn (e) Atromitos FC, Getafe CF B, Atromitos FC, FAS Naousa, Makrochori, Nireas Verias

*** Kotula - Juraj Kotula (a) 30/09/1995, Bratislava (Slovakia) (b) 1,83 (c) D - right back (d) MFK Ružomberok (e) Michalovce, Zbrojovka Brno, Slovan Bratislava, FK Senica, Slovan Bratislava, Zlaté Moravce, Slovan Bratislava, FK Senica, Slovan Bratislava

*** Kotzke - Jonatan Kotzke (a) 18/03/1990, Pinneberg (Germany) (b) 1,84 (c) M - pivot (d) - (e) Górnik Zabrze, FC Ingolstadt, Ingolstadt II, SC Teutonia, VfR Aalen, Wehen Wiesbaden, Jahn Regensburg, 1860 München, Nurernberg II, 1.FC Nürnberg, Nurernberg II

*** Kouadio - Cedric Kouadio (Alain Cedric Herve Kouadio) (a) 19/05/1996, ¿? (Ivory Coast) (b) 1,83 (c) F - center forward (d) RFS (e) Daugavpils

*** Kouadio - Cedric Kouadio (Cedric Khaleb Kouadio) (a) 25/07/1997, Petit Badien (Ivory Coast) (b) 1,75 (c) F - center forward (d) Dynamo Brest (e) Neman Grodno, Shakhter K., FK Slutsk, Torpedo Minsk, FK Slutsk, Slovan Liberec B, ES Bingerville

*** Kouakou - Christian Kouakou (Onil Christian Kouakou) (a) 20/04/1995, ¿? (Sweden) (b) 1,81 (c) F - center forward (d) Kocaelispor (e) Sirius, IFK Göteborg, Brage, Nyköpings BIS, Brommapojkarna, AIK, Mjällby AIF, AIK, Akropolis IF, AIK

*** Kouakou - Kouadio Yann Kouakou (Kouadio Yann Marie Bernard Kouakou) (a) 17/08/1999, Treichville (Ivory Coast) (b) 1,88 (c) M - central midfielder (d) FCD LMM Montemiletto (e) Penya Encarnada, LZS Starowice, Red Star FC B, SD Huesca B

*** Kouame - Prince Isaac Kouame (a) 20/10/2000, ¿? (Sweden) (b) 1,85 (c) F - left winger (d) Brattvåg IL (e) Elfsborg, Skövde AIK, Elfsborg, Motala AIF, Elfsborg, GAIS, Elfsborg

*** Kouamé - Christian Kouamé (Christian Michael Kouamé Kouakou) (a) 06/12/1997, Abidjan (Ivory Coast) (b) 1,85 (c) F - center forward (d) Fiorentina (e) RSC Anderlecht, Fiorentina, Genoa, Fiorentina, Genoa, Cittadella, Prato, Cittadella, Prato, Prato

*** Kouamé - Rominigue Kouamé (Nguessan Rominigue Kouamé) (a) 17/12/1996, Lopou (Ivory Coast) (b) 1,77 (c) M - central midfielder (d) ESTAC Troyes (e) Lille, Troyes, Lille, Troyes, Lille, Cercle Brugge, Lille, Paris FC, Lille, LOSC Lille B, AS Real Bamako, JMG Bamako

*** Kouao - Denis Kouao (Denis Christ Damsen Kouao) (a) 23/11/1996, ¿? (Ivory Coast) (b) 1,79 (c) D - right back (d) Sliema Wanderers (e) Tabor Sezana, AFAD Djékanou, ASEC Mimosas

*** Kouassi - Eboue Kouassi (Jules Christ Kouassi Eboue) (a) 13/12/1997, Acocra-Dabou (Ivory Coast) (b) 1,85 (c) M - pivot (d) FC Arouca (e) KRC Genk, Arouca, KRC Genk, Celtic FC, KRC Genk, Celtic FC, Krasnodar, Krasnodar II, Krasnodar 3, Shirak Gyumri, Ivoire Academie

*** Kouassi - Jean Evrard Kouassi (a) 25/09/1994, N'Damien (Ivory Coast) (b) 1,80 (c) F - left winger (d) Zhejiang FC (e) Trabzonspor, Karagümrük, Trabzonspor, WH Yangtze, SH SIPG, SH Port Reserves, SH SIPG, Hajduk Split, Moossou FC
*** Kouassi - Yao Kouassi (Yao Assamoi Kouassi) (a) 12/08/2002, Abidjan (Ivory Coast) (b) 1,85 (c) M - attacking midfielder (d) - (e) FK Slutsk, FC Saksan
*** Kouassivi-Benissan - Kevin Kouassivi-Benissan (a) 25/01/1999, Helsinki (Finland) (b) 1,85 (c) D - right back (d) HJK Helsinki (e) FC Lahti, HJK Helsinki, FC Inter, HJK Helsinki, RoPS, HJK Helsinki, HJK Klubi 04
*** Kouba - Marek Kouba (a) 01/11/1998, ¿? (Czech Rep.) (b) - (c) G (d) SK Sokol Brozany (e) Bohemians 1905, Vysehrad, Bohemians 1905
*** Koubek - Matej Koubek (Matěj Koubek) (a) 10/01/2000, ¿? (Czech Rep.) (b) 1,88 (c) F - center forward (d) FC Hradec Kralove (e) Bohemians 1905, Usti nad Labem, Bohemians 1905, Jihlava, Bohemians 1905
*** Koubek - Tomas Koubek (Tomáš Koubek) (a) 26/08/1992, Hradec Králové (Czechoslovakia, now in Czech Rep.) (b) 1,97 (c) G (d) FC Augsburg (e) Stade Rennes, Sparta Praha, Slovan Liberec, Sparta Praha, Hradec Kralove
*** Koubemba - Kevin Koubemba (a) 23/03/1993, Coulommiers (France) (b) 1,92 (c) F - center forward (d) - (e) FC Arges, Chornomorets, Kuala Lumpur, KF Teuta, Sabah FK, FK Sabail, Bourg-en-Bresse, CSKA-Sofia, Sint-Truiden, Lille, Stade Brestois, Lille, LOSC Lille B, Amiens SC, Amiens SC B
*** Koudossou - Henri Koudossou (a) 03/09/1999, München (Germany) (b) 1,80 (c) D - right back (d) ADO Den Haag (e) ADO Den Haag, FC Augsburg, Austria Lustenau, FC Augsburg, FC Augsburg II, SV Pullach
*** Koudou - Thérence Koudou (Thérence Ange Koudou) (a) 13/12/2004, Livry-Gargan (France) (b) 1,78 (c) D - right back (d) Stade Reims B (e) -
*** Kougbenya - Didier Kougbenya (a) 12/11/1995, Kpalimé (Togo) (b) - (c) F - left winger (d) - (e) FC Dila, Hapoel Hadera, Maccabi Netanya, FC Dila, Maccabi Netanya, I. Kiryat Gat, FC Ashdod, Beitar TA Ramla
*** Koukola - Tomas Koukola (Tomáš Koukola) (a) 16/02/2002, ¿? (Czech Rep.) (b) - (c) D - left back (d) FK Pardubice B (e) Usti nad Orlici
*** Koulibaly - Kalidou Koulibaly (Kalidou Koulibaly) (a) 20/06/1991, Saint-Dié-des-Vosges (France) (b) 1,86 (c) D - central defense (d) Al-Hilal SFC (e) Chelsea, Napoli, KRC Genk, FC Metz, FC Metz B, SR Saint-Dié
*** Koulierakis - Konstantinos Koulierakis (Κωνσταντίνος Κουλιεράκης) (a) 28/11/2003, Chania (Greece) (b) 1,88 (c) D - central defense (d) PAOK Thessaloniki (e) PAOK B
*** Koulis - Serafim Koulis (Σεραφείμ Κούλης) (a) 16/10/2003, Athina (Greece) (b) 1,89 (c) G (d) Enosis Neon Paralimniou (e) -
*** Koulouris - Efthymios Koulouris (a) 06/03/1996, Skydra (Greece) (b) 1,86 (d) Pogon Szczecin (e) LASK, Alanyaspor, LASK, Atromitos FC, Toulouse, PAOK, Atromitos FC, PAOK, Anorthosis, PAOK
*** Koumetio - Billy Koumetio (Billy Dawson Koumetio) (a) 14/11/2002, Villeurbanne (France) (b) 1,95 (c) D - central defense (d) - (e) Austria Viena
*** Koumouris - Michalis Koumouris (Μιχάλης Κουμουρής) (a) 31/10/1994, Mathiatis (Cyprus) (b) 1,78 (c) F - right winger (d) Nea Salamis (e) Othellos Athien, Chalkanoras, Adonis Id.
*** Koundé - Jules Koundé (Jules Olivier Kounde) (a) 12/11/1998, Paris (France) (b) 1,80 (c) D - central defense (d) FC Barcelona (e) Sevilla FC, Girondins Bordeaux, Girondins Bordeaux B
*** Koupepidis - Ioannis Koupepidis (Ιωάννης Κουπεπίδης) (a) 01/06/2005, Nicosia (Cyprus) (b) 1,82 (c) G (d) APOEL FC (e) -

*** Kourbelis - Dimitrios Kourbelis (Δημήτριος Κουρμπέλης) (a) 02/11/1993, Tripoli (Greece) (b) 1,81 (c) M - pivot (d) Trabzonspor (e) Panathinaikos, Asteras Tripoli
*** Kouros - Alexandros Kouros (Αλέξανδρος Κούρος, Aleksandër Kuro) (a) 21/08/1993, Poliçan (Albania) (b) 1,84 (c) D - left back (d) Floriana FC (e) KF Teuta, Doxa Katokopias, PAEEK Kyrenia, KF Teuta, AOK Kerkyra, Apollon Smyrnis, Iraklis, Atromitos FC, Panionios
*** Kous - Ziga Kous (Žiga Kous) (a) 27/10/1992, Murska Sobota (Slovenia) (b) 1,78 (c) M - right midfielder (d) NS Mura (e) NK Celje, Domžale, NS Mura, Domžale, NS Mura
*** Kousal - Jakub Kousal (a) 06/09/2002, Štěchovice (Czech Rep.) (b) - (c) M - attacking midfielder (d) MFK Skalica (e) Ceske Budejovice B, Skalica, Ceske Budejovice B
*** Kousoulos - Ioannis Kousoulos (Ιωάννης Κούσουλος) (a) 14/06/1996, Limassol (Cyprus) (b) 1,82 (c) M - pivot (d) Omonia Nicosia (e) Nea Salamis
*** Koussa - Mehdi Koussa (a) 07/02/2005, ¿? (France) (b) - (c) M (d) - (e) Racing FC Union Luxembourg
*** Kouter - Nino Kouter (a) 19/12/1993, Murska Sobota (Slovenia) (b) 1,70 (c) M - central midfielder (d) NK Celje (e) Manisa FK, NS Mura, Bad Radkersburg, Verzej, DNŠ Zavrč, NS Mura, NK Carda, NS Mura
*** Koutris - Leonardo Koutris (Λεονάρντο Πάμπλο Κούτρης) (a) 23/07/1995, Ribeirão Preto (Brazil) (b) 1,70 (c) D - left back (d) Pogon Szczecin (e) Olympiakos, Fortuna Düsseldorf, Olympiakos, RCD Mallorca, Olympiakos, PAS Giannina, Ergotelis
*** Koutsias - Georgios Koutsias (Γεώργιος Κούτσιας) (a) 08/02/2004, Thessaloniki (Greece) (b) 1,80 (c) F - center forward (d) Chicago Fire FC (e) PAOK, Volos NPS, PAOK
*** Koutsou - Theodoros Koutsou (Θεόδωρος Κουτσού) (a) 19/04/2004, Frenaros (Cyprus) (b) 1,87 (c) G (d) Enosis Neon Paralimniou (e) Frenaros
*** Kouyaté - Cheikhou Kouyaté (a) 21/12/1989, Dakar (Senegal) (b) 1,89 (c) M - pivot (d) Nottingham Forest (e) Crystal Palace, West Ham Utd., RSC Anderlecht, KV Kortrijk, RSC Anderlecht, FC Brüssel, ASC Yeggo
*** Kouyaté - Kiki Kouyaté (Boubakar Kouyaté) (a) 15/04/1997, Bamako (Mali) (b) 1,92 (c) D - central defense (d) Montpellier HSC (e) FC Metz, Troyes, Sporting B, Kawkab Marrak., AS Bamako
*** Kovac - Adam Kovac (Adam Kováč) (a) 08/06/2000, Levice (Slovakia) (b) 1,91 (c) G (d) - (e) Olympiakos N., Ypsonas FC, Olympiakos N., THOI Lakatamias, Othellos Athien, FK Senica
*** Kovac - Stefan Kovac (Стефан Ковач) (a) 14/01/1999, Beograd (RF Yugoslavia, now in Serbia) (b) 1,85 (c) M - central midfielder (d) FK Čukarički (e) IMT Beograd
*** Kovacev - Milan Kovacev (Милан Ковачев) (a) 10/08/2005, Vrbas (Serbia and Montenegro, now in Serbia) (b) 1,78 (c) F - right winger (d) FK Vojvodina Novi Sad (e) -
*** Kovacevic - Adnan Kovacevic (Adnan Kovačević) (a) 09/09/1993, Kotor Varoš (Bosnia and Herzegovina) (b) 1,89 (c) D - central defense (d) Rakow Czestochowa (e) Ferencváros, Korona Kielce, FK Sarajevo, Travnik
*** Kovacevic - Beno Kovacevic (Benjamin Kovacevic) (a) 17/04/2002, ¿? (Sweden) (b) - (c) M (d) FC AS Hosingen (e) FC Wiltz 71
*** Kovacevic - Bojan Kovacevic (Бојан Ковачевић) (a) 22/05/2004, Užice (Serbia and Montenegro, now in Serbia) (b) 1,93 (c) D - central defense (d) FK Čukarički (e) -

*** Kovacevic - Bojan Kovacevic (Бојан Ковачевић) (a) 28/04/1996, Novi Sad (Yugoslavia, now in Serbia) (b) 1,86 (c) D - left back (d) Karmiotissa Pano Polemidion (e) Doxa Katokopias, Proleter, Kaspiy Aktau, Proleter, Vozdovac, FK Indjija

*** Kovacevic - Daniel Kovacevic (Danijel Kovačević) (a) 04/04/2002, ¿? (Bosnia and Herzegovina) (b) 1,86 (c) D - right back (d) FC Kufstein (e) Sloga Meridian, ZFC Meuselwitz, CZ Jena II

*** Kovacevic - Denis Kovacevic (Denis Kovačević) (a) 12/12/2002, Wien (Austria) (b) 1,81 (c) D - left back (d) - (e) Istanbulspor, Zeljeznicar, SV Kapfenberg, Traiskirchen

*** Kovacevic - Franko Kovacevic (Franko Kovačević) (a) 08/08/1999, Koprivnica (Croatia) (b) 1,86 (c) F - center forward (d) SV Wehen Wiesbaden (e) Domžale, Hoffenheim II, Pafos FC, Hoffenheim II, Cincinnati, Hoffenheim II, NK Rudes, Hajduk Split, NK Rudes, Hajduk Split, Hajduk Split II

*** Kovacevic - Ljubomir Kovacevic (Ljubomir Kovačević) (a) 23/02/2000, Herceg Novi (RF Yugoslavia, Montenegro) (b) 1,86 (c) F - center forward (d) Rudar Pljevlja (e) Radnik Bijelj., S. Novi Grad, Radnicki Srem, Rudar Pljevlja, Rad Beograd, OSK Igalo, OFK Grbalj

*** Kovacevic - Mladen Kovacevic (Младен Ковачевић) (a) 23/09/2002, ¿? (RF Yugoslavia, now in Serbia) (b) - (c) M - attacking midfielder (d) Jedinstvo Bijelo Polje (e) FK Brodarac

*** Kovacevic - Nikola Kovacevic (Никола Ковачевић) (a) 14/04/1994, Kragujevac (RF Yugoslavia, now in Montenegro) (b) 1,92 (c) M - pivot (d) Persikabo 1973 (e) Al-Nasr Bengh., Radnicki 1923, Novi Pazar, Macva, Radnik, Spartaks, Radnicki Niš, Vojvodina, Spartak, Vojvodina, Radnicki 1923, Šumadija 1903

*** Kovacevic - Novak Kovacevic (Новак Ковачевић) (a) 21/10/2001, ¿? (RF Yugoslavia, now in Montenegro) (b) - (c) M (d) FK Internacional (e) Kom Podgorica, Jedinstvo, FK Drezga

*** Kovacevic - Vladan Kovacevic (Владан Ковачевић) (a) 11/04/1998, Banja Luka (Bosnia and Herzegovina) (b) 1,92 (c) G (d) Rakow Czestochowa (e) FK Sarajevo, Mrkonjic, FK Sarajevo

*** Kovacevic - Vladimir Kovacevic (a) 11/11/1992, ¿? (Yugoslavia, now in Serbia) (b) 1,90 (c) D - central defense (d) Dinamo Makhachkala (e) Mladost GAT, Vojvodina, KV Kortrijk, FC Sheriff, KV Kortrijk, Vojvodina, Spartak, Vojvodina, Proleter, Vojvodina, Hajduk Kula, Vojvodina

*** Kovachev - Svetoslav Kovachev (Светослав Светозаров Ковачев) (a) 14/03/1998, Pleven (Bulgaria) (b) 1,72 (c) F - right winger (d) Akhmat Grozny (e) Akhmat Grozny, Arda Kardzhali, Ludogorets, Arda Kardzhali, Ludogorets, Etar, Ludogorets, Dunav, Ludogorets, Ludogorets II

*** Kovaci - Elvis Kovaci (a) 03/10/1998, Korfu (Greece) (b) 1,70 (c) M - central midfielder (d) - (e) KF Erzeni, FK Apolonia, KF Vora, KF Korabi, KF Vora, KF Korabi, KF Teuta, KS Besa

*** Kovacic - Dominik Kovacic (Dominik Kovačić) (a) 05/01/1994, Zagreb (Croatia) (b) 1,92 (c) D - central defense (d) Kisvárda FC (e) FC U Craiova, NK Lokomotiva, Vejle BK, NK Lokomotiva, Siroki Brijeg, FC Sheriff, FC Lugano, NK Zagreb

*** Kovacic - Mateo Kovacic (Mateo Kovačić) (a) 06/05/1994, Linz (Austria) (b) 1,77 (c) M - central midfielder (d) Manchester City (e) Chelsea, Real Madrid, Chelsea, Real Madrid, Internazionale Milano, Dinamo Zagreb

*** Kovacik - Peter Kovacik (Peter Kováčik) (a) 01/12/2001, Banská Bystrica (Slovakia) (b) - (c) D - right back (d) FK Zeleziarne Podbrezova (e) Jupie FSMH

*** Kovács - Barnabás Kovács (a) 14/11/2002, Dunaújváros (Hungary) (b) 1,81 (c) M - central midfielder (d) Zalaegerszegi TE FC (e) Tiszakécske, Zalaegerszeg, Dunaújváros

*** Kovács - Bence Kovács (a) 14/01/2004, Galanta (Slovakia) (b) 1,86 (c) M - central midfielder (d) Fehérvár FC (e) Fehérvár II, Kazincbarcika, Fehérvár II

*** Kovács - Dániel Kovács (a) 16/01/1994, Gyula (Hungary) (b) 1,90 (c) G (d) Fehérvár FC (e) Soroksár, Zalaegerszeg, Csákvár, Zalaegerszeg, Kecskeméti TE

*** Kovács - Dominik Kovács (Kovács Dominik László) (a) 18/02/2001, ¿? (Hungary) (b) 1,80 (c) D - right back (d) Újpest FC (e) Kazincbarcika, Újpest FC, Újpest II

*** Kovács - Marcell Kovács (a) 09/02/2003, Nyíregyháza (Hungary) (b) 1,85 (c) G (d) Kisvárda FC (e) Ferencváros II, Soroksár, Ferencváros II

*** Kovács - Nikolasz Kovács (a) 27/02/1999, Karcag (Hungary) (b) 1,78 (c) D - right back (d) Budapest Honvéd FC (e) Paksi FC, FC Ajka, Paksi FC, Honvéd, FC Ajka, Honvéd, Balmazújváros, Honvéd, Honvéd II

*** Kovács - Péter Kovács (Kovács Péter Ákos) (a) 10/02/2000, Debrecen (Hungary) (b) 1,91 (c) G (d) - (e) Debrecen, Pécsi MFC, Debrecen, Szolnok, Debrecen, Budaörs, Debrecen, Budaörs, Debrecen, Debrecen II

*** Koval - Maksym Koval (Коваль Максим Анатолійович) (a) 09/12/1992, Zaporizhya (Ukraine) (b) 1,88 (c) G (d) FC Sheriff Tiraspol (e) Al-Fateh, Dinamo Kyïv, Al-Fateh, Dinamo Kyïv, RC Deportivo, Dinamo Kyïv, Odense BK, Dinamo Kyïv, Goverla, Dinamo Kyïv, Goverla, Dinamo Kyïv, Metalurg Z., Zaporizhya II

*** Kovalchuk - Maksim Kovalchuk (Ковальчук Максим Сергеевич) (a) 05/03/2000, Brest (Belarus) (b) 1,87 (c) M - pivot (d) Niva Dolbizno (e) Dynamo Brest, Energetik-BGU, Dynamo Brest, Dynamo Brest II, Energetik-BGU, Dynamo Brest II

*** Kovalenko - Aleksandr Kovalenko (Коваленко Александр Игоревич) (a) 08/08/2003, Moskva (Russia) (b) 1,77 (c) M - central midfielder (d) Zenit de San Petersburgo (e) Sochi, KS Samara, Sochi, KS Samara, Chertanovo, Chertanovo II

*** Kovalenko - Ilya Kovalenko (Коваленко Ілля Олександрович) (a) 20/03/1990, Kalanchak, Kherson Oblast (Soviet Union, now in Ukraine) (b) 1,78 (c) F - left winger (d) - (e) LNZ Cherkasy, Akzhayik, LNZ Cherkasy, FK Ekranas, LNZ Cherkasy, Ingulets, Desna, Ingulets, Desna, PFK Sumy, Desna, Obolon-Brovar, FK Poltava, Kryvbas II, Girnyk KR, Kryvbas II, Naftovyk, Kryvbas II, Stal D.

*** Kovalenko - Ivan Kovalenko (Коваленко Іван Олександрович) (a) 10/03/1999, ¿? (Ukraine) (b) 1,79 (c) D - left back (d) Metalist 1925 Kharkiv (e) Metalist Unior, SK Metalist

*** Kovalenko - Mikhail Kovalenko (Коваленко Михаил Вадимович) (a) 25/01/1995, St. Petersburg (Russia) (b) 1,81 (c) D - central defense (d) FC Pyunik Yerevan (e) Dolgoprudnyi, FC Noah, Tyumen, Sochi, Dinamo S-Pb, Zenit St. Peterburg II, DYuSSh Kolomyag

*** Kovalenko - Viktor Kovalenko (a) 14/02/1996, Kherson (Ukraine) (b) 1,82 (c) M - attacking midfielder (d) Atalanta de Bérgamo (e) Spezia, Atalanta, Spezia, Atalanta, Shakhtar Donetsk, Shakhtar II

*** Kovalets - Kyrylo Kovalets (Ковалець Кирило Сергійович) (a) 02/07/1993, Kyiv (Ukraine) (b) 1,84 (c) M - attacking midfielder (d) FK Oleksandriya (e) Chornomorets, Shakhtar 3, Obolon 2 Kyiv, Obolon Kyiv II

*** Kovalev - Anton Kovalev (Ковалев Антон Владимирович) (a) 19/04/2000, Belynichi (Belarus) (b) 1,78 (c) M - right midfielder (d) Torpedo-BelAZ Zhodino (e) Soligorsk II, Isloch, Soligorsk II, Tukums, Soligorsk II

*** Kovalev - Oleg Kovalev (Ковалёв Олег Николаевич) (a) 24/05/1987, Gomel (Soviet Union, now in Belarus) (b) 1,92 (c) G (d) FK Gomel (e) Rechitsa, FK DSK-Gomel, Gomel, Gomel II, FK DSK-Gomel

*** Kovalev - Yuriy Kovalev (Ковалёв Юрий Владимирович) (a) 27/01/1993, Belynychi (Belarus) (b) 1,74 (c) M - right midfielder (d) FK Orenburg (e) Arsenal Tula, Soligorsk, Soligorsk II

*** Kovalevich - Vladislav Kovalevich (Ковалевич Владислав Васильевич) (a) 04/08/2000, Gomel (Belarus) (b) 1,78 (c) M - right midfielder (d) FK Smorgon (e) Dzerzhinsk, FK Smorgon, Dzerzhinsk, Svetlogorsk, Gomel II

*** Kovalevskiy - Denis Kovalevskiy (Ковалевский Денис Витальевич) (a) 02/05/1992, Orsha (Belarus) (b) 1,85 (c) D - central defense (d) - (e) BK Maxline, Znamya Truda OZ, FK Minsk, Belshina, Slavia, Dynamo Brest, Slavia, Dinamo Minsk II, Slavia, Dinamo Minsk II

*** Kovalkov - Marat Kovalkov (Ковальков Марат Владимирович) (a) 30/11/2004, ¿? (Russia) (b) 1,76 (c) M - attacking midfielder (d) FK Rostov II (e) -

*** Kovaltsuk - Arseni Kovaltsuk (Arseni Kovaltšuk) (a) 07/01/2001, Narva (Estonia) (b) - (c) M - left midfielder (d) Kalev Tallinn (e) JK Trans Narva

*** Kovalyov - Maksym Kovalyov (Ковальов Максим Сергійович) (a) 20/03/1989, Alchevsk, Lugansk Oblast (Soviet Union, now in Ukraine) (b) 1,88 (c) D - central defense (d) LNZ Cherkasy (e) Ingulets, Zirka, Stal Alchevsk, Illichivets, Shakhtar II, Illichivets, Shakhtar II, Zorya Lugansk, Shakhtar II

*** Kovalyov - Maksym Kovalyov (Ковальов Максим Юрійович) (a) 11/07/2000, Odesa (Ukraine) (b) 1,88 (c) G (d) Pirin Blagoevgrad (e) Peremoga Dnipro, Krystal Kherson, FK Viktoriya, Zimbru Chisinau

*** Kovalyuk - Kirill Kovalyuk (Ковалюк Кирилл Сергеевич) (a) 19/09/2003, Brest (Belarus) (b) 1,90 (c) M (d) Naftan Novopolotsk (e) Dynamo Brest, FK Slutsk, FK Malorita, Dynamo Brest II

*** Kovaqi - Gentrit Kovaqi (a) 04/02/1999, Jyväskylä (Finland) (b) - (c) D - central defense (d) - (e) JJK Jyväskylä, HJK Klubi 04, IF Gnistan, Ekenäs IF, SalPa, JJK Jyväskylä

*** Kovar - Matej Kovar (Matěj Kovář) (a) 17/05/2000, Uherské Hradiště (Czech Rep.) (b) 1,96 (c) G (d) Manchester United (e) Sparta Praha, Manchester Utd., Burton Albion, Swindon Town

*** Kovarik - Jan Kovarik (Jan Kovařík) (a) 19/06/1988, Most (Czechoslovakia, now in Czech Rep.) (b) 1,83 (c) M - left midfielder (d) Bohemians Praha 1905 (e) Viktoria Plzen, FK Jablonec, Slavia Praha, Slavia Praha B, Ceske Budejovice, Slavia Praha B

*** Kovel - Maksim Kovel (Ковель Максим Павлович) (a) 12/01/1999, Minsk (Belarus) (b) 1,83 (c) D - central defense (d) Isloch Minsk Region (e) BATE II, Smolevichi, BATE II, Dzerzhinsk, BATE II, Sputnik, BATE II

*** Kovinic - Nedjeljko Kovinic (a) 07/02/2002, Tivat (RF Yugoslavia, now in Montenegro) (b) 1,90 (c) F - center forward (d) FC Zlin (e) FK Bokelj, Radnicki 1923

*** Kovruk - Matvey Kovruk (Коврук Матвей Игоревич) (a) 10/04/2005, Petralevichi (Belarus) (b) 1,90 (c) G (d) BATE Borisov II (e) BATE II, Tsentr Futbola, Dynamo Brest, Tsentr Futbola, Rukh II

*** Kovtalyuk - Mykola Kovtalyuk (Ковталюк Микола Андрійович) (a) 26/04/1995, Sambir, Lviv Oblast (Ukraine) (b) 1,91 (c) F - center forward (d) FC Dila Gori (e) Shakhter K., Akzhayik, FC Dila, FC Anyang, FC Dila, Dinamo Tbilisi, Kolos Kovalivka, Kolkheti Poti, Kolos Kovalivka, Arsenal Kyiv, Michalovce, FK Poltava

*** Kovtunovits - Dmitri Kovtunovits (Dmitri Kovtunovitš) (a) 11/05/1991, Tallinn (Estonia) (b) 1,78 (c) D - central defense (d) Tallinna FC Pocarr (e) TJK Legion,

Sillamäe Kalev, FC Ararat, Paide, JK Nomme Kalju, FC Infonet, JK Nomme Kalju, FC Infonet, JK Nomme Kalju, Kalju Nömme II, TVMK Tallinn II

*** Kowal - Maciej Kowal (Maciej Kowal) (a) 09/12/2002, Dzierżoniów (Poland) (b) 1,95 (c) G (d) Pogon Szczecin (e) Siarka T., S. Kolbuszowa, Stal Rzeszow II

*** Kowalczyk - Sebastian Kowalczyk (Sebastian Kowalczyk) (a) 22/08/1998, Szczecin (Poland) (b) 1,70 (c) M - attacking midfielder (d) Houston Dynamo FC (e) Pogon Szczecin, Pogon II, AP Pogon

*** Kowalski - Mateusz Kowalski (Mateusz Kowalski) (a) 21/07/2005, Tczew (Poland) (b) 1,95 (c) F - center forward (d) - (e) Jagiellonia

*** Köylü - Kubilay Köylü (a) 04/05/1999, Deventer (Netherlands) (b) 1,77 (c) F - left winger (d) Istanbulspor (e) M. Arguvan SK, TEC, Racing Murcia, Kozakken Boys, FC Lisse, De Dijk

*** Koyuncu - Efe Arda Koyuncu (a) 08/07/2005, Istanbul (Turkey) (b) 1,80 (c) D - central defense (d) Basaksehir FK (e) -

*** Kozak - Libor Kozak (Libor Kozák) (a) 30/05/1989, Brumov-Bylnice (Czechoslovakia, now in Czech Rep.) (b) 1,93 (c) F - center forward (d) SS Arezzo (e) Zlin, Slovácko, Puskás AFC, Sparta Praha, Slovan Liberec, AS Livorno, Bari, Aston Villa, Lazio, Brescia, Lazio, SFC Opava

*** Kozak - Matyas Kozak (Matyáš Kozák) (a) 04/05/2001, ¿? (Czech Rep.) (b) 1,77 (c) F - center forward (d) Bohemians Praha 1905 (e) Bohemians 1905, Sparta Praha, Slovan Liberec, Sparta Praha, Sparta Praha B, Teplice, Sparta Praha B

*** Kozak - Milosz Kozak (Miłosz Kozak) (a) 23/05/1997, Gostyń (Poland) (b) 1,76 (c) F - right winger (d) Gornik Leczna (e) Spartak Trnava, Radomiak, Podbeskidzie, Chrobry Glogow, Podbeskidzie, Legia II, Podbeskidzie, Legia II, Wigry Suwalki, Legia II, Z. Sosnowiec, Legia II, Lech Poznan II

*** Kozak - Oleksandr Kozak (Козак Олександр Сергійович) (a) 25/07/1994, Kyiv (Ukraine) (b) 1,74 (c) F - left winger (d) Ingulets Petrove (e) Obolon-Brovar, Stal Kamyanske, Illichivets, Stal Kamyanske, Metalurg Donetsk

*** Kozakevich - Mikhail Kozakevich (Козакевич Михаил Александрович) (a) 19/05/2002, Zhabinka (Belarus) (b) 1,88 (c) G (d) Dynamo Brest (e) Dynamo Brest II, RUOR Minsk

*** Kozar - Alen Kozar (a) 07/04/1995, ¿? (Slovenia) (b) 1,74 (c) M - pivot (d) Balestier Khalsa (e) NS Mura, NK Aluminij

*** Kozel - Evgeniy Kozel (Козел Евгений Сергеевич) (a) 22/02/2001, Stolin (Belarus) (b) 1,93 (c) F - center forward (d) FK Baranovichi (e) Shakhter P., Soligorsk II, Dynamo Brest, Soligorsk II, DYuSSh-2 Rechitsa, Soligorsk II, Gorodeya, Soligorsk II, Tukums, Soligorsk II

*** Kozeluh - Josef Kozeluh (Josef Koželuh) (a) 15/02/2002, Plzeň (Czech Rep.) (b) 1,79 (c) D - right back (d) FC Zbrojovka Brno (e) Zbrojovka Brno, Viktoria Plzen, Chrudim, Viktoria Plzen, Viktoria Plzen B, Chrudim, Viktoria Plzen B, Viktoria Zizkov, Viktoria Plzen B

*** Kozhamberdy - Zhakyp Kozhamberdy (Қожамберді Жақып Есімұлы) (a) 26/02/1992, Taraz (Kazakhstan) (b) 1,83 (c) F - right winger (d) FK Taraz (e) Taraz, Kyran, Taraz, Zhetysu, Taraz, FC Astana, Okzhetpes, FC Astana, Taraz, Taraz-Karatau

*** Kozhemyakin - Oleg Kozhemyakin (Кожемякин Олег Андреевич) (a) 30/05/1995, Kryvyi Rig, Dnipropetrovsk Oblast (Ukraine) (b) 1,84 (c) D - central defense (d) SKA Khabarovsk (e) Torpedo Moskva, Rotor Volgograd, Shinnik Yaroslav, Loko-Kazanka M., M. Lipetsk, Quasar Moskva, Smena Moskva

*** Kozhevnikov - Oleksandr Kozhevnikov (Кожевніков Олександр Дмитрович) (a) 17/04/2000, Poltava (Ukraine) (b) 1,77 (c) F - right winger (d) - (e) JK Trans

Narva, Vorskla Poltava, Girnyk-Sport, Vorskla Poltava, Vorskla II, FK Mariupol II, Vorskla II

*** Kozhukhar - Andriy Kozhukhar (Кожухар Андрій Юрійович) (a) 20/07/1999, Tiraspol (Moldova) (b) 1,97 (c) G (d) Karpaty Lviv (e) Michalovce, Valmiera, Chornomorets, Chornomorets II

*** Kozhushko - Oleg Kozhushko (Кожушко Олег Олександрович) (a) 17/02/1998, Mykolaiv (Ukraine) (b) 1,73 (c) F - center forward (d) Kryvbas Kryvyi Rig (e) FK Oleksandriya, Pyunik Yerevan, Kolos Kovalivka, Chornomorets, Kolos Kovalivka, SK Dnipro-1, Kolos Kovalivka, SK Dnipro-1, Dnipro, Dnipro II

*** Kozi - Leon Kozi (a) 04/02/2003, Tiranë (Albania) (b) - (c) G (d) - (e) KF Drenica

*** Koziello - Vincent Koziello (Vincent Edouard André Koziello) (a) 28/10/1995, Grasse (France) (b) 1,68 (c) M - central midfielder (d) KV Oostende (e) RE Virton, KV Oostende, 1.FC Köln, Nacional, 1.FC Köln, Paris FC, 1.FC Köln, OGC Nice, OGC Nice B

*** Kozik - Eduard Kozik (Козік Едуард Сергійович) (a) 19/04/2003, Grudky, Volyn Oblast (Ukraine) (b) 1,83 (c) D - central defense (d) Shakhtar Donetsk (e) FK Mariupol, Shakhtar II

*** Kozlov - Aleksey Kozlov (Козлов Алексей Евгеньевич) (a) 23/01/1999, Sergiev Posad, Moskau Oblast (Russia) (b) 1,86 (c) G (d) Naftan Novopolotsk (e) Kaspiy Aktau, FK Minsk, Gomel, Torpedo Zhodino, Irtysh Omsk, Utenis, Spartaks, Spartak Moskva II

*** Kozlov - Danila Kozlov (Козлов Данила Сергеевич) (a) 19/01/2005, St. Petersburg (Russia) (b) 1,83 (c) M - attacking midfielder (d) Zenit 2 St. Petersburg (e) Zenit St. Peterburg II

*** Kozlov - Evgeniy Kozlov (Козлов Евгений Евгеньевич) (a) 04/02/1995, Sergiev Posad, Moskau Oblast (Russia) (b) 1,78 (c) F - left winger (d) FK Atyrau (e) Qyzyljar, Akzhayik, JFK Ventspils, Soligorsk, Spartaks, Zenit 2 St. Peterburg, Dinamo SPb, Zenit 2 St. Peterburg, Volga Nizhny NovgorodII, Vityaz Podolsk, Rubin Kazán II, Vityaz Podolsk, Vityaz P. II

*** Kozlov - Mikhail Kozlov (Козлов Михаил Михайлович) (a) 12/02/1990, Mogilev (Soviet Union, now in Belarus) (b) 1,77 (c) M - pivot (d) Neman Grodno (e) Dinamo Minsk, Vitebsk, Dnepr Mogilev, Mogilev II

*** Kozlov - Yuriy Kozlov (Козлов Юрий Сергеевич) (a) 21/05/1991, Vitebsk (Soviet Union, now in Belarus) (b) 1,88 (c) M - attacking midfielder (d) FK Molodechno (e) Naftan, FK Minsk, Neman Grodno, FK Slutsk, Dnyapro Mogilev, Luch, Slonim, FK Minsk II

*** Kozlovskiy - Denis Kozlovskiy (Козловский Денис Анатольевич) (a) 15/05/1993, Bobruisk (Belarus) (b) 1,75 (c) F - center forward (d) FK Gomel (e) Soligorsk, Gomel, Soligorsk, Lokomotiv Gomel, Osipovichi, Lokomotiv Gomel, Osipovichi, Belshina II

*** Kozlovsky - Samuel Kozlovsky (Samuel Kozlovský) (a) 19/11/1999, Bratislava (Slovakia) (b) 1,82 (c) D - left back (d) AS Trencin (e) FC Petrzalka, Slovan B, FC Petrzalka, Slovan Bratislava, Slovan B

*** Kozlowski - Kacper Kozlowski (Kacper Szymon Kozłowski) (a) 16/10/2003, Koszalin (Poland) (b) 1,82 (c) M - central midfielder (d) Vitesse Arnhem (e) Vitesse, Brighton & Hove Albion, Union St. Gilloise, Brighton & Hove Albion, Pogon Szczecin, Pogon II, AP Pogon

*** Kozoronis - Chrysovalantis Kozoronis (Χρυσοβαλάντης Κοζορώνης) (a) 03/08/1992, Heraklion (Greece) (b) 1,79 (c) M - central midfielder (d) Anagennisi Karditsas (e) Panevezys, APO Levadiakos, Petrolul, Ergotelis, PAS Giannina, Ergotelis

*** Kozubal - Antoni Kozubal (Antoni Kozubal) (a) 18/08/2004, Krosno (Poland) (b) 1,77 (c) M - pivot (d) GKS Katowice (e) GKS Katowice, Lech Poznan, Gornik Polk., Lech Poznan, Lech Poznan II

*** Kozuki - Soichiro Kozuki (上月 壮一郎) (a) 22/12/2000, Uji, Kyoto (Japan) (b) 1,82 (c) F - right winger (d) FC Schalke 04 (e) Schalke 04 II, 1.FC Düren, Kyoto Sanga

*** Kozyrenko - Yuriy Kozyrenko (Козиренко Юрій Сергійович) (a) 27/11/1999, Kostopil, Rivne Oblast (Ukraine) (b) 1,72 (c) M - attacking midfielder (d) Ingulets Petrove (e) Vorskla Poltava, Isloch, Vorskla Poltava, Girnyk-Sport, Vorskla Poltava, Vorskla II

*** Kpan - Cyrille Kpan (Cyrille Dominique Kpan) (a) 30/05/1998, Dabou (Ivory Coast) (b) 1,70 (c) F - right winger (d) NK Siroki Brijeg (e) NK Neretvanac, Sertanense, Salitas, Kawkab Marrak., Ouagadougou

*** Kpozo - Patrick Kpozo (a) 15/07/1997, Accra (Ghana) (b) 1,81 (c) D - left back (d) FC Banik Ostrava (e) FC Sheriff, Östersund, IFK Luleå, Östersund, AIK, Tromsø, AIK, Inter Allies

*** Kqiku - Edison Kqiku (a) 16/01/1999, ¿? (RF Yugoslavia, now in Kosovo) (b) 1,79 (c) M - right midfielder (d) SC Gjilani (e) FC Drita

*** Krachkovskiy - Anton Krachkovskiy (Крачковский Антон Романович) (a) 22/06/2002, ¿? (Russia) (b) 1,70 (c) M - central midfielder (d) Kairat Almaty (e) CSKA Moskva II, Kairat Moskva, CSKA Moskva II

*** Krachunov - Plamen Krachunov (Пламен Николов Крачунов) (a) 11/01/1989, Plovdiv (Bulgaria) (b) 1,89 (c) D - central defense (d) Arda Kardzhali (e) Lokomotiv Sofia, Etar, Lokomotiv Sofia, Z. Sosnowiec, Stomil, Sandecja, Ethnikos, St. Johnstone, Slavia Sofia, CSKA Sofia, Lokomotiv Plovdiv, CSKA Sofia, Lokomotiv Plovdiv, Maritsa

*** Kraev - Andrian Kraev (Андриан Бойков Краев) (a) 14/02/1999, Vetren (Bulgaria) (b) 1,91 (c) M - pivot (d) Levski Sofia (e) Hebar P., Botev Vratsa

*** Krafth - Emil Krafth (Emil Henry -Kristoffer Krafth) (a) 02/08/1994, Ljungby (Sweden) (b) 1,84 (c) D - right back (d) Newcastle United (e) Amiens SC, Bologna, Amiens SC, Bologna, Helsingborgs IF, Östers IF

*** Kragl - Oliver Kragl (a) 12/05/1990, Wolfsburg (Germany) (b) 1,79 (c) M - left midfielder (d) FC Trapani 1905 (e) ACR Messina, SV Ried, Avellino, Benevento, Ascoli, Benevento, Foggia, Crotone, Foggia, Crotone, Frosinone, SV Ried, Babelsberg 03, G. Halberstadt, Eintracht Braunschweig, Eintracht Braunschweig II

*** Kraizmer - Aleksandr Kraizmer (a) 14/10/2000, Tallinn (Estonia) (b) - (c) G (d) JK Trans Narva (e) FCI Tallinn, FCI Tallinn III

*** Krajci - Tomas Krajci (Tomáš Krajčí) (a) 07/11/2006, ¿? (Slovakia) (b) - (c) M (d) - (e) Tatran Liptovski Mikulas

*** Krajcirik - Ivan Krajcirik (Ivan Krajčírik) (a) 15/06/2000, Handlová (Slovakia) (b) 1,89 (c) G (d) MFK Ružomberok (e) -

*** Krajcsovics - Ábel Krajcsovics (Krajcsovics Ábel György) (a) 17/08/2004, Debrecen (Hungary) (b) 1,81 (c) F - left winger (d) Budapest Honvéd FC (e) Honvéd II

*** Krajinovic - Nikola Krajinovic (Nikola Krajinović) (a) 09/11/1999, Karlovac (Croatia) (b) 1,76 (c) D - left back (d) FC Koper (e) Hrv Dragovoljac, NK Osijek II, NK Lokomotiva, NK Rudes, NK Lokomotiva, Karlovac 1919

*** Krajisnik - Damjan Krajisnik (Дамјан Крајишник) (a) 24/04/1997, Bijeljina (Bosnia and Herzegovina) (b) 1,75 (c) M - central midfielder (d) FK Radnicki 1923 Kragujevac (e) Metalac, Mladost, Naestved BK, Zvijezda 09, Po-dri-nje, FK Sarajevo

*** Krajnc - Alen Krajnc (a) 01/07/1995, ¿? (Slovenia) (b) 1,80 (c) F - left winger (d) FK Velez Mostar (e) ND Gorica, NK Rogaska, NK Aluminij, DNŠ Zavrč, NK Dekani, Koper
*** Kral - Alex Kral (Alex Král) (a) 19/05/1998, Košice (Slovakia) (b) 1,86 (c) M - pivot (d) 1.FC Union Berlin (e) Union Berlin, Spartak Moskva, FC Schalke 04, Spartak Moskva, West Ham Utd., Spartak Moskva, Slavia Praha, Teplice, Slavia Praha B
*** Kral - Jan Kral (Jan Král) (a) 05/04/1999, Česká Lípa (Czech Rep.) (b) 1,94 (c) D - central defense (d) KAS Eupen (e) Jablonec, KAS Eupen, Hradec Kralove, Mlada Boleslav, Erzgebirge Aue, Mlada Boleslav, Varnsdorf, Mlada Boleslav, Mlada Boleslav B
*** Kralik - Martin Kralik (Martin Králik) (a) 03/04/1995, Prievidza (Slovakia) (b) 1,86 (c) D - central defense (d) SK Dynamo Ceske Budejovice (e) MSK Zilina
*** Kralj - Anton Kralj (Anton Sebastian Kralj) (a) 12/03/1998, Malmö (Sweden) (b) 1,65 (c) D - left back (d) Hammarby IF (e) Degerfors, Sandefjord, Malmö FF, Gefle, Malmö FF, Gefle
*** Kramar - Denis Kramar (Denis Kramář) (a) 08/08/2003, ¿? (Czech Rep.) (b) 1,85 (c) F - center forward (d) SK Sigma Olomouc (e) SFC Opava
*** Kramaric - Andrej Kramaric (Andrej Kramarić) (a) 19/06/1991, Zagreb (Yugoslavia, now in Croatia) (b) 1,77 (c) F - center forward (d) TSG 1899 Hoffenheim (e) Leicester City, Hoffenheim, Leicester City, HNK Rijeka, Dinamo Zagreb, NK Lokomotiva, Dinamo Zagreb, NK Lokomotiva, Dinamo Zagreb
*** Kramaric - Martin Kramaric (Martin Kramarič) (a) 14/11/1997, ¿? (Slovenia) (b) 1,78 (c) F - left winger (d) FK Sochi (e) NK Bravo, NK Maribor, NK Bravo, NK Maribor, NK Krsko, NK Krka
*** Kramaric - Mirko Kramaric (Mirko Kramarić) (a) 27/01/1989, Zagreb (Yugoslavia, now in Croatia) (b) 1,84 (c) D - left back (d) FC Etzella Ettelbruck (e) Steinsel, NK Brezice 1919, NK Radomlje, Zeljeznicar, Haugesund, NK Istra, Inter Zaprešić, NK Lokomotiva
*** Kramarz - Filip Kramarz (Filip Kramarz) (a) 22/06/2004, ¿? (Poland) (b) 1,88 (c) G (d) Cracovia (e) Cracovia II
*** Kramens - Klavs Kramens (Klāvs Kramēns) (a) 07/07/2000, ¿? (Latvia) (b) 1,90 (c) D - central defense (d) DFK Dainava Alytus (e) Spartaks, Noah Jurmala, Spartaks, Valmiera, JDFS Alberts
*** Kramer - Blaz Kramer (Blaž Kramer) (a) 01/06/1996, Celje (Slovenia) (b) 1,91 (c) F - center forward (d) Legia de Varsovia (e) FC Zürich, Wolfsburg II, NK Aluminij, Sampion Celje
*** Kramer - Christoph Kramer (a) 19/02/1991, Solingen (Germany) (b) 1,91 (c) M - pivot (d) Borussia Mönchengladbach (e) Bayer Leverkusen, Borussia Mönchengladbach, Bayer Leverkusen, VfL Bochum, Bayer Leverkusen, Bayer Leverkusen II
*** Kramer - Joris Kramer (a) 02/08/1996, Heiloo (Netherlands) (b) 1,87 (c) D - central defense (d) Go Ahead Eagles Deventer (e) NEC Nijmegen, AZ Alkmaar, Go Ahead Eagles, AZ Alkmaar, SC Cambuur, AZ Alkmaar, FC Dordrecht
*** Kramer - Lars Kramer (a) 11/07/1999, Zaandam (Netherlands) (b) 1,92 (c) D - central defense (d) Aalborg BK (e) Viborg FF, FC Groningen
*** Kramer - Michiel Kramer (a) 03/12/1988, Rotterdam (Netherlands) (b) 1,96 (c) F - center forward (d) RKC Waalwijk (e) ADO Den Haag, FC Utrecht, Maccabi Haifa, Sparta Rotterdam, Feyenoord, ADO Den Haag, FC Volendam, NAC Breda
*** Krancmanis - Arturs Krancmanis (a) 15/08/2003 (b) 1,88 (c) F - right winger (d) FK Tukums 2000 (e) Auda, Spartaks, Auda, Riga II, Auda

*** Krapka - Antonin Krapka (Antonín Křapka) (a) 22/01/1994, Mladá Boleslav (Czech Rep.) (b) 1,83 (c) D - central defense (d) Bohemians Praha 1905 (e) Karvina, Mlada Boleslav, Pardubice, Mlada Boleslav, Pardubice, Mlada Boleslav, Bohemians 1905, Mlada Boleslav, Usti nad Labem, Mlada Boleslav, Mlada Boleslav B

*** Krapukhin - Stanislav Krapukhin (Крапухин Станислав Авенирович) (a) 28/03/1998, St. Petersburg (Russia) (b) 1,91 (c) F - center forward (d) - (e) Kaspiy Aktau, Auda, Riga, Auda, Riga, Zenit 2 St. Peterburg, Zvezda St. Peterburg, Tom Tomsk, Novosibirsk, Tom Tomsk, Zenit 2 St. Peterburg, Zenit St. Peterburg II

*** Krasnikov - Yegor Krasnikov (Красніков Єгор Євгенійович) (a) 05/02/2006, ¿? (Ukraine) (b) 2,00 (c) F - center forward (d) Metalist Kharkiv (e) -

*** Krasniqi - Albin Krasniqi (a) 03/06/2001, Kaçanik (RF Yugoslavia, now in Kosovo) (b) 1,71 (c) F - attacking midfielder (d) FC Prishtina (e) KF Ferizaj, FC Drita, KF Ferizaj, FC Drita, KF Ferizaj

*** Krasniqi - Besnik Krasniqi (a) 01/02/1990, Prishtinë (Yugoslavia, now in Kosovo) (b) 1,81 (c) D - right back (d) FC Drita Gjilan (e) FC Prishtina, FC Ballkani, KF Vëllaznimi, Flamurtari FC, KF Gjilani, KF Istogu, KF Teuta, FK Partizani, FC Prishtina

*** Krasniqi - Bledian Krasniqi (a) 17/06/2001, Zürich (Switzerland) (b) 1,73 (c) M - attacking midfielder (d) FC Zürich (e) FC Wil 1900, FC Zürich

*** Krasniqi - Blendrit Krasniqi (a) 31/01/2006, ¿? (Serbia and Montenegro, now in Kosovo) (b) - (c) D (d) FC Prishtina (e) -

*** Krasniqi - Blerim Krasniqi (a) 05/07/1996, Kavajë (Albania) (b) 1,87 (c) F - center forward (d) FC Drita Gjilan (e) CS Mioveni, SC Gjilani, KF Teuta, KF Skënderbeu, FK Apolonia

*** Krasniqi - Dion Krasniqi (a) 24/08/2003, ¿? (Sweden) (b) 1,88 (c) F - center forward (d) Varbergs BoIS (e) Lunds BK

*** Krasniqi - Endrit Krasniqi (a) 26/10/1994, Therandë (RF Yugoslavia, now in Kosovo) (b) 1,77 (c) M - attacking midfielder (d) Shkëndija Tetovo (e) FC Prishtina, FC Drita, FC Prishtina, FC Drita, FC Prishtina, KF 2 Korriku

*** Krasniqi - Ermal Krasniqi (a) 07/09/1998, Tërpezë (RF Yugoslavia, now in Kosovo) (b) 1,88 (c) F - left winger (d) CFR Cluj (e) FC Ballkani, KF Ferizaj, FC Llapi, FC Malisheva

*** Krasniqi - Gezim Krasniqi (Gëzim Krasniqi) (a) 05/01/1990, Kavajë (Albania) (b) 1,95 (c) D - central defense (d) KF Erzeni (e) KF Egnatia, FK Kukësi, Rabotnicki, FK Partizani, Flamurtari FC, FK Partizani, KS Besa

*** Krasniqi - Ilir Krasniqi (a) 02/04/2000, Bocholt (Germany) (b) 1,89 (c) M - pivot (d) KF Llapi (e) Kek-U Kastriot, KF Fushë Kosova

*** Krasniqi - Kreshnik Krasniqi (Kreshnik Krasniqi Dervishaj) (a) 22/12/2000, Oslo (Norway) (b) 1,83 (c) M - central midfielder (d) Strømsgodset IF (e) Strømsgodset II

*** Krasniqi - Laurit Krasniqi (a) 14/07/2001, Ferizaj (RF Yugoslavia, now in Kosovo) (b) - (c) D - left back (d) Roda JC Kerkrade (e) Roda JC, Royal Antwerp, Young Reds

*** Krasniqi (c) D (d) SC Gjilani (e) - - Blend Krasniqi (c) D (d) SC Gjilani (e) -

*** Krasnov - Evgeniy Krasnov (Краснов Евгений Владимирович) (a) 09/02/1998, Mogilev (Belarus) (b) 1,76 (c) M - central midfielder (d) FK Vitebsk (e) Isloch, Dnepr Mogilev, Mogilev II

*** Krasnov - Nikita Krasnov (Краснов Никита Владимирович) (a) 09/07/2004, ¿? (Belarus) (b) - (c) M - central midfielder (d) Dnepr Mogilev (e) Mogilev II, Dnepr-Yuni Mogilev

*** Krasotin - Anatoliy Krasotin (Красотин Анатолий Анатольевич) (a) 21/02/2000, Ekibastuz, Pavlodar Region (Kazakhstan) (b) 1,73 (c) M - central midfielder (d) FK Ekibastuz (e) FK Aksu, FK Ekibastuz, FK Ekibastuz II

*** Krastev - Boris Krastev (Борис Красенов Кръстев) (a) 08/01/2004, ¿? (Bulgaria) (b) - (c) M - central midfielder (d) Kostinbrod (e) Lokomotiv Sofia

*** Krastev - Dimo Krastev (Димо Николаев Кръстев) (a) 10/02/2003, Burgas (Bulgaria) (b) 1,95 (c) D - central defense (d) US Catanzaro (e) Catanzaro

*** Krastev - Filip Krastev (Филип Кръстев) (a) 15/10/2001, Sofia (Bulgaria) (b) 1,78 (c) M - central midfielder (d) Los Ángeles FC (e) LAFC, Lommel SK, Levski Sofia, Lommel SK, SC Cambuur, Lommel SK, Troyes, Lommel SK, Slavia Sofia, Lommel SK, Slavia Sofia

*** Krastev - Kaloyan Krastev (Калоян Ивайлов Кръстев) (a) 24/01/1999, Sofia (Bulgaria) (b) 1,89 (c) F - center forward (d) Lokomotiv Sofia (e) CSKA-Sofia, Beroe, CSKA-Sofia, Slavia Sofia, Slavia Sofia, Slavia Sofia

*** Kratkov - Dmitriy Kratkov (Кратков Дмитрий Викторович) (a) 15/01/2002, Stavropol (Russia) (b) 1,75 (c) M - pivot (d) FK Krasnodar-2 (e) Krasnodar II

*** Kratochvil - Milos Kratochvil (Miloš Kratochvíl) (a) 26/04/1996, Karlovy Vary (Czech Rep.) (b) 1,86 (c) M - central midfielder (d) FK Jablonec (e) Viktoria Plzen B, Zbrojovka Brno, Viktoria Plzen B, FK Senica, Viktoria Plzen B, Banik Sokolov, Viktoria Plzen B

*** Kratochvila - David Kratochvila (David Kratochvíla) (a) 09/06/2002, ¿? (Czech Rep.) (b) - (c) F (d) 1.FC Slovácko B (e) MFK Vyskov, Slovácko B

*** Kräuchi - Alessandro Kräuchi (Alessandro Samuele Kräuchi) (a) 03/06/1998, St. Gallen (Switzerland) (b) 1,76 (c) D - right back (d) FC Vaduz (e) FC St. Gallen, FC Wil 1900, FC St. Gallen

*** Krauß - Tom Krauß (a) 22/06/2001, Leipzig (Germany) (b) 1,82 (c) M - central midfielder (d) 1.FSV Mainz 05 (e) RB Leipzig, FC Schalke 04, RB Leipzig, 1.FC Nürnberg, RB Leipzig

*** Krautmanis - Janis Krautmanis (a) 22/04/1997, Tukums (Latvia) (b) - (c) D - left back (d) Grobinas SC/LFS (e) Liepaja, Tukums, RFS, Spartaks, Super Nova, Spartaks, Nevezis, Spartaks, Tukums, Spartaks, Valmiera, Liepaja II, RTU, Grobinas, Liepaja II

*** Kravchenko - Anton Kravchenko (Кравченко Антон Сергійович) (a) 23/03/1991, Dnipropetrovsk (Soviet Union, now in Ukraine) (b) 1,90 (c) D - central defense (d) - (e) Kisvárda, Olimpik Donetsk, Karabükspor, Olimpik Donetsk, Stal Kamyanske, Tytan Armyansk, Gelios Kharkiv, Dnipro II, Volyn Lutsk, Dnipro II, Naftovyk, Dnipro II

*** Kravchenko - Dmytro Kravchenko (Кравченко Дмитро Андрійович) (a) 25/02/1995, Poltava (Ukraine) (b) 1,77 (c) M - pivot (d) Metalist 1925 Kharkiv (e) Vorskla Poltava, Vorskla II

*** Kravchenko - Mykyta Kravchenko (Кравченко Микита Якович) (a) 14/06/1997, Zugres, Donetsk Oblast (Ukraine) (b) 1,82 (c) D - right back (d) FK Polissya Zhytomyr (e) FK Polissya, Dinamo Kyïv, Kolos Kovalivka, Dinamo Kyïv, SK Dnipro-1, Dinamo Kyïv, Kolos Kovalivka, Dinamo Kyïv, Olimpik Donetsk, Dinamo Kyïv, Dinamo Kiev II, Illichivets II

*** Kravchenko - Nikita Kravchenko (Кравченко Никита) (a) 11/07/2004, ¿? (Kazakhstan) (b) 1,80 (c) M (d) Kyzylzhar SK Petropavlovsk II (e) -

*** Kravchenko - Sergiy Kravchenko (Кравченко Сергій Сергійович) (a) 24/04/1983, Donetsk (Soviet Union, now in Ukraine) (b) 1,81 (c) M - central midfielder (d) - (e) Chornomorets, SK Dnipro-1, Dnipro, Volyn Lutsk, Dnipro, Dinamo Kyïv, Vorskla Poltava, Qarabag FK

*** Kravchenko - Vladislav Kravchenko (Кравченко Владислав Валерьевич) (a) 15/04/2003, Temirtau (Kazakhstan) (b) 1,83 (c) D - central defense (d) Kairat-Zhas (e) -

*** Kravchuk - Andriy Kravchuk (Кравчук Андрій Сергійович) (a) 26/02/1999, Chernivtsi (Ukraine) (b) 1,87 (c) M - central midfielder (d) - (e) Vorskla Poltava, Torpedo Moskva, Olimpik Donetsk, Ol. Donetsk II

*** Kravchuk - Danylo Kravchuk (Кравчук Данило Вікторович) (a) 02/07/2001, ¿? (Ukraine) (b) 1,80 (c) F - right winger (d) Vorskla Poltava (e) Ingulets, Vorskla Poltava, Vorskla II

*** Kravchuk - Yuriy Kravchuk (Кравчук Юрій Вячеславович) (a) 06/04/1994, Odesa (Ukraine) (b) 1,92 (c) D - central defense (d) FK Minaj (e) Metalist, FK Minaj, Metalist, Girnyk-Sport, Metalist, Girnyk-Sport, PFC Lviv, Girnyk-Sport, Zhemchuzhyna O., Energiya NK, SKA Odessa, Chornomorets 2

*** Kravets - Vasyl Kravets (a) 20/08/1997, Lviv (Ukraine) (b) 1,85 (d) SK Dnipro-1 (e) Vorskla Poltava, CD Leganés, Real Sporting, CD Leganés, Lech Poznan, CD Leganés, CD Lugo, CD Leganés, CD Lugo, Karpaty, CD Lugo, Karpaty

*** Kravtsov - Kirill Kravtsov (Кравцов Кирилл Сергеевич) (a) 14/06/2002, St. Petersburg (Russia) (b) 1,87 (c) M - pivot (d) FK Sochi (e) Zenit, Nizhny Novgorod, Zenit, Zenit 2 St. Peterburg, Zenit St. Peterburg II

*** Kravtsov - Maksim Kravtsov (Кравцов Максим Игоревич) (a) 20/06/2002, Grodno (Belarus) (b) - (c) F - center forward (d) Neman Grodno (e) Neman II, FK Smorgon, Neman II

*** Krawczyk - Piotr Krawczyk (Piotr Krawczyk) (a) 29/12/1994, Siedlce (Poland) (b) 1,87 (c) F - center forward (d) Górnik Zabrze (e) Legionovia, Pogon Siedlce, Orleta R.P., Pogon Siedlce, Swit N.D.M., Pogon Siedlce, Naprzod Skorzec, Pogon Siedlce, Naprzod Skorzec

*** Krch - Daniel Krch (Daniel Krch) (a) 20/03/1992, Tábor (Czechoslovakia, now in Czech Rep.) (b) 1,80 (c) D - central defense (d) FK Dukla Praga (e) Bohemians 1905, Sparta Praha B, Bohemians 1905, Sparta Praha B, FC MAS Taborsko, Sparta Praha B

*** Krch - David Krch (a) 30/06/2003, ¿? (Czech Rep.) (b) - (c) M - attacking midfielder (d) FK Pribram (e) Pribram, Ceske Budejovice B, FC MAS Taborsko, Ceske Budejovice B

*** Krcik - Adam Krcik (Adam Krčík) (a) 16/03/1996, Prievidza (Slovakia) (b) 1,80 (c) D - right back (d) MFK Skalica (e) Karvina, Skalica, Karvina, Liptovsky Mik., Banik Prievidza, 1.SC Znojmo, Banik Prievidza, Ostbahn XI, Duslo Sala

*** Krcik - David Krcik (Dávid Krčík) (a) 28/06/1999, Prievidza (Slovakia) (b) 1,89 (c) D - central defense (d) MFK Karvina (e) Liptovsky Mik., Jihlava, Liptovsky Mik., Banik Prievidza

*** Krdzalic - Anes Krdzalic (Anes Krdžalić) (a) 28/08/2004, Doboj (Bosnia and Herzegovina) (b) 1,80 (c) M - pivot (d) GNK Dinamo Zagreb (e) NK Kustosija, Olimpija, NK Kustosija

*** Krebs - Florian Krebs (a) 04/02/1999, Berlin (Germany) (b) 1,88 (c) M - central midfielder (d) FC Honka (e) Borussia Dortmund II, Chemnitzer FC, Hertha BSC II

*** Krebs - Kristoffer Krebs (a) 06/04/2003, ¿? (Sweden) (b) - (c) F - center forward (d) Europa Point FC (e) Ekenäs IF, Europa Point FC, Denver Pioneers, IFK Stocksund

*** Krefl - Aljaz Krefl (Aljaž Krefl) (a) 20/02/1994, ¿? (Slovenia) (b) 1,73 (c) D - left back (d) NK Olimpija Ljubljana (e) NK Aluminij, Rudar Velenje, Olimpija, Spartak, Olimpija, Rudar Velenje, NK Smartno 1928, Rudar Velenje

*** Kreida - Vladislav Kreida (a) 25/09/1999, Tallinn (Estonia) (b) 1,79 (c) M - central midfielder (d) FC Flora Tallinn (e) St. Patrick's Ath., FC Flora, Skövde AIK, FC Flora, Veres Rivne, FC Flora, Helsingborgs IF, FC Flora
*** Kreidl - Johannes Kreidl (a) 07/03/1996, Hart im Zillertal (Austria) (b) 1,94 (c) G (d) Kuopion Palloseura (e) SV Ried, Nurernberg II, Hamburg II, KuPS, Hamburg II, FC Wacker II
*** Kreiker - Dario Kreiker (a) 07/01/2003, ¿? (Austria) (b) 1,85 (c) M - left midfielder (d) SV Stripfing (e) SV Stripfing, Austria Viena, Young Violets, SC Ortmann, Wiener Neustadt II
*** Krejci - Ladislav Krejci (Ladislav Krejčí) (a) 05/07/1992, Praha (Czechoslovakia, now in Czech Rep.) (b) 1,79 (c) M - left midfielder (d) FC Hradec Kralove (e) Sparta Praha, Bologna, Sparta Praha, Sparta Praha B
*** Krejci - Ladislav Krejci (Ladislav Krejčí) (a) 20/04/1999, Rosice (Czech Rep.) (b) 1,91 (c) M - pivot (d) AC Sparta Praga (e) Zbrojovka Brno
*** Krekovic - Leon Krekovic (Leon Kreković) (a) 07/05/2000, Knin (Croatia) (b) 1,82 (c) F - left winger (d) FC Lahti (e) HNK Sibenik, Beerschot V.A., Hajduk Split, NK Dugopolje, Hajduk Split, Hajduk Split II, NK Dinara Knin
*** Kremenovic - Milan Kremenovic (Милан Кременовић) (a) 08/03/2002, Berlin (Germany) (b) 1,91 (c) D - central defense (d) - (e) NK Dekani, Frosinone, Hebar P., Frosinone, Graficar, Macva, Graficar
*** Kren - Andrey Kren (Крень Андрей Александрович) (a) 11/11/2003, Ivatsevichi (Belarus) (b) 1,70 (c) M - pivot (d) FK Slutsk (e) Slutsk II
*** Kresic - Anton Kresic (Anton Krešić) (a) 29/01/1996, Dieburg (Germany) (b) 1,98 (c) D - central defense (d) CFR Cluj (e) CFR Cluj, HNK Rijeka, Atalanta, HNK Rijeka, Atalanta, Padova, Atalanta, Carpi, Atalanta, Cremonese, Atalanta, Avellino, Atalanta, Trapani, NK Naftas - IG
*** Kresic - Ivor Kresic (Ivor Krešić) (a) 14/03/2001, Mostar (Bosnia and Herzegovina) (b) 1,86 (c) D - central defense (d) NK Zrinski Jurjevac Punitovacki (e) HSK Posusje, Croat. Zmijavci, Jadran Luka Ploce, Zrinjski Mostar, Jadran Luka Ploce, Neretva Metkovic
*** Kreslovs - Deniss Kreslovs (a) 27/03/2007, ¿? (Latvia) (b) - (c) D (d) Spartaks Jurmala II (e) -
*** Kreuzriegler - Martin Kreuzriegler (a) 10/01/1994, ¿? (Austria) (b) 1,82 (c) D - central defense (d) Vålerenga Fotball (e) Widzew Lódz, Sandefjord, Blau Weiss Linz, Hibernians FC, FAC, Austria Lustenau, SV Horn, Blau Weiss Linz, Reichraming Jd.
*** Krezic - Daniel Krezic (Даниел Крезиќ) (a) 03/05/1996, Göteborg (Sweden) (b) 1,86 (c) M - left midfielder (d) - (e) Cork City, Degerfors, Varbergs BoIS, IK Oddevold
*** Kriaf - Ofir Kriaf (קריאף אופיר) (a) 17/03/1991, Jerusalem (Israel) (b) 1,78 (c) M - pivot (d) Beitar Jerusalem (e) Kiryat Shmona, Maccabi Haifa, B. Jerusalem
*** Kricak - Ivan Kricak (Иван Кричак) (a) 19/07/1996, Beograd (RF Yugoslavia, now in Serbia) (b) 1,82 (c) D - central defense (d) Mjällby AIF (e) Radnik, Sindjelic Bg, Rad Beograd, Sindjelic Bg, Rad Beograd, Zarkovo, Rad Beograd
*** Kricfalusi - Ondrej Kricfalusi (Ondřej Kričfaluši) (a) 29/03/2004, ¿? (Czech Rep.) (b) 1,95 (c) D - central defense (d) FC Sellier & Bellot Vlasim (e) Vlasim, Slavia Praha, Slavia Praha B
*** Kriisa - Ranon Kriisa (a) 28/01/1996, Saue ((c) D - central defense (d) Saue JK (e) Kuressaare, Kalev, Saue JK Laagri, Kalev, Kalev Tallinn II, Saue JK Laagri
*** Kriještorac - Eniks Kriještorac (a) 17/01/1999, ¿? (RF Yugoslavia, now in Montenegro) (b) - (c) F - left winger (d) KF Vëllaznimi Gjakovë (e) Jedinstvo, FK Berane, Jedinstvo, Rudar Pljevlja, Jedinstvo

*** Krisjanis - Renards Krisjanis (Renards Krišjānis) (a) 04/04/2002, ¿? (Latvia) (b) - (c) M - attacking midfielder (d) JDFS Alberts Riga (e) Tukums, Ventspils II
*** Kristan - Jakub Kristan (Jakub Křišťan) (a) 05/07/2002, Praha (Czech Rep.) (b) 1,83 (c) M - pivot (d) FK Teplice (e) Vlasim, Teplice, Slavia Praha B, Vlasim, Slavia Praha B
*** Kristensen - Bjorn Kristensen (Bjørn Kristensen) (a) 05/04/1993, Marsaskala (Malta) (b) 1,81 (c) M - pivot (d) Hibernians FC (e) -
*** Kristensen - Bjørn Martin Kristensen (a) 04/05/2002, ¿? (Norway) (b) 1,83 (c) F - center forward (d) Aalesunds FK (e) Grorud, Grorud IL II, Nordstrand IF
*** Kristensen - Mathias Kristensen (a) 24/06/1993, ¿? (Denmark) (b) 2,01 (c) F - center forward (d) Kolding IF (e) Kolding IF, Lyngby BK, Nyköbing FC, AC Horsens, Tarup-Paarup IF, Lolland Falster
*** Kristensen - Mikkel Kristensen (Mikkel Kannegaard Kristensen) (a) 05/07/2006, ¿? (Denmark) (b) - (c) D - central defense (d) Aarhus GF (e) -
*** Kristensen - Rasmus Kristensen (Rasmus Nissen Kristensen) (a) 11/07/1997, Brande (Denmark) (b) 1,87 (c) D - right back (d) AS Roma (e) AS Roma, Leeds Utd., RB Salzburg, Ajax, Midtjylland
*** Kristensen - Thomas Kristensen (Thomas Thiesson Kristensen) (a) 17/01/2002, Aarhus (Denmark) (b) 1,98 (c) D - central defense (d) Aarhus GF (e) -
*** Kristiansen - Anders Kristiansen (a) 17/03/1990, Stavanger (Norway) (b) 1,83 (c) G (d) Sarpsborg 08 FF (e) Union St. Gilloise, Sarpsborg 08, Bryne, Viking, Bryne, Viking
*** Kristiansen - Bendik Kristiansen (a) 20/11/2002, Teie (Norway) (b) 1,85 (c) M - central midfielder (d) Vindbjart FK (e) Ørn Horten, Jerv
*** Kristiansen - Victor Kristiansen (a) 16/12/2002, Copenhagen (Denmark) (b) 1,81 (c) D - left back (d) Leicester City (e) FC København
*** Kristinsson - Arnór Ingi Kristinsson (a) 23/06/2001, ¿? (Iceland) (b) - (c) D - right back (d) Leiknir Reykjavík (e) Leiknir, Valur, Leiknir
*** Kristinsson - Ögmundur Kristinsson (a) 19/06/1989, Reykjavík (Iceland) (b) 1,93 (c) G (d) AE Kifisias (e) Olympiakos, AE Larisa, Excelsior, Hammarby IF, Randers FC, Fram Reykjavík
*** Kristinsson - Sverrir Thór Kristinsson (Sverrir Þór Kristinsson) (a) 06/11/2003, ¿? (Iceland) (b) - (c) D (d) Valur Reykjavik (e) -
*** Kristjánsson - Gudmundur Kristjánsson (Guðmundur Kristjánsson) (a) 01/03/1989, Kópavogur (Iceland) (b) 1,81 (c) D - central defense (d) Stjarnan Gardabaer (e) Hafnarfjördur, Start, Breidablik, Start, Breidablik, Haukar, Breidablik
*** Kristo - Dario Kristo (Dario Krišto) (a) 05/03/1989, Tomislavgrad (Yugoslavia, now in Bosnia and Herzegovina) (b) 1,90 (c) D - central defense (d) HSK Posusje (e) NK Dugopolje, GKS Tychy, Widzew Lódz, NK Dugopolje, Fotbal Trinec, Frydek-Mistek, Dunajska Streda, NK Dugopolje, NK Lucko, Zrinjski Mostar, HNK Sibenik, NK Omis, Zmaj Makarska, NK Rudes, Inter Zaprešić
*** Kristof - Matus Kristof (a) 10/08/2004, ¿? (Slovakia) (b) 1,93 (c) D (d) MSK Rimavska Sobota (e) Ružomberok
*** Kristoffersen - Julian Kristoffersen (a) 10/05/1997, Horten (Norway) (b) 1,98 (c) F - center forward (d) US Salernitana 1919 (e) Virtus Verona, Salernitana, Cosenza, Salernitana, Jeonnam Dragons, Hobro IK, Djurgården, FC København, Ørn Horten
*** Kritsyuk - Stanislav Kritsyuk (a) 01/12/1990, Togliatti, Samara Region (Soviet Union, now in Russia) (b) 1,92 (c) G (d) Gil Vicente FC (e) Zenit, Gil Vicente, B SAD, Krasnodar, SC Braga, Krasnodar, SC Braga, Braga B, Rio Ave, Braga B, Akad. Togliatti, FC Togliatti, Ak. Dimitrovgrad, Akron Konoplev

*** Krivak - Fabijan Krivak (a) 24/02/2005, Zabok (Croatia) (b) 1,82 (c) M - attacking midfielder (d) - (e) Ivancica ZB

*** Krivanjeva - Besart Krivanjeva (a) 28/02/1996, Skopje (North Macedonia) (b) 1,82 (c) D - central defense (d) Struga Trim & Lum (e) SC Gjilani, KF Egnatia, FC Shkupi, Metalurg Skopje

*** Krivicic - Marko Krivicic (a) 01/02/1996, Koper (Slovenia) (b) 1,78 (d) Flamurtari FC (e) KF Erzeni, Tabor Sezana, NK Dekani, Koper, Bologna, Koper

*** Krivitskiy - Vladislav Krivitskiy (Кривицкий Владислав Анатольевич) (a) 03/07/1995, Minsk (Belarus) (b) 1,94 (c) D - central defense (d) - (e) Dynamo Brest, Kyran, Energetik-BGU, FK Minsk II, Granit, FK Minsk II, Torpedo Minsk, FK Minsk II

*** Krivokapic - Matija Krivokapic (a) 19/03/2003, Nikšić (Montenegro) (b) 1,87 (c) F - center forward (d) ETO FC Győr (e) ETO FC Győr, Dunajska Streda, Michalovce, Dunajska Streda, FK Podgorica

*** Krivtsov - Nikita Krivtsov (Кривцов Никита Сергеевич) (a) 18/08/2002, Volodarsk, Nizhny Novgorod Oblast (Russia) (b) 1,86 (c) M - attacking midfielder (d) FK Krasnodar (e) Torpedo Vlad., Tom Tomsk, Torpedo Vlad., Murom, Sokol Moskva, DFK TS

*** Kriwak - Rene Kriwak (a) 30/04/1999, ¿? (Austria) (b) 1,98 (c) F - center forward (d) FC Dordrecht (e) Rapid Wien, TSV Hartberg, Rapid Wien, Rapid Wien II, Wiener SC, FC Marchfeld, SV Stripfing, FC Admira II

*** Krizan - Mitja Krizan (Mitja Križan) (a) 05/06/1997, ¿? (Slovenia) (b) 1,95 (c) D - central defense (d) Rodina Moscow (e) NK Bravo, Lommel SK, NK Bravo, Lommel SK, NK Bravo, NK Fuzinar, NK Celje, Drava Ptuj, NK Celje, NK Aluminij

*** Krizan - Richard Krizan (Richard Križan) (a) 23/09/1997, Plášťovce (Slovakia) (b) 1,90 (c) D - central defense (d) Slovan Bratislava (e) AS Trencin, Puskás AFC, FC Nitra

*** Krizevac - Benjamin Krizevac (Benjamin Križevac) (a) 17/12/2003, Sarajevo (Bosnia and Herzegovina) (b) - (c) F - center forward (d) FK Slavija Sarajevo (e) Zeljeznicar

*** Krizmanic - Kresimir Krizmanic (Krešimir Krizmanić) (a) 03/07/2000, Zagreb (Croatia) (b) 1,88 (c) D - central defense (d) HNK Gorica (e) -

*** Krjauklis - Ritus Krjauklis (a) 23/04/1986, Ilūkste (Soviet Union, now in Lithuania) (b) 1,88 (c) D - central defense (d) Sperre (e) Sperre) Daugavpils, NJ City, XJ T. Leopard, Perak II, RFS, JFK Ventspils, Spartaks, Ajax Cape Town, Golden Arrows, Metalurgs, JFK Ventspils, Dinaburg, AZAL

*** Krkanovic - Demir Krkanovic (a) 19/08/1996, ¿? (RF Yugoslavia, now in Montenegro) (b) 1,84 (c) D - left back (d) FK Decic Tuzi (e) Kom Podgorica, FK Decic Tuzi, FK Jezero, FK Decic Tuzi

*** Krnic - Alija Krnic (Alija Krnić) (a) 02/01/1998, Podgorica (RF Yugoslavia, Montenegro) (b) 1,75 (c) F - right winger (d) Jedinstvo Bijelo Polje (e) FK Kukësi, Javor-Matis, FK Iskra, Javor-Matis, AD Almudévar, FK Decic Tuzi

*** Krob - Jan Krob (Jan Krob) (a) 27/04/1987, Beroun (Czechoslovakia, now in Czech Rep.) (b) 1,75 (c) D - left back (d) - (e) Jablonec, Teplice, Tatran Presov, Teplice, Tatran Presov, Sparta Praha B, Graffin Vlasim, Sparta Praha B, Sparta Praha, Tatran Presov, Sparta Praha, Ceske Budejovice, Sparta Praha, SK Kladno, Sparta Praha, Sparta Praha B

*** Krobot - Ladislav Krobot (a) 01/04/2001, ¿? (Czech Rep.) (b) 1,81 (c) F - center forward (d) FK Pardubice (e) Mlada Boleslav, Pardubice, Mlada Boleslav, Mlada Boleslav B, Usti nad Labem, Mlada Boleslav B, Slavia Praha B, Vysehrad

*** Kroesen - Jaimy Kroesen (a) 27/03/2003, Hellevoetsluis (Netherlands) (b) 1,84 (c) G (d) - (e) Heerenveen
*** Krollis - Raimonds Krollis (a) 28/10/2001, Riga (Latvia) (b) 1,86 (c) F - center forward (d) Spezia (e) Valmiera, Metta, FS Metta II
*** Krolo - Ivan Krolo (a) 23/01/2003, Split (Croatia) (b) 1,89 (c) M - pivot (d) NK Radomlje (e) Hajduk Split, HNK Sibenik, Hajduk Split, Adriatic Split
*** Kronaveter - Rok Kronaveter (a) 07/12/1986, Maribor (Yugoslavia, now in Slovenia) (b) 1,87 (c) M - attacking midfielder (d) SV Allerheiligen (e) NK Maribor, Olimpija, Petrolul, ETO FC Győr, Energie Cottbus, Rudar Velenje, Drava Ptuj, Zeleznicar
*** Kronberg - Claes Kronberg (Claes Philip Kronberg) (a) 19/04/1987, Nykøbing Falster (Denmark) (b) 1,77 (c) D - right back (d) KÍ Klaksvík (e) Sandnes Ulf, Viking, Sarpsborg 08, Lolland Falster
*** Kronberger - Luca Kronberger (a) 15/02/2002, Schwarzach im Pongau (Austria) (b) 1,79 (c) F - left winger (d) WSG Tirol (e) WSG Tirol, Sturm Graz, SV Ried, Sturm Graz, Admira Wacker, FC Admira II
*** Kronus - Adam Kronus (a) 29/07/2002, ¿? (Czech Rep.) (b) - (c) F - right winger (d) FC Zbrojovka Brno (e) Viktoria Plzen B, SILON Taborsko, Viktoria Plzen B
*** Kroos - Toni Kroos (a) 04/01/1990, Greifswald (East Germany, now in Germany) (b) 1,83 (c) M - central midfielder (d) Real Madrid CF (e) Bayern München, Bayer Leverkusen, Bayern München
*** Kröpfl - Mario Kröpfl (a) 21/12/1989, Klagenfurt (Austria) (b) 1,82 (c) M - left midfielder (d) TSV Hartberg (e) SV Lafnitz, SV Horn, Wolfsberg II, Wolfsberger AC, FC Gratkorn, Austria Kärnten, SKA Kärnten II
*** Krotov - Vyacheslav Krotov (Кротов Вячеслав Александрович) (a) 14/02/1993, Astrakhan (Russia) (b) 1,83 (c) F - center forward (d) FC Pari Nizhniy Novgorod (e) Ufa, Spartak Moskva, Spartak-2, Spartak Moskva II, Volgar
*** Kroupi - Eli Junior Kroupi (Eli Junior Eric Anat Kroupi) (a) 23/06/2006, Lorient (France) (b) 1,79 (c) M - attacking midfielder (d) FC Lorient (e) Lorient B
*** Krovinovic - Filip Krovinovic (Filip Krovinović) (a) 29/08/1995, Zagreb (Croatia) (b) 1,75 (c) M - attacking midfielder (d) HNK Hajduk Split (e) Benfica, Nottingham Forest, Benfica, West Bromwich Albion, Benfica, West Bromwich Albion, Benfica, Rio Ave, NK Zagreb
*** Krpic - Miljan Krpic (Миљан Крпић) (a) 03/07/2003, Vrbas (Serbia and Montenegro, now in Serbia) (b) 1,90 (c) M - pivot (d) FK TSC Backa Topola (e) -
*** Krpic - Sulejman Krpic (Sulejman Krpić) (a) 01/01/1991, Brčko (Yugoslavia, now in Bosnia and Herzegovina) (b) 1,87 (c) F - center forward (d) FK Zeljeznicar Sarajevo (e) Western Sydney, FK Tuzla City, Astra Giurgiu, Suwon Bluewings, Zeljeznicar, Tractor Sazi, Sloboda Tuzla, AIK, Sloboda Tuzla, Metalac, FK Sarajevo, HNK Orasje, LASK II
*** Krsmanovic - Nemanja Krsmanovic (Немања Крсмановић) (a) 09/05/2003, Šabac (Serbia and Montenegro, now in Serbia) (b) 1,81 (c) D - left back (d) FK Teplice (e) FK TSC
*** Krstanovic - Ivan Krstanovic (Ivan Krstanović) (a) 05/01/1983, Tomislavgrad (Yugoslavia, now in Bosnia and Herzegovina) (b) 1,96 (c) F - center forward (d) Slaven Belupo Koprivnica (e) NK Lokomotiva, Siroki Brijeg, NK Zadar, HNK Rijeka, Dinamo Zagreb, NK Zagreb, HSK Posusje, NK Drinovci, HNK Tomislav T.
*** Krstevski - Strahinja Krstevski (Страхиња Крстевски) (a) 08/06/1997, Novi Sad (Yugoslavia, now in Serbia) (b) 1,93 (c) F - center forward (d) FC Metaloglobus Bucharest (e) Borac Sajkas, Gravina, FCI Levadia, Crvena zvezda Beograd II, FC

Samtredia, Crvena zvezda Beograd II, Rabotnicki, Crvena zvezda Beograd II, Graficar, Crvena zvezda Beograd II, Lokomotiv Sofia, Proleter, Kovilj, Proleter
*** Krstevski - Vane Krstevski (Ване Крстевски) (a) 28/04/2003, Stip (North Macedonia) (b) 1,78 (c) F - left winger (d) AP Brera (e) -
*** Krstic - Boris Krstic (a) 25/06/2003, Niš (Serbia and Montenegro, now in Serbia) (b) 1,93 (c) F - center forward (d) MSK Zilina (e) MSK Zilina B
*** Krstic - Nemanja Krstic (Немања Крстић) (a) 05/08/1994, Ljubovija (RF Yugoslavia, now in Serbia) (b) 1,78 (c) M - pivot (d) Hamrun Spartans (e) Napredak, Zlatibor, Backa, Metalac, Borac Cacak, Macva, FK Loznica, Kolubara, Napredak, FK Indjija
*** Krstic - Vukasin Krstic (Вукашин Крстић) (a) 13/04/2003, Novi Sad (Serbia and Montenegro, now in Serbia) (b) 1,84 (c) D - central defense (d) FK TSC Backa Topola (e) -
*** Krsticic - Nenad Krsticic (Ненад Крстичић) (a) 03/07/1990, Beograd (Yugoslavia, now in Serbia) (b) 1,82 (c) M - central midfielder (d) - (e) Crvena zvezda, AEK Athína, Crvena zvezda, Alavés, Sampdoria, Bologna, Sampdoria, OFK Beograd
*** Krstonijevic - Veljko Krstonijevic (a) 30/12/2001, ¿? (RF Yugoslavia, now in Montenegro) (b) - (c) F - left winger (d) Rudar Pljevlja (e) FK Pljevlja, Rudar Pljevlja
*** Krstovic - Nikola Krstovic (Никола Крстовић) (a) 05/04/2000, Golubovac (RF Yugoslavia, now in Serbia) (b) 1,85 (c) F - center forward (d) DAC Dunajska Streda (e) Crvena zvezda, Graficar, Crvena zvezda, Zeta Golubovac, Crvena zvezda, Zeta Golubovac
*** Krstovic - Srdjan Krstovic (Срђан Крстовић) (a) 05/08/2000, ¿? (RF Yugoslavia, now in Montenegro) (b) - (c) M - pivot (d) FK Sutjeska Niksic (e) Zeta Golubovac
*** Krstovski - Mario Krstovski (Марио Крстовски) (a) 03/04/1998, Kocani (North Macedonia) (b) 1,83 (c) F - center forward (d) NK Domžale (e) Sloga Meridian, Zrinjski Mostar, Leotar Trebinje, Zrinjski Mostar, Makedonija, Zrinjski Mostar, AP Brera, Rabotnicki, AP Brera, Horizont
*** Krüger - Florian Krüger (a) 13/02/1999, Staßfurt (Germany) (b) 1,86 (c) F - center forward (d) FC Groningen (e) Arminia Bielefeld, Erzgebirge Aue
*** Kruglauzs - Markuss Kruglauzs (Markuss Kruglaužs) (a) 28/01/2002, ¿? (Latvia) (b) - (c) F - center forward (d) FK Liepaja (e) Tukums, Spartaks II, FS Jelgava II
*** Krugovoy - Danil Krugovoy (Круговой Данил Владиславович) (a) 28/05/1998, Siversky, St. Petersburg Region (Russia) (b) 1,76 (c) D - left back (d) Zenit de San Petersburgo (e) Ufa, Zenit, Ufa, Zenit 2 St. Peterburg, Zenit St. Peterburg II
*** Kruja - Arsid Kruja (a) 08/06/1993, Shkodër (Albania) (b) 1,80 (c) M - right midfielder (d) KF Teuta (e) KF Vllaznia, KF Teuta, KF Vllaznia, Hajer, KF Laçi, Hajer, Flamurtari FC, Hajer, KF Vllaznia
*** Kruk - Kamil Kruk (a) 13/03/2000, Drezdenko (Poland) (b) 1,85 (c) D - central defense (d) Zagłębie Lubin (e) Stal Mielec, Zagłębie, Zaglebie Lubin II
*** Krul - André Krul (a) 08/05/1987, Grootschermer (Netherlands) (b) 1,86 (c) G (d) - (e) Glacis United, Katwijk, Alemannia Aachen, Ajax B, Preston Lions FC, Spakenburg, Iwaki FC, SC Cambuur, KFC Turnhout, Bayamón FC, Gron./Cambuur B, Boyacá Chicó, Valletta, FC Utrecht, AGOVV, FC Utrecht, Sparta Rotterdam, FC Utrecht, Telstar, FC Utrecht
*** Krulanovic - Radule Krulanovic (a) 30/06/1999, ¿? (RF Yugoslavia, now in Montenegro) (b) - (c) D - right back (d) Jedinstvo Bijelo Polje (e) Sutjeska Niksic, Jedinstvo, Sutjeska Niksic, OSK Igalo, Sutjeska II, Sutjeska Niksic
*** Krumov - Plamen Krumov (Пламен Асенов Крумов) (a) 04/11/1985, Sofia (Bulgaria) (b) 1,80 (c) D - central defense (d) - (e) Vitosha, Hebar P., Tsarsko Selo,

Arda Kardzhali, Lokomotiv Plovdiv, Slavia Sofia, Levski Sofia, Beroe, Universitatea Cluj, Concordia, Chern. Burgas, Minyor Pernik, Lokomotiv Sofia, Banants, Lokomotiv Sofia, Rilski Sportist, Lokomotiv Sofia
*** Krumrey - Jonas Krumrey (a) 25/11/2003, Prien am Chiemsee (Germany) (b) 1,94 (c) G (d) Red Bull Salzburg (e) FC Liefering
*** Krunic - Milos Krunic (Милош Крунић) (a) 22/11/1996, Beograd (RF Yugoslavia, now in Serbia) (b) 1,98 (c) G (d) Hajer Club (e) Vozdovac, FK Zemun, FK Bezanija, FK Zemun, Rakovica, FK Zemun, Srem Jakovo, FK Zemun
*** Krunic - Rade Krunic (Rade Krunić) (a) 07/10/1993, Foča (Bosnia and Herzegovina) (b) 1,84 (c) M - central midfielder (d) AC Milan (e) Empoli, Borac Cacak, Hellas Verona, Donji Srem, Hellas Verona, Donji Srem, Sutjeska Foca
*** Krupic - Edvin Krupic (a) 03/03/2004, Jesenice (Slovenia) (b) 1,84 (c) M - central midfielder (d) NK Kety Emmi Bistrica (e) Kety Bistrica, Domžale, NK Dob
*** Krupskyi - Ilya Krupskyi (Крупський Ілля Олексійович) (a) 02/10/2004, Vinnytsya (Ukraine) (b) 1,80 (c) D - right back (d) Vorskla Poltava (e) -
*** Kruse - David Kruse (David Kjær Kruse) (a) 15/05/2002, Torrung-Uldum (Denmark) (b) 1,84 (c) M - central midfielder (d) Valenciennes FC (e) AC Horsens
*** Kruse - Fayo Kruse (Fayo Janmon Kore Kruse) (a) 16/04/2004, ¿? (Faroe Islands) (b) - (c) G (d) EB/Streymur (e) -
*** Kruse - Max Kruse (Max Bennet Kruse) (a) 19/03/1988, Reinbek (Germany) (b) 1,80 (c) F - attacking midfielder (d) SC Paderborn 07 (e) VfL Wolfsburg, Union Berlin, Fenerbahce, Werder Bremen, VfL Wolfsburg, Borussia Mönchengladbach, SC Freiburg, FC St. Pauli, Werder Bremen
*** Kruse - Niklas Kruse (Niklas Tummasarson Kruse) (a) 11/05/1999, ¿? (Faroe Islands) (b) - (c) F - right winger (d) EB/Streymur (e) EB/Streymur, HB Tórshavn, EB/Streymur
*** Kruselj - Filip Kruselj (Filip Krušelj) (a) 30/03/2005, Koprivnica (Croatia) (b) 1,82 (c) D - left back (d) Slaven Belupo Koprivnica (e) Koprivnica, Koprivnica, NK Podravina
*** Krushynskyi - Borys Krushynskyi (Крушинський Борис Миколайович) (a) 10/05/2002, Sadkovychi, Lviv Oblast (Ukraine) (b) 1,90 (c) D - central defense (d) FK Polissya Zhytomyr (e) PFK Lviv, PFK Lviv II
*** Krusnauskas - Rokas Krusnauskas (Rokas Krušnauskas) (a) 04/11/1995, Kaunas (Lithuania) (b) 1,90 (c) F - center forward (d) Marijampole City (e) Neptunas, Dziugas, Csikszereda, Hegelmann, Siena, Gandzasar, FC Noah, Kauno Zalgiris, Banga, Kauno Zalgiris, Jonava, Atlantas, Kauno Zalgiris, Atlantas, Spyris
*** Krusnell - Oscar Krusnell (a) 17/02/1999, Stockholm (Sweden) (b) 1,87 (c) D - left back (d) FK Haugesund (e) Brommapojkarna, Hammarby IF, IK Frej Täby, Hammarby IF, Team TG, Hammarby IF, IK Frej Täby, Hammarby IF
*** Krutogolov - Anton Krutogolov (a) 05/04/2001, Tallinn (Estonia) (b) 1,80 (c) M - left midfielder (d) - (e) FCI Levadia, Pärnu Vaprus, FCI Levadia
*** Kruusalu - Mikk Kruusalu (a) 06/12/2000, Tallinn (Estonia) (b) - (c) M - pivot (d) - (e) Kalev Junior, Kalev, Kalev, Kalev Tallinn II
*** Kruzikas - Ignas Kruzikas (Ignas Kružikas) (a) 14/12/1998, Sirvintos (Lithuania) (b) 1,93 (c) F - center forward (d) - (e) Csikszereda, Hegelmann, Panevezys, Riteriai B, Zalgiris B, MRU-TiuMenas, Vilniaus FM
*** Kruzliak - Dominik Kruzliak (Dominik Kružliak) (a) 10/07/1996, Liptovský Mikuláš (Slovakia) (b) 1,85 (c) D - central defense (d) Volos NPS (e) Dunajska Streda, Ružomberok

*** Kryeziu - Almir Kryeziu (a) 14/12/1998, Xërxë (RF Yugoslavia, now in Kosovo) (b) 1,72 (c) F - left winger (d) FC Ballkani (e) FC Drita, KF Arbëria, KF Xërxa, KF Liria, KF Rahoveci, KF Liria

*** Kryeziu - Altin Kryeziu (a) 03/01/2002, Kranj (Slovenia) (b) 1,84 (c) M - pivot (d) - (e) NK Maribor, Torino, Tabor Sezana, RE Virton

*** Kryeziu - Dreni Kryeziu (a) 15/04/1996, Prishtinë (RF Yugoslavia, now in Kosovo) (b) - (c) D - central defense (d) FC Malisheva (e) -

*** Kryeziu - Hekuran Kryeziu (a) 12/02/1993, Luzern (Switzerland) (b) 1,81 (c) M - pivot (d) - (e) FC Winterthur, FC Zürich, FC Luzern, FC Vaduz, FC Luzern

*** Kryeziu - Leotrim Kryeziu (Leotrim Kryeziu) (a) 25/01/1999, Rogaçicë (RF Yugoslavia, now in Kosovo) (b) 1,81 (c) F - center forward (d) FC Prishtina (e) FC Lugano, FC Prishtina, FC Lugano, FC Chiasso, FC Lugano, FC Drita

*** Kryeziu - Mirlind Kryeziu (a) 26/01/1997, Zürich (Switzerland) (b) 1,96 (c) D - central defense (d) FC Zürich (e) SC Kriens, FC Zürich, FC Biel-Bienne

*** Krygård - Kevin Martin Krygård (a) 17/05/2000, Haugesund (Norway) (b) 1,84 (c) M - pivot (d) FK Haugesund (e) -

*** Krymi - Ardit Krymi (a) 02/05/1996, Shkodër (Albania) (b) 1,81 (c) M - pivot (d) KF Vllaznia (e) Soligorsk, KF Vllaznia

*** Kryparakos - Christos Kryparakos (Χρήστος Κρυπαράκος) (a) 12/06/2003, Athen (Greece) (b) 1,74 (c) M - attacking midfielder (d) Panathinaikos Athina B (e) -

*** Kryskiv - Dmytro Kryskiv (Криськів Дмитро Ігорович) (a) 06/10/2000, Kharkiv (Ukraine) (b) 1,80 (c) M - central midfielder (d) Shakhtar Donetsk (e) Shakhtar II, Metalist 1925, Shakhtar II, FK Mariupol, Shakhtar II

*** Krytsa - Aleksandr Krytsa (Крыца Александр) (a) 15/08/2002 (b) 1,77 (c) D - central defense (d) Tobol Kostanay II (e) -

*** Kryvotsiuk - Anton Kryvotsiuk (Anton Viktor oğlu Krivotsyuk (ukr. Кривоцюк Антон Вікторович)) (a) 20/08/1998, Kyiv (Ukraine) (b) 1,86 (c) D - central defense (d) Daejeon Hana Citizen (e) Wisła Płock, Neftchi Baku

*** Kryvotsiuk - Denys Kryvotsiuk (a) 01/10/2004, ¿? (Ukraine) (b) - (c) M - pivot (d) Tiszakécskei LC (e) Zalaegerszeg II

*** Kryvtsov - Sergiy Kryvtsov (Кривцов Сергій Андрійович) (a) 15/03/1991, Zaporizhya (Soviet Union, now in Ukraine) (b) 1,86 (c) D - central defense (d) Inter Miami CF (e) Shakhtar Donetsk, Metalurg Z., Zaporizhya II

*** Krzyzak - Oskar Krzyzak (Oskar Krzyżak) (a) 24/01/2002, Częstochowa (Poland) (b) 1,90 (c) D - central defense (d) Warta Poznań (e) Warta Poznań, Rakow, Skra Czestochowa, Rakow, Skra Czestochowa, Rakow, Bytovia Bytow, Rakow

*** Krzyzanski - Dawid Krzyzanski (Dawid Krzyżański) (a) 08/11/2001, Radziejów (Poland) (b) 1,75 (c) M - attacking midfielder (d) Wisła Płock (e) Wigry Suwalki, Wisła Płock, Wisla Plock II, Lider Wloclawek

*** Ksenofontov - Aleksandr Ksenofontov (Ксенофонтов Александр Витальевич) (a) 05/05/1999, Minsk (Belarus) (b) 1,80 (c) M - left midfielder (d) Torpedo-BelAZ Zhodino (e) Torpedo Zhodino, Rodina Moskva, Vitebsk, Dinamo Minsk II, Vitebsk, Dinamo Minsk II, Underdog, Dinamo Minsk II

*** Kuantaev - Ermek Kuantaev (Куантаев Ермек Болатханұлы) (a) 13/10/1990, Kostanay (Soviet Union, now in Kazakhstan) (b) 1,74 (c) D - right back (d) FC Khan Tengri (e) Taraz, FK Turan, Zhetysu, Kairat Almaty, Zhetysu, Kairat Almaty, Tobol Kostanay, Tobol II

*** Kuat - Islambek Kuat (Куат Исламбек Ержан-Улы) (a) 12/01/1993, Agadyr, Karaganda Region (Kazakhstan) (b) 1,79 (c) M - pivot (d) FC Astana (e) Khimki, Orenburg, Kairat Almaty, FC Astana, Aktobe, FC Astana, Okzhetpes, Lokomotiv Astana, Astana-Zhas

*** Kuavita - Léandre Kuavita (Léandre Filipe Kuavita) (a) 31/05/2004, ¿? (Belgium) (b) - (c) M - central midfielder (d) Standard de Lieja (e) SL16 FC

*** Kubala - Filip Kubala (a) 02/09/1999, Třinec (Czech Rep.) (b) 1,81 (c) F - attacking midfielder (d) FC Banik Ostrava (e) Hradec Kralove, Slovácko, Hradec Kralove, Slovácko, Karvina, Slovácko, Fotbal Trinec, Slovácko, Viktoria Zizkov, Slovácko

*** Kubica - Krzysztof Kubica (a) 25/05/2000, Żywiec (Poland) (b) 1,93 (c) M - central midfielder (d) Benevento (e) Górnik Zabrze, Chrobry Glogow, Górnik Zabrze, Gornik II, C-G Zywiec

*** Kubicki - Jaroslaw Kubicki (Jarosław Kubicki) (a) 07/08/1995, Lubin (Poland) (b) 1,80 (c) M - pivot (d) Jagiellonia Białystok (e) Lechia Gdánsk, Zagłębie, Zaglebie Lubin II

*** Kubik - Tobiasz Kubik (a) 29/01/2003, ¿? (Poland) (b) - (c) M - attacking midfielder (d) Skra Czestochowa (e) Rakow, Rakow II

*** Kubilinskas - Dominykas Kubilinskas (a) 09/01/1999, ¿? (Lithuania) (b) 1,79 (c) M - attacking midfielder (d) FC Dziugas Telsiai (e) Dziugas, FA Siauliai, Utenis

*** Kubin - Tomas Kubin (Tomáš Kubín) (a) 17/02/2004, ¿? (Czech Rep.) (b) - (c) M (d) FK Jablonec B (e) -

*** Kubista - Vojtech Kubista (Vojtěch Kubista) (a) 19/03/1993, Jablonec nad Nisou (Czech Rep.) (b) 1,92 (c) M - central midfielder (d) FK Mlada Boleslav (e) Jablonec, Mlada Boleslav, Jablonec, Karvina, FK Jablonec, Jihlava, FK Jablonec, FK Jablonec B

*** Kübler - Lukas Kübler (a) 30/08/1992, Bonn (Germany) (b) 1,82 (c) D - right back (d) SC Freiburg (e) SV Sandhausen, 1.FC Köln, 1.FC Köln II

*** Kublickas - Darius Kublickas (a) 16/05/2003, Rokiskis (Lithuania) (b) 1,91 (c) G (d) Marijampole City (e) FK Ekranas, Tukums, Panevezys, Panevezys B

*** Kubo - Takefusa Kubo (久保 建英) (a) 04/06/2001, Kawasaki, Kanagawa (Japan) (b) 1,73 (c) F - right winger (d) Real Sociedad (e) Real Madrid, RCD Mallorca, Real Madrid, Getafe CF, Real Madrid, Villarreal CF, Real Madrid, RCD Mallorca, Real Madrid, FC Tokyo, Yokohama F. M., FC Tokyo

*** Kubr - Lucas Kubr (a) 25/02/2004, Tongeren (Belgium) (b) 1,79 (c) D - left back (d) FK Bodø/Glimt (e) -

*** Kuc - Adis Kuc (Адис Куч) (a) 30/11/1998, ¿? (RF Yugoslavia, now in Montenegro) (b) - (c) G (d) Arsenal Tivat (e) FK Berane, FK Ibar, Rudar Pljevlja, FK Ibar, Rudar Pljevlja, Rudar Pljevlja, FK Ibar, Rudar Pljevlja, FK Ibar

*** Kuc - Edvin Kuc (Едвин Куч) (a) 27/10/1993, Tuzi (RF Yugoslavia, now in Montenegro) (b) 1,79 (c) M - pivot (d) FC Ballkani (e) SC Gjilani, FC Ballkani, Rudar Pljevlja, FK Decic Tuzi, FK Mladost, Usti nad Labem, FK Decic Tuzi

*** Kucera - Jakub Kucera (Jakub Kučera) (a) 28/01/1997, ¿? (Czech Rep.) (b) 1,84 (c) M - central midfielder (d) FC Hradec Kralove (e) SK Lisen, 1.SC Znojmo, Vitkovice, Blansko, Zbrojovka Brno

*** Kucera - Tomas Kucera (Tomáš Kučera) (a) 20/07/1991, Havlíčkův Brod (Czechoslovakia, now in Czech Rep.) (b) 1,85 (c) M - central midfielder (d) - (e) Teplice, Viktoria Plzen, Teplice, Viktoria Plzen, Jihlava, Viktoria Plzen, Jihlava, Hradec Kralove, Jihlava, Jihlava B

*** Kuchaev - Konstantin Kuchaev (Кучаев Константин Витальевич) (a) 18/03/1998, Ryazan (Russia) (b) 1,83 (c) M - attacking midfielder (d) CSKA Moskva (e) Rubin Kazan, CSKA Moskva, CSKA Moskva II, Master-Saturn

*** Kucharczyk - Michal Kucharczyk (Michał Kucharczyk) (a) 20/03/1991, Warszawa (Poland) (b) 1,78 (c) F - right winger (d) Pakhtakor Tashkent (e) Pogon Szczecin, Ural, Legia Warszawa, Swit N.D.M., Legia Warszawa, Swit N.D.M.

*** Kucharik - Samuel Miroslav Kucharik (Samuel Miroslav Kuchárik) (a) 24/06/2004, ¿? (Slovakia) (b) - (c) D (d) Tatran Liptovsky Mikulas (e) -

*** Kucher - Danylo Kucher (Кучер Данило Олегович) (a) 25/01/1997, Kryvyi Rig, Dnipropetrovsk Oblast (Ukraine) (b) 1,93 (c) G (d) UTA Arad (e) Ingulets, FK Minaj, RFS, Daugavpils, Girnyk KR, Dnipro, Dnipro II

*** Kucherenko - Oleksandr Kucherenko (Кучеренко Олександр Євгенович) (a) 01/10/1991, Slovyansk, Donetsk Oblast (Ukraine) (b) 1,85 (c) M - pivot (d) NK Veres Rivne (e) Ingulets, Volyn Lutsk, Ingulets, Zirka, FC Veris, FC Costuleni, Nistru Otaci, Avangard K., Stal II, Slovkhlib

*** Kucherenko - Yevgeniy Kucherenko (Кучеренко Євгеній Ігорович) (a) 27/08/1999, Kyiv (Ukraine) (b) 1,92 (c) G (d) FC Dila Gori (e) Kolos Kovalivka, FK Aksu, Kolos Kovalivka, Podillya Kh., Kolos Kovalivka, Leiria, Shakhtar II

*** Kucherov - Valeriy Kucherov (Кучеров Валерій Володимирович) (a) 11/08/1993, Stakhanov, Lugansk Oblast (Ukraine) (b) 1,75 (c) M - pivot (d) NK Veres Rivne (e) FK Kalush, Arsenal Kyiv, Veres Rivne, Stal Kamyanske, Stal Alchevsk, Stal II

*** Kucheruk - Vladyslav Kucheruk (Кучерук Владислав Вікторович) (a) 14/02/1999, Vinnytsya (Ukraine) (b) 1,91 (c) G (d) - (e) Zorya Lugansk, Dinamo Kyïv, Chornomorets, Dinamo Kyïv, Dinamo Kiev II, Kolos Kovalivka, Dinamo Kiev II

*** Kucheryavyi - Maksym Kucheryavyi (Кучерявий Максим Сергійович) (a) 09/05/2002, Kyiv (Ukraine) (b) 1,76 (c) M - attacking midfielder (d) St. Johnstone FC (e) Falkirk FC, St. Johnstone, St. Johnstone B, Kelty Hearts, St. Johnstone B, Brechin City, St. Johnstone B

*** Kuchinskiy - Konstantin Kuchinskiy (Кучинский Константин Алексеевич) (a) 15/07/1998, Minsk (Belarus) (b) 1,72 (c) D - right back (d) FK Gomel (e) Dinamo Minsk, Dinamo Minsk II, Belshina, Dinamo Minsk II, Belshina, Dinamo Minsk II, FK Lida, Dinamo Minsk II, BGU Minsk II, Dinamo Minsk II, BGU Minsk II

*** Kuchko - Gleb Kuchko (Кучко Глеб Алексеевич) (a) 03/06/2005, Minsk (Belarus) (b) 1,80 (c) M - pivot (d) Wisła Płock (e) Wisla Plock II

*** Kuchta - Jan Kuchta (a) 08/01/1997, Liberec (Czech Rep.) (b) 1,85 (c) F - center forward (d) AC Sparta Praga (e) Lokomotiv Moskva, Sparta Praha, Lokomotiv Moskva, Slavia Praha, Slovan Liberec, Slavia Praha B, Slovan Liberec, Slavia Praha B, Teplice, Slavia Praha B, Slovácko, Slavia Praha B, Viktoria Zizkov, Slavia Praha B, Bohemians 1905, Slavia Praha B

*** Kuciak - Dusan Kuciak (Dušan Kuciak) (a) 21/05/1985, Žilina (Czechoslovakia, now in Slovakia) (b) 1,94 (c) G (d) KS Lechia Gdańsk (e) Hull City, Legia Warszawa, FC Vaslui, MSK Zilina, West Ham Utd., MSK Zilina, AS Trencin

*** Kucka - Juraj Kucka (a) 26/02/1987, Bojnice (Czechoslovakia, now in Slovakia) (b) 1,86 (c) M - central midfielder (d) Slovan Bratislava (e) Parma, Watford, Parma, Trabzonspor, AC Milan, Genoa, Sparta Praha, Ružomberok, Podbrezova, Podbrezova B

*** Kuckar - Baver Kuckar (Baver Kuçkar) (a) 15/02/2003, Mus (Turkey) (b) 1,86 (c) G (d) Sivasspor (e) -

*** Kudela - Martin Kudela (a) 29/01/2003, ¿? (Czech Rep.) (b) - (c) M (d) SK Hanacka Slavia Kromeriz (e) HS Kromeriz, Slovácko B

*** Kudelkins - Aleksejs Kudelkins (Aleksejs Kudeļkins) (a) 08/05/2002, ¿? (Latvia) (b) - (c) D - central defense (d) BFC Daugavpils (e) -

*** Kudev - Ljupche Kudev (Љупче Кудев) (a) 07/12/2003, Stip (North Macedonia) (b) 1,75 (c) F - right winger (d) Bregalnica Stip (e) Pehcevo, Bregalnica Stip

*** Kudijan - Andrej Kudijan (Андреј Кудијан) (a) 04/09/1997, Skopje (North Macedonia) (b) 1,85 (c) F - center forward (d) Detonit Plackovica (e) Pobeda Prilep, Kozuf, Gostivar, Bregalnica Stip, Plackovica, FK Skopje, Borec Veles, Rabotnicki, Euromilk GL, Rabotnicki
*** Kudravets - Andrey Kudravets (Кудравец Андрей Русланович) (a) 02/09/2003, Borisov (Belarus) (b) 1,91 (c) G (d) BATE Borisov (e) BATE II
*** Kudrjavcevs - Vjaceslavs Kudrjavcevs (Vjačeslavs Kudrjavcevs) (a) 30/03/1998, Riga (Latvia) (b) 1,89 (c) G (d) SK Super Nova (e) Liepaja, Valmiera, Stomil, Widzew Lódz, Stomil, JFK Ventspils, Legia Warszawa, Riga, Babite, FC Jurmala, Tukums
*** Kudryashov - Fedor Kudryashov (Кудряшов Фёдор Васильевич) (a) 05/04/1987, Mamakan, Irkutsk Region (Soviet Union, now in Russia) (b) 1,84 (c) D - central defense (d) Fakel Voronezh (e) Antalyaspor, Sochi, Basaksehir, Rubin Kazan, Rostov, Terek Grozny, Spartak Moskva, Krasnodar, Spartak Moskva, Tom Tomsk, Spartak Moskva, Spartak Moskva II, Khimki, Spartak Moskva II, Sibiryak Bratsk
*** Kudryashov - Viktor Kudryashov (a) 29/10/2005, ¿? (Estonia) (b) - (c) M - left midfielder (d) JK Trans Narva (e) -
*** Kudsk - Jeppe Kudsk (Jeppe Kudsk Pedersen) (a) 25/02/2003, ¿? (Denmark) (b) 1,88 (c) D - central defense (d) Randers FC (e) -
*** Kudus - Mohammed Kudus (a) 02/08/2000, Accra (Ghana) (b) 1,77 (c) M - attacking midfielder (d) Ajax de Ámsterdam (e) Nordsjælland, Right to Dream
*** Kuek - Akon Kuek (a) 10/05/2004, ¿? (Finland) (b) 1,78 (c) M - central midfielder (d) Vaasan Palloseura (e) -
*** Kuen - Andreas Kuen (a) 24/03/1995, Zams (Austria) (b) 1,75 (c) M - central midfielder (d) Atromitos FC (e) Sturm Graz, SV Mattersburg, Rapid Wien, FAC, Rapid Wien, FC Wacker, FC Wacker II
*** Kuete - Dylan Kuete (Dylan Loic Nsidjine Kuete) (a) 12/07/2000, Duala (Cameroon) (b) 1,77 (c) D - left back (d) F91 Dudelange (e) RFCU Luxembourg, US Mondorf, RFCU Luxembourg, Kaiserslautern II
*** Kühn - Nicolas Kühn (Nicolas-Gerrit Kühn) (a) 01/01/2000, Wunstorf (Germany) (b) 1,74 (c) F - right winger (d) SK Rapid Wien (e) FC Bayern II, Erzgebirge Aue, FC Bayern II, Ajax B, FC Bayern II, Ajax B
*** Kuijpers - Roy Kuijpers (a) 17/01/2000, Zwolle (Netherlands) (b) 1,75 (c) F - right winger (d) RKC Waalwijk (e) FC Den Bosch, FC Den Bosch
*** Kuiper - Pascal Kuiper (a) 17/03/2004, Papendrecht (Netherlands) (b) 1,94 (c) G (d) Excelsior Rotterdam (e) -
*** Kuipers - Bas Kuipers (Bas Edo Kuipers) (a) 17/08/1994, Amsterdam (Netherlands) (b) 1,80 (c) D - left back (d) Go Ahead Eagles Deventer (e) NEC Nijmegen, FC Viitorul, ADO Den Haag, Excelsior, Ajax B, Excelsior, Ajax B
*** Kuittinen - Luka Kuittinen (a) 29/03/2003, Rovaniemi (Finland) (b) 1,90 (c) D - central defense (d) FC Inter Turku (e) RoPS, RoPS II
*** Kujanpää - Aatu Kujanpää (a) 27/07/1998, ¿? (Finland) (b) 1,85 (c) M - attacking midfielder (d) Helsinki IFK (e) SJK Seinäjoki, VPS, SJK II
*** Kujasalo - Niilo Kujasalo (a) 17/03/2004, ¿? (Finland) (b) - (c) M - pivot (d) Kokkolan Pallo-Veikot (e) Kokkolan PV, HJK Klubi 04
*** Kujundic - Marko Kujundic (Marko Kujundžić) (a) 14/10/2002, Banja Luka (Bosnia and Herzegovina) (b) 1,79 (c) D - left back (d) FK BSK Banja Luka (e) BSK Banja Luka, Borac Banja Luka, Sloga Meridian, Borac Banja Luka
*** Kuka - Enes Kuka (a) 14/01/2002, ¿? (Albania) (b) 1,80 (c) M - pivot (d) KF Tirana (e) KS Besa, KF Tirana

*** Kuka - Klajdi Kuka (a) 29/03/1990, Tiranë (Albania) (b) 1,91 (c) G (d) AF Elbasani (e) KF Laçi, Flamurtari FC, KF Laçi, KF Tërbuni, KS Besa, FC Dinamo, KF Turbina, KF Vora, KS Kastrioti, KF Tërbuni, SF Düren, FK Tomori Berat, KF Tërbuni, KF Tirana, FK Tomori Berat, KF Tirana
*** Kuka - Viktor Kuka (a) 25/06/1990, Prishtinë (Yugoslavia, now in Kosovo) (b) 1,82 (c) D - right back (d) FC Suhareka (e) KF Drenica, KF Flamurtari, KF Liria, KF Vëllaznimi, FC Malisheva, KF Feronikeli, KF Ferizaj, FC Drita, KF Ferizaj, FC Drita, FC Llapi, KF Teuta, FC Prishtina
*** Kukavica - Ivan Kukavica (a) 02/02/2004, Split (Croatia) (b) - (c) D (d) NK Lokomotiva Zagreb (e) -
*** Kukharchik - Ilya Kukharchik (Кухарчик Илья Сергеевич) (a) 10/03/1997, Baranovichi (Belarus) (b) 1,72 (c) M - right midfielder (d) Belshina Bobruisk (e) Torpedo Zhodino, Belshina, Torpedo Zhodino, Belshina, Vitebsk, FK Baranovichi, Vitebsk, BATE II, FK Baranovichi, BATE II
*** Kukharchuk - Ilya Kukharchuk (Кухарчук Илья Владимирович) (a) 02/08/1990, Kostroma (Soviet Union, now in Russia) (b) 1,86 (c) F - right winger (d) FC Pari Nizhniy Novgorod (e) Torpedo Moskva, Khimki, Tom Tomsk, Tambov, Baltika, Enisey, Volga Nizhny Novgorod, Shinnik Yaroslav, Spartak Nalchik, Ural, Anzhi, Ural, Anzhi, Rubin Kazán II, Shinnik Yaroslav
*** Kukharev - Aleksandr Kukharev (Александр Кухарев) (a) 02/05/2002, ¿? (Russia) (b) - (c) F - right winger (d) - (e) JK Tammeka
*** Kukharevych - Mykola Kukharevych (Кухаревич Микола Ігорович) (a) 01/07/2001, Udrytsk, Rivne Oblast (Ukraine) (b) 1,91 (c) F - center forward (d) Swansea City (e) Troyes, Hibernian FC, Troyes, OH Leuven, Troyes, Rukh Lviv
*** Kukharuk - Andriy Kukharuk (Кухарук Андрій Олегович) (a) 13/12/1995, Ternopil (Ukraine) (b) 1,73 (c) M - central midfielder (d) NK Veres Rivne (e) Ingulets, FK Mariupol, Rukh Lviv, Agrobiznes V., WSC Hertha Wels, FK Sambir, Nyva Ternopil, Sevastopol II, FK Sevastopol 2
*** Kukhianidze - Giorgi Kukhianidze (გიორგი კუხიანიძე) (a) 01/07/1992, Kutaisi (Georgia) (b) 1,80 (c) M - attacking midfielder (d) FC Qizilqum (e) Torpedo Kutaisi, Qizilqum, Dinamo Tbilisi, Torpedo Kutaisi, FC Locomotive, Torpedo Kutaisi, Shukura, FC Zestafoni, Torpedo Kutaisi, Torpedo Kutaisi II
*** Kukhianidze - Sergo Kukhianidze (სერგო კუხიანიძე) (a) 23/04/1999, Kutaisi (Georgia) (b) 1,79 (c) F - center forward (d) FC Dila Gori (e) Samgurali, Merani Martvili, Torpedo Kutaisi II
*** Kukic - Luka Kukic (Luka Kukić) (a) 16/05/1996, Mostar (Bosnia and Herzegovina) (b) 1,89 (c) G (d) FC Buxoro (e) HSK Posusje, Zrinjski Mostar, Novi Pazar, Zrinjski Mostar, Sloboda Tuzla, Korona Kielce, NK Osijek II, RNK Split, NK Imotski, RNK Split, NK Imotski
*** Kukk - Christopher Kukk (a) 24/08/2003, Tallinn (Estonia) (b) - (c) D - central defense (d) Kalev Tallinn Junior (e) Keila JK
*** Kuklys - Mantas Kuklys (a) 10/06/1987, Šiauliai (Soviet Union, now in Lithuania) (b) 1,86 (c) M - central midfielder (d) FA Siauliai (e) Zalgiris, Zhetysu, Zalgiris, Bohemians 1905, Zalgiris, KV Turnhout, Siauliai
*** Kukoc - Marino Kukoc (Marino Kukoč) (a) 11/07/2004, Split (Croatia) (b) 1,82 (c) M - pivot (d) - (e) NK Kustosija, Hrv Dragovoljac, RNK Split
*** Kukol - Vladimir Kukol (Vladimír Kukoľ) (a) 08/05/1986, Levoča (Czechoslovakia, now in Slovakia) (b) 1,72 (c) M - right midfielder (d) FK Podkonice (e) Podbrezova, FK Poprad, Spartak Myjava, Jihlava, Spartak Myjava, Zawisza, Jagiellonia, Sandecja, Ružomberok, Spisska N. Ves

*** Kukucka - Michal Kukucka (Michal Kukučka) (a) 12/04/2002, Nové Mesto nad Váhom (Slovakia) (b) 1,91 (c) G (d) AS Trencin (e) -
*** Kukucka - Ondrej Kukucka (Ondřej Kukučka) (a) 23/03/2004, ¿? (Czech Rep.) (b) 1,90 (c) D - central defense (d) FK Pardubice (e) Sparta Praha B
*** Kukulis - Roberts Kukulis (a) 25/05/2007, Ventspils (Latvia) (b) 1,87 (c) F - center forward (d) - (e) Super Nova
*** Kulach - Vladyslav Kulach (Кулач Владислав Ігорович) (a) 07/05/1993, Donetsk (Ukraine) (b) 1,78 (c) F - center forward (d) Zira FK (e) Dinamo Kyïv, Vorskla Poltava, Shakhtar Donetsk, Honvéd, Shakhtar Donetsk, FK Oleksandriya, Shakhtar Donetsk, Vorskla Poltava, Shakhtar Donetsk, Shakhtar II, Zorya Lugansk, Shakhtar II, Eskisehirspor, Shakhtar II, Stal D., Shakhtar II, Metalurg Z., Shakhtar II, Illichivets, Shakhtar II
*** Kulakov - Andriy Kulakov (Кулаков Андрій Андрійович) (a) 28/04/1999, Verkhnyobogdanivka, Lugansk Oblast (Ukraine) (b) 1,84 (c) F - center forward (d) FK Oleksandriya (e) Shakhtar Donetsk, Tuzlaspor, Shakhtar Donetsk, FK Mariupol, Shakhtar Donetsk, Shakhtar II
*** Kulakov - Denys Kulakov (Кулаков Денис Єрмилович) (a) 01/05/1986, Izyum, Kharkiv Oblast (Soviet Union, now in Ukraine) (b) 1,85 (c) D - right back (d) Ural Ekaterimburgo (e) Metalist, Dnipro, Vorskla Poltava, Shakhtar Donetsk, Vorskla Poltava, Shakhtar Donetsk, Illichivets, Shakhtar Donetsk, Shakhtar II, UFK Kharkiv
*** Kulakovskyi - Artem Kulakovskyi (Кулаковський Артем Валерійович) (a) 11/02/2002, Komsomolsk, Poltava Oblast (Ukraine) (b) 1,74 (c) M - central midfielder (d) Vorskla Poltava (e) Vorskla II, Girnyk-Sport, Vorskla II, Dinamo Kiev II
*** Kulasin - Enver Kulasin (Enver Kulašin) (a) 11/09/2003, Travnik (Bosnia and Herzegovina) (b) 1,68 (c) F - right winger (d) FK Borac Banja Luka (e) -
*** Kulchitskiy - Vladislav Kulchitskiy (Кульчицкий Владислав Николаевич) (a) 25/01/2002, Slutsk (Belarus) (b) - (c) M - attacking midfielder (d) FK Slutsk II (e) -
*** Kulenovic - Luka Kulenovic (Luka Kulenović) (a) 29/09/1999, Toronto, Ontario (Canada) (b) 1,90 (c) F - center forward (d) FC Slovan Liberec (e) Sloga Meridian, Rudar Prijedor, NK Kustosija, NK Osijek II, Zeljeznicar BL
*** Kulenovic - Sandro Kulenovic (Sandro Kulenović) (a) 04/12/1999, Zagreb (Croatia) (b) 1,91 (c) F - center forward (d) GNK Dinamo Zagreb (e) NK Lokomotiva, Dinamo Zagreb, HNK Rijeka, Dinamo Zagreb, Legia Warszawa, Legia Warszawa
*** Kuleshov - Roman Kuleshov (Кулешов Роман Юрьевич) (a) 14/06/2003, ¿? (Belarus) (b) 1,73 (c) M - pivot (d) FK Slonim 2017 (e) Dnepr Mogilev
*** Kuliev - Eldar Kuliev (Кулієв Ельдар Шахбазович) (a) 24/03/2002, Kyiv (Ukraine) (b) 1,82 (c) M - central midfielder (d) Zira FK (e) FK Minaj, FK Mariupol, FK Mariupol II
*** Kulikov - Daniil Kulikov (Куликов Даниил Михайлович) (a) 24/06/1998, Reutov, Moskva Region (Russia) (b) 1,78 (c) M - pivot (d) Lokomotiv Moskva (e) Loko-Kazanka M., Lokomotiv Moskva II
*** Kulikov - Denis Kulikov (קוליקוב דניס) (a) 24/08/2004, ¿? (Israel) (b) - (c) D - central defense (d) - (e) Maccabi Netanya
*** Kulinits - Aleksandr Kulinits (Aleksandr Kulinitš) (a) 24/05/1992, Tallinn (Estonia) (b) 1,86 (c) D - left back (d) JK Trans Narva (e) Rostocker FC, Kalju FC, NK Krsko, FCI Tallinn, Levadia
*** Kulisek - Patrik Kulisek (Patrik Kulíšek) (a) 14/05/2003, ¿? (Czech Rep.) (b) 1,88 (c) D - central defense (d) FC Zlin B (e) -
*** Kulpeisov - Vyacheslav Kulpeisov (Кульпеисов Вячеслав) (a) 24/12/2001, Kostanái (Kazakhstan) (b) 1,75 (c) M - pivot (d) Tobol Kostanay (e) Tobol II

*** Kulusevski - Dejan Kulusevski (Дejaн Kулушевски) (a) 25/04/2000, Stockholm (Sweden) (b) 1,86 (c) F - right winger (d) Tottenham Hotspur (e) Juventus, Tottenham Hotspur, Juventus, Parma, Juventus, Atalanta, Parma, Atalanta
*** Kulzhanov - Izat Kulzhanov (Кулжанов Изат Бакыевич) (a) 18/07/2001, Aksu (Kazakhstan) (b) 1,71 (c) M - attacking midfielder (d) - (e) FK Aksu, Nosta, Pavlodar II
*** Kumado - Willy Kumado (William Kumado) (a) 16/10/2002, ¿? (Ghana) (b) - (c) D - right back (d) Lyngby BK (e) Nordsjælland, Right to Dream
*** Kumarov - Aydos Kumarov (Құмаров Айдос) (a) 27/02/2002, ¿? (Kazakhstan) (b) 1,75 (c) D - left back (d) Qyzyljar Petropavlovsk (e) Astana-M
*** Kumbedi - Saël Kumbedi (Saël Kumbedi Nseke) (a) 26/03/2005, Stains (France) (b) 1,75 (c) D - right back (d) Olympique de Lyon (e) Le Havre AC
*** Kumbulla - Marash Kumbulla (a) 08/02/2000, Peschiera del Garda (Italy) (b) 1,91 (c) D - central defense (d) AS Roma (e) Hellas Verona, AS Roma, Hellas Verona
*** Kumburovic - Nikola Kumburovic (a) 13/11/1999, Podgorica (RF Yugoslavia, Montenegro) (b) 1,87 (c) D - central defense (d) Chernomorets Novorossijsk (e)'FK Turon, FK Iskra
*** Kumru - Arda Kumru (a) 05/07/2005, ¿? (Turkey) (b) - (c) F - center forward (d) MKE Ankaragücü (e) -
*** Kums - Sven Kums (a) 26/02/1988, Asse (Belgium) (b) 1,76 (c) M - central midfielder (d) KAA Gent (e) RSC Anderlecht, KAA Gent, RSC Anderlecht, Watford, Udinese, Watford, KAA Gent, Zulte Waregem, Heerenveen, KV Kortrijk, RSC Anderlecht, KV Kortrijk, Lierse SK
*** Kun - Dominik Kun (a) 22/06/1993, Giżycko (Poland) (b) 1,71 (c) M - pivot (d) RTS Widzew Łódź (e) Sandecja, Stomil, Wisła Płock, Pogon Siedlce, Wisła Płock, Pogon Szczecin, Stomil, V. Wegorzewo
*** Kun - Patryk Kun (Patryk Kun) (a) 20/04/1995, Giżycko (Poland) (b) 1,65 (c) M - left midfielder (d) Legia de Varsovia (e) Rakow, Rozwój Katowice, Arka Gdynia, Rozwój Katowice, Stomil, Rozwój Katowice, V. Wegorzewo, Stomil, St. Olsztyn II, V. Wegorzewo
*** Kunde - Pierre Kunde (Pierre Kunde Malong) (a) 26/07/1995, Limbé (Cameroon) (b) 1,80 (c) M - central midfielder (d) Olympiakos El Pireo (e) VfL Bochum, Olympiakos, Mainz 05, At. Madrid B, Granada CF, At. Madrid B, Extremadura, At. Madrid B, Alcobendas CF, Best Stars
*** Kundrák - Norbert Kundrák (a) 18/05/1999, Miskolc (Hungary) (b) 1,80 (c) F - center forward (d) Budapest Honvéd FC (e) Debrecen, Szeged, Debrecen, Debreceni EAC, Debrecen, Ferencváros, Soroksár, Ferencváros, Soroksár, Ferencváros
*** Küng - Hannes Küng (a) 02/02/2003, Bludenz (Austria) (b) - (c) D - central defense (d) Wiener Sport-Club (e) Austria Lustenau
*** Kuni - Kuni (邦本 宜裕, Takahiro Kunimoto) (a) 08/10/1997, Kitakyushu, Fukuoka (Japan) (b) 1,72 (c) M - attacking midfielder (d) Johor Darul Ta'zim (e) Casa Pia, Jeonbuk Hyundai, Gyeongnam FC, Avispa Fukuoka
*** Kunic - Petar Kunic (Petar Kunić) (a) 15/07/1993, Drvar (Bosnia and Herzegovina) (b) 1,89 (c) F - center forward (d) FK Radnik Surdulica (e) Napredak, Atyrau, Zrinjski Mostar, AE Larisa, Borac Banja Luka, Novi Pazar, Rudar Prijedor, Dukla B, Radnik Bijelj., Dukla B, Borac Banja Luka
*** Kunskiy - Maksim Kunskiy (Кунский Максим Сергеевич) (a) 09/01/2003, Minsk (Belarus) (b) - (c) F - left winger (d) Shakhter Soligorsk II (e) Shakhter P., Soligorsk II, Energetik-BGU, Soligorsk II
*** Kunst - Des Kunst (a) 12/10/1999, IJmuiden (Netherlands) (b) 1,90 (c) F - left winger (d) VV Katwijk (e) Varbergs BoIS, AZ Alkmaar

*** Kuol - Alou Kuol (a) 05/07/2001, Khartum (Sudan) (b) 1,81 (c) F - center forward (d) Central Coast Mariners (e) VfB Stuttgart, Stuttgart II, SV Sandhausen, Stuttgart II, Central Coast, Goulburn V. S.

*** Kuol - Garang Kuol (Garang Mawien Kuol) (a) 15/09/2004, Cairo (Egypt) (b) 1,75 (c) F - right winger (d) FC Volendam (e) Newcastle Utd., Heart of Midlothian, Newcastle Utd., Central Coast, Goulburn V. S.

*** Kupanov - Filip Kupanov (Филип Купанов) (a) 09/09/2002, Gevgelija (North Macedonia) (b) 1,94 (c) G (d) AP Brera (e) Belasica, AP Brera, Detonit Junior, AP Brera

*** Kupatadze - Lazare Kupatadze (ლაზარე კუპატაძე) (a) 08/02/1996, Chiatura (Georgia) (b) 1,95 (c) G (d) FC Saburtalo (e) Dinamo Batumi, Saburtalo, Jeunesse Esch, Saburtalo, FC Locomotive, Saburtalo

*** Kupcik - Lubos Kupcik (Luboš Kupčík) (a) 03/03/1989, Trstená (Czechoslovakia, now in Slovakia) (b) 1,87 (c) D - central defense (d) FK Pohronie (e) Banska Bystrica, Podbrezova, Banska Bystrica, MSK Zilina B

*** Kupczak - Mateusz Kupczak (Mateusz Kupczak) (a) 20/02/1992, Żywiec (Poland) (b) 1,87 (c) M - pivot (d) Warta Poznań (e) Nieciecza, Podbeskidzie, Nieciecza, Podbeskidzie, GKS Tychy, Podbeskidzie, Skalka Zabnica, Podbeskidzie, C-G Zywiec

*** Küpelikilinc - Berkan Küpelikilinc (Berkan Küpelikılınç) (a) 14/01/2003, Frankfurt am Main (Germany) (b) 1,72 (c) D - right back (d) Gaziantep FK (e) Karaman FK, Gaziantep FK, E. Frankfurt II

*** Kupisz - Tomasz Kupisz (Tomasz Mateusz Kupisz) (a) 02/01/1990, Radom (Poland) (b) 1,80 (c) F - right winger (d) Jagiellonia Białystok (e) Pordenone, Reggina, Pordenone, Salernitana, Bari, Salernitana, Bari, Trapani, Bari, Ascoli, AS Livorno, Ascoli, RC Cesena, Chievo Verona, Novara, Chievo Verona, Brescia, Chievo Verona, Cittadella, Chievo Verona, Jagiellonia, Wigan Ath., MKS Piaseczno

*** Kupresak - Mihael Kupresak (Mihael Kuprešak) (a) 15/05/2001, Orašje (Bosnia and Herzegovina) (b) 1,78 (c) D - left back (d) NK Siroki Brijeg (e) NK Osijek II

*** Kuptsov - Ilya Kuptsov (Купцов Илья Александрович) (a) 25/01/2002, Moskva (Russia) (b) 1,98 (c) G (d) Dinamo 2 Moskva (e) Dinamo Moskva II

*** Kupusovic - Njegos Kupusovic (Његош Купусовић) (a) 22/02/2001, Bijeljina (Bosnia and Herzegovina) (b) 1,79 (c) F - center forward (d) AS Trencin (e) Türkgücü Münch., Eintracht Braunschweig, Erzgebirge Aue

*** Kuqi - Hamdi Kuqi (a) 15/06/2002, ¿? (Italy) (b) - (c) F - center forward (d) AC Libertas (e) -

*** Kuqi - Rinor Kuqi (a) 27/04/1997, ¿? (RF Yugoslavia, now in Kosovo) (b) - (c) D - central defense (d) KF Dukagjini (e) KF Istogu, KF Dukagjini, KF Onix

*** Kuquku - Shaban Kuquku (a) 18/09/2001, Visp (Switzerland) (b) 1,93 (c) G (d) FC Salgesch (e) -

*** Kur - Kur Kur (Kur Gai Kur) (a) 20/02/2000, Kakuma (Kenya) (b) 1,88 (c) M - attacking midfielder (d) - (e) Novi Pazar, Adelaide City, Croydon Kings, Modbury SC

*** Kurakins - Antons Kurakins (a) 01/01/1990, Rīga (Soviet Union, now in Latvia) (b) 1,84 (c) D - left back (d) FK Beitar (e) Riga, JFK Ventspils, Stranraer, Brechin City, Blazma, Dizvanagi

*** Kurakins - Vladislavs Kurakins (a) 09/07/1996, Daugavpils (Latvia) (b) 1,85 (c) G (d) BFC Daugavpils (e) Egersund, Dinamo Riga, Albatroz/Jelgava, Mauerwerk, Riga, Spartaks, Daugavpils

*** Kuraksin - Danil Kuraksin (a) 04/04/2003, Tallinn (Estonia) (b) 1,82 (c) F - left winger (d) FC Flora Tallinn (e) -

*** Kuralbekov - Olzhas Kuralbekov (Куралбеков Олжас Нуржанулы) (a) 04/10/2003, Shymkent (Kazakhstan) (b) 1,80 (c) M (d) FK Turan II (e) -

*** Kurdadze - Beka Kurdadze (ბექა ქურდაძე) (a) 24/01/1997, Tbilisi (Georgia) (b) 1,88 (c) G (d) FC Telavi (e) Saburtalo, FC Gagra, FC Samtredia, Samgurali, FC Gagra, Saburtalo, FC Locomotive, Saburtalo

*** Kurdadze - Levan Kurdadze (ლევან ქურდაძე) (a) 03/09/1990, Tbilisi (Soviet Union, now in Georgia) (b) 1,88 (c) D - central defense (d) Sioni Bolnisi (e) Shukura, Samgurali, FC Dila, Tskhinvali, FC Locomotive, FC Gagra, Guria, Mertskhali, FK Zugdidi, Guria, Tskhinvali

*** Kurdic - Numan Kurdic (Numan Kurdić) (a) 01/07/1999, Tesanj (Bosnia and Herzegovina) (b) 1,89 (c) D - central defense (d) Araz-Naxcivan Nakchivan (e) RWDM, Novi Pazar, RWDM, FK Sarajevo, FK Kukësi, FK Sarajevo, Novi Pazar, FK Sarajevo

*** Kurej - Nicolas Kurej (a) 07/04/2004, Bardejov (Slovakia) (b) - (c) D (d) Dynamo Malzenice (e) Dyn. Malzenice, Spartak Trnava

*** Kurez - Gal Kurez (Gal Kurež) (a) 27/04/2001, ¿? (Slovenia) (b) 1,81 (c) M - attacking midfielder (d) Tikves Kavadarci (e) NK Bravo, Olimpija

*** Kurganskiy - Sergey Kurganskiy (Курганский Сергей Игоревич) (a) 15/05/1986, Grodno (Soviet Union, now in Belarus) (b) 1,91 (c) G (d) BK Maxline Vitebsk (e) Neman Grodno, FK Lida, Slonim, Dnepr Mogilev, Partizan Minsk, Dinamo Brest, Partizan Minsk, Neman Grodno, Savit, Neman Grodno, Neman II

*** Kurgin - Lev Kurgin (Кургин Лев Олегович) (a) 06/06/2002, Taldykorgan (Kazakhstan) (b) 1,83 (c) D - left back (d) Kairat Almaty (e) Kairat Moskva, Kairat-Zhas

*** Kurim - Kristjan Kurim (a) 10/08/1998, Tallinn (Estonia) (b) - (c) D - central defense (d) - (e) Kuressaare, FC Kuressaare II, JK Tabasalu, Kalju FC, Paide, FC Flora III, JK Ganvix

*** Kurka - Petr Kurka (a) 04/07/2002, Vysoké Mýto (Czech Rep.) (b) 1,81 (c) D - left back (d) FK Pardubice (e) Varnsdorf, Pardubice, Usti nad Labem, Pardubice

*** Kurko - Vasyl Kurko (Курко Василь Миколайович) (a) 25/04/1995, Illichivsk, Odesa Oblast (Ukraine) (b) 1,90 (c) D - central defense (d) NK Veres Rivne (e) Livyi Bereg, Prykarpattya, Volyn Lutsk, Zhemchuzhyna O., Metalist II, Chornomorets II

*** Kurminowski - Dawid Kurminowski (a) 24/02/1999, Śrem (Poland) (b) 1,82 (c) F - center forward (d) Zagłębie Lubin (e) Aarhus GF, Zagłębie, Aarhus GF, MSK Zilina, Lech Poznan, MSK Zilina B, Lech Poznan, Michalovce, Lech Poznan, Lech Poznan II

*** Kurnaz - Fatih Kurnaz (Mehmet Fatih Kurnaz) (a) 11/07/2001, Erzurum (Turkey) (b) - (c) M - central midfielder (d) Fatih Karagümrük (e) -

*** Kurt - Mert Kurt (Mert Han Kurt) (a) 25/10/2002, ¿? (Belgium) (b) 1,80 (c) F - center forward (d) Giresunspor (e) Jong Cercle

*** Kurtaj - Albion Kurtaj (a) 02/11/1998, Kaçanik (RF Yugoslavia, now in Kosovo) (b) 1,75 (c) F - left winger (d) FC Prishtina (e) KF Llapi, KF Ferizaj, KF Vitia, KF Ulpiana

*** Kurtalic - Alen Kurtalic (Alen Kurtalić) (a) 28/10/1999, Tuzla (Bosnia and Herzegovina) (b) - (c) M - pivot (d) FK Sloboda Tuzla (e) Jihlava B, Sloboda Tuzla, Zvijezda G., Sloboda Tuzla

*** Kurtanidze - Revaz Kurtanidze (a) 11/01/2005, ¿? (Georgia) (b) - (c) G (d) FC Saburtalo II (e) -

*** Kurtanidze - Tornike Kurtanidze (თორნიკე კურტანიძე) (a) 01/04/2001, ¿? (Georgia) (b) - (c) F - left winger (d) FC Locomotive Tbilisi (e) Merani Tbilisi, Tatran Presov, Merani Tbilisi, WIT Georgia II
*** Kurti - Arlind Kurti (a) 24/01/2005, Fier (Albania) (b) - (c) D - central defense (d) KF Laçi (e) FK Apolonia
*** Kurti - Reild Kurti (a) 17/10/2002, Peshkopi (Albania) (b) - (c) D - right back (d) KF Teuta (e) KF Korabi
*** Kurtic - Jasmin Kurtic (Jasmin Kurtić) (a) 10/01/1989, Crnomelj (Yugoslavia, now in Slovenia) (b) 1,86 (c) M - central midfielder (d) Universitatea Craiova (e) Parma, PAOK, Parma, SPAL, Parma, SPAL, Atalanta, SPAL, Atalanta, Sassuolo, Fiorentina, Sassuolo, Torino, Sassuolo, US Palermo, Varese, US Palermo, ND Gorica, Bela Krajina
*** Kurtiss - Marks Kurtiss (Marks Kurtišs) (a) 26/01/1998, ¿? (Liepaja) (b) 1,82 (c) F - center forward (d) Grobinas SC/LFS (e) Liepaja, JFK Ventspils, Albatroz/Jelgava, Liepaja, Liepaja II
*** Kurtovic - Almin Kurtovic (Almin Kurtović) (a) 16/03/2000, Ljubljana (Slovenia) (b) 1,77 (c) M - central midfielder (d) NS Mura (e) NK Bravo
*** Kurtovic - William Kurtovic (William Albin Kurtović) (a) 22/06/1996, Karlskrona (Sweden) (b) 1,90 (c) M - pivot (d) Hamarkameratene (e) Sandefjord, Ullensaker/Kisa, Sandefjord
*** Kurtulan - Arda Kurtulan (Arda Okan Kurtulan) (a) 19/11/2002, Istanbul (Turkey) (b) 1,83 (c) F - left winger (d) Tuzlaspor (e) Tuzlaspor, Adana Demirspor, Karacabey Belediye, Adana Demirspor, Fenerbahce
*** Kurtulus - Edvin Kurtulus (a) 05/03/2000, Halmstad (Sweden) (b) 1,87 (c) D - central defense (d) Hammarby IF (e) Halmstads BK
*** Kurucay - Hasan Kurucay (Hasan Kuruçay) (a) 31/08/1997, Odense (Denmark) (b) 1,87 (c) D - central defense (d) Eintracht Braunschweig (e) HamKam, Strømmen, Florø SK, BK Marienlyst, A. Selcukspor, Naestved BK
*** Kurukalip - Cagtay Kurukalip (Çağtay Kurukalıp) (a) 24/02/2002, Gaziosmanpasa (Turkey) (b) 1,72 (c) D - left back (d) Iskenderunspor (e) Iskenderunspor, Fenerbahce, Igdir FK, Fenerbahce, Kasimpasa
*** Kurylo - Igor Kurylo (Курило Ігор Михайлович) (a) 03/05/1993, Zboriv, Ternopil Oblast (Ukraine) (b) 1,87 (c) D - central defense (d) Metalist 1925 Kharkiv (e) Agrobiznes V., FK Ternopil
*** Kurzawa - Layvin Kurzawa (Layvin Marc Kurzawa) (a) 04/09/1992, Fréjus (France) (b) 1,82 (c) D - left back (d) París Saint-Germain FC (e) Fulham, Paris Saint-Germain, AS Monaco, AS Monaco B
*** Kurzawa - Rafal Kurzawa (Rafał Kurzawa) (a) 29/01/1993, Wieruszów (Poland) (b) 1,82 (c) M - pivot (d) Pogon Szczecin (e) Amiens SC, Esbjerg fB, Amiens SC, Midtjylland, Amiens SC, Górnik Zabrze, ROW Rybnik, Górnik Zabrze, Gornik II
*** Kusej - Vasil Kusej (Vasil Kušej) (a) 24/05/2000, Ústí nad Labem (Czech Rep.) (b) 1,68 (c) F - left winger (d) FK Mlada Boleslav (e) 1.SK Prostejov, Dynamo Dresden, Usti nad Labem, Dynamo Dresden, FC Wacker, Dynamo Dresden, Usti nad L. Jdg
*** Kushkumbaev - Dias Kushkumbaev (Кушкумбаев Диас Саятович) (a) 30/04/2003, Botokara, Karaganda Oblast (Kazakhstan) (b) 1,74 (c) M - attacking midfielder (d) Kairat-Zhas (e) -
*** Kusk - Kasper Kusk (Kasper Kusk Vangsgaard) (a) 10/11/1991, Aalborg (Denmark) (b) 1,80 (c) F - right winger (d) Silkeborg IF (e) Aalborg BK, FC København, FC Twente, Aalborg BK

*** Kusnyír - Erik Kusnyír (a) 07/02/2000, Nyzhniy Koropets, Zakarpattya Oblast (Ukraine) (b) 1,77 (c) D - right back (d) Debreceni VSC (e) Tarpa
*** Kuster - Markus Kuster (a) 22/02/1994, Kittsee (Austria) (b) 1,95 (c) G (d) FC Winterthur (e) Karlsruher SC, SV Mattersburg, Mattersburg II
*** Kustosz - Mateusz Kustosz (a) 13/01/2003, ¿? (Poland) (b) 1,92 (c) G (d) Unia Swarzedz (e) Warta Poznań, Unia Swarzedz, Warta Poznań, Sokol Kleczew, Warta Poznań, Lechia Kostrzyn, Warta Poznań, Lubonski 1943, Warta Poznań
*** Kusyapov - Talgat Kusyapov (Кусяпов Талгат) (a) 14/02/1999, Aktau (Kazakhstan) (b) 1,86 (c) D - central defense (d) Kaspiy Aktau (e) Kaspiy Aktau, FC Astana, Kaspiy Aktau, FC Astana, Okzhetpes, FC Astana, Kaspiy Aktau, FC Astana, Okzhetpes, Astana-Zhas
*** Kutaladze - Luka Kutaladze (ლუკა კუტალაძე) (a) 27/04/2001, Tbilisi (Georgia) (b) 1,90 (c) G (d) Dinamo Tbilisi (e) -
*** Kutalia - Levan Kutalia (ლევან კუტალია) (a) 19/07/1989, Zugdidi (Soviet Union, now in Georgia) (b) 1,84 (c) F - center forward (d) Alashkert Yerevan CF (e) Ness Ziona, H. Umm al-Fahm, Hapoel Tel Aviv, Irtysh, Dinamo Tbilisi, Torpedo Kutaisi, Shukura, FC Odishi, Merani Martvili, FK Zugdidi, Shukura, FC Zestafoni, FK Zugdidi, Zrinjski Mostar, Slavija S., Zugdidi
*** Kutepov - Ilya Kutepov (Кутепов Илья Олегович) (a) 29/07/1993, Stavropol (Russia) (b) 1,92 (c) D - central defense (d) - (e) Torpedo Moskva, Spartak Moskva, Spartak-2, Spartak Moskva II, Akad. Togliatti, Akron Konoplev
*** Kutesa - Dereck Kutesa (Dereck Germano Kutesa) (a) 06/12/1997, Genève (Switzerland) (b) 1,77 (c) F - left winger (d) Servette FC (e) Stade Reims, Zulte Waregem, Stade Reims, FC St. Gallen, FC Basel, FC Luzern, FC Basel, Servette FC, FC Basel, Servette FC
*** Kutik - Daniel Kutik (Daniel Kutík) (a) 12/05/2004, ¿? (Czech Rep.) (b) 1,84 (c) D - left back (d) MFK Chrudim (e) Hradec Kralove B
*** Kutitskiy - Aleksandr Kutitskiy (Кутицкий Александр Олегович) (a) 01/01/2002, Moskva (Russia) (b) 1,84 (c) M - pivot (d) Dinamo Moskva (e) Dinamo 2, Dinamo Moskva II
*** Kutlu - Berkan Kutlu (Berkan İsmail Kutlu) (a) 25/01/1998, Monthey (Switzerland) (b) 1,86 (c) M - central midfielder (d) Galatasaray (e) Alanyaspor, FC Sion, FC Monthey
*** Kutovoy - Maksim Kutovoy (Кутовой Максим Александрович) (a) 01/07/2001, Slavyansk-na-Kubani, Krasnodar Region (Russia) (b) 1,87 (c) F - center forward (d) SKA Khabarovsk (e) Krasnodar-2, Krasnodar II
*** Kutsia - Giorgi Kutsia (გიორგი კუცია) (a) 27/10/1999, Tbilisi (Georgia) (b) 1,75 (c) M - central midfielder (d) FK Liepaja (e) Liepaja, Dinamo Tbilisi, Rabotnicki, Dinamo Tbilisi, FC Dila, Dinamo Tbilisi
*** Kütt - Roland Kütt (a) 22/04/1987, Kingissepa (Soviet Union, now in Estonia) (b) 1,90 (c) G (d) - (e) Kuressaare, Port Darwin FC, Sörve JK, Kuressaare
*** Kuttin - Manuel Kuttin (a) 17/12/1993, Spittal an der Drau (Austria) (b) 1,95 (c) G (d) Grasshopper Club Zürich (e) Grasshoppers, Wolfsberger AC, Admira Wacker, FC Admira II
*** Kütük - Furkan Kütük (a) 07/12/2002, Kocaeli (Turkey) (b) 1,80 (c) M - pivot (d) Giresunspor (e) 52 Orduspor FK, Giresunspor
*** Kuusk - Märten Kuusk (a) 05/04/1996, Tallinn (Estonia) (b) 1,82 (c) D - central defense (d) FC Flora Tallinn (e) FC Flora, Újpest FC, FC Flora, Kalju FC, Rakvere Tarvas, Kalju FC, Kalju Nõmme II

*** Kuveljic - Nikola Kuveljic (Никола Кувељић) (a) 06/04/1997, Beograd (RF Yugoslavia, now in Serbia) (b) 1,94 (c) M - central midfielder (d) FK TSC Backa Topola (e) Wisla Kraków, FK TSC, Wisla Kraków, Javor-Matis, Wisla Kraków, Javor-Matis, Jedinstvo Sur, IMT Beograd

*** Kuwas - Brandley Kuwas (Brandley Mack-Olien Kuwas) (a) 19/09/1992, Hoorn (Netherlands) (b) 1,81 (c) F - right winger (d) - (e) Giresunspor, Maccabi Tel Aviv, Al-Nasr SC, Al-Jazira, Al-Nasr SC, Heracles Almelo, Excelsior, FC Volendam, KFC

*** Kuzma - Marek Kuzma (a) 22/06/1988, Dubnica nad Váhom (Czechoslovakia, now in Slovakia) (b) 1,82 (c) F - center forward (d) FK Zeleziarne Podbrezova (e) Dubnica, SKF Sered, P. Niepolomice, Cherno More, Zlaté Moravce, Iskra Borcice, Spartak Myjava, Slovan Bratislava, Banska Bystrica, Slovácko, Banska Bystrica, Slovan Bratislava, Dubnica, Slovan Bratislava, Banska Bystrica, Dubnica

*** Kuzmanovic - Mico Kuzmanovic (Мићо Кузмановић) (a) 18/03/1996, Doboj (Bosnia and Herzegovina) (b) 1,78 (c) F - left winger (d) Araz-Naxcivan Nakchivan (e) FK Tuzla City, NK Celje, Rudar Velenje, Excelsior Mouscron, FK Sarajevo, Mladost Kakanj, Drina Zvornik, Borac Banja Luka, Jagodina, Zvijezda G., Modrica Maxima

*** Kuzmanovic - Nemanja Kuzmanovic (Немања Кузмановић) (a) 27/05/1989, Šabac (Yugoslavia, now in Serbia) (b) 1,80 (c) M - attacking midfielder (d) Nea Salamis (e) Banik Ostrava, SFC Opava, Bohemians Prag, Banik Sokolov, Bohemians Prag, Leobendorf, Slovan HAC, FK Srem, Dinamo II, FK Bane Raska, FK Jezero

*** Kuzmenok - Igor Kuzmenok (Кузьменок Игорь Андреевич) (a) 06/07/1990, Zhlobin (Soviet Union, now in Belarus) (b) 1,91 (c) D - central defense (d) FK Gomel (e) Isloch, Torpedo Zhodino, Soligorsk, Dinamo Minsk, Soligorsk, Dinamo Minsk, Soligorsk, Dinamo Minsk, Gomel, Gomel II

*** Kuzmic - Srdjan Kuzmic (Srđan Kuzmić) (a) 16/01/2004, ¿? (Slovenia) (b) 1,83 (c) D - left back (d) Viborg FF (e) NS Mura

*** Kuzmic - Zeljko Kuzmic (Željko Kuzmić) (a) 02/11/1984, Aranđelovac (Yugoslavia, now in Serbia) (b) 1,94 (c) G (d) Radnicki Obrenovac (e) Sol de Mayo, Radnicki 1923, Stadl-Paura, Borac Cacak, Tai Po, Deren FC, Mihajlovac, SV Donaustauf, Svilajnac, FK Topola, NK Jajce, Nybro IF, Travnik, Rudar Prijedor, FK Berane, FK Mladost, KF Himara, Velez Mostar, Saint George SA, Smederevo 1924, Pobeda Prilep, Kania Gostyn, Mornar Bar, Zeleznik Belgr.

*** Kuzmichev - Ivan Kuzmichev (Кузьмичев Иван Александрович) (a) 20/10/2000, Togliatti, Samara Oblast (Russia) (b) 1,96 (c) D - central defense (d) Lokomotiv Moskva (e) Ural, Ural 2, Lada Togliatti

*** Kuznetsov - Yuliy Kuznetsov (Кузнецов Юлий Андреевич) (a) 02/08/2003, Novopolotsk (Belarus) (b) 1,79 (c) M - pivot (d) FK Minsk (e) Naftan, FK Minsk, FK Minsk II

*** Kuzyaev - Daler Kuzyaev (Кузяев Далер Адьямович) (a) 15/01/1993, Naberezhnye Chelny, Tatarstan Republic (Russia) (b) 1,82 (c) M - central midfielder (d) Le Havre AC (e) Zenit, Akhmat Grozny, Neftekhimik, Karelia

*** Kuzyk - Denys Kuzyk (Кузик Денис Вікторович) (a) 18/09/2002, Bogdanivka, Ternopil Oblast (Ukraine) (b) 1,79 (c) D - left back (d) FC Dinamo de Kiev (e) PFK Lviv, Dinamo Kyïv, Kolos Kovalivka, Dinamo Kyïv, Chornomorets, Dinamo Kyïv, Dinamo Kiev II

*** Kuzyk - Orest Kuzyk (Кузик Орест Тарасович) (a) 17/05/1995, Lviv (Ukraine) (b) 1,74 (c) F - left winger (d) Chornomorets Odessa (e) Rukh Lviv, Pafos FC, PAS Giannina, Desna, PAS Giannina, SK Dnipro-1, PAS Giannina, Stal Kamyanske, Dinamo Kiev II, Goverla, Dinamo Kiev II

*** Kvakic - Amar Kvakic (Amar Kvakić) (a) 30/10/2002, Graz (Austria) (b) 1,92 (c) D - central defense (d) FC U Craiova 1948 (e) Velez Mostar, Metalist 1925, FAC, Metalist 1925, SV Kapfenberg, Kapfenberg II, AKA Kapfenberg

*** Kvaratskhelia - Khvicha Kvaratskhelia (ხვიჩა კვარაცხელია) (a) 12/02/2001, Tbilisi (Georgia) (b) 1,83 (c) F - left winger (d) SSC Nápoles (e) Dinamo Batumi, Rubin Kazan, Rustavi, Lokomotiv Moskva, Rustavi, Dinamo Tbilisi

*** Kvaratskhelia - Lasha Kvaratskhelia (ლაშა კვარაცხელია) (a) 27/02/2002, ¿? (Georgia) (b) - (c) F - right winger (d) Shukura Kobuleti (e) Daugavpils, Shukura

*** Kvaskhvadze - Roin Kvaskhvadze (როინ კვასხვაძე) (a) 31/05/1989, Kutaisi (Soviet Union, now in Georgia) (b) 1,83 (c) G (d) Dinamo Batumi (e) Torpedo Kutaisi, Dinamo Tbilisi, Torpedo Kutaisi, Pafos FC, Othellos Athien, Torpedo Kutaisi, FC Zestafoni, Torpedo Kutaisi II

*** Kvasnyi - Mykola Kvasnyi (Квасний Микола Петрович) (a) 04/01/1995, Dolyna, Ivano-Frankivsk Oblast (Ukraine) (b) 1,83 (c) D - left back (d) Agrobiznes Volochysk (e) Veres Rivne, Prykarpattya, Ingulets, PFC Lviv, Prykarpattya, PFK Sumy, Vorskla II, SK Tavriya II

*** Kvasnytsya - Ilya Kvasnytsya (Квасниця Ілля Сергійович) (a) 20/03/2003, Doroshivtsi, Chernivtsi Oblast (Ukraine) (b) 1,74 (c) F - right winger (d) Rukh Lviv (e) UFK Lviv

*** Kvekveskiri - Irakliy Kvekveskiri (Квеквескири Ираклий Анатольевич) (a) 12/03/1990, Ochamchire, Georgian SSR (Soviet Union, now in Georgia) (b) 1,78 (c) M - pivot (d) Fakel Voronezh (e) SKA Khabarovsk, Ararat Moskva, Alashkert CF, Guria, MIKA Aschtarak, SZTK, Dinamo Batumi, Pécsi MFC, SZTK, Pécsi MFC, Kuban II

*** Kvekveskiri - Nika Kvekveskiri (ნიკა კვეკვესკირი) (a) 29/05/1992, Gali (Georgia) (b) 1,86 (c) M - pivot (d) Lech Poznan (e) Tobol Kostanay, FK Qabala, Inter Baku, FC Dila, Dinamo II, Dinamo Tbilisi, Tskhinvali, Dinamo Tbilisi, Baia Zugdidi, Dinamo Tbilisi, Baia Zugdidi, Baia

*** Kveladze - Giorgi Kveladze (გიორგი ქველაძე) (a) 14/12/2001, ¿? (Georgia) (b) - (c) D - left back (d) - (e) FC Locomotive

*** Kvernadze - Giorgi Kvernadze (გიორგი კვერნაძე) (a) 07/02/2003, Samtredia (Georgia) (b) 1,88 (c) F - left winger (d) Frosinone Calcio (e) Frosinone, Kolkheti Poti, Dinamo Batumi, Kolkheti Poti, Saburtalo, FC Saburtalo II, FC Telavi, FC Saburtalo II

*** Kvernadze - Otar Kvernadze (ოთარ კვერნაძე) (a) 10/09/1993, Kutaisi (Georgia) (b) 1,91 (c) F - center forward (d) FC Bakhmaro Chokhatauri (e) Sioni Bolnisi, Torpedo Kutaisi, Vytis Vilnius, Kolkheti Poti, Chikhura, Dinamo Tbilisi, Torpedo Kutaisi, FC Zestafoni, Zestafoni II

*** Kvesic - Josip Kvesic (Josip Kvesić) (a) 21/09/1990, Mostar (Yugoslavia, now in Bosnia and Herzegovina) (b) 1,79 (c) D - left back (d) HNK Sibenik (e) Siroki Brijeg, Hajduk Split, Antalyaspor, Karsiyaka, Antalyaspor, Zeljeznicar, NK Varazdin, MSK Zilina, Siroki Brijeg

*** Kvesic - Mario Kvesic (Mario Kvesić) (a) 12/01/1992, Siroki Brijeg (Yugoslavia, now in Bosnia and Herzegovina) (b) 1,75 (c) M - attacking midfielder (d) NK Celje (e) Olimpija, Pohang Steelers, Olimpija, 1.FC Magdeburg, Erzgebirge Aue, RNK Split, Baník Ostrava B, RNK Split, Siroki Brijeg

*** Kvet - Roman Kvet (Roman Květ) (a) 17/12/1997, ¿? (Slovakia) (b) - (c) M - central midfielder (d) Sivasspor (e) Sivasspor, Viktoria Plzen, Bohemians 1905, 1.FK Pribram, Bohemians 1905, 1.FK Pribram

*** Kvia-Egeskog - Simen Kvia-Egeskog (a) 26/05/2003, Stavanger (Norway) (b) 1,75 (c) F - left winger (d) Skeid Oslo (e) Viking, Hødd, Viking, Skeid, Viking
*** Kvida - Josef Kvida (Josef Kvída) (a) 23/01/1997, Příbram (Czech Rep.) (b) 1,96 (c) D - central defense (d) Pafos FC (e) NEC Nijmegen, PEC Zwolle, Almere City, PEC Zwolle
*** Kvile - Sigurd Kvile (a) 26/02/2000, Bergen (Norway) (b) 1,90 (c) D - central defense (d) FK Bodø/Glimt (e) Sarpsborg 08, Bodø/Glimt, Kristiansund, Bodø/Glimt, Kristiansund, Bodø/Glimt, Åsane, Sarpsborg 08 II, Fana IL II
*** Kvilitaia - Giorgi Kvilitaia (გიორგი ქვილითაია) (a) 01/10/1993, Abasha (Georgia) (b) 1,93 (c) F - center forward (d) APOEL FC (e) KAA Gent, Anorthosis, KAA Gent, Rapid Wien, Dinamo Tbilisi, ETO FC Győr, FC Dila, ETO FC Győr, FC Sasco
*** Kvilitaia - Maksime Kvilitaia (მაქსიმე ქვილითაია) (a) 17/09/1985, ¿? (Georgia) (b) 1,86 (c) G (d) - (e) Samgurali, Shahin Bushehr, Torpedo Kutaisi, FC Liakhvi, Chikhura, FK Zugdidi, Torpedo Kutaisi, FC Locomotive, Spartaki, Torpedo Kutaisi, FC Meshakhte
*** Kvirkvelia - Solomon Kvirkvelia (სოლომონ კვირკველია) (a) 06/02/1992, Samtredia (Georgia) (b) 1,96 (c) D - central defense (d) Al-Okhdood Club (e) Neftchi Baku, FC Gagra, Metalist 1925, Lokomotiv Moskva, Rotor Volgograd, Lokomotiv Moskva, Rubin Kazan, Lokomotiv Moskva, Rubin Kazan, Neftekhimik, Rubin Kazan, Rubin Kazán II, Zenit St. Peterburg II
*** Kvirkvia - Mate Kvirkvia (მათე კვირკვია) (a) 14/06/1996, Tsalenjikha (Georgia) (b) 1,72 (c) F - right winger (d) Kapaz PFK (e) FC Gagra, FC Samtredia, Dinamo Tbilisi, Dinamo Batumi, Rustavi, Torpedo Kutaisi, FC Dila, FC Zestafoni, WIT Georgia
*** Kvist - Bertram Kvist (Bertram Bangsted Kvist) (a) 19/03/2005, ¿? (Denmark) (b) 1,72 (c) M - attacking midfielder (d) Brøndby IF (e) -
*** Kvistgaarden - Mathias Kvistgaarden (Mathias Damm Kvistgaarden) (a) 15/04/2002, Birkerød (Denmark) (b) 1,74 (c) F - center forward (d) Brøndby IF (e) -
*** Kvocera - Milan Kvocera (a) 01/01/1998, Považská Bystrica (Slovakia) (b) 1,75 (c) F - right winger (d) ViOn Zlate Moravce-Vrable (e) Wisła Płock, Michalovce, Banska Bystrica, Radomiak, Michalovce, AS Trencin
*** Kvrzic - Zoran Kvrzic (Zoran Kvržić) (a) 07/08/1988, Teslić (Yugoslavia, now in Bosnia and Herzegovina) (b) 1,80 (c) F - right winger (d) FK Borac Banja Luka (e) HNK Sibenik, Slaven Belupo, Kayserispor, HNK Rijeka, FC Sheriff, HNK Rijeka, Spezia, HNK Rijeka, Spezia, HNK Rijeka, NK Osijek, HNK Rijeka, NK Osijek, HASK Zagreb, Proleter Teslic
*** Kwasigroch - Robert Kwasigroch (a) 26/06/2004, Berlin (Germany) (b) 1,89 (c) G (d) Hertha Berlín (e) Hertha BSC II
*** Kwasniak - Valdemar Kwasniak (Valdemar Manley Kwasniak) (a) 12/06/2003, Odense (Denmark) (b) 1,79 (c) M - pivot (d) Middelfart Boldklub (e) -
*** Kwateng - Enock Kwateng (a) 09/04/1997, Mantes-la-Jolie (France) (b) 1,81 (c) D - central defense (d) MKE Ankaragücü (e) Girondins Bordeaux, FC Nantes
*** Kwelele - Ebuka Kwelele (a) 11/06/2002, ¿? (Ireland) (b) - (c) F - center forward (d) - (e) Newry City, Dundalk FC
*** Kwiecien - Bartosz Kwiecien (Bartosz Kwiecień) (a) 07/05/1994, Starachowice (Poland) (b) 1,89 (c) D - central defense (d) Korona Kielce (e) Resovia, Jagiellonia, Arka Gdynia, Jagiellonia, Korona Kielce, Chrobry Glogow, Korona Kielce, Gornik Leczna, Korona Kielce, Juventa Starachowice, Korona Kielce, Juventa Starachowice

*** Kyabou - Moussa Kyabou (a) 18/04/1998, Bamako (Mali) (b) 1,83 (c) M - pivot (d) FC Sheriff Tiraspol (e) USC Kita
*** Kybyray - Eskendir Kybyray (Кыбырай Ескендир Дастанулы) (a) 14/08/1997, Talgar (Kazakhstan) (b) 1,83 (c) D - right back (d) FK Aktobe (e) Shakhter K., Zhetysu, Zhetysu B, Kairat II
*** Kyei - Grejohn Kyei (a) 12/08/1995, Gonesse (France) (b) 1,87 (c) F - center forward (d) Clermont Foot 63 (e) Servette FC, Stade Reims, RC Lens, Stade Reims, Stade Reims B
*** Kyereh - Daniel-Kofi Kyereh (a) 08/03/1996, Accra (Ghana) (b) 1,79 (c) M - attacking midfielder (d) SC Freiburg (e) FC St. Pauli, Wehen Wiesbaden, TSV Havelse
*** Kyereh - Frederick Kyereh (a) 18/10/1993, Saarbrücken (Germany) (b) 1,85 (c) F - right winger (d) FC Etzella Ettelbruck (e) FC UNA Strassen, Jeunesse Esch, Energie Cottbus, SV Elversberg, Elversberg II
*** Kyeremeh - Francis Kyeremeh (Francis Kyeremeh) (a) 23/06/1997, Nsoatre (Ghana) (b) 1,80 (c) F - right winger (d) FK Sarajevo (e) Zalgiris, Hapoel Tel Aviv, Radnik, Jagodina, BA United
*** Kyllönen - Leo Kyllönen (a) 22/01/2004, ¿? (Finland) (b) 1,80 (c) D - right back (d) Ilves Tampere (e) Ilves II
*** Kyriakidis - Alexandros Kyriakidis (Αλέξανδρος Κυριακίδης) (a) 12/01/2004, Nicosia (Cyprus) (b) - (c) G (d) Nea Salamis (e) -
*** Kyriakidis - Charalampos Kyriakidis (Χαράλαμπος Κυριακίδης) (a) 30/11/1998, Páfos (Cyprus) (b) 1,88 (c) G (d) Omonia Nicosia (e) Omonia Aradippou, Omonia Nicosia, Aris Limassol, Akritas Chlor.
*** Kyriakidis - Loukas Kyriakidis (Λούκας Κυριακίδης) (a) 01/06/2004, Pafos (Cyprus) (b) - (c) M - attacking midfielder (d) Akritas Chlorakas (e) -
*** Kyriakidis - Nikolas Kyriakidis (Νικόλας Κυριακίδης) (a) 20/09/2004, Aglantzia (Cyprus) (b) 1,77 (c) D - right back (d) MEAP Pera Choriou Nisou (e) MEAP Nisou, Omonia Nicosia, THOI Lakatamias, Latsion
*** Kyriakopoulos - Georgios Kyriakopoulos (Γεώργιος Κυριακόπουλος) (a) 05/02/1996, Patras (Greece) (b) 1,86 (c) D - left back (d) AC Monza (e) Monza, Sassuolo, Bologna, Sassuolo, Asteras Tripoli, Sassuolo, Asteras Tripoli, PAS Lamia, Asteras Tripoli, Ergotelis, Asteras Tripoli
*** Kyriakou - Charalampos Kyriakou (Χαράλαμπος Κυριάκου) (a) 09/02/1995, Limassol (Cyprus) (b) 1,81 (c) M - pivot (d) Apollon Limassol (e) Estoril Praia, Apollon Limassol
*** Kyriakou - Michalis Kyriakou (Μιχάλης Κυριάκου) (a) 30/12/2002, Limassol (Cyprus) (b) 1,93 (c) G (d) AEL Limassol (e) ASIL Lysi, AEL Limassol
*** Kyriakou - Panagiotis Kyriakou (Παναγιώτης Κυριάκου) (a) 05/05/2004, Nicosia (Cyprus) (b) 1,93 (c) G (d) Doxa Katokopias (e) Doxa Katokopias, AEL Limassol
*** Kyriakou - Vangelis Kyriakou (Βαγγέλης Κυριάκου) (a) 03/02/1994, Nicosia (Cyprus) (b) 1,83 (c) D - right back (d) Doxa Katokopias (e) Olympiakos N., Anagen.Derynias, EN Paralimniou, Aris Limassol, Othellos Athien, Olympiakos N.
*** Kyriopoulos - Georgios Kyriopoulos (Γεώργιος Κυριόπουλος) (a) 24/08/2004, ¿? (Greece) (b) 1,76 (c) F - right winger (d) Panathinaikos Athina B (e) -
*** Kyritsas - Petros Kyritsas (Πέτρος Κυριτσάς) (a) 06/08/2003, ¿? (Greece) (b) 1,86 (c) G (d) GS Marko (e) Ionikos Nikeas, Apollon Smyrnis
*** Kyrkos - Iason Kyrkos (Ιάσων Κύρκος) (a) 21/03/2003, ¿? (Greece) (b) 1,69 (c) M - attacking midfielder (d) PAS Giannina (e) -

*** Kyrychok - Mykola Kyrychok (Киричок Микола Вячеславович) (a) 16/05/2006, Yampil, Vinnytsya Oblast (Ukraine) (b) 1,84 (c) D - right back (d) - (e) PFK Lviv

*** Kyryukhantsev - Igor Kyryukhantsev (Кирюханцев Ігор Олегович) (a) 29/01/1996, Makiivka, Donetsk Oblast (Ukraine) (b) 1,70 (c) D - right back (d) Zorya Lugansk (e) Shakhtar Donetsk, FK Oleksandriya, Shakhtar Donetsk, FK Mariupol, Shakhtar Donetsk, Shakhtar II

*** Kysil - Yaroslav Kysil (Кисіль Ярослав Валентинович) (a) 31/05/2003, ¿? (Ukraine) (b) 1,70 (c) D - right back (d) - (e) Zorya Lugansk

*** Kyziridis - Alexandros Kyziridis (Αλέξανδρος Κυζιρίδης) (a) 16/09/2000, Skydra (Greece) (b) 1,79 (c) F - left winger (d) Debreceni VSC (e) Zlaté Moravce, Volos NPS, Iraklis

*** Laabus - Reio Laabus (a) 14/03/1990, Tartu (Soviet Union, now in Estonia) (b) 1,88 (c) M - central midfielder (d) Jalgpallikool Tammeka (e) VfR Neumünster, JK Tammeka, FC Flora, Tammeka Tartu, JK Tammeka II

*** Laaksonen - Oiva Laaksonen (a) 19/09/2003, ¿? (Finland) (b) 1,81 (c) F - left winger (d) FC Haka (e) HJS, FC Haka

*** Läänelaid - Karl Läänelaid (a) 07/07/2003, Tartu (Estonia) (b) - (c) D - right back (d) FC Nomme United (e) JK Tammeka

*** Laaneots - Dominic Laaneots (a) 16/06/2001, Tartu (Estonia) (b) - (c) M - central midfielder (d) Jalgpallikool Tammeka (e) -

*** Laasner - Kenlou Laasner (a) 25/12/1999, Tallinn (Estonia) (b) - (c) M - central midfielder (d) - (e) Kalev III

*** Laâziri - Achraf Laâziri (a) 08/07/2003, Hay Hassani (Morocco) (b) 1,77 (c) D - left back (d) Olympique Lyon B (e) FUS Reserve

*** Lababidi - Diaa Lababidi (לבאבידי דיאא) (a) 26/07/1992, ¿? (Israel) (b) 1,73 (c) D - right back (d) Hapoel Hadera (e) Hapoel Acre, Ironi Nesher, Hapoel Acre, Hapoel Herzliya, Hapoel Acre, Beitar Nahariya, Hapoel Acre

*** Labadze - Avtandil Labadze (ავთანდილ ლაბაძე) (a) 09/05/1998, Borjomi (Georgia) (b) 1,89 (c) G (d) FC Samtredia (e) Torpedo Kutaisi, Shakhter P., Svetlogorsk, Osipovichi

*** Laban - Luka Laban (Лука Лабан) (a) 07/04/2004, ¿? (Serbia and Montenegro, now in Serbia) (b) - (c) M - central midfielder (d) FK Napredak Krusevac (e) -

*** Labata - Anthony Labata (Anthony Guy Marie Jo Labata) (a) 26/08/2003, ¿? (Luxembourg) (b) - (c) D - central defense (d) Union Titus Petange (e) -

*** Labeau Lascary - Rémy Labeau Lascary (a) 03/03/2003, Les Abymes (Guadaloupe) (b) 1,84 (c) F - center forward (d) Stade Lavallois (e) RC Lens, RC Lens B

*** Labik - Albert Labik (Albert Labík) (a) 13/05/2004, ¿? (Czech Rep.) (b) 1,78 (c) D - left back (d) FC Sellier & Bellot Vlasim (e) Vlasim, Slavia Praha B

*** Laborda - Míguel Laborda (Miguel Ángel Laborda Gil) (a) 18/02/1995, Tíjola (Spain) (b) 1,81 (c) M - left midfielder (d) - (e) FC Santa Coloma, UE Engordany, Benferri, Estudiantes, Blackfield, CD Plus Ultra

*** Laborde - Gaëtan Laborde (a) 03/05/1994, Mont-de-Marsan (France) (b) 1,81 (c) F - center forward (d) OGC Niza (e) Stade Rennes, Montpellier, Girondins Bordeaux, Clermont Foot, Girondins Bordeaux, Stade Brestois, Girondins Bordeaux, Girondins Bordeaux B, Red Star FC, Girondins Bordeaux B

*** Labra - Labra (Juan Manuel Labrador Aguilar) (a) 24/06/1995, La Línea de la Concepción (Spain) (b) 1,79 (c) F - center forward (d) Europa FC (e) Lions Gibraltar, Cabecense, Lions Gibraltar, Europa FC, Gibraltar Phoenix, Los Barrios, At. Onubense, At. Madrid B, R. B. Linense, Atlético Zabal

*** Labrovic - Nediljko Labrovic (Nediljko Labrović) (a) 10/10/1999, Split (Croatia) (b) 1,96 (c) G (d) HNK Rijeka (e) HNK Sibenik, Junak Sinj, Adriatic Split

*** Labyad - Zakaria Labyad (لبيض زكريا) (a) 09/03/1993, Utrecht (Netherlands) (b) 1,75 (c) M - attacking midfielder (d) FC Utrecht (e) Ajax, FC Utrecht, Sporting Lisboa, Fulham, Sporting Lisboa, Vitesse, Sporting Lisboa, PSV Eindhoven

*** Lacava - Matías Lacava (Matías Rafael Lacava González) (a) 24/10/2002, Caracas (Venezuela) (b) 1,67 (c) F - right winger (d) FC Vizela (e) Vizela, Puerto Cabello, Tondela, Puerto Cabello, Santos, Puerto Cabello

*** Lacazette - Alexandre Lacazette (a) 28/05/1991, Lyon (France) (b) 1,75 (c) F - center forward (d) Olympique de Lyon (e) Arsenal, Olympique Lyon, Olymp. Lyon B

*** Laci - Ziga Laci (Žiga Laci) (a) 20/07/2002, Murska Sobota (Slovenia) (b) 1,89 (c) D - central defense (d) AEK Athína FC (e) Koper, AEK Athína

*** Laçi - Qazim Laçi (a) 19/01/1996, Peshkopi (Albania) (b) 1,73 (c) M - central midfielder (d) AC Sparta Praga (e) AC Ajaccio, Olympiakos, AC Ajaccio, Olympiakos, APO Levadiakos, Olympiakos, APOEL FC, Olympiakos

*** Lackner - Markus Lackner (a) 05/04/1991, Baden (Austria) (b) 1,91 (c) D - central defense (d) SV Stripfing (e) SV Ried, Sturm Graz, Admira Wacker, Sturm Graz, Admira Wacker, FC Admira II, SV Horn, FC Admira II, Admira Wacker, First Vienna FC, Admira Wacker, FC Admira II

*** Lacroix - Maxence Lacroix (a) 06/04/2000, Villeneuve-Saint-Georges (France) (b) 1,90 (c) D - central defense (d) VfL Wolfsburg (e) FC Sochaux

*** Ladra - Tomas Ladra (Tomáš Ladra) (a) 24/04/1997, Česká Lípa (Czech Rep.) (b) 1,78 (c) F - center forward (d) FK Mlada Boleslav (e) Jablonec, Mlada Boleslav, Pardubice, Mlada Boleslav, Pardubice, Mlada Boleslav

*** Lafferty - Danny Lafferty (Daniel Patrick Lafferty) (a) 18/05/1989, Derry (Northern Ireland) (b) 1,82 (c) D - left back (d) Sligo Rovers (e) Derry City, Shamrock Rovers, Sheffield Utd., Peterborough, Sheffield Utd., Burnley, Sheffield Utd., Burnley, Oldham Athletic, Burnley, Rotherham, Burnley, Derry City, Celtic Reserves, Ayr United, Celtic Reserves

*** Lafferty - Kyle Lafferty (Kyle Joseph George Lafferty) (a) 16/09/1987, Enniskillen (Northern Ireland) (b) 1,93 (c) F - center forward (d) Johnstone Burgh FC (e) Linfield, Kilmarnock FC, Anorthosis, Kilmarnock FC, Reggina, Sunderland, Sarpsborg 08, Rangers FC, Heart of Midlothian, Norwich City, Birmingham City, Norwich City, Çaykur Rizespor, Norwich City, US Palermo, FC Sion, Rangers FC, Burnley, Darlington, Burnley, Ballinamallard

*** Laffont - Quentin Laffont (Quentin Pierrick Laffont) (a) 17/01/1996, Montauban (France) (b) 1,73 (c) D - left back (d) - (e) Penya Encarnada, Sant Julià, CE Carroi, Penya Encarnada, AS Gosier, CS Sedan, CS Sedan B, Choisy-au-Bac, Grisolles, Rodez AF B

*** Lafont - Alban Lafont (a) 23/01/1999, Ouagadougou (Burkina Faso) (b) 1,96 (c) G (d) FC Nantes (e) Fiorentina, FC Nantes, Fiorentina, Toulouse

*** Lafont - Morgan Lafont (a) 22/11/1996, Marseille (France) (b) 1,85 (c) F - left winger (d) UE Sant Julia (e) UE Engordany, AC Escaldes, UE Engordany

*** Lagae - Bram Lagae (a) 14/01/2004, ¿? (Belgium) (b) - (c) D - central defense (d) KAA Gent (e) Jong KAA Gent

*** Lagator - Dusan Lagator (Душан Лагатор) (a) 29/03/1994, Cetinje (RF Yugoslavia, now in Montenegro) (b) 1,90 (c) D - central defense (d) Debreceni VSC (e) Wisła Płock, Sochi, Čukarički, Dinamo SPb, Čukarički, FK Mladost, Mogren

*** Lagerbielke - Gustaf Lagerbielke (Gustaf Johan Lagerbielke) (a) 10/04/2000, Stockholm (Sweden) (b) 1,93 (c) D - central defense (d) IF Elfsborg (e) Degerfors, Elfsborg, Västerås SK, Sollentuna FK, Sollentuna FK, Vasalunds IF
*** Lagerlund - Sebastian Lagerlund (a) 14/09/2002, ¿? (Sweden) (b) 1,86 (c) D - central defense (d) Utsiktens BK (e) Häcken
*** Lago - Ramiro Lago (Ramiro Martín Lago) (a) 14/10/1987, Rosario (Argentina) (b) 1,73 (c) F - right winger (d) - (e) La Fiorita, Domagnano, La Fiorita, Cervia, La Fiorita, Cattolica, Virtus, Tre Fiori, Domagnano, SS Folgore, Pennarossa, Marignanese, Tre Fiori, Naturns, Salurn, CA Argentino, AS Sourmena, Tiro Federal, Polideportivo
*** Laguea - Julian Laguea (Julian Paul Laguea) (a) 27/11/2003, ¿? (Gibraltar) (b) - (c) D - right back (d) Lincoln Red Imps FC Reserve (e) FC College 1975, Red Imps Reserves, FC College 1975, Red Imps Reserves
*** Lagundzic - Ivan Lagundzic (Ivan Lagundžić) (a) 14/06/1999, Zagreb (Croatia) (b) 1,73 (c) D - right back (d) - (e) Borac Banja Luka, Olimpija, NK Kustosija, Spansko, Hrv Dragovoljac, HASK Zagreb
*** Laguns - Jekabs Laguns (Jēkabs Lagūns) (a) 16/01/2002, ¿? (Latvia) (b) 1,82 (c) M - attacking midfielder (d) - (e) Bischofshofen, RFS, Valmiera, RFS, Metta, FS Metta II
*** Lagutin - Ilya Lagutin (Лагутин Илья) (a) 14/06/2003, ¿? (Kazakhstan) (b) 1,84 (c) M - pivot (d) Kyzylzhar SK Petropavlovsk II (e) -
*** Lahdo - Mayckel Lahdo (a) 30/12/2002, ¿? (Sweden) (b) 1,71 (c) F - right winger (d) AZ Alkmaar (e) Hammarby IF, Hammarby TFF, Hammarby IF, IK Frej Täby
*** Lahne - Jack Lahne (Jack Daniel Kalichi Lahne) (a) 24/10/2001, Lusaka (Zambia) (b) 1,74 (c) F - center forward (d) IK Start (e) Start, Amiens SC, Újpest FC, Amiens SC, Botev Plovdiv, Amiens SC, Häcken, Amiens SC, Örebro SK, Amiens SC, Brommapojkarna, AIK, Brommapojkarna, Brommapojkarna
*** Lahrach - Yanis Lahrach (a) 02/09/2002, ¿? (Belgium) (b) 1,78 (c) F (d) CS Fola Esch (e) -
*** Lahssaini - Sami Lahssaini (a) 18/09/1998, Liège (Belgium) (b) 1,79 (c) M - central midfielder (d) FC Metz (e) RFC Seraing, FC Metz, RFC Seraing, FC Metz, RFC Seraing, FC Metz, RFC Seraing
*** Laht - Sander Laht (a) 26/09/1991, Kuressaare ((b) 1,83 (c) F - left winger (d) FC Kuressaare (e) FC Flora, Kuressaare, Viljandi, FC Flora, Kuressaare, Sörve JK
*** Lahti - Timi Lahti (Timi Tapio Lahti) (a) 28/06/1990, Jyväskylä (Finland) (b) 1,85 (c) D - central defense (d) IFK Mariehamn (e) FC Lahti, VPS, HJK Helsinki, FC Haka, HJK Helsinki, FC Haka, Padova, Belluno, Padova
*** Lahtimi - Montasser Lahtimi (منتصر لحتمي) (a) 01/04/2001, Rabat (Morocco) (b) 1,85 (c) F - right winger (d) Wydad Casablanca (e) Wydad AC, Trabzonspor, FUS Rabat, FUS Reserve
*** Lahure - Romain Lahure (a) 24/03/2004, ¿? (Luxembourg) (b) - (c) M (d) - (e) F91 Dudelange
*** Laidlaw - Ethan Laidlaw (Ethan James Laidlaw) (a) 02/01/2005, Edinburgh (Scotland) (b) - (c) F - center forward (d) FC Brentford B (e) -
*** Laidlaw - Ross Laidlaw (a) 12/07/1992, Livingston (Scotland) (b) 2,01 (c) G (d) Ross County FC (e) Hibernian FC, Dundee United, Hibernian FC, Raith Rovers, Elgin City, Raith Rovers, St Andrews Utd.
*** Laïdouni - Aïssa Laïdouni (Aïssa Bilal Laïdouni) (a) 13/12/1996, Montfermeil (France) (b) 1,81 (c) M - central midfielder (d) 1.FC Union Berlin (e) Ferencváros, FC Voluntari, Angers SCO B, FC Chambly Oise, Angers SCO B, Les Herbiers VF, Angers SCO B

*** Laifis - Konstantinos Laifis (Κωνσταντίνος Λαΐφης) (a) 19/05/1993, Paralimni (Cyprus) (b) 1,86 (c) D - central defense (d) Standard de Lieja (e) Olympiakos, Standard Liège, Olympiakos, Anorthosis, Alki Larnaca, Anorthosis
*** Laimer - Konrad Laimer (a) 27/05/1997, Salzburg (Austria) (b) 1,80 (c) M - central midfielder (d) Bayern München (e) RB Leipzig, RB Salzburg, FC Liefering
*** Laine - Janne-Pekka Laine (a) 25/01/2001, Tampere (Finland) (b) 1,84 (c) M - central midfielder (d) FC Haka (e) Ilves
*** Laine - Lauri Laine (a) 30/05/2005, ¿? (Finland) (b) 1,80 (c) F - right winger (d) FC Honka (e) FC Honka II
*** Laine - Nooa Laine (a) 22/11/2002, Jyväskylä (Finland) (b) 1,77 (c) M - central midfielder (d) SJK Seinäjoki (e) HJK Klubi 04, JJK Jyväskylä
*** Lainer - Stefan Lainer (a) 27/08/1992, Salzburg (Austria) (b) 1,75 (c) D - right back (d) Borussia Mönchengladbach (e) RB Salzburg, SV Ried, FC Liefering, Grödig
*** Lainez - Diego Lainez (Diego Lainez Leyva) (a) 09/06/2000, Villahermosa (Mexico) (b) 1,67 (c) F - right winger (d) Tigres UANL (e) Real Betis, Tigres UANL, Real Betis, SC Braga, Real Betis, CF América
*** Laizans - Olegs Laizans (Oļegs Laizāns) (a) 28/03/1987, Riga (Soviet Union, now in Latvia) (b) 1,86 (c) M - central midfielder (d) SK Super Nova (e) Spartaks, Riga, Auda, Riga, JFK Ventspils, Enisey, ŁKS, JFK Ventspils, FB Gulbene-2005, Skonto, Lechia Gdánsk, Skonto
*** Lajthia - Xhonatan Lajthia (a) 01/02/1999, Kavajë (Albania) (b) 1,83 (c) M - right midfielder (d) FK Bylis (e) KS Lushnja, KF Egnatia, KF Teuta, KF Erzeni, KF Teuta, KF Egnatia, KF Teuta, KF Erzeni, KF Teuta
*** Lakic - Nikola Lakic (Nikola Lakić) (a) 01/10/1995, Loznica (RF Yugoslavia, now in Serbia) (b) 1,90 (c) G (d) FK Radnik Bijeljina (e) Borac Banja Luka, Rudar Prijedor, Borac Banja Luka, Sloboda Tuzla, Dinamo Vranje, Zvijezda 09, Radnik Bijelj.
*** Lakic-Pesic - Nemanja Lakic-Pesic (Немања Лакић-Пешић) (a) 22/09/1991, Beograd (Yugoslavia, now in Serbia) (b) 1,91 (c) D - central defense (d) - (e) Riteriai, Javor-Matis, Backa, FCI Levadia, Napredak, Vozdovac, Kerala Blasters, SV Kapfenberg, Radnicki Niš, Donji Srem
*** Lakomy - Lukasz Lakomy (Łukasz Łakomy) (a) 18/01/2001, Puławy (Poland) (b) 1,81 (c) M - central midfielder (d) BSC Young Boys (e) Zagłębie, Legia II
*** Lakvekheliani - Luka Lakvekheliani (ლუკა ლაკვეხელიანი) (a) 20/10/1998, Tbilisi (Georgia) (b) 1,75 (c) D - left back (d) Dinamo Tbilisi (e) Mezőkövesd, Saburtalo
*** Lala - Kenny Lala (a) 03/10/1991, Villepinte (France) (b) 1,78 (c) D - right back (d) Stade Brestois 29 (e) Olympiakos, Racing Club Strasbourg, RC Lens, Valenciennes FC, Paris FC
*** Lalic - Milan Lalic (Милан Лалић, Milan Lalić) (a) 25/07/1995, Vogosca (Bosnia and Herzegovina) (b) 1,80 (c) D - right back (d) - (e) Sloga Meridian, FC Van, S. Novi Grad, FC Samtredia, Mladost Kakanj, Dinamo Vranje, Dobanovci, Radnicki 1923, Pazova, Slavija S., Sloga Doboj, FK Zemun
*** Lallana - Adam Lallana (Adam David Lallana) (a) 10/05/1988, St Albans (England) (b) 1,72 (c) M - attacking midfielder (d) Brighton & Hove Albion (e) Liverpool, Southampton, Bournemouth, Southampton
*** Lamanje - Abdel Lamanje (Abdel Aziz Lamanje Ngapout) (a) 27/07/1990, Douala (Cameroon) (b) 1,85 (c) D - central defense (d) - (e) Shakhter K., Astra Giurgiu, Shakhter K., Kaysar, Atyrau, Shinnik Yaroslav, Rotor Volgograd, Shinnik Yaroslav, Grenoble, Grenoble B

*** Lamanna - Eugenio Lamanna (a) 07/08/1989, Como (Italy) (b) 1,87 (c) G (d) AC Monza (e) Spezia, Genoa, Robur Siena, Genoa, Bari, Genoa, AS Gubbio, Genoa, Como
*** Lamba - Chico Lamba (Chico Faria Camará Lamba) (a) 10/03/2003, Bissau (Guinea-Bissau) (b) 1,90 (c) D - central defense (d) Sporting CP B (e) -
*** Lambarskiy - Igor Lambarskiy (Ламбарский Игорь Анатольевич) (a) 26/11/1992, Edineț (Moldova) (b) 1,78 (c) M - attacking midfielder (d) FC Milsami Orhei (e) Mashuk, Olimp Khimki, Urozhay, Nizhny Novgorod, Ural, Tyumen, Ural, Krasnodar, Enisey, Krasnodar, Ac. Chisinau
*** Lambert - Boris Lambert (Boris Luc Lambert) (a) 10/04/2000, Han-sur-Lesse (Belgium) (b) 1,87 (c) D - central defense (d) KAS Eupen (e) -
*** Lambulic - Lazar Lambulic (Лазар Ламбулић) (a) 12/03/2000, Golubovci (RF Yugoslavia, now in Montenegro) (b) 1,93 (c) M - attacking midfielder (d) OFK Petrovac (e) Mornar Bar, FK Jezero, Zeta Golubovac
*** Lambulic - Zarija Lambulic (Зарија Ламбулић) (a) 25/05/1998, Peć (RF Yugoslavia, now in Kosovo) (b) 1,93 (c) D - central defense (d) FK IMT Belgrad (e) Beroe, Mladost GAT, Mladost, Zlatibor, Soligorsk, Zrinjski Mostar, Soligorsk, Proleter, FK Brodarac
*** Lamce - Franko Lamce (Φράνκο Λάμτσε) (a) 30/07/1998, Çorovodë (Albania) (b) 1,84 (c) D - central defense (d) FK Kukësi (e) AO Episkopi, Ast. Vlachioti, PAE Chania, AO Episkopi, PAE Chania, AEEK SYNKA, Platanias, AO Paleochoras, Platanias
*** Lameiras - Rúben Lameiras (Rúben Barcelos de Sousa Lameiras) (a) 22/12/1994, Lisboa (Portugal) (b) 1,74 (c) F - right winger (d) Vitória Guimarães SC (e) Famalicão, Plymouth Argyle, Coventry City, Åtvidabergs FF
*** Lamela - Erik Lamela (Érik Manuel Lamela) (a) 04/03/1992, Carapachay (Argentina) (b) 1,84 (c) F - right winger (d) Sevilla FC (e) Tottenham Hotspur, AS Roma, River Plate, River Plate II
*** Lamhauge - Mattias Lamhauge (Mattias Heðinsson Lamhauge) (a) 02/08/1999, ¿? (Faroe Islands) (b) 1,94 (c) G (d) B36 Tórshavn (e) B36 II, HB Tórshavn, AB Argir, HB Tórshavn, AB Argir, HB Tórshavn, HB Tórshavn II
*** Lamie - Ricki Lamie (a) 20/06/1993, Shotts (Scotland) (b) 1,85 (c) D - central defense (d) Motherwell FC (e) Livingston FC, Morton, Airdrieonians, East Stirlingshire FC, Airdrieonians, Queen's Park, Clyde FC, Airdrie United, Bathgate, Airdrie United
*** Lamine Yamal - Lamine Yamal (Lamine Yamal Nasraoui Ebana) (a) 13/07/2007, Esplugas de Llobregat (Spain) (b) 1,80 (c) F - right winger (d) FC Barcelona (e) Barcelona Atlètic
*** Lamkel Zé - Didier Lamkel Zé (a) 17/09/1996, Bertoua (Cameroon) (b) 1,92 (c) F - left winger (d) Hatayspor (e) KV Kortrijk, Wydad AC, KV Kortrijk, Royal Antwerp, FC Metz, Royal Antwerp, Khimki, Royal Antwerp, Dunajska Streda, Royal Antwerp, Chamois Niort, LOSC Lille B
*** Lammens - Senne Lammens (a) 07/07/2002, Zottegem (Belgium) (b) 1,93 (c) G (d) Royal Antwerp FC (e) KV Brugge, Club NXT
*** Lammers - Sam Lammers (Sam Adrianus Martinus Lammers) (a) 30/04/1997, Tilburg (Netherlands) (b) 1,91 (c) F - center forward (d) Rangers FC (e) Atalanta, FC Empoli, Sampdoria, FC Empoli, Atalanta, Eintracht, Atalanta, PSV Eindhoven, Heerenveen, PSV Eindhoven
*** Lampinen - Pyry Lampinen (a) 07/03/2002, Lahti (Finland) (b) 1,78 (c) F - center forward (d) Kuopion Palloseura (e) FC Lahti

*** Lampinen-Skaug - Simo Lampinen-Skaug (a) 09/04/2005, ¿? (Norway) (b) 1,88 (c) G (d) Strømsgodset IF II (e) -

*** Lampropoulos - Konstantinos Lampropoulos (Κωνσταντίνος Λαμπρόπουλος) (a) 21/04/2003, ¿? (Greece) (b) 1,90 (c) D - central defense (d) PAS Lamia 1964 (e) -

*** Lampropoulos - Vasilios Lampropoulos (Βασίλειος Λαμπρόπουλος) (a) 31/03/1990, Pyrgos (Greece) (b) 1,85 (c) D - central defense (d) OFI Creta (e) VfL Bochum, RC Deportivo, VfL Bochum, RC Deportivo, AEK Athína, Panionios, Ethn. Asteras, Asteras Tripoli, GS Ilioupolis, Asteras Tripoli, Olympiakos, Apol. Kalamarias, Olympiakos

*** Lamprou - Lazaros Lamprou (Λάζαρος Λάμπρου) (a) 19/12/1997, Katerini (Greece) (b) 1,83 (c) F - left winger (d) Excelsior Rotterdam (e) PAOK, OFI Creta, PAOK, FC Twente, PAOK, Fortuna Sittard, PAOK, Panionios, PAOK, Iraklis, Panathinaikos

*** Lamprou - Nikolas Lamprou (Νικόλας Λάμπρου) (a) 28/09/2004, Larnaca (Cyprus) (b) - (c) D (d) - (e) Agia Napa

*** Lamptey - Tariq Lamptey (Tariq Kwame Nii-Lante Lamptey) (a) 30/09/2000, Hillingdon (England) (b) 1,63 (c) D - right back (d) Brighton & Hove Albion (e) -

*** Lamy - Hugo Lamy (a) 16/01/2004, Lagny-sur-Marne (France) (b) 1,76 (c) D - right back (d) AC Bellinzona (e) -

*** Lamy - Julien Lamy (Julien Elie Lamy) (a) 06/11/1999, Brest (France) (b) 1,85 (c) F - left winger (d) NK Celje (e) EN Paralimniou, Grimsby Town, Rotherham, AFC Wimbledon, Rotherham, Plabennec

*** Lancely - Ollie Lancely (Oliver Lancely) (a) 01/07/2000, ¿? (Wales) (b) - (c) F - center forward (d) Airbus UK Broughton (e) -

*** Landakov - Dmitriy Landakov (Ландаков Дмитрий Андреевич) (a) 21/05/1999, Moskva (Russia) (b) 1,98 (c) G (d) Ural 2 Ekaterinburg (e) Orenburg II, Lokomotiv Moskva II

*** Landau - Elay Landau (לנדוי אילאי) (a) 11/09/2000, ¿? (Israel) (b) - (c) M (d) Sekzia Ness Ziona (e) Ironi Ashdod, Ness Ziona

*** Landeka - Davor Landeka (a) 18/09/1984, Imotski (Yugoslavia, now in Croatia) (b) 1,79 (c) M - central midfielder (d) Josip Landeka (e) HSK Posusje, NK Imotski, Siroki Brijeg, Grasshoppers, HNK Rijeka, Zrinjski Mostar, Dinamo Zagreb, Zrinjski Mostar

*** Landgren - Andreas Landgren (Sven Andreas Landgren) (a) 17/03/1989, Helsingborg (Sweden) (b) 1,76 (c) D - right back (d) Helsingborgs IF (e) Fredrikstad, Halmstads BK, Fredrikstad, Udinese, Fredrikstad, Udinese, Willem II, Helsingborgs IF

*** Landi - Gianmaria Landi (a) 29/11/1992, Rimini (Italy) (b) - (c) G (d) - (e) Cailungo, Pennarossa, Riccione, Promosport, Rimini, Saludecio

*** Lang - Ádám Lang (a) 17/01/1993, Veszprém (Hungary) (b) 1,86 (c) D - central defense (d) Omonia Nicosia (e) CFR Cluj, Dijon, AS Nancy, Dijon, Videoton FC, ETO FC Győr, VLS Veszprém

*** Lang - Alex Lang (a) 10/10/1999, ¿? (Wales) (b) - (c) G (d) Cardiff Metropolitan University (e) -

*** Lang - Christoph Lang (a) 07/01/2002, Deutschlandsberg (Austria) (b) 1,83 (c) F - center forward (d) TSV Hartberg (e) TSV Hartberg, Sturm Graz, SV Ried, Sturm Graz, Sturm Graz II

*** Lang - Michael Lang (Michael Rico Lang) (a) 08/02/1991, St. Gallen (Switzerland) (b) 1,85 (c) D - right back (d) FC Basel (e) Borussia Mönchengladbach, Werder Bremen, Borussia Mönchengladbach, FC Basel, Grasshoppers, FC St. Gallen

*** Lang - Noa Lang (Noa Noëll Lang) (a) 17/06/1999, Capelle aan de IJssel (Netherlands) (b) 1,70 (c) F - left winger (d) PSV Eindhoven (e) KV Brugge, Ajax, KV Brugge, Ajax, FC Twente, Ajax, Ajax B

*** Lang - Tanel Lang (a) 15/08/1995, Viljandi (Estonia) (b) 1,83 (c) M - pivot (d) Jalgpallikool Tammeka (e) JK Viljandi, JK Viljandi II

*** Langa - Bruno Langa (Bruno Alberto Langa) (a) 31/10/1997, Maputo (Mozambique) (b) 1,78 (c) D - left back (d) GD Chaves (e) Amora FC, Black Bulls, Amora FC, Black Bulls, Maxaquene

*** Langer - Michael Langer (a) 06/01/1985, Bregenz (Austria) (b) 1,95 (c) G (d) FC Schalke 04 (e) Norrköping, TB Rowdies, Vålerenga, SV Sandhausen, FSV Frankfurt, SC Freiburg, VfB Stuttgart, Stuttgart II, V. Bregenz, FC Hard

*** Langer - Stepan Langer (Štěpán Langer) (a) 16/08/2000, ¿? (Czech Rep.) (b) - (c) M - central midfielder (d) SK Sigma Olomouc B (e) 1.SK Prostejov, Sigma Olomouc B

*** Langgaard - Dávid Langgaard (a) 30/03/1995, ¿? (Faroe Islands) (b) 1,88 (c) D - central defense (d) - (e) KÍ Klaksvík, AB Argir, ÍF Fuglafjördur, KÍ II, KÍ Klaksvík, KÍ II

*** Langmo - Elias Langmo (a) 06/04/2005, ¿? (Norway) (b) - (c) M (d) Tromsø IL II (e) -

*** Langovich - Andrey Langovich (Лангович Андрей Владимирович) (a) 28/05/2003, Rostov-na-Donu (Russia) (b) 1,80 (c) D - right back (d) FK Rostov (e) Rostov II

*** Lani - Georg Lani (a) 02/04/2004, Tartu (Estonia) (b) - (c) D - left back (d) Jalgpallikool Tammeka (e) JK Tammeka III

*** Lansing - Michael Lansing (Michael Ryan Lansing) (a) 13/06/1994, Randolph, New Jersey (United States) (b) 1,93 (c) G (d) Aalesunds FK (e) AC Horsens, Aalborg BK, Vejle BK, Bucknell Bison, NYRB U-23, Bucknell Bison

*** Lantratov - Ilya Lantratov (Лантратов Илья Валерьевич) (a) 11/11/1995, Prokhorovka, Belgorod Region (Russia) (b) 1,94 (c) G (d) Lokomotiv Moskva (e) Khimki, Fakel Voronezh, Baltika, Shinnik Yaroslav, Lokomotiv Moskva II, Loko-Kazanka M., Salyut Belgorod

*** Lanzini - Manuel Lanzini (a) 15/02/1993, Ituzaingó (Argentina) (b) 1,67 (c) M - attacking midfielder (d) CA River Plate (e) West Ham Utd., Al-Jazira, West Ham Utd., Al-Jazira, River Plate, Fluminense, River Plate, River Plate II

*** Lapa - Kristen Lapa (a) 11/02/2000, Tallinn (Estonia) (b) 1,90 (c) G (d) FC Flora Tallinn (e) Kuressaare, FC Flora, Kuressaare, FC Flora

*** Lape - Matteo Lape (a) 15/10/2003, Varese (Italy) (b) - (c) D - right back (d) FC Lugano II (e) -

*** Lapierre - Emmanuel Lapierre (a) 05/08/1993, Rouen (France) (b) - (c) D - left back (d) Jeunesse Esch (e) Hamm Benfica, CS Sedan B

*** Lapira - Paul Lapira (a) 05/02/1998, ¿? (Malta) (b) 1,67 (c) F - left winger (d) Marsa FC (e) Pietà Hotspurs, Marsa FC, Santa Lucia FC, Zejtun C.

*** Laporte - Aymeric Laporte (Aymeric Jean Louis Gerard Alphonse Laporte) (a) 27/05/1994, Agen (France) (b) 1,89 (c) D - central defense (d) Manchester City (e) Athletic, Bilbao Athletic, CD Basconia

*** Laporte - Julien Laporte (a) 04/11/1993, Aurillac (France) (b) 1,85 (c) D - central defense (d) FC Lorient (e) Clermont Foot, Clermont B, Aurillac FC Auv.

*** Lapoukhov - Fedor Lapoukhov (Лапоухов Фёдор Юрьевич) (a) 20/06/2003, ¿? (Belarus) (b) - (c) G (d) Dinamo Minsk (e) Dinamo Minsk II, FK Lida

*** Lapoussin - Loïc Lapoussin (a) 27/03/1996, Rosny-sous-Bois (France) (b) 1,81 (c) M - left midfielder (d) Royale Union Saint Gilloise (e) RE Virton, Red Star FC, US Créteil B

*** Laptev - Denis Laptev (Лаптев Денис Игоревич) (a) 01/08/1991, Mozyr (Soviet Union, now in Belarus) (b) 1,94 (c) F - center forward (d) BATE Borisov (e) Torpedo Moskva, Rukh, Dynamo Brest, Soligorsk, Tosno, Soligorsk, Tosno, Slavia, Tosno, Slavia, Vertikal, Slavia

*** Lara - José Alonso Lara (José Alonso Lara) (a) 07/03/2000, Sevilla (Spain) (b) 1,62 (c) F - left winger (d) - (e) Betis Deportivo, Sevilla FC, RC Deportivo, Sevilla FC, Sevilla At.

*** Lara - Santiago Lara (Santiago Lara Vargas) (a) 14/06/2003, Sabanalarga (Colombia) (b) - (c) M - pivot (d) FC Ordino (e) Ordino B

*** Larade - Lucas Larade (Lucas Alexis Larade) (a) 26/06/1999, Villeneuve-Saint-Georges (France) (b) 1,85 (c) D - central defense (d) FK Jerv (e) Cercle Brugge, US Créteil-Lusitanos, US Créteil B

*** Largo - Largo (José Miguel Alias Trigos) (a) 07/03/1993, Málaga (Spain) (b) 1,70 (c) M - central midfielder (d) - (e) UE Santa Coloma, CD El Palo, At. Porcuna, UD San Pedro

*** Larie - Ionut Larie (Ionuț Justinian Larie) (a) 16/01/1987, Constanța (Romania) (b) 1,91 (c) D - central defense (d) FCV Farul Constanta (e) Gaz Metan, Tobol Kostanay, FCSB, CFR Cluj, FC Viitorul, Farul Constanta, Delta Tulcea, Farul Constanta, Delta Tulcea, Farul Constanta, Rm. Valcea, Farul Constanta

*** Larin - Cyle Larin (Cyle Christopher Larin) (a) 17/04/1995, Brampton, Ontario (Canada) (b) 1,88 (c) F - center forward (d) RCD Mallorca (e) Real Valladolid, KV Brugge, Real Valladolid, KV Brugge, Besiktas, Zulte Waregem, Besiktas, Orlando, UConn Huskies, Sigma FC, UConn Huskies

*** Larios - Juan Larios (Juan Larios López) (a) 12/01/2004, Tomares (Spain) (b) 1,70 (c) D - left back (d) Southampton FC (e) -

*** Larkin - Ross Larkin (a) 10/06/1999, Newry (Northern Ireland) (b) 1,88 (c) D - central defense (d) - (e) Linfield, Portadown

*** Larmour - Daniel Larmour (a) 03/09/1998, Castlereagh (Northern Ireland) (b) 1,86 (c) D - central defense (d) Crusaders FC (e) Glenavon, Carrick Rangers, Carrick Rangers

*** Laroshi - Vokli Laroshi (a) 06/08/2001, Elbasan (Albania) (b) 1,89 (c) G (d) KF Llapi (e) KF Turbina, FK Partizani, KF Turbina

*** Larouci - Yasser Larouci (العروسي ياسر) (a) 01/01/2001, El Oued (Algeria) (b) 1,76 (c) D - left back (d) Sheffield United (e) Sheffield Utd., Troyes

*** Larriere - Alexis Larriere (a) 20/03/1997, Metz (France) (b) 1,80 (c) M - central midfielder (d) Jeunesse Esch (e) FC Rodange 91, FC Metz B, US Avranches, FC Metz B

*** Larsen - Jörgen Strand Larsen (Jørgen Strand Larsen) (a) 06/02/2000, Halden (Norway) (b) 1,93 (c) F - center forward (d) RC Celta de Vigo (e) FC Groningen, Sarpsborg 08, Sarpsborg 08

*** Larsen - Kasper Larsen (a) 25/01/1993, Odense (Denmark) (b) 1,92 (c) D - central defense (d) Fehérvár FC (e) Odense BK, Fehérvár, Odense BK, Norrköping, FC Groningen, Odense BK, FC Astana, Odense BK

*** Larsen - Lars Olden Larsen (a) 17/09/1998, Oslo (Norway) (b) 1,75 (c) F - left winger (d) NEC Nijmegen (e) Pari Nizhny Novgórod, Häcken, Nizhny Novgorod, Mjøndalen, KFUM, Vålerenga II

*** Larsen - Lukas Larsen (Lukas Mosgaard Sloth Larsen) (a) 12/01/2004, Odense (Denmark) (b) 1,90 (c) D - central defense (d) TVD Velbert (e) -

*** Larsen - Marinus Larsen (Marinus Frederik Løvgren Larsen) (a) 30/12/2003, ¿? (Denmark) (b) - (c) M - central midfielder (d) AC Horsens (e) Brøndby IF
*** Larsen - Nicolai Larsen (Nicolai Oppen Larsen) (a) 09/03/1991, Herlev (Denmark) (b) 1,87 (c) G (d) Silkeborg IF (e) Guingamp, Nordsjælland, Aalborg BK
*** Larsen - Tor Erik Larsen (a) 28/09/1998, Ålesund (Norway) (b) 1,90 (c) G (d) Aalesunds FK (e) Stjørdals-Blink, Aalesund, SIUE Cougars, Reading United, SIUE Cougars, Spjelkavik IL, Aalesund II, Spjelkavik IL
*** Larson - Karl Larson (a) 16/09/1991, ¿? (Sweden) (b) 1,76 (c) D - right back (d) - (e) Sirius, Brommapojkarna, Gröndals IK
*** Larsson - Adam Larsson (Adam Mikael Larsson) (a) 05/09/1999, Motala (Sweden) (b) 1,72 (c) F - center forward (d) Ilves Tampere (e) AFC Eskilstuna, Ekenäs IF, AFC Eskilstuna, Linköping City, AFC Eskilstuna, Åtvidabergs FF, AFC Eskilstuna, Linköping City, Motala AIF
*** Larsson - Alexander Larsson (a) 14/01/2004, Sundsvall (Sweden) (b) 1,84 (c) F - center forward (d) GIF Sundsvall (e) -
*** Larsson - Eric Larsson (a) 15/07/1991, Gävle (Sweden) (b) 1,75 (c) D - right back (d) OFI Creta (e) Malmö FF, GIF Sundsvall, Gefle
*** Larsson - Hugo Larsson (Hugo Emanuel Larsson) (a) 27/06/2004, Svarte (Sweden) (b) 1,87 (c) M - central midfielder (d) Eintracht Frankfurt (e) Malmö FF
*** Larsson - Johan Larsson (Johan Erik Larsson) (a) 05/05/1990, Kinna (Sweden) (b) 1,82 (c) D - right back (d) IF Elfsborg (e) Brøndby IF, Guingamp, Brøndby IF, Elfsborg
*** Larsson - Jordan Larsson (Carl Henrik Jordan Larsson) (a) 20/06/1997, Rotterdam (Netherlands) (b) 1,75 (c) F - center forward (d) FC Copenhague (e) FC Schalke 04, FC København, FC Schalke 04, Spartak Moskva, AIK, Spartak Moskva, Norrköping, NEC Nijmegen, Helsingborgs IF, Högaborgs BK
*** Larsson - Sam Larsson (Sam Andreas Larsson) (a) 10/04/1993, Göteborg (Sweden) (b) 1,80 (c) F - left winger (d) Antalyaspor (e) Dalian PFC, Feyenoord, Heerenveen, IFK Göteborg
*** Larsson - Sebastian Larsson (Bengt Ulf Sebastian Larsson) (a) 06/06/1985, Eskilstuna (Sweden) (b) 1,78 (c) M - central midfielder (d) - (e) AIK, Hull City, Sunderland, Birmingham City, Arsenal, Birmingham City, Arsenal, IFK Eskilstuna
*** Larsson - Victor Larsson (a) 19/04/2000, ¿? (Sweden) (b) - (c) D - central defense (d) IFK Värnamo (e) Torns IF
*** Lárusson - Aron Kristófer Lárusson (a) 17/09/1998, Akureyri (Iceland) (b) - (c) M - pivot (d) KR Reykjavík (e) ÍA Akranes, Thór, Völsungur ÍF, Thór
*** Lárusson - Sigurdur Egill Lárusson (Sigurður Egill Lárusson) (a) 22/01/1992, ¿? (Iceland) (b) 1,82 (c) F - left winger (d) Valur Reykjavík (e) Víkingur, Valur, Víkingur
*** Lasagna - Kevin Lasagna (a) 10/08/1992, Suzzara (Italy) (b) 1,81 (c) F - center forward (d) Hellas Verona (e) Udinese, Hellas Verona, Udinese, Carpi, Udinese, Carpi, Cerea, Este, Cerea, Governolo
*** Lascelles - Jamaal Lascelles (a) 11/11/1993, Derby (England) (b) 1,88 (c) D - central defense (d) Newcastle United (e) Nottingham Forest, Newcastle Utd., Nottingham Forest, Stevenage, Nottingham Forest
*** Lasic - Mate Lasic (Mate Zvonimir Lasić) (a) 29/03/2002, Siroki Brijeg (Bosnia and Herzegovina) (b) 1,84 (c) D - central defense (d) HNK Cibalia Vinkovci (e) Siroki Brijeg, HNK Tomislav T., Siroki Brijeg, NK Neretvanac, Siroki Brijeg
*** Lasickas - Justas Lasickas (a) 06/10/1997, Vilnius (Lithuania) (b) 1,78 (c) D - right back (d) NK Olimpija Ljubljana (e) Vozdovac, Jagiellonia, Zalgiris, FK Zemun, Zalgiris, Zalgiris B

*** Laski - Wojciech Laski (Wojciech Łaski) (a) 21/05/2000, Wodzisław Śląski (Poland) (b) 1,86 (c) M - attacking midfielder (d) Jagiellonia Białystok (e) GKS Jastrzebie, Pniowek P., GKS Jastrzebie, Pniowek P., GKS Jastrzebie, Płomień P., GKS Jastrzebie

*** Laskowski - Adrian Laskowski (a) 16/03/1992, Poznań (Poland) (b) 1,88 (c) D - central defense (d) Unia Swarzedz (e) Lech Poznan II, Warta Poznań, Polonia Bytom, Warta Poznań, GKS Dopiewo, Warta Poznań

*** Lassen - Mikkel Lassen (Mikkel Møller Lassen) (a) 19/06/2001, ¿? (Denmark) (b) 1,81 (c) D - right back (d) AC Horsens (e) Aarhus GF, AC Horsens, Aarhus GF, Skive IK, Aarhus GF

*** Lasso - Forrest Lasso (Forrest Baldwin Lasso) (a) 11/05/1993, Raleigh, North Carolina (United States) (b) 1,96 (c) D - central defense (d) Tampa Bay Rowdies (e) GIF Sundsvall, TB Rowdies, Cincinnati, Nashville SC, Cincinnati, Charleston, Wofford, GPS Portland, Wofford, RailHawks

*** Lastuvka - Jan Lastuvka (Jan Laštůvka) (a) 07/07/1982, Havířov (Czechoslovakia, now in Czech Rep.) (b) 1,89 (c) G (d) - (e) Banik Ostrava, Slavia Praha, Karvina, Dnipro, Shakhtar Donetsk, West Ham Utd., Shakhtar Donetsk, VfL Bochum, Shakhtar Donetsk, Fulham, Shakhtar Donetsk, Banik Ostrava, Baník Ostrava B, FC Karvina, Baník Ostrava B

*** Latal - Radek Latal (Radek Látal) (a) 16/12/1997, ¿? (Czech Rep.) (b) 1,85 (c) D - right back (d) FK Mlada Boleslav (e) Sigma Olomouc, Karvina, Sigma Olomouc, Sigma Olomouc B, MFK Vyskov, Sigma Olomouc B, Pardubice, Sigma Olomouc B

*** Lataria - Zurab Lataria (a) 18/05/2002, ¿? (Georgia) (b) - (c) D - central defense (d) FC Saburtalo II (e) Merani Martvili, FC Saburtalo II

*** Latasa - Juanmi Latasa (Juan Miguel Latasa Fernández Layos) (a) 23/03/2001, Madrid (Spain) (b) 1,92 (c) F - center forward (d) Getafe CF (e) Getafe CF, Real Madrid, RM Castilla

*** Laterza - Tom Laterza (a) 09/05/1992, Mondercange (Luxembourg) (b) 1,79 (c) D - right back (d) FC Schifflange 95 (e) Mondercange, Progrès Niederkorn, CS Fola Esch, CS Sedan B

*** Lathouwers - Robin Lathouwers (a) 09/03/2000, Amsterdam (Netherlands) (b) - (c) D - right back (d) VVV-Venlo (e) -

*** Latic - Irvin Latic (Irvin Latić) (a) 24/05/2002, Niederkorn (Luxembourg) (b) 1,82 (c) M - pivot (d) Jeunesse Esch (e) Progrès Niederkorn, UN Käerjeng 97

*** Latifi - Fatbardh Latifi (a) 12/03/1999, Prishtinë (Yugoslavia, now in Kosovo) (b) 1,92 (c) D - central defense (d) - (e) KF Llapi, Ramiz Sadiku, FC A&N, Flat Earth FC, AD Alcorcón B, FC Llapi, Ramiz Sadiku, FC Llapi, Ramiz Sadiku

*** Latifi - Liridon Latifi (a) 06/02/1994, Prishtinë (Yugoslavia, now in Kosovo) (b) 1,76 (c) F - left winger (d) KF Tirana (e) KF Vllaznia, Puskás AFC, FC Sheriff, Puskás AFC, KF Skënderbeu, FK Kukësi, KF Skënderbeu, FC Prishtina, KF Flamurtari

*** Latik - Eldin Latik (a) 22/12/2002, ¿? (Luxembourg) (b) 1,98 (c) G (d) FC Progrès Niederkorn (e) FC Rodange 91

*** Lato - Toni Lato (Antonio Latorre Grueso) (a) 21/11/1997, La Pobla de Vallbona (Spain) (b) 1,71 (c) D - left back (d) RCD Mallorca (e) Valencia CF, CA Osasuna, Valencia CF, PSV Eindhoven, Valencia CF, Valencia Mestalla

*** Latonen - Joakim Latonen (a) 24/02/1998, Turku (Finland) (b) 1,73 (c) M - attacking midfielder (d) IF Gnistan (e) IFK Mariehamn, TPS

*** Latovlevici - Iasmin Latovlevici (a) 11/05/1986, Moldova Nouă (Romania) (b) 1,75 (c) D - left back (d) - (e) Petrolul, FC Arges, CFR Cluj, Kisvárda, Bursaspor, Galatasaray, Karabükspor, Genclerbirligi, Steaua Bucuresti, FC Timisoara, Gloria Bistrita, FC Timisoara, CFR Timisoara, Poli Timișoara

*** Latsabidze - Giorgi Latsabidze (გიორგი ლაცაბიძე) (a) 15/05/1995, ¿? (Georgia) (b) 1,82 (c) D - left back (d) FC Gareji (e) FC Gagra, Saburtalo, FC Dila, Rustavi, WIT Georgia, Tskhinvali

*** Latte Lath - Emmanuel Latte Lath (Junior Emmanuel Delan Latte Lath) (a) 01/01/1999, Anoumalo Marcory (Ivory Coast) (b) 1,76 (c) F - center forward (d) Atalanta de Bérgamo (e) FC St. Gallen, Atalanta, SPAL, Atalanta, Pro Patria, Atalanta, Pianese, Atalanta, Imolese, Atalanta, Carrarese, Atalanta, Pistoiese, Pescara

*** Latva-Kivistö - Antti Latva-Kivistö (a) 03/01/2003, ¿? (Finland) (b) 1,81 (c) G (d) Vaasan Palloseura (e) VPS II

*** Latykhov - Dmitriy Latykhov (Латыхов Дмитрий Денисович) (a) 25/03/2003, Minsk (Belarus) (b) 1,88 (c) F - center forward (d) Isloch Minsk Region (e) Dinamo Minsk, Dinamo Minsk II

*** Latza - Danny Latza (a) 07/12/1989, Gelsenkirchen (Germany) (b) 1,79 (c) M - central midfielder (d) FC Schalke 04 (e) Mainz 05, VfL Bochum, Darmstadt 98, Schalke 04 II, FC Schalke 04, Schalke 04 II

*** Lau - Sebastian Lau (Sebastian Lau Nielsen) (a) 02/07/1996, ¿? (Denmark) (b) - (c) F - center forward (d) B68 Toftir (e) Holstebro BK, Stenlöse BK, Hellerup IK

*** Lauenborg - Frederik Lauenborg (a) 18/05/1997, ¿? (Denamrk) (b) 1,81 (c) M - central midfielder (d) Randers FC (e) -

*** Laukart - Alexander Laukart (a) 25/10/1998, Hamburg (Germany) (b) 1,86 (c) M - attacking midfielder (d) Union Titus Petange (e) Türkgücü Münch., FC Den Bosch, FC Twente

*** Laukzemis - Karolis Laukzemis (Karolis Laukžemis) (a) 11/03/1992, Palanga (Lithuania) (b) 1,88 (c) F - center forward (d) Ayutthaya United (e) Banga, Suduva, UTA Arad, Kaysar, Hibernians FC, NK Istra, Tabor Sezana, NK Istra, Suduva, Jelgava, Suduva, Granitas, Atlantas, Lok Vilnius, Atlantas

*** Lauper - Sandro Lauper (Sandro Mike Lauper) (a) 25/10/1996, Oberdiessbach BE (Switzerland) (b) 1,85 (c) M - pivot (d) BSC Young Boys (e) FC Thun

*** Laur - Kaspar Laur (a) 08/04/2000, Tallinn (Estonia) (b) 2,04 (c) D - central defense (d) Kalev Tallinn (e) Kalev

*** Laura - Luboslav Laura (Ľuboslav Laura) (a) 05/07/1994, Dolný Kubín (Slovakia) (b) 1,84 (c) F - right winger (d) Tatran Liptovsky Mikulas (e) SKF Sered, Dolny Kubin

*** Lauridsen - Jesper Lauridsen (a) 27/03/1991, ¿? (Denmark) (b) 1,82 (c) D - left back (d) Esbjerg fB (e) Randers FC, Esbjerg fB, Midtjylland, Hobro IK, Midtjylland, Hobro IK, Midtjylland

*** Laurienté - Alexandre Laurienté (a) 19/11/1989, Villiers-le-Bel (France) (b) 1,74 (c) D - left back (d) Armand Laurienté (e) RFCU Luxembourg, Union Titus Petange, RE Virton, F91 Dudelange, Francs Borains, KV Oostende, FCV Dender EH, Châteauroux B

*** Laurienté - Armand Laurienté (Armand Gaëtan Laurienté) (a) 04/12/1998, Gonesse (France) (b) 1,71 (c) F - left winger (d) US Sassuolo (e) FC Lorient, Stade Rennes, FC Lorient, Stade Rennes, Stade Rennes B, US Orléans, Stade Rennes B

*** Lauritsen - Mads Lauritsen (a) 14/04/1993, ¿? (Denmark) (b) 1,95 (c) D - central defense (d) Viborg FF (e) Vejle BK, Viborg FF, Vejle BK, Thisted FC, Viborg FF

*** Lauritsen - Mads Lauritsen (Mads Nyboe Lauritsen) (a) 21/03/2005, ¿? (Denmark) (b) 1,80 (c) D - central defense (d) CD Mafra (e) -

*** Lauritsen - Rasmus Lauritsen (Rasmus Steensbæk Lauritsen) (a) 27/02/1996, Brande (Denmark) (b) 1,88 (c) D - central defense (d) Brøndby IF (e) Dinamo Zagreb, Norrköping, Vejle BK, Skive IK, Midtjylland

*** Lauritsen - Tobias Lauritsen (a) 30/08/1997, ¿? (Norway) (b) 1,96 (c) F - center forward (d) Sparta Rotterdam (e) Odd, Pors Fotball, Odd II, Urædd FK, Herkules Fotbal

*** Laursen - Andreas Laursen (Andreas Bækskov Laursen) (a) 21/08/1998, ¿? (Denmark) (b) - (c) D - central defense (d) Odder IGF (e) Hibernians FC, Odder IGF, Horsens FS

*** Laursen - Jacob Barrett Laursen (a) 17/11/1994, Arden (Denmark) (b) 1,79 (c) D - left back (d) Standard de Lieja (e) Arminia Bielefeld, Odense BK

*** Laus - Tino Blaz Laus (Tino Blaž Lauš) (a) 17/03/2001, Split (Croatia) (b) 1,83 (c) M - attacking midfielder (d) HNK Hajduk Split (e) Velez Mostar, Hajduk Split, NK Istra, Hajduk Split, HSK Posusje, Hajduk Split, Hajduk Split II, HNK Mravince

*** Lausic - Marin Lausic (Marin Laušić) (a) 26/06/2001, Split (Croatia) (b) 1,87 (c) M - central midfielder (d) NK Maribor (e) Slaven Belupo, NK Solin, Adriatic Split

*** Lauva - Klavs Lauva (Klāvs Lauva) (a) 30/06/2004, ¿? (Latvia) (b) 1,88 (c) G (d) Valmiera FC (e) Jelgava, Liepaja II

*** Lauwers - Barry Lauwers (a) 29/11/1999, Purmerend (Netherlands) (b) 1,87 (c) G (d) FC Volendam (e) -

*** Laux - Lucas Laux (a) 14/10/2002, Koblenz (Germany) (b) - (c) D - central defense (d) SV Sandhausen (e) SV Sandhausen, Mainz 05, FSV Mainz 05 II

*** Lavalée - Dimitri Lavalée (Dimitri Dominique Lavalée) (a) 13/01/1997, Soumagne (Belgium) (b) 1,87 (c) D - central defense (d) KV Mechelen (e) Mainz 05, Sint-Truiden, Mainz 05, Standard Liège, MVV Maastricht, Standard Liège

*** Lavallée - Lucas Lavallée (Lucas Michel Daniel Lavallée) (a) 18/02/2003, Armentières (France) (b) 1,95 (c) G (d) USL Dunkerque (e) USL Dunkerque, Paris Saint-Germain, LOSC Lille B

*** Lavanchy - Numa Lavanchy (a) 25/08/1993, Morges VD (Switzerland) (b) 1,74 (c) D - right back (d) FC Sion (e) FC Lugano, Grasshoppers, Lausanne-Sport, Le Mont LS, Lausanne-Sport

*** Lavi - Neta Lavi (לביא נטע) (a) 25/08/1996, Ramat haShofet (Israel) (b) 1,77 (c) M - pivot (d) Gamba Osaka (e) Maccabi Haifa

*** Lavia - Roméo Lavia (a) 06/01/2004, Brussels (Belgium) (b) 1,81 (c) M - pivot (d) Southampton FC (e) -

*** Lavrenyuk - Kirill Lavrenyuk (Лавренюк Кирилл) (a) 09/08/2003, ¿? (Kazakhstan) (b) 1,72 (c) F - right winger (d) Shakhter-Bulat (e) -

Printed in Great Britain
by Amazon

27111609R10397